Oxford Dictionary of National Biography

Volume 55

Oxford Dictionary of National Biography

IN ASSOCIATION WITH
The British Academy

From the earliest times to the year 2000

Edited by
H. C. G. Matthew
and
Brian Harrison

Volume 55
Tonson–Usher

OXFORD
UNIVERSITY PRESS

OXFORD
UNIVERSITY PRESS

Great Clarendon Street, Oxford OX2 6DP

Oxford University Press is a department of the University of Oxford.
It furthers the University's objective of excellence in research, scholarship,
and education by publishing worldwide in

Oxford New York

Auckland Bangkok Buenos Aires Cape Town
Chennai Dar es Salaam Delhi Hong Kong Istanbul Karachi
Kolkata Kuala Lumpur Madrid Melbourne Mexico City Mumbai Nairobi
São Paulo Shanghai Taipei Tokyo Toronto

Oxford is a registered trade mark of Oxford University Press
in the UK and in certain other countries

Published in the United States
by Oxford University Press Inc., New York

First published 2004

British Library Cataloguing in Publication Data
Data available

Library of Congress Cataloging in Publication Data
Data available: for details see volume 1, p. iv

ISBN 0-19-861405-5 (this volume)
ISBN 0-19-861411-X (set of sixty volumes)

Text captured by Alliance Phototypesetters, Pondicherry
Illustrations reproduced and archived by
Alliance Graphics Ltd, UK
Typeset in OUP Swift by Interactive Sciences Limited, Gloucester
Printed in Great Britain on acid-free paper by
Butler and Tanner Ltd,
Frome, Somerset

LIST OF ABBREVIATIONS

1 General abbreviations

AB	bachelor of arts
ABC	Australian Broadcasting Corporation
ABC TV	ABC Television
act.	active
A$	Australian dollar
AD	*anno domini*
AFC	Air Force Cross
AIDS	acquired immune deficiency syndrome
AK	Alaska
AL	Alabama
A level	advanced level [examination]
ALS	associate of the Linnean Society
AM	master of arts
AMICE	associate member of the Institution of Civil Engineers
ANZAC	Australian and New Zealand Army Corps
appx *pl.* appxs	appendix(es)
AR	Arkansas
ARA	associate of the Royal Academy
ARCA	associate of the Royal College of Art
ARCM	associate of the Royal College of Music
ARCO	associate of the Royal College of Organists
ARIBA	associate of the Royal Institute of British Architects
ARP	air-raid precautions
ARRC	associate of the Royal Red Cross
ARSA	associate of the Royal Scottish Academy
art.	article / item
ASC	Army Service Corps
Asch	Austrian Schilling
ASDIC	Antisubmarine Detection Investigation Committee
ATS	Auxiliary Territorial Service
ATV	Associated Television
Aug	August
AZ	Arizona
b.	born
BA	bachelor of arts
BA (Admin.)	bachelor of arts (administration)
BAFTA	British Academy of Film and Television Arts
BAO	bachelor of arts in obstetrics
bap.	baptized
BBC	British Broadcasting Corporation / Company
BC	before Christ
BCE	before the common (*or* Christian) era
BCE	bachelor of civil engineering
BCG	bacillus of Calmette and Guérin [inoculation against tuberculosis]
BCh	bachelor of surgery
BChir	bachelor of surgery
BCL	bachelor of civil law
BCnL	bachelor of canon law
BCom	bachelor of commerce
BD	bachelor of divinity
BEd	bachelor of education
BEng	bachelor of engineering
bk *pl.* bks	book(s)
BL	bachelor of law / letters / literature
BLitt	bachelor of letters
BM	bachelor of medicine
BMus	bachelor of music
BP	before present
BP	British Petroleum
Bros.	Brothers
BS	(1) bachelor of science; (2) bachelor of surgery; (3) British standard
BSc	bachelor of science
BSc (Econ.)	bachelor of science (economics)
BSc (Eng.)	bachelor of science (engineering)
bt	baronet
BTh	bachelor of theology
bur.	buried
C.	command [identifier for published parliamentary papers]
c.	*circa*
c.	*capitulum pl. capitula*: chapter(s)
CA	California
Cantab.	Cantabrigiensis
cap.	*capitulum pl. capitula*: chapter(s)
CB	companion of the Bath
CBE	commander of the Order of the British Empire
CBS	Columbia Broadcasting System
cc	cubic centimetres
C$	Canadian dollar
CD	compact disc
Cd	command [identifier for published parliamentary papers]
CE	Common (*or* Christian) Era
cent.	century
cf.	compare
CH	Companion of Honour
chap.	chapter
ChB	bachelor of surgery
CI	Imperial Order of the Crown of India
CIA	Central Intelligence Agency
CID	Criminal Investigation Department
CIE	companion of the Order of the Indian Empire
Cie	Compagnie
CLit	companion of literature
CM	master of surgery
cm	centimetre(s)

Cmd	command [identifier for published parliamentary papers]
CMG	companion of the Order of St Michael and St George
Cmnd	command [identifier for published parliamentary papers]
CO	Colorado
Co.	company
co.	county
col. *pl.* cols.	column(s)
Corp.	corporation
CSE	certificate of secondary education
CSI	companion of the Order of the Star of India
CT	Connecticut
CVO	commander of the Royal Victorian Order
cwt	hundredweight
$	(American) dollar
d.	(1) penny (pence); (2) died
DBE	dame commander of the Order of the British Empire
DCH	diploma in child health
DCh	doctor of surgery
DCL	doctor of civil law
DCnL	doctor of canon law
DCVO	dame commander of the Royal Victorian Order
DD	doctor of divinity
DE	Delaware
Dec	December
dem.	demolished
DEng	doctor of engineering
des.	destroyed
DFC	Distinguished Flying Cross
DipEd	diploma in education
DipPsych	diploma in psychiatry
diss.	dissertation
DL	deputy lieutenant
DLitt	doctor of letters
DLittCelt	doctor of Celtic letters
DM	(1) Deutschmark; (2) doctor of medicine; (3) doctor of musical arts
DMus	doctor of music
DNA	dioxyribonucleic acid
doc.	document
DOL	doctor of oriental learning
DPH	diploma in public health
DPhil	doctor of philosophy
DPM	diploma in psychological medicine
DSC	Distinguished Service Cross
DSc	doctor of science
DSc (Econ.)	doctor of science (economics)
DSc (Eng.)	doctor of science (engineering)
DSM	Distinguished Service Medal
DSO	companion of the Distinguished Service Order
DSocSc	doctor of social science
DTech	doctor of technology
DTh	doctor of theology
DTM	diploma in tropical medicine
DTMH	diploma in tropical medicine and hygiene
DU	doctor of the university
DUniv	doctor of the university
dwt	pennyweight
EC	European Community
ed. *pl.* eds.	edited / edited by / editor(s)
Edin.	Edinburgh

edn	edition
EEC	European Economic Community
EFTA	European Free Trade Association
EICS	East India Company Service
EMI	Electrical and Musical Industries (Ltd)
Eng.	English
enl.	enlarged
ENSA	Entertainments National Service Association
ep. *pl.* epp.	*epistola(e)*
ESP	extra-sensory perception
esp.	especially
esq.	esquire
est.	estimate / estimated
EU	European Union
ex	sold by (*lit.* out of)
excl.	excludes / excluding
exh.	exhibited
exh. cat.	exhibition catalogue
f. *pl.* ff.	following [pages]
FA	Football Association
FACP	fellow of the American College of Physicians
facs.	facsimile
FANY	First Aid Nursing Yeomanry
FBA	fellow of the British Academy
FBI	Federation of British Industries
FCS	fellow of the Chemical Society
Feb	February
FEng	fellow of the Fellowship of Engineering
FFCM	fellow of the Faculty of Community Medicine
FGS	fellow of the Geological Society
fig.	figure
FIMechE	fellow of the Institution of Mechanical Engineers
FL	Florida
fl.	*floruit*
FLS	fellow of the Linnean Society
FM	frequency modulation
fol. *pl.* fols.	folio(s)
Fr	French francs
Fr.	French
FRAeS	fellow of the Royal Aeronautical Society
FRAI	fellow of the Royal Anthropological Institute
FRAM	fellow of the Royal Academy of Music
FRAS	(1) fellow of the Royal Asiatic Society; (2) fellow of the Royal Astronomical Society
FRCM	fellow of the Royal College of Music
FRCO	fellow of the Royal College of Organists
FRCOG	fellow of the Royal College of Obstetricians and Gynaecologists
FRCP(C)	fellow of the Royal College of Physicians of Canada
FRCP (Edin.)	fellow of the Royal College of Physicians of Edinburgh
FRCP (Lond.)	fellow of the Royal College of Physicians of London
FRCPath	fellow of the Royal College of Pathologists
FRCPsych	fellow of the Royal College of Psychiatrists
FRCS	fellow of the Royal College of Surgeons
FRGS	fellow of the Royal Geographical Society
FRIBA	fellow of the Royal Institute of British Architects
FRICS	fellow of the Royal Institute of Chartered Surveyors
FRS	fellow of the Royal Society
FRSA	fellow of the Royal Society of Arts

FRSCM	fellow of the Royal School of Church Music		ISO	companion of the Imperial Service Order
FRSE	fellow of the Royal Society of Edinburgh		It.	Italian
FRSL	fellow of the Royal Society of Literature		ITA	Independent Television Authority
FSA	fellow of the Society of Antiquaries		ITV	Independent Television
ft	foot *pl.* feet		Jan	January
FTCL	fellow of Trinity College of Music, London		JP	justice of the peace
ft-lb per min.	foot-pounds per minute [unit of horsepower]		jun.	junior
FZS	fellow of the Zoological Society		KB	knight of the Order of the Bath
GA	Georgia		KBE	knight commander of the Order of the British Empire
GBE	knight or dame grand cross of the Order of the British Empire		KC	king's counsel
GCB	knight grand cross of the Order of the Bath		kcal	kilocalorie
GCE	general certificate of education		KCB	knight commander of the Order of the Bath
GCH	knight grand cross of the Royal Guelphic Order		KCH	knight commander of the Royal Guelphic Order
GCHQ	government communications headquarters		KCIE	knight commander of the Order of the Indian Empire
GCIE	knight grand commander of the Order of the Indian Empire		KCMG	knight commander of the Order of St Michael and St George
GCMG	knight or dame grand cross of the Order of St Michael and St George		KCSI	knight commander of the Order of the Star of India
GCSE	general certificate of secondary education		KCVO	knight commander of the Royal Victorian Order
GCSI	knight grand commander of the Order of the Star of India		keV	kilo-electron-volt
GCStJ	bailiff or dame grand cross of the order of St John of Jerusalem		KG	knight of the Order of the Garter
GCVO	knight or dame grand cross of the Royal Victorian Order		KGB	[Soviet committee of state security]
			KH	knight of the Royal Guelphic Order
GEC	General Electric Company		KLM	Koninklijke Luchtvaart Maatschappij (Royal Dutch Air Lines)
Ger.	German		km	kilometre(s)
GI	government (*or* general) issue		KP	knight of the Order of St Patrick
GMT	Greenwich mean time		KS	Kansas
GP	general practitioner		KT	knight of the Order of the Thistle
GPU	[Soviet special police unit]		kt	knight
GSO	general staff officer		KY	Kentucky
Heb.	Hebrew		£	pound(s) sterling
HEICS	Honourable East India Company Service		£E	Egyptian pound
HI	Hawaii		L	lira *pl.* lire
HIV	human immunodeficiency virus		l. *pl.* ll.	line(s)
HK$	Hong Kong dollar		LA	Lousiana
HM	his / her majesty('s)		LAA	light anti-aircraft
HMAS	his / her majesty's Australian ship		LAH	licentiate of the Apothecaries' Hall, Dublin
HMNZS	his / her majesty's New Zealand ship		Lat.	Latin
HMS	his / her majesty's ship		lb	pound(s), unit of weight
HMSO	His / Her Majesty's Stationery Office		LDS	licence in dental surgery
HMV	His Master's Voice		*lit.*	literally
Hon.	Honourable		LittB	bachelor of letters
hp	horsepower		LittD	doctor of letters
hr	hour(s)		LKQCPI	licentiate of the King and Queen's College of Physicians, Ireland
HRH	his / her royal highness		LLA	lady literate in arts
HTV	Harlech Television		LLB	bachelor of laws
IA	Iowa		LLD	doctor of laws
ibid.	*ibidem*: in the same place		LLM	master of laws
ICI	Imperial Chemical Industries (Ltd)		LM	licentiate in midwifery
ID	Idaho		LP	long-playing record
IL	Illinois		LRAM	licentiate of the Royal Academy of Music
illus.	illustration		LRCP	licentiate of the Royal College of Physicians
illustr.	illustrated		LRCPS (Glasgow)	licentiate of the Royal College of Physicians and Surgeons of Glasgow
IN	Indiana		LRCS	licentiate of the Royal College of Surgeons
in.	inch(es)		LSA	licentiate of the Society of Apothecaries
Inc.	Incorporated		LSD	lysergic acid diethylamide
incl.	includes / including		LVO	lieutenant of the Royal Victorian Order
IOU	I owe you		M. *pl.* MM.	Monsieur *pl.* Messieurs
IQ	intelligence quotient		m	metre(s)
Ir£	Irish pound			
IRA	Irish Republican Army			

m. *pl.* mm.	membrane(s)
MA	(1) Massachusetts; (2) master of arts
MAI	master of engineering
MB	bachelor of medicine
MBA	master of business administration
MBE	member of the Order of the British Empire
MC	Military Cross
MCC	Marylebone Cricket Club
MCh	master of surgery
MChir	master of surgery
MCom	master of commerce
MD	(1) doctor of medicine; (2) Maryland
MDMA	methylenedioxymethamphetamine
ME	Maine
MEd	master of education
MEng	master of engineering
MEP	member of the European parliament
MG	Morris Garages
MGM	Metro-Goldwyn-Mayer
Mgr	Monsignor
MI	(1) Michigan; (2) military intelligence
MI1c	[secret intelligence department]
MI5	[military intelligence department]
MI6	[secret intelligence department]
MI9	[secret escape service]
MICE	member of the Institution of Civil Engineers
MIEE	member of the Institution of Electrical Engineers
min.	minute(s)
Mk	mark
ML	(1) licentiate of medicine; (2) master of laws
MLitt	master of letters
Mlle	Mademoiselle
mm	millimetre(s)
Mme	Madame
MN	Minnesota
MO	Missouri
MOH	medical officer of health
MP	member of parliament
m.p.h.	miles per hour
MPhil	master of philosophy
MRCP	member of the Royal College of Physicians
MRCS	member of the Royal College of Surgeons
MRCVS	member of the Royal College of Veterinary Surgeons
MRIA	member of the Royal Irish Academy
MS	(1) master of science; (2) Mississippi
MS *pl.* MSS	manuscript(s)
MSc	master of science
MSc (Econ.)	master of science (economics)
MT	Montana
MusB	bachelor of music
MusBac	bachelor of music
MusD	doctor of music
MV	motor vessel
MVO	member of the Royal Victorian Order
n. *pl.* nn.	note(s)
NAAFI	Navy, Army, and Air Force Institutes
NASA	National Aeronautics and Space Administration
NATO	North Atlantic Treaty Organization
NBC	National Broadcasting Corporation
NC	North Carolina
NCO	non-commissioned officer
ND	North Dakota
n.d.	no date
NE	Nebraska
nem. con.	*nemine contradicente*: unanimously
new ser.	new series
NH	New Hampshire
NHS	National Health Service
NJ	New Jersey
NKVD	[Soviet people's commissariat for internal affairs]
NM	New Mexico
nm	nanometre(s)
no. *pl.* nos.	number(s)
Nov	November
n.p.	no place [of publication]
NS	new style
NV	Nevada
NY	New York
NZBS	New Zealand Broadcasting Service
OBE	officer of the Order of the British Empire
obit.	obituary
Oct	October
OCTU	officer cadets training unit
OECD	Organization for Economic Co-operation and Development
OEEC	Organization for European Economic Co-operation
OFM	order of Friars Minor [Franciscans]
OFMCap	Ordine Frati Minori Cappucini: member of the Capuchin order
OH	Ohio
OK	Oklahoma
O level	ordinary level [examination]
OM	Order of Merit
OP	order of Preachers [Dominicans]
op. *pl.* opp.	opus *pl.* opera
OPEC	Organization of Petroleum Exporting Countries
OR	Oregon
orig.	original
OS	old style
OSB	Order of St Benedict
OTC	Officers' Training Corps
OWS	Old Watercolour Society
Oxon.	Oxoniensis
p. *pl.* pp.	page(s)
PA	Pennsylvania
p.a.	per annum
para.	paragraph
PAYE	pay as you earn
pbk *pl.* pbks	paperback(s)
per.	[during the] period
PhD	doctor of philosophy
pl.	(1) plate(s); (2) plural
priv. coll.	private collection
pt *pl.* pts	part(s)
pubd	published
PVC	polyvinyl chloride
q. *pl.* qq.	(1) question(s); (2) quire(s)
QC	queen's counsel
R	rand
R.	Rex / Regina
r	recto
r.	reigned / ruled
RA	Royal Academy / Royal Academician

RAC	Royal Automobile Club		Skr	Swedish krona
RAF	Royal Air Force		Span.	Spanish
RAFVR	Royal Air Force Volunteer Reserve		SPCK	Society for Promoting Christian Knowledge
RAM	[member of the] Royal Academy of Music		SS	(1) Santissimi; (2) Schutzstaffel; (3) steam ship
RAMC	Royal Army Medical Corps		STB	bachelor of theology
RCA	Royal College of Art		STD	doctor of theology
RCNC	Royal Corps of Naval Constructors		STM	master of theology
RCOG	Royal College of Obstetricians and Gynaecologists		STP	doctor of theology
			supp.	supposedly
RDI	royal designer for industry		suppl. *pl.* suppls.	supplement(s)
RE	Royal Engineers		s.v.	*sub verbo / sub voce*: under the word / heading
repr. *pl.* reprs.	reprint(s) / reprinted		SY	steam yacht
repro.	reproduced		TA	Territorial Army
rev.	revised / revised by / reviser / revision		TASS	[Soviet news agency]
Revd	Reverend		TB	tuberculosis (*lit.* tubercle bacillus)
RHA	Royal Hibernian Academy		TD	(1) *teachtaí dála* (member of the Dáil); (2) territorial decoration
RI	(1) Rhode Island; (2) Royal Institute of Painters in Water-Colours		TN	Tennessee
RIBA	Royal Institute of British Architects		TNT	trinitrotoluene
RIN	Royal Indian Navy		trans.	translated / translated by / translation / translator
RM	Reichsmark		TT	tourist trophy
RMS	Royal Mail steamer		TUC	Trades Union Congress
RN	Royal Navy		TX	Texas
RNA	ribonucleic acid		U-boat	*Unterseeboot*: submarine
RNAS	Royal Naval Air Service		Ufa	Universum-Film AG
RNR	Royal Naval Reserve		UMIST	University of Manchester Institute of Science and Technology
RNVR	Royal Naval Volunteer Reserve		UN	United Nations
RO	Record Office		UNESCO	United Nations Educational, Scientific, and Cultural Organization
r.p.m.	revolutions per minute			
RRS	royal research ship		UNICEF	United Nations International Children's Emergency Fund
Rs	rupees			
RSA	(1) Royal Scottish Academician; (2) Royal Society of Arts		unpubd	unpublished
			USS	United States ship
RSPCA	Royal Society for the Prevention of Cruelty to Animals		UT	Utah
			v	verso
Rt Hon.	Right Honourable		v.	versus
Rt Revd	Right Reverend		VA	Virginia
RUC	Royal Ulster Constabulary		VAD	Voluntary Aid Detachment
Russ.	Russian		VC	Victoria Cross
RWS	Royal Watercolour Society		VE-day	victory in Europe day
S4C	Sianel Pedwar Cymru		Ven.	Venerable
s.	shilling(s)		VJ-day	victory over Japan day
s.a.	*sub anno*: under the year		vol. *pl.* vols.	volume(s)
SABC	South African Broadcasting Corporation		VT	Vermont
SAS	Special Air Service		WA	Washington [state]
SC	South Carolina		WAAC	Women's Auxiliary Army Corps
ScD	doctor of science		WAAF	Women's Auxiliary Air Force
S$	Singapore dollar		WEA	Workers' Educational Association
SD	South Dakota		WHO	World Health Organization
sec.	second(s)		WI	Wisconsin
sel.	selected		WRAF	Women's Royal Air Force
sen.	senior		WRNS	Women's Royal Naval Service
Sept	September		WV	West Virginia
ser.	series		WVS	Women's Voluntary Service
SHAPE	supreme headquarters allied powers, Europe		WY	Wyoming
SIDRO	Société Internationale d'Énergie Hydro-Électrique		¥	yen
			YMCA	Young Men's Christian Association
sig. *pl.* sigs.	signature(s)		YWCA	Young Women's Christian Association
sing.	singular			
SIS	Secret Intelligence Service			
SJ	Society of Jesus			

2 Institution abbreviations

All Souls Oxf.	All Souls College, Oxford
AM Oxf.	Ashmolean Museum, Oxford
Balliol Oxf.	Balliol College, Oxford
BBC WAC	BBC Written Archives Centre, Reading
Beds. & Luton ARS	Bedfordshire and Luton Archives and Record Service, Bedford
Berks. RO	Berkshire Record Office, Reading
BFI	British Film Institute, London
BFI NFTVA	British Film Institute, London, National Film and Television Archive
BGS	British Geological Survey, Keyworth, Nottingham
Birm. CA	Birmingham Central Library, Birmingham City Archives
Birm. CL	Birmingham Central Library
BL	British Library, London
BL NSA	British Library, London, National Sound Archive
BL OIOC	British Library, London, Oriental and India Office Collections
BLPES	London School of Economics and Political Science, British Library of Political and Economic Science
BM	British Museum, London
Bodl. Oxf.	Bodleian Library, Oxford
Bodl. RH	Bodleian Library of Commonwealth and African Studies at Rhodes House, Oxford
Borth. Inst.	Borthwick Institute of Historical Research, University of York
Boston PL	Boston Public Library, Massachusetts
Bristol RO	Bristol Record Office
Bucks. RLSS	Buckinghamshire Records and Local Studies Service, Aylesbury
CAC Cam.	Churchill College, Cambridge, Churchill Archives Centre
Cambs. AS	Cambridgeshire Archive Service
CCC Cam.	Corpus Christi College, Cambridge
CCC Oxf.	Corpus Christi College, Oxford
Ches. & Chester ALSS	Cheshire and Chester Archives and Local Studies Service
Christ Church Oxf.	Christ Church, Oxford
Christies	Christies, London
City Westm. AC	City of Westminster Archives Centre, London
CKS	Centre for Kentish Studies, Maidstone
CLRO	Corporation of London Records Office
Coll. Arms	College of Arms, London
Col. U.	Columbia University, New York
Cornwall RO	Cornwall Record Office, Truro
Courtauld Inst.	Courtauld Institute of Art, London
CUL	Cambridge University Library
Cumbria AS	Cumbria Archive Service
Derbys. RO	Derbyshire Record Office, Matlock
Devon RO	Devon Record Office, Exeter
Dorset RO	Dorset Record Office, Dorchester
Duke U.	Duke University, Durham, North Carolina
Duke U., Perkins L.	Duke University, Durham, North Carolina, William R. Perkins Library
Durham Cath. CL	Durham Cathedral, chapter library
Durham RO	Durham Record Office
DWL	Dr Williams's Library, London
Essex RO	Essex Record Office
E. Sussex RO	East Sussex Record Office, Lewes
Eton	Eton College, Berkshire
FM Cam.	Fitzwilliam Museum, Cambridge
Folger	Folger Shakespeare Library, Washington, DC

Garr. Club	Garrick Club, London
Girton Cam.	Girton College, Cambridge
GL	Guildhall Library, London
Glos. RO	Gloucestershire Record Office, Gloucester
Gon. & Caius Cam.	Gonville and Caius College, Cambridge
Gov. Art Coll.	Government Art Collection
GS Lond.	Geological Society of London
Hants. RO	Hampshire Record Office, Winchester
Harris Man. Oxf.	Harris Manchester College, Oxford
Harvard TC	Harvard Theatre Collection, Harvard University, Cambridge, Massachusetts, Nathan Marsh Pusey Library
Harvard U.	Harvard University, Cambridge, Massachusetts
Harvard U., Houghton L.	Harvard University, Cambridge, Massachusetts, Houghton Library
Herefs. RO	Herefordshire Record Office, Hereford
Herts. ALS	Hertfordshire Archives and Local Studies, Hertford
Hist. Soc. Penn.	Historical Society of Pennsylvania, Philadelphia
HLRO	House of Lords Record Office, London
Hult. Arch.	Hulton Archive, London and New York
Hunt. L.	Huntington Library, San Marino, California
ICL	Imperial College, London
Inst. CE	Institution of Civil Engineers, London
Inst. EE	Institution of Electrical Engineers, London
IWM	Imperial War Museum, London
IWM FVA	Imperial War Museum, London, Film and Video Archive
IWM SA	Imperial War Museum, London, Sound Archive
JRL	John Rylands University Library of Manchester
King's AC Cam.	King's College Archives Centre, Cambridge
King's Cam.	King's College, Cambridge
King's Lond.	King's College, London
King's Lond., Liddell Hart C.	King's College, London, Liddell Hart Centre for Military Archives
Lancs. RO	Lancashire Record Office, Preston
L. Cong.	Library of Congress, Washington, DC
Leics. RO	Leicestershire, Leicester, and Rutland Record Office, Leicester
Lincs. Arch.	Lincolnshire Archives, Lincoln
Linn. Soc.	Linnean Society of London
LMA	London Metropolitan Archives
LPL	Lambeth Palace, London
Lpool RO	Liverpool Record Office and Local Studies Service
LUL	London University Library
Magd. Cam.	Magdalene College, Cambridge
Magd. Oxf.	Magdalen College, Oxford
Man. City Gall.	Manchester City Galleries
Man. CL	Manchester Central Library
Mass. Hist. Soc.	Massachusetts Historical Society, Boston
Merton Oxf.	Merton College, Oxford
MHS Oxf.	Museum of the History of Science, Oxford
Mitchell L., Glas.	Mitchell Library, Glasgow
Mitchell L., NSW	State Library of New South Wales, Sydney, Mitchell Library
Morgan L.	Pierpont Morgan Library, New York
NA Canada	National Archives of Canada, Ottawa
NA Ire.	National Archives of Ireland, Dublin
NAM	National Army Museum, London
NA Scot.	National Archives of Scotland, Edinburgh
News Int. RO	News International Record Office, London
NG Ire.	National Gallery of Ireland, Dublin

NG Scot.	National Gallery of Scotland, Edinburgh
NHM	Natural History Museum, London
NL Aus.	National Library of Australia, Canberra
NL Ire.	National Library of Ireland, Dublin
NL NZ	National Library of New Zealand, Wellington
NL NZ, Turnbull L.	National Library of New Zealand, Wellington, Alexander Turnbull Library
NL Scot.	National Library of Scotland, Edinburgh
NL Wales	National Library of Wales, Aberystwyth
NMG Wales	National Museum and Gallery of Wales, Cardiff
NMM	National Maritime Museum, London
Norfolk RO	Norfolk Record Office, Norwich
Northants. RO	Northamptonshire Record Office, Northampton
Northumbd RO	Northumberland Record Office
Notts. Arch.	Nottinghamshire Archives, Nottingham
NPG	National Portrait Gallery, London
NRA	National Archives, London, Historical Manuscripts Commission, National Register of Archives
Nuffield Oxf.	Nuffield College, Oxford
N. Yorks. CRO	North Yorkshire County Record Office, Northallerton
NYPL	New York Public Library
Oxf. UA	Oxford University Archives
Oxf. U. Mus. NH	Oxford University Museum of Natural History
Oxon. RO	Oxfordshire Record Office, Oxford
Pembroke Cam.	Pembroke College, Cambridge
PRO	National Archives, London, Public Record Office
PRO NIre.	Public Record Office for Northern Ireland, Belfast
Pusey Oxf.	Pusey House, Oxford
RA	Royal Academy of Arts, London
Ransom HRC	Harry Ransom Humanities Research Center, University of Texas, Austin
RAS	Royal Astronomical Society, London
RBG Kew	Royal Botanic Gardens, Kew, London
RCP Lond.	Royal College of Physicians of London
RCS Eng.	Royal College of Surgeons of England, London
RGS	Royal Geographical Society, London
RIBA	Royal Institute of British Architects, London
RIBA BAL	Royal Institute of British Architects, London, British Architectural Library
Royal Arch.	Royal Archives, Windsor Castle, Berkshire [by gracious permission of her majesty the queen]
Royal Irish Acad.	Royal Irish Academy, Dublin
Royal Scot. Acad.	Royal Scottish Academy, Edinburgh
RS	Royal Society, London
RSA	Royal Society of Arts, London
RS Friends, Lond.	Religious Society of Friends, London
St Ant. Oxf.	St Antony's College, Oxford
St John Cam.	St John's College, Cambridge
S. Antiquaries, Lond.	Society of Antiquaries of London
Sci. Mus.	Science Museum, London
Scot. NPG	Scottish National Portrait Gallery, Edinburgh
Scott Polar RI	University of Cambridge, Scott Polar Research Institute
Sheff. Arch.	Sheffield Archives
Shrops. RRC	Shropshire Records and Research Centre, Shrewsbury
SOAS	School of Oriental and African Studies, London
Som. ARS	Somerset Archive and Record Service, Taunton
Staffs. RO	Staffordshire Record Office, Stafford

Suffolk RO	Suffolk Record Office
Surrey HC	Surrey History Centre, Woking
TCD	Trinity College, Dublin
Trinity Cam.	Trinity College, Cambridge
U. Aberdeen	University of Aberdeen
U. Birm.	University of Birmingham
U. Birm. L.	University of Birmingham Library
U. Cal.	University of California
U. Cam.	University of Cambridge
UCL	University College, London
U. Durham	University of Durham
U. Durham L.	University of Durham Library
U. Edin.	University of Edinburgh
U. Edin., New Coll.	University of Edinburgh, New College
U. Edin., New Coll. L.	University of Edinburgh, New College Library
U. Edin. L.	University of Edinburgh Library
U. Glas.	University of Glasgow
U. Glas. L.	University of Glasgow Library
U. Hull	University of Hull
U. Hull, Brynmor Jones L.	University of Hull, Brynmor Jones Library
U. Leeds	University of Leeds
U. Leeds, Brotherton L.	University of Leeds, Brotherton Library
U. Lond.	University of London
U. Lpool	University of Liverpool
U. Lpool L.	University of Liverpool Library
U. Mich.	University of Michigan, Ann Arbor
U. Mich., Clements L.	University of Michigan, Ann Arbor, William L. Clements Library
U. Newcastle	University of Newcastle upon Tyne
U. Newcastle, Robinson L.	University of Newcastle upon Tyne, Robinson Library
U. Nott.	University of Nottingham
U. Nott. L.	University of Nottingham Library
U. Oxf.	University of Oxford
U. Reading	University of Reading
U. Reading L.	University of Reading Library
U. St Andr.	University of St Andrews
U. St Andr. L.	University of St Andrews Library
U. Southampton	University of Southampton
U. Southampton L.	University of Southampton Library
U. Sussex	University of Sussex, Brighton
U. Texas	University of Texas, Austin
U. Wales	University of Wales
U. Warwick Mod. RC	University of Warwick, Coventry, Modern Records Centre
V&A	Victoria and Albert Museum, London
V&A NAL	Victoria and Albert Museum, London, National Art Library
Warks. CRO	Warwickshire County Record Office, Warwick
Wellcome L.	Wellcome Library for the History and Understanding of Medicine, London
Westm. DA	Westminster Diocesan Archives, London
Wilts. & Swindon RO	Wiltshire and Swindon Record Office, Trowbridge
Worcs. RO	Worcestershire Record Office, Worcester
W. Sussex RO	West Sussex Record Office, Chichester
W. Yorks. AS	West Yorkshire Archive Service
Yale U.	Yale University, New Haven, Connecticut
Yale U., Beinecke L.	Yale University, New Haven, Connecticut, Beinecke Rare Book and Manuscript Library
Yale U. CBA	Yale University, New Haven, Connecticut, Yale Center for British Art

3 Bibliographic abbreviations

Adams, *Drama* — W. D. Adams, *A dictionary of the drama*, 1: *A–G* (1904); 2: *H–Z* (1956) [vol. 2 microfilm only]

AFM — J O'Donovan, ed. and trans., *Annala rioghachta Eireann | Annals of the kingdom of Ireland by the four masters*, 7 vols. (1848–51); 2nd edn (1856); 3rd edn (1990)

Allibone, *Dict.* — S. A. Allibone, *A critical dictionary of English literature and British and American authors*, 3 vols. (1859–71); suppl. by J. F. Kirk, 2 vols. (1891)

ANB — J. A. Garraty and M. C. Carnes, eds., *American national biography*, 24 vols. (1999)

Anderson, *Scot. nat.* — W. Anderson, *The Scottish nation, or, The surnames, families, literature, honours, and biographical history of the people of Scotland*, 3 vols. (1859–63)

Ann. mon. — H. R. Luard, ed., *Annales monastici*, 5 vols., Rolls Series, 36 (1864–9)

Ann. Ulster — S. Mac Airt and G. Mac Niocaill, eds., *Annals of Ulster (to AD 1131)* (1983)

APC — *Acts of the privy council of England*, new ser., 46 vols. (1890–1964)

APS — *The acts of the parliaments of Scotland*, 12 vols. in 13 (1814–75)

Arber, *Regs. Stationers* — F. Arber, ed., *A transcript of the registers of the Company of Stationers of London, 1554–1640 AD*, 5 vols. (1875–94)

ArchR — *Architectural Review*

ASC — D. Whitelock, D. C. Douglas, and S. I. Tucker, ed. and trans., *The Anglo-Saxon Chronicle: a revised translation* (1961)

AS chart. — P. H. Sawyer, *Anglo-Saxon charters: an annotated list and bibliography*, Royal Historical Society Guides and Handbooks (1968)

AusDB — D. Pike and others, eds., *Australian dictionary of biography*, 16 vols. (1966–2002)

Baker, *Serjeants* — J. H. Baker, *The order of serjeants at law*, SeldS, suppl. ser. 5 (1984)

Bale, *Cat.* — J. Bale, *Scriptorum illustrium Maioris Brytannie, quam nunc Angliam et Scotiam vocant: catalogus*, 2 vols. in 1 (Basel, 1557–9); facs. edn (1971)

Bale, *Index* — J. Bale, *Index Britanniae scriptorum*, ed. R. L. Poole and M. Bateson (1902); facs. edn (1990)

BBCS — *Bulletin of the Board of Celtic Studies*

BDMBR — J. O. Baylen and N. J. Gossman, eds., *Biographical dictionary of modern British radicals*, 3 vols. in 4 (1979–88)

Bede, *Hist. eccl.* — *Bede's Ecclesiastical history of the English people*, ed. and trans. B. Colgrave and R. A. B. Mynors, OMT (1969); repr. (1991)

Bénézit, *Dict.* — E. Bénézit, *Dictionnaire critique et documentaire des peintres, sculpteurs, dessinateurs et graveurs*, 3 vols. (Paris, 1911–23); new edn, 8 vols. (1948–66), repr. (1966); 3rd edn, rev. and enl., 10 vols. (1976); 4th edn, 14 vols. (1999)

BIHR — *Bulletin of the Institute of Historical Research*

Birch, *Seals* — W. de Birch, *Catalogue of seals in the department of manuscripts in the British Museum*, 6 vols. (1887–1900)

Bishop Burnet's History — *Bishop Burnet's History of his own time*, ed. M. J. Routh, 2nd edn, 6 vols. (1833)

Blackwood — *Blackwood's [Edinburgh] Magazine*, 328 vols. (1817–1980)

Blain, Clements & Grundy, *Feminist comp.* — V. Blain, P. Clements, and I. Grundy, eds., *The feminist companion to literature in English* (1990)

BL cat. — *The British Library general catalogue of printed books* [in 360 vols. with suppls., also CD-ROM and online]

BMJ — *British Medical Journal*

Boase & Courtney, *Bibl. Corn.* — G. C. Boase and W. P. Courtney, *Bibliotheca Cornubiensis: a catalogue of the writings … of Cornishmen*, 3 vols. (1874–82)

Boase, *Mod. Eng. biog.* — F. Boase, *Modern English biography: containing many thousand concise memoirs of persons who have died since the year 1850*, 6 vols. (privately printed, Truro, 1892–1921); repr. (1965)

Boswell, *Life* — *Boswell's Life of Johnson: together with Journal of a tour to the Hebrides and Johnson's Diary of a journey into north Wales*, ed. G. B. Hill, enl. edn, rev. L. F. Powell, 6 vols. (1934–50); 2nd edn (1964); repr. (1971)

Brown & Stratton, *Brit. mus.* — J. D. Brown and S. S. Stratton, *British musical biography* (1897)

Bryan, *Painters* — M. Bryan, *A biographical and critical dictionary of painters and engravers*, 2 vols. (1816); new edn, ed. G. Stanley (1849); new edn, ed. R. E. Graves and W. Armstrong, 2 vols. (1886–9); [4th edn], ed. G. C. Williamson, 5 vols. (1903–5) [various reprs.]

Burke, *Gen. GB* — J. Burke, *A genealogical and heraldic history of the commoners of Great Britain and Ireland*, 4 vols. (1833–8); new edn as *A genealogical and heraldic dictionary of the landed gentry of Great Britain and Ireland*, 3 vols. [1843–9] [many later edns]

Burke, *Gen. Ire.* — J. B. Burke, *A genealogical and heraldic history of the landed gentry of Ireland* (1899); 2nd edn (1904); 3rd edn (1912); 4th edn (1958); 5th edn as *Burke's Irish family records* (1976)

Burke, *Peerage* — J. Burke, *A general [later edns A genealogical] and heraldic dictionary of the peerage and baronetage of the United Kingdom [later edns the British empire]* (1829–)

Burney, *Hist. mus.* — C. Burney, *A general history of music, from the earliest ages to the present period*, 4 vols. (1776–89)

Burtchaell & Sadleir, *Alum. Dubl.* — G. D. Burtchaell and T. U. Sadleir, *Alumni Dublinenses: a register of the students, graduates, and provosts of Trinity College* (1924); [2nd edn], with suppl., in 2 pts (1935)

Calamy rev. — A. G. Matthews, *Calamy revised* (1934); repr. (1988)

CCI — *Calendar of confirmations and inventories granted and given up in the several commissariots of Scotland* (1876–)

CCIR — *Calendar of the close rolls preserved in the Public Record Office*, 47 vols. (1892–1963)

CDS — J. Bain, ed., *Calendar of documents relating to Scotland*, 4 vols., PRO (1881–8); suppl. vol. 5, ed. G. G. Simpson and J. D. Galbraith [1986]

CEPR letters — W. H. Bliss, C. Johnson, and J. Twemlow, eds., *Calendar of entries in the papal registers relating to Great Britain and Ireland: papal letters* (1893–)

CGPLA — *Calendars of the grants of probate and letters of administration [in 4 ser.: England & Wales, Northern Ireland, Ireland, and Éire]*

Chambers, *Scots.* — R. Chambers, ed., *A biographical dictionary of eminent Scotsmen*, 4 vols. (1832–5)

Chancery records — chancery records pubd by the PRO

Chancery records (RC) — chancery records pubd by the Record Commissions

CIPM	Calendar of inquisitions post mortem, [20 vols.], PRO (1904–); also Henry VII, 3 vols. (1898–1955)
Clarendon, Hist. rebellion	E. Hyde, earl of Clarendon, The history of the rebellion and civil wars in England, 6 vols. (1888); repr. (1958) and (1992)
Cobbett, Parl. hist.	W. Cobbett and J. Wright, eds., Cobbett's Parliamentary history of England, 36 vols. (1806–1820)
Colvin, Archs.	H. Colvin, A biographical dictionary of British architects, 1600–1840, 3rd edn (1995)
Cooper, Ath. Cantab.	C. H. Cooper and T. Cooper, Athenae Cantabrigienses, 3 vols. (1858–1913); repr. (1967)
CPR	Calendar of the patent rolls preserved in the Public Record Office (1891–)
Crockford	Crockford's Clerical Directory
CS	Camden Society
CSP	Calendar of state papers [in 11 ser.: domestic, Scotland, Scottish series, Ireland, colonial, Commonwealth, foreign, Spain [at Simancas], Rome, Milan, and Venice]
CYS	Canterbury and York Society
DAB	Dictionary of American biography, 21 vols. (1928–36), repr. in 11 vols. (1964); 10 suppls. (1944–96)
DBB	D. J. Jeremy, ed., Dictionary of business biography, 5 vols. (1984–6)
DCB	G. W. Brown and others, Dictionary of Canadian biography, [14 vols.] (1966–)
Debrett's Peerage	Debrett's Peerage (1803–) [sometimes Debrett's Illustrated peerage]
Desmond, Botanists	R. Desmond, Dictionary of British and Irish botanists and horticulturists (1977); rev. edn (1994)
Dir. Brit. archs.	A. Felstead, J. Franklin, and L. Pinfield, eds., Directory of British architects, 1834–1900 (1993); 2nd edn, ed. A. Brodie and others, 2 vols. (2001)
DLB	J. M. Bellamy and J. Saville, eds., Dictionary of labour biography, [10 vols.] (1972–)
DLitB	Dictionary of Literary Biography
DNB	Dictionary of national biography, 63 vols. (1885–1900), suppl., 3 vols. (1901); repr. in 22 vols. (1908–9); 10 further suppls. (1912–96); Missing persons (1993)
DNZB	W. H. Oliver and C. Orange, eds., The dictionary of New Zealand biography, 5 vols. (1990–2000)
DSAB	W. J. de Kock and others, eds., Dictionary of South African biography, 5 vols. (1968–87)
DSB	C. C. Gillispie and F. L. Holmes, eds., Dictionary of scientific biography, 16 vols. (1970–80); repr. in 8 vols. (1981); 2 vol. suppl. (1990)
DSBB	A. Slaven and S. Checkland, eds., Dictionary of Scottish business biography, 1860–1960, 2 vols. (1986–90)
DSCHT	N. M. de S. Cameron and others, eds., Dictionary of Scottish church history and theology (1993)
Dugdale, Monasticon	W. Dugdale, Monasticon Anglicanum, 3 vols. (1655–72); 2nd edn, 3 vols. (1661–82); new edn, ed. J. Caley, J. Ellis, and B. Bandinel, 6 vols. in 8 pts (1817–30); repr. (1846) and (1970)
DWB	J. E. Lloyd and others, eds., Dictionary of Welsh biography down to 1940 (1959) [Eng. trans. of Y bywgraffiadur Cymreig hyd 1940, 2nd edn (1954)]
EdinR	Edinburgh Review, or, Critical Journal
EETS	Early English Text Society
Emden, Cam.	A. B. Emden, A biographical register of the University of Cambridge to 1500 (1963)
Emden, Oxf.	A. B. Emden, A biographical register of the University of Oxford to AD 1500, 3 vols. (1957–9); also A biographical register of the University of Oxford, AD 1501 to 1540 (1974)
EngHR	English Historical Review
Engraved Brit. ports.	F. M. O'Donoghue and H. M. Hake, Catalogue of engraved British portraits preserved in the department of prints and drawings in the British Museum, 6 vols. (1908–25)
ER	The English Reports, 178 vols. (1900–32)
ESTC	English short title catalogue, 1475–1800 [CD-ROM and online]
Evelyn, Diary	The diary of John Evelyn, ed. E. S. De Beer, 6 vols. (1955); repr. (2000)
Farington, Diary	The diary of Joseph Farington, ed. K. Garlick and others, 17 vols. (1978–98)
Fasti Angl. (Hardy)	J. Le Neve, Fasti ecclesiae Anglicanae, ed. T. D. Hardy, 3 vols. (1854)
Fasti Angl., 1066–1300	[J. Le Neve], Fasti ecclesiae Anglicanae, 1066–1300, ed. D. E. Greenway and J. S. Barrow, [8 vols.] (1968–)
Fasti Angl., 1300–1541	[J. Le Neve], Fasti ecclesiae Anglicanae, 1300–1541, 12 vols. (1962–7)
Fasti Angl., 1541–1857	[J. Le Neve], Fasti ecclesiae Anglicanae, 1541–1857, ed. J. M. Horn, D. M. Smith, and D. S. Bailey, [9 vols.] (1969–)
Fasti Scot.	H. Scott, Fasti ecclesiae Scoticanae, 3 vols. in 6 (1871); new edn, [11 vols.] (1915–)
FO List	Foreign Office List
Fortescue, Brit. army	J. W. Fortescue, A history of the British army, 13 vols. (1899–1930)
Foss, Judges	E. Foss, The judges of England, 9 vols. (1848–64); repr. (1966)
Foster, Alum. Oxon.	J. Foster, ed., Alumni Oxonienses: the members of the University of Oxford, 1715–1886, 4 vols. (1887–8); later edn (1891); also Alumni Oxonienses … 1500–1714, 4 vols. (1891–2); 8 vol. repr. (1968) and (2000)
Fuller, Worthies	T. Fuller, The history of the worthies of England, 4 pts (1662); new edn, 2 vols., ed. J. Nichols (1811); new edn, 3 vols., ed. P. A. Nuttall (1840); repr. (1965)
GEC, Baronetage	G. E. Cokayne, Complete baronetage, 6 vols. (1900–09); repr. (1983) [microprint]
GEC, Peerage	G. E. C. [G. E. Cokayne], The complete peerage of England, Scotland, Ireland, Great Britain, and the United Kingdom, 8 vols. (1887–98); new edn, ed. V. Gibbs and others, 14 vols. in 15 (1910–98); microprint repr. (1982) and (1987)
Genest, Eng. stage	J. Genest, Some account of the English stage from the Restoration in 1660 to 1830, 10 vols. (1832); repr. [New York, 1965]
Gillow, Lit. biog. hist.	J. Gillow, A literary and biographical history or bibliographical dictionary of the English Catholics, from the breach with Rome, in 1534, to the present time, 5 vols. [1885–1902]; repr. (1961); repr. with preface by C. Gillow (1999)
Gir. Camb. opera	Giraldi Cambrensis opera, ed. J. S. Brewer, J. F. Dimock, and G. F. Warner, 8 vols., Rolls Series, 21 (1861–91)
GJ	Geographical Journal

Gladstone, *Diaries* | *The Gladstone diaries: with cabinet minutes and prime-ministerial correspondence*, ed. M. R. D. Foot and H. C. G. Matthew, 14 vols. (1968–94)

GM | *Gentleman's Magazine*

Graves, *Artists* | A. Graves, ed., *A dictionary of artists who have exhibited works in the principal London exhibitions of oil paintings from 1760 to 1880* (1884); new edn (1895); 3rd edn (1901); facs. edn (1969); repr. [1970], (1973), and (1984)

Graves, *Brit. Inst.* | A. Graves, *The British Institution, 1806–1867: a complete dictionary of contributors and their work from the foundation of the institution* (1875); facs. edn (1908); repr. (1969)

Graves, *RA exhibitors* | A. Graves, *The Royal Academy of Arts: a complete dictionary of contributors and their work from its foundation in 1769 to 1904*, 8 vols. (1905–6); repr. in 4 vols. (1970) and (1972)

Graves, *Soc. Artists* | A. Graves, *The Society of Artists of Great Britain, 1760–1791, the Free Society of Artists, 1761–1783: a complete dictionary* (1907); facs. edn (1969)

Greaves & Zaller, *BDBR* | R. L. Greaves and R. Zaller, eds., *Biographical dictionary of British radicals in the seventeenth century*, 3 vols. (1982–4)

Grove, *Dict. mus.* | G. Grove, ed., *A dictionary of music and musicians*, 5 vols. (1878–90); 2nd edn, ed. J. A. Fuller Maitland (1904–10); 3rd edn, ed. H. C. Colles (1927); 4th edn with suppl. (1940); 5th edn, ed. E. Blom, 9 vols. (1954); suppl. (1961) [see also *New Grove*]

Hall, *Dramatic ports.* | L. A. Hall, *Catalogue of dramatic portraits in the theatre collection of the Harvard College library*, 4 vols. (1930–34)

Hansard | *Hansard's parliamentary debates*, ser. 1–5 (1803–)

Highfill, Burnim & Langhans, *BDA* | P. H. Highfill, K. A. Burnim, and E. A. Langhans, *A biographical dictionary of actors, actresses, musicians, dancers, managers, and other stage personnel in London, 1660–1800*, 16 vols. (1973–93)

Hist. U. Oxf. | T. H. Aston, ed., *The history of the University of Oxford*, 8 vols. (1984–2000) [1: *The early Oxford schools*, ed. J. I. Catto (1984); 2: *Late medieval Oxford*, ed. J. I. Catto and R. Evans (1992); 3: *The collegiate university*, ed. J. McConica (1986); 4: *Seventeenth-century Oxford*, ed. N. Tyacke (1997); 5: *The eighteenth century*, ed. L. S. Sutherland and L. G. Mitchell (1986); 6–7: *Nineteenth-century Oxford*, ed. M. G. Brock and M. C. Curthoys (1997–2000); 8: *The twentieth century*, ed. B. Harrison (2000)]

HJ | *Historical Journal*

HMC | Historical Manuscripts Commission

Holdsworth, *Eng. law* | W. S. Holdsworth, *A history of English law*, ed. A. L. Goodhart and H. L. Hanbury, 17 vols. (1903–72)

HoP, *Commons* | *The history of parliament: the House of Commons* [*1386–1421*, ed. J. S. Roskell, L. Clark, and C. Rawcliffe, 4 vols. (1992); *1509–1558*, ed. S. T. Bindoff, 3 vols. (1982); *1558–1603*, ed. P. W. Hasler, 3 vols. (1981); *1660–1690*, ed. B. D. Henning, 3 vols. (1983); *1690–1715*, ed. D. W. Hayton, E. Cruickshanks, and S. Handley, 5 vols. (2002); *1715–1754*, ed. R. Sedgwick, 2 vols. (1970); *1754–1790*, ed. L. Namier and J. Brooke, 3 vols. (1964), repr. (1985); *1790–1820*, ed. R. G. Thorne, 5 vols. (1986); in draft (used with permission): *1422–1504*, *1604–1629*, *1640–1660*, and *1820–1832*]

IGI | *International Genealogical Index*, Church of Jesus Christ of the Latterday Saints

ILN | *Illustrated London News*

IMC | Irish Manuscripts Commission

Irving, *Scots.* | J. Irving, ed., *The book of Scotsmen eminent for achievements in arms and arts, church and state, law, legislation and literature, commerce, science, travel and philanthropy* (1881)

JCS | *Journal of the Chemical Society*

JHC | *Journals of the House of Commons*

JHL | *Journals of the House of Lords*

John of Worcester, *Chron.* | *The chronicle of John of Worcester*, ed. R. R. Darlington and P. McGurk, trans. J. Bray and P. McGurk, 3 vols., OMT (1995–) [vol. 1 forthcoming]

Keeler, *Long Parliament* | M. F. Keeler, *The Long Parliament, 1640–1641: a biographical study of its members* (1954)

Kelly, *Handbk* | *The upper ten thousand: an alphabetical list of all members of noble families*, 3 vols. (1875–7); continued as *Kelly's handbook of the upper ten thousand for 1878* [1879], 2 vols. (1878–9); continued as *Kelly's handbook to the titled, landed and official classes*, 94 vols. (1880–1973)

LondG | *London Gazette*

LP Henry VIII | J. S. Brewer, J. Gairdner, and R. H. Brodie, eds., *Letters and papers, foreign and domestic, of the reign of Henry VIII*, 23 vols. in 38 (1862–1932); repr. (1965)

Mallalieu, *Watercolour artists* | H. L. Mallalieu, *The dictionary of British watercolour artists up to 1820*, 3 vols. (1976–90); vol. 1, 2nd edn (1986)

Memoirs FRS | *Biographical Memoirs of Fellows of the Royal Society*

MGH | Monumenta Germaniae Historica

MT | *Musical Times*

Munk, *Roll* | W. Munk, *The roll of the Royal College of Physicians of London*, 2 vols. (1861); 2nd edn, 3 vols. (1878)

N&Q | *Notes and Queries*

New Grove | S. Sadie, ed., *The new Grove dictionary of music and musicians*, 20 vols. (1980); 2nd edn, 29 vols. (2001) [also online edn; see also Grove, *Dict. mus.*]

Nichols, *Illustrations* | J. Nichols and J. B. Nichols, *Illustrations of the literary history of the eighteenth century*, 8 vols. (1817–58)

Nichols, *Lit. anecdotes* | J. Nichols, *Literary anecdotes of the eighteenth century*, 9 vols. (1812–16); facs. edn (1966)

Obits. FRS | *Obituary Notices of Fellows of the Royal Society*

O'Byrne, *Naval biog. dict.* | W. R. O'Byrne, *A naval biographical dictionary* (1849); repr. (1990); [2nd edn], 2 vols. (1861)

OHS | Oxford Historical Society

Old Westminsters | *The record of Old Westminsters*, 1–2, ed. G. F. R. Barker and A. H. Stenning (1928); suppl. 1, ed. J. B. Whitmore and G. R. Y. Radcliffe [1938]; 3, ed. J. B. Whitmore, G. R. Y. Radcliffe, and D. C. Simpson (1963); suppl. 2, ed. F. E. Pagan (1978); 4, ed. F. E. Pagan and H. E. Pagan (1992)

OMT | Oxford Medieval Texts

Ordericus Vitalis, *Eccl. hist.* | *The ecclesiastical history of Orderic Vitalis*, ed. and trans. M. Chibnall, 6 vols., OMT (1969–80); repr. (1990)

Paris, *Chron.* | *Matthaei Parisiensis, monachi sancti Albani, chronica majora*, ed. H. R. Luard, Rolls Series, 7 vols. (1872–83)

Parl. papers | *Parliamentary papers* (1801–)

PBA | *Proceedings of the British Academy*

Pepys, *Diary* — The diary of Samuel Pepys, ed. R. Latham and W. Matthews, 11 vols. (1970–83); repr. (1995) and (2000)

Pevsner — N. Pevsner and others, Buildings of England series

PICE — *Proceedings of the Institution of Civil Engineers*

Pipe rolls — *The great roll of the pipe for . . .*, PRSoc. (1884–)

PRO — Public Record Office

PRS — *Proceedings of the Royal Society of London*

PRSoc. — Pipe Roll Society

PTRS — *Philosophical Transactions of the Royal Society*

QR — *Quarterly Review*

RC — Record Commissions

Redgrave, *Artists* — S. Redgrave, *A dictionary of artists of the English school* (1874); rev. edn (1878); repr. (1970)

Reg. Oxf. — C. W. Boase and A. Clark, eds., *Register of the University of Oxford*, 5 vols., OHS, 1, 10–12, 14 (1885–9)

Reg. PCS — J. H. Burton and others, eds., *The register of the privy council of Scotland*, 1st ser., 14 vols. (1877–98); 2nd ser., 8 vols. (1899–1908); 3rd ser., [16 vols.] (1908–70)

Reg. RAN — H. W. C. Davis and others, eds., *Regesta regum Anglo-Normannorum, 1066–1154*, 4 vols. (1913–69)

RIBA Journal — *Journal of the Royal Institute of British Architects* [later *RIBA Journal*]

RotP — J. Strachey, ed., *Rotuli parliamentorum ut et petitiones, et placita in parliamento*, 6 vols. (1767–77)

RotS — D. Macpherson, J. Caley, and W. Illingworth, eds., *Rotuli Scotiae in Turri Londinensi et in domo capitulari Westmonasteriensi asservati*, 2 vols., RC, 14 (1814–19)

RS — Record(s) Society

Rymer, *Foedera* — T. Rymer and R. Sanderson, eds., *Foedera, conventiones, literae et cuiuscunque generis acta publica inter reges Angliae et alios quosvis imperatores, reges, pontifices, principes, vel communitates*, 20 vols. (1704–35); 2nd edn, 20 vols. (1726–35); 3rd edn, 10 vols. (1739–45), facs. edn (1967); new edn, ed. A. Clarke, J. Caley, and F. Holbrooke, 4 vols., RC, 50 (1816–30)

Sainty, *Judges* — J. Sainty, ed., *The judges of England, 1272–1990*, SeldS, suppl. ser., 10 (1993)

Sainty, *King's counsel* — J. Sainty, ed., *A list of English law officers and king's counsel*, SeldS, suppl. ser., 7 (1987)

SCH — Studies in Church History

Scots peerage — J. B. Paul, ed. *The Scots peerage, founded on Wood's edition of Sir Robert Douglas's Peerage of Scotland, containing an historical and genealogical account of the nobility of that kingdom*, 9 vols. (1904–14)

SeldS — Selden Society

SHR — *Scottish Historical Review*

State trials — T. B. Howell and T. J. Howell, eds., *Cobbett's Complete collection of state trials*, 34 vols. (1809–28)

STC, 1475–1640 — A. W. Pollard, G. R. Redgrave, and others, eds., *A short-title catalogue of . . . English books . . . 1475–1640* (1926); 2nd edn, ed. W. A. Jackson, F. S. Ferguson, and K. F. Pantzer, 3 vols. (1976–91) [see also Wing, *STC*]

STS — Scottish Text Society

SurtS — Surtees Society

Symeon of Durham, *Opera* — *Symeonis monachi opera omnia*, ed. T. Arnold, 2 vols., Rolls Series, 75 (1882–5); repr. (1965)

Tanner, *Bibl. Brit.-Hib.* — T. Tanner, *Bibliotheca Britannico-Hibernica*, ed. D. Wilkins (1748); repr. (1963)

Thieme & Becker, *Allgemeines Lexikon* — U. Thieme, F. Becker, and H. Vollmer, eds., *Allgemeines Lexikon der bildenden Künstler von der Antike bis zur Gegenwart*, 37 vols. (Leipzig, 1907–50); repr. (1961–5), (1983), and (1992)

Thurloe, *State papers* — *A collection of the state papers of John Thurloe*, ed. T. Birch, 7 vols. (1742)

TLS — *Times Literary Supplement*

Tout, *Admin. hist.* — T. F. Tout, *Chapters in the administrative history of mediaeval England: the wardrobe, the chamber, and the small seals*, 6 vols. (1920–33); repr. (1967)

TRHS — *Transactions of the Royal Historical Society*

VCH — H. A. Doubleday and others, eds., *The Victoria history of the counties of England*, [88 vols.] (1900–)

Venn, *Alum. Cant.* — J. Venn and J. A. Venn, *Alumni Cantabrigienses: a biographical list of all known students, graduates, and holders of office at the University of Cambridge, from the earliest times to 1900*, 10 vols. (1922–54); repr. in 2 vols. (1974–8)

Vertue, *Note books* — [G. Vertue], *Note books*, ed. K. Esdaile, earl of Ilchester, and H. M. Hake, 6 vols., Walpole Society, 18, 20, 22, 24, 26, 30 (1930–55)

VF — *Vanity Fair*

Walford, *County families* — E. Walford, *The county families of the United Kingdom, or, Royal manual of the titled and untitled aristocracy of Great Britain and Ireland* (1860)

Walker rev. — A. G. Matthews, *Walker revised: being a revision of John Walker's Sufferings of the clergy during the grand rebellion, 1642–60* (1948); repr. (1988)

Walpole, *Corr.* — *The Yale edition of Horace Walpole's correspondence*, ed. W. S. Lewis, 48 vols. (1937–83)

Ward, *Men of the reign* — T. H. Ward, ed., *Men of the reign: a biographical dictionary of eminent persons of British and colonial birth who have died during the reign of Queen Victoria* (1885); repr. (Graz, 1968)

Waterhouse, *18c painters* — E. Waterhouse, *The dictionary of 18th century painters in oils and crayons* (1981); repr. as *British 18th century painters in oils and crayons* (1991), vol. 2 of *Dictionary of British art*

Watt, *Bibl. Brit.* — R. Watt, *Bibliotheca Britannica, or, A general index to British and foreign literature*, 4 vols. (1824) [many reprs.]

Wellesley index — W. E. Houghton, ed., *The Wellesley index to Victorian periodicals, 1824–1900*, 5 vols. (1966–89); new edn (1999) [CD-ROM]

Wing, *STC* — D. Wing, ed., *Short-title catalogue of . . . English books . . . 1641–1700*, 3 vols. (1945–51); 2nd edn (1972–88); rev. and enl. edn, ed. J. J. Morrison, C. W. Nelson, and M. Seccombe, 4 vols. (1994–8) [see also *STC, 1475–1640*]

Wisden — *John Wisden's Cricketer's Almanack*

Wood, *Ath. Oxon.* — A. Wood, *Athenae Oxonienses . . . to which are added the Fasti*, 2 vols. (1691–2); 2nd edn (1721); new edn, 4 vols., ed. P. Bliss (1813–20); repr. (1967) and (1969)

Wood, *Vic. painters* — C. Wood, *Dictionary of Victorian painters* (1971); 2nd edn (1978); 3rd edn as *Victorian painters*, 2 vols. (1995), vol. 4 of *Dictionary of British art*

WW — *Who's who* (1849–)

WWBMP — M. Stenton and S. Lees, eds., *Who's who of British members of parliament*, 4 vols. (1976–81)

WWW — *Who was who* (1929–)

Tonson, Jacob, the elder (1655/6–1736), bookseller, was born in London, the second son of Jacob Tonson (1620–1668), a barber surgeon, and his wife, Elizabeth Walbancke (*b.* 1631), whose brother was the bookseller Matthew Walbancke; Kathleen Lynch claims that he was baptized at St Andrew's, Holborn, on 12 November 1655. Little is known about Jacob's youth, but his later ease with Latin suggests he was given a good classical education. In 1668 his elder brother Richard (1653–*c.*1700) was apprenticed to the Walbancke firm, and on 6 June 1670 Jacob was apprenticed to the stationer Thomas Basset. Richard Tonson set up his own publishing firm in 1676, and Jacob did the same when he completed his apprenticeship on 7 January 1678. For some time, the brothers published books jointly, and in partnerships with other publishers. Jacob's first publication on his own was an undistinguished, anonymous fictional piece, *God's Revenge Against the Abominable Sin of Adultery* (1678).

Early publishing success Tonson, however, quickly moved to more important books when in 1679 he began publishing the works of John Dryden, soon becoming his exclusive publisher; *Absalom and Achitophel* (1681) was Tonson's first widely celebrated publication. He began to buy up the rights to Dryden's earlier works during the 1680s, and he also began publishing a wide range of the most important writers of the age, including Aphra Behn and the earl of Rochester. During these years Tonson also learned the power of publicity, and he was one of the first booksellers to advertise in the newspapers. This combination of shrewd business practices and first-rate literature soon made Tonsons the most prestigious place for authors to be published. By collecting and reprinting the works of authors like Dryden, he helped turn them into accepted modern classics.

Dryden and Tonson collaborated on a highly significant series of anthologies and compilations of translations. The first was Ovid's *Epistles* (1680), with translations by seventeen different hands; owing to Dryden's literary intelligence and Tonson's business sense, the book had far greater success than translations usually did, going through numerous editions. Between 1683 and 1686 (the year in which he became a liveryman of the Stationers' Company) Tonson and Dryden produced a five-volume set of Plutarch's *Lives*, which employed forty-two translators; it too sold very well, and went into later editions. In the mid-1680s about half Tonson's list consisted of translations; he and Dryden were creating a public taste for such work. Even more important, however, were the anthologies or miscellanies that the two devised. The first, *Miscellany Poems*, included Dryden's 'MacFlecknoe' as well as work by many other contemporary poets. The book's success led to sequels, and it is no exaggeration to say that Tonson created the modern anthology as a genre, one which also whetted the public's appetite for other works by the poets included. One such poet was Alexander Pope, whose first publication came in Tonson's sixth miscellany (1709); Tonson's anthologies guaranteed the poet, especially the young poet, a much wider audience than he might otherwise have been able to find.

Jacob Tonson the elder (1655/6–1736), by Sir Godfrey Kneller, 1717

Milton Another major author associated with Tonson was John Milton. Tonson read Milton's *Paradise Lost* when it was originally published in 1667. When Milton died in 1674, Tonson was still apprenticed to Basset, and he once spent his weekly free day—Sunday—going to the recently deceased poet's house in the hope of buying some books from his library. In 1683 Tonson purchased half the rights to the poem, and acquired the other half in 1690. *Paradise Lost* had had moderate success before Tonson, some 3000 copies having been printed, but it by no means occupied the place it does today in the canon of English literature. Tonson was highly instrumental in creating and nurturing an audience and an appreciation for the poem and for Milton, keeping the poet's reputation alive in a period dominated by a very different literary taste.

Tonson bought not only the rights to the poem but the first edition's corrected manuscript as well, indicating that he saw *Paradise Lost* as having serious, lasting literary value. He did not print the poem, however, until 1688—perhaps because the political atmosphere before that date would not have favoured the work of a puritan revolutionary poet. Tonson approached the 1688 edition with great care: he was careful about the text itself, consulting the three previous printings as well as Milton's manuscript, and making some important emendations. The book was printed, by subscription, in a large folio, with careful and attractive typography. Tonson also paid for illustrations by John Baptist Medina, which, together with the sumptuous look of the book, made a possibly daunting poem more immediately interesting and approachable. As a frontispiece, Tonson printed an engraving of Milton, with six lines by Dryden below it, designed to claim Milton as the great *English* poet, transcending his puritan times and deserving celebration by the new aesthetic and political regime. Tonson remained closely involved with Milton's works for the rest of his life, and in the famous Kneller portrait he is depicted holding the folio edition of *Paradise Lost*. He was protective not only of his copyright but of the quality of Milton's text, and he bitterly criticized an edition put out in the 1730s for its mangling of the poem. Much later in life, when he was asked what poet had made the most money for him, he replied, 'Milton'. There is no doubt that Tonson valued Milton for the money he could make, but it is also clear that he was committed to Milton's literary excellence, which he had perceived early on. Tonson's enthusiasm led him to continue to promote Milton, whom he printed in a variety of editions over the years. His edition of 1695 included scholarly annotations by Patrick Hume, effectively declaring Milton a permanent classic. It is not too much to say that Milton's literary reputation was in large part nurtured and ensured by Tonson's efforts.

Translating the classics After the revolution of 1688 Tonson's political sympathies turned increasingly whiggish, while his most famous living author, the Catholic and pro-Stuart Dryden, fell out of political favour. None the less, their relationship remained strong in the 1690s, though Dryden at least once complained of Tonson's stinginess. He sent Tonson a triplet that served as a threat of the sort of satire he could write if Tonson did not agree to his demands; the lines provide an interesting caricature portrait:

> With leering look, bull faced and freckled fair
> With frowsy pores poisoning the ambient air,
> With two left leggs, and Judas coloured hair.
> (*Poems of John Dryden*, 1766)

'Two left leggs' refers to Tonson's odd manner of walking; he had experienced trouble with his feet since his childhood. Later satirists used the image as well, referring to Tonson's shop as under the sign of two left feet. None the less, for all their occasional quarrelling, Dryden and Tonson remained on good terms.

Dryden continued to do translation work for Tonson. The translation of Juvenal and Persius (1693) ushered in the notion of translation as a kind of modernization, of making the translated author, as Dryden put it, 'speak that kind of *English*, which he wou'd have spoken had he liv'd in *England*, and Written to this Age' (*The Satires of Decimus Junius Juvenalis*, lii). Translation as imitation came to dominate English verse for the next couple of generations; the Persius and Juvenal volume again sold very well, with several succeeding editions. But the most important project Tonson and Dryden undertook was a translation of all of Virgil, first mentioned in 1694. Tonson paid Dryden £200 in advance, a very significant sum, and set about publicizing the work in advance. Using the experience of the Milton volume of 1688, Tonson found over 500 subscribers for the book, which appeared in June 1697 as one of the most eagerly awaited books of the season. The book is one of Tonson's finest achievements in terms of typography, layout, and illustrations (over 100 of them); Dryden added an essay on Virgil, and Joseph Addison contributed a brief introduction to each section. King William was one of the many looking forward to the book, and hinted that he would look favourably on its being dedicated to him, a suggestion that Dryden, naturally, found intolerable. But Tonson cleverly worked around the issue: he had some of his workmen alter the illustrations slightly so that Virgil's Aeneas resembled William. Tonson's main profits from the book came with later, cheaper reprints, but his gain in prestige as the country's finest publisher of literary works was beyond valuation.

The Kit-Cat Club After Dryden's death in 1700 Tonson printed many editions and collections of his works; as with Milton, Dryden's work was a matter of financial profit as well as something to be guarded and promoted for its high literary value. Tonson never abandoned Dryden, despite the political gulf that widened between them. Having become closely involved with the leading whigs during the 1680s, Tonson was a founding member of the Kit-Cat Club, which included virtually all the most powerful whig politicians from 1688 to 1710. An anonymous satire from 1704 calls Tonson the founder of the club, and it quickly became the best-known of the exclusive men's clubs, with much gossip circulating about its members and their doings. Tonson was evidently an enthusiastic and well-liked host, and was nicknamed Bocaj (Jacob backwards) in poems about the club. By 1703 the group had grown too large for Christopher Cat's tavern, and soon thereafter Tonson used the members' dues to build a special clubroom at his residence in Barn Elms, Surrey. Tonson commissioned Sir Godfrey Kneller to paint portraits of forty-eight of the Kit-Cats—including the dukes of Newcastle and Somerset, the earls of Dorset and Essex, and others including Cornwallis and Godolphin—as well as Tonson himself. The club included writers as well, such as Congreve, Addison, and Steele.

Robert Walpole once referred to the Kit-Cats as the men who had saved the kingdom, meaning that they had played a central role in establishing the Hanoverian succession. Tonson himself was never directly involved in politics, but he seems to have been respected by the other members, and it is possible that he at least gathered some intelligence for the group when he went to the continent to purchase paper and other printing necessities. Vanbrugh believed that Tonson secretly went to Hanover in 1703 to carry some messages, and he may have spied on Matthew Prior in France in 1714 when Prior was negotiating between the tory administration and the exiled Stuarts. If the latter is true, there was evidently no ill will between the two men, as Tonson went on to publish a luxurious edition of Prior's poems in 1718. But the exact extent of Tonson's involvement in any espionage remains, not surprisingly, uncertain. In any case, whatever political activity he involved himself in never got in the way of his continuing dedication to his publishing.

Tonson continued to publish plays including the most

popular play of the period, Addison's *Cato* (1713), for whose copyright he paid Addison the then astronomical sum of £107. Tonson spearheaded the Kit-Cats' efforts to fund the building of the new Queen's Theatre in Haymarket, London, as well as other projects, including one to encourage the production of better-quality plays. But the Kit-Cats, despite their cultural endeavours, became increasingly a group dedicated to party politics, and there were purges of anyone in any way connected with the tories. Their strong solidarity, with Tonson as host and organizer, produced some of the whigs' greatest triumphs, such as the Act of Settlement with the Regency (1701), which established the legal basis for the Hanoverian succession, and the Act of Union with Scotland (1707). When George I took the throne in 1714, he rewarded the club members generously; but without the binding pressure of being in opposition the group began to weaken, meeting less and less regularly. When Tonson made an extended trip to France in 1718–20, the club evaporated altogether.

Later publications Among Tonson's major publications during the Kit-Cat years is his great folio edition, in Latin, of the works of Julius Caesar; some nine years in the making, it finally appeared in 1712. No English publisher had ever produced so lavish a book before, with its careful scholarship (the texts were edited by Samuel Clarke), its numerous maps, and its eighty-seven engravings done in superb detail by Dutch artists. The book was dedicated to the duke of Marlborough, and had as its frontispiece Kneller's portrait of Marlborough. Again, this was published by subscription, and in this case Tonson arranged to have each subscriber's coat of arms printed on each double-plate page. He employed John Watts as printer for this edition, and the two worked together on several classical texts over the succeeding decade. In 1713, for instance, Tonson published editions of Lucretius, Terence, Justin, Salust, Pompey, and Aesop, and in 1714 an edition of the Greek New Testament. In the following years he put out editions of Ovid, Catullus, Horace, and Lucan, among many others. His greatest achievement in these years was a sumptuous English edition of Ovid's *Metamorphoses* which, as in the early years of the Dryden partnership, employed a set of different translators. Tonson reprinted many of his existing Ovid translations (including some by Dryden), but he also employed Samuel Garth to find new translators and to oversee the project. Alexander Pope satirized the project in his 'Sandys' Ghost' (1717), referring to George Sandys, the Elizabethan translator of Ovid. Pope finds comedy in the idea of Tonson and Garth beating a drum for volunteer translators:

> I hear the beat of *Jacob's* Drums,
> Poor *Ovid* finds no Quarter!
> (*Minor Poems*, 172)

When the troops of volunteers are finally lined up, Tonson goes out to review them:

> Now, *Tonson*, list thy Forces all,
> Review them, and tell Noses;
> For to poor *Ovid* shall befal
> A strange *Metamorphosis*.
> A *Metamorphosis* more strange

> Than all his Books can vapour;
> 'To what, (quoth 'Squire) shall *Ovid* change?'
> Quoth *Sandys*: *To Waste-Paper*.
> (*Minor Poems*, 174)

The edition appeared in 1717, dedicated to Princess Caroline, with a Kneller portrait of her as frontispiece, in quarto format with numerous illustrations; a nice marketing touch was having each of the fifteen books of the *Metamorphoses* dedicated to a different noblewoman. The edition proved highly successful despite Pope's sneers (Pope himself being engaged in the translation of Homer that was to make his own fortune); indeed, Tonson's Ovid was reprinted as late as the nineteenth century.

Establishing the Tonson dynasty About 1700 Tonson's nephew **Jacob Tonson the younger** (1682–1735) began working for him. The younger Jacob was born in London, the son of Tonson's brother Richard, and over the ensuing fifteen years the younger Jacob increasingly came to run the daily affairs of the Tonson business, until the elder Jacob retired about 1718, with his trip to France in 1718–20 effectively easing him out of it. The younger Jacob had demonstrated energy and ability almost the equal of his uncle's: one of his most important achievements was the purchase of over 100 titles owned by Henry Herringman in 1707, a lot that included three plays by Shakespeare. The elder Jacob had also been actively trying to purchase Shakespeare copyrights, though the details of the sales— and indeed whether some vendors actually owned the copyrights at all—remain unclear.

The elder Jacob Tonson looked on Shakespeare's works as he had Milton's and Dryden's, both as being works of great literary and national value, and as being generators of profit for his firm. He hired Nicholas Rowe, the dramatist, to edit an edition of Shakespeare, which appeared in 1709. Rowe was a responsible editor, if not the most scholarly one, and many of his textual emendations and stage directions remain accepted today. Moreover, his biographical essay was designed to interest the general reader in Shakespeare, and both it and the edition were highly successful in popularizing the plays. The edition was reprinted many times in the coming years.

The younger Jacob Tonson, however, thought the market for Shakespeare insufficiently tapped, and in 1721 he approached Alexander Pope to put together a new edition. The elder Tonson was also enthusiastic about the idea, and he acquired a copy of the First Folio (1623) to help Pope deliver an edition with greater textual integrity than ever before. The Pope edition came out in 1723 (volumes 1–5) and 1725 (volume 6). But Pope, brilliant poet though he was, proved disastrous as an editor: he frequently made 'improvements' in Shakespeare's verse, going as far as dropping entire scenes and soliloquies that he felt violated the plays' unity. Lewis Theobald, an inferior poet but a superior scholar, published an attack on the Pope edition in 1726, entitled 'Shakespeare restored'; Pope was enraged by Theobald's presumption, and set about making him the central figure in his dark satire *The Dunciad*. This left the Tonsons to choose which side they ought to be backing, and to their credit they joined several other publishers in producing Theobald's new edition (1733). In this, however, they were merely facing up to reality, for the Copyright Act of 1709 dictated that their own rights to Shakespeare expired in 1731.

Jacob Tonson the elder, before leaving for his trip to France, signed over all his copyrights—a list that included some twenty-three authors—to his nephew, for £2597 16s. 8d. The younger Tonson hoped he would be heir to his uncle's fortune, even conferring with his uncle's long-time servant about how best to stay on the old man's good side (the servant recommended gifts of food). When the uncle returned in 1720 he gave his Barn Elms estate to his nephew, moving to a new estate, The Hazels, in Ledbury in 1722, where he entertained many of his old Kit-Cat associates. Pope visited him at The Hazels, once inviting his friend the earl of Oxford along, promising him that he would find old Tonson fascinating, 'the perfect Image & Likeness of Bayle's Dictionary [that is, a virtual encyclopedia]; so full of Matter, Secret History, & Wit & Spirit' (Correspondence, 176). During these years Tonson the elder also speculated in the stock market, his canny business sense helping him again: he sold out his shares in the doomed South Sea project before the crash, making a profit on a scheme that ruined many others. The younger Jacob Tonson's hopes for his inheritance came to nothing, for he predeceased his uncle, at Barn Elms on 25 November 1735, leaving a fortune of £100,000. His uncle died soon after, on 18 March 1736, at The Vineyard, an estate between Gloucester and Ledbury; his fortune was reported as much less, £40,000, though it certainly was much greater than that. Tonson the elder was buried at St Mary-le-Strand, London, on 1 April 1736.

With his wife, Mary Hoole, the younger Jacob had two sons, **Jacob Tonson** (1714–1767) and **Richard Tonson** (1717–1772), and they inherited the business. Of the two, Jacob was by far the more engaged in publishing. He carried on his father's and great-uncle's enthusiasm for Shakespeare, hiring William Warburton for his important edition of 1747, and publishing Samuel Johnson's of 1765. Johnson spoke warmly of him, and there are anecdotes of his helping indigent authors such as Henry Fielding with their debts. The firm also produced editions of authors from the old list, such as Milton and Congreve. But the two brothers never had any major impact on publishing, and seemed content to maintain the reputation gained by the preceding generations. Jacob Tonson died on 31 March 1767, in London; he had no children. His brother Richard, who had little to do with the publishing business, was elected MP for Wallingford in 1747, and for New Windsor in 1768. He lived near Windsor, building a special room for the display of Kneller's Kit-Cat portraits. He died on 9 October 1772, also leaving no children. The Tonson copyrights passed on to the Rivington publishing firm. According to the *Dictionary of National Biography*, letters of administration of the goods of Jacob Tonson were left unadministered by his brother and were granted in 1775 to William Baker, MP for Hertfordshire; he too failed to administer and they were granted to Joseph Rogers in 1823.

The Tonson house made significant contributions both to publishing and to English literature. In particular, the elder Jacob Tonson's concern with textual integrity in authors such as Milton and Shakespeare marked his house as one concerned with high-quality publishing defined in the broadest possible way; the typography and layout in his greatest works—such as the Dryden *Virgil* or the edition of Julius Caesar—set new and distinguished standards. Combining such values with excellent business sense made the Tonson company highly profitable for the better part of three generations.

RAYMOND N. MACKENZIE

Sources J. Barnard, 'The large- and small-paper copies of Dryden's *The works of Virgil* (1697): Jacob Tonson's investment and profits and the example of *Paradise lost* (1688)', *Papers of the Bibliographical Society of America*, 92 (1998), 259–71 · S. Bennet, 'Jacob Tonson: an early editor of *Paradise lost*?', *The Library*, 6th ser., 10 (1988), 247–52 · S. L. C. Clapp, *Jacob Tonson in ten letters by and about him* (Austin, TX, 1948) · H. Gardner, 'Milton's first illustrator', *Essays and Studies by Members of the English Association*, new ser., 9 (1956), 27–38 · H. M. Geduld, *Prince of publishers: a study of the work and career of Jacob Tonson* (Bloomington, IN, 1969) · S. Gillespie, 'The early years of the Dryden–Tonson partnership: the background to their composite translations and miscellanies of the 1680s', *Restoration: Studies in English Literary Culture, 1660–1700*, 12/1 (1988), 10–19 · B. W. Kliman, 'Samuel Johnson and Tonson's 1745 Shakespeare: Warburton, anonymity, and the Shakespeare wars', *Reading readings: essays on Shakespeare editing in the eighteenth century*, ed. J. Gondris (Teaneck, NJ, 1998), 299–317 · P. Lindenbaum, 'Milton's contract', *The construction of authorship: textual appropriation in law and literature*, ed. M. Woodmansee and P. Jaszi (Durham, NC, 1994), 175–90 · K. M. Lynch, *Jacob Tonson: Kit-Cat publisher* (Knoxville, TN, 1971) · *Pope's literary legacy: the book-trade correspondence of William Warburton and John Knapton*, ed. D. W. Nichol (1992) · G. F. Papali, *Jacob Tonson, publisher: his life and work (1656–1736)* (Auckland, 1968) [orig. 1933 diss.] · K. Walker, 'Jacob Tonson, bookseller', *American Scholar*, 61/3 (1992), 424–30 · H. B. Wheatley, 'Dryden's publishers', *Transactions of the Bibliographical Society*, 11 (1912), 17–38 · J. A. Winn, *John Dryden and his world* (New Haven, CT, 1987) · D. F. McKenzie, ed., *Stationers' Company apprentices*, [2]: *1641–1700* (1974) · will, PRO, PROB 11/328, sig. 147 [Jacob Tonson (1620–1668)] · will, PRO, PROB 11/676, sig. 91 [Jacob Tonson (1655/6–1736)] · will, PRO, PROB 11/674, sig. 257 [Jacob Tonson (1682–1735)] · will, PRO, PROB 11/983, sig. 461 [Richard Tonson] · *The poems of John Dryden*, ed. J. Kinsley, 4 (1958), 1766 · *Minor poems*, ed. N. Ault (1954), vol. 6 of *The Twickenham edition of the poems of Alexander Pope*, ed. J. Butt (1939–69); repr. (1964), 170–74 · *The correspondence of Alexander Pope*, ed. G. Sherburn, 3 (1956)

Archives BL, papers, Add. MSS 28275–28276 | Bodl. Oxf., letters to Jacob Tonson the younger

Likenesses G. Kneller, oils, 1717, NPG [*see illus.*] · G. Kneller, oils, c.1720 (J. Tonson the younger), NPG

Wealth at death £40,000—Jacob Tonson (1655/6–1736): *GM*, 5 (1736), p. 168 · £100,000—Jacob Tonson (1682–1735)

Tonson, Jacob, the younger (1682–1735). *See under* Tonson, Jacob, the elder (1655/6–1736).

Tonson, Jacob (1714–1767). *See under* Tonson, Jacob, the elder (1655/6–1736).

Tonson, Richard (1717–1772). *See under* Tonson, Jacob, the elder (1655/6–1736).

Tonyn, Patrick (1725–1804), army officer and colonial governor, was the son of Charles William Tonyn (*d.* 1754), a

Patrick Tonyn (1725–1804), by George Clint, pubd 1804 (after Sir Martin Archer Shee)

colonel in the 6th dragoons. By the age of nineteen he had joined his father's unit, and rose to the rank of captain in May 1751. During the Seven Years' War this 'pugnacious Irishman' (Bailyn, 459) gained combat experience in Prussia and by 1761 had achieved the rank of lieutenant-colonel in the 104th regiment. He continued to earn promotions in subsequent decades, being appointed a colonel in 1777, a major-general four years later, and a full general in 1798, despite his withdrawal from active service with his unit more than two decades previously.

Tonyn's departure from his regiment coincided with his appointment as royal governor of East Florida, a province created out of the southernmost lands of North America that Great Britain obtained from Spain via the treaty of Paris (1763). He arrived in the colony's capital of St Augustine on 1 March 1774, just as revolutionary sentiment was peaking among many colonists in North America. Soon after his arrival the stridently loyal governor clashed with certain members of East Florida's population over the necessity of summoning a legislative assembly, thereby alienating, among others, the colony's chief justice and principal landowners. These tensions escalated as warfare broke out in the colonies to the north, although the relatively small population, geographical isolation, and economic insufficiency of East Florida ensured that as a whole the inhabitants remained loyal to the king.

Governor Tonyn energetically pursued measures to maintain his province's allegiance and defend it against American patriot agitators from the north. Responding to orders from the British government, he issued in November 1775 a proclamation inviting loyalists from the rebelling colonies to emigrate to East Florida, where for a ten-year period they would be eligible for land grants free of quitrents. As the number of loyalists inhabiting the province consequently increased, he initiated military preparations as well. In June 1776 Tonyn authorized the formation of the 'East Florida rangers', a loyalist regiment, to assist regular British troops in the colony's protection from opposing forces. Over the course of the war members of this regiment participated in both defensive and offensive actions, at times invading the Georgia backcountry where they stole cattle, harassed settlements, and obtained information on American troop movements and supplies. In addition the governor held several meetings with local Seminole and Creek leaders in which he enlisted American Indian support for the East Florida rangers and defence of the province. As a further precaution Tonyn issued several letters of marque to local shipowners and encouraged privateering while concurrently obtaining for the provincial navy dozens of brigs and schooners to patrol the coastal waters and inland rivers.

Tonyn's efforts succeeded in protecting East Florida from any significant incursion from either the American patriots or Spanish forces who had entered the war in 1779 hoping to re-obtain possession of the Floridas. Nevertheless, as the conflict turned badly for British armies, the governor's superiors called for the military to evacuate the region in May 1782. Despite protests against such a move by both the governor and the loyalist citizens of East Florida, British diplomats relinquished control of the colony to Spain in the peace agreements ending the conflict. Over the next three years Tonyn presided over the relocation of loyalist residents and property to Jamaica, Nova Scotia, the Bahamas, and Britain while negotiating, often heatedly, with the incoming Spanish administrators over transference of political control in the province. Tonyn himself departed from East Florida on 19 November 1785 and returned to Britain, where he resided in Park Street in London. There, like many displaced American loyalists, he petitioned the government for compensation of property losses sustained upon evacuating North America. The almost £6000 he was awarded, along with his military pension, allowed Tonyn to live comfortably until 1804, when he died in London on 30 December at the age of seventy-nine.

DANIEL S. MURPHREE

Sources W. H. Siebert, *Loyalists in East Florida, 1774–1785; the most important documents pertaining thereto, edited with an accompanying narrative*, 2 vols. (Deland, Florida, 1929) · C. L. Mowat, *East Florida as a British province, 1763–1784* (Berkeley, California, 1943) · colonial office papers, PRO, 5/548–571 · J. L. Wright, *Florida in the American Revolution* (Gainesville, Florida, 1975) · British headquarters (Sir Guy Carleton) papers, PRO · Henry Clinton papers, U. Mich. · B. Bailyn, *Voyagers to the west: a passage in the peopling of America on the eve of the Revolution* (New York, 1986) · W. S. Coker and T. D. Watson, *Indian traders of the southeastern Spanish borderlands* (1986) · J. B. Lockey, *East Florida, 1783–1785* (Berkeley, California, 1949) · *Report on American manuscripts in the Royal Institution of Great Britain*, 4 vols., HMC, 59 (1904–9) · M. C. Searcy, *The Georgia–Florida contest in the American Revolution, 1776–1778* (Alabama, 1985) · L. K. Williams, 'East Florida as a loyalist haven', *Florida Historical Quarterly*, 54 (1976), 465–78

Archives PRO, corresp., PRO 30/55 | PRO, British headquarters (Sir Guy Carleton) papers · PRO, colonial office papers, 5/548–571 · U. Mich., Henry Clinton papers

Likenesses G. Clint, mezzotint, pubd 1804 (after M. A. Shee), BM, NPG [*see illus.*] · portrait, St Augustine Historical Society, St Augustine, Florida; repro. in Wright, *Florida in the American Revolution*

Tonypandy. For this title name *see* Thomas, Thomas George, Viscount Tonypandy (1909–1997).

Took, Steve (1949–1980). *See under* Bolan, Marc (1947–1977).

Tooke, Andrew (*bap.* 1673, *d.* 1732), schoolmaster and university professor, was baptized in the parish of St Gregory by Paul, London, on 22 January 1673, the second of the three sons of Benjamin Tooke, citizen and stationer, and his wife, Mary, *née* Juell. He attended Charterhouse School from 1686 until 1690, when he entered Clare College, Cambridge, as a scholar; he graduated BA in 1693 and commenced MA in 1697. In 1695 he became usher, or assistant master, at Charterhouse, a post he retained when on 5 July 1704 he was appointed to succeed Robert Hooke as professor of geometry at Gresham College, London. In November that year he was elected fellow of the Royal Society, whose members met in his rooms at the college until 1710, when they acquired premises elsewhere.

On the death of his brother Benjamin (1671–1723), Tooke inherited an estate of several thousand pounds. He continued to teach at Gresham College and at Charterhouse, where he was effectively in charge from 1723 during the terminal illness of the headmaster, Thomas Walker (*d.* 1728), whom he succeeded on 17 July 1728. Having taken deacon's orders, he occasionally preached and officiated in the Charterhouse chapel, but most of his time was spent teaching the boys. On 7 May 1729 he married Elizabeth, widow of Henry Levett (1668–1725), the former physician at Charterhouse, and resigned as Gresham professor on 26 June that year.

A prolific writer, Tooke was best known for *The pantheon, representing the fabulous histories of the heathen gods and most illustrious heroes* (1698), translated from the *Pantheum mythicum* of the Jesuit father François Antoine Pomey, which went through twenty-two editions. He probably intended his *Synopsis Graecae linguae* (1711) and his edition of William Walker's *Treatise of English Particles* (1720) for his students. He also reprinted some accounts of Gresham College and a copy of Sir Thomas Gresham's will, which he had contributed to Stowe's *Survey of London*. His other publications were translations from French and Latin works of a moral or religious nature. Tooke died of dropsy on 20 January 1732 and was buried in the Charterhouse chapel, where a monument was erected to his memory. His large library was sold by auction in May 1732, and his estate passed to his brother Richard (1685–1737).

THOMPSON COOPER, *rev.* ANITA MCCONNELL

Sources J. Ward, *The lives of the professors of Gresham College* (1740); repr. (1967), 193–7 · B. Marsh and F. A. Crisp, eds., *Alumni Carthusiani: a record of the foundation scholars of Charterhouse, 1614–1872* (1913) · *GM*, 1st ser., 2 (1732), 586 · F. Collins, ed., *The registers and monumental inscriptions of Charterhouse chapel*, Harleian Society, Register Section, 18 (1892), 85 · A. Quick, *Charterhouse: a history of the school* (1990), 28 · parish register, St Gregory by Paul, London, 22 Jan 1673 [baptism]

Tooke, George (1595–1675), army officer and writer, was the fifth son of Walter Tooke (*d.* 1609), administrator, and his wife, Angelet (*d.* 1598), second daughter and coheir of William Woodcliffe, citizen and mercer of London. He was the grandson of William Tooke, auditor-general of the court of wards and liveries for forty-four years until his death in 1588, an office which his father, Walter, inherited.

In 1625 Tooke took part in the unsuccessful expedition against Cadiz, led by Sir Edward Cecil, commanding a company of eighty volunteers. Tooke's own account, *The History of Cales Passion*, written in prose and verse, appears not to have been published until 1652, with new editions in 1654 and 1659. Detailing the shortcomings of logistical preparations prior to the expedition, Tooke wrote 'lest After-ages might unhappily wander into the same gravily way' (*Cales Passion*, 'To the reader'), and did not shrink from acknowledging the errors nor pass over the unfortunate exigencies which all helped contribute to the adventure's miserable outcome. Tooke's role in the débâcle merits no mention in the official relation written by John Glanville, Cecil's secretary, and he seems to have taken greatest pride in having brought his men home without loss.

A lengthy illness, contracted during the expedition's return, put paid to Tooke's own active military career. He took up residence on the family estate of Popes, at Essenden, near Hatfield, Hertfordshire, and there enjoyed the illustrious company of John Selden and John Hales. Tooke succeeded to the estate on the death of his eldest brother, Ralph, on 22 December 1635. That year he published his *Legend of Brita-Mart: otherwise Britaines Mars*, dedicated to his Hertfordshire neighbour, William, second earl of Salisbury, kinsman of the English commander at Cadiz in 1625. In the dedicatory epistle Tooke addressed Salisbury, remarking that 'the manage of a reall war is now familiarly every mans tract; the premises unconsulted, and our provisionall musters and militia still left at large, without any paraphrase' (*The Legend*, A3). The tract was written in the form of a conversation between three characters, Publicola, Infortunio, and Epimetheus, on the subject of England's military defences. The argument was first that it was mistaken to rely on either the kingdom's natural defences, or its military establishments overseas in Ireland and on the continent; and second that the ancient system of trained bands was in serious need of reform. In an extended passage Infortunio defended the emergence of that controversial figure in Caroline military reform, the county muster-master. The whole reads very much as a justification of Charles I's ambitious design to establish a 'perfect militia'. The tract was published a second time in 1646, this time offering 'a paraphrase upon our provisionall British discipline. Inditing it of many severall distempers and prescribing to[o] the cure', and with the conversants renamed 'Mickle-Worth the Patriot, Peny-Wise the Worldling, and Mille-Toyle the Souldier' (title-page).

Tooke also composed eulogies to some of the heroes of

early modern protestant internationalism. In 1647 he published *The Eagle Trussers Elegie*, an encomium on the career of King Gustavus Adolphus of Sweden which he dedicated to Ferdinando, Lord Fairfax, as well as a eulogy to Captain (or Major) William Fairfax, slain at Frankenthal in the Palatinate in 1621. Tooke also ventured some thoughts on Dutch history, in his *Chronological revise, of those three successive princes of Holland, Zeland and Freisland, Floris the fourth, his sonne William king of the Romans, and Floris the fifth* (1647), dedicated to Charles Fairfax. Verses written on John, Lord Harrington, baron of Exton, keeper of the household of Princess Elizabeth, daughter of James I, were also published in 1647. Rounding off an extremely fruitful year Tooke then published a volume of poetry, *Annoe-dicata, or, A miscelanie of some different cansonets, dedicated to the memory of my deceased very deere wife* (1647). Anne, or Anna, Tooke (*bap.* 1615, *d.* 1642) was the daughter of Thomas Tooke of Bere Court in Kent, a distant relation of the Tookes of Hertfordshire. It is not known when she and George Tooke married. Anne died on 9 December 1642 and was buried at Wormeley church in Hertfordshire. Tooke's second wife was Margery, daughter of Thomas Coningsbry of North Mimms, Hertfordshire.

Although Tooke lived for many more years little else is known of him. His allegiance during the civil war is difficult to ascertain, as he was neither appointed to administrative office by parliament nor punished for delinquency. Most of the historical works of 1647 found their way back into print in 1659 or 1660. Tooke died without issue at Popes in 1675. He has not inspired as a writer. Both his prose and his poetry are undoubtedly impaired by a love of far-fetched metaphor and obscured by a painfully involved style, though some have claimed that he has been unduly disparaged.

E. I. CARLYLE, *rev.* SEAN KELSEY

Sources G[eorge] T[ooke], *The history of Cales passion, or, as some will by-name it, The miss-taking of Cales presented in vindication of the sufferers and to forewarne the future* (1652) · G[eorge] T[ooke], *The legend of Brita-Mart: otherwise Britaines Mars, or, A paraphrase upon our provisionall martial discipline* (1653) · Nichols, *Lit. anecdotes*, vol. 9 · R. Clutterbuck, ed., *The history and antiquities of the county of Hertford*, 2 (1821), 352 · W. Mitford, 'George Tooke's poems', *GM*, 2nd ser., 12 (1839), 484
Likenesses J. Brand, pen-and-ink drawing (after engraving by E. Marmion), NPG · engraving (eighteenth century), BL, Add. MS 32350, fol. 141

Tooke, John Horne [*formerly* John Horne] (**1736–1812**), radical and philologist, was born on 25 June 1736 in Newport Street, Westminster, the third of the seven children and the youngest son of John Horne, a prosperous poulterer, and Elizabeth, *née* Horne. He was baptized John Horne at St Anne's, Soho, on the following day.

Background, education, and early career Horne was born into a respectable middle-class family. His mother was a benevolent figure, persuading her husband to donate money to the Middlesex Hospital, of which he later became one of the first treasurers. Horne's father was a man of singularly independent character, exemplified by a lawsuit with Frederick, prince of Wales, who lived next door to the Horne family in Leicester House. When some

John Horne Tooke (1736–1812), by Thomas Hardy, 1791

of the prince's officials sought a passage to Newport market by making an opening through a wall belonging to the Horne property without seeking permission, Horne's father brought the case to court and won. Having achieved his purpose, John Horne senior allowed the doorway to be reopened and was accordingly appointed by the prince as the official supplier of poultry to his household. Despite the immediate honour of this appointment, the prince's sudden death in 1751 saw a debt of several thousand pounds unrecovered.

Horne as a child was decidedly unique, possessing a maturity beyond his age. An old lady who knew him in his youth recollected how he 'never was a boy: with him there was no interval between childhood and age; he became a man all at once upon us' (Stephens, 1.22). He had no particular interest in games or sport, finding instead the most exciting moment of his childhood to be a military expedition on which he joined his father, who was a commissioned officer of the trained bands. As to education, Horne was well grounded yet never really showed signs of distinction. At the age of seven he was sent to Soho Square Academy, and a year later found himself attending school in Westminster. In 1746 Horne entered Eton College, where he spent the next six years. He was elected to the distinction of king's scholar and lived in the college. While his origins distinguished him from so many of the boys at Eton whose families were of the upper classes, Horne apparently felt for the most part at ease among his peers. As a scholar he was bright—more so than brilliant—and as an adult admitted to employing some of the other boys to do his homework. While he neglected the set curriculum, Horne prescribed his own readings, and it is no surprise therefore to find him later advocating that it 'is best to let children read what they like best, till they have formed a taste for reading; and not to direct what books they shall read' (Rogers, 165). In his youth, Horne's imagination was captured by the writings of Shakespeare and Milton, although reading would have become something of a chore following an accident during his schooldays in which he lost the sight of his right eye during a struggle with a fellow student. He was subsequently sent to school in Kent for a time, but disliked the institution intensely and ran away from his tutor, justifying his actions to his father on the grounds that his mentor was ignorant of grammar.

In 1753 Horne was sent to private tutors at Sevenoaks and, the following year, at Ravenstone in Northamptonshire in preparation for admission to Cambridge University. On 12 January 1754 he was admitted as a sizar to St John's College and was senior optime in the tripos of 1758, graduating that year with a BA honours degree in mathematics. During his undergraduate years Horne became well acquainted with Richard Beadon, tutor to the future duke of Gloucester, who later became master of Jesus College, bishop of Gloucester, and finally bishop of Bath and Wells. Despite their divergent careers after university, Horne and Beadon remained close friends. Like Beadon, Horne was reared for the clergy, that being the wish of his father, who was a devout member of the Church of England. But Horne had ambitions for a legal career, and as early as 9 November 1756, while an undergraduate, he enrolled as a member of the Inner Temple, during which time his parents refused to support him.

After graduating from Cambridge, Horne worked briefly as an usher in a school at Blackheath. As a young man at this stage he had a fairly regular physical appearance, with an athletic build, a high forehead, and brown hair. He enjoyed the company of women, but during his time at Blackheath was involved in a love affair with a young woman living in the same house. The relationship was aborted and Horne later recalled how he 'luckily escaped from two evils—matrimony and misery at the same time' (Stephens, 1.28). During this time his father continued to insist on his religious calling, and Horne finally conceded, being ordained deacon on 23 September 1759 and becoming a curate in Kent. He was not, however, fully committed to his post and resigned within a few months following a sudden attack of ague. On his recovery, Horne began to frequent his inn of court on a daily basis, determined 'to eat his way to the bar' (ibid., 1.30). He was befriended at this time by John Dunning, who would later act as his defence counsel, as well as Lloyd Kenyon, who ironically later presided at a trial of Horne and became chief justice of the king's bench and master of the rolls.

Pecuniary circumstances forced Horne to abandon his legal interests, and on 23 November 1760 he was ordained a priest. His father purchased him a living at New Brentford said to be worth between £200 and £300 a year and he was offered further inducements to remain in the church. Although as a preacher Horne was said to be proficient, his sermons were orthodox discourses, as exemplified by the one published in 1769 and entitled simply *A Sermon*. His religious creed is indeed elusive, perhaps on account (as he later admitted) of having no real interest in theological issues. He was, however, a fervent opponent of Roman Catholicism and had no desire to advocate the cause of dissenters. Apart from these convictions, Horne's creed was, according to John Wilkes, believed 'to be *non credo*' (Wilkes, *Controversial Letters*, 29). Nevertheless, Horne conducted his duties with characteristic professionalism and care. With only a half-hearted interest in spiritual matters at best, he studied medicine in the hope of improving the physical well-being of his parishioners and opened a dispensary for their benefit. Despite these efforts and his sobriety at this time, some of his flock found cause to criticize him for what they saw as inappropriate enthusiasm for whatever entertainment the neighbourhood offered and, more particularly, for his fondness for playing cards.

Horne was never completely settled in his duties as curate and in February 1763, not long after the end of the Seven Years' War with France, he eagerly accepted the position of travelling companion to France of the son of the eccentric John Elwes, MP for Berkshire. The sojourn lasted for around twelve months, nine of which Horne spent learning the French language. While there he was introduced to Jean le Rond d'Alembert, the mathematician and *philosophe*, and by chance became acquainted with the Scottish philosopher David Hume. On his return to England, Horne was promised an appointment as king's chaplain, principally through the influence of Demainbray and Elwes, but his interests were captured by prevailing politics.

Horne and the Wilkesite cause When Horne returned from France in 1764 he was imbibed with patriotism, a detestation of Lord Bute, a delight in the popular apotheosis of William Pitt at the time, and a sense of outrage at the treatment of Wilkes over the infamous *North Briton* affair. In the following year he published an anonymous pamphlet, *The Petition of an Englishman*, which comprised twenty-three pages of bold and vindictive satire against Bute and Lord Mansfield and offered a defence of Wilkes. It was a deliberately provocative piece, openly inviting prosecution, and as such was not welcomed by most printers. While the work was offensively critical in its rhetoric, Horne remained unprosecuted—perhaps, as Alexander Stephens contended, owing to the government's desire not to publicize Horne's insinuations about Bute's insidious relationship with the dowager princess of Wales, which the author supported by including a map of Kew Gardens showing the path by which Bute could discreetly attend upon the princess.

In the autumn of 1765 Horne once more ventured overseas, this time in the company of the son of a Mr Taylor, a gentleman from near Brentford. Having abandoned his clerical dress, Horne began 'flaunting through the continent in very unclerical suits of flowered silk and gold lace' (Bleackley, 176). At Calais he met Thomas Sheridan and his wife, and at Paris met Wilkes for the first time through an introduction he carried from Humphrey Cotes, a West-minster wine merchant. Both men soon struck a close relationship, which Wilkes conveyed to Cotes in a letter dated 7 October 1765: 'I have had the pleasure several times of seeing Mr Horne, and I thank you heartily for so valuable an acquaintance' (*Letters of John Wilkes*, 2.207). Before Horne left Paris the two men agreed to remain in contact with each other.

From Paris, Horne travelled to Ferney to meet Voltaire, but the influential French writer did not inspire Horne, who later declared him to be 'inferior in everything' (Stephens, 2.435). He then visited Lyons for a week, where he was frequently in the company of Laurence Sterne, with whom Horne acquired a friendship despite the former being 'clearly bored' by the latter's constant praise of Wilkes (Cross, 375). In Italy, Horne probably got to know the Italian language and became fascinated with Machiavelli. He visited all the principal cities but spent most of his time in Genoa, where he fraternized with a distinguished local family. During this time he became fascinated by a Genoese beauty, Signora Durazzo, but not all of her family approved of his affections. On leaving the city Horne was fortunate to escape death when some of the signora's family mistakenly shot another Englishman.

Back in France, Horne and his companion went to Montpellier, where they became known to Adam Smith, who was then tutor to the duke of Buccleuch. Horne, however, was not well disposed towards Smith, remarking later that he was inferior to Hume and that some of his writings were 'nonsense' and 'written with wicked views' (Rogers, 160). It was from this resort city that Horne also decided to write to Wilkes, on 3 January 1766, in a language not befitting his clerical standing: 'It is true I have suffered the infectious hand of a bishop to be waved over me; whose imposition, like the sop given to Judas, is only a signal for the devil to enter' (Stephens, 1.76). Wilkes never replied, and when Horne reached Paris in 1767 he questioned Wilkes as to his reticence. Wilkes at first tried dismissing Horne's enquiries as a joke, then denied ever receiving the letter, even though it was known to Horne that he had seemed determined to publish it on several occasions. Despite this incident the two men remained on friendly terms, and it was to Wilkes that Horne entrusted five of his fashionable suits upon his departure for England on 25 May 1767, presumably on the assumption he would be soon returning.

During summer 1767 Horne made an effort to apply himself to his clerical duties at Brentford, preaching popular charity sermons and often accepting invitations to speak at London churches. Yet his real enthusiasm was for the world of politics, and it was the return of Wilkes in spring 1768 in time for the general election which rekindled his political passions. When Wilkes decided to stand for Middlesex, Horne was in a position to promote the Wilkesite cause. He organized the use of the two best inns at Brentford by Wilkes's supporters and threw himself earnestly into the political fray, covering the whole constituency on foot or horseback. Under the rousing banner of 'Wilkes and Liberty', Horne used his powerful oratory to sway the electors and his virulent wit to attack the sitting members, George Cooke and Sir William Beauchamp Proctor, in the press. In the end Wilkes won the election, but was soon after arrested on outstanding charges and imprisoned.

As the government continued to refuse Wilkes the right to take his seat in parliament, Horne became an outspoken activist in the ensuing agitations. He made concerted efforts to have a magistrate, Gillam, prosecuted for ordering soldiers to shoot innocent bystanders on 10 May 1768 during the riots in St George's Fields. In the autumn he helped Wilkes draw up a petition to parliament, and during the next Middlesex election campaign, following the death of Cooke, Horne published a series of sarcastic letters in the *Oxford Magazine* attacking Proctor and upholding the Wilkesite candidate. The death of another innocent bystander, George Clarke, in an election riot in December 1768, again saw Horne rally for justice by calling for the prosecution of Edward M'Quirk. A pamphlet entitled *An Appeal to the Public Touching the Death of Mr George Clarke* (1769) was published under the name of the surgeon who examined Clarke, John Foot, but was apparently written by Horne.

In 1769 Horne was elected burgess of Brentford and on 20 February of that year, under Horne's auspices, the Society of Supporters of the Bill of Rights was formed at the London tavern. An advertisement for the society drawn up by Horne states that 'their *sole aim* is to maintain and defend the *legal, constitutional liberty*' of the people (Wilkes, *Controversial Letters*, 150–51), but its primary objective was to assist a financially crippled Wilkes through subscriptions. Supported by some of London's wealthiest and most prominent agitators, the society managed to raise considerable amounts towards retrieving Wilkes's finances. Horne was at this time occupied with an exhausting interest in political contests, such that one critic later commented that he was acting 'as a kind of travelling counsel to every man who thought himself capable of being made an object of public commiseration' (*Blackwood*, 969). Horne, however, had a genuine interest in public liberty and justice. On several occasions he disclosed violations of justice in the courts, including the case of two Spitalfields weavers hanged for murder, which Horne published as *Genuine Copies of All the Letters … Relative to the Execution of Doyle and Valine* (1770). He was even more frequently concerned with political grievances, for instance attacking George Onslow, a former friend of Wilkes and MP for Surrey, in a letter published in the *Public Advertiser* on 11 July 1769 in which he accused Onslow of accepting a bribe in the process of making an appointment to a position in America. On 24 August, Onslow initiated a civil suit against Horne which was tried at Kingston before William Blackstone on 6 April 1770, but the case was deemed nonsuited on legal technicalities. A new trial was brought before Lord Mansfield on 1 August 1770 with the added charges of Horne using defamatory words at a meeting of Surrey freeholders. The jury acquitted Horne over the letters, but ordered he pay £400 in damages for his words. Horne appealed against the judgment, and the case was finally set aside in the court of common pleas on 17 April 1771.

Despite the distractions of these legal engagements, Horne remained active in the political scene. On 30 March 1770 he made a speech to Middlesex freeholders, published as an *Oration Delivered by the Rev. Mr Horne* (1770), in which, *inter alia*, he humorously foreshadowed his legal battle with Onslow. He was also co-author of an address presented to George III by the City of London on 14 March 1770 and the author of another remonstrance presented on 23 May 1770. There is some unlikely speculation that Horne wrote the reply often attributed to William Beckford to the king's answer to the last petition. By the end of 1770 a rift between Horne and Wilkes had opened. It seems that hostilities between the two began after a meeting of Westminster electors on 31 October when Horne published in the newspapers a slighting account of Wilkes's performance. An exchange of written retorts continued until the end of 1770. At much the same time there were suggestions among some Bill of Rights Society members that Wilkes was abusing the society's financial generosity, which came to a head on 12 February 1771 when Horne carried a motion that £500 be raised to help William Bingley, a printer imprisoned in 1768 for publishing the *North Briton*. Two weeks after Horne's motion was passed, another resolution was made that no new subscriptions would be entered into until Wilkes's debts were discharged. On 9 April 1771 Horne moved that the Bill of Rights Society should be disbanded, and when his proposal was rejected by a vote of twenty-six to twenty-four, the minority withdrew and soon formed the Constitutional Society.

In May 1771 Horne published two articles in the *North Briton* on electoral reform advocating annual parliaments, but stopping short of calling for universal suffrage. It was at this time, as Wilkes announced his candidacy for the office of sheriff of London, that Horne reopened their dispute. For two months the men again exchanged offensive letters, in which Horne was variously accused of misappropriating Bill of Rights Society funds and his letter to Wilkes from Montpellier in 1766 was brought to public attention. Horne reacted by accusing Wilkes of pawning his suits left in his possession in 1767 and revealing details of his personal extravagances and financial dishonesty. The combatants were, as Horace Walpole observed, engaged in 'a civil war between themselves' (Walpole, *Corr.*, 31.151). In the ensuing election of sheriffs Horne supported Richard Oliver, who was defeated. Horne's effigy was burned before the Mansion House, indicative of the damage his moral and political reputation had suffered in the course of his dispute with Wilkes.

Soon after this controversy had subsided Horne applied for his MA at Cambridge, and despite opposition from the likes of William Paley, Lord Sandwich, and other religious colleagues the degree was conferred. It was not long before Horne was again embroiled in a heated debate, this time with the scathing critic who published under the pseudonym Junius. Horne was accused of working secretly for the government in the recent election of City sheriffs and was advised to 'go back to his cloisters' (Junius, 253). Horne was quick to react to Junius's claims, and in the written exchanges that followed it was Horne who emerged the victor, having 'sunk Junius at last by law arguments', as William Godwin remarked (Bewley and Bewley, 48).

Amid the political controversies and legal entanglements, Horne remained a popular social figure. His political clique met at the house of Richard Liver, and he kept rooms in Frith Street near his friends Michael Moser, keeper of the Royal Academy, and Thomas Sheridan. Horne was also a keen backgammon and whist player, and as such became known to Domenico Angelo and his son, Henry, doyen of fencing masters, as well as the musicians Johann Christian Bach and Karl Abel. Despite his affability, Horne's personal life remained somewhat unsettled. By the early 1770s he had fathered a son, Sidney Montague, the eldest of his three children, who later served in the East India Company. He was also the father of two daughters, Mary and Charlotte, both of whom used their mother's surname of Hart, but he never married. He seems to have held a rather facetious attitude towards the virtues of matrimony and monogamy, once asserting that he would never marry a pretty woman since 'she would be studious to be admired by others and to please anybody more than her husband' (Rogers, 154–5). Horne had a certain courtly charm with women and he perhaps revelled in a bachelor's lifestyle. It has also been suggested that Horne's avoidance of marriage may be due to his sensitivity over a lifelong bowel problem. Whatever the reason, Horne was definitely shy of marriage, a fact captured by an amusing anecdote which recounts how he had proposed marriage to a Miss Arabin in a letter, but suddenly realized what he had done and returned to the post office to destroy the note.

While his personal life was unsettled, Horne's professional career remained equally uncertain. In 1773 he resigned from his clerical post and moved to a house in Windmill Lane in New Brentford, where he studied philology and again determined to study law. His friends offered him an annuity of £400 until he was called to the bar, but Horne never took advantage of their offer. Not long after settling into his new residence, Horne was called to the aid of his friend William Tooke, whose property at Purley, near Croydon, was to be affected by an enclosure bill which his neighbour, Thomas de Grey, was petitioning to present to parliament. Realizing that it was too late to counter-petition, Horne published a letter in the *Public Advertiser* attacking the speaker, Fletcher Norton, with accusations of partiality in this case and implying that he had been bribed. After the printer of the newspaper gave up the author's name, Horne was ordered to the bar in February 1774. After much deliberation Horne was discharged, de Grey's bill removed, and a measure passed to prevent such bills being so readily presented in future. While Charles James Fox strongly opposed Horne throughout this contest, earning him the lasting wrath of Horne, Tooke was eternally grateful for his assistance and showered him with gifts and promises of inheritance.

The middle years, 1775–1788 As the Wilkesite cause slowly faded, Horne's attentions were soon focused on the American War of Independence. Although he generally regarded Americans to be 'of a very inferior cast' (Stephens, 2.337), Horne was sympathetic to their constitutional demands, realizing that when 'the people of America are enslaved [Britons] … cannot be free' (Horne, *Oration*, 36). Following a clash between the colonists and British troops at Lexington and Concord in April 1775, the Constitutional Society, at Horne's suggestion, raised a subscription for the Americans concerned. Horne was to convey the money to Benjamin Franklin, and the society's resolutions were drawn up by Horne and published in the newspapers to announce that the subscription was for 'our beloved American fellow-subjects, who … preferring death to slavery, were … inhumanly murdered by the King's troops' (Bewley and Bewley, 60). Horne's efforts in this transaction were recognized on 17 June 1919, when the New England Society of Brooklyn unveiled in St Mary's Church, Ealing, a memorial tablet in his honour and paid for a refurbishment of his grave. Far from being honoured at the time, Horne found himself charged with libel for the advertisement he prepared, and on 4 July 1777 was tried before Lord Mansfield. He defended himself with characteristic forcefulness and audacity but was found guilty and sentenced to one year in prison, to pay a fine of £200, and to find sureties for three years of £400 from himself and £200 from two others. In 1778 he brought a writ of error in parliament to reverse the verdict, which was argued by John Dunning, but the judgment was affirmed on 11 May 1778.

Horne was confined in the king's bench prison, where he contracted gaol fever and started drinking claret as a cure, although he later attributed the gout from which he suffered for the rest of his life to the alcohol he consumed in prison. He was permitted to pay for decent accommodation outside the prison walls but 'within the rules', and was frequently visited by friends and dined on a weekly basis at the Dog and Duck public house in St George's Fields. During his imprisonment Horne wrote *A Letter to Mr Dunning on the English Particle* (1778), in which he devotes much attention to the etymologies of words and grammatical standards concerning prepositions and conjunctions. The letter was originally conceived as a means of arguing that his conviction was wrong on account of some grammatical infelicities in the indictment. In time the *Letter* formed an integral part of Horne's major work, *Diversions of Purley*.

After serving eight months of his sentence, Horne was released and rented a room in Vine Street, London, where he continued his legal studies. With promises of many briefs from eminent lawyers, he applied in Trinity term 1779 for admission to the bar, but was rejected by a majority of eight to three benchers of the Inner Temple on the grounds that he was a clergyman. He reapplied in 1782, when Lord Shelburne supported his application, but it was again rejected. In 1794 Horne was once more among the candidates, but no bencher moved for his call. The constant rejections and the inability to fulfil his vocational desires apparently left Horne disgruntled for the remainder of his life, going so far as to sour his relationship with Lord Shelburne, whom Horne held responsible for his rejection. Soon after his unsuccessful application in 1779 Horne moved to a small estate at Witton, near Huntingdon, where he applied himself to farming and spent some of his father's legacy improving the property. Ill health, however, forced him to sell the estate back to the previous owner, and while Horne's movements shortly thereafter remain obscure it is known that at various times during the next nine years he worked as an accountant in Huntingdon for Sir Robert Bernard, lived at 12 Paper Buildings, Temple, and rented a house in Dean Street, London, with his two daughters. Horne also spent time during this period residing with William Tooke at Serjeants' Inn and Purley, and in 1782 added the name of Tooke to his own, which was supposedly an indication that Horne was to be Tooke's heir.

While Horne Tooke's time, especially in the early 1780s, was divided between London and the country, he remained active in City politics. In 1780 he collaborated with Richard Price to expose the financial corruption associated with the British war effort in America, which was written up as *Facts addressed to landholders, stockholders … and all the subjects of Great Britain and Ireland* (1780) and was published in eight editions. He was also a prominent member of the extra-parliamentary reform groups that formed around London, including the committees known as the Quintuple Alliance, and he was nominated for membership of the Society for Constitutional Information on 6 July 1781 by its founder, John Cartwright. Horne Tooke was a supporter of William Pitt's calls for parliamentary reform and in May 1782, as head of some Westminster delegates, called on Pitt to congratulate him on his reform stance. That same month he was present at the Thatched House tavern with Pitt, the duke of Richmond, the earl of Surrey, and other leading reformers of the day when it was decided to petition parliament in support of Pitt's reform proposals. Around this time Horne Tooke published *A Letter to Lord Ashburton* (1782), a work that was published in several editions and republished in 1793, in which he expressed the idea that the aim of good government is the greatest happiness of the individual, a tenet which later became central in Jeremy Bentham's theory of utilitarianism. Although an active reform campaigner at this time, Horne Tooke's political interests were somewhat narrow. He was not inclined to oppose the Test Acts despite having numerous dissenting friends, nor did he take much interest in the Irish cause or the anti-slave trade movement.

The time Horne Tooke spent residing in London gave him the chance of becoming a member of the Speculative Society, a literary and philosophical debating club, where he came to know Richard Sharp and James Mackintosh. He also fraternized during the 1780s with Edward Topham, founder of *The World* newspaper (to which Horne

Tooke contributed), as well as James Perry, the Scottish journalist, and Joseph Johnson, proprietor of the *Analytical Review*. It was, however, the friendship between William Tooke and Horne Tooke which was commemorated in the latter's most significant writing, *Epea Pteroenta, or, The Diversions of Purley*, the first part of which was published in 1786 and revised in 1798, with part two published in 1805. A third volume was planned, but Horne Tooke burnt all his personal papers shortly before his death. Aimed at well-educated readers, *Diversions* was an attempt to democratize language, and as a philological treatise was influential on contemporaries such as the radical grammarians William Cobbett and William Hazlitt and was read by many including Henrietta, countess of Bessborough, who described the second part of the work as a 'strange book', which she thought 'imprudent, ingenious, indecent and entertaining' (*Private Correspondence*, 2.136–8). Horne Tooke profited from the publication, having received subscription payments of 2 guineas that he never returned for the unpublished third volume and making a sum of £4000–£5000 from royalties and subscriptions on the first two volumes.

Although Horne Tooke was never a prolific writer he soon followed *Diversions* with another work, entitled *A Letter to a Friend on the Reported Marriage of HRH Prince of Wales* (1787). This eight-page pamphlet was published in London and Dublin and focused on the assumed scandalous marriage of the prince and Maria Fitzherbert. The following year Horne Tooke produced another work, *Two Pair of Portraits* (1788), in which he derided Charles James Fox and praised Pitt in a satire that was as scurrilous as it was persuasive. At this time Horne Tooke belonged to the Revolution Society and was also involved in the Constitutional Club formed to support Admiral Samuel Hood during the Westminster election of 1788. He had also assumed greater control of a waning Society for Constitutional Information, helping to revive the group with younger members such as the radical Count Alvise Zenobio, Thomas Walker, and Thomas Cooper.

The radical years, 1789–1794 Following the outbreak of revolution in France, Horne Tooke was present at a meeting of the Society for Constitutional Information on 27 November 1789, when a message of congratulations was agreed to be sent to the French national assembly. The following year he opposed Fox in the election for Westminster, and although a popular candidate his campaign suffered from a lack of official backing. He polled last of the three candidates, receiving 1679 votes, but he claimed a moral victory, attracting nearly half as many votes as Fox or Hood but outlaying only £28 on advertising. John Thelwall served as Horne Tooke's assistant during the election and came to admire him as the first person of 'capacious and highly-cultivated mind' with whom he had associated (Thelwall, 76). Horne Tooke was also unrelenting, and petitioned parliament on 12 December 1790 on the grounds that the Westminster electors were disenfranchised, but by a vote of the house the petition was laid on the table. By an act of 1789 Horne Tooke was liable for the costs incurred, and Fox accordingly brought an action against him for the taxed cost of his expenses. The case was heard before Lord Kenyon on 30 April 1792, and despite Horne Tooke's able harangue on corrupt electoral practices a verdict was found in favour of Fox. The trial proceedings were published as a pamphlet and reissued in 1812 and 1819.

As the Society for Constitutional Information rose to prominence in the burgeoning reform movement of 1791, so too did Horne Tooke. He was instrumental in organizing the distribution of Thomas Paine's first part of *The Rights of Man* through the society, and in 1792 he became a member of the Friends to the Liberty of the Press and helped draft the constitution of the London Corresponding Society at the request of its founder, Thomas Hardy. In June 1792 he moved to Wimbledon, where he had earlier purchased a house, later called Chester Lodge, on the west side of Wimbledon Common, and where his neighbours included Henry Dundas and William Wilberforce. His residence became the rendezvous for weekly Sunday dinners, the conversations at which catered for the broad spectrum of political views held by Horne Tooke's guests. Despite the convivial nature of these soirées, the government viewed such gatherings with increasing suspicion, and Horne Tooke himself came under close scrutiny. When he met Charles-Maurice Talleyrand during his diplomatic missions in 1791 and 1792, the authorities declared Horne Tooke's mail to be opened as a suspect person along with Paine and Talleyrand. Horne Tooke's activities during 1792–4 did not give the government any reason to offer mitigation. During 1792 Horne Tooke helped found reform clubs in Aldgate and Southwark calling themselves after the Friends of the People, and with expanding numbers of the Society for Constitutional Information Horne Tooke moved the group's meetings to the Crown and Anchor, where he also organized a dining club every Friday evening before meetings of the society. His failing health and move to Wimbledon did not dampen his enthusiasm, as he continued to attend all the society's meetings and co-authored with John Martin, a lawyer, *An Address to the People of Britain* (1794), approved on 20 January by the London Corresponding Society. An increasingly nervous government had spies working within Horne Tooke's circle by this time, and the suspicion of him as a subversive is reflected in the many caricatures in which he is portrayed as a revolutionary sansculotte.

By 1794 Horne Tooke had emerged, according to one scholar, as 'the heart of the reform movement' (Brown, 52), and as such it is little surprise that the authorities kept a close eye on his movements. Soon after the apprehension of Hardy on 12 May 1794, a letter to Horne Tooke from Jeremiah Joyce was intercepted which posed the question: 'Is it possible to get ready by Thursday?' The reference, as Horne Tooke subsequently proved, was to the preparation of a pamphlet listing sinecure places, but the government apparently interpreted the phrase as referring to an insurrection, and Horne Tooke was duly arrested on 16 May 1794.

On 19 May 1794 Horne Tooke was sent to the Tower along with other radical suspects including Thelwall and Hardy.

A personal diary kept by Horne Tooke in his interleaved copy of *Diversions* records the daily inconveniences and hardships of a regimented prison life, his concerns for the welfare of his daughters, and the physical agony which accompanied the constant and painful treatment of testicular and intestinal problems. Despite the adversities, the veteran reformer was both defiant and heroic. In July he recorded that his confinement had given him

> time to review my life that is passed; and I cannot find any one Action that I have committed, any word that I have written, any syllable that I have uttered, or any single thought that I have entertained, of a political nature, which I wish either to conceal or to recall.　(Tooke, *Diary*, 57)

Such a spirit made Horne Tooke a role model for his imprisoned colleagues, with Thelwall encouraged by his 'philosophic firmness' and 'playful vivacity' (Thelwall, 193), and Stewart Kyd dedicating the second volume of his *Treatise on the Law of Corporations*, written within the Tower, to Horne Tooke's friendship and scholarship.

Horne Tooke and the other prisoners remained in the Tower for five months before being transferred to Newgate on 24 October 1794 to await their trials on charges of high treason. Like most radicals Horne Tooke was prone to self-dramatization, declaring to Thomas Holcroft 'that the best thing our prosecution could have done, for the cause of freedom, was that which they had done: imprison and indict us; except the still better thing which they had yet to do: namely hang us' (Holcroft, 87). Hardy was the first tried, but was acquitted on 5 November 1794. Twelve days later the government proceeded against Horne Tooke, who was ably defended by Thomas Erskine and Vicary Gibbs. The trial lasted six days before Sir James Eyre, with Horne Tooke conducting himself in a 'very cool, clever and witty' manner (*Private Correspondence*, 1.105) and playing a part in examining witnesses. He was 'like some amateur actor pleased with his part and resolved to make the most of it … he rarely laughed himself, but glanced around from his keen and arch eyes a satirical look of triumph' (Townsend, 2.24). On 22 November the jury retired for just two minutes before returning a verdict of not guilty. Horne Tooke's acquittal was the cause of celebration, with newspapers printing trial accounts and his portrait for free. The London Corresponding Society issued commemorative medals, and anniversary dinners became a regular event among reformers, ensuring that the treason trials of 1794 and the hardships endured by the accused remained etched in radical memory.

Later years Following his release Horne Tooke withdrew to Wimbledon, his conduct now more cautious as a result of his failing health, dwindling finances, and the sobering effects of prosecution. According to his own calculations, he had spent a total of 519 days in prison since 1774, which would have had a significant financial and emotional impact. It was not until the general election of 1796 that he showed some renewed passion for politics, when he stood for Westminster against Fox and Sir Alan Gardner. He campaigned against war, taxation, economic depression, and repressive legislation, and held himself out to the electorate as a political martyr who had progressed

'from the hustings to Newgate and from Newgate back to the hustings' (Bewley and Bewley, 192). Horne Tooke polled last of the three candidates, and was fortunate that the £1000 which his campaign cost was offset by a donation from a patron. Around this time Sir Francis Burdett was introduced to the Wimbledon circle, and it was not long before Burdett emerged with 'some degree of intellectuality' from the political initiation offered by Horne Tooke (*Works of Jeremy Bentham*, 10.404), whom he admirably referred to as the 'Wizard of Wimbledon' (Bewley and Bewley, 256). More revolutionary elements were also in the habit of visiting Horne Tooke. The new London Corresponding Society leaders, John Gale Jones, Francis Place, and John Binns, were acquainted with the veteran reformer, and several United Irishmen became regular guests at Wimbledon. The weekly dinners at Horne Tooke's house were a haven for plebeian radicals, as well as popular writers such as Anna Barbauld and John Wolcot and liberal-minded literati including William Godwin, Jeremy Bentham, Joel Barlow, and Samuel Taylor Coleridge.

Despite the popularity of the Wimbledon gatherings their meeting did not raise the same conspiratorial suspicions as those earlier in the decade, perhaps owing to the waning political enthusiasms of the host. Horne Tooke filled his time with gardening, reading, and enjoying the companionship of his daughters and tom cat. He nevertheless maintained an interest in prison reform, campaigning in particular for changes in Cold Bath Fields prison, and took an interest in the case of Gilbert Wakefield, who was imprisoned for libel. Horne Tooke himself was involved in a libel case in 1799, this time prosecuting John Wright, a bookseller, who printed a record of the secret committee of the House of Commons which in the run-up to the treason trials of 1794 had concluded Horne Tooke to be a subversive. Horne Tooke argued that this was a libel since it accused him of a crime of which he had been acquitted, but Lord Kenyon judged that a report of the Commons could not be a libel.

By the end of the 1790s Horne Tooke was living on slender means, having endured the financial strains of infrequent employment, legal engagements, and imprisonment. He had resigned himself to giving up his Wimbledon home and renting a small cottage, but in 1799 he was the timely recipient of a legacy from Felix Vaughan, and his friends raised a subscription and bought an annuity of £600 from Sir Francis Burdett. Horne Tooke soon after involved himself in organizing a fund to support Marcus Despard and his conspirators, who were arrested in 1801 for planning the assassination of George III. James Moody, Horne Tooke's secretary at the Westminster election of 1796 and government spy, reported that Horne Tooke's house served as the 'Headquarters' for organizing the Despard subscription and that Horne Tooke was 'the High Priest' (Hone, 114). At much the same time he met Lord Camelford, who encouraged him to accept his pocket borough of Old Sarum. Although the two men held opposing political views, they remained friends until Camelford was killed in a duel in 1804. For Horne Tooke the offer to sit in parliament came too late to change his life, but it was still an attraction, and he appreciated the irony and challenge of a political reformer representing a rotten borough. On 16 February 1801 Horne Tooke sat in parliament for the first time. By this time, however, he had lost much of his vigour. Age and ill health made him appear in parliament as 'pale and sickly', although he maintained an 'expression of sagacity and energetic resolution' (Bewley and Bewley, 212).

Horne Tooke's position in parliament was soon challenged by Lord Temple on the grounds that he held holy orders, and a select committee was appointed to investigate precedents. The committee's report on 4 May 1801 was not favourable, and Addington introduced a bill to exclude clergymen from election to parliament. Horne Tooke proposed an amendment, but the bill was passed on 19 May despite its opposition by Fox, Sheridan, and Erskine, as well as by Thurlow in the Lords. While the process of determining Horne Tooke's eligibility drew on, he took part in proceedings and made his maiden speech before parliament on 18 February 1801. While his speeches lacked the persuasive effect one might anticipate, Horne Tooke managed to impress some with his oratories, including William Cobbett, who thought they contained 'more good sense on political economy than I ever heard of being uttered in that House for the last 30 years' (*Cobbett's Weekly Political Register*, 193). Horne Tooke kept his seat until parliament was dissolved in June 1802, and in an address to the Westminster electors he declared that 'nothing short of another miracle could possibly enable me to render you any service' in parliament (*Morning Chronicle*, 29 June 1802).

At the election of 1802 Horne Tooke maintained his interest in City politics, appearing in the Westminster hustings in support of Fox for a time and then John Graham. At Brentford he rallied in support of Burdett. Later that year William Tooke died, but instead of making Horne Tooke his heir he decided to discharge some personal debts and bequeathed his old friend the sum of £500. William Tooke's nephew, William Harwood, and great-nephew, John Beaseley, were to share the greater part of the fortune, although Horne Tooke claimed a verbal agreement was in place to divide the legacy equally between the three men. By this time, Horne Tooke had acquired an advance from Burdett to cover annuities for his daughters, and when Harwood refused Horne Tooke's claim Burdett sued and Harwood counterclaimed in chancery. After ten years the case was finally concluded in favour of Burdett.

Despite the freedom afforded by Horne Tooke's financial security and semi-retirement from public life, he still laboured under the effects of gout. Indeed the desperate search for a cure perhaps accounts for his eccentric belief that jolting removed impurities from the human body. Thus he was in the habit of hiring a carriage and riding the roughest roads for several hours when he felt it necessary for his health. His infirmities, however, proved so debilitating that at the Westminster election of 1806 he was unable to campaign for James Paull in spite of his desire to help. The following year, after Paull and Burdett duelled, Horne Tooke published his last pamphlet, *A Warning to the Electors of Westminster* (1807), in which he denounced Paull. Horne Tooke was by this time restricted from playing an active role in politics—more so by his body than his mind. Rheumatism and other problems had made him a virtual prisoner in his own home, and in January 1808 he was so ill it appeared he would die. Horne Tooke, however, slowly recovered only to relapse in August 1809. Within weeks the Old Price riots at Covent Garden theatre were in the public spotlight, and Horne Tooke was a passive supporter of the rioters' cause. As he continued to struggle for his life in the next three years, he maintained an insatiable appetite, especially for grapes, and lost none of his mental alertness.

Death and reputation Despite his will to live, Horne Tooke knew his time was quickly passing. He prepared a tomb in his garden and had a tombstone inscribed. In his last eighteen months he treated himself to a refurnished parlour and refurbished parts of his house, but was characteristically benevolent in discharging the taxes of struggling cottagers behind his property. Horne Tooke's last days were spent in suffering, as he endured kidney stones and gangrene in the legs. Under the constant care of his daughters and Burdett, Horne Tooke refused any visit by the clergy and passed his last days correcting a copy of Shakespeare. He died on 18 March 1812 in Wimbledon and, despite his wish to be buried in his garden, his daughters and sister insisted on a traditional Christian funeral, which took place on 30 March 1812 at St Mary's Church in Ealing. His will bequeathed his estate and possessions to his eldest daughter, Mary Hart.

After his death Horne Tooke was as much revered and reviled as he was during his life. A writer in the *Quarterly Review* thought his life was 'an unavailing and ungraceful struggle' (p. 315), while the *Critical Review* found no reason to distinguish Horne Tooke 'among the principal actors in the political theatre during the last half century, yet he has certainly [made] … his influence strongly felt' (p. 462). Lord Brougham, in referring to Horne Tooke's political career, thought that 'no man out of office all his life and out of Parliament all but a few months … ever acted so conspicuous a part in the political warfare of his times' (Bewley and Bewley, 275). Horne Tooke was indeed a central figure in the burgeoning reform movement of the eighteenth century and his name appears in the chronicles of many of the seminal events of British political history during this period. He is perhaps best remembered by historians for his intrepid roles in the Wilkesite cause, in support of the American revolutionaries, and in the treason trials of 1794. While his political career remains well recognized, Horne Tooke's contributions as a philologist are less significant. Despite the contemporary success and influence of his main treatise on the subject, *Diversions* was outdated by the mid-nineteenth century. Arguably his greatest claim in this respect, as Leigh Hunt suggested, is the fact that he was 'perhaps the first philologist of his nation' (ibid., 275). What cannot be denied is that Horne Tooke, irrespective of the success of his labours in pursuit of his political ideals or philological ideas, was a man whose character ensured he would be influential. His open and hospitable personality attracted to him many friends and disciples, who enjoyed his conversations that could fluctuate freely between humorous wit and caustic criticism. While his physical presence was never particularly imposing and his body fragile and lame in the end, it was his intelligence and mannerisms which ensured him respect in all forums. He was 'a man of independent spirit and upright character' (*Monthly Review*, 424), and it is that unchanging feature under all circumstances which remains so memorable about Horne Tooke.

MICHAEL T. DAVIS

Sources DNB · *Letters of John Wilkes to his friends*, ed. J. Almon (1805) · *The works of Jeremy Bentham*, ed. J. Bowring, [new edn], 11 vols. (1843–59), vol. 10 · C. Bewley and D. Bewley, *Gentleman radical: a life of John Horne Tooke, 1736–1812* (1998) · 'The life of a democrat, a sketch of John Horne Tooke', *Blackwood*, 33 (1833), 963–83 · H. W. Bleackley, *Life of John Wilkes* (1917) · P. A. Brown, *The French Revolution in English history* (1918) · *Cobbett's Weekly Political Register*, 19 (1811), 193–4 · *Critical Review*, 4th ser., 4 (1813), 460–82 · W. L. Cross, *Life and times of Laurence Sterne* (1909) · *Lord Granville Leveson Gower: private correspondence, 1781–1821*, ed. Castalia, Countess Granville [C. R. Leveson-Gower], 2nd edn, 2 vols. (1916) · T. Holcroft, *A narrative of the facts relating to a prosecution for high treason* (1795) · J. A. Hone, *For the cause of truth: radicalism in London, 1796–1821* (1982) · *The letters of Junius*, ed. J. Cannon (1978) · *Monthly Review*, new ser., 12 (1793), 423–5 · *Morning Chronicle* (29 June 1802) · H. Putnam, ed., *Memorial to John Horne Tooke unveiled by the New England Society of Brooklyn* (1920) · review, QR, 7 (1812), 313–28 · S. Rogers, *Recollections*, ed. W. Sharpe (1859) · A. Stephens, *Memoirs of John Horne Tooke*, 2 vols. (1813) · Mrs Thelwall, *The life of John Thelwall* (1837) · J. Horne Tooke, *An oration delivered by the Rev. Mr. Horne* (1770) · J. Horne Tooke, *The prison diary (16 May–22 November 1794) of John Horne Tooke*, ed. A. V. Beedell and A. D. Harvey (1995) · W. C. Townsend, *The lives of twelve eminent judges*, 2 vols. (1846) · *Walpole, Corr.*, vol. 31 · J. Wilkes, *Controversial letters of John Wilkes, esq., the Rev. John Horne Tooke and their adherents* (1771) · M. C. Yarborough, *John Horne Tooke* (1926)
Archives BL, diary, MS C60.i.15 · BL, papers relating to proceedings against him in parliament, Add. MSS 27778, 41065 · PRO, PC 1/21/35A · PRO, TS 11/955 · PRO, TS 24/3/3 | PRO, PC 1/21/35A · PRO, TS 11/955
Likenesses R. Houston, group portrait, oils, c.1768, NPG · R. Brompton, oils, 1777, Man. City Gall. · J. Corner, line engraving, 1791 (after R. Brompton), BM; repro. in *European Magazine* (1791) · T. Hardy, oils, 1791, NPG [*see illus.*] · plaster medallion, 1793 (after J. Tassie), Scot. NPG · sculpture token, 1794, NPG · mezzotint, pubd 1795 (after unknown artist), NPG · J. Gillray, caricature, etching, pubd 1798, NPG · F. Chantrey, marble bust, 1811, FM Cam. · F. Chantrey, terracotta bust, 1811, Sheffield City Museum · F. Chantrey, pencil drawing, NPG

Tooke, Thomas (1774–1858), economist, born at Kronstadt, Russia, on 28 February 1774, was the eldest son of William *Tooke (*bap.* 1744, *d.* 1820), then chaplain to the British factory at Kronstadt, and his wife, Elizabeth, daughter of Thomas Eyton. William *Tooke was his younger brother. Thomas began working at the age of fifteen in a house of business at St Petersburg, and subsequently became a partner in the London firms of Stephen Thornton & Co. and Astell, Tooke, and Thornton. On 8 September 1802 he married Priscilla (*d.* 1837), daughter of Charles Combe MD of Bloomsbury, London.

Tooke apparently did not take part in any public discussion of economic questions until 1819, in which year he gave evidence before committees of both houses of parliament on the resumption of cash payments by the Bank of England. He began his career as an economist as a supporter of the principles embodied in the report of the bullion committee of 1810. Those principles, advocated by Ricardo, Horner, Thornton, and Huskisson, were to become the basis of the bullionist position and were later adopted by the currency school. Tooke's approach to monetary issues changed later in his career, and in the 1840s he became a leading figure in the famous banking school.

During the three years which followed the Resumption Act of 1819 prices of nearly all commodities decreased, and the opinion that the fall in prices was the result of the return to cash payments gained support. Tooke's efforts during his early years as an active economist were devoted to the defence of the resumption and the refutation of the claims that it was responsible for the decline in prices and associated crises. In his first book, published in 1823, *Thoughts and Details on the High and Low Prices of the Last Thirty Years*, he presented data to support his point of view. He pursued the argument in his *Considerations on the State of the Currency* (1826), which also included an innovative discussion of interest rates, and in his *Letter to Lord Grenville* (1829), followed by another letter addressed to Grenville in that year, *On the Currency in Connection with the Corn Trade*. His object was to negate 'the alleged influence of the bank restriction and resumption in raising or depressing general prices beyond the difference between gold and paper', and to show that the act of 1819 was practically inoperative so far as any contraction of the currency was concerned. This line of research led to a detailed examination of the causes which might affect prices, and Tooke claimed to establish the conclusion that the variations, both during the period of restriction and after the resumption, were due to 'real' causes, directly connected with the commodities themselves, and not to monetary factors.

The same views were maintained in the first two volumes of the *History of Prices*, dealing with the period from 1793 to 1837, which were published in 1838. His conclusions as regards that period were that the high prices which, generally speaking, ruled between 1793 and 1814 were due to a relatively large number of unfavourable seasons, coupled with the obstructions to trade which were created by the Napoleonic wars; while the lower range of prices in the subsequent years was attributable to a series of more prolific seasons, the removal of the adverse influences arising out of a state of war, and the consequent improvement in the processes of manufacture and industry.

The *History of Prices* was completed in six volumes; the third, dealing with the years 1838–9, was published in 1840 and contained already some of the formulations of Tooke's transition into a banking school's position. The fourth volume was published in 1848, and the fifth and sixth, in the compilation of which Tooke was assisted by William Newmarch, in 1857, the year before Tooke's death.

The whole work is an admirable analysis of the financial

and commercial history of the period which it covers; and the subject was one with which Tooke was peculiarly well fitted to deal, possessing as he did the rather rare combination of a wide practical knowledge of mercantile affairs with considerable powers of reflection and reasoning. Whatever may be thought of his conclusions, the value of his methods of investigation is beyond dispute.

The chief interest of the later volumes lies in their record of the steps by which Tooke gradually severed himself from the supporters of the currency theory, who may be regarded as the direct heirs of the bullionists of 1810 and 1819. There is a general agreement that Tooke's early publications, before 1840, reflect an approach to monetary issues quite different from that which characterizes his later works. Tooke's 1844 pamphlet, *An Inquiry into the Currency Principle*, marked a complete departure from the monetary views of his first period. These new views constituted a theoretical declaration of the principles of the banking school. In brief, he now argued that there was no theoretical or empirical basis for the currency school's distinction between banknotes and other means of payment, such as cheques and bills of exchange. Secondly, he argued that the quantity theory of money, which stated that prices were determined by the quantity of the medium in circulation, was wrong. Tooke and the banking school thought that, on the contrary, the quantity of the medium in circulation was determined by prices. Prices, he contended, were determined by the incomes of the consumers.

The Resumption Act passed in 1819 was a practical recognition of the instability associated with an inconvertible paper currency. But it did not take long to convince policy makers that the measure was incomplete. The experience of the great crisis of 1825, followed by those of 1836–9, showed that it was not enough to impose on the Bank of England the liability of payment in gold unless there was also security that the bank had the means of discharging the liability. Both in 1825 and in 1839 the danger of another suspension of cash payments was imminent. But while all agreed that the management of the currency, so far as it rested with the bank, was unsatisfactory, there was great difference of opinion as to the remedy which should be applied.

Out of the controversy emerged the act of 1844, the main object of which was to prevent the over-issue of notes and to regulate their quantity so that the volume of the currency should at all times conform in amount to what it would have been under a purely metallic system. Thus, the Bank Act, which separated the issuing of notes from other banking activities, implemented the currency school's analysis.

Tooke was resolutely opposed to the provisions of the act, holding them to be either superfluous or mischievous. He did not dispute that the affairs of the bank had been mismanaged; but he attributed this less to the system than to want of prudence in administering it. He thought that by some changes in the management of the bank, coupled with the compulsory maintenance of a much larger reserve of bullion, more satisfactory results would be achieved than under the inelastic system prescribed by the act.

The supporters of the 'currency theory', whose principles were adopted by Peel and embodied in the act, were represented by Samuel Jones Loyd, Baron Overstone, Robert Torrens, and George Warde Norman. They contended that banks of issue, by the arbitrary extension of their circulation, could produce a direct effect upon prices, and thus stimulate speculation, with the consequent fluctuations and revulsions of credit; that the mere enactment of convertibility on demand was not a sufficient safeguard against these evils; and that the only adequate remedy was to separate the business of issue from that of banking in such a way that the former should regulate itself automatically, and that the discretion of the directors should be confined to the latter alone.

Tooke, on the other hand, reinforced later on by John Fullarton and James Wilson, maintained from 1844 that a paper currency which was readily convertible on demand must necessarily conform, so far as its permanent value was concerned, to the value of a purely metallic currency; that for this purpose no other regulation was required beyond ready and immediate convertibility; that under these conditions banks had no power of arbitrarily increasing their issues; and that the level of prices was not directly affected by such issues.

Tooke's views on the application of free-trade principles to note-issuing were the last to change during his transition from a 'moderate bullionist' to a banking school advocate. Whereas in his early conceptualization he totally rejected the application of *laissez-faire* to note-issuing, in 1844 he came to the conclusion that, in fact, competition, under certain restrictions, might work.

In Tooke's earlier writings there were many passages inconsistent with his later opinions; and the process of development was very gradual (see J. Fullarton, *On the Regulation of Currencies*, 2nd edn, 1845, 18). Overstone also observed before the 1857 select committee on the Bank Acts that 'Mr. Tooke is upon this subject of science very like our great artist Mr. Turner upon the subject of art: he has his later manner as well as his middle manner.'

Tooke was one of the earliest supporters of the free-trade movement, which first assumed a definite form in the petition of the merchants of the City of London presented to the House of Commons by Alexander Baring (later Baron Ashburton) on 8 May 1820. This document, which contains an admirable statement of the principles of free trade, was drawn up by Tooke; and the circumstances which led to its preparation are described in the sixth volume of the *History of Prices*. The substantial advances in the direction of free trade made by Lord Liverpool's government, especially after the accession of William Huskisson in 1828, were no doubt largely due to the effect produced by the petition; and it may fairly be claimed for it that it gave the first impulse towards that revision of commercial policy which was the work of the next half-century.

It was to support the principles of the merchants' petition that Tooke, with Ricardo, Malthus, James Mill, and others, founded the Political Economy Club in April 1821. From the beginning he took a prominent part in its discussions, and he continued to attend its meetings until within a few weeks of his death, his last recorded attendance being on 3 December 1857.

Besides giving evidence on economic questions before several parliamentary committees, such as those of 1819 on the resumption of cash payments, of 1821 on agricultural depression and on foreign trade, and of 1832, 1840, 1841, and 1848 on the Bank Acts, Tooke was the chief commissioner of the children's employment commission and a prominent member of the factories inquiry commission of 1833. He retired from active business on his own account in 1836, but was governor of the Royal Exchange Assurance Corporation from 1840 to 1852, and was also chairman of the St Katharine's Dock Company.

Tooke was elected a fellow of the Royal Society in March 1821, and a corresponding member of the Institut de France (Académie des Sciences Morales et Politiques) in February 1853. He lived in London at 12 Russell Square, afterwards in Richmond Terrace, and at 31 Spring Gardens, where he died on 26 February 1858. He was survived by his second son, two other sons having predeceased him.

In the year after Tooke's death the Tooke professorship of economic science and statistics at King's College, London, was founded in his memory, the endowment being raised by public subscription.

G. H. MURRAY, rev. ARIE ARNON

Sources *Parl. papers* (1819–48) · *The Economist* (March 1858) · *The Athenaeum* (6 March 1858), 306 · *The Athenaeum* (8 June 1858), 595 · A. Arnon, 'The transformation in Thomas Tooke's monetary theory reconsidered', *History of Political Economy*, 16 (1984), 311–26 · A. Arnon, *Thomas Tooke: pioneer of monetary theory* (1991) · D. Laidler, 'Thomas Tooke on monetary reform', *Essays in honour of Lord Robbins*, ed. M. Peston and B. Corry (1972) · F. W. Fetter, *Development of British monetary orthodoxy, 1797–1875* (1965) · T. E. Gregory, introduction, in T. Tooke and W. Newmarch, *A history of prices* (1928) · M. D. Bordo and A. J. Schwartz, 'Money and prices in the nineteenth century: was Thomas Tooke right ?', *Explorations in Economic History*, 18 (1981), 97–127 · Burke, *Gen. GB* [Padwick of Horsham]
Archives BL, corresp. with Lord Grenville, Add. MS 69082 · Derbys. RO, letters to Sir Robert Wilmot-Horton
Likenesses R. Dighton, coloured etching, pubd 1823, NPG, V&A · M. A. Shee, portrait; known to be in possession of his granddaughter in 1898 · J. Stephenson, line engraving (after unknown artist), NPG · watercolour sketch; known to be at the Royal Exchange Assurance Corporation in 1898
Wealth at death under £60,000: administration, 18 March 1858, *CGPLA Eng. & Wales*

Tooke, William (*bap.* 1744, *d.* 1820), writer and translator, was baptized at St John, Clerkenwell, on 26 January 1744, the second son of Thomas Tooke (1705–1773), vintner, of that parish and his wife, Hannah, only daughter of Thomas Mann of St James's, Clerkenwell, whom he married in March 1737. The Tookes claimed descent from Le Sieur de Touque, who arrived in Britain with William the Conqueror. After a liberal classical education at John Shield's reputable Islington academy, William Tooke and his lifelong friend the future publisher John Nichols were apprenticed to William Bowyer the younger. Two years

later, in 1760, Tooke was turned over to James Harrison: he became free of the Stationers' Company in May 1765. His correspondence from this period gives a unique insight into Tooke's life as a journeyman typographer and printer, his love entanglements, writing potential, and his earliest decision, in September 1767, to enter the church. During 1767 he edited and printed an impressive third edition of John Weever's *Antient Funeral Monuments of Great-Britain*. Two years later he printed *The Loves of Othniel and Achsah: Translated from the Chaldee*, described by the *Gentleman's Magazine* as 'a moral poem, in prose, in the manner of Klopstock and Gesner' (*GM*, 1st ser., 39, 1769, 261).

The year 1771 marked a milestone for Tooke, then a resident of St John's Square, Clerkenwell. On 24 February he obtained letters of ordination as a deacon and priest from the bishop of London. He married Elizabeth (*b. c.*1749), daughter of Thomas Eyton of Llangynhaval, Denbighshire, and his wife, Alice Robert. They had two sons: Thomas *Tooke (1774–1858), economist, and William *Tooke (1777–1863), lawyer. Tooke turned down John Duncombe's offer of the living of West Thurrock in Essex when the Russia Company elected him chaplain to the English Factory's church at Kronstadt, St Petersburg's commercial harbour, on 22 March. A year later he was admitted to a master mason's degree at the 'Perfect Union' lodge in the Russian capital. His edition of *Mary Magdalene's Funeral Tears*, by the Jesuit poet Robert Southwell, was published in 1772.

In March 1774 Tooke succeeded John Glen King, his influential friend, as chaplain of the English Factory's St Petersburg church, located at the centre of the Galley, or English Quay. He held the post until 1792 and during this time became friendly with the clergy of several different denominations and with many leading writers and academics, stimulating his ambition to make their works known in Britain. In 1777 Nichols printed Tooke's translation, with additional notes, of *Pieces Written by Mons. Falconet and Mons. Diderot on Sculpture in General*, with special reference to Étienne Falconet's sculpting of his famous equestrian statue of Peter the Great. Then, between 1780 and 1783, Nichols published the four volumes of Tooke's anonymous translation of J. G. Georgi's German work, *Russia, or, A Compleat Historical Account of All the Nations which Compose that Empire*. Extensively reviewed in the *Gentleman's Magazine*, under Nichols's editorship, it provided English readers with their first comprehensive knowledge of the subject. Furthermore, by including Tooke's translation of Pallas's dissertation on the formation of mountains, read in 1777 to the Russian Academy of Sciences, it publicized what Cuvier regarded as the cornerstone of modern geology.

On leave of absence from October 1783 to June 1784, Tooke travelled overland to Britain, visiting Emanuel Kant at Königsberg and the Berlin Academy of Sciences *en route*. He was elected a fellow of the Royal Society of London on 5 June 1783 and signed its charter book on 21 January 1784. He was admitted to Jesus College, Cambridge, as a sizar in May 1784, and was appointed a corresponding member of the Society of Antiquaries of Scotland on 12 June. An informative letter from Tooke to Glen King about ancient Tartar burial sites was read on 25 March at the Society of Antiquaries of London.

Launching a major project on his return to Russia, Tooke contributed thirty-one letters describing fictitious journeys through central and southern Russia and the Ukraine to the *Gentleman's Magazine* (1785–9 and 1794–1816). He wrote as M. M. M., from his family motto, 'Militia mea multiplex', and adopted the persona of a pseudo-military traveller with a peripatetic lifestyle. Most of his material was drawn from travel accounts by Pallas, Georgi, Gmelin, and other historical, cultural, and ethnographic sources.

Tooke was a voluminous correspondent, mostly with Nichols, and his letters, both published and unpublished, provide a remarkable picture of the life of an intelligent and observant Russophile. Among unpublished writings that are discussed in his correspondence are a guide to teaching Greek in schools, via Latin (1785), and his translation in 1783 of Carl Friedrich Bahrdt's version of the New Testament from the third Berlin edition, which Tooke presented to Dr Williams's Library (MS Mod., fol. 43) in 1816. Other letters reflect what resulted in two series of Tooke's didactic lectures, published by Benjamin White, in four volumes each, as *Moral and philosophical estimates of the state and faculties of man; and of the nature and source of human happiness* (1789) and *Moral and philosophical suggestions on various subjects related to human perfection and happiness* (1790); both were well received. Earlier Daines Barrington had relied on the accuracy of Tooke's data when quoting from his letters of 1774 and 1775 in support of his view that the north pole was navigable from the Arctic Ocean throughout the year. Tooke also supplied Richard Gough and Joseph White with scientific and scholarly material in 1784 and 1785. However, his correspondence with Sir Joseph Banks in 1785, 1786, and 1791 is the clearest evidence of his productive liaison between the Royal Society and the Imperial Academy of Sciences at St Petersburg. In his letter dated 23 September 1791 Tooke informed Banks that over the past four years he had compiled several thousand folio pages of items, not published in English, from every branch of literature. 'I take dry dissertations', he writes,

> and give them an easy dress and entertaining air. I compress elaborate works into a legible compass. I stew down old German professors into a potable soup, distill dull lectures into volatile essence, and extract the marrow of every critical bone. (BL, Add. MS 33982, fols. 320–21)

In December 1791 Tooke told Nichols that he wanted to leave Russia and set up a periodical along the lines of James Anderson's well-known *Bee, or, Literary Intelligencer*, a move that was made possible in 1792 by a substantial legacy from his uncle William Mann of the Middle Temple. At his departure Tooke was elected a member of the Free Economic Society of St Petersburg and, on 3 September 1792, a corresponding member of the Imperial Academy of Sciences. Tooke bought a house in Great Ormond Street, where he lived from 1795 to 1820. He frequently attended meetings at the Royal Society, where he introduced many

visitors, signed proposal certificates, and presented the library with nine of his works. He continued to keep Banks posted on Russia through Matthew Guthrie, his St Petersburg correspondent. He composed a memoir of Sir Hans Sloane and his collections, written in French, with English annotations, on Chinese paper from Canton (Guangzhou) made from bamboo cane. He and his son Thomas subscribed to proprietors' shares in the Russell Institution for the Promotion of Literary and Scientific Knowledge, founded in 1808 at Great Coram Street, Brunswick Square.

Tooke continued to make good use of the eclectic material he had accumulated from Russia. In 1795 *The Repertory of Arts and Manufactures* published his letter (reprinted in the *Annual Register* and the *Pocket Magazine*) about the fires during the 1780s on a Russian frigate and to hemp at a ropewalk plant caused by self-igniting substances. That year he also published the two volumes of his *Varieties of literature from foreign literary journals and original MSS.*, a broad selection which included Gregory Shelekov's account of his epic voyage from Okhotsk to America between 1783 and 1787. It was followed in 1798 by *Selections from the most celebrated foreign literary journals and other periodical publications*, the second volume of which contained A. L. Schloezer's pioneering dissertations on Russian history. In the same year a new edition of *The General Biographical Dictionary*, revised and enlarged in fifteen volumes, was published under Tooke's overall editorship. Between 1798 and 1801 he translated or compiled four major works about Russia. Jean-Henri Castéra's French biography, rendered by Tooke as *The Life of Catharine II, Empress of Russia: an Enlarged Translation* (1798), appeared in six editions; over half the text consisted of Tooke's additions. Castéra incorporated most of these, with his own new findings, in another edition of his biography, from which Tooke produced a fourth edition (1800), exemplifying his firmly held belief that a translator–compiler becomes part owner and author of a translated work in his own right. He also supervised the translation of F. C. P. Masson's anonymous *Mémoires secrètes*, published in 1800 by Longman and Rees, as a supplement to *The Life of Catharine II*, under the title of *Secret Memoirs of the Court of Petersburg*. His next compilation, *View of the Russian empire during the reign of Catharine the Second, and to the close of the present century* (1799), was translated into French from the second edition in 1801. Much praised by contemporaries, this comprehensive work succeeded in promulgating Russia through the systematic translation and reconfiguration of source materials. Tooke followed it up in 1800 with a diligent *History of Russia from the foundation of the monarchy by Rurik to the accession of Catharine the Great*. His final major translation on a Russian theme, *The Picture of Petersburg: from the German of Henry Storch* (1801), gave the British reader a well-informed survey of contemporary Russian life, personalities, and institutions, to which Tooke added his own innovatory Russian verse translations.

An excellent preacher, Tooke published at his own expense the sermon he delivered on Ash Wednesday in 1808 as honorary chaplain to the Stationers' Company. In

1814 the corporation of London printed the five sermons which he preached as the lord mayor's chaplain, prompting Nichols to remark that if he could dispense ecclesiastical preferment, 'Mr. Tooke would not be long without at least a Prebendal Stall' (*GM*, 1st ser., 84/2, 1814, 48). Between 1802 and 1814 he published translations of the sermons by Georg Joachim Zollikofer, the celebrated Leipzig reformed church minister, and also translated his *Devotional Prayers and Exercises* (1815). His wittily prefaced translation *Private History of Peregrinus Proteus the Philosopher … from the German* (by Christoph Martin Wieland) appeared in 1796. In 1820 Nichols printed the two quarto volumes of Tooke's translation *Lucian of Samosata: from the Greek. With the Comments of Wieland and Others*. In a long introduction Tooke clearly defined his guiding principles as a translator, enshrined in his *Illustrations* of Horace's epistles and satires, over 300 pages of which appeared in the *Gentleman's Magazine* between September 1806 and November 1811. In what would have been a key work, he was revising these for separate publication at the time of his death.

Tooke died in Guilford Street, London, on 17 November 1820 following a short illness, and was buried on the 23rd in the new burial-ground adjoining the St Pancras churchyard. He was survived by his wife. Nichols was a pallbearer at his funeral.
JOHN H. APPLEBY

Sources Nichols, *Lit. anecdotes*, vol. 9 • A. G. Cross, 'The Reverend William Tooke's contribution to English knowledge of Russia', *Canadian Slavic Studies*, 3/1 (1969), 106–15 • J. M. Kuist, *The Nichols file of the Gentleman's Magazine* (1991) • J. M. Kuist, 'A collaboration in learning: *The Gentleman's Magazine* and its ingenious contributors', *Studies in Bibliography*, 44 (1991), 302–17 • Bodl. Oxf., MS Eng. lett. c. 366, fols. 116–94 • Bodl. Oxf., MS Film 1529/1–2 • A. G. Cross, *By the banks of the Neva* (1997) • *GM*, 2nd ser., 12 (1839), 605 • D. F. McKenzie, ed., *Stationers' Company apprentices*, [3]: *1701–1800* (1978) • *The Banks letters*, ed. W. R. Dawson (1958) • *An account of the proceedings … of the Russell Institution for the Promotion of Literary and Scientific Knowledge* (1808) • registers, St John the Baptist, Clerkenwell, etc., LMA, Microfilm X 102/029 [index to transcripts] • *DNB*
Archives Bodl. Oxf., MS Eng. Lett. c.366, fols. 116–94 • Bodl. Oxf., MS Film 1529/1–2 • DWL, notebook and papers
Likenesses J. Collyer junior, engraving, *c*.1816 (after M. A. Shee), BM, NPG; repro. in W. Tooke, *Lucian of Samosata* (1820), vol. 1, frontispiece
Wealth at death Considerable property, in London and Essex, investments and securities: will, PRO, PROB 11/1636, 341r–342/sig. 644

Tooke, William (1777–1863), lawyer and promoter of arts and literature, was born in St Petersburg, Russia, on 22 November 1777. He was the younger son of William *Tooke (*bap.* 1744, *d.* 1820), historian of Russia and chaplain to the factory of the Russia Company at St Petersburg, and his wife, Elizabeth, daughter of Thomas Eyton of Llangynhafal, Denbighshire. Thomas *Tooke (1774–1858), economist, was his elder brother. William went to England in 1792, and was articled to William Devon, solicitor, in Gray's Inn, with whom he entered into partnership in 1798. Subsequently he went into partnership with Charles Parker at 39 Bedford Row. He remained there for many years before practising instead in the firm of Tooke, Son,

and Hallowes. In 1807 he married Amelia (*d.* 1848), youngest daughter of Samuel Shaen, landowner, of Crix Hall, Hatfield Peverel, near Colchester, Essex. Through her nieces' marriages, he was related to Henry Solly, Unitarian social reformer, G. J. Allman, botanist and zoologist, and the archaeologist W. C. Perry.

In 1825 Tooke took a prominent part in the formation of the St Katharine's Dock. He was the London agent of George Barker, the solicitor of the London and Birmingham Railway. He also acted for the Society for the Suppression of Mendicity. He assisted in the foundation of University College, London, and was one of the first council (19 December 1823). He represented the interests of the college in the 1830s, pressing in the Commons for legislation to enable London to grant degrees, rather unwillingly accepting the ambivalent title of the college which was granted its charter in 1836. He was its treasurer until 1841. Tooke procured the charter for the Royal Society of Literature without payment for his professional services. For many years he was an active member of the council of the society, and one of the chief promoters of Thomas Wright's *Biographia Britannica literaria*. In 1826, with Lord Brougham, Dr Birkbeck, George Grote, and others, he took part in the formation of the Society for the Diffusion of Useful Knowledge; but in 1846, like many others, he disapproved of the publication of the society's *Biographical Dictionary* on the grounds that it was too ambitious a project, both intellectually and financially.

Tooke was elected a fellow of the Royal Society on 12 March 1818. He was present at the first annual meeting of the Law Institution on 5 June 1827, and was mainly instrumental in obtaining its royal charter of incorporation in January 1832. For some years he was the usual chairman of the meetings and dinners, and when Lord Brougham was considering a measure for the establishment of local courts, he addressed to him a letter in defence of the profession of an attorney. From an earlier period he was a leading member of the Society of Arts; in 1814 he was the chairman of the committee of correspondence and editor of the *Transactions*, and in 1862 he was elected president of the society. For services rendered to the Institution of Civil Engineers he was elected an honorary member of that corporation. From 1824 he was honorary secretary and from 1840 one of the three treasurers of the Royal Literary Fund Society.

At the general election of 1830, in conjunction with his friend Sir John William Lubbock, Tooke unsuccessfully contested the close borough of Truro. After the passing of the Reform Bill, however, he was elected on 15 December 1832, and represented the borough until July 1837. He was afterwards a candidate for Finsbury, but did not proceed to a poll, and on 30 June 1841 he unsuccessfully contested Reading. During the five sessions that he sat in parliament he supported reform, and gave his vote for measures for the promotion of education and for the abolition of slavery; but in later life his views were said to have become more conservative. He died at his London residence, 12 Russell Square, on 20 September 1863, and was buried in Kensal Green cemetery. He left two daughters and a son,

Arthur William Tooke of Pinner, Middlesex. Tooke was fond of literature and wrote several works, ranging from texts on the poet Charles Churchill and the *ancien régime*, to private publications of his own verse. He was a contributor to the *New Monthly Magazine*, the *Annual Register*, and the *Gentleman's Magazine*.

G. C. BOASE, rev. ERIC METCALFE

Sources WWBMP, 1.379 · GM, 3rd ser., 15 (1863), 656–9 · *Men of the time* (1862), 753 · *ILN* (10 Oct 1863), 373 · H. H. Bellot, *University College, London, 1826–1926* (1929)
Archives BL, letters; memoir of Sir Hans Sloane | UCL, letters to James Loch · UCL, letters to Society for the Diffusion of Useful Knowledge
Likenesses C. Turner, mezzotint, pubd 1836 (after J. White), BM · J. White, group portrait (governors of the parishes of St George's, Bloomsbury, and St Andrew, Holborn) · wood-engraving, BM; repro. in *ILN*
Wealth at death under £140,000: probate, 21 Oct 1863, *CGPLA Eng. & Wales*

Tooker, William (1553/4–1621), dean of Lichfield and author, was born in Exeter, the second son of William Tooker and Honora Erisey. He received his early education at Winchester College, and proceeded to Oxford, where his matriculation from New College aged eighteen, was entered under the year 1572. He was elected a scholar of New College in 1575 and was a full fellow from 1577 to 1585. On 16 October 1579 he graduated BA, and he incepted MA in 1583. He was admitted BTh and licensed DTh on 4 July 1594.

From 1580 Tooker was a canon of Exeter Cathedral. He was installed as rector of St James-the-Great, Kilkhampton, Cornwall, in 1584. The following year he resigned his fellowship at New College and took up the position of archdeacon of Barnstaple in Exeter diocese. In 1588 he was made rector of St Andrew's, West Dean, Wiltshire, a position he held until his death. In the same year he was appointed one of the chaplains royal, and probably was also collated prebendary of Salisbury Cathedral. In 1590 Tooker was appointed rector of St Peter's, Clovelly, Devon, a position he held until 1601.

A loyal supporter of the monarchy, Tooker compiled a Latin refutation of the excommunication of Elizabeth I by Pope Pius V, *Charisma, sive, Donum sanationis* (1597). In a historical overview from the times of Edward the Confessor to his own age he advocated that English monarchs were endowed with the same gift of kingship that the rulers of biblical times had received. This 'they have accepted directly from God, and have been using from the times of the early Christians' ('immidiate … ab ipso Deo acceperunt, & a primo christianitatis tempore … exercuerunt'; Tooker, *Charisma*, sig. M 3r).

In an age that saw regular debates on whether the Church of England should be remodelled on presbyterian principles Tooker was a firm defender of the establishment of the church, a subject he addressed at length in his *Of the Fabrique of the Church and Church-Mens Livings* (1604). Advocating that the good estate of the established church depended on the well-being of the state, he emphasized that 'Parity in the Church once established in the governement Ecclesiasticall, will draw on paritie in the

politicall and civill estate' (Tooker, *Fabrique*, sig. A 3r). Indeed, clergy derived the necessary freedom to exercise their ministry directly from the monarch: 'onely the Prince giveth them publique liberty, without let or disturbance, to doe that which Christ hath commanded' (ibid., sig. H 4r).

In a later publication against the German Jesuit Martin Beck (Becanus), *Duellum, sive, Singularis certamen cum Martino Becano Jesuita* (1611), he reiterated his strong belief that, although the monarch was the rightful governor of the church, he made no claims to be a spiritual leader of the church:

> God did not bestow ecclesiastical rights on king or emperor. Though a number of church members are subjects of the monarch, the king does not stand above the sacraments, or the Word, or above the spiritual gifts of the church. Therefore he can only ever be her supreme governor.
>
> (Res ecclesiae Deo dandae sunt, non caesari vel Regi: partes vero Ecclesiae sunt homines … qui sunt regis; … rex non est supra sacramenta, et verbum, nec super Ecclesiae spiritualia charismata, et tamen supremus est in Ecclesia gubernator.) (Tooker, *Duellum*, 23)

In recognition of his loyalty to the monarchy Tooker was made dean of Lichfield Cathedral in February 1605. Nine months later, on 25 November 1605, he resigned his archdeaconry. He died at Salisbury on 19 March 1621, and was buried in Salisbury Cathedral on 21 March. He was survived by his son Robert.   J. ANDREAS LÖWE

Sources Wood, *Ath. Oxon.*, new edn, 2.288 · Foster, *Alum. Oxon.* · *Fasti Angl.* (Hardy), 1.407, 1.563 · *Reg. Oxf.*, 1.139, 2.54, 2/3.85 · *DNB*

Toole, John Lawrence (1830–1906), actor and theatre manager, was born on 12 March 1830 at 50 St Mary Axe in the City of London, the younger son of James Toole and his wife, Elizabeth. On 25 July he was baptized at the church of St Andrew Undershaft in the same street. He did not come from a theatrical family: his father was variously an India House messenger, an usher at the Old Bailey, and in the 1840s toastmaster to the City corporation; and Toole, after attending the City of London School (1841–5), was sent to work as a City wine-merchant's clerk.

Early acting career The City largely defined him. An English patriot of conventional outlook, Toole prided himself on his business sense, and applied it with zest and much personal profit to a career on the stage, to which he turned with a driven sense of vocation at the age of twenty-two, having during the preceding two years divided his time outside office hours between the galleries of theatres, the evening classes of the City Histrionic Club—whose members were coached in elocution and gave theatrical performances at Sussex Hall—and the stages of mechanics' institutes, where he sharpened his acting techniques in monologues, imitations of famous actors, and excerpts from plays. Charles Dickens saw one such entertainment by Toole at the Walworth Institute on 23 February 1852 and afterwards vouchsafed his view to Toole's brother, Francis Frederick, that the young amateur would have a strong chance of success on the professional stage. Francis, eleven years Toole's senior and a clerk in the East and

John Lawrence Toole (1830–1906), by John Collier, 1887

West India Dock Company, was to act as Toole's theatrical agent and business adviser for the next fifteen years. To Walworth he had attracted—besides Dickens and other literary and theatrical figures—Benjamin Webster (a future West End employer of Toole's), E. L. Blanchard (soon to contribute scripted material for the one-man shows), and reporters from the national press, each of whom wrote in the amateur's praise—the *Morning Chronicle*, for example, of 26 February attesting to the 'sensation' produced by Toole's acting. Though more than seven months short of his professional début (at the Queen's Theatre, Dublin, on 2 October) he had been acclaimed by members of the theatrical establishment, of which in due course he would become a leader and an ornament. From the 1870s to the 1890s he and Henry Irving were the complementary joint figureheads of the British stage. 'Mr J. L. Toole', as he styled himself—or 'Toole', as he was spontaneously known—sustained for nearly forty years, with almost unbroken success, a position at or near the summit of his adopted profession. To have been known universally by his surname alone was a mark of his fame and singular appeal among all classes of people. For most of the second half of the nineteenth century no actor proved more popular than he throughout the British Isles.

A notable farceur Toole's forte was farce. In this he was assisted by the peculiarities of his physique, physiognomy, and voice. Short of stature, with short legs, he had the head and body of a tall man. His face was broad and open, an ideal canvas for greasepaints, with shining eyes, a long upper lip, and a wide crack of a mouth, the astonishing flexibility of which could induce uncontainable mirth when pursed with false pride, distended in indignation, or in any way awry. The voice, deep and dry, swooping and cockney, was alone sufficient to set a whole theatre in a roar. Toole shared with John Baldwin Buckstone but very few others the ability to make an audience laugh by croaking a remark from off-stage before he came into view. He made free with the audience no less than the text, and they loved him for it—especially in the provinces, where he undertook lengthy annual tours, sometimes alluding to local people, places, and events, regardless of dramatic context but to general delight. Effusive and instinctive, his 'gagging', unlike that of some comedians, was never indecent: it was a sunny propensity that carried over into his private life, where, sporting a spurious monocle, he affected the air of a 'swell' and indulged in notorious practical jokes, as recorded in the *Reminiscences* he published in collaboration with Joseph Hatton in 1889. People thought him quaint, even in his youth. Increasingly he was seen as the last of the old school of English comic actors that had included Buckstone, Edward Richard Wright (from whom he took over as principal low comedian at the Adelphi on 27 December 1858, remaining there nine years), and John Liston, whose famous role of Paul Pry, first acted by Liston in John Poole's farce of that name in 1825, was attempted by Toole to great effect while still an amateur (at the Red Lion Assembly Room, Dorking) on 2 October 1850 and was retained in his repertory for forty-five years. Toole acquired the umbrella that Liston had carried in the part, and deemed it an honour to use it too.

Shortly before becoming a professional actor Toole played Simmons in T. H. Bayly's *The Spitalfields Weaver* for one night at the Theatre Royal, Haymarket. The farce was added to an already copious programme on 22 July 1852, and Toole did not make his first entrance until after one o'clock. (Fifty years later, Edward VII sent him a telegram congratulating him on the golden jubilee of his appearance on the London stage.) After apprenticeship in Dublin, where he was paid £2 a week, he transferred to Edinburgh on 9 July 1853 as principal low comedian, and on 2 October 1854 began his London campaign at the St James's. After six months, having failed to win the West End plaudits he had sought, he returned to Edinburgh; but in the autumn of 1857 he was back in London, at the Lyceum under Charles Dillon (who had employed him at Dublin), frequently acting with Marie Wilton (the future Lady Bancroft), and on 10 March 1858 scored a notable hit as Tom Cranky in the first presentation of John Hollingshead's farce *The Birthplace of Podgers*. At the Adelphi from 1858 to 1867 he was recognized as the foremost English farceur of his generation. The stage partnership he enjoyed throughout that period with Paul Bedford—Toole dwarfish and capering, Bedford tall and sedate—ranked among the most effective comic duos ever seen. It was epitomized in *The Area Belle* of William Brough and Andrew Halliday (7 March 1864), in which the contrasting but complementary comedians were seen as rival suitors, and Toole sang a comic ballad, 'A Norrible Tale', specially written for him by Blanchard.

From burlesque to management At the Gaiety, where he was principally based from 1869 to 1877, Toole, while continuing to appear in farce, was cast more frequently than before in musical extravaganza and burlesque. On 26 December 1871 he took the leading part in *Thespis*, the first collaborative venture of Gilbert and Sullivan. He became so strong a draw for the Gaiety that in 1873, when theatrical chorus singers at the same house were paid a pound or two a week, Toole commanded a weekly salary of £100—a threefold increase upon the sum he had attracted at the Adelphi. As the Irishman Brulgruddery in the younger Colman's *John Bull* and Bob Acres in Sheridan's *The Rivals* he co-starred at the Gaiety during the winter of 1873–4 with the eminent veterans Charles James Mathews and Samuel Phelps. He took the Globe for occasional seasons, and originated the barrister Hammond Coote in James Albery's *Wig and Gown* (6 April 1874) and Charles Liquorpond, a retired footman unexpectedly overtaken by wealth, in H. J. Byron's *A Fool and his Money* (17 January 1878), a character whose affectedly superior pronunciation, particularly of his own name, so seized the public that Toole renamed the piece *Chawles*. On 17 November 1879, having taken control of the snug Folly Theatre near Charing Cross, he realized at the age of forty-nine his ambition of securing a resident managership in London. The Folly, after refurbishment, was relaunched on 16 February 1882 as Toole's Theatre, Toole thereby becoming the first actor to see a West End theatre named after him. Toole's, while reviving its master's old repertory, produced the first solo theatrical writings of J. M. Barrie: *Ibsen's Ghost, or, Toole up to Date* (30 May 1891)—a satire upon London productions of Ibsen—and *Walker, London* (25 February 1892), which logged more than a thousand performances in town and country.

Melodrama and sentiment Toole's supremacy in farce was matched by a genius of another order. When he played the old toymaker Caleb Plummer in *Dot* (which Dion Boucicault had adapted from Dickens's 'Christmas book' *The Cricket on the Hearth* for performance at the Adelphi on 14 April 1862) he touched the heart. Involuntary sobbing by men and women was heard from all parts of the house. Toole's characterization instantly established his reputation as a great actor. Dickens was struck by 'a power of passion very unusual indeed in a comic actor, as such things go, and of a quite remarkable kind' when Balzac's *Le Père Goriot* was brought to the English stage by John Oxenford in 1864—retitled *Stephen Digges*, with Toole as Stephen. That power was further evinced in Walter Gordon's *Through Fire and Water* (29 June 1865), in *Dearer than Life* (Alexandra Theatre, Liverpool, 25 November 1867, transferring to the Queen's, Long Acre, 8 January 1868), and in *Uncle Dick's Darling* (Gaiety, 13 December 1869)—the last two written specially for him by Byron. In the Long Acre company he was supported by Henry Irving, Charles Wyndham, and Lionel Brough; and Irving (with whom he had first acted in 1857, and who became a friend for life)

remained for *Uncle Dick's Darling*. Toole's physical appearance proved as well suited to tender-hearted victims of fate as to farcical upstarts. In his 'serio-comic' vein, combining homely humour with pathos, he drew much from the 'great little tragedian' at the Olympic, Frederick Robson, who died in 1864; but his total mastery of the twin staples of Victorian mass entertainment—farce and domestic melodrama—gave him a dominance unknown to Robson over much of the central ground of English popular culture.

Marriage, family, death, and reputation Toole married Susan Hale, *née* Caslake, a widow five years older than he, on 27 April 1854 at the parish church of St Dunstan and All Saints, Stepney. Susan Toole, a butcher's daughter, had no connection with the stage, but for several months in every year she accompanied her husband and his company about the country. They had a son, Frank Lawrence, born in 1856, and ten years later a daughter, Florence Mabel. Both children predeceased them: Frank on 4 December 1879, aged twenty-three; and Florence on 5 November 1888, aged twenty-two, from typhoid fever contracted at Cork in the previous week when visiting her itinerant parents. Susan died three and a half months later, on 20 February 1889. Toole was desolate, and his health broke. No longer was it natural to be larky and droll, though sporadically he sustained the illusion; and revivals of *Dot*, in which Toole as the gentle, oppressed old father cared tenderly for his sightless daughter, now bore the stamp of the actor's grief. His public gallantly rallied him, but too often in the 1890s found the farces unfunny. Gout left him sometimes unable to walk, and made acting a physical ordeal. Though the lease on his theatre expired on 28 September 1895, bringing his London career to an end (the building was demolished in the following year for an extension to Charing Cross Hospital), he held his troupe together for a final tour, which ended at Rochdale on 19 December 1896; but growing incapacity in the new year prevented his ever acting again. He spent his retirement variously at continental spas, his London home in Maida Vale, and Sea View, a hotel at 129 King's Road, Brighton, where, suffering from Bright's disease, and after protracted physical and mental debilitation, he died on 30 July 1906, aged seventy-six. He was buried on 3 August at Kensal Green cemetery, London, beside his wife and children.

Tributes paid him at his death were echoed, with provisos, in the United States and Canada (where he acted in 1874–5) and Australia and New Zealand (1890–91). The paternalism of his manner towards the 'colonies' and the New World had not gone down as well there as at Charing Cross, where regular patrons were accustomed to the whimsical style of his curtain speeches. He was as much of a caricaturist in his way as were Cruikshank and Dickens in theirs. Toole's Dickensian and quasi-Dickensian portraits supplied a public need. Dickens himself was instrumental in bringing him to the Adelphi. The Garrick Club welcomed him as one of its youngest members. Three times in the 1880s he and his company were commanded to act at Sandringham by the prince and princess of Wales. His popularity was such that in 1870 he starred nightly at two theatres in different plays—but his repertory died with him, and in the twentieth century he was all but forgotten. The profession he served for so long, however, stood in his debt, materially as well as artistically, since by his large donations to theatrical charities and benevolent funds he had helped to support many needy actors and their dependants. MICHAEL READ

Sources *Reminiscences of J. L. Toole*, ed. J. Hatton, 2 vols. (1889) · *Daily Telegraph* (31 July 1906), 2 · *The Times* (31 July 1906), 5 · *The Times* (4 Aug 1906), 12 · A. Goddard, *Players of the period*, 2 vols. (1891) · J. Hollingshead, *Gaiety chronicles* (1898) · J. Forster, *The life of Charles Dickens*, 3 vols. (1872–4) · private information (1912) · C. E. Pascoe, ed., *The dramatic list*, 2nd edn (1880) · I. Vanbrugh, *To tell my story* (1948) · L. Irving, *Henry Irving: the actor and his world* [1951] · R. Foulkes, ed., *British theatre in the 1890s* (1992) · *DNB* · m. cert. · d. cert. · Kensal Green cemetery, London, records
Archives Garr. Club, MSS · Harvard TC · Harvard U., Houghton L., corresp. and papers · Theatre Museum, London, letters [copies] · U. Texas · University of Rochester, New York, Rush Rhees Library, corresp. and papers | Museum of London, F. J. Arlton MSS
Likenesses J. Collier, oils, 1887, Garr. Club [*see illus.*] · S. Goetze, oils, exh. Guildhall Art Gallery, London 1893 · Barraud, photograph, NPG; repro. in *Men and Women of the Day*, 2 (1889) · R. Bell, bust, Garr. Club · A. Bryan, chalk caricature, NPG · W. & D. Downey, woodburytype photograph, NPG; repro. in W. Downey and D. Downey, *The cabinet portrait gallery*, 3 (1892) · H. Furniss, pen-and-ink sketch for a caricature, NPG · S. P. Hall, pencil sketch, NPG · F. Pegram, pencil sketch, V&A · Spy [L. Ward], chromolithograph caricature, NPG; repro. in *VF* (29 July 1876) · photographs, NPG, Harvard TC
Wealth at death £81,346 10s. 10d.: resworn probate, 20 Sept 1906, CGPLA Eng. & Wales

Tooley, Henry (*d.* 1551), merchant adventurer and burgess, about whose early life little is known, is first heard of as a merchant in 1515, but it is likely that he was born in the 1470s, possibly in Catton, near Norwich. The Tooley family marriages suggest a comfortable background, with good Suffolk and Norfolk connections. Tooley's sister Joan was married twice to Yarmouth merchants, the second of whom, Ralph Dene, was three times bailiff of Yarmouth. Another sister, Margaret, married about 1500 William Rede, a merchant of Beccles with wealthy Norwich merchant relations. Margaret's children provided Tooley with useful connections: her son, William (*d.* 1543), became a London mercer who did business for Tooley in the Low Countries and married Anne Fernely of West Creeting; Anne Fernely's sister married Sir Nicholas Bacon and Anne herself married Thomas Gresham as her second husband. Tooley's subsequent connections with the Greshams included assistance with a court case involving Sir Richard Gresham in 1544, and financial dealings with Thomas Gresham, to whom Tooley lent money between 1547 and 1551 and left his only non-family legacy. Margaret's daughter Jane married Robert Daundy (*d.* 1558), a member of a leading merchant family in Ipswich; he became a business colleague of Tooley's and was an executor of his will. Henry Tooley was married by 1525 to Alice Purpet (*d.* 1566), daughter of John Purpet, a yeoman of Ipswich, and his wife, Alice. They had one son and two daughters, none of whom survived adolescence. Alice's family was sufficiently wealthy to use Sir Humphrey Wingfield

(*d.* 1545) as its lawyer. Alice's brother, John, also exported goods from Ipswich.

Tooley's business life is exceptionally well documented. Ipswich town records show his official activities in the town from the 1520s to his death, customs accounts show his imports and exports, and taxation returns give information about his rising level of wealth. There are about twenty surviving business letters. His many legal cases illustrate the nature, scope, and problems of his dealings, in particular two cases involving his factors: the first one affected Simon Cowper, a merchant tailor of London, who traded for Tooley in Bilbao, San Sebastian, Pasajes, and Bordeaux from 1520 to 1522; the second case involved John Armiger in Antwerp between 1541 and 1544. A more unusual survival is his account book of 1521–51, which includes rare details of retail trade and the crewing, provisioning, and use of his ship, the *Mary Walsingham*, bought in Bordeaux in 1521, which Tooley used for trade with the Spanish and the French, and also for Icelandic fishing and trading.

By 1520 Tooley was established in several areas of merchant activity. In the 1520s and 1530s his business was based on the annual import of wine and its sale to retailers and households in the Ipswich hinterland. He also dealt in fish, iron, woad, and salt. In this traditional trade the woad was used to buy coloured woollen cloth from Suffolk, and the salt was used for the fishing trade. The wine, woad, and iron were paid for by the sale of cloth in local currencies or by direct barter of the cloths. Profits came from the retail sales of the wine, fish, miscellaneous household commodities, and dyestuffs, which were distributed largely through local carriers, who also collected payments and took orders. Goods also went by local water traffic to Norfolk, Suffolk, and Essex ports. In the 1540s this trade was disrupted by the war with France. Thereafter Tooley increased his cloth exports through London, to include Antwerp. He also expanded his imports of luxury goods, hitherto a lesser interest, and acted as a middleman in the cloth trade. He lent money at interest. At all periods he traded in miscellaneous goods, dyestuffs, and grain, where the opportunity arose.

Three business letters and entries in Tooley's account book suggest that his wife, Alice, also played an active role in his business, supervising shipments, negotiating payments and deliveries, and collecting debts. Later, as a widow in Mary's reign, Alice suffered for her protestant beliefs. Foxe's *Actes and Monumentes* of 1563 says that Mistress Tooley, widow, was persecuted out of Ipswich and her name was on a list of the town's active protestants in 1558 who had fled the town. However, there is no evidence that Henry, who died two years before Mary came to rule, had suffered for his religious beliefs.

Tooley was first chosen for a town office in 1521; in 1523 he was elected to the Twenty Four (as the town's governing body or corporation was called); and then he became one of the twelve portmen. In 1534 possibly, and in 1542 and 1548 definitely, he served as one of the two bailiffs. In 1546 and 1549 he was one of the six town justices. In the

1540s taxation lists he was the highest burgess taxpayer in Ipswich.

Tooley died at Ipswich in August 1551, and was buried there in the church of St Mary Quay. At the time of his death, he was owed over £2000, and had about £400 in goods, £200 in plate, and £500 in gold money. His land was valued at £46 per annum from two manors totalling 900 acres (in 11 villages) purchased in 1548; he also had four properties let in Ipswich to two brewers, a clothmaker, and the master of the grammar school, in addition to his own house in the parish of St Mary Quay. In his will of November 1550 Tooley bequeathed about £100 to his relatives, £100 to the poor, and £220 for road and bridge repairs; he left a fifth of his income to his wife for her life, while the remainder of his wealth and all his property went to found a philanthropic trust, which became known as Tooley's Foundation. Not surprisingly, his family challenged his will, but in 1556 a start was made on almshouses for ten disabled persons. In 1562 an indenture was drawn up by Lord Keeper Bacon, setting out arrangements for the management of the trust by wardens chosen annually from the aldermen and the Twenty Four and for regular inspections by writ of chancery. In 1569 money from the Tooley fund was used to buy an old Dominican friary and in it to establish Christ's Hospital for the sick, a school for the poor, and a workhouse. Other donors to the trust contributed further almshouses and a library. The nearby grammar school eventually used part of the site. Individual grants from the fund were made for medicine, pensions, for outdoor poor relief, and for education. This provided the bulk of the social provision in the town until the Municipal Reform Act of 1835.

The almsmen thanked God daily that it pleased his 'holy spyryte to move and styrre the harte of Henry Tooley … to gyve landes and possessyons suffycent for a necessarye relesse of us thy poore servantes and to the performance of dyvers other dedes of charytie about this town' (Webb, 159). In February 1566 a memorial tomb for Henry Tooley was erected in the church of St Mary Quay, with a brass of the Tooley family and the epitaph, 'A marchant welthye, whose affayres God furtherid with successe' (ibid., 153). An important Suffolk merchant, Tooley made full use of his offices, of good lawyers, and of his family, his friends, and their connections, to amass a solid provincial fortune.

F. ASHBURNER

Sources J. Webb, *Great Tooley of Ipswich* (1962) · N. Bacon, *The annalls of Ipswche*, ed. W. H. Richardson (1884) · *Select cases concerning the law merchant*, 2, ed. H. Hall, SeldS, 46 (1930) · L. J. Redstone, *Ipswich through the ages* (1948) · account book, Suffolk RO, Ipswich **Archives** Suffolk RO, Ipswich, Tooley's papers [incl. account book, executor papers, correspondence, will] **Wealth at death** £4000–£4500 total; total goods, plate, money approx. £1100; over £2000 owed to him; land probably £46 p.a. (£920?): inquisition post mortem; will, Suffolk RO, Ipswich

Tooley [Wilkinson], **Nicholas** (1583–1623), actor, was born in Antwerp, the only child of William Tooley, freeman of the Leathersellers' Company and merchant adventurer, and his wife, Susan, daughter of Hans Lanquart. William Tooley died in Lanquart's house between 27 October and

26 November 1583, when his will was made and proved. As instructed in the will, Susan took their son to London shortly afterwards, to be cared for according to the custom of the city, whereby the lord mayor and aldermen, sitting as a court of orphans, assumed oversight and responsibility for children of freemen during their minority. Orphan Tooley appears often in the repertories (minutes) of the court of aldermen, and as the only child was entitled to one third of his well-to-do father's estate. His Flemish mother remarried in 1584, and twice more after that, the English husbands being prominent freemen of city livery companies.

Tooley came of a family of landed gentry settled at Burmington in Warwickshire, a few miles from Stratford on the road to London; Shakespeare would have known them from boyhood, and it is reasonable to suppose that it was he who introduced Nicholas to the world of the London theatre. He was apprenticed to Richard Burbage, and Richard's elder brother Cuthbert and his wife, Elizabeth, gave him a home. There is no substantial evidence about what parts he may have played. It seems likely that he was not robust: he consulted the doctor Simon Forman twice in 1599, complaining of 'melancholy … moch gnawing in his stomak & stuffing in his Lungs' (Bodl. Oxf., MS Ashmole 219, fols. 101v, 205r). Tooley was one of the King's Men by May 1605, when his 'fellow' Augustine Phillips made a bequest to him; and he is named in the company's second royal patent of 1619, and among the twenty-six 'Principall Actors' listed in the first folio of 1623. The Burbages had just moved from Shoreditch to the parish of St Giles Cripplegate, and Tooley was buried there on 5 June 1623. His long and interesting will of 3 June, to which a codicil specifies his alternative name of Wilkinson, thanks Elizabeth for her 'motherlie care'. It was proved by his executors and 'loving friends' Cuthbert Burbage and Henry Condell on 17 June 1624 (Honigmann and Brock, 125–6).

MARY EDMOND

Sources M. Edmond, *Rare Sir William Davenant* (1987), chaps. 1–2 · M. Edmond, 'Yeomen, citizens, gentlemen and players: the Burbages and their connections', *Elizabethan theater: essays in honor of S. Schoenbaum*, ed. R. B. Parker and S. P. Zitner (1996), 30–49 · C. Carlton, *The court of orphans* (1974), chap. 3, pp. 42–55 · *VCH Warwickshire*, 5.26–8 · E. K. Chambers, *William Shakespeare: a study of facts and problems*, 2 (1930), 73–80 · Huguenot Society, quarto series, 8, 233 · Simon Forman casebook, Bodl. Oxf., MS Ashmole 219, fols. 101v, 205r [7 July and 1 Dec] · repertories of the court of aldermen, CLRO · parish register, London, St Giles Cripplegate, 5 June 1623, GL, MS 6419/2 · will of Nicholas Tooley, 1582, PRO, PROB 11/64/31 [grandfather] · will of William Tooley, 1583, PRO, PROB 11/66/10 [father] · will of Nicholas Tooley, 1624, PRO, PROB 11/143/53 · E. A. J. Honigmann and S. Brock, eds., *Playhouse wills, 1558–1642: an edition of wills by Shakespeare and his contemporaries in the London theatre* (1993), 72–5, 113–15, 124–8

Toosey, Sir Philip John Denton (1904–1975), merchant banker and army officer, was born on 12 August 1904 at 8 South Bank, Oxton, Birkenhead, Cheshire, the eldest son of Charles Denton Toosey, shipbroker and proprietor of the shipping agency Ross, Skolfield & Co., and his wife, Mabel Caroline Augusta, *née* Percy. He was educated by a governess, then at Birkenhead preparatory school, Birkenhead School, and Gresham's School, Holt, Norfolk

(1917–1922)—then ascendant under its Mertonian headmaster G. W. S. Howson, who transformed it from a small grammar school to a flourishing public school—where he was successful at games, a house prefect, and served in the OTC. The headmaster recommended that he go to Cambridge but, to Toosey's lasting regret, his father refused.

Toosey was apprenticed to his uncle Philip Brewster Toosey's firm, Newall and Clayton, Liverpool cotton merchants, and he played rugby football and shot. In 1926, with others from his rugby club, he made his contribution towards breaking the general strike by unloading a refrigerated ship. In 1927 he was commissioned second lieutenant in the 359 (4th West Lancashire) medium regiment, Royal Artillery, Territorial Army (TA), commanded by Lieutenant-Colonel A. C. Tod, a Liverpool businessman. In 1928 he was sent to Peru on business but the firm went bankrupt and he returned home. In October 1929 Tod appointed him his assistant at the Liverpool branch of Baring Brothers, merchant bankers. Toosey also resumed his TA service. He married on 27 July 1932 Muriel Alexandra (Alex) (1903–1978), daughter of Henry Eccles, Liverpool cotton merchant; they had two sons and one daughter. They resided at Heathcote, Oakfield Road, Hooton, Birkenhead, their home for the rest of their married life.

Toosey was promoted captain in the TA in 1931 and major in 1934. His 236 battery, 359 regiment, won the Royal Artillery king's cup in 1935. The regiment was mechanized but still had First World War 6 inch howitzers. In August 1939 it was mobilized, and in October it was the first TA artillery in France. It served on the Franco–Belgian frontier in the 'phoney war', advanced into Belgium in May 1940, and after brief action retreated, under aerial attack, back into France. Near Dunkirk they fired their ammunition and spiked their guns, then moved to the beach, whence they were evacuated by sailing barge and minesweeper. Following a course at the Senior Officers' School, in 1940–41 he commanded and trained the new 902 home defence battery at Cambridge. In 1941, promoted lieutenant-colonel, he was appointed to command the 135th (Hertfordshire yeomanry) field regiment. In October 1941, part of the 18th division, they sailed for an unknown destination.

While at sea Toosey and his men learned that the Japanese had attacked Pearl Harbor and Malaya. They sailed via Cape Town to Singapore, landing on 13 January 1942. The campaign against the Japanese was already failing disastrously. Toosey's unit, armed with 25-pounders towed by miscellaneous vehicles including municipal dustcarts, was attached to the 11th Indian division and fought in Johore, then retreated to Singapore Island, fought against the Japanese attacks, and again had to withdraw. On 12 February Toosey was ordered to leave Singapore so that his experience could be used elsewhere. Arguing he was a Territorial, he refused to abandon his unit. On 15 February, as ordered, Toosey's unit destroyed its guns. On that day the British imperial forces surrendered to the Japanese and became prisoners of war.

In the Second World War Japanese maltreatment of prisoners of war was such that, whereas only 4 per cent of

British and United States prisoners of war died in German captivity, nearly a third of British, dominion, and United States prisoners of war died in Japanese captivity. Toosey's unit was held at Changi camp, Singapore Island, then at Bukit Timah, where Toosey was initially second in command. From July 1942 to October 1943 the Japanese forced the construction of the Burma–Siam railway, 260 miles across very unhealthy mountain and jungle terrain, to supply their army in Burma, using largely prisoner-of-war labour: their biggest single use of prisoners of war. A total of over 12,000 prisoners of war died on the 'death railway'. The Japanese decided to bridge the Kwae Yai, in Thailand, at Tamarkan, and established a prisoner-of-war camp there. In October he was ordered to take 650 men to Singapore station for an unknown destination. He selected his own unit, some infantry, and elements from the Royal Army Service Corps; they reached Tamarkan on 26 October 1942. He commanded the prisoners, and they were ordered to build two bridges.

Toosey attempted to understand the Japanese mentality, and in the inherently unfavourable situation of the prisoners, knowing that in a confrontation they would lose and might well be tortured and killed, he tried to ensure his men's survival. He protested that the use of prisoners of war as forced labour was illegal, but adopted a policy of limited co-operation with the Japanese, negotiating to the best possible advantage and developing a working relationship with them. Though he had to compromise, he was never 'Jap-happy' (Davies, 204). Known as the 'man to handle the Nips' (ibid., xii) he was diplomat, schemer, and businessman, retained his men's loyalty, and was considered the outstanding British officer on the railway. He insisted on maintaining discipline in the camp and, as far as possible, cleanliness and hygiene: he prohibited beards lest they harbour lice. His policy was equality of sacrifice of officers and other ranks. He refused to allow a separate officers' mess or officer accommodation as these would undermine unity, and he ordered officers to accompany working parties to intervene if necessary.

Malnourished and brutally treated by the Japanese and Korean guards, the prisoners were overworked and many died. They constructed a temporary wooden bridge, then a 'permanent' steel and concrete bridge, completed in May 1943. The railway was militarily successful, transporting many troops and supplies and so prolonging the war in Burma. In 1944 and 1945 the Kwae Yai bridges were damaged by US and RAF bombing, but traffic was not entirely stopped. Unlike in the *River Kwai* film, they were not attacked by allied troops.

After completion of the steel bridge the majority of fit men were moved to camps further up the line. Toosey was ordered to organize Tamarkan as a base hospital, which he did despite difficulties including minimal food and medical supplies. The Japanese considered it the best-run prisoner-of-war camp on the railway and left him considerable autonomy. He kept the highest standards possible. One prisoner later stated that he 'cared for his troops … he was concerned about other people more than himself'

(Davies, 123). He co-operated with the secret 'V' organization of Thais, neutrals, and interned civilians, which smuggled money and drugs into the camps. In December 1943 he was transferred to command Nong Pladuk camp, and in December 1944 he was moved to the allied officers' camp at Kanchanaburi where he was the liaison officer with the Japanese: a difficult task was the commandant was, in Toosey's words, 'an arrogant sadist of the worst type' (ibid., 148). Toosey was moved to Nakhon Nayok camp and was there when Japan surrendered in August 1945. Before the war he had weighed 12 stone; when liberated he weighed only 7½ stone. He rejoined his unit, receiving 'the most wonderful reception' (ibid., 180), and they sailed home from Rangoon.

After the war Toosey successfully resumed his career with Barings in Liverpool, diversifying from their cotton business into a variety of financial services. He also resumed his TA Royal Artillery service, was promoted brigadier, retired in 1954, and was awarded a CBE in 1955. He was awarded a disability pension for the harm to his health during the war. He took a leading role, as Lieutenant-General Percival's deputy, in the Far East Prisoners of War Association, which campaigned for former prisoners of the Japanese, and was determined it should not fall into the 'wrong hands' and be used for political purposes. Following Percival's death in 1966 Toosey became its president. In 1971 he opposed demonstrations against the visit to England by the Japanese emperor Hirohito. He was a JP, high sheriff of Lancashire, active in voluntary organizations, and raised funds for the Liverpool School of Tropical Medicine. In 1974 he was awarded an honorary LLD by Liverpool University and was knighted.

Pierre Boulle, a French writer who had served in the Far East and been a prisoner of war, used Toosey's story as the basis for his novel *Le pont de la Rivière Kwai* (1952), which was filmed as *The Bridge on the River Kwai* (1957) with Alec Guinness as Colonel Nicholson, the character based on Toosey. The fictional Nicholson—reportedly an amalgam of Boulle's memories of collaborationist French officers, the director David Lean's view of the military mind, and Guinness's interpretation of Nicholson as mad—differed greatly from Toosey. He and other former prisoners believed the film a distortion, and Percival helped secure a screen statement of its fictionality. In response to the film Toosey, urged by his friends, agreed to the publication of a biography of himself based on his unpublished autobiography, and co-operated with his chosen biographer, Peter N. Davies, whose sympathetic account showed the reality behind the novel's and the film's fictions. Toosey died at Sefton General Hospital, Sefton Park, Liverpool, on 22 December 1975. After cremation his ashes were scattered at Landican cemetery, Birkenhead.

ROGER T. STEARN

Sources P. N. Davies, *The man behind the bridge: Colonel Toosey and the River Kwai* (1991) · *The Times* (23 Dec 1975) · C. L. S. Linnell and A. B. Douglas, *Gresham's School history and register, 1555–1954* (1955) · *Army List* (1930–31) · *Army List* (1938) · *Army List* (1940) · *Army List* (1952) · *Army List* (1957) · C. Kinvig, *River Kwai railway: the story of the Burma–Siam railroad* (1992) · G. Daws, *Prisoners of the Japanese: POWs of World War II in the Pacific* (1994) · M. H. Murfett and others, *Between two oceans: a military history of Singapore from first settlement to final British withdrawal* (1999) · b. cert. · m. cert. · d. cert.
Archives SOUND BL NSA, documentary recording
Likenesses photograph, 1950–59, repro. in Davies, *Man behind the bridge*, frontispiece
Wealth at death £89,596: probate, 13 Jan 1976, CGPLA Eng. & Wales

Tooth, Arthur (1839–1931), Church of England clergyman, was born on 17 June 1839 at Swift's Park, Cranbrook, Kent, the eighth son of Robert Tooth, a wealthy businessman, and his wife, Mary Anne. Arthur was educated at Tonbridge School and, from 1858, at Trinity College, Cambridge. He graduated in science in 1862 and then travelled round the world twice (he became a first-class horseman and crack shot).

While in Australia, Tooth discovered a vocation to the priesthood (although there are no clues as to when or why he became attracted to ritualism). He was ordained deacon in 1863 by Bishop Charles Sumner to a title at St Mary-the-Less, Lambeth, but he spent only a year there, his vicar finding his churchmanship too 'advanced'. He was ordained priest by Archbishop Longley in 1864 and served a second curacy at St Mary's, Folkestone. From 1865 to 1868 he was minister of St Mary Magdalene's mission church in the parish of St Nicholas, Chiswick. He then embarked on his first entirely independent cure as vicar of St James's, Hatcham, in south-east London, to which he had been appointed by his brother Robert. He was inducted on 18 September 1868.

Tooth at once took steps to renew the church life of his largely artisan parish, setting up many clubs and committees to cater for the needs of his poorer parishioners. Congregations rapidly increased in size. Tooth was an able preacher, and reinforced his simple teaching by various ceremonial practices thought by many to be dangerous innovations reeking of popery. The passing of the Public Worship Regulation Act in 1874 gave his protestant-minded opponents their chance. Three 'aggrieved parishioners' charged him with eighteen offences under the act, including the use of incense, vestments, and altar candles. The case came before Lord Penzance at Lambeth Palace on 13 July 1876. Tooth was not among those present, as he refused to recognize the court's competence to try him. Penzance issued a monition (warning) that the practices objected to must cease forthwith, which Tooth ignored. Penzance summoned him again to appear on 2 December, but again Tooth declined to do so. The judge thereupon inhibited him from conducting services in his church for the next three months. Tooth carried on as before, although services were increasingly interrupted by crowds of rowdies hired by his opponents. Eventually, on 22 January 1877, he was taken into custody and lodged in Horsemonger Lane gaol for contempt of court. His imprisonment changed him in a flash, in the eyes of Anglo-Catholics, from rebel priest to Christian martyr, and he became headline news throughout the country. His name provided scope for endless puns—Bishop Magee of Peterborough referred to 'this wretched Tooth-drawing'. The Home Office authorities became worried by the growing agitation and persuaded the three original complainants to apply for his release. He left prison on 17 February, and eventually his conviction was quashed on a point of law: Lambeth Palace was not one of the places where the trial could legally have been held. The fiasco of his prosecution was the first nail in the coffin of the Public Worship Regulation Act.

By this time, however, Tooth's health was broken. Though he remained nominally in charge of St James's until 21 November 1878, he took little part in its affairs. He lived for a further fifty-two years after his resignation, but was never again entrusted with the charge of a parish. After his brief hour of fame he eschewed the limelight, devoting himself to running a school for orphan boys, a sisterhood, and a home for drunkards at Woodside, a suburb of Croydon. He was described by locals as a tall, grey, dignified man with a slanted mouth, as if he had suffered a stroke. In 1924 the property in which his three institutions were housed was compulsorily purchased by Croydon borough council, and Tooth moved the school, St Michael's, to a new site at Otford, Kent. Towards the end of his life he seemed more and more a figure from a bygone age, having outlived almost all his contemporaries. He died at Otford, unmarried, on 5 March 1931, and was buried in Crystal Palace District Cemetery.

BERNARD PALMER

Sources J. Coombs, *Judgement on Hatcham* (1969) · *Arthur Tooth* (1931) · D. Morse-Boycott, 'Arthur Tooth, 1839–1931', *Lead, kindly light* (1932), 198–205 · B. Palmer, 'Prisoner of conscience', *Reverend rebels: five Victorian clerics and their fight against authority* (1993), 117–57 · private information (2004)
Archives Pusey Oxf., letters, press cuttings | LPL, corresp. with A. C. Tait
Likenesses Spy [L. Ward], caricature, repro. in *VF* (10 Feb 1877) · effigy on cenotaph, shrine of Our Lady, Walsingham, Norfolk
Wealth at death £37,736 18s. 8d.: resworn probate, 18 April 1931, *CGPLA Eng. & Wales*

Toothaker, Roger (d. 1692). *See under* Salem witches and their accusers (act. 1692).

Toothill, Sir John Norman (1908–1986), industrial manager and government adviser, was born at 13 Trafford Road, Leicester, on 11 November 1908, the only son of John Harold Toothill, an engineer's fitter, and his wife, Helena Gibbins. He was educated at Beaminster grammar school, Dorset, following which he undertook an engineering apprenticeship, initially at Tilling, Stevens Ltd and later at Harris Lebus Ltd, the furniture manufacturer. During this apprenticeship he also undertook a course in cost (or management) accounting, qualifying as a cost accountant at the same time as he became an engineer. This dual expertise proved useful in a career that involved managing highly innovative engineering projects. While resident at Perivale, Middlesex, he married, on 4 May 1935, Ethel Amelia, the daughter of George Arthur Stannard, an engineer.

In 1935 Toothill was recruited to become chief cost accountant at Ferranti Ltd. Founded by Sebastian Ziani de Ferranti in 1882, this firm wanted to improve the efficiency of its radio factory at Moston, near Manchester. Given his engineering background, Jack Toothill proved to be highly suitable. He consequently moved to Moston to take up this challenging role.

Although Toothill started at Ferranti Ltd as chief cost accountant, it was as general manager of the firm's Scottish division that he made his biggest contribution. Early in 1943 the decision to produce gyro-gunsights (GGS) in quantity for D-day was made, and as Ferranti had made several prototypes for the Royal Aircraft Establishment they secured a large contract. Moston, however, was already overloaded with contracts, but as Edinburgh had a good pool of female labour Toothill was sent to report on the suitability of available premises. He reported to Stafford Cripps at the Ministry of Aircraft Production that none was suitable, resulting in a campaign to build a new factory. Working twenty-four hours a day, the factory at Crewe Toll, Edinburgh, was built using funds supplied by the Ministry of Aircraft Production and first started production deliveries later in 1943. Crucially, the chairman chose Jack Toothill to run the new operation, giving him permission to recruit sufficient engineering and managerial staff from the instrument and fuze departments in Moston.

By the time the war ended, the Crewe Toll team had become very proficient in this respect, manufacturing 9594 GGS units for the RAF. This also provided the basis of a business that over the following decades became a highly successful supplier of avionic equipment to air forces and civil airlines around the world. With the slump in defence orders after 1945, however, Vincent de Ferranti wanted to repatriate all outlying operations to the main factory, placing an enormous question mark over the Crewe Toll activity. Toothill, on the other hand, was so keen to stay in Scotland and make a great success of his burgeoning avionics business that he lobbied hard for a stay of execution. He also devised a strategy aimed at combining precision engineering with advanced electronics technologies, opening up four laboratories (radar, instruments, vacuum physics, and applications) to develop a viable product range. This was accompanied by the recruitment of a highly talented engineering team, using his contacts in government laboratories to ensure a steady supply of innovative thinkers. Some have claimed that his love of sporting activities like fishing and golf was the key reason why Toothill wanted to stay in Scotland; whatever the case, neither Ferranti Ltd nor Edinburgh regretted the decision to allow Crewe Toll to flourish.

While the late 1940s proved to be highly challenging, given the limited demand for military avionics, once the Korean War had started in 1950 and Britain participated in the rearmament of that decade, driven by the cold war, Crewe Toll generated a substantial business. The most successful product was the AI23 monopulse radar that originated in the instrument and fire-control department, while inertial navigation equipment was also developed as another long-term business. Jack Toothill was often able to secure contracts for this advanced equipment because he committed a lot of effort to meeting with people in the defence world, frequently at cocktail parties and trade fairs.

The shortage of skilled labour in Edinburgh also prompted the work on numerical control, another technology in which Crewe Toll developed a prominent position. Toothill always remained confident that his engineering team could take on any project in their chosen areas, a reflection of which was the rapid growth of Crewe Toll's order book. Indeed, by 1958 Crewe Toll had reported its first profit in excess of £1 million, on a turnover of £5.6 million. This growth also continued over the next thirty years, making the Scottish group the most important division within the expanding Ferranti empire. As a reward for this work Toothill was elevated to the main board of Ferranti Ltd in 1958.

Apart from establishing and building a highly successful avionics business in Edinburgh, another major aspect of Toothill's work was his vision for Scottish industry's future development. In the first place, he established a training school at Crewe Toll that was renowned across Scotland, starting the first Scottish higher national certificate in electronics. He also wanted to encourage further diversification away from traditional industries like coal and heavy engineering. After he was invited in 1949 to join the executive committee of the Scottish Council (Development and Industry), an advisory body on economic development, Toothill proposed in 1951 the construction of a central laboratory at Crewe Toll that would act as a core facility for other Scottish electronics firms in need of development facilities. The Ministry of Supply accepted this plan and provided £513,000 for the new facility opened by the duke of Edinburgh in 1954.

In addition to his work for the Scottish Council, for which he was appointed CBE in 1955, Toothill also sat on the National Economic Development Council, after its formation in 1962, as a representative of Scottish interests. This appointment was prompted by the impact of the Toothill report on the Scottish economy (1961), in which he argued for greater government support for diversification and regeneration. This led to a knighthood in 1964, as well as a host of directorships at Scottish firms like AI Welders Ltd, Fochabers, Moray, the Edinburgh Investment Trust, and Brand-Rex Ltd. By the 1960s Sir John had become a leading Scottish figure in the industrial world, reflecting both the enormous growth of his Crewe Toll operation and his work on behalf of the Scottish economy. Other honorary awards were an LLD from Aberdeen University (1966) and a DSc from Heriot-Watt University (1968).

In 1968 Toothill's health deteriorated to such an extent that he was obliged to retire as general manager of the Crewe Toll division and pass on the reins to his highly successful successor, Sir Donald McCallum. He remained a director of Ferranti Ltd for another seven years, eventually retiring from business in 1975, spending his retirement in his beloved bungalow at Ordiequish overlooking the River Spey at Fochabers, Morayshire. He died in Spynie Hospital, Elgin, on 5 July 1986. By that time, the Scottish electronics industry had become a major player on the European scene, building dynamically on the foundations Sir John had laid at Crewe Toll.　　　　JOHN F. WILSON

Sources WW (1970) · J. F. Wilson, *Ferranti: a history. Building a family firm, 1882–1975* (2000) · personal knowledge (2004) · T. Geiger, *Britain and the economic problem of the cold war* (2002) · private information (2004) [Sir Donald McCallum] · Museum of Science and Industry, Manchester, Ferranti archives · b. cert. · m. cert. · d. cert. · CCI (1986)
Wealth at death £405,245.46: eik corrective confirmation, 15 July 1987, CCI (1986)

Topcliffe, Richard (1531–1604), interrogator and torturer, was born on 14 November 1531, the eldest son of Robert Topcliffe of Somerby, Lincolnshire, and his wife, Margaret, daughter of Thomas, third Baron Burgh of Gainsborough. Orphaned at twelve, Topcliffe's wardship was granted to his uncle Sir Anthony Neville. In 1548 he was admitted to Gray's Inn, but he does not seem to have attended university, concentrating instead on administering his inherited estates in Lincolnshire, Nottinghamshire, and at Topcliffe in the North Riding of Yorkshire. By his own account Topcliffe entered the queen's service shortly before her accession. This introduction may have been secured through the family of his wife, Jane Willoughby of Wollaton, one of whose nieces was an attendant to Princess Elizabeth at Hatfield; it may also help to explain the royal favour that Topcliffe enjoyed throughout his life and the peculiar political licence, in more than one sense, that he came to exercise.

Through the Willoughbys, Topcliffe also had access to the patronage of the earls of Leicester and Warwick. These connections, added to those derived from the service of his guardian Neville to successive earls of Shrewsbury, laid the basis for a career which was relatively unremarkable until Topcliffe was well into his fifties. In January 1570 he raised a band of thirty horses and men at Kenilworth in response to the northern rising, and was later rewarded with stewardship of the lands confiscated from the rebel leader Richard Norton. In 1572 it was probably Leicester who secured for him the parliamentary seat of Beverley and most of what is known of his activities in the 1570s—in parliament and elsewhere—relates to the aftermath of the rising and the investigation of the rebels. It seems to have been this line of work, secured for him by Shrewsbury in 1578 and made more widely applicable by the arrival of the Jesuit mission to England in 1580, that set Topcliffe on the road to becoming the most notorious of those government servants who sought out and interrogated enemies of the crown. The queen's encouragement was a spur. In 1578 Topcliffe related how, during one of many royal progresses at which he was present, she informed him personally of 'sundry lewde Popishe beasts' who were resorting to Buxton (Nichols, 217). It was a theme to which he returned in parliament nine years later, blaming religious superstition in Derbyshire on 'ignorance for lacke of learned ministers' (Hartley, 391). This strongly protestant tone was echoed on other occasions. He complained that Staffordshire was 'backwod' in terms of reformed religion (Hammer, 174), and in correspondence with Shrewsbury deplored the silencing of 'good preachers' in East Anglia merely for 'a lytell nycenes' in their theology (Nichols, 217).

Topcliffe's pursuit of Catholics escalated from the beginning of 1582, and in October of that year he began to be named in Catholic correspondence not just as an interrogator of suspects but also as a torturer. Such work was sanctioned in two ways. Topcliffe was appointed to official commissions, such as those of August 1588 and January 1592, charged with examining imprisoned recusants and priests. Meanwhile, in particular cases he was issued with conciliar warrants authorizing interrogation through the use of torture. In support of these duties Topcliffe was also involved in the search for suspects and in their arrest. This could be as a result of his own initiative, at the behest of the council, or at the request of the House of Commons, as in February 1587, or through official commissions such as that of March 1593.

Evidence directly linking Topcliffe with the use of torture is sparse in the 1580s. He was reported to have racked a prisoner named John Getter in the Tower in 1582 (Caraman, *The Other Face*, 243) but it was as an interrogator who cowed and bullied victims 'in most railing manner, as is always usual with him' that Topcliffe became widely known in the mid-1580s (Caraman, *Gerard*, 270). By now he was a Lincolnshire justice and MP for Old Sarum, a borough in the patronage of the Shrewsburys. Outside politics he had interests in peat extraction and droving, but at Westminster during the Commons sessions of 1584–5 and 1586–7 he was most active in those committees and debates that discussed the Catholic menace, religious disorders, and state security. His absence from parliament after 1587 seems to have been the result of a rift with Shrewsbury, which may in turn have derived from Topcliffe's developing reputation. From September 1588 privy council records show him regularly employed in torturing government prisoners.

Torture authorized by government had been in steady use in England since the mid-1530s but it seems to have increased markedly in the 1580s as Catholic missionary activity escalated. Many were now involved in its authorization—councillors, legal officers, even bishops—yet it was Topcliffe who in the decade from 1588 came primarily to symbolize this most wretched aspect of the Tudor regime. Catholic correspondents were sickened by the relish with which 'the cruellest tyrant of all England' undertook his duties (Caraman, *Gerard*, 230), while in court circles in the mid-1590s the rack and other officially sanctioned instruments of torture were referred to as 'our Topcliffian customs' (Birch, 160). Questions concerning the legality of these customs, their authorization, and the limits to which they could be taken came together in the case of the Jesuit missionary Robert Southwell. In June 1592 Topcliffe graphically sought the queen's permission for the course he intended to take: the prisoner should be manacled at the wrists with 'his feett standinge upon the grounde, & his hands But as highe as he can wratche [reach] against the wawle [wall]' (BL, Lansdowne MS 72). At

his trial in February 1595 Southwell stated that he had been tortured on ten occasions, whereupon, according to Catholic reports, Attorney-General Coke commented that 'Mr Topcliffe has no need to go about to excuse his proceedings in the manner of his torturing' (Heath, 143), and Topcliffe himself justified his own actions by reference to a conciliar warrant authorizing Southwell's torture short of death or maiming.

This was Topcliffe's most notorious case. In the last years of Lord Burghley, the harshest rigours of conciliar policy against Catholics diminished, as did Topcliffe's protected position. He was briefly imprisoned in 1595 for maligning privy councillors, and while in the Marshalsea complained to the queen of his treatment in characteristic terms: 'by this disgrace … the freshe deade boanes of Father Southwell at Tyburne and Father Wallpoole at Yorke, executed bothe since Shrovetyde, wyll daunce for joye' (BL, Harley MS 9889). Once released, Topcliffe was in further trouble, councillors examining him early in 1596 about his arbitrary treatment of prisoners in the Gatehouse. Nevertheless, now in his mid-sixties and in the eyes of his victims 'hoary and a veteran in evil' (Caraman, *Gerard*, 68), Topcliffe was employed by the council for a further four years in applying the manacles to various of its prisoners in Bridewell—plotters, thieves, murderers, 'Egipcians and wanderers' (*APC*, 1596–7, 325). In August 1597 he was also responsible for initiating a government inquiry into the scandalous play *The Isle of Dogs*, during which he was required to interview Thomas Nash and his fellow players in the Fleet prison.

Topcliffe's last years were clouded by lameness and domestic troubles. His nephew Edmund renounced the now odious family name, and his eldest son, Charles, was twice convicted of felony. Nevertheless Elizabeth continued to receive Topcliffe and seek his views on security matters. He retained his house at Westminster churchyard where he kept a 'stronge chamber' and detained suspects in 'hande gyves [fetters]' (BL, Lansdowne MS 72), but increasingly withdrew to his estates at Somerby and Padley Hall, Derbyshire, the latter acquired from the impecunious Catholic Thomas Fitzherbert as part of a contract under which Topcliffe undertook to use persecution as a means of bringing about the early deaths of Fitzherbert's father, uncle, and cousin. Topcliffe died in November or December 1604, leaving most of his possessions to his son Charles. He had three other sons and two daughters.

WILLIAM RICHARDSON

Sources HoP, *Commons, 1558–1603*, 3.513–15 · J. Heath, *Torture and the English law* (1982) · *CSP dom.*, 1547–1625 · *APC*, 1571–97 · *The letters and despatches of Richard Verstegan, c. 1550–1640*, ed. A. G. Petti, Catholic RS, 52 (1959) · J. H. Pollen, ed., *Unpublished documents relating to the English martyrs*, 1, Catholic RS, 5 (1908) · T. E. Hartley, ed., *Proceedings in the parliaments of Elizabeth 1, 1584–1589* (1995) · *Calendar of the manuscripts of the most hon. the marquis of Salisbury*, 24 vols., HMC, 9 (1883–1976), vols. 5–13 · J. Nichols, *The progresses … of Queen Elizabeth*, 2 (1823) · T. Birch, *Memoirs of the reign of Queen Elizabeth*, 1 (1754) · BL, Lansdowne MS 72, fol. 133 · BL, Harley MS 9889, fol. 185 · P. Caraman, *John Gerard: the autobiography of an Elizabethan* (1951) · P. Caraman, *The other face: Catholic life under Elizabeth I*

(1960) • P. E. J. Hammer, *The polarisation of Elizabethan politics: the political career of Robert Devereux, 2nd earl of Essex, 1585–1597* (1999) **Archives** BL, corresp., Add. MSS • BL, corresp., Harley MSS • BL, corresp., Lansdowne MSS • PRO, corresp., state papers, domestic

Topham, Edward (1751–1820), journalist and playwright, was born in York in 1751 and baptized there on 17 June 1751, probably the sixth of at least eight children of Francis *Topham LLD (*c.*1713–1770), master of faculties and commissar of the exchequer and prerogative court of the York diocese. When Topham was seven his father, an ambitious and powerful church lawyer, tried to procure, and believed he had obtained, for him the promise of the reversion of his lucrative commissaryship. Dean Fountayne, supported by Archbishop Hutton, flatly denied any such undertaking, and Dr Topham's self-righteous anger at being forsworn erupted into a pamphlet war, initiated by his *Letter address'd to the dean of York; in which is given a full detail of some very extraordinary behaviour* (1758). Employed by the dean to reply was the vicar of Coxwold, Laurence Sterne, who launched into his own literary career with *A Political Romance, Addressed to ——, Esq., of York* (1759; reissued 1769, reprinted as *The History of a Good Warm Watchcoat*), an extended lampoon, in which Dr Topham was cast as Trim, a village sexton.

Edward Topham was sent to Eton College in 1756 or 1757 and remained there eleven years. There is some doubt over his reported involvement in the boys' mass protest against Dr Foster's rule in November 1768. Frederick Reynolds, who became a close friend through Topham's interest in the theatre, recounts Topham's story of participation in a subordinate role, but the claims that he was a leader of the rebellion (including in his own over-embellished account in 'The schools', *World*, 15 November 1787) are not substantiated in other sources. Moreover, the Cambridge University records state that he was enrolled as a pensioner at Trinity College (22 April 1767), over a year before the revolt took place, though Topham may not have taken up residence until his admission as fellow-commoner on 23 October 1769. Topham did not study very seriously at Cambridge, where he became known for his ability as an engraver of humorous subjects: his reputation was sufficient for Horace Walpole to want to add examples of his work to his growing collection. He left without taking a degree.

After a period travelling on the continent Topham spent six months in Scotland, mainly in Edinburgh, and then published *Letters from Edinburgh, 1774 and 1775* (1776), containing 'Observations on the diversions, customs, manners, and laws of the Scotch nation'. In 1777 he published the tory pamphlet 'Address to Edmund Burke on affairs in America'. In the same year he purchased an army commission, as cornet in the King's 2nd Horse Guards, of which regiment he served for about seven years as adjutant. Having earned the gratitude of George III for his efficiency in bringing his soldiers up to scratch, he was caricatured in print shops as 'the tip-top adjutant'.

Topham was a leader of fashion of the day. Reynolds describes his 'short scarlet coat, with large cut steel buttons; a very short white waistcoat, top-boots, and leather breeches, so long in their upper quarters, as almost to reach his chin', in contrast to the long coats and waistcoats and short breeches normally worn at this period (Reynolds, 2.39). Conspicuous as a man of fashion even at a period when singularity of dress or manner was not unusual, Topham featured in several of Reynolds's comedies and the playwright later commented that his 'profits on Topham alone … must have amounted to upwards of one thousand pounds' (ibid., 2.46).

During the Gordon riots in London in June 1780 Topham distinguished himself in command of a small detachment of cavalry, though accounts vary as to whether he acted in defence of Parliament Square or Buckingham House. He was promoted to captain in 1782. In 1783 he acted as second to Captain George Riddell of the Horse Grenadiers in his (illegal) duel with Captain Cunningham of the Scots Greys. Seriously wounded, Riddell was conveyed to Topham's house in Bryanstone Street, where he shortly afterwards died. On his retirement Topham acquired the rank of major.

Topham was well acquainted with many prominent political and theatrical personalities, including Wilkes, Pitt, the Colmans, and Sheridan. His direct association with the theatre began in the summer of 1779, when he contributed a prologue to *A Widow and No Widow* by his friend R. P. Jodrell, the first of many prologues and epilogues for plays by Miles Peter Andrews, Mrs Inchbald, Reynolds, Thomas Morton, and others, which (apart from a break between 1786 and 1791) he continued to write on a fairly regular basis until 1795. For his efforts in this vein he became known as Captain Epilogue. Topham turned to playwriting in 1780. He wrote several farces, the earliest of which, *Deaf Indeed* (1780), was damned on the first night and never performed again. More successful were *The Fool* (1785), *Small Talk, or, The Westminster Boy* (1786), and *Bonds without Judgement* (1787). In all three pieces there were roles for the actress Mary Stephens (Becky) *Wells (1762–1829), with whom Topham began a liaison during the mid-1780s. The dedicatee of the published text of his second play, *The Fool*, in which she had a big success as Laura, Mrs Wells also spoke a specially written 'Epilogue-Prologue' in the character of Macheath, her principal role in the main piece of the evening, *The Beggar's Opera*. In Topham's third play, chosen for a benefit performance, her appearance in the second act dressed as a Westminster scholar caused uproar from the claque of Westminster boys, purposely present, and the remainder of the play could not be heard.

On 1 January 1787 Topham began a daily newspaper entitled the *World and Fashionable Advertiser*. Originally it was designed to puff Mrs Wells, but according to James Winston, she took over a large part of its conduct over several years, including sending reports from the Hastings trials. Other associates on the paper included Miles Peter Andrews, the Revd Charles Este, and the publisher John Bell (1745–1831), who had a share in the management. Hannah More, referring to its emphasis on 'elopements, divorces, and suicides', described the paper as full of 'elegant periods and sublimated nonsense' (Walpole, 31.265).

The first productions of the mainly Florentine-based band of English poets noted for their flamboyant sentimental verse, known as the Della Cruscans, made their first appearance in the *World*. Among Topham's own contributions were his sometimes unreliable recollections of Eton and the earliest version of his *Life of the Late John Elwes* (first published 1790 in book form; 12th edn, 1805), the memoir of a notorious miser who lived at Stoke in Suffolk, close to Topham's villa Cowslip Hall (so-called after the nickname Mrs Wells acquired as heroine of O'Keeffe's *The Agreeable Surprise*, 1781). Topham was proud of his achievement in having persuaded Elwes to settle his money on his children. In Reynolds's opinion this biography exhibited 'so perfect a picture of character and eccentricity, as ever to render any other account of its subject wholly supererogatory' (Reynolds, 2.36).

The proclivities of Topham's newspaper the *World* for scandal and gossip eventually and inevitably landed him in trouble with the courts. He was accused of libelling the memory of the late George Nassau Clavering, third Earl Cowper (*d*. Florence, 22 December 1789). When a guilty verdict was returned, Topham appealed, on grounds of misdirection of the jury. After protracted legal wrangling it was allowed (*King* v. *Topham*, 1791) on the grounds that there had been no intention 'to create any ill blood, or to throw any scandal on the family and posterity of Lord Cowper, or to induce them to break the peace in vindicating the honour of the family' (Pollock, 347), a judgment still applied as precedent. Meanwhile, by autumn 1790, the partnership between Topham and Este had broken up after a quarrel over the financial arrangements, Este having allegedly surrendered his quarter share in the paper in 1788 in return for an annuity. A dispute ensued through Topham's refusal to pay, largely conducted through the columns of *The Oracle*, and, in January 1793, by reference to the courts. The British Library copy of Este's *My Own Life* (1787) includes cuttings of *The Oracle* letters, headed in manuscript 'The Rev. Mr Este's appeal to the publick'.

Topham disposed of the encumbrance of the *World* in 1792, at about the same time abandoning Mrs Wells for another actress. He retreated with their three children (Maria Cowslip, Harriet, and Juliet)—a fourth died at birth—to his native Yorkshire, to Wold Cottage, a substantial dwelling near Thwing, where he took to farming several hundred acres of land and breeding greyhounds, among them the pre-eminently swift black greyhound called Snowball. A product of this period of semi-retirement was his publication of a new annotated edition of Somerville's poem *The Chase* (1804), with a sketch of the author's life.

An event of major astronomical significance took place on Topham's property at Wold Cottage about 3 p.m. on Sunday 13 December 1795, when a large meteorite weighing 56 lb fell to earth two fields from the house, the noise of impact being heard as far away as Bridlington. Topham was absent in London at the time but his estate workers retrieved the object and Topham soon realized its significance both as a phenomenon worthy of exhibition and as a money-making enterprise. The circumstances of the fall were recounted in Topham's letter to James Boaden's newspaper *The Oracle* (12 February 1796; later reprinted in the *Gentleman's Magazine*, 1797, with additional testimonials and an engraving). Handbills were distributed and advertisements taken out in newspapers advising of the stone's public exhibition 'for the inspection of the curious' (*The Times*, 7 July 1796). It was transported to London, where, opposite the Gloucester Coffee House, at 2 Piccadilly, it was shown to visitors on payment of a shilling fee, for which they received as a souvenir 'an exact Engraving of the Stone' and copies of authenticating testimonials by witnesses (ibid.). A quarto pamphlet entitled 'An account of a remarkable stone which fell from the clouds' was published by Topham in 1798 and in 1799 he erected a brick column on the spot, within sight of Wold Cottage, where the meteor had landed. Several years later, in 1804, Topham sold what was left of the stone—substantial pieces having already been given away—to James Sowerby for his private museum in London. After 1837 it eventually passed, via the British Museum and former South Kensington Museum, to the Natural History Museum, London, where it is still exhibited as the 'Wold Cottage meteorite'. In the collections are contemporary illustrations of the meteor, including the tinted engraving originally done by Topham's daughter Harriet for Sowerby's museum. The event's continuing importance lies in the fact that it is 'the oldest recorded fall on the British mainland for which a sample remains' and because it played a significant part in the acceptance of meteorites as stones from the sky (Pillinger and Pillinger, 589).

A self-described wit and noted conversationalist, Topham was active in the exclusive Lion Club (of which there were only thirteen members, including Reynolds, Miles Peter Andrews, and Robert Merry). He was known to a very wide circle and was described as in temper 'easy and companionable' and 'a warm and zealous friend' (*GM*, 1820, 469). In physical appearance he was distinguished by a set of 'immense whiskers', often referred to by the future George IV as 'his great bird's nests' (Reynolds, 2.29). Politically prominent, man of fashion and womanizer, Topham was in youth a continual subject of caricature. He was, for instance, depicted in James Gillray's 'Thunderer' (20 August 1782) as a windmill, together with the prince of Wales and the actress Mrs Perdita Robinson, with whom he had a short relationship in the early 1780s, after she was cast off by her royal lover; and Rowlandson shows him (5 October 1785) as 'Captain Epilogue to the [Mrs] Wells'.

A more sober side to Topham's personality made him active in the magistracy in Suffolk and in the north and east ridings of Yorkshire, where he was also deputy lieutenant. A devoted father to his daughters and a liberal landowner, he was a keen promoter of the science of agricultural improvement. Topham died unmarried in his sixty-ninth year at Doncaster on 26 April 1820. He was survived by two daughters, Maria and Juliet, who, like their deceased sister Harriet (*d*. 1810), were renowned Yorkshire beauties and accomplished horsewomen.

JOHN RUSSELL STEPHENS

Sources F. Reynolds, *The life and times of Frederick Reynolds, written by himself*, 2nd edn, 2 vols. (1827) · *GM*, 1st ser., 90/1 (1820), 469 · A. H. Cash, *Laurence Sterne: the early and middle years* (1975) · S. Morison, *Edward Topham, 1751–1820* (1933) · *GM*, 1st ser., 67 (1797), 549–51 · C. T. Pillinger and J. M. Pillinger, 'The Wold Cottage meteorite: not just any ordinary chondrite', *Meteoritics and Planetary Science*, 31 (1996), 589–605 [illustrated] · C. B. Hogan, ed., *The London stage, 1660–1800*, pt 5: *1776–1800* (1968) · Walpole, *Corr.* · Venn, *Alum. Cant.*, 2/6 · H. C. Maxwell Lyte, *A history of Eton College, 1440–1875* (1875) · *The Times* (17 Jan 1793), 3 · C. Este, *My own life* (1787) [BL copy] · F. Pollock, ed., *The revised reports*, 152 vols. (1891–1920), 1.343–7 · Highfill, Burnim & Langhans, *BDA*, vol. 15 [Mary Wells] · D. E. Baker, *Biographia dramatica, or, A companion to the playhouse*, rev. I. Reed, new edn, rev. S. Jones, 3 vols. in 4 (1812) · Nichols, *Illustrations*, 7.484 · [J. Watkins and F. Shoberl], *A biographical dictionary of the living authors of Great Britain and Ireland* (1816) · F. Ross, *Celebrities of the Yorkshire wolds* (1878), 163–6 · *Public characters of 1804–1805* (1805), 198–212 · *Annual Biography and Obituary*, 5 (1821), 267–79 · C. Redding, *Fifty years' recollections, literary and personal*, 2nd edn, 1 (1858), 80–82 · J. Taylor, *Records of my life*, 2 (1832), 292–6 · T. Wright and R. H. Evans, *Historical and descriptive account of the caricatures of James Gillray* (1851), 26, 378, 382–4 · M. D. Wells, *Memoirs of the life of Mrs Sumbel, late Wells*, 3 vols. (1811) · last will and testament, Borth. Inst.
Likenesses P. W. Tompkins, stipple, pubd 1790 (after Russell), BM, NPG · J. Russell, group portrait, 1791 (with Mary Stephens Wells and their three children) · stipple, pubd 1803, BM, NPG; repro. in *Public characters of 1804–1805* · Gillray, caricature, repro. in *The Thunderer* (20 Aug 1782) · F. Jukes, aquatint (after Rowlandson) · R. Pollard, etching (after Rowlandson), repro. in *Vauxhall Gardens* (28 June 1785) · J. Russell, portrait

Topham, Francis (*c*.1713–1770), ecclesiastical lawyer, son of Edward Topham, esquire, and his wife, possibly named Susan, was born at Cowton Grange in the parish of Middleton Tyas, near Richmond, Yorkshire, and attended Mr Close's school at Richmond. He matriculated at the University of Cambridge in 1729 and was admitted a pensioner at Sidney Sussex College on 24 June, proceeding LLB in 1734 and LLD in July 1739. Topham's career lay in the civil law. By the late 1730s he had acquired property in the parish of St Helen's, Stonegate, York, and was admitted an advocate in the ecclesiastical courts of York by Archbishop Lancelot Blackburne on 17 January 1737. He secured patronage at York from archbishops Thomas Herring and Matthew Hutton in succession, and benefited from the translation of both to Canterbury. Topham also married, probably in 1737 or before (his wife was called Charlotte), and they had a family of eleven, possibly twelve children, one of whom was the journalist and playwright Edward *Topham.

Topham's legal career in York progressed well enough during the 1740s for him to begin work in the Canterbury province. He was appointed master or commissary of the faculties on 9 December 1747 by Archbishop Herring's letters patent (Herring had been translated from York to Canterbury that same year) and he was admitted to practise as an advocate at the court of arches on 11 January 1748. In the former role Topham became well known to successive archbishops of Canterbury and, on occasion, offered legal advice, or sought their opinion. There was considerable rivalry between Topham and the vicar-general of Canterbury, George Paul, over their respective powers to issue marriage licences. Topham's determination to protect his office's powers to issue special licences for the solemnization of matrimony was upheld in a case of 1755 heard by the dean of the arches, Sir George Lee, who ruled that the vicar-general's power to issue them in either province had ceased following Hardwicke's Marriage Act of 1754. As commissary Topham was ever watchful of the established church's interests, for instance displaying a reluctance in 1760 to concede a Quaker's petition to become a public notary on the grounds that 'this seemingly peaceful & inoffensive sect are very apt to be very clamorous about Tythes, Church Powers, and other ecclesiastical matters' (to Archbishop Secker, 5 March 1760, LPL, Secker MSS vol. 4, fol. 250).

Though he spent long periods in London, Topham passed most of his time in York and as early as 21 November 1749 appointed John Bettesworth, an advocate general in the court of arches, to be his surrogate. He accumulated most of the major legal offices connected with the archdiocese of York between 1747 and 1751, crowning his progress with appointment by Archbishop Hutton of York as commissary and keeper-general of the exchequer and prerogative court of the archbishop on 28 June 1751. Topham was thus the holder of the major office in the ecclesiastical courts for the northern province, but he remained unsatisfied. His unrelenting search for patronage was judged excessive by some members of the York chapter and matters came to a head early in John Fountayne's deanship. Topham angled for the commissaryship of the peculiar court of Pickering and Pocklington (in the dean's gift), and the commissaryship of the dean and chapter of York (where the dean had a leading voice). Neither materialized, and the former was awarded to Laurence Sterne, despite Topham having the patent for it made out with his name written in, ready for the dean's seal. The affair resulted in a public quarrel between him and Dean Fountayne at York after a dinner party which Sterne attended. Topham was meanwhile denied permission to pass the office of commissary and keeper-general of the exchequer and prerogative court of the archbishop on to one of his sons. He attacked Fountayne in print in December 1758 for this supposed outrage with the anonymous *A Letter Address'd to the Reverend the Dean of York* and followed it up with a second pamphlet, *A Reply to the Answer to a Letter Lately Address'd to the Dean of York* (January 1759).

At this point Sterne joined the quarrel with his allegorical *A Political Romance* (1759), perhaps better known as *A History of a Good Warm Watch-Coat*, where Topham is cast as Trim, the sexton and dog-whipper of the parish, trying to obtain an old watch coat for his family's use. Together with some accompanying letters it constituted a final, brilliant rejoinder. Sterne, in his letter of 20 January 1759, noted the many 'coarse and unchristian Insinuations' in the *Reply*, which he believed would grieve Topham equally 'when the first Transport of Rage is a little over' (*Letters*, 72). Topham was subsequently immortalized by Sterne in *Tristram Shandy* as Didius, the great church lawyer, who had 'a particular turn for taking to pieces and new framing over again, all kinds of instruments to insert his legal whim-wham'. However, Sterne later had second thoughts about the 'ridiculous light' in which he had depicted Topham in the *Political Romance*, telling his half-cousin by marriage, Mrs Elizabeth Montagu (in a memorandum for Mrs Sterne should he die abroad), that he doubted 'whether he deserves it' (28 Dec 1761, *Letters*, 147).

Topham suffered for much of his life from gout, and his health declined sharply in the late 1760s, when he was obliged to rely on surrogates acting for him in the York exchequer and prerogative court. In the Canterbury province relations between himself and Archbishop Thomas Secker, who succeeded Hutton in 1758, were respectful but more distant than had been the case with earlier primates. Perhaps the climax of Topham's career was the issuing of a mandate from Archbishop Secker in 1764 for a marriage licence between Princess Augusta, George III's eldest sister, and Charles, hereditary prince of Brunswick-Wolfenbüttel. Only two years later Topham's reputation further suffered when his office unaccountably held up the issue of a licence to the Hon. and Revd Henry Egerton and the case was referred to the king's bench.

This furore did not prevent Topham from being nominated to the officiality of the archdeaconry of Nottingham on 27 February 1770. He died on 17 October following. Topham was an experienced, dedicated lawyer, but not one of the most learned, and his excessive ambition did him no favours. His will was dated 15 October 1770, but was neither signed nor sealed; probate was granted on 15 June 1772. Mrs Topham died on 4 August 1771. Topham was allegedly the author of *Some observations on the statute of the 26th of his late majesty King George II intitled An act for the better prevention of clandestine marriages* (n.d.). It argued that evidence from the parish registers of Sheffield, Leeds, Liverpool, and Manchester showed that fears Lord Hardwicke's Marriage Act would cause marriages to decline were groundless.   NIGEL ASTON

Sources W. Dugdale, *The visitation of the county of Yorke*, ed. R. Davies and G. J. Armytage, SurtS, 36 (1859) [Topham family tree] · *VCH Yorkshire North Riding*, 1.247, 304 · *GM*, 1st ser., 40 (1770), 487 · Venn, *Alum. Cant.*, 2/6.355 · F. Reynolds, *The life and times of Frederick Reynolds, written by himself*, 2 (1826), 190–92 · *N&Q*, 2nd ser., 12 (1861), 474 · Nichols, *Illustrations*, 2.673, 682–3 · E. H. W. Dunkin and C. Jenkins, eds., *Index to the act books of the archbishops of Canterbury, 1663–1859*, pt 2, British RS, 63 (1938), 383–4 · B. D. Till, 'The administrative system of the ecclesiastical courts in the diocese and province of York', vol. 3: '1660–1883: a study in decline' (typescript), 1963, Borth. Inst. · *An inventory of the historical monuments in the city of York*, Royal Commission on Historical Monuments (England), 5 (1981) · W. L. Cross, *The life and times of Laurence Sterne* (1909), 155–88, 244–5 · *Letters of Laurence Sterne*, ed. L. P. Curtis (1935) · A. H. Cash, *Laurence Sterne: the early and middle years* (1975), 228–33, 245–51, 269–76 · *York Courant* (6 Aug 1771) · MS notes of Richard Forrester, York City Archives, acc. 492

Archives BL, letters to Andrew Ducarel, Add. MS 23990, fols. 36, 38, 50, 68, 87 · Borth. Inst., Bishopthorpe MSS, C&P XX · Borth. Inst., consistory court book, 26 Jan 1738 · Borth. Inst., precedent books, P24, P25; ADM A./20; EXCH. AB30, 1757–69 · LPL, FI/K, fols. 17–18, 84; Kkk 14/42, Kkk 2/48; Secker MSS, vol. 4, fols. 250–62; archbishops' MSS, MS 1119 · York City Archives, MS notes of Richard Forrester, acc. 492 · York Minster Library, register of deeds, Wh, fol. 16*r*–16*v*

Wealth at death several small estates, incl. Cowton, Yorkshire, and lease at Downham, Cambridgeshire: will, Borth. Inst., Prog. 3 July 1772

Topham, Francis William [Frank] (1808–1877), watercolour painter, was born at Leeds, Yorkshire, on 15 April 1808, the son of Richard Topham (1781–1834), pawnbroker, and his wife, Elizabeth Rawson (1784–1861). Apprenticed to an uncle, Samuel Topham, an engraver and future pioneer of portrait photography, he first engraved lettering for cards and monograms for cutlery and, with a few flourishes, commercial bills. In 1830 he moved to London with savings of £5 to take up heraldic engraving, before joining the publishers Fenner and Sears as an engraver of title-pages and illustrations. This led to original illustrative work for books, including Walter Scott's Waverley novels, S. C. Hall's *Book of Gems* (1836), and George Tattersall's *The Lakes of England* (1836)—which was republished in colour under Topham's name in 1869—and for the *Illustrated London News*. In 1851 he engraved frontispieces for the three volumes of Charles Dickens's *A Child's History of England*.

In March 1832 Topham married Mary Anne Beckwith (1811–1873) of Clerkenwell, London, the sister of a fellow engraver, Henry Beckwith; they had ten children. The couple lived at 32 Fortess Terrace, Kentish Town and, from about 1854, at 1 Bloomfield Villas, Tufnell Park West. Soon after his arrival in London, Topham joined the Artists' Society, which met in Clipstone Street to draw models picked from street vagabonds. He began to exhibit in 1832 and had seven paintings shown at the Royal Academy. In 1842 he was elected an associate of the New Society of Painters in Water Colours, becoming a full member in the following year. He moved to the Society of Painters in Water Colours in 1848.

Working almost exclusively in watercolour, Topham proved himself a remarkable colourist. Joseph Jenkins, secretary of the Society of Painters in Water Colours, wrote that:

> Topham's shadows are rich and transparent because he saw light in shadow. … He put on colour and took off colour, rubbed and scrubbed, sponged out, repainted, washed, plastered and spluttered his drawings about in a frenzied sort of way in the effort to produce something lurking in his mind. … Every drawing seemed something like an experiment. (Roget, 2.325)

He soon took peasant life as a favourite—sometimes sentimental—subject, and in 1844 and 1845 he visited the west of Ireland with his fellow painters Frederick Goodall and Alfred Fripp. This led to further tours in Ireland in 1860 and 1862 and to Scotland and Snowdonia, where from 1852 he was a regular member of the artists' colony at Betws-y-coed.

Topham's illustrations for Charles Dickens were not followed by more such commissions; however, he painted a number of Dickensian subjects and presented the author with a watercolour of *Barnaby Rudge* which eventually hung in Dickens's homes at Broadstairs and Gad's Hill. Dickens recruited Topham to his amateur theatrical company, the Guild of Literature and Art, and the painter frequently performed with Dickens, Wilkie Collins, and the artists Clarkson Stanfield and John Tenniel. The company appeared before Queen Victoria and in country houses, as well as in London and provincial theatres. Topham earned

Dickens's praise for his portrayal of Goodenough Easy in Edward Bulwer-Lytton's *Not so Bad as we Seem* in 1851, and he also shone in Douglas Jerrold's *The Rent Day*.

Topham missed most of the following two years' productions as he was touring Spain: in search of the picturesque, he visited Madrid, Toledo, Segovia, Córdoba, Granada, and Seville. He travelled rough and caused bewilderment among innkeepers, who could not understand why he should pay peasants to sit for him instead of charging them for painting their portraits. The squalor of Spain appalled him: '"There is *but one Madrid*", says the Spaniard; "So much the better," says the Englishman,' he wrote in a letter home; he hated, too, the cruelty of the bull-fight. However, he considered, 'Such glorious combinations of landscape and architecture I don't think are to be found in any other country' (Roget, 2.322). Topham's larger Spanish works were painted from sketches on his return to London, his subjects being figures in brightly coloured native dress in settings indicated by such titles as *The Eve of the Fiesta*, *The Andalusian Letter-Writer*, and *Spanish Gossip*. French subjects dating from 1857, and Italian from 1864, resulted from subsequent visits to Brittany, Venice, and Capri. His paintings commanded good prices from the growing urban middle class avid for colourful paintings of rural life: *The Gipsy Toilet* fetched £498 in 1865, *The Picador, Seville* £378 in 1873, and *Preparing for the Bullfight* £341 in 1874.

Topham was said to be an amusing companion, and a skilled amateur conjuror and juggler, which caused difficulties in Ireland when the superstitious accused him of casting magic spells, even making coins appear inside potatoes. This talent surprised Charles Dickens, who wrote that 'Topham has suddenly come out as a Juggler and swallows candles and does wonderful things with the Poker' (*Letters of Charles Dickens*, 6.539). In appearance Topham was bearded and, when going bald, always wore a skull-cap; retaining his stubborn but humorous Yorkshire character, he was a founder member and vice-president of the Savage Club.

In 1862 Topham moved to Warwick House, 86 Adelaide Road, London; then in 1873 he built himself a large house and studio at 4 Arkwright Road, Hampstead, which he named Dinas after one he had rented for his family near Betws-y-coed. His happy family life was shadowed by bereavement; one of his children died in 1857, his wife in 1873, and a favourite daughter, Polly, soon afterwards. His eldest son, Francis William Warwick (Frank) Topham (1838–1924), also a painter, married, on 3 May 1870, Helen Lemon, daughter of Topham's friend Mark Lemon, the first editor of *Punch*.

In 1877 Topham, whose own health had been failing, made a final visit to Spain, travelling with two friends. In Madrid he was taken ill, but he continued to Córdoba by train, making the seventeen-hour journey with only two biscuits to share between the three of them. On arrival he collapsed and died at the Fonda Suiza, a hotel in the strada Torrijos, on 31 March. He was buried in the protestant cemetery outside Córdoba; when that fell into dereliction

he was re-interred on 16 December 1959 at the municipal cemetery of San Rafael in the city, where, in 1994, a nearby square was renamed plaza del Pintor Topham. Examples of his work are in the collections of the British Museum and the Victoria and Albert Museum, London; the Williamson Art Gallery and Museum, Birkenhead; the Art Gallery and Museum, Bury; the Reading Museum and Art Gallery; the Ulster Museum, Belfast; and the municipal collection in Córdoba.   TOM POCOCK

Sources J. L. Roget, *A history of the 'Old Water-Colour' Society*, 2 vols. (1891) · T. Pocock, *Topham and son* (1985) [exhibition catalogue, Hampstead Museum, London, 1985] · T. Pocock, 'The quest for F. W. Topham', *Country Life*, 170 (1981), 1860–61 · *The letters of Charles Dickens*, ed. M. House, G. Storey, and others, 6–7 (1988–93) · P. Lord, *Clarence Whaite and the Welsh art world: the Betws-y-Coed artists' colony, 1844–1914* (1998) · *The reminiscences of Frederick Goodall* (1902) · A. A. Adrian, *Mark Lemon: first editor of 'Punch'* (1966) · *The letters of Charles Dickens*, ed. M. House, G. Storey, and others, 12 (2002) · F. G. Kitton, *Dickens and his illustrators* (1899) · Mallalieu, *Watercolour artists*, vols. 1–2 · Bryan, *Painters* (1909–10) · Wood, *Vic. painters*, 3rd edn · *CGPLA Eng. & Wales* (1877) · private information (2004) [family, friends; British embassy, Madrid] · Registro Civil de Córdoba, 1877 [copy, 1995] · grave, cemetery of San Rafael, Córdoba, Spain · J. W. T. Ley, *Dickens and his circle* (1918)
Archives Bankside Gallery, London, Royal Watercolour Society archive · Col. U., Rare Book and Manuscript Library, corresp.
Likenesses photograph, *c.*1855, priv. coll.; repro. in J. Maas, *The Victorian art world in photographs* (1984) · Elliott & Fry, carte-de-visite, NPG · group portrait, woodcut (*Our Artists — Past and Present*), BM, NPG · wood-engraving, NPG; repro. in *ILN* (6 May 1848) · wood-engraving (for *ILN*, 14 April 1877; after photograph by Elliott & Fry), BM, NPG · (*The selection committee of the R.W.S.*), Royal Watercolour Society archive
Wealth at death under £10,000: resworn probate, June 1878, *CGPLA Eng. & Wales* (1877)

Topham, John (1746–1803), antiquary, was born on 6 January 1746 at Emley, in the West Riding of Yorkshire, the third son of Matthew Topham (d. 1773), vicar of Withernwick and Mappleton, in Holderness, and his wife, Ann, daughter of Henry Willcock of Thornton in Craven. He spent his childhood at Malton, in the East Riding. His father was the fifth son of Christopher Topham of Caldbergh and Withernwick, and was probably able to use family connections to secure a post for John under Philip Carteret Webb, then joint solicitor to the treasury. Webb, a busy and often unpopular politician, was also a prominent and influential member of the Society of Antiquaries. He thought well of John, who was inclined to historical studies, and found him a place in the state paper office under Sir Joseph Ayloffe and Thomas Astle, later the keeper of records in the Tower of London.

Webb was keenly interested in the ordering and preservation of the public records, and particularly at that time in printing the parliament rolls, the records of parliament in the middle ages from 1278 to 1503. He may well have introduced Topham to the state paper office to further his campaign. Topham was certainly engaged in the work from its inception in 1767 (when he was elected a fellow of the Society of Antiquaries) to the completion, printing, and distribution of the six folio volumes of *Rotuli parliamentorum* in 1776-7. Together with Astle and Philip Morant he was responsible for a remarkably successful edition of a forbidding mass of parchment.

Topham was admitted a member of Lincoln's Inn in 1771, and in April 1779 he was elected a fellow of the Royal Society. In May 1781, having served as secretary to the commission reviewing the records, he was appointed a deputy keeper of the state papers. A year later the papers became a historic archive when responsibility for foreign and home affairs was formally divided between the two secretaries of state, and the new Foreign and Home offices—the first modern departments of government—began to keep their own records. In 1771 Topham was made a commissioner in bankruptcy and in 1787 he became a bencher of Gray's Inn; in 1788 he was treasurer of the Society of Antiquaries for the second time, having served briefly in 1783-4. He was not a prudent treasurer, yet regularly attended the committee meetings of the society. He also acted as registrar to a charity for the relief of poor widows and children of the clergy, and was treasurer of the orphan charity school. In 1790 he was appointed librarian to the archbishop of Canterbury, in succession to Michael Lort, canon prebendary of Tottenham in St Paul's.

On 20 August 1794 Topham married Mary, daughter and coheir of Samuel Francis Swinden (*d.* 1764) of Wimpole Street, London, and Greenwich. Besides his official duties and charitable work he pursued his own studies, contributing a series of papers to *Archaeologia* and editing texts, including Francis Gregor's translation of Sir John Fortescue's *De laudibus legum Angliae* (1775) and, with Richard Blyke, Sir John Glanvill's *Reports of certain cases determined in parliament in the twenty-first and twenty-second years of James I.* He added a historical preface to that volume on the law and practice of determining disputed elections. He also published the daybook of the comptroller of the wardrobe in Edward I's reign, *Liber quotidianus contrarotulatoris garderobae, AD 1299-1300* (1787), with a useful introduction.

Topham died at Cheltenham on 19 August 1803 and was buried in the cloisters of Gloucester Cathedral; there is a memorial tablet to him on the wall of the north aisle. His marriage was childless, and his books and collections were sold in 1804. The British Museum acquired numbers of his manuscripts, now in the British Library, including more than fifty volumes of deeds known as the Topham charters, relating to English monastic houses. Topham was learned in the law, and in the middle ages at large, but his chief contribution to scholarship was his work on the rolls of parliament, which served the most rigorous purposes of historical enquiry for more than two centuries.

G. H. MARTIN

Sources *DNB* · Nichols, *Lit. anecdotes* · Nichols, *Illustrations* · M. M. Condon and E. M. Hallam, 'Government printing of the public records in the eighteenth century', *Journal of the Society of Archivists*, 7 (1982-5), 348-88 · *IGI*

Archives BL, transcripts and editorial papers, Add. MSS 4631-4659 · S. Antiquaries, Lond., antiquarian notes and papers | BL, letters to Lord Hardwicke, Add. MSS 35617-35624, *passim* · Bodl. Oxf., corresp. with J. C. Brooke · Bodl. Oxf., letters to John Nichols and J. B. Nichols

Topham [*née* Hillier], **Mirabel Dorothy** (1891–1980), racecourse owner, daughter of Henry Hope Hillier, a licensed victualler, and his wife, Nellie, was born on 14 August 1891 at the Baron's Court Hotel, Connaught Road, Fulham, London, which her father ran. There Mirabel spent her childhood. Henry Hillier later became manager of the Haymarket Theatre, where Mirabel went on stage as Hope Hillier, a gaiety girl. She appeared in several West End productions.

This career wound up in 1922, when on 19 April Mirabel Hillier married Arthur Ronald Topham (*b.* 1885/6), a leading member of the family which had long run Aintree racecourse near Liverpool. In 1935 she was elected to the board of the family company, Topham Ltd, which ran Aintree. Three years later she became managing director of the company, and in her attempts over the next three decades to make Aintree financially viable, displayed immense enthusiasm and real business skill. Taking an immense pride in staging the Grand National, the world's greatest steeplechase, she purchased the freehold of the 270 acre racecourse from Lord Sefton in 1949 for £275,000. Mirabel Topham then restored a derelict cottage on the course and lived there in what she subsequently described as her 'padlocked house' (*The Times*, 2 June 1980).

Unfortunately, a significant decline in attendances at the hurdle and flat races at Aintree, caused in large part by the emergence of television as a medium for popular entertainment, put the future of the racecourse in jeopardy. In a bid to generate new income Mirabel Topham devised new attractions, including the opening of a motor-racing circuit. This allowed the European grand prix to be staged there in 1954.

Mirabel Topham learned to negotiate quickly and effectively with a wide range of individuals and groups, including stable lads, trainers, accountants, and bookmakers. A redoubtable person, she gained a reputation as a no-nonsense woman. In her business dealings she did not suffer gladly those whom she perceived as fools or opportunists. A number of outside trainers were known to harbour resentment towards her, and she was occasionally in dispute with the Jockey Club. She could be tough where corporate interests were concerned. Mirabel Topham caused a number of newspaper headlines over her attacks on commentary rights and lack of television revenue from the BBC. Throughout the 1950s and 1960s, moreover, as attendances at Aintree fell, she reduced its racing calendar, so that by the early 1970s Aintree was reduced to a single annual three-day meeting, the highlight of which was the Grand National. As a number of obituaries later put it, Mirabel Topham found the Aintree going heavy.

Mirabel Topham's combative spirit inevitably made her a public figure, and the battles in which she engaged 'gave the public a picture of a tough, unapproachable and obstinate impresario' (*The Times*, 2 June 1980). Yet that was far from being the whole picture, and friends and family remarked that she possessed 'an engaging charm and a

Mirabel Dorothy Topham (1891–1980), by unknown photographer, 1970

sense of humour' (ibid.). In addition Mirabel Topham could never be called a philistine: she was a patron of the arts, and a generous benefactor of the Walker Art Gallery in Liverpool. She initiated an annual competition from 1949 for the design and manufacture of a trophy for the Topham Trophy steeplechase, a race held during the Grand National meeting.

From at least the early 1960s Mirabel Topham was involved in attempts to sell the racecourse. In 1964 Lord Sefton took legal action against her sale of the land for residential purposes (on the grounds of a restrictive covenant in the 1949 agreement). Mirabel Topham finally won the action, after the House of Lords ruled in her favour; but the sale fell through. Mirabel Topham's reign at Aintree finally ended in 1973, when the course was purchased by the Merseyside property dealer and prominent member of the turf, William Davies, for an estimated £3 million. In retirement Mirabel Topham lived at her beloved Paddock Lodge home at Aintree. She also had a house at 18 Hanover Terrace, Regent's Park, London.

Mirabel Topham died of cancer, aged eighty-eight, on 29 May 1980 in Paddock Lodge. She was buried in the family vault in north Wales. Although Mirabel Topham had no children of her own, she adopted a cousin's children, Patricia and James Bidwell; they inherited most of her estate. In a long and appreciative obituary, *The Times* described Mirabel Topham as one of the turf's most forceful and controversial personalities. 'Mrs Topham will be remembered', it added, 'as a large, formidable figure of eighteen stone, dressed in tweeds and prepared to stand

firmly by decisions, however unpopular. She enjoyed the scent of battle and was always ready to champion David against Goliath' (*The Times*, 2 June 1980).

MARK CLAPSON

Sources *The Times* (2 June 1980) · *The Times* (16 June 1980) · *The Times* (1 Dec 1980) · *Sporting Life* (2 June 1980) · b. cert. · d. cert. · m. cert. · *CGPLA Eng. & Wales* (1980)
Likenesses photograph, 1970, Empics Sports Photo Agency [*see illus.*]
Wealth at death £181,850: probate, 19 Nov 1980, *CGPLA Eng. & Wales*

Topham, Thomas (1710–1749), strong man and publican, was born in London; all that is known about his parents is that his father was a carpenter. In 1734, having just completed his apprenticeship in carpentry, Thomas determined to become a publican and began his new career as the landlord of the Red Lion inn near old St Luke's Hospital, London. It seems likely that this change of career was prompted by an awareness of the commercial potential of his feats of strength. These had first come to public attention when, despite lying on his back with his feet against the dwarf wall that divided Upper and Lower Moorfields in London, he had succeeded in winning a tug-of-war against a horse. It was certainly the case that within a very short time of becoming a publican Topham was conducting commercial exhibitions of his feats, notably at Stationers' Hall on 10 July 1734. A woodcut of the event shows him lying extended between two chairs, with a glass of wine in his right hand, and five gentlemen standing on top of his body.

Topham embarked on numerous provincial tours, as well as exhibiting feats of strength in Ireland and Scotland. During these tours he was often lauded. For instance, at Macclesfield in Cheshire the corporation were so impressed by his feats that they gave him a purse of gold coins and made him a free burgess. On 3 April 1737, as part of an exhibition to which he charged 1s. admission per head, Topham rolled up a pewter dish of 7 lb 'as a man rolls up a sheet of paper' (Wilson, 8). This astonishing achievement was witnessed by many influential people, including the natural philosopher Jean Theophilus Desaguliers, who had their names inscribed on the dish, which was donated to the British Museum. Later during the exhibition, while lying on two chairs with four people standing on his body, Topham, using just one hand, lifted the 27 stone vicar of All Saints' Church up—a truly amazing feat. At the end of this exhibition Topham sang 'Mad Tom', though his voice was described as 'more terrible than sweet' (Pinks, 78).

During his long periods of absence Topham's publican business failed, and although over the next eight years he took on the leases of at least three other London pubs, the Golden Lion and Duke's Head in Islington, and the Bell and Dragon in Shoreditch, all proved commercial failures. This appears surprising because he would sometimes stage public performances of feats of strength, charging 1s. admission. His most celebrated performance was on 28 May 1741 at the Apple Tree inn (opposite Coldbath Fields prison), a London pub that he might have been running, though this is unclear. The event was a celebration of Admiral Edward Vernon's election to parliament on an anti-Walpole ticket. Standing on a wooden stage Topham on this occasion raised three hogsheads of water weighing 1836 pounds, via a strong rope and tackle that passed over his shoulders.

Topham appears to have been convivial, joining both the freemasons and the Strong Man Lodge, but despite his 'good nature' (Nelson, 130) much of his life was very unhappy. The chief cause of this was his perpetually unfaithful wife, though this anguish was amplified by his many business difficulties. He seems to have been rather simple and suffered two serious accidents through behaving stupidly. In the first, a failure to assess the dangers of a feat involving two horses led to his knees' becoming damaged, leaving him with a slight limp. In the second, as a joke, he began to tug away scaffolding (much to the anxiety of the builders on top), and a large post struck him on the head. He was also easily duped and lost a bet to an archer in a Finsbury pub when he failed to realize that the only way to hold a bow in order to draw an arrow two thirds of its length was to point it towards his ear not his breast. Tales of such naïvety lend credibility to Topham's feats of strength; although he was only 5 ft 10 in., and it was well established that skilful conmen, such as those functioning in Germany, could accomplish some of the stunts that he performed, even the most sceptical contemporaries were convinced that his achievements were 'genuine' (Fairholt, 49).

In 1745 Topham became master of the Shoreditch pub the Bell and Dragon and supplemented his income by performing exhibitions of strength for public amusement. Unfortunately, his generally mild disposition was excited to frenzy by his unfaithful wife and in early August 1749 he stabbed both her and himself. Topham's wife, whose name is unknown, survived the assault, but after languishing for a few days he died at the Bell and Dragon, and was buried in the church of St Leonard, Shoreditch, on 10 August 1749.   W. W. WROTH, *rev.* ADRIAN N. HARVEY

Sources F. W. Fairholt, *Eccentric and remarkable characters* (1849) · G. H. Wilson, *The eccentric mirror*, 4 vols. (1807), vol. 3 · W. J. Pinks, *The history of Clerkenwell*, ed. E. J. Wood, 2nd edn (1881) · T. Cromwell, *Walks through Islington* (1835) · *Kirby's wonderful … museum*, 6 vols. (1803–20), vol. 1, p. 157 · J. Nelson, *The history and antiquities of the parish of Islington*, 2nd edn (1823) · W. Hutton, *The history of Derby*, 2nd edn (1817) · *N&Q*, 5th ser., 6 (1876)

Likenesses W. H. Toms, line engraving, pubd 1741 (after C. Leigh), BM · illustrations, repro. in *Kirby's wonderful … museum*, vol. 1, p. 157

Toplady, Augustus Montague (1740–1778), Church of England clergyman and hymn writer, was born on 4 November 1740 at Farnham, Hampshire, the only surviving child of Richard Toplady (1713?–1741), army officer, and Catherine (1704–1770), the daughter of Richard Bate (*d.* 1736), incumbent of Chilham, near Canterbury, from 1711 until his death. On his maternal side he was a grandson of the Stanhopes of Mellwood in Lincolnshire. His parents had been married by his mother's brother, Julius Bate

Augustus Montague Toplady (1740–1778), by John Raphael Smith, pubd 1777

(1711–1771), at his church of St Paul's, Deptford, on 31 December 1737. His father, who was from Ireland, probably Enniscorthy in co. Wexford, took a commission first in Moreton's marines in 1739 and then transferred to Cottrell's regiment, serving with which he met his death, probably from yellow fever, at Cartagena in May 1741. Toplady never knew his father and thus came entirely under the care of his mother, who settled in Petty France, London. He became a scholar of Westminster School probably in 1750 (he himself records his attendance there in 1751), where he remained until 1755.

Toplady and his mother moved to Ireland, perhaps in pursuit of legal claims to her husband's family estate. Toplady matriculated from Trinity College, Dublin, on 11 July 1755 and proceeded BA in 1760. In August 1756 he heard the itinerant James Morris, a follower of Wesley, preaching on Ephesians 2: 13 in a barn at Codymain in the parish of Ballynaslaney, co. Wexford, an occasion which he later recorded in his diary on 29 February 1768 as 'that memorable evening of my effectual call by the grace of God' (A. Toplady, *The Posthumous Works of A. M. Toplady*, 1780, 275). There is a deep irony in this early link with Wesley, for it would not be long before their lifelong controversy would erupt. In a sermon at St Ann Blackfriars on 25 May 1774 Toplady claimed, 'It pleased God to deliver me from the Arminian snare before I was quite eighteen' (*Works*, 1825, 3.170), mainly, he asserted, by reading the seventeenth-century puritan Thomas Manton on St John's gospel, chapter 17, and then Zanchius of Heidelberg's *Confession of the Christian Religion* (1562), which he translated and later published in an edited version as *The Doctrine of Absolute Predestination Stated and Asserted* (1769).

After graduation Toplady returned to England with his mother; she took up residence once again in Westminster at New Way, where she remained until her death in 1770. He met and was influenced by various Calvinistic ministers, not only Whitefield but also the Baptist John Gill of Horsleydown in Southwark and William Romaine, who preached at the New Way Chapel. Toplady was ordained deacon by Edward Willes, the bishop of Bath and Wells, on 5 June 1762 to serve the curacy of Blagdon, Somerset, in the Mendip hills; he was priested two years later in June 1764. Near to Blagdon is Burrington Combe, a spectacular ravine, where legend and now a metal plaque have it that Toplady wrote 'Rock of ages'—a very unlikely story. He preached his last sermon at Blagdon on 29 April 1764, returned briefly to London, and was then licensed as curate of Farleigh Hungerford, some 7 miles from both Bath and Frome, where he remained for just over a year. He was back with London friends in the winter of 1765–6, but in May 1766 he began a two-year incumbency of the Devon villages of Harpford and Venn Ottery. Being troubled by the circumstances under which this living had apparently and without his knowledge been purchased for him, Toplady exchanged it for Broad Hembury, also in Devon, to which he was instituted on 6 April 1768. Despite several absences he remained vicar there for the rest of his life.

Toplady never married, but two women of very different character and interests appear to have attracted him. One, not surprisingly, was Selina, countess of Huntingdon, whom he first met in 1763 and in whose chapels, and in whose presence, he preached several times after leaving Broad Hembury in 1775. The other, much more surprisingly, was the worldly Catharine Macaulay, historian and egalitarian controversialist, whom Toplady met probably in 1773 and with whom he spent some time in May 1774. She was in Devon for three months in that year and heard him preach in Wells Cathedral in October, and he expressed the hope of staying in Bath near to her house in the winter of 1774–5. He even warned her against her friend, 'the dapper doctor', Thomas Wilson, rector of St Stephen Walbrook, who had placed his house in Bath at her disposal. Toplady also saw her later when she lived in Berners Street, London, but by 1777 he could dismiss her with what he called her 'such contemptible vanity and such childish affectation' (*Works*, 6.290–91). At this time Toplady upbraided himself for having been 'unusually idle, both as a preacher and as a writer' (ibid., 281). That judgement must have been very relative in one so prolific. Of his preaching it has been said that 'his voice was melodious and affecting; his manner of delivery and action were engaging, elegant and easy. His explanations were distinct and clear; his arguments strong and forcible; and his exhortations warm and animating' (A. C. H. Seymour, *Life and Times of Selina, Countess of Huntingdon*, 1840, 2.63–4).

The Calvinism which Toplady preached from the pulpit suffused his polemical writings. *The Church of England Vindicated from the Charge of Arminianism* (1769) was directed against Thomas Nowell, the professor of modern history at Oxford, who had criticized the six students expelled from St Edmund Hall for their evangelical views. This apart, most of Toplady's work formed a protracted quarrel with Wesley, who had dismissed his *Doctrine of Absolute Predestination* as suggesting that only one in twenty would be saved and that 'The elect shall be saved, do what they will—the reprobate shall be damned, do what they can' (J. Wesley, *The Works of the Rev. J. Wesley*, 14 vols., 1872, 10.370). Toplady replied with *A Letter to Mr John Wesley Relating to his Pretended Abridgement of Zanchius on Protestantism* in March 1771. Wesley responded with *The Consequence Proved* (August 1771) and Toplady came back with *More Work for Mr Wesley* (28 November 1771). Others joined in and the controversy culminated in Toplady's greatest work, *The Historic Proof of the Doctrinal Calvinism of the Church of England* (1774), a massive study tracing the doctrine from the early church and devoting 500 of its 700 pages to the Reformation and the Laudian reaction. In 1775 he published his *Scheme of Christian and Philosophical Necessity Asserted* in reply to Wesley's *Thoughts upon Necessity* (May 1774) and followed it in the same year with *An Old Fox Tarred and Feathered*, a scurrilous attack exposing Wesley's alleged plagiarism. In his footnote on the Synod of Dort in *The Historic Proof*, Toplady isolated his five fundamental tenets of Calvinism as election, limited redemption, the spiritual incapacity of the human will because of sin, the invincible efficacy of regenerating grace, and the final perseverance of the truly converted.

Toplady took over the editorship of the *Gospel Magazine* from Charles de Coetlogon in December 1775 and ran it until July 1777, continuing here also his attacks on Wesley. It was in this publication that the first verse of 'Rock of ages' appeared in September 1775, to be followed by the full hymn in March 1776. Toplady had written verses from his youth, his first book being *Poems on Sacred Subjects* (1759), but the main body of his work is to be found in *Psalms and Hymns for Public and Private Worship* (1776). Toplady's last three years were spent mainly in London, where he occupied the pulpit of the French Calvinist chapel in Orange Street. There on 14 June 1778, during his final illness, he made a dramatic entry to deny reports being spread about by Wesley and his followers that he had renounced his Calvinistic beliefs. This final address was published as *The Rev. Mr Toplady's Dying Avowal of his Religious Sentiments* (1778). He died, a victim of tuberculosis, at Knightsbridge, on 11 August 1778 and was buried six days later at Whitefield's Tabernacle (later the Whitefield Memorial Church) in Tottenham Court Road, London.

Most of Toplady's hymnody is now forgotten. Three pieces still minimally survive—'A debtor to mercy alone', 'Deathless principle, arise', and 'Object of my first desire'. Only in 'Rock of ages' are the dramatic power, emotional tension, and sheer vividness of physical suffering so compelling. It is a hymn so well known that it is almost standard for those film scenes of the kind found, for example, in John Ford's westerns where, as the congregation is singing it confidently, there is suddenly threat and danger from the enemy at the door. Toplady's hymns match his preaching; there are no half measures. For him assurance was complete; his was faith in the furnace, religion at perpetual white heat.   ARTHUR POLLARD

Sources The works of Augustus M. Toplady, new edn, 6 vols. (1825) · G. Lawton, Within the Rock of ages: the life and work of Augustus Montague Toplady (1983) · T. Wright, The life of Augustus M. Toplady (1911) · P. E. G. Cook, Augustus Toplady: the saintly sinner (1978) · A. Pollard, 'Restless endeavour: a study of the hymns of A. M. Toplady', The Churchman, new ser., 73 (1959), 23–8 · J. Julian, ed., A dictionary of hymnology, rev. edn (1907), 1182–3 · H. D. Rack, Reasonable enthusiasm: John Wesley and the rise of Methodism, 2nd edn (1992) · DNB · Burtchaell & Sadleir, Alum. Dubl.
Archives Cowper Memorial Library, Olney, Northamptonshire, sermon drafts and other MSS · Emory University, Atlanta, Georgia, Robert W. Woodruff Library, papers
Likenesses J. R. Smith, engraving, pubd 1777, NPG [see illus.] · engraving, 1777, repro. in Wright, Life of Augustus M. Toplady; in possession of Whitefield's Tabernacle, 1911 · C. Blackberd, line engraving (after C. R. Ryley), BM; repro. in Memoirs (1794) · pencil-and-gouache drawing (after J. R. Smith), NPG
Wealth at death see Lawton, Within the Rock of ages, 134

Topley, William (1841–1894), geologist, was born on 13 March 1841 in Greenwich, Kent, the son of William Topley and his wife, Carolina Georgina Jeans. He was educated at local private schools and entered the Royal School of Mines for three years' study in 1858. He was appointed assistant geologist to the geological survey of England and Wales in 1862 and started fieldwork in the weald of southeast England under the supervision of Clement le Neve Foster (1841–1904). The survey of the weald had begun in 1855 under H. W. Bristow, and eventually involved nine geologists over a period of twenty years. Topley mapped the Hastings beds of the central weald as well as river deposits of the Darent, Stour, and Medway. His work on the river deposits led to an abiding interest in denudation, and to an important joint paper with Foster in the Quarterly Journal of the Geological Society (1865) which gave convincing evidence that the land surface of the weald was shaped by rain and rivers rather than by the sea. He thus became part of a group of survey geologists, including Archibald Geikie, Joseph Jukes, and Andrew Ramsay, who opposed Roderick Murchison, then survey director, on this topic.

In 1867 Topley married Ruth Whiteman. The following year he was promoted to the rank of geologist and sent north to work in Northumberland under Henry H. Howell. There he mapped considerable areas of Carboniferous rock and the overlying glacial drift, and gave the name Rothbury Grits to one of the subdivisions of the Carboniferous Limestone. He also mapped part of the Whin Sill, and published a paper with G. A. Lebour demonstrating that it is an intrusion and not a lava flow. Between 1871 and 1874 Topley took what spare time he had to write up a comprehensive memoir on the geology of the weald from the notes left by the geologists who had worked on the project, seven of whom either were dead or had resigned from the survey. The work was published as a memoir of the geological survey in 1875, and is his chief memorial. In 1880 he was recalled to survey headquarters in Jermyn Street, London, to superintend the publication of maps and memoirs, and in 1893 he succeeded Edward Best with the entire charge of the office. Although not a great traveller, Topley paid geological visits to France, Belgium, Switzerland, Canada, and Algeria at different times.

Topley had many interests and commitments outside his official duties. He assisted with, and later edited, the enormously time-consuming Geological Record, he was secretary to the geological section at fifteen meetings of the British Association between 1872 and 1880, and sat on the committee on sub-wealden exploration, and on that enquiring into the rate of erosion of sea coasts. Topley was president of the Geologists' Association from 1885 to 1887 and was secretary of the London International Geological Congress in 1888, in which capacity he contributed to the congress's geological map of Europe. He was elected a fellow of the Royal Society in 1888. He was also interested in the engineering aspects of geology, and published on landslips and on plans for a channel tunnel, as well as in mineral resources and water supply. The relationship of water supply to human health also concerned him, and he lectured to the Sanitary Institute Congress on geology in its relation to hygiene in 1890. Finally, the influence of geology on agriculture had interested Topley since his early work in the weald, and he published papers on the agricultural geology of that area (1872) and on the comparative agriculture of the counties of England (1871). Topley died at his home, 13 Havelock Road, Croydon, on 30 September 1894 of disease thought to have been caused by drinking contaminated water while in Algeria.

JOHN C. THACKRAY

Sources H. B. [H. B. Woodward], Quarterly Journal of the Geological Society, 51 (1895), lvii–lxi · H. B. Woodward, 'William Topley', Geological Magazine, new ser., 4th decade, 1 (1894), 570–75 · A. H. G. [A. H. Green], PRS, 59 (1895–6), lxix–lxxi · W. W. [W. Whitaker], 'William Topley', Nature, 50 (1894), 579–80 · J. F. Kirkaldy, 'William Topley and The geology of the weald', Proceedings of the Geologists' Association, 86 (1975), 373–88 · CGPLA Eng. & Wales (1894) · DNB
Archives BGS, notebooks
Likenesses photograph, repro. in Woodward, 'William Topley', 570 · photograph, BGS
Wealth at death £1583 16s. 10d.: probate, 15 Nov 1894, CGPLA Eng. & Wales

Topley, William Whiteman Carlton (1886–1944), bacteriologist, was born at 61 Wickham Road, Lewisham, London, on 19 January 1886, the eldest of the three sons of Ebenezer Topley (1851–1916), wholesale grocer, and his wife, Elizabeth Whiteman. The geologist William Topley was his uncle. He was educated at the City of London School and at St John's College, Cambridge, of which he was a scholar and where he gained a first-class award in the natural sciences tripos of 1907. He completed his medical training at St Thomas's Hospital, London, qualifying in 1909. After serving in 1910 as house physician, demonstrator of morbid anatomy, and assistant director of the pathological laboratory, at St Thomas's Hospital, he was bacteriologist to the Samaritan Free Hospital for Women, and director of the clinical pathological department and lecturer on bacteriology at Charing Cross Hospital, from 1911 to 1922. In 1912 Topley married Kate, daughter of

Frederick W. Amsden, of Sevenoaks, Kent; they had twin daughters in 1916.

During the First World War, Topley served as a captain in the Royal Army Medical Corps, and in 1915 he was bacteriologist to the British Sanitary Commission in Serbia. He was professor of bacteriology at the University of Manchester from 1922 to 1927, and professor of bacteriology and immunology at London University and director of the division of bacteriology and immunology at the London School of Hygiene and Tropical Medicine from 1927 to 1941. He was a member of the Medical Research Council from 1938 to 1941, and early in 1939 he took a leading part in the organization of the Emergency Public Health Laboratory Service, to meet the needs of impending war. In 1941 Topley was appointed secretary of the Agricultural Research Council. He was also a member of the war cabinet scientific advisory committee and of the colonial research advisory committee.

At the Royal College of Physicians, Topley was Murchison scholar in 1910; he was admitted a fellow in 1918; and he delivered the Goulstonian lectures in 1919 and the Milroy lectures in 1926. In 1930 he was elected FRS, served on the council of the Royal Society in 1936–7 and 1938–40, was Croonian lecturer in 1941, and received a Royal medal in 1942 for his work on experimental epidemiology and immunology. In 1942 he was elected an honorary fellow of St John's College, Cambridge.

Topley began his career combining clinical pathology, lecturing, and private practice, but his experiences of the typhus epidemic, which he witnessed with the sanitary commission in Serbia, persuaded him to give up medical practice and to pursue research. He was convinced that the study of epidemiology required a more experimental basis, rather than the usual descriptive or historical methods. His principal research consisted of carefully controlled laboratory experiments to chart the spread of disease in populations of mice under different conditions. He was one of the first to use such experimental methods. Much of this work was summarized in the Special Report 209 issued by the Medical Research Council in 1936. *The Principles of Bacteriology and Immunity*, which he wrote with Graham Selby Wilson (2 vols., 1929), rapidly established itself as the standard work of reference in the English language and by its eighth edition had become known popularly as 'Topley and Wilson'. His *Outline of Immunity* (1933) was a shorter review of the then state of knowledge of this subject.

Increasingly, Topley took on administrative responsibilities at the London School of Hygiene and Tropical Medicine, at the Medical Research Council, and in war work. In 1941 he became secretary to the Agricultural Research Council, a change of field which surprised many of his contemporaries but to which he devoted customary energy and enthusiasm.

Colleagues found it difficult to describe Topley's character. He was a well-respected figure in British medicine, very supportive of younger colleagues, with little time for laxity or posturing, especially in scientific matters. He could also, occasionally, be highly critical of some small

point, or deliberately provocative in conversation. Most of his leisure time was spent with his family, and they enjoyed rare boating holidays; generally, however, Topley was absorbed in science, which he regarded as a pleasure as well as a vocation, and he had few other interests. He worked himself extremely hard, to which most of his obituarists attributed his sudden death at his office at 6A Dean's Yard, Westminster, London, on 21 January 1944. He was survived by his wife.

W. J. BISHOP, *rev.* KEITH VERNON

Sources H. R. Dean and G. S. Wilson, *Journal of Pathology and Bacteriology*, 56 (1944), 450–69 · M. Greenwood, *Obits. FRS*, 4 (1942–4), 698–712 · *Nature*, 153 (1944), 215–16 · *The Lancet* (5 Feb 1944) · *BMJ* (5 Feb 1944), 201–2 · *The Times* (22 Jan 1944) · *WWW* · b. cert. · *CGPLA Eng. & Wales* (1944)
Archives PRO, corresp. with Sir Henry Dale, Cab 127/227
Likenesses Hill and Saunders, photograph, 1938, repro. in Dean and Wilson, 450 · J. Russell & Sons, photograph, repro. in *The Lancet*, 198 · W. Stoneman, photographs, NPG · photograph, repro. in Greenwood, *Obits. FRS*, 698 · photomechanical print (after Hill and Saunders), Wellcome L.
Wealth at death £10,125 16s. 1d.: probate, 14 April 1944, *CGPLA Eng. & Wales*

Toplis, (Francis) Percy [called the Monocled Mutineer] (1896–1920), confidence trickster and mutineer, was born on 22 August 1896 at Sanforth Street, Newbold, Chesterfield, Derbyshire, the son of Herbert Toplis, assurance collector, and his wife, Rejoice Elizabeth Webster. In 1908, at the age of eleven, he tricked a clothier at Sutton in Coldfield into giving him two suits on approval, and pawned one for 5s. His crime was detected, and he was sentenced at Mansfield petty sessions to six strokes of the birch. Three months later he was put on a year's probation by Chesterfield magistrates for tricking a street vendor out of thirty-six newspapers. Among other delinquencies while a pupil at South Normanton elementary school he circulated a bottle of laudanum which put several classmates to sleep during a geography lesson. He had a strong, even compelling character in boyhood but a rough manner. On leaving school in 1910 he was apprenticed as a blacksmith at Blackwell colliery, but after quarrelling with the pit manager he decamped to Scotland. There he was imprisoned for ten days after travelling on a railway without a ticket. In 1912 he was sentenced to two years' hard labour for a sexual assault on a Lincolnshire girl.

Percy Toplis, as he was always known, was released from Lincoln gaol in the autumn of 1914 and volunteered for the army in the following year. He served in France as a stretcher-bearer in the Royal Army Medical Corps before obtaining compassionate leave after reporting the death of his non-existent wife in childbirth. On reaching England he bemedalled himself as a hero and was lionized in his native Mansfield. Later, while absent without leave in London, masquerading as an officer, he had various amorous adventures. He was much given to brandishing, and perhaps even to firing, his revolver to impress or intimidate. His vanity, excitability, and dishonesty were incorrigible.

In 1917 Toplis was sent to the British army base camp at Étaples. There he continued to defy discipline and to dress as a monocled officer, although he remained merely a private in the medical corps. On 9 September the soldiers at Étaples mutinied: among other acts a thousand marauding deserters released fifty prisoners from a detention compound. Toplis, who always liked to cut a fine figure, was one of five insurgents who formed a deputation to the mountebank patriot Horatio Bottomley, then paying a self-publicizing visit to the front. When the mutiny petered out after six days, Toplis, who had earned the nickname the Monocled Mutineer, went missing. Although soon captured, he tunnelled out under the sand of his barbed wire compound, and returned by subterfuge to England.

There Toplis evaded detention as a deserter by the bold stroke of enlisting in the Royal Army Service Corps. However, around the time of the armistice in 1918, he was convicted in the name of Williams before Nottinghamshire Hall bench for obtaining a watch by false pretences, and served six months' hard labour. On his release he managed to re-enlist yet again in the Royal Army Service Corps in August 1919. He became involved in various army rackets, including the theft and resale of petrol, and continued his career as a confidence trickster and Don Juan when on leave in London. He had a ready supply of badges and uniforms of different ranks and regiments, and sported a gold-rimmed monocle when impersonating army officers. Having stolen a military Sunbeam motor car on Boxing night of 1919, he was again detained and again escaped confinement. In January 1920 he enlisted under his own name in the RAF, but soon deserted. His self-destructiveness now became lethal.

On 25 April the corpse of Sidney George Spicer, a young Salisbury taxi driver, was discovered with a bullet wound to the head under a hedge at Thruxton Down, near Andover. Spicer's grey Darracq five-seater was later found abandoned at Swansea. Evidence accumulated indicating Toplis as the perpetrator. An intense and heavily publicized hunt was raised for him even before a verdict of wilful murder was returned against him on 26 May. During his six weeks on the run, sightings of him were reported from 107 different places. At the start of June he shot and gravely wounded a policeman and gamekeeper who together challenged him with being in unlawful occupation of a lonely shooting lodge in Banffshire. He then fled south as an even more desperate fugitive. On the evening of 6 June he was ambushed and shot dead by police outside Plumpton church in Cumberland. The police gave no quarter. Toplis, who was 5 feet 8 inches, slender, with small blue eyes, a ruddy complexion, reddish hair, and thin ginger moustache cut à la Charlie Chaplin, was buried (with his monocle secreted in the coffin) in a pauper's grave in Penrith cemetery on 9 June.

RICHARD DAVENPORT-HINES

Sources W. Allison and J. Fairley, *The monocled mutineer* (1978) · *The Times* (26 April 1920) · *The Times* (27 April 1920) · *The Times* (30 April 1920) · *The Times* (27 May 1920) · *The Times* (4 June 1920) · *The Times* (5 June 1920) · *The Times* (7 June 1920) · b. cert.
Likenesses photograph, 1917, IWM · photograph, 1920, repro. in Allison and Fairley, *The monocled mutineer*, facing p. 97; formerly at Penrith police station, 1977

Topolski, Feliks (1907–1989), artist and stage designer, was born in Warsaw on 14 August 1907, the only child of Edward Topolski, actor and manager, and his wife, Stanislawa Drutowska, who later divorced her husband and married an army officer. Topolski matriculated from Mikolaj Rey School in 1925, his artistic talent already evident and fostered by his mother. He was encouraged to develop his artistic abilities by Tadeus Pruszkowski, principal of the Warsaw Academy of Art, where Topolski studied from 1927 to 1932. A summer school at Kazimierz, over which Pruszkowski presided, was described by Topolski in his autobiography, *Fourteen Letters* (1988), as an important liberating influence, both artistically and socially. He made many friends, and began to enjoy the free love affairs with women which were a currency of his milieu, and which were woven into the pattern of his life.

In Warsaw Topolski joined the artillery reserve, in which he was commissioned as a second lieutenant. He became active in the city's artistic and literary life, besides during the early 1930s making extensive travels in Europe which began with a trip that included Vienna, Italy, France, and England in 1933.

In 1935 Topolski went to London with an assignment to record the jubilee of George V. He found England enjoyably exotic, and was quickly accepted into a congenial set of talented people. An early commission was to draw the first cover of *Night and Day*, a short-lived periodical through which he gained literary friendships, including that of Graham Greene. Drawings for the *News Chronicle* formed the basis for his first English book, *The London Spectacle* (1935). His fluent graphic style was from the first equally effective in newspapers, magazines, or books; for example, George Bernard Shaw became a firm admirer, and commissioned him to produce illustrated editions of three of his plays. Shaw described him as 'an astonishing draughtsman; perhaps the greatest of all the impressionists in black and white'. He was also commissioned by Shaw to design stage sets.

The war years of 1939–45 consolidated Topolski's British reputation as an exceptionally gifted draughtsman, adept at recording history as it happened. He became an official war artist in 1940 and began by making drawings of the London blitz. In 1941 he was sent on an Arctic convoy to Russia to draw for both the Polish authorities and the *Picture Post*. He was subsequently employed by both the Polish and British authorities, as works in the Imperial War Museum and in Warsaw testify.

Topolski published three wartime books of drawings (*Britain in Peace and War*, 1941; *Russia in War*, 1942; and *Three Continents, 1944–5*, 1946), and worked extensively for magazines in Britain and the United States. From 1944 he was officially posted variously to draw convoys, to Egypt, the Levant, east Africa, Burma, China, and Italy. After the invasion of France he followed the armies into Germany, where he was one of the witnesses of Belsen concentration camp, and later he attended the Nuremberg trials. He was naturalized in 1947.

Topolski had become internationally celebrated and remained so. He scored a popular success with portraits used for the British television programme *Face to Face*, published as a book in 1964. Topolski had also undertaken a series of twenty portraits in 1961–2 of great literary figures of the twentieth century for the University of Texas (now held in the Harry Ransom Humanities Research Center), including T. S. Eliot, E. M. Forster, Edith Sitwell, and Evelyn Waugh. In all he produced twenty-two books. His gifts as a painter on a large scale were also recognized by commissions beginning with a mural for the Festival of Britain in 1951—*Cavalcade of the Commonwealth*, later placed for ten years in the Victoria Memorial Hall, Singapore. In 1958 Philip, duke of Edinburgh, commissioned a record of the coronation of Elizabeth II for a corridor in Buckingham Palace. His culminating mural work was *Memoir of the Century*, begun in 1975, a vast panoramic interior under the railway arches of Hungerford Bridge on London's South Bank, where he also had his post-war studio. A graphic published parallel was *Topolski's Chronicle* (1953–79 and 1982–9), which reproduced drawings from the artist's extensive travels throughout the world. Nine of his portraits are in the National Portrait Gallery, and a substantial collection of his work (30 paintings and 550 drawings) is in the Muzeum Narodowe w Warszawie, the national museum of Poland in Warsaw. Further examples of his work are in the British Museum, the Victoria and Albert Museum, the Tate Gallery, and the Imperial War Museum.

Topolski was small in stature with brown eyes, and a charm of manner which made him welcome at every level of society. In 1944 he married Marion (d. 1985), daughter of Tom Mason Everall, businessman. They had a son and a daughter, Daniel and Teresa. Daniel became well known as the coach of the Oxford University boat crews which gained a succession of wins over Cambridge. Topolski's first marriage was dissolved in 1975, in which year he married Caryl Jane, architect, daughter of Theodore Stanley, company director.

Topolski received many awards for his work, about which four television programmes were made. He was awarded a doctorate by the Jagiellonian University of Cracow in 1974, and was elected RA in 1989. He died in St Thomas's Hospital, London, from heart disease and diabetes, on 24 August 1989, and was survived by his wife.

JOSEPH DARRACOTT, rev.

Sources F. Topolski, *Fourteen letters* (1988) · *The Times* (25 Aug 1989) · private information (1996)

Archives BFI, corresp. with Ivor Montagu

Likenesses photographs, 1941–68, Hult. Arch. · photograph, repro. in *The Times* · photograph, repro. in *Sunday Telegraph* (15 April 1979)

Wealth at death £460,197: probate, 25 May 1990, *CGPLA Eng. & Wales*

Topping, Andrew (1890–1955), public health physician, was born on 20 December 1890 at 82 Stanley Street, Aberdeen, one of the eight children of Robert Topping, an assistant inspector of schools in the Scottish education department, and his wife, Robina Bayne. He was educated at Robert Gordon's College, Aberdeen, and the University of Aberdeen, where he graduated MA in 1911 and MB ChB

in 1914. While a student he was a colour-sergeant in the 4th battalion of the Gordon Highlanders (TA), and he took an active part in university sports as a member of the football, golf, and water-polo teams. On 9 August 1913 Topping married another graduate of Aberdeen, Alfreda Margaret Wood (b. 1891/2), daughter of Alfred Lyon Wood, a pharmacist, with whom he had two sons and a daughter. The younger son died in an accident while still a child. During the First World War, Topping served in the Royal Army Medical Corps in France, Gallipoli, and Mesopotamia, and was mentioned in dispatches. After demobilization in 1919 he was appointed senior medical officer to the Anglo-Persian Oil Company at Abadan, but in 1923 he returned to Aberdeen to take the diploma in public health; he also graduated MD with a thesis, entitled 'Notes on the protean nature of smallpox, with an investigation of the theory that alastrim is a separate entity', for which he gained a commendation.

Topping took up his first public health appointment in 1923, as assistant medical officer of health for Woolwich. He transferred to a similar post in Lancashire in 1927. Between 1930 and 1932 he was medical officer of health for Rochdale, where he organized what later became known as the Rochdale experiment, during which he displayed his ability as a co-ordinator by persuading a group of general practitioners, consultants, and public health personnel to investigate the causes of maternal mortality. He publicized the advantages of antenatal care, recommended conservative treatment in confinements, and obtained provision of new maternity and paediatric wards by Rochdale council. This lowered maternal mortality from 8 per thousand to 3.5 per thousand. In 1932 Topping returned to London as medical superintendent of the Southern Fever Hospital at Dartford, and in 1933 he joined the London county council to become senior medical officer in charge of special hospitals and subsequently of the laboratory services. In 1940 he took up the post of deputy medical officer of health for London, and in 1942 he became director of the London Ambulance Service. He encouraged his fellow Scots to join the London county council's service, causing a colleague to remark that 'County Hall always had a strong smell of haggis.'

Towards the end of the Second World War, at the request of the Ministry of Health and in association with Sir Archibald Gray, Topping visited all the hospitals in London and the home counties to prepare a survey which was published as a blue book in 1944 and which was described in his obituary in *The Lancet* as a 'minor classic'. In 1944 he accepted the temporary post of director of the European division of the United Nations Relief and Rehabilitation Administration, and in the following year he became the deputy director of the relief services. One of his Polish colleagues, Dr H. Zborowski, said in a tribute that 'he was well known to us as a man of noble character and outstanding qualifications for his important post … His handling of the difficult international personnel proved his excellent judgement' (Zborowski, 569).

At the end of the war Topping worked briefly for the Ministry of Health and was also a lecturer at Charing Cross medical school, but in 1947 he returned to Lancashire to become the first professor of preventive and social medicine at the University of Manchester. In 1950 he returned to London once more as the first full-time dean at the London School of Hygiene and Tropical Medicine. In 1952 Topping served as president of the Society of Medical Officers of Health, having been elected unanimously; he used his presidential speech to call for money to be spent on educating the public in the prevention of disease rather than on its cure. He was appointed CMG in 1954 and in the early part of that year, during a visit to Accra in the Gold Coast, he was involved in a car accident which physically disabled him and left his health permanently impaired. He returned to work in May 1954 but fell ill again in January 1955; he died in the Whittington Hospital, Highgate Hill, Islington, London, from a malignant cerebral glioma on 28 August 1955. He was cremated at Golders Green crematorium on 2 September 1955. His wife, daughter, and elder son survived him.

Topping was noted for his administrative abilities, but he was not afraid to court controversy or to state his opinion, which was usually in favour of radical change. Despite this he remained approachable and genial, and no bad feeling was left after disagreements. Topping was also a notable public speaker and raconteur, with a fund of witty stories which he told with great effect.

MARY E. GIBSON

Sources *BMJ* (1955), 2.622–3 · *The Lancet* (3 Sept 1955), 511–13 · *Aberdeen University Review*, 36 (1955–6), 325–7 · Munk, *Roll* · J. M. Mackintosh, *Year Book of the Royal Society of Edinburgh* (1954–5), 54–6 · *Public Health*, 49 (1 Oct 1955), 19 · J. M. Mackintosh, *BMJ* (3 Sept 1955), 673–4 · R. Cruikshank, *BMJ* (10 Sept 1955), 684 · P. Manson-Bahr, *The Lancet* (10 Sept 1955), 568–9 · H. Zborowski, *The Lancet* (10 Sept 1955), 569 · b. cert. · m. cert. · d. cert. · *CGPLA Eng. & Wales* (1955) · *Medical Directory* (1926–50)
Archives London School of Hygiene and Tropical Medicine, personal file
Likenesses photograph, c.1950, London School of Hygiene and Tropical Medicine · Elliott & Fry, photograph, c.1952
Wealth at death £6319 3s. 2d.: probate, 5 Oct 1955, *CGPLA Eng. & Wales*

Topsell, Edward (*bap.* 1572, *d.* 1625), Church of England clergyman and author, was born in Sevenoaks, Kent, and was baptized there on 3 February 1572, the son of John Topsell (*d.* 1573). He matriculated as a sizar at Christ's College, Cambridge, in 1587, graduated BA in 1591 or 1592, and probably proceeded MA, though there is no record of this. He held a variety of cures and livings in Sussex (Hartsfield, 1592; Framfield, 1593–6; East Hoathly, 1596–8; Mayfield, 1605–6; East Grinstead, 1610–15), Hertfordshire (Datchworth, 1598–1601), and Northamptonshire (Syresham, 1602–8). The name of his first wife is not known, but a daughter, Mary, was baptized at Datchworth in 1600 and a son, Abel, matriculated at Trinity College, Oxford, in 1617, aged fifteen; both survived him. From 7 April 1604 Topsell was perpetual curate of St Botolph, Aldersgate, London, and on 12 August 1612 he married Mary, widow of Gregory Seaton, stationer, of the adjacent parish of St Anne and St Agnes.

Topsell's early publication *The Reward of Religion: Delivered in Sundrie Lectures upon the Booke of Ruth* (London, John Windell, 1596) is addressed to Margaret, Lady Dacre of the South, whose husband, Sampson Lennard of Chevening, promoted his early studies. The book reflects upon marriage and duty; it was reissued in 1601 and in 1613. *Time's Lamentation, or, An Exposition of the Prophet Joel in Sundry* [42] *Sermons or Meditations* (London, by E. Bollifant for G. Potter, 1599), dedicated to Charles Blount, Lord Mountjoy (described by Topsell as 'the meane of my preferment'), condemns 'vanity and frivolity', that is, worldly preoccupations of all kinds. Topsell warns his audience not to doubt plagues or grow impatient at these tales of 'a muster of fraybugs, and little worms an inch long'; we must not 'weigh [such matters] in the ballance of natural reason but lay them to a sound spirituall judgement. The waies of God are not like the waies of men' (p. 68). The same note is struck in *The Householder, or, Perfect Man: Preached in Three Sermons* (London, by Henry Rockyt, 1610, 16mo), addressed to Richard Sackville, third earl of Dorset, his wife, Anne, and to four other noblemen of Topsell's acquaintance.

Insistence upon a spiritual reading of the book of nature is to be found prominently in the prefatory material, and less prominently in the text, of Topsell's most celebrated publications, *The Historie of Foure-Footed Beastes* (London, W. Jaggard, 1607) and *The Historie of Serpents* (London, W. Jaggard, 1608), both dedicated to Richard Neile, dean of Westminster. Topsell's declared purpose in collecting together pictures of animals, and stories about their ways, is to entertain, to inform, and above all to edify. He envisages *The Historie of Foure-Footed Beastes* as suitable sabbath reading-matter in the godly home (epistle dedicatory, final paragraph). These books have usually been seen, and criticized, as contributions to natural history—indeed, it was in this light that they were reissued by John Rowland, together with Thomas Mouffet's *History of Insects*, in 1658. But Topsell made no claim to be a naturalist. He was an industrious compiler, collecting information out of 'divine Scriptures, fathers, Philosophers, Physitians and Poets' amplified with 'sundry accidental Histories, Hierogliphycks, Epigrams, Emblems, and Aenigmatical Observations'. He relied heavily on the *Historia animalium* of the mid-sixteenth-century Swiss protestant encyclopaedist Conrad Gesner, from whose work most of the text and the pictures in both books is derived. He reproduces much of Gesner's text verbatim, but also paraphrases, digests, or omits passages without warning. He adds material from the English writers John Caius (on dogs), Thomas Blundeville and Gervase Markham (on the horse), and Thomas Penny via Thomas Mouffet (on insects), as well as remarks of his own.

Topsell has rightly been judged to have been 'a man of very little originality, who reproduced what his authorities gave to him', and who was guilty on occasion of blurring the distinction between citation and commentary, in such a way as to lay himself open to the charge of plagiarism (Raven, 218, 167, 223–6). His work is ignored by the later seventeenth-century naturalist John Ray. When Topsell and the printer William Jaggard collaborated on the *Foure-Footed Beastes* it was, no doubt, on the assumption that 'there was a public ready to enjoy and able to pay for large illustrated books of this kind' (Raven, 218). That this public was ready to complain about printers' errors was perhaps an unwelcome surprise. In his preface to *The Historie of Serpents* Topsell apologizes for the shortcomings of the first volume, and explains that neither he nor the printer could afford to pay for a scholarly proof-corrector. Clearly, the project had proved to be both expensive and difficult. Signs of haste, and perhaps of boredom, are evident already in the book on serpents. Despite the fact that Topsell lived on for another twenty years, the intended volumes on birds and fishes never appeared. He died, probably in London, in 1625, and was buried at St Botolph.   G. LEWIS

Sources Venn, *Alum. Cant.* · E. Carter, *The history of the University of Cambridge* (1753), 234 · J. Peile, *Biographical register of Christ's College, 1505–1905, and of the earlier foundation, God's House, 1448–1505*, ed. [J. A. Venn], 1 (1910), 191 · C. E. Raven, *English naturalists from Neckam to Ray: a study of the making of the modern world* (1947) · A. C. Jenkins, *The naturalists* (1978), 21–3 · N. Jardine, J. A. Secord, and E. C. Spary, eds., *Cultures of natural history* (1996), 72 · W. Ley, introduction, in E. Topsell, *The history of four-footed beasts and serpents and insects*, 1 (1967) · PRO, PROB 11/145, sig. 62 · parish register (baptism), 3 Feb 1572, Sevenoaks

Torch, Sidney (1908–1990), organist, conductor, and composer, was born on 5 June 1908 at 27 Tottenham Court Road, London, the son of Morris Torchinsky and his wife, Annie Hoppen. His father, an orchestral trombonist, sent him to study piano at the Blackheath Conservatoire. Clearly Torch must have been a talented pianist because his first professional engagement was as accompanist to the celebrated violinist Albert Sandler. He then moved into several cinema orchestras playing for silent films, but the arrival of talking pictures towards the end of the 1920s meant that full orchestras were no longer needed, and even prestigious ensembles such as Emanuel Starkey's orchestra at the Regal, Marble Arch (in which Torch also played piano), were disbanded. At the Regal a Christie organ was built in 1928, and Torch was full-time organist there from 1932 to 1934.

Despite the popularity of his jazzy arrangements with cinema-goers who heard him in person, and the thousands of record buyers who purchased his 78s, the BBC did not invite Torch to broadcast regularly until late in 1934. Microphones of the period had great difficulty coping with the wide dynamics and timbral range of modern organs. In 1936 he joined Union Cinemas and recorded at their flagship theatre, the Regal in Kingston upon Thames. The following year he opened the magnificent Wurlitzer organ at the Gaumont State, Kilburn, then the largest cinema organ in England.

The Second World War affected, but did not curtail, Torch's promising career; in 1940 he joined the Royal Air Force, initially being stationed near Blackpool, Lancashire, where he continued to record at the opera house.

After training as an air gunner he was commissioned and attained the rank of squadron leader. He became conductor of the RAF Concert Orchestra, thus allowing him to study more closely the intricacies of orchestral scoring. This proved invaluable when he resumed civilian life after the war. He turned to light orchestral composing, arranging, and conducting, in which he quickly established himself through his BBC radio broadcasts and commercial recordings for Parlophone and Columbia.

Torch's composing talents were ideally suited to the requirements of the production music (mood music) publishers, who were rapidly establishing libraries of recorded orchestral music in London. Chappells had already started recording light music on 78 r.p.m. discs for the use of radio, film, newsreel, and eventually television companies as early as 1942, and from 1946 onwards Torch contributed more than a hundred varied works to the Chappell catalogue, both under his own name and as Denis Rycoth (an anagram). He also conducted the Queen's Hall Light Orchestra on these special recordings, and was similarly engaged by rival publishers Francis, Day, and Hunter.

The climax of Torch's career came in 1953, when he helped the BBC devise *Friday Night is Music Night*. The BBC Concert Orchestra had been formed the previous year, and Torch conducted them for almost twenty years in this radio series on the Light Programme (and later Radio 2), until his retirement in 1972. His inventive arrangements continued to be heard long after his departure from the programme. During this period he became one of the most popular and respected conductors of light music in Britain. His countless broadcasts included many celebrity concerts, often at London's Royal Festival Hall as part of the BBC's regular light music festivals.

Torch had a reputation as something of a martinet, according to the musicians and singers who performed under his baton. One described the crackle that emanated from his starched shirt-cuffs on some of his rapier-like downbeats. Singers dreaded 'the glare of the Torch' if they failed to please the maestro. Yet he was also remembered for various acts of kindness, seldom made public, but nevertheless appreciated by some of his musicians who needed temporary financial assistance. He demanded smartness in the dress sense from his musicians, and always had in reserve an extra pair of gloves or black socks in case of need. His music was also often entertaining to watch as well as to hear: his *London Transport Suite* and *Duel for Drummers* are ideal examples requiring athletic participation from the percussion section. Among his best-known compositions were *Shooting Star*, *Samba sud*, *Going for a Ride*, *On a Spring Note*, and *The Trapeze Waltz*. Torch was married to Eva Elizabeth Tyson (1915–1990), a BBC producer.

Following his retirement Torch seemed to lose interest in his previous musical activities. He rarely wanted to talk about his pre-war stardom as a cinema organist, and similarly dismissed most attempts to get him to recall his great moments in light music. In a rare radio interview in 1983 he admitted that he had been cruel to most of his producers, although he felt that many of them probably benefited from the experience. He was appointed MBE in 1985. Torch died at his Sussex home, Flat 3, The Moorings, St Johns Road, Eastbourne, on 16 July 1990 at the age of eighty-two, having taken an overdose. His wife had died on 1 March 1990.

DAVID ADES

Sources *The Times* (19 July 1990) · b. cert. · d. cert. · private information (2004) · *Sidney Torch*, EMI, HMV 2 [audio CD] · *Sidney Torch*, Marco Polo 8223443 [audio CD] · *Journal into Melody* (1956–82) · *Daily Telegraph* (19 July 1990) · b. cert. [E. Tyson] · d. cert. [E. Torch]
Archives FILM BFI NFTVA, news footage · BFI NFTVA, performance footage · BFI NFTVA, propaganda film footage (National Savings Committee) |SOUND BL NSA, performance recordings · BL NSA, 'A tribute to Sidney Torch'
Likenesses photographs, BBC Picture Archive, London · photographs, EMI Records
Wealth at death £163,849: probate, 10 Oct 1990, *CGPLA Eng. & Wales*

Torday, Emil (1875–1931), anthropologist, was born in Budapest, Hungary, on 22 June 1875. His family were landowners, with estates in the town of Torda which subsequently, with boundary changes, became part of Romania. Little is known of his early life or his education, which he received in both Hungary and Germany. He was enrolled as a student at the University of Munich, but left without completing his degree and moved to Brussels where he worked for a time in a bank. Torday was an excellent linguist who learned to speak fifteen languages, eight of them African, and had already developed the engaging, maverick personality which became apparent in his later activities and in his more popular writing.

Torday's reputation rests largely on his experiences in equatorial Africa, where he travelled and worked almost continuously from 1900 to 1910. He first took up a colonial administrative post at Lake Mweru in the south-east of Congo Free State. He had few formal duties and spent his time learning local dialects and developing an interest in Luba culture. In 1904 his appointment came to an end and he voyaged back to Europe, but sought a way of returning to central Africa at the earliest opportunity. On a visit to London he met Thomas Athol Joyce, a curator at the British Museum, and formed an association with this institution which influenced his whole career. When he returned to the Belgian Congo—this time as an employee of the Compagnie du Kasai, and later when mounting his own expedition in 1907—he increasingly came to act as an agent of the British Museum. In this capacity he undertook ethnographic surveys of the people of the Kwango-Kwilu river basin and of the Kasai, formed comprehensive ethnographic collections, and created photographic and phonographic records. Over 3000 objects collected by Torday are now in the British Museum collections.

The centre point of Torday's ethnographic work was his engagement with the Kuba peoples, and especially his relationship with the nyimi (king) Kot aPe (or Kwete in Torday's spelling). Always an advocate of indigenous views, Torday found in the Kuba a sumptuous kingdom with a sumptuous artistic tradition, and in Kot aPe an impressive ruler. Furthermore, the Kuba had a dynastic history which could be related to European chronologies: it was founded in the early seventeenth century, dated in oral tradition to a known passage of Halley's comet. In Congo, the very heart of Conrad's 'heart of darkness', Torday believed he had 'discovered' a kingdom on a parallel with European dynasties. 'Have the staff of police at the British Museum been doubled to keep out the publishers?', he wrote to enquire of Joyce (letter, 1909). Here was a culture to overthrow many western stereotypes.

When he returned to Europe in 1909 Torday began publicizing his expedition's achievements. He was awarded the imperial gold medal for science and art by the emperor of Austria in 1910. In 1913 he spent several months as a lecturer and curator in Philadelphia, but based himself mainly in London. A series of articles, monographs, and popular books appeared, of which the best-known was *On the Trail of the Bushongo* (1925). On 17 March 1910 Torday married Gaia Rose Macdonald (*b.* 1884/5), a Scotswoman, and had a daughter, Ursula (1912–1997), who subsequently became a romantic novelist under the pseudonym, among others, of Paula Allardyce. A medical career at the London Hospital was cut short by the outbreak of war, during which Torday engaged in relief work for prisoners of war. He subsequently continued as an anthropologist through his writing, his involvement with the International African Institute, the Royal Anthropological Institute, and Save the Children International. His last substantial work was another ethnographic survey, *Descriptive Sociology: African Races* (1930). Torday died in London on 9 May 1931 of heart failure, following an operation, at the French Hospital, Shaftesbury Avenue, close to the British Museum.

Torday's influence on subsequent anthropology has not been extensive. He held no formal position, and was not interested in big theories, like his contemporary and adversary Leo Frobenius. Yet the extent and value of his documentary work on the cultures of Congo remains a primary point of reference. An exhibition of his collection at the Museum of Mankind, London (part of the British Museum), in 1990 attracted new attention to his work. His photographic archive is divided between the latter depository and the Royal Anthropological Institute, which is the custodian of his manuscripts.

JOHN MACK

Sources J. Mack, *Emil Torday and the art of the Congo, 1900–1909* (1990) · M. W. Hilton-Simpson, *Man*, 54 (1932), 48; 55 (1932), 48–9 · B. Malinowski, *The Times* (14 May 1931) · Lord Noel-Buxton, *The Times* (14 May 1931) · 'Torday, Emil', *Biographie coloniale Belge* (1955), 4.883–5 · d. cert. · m. cert.
Archives Museum of Mankind, London, photographs (anthropological) · Royal Anthropological Institute, London, anthropological notes, lectures, and papers · Royal Anthropological Institute, London, photographs (anthropological), MSS, MSS 192–198
Likenesses photograph, repro. in Mack, *Emil Torday*, cover

Torel, William (*fl.* 1291–1303), goldsmith and bronze caster, was a London goldsmith employed by Edward I to execute the gilt-bronze effigies of Henry III and Queen Eleanor of Castile for their tombs at Westminster Abbey and Lincoln Minster. One of the most important documented English medieval metalworkers whose work survives, Torel was given the commission for the three effigies in 1291 and had completed the work by 1293, having established a temporary workshop in the abbot's cemetery at Westminster for the purpose. The metal was supplied by William Sprot and John of Ware, the gold by merchants of Lucca. The total remuneration to Torel for the work was nearly £140. The employment at court of a goldsmith for major metalwork commissions was normal, and Torel's techniques for manufacturing the effigies, using the lost-wax process with mercury gilding, were also well established. The indications are that Torel was himself responsible for making the wax models from which the casts were made. The Westminster effigies of Henry and Eleanor survive. That of Eleanor for her entrail tomb at Lincoln is lost, but known from a seventeenth-century representation which shows that it closely resembled the Westminster example. Although almost certainly not portraits, the effigies, cast in metal of unusual thickness, are among the finest bronze castings of their date in western Europe. Torel's work compares extremely favourably with contemporary French and German effigial bronze work of the type found at St Denis in Paris, or at Cologne. His documented career ends on a picaresque note: in 1303, after the burglary in that year of the king's treasury at Westminster Abbey, William Torel *aurifaber* is noted as having bought two gold rings from one of the principal suspects in the case.   PAUL BINSKI

Sources Chancery records · PRO, exchequer, queen's remembrancer, accounts various, E101 · F. Devon, ed. and trans., *Issues of the exchequer: being payments made out of his majesty's revenue, from King Henry III to King Henry VI inclusive*, RC (1837), 99, 105 · [B. Botfield and T. H. Turner?], eds., *Manners and household expenses of England in the thirteenth and fifteenth centuries, illustrated by original records*, Roxburghe Club, 57 (1841), 95–139 · R. Brown, H. M. Colvin, and A. J. Taylor, eds., *The history of the king's works*, 1 (1963), 479–82 · J. Alexander and P. Binski, eds., *Age of chivalry: art in Plantagenet England, 1200–1400* (1987), nos. 377, 379 [exhibition catalogue, RA] · F. Palgrave, ed., *The antient kalendars and inventories of the treasury of his majesty's exchequer*, RC, 1 (1836) · T. F. Tout, 'A medieval burglary', *Bulletin of the John Rylands University Library*, 2 (1914–15), 348–69

Torigni, Robert de [called Robert de Monte] (*c*.1110–1186), chronicler and abbot of Mont-St Michel, was born *c*.1110, the son of Teduin and Agnes of Torigni-sur-Vire, near St Lô in Normandy. But knowledge of both Robert's birth date and his parentage is flawed: the date is based on the assumption that he would not have entered Bec before his eighteenth birthday, while his parents are identified in documents, now lost, transmitted only through the writings of a seventeenth-century antiquarian. Torigni was successively a monk of Bec (1128), prior of Bec (1149), and finally abbot of Mont-St Michel from 1154 until his death in 1186; it was his position as abbot that has led some modern historians to call him Robert de Monte, but Robert de Torigni is preferable, since that is what he called himself.

Robert de Torigni wrote two works of history—an account of the Norman dukes (the *Gesta Normannorum ducum*), and a chronicle of the world (called *Roberti accessiones ad Sigebertum*)—that make him an important figure in understanding English and Norman affairs of the twelfth century. Both these works were continuations of the historical writings of others, and are notably wide-ranging. The *Gesta Normannorum ducum* was begun by Dudo of St Quentin, and later added to by William of *Jumièges. Torigni shortened some sections, interpolated others, and continued the work to the year 1138. His most original contribution is chapter 8, which covers the reign of Henry I (1100–35). Torigni's world chronicle closely followed Sigebert of Gembloux's *History of the World* (which in turn borrowed heavily from Eusebius, Jerome, and Prosper), although for the period 1112–86 much of the material was Torigni's own. His attention was necessarily fixed on western Europe, especially England and France, but he was also well informed about the crusades. After his death both histories circulated widely, and later historians like Ralph de Diceto, Matthew Paris, and Nicholas Trevet borrowed generously from him.

Robert de Torigni also wrote several other works of lesser significance: the *De immutatione ordinis monachorum*, a treatise both on the Cistercian order and a listing of the Norman religious houses and their abbots; a catalogue of the archbishops, bishops, and abbots of France and England; probably a chronicle of the abbots of Bec; the annals of Mont-St Michel; various prologues, letters, and charters; and even a list of the books in the library at Bec. His style, however, was undistinguished, his most recent editor, E. M. C. van Houts, maintaining that 'he is by far the least skilled Latinist among the authors of the *Gesta Normannorum ducum*' (*Gesta Normannorum*, 1.xci).

Modern assessments of Torigni's abilities as a historian are mixed. On the one hand his writings add immeasurably to the basic chronological and factual knowledge of the lives of the twelfth-century English kings, especially since Torigni (unlike other monk–historians) had personal contact with the royal court. Moreover, Torigni makes relatively few factual errors. And he occasionally includes supporting documents in his text, such as the treaty of 1158 between Henry II and Theobald, count of Blois. On the other hand his work lacks the critical and synthetic abilities shown by such contemporary historians as Orderic Vitalis and Henry of Huntingdon. His political narratives are often interrupted by records of bizarre events such as the skeleton of a 50 foot giant washing up on the shores of England. It is not surprising that Torigni's work favours the Angevin royal family with whom he was acquainted: he thrice received Henry II at Mont-St Michel; he stood sponsor to Henry II's daughter Eleanor at her baptism in 1161; and he encouraged a colleague to write a biography of Henry II's father, Geoffrey of Anjou (d. 1151). But Torigni's loyalty sometimes goes too far: the events of the Becket controversy are never mentioned, and Thomas Becket's embarrassing murder merits but a sentence. This is silence bordering on the disingenuous.

Robert de Torigni deserves unqualified praise for his many other achievements. When he was elected abbot, Mont-St Michel was suffering severe difficulties. Yet Torigni was able to restore its dispersed estates by obtaining royal and papal grants; by travelling widely to administer its lands in Normandy, on the Channel Islands, and in England; and by serving as castellan of nearby Pontorson. He quelled internal dissension within his monastery, increased the number of monks, reinvigorated the cults of several saints (especially Aubert and Lawrence) by rehousing their relics, and built new sections of the abbey. A lifelong bibliophile, Torigni also augmented the monastery's library. Indeed, it was Torigni who in 1139 first showed to the historian Henry of Huntingdon a copy of Geoffrey of Monmouth's influential *History of the Kings of Britain*.

Robert de Torigni was, in sum, an effective and energetic abbot whose love for order and for books compelled him to write history. He died in 1186, either on 23 or 24 June, and was buried in the (now roofless) west end of the upper nave at the abbey church of Mont-St Michel.

DAVID S. SPEAR

Sources *Chronique de Robert de Torigni*, ed. L. Delisle, 2 vols. (Rouen, 1872–3) • R. Howlett, ed., *Chronicles of the reigns of Stephen, Henry II, and Richard I*, 4, Rolls Series, 82 (1889) • *The Gesta Normannorum ducum of William of Jumièges, Orderic Vitalis, and Robert of Torigni*, ed. and trans. E. M. C. van Houts, 2 vols., OMT (1992–5) • *Chronique du Bec*, ed. A. A. Porée, Société de l'Histoire de Normandie (1883) • R. Foreville, 'Robert de Torigni et "Clio"', *Millénaire monastique du Mont-Saint-Michel*, 2 (1967), 141–53 • A. Gransden, *Historical writing in England*, 1 (1974) • A. A. Porée, *Histoire de l'abbaye du Bec*, 2 vols. (1901) • E. M. C. van Houts, 'Robert of Torigni as genealogist', *Studies in medieval history presented to R. Allen Brown* (1989), 215–33 • M. Chibnall, 'Orderic Vitalis and Robert of Torigni', *Millénaire monastique du Mont-Saint-Michel*, 2 (1967), 133–9 • *Trésors des abbayes Normandes* (1979), no. 281 • M. Gibson, 'History at Bec in the twelfth century', *The writing of history in the middle ages*, ed. R. H. C. Davis and J. M. Wallace-Hadrill (1980), 167–86 **Archives** Mont-St Michel, Avranches MS 159, MS 210 [copy] • Universiteitsbibliotheek, Leiden, MS BPL20 [copy]

Torkington, Richard (*fl.* 1511–1518), Catholic priest and pilgrim, is of unknown origins. In 1511 he was presented by Sir Thomas Boleyn, later earl of Wiltshire, to the Norfolk rectory of Mulberton, and he was still parson there when in 1517 he undertook a pilgrimage to the Holy Land. According to his own account of his experiences he left Rye on 20 March, and passed through France to northern Italy. After some time in Turin, Milan, and Pavia (where he noted the tomb of Lionel of Antwerp, second son of Edward III), on 29 April he arrived in Venice. There he witnessed the ceremony of the city's 'marriage to the sea' and also observed the building of new ships in the arsenal, recording that twenty-three new ships were then being constructed by over a thousand workmen; a hundred hands were busy at rope making alone.

On 14 June Torkington sailed from Venice with other pilgrims. They travelled by way of Corfu, Zante, Cerigo, and Crete, sighted the Holy Land on 11 July, and landed at Jaffa four days later. On 18 July they reached Jerusalem and stayed for just over a week, until the 27th. Torkington lodged in the hospital of St James on Mount Sion and visited all the holy places, both in Jerusalem and in Bethlehem. His response to the various shrines and relics seems to have been uncritical, recording without comment the legends attached to them; thus he accepts that the Dome of the Rock was the veritable Temple of Herod. He notes many times his fear of Muslim attack, and expresses strong views on Turkish misrule in Palestine. Nevertheless, it was in a spirit of rejoicing and gratitude that his company sailed for home on 31 July.

Torkington's return to England was considerably more troubled than his outward passage. The ship was detained for a month in Cyprus, and he was later left behind ill in Rhodes, where he stayed for about six weeks in September and October, in the care of the knights of St John. Further progress was hampered by storms, which drove his ship back down the Adriatic. On 20 February 1518 he witnessed a Jewish wedding on Corfu, but eventually returned north by way of Sicily and the west coast of Italy, where he visited Naples and Rome. He did not reach Dover until 17 April, when he reckoned that he had been out of England for one year, five weeks, and three days. He concluded his pilgrimage at the shrine of St Thomas in Canterbury Cathedral on 18 May following.

The rest of Torkington's life is as obscure as its earlier years, and it is only possible to say that he was no longer rector of Mulberton by 1526, when a successor was appointed. His account of his pilgrimage remained in manuscript until the late nineteenth century. Two transcripts survive in the British Library, London, as Add. MSS 28561 and 28562: the former is of the sixteenth century, the latter is the work of Robert Bell Wheler, who also published an account of the text in the *Gentleman's Magazine* for October 1812. The journal was finally edited for publication by W. J. Loftie in 1884, with the title *Ye Oldest Diarie of Englysshe Travell … the Pilgrimage of Sir Richard Torkyngton*. Subsequent comparisons have revealed a marked lack of originality on Torkington's part. His descriptions of Candia seem to have been copied from early editions of *Informacon for Pylgrymes unto the Holy Londe* (editions of 1498, 1515, 1524), including an erroneous reference to Acts instead of Titus for St Paul's condemnation of the Cretans. And his account of the wonders of Venice and the Holy Land, and of what he saw between the two, agrees almost verbatim with that written by the chaplain of Sir Richard Guildford, as it was published by Pynson in 1511. Torkington does, however, add the occasional observation of his own, especially on the subject of relics.

C. R. BEAZLEY, rev. ANDREW A. CHIBI

Sources *Ye oldest diarie of Englysshe travell … the pilgrimage of Sir Richard Torkyngton*, ed. W. J. Loftie (1884) • C. Tyerman, *England and the crusades, 1095–1588* (Chicago, 1988) • F. Blomefield and C. Parkin, *An essay towards a topographical history of the county of Norfolk*, [2nd edn], 11 vols. (1805–10), vol. 5, p. 80 **Archives** BL, Lansdowne MS 979

Torphichen. For this title name *see* Sandilands, James, of Calder, first Lord Torphichen (*d.* 1579); Sandilands, James, seventh Lord Torphichen (*d.* 1753).

Torporley, Nathaniel (1564–1632), mathematician, was born in Shropshire of unknown parentage and admitted to Shrewsbury's Free Grammar School as an 'oppidan' in 1571. He matriculated at Christ Church, Oxford, on 17 November 1581 as a 'plebeian' and graduated BA on 5 February 1584. He then departed to France where his mathematical knowledge equipped him to serve as secretary to the famous French mathematician François Viète (1540–1603). He was probably the link between Viète and the English mathematician Thomas Harriot; in a letter to Harriot from Paris, probably written in 1586, Torporley refers to his journey via Gravesend, Calais, and Amiens. He probably returned to Oxford in 1587 or 1588, and proceeded MA from Brasenose College on 8 July 1591.

Torporley entered holy orders and was appointed rector of Salwarpe, Worcestershire, on 14 June 1608, a living he held until 1622. He was also rector of Liddington, Wiltshire, in 1611. For most of the time, however, he resided chiefly at Sion College, on London Wall. Torporley's knowledge of mathematics and astronomy attracted the notice of Henry Percy, ninth earl of Northumberland, who may have supported him, although the only recorded payment dates from 1627. On 27 November 1605, just after the discovery of the Gunpowder Plot, Torporley was examined by the council for having cast the king's nativity. At Harriot's death in 1621 he was named in the will as overseer of Harriot's mathematical writings.

Apart from several mathematical works left in manuscript, Torporley published *Diclides coelometricae* (1602), in which he expounded a simplified spherical trigonometry designed for computing astronomical tables. While accepting the Copernican system, he briefly presented a bizarre explanation for the planetary orbits. The French astronomer J. B. J. Delambre, writing in 1821, found the entire book tedious, and described Torporley's so-called new and simplified astronomical tables as the most obscure and difficult which he had ever encountered. Torporley also designed a new type of semicircle, and his sundial and perpetual calendar was constructed by the instrument maker Charles Whitwell (d. 1611).

Torporley died in Sion College and was buried in the adjacent church of St Alphege on 17 April 1632. He left a nuncupative will dated 14 April, by which he bequeathed to Sion College all his mathematical books and manuscripts, astronomical instruments, notes, maps, and a brass clock. Administration was granted to his married sister, Susanna Tasker.　　　　ANITA MCCONNELL

Sources M. Feingold, *The mathematicians' apprenticeship: science, universities and society in England, 1560–1640* (1984), 111–12, 137, 211 · J. V. Pepper, 'A letter from Nathaniel Torporley to Thomas Harriot', *British Journal for the History of Science*, 3 (1966–7), 285–90 · *Brief lives, chiefly of contemporaries, set down by John Aubrey, between the years 1669 and 1696*, ed. A. Clark, 1 (1898), 263 · E. G. R. Taylor, *The mathematical practitioners of Tudor and Stuart England* (1954); repr. (1970), 187 · J. W. Shirley, *Thomas Harriot: a biography* (1983) · *Reg. Oxf.*, 2/3.118 · J. B. J. Delambre, *Histoire de l'astronomie moderne*, 2 vols. (Paris, 1821) · F. R. Johnson, *Astronomical thought in Renaissance England* (1937), 234–5

Torr, Dona Ruth Anne (1883–1957), historian, was born on 28 April 1883 at Carlett Park, Eastham, Chester, the third daughter in the family of four daughters and two sons of William Edward Torr (1851–1924) and his wife, Julia Elizabeth Holmes. Her father, a clergyman, inherited the estate of Carlett Park, Eastham, Cheshire, in 1880, when he also became the vicar of Eastham. He was later an honorary canon of Chester Cathedral. Her second brother, William Wyndham Torr, became a brigadier and served as British military attaché at several embassies.

Scarcely anything more is known about her family. She seems to have kept her private self under a veil, and remained throughout a somewhat 'reticent' figure (Schwarz, 67). It may be guessed that, like a good many left-wing sectaries of her time, she inherited from a religious upbringing a Christian ethic of her own shaping.

Dona Torr was growing up at a time when educated young women were beginning to strike out on their own. She was educated by private tuition at home at Carlett Park, but went on to study at Heidelberg and at University College, London, where she studied English and Greek philosophy. At University College between 1911 and 1914 she helped to organize student debates, was vice-president of the women's union committee, and was on the editorial board of the union magazine. Her wide education gave her a good knowledge of languages and the arts; in her youth she was also an enthusiast for horse-racing. She reacted strongly against the First World War and soon after the war joined the Labour Party. Her first employment was on the staff of the pro-Labour *Daily Herald*. She became a member of the Communist Party of Great Britain on its founding day, 31 July 1920, and proved an exemplary party member, taking on whatever responsibilities came her way, including editorial work on the party's weekly organ, *Workers' Life*, and acting as a translator at the Fifth Congress of the Communist International. In 1926 during the general strike she could be seen on a bicycle distributing leaflets. Unassuming on her own account, she could be a stickler for observance of party rules when she felt they were being neglected. She married one of her comrades, Walter Milton Holmes, a journalist; they were both given places on the colonial committee set up in 1925 to improve contacts with the small struggling communist parties or groups in India, Egypt, and elsewhere.

Torr's own special interest was history, and a cluster of young historians in the party owed much to her encouragement. She helped to keep them from theorizing too much on mechanical lines, a temptation into which the Marxist concept of history-writing as a science has sometimes led its students. One initiative of hers was a plan for a series of small books made up of extracts from important Marxist texts. It was designed to show ordinary readers how great a part the people had played in events. Unluckily her own contribution, *Marxism, Nationality and War*, came out in 1940, when the party was committed—an astounding *volte-face*—to the Moscow line of opposing war against Nazi Germany.

Far more helpful were her translations from German. Here her biggest undertaking was an anthology of letters of Marx and Engels, to each other and to numerous friends. Her edition, which came out in 1934, shines by the way it turns into idiomatic English the colloquial writing of two foreigners, both gifted writers, who spent most of their lives in England. The volume is moreover an invaluable storehouse of Marxist thinking. But it was to the recent history of her own country, and the struggles of its working class, that Torr's thoughts were increasingly turning. She had begun early to plan a life-and-times, on a grand scale, of Tom Mann, one of the outstanding heroes of British labour, whom she came to know and greatly admired. He was remembered above all for leading the great London dock strike of 1889. It cost Torr twenty years to get a first volume nearly ready; by then some help was needed from two of her closest allies, Christopher Hill and A. L. Morton. It was a well-earned return for her generosity in helping other writers. *Tom Mann and his Times* appeared in 1956.

In 1954 a collection of essays, *Democracy and the Labour Movement*, edited by John Saville, was presented to Torr by some of the historians among whom she had worked. Its preface described her as 'a pervading influence for a whole generation of Marxist historians'. In July of that year a week-long conference on English history was held at Hastings, with many of her disciples among the participants. She was too unwell by then to be one of the speakers; someone carried away an image of her as a benign lady abbess among her flock. But nemesis was hanging over the party to which she had given so much. In 1956 the Hungarian rising against Soviet rule broke out, and was suppressed by force. The party leadership dutifully endorsed Moscow's mailed fist; a large minority of the membership refused to follow. The shock to Dona, still loyal to the old faith, must have been very severe. She died at Edgware General Hospital, Hendon, Middlesex, on 8 January 1957, and was cremated six days later at Golders Green. Her husband survived her. Their partnership had proved happy. Dona did most of her work at home, while Walter did most of the housework and all the cooking. The atmosphere was recalled by the historian Dorothy Thompson, a close friend who often stayed with them, as 'always warm and friendly' (private information).

V. G. KIERNAN

Sources *Daily Worker* (9 Jan 1957) · D. Renton, 'The history woman', *Socialist Review* (Nov 1998) · B. Schwarz, 'The people in history', *Making histories: studies in history-writing and politics*, ed. R. Johnson (1982) · D. Renton, 'Opening the books: the personal papers of Dona Torr', *History Workshop Journal*, 52 (2001), 236–45 · D. Torr, letters, 1940–49, priv. coll. · private information (2004) [Dorothy Thompson] · UCL, Archives · Burke, *Gen. GB* (1955) · b. cert. · d. cert.
Archives People's History Museum, Manchester, Communist Party of Great Britain archive
Likenesses photograph, repro. in *Daily Worker*
Wealth at death £2072 10s. 11d.: probate, 1958, CGPLA Eng. & Wales

Torr, William (1808–1874), agriculturist, was born on 22 December 1808, one of at least two sons of a yeoman family which had been settled for several generations at Riby in north Lincolnshire. His education was interfered with by a severe strain affecting the spine while pole-jumping, and he gave up plans to study law. He left school at sixteen and travelled through various parts of Great Britain and the continent.

Torr began farming in his native parish of Riby in 1833. In 1848 he moved to Aylesby Manor Farm, which had been well known for eighty years for its breed of Leicester sheep. Its reputation was successfully maintained and increased under Torr's management. Animals from the Aylesby flocks and herds were sent to all parts of the United Kingdom and to the continent, the colonies, and even Japan. In 1854 Torr also took a farm of 420 acres at Rothwell. In 1856 he succeeded his uncle in the occupation of the Riby Grove farm. The total area of his three farms was over 2400 acres, most of which had been rented by his family for 150 years. He managed all three farms himself.

The main feature of Torr's farms consisted in his magnificent breeds of livestock. He was especially proud of his flock of Leicester sheep, direct descendants of Robert Bakewell's original Leicester. He had also a stud of thoroughbred ponies, which had been bred at Riby since 1804. But what gives Torr's name its importance in the history of agriculture was his famous breed of shorthorn cattle, carefully bred over a thirty-year period. Torr began to lay the foundations of his herd in 1844, hiring bulls from Richard Booth of Worlaby, another famous shorthorn breeder of the time. After his death 84 animals, from stock bred (for several generations) on his farm, were sold, in the presence of about 3000 people, for a total of £42,919 16s. This sale resulted in the scattering of Torr's herd over the whole of the United Kingdom.

Torr acquired a well-deserved reputation as an agriculturist, and was widely in demand as a judge of livestock at agricultural shows. He became a member of the Royal Agricultural Society in 1839, and continued to be closely connected with it throughout his life. In May 1857 he was elected to the council. He was a regular member of the inspection committee appointed to visit the sites offered for the annual country meetings, and he was one of the judges of farms in the first competition carried out under the auspices of the society in connection with the Oxford meeting of 1870. Torr was also an active member and trustee of the Smithfield Club, as well as honorary director of the Lincolnshire Agricultural Society, and a member of the Highland Agricultural Society.

Following the outbreak of cattle plague in 1865, Torr gave expert evidence to select committees of the House of Commons on the various ways of transporting live cattle and dead meat. He also invented many improvements in the details of farm management, and designed one of the first convex mould-board ploughs, a farm gate (which won a prize at the Warwick meeting of the Royal Agricultural Society in 1859), a spring wagon, and a pig trough. Torr died at Aylesby Manor on 12 December 1874, and was buried in Riby churchyard.

ERNEST CLARKE, *rev.* ANNE PIMLOTT BAKER

Sources *Journal of the Royal Agricultural Society of England*, 2nd ser., 11 (1875), 303–9, 345 · *Agricultural Gazette* (19 Dec 1874), 1627 · C. J. Bates, *Thomas Bates and the Kirklevington shorthorns* (1897) · private information (1898) · *Journal of the Royal Agricultural Society of England*, 2nd ser., 2 (1866), 541, 549 · *Journal of the Royal Agricultural Society of England*, 2nd ser., 3 (1867), 351 · *Journal of the Royal Agricultural Society of England*, 2nd ser., 5 (1869), 415 · The Druid [H. H. Dixon], *Saddle and sirloin, or, English farm and sporting worthies* (1870), 474 · d. cert.
Likenesses Knight, portrait, c.1864, priv. coll.
Wealth at death under £60,000: resworn probate, Aug 1876, CGPLA Eng. & Wales (1875)

Torrance, George William (1835–1907), Church of Ireland clergyman and composer, was born at Rathmines, Dublin, the eldest son of George Torrance, a merchant tailor. He was a chorister in Christ Church, Dublin, from 1847 to 1851 under Sir Robert Prescott Stewart, and became an organist for a short time at Blackrock, followed by St Andrew's (1852) and St Anne's (1854) in Dublin. A Te Deum and Jubilate which he composed in early youth showed promise, and in 1854 he composed an oratorio, *Abraham*, which was performed the following year with Stewart at the organ and the composer conducting, at the Antient Concert Rooms, Dublin. In order to complete his musical studies Torrance went to Leipzig in 1856. In 1858, having returned to Dublin, he produced an opera, *William of Normandy*. A second oratorio, *The Captivity* (words by Goldsmith), was given at the Antient Concert Rooms on 19 December 1864. Meanwhile, drawn towards the ministry, Torrance entered Trinity College, Dublin, in 1859; he graduated BA in 1864 and MA in 1867. He was ordained deacon in 1865 and priest in 1866, and was curate of St Michael's, Shrewsbury (1865–7), and of St Anne's, Dublin (1867–9).

In 1869 Torrance went for health reasons to Australia, and held successively the curacies of Christ Church, Melbourne (1870–71), and St John's, Melbourne (1871–7), and the incumbencies of All Saints, Geelong (1877–8), Holy Trinity, Balaclava (1878–94), and St John's, Melbourne (1894–7). In 1879 he received the degrees of MusB and MusD from Dublin University on the recommendation of Stewart, then professor of music, and in 1880 Melbourne University conferred on him a doctorate. His third oratorio, *The Revelation*, was produced with great success at Melbourne in June 1882.

About 1897 Torrance returned to Ireland and was appointed chaplain to the bishop of Ossory. He was bishop's vicar-choral and librarian of St Canice's Cathedral Library in 1899 (1898 according to the *Musical Times*), and in 1900 became prebendary of Killamery and canon of St Canice's, Kilkenny. He was also registrar for the united dioceses of Ossory, Ferns, and Leighlin. He continued to compose much sacred and secular music. In January 1902 he won the prize (10 guineas) offered by the *School Music Review* for the best coronation song for school singing with his 'Come, raise we now our voices', published as no. 676 of Novello's School Songs. In 1903 his madrigal 'Dry be that tear' won the Molyneux prize and the medal offered by the Madrigal Society (London). Two of his anthems, 'Who shall roll us away the stone?' and 'I will pray the father', were published in Novello's Octavo Anthems and appeared in the *Musical Times*, and ten of his hymns were included in *The Church Hymnal* (Ireland), including the favourite 'Euroclydon' (1886). Torrance died in Kilkenny on 20 August 1907. He was married, and his wife died three days before him.   W. H. G. FLOOD, rev. DAVID J. GOLBY

Sources *MT*, 48 (1907), 609 · R. J. Pascoll, 'Torrance, George William', *New Grove* · private information (1912) · personal knowledge (1912)

Torré, Giovanni Battista (*fl.* 1753–1776), pyrotechnician and print publisher, was born in Italy and studied under the scene-painter Servandoni. He first travelled to London in 1753 to work with the Brock family on their firework displays at Marylebone Gardens. However, until 1771 he resided mostly in Paris, where in 1760 he opened a shop called the Cabinet de Physique Experimentale, from which he made and sold barometers, other scientific instruments, and books. The culmination of his pyrotechnic career in France came in 1770, when he oversaw the fireworks for the marriage of Marie Antoinette and the future Louis XVI. In 1771 he left France for London to escape political tensions. His invitation to England had been arranged in part by David Garrick, who had set up a meeting between Torré and the managers of Ranelagh Gardens. They did not agree terms, but Torré quickly found work with Messrs Arnold and Berry, who were promoting entertainments in Marylebone Gardens. Torré moved in with his son Anthony, who had set up his printselling business in Market Lane in the early 1760s.

Torré's pyrotechnic exhibitions were innovatory to Britain, for, rather than being simply a display of fireworks in front of an ornamental structure, they involved performers, revolved around a narrative (usually taken from myth), and fully integrated the pyrotechnics into a highly visual setting, thus cleverly creating entertainments that drew as much on stage effects as on conventional fireworks. In one of his pieces, *The Forge of Vulcan*, we are told that Torré made use of rockets directed by ropes to give the effect of moving fire and transparent troughs of water lit from underneath to suggest flowing lava. It was his use of performers, theatrical devices, and scenery that set Torré apart from others in his profession; he was seen to draw upon the Italian tradition of decorative pyrotechnic adornment to architectural designs as well as a more theatrical heritage.

Torré certainly had contact with the theatre: he developed the lycopodium torch for Garrick, which created spectacular stage effects, and had apparently worked as a scene-painter in Paris. His work in Marylebone Gardens seems to have had elements in common with Loutherbourg's scenic innovations for the theatre; indeed, Torré had staged mechanical performances, in some ways similar to Loutherbourg's *Eidophusikon*, in Paris in 1760. The two men certainly knew each other, having journeyed to England together, and later Torré became Loutherbourg's first publisher. Torré produced exhibitions at Marylebone Gardens for the summer seasons of 1772, 1773, and 1774; among his offerings were *Hercules Delivering Theseus from Hell*, *Orpheus and Eurydice*, which made use of transparencies, *The Emperor of China*, advertised with new settings and costume, and further additions to *The Forge of Vulcan*, which became his most famous piece and which he produced for the king's birthday in 1772 and for Garrick's *fête champêtre* in 1774.

However significant his innovations, Torré had some detractors. A Mrs Fountayne, after being disturbed by his fireworks, petitioned for the closure of the entertainments. In the proceedings that followed, Mrs Fountayne repeated the popular rumour that Torré had blown up his wife and child, and rumours circulated that he had killed

900 at Marie Antoinette's wedding. Torré rejected both allegations: no one had been killed at the wedding, his wife was living with him, and his child was at boarding-school. Dr Johnson too had a disagreement with Torré when an exhibition was cancelled because of wet weather. The disappointed Johnson suggested the cancellation was merely to save money, and incited men to light the fireworks with torches. They failed to go off, because, as Torré had pointed out, the pyrotechnics were too damp.

It is probable that Torré was as much an impresario as a pyrotechnician. He certainly had a mind for commerce; indeed, he seems to have been as often found collecting money at the gate to his attractions as overseeing their presentation. After his career as a pyrotechnician he returned to selling scientific instruments and publishing prints, including those of Loutherbourg and Bartolozzi. The shops that he founded in Paris and London were later identified as the original locations for the fine art dealers Colnaghi, a firm formally established by Torré's son Anthony in partnership with Paul Colnaghi.

Torré probably died in the early 1780s, but even here there is some doubt, since Brock suggests that he was active in 1792, producing *The Forge of Vulcan* in Ranelagh Gardens. *The Times* of 10 August 1792 certainly advertised the event, but made no mention of Torré's name, and this may have been a revival undertaken by others. There is no parish record of his burial in London between 1780 and 1784, but he may, of course, have returned to Paris.

GAVIN CARVER

Sources M. Sands, *The eighteenth-century pleasure gardens of Marylebone, 1737–1777* (1987) · A. St H. Brock, *A history of fireworks* (1949) · *The letters of David Garrick*, ed. D. M. Little and G. M. Kahrl, 3 vols. (1963) · C. Baugh, *Garrick and Loutherbourg* (1990) · W. Wroth and A. E. Wroth, *The London pleasure gardens of the eighteenth century* (1896) · Highfill, Burnim & Langhans, *BDA* · F. Hedgcock, *Garrick and his French friends* (1912) · J. T. Smith, *A book for a rainy day, or, Recollections of the events of the years 1766–1833*, ed. W. Whitten (1905) · G. M. Bergman, *Lighting in the theatre* (1977) · G. W. Stone and G. M. Kahrl, *David Garrick: a critical biography* (1979)

Torre, James (1649–1699), antiquary, was the son of Gregory Torre of Bourne, Lincolnshire, and Anne, the daughter of John Farr of Epworth, Lincolnshire. He was born in April 1649 and baptized at Haxey, Lincolnshire, on 30 April 1649. He was educated at Belton School and entered Magdalene College, Cambridge, in June 1666. He matriculated in 1667 and was admitted to the Inner Temple the following year. Among his contemporaries at the Inner Temple was the London antiquary Henry Keepe, who shared Torre's interest in ecclesiastical antiquities and genealogy and whose works include a manuscript account of the city of York compiled in the 1680s. It is uncertain when or why Torre settled at York, but the reason may be linked to his marriage to Elizabeth, daughter of William Lincoln DD of Bottesford, Lincolnshire.

In York, Torre devoted himself to research on the ecclesiastical antiquities of Yorkshire. The first of the resulting five folio volumes of his collections is entitled 'Antiquities ecclesiastical of the city of York concerning churches, parochial conventual chapels, hospitals, and gilds, and in them chantries and interments, also churches parochial and conventual within the archdeaconry of the West Riding, collected out of publick records and registers, AD 1691'. The subsequent volumes cover the other archdeaconries in the county and the peculiar jurisdictions. All the volumes are indexed and provide indexes for the ecclesiastical records he used as well as preserving material that would otherwise have been lost. He compiled lists of parochial incumbents from the records of institutions in the registers of the archbishops of York and supplemented this material from the registers of the dean and chapter. He also searched the wills proved at York, extracting from them all clauses relating to the interments of testators and appending these to the accounts of the relevant churches. He omitted little and his errors in relation to dates are rare, although he is less reliable on names. The date given in the first volume corresponds with the appointment of John Sharp as archbishop of York; this consolidation of Torre's researches was presumably instigated by the archbishop, who shared his antiquarian interests and subsequently acquired the volumes. Sharp used Torre's collections in the production of his own account of the rights and revenues of his office, and after the archbishop's death they were presented to the chapter library by his executors. Torre was never a purely ecclesiastical antiquary, as is suggested by his interest in the location of interments, and his interest in genealogy led him to compile five folio volumes entitled 'English nobility and gentry, or, Supplemental collections to Sir William Dugdale's *Baronage*'. These represented amended transcriptions of Dugdale's work with the addition of the genealogies of less socially elevated families. Torre was a friend of Ralph Thoresby, who used his manuscripts in the compilation of *Ducatus Leodiensis* (1715), and they have been widely used by subsequent topographers of Yorkshire and those working in neighbouring counties. Francis Drake, who was particularly beholden to his predecessor's work, described his own history of York as 'but a key to some part of Torre's collections' (*Eboracum*, 1736, preface).

Torre's first marriage was childless. On 24 April 1694 he married Anna, the daughter of Nicholas Lister of Leeds, and a son, Nicholas, was born the following year. In 1699 he purchased the manor of Syndale, near Wakefield, but died on 31 July 1699 of a contagion then prevalent in the area. He was buried at Normanton, Yorkshire. His continuing status as a local antiquary is attested by the association of his name with a slim volume entitled *The Antiquities of York* (1719), presumably to give the work spurious authority twenty years after his death.

JAN BROADWAY

Sources Venn, *Alum. Cant.* · W. T. Lancaster, ed., *Letters addressed to Ralph Thoresby* (1912) · A. Hamilton Thompson, 'The registers of the archbishops of York', *Yorkshire Archaeological Journal*, 32 (1936), 245–63 · *VCH Yorkshire City of York* · *DNB*

Archives BL, estate notebook, Add. MS 34146 · BL, genealogical and heraldic collections relating to Yorkshire and north of England, Egerton MSS 2573–2577 · Bodl. Oxf., notes, pedigrees, and extracts from MSS relating to Yorkshire and annotated copy of the

English traveller, MS Gen. Top. 8 6281; MS Top. Yorks. b 14 · York Minster archives, heraldic and genealogical MSS, Add. 57–64
Likenesses oils; in possession of H. J. Torre, in 1898

Torrens, Sir Arthur Wellesley (1809–1855), army officer, second son of Major-General Sir Henry *Torrens (1779–1828) and his wife, Sarah (*c*.1781–1863), daughter of Robert *Patton [*see under* Patton, Philip], governor of St Helena, was born on 18 August 1809, and was a godson of the duke of Wellington. In 1819 he was appointed a page of honour to the prince regent. After attending the Royal Military College, Sandhurst, he was commissioned ensign in the Grenadier Guards and lieutenant on 14 April 1825. He was appointed adjutant of the 2nd battalion with the temporary rank of captain on 11 June 1829. He was promoted lieutenant in the Grenadier Guards and captain on 12 June 1830. He continued to serve as adjutant of his battalion until 1838, when he was appointed brigade major at Quebec on the staff of Major-General Sir James Macdonell, commanding a brigade in Canada, and took part in the operations against the rebels in late 1838. He was promoted captain in the grenadiers and lieutenant-colonel on 11 September 1840, when he returned to England.

Torrens exchanged into the 23rd Royal Welch Fusiliers, and obtained the command on 15 October 1841. On the augmentation of the army in April 1842 a second battalion was given to the regiment. The depot was moved from Carlisle to Chichester, where, with two new companies, it was organized for foreign service under Torrens, who embarked with it at Portsmouth for Canada on 13 May, arriving at Montreal on 30 June. In September 1843 he went, in command of the 1st battalion, from Quebec to the West Indies, arriving at Barbados in October 1843. The battalion was moved from time to time from one island to another, but for two and a half years Torrens commanded the troops in St Lucia and administered the civil government of that island. The sanitary measures he adopted to preserve the troops' health met with unprecedented success, and were considered so admirable that correspondence on the subject was published in November 1847 by order of the duke of Wellington, commander-in-chief, for the guidance of officers commanding overseas. Torrens declined the offer of the lieutenant-governorship of St Lucia as a permanent appointment, preferring to continue his service in the Royal Welch Fusiliers.

Torrens sailed with his battalion from Barbados in March 1847, arriving at Halifax, Nova Scotia, in April. The battalion returned to England in September 1848; it was initially stationed at Winchester, and from 1850 at Plymouth. In 1851 Torrens relinquished the command, and in 1852 published *Notes on French infantry and memoranda on the review of the army in Paris at the Feast of Eagles in May 1852*. On 1 January 1853 he was appointed assistant quartermaster-general at the Horse Guards, and became a member of a commission which in the spring of that year investigated the organization of the French, Austrian, and Prussian armies.

On his return Torrens was nominated a brigadier-general to command an infantry brigade in the British army in Turkey in the war with Russia. He joined the 4th division under Sir George Cathcart at Varna just before its embarkation for the Crimea. He was at the head of his brigade at the battles of the Alma and of Balaklava, where he was engaged in support of the cavalry and lost some men in recapturing two redoubts. On the morning of 5 November 1854 he had just returned from the trenches when he was told of the enemy's attack from the valley of Inkerman, and, under the direction of Cathcart, he attacked with success the left flank of the Russians, his horse falling under him, pierced by five bullets. Just before Cathcart was struck down by his mortal wound he called out, 'Nobly done, Torrens!' Torrens was still in front, cheering on his men, when he was struck by a bullet, which passed through his body, injured a lung, splintered a rib, and was found lodged in his greatcoat. He was invalided home. He received the thanks of parliament, was promoted a major-general for distinguished service in the field on 12 December 1854, and was made a KCB, military division.

On 2 April 1855 Torrens was appointed deputy quartermaster-general at headquarters, and on 25 June the same year was sent as a major-general on the staff to Paris as British military commissioner. His health, enfeebled by his wound, broke down, and he died in Paris on 24 August 1855; he was buried in the cemetery of Père Lachaise. His widow, Maria Jane, youngest daughter of General John Murray, whom he had married in 1832, erected a monument to him in St Paul's Cathedral.

R. H. VETCH, *rev.* JAMES LUNT

Sources War office records, dispatches · A. W. Kinglake, *The invasion of the Crimea*, 8 vols. (1863–87) · *GM*, 2nd ser., 44 (1855), 430–31 · M. F. Conolly, *Fifiana, or, Memorials of the east of Fife* (1869) · R. Cannon, ed., *Historical record of the twenty-third regiment, or the royal Welsh fusiliers* (1850) · Fortescue, *Brit. army*, vol. 13 · R. Broughton-Mainwaring and R. Cannon, eds., *Historical record of the Royal Welch fusiliers, late the twenty-third regiment, or, Royal Welsh fusiliers … in continuation of the compilation … by R. Cannon* (1889) · W. H. Russell, *The war in the Crimea* (1855) · Boase, *Mod. Eng. biog.*
Likenesses G. Sander, mezzotint, pubd 1864 (after L. Dickinson), NPG

Torrens, David Smyth (1897–1967), physiologist and horologist, was the eldest of the three sons of David Smyth Torrens (*d.* 1936) and his wife, Margaret, *née* Hogg (*d.* 1948); there was also a daughter. He was born on 10 September 1897 on the family's small farm The Carragh, Coolnaman, near Garvagh, co. Londonderry, and attended Drumeene national school and Moneydig public elementary school. His family forced him to leave school to work on the farm; he found the life to be very uncongenial, but after attending local evening classes in agriculture, he won a scholarship to the Albert Agricultural College in Dublin. His parents disapproved very strongly, and it was left to a local shopkeeper to give him a suit when he left home in 1915. In 1916 he was awarded a first-class diploma in agriculture; from 1916 to 1920 he attended the Royal College of Science in Dublin, and on graduating as an associate, was appointed demonstrator in zoology in Trinity College, Dublin.

In 1924 Torrens became demonstrator in the department of physiology, where his professor, Harold Pringle, encouraged him to undertake a degree in natural sciences. He graduated in 1928 with a first-class degree, placed first in the list; then, while still working as a junior assistant in the physiology department, he registered as a medical student in Trinity College, graduating MB, BCh, BAO in 1934. Torrens became a lecturer there in 1933, and in July 1934 Professor Pringle had him appointed assistant professor. Two years later Torrens succeeded Pringle in the chair of physiology and as King's professor of the institutes of medicine; the rest of his life was spent living and working in Trinity College. He was a dedicated and much loved teacher, whose deep concern for his students' progress and welfare outweighed his legendary shyness and reserve. He ran his department efficiently and sometimes almost single-handed, and was dean of the college's medical school from 1950 to 1959, and vice-dean from 1959 to 1967. The heavy teaching and administrative load left little time for research, especially since he sat on many public bodies and regulatory boards, including the General Medical Council of Ireland. He was no conversationalist; his manner could be sharp to the point of rudeness. He preferred to listen rather than talk.

Many former colleagues and students wrote to the organizer of a ceremony to mark 'Davy' Torrens's retirement on 10 June 1967; their letters were full of the deepest admiration and esteem for a man who had been totally—and to their knowledge solely—committed to his department and college. Few in Ireland knew that he had somehow found time and energy to devote to his lifelong passion for the history and craft of horology, or realized that in that field he had achieved an international reputation and amassed an outstanding, irreplaceable collection of horological tools and books; at his death, the collection weighed 9 tons. In vacations he visited famous clockmakers in Britain and Europe, learned their skills, and as the craft industry died with them, acquired their outmoded tools. He served as special technical adviser to the British Horological Institute, helped to translate classic watchmaking treatises, and was recognized as the world's leading authority on the history of horology. His published output was not commensurate with his vast knowledge; fewer than twenty-five slight but elegant articles represent a lifetime of study, travel, and practical experience. If he had been able to do no more than catalogue his collection, antiquarian horology and allied historical disciplines would have profited greatly.

Torrens retired from Trinity College in June 1967, was admitted to the freedom of the Worshipful Company of Clockmakers of London in the same year, and died, unmarried, of cerebral embolism in the Merrion Nursing Home, Dublin, on 24 November 1967. He died intestate, and his collection was dispersed, though parts of it were kept together in the British Museum and elsewhere. A strongly religious man, he was buried beside Moneydig Presbyterian Church near his childhood home.

LINDE LUNNEY

Sources P. Froggatt and A. C. Davies, 'David Smyth Torrens: physiologist and horologist', *Hermathena*, 140 (1986), 11–31 · P. Froggatt and A. C. Davies, 'David Smyth Torrens (1897–1967): a biographical note', *Hermathena*, 146 (1989), 49–52 · A. C. Davies, 'David Smyth Torrens, 1897–1967: an horological memoir', *Antiquarian Horology and the Proceedings of the Antiquarian Horological Society*, 14 (1983–4), 564–84 [incl. list of Torrens's horological writings, and writings about him] · private information (2004) · *BMJ* (9 Dec 1967), 624
Archives TCD | King's AC Cam., corresp. with John Saltmarsh
Likenesses photograph, repro. in Froggatt and Davies, 'David Smyth Torrens' · photograph, repro. in Davies, 'David Smyth Torrens'

Torrens, Sir Henry (1779–1828), army officer, was reportedly, but questionably, descended from a Swedish Count Torrens, a cavalry captain in the army of William III who settled in Ireland after the battle of the Boyne (1690). Sir Henry's great-grandfather Thomas Torrens, of Scottish descent, was settled at Dungiven, co. Londonderry, early in the eighteenth century. Thomas's third son, Dr John Torrens (d. 1785), Sir Henry's grandfather, was prebendary of Derry, headmaster of Derry diocesan school, and rector of Ballynascreen. Sir Henry's father, the Revd Thomas Torrens, married Elizabeth, daughter of Samuel Curry of Londonderry. The eldest son, John (1761–1851), was archdeacon of Dublin; the second, Samuel, captain of the 52nd regiment, died of wounds received in action at Ferrol in 1800. The third son, Robert (1776–1856), was a justice of the court of common pleas in Ireland.

Henry, the fourth son, was born in Londonderry. Both his parents died during his infancy. He and his brothers were brought up by their maternal grandfather, the Revd Dr Thomas, before Henry went to his father's cousin, Thomas Torrens. He was educated at the military academy of Dublin where 'from the hilarity of his disposition, he was universally designated "Happy Harry"' (*GM*, 374). He received a commission as ensign in the 52nd (Oxfordshire) foot on 2 November 1793, became a lieutenant in the 92nd on 14 June 1794, and was transferred to the 63rd on 11 December 1795. He accompanied the 63rd to the West Indies and took part in the expedition under Abercromby against St Lucia; he was also present at the attack on Morne Chabot on 29 April 1796, and at the siege of Morne Fortuné and its surrender on 26 May, before which he was severely wounded in the right thigh. Despite this wound Torrens joined the 63rd in time for the attack on St Vincent, and on 8 June took a prominent part in the assault of three French redoubts, when the French were driven out and took refuge in the New Vigie; they capitulated on the following day. He was employed for seven months in command of an outpost in the forests of St Vincent against the Charib Indians of the island, and, on their defeat on 28 March 1797 the commander of the forces rewarded him with promotion to a company, with which he served in Jamaica as captain and paymaster until June 1798, when he returned to England.

In August 1798 Torrens was appointed aide-de-camp to Major-General John Whitelocke, second in command under the earl of Moira and lieutenant-governor of Portsmouth. In November he went to Portugal as aide-de-camp

Sir Henry Torrens (1779–1828), by James Thomson, pubd 1820 (after Sir Thomas Lawrence, 1815)

to Major-General Cornelius Cuyler, who commanded the auxiliary troops sent by the British government against the threatened Spanish invasion. On 8 August 1799 he was transferred to the 20th foot, then forming part of the force under the duke of York for the expedition to The Helder. Torrens served with the 20th throughout the campaign; he landed on 28 August, and took part in the repulse of the French attack at Crabbendam, under General Daendels, on 10 September, when the regiment was complimented by Sir Ralph Abercromby for its gallantry; he was also engaged in the battle of Hoorne on 19 September, and in the two battles of Egmont-op-Zee on 2 and 6 October. At the latter Torrens was wounded by a bullet which passed through his right thigh and lodged in his left thigh; the bullet was never extracted.

Torrens returned to England in November 1799, and was promoted on 3 November to a majority in the Surrey rangers, a fencible regiment then being raised. Its formation devolved upon Torrens, who subsequently embarked with it for North America. He commanded it for a year in Nova Scotia, and returned to England in the autumn of 1801.

On 4 February 1802 Torrens exchanged, as major, into the 86th foot, then forming part of the Indian force in Egypt under Sir David Baird. He accompanied it across the desert to the Red Sea, and embarked with it on the return to India of Baird's expedition in the summer. On arrival at Bombay, Torrens was so ill from sunstroke that he was obliged to sail at once for Europe. The ship touched at St Helena; he remained there, recovered his health, and married, about May 1803, Sarah (c.1781–1863), daughter of

the governor, Colonel Robert Patton of Kirkcaldy, Fife; they had four sons, including Sir Arthur Wellesley *Torrens and Henry Whitelocke *Torrens, and two daughters.

Torrens rejoined his regiment in India in 1804, and commanded in the field during the Second Anglo-Maratha War. He was promoted brevet lieutenant-colonel on 1 January 1805, and returned to England. Torrens was made assistant adjutant-general on 17 October 1805, and was employed on the staff of the Kent military district. He was transferred as regimental major to the 89th foot on 19 February 1807. On 11 May he was appointed military secretary to Major-General John Whitelocke, who had been nominated to the command of the army in South America. Torrens arrived at Montevideo in June, and took part in the disastrous attack on Buenos Aires on 5 July, when he received a contusion from a bullet which shattered his sabretache. He returned to England with Whitelocke, and was reappointed on 27 November an assistant adjutant-general on the staff in Great Britain; in December he became assistant military secretary to the commander-in-chief, the duke of York. He gave evidence at Whitelocke's court martial in January, February, and March 1808. His position as a member of Whitelocke's personal staff was a delicate one, but he acquitted himself with credit at the hearing.

In June 1808 Torrens was appointed military secretary to Sir Arthur Wellesley (later Viscount Wellington), and accompanied him to Portugal; they arrived in July. He was present at the action of Roliça on 17 August and at the battle of Vimeiro on 21 August. Torrens received the gold medal for these victories, and was made a knight of the order of the Tower and Sword by the Portuguese regency. He returned to England in October with Wellesley on the latter's supersession, and resumed his duties as assistant military secretary at headquarters.

Torrens was promoted military secretary to the commander-in-chief on 2 October 1809. On 13 June 1811 he was transferred from major of the 89th foot to a company (captain and lieutenant-colonel) in the 3rd foot guards. On 11 January 1812 he was appointed aide-de-camp to the prince regent, and promoted colonel in the army; and on 4 June 1814 he was promoted major-general. In 1815 he was made a KCB, military division (15 January), and appointed to the colonelcy of the second garrison battalion (5 April); later that year (27 November) he was transferred to the colonelcy of the Royal African Colonial Corps. On 21 September 1818 he was transferred to the colonelcy of the 2nd West India regiment, and on 25 March 1820 he was appointed adjutant-general of the forces. Because he now earned less than when a military secretary, a civil-list pension of £800 a year was bestowed on his wife to compensate him.

In 1824 was published Torrens's revision of the official *Regulations for the Exercise and Field Movements of the Infantry of the Army*. Intended to consolidate, not innovate, it incorporated changes made by regiments during the war, so that drill would again be uniform. It retained repetitive movements and long words of command, and its main provision was for a line of two ranks, not three. It was criticized, and again revised in 1833.

On 26 July 1822 Torrens was transferred to the colonelcy of the 2nd or Queen's Royal regiment of foot. On 23 August 1828 he was out riding with his wife and two daughters while on a visit to a friend at Danesbury, Hertfordshire, when he was 'seized with apoplexy' (*GM*, 375) and died two hours later. He was buried in Welwyn church, Hertfordshire, on 28 August.

R. H. VETCH, rev. ROGER T. STEARN

Sources *Memoir of Sir Henry Torrens* (privately printed) • War Office records, PRO • J. Philippart, ed., *The royal military calendar*, 3rd edn, 5 vols. (1820) • *GM*, 1st ser., 98/2 (1828) • *Annual Register* (1828) • *Naval and Military Magazine*, 4 (1828) • E. Cust, *Annals of the wars of the eighteenth century*, 5 vols. (1857–60) • E. Cust, *Annals of the wars of the nineteenth century*, 4 vols. (1862–3) • H. Strachan, *From Waterloo to Balaclava: tactics, technology and the British army, 1815–1854* (1985) • T. C. W. Blanning, *The French revolutionary wars, 1787–1802* (1996) • A. J. Guy, ed., *The road to Waterloo: the British army and the struggle against revolutionary and Napoleonic France, 1793–1815* (1990) • R. Muir, *Britain and the defeat of Napoleon, 1807–1815* (1996) • private information (1997) [Peter Moore of Darlington, NSW, Australia]
Archives BL, corresp., Add. MSS 62096–62097 • BL, corresp. and letter-book, Add. MSS 61831–61834 | BL, corresp. with Mrs Abell, Add. MS 62069 • BL, corresp. with Sir Hudson Low, Add. MSS 20113–20197 • BL, corresp. with earl of Liverpool, Add. MSS 38246–38323, 38474, 38573 • BL, letters to Sir Robert Peel, Add. MS 62096 • BL, corresp. with Sir James Willoughby Gordon, Add. MS 49485 • NL Scot., corresp. with Sir George Brown • NL Scot., corresp. with Lord Lynedoch • U. Nott., Hallward Library, letters to Lord William Bentinck
Likenesses T. Lawrence, oils, 1815; formerly at Londonderry town hall; destroyed • C. Turner, mezzotint, pubd 1817 (after T. Lawrence), BM • J. Thomson, stipple, pubd 1820 (after T. Lawrence), NPG [*see illus.*] • T. A. Dunn, engraving (after T. Lawrence)

Torrens, Henry Whitelocke (1806–1852), administrator in India and author, eldest son of Major-General Sir Henry *Torrens (1779–1828) and his wife, Sarah (*c.*1781–1863), daughter of Robert *Patton [*see under* Patton, Philip], onetime governor of St Helena, was born on 20 May 1806 at Canterbury, Kent. Sir Arthur Wellesley *Torrens was his brother. He was educated at Charterhouse School and Christ Church, Oxford, where he was rusticated along with the duke of Wellington's sons for painting the doors of the college red. He left a more lasting mark on the college as one of the founders of its choral society. In 1828, having first tried law and a Foreign Office clerkship, he accepted a writership in the East India Company's service.

Torrens arrived in Calcutta in November 1828 and by the following July had made sufficient progress in Arabic, Persian, and Hindustani to be given an appointment in Meerut district as assistant to the magistrate. He remained in Meerut until 1835 and, with Henry Miers Elliot, helped found the *Meerut Observer*, one of the North-Western Provinces' first newspapers. In this period, he was twice married: firstly, in 1832, to Eliza Mary (*d.* 1834), daughter of Sir Walter Roberts, bt, with whom he had one son; and secondly, in 1835, to Louisa Anne Rebecca, daughter of George Law of the Bengal civil service, with whom he had two sons and three daughters.

In 1835 he returned to Calcutta to a place in the secretariat and while there threw himself into the agitation for greater freedom for the press. From October 1837 until

February 1840 he accompanied Lord Auckland on his extensive up-country tour as deputy secretary in all the civil departments in attendance on the governor-general. His linguistic skills shone brilliantly on this tour, and many of the princes and dignitaries meeting Auckland asked specifically for Torrens as their interpreter. It was while in this post, according to J. W. Kaye, that Torrens exercised a baneful influence on Auckland and, along with John Colvin and William Macnaghten, persuaded him to invade Afghanistan. Kaye's portrait of Torrens in his *History of the War in Afghanistan* (1851) is a somewhat catty one, noting, for example, his popularity with the women of the governor-general's suite. In a reply published posthumously in the *Friend of India* in September 1852, Torrens stated that although he had supported the decision to reinstate Shah Shuja in Afghanistan, at least until it transpired that an army of occupation would be required to keep him there, he had never been sufficiently close to Auckland actually to influence the content of the policy.

In October 1840 Torrens became secretary to the board of customs in Calcutta. In April 1847 he was shunted into a dead-end job as agent to the governor-general at Murshidabad, where he remained until his death in 1852. Torrens's friends lamented this snubbing of an extremely talented officer, but Torrens himself had never made any secret of his antipathy for the service and had disdained to cultivate the patrons necessary for promotion.

Torrens had always devoted much of his leisure to literature. In 1838 he published what would eventually be seen as his most substantial work, the first volume of a translation of the *Arabian Nights*. Torrens's version is noteworthy for its liveliness and the absence of the earnestness and scholarly pretensions that characterized other translations of the day. He contributed several articles on ancient coins, inscriptions, and gems to the journal of the Asiatic Society of Bengal, and also served as secretary to the society from 1840 to 1846. In 1846 the *Eastern Star* began publishing instalments of his wide-ranging *Remarks on the Scope and Uses of Military Literature and History*, which was subsequently reissued as a book, and in 1848 he published a novel, *Madame de Malguet*, which was favourably received in London. A collection of his shorter pieces along with a memoir of his life was published by James Hume in London in 1854.

Torrens died at Calcutta on 16 August 1852, and was buried the next day in the Lower Circular Road cemetery there.

KATHERINE PRIOR

Sources J. Hume, *A selection from the writings, prose and poetical, of the late Henry W. Torrens, Esq., B.A., Bengal civil service, and of the Inner Temple with a biographical memoir*, 2 vols. (1854) • R. L. Arrowsmith, ed., *Charterhouse register, 1769–1872* (1974) • BL OIOC, Haileybury MSS • Foster, *Alum. Oxon.* • C. R. Wilson, ed., *List of inscriptions on tombs or monuments in Bengal* (1896) • *DNB* • Burke, *Peerage* (1939)
Archives BL OIOC, Courtenay MSS
Likenesses C. Grant, lithograph (after his portrait, 1846), repro. in C. Grant, *Lithographic sketches of the public characters of Calcutta* [1850] • lithograph, repro. in Hume, *Selection from the writings*, vol. 1, frontispiece

Torrens, Robert (1780?–1864), political economist, was the first of three children of Robert Torrens (*fl.* 1758–1790) and his wife, Elizabeth (*fl.* 1762–1790), third daughter of the Revd Skeffington Bristow and his wife, Elizabeth Gore Grattan. He was born either at his paternal grandfather's house, Hervey Hill rectory, near Kilrea, Londonderry, or at the house of his maternal grandfather, Hazelwood, Resharkin, co. Antrim. He was probably educated at Derry diocesan school.

Military career On 1 February 1796 Torrens was commissioned second lieutenant in the corps of marines; he was promoted first lieutenant on 18 November 1797. He served at Plymouth, Chatham, and Woolwich divisions and in detachments aboard Royal Navy ships on escort service and policing British waters. He was with HMS *Glenmore* on the Cork station when he married Charity Herbert (*c.*1784–1854), second daughter of Richard Chute (*fl.* 1770–1820), of Chute Lodge, Cork City, and Chute Hall, Roxborough, co. Kerry, at St Fin Barre's Cathedral, Cork, on 8 November 1801. Their four children, born in Cork and co. Kerry, included Robert Richard Chute *Torrens, first premier of South Australia and author of the Torrens Act. By September 1819 Torrens had 'long been separated and for some time divorced' and was robbed of 'a fortune more than sufficient' by the death of his intended second wife (Torrens to Place, 30 Sept 1819, BL, Add. MS 37949, fol. 79). He somehow nullified his Irish marriage (but legitimized his children by having them rebaptized at St Mary's, Woolwich, in 1819). On 12 December 1820 he married a minor English heiress, Esther Sarah Serle (1778–1874), second daughter of Ambrose *Serle RN, commissioner of transport, and his wife, Martha Priaulx.

Torrens was promoted captain on 26 July 1806. While participating in the economic warfare of Britain's 'continental blockade', he began writing the first of about ninety books and pamphlets on economics, politics, and social questions. *Thoughts on the Catholic Question* (1808) supported Catholic emancipation and described his Irish nationalism. Six months later his début in political economy, *The Economists Refuted* (1808), grounded his thinking on free trade and colonies. Two 'delightfully naïve' (Corry), 'very bad' (Allibone, *Dict.*) novels followed. *Coelibia Choosing a Husband* (1809), the heroine of which is a budding political economist, advocated higher education for women and pilloried Hannah More's *Coelebs Choosing a Wife* (1808) and its imitators. *The Hermit of Killarney: a Catholic Tale* (1813) fictionalized Torrens's frustration at the failure of emancipation, his support for which cost him a seat in the Commons. 'Habits of patient investigation' were interrupted by Torrens's appointment in August 1810 to the Isle of Anholt in the Kattegut off Copenhagen under Captain J. W. Maurice RN. On 27 March 1811 Torrens's 380 marines repelled a Danish landing involving 4000 personnel. Wounded slightly, he was gazetted brevet major on 9 April and the Admiralty promised him a major's pay and the Anholt command after Maurice. Relations with Maurice soured and Torrens was relieved in January 1812 for insubordination, yet pressed charges against Maurice; Torrens

Robert Torrens (1780?–1864), by unknown photographer, *c.*1860 [seated, with his son Sir Robert Torrens]

used his accommodating withdrawal in August for patronage over the next twenty years. He led his marines at the storming of Antwerp in February 1814 and sought, unsuccessfully, a variety of commands and staff appointments. Recruiting (mainly) and a new bayonet drill (briefly) were all the corps offered after 1815 as duties collided with aspirations. Annual applications (1815–22) to retire owing to ill health were denied. He became lieutenant-colonel by brevet on 12 August 1819. 'Private interests' forced the Admiralty to give him half-pay in September 1823. He returned to full pay in 1830 and on 4 June 1831 was appointed major. Three times he tried to sell out as a lieutenant-colonel, but was allowed to dispose only of a majority (17 October 1834).

Political career and economic thought Meanwhile, fuelled by his brand of Irish nationalism and a thinly veiled desire for personal advancement, Torrens consolidated his contemporary reputation. The anti-bullionist *Essay on Money* (March 1812) led to an offer of a Treasury borough that lapsed because of his refusal to abandon emancipation. Converted to the bullionist credo by 1826, Torrens went on to lead the currency school. More important in his early career was his systematic and creative critique of Ricardo, which asserted that capital rather than labour was the better measure of value. *An Essay on the External Corn Trade* (1815) discovered the principle of comparative advantage in international trade and shared with Ricardo and Malthus the discovery of the law of diminishing returns. Torrens also subverted Malthus by advocating colonization to alleviate overpopulation. His publications of this period culminated in his most general treatise, *An Essay on the Production of Wealth* (1821), but this neither lived up to earlier promise nor received its advertised sequel on distribution.

Torrens was politically unorthodox too, as he courted men of all parties to have his economic views pass into public policy. He endorsed Francis Burdett's reform proposals in 1809 and, after failing to win Rochester in June 1818, bore them out in his justificatory *Letter to the Freemen* (1819). He won Ipswich for the whigs in mid-June at a cost of £5000, determined to be independent, though friends feared he would 'feel his way to some place'. His maiden speech occurred during a corn law debate (24 November 1826), but he was unseated the following February. Unsuccessful at Pontefract (July 1830), he won Ashburton for its owner, without party support (June 1831). King William wanted him cashiered for suggesting, in September 1832, the abolition of the House of Lords. Instead, the Reform Act abolished Torrens's seat at Ashburton—not before a 'tipsy speech' preceded being 'as sick as a dog in the Long Gallery' (*Letters of Thomas Babington Macaulay*, 11 March 1833, 2.232). He topped the polls at Bolton in December 1833 but was defeated in January 1835 and did not contest a further seat. He was 'generally listened to with attention in the house', though an 'unmusical' voice (his Ulster burr?) and affected manner detracted from his otherwise 'effective speeches' (Grant, 188–91).

Newspapers gave Torrens his livelihood and his chief conduit for receiving and giving patronage, as a publicist for reform and economics. During 1820 Torrens led a syndicate that made *The Traveller*, a London evening paper, whig and a mouthpiece of political economy. Merging it with *The Globe* (30 December 1822) also made it England's second-largest daily; by 1828 it monopolized the evening paper market. Torrens retired as manager by mid-1826 but, 'chief though dormant partner' still, he continued to influence policy and management as late as 1858. Even under Brougham's sway, the paper was usually 'ministerial' on the Liberal side. For professional debate—fellowship of the Royal Society (10 December 1819) being inadequate to the purpose—Torrens helped form the Political Economy Club, and chaired its inaugural meeting on 30 April 1821. The club broke Ricardo's dominance of discussion.

Ricardo's death (September 1823) enhanced Torrens's standing as a theoretician and freed him to do his greatest work: to force the Colonial Office's hand on colonization and emigration, thereby modernizing the empire. From March 1825 he promoted the idea of commercial colonization through the New Zealand Company and kept the government's focus on the subject throughout 1826–31. He had petitioned (1816) to be governor of New South Wales or Van Diemen's Land; to a renewed application for the latter he added another for a large land grant and a senior post at Swan River (1828–31). Under-secretary Wilmot Horton promised him a seat on any 'colonial board' that eventuated (1826) and, in the Commons on 15 February 1827, Torrens supported Horton's successful motion for another emigration committee. Torrens sought 'parliamentary or official employment' from liberal ministers (1827–32) but received only the contract for the new *Police Gazette* (28 January 1828). Denied membership of the colonial land board (1828) and the Irish and emigration commissions (1831), Torrens was by 1832 the acknowledged leader of the 'systematic colonisers' clandestinely dominated by E. G. Wakefield, though Torrens's variant, 'self-supporting colonisation', encouraged the peasant proprietorship that Wakefield abhorred. He chaired the National Colonization Society (formed in 1830), led its negotiations with the Colonial Office, and helped float the South Australian Land Company (1832–3). He was integral to the South Australian Association's wrangles with four successive colonial secretaries (1833–5). When the South Australia Act established a commission to sell colonial land and dispatch emigrants (August 1834), he used political credit to be gazetted chairman (5 May 1835). Three weeks later he completed *The Colonization of South Australia* and the commissioners set about preliminary land sales, recruiting emigrants and raising loans. Torrens alienated Wakefield over the appropriate price for land and became the experiment's chief manager.

Torrens then proposed additional remedies for Ireland. Early in 1836 he lobbied to set aside a portion of all colonial land revenues for an Irish emigration fund. The resulting select committee on the disposal of colonial lands was a victory for Wakefield's opinions over Torrens's. Wakefield went on to colonize New Zealand, though he had to compromise with Torrens's New Zealand Company of 1825. Torrens failed to have emigration included in the new Irish poor law (1837–8), so in Dublin, in July 1839, he helped form the South Australian Colonization Society. Adversaries called him the 'Irish exterminator', as Irish investment and emigration picked up during 1840–42 to Torrens's envisioned 'New Hibernia'. By then Lord John Russell had replaced the South Australian commission with the colonial land and emigration commission (15 January 1840). Torrens was chairman, making him (briefly) the chief executive officer of the British empire. When South Australia's bankruptcy was clear (January 1841), he agreed to resign for purchasing land in the colony contrary to an 1835 ruling by Lord Glenelg. He gave up office when Russell's committee of inquiry reported unfavourably (9 April), though without indicting him. He began lobbying immediately for reinstatement and compensation, relenting only when, on Torrens's resignation from the Political Economy Club in February 1851 owing to ill health, Russell granted him a civil-list pension of £200 p.a. (July 1851) not as South Australian compensation but for 'services to political economy'.

In 1841 Torrens began the notorious series of pamphlets *The Budget: on Commercial and Colonial Policy* (1844), which abrogated classical doctrine by proposing a theory of reciprocity of import tariffs as a protectionist exception to international free trade. Torrens cultivated Benjamin Disraeli along these lines (1847–52). He also renewed pressure for colonization to aid famine-stricken Ireland in *Ireland Saved* (1847, 1849). But it was banking that dominated

Torrens's last twenty years. Peel's Bank of England Charter Act 1844 owed much to Torrens's 'currency scheme' and 'bank arrangement' of 1836 (for which he sought a £10,000 gratuity from the Bank of England), and to his currency controversy with Thomas Tooke, 1840–44. Torrens's classic defence of the act went through six manifestations (1847–58). During 1856–7 he worked on 'a treatise on money' and in July 1860 on a reply to Michael Chevalier on the value of gold, but he admitted to 'failing powers'. His last original work was his review of 'Lord Overstone on metallic and paper currency' in the *Edinburgh Review* (January 1858). His final public activity was to dispute the withdrawal of his *Police Gazette* contract, and compensation, with the Treasury and Home Office (1858–62).

Torrens settled at 36 Regency Square, Brighton, in 1857 after living in London in coffee houses, hotels, clubs, and rooms, and since the age of sixty in Welsh mountain towns and at the English seaside to combat perennial bronchitis. In 1861 he moved to 16 Craven Hill, Bayswater. He died there of an abscess on the lung on 27 May 1864 and was buried at Kensal Green cemetery on 30 May. His estate, 'under £16,000', consisted of annuity interests in a freehold estate, considerable funds, and some railway shares, his colonial investments having been long since realized or conveyed to his surviving son, Robert.

Torrens has undergone a respectable rehabilitation since his work was adjudged 'devoid of interest' (Harris, 550). His writings may be grandiloquent, pompous, and clogged with arithmetical examples, but his intellectual positions place him 'high up in the second class' among classical economists (Robbins, 1–2). Torrens, 'gentlemanly and prepossessing', had a 'finely proportioned figure' and 'an intellectual expression' (Grant, 191). Politicians did not always esteem his support yet they underrated his tenacity; economists found him combative though courteous in debate; colonizers found him inconsistent and indecisive; South Australian historians blame him for corrupting Wakefield's vision and bringing the colony to its knees. Friends and family thought him tender and generous, and his great-nephew William Torrens McCullagh Torrens, a reforming politician and writer on free trade, added Torrens to his surname in 1863 as a mark of respect.   PETER MOORE

Sources L. C. Robbins, *Robert Torrens and the evolution of classical economics* (1958) [incl. extensive work list] · F. W. Fetter, 'Robert Torrens: colonel of marines and political economist', *Economica*, new ser., 29 (1962), 152–65 · D. Pike, *Paradise of dissent: South Australia, 1829–1857*, 2nd edn [1967] · P. L. Moore, 'Colonel Robert Torrens: some bicentennial observations', *Journal of the Historical Society of South Australia* (1980), 68–83 · M. Blaug, *Great economists before Keynes* (1986) · M. Blaug, ed., *McCulloch, Senior and Torrens*, Pioneers in economics, 17 (1991) [repr. most scholarly articles about Torrens] · B. A. Corry, 'Torrens, Robert', *The new Palgrave: a dictionary of economics*, ed. J. Eatwell, M. Milgate, and P. Newman, 4 vols. (1987) · Allibone, *Dict.* · [J. Grant], *Random recollections of the House of Commons*, 5th edn (1837) · C. A. Harris, 'Robert Torrens', in R. H. I. Palgrave, *Dictionary of political economy*, 3 vols. (1894–9) · R. Torrens, *The economists refuted 1808 and other early writings*, ed. P. Groenewegen (1984) · *Collected works of Robert Torrens*, ed. G. de Vivo, 8 vols. (2000) · R. D. C. Black, *Economic thought and the Irish questions, 1817–1870* (1960) · *The correspondence of Lord Overstone*, ed. D. P. O'Brien, 3 vols. (1971) · *The works and correspondence of David Ricardo*, ed. P. Sraffa and M. H. Dobb, 11 vols. (1951–73) · *The letters of Thomas Babington Macaulay*, ed. T. Pinney, 2 (1974) · *Kerry Evening Post* (1 Feb 1854) [death of first wife] · d. cert. [Esther Torrens] · *The Times* (31 May 1864) · d. cert. · R. Torrens to Francis Place, 30 Sept 1819, BL, Add. MS 37949, fol. 79
Archives Bodl. Oxf., letters to Benjamin Disraeli · Borth. Inst., letters to Sir Charles Wood · CKS, Norman MSS · Derbys. RO, letters to Robert J. Wilmot-Horton · Duke U., Perkins L., Croker MSS · LUL, letters to Lord Overstone · NA Scot., Melville muniments · UCL, letters to Lord Brougham
Likenesses E. Boyden, portrait, exh. Royal Hiberniana Academy, Adelaide 1827 (*Colonel Torrens*) · double portrait, photograph, c.1860, State Library of South Australia, Adelaide, Mortlock Library of South Australiana [*see illus.*]
Wealth at death under £16,000: probate, 7 July 1864, *CGPLA Eng. & Wales*

Torrens, Sir Robert Richard Chute (1812–1884), land reformer, was the second son of Lieutenant-Colonel Robert *Torrens (1780?–1864) and his first wife, Charity Herbert Chute. He was born in Cork on 31 May 1812, educated at Trinity College, Dublin (BA, 1835), and became a customs officer. On 19 February 1839, at St James's Church, Westminster, he married Barbara Ainslie, *née* Parks, the widow of George Augustus Anson. In 1840 they emigrated to South Australia, where he became collector of customs at £350 a year and built a handsome house, St Clair, at Woodville. Successive governors of the colony repeatedly censured him for irregularities, but he was answerable only to the customs board in London, which rebuked but did not displace him. While his quarrelsome, sometimes violent, behaviour and his land speculations throughout Australasia made him despised as a rogue and swindler, by 1850 he had a bank balance of £18,000.

Appointed a legislative councillor in 1851 and colonial treasurer in 1852, Torrens emerged as the most reactionary of the colony's legislators. After building the mansion Torrens Park (later Scotch College) at Mitcham, he was so disgusted by the introduction of manhood suffrage, the ballot, and an elected upper house when a new constitution was adopted in 1855–6 that he decided to quit the colony. He found, however, that he could not sell his land because so many of his deeds were of dubious validity. So in 1857 he joined a twenty-year-old crusade to simplify, cheapen, and expedite all dealings in land, by introducing the registration of titles, and won election to the house of assembly promising to champion that cause. Several colonists had drafted bills to implement the reform. Torrens took up one of these, the handiwork of a German immigrant, Dr Ulrich Hübbe, who had modelled it on the system operating in the Hanseatic cities. Torrens effectively countered criticisms from lawyers fearing a loss of income and secured the bills' enactment in January 1858. He then resigned from parliament to become registrar-general, with a salary of £1000. He incurred fresh censures because his continued land-jobbing seemed inappropriate now that he could definitively determine ownership disputes. When he travelled to other colonies badgering their parliaments to copy the Real Property Act, members of the Adelaide chamber of commerce claimed he was doing so to make his own bad titles indefeasible.

Having realized his Australasian assets, Torrens

returned to England in 1862 and undertook lecture tours advocating land-title reform. After two unsuccessful attempts he was elected MP for Cambridge in 1868, but he won little support for the registration of land titles in Britain. He lost his seat in 1874. At his country home, Hannaford, near Ashburton, Devon, he engaged in ceaseless self-promotion and fruitless attempts to secure a pension from the South Australian parliament. Despite a warning from Governor Sir Dominick Daly in Adelaide that he had been 'the occasion of much mischief in this community and honours conferred on him would certainly not give general satisfaction' (Adelaide, State Records Office, GRG 2/14/1/30–31), Torrens was appointed KCMG in 1872 and GCMG in 1884. He died, of pneumonia, at Falmouth, Cornwall, on a journey from the Isles of Scilly, on 31 August 1884 and was buried in Leusdon churchyard, Devon. His wife died in 1899 and was interred with him. They had no children.

In a series of pamphlets explaining the South Australian system of conveyancing by registration of title, Torrens claimed to be the originator of the reform. This influenced his first biographers and writers of legal textbooks. South Australians, knowing that some twenty other people had prepared the way, long before Torrens became interested, and had helped to get Hübbe's bill enacted, for more than a century insisted on speaking of their 'Real Property Act titles'. Wherever the legislation was copied, the terms 'Torrens Act' and 'Torrens titles' were prevalent from the beginning. Since the 1970s those usages have gained general currency in South Australia too.

P. A. HOWELL

Sources K. Preiss and P. Oborn, *The Torrens Park estate* (1991) · *South Australian parliamentary debates* (1880), cols. 422–8 · D. Day, *Smugglers and sailors* (1992), 363–77 · P. A. Howell, 'Constitutional and political development, 1857–1890', *The Flinders history of South Australia*, ed. D. Jaensch, 2: *Political history* (1986), 95–177, esp. 157–63, 177 · *AusDB* · baptism record, St Mary Magdalene's Church, Woolwich, Kent, 18 July 1819

Archives State Records, Adelaide, South Australia, GRG2

Likenesses double portrait, photograph, *c.*1860 (with his father, Robert Torrens), State Library of South Australia, Adelaide, Mortlock Library of South Australiana; *see illus. in* Torrens, Robert (1780?–1864) · C. Hill, drawing, State Library of South Australia, Adelaide, Mortlock Library of South Australiana · oils, Art Gallery of South Australia, Adelaide · photographs, State Library of South Australia, Adelaide, Mortlock Library of South Australiana

Wealth at death £17,292: *AusDB*

Torrens, (William) Torrens McCullagh (1813–1894), politician and author, born at Delville House, near Dublin, on 13 October 1813, was the eldest son of James McCullagh of Delville, near Dublin, and Jane, daughter of Andrew Torrens of Dublin, the brother of Robert Torrens. Torrens McCullagh—as he was known until 1863—was educated at Trinity College, Dublin (BA, 1833; LLB, 1842). On 31 October 1832 he was admitted a member of Lincoln's Inn; in 1836 he was called to the Irish bar at King's Inns, Dublin, and on 6 June 1855 was called to the English bar. He married in 1836 Margaret Henrietta, daughter of John Gray of Claremorris, co. Mayo, and sister of Sir John Gray MP.

Brought to the attention of Archbishop Whately for his support of Irish poor relief, in 1835 McCullagh was given the post of assistant commissioner to the special commission on relief of the Irish poor. He travelled extensively through Ireland, and presented thorough and valuable reports on the condition of the destitute poor, which contributed to the decision in 1838 to extend the workhouse system to Ireland.

In 1842 McCullagh assisted Sir Robert John Kane in founding the first Irish mechanics' institute, in Dublin; on its opening he delivered a course of lectures on the use and study of history, published in 1842. He joined the Anti-Corn Law League, and at the suggestion of Cobden published *The Industrial History of Free Nations* (1846), which attempted to prove that world progress had been achieved only by the industry of urban, non-feudal peoples and that the corn laws were restrictive of independence and self-culture.

From 1847 to 1852, when he and Sir Charles Napier failed to win Great Yarmouth, McCullagh was MP for the borough of Dundalk. In 1857 he was returned for Yarmouth, and in 1865 (having adopted his great-uncle's surname) for the old and undivided borough of Finsbury, where he retained the seat for twenty years. In parliament he was an independent Liberal, opposed to the introduction of a branch-based mass party, and his independence was to cause severe financial problems in later life. Though winning Finsbury on a platform of extension of the suffrage, the ballot, and the abolition of church rates, from 1865 he earned a reputation as a campaigner for metropolitan social reform. He supported Disraeli's proposal for household suffrage in 1867, and in committee on the bill moved and carried an amendment establishing the lodger franchise. In 1868 he introduced the landmark Artisans' Dwellings Bill, enabling local authorities to clear away overcrowded slums and erect decent dwellings for the working classes, which was passed despite a powerful opposition. In 1869 he obtained for London boards of guardians the power to board out pauper children. He was a defender of the right of political asylum; the Extradition Act of 1870, which prevented prisoners from being extradited on one plea and tried on another, was based on the report of a select committee appointed at his suggestion. During the discussions in committee of William Edward Forster's Education Act of 1870, he proposed and carried an amendment establishing a school board for London, and he served on the Finsbury school board from 1870 to 1872. In 1885 he carried an act making the charge for water rates in the metropolis leviable only on the amount of the public assessment.

McCullagh Torrens was a tireless lobbyist and pamphleteer. He was a founder member of the Liberty and Property Defence League, established in 1882 to combat state socialism, the Clerkenwell Emigration Club, and the National Emigration League, set up in 1870. He also served on the Jamaica Committee and was vice-president of the Aborigines' Protection Society. He was a member of the executive of the Association for the Improvement of London Workhouse Infirmaries in 1866 and the executive of the Travelling Tax Abolition Committee from its inception in 1877. He was also a member of the Reform Club. His

1872 publication *Our Empire in Asia: how we Came by it* served as a critique of imperialism and a manifesto for self-rule.

McCullagh Torrens wrote several works of history and biography, including memoirs of R. Lalor Sheil (1855), Sir James Graham (1863), Viscount Melbourne (1878), and Lord Wellesley (1880), as well as the autobiographical *Twenty Years in Parliament* (1893) and the posthumous *History of Cabinets* (1894); the latter was based on twenty years' work, and to it he had devoted the last seven years of his life.

In 1878 McCullagh Torrens married his second wife, Emily, widow of Thomas Russell of Leamington Spa, and the third daughter of William Harrison of the same town. In 1885 he withdrew from parliament, the expense of which precipitated his bankruptcy, owing £6630, in 1886. On 25 April 1894 he was knocked down by a hansom cab in London and severely injured. He died the following day at 23 Bryanston Square, the residence of his daughter.

MICHAEL MACDONAGH, rev. MATTHEW LEE

Sources G. T. Bettany, 'Biographical sketch of Torrens', in W. T. M. Torrens, *Melbourne* (1890) · J. Davis, *Reforming London* (1988) · W. T. M. Torrens, *Twenty years in parliament* (1893) · *Debrett's Illustrated House of Commons and the Judicial Bench* (1867), 226–7 · Boase, *Mod. Eng. biog.* · *The Times* (27 April 1894) · H. L. Molchow, 'Torrens, William Torrens McCullagh', *BDMBR*, vol. 2
Archives Bodl. Oxf., letters to Disraeli
Likenesses Spy [L. Ward], caricature, chromolithograph, NPG; repro. in *VF* (8 Dec 1883)

Torrie [*née* Dighton], (**Ellen**) **Margaret** (1912–1999), social worker and charity founder, was born on 17 March 1912 at 61 Melrose Avenue, Wimbledon, London, the daughter of Ernest John Cornfield Dighton, a civil servant in the Board of Education, and his Swiss wife, Marie, *née* Delger (d. 1977). After leaving school in Chertsey, Surrey, she worked for the Greenwich branch of the Charity Organization Society in the dockland slum areas, before training as a secretary. A Quaker and a pacifist, she joined the Peace Pledge Union, and with John Barclay she opened the Dick Sheppard Centre in London, organizing meetings and lectures on peace and international affairs. At the beginning of the Second World War she started the Dick Sheppard Club in Paddington for local families and old people, and also helped Jewish refugees. She was a founder of the International Arts Centre in Bayswater, set up to encourage the arts in wartime, and she organized lectures, concerts, and exhibitions.

On 14 July 1943 Margaret Dighton married Alfred Malcolm Torrie (1898–1972), a psychiatrist then serving as a captain in the Royal Army Medical Corps. A Scot, from Deeside, he was a widower. They had one son (d. 1988) and one adopted daughter. When Dr Torrie was appointed medical superintendent of a Quaker mental hospital in York in 1951, they moved north: while there she helped to establish a headquarters for the York branch of the family service unit, and also became interested in the work done at Spofforth Hall, a centre for the rehabilitation of problem families. They moved back to London in 1956, settling close to Kew Gardens, and she began to work for the Citizens' Advice Bureau. In 1956 some of the nerves in her face were paralysed after a dental injection, and she struggled with speech difficulties for the rest of her life, despite an operation in 1970 to ease the discomfort.

In 1959 Margaret Torrie turned her attention to the problems facing the 3 million widows in the United Kingdom. After placing an advertisement in the local newspaper inviting widows to write to her, she formed a pilot group of twenty-five widows, and from there set up Cruse, the first organization in Britain for widows and their children. The name was inspired by the Old Testament story of the widow who shared her last cruse (jar) of oil with a stranger, only to find that it instantly replenished itself. At first she was mainly concerned with widows with children, who not only had to deal with their grief but also faced a drop in their standard of living. For many years she found it difficult to raise funds, finding that most people shrank from the subject of death and bereavement, and financed the organization herself, as well as running it, for sixteen years, from her home in Lion Gate Gardens, Richmond. The emphasis was on practical help, rather than self-help, and she built up a panel of professional people who came to meetings to give advice on legal and financial matters. In the first year she started fact sheets for widows and the *Cruse Chronicle*, a monthly newsletter. Using information supplied in detailed questionnaires, she was able to get an accurate picture of widows and their predicament with which to back her campaign to improve their statutory position, and she drew up a widows' charter which she sent to all MPs. The issues included abolishing the earnings rule, by which widows could not receive benefits in addition to earnings; increasing widows' pensions; and reducing the age at which a widow could receive her pension. She managed to generate a good deal of publicity on the radio and in the press, and an early champion of her cause was the journalist Katharine Whitehorn, whose article 'Widow's Might' appeared in *The Spectator* in 1960, while Dr Torrie published an important article, 'The Community Care of the Widow', in the *British Medical Journal* for the same year. It was he who began training bereavement counsellors and providing seminars in bereavement work for professional people, including social workers, doctors, and clergymen. Parents' circles were set up, with group counselling, and Cruse reached far beyond anything provided by the statutory services. In 1970 she published *Begin Again: a Book for Women Alone* (rev. edn, 1975), written as a textbook for widows and those wanting to help them.

After the death of her husband in 1972, and as the number of branches grew, Torrie found it increasingly difficult to run the administration from her own home, and in 1973 she secured the first government grant, which enabled Cruse to buy a house in Richmond; it opened its own headquarters, Cruse House, in 1975. The first national organizer was appointed in 1975, and in 1977 Torrie retired from day-to-day administration and moved to Grayshott, in Surrey; she was appointed MBE in June 1977. In the next few years she wrote a number of pamphlets for widows and those helping them, including *Early Days in Widowhood*, *Living through Loss*, and *Helping the Widowed*; and also

The Art of Listening, a booklet for counsellors. In 1979 she gave up editing the *Cruse Chronicle*. Cruse extended its service to include widowers in 1980, and in 1987 it became Cruse Bereavement Care, providing information and support for all bereaved people. By 2000 there were over 200 branches in the United Kingdom, and it helped 100,000 people a year.

In her retirement Torrie published several volumes of poetry, including *Selected Poems* (1979), *New Poems* (1986), and *Poems for Today* (1992). She also wrote *Completing the Circle: New Ways of Life After Fifty* (1982), *My Years with Cruse* (1987), and *Living Awake: some Reflections on Life in the Nineties* (1993). She enjoyed painting, having studied art at St Martin's School of Art during the war and at York College of Art while living in Yorkshire, and held exhibitions of her work. She spent her final years in Grayshott Nursing Home, Boundary Road, Grayshott, Hindhead, Surrey, where she died on 8 September 1999. She was cremated on 16 September.   ANNE PIMLOTT BAKER

Sources M. Torrie, *My years with Cruse* (1987) · M. Torrie, *Begin again: a book for women alone* (1970) · *The Independent* (11 Sept 1999) · *The Times* (10 Sept 1999) · b. cert. · m. cert. · d. cert.
Likenesses D. Wilding, photograph, 1969, repro. in M. Torrie, *New poems* (1986), vi · photograph, repro. in *The Independent*
Wealth at death £200,000: probate, 11 Oct 1999, *CGPLA Eng. & Wales*

Torrigiani [Torrigiano], **Pietro** (1472–1528), sculptor and draughtsman, was born 'sopr' Arno' at noon on Sunday 22 November 1472 and began life probably in the family town house (first rented, later purchased by 1480) at the top of Borgo San Jacopo (near the Ponte Vecchio), Florence. Pietro, or Piero as he was baptized in Florence Cathedral on 24 November 1472, was the fifth of the eight children of Torrigiano di Antonio Torrigiani (1429–c.1500) and Dianora di Francesco Tucci (b. c.1449). His parents were both Florentine, and Pietro's uncle, Luca di Antonio Torrigiani, was responsible for establishing the main branch of the well-known Torrigiani family in Florence, whose roots can be traced back to 1258. Pietro's father worked as a silk merchant in Florence and also owned smaller country homes and vineyards in nearby Signa, known for the production of clay and terracotta.

Although several new documents have been discovered, still relatively little information about Pietro Torrigiani's family background, youth, and early training is known. According to the later sixteenth-century Florentine source Giorgio Vasari, as an adolescent Pietro Torrigiani studied drawings and terracotta, bronze, and marble sculpture with Bertoldo di Giovanni in the Florentine academy of Lorenzo de' Medici in the gardens near San Marco until about 1492. Vasari described Pietro's early works as 'very beautiful' and thought his personality was strong and powerful, even haughty (*superbo*), overbearing, and prone to violence. The rivalry between Torrigiani and Michelangelo (nearly four years younger) led to the famous fist fight probably just before or during early 1492 in the Brancacci chapel in Santa Maria del Carmine, Florence, where Torrigiani broke Michelangelo's nose, permanently disfiguring him (an incident recorded by Vasari

and Benvenuto Cellini). Consequently, Vasari reports that Lorenzo de' Medici banished Torrigiani from Florence; by August 1492 he is recorded in Bologna making a terracotta bust of a physician, Stefano della Torre. Vasari further records that Torrigiani then moved to Rome to work with Andrea Bregno and Bernardino Pinturicchio and their workshops on the stucco and marble decoration of the Torre Borgia apartments in the Vatican for Pope Alexander VI (who reigned from 1492 to 1503). Recently discovered documents dating between 1493 and 1506 establish that Torrigiani was active as a sculptor in Rome, Florence, Siena, and elsewhere in Italy and in Avignon, and that he may not have moved northwards to northern Europe and England until after 1506.

Documented in Rome as 'Magistro Petro Scarpelino Florentino', and also called 'Petrus Scarpelinus florentinus', Torrigiani was commissioned by Cardinal Adriano Castellesi, Pope Alexander VI's papal secretary, to produce a series of large marble sculptural monuments and architectural sculptures, including a cantoria, marble doorways, tombs, and monuments for San Giacomo degli Spagnoli, now called Nostra Signora del Sacro Cuore, on Piazza Navona in Rome. Torrigiani also produced at least three finely carved busts, of Santa Fina, St Gregory, and Christ for his landlord in Rome, the priest Stefano Coppi, who later donated these to his native town of San Gimignano. These were produced about 1498 in Rome, the same year Torrigiani wrote his will with Coppi as executor. Vasari records that concurrently Torrigiani supplemented his income by enlisting as a mercenary in Cesare Borgia's army in the war of Romagna (1499–1500); he then joined the Florentines in their battle against Pisa (autumn 1499) and later fought at Gagliano, in December 1503, with Piero de' Medici and the French forces. He was lauded as a valiant soldier and returned to Florence at least by early to mid-1503, when he married Felici di Francesco di Niccolò Mori Ubaldini (d. 1541), with whom he had one child, a son, Torrigiano (1503–1528). During this time Torrigiani carved the marble statue of St Francis (c.1501) for Cardinal Francesco Piccolomini's family altar (Siena Cathedral, completed by Michelangelo). Francesco Todeschini Piccolomini (d. 1503), the cardinal protector of England from 1492 to 1503, before being elected as Pope Pius III, and Cardinal Castellesi, Torrigiani's two main patrons during his formative years in Rome, were highly influential with the church and courts in England and Spain. They, along with the Florentine banking families Baroncelli, Bardi, Cavalcanti, and Frescobaldi, who also had branches in Rome, London, and throughout Europe, helped to arrange a network for the necessary introductions for the prestigious commissions Torrigiani would later receive in England.

In February 1504 Torrigiani is documented in Avignon, where he was commissioned to sculpt three statues for a *Crucifix with the Virgin and St John* for members of the Baroncelli family. In and out of Florence also during these years, Torrigiani made many drawings and marble and bronze sculptures 'with nobility and good style' (Vasari, 4.260) for merchants. In January 1506 he purchased in Rome two large blocks of marble which Michelangelo had previously owned, suggesting the two sculptors maintained professional contacts during this period. Thus, until 1506 Torrigiani travelled and worked as a talented sculptor throughout Italy and southern France while remaining active in Rome and Florence, probably with the workshops of Andrea Bregno, Giuliano da Maiano, and Antonio Pollaiuolo.

About 1506–7 Torrigiani travelled north, perhaps with Florentine merchants or members of banking families. In April 1510 he is documented working for Margaret of Austria, regent of the Netherlands. In Bruges he repaired a bust of Mary Tudor, the daughter of Henry VII, king of England, and advised Margaret on the tomb of Mary of Savoy and unnamed funerary commissions, most probably for her priory church at Brou. He is first recorded in England on 23 November 1511, when he received the commission to make the tomb of the mother of Henry VII, Lady Margaret Beaufort (d. 1509), in the newly built Henry VII chapel in Westminster Abbey, London.

Torrigiani was, however, probably in London by about 1507, from which date he is thought to have advised Henry VII on plans for the king's family monuments, modelled the bust of Mary Tudor for her proposed marriage of 1507–8 to Margaret of Austria's nephew Charles I, and then produced about 1509–11 the three superb polychromed terracotta busts *King Henry VII* (V&A), the young *Henry VIII*, and *John Fisher, Bishop of Rochester* (Metropolitan Museum of Art, New York), as well as the polychrome plaster and wood *Death Mask* and *Funeral Effigy of Henry VII* (Westminster Abbey Museum, London), on the king's death in April 1509.

The documented sculptures Torrigiani produced in England were all made for Westminster Abbey between 1511 and 1522/5, when he left to work in Spain. Working in the abbey precinct, Torrigiani collaborated with various northern craftsmen on the distinctive black touchstone, white marble, and gilt bronze tomb of Lady Margaret Beaufort. Verrocchio's earlier Medici tomb in San Lorenzo, Florence, and Pollaiuolo's papal tombs in St Peter's, Rome, probably inspired this new combination of precious materials. The surviving contract and documents establish that, for Lady Margaret's tomb, for a fee of £500 Torrigiani designed and carved a new Italianate-inspired timber model of the tomb chest and the chest itself, incorporating Italian Renaissance decorations. He also made the life-like gilt bronze effigy and canopy based upon a two-dimensional design by Maynard Vewicke, a London painter. This system follows the more traditional medieval collaborative process then prevalent for the production of late Gothic tombs in England and northern Europe rather than the Italian Renaissance practice of allowing the sculptor greater artistic autonomy. As a result, the design of the Beaufort tomb is somewhat unbalanced, and the monument exhibits an uneven visual tension between the northern late Gothic tabernacle and the new Italianate-inspired tomb chest.

However, Torrigiani's next major work, the tomb of Henry VII and Elizabeth of York, commissioned on 26 October 1512 from Henry VIII, his next English patron, allowed Torrigiani considerably more freedom in design and execution to demonstrate further his many artistic talents. Torrigiani agreed

to make and worke, or doo to be made and wrought, well, surely, clenly, workemanly, curiously and substancyally, for the sum of £1,500 sterling, a tombe or sepulture of whit marbill and of black touchstone wt. ymags, figures, beasts and other things of cuppure gilt. (*LP Henry VIII*, 3/1, no. 7)

For this central monument in the newly built chapel of Henry VII in Westminster Abbey, Torrigiani rejected the earlier estimate and design of 1506 which Guido Mazzoni had submitted based on the tomb of *Charles VIII of France* (St Denis, Paris). For the Henry VII tomb Torrigiani designed four elegant gilt bronze Italianate seated angels holding the epitaph and royal arms to flank the two gilt bronze life-size effigies which lie on a sarcophagus with Italian Renaissance motifs (naked Verrocchiesque putti, grotesques, garlands, and birds) and six roundels with reliefs representing pairs of the king's patron saints. The Henry VII monument and chapel were lauded as early as 1530 as one of 'the wonders of the world' (*orbis miraculum*) in John Leland's description of Westminster Abbey (*De rebus Britannicis collectanea*, 6 vols., 1530, ed. T. Hearne, 1715). More recently it was described as 'the finest Renaissance tomb north of the Alps' (Pope-Hennessy, 219). Its Italian Renaissance design was influential on tombs in sixteenth- and seventeenth-century England.

The success of this tomb led Torrigiani to receive other important commissions in England. On 5 January 1519 he was commissioned by the king to design and produce for a fee of £2000 an even larger and more monumental tomb (later abandoned) for Henry VIII and Katherine of Aragon. On 5 March 1517 he received the commission for £1000 to produce the high altar for Henry VII's chapel (mainly destroyed 1644, but reconstructed with surviving pieces, 1932–5). This was a sumptuous monument of gilt bronze reliefs, polychrome and white glazed terracotta statues, marble, and black touchstone. In June 1519 Torrigiani travelled from London to Florence and later that year returned with additional assistants and collaborators to work on these and other commissions, one of whom was probably Benedetto da Rovezzano. He contracted the painter Antonio Toto del Nunziata and the sculptors Antonio di Piergiovanni di Lorenzo da Settignano and Giovanni Luigi di Bernardo di Maestro Jacopo da Verona to return with him to London. Cellini refused Torrigiani's invitation to the Tudor court but described their meeting in his *Vita*, where he records that Torrigiani unsuccessfully attempted to enlist him to make 'a great work for my king', and boasted of his 'gallant feats among those beasts of Englishmen' (Cellini, 18). During these years Torrigiani designed and produced several other distinguished portrait busts and tombs in England in marble, bronze, and terracotta, including the wall tomb of Dr John Yonge (d. 1516) for the Rolls Chapel, Chancery Lane, the first completely Renaissance-style monument in England; the wall tomb of Dean John Colet (d. 1519) in St Paul's, Covent Garden (destroyed); the marble head and roundel of Christ the redeemer (c.1520/22; set before 1532 in the western exterior wall of Abbot Islip's chapel, Westminster Abbey, now in the Wallace Collection); the bronze profile bust of Sir Thomas Lovell (d. 1524); and other works, for example, at Hampton Court. Torrigiani's Florentine followers, including Giovanni da Maiano the younger and Benedetto da Rovezzano, continued to produce Italianate sculpture at the Tudor court for several decades after his departure.

Torrigiani left England for Spain either in 1522, when Charles V visited Henry VIII and his aunt, Katherine of Aragon, in London, or about 1525, when he is recorded after modelling a terracotta bust of Empress Isabella of Portugal (1503–1539) for her marriage in 1526 to Charles V in Seville. Torrigiani may have worked for Isabella in Portugal and/or also on the Spanish royal tombs in Granada Cathedral. He is documented at the royal monastery of Guadalupe (Extremadura, Spain) in 1526 producing a polychrome terracotta statue of St Jerome (now in the sacristy), originally placed on the high altar. In Seville, Torrigiani modelled and painted masterful and influential lifesize polychrome terracotta statues of the *Penitent St Jerome* and two *Virgin and Child* groups (one of these for the Hieronymite convent of San Jerónimo de Buena Vista outside Seville—both it and the *St Jerome* are now in the Museo de Bellas Artes, Seville). These powerful, expressive statues influenced later Spanish sculptors and painters, especially Montañes, Velásquez, Zurbarán, and Goya.

While in Spain in 1525, Torrigiani transferred ownership of a family farm in Tuscany to his nephew for 1100 gold Florentine ducats. According to Vasari, Torrigiani was so incensed after being tricked with an inadequate payment of sacks full of worthless 'maravedis' as payment from the duque de Arcos in Seville that he destroyed a life-size terracotta statue of the Virgin and child that he was creating. He was imprisoned for this sacrilege, and due to his melancholic spirit he then starved himself to death. While this story remains unsubstantiated, estate documents refer to Torrigiani's widow receiving restitution of her inheritance, including various properties, and indicate that he died in the summer (July or August) of 1528.

Although Vasari, Cellini, and other supporters of Michelangelo created an unsympathetic image of Torrigiani and his work in Italy, his modelled and carved sculptures, especially his sepulchral monuments in Westminster Abbey and his polychrome sculptures made in England and Spain, are among the best Florentine Renaissance sculptures anywhere. He may rightly be credited as being one of the first Italian Renaissance artists to bring the new Italianate style and new combinations of sculptural materials and techniques into Tudor England. His influence in England continued with the work of other Italian sculptors and inspired later tomb monuments by Hubert Le Sueur, court sculptor to Charles I, in the Henry VII chapel in Westminster Abbey. Torrigiani was a brilliant and versatile Florentine Renaissance artist, whose most significant, innovative, and influential works were produced in early sixteenth-century England and Spain.

ALAN PHIPPS DARR

Sources A. P. Darr, 'Pietro Torrigiano and his sculpture for the Henry VII chapel, Westminster Abbey', PhD diss., Institute of Fine Arts, New York University, 1980 · A. P. Darr, 'New documents for Pietro Torrigiani and other early cinquecento Florentine sculptors active in Italy and England', *Kunst des Cinquecento in der Toskana*, ed. M. Cammerer (Munich, 1992), 108–38 · A. P. Darr, 'The sculpture of Torrigiano: the Westminster Abbey tombs', *Connoisseur*, 200 (1979), 177–84 · A. P. Darr, 'From Westminster Abbey to the Wallace collection: Torrigiano's *Head of Christ*', *Apollo*, 116 (1982), 292–8 · A. P. Darr, 'Verrocchio's legacy: observations regarding his influence on Pietro Torrigiani and other Florentine sculptors', *Verrocchio and late Quattrocento Italian sculpture*, ed. S. Bule, A. P. Darr, and F. S. Gioffredi (Florence, 1992), 125–39 · A. P. Darr, 'Torrigiani, Pietro', *The dictionary of art*, ed. J. Turner (1996) · J. Turner, ed., *Encyclopedia of Italian Renaissance and mannerist art* (2000), vol. 2, pp. 1628–30 · G. Vasari, *Vite*, ed. G. Milanesi (1878–85), vol. 4, pp. 255–65 · B. Cellini, *Vita* (c.1558–1567); trans. J. A. Symonds as *The life of Benvenuto Cellini written by himself* (1949), 18–19 · A. Higgins, 'On the work of Florentine sculptors in England in the early part of the sixteenth century: with special reference to the tombs of Cardinal Wolsey and King Henry VIII', *Archaeological Journal* (1894), 129–220, 367–70 · R. S. Scott, 'On the contracts for the tomb of the Lady Margaret Beaufort, Countess of Richmond and Derby', *Archaeologia*, 46 (1914–15), 365–76 · A. Ferrajoli, 'Un testamento dello scultore Pietro Torrigiano e ricerche sopra alcune sue opere', *Bollettino d'Arte* (1915), 181–92 · F. Grossmann, 'Holbein, Torrigiano and some portraits of Dean Colet', *Journal of the Warburg and Courtauld Institutes*, 13 (1950), 202–36 · P. G. Lindley, 'Una grande opera al mio re: gilt-bronze effigies in England from the middle ages to the Renaissance', *Journal of the British Archaeological Association*, 143 (1990), 112–30 · C. Galvin and P. G. Lindley, 'Pietro Torrigiano's portrait bust of King Henry VII', *Burlington Magazine*, 130 (1988), 892–902 · G. Calvin and P. G. Lindley, 'Pietro Torrigiano's tomb for Dr Yonge', *Church Monuments*, 3 (1988), 42–60 · P. G. Lindley, 'Playing check-mate with royal majesty? Wolsey's patronage of Italian Renaissance sculpture', *Cardinal Wolsey: church, state and art*, ed. S. J. Gunn and P. G. Lindley (1991), 261–85 · *LP Henry VIII*, 3/1, no. 7 · J. Pope-Hennessy, 'The tombs and monuments', *Westminster Abbey*, ed. A. Rowse (1972), 219 · C. M. Sicca, 'Consumption and trade of art between Italy and England in the first half of the sixteenth century: the London house of the Bardi and Cavalcanti company', *Renaissance Studies*, 16/2 (June 2002), 163–201 · F. Hepburn, 'Three portrait busts by Torrigiano: a reconsideration', *Journal of the British Archaeological Association*, 154 (2001), 150–69

Archives Archive de Vaucluse, Avignon · Archive du Nord, Lille · Archivio Comunale di Roma · Archivio Comunale di Siena · Archivio del real Monasterio de Nuestra Señora de Guadalupe, Guadalupe, Spain · Archivio dell'Opera del Duomo, Firenze · Archivio di Stato di Firenze · Archivio di Stato di Pesaro · Archivio di Stato di Roma · Archivio Notarile di Bologna · Archivio Notarile di Fossombrone · Archivo di S. Maria di Monserrato, Roma · Biblioteca Comunale di Siena · Biblioteca Nazionale, Firenze · BL, sources and travel diaries on Henry VII Chapel cited in Darr, 'Pietro Torrigiano and his sculpture', II · BL, St John's College, Cambridge, accounts, Add. MS 7099 · BL, Harleian MS 297, fol. 28 · BL, Cotton MS Titus B, vii, no. 324 · BL, Lansdowne MS 116, fol. 13 · BL, Cotton MS, Augustus II · BM, Phillipps MS 4104 · BM, Welbeck Abbey MS · PRO, PROB 11/16–18 · PRO, Exchequer E 36/214, pp. 15, 39, 52 · Westminster Abbey Muniments, London, no. 6638, 30626, 44026 · Cambridge, treasury muniments from St John's College and Christ's College, Cambridge: accounts of the executors of Lady Margaret

Torrington. For this title name *see* Herbert, Arthur, earl of Torrington (1648–1716); Byng, George, first Viscount Torrington (1663–1733); Byng, John, fifth Viscount Torrington (1743–1813).

Torry, Patrick (1763–1852), Scottish Episcopal bishop of St Andrews, Dunkeld, and Dunblane, born on 27 December 1763 in the parish of St Edward, Aberdeenshire, was the son of Thomas Torry, a woollen cloth manufacturer at Garneston, and his wife, Jane, *née* Watson, daughter of a farmer in the same parish. He was raised as a member of the Church of Scotland, but his uncle James Watson, who had joined the Jacobite rebellion of 1745, influenced him in the direction of Episcopalianism. After schooling at Lonmay, Aberdeenshire, Torry began teaching at the age of eighteen, first in Selkirk parish school under his uncle, and then at Lonmay. In June 1782 he went to live with John Skinner of Linshart (1721–1807), under whose tutoring he read for Episcopalian orders, and in the following September he was ordained deacon of the Scottish Episcopal church by Bishop Robert Kilgour of Aberdeen. Though only nineteen years old, Torry was put in charge of a congregation at Arradoul, Banffshire, and in 1783 he was ordained priest. In 1787 he married Kilgour's daughter, Christian, who died childless in 1789. In the same year Torry became Kilgour's assistant in his charge at Peterhead, and on Kilgour's death in 1791 Torry succeeded to his charge, which he held until 1837. He married his second wife, Jane, daughter of Dr William Young of Fawsyde, Kincardineshire, in September 1791; they had three sons and four daughters, of whom the eldest son, John, became dean of St Andrews. In 1807 Torry was made treasurer of the Scottish Episcopal Friendly Society.

On 6 October 1808 Torry was elected bishop of Dunkeld in succession to Jonathan Watson, and was consecrated bishop on 12 October at Aberdeen. As bishop he retained his pastoral charge at Peterhead, where he lived. George Gleig was originally chosen bishop, but the hostility of Bishop John Skinner (1744–1816) kept Gleig out of the see. Torry retained his bishopric for forty-four years; towards the end of his life he was one of the last survivors of the penal years of Scottish Episcopalianism and the nonjuring tradition of the eighteenth century. In 1837 he resigned his charge of the congregation at Peterhead, though he continued to reside there. Torry's age prevented his being elected in 1841 as primus in succession to Bishop James Walker. Following the revival of the medieval episcopal title of St Andrews at a synod held at Edinburgh in September 1844, Torry was henceforth known as bishop of the united dioceses of St Andrews, Dunkeld, and Dunblane.

The most important incident of Torry's episcopate was the publication in April 1850 of his *Prayer-Book*, which claimed to be the embodiment of the usages of the Scottish Episcopal church. Torry had throughout his life been a staunch champion of the Scottish communion office, which was derived, through Laud's prayer book of 1637, from the first prayer book of Edward VI. The office was used by those Episcopalians in communion with the Scottish bishops who remained illegal nonjurors until the death of Prince Charles in 1788, when they took the oath to George III and were subsequently joined by the juring Episcopalian congregations in Scotland. The latter, while becoming members of the Scottish Episcopal church,

Patrick Torry (1763–1852), by unknown engraver

retained the use of the English prayer book and looked to conformity with the Church of England. In 1847 a petition was presented to Torry from some of his clergy requesting that he patronize the compilation of a service book comprising the nonjuring liturgical usages. Torry's *Prayer-Book*, as it was known, was recommended by him and published in April 1850 as though it were the authorized service book of the Scottish Episcopal church. A storm of opposition led by Charles Wordsworth at once arose because of the minority use of the Scottish communion office among Episcopalians, the threat to Episcopalian similarity with the Church of England, and the lack of canonical sanction for some of its usages. During a struggle between the formerly nonjuring and Anglicized traditions of the Scottish Episcopal church, the publication was censured by a majority of the Scottish Episcopal synod, by the St Andrews diocesan synod on 19 June 1850, and again, after Torry had published a protest, by the Episcopal synod on 5 September.

Other questions on which Torry came into conflict with his fellow bishops were the support he gave to the European mission to Anglicans of Bishop Michael Luscombe and his favourable reception of the appeal of William Palmer (1811–1879) in connection with Palmer's exploration of the intercommunion of Anglicanism and Eastern orthodoxy. Torry was regarded by English Tractarians as the most sympathetic figure among the Scottish bishops, apart from Bishop Alexander Forbes of Brechin. They therefore sponsored a number of initiatives in his diocese, including the foundation of Trinity College, Glenalmond, and the building of St Ninian's Cathedral, Perth, an early outpost of Anglo-Catholic ritualism in Scotland, the statutes of which Torry formally approved on 6 January 1851. Torry died at Peterhead on 3 October 1852, and was buried in St Ninian's Cathedral on 13 October.

A. F. POLLARD, rev. ROWAN STRONG

Sources J. M. Neale, *Life and times of Patrick Torry* (1856) · G. Grub, *An ecclesiastical history of Scotland*, 4 vols. (1861), vol. 4 · J. Skinner, *Annals of Scottish episcopacy* (1818) · Torry MSS, NA Scot. · P. Torry, *A pastoral letter* (1846) · registers of the College of Bishops, Scottish Episcopal Church · M. Lochhead, *Episcopal Scotland in the nineteenth century* (1966) · F. Goldie, *The Episcopal Church in Scotland* (1955) · R. Strong, *Alexander Forbes of Brechin* (1995) · J. Wordsworth, *The episcopate of Charles Wordsworth, bishop of St Andrews* (1899), 42
Archives LPL, corresp. with the bishop of London · NA Scot., corresp. · NRA Scotland, priv. coll., corresp. | University of Dundee, Brechin diocesan archives
Likenesses engraving, repro. in Neale, *Life and times*, frontispiece · engraving, repro. in J. F. S. Gordon, *Ecclesiastical chronicle for Scotland* (1867), vol. 2, p. 330 [see illus.]

Torshell, Samuel (1605–1650), Church of England clergyman, was born on 4 June 1605, the son of Richard Torshell, a London merchant tailor, and his wife, who was a midwife. He was at Merchant Taylors' School from 1617 until 1620 and matriculated as a sizar at Christ's College, Cambridge, at Easter 1621. He graduated BA in 1625 and proceeded MA in 1628. In 1628 Torshell was appointed lecturer at St Bartholomew by the Exchange in London with a salary of £50. The following year he was appointed preacher at Bunbury in Cheshire by the London Haberdashers' Company. His first publication, *The Three Questions of Free Justification, Christian Liberty, the Use of the Law* (1632), was dedicated to the company. The following year he published nine sermons preached at Bunbury, under the title *The Saints Humiliation* (1633), and dedicated them also to the master and wardens of the company. It was probably Torshell who on 25 July 1632 had married Prudence Stock, at St Vedast, Foster Lane, or St Michael-le-Querne. A Prudence, daughter of Richard Stock, had been baptized in 1608 at St Matthew, Friday Street, and it is likely that the 1632 bride was the daughter Prudence mentioned in the will of Richard *Stock (1568/9–1626), rector of All Hallows, Bread Street, and famed puritan minister.

In 1633 Archbishop Neile complained that as a result of the company's patronage Bunbury was 'a good nursery of Novelists' (Richardson, 12). Torshell himself was later to assert that 'I never thought Episcopacie to be Divine Right … yet I looked upon it as the most antient and prudentiall way of government, and so obeyed it and spoke well of it, though not its mad and furious ways.' In particular Torshell disliked the altar policy of the 1630s, the suppression of godly preachers, and the overuse of excommunication. He claimed that he was finally persuaded of the 'inconveniencies and mischiefes' of episcopacy by John White's speech against it in parliament (*The Hypocrite Discovered and Cured*, 1643, A3v). Torshell was also entrusted with Richard Stock's papers. In 1641 he prepared Stock's *A Learned and Very Usefull Commentary upon the Whole Prophesie of Malachy* (1641) for the press and it appeared in the same volume as Torshell's own *Exercitation upon the Same Prophesie of Malachy*.

At the end of 1642 Torshell left Bunbury for London 'to seeke refuge in these more safe coverts' (Torshell, *A Helpe to Christian Fellowship*, 1644, foreword). In 1643 he clarified his support for parliament in two publications, *The Hypocrite Discovered and Cured* and *A Case of Conscience, Concerning Flying in Times of Trouble*, in which he complained of those who 'came up to the Parliaments sense in the head of the Tyde, [but] are willing to shrinke away in the Ebbe of things' and argued that 'if we love the publicke cause, wee must not onely keepe it company in its health, but stand by it and comfort it in its faintings' (*A Case of Conscience*, A2r–v). Torshell had not forgotten his godly contacts in Cheshire, however, and in the following year he published two sermons dedicated to Jane Done of Utkinson in testimony of 'how deare your religious family and all our Christian neighbourhood, are unto my thoughts' (*A Helpe to Christian Fellowship*, foreword).

In the spring of 1644 Torshell was appointed tutor to the king's two youngest children when they were committed by parliament to the custody of Algernon Percy, tenth earl of Northumberland. His sermon delivered that year on 28 December on the birthday of Princess Elizabeth was published as *The Womans Glorie: a Treatise, Asserting the Due Honour of that Sexe* (1645), in which he argued that women were 'capable of the highest improvements' and that 'the whole Sexe [was] unduly reproached'. Although Torshell took a positive view of women's abilities, he was also wholly conventional in arguing that these could best be developed by the pursuit of piety and that women were in subjection to men. On 12 May 1646 he delivered a sermon, *The Palace of Justice*, to the House of Commons in thanksgiving for the taking of several garrisons as the first civil war reached its close. That year Torshell was admitted as vicar of St Giles Cripplegate, London, but a successor was admitted the following year. He also published *A Designe about Disposing the Bible into an Harmony* (1647), a plan for transposing the order of biblical books and chapters to create a continuous history. On his deathbed he appointed his wife, Elizabeth, as his executor. He had already provided for his eldest son, Richard, who had been apprenticed at the cost of £50, and he left £40 each to his four other children. Torshell died on 22 March 1650.

JACQUELINE EALES

Sources R. C. Richardson, *Puritanism in north-west England: a regional study of the diocese of Chester to 1642* (1972) · P. S. Seaver, *The puritan lectureships: the politics of religious dissent, 1560–1662* (1970) · will, PRO, PROB 11/212, fol. 92 · Mrs E. P. Hart, ed., *Merchant Taylors' School register, 1561–1934*, 2 (1936) · Venn, *Alum. Cant.* · *The obituary of Richard Smyth … being a catalogue of all such persons as he knew in their life*, ed. H. Ellis, CS, 44 (1849), 29 · J. Peile, *Biographical register of Christ's College, 1505–1905, and of the earlier foundation, God's House, 1448–1505*, ed. [J. A. Venn], 1 (1910), 338 · *IGI* · *Walker rev.*, 48
Wealth at death bequests of £160: will, PRO, PROB 11/212, fol. 92

Tosny, Ralph de [Ralph de Conches] (*d.* 1102?), baron, was the son of Roger de Tosny and Godehildis, and thus from one of the most powerful families on the southern frontier of Normandy. The viking ancestor claimed for them, an otherwise unknown uncle of Rollo, first duke of Normandy, called Malahulc, was added to the family tree only in the twelfth century; during Ralph's lifetime his ancestry was traced to a Frankish great-grandfather. Tosny, in the Seine valley, was in the family's hands by the 980s and gave them a hereditary territorial surname by the 1010s, probably the first in the duchy. Roger founded one of the earliest baronial abbeys at Conches, which provided an alternative surname over several generations. An outsider as far as Duke William's relatives were concerned, Roger and two sons older than Ralph were killed in a bloody feud with the Beaumonts c.1040. Afterwards his widow was married into the ducal kin in the person of Richard, count of Évreux, in whose household Ralph was presumably raised.

Ralph de Tosny's own career began in the 1040s, witnessing charters, first alongside his mother and then from 1050 alone, at a time when his family was being drawn closer to the ducal kin through his sister Adelize's marriage to *William fitz Osbern. When the French attacked Normandy in 1054 he was Duke William's standard-bearer and trusted envoy, but as he grew older he became like his father, proud and reckless, a typical Norman (except that his ancestry was Frankish). Physically brave into his old age, he was simply incapable of subordinating his will to anyone else, even his lord, for any length of time.

Ralph's power was based on large estates around Conches, Tosny, and Acquigny, with other fiefs scattered north of the Seine and even in the Cotentin. By the early 1060s he had married, and significantly it was outside the duchy. His bride, Isabel (or Elizabeth; d. in or after 1102), was the daughter of Simon de Montfort l'Amaury and at least Ralph's match in character: adored by her knights, she rode to war with them, armed as they were.

Ralph de Tosny's belligerence had a frequent outlet in violent quarrels with neighbouring barons. One, about 1060, involved the Montgomerys; Duke William took their side, confiscated Ralph's lands, and exiled him. In retaliation, Ralph and other dispossessed lords razed the town of St Evroult, but in 1062 or 1063, at the prompting of Simon de Montfort and because the duke needed all the friends he could get in the southern marches, William reinstated him. For the rest of the 1060s Ralph was at the centre of things in Normandy, present both at the ducal court and in the army which invaded England. Tradition later had it that he declined to carry the Norman banner at Hastings so that he could join the thick of the fight.

The rewards which Ralph de Tosny found in England were modest for a lord of his standing. Other and lesser members of his family, Robert of Stafford and Robert de Tosny of Belvoir, were treated at least as well. Perhaps he preferred Normandy, or it may be that more expansive gifts were ruled out by his earlier rebellion and then by his support for Robert Curthose in 1078–9, when again his lands were briefly confiscated. At first he probably received only the big scattered soke of Necton in Norfolk and a handful of manors in Essex and Hertfordshire, including Flamstead, later capital of the Tosny barony. More came his way after the fall in 1075 of his nephew

Roger de *Breteuil, earl of Hereford, in Berkshire, Gloucestershire, Worcestershire, and Herefordshire, with Clifford Castle. Ralph is only once known to have visited England after 1066 (though the documentation may be misleading) and took little interest in his English gains, subinfeudating half, including Clifford. Few of the principal families of the Norman honour became his tenants in England. On the other hand he gave generously there, to his own abbey of Conches, to St Taurin at Évreux, and to St Evroult, the last as belated amends for his earlier crimes and after he returned from Spain c.1075 (whether from pilgrimage or a military campaign is unclear). In Normandy he husbanded his resources more carefully, but made many small gifts to those and other houses.

On the death of William I in 1087, Ralph de Tosny was among the Norman lords who threw off Duke Robert Curthose's authority by expelling his garrisons from their castles, but then fought alongside him in the successful 1088 campaign in Maine. In the early 1090s Ralph witnessed several of the duke's charters, but he was alert to his own interests, and when Curthose failed to defend him in another of those nasty private wars along the march, this time against his wife's nephew Guillaume, count of Évreux, he switched to William Rufus, who willingly sent help. When peace came in 1091 or 1092, Curthose formally transferred the Tosny fiefs to Rufus's lordship. Ralph was then a Rufus loyalist, more or less, probably joining his 1098 campaign against the French, but taking the opportunity of his death in 1100 to settle a grudge against his Beaumont neighbours. He died an old man, pugnacious almost to the last, on 24 March, probably in 1102, and was buried at Conches Abbey. All the Tosny lands passed to his oldest surviving son, another Ralph.

C. P. LEWIS

Sources L. Musset, 'Aux origines d'une classe dirigeante: les Tosny, grands barons normands du Xe au XIIIe siècle', *Francia*, 5 (1977), 45–80 · Ordericus Vitalis, *Eccl. hist.* · A. Farley, ed., *Domesday Book*, 2 vols. (1783) · E. Searle, *Predatory kinship and the creation of Norman power, 840–1066* (1988) · D. Bates, *Normandy before 1066* (1982)

Tosti, Sir (Francesco) Paolo (1846–1916), songwriter and singing teacher, was born on 9 April 1846 in Ortona sul Mare, Abruzzi, Italy. In 1858 he went to Naples, where he entered the Conservatorio di San Pietro a Majella. There he studied the violin under Pinto. His teachers of composition were Saverio Mercadante, the director of the Collegio di San Sebastiano, the leading conservatory in Naples, and a prolific composer of operas, and Carlo Conti, professor of counterpoint and composition at San Pietro a Majella until 1858, and later director, regarded by Rossini as the most remarkable Italian contrapuntal composer of the time. His success as a pupil led Mercadante to appoint Tosti 'maestrino' (pupil teacher) at a salary of 60 lire a month. His health broke down under the strain of overwork, however, and he returned to Ortona in 1869 to convalesce. During the seven months he spent there he wrote two songs, 'Non m'ama più' and 'Lamento d'amore', which he had difficulty in publishing at the time, but which later became popular.

In 1870 Tosti went to Rome, where the pianist Giovanni

Sir (Francesco) Paolo Tosti (1846–1916), by Walery, pubd 1890

Sgambati, a pupil of Liszt and a leading figure in the musical life of Rome, recognized his talent and encouraged him. A crucial event in launching his career was a concert at the Sala Dante in Rome, at which Tosti sang a ballad composed specially for the concert by Sgambati, 'Eravi un vecchio', as well as some of his own songs. In the audience was Princess Margherita of Savoy (later queen of Italy), who appointed him as her singing teacher and later keeper of the musical archives of the Italian court. His reputation as a songwriter meanwhile grew rapidly.

In 1875 Tosti made his first visit to London, and after this returned every year to the city, where he became very popular in fashionable circles. In 1880 he decided to settle in London permanently, and that same year Queen Victoria appointed him teacher of singing to the royal family. He gave lessons to the princess of Wales, and sang duets with the queen. In 1894 he became teacher of singing at the Royal Academy of Music; many of his pupils there became famous singers.

Tosti's popularity as a songwriter rested mainly on his English ballads, much used in drawing-rooms. The most famous, 'Goodbye', with lyrics by George Whyte-Melville, is a prime example of the genre:

> What are we waiting for? Oh, my heart!
> Kiss me straight on the brows! And part!
> Again! Again! my heart! my heart!
> What are we waiting for, you and I?
> A pleading look—a stifled cry.
> Goodbye, for ever! Goodbye, for ever!
> Goodbye, Goodbye, Goodbye.

Other popular English ballads included 'Parted', with words by F. E. Weatherly, the librettist for many of Tosti's songs, 'Mother', 'Forever', 'Beauty's Eyes', 'At Vespers', 'My Dreams', and 'That Day'. He also continued to write Italian songs, including fifteen duets, *Canti populari abruzzesi*. His later songs, 'Mattinata' and 'Serenata', were particularly successful. Of his French songs, 'Ninon', 'Chanson de l'adieu', and 'Pour un baiser' were all great favourites in England.

Tosti was appointed KCVO in 1908. Homesick for Italy, he returned there in 1913, and he died in Rome on 2 December 1916. ANNE PIMLOTT BAKER

Sources *The Times* (4 Dec 1916) · H. Simpson, *A century of ballads, 1810–1910* (1910) · E. A. Mario, *Francesco Paolo Tosti* (1947) · M. Turner, *The parlour song book* (1972) · *New Grove*

Likenesses Walery, photograph, pubd 1890, NPG [*see illus.*] · J. Lavery, oils, 1903, Royal College of Music, London · M. Beerbohm, caricature, ink and watercolour over chalk, 1908, BM · Ape [C. Pellegrini], lithograph, repro. in *VF*, 17 (1885), pl. 344 · G. W. Lambert, pencil drawing, NPG

Wealth at death £102 10s.: administration, 28 Nov 1917, *CGPLA Eng. & Wales*

Tostig, earl of Northumbria (*c*.1029–1066), magnate, was the third son of *Godwine, earl of Wessex (*d*. 1053), and *Gytha [*see under* Godwine]. He had two elder brothers, *Swein and Harold (later King *Harold II), and at least four younger ones, Ælfgar, *Gyrth, *Leofwine, and Wulfnoth. He also had at least two sisters, *Edith and Gunnhild, and perhaps one more. In 1051 Tostig married *Judith of Flanders, daughter of Baudouin (IV), count of Flanders, and his second wife, Eleanor of Normandy, who was first cousin to Edward the Confessor. The marriage seems to have been contracted during the exile of Tostig's father, Earl Godwine, at the court of Count Baudouin (V) in the autumn of 1051. Although the author of the life of King Edward calls Tostig 'earl', it is the sole direct evidence for his status at his wedding. If he had not yet attained this rank, then the marriage contracted was a considerable coup for the Godwine clan. At Easter 1053 Tostig and his brothers Harold and Gyrth carried their father's body into the king's chamber at Winchester after Godwine had collapsed and died.

Before mid-Lent 1055 Tostig had succeeded Siward as earl of Northumbria and his accession may have earned the Godwine family the enmity of Ælfgar of Mercia, who coveted the earldom for himself. The life of King Edward claims that Tostig was held in special affection by Edward the Confessor and his appointment may have owed much to the combined influence of his elder brother Harold and his sister Queen Edith. Tostig is described as a man of courage, endowed with great wisdom and shrewdness of mind. He was favourably compared with his brother Harold, both being distinctly handsome and graceful, similar in strength and bravery. The life of King Edward goes on to add that Tostig was endowed with very great and prudent restraint, although he tended to be rather overzealous in attacking malefactors. He carefully weighed up situations and once he had decided on a course of action he embarked upon it without discussing matters further with his fellows. Occasionally it seemed that he acted without planning and so caught his opponents unawares. He shared with his brother Harold the ability to disguise his true feelings, thus keeping people guessing as to their intentions. For the biographer of King Edward, Tostig and Harold were the twin pillars upon which peace in England rested.

Religious, diplomatic, and military activity Tostig and his wife were well known for their alms giving. During the period of Tostig's rule in Northumbria, they forged close links with the community of St Cuthbert at Durham. The *Libellus de exordio atque procursu istius hoc est Dunelmensis ecclesie* of Symeon of Durham (written between 1104 and 1107) describes the gifts they made to St Cuthbert, among which was a crucifix and images of the Virgin and of St John the Evangelist executed in gold and silver, together with many other precious ornaments for the church. Symeon also preserves the story of Judith's desire to worship at Cuthbert's shrine. Owing to an injunction against women entering the precincts of the church, Judith sent one of her maidservants to attempt an entry. On crossing the boundary of the churchyard the girl fell ill and died soon afterwards. It was in order to make amends for her temerity that Judith and Tostig made their gifts to the community. The links with Durham seem to have been close and Bishop Æthelwine provided Judith with some of St Oswine's hair. Judith was famed as a patron of the arts and at least four gospel books have been associated with her. In one of these (New York, Pierpont Morgan Library, Morgan MS 709, fol. 16) she is depicted in a line drawing. It does not seem likely that the community of St Cuthbert led the attack upon Tostig in 1065, as under him it had enjoyed the benefits of his strong rule. Durham tradition also preserved the story of the escape from prison of a certain Aldan-hamal whom the earl had incarcerated for robbery. The thief invoked St Cuthbert's aid, escaped his prison, and claimed sanctuary within the cathedral. One of Tostig's officers, Barcwith, was struck down by the saint for daring to violate the sanctuary. Despite this attack on the church, Tostig and his wife are commemorated in the Durham *Liber vitae*.

The author of the life of King Edward suggests that Tostig remained faithful to his wife and that their marriage was chaste. In 1061 they led an embassy to Rome which included Ealdred, archbishop-elect of York, who was journeying there for his pallium. On the outward and return journeys Tostig demonstrated his piety by worshipping at each shrine he came across. Pope Nicholas II (r. 1059–61) received Tostig and his companions honourably and invited the earl to attend a synod, presumably that of Easter (15 April) 1061, called to deal with the problem of simony in the church, at which, it is said, Tostig sat immediately next to the pontiff. During the dispute over Ealdred's election to York, it seems that the earl threatened to withhold the Peter's Pence which he had brought with him from England. Tostig's embassy became embroiled in the local struggle between the Tuscan nobility and the papacy when members of his party were attacked on the via Cassia shortly after leaving for home. The earl had sent Judith and most of his retinue on ahead

and they were unaware of what had happened to their fellows. The attackers were led by Gerard, count of Galeria, who was later excommunicated by Pope Nicholas II for this act of aggression. During the attack a certain nobleman, Gospatric, enabled his lord, Tostig, to escape by pretending that he was the earl. The name Gospatric was common in the north in this period and this holder of it cannot be identified with certainty, but it is possible that he was either the post-conquest earl of Northumbria or the Gospatric, son of Uhtred, who was slain on Queen Edith's orders in 1064. On their return to Rome, Tostig and his companions were treated with compassion by the pope, who gave them gifts from the treasury of St Peter, whereupon they departed with the apostolic benediction. The party reached England safely in the autumn of 1061.

During Tostig's absence, Malcolm III of Scotland had attacked the north of England, pillaging Holy Island in particular. It has been suggested that Malcolm timed the raid to coincide with Tostig's journey to Rome so that, apart from the military advantage, he might not break his oath of sworn brotherhood with the earl. The life of King Edward suggests that earlier, perhaps in 1058, the Scots had made raids on Tostig's earldom in order to test him. Tostig had responded by wearing the Scots down by cunning schemes rather than by military campaigns, until Malcolm agreed to serve Tostig and King Edward. Malcolm is said to have given Tostig hostages and it may have been at this time that he became the earl's sworn brother. In 1059 Malcolm was conducted to Edward's court by Tostig, the archbishop of York, and the bishop of Durham, and it seems likely that the agreement was made on this occasion. Some time after his return from Rome, in the last week of May 1063, Tostig invaded north Wales, probably from Chester, in support of his brother Harold's campaign launched from Bristol. The success of the campaign probably induced the Welsh to kill their king, Gruffudd ap Llywelyn, and present his head to Harold and Tostig.

Victim of rebellion Tostig seems to have been a trusted minister of the crown and was at Edward's court in 1065, either hunting with the king or possibly completing a task that Edward had entrusted to him, when revolt broke out in his earldom. Tostig had delegated the government of Northumbria north of the River Tyne to his lieutenant, the Yorkshire thegn Copsi, but their regime seems to have provoked a violent rebellion. According to the life of King Edward, some of the Northumbrian nobles who had suffered under Tostig's rule conspired to bring him down late in 1065, after Michaelmas or perhaps in October. The Anglo-Saxon Chronicle charges Tostig with robbing churches, depriving men of their lands and lives, and acting against the law. As King Edward promised the rebels that he would restore the laws of Cnut to the north, it may be that Tostig had tried to introduce West Saxon law into the region. John of Worcester suggests that the combination of a great tax levied on the Northumbrians and the murder of the Northumbrian nobles Gamel, son of Orm, and Ulf, son of Dolfin, who were linked to the house of Bamburgh, was at the heart of the revolt. The murder of another Northumbrian noble, Gospatric, at the behest of Queen Edith on 28 December 1064 has also been seen as a contributing factor. It is possible that during the Northumbrian revolt against the Normans in 1069–70, the memory of this murder provoked the earl of Northumbria, who was Gospatric's nephew and namesake, to despoil the gilded cross which Tostig and his wife had presented to the community of St Cuthbert.

On 3 October 1065 the rebels, led by Gamelbearn, Dunstan, son of Æthelnoth, and Glonieorn, son of Heardwulf, who may have been intriguing with Earl Eadwine of Mercia and his brother Morcar, broke into Tostig's residence in York and killed those of his soldiers who did not escape. John of Worcester names two of the victims, the housecarls Amund and Reavenswart, and suggests that some 200 men lost their lives. The rebels then nominated Morcar as their earl, invited his brother Eadwine to join them, and marched south. Anyone associated with Tostig's regime was killed and there was much slaughter both in York and in Lincoln. The life of King Edward sees the revolt as heralding the return of the robber bands that had dominated the north before the imposition of order by earls Siward and Tostig. The rebels marched to Northampton, where they were met by Earl Harold, and then as far as Oxford where, on 28 October 1065, they were met by envoys from King Edward. The rebels demanded the exile of Tostig, charging him with being too cruel in the exercise of his authority and with punishing miscreants more out of a desire to confiscate their property than out of a love of justice. They also demanded that the king accept Morcar as earl of Northumbria. According to the biographer of King Edward, Tostig alleged that his brother Harold had conspired with the rebels against him. Tostig made the accusation in the presence of the king but Harold purged himself with a public oath of exculpation. Edward decided to crush the rebellion, in support of his brother-in-law, but was deserted by Earl Harold and the English thegns, who refused to provoke a civil war. Harold conveyed Edward's acceptance of the rebels' terms and agreed that the laws of Cnut would be re-established in Northumbria.

Exile, return, and death This was a pragmatic response to the situation but it marked a final fissure between Harold and his brother. The twelfth-century historian Henry of Huntingdon believed that the rift between Harold and Tostig had occurred shortly after their successful invasion of Wales in 1063. Jealous of his brother's higher place in the king's affections, Tostig went to Hereford, where Harold was preparing a banquet to entertain the king, and had Harold's servants dismembered and served up for the royal guest. Tostig was thus forced into exile along with his wife, Judith, and his lieutenant, Copsi. It may be at this date that the shires of Northampton and Huntingdon were detached from the earldom and granted to Siward's son, Waltheof, who had been denied the earldom of Northumbria in 1055 and now again in 1065. The author of the life of King Edward sees the failure of Edward to reinstate Tostig as marking the beginning of his physical decline. Queen Edith also tried to intervene on her brother's behalf, but in vain. Tostig took leave of his mother and crossed the channel, with his wife and infant children and members of his immediate retinue, after 1 November 1065. According to the life of King Edward the exiles were welcomed by Count Baudouin (V) of Flanders a few days before Christmas and given a house and estate in St Omer, together with the revenues of the town as maintenance. Orderic Vitalis, writing in the early twelfth century, believed that during his exile Earl Tostig had visited Duke William of Normandy in an attempt to forge an alliance against Harold. Similarly Snorri Sturluson's *King Harald's Saga*, written at the end of the twelfth century, suggests that Tostig had travelled to Denmark and then Norway in order to enlist the aid of kings Swein and Harald in his attack on England. After Tostig's departure, his brother Harold may have formed an alliance with earls Eadwine and Morcar and began to advance his own claims to the English throne. The enmity between the brothers was not ended by Harold's coronation and Tostig was absent from the ceremony.

Shortly after the appearance of Halley's comet on 24 April 1066, Tostig attempted to recover his place by making raids on England. He attacked the Isle of Wight, taking plunder and provisions before moving along the coast to Thanet, where, according to Gaimar, he was met by Copsi. They attacked 'Brunemue' before entering the Humber. Driven out of Lindsey by earls Eadwine and Morcar and deserted by his Flemish allies, Tostig made his way to Scotland. He seems to have joined up with King Harald Hardrada of Norway at the mouth of the River Tyne early in September 1066. The two entered the Humber and by way of the Ouse landed at Riccal. On 20 September they defeated the forces of earls Eadwine and Morcar at Gate Fulford but were themselves defeated and killed by King Harold at Stamford Bridge, on the Derwent, on 25 September. Tostig's lieutenant, Copsi, may have been with his master at the battle, but he survived and was later to hold the earldom under William I. After Tostig's death, his widow, Judith, remained in Flanders until late 1070 or early 1071, when she married Welf (IV), duke of Bavaria.

Domesday Book records lands held by Earl Tostig and values them at £492, which ranks him among the wealthiest landholders of Edward's reign. This figure is almost certainly an underestimate, as the survey probably failed to record every instance of the transference of Tostig's manors after his exile. In addition, the northern half of his earldom was not surveyed by the Domesday commissioners. Apart from his estates in the earldom of Northumbria, which seems to have included Nottinghamshire, Tostig held land in the south, mainly in Hampshire, the south-west, and the east midland shires, particularly Northamptonshire and Huntingdonshire.

WILLIAM M. AIRD

Sources F. Barlow, ed. and trans., *The life of King Edward who rests at Westminster*, 2nd edn, OMT (1992) · *ASC*, s. a. 1055, 1061, 1063, 1065, 1066 · John of Worcester, *Chron.* · *L'estoire des Engleis by Geffrei Gaimar*, ed. A. Bell, Anglo-Norman Texts, 14–16 (1960) · Symeon of Durham, *Opera* · J. Raine, ed., 'Vita Oswini regis deirorum', *Miscellanea biographica*, SurtS, 8 (1838), 1–59 · [J. Stevenson], ed., *Liber vitae* *ecclesiae Dunelmensis*, SurtS, 13 (1841) • *AS chart.*, S 1137 • A. J. Robertson, ed. and trans., *Anglo-Saxon charters*, 2nd edn (1956) • F. Barlow, *Edward the Confessor* (1970) • P. A. Clarke, *The English nobility under Edward the Confessor* (1994) • W. E. Kapelle, *The Norman conquest of the north: the region and its transformation, 1000–1135* (1979)

Wealth at death over £492, value of manors recorded in Domesday Book: Clarke, *English nobility*, 191–4

Totnes. For this title name *see* Carew, George, earl of Totnes (1555–1629).

Totney, Thomas [*later* Theaurau John Tany] (*bap.* **1608**, *d.* **1659?**), prophet and visionary, was baptized on 21 January 1608 in the parish of South Hykeham, Lincolnshire, the third, but eldest surviving, son of John Totney (*d.* 1638) and Anne, *née* Snell (*d.* 1642). John Totney, although never of the parish élite, was a substantial farmer and respectable member of the local community.

Early life Nothing is known of Thomas's education. On 24 April 1626 he was bound as an apprentice for eight years to Thomas Letchworth, fishmonger of the City of London. Members of the Fishmongers' Company were, however, able to transfer, for a fee, to the Goldsmiths' Company, and it was as a maker of silver and gold trinkets that he was trained by Letchworth. On 29 April 1633 he was discharged from his apprenticeship and became a freeman of the Fishmongers' Company. At some point in the next twelve months he married a daughter (her name is unknown) of Richard Kett (*c.*1571–1653) of Crownthorpe, Norfolk, and a landowner on the cusp of gentry status. Richard Kett's grandfather had been the brother of Robert Kett, leader of the 1549 rebellion; his uncle Francis Kett was burnt for heresy in 1589 and his father imprisoned for the same offence. Perhaps with the help of his wife's dowry, Totney did not serve as a journeyman, but set up his own shop in the parish of St Katherine Creechurch. He was one of several downmarket goldsmiths in the low-rent first precinct of Aldgate ward; and he took on his first apprentice. His formal incorporation into the Goldsmiths' Company is registered on 17 January 1634.

Totney lived in St Katherine Creechurch at the time when Stephen Denison (*c.*1581–1649) was delivering thunderous sermons on the immutability of God's decrees of predestination, and his texts—especially Romans 9: 11–13—were those that Totney later recalled as being those which in the days 'when he knew not God' he was 'much troubled at' (T. J. Tany, *Second Part of his Theos-ori apokolipikal*, 1653, 22, 24). When his first son was born in the second week of December 1634, despite Denison's best efforts Totney refused to have him baptized. On 6 February 1635 he was hauled before the consistory court, and the bishop's commissary ordered the child to be baptized notwithstanding Totney's (unspecified) objection. Shortly afterwards his wife died, and on 25 March 1636 he married, by special licence (it being Lady day and in Lent), Alice (1615–1648), daughter of Francis Burton (*c.*1578–1617), a freeman of the Stationers' Company. The couple seem to have had five children between 1639 and 1648, all of whom were baptized.

At some point John Totney inherited from his brother a farm in Little Shelford, Cambridgeshire. In the spring of 1640 Thomas and Alice moved to live there. Thomas arrived—according to his own later account—just in time to play a leading part in resisting the payment of ship money. He claims to have been imprisoned for his pains and to have had his goods distrained—'I ever stood against the Thing Tyranny', he wrote, with specific reference to this (Tany, *The Nation's Right in Magna Charta Discussed*, 8). Independent evidence identifies him as constable of Little Shelford that year, so it may have been for failure to collect ship money rather than failure to pay it that he was distrained. There are a series of payments in 1642 that showed support for those opposed to Charles I—for example, 16*s.* for the relief of distressed protestants in Ireland (spring 1642) and a £3 loan to the parliamentary cause (September 1642). And he claimed that in January 1643 he volunteered to serve in the troop of horse raised by Captain Oliver Cromwell, deeply moved by an appeal by the future lord protector in front of the 'Market-house' in Huntingdon where 'you sought not ours but us; and our welfare, and to stand with us for the liberty of the Gospel and the Law of the Land' (T. J. Tany, *Theauraujohn High Priest to the Jewes*, 1652, 6). His later possession of a great saddle, a musket, two pistols, and a sword confirms that he served as a harquebusier. However, his military career was over by the end of 1644 when he was back in Shelford acting as a local tax official and agent for sequestered royalist land. The records suggest a dedicated supporter of parliament, a willing russet-coated servant at the bottom of the administrative pyramid erected by the Long Parliament.

Calling as a prophet In the spring of 1648 Totney uprooted and returned to London, setting up a small shop under the sign of 'the three golden lions' in the parish of St Clement Danes. Shortly afterwards his wife died. And something—possibly the grief—triggered a great spiritual crisis that was to change his life.

In August 1649 Totney began a ritual of purification, a penitential process that culminated on Friday 23 November:

> after fourteen weeks in humiliation and fasting … and praying divers days, seeking earnestly to God … the Lord came upon me in power … and fell upon me in my shop … overpowering my understanding, and manhood, wisdom … and he struck me dumb, then after blind, and then dead, in the beholding of hundreds of men, then I was corded and bound in my bed … and my sufferings were inexpressible … Then I saw the sufferings of the body of that man Jesus my brother … I was made hands, feet, food, eyes, and clothing to many … emptied to temporals but filled with eternal being which loved me with everlasting love … Then I saw the great light shine in me and upon me, saying *Theaurau John* my servant, I have chosen thee my Shepherd, thou art adorned with the jewel of Exceliency … The Lord spake unto me by Voice: whose voice I heard, but saw no appearance, and *He* changed my name from *Thomas* to *Theaurau John*.   (This collage is assembled from several of his own descriptions of his ecstatic vision: T. J. Tany, *Theos-ori apokolipikal*, sig. A2v, 33; *Second Part*, 53; *High Priest*, 5, 6; *Nation's Right*, 6.)

Totney believed himself called in the manner of Moses to assemble the children of Israel—the 144,000 of them, the thirteen tribes of Israel. He was to prepare for the second coming of Christ. He saw himself as the new Abraham—and so he circumcised himself as a sign of the renewed covenant; as the new Moses, to lead God's chosen people from Egypt to Canaan; he was sent forth to preach everlasting love to those who would listen, and woe and destruction to those who would not listen: for the day of judgment was coming, when 'the earth shall burn as an oven' and all the proud, the wicked, and the 'ungodly shall be as stubble to his flame' (T. J. Tany, *Theauraujohn his Aurora in tranlogorum in Salem gloria*, 1650, 49—citing Malachi 4: 1). He went armed with his rusting sword from the war, and the London press was soon mockingly reporting his doom-laden preaching.

He also had a new name—Thomas became The-aurora-John, or Theaurau John; and Totney became Tany after one of the knights listed by Raphael Holinshed as a follower of William the Conqueror; and with this new name came a new noble identity—Totney or Tany (respectively pronounced Tawtney and Tawney) designed for himself a coat of arms based on that of the de Tany family as listed in the papers of Robert Glover, the sixteenth-century Somerset herald. He believed himself to be the high priest of the lost tribe of Israel, the high priest of the order of Aaron, and he created a fantastic genealogy to prove it. He believed himself to be the prophet foretold by the book of Malachi (Malachi 3: 1), for he took himself to be one who 'is like a refiner's fire, and like fuller's soap. And he shall sit as a refiner and purifier of silver.' The one who purifies the silver, the one who purifies the gold: to Tany, it was the same thing. Like the prophets of the Old Testament, he claimed that his authority as a prophetic messenger rested with the one who sent him, God.

In addition to all this, Tany set out to develop a new linguistic system, based on imperfectly grasped syntactical knowledge of Hebrew, Greek, and Latin: these changes, he claimed, 'are the key and inlet to the deity, and the outlet of his creatived creation and creations' (T. J. Tany, *Aurora*, 2). This does not make him easy to read, although buried away in his obscurantist pamphlets (quite likely mercurial in the precise sense) is strong, clear radical preaching against 'the diabolical dumb dogs [and] tythe-mongers' (Isaiah 56: 10) who fleece rather than 'feed my people' (Micah 7: 14) (T. J. Tany, *Theos-ori apokolipikal*, 34). And he cried down formal religion and cried up social justice—the imperative to 'feed the hungry, clothe the naked, oppress none, set free the bounden, if this be not, all your religion is a lye, vanity, a cheat, deceived and deceiving' (T. J. Tany, *Second Part*, 90).

Public ministry, 1650–1655 But such obscurantism did not deter others from believing in Tany and supporting him: it is likely that his mercurial pamphlets were subsidized by Captain Robert Norwood, an army radical, and that he became involved not later than September 1650 in the radical group gathered around John Pordage in Bradfield rectory and including men like William Everard. His main publications were concentrated into the period 1650–53. His 1650 publications included *I Proclaime from the Lord of Hosts the Returne of the Jewes from their Captivity* (25 April

1650); *Whereas Theauraujohn Taiiijour my Servant* (15 November 1650); *The Nation's Right in Magna Charta Discussed* (28 December 1650); *Theauraujohn his Aurora in tranlogorum in Salem gloria* (December 1650). All appear to have been printed by printers with radical credentials like Henry Hills, a member of William Kiffin's congregation, and distributed through Giles Calvert's shop near St Paul's. In 1651 and 1653 he published the two parts of his *Theauraujohn his Theos-ori apokolipikal*, but from new year's day (25 March) 1651 he began a new life as an evangelist, pitching his tent in public places and preaching to curious crowds. His first pitch was in the Middle Park at Eltham, Kent, and after that he pitched in or near Robert Norwood's house in the parish of St Mary Aldermary in the City of London. This led to the arrest of Tany and Norwood for spreading ranter ideas, and to their imprisonment and trial, as reported lucidly by Norwood (*The Case and Trial of Capt. Robert Norwood*, 1652) and fantastically by Tany (*Theos-ori apokolipikal*, 69–74). They were indicted by a grand jury on 25 June 1651. The charge was blasphemy, and specifically that they denied the existence of heaven and hell—no salvation and no damnation. Under the recently passed Blasphemy Act this carried a penalty of six months in prison.

After the hearing they were released on bail. But there was no silencing Tany, who resumed his evangelization of Eltham. When he and Norwood reappeared before the sessions on 13 August, they were convicted of blasphemy, and sentenced to six months' imprisonment in Newgate. They and (unnamed) friends lodged an appeal under a writ of habeas corpus, which was first heard on 27 October 1651 and several times adjourned until, on 22 February 1652, Lord Chief Rolle ruled the writ out of time. They were then released on a recognizance for good behaviour (aimed at muffling them) for one year. Still incensed at their treatment Norwood brought a writ of error to the court of upper bench to have his conviction quashed. And his persistence paid off. The court determined that although they denied the existence of hell and damnation, they had not denied heaven and salvation, and however logically the latter flowed from the former, the law could not infer it. Thus 'the Judgement ag[ainst] the defend[an]ts be reversed and the p[ar]tie restored' (PRO, KB21/13, fol. 212b).

Flushed with triumph, Tany now published a pamphlet entitled *Theauraujohn high priest to the Jewes, his disputive challenge to the universities of Oxford and Cambridge and the whole hirach of Roms clargical priests* (March 1652). This was the least coherent of his anti-clerical tracts. But it does reveal a little more about his way of life, as he alternated between a lodging house in Bow and what he referred to as 'the Tent of *Judah*' at Eltham (T. J. Tany, *Tharam Taniah, Leader of the Lords Hosts*, probably published in 1655). It is clear that this tent was modelled on the tabernacle of ancient Israel—or so he claimed and so Lodowick Muggleton maintained, in a manuscript tract denouncing Tany as a false prophet (L. Muggleton, *The Acts of the Witnesses of the Spirit*, 1699, 44).

On 1 January 1653 Tany was ordered by God to 'retract from speaking unto any person for 34 dayes, and 21 of the same dayes to see no person' (T. J. Tany, *High News for Hieru-salem*, no date, 2). During this fiercely purgative retreat he was given a new name—Theauroam Tanijahhh—and a new commission, to address the Jews of the world, and he began by writing (and, according to his own account, sending an edict engraved in brass) to the Jews of Amsterdam. This provoked no response, so he issued a second edict to the people of England, Wales, Scotland, and Ireland 'desiring those that would go up to Herusalem' to build 'the Temple unto our Jah the Great Jehovah' (T. J. Tany, *High News*, p. 3, 7). He then retreated into silence, 'to be taught a pure language' (after Zephaniah 3: 9), and was (so far as the records go) invisible. Perhaps this is connected with the fact that at just this time a list of thirty 'Grand Blasphemers and Blasphemies' was submitted to the committee of religion, the nineteenth of which cited 'a Goldsmith that did live in the *Strand* and after in the City, and then at Eltham; who called his name Theaurau-John Tany, the High Priest &c. Published in Print That all Religion is a lie, a deceit, and a Cheat' (*A List of some of the Great Blasphemers and Blasphemies*, 1654).

Tany becomes visible again on Good Friday (24 March) 1654, writing from the 'Tent of Judah' to commend the Quakers as 'the children of Abraham, Isaac and Jacob; who are circumcised in Heart' (T. J. Tany, *Tharam Taniah*). He then launched himself into a frenzy of preaching and publishing, proclaiming himself the king of seven kingdoms (including France, Rome, England, and Jerusalem). In the middle of all this he burnt his tent together with all his military paraphernalia (except for his sword) and all his books (including his Bible—which led to his being stoned and having to take flight in a rowing boat fortuitously moored near the bonfire).

On 30 December 1654 the regicide Augustine Garland and Sir Anthony Ashley Cooper moved that Lord Protector Oliver Cromwell be crowned. This provoked a furious response. Tany denounced them in *My EDICT Royal* (probably published in 1655) and then went on the rampage in the lobby of the House of Commons, slashing at the doorkeeper and at many more present. Overpowered, he was brought to the bar of the House where he refused to remove his hat, but reproved the assembled MPs and was remanded to the Gatehouse prison. On 3 January he was interrogated by a committee of MPs, and asserted that his 'office is to gather the dispersed Jews' and 'to carry them to the Holy Land' (*Mercurius Politicus*, no. 238, p. 5033). He was remanded for trial before the court of upper bench, but when parliament was dissolved at the beginning of February, he was released on a writ of habeas corpus.

On Sunday 23 September 1655 it was reported that Tany 'in one of his old whimsies' had, with the help of some of his disciples, pitched a tent in the large tract of open ground between Lambeth Marsh and Southwark known as St George's Fields. Tany, it was said,

> propounds again the wild tenets he doth hold in Religion, and is resolved to defend them against all opposition; but take heed of him, for if you cross him, he will so lay about him, and rebuke you with his Monumentall sword. (*Weekly Intelligencer*, no. 28, 23 Sept 1655, last page)

On 28 September the council of state received a complaint about him from a local inhabitant (John Balderson) and the council ordered the local justices to remove him and his tent, which they appear to have done with relish and excessive force.

Last years and significance Tany then seems to have gone down into Kent and at some point in the summer of 1656 crossed the English Channel and arrived in the United Provinces 'to call the Jews there' (L. Muggleton, *The Acts of the Witnesses of the Spirit*, 44). Very little is known of his activities in the Netherlands, except that at some point he made his way to Brill, a port on the island of East Voorne. A newspaper report in December 1659 seems to indicate his fate: 'In a letter from Brill unto Mr Henry Jessey … tis certified that John Tanni as he was called here, or Ram Johoram as he lately called himself, was cast away in his passage in a ship as he came from the Brill for London' (*A Particular Advice from Foreign Parts*, no. 52, p. 558). If he did not die in this way, then we can be sure that he was dead by 28 September 1663 when his daughter was married by a licence that recorded both her parents as dead.

It is plausible but inadequate to see Tany as a crazy man, all too likely maddened by the mercury in the goldsmith's refinery, and allowed to make his voice heard because of the special circumstances of the English revolution and a world made free to listen to crazed voices. But this would be to underestimate and to overlook the significant number of remarkable but elusive works that he wrote and that can fairly be said to be unlike anything else in the English language. His sources were varied, although they seem to have included almanacs, popular prophecies, and legal treatises, as well as *The Testament of the Twelve Patriarchs, the Sonnes of Jacob* (1647), Jacob Boehme's *A Description of the Three Principles of the Divine Essence* (English translation, 1648) and *Mercurius Teutonicus* (1649), *Theologica Germanica, or, Mysticall Divinitie* (1648), *Paracelsus of the Nature of Things* (1650), Henry Cornelius Agrippa's *Three Books of Occult Philosophy* (1650), and Menasseh ben Israel's *The Hope of Israel* (1650). Indeed Tany's writings embrace currents of magic and mysticism, alchemy and astrology, numerology and angelology, Neoplatonism and gnosticism, hermeticism and Christian Cabbala—a ferment of ideas that fused in a millenarian yearning for a return of Christ to earth. The English revolution freed crazy, learned men and women to speak their minds and challenge their times. Tany had a few loyal followers but—unlike Lodowick Muggleton and others—he failed to found a sect. His vision was like molten gold, untouchable, malleable, redolent of possibility; and the trinkets he made with his words are as worthy of preservation as much of the solemn and weighty pronouncements of heavyweight puritans that have crumbled to dust with the passage of time.   ARIEL HESSAYON

Sources A. Hessayon, *'Gold Tried in the Fire': the prophet Theaurau John Tany and the puritan revolution* [forthcoming] • T. J. Tany [T. Totney], *The nation's right in Magna Charta discussed with the thing called parliament* (1650)

Toto, Anthony (1499–1554), artist, was the son of the Florentine artist Toto del Nunziata, whom Vasari described as a 'dipintore di fantocci', as a maker of fireworks, and as a practical joker. In Florence Toto was a pupil of the painter Ridolfo Ghirlandaio at the same time as Perino del Vaga. With his master he painted an altarpiece of the Virgin and child with two saints in San Piero Scheraggio, while in friendly competition with del Vaga he painted a figure on the triumphal arch erected for the entry of Pope Leo X into Florence in 1515. In 1519 he was engaged by the sculptor Pietro Torrigiano to come to England and work on a projected tomb for Henry VIII and his queen.

Although this tomb was never executed Toto entered the service of the king as a painter, and his name subsequently appears in the account books of the royal household in conjunction with that of another Florentine painter, Bartolommeo Penni. Vasari states that Toto executed numerous works for the king of England, some of which were in architecture. In particular he refers to Toto's work on the 'principal palace' of Henry VIII (probably Nonesuch Palace, near Cheam in Surrey). In 1530 Toto painted nine religious pictures for the library and the king's closet of Hampton Court Palace, and in the same year he also painted and gilded four antique heads brought from Greenwich to 'Hanworthe'. Two years later he was paid with 'John de la Mayn' (perhaps Giovanni da Maiano) for work on 'certen antique hedes'. From at least 1536–7 Toto lived in the parish of St Bride, Fleet Street, London, and in the latter year he executed a heraldic painting for the funeral of Jane Seymour.

Toto was married twice, first to Ellen, and then to Katherine. Presumably with his first wife he had three children, Anthony (also a painter), Ellen (who married the painter Lewes Williams), and Winifred (who married Sir Charles Calthrope, attorney-general for Ireland). Toto received letters of naturalization and free denization in June 1538, in which year he and his first wife also received a grant of two cottages at Mitcham in Surrey as well as the lease of the manor of Ravesbury.

In 1540 Toto received payment from Henry VIII for 'a table of the story of King Alexander' and for a 'table of Calomia' (probably a 'Calumny of Apelles'). In 1541 he received a licence to export 600 tons of beer which he later sold on. Toto is perhaps the 'Mr. Anthony, the kynge's servaunte of Grenwiche', bequeathed 10 pounds in the will of Hans Holbein in 1543. In 1544 he succeeded Andrew Wright as the king's serjeant-painter and he also became a member of the king's privy chamber. In the same year he produced heraldry and other decorations for Sir Thomas Cawarden, master of the king's tents. The document that records this commission carries the only known example of Toto's signature and, on the reverse, a drawing of a prancing horse presumably although not certainly, by the artist. In 1547 Toto worked on the decorations for the funeral of Henry VIII as well as those for the coronation of Edward VI, during whose reign he worked on costumes and settings for revels at court. Ultimately he also designed decorations for Edward's funeral. As a new year's gift in 1552 Toto presented Edward VI with a portrait of a duke, 'steyned upon cloth of silver' (Auerbach, 66–7).

In 1551 he and John Leades supervised two teams of painters who erected a temporary banqueting house in Hyde Park for the reception of a French embassy. Toto died intestate before 1 November 1554 and the following year the crown paid his widow, Katherine, outstanding debts for the painting of ships.

Anthony Toto was the most prominent of a number of Italian artists who worked at the English court during the sixteenth century, nearly all of whom showed extreme versatility in the range of commissions they were willing to undertake. The artist's career demonstrates this quality, encompassing work on sepulchral monuments, the design of architecture, religious and secular painting on both walls and independent supports, and the decoration of sculpture, as well as the design of revel and funeral decoration.   P. G. MATTHEWS

Sources G. Vasari, *Le vite de' più eccelenti pittori scultori e architetti: nelle redazioni del 1550 e 1568*, ed. R. Bettarini (Florence, 1967) · E. Auerbach, *Tudor artists* (1954) · Thieme & Becker, *Allgemeines Lexikon*, vol. 33 · J. G. Nichols, 'Notices of the contemporaries and successors of Holbein', *Archaeologia*, 39 (1863), 19–46, esp. 36 · E. Croft-Murray, *Decorative painting in England, 1537–1837*, 1 (1962), 17–18, 21, 26, 164–5, 176 · R. Strong, 'More Tudor artists', *Burlington Magazine*, 108 (1966), 83–5 · *Literary remains of King Edward the Sixth*, ed. J. G. Nichols, 2 vols., Roxburghe Club, 75 (1857), vol. 1, p. cccv; vol. 2, p. 590

Tottell [Tottel, Tothill], **Richard** (*b.* in or before **1528**, *d.* **1593**), printer and bookseller, was the third son of William Tothill, fishmonger and citizen of Exeter, and his wife, Elizabeth (*née* Matthew). Richard was one of eleven children, with seven sisters and three brothers, Geoffrey (*d.* 1574), who would later become recorder and MP for Exeter, John, and Robert. Their father was prosperous, becoming bailiff, sheriff, and eventually mayor of Exeter in 1552. The family name was written variously as Tathill, Tothill, Tottel, Tottell, Tottle, Tottyll, or Toutell; Richard referred to himself as Tothill but signed himself Tottyl.

Tottell served his apprenticeship successively with the printers William Middleton (*d.* 1547) and William Powell, who married Middleton's widow, Elizabeth, and he was admitted as a freeman of London and a member of the Stationers' Company on 19 January 1552. His career flourished from the outset. He seems to have been well connected with the London legal élite and on 12 April 1553, a few months before Edward VI's death, he was granted the exclusive right to print for seven years 'almaner bokes of oure temporall lawe called the Common lawe' (*CPR, Edward VI*, 5.47); in 1582 the city's remembrancer, Thomas Norton, claimed that Tottell had gained the privilege 'at [the] sute of the Judges' (Arber, *Regs. Stationers*, 2.775). When Mary came to the throne in 1553, Tottell was able to benefit openly from the patronage of a clique of eminent lawyers hitherto in exile on the continent, among them William Rastell, Thomas More's nephew, and Tottell's patent for common-law books was renewed on 1 May 1556.

When the Stationers' Company was formally incorporated on 4 May 1557, Tottell was listed sixty-seventh out of the ninety-seven members named in the charter. A month later he printed the work with which he has since become most associated, a collection of early Tudor court poetry that included poems by Sir Thomas Wyatt and Henry Howard, earl of Surrey; entitled *Songes and Sonettes*, it is better known today as 'Tottell's Miscellany'. It was reprinted at least eight times before 1600 and it was one of seven titles whose rights of publication were yielded by Tottell to the company in 1584 for 'the reliefe of the poore of the saide Companie' (Arber, *Regs. Stationers*, 2.786). The year 1557 also saw the publication by Tottell, John Cawood, and John Walley of the first English edition of the works of Thomas More, and the printing by Tottell of Surrey's translation of the *Aeneid*, and Thomas Tusser's *A Hundreth Good Pointes of Husbandrie*.

On 12 January 1559, Tottell's common-law patent was renewed by Elizabeth for as long 'as he shall behave and demesne him selfe well in using of the said priviledge', effectively for life; his name also appears in her general coronation pardon dated three days later (Byrom, 223). It seems to have been at about this time that he married Jane, or Johan (that is, Joan), the daughter of Richard Grafton, who had been the king's printer during the reign of Edward VI and whose *Chronicle* Tottell would later publish. A son, William, was born in 1560, who entered Middle Temple in 1576 with Richard Grafton the younger, and later became one of the six clerks in chancery; he married Catherine, the daughter of Sir John Denham. Tottell's other known children were Alice (who married Thomas Colthurst in 1582), James, Anne (who married William Pennyman in 1594), Judith, and Richard.

To the aggrievement of other less prosperous stationers who claimed in a 1577 petition that he sold law books 'at excessive prices, to the hinderance of a greate number of pore studentes', Tottell profited over the years by shrewdly taking advantage of his law-book monopoly, publishing *The Bookes of Yeares and Termes* and other innovative and improved educational legal texts such as an annotated Magna Carta; in all he published over 100 items relating to the common law (Arber, *Regs. Stationers*, 1.111). In 1577 a dispute with the newly appointed queen's printer, Christopher Barker, over the publishing rights of abridgements of statutes was resolved by the Stationers' Company: Barker was 'to have but half the benefitt During his lief' and all copies were to carry his imprint only (ibid., 1.115). Barker's own report on printing privileges submitted to Lord Burghley in December 1582 claimed that 'the patent of the Common Lawe hath ben very beneficiall … but nowe it is of much lesse value then before': in other words, Barker felt that Tottell had effectively exploited it to the full (ibid., 1.116). It was perhaps in response to this report that on 18 February 1583 Tottell took the precaution of retrospectively entering, at a cost of 17s. 6d., at least fifty titles in the company's register, most having been printed under his patent, and some published many years before. As Christopher Knott argues, the increasing value of Tottell's patent meant that he was 'less willing to risk capital on other types of publishing' as his career progressed (Knott, 311). However, he did make unsuccessful attempts to gain patents for the printing of cosmographical books and tables, and for the domestic manufacture of paper which was at this time all imported; an earlier effort to set up a paper mill with other stationers had failed. In 1583 he was noted as having three printing presses although he 'useth but one' (Arber, *Regs. Stationers*, 1.248). After 1587 he printed very little.

Throughout his career Tottell was a man of considerable substance, able to make sizeable financial contributions to the Stationers' Company and other official causes. In 1588 he was one of only two members of the company able to contribute £100 towards a royal loan, in addition to £30 he had already contributed through the company. He was also an important member of the company, rising swiftly through the corporate offices and serving as master in 1578–9 and 1584–5. In 1587–8 he was noted as having joined with other wealthy stationers in promoting the passage of the 1586 decrees of Star Chamber for the regulation of printing, paying £5 towards the company's costs.

For all of his career Tottell worked at the sign of the Hand and Star, formerly the premises of Henry Smith (d. 1550), located on the north side of Fleet Street, within Temple Bar and conveniently close to the inns of court and the law courts. In 1556 he bought two houses and three shops near the Hand and Star; in July of that same year Ellen Cowper was indicted for stealing £3 from his house. From 1572 onwards he also began to acquire land piecemeal in Little Missenden and Amersham, Buckinghamshire, hoping to found a family estate. In July 1580 he leased a mansion house, Pury Place, in Harmondsworth, Middlesex, and in 1588 he retired to Wiston, Pembrokeshire. In September 1589 his absence from London led him to be formally discharged of his responsibilities as a member of the Stationers' Company's governing body but 'havinge bene always a lovinge & orderly brother in the cumpany, & nowe absent [not] for any cause savinge his infyrmytie & farr dwelling from the cyty', these were to be restored to him whenever he was in the city (Greg and Boswell, 33). As late as 1591 he was still able to contribute towards a company assessment for the provisioning of royal ships. He died in Wiston, either in early July or on 1 September 1593, survived by his mother, his wife and six children, and a brother, John. The common-law patent passed to Charles Yetsweirt, to whose father, Nicasius, one of the clerks of the signet, a reversion had been granted in 1577.

During his lifetime Tottell had benefited from friends on both sides of the Tudor religious divide and had proved himself both cautious and clever in politically unstable times. Probably a Roman Catholic, he chose to settle his affairs by means of a family settlement rather than will and testament, although this may merely have been because he preferred to keep his affairs private. An extremely prosperous 'new man' of much influence in his day, he ultimately failed in his great venture to found a county dynasty, his hard-won estates eventually leaving the Tottell family through his granddaughter Joan's marriage into the Drake family. His legacy lies in his reputation and achievements as an innovative publisher.

ANNA GREENING

Sources H. J. Byrom, 'Richard Tottell: his life and work', *The Library*, 4th ser., 8 (1927–8), 199–232 · Stationers' Company, London, Tottell papers · Arber, *Regs. Stationers* · W. W. Greg and E. Boswell, eds., *Records of the court of the Stationers' Company, 1576 to 1602, from register B* (1930) · *STC, 1475–1640* · liber A, Stationers' Company, London · M. Pearson, 'An index to "liber A": a volume of the records of the Stationers' Company of London for the period 1559–1791', MA diss., Victoria University of Wellington, 1980 · H. R. Plomer, *Abstracts from the wills of English printers and stationers from 1492 to 1630* (1903) · *DNB* · E. G. Duff, *A century of the English book trade* (1905) · catalogue, Bucks. RLSS, Drake papers · A. Greening, 'A 16th-century stationer and his business connections: the Tottell family documents (1448–1915) at Stationers' Hall', *The book trade and its customers, 1450–1900: historical essays for Robin Myers*, ed. A. Hunt, G. Mandelbrote, and A. Shell (1997), 1–8 · BL, Lansdowne MS 56, fols. 7r–8v · P. Blayney, 'William Cecil and the stationers', *The Stationers' Company and the book trade, 1550–1990*, ed. R. Myers and M. Harris, St Paul's Bibliographies (1997), 11–34 · C. A. Knott, 'Richard Tottell', *The British literary book trade, 1475–1700*, ed. J. K. Bracken and J. Silver, DLitB, 170 (1996), 308–13 · *CPR* · B. Dickins, 'Stationers made free of the city in 1551/2 and 1552', *Transactions of the Cambridge Bibliographical Society*, 1 (1949–53), 194–5 · P. W. Hasler, 'Tothill, Geoffrey', HoP, *Commons, 1558–1603* · S. Clark, 'Wisdom literature of the seventeenth century: a guide to the contents of the "Bacon-Tottel" commonplace books', *Transactions of the Cambridge Bibliographical Society*, 6 (1972–6), 291–305; 7 (1977–80), 46–73
Archives Worshipful Company of Stationers and Newspaper-makers, London, documents | Worshipful Company of Stationers and Newspaper-makers, London, Stationers' Company archives

Tottenham, Charles (1685–1758), politician, was the only child of Edward Tottenham (*d.* 1712), landowner, of Tottenhamgreen, Ballyloskeran, near Taghmon, co. Wexford, and his wife, Elizabeth, daughter of Samuel Hayman (*d.* *c.*1713) of Youghal, co. Cork. By 1713 he had married Ellinor (*d.* 1745), the daughter of John Cliffe, of Mulrankin, co. Wexford, a prominent tory member of the Irish House of Commons. Tottenham had to wait until the general election of 1727 before he himself acquired a seat in the Irish parliament, for the borough of New Ross, possibly on the interest of Arthur Annesley, fifth earl of Anglesey.

Except for one famous incident, Tottenham made little mark in public life. It seems likely that he shared the high-church proclivities of his family and connections, who included the Wexford families of Loftus and Colclough. By 1727 their brand of toryism had been transmuted into die-hard support for the 'patriot' opposition. Tottenham's moment of glory probably came in November 1731, when it would appear that he gave the crucial vote to defeat a proposal from government to secure long-term funding of the Irish national debt. According to legend (which does not identify correctly the particular division concerned), he had only arrived at the last minute to vote, after an overnight ride from co. Wexford, having heard that the question was to come on sooner than expected. He had been obliged to force his way past the serjeant-at-arms, since he was 'undressed, in dirty boots, and splashed up to his shoulders', and it was contrary to the rules of the House of Commons for a member to appear improperly attired. But, so the story went, the speaker decided that he had no power to exclude Tottenham, who strode into the chamber in his riding boots 'to vote for the country'. Little was heard of this curious episode at the time, and nothing subsequently until 1749, when an engraving was made of 'Tottenham in his boots', carrying a riding crop, on the steps of the Parliament House. This was based on a portrait by Justin Pope Stevens, evidently painted in 1749 but dated as 1731. The probable occasion for the engraving was a parliamentary fracas in the 1749 session over the appropriation of the surplus in parliamentary funds. Tottenham was briefly to regret his renown when he voted with the government in favour of the altered money bill four years later, in 1753, and was subjected to a stinging rebuke in the *Dublin Spy*, which accused him of exchanging his hallowed boots for 'Court stilts and dirty spatter-dashes' and declared that his name would 'stink on the dunghill of bad fame to all ages' (*Dublin Spy*, 24 Dec 1753, 7). In fact, this indiscretion was soon forgotten, and in the later eighteenth century his reputation not only recovered but steadily grew. Indeed, the toast 'Tottenham in his boots' became a staple of Irish patriotic conviviality. Though his was not the only vote delivered in boots in the Irish parliament, it was by far the most often remembered. 'This anecdote could not die while the Irish parliament lived' (Barrington, 1.105–6), wrote Sir Jonah Barrington, whose account of the episode related it to a division on the appropriation of a revenue surplus. Later still, opponents of the Anglo-Irish Union of 1801 depicted 'Tottenham and his boots' as having successfully resisted the efforts of an English minister 'to deprive Ireland of a resident legislature' (obituary notice of Lord Arran, *c.*1809, Arran MSS, T 3200/2/48).

Tottenham and his first wife had six sons and two daughters. His second marriage, in 1746, to Mary (*c.*1694–1777), the twice-widowed daughter of John Grogan of Johnstown, co. Wexford, who had been previously married to two other Wexford gentlemen, Major Andrew Knox and William Hore of Harperstown, produced no children. Tottenham died on 20 September 1758 and his eldest son, John, later first baronet, succeeded him and served as MP for New Ross and Fethard in the Irish parliament. His son Charles Tottenham (afterwards Loftus) enjoyed a long and successful political career, but as a ministerialist and pro-unionist rather than a patriot, and received no less than five separate peerage creations, as Baron and Viscount Loftus, then earl (1794) and marquess (1800) of Ely in the Irish peerage, and Baron Loftus (1801) in that of the United Kingdom. D. W. HAYTON

Sources *DNB* · Burke, *Gen. Ire.* (1904), 594–5 · H. L. Tottenham, 'Tottenham in his boots', *N&Q*, 7th ser., 6 (1888), 41–2 · J. Barrington, *Personal sketches of his own times*, 1 (1827), 105–6 · W. E. H. Lecky, *A history of Ireland in the eighteenth century*, 1 (1892), 459–60 · *The journals of the House of Commons of the kingdom of Ireland*, 3–6 (1753) · R. E. Burns, *Irish parliamentary politics in the eighteenth century*, 2 (1990), 8 · *The king's business: letters on the administration of Ireland, 1740–1761, from the papers of Sir Robert Wilmot*, ed. J. Walton (1996), 134 · PRO NIre., Arran MSS, T 3200/2/48 · *Engraved Brit. ports.*, 4.294 · A. Crookshank and the Knight of Glin [D. Fitzgerald], eds., *Irish portraits, 1660–1860* (1969), 35 [exhibition catalogue, Dublin, London, and Belfast, 14 Aug 1969 – 9 March 1970]

Likenesses attrib. J. Latham, oils, 1731, NG Ire. • A. Miller, mezzotint (after oil painting by J. Pope Stevens, 1749), BM, NG Ire.

Touche [*formerly* Touch], **Sir George Alexander, first baronet** (1861–1935), accountant, was born in Edinburgh on 24 May 1861 as George Alexander Touch (the 'e' was added in 1906 by royal licence and authority because of annoyance with the persistent mispronunciation of his name), the third of the seven children of Anthony Murray Touch, a banker, an agent with the Edinburgh branch of the Union Bank of Scotland, and his wife, Margaret, daughter of Alexander Guild. He was educated at the Bonnington Academy, the Edinburgh Institute, and Edinburgh University before becoming indentured to the Scottish chartered accountant Alexander Thomas Niven in 1878. He was admitted to membership of the Society of Accountants in Edinburgh in 1883, having distinguished himself in actuarial science, and then, in common with many other Scots at that time, set off immediately for London, where he joined Broads, Paterson, and May, chartered accountants. On 4 June 1887 he married Jessie (1862/3–1917), daughter of Isaac Brown, wine merchant; they had four sons.

In addition to accountancy, Touche's career encompassed politics and the management of investment trusts. He was appointed secretary of the newly formed Industrial and General Trust in 1889 which, in common with many other investment trusts, suffered following the Baring crisis of 1890, with the result that its capital was reduced in 1894. Following his appointment as manager, he worked to place the trust on a profitable basis and was subsequently appointed director in 1898 and chairman in 1908. He quickly became prominent in the investment world, and the restoration to prosperity of the Winchester House group of companies, as his investment trusts came to be known, formed a large and perhaps principal part of his life's work. It has been said that he did a great deal to lay down the principles on which investment trusts have been run ever since, and his obituary notice in the *Accountants' Magazine* saw him principally as a creator and restorer of the trust company movement. At the time of his death in 1935 he was director of twelve major trust companies and chairman of nine of them. His many directorships outside the investment trust movement included also chairmanships of the Anglo-Argentine Tramways Company, the Midland Railway Company of Western Australia, and the Mexican Southern Railway.

When called in by companies in difficulty, Touche saw himself as a reconstructor rather than a liquidator, and work in this area encouraged him to found an accountancy practice, George A. Touch & Co. (now Deloitte and Touche), in London in 1899. The firm was initially located in Bartholomew Lane but moved to Basildon House, Moorgate, in 1901. He later opened an office in Birmingham but his main energy was devoted to developing the firm's overseas operations. The first branch in Canada (in Toronto) was opened in 1909 and in the 1920s and 1930s his firm was one of the leading accountancy practices in that country. His first branch in the United States, Touch, Niven & Co., was established jointly with John B. Niven, the son of his own principal; this was set up in New York in 1900, and further offices were opened in Minneapolis, Chicago, St Louis, and Cleveland between 1913 and 1919. A Paris office was opened in 1920. At home, the firm remained relatively modest in size, having a staff of just 67 in 1939, which may be contrasted with the 345 partners and 4303 professional staff located in 22 offices in the United Kingdom in 1995.

Touche was a staunch Conservative who was returned to parliament for North Islington in 1910; he retired because of ill health in 1918. He was an accomplished speaker who spoke with authority on financial matters. He became an alderman of the City of London in 1915 and was sheriff in 1915–16. Knighted in 1917, he was created a baronet in 1920 and was also one of his majesty's lieutenants for the City of London. In addition, he was made a knight of the Serbian order of St Sava.

Touche served on the council of the Society of Accountants in Edinburgh from 1904 to 1908. Outside his business life, his recreations included riding and swimming. He also wrote poems which he sent in printed form to his friends at Christmas. Soon after his wife died in 1917, his health deteriorated. His public appearances became increasingly rare, as he worked mainly from his home near Dorking, Surrey, and travelled up to London only for board meetings. He died at Broomfield, Westcott, near Dorking, Surrey, on 7 July 1935. He was succeeded as second baronet by his eldest son, Norman George Touche.

JOHN RICHARD EDWARDS

Sources A. B. Richards, *Touche Ross & Co., 1899–1981: the origins and growth of the United Kingdom firm* (1981) • A. B. Richards, 'Touche, Sir George Alexander', *DBB* • M. E. Murphy, 'Sir George Touche, Bart, CA, 1861–1935: a memoir', *Business History Review*, 34 (1960), 467–77 • *Accountancy*, 116 (1995), 18 • *Accountants' Magazine*, 39 (1935), 493–5 • *CGPLA Eng. & Wales* (1935) • m. cert. • d. cert.
Archives HLRO, corresp. with A. Bonar Law
Likenesses portrait, repro. in Richards, *Touche Ross & Co.*
Wealth at death £187,285 19s. 5d.: probate, 6 Aug 1935, *CGPLA Eng. & Wales*

Touchet, Anne, countess of Castlehaven. *See* Brydges, Anne, Lady Chandos (1580–1647).

Touchet, George [*name in religion* Anselm] (*d.* before **1689**?), Benedictine monk, was born at Stalbridge, Dorset, the second son of Mervin *Touchet, twelfth Baron Audley and second earl of Castlehaven (1593–1631), who was convicted and executed for rape and sodomy in 1631, and his first wife, Elizabeth Barnham (1592–1622x4). He made his monastic profession at the English Benedictine priory of St Gregory, Douai, on 22 November 1643, taking the name Anselm in religion. He worked on the English mission and may have taught, from 1657, at the College of St Vedast in Douai. However, it is possible that he remained in England, as he became chaplain to Queen Catherine of Braganza with rooms at Somerset House and a stipend of £100 a year; he was performing weddings at St James's from 1662 until 1672 and at Somerset House during 1674–5. In 1675 Touchet was banished, and in 1678 he was expressly excluded by an act of parliament from the succession to the earldom of Castlehaven, which passed to his brother

Mervyn, in 1684. In 1682 Touchet wrote a letter to the Brussels nuncio concerning the oath of allegiance, but was 'never employed in official [monastic] life and appears to have died before the Chapter of 1689' (Athanasius, 1999, 103).

Touchet was the author of a work of Catholic controversy, *Historical collections out of several grave protestant historians concerning the changes of religion and the strange confusions following from thence*, first published (without a place of publication) in 1674; an amended edition appeared in London in 1684. Such historical work was typical of the Benedictine approach of the time: an assertion that England could be saved from perdition not so much by theology as by an exploration of historical continuity and by a demonstration of Catholic authority. In this Touchet was in the company of Hugh Serenus Cressy, James Maurus Corker, and John Dryden's *Defence* of the duchess of York's conversion. A copy of a manuscript of Touchet's, a translation of the work of the Capuchin Constantine Pauret de Barbanson (1581–1632), was published in an abridged form in 1928 as *The Secret Paths of Divine Love*. Touchet's spiritual writing associates him closely with the tradition of the English Benedictine mystic, Augustine Baker.

THOMPSON COOPER, *rev.* DOMINIC AIDAN BELLENGER

Sources A. Allanson, *Biography of the English Benedictines* (1999) · Athanasius [P. A. Allanson], 'Biography of the English Benedictines', Ampleforth Abbey, Yorkshire · D. Lunn, *The English Benedictines, 1540–1688* (1980) · GEC, *Peerage* · T. A. Birrell, 'James Maurus Corker and Dryden's *Conversion*', *English Studies*, 54 (1973), 461–9, esp. 467 · J. C. M. Weale, ed., *Registers of the Catholic chapels royal and of the Portuguese embassy chapel, 1662–1829*, Catholic RS, 38 (1941) · *The old brotherhood of the English secular clergy: catalogue of part of the archives* (1968), 31

Touchet, James. *See* Tuchet, James, seventh Baron Audley (*c*.1463–1497).

Touchet, James, **third earl of Castlehaven** (*bap.* 1612, *d.* 1684), army officer, was the eldest son and heir of Mervin *Touchet, second earl of Castlehaven (1593–1631), and his first wife, Elizabeth (1592–1622x4), daughter and heir of Benedict Barnham, alderman of London. In 1631, after a trial in the House of Lords, his father was executed for 'unnatural offences' involving gross sexual misconduct against his second wife, Lady Anne Brydges, *née* Stanley, daughter of the fifth earl of Derby, and her daughter from her first marriage, Elizabeth Brydges (1614/15–1679), who had been thirteen years old when she was married to James, her stepbrother, in 1628. Arrangements in the Touchet household were not conducive to filial piety, and James was instrumental in bringing his father to justice. He succeeded to the Irish earldom of Castlehaven with the swing of the headsman's axe, but most of his father's English patrimony was lost to Lord Cottington. The title Baron Audley of Hely was granted to him in 1633, but in so far as the creation was virtually a restoration to an ancient dignity it lay outside the power of the crown alone to make it, and it was not confirmed until parliament passed an act in 1678.

Military career Castlehaven began a military career on the continent before returning home in 1638 by royal command and attending the king to Berwick. After another season on the continent the earl was in Ireland at the outbreak of the rising there on 23 October 1641. When he offered his assistance to put down the rising, his treatment at the hands of the protestant lords justices Sir William Parsons and Sir John Borlase contributed to the growing mistrust between the Catholics of the pale and the Dublin administration, helping to propel the former into the rebel camp. Indicted of high treason in May 1642, Castlehaven was placed in the custody of one of the sheriffs of Dublin, whence he fled the following September, having learned of an intention to place him under more strict confinement in the castle. He later professed that he had intended to go to England via France, but in the event he was persuaded to accept a command as general of horse under Sir Thomas Preston in the army of the confederate Catholics when he came to their headquarters at Kilkenny. Suspicious of the confederate organization, the Ulstermen believed that Castlehaven was, in effect, an Ormondist plant, and that his 'escape' had been contrived as a means of opening a line of communication between Dublin and Kilkenny whereby Ormond, Castlehaven's kinsman by marriage, might reach an agreement with the confederates.

Castlehaven served with Preston at the capture of Burros Castle on 30 December 1642, and of Birr on 19 January 1643. Entrusted with the execution of the articles of capitulation of the latter, he conveyed the garrison safely to Athy. On 18 March he commanded the horse at the battle of Ross, where the confederates were defeated by Ormond. When Preston, having rallied his forces, sat down before Ballynekill, Castlehaven intercepted and routed a strong detachment sent to raise the siege under Colonel Crawford near Athy on 13 April. Although he was primarily concerned with the defence of Kilkenny, he was sent into Munster later in the spring to counter Murrough O'Brien, earl of Inchiquin, scourge of the rebellious southwest. On 4 June he fought with the forces of Sir Charles Vavasour near Castle Lyons, inflicting very heavy losses and capturing Vavasour himself, as well as his cannon and baggage. Having returned to Kilkenny, he was afterwards employed in reducing the outstanding fortresses in co. Kildare between the Barrow and the Liffey, but his further progress was stopped by the conclusion of the cessation, in promoting which he had taken an active part, on 15 September.

Having helped in the shipment of Ormond's Irish forces to assist the king in England, in 1644 Castlehaven commanded a force of 6000 foot and 600 horse sent to Ulster to aid Owen Roe O'Neill against the New Scots commander there, Major-General Robert Monro, who refused to recognize the cessation. After suppressing a rising in co. Mayo *en route*, Castlehaven joined up with O'Neill at Portlester, and towards the end of July both armies marched towards Tanderagee. Failing to engage Monro, the campaign fizzled out in the trenches before Charlemont, ending in mutual recrimination when Castlehaven withdrew his forces, their supplies exhausted, into co. Cavan. Having seen his army into winter quarters, and having arrived at Kilkenny, he found the supreme council in a state of consternation owing to the defection of Lord Inchiquin and the surrender of Duncannon fort by Sir Laurence Esmonde. Castlehaven served as a volunteer under Preston at the siege of Duncannon, and was present at its rendition on 18 March 1645. The truce with Inchiquin drawing near its expiration, Castlehaven was sent with 5000 foot and 1000 horse into Munster, speedily reduced all the castles in the baronies of Imokilly and Barrimore, and, having wasted the country up to the walls of Cork, sat down before Youghall, 'thinking to distress the place' into a surrender (*DNB*). But the town was relieved, leaving Castlehaven little to do beyond destroying the harvest until placing his army in winter quarters. He returned to Kilkenny in late November. He was one of the signatories to the contract made with Rinuccini on 19 February 1646, agreeing not to conclude a peace until provision had been made for the full exercise of the Catholic religion. Predictably, however, he supported the subsequent first Ormond peace, and was even employed by the lord lieutenant in a futile attempt to persuade the nuncio to accept it. Castlehaven then accompanied Ormond on his withdrawal to Dublin, bearing the sword of state before him at his entrance on 13 September.

Castlehaven lent his support to Ormond's negotiation with the Westminster parliament, and had already left Ireland by the time the English commissioners arrived. He went to France, and was present at the battle of Landrecies, fighting in Prince Rupert's troop. Afterwards he retired to St Germain, and remained in attendance on the queen and prince of Wales until returning with Ormond into Ireland. When the lord lieutenant secured his second treaty with the confederates in January 1649, Castlehaven took command of the horse, and with an army of 5000 foot and 1000 cavalry he was sent to reduce O'Neill's outposts in the Irish midlands. After seeing off a challenge for his command from Lord Taaffe, whom some members of the general assembly plainly preferred to Castlehaven, the earl was on hand to share in the ignominy of Ormond's defeat at Rathmines in August 1649. He signed the order for the defence of Drogheda, and, having been entrusted with a special command over forces destined for the relief of the southern towns, he succeeded on 6 October in throwing 1500 men into Wexford, a dubious achievement which enabled the commander of that place, Synnot, to break off his correspondence with Cromwell. A few days later Castlehaven forced Ireton to raise the siege of Duncannon. He was then appointed governor of Waterford, with 1000 men under his command to reinforce the garrison, and was refused admittance by the citizenry.

In the following year Castlehaven was appointed commander-in-chief of the Leinster forces, taking the field in March with some 4000 men. But he was too weak to confront Hewson, contenting himself with watching his movements, and when Kilkenny fell to Cromwell at the end of the month, he withdrew to the borders of King's county, and in June made an unsuccessful attempt to relieve Tecroghan, which 'was by the confession of all parties, even of the enemy, allowed to be the gallantest action that had been performed since the beginning of the war' (*DNB*). Afterwards finding it impossible to keep an army together, he granted commissions for horse and foot to all who applied for them, whereby, although managing to keep up an appearance of war, he gave to it the character of a freebooting campaign, which caused as much harm to his own party as to the enemy. When the citizens of Limerick refused to co-operate with the lord lieutenant, Castlehaven did what he could to deflect Ormond's growing determination to quit the kingdom, but to no avail. Having appointed Clanricarde his lord deputy, and Castlehaven commander-in-chief in Munster and Clare, Ormond sailed for France in December. The approach of Ireton persuaded the townsmen of Limerick of the need to co-operate with the confederate command, enabling Castlehaven to undertake a successful offensive into co. Kerry. Early in the following year he crossed the Shannon into co. Tipperary, but the object of the expedition was frustrated by the plundering propensities of his officers, and, being compelled to retreat before Ireton and Broghill, he recrossed the Shannon at Athlone. He failed to prevent Ireton from besieging Limerick, and the capitulation of that city on 27 October, followed by the loss of Clare, forced him and Clanricarde into Iar Connaught. But with the situation growing daily more desperate, he was on 10 April dispatched by the lord deputy into France for the purpose of soliciting aid to enable the latter to maintain 'a mountain war' (ibid.).

Continental campaigns Castlehaven reached Brest after a sharp encounter with an English vessel in the channel, and was posted to St Germain. Having failed to obtain the supplies required, he was granted permission to enter the service of the prince of Condé in the war of the Fronde. He was appointed to the command of a regiment of horse and was present at the fight in Faubourg St Antoine on 2 July 1651; after quitting Paris with Condé, he was taken prisoner at Comercy by Turenne. Thanks to the intervention of the duke of York he was shortly afterwards exchanged and was placed at the head of the Irish regiments fighting for the French crown in the war with Spain, holding the rank of *maréchal-de-camp*, or major-general. He was present at the sieges of Rocroi in 1653 and of Arras in 1654, the relief of Valenciennes and the capture of Condé in 1656, the siege of St Guislain and the relief of Cambrai in 1657, and the battle of the Dunes in 1658. He returned to England with Charles II. On the outbreak of the war with the Netherlands, Castlehaven served as a volunteer in several naval actions, and in June 1667 landed at Ostend with 2400 recruits for the Old English regiment, of which he was appointed colonel. His men were used to strengthen the garrisons at Nieuport, Lille, Courtrai, Oudenarde, and other places. He returned to England with the conclusion of the peace of Aix-la-Chapelle on 2 May 1668. He took a commission in the Spanish army in 1676, serving in the trenches before Maastricht—'by much the bloodiest siege that I ever saw'

(*DNB*)—and was at the siege of Charleroi in 1677 and the battle of Mons in 1678. After the peace of Nijmegen, he returned to England. On 19 or 20 June 1679 Castlehaven obtained a settlement for his second marriage—to Elizabeth (*d.* 1720), apparently daughter of one Graves—within just over three months of burying his first wife.

In 1680 Castlehaven published his *Memoirs*, in which he described the Irish wars, discussing at length the various cessations and treaties between Charles I and Charles II, their lord lieutenant, and the Catholic rebels in Ireland during the 1640s. The publication at the time of the crisis over the Popish Plot was somewhat inopportune, although not without calculation. The earl's dedication of the book to the king was described as presumptuous. The *Memoirs* sparked a violent controversy when the lord privy seal, Arthur Annesley, earl of Anglesey, stung by the imputations of treason and disloyalty which Castlehaven laid at the door of New English protestants in Ireland, replied to Castlehaven's recollection of the events of the 1640s in *A Letter from a Person of Honour in the Country*. Anglesey's own recollections were felt to have calumnied the late king, and at the request of Charles II the duke of Ormond replied to Anglesey in turn. When Anglesey retorted in another *Letter*, the duke appealed to the privy council to appoint a committee to examine the matter, which eventually ended with Anglesey's dismissal and the transfer of the privy seal to Lord Halifax. Coincidentally, about the same time there was a move to have Castlehaven struck off the Irish establishment. His one reliable source of post-Restoration income in jeopardy, in the spring of 1683 it was rumoured that the earl intended to join several other noblemen in volunteering to take up arms in the 'holy war' with the Turks in Hungary. However, he appears never to have set out, and died at Kilcash, co. Tipperary, his sister's house, on 11 October 1684, and was succeeded by his youngest brother, Mervyn—the second son, George *Touchet (*d.* before 1689?), a Benedictine monk, having been expressly passed over in the act formally restoring the barony of Audley in 1678.

SEAN KELSEY

Sources DNB · GEC, *Peerage*, 3.86–8 · *CSP dom.*, 1682–3
Archives BL, letters to Sir Robert Southwell, Add. MS 34345

Touchet, Mervin, second earl of Castlehaven (1593–1631), convicted rapist and sodomite, was the eldest son of George Touchet, eleventh Baron Audley in the English peerage and from September 1616, for the last five months of his life, first earl of Castlehaven in the peerage of Ireland (1550/51–1617), and his first wife, Lucy Mervyn (*d.* 1609/10), daughter and heir of Sir James Mervyn of Fonthill Gifford, Wiltshire, and his wife, Amy Clarke. Little is known of Mervin Touchet's early life and education. From 1600 his family lived mostly in Ireland on estates in Munster and, after the planting of Ulster, in co. Tyrone and Armagh, but Mervin apparently preferred life in England. In 1608, allegedly because of this (and to prove his own commitment to Ireland), George Touchet conveyed to Mervin the family's major English properties: Nether

Stowey in Somerset and Stalbridge in Dorset. In the same year Mervin was knighted.

In 1611 Touchet was admitted to the Middle Temple (where his father had been a member); that same year, Sir James Mervyn left his 'well-beloved' grandson the Wiltshire estates of Compton Bassett and Widcombe (Herrup, 11). Also about 1611 Touchet married Elizabeth Barnham (1592–1622×4), eldest of four coheirs of the wealthy London alderman Benedict *Barnham. Her inheritance included properties in Middlesex, Essex, Hampshire, and Kent as well as London. Their first son, James *Touchet, was baptized in 1612. The couple had three daughters (Lucy, Dorothy, and Frances) as well as two more sons (George *Touchet and Mervin).

Mervin Touchet inherited his father's Irish lands and title in 1617. In 1620 his estate again expanded. Despite Sir James Mervyn's desire that Fonthill Gifford remain in the male Mervyn line, Castlehaven purchased it from his cousin Sir Henry *Mervyn for £25,000. According to the diarist Walter Yonge, in the early 1620s Castlehaven and his wife became Roman Catholics. The earl repeatedly denied this, yet most and perhaps all of his children were active Catholics. Catholic histories suggest that the earl returned to the Church of England only when as a widower he decided to remarry.

Castlehaven married his second wife, Lady Anne *Brydges, *née* Stanley (1580–1647), eldest of the three daughters and coheirs of Ferdinando *Stanley, fifth earl of Derby, and widow of Grey *Brydges, fifth Baron Chandos, on 22 July 1624. Anne was significantly older than Mervin but, like him, was recently widowed with several children. Her two sons (George and William) and perhaps her youngest daughter (Frances) with Chandos remained in the care of their grandmother Alice Egerton, dowager countess of Derby [see Spencer, Alice]; their eldest daughter, Elizabeth, joined her mother at Fonthill Gifford. In 1628, aged thirteen, Elizabeth was married to Castlehaven's heir, James, Lord Audley.

The marriage was not happy. Within a year Audley had left Fonthill Gifford and his wife was involved (whether willingly or not remains unclear) with a favourite of Castlehaven's named Henry Skipwith. This adultery, exacerbated by the earl's excessive generosity to Skipwith, precipitated a confrontation between father and son that ended with the son's complaint to the king in the 'hope to find him a father when my own forsakes me' (PRO, SP 16/175/2). Between November 1630 and April 1631 what began as familial tension over property broadened into a story that implicated virtually everyone at Fonthill Gifford in disorder, promiscuity, or pandering.

The privy council found evidence of 'crimes too horrid for a Christian man to mention' (Northants. RO, Isham-Lamport MS 3339, p. 12), the most legally serious of which were the felonies of rape and sodomy. On 25 April 1631 the earl was tried for helping one manservant (Giles Broadway) to rape the countess of Castlehaven and for committing sodomy with another servant (Florence Fitzpatrick). Henry Skipwith was never formally accused of any crime. Castlehaven became the first peer tried for felony under

Charles I. The king hoped that women in particular would avoid the 'obscene tragedy' of the trial (Hunt. L., Hastings MSS, legal box 5, folder 2(1)), but special scaffolds were built in Westminster Hall to accommodate the inevitable crush of spectators. News writers throughout England and as far away as Massachusetts Bay speculated about the outcome.

Because parliament was not in session Thomas Coventry (the lord keeper) presided over an *ad hoc* court as lord high steward; twenty-seven peers (including virtually the entire privy council) acted as judge and jury. Half a dozen or so testimonies (including those of the countess of Castlehaven and her daughter) graphically detailed a household infested with debauchery. The countess said that her rape was the final act in abuse dating from the beginning of her marriage. Two or three days after they were married, she deposed, Castlehaven abandoned her bed for those of prostitutes and serving boys, ordered servants to expose themselves before her, and encouraged her into sexual intercourse with various of his favourites. The earl's minions controlled household finances and enriched themselves with goods and properties. One married Castlehaven's eldest daughter, a second slept with the heir's wife, and a third was told that he might eventually marry the countess. To further humiliate James, the earl, it was said, intended that the still virginal Elizabeth bear a bastard to be accepted as his son's heir. 'I shall be bold to give your Grace a reason why he became so ill', the attorney-general explained, 'he believed not God' (Northants. RO, Isham-Lamport MS 3339, p. 7). Impiety made Castlehaven unsafe: as the head of a household he contaminated not only his inferiors, but also the patriarchal ideal upon which early modern families and governance were based.

Castlehaven insisted that he was not guilty, that in pursuit of a hastened inheritance and new husband his son and wife had conspired to commit judicial murder. The earl admitted generosity towards his servants, but little else. He accused the countess of adultery and infanticide, his son and daughter-in-law of lust and greed. All the witnesses against him, he reminded the court, would gain materially from his demise; the testimony about rape was inconsistent; and the evidence on sodomy denied the definitive act of penetration. Against common practice the only witnesses against him were his wife and servants. 'It is my estate, my Lords, that does accuse me this day, and nothing else' (Folger Shakespeare Library, MS Vb328/21), the earl insisted. He presented himself as a man in danger from disgruntled inferiors, the victim of a dilemma that illustrated both the need for and the tensions inherent in all hierarchy.

Fantastical as that might seem, the case does have distinctive oddities. The testimony did not fit received definitions of rape or sodomy, and there were contemporary suspicions of suborned evidence. The servants who had figured prominently in the first accusations escaped unharmed; Castlehaven's co-defendants were two more lowly men. The counter-charges included not only conspiracy and corruption, but also perjury, infanticide, and petty treason. The jury debated the case for several hours before returning their convictions, and the final answer was unusually divided: twenty-six votes to convict on rape, but a barely sufficient fifteen to convict on sodomy.

Three weeks separated the trial from Castlehaven's execution. The earl's family petitioned for his pardon, but the king refused to investigate allegations of corruption, and the earl (who disclaimed any interest in mercy) refused to confess guilt. Sir Edward Hyde found Castlehaven on the eve of his death as 'full of pity as ever any martyr was' (BL, Add. MS 17017, fol. 1*v*). On the scaffold at Tower Hill on 14 May, before his beheading, Castlehaven affirmed his faith in the Church of England and in the king's right to try him, but reiterated his protests against the verdict. He was buried the same day in the chapel of the Tower of London. The trial and execution of his co-defendants in July settled few questions since both confessed yet qualified their confessions in ways that supported some of their master's allegations. And by then libels had already begun to appear recasting the story as one of adultery.

James Touchet lost Fonthill Gifford (now in the king's gift) to Frances Cottington, but Charles I returned to the new earl his father's other English lands and titles. On the insistence of the dowager countess of Derby the king pardoned both Anne and Elizabeth. The elder countess of Castlehaven did not remarry; the younger was never permanently reconciled with her husband. The scandal, however, had a continued life. Throughout the 1630s poetry and manuscripts about the story circulated widely, some emphasizing Castlehaven's guilt, others focusing more on his denials. Castlehaven's sister, the prophet Lady Eleanor *Davies, published in 1633 the first of three tracts written by her to exonerate him. The case influenced the plot of Milton's *Masque at Ludlow Castle, or, Comus* (performed originally in 1634 for Castlehaven's in-laws). In 1643, 1679, 1699, and 1708 anonymously authored pamphlets appeared, each rescripting the case to suit contemporary anxieties. From its first edition (1719) on, the editors of *State Trials* included those of Castlehaven, Broadway, and Fitzpatrick. By the early eighteenth century most commentators understood Castlehaven's as a case of sodomy rather than one about discipline, piety, and household order. An extreme example of a generic problem about self-control had become a story about deviant identity. As such it is often cited in histories of male homosexuality.

The law provided the case with a legacy closer to its origins. As early as 1631 at least one practising lawyer, Sir William Drake, privately questioned the court's willingness to accept non-penetrative sex as sodomy; Hutton's law reports (the first one to include the case) agreed. And Sir Matthew Hale used Castlehaven's situation to warn of what he saw as the dangers inherent in the law of rape. The trial was most influential, however, as a precedent in spousal rights; until made redundant by legislation, it was the leading case behind an injured wife's right to testify against her husband.

CYNTHIA B. HERRUP

Sources C. Herrup, *A house in gross disorder: sex, law and the 2nd earl of Castlehaven* (1999) · GEC, *Peerage* · W. Drake, *Fasciculus Mervinensis, being notes historical, genealogical, and heraldic, of the family of Mervyn*

(1873) • Northants. RO, Isham-Lamport papers, MS 3339 • PRO, SP Charles I • Baga de Secretis, PRO • *APC* • *State trials* • *The tryal and condemnation of Mervin, Lord Audley Earl of Castle-Haven, at Westminster, April the 5th 1631, for abetting a rape upon his Countess, committing sodomy with his servants, and commanding and countenancing the debauching his daughter* (1699) • *The trial of Lord Audley, earl of Castlehaven for inhumanely causing his own wife to be ravished and for buggery* (1679) • *The arraignment and conviction of Mervin, Lord Audley, earl of Castlehaven, (who was by 26 peers of the realm found guilty of committing rapine and sodomy) at Westminster, on Monday, April 25, 1631* (1642/3) • *The case of sodomy, in the trial of Mervin, Lord Audley, earl of Castlehaven, for committing a rape and sodomy with two of his servants* (1708) • H. A. C. Sturgess, ed., *Register of admissions to the Honourable Society of the Middle Temple, from the fifteenth century to the year 1944*, 3 vols. (1949)

Archives HLRO, main papers • NL Scot. | Hunt. L., Ellesmere MSS • Hunt. L., Hastings MSS • Leics. RO, Braye MSS • Northants. RO, Finch-Hatton MSS • Northants. RO, Isham-Lamport MSS

Likenesses woodcut, repro. in *Arraignment and conviction*, frontispiece

Wealth at death moveables and rents as high as £50,000 plus significant confiscated estates: Herrup, *A house*, 101–2

Touchet, Samuel (*c*.1705–1773), merchant and politician, was born about 1705, the eldest son of Thomas Touchet (*d*. 1745), a merchant and manufacturer of Manchester, and his wife, Mary, *née* Sworton. Although they thought otherwise, the Touchets of Manchester were not of the same family as the Touchets, lords Audley and earls of Castlehaven. The Manchester Touchets began with Thomas, a pin maker of Warrington, who married well, moved to Manchester, and became the town's wealthiest merchant and manufacturer of linen and cotton goods. The Touchets were Unitarians, and several were trustees of the Cross Street Chapel. Thomas's younger sons continued the business in Manchester, while his eldest son, Samuel, represented the firm in London. Samuel married Dorothy Hallows and had several children, including at least two sons.

Samuel Touchet's business career prospered with interests in the import of raw cotton from the Levant and the West Indies, and linen yarn from Europe. He was so successful in the import of cotton that he was suspected by the Manchester manufacturers of seeking a monopoly. His ambitions in this regard are unclear, but an attempted alliance in the early 1740s with Lewis Paul, the inventor of the first roller-spinning machine, could have given him a monopoly of cotton spinning by means of powered machines. In any case he became personally wealthy, and his business interests diversified during the 1750s into shipping, insurance broking, speculation in naval prizes, and the sugar and slave trades. Like most merchants with wide connections and considerable assets abroad, he became a government contractor and financier, and he stood fifth on the list of subscribers who underwrote the loan of £8 million floated in 1759. Long before entering parliament he was a prominent public figure, representing Lancashire's commercial interests in London and leading parliamentary agitations such as that in 1751 for a bounty on checked and striped linens.

Touchet's exploits in commercial politics were as ambitious as his trading ventures. As early as 1749 he was among a group of merchants who unsuccessfully tried to secure a monopoly of the trade to Labrador. At the outbreak of war with France in 1756 he made an even bolder bid for a trading monopoly, this time with Senegal. This French trading station in west Africa exported slaves, ivory, gold, wax, and a gum indispensable in linen and cotton printing. Touchet had a half-share in Thomas Cumming's expedition which captured Fort St Louis in 1758. The claim to the Senegal trade, although supported by Pitt and repeatedly pressed by Touchet himself, was opposed by the Royal African Company and disallowed on the advice of the law officers of the crown. Touchet became an MP in the general election of 1761, coming second in the poll at Shaftesbury. Meanwhile his business career had foundered in the financial crisis of that year, and attempts to stave off the creditors finally failed in 1763. The Manchester firm escaped bankruptcy and privilege of parliament protected Touchet. However, in 1765, largely as a result of his case, parliament removed that privilege from future cases of insolvency, although the legislation was not restrospective; Touchet remained in the Commons until 1768.

Touchet's political career was relatively low key. In Bute's parliamentary list he was classed as 'Government', but his several interventions in Commons business dealt with matters strictly within his own sphere of competence rather than with problems of high policy. However, he continued to work closely with his political friends. He was consulted by Fox on the commercial aspects of the peace preliminaries with France in 1763 and, in by far the most significant incident of his political life, advised Charles Townshend on his plans for taxing the Americans. Among Townshend's papers survives an undated draft in Touchet's handwriting of the American duties exactly as introduced into the house in 1767 with such serious later repercussions. In Namier's view there can be no doubt of his importance as friend and adviser to Townshend, but Townshend died in 1767. Although Touchet continued to act as adviser and go-between for the Fox family and others, he had lost his chief patron. A supporter in his later days was Sir Edward Walpole, with whom he conducted his last ambitious scheme for mineral rights in and about Lake Superior in Canada. When eventually a charter was forthcoming in 1772, Walpole emerged as governor of the company with Touchet as deputy governor. Fox was among the proprietors.

Touchet died suddenly of apoplexy on 28 May 1773 at his house in Westminster.   ALAN J. KIDD

Sources A. P. Wadsworth and J. de Lacy Mann, *The cotton trade and industrial Lancashire, 1600–1780* (1931) • HoP, *Commons* • E. Axon, 'Harrison Ainsworth's maternal ancestors', *Transactions of the Lancashire and Cheshire Antiquarian Society*, 29 (1911), 103–53 • *Manchester Guardian* (23 Nov 1874) • *Manchester City News* (1 Dec 1923) • *Letter from a merchant in Bristol to a merchant in London* (1762) • *Manchester Mercury* (1 June 1773) • J. Hunter, *Familiae minorum gentium*, ed. J. W. Clay, 1, Harleian Society, 37 (1894) • T. Baker, *Memorials of a dissenting chapel* (1884) • G. Ormerod, *The history of the county palatine and city of Chester*, 3 vols. (1819) • T. Perceval, *Letter to a friend* (1759)

Archives BL, letters to duke of Newcastle • PRO NIre., letters to Sir G. MacCartney

Toulmin, Camilla Dufour. *See* Crosland, Camilla Dufour (1812–1895).

Toulmin, David. *See* Reid, John (1913–1998).

Toulmin, Joshua (1740–1815), Unitarian minister and historian, was born in Aldersgate Street, London, on 30 April 1740. He was the son of Caleb Toulmin of Aldersgate Street and his wife, Mary, daughter of Thomas Skinner. In later life he acknowledged his debt to the religious values of his nonconformist upbringing. In 1748 he entered St Paul's School, London, where he acquired a classical education. In 1756, his early inclination towards the dissenting ministry having been confirmed, he spent five years in training for that profession in London, under the tuition of David Jennings and Samuel Morton Savage, with the latter of whom he had a family connection. The classes were conducted under the auspices of the Coward Trust at Savage's residence in Wellclose Square. Like several of his fellow students Toulmin began to depart from Calvinist orthodoxy and encountered 'severe remonstrances' from his parents, together with the disapproval of Jennings (*Monthly Repository*, 10.665).

On leaving Hoxton, Toulmin became minister of the Presbyterian congregation of Colyton, Devon, in succession to an Arian, Samuel Slater. He quickly acquired a wide circle of friends, notably in Exeter and Bridport. In 1764 he married Jane (*d.* 1824), the youngest daughter of Samuel Smith of Taunton; they had twelve children, of whom their eldest son, Henry (Harry) Toulmin (1766–1823), served as a dissenting minister in Lancashire before emigrating to the United States where he became a judge of the Mississippi territory and a member of the Alabama state assembly.

According to Murch, Toulmin's efforts increased the size of his flock at Colyton. But he disturbed some of its members by his opposition to infant baptism and his adoption of Baptist opinions. Consequently he left Colyton in March 1765 to become minister of Mary Street General Baptist Chapel, Taunton. Here he remained for almost thirty-nine years. The small (and declining) size of the congregation obliged Toulmin to augment his income by taking pupils, while his wife ran a successful bookshop. He also maintained a steady stream of publications; his obituary in the *Monthly Repository* lists fifty-eight separate items. By his revision and enlargement of Daniel Neal's *History of the Puritans* (1793–7), Toulmin earned a reputation as a historian of dissent, while his *History of the Town of Taunton* was published with a respectable list of subscribers in 1791; subsequent editions appeared in 1810 and 1822. He published numerous sermons, including collected editions in 1789 and 1810. His sermon 'The American War Lamented' (February 1776) deplored the government's use of force against the colonists and placed Toulmin firmly in the radical camp.

Like many General Baptists of the later eighteenth century Toulmin came to adopt anti-Trinitarian opinions. In 1777 he published an admiring biography of Faustus Socinus and subsequently defended Socinian opinions in a

Joshua Toulmin (1740–1815), by George Clint, pubd 1810 (after Richard Bonington)

pamphlet controversy with Andrew Fuller. He demonstrated his commitment to philanthropy by his promotion of Sunday schools, on which subject he published a sermon in 1789. He was a founder member of the Western Unitarian Society in 1792 and won the respect of Joseph Priestley and Theophilus Lindsey; it was partly through their influence that he was awarded the degree of DD by Harvard College in 1794. He was already (1769) the holder of an MA from Brown University, a Baptist institution.

Toulmin involved himself fully in the political campaigns of the Unitarians. His *Letter to the Bishops* (1789) strongly advocated the repeal of the Test and Corporation Acts, and he obtained more than 200 signatures in Taunton for the Unitarian petition for improved legal rights in 1792. He shared in the opprobrium which fell upon Unitarians during the French Revolution and, like Priestley at Birmingham, he encountered mob violence. According to one report an effigy of Thomas Paine was burnt outside his door, his windows were broken, and his house threatened with fire. His life was thought to be in danger and his wife was obliged to relinquish her bookselling enterprise. Unlike Priestley, however, he was not obliged to leave his chapel, and he remained in Taunton until 1804, although he made no secret of his opposition to the war with revolutionary France, declining to contribute to patriotic subscriptions.

In 1803 Toulmin received an invitation to the New Meeting at Birmingham, which had previously been Priestley's chapel. After some thought, and after other invitations from Gloucester and Great Yarmouth, he accepted and moved to Birmingham in January 1804. His pastoral efforts at the New Meeting seem to have been much appreciated. He continued to preach and write in defence of Unitarianism and to travel extensively in its support. On

15 July 1802 he preached before the Southern Unitarian Society at Portsmouth, and published his sermon under the title *The Doctrine of the Scriptures Concerning the Unity of God and the Character of Jesus Christ* (1802). It is said to have converted Robert Aspland from Arianism to the belief in 'the simple humanity of Christ' that characterized the Unitarian theology of this period (Aspland, 122–3). While in London for a meeting of the British and Foreign Bible Society in 1815 Toulmin aggravated his physical ailments, of which the chief was 'an affection of the lungs' (Kentish, 34). He died in Birmingham on 23 July of that year at the age of seventy-five, having previously indicated his intention to retire, and was buried with full dissenting honours in the burial-ground of the Old and New Meetings, Birmingham, on 1 August. His widow died on 8 July 1824. Toulmin was an important figure in the development of English Unitarianism as a separate denomination, and was a significant, if relatively minor, figure in the history of radicalism. It was characteristic of him that he disapproved of George III's jubilee in 1809 and that he wrote in that year: 'Our Dissenters and Whigs are timid. They fear the influence of the clergy' (Aspland, 237).

G. M. DITCHFIELD

Sources J. Kentish, *Monthly Repository*, 10 (1815), 665–74 · *Monthly Repository*, 11 (1816), 496, 653–4 · *Monthly Repository*, 19 (1824), 481 · J. Kentish, *The counsel of a deceased Christian pastor … a sermon … on occasion of the death of Joshua Toulmin* (1815) · R. B. Aspland, *Memoir of the life, works and correspondence of the Rev. Robert Aspland* (1850) · I. Worsley, *A sermon on the death of the Rev. Dr Joshua Toulmin* (1816) · J. E. Bradley, *Religion, revolution and English radicalism: nonconformity in eighteenth-century politics and society* (1990) · K. Haakonssen, ed., *Enlightenment and religion: rational dissent in eighteenth-century Britain* (1996) · R. B. Gardiner, ed., *The admission registers of St Paul's School, from 1748 to 1876* (1884) · Allibone, *Dict.* · J. Murch, *A history of the Presbyterian and General Baptist churches in the west of England* (1835) · *The theological and miscellaneous works of Joseph Priestley*, ed. J. T. Rutt, 1/1 (1831–2) · *GM*, 1st ser., 85/1 (1815), 187, 473–4 · Nichols, *Illustrations*, 4.845–6 · G. M. Ditchfield, 'Public and parliamentary support for the Unitarian petition of 1792', *Enlightenment and Dissent*, 12 (1993), 28–48 · Dr Williams Registry, vol. A, PRO, RG4/4658

Archives DWL, letters to John Sturch · N. Yorks. CRO, Wyvill MSS

Likenesses G. Clint, mezzotint, pubd 1810 (after R. Bonington), AM Oxf., BM [*see illus.*] · J. Partridge, stipple, NPG; repro. in *Monthly Repository*, 11 (1816), frontispiece

Wealth at death personal estate valued at over £1000; some land and real estate, profits from which were bequeathed to wife; monetary bequests to children; manuscripts to his son; £800 bequeathed to his daughter: will, 19 Aug 1815, PRO, PROB 11/1572, fol. 238v

Toulouse. For this title name *see* Joanna, countess of Toulouse (1165–1199).

Toup, Jonathan (1713–1785), classical scholar and Church of England clergyman, was born in December 1713 at St Ives, Cornwall, where he was baptized on 5 January 1714, the only son of Jonathan Toup (*d.* 1721), curate and lecturer of St Ives, and Prudence (1691–1773), daughter of John Busvargas of St Just, Penwith. His father's family came from Dorset and his grandfather Onesiphorus Toup, rector of Bridport, appears to have lost most of the family property. Following his mother's marriage in September 1723 to John Keigwyn (*d.* 1761), vicar of Landrake and St Erney, Toup was adopted by his maternal uncle William Busvargas. He was educated at St Ives grammar school and afterwards at the Revd John Gurney's private school at St Merryn. From March 1733 to November 1739 he was a batteler of Exeter College, Oxford, where John Upton (1707–1760) was his tutor throughout. He graduated BA on 14 October 1736 but did not proceed MA until 1756, when he took the degree from Pembroke College, Cambridge. He was ordained deacon on 6 March 1736 and three days later was licensed curate of Philleigh in Cornwall. There he remained until 29 May 1738, when he was licensed as curate of Buryan in the same county, having been ordained priest the previous day. Through his uncle's influence he was presented on 28 July 1750 to the rectory of St Martin by Looe, which he held until his death.

Toup's tenure of a curacy in a remote village gave him ample leisure to pursue his researches. His first publication was devoted to a recondite encyclopaedia containing important information of value for specialists, *Emendationes in Suidam* (3 pts, 1760–66), and it established his reputation as a textual critic. The first two parts, dedicated respectively to George Lavington, bishop of Exeter, and Jacob Harris, brought him to the notice of William Warburton, bishop of Gloucester, who recommended him for preferment to Archbishop Secker, Lord Shelburne, and Frederick Keppel, bishop of Exeter. It is said that Warburton asked Keppel whether he had taken care of Toup. 'Toup, who is Toup?' replied the bishop. 'A poor curate in your diocese', said Warburton, 'but the first Greek scholar in Europe' (W. Warburton, *Works*, new edn, 1811–41, 14.247–8). In return for his support Toup dedicated the third part of the *Emendationes* to Warburton. His *Epistola critica* (1767), addressed to Warburton, is generally considered as the fourth part of the *Emendationes*.

Toup contributed to an edition of Theocritus by Thomas Warton in 1770 and made similar contributions to various other editions issued later in that decade. His best-known work appeared in 1778; it was an edition of Longinus's *On the Sublime* and made this outstanding essay of ancient literary criticism far more accessible than it had been hitherto. It was the gift of a copy of this edition that stimulated Richard Porson to take up research in Greek. Toup's scholarship was greatly admired both at home and abroad but his critics claimed that his reputation was marred by a churlish, conceited, and supercilious nature. He praised few classicists other than Bentley, and his intemperate attacks on fellow scholars such as Robert Lowth, Benjamin Kennicott, and Johann Jacob Reiske led the last to describe him as 'homo truculentus et maledicus' (Brink, 93).

Following his mother's death in 1773 Toup inherited the property formerly owned by his stepfather and by his uncle and thus enjoyed a handsome income; at his own death his personal wealth was estimated at over £12,000. Warburton's patronage finally won him further preferment in the church in May 1774, when he was appointed to a prebend at Exeter by Bishop Keppel. Keppel then nominated him to the vicarage of St Merryn, which he held from 29 July 1776 until his death. In the same month he was appointed chaplain to his old friend Bishop Hurd of Lichfield. Toup never married and from 1763 he had shared his house with his half-sister Ann (1730/31–1814), widow of John Blake (*d.* 1763), and her three daughters, all of whom married into the Nicolas family. His sister Mary had married Charles Worth, an attorney of St Ives, who then married Toup's other half-sister, Prudence (*b.* 1727). Toup spent his last twenty-five years in St Martin and declined all inducements to move to London or Oxford. From 1780 his mental faculties deteriorated markedly and in his final months he was unable to perform his ministerial duties. He died at St Martin rectory on 19 January 1785 and was buried under the communion table of the church: his eldest half-niece, Phillis Blake, erected a small marble tablet to his memory in the church. His property passed to John Toup *Nicolas (1788–1851), eldest son of his youngest half-niece, Margaret Blake. His library of classical, historical, and critical works, many of which contained manuscript notes by him, was sold by Leigh and Sotheby between 10 and 13 May 1786. Toup had left his manuscript notes on Polybius to the Clarendon Press in Oxford and Phillis Blake bequeathed the rest of his manuscripts to the Bodleian Library.

W. P. COURTNEY, rev. M. J. MERCER

Sources Nichols, *Lit. anecdotes*, 2.339–46 · Boase & Courtney, *Bibl. Corn.*, 2.730–32 · T. Bond, *Topographical and historical sketches of the boroughs of East and West Looe* (1823), 18–20 · Allibone, *Dict.* · Foster, *Alum. Oxon.*, 1715–1886, 4.1428 · *GM*, 1st ser., 55 (1785), 79, 340 · *GM*, 1st ser., 56 (1786), 525–6, 652–4, 860–61 · *GM*, 1st ser., 57 (1787), 216–17 · *GM*, 1st ser., 63 (1793), 811, 1078–80, 1193 · *GM*, 2nd ser., 15 (1841), 349–51 · J. Aikin and others, *General biography, or, Lives, critical and historical of the most eminent persons*, 10 vols. (1799–1815) · A. Chalmers, ed., *The general biographical dictionary*, new edn, 32 vols. (1812–17) · C. O. Brink, *English classical scholarship: historical reflections on Bentley, Porson, and Housman* (1986), 93–4 · M. L. Clarke, *Greek studies in England, 1700–1830* (1945)
Archives BL, corresp., Add. MS 32565 · Bodl. Oxf., corresp. and papers | BL, letters to Revd T. Warton, Add. MSS 42560, fols. 162, 222; 42561, fols. 7, 12, 53, 62
Wealth at death over £12,000: *GM*, 1st ser., 55 (1785), 340

Touraine. For this title name *see* Douglas, Archibald, fourth earl of Douglas, and first duke of Touraine in the French nobility (*c.*1369–1424); Douglas, Margaret, countess of Douglas, and duchess of Touraine in the French nobility (*b.* before 1373?, *d.* 1450/51); Douglas, Archibald, fifth earl of Douglas, and second duke of Touraine in the French nobility (*c.*1391–1439); Douglas, William, sixth earl of Douglas, and third duke of Touraine in the French nobility (1422/3–1440).

Tournai, Simon de (*c.*1130?–1201?), schoolman and theologian, undoubtedly took his name from Tournai in what is now Belgium. However, although Matthew Paris styles him 'a Frenchman by birth named Simon, taking his *cognomen* from Tournai' (Paris, *Chron.*, 2.476), he was often considered by English scholars before the nineteenth century to have been a native of Cornwall, who was educated at Oxford before he went to Paris. Polydore Vergil, in his *Anglica historia*, published in 1534, lists Simon Thuruaius as a celebrated man of learning who lived in the reign of King John, and implies that he was English. Surnames

such as Torney and Torway are found in Cornwall in the sixteenth century, and this might be the reason why John Bale, in his *Illustrium maioris Britanniae scriptorum … summarium* of 1548 (Bale, *Summarium, centuria secunda*, fols. 99b–100a), as well as following Vergil in claiming Simon for England, also reports the suggestion—albeit as one made by others—that Simon Thuruaius (as he follows Vergil in styling Simon) was Cornish, and moreover that the alternative name, Simon de Tornaco or Simon de Tournai, rested on a confusion caused by the similarity of the two names. By the time the first volume of his *Scriptorum illustrium maioris Brytanniae … catalogus* was published in 1557, Bale had abandoned conjecture for certainty, and he listed Simon simply as 'an English priest, a native of Cornwall' (Bale, *Cat.*, 1.243). In this he was followed by such seventeenth- and eighteenth-century bibliographers as Thomas Fuller, Anthony Wood, and Thomas Tanner.

Simon is named in contemporary sources as 'of Tournai' because he received his early education at that city's chapter school. Probably born about 1130, before 1155 he entered the cathedral school of Notre-Dame in Paris, perhaps initially as a student under Odo of Soissons. He writes of himself as a grammarian as well as a theologian. Odo complained to Pope Alexander III in 1166 or 1167, after his retirement in 1165, that Bishop Maurice had gone back on a promise to grant his canonry or another benefice to one of his former students. This student, who may well have been Simon, was provost of the schools, and had taken over Odo's teaching. Odo writes that he taught scripture vigorously and orthodoxly, and that he himself had supported him financially for twelve years. The pope was asked to intervene with the bishop or to provide a prebend for him. It appears likely that it was at about this time that Simon obtained a canonry at Tournai. Peter Comestor was appointed in Paris, but Simon none the less stayed in the city, using his revenues from Tournai to support himself, contrary to a diocesan statute forbidding non-residence. For doing this the bishop and chapter tried to deprive him of his office. The abbot of Ste Geneviève, Étienne de Tournai (1176–92), intervened on his behalf with Guillaume, the archbishop of Rheims, and wrote warmly of his good name and scholarship. He appears as a master in 1172–3 in the cartulary of Ste Geneviève and is recorded as having assisted Cardinal Pietro da Pavia in formulating a settlement favourable to Ste Geneviève in 1174–8. He also appears, along with Gerard Pucelle, as Magister Symon de Tornaeo in the witness list of an undated document of *c.*1180. Simon may have taught theology in Paris until almost the end of the century.

Simon de Tournai shows himself in his surviving writings to be one of the influential group of Porretani who followed in the tradition of Gilbert de la Porrée rather than in that of Peter Lombard. It is not known whether Gilbert, bishop of Poitiers from 1142 until his death in 1154, ever taught him; this seems unlikely, but in his *Sentences* Simon sometimes copied closely from Gilbert's writings, though without revealing his source. He was well acquainted with, and liked to cite as other Porretans also did, the works of Boethius, St Augustine, St Hilary, and

John the Scot (Eriugena). His major theological writings include a collection of 102 theological *Disputationes* with 371 questions, written after 1160, and the earlier *Institutiones in sacra pagina* or *Summa*, which may not have been finished and is largely unpublished but is found in the Bibliothèque Nationale, Paris (MSS Lat. 3114A and 14886). The former manuscript is incomplete; a portion of it, *Sermo de Deo et divinis*, has often been cited as a separate work. The relationships, chronological and other, between Simon's works and those of his contemporaries (such as Ralph Ardens and Alain de Lille) who shared many of his outlooks, present complex problems, but if his *Summa* is dated to 1160–65, then Simon was an especially influential teacher of theology at a time when the numbers of identifiable teachers of theology at Paris were increasing. The part of the *Summa* that concerns the Trinity influenced closely the *Sentences* of Pierre de Poitiers. Simon drew upon the teaching on marriage of the *Summa decretorum* of the Bolognese master, Rufinus of Assisi, and of the anonymous *Speculum ecclesiae*; and he influenced the writing of the *Summa* of another Porretan, Master Martin, which survives in the Bibliothèque Nationale, Paris (MS Lat. 14526), and was written after about 1195. His writings also influenced Lothar of Segni, who was to become Pope Innocent III (*r.* 1198–1216).

Only one of the sermons of Simon de Tournai survives. An exposition of the Athanasian creed, written in the 1160s, it enjoyed a certain popularity until the mid-thirteenth century. Simon began this work with an observation that prompted discussion of the relationship between faith and reason during the thirteenth century: for Aristotle an argument is a reason that generates faith, but for Christ an argument is faith that gives a reason which leads to understanding. Also ascribed to him, but tentatively, are commentaries on the Lord's prayer and on the apostles' creed.

Simon de Tournai did not gain further promotion. He occasionally shows a mordant wit—'I would rather be a Catholic yokel than a heretical curialist' (*Disputationes*, 39); 'the church has canonized in error many of the damned' (ibid., 267). He fell victim to gossip by other writers. According to the Monk of Afflighem in his *Catalogue of Illustrious Authors* (written *c.*1270–73), Simon's favourite master was Aristotle, and his adherence to Aristotle's views led to accusations of heresy against him 'by some moderns'. Simon was, in fact, one of the earliest theologians to study the newly available translations of Aristotle's books on *Physics*, the *Soul*, and *Metaphysics*. At the end of the twelfth century, and later, stories circulated that attributed to him, but in conflicting detail, arrogance, blasphemy, and the possession of a concubine named Adelaide. Many of them appear in British sources, demonstrating not only Simon's own notoriety, but also the way in which leading masters in the Parisian schools became celebrities on the English side of the channel. According to Gerald of Wales, Simon wondered how long the superstition of Christianity could endure, and also brashly criticized the venality of the papal curia, on the occasion of a visit there, by saying publicly that access to

Simon Peter was through Simon Magus. Gerald also reports that God punished him with loss of speech and memory; this probably followed a severe stroke. The Dominican friar Thomas de Cantimpré (1201–1270) wrote that Simon spoke of Moses, Christ, and Muhammad as alike impostors.

Matthew Paris sketches the career of Simon de Tournai in terms of rise and fall: for ten years regent of arts at Paris, he then turned his attention to theology, in which he showed a speculative bent and achieved so much proficiency that he obtained the master's chair in a few years. His tenacity of memory, natural abilities, and the brilliance with which he solved disputed theological questions, brought to his lectures audiences that more than filled the largest available room in the schools. But, while lecturing one day, he was so much elated at the acclaim that greeted his orthodox determination of questions concerning the Trinity, that he exclaimed that he could demolish his own solutions with stronger arguments if he wished to be mischievous. Whereupon he was suddenly struck dumb and bereft of his mental faculties, so that he never taught again. Nearly two years later he could barely learn from his son, or say, the Pater noster and the creed. This story, in which suspicion is also cast on Simon's orthodoxy, Matthew says came from an eyewitness, Nicholas of Farnham, afterwards bishop of Durham—one of the many English students who went abroad and attended lectures given by famous masters in Paris and elsewhere. Matthew Paris places Simon's death in 1201.

DAVID LUSCOMBE

Sources Les 'Disputationes' de Simon de Tournai: texte inédit, ed. J. Warichez, Spicilegium Sacrum Lovaniense, 12 (1932) · 'Simon of Tournai's *Commentary on the so-called Athanasian creed*', ed. N. Haring, *Archives d'Histoire Doctrinale et Littéraire du Moyen Âge*, 43 (1976), 135–99 · N. Haring, 'Simon of Tournai and Gilbert of Poitiers', *Mediaeval Studies*, 27 (1965), 325–30 · M. Schmaus, 'Die Texte der Trinitätslehre in den *Sententiae* des Simon von Tournai', *Recherches de Théologie Ancienne et Médiévale*, 4 (1932), 59–72, 187–98, 294–307 · *Sententiae Petri Pictaviensis*, ed. P. S. Moore, M. Dulong, and others, 2 (Notre Dame, IN, 1950), xxxvi–xliii · D. Van den Eynde, 'Deux sources de la Somme théologique de Simon de Tournai', *Antonianum*, 24 (1949), 19–42 · J. B. Pitra, ed., *Analecta novissima spicilegii Solesmensis*, 2 (Paris, 1888); facs. edn (1967), xxxix–xl · F. Stegmüller, ed., *Repertorium biblicum medii aevi*, 5 (Madrid, 1955), 8880 · Stephanus Tornacensis, 'Epistola LIX', *Patrologia Latina*, 211 (1855), 353A · *Gir. Camb. opera*, 2.148 · Paris, *Chron.*, 2.476–7 · J. W. Baldwin, *Masters, princes and merchants: the social views of Peter the Chanter and his circle*, 2 vols. (1970), vol. 1, pp. 18, 43–4; vol. 2, p. 33 · P. Vergil, *Anglicae historiae* (Basel, 1534), 284 · J. Bale, *Illustrium Maioris Britannie scriptorum … summarium* (1548), fols. 99b–100a · Bale, *Cat.*, 1.243 · Fuller, *Worthies* (1662), 1.203 · Tanner, *Bibl. Brit.-Hib.* · A. Wood, *The history and antiquities of the University of Oxford*, ed. J. Gutch, 1 (1792), 54
Archives Bibliothèque Nationale, Paris, MSS Lat. 3114 A, 14886

Tournay, Simon of. *See* Tournai, Simon de (*c.*1130?–1201?).

Tourneur, Cyril (*d.* 1626), writer and soldier, is of obscure origins. It seems possible that he was either a son of Edward Tournor of Canons, Great Parndon, Essex, and his second wife, Frances Baker (*d.* 1600), or (less likely) a grandson, his father, also named Edward (1559–1623), a barrister of the Middle Temple, being a son of Tournor's first marriage. What suggests this (summarized by Nicoll, 2–4) is twofold. First, both Cyril Tourneur and a Captain Richard Turnor, of Canons, brother of the younger Edward Tournor, were closely associated with Sir Francis Vere and with the Cecil family: Richard Turnor serving in the Low Countries under Sir Thomas Cecil (later earl of Exeter) and Sir Francis Vere, and Cyril Tourneur under Vere and Sir Edward Cecil, later Viscount Wimbledon, third son of Sir Thomas. Second, Cyril is an exceedingly rare name in Elizabethan England, and the Tournor / Tourneur family (whose name was variously spelt, as was Cyril Tourneur's) were given to naming their children unusually as the unfortunately incomplete parish register of Great Parndon indicates: thus Nicoll (pp. 4–5) lists, among others, a Maurice, a Joshua, a Lydia, and a Demetrius.

Early literary career The little that is known of Tourneur's life indicates two aspects to his career: literary and military. He first appears in 1600 as author of *The Transformed Metamorphosis*, an obscurely allegorical poem about the state of the arts in England. Showing the influence of Edmund Spenser and John Marston, the poem is in some respects obscure, and there has been considerable debate (see Schuman, 41–6) over the identification of the island of Delta, almost certainly England, and of the figure of Mavortio, most plausibly Henry VIII. But the general drift seems clear enough: Mavortio rid Delta of the corruption of Roman Catholicism, and under his protection '*Mars* and the Muses had their dignity'. After Mavortio's death, however, corruption set in once more and the muses were reinfected, with '*Nilus Crocodiles … bathing in the pure Castalian* head' (548–9). But in the last four of the poem's eighty-seven stanzas, the rock of truth on which the poet has taken refuge metamorphoses into Eliza (Elizabeth I), who effects a new metamorphosis. Tourneur's 'Epilogue', with its emphatic contrast between now, when

Heav'ns sacred lights agree in one consent
To drive the cloudes from foorth the firmament
(13–14)

and the dark night of the soul in which he originally wrote, suggests that circumstances might have changed before the poem's publication, with a call for reform somehow transformed into a statement of hope, perhaps by an event such as the calling in and burning by the ecclesiastical authorities in June 1599 of satiric and erotic works by Marston and others.

Following *The Transformed Metamorphosis* nothing certain is heard of Tourneur until 1609, with the publication of his *Funerall Poeme upon the Death of the most Worthy and True Souldier, Sir Francis Vere*, but two works published in the interim have with varying degrees of confidence been attributed to him. *Laugh and Lie Downe* (1605) is a prose pamphlet in the dream-vision tradition, in which C. T. exposes folly in such figures as the lover, the henpecked husband, the profligate, the soldier, and the whore. In its didacticism it sorts well with works undoubtedly by Tourneur. Whether *The Revenger's Tragedy* (1607) was also Tourneur's has long been debated. Published anonymously, it was first attributed to him in a play list of 1656, and until recently it constituted his chief claim to fame,

since of its kind—a tragedy of blood shot through with black comedy, which indeed employs many of the techniques of comedy in presenting a fierce critique of revenge and revengers, along with a bitter exposé of court corruption—it is a masterpiece. There now, however, appears to be an overwhelming case for the authorship of Thomas Middleton. The earlier balance of pro-Tourneur and pro-Middleton articles was based on impressionistic assessments, on parallels, and on literary judgement (see Schuman, 62–76), but these approaches have given way to an impressive series of analyses, computer-assisted since the 1970s, of the language of *The Revenger's Tragedy*, and its likeness to that of Middleton (see Lake, 136–57, and Jackson, 33–40 and 161–8).

A Funerall Poeme upon the Death of … Sir Francis Vere is a plain but eulogistic memorial to a great soldier. It displays a close knowledge of Vere's methods of command, and it shrewdly analyses what made them so successful, but Tourneur's primary focus is on the man, and on the personal qualities that marked him as exceptional. 'His *Minde*', Tourneur writes, 'was like an *Empire*, *rich* and *strong*': he was modest, temperate in judgement, and flexible in his approach to commanding men, and waging war. It is this, for Tourneur, that makes Vere great.

The Atheist's Tragedy In 1611 there appeared Tourneur's first (as it now seems) play, *The Atheist's Tragedy*. Strongly didactic, it demonstrates in terms both comic—the subplot involving Levidulcia and Sebastian—and serious, the fatal implications of atheism (embodied in the villainous D'Amville), and the rewards that accompany a patient adherence (by the hero, Charlemont) to Christian principles. As with *The Transformed Metamorphosis* it may be that Tourneur is responding to a particular stimulus, in this case *The Revenge of Bussy D'Ambois* by George Chapman. For, as H. H. Adams has argued ('Cyril Tourneur on revenge', *Journal of English and Germanic Philology*, 48, 1949, 82–6), Charlemont, the hero who refuses to revenge, seems to be a remodelling in Christian terms of Chapman's Clermont, who likewise abstains from revenge, but on Stoic principles. Clifford Leech, taking the case further, suggests ('*The Atheist's Tragedy* as a dramatic comment on Chapman's *Bussy* plays', *Journal of English and Germanic Philology*, 52, 1953, 525–30) that D'Amville, Tourneur's supreme atheist, may be based on Chapman's Bussy, whose surname he echoes.

Viewed realistically, the principal characters in *The Atheist's Tragedy* seem somewhat stiff and lifeless, but as dramatic exempla they serve Tourneur's purposes well. The ending, in which D'Amville brains himself as he attempts to execute Charlemont, marks the summation of the nonnaturalistic mode that *The Atheist's Tragedy* employs. It is unfortunate that there has been only one modern production to test the dramatic viability of Tourneur's one undoubted surviving play, since it might well succeed if sympathetically produced. There is no shortage of dramatically effective scenes, and plenty of humour, associated particularly with the hypocritical tallow-chandler turned preacher, Languebeau Snuffe.

Later literary career   Hard on the heels, it seems, of *The Atheist's Tragedy* came Tourneur's second play, a tragicomedy entitled *The Nobleman*. Ironically, given that it has not survived, save for a single piece of incidental music, more is known about the stage history of *The Nobleman* than about any other play with which Tourneur is associated. Performances at court by the King's Men were recorded on 23 February 1612 and at Christmas of that year, and the play was still in the repertory of the company in 1641 (Bentley, 1.65–6).

The death on 24 May 1612 of the great Robert Cecil provided the occasion for Tourneur's prose *Character of Robert Earle of Salesburye*, probably written for the family and never published, though extant in five manuscript copies. The *Character* demonstrates close personal knowledge of Cecil, such as the ruin to which devotion to affairs of state nearly brought him—ruin from which he was rescued by the good management of his steward. The importance of Cecil's service to the realm is declared, but as in the elegy on Sir Francis Vere, Tourneur is more interested in praising his subject's character: his generosity, prudence, self-control, and denial of self in the interests of the state. It is a moral summation of the man, rather than an account of his statesmanship, and accordingly it stresses Cecil's religious faith declared (as Tourneur must have known) in his will, and his peaceful end, in the tradition of the 'good death'.

Later in 1612 another death, that of Henry, prince of Wales, occasioned deep national grief. Tourneur was one of many poets who marked the event, his *A Griefe on the Death of Prince Henrie*, published in January 1613, appearing both separately and with elegies by John Webster and Thomas Heywood. In *A Griefe* Tourneur again dwells on the personal and the moral. Without ignoring the loss to the realm—indeed including a poem 'On the Succession', in which he develops the imprudent conceit of Henry's dying in order to simplify and thus strengthen the succession to the throne, a poem deleted from most surviving copies of the elegy—he makes Henry's death the occasion for what Ruth Wallerstein (*Studies in Seventeenth Century Poetic*, 1950, 84) calls 'spiritual drama', in which the death of the exemplification of Virtue exposes the world for the worthless thing it is, and in which the primary focus is on Henry's exemplary life and death.

The final literary record relating to Tourneur is a mention in a letter written in June 1613 by Robert Daborne to Philip Henslowe, the theatrical entrepreneur, that he had 'given Cyrill Tourneur an act of the Arreignment of london to write' (W. W. Greg, *The Henslowe Papers*, 1907, 72). If completed, the play has not survived. It may have been based on *The Bellman of London*, a prose pamphlet by Thomas Dekker. Though there are no records to support the supposition, it is possible that in the same year, 1613 (see Chambers, 3.227), Tourneur may also have been collaborating on another, extant play, *The Honest Man's Fortune*, this time with Nathan Field and John Fletcher. Gerritsen argued Tourneur's authorship of the first four scenes (assigned by Hoy, 100–08, to Field), and Jackson (pp. 216–20) has strongly supported the case for Tourneur's part-

authorship of the tragicomedy, which has as its hero a paragon of Christian patience akin to Charlemont, and a title intriguingly like the subtitle of *The Atheist's Tragedy*, 'The Honest Man's Revenge'.

Military career   The remaining records relating to Tourneur all concern military or diplomatic activity. On 23 December 1613 Tourneur was granted £10 for 'his chardges and paines in carrying letters for his Ma^ts service to Brussels' (Cunningham, xliii); in August 1614 he is mentioned in a letter written from Nijmegen by James Bathurst as having been there and at Brussels, but now 'gone to the army with his Colonel' (J. R. Sutherland, 'Cyril Tourneur', *TLS*, 16 April 1931, 307). In 1617 he was, for unknown reasons, arrested on the order of the privy council, but he was shortly released on the bond of Sir Edward Cecil. Then, in 1625, Tourneur was appointed secretary to the council of war on the Cadiz expedition, though he was later displaced by a royal appointee. The expedition was a dismal failure, and it returned to Britain with its ships ravaged by fever. One of those put ashore at Kinsale, Ireland, was Cyril Tourneur, who died there on 28 February 1626, leaving a widow, Mary, who petitioned the council of war for a pension, and was supported by Sir Edward Cecil, now the earl of Wimbledon, who attested to her husband's good service.

Since all the records relating to Tourneur's literary activity predate those concerning his military and diplomatic service, it may appear that he lived a life in two halves, literary and then military, but there is fortunately enough in the later documentary evidence to contradict this. Bathurst's letter, for instance, relates that 'Mr Cirrill Turner … belongs to General Cecil and was in former times Secretary to Sir Francis Vere', thus confirming that he was in the Low Countries in the first years of the seventeenth century, and may even have been in the service of Vere as early as the Cadiz expedition of 1598. That he served long and well in the Netherlands is also attested by Mary Tourneur's statement in her petition that her husband 'heretofore was ymployed under the States of Holland, & had settled meanes of 60^li p annum by his place, beside the dayly hopes he had of some greater pferment there' (Nicoll, 31).

Literary reputation   With the attribution of *The Revenger's Tragedy* to Middleton, Tourneur's literary standing has shrunk markedly. But the loss of what was once regarded as his masterpiece enables modern readers to see him in a clearer light. The author of *The Revenger's Tragedy* was long regarded (if wrongly) as cynical and nullifidian, but the Cyril Tourneur of *The Atheist's Tragedy*, of the lucid and thoughtful elegies on Sir Francis Vere and Henry, prince of Wales, and of that confusing but powerful outcry against the prostitution of the muses, *The Transformed Metamorphosis*, shows himself to be a traditional Christian moralist, with a consistent didactic bent. As such, he has a deserved, if minor, place in English literary history, appropriate to a man who seems to have written for gain only when not employed in his chosen profession of soldier.

DAVID GUNBY

Sources A. Nicoll, 'Introduction', in *The works of Cyril Tourneur* (1929), 1–49 • S. Schuman, *Cyril Tourneur* (1977) [incl. descriptive bibliography] • M. P. Jackson, *Studies in attribution: Middleton and Shakespeare* (1977) • D. J. Lake, *The canon of Thomas Middleton's plays* (1975) • *The honest man's fortune*, ed. J. R. Gerritsen (1952) • P. Cunningham, *Extracts from the accounts of the revels at court* (1842) • C. Tourneur, *The atheist's tragedy*, ed. I. Ribner (1964) • B. Wagner, 'Elizabethan dramatists', *TLS* (28 Sept 1933), 651 • E. K. Chambers, *The Elizabethan stage*, 4 vols. (1923) • C. R. Forker, 'Cyril Tourneur', *The new intellectuals*, ed. T. P. Logan and D. S. Smith (1977), 248–80 [incl. comprehensive bibliography] • C. Hoy, 'The shares of Fletcher and his collaborators in the Beaumont and Fletcher canon [pt 4]', *Studies in Bibliography*, 12 (1959), 91–116, esp. 100–08 • P. B. Murray, *A study of Cyril Tourneur* (1964) • G. E. Bentley, *The Jacobean and Caroline stage*, 7 vols. (1941–68)

Tours, Berthold (1838–1897), composer and music editor, whose baptismal name was Bartolomeus, was born on 17 December 1838 in Rotterdam, the son of Bartolomeus Tours, organist of the church of St Laurent in that city. He was a pupil of, and assistant to, his father and also studied under J. J. H. Verhulst; later he became a student at the conservatories of Brussels and (in 1857) Leipzig. After accompanying the music-loving Prince Yury Galitzin to Russia, he remained there in the prince's service from January 1859 to April 1861. He then migrated to London, where he remained for the rest of his life, though he retained his Dutch nationality. In June 1868 he married Susan Elizabeth Taylor, a native of Hackney; they had a daughter and five sons.

Besides writing and teaching, Tours played the violin in various theatre and concert orchestras, and in 1862 joined the orchestra of the Royal Italian Opera at Covent Garden. He also held the post of organist at St Helen's, Bishopsgate (1864–5), St Peter's, Stepney (1865–7), and the Swiss church in Soho (1867–79). In 1872 he joined the editorial staff of the music publishing house of Novello, Ewer & Co., as assistant initially to Joseph Barnby and then, from 1875, to John Stainer. In 1877 he became chief editor, an influential position which he held until his death and in which he was able to use his critical acumen, judgement, and perseverance to considerable effect. For Novello he made many piano reductions from full scores of operas, oratorios, and the like, and he was himself a prolific composer of services, anthems, songs, and instrumental pieces. He also produced a *Primer of the Violin* (1879) for Novello that was highly regarded. Of his instrumental compositions, the *Gavotte moderne en ut* (1870) achieved some popularity, but it was above all for his morning and evening service in F (1885) that he became esteemed as a composer. However, the currency of his compositions faded with that of Victorian music generally. According to his obituary in the *Musical Times*, Tours was a modest, retiring man and a natural editor, being 'learned, laborious and accurate in a remarkable degree'. He died at his home, 26 Rivercourt Road, Ravenscourt Park, on 11 March 1897 and was buried in Highgate cemetery.

His fourth son and fifth child, **Frank Edward Tours** (1877–1963), music director and composer, was born on 1 September 1877 at 210 The Grove, Hammersmith. He received musical training from his father and at the Royal College of Music from Charles Stanford, Walter Parratt, and Frederick Bridge. He was organist at St John's, Hammersmith, and, after conducting Stanford's opera *Shamus O'Brien* in 1897, for several years musical director at Daly's, the Prince of Wales's, Gaiety, Aldwych, and other theatres. He contributed additional numbers to numerous Edwardian musical shows, collaborated with Paul A. Rubens on *The Dairymaids* (1906), and composed the score of *The Dashing Little Duke* (1909). He also wrote many independent ballads, of which it was above all his setting of Kipling's 'Mother o' Mine' (1903) that made his name as a composer and which has remained his most performed work. He collaborated closely with Jerome Kern in the latter's early days in London, and from 1912 Tours began to divide his time between London and New York. During the 1920s he was for a time conductor at the Plaza Picture Theatre in Lower Regent Street, but increasingly he concentrated on work in the USA. He conducted on Broadway for several editions of the *Ziegfeld Follies* as well as for George M. Cohan and other American impresarios. A companionable, witty *bon vivant*, Tours was regarded by his friends as a confirmed bachelor until, in his mid-forties, he married an American, with whom he had six daughters and a son. With the coming of musical films he moved to Hollywood, and he spent the final years of his life as an orchestral consultant to various film companies. He died in Los Angeles on 2 February 1963.   ANDREW LAMB

Sources *DNB* • B. C. Hilliam, *The Times* (9 Feb 1963) • J. Parker, ed., *Who's who in the theatre* (1912) • J. Parker, ed., *Who's who in the theatre*, 9th edn (1939) • *MT*, 38 (1897), 238–9 • K. Gänzl, *The encyclopedia of the musical theatre* (1994) • E. A. Weinandt and R. H. Young, *The anthem in England and America* (1970) • F. Blume, ed., *Die Musik in Geschichte und Gegenwart*, 17 vols. (Kassel and Basel, 1949–86) • B. C. Hilliam, *Flotsam's follies* (1948) • *CGPLA Eng. & Wales* (1897)
Likenesses portrait, repro. in *MT*
Wealth at death £2445 18s. 6d.: probate, 29 April 1897, *CGPLA Eng. & Wales*

Tours [Marçay], **Étienne de** (d. 1193), administrator, was a member of the lesser baronage of the south Touraine. He appears as a royal chamberlain in the pipe roll of 1158, and was keeper of the king's treasure at Chinon. He became seneschal of Anjou in 1163, and still held that post on 12 June 1189, when he fired Le Mans to defend it from Philip Augustus. Richard I, on his accession, imprisoned Étienne and compelled him to surrender the royal treasure in his charge. Richard of Devizes, who calls him Étienne de Marçay, says that he was imprisoned at Winchester, and had to pay a heavy fine for his release (*Chronicon Richardi Divisensis*, 4–5). William of Newburgh relates that he had been raised from a humble position by Henry II, and was after his release kept in authority by Richard I. Believing that Richard would never return from the crusades, and relying on the prophecy of a wizard, Étienne exercised his power in an arbitrary fashion. The wizard foretold that he would die 'in pluma', and he duly met his death at a fortress of that name in 1193, shortly before Richard's return. Étienne has sometimes been identified wrongly with Stephen of *Thornham (d. 1213/14).

C. L. KINGSFORD, rev. THOMAS K. KEEFE

Sources *Pipe rolls*, 4 Henry II, 125, 137, 168; 18 Henry II, 125, 137, 168 • W. Stubbs, ed., *Gesta regis Henrici secundi Benedicti abbatis: the* *chronicle of the reigns of Henry II and Richard I*, AD 1169–1192, 2 vols., Rolls Series, 49 (1867), 2.9, 67, 71 • *Chronicon Richardi Divisensis / The Chronicle of Richard of Devizes*, ed. J. T. Appleby (1963), 4–5, 85 • P. Meyer, ed., *L'histoire de Guillaume le Maréchal*, 3 vols. (Paris, 1891–1901), lines 9173–211 • R. Howlett, ed., *Chronicles of the reigns of Stephen, Henry II, and Richard I*, 2, Rolls Series, 82 (1885), 424–6 • J. Boussard, *Le comté d'Anjou sous Henri Plantegenêt et ses fils, 1151–1204* (1938), 114–28 • J. Boussard, *Le gouvernement d'Henri II Plantegenêt* (1956), 357–8 • L. Delisle and others, eds., *Recueil des actes de Henri II, roi d'Angleterre et duc de Normandie, concernant les provinces françaises et les affaires de France*, 1 (Paris, 1909–27), 459–63; 2 (1916), 240; 3 (1920), 6 • J. H. Round, ed., *Calendar of documents preserved in France, illustrative of the history of Great Britain and Ireland* (1899), 378 • R. W. Eyton, *Court, household, and itinerary of King Henry II* (1878), 297

Tours, Frank Edward (1877–1963). *See under* Tours, Berthold (1838–1897).

Tours, John of [John de Villula] (d. 1122), bishop of Bath, was the diocesan in Somerset at the time when the cathedral moved from Wells to Bath. A native of Touraine, and a priest of the church of Tours, during his early life he practised as a physician. It is possible that he was the 'Johannes medicus' who attended William I on his deathbed, and that his medical knowledge helped him to secure preferment at William II's court where, like several other physicians, he was a chaplain at the time of his promotion to the episcopate. The central interest of John's activities as bishop lies in the transfer of his episcopal seat from Wells to Bath and in his subsequent relations with both churches. He was consecrated in July 1088, and within about a year had secured from Rufus the gift of the abbey at Bath which he established as a cathedral priory. William of Malmesbury saw the act as inspired by greed for the landed wealth of the abbey, though it does of course fit into a pattern of similar moves that occurred at this time, whereby cathedral churches were transferred to larger and more easily defensible places. By 1091 the bishop was able to consolidate his position by the purchase from the king of the city of Bath—William of Malmesbury and the *Historiola de primordiis episcopatus Somersetensis* record money (in differing amounts) as having changed hands, though the royal charter itself speaks only of a grant made in alms.

At Bath, Bishop John's dealings with the monastic church seem to have been mixed. According to William of Malmesbury, he was at first inclined to consider the monks as poorly educated barbarians and, having seized all that they had, required his lay servants to dole them out only a meagre living. Later, however, he made restitution (though not the full restoration of the monastic revenues that his charter of 1106 purports to make) and exhibited considerable generosity in his gifts to the convent. Despite the bishop's own shortcomings in the field (William of Malmesbury says that although he enjoyed the company of scholars, his speech was so artless as to invite the derision of children), the monks became renowned for their learning. He also rebuilt the priory church on an impressive scale.

At Wells the historical tradition surrounding Bishop

John, represented above all by the *Historiola*, is more uniformly critical. Under Bishop Giso (d. 1088) the clergy of Wells had come to adopt the common life and had received considerable endowments from Edward the Confessor, his queen, and the bishop himself. John's episcopate saw a reversal of their fortunes as, presumably wishing to make good his move to Bath by a reduction of the establishment at Wells, he destroyed the canons' communal buildings and gave away much of their revenue to his brother and steward, Hildebert.

In ecclesiastical matters more generally John of Tours played a part familiar in the late eleventh and early twelfth centuries. Within the diocese his episcopate witnessed the emergence of the bishop's court and the appearance of three archdeacons (who do not, however, appear to have received territorial designations at this time). As a former royal chaplain, he maintained close links with the court: he witnessed royal grants and attended councils. In Eadmer's account he was one of four bishops who at Winchester in 1097 protested their worldly interests and loyalty to the king and refused to assist Anselm in his determination to visit Rome. In a similar vein, Orderic Vitalis lists him among those to whom Rufus had given ecclesiastical honours 'like hireling's wages' (Ordericus Vitalis, *Eccl. hist.*, 5.203). On Christmas day 1122 Bishop John was seized by a pain in the heart and he died the following day. He was buried in the middle of the choir at Bath. William of Malmesbury comments upon his good health during life and his great age at death. The toponymic 'de Villula' by which John was previously known derives from Henry Wharton's misreading of his episcopal profession.   FRANCES RAMSEY

Sources 'A brief history of the bishoprick of Somerset from its foundation to the year 1174', *Ecclesiastical documents*, CS, 8 (1840) • *Willelmi Malmesbiriensis monachi de gestis pontificum Anglorum libri quinque*, ed. N. E. S. A. Hamilton, Rolls Series, 52 (1870) • F. M. R. Ramsey, ed., *Bath and Wells, 1061–1205*, English Episcopal Acta, 10 (1995) • *Reg. RAN*, 1066–1100 • Ordericus Vitalis, *Eccl. hist.* • *Eadmeri Historia novorum in Anglia*, ed. M. Rule, Rolls Series, 81 (1884) • Symeon of Durham, *Opera* • William of Jumièges, *Gesta Normannorum ducum*, ed. J. Marx (Rouen and Paris, 1914) • R. A. L. Smith, 'John of Tours, bishop of Bath, 1088–1122', *Downside Review*, 60 (1942), 132–41 • *The itinerary of John Leland in or about the years 1535–1543*, ed. L. Toulmin Smith, 3: *The itinerary in Wales* (1906), 143 • J. Manco, *Bath Abbey* [forthcoming]

Tourtel [*née* Caldwell], **Mary** (1874–1948), illustrator and author, was born on 28 January 1874 at 52 Palace Street, Canterbury, Kent, the youngest child of Samuel Austen Caldwell, a stained-glass designer and stonemason, and his wife, Sarah, formerly Scott. Mary's father, and later his son Samuel, restored stained glass for Canterbury Cathedral. Her elder brother Edmund was a talented animal painter and book illustrator who exhibited at the Royal Academy. In this artistic environment, it is not surprising that Mary showed an early talent for drawing, and she was educated at the prestigious local Sidney Cooper School of Art, where she won the coveted Prince of Wales scholarship. Her forte was animal drawing, and her illustrations for children's books were first published in 1897. A handsome, strong-featured woman, in the late 1890s she married the journalist Herbert Bird Tourtel (*d*. 1931).

Mary and Herbert Tourtel remained childless, and travelled extensively together in Italy, Egypt, and India. Later they were to develop a shared passion for flying, and Mary Tourtel was then able to sketch from the air unusual angles and aspects of landscape which were to enrich many of her picture-strips.

It is as the creator of Rupert Bear that she attained distinction. Despite her talents and successful early career, Mary Tourtel's anthropomorphic animal drawings had considerably less panache than those of several gifted contemporaries (notably the Teddy Tail originator, Charles Folkard, and H. S. Foxwell, the most brilliant of the Amalgamated Press's Tiger Tim illustrators). Nevertheless she created Britain's longest-running newspaper-strip hero. Now frequently dubbed 'Britain's answer to Mickey Mouse', Rupert owed his existence to the Fleet Street circulation battles. The *Daily Mail* launched Folkard's sale-boosting mouse, Teddy Tail, in 1915 and the *Daily Mirror* followed suit with A. B. Payne's extremely successful penguin and dog twosome, Pip and Squeak, who were soon joined by Wilfred, their rabbit foster child. The *Daily Express*'s proprietor Lord Beaverbrook instructed his editor, R. D. Blumenfeld, to find and develop an animal character to eclipse those of the *Daily Mail* and *Daily Mirror*. One or two experimental strips were tried and rejected, and Herbert Tourtel, then a sub-editor on the paper, suggested that Mary could produce what was required.

Mary Tourtel's first Rupert serial, *The Little Lost Bear*, began as a single-frame picture with verse narrative on 8 November 1920: Rupert's neat appearance (his scarf, sweater, checked trousers, and upright stance) was immediately established. He was pictured with his parents, and thus tenuously linked with magical elements of *The Three Bears* fairy-tale, but a cosy, domestic atmosphere was also conveyed. All this, plus the fact that Rupert, despite his furry head and hands, was always in essence a small boy (in fact a juvenile version of Everyman) ensured his success. Adult readers as well as children empathized with his wonderfully wide-ranging adventures in which he was frequently the innocent abroad, beset by but always triumphing over evil in the shape of Tourtel's colourful ogres, giants, and monsters. Her balladic style and rustic but Gothic-spiced settings launched not only Rupert but his assorted animal chums, and arguably her most intriguing character, the Merlin-esque Wise Old Goat.

Mary Tourtel drew, and contributed most of the slightly lumpy verse to, the daily Rupert strip until 1935, giving it up then because of failing eyesight. Her husband had died from a heart condition in 1931, and on her retirement Mary returned to Canterbury. She developed a brain tumour, and died in Kent and Canterbury Hospital on 15 March 1948; she was buried in St Martin's churchyard, Canterbury.

In the hands of subsequent artists Rupert has continued in the *Daily Express*, in books, and on television, giving rise to a whole line of merchandise. There has been some slight updating in deference to new social attitudes, and, despite occasional accusations of anti-feminism, racism, and class prejudice, Rupert has survived, holding an appeal for a varied readership.   MARY CADOGAN

Sources W. Lofts, D. Adley, and J. Beck, *The new Rupert index* (privately printed, Lewes, Sussex, 1991) • M. Cadogan, 'Rupert: sixty years in the same trousers', *Sunday Times* (9 Nov 1980) • M. Cadogan, 'The bear facts', *Times Educational Supplement* (15 Nov 1985) • Canterbury City Council Art Heritage Museum, *Rupert* (1988) • G. Perry and A. Bestall, *A bear's life* (1985) • *Nutwood: The Journal of 'The Followers of Rupert'*, 1–13 (1983–90) • *Nutwood News Letter: 'The Followers of Rupert'*, 1–22 (Nov 1990–Dec 1996) • b. cert. • d. cert.

Wealth at death £21,621 14s. 5d.: probate, 7 July 1948, *CGPLA Eng. & Wales*

Tout, Thomas Frederick (1855–1929), historian, was born at Norwood, Surrey, on 28 September 1855, the only child of Thomas Edward Tout, wine merchant—whose father, of a Somerset family, had settled in London—and his wife, Anne Charlotte Finch (*b*. 1821). Educated at St Olave's Grammar School (1869–74), Southwark, he became head of the school and in 1874 won the Brackenbury history scholarship at Balliol College, Oxford, where he went into residence in January 1875. Among his contemporaries at Balliol were Charles Harding Firth, Reginald Lane Poole, John Horace Round, Sidney Lee, Richard Lodge, Arnold Toynbee, William Ashby, Sidney Low, W. Piker, F. C. Montagu, and Charles Edwyn Vaughan. In 1877 Tout was ranked alone ('Unus Solus, Totus', as the regius professor noted) in the first class in modern history, and gained a second class in *literae humaniores* in 1879. From the first his interests centred in medieval history, and the teacher to whom he owed most was William Stubbs, whose preeminence in English medieval studies he was later to match.

After graduation Tout turned down a career in the civil service, in favour of teaching. He worked in Oxford as a private tutor for two years before being appointed professor of modern history at St David's College, Lampeter, where he remained until his election, nine years later, to the chair of medieval and modern history at Owens College, Manchester. The years at Lampeter were the making of Tout, and most of the ideas with which he was later associated at Manchester received trial there. While studying Welsh history, he also took a large part in reconstituting and reviving the college, and developed the self-confidence which his Oxford contemporaries had found lacking. In 1883 he was elected to a prize fellowship at Pembroke College, Oxford, and from 1889 to 1891 he was an examiner in the Oxford school of modern history.

Teaching history in Manchester Tout went to Owens College, in 1890 and remained there until his retirement in 1925, building an impressive career as an administrator, teacher, and writer. As an administrator, he took a prominent part in the successful campaign to divorce Owens College from the federal Victoria University (which also included University College, Liverpool, and Yorkshire College, Leeds) and to turn it into the Victoria University of Manchester. To the task of building up the new university Tout brought tireless energy, vision, and a strength of will

Thomas Frederick Tout (1855–1929), by Walter Stoneman, 1917

colleague James Tait. It was Tout's conviction—shared by other English historians such as Sir Charles Firth, J. B. Bury, and George Prothero—that an undergraduate programme which trained students to be historians and researchers was also an excellent intellectual training for any walk of life. From 1892 onwards Tout ensured that the last year of the undergraduate course should offer students a grasp of the original sources of history through the detailed study of a special subject. From the year 1907 this was achieved by means of a thesis, which occupied a large part of the third year and was closely related to the special subject studied intensively with plenty of expert guidance. Tout's approach thus combined an Oxford-style broad coverage of general European history with early but limited specialization in a special subject. Its success depended on Tout's splendid gifts as a teacher: a fine lecturer, he carried his subject in his head, speaking always without notes or even immediate preparation but with illuminating digressions suggested by his own special studies or his travels. A cyclist and a walker, he had a life-long interest in medieval antiquities and archaeology: England and Wales he knew through and through, and there were no *départements* in France and few countries in Europe which he had not visited.

Tout's highest gifts, however, lay in his personal relations with his students. Wholly without vanity, he met them on a footing of equality, as interested in them and their future as he was in their work. Through his teaching he brought the subject to life, and his own energetic example and his faith in learning inspired a substantial number to pursue historical studies. His success as teacher was made evident by the character of these graduates, who were trained in historical techniques which were developed to a level rarely aspired to in the other English universities at that time. Of the 123 students taught in Manchester between 1890 and 1914, 6 became professional historians and over 20 others published historical work. From these beginnings there slowly grew a postgraduate school, the work of which gained increasing recognition through the publications of the Manchester University Press. In 1920 Tout gave up most of his active teaching, and devoted himself to the organization of this postgraduate school.

The DNB and other writings Tout's writings fall into two well-marked groups, divided from each other by the year 1908. Before this year the easy adaptation to circumstances which marked his whole life was accurately reflected in his work. He filled in some of the gaps faced by all school and university students of history by writing a number of successful textbooks, including a standard *History of England* for schools (in conjunction with F. York Powell; part 3, 1890; part 2, 1898), and threw himself with enthusiasm into the two great new historical ventures of his time: the *English Historical Review*, founded in 1886 as Britain's first specialist historical periodical, for which he was a regular and respected reviewer, and the *Dictionary of National Biography*, of which the first volume appeared in 1885. Tout's 240 contributions—spread out over more than 40 volumes in the original edition, and together

which was almost ruthless. His robust and practical sense made him an extremely useful counsellor, while his criticisms were always of the constructive kind, not sceptical and discouraging. He was a hard fighter who, it was said, developed 'an irritable roughness' in debate. But he had a faith in his ideas which inspired respect, and in all personal relations a warm-hearted, human sympathy which often helped his opponents to overlook his wilder side. It was this almost paradoxical contrast which prompted the *bons mots* 'Tout comprendre c'est Tout pardonner.' Apart from the campaign for the new university, Tout was also significant as an administrator for his work on the building up of the faculty of arts, in the establishment of the non-denominational faculty of theology and the introduction of technological subjects, in the founding of the Manchester University Settlement, in insisting upon the same opportunities in the university for women as for men, and by his creation of the Manchester University Press. He also did invaluable and characteristic work in securing better conditions of pay and service for university lecturers and administrative officers, and, as chairman of the governors of Manchester High School for Girls between 1904 and 1924, in establishing 'sabbatical' terms for the staff, on full salary.

These tasks, to which Tout devoted considerable time and energy, never overshadowed his main aim, which was to develop the history school at Manchester. Here, he built upon the solid foundation of his predecessor, Sir Adolphus William Ward, and secured the full support of his amounting to a whole volume—ranged over the whole of the middle ages and occasionally beyond; they included an entry of nearly 6000 words on Catherine of Braganza. His medieval entries included three English kings (Edward II, Henry IV, and Henry VI), but were predominantly on magnates and senior ecclesiastics, rather than on the administrators upon whom he was to concentrate later in his career. They showed a pronounced geographical bias towards Wales and the Welsh marches: Tout provided articles on many Welsh princes and members of the Anglo-Welsh nobility, for instance on eight Fitzalans and ten Mortimers. It was good work, conceived at first on old-fashioned and optimistic lines, and largely drawn from printed primary sources, especially chronicles, of which he displayed from the first an impressive knowledge, but broadening and deepening with the years as he became increasingly familiar with the manuscript sources. Apart from these articles, Tout's early researches are demonstrated in three specialist studies: an article 'The Welsh shires', published in *Y Cymmrodor* in 1888; volume 3 (1216–1377) in Longman's *Political History of England* (1905), and *State Trials of the Reign of Edward I, 1289–1293*, written in conjunction with his sister-in-law Hilda Johnstone (1882–1961) and published in 1906 in the Camden series of the Royal Historical Society. The last of these brought Tout into immediate touch with the unexplored materials in the Public Record Office and foreshadowed the work of his second period.

In 1912, in evidence before the royal commission on public records, Tout set out in considerable detail certain conclusions to which work among archives had led him. The actual stimulus was supplied by Eugène Déprez's *Études de la diplomatique anglaise, 1272–1485*, which Tout reviewed in the *English Historical Review* (1908). For the rest of his life he focused on administrative history, and his work in this area is his most significant contribution to medieval history. It was embodied in two books, *The Place of the Reign of Edward II in English History* (1914) and *Chapters in the Administrative History of Medieval England* (6 vols., 1920–31). The first of these works grew out of his Ford lectures delivered at Oxford in 1913; of the *Chapters*, the last two volumes, although virtually finished before his death, were published posthumously. Before then Tout's originality had lain in his advanced conception of historical teaching. He was now to develop an entirely new direction for the study of institutional history as profound as that initiated by Stubbs in the 1870s, and to supply the first constructive criticism of that great historian's interpretation of the middle ages. Tout's basic argument was that, owing to the prevailing absorption in the constitutional history of parliament, English medieval history had been seen out of focus, since to contemporaries the administrative side of government was more important. Tout's object was to supplement Stubbs's work by detailing the history of the great administrative departments and their off-shoots, thus shifting the prevailing focus away from traditional notions of power and authority invested in king and parliament to the day-to-day running and maintenance of the administrative machinery of government. Not only did Tout's approach inspire other historical research, but his pioneering work at the Public Record Office—which H. W. C. Davis called 'blazing a track through … jungle'—also increased the productivity of other historians through his systematic calendaring and indexing of hitherto neglected sources. Recent scholarship has tended to regard Tout's concentration upon administrative procedure as apt to be misleading, in that it neglects the importance of patronage and personal relationships to the conducting of government business, but his work has nevertheless proved of lasting value to the understanding of the machinery of administration which kings and magnates aspired to exploit and control.

To a great extent Tout was applying to English institutional history ideas which had already been worked out with remarkable results by French historians, and one effect of his work was to emphasize the underlying similarity of French and English institutions. He developed the idea of this 'common heritage' in his *France and England: their Relations in the Middle Ages and Now* (1922), based mainly upon four lectures given at Rennes, at the invitation of the University of Rennes, in 1921. In this book and in a number of vigorous popular lectures given during the last fifteen years of his life he generalized the results of his special studies, to which they form an excellent introduction. To the end of his life Tout was also closely connected with the *English Historical Review*, the *Scottish Historical Review*, and *History*. To each of these journals he contributed many valuable articles, notably that on 'Firearms in England in the fourteenth century' in volume 26 of the *English Historical Review* (1911). A careful list of all his writings up to 1925, compiled by his wife, was included in the *Essays in Medieval History* presented to him by friends and pupils in that year; a note appended to A. G. Little's memoir in *History* (January 1930) carried the list down to Tout's death. A collection of his miscellaneous writings, historical articles, and public lectures was published posthumously as *The Collected Papers of Thomas Frederick Tout* (3 vols., 1932–4).

Character and final years Behind all these activities lay the force and charm of a remarkable personality. Of middle height and thickset, Tout was an excellent talker and raconteur, with slow and emphatic utterance, delighting in pungent epithets. Warm-hearted and kindly, he shared naturally the joys and troubles of his friends, and he had the understanding which won the devotion of all who worked with him or for him. Although the busiest of people, there was no limit to the time he could spare to help and counsel all who sought his advice. His life's work was underpinned by a happy private life: on 18 December 1895 he had married Mary Johnstone (*b.* 1872/3), one of his first students and daughter of Herbert Alison Johnstone, a schoolmaster from Stockport. She shared his public work as well as his personal interest in historical scholarship and his students, and their home became the centre of an ever-widening circle of friends.

Tout resigned his chair at Manchester in 1925. He returned to London, and settled at Hampstead, where he had all but completed his *Administrative History* at the time of his death. In these years he maintained his public interests to the full: he was president of the Royal Historical Society from 1926; he directed the medieval publications of the British Academy, of which he had been elected a fellow in 1911 and which, as an active member of the council, he represented at the meetings of the Union Académique Internationale at Brussels in 1920 and 1921; he was elected a member of the Athenaeum under rule 2; he was a member of the committee of the Institute of Historical Research and of the advisory committee of the BBC for national lectures. In 1928 he travelled in the USA, where he delivered the Messenger lectures at Cornell University, and in Canada. The last ten years of his life were marked by widening recognition of his pre-eminent position in medieval studies. Honorary degrees were conferred on him by the universities of Durham (1921), Liverpool, Edinburgh (both 1925), Oxford (1926), and Colorado (1928), and he was made an honorary fellow of Pembroke College, Oxford, and a corresponding fellow of the academy of Caen and of the Mediaeval Academy of America. These years were also marked by an ever-increasing interest in the development of history as a profession and particularly international co-operative ventures, such as the International Congress of Historical Studies. He had much to do with its development from the beginning, and was president of the medieval section at the international congress held in London in 1913 and again at Brussels in 1923. He was an active member of its standing committee, president of the British national committee, and was arranging for the annual meeting in England in 1930 at the time of his death. He died at his home, 3 Oak Hill Park, Hampstead, London, on 23 October 1929, and was survived by Mary Tout and by two sons and a daughter; the first son had died in infancy.

V. H. GALBRAITH, *rev.* PETER R. H. SLEE

Sources JRL, T. F. Tout MSS · *The collected papers of Thomas Frederick Tout*, 3 vols. (1932–4) [incl. memoir and bibliography] · P. B. M. Blaas, *Continuity and anachronism* (1978) · P. R. H. Slee, *Learning and a liberal education: the study of modern history in the universities of Oxford, Cambridge and Manchester, 1800–1914* (1986), 153–4 · A. G. Little, *History*, new ser., 14 (1929–30), 313–24 · J. Tait, 'Thomas Frederick Tout', *EngHR*, 45 (1930), 78–85 · H. Guppy, 'Proposed memorial to Professor Tout', *Bulletin of the John Rylands University Library*, 14 (1930), 305–6 · personal knowledge (1938) · m. cert. · d. cert. · *CGPLA Eng. & Wales* (1930)
Archives Hunt. L., letters · JRL, corresp., papers, and notebooks · NL Wales, letters | NL Wales, corresp. with J. Goronwy Edwards
Likenesses W. Hoffert, photograph, *c.*1880, repro. in *Collected papers*, vol. 3, frontispiece · Elliott & Fry, photograph, *c.*1916, repro. in *Collected papers*, vol. 2, frontispiece · W. Stoneman, photograph, 1917, NPG [*see illus.*] · Lafayette, photograph, Pembroke College, Oxford; repro. in *Collected papers*, vol. 1, frontispiece · oils, St David's University College, Lampeter, Cardiganshire
Wealth at death £12,995 14*s.* 1*d.*: probate, 17 Feb 1930, *CGPLA Eng. & Wales*

Tovey, D'blossiers [Bloshier] **(1692–1745)**, historian and antiquary, son of John Tovey, a citizen and apothecary of London, was born in the parish of St Martin-in-the-Fields on 1 March 1692. He matriculated from Queen's College, Oxford, on 12 March 1709, and graduated BA in 1712. He was elected fellow of Merton College in the same year and

proceeded MA in 1715. He was called to the bar of the Inner Temple in 1717 and took the degree of DCL at Oxford in 1721. He was ordained in the Church of England soon afterwards. From 1723 to 1727 he was rector of Farleigh, Surrey, and from 1727 to 1732 vicar of Embleton, Northumberland. In 1732 he returned to Oxford on his election as principal of New Inn Hall, and he held that office until his death in 1745.

Tovey was interested in history and archaeology, and devoted much time to a history of the Jews in medieval England. He freely utilized the numerous documents which William Prynne had first published in *A Short Demurrer to the Jews' Long Discontinued Remitter into England* (1656), but he supplied much additional information derived from his own research. His book, published in Oxford in 1738, was entitled *Anglia Judaica, or, The history and antiquities of the Jews in England, collected from all our historians, both printed and manuscript, as also from the records in the Tower and other publick repositories*. It was dedicated to George Holmes, deputy keeper of the records in the Tower of London.

Tovey's work has remained a major source for the history of the Jewish community in Britain. He estimated that the number of Jews in London (both Ashkenazim and Sephardim) totalled 6000, and that in 1738 there were no permanent settlements outside the capital. *Anglia Judaica* continues to be cited in modern histories of British Jewry. A letter from Tovey to Dr R. Rawlinson, dated 18 June 1744, 'concerning a Roman brick found in Market Lane', was printed in *Archaeologia* in 1770.

SIDNEY LEE, *rev.* ROBERT BROWN

Sources T. M. Endelmann, *The Jews of Georgian England, 1714–1830: tradition and change in a liberal society* (1979) · D. S. Katz, *The Jews in the history of England, 1485–1850* (1994); repr. (1997) · Bodl. Oxf., MS Rawl. C. 369, fol. 55 · *Archaeologia*, 1 (1770), 139 [extract of letter from Tovey to Dr R. Rawlinson, 18 June 1744] · Watt, *Bibl. Brit.* · Foster, *Alum. Oxon.*

Tovey, Sir Donald Francis (1875–1940), music scholar and composer, was born on 17 July 1875 at 23 High Street, Eton, Buckinghamshire, the youngest of the four children of the Revd Duncan Crookes Tovey (1842–1912), and his wife, Mary Fison (*d.* 1908). Two sisters had died in infancy, but Donald grew up with an admired elder brother, Duncan (1872–1918), who later became an actor, writer of light verse, and sergeant in the London Scottish regiment.

Tovey's childhood circumstances were comfortable and book-lined. His mother was well-read, witty, eccentric, and valetudinarian. His father, in succession chaplain of Trinity College, Cambridge (1871–4), assistant classics master at Eton College (1874–86), and rector of Worplesdon, near Guildford (1886–1912), was a biblical commentator, literary essayist, and scholar of eighteenth-century poetry. Neither parent was musical, however; so when Sophie Weisse (1851–1945), a pianoforte teacher who had a dame-school in Eton, discovered that their four-year-old son had startlingly precocious gifts in that direction, she was allowed to take charge of his education, musical and general. Thus began a close and crucial relationship—mutually affectionate and admiring at first, but later

Sir Donald Francis Tovey (1875–1940), by Sir William Rothenstein, c.1936

tinged quite often with resentment and irritation—which was to last until Tovey's death sixty years later.

Tovey never attended school in the conventional sense, but this did not stop him becoming knowledgeable about languages and literatures, mathematics and astronomy. He had solid musical instruction from Weisse herself (pianoforte, by Deppe's method), Walter Parratt and James Higgs (counterpoint, for which he had an innate gift), and Hubert Parry (composition). There was fruitful contact too with A. J. Hipkins, the expert on keyboard instruments; but most importantly, Weisse—German in origin herself and Germanic in musical outlook—introduced him, aged seven or eight, to the violinist Joseph Joachim, the great ambassador to Britain of the German 'classical' tradition of Bach, Beethoven, Schumann, and Brahms. Joachim was impressed. Though separated in age by over forty years, he and Tovey developed an intense mutual musical admiration, appearing in recitals and chamber concerts together from 1894 until the older man's death in 1907. Joachim and Sophie Weisse became in effect a second pair of highly influential parents for Tovey, though he never lost his affection for and contact with his natural pair.

Weisse groomed her eager pupil in his teens for the career of an international concert pianist: one who would have a formidably large, distinctly high-minded repertory and a self-abnegating concern to serve the intentions of the composers he played. By the 1890s he was himself composing energetically, mainly in traditional instrumental and orchestral forms; and he was able to complete his general education in style, since from 1894 to 1898 he

was the first holder of the Lewis Nettleship memorial scholarship at Balliol College, Oxford, a scholarship designed to give a musician of promise a grounding in the humanities. Though he left Oxford with only a third in Greats, his time there gained him several admiring and well-placed friends, notably Denys Bray, to whom he became deeply attached. It gave him too a training in classical literature and philosophy which led to his contemplating the 'metaphysics of tonality' and starting to write a grand treatise, *The Language of Music*. This was never finished—a failing which was to be characteristic of Tovey's big book projects—but his work on it from 1896 to 1900 gave him the fluency and argumentative resource to become a published writer at the turn of the century, initially with a few general pieces on music and some hugely extended programme notes (or 'analytical essays' as they were called) on particular concert works.

After a spell of recital playing out of town, Tovey was launched on the capital as a pianist by Sophie Weisse in November 1900. 'Now he comes to London', wrote the *Musical Standard*, 'a new Schumann—pianist, critic, and composer' (24 Nov 1900). For the next fourteen years he was visibly and vigorously active in each of those roles, though he was based at some distance from the capital in one or other of the houses provided for him by Weisse close to Northlands, the school she had established for well-connected young ladies in 1892 at Englefield Green, near Egham. As composer Tovey completed a piano concerto (1903), a quantity of chamber music, and a symphony (1913), as well as beginning an ambitious 'music drama' in 1907 on the Theseus–Phaedra–Ariadne myth: *The Bride of Dionysus*, to a text by his close friend R. C. Trevelyan. His concert pieces, with their serious craftsmanship and a markedly Teutonic cast uncharacteristic of the younger generation of English composers at the time, were heard with respect in Britain and more especially on the continent. As concert pianist, he played concertos, his own and other people's, and in London, Berlin, Vienna, and elsewhere gave recitals more challenging than the norm. Favourite items of his such as Bach's 'Goldberg' variations and Beethoven's 'Hammerklavier' sonata were not standard concert fare in the 1900s; and audiences needed stamina when, warmly applauding his performance of book 1 of the Brahms–Paganini variations, they found themselves rewarded with all of book 2 as an encore.

Tovey was also involved in several London chamber music series, as well as Weisse's Northlands concert seasons, playing *inter alios* with those musicians who after the death of Joachim became his closest friends in the profession: the violinist sisters Jelly d'Aranyi and Adila Fachiri (Joachim's great-nieces) and the cellist Pablo Casals. In 1912 the brothers Fritz and Adolph Busch, conductor and violinist, were added to his circle of musical intimates. He also conducted some out-of-town choral and orchestral concerts, Bach cantatas being a speciality. His memory for musical scores was held, by Joachim and Parry among others, to be prodigious—his memory for musical facts and ideas also. So he lectured on music at Northlands and elsewhere; and his early published writings led to further journalistic and discursive essays, to the beginnings of a book on his musical hero, Beethoven, and most influentially to the contribution of many substantial articles on musical forms and the achievements of major composers to the eleventh edition of the *Encyclopaedia Britannica* (1910–11).

However, this freelance life proved a considerable strain, something exacerbated on an intimate level by unrequited feelings for the sister of Tovey's successor as Nettleship scholar, F. S. Kelly, by a period of especially tense relations with Weisse (who was becoming increasingly possessive and resentful of any activities outside her control), and by a woundingly hot-blooded triangular misunderstanding with Casals and Guilhermina Suggia during a visit to Spain in 1912. So it is not surprising that Tovey should decide on a change of direction, applying in 1914 to become Friedrich Niecks's successor in the Reid chair of music at Edinburgh University. Appointed that summer, he began a notable twenty-six-year tenure which, though no more to the taste of some staid Scottish music lovers than his London career had been to those critics who dismissed him as far too earnest and cerebral, led to something of a golden age in Edinburgh music-making and to an international reputation for Tovey himself.

From 1914 until his death (and for a considerable time thereafter), that reputation was not founded on his compositions. These had their admirers, but they were not a large band. To make things worse, Tovey's compositional flow came close to drying up, partly because of personal and professorial pressures, partly out of a sense of isolation: the works of most of his composer contemporaries, he felt, spoke a language he did not understand. After the completion of *The Bride of Dionysus* in 1918—its première did not occur until 1929 in Edinburgh—he composed very little apart from the cello concerto in C, begun in 1933 and first given the following year by the reconciled Casals. Rather, it was as a performer, a lecturer, and especially a writer on music that Tovey became widely known.

Tovey's teaching terms as Reid professor ran from October to March only; so for the rest of the year he could carry on his recital work, which in the 1920s and early 1930s took him to the USA, notably New York and Boston, as well as to a range of British and continental venues. Fruits of his preparation for such recitals were the influential editions-with-commentary of Bach's forty-eight preludes and fugues and the Beethoven pianoforte sonatas which he published collaboratively in 1924 and 1931. During teaching terms he organized and often played at 'historical concerts' for students, Sunday 'pops' for town and gown, and from 1917 onwards (as a result of his founding the semi-professional Reid Symphony Orchestra the previous year) the annual series of Reid orchestral concerts at the Usher Hall. For these he trained the orchestra (with his orchestration students observing), conducted it with great musicality if not quite such great technical efficiency, played concertos with it, and brought in distinguished soloists and composer–conductors to round out a wide if rather conservative repertory.

The Reid concerts generated a host of extended programme-book essays by Tovey on the works performed, supplementing those he had written earlier for his London concerts and for the London visit of the Meiningen orchestra in 1902. The essays began to attract a following of their own, especially when Tovey in collaboration with Hubert Foss brought together and republished a large selection of them as the six volumes of *Essays in Musical Analysis* (1935–9). These had a huge success. All over the English-speaking world for a generation or more, 'looking it up in Tovey' became the way of finding out the most useful things about particular pieces of music from Palestrina to William Walton: acute and illuminating things, literately, wittily, and companionably expressed.

Aside from all this activity, Tovey saw his professorial role less as a musicologist—though he did edit Bach's *Art of Fugue* (1931)—than as a stimulating teacher. He lectured to undergraduates and Workers' Educational Association classes in Edinburgh and to academic audiences in California (visiting Santa Barbara in 1924, 1925, and 1926). A wider music-loving public heard him in BBC radio talks in the 1920s and 1930s: talks some found inspiring, some bemusing. And at Glasgow, Oxford, Liverpool, and London he gave several prestigious 'named' lectures and lecture series, their titles indicating some of his recurrent concerns: 'Music in being' (1925), 'Musical form and matter' (1934), 'The integrity of music' and 'Normality and freedom in music' (1936), and 'Musical textures' and 'The main stream of music' (1938).

Tovey's public outreach and acclaim—he was knighted in 1935—hid much personal sorrow and physical distress. On 22 April 1916, not long after his arrival in Edinburgh, he had impulsively married Margaret Cameron, the daughter of a Scottish painter, but the couple proved incompatible and she became mentally ill. A baby boy was adopted in 1919 and named John Wellcome Tovey, but could not save the situation. Margaret Tovey turned vindictively against her husband, and they were divorced in 1922. On 29 December 1925 Tovey married Clara Georgina Wallace (*c*.1875–1944), a friend since childhood and more recently guardian to John. Theirs was a much happier union, but before it began Tovey's health, never very strong in spite of his big physique and formidable energy, had a phase of near total collapse, the result of a long-undiagnosed attack of amoebic dysentery contracted in the USA in 1924. Though he seemed to recover, some permanent damage may have been done, compounding the effects of growing cardiovascular problems—he had a heart attack in 1932—and of arthritis of the hands and arms, which was seriously affecting his keyboard technique by the mid-1930s. He died from heart disease and nervous exhaustion at his home, 39 Royal Terrace, Edinburgh, on 10 July 1940, a week before his sixty-fifth birthday; after his cremation (between 10 and 16 July) a report in *The Scotsman* announced that his ashes were to be interred at Worplesdon. The shock to the musical world was the greater because he was at the height of his fame and seemed to be at the peak of his powers—though these were his analytical, critical, educational, literary, and scholarly powers, rated by Tovey himself well below his abilities as composer and pianist, which time and circumstance had thwarted. ROGER SAVAGE

Sources M. Grierson, *Donald Francis Tovey: a biography based on letters* (1952) • M. Tilmouth, introduction, in D. F. Tovey, *The classics of music*, ed. M. Tilmouth (2001) • U. Edin. L., Tovey archive • *DNB* • H. Havergal, 'Donald Francis Tovey: musician and teacher', Cramb lectures, U. Glas., 1963, U. Edin. L., Tovey Archive [unpubd typescript; copy] • S. Deas, 'Donald Francis Tovey: the creative scholar', *Recorded Sound*, 59 (1975), 456–60 [incl. discography] • M. Tilmouth, 'Tovey, Sir Donald (Francis)', *New Grove*, 2nd edn • *The Scotsman* (17 July 1940) • b. cert.
Archives U. Edin. L., corresp; papers and collections | BBC WAC, corresp. and scripts • priv. coll., letters to C. G. Barkla • Worcs. RO, letters to Sir Granville Bantock | SOUND BBC WAC • BL NSA, oral history interview • BL NSA, performance recording • BL NSA, recorded talk
Likenesses pencil drawing, 1885 • F. Yates, portrait, charcoal, 1900 • C. Kunwald, chalk drawing, 1907, Balliol Oxf. • P. A. de Laszlo, oils, 1913, U. Edin., faculty of music • D. Foggie, pencil drawing, 1933, U. Edin. • W. Rothenstein, sanguine and pencil drawing, c.1936, NPG [*see illus.*] • A. Campbell, ink drawing, 1938, U. Edin., Tovey archive • O. Schlapp, gouache drawing, U. Edin. • photographs, repro. in Grierson, *Donald Francis Tovey* • photographs, repro. in Tovey, *Classics of music*
Wealth at death £3994 2s. 1d.: confirmation, 12 Aug 1940, CCI

Tovey, Douglas Arnold Robert (1908–1991), property developer, was born on 21 March 1908 in Portishead, Somerset, the son of George Arnold Tovey, ironmonger, and his wife, Lilian Mary, *née* Nott. He won a scholarship to the choir school at Wells Cathedral, leaving at sixteen to work as a clerk in the Great Western Railway's surveyors' office. He later became the right-hand man of the assistant chief surveyor, Reginald Scarsbrook. On 9 September 1930 he married Norah Scott (*b.* 1905/6), secretary, and daughter of Edward Scott. They enjoyed more than sixty years of a happy marriage. In 1938 Tovey moved to Edward Lotery's company, Greater London Properties—one of London's most important developers of suburban shopping parades. He was put in charge of shop letting, bringing him into contact with Healey and Baker, Britain's leading estate agents for retail property. At the start of the Second World War, Lotery emigrated to the USA and Tovey was invited by Aubrey Orchard-Lisle of Healey and Baker to join the practice; in 1945 he was made a partner. During the following twenty years Britain experienced an unprecedented boom in commercial property development, in which he was to play a leading role. Known to colleagues as Dart—an acronym of his initials—he acquired a reputation for forthrightness in business, especially in his letters, which abandoned the staid style of contemporary business correspondence in favour of a hard-sell line, with the important words and phrases in capitals. His business propositions justified this bullish tone, proving key to the fortunes of several of Britain's most important post-war property entrepreneurs.

Tovey had a remarkable flair for creating the 'big deal', which led him to play a major role in the 1950s takeover boom. He often arranged a large part of the business transactions for his clients, offering them proposals as a full package, including acquisition, occupiers, and institutional funding. His three most important clients were Montague Burton, Hugh Fraser, and Charles Clore. Burton had been one of the pioneers of leaseback finance, in which properties were sold to financial institutions to realize their value, while being simultaneously leased back to their occupiers on very long, fixed rent, leases. During the early 1950s Tovey applied this technique on behalf of Fraser and Clore to acquire entire companies that were rich in property assets. Tovey had the original idea for Clore's acquisition of the J. Sears Trueform Boot Company in 1953, establishing Clore as the leading figure of the takeover boom. This chain owned some 800 shops, the value of which was quickly realized via sale and leaseback deals, providing Clore with £10 million for further takeovers, many of which Tovey also arranged. In September 1960 Clore sent Tovey, in company with Clore's right-hand man, Leonard Sainer, to New York to purchase the biggest skyscraper he could find. He bought, from the legendary American developer Bill Zeckendorf senior, 40 Wall Street, a 71 storey, 1 million sq. ft block which, at the time, was the tallest on Wall Street.

In the same year, while crossing the Atlantic, Tovey came up with the idea for the merger of Clore's property company, City and Central Investments, with City Centre Properties, owned by Jack Cotton, probably the most famous property developer of the 1950s. Tovey believed that merging the two property empires would avoid the duplication of effort involved in himself and Aubrey Orchard-Lisle (his fellow partner at Healey and Baker, who represented Cotton) separately searching for developments for the two companies. The merger—which created the world's largest property company—proved ill fated. Tensions between Clore and its other leading lights, Jack Cotton and Walter Flack, culminated in a notorious boardroom battle in which Cotton and Flack were outmanoeuvred by Clore. Both Cotton and Flack died tragically shortly afterwards, while the merged concern was eventually acquired by Harold Samuel's Land Securities.

Tovey's career coincided with the heyday of the British property development industry, in which its leading figures were household names and lived in considerable style. This was reflected in Tovey's business and social life; he would often put forward deals for Hugh Fraser, with whom he became close friends, while on holiday with him at St Moritz in the winter or Monte Carlo in the summer. Another leading commercial estate agent, Edward Erdman, recalled that 'Douglas was exhilarating company. He had an engaging warm personality and an uninhibited flow of conversation and was a complete extrovert' (*The Independent*). Tovey was also famously superstitious: his favourite talisman was a spotted Dalmatian dog which was constantly at his side. He retired from Healey and Baker in 1968, at the age of sixty. By then he owned Highmoor Park, a 110 acre estate near Henley-on-Thames, and a house in the Bishop's Avenue, Hampstead. However, he continued to lunch at Claridge's once a week, arriving in his chauffeur-driven Rolls-Royce. He died at the Dunedin Hospital, Bath Road, Reading, on 9 July 1991, leaving an estate valued at £3,872,860. He was survived by his wife, Norah. A memorial service was held at St George's, Hanover Square, on 23 September 1991.

PETER SCOTT

Sources C. Gordon, *The two tycoons* (1984) · D. Clutterbuck and M. Devine, *Clore: the man and his millions* (1987) · E. L. Erdman, *People and property* (1982) · O. Marriott, *The property boom* (1967) · *The Times* (15 Aug 1991) · *The Independent* (28 Aug 1991) · *Estates Times* (16 Aug 1991) · private information (2004) · b. cert. · m. cert. · d. cert.
Likenesses photograph, repro. in P. Scott, *The property masters: a history of the British commercial property sector* (1996) · photographs, repro. in Gordon, *The two tycoons* · portrait, repro. in *The Times*
Wealth at death £3,872,860: probate, 15 Jan 1992, *CGPLA Eng. & Wales*

Tovey, John Cronyn, Baron Tovey (1885–1971), naval officer, was born on 7 March 1885 at Borley Hill, Rochester, Kent, the youngest of the eleven children (four girls and seven boys, one of whom was killed in the First World War) of Colonel Hamilton Tovey, Royal Engineers, and his wife, Maria Elizabeth Goodhue of London, Ontario. Tovey was educated at Durnford House School at Langton Matravers in Dorset, from where in January 1900 he joined the Royal Navy as a cadet in the training ship *Britannia*.

Tovey's first sea appointment was as a midshipman for a year in the battleship *Majestic*, flagship of the channel squadron. This was followed by three years in the cruiser *Ariadne*, flagship of the North America and West Indies station under Vice-Admiral Sir A. L. Douglas. In 1905–6 he undertook sub-lieutenant's courses in gunnery, torpedo, navigation, and pilotage. There followed various appointments, mainly seagoing, during the years leading to the outbreak of the First World War in 1914.

Tovey received his first command on 13 January 1915 when appointed to the 750 ton oil-fired destroyer *Jackal*. He was already a dedicated destroyer man, being described in a report by his flotilla captain as 'entirely to my satisfaction. A good destroyer officer. Keen and zealous' (private information). Tovey was given another destroyer command on 7 May 1916 when appointed to the new destroyer *Onslow* in which he was soon to make his name at the battle of Jutland on 31 May 1916. Tovey was acclaimed for his great courage. In addition to his being appointed to the DSO (1919), he was given special promotion to commander 'for the persistent and determined manner in which he attacked enemy ships'. Although only thirty-one he had established a reputation of star quality, particularly as a destroyer man.

On 28 March 1916 Tovey married Aida (d. 1970), daughter of John Rowe, an independent gentleman, of Plymouth, Devon. There were no children from the marriage.

Tovey remained in command of the *Onslow* until October 1917 when he was given *Ursa*, a new destroyer of 1000 to 1200 tons. His subsequent command of *Wolfhound* gave him still more experience until May 1919 when he joined the Royal Naval College, Greenwich, for a year.

A spell of duty for Tovey in the Admiralty operations division from June 1920 until June 1922, as a young commander, showed that he was already marked as an officer of promise. Tovey's promotion to captain came in December 1923 at the early age of thirty-eight at a time when the number of promotions was tending to diminish because of disarmament. Then followed a number of shore appointments, interspersed with further destroyer work as captain (D). In 1925 his flotilla was based on Port Edger in the Firth of Forth, where another promising officer, Andrew Cunningham, later Viscount Cunningham of Hyndhope, was captain in charge. Cunningham and Tovey between them developed a scheme which increased exercises at sea and rectified lapses in training.

A year at the Imperial Defence College in 1927 was followed by the senior officers' technical course, and then by a testing two years as naval assistant to the second sea lord at the Admiralty. In April 1932 Tovey was given command of the 35,000 ton 16 inch battleship *Rodney*. A responsible appointment, this marked him as a candidate for flag rank, at a time when the navy was recovering from the shock of mutiny at Invergordon. From the *Rodney* Tovey was appointed commodore of the royal naval barracks, Chatham, at the beginning of 1935, and seven months later was promoted rear-admiral.

After other courses, in March 1938 Tovey received his first seagoing flag appointment, becoming rear-admiral (destroyers) in the Mediterranean, and flying his flag in the cruiser *Galatea*. He was promoted vice-admiral in May 1939.

From the outbreak of the Second World War there was great mutual admiration between Cunningham, the commander-in-chief of the Mediterranean fleet, and Tovey. Both were destroyer men and had highly developed qualities of leadership. With the fall of France and the entry of Italy into the war it was necessary at once to adopt the offensive. Gradually the fleet was increased, in support of the policy of retaining the Mediterranean and control of the sea routes at all costs. In late June 1940 Cunningham gave Tovey command of all the allied light forces in the Mediterranean and made him second in command of the fleet.

Protracted discussion ensued between the French and the British as to the policy to be adopted concerning those French ships at Alexandria. It was imperative that they should not fall into enemy hands. But French co-operation seemed unlikely until Cunningham obtained an agreement that the ships should be immobilized for the duration. Widespread gloom changed to relief. The situation was briefly summarized by a smiling Tovey who, when calling on Cunningham, said: 'Now I know we shall win the war, sir. We have no more allies' (private information).

Tovey had established a great fighting reputation for the destroyer flotillas in the Mediterranean, and was now to do the same for his light forces of five cruisers and seventeen destroyers, which he handled magnificently in action against the Italians off Calabria on 9 July 1940. The main action between rival fleets was brief and indeterminate, each side being much concerned about the safety of its own convoy. Although the Italians sustained only minor damage at Calabria, it was to be the beginning of a British campaign in which the British fleet maintained an ascendancy in the Mediterranean that lasted through years of both triumph and adversity. Ten days after Calabria, Tovey's force sank the Italian cruiser *Bartolomeo Colleoni*.

Tovey's distinguished service in the Mediterranean in command of the light forces came to an abrupt end late in 1940 when he was given the acting rank of admiral and transferred to the Home Fleet as commander-in-chief, in succession to Admiral Sir Charles Forbes. Tovey, though not yet fifty-five, was approaching the peak of his active service career.

Tovey faced a very difficult situation in the first part of 1941. Britain was still alone, and the possibility of a German invasion remained, though no longer imminent. More serious, however, was the threat to Britain's Atlantic lifeline, and also the increasing production of German submarines and aircraft. In spite of Britain's blockade of the northern passages, German warships were able to break out from the Baltic and roam the high seas, largely sustained by the supply bases acquired in western France. The new battle cruisers *Scharnhorst* and *Gneisenau* were both at large. Admiral Richard Onslow recorded that in those long hard days of 1941 Tovey's leadership was of the finest: it stemmed from strength of character and fearlessness.

The German admiral Raeder planned for a rendezvous in April 1941, whereby the 'unsinkable' battleship *Bismarck* and the heavy cruiser *Prinz Eugen* should escape unseen from the Baltic, and join forces in the Atlantic with the battle cruisers *Scharnhorst* and *Gneisenau* from Brest. Such a force could cope with almost any likely situation, and would pose a powerful threat to Britain's lifeline. Tovey was aware of the plan and disposed his fleet accordingly, ordering his cruisers to keep a particularly close watch on the Denmark Strait. He had received a great accretion of strength in the new aircraft-carrier *Victorious* which joined him at Scapa Flow. Bomb damage prevented the sailing of those German ships at Brest, but the *Bismarck* and *Prinz Eugen* were reported on 22 May 1941 as having left Bergen, indicating that a break-out was imminent. Tovey had already sailed the battle cruiser *Hood* and the battleship *Prince of Wales* for the Denmark Strait, and at 7.45 p.m. on 22 May with his flag in battleship *King George V*, Tovey sailed the rest of the Home Fleet, including *Victorious* and the battle cruiser *Repulse*, from Scapa Flow. In view of the vast distances to be covered, due care had to be taken over fuel supply.

At 7.22 p.m. on 23 May, in spite of sleet and snow which impaired the visibility, the cruiser *Suffolk* sighted and reported the *Bismarck* and the *Prinz Eugen* as 7 miles ahead of her in the Denmark Strait, steering a south-westerly course. Action was joined at 5.53 a.m. on 24 May. All four ships opened fire. Within seconds the *Hood* was straddled by the *Bismarck* and blew up with a huge explosion. There were only three survivors. With her own fighting capacity drastically reduced by breakdowns and accurate enemy fire, the *Prince of Wales* withdrew under cover of smoke. The German ships continued to steer a south-westerly course. But the *Prince of Wales* had obtained two hits on the *Bismarck*, one of which caused a leak of oil fuel and was to

have dire consequences. Reduction of endurance might have compelled the *Bismarck* to make for a French port.

Tovey, with the *King George V*, *Repulse*, and *Victorious*, was still 300 miles away steaming westward, intent on intercepting the *Bismarck*. Meanwhile the Admiralty diverted various ships to come under Tovey's command so as to be in areas where a renewal of action appeared likely. These included the aircraft-carrier *Ark Royal* (from force H), and the *Rodney* and *Ramillies* with various cruisers and destroyers. Late on 24 May, torpedo reconnaissance bombers from the *Victorious* found the *Bismarck* and delivered with great gallantry, in squally weather, an attack which scored a hit. *Bismarck* escaped yet again.

Tovey had great anxiety at the prospect of fuel shortage in so many of his ships, in an area favourable both for German aircraft and submarines. He decided that if the *Bismarck* had not been slowed down before midnight on 26 May he would be compelled to break off the chase. His margin of success was slender, for at 8.47 p.m. on 26 May, *Ark Royal*'s striking force scored a hit which damaged *Bismarck*'s propellers, jammed her rudder, and effectively stopped her. On the morning of 27 May she faced the combined fire of *King George V* and *Rodney* and sustained overwhelming damage, though gallantly returning fire to the end. Tovey ordered that she should be finished off by torpedoes.

Tovey remarked favourably on the speed and accuracy of the information signalled by the Admiralty. He was however soon to come into conflict with the Admiralty, and with Winston Churchill too. He was much concerned at the lack of air support, and never hesitated to stress the point, thereby earning Churchill's description of him as 'stubborn and obstinate' (private information). Interference by the Admiralty reached a climax in July 1942 when a valuable British convoy, PQ 17 in the Barents Sea, was ordered by the Admiralty (without Tovey's concurrence) to scatter. It resulted in disastrous losses. However, Tovey's forthright opinions, and his utter integrity and courage, inspired confidence throughout the fleet. In July 1943, after two and a half years in command, he relinquished the Home Fleet to become commander-in-chief, the Nore. Preparations were already in hand, not only for the 1943 allied invasion of Sicily, but also for the 1944 entry into Europe.

Tovey was appointed KBE in 1941 after sinking the *Bismarck*. Also in 1941 he was promoted KCB, having been appointed CB in 1937. In 1943 he was further advanced to GCB and also promoted to the highest rank, admiral of the fleet, having been confirmed full admiral in 1942. He was made a baron in 1946.

Tovey was for four years (1948–52) third church estates commissioner, an appointment made by the archbishop of Canterbury, and one which Tovey enjoyed to the full, and carried out with efficiency. He died at Funchal, Madeira, on 12 January 1971, and the barony became extinct.   S. W. C. PACK and C. S. NICHOLLS, *rev.*

Sources *The Times* (13 Jan 1971) · *The Times* (18 Jan 1971) · private information (1986) · *WWW* · S. W. Roskill, *The war at sea, 1939–1945*, 3 vols. in 4 (1954–61) · *CGPLA Eng. & Wales* (1971)

Archives NMM, papers |FILM BFI NFTVA, news footage · IWM FVA, actuality footage · IWM FVA, news footage |SOUND IWM SA, oral history interview

Likenesses W. Stoneman, photograph, 1943, NPG · O. Birley, oils, c.1945–1946, Royal Naval Staff College, Greenwich · W. Dring, pastel drawing, IWM

Wealth at death £66,420: probate, 10 May 1971, CGPLA Eng. & Wales

Tovey, Nathaniel (*bap.* 1597, *d.* 1658), Church of England clergyman, was born in Coventry and baptized there on 23 October 1597 in Holy Trinity Church, son of John Tovey (*d.* c.1614), schoolmaster of the free school in Coventry, who, according to William Dugdale, 'had for his habitation the mansion house'. In 1602 John Tovey resigned his post and the following year moved 2 miles to Combe Abbey, Warwickshire, in order to assume the post of tutor to John Harington, the son of Baron Harington of Exton. Nathaniel Tovey lived in the Harington household until 1612, when he matriculated as a sizar at Sidney Sussex College, Cambridge. The following year John Tovey and the younger Harington travelled to Italy; both died shortly after their return to England. The responsibility for Nathaniel Tovey's education was then assumed by Lucy, countess of Bedford (Harington's sister).

Tovey graduated BA in 1616 and proceeded MA in 1619. In 1621 he was incorporated MA at Oxford and he was ordained, in London, as a deacon and elected to a fellowship and a lectureship in logic at Christ's College, Cambridge. He was dean of the college from 1621 to 1623, and in 1624 served as praelector, so the entries in the admissions book for that year are in his hand. The triers' admission book for 1654 credits Tovey with a BD, but there is no record in the university lists for the relevant period of his receiving this degree.

Probably in Michaelmas term 1627, Tovey became tutor to John Milton on his readmission to college after quarrelling with his original tutor, William Chappell. There may well have been an existing link between them, since the younger Harington's funeral sermon had been preached by Richard Stock, rector of All Hallows, Bread Street, London, where the Miltons worshipped. When Milton's brother Christopher came up to Christ's College in 1631, he too was assigned to Tovey. The Milton brothers left Cambridge in July 1632.

In 1630 Tovey was appointed rector of Lutterworth, Leicestershire, and in 1634 he left Cambridge to take up the appointment. In the autumn of 1634 he travelled to London to appear with five other fellows of Christ's before the court of high commission. The nature of the accusations is nowhere specified, though it may have been related to the conduct of services in the Christ's College chapel, but in any case the six fellows were discharged on 19 November, and Tovey returned to Lutterworth.

On 30 June 1636 Tovey married Elizabeth Warner (*d.* 1658), daughter of Silvester Warner of Wolston Manor and niece of the mathematician Walter Warner. As Wolston Manor was about a mile from Combe Abbey it seems likely that Nathaniel and Elizabeth had known each other for many years. A cache of letters from Tovey to his brother-in-law George Warner in London constitutes a fascinating window into the life of a seventeenth-century Leicestershire rector. Tovey lived quietly in Lutterworth until 1646, when his glebe land was sequestered and a series of charges was laid by the county committee: he was accused of assisting the king's forces in the garrisons at Worcester, Lichfield, and elsewhere, refusing to use the *Directory for the Publique Worship of God* instead of the Book of Common Prayer, railing in the altar, and raising the steps in the chancel. Tovey was ejected, and in 1647 an intruder was installed in Lutterworth. Tovey's whereabouts during his ecclesiastical exile are not known, but in 1654 he secured the patronage of John Manners, earl of Rutland, a prominent supporter of the parliamentary cause, and was appointed rector of Aylestone, Leicestershire, where he recorded in the register that the amendment of the Marriage Act in June 1657 restored the right of ministers to conduct weddings.

In 1658 Tovey and his wife both succumbed to a visitation of plague, and were buried in Aylestone on 9 September 1658. Their son, John, had predeceased them, but they were survived by their daughter, Elizabeth Vincent.

GORDON CAMPBELL

Sources G. Campbell, 'Nathaniel Tovey: Milton's second tutor', *Milton Quarterly*, 21 (1987), 81–90 · J. Goodacre, 'Letters from a seventeenth century rector of Lutterworth: Nathaniel Tovey as marriage agent', *Leicestershire Historian*, 3/2 (1983–4), 9–16 · W. Dugdale, *The antiquities of Warwickshire illustrated* (1656) · Walker rev., 246–7 · first fruits composition books, PRO, E 334/18, fol. 238v · minute books of the court of high commission, PRO, SP 16/261 · proceedings of the committee for sequestrations, PRO, SP 20/4/168, fol. 117v · administration act books, PRO, PROB 6/34/337 · John Scott, 'The foundation of the University of Cambridge', BL, Add. MS 11720 · proceedings of the committee for plundered ministers, BL, Add. MS 15671 · Bodl. Oxf., MS Aubrey 8, fols. 63–8 · Bodl. Oxf., MS Walker C 5/6, fol. 1r [sequestration of glebe land] · Bodl. Oxf., MS Walker C 11, fol. 4r [records of articles being presented to Tovey] · Bodl. Oxf., MS Walker C 17/81 ['articles exhibited against Mr Nathaniel Tovey'] · Bodl. Oxf., MS Walker C 17/119 [record of Elizabeth Tovey's deposition] · parish register, Aylestone church, 9 Sept 1658, Leics. RO, DE 3437/1 [burial] · induction mandates, Leicestershire, Leics. RO, 1D41/28/45 · triers' admission book, 1654, LPL, MS Comm. III/3/Lib2, p. 32 · parish register, Coventry, Holy Trinity Church, 23 Oct 1597 [baptism] · parish register, Wolston parish church, 30 June 1636 [marriage]

Archives PRO, letters, incl. one from his wife, Elizabeth, SP 46/38

Tovi the Proud (*fl.* 1018–1042), nobleman and administrator, was probably of Danish descent. He is remembered as the founder of the college of secular canons at Holy Cross, Waltham, in Essex. The Waltham chronicle, composed between 1177 and 1189, describes the miraculous discovery of the 'Black Rood', a life-sized figure of the crucified Christ, at Tovi's manor of Lutgaresberi (Montacute), Somerset, and its removal to Waltham, described as Tovi's hunting-lodge. The foundations of three earlier churches have, however, been found beneath the present building, and the settlement may date back to the ninth century. Tovi established the rood, girded with his own sword, in the church of Waltham, endowed the church with land and treasures, and established livings for two priests.

The Waltham chronicle exaggerates in describing Tovi

as 'the first man in England after the king' (*Waltham Chronicle*, 13), but there is no reason to doubt its assertion that he was a staller (someone with special functions in the royal administration), for in the reign of Cnut (*r.* 1016–35) he attended a shire-court at Aylton, Herefordshire, 'on the king's business' (*AS chart.*, S 1462). He attests Cnut's charters between 1018 and 1035, often alongside *Osgod Clapa (*d.* 1054), another man known to be a staller; in 1033 they are actually distinguished by their bynames (*AS chart.*, S 968). In 1042 Tovi married Osgod's daughter Gytha, almost certainly as his second wife; it was at their wedding feast, held at Lambeth, that King Harthacnut collapsed and died 'as he stood at his drink' (*ASC*, s.a. 1042, Texts C, D).

In 1042–3 Tovi was among the executors of the will of Ælfric Modercope, an east midlands thegn (*AS chart.*, S 1490), but it is not certain that he is the Tovi who attests charters of Harthacnut and Edward between 1042 and 1044, in every case in a rather lowly position (*AS chart.*, S 993, 998–9, 1003); his name is not uncommon and two men bearing it, Tovi the White and Tovi the Red, attest a charter in 1034 (*AS chart.*, S 961). Tovi the Proud probably died soon after 1042 and may well have been buried at Holy Cross, Waltham. He is commemorated in the *Liber vitae* of Thorney Abbey, as well as at Waltham itself.

Apart from Montacute, Tovi's recorded lands (about 140 hides on the Domesday figures) lay in Essex (Waltham, Loughton, and Alderton), Hertfordshire (Cheshunt, Hitchin), and Middlesex (Edmonton and Enfield); he also had property at Reading, Berkshire. Lambeth, which he gave to Waltham, was probably his wife's marriage portion. Gytha herself provided the rood with a golden crown and gem-encrusted girdle, as well as plate commissioned from the king's goldsmith, Theodoric of London. Tovi left a son Æthelstan—possibly Ælfstan the Staller, recorded *c.*1045 (*AS chart.*, S 1471), for the names were sometimes confused—who lost much of his father's estate through incompetence. The beneficiary was Harold Godwineson (*d.* 1066), who also took on Tovi's role as patron of Waltham: he increased the number of canons, greatly augmented the endowment, and rebuilt the church in the German style. Tovi's grandson *Asgar the Staller was still a wealthy and powerful man around the time of the conquest.　　　　　　　　　　　　　ANN WILLIAMS

Sources *AS chart.*, S 961, 968, 993, 998–9, 1003, 1462, 1471, 1490 • L. Watkiss and M. Chibnall, eds. and trans., *The Waltham chronicle: an account of the discovery of our holy cross at Montacute and its conveyance to Waltham*, OMT (1994) • John of Worcester, *Chron.* • A. Farley, ed., *Domesday Book*, 2 vols. (1783), 1.34, 129v, 137; 2.15v, 16 • P. J. Huggins, 'The excavation of an eleventh-century Viking hall … at Waltham Abbey', *Medieval Archaeology*, 20 (1976) • P. Nightingale, 'The origin of the court of husting and Danish influence on London's development into a capital city', *EngHR*, 102 (1987), 559–78, esp. 564–6 • A. Williams, 'The king's nephew: the family, career, and connections of Ralph, earl of Hereford', *Studies in medieval history presented to R. Allen Brown*, ed. C. Harper-Bill, C. J. Holdsworth, and J. L. Nelson (1989), 327–43 • S. Keynes, *An atlas of attestations in Anglo-Saxon charters, c.670–1066* (privately printed, Cambridge, 1993) • A. J. Robertson, ed. and trans., *Anglo-Saxon charters*, 2nd edn (1956) • *ASC*, s. a. 1042 (texts C, D) • D. Whitelock, 'Scandinavian names in the *Liber Vitae* of Thorney Abbey', *Saga-Book of the Viking Society*, 12/2 (1937–8), 127–53 [repr. *History, law, and literature in tenth- and eleventh-century England* (1981)] • P. J. Huggins and K. N. Bascombe, 'Excavations at Waltham Abbey, Essex, 1985–91: three pre-conquest churches and Norman evidence', *Archaeological Journal*, 149 (1992), 287–320 • P. A. Clarke, *The English nobility under Edward the Confessor* (1994)

Towers, John (*d.* 1649), bishop of Peterborough, was born in Norfolk; his parents are unknown. In 1595 he went up to King's College, Cambridge, but migrated to Queens' College, graduating BA in 1602, proceeding MA in 1606, and being elected a fellow in 1608. In 1615 he proceeded BD and by 1616 the courtier William Compton, later first earl of Northampton, had employed him as his domestic chaplain, a position which continued under Spencer Compton, the second earl, after 1630. Before 1617 Towers married Mary (*d.* 1672); they had nine children, one of whom was called Spencer and another, Compton. On 26 March 1617 Compton appointed Towers rector of Castle Ashby, Northamptonshire, whereupon he resigned his fellowship. Here he first encountered King James I, who promoted him to royal chaplain in appreciation of a sermon on the sanctity of the material church. Towers joined a clique of avant-garde conformists led by John Lambe which dominated the Peterborough church courts. Through David Owen's influence, Northampton presented Towers to the rectory of Yardley Hastings on 12 August 1623. Having proceeded to DD by royal edict dated 13 December 1624, Towers acquired the living of Halifax, Yorkshire, on 4 July 1628. He next obtained from the crown the deanery of Peterborough, to which he was instituted by John Pocklington on 14 November 1630.

The vacancy of the see in 1634 encouraged Towers to lobby for the position, suggesting that another conformist friend, Robert Sibthorpe, replace him as dean. The strategy failed, but Towers achieved a prebendal stall at Westminster on 3 April 1634. He was known at the new court of Charles I and contributed to a series of Lenten lectures there. As Peterborough's dean he strictly regulated the cathedral clergy and charged £5 for burial before the altar. A zealous supporter of the royal prerogative, he requested in 1637 that he, and not the bailiff, be put in charge of the collection of ship money in the town. He succeeded his friend, Francis Dee, as bishop in 1639, being consecrated on 13 January after resigning his prebend.

Towers ranks among the most combative of Laudian bishops. An aggressive consecration sermon preached by Peter Heylin was echoed by the bishop when he launched a tirade against the 'puritan faction' at his visitation of 1639 (PRO, SP 16/474/80). His piety emphasized compulsory participation in altar-centred worship while downplaying the word-centred piety most characteristic of the Jacobean episcopate. His visitation articles, which were borrowed from Matthew Wren's notorious set for Norwich in 1636, stipulated the full Laudian ceremonial—the priest administering communion from within the rails of an east-end altar to communicants receiving there kneeling. Dee had enforced this during his episcopate, but had never openly published the requirement, and the result of Towers's doing so was open opposition by the local magistracy. Towers also recommended the pre-Reformation practice of confession and enjoined all parishes to purchase silver communion services. William Prynne singled out Towers as a threat to the favourite Jacobean ordinance of preaching and, indeed, Towers's policy was one of severe regulation. He intervened in a local dispute between Sibthorpe and opponents at Brackley by erecting a new combination lecture but one whose continued existence he linked, uniquely, to performance of the liturgy in the Laudian fashion. He was a vigorous enforcer of the regime's position during the bishops' wars; prosecutions were initiated against one minister accused of holding a fast in support of the invading Scots and against a ministerial conference which met at Kettering to support the Scots and condemn the oath legitimizing the new canons.

The Long Parliament impeached Towers on 4 August 1641 (with twelve other bishops) for approving in convocation the clerical benevolence to fund the bishops' wars and the canons of 1640, which were regarded as illegal. He was also a signatory of the protest signed by twelve bishops in December complaining that it was not safe for them to attend parliament and that, in their absence, all votes taken were void. The protesters were impeached for high treason for this attempted veto, and were committed to the Tower, but in April 1642 Towers, having been released, returned to Peterborough and soon after joined the king's headquarters at Oxford where he remained during the civil war until the city's surrender in 1646. By that time he had been ejected by parliament from his livings and was reported in 1647 for harassing one replacement minister. Returning to Peterborough he died in obscurity on 10 January 1649 and was buried the next day in the cathedral.

The bishop's eldest son, **William Towers** (1617?–1666), Church of England clergyman and author, was educated at Westminster School as a king's scholar. Having matriculated on 1 September 1634 from Christ Church, Oxford, he graduated BA on 11 April 1638 and proceeded MA on 22 May 1641. His father ordained him a priest on 19 April 1641 and instituted him to a prebendal stall the next day. In 1644 he was appointed rector of Barnack, Northamptonshire, but the course taken by the war led him to move to Oxford, where he obtained a BD in 1646. Ejected from his preferments by parliament in 1646, he supported himself by serving as curate to Edward Reynolds at Upton near Northampton, and obtained additional patronage from Sir Justinian Isham of Lamport. He published three works in the 1650s—*Atheismus Vapulans, or, A Treatise Against Atheism* (1654), *Polytheismus Vapulans* (1654?), and *A sermon against murder: by occasion of the Romanists putting the protestants to death in the dukedom of Savoy* (1655).

At the Restoration, Towers published two sermons of thanksgiving, the first preached on 29 May, the day of Charles II's entry to London, and the second, *Obedience Perpetually due to Kings* (1660), a month later. Towers himself was restored to his preferments through the friendship of the former royalist Mountjoy Blount, earl of Newport, while maintaining the family connection with the Comptons by dedicating his edition of his father's *Four Sermons*

(1660) to James, the third earl of Northampton. In 1662 he was appointed rector of Fiskerton, Lincolnshire, and the following year published a sermon preached at the bishop of Lincoln's visitation. He died on 20 October 1666 while visiting nearby Uffington, where he was buried.

J. FIELDING

Sources A. J. Fielding, 'Conformists, puritans and the church courts: the diocese of Peterborough, 1603–1642', PhD diss., U. Birm., 1989 · dean and chapter act book, 1585–1646, Northants. RO, M (T) 18, MS, fols. 165–99 · H. I. Longden, *Northamptonshire and Rutland clergy from 1500*, ed. P. I. King and others, 16 vols. in 6, Northamptonshire RS (1938–52), vol. 14, pp. 5–7 · W. Prynne, *Canterburies doome, or, The first part of a compleat history of the commitment, charge, tryall, condemnation, execution of William Laud, late arch-bishop of Canterbury* (1646), 378–80 · *Walker rev.*, 13, 285 · PRO, LC 5/132–3; SP 16/474/80 · P. Heylin, *The parable of the taxes* (1659), 311–36 · BL, Lansdowne MS 985, fols. 127–30 · BL, Add. MS 985, fol. 89 · *DNB* · Northants. RO, Isham correspondence, 476 · J. Davies, *The Caroline captivity of the church: Charles I and the remoulding of Anglicanism, 1625–1641* (1992) · S. R. Gardiner, *History of England from the accession of James I to the outbreak of the civil war*, 10 (1884), 122–5

Towers, John (*c*.1747–1804). *See under* Towers, Joseph (1737–1799).

Towers, Joseph (1737–1799), biographer and Presbyterian minister, was born on 31 March 1737 in Southwark, where his father was a secondhand bookseller. At the age of twelve he was employed as an errand-boy to a stationer at the Royal Exchange and in 1754 was apprenticed to Robert Goadby, a printer of Sherborne, Dorset. Here he taught himself Latin and Greek and, under Goadby's influence, became an Arian.

In 1764 Towers returned to London, where he worked for a short time as a journeyman printer. On 19 August 1767 he married Margaret Lomas, a relative of Caleb Fleming, at St Luke Old Street, Finsbury. With the money acquired from his wife's marriage settlement he bought a bookshop in Fore Street, Cripplegate, in London. He continued in this business for nine years, but with no great success. During this time he began to acquire a reputation as a biographer and writer of political pamphlets. He was appointed editor of the *British Biography*, the first seven volumes of which were compiled by him (1766–72). The biography was based on information in *Biographia Britannica*, but also contained much original work, the fruit of his research in the British Museum.

In 1774 Towers gave up his business and was ordained as a dissenting minister; he became pastor of the Presbyterian congregation in Southwood Lane, Highgate, but the opening of a rival meeting-house in the same street (1778) saw his congregation dwindle away. He left Highgate to become, in 1778, morning preacher at Stoke Newington Green, where Richard Price preached in the afternoons. While at Newington Green he assisted Andrew Kippis in the production of a new edition of *Biographia Britannica* (1778–93), to which he contributed between fifty and sixty articles which were signed 'T'. On 19 November 1779 he was awarded the degree of LLD from Edinburgh University and from 1790 to 1799 was a trustee of Dr Williams's foundation.

Towers's contributions to the biographies mentioned

above were but a small part of his literary output. He was a prolific writer of pamphlets and treatises, which reflected his passionate belief in liberty, both religious and political. Many of these were republished in 1796 in a three-volume collection entitled *Tracts on Political and other Subjects*. His most respected single work was *The Life and Work of Frederick the Great* (2 vols., 1788), which ran to a second edition in 1795. Towers's health began to decline from the beginning of 1795 and he began to suffer in particular from jaundice. He died on either 18 or 20 May 1799 at his home in St John's Square, Clerkenwell.

His only son, **Joseph Lomas Towers** (*bap.* 1770, *d.* 1831), Unitarian preacher, was baptized on 18 April 1770 at Bartholomew Close and Pinner's Hall Independent Chapel, and was educated at St Paul's School, London, and New College, Hackney, which he entered in September 1786. He preached for a short time as a Unitarian minister, but without a settled congregation. In 1792 he succeeded Roger Flexman as librarian of Dr Williams's Library. After resigning this post in 1804 he led an eccentric life, busy with literary schemes and the collection of books and prints. He became insane in 1830, and died on 4 October 1831 at the White House, Bethnal Green. He was buried in a vault at Elim Chapel, Fetter Lane. Although allegedly the author of several publications, only two can be credited to him with certainty. These are *Illustrations of Prophecy* (2 vols., 1796) and *The Expediency of Cash Payments by the Bank of England* (1811).

John Towers (*c.*1747–1804), Independent minister, younger brother of Joseph Towers, was born in Southwark. He went to sea as a lad, but after two voyages was apprenticed to a packer of Turnwheel Lane, Cannon Street, London. He taught himself Greek and Hebrew, and began to preach as an Independent. A secession from Jewin Street Independent congregation chose him as pastor and leased the Presbyterian meeting-house in Bartholomew Close, where he was ordained in 1769. For some years he also conducted a day school. In 1784 the congregation moved to a new meeting-house in the Barbican, where his ministry proved remarkably successful. He was twice married: first to Miss Reynolds of Bridewell precinct on 10 October 1769 and for a second time in September 1782. He published *Polygamy Unscriptural* (1780), an answer to Martin Madan's *Thelephera*, and several sermons. He died on 9 July 1804 and was buried on 17 July in Bunhill Fields.   ALEXANDER GORDON, *rev.* M. J. MERCER

Sources W. D. Jeremy, *The Presbyterian Fund and Dr Daniel Williams's Trust* (1885) · A. Chalmers, ed., *The general biographical dictionary*, new edn, 32 vols. (1812–17) · *Public characters*, 10 vols. (1799–1809) · C. Surman, index, DWL · W. Wilson, *The history and antiquities of the dissenting churches and meeting houses in London, Westminster and Southwark*, 4 vols. (1808–14), vols. 3–4 · *GM*, 1st ser., 69 (1799), 528–9 · *GM*, 1st ser., 52 (1782), 502 · Allibone, *Dict.* · [J. Watkins and F. Shoberl], *A biographical dictionary of the living authors of Great Britain and Ireland* (1816) · J. A. Jones, ed., *Bunhill memorials* (1849) · IGI

Archives Bodl. Oxf., notebook

Likenesses B. Duterreau, stipple, pubd 1796 (after C. Borckhardt), NPG · Farn, stipple (after S. Drummond), BM, NPG; repro. in *European Magazine* (1796) · engraving (John Towers), NPG; repro. in Wilson, *History … of the dissenting churches*, vol. 3, facing p. 223 · outline sketch (after portrait), repro. in *Public characters* · portrait, repro. in J. Towers, *Tracts on political and other subjects* (1796), frontispiece

Towers, Joseph Lomas (*bap.* 1770, *d.* 1831). *See under* Towers, Joseph (1737–1799).

Towers, William (1617?–1666). *See under* Towers, John (*d.* 1649).

Towerson, Gabriel (*bap.* 1576, *d.* 1623), naval officer and agent for the East India Company, was baptized on 27 February 1576 in the parish church of St Michael Cornhill, London, the tenth of twelve children of William *Towerson (*d.* 1584), member of the Skinners' Company and common councilman of London. His father led three pioneering voyages to equatorial west Africa in the years 1555–8 and was subsequently a prominent member of the Muscovy, Eastland, and Spanish companies, and a principal promoter of the Fenton expedition of 1582. Towerson's mother, William's second wife, was Parnell (*d.* 1615), a younger daughter of Nicholas Wilford (*d.* 1551), gentleman, merchant tailor, and member of parliament for London. Her eldest brother, and William Towerson's close associate, was Thomas Wilford, esquire, of Wandsworth, Surrey, common councilman, 1561–99, and City chamberlain, 1591–1603. The marriage, in 1565, produced four daughters and four sons. Gabriel outlived all but two of his siblings and his half-brothers and sisters: William the younger (1563–1630), the commander of a privateer in 1587 and later a City alderman, member of parliament, and director of the Spanish Company, 1604, and the East India Company, 1619; and Robert (*b.* 1580), the youngest child, who in 1621 sought employment with the East India Company.

Towerson's early life is obscure. About 1580 his father moved the family to St Gabriel Fenchurch, London, where his mother lived as a widow until her death. Under the terms of William Towerson's will Parnell was to have the custody and bringing up of his children, with the benefit of their portions until each reached the age of majority. For Gabriel, this date was February 1597. His equal share of the estate would have been substantial, but was in large measure delayed until his mother's decease. Parnell Towerson exercised her widow's right to engage in commerce and register apprentices up to at least 1614, and all her sons sought out their freedoms by patrimony in the Skinners', Spanish, and other companies, although specific information for Gabriel has not come to light. William the younger was a founding member of the East India Company in 1600. Gabriel Towerson sailed to the East on the first company voyage; he is mentioned in the last will of John Badby, William Towerson's apprenticed factor, composed at Sumatra on 6 July 1602, and at Bantam in the wills of other factors, composed on 30 January and 12 April 1604. He was, therefore, one of the first resident factors, and remained at Bantam until he returned to England in November 1609 aboard the *Red Dragon*. In 1611 Towerson sailed from London as captain of the *Hector*, and resumed his work at Bantam, returning home in the *Hector* in September 1613 in company with Nicholas Downton. In January 1614 he was accused of private trading, but the penalty was remitted upon his payment of freight charges. Later in the year, with his account not yet cleared, Towerson was none the less admitted to the freedom, in reward for his long service. By 1617 he was in India, and active in the Red Sea ports, where he provoked the ire of Sir Thomas Roe, the English ambassador. He apparently married and maintained an Armenian wife at Agra, but returned to England alone in 1618.

On 24 January 1620 Towerson was ordered to proceed to the East as a principal factor. Lengthy delays ensued. During the voyage out the experienced captain was placed in command of the *Lesser James*, after quarrels between the master, John Wood, and the pilot, John Davis, proved to be irreconcilable. The situation in the Indies was perilous. On 29 June 1621 the council at Jakarta had observed 'the Dutch … never will performe annie thing on the Agreement [with the English], further then to serve their own purposes' (BL OIOC, G/40/1, p. 81). Meanwhile the junior factors refused to continue at their posts beyond the expiration of their apprenticeships, and the factories and vessels were convulsed with infighting and personal recriminations. The letter sent home from Jakarta on 6 November 1621 by Towerson and the council despaired of peaceful co-existence with the Dutch, a sentiment repeated in every dispatch over ensuing months. On 11 January 1622 the council at Jakarta dispatched Towerson to Amboyna 'for a linguist and an accomptaunt' to replace the departing George Muschamp. This communication concluded ominously: 'The dutch growne a most evell and bloudy nation & murthering all they take, and take all they meete friende and foes' (BL OIOC, G/40/1, p. 104).

The English narrative of events at Amboyna in February of 1623 is straightforward. On 15 February Towerson and his colleagues were arrested by Dutch authorities on suspicion of plotting to seize the castle of Amboyna. Confessions were extracted under torture. The English commander and nine countrymen, one Portuguese, and nine Japanese were executed on 27 February, all except Towerson being buried in a common grave. The East India Company departed the Moluccas, leaving the spice trade to their rivals. Survivors claimed English innocence and Dutch perfidy and this cry was reported at the court of directors and at Whitehall, with calls for reparations. Amboyna was long a byword in the British Isles for Dutch dishonesty and cruelty. John Dryden played upon these sentiments with his propaganda drama, *Amboyna*, of 1673; the play reflected the context of the Third Anglo-Dutch War, rather than the events of 1623, but Gabriel Towerson was immortalized as a devout, honest protestant. All those executed died intestate; when the administration of Towerson's estate was secured by his brother William in November 1624 the deceased was described as unmarried. The fate of his wife is unknown, although in the following January it was noted that the company would pay to send Towerson's son to the Indies. J. D. ALSOP

Sources J. D. Alsop, 'The career of William Towerson, Guinea trader', *International Journal of Maritime History*, 4 (1992), 45–82 · will, PRO, PROB 11/67, fols. 101r–101v [William Towerson the elder] · *CSP col.*, vols. 2–4 · G. Birdwood, ed., *East India Company letterbook, 1600–* 1619 (1893) · F. C. Danvers and W. Foster, eds., *Letters received by the East India Company from its servants in the east*, 6 vols. (1896–1902), vol. 1 · abstracts of letters from factories, 1617–32, BL OIOC, G/40/1 · S. Purchas, *Purchas his pilgrimes*, 4 vols. (1625) · journal of the *Lesser James*, 1621, BL OIOC, L/MAR/A33 · *A remonstrance of the directors of the Netherlands East India Company, presented to the States General touching the proceedings against the English merchants, executed at Amboyna, together with the acts of the processe, and the reply of the English East India Company* (1632) · D. K. Bassett, 'The "Amboyna Massacre" of 1623', *Journal of Southwest Asian History*, 1 (1960), 1–19 · A. B. Gardiner, 'Dating Dryden's *Amboyna*: allusions in the text to 1672–1673 politics', *Restoration and Eighteenth-Century Theatre Research*, 2nd ser., 5 (1990), 18–27 · parish register, St Michael Cornhill, 27 Feb 1576, GL [baptism] · P. Croft, ed., *The Spanish Company* (1973) · J. H. Morrison, ed., *Prerogative court of Canterbury, letters of administration, 1610–1630* (1935), 107 · will, PRO, PROB 11/128, fol. 149 [Robert Towerson] · will, PRO, PROB 11/159, fol. 14 [William Towerson the younger]

Archives BL OIOC, abstracts of letters from factories, G/40/1 · BL OIOC, original corresp., E series

Towerson, Gabriel (*bap.* 1635, *d.* 1697), Church of England clergyman, was baptized at Stoke Newington, Middlesex, on 2 July 1635, the son of William Towerson. After attending St Paul's School, Westminster, he was admitted to Queen's College, Oxford, in Michaelmas term 1650, where he was the Pauline exhibitioner until 1659. He matriculated on 27 February 1651, graduating BA on 17 June 1654 and proceeding MA on 21 April 1657. In 1657 his father petitioned Richard Cromwell, then chancellor of the university, to use his influence with the warden and fellows of All Souls to admit his son to a fellowship. He was admitted fellow there in 1659, losing his fellowship in 1663 following his appointment to the college rectory of Welwyn in Hertfordshire, a living he held until his death. At some point he married, and between 1670 and 1687 he baptized fourteen of his children at Welwyn, seven of whom survived him. From 1680 their mother is named in the register, Ann, though it is not as yet known whether she was his only, or a second, wife; Towerson was a widower by the time he died.

Towerson regarded writing as an important part of his ministry and pursued a long-term goal of adult education in the basics of the Christian religion. His work *An Explication of the Catechism of the Church of England* (published in four parts between 1676 and 1688) was rewarded with a Lambeth DD in 1678. He felt this huge compendium to be necessary because the prayer book catechism was 'written only for the younger sort', and that therefore something more substantial was required for adults (Towerson, *Explication*, pt 1, introduction). He wrote that catechists should require from their audience as they grew 'some further deductions, and applications, and illustrations, so, to contribute to so useful a work, as well as to build men up in their most holy Faith, I have undertaken the following Explication' (ibid.). Towerson defined belief as primarily an 'inevident perswasion of the mind' (ibid., 1.20), but asserted that belief needed to be supported by a secondary appeal to evidence, to provide which he engaged in an expansive and reflective use of quotations from the Bible and the fathers.

Towerson's *Explication* reached nearly 1500 pages in

folio. Repeat editions of various sections of the work, in both folio and octavo, showed that he succeeded in supporting adult readers anxious to grow in their understanding of the faith. Out of the strong catechetical tradition in the literature of English Christianity, Towerson was one of the few authors who abandoned the pattern of question and answer and opted for a text in continuous prose. His work evinces the didactic drive of the Church of England in this era. There was a determination to resource the faithful with the means of their own improvement. The *Explication* also underlined the commitment of the Church of England to the Book of Common Prayer. When the *Explication* is considered in conjunction with Thomas Comber's *Companion to the Temple*, which explained church services, the Anglican prayer book was reaffirmed in grand style in a century within which it had not only been doubted but even proscribed, in the 1640s and 1650s. Even though his work was not reprinted after his death Towerson remains important because his massive work, for all its discursiveness, showed the effort that the Church of England was willing to expend in an age that was regarded as being marked by popular ignorance and apathy.

Towerson received an additional appointment as rector of St Andrew Undershaft, London, in 1692. He was alarmed at the inability of most people there to sing and an organ was installed. His *Sermon Concerning Vocal and Instrumental Musick in the Church* (1696) was delivered on the day that the new organ was first used. He remarked that 'The Organ … both by the Lowdness, and the Harmoniousness thereof doth, with a kind of grateful Violence, carry the Voices of Men along with it' (p. 26). Towerson not only wanted people to have an informed faith, but he also wanted them to be able to express themselves as a congregation as part of their duty to God. Towerson died on 14 October 1697 and was buried at Welwyn a week later. The funeral sermon, delivered by George Stanhope, recalled that Towerson had only ever sought preferment so that he could better provide for his family. His estate was divided among his surviving children.   **RICHARD J. GINN**

Sources *DNB* • Foster, *Alum. Oxon.* • I. Green, *The Christian's ABC: catechisms and catechising in England, c.1530–1740* (1996) • G. Towerson, *An explication of the catechism of the Church of England*, 4 pts [1676–88] • G. Towerson, *A sermon concerning vocal and instrumental musick in the church* (1696) • G. Stanhope, *The Christian's inheritance: a sermon … at the funeral of … G. Towerson … preach'd at Welwyn, Octob. 21, 1697* (1698) • will, PRO, PROB 11/440, sig. 214 • Wood, *Ath. Oxon.*, new edn, 4.582–3 • *IGI* • private information (2004)

Towerson, William (*d.* 1584), merchant, was the son of Robert Towerson, yeoman, of Calder in Cumberland. In 1551 he was apprenticed for seven years to Miles Mording, a London skinner. On 15 January 1560 he married Margery, eldest daughter of James Hawes, a prominent and well-connected London merchant, with whom he had four children. After the death of Margery on 18 January 1565, he married Parnell Wilford (*d.* 1615), whose brother Thomas had been involved in the Guinea trade; they had twelve children, one of whom was the naval officer Gabriel *Towerson (*bap.* 1576, *d.* 1623).

During the 1550s Towerson played an important role in the development of the African trade, leading three trading voyages to Guinea. His first voyage, made with the *Hart* and the *Hind*, each of about 60 tons burden, set out on 30 September 1555. After trading peacefully along the coast of west Africa, he returned to London with a profitable cargo of about fifty ivory tusks and 127 lb of gold. His second voyage, set out in September 1556, was a more ambitious undertaking, being made up of the *Tiger* of 120 tons, the *Hart* of 60 tons, and a small pinnace. In Guinea he entered into an informal alliance with a French captain, Denis Blondel (or Blundell), who was in charge of an expedition of five vessels. The combined fleet sailed on to the Gold Coast, where an indecisive battle was fought with five Portuguese ships, though the latter succeeded in scattering the Anglo-French fleet. Despite quarrelling between the English and French leaders, Towerson continued trading along the coast, possibly reaching Beraku, east of the Portuguese fort at São Jorge da Mina, where one of the native chiefs, described by the English as King Abaan, apparently invited the English to build a fort in his territory. He returned to London in April 1557 with a lading of 69 lb of gold and various amounts of ivory and pepper.

Towerson's last recorded voyage to Guinea, which set out in January 1558, was made with the *Minion*, the *Christopher*, the *Tiger*, and a small pinnace. The *Minion* and *Christopher* were both owned by the queen, and according to the Spanish ambassador the expedition sailed with the approval of the lord admiral, William Howard, despite objections from the Portuguese. After a skirmish with five Portuguese vessels along the Guinea coast, Towerson attacked three French ships, seizing one as prize, though it was so leaky that it was sunk. Towerson wanted to sail on to Benin, to test the commercial openings in a region as yet little known to the English, but was prevented from doing so by his company. Unfortunately, his late arrival in Guinea that year meant that many African rulers had already disposed of their limited gold supplies to rival French traders. Though some trade occurred, it was also limited by African suspicions of the English, and fear of Portuguese retaliation. After burning the town of Shama, sickness and disease broke out among Towerson's men. The *Tiger* had to be abandoned because the crew were too weak to man her. Shortly afterwards the *Christopher* was lost at sea. The two surviving vessels reached the Isle of Wight on 20 October 1558. Though Towerson may have returned with more gold than in 1557, the difficulties he encountered during this voyage led him to abandon the Guinea trade. The accounts of Towerson's Guinea voyages, which Richard Hakluyt published in *The Principall Navigations* of 1589, were almost certainly written by Towerson himself shortly after the voyages ended. They contain valuable information about commercial and political conditions along the Guinea coast. Towerson's account of the second voyage is also of some importance in naval history, providing the earliest description in English of a broadside artillery duel at sea.

Towerson was made free of the Skinners' Company in 1559, and sat on the common council of London from 1561 to 1583. During the 1560s he was heavily involved in trading with Antwerp. In 1564 he wrote a useful, though unpublished, account of the navigation to Friesland. He was active in the Iberian trades, becoming a leading member of the Spanish Company, established in 1577. He was also a member of the Russia Company, and one of the original members of the Eastland Company, incorporated in 1579. During the early 1580s he was involved in developing English trade with Constantinople. In 1582 he was one of the commissioners appointed by the Russia Company to supervise the preparations for Edward Fenton's (abortive) voyage to the East Indies. The following year he met John Dee, Adrian Gilbert, and John Davis to discuss the north-west passage. Soon afterwards he was appointed to a committee of Merchant Adventurers to examine Christopher Carleill's plans for a voyage of discovery to North America. Towerson was buried in St Michael's Church, Cornhill, beside his first wife, on 17 June 1584. One of his sons, William, sailed with Fenton in 1582 and went on to become a prominent merchant in the City of London.

JOHN C. APPLEBY

Sources R. Hakluyt, *The principall navigations, voiages and discoveries of the English nation*, 3 vols. in 2 (1589); facs. edn, Hakluyt Society, extra ser., 39 (1965) · J. W. Blake, ed. and trans., *Europeans in west Africa, 1450–1560*, 2, Hakluyt Society, 87 (1942) · *CPR, 1569–80* · *CSP col.*, vol. 1 · *CSP dom., 1601–3, with additions, 1547–65* · *CSP Spain, 1554–8* · B. Dietz, ed., *The port and trade of early Elizabethan London: documents*, London RS, 8 (1972) · J. D. Alsop, 'The career of William Towerson, Guinea trader', *International Journal of Maritime History*, 4 (1992), 45–82 · J. D. Alsop, 'William Towerson's rutter for the Margate–Emden navigation, 1564', *Mariner's Mirror*, 82 (1996), 154–8 · A. Brown, ed., *The genesis of the United States*, 2 vols. (1890) · *An Elizabethan in 1582: the diary of Richard Madox, fellow of All Souls*, ed. E. S. Donno, Hakluyt Society, 2nd ser., 147 (1976) · A. Texeira da Mota and P. E. H. Hair, *East of Mina: Afro-European relations on the Gold Coast in the 1550s and 1560s*, Studies in African Sources, 3 (1988) · J. A. Williamson, *Maritime enterprise, 1485–1558* (1913) · K. R. Andrews, *Trade, plunder and settlement: maritime enterprise and the genesis of the British empire, 1480–1630* (1984) · J. W. Blake, *West Africa: quest for God and gold, 1454–1578*, 2nd edn (1977) · J. Stow, *A survay of London* (1603); repr. with introduction by C. L. Kingsford as *A survey of London*, 2 vols. (1908), vol. 1 · will, PRO, PROB 11/67, sig. 13
Archives Bodl. Oxf., Tanner MS 79 · Guildhall, London, Skinners' Company records · PRO, customs accounts, E 190 · PRO, state papers, domestic and colonial
Wealth at death see will, PRO, PROB 11/67, sig. 13

Towgood, Matthew (*c*.1690–1757). *See under* Towgood, Michaijah (1700–1792).

Towgood, Michaijah (1700–1792), Presbyterian minister and religious controversialist, was born on 17 December 1700 at Axminster, the second son of Matthew Towgood MD (*d*. 1715) and the grandson of Matthew Toogood, an ejected minister. He attended Thomas Chadwick's Grammar School at Taunton with Thomas Amory (1701–1774) until 25 March 1717. They were both educated for the nonconformist ministry at Taunton Academy under Stephen James and Henry Grove.

On the death of Angel Spark in October 1721, Towgood succeeded him as minister of the Presbyterian meeting at Moreton Hampstead, Devon, where he was ordained on 22 August 1722 under the authority of the Exeter assembly.

The charge by John Withers was afterwards published. Towgood fell ill with what was feared to be consumption, but he recovered and devoted himself systematically to pastoral work. He maintained a religious exercise in his own house, engaged in regular pastoral visiting, and catechized the children of the town by rotation. As a result of the Exeter controversy Towgood came to examine the doctrine of the Trinity, and became convinced that 'the commonly received opinion' could not reasonably be considered a fundamental article of faith, especially as it was not required by scripture. 'He did not call in question its truth, but the subject seemed to him so abstruse and difficult, that he could not imagine God had made the salvation of men' to depend upon holding it exactly (Manning, 9). He therefore suspended his judgement. Originally orthodox, in time he became a high Arian, still regarding Christ as a proper object of worship. On 28 May 1723 he married Mary (*d*. 1759), the daughter of James Hawker of Luppit. They had four children, but only a daughter survived him. His son Matthew (1732–1791), educated at Bridgwater under John Moore, was minister at Bridgwater (1747–55), and afterwards a merchant and, ultimately (1773), a banker in London. He was a manager of the Presbyterian Fund (1773–91) and a trustee of Dr Williams's Trust (1780–91). Matthew died in January 1791, and his son, John, also a banker, succeeded him as a Dr Williams's trustee (1791–1837).

At Christmas 1736 Towgood accepted a call to Crediton, Devon, to succeed Josiah Eveleigh who had died in September 1736. He maintained there the same vigorous pastoral ministry. Shortly afterwards he published his first work in defence of dissenting principles, *High-Flown Episcopal and Priestly Claims Freely Examin'd* (1737), followed by *The Dissenters Apology* (1739). His reputation was established with *The Dissenting Gentleman's Answer* (1746) in reply to the charge of schism made by John White, perpetual curate of Nayland, Suffolk, which became a classic digest of nonconformist argument. In response to White's replies he published *The Dissenting Gentleman's Second Letter to … Mr White* (1747) and *The Dissenting Gentleman's Third Letter to … Mr White* (1748). These three letters went through many editions and were abridged by Towgood as a *Dissent from the Church of England Fully Justified* (1753; 11th edn, 1809) and also as *A Calm and Plain Answer* (1772, 1798). Anglicans were still trying to refute the arguments more than fifty years after the original was published. He also published a number of practical works. His *Recovery from Sickness* (1743) was reprinted many times in Britain and America. His *Baptism of Infants, a Reasonable Service* (1750) and *Dipping not the Only Scriptural and Primitive Manner of Baptizing* (1751) were more controversial and provoked responses from Grantham Killingworth and John Gill. He was the author of three papers in *The Old Whig* (1739) under the pseudonym Paulus.

In 1750, following the death of James Green, Towgood was chosen joint minister of James's Meeting in Exeter with his first cousin, Stephen Towgood. With John Lavington and John Walrond of Bow Meeting, Exeter, the four ministers preached to the two united congregations in rotation. Opposing all religious tests, Towgood persuaded James's Meeting to drop the formal account of faith required of candidates for admission to communion. As a consequence Bow Meeting would allow its own ministers to officiate only in the latter. But Towgood was ideally suited to oversee the doctrinal changes in his congregation. A less charitable man would have brought about a secession of one party or the other. He published for the use of James's Meeting a *Collection of Psalms and Hymns* (1757), with the second edition in 1779, which was extensively used by other Presbyterian congregations.

In 1760 James's Meeting was replaced by a new chapel in South Street, called George's Meeting after George III. The same year Towgood helped establish an academy at Exeter following the closure in October 1759 of the nonconformist academy at Taunton. There he taught biblical exegesis. It closed in December 1771 on the death of the divinity tutor, Samuel Merivale. The academy was briefly revived under Timothy Kenrick, Towgood's successor at George's Meeting. The names of forty-eight students are known, but only twelve entered the ministry; the majority entered trade or the professions. They included two future ministers of George's Meeting, Joseph Bretland and Merivale's stepson, James Manning. Towgood resigned as minister in 1782, when he was presented with a magnificent silver cup by the two congregations, engraved 'in testimony of respect' for Towgood's 'eminent and faithful service … during the course of more than thirty years' (Manning, 74). He was a person 'above the middle size, and extremely slender; his eye lively and penetrating. … He had, in early life, a little impediment in his speech, but he almost entirely conquered this defect' (ibid.). On 26 February 1791 he had a stroke which affected his speech. He died in Exeter on 1 February 1792. His portrait by John Opie and the silver cup were presented by his great-grandson to Dr Williams's Trust. The cup is displayed at the trustees' dinner after every general meeting of the trust.

Matthew Towgood (*c*.1690–1757), Presbyterian minister and tutor, was the eldest son of Stephen Towgood (*d*. 1722), dissenting minister at Axminster, and the first cousin of Michaijah Towgood. His place of education is unknown, but he kept an academy first at Colyton, where he also assisted the minister, Samuel Short, and then at Shepton Mallet, offering a classical and theological education. It has been suggested that it was a continuation of the academy established at Lyme Regis by Samuel Short's brother John, and brought by him to Colyton some time before 1698.

In 1715 Towgood was minister at Wilton, Wiltshire, but moved to the much larger congregation at Shepton Mallet, Somerset, in 1716, where he was ordained on 24 October. According to the Evans List there were 700 hearers in 1715. Something of his religious sentiments is evident from his willingness to allow the ordination of the avowed Arian Hubert Stogdon to take place in his meeting-house in August 1718. He continued the academy, and among his students was William West, minister of the Mint Meeting, Exeter (1744–61). In 1729 he moved to Poole to become assistant to William Madgwick, on whose death in 1734 he became sole minister. He quarrelled, however, with those members who, in order to qualify under the Corporation Act, were occasional conformists. In 1739 he preached a bitter sermon from Proverbs 26: 11 directed against them. They locked him out, and he and his supporters established a new meeting, which they registered in March 1739, but it lasted but a few years. Towgood received a grant of £10 a year from the Presbyterian Fund between 1741 and 1743, but in March 1744 it was 'not paid for this time', probably because he had left the ministry and moved to Swanage. He became a brewer, but 'by his habits of study, he was ill-qualified for trade, and did not succeed in it' (Toulmin, 242). He supplied Wimborne, Dorset, but refused an invitation to become minister. Shortly afterwards, in 1753, he became minister of Swanage, where he remained until his death in 1757. He was buried in St James's parish, Poole, on 24 June 1757. He published a defence of William Nation, the Presbyterian minister of Puddington, who had attacked the orthodox sentiments of the four Exeter ministers over the doctrine of the Trinity. In 1734 he published *A Letter to the Reverend Dr Waterland*, who became involved in the reappearance of the earlier Exeter controversy of 1718. He is remembered principally for his *Remarks on the Profane and Absurd Use of the Monosyllable Damn* (1746). DAVID L. WYKES

Sources J. Manning, *A sketch of the life and writings of the Rev. Micaiah Towgood* (1792) · J. Murch, *A history of the Presbyterian and General Baptist churches in the west of England* (1835), 168, 170–71, 292, 296, 335, 404, 412ff., 432, 457, 459, 473, 475 · A. Brockett, *Nonconformity in Exeter, 1650–1875* (1962), 55, 105–8, 139–40 · A. P. F. Sell, 'A little friendly light: the candour of Bourn, Taylor and Towgood', pts 1–2, *Journal of the United Reform Church History Society*, 4 (1991–2), 517–40, 580–613 · W. D. Jeremy, *The Presbyterian Fund and Dr Daniel Williams's Trust* (1885), 170, 175, 206 · H. McLachlan, *English education under the Test Acts: being the history of the nonconformist academies, 1662–1820* (1931), 75, 230–32, 278 · 'Memorial by Mr Manning of dissenting academies in the west of England', *Monthly Repository*, 13 (1818), 89–90 · minute book B, Exeter assembly, 1722, 1744–53, Devon RO, Clay · [M. Towgood], *Ecclesiastica, or, A book of remembrance wherein the rise, constitution, rule, order, and discipline of the church of Christ, ordinarily assembling at Wykecroft, in the parish of Axminster, is faithfully recorded* [1874] [copy at DWL, shelf mark 5106.Dn.4 (MS family pedigree, p. vii)] · J. T. [J. Toulmin], 'Scraps of biography', *Protestant Dissenter's Magazine*, 5 (1798), 241–7 · W. Densham and J. Ogle, *The story of the Congregational churches of Dorset* (1899), 148, 193, 309, 393 · G. E. Evans, *Colytonia: a chapter in the history of Devon being some account of the Old and George's meetings, Colyton, from 1662 to 1898* (1898), 15 · J. W. Ashley Smith, 'Notes: where was John Short?', *Transactions of the Unitarian Historical Society*, 10/1 (1951–4), 43 · 'Early nonconformist academies: VII, Lyme, Colyton, Shepton Mallet', *Transactions of the Congregational Historical Society*, 5 (1911–12), 157–8 · minute book A, Exeter assembly, 1655–9, Devon RO, 3542D M 1/1 [incl. list of students educated by Matthew Towgood at Shepton Mallet] · J. Evans, 'List of dissenting congregations and ministers in England and Wales, 1715–1729', DWL, MS 38.4, pp. 99, 123 · 'Succession of ministers at Portsmouth and Shepton Mallet', *Protestant Dissenter's Magazine*, 4 (1797), 364–5 · E. J. Wilkins, 'Hill-Street Church, Poole', *Christian Life*, 16 (3 May 1890), 207–8 · Poole quarter session records, meeting-place registrations (1739–42), Poole Borough Records, D5–7 · Presbyterian Fund board minutes, vol. 3, 1722–51, DWL, MS OD69, pp. 327, 344, 360, 363 · *DNB* · will, PRO, PROB 11/1215, fols. 157r–159r · parish registers, St James's Church, Poole, 24 June 1757 [burial: Matthew Towgood] · registers, St Peter's Cathedral, Exeter, 28 May 1723 [marriage]

Archives DWL, papers

Likenesses J. Opie, oils, *c.*1783, DWL · engraving (after J. Opie), repro. in M. Towgood, *Letters to Mr White*, 7th edn
Wealth at death substantial benefactions and estate at Lupset, Devon: will, PRO, PROB 11/1215, fols. 157*r*–159*r*

Towgood, Richard (1594/5–1683), dean of Bristol, was born near Bruton, Somerset. He entered Oriel College, Oxford, as a servitor in 1610 and matriculated on 19 April 1611, aged sixteen. He graduated BA on 1 February 1615. Ordained about 1615 he preached in the Oxford neighbourhood and pursued his studies, proceeding MA on 4 February 1618. For a period he was master of the grammar school in College Green, Bristol, and then successively vicar of the Bristol churches of All Saints, from 1619, and of St Nicholas, from 1626. He became a chaplain to Charles I about 1633; that year, on 7 November, he proceeded BD. At an unknown date he married Elizabeth, a daughter of the Hickes family. They had two sons, Richard and William.

Towgood published his sermon *Disloyalty of Language Questioned and Censured* in 1643. On 20 February 1645 he was sequestered from his vicarage 'for his great disaffection to the parliament' (Walker, 4). He was several times imprisoned, under unusually severe conditions, was ordered to be shot, and with difficulty reprieved. Once released he retired to Wotton under Edge, Gloucestershire. Through Archbishop James Ussher's mediation he preached at Kingswood chapel, near Wotton (using the Anglican prayer book), and in 1654 was presented to the neighbouring rectory of Tortworth.

At the Restoration, Towgood returned to St Nicholas at the parishioners' request. He was installed on 25 August 1660 in the sixth prebend in Bristol Cathedral, to which he was nominated before the civil war, and was sworn chaplain to Charles II. In 1664 he was presented to the vicarage of Weare, Somerset. On 1 May 1667 he became dean of Bristol in succession to Henry Glenham, and in October 1671 he declined the bishopric. He published *The Almighty's Gracious Token of Love* in 1676. He died on 21 April 1683, aged eighty-nine or in his eighty-ninth year, and was buried in the north aisle of the cathedral choir. The main beneficiaries in his will were his wife, his surviving son, Richard, and his grandchildren.

ALEXANDER GORDON, *rev.* S. L. SADLER

Sources *CSP dom.*, 1660–61, 222 · will, PRO, PROB 11/373, fols. 207–8 · J. Walker, *The sufferings of the clergy during the Great Rebellion*, ed. [W. E. Flaherty] (1862), 4–5 · W. Kennett, *A register and chronicle ecclesiastical and civil* (1728), 210, 333 · Wood, *Ath. Oxon.*, new edn, 4.86 · Foster, *Alum. Oxon.* · P. Leversage, *A history of Bristol Cathedral* (1853), 68, 71, 87 · W. P. W. Phillimore, ed., *Gloucestershire parish register: marriages* (1901), 7.125 · *Walker rev.*, 178 · Wing, *STC*
Archives Bodl. Oxf., MSS relating to sequestrations in Bristol, W. MS. C. I, 248, 249, 251

Towle, James (1780–1816), stocking knitter and machine breaker, was a native of Basford, Nottingham. Almost nothing is known about his private life except that he had a wife and four children. Luddism—attacking machines in the name of 'King Ludd'—had broken out in the cloth-finishing trade of the West Riding and cotton hand-loom weaving in Lancashire in 1811–12. It erupted anew in April 1814 in the hosiery and lace trades of the east midlands, where offending employers and machine operators were again selected for attack. In a raid in September 1814 one of the attackers and a bystander were shot dead, and Towle was apprehended on the information of the victim of the attack, Thomas Garton, and tried for his alleged part. To the disgust of the town clerk of Nottingham, George Coldham, however, he was acquitted. Coldham reported that there had been many threats against the prosecution witnesses and that the judge himself had been intimidated by the crowds present in court, who had demonstrated in Towle's favour.

There followed a relatively peaceful phase of industrial relations in the hosiery and lace trades, which ended with an attack on Heathcoat and Boden's mill at Loughborough on 28 June 1816, when bobbin net lace machinery to the value of £6000 was destroyed and shots were fired at a guard. James Towle's involvement was easily established: he had been seen and heard boasting of the forthcoming event in a local pub; he used no disguise other than a silk handkerchief over his lower jaw and his face became fully exposed during his exertions, allowing two witnesses a sufficient sighting to enable them to swear positively to his identity after the event; and he was met by a police constable in Beeston after the attack, apparently on his way home tired and wet from his adventures. This time there was no successful intimidation. Towle was convicted, sentenced, and eventually executed. While he awaited death, strenuous efforts were made to extract information from him about the organization of Luddism, but his so-called confession told the authorities nothing of value; he denied knowledge of oaths of secrecy and arming, and named no leaders. He did reveal that when attacks were to be carried out, collections were made among those in work and machine breakers were paid for their services. But this statement was not enough to save him, and he was hanged at Leicester gaol on 20 November 1816. Despite an edict from the rector of St Nicholas's, Nottingham, forbidding the reading of the burial service, his funeral was supposedly attended by some 3000 people, in itself a demonstration of the emotions that his fate generated.

Little is known about his life, but James Towle was, if nothing else, an identified figure among a host of mainly nameless social protesters. According to E. P. Thompson, Towle was of 'heroic stature', an opinion not universally shared. He also maintains that both the evidence and folk tradition show Towle, like James Mellor in Yorkshire, to have been a local Luddite captain, exercising district leadership and providing Luddism with its strongest and most coherent form of organization. However, the fullest existing account of the Loughborough riot, contained in the rambling confession of another Nottingham framework knitter, John Blackburn, seems to suggest otherwise. James Towle is mentioned only three times (once for shooting a dog), whereas there are six references to his brother Bill, a man who had to be restrained from stealing. Blackburn did not suggest any organizing role for Towle and named others who appear to have provided such leadership as there was. It seems possible that James Towle's life and role have been romanticized and that his posthumous reputation has exceeded historical reality.

MALCOLM I. THOMIS

Sources J. L. Hammond and B. Hammond, *The skilled labourer, 1760–1832* (1919) · E. P. Thompson, *The making of the English working class* (1963) · J. F. Sutton, *The date book of Nottingham* (1852) · F. O. Darvall, *Popular disturbances and public order in Regency England* (1934) · *Nottingham Review* · *Nottingham Journal*

Towne [Town], **Charles** (*bap.* 1763, *d.* 1840), animal painter, was born in Wigan and baptized there on 7 July 1763, the third of the five children of Robert and Mary Town. The family were poor, but probably had artistic leanings, for Charles was selling drawings to bring in money by the age of eight, and at twelve he walked to Leeds to work for the landscape artist John Rathbone. His elder brother Robert having moved to Liverpool, Charles joined him there, becoming a coach-painter and for a time a japanner and ornamental painter. He worked for periods in Lancaster and Manchester but by 1785 he had returned to Liverpool, where on 8 May he married a widow, Margaret Harrison.

In the marriage register Towne's occupation is given as coach-painter, but the register recording the birth of the first of his five children, Ellen, in 1786, calls him 'painter', and by 1789, at the birth of his second daughter, Elizabeth, he is described as a horse painter. This turn perhaps reflects a conscious decision on Towne's part to follow in the footsteps of Liverpool's most famous artistic son, George Stubbs. In 1787, at the second exhibition of the Liverpool Society for Promoting Painting and Design, Towne showed a small landscape, but he created a greater stir by copying from memory Stubbs's exhibits, *Haymakers* and *Reapers*. The equestrian portraits of 1792–4 which are his earliest securely dated works are clearly indebted to Stubbs's example.

Although Towne is recorded at a Liverpool address in 1796, he had for several years been working extensively around Manchester. Joseph Farington, on a trip to the town in November 1796, noted that Towne had copied a painting by Richard Wilson at Platt Hall as part of a commission from Henry Blundell of Ince (Farington, *Diary*, 3.687), and the following July he reported that 'Towne is much employed at Manchester, has 6 months work bespoke' (ibid., 3.872). Towne had in the meantime been to London, where he had 'improved much' (ibid.) from seeing the 1797 Royal Academy exhibition and had visited the studio of Philip de Loutherbourg. The latter's influence is manifest in Towne's *The Monarch of the Glen* of 1797 (Walker Art Gallery, Liverpool), a grand view of highland cattle in a mountain landscape.

Towne appears to have lived in London from 1799 to 1804, for he showed nine works, chiefly cattle in landscapes, at the Royal Academy between these dates from addresses in the city and in Camberwell. In 1799 he began adding the 'e' to his surname (although the form Town is found on signed works after this date). At this time too, as a Liverpool obituarist later put it, 'he associated intimately with the celebrated George Morland, mastering his

principles of composition, and imbibing much of his feeling for colour' (*Liverpool Mail*, 9 Jan 1840). This influence extended beyond the artistic to the whole tenor of Towne's later life; for like Morland, Towne appears to have chased work continuously, to have spent money as quickly as he earned it, and to have had regular encounters with burglars, bailiffs, and unscrupulous dealers. Farington stated that Towne was making as much as £600 a year in 1798 (Farington, *Diary*, 3.990) and thereafter his output of work, carefully tailored to the tastes of conservative provincial patrons, was prodigious; yet in later life he operated from the small parlour of a two-room house, and he died—according to the testimony of Catherine King, who was perhaps his second wife—worth less than £300.

Towne worked in the home counties before returning to Liverpool in or shortly before 1810. He was probably drawn back by news of the imminent creation of the Liverpool Academy, under the patronage of Henry Blundell. Towne is listed as one of the academy's founder members, showed at its first four exhibitions, 1810–13, and served as vice-president in 1812–13. His failure to exhibit in the following year was probably connected with the academy's impending temporary demise; when it was revived in 1822, he showed at its next three exhibitions. After 1825, however, he withdrew from its affairs altogether, and between 1827 and 1833 he sent to the exhibitions of the Royal Manchester Institution instead.

An advertisement in the *Liverpool Mercury* in January 1813 announced that Towne was setting up as a picture restorer.

> He also continues to paint Portraits of Horses, Dogs and Cattle in general, at various prices from Six, to Sixty Guineas, according to the size of the Picture, style of finishing, &c.— Views of Park and other Scenery, painted in a superior style.

For the next twenty-five years (although there are signs of increasing delicacy and refinement and a gradual abandonment of warm 'old master' tonalities in the 1820s and 1830s) his art scarcely altered. Some of the buildings in his later works suggest that patrons came from as far afield as Yorkshire and Scotland, but the majority of them were from Lancashire and Cheshire; and although Towne may have travelled to visit them, he remained based in Liverpool. His latest known dated paintings, from 1838, show no sign of decline, although by then he must have been seriously afflicted by the dropsy from which he died at his home in Norton Street, Liverpool, on 6 January 1840. Ninety-seven paintings by Towne, covering all aspects of his career, are in the Walker Art Gallery, Liverpool.

ALEX KIDSON

Sources M. Bennett, *Merseyside painters, people and places*, 2 vols. (1978) · W. S. Sparrow, 'Charles Towne of Liverpool: his youth', *The Connoisseur*, 85 (1930), 286–93 · W. S. Sparrow, 'Charles Towne of Liverpool: early bitterness', *The Connoisseur*, 85 (1930), 370–76 · W. S. Sparrow, 'Towne–Morland–Bailiffs', *The Connoisseur*, 86 (1930), 9–16 · W. S. Sparrow, 'Charles Towne: the last phase', *The Connoisseur*, 86 (1930), 90–97 · W. S. Sparrow, 'Charles Town of London and the Town painters on velvet', *The Connoisseur*, 88 (1931), 80–87 · Farington, *Diary*, 3.682, 687, 872, 964, 990 · E. Morris and E. Roberts, *The*

Liverpool Academy and other exhibitions of contemporary art in Liverpool, 1774–1867 (1998) • E. R. Dibdin, 'Liverpool art and artists in the eighteenth century', *Walpole Society*, 6 (1917–18), 59–91 • J. T. Danson, 'When I was 6 years old', 1823, National Museums and Galleries on Merseyside Archives, Danson MSS, III/4/2.2 • 'Mr Charles Towne, animal-portrait, pastoral and landscape painter', *Liverpool Mercury* (29 Jan 1813) • *Liverpool Mail* (9 Jan 1840)

Likenesses C. Towne, self-portrait, oils, *c.*1790, Walker Art Gallery, Liverpool • C. Towne, self-portrait, watercolour, *c.*1810, Walker Art Gallery, Liverpool • print, stipple, pubd 1824, BM, NPG

Wealth at death under £300: will, District Probate Registry, Chester, 14 Feb 1839

Towne, Francis (*bap.* **1739**, *d.* **1816**), landscape painter, was baptized at All Saints, Isleworth, Middlesex, on 19 August 1739. His parents, William Towne, a corn chandler, and his wife, Lydia, had four other children, three certainly older than Francis. Towne must have shown early evidence of an inclination towards the arts, for on 5 August 1752 (probably his thirteenth birthday), he was apprenticed for seven years to the London coach-painter Thomas Brookshead. In 1759, just as his indenture was coming to an end, Towne won the first prize of 15 guineas awarded by the Society of Arts for 'an original design', which Towne later recalled as 'the best drawing of landscape' (letter to O. Humphrey, 1803; Wilcox, 163).

Towne is then said to have studied under the court portraitist John Shackleton, but he also continued to earn his living in the trade of the coach-painter. In 1763 he was working for Thomas Watson in Long Acre, London, and it was probably not long after this that he went to Exeter, initially to work in the same line. The reasons for Towne's departure to Exeter, the city with which he remained associated for the rest of his life, are obscure. The city's low cost of living certainly suited his frugal habits; yet his friend James White commented in 1781, 'As to painting, you know this is no place for it' (Wilcox, 31), and Towne resented any suggestion that he was merely a provincial. He had begun to contribute landscapes to the exhibitions of the Free Society in 1762, followed in 1763 by a 'large landscape, with a scene from Shakespear's Cymbeline' (Bury, *Towne*, 115). Later in life, Towne appeared to claim he had been invited to become one of the founder members of the Royal Academy in 1767, but had declined. Although he made ten subsequent applications for membership as an associate between 1788 and 1803, he was never admitted, a source of evident bitterness.

Towne's first Devon landscape was shown at the Free Society in 1767. He became the preferred artist of the county's great estates, painting views of their parks and often newly remodelled gardens. At Ugbrooke Park, Devon, he drew or painted a dozen views for Hugh, fourth Lord Clifford, between 1774 and 1780. Towne was also popular as a teacher of drawing to leisured amateurs. These were mainly young women, but in John White Abbott (1763–1851), an Exeter apothecary, he found a committed and assiduous pupil whose reputation even outstripped his teacher's. Abbott's uncle, James White, a local lawyer and leading nonconformist, accompanied Towne on a tour of north Wales in 1777. The drawings, chiefly of waterfalls and castles, have a spare, tense quality which sets them apart from the conventions of the picturesque.

In 1780 Towne travelled to Rome. He joined the artist William Pars, an old friend, and also painted alongside the much younger John (Warwick) Smith. James Irvine, another British traveller who encountered him there, described him as

> one of the strangest genius's I have seen. With a very indifferent understanding he has all the gravity and formality of a profound philosopher and deep reasoner, but he is I believe what we call a good sort of man and applies his art with great industry.   (letter to George Cumberland, 16 Dec 1780; Wilcox, 56–7)

In March 1781 Towne was being shown around the Bay of Naples by the painter Thomas Jones, but, unlike Jones and many other British artists who remained for several years in Italy, Towne was unhappy and after spending the late spring and early summer in and around Rome he decided to return home. He did, however, time the journey to have the best opportunity of visiting the Alps, inspired, no doubt, by the account by Pars of his tour of 1770. Towne travelled with Warwick Smith via the Italian lakes and the Splügen Pass to Lucerne, then on to Geneva. The climax of the tour was reached in the Vale of Chamonix with two watercolours of the source of the Arveyron (Tate collection and V&A). Never before had the medium evoked such hugeness of scale and such a heart-stopping sense of awe.

Far from capitalizing on these experiences, Towne failed to exhibit any continental views until 1788. He had by then also made a tour of the Lake District in 1786, in the company of White and another Exeter nonconformist, John Merivale. The sketchbook pages fully worked up in watercolour (now scattered), and the larger sheets probably painted on the spot, are among his most vibrant creations. In their lengthy inscriptions, Towne left evidence of a modern preoccupation with the authenticity of the painted image. This emerges forcibly in the one-man exhibition of his watercolours he mounted at 20 Lower Brook Street, London, in February 1805, where some 200 of his original sketches were shown, individually mounted by the artist. This singular event, presented in the rooms which two months later were to house the first exhibition of the Society of Painters in Water Colours, attracted very little attention.

On 5 August 1807 Towne married Jeannette Hilligsberg, a French dancer aged only twenty-seven, who had been a dancing-mistress in Exeter since about 1801. The couple took up residence in London but only eight months later, in April 1808, she died. Towne then began a series of annual summer sketching tours which took him to Wales, Cornwall, and Devon in 1809, to Wales again in 1810, to Scotland in 1811, to Oxford in 1813, and finally to Devon in 1815. Towne died on 7 July 1816 at 31 Devonshire Street, his London home, following two years of failing health. He left provision in his will for his body to be conveyed with great pomp to Exeter, to be laid beside his wife in Heavitree church. This was accomplished on 22 July. He also instructed his executors to deposit his Italian drawings in the British Museum (where they remain), to be housed with the works of Pars, a further sign of his self-awareness as an artist and sure expectation that posterity would accord him the recognition denied to him in life.

TIMOTHY WILCOX

Sources T. Wilcox, *Francis Towne* (1997) · R. Stevens, 'New material for Francis Towne's biography', *Burlington Magazine*, 138 (1996), 500–05 · A. Bury, *Francis Towne: lone star of water-colour painting* (1962) · M. Hardie, 'Early artists of the British watercolour school: Francis Towne', *The Collector* (Sept 1930), 10–16; (Oct 1930), 77–83 · A. Bury, 'Some Italian views by Francis Towne', *The Connoisseur*, 102 (1938), 11–14 · P. Oppé, 'Francis Towne, landscape painter', *Walpole Society*, 8 (1919–20), 95–126 · F. W. Hawcroft, *Travels in Italy, 1776–1783: based on the memoirs of Thomas Jones* (1988) · Farington, *Diary* · J. Ingamells, ed., *A dictionary of British and Irish travellers in Italy, 1701–1800* (1997) · Devon RO, Andrews, Son & Huxtable papers, Ref. 3459M [Towne's solicitors] · record of baptisms, Hounslow Public Library

Archives Tate collection, Paul Oppé archive

Likenesses J. Downman, black chalk drawing, *c.*1780, repro. in Oppé, 'Francis Towne, landscape painter', pl. lix · J. Downman, black chalk and watercolour drawing, 1795, BM

Wealth at death £10,000 estate; £1000 in pictures: will, Stevens, 'New material', 503, n. 53

Towne, John (*bap.* 1711, *d.* 1791), religious controversialist, son of Leonard Towne, Church of England clergyman, and his wife, Margaret Hill, was born in Boothby Graffoe, Lincolnshire, where he was baptized on 23 October 1711. He matriculated as a sizar at Clare College, Cambridge, on 26 July 1729, and graduated BA in 1733 and MA in 1736. He was ordained deacon on 22 December 1734 and priest on 21 September 1735. At about this time he became rector of Little Ponton in Lincolnshire, where he lived for the rest of his life. On 22 June 1740 he also became vicar of Thorpe-Ernald in Leicestershire, a post he likewise held until his death. Towne married Anne Parnham on 3 November 1741. They had three daughters, Margaret, Anne, and Martha, and two sons, John, who died young, and Benjamin, who became a painter. Towne's wife died on 31 January 1754.

In 1747 Towne published his first work, *A critical inquiry into the opinions and practice of the ancient philosophers concerning the nature of the soul*, the preface of which was written by his friend William Warburton, whom the work defended. Warburton held Towne, whom he described as a 'reasoning engine', in high esteem (Warburton, 49). According to Bishop Richard Hurd, Towne was 'an ingenious and learned man, and so conversant in the bishop's writings, that he used to say of him, "he understood them better than himself"' (*Works of Richard Hurd*, 1.114). Most of the rest of Towne's works, such as *The Argument of the 'Divine Legation' Fairly Stated* (1751), were likewise devoted to supporting Warburton against Robert Lowth and others.

Towne became archdeacon of Stowe on 5 September 1765, and was collated as a prebendary of Lincoln, probably through Warburton's influence. He died on 15 March 1791 at Little Ponton, where he was buried and 'universally lamented' (*GM*, 61, 1791, 286). A mural tablet to his memory was erected in the church.

ADAM JACOB LEVIN

Sources Venn, *Alum. Cant.* · IGI · *The works of Richard Hurd*, 8 vols. (1811), 1.113–14 · [W. Warburton], *Letters from a late eminent prelate to one of his friends*, ed. R. Hurd, 3rd edn (1809), 49, 53–4 · A. W. Evans, *Warburton and the Warburtonians: a study in some eighteenth-century controversies* (1932), 19–20, 194–5, 250, 292 · Nichols, *Lit. anecdotes*, 2.283–4, 371; 7.426, 693 · *Fasti Angl.* (Hardy), 2.81 · *GM*, 1st ser., 61 (1791), 286 · J. Nichols, *The history and antiquities of the county of Leicester*, 2 (1795–8), 371 · will, PRO, PROB 11/1205, sig. 257 · DNB

Wealth at death see will, PRO, PROB 11/1205, sig. 257

Towne, Joseph (1806–1879), anatomical modeller, was born in Royston, near Cambridge, on 25 November 1806, the middle of the five sons of the Revd Thomas Towne (*d.* 1830), pastor to the New Meeting-House and also a director of the London Missionary Society, and his wife, Mary (*d.* 1839), a schoolteacher. His father was an accomplished painter and in his later years a writer on painting and the camera obscura. Little is known of the youth of Joseph Towne but almost certainly he benefited from the teaching of both his father and his mother. The former, as well as being a minister, ran the local boys' school, and the latter a school for middle-class young ladies.

Through his literary work and his great interest in art, his father would have encouraged Joseph Towne's enthusiasm as a child for modelling animals in clay. He later arranged for Joseph to take his 33 inch high wax model of a human skeleton to Cambridge to show the professor of anatomy, William Clark. Encouraged by his favourable reception in Cambridge, at the age of nineteen Towne travelled to London intending to enter the Society of Arts competition in wax modelling. His brother Jireh and cousins Jonah and Alexander (the latter training as a surgeon at the Webb Street school) were living in the City area. On 17 February 1826 Towne was introduced to three doctors, including W. O. Grainger, lecturer in anatomy and physiology in Webb Street, who referred him to Sir Astley Cooper, a surgeon at Guy's Hospital. Cooper responded positively to Towne's evident skill and authenticated his wax model as an accurate rendition of the human skeleton. Towne was given a letter of recommendation to Mr Harrison, the treasurer of Guy's Hospital, who engaged him as the modeller for the new medical school. He was to remain at Guy's for fifty-three years.

Towne's skeleton in wax was subsequently entered in the Society of Arts' competition and won second prize, the silver medal. A year later Towne exhibited models of the brain, highly praised by Astley Cooper, which secured him the gold medal. He settled into his work at Guy's and five years later, in 1832, he married Mary Butterfield.

During the many years he worked at Guy's Hospital Towne completed a prodigious amount of work. Modelling human anatomy in wax from the careful dissections of John Hilton, who was appointed lecturer in anatomy in 1828, he produced in the next ten years over two hundred anatomical wax models. The work was carried out in a room in the old anatomy theatre at Guy's which he always kept locked. During this time he trained his younger brother Elihu who became a wax modeller himself. No one else was privy to the technique that was used and the secrets of his skills in preparing and colouring the wax died with him. His brother Elihu died at an early age in 1834.

In the middle period of his work at Guy's, Towne produced in association with Dr Addison, physician to Guy's, over five hundred models of skin diseases. In 1834 he exhibited for the first time a marble bust at the Royal Academy. Throughout his working life he exhibited altogether thirteen sculptures in marble at the Royal Academy and another seven which were privately commissioned. Included among these were two busts of the duke of Wellington (one, exh. 1837, is in Guy's Hospital, London; the other, exh. 1842, is in the Junior United Service Club, London), and busts of Benjamin Harrison, Sir Astley Paston Cooper (1841), and the physician Addison (1852) (the last two in Guy's Hospital, London). His bust of Florence Nightingale (marble, 1850) is in the Russell-Cotes Art Gallery and Museum, Bournemouth. He produced a small equestrian statue of the duke of Kent, which was presented to Queen Victoria by Benjamin Harrison on 1 November 1837. Towne himself was presented to the young queen.

In his later years Towne gave a course of lectures at Guy's on the brain and intellect. From 1862 to 1870 he gave lectures on stereoscopic and binocular vision and was still exhibiting at the Royal Academy at the age of sixty. Towne died at his home, Sefton House, Eltham, Kent, on 25 June 1879, and was buried in Norwood cemetery in a grave next to that of his father. His wife and descendants are buried close by. Thomas Bryant (1828–1914), surgeon to Guy's Hospital, wrote a memorial and short biography:

> of my old friend Joseph Towne, the late well-known, highly esteemed, skilled modeller of Guy's Hospital … all who ever walked round Guy's Hospital can testify … the magnitude of the work he has left behind … [the] magnitude in respect to the number of works executed, upwards of one thousand … [and] with respect to their importance and scientific value …

Whereas France was the main source of expertise in this medium, with skills being transferred to England via Madame Tussaud who arrived in England in 1802, Towne's wax models are some of very few nineteenth-century British anatomical waxes to survive. The majority of his models are on display in the Guy's Hospital medical school museum. JOHN MAYNARD

Sources T. Bryant, 'In memoriam Joseph Towne—modeller to Guy's Hospital for fifty three years', *Guy's Hospital Reports*, 3rd ser., 26 (1883), 1–12 · Guy's Hospital medical school, London, Rupert Towne MSS · R. Gunnis, *Dictionary of British sculptors, 1660–1851* (1953); new edn (1968) · D. Petherbridge and L. Jordanova, *The quick and the dead: artists and anatomy* (1997), 93 [exhibition catalogue, London, Warwick, and Leeds, Oct 1997 – May 1998] · *CGPLA Eng. & Wales* (1879)

Likenesses watercolour, 1830, Guy's Hospital, London

Wealth at death under £20,000: probate, 28 July 1879, *CGPLA Eng. & Wales*

Towne, Robert (1592/3?–1664), clergyman and ejected minister, matriculated as from Yorkshire at Oriel College, Oxford on 4 December 1612 when he was said to be aged nineteen; his parents are unknown. He graduated BA in 1614 and was subsequently in London associated with the followers of the antinomian John Eaton. After Eaton's death Towne engaged in controversy with the puritan

preacher Thomas Taylor late in 1630, when many of his associates were being prosecuted before the high commission. Taylor produced an exposé of the antinomians, entitled *Regulae vitae*, to which Towne's *An Assertion of Grace*, written in 1632, was intended as a reply, though it remained unpublished until 1644.

During the 1630s Towne withdrew from London, and was for a time curate at Accrington in Lancashire. He was at Heywood by 1640, when his antinomian views brought him before the bishop of Chester and the court of high commission, which imprisoned and suspended him before his case was dismissed following a disclaimer written by Towne to the bishop on 31 July 1640. His antinomian position, which he expressed as an obedience which 'issueth from the lively spring of free Justification joyfully apprehended and not from the outward dispensation and precepts of the Law' (Towne, *Assertion*, 43), insisted that the individual conscience enlightened by the scriptures was above the moral law. This position remained firmly held. Similar views had been circulating in the north since the ministry of Roger Breareley, curate of Grindleton in the Craven district of Yorkshire, had attracted the attention of the high commission in 1615, and Towne arrived to minister in that region of the county in the early 1640s. In 1643, by which time he was curate at Todmorden on the border between Lancashire and Yorkshire, he was one of those whose antinomian views were complained of before the Westminster assembly. In the following year he finally set out his opinions in *The Assertion of Grace, or, A Defence of the Doctrine of Free Justification*. Soon after its publication, he was summoned before the Manchester classis as a result of a sermon preached at Stopworth. His book was attacked in Samuel Richardson's *A Survey of the Spirituall Antichrist*, published in 1648. On 10 February of that year the Bury classis ordered Towne's removal from Todmorden.

Towne then went to London with the intention of petitioning to be restored to his post. Instead he was offered support in Yorkshire and moved back up north, preaching at the Bingley exercise in 1651. By 1652 Towne had been installed as minister at Elland in the parish of Halifax, where he also preached, along with his son, at the famous exercise held in that town. Described by Oliver Heywood as 'the famous Antinomian who writ some books: he was the best scholar and soberest man of that judgement in the country, but somewhat unsound in principles' (*Autobiography*, 4.7), Towne published in 1654 *A Re-assertion of Grace, or, Vindiciae evangelii* with a preface by Seth Bushell in which were recounted Towne's persecutions by ecclesiastical authority, whether episcopal or not. This second volume constituted a reply to the writings of Anthony Burgess and other presbyterian opponents of antinomianism and was lengthier than Towne's earlier work. By 1655, when he was described as a constant preacher of God's word, Towne had moved to Haworth, but he was ejected from the living in 1662. He continued to minister to a dissenting congregation there until his death; he was buried at Haworth on 10 June 1664. Towne was married, although nothing is known of his wife, and had at least three surviving daughters—Hester, who married John Merrill of London, and Mary and Sarah, neither of whom was married at the time of his death—and two sons, Daniel, who was a nonconformist minister at nearby Heptonstall, and Robert. From his will, proved in July 1664, it is known that Towne had a small estate in Addingham in the Craven district of the Yorkshire dales, which may have been where the family originated.

WILLIAM JOSEPH SHEILS

Sources Calamy rev. · R. Towne, *A re-assertion of grace* (1654) · R. Towne, *An assertion of grace* (1644) · *The Rev. Oliver Heywood … his autobiography, diaries, anecdote and event books*, ed. J. H. Turner, 4 (1885) · B. Dale, *Yorkshire puritanism and early nonconformity*, ed. T. G. Crippen [n.d., *c*.1909] · J. H. Turner, *Haworth past and present* (1879) · original wills, prerogative, July 1664, Borth. Inst. [Robert Towne] · S. Foster, 'New England and the challenge of heresy, 1630 to 1660: the puritan crisis in transatlantic perspective', *William and Mary Quarterly*, 38 (1981), 624–60

Wealth at death small estate in Craven: will, original wills, prerogative, July 1664, Borth. Inst.

Towneley, Christopher (1604–1674), antiquary, the third surviving son of Richard Towneley (1566–1628) of Towneley Hall, Lancashire, and his wife, Jane (*d*. 1634), daughter of Ralph Ashton of Great Lever in the same county, was born at Towneley on 9 January 1604. As the family was Roman Catholic, his education was probably provided privately; he may also have gone abroad for the purpose, as his elder brother did. The statement in the *Dictionary of National Biography* that he became 'an attorney, but probably did not long follow his profession … disabled by being a recusant' derives from the nineteenth-century local historian F. R. Raines, who did not note his sources (Raines, *Journal of Nicholas Assheton*, 26–7n.).

After his father's death in 1628 Towneley probably lived with his mother at Hapton, helping her to run her estates, until her death in 1634; an inventory of her goods assigns his name to a chamber there, and notes that he owed his mother over £60. He was one of her executors. He then lived at Moor Isles, about 4 miles north of Towneley, until his marriage towards the end of 1640 (or early in 1641). His wife was Alice (*bap*. 1593), daughter of John Bradyll of Portfield, Whalley; she was Towneley's second cousin on his mother's side, and the widow of his distant relation Richard Towneley of Barnside and Carr. In 1644 Towneley is again described as of Hapton, but soon afterwards he and his wife moved to Carr Hall, south-west of Colne, where they lived until her death (which is said to have occurred in 1657). He then returned to Moor Isles.

In the civil war Towneley's brother Charles died in the royalist cause 'at the battle of Hesom Moor, at the raising of the siege of York, 2 or 3 August 1644' (Whitaker, 2.190). Christopher also fought (Webster says he was captured at Marston Moor) and the estates of both were sequestered, with respectively a third and a fifth of the annual profits allowed for the support of their families. Alice's receipt of £80 indicates that Towneley was reckoned to enjoy an annual income of £400. He petitioned to compound on 30 April 1646, but was listed among 'imperfect cases' when

his petition could not be found. Family property in Lincolnshire and Lancashire was subsequently declared forfeit and sold, but Towneley Hall was preserved; Towneley seems to have had charge of it as a trustee for his nephew Richard until the latter came of age in 1649. In 1650 Towneley was in the Upper Bench prison, presumably as a royalist.

Towneley is remembered for two of his intellectual interests: the encouragement of astronomy and the collection of documentary evidence for local history. Both these pursuits were aided by resident amanuenses. The young Jeremy Shakerley lived at Carr Hall in the late 1640s and complained that, in return for his work, 'meat and drinke is all I can expect'; one of his letters to William Lilly also records that Towneley was committed to a highly mathematized astrology, 'loves Calculations well, and … will scarcely so much as erect a figure (though about any trivial occasion) without his Diagrams and Logarithms' (Bodl. Oxf., MS Ashmole 423, fol. 121*r*). An unfinished list of Towneley's books compiled between 1647 and 1649 confirms his interest in mathematics, astronomy, and astrology; the same volume also contains medical notes. The benefits of access to the books were acknowledged by Jonas Moore in the preface to one of his treatises, which said the content was translated from an original supplied by 'Mr Christopher Towneley of Carr (a great promoter of Arts and lover of all Ingenuity and ingenuous men', who had given 'not only the use of his Library, but Copies of such Mathematical Manuscripts as he had by him' (*Conical Sections*, appended to *Moor's Arithmetick*, 2nd edn, 1660).

A later account in Edward Sherburne's historical catalogue of astronomers makes Towneley the pivotal figure linking Jeremy Horrocks, William Crabtree, William Gascoigne, and William Milburne:

> happily brought to the Acquaintance of one another by the means of Christopher Townley of Carr in Lancashire Esquire, who stuck not for any cost or labour to promote as well Astronomical as other Mathematical Studies by a diligent Correspondence kept and maintained with the learned Professors in those Sciences; upon which account he was very dear to All the Four; and for which Reason, as for the Particular Respect I owe him, he merits to be named in this Catalogue. (Sherburne, 92–3)

Sherburne was a biased witness, but his claims were not without foundation. Towneley certainly helped to make the astronomical work of some of this group known, as Flamsteed later recalled: 'after all their deaths Mr Christopher Towneley of the Car in Lancashire and Sir Jonas More went to Mr Crabtree's house where his Widdow gave them all his papers these they secured and afterwards sorted' (CUL, RGO 1/65A, fol. 112*v*). Letters passed on to Richard Towneley included the final version of Horrocks's lunar theory, which Flamsteed eventually published in Horrocks's *Opera posthuma* (1673).

Towneley's passion for collecting documentary evidence found its main expression in antiquarian studies. He assembled material for a history of Lancashire in collaboration with Dr Richard Kuerden, who reported about the end of 1659: 'We muster our Antiquityes or paper forces (I mean Mr T. and myself) very neare an Hundred Thousand strong, in transcript' (Ormerod, 8). No publication resulted, but Towneley shared information with other antiquaries, particularly Roger Dodsworth and William Dugdale; he was also a friend of John Hopkinson of Lofthouse, Yorkshire. The collection he built up has been much used by later local historians, especially Thomas Whitaker, who dubbed Towneley 'the indefatigable transcriber'. It was dispersed on the sale of the Towneley library in 1883, and is now divided between Chetham's Library, Manchester Central Library (the Farrar collection), and the British Library.

Towneley died at Moor Isles in August 1674 and was buried at Burnley on 30 August 1674. An inventory of his goods survives; his manuscripts were valued at 40s. (the figure of 11s. in the *Dictionary of National Biography* derives from a misreading), a further 80s. was included for printed books, £3 6s. 8d. for a clock, and 10s. for surveying instruments.　　　　　　　　　　　　FRANCES WILLMOTH

Sources G. C. Yates, 'The Towneleys of Towneley', *Transactions of the Lancashire and Cheshire Antiquarian Society*, 10 (1892), 86–91 · J. H. Lumby, *Calendar of De Hoghton deeds and papers*, Lancashire and Cheshire RS, 88 (1936), appx 4, 'Christopher Towneley's transcripts' · T. D. Whitaker, *An history of the original parish of Whalley*, rev. J. G. Nichols and P. A. Lyons, 4th edn, 2 vols. (1872–6) · J. H. Stanning and J. Brownbill, eds., *The royalist composition papers ... related to the county of Lancaster*, 7 vols., Lancashire and Cheshire RS, 24, 26, 29, 36, 72, 95, 96 (1891–1942), vols. 3, 5–6 · G. Ormerod, ed., *Epistolary relics of Lancashire and Cheshire antiquaries, 1653–1673*, Chetham Society, 24 (1850) · *The journal of Nicholas Assheton*, ed. F. R. Raines, Chetham Society, 14 (1848), 26–7n. · E. Sherburne, *The sphere of Marcus Manilius: made an English poem with annotations and an astronomical appendix* (1675) · W. Dugdale, *The visitation of the county palatine of Lancaster, made in the year 1664–5*, ed. F. R. Raines, 3 vols., Chetham Society, 84–5, 88 (1872–3) · E. Baines and W. R. Whatton, *The history of the county palatine and duchy of Lancaster*, new edn, ed. J. Croston and others, 3 (1890), 379–85 · F. Willmoth, *Sir Jonas Moore* (1993) · *DNB* · C. Webster, 'Richard Towneley (1629–1707), the Towneley group and seventeenth-century science', *Transactions of the Historic Society of Lancashire and Cheshire*, 118 (1966), 51–76 · inventory of the goods of Jane Towneley, 1634, Lancs. RO, WCW · inventory of goods, 1674, Lancs. RO, WCW
Archives BL, family charters, Add. MS 30145 [transcripts] · BL, antiquarian and heraldic notes, Add. MSS 32097–32116 · Bodl. Oxf., genealogical MSS [transcripts] · Bodl. Oxf., notes and letters to Nathaniel Johnston · Chetham's Library, Manchester, commonplace book, recipes, astronomical MSS, material for proposed history of Lancashire, and catalogue of books · JRL, corresp. · Lancs. RO, antiquarian papers · Lancs. RO, genealogical and heraldic papers · W. Yorks. AS, Leeds, genealogical papers relating to Plumpton family · Wigan Archives Service, Leigh, historical transcripts | Man. CL, Farrar collection; antiquarian collection
Likenesses Waddington, portrait; formerly at Towneley Hall, Lancashire, in late nineteenth century · engraving (after photograph by W. Waddington of portrait by Mr Langton), repro. in Yates, 'The Towneleys of Towneley', 87
Wealth at death over £220: inventory, 24 Sept 1674, Lancs. RO, WCW

Towneley, Francis (1709–1746), Jacobite army officer, was born on 8 June 1709 at Towneley Hall, Lancashire, the fifth and youngest son of Charles Towneley (1658–1712) and

Ursula, *née* Fermor, who married in 1685. Towneley's family were Roman Catholics with a strong attachment to the Jacobite cause. His uncle Richard took part in the rising of 1715. As was common in recusant families Francis, as a younger son, sought his fortune abroad. In August 1721 he was admitted to Douai College, though further details of his education are unknown. Six years later he returned to France and in 1728 he was commissioned into the French army as his elder brother John *Towneley had been before him.

Towneley served with distinction at the siege of Phillipsburg in 1734 under the duke of Berwick and was ultimately promoted to a colonelcy by Louis XV. He returned to Britain about 1743 and would doubtless have married and settled but for the second Jacobite rising of 1745. Reviving his French rank he recruited some three hundred men in Manchester and formed them into a regiment of foot and joined Prince Charles's army (in which John Towneley was also serving) on its southward march to Derby and its almost immediate retreat in December. The Jacobites withdrew from Carlisle into Scotland on 21 December leaving Towneley, who had volunteered to act as rearguard, to hold the city with his regiment, now reduced to 117 men, and Captain John Hamilton, governor of the castle, in command of 275 Scots and eight Frenchmen.

On 22 December the duke of Cumberland came up and laid siege to the city. Towneley, well known for his soldierly language, declared that 'it would be better to die by the sword than fall into the hands of those damned Hanoverians' (*State trials*, vol. 18, 339) and prepared to hold out to the last man. Cumberland requisitioned artillery from Whitehaven and on 27 December he began a bombardment of the castle. Three days later, in the face of relentless and overwhelming firepower, Hamilton capitulated, asking only that the garrison be accorded the status of prisoners of war. Cumberland, however, demanded unconditional surrender. At a heated council of war Towneley vehemently opposed such ignominious terms and, though he at last yielded, he did not sign the surrender. He and the officers of his regiment were indicted for high treason at the court house, St Margaret's Hill, Southwark, on 15 July 1746. Towneley disputed the court's jurisdiction, maintaining that since he held the French king's commission, not that of Prince Charles, he should be treated as a prisoner of war, not a traitor. His argument was dismissed and he was found guilty. Towneley was hanged, drawn, and quartered on 30 July 1746 on Kennington Common. His body was buried in the churchyard of St Pancras; his head was displayed at Temple Bar but was recovered and interred in the family crypt at Towneley Hall.　　　　　　　　　　　　　　　　LEO GOOCH

Sources *DNB* · *State trials*, vol. 18 · D. J. Beattie, *Prince Charlie and the borderland* (1928) · J. A. Wheatley, *Bonnie Prince Charlie in Cumberland* (1903) · J. Gillow, ed., 'Catholic registers of Towneley Hall, Lancashire (baptisms and marriages), by the Rev. Thomas Anderton, 1705–1727', *Miscellanea, II*, Catholic RS, 2 (1906), 306–11 · E. H. Burton and E. Nolan, *The Douay College diaries: the seventh diary, 1715–1778*, Catholic RS, 28 (1928) · Burke, *Gen. GB* (1965)

Towneley, John (*bap.* 1697, *d.* 1782), translator, was baptized on 1 January 1697 at St Peter's Church, Burnley, Lancashire, the second son of Charles Towneley (1658–1712) of Towneley Hall, Lancashire, and his wife, Ursula, daughter of Richard Fermor of Tusmore, Oxfordshire. His brother was the Jacobite officer Francis *Towneley, executed in London in 1746. John Towneley entered Gray's Inn on 14 March 1715 and studied law under William Salkeld, serjeant-at-law. At his father's death in 1711 he was left with an allowance of only £60 a year. About 1728 he moved to Paris where female members of his family had been pupils or nuns. There, according to his great-nephew Charles Towneley, he frequented literary society and joined the salon of Madame Doublet de Breuilpont.

In 1731 Towneley entered Rothers's Franco-Irish infantry regiment as lieutenant; he distinguished himself at the siege of Phillipsburg in 1734, and became a captain in 1735. In 1745 his regiment, or a detachment of it, was sent to Scotland to assist Charles Edward Stuart, the Young Pretender, and Towneley took part in the battle of Falkirk. The French envoy, the marquis d'Éguilles, in a dispatch to Bachaumont, wrote on 20 February 1746: 'M. Towly, who will have the honour of delivering my despatches to you, is the man of most intelligence and prudence amongst those here with the prince: you may question him on any subject' (Cottin, 28). In the autumn of 1746 Towneley, with forty-two other Jacobite officers, received a grant of 1200 livres from Louis XV. In December he received the order of St Louis.

According to Charles Towneley, on the publication of Samuel Butler's *Hudibras* (1662–80) 'every real or pretended man of letters chattered on the subject' (*Palatine Note-Book*, 1.27), no doubt thanks to Voltaire's discussion of the poem in two articles of the *Dictionnaire philosophique*. Piqued by Voltaire's description of it as untranslatable except by reducing 'three quarters of the passage to be translated' (*Mélanges*, 174), Towneley began translating passages for the amusement of Madame Doublet's society. John Turberville Needham, his great-nephew's tutor, eventually persuaded him to complete the translation and to publish it. Towneley's *Hudibras* was published anonymously in Paris in 1757, although the frontispiece indicated London as the place of publication, a stratagem to avoid censorship. The English original is given on parallel pages, and Hogarth's engravings are reproduced. The preface is by Towneley while the explanatory notes appended are by Pierre Larcher, the translator of Herodotus. A second edition, with the English text revised by Sir John Byerly and the French spelling modernized, was printed by Firmin-Didot in Paris in 1819. This also included a 'Notice sur J. Towneley', translated from an appendix to the *Critical Review*.

Although the editor of the 1815 edition calls Towneley's work 'rather an imitation than a translation', it aims at being very close to the original. It was extravagantly praised by Horace Walpole. The *Nouvelle bibliothèque d'un homme de goût* (1777) taxed it with bad rhymes and faulty French (1.216–17), while Suard, in the *Biographie universelle*, though acknowledging its fidelity, pronounces the diction poor and the verses unpoetical, 'the work of a foreigner familiar with French but unable to write it with elegance'. It lacks the swing and burlesque rhymes of the original and Towneley himself declared the 'humour untranslatable'.

Towneley died at Chiswick in 1782, at the residence of his nephew and namesake, and was buried in Chiswick churchyard. His library was sold in 1883; he also possessed a considerable collection of Wenceslaus Hollar's prints, which were sold by auction in 1818. The sale also included some fragmentary manuscripts by Towneley.

J. G. ALGER, *rev.* ANTONELLA BRAIDA

Sources Burnley parish register, Lancashire, Society of Genealogists, LA/REG/86330/1–111 (PR 30271/1/2) · J. Foster, *The register of admissions to Gray's Inn, 1521–1889, together with the register of marriages in Gray's Inn chapel, 1695–1754* (privately printed, London, 1889), 360 · *Palatine Note-Book*, 1 (1881), 26–7 · J. G. Alger, 'The Towneleys in Paris, 1709–80: the translator of *Hudibras*', *Palatine Note-Book*, 3 (1883), 84–6 · J. G. Alger, 'The Towneley library', *Palatine Note-Book*, 3 (1883), 187–92 · J. G. Alger, 'The Towneleys in Paris, 1683–1780', *Palatine Note-Book*, 3 (1883), 144–6 · E. E. Estcourt and J. O. Payne, eds., *The English Catholic nonjurors of 1715*, [8 vols.] (1886), 99 · P. Cottin, *Un protégé de Bachaumont: correspondance inédite du marquis d'Éguilles* (1887), lxxi, 28 · F. Michel, *Les écossais en France, les français en Écosse*, 2 vols. (1862), vol. 2, p. 447 · T. D. Whitaker, *An history of the original parish of Whalley* (1801), 466–7 · J. Kirk, *Biographies of English Catholics in the eighteenth century*, ed. J. H. Pollen and E. Burton (1909) · *Correspondance littéraire, philosophique et critique de Grimm et de Diderot*, ed. J. A. Taschereau (1829), 1.290–91 · *Bibliotheca Towneleiana* (1814–15) · *European Magazine and London Review*, 41 (1802), 22–3 · Gillow, *Lit. biog. hist.* · *Œuvres complètes de Voltaire*, new edn, 50 vols. (1877–92)

Likenesses Peronneau, portrait; formerly in possession of Charles Towneley, 1868 · W. Skelton, line engraving, NPG

Townesend, William (*bap.* 1676, *d.* 1739), master mason, was baptized on 17 December 1676 at St Giles's Church, Oxford, the second child and eldest of the three sons of John Townesend (1648–1728), a mason of Oxford, and his wife, Elizabeth Morrell or Morall. His brothers, John (1678–1742) and George (1681–1719), were also masons—the former practised in London and the latter in the Bristol area—but William, the most successful member of the family, remained in Oxford and became the leading master mason in the town during a particularly active phase in its architectural history. Alongside its other main protagonists, the amateur architects Dr Henry Aldrich of Christ Church and Dr George Clarke of All Souls, and the professional Nicholas Hawksmoor, he was a prominent figure in this development; and the statement of the antiquary Thomas Hearne in 1720, that he 'hath a hand in all the Buildings of Oxford, and gets a vast deal of Money that way' (quoted in Colvin, *Biographical Dictionary of British Architects*, 3rd edn, 1995, p. 985), was no exaggeration. His first major undertakings were the erection of Peckwater quadrangle at Christ Church (1706–14) to the design of Aldrich and the fellows' building and cloister at Corpus Christi College (1706–12); and from then on until his death, occasionally working in partnership with another Oxford mason, Bartholomew Peisley (*d.* 1727), he was involved in virtually every significant building project in the university. He also worked elsewhere in the neighbourhood, notably at Radley Hall, Berkshire (1721–5), and as a contractor at Blenheim Palace (1720–39), while other aspects of his business were quarry-working and the production of funerary monuments.

In the building accounts of Queen's College, Oxford, Townesend is referred to as 'architecto', whereas his father, who had worked there previously, was described as 'lapicidae', a distinction which reflects the fact that, like others of his kind, he was certainly able to design as well as to build; but the extent to which he did so unaided is not entirely clear, many of the projects in Oxford at this time evidently being the work of more than one mind. In two cases where he executed designs by Hawksmoor, the Clarendon Building (1712–15) and the north quadrangle of All Souls (1716–35), he had submitted alternative proposals himself; and at Christ Church Library (1717–38) he acted as Clarke's architectural amanuensis, drawing out his designs as well as executing them. More complicated was the situation at Queen's, where designs for the front quad were prepared by Hawksmoor, but the scheme executed by Townesend (1710–21) appears to have been almost entirely the joint work of himself and Clarke; while for the new building at Magdalen, the original design by Edward Holdsworth was revised by Townesend in 1731 under Clarke's direction.

In these circumstances Townesend's own architectural identity is not very clearly defined. His predominant mode, in the Clarendon Building and All Souls designs and at Queen's, as well as in other works, such as the Christ Church buttery (1722) and his Durham quadrangle range at Trinity College (1728), was a simplified version of the baroque of Hawksmoor and Sir John Vanbrugh; but the fellows' building at Corpus Christi College, of which he may have been the designer as well as the builder, was close to the proto-Palladian manner of the Peckwater quadrangle, while his Radcliffe quadrangle at University College (1717–19)—again devised under Clarke's direction—and his Robinson Buildings at Oriel College (1719–20) were faithful copies of the traditional Jacobean style of the adjoining fabric, the former including a skilfully executed Gothic vault.

Townesend and his wife, Mary, had two children who survived their father: a son, John, who carried on the business, and a daughter. William Townesend died in September 1739 and was buried at St Giles's Church on 22 September.　　　PETER LEACH

Sources Colvin, Archs. · H. Colvin, Unbuilt Oxford (1983) · R. Gunnis, Dictionary of British sculptors, 1660–1851 (1953) · W. G. Hiscock, 'William Townesend, mason and architect of Oxford', ArchR, 98 (1945), 99–107 · IGI

Townley, Sir Charles (1713–1774), herald, was born on Tower Hill, London, on 7 May 1713, the eldest son of Charles Townley of Clapham, Surrey, and descended from a younger branch of the ancient family of Towneley Hall, near Burnley, Lancashire. James *Townley (1714–1778) was his younger brother. He was sent to Merchant Taylors' School, London, in 1727. He entered the College of Arms and was appointed York herald in July 1735, Norroy king-

of-arms on 2 November 1751, Clarenceux king-of-arms on 11 January 1755, and Garter principal king-of-arms on 27 April 1773. He was knighted at George III's coronation in 1761. On 24 June 1748 he married Mary, daughter of George Eastwood of Thornhill, Yorkshire. They had three sons and a daughter.

Townley died at his home in Camden Street, Islington, London, on 7 June 1774, and was buried, according to the terms of his will, in the family vault in the church of St Dunstan-in-the-East; his wife survived him. His eldest son, Charles Townley (1749–1800), became Bluemantle pursuivant on 31 December 1774 and Lancaster herald on 24 December 1781.

THOMPSON COOPER, rev. J. A. MARCHAND

Sources M. Noble, A history of the College of Arms (1804), 383, 386, 388, 414, 418, 439, 441 · GM, 1st ser., 44 (1774), 287 · C. J. Robinson, ed., A register of the scholars admitted into Merchant Taylors' School, from AD 1562 to 1874, 1 (1882), 70 · IGI · will, PRO, PROB 11/999, sig. 245, fols. 93v–96v

Wealth at death see will, PRO, PROB 11/999, sig. 245

Townley, Charles (1737–1805), collector of antiquities, was born on 1 October 1737 at Towneley Hall, near Burnley, Lancashire, the eldest in the family of three sons and a younger daughter of William Towneley (1714–1742) and his wife, Cecilia (1714–1777), the fifth daughter and eventual heir of Ralph Standish and his wife, Lady Philippa Howard, the daughter of Henry, sixth duke of Norfolk. The spelling Towneley is now usual for both the family and the place, but Charles, his brother Edward, and their mother all signed themselves Townley.

Townley was four when his father died on 2 February 1742, and he did not take control of the estate until he came of age. The family had remained Catholic after the Reformation, and Townley was sent abroad to the English College at Douai, entering with his brother Ralph (1739–1766) in 1747. After leaving Douai in 1753, he was tutored in Paris by the Revd John Turberville Needham and was introduced to Parisian society by an uncle of his father's, the Chevalier John *Towneley (bap. 1697, d. 1782). Having taken possession of Towneley Hall about 1758, he spent some years in the social and sporting activities of a country squire before undertaking the grand tour.

Townley arrived in Rome on 25 December 1767 and stayed until the following August, visiting Naples and Paestum during March. In Rome he began to collect antiquities, especially marble sculptures. Many early acquisitions were mere tourist souvenirs or outright fakes, but he gradually established himself as a serious collector with purchases from the printmaker Giovanni Battista Piranesi and other Roman dealers, and especially from the English dealer in art and antiquities Thomas Jenkins. Shortly before leaving Rome he paid Jenkins £400 for a fragmentary group of two boys quarrelling over a game of knucklebones, Astragalizontes.

During Townley's second and longest visit to Italy, in 1771–4, he spent a year in Rome and nine months based in Naples, and made extended journeys in southern Italy and

Charles Townley (1737–1805), by Johan Zoffany, 1781–3 [seated (right) in his library in Park Street with Pierre Hughes (seated, left), Charles Greville, and Thomas Astle]

Sicily. In Naples he acquired from the family of Prince Laurenzano a marble bust traditionally identified as the nymph Clytie, which later appeared with busts of Homer and Pericles on an ornate calling card engraved by William Skelton. In Rome he bought antiquities including sculptures from Jenkins, Thomas Byres, and several Italian dealers, and began to buy direct from the painter and excavator Gavin Hamilton. From 1773 some expensive items were bought on credit from Jenkins, on whose death in 1798 Townley was hard pressed to settle a debt of over £500 with his heir. Among these expensive sculptures were a statue of Diana at £250 and a group with a nymph struggling to escape the attentions of a faun, for which Townley paid £350, perhaps influenced by the group's erotic qualities. Although this work doubtless had a certain piquancy for an eighteenth-century collector, in a British Museum inventory of 1848 the group is annotated 'not exhibited'.

After returning to London, Townley corresponded regularly with Jenkins and Hamilton and expanded his collection with purchases from both, especially with sculptures excavated by Hamilton at Monte Cagnolo, Ostia, and elsewhere. Correspondence with Hamilton was sometimes acrimonious, as Townley complained of the quality of the sculptures he sent. With Jenkins he was on better terms: for many years Jenkins supplied Roman gossip as well as sculptures, and Townley undertook purchases in London for him and his friends, obtaining anything from scientific instruments to silk stockings. In 1777 Townley spent another three months in Italy, mainly in Rome, buying as

before from Jenkins, Hamilton, and Italian dealers. Following this last trip to Italy the rate of Townley's acquisitions decreased, but he continued to receive consignments of antiquities of all kinds from Jenkins, including a monumental caryatid (BM), similar to one retained for the papal collection, and other sculptures from the Montalto collection at Villa Negroni in 1786 and a Roman marble copy of the bronze discus-thrower (*discobolus*) by the Greek sculptor Myron (fifth century BC), found in Hadrian's villa in 1791. He also bought sculptures, coins, and other antiquities in London, either privately (for example, from Lyde Browne in 1773) or at auction. Over a period of more than twenty years Townley bought at some of the most important public sales of antiquities, among them those of Henry Constantine Jennings (1778), the duchess of Portland's museum (1786), Lord Cawdor (1800), and Lord Bessborough (1801).

From about 1771 Townley lived in a house in Crown Street (now Whitehall). Early in 1778 he moved into 7 Park Street (now 14 Queen Anne's Gate), designed by Samuel Wyatt and built for him by Michael Barrett. Townley was a compulsive collector. A financial summary drawn up in 1779 shows that he had by then spent about £11,600 on his collections and almost as much on successive houses, accounting for almost three-quarters of the £27,700 that he had borrowed on mortgage and bonds. With experience he became discriminating in his purchases, rejecting objects wrongly restored with alien heads.

In 1783 Johan Zoffany painted Townley in the midst of an imaginary arrangement of his sculptures in the library at Park Street, along with the Hon. Charles Greville, Thomas Astle, and Pierre Hugues, better known as the Baron d'Hancarville. Having fallen under the spell of d'Hancarville's over-ingenious speculations on ancient religion and mythology, Townley engaged him to catalogue his marbles and supported him for some years from 1777 with hospitality and frequent 'loans'.

Townley was elected fellow of the Society of Antiquaries in 1786 (and to its council in 1798) and fellow of the Royal Society in 1791. In 1786 he was also elected to the Society of Dilettanti, and from 1799 served on a committee appointed to publish engravings and descriptions of *Specimens of Antient Sculpture* (drawn largely from his own collection and that of Richard Payne Knight), which eventually appeared in 1809. In 1791 he was elected a trustee of the British Museum, where he influenced the design of the extension planned to house the museum's growing collection of antiquities.

Townley's youthful sojourn in Paris has been seen as the origin of a dissolute lifestyle. To his mother's distress he remained unmarried, but very explicit letters from Richard Payne Knight and various ladies confirm a hint in his travel diary that he led a far from celibate life. He even became a freemason, but towards the end of his life he returned to the practice of his childhood faith.

Townley was reputed a good landlord, considerate of his tenants. He improved the estate, overseeing the planting of many trees, and was involved in the construction of the

Leeds–Liverpool canal. In London he lived relatively frugally, having few servants and keeping no carriage (his coach house provided storage for sculptures). He was, however, a generous host, his Sunday dinners being highly praised by the sculptor Joseph Nollekens. Other members of his circle included Sir Joseph Banks, Richard Payne Knight, Sir Joshua Reynolds, and Richard and Maria Cosway.

Townley's collection became one of the sights of London. Dr Johnson wrote for an appointment in May 1792, and in *The Picture of London for 1802* visitors to the metropolis were advised to apply at the house to learn the hours of admission to 'the finest collection of antique statues, busts, etc, in the world … collected with the utmost taste and judgment' (Cook, *The Townley Marbles*, 7). While no private collector outside Italy could in fact hope to rival the great Roman collections, it remains true that the Townley marbles could bear comparison with any collection in the noble houses of England, even Lansdowne House and Petworth, both of which included sculptures rejected by Townley's taste and judgement. Visitors were freely admitted to see the collection. Some were given conducted tours by Townley himself; for others from about 1786 he provided manuscript catalogues, which were rewritten as the collection grew and the arrangement changed.

Barred from public life for his religion, Townley devoted much time and energy to learning, but his only publication was an account of an ornate Roman helmet found in 1796 at Ribchester in Lancashire, first issued in 1799, and later appearing in *Vetusta monumenta* (4, 1815, 1–11, pl. 1–4). He was also a talented amateur artist. Some of his sculptures are now known only from the drawings he made before disposing of them, and a miniature of the Medici Venus on ivory remains in the possession of the Towneley family.

Townley died without legitimate issue at his house in Park Street on 3 January 1805 and was buried in the family vault at St Peter's Church, Burnley, on 17 January. His estates passed first to his brother Edward Townley Standish (1740–1807), to whom he had already made over the Standish estates when their mother died, and then to an uncle, the bibliophile John Towneley (1731–1813).

In his will, dated 29 November 1802, his marbles were bequeathed to the British Museum, but in a codicil dated 22 December 1804 he left them in trust for his brother or his uncle on condition that a gallery be built to display them either at Towneley Hall or in London, and failing that for the British Museum. John Towneley wished to build a gallery, but Edward was unwilling to undertake the expense, and a compromise was eventually negotiated under which the marbles (including all those mentioned above), with some terracottas and bronzes, passed to the British Museum for £20,000 and (until the passage of the British Museum Act, 1963) the right to nominate a trustee. After John Towneley's death the small antiquities and drawings were sold to the British Museum by his son Peregrine Edward Towneley (1762–1846). The arrival at the British Museum of more than 300 antiquities transformed

its collection. From 1808 the marbles and terracottas were exhibited in a new wing, which had been planned in Townley's lifetime, but within a decade Townley's mainly Roman sculptures, many of them copies of earlier Greek works, were overshadowed by the museum's acquisition of Greek originals, the Bassae frieze and the Elgin collection. New acquisitions were merged with Townley's sculptures, and, although they remained 'the nucleus of the Graeco-Roman series' (Smith, 3.v), it was many years before the intrinsic value of Roman sculptures was fully appreciated, and it was not until 1984 that the museum again had a gallery dedicated to the Townley marbles.

B. F. COOK

Sources Nichols, *Illustrations* · T. D. Whitaker, *An history of the original parish of Whalley, and honor of Clitheroe, in the counties of Lancaster and York* (1801) · G. Vaughan, 'Townley, Charles', *The dictionary of art*, ed. J. Turner (1996) · B. F. Cook, *The Townley marbles* (1985) · S. J. Hill, *Catalogue of the Townley archive at the British Museum*, British Museum Occasional Papers, 138 (2002) · J. Ingamells, ed., *British and Irish travellers in Italy* (1997) · P. R. Harris, ed., *Douai College documents, 1639–1794*, Catholic RS, 63 (1972) · B. F. Cook, 'The Townley marbles in Westminster and Bloomsbury', *British Museum Yearbook*, 2 (1977), 34–78 · L. Cust and S. Colvin, *History of the Society of Dilettanti* (1914) · B. F. Cook, 'A miniature of the Medici Venus executed by Charles Townley, FSA, 1786–1805', *Antiquaries Journal*, 58 (1978), 383 · personal knowledge (2004) · private information (2004) [Sir Simon Towneley] · A. H. Smith, *A catalogue of sculpture in the department of Greek and Roman antiquities, British Museum*, 3 (1904) · A. Wilton and I. Bignamini, *Grand tour* (1996) [exhibition catalogue, Tate Gallery, 1996]

Archives BM, department of Greek and Roman antiquities · BM, archives · Bodl. Oxf., archives · priv. coll. · Towneley Hall, Museums and Art Gallery, Burnley, archive

Likenesses C. Hewetson, marble bust, 1769, BM; repro. in A. Dawson, *Portrait sculpture: a catalogue of the British Museum collection c. 1675–1975* (1999), 218–20, no. 81 · R. Cosway, group portrait, oils, 1771–5, Towneley Hall, Burnley · J. Brown, pencil drawing, 1772?, NG Scot. · factory of J. Wedgwood, ceramic medallion, 1780, BM; repro. in M. Clarke and N. Penny, eds., *The arrogant connoisseur: Richard Payne Knight, 1751–1824* (1982), 146, no. 74 · attrib. W. Tassie, Wedgwood medallion, *c.*1780, Wedgwood Museum, Stoke-on-Trent · J. Zoffany, group portrait, oils, 1781–3, Towneley Hall, Burnley [*see illus.*] · J. Opie, oils, *c.*1783, repro. in A. Earland, *John Opie and his circle* (1911); 319; in possession of J. Smith Barry, 1911 · W. Owen, oils, exh. RA 1799 · J. Flight, miniature?, exh. RA 1802 · J. Nollekens, bust, modelled 1805 (from a death mask), repro. in M. Clarke and N. Penny, eds., *The arrogant connoisseur: Richard Payne Knight, 1751–1824* (1982), 143, no. 60 · J. Nollekens, marble bust, before 1805, BM; version, 1807, Towneley Hall, Burnley · P. Turnerelli, marble bust, exh. RA 1805 · J. Godby, stipple, pubd 1812 (after J. Tassie, Wedgwood medallion), BM; repro. in *General Chronicle and Literary Magazine*, 5 (1812), facing p. 35 · attrib. T. Gainsborough, oils; photograph in NPG, Heinz archive; formerly at Leger, 13 Old Bond Street, London · W. H. Worthington, engraving (after drawing by T. Baxter), repro. in Nicholls, *Illustrations*, facing p. 721 · W. H. Worthington, engraving (after Zoffany), BM · line engraving, repro. in F. Hugues, Baron d'Hancarville, *Recherches sur l'origine, l'esprit, et le progrès des arts de la Grèce*, 3 vols. (1785), xxv

Wealth at death £15,636 6*s.* 10*d.*: PRO death duty registers, IR 26/95 · Standish received £2000 (value of lease on 7 Park Street), £1464 (household contents of 7 Park Street), and residue of £12,172 6*s.* 10*d.*; excl. collection of antiquities and contents of Towneley Hall

Townley, James (1714–1778), playwright and Church of England clergyman, was born in the parish of All Hallows, Barking, Essex, on 6 May 1714, the second son of Charles

Townley, a merchant of Tower Hill and Clapham, and the younger brother of Sir Charles *Townley. He entered Merchant Taylors' School, London, in 1727 and matriculated as a commoner at St John's College, Oxford, on 15 May 1732; he graduated BA (1735) and MA (1738). Townley simultaneously pursued a vocation in the church; he took priest's orders in May 1738, having taken deacon's orders at Grosvenor Chapel, Westminster, from Bishop Hoadly of Winchester on 6 March 1736.

Townley was chosen as lecturer of St Dunstan-in-the-East, London, on 12 October 1738 and only three years later he was appointed chaplain to Lord Mayor Daniel Lambert. He returned to Merchant Taylors' as third under-master, from 22 December 1748 until July 1753, when he was made grammar-master at Christ's Hospital. Townley again returned to Merchant Taylors', to serve as headmaster in 1760 after a brief stint as morning preacher at Lincoln's Inn (1759–60). While headmaster at Merchant Taylors' he attempted to reconfigure and to modernize the curriculum by introducing mathematics and emphasizing drama. Townley's efforts were greatly assisted by the public support of his friend David Garrick and by his ability to integrate his own playwriting skills. Indeed, Townley's curriculum reform provided him with a forum to commence his career, as Merchant Taylors' staged productions of his pieces *Eunuchus of Terence* and *Senecae Troades et ignoramus abbreviatus, in schola mercatorum scissorum.*

Following these amateur stagings Townley wrote three original, professionally produced dramatic works: *High Life below the Stairs* (1759), *False Concord* (1764), and *The Tutor* (1765). *High Life below the Stairs*, a two-act farce first staged at Drury Lane on 31 October 1759, garnered immediate public and critical acclaim, although some believed the play to be the work of Garrick. Further research and review unequivocally establishes that Townley wrote this piece and that Garrick probably contributed editorial assistance—as Townley did in turn for Garrick, most notably on *The Clandestine Marriage*. Regardless of the question of authorship, *High Life* emerged as a smashing popular success; the standard plot of a master who dons the functional yet humorous disguise of a servant to witness and to assess the behaviour of his employees received a great deal of attention—and protest—from its audience, since it became a prominent attraction for all of London society. The play appeared in many editions, was translated into German and French, and was performed on a great many of the world's stages.

Neither of Townley's final two plays, *False Concord* and *The Tutor*, approached the commercial and artistic success of *High Life*. Years after the production of *False Concord*, which had not been particularly well received on its appearance at Covent Garden on 20 March 1764 for the benefit of Woodward, Townley's son-in-law John Roberdeau alleged that Garrick plagiarized Townley's dialogue and characters in the 1767 staging of *The Clandestine Marriage*. Specifically Roberdeau claimed, in an 1805 edition of the *Gentleman's Magazine*, that Garrick's characters Lord Ogleby, Mr Sterling, and Brush in *The Clandestine Marriage* were exact copies of Townley's Lord Lavender, Mrs Sudley,

and a pert valet in *False Concord* (Roberdeau, *GM*, 110). Because no print version of *False Concord* exists this claim can neither be refuted nor substantiated yet the allegation itself has emerged as more noteworthy than Townley and any of his plays.

Attempts to determine the truth of Roberdeau's charge have, however, unearthed evidence that Townley received critical assistance from David Garrick and William Hogarth. Townley's professional relationship with both Garrick and Hogarth had always been assumed, yet remained speculative, but it is now clear that Townley was a constructive influence on various works of Garrick and Hogarth.

As Townley pursued a dramatic career and became increasingly active in London literary circles he continued to advance in his clerical career. In addition to the early appointments he held in the church he received preferments at the rectory of St Benet Gracechurch (22 July 1749) and St Leonard Eastcheap (1749), as well as the vicarage of Hendon in Middlesex (from 2 November 1772 to 1777). Clearly he benefited in his professional advancements from his marriage in 1740, to Jane Bonnin of Windsor, a descendant of the Poyntz family and a relative of Lady Spencer. Townley had two children: a son, James, who upheld the traditional educational association with Merchant Taylors' and eventually became a proctor in Doctors' Commons, and a daughter, Elizabeth, whose marriage to John Roberdeau is noteworthy because of his aforementioned allegation of plagiarism levied against Garrick. Townley died on 15 July 1778; a tablet was erected in his honour in St Benet Gracechurch.

L. LYNNETTE ECKERSLEY

Sources G. W. Stone, ed., *The London stage, 1660–1800*, pt 4: 1747–1776 (1962) • C. B. Hogan, ed., *The London stage, 1660–1800*, pt 5: 1776–1800 (1968) • J. M. Beatty, 'Garrick, Coleman, and *The clandestine marriage*', *Modern Language Notes*, 36 (1921), 129–41 • E. L. Bergman, 'David Garrick and *The clandestine marriage*', *Publications of the Modern Language Association of America*, 67 (1952), 148–62 • *The letters of David Garrick*, ed. D. M. Little and G. M. Kahrl, 3 vols. (1963), 188, 323, 329, 336, 341 • M. A. Goldsmith, 'James Townley and *The clandestine marriage*', *Review of English Studies*, new ser., 29 (1978), 169–77 • Highfill, Burnim & Langhans, *BDA* • R. D. Hume, ed., *The London theatre world, 1660–1800* (1980) • J. R. Roberdeau, 'Fugitive verse and prose', *GM*, 1st ser., 75 (1805), 110, 180, 389 • A. T. Straulman, 'George Coleman and David Garrick, *The clandestine marriage*: a critical edition', PhD diss., University of Wisconsin, 1968 • *DNB* • archives, Merchant Taylors' School, London
Archives Merchant Taylors' School, London, MSS • St John's College, Oxford | Hunt. L., Larpent collection
Likenesses C. Townley, stipple, pubd 1794, BM • H. D. Thielcke, stipple, NPG

Townley, James (1774–1833), Wesleyan Methodist minister and religious writer, was born on 11 May 1774 in Manchester, the son of Thomas Townley, a local businessman. His mother, Mary, a devout churchwoman, was also an occasional attender at Methodist meetings. Townley was educated in Macclesfield by the evangelical incumbent, the Revd David Simpson (1745–1799), whose death and funeral deeply affected the young man. He joined the Wesleyan Methodists in 1790, giving up a promising career in the cotton industry in 1796 to become an itinerant preacher. According to his biographer, Townley was a sensitive and able minister, adept at resolving problems, clearing debts, and strengthening churches (Hoole, 323). Even the acerbic James Everett, no friend to the Wesleyan establishment, commented on Townley's 'steady piety; acceptable pulpit talents; ... [and] deep sympathy' (Everett, 345). His name was canvassed unsuccessfully for the post of connexional editor in 1824 in succession to Jabez Bunting, but three years later he was appointed general secretary of the Wesleyan Missionary Society, retaining this position until his retirement. Elected president of the Wesleyan Methodist conference at Sheffield in 1829, his year of office took a heavy toll on his health, and he was compelled to retire as a minister in 1832.

Townley steadily established a reputation within Methodism for biblical, historical, and linguistic scholarship. He was a member of the Manchester Philological Society founded by Adam Clarke, and his published works included the three-volume *Illustrations of Biblical Literature* (1821) and a critical edition of Maimonides's *Mose nevochim* (1827). A projected history of Christian missions was never completed, and bore fruit only in four articles published posthumously in the *Wesleyan Methodist Magazine* in 1834. His academic and literary achievements were recognized in the award of a DD by Princeton in 1822.

Townley was married twice. His first wife, Mary Marsden (1770–1827), to whom he was married in September 1798, came from a prominent Methodist family in London and was admitted to the Methodist society at the age of seven by John Wesley. Memoirs of her parents, John and Hannah Marsden, written by Townley, were published in the *Methodist Magazine* in 1808. The eldest of the Townleys' eight children died in 1823, and Mary Townley herself died in 1827. His second wife was Dinah Ball, also of London. After an extended period of ill health, James Townley died in retirement at Ramsgate on 12 December 1833.

MARTIN WELLINGS

Sources E. Hoole, 'Memoir of the late Rev. James Townley DD', *Wesleyan Methodist Magazine*, 58 (1835), 321–31 • *Minutes of the Methodist conferences, from the first, held in London by the late Rev. John Wesley* ..., 7 (1838), 343 [1831–5 conferences] • *Wesleyan Methodist Magazine*, 57 (1834), 78–9 • J. Everett, *Wesleyan takings* (1841), 344–5 • *The early correspondence of Jabez Bunting, 1820–1829*, ed. W. R. Ward, CS, 4th ser., 11 (1972), 94, 204 • *Early Victorian Methodism: the correspondence of Jabez Bunting, 1830–1858*, ed. W. R. Ward (1976), 38–40 • *DNB* • J. Townley, 'The grace of God manifested in an account of Mr John Marsden', *Methodist Magazine*, 31 (1808), 32–40 • J. Townley, 'The grace of God manifested in an account of Mrs Hannah Marsden', *Methodist Magazine*, 31 (1808), 77–85 • *Wesleyan Methodist Magazine*, 50 (1827), 720

Archives JRL, Methodist Archives and Research Centre, corresp.
Likenesses J. Thomson, stipple (after J. Jackson), BM; repro. in *Wesleyan Methodist Magazine* (June 1830)

Townsend. *See also* Townshend.

Townsend, Aurelian. *See* Townshend, Aurelian (*fl.* 1583–1649?).

Townsend, Charles Harrison (1851–1928), architect, was born on 13 May 1851 in Birkenhead, Cheshire, the son of Jackson Townsend, solicitor, and his wife, Pauline, the

Charles Harrison Townsend (1851–1928), by Francis Derwent Wood, 1903

daughter of Felix *Yaniewicz, a well-known Polish violinist; he had five brothers and one sister. After attending Birkenhead School, he was articled to the architect Walter Scott of Liverpool from 1867 to 1872. From 1873 to 1875 he was a draughtsman in the office of Charles Barry, and in 1875 he joined Edward Robert Robson's office at the recently formed London school board. In the same year he made the first of many visits to Europe, to which he returned throughout his life, especially to northern Italy, where he developed a lifelong interest in architectural mosaics.

In 1877 Townsend started practice on his own in London, and between 1884 and 1886 was in partnership with Thomas Lewis Banks. When the partnership was dissolved he moved his office to 29 Great George Street, Westminster, where it remained for the rest of his life. In 1888 he was elected a fellow of the Royal Institute of British Architects. He also designed furniture and wallpaper and was elected, also in 1888, to the Art Workers' Guild, of which he was to be an enthusiastic and devoted member, and which provided his main circle of friends; he was elected master of the guild for the year 1903.

Until 1892 Townsend's practice was made up of minor domestic and ecclesiastical work, but in that year he won the competition for the design of the Bishopsgate Institute, the first of the three outstanding public buildings that were to make his reputation. In 1897 he was commissioned to design the Whitechapel Art Gallery and the Horniman Museum in Lewisham, south London, both of which were completed in 1901. These were exceptionally original buildings, and belonged to no recognizable architectural tradition. Writing in 1900, the German architect and critic Hermann Muthesius identified as one of the most significant developments in European architecture the tendency of certain British architects towards what he described as a 'modern' style, which referred to no tradition, and created a new architectural language of space and mass. Foremost among the representatives of this new school he placed Townsend, whom, next to Charles Voysey, he regarded as one of 'the prophets of the new style' (H. Muthesius, *Die englische Baukunst der Gegenwart*, 1, 1900, 30).

Although the unquestionable and striking originality, particularly of the last two buildings, made this a valid assessment in 1900, Townsend never again produced anything of equal quality. After 1901 his practice was limited to relatively uninteresting private houses in southern England. Why he did not sustain the promise of the works of the 1890s is not clear, though it is certainly connected with the change to a much more conservative and less experimental architectural climate in Britain in the 1900s, when there was a revival of baroque and French Renaissance architecture; it may also be to do with Townsend's own equivocal and confused attitude towards the value of architectural traditions.

In 1915 Townsend was appointed assistant director of the London county council's civic survey, a scheme to employ architects deprived of work by the war in the collection of social and physical data on the structure of the city. In 1917 he was employed as a Royal Naval Volunteer Reserve lieutenant in Avonmouth on the dazzle-painting of ships. In 1918 he virtually ceased to practise, and in the early 1920s moved to live with his sister in Northwood, Middlesex, where he died, at his house, 30 Murray Road, on 26 December 1928. He never married and had no children. He is said to have been convivial, widely knowledgeable, with a fertile imagination and a whimsical sense of humour. His most regular companions were artists, several of whom, such as Walter Crane, Sir George Frampton, and Robert Anning Bell, collaborated with him on his buildings.   ADRIAN FORTY, rev.

Sources A. Service, 'Charles Harrison Townsend', *Edwardian architecture and its origins*, ed. A. Service (1975), 162–82 • RIBA BAL • J. Lever, ed., *Catalogue of the drawings collection of the Royal Institute of British Architects: T–Z* (1984) • *CGPLA Eng. & Wales* (1929)
Likenesses F. D. Wood, sculpture, 1903, Art Workers' Guild, London [*see illus.*]
Wealth at death £169 5s. 6d.: probate, 16 Feb 1929, *CGPLA Eng. & Wales*

Townsend, George (1788–1857), writer and Church of England clergyman, was born at Ramsgate, Kent, the son of George Townsend, independent minister, and his wife. He was educated at Ramsgate and attracted the attention of the playwright Richard Cumberland (1732–1811), who encouraged and helped him to go to Trinity College, Cambridge. He matriculated at Trinity in the Lent term of 1808, and graduated BA (1812) and MA (1816). He was ordained deacon in 1813 and priest in 1814. He became curate of Littleport, Cambridgeshire, in 1813, before moving to Hackney as curate to John James Watson, archdeacon of Colchester. In 1816 he was appointed professor at Sandhurst and became curate at Farnborough, Hampshire.

Townsend's first publication was *Oedipus Romanus* (1811), a controversial tract which followed the logic of Sir William Drummond's *Oedipus Judaicus* (which had argued that most of the Old Testament was an astronomical allegory) in order to suggest that the twelve Caesars represented the signs of the zodiac. *Oedipus Romanus* was reissued in 1819, and it also led Townsend to pursue with vigour the

research which was to lead to his great work *The Old Testament Arranged in Historical and Chronological Order*, whose first part was published in London in 1821. This work obtained the notice of, among others, Shute Barrington, bishop of Durham, who appointed him his domestic chaplain in 1822. This position gave Townsend enough free time to bring out the second part of his work, entitled, *The New Testament, Arranged in Chronological and Historical Order* (1825).

During heated arguments over the pending issue of Catholic emancipation, and with Barrington's encouragement, Townsend published a reply to the Catholic Charles Butler's *Historical Memoirs of the English, Scottish and Irish Catholics since the Reformation* (1822) with his own *Accusations of History Against the Church of Rome* (1825; new edn, 1845). He was rewarded for his controversial work and received, on 25 August 1825, the tenth prebendal stall in the see of Durham, which he retained until his death. He also obtained, on 26 April 1826, the chapter living of Northallerton, which he left on 22 February 1839 to become perpetual curate of St Margaret, Durham. In 1836 he compiled a 'Life and vindication of John Foxe', the martyrologist, which was prefixed to the first volume of an edition of S. R. Cattley's *Acts and Monuments of John Foxe* (8 vols., 1837–41).

In 1850 Townsend undertook an unusual journey to Italy with the intention of converting Pope Pius IX to protestantism. He failed in his efforts, but on his return published an account of the mission, *Journal of a tour in Italy in 1850, with an account of an interview with the pope in the Vatican* (1850). During his lifetime Townsend also published a variety of poems, sermons, theological studies, and historical works. He brought out *Flowers from the Garden of the Church, or, The Collects of the Church of England Versified* in 1854.

Townsend, who was twice married, died at The College, Durham, on 23 November 1857, and has been described by one historian as an 'old-style Durham High Churchman' (Wolffe, 112). A son from his first marriage, George Fyler Townsend, later became perpetual curate of St Michael's, Burleigh Street, Westminster, London.

E. I. CARLYLE, *rev.* SINÉAD AGNEW

Sources Venn, *Alum. Cant.* • *GM*, 3rd ser., 4 (1858), 101 • Boase, *Mod. Eng. biog.* • Ward, *Men of the reign*, 891 • J. Foster, ed., *Index ecclesiasticus, or, Alphabetical lists of all ecclesiastical dignitaries in England and Wales since the Reformation* (1890), 175 • Allibone, *Dict.* • J. Wolffe, *The protestant crusade in Great Britain, 1829–1860* (1991)
Likenesses T. Saulini, copper electrotype medallion, 1850, BM • W. Drummond, lithograph, BM, NPG; repro. in *Athenaeum Portraits* (1836) • E. Hastings, oils, University College, Durham

Townsend, George Henry (*d.* 1869), compiler of reference works and journalist, was grandson of John *Townsend (1757–1826), and nephew of George Townsend (1788–1857). Townsend was a prominent tory journalist. He edited *The Herald* during the minority tory government of 1858–9, being dismissed, despite tory protests, about November 1859. As editor, he had close contacts with Lord Malmesbury, the foreign secretary (Earle to Disraeli, November 1859, MS Hughenden B/XX/E177). Townsend then recommended the foundation of a joint-stock company to develop the tory press in London, a proposal too adventurous even for Disraeli. He was editor and manager of *The Press* from about 1865. He worked consistently for his party and understood that following the general election in 1868 he would receive some preferment—perhaps a civil-list pension—as his reward. However, Disraeli resigned without finding anything for him and Townsend, deeply disappointed, committed suicide at Kennington, London, on 23 February 1869 by stabbing himself.

Townsend wrote *Shakespeare not an Impostor* (1857), but his chief literary contribution was as a compiler and editor. He produced an epitome in 1857 of William Russell's *History of Modern Europe*, and edited several literary volumes. His *Manual of Dates* was published in 1857 and, in its fifth edition, by Frederick Martin (1877), remains useful, though largely superseded by Haydn's *Dictionary of Dates*. Townsend edited the seventh edition of *Men of the time* in 1868.

Besides these works, Townsend between 1860 and 1866 wrote several pamphlets containing selections of madrigals and glees for John Green, the proprietor of Evans's music and supper rooms, 43 Covent Garden. As these pamphlets purport to be compiled by John Green, confusion arose, and Green was sometimes regarded as a pseudonym of Townsend. The two were, however, entirely distinct. **John** [Paddy] **Green** (1801–1874) was an actor at the Old English Opera House, London, and at Covent Garden. He became manager of the Cider Cellars in Maiden Lane, the Strand, and took part as a singer in the entertainments there. In 1842 he became chairman and conductor of music at Evans's Hall, and in 1845 succeeded W. C. Evans (*d.* 1855) as proprietor. In 1865 he sold the concern to a joint-stock company for £30,000. In 1866 he gave evidence before a parliamentary committee on theatrical licences. He died in London at 6 Farm Street, Mayfair, on 12 December 1874. His collection of theatrical portraits was sold at Christies on 22 July 1871. The Cider Cellars and Evans's Hall were the originals of W. M. Thackeray's 'Cave of Harmony'.   E. I. CARLYLE, rev. H. C. G. MATTHEW

Sources Boase, *Mod. Eng. biog.* · *Register and Magazine of Biography*, 1 (1869), 317 · *London Review* (27 Feb 1869) · Allibone, *Dict.* · S. E. Koss, *The rise and fall of the political press in Britain*, 2 vols. (1981–4) · L. Brown, *Victorian news and newspapers* (1985) · Bodl. Oxf., Dep. Hughenden

Townsend [Townshend], **Horace** [Horatio] (1750–1837), writer, was the son of Philip Townshend of Ross, co. Cork, and was born in Ross. He entered Trinity College, Dublin, about 1768. He graduated BA in 1770 and MA in 1776. He was incorporated at Magdalen College, Oxford, on 15 April 1776. He took orders and was given the living of Ross Carbery, co. Cork, where he lived for the rest of his life. He is thought not to have married.

Townsend was a writer of some local fame, not to say notoriety. He wrote much verse and occasional articles for *Blackwood's Magazine* under the name Senex, and for *Bolster's Cork Magazine* between 1828 and 1831. His most famous publication was *A Statistical Survey of the County of Cork, with Observations on the Means for Improvement* (1810). The work was drawn up under the auspices of the Dublin Society. It was not a quantitative survey, but a prose description of the county. Townsend systematically described the geology, physical geography, inhabitants, antiquities, and the state of the church and agriculture in the first part of the book, following it with a topographical description barony by barony. Finally came addenda which were lists of miscellaneous items such as observations on bees and eggs.

Townsend in his *Survey* proved a systematic and industrious compiler and could show sympathy towards those whom he observed. He found the local people engaging in some respects and could describe them wittily, comparing for example Englishmen in an inn who would barely exchange one word over their drink with a similar gathering of Irishmen where 'the difficulty is to find a listener' (p. 75). He also wrote sympathetically about the alleged thievish tendencies of the Irish, ascribing these largely to poverty. He perceptively observed that underemployment stemmed from overpopulation in Irish rural districts, and identified the ease with which potatoes could provide for a family as the key to early marriage and further population growth in such districts.

Townsend's survey did, however, show the conventional prejudices of his class and time. In comparing English and Irish peasantry, he proclaimed 'the superiority of the English in cleanliness, decorum, the order and decencies of life' (p. 74). He described the violent attacks among Irish peasants and attributed them to the persistence of their ancient tribal quarrels. What the *Survey* became most immediately known for, however, was its comment, repeated in the second edition of the work, entitled *A General and Statistical Survey of the County of Cork* (1815), on the state of the Roman Catholic clergy in the county. His remarks, particularly criticisms of the clergy's role in education, led to a bitter and protracted correspondence with the Dublin Society and in the Cork press. Townsend's anti-Catholicism became manifest also in his *Observations on the Catholic Claims* (1812), in which he argued against Catholic emancipation chiefly on the grounds that Roman Catholics were claiming a right to freedom of conscience which they denied their own members. While such arguments dominated the immediate and local reception of his work, later readers have valued his detailed and often perceptive descriptions of the county, not least because his was one of the earliest such surveys in Ireland. Townsend died on 26 March 1837 and a memorial in the form of a relief of the Good Samaritan by the noted sculptor Thomas Kirk was raised in Ross Carbery church.

ELIZABETH BAIGENT

Sources Foster, *Alum. Oxon.* · D. J. O'Donoghue, *The poets of Ireland: a biographical and bibliographical dictionary* (1912); repr. (1970) · A. M. Brady and B. Cleeve, eds., *A biographical dictionary of Irish writers*, rev. edn (1985) · H. Potterton, *Irish church monuments* (1975) · *DNB*
Archives NL Scot., corresp. with Blackwoods and poems

Townsend, Isaac (1684/5–1765), naval officer and politician, was the nephew of Sir Isaac Townsend (*d.* 1731), captain in the navy, and for many years resident commissioner at Portsmouth. He may have entered the navy in

1696, as servant to his uncle, captain of the *Ipswich*. He was warranted as a volunteer on that ship in December of this year. Afterwards he was in the *Severn*, *Lincoln*, *Royal William*, *Russell*, and again the *Ipswich* as a seaman or midshipman. Townsend passed his lieutenant's examination on 15 January 1706. It is possible that he was both at Vigo in 1702 and in the action off Malaga in August 1704. He received his first commission, as third lieutenant of the *Resolution*, on 29 July 1707. On 24 September 1707 he was appointed lieutenant of the *Hastings* with Captain John Paul, employed on the Irish station, apparently until the peace. Townsend became second lieutenant of the *Dorsetshire* on 3 March 1718. On 30 June 1719 he was appointed commander of the fireship *Poole*, and on 9 February 1720 he achieved post rank as captain of the *Success* (20 guns), which he commanded on the Irish station for the next ten years. In February 1734 he was given command of the newly commissioned *Plymouth* on the home station. In mid-1738 Townsend was ordered to join Nicholas Haddock's squadron in the Mediterranean. In June 1739 Haddock appointed Townsend to the *Berwick*. In March 1740 Townsend was sent home with a convoy. Along with his ship's company, he was then turned over to the *Shrewsbury* in April 1740, one of the fleet in the channel, with Sir John Norris, and for some time the flagship of Sir Chaloner Ogle, with whom, at the end of the year, she went out to the West Indies. In the operations against Cartagena in March–April 1741 the *Shrewsbury*, with the *Norfolk* and *Russell*, all 80-gun ships, captured the small forts of St Iago and St Philip, at the entrance to the outer harbour. The *Shrewsbury* suffered heavy damage with over 60 dead and wounded. After the failure of the operation against Cartagena the *Shrewsbury* returned to England with a number of other ships under Commodore Richard Lestock.

On 19 June 1744 Townsend was promoted rear-admiral of the red and in December he was elected MP for Portsmouth in the Admiralty interest. On 23 April 1745 he advanced to vice-admiral of the blue. Early that year he went out to the Mediterranean as third in command, with his flag in the *Dorsetshire*. Shortly afterwards news arrived of the departure of a French squadron for the Americas and Townsend was detached with eight ships of the line to protect the British West Indian islands. He had further instructions to try to capture St Lucia or Puerto Rico. In the event the French were not threatening the British islands and the capture of enemy islands proved impracticable. However, Townsend intercepted a convoy of French merchant ships off Martinique on 31 October 1745, capturing or destroying over thirty of the vessels.

Towards the end of 1745 rumours reached London of French preparations to retake Louisbourg, which had been captured by a force of New Englanders, supported by Commodore Peter Warren, in August 1745. Townsend was ordered to take over command of Louisbourg from Warren, who was anxious to return to England. Townsend sailed from Antigua on 31 January 1746 and arrived on 9 May. He remained at Louisbourg with the squadron while the French squadron approached, but failed to attack, the town.

On 17 July 1747 Townsend was promoted admiral of the blue and in 1754 he became governor of Greenwich Hospital. In this position he had to undertake the custody of Admiral John Byng after his arrest in July 1756. He is said by Byng's friends to have performed this duty with needless, even brutal, severity. It is impossible to be certain of Townsend's attitude to Byng, but he had no reservations about succeeding to Byng's parliamentary seat at Rochester after the latter's execution in March 1757.

In February 1757 Townsend was promoted admiral of the white, and following the death of Lord Anson in 1762 he became the senior admiral on the list. He married Elizabeth (1699/1700–1754), daughter of William Larcum, a surgeon of Richmond, and half-sister (on the mother's side) of Elizabeth, daughter of Anthony Storey, apothecary of London, and wife of Sir Isaac Townsend, Townsend's uncle. The fact that uncle and nephew shared the same name has caused frequent confusion, which this curious marriage with sisters of the same Christian name easily intensifies. Townsend has also been confused with George Townsend (1715–1769), a contemporary in rank, though a younger man. Townsend's wife died on 1 April 1754. His only son, Charles, died on 13 January 1764. Townsend himself died on 21 November 1765, aged eighty, and he was buried the next day with his wife and son in the chancel of St Mary, Thorpe, Surrey. A daughter, Elizabeth, survived him.

RICHARD HARDING

Sources commissions and warrants, PRO, ADM 6/6, fol. 50 · PRO, ADM 6/4, fol. 53*v* · PRO, ADM 6/9, fols. 84*v*, 92*v* · PRO, ADM 6/12, fols. 156*v*, 173, 193 · PRO, ADM 6/13, fol. 148*v* · PRO, ADM 6/14, fol. 166 · PRO, ADM 6/15, fols. 254, 324 · PRO, ADM 6/16, fols. 325, 376, 469 · log of the *Shrewsbury*, PRO, ADM 51/943 · *The Royal Navy and North America: the Warren papers, 1736–1752*, ed. J. Gwyn, Navy RS, 118 (1975) · commander-in-chief, Jamaica, to admiralty, Dover to Newcastle, 4 Dec 1745, PRO, SP 42/89, fol. 277 · J. Charnock, ed., *Biographia navalis*, 4 (1796), 85–9 · PRO, PROB 11/914, fol. 343 · M. M. Drummond, 'Townsend, Isaac', HoP, *Commons, 1754–90* · O. Manning and W. Bray, *The history and antiquities of the county of Surrey*, 3 (1814), 245 · J. Williams, transcript, index of registers of St Mary, Thorpe, 1990

Archives PRO, ADM 6/4; 6/9–16; ADM 51/943 · PRO, SP 42/89

Likenesses oils, *c*.1706–1707, NMM

Wealth at death see PRO, PROB 11/914, fol. 343

Townsend, James (*bap.* 1737, *d.* 1787), politician, was baptized on 8 February 1737 at St Christopher-le-Stocks, London, the eldest surviving son of Chauncy Townsend (*bap.* 1708, *d.* 1770), MP, and Bridget, daughter of James Phipps of Wiltshire. His father was a London entrepreneur with interests ranging from linen drapery to coal mines. Townsend did not follow his father into business, for, after attending Hertford College, Oxford, in 1756, he achieved financial independence by his marriage on 3 May 1763 to Rosa Peregrina du Plessis (1745–1785), the illegitimate daughter of Henry *Hare, third and last Baron Coleraine (1693–1749), antiquary, and Rose du Plessis (or Duplessis; 1710–1790). Townsend secured possession of Hare's estate in Tottenham, Middlesex, which had escheated to the crown on his death on the grounds that his daughter was an alien.

Townsend sought a political career, and soon formed a

connection with Lord Shelburne, whose influence as secretary of state in the Chatham ministry of 1766–8 enabled him to enter parliament for the government borough of West Looe at a by-election in 1767 and to retain the seat at the 1768 general election. In that year Shelburne went into opposition; possession of a government seat did not inhibit Townsend from doing likewise. In 1769 he was involved in a scheme of Shelburne's to split East India Company stock to influence the choice of directors, and he helped Shelburne to meet the financial losses caused by a fall in the stock price.

Townsend was a vigorous supporter of John Wilkes during the Middlesex election case of 1768–9, and proposed Wilkes for re-election after his first expulsion. He was a founder member of the Society of Supporters of the Bill of Rights, formed in February 1769 to support Wilkes, and Wilkite power in the City of London brought him election in June 1769 as a lifetime alderman and annual sheriff. But Townsend was one of those who wished to make the society a radical organization and not merely a milch-cow for Wilkes to exploit, and, with other Shelburne men, he seceded under John Horne in April 1771 to form a new Constitutional Society. In City politics this radical split let in a government supporter as lord mayor in 1771, and so in 1772 Wilkes stood with Townsend on a joint ticket, for the mayor was chosen by the court of aldermen from the two top candidates. Townsend's role was merely to facilitate the election of Wilkes, but he played Wilkes false. Always ambitious for a leading position in London politics, in 1771 he had won cheap popularity by refusing to pay land tax on his Tottenham estate, claiming that Wilkes's exclusion left Middlesex unrepresented in parliament; as a result he had suffered distraint on his goods to the value of £200. Now, in 1772, a coalition of Hornites and courtiers secured his election as mayor. The resulting animosity between the two men led Townsend, according to Horace Walpole, to become 'as active an enemy of Wilkes as the Scotch' (Last Journals, 1.250). His treachery led to a riot on his lord mayor's day, and made him so unpopular in London that when he was due to forfeit his government seat at the 1774 general election, and appeared on the hustings, vehement abuse forced his withdrawal.

By the late 1770s mutual self-interest led surviving London radicals to re-unite, and Townsend canvassed for Wilkes in his successful election as city chamberlain in 1779. But he did not seek re-election to parliament until Shelburne returned him for his pocket borough of Calne in April 1782. He then again displayed his radical credentials by speaking for both parliamentary reform and annual parliaments, the latter a cause he had championed in the 1770s. He supported both Shelburne and Pitt against the Fox–North coalition of 1783, but voted against the subsequent Pitt ministry on several occasions. On 9 May 1787 he strongly opposed the impeachment of Warren Hastings, as a man who deserved not the condemnation but the thanks of his country. The diarist Nathaniel Wraxall recalled that 'though he seldom mingled in debate, he manifested whenever he spoke a manly mind, great facility of expression, strong sense, combined with upright

principles of action' (Wraxall, 2.329). Townsend died at Bruce Castle, Tottenham, his residence, on 1 July 1787, after a cold turned into fever; he was buried privately in the churchyard of Tottenham church. His wife had died on 8 November 1785 and he was survived by their son, Henry Hare Townsend, and daughter.

PETER D. G. THOMAS

Sources HoP, Commons, 1754–90 · P. D. G. Thomas, John Wilkes: a friend to liberty (1996) · L. S. Sutherland, The East India Company in eighteenth century politics (1952) · The last journals of Horace Walpole, ed. Dr Doran, rev. A. F. Steuart, 2 vols. (1910) · N. W. Wraxall, Posthumous memoirs of his own time, 2nd edn, 3 vols. (1836) · GM, 1st ser., 57 (1787), 640–41 · IGI

Likenesses R. Hounton, group portrait, mezzotint, c.1768–1770, repro. in H. Bleackley, Life of John Wilkes (1917), 238

Wealth at death Tottenham estate

Townsend, John (1757–1826), benefactor, was born in Whitechapel, London, on 24 March 1757, the son of Benjamin and Margaret Townsend. His father, a pewterer, was disinherited for his attachment to the Calvinistic Methodist leader George Whitefield and, as a result, the family lived a 'humble life' (Congregational Magazine, 226). John was educated at Christ's Hospital, London, which he entered on 6 March 1766 and left on 8 April 1771 at the instruction of his father, who wished him to serve as his apprentice at Swallow Gardens, London. It was during the time of his apprenticeship that he began attending services at Tottenham Court Chapel and was drawn to preaching. After an eight-month position at Lewes, Sussex, he was ordained minister of the Independent church at Kingston, Surrey, in June 1781. He married in the same month Cordelia Carhusac; they had at least one child. Much to Townsend's disapproval members of his Kingston congregation came under the influence of William Huntington's antinomianism, forcing Townsend to resign his position. On 28 October 1784 he became minister of the newly founded Independent church in Jamaica Row, Bermondsey, and from March 1787 he also preached weekly at the Orange Street Chapel.

In 1792 Townsend was responsible, along with Henry Cox Mason, rector of Bermondsey, and the MP Henry Thornton, for the establishment of an asylum for deaf mute children of the poor in Bermondsey. What began as a parish institution attracted a number of subscribers and grew to become a national charity. Plans were laid for the construction on Old Kent Road of a purpose-built asylum, which was begun in July 1807, and for which Townsend, by 'his own individual efforts and personal applications', was able to contribute £6000. In the period between the asylum's foundation and the erection of its new premises Townsend was also involved in the creation of the London Missionary Society (1794) and the British and Foreign Bible Society (1804), for which he provided the name.

In September 1810 Townsend published a Letter to the ministers, officers, and all other members and friends of the congregational churches in England, in which he drew attention to the poverty of his fellow ministers and the inadequacy of the education provided for their children. Townsend received a poor response to his appeal, raising just £200 in four months. As a result he limited his plans to the building of a free school for the sons of poor Independent ministers; this opened as the Congregational school in October 1811. In 1815 the school moved to a house in Lewisham, for which Townsend helped to pay by undertaking a lecture tour of Yorkshire and Lancashire intended 'to excite the churches there to assist it by their patronage'. As well as the *Letter to the Ministers* he also published a collection of sermons on prayer, some *Hints on Sunday-Schools and Itinerant Preaching* (1801), an abridgement of John Bunyan's *Pilgrim's Progress* (1806), and a *Defence of the Reformation* (1815). Townsend, a man of 'eminent philanthropy' (*Congregational Magazine*, 229), was engaged in raising funds to build an almshouse when he died in Bermondsey on 7 February 1826.   PHILIP CARTER

Sources DNB · *Congregational Magazine*, 9 (1826) · D. E. Owen, *English philanthropy, 1660–1960* (1964) · R. Lee, *Bermondsey, 1795* (1993)

Townsend, John (1760–1832), Bow Street runner, was born in the Middlesex Hospital and educated at St Clement Danes school, to both of which charitable institutions he later became a subscriber. As a young man he frequented the Bow Street court, making notes on the cases, and Sir John Fielding, the chief magistrate, appointed him an officer of the court in 1781. In addition to attendance on the magistrates, he was responsible for the serving of writs and for criminal investigations and arrests within the metropolitan area. He was responsible for the first detachment of prisoners to be sent to Botany Bay in 1789, and he recorded that in 1786 he travelled to Dunkirk to arrest four men who were later hanged. As he also told the parliamentary committee on the state of the police of the metropolis in 1816, it was he who arrested the famous highwayman Jerry Abershaw in 1795 and also Broughton, who had robbed the York mail in 1794. His services as detective and security man were also in demand by private hire within and beyond London. He found regular employment at places as diverse as the Bank of England and Vauxhall Gardens, and built up a reputation for efficiency based on a detailed knowledge of the criminal fraternity and for his discretion and loyalty to his employers.

In 1792, following an attack on George III, Townsend was given responsibility for the security of the royal family during their public engagements, and for these services, which he continued to perform until 1831, he received £200 per annum. He became a favourite of George III and of the prince of Wales, later George IV, whom he attended at Carlton House and accompanied to Brighton for many years. He enjoyed what was evidently a licensed familiarity with both monarchs, and his last public employment was to attend William IV on his coronation in September 1831. He provided protection for Lord Eldon, the lord chancellor, during the corn law riots of 1815, and Eldon's testimony to his qualities was one of several records in contemporary memoirs.

Townsend was a principal witness before the parliamentary select committee inquiring into policing in the metropolis in 1816, and his distinctive character is evident in his testimony, in which he clearly enjoyed expatiating on his successes, and his familiarity with those he called 'the first people of the nation'. In his evidence he told the committee that in his early days 'we never had an execution where we did not grace the unfortunate gibbet with between ten and forty criminals'. He expressed firm opposition to the system of blood money, whereby police officers were paid £40 for a successful capital conviction, because he believed it made juries unwilling to convict; he argued that police officers should be remunerated only by increased salaries. Short and corpulent, he had a powerful personality which, it is evident, made a strong impression on both the criminal classes and the ruling classes. He became known as a 'public character' early in his career, and appeared in caricatures over a period of forty years, frequently identified by his smart dress with a characteristic wide-brimmed hat, in a style favoured by his master, the prince of Wales, and by his addiction to the flash or cant slang of the criminal and sporting classes. He remained an officer of Bow Street for over fifty years. He lived in the Strand for a number of years, but it was at his home in Pimlico that he died on 10 July 1832. He was survived by his wife, Ann.   JOHN FORD

Sources 'Select committee on the state of the police of the metropolis', *Parl. papers* (1816), vol. 5, no. 510 · GM, 1st ser., 102/2 (1832) · *The Times* (11 July 1832) · *Bell's Life in London* (5 Aug 1832) · *The reminiscences of Henry Angelo*, ed. H. Lavers Smith, 2 (1904) · *The reminiscences and recollections of Captain Gronow*, 2 (1900) · *The Farington diary*, ed. J. Greig, 3 (1924) · *The public and private life of Lord Chancellor Eldon, with selections from his correspondence*, ed. H. Twiss, 1 (1844) · P. Egan, *Life in London* (1821) · P. Egan, *A trip to the Ascot races* (1826) · B. Blackmantle [C. M. Westmacott], *The English spy*, 2 (1826) · F. G. Stephens and M. D. George, eds., *Catalogue of political and personal satires preserved … in the British Museum*, 7–10 (1942–52) · P. Fitzgerald, *Chronicles of Bow Street police-office*, 1 (1888) · will, PRO, PROB 11/1803, sig. 475

Likenesses H. St C. B, engraved caricature, 1797, BM · R. Dighton, caricature, etching, 1804, BM · oils, c.1815, Metropolitan Police Museum, London · H. B. [J. Doyle], lithograph caricature, 1829, BM

Wealth at death will, 1809, PRO, PROB 11/1803, sig. 475 · apocryphal story that he died with estate valued at £20,000

Townsend, Sir John Sealy Edward (1868–1957), physicist, was born on 7 June 1868 at Galway, Ireland, the second son of Edward Townsend, professor of engineering at Queen's College, Galway, and his wife, Judith, daughter of John Sealy Townsend, a Dublin barrister. He was educated at Corrig School, and in 1885 entered Trinity College, Dublin, where he studied mathematics, mathematical physics, and experimental science. In 1888 he was elected to a foundation scholarship in mathematics at Trinity where in 1890 he graduated BA and, as the best candidate in mathematics and physics, was awarded a double senior moderatorship. For the next five years he taught mainly mathematics, probably in a private capacity, though perhaps based in Trinity where in 1893 and 1894 he won a fellowship prize. Chagrined at failing to gain a fellowship, in 1895 he left Dublin for Cambridge where he entered Trinity College as a pensioner and, like Ernest Rutherford, was

Sir John Sealy Edward Townsend (1868–1957), by unknown photographer

one of the first advanced students in the Cavendish Laboratory who were admitted under the new regulations which permitted non-Cambridge graduates to work for a research degree.

Under J. J. Thomson's guidance Townsend took up research on gaseous ions, that is, electrically charged particles. In 1897 he became the first person to measure the elementary ionic charge. This coup led to his election in 1898 to the coveted Clerk Maxwell scholarship and in 1899 to a research fellowship at Trinity tenable for six years. In 1900 he was appointed assistant demonstrator in the Cavendish Laboratory. In November that year, having been an unsuccessful candidate for the chairs of physics at Glasgow and Liverpool universities, Townsend was unanimously appointed the first holder of the Wykeham chair of experimental physics at Oxford which had been established to remedy the inadequacy of R. B. Clifton, Dr Lee's professor of experimental philosophy, who ran the Clarendon Laboratory. Townsend was statutorily responsible for magnetism and electricity, with the rest of physics being left to Clifton. They soon became bitter rivals. Clifton denied Townsend access to the Clarendon so that for ten years Townsend researched on gaseous ions in makeshift accommodation in the university observatory, in the comparative anatomy department, and in the university museum. Elected FRS in 1903, Townsend pressed for proper accommodation which he secured in 1910 when the electrical laboratory, paid for by the Drapers'

Company and costing £23,000, was opened. A two-storeyed building, it was lavishly provided with stone pillars for sensitive instruments. Next year Townsend enjoyed another success: he married Mary Georgiana, daughter of Peter Fitzwalter Lambert, of Castle Ellen, co. Galway. She was an accomplished hostess who provided a happy family life for Townsend and their two sons.

Until the First World War Townsend was a leader in his research field. Though Thomson attacked Townsend's theory of 1900 that ionization occurred as a result of the collision between electrons and the molecules of gases, two friends from his Cavendish days praised it. In Paris Paul Langevin stressed its explanatory power and in Manchester Rutherford, whom Townsend had helped in 1896 with experiments on radio waves, exploited it in devising in 1908 the famous Rutherford–Geiger counter for detecting alpha particles. Within Oxford Townsend fought successfully for engineering to be recognized in the university, and he gave accommodation to Harry Moseley in 1913. At this time his chief research associates were H. T. Tizard, E. W. B. Gill (fellow of Merton College), and F. B. Pidduck, his theoretician. On the outbreak of war the electrical laboratory provided eight physicists for military research. From 1915 Townsend himself worked on wireless telegraphy, especially on wave meters and mainly at Woolwich, as a major in the Royal Naval Air Service.

After the war Townsend became an isolated figure who lost contact with his Cavendish colleagues and rarely attended scientific meetings. His inability to appreciate others had been shown, it was said, in 1914–15 when George V visited the electrical laboratory: Townsend, who was deep in literary composition, refused to be interrupted and was not presented to the monarch. While many physicists moved on from research on ions, Townsend never strayed from the study of ionization in gases. He not only ignored but was even unfamiliar with the results obtained by other researchers. He continued to use his familiar apparatus and saw the natural world through his own increasingly outmoded terminology. As a believer in classical statistical mechanics, he rejected vehemently relativity and quantum theory. Though Townsend discovered a new phenomenon in the early 1920s—that monatomic gases offer no resistance to low-energy electrons—it became known as the Ramsauer effect because most physicists then accepted the quantum theory and agreed with Ramsauer that it was a quantum phenomenon. Feeling robbed of a discovery which was subsequently important in understanding the wave-like nature of the electron, Townsend never attended after 1924 any international meeting while a professor and he withdrew from commercial work.

Between the wars Townsend led a small group of researchers, often Rhodes scholars, three of whom (V. A. Bailey, L. G. H. Huxley, and C. M. Focken) became leaders in academic physics in the antipodes. Another of his research students, Van de Graaf, became famous later for his high voltage generator. In Britain S. P. MacCallum became a fellow of New College, Oxford, F. Llewellyn

Jones rose to academic and administrative distinction at University College, Swansea, while C. A. J. Young led ICI's central instrument research laboratory.

However, by the 1930s Townsend was a sad figure. A dreary lecturer, a dogmatic supervisor of research, and so out of touch with physics as a whole as to be culpably negligent, he was upstaged in electronics by E. B. Moullin, the reader in electrical engineering in the engineering science department at Oxford. No German refugee sought accommodation in the electrical laboratory before the Second World War, while next door, Lindemann, Dr Lee's professor, provided sanctuary in the Clarendon Laboratory for eight refugee physicists, some of whom stayed and put it on the international map for its low temperature physics. Once the university had decided in the late 1930s to build a new Clarendon, it examined the relations between the two physics laboratories and their professors. It wished to convert Townsend's chair into one for theoretical physics but shelved the issue. In 1941 his career at Oxford ended. His intransigence about helping in the war effort by teaching servicemen provoked the university to take the drastic step of establishing a visitatorial board. It found him guilty of grave misconduct and advised that he resign or be sacked. Townsend, who had been knighted in January, perhaps as a hint to depart, retired in September on condition that the decision of the board would remain confidential. He continued to live in Oxford, and died on 16 February 1957 in the Acland Nursing Home. He was buried on 20 February, at St Philip and St James, Oxford. He was survived by his wife.

Townsend's sporting Hibernian argumentativeness was embarrassing in formal university business but his gifts as a raconteur made him good company. His hobbies were tennis, riding, shooting, and fox-hunting. In his early Oxford days he rode his horse to his laboratory. He did not go to the Clarendon Laboratory to meet physicists, but characteristically he frequently visited it to talk about fox-hunting with D. A. Jackson, a spectroscopist who was a fanatical horseman. As in science Townsend was also deeply conservative in politics, an interest he shared from the thirties with Lindemann and especially with his wife. She became a councillor, an alderman, twice mayor, and an honorary freeman of the city of Oxford.

JACK MORRELL

Sources J. Morrell, *Science at Oxford, 1914–1939: transforming an arts university* (1997) · private information (2004) · *Oxford University Gazette* (1900–41) · A. von Engel, *Memoirs FRS*, 3 (1957), 257–72 · F. L. Jones, 'Townsend', *Year Book of the Physical Society* (1957), 106–10 · J. L. Heilbron, *H. G. J. Moseley: the life and letters of an English physicist, 1887–1915* (1974) · A. von Engel, 'Townsend', *Nature*, 179 (1957), 757–8 · G. S. Im, 'The formation and development of the Ramsauer effect', *Historical Studies in the Physical and Biological Sciences*, 25 (1994–5), 269–300 · D.-W. Kim, 'J. J. Thomson and the emergence of the Cavendish school, 1885–1900', *British Journal for the History of Science*, 28 (1995), 191–226 · TCD, archives · Trinity Cam. · Townsend letters, CUL, Rutherford MSS · Townsend letters, CUL, Kelvin MSS · Townsend letters, CUL, Stokes MSS · D. Wilson, *Rutherford: simple genius* (1983) · Bodl. Oxf., MSS Townsend · Brasenose College, Oxford, I. O. Griffith MSS · election certificate, RS · *The Times* (18 Feb 1957) · *CGPLA Eng. & Wales* (1957)

Archives Bodl. Oxf., papers | CUL, letters to Lord Rutherford · CUL, corresp. with Lord Kelvin · Nuffield Oxf., corresp. with Lord Cherwell

Likenesses photograph, repro. in von Engel, *Memoirs FRS* · photograph, RS [*see illus.*]

Wealth at death £1735 7s. 2d.: probate, 6 May 1957, *CGPLA Eng. & Wales*

Townsend, Joseph (1739–1816), geologist and writer, fourth son of Chauncy Townsend MP (d. 1770), a linen merchant and mining speculator, and his wife, Bridget (d. 1762), daughter of James Phipps, governor of Cape Coast Castle, was born in London on 4 April 1739. He matriculated from Clare College, Cambridge at Michaelmas 1758, and graduated BA in 1762 and MA in 1765. There is an unsubstantiated report that he was elected a fellow of the college. For a time Townsend studied medicine in Edinburgh under William Cullen. He was ordained deacon (London) on 21 December 1763, and showed some sympathy with Calvinistic Methodists, occasionally preaching in the countess of Huntingdon's chapel at Bath. As a preacher, Townsend appeared as 'a gaunt, upright, gigantic figure', having 'long arms with which he gesticulated wildly when he was seized with religious fervour' (Morris, 472). In 1767 he visited Scotland on a mission from Lady Huntingdon. There he was met by a number of 'pious and able ministers of the Established Church'. He preached at a small village, Coldstream, and soon thereafter went to Edinburgh, where he preached to multitudes, remaining there for two months (*Life and Times*, 1.410–11). Either in late 1767 or early 1768 he went to Dublin at Lady Huntingdon's request, and on his representing to her 'the deplorable state of spiritual destitution prevailing in Dublin, she commissioned them [Townsend and a Mr Shirley] to purchase, build, or hire some sound commodious edifice, for the performance of divine worship, *according to the forms of the Established Church*' (*Life and Times*, 2.159–60). Townsend was appointed chaplain to the duke of Atholl in 1769, and in that year and 1770 he visited France, the Netherlands, and Flanders. His first publication, *Every True Christian a New Creature* (1765) reflects his religious beliefs, but, as with some of his other works, attracted little notice. At one time it was thought, wrongly, that Townsend's Methodistical tendencies had made him the satiric butt of *The Spiritual Quixote* by his neighbour Richard Graves. Townsend became rector of Pewsey, Wiltshire, a living he kept until he died. He also became one of the commissioners of the turnpike roads in Wiltshire, an appointment which earned him the nickname the Colossus of Roads.

Townsend's *Free Thoughts on Despotic and Free Government* and *The Physician's Vade Mecum* both appeared in 1781, the latter running to ten editions by 1807. Townsend published two influential works on the poor laws. The first of these, *A Dissertation on the Poor Laws* (1785), though largely forgotten for almost 200 years, was given new life in a 1971 edition. Townsend, who was a friend of Jeremy Bentham, argued in *Observations on Various Plans for the Relief of the Poor* (1788) that the existing poor laws 'so beautiful in theory, promote the evils they were meant to relieve' (Morris, 474). Townsend advocated the abolition of outdoor relief for the able-bodied and went on to propose the compulsory establishment of friendly societies to cover the costs of medical treatment and burial of their members. Thomas Malthus acknowledged Townsend's influence on his own thinking, while the political economist J. R. McCulloch considered that 'Townsend's ideas were not so much a foreshadowing of Malthus's theory as the theory itself' (ibid.).

The work for which Townsend seems to have been best known was his *Journey through Spain in the Years 1786 and 1787* (1791, with a third edition in 1814). He dedicated the work to the earl of Wycombe. The reviewer for the *Monthly Review* blew hot and cold: 'Not withstanding our warm approbation of Mr. Townsend's work, justice obliges us to say, that he indulgences himself too frequently in repetitions, and that there is a considerable degree of obscurity in many of his descriptions'; he also complained that there was too much emphasis on chemistry and not enough on natural history (*Monthly Review*, 1791). J. R. McCulloch describes the *Journey* as 'one of the best works of the kind that has ever appeared, throwing a great deal of light upon the political economy of Spain, and on the causes of her decline' (McCulloch, 215). The sight of beggars in Spain also served to strengthen Townsend's views about how best to tackle poverty. The *Journey* was followed by *A Guide to Health* (1795–6). Both the *Guide* and the *Vade mecum* enjoyed American editions. Townsend also published a volume of sermons in 1805, and concluded his writing career with *The Character of Moses Established* (2 vols., 1812–15). He built up one of the largest fossil collections in Britain and devoted many years to trying to amass evidence to support the Mosaic story of creation. His geological researches led him to form a friendship with William Strata Smith (1769–1839), and he was made an honorary member of the Geological Society of London.

Townsend was twice married, first to Joyce, daughter of Thomas Nankivell of Truro, on 27 September 1773; she died on 8 November 1785. On 26 March 1790 he married Lydia Hammond, the widow of Sir John Clerke; she died in 1812. Townsend died on 9 November 1816 and was buried within the precincts of St John's Church, Pewsey, where a tablet was erected to his memory. He left four sons, Thomas, Charles, James, and Henry, and two daughters, Charlotte and Sophia, from his first marriage. Townsend's obituarist in the *Gentleman's Magazine* claimed pre-eminence for him as 'a mineralogist, a fossilist, and conchologist', and stated that 'As a preacher, he was sound in doctrine and consistent in practice'. He was also 'one of the principal projectors of, and a very considerable shareholder in, the Kennet and Avon Canal' (*GM*). Townsend's *Etymological researches, wherein numerous languages apparently discordant have their affinity traced and their resemblance so manifest as to lead to the conclusion that all languages are radically one* was published posthumously in 1824.

ARTHUR SHERBO

Sources *GM*, 1st ser., 86/2 (1816), 477 • *Monthly Review* (1791), 120–28 • *Monthly Review* (1795), 299–300 • *Monthly Review* (1814), 225–38 • J. Townsend, *A dissertation on the poor laws* (1971) • J. R. McCulloch, *The literature of political economy: a classified catalogue* (1845) • *DNB* • *The life and times of Selina, countess of Huntingdon*, 2 vols. (1844) • A. D. Morris, 'The Reverend Joseph Townsend, MA, MGS (1739–1816): physician and geologist, "Colossus of Roads"', *Proceedings of the Royal Society of Medicine*, 62 (1969), 471–7 [incl. illustration]
Archives Oxf. U. Mus. NH, corresp., mostly letters to William Smith, and strata collection
Likenesses Milton, print, stipple (after J. Townsend), NPG

Townsend [*née* Jesse], **Lucy** (1781–1847), slavery abolitionist, was born on 25 July 1781, the daughter of William Jesse, a Church of England clergyman in West Bromwich, Staffordshire. On 6 July 1807 she married the Revd Charles Townsend (1780–1865), rector of Calstone, Wiltshire, and perpetual curate of West Bromwich, Staffordshire; they had at least three daughters and three sons.

Charles Townsend was an anti-slavery campaigner, and his wife too became active in the movement. The Ladies' Society for the Relief of Negro Slaves (later the Female Society for Birmingham [etc.] for the Relief of British Negro Slaves, then the Ladies' Negro's Friend Society) was founded at a meeting held at her home in West Bromwich on 8 April 1825. Lucy Townsend and Mary Lloyd, whom she had met at meetings of the Bible Society, became joint secretaries of the society which was, from its foundation, independent of both the national Anti-Slavery Society and of the local men's anti-slavery society. It acted as the hub of a developing national network of female anti-slavery societies, rather than as a local auxiliary. It also had important international connections, and publicity on its activities in Benjamin Lundy's abolitionist periodical *The Genius of Universal Emancipation* influenced the formation of the first female anti-slavery societies in America.

Under Lucy Townsend's and Mary Lloyd's leadership the society developed the distinctive forms of female anti-slavery activity, involving an emphasis on the sufferings of women under slavery, systematic promotion of abstention from slave-grown sugar through door-to-door canvassing, and the production of innovative forms of propaganda, such as albums containing tracts, poems, and illustrations, embroidered anti-slavery workbags, and seals bearing the motto 'Am I not a woman and a sister?'. The society was at the height of its influence during the 1823–33 campaign against British colonial slavery, which culminated in the passage of the Emancipation Act in 1833. From 1839 it aligned itself with the newly formed British and Foreign Anti-Slavery Society, and combined support for the universal abolition movement with support for educational work among freed slaves; the society continued to be active until 1919. Lucy Townsend acted as joint secretary of the society until 1836, resigning this post when she moved with her husband to Thorpe, Nottinghamshire, but continuing as a committee member until at least 1845. She was the author of an anti-slavery pamphlet *To the Law and to the Testimony* (1832).

While anti-slavery was her main concern Lucy Townsend was also involved in a variety of other voluntary activities. With Mary Lloyd she established the Juvenile Association for West Bromwich and Wednesbury in Aid of Uninstructed Deaf Mutes in 1834, and she was also involved in

Dorcas meetings, in the Ladies' Bible Association, and, with her husband, in campaigns to abolish bull baiting and other cruel sports.

Lucy Townsend was founder and co-secretary of the first women's anti-slavery society in Britain. Women's contributions to the anti-slavery movement in Britain received little attention from historians until the late 1980s, but their national significance and distinctive contributions to both the ideology and campaigning methods of the movement are now apparent. There are no known portraits of Lucy Townsend, despite the attempt by her friend and fellow campaigner Anne Knight to persuade her that, as 'the person who established woman agency' in the movement and 'the chief lady' of the anti-slavery campaign, she should 'in justice to history and posterity' put herself forward for inclusion in B. R. Haydon's commemorative group portrait of the 1840 World Anti-Slavery Convention (A. Knight to L. Townsend, 20 Sept 1840; Townsend, 'Autographs', MSS Brit. Emp.s., vol. 5, 102). She was described by her fellow anti-slavery campaigners as skilful in devising plans and prompt in their execution, as energetic and persistent, and as successful in stimulating others to action. Lucy Townsend died on 20 April 1847 at the rectory at Thorpe, near Southwell, in Nottinghamshire. CLARE MIDGLEY

Sources C. Midgley, *Women against slavery: the British campaigns, 1780–1870* (1992) · *Report of the Ladies' Negro's Friend Society for Birmingham, West Bromwich, Wednesbury, Walsall, and their Respective Neighbourhoods*, 22 (1847), 12–19 [see also vols. 7–9 (1832–4), 11 (1836) and 20 (1845)] · *Ladies' Society for the Relief of Negro Slaves: at a meeting of ladies, held in West-Bromwich on the 8th of April, 1825, the following resolutions were read and approved* [1825] · *Annual Report* [The Female Society for Birmingham … and their Respective Neighbourhoods, for the Relief of British Negro Slaves], 1–3 (1826–8) · *Annual Report* [The Female Society for Birmingham … and their Respective Neighbourhoods, for the Relief of British Negro Slaves], 5 (1830) · d. cert. · L. Townsend, 'Autographs', Bodl. RH, MSS Brit. Emp.s. · *IGI* · *Clergy List* (1850) · Foster, *Alum. Oxon.*

Archives Bodl. RH, Anti-Slavery Society MSS

Townsend [*née* Butler], **Mary Elizabeth** (1841–1918), philanthropist, was born on 23 July 1841 at St John's vicarage, Kilkenny, the only child of the Revd Robert Butler (*d.* 1847) and his wife, Grace (*d.* 1843), daughter of the Revd James Hamilton of Trim, co. Meath. At the time of her birth, her father was vicar of St John's and domestic chaplain to the earl of Ormond. Left an orphan at an early age, Mary Butler was brought up in England by her father's sisters. On 21 July 1863 she married Frederick Townsend (1823–1905), a serious-minded amateur artist and botanist eighteen years her senior. The marriage was a happy one: Mary Townsend later recalled 'I was free indeed with one who was all in all to me. Then life began to open out in fair colours and every gift I had began to grow and develop under his care' (M. E. Townsend, 'Memories', 7).

In 1875 Frederick Townsend inherited his uncle's estate of Honington Hall, but the couple's early married life was spent at Shedfield Lodge, near Wickham, in Hampshire. Taking a keen interest in the people living on the estate,

Mary Elizabeth Townsend (1841–1918), by unknown photographer, *c.*1865

Frederick organized support for the local cottage hospital, the building of a recreation and reading-room, and a library for working men, and ran village penny-savings banks, while Mary started working classes for girls whose education had finished at elementary school, looked after the ill and the aged, and became involved in the work of the local orphanage for girls. Through these activities she became aware of the problems faced by girls going into domestic service, including loss of communications with their families and unwanted pregnancies resulting in dismissal.

A friend and frequent visitor at Shedfield was the Revd T. V. Fosbery, chaplain to Bishop Samuel Wilberforce; in 1873 the bishop invited Mary Townsend to assist in some diocesan 'rescue work' among 'fallen women'. She soon perceived that prevention was better than cure: realizing that servant girls were often friendless and had no respectable place to go on their half-days off, she argued that they needed 'a little love, a few kind words, a look, a smile of interest to show that they are cared for; that they are expected to do well and that their career is watched with hope' (Money, 7). Fosbery encouraged Mary Townsend to take on this work herself, and through his interest drew in Catharine Tait (1819–1878), Elizabeth Browne (wife of the bishop of Winchester), and Jane Nassau Senior (1828–1877). They all met at Lambeth Palace in May 1874 and resolved to establish the Girls' Friendly Society (GFS), which officially began its work on 1 January 1875.

Although avowedly non-sectarian, the GFS was organized in parish, deanery, and diocesan groups (with a central office in London), reflecting its Anglican origins. It aimed to maintain a high standard of morals among its members (aged from fourteen upwards and unmarried), supplying 'for every working girl of unblemished character a friend in a class above her own' (Money, 36). Both classes of membership—known as members and associates—paid an annual subscription, half of which went to the branch and half to central funds. Recreation rooms, supervised by associates, provided opportunities for working-class girls to meet, read, sew, sing, and enjoy simple refreshments. Mary Townsend worked tirelessly in the early days of the movement. She served as president from 1876 to 1883 and again from 1891 to 1894, and also acted as head of various departments; she was directing the candidates department in 1879 when, by popular demand, it was decided to admit girls as young as eight years old. She wrote copiously for the various GFS journals—such as *Friendly Leaves*, *Friendly Work*, and the *Associates Journal*—and compiled best-selling collections of prayers and hymns. She succeeded in persuading popular writers to contribute to GFS publications, most notably recruiting Charlotte M. Yonge (1832–1901), who opened and ran a branch of the GFS at her home in Elderfield and featured the GFS in such novels as *The Two Sides of the Shield* (1885). Mary Townsend developed lifelong friendships with many of the early associates and paid workers of the GFS, and she was consulted by the general committee even when she held no office.

The GFS encountered some difficulties—the mistresses of households were sometimes suspicious of what they saw as interference between themselves and their servants—but it grew with a speed that astonished the founder. By 1878, when the first report was published, the GFS was active in nineteen dioceses and Gibraltar, with 10,678 members and 4442 associates. A wide range of departments had been established, including those supervising shop and factory workers, publications, houses of rest, and affiliated societies, and services included a circulating library and an employment exchange. Thirty years later, other new departments—including those overseeing the welfare of sick and blind members and the safety of emigrating girls and women—had been established, and the GFS was offering training of various descriptions to members. From 1880 the society enjoyed royal patronage, and Queen Victoria herself acted as an associate and admitted servant girls at Balmoral to membership. In 1911 Mary Townsend celebrated the success of the GFS in expanding its original remit and transcending class boundaries:

> We are no longer an Association of Ladies working for girls chiefly of one class, but a band of women of all ranks, ages and occupations, invited to share in the same work, to uphold the same principles, each according to her power. (Money, 200)

By 1913 the society had 197,493 members and 39,926 associates in England and Wales alone, with 80,274 candidates. When war broke out in 1914 the government sought the assistance of the GFS in recruiting and caring for women war workers, running canteens, and providing comforts for the troops. Mary Townsend herself organized a guild of church needlework to provide linen and paintings for army chaplains in France. She died suddenly on 14 June 1918 at Homewood, Hindhead, Surrey, shortly before the society received commendation for its war efforts in a government white paper, with honours for the president and secretary. She was buried beside her husband in Honington churchyard. Childless herself, Mary Townsend had influenced the lives of many girls and women of all classes, and her ability to motivate, delegate,

and promote essential change ensured that the GFS survived her own death. At the close of the twentieth century it was still active in twenty-five countries worldwide, mainly those in the Anglican communion.

G. M. HARRIS

Sources K. M. Townend, *Some memories of Mrs Townsend* (1923) · M. E. Townsend, 'Memories of a life', Girls Friendly Society archives, GFS Townsend House, Queensgate, London · F. Townsend, 'Memories of early years', Girls Friendly Society archives, GFS Townsend House, Queensgate, London · A. Money, *The story of the GFS*, new edn (1913) · E. V. Jones, *One hundred years of the Girls' Friendly Society: 1875–1975* (1975) · M. E. Townsend, *First report of the work and progress of the GFS* (1878) · M. Heath-Stubbs, *Friendship's Highway (1875–1935)* [GFS Journal] · *Friendly Leaves (1877–1918)* [GFS Journal] · M. Mare and A. C. Percival, *Victorian best-seller* (1947) · C. M. Yonge, *The two sides of the shield*, new edn (1886); repr. (1889) · M. E. Townsend and F. Townsend, 'Sketches and impressions', GFS archives, GFS Townsend House, Queensgate, London, 2 vols. · *Atherstone Parish Magazine* (1884–5) · d. cert.
Archives Girls' Friendly Society, London, archives
Likenesses watercolour, c.1844 (aged three), Girls' Friendly Society, Queensgate, London · photograph, c.1865, Girls' Friendly Society, Queensgate, London [*see illus.*] · photographs, Girls' Friendly Society, Queensgate, London
Wealth at death £26,499 18s. 6d.: probate, 29 July 1918, CGPLA Eng. & Wales

Townsend, Meredith White (1831–1911), newspaper editor and proprietor, born on 1 April 1831, in London, was the only son of William Townsend, gentleman farmer of north Essex, and Alicia, daughter of John Sparrowe. He was educated at Queen Elizabeth's Grammar School, Ipswich; he left, aged sixteen, in 1847, to become an assistant master at a school in Scotland. However, he was almost immediately saved from life as a teacher, a prospect he did not savour, when a family friend, John Clark Marshman, invited Townsend to India to become sub-editor of the *Friend of India* in Calcutta. Townsend engaged in his new career with such enthusiasm, energy, and ability that within five years he was editor, and, by 1853, had become proprietor. The *Friend of India* was essentially a one-man newspaper; Townsend was later to recall how he often wrote the whole paper except the advertisements. Unlike so many other expatriates, Townsend went to considerable pains to improve his knowledge and understanding of India and its peoples. His *munshi*, Pandit Commacanto Mukaji, taught Townsend several Indian languages and he became fluent in Bengali. Never a government stooge, Townsend gave his editorial approval when Dalhousie and Canning as pro-consuls pursued enlightened legislation; they, in their turn, recognized and valued his support. In addition to the *Friend*, Townsend temporarily edited the *Calcutta Quarterly Review*, the *Annals of Indian Administration*, and a vernacular journal, *Satya Pradip*, all the while acting as a correspondent on Asian and Indian affairs for *The Times*. His health eventually broke down and he returned to England. The Indian mutiny in 1857 prompted a swift return to India; throughout that troubled period, Townsend remained at Serampore. He raised his newspaper to the zenith of its influence so that, according to H. H. Asquith in his memoirs, it constituted 'an interesting and powerful factor' in India's affairs (Asquith, 1.67). Then

Meredith White Townsend (1831–1911), by Frederick Hollyer, 1900

overwork and domestic tragedy caused Townsend's health once more to collapse; in 1859, his doctors ordered him to return to England.

Before leaving India, Townsend met James Wilson MP, founder and first editor of *The Economist*, and told him that he wished to start a newspaper in England. Wilson's not entirely disinterested advice was that he should recruit the services of Richard Holt Hutton, Wilson's young successor as editor of *The Economist*. Townsend, however, did not meet Hutton until he had purchased the ailing *Spectator*. So impressed was he that he offered Hutton joint editorship and co-proprietorship of his newly acquired magazine. Hutton accepted, and thus began a journalistic partnership that was generally recognized by fellow journalists as 'the happiest conjunction'. Each complemented the other's gifts and interests: Townsend concentrated on politics, Hutton on literature. Their partnership flourished, harmonious and successful, perfectly realizing the intention of Robert Stephen Rintoul, founder of *The Spectator*, 'to humanise Radicalism by instructing the educated Englishman in ethics, theology, society and statesmanship'. Asquith, who counted Townsend and Hutton his mentors in journalism, recalled in *Memories and Reflections* that the twin denizens of 1 Wellington Street, the Strand, 'frequently engaged in animated clashes in discussion', but that they 'always ended in *entente cordiale*. They would return to their separate offices each to hammer out in their totally different styles their

joint handiwork' (Asquith, 1.68). Their outstanding literary alliance and friendship was sundered after thirty-six years by Hutton's death.

Townsend wrote with zest and ease. Nor would he ever allow the spirit of a piece to be unduly confused by an over-zealous concern for factual exactitude. That is to say, he was a romantic dogmatist, never a self-indulgent pedant. The happy, familiar relationship that existed between *The Economist* and *The Spectator* meant that Walter Bagehot and Townsend contributed to each other's journals to everyone's advantage. In 1898 Townsend asked John St Loe Strachey, who had been *The Spectator's* assistant editor since 1886, to take over editorial and proprietorial control. Strachey agreed, and for a further ten years Townsend contributed to the paper with little abatement of his powers. Townsend, who wrote little except for the press, collaborated with a friend, John Langton Sanford, in compiling a two-volume work, *The Great Governing Families of England* (1865). A collection of articles contributed to various journals was republished as a single volume, *Asia and Europe* (1901).

Townsend married three times: in 1853 he married his cousin, Miss Colchester, but she died the same year; in 1857 he married Isabel Collingwood, but she died shortly after the birth of their son in 1858; finally, in 1861, he married Ellen Frances Snell, who outlived him. They had a son and two daughters. Townsend was not a clubbable man and went very little into society. Friends he received regularly on Mondays at his house in Harley Street. To young or old, humble or powerful, he was invariably genial and courteous. In 1909, his health failed. A long illness with steady mental as well as physical deterioration left him for the last six months of his life in a state of almost perpetual delirium. He died on 21 October 1911, at his home, the Manor House, in Little Bookham, Surrey, where he had lived since 1899. He was buried in Little Bookham churchyard.

John St Loe Strachey, who had known Townsend as friend and colleague for the last quarter-century of his life, recorded in his autobiography, *The Adventure of Living* (1922), his affection and admiration for Townsend's many fine qualities as a man: his kindliness, generosity, and honourable high-mindedness. On occasion, his tongue could be sharp, but although 'he barked, he never bit'. His conversation was notable for his 'mastery of the felicitous epigram'. As a journalist, Strachey considered Townsend 'the greatest leader writer who has ever appeared in the English press'. This is a large claim. But more than 10,000 articles written by Townsend against which the claim may be judged, demonstrate beyond doubt that he was 'never pompous, never dull or common and never trivial' (Strachey, 221, 224, 234). A. J. A. MORRIS

Sources J. St L. Strachey, *The adventure of living: a subjective autobiography* (1922) · W. B. Thomas, *The story of The Spectator, 1828–1928* (1928) · R. D. Edwards, *The pursuit of reason: The Economist, 1843–1993* (1993) · *The Times* (24 Oct 1911) · *Manchester Guardian* (24 Oct 1911) · *DNB* · H. C. G. Matthew, 'H. H. Asquith's political journalism', *BIHR*, 49 (1976), 146–51 · H. H. Asquith, *Memories and reflections, 1852–1927*, ed. A. Mackintosh, 2 vols. (1928)

Archives *The Spectator*, London, register of articles · HLRO, corresp. and papers
Likenesses F. Hollyer, photograph, 1900, V&A [*see illus.*] · photograph, repro. in Strachey, *Adventure of living* · woodcut, repro. in Thomas, *Story of the Spectator*
Wealth at death £36,642 15s. 11d.: probate, 22 Nov 1911, *CGPLA Eng. & Wales*

Townsend, Peter Woolridge (1914–1995), air force officer and official in the royal household, was born in Burma on 22 November 1914, into the large family of Lieutenant-Colonel Edward Copleston Townsend (*b.* 1864), an officer in the Indian army and district commissioner in Burma. He was educated at Haileybury College (which he loathed, and where he was remembered as shy and studious) before entering the Royal Air Force College at Cranwell in 1933. By the age of twenty-seven he held the rank of wing commander, and following the outbreak of the Second World War he proceeded to display gallantry of the highest order. Flying initially in a Hurricane, later in a Spitfire, he brought down the first German bomber to crash in England since the First World War, and in the space of three years he was mentioned in dispatches and received the DSO and the DFC and bar. He was ultimately promoted group captain.

On 17 July 1941 Townsend married (Cecil) Rosemary Pawle (*b.* 1920/21), the daughter of Colonel Hanbury Pawle, of Widford, Hertfordshire. The marriage resulted in the birth of two sons, but it was soon under strain. Meanwhile, Townsend was seconded in 1944 on what was initially to have been a three-month appointment as an equerry to George VI. In 1947, his secondment having been extended (he eventually served at court for nine years), Townsend accompanied the king and queen and the two princesses on their strenuous tour of South Africa. There was at this time no question of any romance between Townsend and Princess Margaret. After only three years with the king he was appointed CVO in recognition of his contribution to the success of the tour, and in 1950 he became deputy master of his majesty's household. Meanwhile, Townsend's marriage had ended in divorce, although he had been the 'innocent party'.

On the death of George VI in 1952 Townsend moved to Clarence House as comptroller to Queen Elizabeth the queen mother, and was appointed an equerry to the new queen, Elizabeth II. Now in even closer proximity than before to Princess Margaret, who was also living at Clarence House, Townsend and the princess fell in love; the intimate nature of their relationship was provocatively broadcast to the world on coronation day 1953, when the princess brushed some fluff from Townsend's uniform. The man in whom Townsend chose to confide was Sir Alan Lascelles, private secretary to the king and someone who had played a prominent part only seventeen years before in the abdication crisis. 'Either you're mad or bad', Lascelles told him (*The Times*, 21 June 1995). He was neither, and in later years, when Lascelles lived in retirement at Kensington Palace, Princess Margaret declined to speak to him on the grounds that she considered him to have been the man who had ruined her life.

Peter Woolridge Townsend (1914–1995), by unknown photographer

With memories of the abdication still raw, the establishment moved swiftly to separate the 39-year-old group captain and the 23-year-old princess, only third in line of succession to the throne. On the eve of a visit to Rhodesia by the queen mother and Princess Margaret, Townsend, instead of accompanying them, was whisked away to Brussels as air attaché. Under the Royal Marriages Act of 1772 Princess Margaret required the consent of the monarch to marry, and to her grandmother Queen Mary and to her mother the situation which had resulted in the abdication had been anathema. Such were the social rules at the time that as a divorcee Townsend would not even have been granted entrance to the royal enclosure at Ascot. A cooling-off period was the best the royal family could hope for at this stage, but Townsend and the princess remained in constant touch, with the princess turning for advice not to the impetuous archbishop of Canterbury, Geoffrey Fisher, but to a young Cambridge chaplain, Simon Phipps, later bishop of Lincoln and godfather to her son.

Although on attaining the age of twenty-five Princess Margaret could have sought the consent of parliament to her marriage had permission been withheld by the queen, there was never any question of such a constitutional hiatus; there was, indeed, no serious possibility of the marriage ever taking place without the princess renouncing her rights to the throne, which Townsend would never have allowed her to do. In 1955, with Townsend's support and in the face of intense press speculation, the princess issued a dignified announcement that 'mindful of the

Church's teaching that marriage is indissoluble' she had decided not to marry Group Captain Townsend. The irony of her later failed marriage to Lord Snowdon only added poignancy to the memories of a genuine but sadly unrealistic love affair.

Group Captain Peter Townsend left England shortly after the princess's announcement, and travelled round the world, working on a book, *Earth my Friend*, which was published in 1959. In the same year he made a second, very happy, marriage, to Marie-Luce Jamagne, the daughter of Franz Jamagne of Brussels, with whom he had a son and two daughters. He travelled extensively in Africa, India, South America, Canada, and the United States, and eventually settled down with his wife in France, where he commenced a successful career as a writer, producing a number of books about the battle of Britain and about the impact of war on the individual, and, in 1978, a balanced and charitable autobiography, *Time and Chance*. Possessed of natural diffidence, generosity, charm, and the modesty that became a hero, he made no secret in old age of his relief that things had turned out the way they did. He died at his home, La Mare aux Oiseaux, Route des Grands Coins, Saint-Léger-en-Yvelines, France, on 19 June 1995. He was survived by his wife, his two sons from his first marriage, and his three children from his second.

MICHAEL DE-LA-NOY

Sources P. Townsend, *Time and chance* (1978) · private information (2004) · *The Times* (21 June 1995) · *WWW* · *Army List*
Archives SOUND BL NSA, documentary recording
Likenesses photograph, News International Syndication, London [*see illus.*] · photographs, Hult. Arch.

Townsend [Townesend], **Richard** (1618/19–1692), parliamentarian army officer, is of obscure origins and unknown parentage. According to tradition he was descended from the Townshends of Raynham, Norfolk, and he evidently laid claim to such kinship, adopting the arms of Sir Roger Townshend (1588–1637), the head of that family. It has been suggested, rather doubtfully and owing to no more than a rough similarity in age, that he was the Richard Townesend, son of John Townsend of Dichford, Warwickshire, who matriculated from Hart Hall on 16 May 1634, aged nineteen. However, he may have come from Dorset, where he served for much of the first civil war. His first wife, Hildegardis Hyde, may well have been a kinsman of Edward Hyde, earl of Clarendon—again suggesting a west-country connection. Of his second wife nothing is known beyond her forename, Mary.

In 1643 Townsend received the commission of captain in a regiment of ten companies raised to garrison Lyme Regis, which was threatened by the approach of Prince Maurice, then in the midst of his triumphant western campaign. On 3 March 1644 he surprised and routed 150 horse at Bridport. Townsend distinguished himself in the defence of Lyme, serving under Robert Blake, when it was besieged from 20 April until its relief on 13 June. Townsend was shot in the head, and promoted to the rank of major. The following year he accompanied his colonel, Thomas Ceeley, against the clubmen of Dorset, defeating them at Bridport on 3 July. When Ceeley was returned as

MP for Bridport that year, Townsend succeeded him in command of the regiment with the rank of lieutenant-colonel. In 1646 he assisted at the siege of Pendennis Castle, near Falmouth, and in August in the negotiations for the surrender of the castle.

The following month Townsend was made colonel of a regiment of 1000 foot to be raised for service in Ireland, with Robert Phayre as his lieutenant-colonel. In March the regiment was still in England, camped at Bath. It had reached Ireland by 15 June 1647, when parliament ordered Townsend and his regiment, which was in a state of some disorder, apparently owing to the presence of native Irish in the ranks, to the assistance of Murrough O'Brien, first earl of Inchiquin, the parliamentarian commander. He joined him in September, and on 13 November, when Inchiquin defeated Lord Taaffe, the royalist leader, near Mallow, Townsend commanded the English centre. Dissatisfied with the treatment accorded to the soldiers in Ireland by the predominant Independent party there, he joined early in 1648 in presenting a strong remonstrance to the English parliament against their neglect of the welfare of the troops. Failing to obtain redress, he soon afterwards joined Inchiquin, who disliked the Independents, in deserting the parliamentarian cause, and in coming to an understanding with Lord Taaffe. In a short time, however, his new associates became distasteful to him, and he entered into communications with parliament.

In December 1648, in consequence of his endeavour to negotiate the surrender of Munster with parliamentary commissioners, Townsend was compelled to take refuge in England. On the execution of Charles I he returned to Ireland, professing that resentment at the king's death had finally determined him to loyalty. In reality, however, according to Thomas Carte, he was sent by Cromwell as a secret agent to corrupt the Munster army. In October 1649 he was arrested and thrown into prison for being concerned in a plot to seize the person of Inchiquin and take possession of Youghal. He was exchanged for an Irish officer, but was no sooner liberated than he engaged in a similar plot, was again taken prisoner, and conveyed to Cork. Inchiquin intended to shoot him as an example, and he was saved only by a timely mutiny of the garrison of Cork, who rose on the night of 16 October and drove the Irish out of the town. Townsend received special praise from Cromwell in a letter to the speaker, William Lenthall, as 'a very active instrument for the return both of Cork and Youghal to their obedience' (Abbott, 2.163).

Townsend retired from service shortly afterwards, and before 1654 settled at Castletownshend, near West Carbery, co. Cork. At the Restoration he was pardoned and hence escaped the forfeitures which overtook many Cromwellian soldiers, having his lands confirmed to him by royal patents in 1666, 1668, and 1680. His good fortune was perhaps owing to the possible Clarendon connection through his first wife. Townsend sat in the Irish parliament of 1661 as member for Baltimore. In 1666 the apprehension of a French invasion caused the lord lieutenant, Roger Boyle, first earl of Orrery, to form the English in Ireland into companies of militia. Townsend was appointed a captain of foot, and in 1671 was appointed high sheriff of the county.

The accession of James II ushered in a period of anxiety for the protestants of southern Ireland. Many took refuge in the north or crossed the sea to England. Townsend, however, stood his ground, and organized the protestant defence in co. Cork. On 18 October 1685 he was appointed 'sovereign', or mayor, of Clonakilty, in spite of the efforts of James to prevent the election of protestants. In November 1690 Townsend's mansion house of Castletownshend was unsuccessfully besieged by 500 Irish under Colonel Driscoll, but a little later it was compelled to surrender to MacFineen O'Driscoll. In compensation for his sacrifices and services Townsend received from government a grant of £40,000.

Townsend died in the latter part of 1692, and was buried in the graveyard of Castlehaven. He had children with both his wives, leaving seven sons and four daughters. The eldest surviving son, Bryan, who served with the English army at the battle of the Boyne, was ancestor of the family of Townshend of Castletownshend.

E. I. CARLYLE, rev. SEAN KELSEY

Sources R. Townshend and D. Townshend, eds., *An officer of the Long Parliament and his descendants, being some account of the life and times of Colonel Richard Townesend of Castletown (Castletownshend) and a chronicle of his family* (1892) · D. Murphy, *Cromwell in Ireland: a history of Cromwell's Irish campaign* (1883), 196–7, 398 · J. P. Prendergast, *The Cromwellian settlement of Ireland* (1870), 192 · *JHC*, 5 (1646–8), 211 · E. Milward, ed., *A collection of the state letters of … Roger Boyle, first earl of Orrery* (1742) · C. H. Firth and G. Davies, *The regimental history of Cromwell's army*, 2 vols. (1940) · R. Townsend, letter to T. Ceeley, Aug 1646, Bodl. Oxf., MS Tanner 59, fol. 481 · *CSP Ire.*, 1633–47 · *The writings and speeches of Oliver Cromwell*, ed. W. C. Abbott and C. D. Crane, 2 (1939)

Townsend, Richard (1821–1884), mathematician, was born on 3 April 1821 at Baltimore, co. Cork, Ireland, the eldest son of Thomas Townsend (d. 1848) of Smithville, a commodore in the Royal Navy, and his wife, Helena, daughter of John Freke of Baltimore. After attending local schools in Castletownsend and Skibbereen, he entered Trinity College, Dublin, on 13 October 1837; he graduated BA in the spring of 1842 as first senior moderator (equivalent to Cambridge wrangler) in mathematics and physics. His entire career was spent as an academic at Dublin University where he gained gradual promotion. He prepared for the college fellowship under the professors of mathematics, James MacCullagh (until 1843) and Charles Graves (from 1843). Success in the highly competitive fellowship examination led to his election as a junior fellow in May 1845 and appointment as college tutor in October 1847. In the spring of 1852 he received the degree of MA and on 25 June 1870 he was appointed professor of natural philosophy, after he had acted as assistant from October 1862 and examiner in mathematics and mathematical physics. Having advanced through the ranks of the junior fellows, he finally became a senior fellow with a seat on the board of the college in the last year of his life. On 7 June 1866 he was elected a fellow of the Royal Society. He was married to his first cousin, Mary Jane Barrett (d. 1881). They had no children.

In the *Cambridge and Dublin Mathematical Journal* (nine volumes, 1846–54) Townsend published a series of articles, mainly on geometrical topics reflecting the research interests of the Dublin mathematical school that flourished under James MacCullagh. His greatest success, however, was as a teacher and he enjoyed popularity as a tutor, having up to two hundred pupils at times. His most important publication was a textbook, *Chapters on the Modern Geometry of the Point, Line and Circle* (2 vols., 1863–5), based on his lectures. This work achieved considerable, even international, recognition, providing, for example, the first elementary treatment of inversive geometry and giving an exposition of the theory of inverse points, figures, and methods of geometrical transformation. A further work entitled 'Lectures on attractions' was left unfinished at his death.

Townsend was a benefactor of the protestant episcopal Church of Ireland. When Gladstone's Irish Church Act of 1869 (effective 1 January 1871) disestablished and partly disendowed the church, Townsend's native parish in west Cork was perceived as a beleaguered outpost in a depressed region where more than 90 per cent of the population was Roman Catholic. He used his influence among college friends and former pupils to raise a considerable sum (perhaps £2500) as the nucleus of a permanent endowment of the parish. Having suffered from heart disease (cardiac dropsy) he died on 16 October 1884 at his house, 54 Upper Leeson Street, Dublin, and was buried at Mount Jerome cemetery. A mathematical exhibition was founded in his memory at the college. In an obituary a former pupil, J. P. Mahaffy, while praising the altruism of the deceased, hinted also at imperfections and psychological curiosities or idiosyncrasies in his character.

JAMES G. O'HARA

Sources *DNB* · Burtchaell & Sadleir, *Alum. Dubl.* · *Dublin University Calendar* · J. P. Mahaffy, *The Athenaeum* (25 Oct 1884), 532 · 'Royal commission on … the University of Dublin, and of Trinity College', *Parl. papers* (1852–3), vol. 45, no. 1637 · *The Times* (18 Oct 1884), 5 · T. W. Moody and others, eds., *A new history of Ireland*, 10 vols. (1976–96), vols. 8–9 · A. J. McConnell, 'The Dublin mathematical school in the first half of the nineteenth century', *Proceedings of the Royal Irish Academy*, 50A (1944–5), 75–88 · J. G. O'Hara, 'Humphrey Lloyd, 1800–1881, and the Dublin mathematical school of the nineteenth century', PhD diss., University of Manchester Institute of Science and Technology, 1979

Archives CUL, letters to Lord Kelvin

Likenesses S. Purser, oils (after photograph), TCD

Wealth at death £7057 9s. 11d.: probate, 21 Nov 1884, *CGPLA Ire.*

Townsend, Theophila (d. 1692), Quaker activist and writer, of unknown parentage, was married to Richard Townsend (1629–1715), a bodice-maker and Quaker of Cirencester, Gloucestershire. Richard, who was the son of Roger and Elizabeth Townsend of Cirencester, had a brother named Roger. His public association with Quakerism is dated first to his arrest in November 1660, and lasted well into the first decade of the eighteenth century; his name appears frequently in the literature of Quaker suffering. The couple were apparently childless.

Theophila Townsend became involved in public professions of faith when, having absented herself for some years from her local parish church, her name became linked to the Quakers. From early in the 1670s through to her death in 1692 she tirelessly protested against anti-Quaker laws: during the 1680s, particularly, she seemed rarely out of prison. The first significant period of incarceration, lasting eleven weeks, was occasioned by an act of public preaching in May 1682. Between that time and April 1686, when she was released, Townsend was frequently castigated by the authorities. By arresting her for minor offences, then committing her for the refusal either to provide sureties for good behaviour or to swear the oath of allegiance, the authorities succeeded in restraining her liberty for much of this four-year period. She was released alongside fifty-six other Quakers freed from Gloucester Castle, after James II issued a declaration of indulgence that brought a level of religious tolerance to nonconformists nationwide.

Townsend's life as a Quaker was therefore shaped by her experiences of 'suffering'; however, only one of her published texts refers extensively to imprisonment—the rest being concerned with more general aspects of Quaker policy. When writing to the 'persecuting magistrates' in *A Word in Councel* (1687), Townsend openly expresses a common antinomian idea that it is better to 'obey God then [sic] Man' (p. 4). Indeed, her usage of Old Testament topoi here and elsewhere is indicative of a prophetic impulse in her writing. In *A Testimony Concerning the Life and Death of Jane Whitehead*, for example, Townsend draws on Revelation to predict the second coming of Christ. She also wrote in praise of other deceased Quakers—Joan Vokins, Amariah Drewet, and Anne Whitehead. Her tribute to Anne Whitehead (*An Epistle of Love*), who was a central member of the London women's meetings, was combined with a more general explanation of women's public work in the separate meetings.

Perhaps the most enduring testimony to Theophila Townsend came from the Quaker martyrologist Joseph Besse who, writing of her many sufferings, pithily described her as 'a virtuous Woman, and of great Understanding' (Besse, 1.225). Townsend's death in Cirencester, through unknown causes, was recorded in the Quaker registers, and she was buried there on 15 June 1692.

CATIE GILL

Sources 'Dictionary of Quaker biography', RS Friends, Lond. [card index] · Quaker index of births, marriages and deaths, RS Friends, Lond., reel 30 · J. Besse, *A collection of the sufferings of the people called Quakers*, 2 vols. (1753) · R. Foxton, 'Hear the word of the Lord': a critical and bibliographical study of Quaker women's writing, 1650–1700 (Melbourne, 1994) · B. Hawkins, *The Quakers in Cirencester: the first fifty years (1655–1705)* (1998) · B. Hawkins, *Taming the phoenix: Cirencester and the Quakers, 1642–1686* (1998) · P. Mack, *Visionary women: ecstatic prophesy in seventeenth-century England*, new edn (Berkeley, CA, 1994) · D. Roberts, *A Quaker of olden time*, ed. E. T. Lawrence (1898)

Townsend, William Charles (1804–1850), legal historian, born in Liverpool, was the second son of William Townsend of Walton, Lancashire. He matriculated from Queen's College, Oxford, in July 1820, graduating BA in 1824 and MA in 1827, and began his publications at an early age by contributing several poems to Fisher's *Imperial Magazine*

about 1820, and publishing *The Paean of Orford: a Poem* in 1826. In November 1828 he was called to the bar at Lincoln's Inn. He attached himself to the northern circuit, before practising at the Cheshire and Manchester assizes. Later he obtained a large practice on the north Wales circuit. In 1833 he was elected recorder of Macclesfield, and in 1834 he married Frances Wood (*d.* in or after 1850), the second daughter of Richard Wood of Macclesfield. In March 1850 he was appointed a queen's counsel, and in the same year became a bencher of Lincoln's Inn.

The publications of Townsend's mature years reflected his keen interest in legal history: *The History and Memoirs of the House of Commons* appeared in 1843–4, followed by *The Lives of Twelve Eminent Judges of the Last and of the Present Century* (1846), and *Modern State Trials* (1850). He died of heart disease on 8 May 1850, at Burntwood Lodge, Wandsworth Common, Surrey, the house of his elder brother, Richard Lateward Townsend, vicar of All Saints', Wandsworth. He was buried on 13 May 1850, in the vaults of Lincoln's Inn, London. He was survived by his wife; they had no children.

E. I. CARLYLE, rev. NILANJANA BANERJI

Sources *GM*, 2nd ser., 34 (1850), 218 · Foster, *Alum. Oxon.* · Allibone, *Dict.* · *Chester Chronicle* (11 May 1850) · *Chester Courant* (15 May 1850) · *Blackwood*, 68 (1850), 373

Townshend. *See also* Townsend.

Townshend [Townsend], **Aurelian** (*fl.* 1583–1649?), poet, was the son of John Townshend of Dereham Abbey, Norfolk, and his wife, Anne, daughter of Sir Robert *Catlin (*d.* 1574), chief justice of the queen's bench. Aurelian and his sister Franceline (or Francelliana) were both born some time before 12 December 1583, when they are mentioned in the will of Thomas Townshend, yeoman of Crimplesham, Norfolk. Aurelian was third cousin of the Armada veteran Sir Roger Townshend (1543?–1590) of Raynham, and of the parliamentary historian Hayward Townshend (*c.*1577–1603×21).

Early career and association with the court In 1600 Aurelian attracted the attention of the secretary of state, Sir Robert Cecil, who proposed to train him for the service of his young son William. A warrant by Cecil dated 1 April 1600 authorizes travelling expenses for 'Aurelianus Townesend' as the queen's messenger to Sir Henry Neville, English ambassador in France (Pipe Office, declared accounts, roll 543, m. 57v; *Aurelia Townshend's Poems and Masks*, xxxvii). In a letter to Neville at the same time Cecil described Townshend as 'a young gentleman' who 'hath bin well bredd, and by his owne industrie attayned to a good superficiall knowledge in the French and Italian tongues' and who also showed promise of being able to 'write faire hands'; he accordingly entrusted him to Neville's care, both linguistic and moral (R. Winwood, *Memorials*, ed. E. Sawyer, 1725, 1.167; *Aurelia Townshend's Poems and Masks*, xxxvii–xxxviii). After he had been a year in Paris, Cecil sent the young Townshend on to Venice, whence he continued, in a spirit of dutiful gratitude, to keep his patron informed of such local and diplomatic news as he might encounter. He does not seem, however, to have been very discreet in his choice of acquaintances. One man he recommended to Cecil, Dr John Thornil, canon of Vicenza, would soon turn out to be a Catholic emissary, harboured in London by the Venetian ambassador, while yet another, the adventurer and intriguer Sir Anthony Sherley, succeeded in tricking Townshend out of 200 *scudi* of Cecil's money. Townshend himself was obliged to borrow 100 *scudi* from the merchant John Brown in order to complete a journey through Tuscany and the Romagna and get back to Venice, but Cecil refused to pay this bill and summoned him home. Townshend's misfortunes were compounded when, on the way back through France, he sprained his ankle, fell ill, spent all his money, and could complete his journey only by imploring Cecil, on 7 February 1603, once again for funds.

Townshend is next heard of in the company of the philosophical writer, poet, and diplomat Sir Edward Herbert on a mission to the king of France, Henri IV, in 1608–9. Herbert describes him in his autobiography as 'a Gentleman That spake the Languages of Frensh Italian and Spanish, in greate Perfection'; as the man who was entrusted to deliver a challenge to a Frenchman with whom Herbert had quarrelled, but also as one of those companions who failed to come to Herbert's assistance when he was cornered by a boar on a hunt (*The Life of Edward, First Lord Herbert of Cherbury, Written by Himself*, ed. J. M. Shuttleworth, 1976, 41–2, 47). Passing references suggest that he may still have served Herbert in some connection as late as 8 April 1615, when, in a letter to Herbert, his stepfather Sir John Danvers refers to 'the hundred pounds imployed' by Herbert 'for Mr. Townsend' ('Old Herbert papers at Powis Castle and in the British Museum', *Collections Historical & Archaeological Relating to Montgomeryshire and its Borders*, 20, 1886, 84). He may also have continued to serve Cecil up to the time of his death in 1612 for, in his account of Cecil's last days, his chaplain John Bowles mentions an afternoon when Cecil 'had noe companie with him, but onely Master Townsend' (Francis Peck, *Desiderata curiosa*, new edn, 2 vols., 1779, 1.208). Nevertheless, positive evidence of Townshend's employment during most of his early years is lacking.

An autograph letter signed by Townshend ('A Tounshend') to William Trumbull, English resident in Brussels, dated from Hampton Court on 13 March 1621 (BL, Add. MS 72360, fols. 136r–137v), indicates that he was then still connected with the court and very much *au courant* with court news and gossip. Townshend refers in passing to his sister (Franceline, who would be reported by James Wadsworth in *The English Spanish Pilgrime*, 1629, 69, to be playing 'the shee Physitian in the Archdutches Court' in Flanders) and to 'my L[ord] of Westmerland' (her lover in exile, the bigamous Edmund Neville, conspirator and unsuccessful claimant to the earldom of Westmorland). Townshend excuses himself from coming over again to Brussels himself 'this somer' because his passport must be signed by 'too many handes' ('for I see a poore man that hath many frends, hath almost no tyme of his owne'). Parish registers reveal that between 1622 and 1634 'Aurelian Townsend gentleman' was living in the parish of St Giles Cripplegate, where his Norfolk kinsmen had once maintained

town residences. Some time between 1619 and 1622 he married Anne (*c.*1597–*c.*1667), daughter of Edward Wythies of Copgrave, Yorkshire. She was the widow of William Agborough (d. 1619), with whom she had one son, Robert, who later adopted Townshend's surname and was knighted in 1660. She bore Townshend five recorded children: George (*bap.* 17 Dec 1622), Mary (*bap.* 8 April 1626), James (*bap.* 15 Dec 1627), Herbert (*bap.* 23 Sept 1631; *bur.* 26 Feb 1634), and Frances (*bap.* 17 Nov 1632). On 3 June 1629 the king granted a petition by Townshend allowing him custody and administration of the estate of the deranged Philippa Ivatt, widow of Thomas Ivatt, searcher of London (*CSP dom.*, 1628–9, 143/40, 144/34).

Writer of court masques and poet Early in 1632 Townshend suddenly came to prominence as a writer of court masques, as temporary successor to Ben Jonson, who had fallen out of favour. On 8 January the king's twelfth night masque *Albions Triumph* was presented, for which Townshend wrote the verses and description (modestly referring to himself in the printed edition as being 'as loath to be brought upon the Stage as an unhansom Man is to see himselfe in a great Glasse', but that he had obeyed the command of the king). The elaborate scenery, machinery, and costumes were devised by Jonson's old rival Inigo Jones, who was also chiefly responsible for the queen's shrovetide masque a month later, *Tempe Restor'd*, to which Townshend contributed the verses. Although some of Townshend's poems were undoubtedly written earlier, it is from the years immediately following these two masques that the bulk of his surviving works can probably be dated. He contributed to further court masques: one on 21 December 1635, when he supplied the antimasques after the French pastoral *Florimène* performed by the queen's ladies; another when he contributed a 'Bacchanall' song to a 'maske before their Majestys', probably the court revival on 12 January 1637 of William Cartwright's *The Royal Slave*. He also contributed some time in this period to an entertainment presented before the king by the Merchant Adventurers' Company.

Townshend's attachment to the court and to the aristocratic, fashionable society of his day is evident in various of his poems, addressed or paying tribute not only to the king and queen themselves but also to the likes of Lady Judith May, wife of the vice-chamberlain of the household Sir Humphrey May, Sir Kenelm Digby, Henry Carey, earl of Monmouth, and the court musician Henry Lawes and his brother William. One of his neighbours in the Barbican was apparently John Egerton, first earl of Bridgewater, to whom he presented a copy of *Albions Triumph* (now in the Huntington Library). Egerton's children took part in *Tempe Restor'd*, and his wife was mourned by Townshend in March 1636 in a funeral elegy. Like his daughter, Townshend may also have been on good terms with members of the Sackville family, one of whom, the fourth earl of Dorset's son Edward, he mourned in an elegy in 1645. Other friends included the court poet Thomas Carew, whose 'sweet' wit and manly spirit Townshend praised in his elegy on Gustavus Adolphus (killed 6 November 1632). Carew warmly responded in his elegy on the same subject by addressing Townshend as 'my dear Aurelian'; the poem notes that Townshend was living in the Barbican at this time. On 8 August 1633 'Aurelian Towneshend, Esq.' was also admitted to the fellowship of Gray's Inn, then a privileged society of gentlemen as much noted for its literary activities as its legal pursuits.

The civil war By the time of the civil war Townshend's luck may have been waning. According to a reported but unverifiable inscription supposedly by Philip Herbert, earl of Pembroke, in a book apparently dated 1642, the 'poore & pocky Poett' Townshend, 'but a marryed man & an howsekeeper in Barbican', would have been 'glad to sell an 100 verses now at sixepence a piece, 50 shillings an 100 verses' (cited in Alexander Dyce's edition of *The Works of Beaumont and Fletcher*, 1843–6, 1.xvii). It must have been financial straits which made Townshend petition the House of Lords for protection (granted 3 March 1643) against arrest by Isaak Tulley, silkman, on a claim of £600 for silk and fringes he bespoke for the use of Lewis Boyle, Viscount Kinalmeaky (*JHL*, 5.632). Nevertheless, he described himself in that petition as 'the King's Ordinary Servant', and his association with the court persisted. This may, perhaps, be linked to the court successes in another sense of his daughter Mary, to whom he addressed the gently admonitory 'Let not thy beauties make thee proud'. Before she was twenty she was successively mistress of Charles Louis, elector palatine (1617–1680), and Edward Sackville, fourth earl of Dorset (1590–1652), and was even rumoured in 1647 to have dallied with the elector palatine's younger brother, Prince Maurice (1620–1652) ('Divers remarkable passages of the ladies at Spring-Garden, in parliament assembled', *Scarce and Valuable Tracts … Lord Somers*, 2nd edn, 5.472–3). On 26 February 1646 she married, as his second wife, George Kirke, a groom of the bedchamber and gentleman of the robes, at Christ Church, Oxford, where, according to William Dugdale, 'The King gave her; she being the admired beauty of the tymes' (*The Life, Diary, and Correspondence of Sir William Dugdale*, ed. W. Hamper, 1827, 84). The king even settled upon her a jointure of £500 (*CSP dom.*, 1676–7, 132). The couple remained loyal to Charles during the upheavals of the war—as did Townshend's eldest son, George, and his stepson, Robert, who both fought and suffered imprisonment for the king. George and Mary Kirke received various royal favours and allowances after the Restoration before George Kirke's death in 1675; his widow, who was generously pensioned, lived on to 1702.

Townshend himself, however, may not have stayed the course of the war in England, but was possibly the 'Mr. Townshend, Gent.' who was among the seventy 'servants and attendants' of princes Rupert and Maurice allowed by Sir Thomas Fairfax, on 19 June 1646, to leave for the continent after the fall of Oxford (E. Warburton, *Memoirs of Prince Rupert, and the Cavaliers*, 1849, 3.234). It is possible that in this period he supported himself by serving as a tutor to one or more younger exiles, including Sir Roger Townshend (1628–1648) and his brother Horatio, later Baron and Viscount Townshend (*bap.* 1630, *d.* 1687), who, on 16 December 1646, had leave from parliament to travel abroad for three years. The grant of arms to Horatio by Sir Edward Walker in 1663 mentions Horatio's having received his education under Aurelian Townshend (BL, Add. MS 37675, fol. 49r).

Townshend is next heard of in a poem by one C. R. 'To my Worthy Friend A:T:', inviting him to write an elegy on Lord Francis Villiers, who was killed by parliamentary forces at Kingston on 7 July 1648. Hailing Townshend as 'the last of all the Poets race' with 'the ablest Pen' the writer stresses how 'old' the poet is ('Your health a sicknesse, & your Muse growne cold'), his 'Long-spun Thread' almost 'become a shread' (University College, London, Ogden MS 42, 3–4). It is possible (from the attribution in a fragment of the poem formerly among the Sackville papers) that Townshend lived to write one more notable poem: a heroic elegy on Charles I's execution, on 30 January 1649, the complete text of which (Ogden MS 42, 1–3) is signed 'Philobasile' (lover of the king). Otherwise, unless he is the 'Tounshend' who contributed a slight, eight-line dialogue to the commendatory poems in Clement Barksdale's *Nympha libethris* in 1651, no more is heard of him.

Townshend's reputation Apart from the three main court masques in which he was involved in 1632 and 1635, and two or three sets of commendatory verses, Townshend's writings remained unpublished in his lifetime. They were written for, and confined to, coterie manuscript circulation, and various of the poems were also given musical settings by Henry Lawes and others. Judging by the number of copies surviving in seventeenth-century manuscript miscellanies, a few of his lyrics achieved considerable popularity, especially 'Victorious Beauty', addressed to Catherine Howard, wife (in 1608) of his first patron's son, William Cecil, second earl of Salisbury.

Townshend's literary canon was first established by Chambers in his collected edition (1912). Additions and modifications to it were made, from both manuscript and printed sources, in Cedric C. Brown's edition (1983). Yet further additions (including the two elegies of 1648–9) can be made from a royalist anthology of the 1650s now at University College, London (Ogden MS 42), from manuscripts of verse tributes by him to Lord North and to the newly born Prince Charles (BL, Add. MSS 27407, fol. 5r, and 27408, fols. 112r–113r), and from Sir Henry Herbert's copy of verses for a masque now in the National Library of Wales (NL Wales, MS 5308E, fols. 12r–13v).

With the exception of a perfunctory reference in Sir John Suckling's 'Session of the Poets' (1637), which is heavily outweighed by C.R.'s eulogy in 1648, evidence of the poet's contemporary reputation is otherwise meagre. In his 1633 elegy on Gustavus Adolphus, Thomas Carew (author of the much more ambitious and successful court masque *Coelum Britannicum*, performed 18 February 1634) praised Townshend's ability, in his elegy on Gustavus Adolphus, to 'soar' to 'a loftier pitch' and make a 'noble flight', while at the same time implying that his customary level was to sing 'harmless pastimes' to 'rural tunes'.

Townshend's verse is not generally comparable to the more richly textured poems of his more prolific friend Carew, let alone to the metaphysical complexities of John

Donne, whose influence nevertheless extended to him as to so many of his contemporaries. But neither is it fair to dismiss him, as T. S. Eliot did, as merely a 'faint, pleasing tinkle' ('The metaphysical poets', 1921). Townshend's voice was distinctive enough, and somewhere in the rich canon of seventeenth-century English verse is a respectable niche for him where the virtues of accomplished lyricism, charm, sophisticated (if obsequious) gallantry, tact, and courtesy may receive due homage.   PETER BEAL

Sources *Aurelian Townshend's poems and masks*, ed. E. K. Chambers (1912) · *The poems and masques of Aurelian Townshend*, ed. C. C. Brown (1983) · P. Beal, 'Songs by Aurelian Townshend, in the hand of Sir Henry Herbert, for an unrecorded masque by the Merchant Adventurers', *Medieval and Renaissance Drama in England*, 15 (2002), 243–60 · GEC, *Peerage*, new edn, 12/1.802–4, 12/2.560–65 · J. Foster, *The register of admissions to Gray's Inn, 1521–1889, together with the register of marriages in Gray's Inn chapel, 1695–1754* (privately printed, London, 1889) · W. Scott, ed., *A collection of scarce and valuable tracts … Lord Somers*, 2nd edn, 13 vols. (1809–15) · parish register, London, St Giles Cripplegate, GL, MS 6419, vol. 2 · will of Thomas Townshend of Crimplesham, Norfolk, PRO, PROB 11/69, sig. 42
Archives BL, Add. MSS 27407, fol. 5r; 27408, fols. 112r–113r; 37675, fol. 49; 72360, fols. 136r–137v · Coll. Arms, MS K.3 · GL, MSS 6419, 4097 · Hatfield House, Hertfordshire, library of the marquess of Salisbury, Cecil papers 84–87, 91, 93, 96 · NL Wales, MS 5308E, fols. 12r–13v · UCL, Ogden MS 42

Townshend [née Campbell], **Caroline**, *suo jure* **Baroness Greenwich** [*other married name* Caroline Scott, countess of Dalkeith] (**1717–1794**), landowner, was born on 17 November 1717, the first of the five children of John *Campbell, second duke of Argyll and first duke of Greenwich (1680–1743), and his second wife, Jane Warburton (*d.* 1767), daughter of Thomas Warburton of Winnington, Cheshire. The duke, 'warm-hearted, frank, honourable, magnanimous but fiery-tempered, rash, ambitious, haughty and impatient of contradiction' (*Scots peerage*, 1.376), was successively commander-in-chief of the government forces in Scotland and high steward of the household. His second wife, a plain, unsophisticated country woman of much lower rank than he, had been maid of honour to Queen Anne and subsequently served in the same capacity in the household of Caroline of Ansbach, princess of Wales, wife of the future George II. Their eldest daughter was born at 27 Bruton Street, their London house, and christened Caroline, for the princess, who acted as godmother.

The family visited the duke's Scottish estates each summer, but Caroline and her four younger sisters were brought up at Sudbrook, an elegant mansion built by their father on the west side of Richmond Park. Accommodated in a special wing known as 'The Young Ladies' House', they were left to do much as they pleased. Having no son, their father treated Caroline as his heir and summoned her to dine with him on Sundays, but at other times the sisters had little discipline and ran wild. As a result, they were known to contemporaries as 'the bawling Campbells' and 'the screaming sisterhood' (Lindsay and Cosh, 5). Even so, Caroline was attractive and extremely eligible. Introduced into London society, she had a brief romance with the earl of Lichfield's son, Lord Quarendon, a personable young man not wealthy enough to be acceptable to her

Caroline Townshend, *suo jure* Baroness Greenwich (1717–1794), by Sir Joshua Reynolds, 1756–7

father. Meanwhile, Francis Scott, second duke of Buccleuch, had decided that she would make an appropriate wife for his elder son, Francis, earl of Dalkeith (1721–1750). The dukes met in May 1742 and the match was made. 'Lord Dalkeith likes the lady extreamly well, and I don't doubt they will be very happy together', the duke of Buccleuch commented with satisfaction (Fraser, 1.487). Caroline's tearful protests and Lord Quarendon's angry assertions that he had been jilted were ignored, and the wedding took place at Bruton Street on 2 October 1742.

Just over a year later, on 4 October 1743, the duke of Argyll died. Because he had no son, his English honours became extinct and his dukedom, which was entailed on the male line, passed to his younger brother. Caroline, however, inherited various properties, including Adderbury, a large seventeenth-century mansion in Oxfordshire, and Caroline Park, Granton, now part of Edinburgh. Originally known as Royston House, the latter had been purchased in 1739 by the duke, who had changed its name in his daughter's honour. Caroline and her husband divided their time between London, Adderbury, and their Scottish properties. Lord Dalkeith was not as handsome as Lord Quarendon, but he was dignified and sincere, and he made an agreeable husband. He represented Boroughbridge in parliament from 1746 to 1747. Caroline gave birth first to a daughter, born in 1743 and named after herself, and then to four sons, including Henry *Scott, third duke of Buccleuch (1746–1812). The family's happy life was shattered when, at the age of twenty-nine, Lord Dalkeith contracted smallpox and died at Adderbury on 1 April

1750, leaving his estate and the guardianship of the children to his wife. Caroline was five months pregnant, and gave birth to their second daughter, Frances, later Lady Frances *Douglas, on 26 July.

For the next five years Caroline remained a widow, and during that time her eldest son and daughter both died. In 1755, however, she remarried and began a second family. The wedding took place at Adderbury on 15 August. Her new husband, Charles *Townshend (1725–1767), eight years her junior, was the brother of George, first Marquess Townshend. Variously described as a brilliant orator able to intoxicate the House of Commons with his witty irrelevancies, and as 'the consummate self-seeking political insider' (note, Charles Townshend MSS), Charles was already MP for Great Yarmouth. With the help of Caroline's connections, he became lord of the Admiralty, secretary at war during the Seven Years' War, and, finally, chancellor of the exchequer. Their first child, Anne, was born the year after their marriage, when Caroline was thirty-nine, and she went on to have three more sons.

In recognition of the fact that Caroline had been unable to inherit her father's titles and principal estates, she was appointed ranger of Greenwich Park, and then, on 19 August 1767, she was created a peeress in her own right, with the title of Baroness Greenwich. Just over a fortnight later, on 4 September 1767, Townshend died suddenly at the age of forty-two. Caroline lived on for almost thirty years more, looking after her property, interesting herself in her family, and enjoying London society. She died at Sudbrook on 11 January 1794. Her title of Baroness Greenwich had been created with remainder to the male issue of her second marriage, but her sons by Townshend had predeceased her, leaving no male children themselves, and so her title became extinct. She was buried in Westminster Abbey, in the Argyll family vault in Henry VII's chapel, on 25 January 1794.   ROSALIND K. MARSHALL

Sources *Scots peerage* · W. Fraser, *The Scotts of Buccleuch*, 2 vols. (1878) · I. G. Lindsay and M. Cosh, *Inveraray and the dukes of Argyll* (1973) · P. Dickson, *Red John of the battles* (1973) · GEC, *Peerage* · *Edinburgh*, Pevsner (1984) · some legal correspondence and papers of Viscountess Greenwich, 1784 and 1754–89, U. Mich., Clements L., Charles Townshend MSS, 295/1, 298
Archives NA Scot., corresp. and two plans of Caroline Park area in dispute between Viscountess Greenwich and William Davidson of Muirhouse, GD 24/5, RHP 713 and 714 | U. Mich., Clements L., Charles Townshend MSS 295/1, 298
Likenesses J. Reynolds, oils, 1756–7, priv. coll. [*see illus.*] · T. Bardwell, pencil drawing, Scot. NPG · T. Bardwell, two portraits, oils, priv. coll.

Townshend, Charles, second Viscount Townshend (1674–1738), politician, diplomatist, and agricultural innovator, was born on 18 April 1674 at Raynham, Norfolk, and baptized on 2 May at St Martin-in-the-Fields, London. He was the eldest of the three sons and heir of Horatio *Townshend, first Viscount Townshend (*bap.* 1630, *d.* 1687), politician, and his second wife, Mary (*d.* 1685), the daughter of Sir Joseph Ashe, of Twickenham, Middlesex. His two brothers were Roger (*d.* 1709), a colonel of a foot regiment and MP for Norfolk and later Great Yarmouth;

Charles Townshend, second Viscount Townshend (1674–1738), by Sir Godfrey Kneller, 1704?

and Horatio (*c.*1683–1751), who was MP for Great Yarmouth and later Heytesbury, a director of the South Sea Company, a governor and director of the Bank of England, and a commissioner of the excise. Townshend took his seat in the House of Lords in December 1687 following the death of their father.

Early life and career Townshend was educated at Eton College and matriculated at King's College, Cambridge, at Easter 1691. After travelling abroad for three years from August 1694 to October 1697 he married, on 3 July 1698, Elizabeth (*d.* 1711), the second daughter of Thomas *Pelham, first Baron Pelham. During their thirteen-year marriage they remained devoted to one another and were rarely separated. The couple had nine children; the first, Horatio, was born in August 1699 and was followed by two girls and six boys. Only five of the children, four sons and one daughter, survived to adulthood.

Although his father had been a staunch tory, Townshend favoured the whigs and quickly became active in politics. In 1701 he was appointed high steward of King's Lynn (21 April) and of Norwich Cathedral (21 or 30 April), offices he held until his death. In addition he served as lord lieutenant of Norfolk, a position he held twice (1701–

13 and 1714–30), and as *custos rotulorum*, to which he was appointed on 31 May 1701. These offices and his stature in the community gave Townshend considerable political influence. In May 1701 he also delivered his maiden speech in the House of Lords. Unfortunately he was not a skilled orator. Even one of his friends, the fourth earl of Chesterfield, noted that, although Townshend always 'spoke materially, with argument and knowledge … [he] never pleased … [because] his diction was not only inelegant, but frequently ungrammatical, always vulgar: his cadences false; his voice unharmonious, and his actions ungraceful' (*Letters of … Chesterfield*, 4.1454). He went on to observe that 'Nobody heard him with patience' and that some individuals 'used to joke upon him and repeat his inaccuracies' (ibid., 4.1455). In spite of this failing, Townshend played an important political role, in part because of his and Robert Walpole's control of the Norfolk whigs, who usually acted with the junto leadership.

During the early years of Queen Anne's reign Townshend protested against the Occasional Conformity Bill, defended the rights of the electorate in the Aylesbury election, and helped to defeat the proposal to invite Princess Sophie of Hanover to England. In 1706 he became a member of the Royal Society and was nominated to serve as one of the commissioners to negotiate the treaty of union between England and Scotland. The following year he was appointed captain of the yeomen of the guard (25 November) and was sworn of the privy council (1 December), and in 1708 he was elected to serve on a committee of seven peers investigating charges of treason against William Gregg, Robert Harley's secretary.

Diplomatic career In 1709 the queen appointed Townshend to his most important diplomatic post, at The Hague, the main artery of British diplomacy. This post was crucial not only because of the importance of maintaining good relations with Britain's closest ally but also because it was the 'whispering gallery' of Europe (Horn, *British Diplomatic Representatives*, 19–20), where the most extensive information on European politics was available. At that time the British, embroiled in the War of the Spanish Succession (1702–13), feared that the Dutch might conclude a separate peace with France. Many whigs were delighted with the selection of Townshend. Bishop Burnet for one thought him 'a man of great integrity, and of great principles in all respects; free from all vice and of an engaging conversation' (*Burnet's History*, 6.18–19).

The impetus for the appointment had come from John Churchill, duke of Marlborough, who had pressed the government to appoint a colleague to aid him in concluding a treaty with the Dutch. The ministry had first chosen Charles Montagu, earl of Halifax. Justifiably suspicious of the duke's motives, Halifax had refused, whereupon the ministry turned to Townshend, one of the protégés of John, Lord Somers, who as early as 1707 had been promised the post at The Hague. Negotiations with the Dutch had been ongoing for several years at the time of Townshend's appointment. Plans for a barrier treaty, to construct a string of fortresses in the Southern Netherlands, had been discussed in 1706 but came to nothing. Only

when the British learned that France had begun talks with the continental allies did they, fearing that the Dutch might conclude a separate peace, authorize Marlborough to reopen discussions for a barrier. Marlborough, realizing that the other allies, notably Prussia and Austria, would oppose this barrier, and that a barrier treaty was too high a price for the British to pay for Dutch adherence to the war effort, distanced himself at the outset from the negotiations. Such was the situation that Townshend confronted when he arrived at The Hague on 17 May 1709.

Fortunately, many of the Dutch leaders, including Anthonie Heinsius, the grand pensionary, befriended the popular young diplomatist. As ambassador-extraordinary and plenipotentiary to the United Provinces (13 May 1709 to 21 March 1711) Townshend helped to draw up the harsh peace terms that Louis XIV rejected. In 1709 he also concluded a treaty with the Dutch guaranteeing the Hanoverian succession and allocating the Dutch a barrier of fortifications in the Spanish (later the Austrian) Netherlands. His conviction that Dutch security depended on the acquisition of a good barrier and that a more generous treaty would secure Dutch allegiance to Britain and the ongoing war led him to exceed his instructions and make strategic, financial, and commercial concessions not outlined in the British project. Among the proposals offered to the Dutch by Townshend were the cession of Upper Gueldres, territory which the king of Prussia claimed as part of his inheritance from his mother, and the inclusion of other fortresses in the barrier, such as Dendermonde, which were of economic but not strategic importance.

The reaction of Britain's allies was explosive: Frederick I of Prussia was furious because the treaty ignored his claims to Gueldres, and Joseph I of Austria because the treaty implied Dutch military and economic domination of the Netherlands. In Great Britain the treaty provoked an uproar because many believed that it constituted more of a barrier against British trade than a military barrier against France. Merchants objected in particular to the clauses which gave the Dutch an equal share in the concessions of the Spanish empire and greater trade advantages in the Netherlands. The infamous double duty which the British had to pay on goods imported into the Netherlands amounted to a potent trade weapon. A lively pamphlet war soon erupted. On one side Francis Hare, in *The Barrier Treaty Vindicated*, attempted to justify the treaty by arguing that it had fulfilled its main purpose, the securing of a sufficient barrier for the Dutch and the safeguarding of the protestant succession. On the other, Jonathan Swift attacked the treaty for ignoring the rights of the allies and for endangering British trade, making Britain 'a Province to Holland, and a Jest to the whole world'. Henry St John reflected the tory attitude when he remarked that it was the 'last and great sale of British interests' (Feiling, 404). The conclusion of the treaty, which Marlborough cannily refused to sign, marked a far from edifying chapter in the diplomatic history of the United Provinces. The Dutch, ignoring the larger issue of peace or war, crudely squeezed concessions out of their unwilling ally.

None the less, Townshend's mission marked the high

point of Anglo-Dutch relations during the war. Although the Dutch had forced the British to consent to Townshend's treaty, they had in the process tied themselves to Britain and had given up their last chance of a separate peace with France. Townshend's mission and the conclusion of the barrier negotiations exemplify the British policy of 'appeasing' the Dutch to prevent their defection to France. However, Dutch gains were largely illusory. With its extensive military and economic advantages, the barrier did not necessarily form a strong defence, since it later alienated both France and the inhabitants of the Southern Netherlands. Equally, it was highly improbable that either the king of Prussia or the Habsburgs would accept a treaty so detrimental to their own interests. Lastly, the extensive commercial concessions which the Dutch obtained would invariably lead to conflict with Great Britain, the treaty's guarantor.

In 1709 Townshend, along with Marlborough, negotiated the peace preliminaries with Anthonie Heinsius and the French representatives, Jean Baptiste Colbert, marquis de Torcy, and Pierre Rouillé de Marbeuf. The basis of the preliminaries was the cession of the whole Spanish monarchy to the Habsburgs and the acknowledgement of Archduke Charles as king of Spain. Louis XIV was to restore all the towns and forts conquered in the Spanish Netherlands. He was also required not only to withdraw all French troops from Spain but also to help the allies to remove Philip V. If the whole Spanish monarchy were not ceded within two months of the treaty's conclusion, the armistice would expire. It was these demands, presented in the infamous articles 4 and 37, that doomed the talks. Subsequent meetings in Gertruydenberg underscored Louis XIV's refusal to make all the sacrifices without receiving anything more than a promise of peace negotiations in return. Louis continued to maintain that he would rather wage war against his enemies than his children. These negotiations, though ultimately futile, proved that the barrier treaty had indeed secured Dutch allegiance to Britain and the war. In the spring and summer of 1710 the British government, fearing that the Great Northern War might spill over and merge into the War of the Spanish Succession, authorized Townshend to sign the conventions of 31 March and 4 August which guaranteed the peace in the Holy Roman empire, Poland, and the duchies of Schleswig and Jutland.

Fall of the whigs and opposition By 1710 Britain, as well as France, was weary of the war. The ministerial revolution which ushered the tories back into power ultimately meant the recall of Townshend on 21 March 1711 and a repudiation of the barrier treaty in 1712. Although the tories at this time paraded their co-operation with the Dutch and simulated a desire to continue the war to ensure stability at home and to obtain the best possible terms from France, St John in particular bombarded Townshend with complaints about the failure of the Dutch to fulfil their treaty obligations. These demands were a hint of Britain's coming withdrawal from the conflict, and marked the beginning of British abandonment and eventual renunciation of their Dutch allies.

Townshend was not only recalled from his post but also dismissed as captain of the yeomen of the guard (13 June 1711). In addition to these political trials he was grief-stricken by the loss, between April and June 1711, of his newborn daughter Elizabeth, his wife—in his 'first irreparable misfortune' (7 July 1711, BL, Stowe MS 224)—and his eldest son, Horatio. On 14 February 1712 he was censured by the tory-dominated House of Commons for exceeding his instructions and condemned as a public enemy. Gilbert Burnet, an admirer of Townshend, in commenting on this incident, sardonically noted that 'reason is a feeble thing to bear down resolutions already taken' (*Burnet's History*, 6.123). In 1713 the tories forced the Dutch to renegotiate the treaty and drastically reduced the number of fortresses. Locally Townshend retained his position as lord lieutenant of Norfolk until April 1713, when James Butler, duke of Ormond, replaced him. By that time Townshend had lost his ability to influence local appointments or to protect his appointees.

While in opposition Townshend spent his time harassing the government. In particular he worked with other whigs on the bill which declared enlisting and recruiting individuals for the Pretender to be high treason, and he protested against the now infamous restraining orders (10 May 1712) in which Bolingbroke ordered Ormond not to engage in any further continental military action. These orders meant in effect an abandonment of Britain's allies. In the midst of this political manoeuvring Townshend married, on 6 July 1713, Dorothy (d. 1726), known as Dolly, the charming and beautiful sister of his boyhood friend and whig colleague Robert Walpole. The marriage, which produced eleven children, the eldest of them being George *Townshend, was a happy one for Townshend and helped to cement the friendship of this unlikely political duo. At the same time Townshend strengthened his ties with Hanoverian agents, especially Johann Kaspar von Bothmer, in preparation for the accession of George I. Townshend was able to win over George I because of his reputation for integrity and hard work and his staunch adherence to the cause of the Hanoverian succession. His friendship with influential Dutch officials, such as Heinsius and Slingelandt, also helped him. After the death of Queen Anne in August 1714 George chose Townshend as one of the eighteen regents to prepare for his accession.

The early reign of George I Once in power George I appointed Townshend secretary of state for the northern department, a post he held from 17 September 1714 to 12 December 1716. On 1 October he was again sworn of the privy council and began his second term as lord lieutenant of Norfolk. George's accession also saw Townshend's brother-in-law Robert Walpole appointed first lord of the Treasury and chancellor of the exchequer. Although he advised against the prosecution of Robert Harley (now earl of Oxford) for treason and later favoured pardoning Henry St John (now Viscount Bolingbroke), Townshend generally supported the proceedings against those who concluded the treaties of Utrecht and urged the seizure of the papers of Lord Strafford, one of the British envoys. He energetically helped to suppress the Jacobite rising in 1715, supported the Septennial Act of May 1716 which extended the legal life of the existing and subsequent parliaments from three to seven years, and tried to restrict British involvement in the naval war between Sweden and Denmark.

In his capacity as secretary of state Townshend promoted defensive alliances with both the Holy Roman emperor and the king of France and, with James Stanhope's assistance, concluded a definitive barrier treaty with the Dutch on 14 November 1715. His delay in signing a treaty with France because of difficulties over the Pretender and over the destruction of the fortifications at Mardyke, a pirate haven, irritated George I, who, deeply involved in the Great Northern War, wanted the French treaty speedily concluded. Townshend's belief that an aggressive policy in northern Europe would be expensive and contrary to Britain's interests caused him to lose influence with both the king and his minions, including Stanhope, who wanted Britain to take an active role in the Baltic. George I also opposed Townshend's plan to re-establish the balance of power between Russia and Sweden.

Although the main cause of Townshend's fall was a difference over foreign policy, personal rivalries also played a role. The fissure present at the outset in the government progressively widened. George's increasing favouritism towards both Stanhope and the earl of Sunderland worsened relations among the whigs. Sunderland, who had been lord lieutenant of Ireland and then lord privy seal, envied Townshend, who, though less experienced, held the more influential office. Sunderland convinced George I and Stanhope that Townshend and Walpole were plotting with the prince of Wales. Townshend's procurement of an Irish rather than a British title for the king's mistress, Melusine von der Schulenberg, angered her and worsened his position.

The rift in the government over foreign policy led Townshend on 26 December 1716 to exchange the office of secretary of state for that of the lucrative but politically powerless office of lord lieutenant of Ireland, to which he was appointed on 24 February 1717, although he never visited the country. While Townshend was reluctant to accept this position, widely regarded as a form of political exile, he did so in order to avoid further splits within whig ranks. However, the attempt to appease Townshend and to prevent additional divisions ultimately failed, as Walpole joined the opposition to Stanhope and Sunderland. Walpole presciently told Stanhope that he was quite mistaken in believing that removing his brother-in-law would 'meet with no objection from the Whigs' (Plumb, 1.237). Walpole, who whatever his faults proved loyal on this occasion, pointed out that 'Such sudden changes to old sworn friends are seldom look'd upon in the world with a favourable eye' (Coxe, *Walpole*, 2.143). Townshend himself opposed the king's favoured ministers and continued to criticize the ministry's policies, for example the crucial Mutiny Bill. This stand led to his dismissal on 20 April 1717.

Walpole resigned shortly after, as did William Pulteney, Paul Methuen, and the duke of Devonshire. After Townshend's other supporters, including Sir Charles Turner, were dismissed, the king reconstructed the cabinet under Stanhope's leadership.

Townshend did not, however, remain out of power for long. In concert with Walpole and other opposition whigs he adopted the effective tactic of showing the ministry his political importance while at the same time making himself so troublesome that the king would be forced to bring him back into the government. Such measures included the support offered by the Townshend–Walpole whigs to Lord Oxford in May 1717 and opposition to the Peerage Bill in 1719. More positively, Townshend, along with Walpole, also reconciled the prince of Wales to his father. This and the successful piloting of the civil list through the House of Commons ensured Townshend's and Walpole's return to power.

Political career, 1720–1729 Early in 1720 Townshend was partially reconciled to Stanhope, and on 22 June George I appointed Townshend president of the council and Walpole paymaster-general of the forces. Following Stanhope's death from a stroke on 5 February 1721, Townshend was reappointed secretary of state for the northern department on 21 February. The forced retirement of Sunderland, who still held a court appointment as groom of the stole, and the latter's death on 19 April 1722, left Townshend and Walpole only one powerful enemy at court: John Carteret, then secretary of state for the southern department. Carteret, who spoke fluent French and German and was very knowledgeable about European affairs, in part because of his earlier position as ambassador to Sweden, wanted to protect Hanoverian interests by blocking Russian ambitions in the Baltic and securing the friendship of the emperor. Carteret's enforced move in April 1724 to become lord lieutenant of Ireland nullified this threat but also rid the ministry of its last common enemy. Walpole's skilful handling of the South Sea Bubble crisis marked a change in the equilibrium between Walpole and Townshend, although George I still favoured Townshend over his brother-in-law. The king granted his eldest son, Horatio, a peerage in May 1723 and made Townshend a knight of the Garter in July the following year.

The first major clash between Townshend and Walpole occurred over the treaty of Hanover, which Townshend concluded with France and Russia in order to counteract the Austro-Spanish treaty of Vienna (1725). Townshend insisted on retaining Gibraltar, which the Spanish had hoped to recover. Walpole, however, thought that Townshend was overstating the threat from the Austrians and attempting to overturn Britain's traditional alliance. As the political relationship between the two men unravelled, the death of Townshend's second wife on 29 March 1726 also weakened the ties that had bound them. Dolly, who died of smallpox, had been devoted to both her husband and her brother. Thereafter the rift between the two widened, with Townshend and Walpole now vying for power not only at court but also in Norfolk.

By the time George II ascended the throne in June 1727 the political pendulum had swung in favour of Walpole, who had assiduously courted the queen and spent a great deal of time with the king. Townshend's position at court had been further weakened during the years 1727–8 because of his severe ill health. A struggle for power between the two men ensued. Chesterfield, who knew Townshend well, observed that the latter was 'not of a temper to act a second part, after having acted a first' (BL, Stowe MSS, Chesterfield characters). The same was even truer of Walpole, who wanted more influence in foreign policy and differed with Townshend over its direction. Townshend, for example, remained suspicious of Prussia, while both Walpole and the queen sought a closer alliance with that power. Townshend remained loyal to the Dutch. Although he believed that the territorial integrity of Austria was essential for Britain's long-term interests, he distrusted the Austrians, whom he regarded as ungrateful, obstinate, and likely to threaten the European system. He was fully aware too of the fragility of Britain's alliance with France. Walpole, in contrast, did not appreciate how divergent Britain's and France's long-term interests and aims were.

The relations between Townshend and his fellow secretary for foreign affairs, the duke of Newcastle, also worsened over time. In the early years of his ministry Newcastle, who had no diplomatic experience, was dependent on his colleague. After Townshend's illness Newcastle became increasingly confident and ambitious. It was Newcastle who helped to ignite the crisis that led to Townshend's resignation. The conclusion of the treaty of Seville in 1729 was undoubtedly the *coup de grâce*. While Townshend was in Hanover with the king, Walpole and Newcastle outmanoeuvred him. They dispatched William Stanhope to Spain to conclude a peace which provided that, in return for recognizing their claims to Parma and Piacenza, the Spanish would restore the privileges of the *asiento* and allow commissioners to adjudicate difficulties over trade in the Caribbean. Stanhope's reward was elevation to the peerage and later appointment to Townshend's position. This treaty solved nothing. Walpole never really appreciated the long-term consequences of his actions, nor did he comprehend the clash between British, French, and Spanish long-term interests or understand that not all problems could be resolved diplomatically.

When Townshend failed to obtain an appointment for either Chesterfield or Paul Methuen, he realized how little influence he retained. None the less, Walpole could not force him out and had to wait for him to resign. By 1730 it was clear that Townshend and Walpole could no longer work together; Walpole baited Townshend and quarrelled openly with him. Walpole's gratitude to Townshend for his past aid and support now counted for little. Although both were ambitious and hard-working, they shared little else. Townshend, a nobleman of a second generation, was scrupulously honest and frugal, while Walpole, a squire's son, was venal, lecherous, vulgar, and prodigal. Townshend was often forceful and blunt while Walpole was devious and frequently ingratiating. Walpole's allegation that Townshend did not pay enough attention to parliamentary opinion was unfounded. Nor is it true that fundamental policy clashes triggered Townshend's resignation, for policy changed little after his retirement.

Townshend had considered resigning as early as autumn 1729 but eventually took the decision on 15 May 1730, when he 'retired in disgust' (Coxe, *Walpole*, 1.332). Although he had enjoyed the work entailed in his position, he hated the continual intrigues. He never wavered from his resolution not to return to the capital or to become involved once more in political disputes. He never wrote to or saw Robert Walpole again, though he did maintain a tenuous relationship with the latter's brother Horatio. His resignation was tragic in that it marked the end not only of a successful political alliance and a dedicated public career but also the termination of a long friendship.

Retirement: family, farm, and turnips Townshend retired to his Norfolk estate, where he devoted the remainder of his life to his friends, family, and farm, only occasionally serving as justice of the peace. This retirement rejuvenated him. He told a friend that he passed his time 'with great happyness and content' which ought to 'be our chief care whilst we are in this world' (BL, Add. MS 28052, fol. 153). His improvements in agriculture, especially his championing of the value of turnips, a crop whose use he promoted as an integral part of a successful rotation plan, earned him the nickname Turnip Townshend. He also experimented with some of the new methods he had seen in the United Provinces and in Hanover, where the soil resembled that of Norfolk. Instead, for example, of sowing his turnips with the broadcast method, he drilled and hoed them. On his lands he used the four-crop 'Norfolk rotation': turnips, barley or oats, clover or rye, and wheat. This method was especially valuable because farmers did not have to let the land lie fallow and could maintain stock over the winter. In addition, Townshend enclosed, reclaimed, and improved his land through his use of quantities of manure and marl, and fed his cattle and sheep turnips over the winter. His goal was to transform previously unusable acreage into permanent arable through the use of restorative crops. Long-term leases were offered as incentives to his tenants to improve the land. Specific clauses in contracts often required tenants to participate in the cultivation of turnips. He was also interested in the scientific elements of farming and experimented with the breeding of livestock. Townshend's innovations were immortalized by Alexander Pope, who described an individual who 'Ploughs, burns, manures, and toils from Sun to Sun' (A. Pope, *Imitations of Horace*, epistle II, ii).

Contemporaries differed in their assessment. While some regarded Townshend as tall and handsome, others saw him as rough and bucolic. Godfrey Kneller's portrait of about 1704 depicts him as tall, with an oval face, thick eyebrows, and a long nose. John Macky praised him as a 'Gentleman of Great Learning, attended with a sweet Disposition; a Lover of the Constitution of his Country; is beloved by every Body that knows him' (*Memoirs of the Secret Services*, 89). Lord Hervey, a partisan of Walpole known for his malicious pen, detested Townshend whom he called 'rash in his undertakings, violent in his proceedings, haughty in his carriage, brutal in his expressions, and cruel in his disposition; impatient of the least contradiction, and as slow to pardon as he was quick to resent' (Hervey, 1.108). This view was predictably echoed by Matthew Prior, who was indicted for his role in the Utrecht peace, and who described Townshend as 'brusque, arrogant, stubborn' (Eves, 330). William Coxe favoured the middle ground in his description of a man who, 'though impetuous and overbearing, was generous, highly disinterested, of unblemished integrity and unsullied honour' (Coxe, *Walpole*, 1.64). Townshend's 'sweetness of disposition' (*Private Correspondence of Sarah, Duchess of Marlborough*, 2.581) in fact glossed over his other faults and often endeared him to others.

Townshend was undoubtedly capable, determined, and hard-working, but in achieving his goals he sometimes appeared blunt, abrasive, stubborn, impatient, and overbearing. In contrast to many of his contemporaries whose venality was legendary he was scrupulously honest. He was generous to both friend and foe. He was also a passionate man who loved and hated quickly and rarely changed his mind once an opinion had been formed. The astute Lord Chesterfield pointed out that, though in appearance he was often rough and coarse, 'his nature was by no means so; for he was a kind husband to both his wives, a most indulgent father to all his children, and a benevolent master to his servants' (BL, Stowe MSS, Chesterfield characters, fol. 14).

Historians have often underrated Townshend's accomplishments in part because his rival Walpole outmanoeuvred and outlasted him. Townshend died at Raynham on 21 June 1738 and was buried there on 27 June.

Heir and offspring Townshend's eldest surviving son, **Charles Townshend**, third Viscount Townshend (1700–1764), politician and benefactor, was born on 11 July 1700 and baptized at St Martin-in-the-Fields on 15 July. After attending Eton College and King's College, Cambridge, where he was admitted in 1718, he was MP for Great Yarmouth between 1722 and 1723. In addition he held various offices, including lord of the bedchamber (1723–7), master of the jewel house (1730–39), lord lieutenant of Norfolk (1730–38), succeeding his father, and high steward of Norwich Cathedral (from 1738 until his death). On 24 May 1723 he took his seat in the House of Lords as Baron Townshend of Lynn, and on 29 May he married Etheldreda (*c*.1708–1788) [*see* Townshend, Etheldreda], the daughter of Edward Harrison, of Balls Park, Hertfordshire, a woman notorious for her wit and malice as much as for her promiscuity. They had five children, among them George *Townshend (1724–1807), an army officer and later fourth

viscount, and Charles *Townshend (1725–1767), a politician. Although Charles and his wife were both somewhat eccentric, they differed in many ways; the marriage was not happy and the couple formally separated in 1741. He had an affair with his maid and fathered three more children, for whom he provided. Contemporaries praised his wit and imagination as well as his intelligence. In 1751 he published his thoughts on trade in a pamphlet, *National Thoughts, Recommended to the Serious Attention of the Public*. In Townshend's view industry created trade, and trade wealth; drunkenness and idleness were responsible for the miseries of the poor. A decline in trade caused a decline in national greatness. Townshend opposed the export of cheap corn because he believed that it would undercut Britain's trading position. He corresponded extensively with the economist Josiah Tucker and established a prize for the best paper written on trade theory at the University of Cambridge. The prize, intended to stimulate debate on commercial matters, ultimately proved a fiasco and was withdrawn. His endowment of a charity school at Raynham to educate both boys and girls also illustrated his social concern. He died on 12 March 1764 at Raynham and was buried there on 20 March. The bulk of his estate went either by entail or settlement to his eldest son, Charles, or to his estranged wife, who died on 9 March 1788.

The second viscount had three more sons from his first marriage who reached maturity. The Hon. **Thomas Townshend** (1701–1780), politician, was born on 2 June 1701. He entered Eton College in 1718 and King's College, Cambridge, in 1720, graduating MA in 1727, and served as MP for Winchelsea from 1722 to 1727 and for Cambridge University between 1727 and 1774. During the early part of his political career he regularly attended parliament and spoke often on behalf of his constituents. A man of great charm, he acted as his father's secretary before serving as under-secretary of state (1724–30), teller of the exchequer (1727–80), and secretary to the duke of Devonshire, lord lieutenant of Ireland (1739–45). On 2 May 1730 he married Albinia (*d*. 1739), the daughter of John Selwyn, of Matson; the couple had three sons and two daughters before Albinia's death on 7 September 1739. Thomas died on 21 May 1780.

Thomas's younger brother the Hon. **William Townshend** (1702–1738), also a politician, was born on 9 June 1702 and sat as MP for Great Yarmouth from 1723 until 1738. In addition in 1729 he was appointed groom of the bedchamber by Frederick, prince of Wales, with whom he enjoyed a close friendship. On 29 May 1725 William married Henrietta (*d*. 1755), the daughter of Lord William Powlett; they had one son and two daughters. William also served as usher of the exchequer from 1730 until his death, several months before his father, on 29 January 1738. The second viscount's fourth son, the Hon. **Roger Townshend** (1708–1760), an army officer and politician, was born on 15 June 1708. He joined the army as a cavalry officer and served as governor of Great Yarmouth garrison (1744–5) and as an aide-de-camp to George II at the battle of Dettingen (1743). He was by then MP for Great Yarmouth, having been elected in 1737. In 1747 he transferred to represent Lord Cornwallis's pocket borough of Eye. In the following year he left the Commons, having taken up the position of receiver of customs, which he held until his death, on 7 August 1760. He was unmarried.

LINDA FREY and MARSHA FREY

Sources J. H. Plumb, *Sir Robert Walpole*, 2 vols. (1956–60) · W. S. Churchill, *Marlborough: his life and times*, 6 vols. (1933–8) · D. Coombs, *The conduct of the Dutch: British opinion and the Dutch alliance during the War of the Spanish Succession* (1958) · *Memoirs of the duke of Marlborough*, ed. W. Coxe, 3 vols. (1818–19) · W. Coxe, *Memoirs of the life and administration of Sir Robert Walpole, earl of Orford*, 3 vols. (1798) · *The letters and dispatches of John Churchill, first duke of Marlborough, from 1702 to 1712*, ed. G. Murray, 5 vols. (1845) · K. Feiling, *A history of the tory party, 1640–1714* (1965) · R. Geikie and I. S. Montgomery, *The Dutch barrier, 1705–1719* (1930) · L. Frey and M. Frey, *The treaties of the War of the Spanish Succession: an historical and critical dictionary* (1995) · J. T. Rosenheim, *The Townshends of Raynham: nobility in transition in Restoration and early Hanoverian England* (1989) · F. Salomon, *Geschichte des letzen Ministeriums Königin Annas von England (1710–1714) und der englischen Thronfolgefrage* (1894) · J. G. Stork-Penning, *Het grote werk* (1958) · D. B. Horn, *British diplomatic representatives, 1689–1789* (1932) · G. S. Holmes, *British politics in the age of Anne* (1967) · J. Black, *British foreign policy in the age of Walpole* (1985) · *The works of the late right reverend and learned Dr. Francis Hare*, 4 vols. (1746) · HoP, *Commons, 1715–54* · HoP, *Commons, 1754–90* · *Bishop Burnet's History of his own time*, another edn, 6 vols. (Edinburgh, 1753) · S. van Goslinga, *Mémoires relatifs à la Guerre de Succession de 1706–1709 et 1711* (1857) · *Memoirs of the secret services of John Macky*, ed. A. R. (1733) · D. B. Horn, *British diplomatic service, 1689–1789* (1961) · *Private correspondence of Sarah, duchess of Marlborough*, 2 vols. (1838) · C. E. Eves, *Matthew Prior: poet and diplomatist* (1939) · [J. Swift], *Some remarks on the barrier treaty between Her Majesty and the states-general*, 2nd edn (1712) · B. Williams, *The whig supremacy, 1714–1760* (1962) · J. Black, 'Fresh light on the fall of Townshend', *HJ*, 29 (1986), 41–64 · R. Hatton, *George I: elector and king* (1978) · J. F. Chance, *George I and the Northern War* (1909) · J. F. Chance, *The alliance of Hanover: a study of British foreign policy in the last years of George I* (1923) · H. T. Dickinson, *Walpole and the whig supremacy* (1973) · R. Browning, *The duke of Newcastle* (1975) · *The manuscripts of his grace the duke of Portland*, 10 vols., HMC, 29 (1891–1931), vol. 6 · *The letters of Philip Dormer Stanhope, fourth earl of Chesterfield*, ed. B. Dobrée, 6 vols. (1932) · GEC, *Peerage* · N. Riches, *The agricultural revolution in Norfolk* (1967) · H. W. Saunders, 'Estate management at Rainham in the years 1661–1686 and 1706', *Norfolk Archaeology*, 19 (1917), 39–66 · J. R. Raven, 'Viscount Townshend and the Cambridge prize for trade theory, 1754–1756', *HJ*, 28 (1985), 535–55 · N. Kent, 'On Norfolk turnips and fallowing', *Annals of Agriculture*, 22 (1794), 24–30 · J. Hervey, *Memoirs of the reign of George the Second*, ed. J. W. Croker, 2 vols. (1848) · G. Shelton, *Dean Tucker and eighteenth-century economic and political thought* (1981) · E. Sherson, *The lively Lady Townshend and her friends* (1926)

Archives BL, corresp., Add. MSS 63079, 63095, 63103 · BL, diplomatic corresp., Add. MSS 22205–22207 · BL, registers, corresp., and papers, Add. MSS 33273, 36795, 38498–38499; Egerton MSS 892–894 · Bodl. Oxf., diplomatic corresp. and papers; papers · Herts. ALS, letter-book and letters · NL Aus., corresp. and papers · Norfolk RO, corresp. · priv. coll., Townshend MSS · Raynham Hall, Norfolk, MSS · Yale U., Beinecke L., corresp. and papers | BL, letters to J. Dayrole, Add. MSS 15866–15867 · BL, letters to Lord Hardwicke, Add. MSS 35585–36138, *passim* · BL, corresp. with duke of Newcastle, Add. MSS 32686–32992, *passim* · BL, letters to Sir John Norris, Add. MSS 28153–28156 · BL, corresp. with James Stanhope, Add. MS 22510; Egerton MS 3124 · BL, corresp. with Horatio Walpole, Add. MSS 37635, 46856 · BL, corresp. with Charles Whitworth, etc., Add. MSS 37358–37389, *passim* · Bodl. Oxf., corresp. with Henry Boyle · Bodl. Oxf., letters to Lord North · Chewton House, Waldegrave MSS · CUL, letters to R. Walpole · Nationaal Archief, The Hague, Archief Anthonie Heinsius · priv. coll.,

corresp. with Lord Waldegrave · Suffolk RO, Bury St Edmunds, corresp. with duke of Grafton · U. Hull, Brynmor Jones L., corresp. with Sir Charles Hotham · U. Nott. L., Pelham MSS, corresp. with duke of Newcastle

Likenesses G. Kneller, oils, 1704?, NPG [*see illus.*] · oils, *c.*1715–1720 (after G. Kneller), NPG; version, Audley End House, Essex · studio of G. Kneller, oils (as young man), NPG · J. Simon, mezzotint (after G. Kneller), BM, NPG

Townshend, Charles, third Viscount Townshend (1700–1764). *See under* Townshend, Charles, second Viscount Townshend (1674–1738).

Townshend, Charles (1725–1767), politician, was born on 27 August 1725, the second of the four sons and one daughter of Charles *Townshend, third Viscount Townshend (1700–1764) [*see under* Townshend, Charles, second Viscount Townshend], politician, and his wife, Etheldreda *Townshend (*c.*1708–1788), the daughter of Edward Harrison of Balls Park, Hertfordshire, and his wife, Frances Bray. It was not a stable family background, for his parents were as promiscuous sexually as he was to be politically, and they separated in 1741. Charles, then aged fifteen, sided with his father and saw little of his mother for the next decade. As if this were not trauma enough, he was perpetually dogged by ill health—'my crazy constitution'; modern diagnosis has identified epilepsy as his chief ailment. He was intended by his father for the bar, whereas his elder brother, George *Townshend, later fourth Viscount and first Marquess Townshend, was set on a military career. In 1742 Charles both entered at Lincoln's Inn and went to Clare College, Cambridge. After three years in Cambridge he spent a year at Leiden University, the leading centre for the study of Roman law, and then returned for a year in residence at Lincoln's Inn; he was called to the bar in 1747. His relationship with his bullying and parsimonious father was an unhappy one. A letter written when he was twenty shows Charles being driven to defend his weekly game of real tennis as 'more an exercise necessary for my health than as a diversion' (Namier and Brooke, 6), having given up cricket because his father deemed it a waste of time and money. His father was constantly complaining of what Charles cost him, and Charles early acquired the habit of making assurances he would not fulfil.

Political apprenticeship, 1747–1760 At the general election of 1747 Townshend was returned to parliament for Great Yarmouth, a borough where his family had considerable influence. He first had to assure his father that he would not be diverted from a legal career, a promise from which he was released within a year on grounds of ill health. The political stage beckoned. The Townshend family was at the heart of the whig aristocratic oligarchy, and his paternal grandmother a half-sister of the then prime minister, Henry Pelham, and his brother the duke of Newcastle, who was wont to refer to Charles Townshend as his nephew. In 1748 Lord Townshend asked Newcastle to give Townshend a seat on the Board of Admiralty. That was aiming too high for a first ministerial post, and he had to settle for a seat at the Board of Trade and Plantations in

Charles Townshend (1725–1767), by Sir Joshua Reynolds, 1765–7

1749. Here he soon won the favour of Lord Halifax, president of the board, and industriously acquired a knowledge of commercial and colonial matters. His spell at the Board of Trade was the time when he formulated the opinions on America he sought to enact as chancellor of the exchequer. It was Townshend who in 1753 drafted instructions to the governor of New York directing that colony's assembly to make permanent financial provision for official salaries. Here was the germ of the idea behind his revenue duties of 1767, the financial independence from assemblies of colonial administrators and judges, as the key to the maintenance of British control. That was not an idea unique to Townshend, but one he always kept in mind.

As yet Townshend made no mark in parliament. The diarist Horace Walpole later recalled that 'Townshend's speeches for four or five years gave little indication of his amazing parts. They were studied, pedantic' (*Last Journals of Horace Walpole*, 1.82), usually on departmental business. Not until 1753 did Townshend shine in debate, opposing the Marriage Act by championing from his own experience the cause of children against parents. His long and witty speech led Walpole to take note of the:

young man of unbounded ambition, of exceeding application, and, as it now appeared, of abilities capable of satisfying that ambition, and of not wanting that application … His figure was tall and advantageous, his action vehement, his voice loud, his laugh louder.   (Walpole, *Memoirs of … George II*, 1.340–41)

At the ministerial reshuffle of 1754, when Newcastle succeeded his deceased brother as prime minister, Townshend sought a seat on the Treasury board, again aiming a rung too high, and had to settle for one at the Admiralty board. Then came the turning point of his life in a political as well as personal sense—his marriage on 18 September 1755 to Lady Caroline Scott, styled Lady Dalkeith (1717–1794) [see Townshend, Caroline, *suo jure* Baroness Greenwich], the eldest daughter of the late John *Campbell, second duke of Argyll and first duke of Greenwich (1680–1743), and his wife, Jane Warburton. She was the widow of Francis Scott, styled earl of Dalkeith (1721–1750), politician, and the mother of Henry *Scott, third duke of Buccleuch. Apart from considerable expectations, she was already a wealthy woman, possessing a net income of £3000 besides a personal estate of £46,000, out of which she proposed to settle £30,000 on Townshend. The couple had three children: two sons, Charles and William, who both died as unmarried army officers, and a daughter, Anne, twice married. It was the political import of the marriage that caught Horace Walpole's attention: 'Charles Townshend marries the great Dowager Dalkeith. His parts and presumption are prodigious. He wanted nothing but independence to let him loose' (*Letters of Horace Walpole*, 3.321). For Townshend financial security now begat political volatility.

Within a month of his marriage Townshend, hitherto an undoubted ministerial supporter, was rated as 'doubtful' by Newcastle. His new independence coincided with unease over recent cabinet decisions, and not even an offer by the duke of a place on the Treasury board could cement his allegiance. Townshend shared the concern of Pitt about Newcastle's European-orientated policy, contrasting it with the apparent neglect of America. Pitt's dismissal from office was soon followed by his own in the Christmas recess. When parliament reassembled in early 1756 Townshend adopted the American viewpoint, denouncing the defenceless state of the colonies. His displays of verbal pyrotechnics, replete with epigrams and satire, were much admired, and that, according to Walpole's reflections on the session, was their sole purpose: 'Neither caring whether himself or others were in the right, [he] only spoke to show how well he could adorn a bad cause, or demolish a good one' (Walpole, *Memoirs of … George II*, 2.147).

That Townshend, despite his evident talents, was not taken seriously meant that he could be left out of the political reckoning. When Pitt formed a new ministry after the fall of Newcastle in the autumn of 1756, he was the conspicuous exception in not being given active political employment, and was fobbed off with the court post of treasurer of the chamber. Lord Waldegrave, a royal confidant, noted that 'Pitt did not choose to advance a young man to a ministerial office, whose abilities were of the same kind, and so nearly equal to his own' (*Memoirs and Speeches*, 186). Since the Townshend family's hold on Yarmouth had become uncertain, Townshend's re-election on receiving office was for the Admiralty-controlled borough of Saltash. Antipathy to Pitt naturally ensued, as Waldegrave noted: 'Charles Townshend hated Pitt, and disliked his employment which was merely a sinecure' (ibid., 195). During the political manoeuvres of 1757 that were designed to exclude Pitt from office, Townshend was talked of as a possible secretary at war, but he deemed it unwise to join in such an unpopular scheme, and so retained his court office throughout the Pitt–Newcastle coalition ministry that won the Seven Years' War. He became reconciled to Newcastle by 1758, when the duke became godfather to his first son. The next year a possible appointment arose for Townshend as chancellor of the exchequer in a ministerial reshuffle. Newcastle commented to his crony Lord Hardwicke on 31 August 1759: 'if Charles Townshend had not such a character, I would make him Chancellor of the Exchequer at once, but there is no depending upon him, and his character will not go down in the City nor anywhere else' (Namier and Brooke, 59). The former lord chancellor agreed: 'That office should be filled by somebody who may in a particular manner be depended upon, of some gravity, known veracity, whose word may be taken and relied on' (ibid.). No changes of office took place in 1759, and Townshend remained becalmed in the political doldrums until the death of George II in 1760.

The shuttlecock of politics, 1760–1766 Townshend meanwhile had acquired some degree of favour at the court of the prince of Wales, and, following the latter's accession as George III, the new king's favourite, Lord Bute, included him as one of three stipulated nominations for office. Townshend 'had sworn allegiance to him, *for a time*', so he said (*Political Journal of … Dodington*, 414). He accordingly became secretary at war in March 1761, and at the king's behest was given the safe Treasury borough of Harwich. But, before the new parliament met in November, Townshend had taken umbrage at George Grenville's being appointed leader of the House of Commons instead of himself, after the resignation of Pitt in the previous month. He annoyed Bute and the king by implicit criticisms of ministerial policy, notably by warm support for continuing British participation in the German campaign, a strategy favoured by Pitt rather than Bute. Townshend, when introducing the army estimates on 9 December, even commended 'Mr Pitt's divine plan' (Walpole, *Memoirs of … George III*, 1.79). He then fell into line, and during the first half of 1762 maintained a low political profile, devoting himself to the work of the war office, a busy department. But by midsummer he was quarrelling with Bute over army appointments, and threatening resignation, a step the king would have welcomed, as he wrote to Bute on 15 July:

> I fancy though that he will think bullying not the way to get anything but the loss of his employment. Besides his character is so very bad that I believe nothing would

strengthen the opinion of the present government in the eyes of the public so much as that vermin being against it. (*Letters … to Lord Bute*, 120)

Townshend did not resign, and by October, when Grenville had been replaced by Henry Fox to carry the peace terms through parliament, George III was coupling Townshend and Fox as the two men to accomplish that task, but at the same time he denounced as absurd an idea of rewarding him with Grenville's post as secretary of state. Townshend himself for a while aspired to become president of the Board of Trade, but in the end he chose to retain the war office. He was included in ministerial consultations on the peace terms, but simultaneously was assuring Newcastle, now in opposition, that he would not support Fox in parliament, and he certainly thought that Britain had not obtained enough concessions. Townshend at this time justified his behaviour as that of an independent man, without political connections, judging policies on their merits:

> It is my firm resolution to act the part of a man of business and a man of honour; to be decided by things and not men; to have no party; to follow no leader; and to be governed absolutely by my own judgement. (Namier and Brooke, 77)

That he could, as he did in this reflection on 10 November, regard his behaviour as consistent was remarkable self-deception. A less complimentary opinion was penned on 19 October by Richard Rigby, reporting events to the peace envoy in Paris, the duke of Bedford: 'Charles Townshend, that splendid shuttlecock, veers about with all these different gales. He laughs at the ministry at night and assures them in the morning that he is entirely theirs' (ibid., 75).

The next twist in Townshend's career was his sudden resignation from the war office on 8 December 1762, the day before the great House of Commons debate on the peace. He then confounded expectations by defending the terms of the peace in a speech highly rated by friend and foe. The explanation of this double somersault was that he had been afraid of a direct confrontation with Pitt. That fear vanished when Pitt left the house immediately after his own speech, when Townshend made what cynics thought was the second of two alternative speeches he had prepared. Townshend, being out of office, was now courted by Newcastle, but in vain, for the ministry perceived he was the opposition's last parliamentary hope—Pitt having disavowed any alliance with the duke. Early in 1763 Townshend accepted Bute's offer to be president of the Board of Trade, a post he desired through his concern over growing colonial disregard of British authority. His brief tenure of the post, from mid-February to early April, was notable for the first specific proposal of a colonial tax, to meet the promises made on 4 March by the new secretary at war, that America would in future pay its own army costs. On 18 March Townshend moved that this money should be raised by converting into a revenue duty of 2*d.* the existing 1733 prohibitory duty of 6*d.* a gallon on foreign molasses, a sugar product used to make rum. That would allow, he said, legal importation into North America of a commodity notoriously being smuggled. The ensuing legislation, regarded with dismay as premature by

George III and Bute, was killed by a procedural device on 30 March.

Townshend's spell as president of the Board of Trade was cut short by a change of ministry consequent on Bute's decision to resign. The king's intention was that Townshend would be promoted to the Admiralty, a cabinet post vacated by Grenville's elevation to the Treasury. The motives for this change were twofold: the danger of leaving the uncontrollable Townshend in such a sensitive post when American issues would be in the forefront of attention; and a desire to provide for Lord Shelburne, a protégé of Bute but too young for a cabinet post. Townshend, ignorant of the overall plan, was offered the Admiralty on 7 April, and stated his wish to remain at the Board of Trade. On 14 April the king personally persuaded him into accepting the Admiralty: as part of the bargain George III agreed to fulfil a promise of Lord Bute that Lady Dalkeith would be given her father's lapsed British peerage title of Greenwich, with reversion to her male heirs by Townshend. The next day, however, Townshend demanded of the king a seat at the Admiralty board for a friend, Peter Burrell, only to be told that he was too late and to be reminded that he had previously accepted the Admiralty without any such condition. Townshend obstinately refused to give way, and found himself out of the ministry, for Shelburne had already been appointed to the Board of Trade.

For two years Townshend was out of office, but never out of consideration for it. Pitt put him down for secretary of state in his ministerial plan of August 1763, a gesture for which Townshend was long grateful. He was thought of for, but not offered, the Admiralty in September, when his brother George reported to Prime Minister Grenville that Charles seemed determined to continue in opposition. George Townshend, after an active military career, had now entered politics himself, as a courtier supporting the successive ministries of Grenville, Rockingham, and Chatham in the post of lieutenant-general of the ordnance. His political estrangement from Charles continued until 1765. By the autumn of 1763 Charles Townshend was involved in opposition consultations, and spoke frequently against government in debates on the first Wilkes case of general warrants. He was regarded by Newcastle as his colonial expert, but missed the American debates of 1764 for a variety of reasons, including his father's death on 12 March. By the end of the session, dismayed by Pitt's absence from parliament, Townshend was preparing to desert Newcastle. During the recess of 1764 he both wrote opposition propaganda and sounded out Grenville about joining his ministry. After parliament reassembled in 1765 Townshend began to speak for the government, most famously in support of Grenville's American Stamp Bill on 6 February, when the Connecticut agent Jasper Mauduit ascribed to him this peroration:

> And now will these Americans, children planted by our care, nourished up by our indulgence until they are grown to a degree of strength and opulence, and protected by our arms, will they grudge to contribute their mite to relieve us from

the heavy weight of that burden which we lie under? (Namier and Brooke, 129)

On 3 March Townshend had a private interview with Grenville at the house of his brother George, now Lord Townshend, and his public transfer of allegiance was demonstrated by a speech on the Regency Bill on 12 May. Townshend became paymaster-general on 24 May, at a time when George III was already seeking to rid himself of the Grenville ministry. Simultaneously he was being listed for ministerial office in an incoming administration to be formed by Newcastle's friends under Lord Rockingham. In early July he was pressed to become chancellor of the exchequer in that ministry, even by George III himself, but chose to retain the pay office and declined to attend cabinet. He failed to support the ministerial repeal of the Stamp Act in debate.

Chancellor of the exchequer: India and America Townshend's hour came when Pitt was called upon to form a ministry in July 1766. He named the duke of Grafton to the Treasury, and insisted that Townshend should be his chancellor of the exchequer. Townshend was reluctant to exchange his lucrative post at the pay office, worth £7000, for one involving much drudgery and with a salary of only £2500, but was bullied into acceptance by Pitt. Although he did succeed in raising his office to cabinet rank, Pitt, now to become earl of Chatham, retained Henry Conway as leader of the Commons, as he had been under Rockingham, since he was a much more respected figure than Townshend. But as debaters there was no comparison between them. The great Irish parliamentarian Henry Flood opined after hearing a debate on 25 November 1766 that there was 'no one person near Townshend. He is the orator; the rest are speakers' (*Correspondence of William Pitt*, 3.144n).

Illness prevented Chatham giving a lead to his administration, a situation of which the irrepressible, irresponsible Townshend took full advantage, when the ministry faced problems in India and America. The recent acquisition of Bengal by the East India Company raised the linked questions of ownership of that territory and allocation of the anticipated revenue of £2 million. The view of Chatham was that the crown possessed the sovereign authority, and should therefore claim the lion's share of the revenue. But Townshend and Conway, his chief Commons spokesmen, both championed the rights of the company, and Chatham's prolonged ill health early in 1767 allowed them to thwart his policy in a divided cabinet. On 4 March Chatham was driven to offer Townshend's post to Lord North, whose refusal only strengthened Townshend's hand. Even the revelation that Townshend had a pecuniary motive did not destroy his position. By the spring it was known that the chancellor of the exchequer had been successfully speculating in East India stock, and with government money too, left temporarily in his hands from the pay office. Walpole wrote on 19 March that the secret was out:

> Charles Townshend's tergivisations appear to have been the result of private jobbing. He had dealt largely in India stock, cried up the Company's right to raise that stock, has sold out

most advantageously, and now cries it down. What! and can a Chancellor of the Exchequer stand such an aspersion? Oh, my dear Sir, his character cannot be lowered. (*Letters of Horace Walpole*, 7.97)

Having made over £7000 for himself Townshend was now concerned to obtain good terms for the state. This he achieved by avoiding controversy over legal rights and instead pragmatically negotiating with the company an annual payment of £400,000. The ministry coerced the company by legislation to limit its dividend, and a debate over the measure on 8 May was the occasion for Townshend's famous 'champagne speech'. Contemporaries differed on how far he was drunk and his speech unpremeditated. 'It lasted an hour', Walpole wrote, 'with torrents of wit, ridicule, vanity, lies, and beautiful language'. Townshend hit targets all round the political spectrum, including the crown:

> Government, he said, must not continue to be what he himself was always called, a weathercock. Nobody but he could have made that speech, and nobody but he would have made [it], if they could. It was at once a proof that his abilities were superior to those of all men, and his judgement below that of any man. It showed him capable of being, and unfit to be, First Minister. (ibid., 7.105–6)

America was simultaneously under consideration together with India, and it is for his taxation of the colonies that Townshend is above all remembered by posterity. At the time much ministerial attention was also paid to coercion of New York for its defiance of the 1765 Mutiny Act, and it was Townshend's suggestion of preventing that colony's assembly from enacting any legislation until it was willing to pay army costs that was adopted by the cabinet. That was the most moderate of three measures under consideration, adopted in preference to coercive billeting and direct taxation, and it strengthened Townshend's repeated claim to be a friend of America. His taxation plan might seem to invalidate that contention, but longstanding historical myths have clouded the picture. The principle of colonial taxation was always accepted by the Chatham ministry. That Townshend was premature in his announcement, and personally involved in the detailed enactment, has led to his being given full responsibility for the 'Townshend duties'. His personal contribution was not the imposition of American taxation as such, but alteration of the aim from the initial purpose of paying for the army there to the scheme he had suggested in 1753, and again in 1754, of freeing colonial government from financial dependence on the assemblies. The mode of taxation he adopted was the imposition of colonial import duties, thereby exploiting the supposed American distinction of internal and external taxes. After Chatham's failure to replace him on 4 March, Townshend was able to impose his views on the cabinet. It would seem that no contemporary perceived that, since government in America was already financed by the colonial assemblies, Townshend's plan would not save the British taxpayer any money. The eventual targets for his duties were British china, glass, and paper, and, more famously, tea, a duty of 3*d.* a pound calculated to bring in half the estimated £40,000 revenue. That amount was small, derided by

Grenville in opposition, but intended by Townshend to be only a beginning. There was no connection, as was once thought then and later, with a ministerial defeat of 27 February on the land tax that cost the administration £500,000 in revenue. That deficit was made up, not by the levy on the East India Company, but by an assiduous scrutiny by Townshend of government departments that uncovered numerous odd sums of money.

The middle of 1767 saw Townshend in the ascendant, carrying his measures concerning America and India, and being a success as chancellor of the exchequer. Personal matters also went well for him. The inheritance by his wife in April of a further income of £4000 per annum from her mother enabled him to boast to Grafton of his complete financial independence. He capitalized, too, on his political success and seeming indispensability by obtaining at last for his wife on 19 August the long-coveted British peerage title of Greenwich held by her father, albeit as baroness not duchess: since her two sons predeceased her, the title expired on her death. And it was largely through his influence that, in the same month, his brother Lord Townshend was appointed lord lieutenant of Ireland. And then suddenly he died, on 4 September 1767, at Sudbrook, Surrey, of a 'putrid fever', aged forty-two. 'That first eloquence of the world is dumb', wrote Walpole, conveying the sense of shock and loss to the political scene (*Letters of Horace Walpole*, 7.133).

Conclusion Walpole was well aware that Townshend had dazzled to deceive, and wrote a considered judgement to Conway:

> As a man of incomparable parts, and most entertaining to a spectator, I regret his death. His good humour prevented one from hating him, and his levity from loving him; but in a political light I own I cannot look upon it as a misfortune. (*Letters of Horace Walpole*, 7.129)

Throughout his life men saw through Townshend for what he was, brilliant but unreliable. If posterity remembers him for the taxation that set in train the sequence of events that culminated in the American War of Independence, contemporaries were both fascinated and appalled by his behaviour. While perhaps matching Pitt in oratory, he lacked the other's political courage, for all his boasts of independence. To his parliamentary talent he added administrative ability, when he put his mind to it. Yet his capricious character made him his own worst enemy, a phrase used of him by Henry Fox in 1763. To be talked about was his chief aim in life, and Edmund Burke gave him a belated obituary notice which he would have liked, in his famous speech of 19 April 1774 on American taxation, when he declared that Townshend had been 'the delight and ornament of this House, and the charm of every private society which he honoured with his presence' (Simmons and Thomas, 4.222).

PETER D. G. THOMAS

Sources L. Namier and J. Brooke, *Charles Townshend* (1964) · C. P. Forster, *The uncontrolled chancellor: Charles Townshend and his American policy* (1978) · P. D. G. Thomas, *British politics and the Stamp Act crisis: the first phase of the American revolution, 1763–1767* (1975) · *The memoirs and speeches of James, 2nd Earl Waldegrave, 1742–1763*, ed. J. C. D. Clark (1988) · *The political journal of George Bubb Dodington*, ed.

J. Carswell and L. A. Dralle (1965) • H. Walpole, *Memoirs of the reign of King George the Third*, ed. G. F. R. Barker, 4 vols. (1894) • *The letters of Horace Walpole, fourth earl of Orford*, ed. P. Toynbee, 16 vols. (1903–5); suppl., 3 vols. (1918–25) • H. Walpole, *Memoirs of the reign of King George the Second*, ed. Lord Holland, 2nd edn, 3 vols. (1847) • *The last journals of Horace Walpole*, ed. Dr Doran, rev. A. F. Steuart, 2 vols. (1910) • *Letters from George III to Lord Bute, 1756–1766*, ed. R. Sedgwick (1939) • *Correspondence of William Pitt, earl of Chatham*, ed. W. S. Taylor and J. H. Pringle, 4 vols. (1838–40) • R. C. Simmons and P. D. G. Thomas, eds., *Proceedings and debates of the British parliaments respecting North America, 1754–1783*, 6 vols. (1982–7) • GEC, *Peerage* • HoP, *Commons*

Archives BL, corresp., Add. MS 63079 • Bodl. Oxf., papers • Bodl. Oxf., corresp. • NRA Scotland, corresp. • NRA, priv. coll., corresp. and papers • Raynham Hall, Norfolk • U. Mich., Clements L., political and family papers, corresp. | BL, corresp. with Lord Loudoun, Add. MSS 44068–44078 • BL, corresp. with duke of Newcastle, Add. MSS 32720–33071 • Bodl. Oxf., letters to Lord Townshend • CKS, corresp. with Sir J. Amherst • Suffolk RO, Bury St Edmunds, letters to duke of Grafton

Likenesses oils, *c*.1750, Buccleuch estates, Selkirk • J. Reynolds, oils, 1765–7, priv. coll. [*see illus.*] • J. Dixon, mezzotint, pubd 1770 (after J. Reynolds), BM, NPG • attrib. I. Gossett, wax medallion, NPG • Miller, line engraving (after unknown artist), NPG

Townshend, Charles, first Baron Bayning (1728–1810), politician, born on 27 August 1728 in Twickenham, Middlesex, was the only son of the Hon. William *Townshend (1702–1738) [*see under* Townshend, Charles, second Viscount Townshend], politician, and his wife, Henrietta (*d*. 1755), the daughter of Lord William Paulet and his second wife, Anne Egerton. Both his parents came from powerful whig families, for his father was the third surviving son of Charles *Townshend, second Viscount Townshend (1674–1738), and his mother was the granddaughter of Charles *Paulet, first duke of Bolton (1630/31–1699). He was educated at Eton College (1742–5) and Clare College, Cambridge, and graduated MA in 1749. He was appointed secretary to the British embassy at Madrid on 17 September 1751, and remained in Spain for four years. Henceforth he became known as 'Spanish Charles', in contradistinction to his brilliant namesake and cousin, the politician Charles *Townshend (1725–1767).

Townshend left Madrid in January 1755 following his mother's death and returned to England. At the general election of 1756 he succeeded his cousin Charles as member for Great Yarmouth, which his father had previously represented from 1723 to 1738. He remained the city's MP until 1784. He acted generally with the Rockingham whigs, but was not prominent as a speaker, and is reported to have spoken on only three occasions in the 1768–74 parliament. He was present at the great gathering of whigs held at Claremont, Newcastle's house at Esher, on 30 June 1765, and was one of the minority there who advised against taking office without Pitt. When, however, Rockingham became premier, Townshend was made a lord of the Admiralty, on 16 July 1765. In February 1770 he exchanged this office for a commissionership of the Treasury under North, with whom he became closely associated. He was sworn of the privy council on 20 June 1777 and on 17 September was appointed joint vice-treasurer of Ireland. On 21 August 1777 he married his cousin Annabella Smith (*d*. 1825), the daughter of the Revd Richard Smith and his wife, Annabella, who was a granddaughter of Lord William Paulet. They had three sons and five daughters.

In the Fox–North coalition ministry of 1783 Townshend held the office of treasurer of the navy. Faced with an opposition of independents and dissenters who were united against the coalition, he declined to stand for re-election at Great Yarmouth at the 1784 general election. He was returned on the family interest in 1790 and finally retired from parliament in 1796. As one of the Portland whigs, he gave his support to Pitt in 1794, and was created a peer on 20 October 1797, with the title of Baron Bayning of Foxley. In 1807 he was elected high steward of Yarmouth in succession to his uncle George Townshend, first Marquess Townshend.

Townshend died after a few hours' illness on 19 May 1810, aged eighty-one. His widow, who became heir of her brother Powlett Smith-Powlett of Sombourne, Hampshire, died at Chislehurst on 3 January 1825. Of their eight children, the two surviving sons, Charles Frederick Powlett Townshend (1785–1823) and Henry Powlett (1797–1866), who assumed by royal licence the name of his maternal great-grandfather, William Powlett, both died without heirs, and on the death of the younger in 1866 the peerage became extinct.

G. LE G. NORGATE, *rev.* IAN K. R. ARCHER

Sources L. Namier, 'Townshend, Charles', HoP, *Commons* • GEC, *Peerage*, new edn • Venn, *Alum. Cant.* • A. B. Beaven, 'Charles Townshend, MP for Yarmouth, 1756–1761', *N&Q*, 10th ser., 11 (1909), 282–3 • B. Burke, *A genealogical history of the dormant, abeyant, forfeited and extinct peerages of the British empire*, new edn (1883) • *GM*, 1st ser., 80 (1810), 594 • *GM*, 4th ser., 1 (1866), 405–6 • H. Walpole, *Memoirs of the reign of King George the Third*, ed. G. F. R. Barker, 4 vols. (1894) • H. Walpole, *Journal of the reign of King George the Third*, ed. Dr Doran, 2 vols. (1859) • G. Thomas, earl of Albemarle [G. T. Keppel], *Memoirs of the marquis of Rockingham and his contemporaries*, 2 vols. (1852) • N. W. Wraxall, *Historical memoirs of his own time*, new edn, 4 vols. (1836) • N. W. Wraxall, *Posthumous memoirs of his own time*, 2nd edn, 3 vols. (1836) • D. B. Horn, ed., *British diplomatic representatives, 1689–1789*, CS, 3rd ser., 46 (1932), 100, 133–4

Archives BL, diplomatic dispatches, etc., Add. MS 36122, Stowe MS 296 • Gateshead Central Library, Gateshead • Norfolk RO, corresp. and papers • Northumbd RO, Newcastle upon Tyne, letters • Wilts. & Swindon RO, letters | BL, corresp. with duke of Newcastle, Add. MSS 32735–32990 • Norfolk RO, letters to John Reynolds

Likenesses W. C. Edwards, line engraving (after D. Gardner), BM

Townshend, Charles Fox (1795–1817), founder of the Eton Society, born at Balls Park, Hertfordshire, on 28 June 1795, was the eldest son of John Townshend (1757–1833), member of parliament successively for Cambridge University, Westminster, and Knaresborough, and his wife, Georgiana Anne, daughter of William Poyntz of Midgham, Berkshire. George Townshend, second marquess, was his uncle, and John, the fourth marquess, was his younger brother. Charles James Fox was his godfather. Townshend was educated at Eton College (1807–12) under John Keate.

In 1811 Townshend founded the Eton Society, which was both a debating society and a social club. Its members were originally known as the Literati, but afterwards the society was called 'Pop', from *popina*, 'eating-house', because its meetings were held in a room over the shop of Mrs Hatton, a confectioner. In 1846 this house was pulled down and the club removed to the Christopher, one of the inns of court. Keate approved the objects of the society, and the translation of *docti sumus*, 'I belong to the Literati', became one of his stock jokes (Lyte, 403). The original number of members was twenty; it increased to thirty, but by 1816 had sunk to fourteen, and had it not been for the protest of the founder the society would probably have become extinct. Townshend's remonstrations had their effect, however, and the membership immediately recovered. He saw the society as more than merely a school club and in its early years Pop included many distinguished orators; some who had left the school continued to belong—when W. E. Gladstone was a member in the 1820s a number of MPs were among the membership. Remarkable for having been run successfully by boys for more than a century, the Eton Society later assumed the character of a social oligarchy within the school rather than a debating society. Its founder proceeded to St John's College, Cambridge, and graduated MA in 1816. He died unmarried in Grosvenor Place, London, on 2 April 1817, while a candidate for the representation in parliament of Cambridge University. Townshend's early death, caused by consumption, was a severe blow to his father, who, encouraged by his son's achievements at Eton, had grandiose ambitions for his becoming leader of the whig party.

THOMAS SECCOMBE, rev. M. C. CURTHOYS

Sources Venn, *Alum. Cant.* · H. C. Maxwell Lyte, *A history of Eton College, 1440–1910*, 4th edn (1911) · T. Card, *Eton renewed: a history from 1860 to the present day* (1994) · *Commons, 1790–1820*, vol. 408 · Eton Society Membership List, BL, Add. MS 44717, f.105
Likenesses F. Chantrey, marble monument, St John Cam. · bust, Eton · stipple, BM

Townshend, Sir Charles Vere Ferrers (1861–1924), army officer, was born on 21 February 1861 at Great Union Street, Southwark, the eldest son of Charles Thornton Townshend (1840–1889), a railway clerk, and his first wife, Louisa (d. 1878), daughter of John Graham of Melbourne, Australia. Charles Thornton Townshend was the great-grandson of the first Marquess Townshend, and from 1889 until 1916 his son was heir presumptive to the peerage. Townshend was educated at Cranleigh School, Kent, and the Royal Naval College at Dartmouth.

Townshend was commissioned a lieutenant in the Royal Marine light infantry in February 1881. He was sent to Suakin with a battalion of marines in 1884 and was shortly afterwards attached to Sir Herbert Stewart's column when it advanced up the Nile valley to relieve General Gordon, besieged in Khartoum. Townshend fought at the battles at Abu Klea (17 January 1885) and Gubat (19 January 1885). Following the fall of Khartoum he participated in the retreat across the Bayuda Desert. He was later mentioned in dispatches and on 15 January 1886 transferred to the Indian Staff Corps. He was briefly posted to the 7th Madras infantry, but soon after exchanged into the 3rd Sikh infantry and finally into the Central India horse. In 1891 he was selected for service in the Himalayas and was

sent to Gilgit where he assumed command of the 1st (or Raga Pertab) battalion of the imperial Kashmir contingent. During the 1891 Nunza-Nagar expedition he was mentioned in dispatches after taking a prominent part in the capture of the hill forts at Nilt and Hunza, and early in 1892 he was promoted captain.

After briefly serving as military governor of Hunza Townshend returned to his regiment late in 1892. In 1893 he was sent to the Himalayas to command Fort Gupis, located midway between Gilgit and Chitral. A series of murders committed by Sher Afzul, who had usurped the throne of Chitral, and his subsequent disaffection, led to the dispatch of Sir George Scott Robertson, the local political agent, to Chitral, escorted by a detachment of troops led by Townshend from Gupis early in 1895. This small force reached Chitral, but was then besieged in the fortified palace for a period of 46 days (4 March–20 April). Throughout the siege Townshend commanded the garrison and had to surmount difficulties caused by shortages of food, the presence of the political agent, and the fact his own men proved apathetic in the face of enterprising tribal attacks. In April 1895 the fort was relieved by a force of imperial service troops from Kashmir. Townshend received the thanks of government and a brevet majority, and, despite his youth, he was created CB.

Townshend enjoyed celebrity status on his return to England. Hoping to advance his career by further active service, he transferred, with little difficulty, to the Egyptian army. In February 1896 he arrived in Cairo, where he assumed command of the 12th Sudanese battalion. A few weeks later his unit formed part of the Kitchener expedition which had set out to reconquer the Sudan. He participated in the recovery of Dongola province in 1896 and obtained a mention in dispatches and a brevet lieutenant-colonelcy. Throughout 1897 he served in the Nile valley, and in the following year he commanded his battalion during the battle of the Atbara and the battle of Omdurman and was rewarded a DSO for his services. On 22 November 1898 he married Alice Ida (d. 1965), daughter of Count Louis Cahen d'Anvers; they had one daughter, Audrey.

Townshend resigned from the Egyptian army and returned to India in 1899 to take up a staff appointment, but following the outbreak of the Second South African War he applied to be sent to South Africa. In March 1900 he was appointed assistant adjutant-general on the staff of the military governor of the Orange Free State at Bloemfontein. He disliked this appointment, however, and returned to England in September 1900 where he was reinstated in the British army with the rank of major in the Royal Fusiliers. Townshend's military career was marred by his arrogance, egotism, ambition, and intense dislike of routine soldiering, which did not endear him to his fellow officers. Until March 1903 Townshend remained in England; he then exchanged into the battalion of his regiment serving in India. In January 1904 he was promoted colonel and in December he returned to England. During 1905 he briefly acted as military attaché in Paris, but his restlessness prompted him to transfer to the

Shropshire light infantry in March 1906, and again he returned to India. In August 1907 he was appointed assistant adjutant-general of the 9th division and in February 1908 he was promoted substantive colonel. A year later Townshend was appointed commander of the Orange River Colony in South Africa, with the rank of brigadier-general. Following promotion to major-general in July 1911 he returned to England where he was appointed general officer commanding (GOC), home counties, and then GOC, East Anglian division of the Territorial Force. In June 1913 he once again went to India and briefly commanded the Jhansi brigade before taking over the Rawalpindi brigade.

Townshend was at Rawalpindi when the First World War broke out and made frequent attempts to obtain a command at the front. In April 1915 he was appointed GOC of the 6th Indian division, one of two divisions deployed in Mesopotamia under the command of Sir John Nixon. During the ensuing campaign the brunt of the fighting was borne by Townshend's division. His first task was to drive the Turks northwards from Kurna on the River Tigris, despite severe flooding in the area. Townshend organized a fleet of barges, known locally as *bellums*, on which two brigades were embarked, supported by three naval sloops and other assorted craft. On 31 May he delivered a bold frontal attack—dubbed Townshend's regatta—employing this improvised river transport and the action achieved complete success. The defenders were pursued northwards by Townshend and a handful of men, embarked on river craft, until he reached Amara (90 miles up river) where the bulk of the Turkish troops surrendered.

Townshend fell ill shortly afterwards and was sent to India to recover. In September he resumed command of his division which was now deployed along the Tigris in front of an entrenched Turkish force occupying positions astride the river at Kut-al-Amara (150 miles from Amara). Despite growing transport and supply difficulties, a further advance on Baghdad was ordered by Sir John Nixon. On 27 September Townshend attacked the Turkish positions astride the river, skilfully employing a night advance and a turning movement to defeat the enemy. On 29 September Kut was captured, although this victory could not be followed up due to weakness and fatigue among the British forces. Retreating in good order, the Turks took up a new fortified position at Ctesiphon and thus covered Baghdad. Townshend was compelled to halt at 'Aziziyyah, 60 miles beyond Kut, owing to worsening transport problems caused by the shallowness of the Tigris.

Despite his objections Townshend was ordered to resume the advance on Baghdad by Sir John Nixon; the force was numerically weak because promised further reinforcements had not arrived. A successful preliminary attack on a Turkish advanced post, al-Qutuniyyah, encouraged further optimism and helped minimize all the attendant difficulties involved in an offensive. Townshend once again attempted to turn the left flank of the strong Turkish position at Ctesiphon while launching his main attack at a point in their main line of resistance.

After heavy fighting this was secured, but only at great cost in lives. The Turks, bolstered by good quality reinforcements from the Caucasus, counter-attacked on the following day, forcing the British to retreat.

Townshend conducted a skilful fighting withdrawal, bringing with him 1350 Turkish prisoners, and entered Kut on 3 December 1915 where he assumed the defensive. After two attacks, several Turkish divisions closely invested the town and attempted to starve the defenders into submission. Attempts by Lieutenant-General Aylmer and Major-General Gorringe in January and February failed to relieve the beleaguered garrison. The defending troops suffered severely from shortages of food and medical supplies and when Townshend finally opened negotiations with the Turkish authorities, starvation was imminent. Kut finally surrendered on 29 April 1916.

Townshend was separated from his men by his Turkish captors. Although his troops suffered appallingly from neglect and brutality, Townshend himself was well treated, being interned on Prinkipo Island, near Constantinople where he took little apparent interest in the welfare of his men. In October 1917 he was created KCB, while still in captivity. A year later he was released by the Turks in order that he could plead on their behalf for favourable terms of surrender. The armistice with the Turks was signed on 30 October 1918 following which Townshend returned to England.

Townshend did not secure any further military employment: his reputation had been blighted less by the surrender of Kut than by his indifference to the fate of his men in captivity, and by his own vainglorious account of his campaign in Mesopotamia, published in 1920. He retired from the army and was elected to parliament in November 1920 as an independent Conservative, for The Wrekin, Shropshire. He spoke occasionally in the Commons on matters concerning the Middle East or ex-servicemen, but he was not a successful politician and did not seek re-election in October 1922. He sought to act as a mediator between Great Britain and Turkey in the final settlement of questions arising from the war, such as the evacuation of Greek troops from Turkish territory, but his services were curtly declined by the government. Acting on his own initiative, he met Kemal Pasha at Ankara in June 1922, and on his return to London strongly backed the Turkish stance but failed to find any support in official circles. In 1923 he visited Ankara once again, but his health was deteriorating, and despite wintering in the south of France to convalesce, Townshend died of cancer in the Hotel d'Iena, avenue d'Iena, Paris, on 18 May 1924. He was buried with military honours in the family plot at the church of St Mary, East Raynham, Norfolk.   T. R. MOREMAN

Sources *The Times* (19 May 1924) · A. J. Barker, *Townshend of Kut: a biography of Major-General Sir Charles Townshend* (1967) · E. Sherson, *Townshend of Chitral and Kut* (1928) · C. V. F. Townshend, *My campaign in Mesopotamia* (1920) · F. J. Moberly, ed., *The campaign in Mesopotamia, 1914–1918*, 4 vols. (1923–7) · *DNB* · *Indian Army List* · A. J. Barker, *The neglected war: Mesopotamia, 1914–1918* (1967) · Burke, *Peerage* (1967) · *CGPLA Eng. & Wales* (1925)

Archives BL, papers, Add. MSS 63082, 63102 · King's Lond., corresp. · NRA, priv. coll., diaries and papers | CUL, corresp. with Lord Hardinge · U. Durham L., corresp. with Sir Reginald Wingate | S O U N D IWM SA, oral history interview
Likenesses photograph, *c.*1914, repro. in Barker, *Townshend of Kut* · R. G. Eves, repro. in Sherson, *Townshend of Chitral and Kut*
Wealth at death £119 2*s.* 5*d.*: administration with will, 14 July 1924, *CGPLA Eng. & Wales*

Townshend, Chauncy Hare (1798–1868), poet and collector, was born on 20 April 1798, the only son (he had a younger sister) of Henry Hare Townsend (1765?–1827) of Busbridge Hall, Godalming, and Walpole, Norfolk, and his wife, Charlotte Winter Lake (*c.*1770–1831), daughter of Sir James Winter Lake of Edmonton (*b.* 1745). He was educated at Eton College (1811–15) and Trinity Hall, Cambridge (BA, 1821; MA, 1824). He won the chancellor's English medal for his poem 'Jerusalem' (1817). Although ordained, he never took a living, perhaps because of poor health, but he was a self-confessed hypochondriac. Townshend (he changed the spelling of his name in 1828) was determined to be a poet; he approached Robert Southey, the poet laureate, with his work in 1815. Southey offered encouragement and they corresponded for several years, Townshend visiting Southey in Keswick. Townshend's first volume, *Poems* (1821), followed, dedicated to Southey. This was revised and reprinted in 1825 as *The Weaver's Boy*. On 2 May 1826 Townshend married Eliza Frances, eldest daughter of Sir Amos Godsill Robert Norcott, of Hornsey. The marriage ended on 30 August 1843, confirmed by deed of separation on 6 September 1845, with 'unhappy differences' cited as the cause. There were no children.

In 1827 Townshend published anonymously *The Reigning Vice: a Satirical Essay in Four Books*. He also contributed to annuals and other periodicals. Through Southey, Townshend met Wordsworth, but upset their cordial relationship with critical articles on Wordsworth in *Blackwood's* during 1829. Townshend continued to contribute to *Blackwood's*, and, thanks to his friendship with Dickens, to *Household Words*, and later to *All the Year Round*. Dickens came to regard Townshend as a close friend, and was made his literary executor (thereby being required to publish Townshend's *Religious Opinions*, 1869). The two first met in 1840 at the home of Dr John Elliotson, a mesmerist. Mesmerism intrigued both Dickens and Townshend, who published *Facts in Mesmerism* (1840), dedicated to Elliotson, and *Mesmerism Proved True, and the Quarterly Reviewer Reviewed* (1854). In 1851 Townshend published two volumes of verse: *Sermons in Sonnets* and, under the pseudonym T. Greatley, *Philosophy of the Fens*, a lively satirical work drawing on contemporary life. A ballad, *The Burning of the Amazon*, was published in 1852, the profits going to those who suffered by the calamity. A further volume of verse, *The Three Gates*, followed in 1859, reprinted in 1861, dedicated to Dickens.

For long periods Townshend lived abroad for health reasons. When in London (about two months each summer), he dined regularly with Dickens, who also visited Townshend in his Lausanne villa. Dickens skilfully

Chauncy Hare Townshend (1798–1868), by John Boaden, exh. RA 1828

reflects Townshend's character when describing him aboard the Folkestone ferry, in his carriage, which he found 'perforated in every direction with cupboards, containing every description of physic, old brandy, East India sherry, sandwiches, oranges, cordial waters, newspapers, pocket handkerchiefs, shawls, flannels, telescopes, compasses, repeaters … and finger-rings of great value' (*Letters of Charles Dickens*, 8.177).

The latter were part of Townshend's collection of precious stones, which in his will he left to the South Kensington Museum, with collections of Swiss coins, cameos, photographs, drawings, and engravings. His remaining collections were left to the Wisbech and Fenland Museum, including his library, with the manuscript of *Great Expectations*, the novel which Dickens 'affectionately inscribed' to Townshend. Townshend's death in his London home, 21 Norfolk Street, Park Lane, on 25 February 1868, upset Dickens, then in America: 'It is not a light thing to lose such a friend, and I truly loved him' (*Letters of Charles Dickens*, 1880, 372). Townshend was buried in the new cemetery, Godalming.

Bulwer Lytton described Townshend's 'beauty of countenance' as a young man, but noted that he became 'plain in later life—an accomplished man—but effeminate and mildly selfish' (*Letters of Charles Dickens*, 2.110n). Townshend's will hardly supports the latter charge. The bulk of his estate went to found the Burdett-Coutts and Townshend Foundation School in Rochester Street, Westminster, a charity school offering free evening education to 400 children over thirteen. Townshend remained a minor literary figure, with a wide acquaintance in the arts world and a considerable knowledge of the artefacts he collected. His lasting memorial is perhaps Wisbech Museum itself, rather than his writing.

ROSEMARY SCOTT

Sources Wisbech Museum, Townshend papers · P. Cave, ed., *The life and times of Chauncy Hare Townshend* (1998) · W. L. Hanchant, 'Chauncy Hare Townshend', *23rd annual report of the Wisbech Society* (1962) · R. S. Boddington, *Pedigree of the family of Townsend* (1881) · *The letters of Charles Dickens*, ed. M. House, G. Storey, and others, 2–11 (1969–99) · *The Times* (7 April 1868) · *The Athenaeum* (29 Feb 1868) · *The Athenaeum* (11 April 1868) · *GM*, 4th ser., 5 (1868) · *The life and correspondence of Robert Southey*, ed. C. C. Southey, 6 vols. (1849–50), vols. 4–5 · *The letters of Charles Dickens*, ed. [G. Hogarth and M. Dickens], 2 (1880) · H. E. C. Stapylton, *The Eton school lists, from 1791 to 1850*, 2nd edn (1864) · Venn, *Alum. Cant.* · *Wellesley index* · IGI
Archives V&A, bequest · Wisbech Museum, Cambridgeshire, autograph collection, literary papers, and sketchbooks | Herts. ALS, letters to Sir Edward Bulwer Lytton, D/EK C1, C2, C6, C17, C25 · NL Scot., letters to Blackwoods
Likenesses J. R. Smith, crayon drawing, c.1805, V&A · J. Boaden, oils, exh. RA 1828, V&A [*see illus.*] · S. Woodhouse, double portrait (as a child with his sister, Charlotte), V&A · stipple and line engraving, NPG
Wealth at death under £16,000 in England: probate, 27 March 1868, *CGPLA Eng. & Wales*

Townshend [*née* Harrison]**, Etheldreda** [Audrey]**, Viscountess Townshend** (*c.*1708–1788), society hostess, was the daughter of Edward Harrison (1674–1732) and his wife, Frances (*d.* 1758), of Balls Park, Hertfordshire. Her father was governor of Fort St George, Madras, India, from 1711 to 1717, MP for Weymouth and Melcome Regis from 1717 to 1722 and for Hertford from 1722 to 1726, postmaster-general from 1726 until his death, and several times deputy chairman, and in 1729 chairman, of the East India Company. Her mother was the daughter of Reginald Bray, of Great Barrington, Gloucestershire. The deaths of her brother and two sisters in infancy left her an only child. She was presumably named after her paternal grandmother Audrey, *née* Villiers, but always used the form Etheldreda.

On 29 May 1723 Etheldreda married Charles *Townshend (1700–1764) [*see under* Townshend, Charles, second Viscount Townshend], afterwards third Viscount Townshend. On 24 May he had been summoned to the House of Lords as Baron Townshend of Lynn, and until the death of her father-in-law in 1738 she was known as Lady Lynn. From the outset they had a stormy marriage. Her husband was preoccupied with his mistress, a maidservant on the Raynham estate in Norfolk, and they led separate lives, not even seeing each other at dinner. They did cohabit sufficiently to have children: George *Townshend, later first Marquess Townshend (1724–1807); Charles *Townshend (1725–1767); Roger (*d.* 1759), who pursued a military career; Edward, who died of smallpox in 1731, as a young boy; and Audrey (*d.* 1781), who in 1756 eloped with Captain Robert Orme, from Devon.

As Etheldreda lived separately from her husband, she was able to enjoy men's company more than most other ladies in her position. In 1738 John Perceval, first earl of Egmont, wrote that Lady Townshend had 'gained to herself as infamous a character as any lady about town for her

Etheldreda Townshend, Viscountess Townshend (*c.*1708–1788), by Jean Baptiste van Loo, in or before 1742

gallantries' (*Egmont Diary*, 2.510). This was followed by a formal separation about 1740 or 1741, from which time her husband lived at Raynham with his mistress. Following their separation she moved to her own establishment in the Privy Garden near St James's Street, Westminster, where she spent her time hosting leading dignitaries and organizing gorgeous entertainments, which were renowned throughout the country. By 1742 she had taken as her lover the politician Thomas *Winnington (1696–1746), whom she 'used as insolently as if she kept him, not he her' (Walpole, *Corr.*, 30.46). After Winnington's death on 23 April 1746 she fell in love with the Jacobite William Boyd, fourth earl of Kilmarnock, during his trial for treason in 1746, and amused and embarrassed her friends with a sudden, although short-lived, conversion to Jacobitism. Her later lovers included Frederick *Campbell (1729–1816), whom Walpole reported her as pursuing in 1752, and, a few years later, Henry *Fox (1705–1774), to whom she remained a political confidante for several years. Politically she opposed the ministry of Sir Robert Walpole, and later that of Henry Pelham and his followers, but seems to have been ill-disposed to governments in general.

The chief authorities for Etheldreda's career are her friends Horace Walpole and Lady Mary Wortley Montagu. Both tended to portray her as a woman of the world who paid little attention to what people said about her as long as she could amuse herself in the way she liked best, and continued to be surrounded by plenty of lively men and women. Her exploits are supposed to have been the basis for the portrayal of Lady Bellaston in Henry Fielding's *Tom

Jones, and also Lady Tempest in Francis Coventry's *Pompey the Little*.

Following the death of her mother in 1758 Etheldreda inherited a further sum of £1000 per annum to add to the £2000 already settled on her. On 7 July 1759 her son Roger was killed at the battle of Ticonderoga; she erected a monument to his memory in Westminster Abbey in 1762, designed by Robert Adam. She inherited Balls Park from her uncle George Harrison when he died in 1759, but received no legacy from her husband when he died at Raynham on 12 March 1764; he reportedly left £50,000 in trust for his mistress.

Etheldreda continued to lead an eventful life. In 1765, for example, she was arrested in the streets outside the house of a painter whose bill she had refused to pay because it was double the original estimate. She was, however, badly affected in 1767 by the death of her son Charles, and it was several years before her activities were once again a talking point for fashionable London society. In June 1780 Walpole reported her as so 'terrified' by the Gordon riots that she 'talked the language of the Court, instead of Opposition' (Walpole, *Corr.*, 33.195), breaking a habit of decades. She died suddenly on 5 March 1788 and was buried on 12 March in the family vault at All Saints, Hertford, near her own property of Balls Park, which she left to her grandson Lord John Townshend.

Nineteenth-century writers regarded Lady Townshend as exemplifying the loose morals and absence of restraint they deplored in eighteenth-century society: to Justin McCarthy she was 'a whimsical spiteful sprightly oddity' (McCarthy, 3.152) who separated from her husband 'to carry her beauty, her insolence, and her wit through an amazed and amused society'. In the early twentieth century her reputation was defended by her great-great-great-grandson Erroll Sherson, who portrayed her as 'one of the most beautiful, fascinating and witty women of a fascinating and witty age, who held her own, brilliantly and audaciously as a lady of quality' (Sherson, 1), well-bred, ambitious, and accomplished, with a mode of living distinguished by luxury, joviality, and expense. This assessment seems more likely than McCarthy's to be enhanced by further study.   JOHN MARTIN

Sources E. Sherson, *The lively Lady Townshend and her friends* (1924) · J. H. Jesse, *George Selwyn and his contemporaries*, 4 vols. (1843) · GEC, *Peerage* · will, PRO, PROB 11/1164, sig. 160 · J. McCarthy, *A history of the four Georges (and of William IV)*, 4 vols. (1884–1901) · A. N. Newman, 'Harrison, Edward', HoP, *Commons, 1715–54* · Walpole, *Corr.* · A. N. Newman, 'Harrison, George', HoP, *Commons, 1715–54* · R. R. Sedgwick, 'Winnington, Thomas', HoP, *Commons, 1715–54* · *Manuscripts of the earl of Egmont: diary of Viscount Percival, afterwards first earl of Egmont*, 3 vols., HMC, 63 (1920–23) · H. Fox, letters to Lady Townshend, 1742–66, Bodl. Oxf., MS Eng. lett. d. 85

Archives Raynham Hall, Norfolk, MSS

Likenesses J. B. van Loo, oils, in or before 1742; Sothebys, 8 Nov 1995, lot 40 [*see illus.*] · Kneller, oils, repro. in Sherson, *Lively Lady Townshend*, 152 · Zincke, oils, repro. in Sherson, *Lively Lady Townshend*, frontispiece

Wealth at death Balls Park property in Hertfordshire: will, PRO, PROB 11/1164, sig. 160

Townshend, George (1715/16–1769), naval officer, was the eldest son of the politician and agricultural improver Charles *Townshend, second Viscount Townshend (1674–1738), and his second wife, Dorothy (*d.* 1726), sister of Robert Walpole, first earl of Orford. He entered the navy in 1729 in the *Rose* (20 guns), with Captain Weller, apparently on the Carolina station. After two and a half years in her he served for four and a half in the West Indies, in the *Scarborough*—also a 20-gun frigate—with Captain Thomas Durell, and for the first part of the time with Lieutenant Edward Hawke. Townshend passed his examination on 23 October 1736, being then, according to his certificate, nearly twenty-one (PRO, ADM 107/3, p. 304). On 30 January 1739 he was promoted captain of the frigate *Tartar*, which he commanded on the Carolina station until November 1741. In December he was appointed to the *Chatham*, and two years later to the *Bedford* (70 guns), in which he went out to the Mediterranean and took part in the action off Toulon on 11 February 1744; he continued there under Vice-Admiral William Rowley, and in the summer of 1745 Rowley appointed him to command a detached squadron on the coast of Italy, with the rank of commodore.

Townshend's first duty was to co-operate with the insurgent Corsican patriots against the Genoese. Hearing from them that they had 3000 men under arms he posted his ships and bombs before Bastia, and on the night of 6–7 November destroyed the batteries and reduced the town to ruins. It then appeared that the 3000 men had yet to be raised, and it was not until 18 November that the insurgents were able to take possession of the town. Towards the end of the month he reduced the forts of Mortella and San Fiorenzo; but the Corsican patriots were so busy fighting among themselves—'alternately dining together and squabbling' as Townshend told the Admiralty—that nothing could be effectively done. This unsatisfactory situation continued for some months. On 7 April Townshend wrote to the Admiralty that the dissensions were so violent that nothing could be done without a number of regular troops. On 8 May he made clear that, as his whole force was needed to maintain the blockade of the Genoese coast, the revolt in Corsica should be left to itself. To the difficulty of disunion among the patriots was added that of the presence in the neighbourhood of a French squadron reportedly fully equal in force to that with Townshend. In March he had stretched across to Cartagena and, having watered at Mahon, was on his way to Cagliari to consult with the Sardinian viceroy, when he saw four large ships and two French men-of-war. Having with him only one ship, the *Essex*, besides the *Bedford*, and two bombs, Townshend judged against engagement until he could secure the rest of his squadron. With this French squadron on the coast, he concluded that 'nothing can be attempted against Corsica'.

Having received several such communications the Admiralty sent out an order for a court martial to inquire into Townshend's conduct and behaviour. This was carried out on 9 February 1747, with the result that the court was convinced that Townshend 'did not meet with a squadron of the enemy's ships, nor see or chase any ships so as to discover them to be enemies'. They concluded moreover that Townshend's report upon the vicinity of the French squadron was based upon purely hearsay evidence. The court was therefore of the opinion that Townshend's letters were written 'with great carelessness and negligence' and 'contained very false and erroneous accounts of Captain Townshend's proceedings'. He was required by the court to write letters to the Admiralty and to Vice-Admiral Henry Medley, the commander-in-chief, begging pardon for his fault; it was also recommended that he be severely reprimanded by the president. Horace Mann, British representative in Florence, who had formed a very poor opinion of Townshend's capacity and education, wrote to Horace Walpole that if Townshend had been capable of writing an intelligible letter in his own language he would not have found himself suspected of cowardice; and that he had omitted to state that he had only one ship besides his own (J. Doran, *Mann and Manners at the Court of Florence, 1740–1786*, 2 vols., 1876, 1.56). For his part Walpole attributed the court martial entirely to political motives: 'The persecution is on account of the poor boy's relation to my father' (Walpole, *Corr.*, 19.332). Moreover Townshend's letters are perfectly intelligible, and the fact of his having with him only one ship besides his own is clearly stated, and the ship named. None the less Townshend's surprisingly uncouth manner is well attested by Edward Brenton.

After this, Townshend continued in the Mediterranean until towards the end of the year, when he returned to England, and paid the *Bedford* off in December. Because Townshend enjoyed Henry Pelham's 'very powerfull support' (BL, Add. MS 15957, fol. 87), and had been a commodore, Lord Sandwich appointed him to command off the Scheldt in the spring of 1748 with a broad pennant in the *Folkestone*. From November 1748 to November 1752 he was commodore and commander-in-chief at Jamaica, with his broad pennant in the *Gloucester*. On 4 February 1755 he was promoted rear-admiral of the white, and again sent out to Jamaica, as commander-in-chief, with his flag in the *Dreadnought*. Townshend returned to England in 1757 and had no further service, but he became vice-admiral in 1758 and admiral in 1765; and he died, apparently unmarried, in August 1769.   J. K. LAUGHTON, *rev.* RUDDOCK MACKAY

Sources W. L. Clowes, *The Royal Navy: a history from the earliest times to the present*, 3 (1898); repr. (1996) · R. F. Mackay, 'Lord St Vincent's early years, 1735–55', *Mariner's Mirror*, 76 (1990), 51–65, esp. 51–2 · E. P. Brenton, *Life and correspondence of John, earl of St Vincent*, 2 vols. (1838) · R. Pares, *War and trade in the West Indies, 1739–1763* (1936) · J. Charnock, ed., *Biographia navalis*, 4 (1796), 434 · PRO, ADM 107/3 **Archives** U. Mich. | PRO, admiralty records relating to court martial

Townshend, George, first Marquess Townshend (1724–1807),

politician and caricaturist, was born on 28 February 1724 in London, the eldest son of Charles *Townshend, third Viscount Townshend (1700–1764) [*see under* Townshend, Charles, second Viscount Townshend], politician, and his wife, Etheldreda *Townshend (c.1708–1788), the daughter and sole heir of Edward Harrison of Balls Park, Hertfordshire. George I was one of the sponsors at his baptism, at St Martin-in-the-Fields, London, 25 March 1725. The future chancellor of the exchequer Charles

George Townshend, first Marquess Townshend (1724–1807), by Sir Joshua Reynolds, 1778–9

*Townshend was his younger brother. He was educated at Eton College and St John's College, Cambridge, whence he graduated MA on 3 July 1749. Regarded by contemporaries as a very handsome man, Townshend is described by Sir Lewis Namier as 'warm hearted, sensitive and capable of enthusiasms, but unsteady and odd, intermittently ambitious, often disgruntled, quarrelsome, lacking in judgment, and burdened with an insuperable urge to ridicule, the resort of the intelligent under oppression' (Namier 549).

Early military career In summer 1743, while on the grand tour of Europe, Townshend joined the army in Flanders as a volunteer. Two years later he was offered the command of a regiment and in April was appointed captain in the 7th regiment of dragoons. He was serving under the duke of Cumberland, and his Pelhamite relations (his paternal grandmother was a half-sister of the duke of Newcastle) took the opportunity to foster this connection. His parents had separated in March 1741, and, unlike his brother Charles, he had remained close to his mother, a woman known for her wit and promiscuity, her dislike of Cumberland, and her sympathy for the Jacobite cause. To counter her influence, George Townshend was placed in the care of the Cumberland family, a move that was to benefit his military career. He served under Cumberland at Culloden on 16 April 1746, and in the following February he became aide-de-camp to the duke. At the same time he transferred to the 20th foot, and after fighting in the battle of Laufeld on 2 July he moved to the 1st foot; on 8 March 1748 he assumed the office of lieutenant-colonel. However, this stage of his military career was brought to an end by a disagreement with Cumberland, possibly over the treatment of another junior officer.

Parliamentary politics, 1749–1757 In 1747, while in Flanders, Townshend was elected unopposed as MP for Norfolk, and it was politics that occupied his attention on his return to England. His first recorded parliamentary speech, in February 1749, was in the debate on the Mutiny Bill when he supported an attack made on Cumberland by Richard Lyttelton, a fellow officer. In the following year Townshend moved that courts martial should replace the commanding officer as the authority empowered to punish non-commissioned and private officers. This was another thinly disguised attack on Cumberland, and, though it was backed by the prince of Wales's party, it was defeated. This year also saw Townshend leave the army, reputedly over the refusal to allow him to stay and cultivate the whig interest in Norfolk. However, his dispute with Cumberland continued and was compounded in 1751 after the publication of a pamphlet titled *A Brief Narrative of the Late Campaigns in Germany and Flanders*; this criticized Cumberland's military capability, and was thought to have been written, or at least inspired, by Townshend.

For a short period Townshend became allied with the following of the prince of Wales. But after the prince's death in March 1751 he made peace with the Pelhams, and Newcastle counted him among his supporters. His animosity to Cumberland continued though, and when Henry Fox, his political agent, was appointed secretary of state and leader of the house, Townshend and his brother moved into opposition; they joined William Pitt and the Grenvilles in opposing the address on 13 November 1755. In autumn 1756 Townshend gained political prominence as the foremost supporter of an extension of the militia. He was motivated by his dislike of standing armies and by his determination to strike back at Cumberland. As champion of this populist issue and a respected member of the country gentlemen, he was a valuable asset to Pitt.

After the defeat of his Militia Bill in the Lords Townshend was responsible for an important innovation in the way the opinions of the voting public were utilized. He sent a circulating letter to the boroughs and corporations instructing them to advise their members to campaign for another militia bill. He was therefore responsible for popularizing a propaganda weapon that would prove invaluable to the parliamentary reform campaign of the 1780s.

During the early months of 1757 Townshend divided his time between resuscitating the Militia Bill and promoting a parliamentary inquiry into the loss of Minorca. Along with his brother he attempted to encourage opposition 'out-of-doors' to the government, focusing on these two issues. His involvement in the ill-fated inquiry enabled him to score points against Henry Fox, particularly after Pitt's dismissal from the ministry.

On 28 June 1757 Townshend's Militia Bill received royal assent, and he deserved much of the credit for steering it through parliament and for ensuring that it was implemented effectively in the face of strenuous opposition from his father. However, although Townshend remained on good terms with Pitt and had formed a new connection with Bute, his political influence was short-lived, curtailed as it was by the Pitt–Newcastle coalition. Townshend regarded the new administration as a union of competing interests, which had been formed without any declaration of a public system of measures. He was also incensed by the nominal position in the new ministry offered to his enemy Henry Fox. Townshend felt betrayed by his former ally, and he and his brother retired to the country. By now Townshend was married and the father of a growing family. On 19 December 1751 he had married, with a marriage portion of £12,000, Lady Charlotte Compton (*d*. 1770), the second daughter of James Compton, fifth earl of Northampton, and his wife, Elizabeth Shirley, Baroness Ferrers in her own right. His wife, who had succeeded to her mother's title in 1747, inherited her father's title and his fortune on his death in 1754, since she was by then his sole heir.

Political caricaturist Townshend was acutely aware of the importance of propaganda and public opinion, and he used pictorial satire against his enemies to reinforce his political views. During the campaign for the Militia Bill he had adorned 'the shutters, walls, and napkins of every tavern in Pall Mall with caricatures of the Duke [of Cumberland] and Sir George Lyttleton, the Duke of Newcastle and Mr. Fox' (Walpole, *Corr.*, 37.444). Walpole was moved to observe that 'his genius for likenesses in caricature is astonishing' (ibid.). Inspired by the works of Hogarth and Italian *caricatura*, Townshend was said to have invented a new form of political caricature, depicted on cards. More importantly, according to Walpole, he was the first to introduce personal caricature into political prints. However, it is questionable whether this marked a watershed in visual satire. Diana Donald has argued that it is too simplistic to suggest that he initiated a shift which saw the old emblematic tradition being replaced by more sophisticated personal caricature. Yet Townshend does have a legitimate claim to significance in the development of satirical art. Donald states that his 'savage personal lampoons, once engraved and published, transformed *caricatura* from an innocuous amusement into an offensive weapon in the political feuds of the day' (Donald, *Age of Caricature*, 14). Even so, the full extent of his influence would not be seen until the 1780s—when Gillray and Rowlandson reintroduced parody and the mock-heroic into visual satire.

It is doubtful whether Townshend's ability as a caricaturist advanced his career: George II was displeased by his foray into this world of 'low' art, and his pointed satire quickly brought him a number of other enemies. In 1757 a pamphlet titled *An Essay on Political Lying* was published in reaction to a print by Townshend, probably by a hireling of Henry Fox. Moreover, the offence caused by his drawings was compounded by what his enemies regarded as his close association with Grub Street, demonstrated by the sponsorship of caricaturists and printsellers such as Mary and Matthew Darly. It was felt that by ridiculing members of his own class he was inciting the mob, and his support of petitioning as a political weapon gave further ammunition to his opponents.

Serving in Quebec Townshend was compensated for his failure to advance in political circles by the retirement of Cumberland. As Townshend's political estrangement from Pitt had been brief, this meant that a resumption of his military career was both a viable and an attractive option. When he applied to be reinstated in the army he was assisted by Pitt; on 6 May 1758 he was promoted to the rank of colonel and became aide-de-camp to George II. Pitt was also instrumental in securing his appointment in February 1759 as brigadier under Major-General James Wolfe, who was responsible for leading an expedition against French-held Quebec. Townshend sailed with Wolfe, reaching Louisburg harbour in May. The expedition then headed for Quebec and Townshend took part in the attack on Montcalm's camp at Montmorenci in late July. After this point, however, the relationship between Townshend and Wolfe deteriorated. Frustrated by their failure to make any real progress in Quebec, Townshend complained to his wife on 6 September from Camp Levi: 'General Wolfs health is but very bad. His generalship, in my poor opinion, is not a bit better: this only between us. He never consulted any of us till the latter end of August, so that we have nothing to answer for, I hope, as to the success of this campaign' (*Townshend MSS*, 309). When Wolfe did consult his officers an attack on the north side of the St Lawrence above Quebec was agreed upon. Some sources credit Townshend as the originator of this plan, but it has also been suggested that he advised against it as too hazardous. Townshend led the left wing at the battle on the heights of Abraham, and when Wolfe was killed and Monckton disabled, overall command devolved upon his shoulders. He abandoned the pursuit of the French army, preferring to focus on bringing Quebec to a speedy surrender, which it did on 17 September 1759.

Although Townshend returned as a hero, his victory was tainted by accusations that he had endeavoured to embellish his own part in the battle at the expense of Wolfe. Wolfe, killed heroically on the verge of victory, was a more easily accepted saviour of British Canada. Townshend, as a noted satirist, and a subordinate known to have been on bad terms with Wolfe, came out of the affair badly. Henry Fox and Cumberland were both implicated in the minor pamphlet war that ensued. Indeed Townshend was ready to challenge Lord Albemarle, Cumberland's protégé, to a duel, subsequently called off, for his part in the business.

Political career, 1760–1767 Ultimately, Townshend's friendship with Bute prevented the Quebec affair from damaging his political career, and in December 1760 he was sworn of the privy council. He also continued to see military service. Between February and December 1761 he was with the British army in Germany, and he spent much of the second half of 1762 on active service in Portugal. While abroad he corresponded with Bute, and on his return he made it clear that he supported the controversial peace treaty ending the Seven Years' War. However, though he was prepared to speak out on the main issues of the day, when in parliament his primary concern remained the militia.

On 14 March 1763 Townshend became lieutenant-general of the ordnance in the Grenville ministry. He was reasonably firm in his support for Grenville, and in the early days of the administration he did all that he could to persuade his brother to join him in government. However his encouragements succeeded only in alienating Charles. For his own part Townshend avoided becoming involved in the Wilkes affair and general warrants, but as a landowner in a 'malt county' he staunchly supported the Cider Act. This, though, was the end of his career in the Commons as he succeeded his father as fourth Viscount Townshend on 12 March 1764. The death of his father seemed to initiate a process of reconciliation between Townshend and his brother. This was assisted by the fact that Charles was becoming disillusioned with life in opposition and was looking for a place in government. Townshend's own importance was now derived largely from the precocious talents of his brother. Their restored amity allowed him to exert a good deal of influence over his brother's actions. In May 1765 Townshend prepared the way for Charles's inclusion in the Grenville ministry, and on Grenville's fall Townshend was able to persuade Charles to refuse office with the Rockinghams. Charles James Fox claimed that Townshend was motivated by his continued bitterness towards Cumberland and pique at the failure of the Rockinghams to court him.

On the formation of the Chatham ministry, in which Charles was chancellor of the exchequer, Townshend offered his services to the government. After the abortive appointment of Lord Bristol, he became lord lieutenant of Ireland on 19 August 1767, a post to which he had long aspired. He owed his position to the influence of his brother Charles, but contemporaries also cited his connection with Lord Bute.

Irish viceroy, 1767–1772 During the short-lived Bristol administration in Ireland the Chatham ministry had indicated its determination to make inroads into the power of the Irish undertakers, namely the leading parliamentarians and landowners who undertook to manage government business in return for a share of patronage. But research by Thomas Bartlett has demonstrated that Townshend himself was responsible for the radical policies followed during his administration, though it is clear that the British ministry had been preparing for a change in the Irish system of government for some years. Some doubt remains as to whether Townshend was appointed as a resident lord lieutenant—a measure that would make inroads into undertaker influence.

A failure to clarify the government's Irish policy at a succession of cabinet meetings meant that Townshend's administration began in a state of confusion. This situation was made all the more problematic by the death of Townshend's brother Charles on 4 September, thus removing his only genuinely sympathetic ear in the cabinet. As a result, at a time when sensitive handling of Ireland was vital, the British ministry did all it could to inflame the Irish parliament and damage Townshend's credibility.

The popularity of Townshend's administration was immediately dented by the British ministry's delay in appointing a new Irish lord chancellor, and then by its decision to recommend an Englishman for the post, thus alienating senior Irish legal officers. A simultaneous dispute occurred over the Judges' Tenure Bill, giving security of tenure to Irish judges during good behaviour, which Townshend, in his speech to the Commons, had announced would be approved by the British ministry. The secretary of state, Lord Shelburne, denied that Townshend had been given this authority, and when the British privy council altered the bill it was rejected.

Townshend's principal task on appointment was to secure an augmentation of the British army in Ireland, in order to bring Irish regiments up to the same size as their British counterparts. This process of standardization was made necessary by gains in the American mid-west and by the adoption of the fixed rotation of regiments in 1765, whereby regiments would rotate throughout the empire and therefore would have to be the same size. However, in Ireland the augmentation was unpopular, as Irish politicians feared that the army was being increased only in order for regiments to be sent abroad, thus denuding Ireland's defence against the Catholic threat. As a palliative Townshend was allowed to accept a bill to limit the term of the Irish parliament to eight years. But his failure to secure undertaker support—as the British ministry refused to accept their patronage demands—and the approaching general election made necessary by the new Octennial Bill, which made MPs more responsive to public opinion, ensured the defeat of the augmentation on 19 April 1768. Townshend eventually secured its passage on 21 December 1769, after introducing measures to quiet fears of Irish troop losses. But his disagreements with the leading Irish politicians had persuaded him that the reform of the Irish system of government was essential if British influence over its oldest colony was to continue.

Townshend's new system comprised several measures: the viceroy's constant residency; reform of the Irish revenue board; dismissal of recalcitrant office-holders; encouragement of the hereditary revenue; and the creation of a Dublin Castle party loyal to the viceroy. Yet, though parts of this programme were approved by the duke of Grafton, it was not until Lord North was appointed prime minister that Townshend had the full support of the British government. Indeed for a time it seemed likely that Townshend would be replaced by Lord Sandwich, a member of the Bedford group. However, in this case it seems that Townshend received direct support from the king, who had no liking for Sandwich because he was not a man of 'blameless character'. It is probable that Townshend had endeared himself to the king through his determination to cut through factional politics in Ireland, putting himself and the Irish government at the king's service.

On 21 November 1769 the British government was given a clear indication of the need to reassert a measure of control over Ireland when the Irish Commons rejected a money bill, explicitly stating that this was because it had not originated in the Commons. Townshend, with the backing of an incensed British ministry, retaliated by proroguing the Irish parliament. The extended parliamentary interval allowed Townshend the opportunity to begin his reforms, but he was not helped by the unpopularity of the prorogation. The suspension of parliament was a political blow to Irish patriotic sentiment and an economic blow to Dublin's business community. The *Freeman's Journal* printed regular attacks on Townshend and his administration, and Dublin also witnessed a pamphlet war. The anti-Townshend pamphlets written by opposition MPs were published together in *Baratariana*, a collection that included references to his caricatures. He was described as a 'Tyro of the graphic art', a man who mixed 'malevolence with levity ... dedicating even his *smiles* to the injury of his companions' (*Baratariana*, 308, 351).

Townshend tried to repair some of this damage by holding balls in aid of Irish manufacture and by promoting Irish trade concessions. But his personal popularity remained low. He had alienated many Irish politicians through his wit and temper. His habit of carousing into the early hours of the morning in Dublin Castle with those not of the first rank was also frowned upon by the Irish élite.

Nevertheless Townshend used the interval to his advantage, particularly after the North ministry, in cabinet meetings on 21 February and 24 December, approved his reform programme and thereby created a new board of accounts, dismissed John Ponsonby from the revenue board, and approved the revenue board's division. In order to test the paper majority of Townshend's newly formed Castle party, a short parliamentary session was called in February 1771. Townshend's reforms were vindicated, as the opposition was comprehensively defeated in a series of votes, and John Ponsonby resigned as speaker in frustration. However, public dissatisfaction was demonstrated in a riot outside the Commons. Townshend claimed 'that the cry amongst the mob was that the lord lieutenant had got a great majority, and was going to carry away their parliament' (*Calendar of Home Office Papers*, 3.211).

Townshend, having turned away from the undertakers' assistance, was now reliant on an ambitious group of men—many of them with patriotic inclinations—eager for reward. There was insufficient patronage to keep the new Castle party content, and as the next session approached it became clear that his majority was no longer solid. To counteract this problem Townshend began to turn to Lord Shannon, an old-style undertaker, who had never really been reconciled to life in opposition. However, though Townshend laid the groundwork for Shannon's return, he was not able to count on his support, and his government was defeated on several issues, most notably the division of the revenue boards. Shannon refused to return to government under Townshend, partly because of the viceroy's support for bills designed to bring relief to Ireland's Catholics.

Although the session ended quietly it was clear to the North ministry that Townshend's personal standing was preventing the completion of government dominance, and that his removal would restore a measure of calm to Irish politics. Henry Seymour Conway claimed that Townshend 'disdains too much to be a politician and will not take the trouble of managing, or let others do it' (PRO NIre., Annaghmore MSS, T 2812/12/25). Indeed his personal relations with some Irish politicians were at their lowest ebb during his last months in Ireland, and an argument with Lord Bellamont resulted in a duel in which Bellamont was shot and injured. Francis Andrews, provost of Trinity College and a government supporter, observed: 'It is rather odd that a man who had so many great things to give away, and gave them all to the people of the country, should not leave a friend behind him' (*Eighth Report*, HMC, 1.193). In reality, however, his departure was lamented by many Irish politicians, and he was attended by a sizeable crowd when he came to board his ship. Indeed Townshend's Irish friends continued to hold a dinner on the day of his birthday for years after he had left Ireland.

Townshend left behind a much-altered system of government. The lord lieutenant, being now resident, possessed a greater degree of control over his managers; individuals no longer held more than one principal office of the crown, and the lords justices had disappeared. Townshend had also increased the hereditary revenue, although this did not lessen the reliance of the Castle government on the Irish parliament. His reforms were a direct result of his own persistence, but at the same time he had been reliant on the support provided by the North ministry. In essence the British ministry had adopted a policy of direct rule over Ireland, with Townshend responsible for the implementation of this policy and its fine-tuning.

Final years, 1772–1807 On his return from Ireland Townshend was restored to his old office at the Ordnance. He remained a firm supporter of North and went into opposition on the formation of the Rockingham ministry. When the Fox–North coalition was formed he returned again to the Ordnance. Throughout the remainder of his political life he remained exercised by a limited number of issues. The militia still concerned him, and added to this was now Ireland. He spoke on several occasions in the Lords on behalf of Irish trade concessions. This was a service that many Irish politicians recognized as their dislike of him was tempered in the years before his death.

Townshend's wife had died in Ireland, at Leixlip Castle, on 14 September 1770, and he married, on 19 May 1773, Anne (*d.* 1819), the daughter of Sir William Montgomery, first baronet, MP for Ballynekill, and his first wife, Hannah Tomkyns. They had six children. Townshend continued to climb the ranks of the army, becoming colonel of the 2nd regiment of dragoons on 15 July 1773, general on 20 November 1782, and field marshal in 1796. One of his most cherished ambitions was achieved on 31 October 1786, when he was created Marquess Townshend of Raynham. He held a number of other offices during the latter years of his life, including lord lieutenant and vice-admiral of the county of Norfolk, governor of Hull, governor of Jersey, and high steward of Tamworth. His wife was appointed mistress of the robes to the princess of Wales in 1795. But these honours could not disguise a rather lacklustre end to a tumultuous political and military life. He spent much of his time as a county squire, an advocate of the new farming techniques popularized by his grandfather. He died on 14 September 1807 at Raynham, Norfolk, where he was buried on 28 September. His wife survived him and died on 29 March 1819; he was succeeded as second marquess by his eldest son by his first marriage, George *Townshend (1753–1811).

Excepting his Irish post, which in the eighteenth century was regarded as a curse as much as a blessing, Townshend never held high political office; indeed it could be said that he never aspired to it. Yet his achievements were to have a resounding impact. His involvement in introducing a more direct form of government in Ireland in 1767 marked a major step towards union. His sensitivity to propaganda and public opinion is also noteworthy. He was a significant political caricaturist, and his advocacy of the petitioning of MPs challenged the eighteenth-century notion of the relationship between MPs and their electors.

MARTYN J. POWELL

Sources *DNB* · L. B. Namier, 'Townshend, Hon. George', HoP, *Commons, 1754–90* · HoP, *Commons, 1715–54* · T. Bartlett, 'The Townshend viceroyalty, 1767–72', *Penal era and golden age: essays in Irish history, 1690–1800*, ed. T. Bartlett and D. W. Hayton (1979), 88–112 · D. Donald, *The age of caricature: satirical prints in the reign of George III* (1996) · J. Redington and R. A. Roberts, eds., *Calendar of home office papers of the reign of George III*, 4 vols., PRO (1878–99) · H. M. Atherton, 'George Townshend, caricaturist', *Eighteenth-Century Studies*, 4 (1970–71), 437–46 · D. Donald, 'Calumny and caricatura: eighteenth-century political prints and the case of George Townshend', *Art History*, 6 (1983), 44–66 · H. M. Atherton, 'George Townshend revisited: the politician as caricaturist', *Oxford Art Journal*, 8/1 (1985), 3–19 · T. Bartlett, 'Viscount Townshend and the Irish revenue board, 1767–73', *Proceedings of the Royal Irish Academy*, 79C (1979), 153–75 · T. Bartlett, 'The Irish House of Commons' rejection of the "privy council" Money Bill in 1769, a re-assessment', *Studia Hibernica*, 19 (1979), 63–77 · T. Bartlett, 'Opposition in late eighteenth-century Ireland: the case of the Townshend viceroyalty', *Irish Historical Studies*, 22 (1980–81), 313–30 · T. Bartlett, 'The augmentation of the army in Ireland, 1767–1769', *EngHR*, 96 (1981), 540–59 · M. Peters, *Pitt and popularity: the patriot minister and London opinion during the Seven Years' War* (1980) · J. L. McCracken, 'The Irish viceroyalty, 1760–73', *Essays in British and Irish history in honour of James Eadie Todd*, ed. H. A. Cronne, T. W. Moody, and D. B. Quinn (1949), 152–68 · M. J. Powell, 'Managing the Dublin populace: the importance of public opinion in Anglo-Irish politics, 1750–1772', *Irish Studies Review*, 16 (1996), 8–13 · Walpole, *Corr.*, vol. 37 · H. Walpole, *Memoirs of the reign of King George the Third*, ed. G. F. R. Barker, 1 (1894) · [H. Grattan and others], *Baratariana: a select collection of fugitive political pieces*, ed. [Rev. Simpson], 2nd edn (1773) · *The manuscripts of the Marquess Townshend*, HMC, 19 (1887) · PRO NIre., Annaghmore MSS, T 2812/12/25 · *Eighth report*, 1, HMC, 7 (1907–9) · BL, Newcastle MSS, Add. MS 32867, fols. 72–7 · GEC, *Peerage* · IGI

Archives BL, corresp., Add. MSS 63079–63080, 63096, 63099–63100, 63103, 63110–63111 · BL, corresp. and papers, Add. MSS 38497, 38505–38506, 41152, 50006–50012 · Boston PL, corresp. · Duke U., Perkins L., corresp. · Jersey Archive, St Helier, letters to Townshend and outward corresp. as governor of Jersey [copies] · JRL, corresp. and papers · NA Canada, corresp. · NA Ire., corresp. relating to Ireland · NAM, corresp. and papers · NL Ire., corresp. · Norfolk RO, family and personal corresp. and papers · NRA, priv. coll., corresp. and papers · Representative Church Body Library, Dublin, corresp. relating to ecclesiastical patronage · Staffs. RO, corresp. and papers relating chiefly to Tamworth affairs · U. Mich., Clements L., corresp. and papers · Yale U., Farmington, Lewis Walpole Library, account book and corresp. · Yale U., Beinecke L., corresp. and papers | BL, letters to Sir Frederick Haldimand, Add. MS 21709 · BL, letters to Lord Hardwicke, Add. MSS 35663–35732 · BL, corresp. with earl of Liverpool, Add. MSS 38206–38231, 38305–38311, 38416, 38449 · BL, corresp. with duke of Newcastle, Add. MSS 31725–33118 · BL, corresp. with William Windham, Add. MSS 37881–37882, 37908 · Bodl. Oxf., letters to Charles Townshend · CKS, letters to Sir Jeffrey Amherst · Derbys. RO, Catton MSS · Hunt. L., letters to Lord Pery · JRL, letters to Sir James Caldwell · Mount Stuart Trust, Isle of Bute, corresp. with lords Loudon and Bute · NL Wales, corresp. relating to Queen's Dragoon Guards · NL Wales, corresp. with earl of Pembroke · Norfolk RO, letters to Preston family · NRA, priv. coll., corresp. with Robert FitzGerald · priv. coll. · PRO, letters to William Pitt, PRO 30/8 · PRO NIre., letters to Lord Macartney · Queen's Dragoon Guards Museum, Cardiff, corresp. relating to Queen's Dragoon Guards

Likenesses T. Hickey, oils, 1769, Mansion House, Dublin · J. Reynolds, oils, 1778–9, Art Gallery of Ontario, Toronto [*see illus.*] · M. Brown, oils, NA Canada · De Lippe, pen-and-ink drawing, BM · J. Macardell, mezzotint (after T. Hudson), BM, NPG · C. Turner and R. Jose, engraving (after J. Reynolds)

Townshend, George, second Marquess Townshend

(1753–1811), antiquary and politician, the eldest son of George *Townshend, first marquess (1724–1807), and his first wife, Charlotte Compton, Baroness Ferrers and Compton (*d.* 1770), was born on 18 April 1753. He was educated at Eton College from 1 April 1761 to 1770 and at St John's College, Cambridge, which he entered on 20 November 1770, and was created MA on 6 July 1773. As a young man he served in the army; he was gazetted cornet in the 9th dragoons on 29 September 1770, lieutenant in the 4th regiment of horse on 1 October 1771, and captain in the King's light dragoons on 31 December 1771. On his mother's death, on 14 September 1770, he succeeded to the baronies of Ferrers (or, as he preferred it, de Ferrars) and Compton. Relations with his father broke down in 1774 as Lord Townshend, heavily encumbered by debt, attempted to secure the agreement of his son to the breakup of the entail on the family estates. Ferrars agreed, but only on terms which his father found objectionable. On 24 December 1777, at Lambeth Palace chapel, he married Charlotte (*bap.* 1754, *d.* 1802), the second daughter and coheir of Eaton Mainwaring Ellerker of Risby Park, Yorkshire. They had two sons, George Ferrars *Townshend (who succeeded his father in his titles but was disinherited from the Raynham estate in Norfolk) and Charles Vere Ferrars. Their marriage lasted until Charlotte's death, at Bristol Hotwells, on 2 February 1802.

Ferrars did not play a major political role in the House of Lords, although he did speak in a number of debates; in 1775 he spoke on 26 October, when he declared that he

should oppose all the measures of the court, although out of respect to his father he forbore to begin doing so that day. When the whigs returned to office in the spring of 1782 he was made a privy councillor and was nominated captain of the band of gentlemen pensioners. The younger Pitt reappointed him to that post in December 1783, and on 5 March 1784 he was named a member of the committee of the privy council which managed colonial commerce until the Board of Trade was constituted. On 18 May that year Ferrars was created earl of Leicester. His father, from whom he had sought permission to assume the title, had told him that he might take any title but that of Viscount Townshend. The earldom of Leicester had in fact been extinct since 1759. Charles James Fox had wished to give it to his friend Thomas Coke, whose family had possessed it after the Sidneys, and a new earldom of Leicester of Holkham was created for Coke in 1837.

In February 1788 Leicester signed a protest against Lord Thurlow's proposal that the Commons should produce evidence in support of Warren Hastings's impeachment before calling on the defendant. He was master of the Royal Mint from 20 January 1790 to July 1794 and held the office of joint postmaster-general from January 1790 to February 1799. On 20 February 1799 he was named lord steward of the household, an office which he held until August 1802. In January 1806 he wrote to Grenville in anticipation of a new ministry, requesting that he should be reinstated as superintendent of the Post Office—an ambition which fell foul of the need for inclusiveness in the ministry of all the talents. On the death of his father in 1807 he succeeded as second Marquess Townshend.

Leicester was a keen amateur antiquary from his youth, being particularly interested in heraldry and archaeology. Walpole referred to his 'violent passion for ancestry'—which Walpole alleged he preferred to gambling (*Letters*, 7.159). He devoted considerable effort to establishing his own genealogical claim to the earldom of Derby, held in the middle ages by the Ferrers family. After the death in 1784 of the president of the Society of Antiquaries, Jeremiah Milles, he was swiftly elected to the council of the society and made a vice-president, preparatory to his planned election as president. Meanwhile, Edward King was elected temporary president, on the understanding that he would cede his position to Leicester in the official elections to be held in April. King claimed later to have had a completely different understanding of the arrangements, and challenged Leicester for president in the first contested election in the society's history. Leicester won by a majority of two to one, and magnanimously included the defeated King at the top of his house lists. King was less gracious in defeat; he had been accused of underhand dealings in the campaign, and after 1784 rarely attended the meetings of the society.

Leicester provided a good figurehead for the society, offering social and fashionable cachet, as well as having some credibility as an antiquary. The society had recently moved to accommodation in Somerset House, and its membership was rapidly expanding and included increasing numbers of gentlemen from 'polite society'. Although he neither followed up the administrative reforms which King had swiftly implemented nor acted as a dynamic intellectual force, he was conscientious in attending council meetings and was willing to allow his fellow antiquaries to exploit the aristocratic connection. It was through his intervention that Richard Gough gained permission to dedicate his new edition of Camden's *Britannia* to George III in 1789. He particularly associated himself with the antiquities of Leicestershire: John Throsby, the historian of Leicester, dedicated his history to him, and John Nichols acknowledged his assistance in the preface to his history of Leicestershire, the first volume of which was dedicated to the earl. Leicester was also admitted to the Royal Society in 1781 and was made a trustee of the British Museum in 1787. He continued as president of the Society of Antiquaries until his sudden death, at Richmond, Surrey, on 27 July 1811. He was buried at Raynham, Norfolk.

R. H. SWEET

Sources *GM*, 1st ser., 77 (1807), 894–5, 974–5 · *GM*, 1st ser., 81/2 (1811), 93, 664 · GEC, *Peerage*, new edn · J. Evans, *A history of the Society of Antiquaries* (1956) · *The letters of Horace Walpole, earl of Orford*, ed. P. Cunningham, 9 vols. (1857–9); repr. (1891) · Nichols, *Lit. anecdotes*, vol. 6 · *A speech delivered by Edward King* (1784)
Archives PRO, household and estate papers, C 107/38–39 | BL, letters to Lord Grenville, Add. MS 58964 · BL, corresp. with first Marquess Townshend, Add. MSS 50010–50011 · Bodl. Oxf., corresp. with John Charles Brooke · PRO, letters to William Pitt, PRO 30/8
Likenesses W. Lane, group portrait, chalk drawing, *c.*1810 (*Whig statesmen and their friends*), NPG · F. Bromley, mezzotint (after J. Reynolds), BM · J. S. Copley, group portrait, oils (*The collapse of the earl of Chatham in the House of Lords, 7 July 1778*), Tate collection; on loan to NPG · M. Kangue, engraving (after J. S. Copley)
Wealth at death was left £8000 by father: *GM* (1807), 4

Townshend, George Ferrars [alias George Compton], **third Marquess Townshend** (1778–1855), disinherited aristocrat, was the elder son of George *Townshend, second Marquess Townshend (1753–1811), and his wife, Charlotte Ellerker (*d.* 1802), of Risby Park, Yorkshire. He was born on 13 December 1778 in Wimpole Street, London, and was educated at Eton College and at Trinity College, Cambridge, where he matriculated in 1798. He was known as Lord Chartley and Lord Leicester before succeeding as marquess in 1811. He had a serious dispute with his father over the use of the title of earl of Leicester, and was subsequently disinherited by him in favour of his younger brother, Charles. Reasons for the rupture are not made explicit. Farington described him as 'a very effeminate young man—sometimes he wore pink ribbons on his shoes' (*Farington Diary*, ed. Greig, 4.223), and his marriage, to Sarah (*c.*1786–1858), daughter of John Dunn-Gardner of Chatteris, was an unmitigated disaster. They married on 12 May 1807, and by November of the same year were reported to be on the point of separation. They separated in the following year, Lady Chartley accusing him of impotence and 'not being formed as a man should be' (*Farington Diary*, ed. Greig, 5.75). Townshend lived chiefly at Genoa, where he was known as Mr Compton. He died under that name on 31 December 1855 at his home, the Villa Rostan, Pegli, near Genoa, and was buried in the protestant cemetery of San Benigno. His wife went through a ceremony of

marriage at Gretna Green on 24 October 1809 with John Margetts (*d.* 1842) and was known as Mrs Margetts until 1823; they had at least three sons and two daughters. From 1823 she styled herself Marchioness Townshend, a form of address to which she was perfectly entitled, no divorce having taken place. It was under that name that she died, on 11 September 1858, at Brighton, and was buried in Kensal Green cemetery. She had married, on 10 January 1856, James Laidler of Fenton, Northumberland. Her eldest surviving son from her liaison with Margetts, John, called himself Lord John Townshend from 1823 until 1828, when he adopted the title of earl of Leicester. An act of parliament of 1842–3 ruled that these were not legitimate children of the Townshend marriage, overturning the legal doctrine that where a marriage existed, the husband was presumed to be the father of all the children. Thereafter, the son, who was Conservative MP for Bodmin in 1841–6, took his grandmother's name, Dunn-Gardner, by royal licence.

K. D. REYNOLDS

Sources GEC, *Peerage* · *The Farington diary*, ed. J. Greig, 5 (1925)
Likenesses photograph (after miniature, now lost), priv. coll.

Townshend, Hayward (*c.*1577–1603x21), parliamentary diarist, was the eldest son of Sir Henry Townshend (1537?–1621), second justice of Chester and a member of the council of the marches in Wales, and his wife, Susan (*d.* 1592), daughter of the prominent Londoner Sir Rowland *Hayward. He was educated at St Mary Hall, Oxford, where he graduated BA in 1595, and he studied at Lincoln's Inn, being called to the bar in 1601. When he was elected to parliament in 1597 he became one of the youngest men to sit in the Elizabethan Commons. Then and in the 1601 parliament Townshend sat as MP for Bishop's Castle, Shropshire. Criticism of the royal granting of monopolies was voiced in both these parliaments. In 1601 Townshend proposed that the Commons petition the queen for permission to proceed against monopolies by statute, a suggestion that earned him the praise of Sir Francis Bacon. Townshend was an active participant in this parliament, offering his own, ultimately unsuccessful, measures on solicitors and perjury. He spoke eloquently and, on his own report, decisively, in favour of the Painter–Stainers' Company, which was seeking protection against encroachment of their trade by the Plasterers in 1601.

However, it is as a parliamentary diarist that Townshend has earned his reputation. He kept a relatively thin diary for 1597–8, but any previous parliamentary journal is incomparable both in length and substance to his for 1601. The young MP was impressed by the opening and closing ceremonies and was particularly moved to record procedural discussions and matters of privilege. He was also a keen observer of detail, as in 1597 when he noticed that the clerk of the crown received the subsidy bill and 'laid it on a little table standing before the Speaker betwixt ii great wax candles one a plaine greene carpet' (Hartley, 3.241). Townshend often described bills fully and he recorded debates on a wide range of matters. However, it is his joy in the workings of the institution and his fascination with the persons around him that contributes much to modern understanding of an Elizabethan House of Commons. In 1597–8 Townshend refers to those 'in the rebellioues corner in the right hand of the Howse' (ibid., 238) and to how MPs, having waited for thirty minutes to gain access to the closing ceremonies, rushed in with 'the greatest thrust and most disorder that ever I sawe' (ibid., 240–41). Through Townshend it is known that one MP was upset in 1601 because a gentleman usher told those MPs standing outside the door of the House of Lords, trying to hear the lord keeper's speech, that 'yf they ware not quyett they should be sett in the stockes' (ibid., 310); that the house considered ordering a page, who had harassed an MP, to be taken to a barber to have his excessively long hair cut before being discharged, and that one morning, while waiting for the speaker's arrival, older MPs discussed how, in earlier days, special scaffolding had been required to accommodate fashionable breeches. Townshend gives important insights into the processes of lobbying, recording that one town 'openlie in the Howse canvased for voices and procured councellors to speake in the behalfe' of their case in 1597–8 (ibid., 240), and he reported that lists of monopolies circulated while the house debated the matter in 1601. His diary reveals the eloquence and influence of men such as Sir Francis Bacon, Sir Robert Cecil, and Sir Walter Ralegh.

Townshend was certainly dead by 2 April 1621, when his father drew up his own will, and it has been suggested that he died as early as 1603, on the grounds that such an active MP would hardly have failed to seek a seat for the 1604 parliament (HoP, *Commons, 1558–1603*, 517). He was apparently unmarried. Townshend's *Historical collections, or, An exact account of the proceedings of the four last parliaments of Queen Elizabeth of famous memory* was published in 1680.

DAVID DEAN

Sources HoP, *Commons, 1558–1603* · T. E. Hartley, ed., *Proceedings in the parliaments of Elizabeth I*, 3 (1995) · T. Nash, *Collections for the history of Worcestershire*, 2 vols. (1781–2); 2nd edn (1799) · H. T. Weyman, 'The members of parliament for Bishop's Castle', *Transactions of the Shropshire Archaeological and Natural History Society*, 2nd ser., 10 (1898), 33–68 · A. F. Pollard and M. Blatcher, 'Hayward Townshend's journals [4 pts]', *BIHR*, 12 (1934–5), 1–31; 13 (1935–6), 9–34; 14 (1936–7), 149–65; 15 (1937–8), 1–18 · PRO, PROB 11/138, sig. 107 [will of Sir Henry Townshend]
Archives BL, journals, Stowe MSS 362–363, Cotton MSS, Hargrave MSS | BL, Egerton MSS, Harley MSS, journal · Bodl. Oxf., MSS Rawl., journal · CUL, journal · Herts. ALS, Gorhambury MSS, journal · Inner Temple, London, Petyt MSS, journal · Northants. RO, Finch-Hatton MSS, journals · PRO, state papers domestic, journal

Townshend, Horace. *See* Townsend, Horace (1750–1837).

Townshend, Horatio, first Viscount Townshend (*bap.* 1630, *d.* 1687), politician, was baptized on 16 December 1630 at Stiffkey, Norfolk, the second son of Sir Roger Townshend, first baronet (1595–1637), of Raynham, Norfolk, and his wife, Lady Mary (*c.*1611–1669), daughter and coheir of Horace *Vere, Baron Vere of Tilbury. His mother remarried on 21 June 1638, her new husband being Mildmay *Fane, second earl of Westmorland. Townshend and his elder brother, Roger (1628–1648), matriculated at St John's College, Cambridge, on 9 November 1644 and

Horatio Townshend, first Viscount Townshend (*bap.* 1630, *d.* 1687), by Sir Peter Lely, *c.*1665

graduated MA on 27 November 1645. On 16 December 1646 they received leave from parliament to travel abroad for three years. After they had visited France, and with a visit to Rome planned, Roger died in Geneva some time before 13 July 1648. Townshend returned home as the third baronet and shortly after was married (articles, 22 October 1649) to Mary (1634–1673), daughter and sole heir of Edward Lewkenor, of Denham, Suffolk. They had no children.

Townshend began to play a small role in local government, being nominated to parliamentary commissions in 1649 and serving as a JP from 1652. He sat in the protectorate parliaments of 1656 and 1659, but by the latter date he was working in favour of a restoration of the monarchy. Clarendon later recalled that he was 'a gentleman of the greatest interest and credit' in Norfolk, and was 'liable to no reproach or jealousy' because he had been too young to fight in the civil wars (Rosenheim, 19). He seems to have been ready to raise the county in 1659 if there was a successful royalist landing nearby. He was appointed to the council of state on 17 May 1659, but only after receiving royal permission to do so, and never actually took his seat. He played a vital role in ensuring that Lord Fairfax came out in support of General Monck, and on 28 January 1660 he delivered to the Rump an address from Norfolk in favour of a free parliament, which he subsequently presented in February to Monck. He was duly elected to the Convention Parliament for Norfolk in April 1660, and was one of the twelve representatives from the Commons sent to escort Charles II from Breda.

Townshend did not stand at the general election of April 1661, probably because he knew that he would shortly be raised to the peerage (20 April) as Baron Townshend of Lynn Regis. Having been a militia colonel since October 1660, he was made lord lieutenant of Norfolk in August 1661. Other local offices soon followed, including the vice-admiralty of Norfolk, and the high stewardship of King's Lynn. Another reward for his services was the farm of the coal duties, which he was granted by the crown in 1664. In politics he seems not to have been close to the old Presbyterian leadership, and he was a supporter of the lord chancellor, the earl of Clarendon. He may have voted against the Corporation Act, but he then proceeded against conventicles if they seemed a threat to order. He was forecast by Lord Wharton in July 1663 as likely to oppose the motion to impeach Clarendon, and he promoted some measures, such as militia legislation, which the government favoured in the Lords. He was particularly active in the militia during the Second Anglo-Dutch War when invasion threatened the east coast of England.

Townshend buried his first wife on 22 May 1673, and on 27 November 1673 he married Mary (1652/3–1685), daughter of Sir Joseph Ashe, first baronet, of Twickenham, Middlesex. They had three sons. The birth of a male heir in 1675 seems to have changed Townshend's outlook on life and he became concerned to leave his estate in good order, his early years having led to increased indebtedness as he wrestled with outgoings for jointures, portions for his sisters, and the completion of Raynham Hall.

Townshend's position in Norfolk politics changed in the early 1670s when a series of by-elections caused divisions within the county. Townshend supported the candidature of Sir John Hobart, third baronet, in the Norfolk by-election of 1673, which angered the old cavaliers, and in 1675 he opposed the candidate of Lord Treasurer Danby in another by-election at King's Lynn and when the county also faced a contested by-election. At Westminster he was seen as an opponent in April–June 1675 of Danby's proposal for a non-resisting test act, and on 20 November 1675 he voted for an address to Charles II in favour of a dissolution. As a consequence of this opposition to Danby's ministry, he lost his lord lieutenancy on 25 February 1676. For the next few years Townshend was associated with the country party in opposition to Danby and the Court. In 1677 he left his proxy with the earl of Shaftesbury, and was even briefly a supporter of exclusion.

However, Townshend was essentially a moderate figure, and the more extreme Norfolk whigs caused him to draw back towards the court. In January 1682 he disowned the whig county MPs he had helped to get elected. His reward was a step up in the peerage: on 2 December 1682 he was created Viscount Townshend. In August 1683 he signed the loyal address in the wake of the Rye House plot. His political stance in the late 1670s, however, meant that he was never in favour with James II. He spent his last years improving his estates and preparing for the likelihood that his son would succeed him as a minor. Townshend's second wife predeceased him, dying of smallpox on 17 December 1685. Townshend himself died in late November or early December 1687, after making a codicil to his will on 26 November. He was buried on 10 December 1687 at East Raynham, and was succeeded as second viscount by his eldest son, Charles *Townshend.

STUART HANDLEY

Sources J. M. Rosenheim, *The Townshends of Raynham* (1989) · M. W. Helms and E. Cruickshanks, 'Townshend, Sir Horatio', HoP, *Commons, 1660–90*, 3.579–80 · GEC, *Peerage*, new edn · Venn, *Alum. Cant.* · R. Davis, 'The "presbyterian" opposition and the emergence of party in the House of Lords in the reign of Charles II', *Party management in parliament, 1660–1784*, ed. C. Jones (1984), 1–21, 33 · *The manuscripts of the Marquess Townshend*, HMC, 19 (1887), 25–37 · *Denham parish register, 1539–1800, with historical notes and notices* (1904), 53, 137, 259 · Clarendon, *Hist. rebellion*, 6.111–12, 165 · *Calendar of the Clarendon state papers preserved in the Bodleian Library*, 4: *1657–1660*, ed. F. J. Routledge (1932), 205 · A. Swatland, *The House of Lords in the reign of Charles II* (1996), 30, 38, 45–6 · P. Seaward, *The Cavalier Parliament and the reconstruction of the old regime, 1661–1667* (1988), 81–2 · J. Miller, 'A moderate in the first age of party: the dilemmas of Sir John Holland, 1675–85', *EngHR*, 114 (1999), 844–74, esp. 853, 859–70 · will, PRO, PROB 11/389, sig. 157
Archives BL, corresp. and papers, Add. MSS 41654–41656 · Norfolk RO, corresp. and papers · NRA, priv. coll., corresp. and papers · Raynham Hall, Norfolk, MSS | BL, corresp. with William Windham, Add. MS 37911
Likenesses P. Lely, oils, c.1665, NMG Wales [*see illus.*]
Wealth at death £5500 p.a. from lands: Rosenheim *Townshends of Raynham*, 65

Townshend, Sir John (1567/8–1603), landowner and local politician, was the elder son of Sir Roger *Townshend (c.1544–1590), courtier, and his second wife, Jane (c.1547–1618), the eldest daughter of Sir Michael Stanhope of Shelford, Nottinghamshire. In childhood Sir Roger had inherited a house in Stoke Newington, Middlesex; property and land in Suffolk, Oxfordshire, Middlesex, and Essex; and twenty manors around Raynham, Norfolk, acquired by the family at the dissolution of the monasteries. As London agent, first of Thomas, fourth duke of Norfolk (executed in 1572), and then of his son Philip, earl of Arundel (imprisoned in 1585), Roger enjoyed Howard patronage, a determining factor in his son's life.

John Townshend matriculated from Magdalen College, Oxford, aged thirteen, on 24 November 1581, then transferred to Trinity College, Cambridge, where his father and his uncle Michael Stanhope had been; in 1591 Townshend presented Cambridge University with a formidable staff for its senior proctor. Townshend, unexceptionally for a gentleman, never graduated, leaving university for foreign travel. He probably served with his father in July 1588 on the fleet sent against the Armada under Charles Howard, Lord Howard of Effingham, subsequently fighting under Sir Francis Vere in the Netherlands. He took residence at Raynham following his father's death in 1590. His widowed mother in 1598 married Henry Berkeley, seventh Lord Berkeley. Townshend had himself married, towards the end of 1593 or in the first half of 1594, Anne (d. 1622), eldest of the three daughters of Nathaniel *Bacon of Stiffkey, near Raynham, a man of wealth, puritan leanings, and considerable local influence, who was sheriff of Norfolk in 1599 and was knighted in 1604.

Townshend was returned for Castle Rising, Norfolk, to the parliament that met on 19 February 1593. Thereafter he became increasingly active in local affairs, where power struggles tended to reflect court faction. As a Howard client, like his father, his father's friend Sir Edward Coke, and his father-in-law, Townshend opposed the royal favourite, the earl of Essex, supported in Norfolk by Sir Arthur Heveningham. In 1596 Townshend accompanied Lord Thomas Howard on the Cadiz venture, being knighted by him for valour. The following year, in opposition to Heveningham, Townshend was elected to parliament for Norfolk as knight of the shire, and in 1601, again rebuffing Essex partisans, he was returned for Orford, Suffolk, probably through the influence of Coke, the borough's recorder, and of his uncle Michael Stanhope. As his name does not appear in the journals of the House of Commons his parliamentary participation remains conjectural.

Local struggles for power were bitter, bringing violence and instability to the county. About 1598 Townshend became a justice of the peace, but within two years he was dismissed from the bench for quarrelling with Heveningham's supporter Sir Christopher Heydon, a relation of his father's first wife. In 1597 Townshend's appointment to the Norfolk musters commission was successfully blocked by Heveningham, so he was unable to participate until December 1598, thereon frustrating Heveningham's ambitions to increase Norfolk's small number of very large foot companies to thirty-three small ones; about then his father-in-law obtained for him a captaincy of the foot company for the hundreds of Gallow and Brothercross. In 1600 Heydon challenged Townshend to a duel, averted by the privy council, Coke promising surety for Townshend's keeping the peace. Even so, seemingly Townshend was debarred by Heydon from the Norfolk musters commission until July 1601, when the privy council ordered his reinstatement. That same year Theophilus Finche was involved in a serious dispute with Townshend, Sir Robert Cecil acting as peacemaker. Townshend died, possibly at his home at Stoke Newington, on 2 August 1603 from a wound received the previous day in a duel fought on horseback on Hounslow Heath. His opponent, a relative on his father's side, Sir Matthew Browne, was killed on the spot. Browne, the member of parliament for Gatton, Surrey, was also a client of Lord Thomas Howard, which may suggest his quarrel with Townshend was personal. Townshend died intestate, letters of administration being granted the day following his death. His estate passed to Roger, his seven-year-old son, created a baronet in 1617; his younger son, Stanhope, died in London of wounds received duelling in the Netherlands; his daughter, Anne, married John Spelman. His widow, with the

children, took residence at her father's house at Stiffkey, and died there in early November 1622, a few days before her father's death.   CECIL H. CLOUGH

Sources R. Virgoe, 'Townshend, John', HoP, Commons, 1558–1603 · A. Hassell Smith, County and court: government and politics in Norfolk, 1558–1603 (1974), index references · Foster, Alum. Oxon., 1500–1714, vol. 4 · Venn, Alum. Cant. · Cooper, Ath. Cantab., 2.355–6 · F. Blomefield and C. Parkin, An essay towards a topographical history of the county of Norfolk, [2nd edn], 11 vols. (1805–10), vol. 7, pp. 134–5 · G. A. Carthew, The hundred of Launditch and deanery of Brisley, in the county of Norfolk, 2 (1877), 781–2 · S. D'Ewes, The journals of all the parliaments during the reign of Queen Elizabeth, both of the House of Lords and House of Commons, ed. P. Bowes (1682), 507, 552, 553, 555, 557, 559, 561, 562, 567 · APC, 1597–8, 307; 1598–9, 345; 1601–4, 30 · CSP dom., 1591–4 · Calendar of the manuscripts of the most hon. the marquis of Salisbury, 4, HMC, 9 (1892), 485; 10 (1904), 352, 367, 458; 11 (1906), 92; 14 (1923), 280 · The manuscripts of his grace the duke of Portland, 10 vols., HMC, 29 (1891–1931), vol. 9, p. 90 · J. Durham, The Townshends of Raynham (1920), 31 · C. D. Bowen, The lion and the throne: the life and times of Sir Edward Coke (1552–1634) (1957) · The papers of Nathaniel Bacon of Stiffkey, ed. A. H. Smith and others, [4 vols.], Norfolk RS (1979–), vols. 3 and 4 · 'The letters and will of Lady Dorothy Bacon', ed. J. Key, A miscellany, Norfolk RS, vol. 56 (1991)
Likenesses panel, Raynham Hall, Norfolk

Townshend, John (1789–1845), army officer, was the eldest surviving son of Richard Boyle Townshend, high sheriff for co. Cork and MP in the Irish House of Commons, and his wife, Henrietta, daughter of John Newenham of Maryborough. He was born at Castletownshend on 11 June 1789, and on 24 January 1805 was appointed cornet in the 14th light dragoons. He became lieutenant on 8 March 1806, by purchase, and captain on 6 June, without purchase. On 16 December 1808 he sailed from Falmouth with his regiment for Portugal. He served in the Peninsular War, in Portugal and Spain, from 1809 to 1813, and was repeatedly in action, serving at the sieges of Ciudad Rodrigo (December 1811 and January 1812) and Badajoz (March–April 1812), and the battles of Salamanca (22 July 1812) and Vitoria (21 June 1813). On 24 June 1813 he took part in the taking of the enemy's last gun near Pamplona, under the command of Major Brotherton of the same regiment, and was constantly engaged with the enemy until the battle of Orthez on 27 February 1814. On 8 March he was made prisoner of war in an encounter with the enemy near the city of Pau, but was quickly released. He was subsequently present at the battle of New Orleans (8 January 1815).

Townshend was made: brevet major on 21 January 1819, as a reward for his services during the Peninsular War; major in the regiment, by purchase, on 13 September 1821; lieutenant-colonel, by purchase, on 16 April 1829; and aide-de-camp to the queen and colonel in the army on 23 November 1841. In 1827, on the death of his father, he succeeded to the family estates at Castletownshend. In 1831 he was one of the board of officers appointed by the general commanding in chief, under Lord Edward Somerset, for revising the formations and movements of cavalry. He served with his regiment in India for some years, but embarked at Bombay for England in November 1844. He landed in England in January 1845, and died unmarried at Castletownshend on 22 April 1845; he was buried there. A monument was erected to his memory in the church of Castletownshend by the officers of his regiment. He was succeeded in his estates by his brother, the Revd Maurice Fitzgerald Stephens-Townshend.

W. W. WEBB, *rev.* JAMES LUNT

Sources R. Townshend and D. Townshend, *An account of Colonel Richard Townshend and his family* (1892) • Record of Colonel Townshend's services, PRO • record of Colonel Townshend's services, BL OIOC

Townshend [Townesend], **Sir Roger** (*c*.1430–1493), justice and law reporter, was the son of John Townshend (*d*. 1466), a prosperous yeoman farmer of Raynham in Norfolk, and his wife, Agnes. He was probably born in the early 1430s, since he entered Lincoln's Inn in 1454. Within six years he was treasurer of the inn, and he probably gave his first reading around 1462; his second was in 1468 and his third in 1475. During the 1460s he built his practice at the bar, and in the year-books for 1467 we find him confidently disputing with Chief Justice Markham in the king's bench. He was acting as legal adviser to the Paston family by 1465, when he assisted them in the Fastolf will dispute and in a king's bench case reported in the year-books; at the same period he was assisting the duke of Norfolk. His services extended to moneylending, and an unredeemed Paston mortgage brought him the manor of East Beckham in 1470. Townshend served as a justice of the peace for Norfolk from 1466 until his death, and he was twice elected to parliament: first for Bramber in 1466, through the duke of Norfolk's influence, and then for Calne in 1472. By the 1470s he was sufficiently eminent in the law to act for the duke of Buckingham and the queen mother, and on 24 June 1478 he was created serjeant-at-law. Three years later he was appointed a king's serjeant, and he was reappointed to the office by Richard III. He began sitting as an assize judge in the last year of Edward IV's reign, going on the northern circuit until 1488, when he changed to the less arduous home circuit. His appointment as a justice of the common pleas came on 20 September 1485, and he sat in that court until the term in which he died, receiving his knighthood at Whitsun 1486.

In 1467 or 1468, Townshend married Eleanor (*d*. 1499), daughter of William Lunsford of Lunsford, Sussex. Their eldest son, Roger, grandsons Robert and Giles, and great-grandson Henry all made careers in the law and became benchers of Lincoln's Inn. By the time of his death, on 9 November 1493, he had spent around £3800 on land purchases, and was a major sheep farmer, owning 12,000 sheep in 1490 (in a famous judgment of 1487 he held a shepherd liable for negligence in losing a flock of sheep). His worldly success had carried the family into the gentry class; the hall, parlour, and chapel at Raynham were soon filled with armorial glass, and the visitation books garnished with bogus pedigrees. The justice expressed a wish to be buried in St Katherine's Chapel, Raynham, or in the Whitefriars if he died in London. Stow recorded an inscription in the Whitefriars to a Sir Thomas Townshend, which is probably an error for Roger. Roger's widow desired a tomb to be made for herself and her husband's bones at Raynham; the tomb chest survives, but even in the seventeenth century it bore no inscription.

Townshend had some obscure connection with the organization of a library in Lincoln's Inn, and kept over forty books at his home, besides the law library which he must have had in London. His name is remembered by legal historians as that of the first known reporter of cases, discounting the considerably more obscure figure of John Bryt in 1410. The year-books 1–2 Edward IV were printed by Pynson with the explicit 'secundum Townsend', and there are other references to reports under his name from the years 1458, 1460, and 1486. It is clear, therefore, that Townshend started keeping reports soon after joining Lincoln's Inn, and was still doing so as a justice nearly thirty years later. In view of this continuity, it seems highly likely that many of the other year-books during this period were written by him. Only a few personal jottings on circuit survive, in an autograph notebook at Raynham, and it is not clear whether the year-books which formed part of his estate, including a 'boke in papyr of dyverse yeres', were of his own making.

J. H. BAKER

Sources W. P. Baildon, ed., *The records of the Honorable Society of Lincoln's Inn: the black books*, 1 (1897) • C. E. Moreton, *The Townshends and their world: gentry, law, and land in Norfolk, c.1450–1551* (1992) • C. E. Moreton, 'A "best betrustyd frende"?: a late medieval lawyer and his clients', *Journal of Legal History*, 11 (1990), 183–90 • introduction, *The reports of Sir John Spelman*, ed. J. H. Baker, 2, SeldS, 94 (1978) • *The notebook of Sir John Port*, ed. J. H. Baker, SeldS, 102 (1986), 100 • Baker, *Serjeants* • Sainty, *Judges*, 70 • E. W. Ives, *The common lawyers of pre-Reformation England* (1983) • N. Davis, ed., *Paston letters and papers of the fifteenth century*, 2 vols. (1971–6) • N. Doe, 'Legal reasoning and Sir Roger Townshend JCP (d.1493)', *Journal of Legal History*, 11 (1990), 191–9 • J. C. Wedgwood and A. D. Holt, *History of parliament*, 1: *Biographies of the members of the Commons house, 1439–1509* (1936) • HoP, *Commons* • W. Hudson, ed., *The records of the city of Norwich*, 1 (1906), 307 • Dyer's *Reports*, fol. 106a • *CIPM, Henry VII*, 1, nos. 1028, 1136, 1143 • BL, Lansdowne MSS, 874, fol. 137 • Essex RO, D/DQ 14/124/3/343 • Y.B. Hil. 4 Edw. IV, fol. 41, pl. 3; Trin. 7 Edw. IV, fol. 13, pl. 4. • Sainty, *King's counsel*, 12

Archives Norfolk RO • priv. coll., personal accounts, memoranda, etc. | Raynham Hall, Norfolk, Marquess of Townshend MSS

Wealth at death see will, PRO, PROB 11/10, sig. 2

Townshend, Sir Roger (*c*.1544–1590), courtier, was the eldest son of Richard Townshend (*d*. before 1551), landowner, of Brampton, Suffolk, and Katherine, daughter and coheir of Sir Humphrey *Browne, justice of the common pleas. In 1551 he inherited more than twenty manors in the vicinity of Raynham, Norfolk, and other property from his great-grandfather Sir Roger Townshend that was worth £630 per annum in 1546, making him one of the wealthiest gentlemen in East Anglia. He attended Trinity College, Cambridge, in 1553 but did not graduate. A special commission declared him of age to enter into his estates in February 1565, and he received a licence to do so in May. He subsequently followed his grandfather into the service of the Howard family, becoming man of business to Thomas Howard, fourth duke of Norfolk. This service kept him predominantly in London, but he strengthened his ties to his county by marrying Ursula (*d*. before 1564), daughter of Sir Christopher Heydon, one of Norfolk's leading gentlemen. Heydon was protestant and was not a Howard client. In 1563 Townshend was elected MP for Norfolk at a by-election. The duke used his influence effectively but bluntly by virtually ordering the sheriff to oversee the return of Howard clients.

Following his wife's death without children, Townshend married Jane (*c*.1547–1618), daughter of Sir Michael Stanhope of Shelford, Nottinghamshire, and Anne, daughter of Nicholas Rawson of Aveley, Essex. They had two sons, Sir John *Townshend (1567/8–1603) and Sir Robert Townshend (*b*. 1580). Townshend continued in the service of the Howards, taking charge of the affairs of Philip Howard, earl of Arundel, after the execution of his father in 1572. Although Arundel complained about Townshend's zealousness in carrying out his duties, including prudently getting him away from a street brawl in 1582, and they had their differences at various times in the 1580s, the earl remembered his servant in his will with the generous gift of a large gilt bowl (though Townshend predeceased his master). He continued to court protestant families too. He leased the former Robsart estate in Norfolk from Robert Dudley, earl of Leicester, from 1579 and owed him £500 at the latter's death in 1588. Between 1576 and 1584 Townshend appeared with his wife on the list of donors of new year's gifts to Elizabeth I—they may both have held office at court. Following Arundel's imprisonment, Townshend appears to have spent a short period in custody himself. His settlement of his estate through the writing of a will in December 1587 may indicate the transfer of his service to Arundel's half-brother Lord Thomas Howard, a member of the council of war of his kinsman Charles Howard, Baron Howard of Effingham and later earl of Nottingham. He certainly played an active part in the defeat of the Armada, being knighted at sea by Effingham, now lord admiral, on 26 July 1588.

Townshend died at Stoke Newington, Middlesex, a property he had purchased from Thomas Sutton, the founder of Charterhouse, London, on 30 June 1590 and was buried at St Giles Cripplegate. His extensive lands in Norfolk, along with property in Suffolk, Oxfordshire, Middlesex, and Essex left his widow and two sons well provided for. In 1597 she made an advantageous match with Henry Berkeley, seventh Baron Berkeley, whose first wife, Katherine, had been the sister of Townshend's first patron. Lord Thomas Howard was one of Jane Townshend's representatives in the financial settlement of this marriage, reinforcing the Howard connection.   JAN BROADWAY

Sources HoP, *Commons, 1558–1603*, 3.519–20 · PRO, PROB 11/77, sig. 16 · Venn, *Alum. Cant.*, 1/4 · Foster, *Alum. Oxon., 1500–1714* · J. Maclean, ed., *The Berkeley manuscripts*, 3 vols. (1883–5), 2.392–3, 428–9 · W. Rye, ed., *The visitacion of Norffolk ... 1563 ... 1613*, Harleian Society, 32 (1891)
Likenesses tapestry (commemorating the defeat of the Armada); formerly in the House of Lords, but destroyed by fire
Wealth at death considerable; a number of manors and other property in Norfolk, Suffolk, Oxfordshire, and Middlesex; also known to have acquired property in Essex: will, PRO, PROB 11/77, sig. 16; HoP, *Commons, 1558–1603*

Townshend, Roger (1708–1760). *See under* Townshend, Charles, second Viscount Townshend (1674–1738).

Townshend, Thomas (1701–1780). *See under* Townshend, Charles, second Viscount Townshend (1674–1738).

Townshend, Thomas, first Viscount Sydney (1733–1800), politician, was born in London on 24 February 1733, the eldest son of three sons and two daughters of Thomas *Townshend (1701–1780), politician [*see under* Townshend, Charles, second Viscount Townshend], and Albinia (1713/14–1739), daughter of Colonel John Selwyn. He was educated at Eton College (1748) and at Clare College, Cambridge (1750–53), from where he graduated MA in 1753.

Early career and marriage A member of the well-connected Townshend family, with familial links to the Selwyns, Walpoles, and Pelhams, Tommy Townshend was marked out for a political career. His grandfather had been secretary of state under Walpole, the duke of Newcastle was his great-uncle, and his cousin was the brilliant Charles Townshend. He became MP for Whitchurch, in Hampshire, on his father's interest in 1754. With both father and son initially attached to their influential kinsman Newcastle, Tommy was made a clerk to the household of the prince of Wales in 1756. Upon George III's accession in 1760 he was raised to the sinecure of clerk of the board of green cloth. He married, on 19 May 1760, Elizabeth (1736–1826), eldest daughter and coheir of Richard Powys of Hintlesham, Suffolk, and his wife, Mary Brudenell. They had six sons and six daughters. Elizabeth Townshend later served as lady of the bedchamber to Queen Charlotte.

Newcastle resigned in opposition to the king's favourite, Bute, in May 1762, and in November the king dismissed Newcastle's ally the duke of Devonshire. Unlike most Pelhamite officeholders Townshend decided to stay in place. But as a 'young friend' of Newcastle, eager for systematic opposition, he was notable in speaking and voting against the ministry's peace preliminaries after the Seven Years' War. He was ousted in the 'Massacre of the Pelhamite Innocents' in December 1762. George III thought he could not 'be too soon dismissed, that will frighten others' (*Letters ... to Lord Bute*, 174).

Townshend remained close to the Newcastle–Rockingham faction, though he was gravitating towards William Pitt. In December 1762 he acted as intermediary in discussions between the two parties. Rockingham brought him back into office as a lord of the Treasury on 12 July 1765. However, Townshend kept a foot in Pitt's camp and again, during the Stamp Act crisis in January 1766, was commissioned to sound out the great man. When Pitt (now earl of Chatham) formed a ministry in July, with Rockingham replaced by the duke of Grafton at the Treasury, Townshend remained in place; indeed he informed Newcastle that he would not resign. On 23 December 1767 he was rewarded with a share of the potentially lucrative position of paymaster-general of the forces and was sworn of the privy council. By the general election of 1768 it seemed that he had completely drifted away from the Rockinghams; neither Newcastle nor Rockingham now counted him as a supporter.

In 1768 this second phase of Townshend's courtly career came to a premature end. Grafton wanted him to make way for Richard Rigby at the pay office in order to gain support for his ministry from the duke of Bedford's group. But Townshend was not prepared to settle for the second-best of Rigby's vice-treasurership of Ireland (though it was of similar status and value), and, as Rigby reported, was 'obstinately bent to carry his folly so far as to go out of employment' (*Correspondence of John, Fourth Duke of Bedford*, 3.401). On 10 June 1768 he left office and was to remain in opposition for the next fourteen years.

In opposition Rockingham eagerly excused Townshend's earlier behaviour once he had come back into the opposition fold. He told Newcastle 'I have always had a partiality towards Tommy Townshend' and justified his flouncing out of government as a result of 'his never having been quite so satisfied in his own mind since he separated from us'. Townshend himself claimed his actions 'had not arose from any bickering about this or that office' but from a political decision to oppose the Bedfordites (BL, Add. MS 32990, fols. 206–7, 216–18).

Townshend's attachments, however, were never clear-cut in this period and his loyalties were apparently flexible. He never fully re-entered the Rockingham orbit. His father controlled the two parliamentary seats at Whitchurch and his uncle George Selwyn nominated those at Ludgershall; upon their deaths, in 1780 and 1791 respectively, Townshend had control of all four seats. With his family and 'parliamentary interest', as well as his 'very independent fortune', he had the ability to act freely (*Memoirs of … Wraxall*, 2.45). There are reports of him being variously 'a great admirer' of George Grenville, influenced by Lord George Germain (for whom he acted as second in his duel of December 1770; *Correspondence of Edmund Burke*, 3.407), and connected to the king's estranged brother, the duke of Gloucester (Horace Walpole regarded him as Gloucester's only 'sensible' friend; *Last Journals*, 1.165). His most consistent flirtation, though, was with Pitt; never an out-and-out Chathamite he rather hovered between him and the Rockinghams—and always he hoped for conciliation between the two.

In 1769 Townshend was talking optimistically to Edmund Burke about a 'union of the parties', specifically referring to a conversation with Chatham. Burke, now at the heart of Rockinghamite thinking, considered Townshend a 'very honest and safe man'; Rockingham countered that 'our friend' Townshend was 'naïve' (*Correspondence of Edmund Burke*, 3.88–90). Four years later, in January 1773, Burke wondered where Townshend's loyalties lay when he was missing on an important vote against the ministry's East Indian measures. He implied that Townshend might have been led astray by Chatham on this occasion, as he 'is disposed to a great deference to the opinions of those, who are at most but allies'. Burke reassured Rockingham, however, that it was their own party that 'he loves by far the best' (*Correspondence of Edmund Burke*, 3.406–7).

Once in opposition Townshend aimed to show what a nuisance he could be. He was notable in opposing the expulsion of Wilkes in 1769 and became one of the most prominent MPs in opposition to North's ministry; he was the opposition candidate for speaker in 1770. It has been calculated that he spoke 380 times during the 1768–74 parliament; only the Rockinghamite spokesmen Burke and Dowdeswell and the prime minister himself spoke more frequently.

The American crisis The growing crisis in America eclipsed all other issues in this period. Townshend's position was equivocal at first. With the Rockinghams and the Pittites he had opposed the passing of the Stamp Act in 1765 and was in favour of its repeal the following year. However, he had not opposed Charles Townshend's duties on America in 1767, when he was a junior member of the Treasury; he later claimed that if there had been a division he would have done so. In February 1769 he sought to justify his cousin's duties: 'it was not the opinion of one man … It had pervaded the nation that it was absolutely necessary to do something … He desired taxes agreeable to the Americans themselves' (BL, Egerton MS 217, fols. 267–8).

Townshend was later wrong-footed by events in America in 1774. Like many contemporaries he was horrified by the Boston Tea Party. He supported the ministry's Boston Port Bill, the Massachusetts Government Bill, and the Massachusetts Justice Bill, as he believed the Americans should be punished; he only started to question government measures for quelling the problems when no conciliatory measure was announced. He believed that the tea duty on America should be reviewed. With the introduction of the Quebec Bill, Townshend's hostility to the government was on firmer ground, for he found it easy to attack this as a threat to English liberty. After this point he was in line with opposition thinking on America, though he wavered between the Rockinghamite and Chathamite strains. With the Rockinghams he bemoaned the worsening news from America up to the outbreak of war in 1775, while the Chathamites rejoiced, seeing it as a positive opportunity. By 1778 he was with the Chathamites in opposing the acceptance of outright independence, whereas the Rockinghams now reluctantly admitted the reality of the situation.

Townshend was one of the most vociferous opponents of North, who in the debate of 3 June 1774 on the Quebec Bill reportedly 'rose in a terrible passion' (Cobbett, *Parl. hist.*, 17, 1774, 1390) and declared that he did not care what Townshend thought of him, for he was a 'passionate and prejudiced man' (BL, Egerton MS 261, fol. 406).

Townshend was at the centre of opposition thinking and was consulted on matters of parliamentary tactics. What he hoped for most of all was reconciliation between Rockingham and Chatham. In November 1777, when the ministry was reeling from ill success in America, he 'never saw so fair … [a] prospect of union among those in opposition'. He expressed satisfaction that Chatham would not only be consulted but 'referred to for his absolute decision' (*Rutland MSS*, 2.11). Walpole thought Townshend had always been 'chiefly connected' with Chatham (*Last Journals*, 2.491). Townshend did weep openly in the Commons on the announcement of Chatham's death in 1778 and, with outright Chathamites and Rockinghams, was a pall-bearer at Chatham's funeral. He appears, however, to have remained independent of the Chatham–Shelburne connection down to the end of North's ministry.

Townshend tied his fortunes to the Rockinghams and their allies as long as North was in power. The aim was to bring down the government, and he, like them, waited on events in America. Failure in the war meant that by 1780 cracks had started to appear in the ministry. In the economical reform debates in March the opposition hoped for success, and there are reports of Townshend and Charles James Fox vying for who should take the pay office upon a ministerial change. Townshend's debating skills had put him in the running for significant office. By July 1780, with negotiations between the ministry and opposition, even the king accepted that men like Townshend would be a positive acquisition to his government.

In cabinet North's ministry was finally overturned in March 1782 and Rockingham returned to power. Townshend's uncle George Selwyn reported that his nephew had 'a situation fixed in his own mind, as adequate to his consequence' (*Carlisle MSS*, 595). On 27 March he was made secretary at war, and Selwyn believed that 'this was what he hoped for' (ibid., 608). Yet Townshend's cherished whig unity was soon tested with the death of Rockingham just three months later. Shelburne succeeded him and consequently Fox and most of the Rockinghams left office. While others went out with Fox in 1782 Townshend never entertained the idea; echoing Chatham's perennial maxim of 'measures not men' he condemned Fox's 'quitting if measures are right because they cannot fill offices to their wish' (*Later Correspondence of George III*, 6). Walpole considered that Townshend had 'addicted himself' to Shelburne (*Last Journals*, 2.491). More likely, first with the smashing of North's solid ministry and then with Rockingham's death, Townshend felt that the situation was fluid again and that he himself was a free agent. Most of the cabinet having deserted, on 10 July 1782 he replaced Shelburne at the Home Office. Shelburne's ministry soldiered on despite constant opposition from the Rockingham whigs. Townshend played his part, strenuously defending in the Commons the peace with America. But in April 1783 he was ousted, with the Shelburne ministry, as the Fox–North coalition forced themselves into government. Shelburne's parting request to the king was to reward Townshend with a peerage for his parliamentary services to the ministry. He was created Baron Sydney on 6 March.

Sydney's latest exclusion from office was of very short duration. By December 1783 the king had expelled the coalition and placed the young William Pitt at the head of his ministry. With a lack of senior politicians willing to serve with him Sydney was brought back as home secretary on 23 December. Apparently he had 'volunteered', though he 'very much disliked the employment' and hoped for a less taxing position in future (Fitzmaurice, 2.280–81).

Pitt's ministry As early as 1784 Pitt considered replacing Sydney at the Home department. On agreeing to dissolve parliament in March 1784 he wanted to add something to the king's speech about parliamentary reform; Sydney and most of the cabinet notably overruled this. Sydney thought of parliamentary reform for Ireland as 'ruinous' and a 'crude and undigested … proposal' (*Rutland MSS*, 3.78). It appears that he had the same view on reform in England, for when the opposition accused Pitt of being lukewarm on the proposal Sydney confessed 'I could, from my heart, forgive him that crime' (ibid., 81). In May, after success in the general election, Pitt asked Richmond to replace Sydney, who would have taken the privy seal, but Richmond declined.

Now in late middle age, Sydney was fairly conservative. The king confided in this like-minded cabinet ally that he disapproved of Pitt's espousal of parliamentary reform in January 1785. George III had 'unalterable sentiments' about changing the constitution but wanted to deal diplomatically with Pitt's proposals (*Later Correspondence of George III*, 3.119). In March he again sought the advice of Sydney, who confessed to 'lamenting extremely that the subject of a Parliamentary Reform should come into discussion' (ibid., 142) at this difficult time. Though the king had promised Pitt that he would not discuss his views on reform with anyone else Sydney was certainly party to his hostility. He gave only half-hearted support to penal reform and, with Lord Chancellor Thurlow, spoke in opposition to the abolition of the slave trade in June 1788. On this occasion Pitt threatened that if they would not support him on this then he could no longer work with them in cabinet. Anti-abolitionism was obviously strongly felt by Sydney, for he opposed measures to abolish the slave trade in the Lords until as late as July 1799.

By 1789 Pitt felt that the time was right to rid himself of Sydney, who was more expendable for the king than was Thurlow and in June 'received from Mr Pitt your Majesty's gracious determinations regarding me' (*Later Correspondence of George III*, 3.421). Sydney handed over the seals of office on 5 June and was created Viscount Sydney six days later. It was during his period as home secretary, however, that he created for himself his lasting memorial. He had concerned himself with the affairs of the new colony of New South Wales. In particular he had supported the establishment of a penal colony at Botany Bay; in 1788 the settlement was named Sydney in honour of him.

Final years Sydney's removal from office was sweetened with the sinecure of the chief justiceship in eyre, south of the Trent, which was worth £2500 a year; he was also made deputy lieutenant of Kent in 1793. The income from his various offices added to the considerable wealth that he had inherited on the death of his father in 1780, together with the family estate of Frognal, near Chislehurst, in Kent; he was further enriched when he succeeded to the landed estates of his uncle Selwyn on his death in 1791. He appears to have benefited also from the death of the tenth earl of Exeter, in December 1793, for Exeter's late wife had left £70,000 to her husband for his life, with a subsequent reversion to Townshend.

Sydney died at his estate at Frognal on 30 June 1800, of a cerebral haemorrhage, and was buried on 3 July in Chislehurst church. His estate and title passed to his eldest son, John Thomas. For a man who held high office for six years Sydney is an overlooked figure. Even his obituaries were more concerned with the manner of his death than with his achievements in life. Most contemporary commentators seemed to consider him not hugely talented. Storer damned him with the faint praise that he had 'surpassed everybody's expectation in his political career' (*Carlisle MSS*, 376). Wraxall too was convinced that 'his abilities, though respectable, scarcely rose above mediocrity' (*Memoirs of … Wraxall*, 2.45). This view of his worth is echoed by modern historians, in particular Pitt's biographers. Rose was certainly over-generalizing, in relation to Sydney, when he stated that only Pitt and Thurlow in the 1784 ministry 'could make a tolerable speech' (Barnes, 74). Ehrman, while admitting that he was 'assiduous' and 'a fair debater', concluded that he was 'an average politician of the second rank' who was 'seldom impressive' (Ehrman, 2.184–5; 3.125). These judgements are a little harsh. The initial enthusiasm of the principled 'young friend' of Newcastle does seem to have waned first into vocal independence and then settled merely into a desire for office and honours. In this last respect Sydney was successful, and he certainly avoided the permanent, barren opposition of many of his contemporaries.

What can be said is that Sydney was perhaps mistaken in accepting a peerage and thus losing much of the influence that came from being a Commons' man. He had been appointed by Rockingham—and retained by Shelburne and Pitt—for his debating skills, which were notable. His administrative skills, once in high office, were not so readily apparent. Wraxall pronounced:

> the reputation that he had acquired while seated on the opposition bench … he did not preserve or sustain after his elevation to the peerage … Tommy Townshend displayed very considerable talents. Lord Sydney, when removed to the Upper House of Parliament, seemed to have sunk into an ordinary man. (*Memoirs of … Wraxall*, 4.5)

IAN K. R. ARCHER

Sources *The correspondence of Edmund Burke*, ed. T. W. Copeland and others, 10 vols. (1958–78) • E. A. Webb, G. W. Miller, and J. Beckwith, eds., *The history of Chislehurst: its church, manors, and parish* (1899) • *The later correspondence of George III*, ed. A. Aspinall, 5 vols. (1962–70) • *The historical and the posthumous memoirs of Sir Nathaniel William Wraxall, 1772–1784*, ed. H. B. Wheatley, 5 vols. (1884) • *The manuscripts of his grace the duke of Rutland*, 4 vols., HMC, 24 (1888–1905) • *Autobiography and political correspondence of Augustus Henry, third duke of Grafton*, ed. W. R. Anson (1898) • *Letters from George III to Lord Bute, 1756–1766*, ed. R. Sedgwick (1939) • *Correspondence of William Pitt, earl of Chatham*, ed. W. S. Taylor and J. H. Pringle, 4 vols. (1838–40) • P. C. Yorke, *The life and correspondence of Philip Yorke, earl of Hardwicke*, 3 vols. (1913) • J. Brooke, 'Townshend, Thomas', HoP, *Commons, 1754–90* • P. D. G. Thomas, *Tea party to independence: the third phase of the American Revolution, 1773–1776* (1991) • *The manuscripts of the earl of Carlisle*, HMC, 42 (1897) • D. G. Barnes, *George III and William Pitt, 1783–1806: a new interpretation based upon a study of their unpublished correspondence* (1939); repr. (1965) • P. D. G. Thomas, *The Townshend duties crisis: the second phase of the American revolution, 1767–1773* (1987) • *The last journals of Horace Walpole*, ed. Dr Doran, rev. A. F. Steuart, 2 vols. (1910) • *Life of William, earl of Shelburne …*

with extracts from his papers and correspondence, ed. E. G. P. Fitzmaurice, 2nd edn, 2 vols. (1912) • *Correspondence of John, fourth duke of Bedford*, ed. J. Russell, 3 vols. (1842–6) • J. Ehrman, *The younger Pitt*, 3 vols. (1969); (1983); (1996) • *The journal and correspondence of William, Lord Auckland*, ed. [G. Hogge], 4 vols. (1861–2) • P. D. G. Thomas, *British politics and the Stamp Act crisis: the first phase of the American revolution, 1763–1767* (1975) • P. D. G. Thomas, 'Check list of MPs speaking in the House of Commons, 1768–1774', *BIHR*, 35 (1962), 220–26 • *DNB* • Sainty, *Peerage creations* • Burke, *Peerage* • W. Sterry, ed., *The Eton College register, 1441–1698* (1943) • Venn, *Alum. Cant.*

Archives BL OIOC, corresp. relating to India • Hunt. L., corresp. and papers • NA Canada, corresp. and papers relating to Canada • NL Ire., corresp. relating to Ireland • PRO, corresp., PRO 30/55 • RCP Lond., corresp. and papers relating to illness of George III • U. Leeds, Brotherton L., political corresp. • U. Mich., Clements L., corresp. and papers • Wilts. & Swindon RO, letters • Yale U., Beinecke L., accounts | Beds. & Luton ARS, corresp. with Lord Grantham • BL, corresp. with first marquis of Buckingham, Add. MS 40177–40178 • BL, letters to Frederick Haldimand, Add. MSS 21705, 21708, 21734–21736 • BL, letters to Lord Hardwicke and R. M. Keith, Add. MSS 35531–35682 • BL, corresp. with duke of Leeds, Egerton MSS 3498, 3505 • BL, corresp. with Lord Liverpool, Add. MSS 38222–38234, 38309–38311 • BL, corresp. with duke of Newcastle, Add. MSS 32940–33101 • Bodl. Oxf., corresp. with Lord Macartney • CKS, letters to William Pitt • NL Ire., corresp. with Lord Bolton • North Carolina State Archives, Raleigh, James Abercromby's letter-book • NRA, priv. coll., letters to Lord Shelburne • PRO, corresp. with first earl of Chatham and Lady Chatham, PRO 30/8 • Royal Arch., letters to George III • U. Nott. L., letters to duke of Newcastle • U. Nott. L., corresp. with duke of Portland

Likenesses engraving, 1783 (*The state windmill*), BM • attrib. S. Collings, engraving, 1784 (*The British Titans*), BM • J. Sayers, engraving, 1784, BM, NPG • engraving, 1784 (*Dissolution*), BM • W. Dent, engraving, 1785 (*Fox in the block-shop, or, The heads of opposition rejected*), BM • J. Sayers, engraving, 1785 (*Boring a secret of st-e*), BM • J. Gillray, engraving, 1786 (*A new way to pay the national debt*), BM • J. Gillray, aquatint, 1787 (*The Board of Controul, or, The blessings of a Scotch dictator*), BM • J. Gillray, engraving, 1787 (*The Prince in clover*), BM • engraving, 1787 (*Sale of the cabinet stud*), BM • W. Dent, engraving, 1788 (*The slave trade*), BM • W. Dent, engraving, 1788 (*Illustration by Shade*), BM • J. Gillray, engraving, 1788 (*Market day*), BM • J. Gillray, engraving, 1788 (*State-jugglers*), BM • J. Gillray, engraving, 1788 (*Coaches*), BM • J. Gillray, engraving, 1788 (*The Installation Supper, as given at the Pantheon, by the Knights of the Bath on the 26th of May, 1788*), BM • J. Nixon, engraving, 1788 (*Tryal of Hastings Westminster Hall*), BM • engraving, 1788 (*King Pitt a cut purse of the empire and the rule that from a shelf the precious diadem stole and put it in his pocket. Hamlet*), BM • engraving, 1788 (*Deities of the day, or, The gods in their altitudes. A farce now performing*), BM • T. Rowlandson, engraving, 1788–9 (*State butchers*), BM • H. Wigstead, engraving, 1789 (*The propagation of a truth*), BM • engraving, 1789 (*The triumph of liberty*), BM • engraving, 1789 (*Political monsters going to Westminster*), BM • engraving, 1789 (*Irish wolf dogs putting English blood hounds to flight*), BM • J. Gillray, engraving, 1790 (*John-Bull, baited by the dogs of excise*), BM • J. Gillray, aquatint, 1796 (*Promis'd horrors of the French invasion, - or - Forcible reasons for negotiating a regicide peace. Vide, the authority of Edmund Burke*), BM • J. Reynolds, portrait, priv. coll. • J. Scott, mezzotint (after J. Reynolds), BM, NPG • G. Stuart, portrait, repro. in Webb and others, eds., *History of Chislehurst* • engraving (*The delectable Miss Wh-rt-n, the vigilant secretary*), BM

Wealth at death property in Kent, Norfolk, Gloucestershire, Wiltshire, Nottinghamshire, and Hampshire; plus interests in Whitchurch and Ludgershall, all left to eldest son; wife and other children received £34,300 in cash: probate, will, PRO

Townshend, William (1702–1738). *See under* Townshend, Charles, second Viscount Townshend (1674–1738).

Townson, Robert (*bap.* 1576, *d.* 1621), bishop of Salisbury, was born in Cambridge and baptized in St Botolph's

Church there on 8 January 1576, as son of Renould or Renold Toulnesson. Admitted to Queens' College, Cambridge, as sizar on 28 December 1587, he graduated BA in 1592 and proceeded MA in 1595. He became a fellow of his college in September 1597 and took his BD in 1602. He preached at Paul's Cross on 28 November of that year. On 29 March 1604 he was instituted vicar of Wellingborough, Northamptonshire; on 17 June he married Margaret, daughter of John Davenant and widow of William Townley. Townson became vicar of Old, Northamptonshire, on 16 February 1607. In 1613 he proceeded DD.

Townson's 'comely carriage, courteous nature' and fine preaching, later recalled by his nephew Thomas Fuller (Fuller, *Church History*, 3.294), evidently contributed to his preferment, by 1617, as a royal chaplain. Appointed dean of Westminster on 16 December of that year, he was strict in enforcing a dress code for the abbey congregation. He attended Sir Walter Ralegh before and at his execution on 28 October 1618, writing to Sir John Isham on 9 November that the event was already 'almost forgotten' (Hearne, 1.clxxxvi). Townson was expected to replace Harsnett at Chichester, but was elected bishop of Salisbury on 24 March 1620, being consecrated on 9 July. In his subsequent visitation, he was the first to adopt Bishop Overall's articles for Norwich (1619), which included recommendation of auricular confession as preparation for receiving communion.

Townson died (from smallpox by one account, from late-night study by another) on 15 May 1621, and was buried next day by St Edmund's Chapel in Westminster Abbey. His brother-in-law John *Davenant (*bap.* 1572, *d.* 1641) succeeded to the bishopric of Salisbury, allegedly providing for Townson's many children; of these, Robert became prebendary of Salisbury in 1632. Townson's widow died aged forty-nine on 29 October 1634 and was buried in Salisbury Cathedral.   C. S. KNIGHTON

Sources Venn, *Alum. Cant.* · H. I. Longden, *Northamptonshire and Rutland clergy from 1500*, ed. P. I. King and others, 16 vols. in 6, Northamptonshire RS (1938–52) · *Fasti Angl., 1541–1857*, [Salisbury], 2, 49 · *Fasti Angl., 1541–1857*, [Ely], 70 · T. Hearne, ed., *Walteri Hemingford canonici de Gissburne historia de rebus gestis*, 2 vols. (1731), 1.clxxxiv–clxxxvi · T. Fuller, *The church history of Britain*, ed. [J. Nichols], 3 (1837), 294 · Fuller, *Worthies* (1840), 1.231–2 · S. H. Cassan, *Lives and memoirs of the bishops of Sherborne and Salisbury, from the year 705 to 1824*, 2 (1824), 107–11 · K. Fincham, *Prelate as pastor: the episcopate of James I* (1990), 238n, 306, 314 · *The letters of John Chamberlain*, ed. N. E. McClure, 2 (1939), 105, 176, 178, 240, 294, 375 · *Diary of John Manningham*, ed. J. Bruce, CS, old ser., 99 (1868), 93–5 · J. L. Chester, ed., *The marriage, baptismal, and burial registers of the collegiate church or abbey of St Peter, Westminster*, Harleian Society, 10 (1876), 117 · C. Hill, *Economic problems of the church from Archbishop Whitgift to the Long Parliament* (1956), 21 · K. Fincham, ed., *Visitation articles and injunctions of the early Stuart church*, 1 (1994), 157–68, 173

Townson, Robert (1762–1827), natural historian and traveller, was born early in 1762 at Spring Grove, Marshgate, Richmond, Surrey, the youngest child of London merchant and insurer John Townson (1721–1773) and Sarah Shewell (1731–1805), daughter of James Shewell (1708–1786) and Sarah Smith (*d.* 1748). The Shewells were partners in the brewery trade with Samuel Whitbread and the publishing business with Thomas Longman. Sarah Shewell was the wife of Charles Aldcroft (*d.* 1774), a London haberdasher, with whom she had one child, James Aldcroft (1752–1796), who later took the name Townson. This was because John Townson and Sarah Shewell had carried on a concealed 'criminal conversation' since about 1753 which yielded three other children—Mary (1754–1822), Ann (1756–1811), and John (1760–1835)—in addition to Robert before they married in 1766. John Townson died in 1773 at Hackney. A neighbour there, John Witts (1750–1816), who married Robert's sister Ann in 1774, was inducted vicar of Cardington, Shropshire, in 1777, whereon the Townson family took up residence beneath the Lawley, in beautiful countryside which was greatly to influence Robert's later career.

From about 1777 to 1783 Townson was apprenticed in Manchester but finding his interests were not mercantile, he set off to travel, largely on foot, through France and Italy to Sicily. In 1787, on his way home, he studied chemistry and assaying under Balthasar Georges Sage (1740–1824) at the École des Mines in Paris. In 1788 he enrolled as a student of medicine and chemistry, and later of botany, at Edinburgh University. He planned a career in surgery, but Edinburgh soon showed him he should instead become a natural historian. In 1790 he was duly elected president of the student Edinburgh Natural History Society and in 1791 a fellow of the Royal Society of Edinburgh, proposed by James Hutton, the geologist.

In 1791 Townson unsuccessfully applied to become government naturalist to the colony of Upper Canada. In 1792, after he had left Edinburgh without graduating, his paper 'Observations against the perceptivity of plants' was read to the Linnean Society in London. His travel plans having failed, he enrolled late in 1791 as a student of natural history at the University of Göttingen, going there by way of Uppsala and Copenhagen. While in Göttingen he took a year off to travel to Vienna and throughout Austrian Habsburg lands. He returned to Göttingen and published his first works, on reptilian physiology, in 1794 and 1795. He returned home in 1795 and was awarded the degree of LLD in 1796 by Edinburgh University. He settled again in Shropshire where his *Travels in Hungary* (1797) was written. This contained pioneering botanical, entomological, and petrographic observations and spirited descriptions of his exploits, including those in the Tatra Mountains and in Slovakian caves.

Townson then sought the patronage of the East India Company to undertake mineralogical surveys in India, convinced, by his experiences in Germany, of the need for proper encouragement of such science. But this too was unsuccessful, as was a similar 1797 application to the Sierra Leone Company, which it was thought might distract attention from agriculture there. So Townson stayed in Shropshire and wrote his significant *Philosophy of Mineralogy* (1798), *A Poor Man's Moralist* (1798; five editions up to 1804), and *Tracts and Observations in Natural History* (1799). This last was the most important work. It completed the description of his pioneering experiments in reptilian physiology and gave a remarkable account of the geology of Shropshire.

Disillusioned by his failures to obtain patronage, Townson started travelling again, in England and in Europe. Between 1802 and 1805 he spent much time compiling a *History of Yorkshire*, a planned major county history abandoned only through lack of subscribers. In May 1805 his mother died and he decided to follow his Royal Marines officer brother John to Australia. With all his natural history collections gathered in Shropshire, but his manuscripts burnt, he set off in December 1806. Despite promises by the British government of land, and assurances that he was the type of settler most needed, on his arrival he found the governor, William Bligh (1754–1817), of a completely different opinion. Promises made in London were not kept and Townson became one of the 'rum rebels' who helped depose Bligh in 1808. In 1811 he was at last granted land and settled at Varro Ville, near Sydney; but his scientific aspirations to explore Australia had been thwarted by Bligh and the primitive state of democracy in the colony. His attempts to investigate the novel natural history of his new country were equally frustrated.

At Varro Ville Townson became a successful farmer and wine producer, using the scientific methods which had proved so uninteresting to his contemporaries. He was still trying to return to Britain in 1820 but, finding the disposal of his estates impossible, he remained, somewhat embittered, until his death there on 27 June 1827. He was buried in St John's churchyard, Parramatta, on 3 July. He left goods worth under £10,000. **H. S. TORRENS**

Sources P. Rózsa, ed., *Robert Townson's travels in Hungary* (Debrecen, 1999) [Proceedings of the Townson Symposium held in Debrecen, 26 September 1997] · H. S. Torrens and T. G. Vallance, 'The Anglo-Australian traveller Robert Townson and his map of Hungarian 'Petrography'', *Contributions to the history of geological mapping*, ed. E. Dudich (1984), 391–8 · 'Townson, Robert', *AusDB* · C. B. Jørgensen, 'Paddernes vandøkonomi. Robert Townson: En glemt pioner', *Naturens Verden*, 8 (1994), 284–91 · W. A. S. Sarjeant and A. P. Harvey, 'Uriconian and Longmyndian: a history of the study of the precambrian rocks of the Welsh borderland', *History of concepts in Precambrian geology*, ed. W. O. Kupsch and W. A. S. Sarjeant (1979), 181–224 · N. S. R. Maluf, 'Robert Townson and the respiratory movements of the tortoise', *Isis*, 34 (1942–3), 128–32 · C. B. Jørgensen, 'Robert Townson's observations on amphibian water economy revived', *Comparative biochemistry and physiology*, 109A (1994), 325–34 · I. Pisút, 'Botanické Výskumy Roberta Townsona na Slovensku roku 1793', *Zbornik Slovenskeho Narodneho Musea*, 29 (1983) · D. Laing, ed., *A catalogue of the graduates … of the University of Edinburgh*, Bannatyne Club, 106 (1858), 259
Likenesses A. Earle, portrait, Mitchell L., NSW

Townson, Thomas (1715–1792), Church of England clergyman and religious writer, was born at Much Lees, Essex, where he was baptized on 17 April 1715. He was the eldest son of John Townson (d. 1734), rector of Much Lees, and his wife, Lucretia (1683–1760), daughter of Edward Wiltshire, rector of Kirk Andrews upon Esk. He was educated first by Henry Nott, vicar of Terling in Essex, and then at Felsted School. He matriculated as a commoner at Christ Church, Oxford, on 13 March 1733. He was elected a demy of Magdalen College, Oxford, in July 1735, and a probationary fellow in 1737. During his time at Magdalen he wrote several hexameters. He graduated BA on 20 October 1736 and MA on 20 June 1739. He was ordained deacon on 20 December 1741 and priest on 19 September 1742; three days later he embarked on a tour of France, Italy, Germany, and the Netherlands in the company of William Francis Drake and Edward Holdsworth, and on his return in 1745 resumed tutorial work in Oxford. On 25 August 1746 he was instituted to the vicarage of Hatfield Peverel in Essex. He was junior dean of arts in 1748 and 1749, and in the latter year resigned the living of Hatfield. On 6 June 1749 he became senior proctor of the university, and on 29 August he was presented to the rectory of Blithfield in Staffordshire. On 15 June 1750, soon after the end of his term as proctor, he graduated BD, and served as bursar of Magdalen.

Townson was said to be second only to Robert Lowth in scholarship at Oxford. Though he was reluctant to leave the university he did so on 9 December 1751, preparatory to his institution to the lower mediety of Malpas, Cheshire. He took up residence there on 2 January 1752, resigning his fellowship at about the same time, and lived there until his death. He turned down an exchange of livings in Whitechapel in 1756, and after spending some years dividing his time between his two parishes, he resigned Blithfield in February 1759, on receiving a bequest of £8000 from an old friend, William Barcroft, rector of Fairstead and vicar of Kelvedon, Essex. Townson then applied himself more especially to literary pursuits, publishing, in 1767, two works on Francis Blackburne's *The Confessional*. In September 1768 he virtually repeated his European tour of 1742, returning in October 1769 to a joyful welcome from his parishioners.

Townson subsequently published numerous articles in the *Gentleman's Magazine*. In 1778 his *Discourses on the Four Gospels* appeared, which Lowth called a 'capital performance' and which was translated into German (Allibone, *Dict.*, 3.2442). On 30 October 1781 he was collated to the archdeaconry of Richmond in Yorkshire, a position to which was attached a prebendal stall in Chester. In 1783 he was offered the regius professorship of divinity at Oxford, which he declined on account of his age, yet, at seventy-five, he was still capable of writing Latin poetry for his friend William Drake. In 1790, however, he began to suffer a painful disease of the lungs, which eventually killed him. He died, unmarried, at Malpas on 15 April 1792, with his friend and biographer archdeacon Ralph Churton present, and was buried near the north wall of the churchyard on 23 April. His younger brother John Townson, of Gray's Inn, erected a tablet to his memory in the chancel.

In 1793 Townson's *Discourse on Evangelical History* appeared, edited by the Revd Thomas Bagshaw; Ralph Churton published a memoir of Townson, together with his *Works*, in 1810. Bishop John Jebb edited Townson's *Practical Discourses* (1830), which he says 'were admired and valued by the brightest ornaments of the last age' (Allibone, *Dict.*, 3.2442). **ADAM JACOB LEVIN**

Sources R. Churton, 'Account of the author', in *The works of Thomas Townson*, ed. R. Churton, 2 vols. (1810), v–xcii · S. A. Allibone, *A critical dictionary of English literature and British and American* authors, [another edn], 3 (1877), 2442 · *GM*, 1st ser., 80 (1810), 47–52, 100 · *GM*, 1st ser., 100/1 (1830), 238–40 · Foster, *Alum. Oxon.* · *Fasti Angl.* (Hardy), 3.268 · will, PRO, PROB 11/1219, fols. 155–8 · J. Sargeaunt, *A history of Felstead School* (1889), 51–3 · J. R. Bloxam, *A register of the presidents, fellows … of Saint Mary Magdalen College*, 8 vols. (1853–85), vol. 1, p. 151; vol. 2, p. cxcii; vol. 6, pp. 164, 221, 233–40; vol. 7, p. 18 · *DNB*

Archives Staffs. RO, corresp. with Lord Bagot · Warks. CRO, theological notes, letters to Sir Roger Newdigate · Yale U., Beinecke L., corresp. with Walter Bagot

Likenesses J. Russel, group portrait, 1744, priv. coll.; *see illus. in* Holdsworth, Edward (1684–1746) · J. Basire, engraving (after portrait), repro. in *Works*, vol. 1, ed. Churton, frontispiece

Wealth at death over £1200: will, PRO, PROB 11/1219, fols. 155–8

Towry, George Henry (1767–1809), naval officer, born on 4 March 1767, one of a family which for several generations had served in or been connected with the navy, was the son of George Philipps Towry, for many years a commissioner of victualling. His grandfather Henry John Philipps Towry (*d.* 1762), a naval captain, was the nephew of Captain John Towry (*d.* 1757), sometime commissioner of the navy at Port Mahon, and took the name of Towry on succeeding to his uncle's property in 1760. George Henry Towry was for some time at Eton College while his name was on the books of various ships. In June 1782 he joined the *Alexander* as captain's servant with Lord Longford, and was present at the relief of Gibraltar under Lord Howe and the encounter with the allied fleet off Cape Spartel. He afterwards served in the *Carnatic* with Captain Molloy, in the yacht *Royal Charlotte* with Captain William Cornwallis, and in the *Europa*. From October 1784 to March 1786 he was in the *Hebe* with Captain Edward Thornbrough, in which ship Prince William Henry (later William IV) was a lieutenant, and from March 1786 to December 1787 was in the *Pegasus*, with Prince William as captain. On 6 February 1788 Towry passed his examination and on 23 October 1790 was promoted lieutenant. Early in 1793, at Lord Hood's request, he was appointed to the *Victory*, in which he went to the Mediterranean, where on 14 September 1793 he was made commander. On 18 June 1794 he was posted to the frigate *Dido* (28 guns).

On 24 June 1795, with the *Lowestoft* (32 guns), on her way from Minorca to look into Toulon, the *Dido* met two French frigates, the *Minerve* (40 guns) and the *Artémise* (36 guns), both of them larger, heavier, and more heavily armed than the British ships; the *Minerve* alone was superior in broadside weight of shot to the *Dido* and *Lowestoft* together. Seeing this great apparent superiority, the French ships sailed towards the British, the *Minerve* leading. The *Dido* led the British ships and brought the *Minerve* to close action. The *Minerve*, being twice the weight of the *Dido*, attempted to run her down, but the *Dido*, swerving at the critical moment, received the blow obliquely and caught the *Minerve's* bowsprit in her mizen rigging. The heavy swell broke off the *Minerve's* bowsprit and the *Dido's* mizenmast, and the two ships lay by to clear away the wreck, when the *Lowestoft*, coming to the *Dido's* support, completely dismasted the *Minerve*. On this the *Artémise*, which had been firing distant broadsides at the British

ships, fled. Towry, seeing that the *Minerve* could not escape, signalled the *Lowestoft* to chase, but recalled her an hour and a half later, seeing that pursuit was hopeless. When the *Lowestoft* again closed with the *Minerve*, and the *Dido*, having repaired her damages, came up, the Frenchman surrendered. The British success was due largely to the misconduct of the *Artémise's* captain, but the capture of such a ship as the *Minerve* was a brilliant achievement and was praised by Nelson, who wrote to his wife: 'Thank God the superiority of the British navy remains, and I hope ever will: I feel quite delighted at the event' (*Dispatches and Letters*, 2.48).

The *Minerve* was brought into the service and Towry was appointed to command her, but in April 1796 he was moved by Sir John Jervis (afterwards the earl of St Vincent) to the *Diadem* (64 guns). During the year he was detached in the *Diadem* under the orders of Commodore Nelson, who for part of the time hoisted his broad pennant on board her, notably at the evacuation of Corsica in October (*Dispatches and Letters*, 2.300–02). Off Cape St Vincent on 14 February 1797 the *Diadem*, still commanded by Towry, closed the line, but had no very prominent part in the battle. Towards the end of the year she was sent to England. In December 1798 Towry was appointed to command the frigate *Uranie* (38 guns), in which, and afterwards in the *Cambrian*, he continued until the peace. In July 1803 he was appointed to the *Tribune*, which he commanded in the channel during the early months of the winter. Under the severity of the work his health gave way, and in January 1804 he was obliged to take sick leave. From May 1804 to June 1806 he commanded the yacht *Royal Charlotte*, and was afterwards one of the commissioners for the transport service. He married in 1802 a Miss or Mrs Chamberlayne (*d. c.*1806); of their children a son and a daughter survived. Towry died in his father's house in Somerset Place, London, on 9 April 1809, and was buried on 17 April at St Marylebone.　　J. K. LAUGHTON, *rev.* ANDREW LAMBERT

Sources *The dispatches and letters of Vice-Admiral Lord Viscount Nelson*, ed. N. H. Nicolas, 7 vols. (1844–6) · D. Syrett and R. L. DiNardo, *The commissioned sea officers of the Royal Navy, 1660–1815*, rev. edn, Occasional Publications of the Navy RS, 1 (1994) · *GM*, 1st ser., 79 (1809), 475 · naval documents, PRO · J. J. Colledge, *Ships of the Royal Navy: an historical index*, 1 (1969)

Likenesses W. Ridley, stipple (after P. Jean), BM, NPG; repro. in *European Magazine* (1797)

Towse, Sir (Ernest) Beachcroft Beckwith (1864–1948), army officer and campaigner for the welfare of blind people, was born at Regent's Park, London, on 23 April 1864, the elder of the two sons of Robert Beckwith Towse, solicitor, and his Irish wife, Julia Ann Corcoran. The high-spirited and adventurous Towse was educated at Stubbington House, Gosport, and Wellington College, Berkshire, and in 1883 he joined the 3rd Seaforth Highlanders (the Highland rifle militia); he was promoted lieutenant in December 1885. In 1886 he transferred to the Gordon Highlanders; he served with the Chitral relief force (1895), was at the storming of the Malakand Pass, was promoted captain in 1896, and served in the north-west frontier and

Sir (Ernest) Beachcroft Beckwith Towse (1864–1948), by Walter Stoneman

Tirah campaigns (1897–8). Towse had married on 25 October 1892 Gertrude, younger daughter of John Christie, a stockbroker; they had no children. In October 1899 he went with the 1st battalion of his regiment to South Africa and was present at the advance on Kimberley and the battle of Magersfontein (11 December 1899) when the Highland brigade suffered heavy casualties. On 30 April 1900 on Mount Thaba, when rallying his force of twelve men to attack some 150 Boers, he received the wound which blinded him. For his gallantry then and for his attempt at Magersfontein to carry his mortally wounded colonel to safety, he was awarded the Victoria Cross (gazetted 6 July 1900). He was mentioned in dispatches.

His military career over, Towse turned all his vigorous powers to the service of the blind. He joined the council of the National Institute for the Blind (then the British and Foreign Blind Association) in 1901 and became vice-chairman later that year; he was also a member of the committee of the Incorporated Association for Promoting the General Welfare of the Blind. Towse travelled the country to help the work of the institute and foster public interest in the welfare of blind people. When war broke out in 1914 he was soon an honorary staff captain (without pay and allowances) for base hospitals in France and Belgium. He brought comfort to many wounded, writing letters home from his braille notes; he was probably one of the first welfare officers, and was mentioned in dispatches.

Before going to the war Towse suggested to the National Institute for the Blind that they should set up a subcommittee to look after blinded former servicemen. This, under the inspiration of Sir Arthur Pearson, developed into St Dunstan's, but Towse realized that there was still no help available for former servicemen who went blind through causes other than the war, or for the blind dependants of servicemen. In 1923, therefore, he inaugurated a Special Fund for Blind Ex-Servicemen which continued as the Sir Beachcroft Towse Ex-Service Fund. His concern for all who returned from the war led him to help in launching in 1917 the Comrades of the Great War, and as chairman he travelled during two years over 12,000 miles in the British Isles. This organization merged with others to form the British Legion, of which he became a national vice-president in 1927, remaining in office until his death.

Captain Towse's striking figure with its soldierly bearing and immaculate attire, including a tartan waistcoat, was often seen at great functions. In 1900 he was made a sergeant-at-arms in ordinary to the queen, and from 1903 to 1939 he was a member of the Honourable Corps of Gentlemen-at-Arms. In 1920 he was appointed CBE and in 1927 KCVO for services to the blind and to former servicemen. In 1916 he became a knight of grace of the order of St John of Jerusalem.

The Second World War brought Towse into yet another field of service when he made his home at Long Meadow, Goring-on-Thames, available for civilians blinded through air raids. It thus became the first Queen Elizabeth Home of Recovery and he remained there in charge of this important work of rehabilitation. In 1944, on account of continuous ill health and advancing years, he resigned from the chairmanship of the National Institute for the Blind he had assumed in 1923. His resignation was received 'with a sense of personal loss and poignancy of regret almost too deep for words', and he was elected president, an office which had been vacant since the death of Pearson in 1921.

Towse was also a member of the livery of the Fishmongers' Company and of the court of the Clothworkers' Company, health alone preventing him from taking up the mastership of the latter, to which he was elected in 1941. He was also vice-president of Worcester College for the Blind, the Greater London Fund for the Blind, and the Hepburn Starey Blind Aid Society, and chairman of the British Wireless for the Blind Fund. In early life his chief interests, apart from his service career, had been polo, hunting, and big game shooting. After he was blinded he became a fine fisherman and a skilful carpenter and joiner.

Towse's wife, Gertrude, had died in 1935, and in his later years he was cared for by a niece. He died at his home, Long Meadow, Goring-on-Thames, Oxfordshire, on 21 June 1948. BASIL CURTIS, *rev.* ROGER T. STEARN

Sources private information (1959) · personal knowledge (1959) · *WWW* · Burke, *Peerage* (1929) · S. Dark, *The life of Sir Arthur Pearson* [1922] · *The register of the Victoria cross*, 3rd edn (1997) · *CGPLA Eng. &*

Wales (1948) · J. Dunn, *The Parramatta cemeteries: St. John's* (Parramatta, NSW, 1991), 87
Archives FILM BFI NFTVA, documentary footage
Likenesses W. Stoneman, photograph, NPG [*see illus.*] · photograph, repro. in *The register of the Victoria cross*, 313
Wealth at death £25,051 16s. 3d.: probate, 25 Oct 1948, *CGPLA Eng. & Wales*

Towson, John Thomas (1804–1881), scientist and photographer, the son of John Gay Towson (1769–1857) and his wife, Elizabeth Thomas, was born at Fore Street, Devonport, on 8 April 1804, and educated at Stoke classical school. He initially followed his father's trade as a maker of chronometers and watches. When the daguerreotype process was introduced in 1839 he and Robert Hunt (1807–1887) devoted considerable attention to it; it was with the help of Towson's work, published in the *Philosophical Magazine* (November 1839) and entitled 'On the proper focus for the daguerreotype', that the American John William Draper took the first sunlight picture of a human face in 1840. Towson was the first to devise the means of taking a photographic picture on glass and of using the reflecting camera; and, with Hunt, he produced highly sensitive photographic papers, for the sale of which they appointed agents in London and elsewhere. On 19 November 1840 he married at Stoke Demerel church, Devonport, Margaret, daughter of William Braddon, sail maker, of Devonport. At this time Towson described himself as 'watchmaker'.

About 1846 Towson turned his attention to navigation, in which he instructed young men in the naval yard. His investigations led to the suggestion that the quickest route across the Atlantic would be by sailing on the great circle. Sir John Herschel drew the attention of the Admiralty to Towson's discovery, and that department subsequently published Towson's *Tables for Facilitating the Practice of Great Circle Sailing*, and his *Tables for the Reduction of ex-Meridian Altitudes* (1849). The works proved of particular value to the merchant marine. In 1850 he moved to Liverpool on being appointed scientific examiner of masters and mates there; he held the post until 1873, when he retired, still holding an appointment as chief examiner in compasses. In 1853 he brought before the Liverpool Literary and Philosophical Society the subject of the deviation of the compass on board iron ships, and in 1854 he helped William Scoresby (1789–1857) to draw the attention of the British Association to the matter. The result of the discussion was the formation of the Liverpool compass committee, whose three reports, subsequently presented to both houses of parliament, were largely produced by Towson. In recognition of his services to navigation he was on 9 January 1857 presented by the shipowners of Liverpool with a dock bond for £1000 and a gratuity of more than £100. In 1863 he was instructed by the Board of Trade to prepare a manual which was published as *Practical Information on the Deviation of the Compass … [on] Iron Ships*. In 1870 he prepared a syllabus, adopted by the Board of Trade, for examinations in compass deviations. Towson died at his home, 47 Upper Parliament Street, Liverpool, on 3 January 1881, leaving a widow.

Towson wrote prolifically on geography, photography, and history, but it was his works on navigation, which reached several editions and were translated into various languages, for which he is best remembered.

C. W. SUTTON, *rev.* ELIZABETH BAIGENT

Sources *Men of the time* (1875) · Boase, *Mod. Eng. biog.* · *The Times* (4 Jan 1881), 6 · *The Athenaeum* (8 Jan 1881), 59 · W. J. Harrison, *History of photography* (1888) · *Who was who in America: historical volume, 1607–1896*, rev. edn (1967) · *CGPLA Eng. & Wales* (1881) · m. cert. · private information (1898) · S. T. S. Lecky, *Wrinkles in practical navigation* (1894) · R. Hunt, *Manual of photography* (1853) · *Draper Memorial Park: the story of John William Draper and his brother Henry* (1950)
Wealth at death under £1500: probate, 21 Jan 1881, *CGPLA Eng. & Wales*

Toy, Humphrey (*b.* in or before **1537**, *d.* **1577**), bookseller, was the son of the London bookseller **Robert Toy** (*d.* 1556) and his first wife (*d.* in or before 1546); the couple also had a daughter, Rose, who married the London stationer Arthur Pepwell (*d.* 1568/9). The *Dictionary of National Biography* suggested that Robert was originally Welsh—a speculation supported by the bequest by Robert's second wife to another Robert, 'the son of Humfrie Toye of Carmarthen', in 1565 and Humphrey's activities as a publisher of Welsh works (Plomer, 15). Robert was probably freed by the Stationers' Company before 1537 and was assessed at £20 in St Faith's parish, London, in 1541. He was publishing from premises in St Paul's Churchyard probably from 1542 onwards; from 1545 he was operating under the sign of the Bell. On 22 January 1546 he married Elizabeth Scampion (*d.* 1565) of St Margaret's, Westminster. *STC* associates him with the publication of more than forty titles, mostly religious and theological, including two works by Stephen Gardiner, one title by Foxe, and, in 1551, an edition of the Matthew Bible. He also co-published Chaucer's works and two Skelton texts, *Phyllyp Sparowe* and *Why Come ye Nat to Courte*.

Robert's son Humphrey matriculated as a sizar from Queens' College, Cambridge, at Michaelmas 1551, but there is no record of his obtaining a degree. Robert died between 5 February 1556, the date of his will, and 12 February, when Elizabeth rewarded the Stationers' Company for 'commynge to the buryall of hyr husbonde' (Arber, *Regs. Stationers*, 1.35). At his death Robert had property interests throughout St Paul's Churchyard and the nearby Paternoster Row, and left his shop to Elizabeth, his executor, with a reversion to Humphrey upon her death. Other bequests included the Stationers' Company and the poor of the parish of Cleobury Mortimer, Shropshire, where Robert's brother Edward Toy (or Troy) had been vicar since 1551. Elizabeth carried on the bookselling business until at least 1558, most notably entering more than thirty ballad titles with John Walley in the company's register.

On 11 March 1558 Humphrey, who then must have been at least twenty-one, was freed by patrimony into the Stationers' Company. He entered his first work in the company's registers in August 1560, and was admitted to the livery in summer 1561. He served as a renter warden of the company for successive years for 1561–2 and 1562–3, and was living at his shop at the sign of the Helmet in St Paul's

Churchyard (probably opposite the great north door of the cathedral) from 1562 until 1574. In 1564 he brought an action in chancery against Robert Leche, chancellor of West Chester, over money owed for copies of the second book of *Homilies*. Toy's stepmother died in 1565, leaving him most of her estate. Humphrey was evidently married by this time, as Elizabeth's will named Elizabeth and Joan as his children. He was married to Margaret or Margery (*d.* after 1577), daughter of James Revell, surveyor of the works, but neither the date of marriage nor whether she was the mother of these children is known. Toy rose further in the Stationers' Company, serving as under-warden for two terms between 1571 and 1573. In the summer of 1575 he was involved, with three other members of the book trade, in a dispute with the queen's printer, Richard Jugge, over the right to print bibles.

Only about thirty works bearing Toy's imprint survive, including an edition of Grafton's *Chronicle*. Toy was a 'deare Friend' of the Welsh scholar William Salesbury, and in 1567 he published Salesbury's translations of the Bible and the Book of Common Prayer as well as his guide to Welsh pronunciation (Salesbury, sig. A2r). Toy's business also had an important international dimension. Between at least 1566 and 1569 he had links with the printer Christopher Plantin in Antwerp: during the first half of 1568, for example, he received thirty-five reams of books from Antwerp, while a surviving list of 159 books sent to him by Plantin, apparently just after Toy's death, showed that he was using Plantin as an agent to purchase protestant works from across Europe.

Toy may have had Bristol connections as, following his death on 16 October 1577, he was buried in All Saints' Church in that city, where his widow set up a funeral monument. The administration of his estate was granted to Margaret on 26 November and his shop passed to his former apprentice, Thomas Chard. Toy is to be distinguished from a contemporary namesake in the Merchant Taylors' Company who was active in 1583.   I. GADD

Sources STC, 1475–1640 · R. G. Lang, ed., *Two Tudor subsidy assessment rolls for the city of London, 1541 and 1581*, London RS, 29 (1993) · E. G. Duff, *A century of the English book trade* (1905) · H. R. Plomer, *Abstracts from the wills of English printers and stationers from 1492 to 1630* (1903) · Venn, *Alum. Cant.* · administration, PRO, PROB 6/2, fol. 135v · H. G. Aldis and others, *A dictionary of printers and booksellers in England, Scotland and Ireland, and of foreign printers of English books, 1557–1640*, ed. R. B. McKerrow (1910) · P. W. M. Blayney, *The bookshops in Paul's Cross churchyard* (1990), 12–13, 48–50 · B. Dietz, *The port and trade of early Elizabethan London: documents*, London RS, 8 (1972) · private information (2004) [J. A. C. Sewell] · S. F. F. Auchmuty, *The history of the parish of Cleobury Mortimer, Salop* (1911); repr. (1996) · Arber, *Regs. Stationers* · W. Salesbury, *A playne and a familiar introduction* (1567)

Toy, John (1608x11–1663), Church of England clergyman and headmaster, was born in Worcester, the son of John Toy, mercer, of Worcester, sometime clerk of the parish of St Swithun in the city; he had married Fortune Burton, widow, in 1608. Toy was educated at the King's School, Worcester, as a non-foundationer. On 27 April 1627 he received an exhibition of 40s. per annum from the dean and chapter to support three years' further study. He was admitted to Pembroke College, Oxford, the same year (when he was said to be sixteen) as a servitor or batteler. He matriculated on 23 May 1628, graduated BA on 27 January 1631, and proceeded MA on 2 July 1634.

Toy subsequently became chaplain to the bishop of Hereford. In 1638 he published *Worcester's Elegie and Eulogie*, an account of the epidemic which killed 1500 people in the city between June 1637 and 1638. Toy ascribed the plague to God's anger at the citizens' failure to take heed of His (and Toy's) previous warnings, though he conceded that Worcester was no more wicked than the average cathedral city. At Michaelmas 1638 he became gospeller of the cathedral. In the following year of account he was listed as a minor canon. On 22 October 1641 he was instituted to the rectory of Stoke Prior, Worcestershire. A week later he received a lease of a house in the cathedral precinct for the term of his ministry there. He published a sermon given at the funeral in February 1642 of Alice, wife of the cathedral organist, Thomas Tomkins.

At about this time Toy became master of the city school. He moved to the headmastership of the King's School, probably in the summer of 1644. Along with the rest of the collegiate body, he was deprived after the city's surrender to parliament in July 1646. He retired to his vicarage, but was sequestrated from that also in 1649. In the course of this year he sent to the press his *Grammaticae Graecae Enchiridion in usum scholae collegialis Wigorniae*, published the following year, which possibly helped to secure his appointment to the headmastership of Queen Mary's School, Walsall, in 1650. One of his pupils there, Dr Philip Fouke, later commended Toy's teaching as successful 'even among triumphing rebels' ('inter perduelles triumphantes') and without resort to lashings and scourgings ('flagris et verberibus'; inscription in British Library copy of Toy's *Quisquillae poeticae*, 1662; transcribed with translation in Macdonald, 135).

Toy was restored to the headmastership of the King's School in September 1660 and he also regained his living. One of his pupils during his second term at Worcester may have been the future Lord Chancellor Somers. Toy died on 28 December 1663 and was buried two days later in the south transept of the cathedral. His widow, Martha, died on 10 April 1677, aged sixty-nine, and was buried at Stoke Prior.   C. S. KNIGHTON

Sources T. Nash, *Collections for the history of Worcestershire*, 2 (1782), 381 · Wood, *Ath. Oxon.*, new edn, 3.649–52 · J. Chambers, *Biographical illustrations of Worcestershire* (1820), 163–4 · VCH Worcestershire, 4.486–7 · BL, Add. MS 24489, fol. 108v · J. F. D. Shrewsbury, *A history of bubonic plague in the British Isles* (1971) · F. V. Follett, *A history of the Worcester Royal Grammar School* (1951), 54–6 · Foster, *Alum. Oxon.* · D. Robertson, ed., *The old order book of Hartlebury grammar school, 1556–1752*, Worcestershire Historical Society, 17 (1904), 95 · A. Macdonald, *A history of the King's School Worcester* (1936), 123, 129–37 · M. Craze, *King's School, Worcester* (1972), 81–3, 89–108 · I. A. Atkins, 'Notes on John Toy (1609–1663) and Thomas Taylor (1602–1673)', *The Vigornian* (July 1943), 308–9 · I. A. Atkins, 'Notes on John Toy (1609–1663) and Thomas Taylor (1602–1673)', *The Vigornian* (Dec 1943), 324–5

Toy, Robert (*d.* 1556). *See under* Toy, Humphrey (*b.* in or before 1537, *d.* 1577).

Toye, Thomas (1801–1870), minister of the Presbyterian Church in Ireland and revivalist preacher, was born in Clonakilty, co. Cork, on 6 October 1801, the eldest of three children in a prosperous Church of Ireland family. Educated at home and in a local classical school, he was prevented by asthma from entering Trinity College, Dublin, or taking up the legal career planned for him. Following a conversion experience in 1818 he became increasingly involved in church work and in 1825 he joined an Independent congregation in Mallow, co. Cork, having gone to live there with an uncle, Dr Justice, for the sake of his health. He moved to Cork to the home of an aunt, Mrs Captain Nield, and became actively involved in the Independent congregation of the Revd John Burnett.

After his marriage in 1825 to Ellen Hogg (d. 1840), daughter of J. F. Hogg of Clonakilty, Toye returned to Cork to live. He founded local branches of the Bible and London Missionary societies and held evangelistic services in his own home. Ordination as an Independent minister followed in 1836. After his wife's death in 1840 he moved to Belfast where he had preached occasionally and had become the friend of the Secession church leader, the Revd John Edgar. Edgar allowed him to preach in a schoolroom connected with his Alfred Street congregation and this led to regular services in a loft in James Street. So successful was his ministry there that a new Presbyterian congregation was formed in Great George's Street with Toye installed as its first minister by the Belfast presbytery on 3 March 1842. Largely through the generosity of a wealthy Presbyterian lady, Miss Jane Gregg, also a major benefactor of the Presbyterian college, Belfast, a new church building was opened free of debt in 1843.

Always an evangelist, Toye published more than 200 tracts for distribution in his congregation and organized prayer and class meetings to encourage church members to share their spiritual experiences. Some Presbyterians considered that Toye was really a Methodist.

Toye remarried soon after coming to Belfast but his second wife, Harriet Elizabeth Shaw, the daughter of William and Charlotte Shaw of Cork, died on 24 July 1852 and in 1853 he married Jane Galway (d. 1886), the daughter of William Galway of Dundonald, who survived him to publish an account of his life and work, *Brief Memorials of the Rev. Thomas Toye, Belfast* (1873). There were no children of any of his marriages.

Toye was prominently involved in the 1859 Ulster revival. He brought some of the early Ahoghill converts to his pulpit to recount their experiences. Revival meetings continued in Great George's Street until July 1860, and Toye gave stirring accounts of the revival on visits to Scotland, where his preaching was popular.

Although he had subscribed the Westminster formularies, Toye contributed to the softening of Irish Presbyterianism's rigid Calvinism which was taking place under the impact of evangelicalism. His only major speech in the general assembly was during the controversy over assurance of salvation which followed the revival, in which he argued strongly that scripture clearly taught a doctrine of present salvation, that humankind could be saved and know it.

Toye died suddenly of heart failure on 15 May 1870, at his home in Great George's Street, and was buried in the Clifton Street cemetery, Belfast, on 17 May. A *Belfast News-Letter* correspondent reported that, for his funeral service, his church was 'crowded to excess by an audience drawn from all classes in the community, many of them very poor people and some of them to all appearances outcasts of society who felt that they had lost a true friend' (*Belfast News-Letter*, 19 May 1870). His eccentricities—he would slip out of his pulpit to enjoy a smoke during the singing of a long psalm—and his sincerity had endeared him to many. 'His life-work', declared his memorial tablet, 'was the conversion of souls and the revival of vital godliness.'

FINLAY HOLMES

Sources J. E. Toye, *Brief memorials of the Rev. Thomas Toye, Belfast* (1873) · J. M. Barkley, 'Thomas Toye—revivalist preacher', *Bulletin of the Presbyterian Historical Society of Ireland*, 8 (Nov 1978) · *Evangelical Witness*, 9 (1870) · W. B. Kirkpatrick, 'Review of *Brief memorials*', *Evangelical Witness*, 12 (1873) · *Belfast News-Letter* (16–19 May 1870) · R. S. J. Clarke, *Old Belfast families and the new burying ground* (1991), 253–4 · T. Hamilton, ed., *Irish worthies* (1875), 59–63
Archives Presbyterian Historical Society of Ireland, Belfast
Likenesses double portrait, photograph (with his third wife), Presbyterian Historical Society of Ireland, Belfast · photograph, repro. in Toye, *Brief memorials*
Wealth at death £100: probate, 8 June 1870, *CGPLA Ire.*

Toynbee, Arnold (1852–1883), social reformer and political economist, was born at 18 Savile Row, London, on 23 August 1852, the second son of Joseph *Toynbee (1815–1866), an eminent aural surgeon, and his wife, Harriet Holmes. Toynbee owed much in his early years to the influence of his father, who, though he died when his son was only fourteen, had already inspired him with a love of literature and with the foundations of those social ideals which were afterwards the main interest of his life. Toynbee began his education at a preparatory school at Blackheath.

At the age of thirteen or fourteen a fall from his pony resulted in a severe concussion and recurring headaches, which were to plague him especially when he was under strain. Hence, rather than go to Rugby School as planned, Toynbee went to the Revd J. M. Brackenbury's school in Wimbledon, and following his father's death in 1866, spent two unfruitful years in an army preparatory school reading for the military academy at Woolwich. Strained relations with his mother and the lack of a clear sense of purpose meant that he spent the next few years attending some classes at King's College, London, and reading on his own at home and in various lodgings. Finally he came into a small inheritance from his father, enabling him to go to Oxford in 1873. He had a sharp intellect and strongly independent character, which enabled him to acquire an amount of knowledge in certain fields of study, and to develop a strength and originality of opinion very unusual at so early an age. However, according to his friend F. C. Montague, Toynbee at this stage 'imagined himself to have gone deeper and further than was really the case' (Montague, 10).

Arnold Toynbee (1852–1883), by unknown photographer

In January 1873 Toynbee matriculated as a commoner at Pembroke College, Oxford. In November of that year he competed for the Brackenbury (history) scholarship at Balliol. Though he was not successful, his work made a great impression on the examiners, and Benjamin Jowett of Balliol offered him rooms. Toynbee was keen to take up this offer, but the master of Pembroke raised objections. Following Jowett's advice, Toynbee left Pembroke and ceased to be a member of the university, though still residing at Oxford. In January 1875 he matriculated afresh, this time as a commoner at Balliol, though he had to abandon his plan to sit for Greats (the final examination in philosophy and ancient history) and instead read for an ordinary pass degree. As an undergraduate he was a considerable influence among his Balliol contemporaries.

Toynbee came at first under the influence of Ruskin, who may have stimulated Toynbee's initial interest in political economy. He joined with enthusiasm the North Hinksey diggers' project, where Ruskin hoped to teach Oxford men the value of labour in the service of the community. But he soon became an ardent disciple of T. H. Green and adopted Green's gospel of civic duty, which led to Toynbee's joining some of his Balliol contemporaries in tutoring the teacher-trainees of the Oxford Wesleyan Boys' School. Toynbee resolved a crisis of faith through Green's broad-church views, whereby duty replaced dogma as the main expression of faith. This, in turn, resulted in Toynbee's involvement with the Church Reform Union's campaign to strengthen the national character of the established church and democratize its government, especially at the parish level. The desire to assist in raising the material and moral condition of the mass of the population grew more and more to be the absorbing passion of his life, and it was in order to direct his own and others' efforts in this direction that he threw himself with great energy into the study of economics, and especially of economic history. In spite of his poor health, which caused frequent and serious interruption to his studies, Toynbee obtained such a mastery of economics that immediately after taking his degree (1878) he was appointed a tutor at Balliol in charge of the candidates for the Indian Civil Service. In the following year he married (26 June 1879) Charlotte Maria (1841–1931), daughter of William Duncombe Atwood [see Toynbee, Charlotte Maria], who was eleven years his senior.

Toynbee's Oxford lectures, primarily intended for his pupils but soon attracting a wider circle of hearers, dealt with the principles of economics and contemporary economic history. His main interest was the history of the great changes which had come over the industrial system of Great Britain between the middle of the eighteenth century and his own time. Keen to apply the new liberal principles of Green, he took part in charity organization (he was a poor-law guardian from 1881), co-operation, and adult education. He gave public lectures on the industrial problems of the day, which were attended by large working-class audiences in Bradford, Newcastle, Bolton, Leicester, and London.

The posthumously published volume of his works entitled *The Industrial Revolution* (1884) reveals the nature of Toynbee's interests. The first part of it, 'The industrial revolution' proper, consists of the notes of his lectures delivered at Balliol on the industrial history of Great Britain from 1760, a subject on which he was collecting materials at the time of his death. Despite its fragmentary character and occasional inconsistencies, *The Industrial Revolution* is full of valuable research and acute observation. In effect, Toynbee made in his lectures a strong case for the study of economic and social history as deserving specialization in addition to the traditional political and constitutional history. Toynbee has been widely credited with having established the term 'industrial revolution' as a proper historical concept. However, his intention was to extend the application of the whig argument contrasting the peaceful and gradual reformism of the 'English revolution' with the violence of the French Revolution. Toynbee had adopted the positivist view of progress as encompassing all spheres of human activity and tried to show how industrialization had carried with it progressive political change, thereby rejecting the need for revolutionary politics. The popular addresses, including 'Wages and natural law' and 'Industry and democracy', which compose the second half of the volume, are chiefly of interest as illustrations of Toynbee's character and aims as a social missionary. The eloquence, the religious fervour, the enthusiasm for the better organization of industrial society, and the genuine but not uncritical sympathy with working-class aspirations which were characteristic of him, are traceable even in the fragmentary remains of these lectures, which were largely extempore, and could in some instances only be pieced together after his death, from notes or from the reports of provincial newspapers. But the chief source of Toynbee's influence lay in the charm of his personality. His striking appearance, 'a face of almost Greek regularity of feature' (Milner, xiv), winning manners, and great power of expression aided by a melodious voice, above all his transparent sincerity and high-mindedness, won the respect and affection of all with whom he came into contact, whether as pupil, teacher, or fellow worker in social causes.

Since his undergraduate days Toynbee had been a friend of Jowett, master of Balliol. He was also closely associated with T. H. Green and Richard Lewis Nettleship. Following a brief stay in the summer of 1875 in east London, he was also associated with Canon Barnett, vicar of St Jude's, Whitechapel, and became a founder of the first university settlement, Toynbee Hall, which was established soon after Toynbee's death and named after him.

Toynbee belonged to the first generation of new Liberals who strove to preserve the political alliance between labour and Liberalism by means of producing a new mix of updated Liberal ideology. They combined the traditional values of free trade and self-help with Green's advocacy of greater intervention by the state in ensuring its citizens' welfare and with practical reform schemes which were to compete with radical socialism. Following Green's example, Toynbee entered municipal politics in 1882, when he stood unsuccessfully as a Liberal candidate for Oxford's north ward, where Green had held a seat until his death. He was opposed to the extreme individualism of some of the earlier English economists, and he came to reject the validity and utility of classical economics. He believed strongly in the power of free corporate effort, such as that of co-operative and friendly societies and of trade unions, to raise the standard of life among the mass of the people, and in the duty of the state to assist such effort by free education, by the regulation of the conditions of labour, and by contributing to voluntary insurance funds intended to provide for the labourer in sickness and old age.

In the last year of his life Toynbee was deeply interested in the agitation that was provoked by Henry George's book on *Progress and Poverty* (1880) and his lectures in the British Isles. Convinced of the one-sidedness of that remarkable work, and alarmed by what he considered the bad and misleading influence which it was exercising upon the leaders of working-class opinion, he did his best to combat the doctrine of land nationalization by speech and writing. Two lectures which he delivered on the subject, first in Oxford and then at St Andrew's Hall, Newman Street, London, were his last efforts as a teacher on social questions. For some time he had been greatly overworked, and the physical and mental strain of delivering the lectures in London to hostile audiences were held to have contributed to the complete breakdown of his health. He contracted meningitis and died at 3 Thornton Hill, Wimbledon, Surrey, on 9 March 1883 and was buried in Wimbledon churchyard. At the time of his death Toynbee, who had been made bursar of Balliol in 1881, was just about to be appointed a fellow of that college. Following his untimely death he was widely hailed as a modern martyr who had given his life in the service of the masses. In retrospect he is best remembered for having established the academic usage of the term 'Industrial Revolution', and as one of the leaders of early new Liberalism.

ALON KADISH

Sources A. Kadish, *Apostle Arnold: the life and death of Arnold Toynbee, 1852–1883* (1986) · F. C. Montague, *Arnold Toynbee* (1889) · A. Milner, *Arnold Toynbee: a reminiscence* (1895) · G. Toynbee, *Reminiscences and letters of Joseph and Arnold Toynbee* (1910) · b. cert. · m. cert. · d. cert. · CGPLA Eng. & Wales (1883)
Archives Balliol Oxf., letters to his family | Bodl. Oxf., Milner MSS · Derbys. RO, letters to Philip Gell
Likenesses J. E. Boehm, marble medallion (posthumous), Balliol Oxf.; plaster cast, NPG · photograph, Balliol Oxf. · photograph, NPG [see illus.] · photographs, repro. in Toynbee, *Reminiscences and letters*
Wealth at death £777 15s. 3d.: probate, 19 April 1883, CGPLA Eng. & Wales

Toynbee, Arnold Joseph (1889–1975), historian, was born in London on 14 April 1889, the only son and eldest of the three children of Harry Valpy Toynbee (1861–1941) and Sarah Edith Marshall (1859–1939).

Family and education The family occupied a quite prominent position in late Victorian England. H. V. Toynbee was the fourth son of Joseph *Toynbee (1815–1866), a highly successful London doctor, and was the younger brother both of Paget Jackson Toynbee (1855–1932), who became a very well-known expert on Dante, and more importantly of Arnold Toynbee (1852–1883), who at a very early age achieved a wide reputation as a reforming thinker on social problems, was a tutor at Balliol College, Oxford, and died young, at the age of thirty. Toynbee Hall in London was named in his memory, as was his nephew Arnold J. Toynbee, born six years after his death. H. V. Toynbee and his wife had two further children, Jocelyn Mary Catherine *Toynbee (1897–1985), who became an important Roman archaeologist and art historian, and was Lawrence professor of classical archaeology at Cambridge University and a fellow of the British Academy, and Margaret (b. 1900). In later years the two sisters lived together in Park Town, Oxford.

H. V. Toynbee did not have a successful career to match those of the other members of the family. In 1883, following in the family's tradition of high-minded public service, he became district secretary of the Charity Organization Society, a position that neither held any great prominence nor provided an adequate income for the maintenance of an upper-middle-class lifestyle. W. S. McNeill, to whose penetrating and sympathetic biography *Arnold Toynbee: a Life* (1989) all treatments of Toynbee, including this one, owe much, attaches great importance to the strain imposed on the young Toynbee both by the necessity to live up to high expectations and by the sheer practical need, if a fitting education were to be secured, to gain the scholarships that would make this possible. McNeill also stresses the influence of Toynbee's

Arnold Joseph Toynbee (1889–1975), by Yousuf Karsh, 1955

mother, a strong-minded and highly principled person, who had studied history at Cambridge at a time when women were not admitted to degrees, and had gained what would have been classified as a first-class degree.

Toynbee was to show very early the capacity for mastery of languages, for voracious reading, covering a far wider range than would have been suggested by the educational norms of the period (or indeed of any period), and for sheer hard work. One of the most notable characteristics of his achievement over his lifetime was his astonishing productivity in writing. It could well be argued that this capacity, shown perhaps best of all in the annual *Surveys of International Affairs* which he produced in the 1920s and 1930s (see below), in the end served to damage his reputation. The sheer scale of his academic writing, public moralizing, travel writing, and personal comment on world affairs, had the effect of wearying readers and obscuring the true power and originality of his mind.

The course of Toynbee's intensive education up to the outbreak of the First World War serves to illustrate his capacities and to provide some idea of the training which made his later achievements possible, without of course explaining them. For the education that he received represented simply the standard curriculum for the middle and upper classes of the period, focused above all on the intensive early learning of classical Greek and Latin, to a level of proficiency which is now unimaginable, and on the reading of the major classical texts as the keys to the understanding of human nature and history. When Toynbee came, at the end of his *Study of History*, to write a characteristically self-referential chapter entitled 'How this

book came to be written', he went directly back to his classical education in the years before the First World War:

> Thanks to his professional good fortune in being born into a Time of Troubles that was, by definition, a historian's paradise, the present writer was, in fact, moved to interest himself in each of the historical conundrums flung at him by current events. But his professional good fortune did not end there. By the summer of AD 1914 he had been studying Latin for fifteen years and Greek for twelve; and this traditional education had the wholesome effect of rendering its recipients immune against the malady of cultural chauvinism … He could not live through the outbreak of war in AD 1914 without realizing that the outbreak of war in 431 BC had brought the same experience to Thucydides … There was a sense in which the two dates AD 1914 and 431 BC were philosophically contemporaneous. (*A Study of History*, 10, 1954, chap. 13)

It may be doubted whether a classical education in fact generally served to broaden the perspective of Toynbee's contemporaries in this way; the truth was rather that he was able to use it, in a unique manner, towards the wholly admirable end of a perspective which, in its own distinctive way, was to embrace the whole of human history as he saw it.

But the passage also alludes to the concrete details of bourgeois education as then experienced. For it indicates that Toynbee had begun Latin at the age of seven or eight, which was in fact at a day school called Warwick House in Maida Vale, London, situated near where the family lived, in not entirely comfortable circumstances, in a house owned by Toynbee's great-uncle, the brother of Joseph Toynbee. His Greek had begun when he was about ten, when he was sent to a boarding preparatory school, Wootton Court in Kent. From there Toynbee took the crucial step of winning a scholarship to what was intellectually the most prestigious public (that is, fee-paying) school in England, Winchester College. In the competitive scholarship examination in 1901 he just failed, but in 1902 was successful, gaining the third of eleven scholarships. Within the school also the intensity of the linguistic education provided, and the stress on writing, not only in English but also in Greek and Latin, served him extremely well. He was later to be a conspicuously good linguist, able not only to read a variety of modern languages, but to converse and lecture in them. So it is worth noting that among the battery of prizes that he collected at Winchester was one in German. The record also shows, perhaps more surprisingly, that he was already writing extensive essays on wide historical themes, such as Byzantine history or central Asia in the medieval period.

The natural next step for an outstanding classical scholar at Winchester would have been to go on to New College, Oxford, also founded by William of Wykeham. Toynbee did go to Oxford, but characteristically did not quite follow the conventional track; instead he won a scholarship to Balliol College, which under the mastership of Benjamin Jowett (1870–93) had become the embodiment of late Victorian seriousness, with a mission to train the most talented of the young men of each generation for public service.

The emphasis here too, however, was firmly on the classics, and specifically on the four-year course entitled *literae humaniores*, consisting of a first part (moderations) devoted essentially to further study of classical literature, and a second part divided between ancient (meaning Greek and Roman) history and philosophy. Toynbee entered Balliol in October 1907, and took his finals, after a further string of prizes, in the summer of 1911. Two aspects of his personal life in this period deserve particular mention. First, his father, H. V. Toynbee, suffered increasing mental strains, and in 1909 was confined to an institution (he remained in one or another institution until his death in 1941). Second, already as an undergraduate student, Toynbee attracted the attention of Gilbert Murray, who since 1905 had been a fellow of New College, and in 1908 became regius professor of Greek, as he remained until 1936. It was to be very significant for Toynbee's personal history, as explored by W. S. McNeill, that Murray had married Lady Mary Carlisle, the eldest daughter of the earl of Carlisle. At the personal level both Murray and Toynbee represented examples of high-achieving members of the educated bourgeoisie who rose into the orbit of the English aristocracy. Toynbee was invited to the Carlisle family seat, Castle Howard in Yorkshire, while still an undergraduate in 1910.

Travels in the Mediterranean, marriage, and wartime propaganda At the intellectual level Murray's prominent role in making Greek literature and culture intelligible in contemporary terms was surely relevant to Toynbee's development, as was his capacity for ambitious and large-scale categorization. His *Four Stages of Greek Religion* was published in 1912. In the meantime Toynbee had demonstrated his mastery of conventional classical scholarship by publishing an article on Herodotus in the *Classical Review* (1910), again while still an undergraduate. In the fashion of the period, when young men of exceptional talent could be regarded as ready for established teaching posts already at the moment of taking their final exams, he was offered a fellowship and tutorship in ancient history at Balliol for October 1912. Far more important for the future, however, was the fact that by winning the Jenkins prize in 1911 he was provided with the resources that enabled him to spend the year from September 1911 to August 1912 travelling through Italy and Greece, partly with others and partly alone, often walking through remote areas with no modern comforts or facilities.

The experience of direct and intimate contact with the Mediterranean landscape made a powerful impression on Toynbee, vividly reflected in his autobiographical work *Experiences*, published nearly six decades later, in 1969, as it is also in the preface to the first volume of his *Hannibal's Legacy* (1965). While travelling in Greece, he also had one of a series of mystical visions of the past, on the site of the battle of Cynoscephalae (197 BC), as he was to recall in volume 10 of *A Study of History* (1954). It was his capacity for revealing to the public an apocalyptic vision of himself and his relation to human history that was to be one of the factors that were to leave him exposed to so much derision in the 1950s. The fact remains, however, that his demanding journey through Italy and Greece in 1911–12 was no mere post-finals jaunt, but was put by him to profound use in something more than a merely intellectual sense—in giving himself both a deep feeling for the landscapes of the region and their exploitation by peasant farmers over the centuries, and an awareness of the modern condition of both societies.

Whether or not these experiences left him already not entirely content with the conventional role of a tutor at Oxford, Toynbee duly entered on that position in October 1912; he published a very substantial article, 'The growth of Sparta', in the *Journal of Hellenic Studies* in 1913, and gave lectures in 1913–14 that were to serve as the basis of *Hannibal's Legacy* (1965). The lectures, like the two-volume work itself, will have stepped far outside the normal bounds of the story of Hannibal's conflicts with Rome, to look both at the wider history of the world as it was between the fourth and second centuries BC, and at the impact of the war on the Italian countryside. At the same time, with a typical combination of ambition and breadth of vision, he was planning to write a history of Greece which would extend from prehistoric times to the Byzantine period.

It must have seemed that Toynbee was set for an exceptionally successful career within an established framework, and all the more so when in May 1913 he became engaged to Rosalind Murray (d. 1967), the daughter of the regius professor and of Lady Mary Murray. They were married in September 1913, and their first child, Antony Harry Robert Toynbee, was born on 2 September 1914. The future, however, was not to be the untroubled success that might have been expected. Tony Toynbee committed suicide in 1939, and his parents' marriage ended in separation in 1942, and in divorce in 1946. Just before the birth of their first child the First World War had broken out, and for Toynbee, as for millions of others in different ways, the effects were to break up irrevocably a course of life which may have seemed entirely set and predictable. In his case the disturbance did not take the form of military service. He did indeed offer himself for service, but at the same time presented an opinion from a doctor to the effect that, if he did serve, the dysentery which he had contracted during his travels in 1911–12 would be very likely to recur. He was consequently excused. In the view of W. S. McNeill, he was persuaded into finding this pretext by his wife, was subsequently ashamed of having done so, and devoted most of the rest of his life to foreign affairs as a way of performing the public service that the traditions of his class would have expected, and which he had found a means of avoiding.

Naturally, such an interpretation, however convincing, cannot be proved. But the facts show that Toynbee was drawn into government propaganda work from 1915 onwards, and that he also emerged, with astonishing rapidity, as a public commentator on international affairs. His book *Nationality and the War*, a substantial work of 511 pages, was published in 1915, and a vigorous denunciation of Turkish atrocities, *The Treatment of the Armenians in the Ottoman Empire, 1915–16*, in 1916. In 1915 also, to the dismay of his friends and mentors, especially A. D. Lindsay, he resigned his fellowship at Balliol. Though he was to come back very late in life to write major works on Graeco-Roman history, he was never again to hold a teaching post concerned with the classical world. It is surely also of profound relevance to the nature of his most significant and controversial work, *A Study of History*, that when he abandoned the career of a Graeco-Roman historian he was extremely well read in the major historians of Greece and Rome, of whom Thucydides, as already noted, was the most important for the development of his conceptions; and also that he had had time to write precisely one scholarly article on ancient history. His preparation for his *magnum opus* was therefore to take the form of involvement, at quite a junior level, in foreign affairs, during the war and its aftermath, and in bold and controversial writing on current affairs.

In May 1917 Toynbee was formally appointed to the foreign intelligence department of the Foreign Office, and in 1918–19 he was a member of the British delegation to the Paris peace conference. He may well have hoped to have a significant influence at this time, but if so was disappointed; it should be recalled that at this point he was still only reaching his thirtieth birthday. At all events, it was an unexpected opportunity, and one which was highly fortunate financially, since he had no significant private means, and no obvious prospects of secure employment, that just at this moment a group of Greek subscribers had provided the funds for what was eventually to be called the Koraes chair of modern Greek and Byzantine history, language, and literature, to be established at King's College, London. The proposal had the support of the Greek government, but when Toynbee was appointed in May 1919 he was not made aware that a 'subscribers' committee' still existed, or that it expected to receive reports on the work of the professor. The tangled story of the conflicts that subsequently arose is told with great clarity and detail by R. Clogg in *Politics and the Academy: Arnold Toynbee and the Koraes Chair* (1986).

'The tragedy of Greece' Before that story is discussed, two other features of Toynbee's intellectual biography deserve to be stressed. One is the appearance in 1918 of Spengler's *Der Untergang des Abendlandes*, which Toynbee recorded later that he read in 1920. Even more significant is the remarkable lecture entitled 'The tragedy of Greece' which he delivered in Oxford in May 1920 for students reading *literae humaniores*, and which was to be published in 1921. As has often been observed, almost all the features of his later grand design are adumbrated here; given the sonorous tone of the text, it is hard for the reader to recall that at that moment Toynbee was thirty-two. The lecture begins with the pronouncement that 'civilizations are the greatest and rarest achievements of the human mind', and then proceeds to enumerate them, noting that civilizations worth the name are few in comparison with the total of known human societies. It continues by suggesting that great civilizations are like great tragedies, and may all reveal the same plot.

Against this background Toynbee then turns to the current reasons for studying Greek history, as they seemed in 1920. First, and above all, it was because the war had made it impossible to take our civilization for granted. Greek history should be studied because it can be seen as a complete story: because of the fine literary quality of the narratives through which it is approached; because it could provide a form of *katharsis*; and because the study of another language and another political system could serve to put our society in perspective. He then divides the 'plot' of Greek history into three 'acts': from the eleventh century BC to 431 BC (the outbreak of the Peloponnesian War, as described by Thucydides); from 431 to 31 BC; and finally from 31 BC to the seventh century AD. At the end he turns, in explicit comparison to the Bolshevik revolution, to the decline of the Roman empire, with the emergence of an 'internal proletariat' as the bearer of a new civilization, Christianity. But, Toynbee claims, 'the fatal catastrophe had occurred six centuries earlier, in the year 431 BC'. The lecture shows Toynbee's capacity for perspective, combined with an almost mystical acceptance of the validity of a historical turning point, or 'catastrophe', as fashioned for subsequent readers by a literary narrative, that of Thucydides.

Responsiveness to contemporary events was at all times a primary characteristic of Toynbee's mind, and quite shortly after taking the Koraes chair he obtained leave of absence to travel through Greece and Turkey, which he did between January and September of 1921, while employed to act as correspondent for the *Manchester Guardian*. This was a fateful moment in the modern history of the eastern Mediterranean. After the end of the war Greek ambitions had won the support of the allies. A Greek landing had taken place at Izmir in May 1919, while allied forces occupied Constantinople in May 1920. Greek forces advanced steadily, and had occupied large parts of western Turkey before being met by nationalist forces organized by Mustafa Kemal (Atatürk). The Turkish advance between September 1921 and September 1922 ended with the complete expulsion of Greek forces from Turkey, and the forced emigration of the large, long-settled Greek population.

Toynbee's observations of these events resulted both in dispatches to the *Guardian* and, with typical rapidity, in his extremely significant and controversial book *The Western Question in Greece and Turkey: a Study in the Contact of Civilizations*, published in a first edition in 1922 and a second in 1923. In the longer term the importance of the book is that in it Toynbee felt able to use his observations of these events first to express a major thesis: the destructive efforts of a 'Western' conception, nationalism, on societies (those of both Greece and Turkey) to which it was foreign; and second to offer wide-ranging reflections on Greece as embodying the 'Near East' and Turkey the 'Middle East', and on the history of Christianity in the region. The characteristic tones of *A Study of History* are already present: 'The early Christian Church was the last phase of Ancient Hellenic or Graeco-Roman society, which died after it had had intercourse with other societies and had given birth to several children' (Toynbee, *The Western Question*, 328).

The more immediate effect was the furore which resulted from Toynbee's reports of atrocities committed by Greek forces in Turkey (for instance, the section headed 'Narrative written at Yalova on 1st June, 1921', pp. 299–300). His preface to the book shows that he was well aware of the possible reaction:

> It may, I fear, be painful to Greeks and 'Philhellenes' that information and reflections unfavourable to Greece should have been published by the first occupant of the Koraís Chair. I naturally regret this, but from the academic point of view it is less unfortunate than if my conclusions on the Anatolian Question had been favourable to Greece and unfavourable to Turkey. The actual circumstances, whatever personal unpleasantness they may entail for me and my Greek friends and acquaintances, at least preclude the suspicion that an endowment of learning at a British University has been used for propaganda on behalf of the country with which it is concerned.

Toynbee's personal dignity and high-mindedness are perhaps nowhere better shown than here. However, to an extent even greater than he had anticipated (especially as he was not aware of the potential rights of the subscribers' committee in checking on the conduct of the holder of the chair), a major controversy broke out, and in the end he resigned as from 30 June 1924. His letter to *The Times* explaining his position is printed in Clogg's *Politics and the Academy* (p. 116).

Once again Toynbee might potentially have been without employment, a prospect made more serious by the birth of his sons (Theodore) Philip *Toynbee, in June 1916, and Lawrence, in December 1922. Partly, it seems, because of Toynbee's unremitting dedication to work, and partly owing to unresolved and conflicting expectations, even relating to Castle Howard itself, in relation to Toynbee's aristocratic in-laws and their properties, family life was never entirely happy or harmonious. Philip Toynbee proved difficult, resentful, and unsettled.

Survey of International Affairs However, even before Toynbee formally left the Koraes chair in June 1924, the essentials of the position that he was to occupy (with an interval during the Second World War) for the rest of his working life had already been established. A temporary post at the British (later the Royal) Institute of International Affairs had been given to him already in February 1924, and was made permanent, along with a chair of international history at London University, in 1925. Since in the event he did not teach, this latter became a research professorship in 1928. From 1926 onwards he held the post which he kept until retirement, director of studies at the Royal Institute of International Affairs.

Toynbee's principal duty in this position was one which he achieved with a success that none of those who followed him were able to match, namely the publication each year of a volume of the *Survey of International Affairs*. The series began in 1925 with a resumptive volume, *The Survey of International Affairs, 1920–1923*, and thereafter one volume, on an almost unbroken rhythm, came out every year until 1938, which saw published the *Survey* for 1937.

On occasion the volumes focused on a specific area, for example that published in 1927, *The Islamic World since the Peace Settlement*. The fifteen volumes published up to 1938 represent an unparalleled achievement in terms of their scale and scope, and the analytical power required to bring the material, mainly derived from newspaper cuttings, into intelligible order. As an exercise in contemporary history, and as expressing the values and outlook of the inter-war years, they surely deserve a significant place in the history of historiography, and would equally merit detailed analysis.

From the 1929 volume onwards the title-pages indicate that the author was assisted by Veronica Marjorie Boulter (1894–1980), who selflessly took on a larger and larger proportion of the work, eventually writing substantial sections herself. She was to be Toynbee's mainstay and assistant for the rest of his life, and became his wife in 1946. Quite unjustly, her death in 1980 seems to have gone effectively unmarked; there was no *Times* obituary.

A Study of History One of the reasons why Veronica Boulter needed to take on an increasing proportion of the work on the *Survey* was that from 1930 onwards Toynbee was preparing for his *Study of History*. It should be recalled that, strictly speaking, he had at that point written no scholarly history at all, other than one large article in the *Journal of Hellenic Studies* (1913). The bases on which he felt able to launch himself on such a project can hardly be summed up in any definitive way. But they include the overwhelming importance in his educational background of Thucydides, as a historian who set out not only to record but also to offer authoritative explanations of events, in the explicit expectation that they would be useful in the future; the shock of the outbreak of the First World War, and the sense (as he had told Oxford undergraduates in 1920) that our civilization was not to be taken for granted; and the experience, which in his case had begun in his mid-twenties, of commenting publicly, and in sweeping terms, on current affairs. This latter of course still was his main public role when he began work on the *Study* in 1930, at the age of forty-one.

It would be worth research being undertaken to see if there is any evidence on how the vast reading necessary for this project was undertaken, and how the information was filed and stored for use. In the nature of the plan, as laid out very early, the work was not to be in any sense a sequential, narrative, *history* of the world, but an analytical, or moralizing, or even philosophical, study, whose subject was to be 'civilizations'. Nation states, as Toynbee explains in the case of England in the first volume, represented units which had to be seen as parts of larger wholes, and were therefore not in themselves satisfactory objects of study. Nor were all past societies, but only those twenty-one or so which, by virtue of a higher culture, qualified as civilizations. The purpose of the study is to analyse characteristic features of the genesis and then the disintegration of civilizations. A subordinate theme is to ask which civilizations are 'affiliated to', that is, in some sense derive from, earlier civilizations. The characteristic features which are taken as providing the model are very explicitly derived from what he takes to be the story of Hellenic civilization, and of Western society which is 'affiliated' to it. These features are: a universal state (the Roman empire); an 'internal proletariat' (the slaves or former slaves who—it is assumed—formed the earliest Christian churches); an external proletariat (the barbarians); an interregnum, marked by invasions and also the emergence of the church; and then rise of the Western society. Both the attraction, to readers trying to find meaning in history, and the dangers of Toynbee's method, in the eyes of almost all professional historians, arise from the use of such a model to bring out the significance of comparable features allegedly to be found in a whole range of civilizations or societies—some of them, such as Syriac society, essentially a construction by the author.

However, whatever the reservations felt by professional historians, none should feel entitled to denigrate the gigantic intellectual energy which enabled Toynbee to gain at least some intelligible conception of so many different societies, or the underlying moral impulse to rid himself, and his readers, of the parochialism inherent in a conventional Western outlook. Whether the effort to incorporate all that he discovered within models of genesis and disintegration was an equally justifiable project is of course more open to question.

The first three volumes of *A Study of History* were published in 1934, and volumes 4–6 in 1939. With the outbreak that year of the Second World War, Toynbee reverted once again to government service, first as director of the foreign research and press service in 1939–43. In this period he was based in Oxford, while Rosalind Toynbee decided to move back to London. In 1943–6 he was director of the research department of the Foreign Office, and in 1946 was once again a member of the British delegation to the peace conference, held in Paris in April of that year. After the dissolution of his first marriage in August 1946, on 28 September he married Veronica Boulter.

Post-war reputation In 1946 Toynbee returned to his post as director at the Royal Institute. The next few years saw both the high point of his international standing and its rapid decline. The key factor in his (for a time) unparalleled fame was unquestionably the publication in 1946 of an extremely intelligent abridgement by D. C. Somervell of the first six volumes of *A Study of History*. Originally prepared spontaneously, the two-volume abridgement was readily accepted by Toynbee, and was published with his full agreement. It was a success on a scale probably never matched by any other historical work. By September 1947 Oxford University Press had sold 100,000 copies. More striking still, Toynbee had come to be seen in the USA as someone uniquely equipped to give meaning to history in an age of rapid change. A cover story on him in *Time* magazine in March 1947 made him a national figure, and contributed to sales of more than 250,000 copies by the New York office of Oxford University Press.

Toynbee's purpose in writing the *Study* had always been in one sense a moral or propagandistic one, to free himself and his readers from the limits of a parochial, Western

view. But in execution it had been an analytical one, devoted to the discovery of recurrent features in the genesis and disintegration of civilizations. In that sense it represented, in intention at least, an objective and cyclical view of the rise and fall of civilizations. But in the war years and after, while he never returned, in any strictly confessional sense, to the Christianity in which he had been brought up, he certainly became much more religious, even mystical, in outlook, and grew closer to Catholicism. In a more general sense he also began to see his own role as a historian, in the words which he used for the title of the final section of his *Study*, as being 'The quest for a meaning behind the facts of history'. In volume 10, indeed, he even speaks of that meaning as being 'a revelation of God and a hope of communion with him'.

When volumes 8–10 were finally published in 1954, therefore, the underlying logic of the whole project had changed, and Toynbee had come to see history not as a cycle of rises and falls but as a progression towards an end whose nature and meaning were spiritual. There remained, along with the vast sweep of information and the real engagement with different civilizations, the heavily moralizing tone, an ever present tendency to put concepts into capitals (such as 'Time of Troubles'), and an unguarded and all too perceptible self-importance in the representation of himself as author.

It was not surprising, therefore, if critics among professional historians began to assert the view that the entire conception was inflated and overblown, and rested on the evidence of patterns which were not really there. The most pointed criticism, if invariably polite in tone, perhaps came from the major Dutch historian Pieter Geyl in three essays subsequently republished in his *Debates with Historians* (1955): 'Toynbee's system of civilizations' (1948), 'Toynbee once more: empiricism or apriorism' (1952), and 'Toynbee the prophet (the last four volumes)' (1955). But the most devastating and wounding satire on the pretentiousness of the project, and on the inflated tone of the self-representation of its author, came from H. R. Trevor-Roper in his article 'Arnold Toynbee's millennium', published in *Encounter* in June 1957.

From that time on it would be true to say that Toynbee's work has not been much discussed among professional historians, and has gradually faded from view among the educated public. In the face of criticism Toynbee himself remained resolutely polite and reasonable, and published a volume of more than 700 pages, entitled *Reconsiderations*, as volume 12 of the *Study* in 1961 (volume 11 was devoted to maps and a historical gazetteer). In 1955 he retired, and for the next two decades travelled and lectured widely, and retained a considerable public role internationally, especially in Japan. He also wrote incessantly, in part in a moralizing or philosophical vein, but he also published two volumes of an autobiographical character, *Acquaintances* (1967) and *Experiences* (1969).

Later classical and Byzantine studies It should be stressed that in these years, when the fame and perceived significance of the *Study* were receding in the eyes of the public and of professional historians alike, Toynbee showed a truly remarkable energy, and an academic capacity of a highly professional kind, in going back to the classical and Byzantine world, and publishing three very substantial and considerable works, which have not really received their due among historians. The first of these was the massive two-volume work *Hannibal's Legacy*, published in 1965. As mentioned earlier, this theme had formed the subject of lectures in Oxford in 1913–14. The terms in which in the preface Toynbee alludes to the origins of the book are characteristic of him: 'I had meant to follow up my lectures, immediately after I had delivered them, by writing this book; but from August 1914 to August 1957 I was prevented from doing this by other preoccupations'. The book is a massive re-examination, first, of the evolution and structure of Roman domination in Italy in the fourth and third centuries BC, set (as indicated above) against the background of other political formations in the known world of the period. He also stressed, rightly and in a way not matched by others, the profound originality of the Roman system for the incorporation of other communities, beginning in the 330s BC. Similarly, the second volume looks in equal detail at Rome and Italy in the second century, after Hannibal, and at the wider context of Rome's role in the Mediterranean world. The sheer weight and size of the work, and the ponderous prose in which it is written, combined with the relative absence of archaeological, documentary, or epigraphic evidence, have given it, very misleadingly, an old-fashioned appearance, and it has had less impact than it should have. But it is in fact the most important modern work on the period.

Not quite as much could be claimed for *Some Problems of Greek History* (1969). But none the less it is a major original achievement. It is divided into four parts: a discussion of population movements in the post-Mycenaean period, which is indeed out of date; a detailed treatment of a still hotly debated topic, the progress of Hellenization and the use of the Greek language in antiquity in the areas to the north of the Greek peninsula; at the end some *jeux d'esprit* on the question of what would have happened if certain key figures (for instance, Alexander's father, Philip) had lived longer; and, as the centrepiece, 260 pages on the rise and decline of Sparta, admittedly a somewhat old-fashioned subject, but one on which Toynbee showed himself easily the equal (to say the least) of similarly old-fashioned scholars of a much younger generation.

Finally, published in 1973, the year in which Toynbee celebrated his eighty-fourth birthday, there came *Constantine Porphyrogenitus and his World*. Here again, though the whole work makes, inevitably, an old-fashioned impression in style and language, it would be hard to find anywhere else so detailed and comprehensive an overview (in 768 pages) of the tenth-century Byzantine empire or of the life and works of the emperor himself. In the year after the publication of this book Toynbee was ceremoniously received 'at the gates' ('ad portas') at his old school, Winchester, and made a speech in Latin from memory. Shortly after, he suffered a stroke, from which he never recovered; he died the following year, on 22 October 1975,

at Purey Cust Nursing Home, York. He was buried at Terrington, Yorkshire. Veronica Toynbee, who had supported him as his wife for the previous thirty years, and as his assistant for half a century, died five years later.

Toynbee received a number of forms of public recognition, including honorary doctorates, the fellowship of the British Academy in 1937, and appointment as a Companion of Honour in 1956. But given the unprecedented scale of his scholarly achievement, as a historian, as an observer of international affairs, and as what one might call a historical moralist or philosopher of history, he might reasonably have expected more. Nor is there any sign that his unique grasp on international affairs was put to use by successive British governments except during the two world wars.

Toynbee did achieve, for a few years after the end of the Second World War, a level of public recognition not matched by any other historian of his time. But it could not be said, at the end of the century, that his influence had lasted either among the educated public or among professional historians. The twelve volumes of *A Study of History* were long out of print, though D. C. Somervell's two-volume abridgement was still available, as were a very few of his almost innumerable other books (listed in the bibliography by S. Fiona Morton, 1980). Toynbee was always very clearly aware of having been the product of a specific social and educational environment, the late Victorian and Edwardian English upper middle class, steeped from an early age in Latin and Greek. His prodigious output of scholarly work, lasting until the 1970s, would deserve reconsideration in terms of the history of culture and of historiography. But the *Study* itself, the *Surveys* published in the inter-war years, and the three massive contributions to classical and Byzantine history produced in his old age also deserve recognition and re-evaluation as intellectual achievements in their own right.

FERGUS MILLAR

Sources W. H. McNeill, *Arnold Toynbee: a life* (1989) · W. H. McNeill, 'Arnold Joseph Toynbee, 1889–1975', *PBA*, 63 (1977), 441–69 · R. Clogg, *Politics and the academy: Arnold Toynbee and the Koraes chair* (1986) · W. McNeill, *Toynbee revisited* (1993) · C. T. McIntire and M. Perry, eds., *Toynbee: reappraisals* (1989) · P. Geyl, *Debates with historians* (1955), chaps. 5, 7, 8 · A. J. Toynbee, *The tragedy of Greece* (1921) · A. J. Toynbee, *The Western question in Greece and Turkey: a study in the contact of civilisations*, 2nd edn (1923) · A. J. Toynbee, *Reconsiderations* (1961), vol. 12 of *A study of history* · A. J. Toynbee, *Acquaintances* (1967) · A. J. Toynbee, *Experiences* (1969) · S. F. Morton, *A bibliography of Arnold J. Toynbee* (1980) · *CGPLA Eng. & Wales* (1976)

Archives Bodl. Oxf., papers · Corning Community College, Corning, New York, Arthur A. Houghton Jr Library, working papers and drafts for 'A study of history' | Bodl. Oxf., corresp. with L. G. Curtis · Bodl. Oxf., corresp. with Gilbert Murray · Bodl. Oxf., letters to Sir Alfred Zimmern · CUL, corresp. with Sir Herbert Butterfield · HLRO, letters to Herbert Samuel · King's Lond., corresp. with Sir B. H. Liddell Hart · NA Scot., corresp. with Philip Kerr · NRA, priv. coll., letters to Rosalind, countess of Carlisle · Nuffield Oxf., corresp. with Lord Cherwell | SOUND BL NSA, 'A personal memory of Arnold Toynbee', 10 June 1964 · BL NSA, performance recording

Likenesses E. Stillman, wax medallion, 1893, NPG · W. Stoneman, photograph, 1945, NPG · Y. Karsh, bromide print, 1955, NPG [*see illus.*] · W. Bird, photograph, 1959, NPG · G. Argent, photograph, 1969, NPG · J. Pannett, chalk, 1972, NPG · L. Toynbee, oils, Royal Institute of International Affairs, Chatham House, London · photograph, Hult. Arch.

Wealth at death £132,425: probate, 13 Oct 1976, *CGPLA Eng. & Wales* · £8087: further probate, 2 June 1977, *CGPLA Eng. & Wales*

Toynbee [*née* Atwood], **Charlotte Maria** (1841–1931), college administrator and local government official, was born on 30 March 1841 in Muswell Hill, Middlesex, the only daughter of William Atwood and his wife, Charlotte Maria, *née* Hodgskins, of Odiham. She had one brother. Her father was a linguist and clerk in the Foreign Office, and she spent much of her childhood abroad before the family eventually settled in Wimbledon. She was educated at French schools abroad, and at school in London.

The Atwood family was Anglican and Liberal. Charlotte remained a devout and tolerant member of the Church of England. She first took notice of her future husband, Arnold, when he said to her 'the spirituality of life is what we have got to teach men' (C. Toynbee, 'Memoir of Arnold Toynbee'). Liberal reformism created another bond with Arnold. They were both interested, for example, in private pension schemes to promote individual self-reliance.

Charlotte was small, slight, and dignified. She held herself very upright, both when walking—frequently with her dog—and when sitting, 'perched like a pin on her severe sofa' (E. B. M., 28). She had a low, measured pattern of speech, and an independent mind. Her nephew Arnold J. Toynbee thought her indomitable and incisive, and wrote 'her heart was always kind, but her personality was commanding' (A. J. Toynbee, *Acquaintances*, 21).

Charlotte met Arnold *Toynbee (1852–1883) in 1873, when she was thirty-two and he was twenty-one. When they married on 26 June 1879 Arnold was a protégé of Jowett's and a tutor at Balliol College, Oxford. Their marriage was an equal and happy partnership. Charlotte commented that Arnold 'would probably never have married a woman who wished for, or required, much everyday attention' ('Memoir'). They lived first in east Oxford, then from early 1881 at 5 Bevington Road in north Oxford. A year after Arnold's premature death in 1883 she moved to 10 Norham Gardens, Oxford, where her mother came to live with her until the latter's death.

Charlotte edited Arnold's *Lectures on the Industrial Revolution in England* in 1884. She also joined the general committee of Toynbee Hall, the settlement in the East End named in his honour that same year. But she also had work of her own. In November 1883 she became honorary house treasurer of Lady Margaret Hall (LMH), which had been opened four years earlier for the education of women students. She kept the accounts at LMH for nearly forty years, until 1920. She was an active opponent of the campaign for women's suffrage, and like many other members of the LMH council disapproved of the attempts made in 1895–6 at Oxford to open the BA degree to women. However, her careful attention to the finances, buildings, and gardens at LMH made a substantial contribution to the development of women's education at Oxford University. The

Charlotte Maria Toynbee (1841–1931), by Anna Massey Lea Merritt, 1908

LMH council on 27 November 1915 named a new building—the third designed for the hall by Reginald Blomfield—in her honour. She was also a benefactor of LMH, directly and indirectly. She left a bequest to help build the chapel, and in 1921 a group of friends and former students gave £600 collected in her name towards the building fund. She was a member of LMH council from 1883 until 1926, when, with the adoption of new statutes, she was elected as one of the first group of honorary fellows.

In 1893 Charlotte was the first woman elected a guardian of the poor in Oxford, a post Arnold had held before her, which she retained for thirty years. She obviously judged that this responsibility fell within the woman's sphere while national politics did not. In an article, 'Poverty and the poor law', in the *Economic Review* (10/3, 1900, 316–22) she argued uncompromisingly for the gradual abolition of outdoor relief, and its replacement by pensions and other forms of self-help and charity, on the grounds that its perpetuation depressed wages and fostered dependence, that boards of guardians could not discriminate 'accurately and justly' between applicants, and that doling out small sums was degrading to the respectable poor. She had a sustained interest in the children of the poor-law school at Cowley, whom she visited regularly and helped throughout their lives. In 1908 she individually launched a printed appeal for £5000 for the purchase of Bartlemas Field, around the almshouse and chapel, which she described as 'the *one only* bit of picturesque antiquity in all the large and hideous new suburb of Cowley St. John' (Mrs A. Toynbee, *Bartlemas Field*, 1908).

Charlotte was a conservative figure in Oxford, with a wide circle of influential friends, some of whom—like Annie Rogers—were notable feminists. Her two lifelong friends, also important figures in the Association for Promoting the Education of Women in Oxford, were Bertha Johnson and Charlotte Green. She and Mrs Green, both widowed early, attended St Giles' Church in Oxford together every Sunday for very many years. Charlotte Toynbee died at 10 Norham Gardens on 8 January 1931, and was buried two days later at St Sepulchre's cemetery, Oxford.   FRANCES LANNON

Sources *Oxford Magazine* (22 Jan 1931), 332–3 · E. B. M., 'Charlotte Maria Toynbee', *Brown Book* (1931), 28–31 · E. Wordsworth, 'In memoriam Mrs Toynbee', *Brown Book* (1931), 27–8 · A. J. Toynbee, *Acquaintances* (1967), 21–37 · A. Kadish, *Apostle Arnold: the life and death of Arnold Toynbee, 1852–1883* (1986) · C. Toynbee, 'Memoir of Arnold Toynbee', Balliol Oxf., Toynbee MSS · C. M. Toynbee, Prefatory note, in A. Toynbee, *Lectures on the Industrial Revolution in England, popular addresses, notes and other fragments* (1884), 29–31 · A. Milner, 'Reminiscence', in A. Toynbee, *The Industrial Revolution of the eighteenth-century in England*, new edn (1908), 9–30 · *Reminiscences of Joseph and Arnold Toynbee*, ed. G. Toynbee, 100, 162 · 'Address to Mrs Arnold Toynbee', 4 June 1921, Lady Margaret Hall, Deposit 11 · m. cert.
Archives Balliol Oxf., memoir of Arnold Toynbee [with Toynbee MSS]
Likenesses A. M. Lea Merritt, oils, 1908, Lady Margaret Hall, Oxford [*see illus.*] · photographs
Wealth at death £12,884 8s. 1d.: resworn probate, 18 Feb 1931, CGPLA Eng. & Wales

Toynbee, Jocelyn Mary Catherine (1897–1985), archaeologist and art historian, was born at 12 Upper Westbourne Terrace, Paddington, London, on 3 March 1897, the daughter of Harry Valpy Toynbee (1861–1941), secretary of the Charity Organization Society, and his wife Sarah Edith, *née* Marshall (1859–1939). She was educated at Winchester High School for Girls and at Newnham College, Cambridge, where she was awarded firsts in both parts of the classical tripos (1919 and 1920). Her family was noted for its scholarly talents and its social concerns; her mother, who had been a student at Newnham and had taken a first in the Cambridge historical tripos, was a particularly important influence upon her. These family traits were continued in her own generation by her brother Arnold Joseph *Toynbee and her sister Margaret, as well as by herself.

After briefly teaching classics at Cheltenham Ladies' College, at twenty-four Toynbee was appointed tutor in classics at St Hugh's College, Oxford, a post she held from 1921 to 1924, when she resigned along with the other tutors in protest against the dismissal of Cecilia Ady by the principal Eleanor Jourdain. She then became lecturer in classics at Reading University. Her election in 1927 as fellow and director of studies in classics at Newnham and appointment in 1931 as lecturer in classics at Cambridge provided her with a secure post and an ideal base for developing her own research interests. She held these posts until 1951.

Toynbee played a notably supportive role at Newnham. She was a devoted and sympathetic tutor of undergraduates. At first meeting she might appear austere and a little forbidding, but her charm and obvious humanity were quick to emerge. She helped many of her pupils to find posts after graduation. She was also a helpful and careful supervisor of research students, though at no stage did they constitute a school. Her lectures were distinguished by her great powers of exposition as well as by her wide and deep knowledge of her subject. She was not an active excavator or field worker, but she was an accomplished interpreter of archaeological evidence. Her particular forte was Roman art, encouraged by early contacts with Eugénie Strong, though this was as broadly based as it could be, including architecture, coinage, dress, and even hair-styles. In the mid-twentieth century she was the leading British scholar in Roman artistic studies and one of the recognized authorities in this field in the world.

Toynbee's particular interest was the culture of the Roman empire and the continuity of Greek artistic traditions within it. Her major publications began with *The Hadrianic School: a Chapter in the History of Greek Art* (1934), based on the dissertation for which she was awarded an Oxford DPhil in 1930, and *Roman Medallions* (1944). They were greatly augmented after her election to the Laurence chair of classical archaeology at Cambridge in 1951. Her long career as a college tutor and lecturer who could cover a wide academic range in both classics and the archaeology of the classical world and her world reputation as a scholar and expositor made her the obvious choice for the appointment. Over the following eleven years a series of major works appeared, ranging from Rome to Roman Britain. With J. B. Ward Perkins she published *The Shrine of St Peter and the Vatican Excavations* in 1956. As a convert to Roman Catholicism and a devoted Catholic thereafter, this was a project with peculiar significance for her. Her mastery of Roman sculpture and its subtle resonances was brilliantly displayed in *The Flavian Reliefs from the Palazzo della Cancelleria in Rome* (1957).

These monographs were accompanied by many papers on individual discoveries from north Africa to the temple of Mithras in London and the moving early Christian mosaic in the villa at Hinton St Mary in Dorset. Toynbee's interest in the art of Roman Britain revealed a wide appreciation of provincial and Celtic art as well as work in the Graeco-Roman tradition. At the time of her retirement from the Laurence chair, in 1962, she was involved with a major exhibition of Romano-British art at the then Guildhall Museum in London, for which she wrote the catalogue *Art in Roman Britain* (1962). This was shortly followed by *Art in Britain under the Romans* (1964). Her retirement to Oxford, where she joined her sister Margaret, opened another productive phase. *Death and Burial in the Roman World* (1971) covered an immense sweep from Etruscan Italy to the Ostrogothic kingdom. *Animals in Roman Life and Art* (1973) is a delightfully characteristic work which reminded her former Cambridge pupils of lectures in earlier decades. *Roman Historical Portraits* (1977) was more severely technical and lacked the humane insights of her earlier studies.

At the heart of Jocelyn Toynbee's life and work was her devotion to learning, especially classical learning. Given the scholarly nature of her family, this is understandable. For her, scholarship was an essential and unquestionable part of life. She was genuinely distressed by the thought that schools might not provide instruction in Latin. Administration was not a field in which she felt at home, but she met its inevitable demands with dutiful attention. Her wise counsel was deployed at Newnham and in the learned societies to which she belonged. She was a determined fighter for the causes she espoused, but she won many to her side by her total absence of rancour. Long after her formal retirement she was still advising research students and other young scholars, despite increasing deafness. Until shortly before her death she was still eager to hear of new discoveries and reinterpretations.

Toynbee was a fellow of the Society of Antiquaries (1943), which awarded her the Frend medal for her contributions to the archaeology of the Christian church, a fellow and medallist of the Royal Numismatic Society, and a fellow of the British Academy (1952). She also received honorary doctorates from the universities of Newcastle (1967) and Liverpool (1968). She died, unmarried, at 4 Marston Ferry Road, Oxford, on 31 December 1985.

MALCOLM TODD

Sources Newnham College, Cambridge, archive · *The Times* (4 Jan 1986) · personal knowledge (2004) · J. M. Reynolds, 'Jocelyn Mary Catherine Toynbee, 1897–1985', *PBA*, 80 (1993), 499–508 · b. cert. · d. cert.
Archives AM Oxf. · U. Newcastle
Likenesses B. Gaye, photograph, repro. in Reynolds, 'Jocelyn Mary Catherine Toynbee', 500
Wealth at death £108,599: probate, 28 April 1986, *CGPLA Eng. & Wales*

Toynbee, Joseph (1815–1866), ear surgeon, was born at Heckington, Lincolnshire, on 30 December 1815, the second son of George Toynbee, a landowner and large tenant farmer. Educated at King's Lynn grammar school, at the age of seventeen he was apprenticed to William Wade of the Westminster General Dispensary in Gerrard Street, Soho, London. He studied anatomy under George Derby Dermott at the Great Windmill Street school of medicine, and gained a reputation for dissection. He subsequently studied at St George's and University College hospitals, and was admitted a member of the Royal College of Surgeons, London, in 1838. Study of the ear attracted him even during his student life. He was spurred on by the activity of the 'aurists', among whom was John Harrison Curtis, whose claim that one of the commonest causes of deafness was a deficiency of cerumen caused him to take issue in correspondence to *The Lancet* in 1838 under the initials 'J. T.'. In the same year he gained an appointment at the Hunterian Museum of the Royal College of Surgeons under Richard Owen. Among his research activities, using the microscope, was a paper entitled 'On the non-vascularity of articular cartilage, the cornea, crystalline lens and vitreous humour, and of the epidermoid appendages', which secured him election to the Royal Society in 1842 at the age of twenty-six. He was appointed in 1843 as surgeon to the St George's and St James's Dispensary and

Joseph Toynbee (1815–1866), by Maull & Co.

later in the year was elected one of the first fellows of the Royal College of Surgeons of England.

Toynbee realized that the failure to study pathology was the main reason for the disrepute into which aural surgery had fallen, and that the only rational approach to the understanding and treatment of aural disease lay in dissection of temporal bones. Over a period of twenty years he amassed a collection of over 2000 specimens, many of which came as a result of appointments as aural surgeon to the Asylum for the Deaf and Dumb in the Old Kent Road, and to the Asylum for Idiots at Earlswood, Surrey, and others which were derived from patients he had examined. In 1857 he published *A Descriptive Catalogue of Preparations Illustrative of the Diseases of the Ear in the Museum of Joseph Toynbee*. The collection attracted the young Adam Politzer (1835–1920) and was viewed by many, including Anton von Tröltsch (1829–1890). On Toynbee's death the collection was given to the Hunterian Museum, but was destroyed in the Second World War.

In 1853 Toynbee invented his artificial tympanic membrane, which consisted of a disc of gutta-percha to which was attached a fine silver wire; he published his results in a book entitled *On the Use of Artificial Membrana tympani in Cases of Deafness*. There was some rivalry between Toynbee and James Yearsley over the various merits of their respective artificial eardrums. Toynbee's *Diseases of the Ear:*

their Nature, Diagnosis and Treatment (1860) was the most advanced and comprehensive textbook of its kind. It was dedicated to the governors of St Mary's Hospital, Paddington, who in 1851 had had the foresight to appoint him as aural surgeon and to set aside the first beds in a general hospital for diseases of the ear. He resigned from this appointment in 1864. Toynbee noted that the Eustachian tube opened only in swallowing and yawning, and blew air up the tube with a catheter. He practised myringotomy and described osteomata, 'molluscous' tumour (cholesteatoma) and ankylosis of the stapes, which he incorrectly attributed to a 'rheumatic arthritis'. This was later shown by Politzer to be due to otosclerosis. He recognized intracranial spread of otogenic infection, but did not perform mastoidectomy.

Initially living at 12 Argyll Place, St James's, Toynbee moved in 1850 to 18 Savile Row and there conducted a very successful practice. In 1854 he took a country house at Parkside, Wimbledon. Much of his life was devoted to philanthropic work. He started a Samaritan Fund to assist the sick poor of Wimbledon and later a Metropolitan Association for Improving the Dwellings of the Working Classes. In Wimbledon he endowed a village hall and a small museum and published *Hints on the Formation of Local Museums* (1863) and *Wimbledon Museum Notes*. A fountain erected to the memory of Joseph Toynbee by the Working Men's Club still stands. He married, on 4 August 1846, Harriet, daughter of Nathaniel Reynolds Holmes and niece of the antiquary John Holmes; together they had nine children. Their second son, Arnold *Toynbee (1852–1883), shared his father's interest in social welfare and devoted his short life to it. Two years after Arnold Toynbee's death the first University Settlement was founded in Whitechapel by Canon Barnett, and was named Toynbee Hall. The third of the Toynbees' four sons was the Dante scholar Paget Jackson *Toynbee (1855–1932); their daughter Grace Coleridge *Frankland was a bacteriologist.

Joseph Toynbee's life was described by his daughter Gertrude in her books *Joseph Toynbee* (1909) and *Reminiscences and Letters of Joseph and Arnold Toynbee* (1910) as outwardly quiet, uneventful, and hard-working. His inner life, though, showed intensity of love and sympathy, lofty idealism, undying trust, and aspiration. He had a fine bearing and gracious manners and to his children was father, mother, brother, friend, and teacher all in one. Toynbee was devoted to Gothic and Norman architecture and to literature, particularly that of William Wordsworth, John Ruskin, and Samuel Coleridge. He also collected watercolours, especially those of D. G. Rossetti, Edward Burne-Jones, James Holland, and Samuel Palmer—most of whom were his friends. Botanical specimens prepared by him are still in the Kew Gardens collection. Toynbee's secret was not to encumber himself with petty worries but to be free to absorb new experiences and to seek the truth.

Toynbee died at his home in Savile Row on 7 July 1866 as he had lived—enquiring. Believing that tinnitus might be relieved by the inhalation of the vapours of hydrocyanic acid and chloroform, with a subsequent Valsalva insufflation, he fatally subjected himself to the test. He was buried in the churchyard of St Mary's, Wimbledon, and at the time of his death was president of the Quekett Microscopical Society and treasurer of the Medical Benevolent Fund. He was survived by his wife.   NEIL WEIR

Sources N. Weir, *Otolaryngology: an illustrated history* (1990) • J. F. Simpson, 'Joseph Toynbee: his contributions to otology', *Proceedings of the Royal Society of Medicine*, 56 (1963), 97–104 • G. Toynbee, *Reminiscences and letters of Joseph and Arnold Toynbee* (1910) • G. Toynbee, *Joseph Toynbee* (1909) • m. cert. • d. cert. • *CGPLA Eng. & Wales* (1866) • *DNB*
Archives RS, letter
Likenesses Maull & Co., photograph, 1842, RS • Maull & Co., photograph, NPG [*see illus.*] • R. H. Rushton, drawing, Royal Society of Medicine, London • photograph, repro. in Toynbee, *Reminiscences and letters*, frontispiece
Wealth at death under £45,000: probate, 15 Aug 1866, *CGPLA Eng. & Wales*

Toynbee, Paget Jackson (1855–1932), Dante scholar, was born on 20 January 1855 at Beech Holme, Wimbledon, the third of four sons of the ear surgeon Joseph *Toynbee (1815–1866) and his wife, Harriet, daughter of Nathaniel Holmes, and niece of the antiquary John *Holmes (1800–1854). He was younger brother of the social reformer Arnold *Toynbee (1852–1883), and a second cousin of the painter and critic Sir Charles John *Holmes (1868–1936). Paget Toynbee was educated at Haileybury College and at Balliol College, Oxford, where he read classics (1874–8) and in 1901 obtained a DLitt. He worked for some years as a private and travelling tutor, visiting the Cape Colony in 1881, and Japan and Australia in 1886–7. In 1892 he abandoned teaching and devoted himself entirely to research, particularly to the study of Dante. On 23 August 1894 he married Helen Wrigley (1868/9–1910), scholar, and daughter of Edwin Grundy Wrigley, of Bury, Lancashire, who spent her life editing the letters of Horace Walpole.

Toynbee's first publications were two philological textbooks, *Specimens of Old French* (1892), and *A historical grammar of the French language* (1896), an expanded version of Auguste Brachet's work. In 1895 he became a member of the Oxford Dante Society, founded by Edward Moore. His first massive contribution to Dante scholarship was the *Dictionary of Proper Names and Notable Matters in the Works of Dante* (1898; latest edition by C. S. Singleton in 1968), which, with its revised and abbreviated edition, the *Concise Dante Dictionary* (1914), became an indispensable handbook for Dante students. After 1900 he assisted Moore in revising the text for the Oxford Dante, and in 1909 he published *Dante in English Literature from Chaucer to Cary* (2 vols.), which brought together practically all that was written in English about Dante, in an 'amazingly minute survey' (*Oxford Magazine*, 721). For Toynbee, Dante was a 'treasure house full of obscurities and difficulties which needed elucidation and solution, and he spared no pains to provide them' (ibid.). Although he confined himself to the accumulation and elucidation of facts, making no attempt at literary appreciation, his exhaustive memory and tireless energy won him a worldwide reputation as a

Paget Jackson Toynbee (1855–1932), by Walter Stoneman, 1921

Dantist (he was a corresponding member of the Reale Istituto Lombardo di Scienze e Lettere from 1909). His life of Dante, first published in 1900, 'painstakingly' sifted details to 'add so many items of solid information to our knowledge of Dante' (ibid., 722).

After his wife's death in 1910 Toynbee took up her unfinished task of editing Walpole's letters, and Horace Walpole, to whom Dante was 'extravagant, absurd, disgusting, in short a Methodist parson in Bedlam' (letter to William Mason, 1782), from then on shared Dante's place in his activities, which resulted in three supplementary volumes of *Letters* (1918–25) and the *Correspondence of Gray, Walpole, West and Ashton* (2 vols., 1915). Toynbee was described as being both physically and mentally 'ponderous and forceful' in later life, as if 'he intentionally limited his field of activity in order to probe deeper into it' (*Oxford Magazine*, 722). After 1910 Toynbee, who had no children, and who suffered the consequences of typhoid fever, lived the life of a recluse at Fiveways, the house which he built at Burnham, Buckinghamshire, in 1907. Although he rarely had more than a tame robin for companionship, he was never really lonely. He emerged occasionally to stay with his friend and fellow Dantist William Walrond Jackson for meetings of the Oxford Dante Society, of which he was honorary secretary, 'guiding spirit, and almost the benevolent despot' (ibid., 721) from 1916 to 1928. He was one of the very few Englishmen to be made a corresponding member of the Italian Reale Accademia della Crusca in

January 1918, and of the Accademia Lucchese di Scienze, Lettere ed Arti in 1920. His very valuable emended text of Dante's *Epistolae*, with introduction and notes, appeared in 1920.

Toynbee was elected a fellow of the British Academy in 1919, and was awarded the Serena medal in 1921. He was made an honorary fellow of Balliol College in 1922, and in 1923 the University of Edinburgh conferred on him the honorary degree of LLD. Among his last services to Dante scholarship were the revision of the Oxford Dante for its fourth edition (1924) and the bequest of a valuable collection of books, such as early editions of Dante, Petrarch, and Boccaccio, to the Bodleian Library to which he had made notable benefactions between 1912 and 1917 and in 1923. He died at Fiveways on 13 May 1932. He was recognized by his contemporaries as one of the great English Dantists, and a 'giant of scholarship' (*Oxford Magazine*, 723).   C. M. ADY, *rev.* DIEGO ZANCANI

Sources E. G. Gardner, 'Paget Toynbee, 1855–1932', *PBA*, 18 (1932), 439–51 · E. Hilliard, ed., *The Balliol College register, 1832–1914* (privately printed, Oxford, 1914) · Bodl. Oxf., MSS Toynbee d. 23, d. 25 · P. Toynbee, *The Oxford Dante Society: a record of forty-four years (1876–1920)* (1920) · *Verbali*, Accademia della Crusca, Florence, Italy, 16 (1915–23), 332–3 · D. Zancani, 'Una biblioteca di cent'anni fa: la "Dante collection" di Paget Toynbee', *La Bibliofilia*, 100 (1998), 495–512 · *Enciclopedia Dantesca*, 3 · *Oxford Magazine* (26 May 1932), 721–3 · b. cert. · m. cert. · d. cert.

Archives Bodl. Oxf., corresp. and papers · Bodl. Oxf., corresp.

Likenesses W. Stoneman, photograph, 1921, NPG [*see illus.*] · photograph, Bodl. Oxf., Toynbee MS d. 23 · portrait; in the possession of Accademia della Crusca, Florence, in 1923

Wealth at death £10,782 13s. 11d.: resworn probate, 16 July 1932, *CGPLA Eng. & Wales*

Toynbee, (Theodore) Philip (1916–1981), writer, was born at 372 Woodstock Road, Oxford, on 25 June 1916, the second in the family of three sons of Arnold Joseph *Toynbee (1889–1975), historian, and his first wife, the writer Rosalind Murray (d. 1967), daughter of (George) Gilbert Aimé *Murray (1866–1957), scholar, poet, and author, and Lady Mary Howard. As a child Toynbee was aware of the social distinction between his father, whose family included academics and professionals, and the Howards on his mother's side who 'owned so many square miles of Cumberland and the North Riding' (Toynbee, *Part of a Journey*, 89). He grew up, in 'liberal-minded' agnosticism, close to the Chelsea Embankment in London, with holidays spent in the grounds of Castle Howard (ibid., 92). His father's academic celebrity and the baroque splendours of his mother's ancestral home played their parts in a long narrative poem later on, but he was more impressed in youth by his Australian Murray ancestors and their perhaps imaginary background of convict hulks and outlawed bushwhackers on the wallaby trail. They fitted the radical yearnings which, at seventeen, made him run away from Rugby School (where he played for the first fifteen) to join the fifteen-year-old Esmond Romilly, Winston Churchill's nephew, who after a similar flight from Wellington College to the London docks had launched the anti-public-school broadsheet *Out of Bounds*. Toynbee acted as joint editor and, with Romilly, took part in anti-fascist protests,

(Theodore) **Philip Toynbee** (1916–1981), by Jane Bown, 1961

but Toynbee eventually succumbed to family pressure to return to school. The friendship with Romilly was recounted in Toynbee's memoir *Friends Apart* (1954). Expelled from Rugby, then coached by the monks of Ampleforth, Toynbee won a history scholarship to Christ Church, Oxford, where he took a second class in modern history in 1938 and became the first communist president of the Oxford Union. In 1936 he had led an international student delegation on a tour of Spanish republican strongholds and by 1937 had published his first novel, *The Savage Days*, in which an upper middle class man struggles to choose between his débutante girlfriend and the Communist Party.

Toynbee's life was indeed split between left-wing politics, scrapes, the Café Royal and the Gargoyle, the pursuit of 'liberal girls' in London ballrooms, and the beginnings of serious writing: contradictions which he carried off with an engaging assumption of clownish self-mockery. The disparities of his life (while working with miners in the 1930s he disappeared at weekends for parties at Castle Howard) were evident in his appearance: his large frame, shabby clothes, and handsome, rugged face gave him the look of an aristocratic stevedore.

Romilly, meanwhile, back from the Spanish Civil War, had eloped with Jessica Mitford and they all lived for a spell hugger-mugger in Rotherhithe, east London. In 1938–9 Toynbee was editor of the *Birmingham Town Crier*. He left communism early, but retained a lasting commitment to principles of social justice. On 25 November 1939 he married Anne Barbara Denise (*b.* 1919/20), daughter of Colonel George Harcourt Powell. They later settled in the

Isle of Wight and had two daughters, one of whom, Polly, made a name as a writer. But 1939 was otherwise an unhappy year for Toynbee with the suicide of his older brother, Tony.

In the Second World War, via the ranks of the Welsh Guards, Toynbee was commissioned and in 1940–42 served in the intelligence corps. In 1942–4 he was seconded to the Ministry of Economic Warfare; he reached the rank of captain and was on the staff of Supreme Headquarters Allied Expeditionary Force in France and Belgium during 1944–5. Toynbee was characteristically candid about his conduct during the war: his time in Paris and Brussels was brought to an ignominious end when he found himself in detention barracks for a misdemeanour and he 'managed in the shadow of this disgrace to creep out of the army again and back to the last remnants of the war in London' (Toynbee, 'A Writer's Journey', 4).

It was while working at the ministry in London during the central years of the war that Toynbee made headway in his literary career. He had been an early contributor to *Horizon* and was briefly literary editor of Contact Publications after the war. His novels *A School in Private* (1941) and *The Barricades* (1943), about a schoolboy who tries to join the Spanish loyalists, were well received and conventional in style, while the more experimental *Tea with Mrs Goodman* (1947) was greeted with considerable acclaim. The *New Statesman* proclaimed that 'English prose would never be the same again' (Mitford, 6). Of his search for a new means of expression Toynbee said that 'the only way of writing is to string together a necklace of sharp occasions and to conceal as best I can any narrative of explanatory thread' (Toynbee, *Part of a Journey*, 102). *The Garden to the Sea* (1953), a bitter account of the breakup of a marriage, followed the same pattern but failed to excite the critics.

By this time Toynbee's wife had left him. The marriage was under considerable pressure from Toynbee's occasional lapses; long stretches of country diligence were punctuated by brief London spells of brisk intemperance; drink, indeed, remained a bane all his life, although his wide circle of friends, which included the art historian Ben Nicolson and the critic Cyril Connolly, largely forgave him.

In 1950 the marriage was dissolved, though both parties always remained friends, and in the same year Toynbee married Frances Genevieve (Sally), daughter of Charles Stout Smith, oil company executive in the USA. She was a member of the American embassy in Tel Aviv whom he met while he was covering the Levant for *The Observer*. They had a son and two daughters, and after an interlude in Suffolk they settled at Barn House in woodlands near Tintern Abbey. Toynbee became the leading *Observer* literary critic for the rest of his life and helped to raise weekly reviewing to a very high level.

Toynbee spent the rest of his career as a writer working on *The Valediction of Pantaloon*, an astonishing multi-volume series of tragi-comic verse, with the intention of writing a masterpiece to follow *Don Quixote*, *The Prelude*,

Faust, and *A la recherche du temps perdu*, 'for who can write a great book without setting out to write a great book' (Toynbee, 'A Writer's Journey', 4). Continuing with his experiments with narrative, Toynbee hoped to 'develop and change existing media for my entirely new purposes … a Bouvard-like procession through all the major ideas and idiocies of the age' (Mitford, 105). Toynbee's faith in his talent and vision was recognized by Stephen Spender, who thought *A Learned City* (1967) 'one of the most remarkable poems of the century' (ibid.). With imaginative vigour and metrical skill (with only occasional lapses) the *Pantaloon* series encapsulates in epic form the spirit of the first half of the twentieth century. Toynbee struggled until his death to publish the last four volumes after Chatto and Windus rejected them.

Toynbee's deep interest in social and ecological issues led to *Underdogs* (1961) and *The Fearful Choice* (1958), a compilation of answers to a letter he had circulated to seventy-five public figures on the subject of nuclear weaponry (his fear of nuclear war was such that, according to Jessica Mitford, he collected 'euthanasia medicine'). But a Peacockian experiment at turning his roomy Barn House into a commune turned out a disappointment and a failure. While he was committed to the concept, communal living did not suit him and he began to suffer from severe bouts of depression. Meanwhile, to the dismay of fellow agnostics, Toynbee developed the growing intellectual belief in Christian practice which he recounts in *Part of a Journey* (1981) and *End of a Journey* (1988). Visits to London grew rarer; as Brother Philip, he became an extramural associate of the nearby Anglican Tymawr convent, and died of cancer on 15 June 1981 at his home, Woodroyd Cottage, The Hudnalls, St Briavels, near Lydney, Gloucestershire; his wife survived him.

Toynbee achieved his avowed longing 'to become a good man' and it may be thought that *Pantaloon* fulfilled his ambition to write a masterpiece, although it has never received the popular attention it deserves.

P. L. FERMOR, rev. CLARE L. TAYLOR

Sources J. Mitford, *Faces of Philip: a memoir of Philip Toynbee* (1984) • P. Toynbee, *Part of a journey: an autobiographical journal, 1977–1979* (1981) • P. Toynbee, *End of a journey: an autobiographical journal, 1979–81*, ed. J. Bullimore (1988) • P. Toynbee, *Friends apart: a memoir of Esmond Romilly and Jasper Ridley in the thirties* (1954) [repr. 1980] • P. Toynbee, 'A writer's journey', *New Review*, 3/33 (Dec 1976) • *WW* (1957–63) • m. cert. [Anne Powell] • d. cert.
Archives Bodl. Oxf., papers
Likenesses J. Bown, photograph, 1961, repro. in J. Bown, *Men of consequence* (1987) [see illus.]
Wealth at death £100,155: probate, 1981, *CGPLA Eng. & Wales*

Tozer, Aaron (1788–1854), naval officer, entered the navy in June 1801 on the *Phoebe*, with Captain Thomas Baker, on the Irish station. He afterwards served in the East Indies and on the home station, and, again with Baker, in the *Phoenix*, in which on 10 August 1805 he was present at the capture of the French frigate *Didon*, which was carrying important dispatches from Villeneuve at Ferrol to Rochefort. Tozer was dangerously wounded in the shoulder, and, after passing his examination, was specially promoted lieutenant on 11 August 1807. After serving in the

York (74 guns) at the capture of Madeira and in the West Indies, he was appointed, in December 1808, to the *Victorious*, in which he took part in the Walcheren expedition in July and August 1809. The *Victorious* was in the Mediterranean, in the defence of Sicily, from June to September 1810, during which time Tozer was repeatedly engaged in actions between the boats and the vessels of Murat's flotilla, and on 22 February 1812 was at the capture of the *Rivoli*. In February 1813 Tozer was appointed to the *Undaunted*, and during the following months repeatedly commanded her boats in storming the enemy's batteries or cutting out trading and armed vessels from under their protection. On 18 August 1813, in an attack, in force, on the batteries of Cassis, when the citadel battery was carried by escalade and three gunboats and twenty-four merchant vessels were brought out, Tozer was severely wounded by a canister shot in the groin and by a musket shot in the left hand, in consequence of which he was invalided out. On 15 July 1814 he was promoted commander, and in December 1815 was awarded a pension of £150 a year. From 1818 to 1822 he commanded the *Cyrene* (20 guns) in the West Indies and in 1829 the yacht *William and Mary*. He married, on 5 June 1827, Mary, the eldest daughter of Henry Hutton of Lincoln; they had one son, the Revd Henry Fanshawe *Tozer, fellow of Exeter College, Oxford. On 14 January 1830 Tozer was promoted to post rank, but had no further employment, and died at Plymouth, where he was living, on 21 February 1854.

Tozer had an amphibious career, distinguished by bravery and exceptional in intensity, but not untypical of a period of unquestioned British supremacy at sea.

J. K. LAUGHTON, rev. ANDREW LAMBERT

Sources D. Syrett and R. L. DiNardo, *The commissioned sea officers of the Royal Navy, 1660–1815*, rev. edn, Occasional Publications of the Navy RS, 1 (1994) • O'Byrne, *Naval biog. dict.* • J. Marshall, *Royal naval biography*, 3/2 (1832) • *GM*, 2nd ser., 42 (1854), 77 • *Navy List* • W. James, *The naval history of Great Britain, from the declaration of war by France, in February 1793, to the accession of George IV, in January 1820*, [2nd edn], 6 vols. (1826) • P. Mackesy, *The war in the Mediterranean, 1803–1810* (1957)

Tozer, Henry (c.1601–1650), Church of England clergyman, was born in North Tawton, Devon, to unknown parents. Having matriculated from Exeter College, Oxford, on 3 May 1621, when he was said to have been aged twenty, he graduated BA on 18 June 1623, and that year became a fellow of the college. He proceeded MA on 28 April 1626 and was ordained. Two years later he published the very conventional *Directions for a Godly Life: Especially for Communicating at the Lord's Table* (1628), dedicated to Viscount Falkland's son Lorenzo Cary, whose tutor he was, but by May 1630 he had been reported to the vice-chancellor as having discussed the differences disturbing the peace of the church. On 21 October 1632 he was appointed lecturer at St Martin's, Carfax, Oxford, where his sermons were especially frequented by those deemed puritans and he himself gained the reputation of a 'precise puritan'; according to Anthony Wood, Tozer also preached at St Giles, to the north of the city (Wood, *Ath. Oxon.*, 3.273–4). Even so, his second publication, *A Christian Amendment* (1633), originally a St Martin's sermon, was an equally uncontroversial exhortation to holiness, dedicated to his former student Sir Walter Pye the younger of Hereford. On 28 July 1636 Tozer proceeded BD.

Like his college head, John Prideaux, whom he assisted as bursar and sub-rector, Tozer apparently remained a convinced Calvinist and he retained over the next decade his popularity among those keen for 'primitive religion'. However, qualities that could simultaneously gain him acceptance from the Laudian establishment are evident in his *Christian Wisdome* (1639), based on a sermon delivered at the university church of St Mary's in November 1638. Dedicated to Robert Ker, earl of Ancrum, a courtier and apparently a patron of long standing, it located true wisdom—the wisdom of Solomon—in striving to be like God, not in spending time in such activities as 'the curious ordering of thy haire' (*Christian Wisdome*, 7). It firmly rejected 'Romanists, monks and friars' (ibid., 86–7) who locked up, or steered men away from, wisdom, but condemned those who sought Solomons of their own in 'a Parlour, an Anabaptisticall Convention' (ibid., 100). If an incumbent were non-resident, or otherwise unsatisfactory, God would 'put in a better Solomon', but in the meantime it was preferable to stay put than to journey to seek a better, and better to attend the parish church than to read 'in your closet' (ibid., 104).

Tozer was approved by the House of Commons on 25 April 1642 as representative for Glamorgan in the Westminster assembly, but had not attended by 25 October 1643 when he was ordered to do so, and he never complied. In 1644 he became vicar of Yarnton, Oxfordshire, an Exeter College living, but he apparently continued to live in Oxford, where in 1646 he refused a DD degree. In the absence of Exeter's new rector, George Hakewill, Tozer managed the college and was prominent among opponents of the parliamentary visitation of the university. On 21 March 1648 he was called before the commission on a charge of reinstating the use of the Book of Common Prayer in Exeter chapel. On refusing to surrender prayer books and college keys he was expelled from his fellowship in May, and at the end of June, having been forcibly ejected from his pulpit at Carfax by soldiers of the garrison for preaching defiance, was briefly imprisoned in the Boccardo. He was allowed to retain his chamber at Exeter, and was then given permission to travel.

Tozer went to Rotterdam, where he became minister to the Company of Merchant Adventurers. There on 27 August 1650, 'weake in bodie', he made his will, leaving his friend Thomas Marshall and his servant Henry Parr between them French, Spanish, and Italian dictionaries and bibles, 'all my musical instruments' and manuscripts there, and the works of Henry Ainsworth, the leader of English separatists at Rotterdam (PRO, PROB 11/215, p. 84). His former colleague William Standard, who had eventually submitted to the parliamentary visitors, and Exeter College itself also benefited from bequests, including Tozer's manuscripts at Exeter and £50 due from land in Exeter Castle. Tozer died in Rotterdam on 11 September 1650, reportedly aged forty-eight, and was buried locally in the English church. Probate was granted on 6 January 1651 to his executor, George Potter, mercer and mayor of Oxford, who received the residue of the estate.

VIVIENNE LARMINIE

Sources Foster, *Alum. Oxon.* · C. W. Boase, ed., *Registrum Collegii Exoniensis*, new edn, OHS, 27 (1894), cix, cxvii–cxx, 99 · Wood, *Ath. Oxon.*, new edn, 3.273–4 · *Walker rev.*, 300 · *Hist. U. Oxf. 4: 17th-cent. Oxf.*, 728, 760 · *CSP dom.*, 1629–31, 260 · *JHC*, 2 (1640–42), 541 · PRO, PROB 11/215, 84 [will]

Tozer, Henry Fanshawe (1829–1916), geographer and classical scholar, was born in Plymouth on 18 May 1829, the only son (there was also a daughter) of Captain Aaron *Tozer RN and his wife, Mary Hutton of Lincoln. He entered Winchester College in 1842, and University College, Oxford, in 1847, and won a scholarship to Exeter College, Oxford, in 1848; he obtained a second class in *literae humaniores* in 1850. He was elected a fellow of Exeter in 1850, and was ordained deacon in 1852 and priest in 1853. He was classical tutor at Exeter College and remained a fellow (from 1893 honorary fellow) until his death, except for the period from 1868, when he vacated his fellowship on his marriage, until 1882, when the passing of the statutes of the second university commissioners enabled him to be readmitted as fellow. Tozer married Augusta Henrietta, daughter of Hans David Christopher Satow, a Swedish merchant who settled in London in 1825, and his wife, Margaret Mason, an Englishwoman.

A versatile and hardy traveller, Tozer made his first journey to Italy and Sicily, the prelude to an extended and detailed tour of Greece as far as Thessaly. Thereafter he made regular journeys in Greece and Turkey, some of which formed the subject of two of his major travel books, *Researches in the Highlands of Turkey* (2 vols., 1869) and *Turkish Armenia and Eastern Asia Minor* (1881). The first of these described two arduous journeys from Constantinople to Salonika (taking in Mount Athos, which he climbed) across the Scardus and Bertiscus ranges, then further north into Montenegro and across the Mirdita country of central Albania; the second described a journey from Samsun across the Anatolian plateau, through Cappadocia, past Lake Van to Erzurum, and so back to Trebizond, the last stretch roughly along the route taken by Xenophon and the Ten Thousand. On these travels Tozer was usually accompanied by T. M. Crowder, bursar of Corpus Christi College, Oxford, whose sixteen volumes of closely written journals, recording these and many other travels, are preserved in the college library.

Tozer travelled after the pioneer journeys of W. M. Leake in Greece and Macedonia and of W. J. Hamilton in Asia Minor had opened up these countries to archaeologists, and his main interest was not in the discovery of archaeological material but in physical and human geography. He was thus a true follower of Strabo, the author to the dissemination of whose work he contributed most. He was a keen observer of the landscape (including the flora—he was a skilled botanist) and of the people who lived in it and the regimes under which they lived. In Greece especially he absorbed much local folklore, and all his life he continued to write articles on modern Greek legends and folk-songs and allied topics. He was also deeply interested in Byzantine history and literature, and one of his lasting achievements was to re-edit George Finlay's seven-volume *History of Greece* (1877). This was a task of considerable complexity and Tozer's edition became the standard one. The geographers were, however, never far from his thoughts, and in 1893 he produced his admirable *Selections from Strabo* (which remained the most sympathetic introduction to Strabo); this was followed in 1897 by *A History of Ancient Geography*—one of the best, if not the best, handbook on both ancient geography and geographical writers, in Greek and Latin, to the end of the western empire. This is in a way a companion volume, in its emphasis on the geographers, to his much earlier book, *Lectures on the Geography of Greece* (1873), based on lectures given in Oxford in 1872. His later travels in the Aegean formed the subject of his delightful *Islands of the Aegean* (1890). In addition to this intensive work on his special subjects, and the work, such as the study of modern Greek, that arose naturally out of his other activities, Tozer had an abiding love for Dante, and published both an elegant three-volume commentary on the *Divina commedia* (1901) and a prose translation of the poem (1904).

Tozer's writings are invariably simple in style and straightforward in substance, but he had a direct appreciation of landscape, which carries its own charm, and, like his friend Edward Lear, a sharp eye for human foibles and vanities as revealed by the activities of local officials in the Turkish provinces. His main contribution to the understanding of ancient geography lay in his personal knowledge of the topography over a wide area, combined with a natural appreciation of the writings of the geographers themselves, especially Strabo. His eminence in his field was signalled by his inclusion in the original list of fellows of the British Academy in 1903; but in the Oxford of the second half of the nineteenth century, parochial, preoccupied with spiritual and philosophical problems, the Oxford of Jowett, Pater, and Pattison, his interests and experiences must have set him apart. He died childless on 2 June 1916 at his home, 18 Norham Gardens, Oxford. One of his executors was his wife's brother, Sir Ernest Mason Satow.

Tozer is chiefly remembered as a pioneer of the establishment of geography in British universities, which lagged far behind their continental counterparts in this respect. His particular research and lectures proved, like contemporary work in biblical geography, to be something of an academic cul-de-sac. They were regarded as peripheral to classical studies, and geography ultimately drew more on the natural sciences and contemporary exploration which dominated German advances in the subject. None the less, Tozer's work has been consulted by those (admittedly few) geographers interested in the field (see (Coones, 1986)), and his *Ancient Geography* was reprinted as late as 1974. It is his staunch belief in the need for history to have a firm base in geography and in the inherent value of geography that remain of most interest. He strongly advocated 'the intelligent study of historical geography' (his dedication to A. P. Stanley in the *Geography of Greece*), and in the 1880s wrote to John Scott Keltie to say 'it would be a good thing to have a professor or reader in geography [at Oxford] as a definite recognition of the subject and as providing the university with a man who should represent the branch of knowledge', though he recognized that 'the studies of undergraduates are almost entirely regulated by the examination' so that without syllabus reform geography would continue to be 'crowded out' (Baker, 124–5). In 1887, shortly after Tozer wrote, Halford Mackinder became the first reader in geography at Oxford, though the establishment of geography as an honour school was to take longer. This interest in broadening the university curriculum was typical of Tozer, who, unlike many contemporary fellows, was active in learned societies such as the Society for Promoting Hellenic Studies, was a corresponding member of Near-Eastern learned societies, and, as curator of the Taylor Institution in 1869–93, was active in broadening the scope of scholarly enquiry at Oxford.

P. M. FRASER, rev. ELIZABETH BAIGENT

Sources *The Times* (3 June 1916) · W. W. Jackson, 'Henry Fanshawe Tozer, 1829–1916', *PBA*, [7] (1915–16), 566–74 · L. R. Farnell, *Bibliography of the fellows and tutors of Exeter College, Oxford in recent times* (1914) · *WWW*, 1916–28 · T. M. Crowder, journals, CCC Oxf., MSS C.C.C. 453–5 · *Register of convocation of the University of Oxford for 1894–95* (1894) · P. Coones, *Mackinder's 'Scope and methods of geography'*, *Oxford Research Papers* [centenary issue] (1987) · P. Coones, *Euroclydon: a tempestuous wind*, *Oxford Research Papers*, 36 (1986) · J. B. Wainewright, ed., *Winchester College, 1836–1906* (1907) · private information (1994) · J. N. L. Baker, *The history of geography* (1963) · D. I. Scargill, 'The RGS and the foundations of geography at Oxford', *GJ*, 142 (1976), 438–61

Wealth at death £43,531 11s. 6d.: probate, 1916, *CGPLA Eng. & Wales*

Tracey, Sir Richard Edward (1837–1907), naval officer, son of Commander John Tracey, was born on 24 January 1837, and entered the navy in 1852. He served in the Baltic campaign of 1854 as a midshipman of the *Boscawen*, passed his examination in January 1858 while serving in the sloop *Harrier*, on the south-east coast of North America, and was promoted lieutenant on 28 June 1859. After studying on the *Excellent* he was appointed in July 1860 to the *Conqueror* in the channel squadron, and two years later received a supernumerary appointment to the *Euryalus*, flagship of Sir Augustus Leopold Kuper on the East Indies and China station. Tracey took part in the active operations in Japan, especially the engagement with the forts at Kagoshima in August 1863 and the attack on the batteries in the Strait of Simonoseki in September 1864; he was mentioned in dispatches, and on 21 November 1864 was promoted commander. In 1865 Tracey married Janet (d. 1875), daughter of the Revd W. Wingate.

The Japanese government under the Tokugawa Shogunata asked that British naval officers be lent for training purposes to their new navy, and Tracey was placed in charge of the mission. He and his companions set about organizing and superintending the naval school at Tsukiji (1867–8), and while thus employed he was on the books of the *Euryalus*. However, a new Japanese government ended

Tracey's work, which was not resumed until 1873, when Commander Archibald Douglas took out to Japan a second naval mission. Tracey for a short time rendered similar services to the Chinese navy, for which he was decorated by the emperor with the order of the Double Dragon, and in November 1869 he was appointed to command the gunvessel *Avon*, in which he remained on the China station until his promotion to captain on 29 November 1871. In July 1876 he was appointed to the corvette *Spartan*, which he commanded for four years on the East India station, in particular on the east coast of Africa, where he helped to suppress the slave trade. In January 1881 he became flag captain in the battleship *Iron Duke* to Sir George Ommanney Willes, commander-in-chief on the China station.

Having returned home early in 1884 Tracey was appointed to the battleship *Sultan*, which he commanded for a year in the channel squadron. In April 1885 he became an aide-de-camp to Queen Victoria, and in July was appointed to Portsmouth Dockyard. On 30 November 1887 he married Adelaide Constance Rohesia, only daughter of John Constantine de Courcy, twenty-ninth Baron Kingsale in the Irish peerage.

Tracey reached flag rank on 1 January 1888, and first hoisted his flag as second in command of the fleet under Sir George Tryon in the manoeuvres of 1889; in September of that year he was appointed in the same capacity to the channel squadron. In January 1892 he was made admiral superintendent at Malta, and on 23 June 1893 was promoted to vice-admiral. In 1896 he was an umpire for the naval manoeuvres, and for three years from October 1897 was president of the Royal Naval College, Greenwich. He was made KCB in May 1898, was promoted admiral on 29 November following, and retired on 24 January 1901. He died at his home, 8 Sloane Gardens, Chelsea, London, on 7 March 1907, and was buried at Kensal Green cemetery. He was survived by his second wife. Although a highly regarded sea officer Tracey had little impact on the service and had little to contribute ashore.

L. G. C. LAUGHTON, rev. ANDREW LAMBERT

Sources C. Penrose Fitzgerald, *Sir George Tryon* (1898) · Navy List · *The Times* (9 March 1907) · *The Times* (12 March 1907) · A. D. Lambert, *The Crimean War: British grand strategy, 1853–56* (1990) · G. S. Graham, *The politics of naval supremacy* (1965) · G. S. Graham, *The China station: war and diplomacy, 1830–1860* (1978) · CGPLA Eng. & Wales (1907)
Likenesses engraving
Wealth at death £857 5s. 8d.: probate, 7 Oct 1907, CGPLA Eng. & Wales

Tracy, Isolda de (d. in or after 1301). *See under* Cardinan family (*per.* 1066–c.1300).

Tracy, John, seventh Viscount Tracy of Rathcoole (1722–1793), college head, was born on 8 August 1722 at Toddington Manor, Gloucestershire, the third son of Thomas Charles Tracy, fifth Viscount Tracy (1690–1756), but the first child of his second wife, Frances (c.1697–1751), daughter of Sir John Packington, fourth baronet. He was educated at Abingdon School, Berkshire, and matriculated at University College, Oxford, on 9 May 1741; he graduated BA in 1745. He migrated to All Souls that year as a scholar, and in 1746 became a fellow, before proceeding MA in 1749, BD in 1757, and DD in 1761. He held the livings of Lewknor, Oxfordshire (1763–4), Didbrook, Gloucestershire (1765–89), and Farnborough, Berkshire (1768–9).

In 1755 Tracy, as senior proctor of the university, nominated the lawyer William Blackstone, then bursar of All Souls, to a vacancy in the delegacy of the university press, thus asserting a disputed proctorial right to make an appointment without the consent of the vice-chancellor, who was at that time the notorious pluralist George Huddesford. Tracy's justification for so doing was that the abuses in the press were notorious but that the existing authorities had done nothing to confront them. It was a small enough action, but its implications were significant; Tracy had fired the first shot in an assault which 'breached the citadel of power, thitherto occupied by the Heads of Houses, and thrust into it an indomitable fighter against abuses and neglect' (Carter, 327).

Tracy's election as warden of All Souls in June 1766 took place against the background of a running battle between the college and its visitor, the archbishop of Canterbury, over the rights of founder's kin to fellowships at All Souls. Successive visitors tended to support the view that the college was in effect the property of a group defined by kinship, but the fellows wished to recruit more widely, and Tracy—though himself able to lay claim to be founder's kin—was an advocate of openness. Blackstone had argued in his *Essay on Collateral Consanguinity* (1750) that both canon and civil law placed limits on the duration of effective consanguinity, and concluded that the claims of founder's-kinship should be said to have expired. However, when in 1761 the college had petitioned the visitor for a decision on whether collateral consanguinity was to continue indefinitely, the visitor had ruled that the college must adhere strictly to its statutes, with the result that by 1777 the founder's-kin fellows were a majority. In the latter year, however, under Tracy's leadership the college won a concession from the visitor, who permitted them to limit such fellowships provided the number remained always above ten. This limitation was challenged in 1792 by a claimant in Doctors' Commons; but the visitor upheld the previous ruling. Following Tracy's death in 1793 the numbers of founder's-kin fellows again rose significantly.

Tracy appeared on the side of reform also in 1772, when the university was divided over the question of undergraduate subscription to the Thirty-Nine Articles, and he was one of the heads of the party 'desirous of abolishing the present Subscription, without providing any Substitute' (*Hist. U. Oxf.* 5: 18th-cent. Oxf., 175). Otherwise, although he did not cut a conspicuous figure in eighteenth-century Oxford, the records of his activities show Tracy as an able manager of affairs and a judicious amender of abuses. As warden of All Souls he steered a course towards respectable administration. His private papers suggest a discreetly robust, unpretentious, and conscientious temperament with something of a passion for precise detail, as for example in the keeping of accounts or the measurement of distances, an impression fortified by the portrait of him painted by Sir Thomas Lawrence.

In August 1792 Tracy inherited the viscountcy on the death of his half-brother Thomas Charles Tracy. He died unexpectedly in Bath on 2 February 1793 and was buried on 10 February 1793 at Toddington, Gloucestershire. He never married, and was succeeded in the title and family estate at Toddington by his brother Henry Leigh Tracy (1733–1797), although in his will he was able to leave him only £100, with £500 being given to All Souls.

M. ST JOHN PARKER

Sources [J. Tracy and C. Mortimer], *A reply to Dr Huddesford's observations relating to the delegates of the press with a narrative of the proceedings of the proctors with regard to their nomination of a delegate April 28 1756* (1756) • H. Carter, *A history of the Oxford University Press*, 1: *To the year 1780* (1975) • *Hist. U. Oxf.* 5: *18th-cent. Oxf.* • G. D. Squibb, *Founders' kin: privilege and pedigree* (1972) • W. Blackstone, *An essay on collateral consanguinity* (1750) • [J. Tracy], pocket book, Glos. RO, D2153 1101 0/13 • [J. Tracy], note book, Glos. RO, D2153 932 0/12 • parish register, Toddington, Gloucestershire, St Andrew, 8 Aug 1722 [birth] • parish register, Toddington, Gloucestershire, St Andrew, 26 Aug 1722 [baptism] • parish register, Toddington, Gloucestershire, St Andrew, 10 Feb 1793 [burial] • *Jackson's Oxford Journal* (1763–93) • Burke, *Peerage* (1999) [Sudeley] • Foster, *Alum. Oxon.* • GEC, *Peerage* • *GM*, 1st ser., 63 (1793), 187

Archives All Souls Oxf., warden's safe, Warden's MS 6 • Glos. RO, Hanbury-Tracy family MSS

Likenesses T. Lawrence, oils, c.1790–1793, All Souls Oxf. • C. Knight, engraving (after T. Lawrence, c.1790–1793) • portrait (after T. Lawrence, c.1790–1793), All Souls Oxf.

Wealth at death £500 to All Souls College, Oxford; £100 to brother; residue of estate to sister; in 1793 the income of the warden of All Souls College, Oxford, was said to be £375: *Hist. U. Oxf.* 5: *18th-cent. Oxf.*, 238

Tracy, Richard (b. before **1501**, d. **1569**), religious activist, was the fourth of five children of William Tracy of Toddington, Gloucestershire (d. 1530), and his wife, Margaret, née Throckmorton, of Warwickshire. Before 1547 he married Barbara, daughter of Sir Thomas Lucy of Charlecote (d. 1525); they had three sons, Paul, Nathaniel, and Samuel, and three daughters, Hester, Susan, and Judith. He was admitted BA at Oxford on 27 June 1515, and was admitted to the Inner Temple on 6 July 1519; he remained an active member of the Inner Temple, and was governor in 1549–50. In 1529 he was returned to parliament for Wootton Bassett, perhaps as a client of Sir Edward Baynton or of Sir John Bridges; he probably sat for the same borough in the parliament of 1536, and may have done in 1539 and 1542.

The Tracys were one of the leading families of northern Gloucestershire, and during the 1520s they and some others in their circle became associated with early protestantism: the reformist martyr James Bainham was Richard's cousin. Richard himself first came to prominence through the affair of his father's will. William Tracy died on 10 October 1530, leaving a will which was a lengthy, uncompromising, and polemical exposition of his protestant understanding of justification. He was posthumously convicted of heresy by the convocation of Canterbury, and the chancellor of Worcester was ordered to exhume the body. He did so, but he also had the body burnt, and since there was no writ of *de haeretico comburendo*, this was illegal. Richard Tracy and his mother were the sole heirs and executors of the will (no mention is made of the elder son, also William), and Richard took up the cudgels on his father's behalf. In addition to his understandable outrage at the 'greate & abhhominable worldly shame don unto his kyndred in burnyng his roten bones' (PRO, SP 1/74, fol. 36r), he probably already shared his father's beliefs. He succeeded in having a fine of £300 imposed on the over-zealous chancellor, and, perhaps more significantly, he seems in the process to have caught the eye of Thomas Cromwell.

In 1533 Cromwell granted Tracy Tewkesbury Abbey's manor of Stanway, Gloucestershire, against the express wishes of the abbot. Stanway was to form the core of the holdings which Tracy accumulated over the next eighteen years, of which the most important was to be a major part of the lands of Clifford Priory. He sat on the commission of the peace for Worcestershire from 1537 to 1547, and for Gloucestershire in 1547–8; in 1539 he was shortlisted for, but not pricked, sheriff of Worcestershire. He worked closely with Bishop Latimer in the dissolution of the local monasteries, and when the blood of Hailes was declared to be fraudulent in 1538 the relic was left in Tracy's custody. Latimer wrote to Cromwell that he wished there were many more like Tracy.

Tracy's prosperity did not prevent his maintaining a genuine commitment to evangelical reform. One of the most public signs of this was the scriptural names that he chose for his children; his daughters' names in particular betray a distinctively reformist respect for the heroines of the Old Testament. More practically he supported the zealous young Zwinglian Bartholomew Traheron through university after Traheron was orphaned, urging him 'to forsake the puddels of sophisters and to fetche water from the pure fountaynes of the scripture' (Vigo, sig. +2v). In 1540 he published a translation of a Latin work by John Frith, and in 1543 a pamphlet of his own on justification by faith. His *Supplycacion* of 1544, too controversial to be printed in England, combined a demand for doctrinal reform with one for the reform of the Commonwealth; these were themes he had first explored in an unpublished tract in the 1530s. In 1546 Tracy sent a message of encouragement to the imprisoned reformer Edward Crome, although John Foxe noted sourly that Tracy gave no help to the messenger when he was caught and tortured. After the death of Henry VIII, Tracy became more outspoken, publishing two tracts against the mass during 1548. However, his relationship with Edward VI's protectorate regimes was uncomfortable. Although he sat on the Chantries Act commission for Gloucestershire, he was removed from the commission of the peace in 1548, and from May 1551 to November 1552 he was imprisoned in the Tower, after an obscure incident in which he sent a 'seditious lettre and a lewde message'—presumably one derogatory to the duke of Northumberland—to his friend Robert Keilway, MP for Bristol. In Mary's reign he remained in England, and although he was summoned before the privy council twice in 1555 for having 'behaved himself verye stubburnely' in religious matters, both times he submitted (*APC, 1554–6*, 181). In January 1556 he was troubled again, for objecting to the forced loan.

Tracy's fortunes revived with Elizabeth's accession. From 1559 to his death he sat on the commission of the peace for Gloucestershire, and he was sheriff in 1560–61. However, his commitment to religious reform could still be obstinate. He preached weekly in Stanway church for a year early in the reign, in violation of the rubrics; in April 1565 he wrote to Cecil, warning brusquely that if the queen did not refrain from the use of images she courted 'great perrel off goddes wrath & dyspleasure' (PRO, SP 12/36, fol. 77r). He died on 8 March 1569 at Stanway.

ALEC RYRIE

Sources PRO, state papers domestic, Henry VIII, SP 1/74, fol. 36, 1/150, fols. 178–9, 1/153, fol. 60, 1/244, fol. 243 · PRO, state papers domestic, Elizabeth, SP 12/36, fol. 77 · *LP Henry VIII*, 6, nos. 41, 161, 299; 12/2, no. 1304; 13/2, nos. 710, 967(26); 14/1, no. 84; 14/2, no. 728(2); 19/2, no. 527(12) · *APC, 1550–1552*, 220, 272–3, 482; 1552–4, 172; 1554–6, 145, 181; 1556–8, 45 · C. Litzenberger, *The English Reformation and the laity: Gloucestershire, 1540–1580* (1997) · HoP, *Commons, 1509–58*, 3.471–3 · J. Britton, *Graphic illustrations, with historical and descriptive accounts, of Toddington, Gloucestershire* (1840) · J. Vigo, *The most excellent workes of chirurgerye*, trans. B. Traheron (1543) · R. Tracy, *The profe and declaration of thys proposition: fayth only justifieth* (1543) · R. Tracy, *A supplycacion to our moste soveraigne lorde Kynge Henry the eyght* (1544) · R. Tracy, *A bryef & short declaracyon made, wherby eve[ry] Chrysten man maye knowe, what is a sacrament* (1548) · R. Tracy, *A most godly enstruction and very necessarie lesson [of] the communion of the bodie & bloud or our saviour Christe Jesus* (1548) · *The acts and monuments of John Foxe*, ed. S. R. Cattley, 8 vols. (1837–41)

Tracy, Robert (1655–1735), judge, was born at Toddington, Gloucestershire, the fifth son of Robert Tracy, second Viscount Tracy of Rathcoole (c.1592–1662), but the first son with his second wife, Dorothy (*bap.* 1630, *d.* 1685), daughter of Thomas Cocks of Castleditch, Herefordshire. Tracy matriculated at Oriel College, Oxford, on 29 October 1672, aged seventeen, and entered the Middle Temple on 15 April 1673. He was called to the bar on 21 May 1680. He married on 29 August 1683 Anne (*bap.* 1659, *d.* 1714), daughter of William Dowdeswell of Pull Court, Worcestershire. They had three sons and two daughters.

In July 1699 Tracy was appointed a judge in the Irish king's bench. In November 1700 he was made a serjeant-at-law, and on the 15th he was transferred to the court of exchequer in England. Despite a little concern expressed to Robert Harley over his future, following the death of William III, Tracy was transferred to the court of common pleas on 23 June 1702. In July 1705 he was perceived as Harley's candidate to succeed Nathan Wright as lord keeper. He presided over the trials of those indicted for riot during the Sacheverell trial in 1710, and in the hiatus which followed Lord Cowper's resignation of the seals in September 1710 Tracy was one of three men given temporary custody of the great seal.

Tracy was reappointed to common pleas in November 1714 following the accession of George I. In December 1716 he tried the Scottish Jacobite rebels in Carlisle, giving 'a very handsome charge' ('Eight Letters', 523) to the court. In January 1718 he was one of three judges who gave their opinion against the king having the right to educate his grandchildren. In May 1725 Tracy was being talked of for promotion to lord chief baron or lord chief justice, but by December of that year it was rumoured that he would surrender his place in return for a pension. This duly occurred on 26 October 1726 with a pension of £1500 p.a. Tracy died at his 'new built house' (PRO, PROB 11/673/217) at Coscomb, Gloucestershire, on 11 September 1735, and was buried in the local church at Didbrook. His two adult sons having predeceased him, in his will Tracy left his estate to his grandson Robert Tracy, remainder to his daughter Anne, the wife of Thomas Wylde MP, for life, then to his grandson Robert Pratt, the son of his daughter Dorothy and her husband, Sir John Pratt, the former lord chief justice.

Upon Tracy's death the *Gentleman's Magazine* described him as 'a complete gentleman and a good lawyer; of a clear head and an honest heart, and delivered his opinion with that genteel affability and integrity that even those who lost a cause, were charmed with his behaviour'. Dudley Ryder, on the other hand, confided to his diary his distaste for some of Tracy's judicial methods and for favouring certain attorneys that appeared before him.

STUART HANDLEY

Sources Sainty, *Judges*, 79, 127 · Baker, *Serjeants*, 451, 541 · F. E. Ball, *The judges in Ireland, 1221–1921*, 2 vols. (New York, 1927), 64 · J. J. Howard and F. A. Crisp, eds., *Visitation of England and Wales*, 21 vols. (privately printed, London, 1893–1921), vol. 7, p. 65 · will, PRO, PROB 11/673, sig. 217 · Foss, *Judges*, 8.62–4 · IGI · Foster, *Alum. Oxon.* · H. A. C. Sturgess, ed., *Register of admissions to the Honourable Society of the Middle Temple, from the fifteenth century to the year 1944*, 1 (1949), 186 · N. Luttrell, *A brief historical relation of state affairs from September 1678 to April 1714*, 4 (1857), 536, 702; 6 (1857), 572–3, 633 · *The manuscripts of his grace the duke of Portland*, 11 vols., HMC, 29 (1891–1931), vol. 4, pp. 35, 610; vol. 5, p. 553; vol. 6, pp. 7–8; vol. 7, p. 407 · *The Marlborough–Godolphin correspondence*, ed. H. L. Snyder, 1 (1975), 418n. · 'Eight letters by William Nicolson, bishop of Carlisle, to the archbishop of York, 1716', ed. H. Paton, *Miscellany … I*, Scottish History Society, 15 (1893), 523–6 · DNB · GEC, *Peerage* · GM, 1st ser., 5 (1735), 559

Archives Worcs. RO, letters, accounts, and papers | S. Antiquaries, Lond., letters to John Higford

Tracy, Walter Valentine (1914–1995), typographer, was born on 14 February 1914 in Islington, London, the son of Walter Tracy (1882–1938), a seaman in the Royal Navy. His mother, Anne Nunn (1883–1984), worked as a leather machinist before her marriage in 1909. Walter was the elder of two children: his sister, Rose Anne, was born in 1917. She said after her brother's death that they had a happy childhood in a quiet, respectable family, and their parents, within their limited means, provided for all their needs 'with loving but undemonstrative care' (private information). Walter attended Islington elementary and then Shoreditch secondary schools. When his father was demobbed after serving at sea throughout the First World War, he took a job as a warehouseman and his wife worked as a part-time charwoman. Through a friend of his father's in the printing trade, Walter at the age of fourteen became an apprentice in William Clowes, one of the largest printing firms in Great Britain. After training as a printing compositor, Tracy became one of the ablest type designers in Britain, if not the world. He specialized in typefaces for newspapers. After he retired, Walter at the suggestion of a friend recorded his recollections, 'Composing room days—and after', which were published in bulletin 40 (winter 1995–6) of the Printing Historical Society, with two photographs of Walter Tracy without the beard he grew after retiring. Much of the following account is taken from that important source.

When he came out of his time as a compositor Tracy got a job in the typographic design studio of the Baynard Press in London. The firm specialized in designing and printing posters for the London Underground and other bodies, printed from lithographic stones under the direction of Thomas Griffits; Barnett Freedman often worked there on his book jackets and illustrations for the publishers Faber and Faber.

In 1938 Tracy became a print buyer in Notley's, a small but leading advertising agency. He found that he did not enjoy advertising, but had to stay there during the war, having been rejected for active service—he thought unfairly—for health reasons. In 1942 he married (Muriel) Frances Campbell (b. 1913), who survived him: they had no children. In 1946 he left Notley's and became a freelance designer, and succeeded in making a living 'chiefly because' (in his own words) 'the good typographers [of whom at that time there were not many] were still in the services' (Tracy, 'Composing room days', 9). His abilities were seen by James Shand, a Glaswegian printer who now headed the Shenval Press in England, which he had founded in 1930 as a vehicle for high-quality printing. Shand was gifted both as a writer and designer, although he could not draw a straight line or a circle: he was one of the most intelligent and eccentric printers in Britain. With Robert Harling as editor and designer, Shand had before the war produced eight issues of a lively journal, *Typography*, and they now set up a publishing firm, Art and Technics, to produce the sort of work they admired. Shand gave Tracy the job of putting their books together and getting them ready for the press, on a part-time basis of four mornings a week. In Tracy's words

> James Shand was a man of culture and taste, and for me, having no taste at all at that time, his example, his conversation, and his gentle hints of a better way were immensely valuable. His influence on me was strong. My mind expanded (and not before time: after all, I was in my thirties), and I began to take a serious interest in the history and aesthetics of printing, to acquire books on the subject, and to form opinions—and even to learn when to change them. (Tracy, 'Composing room days')

In 1947 Shand, who was a consultant to the Linotype Company, asked Tracy to take over the periodical *Linotype Matrix*, which he had started before the war, and to edit and produce it; Tracy proceeded to write and design most of the first twenty or so issues. He became a full-time member of Linotype, and was soon their manager of typeface development. His technical knowledge and experience made him time and again a better designer than the professional artists. One of his most notable achievements was Jubilee, a face required to replace the famous Times New Roman, whose matrices (the moulds from which the type was cast) were continuously found to need renewal, owing (as Sebastian Carter has pointed out) to

Stanley Morison's requirement for close setting, which made the matrix walls very thin.

Jubilee, introduced in 1953, was used by a number of newspapers, but not by *The Times*. In 1969 Tracy designed Telegraph Modern for the *Daily Telegraph*. But in 1972 he was asked by *The Times* to design a new face to replace Times New Roman: it was called Times Europa, introduced into *The Times* in October 1972, and the *Sunday Times* a year later. Tracy's position as a leading typeface designer was now plain for all to see. He designed two faces for classified (very small) advertisements, Adsans and Maximus; and was then involved in making Arabic faces for Linotype composition. He learned the letters and numerous ligatures used in Arabic typesetting, without having to learn the language. He retired in 1977, but, in his own words 'work did not cease (I knew boredom would be fatal)' (Tracy, 'Composing room days', 14). There were the Arabic Quadi face for Linotype; three weights of Kufic for Letraset; a 90-character Arabic for the Kroy machine, called Oasis; and the Malik, Medina, and Sharif faces for Bitstream; and a headline type, Telegraph New Face Bold, made in partnership with Shelley Winter for the *Daily Telegraph*, which was released in 1989. In 1973 he had been elected a royal designer for industry, and in 1993 he was awarded the Frederic W. Goudy award by the school of printing management at Rochester Institute of Technology.

Tracy also wrote two books: *Letters of Credit: a View of Type Design* (1986), and *The Typographic Scene* (1988), both published by Gordon Fraser, and both modestly but authoritatively written, and still today of great value. His dissection of the differences between 'legibility' and 'readability', discussed in *Letters of Credit*, is one of the first things that must be learned by anyone interested in typography.

Walter Tracy was a deeply kind and honest man, with a real sense of humour, and immensely generous in help to all who came to him. He died at his home, 2 Cedar Court, The Drive, Finchley Way, London, on 28 April 1995 and was cremated at St Marylebone crematorium, Finchley.

RUARI MCLEAN

Sources W. Tracy, 'Composing room days—and after', *Printing Historical Society Bulletin*, 40 (winter 1995–6), 9–14 • private information (2004) [Frances Tracy, wife; and Rose Anne Tracy, sister] • *The Times* (3 May 1995) • W. Tracy, *Letters of credit: a view of type design* (1986) • W. Tracy, *The typographic scene* (1988) • CGPLA Eng. & Wales (1995)

Wealth at death £125,000: probate, 27 June 1995, CGPLA Eng. & Wales

Tracy, William de (d. in or before 1174), one of the murderers of Thomas Becket, has been shown to have been the son of John of Sudeley, and Grace, daughter of William de Tracy, a natural son of Henry I, whose name he took. He thus possessed royal ancestry in both the paternal and the maternal lines, since through his father William de Tracy was descended from Godgifu, daughter of Æthelred II and wife of Drogo, count of the Vexin. Tracy was a man of considerable property. He was lord of at least part of the manor of Bradninch, the Domesday fief of William Capra, which had escheated to Henry I, and been granted by him to his illegitimate son, the elder William de Tracy. He also held Moreton Hampstead, Devon, where the dedication of the parish church was later changed to 'St Thomas Becket'. He came into the possession of Toddington, Gloucestershire, by an exchange with his brother, to whom he gave Burton Dassett, Warwickshire, between 1139 and 1148. The extent of his holdings is indicated by the knight service he owed. In 1165 he answered for scutage on thirty knights. In his return to the Inquest of Knight Service in 1166 he responded as holding 25¾ knights' fees of the old enfeoffment and 2½ in demesne, and later scutages were charged on 25–6 knights' fees.

Although, therefore, Tracy was a man of considerable substance, there is no sign of his having taken an active role in royal service, beyond being described as a courtier and chamber knight. He acted as a witness to at least one royal charter. In 1155 he was one of a large number of witnesses of a confirmation to St Martin of Troarn, made by Henry II at Worcester. Among the other witnesses, mostly of the highest rank, were the current and future archbishops of Canterbury, Theobald and Thomas Becket. As well as acting as a witness in the royal court Tracy also confirmed a charter of his brother Ralph of Sudeley, conferring Yanworth, near Cirencester, on Gloucester Abbey. This grant dates from the period of Gilbert Foliot's abbacy, and therefore cannot be dated after 1148. It is therefore valuable as confirmation that William de Tracy was the brother of Ralph of Sudeley. Tracy also made charitable grants on his own account. One such can be assigned to the period before the murder of Becket, by the wording of the charter itself, which refers to a grant of all the churches on his land to Alan de Tracy, clerk, by William de Tracy 'before his crime against St. Thomas'. Another benefaction which probably, though not certainly, antedates the murder is the founding of a leper hospital at 'Coismas'. An entry in the cartulary of St Étienne de Plessis-Grimoult, executed by Guillaume, bishop of Le Mans (1154–87), records this endowment, and the building of the leper hostel by Tracy. However, the project was evidently of short duration, since by 1187 at the latest the house had been empty for some time, and its revenues had been assigned by Henry II to Alan the Clerk, William de Tracy's brother, who in turn requested that they should be given to the church at Yvrandes, where there was a hermitage linked with Plessis-Grimoult.

There are slight indications, however, that Tracy had earned and enjoyed royal favour in the years before 1170. He is described as having often performed bravely in military action, and presumably this ability was displayed on the king's behalf. On two occasions, in 1155 and 1168, he received pardons by royal writ for payments for scutage and for the aid for marrying the king's daughter amounting to £37 10s., the full amount of his debts.

Tracy was certainly at Henry II's court at Bur-le-Roi, near Bayeux, at Christmas 1170, where Becket's conduct, and above all his excommunication of the bishops who had crowned Henry, the Young King, earlier that year, was angrily discussed. The king's famous outburst, 'What miserable drones and traitors have I nourished and promoted in my household, who let their lord be treated with such shameful contempt by a low-born clerk' (Robertson and Sheppard, 2.429), which later oral tradition renders simply, 'Who will rid me of this turbulent priest?' (Lyttelton, pt 4, 353), prompted the departure of Tracy with Reginald *Fitzurse, Hugh de *Morville, and Richard Brito on their ill-conceived journey to Canterbury. Fitzurse (in whose article the confrontation with Becket is described more fully) took the lead in the initial interview with the archbishop on 29 December, in which Tracy uttered not a word. Unlike the other three knights Tracy did not put on armour before the frenzied pursuit of Becket into the cathedral, but throughout the murder wore a green cloak and a particoloured tunic. So, as he was less encumbered than the others, they tried at one point to hoist Becket onto his back, to carry him out of the cathedral itself, and in the tussle which followed, the archbishop nearly felled him. It has been claimed that both he and Reginald Fitzurse struck the first blow, and nearly cut off the arm of Becket's attendant, Edward Grim—Tracy certainly claimed responsibility for this, in conversation the evening after the murder at Saltwood Castle, though he believed that the wounded man was John of Salisbury. Tracy and the other murderers left the cathedral immediately after completing their pillage of the archiepiscopal palace, and retired that night to Saltwood Castle, Kent. They eventually took refuge at the royal castle of Knaresborough, Yorkshire, then in the custody of Morville.

Tracy seems to have been the first to come to his senses: in a confession to Bartholomew, bishop of Exeter, apparently made in Devon shortly after the murder, he said that his heart sank and he feared that the earth might open up and swallow him. Mythical stories about the fate of all four of the knights involved in Becket's murder appeared rapidly, but especially in the case of Tracy. The most famous of these is that Tracy, on his way to the Holy Land to do penance for the murder, was turned back by adverse winds. Another local legend had it that he spent many years in a hermitage on the Devon coast, expiating his offence. However, an extremely, and apparently deliberately, cryptic letter from Becket's former chaplain, Herbert of Bosham, makes it clear that he had made his way to the papal curia by the latter months of 1171, 'at the time when King Henry went into Ireland' (Robertson and Sheppard, 7.511–12). According to Herbert, Tracy had obtained secret information about the legates Albert and Theodwin, so secret that it should have been known only to the king of England. It is not clear what use Herbert expected Tracy to make of this, but in any case, according to the author of the life of Becket in the Lansdowne manuscript, he was ordered by the pope to continue his journey to the Holy Land. The last certainly established action of his life took place at Cosenza in southern Italy, presumably on his way there, where he executed a charter conferring on the monks of Christ Church, Canterbury, the sum of 100s. a year, to support a monk praying day and night for the living and the dead, from his manor of Daccombe in Devon. This charter was witnessed by the abbot of St Euphemia, where, according to Herbert of Bosham, Tracy lay dying.

Herbert gives horrific details of Tracy's death, and although there is an alternative tradition that he did reach the Holy Land, his account of events is to be preferred. The charter making the grant of Daccombe was confirmed by Henry II between July and October 1174, and this confirmation therefore constitutes an extreme *terminus ante quem* for Tracy's death. His lands at Toddington passed to his elder son Henry: he made provision for his younger son, Alard, by presenting him to the living there.

R. M. FRANKLIN

Sources J. C. Robertson and J. B. Sheppard, eds., *Materials for the history of Thomas Becket, archbishop of Canterbury*, 7 vols., Rolls Series, 67 (1875–85) · E. Magnússon, ed. and trans., *Thómas saga Erkibyskups*, 2 vols., Rolls Series, 65 (1875–83) · G. de Pont-Sainte-Maxence, *La vie de Saint Thomas le martyr*, ed. E. Walberg (Lund, 1922) · St Aelred [abbot of Rievaulx], 'Relatio de standardo', *Chronicles of the reigns of Stephen, Henry II, and Richard I*, ed. R. Howlett, 3, Rolls Series, 82 (1886) · *Pipe rolls*, Henry II · F. Barlow, *Thomas Becket* (1986) · I. J. Sanders, *English baronies: a study of their origin and descent, 1086–1327* (1960) · private information (2004) · GEC, *Peerage* [1887–98] · *The Sudeleys—lords of Toddington*, The Manorial Society of Great Britain (1987) · Burke, *Peerage* (1970) · R. A. L. Smith, *Canterbury Cathedral priory: a study in monastic administration* (1943) · G. Lyttelton, *The history of the life of King Henry the Second*, 6 vols. (1769–73)
Likenesses illumination, 1190–1210, BL, MS Harl. 5102 · enamelled châsse, 13th cent., S. Antiquaries, Lond. · stained-glass window, c.1206, Chartres Cathedral · reliquary, c.1250, Heidal church, Valdres, Norway · ivory plaque, 14th cent., V&A · stained-glass window, c.1350, Christ Church Oxf. · alabaster table, 15th cent., BM · painted panel, 1450–99, Canterbury Cathedral · ceiling boss, Exeter Cathedral · portrait, BL, Cotton MS Claudius Bii, fol. 341*r* · wall painting, S. Maria, Tarrasa, Spain

Tracy, William (*d.* 1530), landowner and religious radical, was the son of Sir Henry Tracy of Toddington, Gloucestershire, and Alice Baldington, daughter and coheir of Thomas Baldington of Oxfordshire. He was married to Margaret Throckmorton, daughter of Thomas Throckmorton of Corse Court in Gloucestershire. His sister, Elizabeth, was married to Sir Alexander Bainham of Westbury-on-Severn in Gloucestershire, a very prominent member of the county's gentry; their youngest son, James, would be burnt at Smithfield for his evangelical beliefs in 1532. William Tracy was an active member of the Gloucestershire élite, serving as sheriff in 1513 and on numerous commissions of the peace. He was also connected to other prominent families in the county, not only serving as a feoffee of the estate of Sir Alexander Bainham and as an executor of Elizabeth Bainham's will, but also as one of the executors of the will of Dame Joan Huddleston, widow of Sir John, daughter of Sir Miles Stapleton of Norfolk, and granddaughter of Sir Thomas de la Pole.

Although nothing is known concerning Tracy's education, he was learned, and by the time of his death had developed a clearly evangelical theology. In the 1520s, while carrying out his duties as a JP, he had become acquainted with William Tyndale, the evangelical biblical scholar who was then residing in the county. Tyndale later described him as 'a learned man and better sene in the workes of Sainct Austine … than ever I knew doctoure in Englande' (*Testament*). Tracy's learning, and more particularly his theology, may well have been influenced by his

contact with Tyndale, and he in turn may have influenced his nephew, James Bainham. The nature of Tracy's beliefs became most apparent after he died at Toddington, on 10 October 1530, when his remarkable will began to circulate all over England. This will, in which he proclaimed his complete assurance in the salvation of his soul and eschewed all works and prayers as means of salvation, was circulating in London by 1531, made available by an unknown hand. That same year it was refused probate by the prerogative court of Canterbury and condemned by convocation; Tracy was declared a heretic and orders were given to remove his body from consecrated soil. The chancellor of the diocese of Worcester had the body exhumed, but overstepped his authority by having it burnt, and was subsequently fined £300 for his actions.

However, William Tracy's words could not be silenced by official or semi-official action. Four years after he was declared a heretic and his body was burnt, his will was published in Antwerp with commentaries by William Tyndale and John Frith, and its influence was soon visible in the religious portions of the wills of others. In 1537 William Shepard, of Mendlesham in Suffolk, incorporated Tracy's will in its entirety into his own, adding explanatory passages and paragraphs to clarify his understanding of its content. New editions of the will were then published in 1546 and 1548, and their influence can be seen in a number of wills written all over England between 1548 and 1640. These appropriated portions of Tracy's will and modified them to create their own distinctive but recognizable evangelical religious preambles. William Tracy thus provided a model of evangelical or protestant rhetoric for those crafting religious statements for their wills, a model that outlived him by over 100 years.

CAROLINE LITZENBERGER

Sources *LP Henry VIII* · J. Craig and C. Litzenberger, 'Wills as religious propaganda: the testament of William Tracy', *Journal of Ecclesiastical History*, 44 (1993), 415–31 · *The acts and monuments of John Foxe*, new edn, ed. G. Townsend, 8 vols., vols. 4–5 · Hockaday abstracts, Gloucester City Library, vol. 228, 1519, unpaginated · C. R. Hudleston, 'Sir John Huddleston, constable of Sudeley', *Transactions of the Bristol and Gloucestershire Archaeological Society*, 48 (1926), 117–32 · J. Maclean and W. C. Heane, eds., *The visitation of the county of Gloucester taken in the year 1623*, Harleian Society, 21 (1885) · PRO, PROB 11/22, fols. 208v–209v · *The testament of Master Wylliam Tracie esquier, expounded both by William Tyndale and Jhon Frith* (1535) · 'The testament of W. Tracie expounded by W. Tindall', *Wyclyffes Wycket* (1546) · 'The testament of W. Tracie expounded by W. Tindall', *Wicklieffes Wicket: faythfully overseene and corrected*, ed. M. C. [M. Coverdale] (1548) · 'The testament of W. Tracie expounded by W. Tindall', [E. Hall], *The union of the two noble and illustre femelies of Lancastre and Yorke*, ed. [R. Grafton] (1548) · D. Wilkins, ed., *Concilia Magnae Britanniae et Hiberniae*, 3 (1737) · S. Tymms, ed., *Wills and inventories from the registers of the commissary of Bury St Edmund's and the archdeacon of Sudbury*, CS, 49 (1850) · *HoP, Commons, 1509–58*, 3.471–3
Archives Glos. RO · PRO

Tradescant, John, the elder (*d.* 1638), gardener and collector, is thought to have been born in England, perhaps in the 1570s. His antecedents are unrecorded but he seems to have had family connections in East Anglia: possible

John Tradescant the elder (*d.* 1638), attrib. Emanuel de Critz [posthumous]

candidates for his parents have been identified at Corton, while his son John *Tradescant (*bap.* 1608, *d.* 1662) was to leave legacies to 'namesakes' (described by his wife as 'kinsmen') at Walberswick, both villages lying on the Suffolk coast. Anthony Wood's often-quoted reference to 'a famous Gardener called Joh. Tredescaut a Dutchman' (Wood, *Ath. Oxon.*, 2, col. 888) is misconceived, since it refers to Tradescant's indisputably English-born son.

The earliest detail known of Tradescant's life is the record of his marriage on 18 June 1607 at Meopham in Kent to Elizabeth Day, daughter of the late vicar of the parish. From two years later there survives a letter written by Tradescant to William Trumbull, British resident in Brussels, outlining difficulties he has encountered on a passage to Flushing—a journey which suggests (although no reason is given for the visit) that he may already have found a wealthy patron who might send him to the continent in search of garden specimens.

Plant collecting abroad Such is the conclusion encouraged by Tradescant's subsequent experience in the service of his first known employer, Robert Cecil, first earl of Salisbury, at Hatfield House. In 1611, at Salisbury's behest, Tradescant travelled on an extended trip through the Low Countries and Flanders to Paris, buying trees, flowering shrubs, vines, and bulbs for the gardens at Hatfield. The relevant bills, detailing in addition to their purchase prices arrangements for the transport of the specimens to Hatfield, survive in the Salisbury archives. Following the death of the first earl in 1612, Tradescant remained in the

employment of the second earl, on whose behalf he again visited France, before transferring his allegiance (by midsummer 1615) to Edward, first Baron Wotton, who then occupied the former monastery of St Augustine at Canterbury.

During the period of his engagement at Canterbury, where his success in growing melons, mandrakes, and other exotics attracted admiring comment from Sir Henry Mainwaring and others, Tradescant was released to accompany an embassy to Tsar Michael Feodorovich, led by Sir Dudley Digges. Tradescant's diary of this 'Viag of Ambusad' via the North Cape to Archangel, written in a rude hand and style, survives among the Ashmole manuscripts in the Bodleian Library; its significance was first recognized by Hamel about 1854 and it has been republished with commentaries by Konovalov and by Leith-Ross. Tradescant's official duties evidently were of a negligible nature and while the ambassadorial party set off for the imperial court he was left to pursue three weeks of uninterrupted fieldwork among the coastal flora, noting the characteristics of plants and other wildlife—the first such investigations recorded on Russian soil—and gathering specimens for shipment back to England. Parkinson (*Paradisi*, 346; *Theatrum*, 705) identifies white hellebores, purple cranesbill, and other plants among those brought to England on that occasion by 'that worthy, curious and diligent searcher and preserver of all natures rarities and varieties, my very good friend, John Tradescante', and the list of introductions is extended by Boulger. The *Rosa Moscovita* later recorded at Lambeth was probably introduced on the same occasion.

Another exotic, the 'Algiers apricot', evidently was a trophy from another expedition, on which Tradescant accompanied the fleet sent in 1620–21 under the command of Sir Robert Mansell to quell the Barbary pirates who were proving an increasing hazard to English shipping. He sailed as a gentleman volunteer on the pinnace *Mercury*, under the command of Captain Phineas Pett, and whatever action he may have seen at sea Tradescant took care to collect such specimens as he could on land, when circumstances permitted: of various 'corne flagges', he later related to Parkinson that he had seen 'many acres of ground in Barbary spread over with them' (Parkinson, *Paradisi*, 190); a variety of starry-headed clover is said to have been collected by him during that same voyage at Formentera and, again according to Parkinson, the wild pomegranate 'was never seene in England, before John Tradescante … brought it from parts beyond the Seas, and planted it in his Lords Garden at Canterbury' (ibid., 430).

In 1623 Tradescant entered the service of George Villiers, first duke of Buckingham, on whose account he again visited the Low Countries and Flanders, buying trees and other plants. In 1625, when the duke was sent to France to provide an escort for Charles I's bride, Henrietta Maria, on her introductory journey to England, Tradescant followed in his wake with 'my Lords stuff and Trunkes &c' (BL, Add. MS 12528, fol. 21, no. 19) and took the opportunity to acquire further specimens for the duke's gardens at New Hall in Essex. Two years later he accompanied the duke again to France in less congenial circumstances when Buckingham mounted his ill-conceived attempt to bring relief to the besieged protestants of La Rochelle, a mission that foundered when Buckingham's army was decimated on the Île de Ré.

The Lambeth garden   Following Buckingham's assassination in 1628 Tradescant installed his family in the then relatively undeveloped environs of South Lambeth in Surrey; the original site of the house and garden that were to become so famously associated with 'Tradescant's Ark' and his gardens, marked approximately by the present-day Tradescant Road and Walberswick Road, has been precisely located (Sturdy). There Tradescant established many of the exotics he had personally imported as well as others which arrived more indirectly. Among the latter was the plant with which his name is most closely linked, *Tradescantia virginiana*, of which Parkinson was to write:

> This Spider-Wort is of late knowledge, and for it the Christian world is indebted unto that painfull industrious searcher, and lover of all natures varieties, John Tradescant … who first received it of a friend, that brought it out of Virginia.   (Parkinson, *Paradisi*, 152)

While the house provided a settled base for Tradescant for the remainder of his life, he was to be favoured with two further appointments. The first of these came in 1630 when he was chosen by the king as 'Keeper of our gardens, Vines and Silke-wormes' at Oatlands Palace in Surrey (a property which was by this time settled on the queen). Among other duties he carried out there was the laying-out of a new bowling green and the provision of sheltered accommodation for 200 orange trees. His gardening career was crowned in 1637 with his appointment as custodian of the Oxford Physic Garden. The post is likely to have been of an advisory nature and there is little or no evidence of any impact he may have made there; in any case he died within a year of his appointment.

The museum which he was to establish at Lambeth brought fame to Tradescant in equal measure to his gardening activities, although without the latter he could hardly have achieved so much. Early inspiration may have been provided by Sir Walter Cope (*d.* 1614), whose extensive cabinet was described by the Swiss Thomas Platter in 1599 and on whose behalf Tradescant bought plants to the value of £38 on his visit to the Netherlands in 1611. The same occasion would have provided him with opportunities to visit the well-known collections housed in the botanic gardens and the anatomy school of Leiden University and he was also on intimate terms with the Morin family in Paris, possessors of a 'rare collection of shells, Flowers and Insects' (Evelyn, *Diary*, c.1–6 April, 1644). The greatest impetus to his collecting career undoubtedly came during his years of service to the duke of Buckingham. A letter of 1625, written by Tradescant in Buckingham's name and addressed to Edward Nicholas, then secretary to the navy, exhorts sea captains, ambassadors, and overseas merchants to furnish the duke with all manner of natural and artificial curiosities. The full significance of this letter is difficult to establish: Buckingham's primary interests as a collector lay in the realms of fine art and classical antiquities rather than curiosities, and it is hard to decide whether he merely allowed his gardener to make use of his influential name or whether it reveals a new area of interest on the part of the duke, the everyday administration of which may have been placed in Tradescant's hands. Similarly, Charles I had no recorded interest in curiosities yet a letter of 1633, sent by the secretary of state, Francis Windbank, to the court of the East India Company, desires the company to 'write for such varieties as are expressed in a paper thereinclosed, and being returned to deliver them to John Tradescant to be reserved by him for His Majesties Service' (Leith-Ross, 97). Here again, Tradescant may conceivably have played a curatorial role in this little-known area of the king's interests.

By 1634 Tradescant's own museum was sufficiently well established for a visitor (Peter Mundy) to spend 'a whole day in peruseing, and that superficially, such as hee had gathered together' (R. C. Temple, ed. *The Travels of Peter Mundy in Europe and Asia, 1608–1667*, Hakluyt Society, ser. 2, vols. 45–6, 1919, 1–3). A description of the collection from 1638 includes the earliest mention of its most famous surviving treasure, 'the robe of the King of Virginia', better known as 'Powhatan's Mantle'. The later history of the collection is discussed in relation to John Tradescant the younger, to whom it passed on his father's death.

The best-known portrait of Tradescant is that by Cornelis de Neve (a relative of Hester Pooks, who was to marry the younger Tradescant shortly after his father's death): it shows a self-assured, keen-eyed figure with a well-tended beard and with a gold ring in his ear. While appealing as an image, it is thought to have been painted posthumously and at second hand, based on a further posthumous portrait by Emanuel de Critz (another kinsman of Hester's), although the fact that both artists were potentially well acquainted with Tradescant before his death encourages the view that they may have produced reasonably accurate likenesses.

Tradescant was buried at St Mary's Church, Lambeth, on 17 April 1638; the churchwardens' accounts record a charge of 5s. 4d. for 'the gret bell and black cloth'. In his will, proven on 2 May of that year, he left the lease of the Lambeth property to his son John, along with another lease held at Woodham Walter, Essex; his grandchildren shared leases on further properties in Long Acre and Covent Garden, as well as £150 then held by Lord Goring. Tradescant's wife predeceased him; she was buried at St Mary's on 1 June 1635. The specimens taken home by Tradescant from his extensive travels, and his skill at raising exotic plants in England, considerably increased the number of foreign edible and decorative species henceforth regularly cultivated in English gardens.

ARTHUR MacGREGOR

Sources P. Leith-Ross, *The John Tradescants* (1984) · A. MacGregor, ed., *Tradescant's rarities: essays on the foundations of the Ashmolean Museum* (1983) · M. Allen, *The Tradescants* (1964) · G. S. Boulger, 'The first Russian botanist', *Journal of Botany, British and Foreign*, 33 (1895), 33–8 · S. Konovalov, 'Two documents concerning Anglo-Russian relations in the early seventeenth century', *Oxford Slavonic Papers*, 2 (1951), 128–44 · D. Sturdy, 'The Tradescants at Lambeth', *Journal of*

Garden History, 2 (1982), 1–16 • W. Watson, 'Some account of the remains of John Tradescant's garden at Lambeth', *PTRS*, 46 (1749–50), 160–61 • J. Parkinson, *Paradisi in sole paradisus terrestris* (1629) • J. Parkinson, *Theatrum botanicum* (1640) • T. Johnson, *The herball, or, Generall historie of plantes gathered by John Gerarde* (1633) • J. Tradescant, *Plantarum in horto Iohannem Tradescanti nascentium catalogus* (1634) • P. J. Jarvis, 'The introduced trees and shrubs cultivated by the Tradescants at south Lambeth, 1629–1679', *Journal of the Society of the Bibliography of Natural History*, 9 (1978–80), 223–50
Archives AM Oxf., artificial rarities • Bodl. Oxf., Russian diary, drawings, and papers • Oxf. U. Mus. NH, natural rarities | Hatfield House, Hertfordshire, Salisbury archives
Likenesses attrib. E. de Critz, oils (posthumous), AM Oxf. [*see illus.*] • W. Hollar, etching, BM, NPG; repro. in J. Tradescant, *Museum Tradescantianum* (1656) • attrib. C. de Neve, oils (posthumous), AM Oxf. • double portrait, oils (with his wife), AM Oxf. • oils (on his deathbed), AM Oxf.

Tradescant, John, the younger

Tradescant, John, the younger (*bap.* 1608, *d.* 1662), gardener and collector, son of John *Tradescant the elder (*d.* 1638) and his wife, Elizabeth Day, was born at Meopham, Kent, and baptized there on 4 August 1608. He was educated between 1619 and 1623 at the King's School, Canterbury, while his father was in the service of Lord Wotton.

Travels to Virginia On 29 February 1628 the younger Tradescant married Jane Hurte (*d.* 1635), who bore him a daughter, Frances (*c.*1628–*c.*1667), and a son, John (1633–1652). No record survives of his having been indentured, the Gardeners' Company records for the relevant period largely having been destroyed, but in 1634 he was admitted a freeman of the company. Three years later he made the first of three recorded visits to Virginia, when it was noted that 'In 1637 John Tradescant was in the colony, to gather all rarities of flowers, plants, shells, &c' (*CSP col.*, 1, no. 11). The presence of this record among the State Papers has been taken to imply that Tradescant's visit to Virginia was undertaken at the instigation of Charles I, a contentious conclusion but one supported by a statement by John Morris, master of the watermills, that he was there under the auspices of the king. The latter author mentions that Tradescant brought back with him 'a couple of hundred plants hitherto unknown to our world'. Parkinson's *Theatrum botanicum* lists several species of these plants (burr reed, columbine, jasmine, cypress, and possibly the Virginian locust tree, as well as a variety of fern) 'which Mr. John Tradescant the younger, brought home with him from Virginia, this present yeare, 1638, presently after the death of his father' (Parkinson, 1045).

Thereafter Tradescant was appointed to his father's former position as gardener at the royal palace of Oatlands, while continuing to develop the garden associated with the family property at Lambeth. Estimates of the son's prowess are more difficult to find than for his father, but Morris accords him the highest honours in this field, describing him as 'most experienced in gardening matters' (Leith-Ross, 103) and delighting in exotic plants, while Hartlib, in his *Universal Husbandry Improved* (1650, p. 72), records that Tradescant 'daily raiseth new and curious things'. Morris goes so far as to bracket Tradescant's name with those of Thomas Johnson and John Parkinson as

'those three great men of our native botanists'—an estimate to which due weight should be given since Morris had no very high opinion of Tradescant at a personal level (Bekkers, 117).

In 1642, on the eve of England's collapse into civil war, Tradescant again took ship for Virginia, this time on his own account. The length of his stay is not known but was probably months rather than years. He continued to carry out his duties at Oatlands, perhaps up until the sale for demolition of the palace in 1650: in a bill dated 12 April 1648, now in the Ashmolean Library, he claims £40 'for work to be don for amending the Walks in the Vineyard Garden & for repairing the Bowling Greene there'. In 1653–4 he made the round trip to Virginia for a third and final time.

The Tradescant museum Throughout this period Tradescant continued to support his family from the proceeds of his gardening activities as well as from income from the museum established by his father at Lambeth. Three years after the death of his wife Jane in 1635, on 1 October 1638, Tradescant married Hester Pooks: an incidental benefit of this match was the series of portraits of all three generations of Tradescants that survives in the Ashmolean Museum, mostly attributed to the brothers Emanuel and Thomas de Critz and to Cornelis de Neve, to all of whom Hester was related. In 1645 the eighteen-year-old Frances Tradescant was to marry Alexander Norman, a widower of fifty-six. Norman's first wife had been a sister of Frances's grandmother and in his capacity as cooper to the ordnance Norman had supplied Buckingham's expedition to the Île de Ré on which his new wife's grandfather had served. Norman's death is recorded in 1657 and Frances is thought to have died ten years later. Tradescant the younger's son John evidently followed in the footsteps of his elders—Hartlib says that he was 'brought up to looke to the Botanical Garden and plants'—but in 1649 Hartlib records that his father was offering to part with the rarities in the museum in return for an annuity of £100, the value of the collection being estimated at ten times that sum. When the youngest John Tradescant died at the age of nineteen in 1652, however, the collection remained unsold.

It is difficult to detect much in the way of tangible contributions made by the younger Tradescant to the museum, beyond a supposed leg-bone of the Hertfordshire giant Jack o' Legs and a fragment of the True Cross (which 'casually had been broken from' a larger relic variously said to have belonged to Charles I or to Henrietta Maria, while it was in Tradescant's care). Tradescant himself, however, was proud to refer to the collection as 'those Rarities and Curiosities which my Father had sceduously collected, and my selfe with continued diligence have augmented, & hitherto preserved together'. The quotation comes from the preface to his *Musaeum Tradescantianum*, a 183-page octavo volume published in 1656—the first museum catalogue to appear in England. The initiative for this volume (and also the funding for it) came from Elias Ashmole, whose influence looms large in later perceptions of the Tradescants' importance. Both Ashmole and

Dr Thomas Wharton (who collaborated in the venture) evidently contributed considerably to the text of the catalogue, which bears a dedication to the president and fellows of the College of Physicians. Interestingly, in 1649 Hartlib recorded in his 'Ephemerides' that the physician George Bate offered to endow a physic garden for the college, one possibility being that its basis would be formed by Tradescant's garden. The plant list included in *Musaeum Tradescantianum* contains a significantly greater proportion of medicinal plants than was grown by the elder Tradescant; however, no formal association with the college was to develop. The presence of significant numbers of food plants in the list may also hint at a degree of purposefulness on Tradescant's part, a conclusion reinforced by his persuasion by the arguments of his collaborators and voiced in the preface to *Musaeum Tradescantianum*, that the catalogue would be 'an honour to our Nation, and a benefit to such ingenious persons as would become further enquirers into the various modes of Natures admirable workes, and the curious Imitators thereof', sentiments which were to have their apotheosis when the collection formed the foundation of the Ashmolean Museum some years later.

Ashmolean Museum The transfer of the Tradescant collection to Oxford was not a straightforward matter. Deprived of his male heir and indebted to Ashmole for the large part he had played in publishing the catalogue of the museum (which was to be reprinted with a new dedication to Charles II in the year of the Restoration), Tradescant drew up in 1659 a deed of gift by which he left the museum collection to Ashmole; Hester was to retain a lifetime's interest in the collection. Almost immediately, it seems, Hester prevailed upon her husband to change his mind in this matter, as a result of which he drew up first one will, in which the collection was to be bequeathed to the king, and then another in which it was to go instead to the University of Oxford or of Cambridge, at the discretion of Hester, his executrix. These documents, whose existence was kept secret from Ashmole, were inevitably to become a source of bitter disagreement following Tradescant's death at Lambeth on 22 April 1662. (He was buried at St Mary's, Lambeth, on 25 April.)

Within a month Ashmole had preferred a bill of complaint in chancery, alleging that Hester was attempting to frustrate the terms laid out in the deed of gift drawn up in his favour; Hester vigorously resisted, citing the subsequent will and declaring her intention that the collection should go to Oxford. In May 1664 the case finally came before the lord chancellor, the earl of Clarendon, who found in favour of Ashmole, decreeing that he should 'have and enjoy all and singular these Bookes, Coynes, Medalls, Stones, Pictures, Mechanicks, Antiquities and all and every other the Raryties and Curiosities of what sort or kind soever' (PRO Chancery Proceedings L33/221/774; Josten, 1966, vol. 3, 987–8). Thereafter the collection remained in Hester's possession and relations seem for a while to have warmed between her and Ashmole, until in 1674 he decided to buy the property adjoining the Tradescant house, after which matters turned sour again with

Hester accusing Ashmole of harassment and he ultimately demanding a written retraction of various alleged slanders. Subsequently Hester prevailed on him to take some parts of the collection into his own property and following her death by drowning in her garden pond on 4 April 1678 Ashmole took possession of the remainder. Thus it was through Ashmole that the collection was donated to Oxford (which intention he had signalled some eight years earlier) where, in 1683, the purpose-built Ashmolean Museum was formally inaugurated.

It has been held by later writers that in founding the institution in which his own name is commemorated, 'the name of Tradescant became unjustly sunk in that of Ashmole'. There can be little doubt, however, that if the collection had passed directly to the university under the terms of Tradescant's second will and without the benefit of the terms Ashmole was able to exact for the provision of new premises and the institution of tightly drafted regulations of his own composition, the benefaction would have proved ephemeral in the extreme in its new environment. However much to the chagrin of the shades of Tradescant and his wife, Ashmole's intervention in their lives contributed not a little to the immortality of their name. ARTHUR MacGREGOR

Sources P. Leith-Ross, *The John Tradescants* (1984) • A. MacGregor, ed., *Tradescant's rarities: essays on the foundations of the Ashmolean Museum* (1983) • M. Allen, *The Tradescants* (1964) • J. Tradescant, *Musaeum Tradescantianum* (1656) • J. Parkinson, *Theatrum botanicum* (1640) • P. J. Jarvis, 'The introduced trees and shrubs cultivated by the Tradescants at south Lambeth, 1629–1679', *Journal of the Society of the Bibliography of Natural History*, 9 (1978–80), 223–50 • *Correspondence of John Morris with Johannes De Laet (1634–1649)*, ed. J. A. F. Bekkers (1970) • S. Hartlib, *Universal husbandry improved* (1650) • R. F. Ovenell, *The Ashmolean Museum, 1683–1894* (1986) • A. G. MacGregor and A. J. Turner, 'The Ashmolean Museum', *Hist. U. Oxf.* 5: *18th-cent. Oxf.*, 639–58 • PRO, PROB 11/308, sig. 72
Archives AM Oxf., artificial rarities • Bodl. Oxf., drawings, journal, and papers • Oxf. U. Mus. NH, natural rarities
Likenesses attrib. E. de Critz, oils, 1652, NPG • attrib. E. de Critz, double portrait, oils (with his friend Zythepsa), AM Oxf. • W. Hollar, etching, BM, NPG; repro. in Tradescant, *Musaeum Tradescantianum* • double portrait, oils (with second wife, Hester), AM Oxf.

Trafford, F. G. *See* Riddell, Charlotte Eliza Lawson (1832–1906).

Trahaearn ap Caradog (d. 1081), ruler in Wales, was, according to the genealogies, the son of Caradog ap Gwyn ap Gollwyn. One textually corrupt genealogy states that he was also the son of Angharad, daughter of Maredudd ab Owain (d. 999). It has alternatively been suggested that his mother was a daughter of Gwerystan ap Gwaithfoed of Powys. Originally lord of Arwystli (the region around Llanidloes), he became in 1075, on the death of his first cousin Bleddyn ap Cynfyn, ruler of the greater part of north Wales. His claim was at once contested by Gruffudd ap Cynan, representing the old line of Gwynedd, who is said to have defeated Trahaearn at Gwaederw in the region of Meirionydd, but appears to have been beaten at Bron-yr-Erw later in the year and forced to return to Ireland. In 1078, at Pwllgwdig, Trahaearn defeated Rhys ab Owain of south Wales, who was soon afterwards slain. His power brought about a coalition between Gruffudd ap Cynan and Rhys ap Tewdwr of Deheubarth, who in 1081 led a joint expedition against him from St David's, and defeated him and his allies, Caradog ap Gruffudd and Meilyr ap Rhiwallon, at 'Mynydd Carn' (probably in south Cardiganshire), where Trahaearn fell. The battle is commemorated in a poem by Meilyr Brydydd. Robert of Rhuddlan's epitaph attributed to him a victory over 'Trehellum'. Trahaearn left four sons: Meurig and Griffri, both slain in 1106; Llywarch (*fl.* 1124), lord of Arwystli, and Owain. The descendants continued to rule in Arwystli and Cedewain until the thirteenth century.

J. E. LLOYD, *rev.* DAVID E. THORNTON

Sources P. C. Bartrum, ed., *Early Welsh genealogical tracts* (1966) · J. Williams ab Ithel, ed., *Annales Cambriae*, Rolls Series, 20 (1860) · T. Jones, ed. and trans., *Brenhinedd y Saeson, or, The kings of the Saxons* (1971) [another version of *Brut y tywysogyon*] · T. Jones, ed. and trans., *Brut y tywysogyon, or, The chronicle of the princes: Peniarth MS 20* (1952); 2nd edn (1973) · D. S. Evans, ed. and trans., *A mediaeval prince of Wales: the life of Gruffudd ap Cynan* (1990) [Eng. trans. of *Historia Gruffud vab Kenan*, with orig. Welsh text] · Ordericus Vitalis, *Eccl. hist.*, 6. 144 (bk VII) · A. French, 'Meilyr's elegy for Gruffudd ap Cynan', *Études Celtiques*, 16 (1979), 263–78 · J. E. Lloyd, *A history of Wales from the earliest times to the Edwardian conquest*, 3rd edn, 2 vols. (1939) · K. L. Maund, *Ireland, Wales, and England in the eleventh century* (1991) · K. L. Maund, 'Trahaearn ap Caradog: legitimate usurper?', *Welsh History Review / Cylchgrawn Hanes Cymru*, 13 (1986–7), 468–76

Traherne, John Montgomery (1788–1860), antiquary, born at Coedrhiglan, St George's-super-Ely, Glamorgan, on 5 October 1788, was the eldest child (of four) and only son of Llewelyn Traherne (1766–1841) and his first wife, Charlotte (d. 1796), daughter of John Edmonds and his wife, Charlotte Dive, of St Hilary, Cowbridge, Glamorgan. The Trahernes traced descent on the female side from the Herberts of Swansea, progenitors of the earls of Pembroke and Powis, and on the male from the Treharnes of Castellau, Llantrisant, Glamorgan. Shrewd marriages had transformed the family from minor gentry to one of the major and best-connected county families by the late eighteenth century. Traherne was educated at private schools in Hammersmith (1800) and Lodiers, near Bridport, Dorset (1801–06), where he first acquired a taste for antiquities. He matriculated from Oriel College, Oxford, on 11 December 1806, proceeding BA in 1810 and MA in 1813. He was ordained deacon in 1811 and priest in 1812, but he served for only six months at St Hilary before ill health forced his resignation. On 21 March 1844 he was installed chancellor of the diocese of Llandaff, his only ecclesiastical office and an appointment which he retained until 1851.

At Oxford, showing no aptitude for classics or mathematics, Traherne was advised to follow lectures in botany, chemistry, and anatomy. He published some scientific work anonymously and pseudonymously and he was elected fellow of the Linnean Society on 21 December 1813, of the Geological Society in 1817, and of the Royal Society on 29 May 1823. He became one of the chief authorities of his time on the genealogies, history, and archaeology of Glamorgan. In 1822 he published *Lists of the Knights of the Shire for Glamorgan and of Members for the Boroughs* and *Abstract of Pamphlets Relative to Cardiff Castle in the Reign of Charles I*. In 1840 he edited *Historical notices of Sir Matthew Cradock, knt., of Swansea, in the reigns of Henry VII and Henry VIII* and also *Stradling correspondence: a series of letters written in the reign of Queen Elizabeth, with notices of the family of Stradling of St Donat's Castle*. The bulk of the letters in this collection were addressed to Sir Edward Stradling (1529–1609), an Elizabethan scholar and literary patron. Traherne was an active member of the Cambrian Archaeological Association, contributing notes and papers to *Archaeologia Cambrensis*, and he was a corresponding member of the Welsh Manuscripts Society. Among his acquaintances and correspondents were a number of leading literary and scientific figures as well as most contemporary Welsh scholars, and his assistance was frequently acknowledged by other workers in the same field. He was elected a fellow of the Society of Antiquaries on 15 February 1838, and he was also an honorary member of the Society of Antiquaries, Newcastle upon Tyne, and of the Society of Antiquaries, Copenhagen. He also played a part in local cultural life, acting as a trustee of the Cowbridge lending library and of the town hall building committee, and as a governor of Howell's School, Llandaff.

Traherne married, on 23 April 1830, Charlotte Louisa (d. 1880), third daughter of Thomas Mansel Talbot of Margam, who was an antiquary and artist in her own right. They had no children. He died on 6 February 1860 at Coedrhiglan, where he had resided most of his life, and which he rebuilt in 1820–23 after taking down the older house of 1767; but he spent the last months of his life at St Hilary, near Cowbridge, Glamorgan, and it was here that he was buried. Traherne's collections of manuscripts contain a great deal of late medieval poetry relating to Glamorgan, histories, records, and genealogies of the county, the papers of the eighteenth-century lexicographer John Walters, numerous transcripts, and his correspondence. A manuscript autobiography to c.1830 is in private hands. A few manuscripts passed on his death to his friend Sir Thomas Phillipps, and are at the central library in Cardiff, but the greater part of the collections, including the papers of William Davies (1756–1823) of Cringell, purchased by Traherne but presented by him to the Neath Philosophical Society Library in 1844, are at the National Library of Wales, Aberystwyth.

D. L. THOMAS, *rev.* BRYNLEY F. ROBERTS

Sources R. Denning, 'The Rev. John Montgomery Traherne', *Glamorgan Historian*, 4 (1967), 46–55 · D. Jones, Anecdotes of Glamorganshire people, 1889, Cardiff Central Library, MS 4.876 · autobiography MSS, 1833, priv. coll. [not seen] · Burke, *Gen. GB* (1865–1972) · handlist of manuscripts, NL Wales, MSS 6511–6615, 11979 · 'Annual Report', 1929, NL Wales, 20 · *Archaeologia Cambrensis*, 3rd ser., 6 (1860), 140 · *The Cambrian* (3 Feb 1860), 4 · D. Rhys Phillips, 'A forgotten Welsh historian: William Davies, 1756–1823', *Journal of the Welsh Bibliographical Society*, 2 (1916–23), 1–43, esp. 22–9 · E. Lewis, 'Cowbridge Diocesan Library, 1711–1848', *Journal of the Historical Society of the Church in Wales*, 4 (1954), 36, 44 · L. J. Hopkin-James, *Old Cowbridge* (1922), 56 · Foster, *Alum. Oxon.* · *CGPLA Eng. & Wales* (1860)

Archives NL Wales, corresp., working papers, collected papers | Bodl. Oxf., corresp. with Sir Thomas Phillipps · Cardiff Central Library, Phillipps MSS · Dorset RO, letters to Thomas Rackett · NL Wales, Clark MSS
Likenesses oils, c.1815, NMG Wales
Wealth at death under £3000: administration, 14 Nov 1860, *CGPLA Eng. & Wales*

Traherne, Thomas (c.1637–1674), poet and writer, was born within the walls of the city of Hereford, the son of a shoemaker, a master craftsman and freeman of Hereford who kept at least two apprentices, and who was very probably John Traherne (*fl.* 1629–1648), of the parish of All Saints. Nothing is known of the identity of Traherne's mother, but he had a younger brother, Philip (1640–1723), with whom he maintained a close relationship throughout his life, and who was to become chaplain to the Levant Company in Smyrna (1670–75), and subsequently minister of Wimborne Minster, Dorset (1684–1723).

Childhood and education Traherne's writing powerfully recreates both the innocence of his infancy, in which he was 'Entertained like an Angel with the Works of GOD', and his fall, as he was 'made to learn the Dirty Devices of this World' (*Centuries*, 3.2, 3). His experience was paralleled by that of Hereford; the royalist city, which had 'seemed to stand in Eden' (ibid., 3.3), was occupied for the first time in 1642 by parliamentary troops, and was finally captured for parliament in December 1645. John Traherne, who had fought as an officer in the local royalist militia, was taken prisoner, and paid a ransom of £4. His fortunes, however, seem to have revived, and in Michaelmas 1648 he completed the purchase of property in the parish of All Saints, almost certainly that in Widemarsh Street which was later to belong to Thomas and after his death to be settled on the city for use as almshouses. Hereford retained a parliamentary garrison, and the clergy of the cathedral and city churches were replaced by puritan nominees, some of whom would later support Traherne's presentation to a living. Probably too they influenced his education; he may have attended Hereford Cathedral school, and although 'Scholes were a Burden' he certainly received the equivalent of a grammar school training. But to the young Thomas, the world was a 'Comfortless Wilderness'; even as a child he had begun 'to long after an unknown Happiness', the attainment and communication of which was to be the object of his life (ibid., 3.14, 15).

On 1 March 1653 Traherne was admitted as a commoner at Brasenose College, Oxford, a college governed with a zealous puritanism, to the requirements of which he must have conformed. He matriculated as a plebeian on 2 April 1653, was admitted to the degree of BA on 13 October 1656, created MA on 6 November 1661, and admitted BD on 11 December 1669. As a student he relished both the 'Beautifull Streets and famous colledges' of Oxford (*Select Meditations*, 3.83), and 'the Taste and Tincture of another Education … Glorious Secrets, and Glorious Persons past Imagination'; but notoriously found that 'There was never a Tutor that did professely Teach Felicity' (*Centuries*, 3.36, 37). His notes on his conventional undergraduate reading are to be found in his 'Early notebook' (Bodl. Oxf., MS Lat.

misc. f. 45). He remained in Oxford at least until Lent 1657, when he took part in the disputations required of a determining bachelor.

Credenhill On 30 December 1657 Traherne was admitted by the commissioners for the approbation of public preachers to the rectory of Credenhill in Herefordshire, to which he had been presented by its patron, Amabella, countess dowager of Kent. He was supported by certificates from some of the county's leading presbyterian clergy, William Voyle, William Lowe, Samuel Smith, and George Primrose, preachers at Hereford Cathedral, who were all to be ejected after the Restoration. Traherne may well have received ordination from them since, although presbyterian classes were never established in Herefordshire, they ordained many ministers in the cathedral in an attempt to stem sectarianism, an aim with which Traherne would certainly have agreed. At this date, therefore, he is probably to be seen as having moderate puritan sympathies. When at the Restoration he sought episcopal ordination long before the eventual church settlement required it, it is not clear whether he did so out of doctrinal conviction, or in order to strengthen his title to his living. He was ordained deacon and priest at Launton, Oxfordshire, on 20 October 1660 by Robert Skinner, bishop of Oxford, the see of Hereford being vacant. On 18 August 1662, unlike his sponsors, he subscribed to the Act of Uniformity.

It seems to have been during this period of uncertainty for the church shortly after the Restoration that Traherne composed his *Select Meditations* (first published in 1997), a series of short reflections on his own vocation 'to teach Immortal Souls the way to Heaven' (3.83), his devotional life, and its relationship to the political and ecclesiastical turmoils of the nation. It juxtaposes a fervent commitment to 'the Beautifull union of my Nationall church' and its 'External Flourishing' (1.85, 3.23) with an intense perception of spiritual realities, including an experience of the infinity of the human soul so powerful 'that for a fortnight after I could Scarsly Think or speak or write of any other Thing' (4.3).

Traherne was to remain rector of Credenhill until he died in 1674; apart from some temporary absences he was, as his churchwarden reported in 1673, 'continualy resident amongst us' until early in the year of his death (Hereford County RO, registrar's files, 1673/488). His parish, 5 miles north-west of Hereford, was a very small one of about two dozen households, about half of them living close to the poverty line, and had neither school nor midwife. Traherne himself, with a living worth £50 a year, was relatively affluent, and there was only one house in the parish larger than his four-hearth rectory: he 'called his Hous the Hous of Paradice' (*Centuries*, 4.22). Ecclesiastical records show him engaged in the usual round of a parish minister, reporting that he 'does duly visit the sick, Instruct the youth' (Hereford County RO, registrar's files, 1673/488), although Traherne did not always find such visiting easy: 'And when I enter into Houses, let me remember the Glory I saw in the feilds' (*Select Meditations*, 2.100). His churchwarden thought him 'a goo[d] and Godlie man well Learned … and a good Preacher of gods word and a very devout liver' (Hereford County RO, registrar's files, 1667/349). On 28 May 1669 a Mr John Traherne was buried in the parish, perhaps his father. Later in his ministry Traherne also had ecclesiastical responsibilities outside his own parish; on 26 July 1667 he was appointed a surrogate for the dean of Hereford in his consistory court, and regularly presided there during 1671 and 1672.

Traherne's church of St Mary, 'the Roffe well covered wth tyle, the wyndowes well glazed' was 'soe decentlie ordered as becometh the howse of God' (Hereford County RO, registrar's files, 1666/36), but of his liturgical practice little is known. Twenty-five years after his death, it was said by an anonymous acquaintance that he 'became much in love with the beautiful order and *Primitive* Devotions of this our excellent Church', and 'never failed any one day either publickly or in his private Closet, to make use of her publick Offices' (*Serious and Pathetical Contemplation*, sig. A4v). Such an affection for the Anglican liturgy must have developed gradually; after the Restoration Traherne had seen not the Book of Common Prayer, but the Lord's prayer as 'the Liturgie of His church' (*Select Meditations*, 3.58b). His 'Church's year-book' (Bodl. Oxf., MS Eng. th. e. 51), a collection of meditations and devotions on the liturgical calendar, which he began before 1670, may have been part of the process by which he familiarized himself with classic Anglican texts.

It was probably at the beginning of Traherne's ministry at Credenhill that, having 'all my Time in mine own Hands', he took the momentous resolution to 'Spend it all, whatever it cost me, in Search of Happiness' (*Centuries*, 3.46). This dedication may have been associated with a period of 'Close Retirements' lasting some years, in which he walked 'with God, as if there had been non other but He and I' (*Select Meditations*, 3.69). As he progressed in 'the study of Felicitie', he achieved the perception which illuminates all his writing, that 'all things were Gods Treasures in their Proper places' (*Centuries*, 3.52, 60), and this discovery in turn led to a burning desire to communicate his vision to others. Indeed, as his anonymous acquaintance remembered, Traherne was 'so wonderfully transported with the Love of God to Mankind' that 'those that would converse with him, were forced to endure some discourse upon these subjects, whether they had any sense of Religion, or not' (*Serious and Pathetical Contemplation*, sig. A4r).

Manuscript works The same acquaintance also recorded that Traherne spent 'most of his time when at home, in digesting his notions of these things into writing' (*Serious and Pathetical Contemplation*, sig. A4r), an assertion amply verified by the quantity of Traherne's original works which survive in manuscript. Definite dates cannot be assigned to most of these works, a number of which remained unfinished at Traherne's death; many of them appear to have been written after the Restoration, and several, including 'Commentaries of heaven' (BL, Add. MS 63054) and 'The kingdom of God' (LPL, MS 1360) were composed at least in part after 1670. It is however primarily Credenhill which must be seen as the context of their composition.

Traherne's major works vary widely in genre, ranging from the ecstatic lyric poems (first published in 1903), which celebrate 'the Old / And Innocent Delights' of Eden and childhood ('Eden', ll. 33–4), to 'Commentaries of heaven', an encyclopaedia of felicity in which 'EVRY BEING' is, with much ingenuity, 'Alphabeticaly Represented As it will appear In the Light of GLORY' (title-page). This latter work, conceived on a vast scale but completed only from 'Abhorrence' to 'Bastard', embraces not only theological topics, but also shows a keen interest in contemporary scientific discoveries and in political and ecclesiastical affairs. In *Centuries* (first published in 1908) Traherne instructs a friend in 'those Truths you Love, without Knowing them' (1.1) by unfolding his own experience of felicity, both as a child and as an adult, through a series of meditations. 'The kingdom of God' is a physicotheological work, which moves from exploration of the attributes of God and the 'Glory & Perfection' of his spiritual kingdom (fol. 177r), to an account, often given in terms of the new philosophy, of the 'World of Mysteries' (fol. 258v) comprehended within the created universe. 'The ceremonial law' (Folger Shakespeare Library, MS V. a. 70) is a biblical poem in heroic couplets, based on the events of Genesis and Exodus, which combines a lively narrative of the journey of the Israelites through the wilderness with typological exposition. All of these works, through Traherne's vivid and often idiosyncratic style and vocabulary, embody his characteristic themes of the infinity of space, the limitless potential of 'This busy, vast, enquiring Soul' ('Insatibleness II', 1.1), our creation in the image of God, the necessity of free will, the 'Permanent and Steddy' treasures of Adam in Eden (*Select Meditations*, 3.12), and their repossession in greater abundance by the redeemed. Although none of these works was published by Traherne, some of them show clear evidence of having been prepared for publication, 'Commentaries of heaven' in particular addressing 'Publick Persons' (fol. 17r. 2).

Traherne however also had a more immediate and intimate audience of 'living Auditors' for his works (*Select Meditations*, 2.45). The ten extant manuscripts of his writings, although chiefly autograph, also contain contributions in some six other hands. These show that a number of other people, one of whom has been identified as Traherne's brother Philip, worked with him in the production of the manuscripts, copying out his own work, making extracts from other authors under his direction, and perhaps occasionally adding short passages of their own selection or composition. The manuscripts also provide evidence that Traherne showed his work to friends for comment. The friend who read the unfinished 'Ceremonial law' responded enthusiastically, 'I like this mightily' (flyleaf), while the marginal annotations to 'A sober view of Dr Twisse his considerations', Traherne's survey of Calvinist and Arminian debate, take a more critical stance: 'all this is Good & True, but y[u] have said it over & over' (LPL, MS 1360, fol. 84r). *Centuries* is addressed to a friend, and 'of the Soul' (Yale University, Beinecke Library, Osborn MS b.

308) written in response to a request. Writing was not a solitary activity for Traherne, and most of the manuscripts can be seen in some degree as communal productions.

Associates and character Traherne placed a high value on the possession of 'Intelligent Friends & Heavenly Companions', although many of the friends mentioned in his writing, such as the 'Knight, & a Traveller' from whom he heard 'som curious Observations' on ants, remain unidentified ('Commentaries', fols. 29v 2, 101r 1). Interestingly, in spite of his vehement attacks on 'Disobedient Hereticks' (*Select Meditations*, 3.23), most of his known associates, including Sir Edward Harley, Thomas Barlow, Thomas Good, and Sir Orlando Bridgeman, were sympathetic to nonconformists, or were actively involved in attempts to comprehend them within the national church. Traherne apparently met John Aubrey, and possibly he also knew the devotional writer Susanna Hopton, who lived at nearby Gattertop, and whose niece and god-daughter Susanna Blount married Philip Traherne in August 1670. Traherne himself never married, but 'led a single and a devout life' (Wood, *Ath. Oxon.*, 2.531). He seems to have made a deliberate choice of celibacy: 'I would be Disentangled from all the World, but God alone. Free to Suffer & to follow Vertue' ('Inducements to retiredness', LPL, MS 1360, fol. 5r).

Contemporary references speak highly of Traherne's character. Thomas Good thought him 'on of the most pious ingenious men that ever I was acquainted with' (Worcester Cathedral Library, MS D. 64), and he was remembered as 'a man of a cheerful and sprightly Temper … ready to do all good Offices to his Friends, and Charitable to the Poor almost beyond his ability' (*Serious and Pathetical Contemplation*, sig. A4v). Traherne himself knew that he also suffered from the weaknesses of a sociable personality: 'Too much openness and proneness to Speak are my Diseas. Too easy and complying a Nature' (*Select Meditations*, 3.65). A contrasting trait in his character was his obvious relish in his skill as a controversialist, as he described an intellectual skirmish in 'the *New-Parks*' at Oxford with a 'Grave Person' committed to 'promoting Popery' (*Roman Forgeries*, 1673, sig. B7r); recounted how he twice questioned the baptist John Tombes 'at his Amsterdam, his Heretical Church in Leominster', leaving that distinguished scholar 'as Blank, & mute as a Fish'; and boasted that 'it is the Easiest thing in the World to convince & confound a Jew, as I my self have done' ('Commentaries', fols. 194r 2–v 1, 139v 1).

Contact with Oxford and London During his residence in Credenhill, Traherne maintained contact with Oxford, returning to take his MA in November 1661 and his BD in December 1669; on both occasions he was dispensed from some of the statutory requirements. In 1664 he donated 20s. towards the completion of the new library and chapel at Brasenose. On at least one of his visits he worked in the Bodleian Library, 'the Glory of *Oxford*, and this Nation', on his *Roman Forgeries* (sig. B7r), a polemical tract exposing the alleged falsification by Roman Catholics of the councils of the first 420 years of the church; one scarce book he discovered in the collection of Thomas Barlow, Lady Margaret professor of divinity. Traherne emphasized the meticulousness of his research: 'I do not trust other mens information, but mine own eyes' (sig. B6v). He was working on *Roman Forgeries* in the early 1670s, but described it in 'Commentaries' as complete, and 'fit to be published' (fol. 104v 2). In autumn 1673 he was in London arranging its publication.

Roman Forgeries was entered in the Stationers' register by the bookseller Jonathan Edwin on 25 September and licensed on 24 November 1673, becoming, by the timing of its publication, a contribution to the anti-Catholic political ferment of that year. Its title-page attributes it simply to a 'Faithful Son of the Church of ENGLAND'. Traherne probably remained in London for some time: he may have made handwritten corrections to the printed copies of his book, and he was apparently absent from Credenhill on 17 October, when the incumbent of a neighbouring parish was acting as its curate. While in London he may have had contact with the latitudinarian divine Edward Stillingfleet, and more importantly with his future patron Sir Orlando Bridgeman, lord keeper of the great seal until his removal from office in November 1672. *Roman Forgeries* dedicates to Bridgeman 'The USE and BENEFIT' of the author's 'Ensuing Labors' (sig. A2r), perhaps indicating a hope of employment in Bridgeman's service.

Final months at Teddington Traherne was apparently back in Credenhill on 15 January 1674, but by 19 February he had 'removed out of the Country' to become domestic chaplain to Sir Orlando Bridgeman at Teddington, Middlesex (*Serious and Pathetical Contemplation*, sig. A4v). How Traherne obtained such a position, which was a recognized step to preferment, is not known, although it could have been through the family connections of Sir Edward Harley. Bridgeman, a man with 'very serious impressions of religion on his mind' (*Burnet's History*, 1.454), had since his dismissal lived in seclusion at his substantial villa in the fashionable village of Teddington, with his second wife, Dorothy, 'a woman that hath no good esteeme by any that knows her' (*Life … of Sir William Dugdale*, 396), and their daughter, Charlotte. As chaplain Traherne would have taken prayers for the family and for the other employees of the house, but he was not the incumbent of Teddington, which was served by its perpetual curate. Nor would he have had any opportunity to take the prominent role in ecclesiastical politics played by Hezekiah Burton, Bridgeman's chaplain when he was lord keeper. He may, however, have met Burton and another former chaplain, Richard Cumberland, both of whom were close friends of Bridgeman, and who shared both his latitudinarian views and his opposition to Hobbes.

The whole of Traherne's brief residence at Teddington was overshadowed by illness and death. His first recorded act in Bridgeman's service was to witness his will; by early May Bridgeman was seriously ill, and on 25 June 1674 he died. After his patron's death Traherne remained at Teddington with Lady Bridgeman, preparing his *Christian Ethics* for the press. This treatise offers a guide to 'the way of *Vertue*' (sig. A2v) neither by presenting moral conduct in terms of duty or expediency, nor by condemning vice, 'which is far the more easie Theme' (sig. A4r), but by making 'as *visible*, as it is possible for me, the lustre of its *Beauty, Dignity*, and *Glory*' (sig. A3r). The work's connection with the Bridgeman household may be reflected both in its engagement with Hobbes's 'arrogant *Leviathan*' (p. 519), and in that it envisages an audience of 'Birth and Breeding' (p. 11). *Christian Ethicks* was entered in the Stationers' register by Jonathan Edwin on 6 August 1674, and was licensed for publication on 25 November, but the 'Author's much lamented Death' (sig. a8v) had taken place before he had been able to correct the proofs.

On 27 September 1674 Traherne was 'lyeing sick at the Lady Bridgmans house', and made a nuncupative will, commenting 'I have not soe much, but that I can dispose of it by word of mouth'. He had apparently already begun transferring his houses in Widemarsh Street to the corporation of Hereford for use as almshouses on 25 August. In his will he left a ring to Lady Bridgeman and to Charlotte, and small bequests to each of the Bridgeman servants. To his brother Philip, absent in Smyrna, he left all his books and 'my best hatt', telling his sister-in-law Susanna, who was present, 'I desire you would keep it for him' (PRO, PROB 10/1061). By 3 October Traherne was dead, although the exact date of his death is unknown. He was buried at Teddington on 10 October 1674 'under the reading Desk in the church, just entering into the Chancell he had no stone laid over him' (Bodl. Oxf., MS Wood F 45, fol. 40).

Reputation and rediscovery of manuscripts At his death, Traherne had only a slight reputation as a scholar 'well read in primitive antiquity' (Wood, *Ath. Oxon.*, 2.531). Neither *Roman Forgeries* nor *Christian Ethicks* was widely read, and when in 1699 his *Serious and Pathetical Contemplation* (now known as *Thanksgivings*) was published 'At the request of a Friend of the Authors', it was thought to be 'to no purpose' to identify its author (title-page, sig. A3v). His other manuscript works remained unpublished, although Philip abortively prepared a volume of poems for the press, and by the early nineteenth century they were widely dispersed. Traherne would have sunk into oblivion had it not been for the extraordinary rediscovery of his manuscript writings which took place during the twentieth century. This story began in winter 1896–7 when W. T. Brooke purchased two manuscripts, *Centuries* and a folio volume containing poems and a commonplace book, from two London book barrows for a few pence. Thought at first to be by Henry Vaughan, they were subsequently identified as Traherne's through the detective work of Bertram Dobell, who published *The Poetical Works* (1903), and *Centuries* (1908). This led to several other discoveries, including some notebooks, and the identification of *Poems of Felicity* in the British Museum (published in 1910). In 1964 *Select Meditations* was identified, and in 1981 'Commentaries of heaven' was recognized as Traherne's, having been rescued about 1967 from a burning rubbish tip in Lancashire, already partly scorched. In late 1996 and early 1997, exactly one hundred years after the first discoveries, two

further manuscripts came to light: 'The ceremonial law', which had been in the Folger Shakespeare Library since 1958; and a large volume in Lambeth Palace Library, containing 'Inducements to retiredness', 'A sober view', 'Seeds of eternity', 'The kingdom of God', and a fragment on 'Love'. Given the fortuitousness of this sequence of discoveries, it is entirely possible that yet more manuscript works may be found.

Partly as a result of the nature of the first discoveries, Traherne was seen for much of the twentieth century primarily as a poet, rather than as a prose writer, and as a radiant and sometimes facile mystic who 'was unaffected by the domination of either king or protector' (Iredale, 2). A tendency to associate his work with that of the earlier metaphysical poets seemed further to distance it from the concerns of the Restoration period in which he actually wrote. More recent major discoveries and changing critical tastes have led to a growing appreciation of the qualities, both literary and intellectual, of his prose, and an increased understanding of the depth of his engagement with the religious and the political issues of his time. None the less a number of major works remain as yet unpublished, so that the comment written in a seventeenth-century hand on the flyleaf of the Lambeth manuscript still stands: 'Why is this soe long detaind in a dark manuscript, that if printed would be a Light to the World, & a Universal Blessing?' JULIA J. SMITH

Sources J. J. Smith, *Thomas Traherne* [forthcoming] · Wood, *Ath. Oxon.*, 2nd edn · T. Traherne, *Centuries, poems, and thanksgivings*, ed. H. M. Margoliouth, 2 vols. (1958) · T. Traherne, *Select meditations*, ed. J. J. Smith (1997) · [T. Traherne], *A serious and pathetical contemplation of the mercies of God* (1699) · P. Beal and others, *Index of English literary manuscripts*, ed. P. J. Croft and others, [4 vols. in 11 pts] (1980–), vol. 2, pt 2 · J. J. Smith, 'Thomas and Philip Traherne', *N&Q*, 231 (1986), 25–31 · will, PRO, PROB 10/1061 · A. Pritchard, 'According to Wood: sources of A. Wood's lives of poets and dramatists', *Review of English Studies*, new ser., 28 (1977), 268–89, 407–20 · R. D. Jordan, 'Thomas Traherne: notes on his biography', *N&Q*, 225 (1980), 341–5 · admission to rectory of Credenhill, 30 Dec 1657, LPL, MS Comm.III/6 · register entry for ordination, 20 Oct 1660, Oxon. RO, Oxford diocesan papers, d. 106 · registers of congregation, Oxf. UA, NEP/supra/17, Qa (1647–59); NEP/supra/18, Qb (1659–69); NEP/supra/19, Bd (1669–80) · documents relating to Traherne property in All Saints, 1647–74, Herefs. RO, charity papers, BH 38/34; 38/36; 59/238; 59/239 · act books of the consistory court of the dean of Hereford, Hereford Cathedral Library, HCA 7002/1/5 (office cases 1670–73); 7002/1/12 (instance cases, 1665–7); 7002/1/13 (instance cases, 1671–2) · J. Aubrey, 'Miscellanies', *Three prose works*, ed. J. Buchanan-Brown (1972) · [C. B. Heberden], ed., *Brasenose College register, 1509–1909*, 2 vols., OHS, 55 (1909) · J. J. Smith and L. Yeandle, '"Felicity disguisd in fiery words": Genesis and Exodus in a newly discovered poem by Thomas Traherne', *TLS* (7 Nov 1997) · G. E. B. Eyre, ed., *A transcript of the registers of the Worshipful Company of Stationers from 1640 to 1708*, 3 vols. (1913–14) · E. Arber, ed., *The term catalogues, 1668–1709*, 3 vols. (privately printed, London, 1903–6) · account book of Joyce Jefferies of Hereford, 1638–48, BL, Egerton MS 3054 · D. Inge and C. Macfarlane, '"Seeds of eternity": a new Traherne manuscript', *TLS* (2 June 2000) · *Burnet's History of my own time*, ed. O. Airy, new edn, 2 vols. (1897–1900) · *The life, diary, and correspondence of Sir William Dugdale*, ed. W. Hamper (1827) · Q. Iredale, *Thomas Traherne* (1935) · Traherne MS, LPL, MS 1360

Traheron, Bartholomew (*c*.1510–1558?), protestant writer and reformer, is of uncertain origins, although he is thought to have been of Cornish stock. The chronology of his university career suggests that he was born about 1510. He was possibly the son of George Traheron, a Herefordshire JP in 1523 who died soon after that year. Bartholomew was then brought up by Richard Tracy of Gloucestershire (son of the famous protestant William Tracy, whose will was commented upon by both William Tyndale and John Frith) under whose tutelage he almost certainly came into contact with evangelical ideas in his early life. He studied at Oxford, possibly at Exeter College or Hart Hall, and was persecuted there by John London, warden of New College. After Oxford he moved to Cambridge, where he graduated BA in 1533. It was at some point after this that he travelled abroad, especially in Italy and Germany, and kept company with John Butler, Nicholas Eliot, and Nicholas Partridge. He met Heinrich Bullinger at Zürich in September 1537, and from there went to Strasbourg in 1538, where he published a treatise exhorting his brother Thomas to convert to the reformed faith.

By March 1539 at the latest, Traheron had entered the service of Thomas Cromwell, but he withdrew from political life after the latter's fall in 1540. Some time about 1542 he married the daughter of a man who 'followed godly doctrine'; she was so poor that her husband was rumoured to have been forced to take up school teaching (Robinson, *Original Letters*, 626). In 1543 he published a translation of an Italian book on surgery, entitled *The most excelent worckes of chirurgery made and set forth by maister John Vigon, head chirurgien of our tyme in Italy, translated into Englishe by Barth. Traheron, whereunto is added an exposition of straunge termes and unknowen symples, belongynge unto the arte* (*ESTC*, no. 24720). Shortly before fleeing once again to the continent in 1546, he was granted three rectories in St Asaph diocese on the recommendation of Lord Chancellor Wriothesley. While he was abroad Traheron stayed in Geneva, where he met Calvin and developed the distinctive views on predestination which were shortly to win him some notoriety. With the accession of Edward VI in 1547 he was summoned back to England and from 22 April 1547 to 1 December 1549 was writer to the great seal and examiner of letters patent. He was elected MP for Barnstaple in 1547, and during the first session of the new parliament campaigned vigorously for the reform of doctrine. In the second session, which began in November 1548, he made a name for himself as one who argued for an unambiguously sacramentarian policy in the reformation of the eucharist. From 14 December 1549 to 22 October 1553 he was keeper of the king's library with a salary of 20 marks, while in February 1550 he was appointed a tutor to the young Henry Brandon, second duke of Suffolk.

At about this time Traheron engaged in a vigorous dispute with John Hooper over the nature of predestination, where his Genevan background set him in opposition to Hooper's eclectic approach which drew on the work of Bullinger and Melanchthon. Their struggle was a conflict between former exiles and reflected differences which existed between various continental protestants. Traheron argued strongly for a double-predestinarian approach, while Hooper tended more towards the synergistic position of Melanchthon, even borrowing significant passages from Melanchthon's writings in order to strengthen his arguments. Traheron is almost certainly one of the unnamed Calvinists whom Hooper excoriates in the preface to the second edition of his *A Declaration of the Ten Holy Commandments*. The debate provoked John ab Ulmis to write to Bullinger on 30 April 1550, marvelling at how far the two men disagreed over predestination. Later that same year, on 31 December, ab Ulmis again wrote to Bullinger about the rough treatment which Traheron thought he was receiving at Hooper's hands.

After Suffolk died on 14 July 1551 Traheron moved once more to the country for a life of quiet scholarship. He contributed to the volume of epigrams published on the death of Bucer in 1551. In September of that year, however, William Cecil proposed that he be made dean of Chichester, and he was nominated to this position on 29 September, though it was not until 8 January 1552 that he was finally elected. In the meantime, on 11 November 1551, he was nominated to the committee for the reform of church law. The chapter at Chichester apparently resented the intrusion of a layman and was consistently obstructive during his tenure. As a result he resigned about the end of 1552 to take up a canonry at Windsor which had been arranged for him in September by the council. He proved himself to be something of a nuisance in this position as well, and this, together with a tendency towards outspokenness which made him few friends in high places, helped ensure that he was not elected to the second parliament of the reign, which began on 1 March 1553. At this point, moreover, he seems once again to have become embroiled in a debate over predestination, writing to Bullinger to canvas Zürich opinion on the issue in order to provide himself with ammunition against a Melanchthonian party (possibly Hooper once again) which was gaining influence. Bullinger's reply was far too equivocal on key issues for Traheron, who made his position clear in a further letter indicating the Calvinistic bent of his thinking:

> I cannot altogether think as you do. For you so state that God permits certain things, that you seem to take away from him the power of acting. We say that God permits many things, when he does not renew men by his Spirit, but gives them up to the dominion of their own lusts. And though God does not himself create in us evil desires, which are born with us; we maintain nevertheless that he determines the place, time, and mode, so that nothing can happen otherwise than as he has before determined it should happen. (Robinson, *Original Letters*, 326)

On Mary's accession, Traheron, like many other protestants, resigned his appointments and went into exile on the continent. He was a firm supporter of Richard Cox during the latter's brief conflict with John Knox and William Whittingham over the use of the Book of Common Prayer in the English church at Frankfurt am Main. Here he was one of the signatories to the famous letter which Cox wrote to Calvin on 20 September 1555 which justified the Book of Common Prayer and the treatment of Knox, claiming in classic *post hoc–propter hoc* style that the

Scotsman's *Admonition to England* was so vitriolic as to require his removal:

> We can assure you, that that insane pamphlet of Knox's added much oil to the flame of persecution in England. For before the pamphlet was published, not one of our brethren had suffered death; and we are sure that you know how many excellent men perished in the flames as soon as it came out.   (Robinson, *Original Letters*, 762)

After Knox's expulsion Traheron appears to have briefly held a theological lectureship in the congregation at Frankfurt before leaving for Wesel, where he published expositions of part of John's gospel and of the book of Revelation, as well as engaging in a small amount of anti-Catholic polemicizing. His treatise *A Warning to England to Repente, by the Terrible Exemple of Calice, Given the 7 of March 1558*, indicates that he was still alive at that date, but he is not recorded thereafter, and probably died at Wesel during that year. He certainly never returned to England.

CARL R. TRUEMAN

Sources H. Robinson, ed. and trans., *Original letters relative to the English Reformation*, 1 vol. in 2, Parker Society, [26] (1846–7) · BL, Lansdowne MS 981 · *The decades of Henry Bullinger translated by H. I.*, ed. T. Harding, 4 vols., Parker Society, 36 (1849–52) · *Opera Calvini* (Brunswick, 1863–1900) · [W. Whittingham?], *A brieff discours off the troubles begonne at Franckford* (1575) · *Fasti Angl., 1541–1857*, [Chichester] · HoP, *Commons, 1509–58*, 3.473–4 · Emden, *Oxf.*, 4.573–4 · S. Brigden, *London and the Reformation* (1989) · C. Litzenberger, *The English Reformation and the laity: Gloucestershire, 1540–1580* (1997) · R. A. Leaver, 'Goostly Psalmes and Spirituall Songes': English and Dutch metrical psalms from Coverdale to Utenhove, 1535–1566 (1991) · Wood, *Ath. Oxon.*, new edn, 1.324 · C. K. Trueman, *Luther's legacy: salvation and English reformers, 1525–1556* (1994)
Archives BL, Lansdowne MSS

Trail, Ann Agnes [*name in religion* Agnes Xavier] (1798–1872), Roman Catholic nun and artist, was born on 16 February 1798 at Panbride, Forfarshire, the second of eleven children of the Revd David Trail (1765–1850), minister of Panbride, presbytery of Arbroath, and his wife, Catherine, daughter of John Bliss of Deptford, Dullan. She had six sisters and four brothers. Her father, grandfather, and great-grandfather had held the charge of Panbride since 1717, the longest period for a charge to be continuously in a single family in the Church of Scotland. Educated by teachers employed by her mother, Trail in turn taught her younger brothers and sisters. At seventeen she went to relatives in northern England for eighteen months. She returned to continue teaching her younger brothers and sisters. Six months later she went to teach at an Irish charity school for two years. She visited the poor and sick, distributing tracts and reading sermons. After training as an artist (1822–4), and having received several commissions in London, she went to Italy in 1826. After travelling through Italy from Rome for six months and to Venice for four months, she returned to Rome early in 1828. Several eligible men paid her attention but none proved acceptable. At one point she travelled with the artist David Wilkie. After painting and reflecting in Florence, Milan, and Parma she returned via Loreto to Rome. After being introduced to Augustine Baines, later vicar apostolic of the western district and founder of Prior Park College, she was received into the Catholic church by Cardinal Odeschali on 16 June 1828. Artistic yearning and religious enquiry had come to a common conclusion.

Trail returned home in the summer of 1829 and spent the next three years mainly in England. In 1832, at the Benedictine convent in Hammersmith, she met James Gillis, later the exuberant vicar apostolic of the eastern district of Scotland. He persuaded her to join his proposed convent. In August 1833 she and her fellow Scot Margaret Clapperton entered the Ursulines of Jesus novitiate at Chavagnes, France, at which time she took the name Agnes Xavier. In 1834 she returned with seven French nuns and two lay sisters to found St Margaret's, Greenhill, Edinburgh, the first post-Reformation convent in Scotland. John Menzies of Pitfodels, an immense benefactor of Scottish Catholicism, gave the convent property. The chapel was designed by A. W. Pugin's master, Gillespie Graham: Pugin himself produced an extraordinary design for a cathedral adjoining St Margaret's in 1849. Sister Agnes spent the rest of her life at the convent. Within a year, five postulants entered; in the next fifty years, nineteen other religious orders came to Scotland. Sister Agnes contributed largely to the Scottish Roman Catholic revival by dispelling anti-Catholic feeling and acting as a funnel to conduct European Romantic Catholic ideas to the circle of upper- and middle-class women in which she moved. Her ultramontanism was in turn reinforced by exiled Bourbons and Catholics and by female converts such as Mrs Hutchison and Wilhelmina Monteith. Her faith was more assertive, self-confident, and enthusiastic than the staid Catholicism of the early nineteenth century. Part of an institutional revolution she, like other female religious including Frances Lescher, Mary Hallahan, Catherine McAuley, and Cornelia Connelly, played a leading role in the expansion of Roman Catholic education by religious orders. She herself gave drawing classes, executing many miniatures, of which several are still in St Margaret's.

At the suggestion of her first spiritual adviser at the church of the Gesù in Rome, Thomas Glover, one of the first restored Jesuits, Sister Agnes wrote a spiritual autobiography. Her considerable religious experience enabled her to instruct many substantial, generous converts. Throughout her life she herself was influenced by two Cambridge converts, Ambrose Phillipps de Lisle and the Passionist Ignatius Spencer. She endorsed their ambitious scheme for the conversion of England through their Association of Prayer. Through them she came into contact with the Cistercians of Mount St Bernard Abbey; Dominic Barberi; and French Franciscan, English Benedictine, and Irish nuns in Galway, Newfoundland, and Australia. Her close confidant, the Canadian-born Bishop Gillis, drew her further into Catholic revivalism through his avid collecting of relics of St Margaret in Spain, his friendship with Bishop Dupanloup, and his promotion of interest in Scottish Catholicism through L'Oeuvre du Catholicisme en Europe. He initiated the first *Quarant'Ore* in Scotland in the convent in 1842, several years before it was used in England, and the first Corpus Christi procession.

After a stroke in later years Sister Agnes gradually withdrew from her duties. She died in Edinburgh on 3 December 1872, the feast of her patron, Francis Xavier. She was buried in the chapel of St Margaret's Convent, Edinburgh and subsequently in Grange cemetery. She can be regarded as a unique Presbyterian feminist contributor to the European Catholic revival. BERNARD ASPINWALL

Sources History of St Margaret's convent, Edinburgh (1897) · Autobiography of Miss Trail (1897) · A. A. Trail, The revival of conventual life (1886) · Fasti Scot., new edn, vol. 5 · W. Ewing, ed., Annals of the Free Church of Scotland, 1843–1900, 2 vols. (1914) · A. Bellesheim, History of the Catholic Church in Scotland, ed. and trans. D. O. H. Blair, 4 vols. (1887–90) · J. F. S. Gordon, Scotichronicon, 2 vols. (1867)
Archives Scottish Catholic Archives, Edinburgh · St Margaret's convent, Edinburgh | Sacra Congregazione di Propaganda Fide, Rome
Likenesses photograph, St Margaret's convent, Edinburgh

Trail, Robert (1642–1716), Presbyterian minister, was born in May 1642 at Elie in Fife, the second son of Robert Trail (1603–1678), minister of Elie and then Old Greyfriars, Edinburgh, and Jean (d. 1680), daughter of Alexander Annand of Auchterallan in Aberdeenshire. He lived in Elie until his father's transference to Edinburgh in 1648, but little is known of his early education with the notable exception that it was closely supervised by his father in the family home. Although the exact dates are unknown, he matriculated and graduated in the late 1650s at the University of Edinburgh, where he distinguished himself in literary and theological studies. He shared his father's resolute presbyterian convictions and sided with the protester party in the Church of Scotland, which was committed to the precepts and principles laid down in the national covenant. He was intimate with William Guthrie of Fenwick and accompanied his father's friend, James Guthrie, minister of Stirling, to his place of execution in the capital in May 1661. Little is known about his whereabouts or activities between then and 1666 but an entry in the Scottish privy council records of 9 October 1667 reveals that he was 'sometyme chaplane to Scotstarvet' (Reg. PCS, 2. 347–8). The Scotstarvit in question was probably the house of Scot of Scotstarvit in Fife. After his father's banishment from Scotland early in 1663 for reminding Charles II of his obligations to the covenant, Trail became increasingly associated with the covenanter and itinerant preacher John Welsh of Irongray. Trail was back living in Edinburgh at some point in 1666, for he was forced to flee along with his mother and elder brother, William, after a copy of John Brown of Wamphray's proscribed work An apologeticall relation of the particular sufferings of the faithfull ministers & professors of the Church of Scotland, since 1660 was discovered during a raid on the family home by the civil authorities. He was declared a rebel and a traitor by the privy council on 4 December 1666 for taking part in the Pentland rising the previous month.

Early in 1667 Trail joined his father in the Netherlands, where he continued to study theology and distinguished himself in assisting Nethenus, the professor of divinity at the University of Utrecht, in the preparation of Samuel Rutherford's Examen Arminianismi (1668) for republication. Nethenus described him as 'a pious, prudent, learned, and industrious young man' (Works, 1.v). In his absence the Scottish privy council exempted him from the Act of Indemnity in October 1667. It was probably for this reason that he settled in England in 1669 and was ordained to the ministry by presbyterian ministers in London the following year and called and inducted to a nonconformist presbyterian charge at Cranbrook in Kent. On 14 December 1676 an official complaint was registered against him by the Scottish privy council after it was discovered that he was among those who 'did preach and exercise the functions of the ministry' on the English side of the border with Scotland (Reg. PCS, 5.79). He is also known to have crossed into Scotland where he preached and officiated at conventicles with John Welsh. He was in Edinburgh in May 1677 and was apprehended by the civil authorities in July. He appeared before the privy council on the 19th of that same month. During his interrogation he admitted to preaching at house conventicles and to assisting John Welsh on the English side of the border, but refused to perjure himself on oath by confessing to preaching at open-air gatherings. The council ordered him detained on the Bass Rock in the Firth of Forth until further notice. On 5 October he petitioned the council to be freed from his incarceration, which plea was granted on 1 November on pain of 2000 merks and re-imprisonment on the Bass if he re-offended. He returned to Cranbrook and remained there for an indefinite period before settling in London. After the Revolution of 1688 he accepted a call to be co-pastor with Nathaniel Mather of an Independent church which met in Paved Alley, Lime Street. After Mather's death in 1697 he is known to have been pastor to another congregation in the city for the remainder of his life.

Trail was an evangelical writer and biblical expositor of some distinction. His exposition of 1 Timothy 4:16 was first published in 1682 under the title By What Means can Ministers Best Win Souls? He made a notable contribution in the Neonomian controversy that followed the publication of the works of Dr Tobias Crisp in 1690. His A vindication of the protestant doctrine concerning justification and of its preachers and professors from the unjust charge of antinomianism (1692) was a judicious and pertinent defence of the Reformed doctrine of grace against antinomianism, Arminianism, and neonomianism. He also wrote a biographical sketch on William Guthrie and penned an endorsement of Walter Marshall's Gospel-Mystery of Sanctification (1692). By far the bulk of his published works consisted of series of sermons. His thirteen sermons on Hebrews 4: 16 were published under the title The Throne of Grace (1696), which was later greatly prized by Ebenezer Erskine and was the inspiration for his The Full Assurance of Faith from the same text. Trail's sixteen sermons on John 17: 24 entitled Concerning the Lord's Prayer; twenty-one on Hebrews 10: 20–24, which were collectively published as a Steadfast Adherence to the Profession of our Faith; eleven sermons on 1 Peter 1: 1–4; and six on Galatians 2: 21 which were printed as the Righteousness of Christ, were all published posthumously. It was testimony to his ongoing popularity as a writer that the first edition of his collective works appeared in 1745 to be followed by further editions in 1776, 1795, 1806, 1810, and 1845. The Banner of Truth Trust published a definitive edition of his works in 1975. He died unmarried on 16 May 1716 in London at the age of seventy-four.   A. S. WAYNE PEARCE

Sources *The works of Robert Trail*, 2 vols. (1975) • *DSCHT*, 827 • *DNB* • R. Wodrow, *The history of the sufferings of the Church of Scotland from the Restoration to the revolution*, ed. R. Burns, 4 vols. (1839–41) • W. H. Carslaw, preface, in J. Howie, *The Scots worthies*, ed. W. H. Carslaw, [new edn] (1870), ix–xv • J. C. Johnston, *Treasury of the Scottish covenant* (1887) • *Reg. PCS*, 1st ser., vols. 2, 5 • *Fasti Scot.*, new edn, 1.38

Trail, Walter (*b.* before 1345?, *d.* 1401), bishop of St Andrews, is of unknown origins. Although one version of Walter Bower's *Scotichronicon* claims that he was almost seventy when he died in 1401, Trail's appearance as a student in Paris in the mid-1360s suggests a date of birth shortly before 1345. He was educated at the universities of Paris and Orléans, where his studies in arts and law extended through much of the 1360s and 1370s. In this period he obtained an MA degree and became a doctor of both civil and canon law. He spent the early part of his ecclesiastical career in the papal curia. Before 26 February 1379 Trail had been appointed auditor of the sacred apostolic palace, and between 25 June and 31 October 1383 he became a referendary in the papal chancery. As a result of his services he obtained a number of papal grants to benefices in his native Scotland, although many of these were never realized.

On 29 November 1385, shortly after the death of William Landel, Trail was papally provided (at Avignon) to the see of St Andrews. The cathedral chapter had elected the prior of St Andrews, Stephen Pa, as Landel's successor, but Pa was captured by English pirates on his way to seek papal confirmation of his election and died in captivity at Alnwick on 2 March 1386. Trail appears to have been consecrated as bishop between 27 January and 15 February 1386. He continued to enjoy considerable papal favour, including a grant of the right to judge first appeals from Scottish diocesan courts to the papacy. In addition, before 1 December 1394, he was appointed papal collector in Scotland.

Trail drew praise from the near contemporary chroniclers Andrew Wyntoun and Walter Bower for his high moral standards and for his role in the governance of the kingdom. Bower describes him as 'a very solid pillar of the church, a vehicle for eloquence, a repository of knowledge and defender of the church' (Bower, 8.37). From about October 1387 he became a regular witness to royal charters under the great seal and, as the premier Scottish bishop, took the leading role in public ceremonies such as the funeral of Robert II and the coronation of his successor, Robert III, in August 1390. Trail was also active as a diplomat, visiting the French court in 1391–2 and taking part in Anglo-Scottish truce negotiations during the 1390s. He may have played a significant role in the easing of strained relations within the royal dynasty in the 1390s. His death in 1401, combined with the near simultaneous demise of Queen Annabella and Archibald, third earl of Douglas, was held to be responsible for the outbreak of hostilities

between Robert, duke of Albany, and his nephew David, duke of Rothesay, in 1401–2. Bower asserts that with the deaths of Trail, Annabella, and Douglas 'dignity departed, honour withdrew and the integrity of Scotland died away' (ibid.).

Apart from his role in the political and social life of the kingdom, Trail was said to have been an active and severe diocesan bishop, and to have been responsible for the building of the episcopal castle in St Andrews. He is last recorded on 5 March 1401, as a witness to a royal charter, and was certainly dead by 1 July 1401 when the St Andrews Cathedral chapter met to elect his successor. According to Bower, Trail was buried close to the high altar of St Andrews Cathedral.   S. I. BOARDMAN

Sources W. Bower, *Scotichronicon*, ed. D. E. R. Watt and others, new edn, 9 vols. (1987–98), vols. 3, 8 • *The 'Original chronicle' of Andrew of Wyntoun*, ed. F. J. Amours, 6, STS, 1st ser., 57 (1908) • J. M. Thomson and others, eds., *Registrum magni sigilli regum Scotorum / The register of the great seal of Scotland*, 2nd edn, 1, ed. T. Thomson (1912) • H. Denifle and A. Chatelain, eds., *Auctarium chartularii universitatis Parisiensis*, 1 (Paris, 1894) • *Chartularium universitatis Parisiensis* (1889–97), vol. 3 • W. H. Bliss, ed., *Calendar of entries in the papal registers relating to Great Britain and Ireland: petitions to the pope* (1896) • D. E. R. Watt, *A biographical dictionary of Scottish graduates to AD 1410* (1977) • D. Laing, ed., *Registrum cartarum ecclesie Sancti Egidii de Edinburgh*, Bannatyne Club, 105 (1859)

Trail, William (1746–1831), mathematician and Church of Ireland clergyman, was born on 23 June 1746 at Logie in the presbytery of Brechin, the second son of the Revd William Trail (1712–1756) and his wife, Mary Trail (1731–1756), the daughter of the Revd Robert Trail, minister of Panbride. Nothing is known of his early life or education, apart from the fact that just prior to turning ten years of age he was orphaned, when both of his parents died on 3 April 1756 of a malignant fever. His father was educated at Marischal College, Aberdeen, and the younger Trail likewise entered Marischal in 1759. In 1763 Trail transferred to the University of Glasgow, where he graduated with his MA degree in the spring of 1766. While studying at Glasgow, Trail was befriended by the distinguished professor of mathematics, Robert Simson (1687–1768), and by the professor of moral philosophy, Thomas Reid (1710–1796), who both had a high opinion of his mathematical talents.

Following the death of Professor John Stewart, the magistrates and town council of Aberdeen invited applications for the vacant chair of mathematics at Marischal College, in an advertisement in the *Aberdeen Journal* for 31 March 1766. In order to avoid any wrangles over the appointment, the magistrates and town council decided to make their choice on the basis of 'a comparative Trial and impartial Examination', which they scheduled for the following August. Trail was one of six candidates whose competence in the various branches of mathematics was assessed from 13 until 28 August by a group of examiners that included Thomas Reid, who was a graduate of Marischal and an accomplished mathematician. Although Trail faced stiff competition from Robert Hamilton and John Playfair (who later went on to teach mathematics at Marischal College and the University of Edinburgh respectively), on 28 August he was judged to be the best qualified for the position. His election was confirmed by the faculty at Marischal on 29 October 1766, and he delivered his inaugural oration as professor in January 1767. In Aberdeen, Trail was an active member of the Aberdeen Philosophical Society, to which he was elected in November 1766. Over the course of the next seven years he read a series of discourses on the mathematical sciences, and proposed discussion questions on morals, astronomy, mathematics, and the physical sciences. In addition he served as president of the society in 1772. During this period Trail also published the *Elements of Algebra*, which was a textbook specifically designed for university students.

Even though his career was flourishing and he was earning approximately £120 per year in salary and class fees, Trail left Marischal College in 1774 to take up a position in the Church of Ireland. It may be that he was uncertain about the wisdom of the move, since he did not officially resign from his chair until the spring of 1779, but whatever doubts he may have harboured he remained in Ireland for roughly the next twenty years. Through the influence of his uncle, the bishop of Down and Connor, James Trail (1725–1783), Trail settled in the diocese of Connor as the prebendary of Cairncastle, where he officiated until 1781, when he became the chancellor of Connor and rector of Lisburn. In 1796 illness forced him to resign as rector, though he retained his post as chancellor. Shortly thereafter, on 29 April 1799, in Edinburgh, he married Lady Frances Charteris (1754–1848), the second daughter of Francis, styled seventh earl of Wemyss; no children resulted from this marriage.

While he was in Ireland, Trail became a fellow of the Royal Society of Edinburgh and a member of the Royal Irish Academy, and thus continued to be involved in the republic of letters. Earlier he had been given an honorary LLD degree by Marischal College, in April 1774. He issued new editions of his algebra textbook in 1779, 1789, and 1796, and at some point he was invited by the second Earl Stanhope to write a brief life of Robert Simson for inclusion in the *Biographia Britannica*. Frustrated by protracted delays in the appearance of his entry, in 1812 Trail published his *Account of the Life and Writings of Robert Simson*, which to this day remains the most detailed biography of Simson.

William Trail died in Bath on 3 February 1831 of unknown causes. He was greatly missed by his wife, who subsequently died in Bath on 1 April 1848.

PAUL WOOD

Sources J. B. Leslie, ed., *Clergy of Connor: from Patrician times to the present day* (1993) · W. I. Addison, ed., *The matriculation albums of the University of Glasgow from 1728 to 1858* (1913) · P. J. Anderson and J. F. K. Johnstone, eds., *Fasti academiae Mariscallanae Aberdonensis: selections from the records of the Marischal College and University, MDXCIII–MDCCCLX*, 3 vols., New Spalding Club, 4, 18–19 (1889–98) · 'Marischal College register of presentations, 1678–1857', U. Aberdeen, MS M93 · H. L. Ulman, ed., *The minutes of the Aberdeen Philosophical Society, 1758–1773* (1990) · *Fasti Scot.*, new edn, vols. 1–9 · B. Ponting, 'Mathematics at Aberdeen: developments, characters, traits, 1717–1860', *Aberdeen University Review*, 48 (1979–80), 162–76

Traill, Anthony (1838–1914), college head, was born on 1 November 1838 at Ballylough, co. Antrim, the eldest son of William Traill, of Ballylough House, and his wife, Louisa, daughter of Robert French, of Monivea Castle, co. Galway. His family, of Scottish origin, descended from Colonel James Traill, a soldier in the Cromwellian army, who settled in Ireland about the year 1660. After attending a day school in Belfast, Traill entered Trinity College, Dublin, in 1856, was first scholar in mathematics in 1858, and graduated BA in 1860, winning first place among the moderators in mathematics and experimental science. In 1865 he was elected to a fellowship, which he held until his appointment to the provostship in 1904. In June 1867 he married Catherine Elizabeth (d. 1909), daughter of Captain James Stewart Moore of Ballydivity, co. Antrim, with whom he had five sons and three daughters.

A man of restless energy, Traill took a share in every department of college life. Although trained principally in applied mathematics, he took degrees both in law (LLB, 1865) and in medicine (MD, 1870). He was keenly interested in the fortunes of the school of physic, and in later life prided himself on being the only *medicus* among the provosts of Trinity. He was equally zealous in fostering the recently founded school of engineering, and for many years was a member of its staff with the title of assistant to the professor of natural philosophy. He was also a member of the university council from its first formation in 1874, sat on innumerable committees, and was an active and somewhat turbulent participator in the college politics of his day. At the same time he was a most successful and hard-working college tutor; the fortunes of his pupils were his personal concern, and he prided himself on their successes. His athletic distinction as captain of cricket, racquets champion, golfer, and mountaineer (he was a member of the Alpine Club) brought him into close touch with the undergraduates, who regarded him with a mixture of affection and amusement, tempered by fear.

College duties far from exhausted Traill's energy. He was a keen politician—a Unionist of the Ulster type. Himself the owner of a small estate in Antrim and deputy lieutenant for that county, he fought the losing battle of the landlords during the eighties and nineties, putting their case in periodical articles and representing them on the royal commission (1897–8) which inquired into the working of the Land Acts. His appointment as provost of Trinity College was generally ascribed to the influence of the Ulster Unionists. It was also, no doubt, in part a reward for his services to the Church of Ireland, to whose material interests he gave a lifelong devotion. He was an original member of its representative body, and for many years was entrusted with the duty of presenting the financial report to the general synod. As a commissioner of national education for Ireland (1901–14), he watched jealously over the church's interests, as he conceived them, in educational matters; and as a member of the educational endowments (Ireland) commission (1885–92), he worked hard to save for the church as large a residue as possible of her legal inheritance.

To these various activities Traill brought prodigious

physical energy and a most tenacious will. Contact with him gave a dominant impression of force, physical and moral. Nothing could less resemble the conventional idea of the college don. His presence was like a perpetual gale of wind; his bearing was aggressive, his gestures unrestrained, his speech uncompromising. He was contemptuous of forms and ceremonies, careless of personal dignity, and indifferent to the amenities of life. Essentially a man of action, he cared only for getting things done. He bore down opposition, or else wore it out by sheer persistence. In his maturer years he lost nothing of his driving power, and gained from experience a shrewd judgement of affairs. Combative and self-confident as ever, he would never own himself beaten or mistaken; but he knew when to make concessions, and was always ready for a fair bargain. If he fought hard, he never lost self-command, and never bore his opponent a grudge. It was his favourite saying that he gave hard knocks, and took them.

During his provostship, from 1904 until his death, Traill's rough-hewn and massive figure was familiar to all Dublin. He steered the college successfully through difficult times. He resisted James Bryce's proposals (1906) for solving the Irish university problem by amalgamating Trinity College with the colleges of the Royal University, and when this danger was averted, he had a principal share in effecting the long-needed reform of the internal constitution of his college, which did so much to renew its vitality. His energetic rule was felt in every department of Trinity College, especially in the science schools, and no detail of administration was too petty for his personal attention.

In character and outlook, Traill was a genuine son of Ulster—in his industry, his self-confidence, his toughness of fibre, his practical view of life, his insistence on material values, his strong prejudices, and his simple and sincere piety. One of his last public acts, at the start of the Ulster campaign against home rule in September 1911, was to put the case for a parliament in Ulster to balance any Catholic parliament in Dublin. Traill died at his home, the Provost's House, Trinity College, Dublin, on 15 October 1914.   E. J. GWYNN, rev. M. C. CURTHOYS

Sources personal knowledge (1927) · E. Gaskell, *Ulster leaders* (1914) · *WWW* · Burke, *Gen. Ire.* (1958) · R. B. McDowell and D. A. Webb, *Trinity College, Dublin, 1592–1952: an academic history* (1982) · P. Bew, *Ideology and the Irish question* (1994) · *Wellesley index* · *CGPLA Ire.* (1915)
Archives TCD, corresp. and papers | CUL, corresp. with Lord Kelvin · TCD, letters to W. J. M. Starkie
Likenesses portrait, repro. in Gaskell, *Ulster leaders*
Wealth at death £3202 8s. effects in England: Irish probate sealed in London, 13 March 1915, *CGPLA Ire.* · £6779 0s. 11d.: probate, 8 Feb 1915, *CGPLA Ire.*

Traill [née Strickland], **Catharine Parr** (1802–1899), author, botanist, and settler in Canada, the fifth of the eight surviving children of Thomas Strickland (1758–1818) and his wife, Elizabeth Homer (1772–1864), was born at Rotherhithe, London, on 9 January 1802. She was named after Henry VIII's sixth wife, with whom the family (wrongly) claimed a connection. Shortly after her birth

the family moved to East Anglia, where Thomas Strickland began his own business, living in Norwich and then at Stowe Hall, near Bungay. In 1808 he bought Reydon Hall, near Southwold in Suffolk, where Catharine was largely brought up. Socially isolated and educated at home, the Stricklands were a close-knit and affectionate family. Catharine's education was a liberal one, covering subjects including history, geography, botany, the natural sciences, and several languages; she was encouraged to read widely and independently. Practically all the Stricklands had a literary turn—her elder sisters Agnes *Strickland and Elizabeth *Strickland [see under Strickland, Agnes (1796–1874)] later became the well-known authors of *The Lives of the Queens of England* (1840–48)—but Catharine was the first of the siblings to have a manuscript published: *The Tell-Tale: an Original Collection of Moral and Amusing Stories* (1818). Over the next fourteen years she published some fifteen or more books for children, often works of didactic fiction, such as *Prejudice Reproved, or, The History of a Negro Toy-Seller* (1826), or reflecting her geographical or botanical interests, such as *The Young Emigrants, or, Pictures of Canada* (1826) and *Sketches from Nature, or, Hints to Juvenile Naturalists* (1830). She also contributed to annuals and periodicals.

About 1829 Catharine Parr Strickland became engaged to Francis Harral, the son of an editor of Suffolk newspapers. When the engagement was broken off in 1831 she went to London to recover: there she and her sister Susanna met their future husbands, both of whom were officers in the 21st Scottish fusiliers. She married Thomas Traill, an Orkney-born widower with two sons, on 13 May 1832 at Reydon; soon after, on 7 July 1832, she and her husband emigrated to Canada, sailing from Greenock. They settled on the River Otonabee, near Catharine's brother Samuel, who had emigrated in 1825, and in 1834 Catharine's sister Susanna *Moodie and her husband, who were also emigrants, came to live near them. Later the Traills lived at Ashburnham, near Peterborough, and on the south shore of Rice Lake, both in the same region of Upper Canada, always in some financial difficulty and dependent on help from family and friends.

The difficulties and discomforts of a settler's life, exacerbated by her husband's periodic fits of depression and commercial failure, made Mrs Traill's life a hard one: however, the struggle for subsistence, the birth of nine children in fourteen years, and the constant need to earn extra income by writing do not seem to have dimmed her innate optimism and ability to enjoy the small delights of everyday life. She wrote for English and Montreal journals, and in 1836 *The Backwoods of Canada* was published by the London publisher Charles Knight; it was a collection of her lively letters home to her family, detailing the journey to Canada, the seasons, sights, flora, and fauna of her new country, and the day-to-day activities of a newly arrived settler. In 1852 she published *Canadian Crusoes: a Tale of the Rice Lake Plains*, again with a London publisher. The tale of three children lost from home for three years, it was at once an adventure story, a piece of contemporary wisdom literature, and a practical survival guide for the

Canadian backwoods. The more mundane accounts of how to dig a root-house and to harvest seasonal fruits were enlivened by such events as a forest fire, the adoption by the party of an outcast Indian girl, and the kidnap of one of their number by Indians. It was well reviewed and the 1852 American edition went through at least nine impressions; it was reprinted as late as 1923 as a commercial concern, and remains one of the founding works of Canadian children's literature.

In 1854 Mrs Traill published *The Female Emigrant's Guide, and Hints on Canadian Housekeeping*, republished as *The Canadian Settler's Guide* from 1855 on. This work was intended to offer advice to lower-class women (and, indeed, men) on a variety of topics, such as what to bring with them to Canada, how to build a log-house, and what to plant in a vegetable garden. Recipes for apple puddings and bread jostled with government statistics on numbers of settlers and the cost of fares for passages to Canada. In 1856 Mrs Traill published *Lady Mary and her Nurse, or, A Peep into the Canadian Forest* in London; in Canada it had already appeared in serial form.

On 26 August 1857 the Traills' home, Oaklands, on Rice Lake, was burnt down; the family lived with a friend, Frances Stewart, for the next two years. Catharine Parr Traill's notes on Canadian wild flowers were among the few items saved from the fire. She attempted to earn money by writing, needlework, and producing albums of pressed flowers and ferns, but her financial difficulties were increased by the death of her husband on 21 June 1859. A grant from the British government of £100—achieved through the influence of Lady Charlotte Greville, who was impressed by one of Mrs Traill's albums—and the help of her family finally enabled her to buy Westove, in Lakefield, in 1860. There she lived for the rest of her life with her devoted daughter Kate.

Mrs Traill's later publications brought to fruition her lifelong interest in botany. In 1868 she published *Canadian Wild Flowers*, which was illustrated by her niece Agnes Dunbar Fitzgibbon, who also illustrated her *Studies in Plant Life in Canada*, which appeared in 1885. These publications were too late to earn Mrs Traill the place she deserved in the history of Canadian botany, which had evolved from the Paleyite perspective and emphasis on gathering and classifying species which characterized her botanical researches. But the charm and detailed observations of her essays in *Pearls and Pebbles, or, Notes of an Old Naturalist* (1894) show that she was no unworthy disciple of Gilbert White, whose *Natural History and Antiquities of Selbourne* (1789) had been her model for *Plant Life*. Mrs Traill's last publication was *Cot and Cradle Stories* (1895).

Catharine Parr Traill had an attractive personality, gentle and humorous, and formed many close friendships, particularly with other women, in her Canadian life. A visitor in 1853 described her appearance and manner: 'a pleasant enough woman, stout with a slightly blue tinge but very frank and made no secret of their having had a great struggle for the bare necessities' (*Selected Correspondence*, 24). In her later years Mrs Traill received several honours, including, at her own request, the grant of Polly Cow

Island in the River Otonabee. A fern was named after her. She died at her home, Westove, on 29 August 1899, and was buried in the cemetery at Lakefield on 31 August.

Catharine Parr Traill's significant role in the development of a Canadian pioneer literature—intent on exploration and discovery, naming and taming the New World—has long been recognized, although her reputation has sometimes been overshadowed by that of her sister Susanna Moodie. The efforts of scholars such as Carl Ballstadt, Clara Thomas, and Michael A. Peterman have succeeded in rescuing Mrs Traill from Northrop Frye's characterization of her as a Wordsworthian sentimentalist. But the essential optimism and equanimity of her outlook on life and her surroundings still provoke criticism from those more impressed by Moodie's more dramatic and complicated reaction to the settler experience. Recent critics such as Marion Fowler and Gaile McGregor have argued that she tended to take refuge from the trials of her Canadian experience in an unconvincingly cheerful and ladylike domesticity. However, Mrs Traill's desire to cultivate a civilized way of life in the Canadian backwoods illustrates her adaptability and resourcefulness at least as much as her conventionality, and does not mean that she underrated either the difficulties or the unexpected pleasures of settlement life. Modern readers may find her proselytizing piety occasionally tiresome, but Catharine Parr Traill's clarity of style and openness to new experiences and natural phenomena ensure that her varied works will continue to retain their appeal and interest.

ROSEMARY MITCHELL

Sources M. A. Peterman, 'Strickland, Catharine Parr (Traill)', *DCB*, vol. 12 · M. A. Fitzgibbon, 'Biographical sketch', in C. P. Traill, *Pearls and pebbles, or, Notes of an old naturalist* (1894), iii–xxxvi · C. P. A. Ballstadt, 'Catharine Parr Traill', *Canadian writers and their works*, ed. R. Lecker, J. David, and E. Quigley, Fiction series, 1 (1983), 149–93 · *I bless you in my heart: selected correspondence of Catharine Parr Traill*, ed. C. Ballstadt, E. Hopkins, and M. A. Peterman (1996) · C. Thomas, 'The Strickland sisters', *The clear spirit: twenty Canadian woodmen and their times*, ed. M. Quayle Innis (1966), 42–73 · M. A. Peterman, '"Splendid anachronism": the record of Catharine Parr Traill's struggles as an amateur botanist in nineteenth-century Canada', *Re(dis)covering our foremothers: nineteenth-century Canadian women writers*, ed. L. McMullen (1990), 173–85 · C. P. Traill, *The backwoods of Canada* (1966) [with introduction by C. Thomas] · M. Fowler, *The embroidered tent: five gentlewomen in early Canada* (1982) · S. Eaton, *Lady of the backwoods: a biography of Catharine Parr Traill* (1969) · A. Morris, *Gentle pioneers: five nineteenth-century Canadians* (1968) · D. Jackel, 'Mrs Moodie and Mrs Traill, and the fabrication of a Canadian tradition', *The Compass*, 6 (1979), 1–22 · W. Gairdner, 'Traill and Moodie: the two realities', *Journal of Canadian fiction*, 2/3 (1973), 75–81 · C. F. Klinck, ed., *Literary history of Canada: Canadian literature in English* (1965), 125–44, 364–88
Archives NA Canada, family papers · Toronto Public Library, family papers and Stewart family papers | PRO, Glyde papers
Likenesses miniature, *c.*1820–1829, repro. in Ballstadt, Hopkins, and Peterman, eds., *I bless you in my heart* · S. S. Tully, watercolour?, 1899, repro. in E. Caswall, ed., *The backwoods of Canada* (1929), frontispiece · photograph (in middle age), repro. in Ballstadt, Hopkins, and Peterman, eds., *I bless you in my heart* · photograph (in her nineties), repro. in Ballstadt, Hopkins, and Peterman, eds., *I bless you in my heart*

Traill, Henry Duff (1842–1900), satirist and journalist, was born at Morden Hill, Blackheath, on 14 August 1842, the

Henry Duff Traill (1842–1900), by unknown photographer

sixth son of James Traill, a magistrate of Greenwich and Woolwich, and his wife, Caroline, *née* Whateley, of Handsworth, Staffordshire. His uncle, George Traill, was Liberal MP for Orkney and Caithness until 1869. Traill was educated from April 1853 at Merchant Taylors' School, London, where he was good at both classics and mathematics and came top of the school. He was elected to St John's College, Oxford, in 1861, as one of the last holders of a fellowship reserved for former pupils of Merchant Taylors' School. Although he gained a first class in classical moderations in 1863, he graduated BA with a second class degree in natural science in 1865. In 1868 he was awarded a BCL degree, and in 1873 the honorary degree of DCL. He relinquished his fellowship on his marriage in 1879.

Traill was called to the bar at the Inner Temple in 1869 and in 1871 he was appointed an inspector of returns under the education office. But journalism particularly attracted him, and he soon found work on the *Yorkshire Post*. After settling in London he contributed to several newspapers, including *The Observer*, and in 1873 joined the staff of the *Pall Mall Gazette*, edited by Frederick Greenwood. When the *St James's Gazette* was founded in 1880 he left the *Pall Mall Gazette* to join the staff of the new journal, and also wrote literary reviews, essays, and leading articles for the *Saturday Review*. He also wrote mainly satirical verses, some of which were republished as *Recaptured Rhymes* (1882) and *Saturday Songs* (1890). His gift for parody can be seen at its best, perhaps, in the pamphlet *The Israelitish Question and the Comments of the Canaan Journals Thereon* (which he published anonymously in 1876), in

which the style of the leading London newspapers was cleverly caricatured.

In 1882 Traill left the *St James's Gazette* to join the *Daily Telegraph*, where he acted as chief political leader writer until 1897. He continued to contribute to the *Saturday Review*, and after 1888 again wrote for the *St James's*. Between 1889 and 1891 he was editor of *The Observer*. In 1897 on its foundation, he became the editor of *Literature*, a post he held until his death.

Traill also published books on a wide variety of subjects. In 1881 he wrote a short account in the English Citizen series, of the British constitution. He also contributed short lives of Sterne (1882) and Coleridge (1884) for the English Men of Letters series, as well as full-scale biographies of Shaftesbury (1886), William III (1888), Strafford (1889), the marquess of Salisbury (1891), and Lord Cromer (1897). A more elaborate and deeply researched biography was his *Life of Sir John Franklin* (1896), the Arctic explorer, which drew on personal documents placed at his disposal by Franklin's family. Between 1893 and 1897 he was editor of an ambitious project, *Social England*, which aimed to give a historical account of the social, industrial, and political development of the nation.

Traill's satirical gifts are exhibited in the collections of his literary and miscellaneous essays, *Number Twenty* (1892) and *The New Fiction* (1897), and particularly in *The New Lucian*, published in 1884. He also used his experience of writing and acting in school and university plays to write for the stage. His *Glaucus: a Tale of a Fish* was performed at the Olympic Theatre in 1865 with the popular burlesque actress Ellen Farren in the title role. His most ambitious play was *The Medicine Man*, written in collaboration with Robert Hichens and produced by Sir Henry Irving at the Lyceum Theatre in May 1898.

Traill was fond of travel, especially to the Mediterranean, and in 1893 and in 1895 he visited Egypt, describing the second journey in animated letters to the *Daily Telegraph*, which were afterwards republished as *From Cairo to the Soudan Frontier* (1896). His last book, an account of recent north-eastern African history, was published posthumously as *England, Egypt, and the Soudan* (1900). Traill died at the Great Western Hotel, Paddington, London, on 21 February 1900 from a wholly unsuspected disease of the heart. He was buried on 26 February 1900 in the Paddington old cemetery, Kilburn. His widow, Emily, was granted a civil-list pension. S. J. Low, *rev.* CHANDRIKA KAUL

Sources *The Times* (22 Feb 1900) • *The Observer* (25 Feb 1900) • *Literature* (3 March 1900) • *WWW*, 1897–1915 • Boase, *Mod. Eng. biog.* • census returns, 1881

Archives NRA, priv. coll., papers | U. Leeds, Brotherton L., letters to Henry Arthur Jones

Likenesses S. P. Hall, portrait, exh. New Gallery 1889 • H. Furniss, caricature, pen-and-ink sketch, NPG • photograph, NPG [*see illus.*]

Wealth at death £2828 13s. 11d.: resworn probate, Oct 1900, CGPLA Eng. & Wales

Traill, Robert (1720–1775), Church of Scotland minister and university teacher, was born in Fordoun, Kincardineshire, and was baptized on 6 March 1720 at Benholm, the second son of the minister of Benholm, William Traill

(1683–1743), and his wife, Marion Hamilton (*d.* 1751). Traill matriculated at the University of Edinburgh in 1733 and was licensed to preach by the presbytery of Brechin on 1 August 1744. On 30 April 1745 he was presented by the crown to the parish of Kettins in Forfarshire. Traill's appointment proved unpopular with those parishioners who defended their right to chose their own minister and those who were Jacobite sympathizers. A mob disrupted his arrival at Kettins, and he had to be ordained at nearby Meigle on 22 January 1746. Having weathered the storm, on 5 November 1747 he married Christian, the daughter of the Revd Thomas Thomson of Auchtermuchty.

Thanks to the patronage of the earl of Findlater and Seafield, on 20 December 1753 Traill was installed as minister of Banff, and joined the circle of enlightened literati centred on Seafield's son, Lord Deskford. The form of polite Presbyterianism cultivated by Deskford's coterie came to public notice two years later through Traill's *The Qualifications and Decorum of a Teacher of Christianity Considered*, a sermon preached on 8 April 1755 before the synod of Aberdeen in which he responded to disparaging remarks made about the clergy in David Hume's essay, 'Of national characters'. This sermon was the first in a series of published salvos against Hume launched by Deskford's associates, and the critical assessment of Hume's writings also figured prominently in the proceedings of the Aberdeen Philosophical Society, of which Traill was a founding member in January 1758. Although he did not attend many of the society's meetings, Traill did submit questions on astronomy, political economy, and philosophy for discussion, and on 12 April 1758 he spoke on Rousseau's *Discours sur l'origine de l'inégalité*. In February 1760 the University of St Andrews awarded him the degree of doctor of divinity.

Due largely to Deskford's political connections Traill became the professor of oriental languages at the University of Glasgow in July 1761, and was unanimously elected to succeed William Leechman in the chair of divinity three months later. Traill was immediately embroiled in the acrimonious politics which divided the faculty, and he had a taste of the factionalism within the Scottish kirk when he served as moderator of the general assembly in May 1762. During his Glasgow years Traill was active in the Glasgow Literary Society, and canvassed topics in political economy, church history, aesthetics, moral philosophy, and geology. He was also one of the professors who welcomed General Pasquale Paoli to the university on 6 September 1772. After his death in Glasgow on 19 October 1775 Hume commented that Traill had infected his students with a spirit of religious bigotry, but Adam Smith had a more complimentary view of Traill while they were colleagues in Glasgow. Traill was buried in Glasgow.

PAUL WOOD

Sources *Fasti Scot.*, new edn · minutes of the Aberdeen Philosophical Society, U. Aberdeen, MS 539/1 · matriculation lists for arts and divinity students, U. Edin. L., special collections division, university archives · faculty meeting minutes, 1761–76, U. Glas., Archives and Business Records Centre, 26650, 26690 · minutes, 1764–79, U. Glas., Glasgow College Literary Society, Murray MS 505 · bap. reg. Scot., General Register Office for Scotland, Edinburgh, old parish record 253/1 · E. C. Mossner, *The life of David Hume* (1954); repr. (1970)
Archives U. Aberdeen · U. Glas., Archives and Business Records Centre | U. Glas., Murray MSS

Traill, Thomas Stewart (1781–1862), physician and specialist in medical jurisprudence, was born at Kirkwall, Orkney, on 29 October 1781, the only son of Reverend Thomas Traill (*d.* 1782), of Tirlet, Orkney, and his wife, Lucia, daughter of James Traill, of Westray, Orkney. Traill's father died soon after his birth and he was educated privately in Orkney by his uncle, Reverend Robert Yule, tutor to the sons of Thomas Balfour, sheriff-substitute for Orkney. Traill took his MA at Edinburgh and graduated MD, Edinburgh, in 1802.

Though Traill expressed a wish to practise medicine in Scotland unknown circumstances led him to set up in general practice in Liverpool in 1804 where, over the next twenty-seven years, he built up a prosperous practice. Liverpool's burgeoning cultural scene offered Traill many opportunities to pursue his keen literary and scientific interests. His ability to absorb and store factual material on diverse subjects helps to account for his prolific output of articles and papers. He became part of the 'Roscoe group' of influential doctors and businessmen devoted to the furtherance of arts and the sciences [*see* Roscoe, William (1753–1831)], and was a founder member and first secretary of the Liverpool Literary and Philosophical Society (1812). He was also a prime mover in the foundation of the Liverpool Royal Institution (1817) where he lectured as titular professor of chemistry and became one of the institute's first presidents. On 26 July 1811 Traill married Christian (*d.* 1842), second daughter of Dr Henry Robertson, parish minister of Kiltearn, Ross-shire. There were two sons and three daughters of the marriage.

In 1829 Traill was appointed physician to Liverpool Infirmary and joined the staff of the Ophthalmic Infirmary. In 1831 he became one of four doctors entrusted by Liverpool town council with combating cholera. However, Traill left Liverpool in 1832 to become regius professor of medical jurisprudence in the University of Edinburgh, a position achieved by direct political patronage, a not uncommon way of acquiring regius medical chairs. Traill originally applied for the vacant chair of materia medica, but Edinburgh town council and magistrates elected Robert Christison, then professor of medical jurisprudence.

Traill was an avowed whig and friend of Henry Brougham from university days, and in 1812 had supported Brougham's failed campaign against Canning to become a member of parliament for Liverpool. Traill's vigorous support lost him many tory patients, and income. Among the many notable names in Traill's testimonials were Brougham, then lord chancellor, and Francis Jeffrey, lord advocate for Scotland. Traill wrote immediately to the home secretary, Lord Melbourne, for Christison's vacant chair, which lay within the gift of the crown, stressing that 'I have the honour to be personally known to the Lord Chancellor Brougham and the Lord Advocate' (Traill to Lord Melbourne, 20 June 1832, NA Scot., HH5/7). Within weeks his warrant for the chair of medical jurisprudence was prepared. Thus, at the age of fifty, Traill returned to Scotland and held the chair until his death in 1862.

Traill reintroduced the chair's tandem subject, medical police (public health), discarded by Christison in 1822. An amiable man with a retentive memory, Traill was an able teacher, and never missed a single lecture. His *Outlines of a Course of Lectures on Medical Jurisprudence*, published in 1836, reached a third edition in 1857. Together with Christison and James Syme, Traill produced the standard work on post-mortem procedure in Scotland, *The Medico-Legal Examination of Dead Bodies*, published in 1839 by request of the lord advocate. The principles expounded are still current practice. Overshadowed by Christison's expertise in toxicology, Traill did not achieve eminence as a medical witness. He was editor of the eighth edition of the *Encyclopaedia Britannica*, contributing some hundreds of articles but, through ill health, much of the editing of the twenty-one volumes was done by others.

Traill remained an Orkney man to the last. It is reported that he never took a class fee from an Orkney student and often revisited his birthplace to deliver chemistry lectures, the fees from which he donated to the islands' poor. Traill was elected fellow of the Royal Society of Edinburgh in 1819 and fellow of the Royal College of Physicians of Edinburgh in 1833, becoming president from 1852 to 1854. Traill was not averse to the principle of admitting women to the medical profession. In 1862 he supported Elizabeth Garrett's (unsuccessful) petition to be admitted to the college's preliminary examination and registration. Traill died at Edinburgh on 30 July 1862.

BRENDA M. WHITE

Sources *The Lancet* (9 Aug 1862) · *The Lancet* (13 Sept 1862) · *BMJ* (23 Aug 1862) · *Edinburgh Medical Journal*, 8 (1862–3), 296, 389–91 · *The Scotsman* (1 Aug 1862) · *Orkney Herald* (5 Aug 1862) · *The Orcadian* (2 Aug 1862) · *The Orcadian* (9 Aug 1862) · parish register (baptisms), Kirkwall and St Ola, 1781, Orkney Archives · E. W. Marwick, 'Notable Orkney centenary', *The Orcadian* (2 Aug 1962) · letter from Thomas Traill, Edinburgh, to William Balfour, 1802, Orkney Archives, Balfour MSS · J. A. Shepherd, *A history of the Liverpool Medical Institution* (1979) · T. Kelly, *For advancement of learning: the University of Liverpool, 1881–1981* (1981) · Evidence to the Committee of Enquiry into the state of Anatomical Studies in these Kingdoms, letter from Thomas Stewart Traill of Liverpool addressed to Henry Warburton, esq., M.P., chairman of the committee, 1 May 1828, appx 10 · R. P. Fereday, *The Orkney Balfours, 1747–99: Trenaby and Elwick* (1990) [Orkney Archives] · testimonials in favour of Dr Thomas Stewart Traill for the chair of materia medica in the University of Edinburgh, 1832, U. Edin. L., special collections division, P. 89. No. 31 · letter from Thomas S. Traill to Lord Melbourne, 20 June 1832, NA Scot., HH5/7 [seeking the chair of medical jurisprudence at U. Edin.] · W. S. Craig, *History of the Royal College of Physicians of Edinburgh* (1976) · M. A. Crowther and B. White, *On soul and conscience: the medical expert and crime* (1988) · parish register (marriage), Kiltearn, Ross and Cromarty, 26 July 1811
Archives Lpool RO, family corresp. · NL Scot., corresp., diaries, and papers | Linn. Soc., letters to Sir James Smith · Linn. Soc., letters to William Swainson · U. Lpool L., corresp. with William Rathbone · U. St Andr. L., corresp. with James David Forbes
Likenesses J. Turmeau, portrait, exh. Liverpool Academy 1811 · J. Lonsdale, oils, 1833, U. Lpool · lithograph, Wellcome L.
Wealth at death £1368 3s. 5d.: confirmation, 20 Nov 1862, NA Scot., SC 70/1/114, 256–61

Traill, William Atcheson (1844–1933), promoter of electric railway traction, was born at Ballylough House, Bushmills, co. Antrim, the third son and sixth child of William Traill, a local protestant landowner, and his wife, Louisa French. His brother Anthony *Traill (1838–1914) became high sheriff of Antrim and, in 1904, provost of Trinity College, Dublin. Educated at private schools, William went to Trinity College, Dublin, taking an engineering degree in 1865 and the master of engineering, M(Ing), in 1873.

Traill joined the geological survey of Ireland in 1868 and became an expert in water supply. He resigned in 1881 to promote his life's work, the electrically powered Portrush, Bushmills, and Giant's Causeway Railway and Tramway Company (to use its final name) founded by himself and Anthony Traill to transport local minerals. Capital was raised from friends at Trinity, although Sir William Siemens (£3500) and Lord Kelvin (£1000) were also shareholders in the £20,000 company. Despite many efforts, the goods business never materialized, and the line became a summer season only tourist business until its closure in 1949.

Steam services began early in 1883, electric cars working sporadically from September 1883. Regular electric services began on 5 November 1883 following the completion of a hydroelectric plant at Walkmills, the railway being the first to use hydroelectric power. The line was initially 6 miles long with another 2 mile extension to Giant's Causeway opening on 1 July 1887. Traill patented (no. 3277, 1883) a conduit system of burying the live rail in a pipe with electrical contact by means of a mechanism he devised. He used a simple third rail system on the rural stretches, but steam trams were used in Portrush until 1900 when a 500 volt overhead cable was installed along the entire route. The conduit patent was sold to an American company 'for a small sum' (McGuigan, *Giant's Causeway Tramway*, 105). Conduits were popular with tramways, but they installed devices independently invented in America in 1884.

Traill showed that electric railways worked, thereby inspiring many more electric railway lines. He devoted his life to his company and local affairs, though he was on the general council of the British Association. Traill was married first to Harriet Jane Wrigley, who died in 1888, then to Elizabeth Greer; they had a son (*b.* 1890) and a daughter (*b.* 1891). He met his third wife, Nora Westwood (*d.* 1953) in 1895, when he rescued her from drowning off Portrush. He died at his home, Rockhaven, Port Stewart, north Antrim, on Thursday 5 July 1933, survived by his third wife, and daughter. His last few weeks had been spent in organizing the railway's jubilee.

R. L. VICKERS

Sources J. H. McGuigan, *The Giant's Causeway tramway* (1964) · *Engineering* (14 July 1933), 47 · *The Engineer* (14 July 1933), 25 · J. H. McGuigan, *Giant's Causeway, Portrush & Bush Valley Railway & Tramway Co. Ltd* (1983) · *Locomotive Railway Carriage and Wagon Review* (14 July 1933) · private information (2004) [R. S. Traill] · 'Giant's Causeway electrical tramway', *The Engineer* (28 Sept 1883), 239 · 'Turbines, Portrush and Bush Valley tramway, diagram', *The Engineer* (28 Sept 1883), 244–5
Archives PRO NIre., Railway Company archives · Ulster Folk and Transport Museum, Holywood, prints · Ulster Museum, Belfast,

R. J. Welch collection, prints | FILM Ulster Folk and Transport Museum, Holywood, short colour film c.1946/7
Likenesses portrait, Ulster Folk and Transport Museum
Wealth at death £1210 1s. 2d.: probate, 11 Jan 1934, CGPLA Eng. & Wales

Train, George Francis (1829–1904), promoter of the horse tramway, was born in Boston, Massachusetts, on 24 March 1829, the son of a merchant, Oliver Train. His father's last traceable act was to send him back alone by sea to England at the age of four after his mother had died of yellow fever in New Orleans. He was brought up by his grandmother on her farm at Waltham.

Train became a grocer's boy at the age of fourteen but then, when he was sixteen, he got a job as shipping clerk with his uncle, Enoch Train. Five years later he was sent to manage the Liverpool end of his uncle's very successful White Diamond shipping line and concurrently seems to have obtained a financial interest in shipping out of California during the Australian gold rush. He was in Melbourne from 1853 to 1855. When Enoch Train's business got into difficulties in 1856–7, his nephew went back to America. On 5 October 1851 he married Wilhelmina Wilkinson Davis (d. 1879) at Louisville, Kentucky, USA; they had four children.

Horse-drawn street railways, known for decades in New York, were then attracting greater attention from entrepreneurs in other cities, some lines being built on the tongue-and-groove system, flush with the road surface, and others using L-shaped rails, along which the cars could run on ordinary wheels; the latter system had the great disadvantage that the vertical part of the 'L' protruded above the road surface and interfered with all other traffic. Whichever system was used, however, the reduced rolling resistance on smooth rails meant that two horses could pull a much larger vehicle, capable of seating forty-eight fare-paying passengers in greater comfort—twenty-four inside and twenty-four more out in the open on top—twice as many as the competing two-horse omnibus.

A self-confident salesman, Train was hired to secure franchises for street railways of the L-type, first in the United States and then in Europe. Here the *chemin de fer américain* had been demonstrated by Alphonse Loubat from 1853 in Paris, where it had been seen by the English engineer William Joseph Curtis while visiting the international exhibition there in 1855. In the following year Curtis took out a patent for a tramcar with two sets of wheels which could be lowered independently, one set flanged to run on grooved lines and one flat to run on paved roads. Vehicles of this adaptable sort were already being run on the busy dock road in Liverpool in 1859 before Train's arrival there. His proposal to operate at lower fares was turned down by the dock board on 3 February 1860.

Having produced a fifty-page publicity pamphlet, Train tried his luck on the other side of the River Mersey with the road authority at Birkenhead. He obtained its consent and managed to get local financial support for the Birkenhead Street Railway Company Ltd, incorporated on 7 May 1860, to lay an L-shaped track from Woodside Ferry to Birkenhead Park, about 1¼ miles away. This took six weeks to lay and was opened on 30 August 1860. Train himself contributed only a quarter of the capital and had nothing to do with the actual construction of the line. The double-deck tramcar was made by Robert Main, a local coach-builder. This tramway managed to survive, but no thanks to Train; the main local shareholder soon replaced the objectionable protruding rails.

Train then turned his attention to London, where Curtis already had a tramway running in Islington and where the London General Omnibus Company had been showing an interest in tramways for three years. Train showered all the road authorities with his pamphlet and also with applications to run demonstration stretches of line. Only three were successful. As at Birkenhead they were all financed and engineered by others but, unlike at Birkenhead, only single-deckers were used and all the rails soon had to be removed. The Bayswater line, running less than a mile west of Marble Arch, down Bayswater Road, was opened on 25 March 1861 but closed before the end of September. The Victoria Street line was laid for a short distance down the road towards the new Victoria Station from Westminster Abbey, and opened on 15 May 1861, but was removed on 7 March 1862. The Surrey Side Tramway, from the south side of Westminster Bridge to Kennington Gate, opened on 15 August 1861 and was removed on 21 June 1862.

Three other tramways were embarked upon in the provinces before the full extent of failure in London was appreciated. One ran for about a mile from the Liverpool borough boundary along the Prescot turnpike to the Old Swan: opened on 2 July 1861, it closed before the end of May 1862, when the track began to be removed. A short and ill-located line was opened in Darlington on 1 January 1862 but closed before November 1865, when the tramway company went into liquidation. The third line ran in the Potteries from Foundry Street, Hanley, to Burslem. It was opened on 13 January 1862 but survived, as at Birkenhead, only after the leading shareholder replaced the protruding step rails.

Train returned to the United States in 1862. The rest of his flamboyant life was concerned mainly with the financing of railway land grants in America, travelling the world, writing, and lecturing, though much of the year 1868 he spent involuntarily in Ireland, in prison for debts owed to English creditors. Egotist to the last, he dictated *My Life in many States and Foreign Lands* in 1902 and died from heart failure on 19 January 1904 at Mills Hotel, New York, which the *Times* correspondent there, in the briefest of obituary dispatches, described as a cheap lodging-house.

THEO BARKER

Sources C. E. Lee, 'The English street tramways of George Francis Train', *Journal of Transport History*, 1 (1953–4), 20–27, 97–108 · S. Gunn, 'Train, George Francis', *DAB* · *WWW* · J. B. Horne and T. B. Maund, *Liverpool Transport*, 2nd edn, 1 (1995) · C. Klapper, *The golden age of tramways* (1961) · *The Times* (20 Jan 1904) · G. F. Train, *My life in many states and foreign lands* (1902)
Likenesses photograph, repro. in Horne and Maund, *Liverpool Transport*, p 23

Wealth at death died in poverty: *The Times*

Train, Joseph (1779–1852), exciseman and antiquary, was born on 6 November 1779 at Gilminscroft in the parish of Sorn, Ayrshire, where his father was land steward. In 1787 the family moved to Ayr, where Train's father became a day labourer. His own schooling was limited. At an early age he was apprenticed to a weaver in Ayr, but he persevered with private study, taking a particular interest in antiquarian and traditional lore.

Train joined the ranks of the 7th North British regiment of militia in June 1798. For almost four years he served as a private at barracks and camps in various parts of Scotland, until the regiment was run down during the peace of Amiens. He then returned to the loom in Ayr, and on 30 April 1803 married Mary (b. 1780), daughter of Robert Wilson, a gardener in that town. The couple had five children.

In 1806 Train published his *Poetical Reveries*, the first fruit of his scholarly and literary pursuits. One of the subscribers was his former company commander, Sir David Hunter Blair. Two years later Blair secured Train an appointment in the Scottish excise, and he entered as an assistant officer. A transfer in 1810 from Ayr to Balnaguard, in Perthshire, pitted him against the whisky bootleggers for a year, after which he was posted back to Ayrshire, as an officer. A period of more stability ensued after he was moved in 1813 from Largs to Newton Stewart, Wigtownshire. His work now ranged over much of Galloway and Carrick, and he began to gather materials for a history of the region. He also turned into verse some of the tales and traditions that he had collected. When these were printed by Ballantyne in 1814, under the title *Strains of the Mountain Muse*, they caught the eye of Walter Scott (an anecdote in the collection eventually provided the outline of Scott's 'Wandering Willie's Tale', in *Redgauntlet*). At this time Scott was working on *The Lord of the Isles* and he asked Train for information about Turnberry Castle, where Bruce landed on his return from Ireland. From then on Train willingly subordinated his pursuits to Scott's interests and was soon sending him pages crammed with antiquarian material. One of the stories that he forwarded was of an astrologer wandering in the wilds of Galloway who predicted the future of a new-born child, and this was woven into the opening chapters of *Guy Mannering*. In the course of their long friendship Train was just as assiduous in finding curiosities for Scott's museum, including Rob Roy's pouch, which was the germ of the novel featuring that outlaw.

Scott did what he could to further Train's career. He passed on to the chairman of the Scottish excise board a paper that Train had produced on the control of distillation of spirits, and the proposals were implemented. In 1816 Train made the first of several visits to Scott in Edinburgh. On this occasion he fired Scott's imagination with his accounts of Robert Paterson—'Old Mortality'—thus suggesting the theme of the novel of that name. Scott's melodrama *The Doom of Devorgoil*, completed in 1817, was based on another of Train's stories. *The Heart of Midlothian*, published in the following year, was indebted to Train for information about the prototype of Madge Wildfire, a figure known as Feckless Fannie who formerly wandered through Ayrshire and Galloway. Other beneficiaries of Train's researches at this time included George Chalmers, who sought his assistance for sections of his bulky historical and topographical work *Caledonia*.

Scott's efforts on Train's behalf bore further fruit in 1820. He was placed on the list for promotion to the grade of supervisor, leading to another succession of postings, to Cupar in Fife, to Kirkintilloch, to Queensferry, and to Falkirk. In September 1823 a single board was created to manage the excise in the United Kingdom as a whole, and Scott turned his attention southwards. In 1824 he recommended his protégé to Peel, the home secretary, who drew in Lord Liverpool, the prime minister, and a 'whisper' was conveyed to the new board. But all did not go smoothly. Many Scottish officers were convinced that they were discriminated against by English officials who occupied some of the key posts in Edinburgh. Train, for one, was found guilty of negligence, on flimsy grounds, and was removed from Falkirk to Wigtown at the end of 1824; he did, however, succeed in an application for a more congenial vacancy in Dumfries a few months later. Robert Burns, who had briefly officiated there as supervisor, described the job as 'an incessant drudgery, and would be nearly a compleat bar to every species of literary pursuit' (*Complete Letters of Robert Burns*, 1987, 715). Train made the best of it. He was able to recover stories of Burns and passed them on to Lockhart when he was working on his life of Burns, while presenting other documents to Scott. He also still found time for visits to Edinburgh and Abbotsford. On one of these he related the story that formed the basis of *The Surgeon's Daughter* in the first series of *Chronicles of the Canongate*. Scott's introduction (1827) to these chronicles complemented his recent public acknowledgement of authorship of the Waverley novels with a tribute to those who had supplied 'hints of subjects and legends'. He gave pride of place to Train's 'unremitting kindness' and 'unwearied industry'.

If Train was as diligent in his official duties as he was in searching for antiquarian lore, he well deserved Scott's lobbying. Once more, however, he met with disapproval on account of a supposed negligence, and was reduced from the rank of supervisor. On appeal he regained his former grade, but at the same time was posted to Castle Douglas late in 1827. Before long Scott's preparations for his *magnum opus* edition of the Waverley novels stimulated a new cycle of activity, and Train began supplying a variety of fresh information, utilized in Scott's introductions and notes. Further recognition came in November 1829, when Train was admitted fellow of the Society of Antiquaries of Scotland. Scott's death in 1832 left a great blank, but Train's interest in his old studies endured. Having retired from the excise on health grounds in 1836, with an annual pension of £112, he remained in Castle Douglas, free to return to authorship on his own account. Scott had long before urged him to undertake a history of the Isle of Man. Train now produced his substantial *Historical and Statistical Account of the Isle of Man*, published in Douglas in four parts in 1842–5. It was followed in 1846 by *The Buchanites from First to Last*, chronicling a peculiar religious sect that had had a following in south-west Scotland. He also kept up an extensive correspondence with a circle of scholarly friends, and among those who applied to him for help was Agnes Strickland, seeking materials for a life of Mary, queen of Scots.

James Hannay visited Train towards the end of 1852, afterwards describing him as 'a tall old man, with an autumnal red in his face, hale-looking, and of simple, quaint manners' (Hannay, 476). The little parlour in Lochvale Cottage, on the banks of Carlingwark Loch, Castle Douglas, was full of antiquities and specimens of ancient furniture, which Train proudly displayed to his visitor. A few weeks later, on 7 December 1852, after a short illness, he died peacefully at his cottage, in his seventy-fourth year.   ANGUS FRASER

Sources J. Patterson, *Memoirs of Joseph Train* (1857) · W. Train, 'Biographical memoir of the author', in J. Train, *An historical and statistical account of the Isle of Man* (1845), 1–29 · R. W. Macfadzean, 'Joseph Train, F.S.A. (Scot.)', *Annual Burns Chronicle and Club Directory*, 13 (1904), 76–88 · *The letters of Sir Walter Scott*, ed. H. J. C. Grierson and others, centenary edn, 12 vols. (1932–79) · W. S. Crockett, *The Scott originals*, rev. 3rd edn (1932) · pay lists, 7th north British regiment of militia, 1798–1802, PRO, WO 13/73–77 · excise minute books, 1808, 1822–5, 1836, NA Scot., CE 2/17, 2/18, 2/40, 2/41, CE 13/3, 13/4 · excise minute books, 1808, 1822–5, 1836, PRO, CUST 47/616, 47/619 · [J. Hannay], 'Joseph Train', *Household Words*, 7 (1853), 475–7 · IGI
Archives NL Scot., corresp. and papers relating to the Buchanites · NL Scot., corresp. with Sir Walter Scott, MSS 874, 3277, 3885–3917 · U. Edin. L., Laing collection, notes on Burns
Likenesses silhouette, repro. in Macfadzean, 'Joseph Train, F.S.A.', 79

Trant, Clarissa Sandford (1800–1844). *See under* Trant, Nicholas (1769–1839).

Trant, Nicholas (1769–1839), army officer, was the son of Thomas Trant and his wife, the daughter of James Trant. His mother and father were probably cousins, living in Dingle, co. Kerry, and his forebears were of Danish origin. His grandfather Dominick Trant, also of Dingle, wrote a tract, *Considerations on the Present disturbance in Munster* (1787).

Trant was educated at a military college in France, but when the Revolutionary War broke out he entered the British army, and on 31 May 1794 he was commissioned lieutenant in the 84th foot. He served with the 84th at Flushing, and went with it to the Cape of Good Hope in 1795. After his return to England he received command of a company in one of the regiments of the Irish brigade. His regiment was sent to Portugal, and he took part in the expedition under Sir Charles Stuart which resulted in the capture of Minorca in November 1798. There Trant was appointed agent-general for prizes, and helped to organize the Minorca regiment, in which he was made major on 17 January 1799. This was the year in which Trant married Sarah Georgina Horsington, an Englishwoman with evangelical connections. A daughter, Clarissa Trant [*see below*],

was born to the couple in 1800, and a son, Thomas Abercrombie, in 1805. Sarah died shortly after Thomas's birth. Thomas was commissioned in the 38th foot in 1820, and was captain in the 28th foot when he died, aged twenty-seven, on 13 March 1832.

Trant served in the expedition to Egypt, and his regiment supported the 42nd and 28th in the battle of Alexandria. It was disbanded after the peace of Amiens, and Trant left the army; but he soon made a fresh start in it, and was commissioned ensign in the Royal Staff Corps on 25 December 1803. He was promoted lieutenant on 28 November 1805, and was sent to Portugal as a military agent in 1808. Because British officers usually received advanced rank in the Portuguese service he was appointed lieutenant-colonel. When Sir Arthur Wellesley (later the duke of Wellington) advanced from the Mondego in August the Portuguese general Bernardin Freire remained behind, but he allowed Trant to accompany Wellesley with a Portuguese corps of 1500 foot and 250 horse. At Roliça his assignment was to turn the French left. His inexperienced troops became jammed in a narrow gorge, however, and did not fully achieve their objective. At Vimeiro he was in reserve with Craufurd's British brigade.

Trant returned to England after the convention of Cintra, but went back to Portugal early in 1809 as part of the quartermaster-general's contingent to arrange details of the evacuation then planned. However, later in the year another British force began landing, and Trant raised a corps from the students of Coimbra University. After the Portuguese defeat at Braga and the French capture of Oporto, fresh recruits flocked to him. With about 3000 men he boldly maintained himself on the Vouga until May. He took part in the advance of Wellesley's army to the Douro, and was made governor of Oporto when it was recovered.

Trant was promoted captain in the staff corps on 1 June 1809, but soon afterwards was told that he would be removed from it unless he gave up his Portuguese employment. The situation was saved by Wellington, who intervened to write, on 9 May 1810, that there was no officer the loss of whose services in Portugal would be more felt. By this time Trant held the rank of brigadier-general.

In the autumn of 1810, while Wellington was falling back on Torres Vedras, Trant twice showed his 'activity and prudent enterprise', as Beresford described it. On 20 September, with a squadron of cavalry and 2000 militia, he surprised the French artillery train in a defile. His men became alarmed, and he had to fall back; but he took 100 prisoners, and caused Masséna to lose two vital days in his advance. On 7 October he marched suddenly upon Coimbra, where Masséna had left his sick and wounded with only a small guard. He met with little or no resistance, and carried off 5000 prisoners to Oporto. Napier described it as the most daring enterprise by any partisan force during the entire war. Some of the French officers who were taken prisoner prepared a letter, printed in an appendix by Napier, in which they defended his humanitarian treatment of the prisoners despite some atrocities committed by a few of his men.

In some respects Trant was ideally suited to lead the Portuguese troops. He was given to derring-do, but he was a steadying influence on his troops, who continued to improve under his guidance despite the handicap that he was always short of money. He seemed to exercise more authority over his troops than the Portuguese officers. In October 1811 the Portuguese government conferred on him the title of knight commander of the Tower and Sword. Both Fortescue and Oman included substantial references to his frequent brilliant accomplishments. In April 1812 he executed a ruse that prevented two French divisions from storming Almeida. He dressed many of his men in red coats, made them visible around the fortress, and at night built many bivouac fires to simulate bodies of British troops. This was convincing enough to cause Marmont to withdraw his forces for a time. On 13 April he was at Guarda with 6000 militia, and had a plan for surprising Marmont in his quarters at Sabugal; but on that night he himself narrowly escaped surprised by Marmont in Guarda. Wellington, while praising his action in the emergency, warned him not to be too venturesome with such troops as his.

In 1813 fresh difficulties were raised about his drawing pay as a staff corps officer while in the Portuguese service. He obtained leave to go to England, and Wellington wrote strongly in support of his claim, expressing once more his appreciation of Trant's services and merits, and stating that he had been employed in a most important situation for the expenses of which his allowances were by no means adequate. He seems to have had no further part in the war. He had a bullet in his side, from which he suffered much for the rest of his life. He was transferred from the staff corps to the Portuguese service list on 25 October 1814, and received a brevet majority on 6 June 1815: scant reward for services so often praised. He was placed on half pay on 25 December 1816, and he resigned his half pay and left the army altogether in 1825. In May 1818, in financial difficulties, he had asked Wellington to write on his behalf to the king of Portugal; but Wellington replied to Beresford that it would be an indelicacy. Trant died on 16 October 1839 at Great Baddow, Essex, where his son-in-law, John Bramston, was vicar.

Trant's daughter, **Clarissa Sandford Trant** [married name Bramston] (1800–1844), diarist, was born in Lisbon on 30 November 1800. Owing to her father's long periods in Portugal in her early years her education was unconventional, frequently by tutors or a governess, though she also attended two schools in London: one at Gough House and the other in Sloane Street. Her mind was nimble and her pen well practised, as demonstrated by her diary. She was a serious-minded young woman who did not read fiction. She travelled extensively while young, and, though not associated with the highest society, she had contact with some of the great names of the period such as Lord John Russell, the prince of Orange, Talleyrand, Sir Charles Stuart, George Canning, the duke of Wellington, and Daniel O'Connell. She had a very close relationship with her brother Thomas and with her father during her early years. Though not wanting to be an 'old maid' she rejected at least twelve suitors before marrying in 1832, at the age of thirty-one, a spiritually compatible clergyman: the Revd John Bramston, pupil of Keble, friend of Newman, and vicar at Great Baddow, Essex. They had three children: Clara (b. 1833), Mary (b. 1841), and John (b. 1843). Her health was fragile in her later years, and she died of pleurisy on 10 April 1844 at the age of forty-three. Her husband remarried a year later. *The Journal of Clarissa Trant*, edited from the twenty-eight volumes of her diary, by a descendant, Miss C. G. Luard, was published in 1925.

E. M. LLOYD, *rev.* GORDON L. TEFFETELLER

Sources *Annual Register* (1839) · Fortescue, *Brit. army* · D. Gates, *The Spanish ulcer: a history of the Peninsular War* (1986) · *GM*, 1st ser., 102/1 (1832), 371 · *GM*, 2nd ser., 12 (1839), 653 · J. J. G. Pelet, *The French campaign in Portugal, 1810–1811*, ed. and trans. D. Horward (1973) · *The Journal of Clarissa Trant*, ed. C. G. Luard (1925) · W. F. P. Napier, *History of the war in the Peninsula and in the south of France*, rev. edn, 6 vols. (1876) · F. F., M. C. D. T. [Frade Fort or, Cunato Monge Cisterciense Doctor Theologo], *Noticias biograficas do Coronel Trant* (1811) · C. W. C. Oman, *A history of the Peninsular War*, 7 vols. (1902–30) · J. Philippart, ed., *The royal military calendar*, 3rd edn, 5 vols. (1820) · A. I. Shand, *Wellington's lieutenants* (1902) · G. L. Teffeteller, *The surpriser: the life of Rowland, Lord Hill* (1983) · *The dispatches of … the duke of Wellington … from 1799 to 1818*, ed. J. Gurwood, 13 vols. in 12 (1834–9) · H. Blodgett, *Centuries of female days: Englishwomen's private diaries* (1989)

Archives LPL, corresp. and papers | Bodl. Oxf., corresp. with Sir William Napier

Likenesses Neri, cameo engraving, 1829, repro. in Luard, ed., *Journal of Clarissa Trant* (1925)

Tranter, Nigel Godwin (1909–2000), writer, was born on 23 November 1909 at 35 Brownlie Street, Glasgow, the only child of Gilbert Tredgold Tranter (1869–1929), insurance agent, and his second wife, Eleanor Annie, *née* Cass (1875–1933). Gilbert Tranter had been a priest of the Catholic Apostolic church but was expelled about 1904 following misplaced speculation in gold shares, deemed gambling and unfitting a priest. Baptized a Catholic Apostolic, Nigel continued to regard himself as such even after the church became defunct, but worshipped as a Scottish Episcopalian from 1938.

Tranter was educated at George Heriot's school, Edinburgh, but straitened family circumstances in the wake of his father's death robbed him of a hoped for career in architecture and he went into the family insurance business. On 11 July 1933 Tranter married May Jean Campbell Grieve (1911–1979), daughter of Thomas Douglas Grieve, nurseryman, and his wife, Hume Speirs, *née* Gray. They had one daughter, Frances-May (b. 1935), and a son, Philip (b. 1937). Tranter's first book, *The Fortalices and Early Mansions of Scotland, 1400–1650*, illustrated with his own drawings, was published in 1935, when he was twenty-five. His first novel, *Trespass*, followed in 1937 and from then on he wrote compulsively, starting the next novel the same day that he finished the last. Most were novels on Scottish subjects and, in the early years, modern adventure stories modelled on Buchan. From the start, virtually everything he wrote was published.

Tranter was called up in 1942 for war service with the Royal Artillery. This brought no break in his writing, however, and he completed four and a half novels on the king's time. It was in the army that he formed the habit, later his hallmark, of taking long solitary walks, writing as he walked. On demobilization in 1946, he became a full-time writer and continued to produce light adventure stories, some of great charm, but financial necessity resulted also in some potboilers of limited merit, including half a dozen Westerns published under the pseudonym Nye Tredgold.

Always a fervent Scottish patriot, Tranter became deeply involved after the war in the campaign for devolution in Scotland. He helped draft the Scottish covenant (1949), which attracted over 2 million signatures, and was vice-convener of the Scottish Convention from 1951 to 1955. He was also involved in the return of the coronation stone after its removal from Westminster Abbey at Christmas 1950. Although frequently assumed to be a Scottish nationalist, he channelled his political energies, when these campaigns failed, into the Scottish Liberal Party, then the only political party favouring devolution without full independence. Tranter engaged actively in more local campaigns, notably as chairman of the Scottish National Forth Road Bridge Committee in the 1950s. His sharp pen and gadfly interventions in politics turned him into a national figure.

Tranter's works *The Fortified House in Scotland* (5 vols., 1962–70) and *The Queen's Scotland* (4 vols., 1971–7) provided valuable insights into Scottish history but he turned increasingly to historical novel writing. The Bruce trilogy (*The Steps to the Empty Throne*, *The Path of the Hero King*, and *The Price of the King's Peace*, published 1969–71), two volumes on Montrose (*The Young Montrose* and *Montrose: Captain General*, published 1972 and 1973), and *Wallace* (1975) marked a high point in his career as a novelist and brought him massive sales. The novels varied in intrinsic interest and in the quality of the writing, but his gift for story-telling fleshed out the dry bones of Scottish history for the man in the street and he taught a whole generation of Scots all the history they knew. The publication of his novels dovetailed with a profound sense of national identity and growing dissatisfaction with Westminster government at all levels of Scottish society. There was a hunger for Scottish history in accessible form, and with his extraordinary industry and careful attention to detail, Tranter was well placed to meet it. He also helped to secure the restoration of some seventy Scottish fortified houses in private hands.

Of average height, fair-skinned, and blue-eyed, Tranter was spare in build, frugal by habit, and a lifelong abstainer and non-smoker, with no taste for the small luxuries of everyday life: these traits and his routine of walking upwards of 10 miles a day into old age kept him strikingly fit. Conservative by inclination, and with a strong religious faith, he was an old-fashioned father, and he was devastated by the sudden death of his son, Philip, in 1966: no other personal relationship or loss affected him so deeply. But he was always strongly attracted to women, and they to him, and after his wife's death he had a number of close women friends before settling down in 1983 with Joan Isobel Esslemont Earle, *née* Paton (*b.* 1920). He

was impatient by nature and at times incautious, plunging into political controversy with scant regard for whom he might offend, driven by a passion which seemed at odds with a generally genial personality. But the passion that drove him was always for Scotland, and his lifetime pleasure, the part he played in the rescue of her little castles. He was appointed an OBE in 1983 and received an honorary DLitt from the University of Strathclyde in 1990.

Nigel Tranter died on 9 January 2000 at his home, 2 Goose Green Mews, Gullane, East Lothian, and was buried in Aberlady churchyard, East Lothian, on 13 January. A memorial cairn was erected at Aberlady Bay, close to Quarry House, his home for almost fifty years. At his death he had published over 130 titles; seven more manuscripts were complete and ready for publication.

RAY BRADFIELD

Sources NL Scot., Tranter MSS · NA Scot. · *WW* (1997) · *Who's who in Scotland* (1998) · R. Bradfield, *Nigel Tranter: Scotland's storyteller* (1999) · *The Times* (11 Jan 2000) · *The Scotsman* (12 Jan 2000) · *The Guardian* (11 Jan 2000) · personal knowledge (2004) · b. cert.
Archives NL Scot., archive, corresp., literary MSS, notes, and newspaper cuttings · NL Scot., further literary papers | FILM *The storyteller*, Wark-Clements production for TV2, 1992
Likenesses photograph, repro. in *The Scotsman* · photograph, repro. in Bradfield, *Nigel Tranter*, cover, facing p. 207, following p. 206

Trapnel, Anna (*fl.* 1642–1660), self-styled prophet, was born in Poplar, Stepney, Middlesex, apparently the only child of William Trapnel (*d.* before 1645?), shipwright, and a godly mother who exerted seminal influence by raising her daughter as a literate woman of middle rank and teaching her to think of herself as uniquely chosen.

Anna experienced her first vision in 1642 at a sermon preached by John Simpson. The harrowing death of her mother, probably in 1645, was followed by an intense quest for salvation and truth, involving phases of suicidal Calvinist despair, fasting, trances, visions, and associations with various puritan congregations. In her pamphlet *The Cry of a Stone* (1654) she records a Damascene illness in 1647 which gave rise to a sequence of successful prophetic visions: weeks prior to the New Model Army's bloodless entry into London on 6 August to quell counter-revolution and mob rule she predicted their 'coming-in *Southwark*-way'; in 1650 she foresaw Cromwell's defeat of the Scots at Dunbar, 'a *Gideon*' provided by God 'so surely should the *Scots* be ruinated' (*Cry*, sigs. A3r, A3v). That year she joined John Simpson's millenarian Baptist congregation at All Hallows-the-Great and forged links with other radical ministers (Henry Jessey, John Greenhill, and Christopher Feake). In 1652 Anna predicted victory over the Dutch and the calling-in of the Jews preparatory to the apocalypse, and in 1653 Cromwell's dissolution of the Barebones Parliament, in which her fellow Fifth Monarchists sat: envisioning four days before it happened 'that suddenly *Gideon* … and M[ajor] G[eneral] *Harrison* came into the Parliament-house and desired removal of them' (*Cry*, sig. B1v). Finally disenchanted with Cromwell when he declared himself protector on 16 December 1653 (which she claimed to have predicted), Anna accompanied

Vavasor Powell, the fiery Welsh Independent minister, during his examination for treason at Whitehall, where, seized by the prophetic afflatus, she was taken to Mr Roberts's hostelry, there to rhapsodize in verse, 'lying in bed with her eyes shut, her hands fixed, seldom seen to move' for eleven days and twelve nights, in bursts of several hours, her inspirations being recorded by a scribe at the bedside, which was visited by sundry notable radical sectaries (*Cry*, sig. A1v). Her prophecies included God's punishment of Cromwell's corruption, spiritual advice to merchants, promises to the 'saints' of becoming 'Potentates' in the coming millennium, and invective against universities and churches. The text was published in *The Cry of a Stone*.

Anna became a celebrity, viewed by the protectorate as seditious. In 1654 she published a spiritual autobiography, *A Legacy for Saints*. Her authenticity was tested by sceptics, such as the anonymous letter-writer of 21 December 1654, who noted that she was 'so stiffened in her body ... one would think her dead' and that 'she cannot make a verse when she is herself', persisting for eight days at a stretch without food, 'save once in twenty-four hours a little ... small beer' (Bodl. Oxf., MS Rawl. A21, p. 325).

In her *Report and Plea* (1654) Anna described her journey to Cornwall at the behest of God and the imprisoned millenarian ministers, Feake and Simpson, to liaise with Fifth Monarchist Captain Langden, MP in the Barebones Parliament, and local militants including John Bawden and Thomas Allen in Truro. She described interrogation while in a trance by JPs who 'pincht me by the nose and caused my pillow to be pull'd from under my head ... but I heard none of all this stir and bussle' (*Report and Plea*, sig. D3r). At her assize's trial she was accused of witchcraft, madness, whoredom, vagrancy, and seditious intent. Anna defended herself nervously but vehemently as a free single woman (and hence masterless), whose right to pray, publish, and travel were founded in common and divine law, backed by her rights as taxpayer.

Following her arrest on 23 March 1654 Anna was sent, via Plymouth, by ship to Portsmouth and then to Bridewell, where she was cared for by women members of the All Hallows congregation, especially Ursula Adman, who 'kept me company seven weeks ... she was a friend born for the day of adversity' (*Report and Plea*, sig. G2v). Anna now set up as a martyr, writing inflammatory letters from prison, and the protectoral government found it prudent to release her on 26 July 1654. In 1656 she revisited Cornwall, canvassed Wales, and was said to be meditating an excursion to the continent. Trance doggerels of 1657 and 1658 were collected in a thousand-page printed folio volume, placed in the Bodleian Library, which, with *A Voice for the King of Saints and Nations* (1658), records her dispute with the Quakers (often mistaken by contemporaries for Fifth Monarchists because of their ecstatic and antijudicial stance). Scathing Quaker representatives were present at these sessions, at which Anna boasted her vintage as God's seasoned chosen prophet ('Poor Instrument hath found thee, Lord, / For fourteen years together'),

urging the scribe to keep up and condemning the culture of literacy ('Antichrist's libraries') as inferior to the unmediated voice. Latterly dissociating herself from the violent militancy of Venner, she loudly espoused politically quietist millenarianism.

Anna was a touchstone for interregnum female seers. Her writing style, close to the spoken word, is quirkily naïve, rapturous, canny, and sublimely innocent of humour, with a vein of nature mysticism and a testamentary realism. Her catatonic trances negotiated the danger of criminal stigmatization as immodest, demented, or demonic, identifying her as the Almighty's supine 'handmaid', 'vessel', and mouthpiece: 'thy Servant is made a voice ... a voice within a voice ... even thy voice through her' (*Cry*). Anna dropped out of public knowledge after the Restoration.   STEVIE DAVIES

Sources A. Trapnel, *The cry of a stone, or, A relation of something spoken in Whitehall* (1654) • A. Trapnel, *A legacy for saints* (1654) • *Anna Trapnel's 'Report and plea, or, A narrative of her journey from London into Cornwall'* (1654) • A. Trapnel, *A voice for the king of saints and nations* (1658) • A. Trapnel, 'Poetical addresses and discourses', 1659?, Bodl. Oxf. • Bodl. Oxf., MS Rawl. A. 21, 325 • C. Burrage, 'Anna Trapnel's prophecies', *EngHR*, 26 (1911), 526–35 • P. Mack, *Visionary women: ecstatic prophecy in seventeenth-century England* (1994) • S. Davies, *Unbridled spirits: women of the English revolution, 1640–1660* (1998) • A. Evans, *A message from God [by a dumb woman] to his highness the lord protector ... by Elinor Channel* (1654) • B. S. Capp, *The Fifth Monarchy Men: a study in seventeenth-century English millenarianism* (1972)
Archives Bodl. Oxf. • LUL • RS Friends, Lond.

Trapp, John (1601–1669), Church of England clergyman and writer on theology, was born at Croome d'Abitot, Worcestershire, on 5 June 1601, the son of Nicholas Trapp, yeoman of Kemsey. He was educated at the free school in Worcester and then at Christ Church, Oxford, where he matriculated on 15 October 1619 and graduated BA in 1622. John Ley, later a colleague in Warwickshire, was one of his tutors. On graduation Trapp became usher of the free school in Stratford upon Avon (where an older kinsman, Simon Trapp, was already curate), succeeding as headmaster in April 1624. Having proceeded MA on 17 June, twelve days later he married Mary Gibbard at Holy Trinity, Stratford; the couple had a large family of at least ten children.

Trapp was preacher at the Stratford chapelry of Luddington in the early 1630s with a salary provided by Edward Conway, second Lord Conway, and in 1636 was presented to the vicarage of Weston-on-Avon, Gloucestershire (2 miles from Stratford), by Lionel Cranfield, earl of Middlesex. His first publication, *God's Love Tokens and the Afflicted Man's Lessons* (1637), was a funeral sermon for Cranfield's daughter. Trapp was active in south Warwickshire puritan circles in the 1630s, discussing sermons and exchanging manuscripts with Samuel Clarke, Thomas Dugard, and others. He joined in the petitioning against the Laudian innovations in 1640, and acted as a chaplain to the parliamentary garrison in Warwick Castle under Colonel John Bridges from 1644 to 1646. In May 1646 he claimed in a letter to friends in New England that he had

One of this Ages Greatest little men,
Great in Good Workes, witnesse his golden Pen.
His Pen hath drawn his Learned Head in part.
His Holy Life proclaimes a Gracious Heart.
Should any mee consult how hee might rise
Vnto Compleatnesse, I would say. Trappize,
                                        T. D. R. B.
Vera Effigies Iohanis Trapp: A. M. Ætat sua 53 1654

John Trapp (1601–1669), by Richard Gaywood, 1654

been held to ransom by royalists in the summer of 1643 and threatened again in the following year. He was contemptuous of his beleaguered royalist patron, denouncing Middlesex from the pulpit of another Cranfield living, Welford-on-Avon, where Trapp had replaced the royalist incumbent. But Trapp was no radical: rather he was committed to a reformed national church and signed the Warwickshire ministers' 'Testimony' against sectarianism and religious liberty in 1648. In 1654–5 he was among the Warwickshire ministers who operated a semi-formal classis centred on Kenilworth.

Trapp's supreme achievement as a writer was his commentaries on all the books of the Bible, issued in parts and then combined editions from the mid-1640s to the 1660s. *A Brief Commentary upon the Gospel According to St John* inaugurated the series in 1646, while *Annotations upon the Old and New Testament* (five volumes in one) completed it in 1662. The many surviving copies suggest that this voluminous and mostly uncontroversial work was a useful reference tool for contemporary clergy in particular. Its topical references to writings against sectarianism and other mid-century polemic did not prevent several reprints being issued in the later seventeenth century and a further edition in the mid-nineteenth.

Trapp was one of the alternative candidates suggested by Richard Baxter when he turned down a bishopric in

1660. Although he lost the Welford living when the previous incumbent returned at the Restoration, Trapp conformed in 1662 and continued to serve at Weston and Stratford. He seems to have accommodated himself to the religious changes of his life with little difficulty, changing the dedicatees in the various editions of his published works to chime with the vagaries of power: he honoured Cranfield before the civil war, Bridges in the 1640s and 1650s, and royalist gentry in the 1660s. Trapp died on 17 October 1669 and was buried at Weston. He was described by his neighbour John Hall, who treated him for melancholy in 1635, as being 'for his piety and learning second to none' (Lane, 344). To his friend Thomas Dugard, in a commendatory verse to Trapp's *Commentary on the Pentateuch or the Five Books of Moses*, he was 'One of this Age's Greatest Little Men': small in stature, yet an imposing religious writer.   ANN HUGHES

Sources A. Hughes, *Politics, society and civil war in Warwickshire, 1620–1660* (1987) · J. Trapp, *Annotations upon the Old and New Testament*, 5 vols. (1654–62) · Cranfield papers among the Sackville manuscripts, CKS, U269 · A. B. Grosart, *Memoir of John Trapp* (1867) · P. Tennant, *The civil war in Stratford upon Avon* (1996) · J. Lane, *John Hall and his patients* (1996) · *The Wyllys papers*, Collections of the Connecticut Historical Society, 21, Hartford, Connecticut, 1926 · Foster, *Alum. Oxon.* · IGI

Archives Kent Archives, Sackville papers · Kent Archives, Cranfield papers · Shakespeare Birthplace Trust, The Stratford Borough records

Likenesses R. Gaywood, etching, 1654, BM, NPG [*see illus.*]

Trapp, Joseph (1679–1747), Church of England clergyman and writer, was born at Cherrington, Gloucestershire, in November 1679, the second son of Joseph Trapp (1638–1698), rector of Cherrington from 1662, and his wife, Elizabeth. He was the grandson of John *Trapp (1601–1669), a parliamentary chaplain. One of six surviving children he was baptized on 18 December 1679 at Cherrington. Educated at first by his father and later at New College School in Oxford, he matriculated on 14 July 1695 at Wadham College, Oxford, where he held a Goodridge exhibition from 1695 to 1700. Elected to a scholarship in 1696 he graduated BA on 22 April 1699 and MA on 19 May 1702. He became a fellow of Wadham in 1703. His early reputation was that of a minor poet: some Latin hexameters, *Fraus nummi Anglicani* (1696), appeared in the *Musae Anglicanae* (2.211), and his work was included in Oxford verse collections commemorating the duke of Gloucester (*d.* 1700) and William III (*d.* 1702). During this time Trapp developed a connection with the London theatre world; his anonymous *Prologue to the University of Oxford*, delivered at the Act in July 1703, was spoken by Thomas Betterton, and his Turkish tragedy, *Abramulè, or, Love and Empire*, which was first performed at Lincoln's Inn Fields in 1704, secured lasting critical acclaim. In 1708 he became the first professor of poetry at Oxford and in 1709 he served as pro-proctor. His appointment to the poetry chair, which he held until 1718, gave 'great satisfaction [to] the whole university', according to Thomas Hearne, the diarist, who regarded him as 'a most ingenious honest gent. and every ways deserving' (*Remarks*, 2.120). Opinion was divided on the merit of Trapp's lectures, which were mainly concerned with the classical poets, particularly those of Rome. Hearne thought that the first lecture, delivered in January 1711, displayed 'much conceit' but others found Trapp's criticisms 'sound and clear' (N&Q, 2nd ser., 11.194). The lectures were well attended and their original Latin text, Praelectiones poeticae (3 vols., 1711–19), was reissued in translation, with additional notes, in 1742. However, Trapp's greatest literary endeavour, a translation into blank verse of the complete works of Virgil (1731), was less successful. Accurate but dull it deserved Dr Johnson's verdict that it 'may continue its existence as long as it is the clandestine refuge of schoolboys' (Johnson, 1.453), although the merit of its explanatory notes and critical observations brought the work to a fourth edition in 1737. Another epic undertaking, Paradisus amissus Latine redditus, published by Trapp at his own expense, in two volumes (1741–4), proved a costly failure.

Among his contemporaries Trapp was noted less for his literary endeavours than as a political writer and as a churchman. From an early age he manifested combative high-church qualities inherited from his father, whose epitaph at Cherrington recorded him thus:

schismaticis ... insensus
Disciplinae fideique ecclesiae Anglicanae tenax.
(GM, 381)

In 1701 he dedicated a flattering poem, Aedes Badmintoniae, to the high tory Henry Somerset, second duke of Beaufort, and at about the same time he became a friend of the high-church champion Dr Henry Sacheverell. This association endured for many years. Trapp acted as a manager for Sacheverell during his celebrated trial before the House of Lords in Westminster Hall in March 1710 and afterwards succeeded him in his lectureship in the parish of Newington, Surrey. Trapp used his talent as a pamphleteer on Sacheverell's behalf more than once with, for example, An Ordinary Journey No Progress, or, A Man doing his Own Business No mover of Sedition (1710) and The case of the patron and rector of St Andrew's, Houlbourn, in answer to a pamphlet entitled, The case of the erectors of a chapel ... in the said parish (1722). When Sacheverell died, in 1724, Trapp inherited the greater part of his library, together with a legacy of £200 and instructions to destroy most of his papers.

Trapp's polemical energies were frequently employed on behalf of the tory administration that came to power in 1710, following Sacheverell's trial. Pamphlets, such as Most Faults on One Side (1710) and The True Genuine Tory-Address, and the True Genuine Whig-Address, Set Against one another (1710), drew responses. As chaplain to the new lord chancellor of Ireland, Sir Constantine Phipps, the leading counsel for Dr Sacheverell at his trial, Trapp followed him to Dublin in 1711, where he generated controversy with a high-flying sermon on Restoration day, 29 May. In the same year he addressed a poem To Mr Harley, on his First Appearing in Publick, after the Wound Given him by Guiscard, and published a satirical pamphlet, The Character and Principles of the Present Set of Whigs. Although Swift thought this 'a very scurvy piece' (Swift, 269), it reached a third edition in 1712, by which time Swift was claiming credit for having secured the post of chaplain to Viscount Bolingbroke

for Trapp, who was said to be 'mighty happy and thankfull for it' (ibid., 550). In 1713 Bolingbroke received the dedication of Trapp's poem Peace. This partisan celebration of the treaty of Utrecht served primarily as a vehicle for a collection of eulogistic portraits of the tory leaders; Swift thought it 'dull' (ibid., 65on.).

Trapp shared his party's disappointment at the accession of George I. He played a leading part in the tory counter-demonstration at Oxford on coronation day, 20 October 1714, when he presented Sir Constantine Phipps, his former patron, for the honorary degree of DCL, but afterwards concentrated on his ecclesiastical career. Having failed to become a lecturer in the high-church parish of St Clement Danes, London, in November 1712, he became lecturer of St Olave Jewry and of St Martin, Ironmonger Lane, in 1714, and lecturer of St Martin-in-the-Fields in 1715. He was presented by the earl of Peterborough to the rectory of Dauntsey, Wiltshire, in 1714, and exchanged this for the London parishes of Christ Church Greyfriars and St Leonard, Foster Lane, in 1722 on the presentation of the high tory governors of St Bartholomew's Hospital. He held this appointment until his death, in 1747, adding to it, in 1733, the rectory of Harlington, Middlesex, a living in the gift of Lord Bolingbroke.

Trapp was a devout and energetic minister. He officiated unfailingly at public daily prayers and was noted for his strict adherence to correct standards of clerical dress. As 'little Parson Dapper' his accomplished pulpit manner earned him an honourable mention in The Tatler (1.457) and he was frequently invited to preach on major occasions, such as before the lord mayor, the Corporation of the Sons of the Clergy, and the charity schools of London and Westminster. He dedicated a tract, entitled Duties of Private, Domestic, and Public Devotion, to his parishioners at Dauntsey, and presented every member of his London congregations with a copy of Thoughts upon the Four Last Things: Death, Judgment, Heaven, Hell, a Poem (1734–5; 3rd edn, 1749). In this latter work Trapp indicated the sense of urgency with which he had come to regard his pastoral vocation and commented: 'I have lived in six reigns, but for about twenty years past, the English nation has been so prodigiously debauched that I am almost a foreigner in my own country' ('Advertisement'). His epitaph included the arresting lines:

Death! Judgment! Heaven! Hell! think, Christian, think!
You stand on vast Eternity's dread Brink!

and concluded with the earnest hope that his flock might 'Hear me at least, oh! hear me from my grave'. After his death a selection of Trapp's parochial sermons were published in a two-volume edition (1752), which afforded further evidence of his efforts to guard his flock against the enticements of both overt and concealed infidelity. Anxious in particular to repudiate deistical claims that a mere 'religion of Nature' furnished a sufficient guide for conduct Trapp condemned the 'absurd presumption' of 'our new Philosophers', whose 'short-sighted Reason' blinded them to the 'Glory of God in his Works of Creation and Providence' (Trapp, Sermons, 1.xi–xii). He also wrote sadly about those who 'make no other Use of Flowers, Herbs,

Fruits and Animals, than to see, smell, and eat them; when, if due Reflection were made upon them, they would serve to the noblest Purposes of … Morality' (ibid., 266). In 1729 and 1730 he gave the lectures on Lady Moyer's foundation, published as *The Doctrine of the most Holy, and Ever-Blessed Trinity, Briefly Stated and Proved*, and his *Explanatory Notes upon the Four Gospels and the Acts of the Apostles* (2 vols., 1747–8) were reprinted in 1775 and 1805.

Throughout his life Trapp remained a strong high-churchman who exemplified all the characteristics of his party. Ever mindful of the experience of the church during the civil war, and the Commonwealth and protectorate that followed, he revered the memory of Charles I and deplored his 'most horrid Murder and Parricide' (Trapp, *Sermons*, 22). He sympathized with some of the nonjurors, particularly Roger Laurence, author of *Lay Baptism Invalid*, whom he presented at Oxford for an honorary MA in 1713 (*Remarks*, 4.212). Believing that the Church of England was a divinely commissioned part of the church catholic Trapp repudiated the Erastian doctrines advanced by Benjamin Hoadly, bishop of Bangor, and noted pointedly that 'in the Primitive Church some of the most noted Heresiarchs were Bishops' (*The Real Nature of the Church or Kingdom of Christ*, 1717, 5). Using texts such as Numbers 16 and Hebrews 5: 4 he maintained a high notion of the divine authority of the regularly constituted ministry and lamented that the 'temporal condition of Spiritual Persons, and of their families … is, upon the whole, very hard and unequal'. This he believed was a consequence of 'unconscionable pillage' during the Reformation (*The Dignity and Benefit of the Priesthood*, 1721, 28, 43). He regarded the dissenters, who had no regular ministerial succession, as dangerous schismatics and attacked plans to comprehend them within the Church of England as 'absurd' and 'wicked' (*A Preservative Against Unsettled Notions, and Want of Principles in Religion*, 1715, xix). In the late 1730s, predictably, Trapp was deeply alarmed by the emergence of the Methodists, whom he likened to the Puritans of the 1640s. In his best-remembered work, *The Nature, Folly, Sin and Danger, of being Righteous over-much*, which went through four editions in 1739, Trapp attacked the mortifications practised by the followers of George Whitefield, who responded, along with others, including William Law and the anonymous author of the satirical *Dr Trapp Vindicated from the Imputation of being a Christian*. Trapp was undeterred and returned to the charge. In an assize sermon preached at Oxford, entitled *The Nature, Usefulness and Regulation of Religious Zeal* (1739), he glanced slightingly at Law: 'to eat nothing but bread and herbs, and drink nothing but water, unless there be a particular reason for it, is folly at best' (p. 7). This sermon was received with marked respect by the vice-chancellor, Dr Theophilus Leigh, who 'stood up all the time of his preaching … to manifest his high sense of so respectable a character' (*GM*, 660). A further piece, *The true spirit of the Methodists and their allies (whether other enthusiasts, papists, deists, Quakers, or atheists) fully laid open* (1740), provided a comprehensive response to Trapp's antagonists, including Whitefield, who was accused of 'Quakerism, Enthusiastic Madness and Malice' (26), and Law,

whose *Grounds and Reasons of Christian Regeneration* was dismissed as an 'Enthusiastical Rhapsody' (p. 38). In common with other high-churchmen Trapp was also a decided critic of the Roman Catholic church. He published *Popery Truly Stated, and Briefly Confuted* (1726; 3rd edn, 1745) in response to 'the late unusual Growth of Popery' (p. 2); it rehearsed familiar arguments in favour of private judgement, as guided by scripture, and against papal supremacy, novel doctrines, and superstitious practices. This work, together with *The Church of England defended against the calumnies and false reasonings of the church of Rome* (1727), a response to *England's Conversion and Reformation Compar'd* by the Catholic controversialist Robert Manning, secured for Trapp the degree of DD by diploma at Oxford in February 1728.

In person Trapp was 'of a middle stature, slender habit, olive complexion, and a countenance of uncommon openness and animation' (*GM*, 383). The three-quarter-length portrait presented to the Bodleian Library in 1755 was considered an excellent likeness. He was naturally irascible but made efforts to control his temper when provoked, 'compressing his lips as he retired, like a true Christian philosopher'. Although it was said that he 'studied harder than any man in England' he could be diverted in convivial company; one memorialist recalled 'his giving us the good old song of *Celebrate this Festival & c*, for which, even in an advanced age, he was not ill-qualified, by the possession of an agreeable tenor-base voice' (ibid., 384). He married, on 7 December 1714, 'Mrs White, a young Girl of about 18 years of age, Daughter of a Widdow in Oxford' (*Remarks*, 5.4), with whom he had two sons. The first, Henry, for whom Lord Bolingbroke stood godfather, died in infancy. The second, Joseph (*d.* 1769), became a fellow of New College, Oxford, in 1734 and rector of Stratfield Saye in Hampshire.

Trapp died at Harlington, of pleurisy, on 22 November 1747 and was buried in the parish church there, at the north side of the entry into the chancel, where he is commemorated by a monument. Another monument, engraved as the frontispiece to the second volume of his *Sermons* (1752), was erected on the east wall of the chancel of Christ Church Greyfriars and paid for by the parishioners.   RICHARD SHARP

Sources DNB · *GM*, 1st ser., 56 (1786), 381–4, 660–63 · *Remarks and collections of Thomas Hearne*, ed. C. E. Doble and others, 11 vols., OHS, 2, 7, 13, 34, 42–3, 48, 50, 65, 67, 72 (1885–1921) · Foster, *Alum. Oxon.* · IGI · D. Lysons, *An historical account of those parishes in the county of Middlesex which are not described in 'The environs of London'* (1800), 129–32 · D. E. Baker, *Biographia dramatica, or, A companion to the playhouse*, rev. I. Reed, new edn, rev. S. Jones, 2 (1812), 2 · D. F. Bond, ed., *The Tatler*, 1 (1987), 457 · J. Swift, *Journal to Stella*, ed. H. Williams, 1 (1948), 158 · J. Trapp, *Sermons on moral and practical subjects*, 2 vols. (1752) · S. Johnson, *Lives of the English poets*, ed. G. B. Hill, [new edn], 3 vols. (1905)

Likenesses R. Clamp, stipple (after portrait), BM, NPG; repro. in E. Harding and S. Harding, *Biographical mirrour* (1796) · C. Grignion, engraving, repro. in Trapp, *Sermons*, frontispiece · oils, Bodl. Oxf. · oils (after portrait), Wadham College, Oxford

Traquair. For this title name *see* Stewart, John, first earl of Traquair (*c.*1599–1659).

Traquair [*née* Moss], **Phoebe Anna** (1852–1936), artist, was born on 24 May 1852 in Kilternan, co. Dublin, the sixth of the seven children of William Moss, surgeon, of Dublin and his wife, Teresa, daughter of John and Jane Richardson of Kilgobbin, co. Dublin. From 1869 to 1872 she studied at the School of Design of the Royal Dublin Society. On 5 June 1873 she married in Dublin the Scottish palaeontologist Ramsay Heatley *Traquair (1840–1912), whose research papers she had illustrated. On his appointment to the Museum of Science and Art, they moved in early 1874 to Edinburgh, where their three children, Ramsay (*b.* 1874), Harry (*b.* 1875), and Hilda (*b.* 1879), were born.

Traquair's earliest surviving works, produced in the late 1870s, are landscape watercolours and embroidered domestic textiles; examples of both are in private collections and in the Victoria and Albert Museum, London. By the mid-1880s her expanding social circle included the biologist and sociologist Patrick Geddes, whose Edinburgh Social Union in 1885 engaged her to decorate the tiny new mortuary chapel of the Royal Hospital for Sick Children. Completed in 1886, the chapel was demolished in 1894 but wall sections survive in a new building. She restored these transferred walls within a new scheme of 1896–8 painted in the simpler style of a child's picture book.

In the later 1880s Traquair worked figural embroidered panels for draughtscreens. The finest is her triptych *The Salvation of Mankind* (1887–93; City Art Centre, Edinburgh). Her style was initially close to the symbolist work of Edward Burne-Jones and D. G. Rossetti, which had been promoted in reviews by Geddes and was also supported by another friend, John Miller Gray, first curator of the Scottish National Portrait Gallery. Gray and Ruskin, with whom she corresponded in 1887, encouraged Traquair to illuminate manuscripts. She also began to work on commercial book design and illustration for Walter Scott of London and T. and A. Constable of Edinburgh.

Traquair's decoration of the song school of St Mary's Episcopal Cathedral, Edinburgh (1888–92), won her national recognition. Illustrating the Benedicite and combining portraiture with a skilful use of colour and decorative pattern, the scheme showed both technical innovation and stylistic independence. Together with the range of her crafts (which now included book cover tooling), her third Edinburgh decoration, at the Catholic Apostolic church (1893–1901), demonstrated a reintegration of art with craft. This major mural scheme turned a neo-Norman church into a 'jewelled crown' and, like her outstanding quartet of silk-embroidered panels *The Progress of a Soul* (1893–1902; National Gallery of Scotland, Edinburgh), it illustrated the journey of the human spirit through life. Her illuminated manuscripts of the 1890s, many of which illustrated Rossetti, Tennyson, the Brownings, and Dante (and some of which are in the National Library of Scotland and priv. coll.), share with them an intensity of colour and tactile values. She was now Scotland's leading arts and crafts artist.

After 1900 Traquair's diverse studio crafts included the

Phoebe Anna Traquair (1852–1936), self-portrait, 1911

fashionable art of enamelling alongside book cover tooling and art embroidery. She produced hundreds of pieces of jewellery and ornamental work. As she had exhibited by invitation at the world fair in Chicago in 1893, so in 1904 she showed *The Progress of a Soul* in St Louis. Her mural work, now on a reduced level, included the chancel of the church of St Peter at Clayworth, Nottinghamshire (1904–5), and the Manners chapel at Thorney Hill in the New Forest, Hampshire (1920–22).

In 1906, on her husband's retirement, the Traquairs moved to the village of Colinton, then developing as an 'arts and crafts' suburb of Edinburgh. In 1920 she was elected an honorary member of the Royal Scottish Academy. Phoebe Traquair died in Edinburgh on 4 August 1936 and was buried at Colinton parish church.

ELIZABETH S. CUMMING

Sources E. S. Cumming, *Phoebe Anna Traquair* (1993) [exhibition catalogue, Scot. NPG, 6 Aug – 7 Nov 1993] • E. S. Cumming, 'Phoebe Anna Traquair, HRSA, (1852–1936) and her contribution to arts and crafts in Edinburgh', PhD diss., U. Edin., 1987 • A. F. Morris, 'A versatile art worker: Mrs Traquair', *The Studio*, 34 (1905), 339–45 • J. L. Caw, 'The art work of Mrs Traquair', *Art Journal*, new ser., 20 (1900), 143–8 • M. Armour, 'Mural decoration in Scotland', *The Studio*, 10 (1897), 100–06 • M. Armour, 'Beautiful modern manuscripts', *The Studio*, special winter number (1896–7), 47–55 • NL Scot., Traquair MSS 8122–8125 • *The Scotsman* (6 Aug 1936) • *The Times* (6 Aug 1936) • *CGPLA Eng. & Wales* (1936) • private information (2004) [family; J. Turpin] • *The Post Office Edinburgh and Leith directory*

Archives NL Scot., corresp. and papers | University of Lancaster, Ruskin Galleries, MSS • V&A, MSS

Likenesses photograph, 1873, U. St Andr. L. • J. P. Macgillivray, marble bust, *c*.1895, Scot. NPG • photograph, 1904, NL Scot. • P. A. Traquair, self-portrait, oils, 1911, Scot. NPG [*see illus.*] • photographs, National Museums of Scotland, Edinburgh

Wealth at death £9191 14s. 2d.: confirmation, 25 Sept 1936, *CCI*

Traquair, Ramsay Heatley (1840–1912), palaeontologist, was born on 30 July 1840 at the old manse, Rhynd, Perthshire, the last of eight children of the Revd James Traquair (1778–1849), Church of Scotland clergyman, and his wife, Elizabeth Mary *née* Bayley (1800–1843), originally from London. Ramsay's father retired shortly after his birth, and the family moved to Edinburgh, where Ramsay was educated at a preparatory school and then at the Edinburgh Institution. Slightly built, quiet, and studious, he did well academically but not on the sports field, although archery later became a hobby. An early interest in natural history led to his discovery of a fossil fish in Lower Carboniferous rocks at Wardie, Edinburgh, an event which was to influence his life.

Ramsay enrolled as a medical student at Edinburgh University in 1857—natural history was not then a separate subject. William S. McIntosh, his contemporary at Edinburgh, described him as 'slight in physique but with a massive head covered with fair hair, and expressive blue eyes which kindled when he spoke' (McIntosh, 1). Traquair's constitution appears to have been quite delicate; his letters frequently refer to periods of illness, and he found long study arduous. Nevertheless, he graduated in 1862 with a gold medal for his thesis on asymmetry in flatfish. He was demonstrator in anatomy at Edinburgh until 1866 when he became professor at the Royal Agricultural College, Cirencester (with a testimonial from T. H. Huxley). Feeling that this post isolated him from research, he left the following year, to become professor of zoology at the Royal College of Science, Dublin. About this time he published his first paper in the *Transactions of the Royal Society of Edinburgh*, the commencement of his work on Scottish fossil fish.

Traquair remained in Dublin for six years and was elected to the Royal Irish Academy in 1871. In 1873 he was appointed as first keeper of natural history at the Museum of Science and Art (later the Royal Museum) in Edinburgh. He brought with him from Dublin a fund of humorous Irish stories and a wife—Phoebe Anna, *née* Moss (1852–1936), [*see* Traquair, Phoebe Anna] the third daughter of a Dublin physician. A very talented artist, she had undertaken many fossil drawings for him and they had married on 5 June 1873. She later became one of Scotland's foremost pre-Raphaelite craftswomen and first woman member of the Royal Scottish Academy. The couple moved to 8 Dean Park Crescent, Edinburgh, in January 1874. Their first son, Ramsay, was born in 1874 and became an architect and designer, collaborating with his mother on enamelling and metalwork. Harry Moss, later an ophthalmic surgeon, was born in 1875, and Hilda in 1879.

Traquair's appointment in Edinburgh was a government move to resolve the increasingly acrimonious relationship between the museum and the university's professor of natural history (Wyville Thomson) who retained control of the museum's natural history collections. The appointment was made during Wyville Thomson's extended absence on a *Challenger* expedition and ended the university's direct control of the specimens. As a result, Traquair could now concentrate his research on the Palaeozoic fish for which Scotland is renowned. The museum's holdings were good, but Traquair enlarged them into one of the finest fossil fish collections in the world. He purchased widely from dealers and amateurs and acquired important comparative material from European localities. Much of the Scottish material was new to science.

Traquair brought a thorough anatomical knowledge of modern fish to his study of fossil forms and, after a few years' work on the Carboniferous Palaeoniscids, rejected Agassiz' classification based on scale appearance and replaced it with one based on detailed skull and skeletal osteology. His results were published in instalments (1877–1914) as a Palaeontographical Society monograph. This volume remains an important reference work today. He was the first to recognize the relationship between the primitive thelodonts from the Silurian of southern Scotland and the Agnatha (jawless fish).

Traquair did much innovative stratigraphical research using the distribution of fossil fish to date rocks and his work led to the recognition of the Scottish Upper and Lower Carboniferous and the distinction of marine from freshwater horizons. His studies on the Scottish Old Red Sandstone fish allowed an extensive revision of stratigraphy and nomenclature and enabled him to correlate them with other worldwide faunas. His second major monograph on the Upper Old Red Sandstone Asterolepidae was published between 1877 and 1912 by the Palaeontographical Society. He published 142 other research papers including descriptions of many new genera and species still valid at the end of the twentieth century.

Traquair retired in 1906 and moved to Colinton, a prosperous suburb of Edinburgh. He was a fellow of the Royal societies of Edinburgh and London and received many honours; the one he prized most was the royal medal from the latter awarded in 1907. Edinburgh University awarded him an honorary LLD in 1893 and he was visiting Swiney lecturer at the British Museum (natural history) from 1883 to 1887 and 1896 to 1900. He was Britain's foremost palaeoichthyologist, his work pivotal to the science of palaeontology, but the government considered research as private work and reduced his pension accordingly. After retirement he continued writing, and published a memoir on Cretaceous fish from Belgium in 1911. He was also compiling a catalogue of type and figured specimens for the museum. This manuscript shows his increasingly shaky handwriting caused by the onset of Parkinson's disease in 1909 but he remained active until a few weeks before his death at his home, The Bush, Spylaw Bank Road, Colinton, Edinburgh, on 22 November 1912. He was buried in Colinton churchyard during 'a storm of wind and rain' (McIntosh correspondence) and the headstone designed by his wife can be seen adjacent to picturesque Colinton Dell.

Traquair was apparently very reserved, but those who got to know him found 'a simple, kindly nature which endeared him to all who knew him' (*Glasgow Herald*, 7 Dec 1912).

ROBERTA L. PATON

Sources J. Horne, *Proceedings of the Royal Society of Edinburgh*, 33 (1912–13), 336–41 • 'Eminent living geologists', *Geological Magazine*, new ser., 5th decade, 6 (1909), 241–50 • W. C. McIntosh, 'In memoriam', *Scottish Naturalist*, 13 (1913), 1–5 • E. S. Cumming, *Phoebe Anna Traquair* (1993) [exhibition catalogue, Scot. NPG, 6 Aug – 7 Nov 1993] • *Glasgow Herald* (7 Dec 1912) • A. S. Romer, N. E. Wright, T. Edinger, and R. van Frank, 'Bibliography of fossil vertebrates exclusive of North America, 1509–1927', *Geological Society of America*

Memoir, 87/2 (1962), 1391–6 · G. N. Swinney, 'A natural history collection in transition', *Journal of the History of Collections*, 11 (1999), 51–70 · U. St Andr. L., special collections department, McIntosh MSS · b. cert. · d. cert. **Archives** BGS, MSS · NHM, MSS · Royal Museum, Edinburgh, drawings and MSS · U. Edin., MSS | BGS, letters to F. L. Kitchin · Elgin Museum, letters to George Gordon · U. St Andr., McIntosh MSS **Likenesses** W. C. McIntosh, photograph, *c*.1862, U. St Andr. · W. C. McIntosh, photograph, *c*.1874, U. St Andr. · photograph, *c*.1900, Royal Museum, Edinburgh · C. Matthew, bronze medallion, Scot. NPG **Wealth at death** £759 1s. 4d.: confirmation, 19 Dec 1912, *CCI*

Traske, John (*c*.1585–1636), Church of England clergyman and separatist minister, was born in Somerset, the son of unidentified parents described only as 'godly'. He began his career as a schoolmaster in his home county. Although he received no university training, Traske managed to acquire a level of scriptural and theological fluency sufficient to convince diocesan authorities that he was fit for ordination, which came in 1611. In September 1611 he assumed the curacy of Chilton Cantelo, Somerset. By October the next year Traske had been presented to the church courts for preaching without licence; he accordingly fled to Axminster, Devon, where he lectured and acted as a local spiritual adviser, operating out of the household of Sir John Drake.

By 1614 Traske's puritanism seems to have taken a radical turn, as he abandoned the parochial structures of the church in favour of a role as a peripatetic, charismatic sect-master. In May 1614 he was preaching to conventicles in and around Ely, while later that year he was accused of itinerating in Somerset. In late 1615 he was arrested for going up and down as a wandering minister in Middlesex.

Traske's legal difficulties were compounded by his increasingly eccentric religious opinions, many of which were laid out in his pamphlets *A Pearl for a Prince* (1615), *Christs Kingdom Discovered* (1615), and *Heavens Joy* (1616). These opinions included the claim that the kingdom of heaven was fully immanent in this world; that believers no longer committed sin; that repentance was unnecessary for those who had entered the state of grace; that the elect could infallibly recognize one another; and that believers should hold goods in common. Most significantly, Traske and his growing band of London followers adopted a host of Mosaic ceremonies, including dietary restrictions, and strictures on lighting fires and dressing meats on Sundays. During 1616 and 1617, under the influence of the tailor Hamlet Jackson, the 'Traskites' took this impulse further, proclaiming Saturday as the true sabbath. Together with his second wife, Dorothy Coome (*c*.1585–*c*.1645), a schoolteacher (whom he married in 1617), his confidant Returne Hebdon, Jackson, and other disciples, Traske created a clandestine, 'Judaical' religious community that briefly subsisted entirely outside the boundaries of the English church. (Nothing is known of his first wife; he and his second wife were both said to be about thirty-two when they married, but they had separated by 1627.)

The Judaizing phase was short-lived, however, in part because of Traske's brash attempts to convert James I. After the king had received several unseemly letters and manuscripts from him, James and his ministers moved to silence Traske. In June 1618 he was convicted in Star Chamber for having given 'detraction and scandal on the King's most excellent Majesty', for 'scandalizing his Ecclesiastical government', and for 'a seditious practice and purpose to divert his Majesty's subjects from their obedience' ('Trask in the star-chamber', 10). He was sentenced to be degraded, fined, whipped, pilloried, branded, to have his ears nailed to the pillory, and to be gaoled at the king's pleasure.

Having endured state torture and facing a lifetime in prison, Traske opted to reassess his theological position. In 1620 he proffered a full recantation and was accordingly readmitted to preach. Traske wasted no time in returning to his heretical ways. Having abandoned his commitment to Jewish ceremonies, he re-embraced other aspects of his early theology—notably the claim that believers were free from sin—arriving ultimately at a frank antinomianism. At this point he attached himself to the growing antinomian protest movement that had developed at the margins of the puritan community in the 1620s, making common cause with well-known London heretics such as John Eaton and Robert Towne. Despite numerous run-ins with the ecclesiastical authorities, Traske was able throughout the 1620s and 1630s to disseminate his message informally and often illegally in London, Dorset, and Gloucestershire. He died in 1636 while tending to the notorious semi-separatist congregation that had been founded by Henry Jacob in Southwark; he was buried in Lambeth churchyard. Traske's life and career stand as an embodiment of the tendency of puritanism to veer off into heterodox, enthusiastic, and sometimes radical forms of religiosity, a tendency that would reach full fruition during the civil wars and interregnum.

DAVID R. COMO

Sources E. Pagitt, *Heresiography, or, A description of the hereticks and sectaries of these latter times* (1661) · E. Norice, *The new gospel, not the true gospel* (1638) · [J. Falconer], *A briefe refutation of John Traskes Judaical and novel fancyes* (1618) · D. R. Como, 'The kingdom of Christ, the kingdom of England, and the kingdom of Traske: John Traske and the persistence of radical puritanism in early Stuart England', *Protestant identities: religion, society and self-fashioning in post-reformation England*, ed. M. McClendon, J. Ward, and M. MacDonald (2000) · B. R. White, 'John Traske (1585–1636) and London puritanism', *Transactions of the Congregational Historical Society*, 20 (1965–70), 223–33 · D. S. Katz, *Philo-Semitism and the re-admission of the Jews to England, 1603–1655* (1982), 18–34 · 'Trask in the star-chamber, 1619', *Transactions of the Baptist Historical Society*, 5 (1916–17), 8–14 **Archives** CUL, Ely diocesan records · NL Scot., Denmilne state MSS · NL Scot., Advocates MSS · PRO, state papers domestic, Charles I · Som. ARS, Bath and Wells diocesan records

Traun, Bertha. *See* Ronge, Bertha (1818–1863).

Travers, Benjamin (1783–1858), surgeon, was born in April 1783, second of the ten children of Joseph Travers, sugar baker in Queen Street, Cheapside, London, and his wife, a daughter of the Revd Francis Spilsbury. After

Benjamin Travers (1783–1858), by Charles Robert Leslie

receiving a classical education at the grammar school of Cheshunt, Hertfordshire, he was taught privately until at the age of sixteen he was placed in his father's counting-house. He soon found commerce uncongenial, and, as his father frequently attended the lectures of the surgeons Henry Cline and Astley Paston Cooper, Travers was articled to Cooper in August 1800 for a term of six years, as his first pupil, residing in his house. During the last year of his apprenticeship Travers gave occasional private demonstrations on anatomy to his fellow pupils and established a clinical society, meeting weekly, of which he was the secretary.

Travers was admitted a member of the Royal College of Surgeons in 1806 and spent the following session at Edinburgh. He returned to London at the end of 1807, and settled at New Court, St Swithin's Lane. He was appointed demonstrator of anatomy at Guy's Hospital, and, with his father's business in decline, he obtained the appointment in 1809 of surgeon to the East India Company's warehouses and brigade; he retained the post until 1814. Also in 1809 he married Sarah, daughter of William *Morgan (1750–1833), actuary. Following her death, he married in 1813 Caroline Millet, whose father was an East India Company director.

Travers succeeded Astley Cooper at the London Infirmary for Diseases of the Eye (later Moorfields Eye Hospital), developing its resources as a teaching institution centre, with many students from England and abroad. Travers was elected a fellow of the Royal Society in 1813, and he was elected surgeon to St Thomas's Hospital, London, in 1815. He retained the post of surgeon to the eye infirmary

until 1816. Astley Cooper moved, in the same year, and Travers took over his house at 3 New Broad Street and soon acquired a fair share of practice. At this time Travers suffered so much from palpitation of the heart that he discontinued his clinical lectures, and in 1819 he resigned his joint lectureship on surgery with Astley Cooper, though he again began to lecture upon surgery in 1834 in conjunction with Frederick Tyrell, at St Thomas's Hospital. Travers was chosen president of the Hunterian Society in 1827, and in the same year he acted as president of the Royal Medical and Chirurgical Society. His third marriage, in 1831, was to Mary Poulett, youngest daughter of Colonel Stevens of Somerset.

Travers filled all the important offices at the Royal College of Surgeons. He was elected a member of the council in 1830; Hunterian orator in 1838; examiner in surgery from 1841 to 1858; chairman of the board of midwifery examiners in 1855; vice-president in the years 1845, 1846, 1854, and 1855; and president in 1847 and 1856. He was a member of the veterinary examining committee in 1833. He was appointed surgeon to Queen Victoria in 1837 and to Prince Albert in 1840.

Travers followed other leading surgeons of the day in adopting the technique of cataract surgery by lens extraction, devised by Jacques Deviel in 1745. These men raised the status of optical surgery from the condition of quackery to which untrained oculists and quacks had brought it. Travers's *Synopsis of the Diseases of the Eye and their Treatment* (1820), one of the earliest systematic treatises in English, went through three English editions, an Italian translation in 1823, and an American edition in 1825. Travers was also a good pathologist, inheriting the best traditions of the Hunterian school, for he worked upon an experimental basis. He died at his house in Green Street, Grosvenor Square, London, on 6 March 1858, and was buried at Hendon in Middlesex. Travers had a large family and his eldest son, Benjamin Travers, followed him in the medical profession.   D'A. POWER, *rev.* ANITA McCONNELL

Sources *Medical Times and Gazette* (13 March 1858), 270–2 · *The Lancet* (11 Jan 1851), 48 · *The Lancet* (13 March 1858), 278 · *GM*, 3rd ser., 4 (1858), 444 · T. J. Pettigrew, *Medical portrait gallery: biographical memoirs of the most celebrated physicians, surgeons … who have contributed to the advancement of medical science*, 4 vols. in 2 [1838–40] · D. M. Albert and D. D. Edwards, eds., *The history of ophthalmology* (1996), 67–8 · J. Hirschberg, *The history of ophthalmology*, trans. F. C. Blodi, 11 vols. (1982–94), vol. 4, pp. 231–2; vol. 8a, pp. 149–56 · *Edinburgh Medical Journal*, 3 (1857–8), 957 · G. Gorin, *History of ophthalmology* (1982), 74–5

Archives RCS Eng., papers · Wellcome L., lecture notes

Likenesses W. Behnes, marble bust, 1858, RCS Eng. · R. J. Lane, lithograph (after Behnes), BM, NPG · C. R. Leslie, oils, RCS Eng. [*see illus.*] · T. H. Maguire, lithograph, BM

Wealth at death under £30,000: probate, 31 March 1858, *CGPLA Eng. & Wales*

Travers, Benjamin (1886–1980), playwright, was born on 12 November 1886 at Lee Crofts, Sunningfields Road, Hendon, London, the elder son and the second of the three children of Walter Francis Travers (*d.* 1927), clerk and later merchant, of London, and his wife, Margaret Travers Burges (*d.* 1908). He was a great-grandson of Benjamin Travers, pioneer in eye surgery and serjeant-surgeon to

Benjamin Travers (1886–1980), by Howard Coster, 1936

Queen Victoria, and could trace his ancestry back to a Travers who had served in William of Normandy's army. Always called Ben by his family and friends, he was educated at the Abbey School, Beckenham, and at Charterhouse School, where his first form master in the lower school was Leonard Huxley, father of Aldous and Julian Huxley. He was an unusually small boy for his age, and to his mind 'was a complete failure at school'. Charterhouse later established a theatre in his name. The only thing he enjoyed there was cricket, having become an enthusiast for the sport when he saw England's legendary batsman W. G. Grace make a century. (He travelled with the England cricket team in 1928 on their tour of Australia.)

On leaving Charterhouse, in 1904, he was sent by his parents to Dresden for a few months to learn German. The performances of Sarah Bernhardt and Lucien Guitry which he saw there gave him a taste for the theatre, so that on his return he informed his parents that he wished to become an actor. This request was promptly vetoed, and instead he was put into the family business, Joseph Travers & Sons Ltd, one of the oldest wholesale grocery firms in the City, dating from 1666. He found the work of 'tea-clearing' uncongenial and after six months he was transferred to the Malayan branch in Singapore. Here the local manager took an instant dislike to him with the result that he was then consigned to the branch in Malacca, where he had practically no work to do but was able to find a complete set of plays of Sir Arthur Wing Pinero in the local library. This further stimulated his interest in the theatre, since he found them an excellent guide to

the technique of stagecraft. In 1908 his mother died, and as his sister Mabel was already married and his younger brother Frank was still at school, he returned home to keep his father company. He unwillingly went back to the family business in the City, which he found as distasteful as before. However, he endured it until 1911 when a literary friend introduced him to the avant-garde publisher John Lane of the Bodley Head. He spent the next three years in Lane's office and Lane took him with him on business visits to the United States and Canada.

In 1914 Travers joined the Royal Naval Air Service (RNAS), in which he served throughout the war, much of the time as a flying instructor (Ivor Novello was one of his pupils), in the rank of flight lieutenant and later as a major when the RNAS was amalgamated with the Royal Flying Corps. For his wartime exploits, which ended with a brief spell of duty in Russia during the allied intervention, he was awarded the Air Force Cross (1920).

On 29 April 1916 Travers was married to (Dorothy Ethel) Violet Mouncey (1894/5–1951), daughter of Daniel Burton William Mouncey, captain of the Leicester regiment. They had two sons and a daughter. His wife had an income of £1000 a year which was a help when he returned to civilian life and decided to become a writer, settling with her in Somerset. He began work on a farce about a dance act which he turned into a novel, *The Dippers* (1922), published by the Bodley Head. He then turned the novel back into a farce and sent it to the actor–manager Sir Charles Hawtrey, who produced it in London, after a try-out in the provinces, at the Criterion Theatre in August 1922 with Cyril Maude in the lead. It had a fair success, running for 173 performances, but public taste was for plays in the style of Gerald Du Maurier and not 'Pinero grandiloquence' (Travers, *Vale of Laughter*, 93). *The Dippers* was followed by another novel, *A Cuckoo in the Nest* (1925), which he also dramatized after the reviewers praised its humour. Then Travers had a stroke of luck. Tom Walls, former policeman, actor–manager, and future Derby winner, chose *A Cuckoo in the Nest* to succeed his current success *It Pays to Advertise* at the Aldwych. It was produced in July 1925, with Yvonne Arnaud, Mary Brough, Ralph Lynn, J. Robertson Hare, and Travers himself in the principal parts. It was an immediate success and notched up 376 performances.

During the next seven years Travers wrote eight more farces for the Aldwych including *Rookery Nook* (1926), *Thark* (1927), and *Plunder* (1928), which had the distinction of being the first farce in which the action centred on a violent death. Travers's refusal to moralize makes him a significant precursor of Joe Orton. There followed *A Cup of Kindness* (1929), 'a Romeo and Juliet story of the suburbs' (Travers, *Vale of Laughter*, 161), *A Night Like This* (1930), *Turkey Time* (1931), *Dirty Work* (1932), and *A Bit of a Test* (1933), a cricket drama which coincided with the body-line controversy. Between 1926 and 1932 the Aldwych box office grossed £1.5 million in receipts, while the aggregate number of performances of the nine farces totalled nearly 2700. Travers used carefully constructed and elaborate plots and recognizable character types with names derived from Restoration comedy, played by a fixed troupe of actors including Tom Walls as a rake and Ralph Lynn as an Edwardian eccentric. The main source of the humour was in the disparity between the innocence of the protagonists and their unambiguously compromising situations. A film was made of *Rookery Nook* (it was one of the first British talking pictures) and of five of his Aldwych farces.

The heyday of the actor–managers, however, was over by the mid-1930s and the control of plays passed into the hands of syndicates. Travers continued to write plays, but with one exception he never repeated the success of the Aldwych farces. His later most successful pre-Second World War play was *Banana Ridge* (1938). The scene was laid in Malaya, and Travers himself played the part of a Chinese servant, whose colloquial Malay, which Travers remembered from his Malacca days, was most convincing. However, he was disappointed by the failure of his only serious play, *Chastity, my Brother* (1936), based on the life of St Paul, which suffered when the author's anonymous identity became known. During the Second World War he was commissioned in RAF intelligence, becoming a squadron leader and being attached to the Ministry of Information as air adviser on censorship. He wrote several more plays, and also some film scripts and short stories. Then, in 1951, his wife died of cancer. Grief-stricken, he lost most of his old zest for writing, and spent more and more time in travelling and staying with friends in Malaya.

Then the removal of the lord chamberlain's censorship of the theatre in 1968 encouraged Travers to write a comedy extolling the joys of sex with urbanity and sophistication; it was in some ways his greatest theatrical triumph. This was *The Bed before Yesterday*, which was produced at the Lyric in 1975 directed by Lindsay Anderson, with Joan Plowright in the lead as a middle-aged woman discovering sex for the first time. During this period he enjoyed something of a renaissance with several of his Aldwych plays revived, including *Plunder*, which had a sell-out run.

Travers also wrote two autobiographies, *Vale of Laughter* (1957) and *A-Sitting on a Gate* (1978), and a volume of cricket reminiscences, *94 Declared* (1981), published posthumously. Travers was vice-president of the Somerset County Cricket Club and belonged to the MCC. He was also an entertaining after-dinner speaker and in 1946 served as prime warden of the Fishmongers' Company, an office which gave full scope to his characteristic wit. In 1976, when he was in his ninetieth year, he was appointed CBE. In the same year he received the *Evening Standard* special award for services to the theatre. Ben Travers died at the Westminster Hospital, London, on 18 December 1980. Shortly before his death he told an interviewer that he would like his last words, engraved on his tombstone, to be 'This is where the real fun starts.'

Travers established the tone for British farce between the wars but has often been ignored by critics for whom the form is too populist. The Aldwych plays continue to attract audiences mainly as period pieces, but Travers should be regarded as an important figure post-Pinero and pre-Orton, and certainly one of the most skilled of British farceurs.

H. MONTGOMERY HYDE, rev. CLARE L. TAYLOR

Sources B. Travers, *Vale of laughter: an autobiography* (1957) • B. Travers, *A-sitting on a gate: autobiography* (1978) • L. Smith, *Modern British farce: a selective study of British farce from Pinero to the present day* (1989) • C. Innes, *Modern British drama, 1890–1990* (1992) • b. cert. • m. cert. • d. cert. • *The Times* (19 Dec 1980)
Archives BL, corresp. with League of Dramatists, Add. MS 63455 • BL, corresp. with Society of Authors, Add. MS 56835 • Ransom HRC, corresp. with John Lane
Likenesses H. Coster, photographs, 1936–8, NPG [*see illus.*] • T. Heinemann, photograph, 1979, NPG • E. I. Halliday, oils, Garr. Club
Wealth at death £56,043: probate, 21 May 1981, *CGPLA Eng. & Wales*

Travers, Sir Eaton Stannard (1782–1858), naval officer, was the third son of John Travers of Hethyfield Grange, co. Cork, Ireland (where he was born) and his wife, Mehetabel, the only daughter of John Colthurst of Dripsey Castle, co. Cork. He entered the navy in September 1798 on the *Juno* in the North Sea, where during the following year he was on boat service along the Netherlands coast. He was similarly employed in the West Indies during 1800–01. In March 1802 he was moved to the *Elephant*, and in October 1803 to the *Hercule*, the flagship of Sir John Thomas Duckworth. In November, while Duckworth remained at Jamaica, the *Hercule* was attached to the squadron under Commodore Loring blockading Cap Français. On 30 November, when the French ships agreed to surrender, Travers was with Lieutenant Nisbet Josiah Willoughby in the launch which took possession of the *Clorinde* after she had got on shore, and claimed to have been the chief agent in saving the ship by swimming to the shore and so making fast a hawser, by which the frigate was hauled off the rocks. In January and February 1804 he was again with Willoughby in the advance battery at the siege of Curaçao, and was afterwards publicly thanked by the admiral for his bravery. On 23 September 1804 Travers was promoted lieutenant and to command the schooner *Ballahou*, but in February 1805, on her being ordered to Newfoundland, he was appointed to the *Surveillante*, in which again he saw sharp boat service on the Spanish main.

In 1806 the *Hercule* returned to England, and in December Travers was appointed to the frigate *Alcmène* off the coast of France, until she was wrecked off the mouth of the Loire on 29 April 1809. He was afterwards in the *Impérieuse*, on the Walcheren expedition, and in 1810 in the Mediterranean, where for the next four years he was engaged in minor operations against the coasting vessels and coast batteries along the shores of France and Italy. He was repeatedly recommended by his captains and the commander-in-chief for his zeal, activity, and gallantry, but it was not until 15 June 1814 that he received the often-earned promotion to commander. He is said to have been upwards of 100 times engaged with the enemy; to have been in command at the blowing up and destruction of eight batteries and three Martello towers; and to have taken part in the capture of about sixty vessels, eighteen or twenty of them armed, and several cut out from under batteries.

The *Impérieuse* was paid off in September 1814. In April 1815 Travers married Anne Palmer, the eldest daughter of William Steward of Great Yarmouth; they had five sons and two daughters. He remained unemployed until the summer of 1828, when he was appointed to command the *Rose* (18 guns). From her he was advanced to post rank on 19 November 1829, mainly, it would seem, at the desire of the duke of Clarence. The latter, who knew of his long and active war service, later, as William IV, made him a KH (4 February 1834) and knighted him on 5 March 1834. Travers had no further employment afloat; he became rear-admiral on the retired list on 9 July 1855, and died at Great Yarmouth, Norfolk, on 4 March 1858. He was a brave and resourceful amphibious officer who achieved belated recognition.   J. K. LAUGHTON, rev. ANDREW LAMBERT

Sources D. Syrett and R. L. DiNardo, *The commissioned sea officers of the Royal Navy, 1660–1815*, rev. edn, Occasional Publications of the Navy RS, 1 (1994) • O'Byrne, *Naval biog. dict.* • *GM*, 3rd ser., 4 (1858), 441 • J. Marshall, *Royal naval biography*, 3/2 (1832) • W. James, *The naval history of Great Britain, from the declaration of war by France, in February 1793, to the accession of George IV, in January 1820*, [2nd edn], 6 vols. (1826) • P. Mackesy, *The war in the Mediterranean, 1803–1810* (1957) • *CGPLA Eng. & Wales* (1858)

Likenesses oils, *c*.1815, NMM

Wealth at death under £18,000: probate, 2 June 1858, *CGPLA Eng. & Wales*

Travers, James (1820–1884), army officer, third son of Major-General Sir Robert Travers KCMG CB of the 10th foot, was born in Cork on 6 October 1820. After Addiscombe College he was commissioned second lieutenant in the Bengal infantry on 11 June 1838. He arrived at Fort William, Calcutta, on 12 January 1839, and served with the 57th native infantry at Barrackpore until posted to the 2nd native infantry at Ferozepore on 12 April 1839.

Travers served with his regiment in the First Anglo-Afghan War in 1841 and 1842, was repeatedly in action, and was mentioned in dispatches. He was promoted first lieutenant on 7 June 1841. He served with Nott's army and returned to Ferozepore on 23 December 1842. For his war service he was recommended for a brevet majority on attaining the rank of captain.

Travers returned to regimental duty in March 1843, and was appointed adjutant of the Bhopal contingent on 15 March. He was promoted captain on 7 January 1846, and brevet major the following day. In the same month he joined the army of the Sutlej. He commanded a Masiri battalion of Gurkhas in Sir Harry Smith's division at the battle of Sobraon on 10 February 1846, and was mentioned in dispatches. On 24 March 1846 he was appointed second in command of the Bhopal contingent, on 13 February 1850 postmaster at Sehore, on 20 June 1854 he was promoted to be lieutenant-colonel, on 22 August 1855 was appointed officiating commandant, and on 15 February 1856 commandant, of the Bhopal contingent. In this year he commanded a force in the field against Sankar Sing, and received the thanks of government. On 6 December 1856 he was promoted colonel.

After the outbreak of the Indian mutiny in 1857 Travers moved in the middle of June from Bhopal to Indore, where Colonel Henry Marion Durand was the resident, and assumed command of the forces there. On 1 July some of Holkar's troops mutinied, and thirty-nine people were massacred. Travers, uncertain of his own men, nevertheless no sooner heard the guns than he formed up the picket where they could most advantageously charge the guns of the mutineers, and at once ordered them to advance. Gallantly leading them, he drove away the gunners, wounded Saadat Khan, the inciter of the mutiny, and for a few moments had the guns in his possession. But he found only five men had followed him, and, as they were completely exposed to a galling infantry fire, he was obliged to retire. The charge, however, by creating a favourable diversion, not only enabled Durand to place the residency guns in position and to make some hurried arrangements for defence, but allowed many persons to escape to the residency. Travers opened fire from the residency guns, but his cavalry were leaving him, and his efforts to induce his infantry to charge were unavailing. The women and children were therefore placed on gun-carriages, and, covered by the cavalry—which, though willing to follow Travers, would not fight for him—the little band moved out of the residency, and arrived at Sehore on 4 July. For his bravery in charging the guns on 1 July, which Durand brought to notice in his dispatches, Travers was awarded the Victoria Cross on 1 March 1861.

Travers returned to duty with his old regiment, the 2nd native infantry, in 1858. On 8 September 1860 he was appointed commandant of the Central India horse, on 25 October 1861 brigadier-general commanding Saugor district, on 23 July 1865 he was promoted major-general, and the same year received a good-service pension. He was given the command of the Meerut division on 5 August 1869, was promoted lieutenant-general on 5 February 1873, and was made a CB, military division, on 24 May 1873. Travers was permitted on 3 July 1874 to reside out of India. He was promoted to be general on 1 October 1877, and was placed on the unemployed supernumerary list on 1 July 1881. He published in 1876 *The Evacuation of Indore*, to refute statements in J. W. Kaye's *History of the Sepoy War*. He died at Pallanza, Lago Maggiore, Italy, on 1 April 1884, and was survived by his widow, Mary Isabella Travers.

R. H. VETCH, rev. M. G. M. JONES

Sources Boase, *Mod. Eng. biog.* • *Bengal Army List* • BL OIOC • dispatches • H. M. Vibart, *Addiscombe: its heroes and men of note* (1894) • J. W. Kaye, *History of the war in Afghanistan*, 2 vols. (1851) • J. W. Kaye and G. B. Malleson, *Kaye's and Malleson's History of the Indian mutiny of 1857–8*, 6 vols. (1888–9) • J. H. Stocqueler, *Memorials of Afghanistan: being state papers, official documents, dispatches, authentic narratives, etc.* (Calcutta, 1843) • *Professional Papers of the Corps of Royal Engineers*, occasional papers, 3 (1879), paper 6 • H. M. Durand, *The First Afghan War and its causes* (1879) • T. E. Bell, ed., *Last counsels of an unknown counsellor* (1877) • *The register of the Victoria cross*, 3rd edn (1997) • *CGPLA Eng. & Wales* (1884)

Archives NAM, department of archives, letters and papers

Likenesses photograph, repro. in *The register of the Victoria cross*

Wealth at death £5880 14s. 8d.: probate, 13 May 1884, *CGPLA Eng. & Wales*

Travers, John (1549/50–1620). *See under* Travers, Walter (1548?–1635).

Travers, John (1703?–1758), organist and composer, was the son of Joseph Travers, shoemaker, of Windsor. He probably sang in the choir of St George's Chapel, Windsor, and in 1719 was apprenticed to the organist and composer Maurice Greene. He also studied with John Christopher Pepusch, whose friend he became and to part of whose musical library he succeeded on Pepusch's death in 1752 (the music has not been traced since it was sold in 1766). On 24 November 1726 Travers was appointed organist of St Paul's, Covent Garden, and was later also organist of Fulham church. On 10 May 1737 he succeeded Jonathan Martin as one of the organists of the Chapel Royal. His pupils included William Jackson of Exeter. He wrote much church music, including *The Whole Book of Psalms* (*c*.1750). His anthem 'Ascribe unto the Lord' was much anthologized and remained in use throughout the nineteenth century. His secular compositions included *Eighteen Canzonets* which enjoyed much popularity in their day. Travers died in London in June 1758, when William Boyce succeeded to his post at the Chapel Royal.

R. H. NEWMARCH, *rev.* K. D. REYNOLDS

Sources C. Cudworth, 'Travers, John', *New Grove* • Brown & Stratton, *Brit. mus.*

Travers, Morris William (1872–1961), chemist, was born on 24 January 1872 in Kensington, London, the second of the four sons of William Travers (1838–1906), a well-known physician, and his wife, Anne Pocock (1854–1928), the daughter of a London solicitor. Travers was educated at boarding-schools, initially in Ramsgate and Woking. In 1884 he was sent to Blundell's School in Tiverton, Devon, where a good chemistry laboratory had been built two years earlier. There he developed his lifelong enthusiasm for science, leaving in 1889 to enter University College, London, to study chemistry under William Ramsay, with whom he was later to collaborate on the discovery and characterization of the noble gases.

Travers intended to specialize in organic chemistry, and discovered an important but overlooked method of making acetylene (*Proceedings of the Chemical Society*, 9, 1893) anticipating Moissan's electric furnace method by several months. After taking his BSc degree in November 1893, he went to France to study with Alban Haller at Nancy, but returned to London in October 1894 to become a demonstrator in Ramsay's laboratory, where argon had been discovered in August. In March 1895 Ramsay discovered terrestrial helium, and asked Travers to join him in determining its properties. From then until the summer of 1900 the two worked continuously to find and identify the other gaseous elements which the periodic law indicated should exist. Travers published a detailed description of the novel research techniques used in *The Experimental Study of Gases* (1901).

In the search for other inert gases, Ramsay and Travers prepared a large quantity of argon by removing oxygen and nitrogen from air. They liquefied the gas, applied the

Morris William Travers (1872–1961), by Walter Stoneman, 1917

technique of fractional distillation at liquid air temperature, and collected the least volatile fractions. Spectrum analysis indicated the presence of three new gases, which they called krypton, neon, and xenon, discovered during the summer of 1898. In order to complete their researches it was necessary to fully separate neon from helium, which they did at the temperature of liquid hydrogen. Travers constructed the required apparatus independently of James Dewar (1842–1923), who had been the first to liquefy hydrogen. This work on the noble gases is fully described in Travers's books *The Discovery of the Rare Gases* (1928) and *William Ramsay and University College, London, 1852–1952* (1952), and in his biography of Ramsay, *A Life of Sir William Ramsay, KCB, FRS* (1956).

In 1898 Travers was appointed assistant professor at University College, London. He left in 1904 to become professor of chemistry at University College, Bristol, where he was deeply involved in the movement which led to the granting of full university status in 1909. In 1909 he married Dorothy, the daughter of Robert James Gray, a London businessman with family links to Australia, and younger sister of Robert Whytlaw-Gray (1877–1958), with whom Travers had worked at University College. They had two children: Dorothy Mary, a linguist, and Robert Morris William, who became professor of educational psychology at the University of Utah. In 1906 Travers went to India to assist in the founding of the Indian Institute of Science at Bangalore, which opened in 1911 with him as its first director. He was unable to do much research because of administrative responsibilities, but engaged in a controversial study of boron, published in pamphlet form as *Some Compounds of Boron, Oxygen, and Hydrogen* (1916). Travers retired at the end of his term of appointment and returned to England in July 1914.

The outbreak of war turned Travers's attention to the needs of industry. He realized that the country would suffer shortages of scientific glassware, which had until then been imported from the continent, and therefore joined the firm of Baird and Tatlock, glass manufacturers. Under his direction glass furnaces were built in a Walthamstow factory and Duroglass Ltd began technical glass production in 1915. In the same year Travers assisted the War Office in developing a factory for the filling of hand grenades with poison liquid. In 1920, with F. W. Clark, he founded Travers and Clark Ltd, intending to construct glass furnaces and plants for the gasification of coal; the company closed in 1926.

Travers returned to Bristol in 1927 as honorary professor and developed a research group that studied the thermal decomposition of organic vapours, expanding and developing the methods of gas analysis that he had used years earlier. In 1937 he retired, but continued his research. At the start of the Second World War he became a consultant to the explosives section of the Ministry of Supply, where he remained until August 1945, advising on technical problems concerning the manufacture of explosives and propellants. He then joined the staff of the National Smelting Company Ltd, Avonmouth, until his retirement, in 1949, to Stroud, Gloucestershire, where he worked to complete his biography of Ramsay.

Travers was a tall, vigorous, and active man who had a special talent for dealing with technological problems. He was president of the Society of Glass Technology (1921–2), vice-president and Melchett medallist of the Institute of Fuel (1930), a member of the Fuel Research Board (1929–32), and president of the Faraday Society (1936–8). He was elected to the Royal Society in 1904, and was the senior FRS at the time of his death. His non-scientific interests lay in his family, music, and travel. He died in Coney Hill Hospital, Gloucester, on 25 August 1961. K. D. WATSON

Sources C. E. H. Bawn, *Memoirs FRS*, 9 (1963), 301–13 · *DSB* · D. McKie, 'Morris William Travers, 1872–1961', *Proceedings of the Chemical Society* (1964), 377–8 · *Nature*, 192 (1961), 1127–8 · *The Times* (29 Aug 1961), 12 · *DNB* · *CGPLA Eng. & Wales* (1961)
Archives UCL, corresp. and papers | Bodl. Oxf., corresp. with Frederick Soddy
Likenesses photographs, *c.*1895–1960, UCL; repro. in Ramsay MSS, UCL · W. Stoneman, photograph, 1917, NPG [*see illus.*] · W. Stoneman, photograph, 1946, RS · Loveday, photograph, RS; repro. in Bawn, *Memoirs FRS*
Wealth at death £3512 1s. 3d.: probate, 14 Nov 1961, *CGPLA Eng. & Wales*

Travers, P. L. [Pamela Lyndon]. *See* Goff, Helen Lyndon (1899–1996).

Travers, Rebecca (*c.*1609–1688), Quaker preacher and writer, was the daughter of a Baptist. She married William Travers, a tobacconist at the Three Feathers, Watling Street, London, who died in 1664. She had been 'a reader of the Scriptures from a child of six' (Sewel, 2.329). Attending the Baptist church in Broad Street, where James Nayler, the Quaker leader, was holding a dispute, she was astonished to see 'the Countryman [who] stood up on a Form over against the Baptists and they were so far from getting victory that she could hear his words smote them' (Travers, 18). She was converted to the Quakers by Nayler after a dinner party where she was moved by his attack on 'forbidden knowledge', and she later claimed to renounce all intellectual pretensions. After Nayler's punishment and humiliation she dressed his wounds, and at his release from prison in 1659 he stayed at her house; she wrote a 'certificate' on his behalf to parliament.

Travers became a leading woman preacher in London, sometimes preaching in the streets and suffering several imprisonments—often for defending Quaker prisoners in her role as prison visitor in London and Ipswich. She acted both as host and minister at the 'six weeks meetings' held at her own house. The leader of the Quakers' women's meeting in London, she issued *A Woman's Paper for Order* to stop gossip and backbiting. She attended at the 'second day morning meeting', the editorial board for Quaker publications. The conducting of Quaker marriages and care for poor Friends were also part of her duties. In her 'unsuitable great house' Travers hosted visiting preachers such as George Whitehead, the Quaker leader, in 1664, and also George Fox: 'I was never better pleased with my house then when hee was in it' (Swarthmore MSS, 1.395).

Travers was the author of ten separate pamphlets as well as some postscripts and testimonies attached to others' writings: 'One Rebecca Trewish in Watling streit is a wryter of books and gets them prented by Widow Dover' (*CSP dom.*, *1664–5*, 148). Adept equally at polemics and theology, she wrote for those both within and outside Quaker society. She directed her quill especially against apostate brethren; in *The Harlot's Vail Rent* (1669) she accused Elizabeth Atkinson of betrayal for inverting Quaker language to attack her former colleagues. Others were attacked for interfering with Friends or denying their principles (*For those that … Worship at … John Evangelist*, 1659). In *A Testimony Concerning the Life and Light of Jesus* (1663) she expounded the Quaker concern for 'inner' life and preached renunciation of earthly power and conflict. Often she rebutted other pamphleteers, but she also took on the government for enforcing the Conformity Act (*This is for All … that Resist the Spirit*, 1664). Later in life she wrote 'testimonies' for Quakers such as William Bayly (1676), Susanne Whitrow (1677), Alice Curwen (1680), and Anne Whitehead (1686).

Travers tried to reconcile the factions that developed between the followers of Fox and John Perrot, an antinomian, who denied all forms of worship. Her own sister Mary Booth became an adherent of Perrot. Travers wrote using feminine imagery: 'My dear Brethren and Sisters … all drawing from the one Breast the milk of the Word … for the Coat of the Lord is seamless' (*Testimony*, 10). Later she assured Fox that she wished only for unity among the Quakers. She wrote to him to clear herself of having worked to 'strengthen that Spirit of Gainsaying' (Travers to Fox, 17 Aug 1676, Gibson MS 8ii.335/119).

Throughout, Travers believed in the primacy of faith over institutions, but she worked within those institutions for unity among Friends. Accused of self-aggrandizement—'being a Great Mother and Governess'—she presented herself instead as 'a servant to this people' (Mack, 320) and defended Fox's party to maintain unity in the face of persecution.

Travers died, aged about seventy-nine, on 15 June 1688 in London. She was survived by a son, Matthew, and at least one daughter. Her funeral sermon was preached by William Penn in 1688.   LOTTE MULLIGAN

Sources 'Dictionary of Quaker biography', RS Friends, Lond. [card index] · P. Mack, *Visionary women: ecstatic prophecy in seventeenth-century England* (1992) · J. Besse, *A collection of the sufferings of the people called Quakers*, 2 vols. (1753) · *A brief relation of the persecutions and cruelties that have been acted upon the people called Quakers in and about the city of London* (1662) · M. R. Brailsford, *Quaker women, 1650–1690* (1915) · R. Foxton, 'Hear the word of the Lord': a critical and bibliographical study of Quaker women's writings, 1650–1700 (1994) · H. Smith and S. Cardinale, eds., *Women and literature of the seventeenth century: an annotated bibliography based on Wing's 'Short-title catalogue'* (1990) · RS Friends, Lond., Gibson papers · RS Friends, Lond., Swarthmore papers · B. Y. Kunze, *Margaret Fell and the rise of Quakerism* (1994) · W. C. Braithwaite, *The beginnings of Quakerism* (1912) · *CSP dom.*, 1664–5 · W. Sewel, *The history of … the Christian people called Quakers*, 2 vols. (1795) · A. R. Barclay, ed., *Letters, &c. of early Friends* (1841) · R. Travers, *For those that meet to worship at the Steeple-House, called John Evangelist in London* (1659)

Travers, Walter (1548?–1635), religious activist and college head, was born in Nottingham, the eldest child of Walter, a goldsmith, and his wife, Anne, who also had three younger sons and a daughter. His father's will suggests that he was both well off, and (assuming that he wrote the will himself) a committed protestant. The oldest of Walter's brothers, Robert, became a fellow of Trinity College, Cambridge, published theological works, and died in Geneva in 1575; his two youngest brothers, John [see below] and Humfrey, both became ministers in the Church of England. Like Robert, Walter was educated at Cambridge, matriculating as a member of Christ's College in 1560, but soon transferring to Trinity, where he was chosen, along with Thomas Cartwright, who was a fellow, to present a formal address to Queen Elizabeth on her famous visit to the university in 1564. Travers graduated BA in 1565–6, was elected a junior fellow of Trinity in 1567, proceeded MA on 25 March 1569, and in the same year was made a senior fellow.

Geneva, Antwerp, and ecclesiastical discipline At this stage Travers seemed set for further academic honours, ordination, and a clerical career. But in 1570 he gave up his fellowship and left England for Geneva, driven out because of his puritan views. John Whitgift, appointed master of Trinity in 1567 to restore order there, commented that he had forced Travers to leave Cambridge by repeated disciplinary procedures, 'other wise he should have been expelled for his want of conformity towards the house and for his pertinacy' (Strype, 3.507).

As with John Knox and countless other religious immigrants, Geneva provided Travers with both a refuge and a model for the ideal Christian polity. Joined there by his brother Robert and by Thomas Cartwright, who shared their puritan views, he became a friend of Theodore Beza, Calvin's successor as leader of the Genevan reformation. And it was in Geneva that he wrote his major work, *Ecclesiasticae disciplinae et Anglicanae ecclesiae ab illa aberrationis, plena e verbo Dei, et dilucida explicatio*. In 1574 this was published anonymously and under a false imprint by Cartwright, who was then at Heidelberg, with a preface by him endorsing its contents. An English translation was published in the same year, also at Heidelberg. The book was closely based on Calvin's system of ecclesiastical government: for both Calvin and Travers, the church of the New Testament was normative; the duty of the theologian was merely to identify its structure and apply it to contemporary circumstances. It was in this last respect that Travers's originality lay, for he subtly adapted Calvin's biblical model to an English context. In order to undermine the diocesan episcopate of the English church, Travers started off with an examination of the role of bishops in the New Testament, showing that they were not part of a separate hierarchy with authority over other clergy, but merely ministers of local congregations. He also differed from Calvin in identifying elders as a type of deacon, rather than a separate kind of minister. Significantly, in view of the later travails of the presbyterians under Elizabeth, Travers did not deal with the crucial issue of the relationship between a presbyterian church and a hostile state.

After the publication of his account of ecclesiastical discipline Travers tested the waters in England again in 1576, returning to have his degree of MA incorporated in Oxford University. But preferment in England was not forthcoming and he had to follow the familiar puritan path to the Netherlands, where in April 1578 he secured a position as chaplain to the English Merchant Adventurers at Antwerp. It was here that he was ordained, not episcopally but according to the presbyterian fashion of the Dutch Calvinist church, by the laying on of hands by twelve ministers. The church in which he served had a wholly presbyterian structure and discipline, and Travers did not use the Book of Common Prayer, an omission challenged by the English governor of the Merchant Adventurers, Nicholas Loddington. The response, a severe reprimand for the governor by Sir Francis Walsingham and a further rebuke from William Davison, the English ambassador to the Netherlands, demonstrated what was to become a notable feature of Travers's career—his close ties to influential courtiers of a Calvinist inclination.

Travers and the English presbyterian movement In July 1580 Travers again returned to England, to be succeeded in his post in Antwerp by Cartwright. He turned down the offer of a professorship in St Andrews from the Scottish presbyterian leader (and fellow Genevan exile) Andrew Melville, and became instead chaplain to Elizabeth's principal minister, Lord Burghley, and tutor to his son, Robert Cecil, later earl of Salisbury. This marked the beginning of a highly important relationship for Travers, as Burghley, always sympathetic to those of a more radical religious bent than himself, repeatedly used his influence to try to protect Travers. The question, of course, was how could an avowedly presbyterian minister find a niche in the episcopal Church of England? The answer was provided by Burghley who steered Travers towards the Temple Church, that curious foundation of the knights templar which served the spiritual needs of the barristers and students of the Inner and Middle Temples in London. In 1581 Travers secured the position of deputy to the frail master, Richard Alvey. Alvey and Travers got on well, sharing as they did similarly precise religious views, and Travers felt able to introduce some audacious changes, including not kneeling (or even sitting) but ambulatory communion, and an attempt to turn collectors and sidesmen into deacons and elders after the manner of Geneva. The benchers, however, proved far from enthusiastic about the innovations, and Travers had to moderate his ambitions. In 1583 he took the familiar path of puritan scholars anxious to ingratiate themselves with the authorities, by taking up anti-Catholic polemic, publishing *An Answere to a Supplicatorie Epistle*, a detailed attack upon a recent piece of Roman Catholic propaganda, replete with extensive scriptural references to prove that the Church of Rome was a false and heretical church.

The appointment of Whitgift as archbishop of Canterbury in 1583 marked a decisive turning point for English puritans in general and Travers in particular. Determined to weed out nonconformists, Whitgift promulgated a set of fifteen articles with which he confronted the godly, offering them an impossible choice between subscription and suspension. The puritans used their influence at court to secure a two-day debate with Whitgift on the issue in December 1584, and Travers was selected as one of their two spokesmen. Unsurprisingly it achieved nothing. The archbishop's continuing dislike of Travers and his opinions was underlined in 1584, when on the death of Alvey Whitgift wrote to the queen to ensure that Burghley failed in his efforts to secure the succession for Travers:

> Travers hath been and is one of the chief and principal authors of dissension in this church, a contemner of the Book of Prayers, and of other orders by authority established; an earnest seeker of innovation; and either in no degree of the ministry at all, or else ordered beyond the seas … Whose placing in that room … would greatly animate the rest of that faction, and do very much harm in sundry respects. (Knox, 67)

The choice of Richard Hooker as master of the Temple in 1585 paved the way for a set-piece confrontation between the two wings of the English Reformation. In Fuller's much quoted words, 'the pulpit spake pure Canterbury in the morning and Geneva in the afternoon' (Fuller, *Worthies*, 1.264), although Richard Bauckham has argued that the main issue at stake, the status of the Church of Rome, did not in fact neatly fit into any simplistic distinction between puritanism and what would become Anglicanism. Finally in March 1586 Whitgift intervened, banning Travers from preaching. When Travers again sought to enlist Burghley's support, Whitgift reiterated his complaint that Travers's lack of episcopal ordination made him unfit for preferment in the Church of England. Travers, for his part, determinedly fought to regain his right to preach, continuing to live in the Temple until late 1586, and publishing in that year a self-justifying account of his dispute with Hooker, *A Supplication Made to the Council*.

The Book of Discipline Disappointed in their efforts to move the queen, Travers and his fellow puritan leaders decided in 1584–5 to change tactics and turned to direct action, seeking to establish a presbyterian structure within the Church of England as a kind of Trojan horse. It was a dangerous policy: not only did it inevitably arouse the deep hostility of Elizabeth, it also required the puritans to reach a consensus about a major issue on which they had so far proved unable to agree—the precise form that presbyterian church discipline and government should take in England. It was to Travers that they turned to produce an agreed formula. It took a considerable time, but finally in 1587 there appeared 'Disciplina ecclesiae Dei verbo descripta', generally known as the Book of Discipline. A relatively short constitution for an English presbyterian church, this was sent out to all the classes—assemblies of ministers—in England.

Written or maybe just drafted by Travers, the book was divided into two parts, the first of which engaged in the familiar puritan task of ransacking the Bible and outlining all the references it contained to church polity. The second and longer section set down more detailed rules for liturgy, worship, and church organization, based upon the models of the Scottish and mainland European presbyterian churches. The Book of Discipline provided an alternative form of church government for England, with local classes choosing representatives for provincial synods, which would in turn select the men who would constitute the national synod. Travers published another self-explanatory title in 1588, a *Defence of the Ecclesiastical Discipline*. In March 1588, after the death of John Field, the organizing genius of the presbyterian movement, Travers took over as corresponding secretary of the presbyterians in London. It was a difficult moment, for the authorities, led by Whitgift, were now determined to take action against the presbyterians, who had been weakened by the death in September of that crucial puritan patron the earl of Leicester. Finally in 1590 the presbyterian ringleaders were brought successively before the high commission and the Star Chamber and charged with seditiously attempting to undermine the queen's supreme authority in the church. Though held and questioned closely during 1591, the government released the presbyterian leaders after 1592, confident now that it had broken the presbyterian movement.

Provost of Trinity College, Dublin It is mysterious that Travers was never arrested and imprisoned. He is known to have been in London in 1590, and Whitgift was certainly aware of his leading role in the movement, yet he remained at large. Clearly, however, he could not remain long in London. As the presbyterian leaders scattered to the remote corners of the land following their release, Travers again turned to Burghley for one last favour, and was again obliged. Burghley may have been powerless to protect the presbyterians from the Star Chamber in London, but he was still highly influential in Ireland, and he found sanctuary there for Travers in the newly founded university of Trinity College, Dublin. Burghley had been instrumental in establishing the college, and his client, Archbishop Adam Loftus of Dublin, had been its first, albeit temporary, provost. He was succeeded on 5 June 1594 by Travers.

Travers, who had strong views on the religious role of universities, surrounded himself in Trinity by such like-minded puritans as Humphrey Fen, and decisively shaped the new university's theology—and probably the theological education of its most notable early graduate, James Ussher—in a Calvinist way. It would be wrong, though, to see Travers as constructing another presbyterian Trojan horse in Dublin: in an address to the new provost Loftus had publicly warned him against introducing dangerous dissensions into the Irish church. Apart from teaching, much of Travers's time was taken up with securing sufficient money to ensure Trinity's survival, a task made especially difficult by the intensification of the Nine Years' War (1594–1603). In October 1598, with the situation in both the college and the country looking increasingly bleak, he gave up the provostship and departed for England.

Retirement Travers must have had hopes of further preferment, since he secured a letter of recommendation from the Dublin authorities praising his efforts as provost and pointedly emphasizing that he had avoided religious contention during his time in Dublin and was worthy of being allowed to resume his ministry in England. But it was not to be. Though he lived on into the reign of Charles I, Travers never gained another post. Instead he passed the remainder of his life in retirement, appearing occasionally in puritan circles, as in 1604 when his name was mentioned as a possible representative at the Hampton Court conference, or in 1610 when he was noted as preaching without a licence at All Saints' Church, Hereford. His last public statement was his book *Vindiciae ecclesiae Anglicanae*, which appeared in 1630 and sought to defend the protestant church of England against the Roman Catholic threat. Travers died in 1635, some time between making his will on 14 January and its being proved ten days later. In it he distributed his assets in cash (amounting to £351) among his nieces and nephews, along with bequests to support students at Trinity College, Dublin, and Emmanuel College, Cambridge, and to pay for a preacher at Sion College, London.

Among the beneficiaries of Walter Travers's will were the sons of his younger brother **John Travers** (1549/50–1620). John became a demy at Magdalen College, Oxford, in 1567, aged seventeen, and was a fellow of the college from 1569 to 1585. He graduated BA there on 23 October 1570 and proceeded MA on 19 May 1574. Like his elder brother he took orders, though apparently in a more orthodox manner, and also like him was frequently at odds with the church establishment. In 1575 he was involved in disputes over the election of a new college

president, while in 1578 he was summoned before the high commission. He became friendly with the second earl of Bedford, being granted six months' leave of absence from Magdalen in April 1576 in order to stay with the earl. Bedford was a pillar of the godly in the southwest, and it was doubtless through his influence that Travers became active in the diocese of Exeter. In 1585 he was suspended for proclaiming unauthorized fasts there, and in 1600 he was among the ministers denounced by Bishop Cotton for their puritan tendencies. Cotton's complaint implies that Travers had no benefice; in 1601, however, he was vicar of Landrake in Cornwall. Four years later he was a leading figure in the resistance to Archbishop Bancroft's drive for conformity. John Travers died in 1620 as rector of Farringdon in Devon. He had married Alice, sister of Richard Hooker, and they had four sons, all of whom took orders.

Although Walter Travers exerted a considerable influence on the development of English presbyterianism, decisively tying the movement to the strict position that their Calvinist framework was the sole biblical church polity, and seeking to Anglicize the presbyterian system of church government, he signally failed in his major aim—to create an established presbyterian church in England. Indeed, his main achievement was probably, and ironically, his role as the irritant that may have stimulated Hooker to produce one of the few great works of English theology, the *Treatise on the Laws of Ecclesiastical Polity*.

ALAN FORD

Sources J. Strype, *The life and acts of John Whitgift*, new edn, 3 vols. (1822) · Fuller, *Worthies* (1840) · P. Collinson, *The Elizabethan puritan movement* (1967) · S. J. Knox, *Walter Travers paragon of Elizabethan puritanism* (1962) · A. F. S. Pearson, *Thomas Cartwright and Elizabethan puritanism, 1535–1603* (1925) · R. Bauckham, 'Hooker, Travers and the Church of Rome in the 1580s', *Journal of Ecclesiastical History*, 29 (1978), 37–50 · Foster, *Alum. Oxon.* · J. R. Bloxam, *A register of the presidents, fellows … of Saint Mary Magdalen College*, 8 vols. (1853–85), vol. 4, p. 170 · Venn, *Alum. Cant.*
Archives TCD, *Justification of the religion now professed in England* (1630) has occasional notes in Travers's hand, MS 327 · TCD, theological commonplace book, MS 324
Wealth at death £351: will, Knox, *Walter Travers*

Travers, William Inglis Lindon [Bill] (1922–1994), actor and conservationist, was born on 3 January 1922 at 16 Grosvenor Road, Newcastle upon Tyne, the son of William Halton Lindon Travers, an actor and theatre manager, and his wife, Florence Wheatley. His older sister was the actress Linden Travers (1913–2001). Aged only seventeen he joined the army and served throughout the Second World War, chiefly in the Far East. Demobbed in 1946 he joined a touring repertory company, making his London début in *Cage me a Peacock* (1949). Subsequent stage roles included *The Damask Cheek* and the musical *Rainbow Square*. He made his film début with a bit part in *Conspirator* (1949). On 2 December 1950 he married actress Patricia Mary Raine (b. 1927/8), daughter of Thomas Foster Raine, actor. They had a daughter. Travers appeared in the film *The Wooden Horse* (1950), and numerous small parts and supporting roles followed, including *The Browning Version* (1951) as the teacher keen on cricket, *The Square Ring* (1953),

Romeo and Juliet (1954) as Benvolio, and *Footsteps in the Fog* (1955). About to join the Windsor Repertory Company, he was cast by Frank Launder and Sidney Gilliat in the lead role in *Geordie* (1955). He played a puny highlander who, after building up his body via a correspondence course, threw the hammer for Britain at the Melbourne Olympic games. This 'charmingly fresh' comedy was a great success, in both Britain and the USA. Ruggedly handsome, with a powerful frame, stardom was predicted for Travers, and he made two films for MGM British. Director George Cukor cast him as the Anglo-Indian railway superintendent in *Bhowani Junction* (1956) from John Masters's novel; Masters had been Travers's brigade major when fighting with the Chindits. He also played Robert Browning in *The Barretts of Wimpole Street* (1957), a tame interpretation of the love story. Henrietta Barrett was played by Virginia McKenna (*b.* 1931), daughter of Terence Morrell McKenna, auctioneer. She divorced her husband, actor Denholm Elliott, and Travers divorced his wife, allowing them to marry on 19 September 1957. They had three sons and a daughter.

Travers and McKenna appeared together in the wonderful *The Smallest Show on Earth* (1957) as a couple who inherit a fleapit cinema and meet competition from the nearby supercinema. Travers starred in MGM's *The Seventh Sin* (1957), a poor remake of Greta Garbo's *The Painted Veil* from Somerset Maugham's novel, then he and McKenna reunited for Rank's overheated melodrama *Passionate Summer* (1958). A number of indifferent films followed, punctuated by another highland film, *The Bridal Path* (1959), which did not repeat the success of *Geordie*, and, on television, *Lorna Doone* (1963) as John Ridd. Travers had joined the Royal Shakespeare Company in 1962 and appeared in Peter Hall's production of *A Midsummer Night's Dream*, and made his Broadway début in the short-running army comedy *A Cook for Mr General*.

In 1966 came the film *Born Free*, which transformed both the careers and lives of Travers and his wife. The film was as successful as the book had been, recounting the exploits of Kenyan gamewarden George Adamson and his wife Joy, who hand-reared abandoned lion cubs, returning them to the wild. In its wake the couple became committed conservationists, although Travers first accepted a Hollywood offer to play a cavalry lieutenant in *Duel at Diablo* (1966) opposite James Garner and Sidney Poitier. He then directed a documentary, *The Lions are Free* (1967), which told what happened to some of the lions of the original film. Subsequently he appeared in further 'animal films', *Ring of Bright Water*, which highlighted the plight of otters and which he also co-wrote, and *An Elephant called Slowly*, which he also co-wrote and co-produced (both 1969). Other later acting appearances included *A Midsummer Night's Dream* (1968) on television, Captain Hook in *Peter Pan* (1969) on stage in London, and the film *The Belstone Fox* (1973). He was involved in producing further animal documentaries such as *The Wild Dogs of Africa* (1973), *Baboons of Gombe* (1974), *The Hyena Story* (1975), and *The Lion at World's End* (1976), which he also directed. He co-produced a television documentary, *The Queen's Gardens*

(1976), on the fauna of the palace grounds. However, Travers virtually gave up films after Pole-Pole (Swahili for slowly), the elephant used in the 1969 film, died from neglect in captivity in 1983.

In 1990 Travers and McKenna established the animal charity the Born Free Foundation, which came to include several animal rights organizations such as the pressure group Zoo Check (founded in 1984), which campaigned ultimately to have all zoos and safari parks abolished, and Elefriends (1989). His passionate and energetic views on animal welfare often brought Travers into conflict with the owners and keepers of wild animals. In 1993 he produced a video, *The Zoochotic Report*, about animals which had gone mad in captivity. And in the year of his death he had lobbied for the killer whale used in the film *Free Willy* (1993) to be returned to the wild. In later years he set up a video distribution company which made available a number of the film successes of both himself and his wife. Travers died of coronary thrombosis on 29 March 1994 at his home, Gamekeeper's Cottage, Anstie Lane, South Holmwood, near Dorking, Surrey. His wife and children survived him.   ROBERT SHARP

Sources *The Times* (1 April 1994), 23 · *The Independent* (1 April 1994), 26 · *Daily Telegraph* (1 April 1994) · *The Guardian* (1 April 1994), 19; section 2, p. 11 · www.uk.imdb.com, 29 Sept 2001

Traversagni, Lorenzo Guglielmo [Laurentius Guilelmus Traversanus Savonensis, Laurence William of Savona] (*c.*1425–1503), Franciscan friar and humanist scholar, was one of three Italian brothers, all authors. Evidence for the exact date of his birth in Savona is confusing; *c.*1425 is most probable. His father, Giacomo Traversagni, was of noble Ligurian stock. Professed at Savona about 1445, Lorenzo Guglielmo attended the University of Padua in 1446 under Gaetano da Thiene and Francesco della Rovere, the future Sixtus IV, and was later DTh. He went on to the University of Bologna, where in 1448–9 he again studied with della Rovere, and then to the university in Vienna, where he was a student from 1450 and DTh in 1457, and where he remained until 1459. A chair for him in *studia humanitatis* was projected in Vienna. He composed there five dialogues on whether the dead should be mourned (1453) and a letter-writing manual, *Modus conficiendi epistolas*, which had wide circulation in manuscript and print north of the Alps during the fifteenth century.

At the beginning of the next decade Traversagni was in Avignon (25 March 1460) and Toulouse, where he read canon law and gave courses in moral philosophy and rhetoric at the university, completing his dialogues *Recta semita ad mentem sanum* ('The right way to a sound mind') in August 1460, and *Directorium mentis ad Deum* ('The pointer of the mind to God') in 1462. He had returned to Liguria by January 1468 when, from Noli near Savona, he dedicated *Libellus de varia fortuna Antiochi* to the marquess of Noli and Finale.

Why, how, and exactly when Traversagni went to England is not known. At Cambridge in 1476 he lectured on Aristotle's *Nicomachean Ethics* in the new translation by Leonardo Bruni (printed at Oxford in 1479), and on the pseudo-Ciceronian *Ad Herennium*, the Italian humanists' chief rhetorical handbook. From the London Greyfriars in 1477 he wrote the preface to a *Triumphus pudicitiae BVM* ('Triumph of the Chastity of the Virgin'). His *Rhetorica nova, sive, Margarita eloquentie castigate ad eloquendum divina accommodata* ('The new rhetoric, or, The pearl of purified eloquence, adapted to the expression of matters divine') was modelled on the *Ad Herennium* and Cicero's *De inventione* but aimed at reconciling pagan Latin rhetoric with the language of scripture and the liturgy. It was printed only in England, twice by Caxton *c*.1478 and once by the St Albans Printer in 1480. Caxton's copy-text, the only extant manuscript, has a colophon noting that the work was completed at Cambridge on 26 July 1478, under the protection of Edward IV. In October 1478 Traversagni preached a pair of university sermons in Cambridge and in the same year lectured at Cambridge on St Augustine's *City of God*, styling himself professor of the sacred page. During 1480 he lived in the Collège de Narbonne in Paris, lecturing on his *Margarita eloquentie* at the university. In Paris on 24 January he completed his *Epitoma* of that work, which survives in a single manuscript and a single copy of Caxton's unique printing of about 1480; and in February the second book of his *Dialogi de vita eterna*, the third being finished in July in London. In 1482 he was again teaching in Cambridge; in November, in Bruges, he finished transcribing the Hermetic *Pimander* in Latin. During 1482 and perhaps in early 1483 he was in London, where he dedicated to Edward IV (who died on 9 April of that year) his *Triumphus justitiae Jesu Christi*. In the London Greyfriars he made the copy now at Lambeth of his *Triumphus amoris Jesu Christi*. Though its dedicatory preface, dated 18 April 1485, extols both William Waynflete (*d.* 1486) and Magdalen College, as well as sacred studies, Traversagni is not recorded as spending time in Oxford.

By 1487 Traversagni was back in the Franciscan convent in Savona, where he spent the rest of his life. He attempted to found a faculty of rhetoric, continuing to preach, to write further sacred *triumphi*, to revise his earlier works, and to copy those of others, his brothers included. In mid-September 1503 he was planning a collected edition of his writings, but died later that year, his moral and religious works unprinted. J. B. TRAPP

Sources Emden, *Cam.*, 593–4 · J. Ruysschaert, 'Lorenzo Guglielmo Traversagni de Savone (1425–1503): un humaniste franciscain oublié', *Archivum Franciscanum Historicum*, 46 (1953), 195–210 · J. Ruysschaert, 'Les manuscrits autographes des oeuvres de Lorenzo Guglielmo Traversagni imprimés chez Caxton', *Bulletin of the John Rylands University Library*, 36 (1953–4), 191–7 · P. O. Kristeller, *Iter Italicum*, 7 vols. (1963–97) [see indices] · L. G. Traversagni, *Margarita eloquentiae castigatae*, ed. G. Farris (1978) · L. G. Traversagni, 'The *Epitoma Margarite castigate eloquentie* of Laurentius Guilielmus Traversanus de Saona', ed. R. H. Martin, *Proc. Leeds Philos. and Lit. Soc., Lit. and Hist. Sect.*, 20, 2 (1986), 131–269 · G. Farris, *Umanesimo e religione in Lorenzo Guglielmo Traversagni, 1425–1505* (Milan, 1972) · M. R. James and C. Jenkins, *Descriptive catalogue of the MSS in the library of Lambeth Palace*, 5 pts in 1 (1930–32), pp. 624–5, no. 450 · R. Weiss, *Humanism in England during the fifteenth century*, 3rd edn (1967), 162–3, 175, 199 · L. G. Traversagni, *De varia fortuna Antiochi*, ed. G. Farris (1972)
Archives Biblioteca Apostolica Vaticana, Vatican City, MSS Vat. lat. 11441, 11607–11608 · Biblioteca Pubblica, Savona, MSS IX. B. 2. 14–15, 17

Travis, Sir Edward Wilfrid Harry (1888–1956), naval officer and cryptographer, was born on 24 September 1888 at 7 Blendon Terrace, Plumstead Common, Kent, the son of Harry Travis (1858–1927), civil engineer, and his wife, Emmeline Hamlyn. He had a younger sister.

Known as Wilfrid to his family and Jumbo to his friends, Travis went to school in Blackheath and joined the Royal Navy in 1906. Commissioned in 1909, on the first day of the First World War in 1914 he was posted to the personal staff of the commander-in-chief, Admiral J. R. Jellicoe, on the flagship HMS *Iron Duke*. Travis's report, countersigned by Jellicoe, refers to his 'zeal and much ability'. His posting to cipher security is said to have been because he demonstrated the vulnerability of Jellicoe's ciphers by breaking them himself.

From 1916 to 1918 Travis worked on royal naval ciphers in the signal division of the naval staff. This work must have included important liaison with France and Italy since in March 1919 he was appointed both chevalier of the Légion d'honneur by the French and an officer of the order of the Crown of Italy by the Italians.

Travis's work continued after the war in the Government Code and Cypher School (GCCS) under the Secret Intelligence Service (SIS) and by 1925 he was deputy to the head of GCCS, A. G. Denniston, with Denniston supervising cipher-breaking and Travis cipher security. Travis was made CBE in 1936.

On the outbreak of World War Two Travis moved with GCCS to Bletchley Park and began to have responsibilities for the cipher-breaking and interception side as well as communications security. In March 1941 he was appointed chairman of a special inter-services Enigma subcommittee. This was to pursue the proposals put forward by Gordon Welchman and Alan Turing, the leading Enigma cryptanalysts, who proposed that GCCS should plan to break on a big scale and currently the German Enigma machine cipher keys, used for high-level German services communications. This would require the development and production of the breaking machines ('bombes') being devised by Welchman, Turing, the Hollerith Company, and others; the recruitment and training of many additional radio operators to intercept the relevant German service radio networks; and the recruitment of a variety of young people who would be capable of breaking the ciphers, deciphering the messages, and understanding, translating, and reporting the resulting texts.

This was the planning which Travis successfully put in train and in February 1942 Menzies, the new chief of the SIS, made Travis effectively head of Bletchley Park. From 1942 to 1945 Bletchley grew to contain at least 9000 civilians and service people. In addition Bletchley directed the work of a large number of service and civilian-manned interception stations in Britain and abroad which were intercepting enemy radio transmissions. GCCS's formal responsibility was only for cipher-breaking, but the authority to direct the work of the interception stations and the services units at Bletchley Park was a prerequisite for the great cipher-breaking and intelligence successes that Bletchley achieved. That this authority was granted

Sir Edward Wilfrid Harry Travis (1888–1956), by Walter Stoneman, 1946

and substantial with it. The brown ink which he used for his directorial minutes was known to some as 'the director's blood'.

Travis's determination to maintain an attractive garden at his home in Pirbright, Surrey, was shown by the fact that when he bought the house he recruited a local man as gardener and immediately arranged for him to go for three months' training in Kew Gardens. He was an excellent bridge player, playing with Iain McLeod, the politician and a bridge international. Travis died of kidney failure and cancer of the bladder on 18 April 1956 at St Thomas's Hospital, London, and was cremated at Woking on 23 April.   D. R. NICOLL

Sources F. H. Hinsley and others, *British intelligence in the Second World War*, 3/1 (1984), 461 · R. Lewin, *ULTRA goes to war: the secret story* (1978), 17, 47, 54, 136–7 · personal knowledge (2004) · private information (2004) · M. Smith, *Station X: the codebreakers of Bletchley Park* (1998) · b. cert. · m. cert. · d. cert. · WWW · CGPLA Eng. & Wales (1956)

Archives NRA, priv. coll., MSS

Likenesses photograph, *c.*1945, priv. coll. · W. Stoneman, photograph, 1946, NPG [*see illus.*]

Wealth at death £8045 14s. 11d.: probate, 10 July 1956, CGPLA Eng. & Wales

Travis, George (*bap.* 1741, *d.* 1797), Church of England clergyman, was baptized on 13 December 1741 at Shaw, Lancashire, the only son of John Travis of Heyside and his wife, Hannah. He was educated by his uncle Benjamin Travis, incumbent of Royton, Lancashire. He entered Manchester grammar school in January 1756 and St John's College, Cambridge, as a sizar, on 17 April 1761, where he matriculated that Michaelmas. He was also admitted at the Middle Temple on 4 May 1761. Having graduated BA in 1765 (fifth senior optime and chancellor's classical medallist) he was ordained deacon on 3 March of that year and priest on 22 December; he commenced MA in 1768. He married, on 29 July 1766 at Manchester collegiate church, Ann Stringfellow, daughter and coheir of James Stringfellow of Whitfield, Derbyshire; they had no children.

Travis's preferments were all in Cheshire: he was vicar of Eastham (1766–97), perpetual curate of Bromborough (1767–97), and rector of Handley (1787–97). Having spent some £2000 on legal actions to secure and augment the emoluments of Eastham and Bromborough he was not surprisingly 'familiarly acquainted with the law of tithes' (*GM*, 433). He was appointed prebendary of Chester on 9 February 1783 and archdeacon on 27 September 1786. The title-page of his *Letters to Edward Gibbon, Esq.* (1784) describes him also as chaplain to the dowager viscountess—and *ci-devant* socialite—Etheldreda Townshend. The second edition (1785) omits this detail.

Travis's *Letters*, three of which the *Gentleman's Magazine* first published in 1782, attacked Gibbon for discrediting the 'three heavenly witnesses' (1 John 5: 7). This disputed verse, commonly accepted as a matter of Christian faith, was indefensible on manuscript evidence, as Travis, if so disposed, could have learned from Wettstein, Michaelis, or Griesbach.

It was Travis's misfortune to be answered by Richard Porson, in his subsequently reprinted letters to the

to the director of GCCS was due largely to his good relations with the services, but above all was made possible through the personality of Travis himself. In *ULTRA Goes to War* (1978) Ronald Lewin wrote that 'gruff, rough and burly, Travis won little love but muted respect' (p. 136). Gruff, rough, and burly he was but it was not only by his family that he was held in some affection. During the war he used to visit areas of Bletchley Park and came to know many of the people involved personally.

Travis was formally appointed director of GCCS in March 1944 and was made a KCMG in June 1944. At the end of the German war he and his wife gave a celebration fancy dress dance for many hundreds of the staff and it is believed that this was entirely at his own expense.

GCCS was renamed government communications headquarters and Travis remained its director until 15 April 1952. The immediate post-war years in which he was director saw the formal introduction of the organizational structure for GCHQ which he had developed during the war. Travis had personally developed close relations with the American navy and army and in 1946 he was awarded the American medal for merit by President Truman for his 'direct and substantial contribution to the Allied victories both in Europe and in Asia'.

On 4 February 1913 Travis married Muriel Irene Fry (1888/9–1963), daughter of William Henry Fry, architect, and his wife, Marion Winifred. They had two daughters, Valerie (*b.* 1916), who later worked for her father in Bletchley, and Betty (*b.* 1919). Travis was 5 feet 7 inches in height,

Gentleman's Magazine (1788–90), and later by Herbert Marsh. Travis's scholarship was derivative and careless, his manner overweening. Porson made a fool of him. But he persevered; on 3 May 1791 Porson wrote, 'Mr. Travis is gone to Paris to examine Greek MSS. for the use, I suppose, of his third Edition' (R. Porson, *Correspondence*, ed. H. R. Luard, 1867, 49). After Travis's return that edition was delayed until 1794—so the preface mysteriously ends—by '*another employment, different in its kind, yet important in its nature and consequences*'. Travis died on 24 February 1797 at Hampstead, where he had moved for its healthy air, and was buried there on 6 March. There is a monument to him in Chester Cathedral.   HUGH DE QUEHEN

Sources Venn, *Alum. Cant.* · *GM*, 1st ser., 67 (1797), 351, 433 · Criticus [W. Orme], *Memoir of the controversy respecting the three heavenly witnesses* (1830) · *Fasti Angl.* (Hardy), vol. 3 · J. F. Smith, ed., *The admission register of the Manchester School, with some notices of the more distinguished scholars*, 1, Chetham Society, 69 (1866) · *DNB* · parish register, Shaw, Lancashire, 13 Dec 1741 [baptism] · parish register, Manchester collegiate church, 29 July 1766 [marriage]
Likenesses portrait on monument, Chester Cathedral · two miniatures; in possession of T. Corser of Stand, 1866

Traynor, Oscar (1886–1963), Irish nationalist and politician, was born on 21 March 1886 at 32 Upper Abbey Street, Dublin, the son of Patrick Traynor (*d.* 1899), bookseller, and his wife, Maria, *née* Clarke. He came from a strongly nationalist background; his father helped to lower Parnell's body into the grave. He was educated at the Christian Brothers' school in St Mary's Lane, which he left at thirteen. He was apprenticed as a woodcarver and became a compositor, a skilled trade similar to that followed by many Fenian and IRA men. He was goalkeeper for Dublin's Strandville Football Club, moving to Belfast Celtic in 1910.

Traynor participated in the Easter rising, when he was in charge of the occupation of the Metropole Hotel before moving to the headquarters at the General Post Office. He was interned in Knutsford and Fron-goch before being among the first batch of those released at Christmas 1916. In 1917 he was a key figure in the reorganization of the Dublin brigade, and in 1918 he spent a period in Dundalk gaol. On 16 September 1918, at St Agatha's Church, Dublin, he married Annie, daughter of Thomas Coyne, a waiter. They had a son and two daughters.

After the capture and killing of the IRA's Dublin brigade commanding officer, Dick McKee, and his deputy, Peadar Clancy, on the 'bloody Sunday' weekend in November 1920, Traynor took over as commanding officer in Dublin, where he was instrumental in organizing street ambushes and in establishing the city active service units. He was in command of the burning of the Custom House on 28 May 1921, and some of that operation's failure was attributed to him. He joined the majority of his brigade in opposing the Anglo-Irish treaty. At the proscribed army convention in March 1922 he became a member of the army executive, which declared opposition to all political authority. He was critical of the decision of the army executive to remain in siege-like conditions when the Four Courts was attacked by pro-treaty forces on the night of 27–28 June 1922, and was against what he later depicted as a determination by republican forces in Dublin to stage a replay of the Easter rising. None the less, Traynor himself could be criticized for failing to prepare adequately for the onset of the civil war. He was arrested by provisional government forces at the end of July 1922 and interned in Gormanstown camp. On 9 September 1922 he was among imprisoned republican IRA leaders who urged that a republican government be formed, acknowledging the error of military contempt for politicians. He was released in the general amnesty of 1924.

Traynor was elected as a Sinn Féin TD in 1925, then defeated in June 1927. He entered the Dáil as a Fianna Fáil TD in 1932. For the rest of his life he was the supreme de Valera loyalist. In 1933 he organized the special protective unit or 'Broy harriers', a unit within the gardai meant to safeguard the de Valera government's position. He was a fixture in three decades of Fianna Fáil governments: he was minister of posts and telegraphs in 1936, minister of defence in 1939–48 and 1951–4, and minister of justice in 1957 until his retirement in 1961. It was he who persuaded de Valera to stand down as taoiseach in 1959.

Traynor long led the poll in his north, later north-east, Dublin Fianna Fáil fiefdom. He was on the board of the de Valera-owned *Irish Press* and was president of the Football Association of Ireland from 1948 until his death. A sturdy, strongly-built man, he had a direct, forceful personality. His qualifications for high office would appear to owe more to his republican pedigree than to administrative or political abilities. He died of cancer on 15 December 1963 at his home, 14 Dollymount Avenue, Clontarf, Dublin: the state funeral took place three days later, and he was buried in Dublin.   MICHAEL HOPKINSON

Sources memoirs of Traynor, University College, Dublin, de Valera MSS 15272 · interviews with Traynor, University College, Dublin, O'Malley notebooks, P17b/96, 98 · M. Hopkinson, ed., *Frank Henderson's Easter rising, recollections of a Dublin volunteer* (1998) · T. P. Coogan, *De Valera: long fellow, long shadow* (1993) · *Irish Press* (16 Dec 1963) · D. Fitzpatrick, *The two Irelands, 1912–1939* (1998) · NA Ire.
Archives NL Ire., Frank Henderson memoirs · University College, Dublin, Mulcahy MSS |FILM BFI NFTVA, documentary footage · BFI NFTVA, news footage
Likenesses photograph, repro. in Skinner, *Politicians by accident*
Wealth at death £4994: probate, 27 Feb 1964, *CGPLA Éire*

Treacy, Eric (1907–1978), bishop of Wakefield and railway photographer, was born on 2 June 1907 at 63 Kings Road, Willesden, London, the surviving twin son of George Treacy (1866–1929), a furniture salesman, and his second wife, Annie Kate, daughter of Alfred Jopp of Aberdeen and his wife, Annie. A younger sister was born three years later. His father had been born in Burma, where his grandfather, an Irishman, had been a district commissioner. His paternal ancestors included William de Tracy, one of the knights responsible for the murder of Archbishop Thomas Becket. He attended a small private school in Willesden Green, and Haberdashers' Aske's School, Hampstead, from 1918 to 1925. He left school with below average matriculation results and remained acutely conscious throughout his life of his 'abysmal lack of education' (Peart-Binns, 8). However, he had excelled at sport, especially rugby and cricket, and had been heavyweight boxing champion for two successive years. Six feet tall and weighing over 14 stones, he was endowed with a burly physique and a craggy, florid complexion, enhanced by piercing blue eyes and well-groomed fair hair. He was mentally agile, genial, and personable and later maintained that he managed to hold his own wherever he found himself owing to 'a quick wit, a good memory, and more than a fair share of curiosity' (ibid.).

Treacy's parents were not churchgoers during his childhood years, but he later dated the beginning of his Christian experience from family seaside holidays in Norfolk, where he attended children's special service missions and first learned 'to pray rather than say my prayers' (Peart-Binns, 11). He was confirmed on 6 July 1922 and subsequently became a server and Sunday school teacher, attending initially the church of St Jude on the Hill, Hampstead Garden Suburb, and subsequently St Anne's Church, Highgate, whose vicar, James Adderley, was a fervent Christian socialist. After leaving school Treacy sought employment as an insurance agent, but soon discovered that he hated office work. Having joined Toc H, he offered his services as a boxing instructor at a boys' club in Kentish Town, where he began to develop a vocation for the Anglican ministry. He entered King's College, London, as an evening student, but after three hopelessly unsuccessful attempts at the Latin examination moved north in 1929 to take charge of the Shrewsbury School mission, a large boys' club and residential home in the socially deprived dockland of Liverpool. There he developed communication and leadership skills that shaped the future course and style of his ministry, which was spent almost entirely in the industrial north. He completed his theological studies at St Aidan's College, Birkenhead, and was ordained deacon in 1932 and priest in 1933, serving as curate at Liverpool parish church from 1932 to 1934.

Treacy married a voluntary social worker, Mary (May) Leyland Shone (1902–1985), the daughter of James Arthur Shone, a Methodist flour miller, magistrate, and member of the Mersey Docks and Harbour Board, at St Luke's Wesleyan Methodist Church, Hoylake, on 16 June 1932. The marriage was one of total mutual dependence, strengthened by the early loss of a stillborn child and the lack of any other children. In 1936 Treacy was appointed vicar of St Mary's, Edgehill, where he remained until he became a chaplain to the forces in 1940. He proved an outstanding army padre, encouraging some 150 men and officers, nearly a quarter of the 59th medium regiment, to join his confirmation classes in 1944. Moreover, during the regiment's service in Normandy, Treacy was mentioned in dispatches for gallantry and subsequently appointed MBE.

After the Second World War, Treacy moved across the Pennines to become successively rector of Keighley (1945–49), archdeacon and vicar of Halifax (1950–61), bishop-suffragan of Pontefract (1961–8), and bishop of Wakefield (1968–76). The translation of a non-graduate to a diocesan see at the age of sixty-one was testimony to the high regard in which he was held throughout the diocese of Wakefield, where he had served for nearly twenty years. A self-styled liberal evangelical, he was regarded widely as a cleric of middle ground views, and was seen by many as a stabilizing force within the Church of England. He was highly articulate, adept at using the media, forthright in his views, and not afraid to address controversial issues.

Although some of Treacy's views were progressive, his instincts were basically conservative. He voted for reunion with the Methodists in 1969 and was willing to accept women priests, but described *Honest to God* as 'a dangerous book likely to disturb the faith of more people than it will stimulate' (Peart-Binns, 164) and did not welcome new translations of the Bible. He encouraged the Church of England to retain the rite of exorcism, but only within stringent safeguards, after a notorious exorcism in his own diocese had resulted in the killing of a young mother by her estranged husband. Similar paradoxes were evident in his pronouncements on social issues. He criticized legislation which allowed eighteen-year-olds to marry without parental consent, but was sympathetic to the remarriage of the innocent victims of broken marriages in church. He advocated the birching of young delinquents in the early years of his ministry at Liverpool, but later regularly visited prisoners serving life sentences at Wakefield and campaigned for penal reform. He condemned the blasphemous rantings of the television comedy character Alf Garnett, but refused to support campaigners trying to prevent a Scandinavian director from entering Britain to make a film purporting to portray the sex life of Christ. In his role as bishop he found it difficult to reconcile synodical government with episcopal authority and tended to act autocratically, but was widely respected for his pastoral concern, rushing to the pithead of Lofthouse colliery in March 1973 in the early hours of the morning when he heard that miners were trapped underground, and declining an increase in stipend in 1974 to empathize with his low-paid parochial clergy.

Treacy's major recreation, railway photography, sprang from his rapport with railwaymen parishioners in Edgehill during the recession of the early 1930s. His photography earned him an unparalleled national reputation and the sobriquet of the 'footplate bishop'. By the late 1930s his technically accomplished style, with an artist's eye for portraying a locomotive in the landscape, had become instantly recognizable. 'I am wanting to do with my camera what I could only do with a box of watercolours', he once proclaimed, 'to catch that indefinable spell of railways, to make visual something that can only be felt' (Thomas, 7). He once perched on the girders of the Forth Bridge to capture the drama of steam locomotive traction crossing the estuary. He published the first of eight collections of railway photographs in 1946, including his finest book, *Steam Up* in 1949, in which he emphasized that his approach was essentially 'emotional' (ibid., 11). As steam locomotion declined he began to photograph diesels, but less enthusiastically, and became a keen supporter of steam preservation societies.

Following Treacy's retirement, on 31 October 1976, to his country retreat at The Ghyll, Applethwaite, on the lower slopes of Skiddaw, near Keswick, he frequently visited Appleby railway station, where he suffered a major coronary attack photographing the *Evening Star*, the last steam locomotive built for British Rail, and collapsed and died on 13 May 1978. His death was widely reported in the national news media and he was buried on 19 May at Crosthwaite parish church, Westmorland. In addition to a memorial service held at Wakefield Cathedral on 27 June 1978, some 4000 people gathered at Appleby Station on 30 September 1978 for an open-air memorial service. Subsequently a new community centre and meeting place for the diocese adjoining Wakefield Cathedral was named in his memory and a new electric railway locomotive was named the *Bishop Eric Treacy* by his widow in May 1979.

JOHN A. HARGREAVES

Sources J. S. Peart-Binns, *Eric Treacy* (1980) · D. St J. Thomas, *The best of Eric Treacy* (1994) · J. A. Hargreaves, *Halifax* (1999) · *The Times* (15 May 1978) · *The Guardian* (15 May 1978) · *Daily Express* (15 May 1978) · *Daily Telegraph* (15 May 1978) · *Evening Courier* [Halifax] (15 May 1978) · B. Palmer, *High and mitred: prime ministers as bishopmakers, 1837–1977* (1992) · private information (2004) [J. S. Peart-Binns] · b. cert. · m. cert. · d. cert. · *CGPLA Eng. & Wales* (1978)
Archives LPL, MSS, inc. autobiographical notes and diaries as army chaplain in Second World War · priv. coll., collection, incl. negatives of railway photographs · priv. coll., MSS · W. Yorks. AS, Calderdale, corresp. and papers, incl. sermon notes · Wakefield Cathedral, sermons | FILM BBC WAC · Yorkshire Television, Leeds, news footage
Likenesses group portrait, 1974, repro. in Peart-Binns, *Eric Treacy* · photograph, *c.*1978, Wakefield Cathedral · line drawing (after photograph, *c.*1978), repro. in *Wakefield Cathedral centenary development programme* (1987) · photographs, repro. in Peart-Binns, *Eric Treacy*
Wealth at death £83,375: probate, 3 Oct 1978, *CGPLA Eng. & Wales*

Trease, (Robert) Geoffrey (1909–1998), author, was born in Nottingham on 11 August 1909, the third son and youngest child of George Albert Trease (*b.* 1873), a wine merchant, and his wife, Florence Dale (1874–*c.*1955), a doctor's daughter. He won a scholarship to Nottingham high school, where he edited magazines, wrote a play produced by the school dramatic society, and published at his own expense a slim book of poems which, by his own account, sold virtually no copies. He won a classics scholarship to Queen's College, Oxford, but after 'one year of Oxford at its dryest, unrelieved by one flash of inspiration, humour or understanding from any don concerned with me', went down without a degree (Trease, *Whiff of Burnt Boats*, 101). After social work in the East End, from which he emerged with strong left-wing convictions, he scraped a living for two years from Grub Street literary work, falling back in the end on private school teaching. Here he met Marian Haselden Granger Boyer (1906–1989), a fellow teacher, and they were married on 11 August 1933, his twenty-fourth birthday: a marriage which lasted until her death fifty-six years later. They had one daughter.

Without money or prospects, but still intent on a literary career, Trease struggled on, pouring out articles and short stories at a guinea or so a time. The turning point was when he came across a book translated from the Russian, *Moscow has a Plan*, in which a Soviet author dramatized the first five-year plan for the benefit of young

(Robert) Geoffrey Trease (1909–1998), by unknown photographer

readers. Trease had not thought of writing for children, but it now struck him that the boys' adventure stories of his day were still reflecting a vanished world of imperialism and unquestioned privilege. Why not a book for children with a proletarian hero and a left-wing message? The idea was put to a Marxist publisher, Martin Lawrence, who immediately offered him a contract; the result was *Bows Against the Barons* (1934), a Robin Hood story meant to show the seamy side of merrie England, with Robin as a champion of the poor.

Although Trease was to write over 100 more books, mostly historical novels for young readers, this was probably the most significant, not only in determining his future career but also in its effect on children's books. It stimulated a growing demand for down-to-earth realism, and its dialogue, in plain contemporary English, helped to do away with the 'gadzookery' that had traditionally characterized historical fiction for the young.

Bows Against the Barons sold in vast numbers in a Russian translation, and produced a sum in blocked roubles that enabled Trease and Marian to spend five months in the Soviet Union. It was followed by a second 'proletarian' novel, *Comrades for the Charter* (1935), and, among much other writing, a play, *Colony*, performed at the left-wing Unity Theatre on the eve of the Second World War. None the less, Trease was gradually getting the propagandist urge out of his system, and there was little trace of it in *Cue for Treason* (1940), which was about a company of strolling players in Shakespeare's day and featured a plot against the first Queen Elizabeth. This was probably his most popular book and was to stay in print for many years.

After wartime service in the army education corps,

Trease continued mainly to write historical fiction for children. He did not like to be thought of as only a children's writer, however, and produced a handful of adult novels, which had modest success, as well as plays for stage and radio. A study of children's books, *Tales out of School* (1949; revised in 1964), made a powerful impact. In it, besides pillorying some outdated attitudes, Trease insisted on the cultural importance of children's literature and urged authors, publishers, and the public to take it seriously. He believed, not unreasonably, that this book helped to bring about the rise in the quality and standing of children's literature which took place over succeeding decades. He himself continued steadily at work and gradually progressed from restless young pioneer to grand old man, becoming the unquestioned doyen of British children's writers. But as the years went by, commentators found newer and younger writers more exciting. Trease's imagination, though serviceable, did not soar. His stories were planted firmly on the ground. He never went in for fantasy, and his evocations of the past did not achieve the intensity of Rosemary Sutcliff or the brilliance of Leon Garfield. But he went on writing and his books continued to sell.

Trease worked indefatigably for his profession. He was the first chairman of the Society of Authors children's writers group, was prominent in the campaign to end outright payment for copyright, and was chairman of the society's management committee in 1972–3. In 1979 he became a fellow of the Royal Society of Literature. He was unfailingly helpful to aspiring writers, and at Colwall, in the Malvern Hills, where he and his wife lived for many years, he was a mainstay of the local writers' circle. He had a lasting interest in Russia and in the theatre, and one of his last novels, *Shadow under the Sea* (1990), was set in the Crimean coastal resort of Yalta in the brief period of Gorbachov's supremacy. Late in life, to be near his daughter, he moved to Yomede Park, Newbridge Road, Bath, where he died on 27 January 1998.

JOHN ROWE TOWNSEND

Sources G. Trease, *A whiff of burnt boats* (1971) · G. Trease, *Laughter at the door* (1974) · G. Trease, *Farewell the hills* (1998) · G. Trease, *Tales out of school* (1949); rev. edn (1964) · M. Meek, *Geoffrey Trease* (1960) · *The Times* (30 Jan 1998) · personal knowledge (2004)

Archives Notts. Arch., corresp. and literary papers | Notts. Arch., letters to D. E. Gerard

Likenesses V. Hume Moody, portrait, 1960–69, priv. coll. · photograph, News International Syndication, London [*see illus.*]

Treby, Sir George (*bap.* 1644, *d.* 1700), judge and politician, was baptized at Plympton St Mary, Devon, on 1 January 1644, the eldest son of Peter Treby (*d.* in or after 1663), an attorney of common pleas, and his wife, Joan, daughter of John Snelling of Chaddlewood. Treby studied at Plympton School before entering Exeter College, Oxford, in June 1660. He left Oxford without a degree, and on 24 October 1663 he was admitted to the Middle Temple, where he was called to the bar on 2 June 1671. He became a bencher of his inn on 28 January 1681 and a reader in 1686, and was treasurer in 1689–90.

Much of Treby's legal work in the 1670s came from his

Sir George Treby (*bap.* 1644, *d.* 1700), by Robert White, 1700

native county. But it was a London widow, Anna Blount, whom he married on 15 November 1675. She was the daughter of Colonel Edward Grosvenor, with whom Treby remained on close terms after Anna's death, at some time before September 1677.

Entry into politics In March 1677 Treby was elected member of parliament for Plympton. His rival Richard Strode petitioned against the result, claiming that Treby had resorted to 'foul means' (Crossette and Henning). None the less, Treby kept his seat. There are signs in this period of Treby's support of nonconformists and their sympathizers in Plympton and elsewhere. He provided legal counsel to John Starkey, a bookseller whose publications were seized from Treby's Middle Temple chambers in late 1677; Starkey's shop would later become a gathering place for the whiggish Green Ribbon Club, with which Treby was associated. Despite Treby's apparent anti-court leanings, Plympton's corporation underscored their support of him when they named him their recorder and when they re-elected him to both parliaments of 1679.

In parliament Treby took the lead in matters concerned with the wool trade and other issues of importance in Devon. He sought wider responsibilities, but failed to win the chair of the committee of elections and privileges early in 1679. However, in November 1678 Titus Oates had revealed details of the Popish Plot, and the house named Treby to lead the committee of secrecy charged with its investigation. In May he reported the committee's evidence concerning James, duke of York, which gave courage to those, like Treby, who supported York's exclusion from the succession to the crown. Talk arose in June 1679 that Treby might be named the new speaker of the Commons. Nothing came of this, 'because being so short sighted, he cannot see to distinguish members in the house' (*Seventh Report*, HMC, 473).

When Charles II convened parliament in October 1680, Treby was named to the committee investigating those who had promoted the 'abhorrences' of petitions to the king for summoning parliament. He also gained the chair of the elections committee, which he used to benefit those who shared his view of 'popery' and the duke of York, and he continued to lead the committee investigating the Popish Plot. Treby again reported their findings to the Commons and then moved for the preparation of the second Exclusion Bill. He opposed any expedients by which York might be allowed to sit on the throne: 'not to make an utter exclusion of a popish successor is in plain English to have our throats cut' (Bodl. Oxf., MS Carte 72, fol. 466).

In early December 1680 Treby was among the eminent lawyers prosecuting William Howard, Viscount Stafford, the first of the so-called 'popish lords' tried in the House of Lords. At the same time he was appointed recorder of London after Sir George Jeffreys resigned. He was knighted on 20 January 1681; the next month the king commissioned him a justice of the peace for London and for his native Devon.

Plympton returned Treby to the third Exclusion Parliament in April 1681, where he helped to bring in the third Exclusion Bill. More sensationally, he reported to the Commons the information he had received from Edward Fitzharris about the plot. Treby and others hoped that by impeaching Fitzharris they might gain further testimony demonstrating the involvement of Thomas Osborne, earl of Danby, and the duke of York. Once the third Exclusion parliament had been dissolved, and thus any impeachment proceeding that might embarrass the king and his allies had been halted, Fitzharris was charged with treason. Treby joined Sir Francis Winnington and Henry Pollexfen to protect their most important witness from destruction. Treby tried to convince king's bench that it could not hear the case since Fitzharris still had an impeachment pending against him in parliament: for king's bench to take the case would be to remove the matter from a higher court into a lower one. These arguments failed to persuade the justices, who ruled that since parliament had been dissolved, the impeachment proceedings had ended. Fitzharris was tried, convicted, and executed in short order. Not long thereafter Francis Hawkins, chaplain of the Tower of London, published Fitzharris's purported confession, in which he alleged that Treby and others had tried to pressure him into giving false testimony. Treby is assumed to be the author of *Truth Vindicated*, in which he vigorously defended himself and others from 'so vain, so unlikely, and so foolish a slander' (Treby, *Truth Vindicated*, 23).

Opponent of the court On 12 April 1681, within days of his return from the failed parliament at Oxford, Treby had made his second marriage, to Rachel (*d.* before December 1684), daughter of James Standish of Hatton Garden.

Throughout this period he was active with the Green Ribbon Club, where he allegedly promoted a 'free state' (*CSP dom.*, 1680–81, 232) and suggested that James Scott, duke of Monmouth, the eldest illegitimate son of Charles II, should be king. In May 1681 Treby presented to the king an address from London requesting another parliament. The king bridled at this advice, remarking that the City meddled in business that did not belong to it.

In part owing to the City's pressure to summon parliament, Charles's legal advisers decided to attack London's charter by *quo warranto*. Treby, perhaps hoping to earn the king's favour for the City, made a most loyal speech when he presented London's new sheriffs at court in September 1682. But the *quo warranto* went on, and in February 1683 Treby 'argued very learnedly' (Luttrell, 1.249) in king's bench on the City's behalf. The heart of his case was that if a wrong had been done, it could only have been done by individuals, not by the corporation itself; such individuals, not the City, should be sued and punished. More creatively, Treby noted that the *quo warranto* was brought against the corporation by name yet charged that the corporation had been destroyed by the illegal acts it had done. He pointed to the logical contradiction of bringing a suit against a body which the same suit said did not exist. The judges brushed this complaint aside, observing that the corporation would only die when judgment was entered against it.

Judgment was indeed given against the City, though the court delayed entering it on record in hopes that London might be convinced to surrender its charter to the king. Some lawyers advised surrender, but Treby counselled the City to fight on, telling City leaders that surrender would violate their oaths to uphold the City's rights and that it would lead to worse legal trouble than enrolment of the judgment. Treby also believed that, given the City's good behaviour, the king would not press for surrender, but judgment against the charter was entered in October 1683 and the City's corporation ceased to exist. Treby thereby lost his recordership and was soon removed as well from the various county benches on which he served. In 1684, faced with *quo warranto* proceedings and seeing London's example, Plympton surrendered its charter and received a new one that left Treby out of the recordership there as well.

In 1683 Treby had worked unsuccessfully with Pollexfen and William Williams to defend the former London lord mayor Sir Patience Ward on charges that he perjured himself when he gave evidence supporting Sir Thomas Pilkington from the *scandalum magnatum* brought against him by the duke of York. In 1685 Treby joined another group of whiggish lawyers arguing on behalf of Thomas Sandys, sued by the East India Company for a breach of their trade monopoly. He argued, 'The prerogative is great; but it has this general and just limitation, that nothing is to be done thereby that is mischievous or injurious to the subject' (*State trials*, 10.386). Treby reasoned that though the king could create a trading company, he could not grant it exclusive commercial powers. Once again

Treby's arguments limiting the king's authority over corporations failed to convince king's bench. These cases aside, Treby did not appear in as many of the politically sensitive trials of the early 1680s as other great lawyer–MPs such as Williams, Pollexfen, and Winnington.

The one bright spot in this period was Treby's third marriage, on 14 December 1684, to Dorothy, daughter of Ralph Grainge of the Inner Temple. Together they had two children, a son, George, and a daughter, Maria, who died in infancy. Dorothy, however, died within a few years of their marriage. On 6 January 1693 Treby married Mary Brinley (b. c.1663), who reportedly brought a £10,000 portion. A second surviving son, Brinley, was born in 1698.

In elections to parliament in 1685 Treby again stood at Plympton against Strode, though this time Strode prevailed, in part because Plympton's 1684 charter had remodelled the corporation and thus destroyed Treby's political base. By then Titus Oates had been charged with perjury for the testimony he had given in the Popish Plot trials. Treby was initially assigned as Oates's counsel, and though Oates wrote pitiful letters pleading for his advice, he finally decided not to help the darling of the whig cause. He also refused, in 1686, to appear in the great test case of the king's claimed power to dispense with the penal laws, *Godden* v. *Hale*. But in 1688 he agreed to join many of England's most prominent lawyers to defend the seven bishops who had opposed James II's policy of religious toleration. Later that year, as the toleration effort unravelled, James sought to reconstitute London's corporation in its pre-surrender form in hopes of winning back lost political support. Twice James offered Treby his old recorder's office, and twice he refused.

In office under William III   The arrival of William of Orange changed Treby's stance, and on 10 December he resumed his place as the City's recorder. The next day he was among those consulted by the provisional government about what should be done in the wake of James II's departure. At a meeting of London's aldermen on 16 December he was chiefly responsible for the defeat of a motion congratulating James II on his return to London, saying it would be inconsistent with the welcome extended to William. Four days later he led a City delegation to the prince of Orange and gave an obsequious oration to the man who, 'led by the hand of heaven, and called by the voice of the people, has preserved our dearest interests'—chiefly law and the protestant religion—'which is primitive Christianity restored' (*Speech to the Prince of Orange*).

Plympton, its old corporation revived, returned Treby to the Convention Parliament in January 1689. In the debate on the state of the crown he lashed out at James for his promotion of Catholics and his destruction of the corporations, adding that James had renounced the kingdom and could not be trusted. Only William, 'who under God, is our only remedy', could now take the throne (Jones, 244). William named Treby solicitor-general in early March, and on 6 May 1689 he promoted him to attorney-general. In the Commons, Treby reported the new form of the oaths of supremacy and allegiance, helped to prepare

the Bill of Rights, and was among those appointed to bring in a bill for reversing the judgment in the London *quo warranto*. More controversially, he joined the whigs who favoured the clause in the abortive Corporations Restoration Bill that would have barred most urban tories from local office. In March 1690 it first appeared that he had been defeated at Plympton's parliamentary election by his old foe Strode, but the Commons voided that return; he won the second vote two weeks later.

On 30 April 1692 Treby was installed as chief justice of common pleas and thereupon resigned the recordership and his seat in the Commons. In 1693 he presided in the trial of William Anderton for seditious libel, and in 1695 and 1696 he was among the justices who tried the association plotters. Treby gave his most important judicial opinion, in the widely watched bankers' case, in June 1695, in which he recommended reversing the exchequer decree for the bankers. He suggested that the court of exchequer had no power to compensate the bankers by ordering payments out of the Treasury. He was joined in this view by Lord Keeper Somers, who reversed the exchequer judgment. But in January 1700 the House of Lords took up the matter. When they consulted the judges, Treby again gave his opinion against the initial decree, but he and Somers were overruled as the Lords restored the original judgment. Throughout these years Treby often presided in the Lords as speaker when the lord keeper was absent or ill. In May 1700 he was among those briefly commissioned to hold the great seal itself after Lord Somers's removal.

In early December 1700 Treby, feeling ill, moved to Kensington for better air. He died there on 13 December, survived by his fourth wife and two sons. He was quietly buried in the Temple Church in an evening ceremony three days later. Sir John Holt, chief justice of king's bench, along with some of the other justices, served as his executor and as trustee for his sons. Treby left his wife and children with extensive properties in Devon, Cornwall, and Lincolnshire, large amounts of cash out on loan, and a house at Hatton Garden. The aldermen of Plympton, the town that gave him his start in law and politics, received rings from their late recorder.

Assessment   Treby did not prevail in the major cases he argued during the 1680s, but this did not lead contemporaries to doubt his powers as a lawyer. Nahum Tate waxed lyrical on his abilities:

> For law, that does a boundless ocean seem,
> Is coasted all, and fathomed all by him …
> His judgments he from Truth's clear fountain draws,
> Respecting not the party, but the cause …

Evelyn too called him 'a learned man' (Evelyn, 5.438), with good cause. Treby's arguments in the London *quo warranto* and the East India Company cases were notable for their creativity and precision, even if they did not succeed in law. His erudition was equally apparent in his annotations of Dyer's *Reports* and in his words from the bench, which showed his attention to procedural propriety and to logical rigour. His widow erected a monument to his finer qualities in the Temple Church. Unsurprisingly, the tory biographer Roger North did not care much for Treby, who he said 'was no fanatic; but, of the fanatic party, true as steel. His genius lay to free-thinking, and, conformably to his fellows at that time, made the scriptures and Christianity, or rather all religion, a jest …' (North, 2.9). Treby's support of foreign protestants as well as English ones suggests that North was probably right about his sympathy for nonconformists. He showed a consistent commitment to whig political goals in the 1680s. His anti-Catholic bigotry made him more credulous in accepting the evidence of a 'popish' plot than his otherwise careful mind might have allowed; his abandonment of Oates in his hour of need points to his sense of political expediency if not to his personal loyalty to one whose wild allegations had fuelled Treby's rise to prominence.

PAUL D. HALLIDAY

Sources J. S. Crossette and B. D. Henning, 'Treby, George', HoP, Commons, 1660–90 · N. Luttrell, A brief historical relation of state affairs from September 1678 to April 1714, 6 vols. (1857) · Burnet's History of my own time, ed. O. Airy, new edn, 2 vols. (1897–1900) · R. North, The lives of … Francis North … Dudley North … and … John North, new edn, 3 vols. (1826) · State trials, vols. 9–14 · Sainty, Judges · Fifth report, HMC, 4 (1876) · Seventh report, HMC, 6 (1879), pt 1 · The manuscripts of the Earl Cowper, 3 vols., HMC, 23 (1888–9), vol. 2 · The manuscripts of Rye and Hereford corporations, HMC, 31 (1892) · The manuscripts of Sir William Fitzherbert … and others, HMC, 32 (1893) · The manuscripts of the earl of Buckinghamshire, the earl of Lindsey … and James Round, HMC, 38 (1895) · The manuscripts of S. H. Le Fleming, HMC, 25 (1890) · Calendar of the manuscripts of the marquess of Ormonde, new ser., 8 vols., HMC, 36 (1902–20), vols. 5, 7 · Report on the manuscripts of the marquis of Downshire, 6 vols. in 7, HMC, 75 (1924–95) · Report on the manuscripts of Allan George Finch, 5 vols., HMC, 71 (1913–2003), vols. 2–3 · CSP dom., 1677–8, 1680–81, 1683, pt 2, 1683–4, 1685, 1686–7, 1689–90, 1691–2, 1693, 1695, 1700–2 · Foss, Judges, vol. 7, pp. 364–6 · J. B. Rowe, A history of the borough of Plympton Erle (1906) · Devon and Cornwall Notes and Queries, 25 (1952–3), 151–3 · F. Hawkins, A narrative: being a true relation of what discourse passed between Dr. Hawkins and Edward Fitzharris (1681) · [G. Treby], Truth vindicated (1681) · Foster, Alum. Oxon. · Wood, Ath. Oxon., new edn · M. Landon, The triumph of the lawyers: their role in English politics, 1678–1689 (Alabama, 1970) · J. Granger, A biographical history of England, from Egbert the Great to the revolution, 2 vols. (1769); suppl. (1774) · C. T. Martin, ed., Minutes of parliament of the Middle Temple, 4 vols. (1904–5) · J. L. Chester and G. J. Armytage, eds., Allegations for marriage licences issued by the dean and chapter of Westminster, 1558 to 1699; also, for those married by the vicar-general of the archbishop of Canterbury, 1660 to 1679, Harleian Society, 23 (1886) · JHC, 9 (1667–87) · A. Grey, Debates from the year 1667 to the year 1694 (1763), vols. 3–9 · M. Knights, Politics and opinion in crisis, 1678–81 (1994) · D. L. Jones, ed., A parliamentary history of the Glorious Revolution (1988) · P. Halliday, Dismembering the body politic: partisan politics in England's towns, 1650–1730 (1998) · R. Beddard, ed., A kingdom without a king: the journal of the provisional government in the revolution of 1688 (1988) · Sainty, King's counsel · Le Neve's Pedigrees of the knights, ed. G. W. Marshall, Harleian Society, 8 (1873) · G. Cokayne and E. A. Fry, eds., Calendar of marriage licenses issued by the faculty office, 1632–1714, Index Library, 33 (1905) · Evelyn, Diary · The speech of the Honorable Sir George Treby, knight, recorder … upon presenting the honorable Dudley North and Peter Rich esquires, sheriffs (1682) · The speech of Sir George Treby, kt., recorder … to his highness the prince of Orange (1688) · The autobiography of Sir John Bramston, 1st ser., 32 (1845) · will, PRO, PROB 11/459, fols. 220v–222v · N. Tate, An essay of a character of the Right Honourable Sir George Treby kt (1699) · H. A. C. Sturgess, ed., Register of admissions to the Honourable Society of the Middle Temple, from the fifteenth century to the year 1944, 1 (1949), 169

Archives Derbys. RO, Matlock, corresp. [copies] · Derbys. RO, Matlock, corresp. and papers, incl. Popish plot papers · Middle Temple, London, MSS
Likenesses R. White, line engraving, 1700, BM, NPG [see illus.] · group portrait, mezzotint (with counsel for the seven bishops), BL
Wealth at death see will, PRO, PROB 11/459, fols. 220–22v

Trechmann, Charles Taylor (1884–1964), geologist and archaeologist, was born at 10 Cliff Terrace, Hartlepool, co. Durham, on 28 June 1884, the son of Karl (Charles) Otto Trechmann (1851–1917) and his wife, Gertrude Elizabeth, née Taylor. His father was a cement manufacturer and mineralogist; the mineral trechmannite was named after him.

Trechmann was educated at Tonbridge School, Kent, and Armstrong College, Newcastle upon Tyne, where he studied chemistry and geology. Following graduation, he continued his studies at the universities of Basel and Paris, before returning to Britain to work as an analytical chemist at the Warren cement works in Hartlepool (a business owned by his father). Here he developed a research interest in the Zechstein of north-east England, and he distinguished different reef palaeoenvironments in the rocks—work for which the University of Durham conferred on him the degree of DSc.

Trechmann's father died in 1917 and the family business was sold to ICI about 1924. With this financial independence, Trechmann was able to devote his time to research. From the family home in Castle Eden, co. Durham, geology took Trechmann to Africa, New Zealand, Australia, and, most frequently, the Caribbean. Trechmann's research programme in the 1920s and 1930s involved working on the archaeology and geology of north-east England during the summer months. Once winter threatened, he returned to the geologically interesting islands of the Antilles. Thus independent means permitted Trechmann to become one of a rare breed, a twentieth-century 'gentleman geologist'.

Trechmann's contribution to the geology of north-east England, New Zealand, and the Caribbean was considerable. His most notable work was undertaken prior to the Second World War. His work on the Palaeozoic and Mesozoic marine deposits of New Zealand, particularly on the marine Triassic of 'Alpine facies', was an important contribution that provided biostratigraphic data for successions whose dating had hitherto been controversial. He also published some of the first detailed descriptions of the geology of many Antillean islands. In Jamaica he made comprehensive studies of many deposits that had originally been identified by nineteenth-century surveyors. Trechmann's studies of fossil molluscs are still standard references for many areas and stratigraphic units. He published over eighty books and research papers on geology and archaeology, including at least forty on the Caribbean.

In his later years Trechmann presented a striking figure—sparely built and craggy, dressed in grey tweed and a Homburg hat, with gold-rimmed spectacles attached to his lapel by a black ribbon. His individuality often led to an unorthodox approach to geology, and, as was noted by Chubb (p. 50), 'Trechmann's fame as a geologist would stand higher today if he had published nothing after the last war.' His later publications, particularly on the Caribbean, lacked rigour. His view that tidal action was an important tectonic force for mountain uplift was typical of the controversial theories put forward in the 1950s, before the acceptance of plate-tectonics. However, the principal expositions of the theory had to be privately published by Trechmann. Although he could be generous to young geologists, Trechmann could also be antagonistic to his peers, particularly in his dealings with geological surveyors in Jamaica, his favourite Caribbean stamping ground.

Trechmann was a life member of the Geologists' Association and in 1913 he was elected a fellow of the Geological Society, which awarded him the R. H. Worth prize in 1956. Trechmann died, unmarried, at the Diagnostic Clinic in Barbados on 18 February 1964, and was buried in Barbados.   STEPHEN K. DONOVAN

Sources P. Davis and C. Brewer, eds., *A catalogue of natural science collections in north-east England* (1986) · C. A. F. W[estoll] and T. S. W[estoll], 'Charles Taylor Trechmann', *Proceedings of the Geological Society* (1965), 207–8 · L. J. Chubb, 'A critical appreciation of the late C. T. Trechmann's contributions to Caribbean geology', *Journal of the Geological Society of Jamaica*, 19 (1980), 47–51 · A. G. Coates, 'Obituary of Dr Charles Taylor Trechmann, DSc, FGS', *Journal of the Geological Society of Jamaica*, 7 (1965), 48–9 · L. J. Chubb and J. B. Williams, 'Zans memorial issue', *Geonotes (Quarterly Journal of the Geological Society of Jamaica)*, 4/3–4 (1961), 1–39 · private information (2004) · *Rules and list of members of the Geologists' Association* (1960) · *CGPLA Eng. & Wales* (1964) · b. cert.
Archives NHM, corresp. · Sunderland Museum, corresp.
Likenesses photograph, 1950–54, repro. in Chubb, 'A critical appreciation', 60
Wealth at death £136,098: probate, 19 June 1964, *CGPLA Eng. & Wales*

Trecothick, Barlow (1718?–1775), merchant and politician, was born either at Stepney or at sea, the son of Captain Mark Trecothick, mariner, and Hannah Greenleaf. From *c.*1724 he lived in Boston, Massachusetts, where he served as an apprentice to Charles Apthorp between 1734 and 1740. Thereafter he moved to Jamaica, and acted as the agent for Apthorp and Thomlinson for seven years. He returned to Boston, married Grizzell Apthorp, the daughter of his former master, on 2 March 1747, and remained there for three years. He settled in London about 1750 as a North American commission merchant. Among other things, he served as the London correspondent for Apthorp and Thomlinson, supplied other American merchants with European manufactures, provided food and provisions to the troops on a victualling contract he held with Thomlinson, and managed the finances of several military companies with Sir George Colebrooke and other Londoners. Like most influential merchants, he subscribed to government loans during the Seven Years' War.

In 1764 Trecothick was elected alderman of London for Vintry ward and he held this post for ten years; in 1766 he served as London's sheriff and in 1770 as its lord mayor. In addition, from 1766 to 1774, he was employed as New Hampshire's colonial agent, acting as its advocate in Whitehall and parliament. Trecothick's best-known service occurred before he took a seat in the Commons. Throughout the Stamp Act crisis in 1765 and 1766, he performed invaluable services for Rockingham and Newcastle: with other colony agents, he opposed the passage of the act; with other London merchants, he led the search for a legislative remedy in the wake of passage; he marshalled the support of American and Caribbean interests in London and the outports for repeal; and he served as an effective witness in house investigations.

Trecothick had been proposed as MP for the City in the early 1760s but, not possessing the freedom of the City, was not nominated. He was next considered in 1765, when the duke of Newcastle offered him the seat at New Shoreham. But he baulked at the cost of buying the support of the constituency (Newcastle mentioned £1050, in addition to the purchase of a ship from local builders), not to mention the venality of the system, and refused the seat. He was returned as one of the members for London in the election of 1768. The fight was fiercely competitive among seven candidates, some of whom openly questioned his American background and his willingness to serve as a tool of the colonies. During the next six years, until he retired with the dissolution of parliament in May 1774, he adopted a stricter attitude towards protest. For instance, he spoke warmly during the strike of the seamen and the 1768 City riots. Yet he continued to vent his outrage at what he believed to be the inept handling of American trade matters. The Boston massacre in 1770 or the subjugation of Native Americans on St Vincent in 1772 were, to Trecothick, only the latest instances of misguided despotism. Throughout his tenure he sided with the opposition.

In 1768 Trecothick purchased an estate of 5000 acres in Addington, Surrey, for £38,500. At the same time, he acquired a share in a plantation in Grenada and several estates in Jamaica. After the death of his first wife on 31 July 1769, he married Anne Meredith, the sister of Sir William Meredith, third baronet, on 9 June 1770. From 1771 onwards, Trecothick's health failed him and, when parliament was dissolved in 1774, he stood down. He died in Addington on 28 May 1775, and was buried in the churchyard at Addington.   DAVID HANCOCK

Sources T. D. Jervey, 'Barlow Trecothick', *South Carolina Historical and Genealogical Magazine*, 32 (1931), 157–69 · D. H. Watson, 'Barlow Trecothick and other associates of Lord Rockingham during the Stamp Act crisis', MA diss., University of Sheffield, 1957 · P. D. Thomas, *British politics and the Stamp Act crisis: the first phase of the American revolution, 1763–1767* (1975) · will, PRO, PROB 11/1009, sig. 253
Archives BL, Egerton MSS · BL, legal papers, Add. MS 36218 · BL, corresp. with duke of Newcastle, Add. MSS 32970–32977, 33070, *passim* · Hants. RO, Malmesbury MSS

Tredenham, John (*bap.* 1668, *d.* 1710), politician, was baptized on 28 March 1668 at St Ewe, Cornwall, the second (but first surviving) son of Sir Joseph Tredenham (1641/2–1707), politician, of Tregonan, St Ewe, and Elizabeth Seymour (*c.*1635–1731), daughter of Sir Edward Seymour, third baronet, of Berry Pomeroy, Devon. Little is known about Tredenham's early life, although he received a conventional education at the Inner Temple (1682) and Christ Church, Oxford (1684). At Oxford he was reputed to have contributed to the collection of verses celebrating the accession of James II.

Tredenham's tory contacts were formidable, not least his uncle, Sir Edward Seymour, fourth baronet. This may explain his early venture into the electoral arena, close to his twenty-first birthday, when he was defeated at Truro for a seat in the Convention Parliament of 1689. On 1 February 1690 he married Anne (*b.* 1671/2), daughter and coheir of Sir John Lloyd, second baronet (*c.*1651?–1674), of Carmarthenshire, and Mary, daughter of the Revd Matthew Smallwood; they had one daughter, who predeceased her father. According to Sir Joseph, the marriage was not a success owing to the personality of Lady Lloyd who (among other things) intercepted letters between father and son. On 9 April 1690 Tredenham entered parliament in a by-election for St Mawes, following his uncle Henry Seymour's decision to sit elsewhere. Although a tory, Tredenham made little impact during his early years in the Commons, being overshadowed by his father. He did, however, refuse to sign the voluntary Association in 1696, although there is no evidence of his ever supporting the Jacobite cause.

Tredenham achieved considerable notoriety following a dinner on 23 September 1701 at the Blue Posts tavern in the Haymarket, London. His companions that night were his fellow tory MPs Anthony Hammond and Charles Davenant; the Spanish envoy, Navarra; and the French chargé d'affaires, Jean Baptiste Poussin. Unfortunately, orders had been issued to expel Poussin from England that day, in response to Louis XIV's recognition of James III (James Francis Edward Stuart). When this was discovered the whigs exploited it to the full, accusing the tories of Jacobitism, and at the subsequent general election appending the label 'Pousineer' to those who had opposed preparations for war with France. A pamphlet war ensued, and both Davenant and Hammond lost their seats. Ironically Tredenham, who was widely blamed for the débâcle and who had reportedly left the tavern with Poussin, was re-elected for his family borough of St Mawes.

Tredenham continued to sit as a tory under Queen Anne, but there is evidence that he was trimming his sails in the pursuit of office. Both he and his father appear to have sneaked off to avoid voting on the tack of the Occasional Conformity Bill in November 1704. Lampooned as 'poet-laureat to Monsieur Poussin' in 1705 he did not stand at the general election of that year, preferring to solicit Robert Harley for a diplomatic posting. In support of his pretensions he wrote 'I may with confidence pretend to understand the Latin tongue and that I'm no stranger to the French', although he laid most stress on his 'fidelity to her Majesty' (Tredenham to Harley, 13 July 1705, BL, Add. MS 70207). Despite reports in October that he would be posted to Denmark, no office was forthcoming, so he took the opportunity to return to the Commons after the death of his father in 1707. He continued to sit as a tory, and

played a full part in the convocation of tinners in 1710, taking over the chair when the speaker fell ill. Tredenham died on 25 December 1710, either 'by a fall from his coach box' (Le Neve, 3.210) or, as one newsletter described it, 'suffocated with excessive fatness and too plentiful a dinner' (Strathmore MSS, box 74, bundle 10). In noticing his death, Abel Boyer pronounced him as 'one of the leading men of the Church party' before referring to his enduring fame as a 'Pousineer' (Boyer, 53).   STUART HANDLEY

Sources 'Tredenham, John', HoP, *Commons, 1690–1715* [draft] · BL, Add. MS 40775, fols. 109–10, 196, 198, 220–21 · BL, Add. MS 15895, fol. 114 · Tredenham to Harley, 13 July 1705, BL, Add. MS 70207 · BL, Add. MS 36707, fols. 90–92 · G. de F. Lord and others, eds., *Poems on affairs of state: Augustan satirical verse, 1660–1714*, 7 vols. (1963–75), vol. 6, pp. 436, 506 · H. Horwitz, *Parliament, policy and politics in the reign of William III* (1977) · A. Boyer, *The political state of Great Britain*, 2nd edn, 1–2 (1711) · J. L. Vivian and H. H. Drake, eds., *The visitation of the county of Cornwall in the year 1620*, Harleian Society, 9 (1874), 456 · IGI · J. L. Chester and J. Foster, eds., *London marriage licences, 1521–1869* (1887) · J. Le Neve, *Monumenta Anglicana*, 3: 1680–1699 (1717), 210 · newsletter, 26 Dec 1710, Glamis Castle, Strathmore MSS, box 74, bundle 10

Tredgold, Alfred Frank (1870–1952), physician, was born at 49 Liversage Street, Derby, on 5 November 1870, the son of Joseph Tredgold, a builder's foreman, and his wife, Bessey Smith. His ancestors belonged to the Cornish family of Tregol, but his own branch of the family came from Lincolnshire. Six of his near relatives were members of the medical profession. He studied medicine at Durham University and the London Hospital, where he won scholarships and prizes in biology, anatomy, physiology, pathology, and medicine. After qualifying in 1899 he married Zoë (*d.* 1947), daughter of F. A. Hanbury, barrister-at-law. In the same year he was offered a research scholarship in insanity and mental disease, recently founded by the London county council. He chose mental deficiency as his subject and worked for two years in the LCC's asylums and newly built Claybury Laboratory under F. W. Mott. When the scholarship expired he entered general practice to earn a living. In 1905 he was appointed as one of the main medical investigators to the royal commission on the care and control of the feeble-minded. His views were largely endorsed in the report of the commission, which was released in 1908. In the same year he published the first edition of his *Mental Deficiency (Amentia)*, which became the standard text on the subject, going through eight editions in his lifetime alone. His ideas and campaigning efforts paved the way for a specialized system of institutional care under the Mental Deficiency Act of 1913.

Tredgold had been commissioned as an officer in the 2nd volunteer battalion of the Queen's regiment in 1905. On the outbreak of the First World War he offered his services as a mental expert to the Royal Army Medical Corps. However, the importance of such skills was not yet recognized and Tredgold remained a combatant. He served at Gallipoli, and in Egypt and Sinai, rising to the rank of major. In 1916 he was invalided home with severe dysentery, but he remained in command of the local Territorial depot in Guildford. Between the wars he was the leading consultant in mental deficiency in the country. He became neurologist to the Royal Surrey County Hospital and physician in psychological medicine to the London Hospital. He lectured at the Bethlem and Maudsley hospitals and at the London School of Economics. He served on the mental deficiency committees of the Board of Education and the BMA, and on the Ministry of Health's (Brock) committee on sterilization. He was elected FRCP in 1929, was president of the psychological section of the Royal Society of Medicine, and in 1927 gave the Galton lecture to the Eugenics Society. He was one of the driving forces behind the Central Association for Mental Welfare, a voluntary organization which provided community supervision for defectives, and he taught on its training courses for social workers and medical officers. His *Manual of Psychological Medicine* (1943) proved to be another widely read textbook.

Tredgold argued that amentia (his preferred term for mental deficiency) was generally caused by the inheritance or acquisition of a defective germplasm, through poor stock or the effect of alcohol, syphilis, and other poisons. This disposition led to below average intelligence, social failure, and immorality. Training could ameliorate but not cure this pathological condition. Tredgold continued to support his germplasm theory, despite mounting evidence for a genetic explanation. Regarding defectives as a danger to society, he was an ardent proponent of lifetime segregation. However, he was at first wary about sterilization, resigning from the Eugenics Society in 1931 over its claim that sterilization would halve the number of defectives over three generations—in his view a wild overestimate. Nevertheless, in 1934 he endorsed the Brock report's proposals for a voluntary scheme and thereafter joined the campaign to legalize voluntary sterilization.

Shortly after the death of his wife, in 1947, Tredgold lost the sight in one eye through glaucoma. Loss of sight in the other eye and a stroke disabled him in his final years, but he still managed to prepare new editions of his books with the assistance of his son, Roger Francis *Tredgold (1911–1975). He died at his home, St Martin's, Clandon Road, Guildford, on 17 September 1952. He was survived by two daughters and a son. The elder daughter, Joan Alison (1903–1989), was principal of Cheltenham Ladies' College in 1953–64, and his son, physician-in-charge of the department of psychological medicine, University College Hospital, oversaw later editions of *Tredgold's Mental Deficiency*.

MATHEW THOMSON

Sources *The Lancet* (27 Sept 1952) · *BMJ* (27 Sept 1952), 726 · B. Hart, *BMJ* (4 Oct 1952), 783 · *The Times* (18 Sept 1952) · Munk, *Roll* · *WWW* · b. cert. · *CGPLA Eng. & Wales* (1952)
Archives Wellcome L., Eugenics Society MSS
Likenesses photograph, repro. in *The Lancet*, 642 · photograph, repro. in *BMJ*, 726
Wealth at death £23,363 18s. 9d.: probate, 3 Dec 1952, *CGPLA Eng. & Wales*

Tredgold, Sir Robert Clarkson (1899–1977), judge in Rhodesia and Nyasaland, was born in Bulawayo on 2 June 1899, the second son and third of the five children of Clarkson Henry Tredgold, later attorney-general and senior judge of Southern Rhodesia, and his wife, (Emily) Ruth, second daughter of John Smith Moffat, missionary of Inyati Mission and later colonial official.

Tredgold was proud of his family's humanitarian traditions and association for four generations with central Africa: his great-grandfather was Robert Moffat, explorer, missionary, and father-in-law of David Livingstone; his mother, aunt, and uncle were the first three white children born in the country; his father had liberalized legal administration under the Chartered Company; and his paternal great-great-grandfather had striven with Thomas Clarkson for the abolition of slavery (generations of Tredgolds bore the forename Clarkson). Tredgold's younger sister Barbara, founder of Harari Mission in Salisbury, continued the humanitarian tradition.

In his autobiography, *The Rhodesia that was my Life* (1968), Tredgold describes himself as growing up with a country, and tells of childhood in early Salisbury, life in a warm, closely-knit community, of friendships with servants, African folklore learned around the campfire, and of exploration of the veld leading to his love of wild flowers, animals, especially dogs, and the remote *bundu* (bush). From Prince Edward School, Salisbury, and Rondebosch Boys' High School, Cape Town, Tredgold arrived in England in spring 1918 to join the Royal Scots, in which his elder brother, John Tredgold, had died at Arras. Before completion of his training war had ended. On demobilization he became a Rhodes scholar and a member of Hertford College, Oxford, of which he became an honorary fellow in 1961 and where the chapel contains a memorial to him. He obtained a second class in jurisprudence in 1922.

After being called to the bar (Inner Temple) in 1923, Tredgold set up practice in Bulawayo. In 1925 he married Lorna Doris (d. 1972), daughter of John Danby Downing Keilor, Anglican clergyman, of Wallingford, Berkshire. She had been the lord chancellor's Richmond Palace gardener, and their common interest in plants contributed to their happy marriage, which ended in July 1972 with her death. They had no children.

At the small Bulawayo bar work came quickly, briefs coming also from Northern Rhodesia, where in 1931 Tredgold became an acting judge. Specialization was impossible, and Tredgold took civil and criminal work. One case, involving the British South Africa Company's mining rights, ultimately purchased by the government, was a factor in a major realignment in Rhodesian politics and the 1933 election victory of Godfrey Huggins on a policy of racial segregation. Huggins, finding his Reform Party unreliable, formed a national government, and under a new United Party banner won an election in November 1934, with Tredgold being returned for rural Insiza, which he represented until 1943.

Tredgold had always held liberal views. In 1936 he opposed a Native Preachers Bill giving the government control over African religious activity. In the same year he took silk and became minister of justice and internal affairs. He influenced Huggins away from segregationist policies towards economic advancement of Africans, persuaded him not to close the voters' rolls to Africans, and mitigated the application of the Land Apportionment Act, particularly between 1941 and 1943, when he was also minister of native affairs. Unhappy about racial policies, Tredgold escaped his dilemma in 1943 by accepting a high court judgeship. In the same year he was appointed CMG.

Tredgold's other significant contributions were to imperial defence. As first minister of defence in 1939 he was unwilling to employ the small group of white Rhodesians as cannon fodder, thereby destroying the country's élite. He formulated the policy of seconding them as officers and NCOs to the regiments of other colonial territories. Tredgold's intervention secured reinforcements from South Africa, which greatly assisted General Alan Cunningham's Abyssinian campaign. Tredgold was probably progenitor of the empire training scheme. In 1936 he had invited the RAF to train pilots in Rhodesia. After war started he sent Air Vice-Marshal C. W. Meredith to persuade the RAF. The idea expanded into the empire scheme, and, after London negotiations by Tredgold, the first air school opened in 1940 in Salisbury. He also established the Rhodesian African rifles, despite pre-war opposition 'to the arming of natives'.

Tredgold's judicial advancement was rapid. In 1950 he became Southern Rhodesian chief justice and in 1951 ex-officio president of the Rhodesia and Nyasaland court of appeal. Knighted in 1951 and appointed KCMG in 1955, he became chief justice of the new Federation of Rhodesia and Nyasaland, inaugurating Lord Llewellin as first governor-general on 4 September 1953. Ironically, Tredgold had warned the secretary of state, Patrick Gordon Walker, that federation could not succeed because divergent territorial policies towards Africans would lead to dissolution. He was sworn of the privy council in 1957.

Tredgold's liberalism found extra-judicial scope. Following an African railway workers' strike, he chaired a commission urging better wages, housing, and negotiating machinery. His 1946 report stimulated United Kingdom insistence on legislation for native labour boards, which became significant in enabling African industrial organization. His 1957 report on the franchise sought to balance just representation and the retention of government in responsible hands. In the Rhodesian context these were enlightened proposals, giving Africans substantial voting power. However, as enacted, many of the generous aspects were discarded.

In 1957 Tredgold gave fateful advice to R. S. Garfield Todd, the Southern Rhodesian prime minister. Todd, facing a party revolt because of his liberal image, was advised that a dissolution would be refused unless he first called a congress. Todd took the advice and was replaced at congress. An election might have altered Rhodesian history.

In Southern Rhodesia a succession of emergency laws, publicly criticized by Tredgold in 1959, was enacted to counter African nationalism. In November 1960, on the introduction of the Law and Order Maintenance Bill, Tredgold resigned as federal chief justice, because, in his words, the bill 'outraged almost every basic human right and is an unwarranted invasion by the Executive of the sphere of the courts' (*The Times*, 2 Nov 1960, 12a).

Tredgold now sought to form a broad national front of all races. He had no success, being regarded as a visionary, and suffered the agonies of a prophet. In July 1964 he warned that it was the duty of the army and police to suppress a unilateral declaration of independence. Had he not resigned, he would have been able to give the governor, Sir Humphrey Gibbs, the unequivocal official support he so lacked in November 1965, and the crucial order to crown servants to co-operate with the regime of Ian Smith would not have been given.

Despite Tredgold's sadness at Rhodesian events, he could treat these with humour, and gave consolation and advice to a stream of visitors and friends. Throughout life he obtained contentment from interests as a naturalist, from poetry, music, the telling of tales, precision carpentry, and an inexhaustible passion for Rhodesian history. He was made an honorary LLD of Witwatersrand in 1953.

Tredgold was a man of lean and ascetic appearance and upright carriage. From his sunburnt face piercing blue eyes, under a broad forehead, looked out with an apparent seriousness that disappeared with a shy but ready smile. He was a great walker, even in his seventies leaving others far behind. In 1956 he had revised a guide entitled *The Matopos*. These were his beloved hills, a place from which to view the world, think of all humanity, and commune with the elemental powers of the universe. Even during the guerrilla war he returned. In 1973 he published *Xhosa: Tales of Life from the African Veld*. This was illustrated by Margaret Helen Phear, who became the second Lady Tredgold in 1974. She was the daughter of Colin Cuthbert Baines, South African police commandant. In a final joint project Tredgold and his wife contributed plants and information for *Rhodesian Wild Flowers* (1979). Tredgold died at Marandellas, Rhodesia, on 8 April 1977.   CLAIRE PALLEY, *rev.*

Sources *The Times* (12 April 1977) · R. C. Tredgold, *The Rhodesia that was my life* (1968) · L. H. Gann and M. Gelfand, *Huggins of Rhodesia: the man and his country* (1964) · R. Blake, *A history of Rhodesia* (1977) · private information (1986) · personal knowledge (1986) · 'Rhodesia chief justice resigns', *The Times* (2 Nov 1960), 12a
Archives Bodl. RH, official corresp. and papers as minister of justice | Bodl. RH, corresp. with Sir R. R. Welensky

Tredgold, Roger Francis (1911–1975), physician and fencer, was born on 23 October 1911 in Guildford, Surrey, the son of Alfred Frank *Tredgold (1870–1952), physician, and his wife, Zoë Hanbury (d. 1947). He was educated at Winchester College and at Trinity College, Cambridge, before completing his medical studies at University College Hospital, London. In 1938 he married (Verity) Micheline Walker, the daughter of Sir Gilbert Thomas Walker, the meteorologist. They had a son and a daughter. As a young doctor in the Royal Army Medical Corps during the war he became adviser in psychiatry to the allied land forces in India and in south-east Asia, then adviser to the National Health Service, and finally to the army at home. He subsequently compiled three updated editions of his father's textbook *Mental Retardation*. In 1948 he was appointed consultant psychiatrist at University College Hospital (UCH), and within three years became head of the department of psychological medicine there, a post he held for over twenty-five years.

During that time the department at UCH became one of the most respected teaching centres in the country. Tredgold's skill and prescience in collaborating with general practitioners, social workers, psychologists, the clergy, and other helping professions enabled him to integrate psychiatric work with other hospital departments and community services long before the concept of psychiatric departments in district general hospitals was generally recognized. He was also a man of deep spiritual convictions, and worked hard to bring medicine and the churches into closer touch. For someone universally respected and popular, he had a liking for controversy and strong opinions, trenchantly held.

Tredgold was a pioneer in the field of industrial mental health. He was also an inspiring teacher and lecturer, as well as the author of the seminal work *Human Relations in Modern Industry* (1949; rev. edn, 1963). He also edited *Bridging the Gap* (1958), for which he chose the subtitle 'From fear to understanding in mental illness', a choice of words which reflected his own approach to psychiatric problems. He was co-editor of *UCH Notes on Psychiatry for Students and General Practitioners* (1970), a revised edition of which appeared in 1975, shortly before his death. One of his papers which is still quoted today is titled 'The "if only" syndrome'. He was a founder member of the International Committee of Occupational Mental Health, and lectured widely on stress associated with industrial management.

As a young man Tredgold was an outstanding fencer, and represented Britain at three Olympic games (1936, 1948, and 1952). He also won the British sabre championship a record six times, stretching from 1937 to 1955, with six years of this period lost to war. Another record he established was to compete in every one of the twenty-three national sabre championships held between 1934 and 1963: he reached the final on every occasion, and finished in the first three on twelve occasions. He won his international spurs in 1934, while still a medical student, in a foil team match against the USA, while he was fifth in the national épée championships the same year. In 1948, the year in which he took up his consultancy at UCH, he became the first editor of a national magazine for fencing, *The Sword*, and continued to produce this thrice-yearly publication for the next five years. Contemporaries recall him as a formidable and towering presence, difficult to reach, let alone hit, with a lightness of hand and speed of foot that belied his off-piste gangling manner.

A story still told in the lecture halls of UCH recalls the period in the late 1940s, when Roger Tredgold was working at the mental hospital at St Pancras. One lunchtime, this 6 foot 4 inch figure, with an imposing head that looked borrowed from the Addams family, emerged from the hospital clutching an ancient fencing bag and already clad in white canvas fencing breeches. He hailed a taxi, and commanded it to make for the fencing club in Hanover Square, where he was already late for an Olympic squad training session. Safely inside the taxi, he was completing his change into duelling kit when he became aware that his driver had completed a full circle, and had pulled up in front of the hospital gates. The cabbie rushed to the front desk, where he breathlessly complained, ''Ere, I've got one of your inmates in my cab.'

If fencing was his principal interest outside medicine, Tredgold found time for several others: visiting ruins, especially in Turkey and Greece (he remained ever the Winchester classicist), birdwatching (on one occasion he was arrested as a suspected spy on the Albanian border), music, and chess. An active fencer until well into his fifties, he was diagnosed in 1975 with prostate cancer. He died on 24 December 1975 at his home, White Cottage, Old Heathfield, Sussex. His wife survived him.

RICHARD COHEN

Sources E. Lloyd, *The Sword* (spring 1976) · T. Fox, memorial address, 19 Jan 1976 [unpubd] · *The Times* (2 Jan 1976) · *BMJ* (17 Jan 1976), 160 · *The Lancet* (10 Jan 1976), 101–2 · personal knowledge (2004) · private information (2004) [Christopher Tredgold, son; R. C. Winton, friend; B. Adams, colleague] · WWW
Wealth at death £39,313: probate, 22 March 1976, *CGPLA Eng. & Wales*

Tredgold, Thomas (1788–1829), engineer, was born at Brandon, near the city of Durham, on 22 August 1788. After receiving a basic elementary education at the village school he was apprenticed at the age of fourteen to a cabinet-maker at Durham. Tredgold remained with him six years, studying mathematics and architecture in his spare time, and taking advantage of the holidays granted on race days to acquire a knowledge of perspective. Following the completion of his apprenticeship in 1808 he went to Scotland where he worked five years as a joiner and journeyman carpenter. His zeal for self-improvement by intensive study affected his health, particularly through lack of sleep and relaxation. He left Scotland to work in the London office of his relative, William Atkinson, architect to the ordnance, with whom he lived for six years. Continuing to work for Atkinson he maintained his abiding interest in engineering construction. He taught himself French to broaden his technical reading, striving to master the latest literature on engineering and architecture. He also avidly read chemistry, mineralogy, and geology, and sought to improve his knowledge of the higher branches of mathematics.

In 1820 Tredgold published *Elementary Principles of Carpentry*, in which he considered the problems connected with the resistance of timber in relation to making floors, roofs, bridges, and other structures. This work was intended to show clearly the principles of construction. He was conscious of the need to write plainly, avoiding, where possible, esoteric technical language. He also wrote an essay on the nature and properties of timber. With the exception of Barlow's *Essay on the Strength of Timber and other Materials* (1817) Tredgold's work was the first serious attempt in England to determine practically and scientifically the data of resistance, rather than relying on formulae calculated in the previous century. Several editions of Tredgold's work were published after his death; the latest edition appeared in 1919. This work was followed in 1822 by *A Practical Essay on the Strength of Cast Iron and other Metals*.

Though they were long the standard textbooks of English engineers, the scientific value of both these works was seriously impaired by Tredgold's insufficient mathematical training, and particularly by his ignorance of the theory of elasticity, which often led him into error and rendered his reasoning obscure.

In 1823 the increase of business and his commitment to his studies led Tredgold to resign his position in Atkinson's office and to set up on his own account. Confident in his all-round abilities as a writer on technical subjects, he also submitted to the Edinburgh publisher Napier in 1823 an article on steel-engraving 'as far as it relates to printing', adding that it was 'not in my line of pursuits' (BL, Marvey Napier MSS). In the same year Tredgold put forward a criticism of Perkins's steam engine, arguing that it would never produce the same effect as the common condensing engine. In the last five years of his life Tredgold published numerous technical articles, in addition to several books and contributions to the *Encyclopaedia Britannica*.

Tredgold died, exhausted by study, on 28 January 1829, and was buried in St John's Wood chapel cemetery. He left an estate valued at under £800 to his widow, Sally, three daughters, and son Thomas, who held the post of engineer in the office of stamps of the East India Company at Calcutta, where he died on 4 May 1853.

E. I. CARLYLE, *rev.* B. P. CRONIN

Sources C. Knight, ed., *The English cyclopaedia: biography*, 6 (1858) · *London and Edinburgh Philosophical Magazine*, 3rd ser., 4 (1834), 394–6 · *Architectural Magazine*, 1 (1834), 208 · *Dictionary of architecture* · C. Singer and others, eds., *A history of technology*, 4: *The industrial revolution, c. 1750 to c. 1850* (1958), 165, 445, 484 · I. Todhunter, *A history of the theory of elasticity and of the strength of materials from Galilei to the present time*, ed. K. Pearson, 2 vols. (1886–93), vol. 1, pp. 105–7, 454–6, 542; vol. 2, p. 649 · Allibone, *Dict.* · L. M. Brown and I. R. Christie, eds., *Bibliography of British history, 1789–1851* (1977) · death duty register, PRO, IR 26/2249

Archives BM, corresp., Add. MSS 34612–34613 · Inst. CE, letters to Francis Bramah · Lincs. Arch., corresp. with J. S. Langton

Likenesses line engraving, BM, NPG · portrait, repro. in Tredgold, *Steam engine*

Wealth at death under £800: PRO, death duty registers, IR 26/2249

Tredway, Letice [Letitia; *name in religion* Mary] (1593–1677), abbess of the Convent of Our Blessed Lady of Syon, Paris, was baptized Letice or Letitia Tredway, and was the daughter of Sir Walter Tredway (*d.* 1604) of Beaconsfield and his wife, Elizabeth Weyman. After the premature deaths within ten years of both her father and her brother she inherited rights to the family property. By the time of her brother's death in 1615 she had already converted to Catholicism and had entered a Flemish Augustinian convent near Douai, where she remained for some years. At the time there were no English houses in France, although a number had been founded in Flanders. With Thomas Carre, a priest at the English College at Douai, she decided to found the first English house in France. At first, the plan was to open a convent in Douai, but by 1632 she had fixed firmly on Paris as the site of the new house. In spite of a lack of contacts in Paris, in 1633 she obtained letters patent from Louis XIII for the founding of the new house under the direction of English secular clergy, subject to the authority of the archbishop of Paris. However, there were objections, not least because she lacked a foundation fund and had only one professed nun, Margaret de Bury, a Walloon, as a committed supporter. The dowries of five postulants, newly arrived from England, would not contribute financially to the house until they were paid a year later on profession. Mary Tredway settled £3000 from family sources to support the new convent financially and by 1635 the first postulants were professed.

From the beginning the main burden of organization rested on Mary Tredway. However, the reputation of the new convent spread and attracted other entrants from England. By 1640 there were nineteen choir nuns, five lay sisters and three novices; new premises which became the convent's home for the next 220 years had been bought and a school for English girls had been established. Within five years the building programme was completed and she turned her full attention to the spiritual and liturgical life of the convent. She had brought St Augustine's rule with her from Douai and this she applied carefully. By the 1640s the convent of Our Blessed Lady of Syon was a flourishing community which had earned a reputation for excellent music and discipline.

The civil wars in England and France deprived the house of both income and recruits, but its reputation secured financial assistance from Seguier, the chancellor of France, which enabled the convent to survive. In spite of the financial difficulties of this period Mary Tredway and Thomas Carre co-operated in the foundation of a small college, St Gregory's, where English secular priests could stay while they studied at the Sorbonne. Mary Tredway included them in as much of the convent life as she was able to. From the first recruits she found a successor to Thomas Carre, who had acted as financial adviser as well as confessor to the convent. Edward Lutton was an excellent choice, able to sort out a number of serious financial problems for them.

Mary Tredway celebrated her jubilee in 1664 with ceremonies that included special services and music, presentations by the boarders from the school, and dinner with most of the English Catholics in Paris. In old age ill health prevented her carrying out her duties as abbess as she wished and, aged over eighty, she suffered a bad fall in 1672 which left her virtually bedridden for the last five years of her life. Lutton was able to negotiate new constitutions which allowed the election of a new abbess every four years and Mary Tredway resigned after forty years as abbess, spending her last years reading the prayers and devotions of St Thomas à Kempis. She died on 13 October 1677 and was buried in the convent chapel (demolished in 1860).

At her death Mary Tredway left a convent with forty-three choir nuns and ten lay sisters. She had created and led a community which would prove strong enough to survive the French Revolution, giving the veil to eighty postulants. The convent had a high reputation as a centre of discipline and musical excellence and for its school, which attracted pupils from a wide area.

CAROLINE M. K. BOWDEN

Sources A. F. Allison, 'The English Augustinian convent of Our Lady of Syon at Paris … 1634–1713', *Recusant History*, 21 (1992–3), 451–96 • F.-M.-Th. Cédoz, *Un couvent de religieuses anglaises à Paris* (1891) • 'The beginning and progresse of this our monastery called Our Blessed Lady of Syon, chanonesses regulars of the order of St Austin established in Paris in the year 1634', Downside Abbey, Augustinian MSS
Archives Downside Abbey, near Bath, Augustinian manuscripts, 'The beginning and progresse of this our monastery called Our Blessed Lady of Syon, chanonesses regulars of the order of St Austin established in Paris in the year 1634'
Likenesses portrait, St Augustine's Priory, Ealing

Tree, Sir Herbert Beerbohm [*real name* Herbert Draper Beerbohm] (**1852–1917**), actor and theatre manager, was born on 17 December 1852 at 2 Pembridge Villas, Kensington, London, the second of the four children of Julius Ewald Beerbohm (1810–1892) and his wife, Constantia Draper. His father, a London corn merchant, was German-Lithuanian and his mother was British. Sir Henry Maximilian (Max) *Beerbohm was his youngest half-brother, from his father's second marriage.

Education and early stage career Beerbohm received his education at various schools in England, including Mrs Adams's Preparatory School at Frant, Dr Stone's school in King's Square, Bristol, and Westbourne collegiate school in Westbourne Grove, London; he then attended the school where his father had been educated, Schnepfeuthal College in Thuringia, Germany. At the age of eighteen he joined his father's business, but he spent his free hours performing with amateur theatrical groups, and after eight years he left his clerical job to pursue a vocation as an actor.

During the late 1870s he assumed the name Herbert Beerbohm Tree, and performed with amateur groups. After a successful appearance as Grimaldi in Boucicault's *The Life of an Actress* at the Globe Theatre (1878), he began his professional acting career when he joined the Bijou Comedy Company for a brief provincial tour. In the autumn of 1878 he secured his first London engagement, at the Royal Olympic Theatre under the management of Henry Neville. Except for an occasional metropolitan stint, by 1880 his experience had been limited mainly to provincial productions of foreign melodramas and farces in which he played German barons, French marquesses, and other eccentric members of the foreign gentry. One such provincial performance, the old Marquis de Ponstable in *Madame Favart*, garnered Tree an invitation from Genevieve Ward to enact Prince Maleotti in a revival of *Forget-me-Not* at the Prince of Wales's Theatre during April and May 1880. For the next four years he continued touring the provinces and had a few unremarkable performances in London theatres. On 16 September 1882 he married an actress, Maud Holt (1863–1937), with whom he had three daughters. Tree enjoyed his first major success on the London stage in March 1884, when Edgar Bruce, the manager of the Prince of Wales's, commissioned him to

Sir Herbert Beerbohm Tree (1852–1917), by Harrington Mann

play the Revd Robert Spalding in Charles Hawtrey's adaptation of *The Private Secretary*. Immediately afterwards, Tree took the part of Paolo Marcari in Hugh Conway's *Called back*, and the contrast between the timid parson and the dashing Italian spy helped to establish his reputation as a versatile character actor. His career then ebbed, and from late 1884 to 1886 his London appearances in such plays as Pinero's *The Magistrate* and W. S. Gilbert's *Engaged* were commonplace and lacked the distinction of his earlier successes. In the autumn of 1886 Tree joined Frank Benson's company for a week at Bournemouth, where he played Sir Peter Teazle and Iago. After this provincial run he returned to London and the Haymarket Theatre, and his career rallied when he turned his minor role of Baron Harzfeld in Charles Young's *Jim the Penman* into a main feature of the production.

Management By the spring of 1887, aged thirty-four and with nine years of both amateur and professional experience, Tree had secured a sufficient reputation to embolden him to venture into theatre management, and in April he took over the Comedy Theatre in Panton Street. He inaugurated his managerial career with a successful run of W. Outram Tristram's Russian revolutionary play *The Red Lamp*, in which he played Demetrius. In the autumn of 1887 he became the lessee and manager of the more prestigious Haymarket Theatre, where he not only raised the theatre's distinction as a major London playhouse (a status it had lost with the departure of the Bancrofts in 1885) but also secured for himself a reputation as one of London's leading actor–managers. During his ten-year management of the Haymarket, Tree produced and acted in approximately thirty plays, mainly melodramas and farces which were standard nineteenth-century fare, such as *Trilby* and *Captain Swift*. *Trilby*, indeed, was the popular sensation of 1895, running to 260 performances. Tree, unlike many West End theatre managers, who eschewed contemporary and potentially controversial social plays, recognized the importance of the new drama, staging Maeterlinck's *The Intruder* (1890), Wilde's *A Woman of No Importance* (1893), and Ibsen's *An Enemy of the People* (1893). And in an effort to support new playwrights and plays with artistic rather than commercial value, he instituted special 'Monday night' performances restricted to the production of new dramas, essentially emulating Grein's work at the newly established Independent Theatre. He also elevated the Haymarket's status as a Shakespearian playhouse, and his productions of *The Merry Wives of Windsor* (1889), *Hamlet* (1892), and *Henry IV, Part 1* (1896) earned him recognition not only as an accomplished actor–manager capable of producing a wide range of genres but also as a solid competitor to Henry Irving and the Lyceum Theatre.

Her Majesty's Theatre Tree's successful career at the Haymarket enabled him to amass sufficient funds to finance in part construction of a new theatre, Her Majesty's Theatre (renamed His Majesty's with the accession of Edward VII in 1901), which opened on 28 April 1897 with Gilbert Parker's *The Seats of the Mighty*. During his management of Her Majesty's, from 1897 until his death in 1917, Tree staged approximately sixty plays, and the diversity of his repertory revealed his interest in classical drama as well as popular genres. In addition to producing contemporary poetic drama, such as Stephen Phillips's *Herod* (1900), *Ulysses* (1902), *Nero* (1906), and *Faust* (1908), he staged plays by prominent British playwrights, including Henry Arthur Jones's *Carnac Sahib* (1899) and the London première of Shaw's *Pygmalion* (1914). Tree also produced and performed in a number of stage versions of popular nineteenth-century novels: Sydney Grundy's *Musketeers*, an adaptation of Dumas's novel (1898); Henri Bataille and Michael Morton's remake of Tolstoy's work, *Resurrection* (1903); Morton's dramatization of Thackeray's novel *The Newcomes* entitled *Colonel Newcome* (1906); and three Dickensian adaptations, *Oliver Twist* (1905), *The Mystery of Edwin Drood* (1908), and *David Copperfield* (1914). In addition he offered his patrons adaptations of foreign plays, such as Louis Parker's *Beethoven*, a reworking of the play by Réné Fauchois (1909), Henry Hamilton's English version of Adolph Glass's *A Russian Tragedy* (1909), and W. Somerset Maugham's adaptation of Molière's *Le bourgeois gentilhomme* entitled *The Perfect Gentleman* (1913). The repertory at Her Majesty's included the classics, such as *The School for Scandal* (1909), as well as numerous melodramas, farces, and romantic comedies.

Tree and Shakespeare While Tree built Her Majesty's Theatre's solid reputation on the successful productions of a variety of dramas, he earned his theatre the international reputation as the premier playhouse for Shakespeare in Britain during the Edwardian era, and it is for this dedication to the production of Shakespeare that his career was most celebrated. During his twenty-year tenure at Her Majesty's he worked indefatigably to popularize Shakespeare with the general theatregoing public, and his success is evinced by an impressive production record unmatched by any West End manager: he put on sixteen Shakespeare plays which averaged initial three-month runs, many of them successful enough for periodic revivals during subsequent seasons, and he instituted an annual Shakespeare festival which featured more than two hundred performances by Her Majesty's Theatre company and other acting corps during its nine-year existence (1905–13). At a time when most theatre managers believed that Shakespeare's plays lacked commercial viability and spelt financial ruin, Tree proved that Shakespeare could be made accessible and appealing to large numbers of patrons. Fittingly, his initial Shakespearian production, *Julius Caesar*, was his first commercial success at Her Majesty's, and during its six-month run (22 January to 10 June 1898) it enjoyed 165 consecutive performances and attracted 242,000 spectators. His next revival, *King John*, ran from 20 September 1899 to 6 January 1900 and brought in 170,000 patrons, and he followed this with one of his most famous and successful comedies, *A Midsummer Night's Dream*, which played to 220,000 spectators from 10 January to 26 May 1900. Tree's longest running revival, *Henry VIII*, was a record breaker, receiving 254 consecutive performances from 1 September 1910 to 8 April 1911. Most of the Shakespeare revivals at Her Majesty's enjoyed equally unprecedented runs. Tree succeeded in popularizing Shakespeare with his audiences because he staged the plays in ways that appealed to spectators' taste for elaborate spectacle and realistic scenery and scenic effects. Working in the tradition of pictorial realism which dominated the nineteenth- and early-twentieth-century theatre, Tree brought this scenographic method to its apogee, staging the most spectacular Shakespearian revivals in British stage history. At Her Majesty's, audiences experienced unprecedented realistic stage pictures, such as the replica of a fourteenth-century list in *Richard II* (1903), the woodland glade with a shepherd's cottage and babbling brook in *The Winter's Tale* (1906), the storm-tossed sixteenth-century vessel in *The Tempest* (1904), the set of an authentic Renaissance ghetto in *The Merchant of Venice* (1908), or such interpolated scenes as Anne Bullen's coronation in Westminster Abbey and King John's granting of Magna Charta. Tree's work with Shakespeare also involved four film projects that spanned his career at Her Majesty's: the opening shipwreck from his 1904 revival of *The Tempest*, captured on film at His Majesty's in 1905 by Charles Urban; a five-scene version of *Henry VIII*, based on his 1910 production featuring himself as Cardinal Wolsey, and filmed in February 1911 at William Barker's Ealing studio; a 1916 *Macbeth*, bearing no direct resemblance to his 1911 stage version, filmed in California by D. W. Griffith with Tree playing the title role; and, though not as extensive as the others but certainly the most important historically, three brief segments from his *King John* revival filmed in 1899—Tree's initial cinematographic venture and the very first record of Shakespeare on film.

Tree as an actor Tree excelled in character roles, and was considered by many to be the best character actor of his day. He possessed an exceptional mimetic genius that enabled him to enact a wide range of roles in which he gave each a unique and differing individuality, and he excelled especially in those characters with idiosyncratic and eccentric natures on which he could build strong, vivid parts, such as Svengali, Fagin, and Falstaff. His greatest strength was his inventiveness in delineating a character by the use of external details. As an expert with make-up, he could transform his nondescript, protean face into myriad roles which made the actor behind them virtually unrecognizable. Tree also had equal mastery over his facial expressions and body. He had remarkably expressive eyes which could project varying emotions within the character, from the dreamy languor of Hamlet during his moments of reflection and the baleful hatred of Shylock towards his persecutors to the nervous fear of Richard II during his surrender at Flint Castle. His hands were extraordinarily eloquent, and the gestures he used were always significant, telling, and illustrative. In addition, he could radically change his carriage and stature to effect a complete physical transformation into a character. Tree was tall, lanky, and graceful in gesture, but for his performance as Beethoven he transformed into a short, pudgy, bull-necked man with an awkward stride and jerky gestures. In selecting his Shakespearian roles he capitalized on these acting strengths by choosing parts that offered definable, observable, or atypical traits which could be made into strong character roles. His Malvolio was a swaggering and conceited fool, King John a superstitious and deceitful coward, and Macbeth a neurotic and self-torturing monarch. Tree built his characters slowly, allowing inspiration to suggest to him the appropriate business and external details, and he relied on that inspiration during performances, which could lead to inconsistent interpretations of a given role. Moreover, impatient and restless by nature, he easily tired of characters after a brief run, and, in an effort to sustain his own interest in a role, he continually added business and details to the part, which in turn led to further inconsistencies in his portrayals of a character over an extended time. The restlessness that spurred him on in his search for new, challenging, and various roles resulted in a degree of histrionic versatility that went unmatched by any of his contemporaries.

Henry Irving's successor As a manager, Tree was regarded as Irving's successor and heir. Tree's theatre, built and decorated for him in the tasteful Louis XV style and deemed the handsomest playhouse in London, was, as Macqueen-Pope described it, 'the very essence of the Edwardian theatre' and 'the last word in everything theatrical at that time' (*Carriages at Eleven*, 31). Her Majesty's epitomized the cultural milieu of the Edwardian era in its opulence, and Tree's productions, with their elaborate and expensive scene designs, costumes, and properties, mirrored the Edwardian taste for luxury and extravagance. Towards the end of his career, Tree's production methods were being criticized by practitioners who favoured the new stage-craft of Appia and Craig's non-illusionistic sets and Poel's Elizabethanism, but Tree, one of the last major actor–managers to work along the lines of pictorial illustration, adamantly rejected the new scenography and defended his methods by referring his critics to the unprecedented attendance records and length of runs set at his theatre. His impressive managerial career at Her Majesty's, however, was not due solely to the spectacular scenery, for Tree offered his patrons a wide range of productions which could suit the different sensibilities and tastes of most Londoners. Most importantly, he appreciated the need for a strong acting ensemble, and, unlike Irving, he commissioned the best actors to join his company. His productions featured such renowned performers as Constance Collier, Ellen Terry, Madge Kendal, Julia Neilson, Violet Vanbrugh, Oscar Asche, Arthur Bourchier, and Lewis Waller. In every aspect of production Tree hired the most expert artists available, including designers (Lawrence Alma-Tadema, Joseph Harker, Walter Hann, Percy Anderson) and musicians (Raymond Roze, Arthur Sullivan, Coleridge Taylor) who helped create, under his direction, some of the most magnificent and artistic theatre productions of the Edwardian era.

A theatrical partnership Tree's management at the Haymarket and Her Majesty's was aided by his wife, Maud, who viewed their union as a theatrical partnership as well as a personal one. In addition to acting in numerous revivals under her husband's direction, Maud Tree lent encouragement and advice on many of his projects and productions, and her support was a significant contributing factor to his continued success. The professional success earned by their partnership gained them and their three daughters entrée into London's élite society: the Tree family became intimately acquainted with some of the most socially prominent and politically powerful members of Edwardian society, including members of parliament and the peerage, as well as London's coterie of élite intellectuals and aesthetes, 'the Souls', particularly the family of Violet Manners, duchess of Rutland. Viola, Felicity, and Iris Tree were fully absorbed by aristocratic society: Iris married Curtis Moffat, becoming Countess Ledebur, and Felicity married Sir Geoffrey Cory-Wright, third baronet. Viola followed the family profession, and eventually married Alan Parsons, a theatre critic.

Final years and death Tree made significant contributions to the growth of the British theatre and the advancement of theatre art. In 1904 he established the Royal Academy of Dramatic Art, which remains one of the most prestigious schools for stage training in the world. He also served as president of the Theatrical Managers' Association and worked in various capacities for the Actors' Benevolent Fund and the Actors' Association. For all these contributions, as well as for his work at Her Majesty's, he was knighted by Edward VII in 1909. His renown in the theatre world earned him invitations to tour his revivals in America, which he did on numerous occasions, and brought him a special invitation from the German Kaiser, to which he responded by performing with his company in various Shakespearian plays at Berlin's Royal Opera House (1907). He also received invitations to lecture on theatre in Great Britain and America; during the war years, he used these opportunities to deliver patriotic addresses. He wrote several books in which he discussed the importance of the theatre and the arts in modern society.

Sir Herbert Beerbohm Tree died on 2 July 1917, at a London nursing home at 15 Henrietta Street, Marylebone, from pulmonary blood clots after undergoing surgery for a leg injury. He was survived by his wife and three daughters, and also by six children from his liaison with (Beatrice) May Pinney (later Reed): among these children were the film director Carol *Reed and Peter Reed, the father of the film actor Oliver Reed. His body was cremated and his ashes were placed in Hampstead cemetery.

B. A. KACHUR

Sources H. Pearson, *Beerbohm Tree: his life and laughter* (1956) · M. Bingham, *The great lover: the life and art of Herbert Beerbohm Tree*, another edn (1979) · B. Kachur, 'Herbert Beerbohm Tree: Shakespearean actor–director', PhD diss., Ohio State University, 1986 · W. Macqueen-Pope, *Carriages at eleven: the story of the Edwardian theatre* (1947) · M. Cran, *Herbert Beerbohm Tree* (1907) · M. Beerbohm, *Herbert Beerbohm Tree* (1917) · *The Times* (3 July 1917) · *The Times* (9 July 1917) · b. cert. · d. cert. · A. Lambert, *Unquiet Souls: the Indian summer of the British aristocracy, 1880–1918* (1984)

Archives Theatre Museum, London, prompt books, records, and typescripts · University of Bristol, Theatre Collection, diaries, letters, and papers | BL, letters to George Bernard Shaw, Add. MS 50551 · Bodl. Oxf., letters to various members of Lewis family · Ellen Terry Museum, Smallhythe, Kent, letters to Ellen Terry · HLRO, letters to R. D. Blumenfeld · Theatre Museum, London, letters to Clement K. Shorter · U. Birm., corresp. with J. Chamberlain · U. Leeds, Brotherton L., letters to Henry Arthur Jones | FILM BFI NFTVA, news footage | SOUND BL NSA, performance recordings

Likenesses Duchess of Rutland, pencil sketch, 1891 · E. Webling, miniature, 1892, Russell-Cotes Art Gallery, Bournemouth · C. Buchel, charcoal drawing, c.1903, V&A · J. Collier, group portrait, oils, 1904, Garr. Club · A. P. F. Ritchie, lithograph, pubd 1905, NPG · M. Beerbohm, caricature drawing, c.1908, AM Oxf. · G. Frampton, plaster cast of death mask, 1918, NPG · M. Beerbohm, caricature drawing, V&A · C. Buchel, oils (as 'The Beloved Vagabond'), Royal Academy of Dramatic Art, London · C. Buchel, oils (as Hamlet), Royal Academy of Dramatic Art, London · C. Buchel, oils (as Richard III?), Royal Academy of Dramatic Art, London · W. & D. Downey, photograph, NPG · W. & D. Downey, woodbury-type photograph (as Hamlet), NPG; repro. in W. Downey and D. Downey, *The cabinet portrait gallery*, 3 (1892) · Ellis & Walery, photogravure, NPG · H. Furniss, pen-and-ink caricature, NPG; repro. in H. Furniss, *The Garrick gallery of caricatures* (1900) · S. P. Hall, pencil sketch, NPG · H. Mann, oils, NPG [*see illus.*] · A. Morrow, watercolour drawing (as Svengali), Garr. Club · NIBS, caricature, Hentschel-colourtype, NPG; repro. in *VF* (5 April 1911) · J. Ross, coloured woodblock · J. S. Sargent, charcoal drawing · J. S. Sargent, oils (as Svengali in *Trilby*), Garr. Club · Spy [L. Ward], caricature, chromolithograph, NPG; repro. in *VF* (12 July 1890) · photographs, University of Bristol, Theatre Collection, Beerbohm Tree collection · photogravures, NPG · postcards, NPG · woodburytype photographs, NPG

Wealth at death £44,085 10s. 8d.: probate, 3 Nov 1917, *CGPLA Eng. & Wales*

Tree [*married name* Bradshaw], **(Anna) Maria** (1801/2–1862), actress and singer, was born in Lancaster Buildings, St Martin's Lane, London, in August 1801 or 1802, the second

(**Anna**) **Maria Tree** (1801/2–1862), by Alexander Pope, c.1820

of the four daughters of Cornelius Tree, of the East India House. One of her sisters, Mrs Quin, was a dancer, and another enjoyed great success as Ellen *Kean. Maria was a pupil of Sir Henry Rowley Bishop and Gesualdo Lanza, who trained her mezzo-soprano voice. After singing in the chorus at Drury Lane, and a short experience in Bath playing Polly in *The Beggar's Opera*, she appeared in 1818 at Covent Garden as Rosina in *The Barber of Seville*. Subsequently she played various parts, including Susanna in *The Marriage of Figaro*, principally as a substitute for Maria Foote and Catherine Stephens. Her first recorded appearance in an original role seems to have been as Princess Stella in Bishop's *The Gnome King*, a spectacular produced at Covent Garden on 6 October 1819. On 11 December of the same year she appeared as Luciana in an opera based on *The Comedy of Errors*. This led to the series of Shakespearian comedy performances, both musical and straight, on which her fame rested. With the exception of a solitary performance at Drury Lane on 19 April 1823, when she was lent by her own management, she appears to have remained at Covent Garden until her retirement on 15 June 1825, despite a squabble about precedence between her and Mary Ann Paton. February 1824 saw her as the original Coelio in Bishop's *Native Land*. Her last roles were Mary Copp in *Charles II*, Clari in the opera of the same name, and *The Maid of the Mill*, when she was the first to sing Bishop's most famous ballad, 'Home, Sweet Home'. Shortly afterwards she married the widowed James Bradshaw, a propertied tea merchant and MP for Canterbury, who died on 4 March 1847. They had one daughter, Harriet Maria.

It was said that, as a singer, Maria Tree was the best

actress of her day; and that, as an actress, she was the best singer. She was of medium height with a pleasing figure and great simplicity, but no special claim to beauty. She died on 17 February 1862 at her home, 11 Queen's Gate Terrace, London, after a long retirement and a blameless life.

JOSEPH KNIGHT, *rev.* J. GILLILAND

Sources *Oxberry's Dramatic Biography*, 3/44 (1825) • Mrs C. Baron-Wilson, *Our actresses*, 2 vols. (1844) • H. B. Baker, *The London stage: its history and traditions from 1576 to 1888*, 2 vols. (1889) • 'Memoir of Miss M. Tree', *Theatrical Inquisitor*, 15 (1820), 167–9 • *The biography of the British stage, being correct narratives of the lives of all the principal actors and actresses* (1824) • L. J. De Bekker, *Black's dictionary of music and musicians* (1924) • Boase, *Mod. Eng. biog.* • Genest, *Eng. stage* • Hall, *Dramatic ports.* • W. C. Lane and N. E. Browne, eds., *A. L. A. portrait index* (1906) • *Drama, or, Theatrical Pocket Magazine*, 5 (1824), 336 • *CGPLA Eng. & Wales* (1862)

Likenesses A. Pope, pastel drawing, *c.*1820, Garr. Club [*see illus.*] • L. Sharpe, miniature, exh. RA 1821, Garr. Club • G. H. Phillips, mezzotint, pubd 1828 (after R. Westall), NPG • S. De Wilde, watercolour drawing (as Susanna in *The Marriage of Figaro*), Garr. Club • De Wilde, miniature, Garr. Club • engraving (as Imogen), repro. in *Oxberry's Dramatic Biography* • portraits, Harvard TC • print (as Rosina), repro. in 'Memoir of Miss M. Tree', *Theatrical Inquisitor*

Wealth at death under £30,000: administration, 4 April 1862, *CGPLA Eng. & Wales*

Tree, Nancy Keene. *See* Lancaster, Nancy Keene (1897–1994).

Treece, Henry William (1911–1966), writer and schoolteacher, was born on 22 December 1911 at Oxford Terrace, Oxford Street, New Town, Wednesbury, Staffordshire, the younger of the two children of Richard Treece (*b. c.*1872), bridge engineer, and his wife, Mary Fisher, *née* Mason (*b. c.*1875). He attended Wednesbury High School for Boys and won a scholarship to Birmingham University, where he read English, history, and Spanish, graduating in 1933. He entered teaching, eventually becoming English master at the grammar school, Barton-on-Humber, Lincolnshire, in late 1938. He married fellow teacher Nelly Mary (1911–1985), daughter of William Woodman, on 6 April 1939. They had three children: David (1945–1946), Jennifer (*b.* 1947), and Richard (*b.* 1949). Treece joined the volunteer reserve of the Royal Air Force in 1941, attaining the rank of flight lieutenant but serving mainly as an intelligence officer. He returned to teaching at Barton in 1946 as senior English master, retiring on health grounds in late 1959.

Treece started to publish poems, and then short stories, from the mid-1930s in journals such as *Seven*. He produced six collections, the first, *38 Poems*, in 1940, and the last, *The Exiles*, in 1952. However, he was best-known for founding with the Scottish poet J. F. Hendry (1912–1986) the short-lived movement which came to be known as the New Apocalypse and, later, the New Romantics. Characterized by its use of myth and imagery, it was a fairly loose association of young poets based mainly outside London. The pair edited three anthologies: *The New Apocalypse* (1939), *The White Horseman* (1941), and *The Crown and the Sickle* (1943). A strong influence was Dylan Thomas, and Treece later produced the first study of him: *Dylan Thomas: Dog among the Fairies* (1949). In late 1941 Treece, with Alan Rook and Stefan Schimanski, took over the editorship of *Kingdom Come*, succeeded in 1943 by *Transformation* (1943–7), a

Henry William Treece (1911–1966), by David Lee, 1964

series of four anthologies of prose, poetry, and plays edited by Treece and Schimanski. In the early 1950s Treece embarked on a new course as a historical novelist, producing ten titles between 1952 (*The Dark Island*) and 1966 (*The Green Man*). He enjoyed his greatest success with his numerous books (including over thirty novels) for children, particularly his viking stories, such as *Viking's Dawn* (1955) and *The Last of the Vikings* (1964). He frequently broadcast on radio, for which he also produced plays and features. He won an Arts Council play prize in 1955 for his *Carnival King*.

Treece was about 5 feet 10 inches tall, well-built, with glasses, and a natural—but not dominating—air of authority. He was very sociable, and mixed well with people from all walks of life. Nominally an Anglican and politically Conservative, he had wide interests, including boxing, music (he was an accomplished pianist and flamenco guitarist), the theatre, and painting. He died in Scunthorpe General Hospital following a heart attack on 10 June 1966 shortly after completing another children's novel, *The Dream-Time*, which was published posthumously in 1967. His body was cremated at Grimsby crematorium.

BRIAN DYSON

Sources M. Fisher, *Henry Treece* (1969) • private information (2004) [J. Treece Jorup, daughter] • H. Treece, *How I see Apocalypse* (1946) • A. T. Tolley, *The poetry of the forties* (1985) • M. Crouch, *The Nesbit tradition: the children's novel in England, 1945–1970* (1972) • G. S. Fraser, *A stranger and afraid: the autobiography of an intellectual* (1983) • J. A. Baggerly, 'Henry Treece and *The new apocalypse*', PhD diss., Texas

Tech University, 1973 • N. Corcoran, *English poetry since 1940* (1993) • A. T. Tolley, *The poetry of the thirties* (1975) • D. Stanford, *Inside the forties: literary memoirs, 1937–1957* (1977) • A. Kamm, ed., *Collins biographical dictionary of English literature* (1993), 474 • J. R. Townsend, *Written for children: an outline of English-language children's literature*, rev. edn (1974)

Archives Ransom HRC, corresp. and literary papers • State University of New York, Buffalo, Lockwood Memorial Library, corresp. and library papers • U. Hull, Brynmor Jones L. | BBC WAC, radio contributors archives • NL Wales, BBC (Wales) archives • Tate collection, letters to Conroy Maddox [microfiche copies] • U. Reading L., letters to the Bodley Head Ltd • U. Reading L., Chatto and Windus Ltd archives • U. Reading L., Hogarth Press archives • UCL, letters to Alex Comfort

Likenesses D. Lee, photograph, 1964, David Lee Photography Ltd, Barton upon Humber [*see illus.*] • D. Lee, photographs, David Lee Photography Ltd, Barton upon Humber

Wealth at death £5991: administration, 26 Sept 1966, *CGPLA Eng. & Wales*

Treffry [*formerly* Austen], **Joseph Thomas** (*bap.* 1782, *d.* 1850), mining industrialist, was baptized Joseph Thomas Austen at St Andrew's Church, Plymouth, on 1 May 1782, the eldest child in the family of one son and two daughters of Joseph Austen (*d.* 1786), of The Friary, Plymouth, brewer and sometime mayor of Plymouth, and his wife, Susanna (*d.* 1842), daughter of Thomas Treffry of Place, Fowey, Cornwall. She and her sister Jane inherited the Treffry estate in Cornwall in 1779 following the death first of their father and then their brother, William Esco Treffry. After the death of her husband in 1786, Susanna and her children moved to Place. Her two daughters died young, Susanna aged sixteen and Sarah in infancy; but she herself lived long, until only eight years before the death of her son.

Nothing is known of Austen's early education. He was at Exeter College, Oxford, from 1801 to 1804, but left without graduating. He returned to Place and became involved in the management of the small family estate, which had been badly neglected for many years. Taking advantage of high wartime agricultural prices he sought to improve the profitability of the estate's farms and acquired more agricultural land. From about 1815 he turned his attention to the more lucrative prospect of mining by adding to the estate's shareholdings in local copper and tin mines. By 1820 he had acquired control of Wheal Treasure, near St Austell, which was later combined with neighbouring mines and renamed Fowey Consols. At its peak in 1837 this was the second largest producer of copper in Cornwall. His other large copper mine, Par Consols, came into production in 1840.

The success of Austen's mining ventures owed much to his investment in good transport facilities. He built and owned ships to handle his business and made a quay at Fowey, on the south coast. Being unable to link his mines to the port with a railway because of opposition from a landowner, he created an entirely new port at Par which was opened in 1833, complete with an inclined plane railway and canal to serve the nearby mines. He further diversified his business interests, though they remained local and related. He built his own smelting works at Par, and

the port was later linked by railway to the Luxulyan granite quarries, which he also owned and developed. In 1836 he bought the pier and harbour of Newquay on the north coast of Cornwall; this was convenient for shipping the lead from the East Wheal Rose mine, and the china clay and stone from his quarries. He also sought to connect Cornwall with the main national railway system. From 1844 to 1846 he was chairman of the provisional committee established for the purpose, and he presided over the board of the Cornwall Railway from 1846 to 1850.

As a young man, Austen entered forcefully into local politics and strengthened his position in the town by purchasing property and allying himself with the enemies of the unreformed municipal corporation of Fowey. While appearing a fiery radical, his politics were individual and never doctrinaire. Although his political activities gave way to business interests, he briefly entered the political arena at a national level in the early 1840s; this led to an unsuccessful campaign by Cornish mine owners against the proposed reduction of import duties on copper ore as part of Robert Peel's tariff reforms.

Austen took great pride in the Treffry heritage, and in 1838 he fulfilled a long-standing wish to take the name Treffry. To ensure the continuation of the name he left the bulk of his estate to a cousin, the Revd Edward John Wilcocks, provided that he also took the family name. Treffry devoted much time to restore and develop Place, which had become partly derelict. The house was visited by Queen Victoria and Prince Albert in September 1846, though Treffry was too ill to receive them. Treffry also improved the estate with a substantial tree-planting programme.

Treffry served as a magistrate and was high sheriff of Cornwall in 1838–9; he was also a committee member of the East Cornwall Agricultural Society, a patron of the Tywardreath Gardening Society, and vice-president of the Royal Cornwall Polytechnic Society from 1849 until his death. He died at Place, unmarried, on 29 January 1850, after several years of serious illness.

JACK SIMMONS, *rev.* EDMUND NEWELL

Sources J. Keast, 'The king of mid-Cornwall': The life of Joseph Thomas Treffry, 1782–1850 (1982) • A. Rideout, *The Treffry family* (1984) • D. B. Barton, *A history of copper mining in Cornwall and Devon* (1981) • E. Newell, 'Cornish miners' petition to Queen Victoria, 1842: a belated reply', *Devon and Cornwall Notes and Queries*, 36 (1987–91), 204–8

Archives Cornwall RO

Likenesses portrait, priv. coll.

Wealth at death £118,749: *DNB*

Trefnant [Trevenant], **John** (*d.* 1404), bishop of Hereford, was from the village of Trefnant, between Denbigh and St Asaph in north Wales. His episcopal chancellor and executor, Master Reginald Wolston, was a kinsman, and a nephew of the bishop had left Agnes Barton as a widow by 1390. Master John Trefnant (John ap Hywel or John Cresset), perhaps a brother of the bishop, was his protégé and Master Hugh Trefnant (Hugh ap Dafydd), his colleague in the St Asaph chapter, may possibly have been kin too. On the other hand, in 1389 Richard II told the pope that Trefnant was related 'in a close degree' to certain nobles 'assisting at our side', presumably from among the lords appellant and, probably explicitly, the earls of Arundel (Perroy, *Diplomatic Correspondence*, 64).

Trefnant was BCL of Oxford University by 7 April 1372, when the pope granted him four years of non-residence from his rectory of Llanwrin, Powys, to study, and DCL by July 1376 when he was involved in a dispute between the law faculty and the rest of the university. He was living in London as a clerk on 1 October 1376; the next six years are undocumented. On 3 January 1382 he was appointed by Archbishop William Courtenay to secure his pallium in the papal curia, an undemanding task which may suggest he was already there, but in April he was thought available to share custody of the spiritualities *sede vacante* of St Asaph (where he was a canon, at least later, and had close friends). However, on 16 July 1383 he was named as a proctor by Florimund, lord of l'Esparre, to ensure a payment into the papal camera, so it does seem likely that he was already permanently in the curia. Probably by 1385, certainly by January 1386, he had become an auditor of causes, continuing in this office until he became a bishop, and being termed a papal chaplain. In these years he acted as proctor in various personal matters for the king and queen, several English bishops, and clerks of the royal household.

On 3 May 1389 Trefnant was papally provided to the see of Hereford and consecrated in Rome on 20 June. It seems unlikely that this represents an independent initiative by the pope, but very likely that the former lords appellant had encouraged the choice, with Richard II himself having no objection. Urban VI gave Trefnant a safe conduct to return to England on 8 August, and he was in London by 16 October when he received his temporalities. He was used by the crown for his legal skills to assist in various sorts of business: for example, to settle disputes in the Anglo-Prussian trade (24 February 1390); to hear a case between the marshal of France and Sir Matthew Gournay (26 April 1390); to execute the sentence of the court in the celebrated *Scrope* v. *Grosvenor* case (28 November 1390); on an embassy to France (18 March – 4 June 1394). According to Edouard Perroy he was an adviser to the king before the re-enactment of the Statute of *Praemunire* in 1393, and does seem a more appropriate choice, at least in terms of recent experience of the papacy, than Bishop John Gilbert of St David's (his predecessor at Hereford), who is named in the issue rolls of the exchequer. On the other hand, Gilbert had had a very long career, including a term as treasurer of the realm, and had pursued business more than once in the papal curia thirty years before. He was one of the few men left who could remember the many different, often unintended, effects which the original statute (enacted in 1353) had had in Edward III's later years.

Whatever his commissions, Trefnant was usually in his own diocese. Between 1389 and 1393 he was in dogged pursuit of the heretics William Swinderby and Walter Bryt, who were evangelizing there and knew how to exploit the clumsy procedures for arrest, their eventual trials before

him being recorded at unique length in his register. He also attended the Council of Stamford, Lincolnshire, which tried the heretic Henry Crump in June 1392. On the other hand, between 1393 and 1396 he opposed vigorously Archbishop Courtenay's attempts to make a visitation of his diocese. Richard II called him to a council at Oxford on 27 January 1399 to have his opinion about the resolution of the great schism.

The circumstances of the deposition of Richard II, especially the events of 29 and 30 September 1399, required the perpetrators to make at least three successive attempts to compose an 'official account' for circulation, each one seeking to improve on the reality and present a coherent and consistent interpretation. Trefnant is always given a significant role. In the earliest, he was said to have been among those who interviewed the king in the Tower of London on the 29th. In the final version, he and Archbishop Richard Scrope headed the deputation that received Richard II's free abdication that day, and presented it as his proctors to the assembly that met on the 30th. Since this was the version which was to be circulated for dissection by a sharply divided political community, it is to be supposed that not only was there indeed such an assembly (a fact that no one was ever to challenge), and there were over 250 parliamentary members-elect from the shires and boroughs in the capital to tell their constituents about any blatant fiction, but that Trefnant and Scrope did enough to qualify for their roles. Indeed, in terms of the public events it describes, this version has been found wanting only in selectivity and interpretation. Its crucial lies are restricted to what happened away from the public eye.

Accordingly, much effort has been invested in finding an explanation for the choice of Trefnant and Scrope in terms of their political affiliation, without much success. The truth seems to be that they were regarded, rightly, as not only the two most substantial lawyers on the episcopal bench but, specifically, the most recently familiar with the papal curia, that those seeking to remove Richard II relied on civil- and especially canon-law principles and precedents to achieve it, and that Scrope and Trefnant need be seen as no more partisan than simply willing to comply in, and lend their authority (perhaps even skilled legal advice) to, a *fait accompli*. Since becoming a bishop, these had been the only reasons why Trefnant had ever been called into public life, but he had been so called, and regularly. In February 1400 he was even sent to the papal curia to explain the deposition.

On 13 February 1401 Trefnant was appointed to help negotiate (in England) the marriage of Princess Blanche to Count Ludwig of the Palatinate; perhaps some canonical difficulty had emerged from close enquiry into the pair's circumstances. After criticism by the Commons in parliament in March 1401 about the thinness of the king's council, he became a regular attender until March 1403. He was a principal escort of Queen Isabella, Richard II's widow, as far as Calais, when she was returned to her royal family of France, from 26 June to 6 August 1401; England's best canon lawyers and experts in the ways of the papacy had certainly to be on hand to make the best of this most sensitive of all the consequences of the deposition. On 16 July and 26 September 1401 he was appointed to hear an appeal in the perennial case of the count of Denia and his ransom.

Such specialist engagements apart, Trefnant appears to have been away from the heart of political life, and much more at home in his diocese. When he made his will on 1 March 1404 at Prestbury, Gloucestershire, he was too sick to do much more than name and give full discretion to ten executors, mainly members of his diocesan staff but headed by Bishop John Trevor of St Asaph, a friend since boyhood but now (as Trefnant surely was too) much troubled by Owain Glyn Dŵr's claims to the allegiance of their kin-groups in that region. In fact, he did not die until 29 March, still at Prestbury. An inventory prepared for probate shows that he owned a library of nearly ninety books, sixty-six of them on canon and civil law. He was buried, as he requested, in St Anne's Chapel on the south side of Hereford Cathedral.   R. G. DAVIES

Sources R. G. Davies, 'The episcopate in England and Wales, 1375–1443', PhD diss., University of Manchester, 1974, 3.cclxiii–vi · W. W. Capes, ed., *Registrum Johannis Trefnant*, CYS, 20 (1916) · Emden, *Oxf.*, 3.1900–01 · register of Thomas Arundel, LPL, 1, fol. 207 [will] · E. Perroy, *L'Angleterre et le grand schisme d'occident* (Paris, 1933) · *The diplomatic correspondence of Richard II*, ed. E. Perroy, CS, 3rd ser., 48 (1933) · J. H. Parry, ed., *Registrum Roberti Mascall*, CYS, 21 (1917)

Trefusis, Violet (1894–1972), writer, was born at 2 Wilton Crescent, London, on 6 June 1894, the elder daughter of Alice Frederica *Keppel, *née* Edmonstone (1868–1947), mistress of Edward VII. On her birth certificate her father is given as George Keppel (1865–1947). In later life she told people that she was the king's daughter but it is likely that her real father was Ernest William Beckett (1856–1917), later Lord Grimthorpe, MP for Whitby (1885–1905) and senior partner in a bank. Nevertheless Violet had a magical childhood; she was occasionally taken to Buckingham Palace and on royal visits to Paris and Biarritz, and the king adored his mistress's beautiful and charming daughter, writing her letters signed 'Kingy'. Her friend Jean Cocteau remarked that she 'rolled her hoop with a sceptre' (Jullian and Phillips, 13).

Violet Keppel was educated by a French governess and at Helen Wolff's school for girls, in London, where Victoria Mary (Vita) Sackville-*West (1892–1962) was also a pupil. Vita thought that she was a brilliant, extraordinary, and 'unearthly creature' (Nicolson, 25). They visited Pisa, Milan, and Florence together in 1908 and had an intense but childish passion, Violet heaping rubies and tuberoses on her friend. Family life changed irrevocably after the king's death, in 1910; Violet was in Ceylon for a few months with her mother, and then at a Munich finishing school with her sister, Sonia (*b.* 1900). Having written a play in German, she began to write poems in English when she returned to London. They were collected in a limited edition for friends, and some appeared in magazines.

Before and during the First World War Violet drifted

Violet Trefusis (1894–1972), by Jacques-Émile Blanche, 1926

away from Vita, who had married Harold Nicolson in 1912, and for a short time was herself fleetingly engaged to Lord Gerald Wellesley. She had a more serious attachment to Julian Grenfell, killed during the war. But on a visit to Vita in April 1918 the two women began an affair, leading to a 'mad irresponsible summer of moonlight nights and infinite escapades, and passionate letters, and music and poetry' (Nicolson, 103). They wrote a novel together in which the character Eve is a pen portrait of Violet: 'difficult, intractable, exasperating, subtle, incomprehensible' (V. Sackville-West, *Challenge*, 1974, 43). Eve's lover Julian is Vita, who used the name when cross-dressed on romantic adventures with Violet. The novel was published under Vita's name, as *Challenge*, in 1923.

From November 1918 to March 1919 Violet and Vita were in France together, but on their return Violet was pressed by her mother to sever all ties with her lover. Reluctantly she married Denys Robert Trefusis (1890–1929), officer (later major) of the Royal Horse Guards, on 16 June 1919. She did so on the understanding that the marriage would remain unconsummated, and she was still resolved to live with Vita. They resumed their affair just a few days after the wedding, and 'eloped' to France in February 1920; Violet led the way, Vita followed with Denys Trefusis in tow. Harold Nicolson caught up with them for a harrowing meeting in Amiens. Finding that they were 'trapped on every side', Vita returned to London (Jullian and Phillips, 53). The women continued to meet in Europe but the relationship had unravelled by 1921, and the Trefusises left England permanently, for Paris, to avoid further scandal.

In *Orlando* (1928), Virginia Woolf's 'love-letter' to Vita, Violet is fictionalized as the Russian Princess Sasha, who, 'faithless, mutable, fickle', deserts Orlando (p. 37). Vita Sackville-West wrote an account of her relationship with Violet that was published after both of their deaths in Nigel Nicolson's *Portrait of a Marriage*. Violet's ardent letters to Vita were also published.

In Paris, Violet was enthusiastically taken up as the lover of Princesse Edmond de Polignac (formerly Winaretta Singer), daughter of the inventor of the sewing machine and heir to a massive fortune. A rather saccharine portrait of Violet by Jacques Émile Blanche was painted at this time, which did not show what Cyril Connolly judged to be her 'magnificent' eyes 'working in close support of her smile to produce an ironical, rather mocking expression'. Vita Sackville-West thought her voice the most entrancing thing about her, and Connolly agreed: it was 'low and quite bewitching, equally at home in French and English and seldom rising above a husky murmur' (Jullian and Phillips, 98–9). She settled down to a life of social engagements at her salon in Auteuil and at a country house at La Tour de St Loup-de-Naud, Provins, a place recommended to her by Marcel Proust. She rarely saw her husband, who died of tuberculosis in 1929.

Trefusis attended classes at the University of Paris and wrote a play, *Les soeurs ennemies*, about Elizabeth I and Mary, queen of Scots. *Sortie de secours* (1929), the first of four novels in French, was about a woman who sought to make her lover jealous by seducing an older man with whom she falls in love. In the end she learns the value of independence. Trefusis later called it a 'mediocre little book' (*Don't Look Round*, 100). *Écho* (1931), drawing on memories of her childhood Scottish holidays, was more favourably received by the critics and sold well. *Tandem* (1933), written in English, drew on her Parisian friends, particularly the sisters Anna de Noailles and Princesse Marthe Bibesco, and captures Trefusis's epigrammatic conversational style; one character says of herself that 'She is the sort of woman she would not ask to her own parties'.

Broderie anglaise (1935) is Trefusis's response, in French, to Woolf's *Orlando*. An intellectually sterile woman, Alexa (Woolf), and an aristocratic man, Lord Shorne (Sackville-West), are having a tepid affair. When Anne (Trefusis), Lord Shorne's former lover, visits Alexa, she corrects Shorne's version of their relationship. Neither Woolf nor Sackville-West is known to have read it. *Hunt the Slipper* (1937), Trefusis's finest book in English, was reassessed by Lorna Sage as a 'splendidly malicious commentary on England, and on the aristocratic culture that she'd escaped' (Sage, 123). *Les causes perdues* (1941), her final novel in French, was set among an unpleasant group of aristocrats and their servants, and *Pirates at Play* (1950), her last in English, among the rich and fashionable English living in Florence. Trefusis's novels are characterized by an energetic narrative and wit, occasionally lapsing into snobbery and excess. Those written in French are on the whole more inventive and subtle.

In 1936 Trefusis visited Russia and wrote about it for *Le Temps*, whose editor then suggested that she meet Mussolini. The meeting started with her tripping over and spilling the contents of her bag on the floor: 'What could Mussolini, who prided himself on his "way" with women, do but help pick them up? We met on all fours, face to face, under the writing table' (*Don't Look Round*, 124). At the outbreak of the Second World War she joined the ambulance brigade, despite being unable to drive. From summer 1940 she spent the next four years in England. Vita Sackville-West now viewed her former lover as 'an unexploded bomb' and kept her at arm's length (Jullian and Phillips, 103). While in England, Trefusis wrote *Prelude to Misadventure* (1941), a book of autobiographical sketches dedicated to the 'faithful French who have left their families in order to fight on our side'. She also broadcast for La France Libre, for which she received the légion d'honneur in 1950.

On returning to Paris, Violet took up her old life and a succession of distinguished male companions; when she became older she acquired 'nephews'. The duke and duchess of Windsor, Prince Paul of Yugoslavia, Christian Dior, and Pierre Balmain signed her guest book at St Loup. The death of her mother in 1947 was a severe blow: 'What has happened to me since is but a post scriptum. It really doesn't count' (Jullian and Phillips, 121). When Vita saw Violet in Paris in 1949 she looked like a 'dowager duchess on two sticks' (Glendinning, 359). In 1952 she published her evasive and fragmentary memoirs, *Don't Look Round*, and in 1960 she was awarded the order of commendatore by the Italian government, an honour rarely conferred on a woman.

An accident in 1950 had aged Violet prematurely, and from 1963 she was in a very poor state of health. She left her home at the rue de Cherche-Midi in Paris for her late mother's villa at l'Ombrellino, in Florence, on 24 December 1971. Unable to digest food, she died there, of starvation, on 1 March 1972, 'surrounded by statues, empty fountains, and dead flowers' (Jullian and Phillips, 144). One of her last visitors was François Mitterand. After her cremation most of her ashes were scattered close to her mother's tomb in the protestant cemetery near Florence, and the rest sealed in the ancient ruins below La Tour de St Loup.

CLARE L. TAYLOR

Sources P. Jullian and J. Phillips, *Violet Trefusis: a biography including correspondence with Vita Sackville-West* (1976) • N. Nicolson, *Portrait of a marriage* (1973) • *Violet to Vita: the letters of Violet Trefusis to Vita Sackville-West*, ed. M. A. Leaska and J. Phillips (1989–90) • V. Trefusis, *Don't look round: her reminiscences* (1952) • H. Sharpe, *A solitary woman: a life of Violet Trefusis* (1981) • D. Souhami, *Mrs Keppel and her daughter* (1996) • V. Glendinning, *Vita: the life of V. Sackville-West* (1983); repr. (1998) • *The last Edwardians: an illustrated history of Violet Trefusis and Alice Keppel*, Boston Athenaeum, Massachusetts (1985) • L. Sage, *Moments of truth: twelve twentieth-century women writers* (2001) • V. Woolf, *Orlando: a biography* (1928); repr. (1992)

Archives Yale U., Beinecke L., letters

Likenesses A. Hughes, double portrait, photograph, 1899, NPG; *see illus. in* Keppel, Alice Frederica (1868–1947) • group portrait, photograph, c.1907, Hult. Arch. • photograph, 1916, Hult. Arch. • J.-E. Blanche, oils, 1926, NPG [*see illus.*] • D. Hills, oils, 1945, NPG • C. Beaton, three pencil drawings, c.1960, NPG • P. Chandler, bromide print (after original negative, 1952), NPG • M. Ferrini, pastel drawing, repro. in Sharpe, *A solitary woman*

Tregellas, Walter Hawken (1831–1894), writer, born at Truro, Cornwall, on 10 July 1831, was the eldest son of John Tabois Tregellas (1792–1863), merchant at Truro, purser of Cornish mines, and author of the popular *Cornish Tales* (1860). His mother was Anne (1801–1867), second daughter of Richard Hawken. He was educated by his uncle, John Hawken, at Trevarth School, Gwennap, from 1838 to 1845, and from 1845 to 1847 at the grammar school of Truro.

Tregellas was fond of drawing from an early age, and won prizes as an artist at the Royal Cornwall Polytechnic Society at Falmouth between 1846 and 1848. He began his career as a draughtsman in the War Office on 10 July 1855, was promoted second draughtsman in February 1860, rose to be chief draughtsman in May 1866, and retained the post until August 1893. Tregellas married at Holy Trinity Church, Brompton, on 2 November 1861, Zoë Wilson (*b.* 1840), third daughter of Charles *Lucas (1808–1869) and his wife, Frances.

Tregellas was also a keen writer, publishing many works including *China, the Country, History and People* (1867) and *The Horse Guards Memoranda* (1880). His interest in military matters was further illustrated in his *Historical Sketch of the Defences of Malta*, printed for the Royal Engineers' Institute at Chatham in 1879, and in a similar study of the coastal defences of England, which was published in 1887, having originally appeared in the engineers' occasional papers series. He contributed several articles to the *Archaeological Journal* (1864–6) and the *Journal of the Royal Institution of Cornwall* (1883, 1891). Many of his publications were inspired by his native county, including *Cornish Worthies* (1884) and his *Tourist Guide to Cornwall* (1878), which reached a seventh edition in 1895. He also wrote many of the articles on Cornish people in the first thirteen volumes of the *Dictionary of National Biography*. His principal work, a history of the Tower of London, was left unpublished after his death.

Tregellas died at Stanley House, Prince of Wales Terrace, Deal, on 28 May 1894, and was buried in Deal cemetery on 30 May. He had no children, and his wife survived him.

W. P. COURTNEY, *rev.* JOANNE POTIER

Sources West Briton and Cornwall Advertiser (31 May 1894) · West Briton and Cornwall Advertiser (7 June 1894) · Boase & Courtney, *Bibl. Corn.*, 2.751–2 · *Journal of the Royal Institution of Cornwall*, 12 (1893–5), 115–16 · W. P. Courtney, *The Academy* (9 June 1894), 475 · Boase, *Mod. Eng. biog.* · *CGPLA Eng. & Wales* (1894)
Wealth at death £923 3s. 7d.: probate, 15 June 1894, *CGPLA Eng. & Wales*

Tregelles, Edwin Octavius (1806–1886), ironmaster and Quaker minister, was born on 19 October 1806 at Falmouth, the youngest of the seventeen children (eight being twins) of Samuel Tregelles (1766–1831), merchant and rope maker, and Rebecca (1766–1811), daughter of Thomas Smith (1725–1792), London silversmith and member of the Quaker banking firm of Smith, Wright, and Gray. His mother's surviving sister had married Thomas Fox (1747/8–1821), a woollen manufacturer and banker at Wellington, Somerset. By 1827, when Tregelles attained his majority, his forty first cousins were nearly all intellectually vigorous as well as active in commerce or industry—including such scientists as Robert Were Fox (1789–1877) and Charles Fox (1797–1878).

Samuel Tregelles had been one of the twelve partners (mainly of the Fox family) in the Perran foundry, near Falmouth, from its establishment in 1791. The following year the partners had leased the Neath Abbey ironworks and in 1820 Edwin Tregelles was apprenticed to his cousin Joseph Tregelles Price (1784–1854) who had succeeded his father, Peter Price, as managing partner of the Neath Abbey Iron Company, as it was called from 1818. Tregelles was joined there by his brother Nathaniel (1803–1887) who remained until 1847. Edwin himself was a man of conscientious—some in the family thought over-conscientious—scruple and in 1831, rather than be a party to supplying machinery for a Newport brewery, he resigned his position.

Tregelles's work for Neath Abbey had involved extensive travelling and at Youghal, co. Cork, he had seen much of Abraham Fisher, a Quaker miller whose daughter Jenepher (1808–1844) he married on 5 July 1832: there were three children. He had meanwhile set up in business on his own account as a civil engineer, superintending the introduction of gas lighting to many towns in the south of England. He was appointed (1835) engineer of the Southampton and Salisbury Railway; he was engaged in surveying for the West Cornwall Railway; and he reported (1849) on the water supply and sewerage of Barnstaple and Bideford. He was elected a member of the Institution of Civil Engineers on 5 March 1850, but resigned in 1861.

By the time of his election Tregelles had become a tinplate manufacturer at Shotley Bridge, co. Durham. On 4 December 1850 he married his second wife, Elizabeth Richardson (1813–1878): there were no children. Her brother Jonathan Richardson (1802–1871) founded in 1841 the Derwent Iron Company of which her brother-in-law Jonathan Priestman (1825–1888) was later managing director. Tregelles also involved himself in the family's coal interests but in 1853 retired from business and devoted himself entirely to Quaker and philanthropic work. He had begun to speak in Quaker meetings about 1828, his spiritual life by then being much affected by the deaths of seven of his brothers and sisters. His gift in the ministry was recorded by South Wales monthly meeting in 1837. His early travels in the ministry included the Isles of Scilly; Ireland (1839) with Robert Were Fox; the West Indies (1843–4) with James Jesup (1796–1868); and Norway (1846) with Isaac Sharp (1806–1897) and John Budge (1787–1864).

Tregelles's interest in temperance developed into advocacy of total abstinence and he served on the council of the United Kingdom Alliance. He was active in 1855 in the relief of distress in the Hebrides and was engaged, often accompanied by his wife, in numerous journeys in the ministry in Scotland and the north of England. Throughout his life he had a particular concern for the children in Friends' schools: his sister Rachel (1805–1874) was from 1853 to 1862 superintendent of the Quaker York Quarterly

Meeting Girls' School, supervising its removal in 1857 from Castlegate to The Mount.

From 1837 Tregelles suffered indifferent health and following the death of his second wife he suffered severe illness, but was able to spend the winter of 1882 visiting the small groups of French Quakers at Nîmes and Congenies. Short attacks of illness continued, however, and he died of 'natural decay [and] cardiac degeneration' on 16 September 1886 at the home of his elder daughter and son-in-law, Gertrude M. (1833–1932) and Charles (1830–1895) Gillett, Wood Green, Neithrop, Banbury, where he had been living: his body was interred in the Quaker burial-ground, Sibford Gower, Oxfordshire, five days later.

EDWARD H. MILLIGAN

Sources *Edwin Octavius Tregelles: civil engineer and minister of the gospel*, ed. S. E. Fox (1892) · L. Ince, *The Neath Abbey Iron Company* (1984) · *Annual Monitor* (1887), 183–92 · Cornwall Quaker Meeting births digest, RS Friends, Lond. · m. certs. · digest of deaths, 1837–1961, RS Friends, Lond.
Archives RS Friends, Lond., letters
Likenesses photograph, c.1875, repro. in Fox, ed., *Edwin Octavius Tregelles*
Wealth at death £6405 4s. 6d.: probate, 10 Dec 1886, *CGPLA Eng. & Wales*

Tregelles, Samuel Prideaux (1813–1875), biblical scholar, son of Samuel Tregelles (1789–1828), merchant, of Falmouth, and his wife, Dorothy (1790–1873), daughter of George Prideaux of Kingsbridge, was born at Wodehouse Place, Falmouth, on 30 January 1813. He was the nephew of Edwin Octavius Tregelles. He was educated at Falmouth classical school from 1825 to 1828 and showed early promise. From 1829 to 1835 he was employed at the Neath Abbey ironworks in Glamorgan, and he devoted his spare time to learning Greek, Hebrew, and Aramaic. He also mastered Welsh, and sometimes preached and published in that language. Finding his work uncongenial he returned to Falmouth in 1835, and supported himself by taking pupils. Although both his parents were Quakers he joined the Plymouth Brethren, but later in life he became a Presbyterian. On 12 March 1839 he married his cousin, Sarah Anna (1807–1882), eldest daughter of Walter Prideaux, banker, of Plymouth. They had no children.

Tregelles's first book was *Passages in the Revelation Connected with the Old Testament* (1836). In 1837, having obtained work from publishers, he settled in London. He superintended the publication of the *Englishman's Greek Concordance to the New Testament* (1839) and the *Hebrew and Chaldee Concordance to the Old Testament* (1843). In 1841 he wrote 'An historical account of the English translations of the scriptures' for Samuel Bagster's *English Hexapla*.

In 1838 Tregelles took up the critical study of the New Testament and decided to publish a new version of the Greek text. This plan resulted from his discovery that the *textus receptus* did not rest on ancient authority and that existing collations were inconsistent and inaccurate. He aimed to produce a text based entirely on ancient manuscripts compared with early versions and patristic citations to the time of Eusebius, and to state clearly the authorities for the readings. Tregelles was for many years

unaware that he was working on the same lines as the German philologist and textual critic, Karl Lachmann. Like Lachmann he minimized the importance of cursive manuscripts, dating from the ninth century onwards, thereby differing from his fellow critic F. H. A. Scrivener.

Tregelles first became generally known through his *Book of Revelation in Greek Edited from Ancient Authorities* (1844). This contained the announcement of his intention to prepare a Greek New Testament. He began by collating the Codex Augiensis (F 010) at Trinity College, Cambridge. In 1845 he went to Rome with the intention of collating codex B 03 in the Vatican, but, though he spent five months there, he was not allowed to copy the manuscript. He nevertheless managed to note some important readings. From Rome he went to Florence, Modena, Venice, Munich, and Basel, reading and collating all relevant manuscripts. He returned to England in November 1846 and settled at Plymouth, and he continued collating manuscripts in the British Museum. In 1849 he went to Paris, but an attack of cholera drove him home. He returned in 1850, finished the laborious task of collating the damaged 'Cyprius' (K 017), and then collated other manuscripts including the minuscule no. 33, 'Queen of the cursives'. Tregelles subsequently went to Hamburg, and from there travelled to Berlin, where he met Lachmann. He also visited Leipzig, where he collaborated with Constantin Tischendorf, Dresden, Wolfenbüttel, and Utrecht, and he returned home in 1851. Until 1857 he was employed collating manuscripts in England. In 1853 he restored and deciphered the uncial palimpsest Z 035 of Matthew's gospel at Dublin.

In 1854 Tregelles published *An Account of the Printed Text of the Greek New Testament*. In 1856 he rewrote for T. H. Horne's *Introduction to the Critical Study and Knowledge of the Holy Scriptures* the section on textual criticism in volume 4, and in 1860 he contributed a postscript, 'Additions'. These publications provide details about the principles on which his subsequent textual work was based.

The first part of the Greek New Testament, St Matthew and St Mark, was published to subscribers in 1857, but proved unremunerative. Tregelles went abroad for his health, and stayed at Geneva and Milan. At Milan he made a facsimile tracing of the Muratorian fragment (Codex Muratorianus), but he was unable to publish it until 1867. On the return journey he visited Christian Bunsen at Heidelberg. In 1860 he went on a tour through Spain, where he showed much interest in the protestant community. The second part of the Greek New Testament—St Luke and St John—appeared in 1861. In 1862 Tregelles went to Leipzig to examine the Codex Sinaiticus, then in Tischendorf's keeping, and from there he travelled to Halle and Erlangen. Tregelles's editions of Acts and the catholic epistles were issued in 1865 (by which date Tischendorf's facsimile of Codex Sinaiticus was available), and the Pauline epistles up to 2 Thessalonians were published in 1869. He was revising the last chapters of Revelation in 1870 when he had a stroke of paralysis, after which he never walked. He continued to work in bed. The remainder of the epistles were published in 1870, but the book of Revelation (the text of which differs about 230 places from that which he published in 1844) was edited from his papers by S. J. B. Bloxsidge and B. W. Newton in 1872. It lacked the long-expected prolegomena, but in 1879 F. J. A. Hort published an appendix containing the materials for the prolegomena that Tregelles's notes supplied, with additions (especially readings from Codex Sinaiticus and Codex Vaticanus in the gospels) and corrections by A. W. Streane. Tregelles's collations and his edition of a Greek New Testament based on the oldest manuscripts available were remarkable achievements and they paved the way for the Greek edition of Westcott and Hort in 1881 and for the Revised Version of the English Bible of the same year.

Tregelles received the degree of LLD from St Andrews in 1850, and in 1862 he was awarded a civil-list pension of £100, which was doubled in 1870. He was a member of the New Testament Revision Company but was unable to attend its meetings. He died at his home, 6 Portland Square, Plymouth, on 24 April 1875, and was buried five days later in Plymouth cemetery. His wife survived him until 1882, receiving half of his civil-list pension. Among Tregelles's other works, his *Collation of the texts of Griesbach, Scholz, Lachmann, and Tischendorf, with that in common use* (1854) and his *Codex Zacynthius, Fragments of St Luke* (1861) have proved to be of enduring value.

E. C. MARCHANT, *rev.* J. K. ELLIOTT

Sources S. P. Tregelles, *An account of the printed text of the Greek New Testament* (1854), 151–74 · *Western Daily Mercury* (3 May 1875) · F. H. A. Scrivener, *A plain introduction to the criticism of the New Testament*, 4th edn (1894), 2.238–41 · *The Academy* (8 May 1875), 475 · Boase & Courtney, *Bibl. Corn.*, 2.757, 3.1348
Archives BL, corresp. relating to Codex Sinaiticus, Add. MS 61835 | JRL, letters to B. W. Newton · NL Wales, letters to Ebenezer Thomas
Likenesses portrait, *c.*1860–1870, Plymouth City Museum and Art Gallery
Wealth at death under £800: administration with will, 12 Nov 1875, *CGPLA Eng. & Wales*

Tregian, Francis (1548–1608), recusant gentleman, was born in 1548 at Golden Manor, near Probus, Cornwall, the son of John Tregian (1520–1575) and his wife, Katherine (*c.*1520–*c.*1580), eldest daughter of Sir John Arundell of Lanherne and his wife, Elizabeth. He received his early education at home before spending the years 1560–72 on the continent. About 1570 he married Mary (*c.*1550–*c.*1620), eldest daughter of Charles, seventh Lord Stourton, and Anne, daughter of Edward, earl of Derby.

At the age of twenty-four Tregian returned from the continent to serve at the court of Elizabeth I. His zeal for the Catholic faith and his refusal to accept awards and advances from the queen led to his dismissal from court. On his return to Golden Manor he sought to strengthen the faith of his fellow Catholics by engaging a seminary priest, Cuthbert *Mayne. Mayne had been recently ordained at the English College in Douai founded by William Allen. The queen summoned Sir George Carey, the knight marshal, to proceed against Tregian. Orders were sent to Richard Grenville, sheriff of Cornwall, who surrounded Golden with more than one hundred armed men

on the feast of Corpus Christi, 8 June 1577. Tregian, Mayne, and thirty-one other Cornish recusants were arrested. The grateful queen bestowed a knighthood on Grenville for the way he had dealt with this 'matter of religion' (Bushnell, 121). Cuthbert Mayne was put to death on 30 November 1577 as a 'terror to the papists' (Anstruther, 226). Initially charged at Launceston on 16 September 1577 Tregian suffered many trials and was eventually found guilty in 1579 of aiding and abetting Cuthbert Mayne. By a sentence of *praemunire* he became the first Catholic under Elizabeth to forfeit all his lands and goods and was ordered to remain in prison for life. From Launceston he was taken to London, and was held at Marshalsea prison in Southwark, the queen's bench, and lastly in the Fleet prison, Ludgate. His wife was able to visit him in prison and altogether there were twelve children of the marriage. After appeals Tregian was given leave to go on parole in Chelsea in 1601.

In 1603, on the accession of James I, Tregian left once again for the continent, visiting the college at Douai in 1603. In Brussels he saw his son Francis again, and on his arrival in Madrid the king of Spain, Philip III, arranged a triumphant procession for him in the royal coach. He lived on a pension of sixty cruzados a month. He died in the Jesuit hospital at St Roque, Lisbon, on 25 September 1608, and was buried in the floor of St Roque church. On 25 April 1625 his grave was opened. According to Ignatius Stafford his body was found perfect and he was re-buried one year later, by English Catholics, standing up in the marble pulpit of the same church to honour the way he had stood up to Elizabeth. The inscription on the tomb describes 'Dom Francisco Tregian', an 'illustrious English gentleman who died in the city of Lisbon with great fame and saintliness'.

Francis Tregian (1574–1617), his eldest son, was born at Golden Manor, and was educated at Eu, Douai, and Rome, where he was described as 'very noble, twenty years old, a happy and natural genius extremely proficient in philosophy, music and the Latin language' (Knox, 356). He worked for Cardinal Allen in Rome and delivered his funeral address there in 1594. He also worked for Albert, archduke of the Spanish Netherlands, and these facts were held against him when he returned to England. When his attempt to regain Golden Manor failed he was imprisoned in the Fleet in 1614. While there he was known to have been working on an important book for two years. Scholars are agreed that he was transcribing and arranging the music for the collection known as the Fitzwilliam virginal book, now kept in the Fitzwilliam Museum, Cambridge. This important document contains works by William Byrd, who wrote the work *Tregian's Ground* for the family. Tregian was buried in St Bride's Church, Fleet Street, on 11 August 1617.

RAYMOND FRANCIS TRUDGIAN

Sources R. F. Trudgian, *Francis Tregian, 1548–1608: Elizabethan recusant* (1998) · P. Boyan and G. Lamb, *Francis Tregian (Cornish recusant)* (1955) · H. Trudgian, 'Histoire d'une famille anglaise: les Tregians', doctoral diss., University of Paris, 1934 · A. L. Rowse, *Tudor Cornwall: portrait of a society* (1941), 342–79 · G. H. Bushnell, *Sir Richard*

Grenville (1936), 107–25 • T. Taylor, 'Francis Tregian: his family and possessions', *Journal of the Royal Institution of Cornwall*, 18 (1910–11), 103–16 • G. Anstruther, *The seminary priests*, 1 (1969) • J. A. Fuller-Maitland and W. B. Squire, eds., *The Fitzwilliam virginal book* (1899) • *The letters and memorials of William, Cardinal Allen (1532–1594)*, ed. T. F. Knox (1882), vol. 2 of *Records of the English Catholics under the penal laws* (1878–82) • J. Morris, ed., *The troubles of our Catholic forefathers related by themselves*, 1 (1872)

Likenesses portrait, 1583, priv. coll.; repro. in Trudgian, *Francis Tregian*, cover

Wealth at death none; all lands and goods forfeit: Trudgian, *Francis Tregian*, 24

Tregonwell, Sir John (*c*.1498–1565), lawyer and ecclesiastical administrator, may have been born of yeoman stock at Tregonnell in the parish of Manaccan in Cornwall; he had a sister, Alice, who married John Southcote. His first wife's maiden name was Kelway; his second wife, Elizabeth Martin, *née* Bruce (*d*. 1581/2), bore him a son, Thomas, and other children, who all appear to have predeceased him. Tregonwell may have been educated at Crantock College, Cornwall. He certainly attended Broadgates Hall, Oxford, obtaining his BCL on 30 June 1516 and his DCL on 21 July 1522. Before about 1527 he was principal of Vine Hall, Oxford, also known as Peckwaters Inn. Tregonwell practised at the court of arches, being admitted to the College of Advocates on 9 December 1522. By 1527 he is identified as a judge of the admiralty.

Evidently Tregonwell demonstrated considerable legal skill because in 1529 King Henry VIII 'called him from the Arches' to assist in the royal divorce from Katherine of Aragon (*LP Henry VIII*, vol. 14/2, appendix 35). Tregonwell appeared as one of the king's proctors at the hearing before Cardinal Campeggi at Blackfriars in June 1529, and in 1530 accompanied Thomas Cranmer and others to dispute the validity of the king's marriage abroad. As a master of chancery, Tregonwell appeared on behalf of the king on 5 April 1533, demanding that the convocation of Canterbury came to a conclusion regarding the king's divorce. On 8 May 1533 he accompanied Cranmer and others to Dunstable as a councillor in law 'for the King's part' and on 23 May 1533 was present when Cranmer declared the king's marriage as 'against the law of God' (*LP Henry VIII*, vol. 6, nos. 661, 525). As a reward for his part in these events he obtained a £40 annuity for life.

Tregonwell was also involved in diplomatic negotiations. In April and May 1532 he accompanied William Knight, archdeacon of Richmond, and John Hackett to Burborough, where mercantile grievances between the Merchant Adventurers and the Netherlands were discussed. In 1534 he was appointed a commissioner in the two treaties of peace with Scotland which he also signed; in the commission he is described as the principal judge of the admiralty. In October 1545 he was appointed, along with Tunstal and Paget, to treat with King François I of France for peace. Illness prevented him from being appointed an ambassador to Flanders in 1546. His status with the king is reflected in his appointment as one of the council remaining at Westminster during Henry's discussions with François at the end of 1532. However, a setback in Tregonwell's career is revealed in May 1534 when, in a

letter to Thomas Cromwell, he states that Cromwell had 'announced that the King has granted me master of the rolls' (*LP Henry VIII*, vol. 7, no. 743); in the event Cromwell obtained the position when it fell vacant in October 1534.

Tregonwell is best-known for his role as monastic visitor and commissioner. In a draft commission for the visitation of the entire English ecclesiastical establishment, dated either the end of November or early December 1534, Tregonwell is named as one of the three vicegerents. However, in January 1535 Cromwell became vicar-general and Tregonwell later was commissioned as a monastic visitor. He is first clearly identified accompanying Richard Layton at the visitation of Oxford University in the second week of September, issuing injunctions 'for the increase of learning there' and ensuring that every scholar took the oath of supremacy (*LP Henry VIII*, vol. 9, no. 351). After Oxford, Tregonwell parted from Layton and continued the visitation in the southern part of Lincolnshire diocese. By 9 November he had visited Athelney, Cleeve, and other Somerset houses and was about to enter Devon. In the monastic visitation he is last identified in early January 1536 at Salisbury Cathedral. Later in the summer he was probably involved with suppressing smaller houses in the west country. In November 1536 Tregonwell, along with Bedyll and Petre, were commissioned to receive from ecclesiastical institutions the bulls, briefs, and faculties previously issued by the papacy.

Early in 1538 Tregonwell had a commission for dissolving certain greater abbeys, including Abingdon. The pressure on abbeys to surrender increased at the end of 1538 and in December he was sent to Shaftesbury Abbey to encourage its submission. From January to March 1539 he was engaged in taking large numbers of monastic surrenders in the south-west and confirming pension arrangements for the redundant religious. In April 1539 he was one of three canon-law experts appointed by the king and Cromwell to frame the Act of Six Articles. From November 1539 to January 1540 he was principally in Lincolnshire diocese during the final tranche of surrenders and dissolutions.

Tregonwell complained to Cromwell in August 1539 that he had been 'a long suitor' for monastic spoils but 'nothing would fall to my lot' (*LP Henry VIII*, vol. 14/2, appendix 35). He had in 1536 pleaded with Cromwell for the lease of a monastic house 'whereby he may have some help toward his living and funding of his wife and children' (*LP Henry VIII*, vol. 10, no. 388). On 23 February 1540 Tregonwell and his nephew John Southcote were granted in fee simple for £1000 the house, site, and lands of the Benedictine abbey of Milton Abbas, Dorset, which a year previously he had suppressed.

Tregonwell was involved with other key events in King Henry's reign. In the first half of 1535 he was present when two Carthusian priests and Sir Thomas More were questioned for rejecting the king's supreme headship of the church. In May 1536 he participated in the proceedings against Anne Boleyn. After the northern risings of 1536–7 he was involved with examining the abbot of Barlings, the abbot of Jervaulx, George Lumley, and others. In the inquiry into the validity of the king's marriage to Anne of Cleves, Tregonwell was a member of the working party which, in July 1540, pronounced its nullity. He was often given legal commissions by the privy council: in 1541, for example, he was sent to Plymouth to untangle the legal complexity of the wreck of a Portuguese ship. However, the summit of his legal skill is reflected in a commission to determine matters in chancery in the absence of the lord chancellor, dated October 1544; in 1547, 1550, and 1555 he had similar commissions. He was also a receiver of petitions to the House of Lords at parliaments in 1536, 1539, and 1541.

During Edward VI's reign, Tregonwell was still active in legal affairs and as a justice of the peace in Dorset. His name appears on a shortlist of three from which the sheriff of Dorset and Somerset was pricked. His career appears to have been revitalized in Mary's reign: on her accession he was one of the first to be knighted (on 2 October 1553), he was MP for Scarborough in her first parliament, a member of the commission examining Bishop Bonner's appeal against deprivation in Edward's reign, sheriff of Dorset and Somerset in 1554, and a House of Lords receiver of petitions in four parliaments. In February 1554 he was sworn one of the king and queen's council. Tregonwell's social position is exemplified by the licence he received to retain thirty gentlemen or yeomen in his household.

It is probably Tregonwell's conservative religious sympathies that account for his absence from important office after Elizabeth's accession, although he continued as a justice of the peace in Dorset. He made his will in December 1563, with an invocation for the prayers of the 'most glorious and blessed Virgin Mary', and, after apparently a lengthy illness, died at Milton Abbas on 13 January 1565, where he was buried in the old abbey church. His grandson John Tregonwell, son of his deceased son Thomas, was heir and had licence to enter the inheritance in July 1571.

ANTHONY N. SHAW

Sources PRO, SP 1/70–1/208 · A. L. Rowse, *Tudor Cornwall: portrait of a society* (1957), 187–93 · J. H. Bettey, 'Sir John Tregonwell of Milton Abbey', *Proceedings of the Dorset Natural History and Archaeological Society*, 90 (1968), 295–302 · HoP, *Commons, 1509–58*, 3.476–8 · *LP Henry VIII*, vols. 5–21, addenda · *APC, 1547–50, 1554–6* · *CPR, 1547–8; 1549–53; 1553–4; 1555–7; 1563–6* · *Reg. Oxf.*, 1.99 · C. S. Gilbert, *An historical survey of the county of Cornwall*, 2 (1820), 283–7 · PRO, PROB 11/48, fols. 125r–134r · BL, Add. MS 32490 FF(54) · [C. Coote], *Sketches of the lives and characters of eminent English civilians, with an historical introduction relative to the College of Advocates* (1804), 19 · W. A. Shaw, *The knights of England*, 2 (1906), 66 · Burke, *Gen. GB* (1838), 404 · *DNB*
Archives BL, Cotton MS Caligula B.v · PRO, SP 1
Likenesses H. H. Meyer, stipple (after H. Holbein), BM, NPG; repro. in Gilbert, *Historical survey*, vol. 2, p. 284
Wealth at death manor, lands, and possessions at Milton Abbas, Dorset; other manors and estates in Dorset and Cornwall: will, PRO, PROB 11/48, fols. 125r–134r

Tregury, Michael (c.1399–1471), archbishop of Dublin, was born at St Wenn in Cornwall and was educated at Oxford (BA by 1426, BTh by 1439, and DTh by 1444). From 1422 to 1427 he was fellow of Exeter College and in 1434–5 he was senior proctor of the university. Henry VI appointed Tregury first rector of the University of Caen in October 1439, a position he had resigned by March 1440.

John Bale attributed to Tregury the authorship of three works, apparently lectures delivered at Caen: *Lectura sententiarum*, *De origine illius studii* (perhaps referring to the University of Caen), and *Ordinariae quaestiones*. None of them is known to have been printed or to be extant. Tregury was said to have been principal of various halls connected with Exeter College in the 1420s and 1430s. He was ordained priest in March 1427 and held a number of different benefices, particularly in the diocese of Exeter, between 1429 and his promotion to the archbishopric of Dublin in 1449; these included canonries of Crediton, Devon (1447–9); of St Martin le Grand, London (1447–9); of Exeter (resigned 1449); and also the archdeaconry of Barnstaple (1445–9). He was appointed chaplain to Henry VI and Queen Margaret of Anjou. About 1447 the latter wrote recommending Tregury's appointment to the vicarage of Corfe Castle or the bishopric of Lisieux. Neither suggestion seems to have been adopted.

On the death of Richard Talbot, archbishop of Dublin, in 1449, Tregury was papally provided to that see; he was suspended by the pope in 1453 for being consecrated before receiving the bull of provision and without taking an oath of fealty. As archbishop he was a member of the Irish privy council, in which capacity he received an annual salary of £20 but he did not hold other governmental positions. He was in Ireland by late 1451 having been shipwrecked *en route*. He had royal licence to be absent from Ireland for three years from 1458 and again for one year in 1461. His tenure of the archbishopric, which lasted twenty-two years, was marked by an active policy of ecclesiastical visitations and disputes with the archbishop of Armagh over the claims to primacy. His predecessor, Talbot, had apparently much depleted the revenues of his see and, finding the metropolitan cross in pawn and much of the archiepiscopal demesne alienated, Tregury obtained a papal indult to hold other benefices to a total value of not more than £200. In 1462 he was violently assaulted and imprisoned in Dublin by some Irishmen, who were excommunicated for the offence. His claims to lands and jurisdiction were resented by Anglo-Irish and Gaelic Irish. In 1465 he was indicted for assault; he subsequently cleared himself, claiming that there was a conspiracy against him.

Tregury died at his manor house of Tallaght, near Dublin, on 21 December 1471 and was buried near St Stephen's altar in St Patrick's Cathedral. The monument erected over his tomb was afterwards buried under the rubbish in St Stephen's Chapel, where it was discovered by Dean Swift in 1730 and re-erected on the wall to the left of the west gate. By his will, which is dated 10 December 1471, Tregury bequeathed to St Patrick's Cathedral his 'pair of organs' and two silver salt-cellars to be made into chalices; he also directed that oblations should be made on his behalf to St Michael's Mount, Cornwall.

A. F. POLLARD, rev. VIRGINIA DAVIS

Sources Emden, *Oxf.* · M. V. Ronan, 'Anglo-Norman Dublin and diocese', *Irish Ecclesiastical Record*, 5th ser., 48 (1936), 170–93, 378–96 · H. F. Berry, ed., *Register of wills and inventories of the diocese of Dublin … 1457–1483* (1898) · *CEPR letters* · W. H. Bliss, ed., *Calendar of* entries in the papal registers relating to Great Britain and Ireland: petitions to the pope (1896) · CPR · C. McNeill, ed., Calendar of Archbishop Alen's register, c.1172–1534 (1950) · F. C. Hingeston-Randolph, ed., The register of Edmund Lacy, bishop of Exeter, 1: The register of institutions, with some account of the episcopate of John Catrik, AD 1419 (1909) · C. W. Boase, ed., Registrum Collegii Exoniensis, new edn, OHS, 27 (1894) · Letters of Queen Margaret of Anjou and Bishop Beckington and others written in the reigns of Henry V and Henry VI, ed. C. Monro, CS, 86 (1863) · Comte A. De Bourmont, 'La fondation de l'Université de Caen et son organisation au XVe siècle', Bulletin de la Société des Antiquaires de Normandie, 12 (1884), 293–641 · A. Bigot, ed., L'Université de Caen: son passé, son présent (Caen, 1932)

Likenesses tomb slab, c.1471, St Patrick's Cathedral, Dublin

Treherne [Treheyron], **George** (d. 1528), lawyer, came from a Welsh family and was perhaps resident in Herefordshire, where he had many professional connections. In 1498 and 1503 he was accused before the king's council of disorder in what seems to have been a fracas involving the inns of court and chancery, and so it appears he was a member of an inn of chancery by the former date, though 1503 is the year of his admission to Lincoln's Inn. He was practising as an attorney of the common pleas, for Herefordshire clients, by 1500, and continued to do so until the 1520s. However, the demarcation between attorneys and counsel was not yet rigid and Treherne also practised as an advocate. He is mentioned as counsel at Buckinghamshire assizes in 1516, at Hereford assizes in 1519, and at Bridgnorth assizes in 1523, and as counsel in the court of requests in 1520. He became a bencher of his inn in 1518 and two years later, in the autumn of 1520, delivered his celebrated reading on the carta de foresta. This was the best-known exposition of the forest law before the publication of the treatise by John Manwood, and still survives in nearly forty manuscript texts, some in law French and some translated into English. One manuscript contains what purports to be a continuation of the reading with a brief exposition of 11 Hen. VII c. 8, concerning usury, but this is not mentioned in any of the other versions.

Treherne read again in 1525, but the subject of his second reading is not known. He held few public offices, though as early as 1501–2 he served as escheator for Herefordshire and by 1513 he was acting steward or under-steward of St Katharine's Hospital near the Tower of London. Although he presumably maintained a home in Herefordshire, where he was on the commission of the peace from 1525 until his death, he is invariably described in records as 'of London'. He seems to have married twice. His first wife, whom he married before 1508, was Elizabeth, widow of Richard Horton of Burford, Oxfordshire. His second wife was called Margaret; she survived him and married Richard Tracy. He died after January 1528, when he acquired a manor in Gloucestershire, and before September 1528, when an action of debt was brought by his widow. He may have left children. A John Treheyron was receiver in London for New College, Oxford, in the 1530s; and a Thomas Treheyron was sued for dues by Gray's Inn in 1539.

J. H. BAKER

Sources J. H. Baker, Readers and readings in the inns of court and chancery, SeldS, suppl. ser., 13 (2000) · PRO, C244/146/74 · PRO, C244/153/137, 149 · W. P. Baildon, ed., The records of the Honorable Society of Lincoln's Inn: the black books, 1 (1897) · PRO, CP 40 · Hunt. L.,

MS EL 2536–2537 · J. Caley and J. Hunter, eds., Valor ecclesiasticus temp. Henrici VIII, 6 vols., RC (1810–34), vol. 2, p. 261 [John Treheyron]

Trelawney [Trelawny], **Charles** (1653–1731), army officer, was the fourth but second surviving son of Sir Jonathan Trelawny, second baronet (c.1623–1681), of Trelawne, Pelynt, Cornwall, and his wife, Mary, daughter of Sir Edward Seymour of Berry Pomeroy, near Totnes, Devon. He was the brother of Sir Jonathan *Trelawny, third baronet (1650–1721), bishop of Winchester, Henry (c.1658–1702), and John (c.1646–1680). Commissioned in 1672 into the duke of Monmouth's royal English regiment, an auxiliary formation in the French army, Trelawney served during the invasion of the Dutch republic and at the siege of Maastricht in 1673. On 16 March 1674 he transferred as captain into the 2nd battalion of the royal English, commanded by Bevil Skelton. He probably saw action at the battle of Enzheim in 1674, and was certainly involved at Altenheim in 1675. He returned to England in 1677 and was commissioned captain-lieutenant of the old battalion of Monmouth's Foot in 1678, and promoted major on 1 November. On 13 July 1680 he was appointed major of the earl of Plymouth's infantry regiment raised for Tangier. Promotion to lieutenant-colonel of Plymouth's followed on 27 November 1680, when Percy Kirke became colonel, and colonel on 23 April 1682. On the evacuation of Tangier in 1684 he sailed to England, and part of his regiment fought at Sedgemoor in 1685. A leading member of the army conspiracy against James II, he deserted to William of Orange from Warminster in November 1688 accompanied by his lieutenant-colonel, Charles Churchill, a number of officers, and 200 men. James immediately dismissed him, but he was reinstated by William of Orange on 31 December 1688. Promoted brigadier-general on 6 March 1689, he served in Ireland leading a brigade across the river at Slanebridge to turn the Jacobite left during the battle of the Boyne on 1 July 1690. During September he took part in Marlborough's operations against Cork and Kinsale and was promoted to major-general on 2 December 1690. A lifelong tory—he was elected tory MP for East Looe from 1685 until 1695 and for Plymouth from 1698 to 1710—he resigned his colonelcy on 1 January 1692 to his brother Henry in protest at William's favouring of Dutch and German general officers. His decision was made easier by his acquisition of the Hengar estate through marriage on 1 May 1690 to Anne Morice (d. 1691), daughter and heiress of Richard Lower MD of Covent Garden, Westminster, and widow of William Morice of Werrington, Devon (c.1660–1688). When Thomas Tollemache died following the Brest expedition in 1694, there was a rumour that Trelawney might succeed him as colonel of the Coldstream Guards but this was opposed by the whigs, John Cutts receiving the appointment. In 1696 Trelawney was made governor of Plymouth, a post he held until 1722. He married, on 25 June 1699, Elizabeth Mitchell, daughter of Thomas Mitchell, rector of Notgrove, Gloucestershire, from 1665 until 1686. They had one daughter. He died at Hengar on 24 September 1731 and was buried at Pelynt.

JOHN CHILDS

Charles Trelawney (1653–1731), by Thomas Forster

Sources DNB · CSP dom., 1673–5; 1685; 1687–90 · P. Watson, 'Trelawny, Charles', HoP, Commons, 1660–90 · N. Luttrell, A brief historical relation of state affairs from September 1678 to April 1714, 6 vols. (1857) · J. C. R. Childs, Nobles, gentlemen and the profession of arms in Restoration Britain, 1660–1688: a biographical dictionary of British army officers on foreign service (1987) · BL, Add. MS 41805 · U. Nott. L., Portland MSS, PWA 2237 · The life of James the Second, king of England, ed. J. S. Clarke, 2 vols. (1816)

Likenesses T. Forster, pencil miniature, Holburne Museum of Art, Bath [see illus.]

Trelawny, Edward (bap. 1699, d. 1754), colonial governor, was baptized on 9 July 1699 at Trelawne, near Looe, Cornwall, the fourth son of Sir Jonathan *Trelawny, third baronet (1650–1721), bishop of Winchester, and his wife, Rebecca Hele (1670–1710), daughter of Thomas Hele of Babcombe, Devon. He was educated at Westminster School, where he was a queen's scholar, from 1713, and Christ Church, Oxford, where he matriculated on 27 June 1717, but did not take a degree. His father had consolidated and extended the Trelawny family's electoral influence in Cornwall, and in 1723 he was returned to parliament as member for West Looe, one of the family boroughs. He supported Sir Robert Walpole's ministry, and was commissioner of victualling from 21 October 1725 until 1732. After Walpole appointed him a commissioner of customs at Edinburgh, he vacated his parliamentary seat in December 1732. He held the Edinburgh position until 1737, but in 1734 he left Scotland to join the British army's campaigns against the French in the War of the Polish Succession. In his absence he was elected MP for East and West Looe, but was disqualified because of his customs position. The next year his brother Sir John Trelawny, bt (1691–1756), transferred the family estates to him in return for Trelawny taking over his brother's debts. To pay the sum Trelawny had to mortgage the Cornish estates to Sir Charles Wager. Details of his first marriage are unknown. His second marriage, on 8 November 1737, was to Amoretta, daughter of John Crawford, with whom he had one son, who died in infancy and was buried with his mother in St Catherine's Church, Jamaica, in November 1741.

In August 1736 Trelawny was offered the position of governor of Jamaica; he was formally appointed in June 1737, and assumed office on 30 April 1738. Involved in the War of Jenkins's Ear and the War of the Austrian Succession, Trelawny favoured attacks on the Spanish guarda-costas to counter their depredations on English shipping. He raised Jamaican independent companies and slaves for the ill-starred attack on Cartagena in 1741. He accompanied Vice-Admiral Edward Vernon and Brigadier-General Thomas Wentworth in the attack on Panama in 1742, a scheme he backed. In the same year he quarrelled with Rear-Admiral Sir Chaloner Ogle over methods of pressing seamen at Jamaica. In 1743 Trelawny was appointed colonel and captain of the 49th regiment of foot in Jamaica. In 1748 he joined Admiral Sir Charles Knowles in the capture of Fort St Louis on Hispaniola.

Trelawny was a successful governor of Jamaica; even though he had little prior administrative experience, he proved to be a tactful, moderate negotiator with various political factions on the island. He consolidated his governorship as early as 1739, when he agreed a settlement with the maroons that helped to secure internal peace in Jamaica. He avoided serious clashes with the planter-dominated assembly, and usually supported them in their disputes with the judiciary and the council. But he considered that the assembly held too much power and advocated changes to imperial governance, notably that parliament should intervene to resolve squabbles between governors and assemblies. Metropolitan authorities did not pursue this suggestion.

In 1751 Trelawny asked to be relieved of his governorship on grounds of ill health. He was by this time a wealthy man. He had paid off the mortgage on the Cornish estates by 1744, and in addition to his salary as governor and the revenues of the estates enjoyed payments from the Pelham ministry, whose candidates he regularly returned at East and West Looe. His financial situation was still further improved when he married, on 2 February 1752, Catherine Penny, née Douce, widow of the former Jamaican attorney-general Robert Penny, from whom she had inherited a fortune estimated at between £30,000 and £40,000 in Jamaican currency. Retirement could now follow. In September 1752 his successor, Sir Charles Knowles, arrived and Trelawny left Jamaica on 25 November. He took with him the gratitude of the house of assembly for his sound administration in Jamaica. Delayed in his homecoming by being shipwrecked off the Isle of Wight, he arrived in London on 28 April 1753. He died at Hungerford Park on 16 January 1754. He bequeathed his Cornwall properties for life to his brother Sir John, and afterwards to Harry Trelawny, his cousin and brother-in-law, who eventually succeeded as fifth baronet.

Sir William Trelawny, sixth baronet (1722/3–1772), colonial governor and naval officer, was the first son of Captain William Trelawny, Edward Trelawny's first cousin, and his wife, Mary, eldest daughter of William Bisset of Westminster. Educated at Westminster School, where he was admitted in 1733 aged ten, William married his cousin Laetitia (d. 1772), daughter and heir of Sir Harry

Trelawny, at some time in or before 1755. They had two children, Harry *Trelawny (*bap.* 1756, *d.* 1834) and Laetitia Anne (*d.* 1845), who married Paul Trehy Ourry MP. William joined the navy early in life, and was appointed lieutenant in 1743, master and commander in 1754, and post captain in 1756. He served in the navy during the Seven Years' War, and was MP for East and West Looe from 16 May 1757 until June 1767. He succeeded Sir Harry Trelawny as baronet in 1762. As head of the Trelawny interest he uneasily co-operated with his cousin James Buller, whose influence in the Looe seats was increasing. In the Commons he usually supported the government of the day. He vacated his seat on being appointed governor of Jamaica, a position he held from 1768 to 1772. Though he knew little about Jamaica before taking up his appointment, he earned the respect of the creole élite in that island for steering a sensible political course at a time when the assembly and council of Jamaica were frequently at loggerheads. He died at Spanish Town from a fever on 11 December 1772, a few months after his wife, who had died on 24 August; the assembly voted him a public funeral at a cost of 1000 guineas, which took place on 13 December 1772 in Spanish Town. The Jamaican parish of Trelawny was named after him.   KENNETH MORGAN

Edward John Trelawny (1792–1881), by Seymour Stocker Kirkup

Sources G. Metcalf, *Royal government and political conflict in Jamaica, 1729–1783* (1965) · F. Cundall, *The governors of Jamaica in the first half of the eighteenth century* (1937) · E. Cruickshanks, 'Trelawny, Edward', HoP, *Commons, 1715–54* · *Journal of the House of Assembly of Jamaica*, 3, 4, and 6 · L. B. Namier, 'Trelawny, William', HoP, *Commons, 1754–90* · W. A. Feurtado, *Official and other personages of Jamaica* (Kingston, Jamaica, 1896) · J. P. Greene, 'Edward Trelawny's "grand elixir": metropolitan weakness and constitutional reform in the mid-eighteenth-century British empire', *West Indies accounts: essays on the history of the British Caribbean and the Atlantic economy in honour of Richard Sheridan*, ed. R. A. McDonald (Kingston, Jamaica, 1996), 87–100 · L. B. Namier, *The structure of politics at the accession of George III*, 2 vols. (1929), 2.399–402 · *Trelawny correspondence: letters between Myrtilla and Philander, 1706–1736* (1884) · R. Pares, *War and trade in the West Indies, 1739–1763* (1936) · will, PRO, PROB 11/807, sig. 60 · W. J. Gardner, *A history of Jamaica from its discovery by Christopher Columbus to the year 1872* (1873) · G. W. Bridges, *The annals of Jamaica* (1828) · J. Charnock, ed., *Biographia navalis*, 6 vols. (1794–8), vols. 4 and 6 · *Old Westminsters* · private information (2004) [Mrs Ann Laver] · GEC, *Baronetage*
Archives BL, Add. MS 19038 · BL, Newcastle MSS, Add. MSS 32724, 32695 · Bodl. Oxf., letters to C. Wagner [copies] · Boston College, Massachusetts, John J. Burns Library · Cornwall RO, letters to J. Howell · Institute of Jamaica, Kingston, letters · L. Cong., Vernon-Wager MSS, vols. 7, 8, 12, 15, 16 · National Library of Jamaica, Kingston, letters to H. Pelham and others · NMM, corresp. with E. Vernon; letters to C. Wagner · PRO, CO 137/22–25, 48, 56, 57, 59 · Surrey HC, corresp. with Edward Garthwaite, 30/1/2
Wealth at death reputedly between £30,000 and £40,000 in Jamaican money, from his wife: E. Cruickshanks, 'Trelawny, Edward'; will, PRO

Trelawny, Edward John (1792–1881), writer and adventurer, was born on 13 November 1792 probably at his grandfather's house at 9 Soho Square, London. His father was Charles Trelawny (1757–1820), formerly a lieutenant colonel in the Coldstream Guards, later MP for Mitchell, who was made rich by the death of a cousin in 1798, and

his wife, Mary (or Maria), *née* Hawkins (1759–1852). Trelawny later described his father as an oafish brute, but he seems to have been fond of his mother. He had one elder brother, Harry, and four younger sisters. In *Adventures of a Younger Son* (see below) he reports how, at the age of five, assisted by Harry, he killed, taking some time over the deed, a clip-winged raven, his father's pet, which had scared a small female friend of his. Both boys were sent to the Royal Fort Boarding School, run by the Revd Samuel Seyer in Bristol, from which (as he reports in *Adventures*) Trelawny was expelled for attacking both an under-master and the headmaster, and for attempting to burn the place down, in revenge for the continuous floggings he had received.

In October 1805 Trelawny joined the navy, in 1806 attended Dr Burney's Navigation School at Gosport (where he was taught no more than he had been in Bristol), and, in various ships, circumnavigated the globe. He took in Mauritius (assisting at its capture from the French), India, Ceylon, the East Indies, Cape Horn, the River Plate, and St Helena. He was wounded in the knee and face in the English attack on Java in August 1811. A musket ball remained in his knee until 1844, when Robert Browning witnessed its removal. He was transferred from ship to ship, guilty (by his own later account) of frequent assaults on his superior officers. He was invalided out of the navy in 1812, a midshipman still, not having been offered a commission. His father gave him an allowance of £300 a year.

In May 1813 Trelawny married Caroline Julia Addison (*b.* 1794), the nineteen-year-old daughter of an East India merchant. They had two daughters, Maria Julia and Eliza, but in 1816 Caroline left him for her lover, the much older Captain Coleman, and Trelawny divorced her in proceedings which lasted from 1817 to 19 May 1819, and involved much humiliating publicity. Once rid of both unfaithful wife and blighted naval career, he started to read books for the first time, Lord Byron and Shakespeare especially. Byron's heroes fascinated him, as more charismatic and successful versions of himself.

In autumn 1819 Trelawny accompanied his mother and sisters to Paris. The ladies returned, but he moved on to Geneva, which bored him. He made friends with the retired naval captain Daniel Roberts, who shared his keenness for hunting and fishing. At Ouchy he first read Percy Bysshe Shelley, with whose politics, as revealed in *Queen Mab*, he could identify. At the house of Sir John St Aubyn near Geneva he met Edward Ellerker Williams, and Shelley's cousin Thomas Medwin. Very briefly, he encountered the Wordsworths. His father's death in 1820 left him no better off. He returned to England, but was soon back hunting with Roberts in the Alps.

Friendship with Shelley and Byron In 1822, at the invitation of Williams, Trelawny left Geneva for Pisa (he arrived on 14 January), where he met Shelley and Byron, and the two legendary episodes in his life began. Byron liked him both despite, and because of, the fact that he seemed to model his physical image and his doubtful autobiographical tales on those of Conrad, protagonist of Byron's *Corsair*—a copy of which he was rumoured to keep beneath his pillow. Trelawny was in fact more attracted to the idealistic Shelley than to the satirical Byron: in Shelley's more overt anti-establishment attitudes he found a theoretical justification for his own juvenile rebelliousness. He became—retroactively—a democrat and a republican (one of his great heroes had always been John Paul Jones).

In the aborted Pisan circle production of *Othello*, Trelawny was to have taken the lead, with Byron as Iago. Mary Shelley found his company delightful, and he escorted her to balls and carnivals. He was present at the Pisan affray on 24 March 1822, when Sergeant-Major Masi knocked Shelley off his horse, though he played no important part in it. (In his old age he would show off a dagger which, he said, a blind beggar had given him to defend himself against Masi.) Byron saw through his fantasizing with ease and amusement: 'Trelawny could not even to save his life tell the truth', he said. However, he admired Trelawny's practical skills. Trelawny arranged, via Daniel Roberts, for the building of the *Don Juan* (in which Shelley, Williams, and Charles Vivian were to drown) and of Byron's schooner the *Bolivar*. Byron employed him as its captain.

Trelawny writes that he was, through his spyglass, the last person to see Shelley and Williams disappear into the squall off Leghorn on 8 July 1822. He took personal charge of the search for their bodies, and planned and carried through the pagan rites in which the disintegrated corpses were cremated, on the shore of Tuscany and at Viareggio, on 15 and 16 August 1822. It was he who snatched Shelley's unburnt heart from the flames. Both

Mary Shelley and Jane Williams found him a great comforter at this terrible time. He would sit with them for hours, speaking in praise of their husbands. In April 1823 he organized the removal of Shelley's ashes to the pyramid of Caius Cestius in the protestant cemetery at Rome, the planting of ten trees next to them, and the addition of three lines from Ariel's song in *The Tempest* ('Nothing of him that doth fade …') to the inscription.

Trelawny had, on first meeting her on 22 February 1822, fallen in love with Claire Clairmont, Mary Shelley's half-stepsister, the mother of Byron's deceased daughter Allegra. He also had a casual affair with Gabrielle Wright, wife of the *Bolivar*'s designer; but Claire meant much more to him. However, though they may briefly have been lovers, Claire would not marry him, and she left Italy for Austria and then Russia.

To Greece with Byron When Byron started on his own terminal Greek adventure, Trelawny was happy to answer the poet's request to go with him. Byron wrote, 'I shall like your company of all things.' They sailed from Genoa on 21 July 1823. Though Trelawny boxed, fenced, and swam with Byron, he would not wear the pretentious Homeric helmet the poet had had designed for him. Once they had arrived in the Ionian Islands, Byron's unwillingness to move annoyed Trelawny, and with James Hamilton Browne he crossed to the mainland on 6 September 1823, with letters of introduction from Byron, to visit the 'seat of Greek government' at Tripolitsa, to investigate the situation as Byron's agent. He was never to see Byron again alive.

Wearing Greek, not western clothes, he arrived at Tripolitsa, where he met the occidentally-clad Alexander Mavrocordato, whom he at once despised, and the Greek-clad Theodore Colocotrones, whom he admired. Passing through to Corinth, he noted the horrible remains of the victims—human and animal—of Colocotrones' victory over the Turks the previous year in the gorge at Dervenakia. Hamilton Browne departed for London to assist in the raising of a loan; at Athens, Trelawny purchased fifteen or so women, and set up a harem, with which, however, he was soon bored. He became an associate of the Greek warlord Odysseus Androutses, whom he was alone in describing as 'a glorious being', and soon became a leader of *klephts* himself, helping Androutses to storm the Turkish fort at Negroponte (Euboea) without success, and burning several Greek villages without conscience. His capacity for endurance, and indifference to discomfort, endeared him to his men.

When Byron's death was announced, Trelawny hurried to Missolonghi, to take care of the funeral arrangements again, and was disappointed by the decision to send the poet's remains home. But he did (as he reports) take the opportunity to look into the coffin at Byron's withered limb (or limbs—he wrote conflicting accounts of what he saw), and wrote letters about his own vital part in the Greek expedition, explaining that it had been he who suggested that Byron should renounce his quiet life in Italy, and go there in the first place.

After the drama of Byron's death had died down, Trelawny affected to despise his memory. Byron had been 'weak and ignoble', where he, Trelawny, had been decisive and active. He now tried to take control of the Greek situation as he thought Byron ought to have, but only succeeded in making himself unpopular and ridiculous, and soon drifted back into the service of Androutses, even though Androutses was now planning to go over to the Turks. In the well-fortified Mavre Troupa ('Black Hole') cave, high on Parnassus, he married Androutses's half-sister Tersitza, whose age was probably thirteen. Bride and groom had no language in common.

Androutses was, however, arrested and imprisoned in the Venetian tower on the Acropolis. Trelawny was now in command, though only of the Black Hole. But he was not safe there. On 11 June 1825, one of two of Mavrocordato's agents, William Whitcombe, shot him twice at point blank range, but missed all vital organs. The gun of the other agent, Thomas Fenton, failed to go off. Trelawny's jaw was shattered and his mouth immobilized, but he refused all medical treatment and insisted that nature be allowed to take her course. His body cured itself in five weeks, assisted by small helpings of water and egg yolk. Fenton had been shot dead on the spot; once Trelawny realized he was going to survive, he magnanimously let Whitcombe go. The dead body of Androutses was found soon after at the foot of the Acropolis.

Emaciated, with his right arm paralysed and three teeth missing, Trelawny left the cave, and was shipped—with a free passage from Mavrocordato, but without the blessing of the Foreign Office—back to the Ionian Islands. Tersitza, now pregnant, went with him. On Cefalonia, in June 1826, she bore a daughter, Zella, but on the conception of another child left him to go into a convent. The second child died, and the seventeen-year-old Tersitza managed to divorce Trelawny. He recovered the full use of his right arm, and only a slight hunch remained to tell of what had happened.

In 1828 Trelawny returned to England, where he proposed marriage to Mary Shelley, who refused him. Also in 1828 he met Claire Clairmont, and proposed to her again, with the same result. In 1829 he decided to go to Florence, where he was joined by all three of his daughters, although Eliza died. He stayed with John Keats's friend Charles Armitage Brown, and met Walter Savage Landor, who put him and Tersitza into one of his *Imaginary Conversations*. Between 1828 and 1831 he called himself John Edward Trelawny.

Adventures of a Younger Son In 1831 Trelawny published, anonymously, his 'autobiography', *Adventures of a Younger Son*, in the style, spelling, and moral editing of which he was assisted by Armitage Brown, Landor, and Mary Shelley. The title was chosen by Mary Shelley and the publisher, Colburn. Each chapter has an epigraph from either Byron, Shelley, or Keats. The book is as imaginative as any poem by Byron (though the early chapters seem trustworthy). There are echoes of *Don Juan*, especially of Canto 2. Trelawny tells of his adventures in the East, and of his *renegado* career as a French-backed anti-British privateer,

led by a Dutch-American, Shakespeare-reading buccaneer called De Ruyter. There are cruel pranks, sea fights, land raids, a shipboard orgy, and a tiger hunt from which only the elephants emerge with credit. Though the protagonist advertises himself as a foe to oppressors, selective oppression is what he excels at. Scotsmen, surgeons, and other human annoyances exist only to be beaten up or dropped into pits of offal, buildings exist only to be burnt or pulled down, and animals only to be hamstrung, shot, or eaten. Remorse is occasionally expressed for the destruction thus caused. There is a teenage heroine called Zela, whom Trelawny marries, and who learns to take violent initiatives by his side. Very little of the material is verifiable or otherwise, and, almost certainly, none of it is true, though Trelawny might have been thrown off balance had such a thing been pointed out at the time. As a self-portrait it is disagreeable; but the book was a great success, and made Trelawny famous at last; it was said that Byron had modelled Conrad, and even Manfred, on him.

In January 1832 Trelawny sailed to America, in search of adventure, but found none. He met Fenimore Cooper, and John Philip and Fanny Kemble, with whom he visited Niagara, where he swam the rapids, in emulation of Byron's more numerous swimming feats. He became very fond of Fanny Kemble, but she was engaged already. He also met and admired the great engineer Christian Detmold. He visited New Haven, New York, Philadelphia, and Charleston, but despite the celebrity status he enjoyed, became bored and disillusioned, and returned to England early in 1835.

Back in England Trelawny found no role. His fame continued, although his dabbling in chic radical politics did him no good. He was friendly with Bulwer, Brougham, and Mrs Jameson, frequented Lady Blessington's dinners, and figures as the Byronic story-telling bore Captain Sumph in William Makepeace Thackeray's *Pendennis*, and as the heroic Borromeo in William Godwin's *Cloudesley*. When Mary Shelley brought out her first edition of her husband's poems in 1839, Trelawny was outraged at the cuts she made—especially in the notes for *Queen Mab*—and their friendship ceased.

In 1839 Trelawny retired from society and lived in Putney, a self-proclaimed vegetarian, teetotaller, and eschewer of both underwear and overcoats. He had in 1838 started the longest relationship of his life, with Augusta, the separated wife of Harry, the future Lord Goring. She was a friend of Mary Shelley. On 5 August 1839 she bore him a son, Edgar (called, to avoid scandal, John Granby). Harry Goring obtained a divorce in 1841. Trelawny and Augusta married, a daughter, Laetitia, was born, and they moved to Usk in Monmouthshire, where Trelawny first built a house and then bought a nearby farm, which he worked with skill and industry, becoming a valued member of the community. Another son, Frank, was born. His Greek daughter Zella, now Mrs Olguin, sometimes came over from Italy. The family lived happily together until 1858, when Trelawny started a liaison with a teenage girl whose identity seems irrecoverable (she was known as Miss B). Augusta left him and went to Italy, and

Trelawny took Miss B to London, where she was to be replaced in turn by another young woman called Emma Taylor.

Recollections of the Last Days of Shelley and Byron In 1858 Trelawny published *Recollections of the Last Days of Shelley and Byron*, and in 1878 a rewritten version, the more confidently entitled *Records of Shelley, Byron and the Author*. In the earlier work he gives Byron two clubbed feet, but in the later, just one shrivelled Achilles tendon. However, these narratives brought him fame all over again, and made him a favourite among the Victorians, who found in him a link to the mighty dead whose early reputations for freethinking and free living they had sanitized. His portrait of Shelley, especially, was recognized as more accurate than the cleaned-up versions produced by the colleagues of Lady Shelley, daughter-in-law to Percy Bysshe. Both his books of reminiscence may, with cross-checking, be used as reliable and vivid first-hand accounts. Trelawny's insistence on Shelley's republicanism and atheism was accepted with tolerance. He was introduced to Benjamin Disraeli. *Adventures of a Younger Son* had been reprinted, to acclaim, its confession of Trelawny's 'desertion' from the navy ignored. Even his most readily disprovable assertion—that he had known Keats—went unchallenged. The positive reading of his character, which made his eccentricity evidence of his sincerity and strength, won the day. Like Teresa Guiccioli (Byron's last mistress), he had come to believe his own fabricated version of the past, but, unlike Teresa Guiccioli, he persuaded the world to believe it too.

Trelawny's last years were spent at 7 Pelham Crescent, Brompton, and in a house at Sompting, near Worthing. He died at Sompting on 13 August 1881. In accordance with his wishes, his corpse was transported to Gotha, Germany, where it was cremated, and his ashes were taken by Emma Taylor to Rome, where they were buried in the protestant cemetery in the plot, next to Shelley's, which he had purchased in 1823.

Trelawny had an imposing, 6 foot physical presence, with dark piercing eyes, tanned Arab features (according to Mary Shelley's description), a long, curling moustache, a deep and gentle though monotonous voice, and an extremely powerful constitution. Robert Browning reports that he endured the extraction of the bullet from his knee with all the equanimity of a man having his hair cut. His sense of humour was rough, not sophisticated. Irony both eluded and defeated him. To both accurate spelling and personal hygiene he was a stranger. In Greece especially, he saw tolerance of dirt and lice as a manly thing, and, although mild dyslexia may be suspected (he often spelt his own name Jhon), his supposed orthographical incompetence may in later years have formed part of a calculated image. His egotism was huge, as was his capacity for revengeful violence, of which he was proud. He despised those who endured suffering meekly. But he was capable of great generosity.

There are portraits of Trelawny by W. E. West and Joseph Severn, and sketches by Sir Edwin Henry Landseer, E. Duppa, Count d'Orsay, Severn, and Seymour Kirkup.

Trelawny figures in *The Cremation of Shelley's Body* by Fournier and Gérôme (he assisted the painters with detailed notes, which they mostly ignored), and as the old man in *The North-West Passage* by Millais. Several photographs were taken in his old age.

Edward John Trelawny was his own worst enemy in the story of the English Romantic movement. If he had not embroidered his role in such confused and dubious ways, he would be known correctly for what he was: one of its most significant and colourful ancillaries.

PETER COCHRAN

Sources DNB · H. J. Massingham, *The friend of Shelley: a memoir of E. J. Trelawny* (1930) · M. N. Armstrong, *Trelawny: a man's life* (1941) · S. J. Locker, *Shelley, Trelawny and Henley: a study of three Titans* (1950) · R. Glynn Grylls, *Trelawny* (1950) · A. Hill, 'Trelawny's family background and naval career', *Keats–Shelley Journal*, 5 (1956) · A. Hill, *Trelawny's strange relations* (privately printed, 1956) · W. St Clair, *Trelawny: the incurable romancer* (1977) · D. Crane, *Lord Byron's jackal: a life of Edward John Trelawny* (1998) · [E. J. Trelawny], *Adventures of a younger son*, 3 vols. (1831) · *Letters of Edward John Trelawny*, ed. H. B. Forman (1910)
Archives Bodl. Oxf., notebook | BL, Ashley MSS, letters to Claire Clairmont · Bodl. Oxf., corresp. with Mary Shelley
Likenesses J. Severn, oils, 1822–3, repro. in St Clair, *Trelawny*; priv. coll. · W. E. West, oils, 1822–3, repro. in St Clair, *Trelawny*; priv. coll. · S. S. Kirkup, portrait, *c*.1830, repro. in *The Field* (Aug 1881) · A. D'Orsay, lithograph, 1836, BM; repro. in St Clair, *Trelawny* · J. Severn, pen-and-ink drawing, 1838, NPG · photograph, 1871, repro. in St Clair, *Trelawny*; priv. coll. · J. E. Millais, group portrait, oils, 1874 (*The north-west passage*), Tate collection · L. Cattermole, oils, repro. in Locker, *Shelley, Trelawny and Henley* · B. E. Duppa, two pencil sketches, NPG · S. S. Kirkup, lithograph, NPG · S. S. Kirkup, oils, priv. coll. [see illus.] · S. S. Kirkup, sketch, repro. in Locker, *Shelley, Trelawny and Henley* · E. H. Landseer, pencil sketch, NPG · D. Lucas, mezzotint, BM; repro. in Armstrong, *Trelawny*
Wealth at death £14,224 2s. 7d.: probate, 23 Nov 1881, CGPLA Eng. & Wales

Trelawny, Sir Harry, seventh baronet (*bap.* 1756, *d.* 1834), dissenting minister, Church of England clergyman, and Roman Catholic priest, was baptized at St Budeaux, Devon, on 26 June 1756, the only son of Sir William *Trelawny, sixth baronet (1722/3–1772) [see under Trelawny, Edward], and his wife and first cousin, Laetitia (*bap.* 1728, *d.* 1772), daughter of Sir Harry Trelawny, fifth baronet. He attended Plympton grammar school before 1770, and entered Westminster School that year when his father left Britain to become governor of Jamaica. On his father's death on 11 December 1772, he succeeded to the baronetcy and inherited the family estates in south-west England, including the family seat at Trelawne, in the parish of Pelynt, Cornwall. He matriculated as a commoner at Christ Church, Oxford, on 2 July 1773, and graduated BA on 26 April 1776. He married, on 28 April 1778, at Kingston St Mary, Ann (*d.* 1822), daughter of the Revd James Brown, rector of Portishead and vicar of Kingston St Mary, both in Somerset. They had four sons and two daughters.

Trelawny from an early age felt himself called to the Christian ministry but could not in conscience subscribe to the Church of England's formularies. After Oxford, having become intimate with Rowland Hill and undertaken itinerant preaching in Cornwall, Trelawny chose to be ordained as a Presbyterian minister on 22 April 1777 at the

Above Bar chapel, Southampton, where he made a Calvinist confession of faith. He returned to Cornwall after ordination where he helped establish a chapel at West Looe. His pulpit message became progressively moderate as he fell under the influence of the more 'rational' faith of the Revd Micaiah Towgood. On 26 May 1779, in a sermon at Taunton, he pleaded for generous behaviour towards Christians of all dispensations, and insisted that even pious Unitarians were not necessarily beyond salvation. In fact Trelawny had moved into that camp, a preference underlined when he participated in an ordination service with Joseph Priestley at Lympstone, Devon, in July 1779. Theophilus Lindsey reported accurately on 27 March 1780 that 'he is now an Arian of a very liberal cast, not holding the doctrine of the Atonement' (T. Lindsey, letter to William Tayleur). But Trelawny was drifting back to Anglicanism. Sir Harry was unable to withstand pressure from his family and 'tampering' by Bishop John Ross of Exeter (T. Lindsey, letter to William Tayleur, 18 July 1780). It was clearly a considerable embarrassment to the hierarchy that the great-grandson of one of the seven bishops should be assorting with rational dissenters. He was still holding out early in 1780, opining that:

> I must think, that religion is a personal concern, and that every man, by the laws of God and reason, is obliged to enquire for himself, to form the best opinions he is able, and to act honestly, according to them. (Trelawny, A Letter ... to ... Alcock, 5–6)

But his protestations only encouraged more answers, and two months later he was back in the establishment fold, his problems with the Thirty-Nine Articles apparently surmounted.

After keeping term at Christ Church to fulfil residency requirements, Trelawny took his MA and received Anglican holy orders from Bishop Ross of Exeter in one day, 22 June 1781. He quickly made his way in the Church of England. On 27 January 1789 he was named a prebendary of Exeter; in 1791 he became vicar of St Allen, Cornwall, and exchanged it for the living of Egloshayle in the same county two years later. He restored the church there and his sermons were so popular that he had to provide additional galleries. He resigned the benefice in 1804 from a combination of ill health and inability to fulfil conditions of residency under the 1803 legislation. He gave up his prebendal stall at Exeter in 1810. Trelawny's parochial duties did not inhibit him from being a successful estate owner at Trelawne. He corresponded with Robert Bakewell over cattle breeds and was a friend of the Revd Robert Walker of St Winnow, a well-known Cornish agriculturalist.

Trelawny's religious restlessness was a recurrent part of his life, but it never seems to have affected the esteem in which most people regarded him. His goodwill towards his former dissenting colleagues was never in doubt, and his tergiversations were forgiven. As Job Orton ruefully observed: 'I never expected any steadiness from him' (Orton to the Revd Mr Hughes, 13 Sept 1780, Orton, 2.20). Preaching was Trelawny's lifelong passion, and he invariably attracted a fair-sized congregation, perhaps because 'his countenance was particularly prepossessing' (GM,

2nd ser., 1/1, 1834, 653). His daughters Mary and Ann Letitia became Catholics and turned the family chapel at Trelawne into a Roman Catholic one. Following the death of his wife (who remained an Anglican) at Trelawne on 18 November 1822, he was persuaded by his daughters to convert to Catholicism in the mid-1820s. By that date he was permanently resident in Rome. He was ordained as a Catholic priest by Cardinal Carlo Odescalchi on 30 May 1830. Trelawny died on 25 February 1834 after an illness of ten days at Laveno on Lake Maggiore in Italy, and was buried at Laveno in a ceremony attended by all the local clergy. NIGEL ASTON

Sources GEC, Baronetage, 2.45 · GM, 1st ser., 48 (1778), 237 · GM, 1st ser., 61 (1791), 878 · GM, 1st ser., 63 (1793), 1063 · GM, 1st ser., 66 (1796), 416, 553 · GM, 1st ser., 80 (1810), 657 · GM, 1st ser., 89/1 (1819), 9 · GM, 2nd ser., 1 (1834), 652–3 · GM, 2nd ser., 1 (1834), 563 · N&Q, 2nd ser., 9 (1860), 472 · N&Q, 2nd ser., 10 (1860), 13–15, 76–7 · Old Westminsters, vol. 2 · Christ Church Oxf. · Foster, Alum. Oxon., 1500–1714 · parish register, Somerset, Kingston St Mary, 28 April 1778, Som. ARS [marriage] · [H. Trelawny], A confession of faith by Sir Harry Trelawny, A.B., late of Christ Church, Oxford. Delivered at his ordination, in the Rev. Mr Kingsbury's meeting-house at Southampton, April 22, 1777. Introductory discourse and questions proposed by Rev. William Kingsbury, MA (1777) · H. Trelawny, A sermon preached at Taunton, May the 26th, 1779, before an assembly of the protestant dissenting clergy (1779) · [H. Trelawny], A letter from the Rev. Sir Harry Trelawny, Bt., to the Rev. Thomas Alcock, vicar of Runcorn and of St Budeaux (1780) · A. Seymour, The life and times of Selina, countess of Huntingdon, 2 vols. (1839), vol. 2, pp. 418–21 · J. Murch, A history of the Presbyterian and General Baptist churches in the west of England (1835), 541–6 · T. W. Aveling, Memorials of the Clayton family (1867), 36, 40–56 · Letters to dissenting ministers and to students for the ministry from the Rev. Job Orton, ed. S. Palmer, 2 vols. (1806), vol. 2, pp. 20, 188, 200–01 · R. Polwhele, The history of Cornwall, new edn, 7 vols. (1816), vol. 5 · F. Hitchins and S. Drew, The history of Cornwall, 2 vols. (1824) · J. Polsue, A complete parochial history of the county of Cornwall, 4 vols. (1867–72), vol. 4, pp. 32–41 · Boase & Courtney, Bibl. Corn., 2.657–8 · G. Oliver, Collections illustrating the history of the Catholic religion in the counties of Cornwall, Devon, Dorset, Somerset, Wilts, and Gloucester (1857), 30 · T. Lindsey, letters to William Tayleur, JRL, Unitarian College Archives, Lindsey letters, vol. 3

Archives Cornwall RO, corresp. with Anthony Jeeves of West Looe, DDX/349 · Cornwall RO, 'Trelawne Book', X/1031

Trelawny, Ian Clarence (1917–1998), docks manager and port consultant, was born on 17 January 1917 at 1 Coltbridge Terrace, Edinburgh, the eldest child in the family of three sons and two daughters of Captain Clarence Walter Eyre Trelawny, an officer in the Royal Navy, and his wife, Barbara Cecil, née Carus-Wilson (d. 1976). The family was from Cornwall, and Trelawny was educated at St Erbyn's School, Penzance, and King's College, Taunton. After working as a clerk for a cold storage firm, in 1938 he started a boat-building and yacht-broking business in London. On 23 September 1939 he married Mary Ethel (b. 1914/15), the daughter of Edgar Frank Eyles, theatrical manager.

On the outbreak of the Second World War Trelawny joined the Royal Navy as a rating, serving in minesweepers and later in an armed merchant cruiser. After he had recovered from severe wounds received in action in August 1942, he was commissioned and was posted to Felixstowe, Suffolk, where he served in the coastal force.

Following promotion to lieutenant-commander he commanded the 11th MTB (motor torpedo boat) flotilla from 1943 to 1945. He was awarded the DSC and bar for his part in many raids against German ships firing on British planes flying over the North Sea, and on E-boats attacking British coastal shipping. During the Normandy invasions in 1944 he worked on salvage, and later he organized the reopening of several ports along the northern European coast. He remained in the Royal Navy after the war, commanding a salvage ship in Hong Kong harbour for a time. On 12 October 1946, his first marriage having ended in divorce, he remarried: his second wife was (Angela) June Wilkinson (b. 1923/4), the daughter of Dr James Howard Wilkinson, medical practitioner. She had served in the Women's Royal Naval Service during the war. They had one son and three daughters.

Trelawny was appointed manager of the Felixstowe Dock and Railway Company in 1955. The company had been founded as the Felixstowe Railway and Pier Company in 1875 by Colonel George Tomline, a local landowner, who had bought 6000 acres of land from the duke of Hamilton in 1867, and obtained parliamentary permission to build a railway line from Ipswich to Felixstowe— then only a small village on the north bank of the River Orwell, about a mile from the North Sea. The railway was completed in 1877. Hoping to develop Felixstowe as a port, he extended the line down to the Orwell and in the early 1880s built a small dock basin opposite the port of Harwich. But although Felixstowe developed as a seaside resort, the port did not prosper except as a centre for flying boats between the wars, and it was requisitioned during the Second World War as a base for air-sea rescues, as well as for coastal defence. In 1951 the nearly derelict docks were handed back to the company, which was bought by Gordon Parker, a Norfolk grain merchant, who became chairman. The docks were flooded during the devastating east coast floods of 1953, causing the dock basin to silt up, and the old wooden piers were destroyed, while the foundations of many buildings, and the railway lines, were undermined.

Starting with a workforce of nine, Trelawny began dredging the docks and salvaging what remained of the infrastructure. This was in the face of opposition from the local council, which did not want the town to expand and tried to purchase compulsorily the docks to use as a rubbish dump. Trelawny was helped by the fact that Felixstowe, as a virtually redundant port, had not been included in the national dock labour scheme of 1947, and so he was not hampered by some of the restrictive practices enshrined in the scheme. Two new piers were completed in 1957, and, always in the forefront of developments in methods of cargo handling, he was the first dock manager to use forklift trucks, in 1956. In order to encourage the expanding plastics industry to import chemicals through Felixstowe, he reclaimed the old admiralty tanks, and built new ones, linked by pipelines to tankers moored on the quay, for the storage of liquid chemicals. An oil jetty was completed in 1964.

The biggest expansion of Felixstowe as a cargo port came in the 1960s with the introduction of container traffic, and Felixstowe was the first East Anglian port to build a container holder for use on roll-on roll-off ferries. A new cold store, the only one on the east coast, opened in 1963 to handle frozen goods passing through the docks, and Trelawny went on to open a tanker terminal. By the mid-1960s work was under way on a scheme to reclaim land in Harwich harbour to build a quay to provide space for more container ships and ferries. The new container terminal was completed in 1968 and extended in 1973. By 1975 Felixstowe docks were able to handle 3 million tons of container traffic. Townsend Thoresen, the ferry company, began operating a regular passenger service to Zeebrugge in Belgium in 1974 and opened a continental ferry terminal in 1978. By the end of the century Felixstowe had been transformed from a quiet seaside town, chiefly a dormitory for Ipswich, into Britain's largest container port. Although the port was bought by European Ferries in 1976, and taken over first by P & O in 1987 and then by Hutchison Whampoa in 1991, the Felixstowe Dock and Railway Company (known as the Dock Company) continued to own and operate most of the cargo handling infrastructure.

Trelawny was appointed OBE in 1967. In 1972 he moved from management to be head of the consultancy side of the company, and he travelled worldwide, advising on the improvement of port facilities. He retired in 1987, and died on 22 April 1998 in the St Elizabeth Hospice, 565 Foxhall Road, Ipswich, Suffolk, of lung cancer. His remains were privately cremated on 30 April. He was survived by his wife, June, and their four children.

ANNE PIMLOTT BAKER

Sources P. Hadwen, J. Smith, P. White, and N. Wylie, *A pictorial history of Felixstowe dock* (1998) · L. C. Reynolds, *Home waters: MTBs and MGBs at war, 1939–1945* (2000) · A. Jobson, *The Felixstowe story* (1968) · G. Kinsey, *Seaplanes–Felixstowe* (1978) · *The Times* (1 May 1998) · *East Anglian Daily Times* (25 April 1998) · private information (2004) [widow] · b. cert. · m. certs. · d. cert.

Likenesses photograph, 1956, repro. in Hadwen, Smith, White, and Wylie, *Pictorial history*, no. 163 · photograph, repro. in *The Times*

Trelawny, Sir John (d. 1433×47), landowner and soldier, was the son of John Trelawny of Trelawny, Cornwall, and his wife, Maud, daughter of Robert Menwenick. It is not easy to distinguish the son from either the father or another, junior, John Trelawny, who may in fact have been the second John's younger brother. All three were members of parliament for Cornish constituencies, the father representing Bodmin in 1397, and the youngest John sitting for Liskeard in 1421 and for Lostwithiel in 1449. But the second John Trelawny was twice knight of the shire for Cornwall in 1421, and probably also in 1413, and by the end of 1414 had been elected coroner in that county. He also served in France, in 1415 (when he probably fought at Agincourt) in the retinue of Edward, Lord Courtenay, and in 1417 under the duke of Exeter. On 27 September 1419, no longer coroner, but with the style of 'king's knight', he was granted an annuity of £20 per annum by Henry V, later confirmed by Henry VI. He added three oak or laurel leaves to his arms, while the figure of Henry V, which once stood over the west gate of Launceston, is said to have had at its feet the inscription: 'He that will do aught for mee, Let hym love well Sir John Tirlawnee' (Polsue, 3.89). Sir John was still receiving his annuity in 1432, and in the following year made arrangements for the descent of some of his Cornish lands. With his wife Agnes, daughter of Robert Tregoddick, he had perhaps two sons, and also two daughters. He was dead by 1447, while his presumed younger brother and namesake lived until at least 1465.

E. L. O'BRIEN

Sources L. S. Woodger, 'Trelawny, John I', 'Trelawny, John II', 'Trelawny, John III', HoP, *Commons, 1386–1421* · J. Polsue, *A complete parochial history of the county of Cornwall*, 3 (1867–72)

Trelawny, Sir John Salusbury Salusbury-, ninth baronet (1816–1885), politician and diarist, was born at Harewood, Cornwall, on 2 June 1816, the elder son of Sir William Salusbury-Trelawny, the eighth baronet (1781–1856), MP for East Cornwall (1832–7), and his wife, Patience Christian (d. 1879), daughter of John Phillips Carpenter. The family, anciently landed in Cornwall, were baronets from 1628, owning 8000 acres in 1873; the third baronet was Sir Jonathan Trelawny, bishop of Bristol and Winchester, one of the seven bishops committed to the Tower by James II. Educated at Westminster School and Trinity College, Cambridge (BA, 1839), John Trelawny, as he liked to be known, was called to the bar (Middle Temple, 1841) but never practised. A captain in the Royal Cornwall Rangers militia (1840), he later commanded the 2nd Cornwall rifles. A cultured man of wide interests, he published in 1842 with R. P. Collier, first Baron Monkswell, the future politician and judge, a translation of the first two books of Lucretius; to which he contributed book 1 (Wright, 449–50). On 25 January the same year he married Harriet Jane (d. 1879), daughter of John Hearle Tremayne MP, of Heligan, Cornwall, with whom he had three children. He first stood for parliament in 1841, when he unsuccessfully contested his father's old constituency. From 1843 to 1852 and again from 1857 to 1865, he represented Tavistock; in the interval he fought Brighton, Liskeard, and Bedford. Finally, he sat for East Cornwall in 1868–74.

By his death Trelawny had largely been forgotten; he rated a very brief obituary in *The Times*. In his day, he was a prominent back-bencher, a humane and usually realistic reformer, whose causes ranged from the deficiencies of Peel's Bank Charter Act, the subject of a pamphlet from him in 1847, to the Contagious Diseases Acts regulating prostitution in naval ports and garrison towns. The almost surreptitious passage of the initial Contagious Diseases Act of 1864 was largely his doing: 'The danger', he observed, 'is not so much in what to say as in what to avoid saying' (*Parliamentary Diaries*, 286). He also championed the Maori against encroaching white settlers in New Zealand (Steele, 356). It was, however, his sponsorship of successive church rates bills (1858–63) on behalf of the Liberation Society that gave him considerable importance in the eyes of party leaders and whips. He is best described as a free-thinking gentry radical, and as such slightly old-fashioned even then. 'Old institutions', he wrote in 1862

'—even though imperfect or, in part, mischievous—give a country, at least, a backbone' (*Parliamentary Diaries*, 219). As a young man he had, however, advocated disestablishment, the basis of his claim in the 1840s to be an 'ultra Radical'. Strongly conservative where individual, as distinct from corporate, property rights were concerned, he was far from orthodox, and a determined libertarian, in matters of belief. 'Desire is prayer, and prayer, if not a kind of blasphemy, is desire', he told himself (ibid., 241). He brought in bills (1861–3) to allow professed unbelievers to give sworn evidence in criminal cases, content, after he had failed to carry them, to be 'thought to sin with Hobbes and Bentham' (ibid., 163). Not surprisingly relations with his dissenting constituents in Tavistock were sometimes difficult. He steadily opposed 'a sour and sectarian observance of ... Sunday' (*Hansard 3*, 113, 31 July 1850, 587), and supported, on political rather than religious grounds, the Maynooth grant. As a result, he felt obliged to give up his seat, consistently with his often stated willingness to do so when he lost his electors' confidence. Tavistock took him back in 1857; he had the duke of Bedford's interest on his side, but he retired again in 1865, following local criticism of his conduct in advocating the Sunday opening of museums, and resisting legislation to close public houses on the same day. His years as a member for his native county were comparatively uneventful; worsening health ended his parliamentary career. A conscientious member of the royal commission on the Contagious Diseases Acts in 1870–71, he defended them against a rising tide of criticism, publishing in 1872 an analysis of the commission's evidence.

It was Trelawny's dedication to religious freedom that made him the Liberation Society's shrewd, if incongruous, choice in 1857 to introduce its annual bills to abolish church rates. Independent but staunchly liberal, landed and titled, well liked in the house, he was more congenial to the Commons than a middle-class nonconformist radical. He never became a member of the society, nor did he by then sympathize with its ultimate goal of disestablishment. His aim, shared by most of those who voted with him, and by a few tories, was to redress a mainly symbolic but emotive grievance as part of a larger policy, deeply rooted in the whig past, of comprehension. 'It seems to me', he reflected, 'the terms of joining the Church should be made as broad and easy as possible' (*Parliamentary Diaries*, 241). He emphasized that the church had many friends among dissenters, who did not wish to see her overthrown; she was in no real danger from the liberationists. He obtained varying majorities for his bill in 1858–60, getting Palmerston's vote from 1859, although the Lords proved an insuperable obstacle. But from 1861 the tories, with the support of Gladstone and a handful of others on the Liberal side, were able to defeat Trelawny in the Commons; church rates were an open question in the Liberal cabinet. Increasingly uncomfortable with the militancy of Dr C. J. Foster, chairman of the liberationists' parliamentary committee, Trelawny desisted after 1863 from his attempts to pass their bill. Nevertheless, his efforts had brought the tories to the point where they introduced bills to exempt dissenters from the rate. Despite the so-called 'Conservative reaction' of the early 1860s, which Trelawny found worrying, abolition was only a matter of time.

Trelawny's surviving diaries, published a century after his death, are a useful source for the period they cover. They preserve the cautiously progressive ambience of Palmerstonian parliaments, in which Trelawny's radicalism mellowed and he became a warm admirer of the premier: 'What a slave to his duty!' (*Parliamentary Diaries*, 239). A master of parliamentary procedure, he was devoted to the house and to the deliberate political process it embodied: 'We educate each other' (ibid., 233).

After the death of his first wife, Trelawny married, in 1881, Harriet Jacqueline, widow of Colonel E. G. W. Keppel. He died at his London home, 25 Albert Gate, Knightsbridge, on 4 August 1885 and was succeeded as baronet by his son William.   DAVID STEELE

Sources *The parliamentary diaries of Sir John Trelawny, 1858–1865*, ed. T. A. Jenkins, CS, 4th ser., 40 (1990) · 'The parliamentary diaries of Sir John Trelawny, 1868–73', ed. T. A. Jenkins, *Camden miscellany, XXXII*, CS, 5th ser., 3 (1994) · *Hansard 3* (1843) · G. I. T. Machin, *Politics and the churches in Great Britain, 1832 to 1868* (1977) · E. D. Steele, *Palmerston and liberalism, 1855–1865* (1991) · *Dod's Parliamentary Companion* · W. H. K. Wright, ed., *West country poets: their lives and works* (1896) · *CGPLA Eng. & Wales* (1885) · Burke, *Peerage* · *The Times* (8 Aug 1885)
Archives BL · Bodl. Oxf., parliamentary diaries | Co-operative Union, Holyoake House, Manchester, letters to George Holyoake
Wealth at death £7229 15s. 0d.: probate, 5 Sept 1885, *CGPLA Eng. & Wales*

Trelawny, Sir Jonathan, third baronet (1650–1721), bishop of Winchester, was the second of the six surviving sons of Sir Jonathan Trelawny, second baronet (*d.* 1681) and his wife, Mary, daughter of Sir Edward Seymour of Berry Pomeroy, Devon. He was born on 24 March 1650 at Trelawne, Pelynt, Cornwall, and baptized in Pelynt parish church on 26 April.

Early years Both Trelawny's father and paternal grandfather had been royalists in arms in the first civil war, a commitment which cost the family dear in the long run. They compounded for their estates but were additionally charged with paying compensation to the parliamentarian Buller family to the tune of £1200. The family were burdened with debts not only during their lives but also after Jonathan Trelawny succeeded to the title of third baronet in 1681. His father was also imprisoned several times during the interregnum but kept up a correspondence with Charles II in exile.

Immediate royal favour at the Restoration began to repair the family's fortunes: Trelawny's father became a gentleman of the privy chamber on 5 June 1660, four years before he inherited the baronetcy. Financial embarrassment did not prevent Trelawny from receiving a good education: he went to Westminster School in 1663 and on to Christ Church, Oxford, in 1668. At the latter he came under the influence of Dr William Jane, with whom he would remain close, an uncompromising defender of the restored Church of England. Trelawny graduated BA on 22 June 1672 and MA on 29 April 1675.

Sir Jonathan Trelawny, third baronet (1650–1721), by Sir Godfrey Kneller, 1720

The Trelawnys emerged as a military gentry family with clear Yorkist affiliations, and Trelawny was the only one among his brothers not to choose a career in the army or the navy. His father was comptroller of the duke of York's household between 1670 and 1674 and served as lieutenant-colonel in the duke of York's regiment of horse until it was disbanded in 1679. His family's dependence on York's favour must have been a complicating factor for Trelawny personally when loyalties became divided after 1685, but in the short term the connection with York promised well for his career prospects. He was appointed a royal chaplain-extraordinary in 1677, less than a year after his ordination as a priest on Christmas eve 1676. Charles II hurried to grant him the living of Calstock in Cornwall, only to discover that it had already been granted to someone else. Instead he was given the rectory of St Ive on 22 September 1677 and his father presented him to the family living of South Hill, to which Bishop Lamplugh instituted him on 4 October. Unfortunately the parsonages of both were in ruins and in need of rebuilding: young Trelawny lived at the family seat of Trelawne, more than 10 miles away from both, and irritated the bishop by seeking a third living—that of Dartington—to make up for the deficiencies of the first two. His plea was refused. Instead, he took on the role of chaplain to Lord Conway.

Much of the next eight years would be taken up with a futile search for further preferment, a search made more urgent when Trelawny inherited his father's debts along with his title in March 1681, following his elder brother's death in October 1680. He lapsed into self-pity and self-dramatization, writing to John Ellis in August 1682: 'the King hath not a gentleman he can entirely confide in but myself, & yet he gives me neither money nor preferment to bear up with against my debts (contracted in the service of the crown)' (Smith, 18). Instead of devoting his energies to the church, an increasing amount of Trelawny's time was spent in the secular government of Cornwall, inspecting his father's old militia troop and succeeding him in his role of vice-admiral of south Cornwall in February 1682, as well as being named on the commission of the peace. He comes across more in this period as a gentry governor of his shire than as any sort of spiritual leader. With his unashamed swearing, his love of good living, and his lack of serious scholarship, it is little wonder that his career in a church led by Archbishop Sancroft was slow to progress. On 31 March 1684, he married the fourteen-year-old Rebecca Hele (1670–1710), daughter of Thomas Hele of Babcombe, Devon, with whom he had a large family. Among their sons was Edward *Trelawny, governor of Jamaica.

Episcopal promotion and the revolution Trelawny's fortunes only began to improve after his family's erstwhile patron, the duke of York, succeeded to the throne as James II in February 1685. Trelawny was not slow to demonstrate his loyalty, soliciting Lord Chief Justice Jeffreys for nominations for seats in parliament, over which he had an influence, even before he was asked; and when Monmouth's rebellion broke out he was notably efficient in mobilizing the Cornish militia, with the help of only one other deputy lieutenant (the rest proving recalcitrant), for which the earl of Sunderland wrote to congratulate him. However, his reward, when it came, fell far below his expectations—the poor bishopric of Bristol. He made no attempt to hide his disappointment, even begging Sunderland to influence the king to change his mind. But it was to no avail and he was consecrated at Lambeth on 8 November 1685, by two archbishops and six bishops then in London to attend parliament.

Despite his misgivings about his new appointment Trelawny was keen to prove himself both as an effective diocesan and as a loyal servant of the king. He achieved the first objective, holding a successful visitation of Bristol Cathedral in January–February 1686, winning over the dean, William Lovett. His primary visitation of Dorset at Easter also went well, gaining Sancroft's warm approval for his injunctions, and his demand that communion tables be set 'altar-wise' at the east end and railed off seems to have been enforced even in Dorchester, despite its long puritan and nonconformist tradition. He also, at this stage, managed to stay in step with royal policy, emphasizing the ill consequences of anti-popish preaching in his visitation charge. However, by 1687 this particular balancing act was proving much harder to sustain and Trelawny found himself increasingly drawn into the episcopal opposition to the king's policies. When called upon by Sunderland to sign an address of thanks for the declaration of indulgence granting toleration to dissenters and Roman Catholics in April 1687, and to promote it among his clergy, his response was equivocal and ultimately disingenuous. Having done nothing for three weeks he communicated to his Bristol clergy, via Dr Jane, that he would not sign the address personally; but when, at a meeting with them, they followed his lead and also demurred, he wrote to Sunderland, claiming that it was their reluctance which had prompted him to refrain from signing. Of the Dorset clergy, only two signed. The king was furious at the disobedience.

Gradually Trelawny became more courageous in his opposition, giving a living to one of the fellows ejected from Magdalen College, Oxford, in December 1687, in clear defiance of the ecclesiastical commissioners' express order. And finally in May 1688 he supported the petition of Sancroft and five other bishops against the order to read the declaration of indulgence in churches and so found himself one of the famous seven bishops who were prosecuted by the angry king. In their tense interview with James II, when he charged them with issuing a trumpet of rebellion, Trelawny fell to his knees and made a self-justifying speech. James found this merely saucy but Trelawny's behaviour sounds more like the *cri de coeur* of a man facing an unbearable tension between his family's traditional royalism and his own commitment to the Church of England. His acquittal along with the others must have been a huge relief and Trelawny responded by paying more than his fair share of the legal costs.

That summer was in many ways Trelawny's finest hour: a moment of moral courage and heroism in a life otherwise marked by self-seeking and conformity. He had every reason to believe that his opposition to the king's policy would be costly to him personally, and he had no way of anticipating the course events would subsequently take. However, a number of myths have grown up around his role in 1688. The 'Song of the Western Men' in support of him at the time of the trial (which Macaulay quotes: 'And shall Trelawney die') probably had nothing to do with him and allegations of his complicity with William of Orange at this time are also, almost certainly, false. James II was probably right to believe as late as mid-November, when he appointed him bishop of Exeter, that Trelawny was still basically loyal to him. On 25 November, when Trelawny's brother Charles, a senior army officer, defected to the prince, Trelawny sent an assurance of his own loyalty to the king, via Bishop Francis Turner, which may well have been sincere.

Military and political realities, however, soon supervened. On 5 December, while Trelawny was at Bristol, the earl of Shrewsbury arrived with a regiment of foot and a letter from the prince of Orange. Trelawny replied cautiously to the latter, expressing approval for the steps taken to secure the protestant religion and the laws and liberties of England. James's flight and in particular his jettisoning of the great seal sabotaged, at least temporarily, Trelawny's translation to Exeter, but he resisted the direction in which political events inexorably moved thereafter. On 31 January and early in February 1689 he voted against the notion that James II had abdicated and against the offer of the crown to William and Mary. However, he stopped short of rejecting the subsequent settlement, took the oaths, and reflected afterwards: 'we thought ourselves obliged to accept the deliverance brought us' (Smith, 58). He seems to have assumed that James II would be implacable to him personally and on that basis was consistently hostile to Jacobitism. Nevertheless, preaching at a thanksgiving service before Queen Anne and both houses of parliament in 1702, in a sermon focusing on national deliverances, he mentioned the Restoration but not the revolution. A reference to 'eighty-eight' turns out to be alluding to the defeat of the Spanish armada in 1588, rather than more contentious events a hundred years later (Trelawny, 30).

Bishop of Exeter, 1689–1706 Perhaps somewhat surprisingly the new sovereigns endorsed and expedited Trelawny's translation to Exeter and he was down in the diocese conducting his primary visitation by August 1689. If Trelawny had been a somewhat incongruous member of the episcopal bench in the Sancroft era, he hardly fitted any better into that of Tillotson and Tenison, although for different reasons. Though appointed to the commission to revise the liturgy in the interests of comprehension in 1689, he took no part in its proceedings and later opposed informal moves designed to placate dissent. He was a staunch defender of church courts and episcopal discipline: in 1704, he wanted convocation (whose revival he fully supported) to censure bishops for neglecting their disciplinary powers. He jealously guarded his episcopal rights, going to law lengthily and expensively several times in the course of the 1690s, especially to uphold his right to regulate education in a number of different spheres. And he was implacably opposed to new developments such as the societies for the reformation of manners, which seemed to undermine the Church of England's status as the guardian of the nation's morals.

Bishop of Winchester and borough-monger Trelawny has gone down in history as a time-server, promoted through the episcopate to the highest level for political services to his masters. This is partly attributable to an acid comment from Gilbert Burnet, a long-standing rival and enemy, that his promotion to the bishopric of Winchester in 1706 was due in part to the electoral interest which he had in west country boroughs. It was certainly remarkable to see an unreconstructed high-church bishop like Trelawny, patron of Atterbury and the convocation movement as he was, becoming a diehard adherent of the increasingly whiggish Marlborough–Godolphin ministry right down to its fall in 1710. But a purely cynical interpretation of this development needs to be put into some sort of context. For one thing, Trelawny was a long-standing friend of the Churchills and of Godolphin before their rise to power. For another, he was genuinely committed to their central policy of energetically prosecuting the war with France, as he showed by the hawkish tone of his thanksgiving sermon of 1702, for all its apparent lack of enthusiasm for the revolution itself (*A Sermon Preach'd before the Queen*). As bishop of Exeter he had a good record of working with

whig clergy across party lines for the good of the church. And, ironically, the move to Winchester made it more difficult for Trelawny to maintain his electoral interest in Cornwall. Beyond this, he did not make his peace with the new tory ministry led by Harley until 1712, quite a long delay for a supposed vicar of Bray, and his subsequent commitment to the Hanoverian succession has all the hallmarks of sincerity.

Nevertheless, Trelawny's status as a borough-monger is not in doubt. He built on his existing family interest and in 1702 boasted, not implausibly, to have had a hand in the return of eleven MPs. Nor can it be doubted that Trelawny could be quite ruthless in defence of his interest, using not only his role as a diocesan but also family connections to extend it. In 1716 he even forced his reluctant daughter Rebecca to marry the disfigured John Buller, in order to extend his influence to the borough of Saltash.

Trelawny's reputation for time-serving has undoubtedly been enhanced by the tone of his correspondence with those in power, which tended to be effusive to the point of flattery. It can be traced as far back as a letter to the earl of Rochester in 1683 and remained a feature of his surviving letters to the end of his life. That it was not purely self-seeking may be inferred from the fact that it was applied equally to long-standing friends and colleagues, like Marlborough and Archbishop Wake, as well as to powerful men with whom he was not previously acquainted. But it certainly sounds craven.

The demands of maintaining a large electoral interest, in a time of frequent polls and spiralling electoral costs, may in part provide the answer to another puzzle about Trelawny: that the proceeds of the enormously lucrative see of Winchester failed to solve his family's financial problems. In the 1690s Trelawny had been financially too embarrassed to incur the additional cost of attending parliament on a regular basis; in 1710 he was still known to be in difficulties, and in 1713 he was compelled to remortgage all his family estates for £9000. He died intestate and after his death nearly £16,000 had to be raised from the sale of Trelawny estates to pay off debts. Yet in his last eight years at Winchester it has been estimated that he must have netted some £25,000, which was brought in by the systematic exploitation of the proceeds of the bishopric, seriously alienating the bulk of its customary tenants. His business manager, Charles Heron, had made a significant start in this area before 1713 and his successor, Edward Forbes, merely continued as Heron had begun.

Again the context of Trelawny's action provides some excuse. The resources of the bishopric had been notably under-exploited, even spoiled, in the final years of his predecessor, Peter Mews, in the opening years of the eighteenth century. And by the time of Trelawny's death at least, other bishops and capitular bodies were beginning to exploit their possessions in a similar way. Maintaining his electoral interest was not the only financial burden on Trelawny at this time. He had a large family to provide for—thirteen children, of whom eleven survived. He did his best for several of them, using the offices which were in his gift as bishop, a nepotism different only in scale from that practised by episcopal colleagues.

Looked at positively, Trelawny could be generous to a fault: his paying more than his share of the legal costs arising from the seven bishops' trial in 1688 was typical, as was his offer to pay for the fitting out of the interior of the meeting-place for the lower house of convocation, though in the latter case, the offer was declined. Negatively, Trelawny could be a spendthrift, building a new chapel at Trelawne, laying out new gardens at his palace at Winchester, and installing a huge episcopal throne in the cathedral there.

No early portrait of Trelawny survives, but a late one (post-1706) is, in its way, quite revealing. He wears the robes of a prelate of the Garter (a role he fulfilled *ex officio* as bishop of Winchester), trappings which he had been particularly keen to acquire on his translation. His nose is straight, the mouth generous but not over-large. Regarding the viewer with a somewhat superior gaze, he has all the air of a gentleman about town, rather than a minister of the church. There was throughout his life a certain incongruity between Trelawny's personal style and the spiritual offices he held, an incongruity felt even during his lifetime. It was savagely satirized in a work called *The Tribe of Levi*, which dubbed him 'Fighting Joshua' and dismissed him as a 'spiritual dragoon' (Strickland, 384). This work focuses on his role in the suppression of Monmouth's rebellion but it could equally have picked out other distinctly unclerical aspects of his life and career, such as his bluntness in speech and in letter writing. His high theology of the apostolic succession sat rather oddly with his very pragmatic attitude to the exploitation of the proceeds of ecclesiastical office for both laudable and questionable purposes.

It is too simple to see Trelawny as a conservative overtaken by changing times; he was in many ways *sui generis* even as a bishop under James II and later as bishop of Winchester he was somewhat ahead of his time, in terms of the vigour with which he exploited the resources of his see and challenged the customary rights of his tenants. His churchmanship and theological views were certainly backward-looking, lifelong campaigner for Laudian-style altars and traditional orthodoxy as he was. He was nevertheless every inch an eighteenth-century borough-monger.

Trelawny died suddenly at his residence in Chelsea on 19 July 1721. His body was moved with great pomp on Thursday 3 August down to Cornwall for interment in the family vault at Pelynt church (where he had been baptized) on 10 August 1721.   ANDREW M. COLEBY

Sources M. G. Smith, *'Fighting Joshua': a study of the career of Sir Jonathan Trelawny, bart., 1650–1721, bishop of Bristol, Exeter, and Winchester* (1985) · Wood, *Ath. Oxon.*, new edn · *The life and times of Anthony Wood*, ed. A. Clark, 5 vols., OHS, 19, 21, 26, 30, 40 (1891–1900) · W. D. Cooper, ed., 'Trelawny papers', *Camden miscellany, II*, CS, 55 (1853) · Sancroft papers, Bodl. Oxf., MSS Tanner · A. Strickland and [E. Strickland], *The lives of the seven bishops committed to the Tower in 1688* (1866) · E. P. Thompson, *Whigs and hunters: the origin of the Black Act* (1975) · G. V. Bennett, *The tory crisis in church and state: the career of Francis Atterbury, bishop of Rochester* (1975) · D. Underdown, *Fire from*

heaven: the life of an English town in the seventeenth century (1992) · G. S. Holmes, *British politics in the age of Anne* (1967) · J. Trelawny, *A sermon preach'd before the queen and both houses of parliament* (1702) · *CSP dom.*, 1687–9 · IGI

Archives Hants. RO, MSS · Royal Institution of Cornwall, Truro, family estate MSS | Bodl. Oxf., MSS Tanner, Sancroft papers · Christ Church Oxf., Wake MSS · U. Nott. L., letters to first earl of Portland

Likenesses G. Bow, silver medal, 1688, NPG · portrait, after 1706, priv. coll.; repro. in Smith, *'Fighting Joshua'* · G. Kneller, oils, 1708, Christ Church Oxf. · G. Kneller, oils, 1720, NPG [*see illus.*] · group portrait, oils (*The seven bishops committed to the Tower in 1688*), NPG · oils, CCC Oxf.

Wealth at death seriously in debt; £15,939 10*s*. raised from sale of Trelawny estates to pay off debts: Smith, *'Fighting Joshua'*

Trelawny, Sir William, sixth baronet (1722/3–1772). *See under* Trelawny, Edward (*bap.* 1699, *d.* 1754).

Treloar, Sir William Purdie, baronet (1843–1923), carpet manufacturer and philanthropist, was born on 13 January 1843 in a room over the gateway of the Patent Coconut Fibre Works in Holland Street, Southwark, London, the second son of Thomas Treloar (1818–1876), a coconut fibre mat manufacturer, formerly of Helston, Cornwall, and his first wife, Elizabeth (1816–1860), the daughter of John Robertson of Pitlochry, Perthshire. Initially brought up in Somerset, Treloar moved with his family to Blackheath, London, and in 1854 he was sent to King's College School, then in the Strand, to which he travelled each day (including Saturdays) by train. He left school at the age of fifteen and entered his father's business as a workman, and when he was sixteen became a foreman. He eventually succeeded to the post of manager, and on his father's death in 1876 inherited the business with its headquarters in Ludgate Circus.

On 20 March 1865, at St Margaret's Church, Westminster, Treloar married Annie (1842–1909), the daughter of George Blake of Mount Street, Grosvenor Square, London. They had no children of their own, but adopted two relatives, Florence Kilner (*d.* 1953, aged eighty-four) and Royson Treloar (1886–1960), Treloar's nephew. Treloar was particularly fond of Florence.

Treloar's civic career began in 1881, when he was elected to the court of common council for the ward of Farringdon Without, and he took an active part in the municipal affairs of the City of London. He instigated action which led to the adoption of ballot elections to the court of common council in 1886 and the opening of the Guildhall Art Gallery on Sunday afternoons in 1894, thus encouraging the activities of the National Sunday League, of which he was president. In 1892 he was elected alderman of the ward of Farringdon Without. In 1899 he became sheriff and helped to raise the City Imperial Volunteers for service in South Africa during the Second South African War. He was knighted on 29 March 1900 following a visit to the City of London by Queen Victoria.

From 1893, for the rest of his life, Treloar administered the annual Guildhall children's Christmas banquet (instigated by Sir Stuart Knill in 1892), and continued the distribution, assisted by the Ragged School Union until 1908, of

Sir William Purdie Treloar, baronet (1843–1923), by Bassano, 1899

Christmas hampers to disabled children in London (commenced by the *Daily Telegraph* in 1892). The Ragged School Union withdrew from the enterprise in 1908 because of possible confusion in the public's mind between itself and Treloar's own charitable foundation, which hurt Treloar's feelings deeply.

In 1906 Treloar was elected lord mayor of London and began a brilliant year of office, during which Edward VII and Queen Alexandra opened the new central criminal court, Old Bailey, and he entertained the monarchs of Norway and Denmark as well as Prince Fushimi of Japan. Treloar himself, as lord mayor, paid an official visit to Berlin, on an occasion which called for unusually tactful exchanges. He wrote a book about his mayoral year, *A Lord Mayor's Diary*, in 1920, to add to his other books, *Ludgate Hill: Past and Present* (1881), *Prince of Palms* (1884), *With the Kaiser in the East, 1898* (1915), and *Wilkes and the City* (1917). In July 1907 he became a baronet, but the title became extinct on his death.

Treloar's most enduring work as lord mayor, however, was the founding of the Lord Mayor's Little Cripples' Fund, launched on 22 November 1906. It received royal support, notably from Queen Alexandra, who opened the queen's fête in aid of the fund at the Mansion House on 13 June 1907, which raised £12,000, and out of which was born the Queen Alexandra League. Treloar collected £60,000 and obtained the Princess Louise Military Hospital, built at Alton, Hampshire, during the Second South

African War, where he established the Lord Mayor Treloar Cripples' Hospital and College, later the Lord Mayor Treloar Orthopaedic Hospital and College. The hospital was transferred to the National Health Service in 1948, but the Lord Mayor Treloar Trust continues to administer the college and the Florence Treloar School (opened 1967) for disabled girls. Treloar devoted to his foundation the greater part of his remaining life, aided greatly by Dr Henry Gauvain, the medical superintendent at the hospital. The institution's pioneering objects were the combined treatment and education of physically disabled children—priority initially being given to children suffering from surgical tuberculosis—and the training of physically disabled young people in suitable trades. The hospital, which opened on 7 September 1908, met a very real need, and many thousands of physically disabled children were successfully treated, educated, and trained there. The college opened on 26 October 1908. In 1919 Treloar founded a seaside branch of the hospital at Hayling Island. As a result of this pioneer work, many other hospital schools were established.

Treloar was viewed by his contemporaries as a genial personality, if rather inclined to self-publicity, and he was a member of many clubs. He was considered a popular, candid, and humorous public speaker, although with a mordant wit, and a formidable opponent. He died at his home, Grange Mount, 13 Beulah Hill, Upper Norwood, on 6 September 1923, and was buried alongside his wife at Shirley churchyard, Surrey, on 11 September.

H. GAUVAIN, *rev.* VIVIENNE ALDOUS

Sources C. E. Lawrence, *William Purdie Treloar: a monograph* (1925) · A. B. Beaven, ed., *The aldermen of the City of London, temp. Henry III–[1912]*, 2 vols. (1908–13) · W. P. Treloar, *A lord mayor's diary, 1906–1907* (1920) · C. E. Lawrence, *William Purdie Treloar: an eightieth birthday tribute* (1923) · A. Lawrence, 'Mr Alderman Treloar', *Cornish Magazine*, 2 (1899), 83–93 · *WWW* · 'Biographical Notes on Sir William Purdie Treloar', CLRO · O. L. Treloar, *Treloar genealogy: tree of Treloar* (1962) · *DNB* · T. L. Sayer, *Gog and Magog and I: some recollections of 49 years at Guildhall* (1931), 69–74 · d. cert. · *CGPLA Eng. & Wales* (1923)

Likenesses Bassano, photograph, 1899, NPG [*see illus.*] · P. T. Cole, oils, 1907, Guildhall Art Gallery, London · H. Furniss, caricature, pen-and-ink sketch, NPG · Spy [L. Ward], chromolithograph caricature, NPG; repro. in *VF* (8 March 1894)

Wealth at death £36,606 19s. 2d.: probate, 26 Oct 1923, *CGPLA Eng. & Wales*

Tremayne, Edmund (*c.*1525–1582), administrator and conspirator, was the second son of Thomas Tremayne, gentleman, of Collacombe, Devon, and Philippa, daughter of Roger Grenville of Stow. Nothing is known of his early life. Late in 1553 he entered the service of Edward Courtenay, earl of Devon, and was sent to the Tower in February or March of 1554 on suspicion of involvement in Wyatt's rebellion. Despite torture, he refused to provide evidence against either Courtenay or the Princess Elizabeth. Released on 18 January 1555 on payment of a fine of £40, he followed Courtenay to the continent where the earl established a household in Venice by mid-January 1556. Tremayne, however, left Courtenay's service soon after, probably as a consequence of his master's refusal to enter more actively into the conspiracies against Mary organized from France by Sir Henry Dudley. Tremayne's brother Nicholas was deeply involved in the conspiracy and had carried proposals from Dudley to Courtenay in Italy, meeting the earl in Ferrara on 21 March 1556, together with Francis Russell, earl of Bedford. However, Courtenay would not commit irrevocably to the conspiracy by joining the rebels.

It is likely that Edmund Tremayne returned with his brother to Paris, where he is recorded by 13 July 1556, but soon after departed for the English rebel camp at Rouen. Despite their adherence to the rebels and their presence in Paris in April 1557 in the company of Christopher Assheton, a leader in the Dudley conspiracy, and the Staffords, neither Edmund nor his brothers followed Thomas Stafford in his assault on Scarborough Castle later that month. Almost simultaneously, the betrayal of the Dudley conspiracy (April 1557) resulted in the dissolution of the rebel faction in France. It is likely that it was at this time that Edmund Tremayne joined the household of the earl of Bedford, who is documented in Calais on 26 July 1557.

The accession of Elizabeth brought Tremayne quick preferment from both Bedford and the queen. He was returned to parliament in 1559 for Tavistock, and appointed deputy butler for Devon in 1561 through the patronage of Bedford who had been named lord lieutenant. Between 1561 and 1574 he served as receiver in nine counties for the duchy of Lancaster, in which office his deputy was Humphrey Michell; Michell, a former servant to Edward Courtenay and a servant to Francis Russell, earl of Bedford, also sat several times in the Commons. William Cecil sent Tremayne to report on Ireland in 1569, and he subsequently wrote a report entitled *Causes why Ireland is not Reformed*. In May 1571 he was sworn clerk of the privy council. In 1572 he was returned MP for Plymouth, and on 13 March he inherited his family's estates on the death of his elder brother Roger. He remained interested in the Irish situation, visiting the island again in 1573; and in 1574 he was granted by the city of Exeter the reversion of Sir Gawen Carew's pension of £40, and was serving as receiver of exchequer revenues for Devon. In that year he also undertook substantial renovations to his house at Collacombe.

Tremayne married in September 1576 Eulalia, daughter of Sir John St Leger (*c*.1516–1593x6) of Annery, Devon; she outlived him. They had a daughter, Elizabeth, and a son, Francis (*d*. 1582), named for his patron, Bedford. In religion Edmund was an adherent of the west-country puritan faction. Much of his political activity was directed towards local issues. He was in 1576 involved in a parliamentary committee on ports, and was appointed piracy commissioner for Devon in 1577. In 1580 he was made a freeman of Plymouth. The close connection between Tremayne and his cousin Sir Francis *Drake is reflected in the queen's instructions to Tremayne to register the treasure unloaded from the *Golden Hind* in October 1580. Charged to investigate the allegations of cruelty made against Drake by the Spanish ambassador, Tremayne found his cousin innocent.

Tremayne died in September 1582, at Collacombe, just weeks before his son. The earl of Bedford oversaw his will. His estates passed to his brother Degory, who erected a monument to five of his brothers, Roger, Edmund, Richard [*see below*], and the twins Andrew and Nicholas. Both the latter had been involved in conspiracy against Mary, and Andrew was implicated with Sir Peter Carew and Sir Anthony Kingston; both brothers were killed at Newhaven in 1563. Edmund's effigy provides an image of the man late in life.

Richard Tremayne (*c*.1530–1584), Church of England clergyman, was born in Devon, the fourth son of Thomas Tremayne and his wife, Philippa Grenville. He graduated BA from Exeter College, Oxford, in 1548 and was elected a fellow on 28 March 1553, proceeding MA on 17 July of that year. The accession of Mary drove Tremayne to flee to Louvain with his pupil, the son of Sir Nicholas Arnold. Early in 1556 he returned to England where he appears to have acted as an agent for the Dudley conspiracy, together with his brother Nicholas. Although discovered, both men escaped to France where they were joined by their elder brother Edmund. Soon afterwards Richard set out for Strasbourg, perhaps as an agent with Arthur Saule to try to convince John Brett to remain on the continent and not perform the queen's commission of searching out the exiles. Failing in that mission, Tremayne returned to France until the reign of Elizabeth.

Named archdeacon of Chichester in April 1559, that summer Tremayne accompanied James Hamilton, third earl of Arran, in secrecy to England from Geneva. In October 1559 he was restored to his fellowship at Oxford, and in January 1560 Bishop Grindal of London ordained him deacon; the following month he was appointed treasurer of Exeter Cathedral. In addition he held several church livings in Cornwall and Devon. His continued absence from Oxford resulted in his losing his fellowship at Exeter College, and in February 1565 he migrated to Broadgates Hall. One year later, on 15 February 1566, he took the degree of BTh, followed on 26 April by that of DTh. On 19 September 1569 Tremayne married Joanna, daughter of Sir Piers Courtenay of Ugbrooke, who outlived him. They had a daughter, Mary, who became wife of Thomas Henslowe.

Richard Tremayne, like his brother Edmund, was a client of the earl of Bedford, who in 1570 recommended him unsuccessfully for the see of Exeter. He sat in convocation for Exeter and endorsed the Thirty-Nine Articles, speaking in favour of substantial revision to the prayer book, reflecting his puritan commitment. He had troubled relations with his bishop, William Alley, over the licensing of an unfit puritan preacher and accusations of nepotism. Richard Tremayne was buried on 30 November 1584 at Lamerton.
KENNETH R. BARTLETT

Sources HoP, *Commons, 1558–1603* · C. H. Garrett, *The Marian exiles: a study in the origins of Elizabethan puritanism* (1938); repr. (1966) · K. Bartlett, *The English in Italy, 1525–1558: a study in culture and politics* (1991) · *CSP dom., 1547–80* · *APC* · D. M. Loades, *Two Tudor conspiracies* (1965) · *The diary of Henry Machyn, citizen and merchant-taylor of London, from AD 1550 to AD 1563*, ed. J. G. Nichols, CS, 42 (1848) · J. L. Vivian, ed., *The visitations of the county of Devon, comprising the herald's visitations of 1531, 1564, and 1620* (privately printed, Exeter, [1895]) · K. R. Bartlett, 'The misfortune that is wished for him: the exile and death of Edward Courtenay, eighth earl of Devon', *Canadian Journal of History*, 14 (1979), 1–28 · *DNB* · J. Brett, 'A narration of the pursuit of English refugees in Germany under Queen Mary', ed. I. S. Leadam, *TRHS*, new ser., 11 (1897), 113–31 · will, PRO, PROB 11/64, fols. 350*v*–352*r*

Archives Devon RO, political and family MSS | BL, Cotton MSS, 'Discourses on Irish affairs' · Hatfield House, Hertfordshire, Burghley MSS, 'Causes why Ireland is not reformed' · Hatfield House, Hertfordshire, Burghley MSS, 'Matters wherewith the queen of Scots may be charged'

Likenesses effigy on monument, probably Lamerton, Devon

Wealth at death unknown, but substantial lands and property specified: will, PRO, PROB 11/64, fols. 350*v*–352*r*

Tremayne, Sir John (*bap.* 1647, *d.* 1694), lawyer and politician, was baptized at Mevagissey, Cornwall, on 16 September 1647, the eldest son of Colonel Lewis Tremayne (*bap.* 1619, *d.* 1685) of Heligan, St Ewe, Cornwall, and Mary (*d.* 1701/2), daughter and coheir of John Carew of Penwarne, Mevagissey. He entered the Inner Temple on 8 December 1666, transferring to the Middle Temple on 30 October 1669, and being called to the bar on 9 May 1673. He must have quickly built up an impressive legal practice because in 1680 he was one of the leading king's bench barristers. No doubt this legal success allowed him to marry, on 13 April 1680, Frances (*bap.* 1655, *d.* 1683), daughter of William Davie, a barrister, of Creedy, Devon, a union which produced one son who died young. It also explains a volume of 'entries, declarations, and pleadings' from the reigns of Charles II and James II which he collected (BL, Lansdowne MS 1142). In 1685 Tremayne succeeded his father to Heligan, and over the next few years embarked on a building programme which saw a new house erected on the site.

The revolution of 1688 gave a further boost to Tremayne's career. On 4 May 1689 he was made a king's serjeant, which increased his legal practice, and he appeared frequently as a counsel before the House of Lords between 1689 and 1693. In May 1689 he was also made a serjeant-at-law, and he was knighted on 31 October. In 1690 he was elected to parliament as a whig for Tregony, but this served only to enhance his legal reputation, as he combined speech-making in the Commons with advocacy in Westminster Hall. He acted as counsel for Richard Graham, Viscount Preston, and others, on trial for treason in January 1691, and for Sir John Germaine in the action for damages brought by the duke of Norfolk; and he prosecuted Lord Mohun for the murder of William Mountfort, the actor, in January 1693. In June 1692 he failed in an attempt to be elected recorder of London, but in the following year he petitioned for, and was granted, the stewardships of several hundred courts in Cornwall.

The exact date of Tremayne's death has not been ascertained, but he made his will on 10 February 1694 and his death was noted on the 20th by Narcissus Luttrell. He was buried in the Temple Church, London, on the 23rd. In 1723 his *Placita coronae, or, Pleas of the Crown in Matters Criminal and Civil* was published, 'digested and revised by the late John Rice of Furnival's Inn'. An English translation by Thomas Vickers in two volumes was published in Dublin in 1793.   STUART HANDLEY

Sources HoP, *Commons, 1690–1715* [draft] · Sainty, *King's counsel*, 23 · Baker, *Serjeants*, 450, 541 · *IGI* · I. J. Herring, *400 years of Tremaynes at Heligan* (1999), 23, 33 · Boase & Courtney, *Bibl. Corn.*, 2.777 · H. A. C. Sturgess, ed., *Register of admissions to the Honourable Society of the Middle Temple, from the fifteenth century to the year 1944*, 1 (1949), 180 · *Register of burials at the Temple Church, 1628–1853* (1905), 28 [with introduction by H. G. Woods] · will, PRO, PROB 11/419, sig. 67 · N. Luttrell, *A brief historical relation of state affairs from September 1678 to April 1714*, 2 (1857), 476; 3 (1857), 272 · D. Lemmings, *Gentlemen and barristers: the inns of court and the English bar, 1680–1730* (1990), 271 · *State trials*, 12.676, 930, 965 · *The manuscripts of the House of Lords*, 4 vols., HMC, 17 (1887–94), vols. 2–4

Archives Cornwall RO, family corresp. · Cornwall RO, MSS | BL, Lansdowne MS 1142

Tremayne, Richard (*c.*1530–1584). *See under* Tremayne, Edmund (*c.*1525–1582).

Tremellius, (Joannes) Immanuel (1510–1580), Hebrew and biblical scholar, was born in Ferrara, Italy, in 1510. His parents were Jews, and he had at least one brother. In Ferrara he received a traditional Jewish education as well as a humanist training in Latin and Greek, and, when he was twenty, proceeded to the University of Padua. There he met Cardinal Alessandro Farnese (the future Pope Paul III), who had him to stay in Rome and visited his father's house in Ferrara. In Padua too he made the acquaintance of Cardinal Reginald Pole and his circle, and was attracted by their beliefs which have come to be known as evangelism. Although Pole remained loyal to the papacy, he and his friends had marked sympathies with the doctrine of justification by faith which had been propagated by Luther. To this seemingly conciliatory form of Catholicism Tremellius converted. He was baptized in Pole's house in Padua in 1540, with Pole himself as his godfather.

The man who was to play the most important part in Tremellius's life was not Pole but a member of his circle, Pietro Martire Vermigli (Peter Martyr), to whom Tremellius may have given Hebrew lessons in Padua. In the summer of 1541 Vermigli, who had in the meantime become prior of the Augustinian canons in Lucca, invited Tremellius to join him and teach Hebrew at the monastic school he had just reorganized. In the society of Vermigli and a number of other distinguished citizens of Lucca, Tremellius moved steadily closer to protestantism. He also issued his first scholarly work, the *Meditamenta*, published in Wittenberg in 1541. In August 1542, after Pope Paul III had introduced the inquisition, Vermigli fled. He subsequently accepted the hospitality of the reformer Martin Bucer in Strasbourg and was soon joined by Tremellius. At this point both men had converted to Reformed protestantism, to which Tremellius was to remain uncompromisingly loyal until his death.

Later Tremellius looked back on his first Strasbourg years as one of the happiest times of his life. He taught Hebrew grammar at the high school founded by Jacob Sturm, with Vermigli as his colleague for Old Testament history. After the traditional trial period of one year he received a permanent appointment. He also met some of the leading reformers. He remained devoted to Bucer, and in the summer of 1543 was introduced to Calvin and Guillaume Farel, two more men who were to be his friends for the rest of their lives. In October 1544 he married a member of the French community, Elisabeth de Grimecieux, a widow from Metz. She already had one daughter from her marriage with Grimecieux, and with Tremellius she was to have a further daughter and a son.

In April 1547 the situation in Strasbourg started to change with the defeat of the protestant forces, the Schmalkaldic League, by the emperor, Charles V. It now appeared that Catholicism might be reimposed in Germany, and Tremellius again looked for a job elsewhere. Backed by Calvin and Farel, he sought employment in Switzerland in November 1547, but could find nothing. Shortly after, however, Tremellius, like Vermigli, received an invitation to England from the archbishop of Canterbury, Thomas Cranmer. Before the year was out they were both staying with their respective families at Lambeth Palace in Surrey.

Tremellius's memories of his stay with Cranmer were just as fond as those of Strasbourg. In April 1549 he was joined by two other refugees from Strasbourg, Bucer and the Hebraist Paul Fagius, and he described the archbishop's court as 'a school, or an arena, of piety and learning' (Tremellius, 6). There he started to write his commentary on the book of Hosea (which he would complete and publish many years later). But his main ambition was an academic post. Late in 1549, while Vermigli was sent to Oxford and created regius professor of divinity, Tremellius, with Bucer and Fagius, was dispatched to Cambridge. He succeeded Fagius as 'king's reader of Hebrew' after Fagius's death on 13 November.

At Cambridge Tremellius made the acquaintance of Princess Elizabeth, the future queen, and developed a lifelong friendship with her two tutors, Matthew Parker, to whose third son he acted as godfather, and her French tutor, a protestant immigrant from Normandy, Anthony Chevallier. Chevallier, who married Elisabeth de Grimecieux, Tremellius's stepdaughter, on 1 December 1550, started on his own distinguished career as a teacher of Hebrew by assisting his father-in-law in his lectures. Tremellius taught with enthusiasm, prepared even to provide tuition free of charge, and it was while he was at Cambridge that he translated the Geneva catechism into Hebrew in the hope of converting other Jews to Christianity. On 24 October 1552 he was granted a prebend in the diocese of Carlisle.

The accession of Queen Mary in July 1553 put an end to the aspirations of Tremellius and his fellow refugees in England. Together with his family, which now included Anthony Chevallier, Tremellius returned to the continent. He stopped in Brussels, hoping to enlist the support of his former protector and godfather Reginald Pole, but the cardinal had no time for apostates. Again like Vermigli, Tremellius returned to Strasbourg. Here, however, the confessional circumstances had altered. Lutheranism was strong, and acceptance of the Augsburg confession a condition for an academic post. Tremellius refused. He then fell back on the support of Calvin, but discovered once more how strong opposition to Calvin and his protégés could be. Having failed to keep a post in Bern or even to obtain one in Lausanne (where he also had the backing of Beza and Viret), Tremellius repaired to Geneva in September 1554 to stay with Calvin. He there received an offer of employment: at the suggestion of his councillor, the jurist Ulrich Sitzinger, the Count Palatine Wolfgang, duke of Zweibrücken, invited him to Germany to act as tutor to his children. Tremellius reached Zweibrücken in November 1554.

The duke, an admirer of Melanchthon, soon regarded Tremellius as indispensable. He refused to let him go when Calvin tried to appoint him professor of Old Testament at the newly founded academy of Geneva, and in December 1558 dispatched him to Hornbach in the hope of turning the former convent school into a high school resembling Sturm's foundation in Strasbourg. Despite his dissatisfaction with the job, Tremellius remained headmaster until 7 March 1561. Shortly before his departure, in January he was sent to Orléans to take part in negotiations concerning the rights of the Huguenots in Metz.

On 4 March 1561 Tremellius had received a summons from the Calvinist elector palatine Frederick III to the University of Heidelberg. First he was entrusted with another mission to France, and it was not until the summer that he could start working at the university. He matriculated on 23 June 1561 after receiving a doctorate in divinity, and was enrolled a member of the academic senate on 9 July. His career at Heidelberg was glorious. He was twice rector; his lectures on Hebrew were enthusiastically attended (his pupils included the French scholar Philippe du Plessis Mornay); and he at last had time to devote himself to scholarship. In 1562 he edited Bucer's lectures which he had heard and copied out in England. In 1563 he published the commentary on Hosea he had started in England. After spending six months with Matthew Parker, now archbishop of Canterbury, in London in 1565, when the University of Heidelberg was closed on account of the plague, he returned to the Palatinate to publish his Latin translation of the Targum Jonathan on the twelve minor prophets in 1567. This was followed in 1569 by an Aramaic and Syriac grammar, in which he made an important distinction between the two languages, and a literal Latin translation and edition of the Syriac New Testament (the second to appear in the sixteenth century), dedicated to Queen Elizabeth. Because of the lack of Syriac types in the workshop of the printer Henri Étienne, however, both the grammar and the New Testament were published in Hebrew characters. Then, with the support of the elector palatine, Tremellius embarked on his major project of translating the Old Testament into Latin, a task which he undertook together with a scholarly Reformed minister of French origin, François du Jon (Franciscus Junius the elder). Junius's contribution was mainly limited to the translation of the Apocrypha.

The work was finally published in Frankfurt in five volumes between 1575 and 1579. It was an important addition to the study of the Old Testament. As the Italian Hebraist Sanctes Pagninus had done before him, Tremellius, in his efforts to produce a Latin translation of the Bible superior to the Vulgate, frequently relied on rabbinic interpretations of difficult words and passages. In doing so he improved on the work of his predecessors and the result of his labours, much admired in the protestant world and even sanctioned, albeit with alterations, at the Catholic universities of Douai and Louvain, had a considerable influence on the English Authorized Version of 1611.

On 5 December 1577 Tremellius relinquished his chair in Heidelberg. Frederick III had died on 26 October 1576. His successor, Louis VI, was a Lutheran who gradually ousted his father's Reformed protégés. Tremellius thus welcomed a call to act as professor of Hebrew at the academy of Sedan, recently founded by Henri de la Tour d'Auvergne, duke of Bouillon. Sedan was to have one of the finest schools of oriental languages in Reformed Europe, and Tremellius did much to contribute to its prestige. He died in Sedan on 9 October 1580.   ALASTAIR HAMILTON

Sources W. Becker, *Immanuel Tremellius: ein Proselytenleben im Zeitalter der Reformation* (1890) · J. Ney, 'Tremellius, Immanuel', *Realencyclopädie für protestantische Theologie und Kirche*, 20 (1908), 95–8 · G. Lloyd Jones, *The discovery of Hebrew in Tudor England: a third language* (1983) · P. McNair, *Peter Martyr in Italy: an anatomy of apostasy* (1967) · *DNB* · B. Hall, 'Biblical scholarship: editions and commentaries', *The West, from the Reformation to the present day*, ed. S. L. Greenslade (1963), vol. 3 of *The Cambridge history of the Bible* (1963–70), 38–93 · I. Tremellius, *In Hoseam prophetam interpretatio* (1563) · S. Adorni-Braccesi, *'Una città infetta': la repubblica di Lucca nella crisi religiosa del cinquecento* (1994)

Tremenheere, Hugh Seymour (1804–1893), civil servant, was born at Wootton House, Gloucestershire, on 22 January 1804, the eldest son of Walter Tremenheere and his wife, Frances, daughter of Thomas Apperley.

Sir Walter Tremenheere (1761–1855), naval officer, was born at Penzance on 10 September 1761, and saw action in the American, French revolutionary, and Napoleonic wars. He was lieutenant-governor of Curaçao, colonel-commandant of the Chatham division of the Royal Marines, and briefly aide-de-camp to William IV, for which last he was made a knight of Hanover. He was known for his Cornish landscape drawings. He died at 33 Somerset Street, Portman Square, London, on 7 August 1855. Two of his sons soldiered in India. George Borlase Tremenheere (1809–1896), lieutenant-colonel of the Bengal Engineers, served in the First and Second Anglo-Sikh wars; in retirement he commanded the western battalion of the Duke of Cornwall's volunteers and was president of the Indian Mutiny Relief Fund. Charles William Tremenheere (1813–1898), major-general of the Bombay Engineers, fought in the Indian mutiny (for which he was made CB), was commandant at Aden, and wrote *Missions in India: the System of Education in Government and Mission Schools Contrasted* (1876). Another son, John Henry Tremenheere (1807–1880), was a prolific contributor to periodical literature.

Hugh Seymour Tremenheere was educated at Winchester College and New College, Oxford (BA 1827, MA 1832), and was called to the bar at the Inner Temple in 1834. Appointed a revising barrister on the western circuit in 1838, he inspected schools for the education department (1839–43), and mines (1843–59) and other industries (1855–71) for the Home Office. He was a fellow of New College from 1824 until his marriage, on 2 April 1856, to Lucy Bernal, third daughter of Ralph Bernal MP, and widow of Vicesimus Knox.

Tremenheere's interest in working-class education began with his membership of the Central Society of Education, a body that published papers on teaching methods and child psychology and lobbied for state-run schools on the Irish model (which kept religious and secular training separate). When the new education committee of the privy council filled its posts in 1839, Tremenheere was appointed to inspect schools of the nonconformist-dominated British and Foreign School Society. His appointment came through the influence of B. F. Duppa, the Central Society's secretary, who knew the lord president of the council Henry Petty-Fitzmaurice, marquess of Lansdowne. A moderate Anglican whig, Tremenheere was not likely to alienate the society. His first mission, to Monmouthshire and Herefordshire in December 1839, officially to survey the state of education, involved an inquiry into the causes of John Frost's Newport rising.

Tremenheere co-operated with the education department's permanent secretary, James Kay-Shuttleworth, in promoting efficient education to teach working-class children their place in society, and aligned himself with non-sectarianism against 'our opponents the High Churchmen & the Newmanites' (Paz, 109). The British and Foreign School Society, however, resented the negative tone of his reports, which criticized its use of the monitorial teaching method. It also felt aggrieved because, unlike the Church of England and the Church of Scotland, it had no control over the appointment of the inspector of its schools. After the defeat of the Peel ministry's Factory Bill in 1843, the government was forced to settle the dispute with the British and Foreign School Society over inspection, and did so by transferring Tremenheere to the Home Office at the end of the year.

At the Home Office Tremenheere was appointed by Sir James Graham as inspector under the Mines Act, 1842. In his annual reports on the mining districts he advocated education to teach obedience, free-market economics, and the evils of trade unions. Education would 'fortify the mind [of the pitmen's children] against attempts at misdirection' from 'agitators of their own class', and promote 'the growth of morality and social order' (Colls, 92). Tremenheere encouraged colliery owners to build schools, and discouraged working-class self-education and schools outside the control of other agencies. Although he interviewed workers and union leaders, his sympathies were on the side of the employers. He saw his main task as the reporting of social conditions in the mining regions, rather than the enforcing of safety regulations. He visited Belgium, France, and Germany to study mining laws and underground inspection in those countries, and recommended that Britain adopt underground inspection. The Mines Act, 1850, of which Tremenheere was the architect, provided for the appointment of inspectors with technical qualifications who would use their expertise to advise colliery managers and encourage them to emulate one another, rather than to force improvements. He was however, energetic in reducing the incidence of the truck system in mining, and the payment of miners' wages in public houses.

The Home Office gave Tremenheere additional tasks in the 1850s and 1860s. He investigated bleaching works (1855), lace works (1861), and bakehouses; he served on royal commissions on the employment of children and young persons in both industry (1862–7) and agriculture (1867–71). In these activities he continued to express his opposition to trade unions, and his beliefs that the state should cajole rather than coerce employers, and that ideologically correct education should be provided to the working classes. He retired from government service in 1871, receiving a CB.

In retirement Tremenheere opposed Irish home rule and church disestablishment, and addressed political pamphlets to a working-class audience, which were published by the Christian Knowledge Society and the Liberal Unionist Association. A contributor to the *Edinburgh Review* (1837–9), *Fortnightly Review* (1881), and *Nineteenth Century* (1880), his other publications included a comparison of the constitutions of Great Britain and the USA (1854), following a tour of North America in 1852, and in *The Political Expertise of the Ancients, in its Bearing upon Modern Times* (1852). He died at Silverdale, Alexandra Road, Farnborough, Hampshire, on 16 September 1893.

D. G. PAZ

Sources R. K. Webb, 'A whig inspector', *Journal of Modern History*, 27 (1955), 352–64 · D. G. Paz, *The politics of working-class education in Britain, 1830–50* (1980) · Robert Colls, '"Oh happy English children!": coal, class, and education in the north east', *Past and Present*, 73 (1976), 75–99 · *The Times* (19 Sept 1893) · *The Times* (22 Dec 1896) · *The Times* (3 Nov 1898) · O. O. G. M. MacDonagh, 'Coal mines regulation: the first decade, 1842–52', *Ideas and institutions of Victorian Britain: essays in honour of George Kitson Clark*, ed. R. Robson (1967), 58–86 · E. L. Edmonds and O. P. Edmonds, *I was there: the memoirs of H. S. Tremenheere* (1964) · E. L. Edmonds and O. P. Edmonds, 'Hugh Seymour Tremenheere, pioneer inspector of schools', *British Journal of Educational Studies*, 12 (1963–4), 65–76 · *Wellesley index* · Boase, *Mod. Eng. biog.*

Archives Morrab Library, Penzance | PRO, home office, registered papers, HO 45 · U. Durham L., letters to third Earl Grey · UCL, letters to E. Chadwick

Wealth at death £4085 10s. 7d.: probate, 20 Oct 1893, *CGPLA Eng. & Wales*

Tremenheere, Sir Walter (1761–1855). *See under* Tremenheere, Hugh Seymour (1804–1893).

Trench, Anthony Chenevix- (1919–1979), headmaster, was born at Kasauli in the Punjab, India, on 10 May 1919, the youngest of four sons (there were no daughters) of Charles Godfrey Chenevix-Trench (1877–1964), revenue commissioner in the Indian Civil Service, and his wife, Margaret May (1888–1981), daughter of John Holmes Blakesley, engineer, of The Avenue, Kew Gardens, London.

The Chenevix-Trenches were of French Huguenot stock who settled in Ireland at the end of the seventeenth century from where they achieved considerable renown in ecclesiastical and military circles; none more so than

Anthony Chenevix-Trench (1919–1979), by Godfrey Argent, 1969

Richard Trench who was appointed archbishop of Dublin in 1864. It was Anthony's father who broke with family tradition by opting for the Indian Civil Service, becoming a much revered figure among the inhabitants of Udaipur. His love of learning and sense of duty duly left their mark upon his children. Introduced to Herodotus at the age of six, Anthony Chenevix-Trench developed a great love for the classics, already evident at Highfield School in Liphook, Hampshire, where he was a pupil from 1927 to 1932. His ability to construct Greek sentences earned him the envy of his fellow pupil Ludovic Kennedy, the writer and broadcaster.

In March 1932, three months before his thirteenth birthday, Chenevix-Trench followed in the footsteps of all three of his brothers by winning a scholarship to Shrewsbury School. Here he continued his effortless rise, gaining a scholarship to Christ Church, Oxford, aged sixteen. He was, according to his esteemed classics master, Jimmy Street, the best pupil he ever taught during his forty-four years at the school. He proceeded to Christ Church in 1937 and the plaudits continued. He gained a first class in classical honour moderations (1939) before the outbreak of the Second World War.

In September 1939 Chenevix-Trench joined the Royal Artillery and was seconded to the 4th mountain battery, frontier force, Indian artillery 22nd mountain regiment. As a senior subaltern he struck up an excellent relationship with his Indian troops, facilitated by his quick mastery of Urdu, and distinguished himself in the retreat through Malaya against the advancing Japanese armies. One of 85,000 imperial troops to surrender at Singapore in February 1942 he was sent to work on the infamous Burma Railway in 1943. There, in the most brutal and degrading conditions imaginable, he proved a fount of inspiration to his fellow captives, translating A. E. Housman's *Shropshire Lad* into Latin and entertaining them with a series of talks on Greek literature.

On his release in 1945 Chenevix-Trench returned to Oxford and was runner-up in the Craven and Ireland scholarships in 1946 before obtaining a first class in *literae humaniores* (1947), with alpha marks in every paper. In January 1948 he accepted an invitation to return to Shrewsbury and in no time established a reputation as a brilliantly inspiring teacher, instilling in his pupils a true appreciation of the ancient civilizations. During the vintage year of 1950–51 ten members of the Shrewsbury classical sixth gained open awards to Oxford or Cambridge.

In 1951 Chenevix-Trench's old tutor, R. H. Dundas, inveigled him back to Christ Church as a classics don but, finding the experience of tutoring undergraduates a more remote and arid one than teaching slightly younger students, he lasted only a year. The housemastership of School House, Shrewsbury, unexpectedly became open and for Chenevix-Trench the opportunity of returning to his old house took precedence over a chance to become headmaster of Charterhouse. At Shrewsbury between 1952 and 1955 his gregarious informality, his deep understanding of boys, and his compassion for those in trouble won him many admirers, although the goodwill was tempered by his unhealthy addiction to corporal punishment, a trait later exposed by one of his former pupils, Paul Foot, in the satirical magazine *Private Eye*. Why such an essentially humane person should on occasions abuse this standard punishment for the time has never been properly explained. What is irrefutable is that his continued dependence on beating when its legitimacy was increasingly being called into question severely undermined his credibility; a point all too readily illustrated by the furore caused by the publication in 1994 of *Eton Renewed*, a modern history of the college, which partially attributed Chenevix-Trench's demise there in 1970 to his predilection for beating.

It was during his time at Shrewsbury that Chenevix-Trench married in 1953 Elizabeth Chalmers (1925–1991), a teacher, eldest daughter of Captain Stewart Dykes Spicer RN. A kind, hospitable person, she willingly supported him both at Shrewsbury and during his subsequent three headmasterships, enabling him to keep open house for all comers. They had twin daughters, and two sons.

In 1955 Chenevix-Trench finally succumbed to the overtures of governing bodies up and down the country by becoming headmaster of Bradfield College, Berkshire, and there now followed the most fulfilling years of his career as he flourished in this arcadian idyll. Eschewing the traditional role of the headmaster as a distant autocrat, he continued to place the interests of the pupils first, teaching, tutoring, and befriending them whenever possible. His enthusiasm, his personal support, combined with his overriding commitment to high academic standards, galvanized the school into raising its sights and acquiring unprecedented prestige in educational circles.

It was against this background of achievement at Bradfield, alongside his membership of the Robbins committee which in 1963 advocated the expansion of higher education, that Chenevix-Trench was appointed headmaster of Eton College as successor to Robert Birley in January 1964 with a view to pouring new wine into old bottles. For the Eton which Chenevix-Trench inherited had changed little in the twentieth century and now, in a less deferential age, the need to transform an élite based on birth to one based on merit was paramount. That much was done to accomplish this at Eton during the next seven years is a measure of his influence. On arrival he oversaw a major review of the curriculum, bringing it into the mainstream of GCE, A and O level studies and achieving unprecedented success in open scholarships at Oxford and Cambridge. At the same time the arts were encouraged, the facilities upgraded, chapel reformed, social services begun, discipline relaxed, and horizons broadened. 'This is the modern Eton', enthused the *Eton Chronicle*, the influential college weekly periodical, in June 1970: 'A school which utilises its facilities to encourage self expression while by no means neglecting its duties as a trainer of the mind and preparer for national exams.' Other independent bodies returned similar verdicts. A BBC documentary in 1965 portrayed the college in a fairly flattering light and the press was supportive of his innovatory agenda.

Despite these undoubted successes Chenevix-Trench's leadership attracted substantial criticism, particularly from those within the college hierarchy who felt that he lacked the *gravitas* expected in an Eton headmaster. Apart from his diminutive stature (Eton headmasters, notwithstanding the renowned Dr John Keate, are traditionally imposing figures) and his dishevelled appearance, they particularly objected to his administrative laxity, and reluctance to follow a consistent line on discipline. On top of this his lack of physical stamina, the legacy of his wartime experiences, his weakness for alcohol, and his penchant for beating were further causes for concern. In March 1969 he was informed by the provost, Lord Caccia, that the academic year ending in July 1970 would be his last. His dismissal was well handled but the damage to his self-esteem was considerable.

In September 1971 Chenevix-Trench became headmaster of Fettes College, Edinburgh, a school of similar size to Bradfield. Back in more familiar surroundings he was in his element and won much support for his reforms which helped usher in a more tranquil period in the school's history after the turbulence of the 1960s. Numbers increased from 420 to 530; girls in the sixth form, first introduced in 1970, became an established component; and a junior school was opened in 1973. It was only during his final years when he was dogged by ill health that his liberal tendencies (beating aside) became something of a liability. He died at his home, The Lodge, Fettes College, 2 Carrington Road, Edinburgh, on 21 June 1979, weeks before his retirement, from a severe internal haemorrhage in his intestine, related to nutritional deprivations in his wartime captivity. His remains were cremated at Warriston crematorium, Edinburgh, on 25 June.　　　　MARK PEEL

Sources M. Peel, *The land of the lost content: the biography of Anthony Chenevix-Trench* (1996) · R. A. Cole Hamilton, *The Fettesian* (Sept 1979) · E. Faulkner, J. Moulsdale, and A. Sopwith, *Bradford College Chronicle* (1979) · F. Coleridge, *Eton College Chronicle* (6 July 1979) · M. Charlesworth, *Old Salopian Newsletter* (1979) · *DNB* · Chenevix-Trench MSS, priv. coll. · Bradfield College, minutes of council meetings at Bradfield, 1955–64 · Edinburgh, Fettes College, minutes of governors' meetings at Fettes, 1971–9 · T. Card, *Eton renewed: a history from 1860 to the present day* (1994)

Archives priv. coll., papers

Likenesses group photograph, 1966, Hult. Arch. · G. Argent, photograph, 1969, NPG [*see illus.*] · J. Brown, oils, 1979, Fettes College, Edinburgh

Wealth at death £35,614: probate, 8 Oct 1979, *CGPLA Eng. & Wales*

Trench, Bridget (*c.*1804–1886). *See under* Knock, visionaries of (*act.* 1879).

Trench, Sir David Clive Crosbie (1915–1988), colonial governor, was born at Quetta, India, on 2 June 1915, the son of William Launcelot Crosbie Trench, an irrigation engineer, and his wife, Margaret Zephanie Huddlestone. He was educated at Tonbridge School and from 1935 to 1937 at Jesus College, Cambridge, where he gained a reputation as a sportsman and respect both as a student journalist and social activist, in his third year running a camp for the unemployed. Joining the colonial service in 1938, he was posted to the British Solomon Islands protectorate. A secondment in Fiji to the secretariat of the western Pacific high commission, to which he was to return as high commissioner, was followed by secondment to Tonga from where he was recalled in September 1942 to be district officer, Guadalcanal, after the Americans under General Vandergrift began the difficult campaign to dislodge the Japanese. Within a year he was acting resident commissioner and commanding officer of the Solomon Islands defence force, the youngest combatant unit in the empire. He remained in this post until 1946. The defence force was responsible for reconnaissance, the rescue of crashed American airmen, and liaison with the 'coast watchers', who manned observation posts behind the Japanese lines. Respected by the islanders whose loyalty was crucial, fluent in the local pidgin, bold and quick-witted, Trench earned the American Legion of Merit in 1943 and the Military Cross in 1944. In 1944 he married Margaret Gould, an American nursing officer. They had one daughter.

The war over, Trench, appointed secretary to the protectorate government in 1947, enthusiastically planned the rehabilitation and development of the Solomons, displaying his strength as a generalist for whom human relationships outweighed institutional structures. He earned a place at the Joint Services Staff College in 1949, after which he was posted to Hong Kong where he worked initially as assistant and deputy defence secretary, and clerk of councils. After promotion in 1956 he served as deputy financial secretary and as commissioner for labour and mines, gaining a valuable insight into both Communist and Kuomintang communities whose politics were powerful in the trade unions movement.

Highly regarded, Trench's attendance at the Imperial Defence College in 1958 was followed by promotion to deputy colonial secretary, Hong Kong, in 1959. His circle of friends was wide, among both Chinese, with whom he spoke Cantonese easily, and expatriates, whose company he particularly enjoyed at the American and foreign correspondents' clubs where his ready humour and deep belly laugh were appreciated. His own background also gave him an empathy with staff transferred from other colonies, sometimes regarded as interlopers. Consolidating his reputation as a forthright and innovative administrator, in 1961 he was given an opportunity to show his paces back in the Western Pacific, where the high commission was now located in the Solomon Islands.

Welcomed enthusiastically as 'ol' friend bilong yumi', Trench encouraged the Solomons to catch up with what was happening elsewhere by accelerating constitutional development. His understanding of Melanesian society and the difficulties of administering isolated communities in a scatter of islands led him to promote progress by a steady series of comparatively short steps, starting with the election of a majority of unofficial members to the legislative council.

In 1964 Trench returned to Hong Kong as governor. Always a social reformer, he actively promoted low-cost housing and the improvement of factory working conditions. He also sought ways to involve the growing and sophisticated middle class, for whom Hong Kong was both home and future, in areas of government which concerned them without creating the democratic institutions which might have encouraged local conflict between the Communist Party of China and the Kuomintang. His attention to tertiary education resulted in the widespread growth of local tertiary institutions and a university grants committee. Seeking a representative and active grass roots level of local administration, Trench appointed a working party of middle seniority staff, some with experience of other dependencies, to report.

To Trench's regret their recommendations had to be shelved when the shock waves of Mao Zedong's cultural revolution spilled over the frontier. Students were among the first both to express dissatisfaction with the *status quo* and to become aware of the reality of 1997 and the end of the New Territories lease. 1966 and 1967 were troubled years in Hong Kong with strikes and spasmodic riots, including demonstrations outside Government House. A big man in every sense, Trench was firm and cool, insisting on a low police profile. With his colonial secretary, Michael Gass, he established under his direct control a strong team of able staff, irrespective of seniority, who effectively began to win the hearts and minds of the people. Trench commented at the time that 'people make an awful fuss about these disturbances because we have so few of them' (*Keesing's Contemporary Archives*, July 1967). There was, indeed, less than a 2 per cent outflow of bank deposits from what was already a significant and fast growing economy.

On retirement to Dorset, despite the ill health of his wife, Trench selflessly put to local use his administrative skills and experience. He served as county councillor, from 1973 to 1981 as chairman of the Dorset Area Health Authority, and as deputy lieutenant. He never commented on those who had followed him in Hong Kong and never lost the respect of those who had served under him. He was appointed CMG in 1960 and advanced to KCMG in 1962 and to GCMG in 1969. He died at his home, 6 Allen Close, Child Okeford, Dorset, on 4 December 1988.

J. H. SMITH

Sources *WWW* · *Colonial Office List* · *The Times* (1966–7) · *Keesing's Contemporary Archives* (July 1967) · *The Times* (6 Dec 1988) · private information (2004) [colleagues] · D. C. Horton, *The happy isles* (1965) · Central Office of Information, *Among those present* (1946) · D. C. Horton, *New Georgia pattern for victory* (1971) · d. cert.

Likenesses photograph, repro. in *The Times* (6 Dec 1988)

Trench, Francis Chenevix (1805–1886), Church of England clergyman and author, was the eldest son of Richard Trench (1774–1860), barrister, and his wife, Melesina *Trench. Richard Chenevix *Trench was his younger brother.

Trench entered Harrow School early in 1818, and matriculated from Oriel College, Oxford, on 12 November 1824, graduating BA in 1834 and MA in 1859. On 4 June 1829 he entered Lincoln's Inn to study law, but in 1834 he was ordained deacon and became curate of St Giles, Reading. The next year he was ordained priest, and on 13 September 1837 he was appointed perpetual curate of St John's, Reading. He married, on 6 December 1837, Mary Caroline, daughter of William *Marsh, the evangelical. They had one son, Richard William Francis (1849–1860), and two daughters, Mary Melesina and Maria Marcia Fanny. From 1857 until 1875, when he retired to London, he was rector of Islip, Oxfordshire. He added the name 'Chenevix' in 1873. Mary Caroline Chenevix Trench died on 4 March 1886 and her husband the next month, on 3 April, in Bursledon, Hampshire.

Trench was a scholarly parson, publishing many sermons, theological works, and travel books, such as *Diary of Travels in France and Spain* (1845), *Scotland: its Faith and Features* (1846), *A Walk around Mont Blanc* (1847), and *A Ride in Sicily, by Oxoniensis* (1851). He contributed to *Macmillan's Magazine* and *Notes and Queries*, published a series of papers as *Islipiana* (1869–70), and wrote *A Few Notes from Past Life* (1862), which includes interesting autobiographical memorabilia.

E. I. CARLYLE, *rev.* H. C. G. MATTHEW

Sources F. Chenevix Trench, *A few notes from past life* (1862) · R. Chenevix Trench, *Letters and memorials*, 2 vols. (1888) · Boase, *Mod. Eng. biog.*

Archives Bodl. Oxf., letters to Lord Lovelace

Likenesses photograph, NPG [*see illus.*]

Wealth at death £13,994 17s. 8d.: probate, 4 June 1886, *CGPLA Eng. & Wales*

Trench, Frederick Chenevix (1837–1894). *See under* Trench, Richard Chenevix (1807–1886).

Trench, Sir Frederick William (*c.*1777–1859), army officer and politician, was the elder son of Michael Frederick Trench (1746–1836) of Heywood, Ballynakill, Queen's county, and his wife, Anne Helena, daughter and heir of Patrick Stewart of Killymoon, co. Tyrone. Richard Le Poer Trench, second earl of Clancarty, was his third cousin. After attending school in Drogheda, Trench entered Trinity College, Dublin, in 1793; he matriculated at Trinity College, Cambridge, aged nineteen, in 1797, when he also enrolled at Lincoln's Inn.

Francis Chenevix Trench (1805–1886), by unknown photographer

Commissioned an ensign and lieutenant in the 1st foot guards on 12 November 1803, Trench became lieutenant and captain on 12 November 1807. In the 1806 general election he was returned as member for Mitchell, Cornwall; the patron of the seat, Sir Christopher Hawkins, having sold this and other seats to men pledged to the Grenville administration. Trench vacated his seat, however, in January 1807, and was appointed to the quartermaster-general's staff in Sicily. He also served in the Walcheren expedition in 1809, and at Cadiz, June–August 1811, under Lieutenant-General Thomas Graham; but after being appointed assistant quartermaster-general in the Kent district, and promoted major, he returned to England.

On 21 February 1812 Lord Roden brought Trench into parliament for Dundalk, on the death of the sitting member, but a series of votes by Trench against the administration and his support for Catholic emancipation caused Roden to drop him at the general election in October, whereupon Trench vainly sought Lord Grenville's assistance. On 23 November 1813 he was made deputy quartermaster-general to the expeditionary force sent to the Netherlands under Graham, with the rank of lieutenant-colonel; this was another speedy promotion, but in 1814, when the war ended, he was placed on half pay.

Trench enjoyed the 'most affectionate' friendship of the fifth duke of Rutland over a period of fifty-five years, 'uninterrupted by one moment of coolness' (will), until the duke's death in 1857. It was the duke who brought him into the Commons again, on a vacancy at Cambridge in November 1819. He retained the seat until 1832. During this period he appears to have been involved in the Ordnance Survey of Ireland. On 27 May 1825 he was promoted colonel and appointed aide-de-camp to the king. In May 1829 Wellington made him storekeeper of the ordnance in the ministerial reshuffle after Huskisson's resignation, an appointment Mrs Arbuthnot regarded as 'so very Tory' (Bamford and Wellesley, 2.277). He was made KCH in 1832, and was automatically promoted major-general on 10 January 1837, lieutenant-general on 9 November 1846, and general on 25 June 1854.

Although Trench was unsuccessful in contesting Scarborough on the Rutland interest in 1832 Peel, whose 'disinterested, and devoted supporter' he avowedly was (BL, Add. MS 40597, fol. 393, 30 Dec 1846), named him secretary to the master-general of the ordnance in his short-lived administration of 1834–5. Trench secured Scarborough in the ensuing general election, held it until 1847, and returned to the Ordnance under Peel's second ministry (1842–6). In the 1842 recess he visited Rome, and in 1845 he toured Spain and Portugal.

Though assiduous in promoting the interests of his Cambridge electors Trench seldom spoke in the Commons and then usually on Irish questions. On 6 April 1827, having performed a *volte face*, he opposed Catholic emancipation: having been 'for years … a daily witness of the evils which arose from the system pursued by the Irish Catholics' (*Hansard 2*, 17.274), he put forward a policy for Ireland that included the employment of the poor by government, measures for improving agriculture and education, paying the Catholic clergy, and widening the franchise; but he was groaned down. It was, he believed, 'the infinite subdivision of land' (ibid., 18.1421) that caused Ireland's ills. But when in March 1829 Peel and Wellington introduced a Roman Catholic relief bill, Trench's devotion to them compelled him to turn again, and give a reluctant consent. (Similarly in 1844 he supported Peel's Maynooth seminary grant.) Opposing the Reform Bill in 1831 as 'rash, improvident, and revolutionary', he defended the character of his Cambridge electors as 'persons of opulence and independence' (*Hansard 3*, 4.743–6).

Trench made his mark, however, as a self-appointed expert on public architecture, a 'Gentleman who fancies Himself a Man of Taste' (BL, Add. MS 38380, fol. 271). Already in 1815 he had proposed a vast pyramidal monument to British naval and military victories over France (designed by Philip and Matthew Cotes Wyatt) on the site that later became Trafalgar Square. In July 1824 he launched a project for a quay or embankment on the north side of the Thames from Westminster to Blackfriars (again drawn out by Philip Wyatt); despite much criticism in March 1825 he introduced a bill to authorize its construction, but he was checkmated by riverine interests. As a member of a select committee on the design of the new

law courts at Westminster early in 1824, Trench employed Philip Wyatt yet again to put on paper his idea, 'far more beautiful and extensive' than that of John Soane, the official architect (Trench). On another committee for the improvement of the Commons' accommodation later in that session he vainly urged a sweeping general plan, but he did secure minor improvements in a revised plan the following year.

Trench was active in Hume's committee for a more commodious Commons in 1831, promoting Benjamin Wyatt's rebuilding proposals. During the same period he joined in the barrage of criticism of Nash's rebuilding of Buckingham Palace, which he proposed converting to a national gallery of art. His hostility to Nash's design had begun in 1825 when he had urged George IV to build, in Hyde Park, a scheme (drawn by Philip Wyatt) that Mrs Arbuthnot (wife of the minister responsible for the crown estate) described as 'the worst plan of a house I ever saw, & quite colossal … It is the most ridiculous plan I ever saw for, added to it, is the idea of a street *200 feet wide* extending from the end of Hyde Park opposite the New Palace to St Paul's!!' (Bamford and Wellesley, 1.420). The king expressed his 'warmest approbation' (BL, Add. MS 38380, fol. 172), but the prime minister rebuffed Trench very sharply.

Trench's hour of triumph came some two decades later and was preceded by two further rebuffs. In 1841, when metropolitan improvement was again being debated, he revived his Thames quay scheme, into which he introduced a railway, in an open *Letter to Lord Duncannon*, the public works minister; he again urged it on the royal commission of 1844, but with complete lack of success. Likewise his projects for improving Piccadilly and the National Gallery in the early 1840s were stillborn. But his long-maturing design for mounting a giant equestrian statue of the duke of Wellington, sculpted by his old friend Matthew Cotes Wyatt, on the Constitution Hill arch (opposite Apsley House), was (thanks to Lord Melbourne's carelessness and the queen's reluctance to embarrass Wellington) carried out in 1846 with the duke of Rutland's support, despite the opposition of *Punch* and the government; there it remained until 1883. Wellington himself, who thought 'that it was the damnedest job from the beginning', was regarded as 'a mere cat's-paw of that impudent Irish pretender' (*Greville Memoirs*, 1.106).

Trench died unmarried, at 81 Marine Parade, Brighton, on 6 December 1859, about a month after making a will bequeathing his Irish property to the eldest of his four sisters, and over £11,000 in 3 per cent consols to his other relatives; he advised his executors to dispose of his letters 'as they may think best, I believe there is no disposal more judicious than the fire' (will).　　　　M. H. PORT

Sources BL, Add MSS 38298, 38300, 38380, 40406, 40495, 40582, 40550, 40579, 40595, 40597 · BL, Egerton MS 3515 · *Hansard 2* (1822–30) · *Hansard 3* (1830–46) · F. W. Trench, *A collection of papers relating to the Thames quay* (1827) · will, 11 Jan 1860, Principal Registry of the Family Division, London · 'Correspondence between commissioners of woods and forests and subscribers … on a statue of the duke of Wellington', *Parl. papers* (1846), 43.345, no. 446 • 'Sub-committee of the Wellington military memorial: report', *Parl. papers* (1846), 43.367, no. 553 • J. Soane, *A brief statement of the proceedings respecting the new Law Courts* (1828) • J. M. Crook and M. H. Port, eds., *The history of the king's works*, 6 (1973) • HoP, *Commons* • F. Barker and R. Hyde, *London, as it might have been* (1982) • J. F. Physick, *The Wellington monument* (1970) • J. Philippart, ed., *The royal military calendar*, 3 vols. (1815–16) • *Boyle's Court Guide* • *CGPLA Eng. & Wales* (1860) • *The journal of Mrs Arbuthnot, 1820–1832*, ed. F. Bamford and the duke of Wellington [G. Wellesley], 2 vols. (1950) • *The Greville memoirs, 1814–1860*, ed. L. Strachey and R. Fulford, 8 vols. (1938), vol. 1, p. 106 • matriculation, Trinity Cam.

Archives BL, letters to his father, Add. MS 53816 • NAM, department of archives, diary | Belvoir Castle, Leicestershire, Rutland MSS • BL, corresp. with second earl of Liverpool, Add. MSS 38298–38380 • BL, corresp. with Sir Robert Peel, Add. MSS 40361–40608, *passim* • BL, corresp. with M. C. Wyatt, Egerton MS 3515 • NL Ire., corresp. with Wellington, Rutland, and others • U. Southampton L., Wellesley MSS

Likenesses oils, *c.*1827, NPG • engraving, in or after 1832 (after portrait by Robson), repro. in T. R. F. C. Trench, *A memoir of the Trench family* (1897) • J. Doyle, caricature, pencil study, BM • J. Doyle, chalk and ink caricature (as Leporello), BM • J. Doyle, pen and chalk drawing, BM • J. H. Robinson, stipple (after J. Robson), BM, NPG; repro. in *Portraits of eminent conservatives and statesmen* [1836–46] • portrait; bequeathed to sixth duke of Rutland

Wealth at death under £25,000: probate, 11 Jan 1860, *CGPLA Eng. & Wales*

Trench, (Frederic) Herbert (1865–1923), poet and playwright, was born at Avoncore, co. Cork, on 26 November 1865, the son of W. W. Trench of Ballater, Bournemouth. In 1880 he went to Haileybury College (Melvill House). At nineteen he first visited Italy, and was to return there often throughout his life. In 1884 he won an open exhibition in modern history to Keble College, Oxford. His university studies were at first hindered by ill health, but he obtained a first class in modern history in 1888 and was elected a fellow of All Souls College, Oxford, in 1889. As an undergraduate he is described by a contemporary as of engaging manners and striking appearance, with fine eyes, straight black hair, a fresh complexion, and a heavy black moustache. In 1891 he married Lilian Isabel, *née* Fox, of Falmouth. They had two sons and three daughters.

Trench was appointed a temporary examiner by the Board of Education in 1891, placed on the permanent staff in 1892, and promoted to senior examiner in 1900. However, he was a man of letters and temperamentally unsuited to administrative work. When the burden of routine at the Board of Education was much increased after the Education Act of 1902, it was probably with feelings of mutual relief that his retirement was arranged.

While working for the Board of Education Trench became increasingly absorbed in his writing. In 1901 he published a translation of a work by Dmitry Merezhkovsky (as *Death of the Gods*), which was admired by contemporaries. But before this he had become known as a 'mystical' poet—first, in 1900 with *Deirdre Wedded and other Poems* and, more definitely, in 1907 with *New Poems*. His best-known and most often anthologized poem, 'Apollo and the Seaman', first appeared in *New Poems*. In 1911 he moved to Settignano, near Florence, and later

poems were inspired by his life in Italy and collected as *Ode from Italy in Time of War* (1915). A later volume, *Poems: with Fables in Prose* (1918), was largely ignored.

From 1909 to 1911 Trench had been artistic director of the Haymarket Theatre in London, and his productions of *King Lear* and Maeterlinck's *The Blue Bird* were well received. Encouraged by his success, he wrote a four-act play, *Napoleon*, which was produced by the Stage Society in 1919, and he was at work upon another, *Talleyrand*, when he died. Having fallen ill on a journey to England, Trench died in hospital at Boulogne, France, on 11 June 1923.

H. GRANVILLE-BARKER, *rev.* KATHERINE MULLIN

Sources H. Williams, 'Memoir', in *The collected works of Herbert Trench*, ed. H. Williams, 3 vols. (1924) • D. Patrick, ed., *Chambers's cyclopedia of English literature*, 3 (1988) • D. C. Browning, ed., *Everyman's dictionary of literary biography* (1958) • *Location register of twentieth-century English literary manuscripts and letters*, BL, 2 (1988) • R. Welch, ed., *The Oxford companion to Irish literature* (1996) • private information (1937)

Archives CUL, corresp., commonplace books, drafts of poems • NRA, corresp. and literary papers • TCD | All Souls Oxf., letters to Sir William Anson • BL, letters to George Bernard Shaw, Add. MS 50551 • Bodl. Oxf., corresp. with Gilbert Murray • U. Glas., letters to D. S. MacColl • U. Leeds, Brotherton L., letters to Clement Shorter

Likenesses A. L. Coburn, photogravure, 1910, NPG • A. Manani, bronze sculpture, 1920, All Souls Oxf. • W. Rothenstein, charcoal drawing, 1921, Keble College, Oxford • photograph, 1924 (after A. Manani, 1920), repro. in Williams, ed., *Collected works of Herbert Trench*, vol. 1

Trench [*née* Chenevix; *other married name* St George], **Melesina** (1768–1827), diarist and letter-writer, was born in Dublin on 22 March 1768, the daughter of Philip Chenevix and his wife, Mary Elizabeth, daughter of Archdeacon Gervais; she was the granddaughter of Richard *Chenevix (1696/7–1779), bishop of Waterford, who owed his see to the patronage of Lord Chesterfield, lord lieutenant of Ireland from 1745 to 1746. After the death of her parents Melesina was brought up by her grandfather Bishop Chenevix and her relative Lady Lifford. After the bishop's death in 1779, she went to live with her maternal grandfather, Archdeacon Gervais, through whose library she rambled at large, and from which, with precocious taste and intelligence, she selected as her favourites Shakespeare, Molière, and Sterne. She developed great personal beauty, and on 31 October 1786 she married Colonel Richard St George of Carrick-on-Shannon and Hatley Manor, co. Leitrim; they had one child before his death in Portugal only two years after the marriage.

For ten years Melesina St George lived in seclusion with her child, and it is not until 1798 that her interesting journal commences. During 1799 and 1800 she travelled in Germany, mixing in the very best society, and noting many items of historical interest. From Berlin and Dresden she proceeded to Vienna, and at Dresden, on her return journey, she met Nelson and Lady Hamilton, of whose lack of refinement some unpleasant instances are afforded. In Germany she also met Rivarol, Lucien Bonaparte, and John Quincy Adams, the sixth president of the United States. An account of this tour was privately issued by her son, Richard, in 1861; it was then incorporated in the *Remains* of 1862.

In July 1802, after a short stay in England, Melesina St George landed from Dover at Calais, on what proved a five years' sojourn in France; she also began exchanging letters with Mary Leadbeater in 1802. In Paris on 3 March 1803 she married Richard Trench (1774–1860), the sixth son of Frederick Trench of Moate, co. Galway. Her husband's eldest brother, Frederic, was created Lord Ashtown in 1800. From his ancestor, Frederick Trench (d. 1669) of Garbally, co. Galway, Richard Le Poer *Trench, second earl of Clancarty (1767–1837), also descended. Both Chenevixes and Trenches were of Huguenot origin.

After this time Melesina Trench's journal writing gave way to a charming correspondence with her husband and her old friends in England and Ireland. After the rupture of the peace of Amiens her husband was detained in France by Napoleon, and was confined to the Loire district. She made repeated visits to Paris to urge his release, and in August 1805 she delivered in person a petition to Napoleon for a passport for her husband; but it was not until 1807 that the requisite document was obtained and they were enabled to make their way to Rotterdam, whence, after a stormy passage, they reached England.

At Dublin, in November, Melesina met her old friend and correspondent, Mary Leadbeater, whom she had employed as almoner among her husband's tenants in Ireland. During a summer visit to the Leadbeaters it is related how she was discovered in the scullery surrounded by a small class of peasant children. The same charm made her much sought after in society, but the frivolities of a 'modish' life became more and more repugnant to her; and her letters become more personal and introspective, lacking external facts and detail. There are, however, some interesting touches respecting Wellington, Jekyll, Hester Piozzi (Mrs Thrale), Mrs Fry, and Lord John Russell, but the references to the political society with which she mixed at Paris under the first empire are tantalizingly brief. No mean judge, Edward Fitzgerald, to whom her son, Richard, submitted her letters and papers in manuscript, classes her letters with those of Walpole and Southey, praising them especially for their 'natural taste and good breeding' (letter dated 3 July 1861).

Apart from the *Remains*, including the journal and correspondence, of which two editions appeared in 1862 under the editorship of Richard Chenevix Trench, then dean of Westminster, Melesina Trench's writings comprise: *Mary Queen of Scots, an Historical Ballad, and other Poems* (n.d., privately issued), *Campaspe, an Historical Tale, and other Poems* (1815), and *Laura's Dream, or, The Moonlanders* (1816). All these were issued anonymously, and show the influence of Byron, Rogers, and especially Thomson, whose *Seasons* she greatly admired. Her *Thoughts of a Parent on Education, by the Late Mrs Richard Trench* (1837) appeared posthumously.

Melesina Trench died at Malvern on 27 May 1827. Her husband survived her many years, dying at Botley Hill, Hampshire, aged eighty-six on 16 April 1860. At that date three of their nine children were still alive: Francis Chenevix *Trench (1805–1886), Richard Chenevix *Trench (1807–1886), afterwards archbishop of Dublin, and Philip Charles (1810–1888) of Botley.

THOMAS SECCOMBE, *rev.* REBECCA MILLS

Sources M. Leadbeater, *The Leadbeater papers*, 2 vols. (1862), vol. 2, pp. 141–332 · Blain, Clements & Grundy, *Feminist comp.*, 1095 · A. J. Webb, *A compendium of Irish biography* (1878), 535–6 · D. J. O'Donoghue, *The poets of Ireland: a biographical dictionary with bibliographical particulars*, 1 vol. in 3 pts (1892–3), 248 · J. S. Crone, *A concise dictionary of Irish biography*, rev. edn (1937), 251 · *GM*, 3rd ser., 8 (1860), 640 · Burke, *Peerage* (1970) · Allibone, *Dict.* · R. Hogan, ed., *Dictionary of Irish literature*, rev. edn, 2 (1996)

Archives Hants. RO, diaries, manuscripts, and corresp.

Likenesses J.-B. Isabey, miniature, 1805 · F. Holl, stipple engraving, in or before 1862 (after portrait by Romney), NPG; repro. in C. Trench, ed., *Remains of the late Mrs Richard Trench* (1862) · F. Engleheart, engraving (after miniature by Hamilton) · T. Lawrence, oils

Trench, Power Le Poer (1770–1839), Church of Ireland archbishop of Tuam, was of Huguenot ancestry, being the third son of William Power Keating Trench, first earl of Clancarty, of the second creation (1741–1805), and Anne, the eldest daughter of the Rt Hon. Charles Gardiner of Dublin. Born in Sackville Street, Dublin, on 10 June 1770, he was educated first at Mr Cormick's school in Wandsworth and Putney, and subsequently, after a few years at Harrow School (1780–84), he attended Mr Ralph's academy in Castlebar, co. Mayo (1784–7). After graduating from Trinity College, Dublin, in July 1791, he was ordained deacon in November and received priest's orders in June 1792. He was immediately appointed to the family benefice of Creagh (Ballinasloe) and in the following year he was authorized to hold this in plurality with the benefice of Rawdenstown, co. Meath. He also acted as his father's business agent on the family's Galway estate. On 29 January 1795 he married his cousin Anne, the daughter of Walter Taylor of Castle Taylor, Galway, with whom he had two sons and six daughters. Initially they took up residence at Raford, near Ballinasloe. Trench was an accomplished horseman; during the uprising of 1798 he was a captain in the local yeomanry raised by his father to resist the French invading army.

In 1802 Trench was consecrated as bishop of Waterford, though family commitments may have contributed to the delay in his removal to the episcopal palace two years later. In 1810 his translation to the see of Elphin brought him back to the vicinity of his family. He was a gifted preacher, noted for his charity, and his diocesan reforms included church and rectory building, diaconal appointments, and administrative improvement.

Unlike his brother the second earl of Clancarty and his sisters Lady Rathdowne and Lady Emily La Touche, Trench was at this stage unsympathetic to the progress of the evangelical movement in Ireland, though he was impressed by the serenity of Lady Emily when he ministered to her at the time of her death in 1816. In the same year, although he valued the work of the evangelical ministers in his diocese, his visitation sermon condemned their doctrines as erroneous. However, a courteously reasoned reply in a letter from Archdeacon William Digby was instrumental in Trench's subsequent identification with the evangelical cause. In 1819 he was advanced to the archdiocese of Tuam but, before this, he had publicly committed himself to support evangelicalism 'by my influence, by my patronage and by my personal countenance' (Sirr, 46).

Although for a time Trench's association with the evangelical societies was somewhat diffident, he made clear to his clergy at their first clerical meeting that in matters of preferment spiritual zeal would be as important a factor as talent. Following his public defence, in 1822, of the Hibernian Bible Society, which had recently lost the support of the Irish primate, Lord John Beresford, Trench became the acknowledged leader of Irish evangelicalism, though this role was not allowed to hinder the vigorous performance of his archiepiscopal duties. Clerical inadequacy which had resulted in some defections to the Roman communion was an immediate cause for concern. Societies for the furtherance of evangelism and education were founded and new churches were established. During the famine of 1822 'he was virtually a proconsul' (Acheson, 1119) in Connaught, where his representations to the government and the relief agencies in London for the distribution of emergency supplies earned him gratitude from protestant and Catholic alike.

Of the evangelical initiatives associated with Trench's archiepiscopacy, Edward Nangle's Achill mission was probably the most celebrated, but not an isolated, example. By establishing his own diocesan branch of the Established Church Home Missionary Society, Trench was able to require his clergy not to obstruct active evangelism among the Catholics in his diocese. The archbishop's unabashed statement in 1827, 'We are proselytisers. We plead guilty to this terrific and unpardonable charge' (Sirr, 487), reflects his sincere commitment to the evangelism of the Bible Society as well as his forceful, uncompromising manner. But such statements were liable to alienate Catholics who had once appreciated his conciliatory spirit. Justly or otherwise, the Catholic *Freeman's Journal* (1824) claimed that when peasants in Trench's archdiocese were forgiven their arrears of rent 'part of the condition is that the tenantry should send their children to the Bible schools; and this is the *questio vexata* between the tenantry and his grace' (Bowen, 73).

The Irish Church Temporalities Act of 1834 (by which, on Trench's death, Tuam became a simple bishopric) resulted in the incorporation of the dioceses of Killala and Achonry into Trench's charge, but the sexagenarian archbishop continued to travel extensively on horseback to discharge these additional responsibilities. He died on 26 March 1839 at his archiepiscopal residence in Tuam, and was buried with his ancestors at Creagh, near Ballinasloe. His wife survived him.   TIMOTHY C. F. STUNT

Sources J. D'A. Sirr, *Memoir of the honourable and most reverend Power Le Poer Trench, last archbishop of Tuam* (1845) · W. Carus, ed., *Memoirs of the life of the Rev. Charles Simeon*, 3rd edn (1848) · Charlotte Elizabeth [C. E. Phelan [Tonna]], *Personal recollections*, 3rd edn (1847) · D. Bowen, *The protestant crusade in Ireland, 1800–70* (1978), 71–4 · A. R. Acheson, 'Trench, Power (Le Poer)', *The Blackwell dictionary of evangelical biography, 1730–1860*, ed. D. M. Lewis (1995) · *GM*, 2nd ser., 11 (1839), 539

Likenesses G. Hayter, group portrait, oils (*The Trial of Queen Caroline, 1820*), NPG

Trench, Richard Chenevix (1807–1886), Church of Ireland archbishop of Dublin, was born on 9 September 1807 at North Frederick Street, Dublin, the third son of Richard Trench (1774–1860), barrister-at-law (brother of Frederic Trench, first Baron Ashtown) and Melesina *Trench (1768–1827), granddaughter of Richard Chenevix, bishop of Waterford. His childhood was spent at Elm Lodge, Burlesdon, near Southampton, purchased by his father in 1810. He attended Twyford School (1816–19) and Harrow School (1819–25), proceeding to Trinity College, Cambridge, in 1825. He took pride in his membership of the Apostles there, and came under the influence of F. D. Maurice and a distinguished group of undergraduates that included Tennyson and Arthur Hallam. While at Trinity he edited and printed a periodical, *The Translator*. He graduated BA in 1829, and proceeded MA in 1833 and BD in 1850.

Trench spent the period immediately following graduation travelling in Europe, much of it in Spain, for whose literature he had developed a passion. He returned home in mid-1830, only to return to Spain within months as part of the somewhat quixotic Torrijos expedition, a group of idealistic volunteers who set out to attack Cadiz in support of the ill-conceived and ineptly executed liberal revolution of José Torrijos, and from which Trench returned unscathed if somewhat embarrassed.

By 1831 his father had taken up residence at Bockley Park, near Stradbally, in Queen's county (co. Laois), where Trench spent much time. On 31 May 1832 he married his cousin Frances Mary Trench (1809–1890), daughter of Francis Trench of Sopwell Hall in co. Tipperary and Mary, daughter of Henry Mason of Shrewsbury. They had seven sons and five daughters.

Trench was ordained deacon in Norwich Cathedral on 7 October 1832, and in 1833 took up the curacy of Hadleigh in Suffolk, under the Tractarian Hugh James Rose, expressing himself glad 'to be quit of Ireland', which was experiencing a period of particular turbulence, largely to do with popular resistance to the payment of tithes to the established church. None the less, in 1847, when the great Irish famine was at its worst, he joined his cousin Frederic Fitzwilliam Trench, rector of Cloughjordan, in relief work, succumbing to fever immediately on his return to England. Years later, as archbishop of Dublin, he was to show himself equally compassionate and energetic during an economic crisis caused by the harvest failure of 1879–80. During the time of Trench's curacy, the Hadleigh conference took place in the parish, attended by Froude and other Tractarian clergy, and convened by Rose to consider the threat that he perceived to lie in the (Irish) Church Temporalities Bill, famously condemned in Keble's 'assize sermon' of 1833.

Rose left that same year for the professorship of divinity at the newly founded University of Durham, and some months later (1834) Trench became curate of St Peter's, Colchester. Ill health soon compelled him to resign and

Richard Chenevix Trench (1807–1886), by George Richmond, 1859

he, his wife, and their daughter (Melesina Mary) spent much of 1834–5 in Italy. His health restored, he returned to England and was ordained priest on 5 July 1835 and in September was made perpetual curate of the newly instituted parish of Curbridge (Winchester).

Trench's six years at Curbridge (his house had once been William Cobbett's) saw the growth of his reputation as a scholar and, equally significant, the development of his friendship with Samuel Wilberforce. His first theological work, *Notes on the Parables of Our Lord* (1841) was a substantial work of exegesis, 467 pages in all. It was well received and, running to fourteen revised editions, his most popular work. It was claimed by his biographer to mark the beginning of 'that other "Cambridge Movement" which reached its zenith and glory in the work of the great New Testament scholars Lightfoot, Westcott and Hort' (Bromley, 70). These years also saw the publication of volumes of poetry that included *Sabbation; Honor Neale; and other Poems* (1838). *Elegiac Poems* (1843) was much influenced by the death of his eight-year-old son, Francis William, in 1841:

> in my hand I feel the grasp
> of that small hand, whose tender clasp
> I shall not feel, oh! any more.

In 1841 Trench was appointed curate to Wilberforce at Alverstoke and although three years later he moved to be rector of Itchen Stoke (1844), Wilberforce, bishop of Oxford from 1845, made him his examining chaplain. He continued to publish theology and poetry and was special preacher at Cambridge (1843) and Hulsean lecturer (1845

and 1846). Evincing a considerable interest in philology, he delivered a series of lectures which he published (1851) as *Study of Words*, which ran into many editions. He followed this with *English Past and Present* (1855) and *A Select Glossary* (1859). These works constituted an important impetus toward the study of the English language. In 1857 he joined the Philological Society, energetically championing the cause of producing a new English dictionary. He read papers on the subject to the society, published as *On some Deficiencies in our English Dictionaries* (1857, 2nd edn 1860) and a resolution of his, put to the society on 7 January 1858, is commonly regarded as having provided the impetus that, the Clarendon Press having been interested in the enterprise, led to the *Oxford English Dictionary*. His seminal role is recorded in the 'Historical introduction' to the work. His reputation was further enhanced by the publication of his second major book, *Notes on the Miracles of Our Lord*, in 1846. In the following year he was appointed professor of divinity at King's College, London, a chair that he held until 1856, when he became dean of Westminster.

Trench was responsible for some innovations, including a Sunday evening service, of which the sermon was a popular component. In 1860 he published his *Sermons Preached in Westminster Abbey* (as in 1873 he would publish *Sermons Preached for the most Part in Ireland*), but he was not regarded as an especially accomplished preacher. It was during his time at Westminster that two of his sons died abroad, Arthur in 1860 and Richard in 1861.

Trench was appointed, not without opposition, in 1863 to succeed Richard Whately as archbishop of Dublin, his consecration taking place on 1 January 1864. His friend F. D. Maurice described the move as 'an awful thing', and indeed the new archbishop came to a church that was entering a particularly turbulent period in its history, in which he was to play a vital, and frequently uncongenial, part. The Established Church of Ireland had already, in the early decades of the century, experienced considerable administrative reform, and continued to be the object of public scrutiny, partly because of its relative wealth, partly because of its minority position. The census of 1861 revealed that of an Irish population of some four and a quarter million, less than three-quarters of a million belonged to the established church. Gladstone identified the Irish church establishment as a major Irish grievance and, in the face of fierce resistance and non-co-operation from its leadership, effected disendowment and disestablishment by the Irish Church Act (1869). None had been more intransigent opponents than Trench, described by the prime minister as 'a dreamer of dreams' (Gladstone, 7.14–15), who 'talks of negotiating at a time when all negotiation will have gone by', though some years later Gladstone's sense of justice caused him to dub Trench 'this excellent man' (Gladstone, 9.264).

It was in the immediate aftermath of disestablishment, when controversy raged about the formulation of a constitution for the Church of Ireland and prayer book revision, that Trench proved to be a highly significant figure. He feared for the catholicity of the newly disestablished church, and that either by its form of government or by liturgical change (the motivation for which had a strongly protestant and anti-ritualist strand) it might cut itself off from the wider Anglican world, or be torn by schism.

In the general convention that met in 1870 to draw up a constitution, Trench argued (successfully) for the bishops to have what amounted to a veto in the general synod. In matters doctrinal and liturgical he had already given opponents in his diocese occasion to attack 'Puseyite Trench', and he fought tenaciously, if not always tactfully—he has been described by a modern though sympathetic commentator as 'the figure who most exacerbated the situation' (Clarke, 284)—in the face of bitter and sometimes ill-informed criticism, for what he believed vital to the survival of the Church of Ireland as part of catholic Christendom. Though an awkward ally at times, he was a key figure among those who ensured that the Irish Book of Common Prayer of 1878 to all intents and purposes retained the integrity of its predecessors.

It can be said with some conviction that Trench's work in Dublin has been more enduring than his theological writing and his poetry, neither of which, however highly rated in their day, can be said to have stood the test of time (though several lines of his kept their place in the second edition of *The Oxford Dictionary of Quotations*, and one survived to the third). But his *On the Study of Words* came out in the Everyman Library in 1927, and in 1994 was included in the series History of Linguistics: British Linguistics in the Nineteenth Century, Trench being described in the introduction to this edition as 'father of the world's best dictionary' and 'one of the foremost advocates of "scientific" [historical] lexicography in Victorian England' (p. ix).

Also of lasting importance was the archbishop's active support for the founding of Alexandra College, Dublin (1866), which pioneered in Ireland the education of women, not only for university courses, but also, from 1880 to 1904, for the degrees of the Royal University of Ireland.

The years of disestablishment and liturgical revision were, for Trench, a time of spiritual and intellectual anguish. To this was added physical suffering when he broke both his legs in a fall on board ship in 1875 when returning from one of his many visits to England. He felt compelled by failing health to resign in November 1884 (waiving his pension rights), and died on 28 March 1886 at 23 Eaton Square, London, where he had spent the winter. He was buried in Westminster Abbey on 2 April, his epitaph composed by Dean Church.

Trench's eldest surviving son, **Frederick Chenevix Trench** (1837–1894), who was born on 10 October 1837, was commissioned in the 20th hussars on 20 January 1857 and was made a lieutenant on 30 April 1858. He had a distinguished military career, being decorated for his service in India (he was present at the capture of Lucknow in 1858) and was made captain in 1867, lieutenant-colonel in 1880, and colonel in 1884. On 17 July 1873 he married Mary Frederica Blanche, the only daughter of Charles Mulville, captain in the 3rd dragoon guards. They had two sons and three daughters. Military attaché at St Petersburg from

1881 to 1886, he retired in the following year with the honorary rank of major-general and died at Braemar on 8 August 1894. He was author of several military works.

KENNETH MILNE

Sources Richard Chenevix Trench: letters and memorials, ed. [M. Trench], 2 vols. (1888) · T. R. F. Cooke-Trench, A memoir of the Trench family (privately printed, 1896) · J. Bromley, The man of ten talents (1959) · Representative Church Body, Dublin, Trench MSS · Gladstone, Diaries · T. Crowley, The politics of discourse: the standard language question in British cultural debate (1989) · H. Aarsleff, The study of language in England, 1780–1860 (1967) · P. M. H. Bell, Disestablishment in Ireland and Wales (1969) · D. H. Akenson, The Church of Ireland: ecclesiastical reform and revolution, 1800–1885 (1971) · R. Clarke, 'The disestablishment revision of the Irish Book of Common Prayer', PhD diss., University of Dublin, 1989 · DNB · A. V. O'Connor and S. M. Parkes, Gladly learn and gladly teach: Alexandra College and School, 1866–1966 (1984) · The Times (29 March 1886)

Archives Hants. RO, corresp. and papers · LPL, corresp. · NL Ire. · Queen's College, London, letters · Representative Church Body Library, Dublin, corresp. | BL, corresp. with W. E. Gladstone, Add. MSS 44374–44478 · BL, corresp. with Macmillans, Add. MS 55096 · Bodl. Oxf., letters to J. W. Croker · Bodl. Oxf., corresp. with Lord Kimberley · Bodl. Oxf., corresp. with Lady Lovelace · Bodl. Oxf., corresp. with Samuel Wilberforce · CKS, corresp. with Lord Stanhope · King's Lond., letters to King's College, London · LPL, corresp. with A. C. Tait · LPL, corresp. with Christopher Wordsworth · NRA, priv. coll., corresp. with T. C. Trench · Pusey Oxf., corresp. with R. W. Randall · Representative Church Body Library, Dublin, corresp. with his agent Thomas Cooke-Trench · Trinity Cam., letters to Lord Houghton; letters to William Whewell

Likenesses S. Lawrence, chalk drawing, c.1841, NPG · H. Watkins, photograph, 1857, NPG · G. Richmond, crayon drawing, 1859, See House, Dublin [see illus.] · G. Richmond, drawing, 1859, Synod Hall, Dublin · J. R. Jackson, mezzotint, pubd 1863 (after G. Richmond), BM, NPG · head, 1881–8, Christ Church Cathedral, Dublin · T. Bridgford, oil drawing, Alexandra College, Dublin · H. Hering, carte-de-visite, NPG · T. Jones, oils, Christ Church Cathedral, Dublin · Mason & Co., carte-de-visite, NPG · W. Walker & Sons, carte-de-visite, NPG · brass effigy on monument, Christ Church Cathedral, Dublin · oils, deanery, Westminster · photograph, NPG · prints, NPG · woodburytype, NPG · woodcuts, NPG

Trench, Richard Le Poer, second earl of Clancarty (1767–1837), diplomatist, born on 18 May 1767, was the eldest surviving son of William Power Keating Trench, first earl of Clancarty (1741–1805), and his wife, Anne (d. 1829), daughter of the Rt Hon. Charles Gardiner MP, of Dublin. His father, who was connected through his mother, Frances Power of Corheen, with Donough *Maccarthy, fourth earl of Clancarty of the first creation, was born in 1741. He sat in the Irish parliament from 1769 to 1797 for the county of Galway, in which his seat, Garbally, was situated. On 29 November 1783 he supported Flood's motion for leave to bring in a reform bill, and on 12 August 1785 he opposed Pitt's commercial propositions when brought forward by Orde; but in 1791 he was attacked by George Ponsonby for supporting the government, in order to preserve its majority (*Irish Parliamentary Debates*, 2nd edn, 11.321–3). He was created an Irish peer on 25 November 1797, with the title of Baron Kilconnel of Garbally; on the occasion of the union and on his son's prompting to Castlereagh, he was further advanced as Viscount Dunlo on 3 January 1801, and earl of Clancarty on 12 February 1803. He died on 27 April 1805.

Richard Trench was called to the Irish bar, and in 1796

Richard Le Poer Trench, second earl of Clancarty (1767–1837), by Joseph Paelinck, 1817

entered the Irish parliament as the member for Newtown-limavady. On 9 February that year he married Henrietta Margaret (d. 1847), daughter of the Rt Hon. John Staples and his first wife, Harriet, daughter of the Rt Hon. William Connolly of Castletown. His wife was 'an excellent, head-aching woman, with none of the representation or insolance of an Ambassadress' (GEC, *Peerage*). They had three sons and four daughters. In 1798 Trench was returned to the Irish parliament for Galway county, which he continued to represent until the union. On 27 June 1798 he seconded the address to the crown; but both he and his brother Charles voted against the proposed union when first brought forward the following year. They were, how-ever, induced to support it in 1800, when Richard was per-suaded by Castlereagh, and Charles was appointed by Cornwallis to the new office of commissioner of inland revenue; their father's advance in the peerage was doubt-less their reward. Richard Trench was elected to the first parliament of the United Kindom for Galway county as a supporter of Pitt, and on 23 November 1802 moved the address, dwelling in the course of his speech on the bene-ficial effects of the union. On 21 May 1804 (by which time he had become known as Viscount Dunlo) he was appoin-ted a commissioner for the affairs of India. In the next par-liament he sat (after his father's death) as earl of Clancarty for the borough of Rye, but on 16 December 1808 he was chosen a representative peer for Ireland. On 13 May 1807 he was sworn of the British, and on 26 December 1808 of the Irish, privy council; and in May 1807 he was appointed postmaster-general in Ireland. He further received the offices of master of the Royal Mint (1812–14) and president of the Board of Trade (September 1812 to January 1818), and joint postmaster-general (1814–16). Between 1810 and 1812 he was a frequent speaker in the House of Lords. On 6 June 1810 he expressed modified approval of the Catholic claims, but criticized severely the attitude adopted by the Irish Catholic hierarchy since 1808. When the question was raised by Lord Wellesley two years later, he declared against unqualified concession, but was in favour of a thorough examination. On 4 January 1811 Clancarty, in a closely reasoned speech, defended the resolutions restricting the powers of the regent.

In November 1813 Clancarty accompanied the prince of Orange to The Hague, and was accredited to him as British ambassador when he was proclaimed William I of the Netherlands. On 13 December he wrote to Castlereagh: 'What with correspondence with two admirals, four gen-erals, British and allied, and your lordship, I am kept so well employed that I have scarcely time to eat or sleep'. On the 14th he wrote urgently demanding the immediate dis-patch of Thomas Graham (Lord Lynedoch) with reinforce-ments to the Netherlands. Early in 1814 he was in commu-nication with Lord Liverpool, the prime minister, on the subject of the Dutch finances. Clancarty was energetic in urging on the prince of Orange the necessary military measures, and succeeded in persuading him to resign the command of the allied forces in the Netherlands to the prince royal of Sweden, Bernadotte. In the succeeding months he was chiefly engaged in formulating a plan for the incorporation of the Belgian and Dutch provinces into the proposed new state of the Netherlands (cf. Yonge, 1.514). Other difficulties were the adjustment of financial relations and the claims of the Belgian clergy and nobility. During the summer months of 1814 his attention was also directed towards the opening up of a reciprocal colonial trade between Britain and the Netherlands, and to the resumption of negotiations for a marriage between Prin-cess Charlotte of England and the hereditary prince of Orange.

Meanwhile Clancarty had kept himself fully informed of the general situation of European affairs. On 11 August he was named one of the four British plenipotentiaries to the Congress of Vienna. Talleyrand, in a letter of 28 December to Louis XVIII, spoke of his zeal, firmness, and uprightness. When Wellington left Vienna for Belgium in March 1815, Clancarty became the senior British plenipot-entiary. He was the British representative on the various commissions respectively appointed to delimit the Polish frontier and to adjust the affairs of Saxony (October 1814); to mediate between Sardinia and Genoa; to regulate the affairs of Tuscany and Parma, and to draw up a prelimin-ary convention (8 February 1815). On 11 March 1815, in an interesting dispatch to Castlereagh, he described the con-sternation of the royalty of Europe at the news of Napo-leon's escape from Elba, but thought it desirable to encourage their fears with the view of bringing to an end the business of the congress. After the peace, on 4 August 1815, he was created Baron Trench of Garbally in the peer-age of the United Kingdom.

At the end of the year Clancarty went to Frankfurt am

Main, and was engaged in resolving the disputes between Bavaria and Baden. On 22 May 1816 he was appointed ambassador to the new kingdom of the Netherlands, but was detained at Frankfurt through the summer. During his second embassy to the Netherlands Clancarty was at first mainly occupied in urging the king to take sufficiently strong measures against the French refugees in the Netherlands, who were plotting against the recent settlement of the country. Subsequently Clancarty devoted his attention to negotiations between Great Britain and the Netherlands for the suppression of the slave trade. During the remainder of the year he was chiefly occupied in negotiations with Prussia relating to frontier disputes and to the evacuation of the Netherlands by Prussian troops. During 1821 he was involved in contradicting Dutch claims that the slave-trade convention of 1818 had been confined to Africa.

In December 1823 Clancarty reluctantly resigned his post in the Netherlands. In 1818 he had received a pension of £2000, and had also been created markies van Heusden by the king of the Netherlands. On retiring from The Hague he was made on 8 December 1823 Viscount Clancarty of co. Cork. He spent most of his retirement on his estates in Ireland, where he was lord lieutenant of co. Galway and vice-admiral of Connaught. On 8 March 1827, speaking in the House of Lords, he censured the negligence of the law officers in Ireland, and declared his opinion that no exceptional measures were necessary for repressing the Catholic Association; but in 1829 he opposed Catholic emancipation on account of the conduct of the Catholics. He said that, like Pitt, he would have granted relief on condition of their good behaviour. In the course of a correspondence with Wellington at this period, Clancarty complained of the lack of support given by the government to the cause of order in Ireland (7 July). Wellington, in reply, charged Clancarty with obstructing the emancipation bill.

Clancarty died at Kinnegad, co. Westmeath, on 24 November 1837, and his wife died on 30 December 1847 at Garbally. Their eldest son, William Thomas Le Poer Trench (1803–1872), succeeded to his father's titles. Clancarty was an important member of Castlereagh's diplomatic team, 'hard-working, if opinionated and reactionary' (Webster, 2.40).

G. Le G. Norgate, rev. H. C. G. Matthew

Sources GEC, *Peerage* · C. K. Webster, *The foreign policy of Castlereagh*, 2 vols. (1925–31) · C. D. Yonge, *The life and administration of Robert Banks, second earl of Liverpool*, 3 vols. (1868) · *Memoirs and correspondence of Viscount Castlereagh, second marquess of Londonderry*, ed. C. Vane, marquess of Londonderry, 12 vols. (1848–53) · S. T. Bindoff and others, eds., *British diplomatic representatives, 1789–1852*, CS, 3rd ser., 50 (1934)
Archives BL OIOC, papers relating to India, Eur. MS F 204 · NA Ire., corresp. with family | BL, corresp. with Sir Robert Gordon, Add. MS 43217 · BL, corresp. with earl of Liverpool, loan 72 · BL, corresp. with earl of Liverpool and Lord Castlereagh, Add. MSS 38250–38298, 38972–38973 · BL, corresp. with Lord Melbourne, Add. MSS 60411–60415 · BL, corresp. with Sir Robert Peel, Add. MSS 40222–40377 · BL, letters to Sir George Rose, Add. MS 42794 · Durham RO, corresp. with Lord Londonderry · Exeter Cathedral, letters to Henry Phillpotts · Northumbd RO, Newcastle upon Tyne, corresp. with Thomas Wallace · PRO NIre., corresp. with Lord Castlereagh · TCD, corresp. with Thomas Conolly
Likenesses J. Paelinck, oils, 1817, NPG [*see illus.*]

Trench, (Richard) William Steuart (1808–1872), land agent and writer, was born on 16 November 1808 at Bellegrove, near Portarlington, Queen's county, Ireland, the fourth son of Thomas Trench (1761–1834), dean of Kildare (brother of Frederic Trench, first Lord Ashtown, and brother-in-law of Melesina Trench), and his wife, Mary, eldest daughter of Walter Weldon of Rahinderry, MP for Athy in 1745. Trench was educated at the Royal School, Armagh, and was admitted to Trinity College, Dublin in 1826, though he does not appear to have taken a degree. In April 1832 he married Elizabeth Susannah (*d.* 1887), daughter of J. Sealy Townsend, master of chancery in Ireland. They had two sons and one daughter.

Trench spent some years preparing to become a land agent, and in 1841 he was awarded the gold medal of the Royal Agricultural Society for his essay, 'Reclamation'. After holding some subordinate positions he was appointed agent to the Shirley estate in co. Monaghan in April 1843. He resigned this post in April 1845. In December 1849 Trench was appointed agent to the extensive estates of the marquess of Lansdowne in co. Kerry, and, in addition to these, he took charge of the property of the marquess of Bath in Monaghan in 1851, and that of Lord Digby in the King's county in 1856. He held these appointments until his death.

Trench's experience of the land management in Ireland ranged from the period immediately before the famine of the 1840s until Gladstone's first Land Act (1870). In 1868 he published *Realities of Irish Life*, a book which was an immediate success and which passed through five editions in a year. The *Edinburgh Review* praised its forcible and impressive description of the Irish peasantry, and likened its popular force, humour, and pathos to that in the early works of Charles Dickens. In 1871 Trench published *Ierne: a Tale*, in which he treated the same topics in fictional form, describing the faith of the Irish peasantry in their indefeasible ownership of the land, but the book did not achieve the success of its predecessor. Trench also wrote a sketch of the history of Ireland from the earliest times to the Act of Settlement in 1870, but the work was suppressed after a large portion had been printed. His final publications were a series of tales, entitled 'Sketches of life and character in Ireland', which appeared in *Evening Hours*, a monthly periodical, in 1871 and 1872.

Trench died at Carrickmacross, co. Monaghan, Ireland, the seat of the marquess of Bath, on 4 August 1872.

C. L. Falkiner, rev. Anne Pimlott Baker

Sources Burke, *Peerage* (1970) · Boase, *Mod. Eng. biog.* · Burtchaell & Sadleir, *Alum. Dubl.*, 2nd edn · P. Bew, *Land and the national question in Ireland, 1858–82* (1978) · B. L. Solow, *The land question and the Irish economy, 1870–1903* (1971) · *CGPLA Ire.* (1872)
Wealth at death under £14,000: probate, 30 Aug 1872, *CGPLA Ire.*

Trenchard, Hugh Montague, first Viscount Trenchard (1873–1956), air force officer, was born at Windsor Lodge, Haines Hill, Taunton, Somerset, on 3 February 1873, the second son and third of six children of Henry Montague

Hugh Montague Trenchard, first Viscount Trenchard (1873–1956), by Sir William Orpen, 1917

Trenchard (1838–1914), solicitor, and his wife, Georgina Louisa Catherine Tower, daughter of Captain John McDowall Skene RN. Many struggling junior officers have been consoled since 1918 by widespread knowledge of two facts: 'the father of the Royal Air Force' found examinations almost impossible to pass, and he did not even begin to become famous until he was well past forty. He was flatly rejected by both Dartmouth and Woolwich, and only just scraped a pass—at the third attempt—in a far less demanding test for militia candidates: these 'last resorts' were placed in whichever regiment would accept them. His difficulties owed much to inept teaching at both navy and army 'crammer' schools, and much to idleness (except at games and riding), but also owed something to the sudden shock of learning, at the vulnerable age of sixteen, that his father's practice had failed. Bankruptcy was a public disgrace hard to bear for a particularly proud member of an old-established family. He was dismayed, rather than inspired, by the knowledge that he owed the rest of his education to the charity of wiser and richer relatives.

Trenchard was granted a commission in September 1893 as a second lieutenant in the 2nd battalion, Royal Scots Fusiliers, and posted to join his regiment in India. An inarticulate, prickly young man, socially inept and without money, he was known as 'the Camel' (did not drink, could not speak), and was far from popular until he revealed a rare combination of talents. He mastered any horse assigned to him; played polo skilfully (fending off Winston Churchill vigorously); traded horses profitably; picked winners regularly; shot accurately; and—not least—organized teams and tournaments efficiently. As

his confidence grew, he began to read voraciously in a determined attempt to educate himself, but he never learned to spell or write with any fluency.

A dashing cavalry officer On the outbreak of the Second South African War in October 1899 Trenchard was sent to South Africa. Promoted to captain in February 1900, he was told to raise and train a mounted company which brought together a bunch of boisterous, aggressive horsemen, many of them Australian. He had the makings of a fine guerrilla leader until his impetuosity led him into an ambush at Dwarsvlei in western Transvaal in October 1900, where he was severely wounded in the chest and spine, and invalided home to England in December. Although his left lung was permanently damaged, he made a remarkable recovery, thanks to a strong constitution and a self-imposed regime of strenuous winter sports in Switzerland, where a heavy fall shook his spine back into place, enabling him to walk freely once more. He returned to South Africa at his own insistence in May 1901 to resume his career as a dashing cavalry officer, fearless in combat, impatient of all orders but his own, and respectful only to those seniors whom he admired. He was full of high Victorian bravado, and his blunt words, boundless energy, and stern discipline of men under his command commended him to Field Marshal Lord Kitchener.

While on leave in England at the end of the war Trenchard accepted an appointment in October 1903 as assistant commandant of the South Nigeria regiment, first as major, then as lieutenant-colonel. He relished the opportunity to lead his own force of irregular cavalry on expeditions against 'unpacified' tribes in the interior, but he also supervised surveys, road building, and drainage projects, and enhanced his reputation as a man of formidable personality who never hesitated to criticize all and sundry in the bluntest terms. Those few who had the courage to answer back were, of course, the men he subsequently valued. In 1906 he was made a member of the Distinguished Service Order, and appointed to command his regiment in 1908. But he fell seriously ill in 1910 and was again invalided home. On recovering, he rejoined his original regiment, dropped in rank to major, and served in Ulster until 1912.

An indifferent pilot and dangerous tutor By 1912 Trenchard was rising forty, unmarried, and discontented. He was respected by good officers and men, but too 'unclubbable' (and too poor) for high rank. After almost twenty years of strenuous military service, he was looking about for new opportunities, in or out of uniform, and his colleagues—wary of his sharp tongue—were more than willing to help him. One of his few friends advised him to learn to fly and he agreed to give it a go. He was promptly granted three months' leave, and boldly spent the considerable sum of £75 on flying lessons at the Sopwith school, Brooklands. After only two weeks of tuition, including no more than sixty-four minutes in the air, he was granted a pilot's certificate (no. 270) by the Royal Aero Club on 31 July 1912.

The Royal Flying Corps having been formed in May 1912,

Trenchard was immediately seconded to it and sent to the Central Flying School at Upavon in Wiltshire, where he met Churchill again (an even worse pilot). Instead of taking a pupil's course—essential if he were to acquire flying skills himself, let alone transmit them to others—his age and military experience saw him appointed to the staff. As assistant commandant, in the rank of lieutenant-colonel, his capacity for effective organization and exacting unquestioned obedience to orders proved of great value to a newly formed school that attracted many would-be free spirits. It was now that his mighty foghorn voice earned him, for the rest of his life, the nickname Boom. Although an indifferent pilot and dangerous tutor, he recognized more quickly than most officers of his age the aeroplane's unlimited military potential.

Constant aggression When war broke out in August 1914 Trenchard took command of Farnborough, Hampshire, where he allegedly found 'one typewriter, a confidential box with a pair of boots in it, and a lot of unpaid bills'. From these small beginnings he began to build an organization capable of supporting a rapidly expanding number of squadrons. As early as November, however, he had escaped from the rear to the front, as an operational commander, and in January 1915 he met General Sir Douglas Haig, who took command of all British forces on the western front from December. Trenchard came to admire Haig without reserve; for his part, Haig declared in 1922 that the First World War had produced only two new things of importance: 'barbed wire and Trenchard' (Boyle, 506).

From 1915 onwards Trenchard pressed hard for the development and quantity production of aircraft of improved design, with more powerful engines and armament, equipped with reliable wireless sets and cameras, and a gadget to permit the accurate dropping of bigger and better-designed bombs. But his main concern, formulated during 1915, was to develop an unflinching spirit of constant aggression among pilots and observers. An opinion that would become an unshakeable doctrine was already forming in his mind. Persistent attack achieved air supremacy, and that supremacy (given aircraft sufficient in quantity and quality) would permit devastating attack upon enemy industrial centres and lines of communication to the fighting fronts. 'The aeroplane', he famously (and mistakenly) asserted 'is not a defence against the aeroplane'. And the use of parachutes, which could have been as readily available for British as well as German airmen by 1918, was forbidden because they might undermine that spirit of aggression. That ruling, made by non-flying members of the air board, was firmly supported by Trenchard.

In August 1915 Trenchard succeeded Sir David Henderson as head of the Royal Flying Corps in France, with the warm approval of both Haig and Kitchener (secretary of state for war) and was promoted to brigadier-general. From Henderson he inherited Maurice Baring—author, linguist, diplomat—as an essential assistant, who translated his incoherent mutterings into fluent prose. 'I can't write what I mean, I can't say what I mean, but I expect you to know what I mean' (Hyde, 57). More poetically, Baring saw his task as 'bottling a mountain torrent while yet preserving the tingling fury of its natural state' (Letley, 174). They visited all squadrons and depots, listened to countless complaints and suggestions, noticed everything, no matter how carefully concealed, and whenever Trenchard's tactless, overbearing manner caused more than usual offence, Baring poured the necessary oil and subtly rebuked his master. His fluent French also made it possible for Trenchard to establish good relations with the French air service. He did it so well that Marshal Foch described him as an incomparable staff officer.

During 1915, however, the Germans produced a Fokker monoplane equipped with a machine-gun that fired safely through the propeller arc and forced Trenchard's technically inferior aircraft onto the defensive. They became 'Fokker fodder' and it was said in parliament that 'our pilots are being murdered rather than killed' (Lee, 214). Until better machines arrived in service early in 1916, he was reluctantly obliged to accept fewer and shorter reconnaissance patrols, and was unable to foster that continuous co-operation between artillery and aircraft (via wireless and photographs) that he and Haig foresaw as the key to accurate hitting of enemy targets. Although British and German machines were evenly matched in quality from 1916 onwards, and the British increasingly outnumbered their opponents, they suffered four times as many casualties as a result of Trenchard's policy of constant offensive. 'To him, as to his staff, and most of his senior commanders', wrote A. S. G. Lee, an able pilot who survived long enough to become experienced, 'for a British aeroplane to be one mile across the trenches was offensive: for it to be ten miles over was more offensive'. What really mattered, however, was not the aircraft's position in the sky but the calibre of its pilot and the quality of his machine. 'The most rashly aggressive pigeon won't get far with a hawk' (Lee, 217–18).

Creation of a new service In England, meanwhile, intense competition between the War Office and the Admiralty for recruits (air and ground), training facilities, factory space, designers, and producers of airframes and aeroengines was harming the war effort. In December 1916, for example, the Royal Flying Corps and the Royal Naval Air Service placed orders for seventy-six varieties of aircraft and fifty-seven of engines (Johns, 10–11). Both air arms were weaker than they should have been, and neither gave serious attention to home defence against aerial attack. Several alarmingly successful daylight raids by German bombers during June and July 1917 revealed the inadequacy of this defence and fuelled powerful demands for a united service, with its own ministry, independent of army or navy control, to make efficient use of aviation resources and frame an effective home defence. General Jan Christian Smuts (South African member of the imperial war cabinet) and Henderson, backed by the prime minister, Lloyd George, were largely responsible for the creation of this independent air service in April 1918. Trenchard agreed with the reformers, but thought it best to struggle on with an unsatisfactory situation until the war ended. He thus had good reason for disliking the title 'father of the Royal Air Force', so often accorded him in later years. If that service had not been created by the heat of battle out of fear of defeat, it would never have emerged out of the chill of calculation when the war to end all war had been won. On the other hand, although he did not father the infant, he certainly deserves credit for protecting it from predators until it was sturdy enough to thrive without anyone's help.

Despite Haig's protests and his own reluctance, Trenchard was appointed chief of the air staff, the first head of the new service, and returned to England in January 1918; he was also knighted (KCB). But the first air minister was Lord Rothermere, younger brother of Lord Northcliffe. These influential newspaper owners, backed by Lloyd George, were vehement opponents of Haig and hoped to procure his dismissal. At that time, Trenchard lacked the political skills, contacts, and even the resolution to counter such men. He simply resigned (bringing Rothermere down with him, to his surprise) in April and sulked for a month. While sitting on a bench in Green Park on 8 May he overheard two naval officers discussing his conduct. 'It's an outrage', said one. 'I don't know why the government should pander to a man who threw in his hand at the height of a battle. If I'd my way with Trenchard I'd have him shot.' Somewhat chastened, he reluctantly agreed to return to France later that month as head of a small force intended to bomb targets in Germany. Neither John Salmond (his successor as head of the RAF in France) nor the French (who feared reprisals, and thought all resources should be devoted to the battlefield) co-operated willingly. 'A more gigantic waste of effort and personnel there has never been in any war', declared Trenchard in November 1918 (Hyde, 44). Nevertheless, the few raids that were mounted convinced him that, in any future war with Germany, a systematic campaign of heavy bombing would shatter the morale of its people. Ignoring evidence to the contrary, he was equally convinced that German bombing would not dismay Britons.

A legendary decade Trenchard was created a baronet in October 1919 and received a handsome cash grant of £10,000. Winston Churchill, minister of war and air, pressed him to resume his post as chief of the air staff, which he did on 15 May, and during the next decade he became a legend. He clearly understood that his new service must be reduced to a shadow of its former strength, and remain small and weak for the foreseeable future, but it could be provided with sound foundations upon which to build a powerful air force, should the need ever arise. A realistic memorandum of September 1919 (converted into a government white paper in December) set out an affordable framework for a service of under 30,000 officers and men. He founded an apprentice school (at Halton, Buckinghamshire) for youths aged fifteen to eighteen who became ground crews, a cadet college (at Cranwell, Lincolnshire) for career officers, and a staff college (at Andover, Hampshire) for future leaders. He set up squadrons at Oxford and Cambridge, introduced short-service commissions and a network of auxiliary squadrons—

rightly believing that many high-spirited young men were eager to spend some exciting years in cockpits, but were not interested in a subsequent, poorly paid career behind desks.

Trenchard also learned to fight in the Whitehall jungle, with Churchill's intermittent support, against persistent attempts by both the War Office and the Admiralty to divide the RAF between them and end its independent existence. He found in 'air policing' of Britain's empire throughout the Middle East, but especially in Mesopotamia (Iraq), an ideal opportunity to demonstrate that the RAF was both effective and cheap. 'Control without occupation' Sir Samuel Hoare, secretary of state for air in the 1920s, called it (Hoare, 265): an irresistible combination for politicians acutely conscious of Britain's financial weakness. A handful of squadrons, equipped with biplanes left over from the war, armed with light machine-guns and small bombs, and supported only by a small number of armoured cars (converted or built out of the RAF's own meagre budget) were usually able to impose a local peace or separate rivals more swiftly and cheaply than large, expensive garrisons of slow-moving soldiers. Trenchard encouraged annual air displays at Hendon, which proved enormously popular, and also fostered the gradual development of air routes which might one day link every part of the empire. At the end of 1923 he was accepted as a member of the chiefs of staff committee—formally equal to the heads of the navy and the army. In 1925 he argued in favour of making the RAF (rather than the Royal Navy, assisted by a garrison of soldiers) primarily responsible for the defence of Singapore. Even before the fall of that base to Japanese attack in 1942 he regarded his failure to win that argument as the low point of his career.

Unfortunately, the success of air policing seduced Trenchard and his successors into ignoring the need to prepare for possible conflict with nations as technically advanced as Britain. The RAF failed to make adequate progress before 1939 in precisely those fields which the offensive doctrine most required: accurate navigation, in daylight or darkness, in large, properly heated and fully armed aircraft capable of carrying heavy loads of efficient bombs (high explosive or incendiary) a long way and dropping them accurately on well-chosen targets. In 1925, however, Trenchard had been impressed by the Fairey Fox, a two-seat, single-engine biplane day-bomber, equipped with an American Curtiss D-12 engine. The Fox outclassed all other British machines of that time, and Trenchard immediately ordered enough to equip a single squadron. Objections—from industry and politicians—to the use of a foreign engine prevented him from ordering more, but the Fox example did encourage a gradual improvement. In the late 1920s, the RAF's success in Schneider trophy races confirmed the high popular regard first earned at Hendon.

Morale was high, thanks partly to team spirit generated by army and navy opposition, partly also to Trenchard's creation in 1919 of a benevolent fund (which has spent millions of pounds since that date relieving distress among servicemen and their families), but mostly to a widespread conviction that aircraft would play a vital part in any future war. That part, according to Trenchard's doctrine, would be primarily as an offensive bomber force, hitting targets of 'strategic' importance, rather than as a defensive fighter force, successfully resisting attempts by enemy bombers to hit British targets. Little attention was paid to co-operation with either the army or the navy, or to practising realistic aerial combat, or to the creation of a fleet of adequate transport aircraft. The doctrine was carefully articulated, confidently asserted, but insufficiently tested, in theory or practice, during (or for long after) Trenchard's term of office.

Trenchard closely supervised the composition of a detailed account of the air war which reflected his own opinions and evaded all controversial issues. Sir Walter Raleigh, Merton professor of English literature at Oxford, wrote the first volume, but he died in 1922, and H. A. Jones, a civil servant who had been Raleigh's chief research assistant, completed the task. Trenchard had offered it first to Baring and then to T. E. Lawrence. Baring wrote an entertaining survey of their wartime partnership, published in 1920, but Trenchard insisted on removing most references to himself, convincing the author that it would be impossible for him to attempt a serious, independent history of the air service. As for Lawrence, although he greatly admired Trenchard, he had the confidence, personal contacts, and intellectual energy to explore those issues—strategy, tactics, equipment, training, inter-service quarrels, political interference, and so on—and make up his own mind about them. Sadly, he too turned it down. Jones left a valuable record; Lawrence might have produced a great one. Instead, we have only *The Mint*, Lawrence's account of recruit life in the early 1920s, which is as vivid and controversial as everything else he wrote.

Trenchard was knighted again (GCB) in January 1924 and became the first marshal of the RAF (equivalent to five-star rank) in 1927. He retired on 31 December 1929 and was made a baron next day. 'You are too big to be the father of a grown-up child', wrote Lawrence on 18 December. 'Let the beast go and make his own mistakes. It's going to be a very splendid service, and will always be proud of you' (Hyde, 233).

Police reformer Trenchard was appointed a director of the Goodyear Tyre and Rubber Company early in 1930 and later a director of Rhodesian Railways. In March 1931 the prime minister, Ramsay MacDonald, invited him to succeed Lord Byng as commissioner of the Metropolitan Police. Morale was held to be low throughout the force, and its organization was clearly in need of reform. He was unwilling to take on a difficult and thankless task, but did so from November, in response to a personal appeal from George V. He had the support of Sir John Anderson, permanent head of the Home Office, and Maurice Drummond, who took on Baring's role as interpreter and writer.

Trenchard made two conditions, revealing his attitude to the new job. One was that he be released at once if his 'life's work' at the Air Ministry seemed in danger; and the other was that he be released as promptly if unrest in India suggested that he would be 'more useful' there in a role for which he considered himself eminently suited—as viceroy.

While awaiting either call, Trenchard submitted to parliament a plan of reform in May 1933 which the government implemented. A police college and forensic laboratory were to be opened at Hendon, and a system of short-service engagements was to be created for a proportion of officers (who, like some young pilots, were assumed to fancy a spell at the sharp end). As in the RAF, he emphasized careful selection, thorough training, and efficient working methods, and recognized a need to widen the social base from which policemen were recruited. He showed an uncommon concern for the overall well-being of the force, rescuing the provident fund from disaster and agitating for both better housing and sporting facilities. He introduced wireless cars and a central control room to deal with the information received.

Unfortunately, Trenchard had long been an enlightened despot and could not change his ways. He issued orders and resented suggestions that he discuss them first. Most senior officers believed he wished to militarize them. He found himself at a loss in dealing with the Police Federation, a powerful and articulate union that had no counterpart in the armed services. By 1934 he was already eager to resign, but he hung on at the king's particular request until July 1935. As a reward he was made a viscount in January 1936. His successor—Sir Philip Game, his own nominee—did not press forward his reforms and most of them quickly lapsed.

Trenchard joined the board of the United Africa Company (part of the Unilever group), which had interests in Nigeria, his old stamping ground, and served as chairman from 1936 to 1953. After his death, Lord Heyworth recalled that he:

> was as interested in the views of a probationer after a first tour as of a senior executive returning from a tour of inspection. He once said that he had no use for people who were not willing to talk 'brain to brain' regardless of status. (*The Times*, 21 Feb 1956)

Backstairs agitator, privileged spectator When war broke out in September 1939, Trenchard was sixty-six: young enough, he believed, to play an important part. Throughout the 1930s he had constantly and volubly asserted the primacy of bombers over fighters, as unconvinced as ever that fighters could successfully resist them. The prime minister, Neville Chamberlain, declined Hoare's recommendation in April 1940 that Trenchard be re-appointed chief of the air staff. Churchill offered him command of Britain's home forces in May and a role in military intelligence in November. Although he wisely refused both offers, Trenchard was not inactive. In alliance with John Salmond, he agitated secretly and effectively during 1940 for the replacement of Newall as chief of the air staff and of Dowding as head of Fighter Command.

Trenchard composed a memorandum in May 1941 which completely misjudged the German character.

British morale, he believed, was secure under bombardment, but 'the German nation is peculiarly susceptible to air bombing', being unable to crack jokes while sheltering: an opinion treated with more respect than it deserved by many admirers, among them Portal, who succeeded Newall in October 1940 (Terraine, 263–4). He wrote three papers on air power issues, published by the Air Ministry in 1946, in which he insisted that the bomber remained the central instrument of air power, and a strategic air offensive the only proper function of that instrument. Most of his senior disciples eventually lapsed (in practice if not in theory) from the true faith, but not Harris, head of Bomber Command, 1942–5.

From 1942 onwards Trenchard enjoyed the role of privileged spectator and potential morale booster. He invited himself to every battlefield in the Mediterranean and north-west European theatres, relishing the deferential company of commanders whom he had encouraged in their early days—Park, Coningham, Tedder, and Douglas—receiving firsthand information about the progress of campaigns, and chatting amiably with awed young airmen. After the war, he often spoke in the House of Lords on air power issues, stoutly defending the RAF point of view, as he interpreted it, against admirals and generals. He became a member of the Order of Merit in January 1951, and received honorary doctorates from Oxford and Cambridge and many other tokens of esteem.

A valiant man In July 1920 Trenchard had married Katherine Isabel Salvin (d. 1959), daughter of Edward Salvin Bowlby and widow of Captain the Hon. James Boyle (killed in August 1914); Baring was his best man. She had three sons from her first marriage (they all served in the armed forces during the Second World War and two were killed) and two more from her second: Hugh (born in 1921), who was killed in north Africa in 1943; and Thomas (1923–1987), who succeeded as second viscount.

Trenchard was a big man, surprisingly clumsy for a successful sportsman. Ruggedly handsome, he had a thick mop of unruly dark hair, shaggy eyebrows, a moustache (which in old age gave him the appearance of a friendly walrus), a direct glance, and a famously loud voice. He had been virtually blind in his right eye since 1937, and was totally blind during the last three years of his life, nearly deaf, sadly crippled, but mentally alert until the end. He died in his London home on 10 February 1956, one week after his eighty-third birthday, and received a magnificent funeral in Westminster Abbey on 21 February. Among the pallbearers were some outstanding airmen—Portal, Tedder, Harris, and Douglas—whose careers owed much to his support. The RAF ensign flew above the abbey while the coffin containing his ashes was conveyed from the Air Ministry's assembly hall in Whitehall Gardens (where it had lain in state) and throughout the service. Overhead flew the RAF's latest strategic bomber, appropriately named Valiant.

If Trenchard 'had not taken up flying when youth had already passed him the Royal Air Force would not have been the bulwark of Britain that it was in either world war' (The Times, 11 Feb 1956; 22 Feb 1956). A bronze statue made by William McMillan and erected in Embankment Gardens, outside the Ministry of Defence, was unveiled by prime minister Harold Macmillan on 19 July 1961 and dedicated by the archbishop of Canterbury. Lord Tedder, a great airman whom Trenchard had always admired, laid a wreath on behalf of all former members of the RAF. A plaque has commemorated his birthplace since September 1973.   VINCENT ORANGE

Sources A. Boyle, Trenchard: man of vision (1962) · H. M. Hyde, British air policy between the wars, 1918–1939 (1976) · G. Lyall, 'MRAF Lord Trenchard', The war lords, ed. M. Carver (1976), 176–81 · M. Baring, RFC headquarters (1920) · Viscount Templewood (Sir Samuel Hoare), Empire of the air: the advent of the air age, 1922–1929 (1957) · W. Raleigh and H. A. Jones, The war in the air, 6 vols. (1922–37) · H. Probert, High commanders of the RAF (1991) · J. Terraine, The right of the line: the Royal Air Force in the European war (1984) · A. S. G. Lee, No parachute: a fighter pilot in World War I (1968) · E. Letley, Maurice Baring: a citizen of Europe (1991) · M. Smith, British air strategy between the wars (1984) · A. Morris, First of the many: the story of the independent force, RAF (1968) · C. G. Grey, 'On the departing chief', The Aeroplane, 37 (1929), 1402–16 · R. Johns, 'Trenchard memorial lecture', RUSI Journal, 142 (Oct 1997), 10–16 · H. A. Taylor, Fairey aircraft since 1915 (1974) · The Times (11 Feb 1956) · Lord Trenchard, Three papers on air power, Air Ministry Publication, 229 (1946)

Archives Royal Air Force Museum, Hendon, department of research and information services, corresp. and papers | BL OIOC, letters to Sir W. R. Lawrence, MS Eur. F 143 · BL OIOC, letters to Lord Reading, MSS Eur. E 238, F 118 · Bodl. Oxf., corresp. with Lord Simon · Bodl. RH, corresp. with Lord Lugard · CUL, corresp. with Samuel Hoare · HLRO, corresp. with Herbert Samuel · King's Lond., Liddell Hart C., corresp. with Sir B. H. Liddell Hart · PRO NIre., letters to Lord Londonderry · U. Glas., Archives and Business Records Centre, letters to Lord Rowallan | FILM BFI NFTVA, news footage

Likenesses F. Dodd, charcoal and watercolour drawing, 1917, IWM · W. Orpen, oils, 1917, IWM [see illus.] · W. Stoneman, two photographs, 1919–32, NPG · O. Birley, oils, c.1926, Royal Air Force Club, London · B. Partridge, chalk caricature, 1927, NPG · H. Green, pencil drawing, 1930, Royal Air Force Staff College, Bracknell, Berkshire · E. Verpilleux, oils, 1936, Royal Air Force College, Cranwell, Lincolnshire · A. R. Thomson, oils, c.1943, Royal Air Force Staff College, Bracknell, Berkshire · F. Beresford, oils, Royal Air Force Bentley Priory, Stanmore, Middlesex, HQ 11 Group · W. McMillan, bronze statue, Embankment Gardens, London; plaster statuette and bronze cast, Royal Air Force Museum, Hendon · photograph, repro. in Boyle, Trenchard, facing p. 609

Wealth at death £3576 12s. 11d.: probate, 11 May 1956, CGPLA Eng. & Wales

Trenchard, Sir John (1649–1695), politician, was born at Lytchett Matravers, near Poole, in Dorset, on 30 March 1649. His father was Thomas Trenchard (1615–1671) of Wolverton and his mother, Hannah Henley (d. 1691), was the daughter of Robert Henley of Bramshill, Hampshire. The family was strongly nonconformist and John Trenchard himself was almost certainly a nonconformist (probably a presbyterian), though a cautious one who avoided prosecution and fulfilled the legal obligations of conformity necessary to hold office. There were other radical connections, two of Trenchard's cousins having married strong supporters of Oliver Cromwell, Colonel William *Sydenham and John Slater. Trenchard himself, in November 1682, married Philip Speke [see Trenchard, Philip (1663/4–1743), under Speke, George], daughter of George *Speke, one of the most outspoken whigs in the south-west, who was to lose one son and nearly a second for participation in the 1685 rebellion.

Exclusionist At the age of fifteen, in 1665, Trenchard matriculated at New College, Oxford, and went on to a career in law, entering the Middle Temple in 1674. He became active in politics. During the Third Anglo-Dutch War he acted as one of Pierre du Moulin's agents in London, a valuable intermediary in gathering political intelligence and helping to co-ordinate the opposition to Charles's pro-French policies. He went on to win one of the borough of Taunton's seats in the first Exclusion Parliament of 1679, a seat he held in the two following elections of 1679 and 1681.

With three other members of the Trenchard family John became a member of the strongly whig and nonconformist Green Ribbon Club. He achieved prominence in the early stages of the Popish Plot, gaining a position on the thirteen-strong committee of secrecy appointed by the Commons to investigate the plot. From the plot, like many other whigs, he moved on to the more dangerous business of attempting to exclude from the succession the heir apparent, James, duke of York, on the grounds that he was a Catholic. Trenchard was one of the seventeen peers and MPs who sensationally presented York as a common popish recusant in June 1680 before the Middlesex grand jury, and in the same year it was he who moved the House of Commons' first Exclusion Bill. He was appointed to the house's committee on the bill, and argued in its third reading that concern for the nation's liberty and religion necessarily overrode any individual's personal rights, even including those of the heir to the throne: 'when a thing is *pro bono publico* we ever step over private Rights' (J. R. Jones, *The First Whigs*, 1961, 138). The high regard in which he was held is indicated by his presence on over thirty Commons committees, from which he was the reporter to the Commons on two (petitioning and the removal of Halifax).

Trenchard was among the core of twenty or so members who were regarded as supporters of the claim of the king's protestant, but illegitimate, son James, duke of Monmouth, to replace the Catholic duke of York as heir to the throne. He had little to do with the earl of Shaftesbury who headed the other, and major, branch of the whigs, which was carefully noncommittal on who should replace York as heir. Trenchard was, however, a regular attender at the King's Head tavern in Fleet Street, the whigs' London headquarters, though he also spent much time waiting on the duke of Monmouth at the latter's house in Soho. While his skills as a lawyer were one reason for Trenchard's prominence in whig circles, no less important was the radical reputation of the town which he represented. Taunton had been strongly parliamentarian during the civil war, harboured many dissenters after it, showed many marks of disrespect for church and crown well into the Restoration, and strongly supported the duke of Monmouth in his rebellion of 1685, providing one-tenth of his total manpower. Trenchard represented the town in all three Exclusion Parliaments, and in the early 1680s was just the man to stoke the fires of opposition there. He

allegedly joked that the Trenchard family had as good a claim to the throne as the family of Stuart, and vowed that the duke of Monmouth would be their general in some unnamed enterprise if the king died. He ran Taunton's (whig) Green Ribbon Club with a Quaker deputy to act in his absence, and used the publican of one of the town's inns as another agent.

Conspiracy and exile When the exclusion movement collapsed after the dissolution of the third Exclusion Parliament of 1681, and a minority of whigs in the next eighteen months began to contemplate armed resistance to the crown, Trenchard was the focus of persistent stories of arms being bought and men being listed in the Taunton area. A former Cromwellian soldier boasted in late 1681 that Trenchard had enlisted him in a troop of horse; a woman claimed to have heard Trenchard around Christmas 1682 speaking of being involved, with others, in some great and secret work; the mayor of Taunton discovered in 1683 that men in his town had been retained and supplied with strong beer to be ready at an hour's notice to fight for Trenchard and Monmouth; and Trenchard persuaded a gunsmith from the village of Trull to move to Taunton, and bought a pair of pistols and muskets from him with the remark that these would do for the king's guards. Confessions and depositions obtained after the discovery of the Rye House plot in 1683, and others following the rebellion of 1685, suggest that Trenchard on several occasions in 1682 and 1683 claimed to be able to raise some 1500 men from the Taunton area to join with other forces from London, Cheshire, and (sometimes) Scotland in ill-defined and shadowy planning for an uprising. However, despite frequent boasts that he had armed men at his disposal, when told by the plot leaders to prepare for action he pleaded that they were not yet ready, and sent word to a meeting of the conspirators in November 1682 requesting a delay of two or three weeks more for his men to make arrangements for their families. Ford, Lord Grey, one of the plotters, believed he plainly saw fear on Trenchard's face when action seemed imminent, and it seems to have been repeated delays in Taunton which made Shaftesbury in December 1682 despair of conspiracy and flee abroad to the Netherlands. There is no clear evidence that Trenchard seriously prepared for a rising, for when the government learned of the Rye House plot (allegedly to assassinate the king), and in summer 1683 launched a series of arrests and house searches, only two or three old firearms and no incriminating papers at all were found in his house, and nothing of significance in those of his Somerset friends. Investigations into talk of arms caches for sixty to eighty men and gunpowder by the barrelful found it to be nothing but talk. But though Trenchard, like most of the whigs caught up in desperate post-exclusion plotting, clearly preferred talk to action, it should be noted that when a genuine rebellion broke out in 1685 several thousand Somerset men did join up in a matter of days, and Taunton was easily the strongest centre of support for the rebel duke.

In July 1683 Trenchard was one of the many whigs arrested following the revelation of the Rye House plot.

Held in the Tower for six months and given pen and paper to make a full confession, he defended himself with considerable skill (helped by the refusal of Lord William Russell to testify against him), and he was released for lack of sufficient evidence in December 1683. With two others he was shown and commented on the draft of the duke of Monmouth's public 'confession' of December 1683, and he was given an enthusiastic welcome in Somerset towns on his way home, but his spell in the Tower had evidently chastened him. He lived quietly at his Dorset home and maintained no contact with fellow conspirators who had fled abroad. His wife was arrested at a conventicle, but not Trenchard himself. By his own account he received word of the duke of Monmouth's planned rising four days before Monmouth landed at Lyme Regis and, estimating correctly that the duke would receive no support at all from the gentry and aristocracy and that the rising would therefore fail catastrophically, he raised what money he could and prepared to leave England. The government, however, sent two privy council messengers to arrest him, and he only just escaped: some time later his father-in-law George Speke was fined 2000 marks for helping him by obstructing the messengers. Angry at the way he had deserted their cause, the rebel leaders captured after the rising, such as Ford, Lord Grey, tried in their confessions to implicate Trenchard as deeply as they could in treasonable conspiracy, while simultaneously labelling him a coward. Possibly because of these accusations his prudence in having nothing whatever to do with the rebellion did him no good with the government and he remained on the wanted list—pardons granted by James II in March 1686 did not include him.

Despairing for the moment of an early return to England Trenchard threw himself into the society of English exiles in the Netherlands, and was accepted by them with surprising ease. He was seen in the company of notorious enemies of James II, boasted that he would now play a leading role rather than see anti-government conspiracies fail yet again, and helped finance a venture to set up a cloth manufacturing business in the Netherlands to provide work for the English exiles. With some other exile leaders he toyed briefly with the idea of setting up a handsome young man who had arrived in the Netherlands from Earl Shilton, Leicestershire, as the late duke of Monmouth's 'son', but decided against trying to run such an improbable pretender. With an eye to his long-term future, however, he continued to assure government agents that he had taken part in neither the Rye House plot nor the 1685 rebellion, and in December 1687 he had his reward when he was finally granted a pardon. He returned to England and early in 1688 returned cautiously to politics. He was among those 'closeted' with James II in 1688, but like other former whigs he had no influence upon the king. The reports of James's election agents described the determination of their local whig collaborators in Taunton to have Trenchard in place as MP there in the intended forthcoming election under a newly restricted franchise. There is no evidence that he played any role in the plotting which climaxed with William of Orange's arrival at Torbay in November 1688, but once the prince was ashore Trenchard worked actively for him, raising £250 from a pair of west country clothiers.

Secretary of state Paying the price for his association with James, Trenchard was rejected by the electors of his old seat of Taunton in 1689. He sat briefly for Thetford and then (from 1690) for Poole. Between the revolution and 1690 he received a series of marks of the king's favour: comptroller of customs for Bristol, chief justice of Cheshire, recorder of Taunton, serjeant-at-law and then king's serjeant, and a knighthood. In parliament he displayed his old vigour, mastery of detail, and fluency in debate, working this time in the interest of the government. By 1693 he had been appointed to a score of parliamentary committees, at the rate of five or six per session, ranging from regulating prisons and attainting rebels to improving the poor law, repairing Dover harbour, and allowing surgeons to prescribe medicines. He managed conferences with the Lords, chaired the Commons committee on elections and privileges from 1691 to 1693, and in the latter year was three times chairman of the Commons ways and means committee. Known as a thoroughly dependable whig, it is no surprise that in the summer of 1693 Sunderland was grooming him to be one of the court managers in the Commons, with particular responsibility for the crucial business of supply.

Trenchard reached the pinnacle of his career in March 1693 when he was appointed one of the two secretaries of state. Though his was the northern (and junior) department, responsibility for naval affairs was added to his office, evidently in the hope that his drive would improve a very lacklustre war at sea against the French. His confidence in office was widely noticed, though opinion about his character was divided: Anthony Wood described him as 'a man of turbulent and aspiring spirit, never contented', though Bishop Burnet saw 'a calm and sedate man … much more moderate than could have been expected, since he was a leading man in a party' (Wood, *Ath. Oxon.*, 4.405; Burnet, 4.193–4). In addition to his naval business he set up a chain of watchers along the French channel coast, pursued Jacobites, and took an interest in Irish affairs. He had a hand in key policy matters, becoming one of the five-man cabinet council set up to take decisions during William's absences abroad. In 1693–4, however, he was involved in two government fiascos, though characteristically he emerged from each formally exonerated of any blame, and still in the government's confidence. In May 1693 a report that French warships had put to sea was not communicated to the fleet, and largely in consequence of this a convoy of merchant ships bound for Smyrna was destroyed. Two admirals and the other secretary of state were sacked, but two parliamentary inquiries found it impossible to apportion blame any further and the matter was dropped. A year later Trenchard took an active, though secondary, part in the investigation of the Lancashire plot, and once again escaped without blame when the government case ignominiously collapsed, though he may have been damaged by allegations that his agents had improperly used search warrants, planted evidence, and taken bribes. By this time he had become ill with tuberculosis, and in August and December 1694 he retired to Dorset to improve his health. He was described as very weak, pale, and thin, and by the spring of 1695 his doctors despaired of his recovery. He died on 27 April 1695 at Kensington. He was buried at Bloxworth church, Dorset, near his house at Lytchett Matravers. His wife, Philippa, lived on until 1743, dying at the age of seventy-nine. Of their four sons and three daughters only one son, George, survived to have children.   ROBIN CLIFTON

Sources R. L. Greaves, *Secrets of the kingdom: British radicals from the Popish Plot to the revolution of 1688–89* (1992) · R. Clifton, *The last popular rebellion: the western rising of 1685* (1984) · K. D. H. Haley, *The first earl of Shaftesbury* (1968) · H. Horwitz, *Parliament, policy and politics in the reign of William III* (1977) · *CSP dom., 1680–95* · *DNB* · P. Earle, *Monmouth's rebels* (1977) · T. Harris, *London crowds in the reign of Charles II* (1987) · HoP, *Commons, 1660–90* · Wood, *Ath. Oxon.*, new edn · Bishop Burnet's History · HoP, *Commons, 1690–1715* [draft] · PRO, PROB 6/71, fol. 93 [grant of administration] · Foster, *Alum. Oxon.* · M. Goldie, 'John Locke's circle and James II', *HJ*, 35 (1992), 557–86
Archives BL, letter-book, Add. MS 35855 · CKS, letter-book, U1515 · Dorset RO, corresp. and papers, D60 | BM, Add. MS 41818 · CKS, letters to first earl of Portland, PWA 1407–1426 · CKS, corresp. with Alexander Stanhope, U1590/052 · PRO, corresp. with George Stepney, SP 105/59, 60 · U. Nott. L., letters to first earl of Portland
Likenesses C. Bestland, stipple, pubd 1789 (after miniature by O. Humphry, after portrait), BM, NPG · C. Bestland, stipple, pubd 1803 (after unknown artist), BM, NPG · J. Watson, mezzotint, BM, NPG
Wealth at death approx. £5000: administration, 1695, PRO, PROB 6/71, fol. 93

Trenchard, John [*pseuds.* Cato, Diogenes] (1668/9–1723), landowner and publicist, was the first son of William Trenchard (1640–1710), landowner, of Cutteridge, Wiltshire, and his wife, Ellen, daughter of Sir George Norton of Abbots Leigh, Somerset. His nonconformist, whig father sat for Westbury in the three exclusion parliaments (1679–81) in which a distant relative, Sir John Trenchard, also sat, representing Taunton. Four decades later that same Somerset borough returned John Trenchard as an independent whig in the general election of 1722. When a student at Trinity College, Dublin—from where he received his first degree on 29 May 1685, aged sixteen—his young tutor, Edward Smith, celebrated 'Mr. Trenchard's Talent of Reasoning', a lastingly esteemed attribute (*Cato's Letters*, preface, xlix). Although a promising young barrister of the Inner Temple, first called to the bar in 1689, his legal career proved brief. With *An Argument Shewing that a Standing Army is Inconsistent with a Free Government* (1697) Trenchard initiated, after the peace of Ryswick, an eventually successful paper war against William III's standing army. In 1699 the House of Commons appointed Trenchard a commissioner of the forfeited Irish lands. When Charles Montagu, then first lord of the Treasury, wanted to take Trenchard into custody for his *Short History of Standing Armies* (1698), William refused. Gratitude for financial support from the Trenchard family at the time of the revolution of 1688 probably contributed to the monarch's decision. Trenchard was privileged from his birth into an ancient,

landed, west country family, and he fell into 'an easy Fortune' from the 'Death of an Uncle', Sir George Norton and from 'his Marriage' (*Cato's Letters*, preface, xlvii). His first wife may have been the daughter of Sir Thomas Scawen who took her own life in November 1718. The following year, on 19 November 1719, Trenchard married Anne (*d*. 15 April 1783), daughter of Sir William Blackett, bt.

Although an aggressive anti-clerical polemicist who denied the Trinity, Trenchard defended the 'Legal Church' and 'was only for pulling down those who would soar above it' (*Cato's Letters*, preface, lix). The established church was in his opinion, a necessary institution and—if committed to Christian love—a socially beneficial one. With an eye to social harmony Trenchard also defended the right of private judgement. The twentieth-century editor of his 'Essays on miracles' describes Trenchard, a Christian deist, as 'an active member of the Anglican Church' throughout his life (Séguin, *Essays*, i).

Trenchard's popular publications were those he produced in collaboration with Thomas Gordon. At the time of the Bangorian controversy Gordon wrote bitingly witty pamphlets endorsing the radical Erastianism of Benjamin Hoadly that apparently caught Trenchard's eye. Gordon always celebrated Trenchard, his 'best Tutor' (*Cato's Letters*, preface, 1), and Trenchard's wealth probably underwrote the beginning of what proved to be an unrivalled success in the annals of early journalism. The *Independent Whig*, which appeared on Wednesdays from 20 January 1720 and ran for almost a year, censured what Gordon, Trenchard, and a third contributor—perhaps Anthony Collins—considered the ubiquitous and corrupt influence of high-church clerics propagating false divinity from their sacerdotal thrones. From November 1720 until September 1722 Trenchard and Gordon submitted letters, usually under the pseudonym Cato, to the 'Author of the *London Journal*'. This new weekly paper, founded by Trenchard and whose foreign correspondents he personally paid, had first appeared in August 1719 as the *Thursday's Journal, with a Weekly Letter from Paris*, and became a Saturday publication early in 1720. The government, frequently vexed at the *London Journal*, finally took it over at the time of the Atterbury conspiracy, just as a letter on standing armies by Trenchard was scheduled to appear. Thereafter, and until 'Cato's Farewell' on 27 July 1723, Trenchard and Gordon sent their letters to the 'Author of the *British Journal*', the *British Journal* being a new weekly that they had started themselves. The Wednesday *Whig* and the Saturday missive enjoyed immediate success, and repeated book-form printings of the *Independent Whig* and *Cato's Letters* during the eighteenth century, speak of an enduring reputation. Readers on both sides of the Atlantic and in the salons of continental *philosophes* found in these publications resonant rhetoric to sound their own causes. Trenchard and Gordon addressed a contemporary context with a strategically deployed discourse that is confined by any presumed distinction between civic republicanism and liberalism. A contemporary's remark about the use of *Cato's Letters* after 1725 as being 'equally quoted by the Advocates and Opposers of Sir R. W. [Robert Walpole]' may serve to encourage further reflection on Cato's signifying practices and the variety of reader responses to 'his' texts (Ralph, 505).

The early essays, appearing just after the plummet of South Sea stock, decried the earl of Sunderland's administration with fit charges of malfeasance and urged angry citizens to call for stern retribution. Severe punishment, argued Cato, would vindicate the natural rights that people had first entered into political society to preserve and would confirm government in its proper role as a trust 'to watch for the Security, and pursue the Interest of All' (*London Journal*, 90, 15 April 1721). Given their profound pessimism about human nature, Trenchard and Gordon challenged any celebration of disinterested virtue. Cato thus exhorted the people, whose interests had been betrayed, to demand legal revenge while members of parliament, whose interests lay in popular policies, were expected to punish the people's betrayers. But Trenchard and Gordon also feared seditious exploitation of righteous anger. Their exhortations were to some extent a strategic deployment of loyalist, libertarian rhetoric to check Jacobitism. Cato's vivid depictions of absolute monarchy also suggest an effort to channel warranted anger along loyal, legal paths grounded in rights theory, articulated in part to counteract those who, Trenchard and Gordon sincerely believed, claimed a divine right to dominion. Trenchard, especially, called for control over the universities and charity schools, which he considered deeply disaffected institutions in the hands of restless rebels to a free state. The Middlesex grand jury condemned Trenchard's 'Of charity, and charity-schools' (*British Journal*, 39, 15 June 1723) as well as three other Cato letters and Bernard Mandeville's *Fable of the Bees* for depicting 'religion and virtue as prejudicial to society, and detrimental to the state' (Gordon, *Cordial*, 2.253). The anti-clerical Trenchard did, indeed, deem clericalism a mental tyranny spelling a civil one. The *British Journal* had advertised the *Fable* and, after Cato's farewell, Gordon and Mandeville published there as Diogenes, a pseudonym that Trenchard used for his more speculative essays. Trenchard only sat in the first session of the second septennial parliament between 1722 and 1723. His brief role there included opposing the suspension of habeas corpus and Walpole's proposal to remit the South Sea Company's debt; a successful motion to impose fines on nonjurors for their presumed sedition; and a vexatious call for attainder against one of the Atterbury conspirators. A well-built but not particularly healthy person, John Trenchard died from a kidney ailment on 16 December 1723 at his residence in Abbots Leigh; the parish church there, where he was buried, holds a monumental Latin inscription to his memory. His three sisters were his heirs. After Trenchard's death, his wife, Anne, married his collaborator, Thomas Gordon.

MARIE MCMAHON

Sources T. Gordon, preface, in *Cato's letters, or, Essays on liberty, civil and religious, and other important subjects*, 3rd edn, 4 vols. (1733), xxx–lx · T. Gordon, *A cordial for low spirits: being a collection of curious tracts*, ed. R. Barron, 3rd edn, 2 (1763), iii, 251–4 · R. Hamowy, foreword, in *The English libertarian heritage: from the writings of John Trenchard and Thomas Gordon in 'The Independent Whig' and 'Cato's letters'*, ed. D. L. Jacobson (San Francisco, CA, 1994) · E. Cruickshanks, 'Trenchard, John', HoP, *Commons, 1715–54* · J. Trenchard and T. Gordon, *A collection of tracts*, 2 (1751), 226–31 · J. Sutherland, *The Restoration newspaper and its development* (1986) · L. G. Schwoerer, *No standing armies! The antiarmy ideology in seventeenth-century England* (1974) · M. McMahon, *The radical whigs, John Trenchard and Thomas Gordon: libertarian loyalists to the new house of Hanover* (1990) · S. Burtt, *Virtue transformed: political argument in England, 1688–1740* (1992), 64–86 · J. A. I. Champion, *The pillars of priestcraft shaken: the Church of England and its enemies, 1660–1730* (1992) · J. A. R. Séguin, *A bibliography of John Trenchard (1662–1723)* (1965) · C. Realey, 'The *London Journal* and its authors, 1720–1723', *Bulletin of the University of Kansas*, 36/23 (1935), 237–74 · S. Pincus, 'Neither Machiavellian moment nor possessive individualism: commercial society and the defenders of the English Commonwealth', *American Historical Review*, 103 (1998), 705–36 · A. Cromartie, 'Harringtonian virtue: Harrington, Machiavelli, and the method of the moment', *HJ*, 41 (1998), 987–1009 · D. R. Lacey, *Dissent and parliamentary politics in England, 1661–1689* (1969) · *N&Q*, 2nd ser., 11 (1861), 215 · *The manuscripts of his grace the duke of Portland*, 10 vols., HMC, 29 (1891–1931) · J. A. R. Séguin, ed., *John Trenchard: essays on miracles* (1964) · [J. Ralph], *A critical history of the administration of Sir Robert Walpole* (1743) · J. M. Bulloch, 'Thomas Gordon, the 'Independent Whig': a biographical bibliography', *University of Aberdeen Library Bulletin*, 3 (Nov 1915–May 1918), 598–612, 733–49

Wealth at death est. £4000: Gordon, 'Preface', *Cato's letters*

Trenchard, Philip (1663/4–1743). *See under* Speke, George (1623–1689).

Trend, Burke Frederick St John, Baron Trend (1914–1987), civil servant, was born on 2 January 1914 in Greenwich, London, the only child of Walter David St John Trend, journalist, and his wife, Marian Gertrude Tyers. He was educated at Whitgift School and at Merton College, Oxford. He obtained first classes in both classical honour moderations (1934) and *literae humaniores* (1936).

In 1936 Trend passed into the civil service and was appointed to the Ministry of Education. A year later he was transferred to the Treasury, where he remained, with a brief interruption, for twenty-five years. His first years at the Treasury were spent on work relating to defence. In 1939, shortly after the outbreak of war, he became assistant private secretary to the chancellor of the exchequer, under Sir John Simon and Sir Kingsley Wood. In 1941, on promotion, Trend returned to dealing with the problems of defence equipment. After the war he again served the chancellor of the exchequer's private office as principal private secretary (1945–9), first to Hugh Dalton and later to Sir Stafford Cripps. During this time the Treasury had the tasks of returning to peacetime levels of expenditure, carrying the reorganization of the civil service, and handling the Labour government's economic policies of Keynesianism and nationalization.

In 1949 Trend became an under-secretary at the Treasury and assumed responsibility for the home finance division, and in 1953 he moved to the central economic planning staff. His Treasury service was interrupted in 1955 for a year in the office of the lord privy seal, then R. A. Butler, followed by three years (1956–9) as deputy secretary to the cabinet, the secretary to the cabinet then being Sir Norman Brook. Much of the day-to-day running of the affairs of the cabinet secretariat was Trend's responsibility. He

Burke Frederick St John Trend, Baron Trend (1914–1987), by Elliott & Fry, 1962

returned to the Treasury in 1959 as third secretary and became second secretary a year later. On Brook's retirement at the end of 1962, he became secretary to the cabinet.

In this capacity Trend served under four prime ministers, Harold Macmillan, Alec Douglas-Home, Harold Wilson, and Edward Heath, and proved himself a civil servant who ably gave an independent, balanced brief to his political masters regardless of their party colour. In particular he accepted responsibility for keeping them informed and advised on all nuclear matters, both civil and military, and maintained contacts on their behalf at the highest level with other governments involved. He also played a major part in organizing the Commonwealth conferences in conjunction with the cabinet secretaries of other member countries. His activities reflected Britain's position in the Commonwealth. He retired in 1973.

An interesting side to Trend's service in the Treasury is that from his early days he undertook the work of the accounting office for the secret vote. His responsibility was to secure value for money in expenditure on MI5 and MI6, but at the same time to ensure the safeguarding of these services. This experience was put to good use in 1974–5, when Trend carried out an official investigation into allegations that Sir Roger *Hollis had been an agent for the Soviet Union. He was unable to reach a definite decision.

In 1974 Trend became a life peer. Between 1973 and 1983

he was rector of Lincoln College, Oxford, and from 1975 to 1983 a pro-vice-chancellor of the university. He served as chairman of the trustees of the British Museum from 1979 to 1986 and was a member of the Advisory Council on Public Records (1974–82). He died holding three other prominent offices: chairman of the managing trustees of the Nuffield Foundation (from 1980), president of the Royal Commonwealth Society (from 1982), and high bailiff of Westminster Abbey and searcher of the sanctuary (from 1983), where during the Second World War he had been a fire-watcher.

Trend had a formidable intellect which he used to penetrate at once to the heart of any problem. At the same time he possessed a constructive and positive approach, which could set out with absolute clarity the possible alternative courses of action in any given situation. His minutes of meetings recorded the proceedings and conclusions with precision and accuracy. He never gave the least indication to those present, either by word or by facial expression, of his personal views or feelings. Tall and serious, he responded to the humour of others but seldom followed it up with his own. Everyone who dealt with him knew that in all circumstances his conduct would undeniably be correct. If to some outsiders he may have appeared somewhat strait-laced in Whitehall, at Oxford it was apparent to everyone that he was thoroughly enjoying himself. With an unchallengeable academic record from his undergraduate years he could hold his own in any assembly. At the same time he was completely relaxed in the company of young people, stimulating them with his conversation and sharing his views with theirs. If in Whitehall it was sometimes said that Trend tended to be academic in his approach, at Oxford he was regarded as very much a man of the world.

Trend was appointed CVO (1953), CB (1955), KCB (1962), and GCB (1968). He was sworn of the privy council in 1972 and became an honorary fellow of Merton College in 1964. He was given honorary degrees by Oxford (DCL, 1969), St Andrews (LLD, 1974), and Loughborough (DLitt, 1984).

In 1949 Trend married Patricia Charlotte, daughter of the Revd Gilbert Shaw, by profession a barrister and later a priest. They had a daughter and two sons, one of whom, Michael, was elected MP for Windsor and Maidenhead at the general election of 1992. Trend died on 21 July 1987 at his London home, 102 Rochester Row. A memorial service was held in Westminster Abbey on 20 October 1987.

EDWARD HEATH, rev.

Sources The Times (22 July 1987) · The Times (20 Oct 1987) · The Independent (24 July 1987) · personal knowledge (1996) · private information (1996) · CGPLA Eng. & Wales (1988)

Archives Bodl. Oxf., corresp. with Attlee

Likenesses Elliott & Fry, photograph, 1962, NPG [see illus.] · photograph, repro. in The Independent

Wealth at death £129,219: probate, 13 Jan 1988, CGPLA Eng. & Wales

Trengrouse, Henry (1772–1854), inventor of life-saving apparatus, was born at Helston, Cornwall, on 18 March 1772, the son of Nicholas Trengrouse (1739–1814) and his wife, Mary Williams (d. 1784). The family had long been the principal freeholders in Helston. Henry was educated at Helston grammar school, and lived in the town all his life. He was a close friend of the Wesleyan preacher, Samuel Drew. On 24 December 1807 he witnessed the wreck of the frigate *Anson* in Mount's Bay, when over a hundred lives were lost, and this disaster led him to devote his life and inheritance to the discovery of some means for saving the lives of shipwrecked seafarers. His first thought was to devise a lifeboat, but when his efforts produced no satisfactory results, he turned his attention to life-saving apparatus.

As early as 1791 Lieutenant John Bell had devised an apparatus for throwing a line to ships from the shore and, concurrently with Trengrouse, Captain George William Manby was engaged in perfecting an apparatus very similar to Bell's. The idea occurred to Manby in February 1807, and in August he exhibited some experiments to the members of the Suffolk Humane Society. He sought to establish communication between the shore and the shipwreck by means of a line fastened to a barbed shot which was fired from a mortar on the shore. By means of this line a hawser was drawn out from the shore to the ship, and along it was run a cradle in which the shipwrecked persons were landed. This invention had been recommended by various committees, and adopted to some extent before 1814. Trengrouse's apparatus, designed in 1808, was similar to Manby's in the use of the line and hawser, but was fired by a rocket fitted to an adapted musket, and a chair was used instead of a cradle. The advantages were that the rocket was much lighter and more portable than the mortar, the cost was much smaller, and there was little risk of the line breaking, because the velocity of a rocket increases gradually, whereas that of a shot fired from a mortar was so great and sudden that the line was frequently broken. Trengrouse's apparatus could, moreover, be packed in a chest 4¼ feet by 1½ feet, and carried on board ship. When stranded, the crew could therefore begin their own rescue, without having to depend on a shore party being available.

It was not, however, until 28 February 1818, after many journeys to London, that Trengrouse could demonstrate his apparatus to Admiral Sir Charles Rowley. A committee was appointed, and on 5 March it reported

> that Mr. Trengrouse's mode appears to be the best that has been suggested for the purpose of saving lives from shipwreck by gaining a communication with the shore; and, so far as the experiments went, it most perfectly answered what was proposed. ('Letter reporting … Trengrouse's invention', 21.361)

It was also suggested that a specimen apparatus should be placed in every dockyard that naval officers might become familiar with its working (ibid.). In the same year a committee of the elder brethren of Trinity House also reported in its favour, and recommended that it should be carried on all vessels. The government ordered twenty sets, but afterwards preferred to have them constructed by the Ordnance department, and paid Trengrouse £50 compensation. In 1821 the Society of Arts awarded him their large silver medal and 30 guineas for the invention.

Alexander I of Russia personally wrote to Trengrouse, presented him with a diamond ring in recognition of the usefulness of his apparatus, and invited him to Russia, but apart from the prize awarded by the Society of Arts and the compensation paid by the government, Trengrouse reaped no pecuniary reward from his invention. An improved rocket was later invented by John Dennett in 1826, another by Colonel Boxer in 1855. The rocket completely superseded the mortar, and became an essential part of the operation of saving lives from shipwrecks.

Trengrouse died at Helston on 14 February 1854, survived by his wife, Mary (1772–1863), daughter of Samuel Jenken, three sons and five daughters.

A. F. POLLARD, rev. R. C. COX

Sources GM, 1st ser., 89/1 (1819), 559–60 · GM, 1st ser., 92/2 (1822), 71 · ILN (23 Oct 1854) · *Encyclopaedia Britannica*, 9th edn (1875–89) · Boase & Courtney, *Bibl. Corn.* · 'Trengrouse, Nicholas', G. C. Boase, *Collectanea Cornubiensis: a collection of biographical and topographical notes relating to the county of Cornwall* (1890) · private information (1898) · 'Letter reporting the results of inspection of Henry Trengrouse's invention', *Parl. papers* (1825), 21.361, no. 415 · 'Report … on experiments at Woolwich', *Parl. papers* (1810–11), 11.111, no. 215 · 'Papers relating to Captain Manby's plan for saving the lives of shipwrecked mariners', *Parl. papers* (1813–14), 11.417–51, no. 48 · J. Bell, 'Some further observations made by Lieutenant Bell upon the application of the mortars intended for threwing a line on shore, in case of a ship being stranded', *Transactions, Society of Arts*, 25 (1807), 139–42 · 'Papers relating to Captain Manby's plan for relief in cases of shipwreck', *Parl. papers* (1816), 19.193–227, no. 409 · H. Trengrouse, 'Apparatus for saving lives in case of shipwreck', *Transactions, Society of Arts*, 38 (1820), 161–5

Archives Cornwall RO, corresp., papers, and journals

Trent. For this title name *see* Boot, Jesse, first Baron Trent (1850–1931); Boot, Florence Annie, Lady Trent (1863–1952); Boot, John Campbell, second Baron Trent (1889–1956).

Tresham, Francis (1567?–1605), conspirator, was the eldest son of Sir Thomas *Tresham (1543–1605) of Rushton, Northamptonshire, and his wife, Meriel Throckmorton (d. 1615), daughter of Sir Robert Throckmorton of Coughton, Warwickshire. Anthony Wood in *Athenae Oxonienses* maintains that he studied at St John's College, Oxford, or Gloucester Hall, 'or both', but there seems to be no corroborating evidence (Wood, *Ath. Oxon.*, 754). In 1593 he married Anne Tufton, elder daughter of Sir John Tufton of Hothfield, Kent. The Jesuit Father John Gerard hints at flaws in Tresham's character; another Jesuit closely involved with the English Catholic families of the time, Oswald Tesimond, generally kinder in his assessments, thought Tresham 'a man of sound judgement. He knew how to look after himself, but was not much to be trusted' (Edwards, 108). At all events, he was long an associate of his cousin Robert *Catesby—their mothers were sisters—and of the brothers John and Christopher Wright, all subsequently conspirators in the Gunpowder Plot.

Tresham was one of the Catholic gentlemen who followed the earl of Essex into rebellion on 8 February 1601. He was among those left by Essex to guard their prisoner, the lord keeper, Sir Thomas Egerton, in Essex House on the afternoon of that tumultuous day. Along with his colleagues, Tresham was arrested and imprisoned, first in the

White Lion, Southwark, and then in the Tower. Freedom cost his father 3000 marks, Tresham being released on 21 June. This ugly experience did not prevent him dabbling in further treasons: he was involved in representations to the king of Spain fronted by Thomas Winter, Guy *Fawkes, and Christopher Wright in 1602 and 1603. Nevertheless, his friends by now had their doubts about Tresham's commitment to the extreme courses they were considering, and they did not trust him with the secret of the Gunpowder Plot until 14 October 1605 (PRO, SP 14/16/63). Sir Thomas Tresham had died in the previous month, and Catesby clearly took this decision with an eye on Francis's newly acquired property, hoping that this wealth could help finance the conspirators' schemes. Although Sir Thomas's debts amounted to more than £11,000, the long-established Rushton estates, among the most prosperous in Northamptonshire, were valued at over £3000 per annum.

Here Catesby made a grave mistake; Tresham had no stomach for the enterprise. He appears to have gone at once into Northamptonshire, shutting up Rushton Hall and taking his family to London. This visit may have provided an opportunity to conceal his muniments in a walled-up closet near the great hall where, more than 220 years later, they were rediscovered by workmen making alterations. Again and again Tresham urged his friends to abandon their scheme. Guy Fawkes says that he was concerned for the safety of Catholic peers attending parliament, and Catesby's airy assurances that the lives of their noble friends would somehow be preserved failed to convince.

Tresham's dilemma was acute. Pressured, and at times openly threatened, by long-standing friends, he was at the same time aware of the immense risks being run, and the probable ruin of himself and every English Catholic should the plot miscarry. Although he never admitted it— the fact would hardly have counted in his favour—Tresham almost certainly wrote the disguised letter to his brother-in-law William *Parker, Lord Monteagle, which, thanks to Monteagle's loyalty or instinct for self-preservation, revealed the conspiracy to the authorities. Another cousin and conspirator, Thomas Winter, clearly suspected as much. Fawkes, in his declaration of 16 November, recalled that Catesby and Winter had told him how Tresham had been 'exceeding earnest' to 'have [Monteagle] warned to be absent from the Parlament' (PRO, SP 14/216/100). Early in November, Winter and Catesby taxed Tresham with the deed at the point of a dagger, and were only half convinced by his anguished protestations of innocence. Tresham salved his conscience by insisting that so far as he could tell, the conspirators had decided to halt their operations as a result of his prompting and his money. At his 'chamber in Clerkenwell' he paid over £190 to Winter, for Catesby's use 'acording to a former agreement between them', in the fortnight before 5 November (PRO, SP 14/216/116). As he himself put it, 'the silence that I used was only to deliver my self from that infamous brand of an accuser, and to save his life which in

all true rules I was bound to do.' He had aimed, he said, 'not only to free his majesty and the state from this present treason, but to shipe them all away that they might have no meanes left them to contrive any more' (PRO, SP 14/16/63). It was, if true, a perilous game, and Tresham knew it. Driven on by his fears, he secured a licence to travel abroad for two years, with servants and horses, granted on 2 November 1605.

Upon the discovery of the treason, Tresham adopted an attitude of innocence. With the extent of the midlands rising still uncertain, and with preparations being made in London against a widespread Catholic revolt, he offered his services against any rebels (Stow, *Annales*, 879–80). On 8 November William Waad, lieutenant of the Tower of London, mentioned in a letter to Salisbury that 'there is one Tresham about the town that was a longue tyme pentioner to the king of Spain, and many others of that crew that would be observed' (PRO, SP 14/216/48B), but it was only when Guy Fawkes—who had never met him and who relied upon what he had heard from Catesby and Winter—named Tresham as a conspirator on 9 November that these suspicions received confirmation. According to Stow, Tresham was committed to the Tower on 12 November. At his first examination he provided a string of evasive answers, but on the following day he set down in his own hand a long account of his efforts to frustrate Catesby's design.

Tresham was, however, past saving, patently guilty of, at the very least, concealment of treason, or misprision. Further examination of other suspects revealed the dark secrets of his past, and by the end of November he was admitting his involvement in the negotiations between English Catholics and the court of Philip III in 1602–3. Like every other prisoner, with the early exception of Guy Fawkes, Tresham was well treated in the Tower. Early in December, however, his health began to deteriorate. The earl of Salisbury described Tresham's complaint as a 'natural sickness, such as he hath been a long time subject to' (*Memorials of Affairs of State … Collected … from the Original Papers of Sir Ralph Winwood*, ed. E. Sawyer, 3 vols., 1725, 2.189). This was almost certainly a strangury. His lingering, painful end was documented at length by his trusted servant William Vavasour, who along with Tresham's wife and a nurse, Joan Sisor, had regular access to the stricken man. The attorney-general Sir Edward Coke, in a list of questions prepared for other conspirators, suggested that Vavasour was thought to be 'Sir Thomas Tresham's base son', but no evidence survives to support this hostile theory (Hatfield House, MS 115/18).

Around the same time, Coke searched Tresham's chambers at the Inner Temple and found there two copies of a Jesuit 'Treatise on equivocation'. He set to work cataloguing the legal and moral pitfalls inherent in equivocation, but appears never to have established that the work was in fact from Henry Garnett's pen. In his last hours, Tresham himself resorted to equivocation, and retracted certain statements he had made implicating Jesuits in the Spanish treason. *Inter alia*, he insisted that he had not seen

Garnett in sixteen years, a manifest falsehood. This assertion, in the very presence of death itself, greatly annoyed and perplexed the investigators.

Tresham died in the Tower early in the morning of 23 December, and was buried there. It suited the government's purposes to interpret his crime as treason. He was attainted along with the other plotters (*Statutes of the Realm*, 4.1068–9), his head was displayed at Northampton, and his lands were forfeited. Tresham was survived by two young daughters—Lucy (1598–1665) and Elizabeth. Lucy became a nun in Brussels; Elizabeth married Sir George Heneage of Hainton, Lincolnshire. Lucy's twin brother, Thomas, had died in 1599. Many of the Tresham lands in Northamptonshire had been entailed by Sir Thomas in 1584, and were inherited—despite the attainder—by Tresham's brother Lewis (*d.* 1639), but Lewis was extravagant and reckless, and the family's economic decline gathered pace. By 1614 the Rushton estate had passed to William Cokayne, in whose family it remained until the nineteenth century. A baronet of the original creation, Lewis was knighted on 9 April 1612. He married in 1603 María Pérez de Recalde, granddaughter of Martín Pérez de Recalde, viceroy of the West Indies, and a stepdaughter of John Moore, alderman of London, and was succeeded in 1639 by their only son, William (*d.* 1643), the second, and last, baronet. MARK NICHOLLS

Sources PRO, SP 14/16 and 216 · Thomas Winter's confession in respect of the Gunpowder Plot, Hatfield House, Salisbury (Cecil) MS 113/54 · M. E. Finch, *The wealth of five Northamptonshire families, 1540–1640*, Northamptonshire RS, 19 (1956) · J. Wake, ed., 'The death of Francis Tresham', *Northamptonshire Past and Present*, 2 (1954–9), 31–41 · *The condition of Catholics under James I: Father Gerard's narrative of the Gunpowder Plot*, ed. J. Morris (1871) · A. E. Malloch, 'Father Henry Garnet's treatise of equivocation', *Recusant History*, 15 (1979–81), 387–95 · A. J. Loomie, 'Guy Fawkes in Spain: the "Spanish treason" in Spanish documents', *BIHR*, special suppl., 9 (1971) [whole issue] · M. Nicholls, *Investigating Gunpowder Plot* (1991) · *The Gunpowder Plot: the narrative of Oswald Tesimond alias Greenway*, ed. and trans. F. Edwards (1973) · Wood, *Ath. Oxon.*, new edn, 1.754–5 · A. Luders and others, eds., *Statutes of the realm*, 11 vols. in 12, RC (1810–28) · J. Stow and E. Howes, *Annales, or, A generall chronicle of England … unto the end of this present yeere, 1631* (1631)

Archives BL, family papers, Add. MSS 39828–39838

Likenesses stipple and line engraving, NPG; repro. in Caulfield, *History of the gunpowder plot* (1804)

Tresham, Henry (*bap.* 1750/51, *d.* 1814), history painter and art dealer, was born in Ireland, but his parentage, and precisely where and when he was born, are so far unknown. On his election to the Royal Academy in 1799 Tresham appears to have given his date of baptism as '21 February 1750 or 1751, in Dublin', while Farington, who recorded Tresham's age in 1794 as forty-six (Farington, *Diary*, 1.135), stated after Tresham's death in 1814 that he was born on 24 February 1750 (ibid., 13.4548). Tresham studied in the Dublin Society's drawing school from 1765 and exhibited with the society between 1768 and 1775. Years later he told Farington that he was 'in great repute in Dublin … for drawing heads', but 'lamented not having practised the mechanical part of painting before He went to Italy' (ibid., 3.1016).

In 1775 Tresham left for Italy, resolved to concentrate on history painting, and by September 1775 had rooms in the middle of the artist colony in Rome. He remained in Rome for thirteen years, increasingly more active as a dealer than as a painter. Occasionally he joined Thomas Jones and Henry Pars in 1777 on sketching excursions in and around Rome, but even on these his instinct to deal was uppermost, as when he bought the antique frescoes in the newly excavated Villa Negroni ('to be taken off the walls at his Own Expence'), selling them within weeks at a large profit to that avid collector Frederick Augustus Hervey, bishop of Derry (Oppé, *Memoirs of Thomas Jones*, 62). Ever the opportunist, Tresham gave 'a grand Entertainment to a large Company' in Rome in January 1780, to celebrate the news of the bishop of Derry's succession to the title of fourth earl of Bristol (ibid., 93).

Tresham's most rewarding patron from 1783 was Colonel John Campbell (later first Baron Cawdor), with whom he travelled in Sicily, 1783–4, and for whom he made landscape drawings, bought pictures and antiquities, and, in particular, acted as Campbell's agent with Canova. Campbell marked the association by commissioning from Hugh Douglas Hamilton *c.*1788–9 a remarkable pastel, *Antonio Canova in his Studio with Henry Tresham and a Plaster Model for 'Cupid and Psyche'* (exh. RA, 1791; V&A). Tresham also acted in Italy as agent for many other collectors, including Frederick Howard, fifth earl of Carlisle, who settled an annuity of £300 on him for life. He was still profiting from sales from his own collection of Etruscan vases in 1809.

Tresham completed several historical paintings in Rome (some sold to the earl bishop, none now known) and some portraits, as well as various weakly Fuseliesque allegorical drawings, such as *A Knight, a Woman and other Figures Cowering from a Serpent in a Cave* (V&A), of which Iolo Williams remarked that 'it is easier to say that it represents something very terrible than to identify the subject exactly' (Williams, 128). More documentarily interesting is a watercolour of an archaeological site (priv. coll.; reproduced in Crookshank and knight of Glin), perhaps depicting Tresham himself as the gentleman-predator who watches anxiously as antique works are hauled into the world of modern dealing. In 1784 he published a volume of eighteen weak but extravagantly mannered aquatints entitled *Le avventure di Saffo*, inspired by Conte Alessandro Verri's *Le avventure di Saffo poetessa di Mitilene*, 1780. On returning to England in 1789 he sent twelve works to that year's Royal Academy exhibition (mostly historical paintings, but also including *A View of Mount Etna from Catania*). From addresses at 9 George Street, Hanover Square, and later 20 Brook Street, London, he continued until 1806 to exhibit paintings mostly drawn from classical or British history, frigid in style and wan in colour. Few of these won praise, but in the 1790s he was commissioned by Robert Bowyer for twenty-four paintings (an example is *The Earl of Warwick Justifies the Title to his Estate*; Manchester City Galleries) to be engraved for David Hume's *History of England*, and by John Boydell for two or three subjects for the *Shakspeare Gallery*. Between 1796 and 1810 Tresham published five volumes of indifferent verse. In London he continued to operate as dealer and agent, notably for William Beckford, for whom he made important purchases, including, in 1799, the two Altieri Claudes.

Tresham was elected an associate of the Royal Academy in 1791 and a member in 1799, and was appointed professor of painting in the Royal Academy Schools in 1807, resigning in 1809 because of failing health. He appears to have been something of a cold fish, neither liked nor wholly trusted by his fellow academicians. Farington recorded that 'Shee [Martin Archer-Shee] said He was a weak man, vain, of no judgment, and acted at the instigation of anybody he happens to associate with' (Farington, *Diary*, 5 Jan 1800). Tresham is not known to have married. After some years of unspecified illness, he died on 17 June 1814 in Bond Street, London. He was buried on 29 June.

JUDY EGERTON

Sources A. P. Oppé, ed., 'Memoirs of Thomas Jones, Penkerrig, Radnorshire', *Walpole Society*, 32 (1946–8) [whole issue] · N. Figgis, 'Irish portrait and subject painters in Rome, 1750–1800', *GPA Irish Arts Review Yearbook*, 5 (1988), 125–36, esp. 128–9, 132 · J. Ingamells, ed., *A dictionary of British and Irish travellers in Italy, 1701–1800* (1997) · N. L. Pressly, *The Fuseli circle in Rome: early Romantic art of the 1770s* (New Haven, CT, 1979) [exhibition catalogue, Yale U. CBA, 12 Sept – 11 Nov 1979] · A. Crookshank and the Knight of Glin [D. Fitzgerald], *The watercolours of Ireland: works on paper in pencil, pastel and paint, c.1600–1914* (1994) · I. O. Williams, *Early English watercolours and some cognate drawings by artists born not later than 1785* (1952) · Farington, *Diary*, 1.135; 3.1016; 4.1344; 13.4548 · directory of membership, RA
Archives Bodl. Oxf., letters to William Beckford
Likenesses H. D. Hamilton, double portrait, oils, exh. RA 1791 (with Antonio Canova), V&A · A. Cardon, stipple, pubd 1814 (after drawing by A. Pope), BM, NPG, NG Ire.; repro. in T. Cadell and W. Davies, *Contemporary portraits* (1822) · G. Dance, drawing, RA · S. Freeman, stipple (after J. Opie), BM; repro. in *Monthly Mirror* (1809) · Mrs D. Tuner, etching (after G. Chinnery), BM, NPG

Tresham, Sir Thomas (d. 1471), administrator and speaker of the House of Commons, was the son of William *Tresham (d. 1450) of Sywell and Rushton, Northamptonshire, and his wife, Isabel, daughter of Sir William Vaux of Harrowden. No doubt his early advancement owed much to his father's influence. In 1443 he shared in William Tresham's appointment to the stewardship and chancellorship of the duchy of Lancaster's estates in those counties in which their family had most interests—Northamptonshire, Buckinghamshire, Bedfordshire, and Huntingdonshire. By 1446 Thomas Tresham was an esquire of Henry VI's hall and chamber: it is his Lancastrian allegiance on the grounds that he had been brought up 'from childhood' in Henry's court. By 1455 he had become an usher of the king's chamber. He was appointed a Huntingdonshire justice of the peace (1446–59) and member of parliament, first for Buckinghamshire (1447), then for Huntingdonshire (1449, twice). In spite of their links with the court, the Treshams had contact enough with Richard, duke of York (d. 1460), to go to meet him on his return from Ireland in 1450; shortly after they had left Sywell on 23 September they were set upon, William Tresham being murdered and Thomas wounded.

Once the court began to regain some ground after its setbacks in 1450, local appointments for Tresham resumed: he was sheriff of Cambridgeshire and Huntingdonshire

(1451–2), justice of the peace (1452–60) and member of parliament (1453), both for Northamptonshire, and commissioner of oyer and terminer in 1453 for the disturbances in north Yorkshire. In January 1454 he was a sponsor of an abortive bill to establish a garrison at Windsor to protect the incapacitated king—as distinct from his 'protection' by the duke of York, upon whom such a measure was doubtless intended to be a reflection. He was probably at the first battle of St Albans on 22 May 1455, and was at first denounced as a principal instigator of the violence, but was ultimately spared Yorkist retaliation. As the court recovered its authority after 1456, offices crowded upon Tresham: he was sheriff of Cambridgeshire and Huntingdonshire again (1457–8), then of Surrey and Sussex (1458–9), but was also elected (probably for Northamptonshire) to the Coventry parliament of 1459. This assembly, packed especially for the attainder of Yorkists, chose him to be its speaker; in reward for his services the crown granted him £40 yearly from rents forfeited by York. He was then appointed to numerous anti-Yorkist commissions of oyer and terminer. Some time before March 1461 he became comptroller of the royal household.

Tresham probably fought at the battle of Northampton on 10 July 1460, but later denied the distinction (peculiarly objectionable to Yorkists) of fighting at Wakefield on 30 December. In January 1461 he had joined Margaret of Anjou by the time she reached Durham, and was then at the second battle of St Albans (where he was knighted) on 17 February, and at Towton on 29 March. Before the latter battle he was one of those on whose head Edward IV put a price of £100. In the event, although captured and attainted, he only suffered forfeiture. He secured a general pardon in 1464, was restored to the Northamptonshire peace commission, and in 1467 again represented the county in parliament. He petitioned Edward IV and negotiated with the beneficiaries of his forfeiture (allegedly pledging 2000 marks) for the return of his 'livelihood', with only partial success. Perhaps as a result he became involved in the Lancastrian intrigues of John de Vere, thirteenth earl of Oxford, and was imprisoned in the Tower of London from November 1468 until Henry VI's readeption in 1470. Rewarded then with grants that included the honour and castle of Huntingdon, all to be held for seven years, Tresham probably served in the readeption parliament as member for the seventh time, and as speaker for the second. In April 1471 he joined Margaret of Anjou at Weymouth and was individually denounced as a traitor in Edward's proclamations. With Edmund Beaufort, duke of Somerset, and others he vainly sought sanctuary in Tewkesbury Abbey after the battle on 4 May 1471, and was beheaded on 6 May. He was buried in Tewkesbury Abbey church. Before 1460 Tresham had married Margaret Lenthall (d. 1483/4), sister of William, Lord Zouche. His heir, John, secured the reversal of his father's attainder and forfeiture on Henry VII's accession in 1485.

JULIAN LOCK

Sources J. S. Roskell, 'Sir Thomas Tresham', *Northamptonshire Past and Present*, 2 (1954–9), 313–23; repr. in *Parliament and politics in late medieval England*, 2 (1981), 267–77 · *CPR, 1232–1509* · R. Jeffs, 'The later medieval sheriff and the royal household: a study in administrative change and political control, 1437–1547', DPhil diss., U. Oxf., 1960 • J. R. Lander, 'Attainder and forfeiture, 1453–1509', *HJ*, 4 (1961), 119–51; repr. in *Crown and nobility, 1450–1509* (1976), 127–58 • K. Dockray, ed., *Three chronicles of the reign of Edward IV* (1988) • *The Paston letters, AD 1422–1509*, ed. J. Gairdner, new edn, 6 vols. (1904) • J. S. Roskell, 'William Tresham of Sywell', *Parliament and politics in late medieval England*, 2 (1981), 137–51 • C. L. Scofield, *The life and reign of Edward the Fourth*, 2 vols. (1923); repr. (1967) • *VCH Northamptonshire* • R. A. Griffiths, *The reign of King Henry VI: the exercise of royal authority, 1422–1461* (1981)

Wealth at death at least £100 p.a., value of Northamptonshire estates forfeited in 1461: *CPR*

Tresham, Sir Thomas (*c*.1500–1559), landowner and prior of the hospital of St John of Jerusalem in England, was the only son of John Tresham (*d*. 1521) of Rushton Hall, Northamptonshire. Following the death of Thomas's mother, his father married Isabel (*d*. 1558), daughter of Sir James Harrington of Hornby, Lancashire. The Treshams were a leading Northamptonshire gentry family: Thomas's eponymous grandfather had served Henry VI as comptroller of the household, and was executed following the battle of Tewkesbury; upon the accession of Henry VII his son John was restored to the family's estates, and was named sheriff of Northamptonshire in 1505. Thomas Tresham married Anne, daughter of William, Lord Parr, and together they had at least three sons and a daughter. Following Anne's death, in November 1540 Thomas married Lettice Lee (*d*. in or before 1557), daughter of Sir Thomas Peniston of Hawridge, Buckinghamshire, and successively widow of Robert Knollys (*d*. 1521) and of Sir Robert Lee (*d*. 1539).

Although an extraordinary esquire of the body as early as 1516 and knighted by 1524, Tresham was no courtier, rarely attending the court save for state occasions such as the arrival of Anne of Cleves (1539) or the reception of the French ambassador (1546). Moreover his military experience under Henry VIII was limited to helping to suppress the Pilgrimage of Grace, and to service in the English army sent into France in 1544. But he was active in the government of his native Northamptonshire, where he was both a JP and gaol delivery commissioner. Pricked four times as sheriff (1524, 1539, 1548, and 1555), Tresham's high standing in his native county was reflected in a recommendation of 1532 to Thomas Cromwell that he would make the sort of 'substantial sheriff' the shire needed. He was also a stalwart member of special county commissions. For example, in 1530 he was responsible for preparing an inventory of the lands held by Cardinal Wolsey within the county, while in 1551 he was a county commissioner for assessing the relief, and one of the commissioners appointed to regulate the price of food in local markets. Tresham represented his native county as a knight of the shire in the parliament of 1539, and again in 1542 (and perhaps 1545). His hostility towards religious reform excluded him from the parliaments of Edward VI, although he continued his service as a JP and county commissioner, and served under the earl of Warwick in the suppression of Kett's rebellion.

Upon the death of Edward VI in July 1553, Tresham moved swiftly to support Princess Mary's claim to the throne. Refusing to muster on behalf of the duke of Northumberland and ignoring the council's orders to recognize Jane Grey as queen, with the support of the citizens of Northampton Tresham proclaimed Mary as queen, and was later placed in command of a company of soldiers which protected her during Wyatt's rebellion. Tresham's decisive actions in July 1553 earned him Mary's gratitude, which took the form of a cash reward, together with the lease of the property of Pipewell Abbey near Rushton. In October 1553 he returned to Westminster as MP for Lancaster, before resuming his rank as first knight for Northamptonshire in the two parliaments of 1554 (as sheriff in 1555 he was ineligible for election). At the same time Tresham served the crown in various unofficial capacities: in May 1554 he escorted Edward Courtenay, earl of Devon, from the Tower to Fotheringhay Castle, while during the summer of 1555 he was called upon to investigate seditious bills circulating in the county. As sheriff in August 1557 he also supervised the burning of a Northamptonshire shoemaker for heresy.

Among the first steps toward the full restoration of the dissolved religious orders in England fervently desired by Queen Mary, in late 1557 it was decided to re-establish the order of St John of Jerusalem in England, with the recently widowed Thomas Tresham as its prior, apparently as a further reward for his earlier loyalty. At Whitehall on 30 November 1557, in the presence of Mary and Cardinal Pole, Tresham and four colleagues took the cross as knights of the order, and Tresham was installed as prior (the order did not receive its landed endowment from the crown, however, until April 1558). Although now a member of the House of Lords, Prior Tresham rarely attended, for he was frequently occupied elsewhere in royal service. In January 1558 he was appointed a commander in the abortive expedition to recover Calais, while in March he was on the Isle of Wight supervising the hasty improvement of defences before an anticipated French invasion.

Throughout the decades of religious turmoil Tresham remained a faithful Catholic. His devotion was shared by his sister Clemence, formerly a nun at Syon, and inherited by his grandson Thomas, who became a notable Northamptonshire recusant. Upon the accession of Elizabeth, an Italian in Tresham's service reported that his master intended 'to observe the old rite secretly', as he had done during the reign of Edward VI (*CSP Venice, 1558–80*, 31). Prior Tresham did not have to conceal his faith for long, however, for he died at Rushton on 1 March 1559, even before the order of St John was dissolved in England and its properties confiscated once more. He was buried on 16 March in St Peter's Church, Rushton, where a fine alabaster monument was erected in the chancel, depicting the prior recumbent in his robes; it was transferred in 1799 to nearby All Saints' Church. Tresham had drawn up his will on 28 November 1557, before embracing the religious life, and amended its contents on 11 September 1558; it was proved by his executors on 4 May 1559. He referred in his will to his buying and selling of lands. He had inherited a rather dispersed estate in Northamptonshire, which he had consolidated into two blocks, centred upon Rushton (his principal seat) and Lyveden respectively. But that was the limit of his achievement, for he made no effort to introduce up-to-date methods of estate management, and it clearly mattered most to him that his heir should come into an unencumbered inheritance. There is an evident note of satisfaction in his reported claim to the latter that 'I shall leave you all your land out of joynture or dower and free from wardshipp, and not a fote of that subject to any statut for inclosure, and verie lytle or none in lease and no part of my rente of inheritance in any sort improved other then my mannor in Houghton' (Finch, 71). All Tresham's sons had predeceased him, and the beneficiary of his outmoded attitude towards his lands was his grandson, another Thomas *Tresham, who inherited a valuable estate ripe for exploitation.   P. R. N. CARTER

Sources M. E. Finch, The wealth of five Northamptonshire families, 1540–1640, Northamptonshire RS, 19 (1956) · HoP, Commons, 1509–58, 3.482 · LP Henry VIII, vols. 2–21 · will, PRO, PROB 11/42B, sig. 19 · CPR, 1547–58 · J. G. Nichols, ed., The chronicle of Queen Jane, and of two years of Queen Mary, CS, old ser., 48 (1850) · The diary of Henry Machyn, citizen and merchant-taylor of London, from AD 1550 to AD 1563, ed. J. G. Nichols, CS, 42 (1848) · D. M. Loades, The reign of Mary Tudor: politics, government and religion in England, 1553–58 (1979) · PRO, state papers domestic, Mary I, SP 11/5, 6, 12 · B. A. Bailey, ed., Northamptonshire in the early eighteenth century: the drawings of Peter Tillemans and others, Northamptonshire RS, 39 (1996) · 'The Tresham monument', Northamptonshire Past and Present, 4 (1966–72), 189–90 · A. G. Dickens, 'Early protestantism and the church in Northamptonshire', Northamptonshire Past and Present, 7 (1983–8), 27–39 · M. A. R. Graves, The House of Lords in the parliaments of Edward VI and Mary I (1981) · CSP Venice, 1558–80

Likenesses attrib. G. and T. Roiley, alabaster effigy on funeral monument, 1562, All Saints' Church, Rushton, Northamptonshire · P. Tillemans, drawing, 1719, repro. in Bailey, Northamptonshire, pl. 239

Tresham, Sir Thomas (1543–1605), gentleman and recusant, was the son of John Tresham (c.1520–1546) and Eleanor (d. 1546), daughter of Anthony Catesby of Whiston. Born in September 1543, Thomas became heir at the age of three to the Northamptonshire estates of his grandfather, Sir Thomas *Tresham (d. 1559). As ward of Sir Robert Throckmorton of Coughton, Warwickshire, whose daughter Meriel (d. 1615) he later married (1566), a religiously conservative upbringing was likely. It was unobtrusive enough, however, for him—after study at the Middle Temple from 1560 to 1568 (Edmund Plowden's inn, and notoriously Catholic)—to become sheriff of Northamptonshire in 1573 and to be knighted at Elizabeth I's visit to Kenilworth in 1575. He was, however, implicated in an assault on an anti-Catholic informer at Kettering in 1576. Robert Persons said he received Tresham into the Roman Catholic church in 1580. If 'scarcely more than a formality' (Anstruther, 112), this moved Tresham to open rejection of the Elizabethan church—until 1578 he was still having his children baptized in the parish church, but not Thomas in 1580.

In 1580 Tresham received the Jesuit Edmund Campion at his house at Hoxton, Middlesex; taken before the privy council and then Star Chamber after Campion's capture the following year, Tresham refused to answer under oath to questions tending to self-incrimination. This began his long career of fines and imprisonment: in 1581–3 in the Fleet prison, then under house arrest at Hoxton (1583–7, 1589–93), except for the tense period of 1587–8, when he was committed again. Finally he was sent to his Northamptonshire house at Rushton, which had the disadvantage that his resort to London for legal and financial business required privy council permission. As a final insult, just as recusants began to enjoy greater liberty, Tresham was subjected to legal harassment (leading to further imprisonment) by the ungrateful Catholic family of his brother-in-law William *Vaux, Lord Vaux of Harrowden, after the latter died in 1595, leaving his intractable financial embarrassments for Tresham to attempt to disentangle.

Tresham became spokesman for lay Catholic loyalism, disavowing that temporal obedience to the crown was compromised by obligations of spiritual obedience to the pope. He was probably associated with a petition to this effect in 1583 and certainly with one in 1585. In 1588 he deplored the denial to Catholic gentlemen of their natural right to defend their sovereign; if not trusted with a weapon, he offered to do so unarmed. Such Catholic loyalism was potentially divisive enough for the government apparently to encourage reports that Jesuits 'regarded him as an atheist' (Renold, 255). But it can be overstated: 'beneath the florid and high-flown prose through which Tresham expressed his obedience was a critique of a government consistently and systematically overstepping its bounds' (Kaushik, 52), from his 1581 arrest onwards.

Despite Tresham's protestations, some of his papers indicate a preference for the dynastic claim of James I, whose accession he hurried to proclaim at Northampton, despite heckling about the pope. He received a promise of an end to recusancy fines and was given a commission for forests—but the first was vitiated by recusants' resort to the Bye plot and their proposal to make Tresham lieutenant of the Tower; the second did not survive complaints about a tactless two-hour 'discourse' to which he subjected his fellows when accused of harsh estate management. Certainly his estates were a particular target for enclosure rioters. Financial problems did not eliminate traditional gentry pursuits, other than public office. From 1593 he substantially remodelled both his Northamptonshire houses, Rushton and Lyveden, building with an 'almost frightening … intensity' (Airs, 22), though spending a relatively modest £970 in seven years. His individual house and garden designs, embodying Catholic religious symbolism, have continued to attract interest, leading to the establishment of a Tresham trail. A Northamptonshire institute of further and higher education has also been named after him.

Tresham died at Rushton Hall after a painful illness on 11 September 1605 and was buried at St Peter's, Rushton, 'the foremost Catholic layman of the old school' (Anstruther, 277)—too old school for the conspiratorial antics of his heir, Francis *Tresham, which ensured the latter survived him by only three months. Sir Thomas Tresham was long cited as the archetypal gentleman ruined by recusancy fines, but this has now been refuted. He was £11,500 in debt at his death, and had £3000 of debts even in 1582. Having paid £7720 for recusancy clearly contributed to the increase, but not as much as his £12,200 spent on marriage portions for six daughters married ambitiously, notably to Catholic peers including William *Parker, Lord Morley. Over £3000 in bribes and fines had gone in 1601 to buy the life of Tresham's son Francis after the Essex rising. Despite an aggressive and far from conservative estate policy, increasing his income to perhaps £3500 p.a., he had failed to economize sufficiently to fund his recusancy. It was his younger son, Sir Lewis Tresham, bt (1578–1639), who succeeded in decisively dissipating the family fortune.

JULIAN LOCK

Sources G. Anstruther, *Vaux of Harrowden: a recusant family* (1953) · *Report on manuscripts in various collections*, 8 vols., HMC, 55 (1901–14), vol. 3 · S. Kaushik, 'Resistance, loyalty and recusant politics: Sir Thomas Tresham and the Elizabethan state', *Midland History*, 21 (1996), 37–72 · A. Morey, *The Catholic subjects of Elizabeth I* (1978) · W. R. Trimble, *The Catholic laity in Elizabethan England, 1558–1603* (1964) · M. E. Finch, *The wealth of five Northamptonshire families, 1540–1640*, Northamptonshire RS, 19 (1956) · G. Isham, *Sir Thomas Tresham and his buildings*, Northamptonshire Antiquarian Society Reports and Papers, 65 (1966) · R. S. Peterson, 'Laurel crown and ape's tail: new light on Spenser's career from Sir Thomas Tresham', *Spenser Studies*, 12 (1998), 1–35 · A. G. Petti, ed., *Recusant documents from the Ellesmere manuscripts, 1577–1715*, Catholic RS, 60 (1968) · J. Morris, ed., *The troubles of our Catholic forefathers related by themselves*, 2 (1875) · *Miscellanea, II*, Catholic RS, 2 (1906) · P. Renold, ed., *The Wisbech stirs, 1595–1598*, Catholic RS, 51 (1958) · P. A. J. Pettit, *The royal forests of Northamptonshire: a study in their economy, 1558–1714*, Northamptonshire RS, 23 (1968) · F. Heal and C. Holmes, *The gentry in England and Wales, 1500–1700* (1994) · *APC, 1578–82, 1587–93, 1595–8, 1600–04* · *Calendar of the manuscripts of the most hon. the marquess of Salisbury*, 17, HMC, 9 (1938); 23 (1973) · J. Strype, *Annals of the Reformation and establishment of religion … during Queen Elizabeth's happy reign*, new edn, 4 vols. (1824) · H. Foley, ed., *Records of the English province of the Society of Jesus*, 2 (1875), 223; 3 (1878), 440; 6 (1880), 717 · M. Airs, *The Tudor and Jacobean country house: a building history* (1995) · J. M. Stean, 'The development of Tudor and Stuart garden design in Northamptonshire', *Northamptonshire Past and Present*, 5 (1973–7), 397–400 · A. Pritchard, *Catholic loyalism in Elizabethan England* (1979), 49–57 · P. Holmes, *Resistance and compromise: the political thought of the Elizabethan Catholics* (1982) · R. B. Manning, 'Richard Shelley of Warminghurst and the English Catholic petition for toleration of 1585', *Recusant History*, 6 (1961–2), 265–74 · F. Edwards, *Guy Fawkes: the real story of the Gunpowder Plot?* (1969) · A. Fraser, *The Gunpowder Plot: terror and faith in 1605* (1996) · W. Weston, *The autobiography of an Elizabethan*, ed. and trans. P. Caraman (1955) · H. A. C. Sturgess, ed., *Register of admissions to the Honourable Society of the Middle Temple, from the fifteenth century to the year 1944*, 1 (1949), 25 · *DNB*
Archives BL, corresp. and papers, Add. MSS 39828–39838 | BL, Add. MS 34394, fol. 38v · BL, Lansdowne MS 68 · Northants. RO, Stopford Stockville MS 234
Likenesses oils, 1578?, repro. in Peterson, 'Laurel crown and ape's tail', 11; priv. coll. · portrait, repro. in Anstruther, *Vaux of Harrowden*
Wealth at death approx. £3500 p.a.; debts of £11,500: Finch, *Wealth of five Northamptonshire families*, 75–6

Tresham, William (d. 1450), lawyer and speaker of the House of Commons, was the son of Thomas Tresham, and was apparently a native of Northamptonshire, where he was to become an influential landowner. Elected one of the two knights of the shire for the county in 1423, he acted again in that capacity in another eleven parliaments (1427, 1429, 1432, 1433, 1435, 1439, 1442, 1445, 1447, and February and November 1449). From 1424 until his death, moreover, he was a Northamptonshire JP. For a man whose origins do not appear to have been particularly distinguished, advancement in his home county went hand in hand with, indeed probably depended upon, advancement at the centre of national affairs. Having trained as a lawyer Tresham was certainly intermittently in the king's service from at least 1415, when he was an auditor of the accounts of royal officials in south Wales.

Little is known of Tresham's activities in the 1420s, when he may have concentrated on his legal career, but that he prospered is shown by his becoming a councillor to the duke of Buckingham in 1430; he continued to receive an annual fee from the duke until at least 1447. In 1432 he was appointed one of his two attorneys-general by Cardinal Henry Beaufort, and during the 1430s was also appointed to a number of commissions by the crown. In 1434, for instance, he was named to a commission to investigate concealments of royal revenues in Northamptonshire, and in 1439 to inquire into the value of crown lands in that county. He also forged a connection with the king's household, possibly by 1434, certainly from 1441. The tie was essentially a legal one: Tresham was employed as an apprentice-at-law, and in that capacity was paid nearly £10 for his work in the parliament of 1435. It was doubtless on the basis of such experience that in 1439 he was elected speaker of the Commons, at a time when there was a call for the reform of the royal household.

In May 1440 Tresham was granted an annuity of £40 by the king, and in September that year was one of the feoffees to whom the estates of alien priories were entrusted, as the endowment for Henry VI's foundation at Eton. Elected speaker again in 1442 and 1447, he continued to be employed by the crown, to an increasing extent through the duchy of Lancaster. Already steward of the duchy estates in Northamptonshire by 1437, he was retained as an apprentice-at-law from 1444 to 1447. In 1446 he was one of the feoffees of the duchy estates reserved for the implementation of Henry VI's will, and in 1448 was appointed chancellor of those feoffees. In 1449 he became chancellor both of the duchy and of the county palatine of Lancaster. Favour at court led to Tresham's being employed in politically sensitive legal cases; in 1444 he was one of the commissioners appointed to investigate charges of treason against Thomas Carver, while in 1447 he heard indictments of treason against members of the household of Humphrey of Gloucester. In August 1450 he was himself indicted in the aftermath of Cade's rebellion, suggesting that he was regarded as a leading member of the regime headed by the duke of Suffolk in the late 1440s.

Shortly after the indictment was made, but in circumstances unconnected with it, Tresham died by violence. When parliament assembled at Westminster in November 1449 he was elected speaker for the fourth time, and so was the spokesman of the Commons in their impeachment of Suffolk in 1450. In 1448 he had been chosen as a feoffee by the duke of York, and in either that year or 1449 had also become a councillor to the duke, but there is no evidence that such Yorkist connections were other than purely professional, or that Tresham's links with the court were weakened thereby. Nevertheless, his ties with York helped to bring Tresham to his death. On 22 September 1450 he was at his Northamptonshire residence of Sywell, intending to meet York as the duke made his way to London. But Tresham was tricked into revealing his movements to a group of his enemies, local men with whom he was engaged in a dispute over property, and early next morning they ambushed him at Moulton and killed him. Perhaps in order to demonstrate his continuing royalism, Tresham was wearing his collar of the king's livery. With his wife, Isabel, daughter of William Vaux of Harrowden, another Northamptonshire lawyer, Tresham had a son, Thomas *Tresham, who was wounded in the attack that killed his father. Thomas had followed William Tresham into the king's household, and remained a staunch Lancastrian for the rest of his life, being executed after the battle of Tewkesbury in 1471. William Tresham's wife also survived him.

HENRY SUMMERSON

Sources J. S. Roskell, 'William Tresham of Sywell', *Parliament and politics in late medieval England*, 2 (1981), 137–51 • R. A. Griffiths, *The reign of King Henry VI: the exercise of royal authority, 1422–1461* (1981) • P. A. Johnson, *Duke Richard of York, 1411–1460* (1988) • R. Somerville, *History of the duchy of Lancaster, 1265–1603* (1953) • B. Wolffe, *Henry VI* (1981) • C. Rawcliffe, *The Staffords, earls of Stafford and dukes of Buckingham, 1394–1521*, Cambridge Studies in Medieval Life and Thought, 3rd ser., 11 (1978)

Tresham, William (1495–1569), priest, was born in the parish of Oakley Magna, Northamptonshire, the son of Richard Tresham of Newton, Northamptonshire, and Rose Billing of Astwell, granddaughter of Sir Thomas Billing, lord chief justice. He studied at Merton College, Oxford, and graduated BA on 16 January 1515, MA in 1520, BTh in 1528, and DTh on 8 July 1532. In 1526 he was ordained priest. From 11 March 1524 to 11 February 1529 he served as registrar of the university. He occupied the office of vice-chancellor in 1532–47, 1550, 1556, and 1558, and was a canon of Cardinal College between 1529 and 1531. In 1527 he was king of the beans at Merton, and was also the college's first bursar (1521–2), third bursar (1526–8), and third dean (1524–6). Upon the transformation of Cardinal College—first to King Henry VIII College, then to Christ Church—Tresham became a canon, occupying the second stall in 1532–5 and in 1546–60. While a canon he oversaw the enlargement of the priory house. He served as vicar of St Mary Magdalen, Oxford, in 1534–7, and of Bampton, Oxfordshire, in 1554–60. He was admitted chancellor of Chichester in 1539, but had been deprived by 1560; he was deprived of his canonry of Lincoln the same year, and of his rectory of Bugbrooke, Northamptonshire. However, he held the Northamptonshire rectory of Towcester until his death.

Occasionally caught up in the religious controversies of his age, Tresham was a theological conservative throughout his career. His preferment in the refoundation of Cardinal College, along with his appointment as a canon of the new diocese of Oxford by royal charter in 1542, are usually seen as connected to his support for the king's divorce from Katherine of Aragon and the subsequent religious policies of Henry's reign. But he may simply have been deft at understanding the system of patronage and promotion within the Tudor church; surviving letters show him appealing to Wolsey, Cromwell, and the king to be generous in their support, and he even informed them of ill incumbents and possible vacancies. This, of course, does not deny a sincere religious conviction, and indeed Tresham appears to have enjoyed a reputation for being forthright, active, and intelligent. In 1535 he was a member of the commission for spiritualities in Oxfordshire, and in 1540 sat on a commission appointed to evaluate the grounding of church rituals in scriptural doctrine; it issued *A Necessary Doctrine and Erudition for any Chrysten Man*, popularly known as the King's Book, in 1543. In 1549 Tresham joined William Chedsey and Morgan Philips in a public debate with Pietro Martire Vermigli (known as Peter Martyr), supporting the doctrine of the real presence in the eucharist against Martyr's more Calvinist position. An account of the debate by Tresham was sent to the privy council with the title *Disputatio de eucharistiae sacramento* (BL, Harley MS 422), and was published under Martyr's name the same year.

Tresham was committed to the Fleet for his conservative religious position and criticism of church policy under Edward VI on 21 December 1551, but returned to freedom and church affairs with the accession of Mary I in 1553. In 1554 and 1555 he was one of the conservatives who debated with Thomas Cranmer, Hugh Latimer, and Nicholas Ridley on issues of orthodoxy and faith. This disputation was represented in an anonymous publication of 1554, later quoted in large part by John Foxe's *Acts and Monuments*. Also in 1554 he met Cardinal Pole to discuss the threatened spoliation of the building that once housed St Mary's College, Oxford, an institution for Augustinian canons which had closed in 1541. On behalf of the university Tresham and Thomas Raynolds, warden of Merton, offered congratulations to Elizabeth I upon her succession. But with his refusal to take the Elizabethan oath of supremacy, Tresham was stripped of all preferments except the rectory of Towcester and placed at Lambeth Palace in the custody of Archbishop Parker. Having made promise upon security that he would not interfere in religious affairs as established by law, he was allowed to retire to Northamptonshire, where he died in 1569. He was buried in the chancel of Bugbrooke church.

GARY G. GIBBS

Sources Emden, *Oxf.*, 4.576–7 • *LP Henry VIII* • R. W. Jeffrey, 'A forgotten college of Oxford', *Brazen Nose*, 4 (1924–9), 260–88

Tresilian, Sir Robert (d. 1388), justice, was a native of Cornwall, owning land at Tresillian, near Merther, though his early career was in Oxfordshire and Berkshire. He received payments for legal advice to Exeter College, Oxford, in 1354–6. On 3 June 1359 Tresilian was recorded as an attorney, and in 1365 as a charter witness in Berkshire. He was a JP in Berkshire in 1367 and in Oxfordshire in 1368. Tresilian maintained links with Cornwall, however, for in 1369 he was probably counsel in a Cornish assize case, and in that year he served as knight of the shire for the county. On 7 December 1369 an order to Hugh Courtenay, earl of Devon, recorded that the admiral had judged a case with two justices and Robert Tresilian, 'all learned in the law' (*CClR, 1369–1374*, 59). By 10 February 1370 Tresilian was serving as JP for Cornwall and he served on many Cornish commissions thereafter. He also accounted for the earl of Stafford's rents in Cornwall in 1372, and on 12 August 1376 was appointed to a commission on the Devon stannary, along with the earl of Devon. Perhaps it was due to his Courtenay connections that on 10 September 1377 Tresilian was appointed to a commission headed by William Courtenay, bishop of London, relating to the custody of the properties of Enguerrand (VII) de Coucy (c.1340–1397). On 21 February 1378 he was described as steward of Cornwall.

By this time Tresilian had become a servant of the crown. In Michaelmas term 1375 he became a king's serjeant, and on 6 May 1378 he was appointed a justice of king's bench. Exactly a month later, on 6 June, he became a knight, being made a banneret at Windsor, with robes given him by the king. Despite his new duties, Tresilian continued to serve in Oxfordshire, where he was again appointed JP on 28 June 1378, and had several other commissions there and in Cornwall. On 10 September 1378, however, he was replaced as steward of Cornwall, though apparently serving again in that capacity before 1385.

Tresilian remained a puisne justice of king's bench until June 1381. On 12 December 1379 he was empowered to receive cognitions and issue certificates even though he was not a justice of common pleas. During these years he served on local commissions not only in the south-west but also in Staffordshire and Wales. These duties were interrupted by the peasants' revolt in June 1381, during which Sir John Cavendish, chief justice of king's bench, was killed. On 22 June Tresilian was appointed to succeed Cavendish, and according to both Knighton and Walsingham he dealt extremely harshly with the rebels, putting heavy pressure on juries to convict, and sentencing those convicted to brutal punishments. Tresilian presided over the execution of John Ball, the rebel preacher, on 14 July 1381, and also that of William Grindcobbe, the leader of the townsmen of St Albans, in October 1381, and of John Wraw, the rebel leader in Suffolk, in May 1382.

As the 1380s progressed Tresilian not only continued to serve as chief justice of king's bench, and as a member of numerous commissions in south and south-west England, but also became increasingly involved in national politics, whose often bitterly partisan character inevitably made him a controversial figure. On 27 May 1384 he was appointed with John, first Lord Montagu, steward of the household, to try Friar John Latimer, who had accused the duke of Lancaster of treason. Before the steward could act, however, Latimer was tortured to death by John Holland, Lancaster's future son-in-law. On 18 July following Tresilian received a pardon, not only for treasons and felonies, but also for sales of the laws of the land and other judicial misconduct of the sort with which he was later charged.

Another controversial case arose on 9 September, when Montagu, Tresilian, and Sir Robert Bealknap, chief justice of common pleas, were ordered to try John Northampton, the former mayor of London, and his allies, who claimed the support of the duke of Lancaster. Tresilian wished to refer the case to the new mayor of London, but was nevertheless present when Northampton was condemned to life imprisonment at Tintagel, Cornwall.

Tresilian took a stronger line against Lancaster the next year. According to Walsingham, the king and his friends planned to arrest the duke, and Robert Tresilian 'boldly mainperned' that he would sentence Lancaster as his crimes deserved. These activities have been identified with a plot in which young courtiers planned to murder Lancaster on 14 February 1385, but the duke escaped. It is a measure of Richard II's trust in Tresilian that at this very time, on 15 February, he should have been retained for life of the king's council, with a yearly fee of 100 marks from the issues of Cornwall and Devon (which he undertook not to collect while receiving other fees), while on 24 February following he was granted the keeping of Conerton Manor in Cornwall. He also appears to have recovered the stewardship of Cornwall, since on 12 December 1385 he was once more replaced in that office.

On 19 November 1386 parliament appointed a commission to restrain the king and his advisers, particularly the chancellor, Michael de la Pole, who was impeached. In the following year it was probably Tresilian who drafted the questions about the commission and impeachment, the so-called 'questions to the judges', which were presented to the other royal justices in meetings at Shrewsbury (1–5 August) and Nottingham (25 August). They all sealed answers declaring that the commission was illegal, the impeachment invalid, and those restricting the royal power punishable as traitors. Later Bealknap and other justices said they signed under threat of death. The response of the king's adversaries was swift and drastic. On 17 November 1387 Thomas, duke of Gloucester, Richard, earl of Arundel, and Thomas, earl of Warwick, later joined by Henry, earl of Derby (son of the duke of Lancaster), and Thomas, earl of Nottingham, appealed Sir Robert Tresilian along with Robert de Vere, duke of Ireland, Michael de la Pole, earl of Suffolk, Alexander Neville, archbishop of York, and Sir Nicholas Brembre (former mayor of London) [see Lords appellant]. The charges against Tresilian were primarily of giving 'aid and counsel' to the chief 'traitors', meaning de Vere, de la Pole, and Neville, but of particular relevance to him were accusations of assembling the justices without the assent of the continual council set up under the commission of 1386, and of making very suspicious demands of them (a reference to the 'questions to the judges'), and also of manipulating legal cases to their own profit (something Tresilian had demonstrably done).

De Vere's attempt to fight the appellants was defeated, and the latter took control. On 4 January 1388 they ordered that Tresilian be imprisoned at Gloucester, but on the same day he was also referred to as a fugitive. Froissart says Tresilian reached Bristol, and there told the king he would return to London to spy on the appellants. But the king was not actually at Bristol, and Tresilian is more likely to have hidden in the London area.

Tresilian was summoned to answer the appeal in parliament and on failing to appear was condemned by default, on 13 February 1388. Six days later he was found hiding in disguise in Westminster. His discovery caused a sensation, coming when proceedings against the king's supporters were at their height. According to Favent, Tresilian was spotted as he observed proceedings from the roof of a house next to Westminster Palace, and was subsequently discovered hiding under a table, heavily bearded and wearing eccentric clothes, so that he looked more like a pilgrim or beggar than a royal justice. Knighton attests the strange clothes and adds that the beard was false, and that Tresilian was recognized by his distinctive voice. He was dragged out to cries of 'We havet hym', and brought before parliament. He claimed the sanctuary of Westminster Abbey, but Gloucester denied the claim. Attempts to argue that the procedure against him had been founded in error were likewise brushed aside, and the original sentence was quickly carried out. Tresilian was drawn on a hurdle to Tyburn, where physical force was needed to make him ascend the scaffold. His clothes, which were found to be filled with protective charms, were stripped off, and he was hanged naked, finally having his throat cut.

Tresilian's wife, Emmaline (Emma), who had screamed and fainted at his arrest, claimed his body for burial at Greyfriars in London. She was the daughter of Richard Hiwish of Devon, and had married Sir Robert by 20 April 1377 as the widow of Richard Recote of Oxfordshire; she later married Sir John Colshull of Cornwall and died in 1403. With Tresilian she had a son, John, and at least two daughters, Joan and Emma. Tresilian had become a wealthy man. Following his execution one of his servants was ordered to answer to the king for 1000 marks from his late master's property, and he had estates in Berkshire, Buckinghamshire, and Oxfordshire, and above all Cornwall. Many of his lands in the latter county had come to him by marriage, but petitions for redress after his death suggest that Tresilian had also added to them by misusing his judicial authority. In spite of such complaints, and despite the opposition of John Tresilian, much of Sir Robert's forfeited land was acquired by John *Hawley the elder, a Dartmouth merchant and pirate, who had married Emma Tresilian.

Sir Robert Tresilian may have been ruthless in his interpretation of the law for private and political ends, but as one of the principal intellectual architects of the 'high' doctrine of the royal prerogative, he had a lasting if often unfortunate influence. JOHN L. LELAND

Sources Chancery records · Calendar of inquisitions miscellaneous (chancery), PRO, 6 (1963) · Knighton's chronicle, 1337–1396, ed. and trans. G. H. Martin, OMT (1995) [Lat. orig., Chronica de eventibus Angliae a tempore regis Edgari usque mortem regis Ricardi Secundi, with parallel Eng. text] · M. McKisack, ed., 'Historia, sive, Narracio de modo et forma Mirabilis Parliamenti apud Westmonasterium', Camden miscellany, XIV, CS, 3rd ser., 37 (1926) · J. Froissart, Chronicles of England, France, Spain, and the adjoining countries, trans. T. Johnes, 2 vols. (1874) · L. C. Hector and B. F. Harvey, eds. and trans., The Westminster chronicle, 1381–1394, OMT (1982) · Foss, Judges · J. Rastell and others, eds., Le livre des assises et pleas del' corone (1679) · C. W. Boase, Registrum Collegii Exoniensis, 2 vols. (1879–94) · N. Saul, Richard II (1997) · S. B. Chrimes, 'Richard II's questions to the judges, 1387', Law Quarterly Review, 72 (1956), 365–90 · R. B. Dobson, ed., The peasants' revolt of 1381, 2nd edn (1983) · J. A. Sparvel-Bayley, 'Essex in insurrection, 1381', Essex Archaeological Society Transactions, new ser., 1 (1878), 205–19 · G. O. Sayles, ed., Select cases in the court of king's bench, 7 vols., SeldS, 55, 57–8, 74, 76, 82, 88 (1936–71), vols. 6–7 · [T. Walsingham], Chronicon Angliae, ab anno Domini 1328 usque ad annum 1388, ed. E. M. Thompson, Rolls Series, 64 (1874) · Thomae Walsingham, quondam monachi S. Albani, historia Anglicana, ed. H. T. Riley, 2 vols., pt 1 of Chronica monasterii S. Albani, Rolls Series, 28 (1863–4), vol. 2
Likenesses portrait?, repro. in www.siue.edu/CHAUCER/14th cent.html, 4 Oct 2002
Wealth at death property forfeited before execution: Calendar of inquisitions miscellaneous, 57–9, 80–87, 93–4, 97–100, 103–5, 118, 122, 136, 138–9, 175–7

Tressell, Robert Philippe. *See* Noonan, Robert Philippe (1870–1911).

Treswell, Ralph (c.1540–1616/17), painter–stainer and surveyor, was the son of Robert Treswell, alias Baker, of St Albans, Hertfordshire, and his wife, Margaret Langley. His date of birth is not known, but the first reference to him at work is 1567–8, and he may therefore have been born about 1540. He was by trade a painter–stainer, a craft which in 1581 included face painters, history painters, arms (heraldic) painters, and house painters; Treswell was probably an arms painter, for he painted streamers and banners for several London companies. He must have become a fairly senior member of his own company, since he was one of the receiving trustees of Painter–Stainers' Hall in 1580, and one of those releasing the hall to others in 1605. He married three times. His first wife was Cicely Cresley, with whom he had three sons: Robert, who became Somerset herald in 1597, Ralph (also a surveyor), and Christopher. His second wife was Anne Kentish, and his third Elizabeth Bachelor.

From at least 1580 Treswell was also drawing pictorial surveys, all of rural estates. These included estates in Northamptonshire of Sir Christopher Hatton, and lands of London institutions such as St Bartholomew's Hospital, Christ's Hospital (of which he was a governor from 1604 to his death), and the Clothworkers' and Leathersellers' companies. Other clients for single surveys included Magdalen College and Christ Church, Oxford. From at least 1607 he also drew up plans of properties in London to accompany leases of Christ's Hospital. In 1610–11 the hospital, and in 1612 the Clothworkers' Company, decided to obtain a comprehensive survey of their London estates. Both these surveys have survived, and they provide an important and unique view of housing conditions in the city before the great fire of 1666.

Treswell, like other heraldic painters, transferred his skills to map making to meet the increasing demand for estate plans in the vigorous property market after the dissolution of the monasteries and the Reformation. Being in London, he could exploit both the court and the merchant community as patrons, and would have been exposed to the new developments in surveying in the published works of Leonard and Thomas Digges and others. He thus became one of the first modern land surveyors.

From 1583 Treswell took part in the administration of Aldersgate ward in the city of London, where he lived; from 1606 he was the ward's senior common councilman. He died intestate between July 1616 and March 1617.

JOHN SCHOFIELD, *rev.*

Sources J. Schofield, ed., *The London surveys of Ralph Treswell* (1987)

Trethowan, Sir (James) Ian Raley (1922–1990), journalist and broadcaster, was born on 20 October 1922 in High Wycombe, the only child of Major James Jackson Raley Trethowan MBE, a retired army officer who combined a life in business and army welfare with writing about sport, and his wife, Winifred Timms. Trethowan followed in his father's footsteps to Christ's Hospital, Horsham, Sussex, where he displayed only modest academic achievement; he left at the age of sixteen to pursue a career in journalism. A short spell as post-boy at the *Daily Sketch* led to a reporting job on the *Yorkshire Post*, before Trethowan joined the Fleet Air Arm during the Second World War in 1941. After the war he rejoined the *Post* in 1946. Working for its London staff he rose rapidly to parliamentary lobby correspondent. There his meticulousness began to be widely noticed. His writing was mostly terse and to the point, and he had a good nose for what constituted a story. He also developed fine contacts within the tory party, about which he made no secret, but which never became so blatant as to diminish his effectiveness as a chronicler of politics across the board.

Trethowan moved to the *News Chronicle* in 1955 and from there was tempted by Geoffrey Cox to join the fledgeling Independent Television News, where he took an on-screen role between 1958 and 1963. Trethowan did not develop into a permanent newscaster, always preferring to involve himself in a little administration. He served as ITN's deputy editor, before moving on to the larger canvas of the BBC in 1963. Trethowan's main work at the BBC was again political, dealing both with Westminster direct and with the broader world of politics through the weekly programme *Gallery*. At the same time he was political commentator for the *Economist* (1953–8 and 1965–7) and *The Times* (1967–8).

In 1968 Baron Hill of Luton, an old political comrade and now chairman of the BBC, needed a new managing director for BBC Radio to succeed F. G. Gillard, the veteran correspondent and administrator. Trethowan, somewhat to his surprise, was asked to apply. He was offered the job and took it—in part, he recorded, because he knew he would never be top-flight on television: 'Not a star', Huw Wheldon had told him, firmly but with kindness.

Trethowan skilfully negotiated the pitfalls of radio management from 1969 to 1975. Radios 1, 2, 3, and 4 were introduced with less pain than had been anticipated. In 1976 Trethowan was switched back to television, this time as managing director, as part of a deliberate grooming for the top job. He succeeded Sir Charles Curran as director-general in late 1977. In his own view he had had 'a lot of luck'.

In his first years at the top, Trethowan was fortunate that his chairman was Sir Michael Swann, a clubbable man of clear view. In Swann's opinion, the BBC would work best if the director-general did the driving, while the chairman and his board assisted in reading the map. Although Trethowan was sometimes suspected by radical broadcasters of acting purely as the 'thirteenth governor', his own memoir, *Split Screen*, analyses in some detail a relationship of sturdy delicacy and shows why it worked well. The political world was sufficiently convinced both to renew the BBC charter, and to sustain the value of the licence fee even during difficult inflationary times. Trethowan suffered a heart attack in 1979, but recovered to continue in office until his official retirement in 1982.

Unlike most BBC directors-general, Trethowan had a full and active life beyond the BBC. He pursued his second love, the turf, as chairman of the Horserace Betting Levy Board between 1982 and 1990, took a directorship at Barclays Bank from 1982 to 1987, and eventually re-emerged in commercial television as director in 1986–7, and then chairman from 1987 to 1990, of Thames Television. There controversy followed him over the 1988 programme *Death on the Rock*, which asked hard questions about the killing of three IRA terrorists. Trethowan stood by the programme and diverted much of the political animus. He again drew on that firm but unfailing courtesy which had stood him in good stead in all his broadcasting and journalistic endeavours. He had a clear vision of the proper province of both commentators and those commentated upon, and throughout his career this enabled him to defuse potentially explosive editorial challenges. In appearance both unassertive and unassuming, he would none the less stand his ground, his determination deepening with each twist and turn of external pressure.

Among his other activities, Trethowan was a trustee of Glyndebourne Arts Trust from 1982 and of the British Museum from 1984, a governor of the Ditchley Foundation from 1985, and on the board of the British Council from 1980 to 1987. The University of East Anglia made him an honorary DCL in 1979, and he was knighted in 1980.

Trethowan's life was cut short by the onset of motor neurone disease, which he bore with good grace, even in its latter wheelchair stages. In 1950 he had married Patricia, daughter of Colonel John Elliott Nelson, retired army officer. They had no children. The marriage was dissolved in 1963 and in the same year he married Carolyn, daughter of Alfred Brian Challen Reynolds, retired army officer and company director. They had three daughters, and it was Trethowan's greatest consolation that he lived to see them into maturity. He died on 12 December 1990 in the Cromwell Hospital, London. A memorial service was held in St Martin-in-the-Fields on 5 March 1991.

BRIAN WENHAM, *rev.*

Sources I. Trethowan, *Split screen: memoirs* (1984) · *The Times* (14 Dec 1990) · *The Times* (6 March 1991) · *The Independent* (14 Dec 1990) · *WWW* · personal knowledge (1996)

Likenesses Barnard, double portraits, photographs, 1966 (with Cliff Michelmore), Hult. Arch. • photograph, repro. in *The Independent* • photograph, repro. in *The Times*

Wealth at death £73,935: probate, 12 April 1991, *CGPLA Eng. & Wales*

Trevaskis, Sir (Gerald) Kennedy Nicholas (1915–1990), colonial official, was born on 1 January 1915 at Hove, Sussex, the eldest of three children of Hugh Kennedy Trevaskis (1882–1962), civil servant in India, and his wife, Eva Gwendolin Constance Mytanwy (1897–1969), daughter of Captain Alfred Ephrot Tizard RN and Mytanwy Tizard. The early retirement of his father from the Indian Civil Service and his ordination in the Church of England gave Trevaskis and his siblings a truly happy family home from 1932 at the rectory, Rusper, Sussex.

Kennedy Trevaskis was educated at Summer Fields School, Oxford, and then at Marlborough College from 1928 to 1933. He was a school prefect, a member of the cricket eleven in 1932 and 1933, and he was described as an extremely useful medium-fast bowler and good batsman. He studied at King's College, Cambridge, from 1933 to 1936, where he was captain of cricket in 1934–6 and of rugby in 1934. He married Sheila James Harrington (*b.* 1920), daughter of Colonel F. J. Harrington, at the Brompton Oratory on 25 August 1945. They had two sons and a daughter.

Trevaskis joined the colonial administrative service in Northern Rhodesia in 1938, at a time when that service was at the peak of its prestige; and the Northern Rhodesia regiment, initially as a sergeant, in September 1939, being taken prisoner by Italian forces in August 1940 in British Somaliland, following one of the last set-piece battles fought in Africa. He learned Italian and was thereby asked to join the British occupied enemy territory administration, Eritrea.

Trevaskis now showed his mettle. He was a big man, physically, but also mentally: to his work he brought a keen intellect, guided by academic rigour. The peoples of his first posting, the Keren, had a strong feudal structure. He presided with skill over mixed-culture tribunals dealing with complex land disputes; later, in his 'left-wing phase', he organized the freeing of the serfs of a combined Keren–Agordat western province from their ancient feudal dues and services. He served in 1947–8 as a member of the British delegation to the four-power commission on former Italian colonies. As political secretary and liaison officer, United Nations commission, he sought in 1950 to secure for Eritrea an independent future; but he was defeated by Haile Selassie's prestige and the United States' need of facilities in Eritrea, which he offered, to monitor communications across the Indian and Pacific oceans. Trevaskis's account of Britain's and his own stewardship is given in *A Colony in Transition: the British Occupation of Eritrea, 1941–52* (1960).

Realizing that he could do nothing further, Trevaskis returned to Northern Rhodesia in 1948, becoming district commissioner of Ndola, headquarters of the immensely wealthy copperbelt region. In 1951 he transferred to the Aden protectorate as political officer, western Aden protectorate, becoming deputy British agent in 1952 and adviser and British agent in 1954. He was back in an environment, essentially Muslim, where his experience, personal qualities, and sympathies were at home.

Trevaskis's first success was the inauguration on 11 February 1959 of the Federation of South Arabia, for which he was appointed CMG. Three years later, largely due to the diplomatic skills of Trevaskis, exercised in fluent Arabic, Aden agreed to join the federation, a necessity if the federation were to cease to be economically dependent on Great Britain. Trevaskis became high commissioner on 16 August 1963 and was advanced to KCMG. Over the following year the colonial secretary, Duncan Sandys, worked at hectic pace, exhausting British officials and Arabian ministers, to bring the Aden–South Arabia Federation to successful birth. This was bitterly opposed by President Nasser of Egypt: a hand grenade was thrown at Trevaskis at Aden airport in December 1963; two lives were lost, and he was wounded.

These efforts were aborted when in late 1964 the general election in Britain was won by the Labour Party, hostile to attempts to maintain British influence east of Suez, and to 'feudal and reactionary' rulers, as one reviewer put it. Anthony Greenwood, Labour's colonial secretary, summoned Trevaskis home. While he waited to see the new minister, his successor, Richard Turnbull, was being dispatched to Aden; Greenwood's order was that the press was to be given no information and that Turnbull's departure was to be secret. Trevaskis had his commission terminated on 23 November 1964.

Trevaskis was subsequently adviser to Sunningdale Oils and was much valued by them on account of his Arabian contacts. He maintained friendly contacts with several Arabian rulers, but his career was, at an age of not yet fifty, effectively at an end. He wrote the history of and the case for the policies he stood for: *Shades of Amber, a South Arabian Episode* (1968) must take its place beside his work on Eritrea as an evocative account of a lost cause. Both gave testimony to his sympathies for the intellectually advanced, though economically under-developed, peoples of the Horn of Africa.

Trevaskis's marriage, a sharing of thirty years abroad and in England, was greatly damaged by the effects of the Aden bombing. He and his wife finally parted in 1976, but did not divorce. Trevaskis had a stable and long-lasting relationship with a young widow, Valentine Sylvia Donovan (1935–1997), who later took his name by deed poll. He bought the Old Rectory, Rusper, where he spent his last years.

In the 1980s, his first love, Eritrea, reclaimed Trevaskis. He became a valued adviser to the Eritrean Peoples' Liberation Front, which in 1993 secured independence. He would have been a principal guest at a conference organized by the Eritrean Peoples' Liberation Front at the beginning of March 1990, but that same March, during an operation for a suspected hiatus hernia, he was found to have

extensive cancer. He died shortly after recovering consciousness on 4 March 1990 at Gatwick Park Hospital, near Crawley, Sussex, and was buried on 21 March in Rusper churchyard.
                                          ANTHONY D'AVRAY

Sources PRO, CO 1055/1–292, esp. 167–9, 268, 271, 273 · PRO, CFO 371/168629–168631, 174487, 179751 · Bodl. RH · *Colonial Office List* (1965) · *WW* (1990) · private information (2004) [family]
Archives Bodl. RH, corresp., diaries, and papers
Wealth at death £400 overdraft: private information

Trevellick, Richard F. (1830–1895), trade unionist and campaigner for social reform, was born on 2 May 1830 to a humble farming family on St Mary's, in the Isles of Scilly. Very little is known of his parents, though his mother was reputed to have had aristocratic ancestors. He had three brothers and a sister. Trevellick had little formal education, and at fourteen was apprenticed in the Southampton shipyards. After a brief attempt to take up farming, he became a ship's carpenter and a lifelong advocate of an eight-hour working day. A devout evangelical Methodist, he also espoused temperance and vegetarianism. In 1851 he sailed to Africa, India, and China. The next year he visited Australia and New Zealand. While in Auckland he organized an Eight-Hour League. In 1854 he went to Melbourne, where organizational efforts bore fruit; the Australian government passed an Eight Hours Bill in 1857. In 1855 he was in San Francisco, then shipped off to Panama with the Pacific Mail Steamship Company. He was in Peru the next year, and served as petty officer first class in the Peruvian navy during a brief war with Chile. Pacific Mail next sent him to New Orleans, where he became president of the local shipcarpenters' and caulkers' union and led a successful strike for a nine-hour working day. While there he married his wife, Victoria.

The American Civil War troubled Trevellick, a lifelong abolitionist. Rather than join the Confederate army, he sought refuge in the British consulate. He planned to return to England, but instead went to New York city, where one of his brothers resided. He remained in the United States, drifting from New York to Pittsburgh, then Detroit, where, in 1865, he became president of the shipcarpenters' and caulkers' union. He was also active in the Michigan Grand Eight Hours League. A powerfully built man who stood 5 feet 8½ inches tall and weighed 180 lb, Trevellick cut a dashing figure, with a moustache that flowed into a long goatee. He regaled colleagues with seafaring stories, and they affectionately nicknamed him Captain.

In 1864 Trevellick held conventions that created the International Industrial Assembly of North America and the Industrial Brotherhood, attempts at a national labour federation. Neither group took root, but the Knights of Labor (KOL) later adopted the statement of principles that Trevellick had written for the brotherhood almost verbatim. Short-lived success came in 1867, when Trevellick helped create America's first post-civil war trade federation, the National Labor Union (NLU). Trevellick penned the NLU's platform and was a lobbyist before the American congress when it passed an eight-hour law for federal labourers in 1868. He served as president of the NLU in 1869, and again from 1871 to 1873. Trevellick publicly agitated for land reform, shorter working days, improved workplace conditions, a ban on Chinese immigration, and an end to employee blacklisting. The NLU, however, disintegrated quickly after electoral defeats in 1872 and the collapse of constituent trades during the economic panic of 1873.

Trevellick supported the Greenback Labor Party, which advocated replacing the gold standard with an inflationary monetary policy based on banknotes. He attended three Greenback conventions between 1876 and 1880, and was active in state and local efforts. Trevellick's wide-ranging reform agenda included calls for women's suffrage, mandatory arbitration laws, land reform, and the application of Christian principles to the workplace. He opposed anarchism, violence, strikes, convict labour, and government intervention in labour disputes. His broad vision found consonance with the KOL, North America's most successful late nineteenth-century labour organization. He served as an organizer-at-large and lecturer from 1878 until his death in 1895, and helped transform the Knights from a Pennsylvania-based organization to one with national prominence. Trevellick's meagre KOL fees were often the sole support for his growing family, as Michigan employers routinely blacklisted him. In 1883 grateful knights helped the Trevellicks build a home, though meeting the mortgage was a constant struggle. Trevellick organized over 200 KOL locals and set up myriad reading-rooms for the education of members. He gave hundreds of lectures on temperance, the Greenback cause, KOL principles, and the eight-hour movement. He wrote at least two pamphlets, *Money and Panics* and *Columbia's Advocate*, as well as numerous poems that appeared in labour journals.

By 1888 Trevellick was troubled and the KOL in decline. He openly bickered with KOL president Terence Powderly over policy, poverty dogged him, the death of a son left him broken, his wife briefly left him, and he abruptly quit as a KOL general lecturer. Many, including Powderly, thought Trevellick's views outmoded, though he was reinstated as a lecturer, and in 1889 the KOL again advanced mortgage assistance. Trevellick was reconciled with Victoria and resumed giving speeches, though they lacked class analysis and his craftwork imagery was increasingly romantic in the age of mass production. By 1893 neither Trevellick nor the KOL were effective advocates for American workers. On 20 February 1895 Trevellick suffered two strokes and died at Fort Street, Detroit, Michigan; he was buried at Woodmere cemetery in Detroit. His wife and four of his five children survived him.
                                      ROBERT E. WEIR

Sources O. Hicks, *Life of Richard F. Trevellick, labor orator* (1896) · *The Advance and Labor Leaf* (17 Feb 1886) · Terence V. Powderly MSS [university microfilms] · Richard F. Trevellick letters, U. Mich., Joseph A. Labadie collection · *Detroit News* (1 Aug 1895) · G. Fink, ed., *Biographical dictionary of American labor* (1984) · N. Ware, *The labor movement in the United States, 1860–1895* (1929) · G. Kealey and B. Palmer,

Dreaming of what might be (1987) • P. Foner, *History of the labor move-ment in the United States*, 1 (1947)

Archives U. Mich., Harlan Hatcher Graduate Library, Joseph A. Labadie collection, letters

Likenesses R. Trevellick, woodcut, repro. in *The Advance and Labor Leaf* (17 Feb 1886)

Wealth at death very few assets: *Detroit News* (15 Aug 1895)

Trevelyan, Sir Charles Edward, first baronet (1807–1886), administrator in India, fourth son of George Trevelyan (1764–1827), archdeacon of Taunton, and Harriet, third daughter of Sir Richard Neave, baronet, was born at Taunton on 2 April 1807. He was educated at Taunton grammar school, at Charterhouse School from 1820, and at East India College, Haileybury. He entered the East India Company's Bengal service as a writer in 1826, having displayed from an early age a great proficiency in Indian languages. On 4 January 1827 he was appointed assistant to Sir Charles Theophilus Metcalfe, the commissioner at Delhi, where, during a residence of four years, he was entrusted with several important missions. His time at Delhi, however, was perhaps most famous for his role in the 'breaking' of the resident, Sir Edward Colebrooke, for corruption. Before leaving Delhi he also contributed from his own funds to the building of a broad street through a new suburb, which subsequently became known as Trevelyanpur. In 1831 he moved to Calcutta, and became deputy secretary to the government in the political department. On 23 December 1834 he married Hannah Moore, sister of Lord Macaulay, who was then a member of the council of the governor-general of India, and one of his closest friends. She died on 5 August 1873, leaving a son, later Sir George Otto *Trevelyan, baronet, and two daughters.

Trevelyan was especially interested in education, and had an important influence on Macaulay's celebrated minute of 1835, promulgating the teaching of European literature and science in India. In April 1836 he was nominated secretary to the Sudder board of revenue, which office he held until his return to England in January 1838. In India Trevelyan was, Macaulay recorded:

> a most stormy reformer … Lord William [Bentinck] said to me … 'That man is almost always on the right side in every question; and it is well that he is so, for he gives a most confounded deal of trouble when he happens to take the wrong one.' (Macaulay to Mrs Cropper, 7 Dec 1834, *Life*, 278)

On 21 January 1840 he became assistant secretary to the Treasury, London, and held this office for the next nineteen years. No civil servant did more to place the Treasury in its modern role of watchdog of the whole of the civil service. Trevelyan's zeal for retrenchment ill equipped him for his role of co-ordinator of relief during the Irish famine of 1845–7 and he gained a reputation for brutal complacency (though his employment schemes had some success). He encouraged the passing of the Poor Law Extension Act in 1847, which gave the Treasury greater influence over the use of poor-law funds. Trevelyan was determined that relief should be financed by the raising of local rates rather than through grants from the Treasury. This involved him in a prolonged dispute with Edward Twistleton of the poor-law commissioners. *The Irish Crisis*

Sir Charles Edward Trevelyan, first baronet (1807–1886), by John Watkins

(1848) summarizes Trevelyan's views. In 1848 Trevelyan was made KCB for his work in Ireland. In 1852–3 he helped with reports on several government departments. One of these, by a Treasury minute written by Gladstone and dated 12 April 1854, led to the brief report known as the Northcote–Trevelyan report ('Report on the organisation of a permanent civil service'), one of the most famous documents of recent British history, which scathingly condemned the patronage system of civil service appointments and recommended open examination and promotion by merit, and sketched what became the administrative grade.

In 1858 Trevelyan was offered the governorship of Madras in succession to Lord Harris, and entered upon his duties in the spring of 1859. He was principally responsible for organizing a new police system and for establishing rights in land, which freed it from encumbrances and made it saleable in fee simple. In February 1860 James Wilson, financial member of the viceroy's council, proposed a plan of severe retrenchment and taxation by which he hoped to improve the financial position of the Indian government. On 4 March Trevelyan and the council of Madras sent a sharply critical response back to Calcutta by open telegram. For this they were censured and, at the same time, the representative of the Madras government in the central legislative council of India was prohibited from following the instructions of his superiors by laying upon the table and advocating the expression of their views. On 21 March a telegram was sent to Madras stating that the bill would be introduced and referred to a committee, which would report in five weeks, whereupon Trevelyan and his council recorded their opinions in a minute and, on the responsibility of Sir Charles alone, passed the document to the newspapers. On the arrival of this intelligence in England Trevelyan was at once recalled. This decision occasioned controversy both in and out of parliament. Palmerston, while defending the recall, spoke in praise of Trevelyan's character; and Sir Charles Wood, the president of the Board of Control, said:

> A more honest, zealous, upright, and independent servant could not be. He was a loss to India, but there would be danger if he were allowed to remain, after having adopted a course so subversive of all authority, so fearfully tending to endanger our rule, and so likely to provoke the people to insurrection against the central and responsible authority. (*Hansard 3*, 11 May 1860, vols. 1130–61)

Trevelyan's temporary disgrace was made more significant by his later triumph. In 1862 he went back to India as finance minister, an emphatic endorsement of the justness of his former views. His tenure of office was marked by increased government expenditure and by extensive measures for the development of public works. On his return home in 1865 he became involved in the question of army purchase, on which he had given evidence before the royal commission in 1857; he developed his views in *The British Army in 1868* (1868). Later his name was associated with a variety of social questions, such as charities and pauperism, on which he published several pamphlets. In 1874 he was created a baronet. He was a staunch Liberal, and gave his support to the Liberal cause in Northumberland, while residing at Wallington in that county, which he had inherited from his cousin Sir Walter Calverley *Trevelyan in 1879. Sir Charles married second, on 14 October 1875, Eleanora Anne (*d.* 1919), daughter of Walter Campbell of Islay. He is drawn by Trollope in *The Three Clerks* (1857) under the name of Sir Gregory Hardlines. He died at his home, 67 Eaton Square, London, on 19 June 1886.   G. C. BOASE, *rev.* DAVID WASHBROOK

Sources *The Times* (21 June 1886) · J. Hart, 'Sir Charles Trevelyan at the treasury', *EngHR*, 75 (1960), 92–110 · E. Hughes, 'Civil Service reform, 1853–5', *History*, new ser., 27 (1942), 51–83 · M. Wright, *Treasury control of the civil service, 1854–1874* (1969) · J. B. Conacher, *The Aberdeen coalition, 1852–1855* (1968) · C. Kinealy, *This great calamity: the Irish famine, 1845–52* (1994) · G. O. Trevelyan, *The life and letters of Lord Macaulay*, [rev. edn], 2 vols. (1908) · *CGPLA Eng. & Wales* (1886) · 'Report on the organisation of a permanent civil service', *Parl. papers* (1854), vol. 27, no. 1713 · H. Trevelyan, *The India we left* (1972) · Burke, *Peerage* (1939)

Archives Northumbd RO, Newcastle upon Tyne, estate and official papers · PRO, papers relating to Ireland, T 64 · U. Newcastle, Robinson L., corresp. and papers | BL, letters to H. Bruce, Add. MS 43994 · BL, letters to W. E. Gladstone, Add. MSS 44333–44334 · BL, Layard MSS · BL, corresp. with Florence Nightingale, Add. MSS 45798–45801 · BL, corresp. with Sir Robert Peel, Add. MSS 40562–40615, *passim* · BL OIOC, letters to Lord Elgin, MS Eur. F 83 · BL OIOC, letters to Sir Richard Temple, MS Eur. F 86 · Bodl. Oxf., letters to Lord Clarendon · Bodl. Oxf., letters to Benjamin Disraeli · Borth. Inst., corresp. with Lord Halifax · Lpool RO, corresp. with Lord Derby · NA Scot., letters to E. W. Hope · NA Scot., corresp. with Sir John McNeill · NL Ire., letters to Lord Emily · PRO, corresp. with Lord John Russell and others, PRO 30/22 · PRO, letters to Lord Granville, PRO 30/29 · Ransom HRC, corresp. with Sir John Herschel · UCL, corresp. with Sir Edwin Chadwick · Wilts. & Swindon RO, Herbert MSS

Likenesses probably by Bourne & Shepherd, albumen print, *c.*1860, NPG · W. & D. Downey, photograph, NPG · E. U. Eddis, portrait · D. J. Pound, stipple and line engraving (after photograph by J. Watkins), NPG · Southwell Bros, carte-de-visite, NPG · J. Watkins, carte-de-visite, NPG [*see illus.*]

Wealth at death £50,801 17*s.* 6*d.*: probate, 6 Sept 1886, *CGPLA Eng. & Wales*

Trevelyan, Sir Charles Philips, third baronet (1870–1958), politician, was born on 28 October 1870 at Ennismore Gardens, Park Lane, London, the eldest of the three sons of Sir George Otto *Trevelyan (1838–1928), politician and historian, and his wife, Caroline (*d.* 1928), daughter of Robert Needham Philips, Liberal MP for Bury. George Macaulay *Trevelyan, the historian, was his elder brother. He was educated at Harrow School (1884–9) and Trinity College, Cambridge (1889–92), where he took a second class in the history tripos.

Family tradition determined for the eldest son a career in politics. Trevelyan was appointed private secretary to Lord Houghton at Dublin Castle, but was bored by underemployment, irked by ceremony, and at odds with his companions. He left Ireland in 1893. Shortly thereafter Trevelyan was adopted as Liberal parliamentary candidate for North Lambeth, but was narrowly defeated in the 1895 general election. In 1896 he was elected to the London school board. Subsequently he was adopted for the West Riding of Yorkshire constituency of Elland, which, like Lambeth, had been secured by family influence. During 1898–9 he toured North America and Australasia, with Sidney and Beatrice Webb as his companions, before entering parliament after a by-election at Elland in March 1899.

Though the scion of a whig family, Trevelyan advertised himself as a Liberal Imperialist. He supported the Second South African War, and looked to Rosebery, and later Asquith, as his leaders. He had earlier called himself a radical Liberal. His changing political ideas were reflected in his contributions to the *Progressive Review* and in his debates with fellow progressive members of a rather self-conscious discussion group called the Rainbow Circle. Membership of the Fabian Society afforded some degree of precision to his political ideas. He never lacked for resolution but, as he disarmingly admitted, he did not possess quickness of mind. Beatrice Webb supposed that Trevelyan enjoyed 'every endowment—social position, wealth, intelligence, an independent outlook and good manners' (Cannadine, 11). H. G. Wells was less impressed by the tyro politician. Undoubtedly high-minded, Trevelyan had little sense of humour or irony, and was only marginally less self-satisfied and endurably boring than his youngest brother, George. (The Trevelyan brothers appear in H. G. Wells's novel *The New Machiavelli* as the Cramptons.) Even his future father-in-law, Sir Hugh Bell, the ironmaster, was amazed at the way in which young Trevelyan pontificated

Sir Charles Philips Trevelyan, third baronet (1870–1958), by Sir William Rothenstein, 1924

earnestly and at inordinate length upon politics, and characterized him, not unfairly, as 'a damned serious gowk' (M. Trevelyan, 40). The person who best understood to what Trevelyan actually aspired in his political career was Mary (Molly) Katharine Bell (1881–1966). They were married on 6 January 1904. They had three sons, including the educationist Sir George Lowthian *Trevelyan, and four daughters.

Trevelyan's laborious instruction of Molly on current political issues included the frequent and anxious admonition that she should not entertain exaggerated notions about his prospects. He acknowledged his knowledge and ability was limited, and consequently he was not likely to rise to a high position. This, however, would allow him to pursue whatever line he thought right. In and out of parliament, Trevelyan's comments upon his party's elders and leaders were often tactless, while his attacks upon policies he considered mistaken were intemperate. Not a trimmer by nature, his demeanour frequently suggested impatience and insensitivity. It was for these reasons, rather than lack of ability, that he was obliged to wait until October 1908 before obtaining even junior office as parliamentary under-secretary at the Board of Education.

On domestic political issues, Trevelyan was a typical radical Liberal. He advocated taxation of land values, Liberal–Labour co-operation on social legislation, and the ending of the House of Lords. On matters of defence and foreign affairs he grew increasingly disillusioned with official policy. In particular, his faith in the capacity and intentions of

the foreign secretary, Sir Edward Grey, was steadily eroded. In 1912 he went so far as to admit to Molly that 'If we begin verging towards war … I will not be party to it' (Morris, 110). On 3 August 1914, if reluctantly, most radical Liberals acquiesced in Britain's ultimatum to Germany. Trevelyan thought Grey's explanation outrageous. Though any commitment to France had frequently been denied, it was clear Britain was condemned to war for no better reason than sentimental attachment to France and hatred of Germany. Trevelyan resigned from the government in protest. By this action he found himself estranged from most of his family, condemned and vilified by a hysterical press, and rejected by his constituency association. Never before or later in his political career was he 'to feel more alone or find criticism more difficult to sustain' (ibid., 126). Around him he rallied those few brave, independent spirits who shared his views. Together they helped to found the Union of Democratic Control, in A. J. P. Taylor's judgement 'the most formidable Radical body ever to influence British foreign policy' (A. J. P. Taylor, *Politicians, Socialism and Historians*, 1982, 103). Trevelyan became the union's principal advocate in the Commons. His stubborn campaign for peace won him grudging respect, if not admiration and support.

On 2 February 1918 Trevelyan published in the radical weekly *The Nation* the assertion that Labour, and not the Liberal Party, was now best fitted to root out the evils of social and economic privilege. He delayed joining the Labour Party himself until November 1918, explaining he had found it extremely difficult to sunder old allegiances and attachments. This change of party further exacerbated already painful divisions, particularly between himself and his parents. His crushing defeat at Elland in the 'coupon' election typically served to strengthen Trevelyan's conviction that he had made the right decision. A year later, he was selected as Labour candidate for the Newcastle upon Tyne Central constituency. He found membership of the Independent Labour Party, a ginger group within Labour, most congenial.

Trevelyan tried to explain to a wider public the reasons for his political conversion. His short book, *From Liberalism to Labour* (1921), was conceived and written to make a bold appeal 'to those who can expect great changes without apprehension', for great experiments were possible and necessary 'in a society where the existing order is patently bankrupt'. It was not he that had abandoned Liberalism, but Liberalism that had abandoned all its chief articles of faith. Trevelyan was accused of playing Judas to his class and betraying his political trust. The charge was exaggerated and false, just as the later claim that he was a communist. His notorious sympathy for Soviet Russia, and his naïve expectation that the Russian Revolution would ensure world peace, was not rooted in any ideology but in a romantic attachment to the Russian people in their epic struggle to throw off the tsarist yoke. It gave pause for thought to Beatrice Webb, that 'an Ultra Whig by tradition and temperament' could so thoroughly metamorphose into an extreme socialist. It was true that he admitted his undiluted joy and confidence in his new cause, and claimed that in the 1922 election, when he was returned to parliament for his Newcastle constituency, 'For the first time I am saying what I truly think' (M. I. Cole, ed., *Beatrice Webb's Diaries, 1912–24*, 1952, 171, 229). He held his seat at the 1923 general election.

To the surprise of no one, when Labour formed its first administration in January 1924, Trevelyan was appointed president of the Board of Education. A sound administrator, he was not overawed, as were many of his colleagues, by his civil servants. As a minister he was popular and successful. Fêted by the Independent Labour Party, his performances at the dispatch box won back his father's approval. He was the first minister of education to address a teachers' conference. In his two periods of office he fought to break down sectarian barriers, to raise the school leaving age, and to make the universities accessible to all young people of ability—even those who were not wealthy. In 1924 he reversed the cuts in education spending imposed in 1922 under the 'Geddes axe', increased the number of free places at grammar schools, and encouraged (but could not require) local authorities to raise the school leaving age to fifteen. Out of office within a year, Trevelyan maintained the experience had been 'enormously worthwhile'. He had achieved 'a good day's work', an opinion shared by H. G. Wells, who asserted 'there has never been a better, more far sighted, harder working, more unselfishly devoted Minister of Education' (Morris, 162).

In opposition, Trevelyan abandoned his former hectoring earnestness for a new, more relaxed parliamentary style that won not only arguments but new friends. He enjoyed an increased majority when re-elected for Newcastle Central in May 1929. But when appointed for a second time Labour's minister for education in June 1929, the confidence of his earlier period in office evaporated. He doubted whether the measures he proposed would succeed in getting through parliament because the party's leaders were so pusillanimous. His central policy was to raise the statutory school leaving age to fifteen. Twice in the summer of 1930 his Education Bill to carry this into effect was withdrawn for lack of parliamentary time. Introduced for a third time in October 1930, the bill was undermined in January 1931 by an amendment carried by John Scurr on behalf of Roman Catholic schools, which sought grants to accommodate increased pupil numbers, and was defeated in the Lords, largely because of the unfavourable financial climate, in February 1931. Trevelyan was at fault in refusing to woo Liberal support; he totally underestimated the intransigence of the Catholic hierarchy and wrongly supposed that Labour's Catholic MPs would put their loyalty to socialism before that to their church. Trevelyan resigned in March 1931, but not only because his bill had been defeated. For months he had wanted to quit the cabinet because he was haunted by the incompetence of his colleagues. At a meeting of the Parliamentary Labour Party to explain his resignation, Trevelyan made a blunt personal attack upon MacDonald.

It was greeted with silence. A few approved, but most resented his criticism, supposing Trevelyan wanted to blame anyone but himself for the failure of his bill. In his letter to his constituents, Trevelyan spoke not of personalities but of the want of constructive socialist measures. Once the initial excitement of rebellion had dissipated, life on the back benches supporting an enfeebled party seemed a complete waste of time. He was bored and impatient with Westminster tactics. But when he was crushingly defeated in the 1931 election, Trevelyan was stunned.

Trevelyan did not pine to return to the Commons. 'I don't want to go back', he assured Molly. In a matter-of-fact way he summed up his parliamentary career: 'The earlier part was only training … I was not worth much … I have nothing to regret … I am not in any way disappointed' (Morris, 190). With clear conscience he could now concentrate all his attention and energy upon his Northumberland estate. He inherited Wallington, along with his father's baronetcy, in 1928. It had been much neglected, but with Molly's vigorous co-operation a plan of wide-ranging reform and improvement was begun that embraced the hall, the garden, the grounds and grouse moors, and the properties and welfare of their tenants. In 1930, as a more congenial prospect than possibly becoming viceroy of India, Trevelyan accepted appointment as lord lieutenant of his county. Many local gentry were scandalized at 'an avowed champion of the rights of democracy' taking the office, traditionally considered an apanage of the Percys, which he retained until 1949.

For a few years after leaving the Commons, Trevelyan continued to attend party conferences. He rather enjoyed the atmosphere of political millenarianism after MacDonald's 'betrayal'. Trevelyan encouraged the Socialist League, gave help both political and material to a number of aspiring and established left-wingers, and seemed quite convinced that the Labour Party was at last committed to socialism. There was a brief moment of personal triumph at the annual party conference in 1933. He successfully introduced a resolution that, if there were even a threat of war, the Labour Party would call a general strike. In the moment of his triumph Trevelyan supposed it to be an 'immensely important decision' (Morris, 191); but he recognized its impracticality long before 1939, when he wholeheartedly supported war against Nazi Germany. In 1934 he lost his place on the party's executive, a decision he accepted with relief. Politics, he avowed, was for the young, bold, and imaginative. They should carry the banner of progress forward. Many were keen to draw him back into national politics: 'Come on! Take up your sword! Alan Breck was not a bonnier fechter than you', pleaded MacNeill Weir, but all to no avail (ibid., 192).

Age did not diminish Trevelyan's physical or intellectual vigour. He remained young at heart and retained an undiminished belief in social progress. His plans for Wallington, that it should become a centre for culture and socialist internationalism, were fully realized. In 1941, subject only to a life interest, he gave Wallington and the estate to the National Trust so that others might enjoy the splendours he had been privileged to know. Trevelyan died at Wallington Hall on 24 January 1958.

A. J. A. MORRIS

Sources A. J. A. Morris, *C. P. Trevelyan, 1870–1958: portrait of a radical* (1977) · D. Cannadine, *G. M. Trevelyan: a life in history* (1992) · C. P. Trevelyan, *Letters from North America and the Pacific*, ed. P. Dower (1969) · K. Trevelyan, *Fool in love* (1962) · M. P. Price, *My three revolutions* (1969) · private information (2004) [family] · U. Newcastle, Robinson L., Trevelyan MSS · M. Trevelyan, *The number of my days* (privately printed, 1963) · *DNB* · 'The odyssey of an anti-war liberal', A. J. A. Morris, *Doves and diplomats*, ed. S. Wank (1978), 85–108 · A. J. A. Morris, 'C. P. Trevelyan', *Biographical dictionary of modern peace leaders*, ed. H. Josephson (1985), 955–8 · M. Swartz, *The Union of Democratic Control in British politics during the First World War* (1971)
Archives U. Newcastle, Robinson L., family corresp. and papers | BLPES, corresp. with E. D. Morel · Bodl. Oxf., letters to Lord Ponsonby · Glos. RO, corresp. with M. Philips Price · HLRO, corresp. with Lloyd George · HLRO, corresp. with Herbert Samuel · JRL, corresp. with James Ramsay MacDonald · London School of Economics, Lansbury Collection · priv. coll., Josiah Wedgwood · Shulbrede Priory, Surrey, corresp. with Lord Ponsonby · U. Hull, Brynmor Jones L., corresp. with E. D. Morel and the Union of Democratic Control · U. Newcastle, Robinson L., corresp. with Walter Runciman
Likenesses W. Rothenstein, sanguine and chalk drawing, 1924, NPG [*see illus.*] · W. Stoneman, photograph, 1930, NPG · J. Parker, portrait, 2001, Wallington House, Northumberland · G. Hermes, bronze bust, Wallington, Northumberland · photograph, repro. in Cannadine, *G. M. Trevelyan*, facing p. 13 · photographs, repro. in Morris, *C. P. Trevelyan* · portraits, Wallington, Northumberland
Wealth at death £95,635 12s. 7d.: probate, 10 March 1958, *CGPLA Eng. & Wales*

Trevelyan, Sir George Lowthian, fourth baronet (1906–1996), educationist, was born on 5 November 1906 at 14 Great College Street, Westminster, the eldest of three sons and the second of seven children of Sir Charles Philips *Trevelyan, third baronet (1870–1958), politician and landowner, and his wife, Mary Katharine *Trevelyan (1881–1966), youngest daughter of Sir Hugh Bell, second baronet. He was the grandson of Sir George Otto *Trevelyan, second baronet, and the nephew of George Macaulay *Trevelyan. His father was Liberal MP for Elland (1899–1918) and Labour MP for Newcastle upon Tyne Central (1922–31), and president of the Board of Education in Ramsay MacDonald's two Labour administrations. George Trevelyan grew up on the family estate at Wallington, Northumberland, attended school at Sidcot, in the Mendips, and in 1925 followed the family tradition by going up to Trinity College, Cambridge, to read history. There he was master of the lake hunt, a chase over the lakeland fells that had been founded by his historian uncle, George Macaulay Trevelyan, and his friend George Winthrop Young, in 1898.

Trevelyan's first interest on leaving Cambridge was making furniture, and he gained experience at the workshops of Peter Waals at Chalford, Gloucestershire. He then spent four years learning and teaching the F. M. Alexander re-education method. Subsequently he moved to Scotland to teach history, literature, woodwork, and outdoor pursuits at Gordonstoun School, when Kurt Hahn was headmaster. He then took up a post at Abinger Hill Preparatory School, near Dorking, Surrey. It was there that he met a fellow schoolteacher and artist, (Editha) Helen Lindsay Smith (1900/01–1994), daughter of Colonel John Lindsay Smith, of the Indian Army Service Corps. They married on 14 August 1940 and later adopted a daughter, Catriona (*b.* 1944). Trevelyan returned to Scotland for most of the Second World War, when, as a captain in the rifle brigade, he was engaged in training home defence forces.

Trevelyan apparently had visions of making Wallington into a centre for adult education. This seemed thwarted when, in 1941, his father announced that he would be handing over the estate to the National Trust (Cannadine, 169); Trevelyan was always reticent in later life in speaking about his ancestors. Nevertheless, on demobilization he gained skills in teaching adults at the army college at Dalkeith, and in 1947 he was appointed first warden of Shropshire Adult College, established at Attingham Park, the eighteenth-century mansion 4 miles east of Shrewsbury that had been the home of the Hill family, barons Berwick, and had formed part of a military base during the Second World War. The college was one of many initiatives launched by H. Martin Wilson, secretary for education for Shropshire county council. Trevelyan proved an inspired appointment. The volume published in 1965 to mark Wilson's retirement commented that Attingham had been 'born of the wartime sense of the unity of the community' and that Attingham was 'an essential part of adult education in the county, particularly reflecting the enthusiasm and devotion of its first and only Warden, Sir George Trevelyan' (*Education in Shropshire*, 77–8).

Attingham was one of more than twenty similar colleges founded in the late 1940s with the aim of providing short courses that would be open to all. Several of these colleges, including Attingham, had a profound, if informal, influence on the development of scholarship. This type of institution effectively disappeared from the educational scene in the last quarter of the twentieth century. Trevelyan promoted the college with much energy. It became a centre for music-making, drama, and film appreciation. Mid-week it was used for teacher training, for business conferences, and by university departments as a base for fieldwork. It was most influential as a location for weekend courses that were open to the public, the first of which began on 21 August 1948 and the last concluded on 25 November 1975, some four years after Trevelyan retired. The college was an independent foundation supported by the local educational charity, the Walker Trust, the University of Birmingham, and Shropshire county council, the organization of courses being part of the duties of some of the staff of the two latter bodies. Trevelyan responded with enthusiasm to suggestions from colleagues for courses of many kinds, often far outside his own spheres of interest. He encouraged courses that stimulated awareness of new directions in scholarship in botany, forestry, the needs of gifted children, film and television studies, folk song, and the workshop approach to theatre. Attingham proved influential in the development of social history, historical demography, industrial archaeology, and garden history.

Trevelyan had a strikingly handsome appearance and resonant speech. His manner was both welcoming and patrician, and some students at the college gained the impression that Attingham was his ancestral home. He himself dispensed cider to students at dinner and conducted short, non-denominational religious services before the start of teaching on Sunday mornings. He was an exuberant participant in field trips and delighted in scrambling up steep slopes. He may have been disappointed that he did not inherit Wallington but found satisfaction, as he wrote in the college prospectus, that 'Attingham has found one of the happiest solutions to the problem of full use of a country house'.

Many of Trevelyan's beliefs sprang directly from Trevelyan family traditions and can also be seen in the life of his uncle the historian. His reading in poetry was wide and deep, and he could quote readily and at length. He had strong commitments to craftsmanship, to the countryside (which he loved to explore on foot), and to adult education. He was also interested in spiritual matters, and in 1942 had been attracted to the ideas of Rudolph Steiner. While he encouraged colleagues to run courses on many subjects he had particular interests of his own about which he permitted no debate during programme planning. Some related to craftsmanship; several of his own, elegantly crafted chairs adorned the college, and for many years he gave great encouragement to the making of mosaics. Such courses were uncontroversial but his courses on spiritual topics did raise some concerns among academic colleagues, particularly when, as with a course entitled 'The significance of the group in the new age', a Michaelmas festival in 1965, it was acknowledged in publicity that they were intended for 'a small and mainly invited group'. Subsequent courses included 'Man know thyself', in 1966, and 'Towards light and love', in 1967. Such topics embarrassed the governing body, which insisted that Attingham would no longer be available for such activities after Trevelyan retired in 1971.

As warden of Attingham Trevelyan facilitated developments in many disciplines. In retirement he came to be regarded as a prophet in the studies that are perhaps best summarized in the title of one of his courses, 'The primal oneness in diversity'. He founded, and from 1971 to 1992 was director of, the Wrekin Trust, whose gatherings carried further the themes of his Attingham courses. He encouraged responsible attitudes to the planet, sought common elements within the great religions of the world, and found spiritual values in literature. Though smitten by arthritis, he travelled extensively, addressing conferences (including an annual gathering of 'Mystics and Scientists'), helped to set up many groups in Britain and overseas, and readily conversed with many who saw themselves as 'New Age' thinkers and acknowledged him as a prophet. He published a succession of books, which included a trilogy entitled *The Aquarian Redemption*, comprising *A Vision of the Aquarian Age* (1977), *Operation Redemption* (1981), and *Exploration into God* (1991), and *Magic Casements: the Use of Poetry in the Expanding of Consciousness*

(1980). He was closely involved with the Findhorn Foundation, the Gatekeeper and Open Gate trusts, the Teilhard de Chardin Society, and the Essene Network. In 1982 he was awarded the Right Livelihood award—established by the Swede Jacob Von Yxkull—for his work in 'educating the adult spirit to a new non-materialistic vision of human nature' and for his contribution to 'healing the planet'. He died, of rheumatoid arthritis and renal failure, on 7 February 1996 at his home, the Old Vicarage, Hawkesbury, near Badminton, Avon. He had succeeded his father as fourth baronet in 1958, and in turn was succeeded by his younger brother, Geoffrey Washington Trevelyan (b. 1920). He was survived by his adopted daughter, Catriona, his wife, Helen, having predeceased him. BARRIE TRINDER

Sources *The Times* (17 Feb 1996) · *The Guardian* (19 Feb 1996) · *The Independent* (26 Feb 1996) · papers relating to Attingham Park, Shrops. RRC · *Education in Shropshire, 1945–65*, Salop county council (1965) · D. Cannadine, *G. M. Trevelyan: a life in history* (1992) · *VCH Shropshire*, vol. 3 · *WWW* [forthcoming] · Burke, *Peerage* · b. cert. · m. cert. · d. cert.
Archives Shrops. RRC, Shropshire county council papers, ephemera relating to Attingham Park
Likenesses photograph, 1976, Hult. Arch. · photograph, repro. in *The Times* · photograph, repro. in *The Independent*
Wealth at death under £145,000: probate, 1996, *CGPLA Eng. & Wales*

Trevelyan, George Macaulay (1876–1962), historian, public educator, and conservationist, was born on 16 February 1876, at Welcombe, near Stratford upon Avon, Warwickshire, the youngest of the three sons of Sir George Otto *Trevelyan, second baronet (1838–1928), who was a historian, landowner, Liberal MP, and cabinet minister, and his wife, Caroline (d. 1928), the daughter of Robert Needham Philips of Manchester.

Ancestry and youth, 1876–1903 Trevelyan's forebears were Cornish gentry, but during the nineteenth century a cadet branch of the family established itself at Wallington in Northumberland, where his father inherited a great estate and the baronetcy in 1886. This place was a formative influence: it was a whig house, which had been remodelled in 1688, the year of the Glorious Revolution; it imbued Trevelyan with a lifelong love of nature and the countryside; and it helps explain his pride in his ancestors. His grandfather Sir Charles Edward *Trevelyan was an Indian pro-consul and reforming civil servant. His great-uncle was Thomas Babington Macaulay, by turns a poet, historian, colonial administrator, and British politician. His father, Sir George Otto Trevelyan, was chief secretary for Ireland in Gladstone's second administration and secretary of state for Scotland in his last. And his elder brother Sir Charles Philips *Trevelyan, third baronet, was secretary of education in the Labour governments of 1924 and 1929.

This was a privileged background, in which the aristocracies of birth and talent converged, and it gave Trevelyan the social confidence and financial security to form his opinions and express his views with fearless independence. From an early age, and as befitted someone bearing his middle name, Trevelyan resolved to write history in the grand manner of his great-uncle. Wherever possible,

George Macaulay Trevelyan (1876–1962), by Edmund H. Nelson, 1946

he would base his work on primary archival research, but his chief concern was to produce big books on large subjects which would be widely read by the educated public that had devoured Macaulay's volumes in an earlier era. History, Trevelyan believed, was an essential element in the public culture of any civilized nation, and he determined to uphold his family tradition by writing that history for his own day. In this endeavour he was astonishingly successful, as the prodigious sales of his books gave him a cultural authority unrivalled among his generation of historians.

In conformity with family precedent, Trevelyan was educated at Harrow School, where Winston Churchill was a near contemporary. In 1893, and again following in the family footsteps, he went up to Trinity College, Cambridge, where he read history. He was soon elected to the Apostles, the university's most exclusive and influential undergraduate society, and his high-toned contemporaries included John Maynard Keynes, Ralph Vaughan Williams, Leonard Wolff, Edward Hilton Young, Bertrand Russell, and E. M. Forster. He never indulged in the homosexual relations that became widespread for a time among some Apostles, but he did absorb their culture of radical agnosticism. Nevertheless, he remained all his life loyal to a secular version of Christian ethics: 'a love of things good, and a hatred of things evil' (Trevelyan, 82). He was much influenced in his historical studies by Maitland and Acton (though he never forgave Sir John Seeley for denouncing Macaulay as a 'charlatan'), and he spent his vacations at Wallington or joining reading parties in the manner of the time. In 1896 he obtained a first in the historical tripos, and soon after (1898) he was elected a fellow of Trinity.

Within a year Trevelyan completed his first book, *England in the Age of Wycliffe* (1899), which was based on his fellowship dissertation, and which was published by Longmans, the imprint under which his father's and his great-uncle's histories had previously appeared. It was a zestful work of confident youth, and the jauntiness of the prose sometimes reads like a parody of Macaulay. But the subject was well suited to Trevelyan's interests and opinions, dealing as it did with the peasants' revolt of 1381; this he interpreted as the first flowering of those impulses towards secular liberty and religious freedom which he regarded as the defining characteristics of English history and the English nation. At this time he was seen as the coming man among young Cambridge historians, and his vigorous, iconoclastic lectures attracted a large undergraduate following. But he found the hypercritical atmosphere of the university inimical to his own more spacious and creative impulses, and he was outraged when in 1903 J. B. Bury denounced literary history in his inaugural lecture as regius professor. Trevelyan promptly resigned his Trinity fellowship, and set off for London.

Liberal and literary London, 1903–1914 Trevelyan's departure from Cambridge virtually coincided with the completion of *England under the Stuarts* (1904), an outstandingly successful general survey, which unfolded the familiar story of the civil war and the revolution of 1688 in more disciplined prose and mature style. As he interpreted it, the seventeenth century witnessed fundamental advances in religious toleration and parliamentary freedom, the forces of Catholic despotism were vanquished, and Great Britain gradually evolved towards the status of a world power. In the same year Trevelyan married Janet Penrose Ward (d. 1956), whose forebears (including Thomas Arnold, headmaster of Rugby) and whose cousins (including the Huxley clan) were almost as illustrious as his own. She was the daughter of the novelist Mary Augusta *Ward and her husband, Thomas Humphry Ward, a journalist. The marriage was happy and fulfilling, not least because Janet Trevelyan was herself a clever and public-spirited woman. She was the author of several works of history and biography, and in 1936 she was made CH in recognition of her work for the preservation of play centres for children in London.

Trevelyan's strong sense of dynastic identity meant his children were very important to him, although he became better at dealing with them when they were adults. His first child, Mary Caroline (1905–1994), inherited her share of the family gifts, pride, and interests, and her many publications included *William III and the Defence of Holland, 1672–73* (1930), a biography of Wordsworth (2 vols., 1957–65), and a memoir of her father (1980). In 1930 Mary Trevelyan married John Richard Humpidge Moorman, a Church of England clergyman with interests in ecclesiastical history, who eventually became bishop of Ripon. By then her father's earlier, militant agnosticism had mellowed into broader tolerance, and his relations with his son-in-law were easier than might have been predicted. The second child of the marriage, Theodore Macaulay (1906–1911), was the apple of his parents' eyes and, as his middle name suggests, he was expected to carry the family name to new heights of distinction in the next generation. But his early death from appendicitis left his father devastated, and the youngest offspring, Charles Humphry (1909–1964), was brought up in Theodore's glowing yet dark shadow. Humphry wrote on Goethe and the Greeks, and became a fellow of King's College, Cambridge, in 1947.

Apart from this one great family tragedy, the years from 1903 to 1914 were probably the most fulfilling of Trevelyan's life. He settled down in Cheyne Gardens in Chelsea, and threw himself into the literary and political life of the metropolis. He taught at the working men's college in Great Ormond Street, and in the company of such like-minded liberals as H. A. L. Fisher and C. R. Buxton he edited a progressive journal entitled the *Independent Review*. But his great work was his Garibaldi trilogy (1907–11), which established his reputation as the outstanding literary historian of his generation. It depicted Garibaldi as a Carlylean hero—poet, patriot, and man of action—whose inspired leadership created the Italian nation. For Trevelyan, Garibaldi was the champion of freedom, progress, and tolerance, who vanquished the despotism, reaction, and obscurantism of the Austrian empire and the Neapolitan monarchy. The books were also notable for their vivid evocation of landscape (Trevelyan had himself followed the course of Garibaldi's marches), for their innovative use of documentary and oral sources, and for their spirited accounts of battles and military campaigns.

In the timing of this trilogy Trevelyan was exceptionally lucky, for the publication of the Garibaldi books almost exactly coincided with the high noon of Edwardian Liberalism. The trilogy also marked a high peak of imaginative intensity and creative endeavour which their author was never quite to scale again. He had now established himself as the master of the two forms of writing about the past which held the field when he was growing up, and to which he devoted the remainder of his working life: narrative national histories and biographies of great men. His next book was a life of John Bright (1913), another Liberal hero who was a high-minded internationalist and campaigner for peace, and a central figure in the making of Victorian England. He was then invited to write (and believed he had been born to write) the biography of the second Earl Grey—whig hero, architect of the Great Reform Act, and another Northumberland patrician. But he had completed only three chapters when the pattern of his own life was changed abruptly.

War and peace, 1914–1927 After much debate with such Liberal pacifists as Bertrand Russell, Trevelyan supported Britain's declaration of war. He disliked continental despotisms, and was sure the Kaiser's Germany came in this category. Late in 1914 he visited Serbia, with the aim of strengthening the resistance to the central powers, and in March 1915 he went on a lecture tour to the United States, putting the British case. His defective eyesight meant he was unfit for military service, but he was determined to

join up somehow, and in the autumn of 1915 he became commandant of the first British Red Cross ambulance unit to be sent to Italy. For three and a half years he served on the mountainous front north-east of Venice, between the rivers Isonzo and Piave, transporting wounded soldiers to hospitals behind the lines. He was conspicuously brave, and insisted on sharing with his drivers the most dangerous tasks under fire. He was decorated by the Italian government, was made CBE in 1920, and recorded his experiences in *Scenes from Italy's War* (1919).

Like many gifted members of the Liberal generation to which he belonged, Trevelyan found the First World War a devastating experience. The easy certainties and confident hopes of the pre-1914 era had turned to dust, the Liberal Party was collapsing, and the European prospect seemed bleak. What, under such changed circumstances, was the role of the public teacher and national historian, which were his self-appointed tasks? Initially, there was some unfinished business which he had to complete. *Lord Grey of the Reform Bill* (1920) was his last piece of partisan whiggery, and *Manin and the Venetian Revolution of 1848* (1923) was his final engagement with Italian history. Meanwhile, Trevelyan and his family had left London for semi-rural Berkhamsted. But this did not imply a withdrawal from public life: rather, it was the prelude to new sorts of involvement. He served on Asquith's royal commission into Oxford and Cambridge universities, and he became active as a conservationist, successfully urging the preservation of the Ashridge estate by the National Trust in 1925.

Trevelyan's post-war histories also exhibited a changed and extended perspective, as his pre-war whiggery broadened into a more inclusive, more tolerant (and more conservative) sense of what he called 'Englishry', first signalled in his *British History in the Nineteenth Century* (1922). This took a less partisan view of politics than his earlier writings, and accepted that it was not only the whigs, but also the tories, who had contributed to the development of the nation. This more consensual approach to the national past reached a fuller flowering in his *History of England* (1926), the first single-volume survey since J. R. Green's account in 1876. Trevelyan had resolved to write such a book during the First World War as a celebration of, and thank-offering to, the English people. In it he set out the essential elements of the nation's evolution and identity: parliamentary government, the rule of law, religious toleration, freedom from continental interference or involvement, and a global horizon of maritime supremacy and imperial expansion.

The book sold exceptionally well, and provided the definitive account of the English past for the inter-war generation and beyond. It also established Trevelyan as the supreme historical commentator on Baldwin's England in the same way that he had earlier been on Asquith's England. Like Trevelyan, Stanley Baldwin was a Harrow School and Trinity College alumnus; like Trevelyan, he believed in the beauty and regenerative values of the countryside; and like Trevelyan, he thought that different classes of English men and women should learn again to live in peace and harmony with each other. By the mid-1920s Trevelyan had become a committed Baldwinite tory, and he was convinced that Macaulay would have taken the same view. He disliked the scornful mockery made fashionable by Lytton Strachey's *Eminent Victorians* (1918), he regretted the eclipse of the traditional territorial aristocracy, and he deplored the corrupt materialism of the Lloyd George coalition and the press lords Northcliffe and Beaverbrook.

Regius professor, 1927–1940 In 1927–8 Trevelyan's life again changed abruptly, when Baldwin appointed him regius professor of modern history at Cambridge, a position that Macaulay had rejected, but which his great-nephew was 'proud as a peacock' to accept. Trevelyan returned in triumph to his Trinity fellowship, and took up residence at Garden Corner, 23 West Road, where he lived for the rest of his life. He was a conscientious lecturer, supervised a clutch of research students, including J. H. Plumb and W. R. Brock, and was chairman of the history faculty board from 1930 to 1934. At about the same time that he returned to Cambridge, Trevelyan inherited from a distant relative a house and small estate at Hallington in Northumberland, where he spent his university vacations and did much of his writing. The death of both his parents in 1928 prompted him to write *Sir George Otto Trevelyan: a Memoir* (1932), and in 1930 he was appointed a member of the Order of Merit, an honour previously enjoyed by his father. He had already, in 1925, been elected a fellow of the British Academy, but he subsequently declined to be president because he had more important and creative things to do.

The major scholarly work of Trevelyan's professorial years was another trilogy, *England under Queen Anne* (1930–34), which took up the national story where Macaulay's history had ended incomplete. It was an appropriate work for a man at the head of his profession, and it was another story with a 'happy ending': the defeat of continental despotism, the consolidation of national liberties, and the union with Scotland. The battle scenes of Marlborough's wars were brilliantly described, and Trevelyan paid even-handed tribute to the achievements of the whigs and the tories, an eirenic view of politics which had been fore-shadowed not only in his *History of England*, but also in his Romanes lecture, published as *The Two Party System in English Political History* (1926). His final work in this mode was *The English Revolution, 1688–89* (1938), published to mark the 250th anniversary of the events it described, and a sort of retrospective prelude to *England under Queen Anne*. For him the true glory of 1688 lay in its tolerant moderation, and in its long-lasting and beneficent effects.

Outside academe, Trevelyan's time was increasingly devoted in these years to public service and conservation work. He was a trustee of the National Portrait Gallery and of the British Museum, he became first president of the Youth Hostels' Association in 1930, and from 1928 to 1949 he was chairman of the estates committee of the National Trust. He became a tireless campaigner for the preservation of the countryside, and it was in support of this cause that he produced *Must England's Beauty Perish?* (1929) and

The Calls and Claims of Natural Beauty (1931). For Trevelyan, as for many members of his generation, it was the countryside which was the repository of national identity, 'spiritual values', and liberty and freedom, and it must be preserved at all costs from bungalows, the motor car, and ribbon development. These feelings also informed his last biography, *Grey of Fallodon* (1937), an elegiac evocation of the British foreign secretary (1905–16), who was another Northumberland landowner and nature-lover, and a firm upholder of decent standards in public life.

Trevelyan had successfully adjusted to the changed and less propitious circumstances of the inter-war years, but he did not find the 1930s an easy decade. He was distressed by Italy's lapse into fascism, and by the rise of Nazi Germany. The first of these developments undermined his belief that Italy was a land of liberty, while the second vindicated his view that the treaty of Versailles had been unduly harsh. Internationally, as well as domestically, he supported the National Governments of Baldwin and Chamberlain, believing in the virtues of appeasement, accompanied by rearmament—the very policies adopted by Sir Edward Grey before the First World War. Although he admired Winston Churchill as a writer and historian, he had no time for Churchill's views on India, Germany, or Edward VIII, and he was a firm supporter of the Munich settlement. But he had little doubt that another war with Germany would come, and that whatever the result, a second such conflict in his lifetime would spell the end of the world as he had known it.

Master of Trinity, 1940–1951 But Trevelyan recognized that Nazi Germany had to be defeated, and he soon became reconciled to, and guardedly admiring of, Churchill's more vigorous leadership. In the autumn of 1940 he accepted the prime minister's offer of the mastership of Trinity, which made his life 'as happy as anyone's can be during the fall of European civilisation' (Trevelyan, 49–50). Despite the straitened circumstances of wartime, he presided with dignity over the fellowship, helped secure the acquisition of Newton's library for the college, was tireless in extending hospitality to visiting American dignitaries, and wrote *Trinity College: an Historical Sketch* (1943). In 1945 he withdrew his name from the final short list for the governor-generalship of Canada. A year later he became high steward of Cambridge, as Macaulay had been before him; in 1947 he was elected president of the Historical Association; in 1950 he was elected FRS; and in 1951 he was president of the English Association. When he reached the age of seventy, the fellows of Trinity unanimously extended his term of office for a further five years.

Trevelyan's most sustained piece of writing during these years was *English Social History* (1944), which was intended to complement his earlier (and mainly political) *History of England*. It surveyed the broad sweep of national social life from the age of Chaucer to the close of the nineteenth century, and although wartime restrictions on paper supply initially held up its production, it soon proved to be the most successful of all his books, confirming his unrivalled position as the nation's historian laureate. Once again, the timing was just right. During the closing months of the Second World War, and in the longer years of Attlee's austerity, Trevelyan presented his readers with a beguiling picture of the past life of the nation, by turns inspiring and nostalgic. Written in the darkest years he had known, he poured out his patriotic feelings for what seemed to him the mortally endangered fabric of English life: landscape and locality, flora and fauna, places and people. Out of his wartime sense of despair and foreboding, he created his final historical masterpiece of public enlightenment, the (substantial) royalties from which he donated to the golden jubilee appeal of the National Trust.

Towards the end of his time as master of Trinity, Trevelyan published *An Autobiography and other Essays* (1949), in which he wrote very guardedly about his inner life, and rather inadequately about his work, his art, and his craft. He admitted that, as befitted the bearer of his name, he was a 'traditional' historian, who had pioneered no new way of seeing or understanding the past. He also conceded his preference for stories with happy endings, and accepted that some of his books (for instance 'the Garibaldis') were 'reeking with bias' (Trevelyan, 69). These venerable admissions seemed to bear out the earlier attacks that had been obliquely mounted on Trevelyan by Herbert Butterfield in *The Whig Interpretation of History* (1931) and by Lewis Namier in his revisionist (that is, antiwhig) work on the reign of George III. And they encouraged a later generation of militant conservative empiricists, led by G. R. Elton and J. P. Kenyon, who were unsympathetic to Trevelyan's politics and envious of his public success, to disparage him as a superficial amateur, with no interest in research, whose books were conspicuously lacking in intellectual bite.

Such attacks merely displayed the lack of scholarly rigour they had mistakenly claimed to find in Trevelyan's own work. For he believed passionately in the importance of primary research, and the Garibaldi books had been much praised for their innovative use of archival material in a work of recent history. He was a great supporter of the Institute of Historical Research in London, and exceptionally generous in his encouragement of younger scholars. For all his early whig and liberal biases, there is no evidence that Trevelyan knowingly distorted historical evidence to support the case he wanted to make. He constantly insisted on the unlikeness of past worlds to the present, and he was much more sympathetic to the power and importance of religion than he is sometimes given credit for. In his imaginative insight and eloquent reconstruction of past people and events he was unrivalled among historians of his generation, and his sense of the transience and tragedy of life gives his best writing a poetic power and a haunting resonance that have never been equalled since.

Last years, 1951–1962 During the closing decade of his life Trevelyan's scholarly reputation went into a prolonged decline among professional academics from which it has only recently begun to recover. His last book, *A Layman's Love of Letters* (1954), was his most personal, and conveyed something of his lifelong delight in English literature. In the public mind he was still regarded as 'the most eminent historian of his time', most of his books remained in print, and further honours were heaped upon him. He was chancellor of Durham University from 1950 to 1958, and he was presented with a Festschrift, *Studies in Social History* (1955), edited by J. H. Plumb. On his eightieth birthday an appeal was launched in *The Times* to found lectures in his honour at Cambridge University. The signatories included Sir John Neale and Sir Winston Churchill, and in their letter they described Trevelyan as 'one of our foremost national figures', who was, like Macaulay before him, 'the accredited interpreter to his age of the English past' (*The Times*, 16 Feb 1956). The first Trevelyan lectures were given in 1958, at which Trevelyan himself made one of his last public appearances. Three years later, in the company of Churchill, he was made a companion of literature.

Throughout his long life Trevelyan drove himself exceptionally hard in pursuit of his chosen calling. His personality was unwarmed by self-indulgence, he cared little about his dress or appearance, and he was wholly devoid of small talk. He was tall, with a wiry frame and austere features, and he enjoyed a well-merited reputation as a tireless walker. He spoke his mind with forthright independence, and to all except his closest friends he could be an intimidating figure. But his youthful ferocity gradually mellowed into a kind of noble grandeur—a greatness of character that matched the greatness of his achievement. He was devoid of vanity, pretence, or pomposity, he was free of envy or small-mindedness, he was outstandingly public-spirited, and he was a generous benefactor to people and causes in which he believed. His wife predeceased him in 1956, and his last years were made harder to bear by failing eyesight. He died at his home in Cambridge on 20 July 1962, and his ashes were scattered in the Lake District.   DAVID CANNADINE

Sources D. Cannadine, *G. M. Trevelyan: a life in history* (1992) · M. Moorman, *George Macaulay Trevelyan: a memoir* (1980) · G. M. Trevelyan, *An autobiography and other essays* (1949) · J. H. Plumb, *G. M. Trevelyan* (1951) · W. O. Chadwick, *Freedom and the historian* (1969) · G. Clark, 'George Macaulay Trevelyan, 1876–1972', *PBA*, 49 (1963), 375–86 · J. M. Hernon, 'The last whig historian and consensus history: George Macaulay Trevelyan, 1876–1962', *American Historical Review*, 81 (1976), 66–97 · G. K. Clark, 'George Macaulay Trevelyan as an historian: charm'd magic casements', *Durham University Journal*, 55 (1962–3), 1–4 · *CGPLA Eng. & Wales* (1962)

Archives BL, corresp. with Sir Sydney Cockerell, Add. MS 52756 · BL, letters to Albert Mansbridge, Add. MSS 65257B–65258 · BL, corresp. with Society of Authors, Add. MS 56835 · Bodl. Oxf., letters to H. A. L. Fisher · Bodl. Oxf., corresp. with Gilbert Murray · CAC Cam., corresp. with C. B. A. Behrens · CAC Cam., corresp. with A. V. Hill · CUL, corresp. with Sir Herbert Butterfield · CUL, letters to V. N. Datta · CUL, letters to Lord Kennet and Lady Kennet · CUL, letters to G. E. Moore · King's AC Cam., letters to Oscar Browning · King's AC Cam., letters to John Maynard Keynes · King's AC Cam., letters to Sir J. T. Sheppard · King's AC Cam., letters and postcards to G. H. W. Rylands · King's Lond., Liddell Hart C., corresp. with

Arthur Bryant · LUL, letters to T. S. Moore · McMaster University, Hamilton, Ontario, letters to Bertrand Russell · Rice University, Houston, Texas, Woodson Research Center, letters to Sir Julian Huxley · Trinity Cam., R. C. Trevelyan MSS · U. Newcastle, G. O. Trevelyan MSS · U. Newcastle, Robinson L., corresp. with Walter Runciman · U. Newcastle, Robinson L., corresp. with G. O. Trevelyan and C. P. Trevelyan | FILM BFI NFTVA, documentary footage | SOUND BL NSA, 'George Macaulay Trevelyan', BBC Radio 3, 17 Feb 1976, NP2673R C1

Likenesses W. Rothenstein, chalk drawing, c.1913, NPG · W. Rothenstein, pencil drawing, 1913, Trinity Cam. · C. Geoffrey, drawing, 1925, priv. coll. · W. Stoneman, photograph, 1930, NPG · F. Dodd, charcoal drawing, 1933, FM Cam. · F. Dodd, pencil drawing, 1933, NPG · E. H. Nelson, oils, 1946, Trinity Cam. [*see illus.*] · W. Stoneman, photograph, 1948, NPG · C. Beaton, photograph, NPG · J. Mansbridge, drawing · J. S. Murray, photograph, repro. in Clark, 'George Macaulay Trevelyan', facing p. 375

Wealth at death £157,765 9s.: probate, 19 Nov 1962, *CGPLA Eng. & Wales*

Trevelyan, Sir George Otto, second baronet (1838–1928),

politician and author, was born on 20 July 1838 at Rothley Temple, Leicestershire, the second of the three children, and the only son, of Sir Charles Edward *Trevelyan, first baronet (1807–1886), and his first wife, Hannah More (1810–1873), daughter of Zachary *Macaulay and sister of Thomas Babington Macaulay, Lord Macaulay.

Childhood and education For the first twenty years of Trevelyan's life his father was in London, serving as assistant secretary to the Treasury, between two periods of an Indian career that culminated in the governorship of Madras. The Trevelyans were a closely knit family, strongly evangelical in religion, and intensely bookish. Trevelyan's bachelor uncle, Lord Macaulay, spent much of his time with them, and had a considerable influence on his young nephew, who was fascinated by him. In 1851 Trevelyan went to Harrow School, then at the peak of its scholarly reputation under C. J. Vaughan, where he became head of the school and won a succession of prizes for English verse. He went up to Trinity College, Cambridge, in 1857 and acquired a lifelong passion for Greek and Latin literature. In 1861 he came second in merit order on the list of candidates for the classical tripos, but unexpectedly failed to secure a college fellowship and instead went to India for a year to act as his father's private secretary.

Early literary and political career, 1863–1880 Trevelyan had established a reputation for satiric verse while at Cambridge, where *Horace at the University of Athens* was published in 1861. When he returned from India he produced two works of a more serious nature. *The Competition Wallah*, which appeared in book form in 1864 after previous serialization in *Macmillan's Magazine*, consisted of a series of letters from an imaginary young Indian civil servant. 'Competition wallah' was the term used to describe an official who had won his post in the competitive examinations which had been introduced by the East India Company in 1853, largely through the efforts of Trevelyan's father. The book was well received in Britain and in India, and nearly seventy years later G. M. Trevelyan was able to

Sir George Otto Trevelyan, second baronet (1838–1928), by Frank Holl, 1886

claim that 'it still remains the most vivid account of the Anglo-Indian world immediately after the Mutiny' (Trevelyan, 65). However, some feathers were ruffled by the comments on the attitudes of British settlers towards the Indian people: 'No one can estimate very highly the moral and intellectual qualities of people among whom he resides for the single purpose of turning them to pecuniary account' (*The Competition Wallah*, letter 9). These settler attitudes had hardened as a result of the mutiny, and in *Cawnpore* (1865), Trevelyan's first historical work, he described the siege and massacre that took place there.

By 1865 Trevelyan had decided on a political career, and in the general election of that year he was returned as a Liberal in a closely fought contest at Tynemouth and North Shields. His father's cousin, Sir Walter Trevelyan, helped him to buy an estate, which was resold after the election, in order to secure tenants' votes. In sharp contrast to this old-style whig paternalism Trevelyan quickly adopted strong radical views, particularly on questions of electoral and administrative reform, to which he adhered firmly and consistently throughout his political career. He often sat next to John Bright during the debates leading up to the second Reform Act in 1867.

In the autumn of that year, while in Paris for the Universal Exhibition, Trevelyan decided on impulse to try to reach Rome in time to witness Garibaldi's invasion of the Papal States. He was on his way south by rail from Florence, then the Italian capital, when he was overtaken by Garibaldi's defeated troops retreating from the battle of Mentana. Trevelyan and his companion Lord Lorne were warmly received by Garibaldi, and after the latter's arrest Trevelyan travelled back to Florence on the same train.

At the 1868 general election Trevelyan was returned unopposed for the Hawick district of the Border burghs, a strongly radical constituency which he represented until the home-rule split in 1886, and he was included, as civil lord of the Admiralty, in Gladstone's first government. Following his father's lead Trevelyan strongly supported Cardwell's army reforms, including the abolition of purchase: indeed he believed that Cardwell had underestimated the scope for reform. In 1870, however, Trevelyan resigned from the government in protest against a proposal, which had been included in W. E. Forster's Education Bill, to increase the rate of grant paid to denominational schools. This had been suggested by Robert Lowe to Gladstone in the hope of defusing the hostility of nonconformist Liberals to the idea of local rate support for church schools, but in his resignation statement of 11 July 1870 Trevelyan called the proposal a parasitical growth which ought never to have been attached to the bill. The resignation was seen as quixotic, and The Spectator (2 July 1870) referred with 'a lurking respect' to 'that extremely rare and inconvenient article, an over-sensitive conscience'. Trevelyan insisted that for him 'there was something stronger than self-interest or fear of ridicule', and throughout his political career he was to attach high priority to the maintenance of a principled independence.

Out of office Trevelyan was freer to pursue a radical agenda. Together with Sir Charles Dilke he campaigned against excessive military and royal expenditure, and he may have written a provocatively titled anonymous pamphlet, What does she do with it?, which appeared in 1871. On 26 April 1872 Trevelyan introduced into the House of Commons a resolution calling for the extension to the counties of the household suffrage which Disraeli had granted to the boroughs in 1867. There was no great enthusiasm for further electoral reform, and the resolution attracted only seventy votes, but with dogged persistence Trevelyan repeated the process during each of the following seven sessions, introducing either a resolution or a private member's bill in an annual succession of quietly persuasive speeches. Trevelyan was not a good impromptu debater, but he had a clear, impressive delivery and was at his best in the set-piece deployment of a logical case. He made the most of the anomaly that by now 3 million urban householders were excluded from the franchise simply because they lived in towns which were not parliamentary boroughs: no one could maintain, he suggested to the House of Commons on 7 July 1875, 'that a man who spins wool at Barnsley would make a worse voter than a man who spins it at Bradford' (Hansard 3, 225, 7 July 1875, col. 1096). Trevelyan argued convincingly that the disfranchisement of rural householders had caused parliament to neglect working and housing conditions in country areas, whereas urban problems had received far more attention. By 1879 Trevelyan's resolution was supported by a significant minority of 226, including Gladstone and many of his senior Liberal colleagues. As Trevelyan put it on 4 March, the issue had 'matured … from the

condition of a not very popular theory to be the most formidable and practical reality'. Thanks to his efforts Gladstone's second administration took office in 1880 with a clear commitment to franchise reform, even though it was 1884 before the third Reform Act was carried.

Like many other radicals who voted for his annual franchise proposals Trevelyan supported W. E. Forster's candidacy for the Commons leadership in 1875 after Gladstone's retirement. But Hartington was chosen, and for the time being caution was the order of the day. During the years of opposition between 1874 and 1880 Trevelyan was not a frequent speaker in parliament, although after the Bulgarian massacres in 1876 he strongly supported Gladstone's crusade against Turkish misgovernment, assuring his leader that on this issue his Hawick constituents neither shared nor understood the folly of the south (BL, Gladstone MSS, Add. MS 44315, fol. 29). Much of Trevelyan's time during these years was taken up with literary work. In 1876 he produced the Life and Letters of Lord Macaulay and in 1880 the Early History of Charles James Fox. Both books were very well received, particularly the life of Macaulay, where Trevelyan's aim was to let his uncle speak for himself, in quasi-autobiographical fashion, through extensive quotations from the correspondence and journals that his nephew had inherited. There is little attempt at critical appraisal, but Macaulay's personality comes across freshly and directly, and the book was praised by many of those who were normally critical of Macaulay's work, including Carlyle and Gladstone, who wrote a long review for the July 1876 issue of the Quarterly Review. Some modern writers on Macaulay (for instance Owen Dudley Edwards) have accused Trevelyan of inaccuracy in transcribing the sources, but it is unlikely that this reflected any conscious desire to exaggerate Macaulay's whiggism. The book on Fox, like that on Macaulay, is elegantly written and enjoyable to read, although it is oddly structured. It covers only the first few years of Fox's career, when he played a minor role as a loyal defender of George III's system of personal government. Trevelyan is constantly reduced to referring to Fox's more distinguished later career in opposition, but it was twenty years before he got round to carrying the story forward. A revealing aspect of the book is its deeply ambivalent attitude towards eighteenth-century politics. As a Gladstonian radical Trevelyan is appropriately shocked by the corrupt patronage and the frivolity, but the classically educated aristocrat in him is fascinated by a society in which 'a few thousand people … thought that the world was made for them … [and] bestowed upon each other an amount of attention quite inconceivable to us who count our equals by millions' (Early History of Charles James Fox, 71).

Ministerial career, 1880–1895 At the April 1880 general election the Conservative candidate at Hawick polled only 553 votes, and the triumphantly re-elected Trevelyan looked forward to being included in the new Liberal government. At the last moment Gladstone rather half-heartedly offered him the vice-presidency of the Board of Trade, but since Joseph Chamberlain would handle all the important departmental business in the House of Commons Trevelyan considered that the junior post would represent political extinction and he refused it, deeply offended by Gladstone's ungracious manner. In November 1880 he agreed to return to his old post of civil lord of the Admiralty, but the episode had left Trevelyan with the unpleasant impression that Gladstone did not rate his qualities highly. This is rather surprising, because Trevelyan had the social and cultural background that Gladstone generally favoured as a basis for a ministerial career: in October 1869 he had sent Gladstone a collection of essays he had written on the work of Aristophanes, a writer they both loved. The over-scrupulous resignation of 1870 and the subsequent radicalism may have counted against Trevelyan in Gladstone's mind, although his loyalty during the crisis over the Eastern question had been beyond doubt.

Trevelyan's opportunity came in May 1882, after the assassination of Lord Frederick Cavendish in Phoenix Park, Dublin. Dilke refused to take over as chief secretary without promotion to the cabinet, so Gladstone offered the post to Trevelyan. This proved to be a brutally tough assignment. W. E. Forster, a much stronger personality, had been worn down by two years spent struggling to uphold law and order in Ireland at the height of the land war, while defending the government's policy in parliament against the relentless attacks of the Irish party. Trevelyan had the advantage of working under Lord Spencer, an experienced lord lieutenant and a cabinet minister, and also, following the release of Parnell from Kilmainham prison, the Irish leader was nominally committed to a policy of co-operation with the Liberal government. Nevertheless the maintenance of law and order and the unremitting pressure in the House of Commons imposed a severe strain on someone as highly strung and sensitive as Trevelyan, and his hair turned white within twelve months. During his two years as chief secretary he answered over 2000 parliamentary questions, many of them fiercely hostile, on every aspect of Irish administration.

On 31 December 1882 Trevelyan confessed to Sir William Harcourt, the home secretary, whom he regarded as his political mentor, that he feared that Dilke's promotion to the cabinet, as a representative of the radical wing of the party, had seriously damaged his own prospects (Harcourt MSS, dep. 92, fol. 13). Harcourt persuaded him not to complain, but on 20 August 1883 Trevelyan suggested to Gladstone that in order to buttress his authority in the House of Commons he ought to be in the cabinet (BL, Gladstone MSS, Add. MS 44335, fol. 122). Gladstone took the hint in surprisingly good part, assuring Trevelyan that his courage in accepting the chief secretaryship after his predecessor's assassination entitled him to favourable consideration when the next opportunity arose. Trevelyan's frustration increased when the cabinet began to prepare the franchise legislation which he regarded as his own special field. In January 1884 he commented in writing to both Harcourt and Dilke on detailed aspects of the proposals, especially in relation to Scotland, while confessing to a feeling of impotence in what he referred to as his

exile. He appreciated Gladstone's gesture in including his name among the sponsors of the third Reform Bill, but by 26 July 1884 he had reached the end of his tether, and wrote to Gladstone asking to be released from a post which was 'not a human life at all'. He felt that he was being used as a decoy to draw the fire of the Parnellites so that his colleagues could get on with more constructive work, and this involved the sacrifice of his 'nerves, health, happiness, and self respect' (BL, Gladstone MSS, Add MS. 44335, fol. 168).

Gladstone realized that Trevelyan could not be left any longer in Ireland, and in October 1884 he at last offered him promotion to the cabinet as chancellor of the duchy of Lancaster, a post without significant departmental duties. The queen initially objected to the appointment, and had to be assured by Gladstone that Trevelyan had modified his old radicalism, and that his removal from Dublin without promotion would be claimed as a victory by the Irish party (Royal Archives, A78/13). The government survived for only eight more months, and was torn for most of this time by disputes over Ireland, Egypt, and the Sudan. As a newcomer to the cabinet Trevelyan found it difficult to make much impression, and Harcourt described him as sitting like a melancholy owl, saying nothing (L. Harcourt, journal, 17 Nov 1884, Harcourt MSS).

After a brief interlude of Conservative government Gladstone returned to power in February 1886, convinced of the need for Irish home rule. Although Hartington remained aloof, most of the other Liberal sceptics were persuaded to join the cabinet on the understanding that they were committed to no more than an inquiry into the feasibility of a home rule scheme. On this basis Trevelyan became secretary for Scotland, a new post created by statute only six months before. With hindsight one can see that this was an important milestone in Scottish constitutional development, for which Rosebery in particular had strongly pressed, and Trevelyan was knowledgeably interested in issues such as disestablishment and home rule for Scotland. Nevertheless the rather miscellaneous administrative functions initially attached to the post (including education, agriculture, fisheries, police, and prisons) were of limited interest to the House of Commons or to an ambitious minister, many of them being carried out by semi-autonomous boards in Edinburgh. Trevelyan made clear his disappointment at not being given a more important post, having unrealistically hoped for the exchequer. However he was able to carry through parliament a bill designed to remedy the grievances of the crofter tenants in the highlands. The short life of the third Gladstone government was overshadowed by Irish home rule, and on 27 March 1886 Trevelyan resigned with Chamberlain when the nature of the proposals began to emerge clearly. In his resignation statement in the House of Commons on 8 April Trevelyan explained that he could not accept the proposed Land Bill under which Irish landlords were to be expensively bought out. He was also concerned about the risks involved in transferring responsibility for law and order to an Irish nationalist government. Spencer and Harcourt had similar reservations, but had come to feel that home rule offered the only remaining hope of pacifying Ireland. Trevelyan was deeply unhappy at being separated from such colleagues, and regretted Gladstone's action in calling for a dissolution of parliament after the rejection of the Home Rule Bill, since this deepened the split in the party. At the election in Hawick in July 1886 Trevelyan was opposed by a Gladstonian Liberal and lost the seat, albeit by only thirty votes. As a mark of their respect his former constituents presented him with a portrait by Frank Holl, now in Trinity College, Cambridge.

Trevelyan was strongly influenced by Chamberlain during the months following their resignation, but he was too much of a radical to be comfortable in the ranks of the Liberal Unionists. At the round-table conference in January–February 1887 he shared Harcourt's optimism about the prospects of negotiating an end to the split, and after the conference failed Trevelyan allowed himself to be coaxed back into the Liberal Party. For once Gladstone treated him with studied consideration. The idea of a major land purchase scheme had been abandoned, and Gladstone was prepared to accept the principle of continued Irish representation at Westminster, thus enabling Trevelyan to maintain that a future home rule bill would differ fundamentally from the proposals to which he had objected. Chamberlain regarded Trevelyan's action as a personal betrayal, and treated him subsequently with savage contempt. Trevelyan returned to parliament in July 1887 after convincingly defeating a Liberal Unionist candidate at Glasgow, Bridgeton, and he retained this seat at the two following general elections in 1892 and 1895.

When Gladstone formed his fourth government in August 1892 Trevelyan returned to the Scottish Office, although Harcourt, in an attempt to increase the number of senior cabinet members in the House of Commons, tried to persuade Gladstone to make him colonial secretary. Trevelyan retained his post after Gladstone's retirement in March 1894, although Rosebery admitted to the queen that he would not himself have appointed Trevelyan as secretary for Scotland (Royal Archives, A70/61). In April 1894 Trevelyan voted for a private member's motion in favour of Scottish home rule: most of his cabinet colleagues abstained.

Family life and final years, 1897–1928 After the return of a Conservative government in 1895 Trevelyan found the House of Commons less congenial, and in 1897 he resigned his seat at the age of only fifty-nine, with over thirty years of life before him. From now on a large part of his time was spent at Wallington, Northumberland, the family seat of which he was proud and deeply fond, and at Welcombe, the house at Stratford upon Avon which his wife had inherited from her father. On 29 September 1869 Trevelyan had married Caroline (d. 1928), the daughter of Robert Needham Philips, a Unitarian merchant from Manchester and Liberal MP for Bury. The marriage of nearly sixty years was a very happy one, and photographs taken at Wallington show Trevelyan as a benevolent, white-bearded patriarch surrounded by his wife and three sons,

Charles Philips *Trevelyan, subsequently a Labour minister for education, Robert Calverley Trevelyan (1872–1951), a poet, and George Macaulay *Trevelyan, who became regius professor of history at Cambridge.

Trevelyan's main achievement in retirement was the completion of a six-volume history of the American War of Independence, which appeared over the years 1899–1914. Like Trevelyan's earlier historical writings this last work is well written and enjoyable to read, but it is overlong and repetitive, with an excessive reliance on the theme that the loss of the American colonies was due to the stubbornness and stupidity of George III and his ministers. The colonists, by contrast, are depicted in a generally heroic light, and it is hardly surprising that the work was much more popular in the United States than in Britain. Trevelyan established a close friendship with Americans such as Theodore Roosevelt and Cabot Lodge.

Although much of Trevelyan's time was devoted to books, especially the Greek and Latin classics, and to country life, it would be wrong to think of him as being wholly detached from national and international politics in his final years. He carried on a regular and detailed correspondence on political affairs with friends such as Lord Bryce. Like many radicals he was deeply unhappy about the methods used by the British in the Second South African War, and although he accepted the necessity for war in 1914 (unlike his son Charles, who resigned from Asquith's government in protest) he recognized that it involved the end of the social world he had known. In 1908 Trevelyan refused Asquith's offer of a peerage, although his name was included three years later on the list of potential peers that was used to overcome the resistance of the House of Lords to the Parliament Bill. In 1911 the Order of Merit was conferred on Trevelyan, and he was an honorary fellow of Trinity College, Cambridge, and Oriel College, Oxford. He died at Wallington on 17 August 1928 at the age of ninety, six months after his wife, and was buried on 20 August at Cambo church. He was succeeded as third baronet by his eldest son.

Assessment Trevelyan is not easy to categorize in terms of political beliefs. His reverence for Macaulay, his intellectual background, and his proud sense of family tradition might have led him to become an orthodox whig. In his writings he certainly looked back nostalgically to the days of Foxite whiggism. But he inherited from his father a more forward-looking interest in administrative reform, and throughout his career there is a consistent strain of genuine radicalism. He liaised with Dilke in campaigning against the royal and military establishments, he supported Forster rather than Hartington for the Commons leadership in 1875, and he took a strongly Gladstonian line over the 'Bulgarian atrocities'. His annual motions in favour of the widening of the county franchise, although in the parliamentary reform tradition of Russell, were radical in the context of the 1870s. Finally, after the home-rule split Trevelyan, unlike many of the whigs, was uncomfortable in the Liberal Unionist camp, and was happy to return to the Gladstonian fold.

In terms of solid achievements Trevelyan cannot be

rated as a major figure in either politics or letters, when compared with the greatest of his contemporaries. Although he served in all four of Gladstone's governments he never held any of the principal offices of state. He was well liked by most of his colleagues, but was too gentle and sensitive to exert a dominant influence on events, and there was a streak of vanity in his nature which led him to overestimate his political claims. At times of crisis he looked for support to more robust characters such as Harcourt and Chamberlain. Under the shadow of Macaulay's example Trevelyan would probably have preferred to be judged as a writer. He produced a series of accomplished and highly civilized books that can still be read with pleasure, but they often lack critical penetration. Perhaps Trevelyan's main claim to be remembered is that his career reflected a consistent integrity that sprang from family pride and from deep-seated radical convictions which were more important to him than ambition or self-interest. The resignations of 1870 and 1886, and the courageous reversal of his position over home rule in 1887, tended to be ridiculed at the time, but such disinterested actions are vital to the health of democratic politics.   PATRICK JACKSON

Sources G. M. Trevelyan, *Sir George Otto Trevelyan: a memoir* (1932) · *DNB* · D. Cannadine, *G. M. Trevelyan: a life in history* (1992) · E. Longford, *Victoria RI* (1964) · O. D. Edwards, *Macaulay* (1988) · J. G. Kellas, *The Scottish political system* (1973) · D. Milne, *The Scottish office* (1957) · *Hansard 3* (1875), 225.1096 · *The Times* (21 Aug 1928) · Bodl. Oxf., Harcourt MSS · Royal Arch.
Archives NRA, priv. coll., corresp. and literary papers · U. Newcastle, Robinson L., corresp. and papers | BL, letters to Lord Gladstone, Add. MSS 46050–46060, *passim* · BL, corresp. with Arthur James Balfour, Add. MS 49792, *passim* · BL, corresp. with W. E. Gladstone, Add. MS 44335 · BL, corresp. with Sir Charles Dilke, Add. MS 43895 · BL, corresp. with Macmillans, Add. MS 55073 · BL OIOC, corresp. with Sir Mountstuart Grant Duff, MS Eur. F 234 · Bodl. Oxf., corresp. with Lord Bryce · Bodl. Oxf., letters to H. A. L. Fisher · Bodl. Oxf., Harcourt MSS · Bodl. Oxf., corresp. with Lord Kimberley · CUL, Royal Commonwealth Society Library, corresp. with Hugh Childers · Glos. RO, letters to Sir Michael Hicks · HLRO, letters to Herbert Samuel · Hove Central Library, Sussex, letters to Lord Wolseley and Lady Wolseley · Hunt. L., letters mainly to James Beck · King's Cam., letters to Oscar Browning · Mass. Hist. Soc., letters to Henry Adams · NL Scot., letters to Sir Charles Dalrymple · NL Scot., corresp. with Lord Rosebery · NL Wales, letters to Lord Rendel · Royal Arch. · Trinity Cam., letters to Lord Houghton · Trinity Cam., letters to R. C. Trevelyan · U. Birm. L., corresp. with Joseph Chamberlain · U. Leeds, Brotherton L., letters to Sir Edmund Gosse · U. Newcastle, Robinson L., letters to Robin Price · U. Newcastle, Robinson L., corresp. with Walter Runciman · U. Newcastle, Robinson L., corresp. with Doris Trevelyan · U. Reading L., letters to George Bell and sons · U. St Andr. L., letters to Sir James Donaldson
Likenesses J. Archer, oils, exh. RA 1872, Wallington, Northumberland · F. Holl, oils, 1886, Trinity Cam. [*see illus.*] · group portrait, photograph, *c*.1900 (with family), repro. in Cannadine, *G. M. Trevelyan* · Fanny, Lady Holroyd, watercolour drawing, 1911, NPG · Spy [L. Ward], caricature, chromolithograph, NPG; repro. in *VF* (2 Aug 1873) · portrait, repro. in *Bookman*, 9 (1899), 116 · portrait, repro. in *Harper's Weekly*, 30 (1886), 108 · portrait, repro. in *Harper's Weekly*, 47 (1903), 1938 · portrait, repro. in *ILN*, 80 (1882), 484
Wealth at death £556,933 17*s*. 11*d*.: probate, 18 Oct 1928, CGPLA Eng. & Wales

Trevelyan, Hilda [*real name* Hilda Marie Antoinette Anna Tucker] (**1877–1959**), actress, was born at West Hackney, London, on 4 February 1877, the daughter of John Joseph Tucker, farmer, and his French wife, Helene Adolphine Marie Foulon. She was educated at the Ursuline convent in Upton, and she made her first stage appearance at the age of twelve as one of the schoolchildren in a revival of H. A. Jones and Henry Herman's *The Silver King* (1889) at the Princess's Theatre, London. When she was sixteen she was touring in the musical comedy *A Gaiety Girl* by Owen Hall and Sidney Jones, and it was not long before she established herself as a provincial leading lady, touring, for example, in *Newmarket*, in which she acted the heroine to the hero of George Arliss, then unknown. Her first serious London engagement, at the Court in 1898, was as understudy to Pattie Browne as Avonia Bunn, cheerful soubrette of the Bagnigge-Wells Theatre in *Trelawny of the 'Wells'*, the comedy by A. W. Pinero. Hilda Trevelyan, who would play Avonia Bunn many times in later life, had the personality for the character's affectionate exuberance. There were few actresses with her special way of gaining and holding the sympathy of an audience; she had no mannerisms but she took listeners into her confidence with a warmth to which they responded at once.

In 1899 she went as Lady Babbie in a touring company of *The Little Minister* by J. M. Barrie, a dramatist who would mean so much to her career. The minister of the play's title was Sydney Blow (stage name of Luke Sydney Jellings Blow; 1878–1961), whom Hilda Trevelyan married in 1910; he became better known as a dramatist, particularly of light comedy and farce. After nearly 700 touring performances in *The Little Minister* Hilda Trevelyan had a variety of London parts. She specialized in the appealing waif or the buoyant soubrette: her comedy and pathos were always very close to each other. She had also the range to succeed the comedian Louie Freear as Fi-Fi in *A Chinese Honeymoon* by George Dance and Howard Talbot at the Strand Theatre during 1903. It was in the following year that she had the kind of East End part in which she would be unrivalled: the cockney Amanda Afflick in *'Op o' me Thumb*, a one-act play by Frederick Fenn and Richard Pryce at the Court. She was so affecting in this that one critic, referring to T. F. Robson, the Victorian actor of the comic-pathetic, called her 'a Robson in petticoats'. Later that year she toured with John Hare as Moira in one of Barrie's lesser-known comedies, *Little Mary*, a character described by the author himself as 'an old-fashioned little girl of twelve, very earnest and practical and quaint, and with all the airs of an experienced mother. She carries the baby with extraordinary rapture.' This was an exact description of Hilda Trevelyan's most telling style. It was not surprising that, later in the year, Barrie cast a player so suited to his work, physically and temperamentally, as Wendy in the Christmas fantasy of *Peter Pan*. It opened at the Duke of York's on 27 December 1904. Hilda Trevelyan would repeat this performance in many revivals and on more than 900 occasions. 'You are Wendy, and there will never be another to touch you,' Barrie wrote to her in 1920.

After this she became, in public imagination, predominantly 'the Barrie actress'. She had the shade of quaintness and whimsicality that Barrie demanded. During her stage life, which lasted for just half a century until retirement in 1939, she appeared in ten other Barrie parts, either new or in a variety of revivals. They included such creations as the resourcefully managing Maggie Wylie, who knew that charm was 'a sort of bloom on a woman', in *What every Woman Knows* (Duke of York's, 1908), and Miss Thing, the cockney maidservant who becomes her own version of Cinderella, in *A Kiss for Cinderella* (Wyndham's, 1916). She was also Tweeny in the 1908 revival of *The Admirable Crichton* at the Duke of York's, Mrs Morland in the 1926 and 1929 Haymarket revivals of *Mary Rose*, and the maid Patty in *Quality Street* at the Haymarket in both 1921 and 1929. Besides Barrie's tribute to 'my incomparable Wendy', various critics called her 'almost magical' and 'unapproachable'. She played for Barrie on one night only, 22 February 1908, the extra scene that he devised for *Peter Pan* as a gift to Charles Frohman, the American manager, who travelled to London for the last night of the 1907–8 run. In this brief episode that followed the ordinary performance of the play the dramatist answered a question often asked: what happened to Wendy when she grew up? Hilda Trevelyan played a Wendy now twenty years older, a real mother with a daughter Jane, who had been the Baby Mermaid. At curtain-fall Barrie slipped the manuscript into Hilda Trevelyan's hands, saying, 'Now you know my afterthought.'

Hilda Trevelyan had various other parts during her sustained career. When she was twenty-eight she played Oliver Twist most winningly in the production by Sir Herbert Beerbohm Tree at His Majesty's (July 1905). She was Lily Wilson in Elizabeth Baker's study of suburban domesticity *Chains* (1910), during the Frohman repertory season at the Duke of York's. She managed the Vaudeville Theatre for a very short time, with Edmund Gwenn, in the summer of 1912. She acted Wish Wynne's original part of Janet Cannot—another of the agreeably managing Maggie characters that she assumed so easily—in a revival of *The Great Adventure* by Arnold Bennett at the Haymarket in 1924, and at the Open Air Theatre, Regent's Park, in June 1936, a surprising place and personage for her, she was—very shrewdly and surely—the Old Lady, Anne Boleyn's confidante, in Robert Atkins's production of *Henry VIII*. After leaving the stage in 1939 she lived for twenty years in happy retirement with her husband at their country house, the Manor House, Witheridge Hill, near Henley-on-Thames, where she died on 10 November 1959. They had no children.

It might be said of Hilda Trevelyan that she played Wendy throughout life. She had no major ambitions and never went beyond the reach of her technique, venturing very seldom indeed into Shakespeare or the classics. A natural actress, she was fortunate enough to live in a period fruitful in the kind of work she could do best. Later generations, demanding a more astringent tone, would find many of the parts unacceptable, but Hilda Trevelyan managed them so sensitively that in her day she had no real rival. In private life she kept her stage charm, and when in 1910 P. P. Howe described her as 'the most reticent and sympathetic of stars' he captured an endearing player's quality.

                                        J. C. TREWIN, rev.

Sources *The Times* (11 Nov 1959) • J. Parker, ed., *Who's who in the theatre*, 6th edn (1930) • S. Blow, *The ghost walks on Fridays* (1935) • D. Mackail, *The story of JMB* (1941) • J. M. Barrie, *When Wendy grew up: an afterthought* (1957) • R. L. Green, *Fifty years of Peter Pan* (1954) • P. P. Howe, *The repertory theatre: a record and a criticism* (1910) • personal knowledge (1971)
Archives NL Scot., letters relating to performances as Wendy in *Peter Pan*
Likenesses C. Buchel and Hassall, lithograph, NPG • postcard, NPG
Wealth at death £15,932 11s. 3d.: probate, 11 Dec 1959, *CGPLA Eng. & Wales*

Trevelyan, Humphrey, Baron Trevelyan (1905–1985), civil servant in India and diplomatist, was born at the parsonage, Hindhead, Surrey, on 27 November 1905, the younger son and fifth of the six children of George Philip Trevelyan (1858–1937), rector of Carshalton, Surrey (and later vicar of St Alban's, Hindhead, and then of St Stephen's, Bournemouth), and his wife, Monica Evelyn Juliet (d. 1962), daughter of Sidney Phillips, vicar of Kidderminster (and later honorary canon of Worcester). John *Trevelyan (1903–1986), secretary to the British Board of Film Censors from 1958 to 1971, was his elder brother.

Trevelyan was educated at Lancing College, Sussex, and Jesus College, Cambridge, where he obtained a second in part one (1926) and a first in part two (1927) of the classical tripos. With a career as a don beckoning, he instead joined the Indian Civil Service in 1929—the family tradition of public service weighing more heavily than the example set by his second cousin, the renowned historian George Macaulay Trevelyan. Assigned to district work in the Madras government, Trevelyan was responsible for sitting as a magistrate, tax collection, and the deciphering of telegrams from Simla (the contents of which, he learned, were not regarded as a priority). Long-standing tensions between the British and the Indians made the work thankless, but what frustrated him most was the rigidly closed expatriate community, which he likened to Surbiton with racial superiority grafted on. After befriending local nationalists, he soon reached the conclusion that wide-reaching social reform needed the impulse of an Indian government.

In 1932 Trevelyan was transferred to the less parochial Indian political service. His first appointment was as under-secretary to the agent to the governor-general in the central Indian princely states, a position that required wide travel during official visits. The purpose of these trips was to encourage good administration, but the nationalists remained convinced that rulers only had to provide a visiting grandee with a tiger or two during a shoot to make everything appear in order. In late 1934 he became under-secretary in the political department of the central government in Delhi. After a few months he moved on to Gwalior, where he acted as guardian to the maharajah, a minor. He married Violet Margaret (Peggy; *b.*

Humphrey Trevelyan, Baron Trevelyan (1905–1985), by Elliott & Fry, 1955

1913), only daughter of General Sir William Henry Bartholomew, chief of the general staff in India, on 10 November 1937. They had two daughters, Susan Anne (*b.* 1941) and Catherine Mary (*b.* 1943).

Trevelyan served as secretary to the resident in Mysore from 1937 to 1940, and deputy commissioner in Bahawalpur state in 1904–41. His career in Indian internal affairs culminated in his appointment as political agent in Mewar and the southern Rajputana states (1941–4). In April 1944 he was sent to Washington as secretary to the agent-general for India. This involved him in international affairs for the first time, as he prepared the way for an Indian embassy in the United States. His last job for the Indian political service returned him to Delhi early in 1946, though it kept him in a diplomatic role as joint secretary in the external affairs department, where he worked closely with Lord Mountbatten (who regarded him as an immensely talented official).

After India's independence in August 1947 Trevelyan entered Britain's foreign service. His first overseas posting was as counsellor in Baghdad from September 1948. Iraq at the time was in the midst of the Arab–Israeli war, which posed internal security problems for the pro-British regime. As counsellor he was responsible for keeping in touch with opposition elements and he was diligent enough to contact some of the men who staged a revolution a decade later. He acted as chargé d'affaires in 1949. A secondment to the Allied Control Commission for Germany followed in November 1950, where he worked as economic and financial adviser to the high commissioner. He was appointed CMG in 1951 (having been made OBE in 1941 and CIE in 1948).

By 1953 Britain was keen to open diplomatic relations with 'red' China, and Trevelyan was assigned to this delicate task. Appointed chargé d'affaires in August 1953, he arrived in Peking to find that the communist government would recognize him only as head of an office for the negotiation of diplomatic relations. But no negotiations were going on and the ministry of foreign affairs refused to receive him after his first formal call. This awkward situation continued until the Geneva conference on Indo-China in early 1954, when Trevelyan's first meeting with Chou En Lai sealed the formalization of diplomatic relations between their two countries. Although relations soon turned sour again, he nevertheless admired Chou En Lai's enormous capacity for work. It was a trait that Trevelyan shared, making it a matter of principle to do any job as well as or better than anyone working with or for him.

In August 1955—two months after being knighted KCMG—Trevelyan became ambassador to Cairo, an appointment that resulted in the severest test of his career. Relations were poor and getting worse because the Egyptian leader, Colonel Gamal Abdul Nasser, objected to Britain's accession to the Iraqi-led Baghdad pact. Trevelyan's scope for diplomatic manoeuvre was severely limited by the direct involvement in Egyptian matters of the prime minister, Anthony Eden. During the winter of 1955–6 the Cairo embassy obtained incontrovertible evidence—from taps on cables running under the Suez Canal—that Nasser was planning to attack Israel and was committed to the Russians. The 'lucky break' intelligence was used to justify a covert Anglo-American operation (code-named Omega) aimed at toppling Nasser, despite Trevelyan's concerns that nationalist extremism would be the lasting result of interference in Egypt's internal affairs.

The long-term strategy of destabilizing Nasser was abandoned after Egypt's nationalization of the Suez Canal Company on 26 July 1956. The Conservative government henceforth wanted quick results. Believing Trevelyan to be gullible, Eden instructed him to avoid anything resembling negotiations; Trevelyan therefore had to content himself with warning London of the difficulties of installing a lasting successor administration. Eden scrawled on one such telegram: 'Tell him to cheer up!' (Thornhill, 17). Trevelyan met Nasser once during the whole crisis—to hand him the Anglo-French ultimatum on 30 October. Nasser's courage in promptly rejecting the terms impressed Trevelyan, unlike Eden's behaviour which he put down to illness.

Expelled from Egypt in November 1956, Trevelyan spent a demoralizing year waiting for a suitable post to become vacant. The first offered was a secondment to the United Nations as under-secretary for special political affairs. It was significant that Egypt raised no objections. Trevelyan accepted the post and moved to New York in January 1958, but he lasted only ten months because he disliked

Secretary-General Dag Hammarskjöld's inability to delegate responsibility. For someone who did his best work when stretched, the situation was untenable. Ironically, the revolution in Iraq in July 1958—which owed much to the impact of Nasserite nationalism after Suez—created a new opening as ambassador in Baghdad.

When Trevelyan arrived in Iraq in December 1958 he was confronted with a chaotic situation. Anti-British feeling was rife—stirred up by the televised show trials of leading figures from the old regime—and there were frequent mob disturbances. It also required a good deal of pragmatism to deal with the regime responsible for the brutal murder of Nuri Said and King Feisal II, Britain's best friends in the Middle East. Nevertheless, within a year Trevelyan had secured compensation for the burning of the embassy premises and the death of a British official during the July revolution. Meanwhile Iraqi politics remained dangerously unstable as plots against the military leader, Brigadier Abdul Karim Qasim, abounded. It amazed Trevelyan that this 'not completely sane' man held on to power for four and a half years before he too was murdered (Trevelyan, *Middle East*, 117). Trevelyan's last year in Iraq was notable for Britain's sending military forces to Kuwait after Qasim had laid claim to the oil-rich emirate. Trevelyan returned to London in November 1961, having been succeeded as ambassador by Sir Roger Allen.

A brief spell in the Foreign Office as deputy under-secretary of state followed before Trevelyan was appointed to the ambassadorship at Moscow. He arrived in the Soviet Union in November 1962 in the wake of the Cuban missile crisis and for the next two years reported on the leadership struggle that culminated in Khrushchov's ousting in October 1964. It was a measure of Trevelyan's work ethic that, in what was meant to be his last overseas post, he learned the Russian language (partly so that he could read Pushkin in the original). Always a talented and supportive hostess, Peggy Trevelyan brought £500 worth of frozen food with her from Britain for entertainment purposes, knowing that food shortages were a frequent problem. Upon retirement from the diplomatic service in August 1965, Trevelyan was offered the job of permanent under-secretary at the Foreign Office but he declined, feeling that it ought to go to a younger man. He was promoted GCMG that year.

In May 1967 the foreign secretary, George Brown, who would not take no for an answer, persuaded Trevelyan to come out of retirement for one last assignment, as high commissioner to Aden. Trevelyan's task was to oversee Britain's withdrawal from the south-west Arabian peninsula, leaving behind an independent government which could ensure stability. 'Poor man,' said Harold Macmillan on hearing of the appointment (Balfour-Paul, 87). The situation was so dangerous—with the British caught in fighting between the Front for the Liberation of South Yemen (which was backed by Nasser's Egypt) and the National Liberation Front—that his wife was not allowed to accompany him. Tensions became even more aggravated following Israel's humiliation of Egypt in the Six Day War of June. Tired of British soldiers being killed by political

gangs, Trevelyan visited London early in September and secured ministerial approval for Britain fixing a date for leaving, whatever the internal situation. He and the last British troops duly left Aden on 29 November as the military band played, to the delight of the press, 'Fings ain't what they used to be'. In the following year he was created a life peer, as Baron Trevelyan, of St Veep.

Trevelyan had a busy retirement on numerous boards, including those of British Petroleum, the British Bank of the Middle East, and the English (later General) Electric Company, but his most fulfilling role was as chairman of the trustees of the British Museum (1971–9). His long connection with Nasser, who had a great respect for him, was a factor in his initial appointment as a trustee in 1970, during the preparations for the Tutankhamun exhibition. Trevelyan also chaired the Royal Institute of International Affairs between 1970 and 1977. Other outlets were also required for his immense energy and he became a prolific writer. His first book, *The Middle East in Revolution* (1970), was followed by *The World Apart* (1971), drawing on his experiences in the Soviet Union and China, *The India we Left* (1972), and *Diplomatic Channels* (1973), an account of the theory and practice of diplomacy. His last book was his most overtly autobiographical, *Public and Private* (1980). As well as becoming an honorary fellow of Jesus College, Cambridge, he received honorary degrees from Cambridge (1970), Durham (1973), and Leeds (1975). In 1974 he was made a member of the Order of the Garter. He died of bronchopneumonia and bulbar palsy at his home, 24 Duchess of Bedford House, Duchess of Bedford's Walk, Kensington, London, on 9 February 1985, and was survived by his wife and two daughters. A memorial service was held at St Margaret's, Westminster, on 19 March 1985. Trevelyan was widely regarded as the outstanding diplomat of his generation—a generation that was obliged to cope with the immense difficulties of Britain's disengagement from empire. It is a testimony to him and his profession that this period is regarded as one of readjustment rather than failure.

MICHAEL T. THORNHILL

Sources H. Trevelyan, *Public and private* (1980) · H. Trevelyan, *The Middle East in revolution* (1970) · *The Times* (12 Feb 1985) · *DNB* · M. T. Thornhill, 'Alternatives to Nasser: Humphrey Trevelyan, ambassador to Egypt', *Contemporary British History*, 13/2 (summer 1999) · G. Balfour-Paul, *The end of empire in the Middle East* (1991) · G. Brown, *In my way* (1971) · P. Gore-Booth, *With truth and great respect* (1974) · K. Hickman, *Illustrated daughters of Britannia* (2001) · O. Miles, 'The British withdrawal from Aden', www.al-bab.com/bys/articles/miles.htm, Sept 2002 · *WWW* · *Foreign Office List* (1965) · B. Urquhart, *Hammarskjöld* (1972) · b. cert. · d. cert. · will

Archives PRO, FO 371, political series

Likenesses Elliott & Fry, photograph, 1955, NPG [*see illus.*] · K. Hickman, photographs, repro. in Hickman, *Illustrated daughters*

Wealth at death £232,754: probate, 14 May 1985, *CGPLA Eng. & Wales*

Trevelyan, John (1903–1986), film censor, was born on 11 July 1903 at 10 Kemerton Road, Beckenham, Kent, the fourth child and elder son in the family of two sons and four daughters of George Philip Trevelyan (1858–1937), Church of England clergyman, and his wife, Monica Evelyn Juliet (*d.* 1962), daughter of Sidney Phillips, Church of

England clergyman. His younger brother was Humphrey *Trevelyan, Baron Trevelyan (1905–1985), diplomatist, and his eldest sister was Mary Trevelyan (1897–1983), founder of International Students' House, London. He was educated at Lancing College and Trinity College, Cambridge, where he was awarded a third class in part one of the history tripos in 1924 and graduated BA in 1925. He was married four times. His first wife, whom he married on 18 September 1928, was Kathleen Margaret Pass (b. 1901/2), daughter of Charles Hallé Pass, gentleman, of Barrow in Furness. They had one son, who was born and died in 1932. Following their divorce in 1949 he married, on 1 June that year, Dr Joan Frieda Scott (b. 1912), medical practitioner and daughter of Francis Clayton Scott, company director, son of Sir James William Schott, later Scott, of Yews in Westmorland, first baronet: they had one son and one daughter. His second divorce, in 1959, was followed by his third marriage, on 7 December that year, to Jean Metcher (1928/29–1972), daughter of Robert Mutch, a railway goods superintendent: they had twin sons. After the death of his third wife he married, in 1974, Rosalie Evelyn Camber (1924/25–1979), daughter of Joseph Lopez-Salzedo, company director.

After teaching in the Gold Coast for a period, Trevelyan in 1929 became an educational administrator, working in Kent and Sussex until his appointment in 1938 as director of education for the county of Westmorland, where, during the Second World War, he had to cope with a huge influx of evacuees from the north-east coast. In 1946 he resigned to take up the post of first director of the British Families Education Service in Germany, where he was responsible for setting up schools for the children of allied servicemen. He left educational administration in 1949 (the year in which he was appointed OBE) to make a living as a freelance writer and lecturer.

In 1951 Trevelyan was invited to join the British Board of Film Censors, which had been set up in 1912 by the film industry in an attempt to stave off interference by local authorities, which had been given legal responsibility for licensing cinemas. In time, the local authorities made it a condition of issuing a licence that the cinema should adopt the board's certificates, although they were able to reverse the decisions of the board, which had no statutory powers. In 1952 Trevelyan was appointed chairman of a new committee, the cinema advisory subcommittee, set up as a forum for discussions between representatives of the licensing authorities, the film industry, and welfare and educational organizations, and in 1958 he was appointed secretary to the board, chosen by representatives of the principal associations of the film industry. Until 1960 the president of the board had sole responsibility for censorship, but in that year the secretary was given joint responsibility with the president, whose role became consultative. Trevelyan served with two presidents: from 1960 to 1965 Lord Morrison of Lambeth held the office, but Trevelyan had a much more successful relationship with his successor, Lord Harlech.

When Trevelyan became a film examiner in 1951, nudity was never allowed in a film: by 1971, when he retired, there were many films which contained material that he considered too pornographic even for adult audiences, and which were consequently refused an X certificate. One of the first films to come to the board after Trevelyan was appointed was *Room at the Top* (1958), regarded as a milestone in the history of British film censorship: in contrast to most British and American films of the 1950s, it dealt with real people and real problems, and despite its explicit dialogue it was passed by the board. This was followed by *Saturday Night and Sunday Morning* (1960), *The L-Shaped Room* (1962), and *A Kind of Loving* (1962), all passed because Trevelyan considered them to be made with good taste and sincerity. In the 1960s, a period of changing attitudes which saw the coming of the 'permissive society', he had to decide what his responsibilities were: he described himself as 'a censor who did not believe in censorship' (*The Times*). But as a former educator he was especially concerned with protecting children from unsuitable material, and he banned films he regarded as pornographic. He also tackled the increasing portrayal of violence on screen, which he thought justified if it was there to show that violence was inhuman. He believed in the importance of establishing good relations with film makers and film-company executives, and he often visited studios to watch films being shot, encouraging producers to show him unfinished scripts so that he could advise on whether acceptance was likely. He managed to keep a balanced view, and was widely respected for his tolerant and reasonable approach.

In his thirteen years as secretary Trevelyan was only involved in one *cause célèbre*, in 1970, when the police raided the Open Space Theatre Club during a showing of Andy Warhol's *Flesh*, which did not have a certificate. Trevelyan, who had suggested the film be shown there as clubs could show films that did not have a certificate, intervened, and when the directors of the theatre were fined by Hampstead magistrates court, he arranged for Warhol to pay the fines. He subsequently gave *Flesh* an X certificate.

Trevelyan was appointed CBE on retirement in 1971. He published *What the Censor Saw*, his reflections on the changing role of censorship, in 1973. He died on 15 August 1986 at his home, 35 Braybrooke Gardens, Upper Norwood, London.   ANNE PIMLOTT BAKER

Sources J. Trevelyan, *What the censor saw* (1973) · *The Times* (18 Aug 1986) · Burke, *Peerage* · b. cert. · m. cert. [Kathleen Margaret Pass] · m. cert. [Joan Frieda Scott] · m. cert. [Jean Metcher] · m. cert. [Rosalie Evelyn Camber] · d. cert.
Archives BFI, corresp. with Joseph Losey · King's Lond., Liddell Hart C., corresp. with Sir B. H. Liddell Hart
Likenesses photograph, repro. in Trevelyan, *What the censor saw*, frontispiece · photograph, repro. in *The Times*
Wealth at death £113.439: probate, 19 Feb 1987, *CGPLA Eng. & Wales*

Trevelyan, Julian Otto (1910–1988), painter and printmaker, was born on 20 February 1910 in Leith Hill, Surrey, the only surviving child (a first son had died at the age of two in 1909 and a daughter had died in infancy) of Robert Calverley Trevelyan, classical scholar and poet (the son of the historian Sir George Otto *Trevelyan and brother of the historian George Macaulay *Trevelyan), and his Dutch wife, Elizabeth, daughter of Jan des Amorie van der Hoeven, of The Hague. He was educated at Bedales School and at Trinity College, Cambridge, where he completed two years of the English tripos (obtaining a second class, division two, in part one, 1930) before leaving, without part two of his degree, to study painting in Paris.

At Cambridge Trevelyan identified himself with the modernist group associated with the magazine *Experiment*, which included William Empson, Jacob Bronowski, Humphrey Jennings, and Kathleen Raine. Through Jennings he was introduced to French painting and surrealist ideas. In Paris, after a false start at the Académie Moderne run by Fernand Léger and Amédée Ozenfant, he enrolled at the printmaking workshop run by Stanley William Hayter (later Atelier 17), and immersed himself in the cosmopolitan nocturnal life of Montparnasse, counting among his friends Massimo Campigli, Vieira da Silva, and Alexander Calder. His training under Hayter was technically and creatively rigorous, and he worked alongside such major contemporaries as Joan Miró, Max Ernst, Pablo Picasso, and John Buckland-Wright. His etchings of this period are wittily surrealistic.

In 1935 Trevelyan established himself at Durham Wharf on the Thames at Hammersmith, where he was to live for the rest of his life. Here, in the mid-1930s, he made his first distinctively original works. Painted and scratched on wood and slate, these spiky linear images of whimsical buildings and transparent cities reflect an awareness of Paul Klee and Miró, but their quirky invention is entirely personal, as is their dreamlike juxtaposition of image and sign. Paintings and etchings in this style were selected for the 1936 International Surrealist Exhibition at the New Burlington Galleries, London, and Trevelyan continued afterwards to take part in English surrealist manifestations and exhibitions. His first one-man show was held at the Lefèvre Galleries in 1935. In 1937-8 he participated in Mass-Observation, run by Tom Harrisson, as a photographer, artist, and observer in Bolton and Blackpool, making *plein-air* collage landscapes of newspaper scraps, ephemera, and coloured paper, in which the fragments of the printed word relate ironically to the topographies depicted. In late 1938, inspired by the expressive authenticity of 'unprofessional painting', and excited by the infernal landscapes of the Potteries, he adopted a deliberately gauche painterly manner and a vehement colourism. This expressionist style matched his response to the vitality and violence of industrialism, and later to the fevered atmosphere of London during the blitz of 1940, the year in which he joined the Royal Engineers as a camouflage officer.

In 1943 Trevelyan was invalided out of the army on psychiatric grounds. His painting in the 1940s became more impressionistic and atmospheric, the handling lighter and less emphatically primitivist, his colours brighter and fresher. The best paintings of this period, the townscapes, riverscapes, and interiors of the late 1940s, have a newly sophisticated looseness of touch, a tonal subtlety and compositional sureness influenced by French painting,

especially by Pierre Bonnard. During the 1950s he moved towards linear depiction and decorative colour, a simplification related to a renewed commitment to etching, which he taught at Chelsea School of Art from 1950 to 1960, and at the Royal College of Art from 1955 to 1963. This developed into the distinctive schematic stylization of his late manner, in which sharply delineated flat planes of colour are deployed across the canvas in jigsaw-like patterns to effect evocative distillations of mood and locale. Unpretentious and charming, this later work avoids false naïvety by disciplined design and a persistent visual wit. As a painter Trevelyan was modest in ambition and achievement, but his work was distinguished always by an authentic innocence of eye, and a spirit by turns passionate, ironic, and humorous. A brilliantly inventive etcher, his linear technique and imaginative texturing, often using found materials and objects, established him as one of the finest printmakers of his generation. He was a much loved and influential teacher.

Trevelyan was a tall, long-faced, and handsome man, whose sweetness of manner disguised a mercurial temperament. From a distinguished family he inherited a wide culture and a love of friendship; parties at Durham Wharf, especially on the day of the Oxford and Cambridge boat race, were famous. He travelled widely throughout his life, constantly recording his impressions in paint, but remained profoundly attached to his studio home by the Thames. In 1963 he suffered an unidentified viral infection of the brain, which badly affected his speech; with regret he had to give up teaching, driving, and playing the oboe. He soon returned to etching, and later to painting. In 1986 he was made a senior fellow of the Royal College of Art and an honorary senior Royal Academician. He had a mini-retrospective exhibition at the New Grafton Gallery in 1977 and his work is represented in the Tate collection and in many other public collections.

In 1934 Trevelyan married Ursula Frances Elinor, potter, the daughter of Bernard Richard Meirion *Darwin, golfing journalist. Their son, Philip Erasmus, was born in 1943. This marriage ended in divorce in 1949, and in 1951 he married (Adye) Mary, painter, daughter of (Harry) Vincent Fedden, sugar broker. There were no children of the second marriage. Trevelyan died in Hammersmith on 12 July 1988. MEL GOODING, *rev.*

Sources J. Trevelyan, *Indigo days* (1957) · *The Independent* (14 July 1988) · *The Times* (14 July 1988) · personal knowledge (1996) · private information (1996)
Archives Tate collection, drawings, papers, and sketchbooks · Trinity Cam., corresp. and papers | Tate collection, corresp. with John Banting
Likenesses J. Trevelyan, self-portrait, 1940, NPG
Wealth at death £1,359,305: probate, 13 Sept 1988, *CGPLA Eng. & Wales*

Trevelyan [*née* Bell], **Mary Katharine** [Molly], **Lady Trevelyan** (1881–1966), political hostess and voluntary worker, was born on 12 October 1881, the youngest of three children of Sir (Thomas) Hugh Bell, second baronet and iron master (1844–1931), and his second wife, Florence Eveleen Eleanore Olliffe, Lady *Bell (1851–1930), the author and social investigator. Her half-sister was the Arabic scholar Gertrude *Bell, and her grandfather was Sir Isaac Lowthian Bell, first baronet, the steel manufacturer and Liberal MP. Molly, as she was universally known, had a comfortable childhood, but her home education consisted primarily of preparation for marriage. She developed a lifelong love of embroidery, music, and languages, and in 1917 she co-wrote a French textbook with her mother, from whom she also acquired an interest in social conditions. After studying briefly at Queen's College, London, she came out in 1899. Although her father was lord lieutenant of the North Riding of Yorkshire, there were few politicians in her family's social circle, so when she began a relationship with the Liberal MP Sir Charles Philips *Trevelyan, third baronet (1870–1958), she regretted her lack of political knowledge. However, he hoped that her youth and beauty could be used for high ends, and after they married on 6 January 1904 and set up house in London she became a successful political hostess, arranging dinners and parties for political friends.

As well as political entertaining Molly Trevelyan pursued a more public role after 1904 as president of the Northumberland Women's Liberal Federation (WLF). She became a popular speaker around the country and favoured women's suffrage, an issue which deeply divided the WLF, but she disliked militancy and did not feel strongly enough to work for the cause. Her husband also supported women's suffrage, but adhered to traditional notions of men's and women's roles, and Molly eventually abandoned her hope that their marriage would be an equal political partnership. She none the less helped him in various ways, from translating German material on land reform to campaigning energetically at every election until his last in 1931, including the difficult election of 1918 when he was attacked for having opposed the war.

After Charles Trevelyan inherited his ancestral home of Wallington Hall, Northumberland, in 1928, they devoted much of the rest of their lives to the estate and the village of Cambo. She and Charles were keenly interested in their tenants' welfare and established a pension plan for schoolchildren. A deeply practical woman, she was not above putting her hand to any work the estate required, and planned and oversaw alterations to the tenants' cottages and farmhouses. In addition to estate work she was a JP and was active with numerous local, national, and international organizations, such as the Workers' Educational Association and the Association of Country Women of the World. She founded branches of the Girl Guides and the Women's Institute in Cambo, and served on the national executive of the National Federation of Women's Institutes for many years. In keeping with her temperance principles she also founded in Cambo a Band of Hope, which local children were pledged to join at a young age. She also played a leading role in the Folk Dance and Northumbrian Pipers societies, and made music an important feature of her family's life. Singing songs, accompanied by Molly on the piano, was a regular part of their domestic routine, and she and Charles also delighted their children, among them George Lowthian *Trevelyan, by regularly

reading to them from a diverse selection of classic literature. Such activities took the place of attending church on Sundays, for while Molly was Unitarian, Charles was agnostic. In appearance her clothes, hairstyle, and pince-nez gave her a Victorian air, and one contemporary described her as attractive in a 'no nonsense' sort of way. Her decades of public service, to politics and various other good causes, were recognized with an OBE in 1963, shortly before her death at St Catherine's Nursing Home, Newcastle upon Tyne, on 8 October 1966. Her ashes were scattered on moorland near Winter's Gibbet on the Wallington estate.

DUNCAN SUTHERLAND

Sources T. Lummis and J. Marsh, *The woman's domain: women and the English country house* (1990) · A. J. A. Morris, *C. P. Trevelyan, 1870–1958: portrait of a radical* (1977) · P. Jalland, *Women, marriage and politics, 1860–1914* (1986) · J. Lees-Milne, *Ancestral voices* (1975) · *WWW* · *The Times* (10 Oct 1966) · K. Trevelyan, *Fool in love* (1962) · private information (2004) · *CGPLA Eng. & Wales* (1967)
Archives U. Newcastle, MSS
Likenesses photographs, Wallington, Northumberland
Wealth at death £30,423: probate, 18 April 1967, *CGPLA Eng. & Wales*

Trevelyan, Paulina Jermyn [Pauline; *née* Paulina Jermyn], **Lady Trevelyan** (1816–1866), art patron and critic, was born on 25 January 1816 at Hawkedon, near Bury St Edmunds, Suffolk, the eldest of the seven children of the Revd Dr George Bitton *Jermyn (1789–1857), vicar of Swaffham Prior, near Newmarket, and his wife, Catherine Rowland (1792–1828), daughter of Hugh Rowland and his second wife, Anne Beck, of Huguenot descent. Her impecunious father was a notable antiquary and naturalist; when only seventeen, she attended with him the 1833 British Association for the Advancement of Science meeting at Cambridge. Here her quick brain and extraordinary memory impressed scientists such as William Whewell, John Stevens Henslow, and Adam Sedgwick, who became lifelong friends. The geologist Walter Calverley *Trevelyan (1797–1879) had come to exhibit fossilized saurian faeces and was struck by her knowledge of botany. He was invited back to Swaffham Prior to look at ferns, and on 21 May 1835 he and Pauline (as she was known) were married. Calverley Trevelyan (as his wife called him)—tall, taciturn, and relatively humourless—was twenty years her senior; reputed to be parsimonious, he was in fact a generous donor to charities of his own choosing and indulgent to his wife's artistic enthusiasms, though he was himself only interested in art if it was 'instructive'. Despite differences of age and character, the marriage was undoubtedly a successful one.

During the first eleven years of their marriage, the couple travelled a great deal in Europe. In Rome, Pauline Trevelyan at once sought out the expatriate artists' colony; in Florence she persuaded her husband to buy her old masters, including a reputed Piero della Francesca. In Switzerland they studied glaciers; in Greece they conducted experiments with the camera lucida, on which Pauline based sketches (now in the British Museum, London). At Corfu she met Louisa Stewart-Mackenzie (later Lady Ashburton), her beloved Loo, who in later years introduced her to Thomas and Jane Welsh Carlyle. From

Paulina Jermyn Trevelyan, Lady Trevelyan (1816–1866), by William Bell Scott, 1864

Portugal they brought back camellias, still in existence in Somerset. The couple also spent much time in Edinburgh, where friendships were forged with leading Scottish scientists, writers, and (for Pauline) theologians. Pauline Trevelyan contributed poems and articles to *The Scotsman* and *Chambers's Edinburgh Journal* and became known in Edinburgh society as an astringent art and literary critic.

In 1846 Trevelyan inherited his baronetcy and with it estates in south-west England, including Nettlecombe Court in Somerset, and in Northumberland, where the family seat was Wallington, which Pauline Trevelyan preferred. Her admiration for the second volume of *Modern Painters* led to a close friendship with John Ruskin, to whom she became 'my monitress-friend in whom I wholly trusted' (*The Works of John Ruskin*, ed. E. T. Cook and A. Wedderburn, 1903–12, 35.457). At his suggestion, she took drawing lessons with William Henry (Bird's Nest) Hunt; she also visited Turner's studio. The Ruskins and Millaises stayed at Wallington on their fateful journey to Glenfinlas in Scotland; when Ruskin's marriage collapsed, Lady Trevelyan unswervingly supported the husband, despite her fondness for Effie Ruskin.

Pauline Trevelyan became a prominent patron of the Pre-Raphaelites, an association reflected in the alterations and embellishments at Wallington. The house's central courtyard was roofed over, with some Ruskinian motifs by the Newcastle architect John Dobson; William Bell Scott was commissioned to paint eight panels with suitably instructive scenes from Northumbrian history, from St Cuthbert to the modern industrial age, while the pilasters were decorated with flowers and plants by Ruskin, Lady Trevelyan, Arthur Hughes, and the future Lady Dilke. Pauline Trevelyan also commissioned a painting from Dante Gabriel Rossetti, and Thomas Woolner began a large marble group for the new central hall; known as *Civilization*, it was only completed after her death in 1866. It was Lady Trevelyan who reputedly saved William Holman Hunt's *Christ in the Temple* from a dramatic fire in a London art gallery. Christina Rossetti and Alexander Munro were among her many guests, and she also recognized the potential genius of Swinburne, when he was still a schoolboy; she became to him a kind of guardian angel or understanding aunt, and in a sonnet written after her death he described her as 'grave-eyed mirth on wings' (*The Poems of Algernon Charles Swinburne*, 5, 1904, 230).

Inspired by her friend Henry Acland, Lady Trevelyan designed capitals for the new Oxford University Museum (while Calverley donated money, a Davy lamp, geological specimens, and a great auk's egg). The architect of the museum, Benjamin Woodward, was invited to 'gothicize' Seaton, near Honiton in south Devon—most of which was owned by Calverley Trevelyan—while Pauline provided Pre-Raphaelite designs for local lace makers (a specimen is now in the Victoria and Albert Museum, London). However, Woodward died, leaving only the plans for a curious piebald 'cottage', in which Lady Trevelyan was to entertain the Carlyles in 1865, and which still stands.

Diminutive, with bright hazel eyes and a protuberant forehead which made her look almost childlike, Pauline Trevelyan was a brilliant and witty woman, enthusiastic, teasing and warm, yet quiet and quaint in manner. William Bell Scott described her as 'light as a feather and quick as a kitten' but 'very likely without the passion of love' (*Autobiographical Notes*, 2.257), which was possibly true. Augustus Hare recalled her eyes twinkling all day long, but 'she is abrupt to a degree and contradicts everyone', he continued, adding that she was not much concerned about home comforts and preferred to sit on the floor (Hare, 2.276). In 1850 she became ill; an ovarian tumour was diagnosed and was lanced with the patient under chloroform, with iodine injections which caused agony. Although Lady Trevelyan suffered recurrent and worsening collapses for the rest of her life, she rarely complained and refused more operations. In April 1866 the Trevelyans somewhat rashly accompanied Ruskin to Switzerland; on 13 May Pauline Trevelyan died at Neuchâtel, with her husband and Ruskin by her bedside; she was buried there on 16 May.   RALEIGH TREVELYAN

Sources U. Newcastle, Robinson L., Trevelyan MSS · priv. coll., Trevelyan family MSS · R. Trevelyan, *A Pre-Raphaelite circle* (1978) · V. Surtees, *Reflections of a friendship* (1979) · R. Trevelyan, 'Effie Ruskin and Pauline Trevelyan', *Bulletin of the John Rylands University Library*, 62 (1979–80), 232–58 · 'Thomas Woolner and Pauline Trevelyan', *Pre-Raphaelite Review*, 2/2 (May 1979) · R. Trevelyan, 'Thomas Woolner: Pre-Raphaelite sculptor', *Apollo*, 107 (1978), 200–05 · *Autobiographical notes of the life of William Bell Scott: and notices of his artistic* *and poetic circle of friends, 1830 to 1882*, ed. W. Minto, 2 vols. (1892) • D. Wooster, *Lady Trevelyan's literary and artistic remains* (1879) • diaries and sketchbooks, University of Kansas, Lawrence, Kenneth Spencer Research Library • M. Lutyens, *Millais and the Ruskins* (1967) • *The Swinburne letters*, ed. C. Y. Lang, 6 vols. (1959–62), vol. 1 • F. O'Dwyer, *The architecture of Deane and Woodward* (1997) • A. J. C. Hare, *The story of my life*, 2 (1896) • R. Trevelyan, 'The Trevelyans at Seaton', *Country Life*, 161 (1977), 1397–400

Archives U. Newcastle, Robinson L., corresp. • University of Kansas, Kenneth Spencer Research Library, diaries and sketchbooks
Likenesses A. Munro, marble medallion, 1855, Wallington, Northumberland; plaster copy, Nettlecombe Court, Somerset • W. Bell Scott, oils, 1864, Wallington, Northumberland [*see illus.*]

Trevelyan, Raleigh (1781–1865), writer, was born on 6 August 1781, the younger son of Walter Trevelyan (1743–1819), sheriff of Northumberland, and his first wife, Margaret, elder daughter and coheir of James Thornton of Netherwitton, Northumberland. Walter was the second son of Sir George Trevelyan, third baronet, of Nettlecombe Court, Somerset.

Raleigh was educated at Eton College and at St John's College, Cambridge, from which he graduated BA in 1804 and MA in 1807. He was an able classical scholar and in 1806 he obtained the senior bachelor's medal for a Latin essay. On 11 November 1801 Trevelyan entered Lincoln's Inn and in 1810 he was called to the bar, but on the death of his elder brother, Walter Blackett Trevelyan, on 3 April 1818, he succeeded to the Netherwitton estates and relinquished his practice. He married, on 14 June 1819, Elizabeth, second daughter of Robert Grey of Shoreston, Northumberland.

Trevelyan passed the remainder of his life chiefly in Northumberland, where he indulged his literary tastes and his conservative tendencies by writing poems and political pamphlets. The former were marked by elegance and scholarship, the latter by unusual moderation. His poems include 'Elegy on the Death of the Princess Charlotte' (1818) and *A Poetical Sketch of the Ten Commandments* (1830?). *Essays and Poems*, a collection of his work, was printed in 1833. Trevelyan died at Netherwitton Hall on 12 May 1865. He was succeeded at Netherwitton by his grandson Thornton Roger Trevelyan.

E. I. CARLYLE, *rev.* M. CLARE LOUGHLIN-CHOW

Sources GM, 3rd ser., 18 (1865) • W. P. Baildon, ed., *The records of the Honorable Society of Lincoln's Inn: the black books*, 2 (1898), 7 • Boase, *Mod. Eng. biog.* • *Law Times* (10 June 1865), 391 • Venn, *Alum. Cant.*
Archives Northumbd RO, Newcastle upon Tyne, letters to Wilson, Chisholme, and Holroyd
Likenesses S. Harding, miniature, FM Cam.
Wealth at death under £8000: resworn administration, 7 Aug 1865, *CGPLA Eng. & Wales*

Trevelyan, Sir Walter Calverley, sixth baronet (1797–1879), naturalist, was born on 31 March 1797 at Newcastle upon Tyne, the eldest son of Sir John Trevelyan, fifth baronet (1761–1846), and his wife, Maria (d. 1852), daughter of Sir Thomas Spencer Wilson. Educated at Harrow School, where W. H. Fox Talbot (1800–1877) was a scientific crony, he proceeded in 1816 to University College, Oxford, becoming a keen geologist under William Buckland's

guidance and an accomplished antiquary who contributed to Hodgson's *History of Northumberland*. Having graduated in 1820 he moved to Edinburgh to extend his scientific interests. In 1821 he visited the Faeroe Islands to study their natural history and in 1823 was the first to demonstrate the intrusive nature of the Whin Sill in Northumberland. From 1822 Trevelyan was an ardent phrenologist who supported a Combeian school in Edinburgh, opposed capital punishment and flogging, argued for state education to prevent crime, and condemned alcohol, tobacco, and opium as morally degrading. Having rejected a possible wife on phrenological grounds, in 1833 he met Paulina Jermyn (1816–1866) [*see* Trevelyan, Paulina Jermyn, Lady Trevelyan], eldest daughter of the Revd G. B. Jermyn, at the British Association for the Advancement of Science; they married on 21 May 1835.

In 1846 Trevelyan succeeded to the title and family estates. As a wealthy landlord he practised scientific agriculture and promoted the well-being of his tenants. In 1853 he refurbished Wallington, Northumberland, as a Pre-Raphaelite showpiece, aided by his artistic wife, a painter and lace designer who was friendly with Ruskin, the Carlyles, and Swinburne. They also developed Seaton, Devon, as a resort.

Trevelyan continued to maintain his antiquarian interests, co-editing a volume of Trevelyan Papers for the Camden Society. He also maintained a large collection for natural history and ethnology at Wallington and generously gave specimens and money to museums. He backed Pitman's movement for spelling reform, becoming president of the derided Phonetic Society. As a political Liberal in 1865 he bought an estate at Tynemouth, where a relative was an election candidate, for £61,000 to secure the tenants' votes; after the election he sold it. As a tolerant Anglican and total abstainer, he collaborated with dissenters in campaigning for the prohibition of alcohol. From 1853 to his death he was president of the United Kingdom Alliance for Suppression of the Liquor Traffic and in 1854 president of the National Temperance Society.

Trevelyan was of foppish appearance, with careless dress and long moustache and hair, but he was a courageous opponent of social and intellectual tyranny and an aristocratic eccentric who fought for causes to the last. Among his eccentricities was a mania for concrete, which culminated in 1877 with the opening of his Axe Bridge at Seaton, England's second concrete bridge. Following the death of his first wife, on 11 July 1867 Trevelyan married Laura Capel, daughter of Capel Lofft, of Troston Hall, Suffolk. He died at Wallington on 23 March 1879 from a cold and was buried simply, as he wished, at Cambo, Northumberland, on 1 April 1879. His wife died the next day. Both his marriages being childless, the title descended to his nephew, Alfred Wilson Trevelyan (1831–1891) but Trevelyan left Wallington to his cousin, Charles Edward *Trevelyan (1807–1886).

JACK MORRELL

Sources R. Trevelyan, *A Pre-Raphaelite circle* (1978) • B. Harrison, *Dictionary of British temperance biography* (1973) • *Proceedings of the Royal Society of Edinburgh*, 10 (1878–80), 354–6 • R. Welford, *Men of mark 'twixt Tyne and Tweed*, 3 vols. (1895) • R. Cooter, *Phrenology in the*

British Isles: an annotated historical biobibliography and index (1989) • D. Wooster, ed., *Selections from the literary and artistic remains of Paulina Jermyn Trevelyan* (1879) • *Northumberland*, Pevsner (1957) • B. Harrison, *Drink and the Victorians: the temperance question in England, 1815–1872* (1971) • R. Trevelyan, 'The Trevelyans at Seaton', *Country Life*, 161 (1977), 1397–400 • J. Hodgson, *A history of Northumberland*, 3 pts in 7 vols. (1820–58) • *Devon*, Pevsner (1989) • *Transactions of the Botanical Society* [Edinburgh], 14 (1883), 8–11

Archives BL, corresp. and papers, Add. MSS 22289, 24965, 27409, 28872, 29708, 29718, 31026–31027 • U. Newcastle, Robinson L., corresp., diaries, and papers | Bodl. Oxf., corresp. with Sir Thomas Phillips • NL Scot., corresp. with George Combe • RBG Kew, letters to Sir William Hooker • U. Edin. L., letters to David Laing

Likenesses G. B. Black, lithograph, 1819, NPG • R. S. Lauder, oils, c.1845, Nettlecombe, Somerset • W. B. Scott, oils, 1850–59, Wallington, Northumberland • Maull & Co., photograph, repro. in T. R. Goddard, *History of the Natural History Society of Northumberland, Durham and Newcastle upon Tyne* (1929) • engraving, repro. in Welford, *Men of mark* • medallion head, Wallington, Northumberland • photograph (with Paulina Trevelyan), repro. in Wooster, ed., *Selections*

Wealth at death under £160,000: probate, 27 May 1879, *CGPLA Eng. & Wales*

Trevenen, James (1760–1790), naval officer in the British and Russian services, was born at Rosewarne, near Camborne, Cornwall, on 1 January 1760, the third son of John Trevenen, curate of Camborne, and Elizabeth, *née* Tellam (d. 1799). He was educated at Helston grammar school and from 1773 at the Royal Naval Academy at Portsmouth, where he studied for three years.

In the spring of 1776 Trevenen was appointed to the *Resolution*, then fitting out for the last voyage of Captain James Cook. From her, in August 1779, he followed Captain James King to the *Discovery*. On 28 October 1780, on the return of the expedition to Britain, he was promoted lieutenant, and early in the following year he was appointed to the *Crocodile*, then commanded by King, in the North Sea and in the channel. In the summer of 1782 he again followed King to the *Resistance*, which went out to the West Indies in charge of convoy. On 2 March 1783 she fell in with and captured the French frigate *Coquette*, then returning from taking possession of Turk's Island. A few days later the *Resistance* and some smaller vessels under the orders of Captain Horatio Nelson in the *Albemarle*, attempted to recapture Turk's Island, but without success. Trevenen returned home in July 1783, and spent most of the next two years in Italy.

In 1786 Trevenen had an idea for a merchant voyage to Nootka Sound, and a small company was discussed, but the project fell through. He considered service in the East India Company and also applied to the Admiralty for employment in connection with the new settlement at Botany Bay. However, opportunities 'out of the common routine of sea duty' as he put it, were limited; thereafter Trevenen developed a disgust for the Admiralty that he thought slow to recognize his—as yet unproved—merit.

In February 1787 Trevenen discussed a scheme to voyage to the north Pacific with the Russian ambassador in London. After approval by the Russian government, Trevenen was ordered to St Petersburg, as he believed, to take command of the project. Before his departure he was warned by friends, including his brother-in-law, Charles Vinicombe Penrose, that should he accept the post he would be required to serve in the Russian navy in the event of war with Turkey. On reaching St Petersburg Trevenen discovered that the Turks had indeed declared war against Russia, that the expedition was postponed, and that he was expected to serve in the navy with the rank of second captain. He agreed to this, subject to the consent of the English Admiralty. Assuming that this would be given, he accepted the command of a ship intended for the Mediterranean. In late 1787 he received the Admiralty's refusal. Considering himself bound to the Russians, he sent a letter in which he resigned his commission. However, his friends did not forward his letter, and it does not appear that the Admiralty ever knew officially of his disobedience.

The outbreak of the war with Sweden in 1788 prevented Trevenen's being sent to the Mediterranean, and in July he took command of the *Rodislav* (64 guns) in the fleet of another British officer in Russian service, Admiral Samuel Greig. In late July Trevenen was involved in the Russians' disappointing engagement with the Swedes near Högland. In the following month he was sent in command of a small squadron to Hangö Head, cutting the communication between Stockholm and the Swedish ports in the Gulf of Finland. This blockade he maintained until the close of the season, and on his return to Kronstadt he was promoted to captain of the first class. In May 1789 Trevenen was again sent to his station off Hangö Head, but during the winter the Swedes had thrown up several batteries. He was therefore recalled, and joined Admiral Chichagoff at Reval. In mid-July they joined a division of the fleet which had wintered at Copenhagen, but on 25 July they found themselves in the presence of the Swedish fleet. A desultory engagement followed, the fleets separated without any result, and Chichagoff joined the Copenhagen squadron and returned to Reval. Trevenen was then sent to occupy Porkala Point and to destroy the batteries in Barö Sound. On his return to Reval at the end of October the *Rodislav* was run on a submerged reef and became a total wreck. A court martial decided that the pilot alone was to blame, and Trevenen was appointed to the *Ne Tron Menya* at Kronstadt under the command of Admiral Kruse. At Kronstadt in February 1789 Trevenen married Elizabeth (d. 1845), daughter of John Farquharson; they had one daughter.

In May 1790 Admiral Kruse put to sea with sixteen ships of the line, wishing to effect a junction with Chichagoff at Reval. The Swedish fleet of twenty-two sail of the line interposed, and on 3 June a sharp action was fought, renewed on the following day, without any decided advantage to either side. Kruse was able to join with Chichagoff, and the Swedes fell back into Viborg Bay. On 3 July 1790 they made an ineffectual attempt to force their way out, but in the action Trevenen received wounds from which he died on board his ship at Kronstadt on 9 July. He was survived by his wife, who later married the editor Thomas Bowdler. J. K. LAUGHTON, *rev.* RICHARD H. WARNER

Sources C. Lloyd and R. Anderson, eds., *A memoir of James Trevenen I* (1959) • V. A. Chistiakov, 'Den *Sisoia Velikogo*' [The day of Sisoia the Great], *Morskoi Sbornik* (July 1988), 78–83 • J. Penrose, *Lives of Vice-Admiral Sir Charles Vinicombe Penrose KCB and Captain James Trevenen* (1850) • R. C. Anderson, 'British and American officers in the Russian navy', *Mariner's Mirror*, 33 (1947), 17–27 • R. C. Anderson, 'Great Britain and the rise of the Russian fleet in the eighteenth century', *Mariner's Mirror*, 42 (1956), 132–46 • F. F. Veselago, *Kratkaia istoriia russkogo flota* [A short history of the Russian fleet] (1939) • R. C. Anderson, *Naval wars in the Baltic during the sailing-ship epoch, 1522–1850* (1910); repr. as *Naval wars in the Baltic, 1522–1850* (1969) • *Obshchii morskoi spisok* [General naval list] (1885–1907) • V. A. Divin and others, eds., *Boevaia letopis' russkogo flota* [Chronicle of the battles of the Russian fleet] (Moscow, 1948) • S. P. Oakley, *War and peace in the Baltic, 1560–1790* (1992) • L. Withey, *Voyages of discovery: Captain Cook and the exploration of the Pacific* (1987)
Archives British Columbia Archives and Records Service, notes on Captain Cook; notes made on HMS *Resolution* • NMM, memoirs
Likenesses lithograph (after portrait by Allingham), repro. in Penrose, *Lives*

Treveris, Peter (*fl.* 1525–1532), printer, was perhaps a foreigner, as many early London printers were, though nothing is known of his birth, early years, private life, or death. According to *The Grete Herball* printed on 27 July 1526 he lived in Southwark at the house called Wodows (wild people). He probably lived here while in London, since he always refers to Southwark whenever he includes his location in an edition. His device, a shield hanging from a tree supported by a wild man and woman, was common at this time. His first dated book is Hieronymus Braunschweig's *Noble Handiwork of Surgery*, printed on 26 March 1525 at Southwark, to which his edition of *The Grete Herball* refers: 'it geveth understandynge of the booke lately prentyd by me' (title-page). Two undated and unsigned volumes, *Arnold's Chronicle* and William Lily's *Rudimenta*, may have been printed by Treveris in 1525.

Treveris's output consisted mainly of small grammatical treatises, which had usually been printed by others before him. His most significant publications were the *Noble Handiwork of Surgery*, possibly translated by the printer and bookseller Lawrence Andrewe, *The Grete Herball*, a reprint of the *Polychronicon* in black letter 'at the expences of J. Reynes' (1527), and John Skelton's *Magnyfycence*, printed for John Rastell (1530). He printed other works for Rastell, including *A C Mery Talys* (1526). He co-operated with other printers: some copies of *The Grete Herball* contain Andrewe's device, and book 4 of Robert Wyer's 1531 edition of Richard Whitford's translation of Thomas à Kempis's *De imitatione Christi* was apparently printed by Treveris. He copied an ornamental compartment used by Thierry Martens of Louvain for his edition of *Magnyfycence* and at least two other editions. A book with the title *This horryble monster is cast of a sowe in a vyllage which is called lebe[n]hayn M.CCCCC & xxxi*, originally printed in Germany, had its original title substituted by Treveris. Two school texts without printer's name from perhaps 1526–7 were said to be for sale at John Thorne's shop ('ap. J. Thorne') in Oxford, though there is no evidence that Treveris ever worked there (*STC, 1475–1640*, 15574, 18833a).

Some of Treveris's grammatical texts were printed with or for Rastell, and others probably for Wynkyn de Worde, as Treveris's border pieces are found in them. Rastell's editions of *Sir Eglamour* (1528?) and *A Dialog of the Poete Lucyan* (1530?) may have been printed by Treveris. The other English works Treveris printed include an edition of *Christmas Carols* (1528?), the verse *A Merry Jest of an Old Fool with a Young Wife* (1530?), and *A Lytell Treatyse agaynst Mahumet and his Cursed Secte* (1530?). Treveris claimed that some of his later editions of grammatical works by John Stanbridge and Robert Whittinton had been carefully emended (for example, 'impressum diligenterque correctum'; *Declinationes nominum*, 1531, title-page), though how far this is true has not been researched.

Treveris seems to have been printing until 1532. Because his material was used by Thomas Raynald from *c.*1539, Treveris probably died in the mid-1530s. Some of his books, especially the *Handiwork of Surgery* and *Polychronicon*, are notable for their woodcuts. Although the latter is neatly printed, most of his work is less attractive.

N. F. BLAKE

Sources E. G. Duff, *A century of the English book trade* (1905) • H. R. Plomer, *Wynkyn de Worde and his contemporaries from the death of Caxton to 1535* (1925), 218–21 • L. Winser, 'The ornamental compartment of *Magnyfycence*, 1530', *The Library*, 5th ser., 31 (1976), 136 • E. G. Duff, *The printers, stationers, and bookbinders of Westminster and London from 1476 to 1535* (1906) • E. J. Devereux, letter, *The Library*, 5th ser., 31 (1976), 251–2 • R. B. McKerrow, 'Border-pieces used by English printers before 1641', *The Library*, 4th ser., 5 (1924–5), 1–37 • E. Hodnett, *English woodcuts, 1480–1535* (1935) • *STC, 1475–1640* • S. O'Connell and D. Paisey, 'This horryble monster': an Anglo-German broadside of 1531', *Print Quarterly*, 16 (1999), 57–63

Treves, Sir Frederick, baronet (1853–1923), surgeon and author, was born at 108 Cornhill, Dorchester, Dorset, on 15 February 1853, the youngest son of William Treves (1812–1867), upholsterer, of that town, and his wife, Jane (1814–1892), daughter of John Knight, of Honiton. His father's family had been settled in Dorset for many generations. In 1860 Treves was sent to the school in Dorchester kept by William Barnes, the Dorset poet, where he remained until 1863. He attended Dorchester grammar school for a few months before entering Merchant Taylors' School, in the City of London. Here he spent seven years, and left in 1871 to begin the study of medicine. There is no record of his having shown special ability during his schooldays.

Treves acquired his medical education at the London Hospital, which offered its students ample opportunities for clinical observation. On its staff were men of scientific distinction, such as John Hughlings Jackson and Jonathan Hutchinson, and others, such as Andrew Clark, who were eminently practical. It was particularly the practical aspects of medicine which appealed to Treves. In 1875 he qualified as a member of the Royal College of Surgeons; in the previous year he had become a licentiate of the Society of Apothecaries. After holding a house surgeonship at the London Hospital, he became in 1876 resident medical officer at the Royal National Hospital for Scrofula (later the Royal Sea Bathing Hospital) at Margate, to which his brother William (Frederick's senior by ten years) was honorary surgeon. Scrofula became the subject of his first research.

Treves became engaged to Anne Elizabeth (1854–1944),

Sir Frederick Treves, baronet (1853–1923), by Sir Luke Fildes,
1896 [reduced replica]

youngest daughter of Alfred Samuel Mason, of Dorchester, and went into practice in Wirksworth, Derbyshire. They married in 1877 and had two daughters. Treves continued to study and passed the examinations for the fellowship of the Royal College of Surgeons in 1878. In the following year he gave up practice in Derbyshire and returned to the London Hospital in order to fill the post of surgical registrar. Later that year a vacancy occurred on the surgical staff of the hospital; he was appointed assistant surgeon in September 1879, and became full surgeon in 1884, at just thirty-one years of age.

Having obtained a place on the surgical staff of his hospital Treves, like other young surgeons in a similar position, had to find a way of earning a living until he had built up a consulting practice. He therefore became a demonstrator of anatomy in the medical school attached to the London Hospital. His reputation as a demonstrator soon spread beyond the walls of the hospital; his clear, incisive style, his power of description, his racy humour, and the applicability of his teaching brought crowds of students to his daily demonstrations. His success as a writer, both of medical treatises and of books on travel, can be traced to his experience as a demonstrator of anatomy. In addition to lecturing in anatomy and surgery, Treves was diligent in the wards of the hospital. He built up a reputation as a leading surgeon, and his consulting room at no. 6 Wimpole Street became one of the best-known in England.

During this period Treves also produced a succession of successful textbooks. In 1883 he published *Surgical Applied Anatomy*; he edited *A Manual of Surgery* (3 vols., 1886) and wrote *A Manual of Operative Surgery* (1891), *The Student's Handbook of Surgical Operations* (1892), and *A System of Surgery* (2 vols., 1895). All these books are characterized by a lively, clear style and many practical observations.

In quite another category are the books which brought Treves fame as an investigator. His early experience with his brother at Margate led him to join in the search into the nature of the condition then known as scrofula. In 1882 he published the results of his research in a book entitled *Scrofula and its Gland Diseases*; ironically in the same year Robert Koch demonstrated that the disorder, which had so greatly puzzled Treves and all previous investigators, was due to the action of a bacillus.

Treves began his surgical career at a time when abdominal surgery was advancing rapidly, and it became Treves's special field of interest. In 1883 the Royal College of Surgeons, of which he was one of the Hunterian professors of anatomy in 1885 and Erasmus Wilson lecturer in pathology in 1881, awarded him the Jacksonian prize for a dissertation on *The Pathology, Diagnosis and Treatment of Obstruction of the Intestine* (1884). In 1885 his Hunterian lectures, on the anatomy of the intestinal canal and peritoneum, appeared as a book which, anatomists agreed, contained his best original work.

When Treves began the study of medicine the condition known as perityphlitis was still obscure. In 1886 R. H. Fitz, of Boston, Massachusetts, published a large series showing that it was not the caecum but its appendix which was the site of the disease; hence he named the condition appendicitis. Treves operated on his first case of perityphlitis (he at first rejected the name appendicitis) in 1887; by 1890 he, too, was convinced that it was the appendix and not the caecum that was the site of the disease. Treves advocated the operative treatment of appendicitis, though he favoured delaying surgery until a quiescent interval had been reached.

So extensive did Treves's private practice become that he retired from the active staff of the London Hospital in 1898 at the age of forty-five. In 1899, on the outbreak of war in South Africa, he volunteered to serve as consulting surgeon to the forces then in the field. On his return to England, he was appointed surgeon-extraordinary to Queen Victoria in 1900; he was made CB and created KCVO in 1901.

In the summer of 1902 Treves's fame became suddenly worldwide. On 24 June, two days before the date fixed for his coronation, Edward VII became acutely ill. His condition was diagnosed as perityphlitis. Treves had been called in by the physicians in attendance. After consultation with Lord Lister and Thomas Smith, he operated to drain the abscess. The king made a good recovery and was crowned on 9 August. Treves was created a baronet in the same year.

In 1900 Treves published an account of his experiences of the Second South African War, under the title *Tale of a Field Hospital*. Thereafter he applied to the description of countries and peoples the qualities which had made him famous as a teacher of anatomy and of surgery. *The other Side of the Lantern* (1905) is based on a tour round the world; *Highways and Byways of Dorset* (1906) is a guide to his native county; a voyage to the West Indies gave him the materials for *The Cradle of the Deep* (1908); *Uganda for a Holiday* (1910) has a self-explanatory title. His impressions of Palestine are vividly reproduced in *The Land that is Desolate* (1912). Treves visited Italy in order to work out the topography of Robert Browning's *The Ring and the Book*, to provide the basis for *The Country of 'The Ring and the Book'* (1913).

After the First World War during which he served at the War Office as president of the headquarters' medical board, Treves chose to live abroad, first in the south of France and afterwards at Vevey on the shores of the Lake of Geneva. His experiences and impressions of these years are published in *The Riviera of the Corniche Road* (1921) and *The Lake of Geneva* (1922). In his last book, entitled *The Elephant Man and other Reminiscences* (1923), he first informed the public about the case of Joseph Merrick.

Treves died at the Clinique de Rosemont in Lausanne, on 7 December 1923, after a few days' illness. His ashes were buried on 2 January 1924 in Dorchester cemetery, his friend Thomas Hardy being present at the ceremony. He was survived by his wife and a daughter. The baronetcy became extinct on his death.

Many honours were conferred upon Treves in addition to those already mentioned. He was appointed sergeant-surgeon to Edward VII (1902) and to George V (1910), and created GCVO (1905). He received honorary degrees from several universities, and was elected rector of Aberdeen University (1905–8). Among many organizations which benefited from his influence were the Boys' Brigade, the Royal National Mission to Deep Sea Fishermen, the British Red Cross Society, and the Star and Garter Home. Treves loved the sea, holding a master's certificate. He was a strong swimmer and fond of bicycling. He avoided social entertainments, preferring to be in bed by ten o'clock so as to be fresh for work at six in the morning. His early morning hours he devoted to study and correspondence.

A. KEITH, *rev.* D. D. GIBBS

Sources S. Trombley, *Sir Frederick Treves the extraordinary Edwardian* (1989) · D. D. Gibbs, 'Sir Frederick Treves, surgeon, author and medical historian', *Journal of the Royal Society of Medicine*, 85 (1992), 565–9 · V. G. Plarr, *Plarr's Lives of the fellows of the Royal College of Surgeons of England*, rev. D'A. Power, 2 vols. (1930), 430–36 · N. Fowler, 'The man with the knife', *Just as it happened* (1950), 109–26 · R. S. Stevenson, 'Appendicitis and King Edward VII', *Famous illnesses in history* (1962), 32–43 · T. P. O'Connor, 'Sir Frederick Treves, a great surgeon', *Daily Telegraph* (10 Dec 1923) · *The Times* (10 Dec 1923) · *BMJ* (15 Dec 1923), 1185–9 · F. Chalfont, 'Fellow-townsmen, Thomas Hardy and Sir Frederick Treves', *The Thomas Hardy Journal*, 6 (1990), 62–78 · 'Passages from the notebooks of Sir Frederick Treves', *Annals of the Royal College of Surgeons of England*, 28 (1961), 384–8; 29 (1961), 265–8 · J. J. Howard and F. A. Crisp, eds., *Visitation of England and Wales*, 21 vols. (privately printed, London, 1893–1921), vol. 13, p. 176 · *The Times* (12 Jan 1944) [obit. of Lady Treves] · d. cert.

Archives Dorset County Museum, Dorchester · RCP Lond., a tour of the world · RCS Eng., reminiscences · Yale U. | Richmond Local Studies Library, London, Sladen MSS · U. Leeds, Brotherton L., letters to Sir Edmund Gosse

Likenesses lithograph, 1884, Wellcome L. · L. Fildes, oils, 1896, St Bartholomew's and the London School of Medicine and Dentistry · L. Fildes, oils, reduced replica, 1896, NPG [*see illus.*] · Spy [L. Ward], coloured lithograph, 1900, Wellcome L. · W. Stoneman, photograph, 1918, NPG · Spy [L. Ward], caricature, chromolithograph, NPG; repro. in *VF* (19 July 1900) · lithograph, Wellcome L. · portrait, repro. in *Toilers of the Deep*, 24 (1909), 84–5

Wealth at death £102,339 13s. 4d.: probate, 20 Feb 1924, *CGPLA Eng. & Wales*

Trevet [Trivet], **Nicholas** (*b.* 1257x65, *d.* in or after 1334), Dominican friar and biblical and classical scholar, was born in Somerset, probably between 1257 and 1265—in the preface to his commentary on Seneca's *Declamations*, written between 1307 and 1314, he reveals his age as forty-nine. He was the second son of Sir Thomas *Trevet (*d.* 1280/81), a Somerset landowner and justice, and his wife, Eleanor.

Education and early travels Nothing is known of Nicholas Trevet's early life, but he appears to have entered the Dominican order in his late teens or early twenties. He joined the prestigious London convent, perhaps through his father's influence, but in the late 1280s he was sent to study at Oxford. The details of his university career are obscure, but he must have been a senior scholar by 1297, when he was appointed to be the Dominican representative to receive royal alms for the order's general chapter. Trevet incepted as doctor of theology c.1302 and remained in Oxford teaching and studying until at least 1307. His six surviving quodlibet collections indicate that he became a prominent figure in the debates of the theology faculty. During this period he also may have been engaged in pastoral work or Dominican business outside the university. He certainly spent some time at Salisbury, because his treatise on the movement of the sun was compiled from observations made there. He seems also to have visited a number of religious houses in southern England and examined their libraries. In his commentary on Seneca's *Tragedies*, completed c.1315, he complained that he had been unable to find the *originalia*, complete and accurate copies of the work of ancient authors, he needed to complete his work. His growing reputation as a scholar as well, perhaps, as a pastor, attracted the friendship and patronage of senior clerical figures and members of the nobility. Their interest shaped the direction of much of his work, and almost all of his later commentaries and treatises were commissioned by or written for one of his patrons.

In the early years of the fourteenth century, perhaps even before 1300, Trevet made the first of several visits to the continent. As a distinguished scholar, he was probably encouraged by his order to advance his studies at foreign *studia*, and he does appear to have spent much of his time abroad in the company of fellow Dominicans. The details of his travels are unclear, but he certainly visited Italy, where he completed his commentary on Boethius's *De consolatione philosophiae*, making, as he recalls in the dedication, two copies which covered 300 folios of vellum, one for the dedicatee, an Italian Dominican, and another for an unidentified man who owned Trevet's source text of Boethius. From c.1307 Trevet settled in Paris, where he studied at the university, but he also continued to travel through France and Italy, visiting Avignon for the Dominican general chapter in 1308, and probably also Florence, Padua, and Pisa.

Trevet's travels had a significant impact on his work as a scholar. He may have already begun to apply his exegetical methods to classical literature while he was still in Oxford, but it was his experiences in France and Italy that really stimulated and confirmed this new direction in his work. His visits to the curia at Avignon, and to cities such as Florence and Pisa, introduced him to new currents in classical scholarship, and in particular to the work of the Paduan scholars who were reviving interest in neglected texts like Seneca's *Tragedies*. He also forged contacts with distinguished curialists such as Cardinal Nicolò da Prato, dean of the Sacred College, who shared his classical interests, and who encouraged him to write new commentaries of his own. Trevet was commissioned by Prato to write a commentary on Seneca's *Tragedies*, and he also appears to have been asked, presumably through other curialists, to write a commentary on Livy's *Ab urbe condita* for Pope John XXII (r. 1316–34).

Return to Oxford Trevet was recalled to Oxford in late 1314. Dominican leaders were concerned to reassert their influence in the schools after a decade of disputes and difficulties, and they were understandably eager to have one of their most distinguished doctors there. He had reached Oxford before 24 December 1314, when he was present at a feast in memory of Piers Gaveston (d. 1312), whose body was resting at the Oxford Blackfriars on its way to Langley for burial. He then appears to have resumed his career as a master in the faculty of theology: in February 1315 his name is recorded alongside other masters involved in the condemnation of a series of heretical theses. But at the same time he worked on a wide range of compositions for his English and continental patrons. He wrote several theological treatises for senior Dominican figures, including the prior provincial, John Bristol, and Edward II's confessor, John Lenham, and chronicles for the Lady Mary (d. 1332), daughter of Edward I, who was a nun at Amesbury, and for Hugues d'Angoulême, archdeacon of Canterbury; he also completed his commissions for the pope and Cardinal Nicolò.

Trevet retired from the schools c.1320, and returned to the London convent. In 1324, although almost seventy years old, he was appointed to be the community's lector, a testimony to his continuing reputation as a theologian. He was still alive in 1334, when he was recorded as a member of the house. Nothing further is known of his career, and it seems likely that he died before the end of the decade.

Theologian and controversialist Trevet was one of the most prolific and influential English scholars in the later middle ages. In three decades he completed almost two dozen lengthy commentaries, chronicles, and other treatises. His intellectual interests were very broad, embracing astronomy, history, literature, theology, and canon law,

but above all he was an exegete, committed to the exposition of ancient Christian and classical texts. His earliest work was a series of commentaries on the books of the Pentateuch, which he began during his first Oxford career. He had completed the commentaries on Genesis and Exodus before 1307 when they were approved by the general chapter of the order meeting in Strasbourg. The chapter urged him to finish the series, but although the commentary on Leviticus was offered to Americ, the Dominican master-general, for approval, the remaining commentaries never appeared. Almost a decade later Trevet sent a revised version of the Genesis commentary to John XXII, suggesting that all five were almost completed. However, there are no surviving copies, and Pits's contention that a Trevetine commentary on Chronicles did exist is unsupported. Even so, he did continue to show an interest in the Old Testament, later composing both a series of notes *De computo Hebraeorum* to complement his Genesis commentary, and a commentary on the Psalms for John Bristol.

Trevet's career coincided with a period of great controversy in the schools and among the orders of the friars, and he devoted several works to current theological and corporate debates. His surviving *quaestiones*, which date from his first Oxford career, address such controversial issues as the nature of salvation through grace and the eternity of the world. He also responded to contemporary concerns over the regulation of the religious life and the work of pastoral care, with a short commentary on the monastic rule of St Augustine and a treatise on the eucharist, *De officio missae*, which he dedicated to John Droxford, bishop of Bath and Wells (d. 1329). Following his return to Oxford in 1314, Trevet became directly involved in academic debates over evangelical poverty, which had already led to bitter clashes between the Dominicans and Franciscans. Before 1320 he completed the now lost treatise *De perfectione vitae spiritualis*, in which he responded to the *De paupertate evangelica*, the work of the Oxford Franciscan Walter Chatton (d. 1343/4). Trevet's work appears to have reignited the debate, and Chatton, together with fellow Franciscan Richard Conington (d. 1330), mounted a formal refutation of the text at the Oxford Greyfriars in 1323.

Histories and classical commentaries For all his involvement in academic controversies, however, Trevet was not a typical schoolman. At the height of his university career, between 1314 and 1320, he completed three chronicles in Latin and French, unusual compositions either for an academic or a friar. His *Cronycles*, written for the Lady Mary, and his *Historia ab origine mundi ad Christum natum*, a Latin version of the same text dedicated to Hugues d'Angoulême, were as much devotional as historical works. But his *Annales sex regum Angliae*, a chronicle from 1135 to 1307, represented a genuine attempt to write contemporary history. Trevet offered detailed accounts of recent events, including the barons' and Scottish wars, and, more importantly, produced perceptive character sketches of both Henry III and Edward I, based on the recollections of the men, the courtiers, counsellors, and soldiers, who had known them. The *Annales* was widely read throughout the late medieval period, and exercised a considerable influence on the work of later historians including Ranulf Higden and Thomas Walsingham.

Trevet's most important and influential works, however, were his classical commentaries. His earliest were the commentaries on Boethius and on the elder Seneca's *Declamations*. The latter, dedicated to the English Dominican John Lenham, may have been completed before Trevet left Oxford *c*.1307. His commentaries on Seneca and on Livy were probably finished shortly after his return to England in 1314: the Livy commentary may have been the 'literary work' for which Trevet received payment from the papal secretary *c*.1318. He is known also to have written, at different points in his career, commentaries on Virgil's *Eclogues*, on Pseudo-Boethius's *De disciplina scholarium*, on the pseudo-classical *Dissuasio Valerii ad Rufinum* attributed to Walter Map, and he is identified in at least one manuscript (Bodl. Oxf., MS Bodley 292) as the author of a commentary on Seneca's *Apocolocyntosis*. His interest in antiquity also led him to compile a commentary on books 11–22 of Augustine's *De civitate Dei*, which was completed by the later Dominican exegete Thomas Waleys.

Influence and reputation Trevet's commentaries were not wholly original, and his critical methods reflected the prevailing view that classical fables must be thoroughly decoded and Christianized to make them safe for modern readers. He was, nevertheless, one of the first English scholars since the twelfth century to develop an extensive knowledge of classical authors, and certainly the earliest northern European writer to absorb the new Italian currents in classical scholarship. Moreover, his commentaries offered European scholars, in many cases for the first time, complete and accurate texts of works of undisputed importance, such as the *De consolatione* and the *De civitate Dei*. The usefulness of his commentaries as sources for the classical texts themselves ensured a wide circulation of his works: almost 300 manuscripts survive from all parts of Europe. His best-known work was probably his commentary on Boethius which alone survives in almost 100 manuscripts. It was especially popular in Italy, where it was translated into the vernacular several times in the later fourteenth century, and was used by both Petrarch and Boccaccio in their works. His commentary on Seneca's *Tragedies* also circulated widely, and there is even evidence that it was cited in a letter attributed to Dante.

Trevet's name became so familiar in some countries that he was frequently identified as the author of works by other writers, such as Thomas Waleys's biblical commentaries and Pierre Bersuire's *Ovidius moralizatus*. In England his commentaries do seem to have inaugurated a tradition of classical scholarship among the mendicant orders that continued well into the fourteenth century in the treatises of Robert Holcot (*d*. 1349), Thomas Waleys (*fl*. 1318–1349), John Lathbury (*d*. 1362), and Thomas Hopeman. In the context of Europe as a whole, however, his legacy was not so much to transform late medieval literary criticism, as to provide later scholars with indispensable

source books on ancient authors which remained the basis of much classical scholarship in Europe until the sixteenth century.

JAMES G. CLARK

Sources Emden, *Oxf.*, 3.1902–3 · R. J. Dean, 'The life and work of Nicholas Trevet with special reference to his Anglo-Norman chronicle', DPhil diss., U. Oxf., 1938 · F. Ehrle, *Gesammelte Aufsätze zur englischen Scholastik* (1970), 303–84 · R. J. Dean, 'Nicolas Trevet, historian', *Medieval learning and literature: essays presented to Richard William Hunt*, ed. J. J. G. Alexander and M. T. Gibson (1976), 328–52 · R. J. Dean, 'Cultural relations in the middle ages: Nicholas Trevet and Nicholas of Prato', *Studies in Philology*, 45 (1948), 541–64 · B. Smalley, *English friars and antiquity in the early fourteenth century* (1960), 58–65 · R. J. Dean, 'The earliest known commentary on Livy', *Medievalia et Humanistica*, 3 (1945), 86–98 · R. J. Dean, 'The dedication of Nicholas Trevet's commentary on Boethius', *Studies in Philology*, 63 (1966), 593–603, 600–03 · R. J. Dean, 'Some unnoticed commentaries on the *Dissuasio Valerii* of Walter Map', *Mediaeval and Renaissance Studies*, 2 (1950), 128–50 · M. L. Lord, 'Virgil's Eclogues, Nicholas Trevet, and the harmony of the spheres', *Mediaeval Studies*, 54 (1992), 186–273 · R. J. Dean, *Medium Aevum*, 10 (1941), 161–8 · Bale, *Cat.*, 1.399–400 · Bale, *Index*, 308–9 · Tanner, *Bibl.-Hib.*, 722–3 · R. Vianello, 'Su un commento virgiliano attribuito a Nichola Trevet', *Studi Medievali*, 3rd ser., 32 (1991), 345–67 · A. Kleinhans, 'Nicholas Trevet OP, *Psalmorum interpres*', *Angelicum*, 20 (1943), 219–36 · B. Smalley, 'Thomas Waleys OP', *Archivum Fratrum Praedicatorum*, 24 (1954), 50–107 · A. Gransden, *Historical writing in England*, 1 (1974), 501–7 · N. Trevet, *Annales sex regum Angliae, 1135–1307*, ed. T. Hog, EHS, 6 (1845) · A. Rutherford, 'The Anglo-Norman chronicle of Nicholas Trevet', PhD diss., U. Lond., 1932 [incl. text of chronicle]

Archives Bodl. Oxf., MS Bodley 292 · Merton Oxf., MS 188

Trevet, Sir Thomas (*d*. 1280/81), justice, came of a small landowning family in Somerset; the Ralph Trevet who preceded him as lord of Durborough in that county must have been his kinsman, but may not have been his father. Thomas is first recorded in 1241, when he made several appearances as an attorney on the bench, and he pursued a legal and administrative career thereafter. In 1255 he was one of two knights instructed to act with commissioners selling woods in Somerset to pay royal debts, and at about this time he was at least twice a colleague of Henry of Bratton as an assize justice in Somerset. He was also steward to the abbots of Athelney and Glastonbury, in 1256 serving the latter as a justice itinerant within the liberty of the twelve hides of Glastonbury. In 1260 he was an assessor of tallage in the south-western counties, and in 1262 he twice headed commissions to deliver Ilchester gaol.

In the political crisis of the mid-1260s Trevet appears to have been regarded at first as a royalist, since in March 1264 he was among those whom Henry III summoned to come armed to Oxford. But he may have seemed to waver in his loyalty to the king, for after the battle of Evesham (4 August 1265) he was suspected of Montfortian sympathies and his lands were taken into the king's hand; his estate at North Barsham in Norfolk was given to a royalist and not recovered until March 1266. But Trevet clearly managed to prove his loyalty to the crown, for on 2 April 1268 he was appointed a justice itinerant, with a salary of £40 per annum, on the circuit of eyres headed by Richard Middleton in the south-west and midlands between then and July 1269, while in 1272 he served in a similar capacity under

Ralph Hengham on eyres in Herefordshire, Staffordshire, and Shropshire. Between the eyres he took assizes in Somerset, Devon, and Dorset, and in 1269 was an assessor of that year's twentieth in Dorset. He did not act as a justice itinerant again after 1272, but during the 1270s he was several times a justice of assize and gaol delivery and a commissioner of oyer and terminer.

Thomas Trevet was still alive in July 1280, when he attended that year's Somerset eyre, but was dead by 5 March 1281. By 1254 he had married Eleanor, daughter of Joan Braunche, who brought him his lands in Norfolk. However, fines from the mid-1250s suggest that this marriage was then fairly recently contracted, and since Trevet's heir at his death was his son William, who was said at that time to be aged forty, it seems likely that Thomas had also made an earlier marriage. The chronicler and Dominican friar Nicholas *Trevet was a younger son, and may have owed something of his religious vocation to his father, since in April 1263 Thomas Trevet gave the black friars of Ilchester a messuage in the suburbs of that town, and was consequently received by the prior 'into all the benefits and orisons in his church' (*Feet of Fines … Somerset*, 1.204).   HENRY SUMMERSON

Sources Chancery records · patent rolls, PRO, C 66/77, mm. 15d, 18d · *VCH Somerset*, vol. 6 · *Curia regis rolls preserved in the Public Record Office* (1922–), vol. 16 · E. Green, ed., *Pedes finium, commonly called, feet of fines, for the county of Somerset*, Somerset RS, 6: *Richard I to Edward I, 1196–1307* (1892) · C. E. H. Chadwyck-Healey and L. Landon, eds., *Somersetshire pleas*, 1, Somerset RS, 11 (1897); 3–4, Somerset RS, 41, 44 (1926–9) · *Rentalia et custumaria Michaelis de Ambresbury … et … Rogeri de Ford … abbatum monasterii beatae Mariae Glastoniae*, ed. C. J. Elton, Somerset RS, 5 (1891) · E. H. Bates, ed., *Two cartularies of the Benedictine Abbeys of Muchelney and Athelney*, Somerset RS, 14 (1899) · A. Watkin, ed., *The great chartulary of Glastonbury*, Somerset RS, 63 (1952) [1952 for 1949] · *F. Nicholai Triveti, de ordine frat. praedicatorum, annales sex regum Angliae*, ed. T. Hog, EHS, 6 (1845), 279 · *CIPM*, 2, no. 414 · *Calendar of the fine rolls*, PRO, 1 (1911), 143
Wealth at death see *CIPM*

Trevet, Sir Thomas (d. **1388**), soldier, was born into a Somerset family with a tradition of royal service extending over several generations. He was probably the son of Sir John Trevet of Otterhampton (b. 1316), who fought in the Crécy campaign of 1346, served regularly as a commissioner of array in Somerset, and represented the county in the parliament of January 1348.

The first records of Trevet's own military career date from the mid-1360s when he was probably in his early twenties. In 1366 he and his brother John took service with Edward, the Black Prince, in Gascony. Both brothers joined the prince's invasion of Castile and fought at the battle of Nájera on 3 April 1367. Thomas Trevet is next heard of in 1370 when he joined the ill-fated expedition of Sir Robert Knolles to France, which was destroyed by Bertrand du Guesclin at the battle of Pontvallain (December 1370). About 1373 he appeared at St Sauveur le Vicomte in the Cotentin peninsula, where Sir Thomas Catterton commanded the principal English garrison of Normandy. Trevet served under Catterton throughout the long siege of St Sauveur by the French which began in the autumn of 1374. By 1375 he had been knighted, and was party to the agreement made with the French on 24 May 1375 by which, unless it was relieved in the meantime, the fortress was to be sold to the besiegers in July. This agreement was performed by the garrison on the date appointed, in spite of the fact that it had been abrogated a week before by the truce of Bruges, an event which caused much controversy in England and led to Catterton's being charged with treason and briefly imprisoned. Trevet's personal share of the payment received from the French was 2000 francs, which was second only to Catterton's own.

In March 1378 the government of the young Richard II sent Trevet to Gascony with a force of eighty men-at-arms and eighty archers to assist his uncle, Matthew Gournay, in the defence of the southern march of the duchy of Aquitaine. However, after his arrival he was diverted to Spain. The English government had promised to put 1000 men at the service of Charles II, king of Navarre, whose kingdom had recently been invaded by the French protégé Enrique da Trastamara, king of Castile. John Neville, the seneschal of Aquitaine, appointed Trevet to command this force. However, he was unable to find more than 240 men in addition to the 160 already in Trevet's service. On 22 October 1378 Trevet was retained by Charles's representatives in Bordeaux and appointed captain of Tudela, a walled town occupying an exposed enclave in the extreme south of the kingdom of Navarre, beyond the Ebro River. In November 1378 he joined Charles II north of the pass of Roncesvalles and crossed the Pyrenees.

Trevet made an impact in Navarre out of all proportion to the small strength of his army. The Castilians, who had overrun a large part of the kingdom in the course of the summer and autumn, abandoned the siege of Pamplona and withdrew most of their forces to their borders. In December 1378 Trevet occupied Tudela, where he assembled a force of Navarrese troops to reinforce his Gascons and English, and launched a raid deep into Castile towards the walled town of Soria. Unfortunately, his men lost their way in a snowstorm in the sierras, and by the time they reached Soria the Castilians had had time to organize its defence. But he burned a number of Castilian villages and severely damaged Enrique da Trastamara's prestige. On 31 March 1378 Charles II made peace with the king of Castile on the terms that all English and Gascon troops were to leave Navarre forthwith. Trevet did his best to obstruct the implementation of the peace. He even endeavoured, in April 1379, to interest Peter III of Aragon in a plan to continue the fight against Castile without the king of Navarre. But Peter was not interested, and Trevet returned to Gascony. By the autumn of 1379 he was back in England.

For the next two years Trevet was fighting almost continuously. In October 1379 he joined the seaborne expedition which left Southampton for Brittany under the command of Sir John Arundel, and survived the storm that wrecked much of the fleet a few days after its departure. In 1380 he took part in the great *chevauchée* of Thomas of Woodstock, earl of Buckingham, from Calais round the west of Paris to Brittany, which was intended to assist John (IV), duke of Brittany, against the French. According to Froissart he fought with great courage in the skirmishes at Cléry-sur-Somme, Fervacques, and Vendôme. He also played a prominent role in the unsuccessful siege of Nantes between November 1380 and January 1381. Trevet served as one of Buckingham's inner council, and was twice sent to complain to John (IV) about the lack of co-operation from the Bretons. In January 1381 John made peace with the French, as the English feared that he would. Trevet went with part of the army into winter quarters at Hennebont and returned to England with the rest of the army in the spring. On his return he was appointed a commissioner of array in Kent and charged with the defence of the coast against invasion. In June and July 1381 he was one of the commissioners charged with the suppression of the peasants' revolt in Kent.

Two years later, in 1383, Trevet was one of the leaders of the so-called 'Norwich crusade', which invaded Flanders in May 1383 under the overall command of Henry Despenser, bishop of Norwich. He left for Flanders late. He supported the ill-judged decision to undertake the siege of Ypres in June, and the decision to abandon it in August, thereby earning himself an enduring reputation for treachery among the Londoners in Despenser's army. When Despenser resolved to turn south and invade Artois, Trevet declined to have anything to do with this adventure. Instead he and other captains shut themselves with a small garrison in the fortress of Bourbourg. When the fortress was besieged by the army of the king of France, Trevet boldly declared their intention of fighting them off. He was grateful, he said, that so powerful an army should do such honour to a mere handful of Englishmen. Shortly afterwards Bourbourg was sold to the enemy and Trevet obtained a substantial part of the bribe which was paid to them. The affair in some ways recalled the surrender of St Sauveur eight years earlier. When he returned to England in the autumn he shared in the obloquy poured on the heads of other leaders of the expedition. In October 1383 he was arrested and brought before parliament to answer charges of treachery. Trevet avoided imprisonment by throwing himself on the king's mercy, but he was made to pay a fine of 1400 francs. His inglorious role in the campaign overshadowed the rest of his career. Even Richard II, to whom he was extravagantly loyal, could call him a 'famous traitor' in a fit of temper.

Nevertheless, Richard listened to Trevet, and the last three years of his life marked the apogee of his political influence at court. In 1385 he served in the king's battalion with a retinue of forty men in the unsuccessful campaign against the Scots. In February 1386 he was appointed admiral of the west at a time of growing concern about the danger of a French seaborne invasion. His only achievement in this office was an operation in the summer in conjunction with his fellow admiral Sir Philip Darcy, which resulted in the unlawful capture of a number of Genoese merchantmen. In December 1386, in the aftermath of the impeachment of the chancellor, Michael de la Pole, Trevet was removed from office.

In the course of 1387 and 1388 Trevet was one of a small group of knights who were closely associated with the king during the growing crisis of his relations with the higher nobility and with parliament. This made him many enemies, and he added to their number by his sneering way with those who crossed him. When the lords appellant accused five of Richard's ministers of treason in November 1387 Trevet was said to have advised the king to take the field against them, and to have tried to ambush them on their way to court. As a result, at the meeting of the great council at Westminster on 1 January 1388 the appellants added Trevet (and several others) to the original five accused. He was arrested and placed in solitary confinement, first in Dover Castle and then in the Tower of London, to await judgment before parliament. For reasons which are unclear Trevet was not tried before the Merciless Parliament which met in February 1388. Instead, at the conclusion of its proceedings at the end of May, he was released on bail to appear before the next parliament. On 6 October 1388 proclamation was made at the sessions of parliament at Cambridge calling on anyone who wished to accuse Trevet of treason or any other capital offence to do so on the following day. But Trevet never confronted his accusers. On the day of the proclamation, as he rode through a ploughed field at Barnwell, his horse stumbled and crushed him. When, early on the following day, he died of his injuries, there was open rejoicing.

Trevet had married twice. He had no children with his first wife, Isabel. After her death he had married about 1379 Elizabeth Lymbery with whom he had two daughters, Anne and Joan. All three survived him. At the time of his death Trevet held land in Somerset and in six other English counties, the fruits of two judicious marriages, and a sound regard for the financial opportunities of war.

JONATHAN SUMPTION

Sources *CClR* · Gascon rolls, Various Accounts E101, PRO, C61 · *Chroniques de J. Froissart*, ed. S. Luce and others, 15 vols. (Paris, 1869–1975) · P. Lopez de Ayala, *Crónicas de los reyes de Castilla*, ed. E. de Llaguno Amirola, 2 vols. (Madrid, 1779–80) · P. E. Russell, *The English intervention in Spain and Portugal in the time of Edward III and Richard II* (1955), ch. 12 · J. Ramon Castro and F. Idoate, eds., *Catalogo del Archivo General de Navarra, Catalogo de la Seccion de Comptos*, 52 vols. (1952–74) · L. C. Hector and B. F. Harvey, eds. and trans., *The Westminster chronicle, 1381–1394*, OMT (1982) · *RotP* · *Knighton's chronicle, 1337–1396*, ed. and trans. G. H. Martin, OMT (1995) [Lat. orig., *Chronica de eventibus Angliae a tempore regis Edgari usque mortem regis Ricardi Secundi*, with parallel Eng. text] · *Thomae Walsingham, quondam monachi S. Albani, historia Anglicana*, ed. H. T. Riley, 2 vols., pt 1 of *Chronica monasterii S. Albani*, Rolls Series, 28 (1863–4) · G. B. Stow, ed., *Historia vitae et regni Ricardi Secundi* (1977) · Rymer, *Foedera* · *CIPM*, 16, nos. 534–7, 764–70

Wealth at death land in seven different English counties: *CIPM*

Trevethin. For this title name *see* Lawrence, Alfred Tristram, first Baron Trevethin (1843–1936); Lawrence, Geoffrey, third Baron Trevethin and first Baron Oaksey (1880–1971).

Trevisa, John (*b.* *c.*1342, *d.* in or before 1402), translator, is of Cornish origins. Though his exact birthplace is unknown, his name implies that he came of a Cornish family from one of the places called Trevessa or Trevease. He was admitted to Exeter College, Oxford, in 1362 and remained as a fellow until 1369, when he became a fellow of the Queen's College. From this date he is referred to as *magister*. In 1370 he was ordained priest to the title of the Queen's College, where from 1376 he became involved in a movement of opposition to the appointment of a new provost, Thomas Carlisle. In 1379 he is named along with the former provost, Henry Whitfield, and others, as excluded from the college 'for unworthiness'; they were required to return property (including twenty-four books whose titles are listed in a separate indenture) which they had removed from the college on their expulsion. Trevisa eventually returned to the college, renting rooms there between 1383 and 1387 and from 1394 to 1396.

It was probably in 1374 that Trevisa became vicar of Berkeley, Gloucestershire, and there is evidence for 1379 as the date of his appointment as the Berkeley family's chaplain in two papal bulls of that date (2 Urban VI) granting Lord Thomas and his wife, Margaret, licence to choose a 'fit and discreet' priest as their confessor. At Berkeley, Trevisa was also a canon of Westbury-on-Trym by 1390, in which year legal documents obscurely record a dispute in 1388–9 over Trevisa's right to his prebend of Woodford and his stall at Westbury; the dispute involved an alleged assault on the dean by a band of Trevisa's supporters, and armed occupation of the disputed stall in Westbury church and of the presbytery at Woodford. Also in 1390 Trevisa granted power of attorney to two fellow clerks in preparation for a journey abroad, the destination of which is unrecorded. This would not have been his first taste of foreign travel, for in two interpolations in his translation of Ranulf Higden's universal history, *Polychronicon*, he claims to have visited Aachen, Aix-les-Bains, and Breisach. It is known that Trevisa had died by May 1402, for a successor to the living of Berkeley, which had become vacant by his death, was appointed at that time. According to local tradition, he was buried in Berkeley church.

Trevisa's original writings are not extensive, comprising some 7000 words of prose interpolation in his translations and in addition the *Dialogue between a Lord and a Clerk* (a fictional representation of a dialogue about translation between his patron and himself) and the dedicatory *Epistle*, which together formed the prefaces to his translation of the *Polychronicon*. His style in these original pieces is strikingly direct, giving the effect of authority and plain-spokenness (in the *Dialogue* dramatically projected in the speech of the lord).

Trevisa's reputation as a writer, however, rests principally on his translations of encyclopaedic works from Latin into English, undertaken with the support of his patron, Thomas (IV), the fifth Baron Berkeley, as a continuous programme of enlightenment for the laity. The *Polychronicon* translation was completed in April 1387 and survives in fourteen manuscripts (of which the two earliest, though not autographs, are assigned a Berkeley provenance) and in a Caxton print of 1482. The scientific encyclopaedia *De proprietatibus rerum* of Bartholomaeus Anglicus was completed in February 1399 and is extant in eight manuscripts; it was printed by Wynkyn de Worde *c*.1495. A third lengthy translation attributed to him, *De*

regimine principum by Giles of Rome, was published in 1997 from the single extant manuscript.

The antagonism towards the regular orders and ecclesiastical establishment displayed in two shorter works translated by Trevisa, Fitzralph's sermon against the friars, *Defensio curatorum*, and the dialogue formerly attributed to William Ockham, *Dialogus inter militem et clericum*, on the limitation of the temporal power of the church, is echoed in some of his interpolations in the *Polychronicon*. In the 1370s and 1380s Trevisa's periods of residence in the Queen's College, Oxford, partly coincided with that of Wyclif and his associates, but there is no evidence that he worked with them on their translation of the Bible (or that he produced at any time a translation of the Bible himself). Like them, however, he was engaged in opening to the laity (in his case the baronial laity), through translation into the increasingly important vernacular, areas of knowledge formerly the preserve of ecclesiastical, Latin learning.   RONALD WALDRON

Sources D. C. Fowler, *John Trevisa* (1993) • Emden, *Oxf.* • *Registrum Simonis de Sudbiria, diocesis Londoniensis, AD 1362–1375*, ed. R. C. Fowler, 2 vols., CYS, 34, 38 (1927–38) • I. H. Jeayes, *Descriptive catalogue of the charters and muniments in the possession of the Rt. Hon. Lord Fitzhardinge at Berkeley Castle* (1892), 175, sel. charters no. 554, 555 [papal bulls] • *Polychronicon Ranulphi Higden monachi Cestrensis*, ed. C. Babington and J. R. Lumby, 9 vols., Rolls Series, 41 (1865–86), vol. 2, p. 61; vol. 6, p. 259 • J. Trevisa, *Dialogus inter militem et clericum*, ed. A. J. Perry, EETS, 167 (1925), lxxv • W. E. L. Smith, ed., *The register of Richard Clifford, bishop of Worcester, 1401–1407: a calendar*, Pontifical Institute of Medieval Studies: Subsidia Mediaevalia, 6 (1976) • J. Smyth, *The Berkeley manuscripts*, ed. J. Maclean, 3 vols. (1883–5), vol. 1, p. 338; vol. 2, p. 22 • A. McIntosh and others, *A linguistic atlas of late mediaeval English*, 4 vols. (1986), vol. 3, pp. 139f. [Berkeley provenance of MSS of the *Polychronicon*: BL, Cotton MS Tiberius D. vii, and Manchester, Chetham's Library MS 11379] • D. C. Fowler, C. F. Briggs, and P. G. Remley, eds., *The governance of kings and princes: John Trevisa's Middle English translation of the De regimine principum of Ægidius Romanus* (1997)

Archives BL, Cotton Tiberius D.vii • Chetham's Library, Manchester, MS 11379

Trevithick, Richard (1771–1833), engineer, was born near Carn Brea in the parish of Illogan, Cornwall, on 13 April 1771, the only son and youngest of the six children of Richard Trevithick (1735–1797) and Anne Teague (d. 1810). The elder Richard, a practical miner, worked in a number of the copper mines in the extensive Camborne–Illogan–Redruth mining district and rose to become captain (manager) of Wheal Chance, Wheal Treasury, East Stray Park, and the famous Dolcoath mine. At Dolcoath he constructed the deep adit (drainage tunnel) in 1765 and about 1775 erected a Newcomen pumping engine.

Early life and marriage It was against this background that the younger Richard Trevithick grew up. He was indulged by his mother Anne, and at his local elementary school in Camborne he soon earned a reputation for obstinacy, disobedience, and truancy. However, it was acknowledged that he was quick-witted in an unconventional way and he showed himself to be good with figures. He was also extremely practical, a gift complemented by his proverbial strength. He grew to be 6 feet 2 inches tall and was powerfully built. As a youth he was a renowned wrestler

Richard Trevithick (1771–1833), by John Linnell, 1816

in the Cornish style, and it was alleged that he could hurl a sledge-hammer from ground level clean over the top of a mine engine-house. In Cornwall and elsewhere he became known as the Cornish Giant. He earned a reputation as being gentle and courteous, but to those who knew him there was also a volatile and rash side to his nature.

Although Trevithick received no theoretical training beyond his basic schooling, he existed in an environment steeped in practical mining and engineering; he learned quickly from his father at the family home at Penponds, near Camborne, and from others active in the local mines. The years of Trevithick's childhood and youth were exciting and innovative ones in Cornwall. The introduction of Watt engines in the Cornish mines in the 1770s made redundant the slower, less reliable, and inefficient Newcomen variety and stimulated a new era of experimentation as Cornish engineers strove to evade the Watt patents. The lapse of the patents in 1800 heralded the great age of Cornish steam engineering, epitomized as it was by the emergence and subsequent perfection of the Cornish engine, the development of which Trevithick was to facilitate.

Trevithick married into another mining and engineering family. On 7 November 1797, at St Erth, he married Jane Harvey (1772–1868/9); they had four sons and two daughters. His wife was the daughter of John Harvey of Hayle foundry, Hayle, Cornwall, which became one of the most significant in the county, producing machinery and components for mines and other establishments at home and abroad. Curiously, however, the relationship between Trevithick and the Harveys never reached its full potential, failing to move beyond that of manufacturer and customer.

As early as 1792 Trevithick was engaged to report on the performance of a new engine at Tincroft mine, near Camborne, and in 1795 he was able to introduce fuel-saving improvements in an engine at Wheal Treasury. By 1797 he was engineer at Ding Dong mine, near Penzance, where he improved an engine designed by William Bull, and shortly afterwards he installed an improved Bull engine at Herland mine. James *Watt had already identified Trevithick as his arch-rival in the patent tussle but to the Cornish people he was now something of a local hero, known affectionately as Cap'n Dick.

High-pressure steam By 1800, in a profound departure from Watt's reliance on low pressure, Trevithick had introduced his double-acting high-pressure steam engine, an innovation which opened the way for both the evolution of the Cornish engine and the invention of the steam locomotive. Although high-pressure engines were more expensive to build than their contemporaries, they were much more efficient in their use of coal—an important consideration in Cornwall, where fuel had to be imported from south Wales. Trevithick's new engines were known as 'puffers' (to distinguish them from the noiseless condensing engines) and were probably first installed at Dolcoath to wind copper-ore to the surface. A whim (winding) 'puffer' is also said to have been installed at the neighbouring Cook's Kitchen in 1800 and was observed to be still in operation there as late as 1870.

About 1802 Trevithick built a small stationary engine for Coalbrookdale in Shropshire (it operated at the unheard-of pressure of 145 lb per sq. in.), but in 1803 he suffered a serious reversal when one of his new high-pressure engines, employed to pump water from the foundations of a mill under construction at Greenwich, exploded with the loss of four lives. Although Trevithick was able to demonstrate that the accident was a result of human error, this did not prevent James Watt and Matthew *Boulton from issuing dire warnings about the dangers of high-pressure steam and the folly of attempting to harness it. Trevithick responded with a range of new safety measures, most notably the 'fusible plug' which has remained a standard feature of steam engine design for over 150 years.

Convinced of the flexibility and potential of high-pressure steam, as early as 1806 Trevithick considered the design of new boilers to improve the performance of existing Boulton and Watt pumping engines. However, he was not able to bring this idea to fruition until about 1812, when he harnessed his new 'Cornish boilers' to existing engines at Dolcoath. Put simply, the Cornish boiler was horizontal and cylindrical, with a fire tube running through the middle. Following the success of the Dolcoath experiment, in 1812 Trevithick further applied the Cornish boiler at Wheal Prosper (in Gwithian parish) when he used high-pressure steam in both expanding and condensing modes, in effect creating the first prototype for what was to be known (and employed) around the world as 'the Cornish engine'. Although others had been experimenting with high-pressure steam, it was Trevithick who had first applied it successfully in an industrial context.

The second outcome of Trevithick's experimentation with high-pressure steam was the steam locomotive. The concept was not new. In 1770 a primitive proto-locomotive had been built in Lorraine, France, by Nicholas Joseph Cugnot, but its tractive effort was virtually non-existent. Similarly, an experimental locomotive constructed by William *Murdock in Redruth, Cornwall, in 1786 proved powerless and unworkable. Trevithick, in contrast, had by 1797 successfully demonstrated at least one working model of a high-pressure steam locomotive. In the previous year he had met Davies Giddy Gilbert, the Cornish technocrat who was to emerge as a major sponsor and advocate of 'improving' and 'progressive' causes, and together the two men worked to produce a full-size version of Trevithick's locomotive. This is said to have been constructed at Stephen Williams' foundry at the Weeth, Camborne, and it was given its first public demonstration on Christmas eve 1801, an event recorded in the words of the well-known Cornish folk-song 'Camborne Hill':

Goin' up Camborne 'ill, Comin' down,
Goin' up Camborne 'ill, Comin' down,
The 'osses stood still, the wheels went aroun',
Goin' up Camborne 'ill, Comin' down!
(Rowse, 128)

A few days later, on 28 December 1801, the locomotive was being driven from Camborne to nearby Tehidy, the seat of the Basset family, when it broke down. The support team adjourned to the local hostelry, allowing the locomotive to overheat and become severely damaged.

Despite this set-back, with the assistance of his cousin Andrew Vivian and the Cornish scientist Sir Humphry *Davy, Trevithick secured a patent for his locomotive on 24 March 1802. Then, in early 1803, a second locomotive was built at Camborne. This version was exhibited in London where it made several successful demonstration runs into the suburbs. However, it suffered a twisted frame, an occurrence which persuaded Trevithick's partners in the project, including Andrew Vivian, to withdraw their support. Undeterred, Trevithick continued the project at the Penydarren ironworks, near Merthyr Tudful in south Wales, where by late 1803 he was employed as engineer.

The first railway locomotive It was at Penydarren that Trevithick constructed what was the first railway locomotive. The first trial of the locomotive took place on 13 February 1804, and on a demonstration run on 21 February it hauled a load of 10 tons of iron, seventy men, and five wagons for a distance of 9½ miles at an average speed of 5 m.p.h. Unfortunately, the permanent way at Penydarren proved unequal to its new task of supporting a railway locomotive, and soon the poorly laid track caused a derailment, after which Trevithick's invention was relegated to the status of stationary engine. However, the locomotive's success was undoubted. It had demonstrated the feasibility of the railway locomotive as a concept, and in so doing

had also proved important principles such as the adhesion to rails, as well as establishing enduring railway engineering practices such as the use of coupling rods.

Four years later a new Trevithick locomotive, 'Catch-me-who-can', was exhibited in July and August of 1808 on a circular railway, or 'steam circus', near Gower Street in London. Rides were available at 1s. a head but the enterprise was not a financial success. It was brought to an end when the track again proved inadequate, resulting in a broken rail. Thereafter, having again successfully demonstrated the inherent capability of the steam locomotive, Trevithick seems to have lost interest in this particular project. However, his contribution had been outstanding. As early as 1805 his assistant John Steele had built a Trevithick-designed locomotive at the Wylam colliery in the north-east of England. It was in the north-east that further innovation was achieved, which led to the emergence of the 'Newcastle school' of George *Stephenson and Robert *Stephenson.

London interlude From 1803 to 1807 Trevithick had been engaged to improve a steam dredger at work in the River Thames, and during this period he became interested in a project to drive a tunnel under the river. In 1805 Robert Vazie (a Cornish engineer) had been contracted to construct a tunnel northwards from Rotherhithe but, encountering certain difficulties, he decided to seek Trevithick's involvement in the scheme. Trevithick took charge of the construction during August 1807, but on 23 September—by which time the tunnel had progressed some 950 feet—water broke in and the work was inundated. Trevithick himself was the last to leave the scene, and was almost drowned. Subsequently, he made a number of suggestions as to how the project might be resumed and improved, but the tunnel was abandoned.

Trevithick remained in London, however, and in 1808 he was joined there by his wife Jane and their family. He went into business with a West Indies merchant, Robert Dickinson, setting up a small works in Limehouse. Various patents and inventions emerged (not least the 'Nautical Labourer', a steam tug and floating crane propelled by a paddle wheel), and iron tanks for storing cargo and water in ships were manufactured. However, the business was not a success. There were disagreements between the two partners, and in 1810 Trevithick was ill with typhus. In February 1811 he and Dickinson were declared bankrupt. Dickinson appears to have escaped most of the ensuing financial burden, Trevithick paying off the majority of the outstanding debt and receiving his discharge in 1814.

Trevithick and his family returned to Cornwall in September 1810, as he began to recover from his illness, and it was during the next few years that he was able to develop the potential of his Cornish boiler and high-pressure 'plunger-pole' engine. In 1812 at Hayle foundry he built a steam engine designed specifically to drive a threshing machine. It was applied with great success on Sir Christopher Hawkins's Trewithen estate at Probus, near Truro, where it was in operation for seventy years.

South American adventure By 1814 Trevithick was beginning to take an interest in the attempts to revive the ancient silver mines of Cerro de Pasco in Peru. He was approached by Francisco Uvillé, one of the promoters of the proposed reworking, with a view to designing and building equipment for the mines. His response was positive and immediate, and on 1 September 1814 four pumping engines, four winding engines, a portable rolling-mill engine, and much else was shipped from Portsmouth for Peru. Although three of Trevithick's associates had travelled with the engines to ensure their effective installation and operation, Trevithick decided that he too should journey to South America. He sailed from Penzance on 20 October 1816, arriving in Lima to an extravagant reception in February 1817. In all, he was to be abroad for some ten years—a decade of turmoil, change, success, and disappointment.

Despite the warm welcome that Trevithick had received, it soon became apparent that his presence was resented by Uvillé. Trevithick decided to explore elsewhere in Peru, inspecting mines and becoming involved in the development of a copper and silver mine in the province of Caxatambo. But this was a time of increasing political volatility in Peru, as the war of independence from Spain became widespread and disruptive. For a time Trevithick was attached to Simón Bolívar's forces, designing a form of carbine for his use, but no sooner was he released from military service than Caxatambo was occupied by the Spanish army. Trevithick was forced to flee, abandoning expensive equipment and some £5000 worth of stockpiled ore. In 1818 Uvillé died and Trevithick returned to Cerro de Pasco to take charge of the workings. However, his efforts were again frustrated by war when in 1820 a battle took place at the mine and there was much damage to the machinery.

After this set-back Trevithick decided to leave Peru, travelling through Ecuador *en route* for Bogota in Colombia. He met a certain James Gerard who informed him of potential mining opportunities in Costa Rica. The two men resolved to investigate these possibilities and they visited a range of sites in Costa Rica, identifying and securing the rights for a number of gold and silver prospects. To raise capital to exploit these finds they decided to return to Britain. They crossed the isthmus of Nicaragua on foot (the first Europeans to do so); this was a traumatic journey in which, on one occasion, Trevithick was almost drowned crossing a river and, on another, was menaced by an alligator. From San Juan de Nicaragua they made their way to Cartagena in Colombia, arriving penniless and half-starved.

By a strange coincidence Robert Stephenson was also in Cartagena. In August 1827 Trevithick and Stephenson met, Trevithick exclaiming, 'Is that Bobby? I've nursed him many a time' (Rolt, 139)—a reference to Trevithick's visit to Newcastle upon Tyne in 1805. Stephenson lent Trevithick £50 to pay his fare home, and Trevithick arrived back in Falmouth on 9 October 1827. After a decade's adventuring in South America, his only possessions were the clothes he wore, a gold watch, a draughtsman's compass, a navigator's compass, and a pair of silver spurs.

Return to Britain Although Trevithick received a hearty welcome home in Cornwall, he had been largely forgotten in the rest of Britain, and his belated attempts to seek royalties from his various patents proved largely unsuccessful. Likewise, a petition presented on his behalf to the government in February 1828 was disregarded. These were blows for Trevithick who, with little personal wealth to promote his endeavours, was largely dependent on income from consultancies, commissions, and sponsorships. James Gerard, meanwhile, had landed in Liverpool in late 1827, and together the two men tried to interest London investors in their Costa Rican proposals. Trevithick turned down what he considered to be a paltry offer of £8000 from one speculator for his mineral rights, but shortly afterwards Gerard died in Paris. Thereafter, the Costa Rican project lost its momentum and was soon abandoned.

Despite these financial failures, Trevithick's energy and capacity for invention remained undiminished. In 1828 he was invited to visit the Netherlands to investigate the possibility of using Cornish engines for drainage purposes. It is said that he had to borrow the £2 fare to make the journey, but once in the Netherlands he made a number of suggestions concerning the drainage of submerged land and the construction of dikes. He subsequently designed equipment for use in the Netherlands; it was built at Hayle foundry but for some reason never delivered.

Among other inventions from this period were a closed-cycle steam engine (1829), a portable room heater which was in effect an early form of storage heater (1830), and a design for a ship propelled by a water-jet (1832). Trevithick also designed an enormous column 1000 feet high to commemorate the Reform Act of 1832, a proposal which aroused considerable public attention but was not taken up. His last patent, dated 22 September 1832 (no. 6308), was in connection with the employment of superheated steam.

Death and subsequent historiographical invisibility At some time in the late 1820s or early 1830s Trevithick entered into an agreement with John Hall of Dartford, Kent, to carry out developmental work on a steam engine of Hall's design. However, Trevithick fell ill and, after a week's confinement in bed in his lodgings at The Bull inn in Dartford, he died on 22 April 1833 at the age of sixty-two. To avoid having a parish funeral for Trevithick, his workmates clubbed together to cover the funeral costs. Trevithick was laid to rest in an unmarked grave in Dartford on 26 April 1833.

Trevithick's wife, Jane, lived to the age of ninety-six. She had remained loyal to him during long years of financial difficulty and separation. (She had received no money from him during his South American sojourn, during which time she was supported by her brother, Henry Harvey.) Of their six children, Francis Trevithick (1812–1877) became chief mechanical engineer of the London and North Western Railway Company, and Frederick Henry

Trevithick constructed the floating steam bridge between Portsmouth and Gosport in 1864. Little is known of Richard (1798–1872), John Harvey (1806–1877), Ann, or Elizabeth.

In June 1888 Trevithick was celebrated in a 'Trevithick window' in the north aisle of Westminster Abbey, London, in which he was depicted in the guise of St Piran, the patron saint of Cornish miners. However, he has remained somewhat historiographically invisible, despite a laudatory biography written by his son Francis in 1872 and more modern biographies by James Hodge (1973; repr. 1995), L. T. C. Rolt (1960), and others. The unsatisfactory aspects of Trevithick's own life and the early demise of Cornwall as a centre of steam engineering no doubt assisted the process by which the 'Newcastle school' of George Stephenson and Robert Stephenson gained general recognition as the 'inventor' of the railway locomotive. Only in Cornwall, where the Saturday nearest to the anniversary of his death is celebrated as Trevithick day, are his achievements widely recognized.

PHILIP PAYTON

Sources J. Hodge, *Richard Trevithick: an illustrated life of Richard Trevithick, 1771–1833* (1973); repr. (1995) · L. T. C. Rolt, *The Cornish giant: the story of Richard Trevithick, father of the steam locomotive* (1960) · H. W. Dickinson and A. Titley, *Richard Trevithick: the engineer and the man* (1934) · W. J. Rowe, *Cornwall in the age of the industrial revolution*, 2nd edn (1993) · A. C. Todd, *Beyond the blaze: a biography of Davies Gilbert* (1967) · E. Vale, *The Harveys of Hayle: engine builders, shipwrights and merchants of Cornwall* (1966) · F. Trevithick, *Life of Richard Trevithick, with an account of his inventions*, 2 vols. (1872) · *DNB* · P. J. Payton, *The making of modern Cornwall* (1992) · D. B. Barton, *The Cornish beam engine: a survey of its history and development in the mines of Cornwall and Devon from before 1800 to the present day* (1969); repr. (1989) · E. K. Harper, *A Cornish giant, Richard Trevithick* (1913) · J. F. Odgers, *Richard Trevithick, 'the Cornish giant', 1771–1833* (1956) · G. N. von Tunzelmann, *Steam power and British industrialization to 1860* (1978) · A. L. Rowse, *A Cornish anthology*, 2nd edn (1982)

Archives Royal Cornwall Museum · Sci. Mus., letter and account books · Sci. Mus., corresp. and papers relating to Thames Driftway, Hayle Foundry | Bodl. Oxf., corresp. with William Smith · Royal Cornwall Museum, corresp. with Davies Gilbert

Likenesses J. Linnell, oils, 1816, Sci. Mus. [*see illus.*] · window, 1888 (*Trevithick window*), Westminster Abbey · L. E. Merrifield, statue, Camborne Public Library, Cornwall · J. F. Skill, J. Gilbert, W. Walker, and E. Walker, group portrait, pencil and wash (*Men of science living in 1807–8*), NPG · bust, Royal Cornwall Museum, Truro · miniature, Sci. Mus.

Trevor, Arthur Hill-, first Viscount Dungannon (d. 1771). *See under* Trevor, Arthur Hill-, third Viscount Dungannon (1798–1862).

Trevor, Arthur Hill-, third Viscount Dungannon (1798–1862), politician, was born in Berkeley Square, London, on 9 November 1798. He was the only surviving son of Arthur Hill-Trevor, second viscount (1763–1837), and his wife, Charlotte, third daughter of Charles Fitzroy, first Baron Southampton.

Trevor's great-grandfather, **Arthur Hill-Trevor**, first Viscount Dungannon (d. 1771), of Belvoir, co. Down, and Brynkinalt, Denbighshire, was the second son of Michael Hill of Hillsborough, and Anne, the daughter and heir of Sir John Trevor (1637–1717). He inherited the Trevor property from his father's half-brother, Marcus Hill (d. 1751), who was son of William Hill and Mary, daughter of Marcus Trevor, first Viscount Dungannon of the first creation. He was chancellor of the Irish exchequer in 1754–5. On 17 February 1766 he was created Viscount Dungannon and Baron Hill of Olderfleet. He died in Dublin on 30 January 1771, and was buried at Belvoir. His second wife, whom he married in January 1737, was Anne, (1715–1799), daughter and heir of Edmund Francis Stafford of Brownstown, co. Meath. She died on 13 January 1799. Their daughter, Anne, married in February 1759 the earl of Mornington, and was mother of the first duke of Wellington and of Marquess Wellesley. There were two other daughters and a son, Arthur, who was father, with Letitia, eldest daughter of Hervey, first Viscount Mountmorres, of Arthur Hill-Trevor, second Viscount Dungannon; he succeeded his grandfather in the title, and died at Brynkinalt on 14 December 1837.

His son, Arthur Hill-Trevor, was educated at Harrow, and matriculated from Christ Church, Oxford, on 17 October 1817, graduating BA in 1820 and MA in 1825. He married, on 10 September 1821, at Livorno, Sophia, fourth daughter of Colonel Gorges Marcus Irvine of Castle Irvine, co. Fermanagh. She died on 21 March 1880.

In 1830 Hill-Trevor was elected as MP for New Romney, and in the following year for the city of Durham. He was a vigorous opponent of the reform bills of 1831–2, both in the house and outside it. On 30 August 1831 he moved an amendment to the effect that the existing non-resident freemen should keep their votes during their lives. In the course of the year Hill-Trevor issued an anti-reform pamphlet in the guise of a *Letter to the Duke of Rutland*. When the bill was reintroduced he again contested it, and published another pamphlet exhorting the peers to stand firm. At the dissolution he lost his seat, but was re-elected at Durham in the election of 1835. He vigorously opposed municipal corporation reform, regarding it as an attempt to extend the parliamentary franchise indirectly, and put himself forward as the defender of the freemen, moving to omit the clause disfranchising them (23 June 1835); he was defeated by a majority of forty-six. In February 1837 he obtained the rejection of the motion of Sir William Molesworth for the repeal of the property qualification for members of parliament. He seconded the motion of Peter Borthwick for the revival of convocation (3 May), and also his proposal for the establishment of a system of national education in connection with the church (2 June). During this parliament he several times introduced a measure for the control of beershops, but met with little support. He forbade any of his tenants to set one up. In the session of 1839 he opposed the Irish Municipal Corporation Bill as an attempt to put down protestantism. In 1841 he joined Sir Robert Harry Inglis in opposing the further restriction of capital punishment, which he thought should still be inflicted in cases of arson, midnight burglary, and some other offences. While a member of the Commons he always singled out for attack the radical section of his opponents. He was more than once denounced by O'Connell, who on one occasion referred to him ironically as 'the meek and modest representative of the clergy of Durham'.

Hill-Trevor, who had succeeded his father as third Viscount Dungannon in 1837, was defeated at the general election of that year and, though elected at a by-election in April 1843 for his former constituency, was immediately afterwards unseated on petition. In September 1855 he was elected a representative peer for Ireland, and henceforth took an active part in the proceedings of the House of Lords. His strongest efforts were directed against legislation dealing with the marriage laws. He himself led the opposition to the Divorce Bill of 1857, and two years later (22 March 1859) moved the rejection of Lord Wodehouse's Marriage Law Amendment (Deceased Wife's Sister) Bill. His speech on the latter bill was printed the same year. On 27 May 1862 he led the opposition to Lord Ebury's motion for the abolition of clerical subscription.

Dungannon was a member of several learned societies. He published, besides several pamphlets, *The Life and Times of William III* (2 vols., 1835–6), dedicated to Edward Nares, regius professor of modern history at Oxford; the book was written with the assistance of Henry John Todd, archdeacon of Cleveland, and with access to the documents at Stowe, but is of slight historical value. Dungannon died at his London home, 3 Grafton Street, on 11 August 1862 and, having no male children, his titles became extinct.

G. LE G. NORGATE, rev. H. C. G. MATTHEW

Sources GEC, *Peerage* · Boase, *Mod. Eng. biog.* · *GM*, 3rd ser., 13 (1862), 360 · *ILN* (23 Aug 1862)
Archives Durham RO, letters to Lord Londonderry · NL Wales, letters to Louisa Lloyd
Likenesses S. C. Smith, oils, *c.*1856, V&A · J. J. Chant, mezzotint, pubd 1858 (after S. C. Smith), NPG, V&A · W. Say, mezzotint (as a boy; after J. Burnet), BM
Wealth at death under £35,000: probate, 6 Dec 1862, *CGPLA Eng. & Wales*

Trevor, George (1809–1888), writer and Church of England clergyman, was born at Bridgwater, Somerset, on 30 January 1809, the sixth son of Charles Trevor, a customs officer. His paternal grandmother, Harriet, was the sister of Horatio and James Smith, the authors of *Rejected Addresses* (1812). Trevor was educated at a day school at Bridgwater, and in 1825 entered the East India Company office in London as a clerk; there he was contemporary with John Stuart Mill. In London he made the acquaintance of the Disraeli family. On 6 February 1832 he matriculated from Magdalen Hall, Oxford, managing to keep his terms while discharging his duties as clerk. He was a prominent speaker at the Oxford Union, where he caused a furore in 1835 by accusing the treasurer, Edward Cardwell, of falsifying the accounts—a charge he was forced to withdraw. On 12 July 1836 Trevor married Elizabeth (*d.* 1879), daughter of Christopher Garrick of Richmond, Surrey, the grandson of George Garrick, brother of David Garrick. They had several children.

Having resigned his clerkship the previous year, Trevor was ordained priest in 1836, and in order to qualify for an East India chaplaincy took an honorary fourth class in civil law. That year he was assigned to the Madras establishment, and from 1837 to 1845 ministered at Bangalore, where he built St Paul's Church and founded a Tamil mission.

On his return to England, Trevor graduated BA in 1846 (MA, 1847) and was appointed resident deputy of the Society for the Propagation of the Gospel in the province of York. In 1847 he was instituted rector of All Saints', Pavement, York, and at the same time received a non-residentiary canonry in the cathedral, with the prebendal stall of Apesthorp. In 1850 he was appointed by the burgesses of Sheffield to be chaplain of their parish church, and took up his residence in the town. He was, however, prevented from preaching in the church by successive vicars, Thomas Sutton and Thomas Sale, who were suspicious of his high-church views on sacramental theology. Responding to their suspicions, he asserted his Anglican orthodoxy in a series of lectures on the Reformation, which drew large crowds. Although his right to the chaplaincy and its endowments was established by proceedings in chancery and the queen's bench, he remained barred from the pulpit and returned to York in 1855.

Since 1847, when he was elected proctor for the chapter of York, Trevor had taken a leading part in the movement for the revival of the northern convocation, whose meetings had become a mere formality, thus depriving the clergy of a forum for debate. His work on the history of the two convocations (*The convocation of the two provinces, their origin, constitution, and forms of proceeding, with a chapter on their revival*, 1852) had considerable influence on clerical opinion, but progress was blocked during the lifetime of Archbishop Thomas Musgrave (1788–1860). The northern convocation finally met on 23 March 1861, and Trevor was appointed synodal secretary the following year. He did much to make the revived body broadly representative.

Trevor was a forceful and popular preacher, but in his latter years at All Saints' found his congregation drawn off by the rival attraction of the services in the minster. In 1868 he retired to the living of Burton Pidsea in Holderness, and in 1871 was translated to the rectory of Beeford. In 1874 he was made an honorary DD by Holy Trinity College, Hartford, Connecticut, in recognition of his work *The Catholic Doctrine of the Holy Eucharist* (1869; 2nd enlarged edn, 1875), a vindication of the older high-church doctrine. A prolific author, Trevor also wrote three works on India, as well as books on the history of Egypt, Rome, and Russia. He was a contributor to *Blackwood's Edinburgh Magazine* from as early as 1833, and was well known for his articles in the national press. In 1886 he was made an honorary DD by the University of Durham.

Trevor died on 18 June 1888 at the rectory of his son, George Wilberforce Trevor, at Marton, near Middlesbrough, Yorkshire, and was buried at Beeford. A memorial tablet was erected to his memory in the north aisle of the choir of York Minster where he had been a canon for forty-one years.

G. MARTIN MURPHY

Sources *The Times* (20 June 1888) • *The Guardian* (27 June 1888) • *Yorkshire Post* (20 June 1888) • *Biograph and Review*, 6 (1881), 195–8 • O. Chadwick, *The Victorian church*, 3rd edn, 1 (1971), 381 • H. A. Morrah, *The Oxford Union, 1823–1923* (1923), 79–83 • A. Patchett Martin, *Life and letters of the Right Honourable Robert Lowe, Viscount Sherbrooke*, 1 (1893), 82–4 • D. A. Jennings, *The revival of the Convocation of York, 1837–1861*, Borthwick Papers, 47 (1975) • *CGPLA Eng. & Wales* (1888) • DNB

Wealth at death £3783 14*s*. 5½*d*.: probate, 24 July 1888, *CGPLA Eng. & Wales*

Trevor, George Rice Rice-, fourth Baron Dynevor (1795–1869), politician, was born on 5 August 1795, the eldest son of George Talbot Rice, third Baron Dynevor (1765–1852), and his wife, Frances (1772–1854), third daughter of Thomas *Townshend, first Viscount Sydney. George Talbot Rice used the surname De Cardonnell between 1793 and 1817. The younger George was educated at Westminster School and at Christ Church, Oxford, where he matriculated in 1812 but did not graduate. The Rice (or Rhys) family was descended from an old Welsh royal line; George Rice Rice, however, assumed the additional name of Trevor by royal licence (28 October 1824) on inheriting the estates of the Trevors of Glynde in Sussex. A month later, on 27 November 1824, he married Frances (1803–1878), eldest daughter of Lord Charles *Fitzroy, with whom he produced four daughters but no male heir.

By this time, Trevor had entered parliament, being returned unopposed for Carmarthenshire on 16 March 1820. An unflinching tory, and a 'thick and thin Church of England man', he opposed both the emancipation of Catholics in 1829 and the Reform Bill in 1831, resigning his seat at that year's general election knowing that he disagreed with a majority of his constituents on the matter. In 1832, however, with the Reform Act a fact of life, he recaptured the seat, having first indicated that he supported the maintenance of the corn laws and a reduction in the malt tax. Although Trevor's parliamentary career was uneventful, his friendship with the duke of Wellington—he received an honorary DCL on the occasion of the duke's election as chancellor of Oxford University in June 1834—gave him a certain status in metropolitan Conservative circles.

Trevor's most important public role, however, came during the Rebecca riots, an outbreak of turnpike gate breaking which swept through south-west Wales in 1842–4. The co-ordination of the official response to the disturbances fell to him when his ageing father, then lord lieutenant of Carmarthenshire, appointed him his vice-lieutenant. His response was uncompromising. He forced the county quarter sessions to establish a professional police force, called in troops of the 73rd infantry regiment and the 4th light dragoons, and worked closely with Colonel James Francis Love, commander of the south Wales military district, to restore order. Nor were the troops simply for show: he assured a meeting of magistrates at Newcastle Emlyn in June 1843 that he would order them to fire on the rioters if necessary. The response of the protesters was predictably fearsome: in September 1843, they audaciously dug a grave within sight of Dinefwr Castle, the

family seat, and announced that Trevor would occupy it by 10 October. Trevor, however, surrounded by soldiers, survived unscathed.

Once tranquillity had been restored, through an upturn in the economy and an act of parliament which addressed the administration of the turnpike trusts, Trevor continued as county MP until 1852, when his father died. His succession to the title released him from a political life of increasing frustration: after the Conservative split of 1846 he confessed, 'I cannot join the staff of Lord George Bentinck, cannot place confidence in Sir Robert Peel, nor join the ranks of Lord John Russell' (*Dod's Parliamentary Companion*, 1847, 246). Although he attended the House of Lords regularly, voting consistently with the Conservative peers, he lost interest in Carmarthenshire politics, passing the administration of his interest to Lord Cawdor. In local affairs, however, he remained active, associating his name with useful projects such as the Carmarthen Literary and Scientific Institution and the Lifeboat Society.

His elevation to the House of Lords as fourth Baron Dynevor, in April 1852, coincided with his appointment as militia aide-de-camp to the queen, with the rank of colonel, and in August 1861, he was appointed honorary colonel of the Royal Carmarthen and Pembroke militia. Dynevor died at Great Malvern on 7 October 1869, from an attack of paralysis, and was interred in the family vault at Barrington Park, in Gloucestershire.

MATTHEW CRAGOE

Sources M. Cragoe, *An Anglican aristocracy* (1996) • D. J. V. Jones, *Rebecca's children* (1989) • Burke, *Peerage* • H. M. Vaughan, *The south Wales squires*, 1st edn 1926 (1988) • *The Times* (9 Oct 1869) • *Carmarthen Journal* (15 Oct 1869) [obit.] • Boase, *Mod. Eng. biog.* • Foster, *Alum. Oxon.*
Archives Carmarthenshire RO, parliamentary sketches and yeomanry papers | NL Wales, letters to his future wife • NL Wales, letters to Johnes family
Likenesses J. Lucas, portrait, 1852–5; on loan to Dinefwr, Carmarthenshire • G. Hayter, portrait, NL Wales • G. Richmond, watercolour, priv. coll. • portrait, repro. in *ILN*, 28 (1856), 72
Wealth at death under £80,000: probate, 15 Jan 1870, *CGPLA Eng. & Wales*

Trevor, Sir John (1596–1673). *See under* Trevor, Sir John (*bap.* 1624, *d.* 1672).

Trevor, Sir John (*bap.* 1624, *d.* 1672), politician and government official, was baptized on 23 August 1624 at St Margaret's, Westminster, the second but eldest surviving son of **Sir John Trevor** (1596–1673), politician, and Anne, the daughter of Sir Edmund Hampden. Sir John Trevor senior was the eldest son of John Trevor of Trefalun (1563–1630), navy official and politician, and Margaret, the daughter of Hugh Trevanion of Trevannion, Cornwall, and from his father inherited Plas Teg, Flintshire. He married Anne Hampden in 1619.

Trevor senior was knighted at Windsor on 7 June 1619 and sat as a member of parliament for Denbighshire in 1621 and Flintshire in the following parliaments. He then moved to Great Bedwyn in 1628 and Grampound in the

Long Parliament. He initially made little mark in the parliaments, and was later named as one of those who had offered bribes to the lord chancellor in the parliament of 1621. A moderate presbyterian, he managed to gain the favour of the court and acquired the keepership of several royal forests and his father's farm of the coal tax, as well as the inheritance of Trefalun in 1638 from his uncle Sir Richard Trevor. He was involved in a number of royal commissions during the 1630s and was a member of the Long Parliament, being noted there as a spokesman for north Welsh affairs. He sat on the committee of both kingdoms from 2 June 1648 and the commission for the propagation of the gospel in Wales in 1650, as well as the republican council of state in 1651 and 1652–3. In addition he sat on local committees for militia and taxation in Middlesex, Westminster, Denbighshire, and Flint. Trevor sat in Cromwell's second parliament of 1656 and supported the offer of the crown to the lord protector. Trevor was a rising man in the 1650s, sensible enough not to be a regicide, and making the most of the financial opportunities of the period, including the purchase of royalists' and recusants' estates. He took no part in the Restoration, but was given a royal pardon on 24 July 1660 and subsequently lived in London, his estate at Plas Teg in Wales being given as a refuge to William Jones, a deprived churchman, as his pensioner. He may have married Margaret Griffith in 1672. He died in 1673 bequeathing some of his property to the establishment of two houses for poor men in Wales.

Sir John Trevor the younger was educated at Leiden in 1643 and entered parliament as a recruiter member for Flintshire on 2 December 1646. He faltered at the possibility of regicide however and was excluded, or retired, in 1648. About 1649 he married his cousin Ruth (1628–1687), fourth daughter of John *Hampden, the puritan politician, and the couple had five sons and one daughter. Ruth remained a presbyterian following the Restoration and attended Thomas Manton's church in London. Trevor returned to public life in the Cromwellian parliaments of the 1650s. He also sat on several county committees from 1657. His politics in the 1650s were clearly moderate, based on ideas of legality and a dislike of innovations. He supported the offer of the crown to Cromwell, and welcomed the constitution of 1656, hoping for the peace of the people as the main basis for the legal settling of the nation. He was a supporter of Richard Cromwell, and on the latter's removal backed George Monck, sitting on the council of state in February 1660. He was rejected by Flintshire in the Convention of 1660 and instead sat for Arundel. In a pamphlet of 1660 Trevor further outlined his political views in that he was against the Rump and called for a broader based settlement than the Rump could ever provide. Significantly he also claimed that absolute uniformity of religion was not essential to any monarchy. With this Trevor made a successful transition into the Restoration.

Trevor was MP for Great Bedwyn from 18 February 1663 to his death in 1672 and was an advocate of leniency in the indemnity debates. He was named to the committee for restoring the dukedom of Norfolk to the Howard family and was concerned to make good relations with the royal regime. Chosen for a diplomatic mission to France in 1663, he had already become attached to the party of Sir Henry Bennet, the future earl of Arlington. The fall of Lord Chancellor Clarendon in 1667 opened up new opportunities to Trevor. With a continued credit among the dissenters and at court because of his attacks on Clarendon he was thought to be useful for a regime planning religious indulgence as part of its policy. Trevor was knighted in 1668 and sent on another mission to France. There he did not behave himself altogether well according to Charles II, who was 'troubled that Trevor carried himself so like an ass' to Henriette-Anne, the king's sister. Charles claimed that he had 'sent him a chiding for it' and put it down to his 'want of good breeding' (Bryant, 1963, 216). None the less with the retirement of William Morrice on 29 September 1668 Trevor was allowed to purchase the junior secretary of state's place for the sum of £8000. Although initially the patent included the usual clause of giving the recipient £100 for life, this was changed—either because of jealousy from other courtiers or through retrenchment—to £100 during pleasure only and such was the limitation on Trevor's power that he did not challenge it.

Indeed, despite his post, Trevor was without any real influence or authority in the regime; it was Arlington, the senior secretary of state, who held the reins of power at this time. Trevor wavered between the clashing forces of Arlington and the duke of Buckingham in this period and some considered him as Buckingham's man as he secured the election of Buckingham as chancellor of the University of Cambridge in May 1671. He continued to support the relief of dissenters, speaking against the continuation of the Conventicles Act in November 1669, was unhappy at having to enforce it, and according to Joseph Williamson in 1671 'Secretary Trevor [was] theirs', that is, wholly in with the dissenters (CSP dom., 1671, 569). He naturally supported the declaration of indulgence of 15 March 1672 and had some share in its administration. Trevor died suddenly of apoplexy and fever on 28 May 1672, allegedly brought on by drinking cold wine with ice when he was very hot. He was buried on 31 May at St Bartholomew-the-Less, Smithfield, in London. His wife died on 1 December 1687, and his second son, Thomas *Trevor, was created Baron Trevor of Bromham.　　ALAN MARSHALL

Sources A. Bryant, ed., *Letters, speeches and declarations of King Charles II* (New York, 1935); new edn (1963) · *CSP dom., 1671* · A. H. Dodd, 'The pattern of politics in Stuart Wales', *Transactions of the Honourable Society of Cymmrodorion* (1948), 8–91 · A. H. Dodd, 'Wales's parliamentary apprenticeship (1536–1625)', *Transactions of the Honourable Society of Cymmrodorion* (1942), 8–72 · F. M. G. Evans, *The principal secretary of state: a survey of the office from 1558 to 1680* (1923) · A. M. Burke, ed., *Memorials of St Margaret's Church, Westminster* (1914) · D. Brunton and D. H. Pennington, *Members of the Long Parliament* (1988) · D. J. Witcombe, *Charles II and the cavalier House of Commons, 1663–1678* (1960) · G. L. Turner, ed., *Original records of early nonconformity under persecution and indulgence*, 3 vols. (1911–14) · *Diary of Thomas Burton*, ed. J. T. Rutt, 4 vols. (1828) · J. Trevor, *The fair dealer, or, A modest answer to the sober letter of his excellency, the Lord General Monck* (1660) · C. G. O. Bridgeman and J. C. Walker, eds., *Supplementary report on the manuscripts of the late Montagu Bertie, twelfth*

earl of Lindsey, HMC, 79 (1942) · J. P. Ferris, 'Trevor, John', HoP, Commons, 1660–90
Archives Bodl. Oxf., corresp. | BL, letters, mainly to Sir W. Temple, Sloane MS 1003 [copies]
Likenesses P. Lely, oils, Glynde Place, East Sussex · engraving (after Lely), repro. in Burke, *Memorials*, facing p. 116 · group portrait, oils (family group), Glynde Place, East Sussex

Trevor, Sir John (*c*.1637–1717), judge and speaker of the House of Commons, was the second son of John Trevor (1602–*c*.1643) of Bryncunallt, Denbighshire, judge on the north Wales circuit, and his wife, Margaret, the daughter of John Jeffreys of Acton, Denbighshire. He married Jane (1643–1704), daughter of Sir Roger *Mostyn, first baronet, of Mostyn in Flintshire and widow of Sir Roger Puleston of Emral, Worthenbury in the same county. They had four sons and two daughters. The Trevor family had long held the Bryncunallt estate but with significant interests in Ireland they were never as influential in Wales as the cadet branch of the family based at Trefalun.

Trevor's education was given direction by his father's brother, Arthur Trevor. He attended Ruthin School as a young boy and proceeded to St Paul's School, London, in 1647. He worked as a clerk in his uncle's legal chambers until he was admitted to the Inner Temple in November 1654. By May 1661 he had been called to the bar. Having acquired a basic knowledge of the 'knavish part of the law' he became a recognized expert at handling gambling transactions (North, 1.286). He ingratiated himself at the Stuart court and was rewarded with a knighthood on 29 January 1671. Two years later he was promoted to become one of the king's counsel. Called to the bench of the Inner Temple in May 1673, he became its treasurer later that year and was a reader by 1675. Promotion in the legal world coincided with political progress. On 10 February 1673 he became MP for Castle Rising in Norfolk. This was a pocket borough of the Howard family and Trevor purchased the seat for £60.

Bishop Gilbert Burnet, a contemporary commentator, described Trevor as 'a bold and dexterous man [who] … knew the most effectual ways of recommending himself to every government' (*Bishop Burnet's History*, 4.76). During the closing years of the Cavalier Parliament (1661–79) Trevor's career justified these words. He was an active debater and a clear government supporter. By the autumn of 1675 his eminence was such that he was chairing both the committee of ways and means and that on the state of the nation. He was an ardent defender of the established church and played a significant part in debates relating to the threat of Catholicism. He was elected chairman of the committee on the growth of popery in the spring of 1678 and took the lead in these inquiries. He was also a member of the committee which investigated the Popish Plot later that year, and presented the draft address to the House of Commons for the removal of all Catholics from London.

Committed to the hereditary succession, Trevor was a vehement opponent of exclusion. He was returned for Bere Alston in Devon in the parliaments of March and October 1679, but he gained a Welsh seat in the third Exclusion Parliament (1681) by securing Denbigh County.

Trevor spent most of his time at his London residence in Clement's Lane but by this time he had inherited the Bryncunallt estate on the death of his brother and certainly made an effort to consolidate his presence in north Wales. He was deputy lieutenant for Denbighshire and Flintshire in 1679–89, and served as mayor of Holt in 1682–3. He was a member of the commission into encroached lands in Denbighshire in 1684 and was made a freeman of Denbigh the following year. Among his charitable bequests was a £100 subscription to Denbigh grammar school.

Trevor was returned for Denbigh boroughs in 1685. At the opening of parliament on 19 May he was proposed for the speakership by the secretary of state, Charles Middleton, and deemed suitable 'by reason of his great integrity, knowledge of the laws of the land and of the rules and orders of this House' (BL, Lansdowne MS, 507, fol. 40). With the support of his cousin Sir George *Jeffreys and the king he was accepted without opposition. As a staunch tory he must have been comfortable presiding over this tory-dominated assembly. On 12 October 1685 he was rewarded for political service with the mastership of the rolls—it is no coincidence that the appointment followed Jeffreys' elevation to the position of lord chancellor. For the last few weeks of the parliamentary session Trevor held both offices simultaneously.

On 6 July 1688 Trevor was appointed to the privy council and he was one of the few who attended James II's last privy council meeting on 16 December. This loyalty led to a temporary loss of favour at the start of the reign of William and Mary. He was elected MP for Bere Alston in 1689 but was deprived of his other influential positions. Still, his legal expertise meant that he was appointed solicitor-general to the queen in 1689 and he became the self-appointed leader of the tories during this parliament. He was elected MP for Yarmouth in the Isle of Wight in 1690. The previous summer William III had commented to the marquess of Halifax that he considered Trevor to be 'such a knave that it would be objected if he was employed' (Foxcroft, 2.228). Despite such concerns Trevor's usefulness could not be ignored and when parliament convened on 20 March 1690 he was proposed for the speaker's chair by Sir John Lowther, the vice-chamberlain, and once again was accepted without opposition. Trevor's career now went from strength to strength. He was appointed first commissioner of the great seal in June 1690 in the place of Sir John Maynard, and on 1 January 1691 he was restored to the privy council. Two years later, on 13 January 1693, he was reinstated as master of the rolls.

As speaker it was Trevor's responsibility to decide who should speak in debate, even though his choice could be overruled by a majority of MPs. Anecdotes about his behaviour exist in plenty. He was very obviously cross-eyed and tales developed about how this meant that during debate more than one member could think that they had 'caught the Speaker's eye'. There is nothing to substantiate these tales in recorded debate; it is more likely that Trevor conformed with the tradition of allowing government spokesmen to take the floor at the most tactically advantageous time, and otherwise ensured that he chose speakers in a way which protected him against any accusations of blatant bias.

The speaker's office was an openly partisan one so in addition to managing debates Trevor was expected to promote the king's business. In the main he seems to have coped successfully with these demands until his speakership came to an abrupt end in 1695 when he found himself at the centre of a House of Commons inquiry into corruption. On 12 March 1695 Paul Foley, reporting from the select committee, informed the house that on 12 February 1693 the common council of London had ordered that 1000 guineas should be given to Sir John Trevor in return for his support in relation to the London Orphans Bill. The order was endorsed with the information that the payment had indeed been made on 22 June in the presence of witnesses. This report led to a four-hour debate on Trevor's behaviour chaired by Trevor himself. At nine o'clock Trevor was placed in the uncomfortable position of stating the question on a motion condemning his own behaviour. The house decided that he was guilty 'of a high crime and misdemeanour' (*JHC*, 11.271).

The following day Trevor was absent from the house, having been 'taken with a violent fit of the colic' and the house was forced to adjourn (*JHC*, 11.271). On 14 March the house received a second letter of apology from the speaker whereupon Thomas Wharton, comptroller of the household, announced that the king gave leave for the election of a new speaker. On 16 March the house passed an order that Trevor should be expelled. As investigations continued it was discovered that Trevor was also one of the members who had accepted gratuities from the East India Company. On 3 May it was decided that the ex-speaker should be impeached for his behaviour but the prorogation of parliament protected Trevor from this fate.

Corruption charges ended his time in the chair but Trevor's career in public office continued. He retained the mastership of the rolls until his death. There is no evidence to suggest that he was anything other than impartial in legal affairs and his decisions were cited by later judges. During the reign of Queen Anne he was sworn of the privy council in June 1702 and was also returned to his Welsh offices. He was constable of Flint Castle from 1705 until his death and *custos rotulorum* for Flintshire (1705–14). He died intestate in London on 20 May 1717 and was buried in the Rolls Chapel in Chancery Lane ten days later. He was reputed to have left a fortune of £60,000 which was divided among his children. Trevor's sons died without heirs and the Bryncunallt estate eventually passed to his daughter Anne.   KATHRYN ELLIS

Sources K. Ellis, '"The squint from the chair": speaker Sir John Trevor, c.1637–1717', *Parliamentary History*, 17 (1998), 198–214 • HoP, *Commons, 1660–90* • *DWB* • *Bishop Burnet's History* • *DNB* • F. A. Inderwick and R. A. Roberts, eds., *A calendar of the Inner Temple records*, 3 (1901) • J. E. Griffith, *Pedigrees of Anglesey and Carnarvonshire families* (privately printed, Horncastle, 1914) • *JHC*, 9–11 (1667–97) • *Le Neve's Pedigrees of the knights*, ed. G. W. Marshall, Harleian Society, 8 (1873) • proceedings on choice of speaker, 1553–1734, BL, Lansdowne MS 507 • R. North, *The lives of … Francis North … Dudley North … and … John North*, new edn, 3 vols. (1826), vol. 1 • H. C. Foxcroft, *A character of the Trimmer: being a short life of the first marquis of Halifax* (1946), vol. 2 • H. O'Sullivan, 'The Trevors of Rostrevor: a British colonial family in seventeenth-century Ireland', MLitt. diss., Dublin, 1985 • K. M. Thompson, *Ruthin School: the first seven centuries* (1974) • M. McDonnell, ed., *The registers of St Paul's School, 1509–1748* (privately printed, London, 1977) • parish registers, Whitford, Flintshire, Denbighshire or Flintshire RO, P/69/1/1 [marriage] • W. Musgrave, *Obituary prior to 1800*, ed. G. J. Armytage, 6, Harleian Society, 49 (1901), 123 • PRO, PROB 6/393

Archives Denbighshire RO, Ruthin, Brynkinalt MSS • NL Wales, Chirk Castle MSS, letters relating to Denbigh elections

Likenesses J. Closterman, portrait, c.1668 (after J. Allen?), Speaker's House, London • J. Allen?, oils, c.1690–1692, priv. coll. • oils, type of c.1690–1692 (after J. Closterman), Palace of Westminster, London • W. Bond, stipple, pubd 1798 (after J. Allen?), BM, NPG; repro. in P. Yorke, *Royal tribes of Wales* (1798)

Wealth at death £60,000—personal estate: *Le Neve's pedigrees*, ed. Marshall, 245; *DNB*

Trevor, John (1855–1930), founder of the Labour church, was born on 7 October 1855 in Liverpool, the younger child and only son of Frederick Francis Trevor, linen draper, and his wife, Harriet, the daughter of John Cripps of Wisbech, a small grocer and linen draper. By the age of nine, he was an orphan; Trevor and his sister were brought up in Wisbech by their maternal grandmother, though eventually his sister went to live with her recently widowed paternal grandmother.

Trevor's grandparents were kindly, but the idiosyncratic and severe Baptist sect to which they belonged left a permanent scar on his mind. After a dame-school and a fly-by-night boarding-school, he entered a second boarding-school that was physically rigorous and educationally sufficient to allow him to pass the Cambridge local examination. In 1870 he was articled for five years to a Norwich architect. After an interlude in Liverpool and a return to Norwich he suffered a physical collapse and eventually a loss of faith, though not of religious impulse.

In 1877 Trevor travelled to Australia. He returned the next year by way of the United States, determined to be a minister, probably among the Unitarians, though he knew little about them. He had introductions to Brooke Herford and Robert Collyer (1823–1912), English Unitarian ministers in Chicago, and they directed him to Meadville Seminary in western Pennsylvania, where he spent a year. In 1879 he returned to England. After a spell at Manchester New College, London, and some experience of preaching, he began practice as an architect in Folkestone. On 28 July 1881 he married his first cousin Eliza, daughter of Franklin Stanley Cripps, a Wisbech shopkeeper; they had four sons, two surviving to adulthood. The Folkestone experiment having failed, in 1884 they moved to Ballingdon, Essex, where he tried but failed to write a novel, and in 1887 they settled in London, where he undertook another year-long course at Manchester New College.

In 1888 Trevor became assistant minister to Philip Henry Wicksteed at the chapel in Little Portland Street. London gave him opportunities to study social problems (which also deeply engaged Wicksteed), and he began to see a relationship between politics and religion. In June 1890 he moved to Manchester to become minister at the fashionable chapel in Upper Brook Street. In April 1891, at a Unitarian conference in London, he heard Ben Tillett (1860–1943) deliver a harsh attack on the alienation of existing churches from the working man. Taking up the challenge, which echoed his own growing feeling about the Unitarians and his sympathy with the Salvation Army, he determined to found a labour church. The initial meeting was held on 4 October 1891 at Chorlton town hall. The initiative was sternly criticized in the Unitarian press, and the difficulty of his position at Upper Brook Street as his commitment to socialism became apparent led to his resignation in the same year.

In 1892 Trevor founded a monthly publication, *Labour Prophet*, and began a series of tracts. In 1893 he became chairman of the Labour Church Union, and the movement spread with remarkable rapidity from Lancashire and Yorkshire to the midlands and south Wales and into Scotland, drawing primarily on upper levels of working men (and some women), with some representation from the lower middle class. There was considerable variation in practice from congregation to congregation: some had readings from secular sources and hymns; a few were licensed for marriages and there were even baptisms. But Trevor was unsuited to exert strong leadership, particularly as his life was darkened by illness and personal tragedy. By the end of the century the movement was in sharp decline.

The loss of a second son in June 1894 was followed by the death of Trevor's wife; in 1895 he married Annie Jones Higham (d. 1919), with whom he had two daughters. In 1897 he moved to a farm in Horsted Keynes, Sussex, where from 1899 to 1902 he encouraged young Labour church members to visit him for informal religious training in his 'school of natural religion'. This project met with little success, and he soon severed his formal ties with the church. In 1902 he lived briefly in Clerkenwell, London, where he tried to establish the Labour Church Settlement as a centre of intellectual and cultural life for what remained of the movement.

In 1909 Trevor moved to Hampstead, working for several years as a professional photographer. In the same year he published a pamphlet, *The One Life*, which revealed his intense interest in questions of sexuality and his idea of forming an independent group modelled on the Oneida community, which he had visited on his American journey.

He never finally severed links with the Unitarians, serving as a supply minister at Newbury in the early 1920s, but he became a lonely and isolated figure, increasingly disillusioned with all churches and convinced that God was working outside such institutions. Trevor died in London on 7 January 1930 and was buried in Highgate cemetery.

R. K. WEBB

Sources J. Trevor, *My quest for God*, 2nd edn (1908) [1st edn, 1897] · J. Saville and R. Storey, 'Trevor, John', *DLB*, vol. 6 · K. S. Inglis, *Churches and the working classes in Victorian England* (1963), chap. 6 · S. Pierson, 'John Trevor and the Labor church movement in England, 1891–1900', *Church History*, 29 (1960), 463–78 · C. H. Herford, *Philip Henry Wicksteed, his life and work* (1931) · J. Trevor, *The one life* (1909) · *Christian Life* (5 Dec 1891) · *Christian Life* (14 Dec 1895) · *DNB* · d. cert.

Archives U. Warwick Mod. RC, biographical corresp. and papers collected by G. W. Brassington
Likenesses photographs, repro. in Trevor, *My quest for God*

Trevor, John Hampden-, third Viscount Hampden (1748–1824), diplomatist, was born in London on 24 February 1748 and baptized John Trevor at St George's, Hanover Square, on 26 March, the second son of Robert *Trevor, later fourth Baron Trevor and first Viscount Hampden (1706–1783), a diplomatist, and his wife, Constantia de Huybert (1726/7–1761). In February 1754 his father added Hampden to the family name on succeeding to John Hampden's Buckinghamshire estates.

Hampden-Trevor was educated at Westminster School, and matriculated from Christ Church, Oxford, on 28 January 1767. He graduated BA on 20 October 1770 and proceeded MA on 9 July 1773. On 5 August 1773 he married at Slapton, Buckinghamshire, Harriet (1750/51–1829), only child of Daniel Burton, a canon of Christ Church and rector of Slapton; they had no children. Following his father's career, he was appointed on 8 April 1780 minister-plenipotentiary at Munich to the elector palatine and minister to the diet at Regensburg. His principal duty was to watch for attempts by France to negotiate a subsidy treaty, which would secure troops, with any part of the empire. He was also charged with investigating the grievances of protestants in the empire. Having performed his duties satisfactorily, he succeeded Lord Mountstuart as envoy to the Sardinian court in March 1783. He arrived at Turin on 15 October 1783 with instructions to assist the Vaudois and other protestant subjects of the Sardinian king, and to this end he received a Vaudois deputation on 27 December. In January 1785 he was ordered to maintain strict neutrality in the struggle between France and Austria, and his numerous dispatches demonstrate the difficulties of the Sardinian kingdom sandwiched between the two great powers. He tried unsuccessfully to be promoted to Florence in December 1786 but later refused missions to both Russia and Vienna. The title of minister-plenipotentiary was conferred on him on 16 June 1789, with additional pay he had requested six years earlier when he declared that he had spent £4000 more than he received from the government. From 1793 to 1796 the critical state of affairs kept him constantly at his post but in May 1797 he took leave; he was never able to return to Turin because the French occupied the city in July 1798. His official recall was delivered to him in Florence in November 1799 and, having failed to be nominated as an intermediary between the Austrian army and the Piedmont government in May 1800 on the grounds of his too strong attachment to the Sardinian court, he went into retirement.

During his time in Turin, or on leave in Switzerland, Hampden-Trevor counted among his friends Horace Walpole, the Berry sisters, Edmund Burke, Lord Sheffield, and Edward Gibbon; the latter wrote of him in 1792 that he was 'par lui-meme un des hommes les plus essentiels et les plus essentiels que j'aye jamais connûs' (*Letters of Edward Gibbon*, 3.245). In the same year Hampden-Trevor published at Parma *Poemata Hampdeniana*, a folio edition of his father's Latin poems, dedicated to George III. Gibbon was also charmed with his wife, as was Benjamin Constant who fell briefly but dramatically in love with her in Lausanne. In retirement, such lustre as accompanied their life in Italy and Switzerland soon faded. When Lord Glenbervie dined with them at Richmond in 1804 he noted:

> He has a great deal of that stiff politeness which a long diplomatic career is so apt to give. His parts are above par, and he is civil but not agreeable. She has still the remains of a most engaging countenance and manner, but too coaxing and adulatory, which by being perpetual and undiscriminating does not flatter. (*Diaries*, 1.362)

Hampden-Trevor succeeded his brother Thomas in the peerage as third Viscount Hampden on 20 August 1824 and died a few weeks later on 9 September 1824 in Berkeley Square, London. He was buried at Glynde in Sussex. The Hampden estates passed to the Hobart family. He was survived by his wife, who died on 26 June 1829 and was also buried at Glynde.   WILLIAM CARR, *rev.* P. J. JUPP

Sources Walpole, *Corr.*, 25.595; 42.397 · *Extracts from the journals and correspondence of Miss Berry from the year 1783 to 1852*, ed. Lady T. Lewis, new edn, 3 vols. (1866), 1.236–9 · *The correspondence of Edmund Burke*, 6, ed. A. Cobban and R. A. Smith (1967), 216–9 · *The letters of Edward Gibbon*, ed. J. E. Norton, 3 vols. (1956), 2.211; 3.33, 51–2, 61, 245 · *The diaries of Sylvester Douglas (Lord Glenbervie)*, ed. F. Bickley, 2 vols. (1928) · *The manuscripts of J. B. Fortescue*, 10 vols., HMC, 30 (1892–1927), vol. 2, p. 436; vol. 3, pp. 85–6; vol. 6, p. 211 · GEC, *Peerage*

Archives Balliol Oxf., letters to James Mallet du Pan · Beds. & Luton ARS, corresp. with Lord Grantham · BL, corresp. with Francis Drake, Add. MSS 46823–46824 · BL, letters to Lord Grenville, Add. MS 59025 · BL, letters to Sir Robert Keith, Add. MSS 35519–35545, *passim* · BL, letters to duke of Leeds, Add. MSS 28060–28065 · BL, letters to Lord Nelson, Add. MSS 34904–34915, *passim* · Hants. RO, corresp. with William Wickham · NMM, letters to Sir William Hamilton · Shrops. RRC, corresp. with Lord Berwick and Joseph Brame

Trevor, Marcus [Mark], **first Viscount Dungannon** (1618–1670), royalist army officer and politician, was born at Rosetrevor, co. Down, on 15 April 1618, the son of Sir Edward Trevor (*d.* *c.*1649) of Rosetrevor and of Brynkynallt, Denbighshire, and his second wife, Rose (*d.* 1623), the daughter of Henry *Ussher, archbishop of Armagh. His father had left his property in Wales for estates in Ireland worth £800 per annum.

Trevor was admitted to the Inner Temple in November 1634. However, his connections to the planter community in Ireland were strong. On 29 September 1633 he was engaged to marry Frances (*c.*1618–1656), the daughter and coheir of Marmaduke Whitechurch of Loughbrickland, co. Down. They married in August 1636 after her parents' deaths; they had two children. His sister married Sir Hans Hamilton of Monella and Hamilton's Bawn. In September 1636 Trevor walked in Lord Montgomery of Ards's funeral procession. In the 1640 Down election he and his father aligned themselves with the planter Hills and the Irish Bagnalls, McGuinesses, and O'Neills against the Montgomery–Hamilton (planter) faction and their Irish allies. He served as MP for Downpatrick (1639–49), while his father was elected for Newtonards in 1640. Following the Irish rising of October 1641 the insurgents imprisoned his

father in Narrowater Castle, Newry, until April 1642. Marcus Trevor became a commander in Down, and received a letter threatening reprisals from the rebel Con Magennis (perhaps a former political ally). He later joined one of the earl of Ormond's regiments. In October 1643 he departed for England to serve the king against the parliamentarians. Following parliamentarian advances in north-east Wales he found himself a major of horse defending Holt Bridge with Ellice's foot. He acquired command of the horse regiment of Arthur, Lord Capel (originally raised in November 1642). On 12 January 1644 he just escaped capture by the parliamentarians when they made a night attack on Ellesmere, Shropshire. By February his regiment mustered just 30 men, but by 5 May its strength had risen to 400. He joined Prince Rupert's army on 16 May.

At the battle of Marston Moor his regiment served with the right wing of the royalist cavalry at the extreme left of the front line. Once the battle started Marcus countercharged Cromwell's horse regiment, hitting it in the right flank. He personally fought Cromwell and wounded him, forcing the future lord protector to leave the action to have his wound dressed. Trevor's horse survived the battle and retreated to north Wales. He became the governor of Ruthin Castle on the River Clywd. His regiment was badly weakened in the action at Montgomery Castle on 18 September. On 19 October Sir Thomas Myddleton's parliamentarian force attacked Ruthin. Trevor and his 120 cavalry fled, but his deputy successfully held the town. In December the inhabitants of the vale of Clywd petitioned Lord Byron against the regiment's excessive requisitions. Before the war's end Trevor's horse was cast into Prince Charles's horse as reinforcements, and it disbanded following the royalist defeat in Cornwall. On 12 April 1646 Trevor surrendered Ruthin Castle to the parliamentarians. He submitted to Fairfax in Oxford in May.

In July 1647 Trevor and his wife, Frances, were in Holywell, Flintshire, on the way to Ireland. Once there he joined Michael Jones's parliamentarian force for service against the Irish confederates. He received the governorship of Carlingford on 13 April 1648. On 3 November while scouting for Jones he prevented the parliamentarians from being surprised when he spotted Owen Roe O'Neill's army crossing a bridge near Clonee, 5 miles from Dublin. He served under Colonel George Monck, perhaps as late as April 1649. On hearing of Charles I's execution he deserted the parliamentarian army and joined Ormond's Irish royalist army. In May he helped Lord Inchiquin, who commanded 2000 foot and 1500 horse, to blockade and capture Drogheda. On 23 July with six horse troops he attacked the Irish confederate Lieutenant-General Richard O'Farrell who was convoying a supply of ammunition received from the parliamentarians. Trevor's cavalry dispersed all but 70 of the 800 largely drunken Irish foot and horse, forcing O'Neill's army to retreat into Monaghan. Subsequently he commanded a food and ammunition magazine at Ardee, but he could not aid Drogheda during Cromwell's siege. On 26 September with 500 horse he attacked Colonel Robert Venables at Dromore. Trevor's initial success turned to failure when the English rallied.

Following a skirmish Trevor retreated west across the River Bann. After Ormond and O'Neill formed an alliance on 12 October Trevor was so excited at the prospects it offered that he travelled to his former enemy's camp to pay his respects. In November, while serving with Inchiquin during the attack on Cromwell at Glascarig near Wexford he was shot in the belly and carried to Kilkenny. On 16 December Monck ordered Major George Rawdon to prohibit Trevor from returning to his estates. In March 1650 Ormond promoted him lieutenant-general of horse, but in April with Viscount Montgomery of Ards and Lord Moore he submitted to Cromwell at Clonmell.

The regicide Colonel John Jones (who hailed from north Wales, as had Trevor's father) had succeeded Trevor as governor of Carlingford, and despite their political differences the two men became friends. As Jones married a sister of Cromwell's in 1655 the connection had potential patronage benefits for Trevor. Meanwhile in October 1651, perhaps in connection with the terms of his submission, he claimed exemption from the common burdens. The Commonwealth government trusted him sufficiently in October 1652 to order him to gather 500 Roman Catholic Irish in Ulster and march them to Carlingford for transportation from the province. Subsequently he supported Henry Cromwell major-general of the forces in Ireland, and from 1657 lord deputy, spent time in Dublin, and even received a hawk from his former oppressor Major Rawdon. As late as November 1654 the lord protector suggested that he be imprisoned, but he changed his policy on 25 April 1655 when he ordered that his former adversary be placed under his protection and permitted to use his Irish estates. Trevor later claimed that as the republic fell apart he had tried to suborn Henry Cromwell to declare for Charles II, promising him 5000 troops from Ulster. Whatever the truth of that story, he certainly maintained close relations with the protectorate regime in Ireland as it entered its final days. Jones arranged for him to receive the lease of the corporation of Carlingford and its lands (600 acres), while in June 1659 the lord lieutenant presented him with a similar grant of Dundalk (1200 acres) as well as further lands in co. Louth, and in co. Kildare, as one of his last acts. In November 1659 with Viscount Montgomery of Ards and Colonel Vere Essex Cromwell he began plotting the restoration of the monarchy in Ireland. In the next month he was involved in the royalist plot against Dublin Castle. In 1660 he kept Ormond, then living in Brussels, apprised of Irish affairs.

After the Restoration Trevor gained a degree of public prominence as a government official. He became ranger of Ulster on 6 December and was appointed to the Irish privy council on 19 December. In 1661 the shire electors of Down returned him to the Dublin parliament. His friendship with Ormond brought him material benefits when on 20 March 1661 the Irish land commissioners confirmed his rights (against those of pre-October 1641 landholders and grantees who had served against the Irish rebels) to the protectorate land grants, a decision confirmed by the privy council on 24 October. He received the office of master of the game and ranger-general of his majesty's woods (including Phoenix Park, where the post had a lodge) on 28 August, the licence for gunpowder manufacture in Down on 16 October, and command of a troop of Irish horse. He was elevated to the Irish peerage on 28 August 1662 as Baron Trevor of Rosetrevor and Viscount Dungannon and entered the Irish House of Lords on 12 September. The citation in his grant of supporters stated the elevation to peerage arose from his wounding Cromwell, but given his subsequent career the patronage of Ormond was most likely the cause of the honour. During the Restoration he alternated his time between Ulster and Dublin. As lord lieutenant of co. Down from 1664 he dealt with tory bands by setting them against each other, as opposed to the more usual policy of allowing them to go into voluntary exile with the profits of their crimes. In June 1666 he helped to suppress a mutiny by the Carrickfergus Castle garrison. That August he travelled to co. Kilkenny, co. Wicklow, and co. Wexford in the company of Ormond. On 14 August 1667 he received the appointment as marshal of Ireland, which brought him an annual salary of £687. In April 1668 he and his wife travelled to Holyhead, Chester, and Coventry with Ormond. In October 1669, along with Viscount Conway, he dealt with the pay stoppage of the Royal regiment in Dublin. He died on 3 January 1670 at Dundalk and was buried in Clanallin church, near Rosetrevor, on 10 January. His first wife had died on 9 February 1656. He was survived by his second wife, Anne (d. 1692), daughter and heir of John Lewis of Anglesey and widow of John Owen of Orieltown, Pembrokeshire.

With his first wife, Frances, Trevor had two sons. Arthur was born in 1644 and died on 1 June 1661. Marcus (1645–3 June 1669), matriculated at Trinity College, Dublin, on 10 June 1661, and served as the MP for Down from November 1665 to August 1666. With his second wife Trevor had four sons. Edward died in March 1666. Lewis succeeded as second viscount. He subscribed for the publication of the fourth edition of Milton's *Paradise Lost*. He died in Spring Gardens, Middlesex, and was buried on 3 January 1692 in Kensington. John, born in Dublin in 1668, matriculated from Christ Church, Oxford, on 27 March 1686 with his brother Marcus (Mark; b. 1669). On 31 December 1687 the younger brother accidentally shot and killed his sibling and fellow student. Mark succeeded as third viscount in 1692. After Oxford he attended the Inner Temple in 1688; he had a reputation for drunkenness. Mark became a soldier as his father had and served as colonel of the foot in Spain from 1704 until his death at Alicante on 8 November 1706 from spotted fever. He had married Arabella Susanna, widow of Sir John Magill, and daughter of Hugh Hamilton of Glenawly. Their daughter Arabella, baptized on 7 February 1667, married the Hon. Henry Bertie on 17 July 1708, and died on 10 December 1708. As the peerage was limited to the male heirs she did not succeed to the title. Eventually the property passed to Arthur Hill-Trevor, Viscount Dungannon.   EDWARD M. FURGOL

Sources *CSP dom.*, 1649–77 · *CSP Ire.*, 1639–70 · *The manuscripts of the earl of Westmorland*, HMC, 13 (1885); repr. (1906) · *The manuscripts of the duke of Beaufort … the earl of Donoughmore*, HMC, 27 (1891) · GEC, *Peerage* · R. Bagwell, *Ireland under the Stuarts*, 3 vols. (1909–16) · The

Montgomery manuscripts, ed. G. Hill (1849) • C. McNeill, ed., *The Tanner letters*, IMC (1943) • H. O'Sullivan, *John Bellew, a seventeenth century man of many parts* (Dublin, 2000) • J. H. Ohlmeyer, *Civil war and Restoration in the three Stuart kingdoms: the career of Randal MacDonnell, marquis of Antrim, 1609–1683* (1993) • A. H. Dodd, *Studies in Stuart Wales* (1952) • H. O'Grady, *Strafford and Ireland: the history of his viceroyalty with an account of his trial*, 2 vols. (1923) • R. Hutton, *The royalist war effort, 1642–1646*, 2nd edn (1999) • S. Reid, *All the king's armies* (1998) • N. Tucker, *North Wales in the civil war* (1958) • P. Young, *Marston Moor* (1970) • J. I. Casaway, *Owen Roe O'Neill and the struggle for Catholic Ireland* (Philadelphia, 1984) • D. Murphy, *Cromwell in Ireland* (1885) • R. Dunlop, *Ireland under the Commonwealth*, 2 vols. (1913) • A. Clarke, *Prelude to Restoration in Ireland* (1999) • J. P. Prendergast, *Ireland from Restoration to revolution* (1887) • TCD, MS F.4.18

Archives Bodl. Oxf., Carte MSS • PRO, state papers, Ireland

Trevor, Richard (1707–1771), bishop of Durham, was born on 30 September 1707 at Peckham, Surrey, the youngest son of Thomas *Trevor, first Baron Trevor (*bap.* 1658, *d.* 1730), judge, and his second wife, Anne (*d.* 1746), the daughter of Colonel Robert Weldon and widow of Sir Robert Bernard. Trevor was educated first at Bishop's Stortford in Hertfordshire, and then at Westminster School. On 6 July 1724 he entered Queen's College, Oxford, as a gentleman commoner; he graduated BA in 1727. In November 1727 he was elected fellow of All Souls, and in 1731 received his MA; he took holy orders in the same year. In 1732 his half-brother Sir John Bernard presented him to the valuable living of Houghton-with-Wilton in Huntingdonshire. He was appointed canon of Christ Church on 8 November 1735, and proceeded DCL in 1736.

Trevor was consecrated bishop of St David's on 1 April 1744, and translated to the see of Durham on 9 November 1752. He owed the former episcopal office to the patronage of the duke of Newcastle, and the latter to Henry Pelham. However, he failed to gain promotion to the primacy when the archbishopric of Canterbury became vacant in 1758; and he was unsuccessful in his attempt to be elected chancellor of Oxford University in 1759, when his two competitors, the earls of Lichfield and Westmorland, combined their votes against him.

Trevor was actively involved in the 'improvement' of his two major places of residence: the palace of the bishops of Durham, in which he lived in summer, and the Sussex family estate where, after 1744, he spent the winter months. Thus he is said to have spent £8000 at Bishop Auckland, in order to begin the south front and build a Gothic gateway to the park. As for his other residence, Glynde Place, near Lewes, he not only improved the mansion, but also had the church rebuilt in Georgian style.

Horace Walpole and his correspondents jokingly referred to Trevor as St Durham—a jest aimed at his reputation for saintliness. His record of ecclesiastical patronage in the long Durham episcopate provides evidence of his consistent concern for the high standard expected of clerics to whom he offered preferments. A very benevolent man, Trevor bequeathed £3450 to several public charities and to the poor of the places he had lived in (PRO). The full-length portrait in oils that is preserved at Glynde Place conveys the confident image of a prelate of great human stature, though not as 'fat-bellied' (Walpole, 10.257) as Horace Walpole's correspondence suggests. Two

of Trevor's five published sermons were in support of the Hanoverian establishment in times of crisis.

Bishop Trevor, who was unmarried, died of gangrene in London on 9 June 1771, and was buried 'very privately (according to his own directions)' (Allan, 24) at Glynde in Sussex on 19 June. A monument by J. Nollekens was erected to him in the chapel at Bishop Auckland in 1775.

FRANÇOISE DECONINCK-BROSSARD

Sources R. F. Dell, ed., *The Glynde Place archives: a catalogue* (1964), xxv–vi • *GM*, 1st ser., 47 (1777), 224–6, 625–7 • G. Allan, *A sketch of the life and character of the Right Honourable and Reverend Richard Trevor lord bishop of Durham with a particular account of his last illness* (privately printed, Darlington, 1776); repr. in W. Hutchison, *The history and antiquities of the county palatine of Durham*, 1 (1785) [repr. in W. Hutchinson, *The history and antiquities of the county palatine of Durham* (1785), 1.580–88] • Walpole, *Corr.*, 5.185; 9.310, 310n.; 10.257; 20.323n. • J. C. Shuler, 'The pastoral and ecclesiastical administration of the diocese of Durham, 1721–1771: with particular reference to the archdeaconry of Northumberland', PhD diss., U. Durham, 1975 • Foster, *Alum. Oxon.* • *Old Westminsters* • Nichols, *Lit. anecdotes* • will, PRO, PROB 11/968, fols. 145–51

Archives U. Durham L., Auckland Castle episcopal records, act book • U. Durham L., AUC 1 box 8 (item 35) | BL, corresp. with duke of Newcastle, Add. MSS 32723–33088, *passim* • E. Sussex RO, Glynde Place archives

Likenesses T. Hudson, portrait, *c.*1750–1760, Glynde Place, Sussex • attrib. J. Hudson, oils, 1756, Christ Church Oxf. • T. Hudson, oils, 1756, Bishop Auckland Palace, Durham • J. Nollekens, marble statue, 1775, Auckland Castle, Durham • J. Bacon sen., marble bust, Christ Church Oxf. • J. Collyer, line engraving (after R. Hutchinson), BM; repro. in Allan, *Sketch of the life* • R. Hutchinson, engraving, repro. in Allan, *Sketch* • oils, Glynde Place, Sussex; repro. in Dell, *Glynde Place archives* • oils, All Souls Oxf.

Wealth at death £3450 to several charities: *GM*, 44 (1774); Allan, *A sketch*, 225

Trevor, Robert Hampden-, first Viscount Hampden (1706–1783), diplomatist, was born on 17 February 1706 in the parish of St Clement Danes, London. He was the third son of Thomas *Trevor, first Baron Trevor (*bap.* 1658, *d.* 1730), a judge, and the first son of his second wife, Anne (*d.* 1746), the daughter of Colonel Robert Weldon and the widow of Sir Robert Bernard. He was educated privately and at Queen's College, Oxford, whence he matriculated as gentleman commoner on 21 February 1723 and graduated BA on 20 October 1725. He was nominated fellow of All Souls on 20 November 1725. In 1729 he was appointed clerk in the secretary of state's office, and from 1734 to 1739 he was secretary of the embassy at The Hague, under Horace Walpole. In September 1739 he was appointed envoy-extraordinary, and in July 1741 was raised to the rank of minister-plenipotentiary. In February 1737 he stood as the parliamentary candidate for Oxford University, but was heavily defeated by William Bromley. He later declined another opportunity to enter the Commons when offered a seat by the duke of Newcastle in October 1743. At The Hague, on 6 February 1743, he married Constantia (*d.* 1761), the daughter of Peter Anthony de Huybert, lord of Kruyningen. They had four children: Maria Constantia, Thomas, John, and Anne.

During the whole period of Trevor's residence in the Netherlands, from 1734 to 1746, he kept up a regular and almost weekly correspondence with Walpole. The difficulties attending his position as minister became greatly increased in May 1744. The Netherlands, disaffected with its ally, became reluctant to apply itself to the war against France and Prussia with any vigour. Trevor's candid reporting of the Dutch government's dissatisfaction with the 'electoral bias' of George II's foreign policy was well received by the Pelham ministry at home, and in July 1745 he was entrusted with some delicate negotiations relating to the bribery of the ministers of the elector of Cologne, and the elector himself. In August 1745 Trevor expressed himself strongly in favour of opening peace negotiations with France, arguing that 'the only string left to our bow … before Europe is absolutely flung off its old hinges, is to try whether there may still be a party left in the French cabinet for peace' (*Buckinghamshire MSS*, 123). He therefore drew up a plan for a settlement through a preliminary treaty between France and the maritime powers. This was generally approved by the ministry, but was not adopted and led to no results, thereby making Trevor's position in the Netherlands almost untenable. It was at first intended that he should act as the British plenipotentiary at the negotiations in Breda, but Lord Sandwich was ultimately sent. On the arrival of the latter's credentials in November 1746, Trevor sent in a request for his recall. On 22 November he was promised a commissionership of the revenue in Ireland, which he received in 1750, and he left the Netherlands early in January 1747.

In 1754 Trevor, whose great-grandmother, Ruth, was the daughter of the patriot John Hampden, succeeded to the estates of John Hampden of Great Hampden, Buckinghamshire, and on 22 February of the same year he took the name of Hampden. On 2 June 1759 he was appointed joint postmaster-general, an office he held until 19 July 1765. Trevor was originally a supporter of Sir Robert Walpole, but from the accession of George III he was a close friend and follower of George Grenville. He protested against the repeal of the Stamp Act, and opposed the proceedings of the House of Commons relating to John Wilkes's election for Middlesex. On the death of his half-brother John Trevor, on 27 September 1764, he became fourth Baron Trevor of Bromham, Bedfordshire. He was created Viscount Hampden on 8 June 1776. According to Walpole, he owed his viscountcy to the influence of his son-in-law Henry Howard, twelfth earl of Suffolk (1739–1779), who had married Maria Constantia Trevor (1744–1767) on 25 May 1764 at St George's, Hanover Square. Following the death of George Grenville, Suffolk had negotiated with North the return of the remnants of the Grenville grouping to the ranks of government.

Trevor was the author of a number of Latin poems and a collector of drawings and prints. He was elected a fellow of the Royal Society on 13 December 1764. He died of palsy on 22 August 1783 at Bromham, where he was buried on 9 September. He was succeeded by his eldest son, Thomas Hampden-Trevor, second Viscount Hampden (1746–1824), who in turn was succeeded by his brother John Hampden-*Trevor, third Viscount Hampden (1748–1824), diplomatist. WILLIAM CARR, *rev.* MARTYN J. POWELL

Sources GEC, *Peerage* · J. E. Doyle, *The official baronage of England*, 3 vols. (1886) · *Memoirs of Horatio, Lord Walpole*, ed. W. Coxe, 2nd edn, 2 vols. (1808) · J. Brooke, *The Chatham administration, 1766–1768* (1956) · *The manuscripts of the earl of Buckinghamshire, the earl of Lindsey … and James Round*, HMC, 38 (1895), 1–154 · *Reports on the manuscripts of the earl of Eglinton*, HMC, 10 (1885) · D. B. Horn, ed., *British diplomatic representatives, 1689–1789*, CS, 3rd ser., 46 (1932), 163–4
Archives Bucks. RLSS, official corresp.; official corresp. relating to service at The Hague | PRO, Trevor dispatches | BL, corresp. with Lord Carteret, Add. MSS 22532–22533, 40846–40847 · BL, letters to earls of Hardwicke, Add. MSS 35407–35693 · BL, corresp. with Benjamin Keene, duke of Newcastle, Add. MSS 32701–33072 · BL, letters to Thomas Robinson and I. Dunant, Add. MSS 23792–23824 · BL, corresp. with Walter Titley, Egerton MSS 2683–2693 · BL, letters to Lord Tyrawley, Add. MSS 23628–23631 · NRA, priv. coll., corresp. with first Earl Waldegrave · U. Cal., Berkeley, Bancroft Library, letters to Lord Chesterfield · Yale U., Farmington, Lewis Walpole Library, letters to E. Weston · Yale U., Beinecke L., letters to Henry Pelham
Likenesses S. Harding, stipple, pubd *c*.1802 (after portrait by W. Gardiner), NPG · J. S. Copley, oils, Glynde Place, East Sussex · attrib. Opie, oils, Bromham House, Bedfordshire · line engraving (after a medal), BM, NPG · vignette portrait, repro. in R. Trevor, *Poematia Hampdeniana*

Trevor, Sir Sackville (1567–1635), naval officer, was the fourth son of John Trevor (*d*. 1589), landowner, of Trevalyn Hall, Trefalun, Denbighshire, and his wife, Mary Brydges, a cousin of the Sackville family. Both of his elder brothers, Sir Richard (1558–1639) and Sir John (1563–1630), enjoyed the patronage of the Howard family, Sir John beginning his career as private secretary to Lord Howard of Effingham. Sackville Trevor's younger brother, Sir Thomas *Trevor (*c*.1573–1656), was a judge. Sackville Trevor first commanded the *Sun*, in the channel guard of 1595, and in the Cadiz expedition of 1596 he commanded the *Charles*. He served under Sir Robert Mansell in the Irish guard of 1599 and from 1600 was one of Sir Richard Leveson's captains, commanding the 340 ton *Adventure* in the 3 June 1602 action which resulted in the capture of a valuable carrack at Cezimba. When Sir William Monson took over Leveson's command Trevor was made vice-admiral on 3 August 1602, serving to the end of the year. He took four prizes, valued at £4500, off the coast of Spain, for which the queen awarded him £500, still unpaid at her death, at which time Trevor was serving under Leveson and Monson in the channel squadron. James I knighted him at Chatham in 1604, and he finally received £300 for his reward in April 1605. His brother Sir John had been surveyor of the navy from 1598, but even with this connection commissions were hard to secure in the new reign. The 1608 commission of inquiry found him to be involved in the corruption prevalent in the navy. He was accused of submitting false returns of crews, sending a ship in for needless repair, accepting payments for appointments, and misappropriating funds. He firmly denied the last charge. Although these malpractices were almost universal at the time, it should not be forgotten that the inquiry was politically motivated and intended to damage the lord admiral, Howard of Effingham. Recalled to service in 1623, Trevor commanded the *Defiance* in the squadron sent to Santander to escort home Charles, prince of Wales. On

12 September Charles, having dined on board the *Prince*, returned to Santander after dark. Seeing that the wind and tide were sweeping his boat out to sea Trevor floated a buoy with a rope attached from the stern of his own ship, which the prince's party seized, rescuing Charles from a perilous situation.

Trevor had married Eleanor, *née* Savage (1557–1625), widow of Sir Henry Bagenall, in 1603 and normally resided at her house of Plas Newydd, Anglesey; he represented Anglesey in the parliament of 1625. After his wife's death in that year he married Elizabeth, *née* Brooke, widow of Kenrick Eyton. When Charles I succeeded in 1625 Trevor used the services of Lewis Bayly, bishop of Bangor and husband of his stepdaughter Anne Bagenall, to recommend himself to the king and to the duke of Buckingham, the king's favourite and a lord high admiral with reforming ambitions. Trevor became an active member of the 1626 commission to inquire into abuses in the navy. In 1627, with England at war with France and Spain, he was given command of a squadron blockading the Elbe to prevent supplies from the Baltic being sent to either country. He had to contend with mutinous conduct and with crews who not only lacked victuals but were desperately short of clothes, being in his words 'very naked' (*CSP dom.*, 1627–8, 243). He was instructed to land the small force commanded by Charles Morgan, sent to support the king of Denmark, and reported to Buckingham on 23 May that it had landed at Stade, but noted that sixty ships had left Hamburg for Spain before his squadron had arrived. The Hamburg merchants complained bitterly of the blockade, as English ships were still trading with Spain. In September 1627 the privy council instructed him to go to the Texel to take or destroy eight or ten French ships under construction there, despite English protests. On the night of 27 September he sailed along the line of Dutch ships at anchor until he found a French ship, the *St Esprit* of 800 tons and 54 guns. His ship, the *Assurance*, fired a broadside and the French vessel hastily surrendered. Although there were other French ships within 4 or 5 miles, he did not attempt to attack them and took his prize back to England, leaving Captain Alleyne in charge of the remainder of the squadron. Both Alleyne and Captain Duppa complained to the council that he could have done more, and had ignored offers of help from Dutch pilots, but most of Trevor's captains came to his support and the privy council gave him its full backing. He received the best piece of ordnance from the *St Esprit*, with the king's approval. The Dutch authorities made no protest at his action, which was the sole naval success of the period.

In April 1632 Edward Nicholas, secretary to the admiralty commissioners, consulted Trevor, with Sir Henry Mervyn, Sir Robert Mansell, and others, about the number of men required for the ships of the navy. About February 1635 Trevor, Monson, Mervyn, Mansell, and others certified that lighthouses were needed at the North and South Forelands. Trevor died in the same year and was buried at St Bride's, Fleet Street. His nephew and correspondent,

the writer James Howell, declared that the operation at the Texel was 'one of the best exploits that was performed since these wars began' (Howell, bk 1, section 5, letter 10).

RICHARD WISKER

Sources *CSP dom.*, 1603–10, 212; 1625–6, 361, 510; 1627–8, 360–62, 366–70, 372–6, 388–9; 1629–30, 463, 495, 518; 1631–2, 313, 328; 1633–4, 104 · *The naval tracts of Sir William Monson*, ed. M. Oppenheim, 1, Navy RS, 22 (1902), 359; 2, Navy RS, 23 (1902), 87–8, 167, 177, 183; 3, Navy RS, 43 (1914), 1.359; 2.87–8, 167, 177, 183; 3.354, 366, appx 3 · E. S. Jones, *The Trevors of Trevalyn* (1955), 25–6, 31–5, 49–58 [incl. family tree] · *The autobiography of Phineas Pett*, ed. W. G. Perrin, Navy RS, 51 (1918), 102, 113, 129, 146–7, 151, 221 · A. P. McGowan, ed., *The Jacobean commissions of enquiry, 1608 and 1618*, Navy RS, 116 (1971), 129, 172, 211, 248 · *APC*, 1627–8, 9, 22, 37, 88, 94 · S. R. Gardiner, *A history of England under the duke of Buckingham and Charles I, 1624–1628*, 2 (1875), 149–50 · *Collins peerage of England: genealogical, biographical and historical*, ed. E. Brydges, 9 vols. (1812) · 'Letter of Lewis Bayly', *Archaeologia Cambrensis*, 4th ser., 2 (1871), 336–8 · A. P. Palmer, *History of the old parish of Gresford* (1903) · *DWB* · J. Howell, *Epistolae Ho-elianae*, ed. J. Jacobs, 2 vols. (1890–92), bk 1, section 5, letter 10 · W. A. Shaw, *The knights of England*, 2 vols. (1906)

Archives E. Sussex RO, Glynde Place archives · Flintshire RO, Hawarden, Trevor of Plas Teg · Flintshire RO, Hawarden, Trevor of Trevalyn

Likenesses attrib. C. Johnson, oils, 1627, Glynde Place, Sussex

Wealth at death was left life interest in mansion and 100 acres, 23 March 1635: Palmer, *History of the old parish of Gresford*, 268 · was left 10s. in father's will: Jones, *The Trevors*, 26

Trevor, Sir Thomas (*c*.1573–1656), judge, was born at Trefalun in Denbighshire, the fifth and youngest son of John Trevor (*d*. 1589) of that place, and his wife, Mary, the daughter of Sir George Brydges of London; Sir Sackville *Trevor (1567–1635) was his elder brother. From 1581 he attended Shrewsbury School and after his father's death was placed in the care of Robert Sackville. After a period at the Inner Temple in November 1592, he was admitted a member of the Inner Temple in November 1592, was called to the bar in 1603, became a bencher in 1617, and was summer-vacation reader of his inn in 1620. Trevor married successively Prudence (*d*. 1615), daughter of Henry Butler; Frances (*d*. 1625), daughter and heir of Daniel Blennerhasset of Norfolk; and Ellen Poyntell (*d*. 1654), widow of Edward Allen, alderman of London.

Early in his career Trevor began to accumulate offices, becoming feodary of Surrey in 1603, an auditor for the duchy of Lancaster in 1604, steward of Windsor Castle in 1605, and deputy steward of Hampton Court by 1610; by 1611 he was solicitor-general to Prince Charles. Probably through the influence of the family of his brother John's wife, Trevor was elected MP for Tregony, Cornwall, in 1601; he represented Harwich in Essex in 1604, Newport iuxta Launceston, Cornwall, in 1614, and Saltash in Cornwall in 1621 and 1624. He was knighted at Whitehall on 19 June 1619. Although, according to William Dugdale, Trevor was not an outstanding lawyer, on 28 April 1625 he was made king's serjeant and on 10 May that year was appointed fourth baron of the exchequer in the place of George Snigge, being sworn into office on 14 May. On 17 December 1633 he was made a member of the court of high commission. On 7 February 1627 Trevor had been one of the twelve judges who returned an answer favourable to the right of the crown to collect ship money, and he followed up his opinion in 1638 by delivering judgment in favour of the government in the case of John Hampden, his niece's husband.

On the meeting of the Long Parliament proceedings were taken against the judges for their declaration in regard to ship money, and in December 1640 Trevor and four others were required to give security in £10,000 each for their appearance when called for. Trevor was impeached the following July with Sir Humphrey Davenport, after Edward Hyde (afterwards earl of Clarendon) had opened the case against them. At the outbreak of the civil war Trevor recognized the authority of parliament. He was one of the three judges who remained in London, presiding at the exchequer, while Sir Francis Bacon was alone in the king's bench and Edmund Reeve was at the common pleas. During Michaelmas term 1643 Trevor and Reeve were served with writs from King Charles requiring their attendance at Oxford, but instead of complying they committed the messengers, one of whom was afterwards executed as a spy. None the less, on 19 October 1643 Trevor was fined £6000 for his ship money judgment, and he was sentenced to imprisonment at the pleasure of the House of Lords. The fine was immediately paid, and Trevor was released and allowed to resume his place in the exchequer. He was finally freed from his impeachment on 20 May 1644.

After the execution of the king, Trevor refused to accept a new commission and he retired to Leamington Hastings in Warwickshire, having by this time acquired extensive properties in Denbighshire, Warwickshire, and Middlesex. He died on 21 December 1656 at his manor of Leamington Hastings and was buried there. His heir was his only son Thomas, from his first marriage, who was created a baronet in 1641 and who died childless on 26 February 1676, when his estate descended to Sir Charles Wheler, baronet, grandson of Trevor's sister Mary.

E. I. CARLYLE, rev. W. H. BRYSON

Sources Foss, *Judges*, 6.367–9 · M. R. Pickering, 'Trevor, Sir Thomas', HoP, *Commons, 1558–1603* · F. A. Inderwick and R. A. Roberts, eds., *A calendar of the Inner Temple records*, 5 vols. (1896–1936) · J. E. Martin, ed., *Masters of the bench of the Hon. Society of the Inner Temple, 1450–1883, and masters of the Temple, 1540–1883* (1883), 25 · *State trials*, 1125 · Baker, *Serjeants*, 182–3, 358–60, 376, 438, 541 · W. H. Bryson, *The equity side of the exchequer* (1975), 184 · W. Dugdale, *The antiquities of Warwickshire illustrated*, rev. W. Thomas, 2nd edn, 2 vols. (1730), 319 · [B. Whitelocke], *Memorials of the English affairs* (1682), 47, 76 · Sainty, *Judges*, 123 · W. R. Prest, *The rise of the barristers: a social history of the English bar, 1590–1640* (1986), 397
Archives LPL, domestic and personal accounts
Likenesses C. Johnson, oils, Glynde Place, Sussex

Trevor, Thomas, first Baron Trevor (*bap.* 1658, *d.* 1730), jurist, was baptized on 8 March 1658 at St Bartholomew-the-Less, London, the second of five sons of Sir John *Trevor (*bap.* 1624, *d.* 1672), MP and secretary of state under Charles II, and his wife, Ruth (*bap.* 1628, *d.* 1687), the daughter of the parliamentary leader John *Hampden and his wife, Elizabeth. Trevor's father was descended from an old and prominent Welsh family and his mother from a wealthy Buckinghamshire family; both his parents

had dissenting sympathies and he was sent to a school operated by the ejected presbyterian clergyman Samuel Birch in Shilton, Oxfordshire, where his classmates included Robert Harley and Simon Harcourt. He matriculated at Christ Church, Oxford, on 7 July 1673. Trevor was admitted to the Inner Temple on 1 May 1672, called to the bar on 28 November 1680, and called to the bench on 21 April 1689. He was appointed queen's attorney and king's counsel on 20 March 1689 and he was treasurer of his inn from 27 October 1689 to 26 October 1690. Trevor was named solicitor-general on 2 May 1692. He was regarded as a protégé of Attorney-General Somers, who recommended Trevor as his replacement when he became lord keeper in 1693; William III, however, chose Edward Ward for the position and a disappointed Trevor had to wait until the office next became vacant before he finally became attorney-general on 8 June 1695. In that office he actively led the prosecution of those accused of plotting to assassinate the king.

Trevor was knighted on 21 October 1692, elected to parliament on 9 November 1692 for Plympton Erle, Devon, and re-elected in 1695. In these two parliaments he generally supported the court whigs—co-sponsoring with Somers an Abjuration Bill, defending Admiral Russell, and opposing the Disbanding Bill—but he also took an independent line on occasion. In 1696 he expressed to his ministerial colleagues misgivings about proceeding against Sir John Fenwick by bill of attainder and he abstained on the bill's final reading. In 1698 he spoke passionately against the whig-initiated bill of pains and penalties against Charles Duncombe. Perhaps disillusioned with parliamentary politics, Trevor did not seek re-election in 1698, though he continued to serve as attorney-general. In 1699–1700 rumours were rife that Trevor was to be given the great seal, but he adamantly refused it, possibly because it might lose him income from a lucrative legal practice (Holmes, 124–5). He re-entered parliament—this time for Lewes, Sussex—in 1701, but served only briefly, being named lord chief justice of the common pleas on 5 July 1701. He was one of the judges who unsuccessfully advised the House of Lords in the case of *Ashby* v. *White* (1704) to support the right of the Commons to determine electors for members of parliament, seeing it as a logical extension of the Commons' right to determine its own membership.

Trevor was sworn in as a member of the privy council on 18 June 1702 and elected fellow of the Royal Society on 7 December 1707. Twice, in 1705 and 1710, he refused offers of the great seal, though he did agree to serve temporarily as first commissioner of the great seal from 26 September to 19 October 1710. He was one of the twelve new peers created at the instigation of Oxford to insure a majority in the House of Lords for the impending peace treaty and he became Baron Trevor of Bromham on 1 January 1712. These new peers were understandably criticized for being selected on grounds other than merit, a criticism that was compounded in Trevor's case by concerns about the appropriateness of a judge who was to advise the House of Lords also serving as a voting member of that body. Trevor soon became caught up in the political struggle between Oxford and Bolingbroke. Edward Harley credited Trevor with dissuading Oxford from resigning in early 1714, but by that summer Trevor seems to have become allied with Bolingbroke. In any case he fell victim to the general purge of tory office-holders that accompanied the Hanoverian accession, being removed as chief justice on 14 October 1714. For the next decade Trevor was one of the leaders of the tory opposition in the Lords: he denounced the Septennial Bill (1716) and various mutiny bills and he signed no fewer than forty-one protests. He stood by his old tory colleagues, presenting Oxford's petition to the Lords for a speedy trial (1717), opposing the bill of pains and penalties against Bishop Atterbury (1723), and supporting the restoration of Bolingbroke's estates (1725). Nevertheless, he received overtures to join the government in 1717 and again in 1721, and he eventually became lord privy seal on 11 March 1726. He was one of the regents during the absence of George I from England in 1727 and he was named lord president of the council on 8 May 1730, one month before his death.

Although he had been subject to dissenting influences in his youth Trevor became a firm Anglican, supporting the Schism Bill (1714) and the Blasphemy Bill (1721) and opposing relief for the Quakers (1722). Some, such as Lord Hervey, have seen Trevor as unprincipled as he switched from the whigs to the tories and then back again to the whigs (Hervey, 1.85), but Trevor did display principled independence in the Fenwick and Duncombe affairs opposing inflicting excessive punishment by extra-legal means, a principle consistent with both his later opposition to offering a reward for killing James Francis Edward Stuart, the Old Pretender and his avowed sentiments when defending Atterbury. Perhaps a more telling criticism is that he lacked either the self-confidence or the fortitude to take on the demands and controversies of high public offices such as the lord chancellorship. Sir Richard Onslow described Trevor as a 'most reserved, grave, and austere judge', but also 'an able and upright one' (Burnet, 4.342). Even Cowper, in recommending Trevor's removal as chief justice, acknowledged that Trevor was 'an able man', though he wryly added that as a judge Trevor had 'grown very wealthy' (Campbell, 4.349). Some of Trevor's judicial decisions have been preserved, principally in *Lord Raymond's Reports*.

Trevor married Elizabeth Searle (c.1672–1702) when she was about eighteen on 5 June 1690. They had two sons, Thomas and John, who were second and third barons Trevor respectively, and three daughters, Ann, Laetitia, and Elizabeth. Lady Trevor died in 1702 and Trevor married Anne Weldon (d. 1746), the widow of Sir Robert Bernard, on 25 September 1704. They had three sons, Robert *Trevor, the future Viscount Hampden, Richard *Trevor, who became bishop of Durham, and Edward, who died young. Trevor purchased an estate at Peckham, Surrey, shortly after the revolution of 1688 and in 1708 he paid over £21,000 for the estate of Bromham, Bedfordshire. Trevor died at his home in Peckham on the morning of 19 June 1730 from 'a sudden pain in his stomach' (*Political State of Great Britain*, 39, June 1730, 664). He was buried at the church in Bromham on 1 July, where his epitaph is inscribed on a large marble monument to him.

ROBERT J. FRANKLE

Sources Cobbett, *Parl. hist.*, vols. 5–8 · GEC, *Peerage*, new edn, vol. 12/2 · *The manuscripts of his grace the duke of Portland*, 10 vols., HMC, 29 (1891–1931), vols. 3–6 · H. Horwitz, *Parliament, policy and politics in the reign of William III* (1977) · B. W. Hill, *Robert Harley* (1988) · HoP, *Commons, 1660–90*, vol. 3 · L. Colley, *In defiance of oligarchy: the tory party, 1714–60* (1982) · *VCH Bedfordshire*, vol. 3 · *VCH Surrey*, vol. 4 · W. L. Sachse, *Lord Somers: a political portrait* (1975) · *Bishop Burnet's History*, vols. 1–4 · John, Lord Hervey, *Some materials towards memoirs of the reign of King George II*, ed. R. Sedgwick, 3 vols. (1931) · G. Holmes, *Augustan England* (1982) · J. Campbell, *Lives of the lord chancellors*, 8 vols. (1845–69), vol. 4, p. 349

Archives LPL, domestic and personal accounts | BL, letters, Portland Loan MS 29/143

Likenesses attrib. T. Murray?, oils, c.1702, NMG Wales · R. White, line engraving, 1702 (after T. Murray), BM, NPG · G. Kneller, portrait, priv. coll. · J. Sympson, line engraving, NPG

Wealth at death manors of Bromham, Carlton, Chellington, and Dylywyk in Bedfordshire, and Bredinghurst Manor, Peckham, Surrey: *VCH Bedfordshire*, 44–49, 96; *VCH Surrey*, 31; will, PRO, PROB 11/639

Trevor, William Spottiswoode (1831–1907), army officer, was born in India on 9 October 1831, the second son of Captain Robert Salusbury Trevor (d. 1841), 3rd Bengal cavalry, and his wife, Mary, youngest daughter of William Spottiswoode, laird of Glenfernate, Perthshire, Scotland. His father was one of the three officers murdered with Sir William Macnaghten at Kabul in 1841. The widow and children were held captive by Akbar Khan for nine months. After their return to England William was educated at Edinburgh Academy and at the East India Company's Addiscombe College. He was commissioned second lieutenant in the Bengal Engineers on 11 December 1849. While under professional instruction at Chatham, he was for some months on special duty at the Great Exhibition of 1851. He arrived in India in 1852 in time to take part in the Second Anglo-Burmese War; he was severely wounded in the storming and capture of the White House Picquet stockade in the operations before Rangoon on 12 April 1852, and was mentioned in dispatches. In the autumn he had sufficiently recovered to join the force under Sir John Cheape in the Danubyu district, and was present in several actions, ending with the attack on the entrenched position at Kym Kazim on 19 March 1853. For his conduct on this occasion, when he was again wounded, Trevor received the thanks of the government. He was promoted lieutenant on 1 August 1854.

After the Second Anglo-Burmese War Trevor was employed on the Pegu survey, and later on the Bassein River in Burma, with a view to constructing a sanatorium at the mouth of the river. The country was in an unsettled state and Trevor's position most insecure. Transferred in October 1857 to Bengal, he accompanied the Darjeeling field force, to intercept the mutineers of the 75th native infantry from Dacca, and engaged them at Cherabandar on the Bhutan frontier. Trevor married, on 19 June 1858, at Darjeeling, Eliza Ann (d. 1863), daughter of the Revd Henry Fisher, East India Company chaplain: they had two daughters. He was promoted captain on 27 August 1858 and was employed in the construction of the Ganges and Darjeeling Road. In 1861 he was appointed garrison engineer at Fort William, Calcutta, and converted a tract of waste land on the bank of the Hooghly into the pleasure resort known as the Eden Gardens. In February 1862 he officiated as superintending engineer of the northern circle, and completed the Ganges and Darjeeling Road to the foot of the mountains. In May 1863 he was appointed controller of accounts, and improved the method of keeping them.

In February 1865 Trevor joined the Bhutan field force as field engineer under Major-General Henry Tombs. At the attack on Dewangiri on 30 April, he and a brother officer, James Dundas, greatly distinguished themselves in forcing their way alone ahead of their Sikh soldiers into a barely accessible blockhouse, the key of the enemy's position, in which some 180 to 200 of the enemy had barricaded themselves after the rest of the position had been carried. He was suffering from illness at the time, and was five times wounded in the desperate encounter. His bravery was rewarded by the VC. After being treated at Gauhati he went on long leave of absence, and on his return became superintending engineer at the Bengal presidency. He was made brevet major on 15 May 1866.

Promoted lieutenant-colonel on 19 August 1874, Trevor was appointed special chief engineer for the famine relief works north of the Ganges. He received the thanks of the government for his work. After serving as inspector-general of military works he was transferred as chief engineer to central India, and in December 1875 was appointed chief engineer of British Burma. In this post, which he held for five years, he helped to draft a scheme for the reorganization of the engineer establishment, for which he was again thanked by the government. He was promoted brevet colonel on 19 August 1879. From February 1882 to February 1887 he was secretary to the government of India in the public works department. He retired with the honorary rank of major-general on 20 February 1887. He was a steady shot with a revolver—to which on several occasions he owed his life—an expert swordsman, and a daring rider. He died on 2 November 1907 at his home, 11 Queen's Mansions, 58 Victoria Street, Westminster, London, and was buried at Kensal Green cemetery. R. H. VETCH, rev. M. G. M. JONES

Sources royal engineers' records · *Royal Engineers Journal*, new ser., 8 (1908) · *The Times* (4 Nov 1907) · *The Times* (7 Nov 1907) · H. M. Vibart, *Addiscombe: its heroes and men of note* (1894) · BL OIOC · Burke, *Gen. GB* · private information (1912) · *WWW, 1897–1915* · Kelly, *Handbk* (1891) · Kelly, *Handbk* (1893) · *CGPLA Eng. & Wales* (1907)

Likenesses G. Brackenbury, portrait, 1901; known to be in family possession, in 1912

Wealth at death £21,310 1s. 5d.: probate, 22 Nov 1907, *CGPLA Eng. & Wales*

Trew, Ethel Mary (1869–1948), headmistress, was born on 24 April 1869 at Lilliput Hall, Oystermouth, Glamorgan, the sixth child of Thomas Trew (b. c.1830), a grocer and later a coal and corn merchant, and his wife, Ellen Mary, née Bradford (b. c.1836). Although the family was living in

Wales in the year that Ethel went to high school they considered their family home to be the Somerset village of South Petherton. She entered the new Manchester high school about 1880, and reputedly lived in lodgings nearby. She appears to have started her teaching career immediately upon leaving school, and in 1894 she was teaching mathematics at the West Cornwall College, in Penzance. There she was influenced by the charismatic headmistress Marion Waller, and when in 1894 Waller became head of Queenswood—a new Methodist girls' school in Clapham Park, London—Trew went with her as an assistant mistress. Miss Waller left the school in 1897, to marry, and Miss Trew was offered the headship. She approached the job reluctantly and seems to have realized that in accepting it she was making a choice between the school on the one hand and marriage and a family of her own on the other. Under pressure from the directors to accept she gave in: 'with a pang of sorrow I realised even then how much I was giving up' (Watson, 20). In future she channelled all her considerable dynastic ambitions and maternal feelings into the making of Queenswood.

Ethel Trew involved herself in every detail of the developing school. Whether it was the minutiae of school management (it was said that she knew the location of every piece of furniture in the school), or the spiritual (she compiled the school prayerbook), or the pastoral—as witnessed by her desire to get to know every girl personally and her habit of kissing them goodnight—she was in complete command. She became the matriarch, the school her extended family. In return for her devotion she demanded unquestioning obedience from staff and students alike.

In her early years at Queenswood Miss Trew's dynamic personality served her well. While still at Clapham Park the school was already noted for its music, but practice sessions brought complaints from the neighbours and on one occasion the matter came to court. Accompanied by several of her girls Miss Trew won the case, apparently by shamelessly charming the judge. This charm worked on fathers too and was often deployed to persuade them to enrol their daughters in higher education. Though she accepted that marriage was the likely career for the majority of her pupils she believed firmly that each should be educated to the highest level permitted by her abilities. Fathers usually gave in to her—she was furious on those rare occasions when she failed to convince them. Under her leadership the school moved in 1925 to its new, more spacious premises in Hatfield, Hertfordshire, and she presided over its building programme, characteristically devoting most attention to the chapel. She also convinced the trustees to establish a preparatory school for the youngest girls.

Miss Trew ruled over her extended surrogate family with a firm but loving hand—one girl described her as 'the benevolent despot … a bit of an emotional blackmailer' (Watson, 27). Her staff was completely at her mercy and she was known to demonstrate her power over them by belittling them in the girls' presence. Yet she was kind in time of illness or family trouble and valiant in her own conduct, surviving both a fire that destroyed her house in 1936 and a bomb that brought down her ceilings in 1944. She had endless supplies of sayings to encourage the development of character: 'find your niche and fill it', 'when you have put your hand to the plough, never turn back', and most famously, 'do your duty and a little more'. Like most teachers of her generation she placed great emphasis upon physical health, mental purity, social conscience, lady-like manners, and especially self-control. Her interest in the latter probably stemmed from her own battles to control her quick temper and impulsive tongue (ibid., 32). Some of her edicts, such as her successful ban on coughing in chapel, reflected her own formidable will-power, which kept her at her post despite frequent bouts of ill health. She recruited a talented staff and generally left them to get on with the business of teaching. Though the quality of instruction was high she never quite appreciated the importance of science teaching. However, this weakness in the curriculum did not prevent many of the girls choosing careers in nursing, although teaching was always the most common choice for Queenswood graduates.

The world moved on between the wars and Miss Trew did not. Increasingly the ageing headmistress, for all her powerful and contradictory charm, was losing touch with the realities of running a modern school. In 1935, under pressure from the trustees, she appointed an assistant headmistress, but allowed her little power. Though she had built a small house for her retirement (on the school estate) she was emotionally too involved with the school to be able to give it up. Her retirement was accomplished in slow and painful stages. She ceded the academic side of the school to her successor in 1943 but kept control of the domestic, social, and spiritual side. She also maintained control of the management of the estate even after she had formally retired in 1944. This proved disastrous, since a plausible estate manager cheated the school. Her final resignation took place in September 1948. She died shortly afterwards, at her home, Mymfield, Kentish Lane, Hatfield, on 7 December 1948 and was buried at South Petherton.

Memoirs of Miss Trew focus on her personality and her sayings rather than on her actions, for it was through the former that she exercised influence. Small in stature, she was nevertheless imposing. With her elegant furs and clothing (she favoured purple) she projected a regal dignity and was often likened to Queen Mary: 'she used to sail around the school' accompanied by her two Cairn terriers (Watson, 24). She had a distinctive voice, rather sharp, with the dropped 'h' peculiar to the west country. She was imperious, charming, cruel when crossed or angered, kind, generous, and unexpectedly forthright and practical. Her rule was benevolent but absolute—when she spoke of 'my girls', 'my staff', and 'my school' she meant precisely what she said (ibid., 22). Her tragedy was in staying on too long when changing times and her own failing powers of judgement let her down. In her prime she could madden with her certainties and her imperious manner,

but she built a modern school, working within a social system that often limited girls' opportunities, using her force of personality to create openings for those who showed promise, and moulding her pupils to fit happily into the world as she found it. She subordinated her entire personality to the school and it is not unreasonable to say that for fifty years Ethel Trew was Queenswood.

ELIZABETH J. MORSE

Sources N. Watson, *In hortis reginæ: the story of Queenswood School, 1894–1994* (1994) · H. M. Stafford, *Queenswood: the first sixty years, 1894–1954* (1954) · b. cert. · d. cert. · census returns, 1881
Likenesses photograph, 1890–94, repro. in Watson, *In hortis reginæ*, 22 · F. Salisbury, oils, *c.*1946, Queenswood School, Hertfordshire; repro. in Watson, *In hortis reginæ*, 25 · photograph, repro. in Watson, *In hortis reginæ*, 20
Wealth at death £35,709 12s. 2d.: probate, 21 Feb 1949, *CGPLA Eng. & Wales*

Trew, John (*fl.* 1563–1590), engineer, whose early life is unknown, was first referred to in the 1560s as a gentleman of Glamorgan; in December 1582 he described himself as 'an old man worn owt in service' (PRO, SP 12/219, no. 52).

Trew is known to have built one of the earliest English canals. In September 1563 he signed a contract with the corporation of Exeter to build a 'Haven' so that boats carrying 10 tons could reach Exeter on all tides rather than having to unload at Topsham and carry the goods to Exeter by land. By 1566–7 the haven, a lateral canal 3110 yards long down the western side of the Exe valley, was complete. The work included the construction of three pound locks, the first such in England. Each lock was of a sufficient size to hold several boats at any one time, and the upper lock was large enough to act as a dock. After completion Trew was not paid immediately, for there were complaints that the canal could be entered only on high tides, and there were problems with silting. It was not until 1573, after litigation, that a settlement was reached whereby Trew received a cash payment of £224 and an annuity of £30, but not the right to monopoly carriage originally agreed.

During this dispute Trew petitioned William Cecil, Lord Burghley, complaining of his mistreatment and financial hardship, and cited his various skills. These included the draining of mines or marshes, the supply of water to towns, the recycling of water to power mills, the construction of canals, the knowledge of where there were deposits of copper and alum, and hints about a secret weapon of war. He also noted a machine to raise great weights 'as I gave the example in Ireland' (BL, Lansdowne MS 107, no. 73), but nothing else has been discovered of his sojourn there. It is also known that in 1576 he was one of the founders of an ironworks at Pont-y-moel in Monmouthshire.

Trew was soon to be employed on projects encouraged by the privy council. He was probably the 'Mr Trewe' who was paid £6 13s. 4d. in 1579 for supervising major repairs to the only other English pound lock, that at Waltham Abbey on the River Lea, built in 1577 as part of an important river improvement scheme (PRO, SP 15/27, no. 6). Soon afterwards he was employed on the improvement of Dover harbour, but his reputation was to suffer as a result. In August 1580 he was already surveyor of the works after submitting the cheapest proposals to the commissioners. He was hired at 10s. a day 'for we could not bring him with good will to take less' (PRO, SP 12/141, no. 36), but within a year a damning report was submitted by Thomas Digges (d. 1595). This criticized Trew's supervision of the hewing of stone at Folkestone, the foundations he had laid for the sea wall at Dover, and the overall conception of the project, on the grounds that his proposed wall was badly placed with regard to the tides. Holinshed's chronicles were to repeat this assessment, and such criticism led to Trew's dismissal and the use of others instead.

Soon afterwards, in December 1582, Trew petitioned Elizabeth I, offering his services in any impending war. He mentioned two inventions, one a type of gun or cannon, the other a shield to be driven before advancing troops; but he also took the opportunity to mention the machinations of unjust persons who had harmed him and his family, and asked for an office with a wage or pension 'to releve myne old yeares'. This is the last documented reference to John Trew (PRO, SP 12/219, no. 52). His career does not seem to have been particularly successful, but he was an early example of British expertise at a time when most engineering skills were imported; and he does deserve better than the description 'a crazy projector' afforded him in the Lansdowne Manuscripts catalogue (*Catalogue of the Lansdowne Manuscripts*, no. 107/73, 206). Nothing is known about his family life or when he died.

K. R. FAIRCLOUGH

Sources P. C. de la Garde, 'On the antiquity and invention of the lock canal of Exeter', *Archaeologia*, 28 (1840), 7–26 · P. C. de la Garde, 'Memoirs of the canal of Exeter from 1563 to 1724', *PICE*, 4 (1845), 90–102 · W. Rees, *Industry before the industrial revolution*, 2 vols. (1968) · K. R. Fairclough, 'The Waltham pound lock', *History of Technology*, 4 (1979), 31–44 · *Holinshed's chronicles of England, Scotland and Ireland*, ed. H. Ellis, 4 (1808), 854–68 · PRO, SP 12/219, no. 52 · PRO, SP 15/27, no. 6 · PRO, SP 12/141, no. 36 · PRO, SP 12/219, no. 52 · BL, Lansdowne MSS · H. Ellis and F. Douce, eds., *A catalogue of the Lansdowne manuscripts in the British Museum*, 1 (1812), 206 · A. Hasenson, *The history of Dover harbour* (1980), 26–32 · W. B. Stephens, 'The Exeter lighter canal, 1566–1698', *Journal of Transport History*, 3 (1957–8), 1–11
Archives BL, Lansdowne MSS · PRO, state papers, 12/219 no. 52 · PRO, court of exchequer, E178/1518 no. 52

Trewavas, Ethelwynn (1900–1993), ichthyologist, was born on 5 November 1900 in Penzance, Cornwall, the eldest of four children (three girls and a boy) of Benjamin James Trewavas (1869–1960), surveyor of borough revenues in Penzance and a Wesleyan Methodist lay preacher, and his wife, Sarah, *née* Hutchings (1877–1964), a primary schoolteacher; both were of Cornish stock. Her schooling in Penzance, at St Paul's infants' school (1905–9) and West Cornwall College for Girls (1909–17), encouraged her interest in natural history and her attendance at Reading University College (1917–21), where she graduated with honours in zoology and a Board of Education certificate in teaching. But she preferred research to schoolteaching, and in 1925 she was awarded a London University research scholarship; this she held at King's College

for Women. After consultation with C. Tate Regan at the British Museum (Natural History) she studied the anatomy of frogs; she was made a London DSc in 1934.

Tate Regan, when appointed director of the British Museum (Natural History), in 1928, engaged Trewavas as his research assistant; together they described, in a paper published in *Oceanographic Reports* in 1932, deep-sea angler fishes collected by the Danish expedition in which J. Schmidt established the life history of the European eel. In 1935 Trewavas was one of the first three women appointed to the established staff of the museum. Her work as assistant keeper entailed naming and incorporating into the national collection fishes collected from many parts of the world. This required constant revision of fish classification and entailed field expeditions to study fish biology, but Trewavas always made time to help a constant stream of visitors to the museum—scientists, students, fisheries officers, and aquarists—in addition to being active on various committees. Her whole research life was devoted to ichthyology, based at the British Museum (Natural History) where her happy disposition made her a stimulating colleague. She was deputy keeper (zoology) from 1958 until her official retirement in 1961 but she continued her research at the museum—renamed the Natural History Museum in 1963—until her death.

In 1935 Trewavas's museum study of fishes collected on the Christy expedition to lakes Nyasa and Tanganyika in 1925–6 led to a lifelong interest in the evolution of cichlid fishes in African lakes. In 1938–9 she spent several months on Lake Nyasa as a member of the fisheries survey mounted by the Colonial Office as part of a nutrition survey, which laid the foundations for post-war studies. During the Second World War she helped to evacuate the museum's collections from London, to escape air raids. She was also honorary secretary of the Council of Women Civil Servants, which campaigned for removal of the marriage bar for women in government and the civil service, for equal opportunities, and for equal pay for equal work—objectives achieved after the war.

Appointed a member of the fisheries advisory committee to the secretary of state for the colonies in 1945 Trewavas helped to train fishery officers for overseas appointments, which led to African visits. In 1947 she spent two months in Nigeria attached to the Fisheries Development Unit, where she became interested in mullets and sciaenid fishes, both of economic importance. In 1965 she made an extensive tour in east and central Africa. In 1970 she investigated cichlid biology in Cameroon crater lakes. She was the world authority on tilapiine cichlid fishes, important in fish culture throughout the tropics. After her official retirement this work culminated in her definitive monograph on these fishes, *Tilapiine Fishes of the Genera Sarotherodon, Oreochromis and Danakilia* (1983). She then continued her 'unfinished' studies of Malawian cichlids by completing a book on these—*Malawian cichlid Fishes, the Classification of some haplochromine genera* (1989)—with the collaboration of David Eccles, a herculean task, as her eyesight was then deteriorating.

Trewavas (Wyn or E. T., as she was affectionately known

by her colleagues) was a member of many scientific societies and served on the councils of the Freshwater Biological Association and the Systematics Association. She was an honorary member of the American Society of Ichthyologists and Herpetologists and of the American Museum of Natural History, and honorary president of the British Cichlid Association. The Linnean Society awarded her their gold medal in 1968 and elected her a fellow *honoris causa* in 1991, the year that the University of Stirling gave her an honorary doctorate. More than a dozen fish species were named in her honour. She set the highest standards of scholarship. During her active scientific career of over sixty years she published more than 120 scientific papers and books and described over 460 fish taxa. While always neat and meticulous, distinguished since her twenties by a halo of silver hair, with a keen but kindly wit and great lucidity of expression, she completed much of her research purely for the interest and fun of it. She never married. In later life she shared a house with her musical sister, Sylvia March, in Tilehurst, near Reading. There former colleagues enjoyed visiting her, for she remained very alert and receptive of new ideas, despite declining hearing and eyesight. She enjoyed music and doing crossword puzzles. She died at her home, Pincents Hill House, Calcot, Tilehurst, of heart failure on 16 August 1993 and was cremated at Reading on 20 August.

ROSEMARY LOWE-MCCONNELL

Sources D. L. G. Noakes, 'The life and work of Ethelwynn Trewavas', *Environmental Biology of Fishes*, 41 (1994), 33–65 [repr. in E. K. Balon, M. N. Bruton, and D. L. G. Noakes, eds., *Women in ichthyology* (1994)] · *The Times* (25 Aug 1993) · *The Independent* (21 Aug 1993) · *The Guardian* (31 Aug 1993) · personal knowledge (2004) · private information (2004) [P. Corbet, S. Corbet]
Archives NHM, papers, specimens, and notebooks
Likenesses photographs, repro. in Noakes, 'Life and work'

Trewin, John Courtenay (1908–1990), writer and drama critic, was born on 4 December 1908 at 15 Woodford Villas, Plymouth, Devon, the only son of Captain John Trewin (1858–1932), master mariner, and his wife, Annie James (1865–1942). Both parents were natives of Cornwall, and with two older sisters he spent his childhood at Kynance Bay House at the tip of the Lizard peninsula, a windswept and sea-girt environment which forever haunted his imagination and inspired a lifelong allegiance to all things Cornish. Educated at Landewednack School, Hoe grammar school and, from 1920, Plymouth College, he secured his first employment in 1926 as a cub reporter with the *Western Independent*, covering the full gamut of local events, including performances at the Plymouth Repertory Theatre and Theatre Royal.

Moving to London in December 1932, Trewin joined the editorial staff of the *Morning Post*, realizing a youthful ambition by becoming an accredited drama critic as second to S. R. Littlewood. On the *Post*'s closure in 1937 he was engaged by *The Observer*, where he again served as deputy reviewer to Ivor Brown and, from 1943 to 1948, as literary editor as well. Over the following decades his preoccupation with the theatre progressively intensified; by 1983 he reckoned he had reviewed some 7000 performances. In addition to a radio drama column for *The Listener* (1951–7), he contributed regular notices to *Punch* (1944–5), *John O'London's* (1945–54), *The Sketch* (1947–59), the *Illustrated London News* (1947–88), and to *The Lady* (from 1949) and the *Birmingham Post* (from 1955) until shortly before his death. He rarely missed a West End first night. Arriving early by tube from his home in Hampstead, he would remain resolutely in his seat throughout the performance as if loath to dispel its atmosphere by the companionship of colleagues or the stalls bar. He was invariably accompanied by his wife, Wendy Elizabeth Monk (1915–2000), whom he had first met in the Plymouth newsroom and married on 4 October 1938. An inseparable couple, whose shared interests also bore fruit in literary collaboration, they had two sons, Ion (*b*. 1943) and Mark Antony (*b*. 1949).

Alongside a busy journalistic career Trewin found time to produce almost a hundred books, as author, co-author or editor. A voracious reader as a child, he wrote stylishly on a range of subjects, from topography to biography (or autobiography) and theatre history. Notable publications in these areas are his *Up from the Lizard* (1948) and *Down to the Lion* (1952), which intertwine evocation of landscape with personal memoir, *Portrait of the Shakespeare Country* (1970), and two colourful miscellanies entitled *The West Country Book* (1949, 1981); his biographical studies of William Macready (1955)—whose journal he also edited (1967)—Robert Donat (1968), and Peter Brook (1971), and his critical monographs on Edith Evans (1954), Sybil Thorndike (1955), Paul Scofield (1956), Alec Clunes (1958), and John Neville (1961); his *The Shakespeare Memorial Theatre* (with M. C. Day, 1932), *The Night has been Unruly* (1957), *Benson and the Bensonians* (1960), *The Pomping Folk in the Nineteenth-Century Theatre* (1968), and *The Edwardian Theatre* (1976). Still more of his output was devoted to the theatre of his own time, his extensive reviewing experience underpinning a synoptic appraisal of the contemporary scene, as in *The Theatre since 1900* (1951), *Dramatists of Today* (1953), *The Gay Twenties* (1958), *The Turbulent Thirties* (1960), *The Birmingham Repertory Theatre, 1913–1963* (1963), *The Arts Theatre, London, 1927–81* (with Wendy Trewin, 1986), *Five & Eighty Hamlets* (1987), and a number of books on modern Shakespearian production, among them *The Stratford Festival* (with T. C. Kemp, 1953), *Shakespeare on the English Stage, 1900–1964* (1964), *Shakespeare's Plays Today* (with A. C. Sprague, 1970) and *Going to Shakespeare* (1978). He also wrote plays for children, poetry, and numerous short stories, compiled several anthologies, and edited many volumes of *Plays of the Year*.

If the success of Trewin's books owed much to their judicious combination of scholarship with journalistic readability, his long spell as a critic was sustained by an unalloyed passion for theatre in all its forms, a sense of excitement as the house lights dimmed, instinct with a perennial hope that something interesting was about to happen. His most characteristic gift was an ability to communicate the precise visual and vocal texture of a performance, particularly an actor's performance—'the quality of speech', he argued, 'is more important than a piece of furniture' (*Five & Eighty Hamlets*, 178)—while his encyclopaedic power of recall for performances past, which lent balance and authority to his discriminating comments on the present, endeared him to the profession. His gentlemanly avoidance of the supercilious or sardonic review—which serves the critic's interests more than his subject's—did little to advance his career in Fleet Street, but appropriate recognition came in other ways: his election to fellowship of the Royal Society of Literature (1954), presidency of the Critics' Circle (1964–5), an honorary MA degree from the University of Birmingham (1978), and in 1981 he was appointed OBE for services to the theatre. Continuously active before suffering a stroke in December 1989, he died in London at the Royal Free Hospital, Hampstead, on 16 February 1990; and was cremated at Golders Green on 23 February.

DONALD ROY

Sources J. C. Trewin, *Up from the Lizard* (1948) · J. C. Trewin, *Down to the Lion* (1952) · J. C. Trewin, 'When you've seen 7000 performances', *Plays and Players*, 353 (Feb 1983), 19–20 · private information (2004) [Ion Trewin] · *The Guardian* (20 Feb 1990), 39 · *The Independent* (23 Feb 1990), 20 · *The Times* (19 Feb 1990), 2 · *The Times* (20 Feb 1990), 14 · *The Times* (23 Feb 1990), 14 · *WWW, 1981–90* · I. Herbert, ed., *Who's who in the theatre*, 1 (1981) · K. Webb, ed., *Christopher Fry: an experience of critics, and the approach to dramatic criticism* (1952) · C. Fry, 'Writers remembered: J. C. Trewin', *The Author* (summer 1990), 57 · P. Hartnoll, ed., *The concise Oxford companion to the theatre* (1972), 562 · J. R. Taylor, *The Penguin dictionary of the theatre* (1966), 272 · *CGPLA Eng. & Wales* (1990) · b. cert. · m. cert.
Archives U. Reading L., notebooks and typescripts · U. Reading L., notebooks, reviews, and papers | Bodl. Oxf., letters to Jack Lambert and Catherine Lambert
Likenesses R. Searle, ink drawing, 1953, repro. in J. C. Trewin, *The gay twenties* (1958), jacket; priv. coll. · photograph, *c*.1980, repro. in Trewin, 'When you've seen 7000 performances' · R. Searle, caricature, priv. coll.; repro. in Webb, ed., *Christopher Fry: an experience of critics* · photograph, repro. in *The Times* (20 Feb 1990) · photograph, repro. in Fry, 'Writers remembered'
Wealth at death £103,294: probate, 6 June 1990, *CGPLA Eng. & Wales*

Trewman, Robert (1738/9–1802), printer and newspaper proprietor, was probably born in Exeter. Details of his parentage are unclear, but the name Trewman is recorded in Exeter from at least the sixteenth century. He was apprenticed to Andrew Brice, the printer of the *Exeter Journal*, for seven years but in 1763 he and Brice's foreman William Andrews quarrelled violently with their master and left him to establish the *Exeter Mercury*, the first issue of which appeared 2 September 1763 from 'the house late the Mitre Tavern in Southgate Street'. In November 1765 Andrews moved to Plymouth, leaving Trewman as sole proprietor of the newspaper which from 1770, after several changes of title, became known as *Trewman's Exeter Flying Post*. On 23 December 1765 Trewman married Mary (*bap*. 1747), the daughter of Zachary and Mary Turner, at St Edmund's Church. They had six sons and seven daughters, the eldest son being Robert, born in 1767, who was taken into partnership in 1790. Mary Trewman died on 24 December 1817.

In December 1764 the premises of the newspaper moved to Waterbeer Street and to the High Street in September 1781. The relocation reflected the growing status and prosperity of Trewman's business, a feature common to many late-eighteenth-century provincial newspapers. In December 1791 he acquired and closed the *Old Exeter Journal*, which had been run by the Brice family. Aside from his newspaper Trewman ran a bookshop which became one of the meeting places of the Exeter literati. He was also a lottery and insurance agent and a proprietor of the Exeter Theatre, being one of those responsible for its rebuilding in Bedford Circus in 1787. He was a leading freemason and author of *The Principles of Freemasonry Delineated*, which he published himself in 1777. He also edited *The Antient History and Description of the City of Exeter* (1765) based on the work of the sixteenth-century antiquary John Hooker and other authorities. A specially bound copy of this work was presented to George III when he visited Exeter in 1789. In 1796 Trewman published *Essays by a Society of Gentlemen at Exeter*, with contributions from the leading scholars in the city, including the historian Richard Polwhele, whose *History of Devonshire* was printed by the Trewmans in three volumes between 1793 and 1806. Trewman also saw through the press the works of many other prominent local authors, for example the poets William Kendall, Hugh Downman, and Joseph Reeve. Trewman's bookshop held a wide-ranging stock, including the works of Thomas Paine before that author was burned in effigy at Exeter; but by 1793 Trewman was printing for the loyalist Constitutional Society. Following his death in Exeter aged sixty-three, on 20 February 1802, after a long illness, he was described as 'a zealous supporter of our present happy Constitution in Church and State' (*Exeter Flying Post*, 25 Feb 1802). He was buried in Bartholomew churchyard. The newspaper was continued 'as a respectable high and dry Tory organ' (Dymond, 'Flying Post', 165) by his widow with his son Robert (*d*. 1816) and then by his grandson Robert James Trewman (*d*. 1860), after which it transferred to James Bellerby. It finally ceased publication in 1917.

IAN MAXTED

Sources R. Dymond, 'Trewman's Exeter Flying Post', *Western Antiquary*, 5/8 (1886), 163–6 · G. Oliver, 'Biography of Exonians, no. 38', *Trewman's Exeter Flying Post* (29 Nov 1849) · I. Maxted, *The Devon book trades: a biographical dictionary* (1991), 132–3 · R. Newton, *Eighteenth-century Exeter* (1984), 121 · R. Dymond, 'Exeter and neighbourhood under George the Third', *Trewman's Exeter Flying Post* (1 Jan 1879) · R. N. Worth, 'Notes on the history of printing in Devon', *Report and Transactions of the Devonshire Association*, 11 (1879), 503–5 · T. N. Brushfield, 'Andrew Brice and the early Exeter newspaper press', *Report and Transactions of the Devonshire Association*, 20 (1888), 163–214, esp. 199 · C. E. Lugard, *The family of Trewman of Exeter* (1947) · *Trewman's Exeter Flying Post* (25 Dec 1817)
Archives Westcountry Studies Library, publisher's file of *Exeter Flying Post*

Trickett, Sir Henry Whittaker (1857–1913), slipper manufacturer, was born on 23 July 1857 at Miller Barn Lane, Newchurch, Waterfoot, in the Rossendale valley, Lancashire, the eldest of five children of Henry Whittaker Trickett (1831–1904), a journeyman woollen carpet printer, and his wife, Alice, *née* Whittaker (1832–1886). At eight years of age, after a very brief education at the local church school, he went to work for his uncle, Joshua Trickett, who ran a small felt-printing works a mile or so from Waterfoot. Starting as a 'tier' boy, supplying printers with colours, he subsequently completed a five-year apprenticeship at the age of twenty-two. Meantime, at Bethel Baptist Church, Waterfoot (where he was baptized on 7 January 1877, and where he later served as deacon, Sunday school superintendent, treasurer, and trustee), he met Elizabeth Alice, daughter of John Ormerod, a cotton weaver; they were married on 23 January 1879.

The Greenbridge carpet works, where Trickett worked, hit hard times, and his career took a different turn. In 1881 he became a commercial traveller for Gregory & Co., one of the small slipper manufacturing concerns which had sprung up in the Waterfoot area in the 1870s and originated from the crude slippers of waste felt worn by block-printers for walking on carpets in the process of manufacture. Trickett stayed with Gregory & Co. for less than two years, crucially learning that the footwear industry (then mainly concerned with boots and shoes) had entered a period of revolutionary change. Large-scale factory production, the emergence of wholesale and retail networks, the rising purchasing power of the working and middle classes, the possibilities of attaining volume sales in mass markets: such developments persuaded Trickett to set up on his own in 1882.

Trickett borrowed £75 from relatives and rented an old weaving shop, measuring barely 10 by 15 yards, and with six employees started making slippers. A vigorous marketing campaign brought orders from all parts of the country. All profits were invested in specialized machinery or stocks of material. Within about twelve months Henry Trickett employed over sixty people. In 1889 he purchased Gaghills Mill, a large disused cotton mill in Burnley Road, Waterfoot, where he installed the latest American machinery: power presses, high-speed sewing machines, heel-fixing machinery. An export drive expanded his sales into Europe (previously supplied by German manufacturers) and the Far East. A decade later he leased the latest machinery from the newly formed and monopolistic British United Shoe Machinery Company. By 1900 the Gaghills factory, with a labour force of about 1000 people, was producing 72,000 pairs of slippers monthly. In 1913 1200 employees produced 2.5 million pairs of slippers annually. Others emulated Trickett, who was widely known as the Slipper King. By 1893 there were ten slipper firms in the Rossendale district and by 1900 thirteen, none of which failed before 1914. However, Trickett's was the largest firm, employing a third of all the district's slipper workers in 1900. Trickett paid close attention to design, new materials, and marketing, including eye-catching and humorous advertisements. He set up a chain of sales offices and depots across the UK, the white-dominated parts of the British empire, and the USA.

Trickett genuinely cared for his workers and for Rossendale. Continuity of employment, payment of better than average wages, and provision of clean working conditions, refreshment rooms, medical facilities, a training school, sick (1893) and holiday (1897) clubs, and a bowling green and gardens next to the mill—as well as a terrace of houses and an arcade of shops in Waterfoot—enhanced Trickett's good reputation, eased his labour relations, and facilitated the introduction of new machinery.

Trickett became a Liberal town councillor for Rawtenstall (of which Waterfoot was part) in 1891, and between 1898 and 1902 he served a record five times as mayor of the borough, being elected alderman in 1900. He declined offers to stand as a parliamentary candidate (supporting Sir William Mather's candidature in 1900) but between 1901 and 1913 he served variously as president of the Rossendale Liberal Association, vice-president of the Lancashire and Cheshire Free Trade League, vice-president of the Lancashire and Cheshire Liberal Federation, and JP. He was knighted in 1909.

Management of his business was entrusted by Trickett to five senior employees to whom he gave a share of net profits. In 1901 the firm was registered as H. W. Trickett Ltd. Trickett relinquished sole ownership for £5335 in cash, £40,000 in 5 per cent cumulative preference shares, and 31 per cent of the issued ordinary share capital of £18,100. His managers bought shares. However, Trickett retained control by limiting share sales and preserving the lifetime right to appoint and dismiss his fellow directors. Trickett died suddenly at the age of fifty-six on 3 August 1913, and was buried in the Baptist graveyard, Waterbarn. He was survived by his wife and two daughters and left an estate valued at £120,907 gross.

DAVID J. JEREMY

Sources C. E. Harvey and D. J. Jeremy, 'Trickett, Sir Henry Whittaker', *DBB* · C. Aspin, 'The slipper king', *Mr Pilling's short cut to China and other stories of Rossendale enterprise* (1983), 65–9 · Lambert Howarth Group History, Lambert Howard PLC · company papers, Newchurch Boot Co, Waterfoot, Rossendale · PRO, Company Registration Office file BT 31 9597/71316 · m. cert. · private information (2004) · W. Arnold, *Bethel Baptist Church and Sunday school* (1954) · R. A. Church, 'The effect of the American export invasion on the British boot and shoe industry', *Economic History Review*, 2nd ser., 18 (1968) · P. Cronkshaw, 'An industrial romance of the Rossendale valley: the development of the shoe and slipper industries', *Transactions of the Lancashire and Cheshire Antiquarian Society*, 60 (1948), 29–46 · W. H. Fraser, *The coming of the mass market, 1850–1914* (1981) · P. Head, 'Boots and shoes', *The development of British industry and foreign competition, 1875–1914*, ed. D. H. Aldcroft (1968) · J. B. Jeffreys, *Retail trading in Britain* (1954) · J. G. Ketchen, 'The art and industry of slipper manufacture', *Gentleman's Journal* (1919) · 'Miss Trickett's coming of age: workpeople's gift at Gaghills', *Rossendale Free Press* (24 Aug 1912) · 'Sir Henry Whittaker Trickett: brief summary of his public and business career', *Rossendale Free Press* (13 Nov 1909) · 'The Sir H. W. Trickett Memorial', *Rossendale Free Press* (13 June 1914) · 'The Sir H. W. Trickett Memorial', *Rossendale Free Press* (20 June 1914) · *WWW*

Archives Rawtenstall Public Library, Rossendale collection, booklets and newspaper cuttings relating to Trickett and his firm
Likenesses photograph, repro. in Ketchen, 'Art and industry'
Wealth at death £120,907 7s. 3d.: probate, 25 Oct 1913, *CGPLA Eng. & Wales*

Trigge, Francis (1547?–1606), Church of England clergyman and writer on social issues, was probably born in Lincolnshire. He matriculated from University College, Oxford, in 1564, graduating BA on 16 February 1569 and MA on 12 May 1572. After taking priest's orders he was appointed rector of Welbourn in Lincolnshire some time before 1589. He married a daughter of Elizabeth Hussey 'of Hunnington', probably the widow of John Hussey of Harrington (W. C. Metcalfe, ed., *The Visitation of the County of Lincoln*, 1592, 69).

While in Lincolnshire Trigge devoted considerable attention to social and economic changes in the country. In 1594 he published *A Godly and Fruitfull Sermon Preached at Grantham 1592*, in which he reproved the commercial practices and values of the time. The treatise revives the prophetic tone and biblical moralism favoured by mid-sixteenth-century protestant reformers, such as Bishop Hugh Latimer and Robert Crowley. Also like the early protestants, Trigge maintained a conservative moral position on a range of related social and economic issues; for example, he opposed all forms of usury, and criticized those who sought to stray from their vocations. This was followed in 1604 by a work entitled *To the kings most excellent majestie, the humble petition of two sisters, the church and Common-wealth for the restoring of their ancient commons and liberties*, a vehement protest against the enclosure of common lands and the conversion of arable land into pasture. Trigge denounced the moral turpitude of such proceedings, and argued forcefully against the depopulation of rural villages. He wrote: 'I have heard an old prophecy, that horn and thorn shall make England forlorn. Enclosers verify this by their sheep and hedges at this day' (sig. D5r).

Besides the works of social criticism, Trigge wrote a number of other texts, in English and Latin, mainly devoted to religious commentary and controversy. Though not closely associated with an Elizabethan puritan movement, he passionately defended the achievements of the Reformation in England, and maintained the Reformation tradition of anti-Catholic polemic. For example, his *An apologie, or, Defence of our dayes, against the vaine murmurings and complaints of manie: wherein is … proved that our dayes are more happie … than the dayes of our forefathers* (1589), presents a sustained celebration of English protestantism.

Trigge was the founder and principal benefactor of the chained library in St Wulfram's Church, Grantham, established in 1598, and now containing about 300 books. The original collection was kept in a chamber over the south porch of Grantham church, and on the wall of the library were formerly some verses recording the gift (B. Street, *Historical Notes on Grantham*, 1857, 157). Trigge died in 1606 at Welbourn and was buried on 12 May in the chancel of the church.   E. I. CARLYLE, rev. ANDREW McRAE

Sources Wood, *Ath. Oxon.*, new edn, 1.759–60 · Foster, *Alum. Oxon.* · J. Thirsk, *The rural economy of England* (1984), 162–3 · A. McRae, *God speed the plough: the representation of agrarian England, 1500–1660* (1996), 71–2

Trigge, Stephen (*fl.* 1660–1690). *See under* Trigge, William (*fl.* 1630–1656).

Trigge, William (*fl.* 1630–1656), empiric, whose origins are obscure, was one of the best-known unlicensed medical practitioners in London and a thorn in the side of the medical and political authorities. The censors' board of the London College of Physicians first heard of the illicit practice of this shoemaker, then living near Coal harbour, on 10 December 1630. When, on 28 January, he appeared at the college to answer the complaint he claimed to be a 'servant to the Queen' (later changed to a servant of God), although also allowing that he practised in cases of rickets, dysentery, gout, and plague, which was then epidemic. The censors solemnly warned him not to practise again, but he plainly continued to do so despite his pledge to obey, since a few months later Mrs Goodridge testified that he had practised on her husband, charging far more than she could afford (20s., with 40 more to be paid upon cure). The censors fined Trigge £10 and confined him to the compter in Wood Street until he paid. On 23 September and 14 October 1631 a surgeon, Mr Cooke, reported to the physicians that Trigge had given a clyster and a cordial, followed by a vomit, to one Mrs Barnabye, who subsequently died. This time Trigge was fined £25 and confined to the Fleet prison until he paid; somehow by early 1632 he had managed to get the warden of the Fleet to let him out, whereupon the two men who had stood surety for him (Phillip Tiller and William Key) were forced to take his place. In June the censors finally forced the warden himself to pay most of Trigge's fine (£20). But, living near the Tower, he continued to practise, and to be complained of.

Toward the end of another plague epidemic, on 10 March 1637, Trigge was accused by Dr Daniel Oxenbridge of having killed one of his patients. Trigge had attempted to cure one Widow Thompson, who had suffered from hydropsy, by paracentesis (inserting a drain), but the patient died fourteen days after Trigge's first ministrations. The college determined to end his practice once and for all, but they had difficulty forcing him to appear. The censors obtained a warrant from the privy council to force him to come before them, but it was his wife who came to a meeting of the censors' board on 5 May to plead for leniency, stating that although he had begun as a shoemaker, 'now he made profession only of distilling waters, and that he did use to give certain powders, and Cordials to such as were infected with the plague' (annals, RCP Lond.). Not satisfied, the censors took further testimony against Trigge's bungling from a surgeon, Henry Aron, on 20 October. The privy council also heard the affidavit of the college's beadle, George Brome, on 1 December, complaining that when presented with the council's warrant Trigge reviled Brome, the warrant, and the college. Finally, on 10 January 1638, a messenger from the privy council brought Trigge in tow to answer the censors. Trigge claimed to have learned how to manage the hydropsy case from witnessing a midwife, Mrs Nokes, dissect the body of someone who had died of dropsy. Besides which, he said, the 'doctor', John Pordage (a minister, and later Behminist), was present. 'Butt the Censors judge it a bold dangerous and unlawfull practise for which they committed him to Newgate and fined him £20' (ibid.). His wife appeared before the censors again on 19 January, explaining that Trigge began to practise physic four years after coming from Canterbury to London, out of necessity, especially by making pills and electuaries, particularly mithridate and London treacle (two panaceas against poison, which was often taken to be the cause of plague). She paid his fine and got his release from Newgate. On 26 January Trigge was formally interdicted from practice, and he agreed that he would go back to his former trade of distiller— although he also offered to prove that many London distillers of aqua vita 'made use of the lees of starch wash and such trash to the great abuse of the Kinges subjects' (ibid.).

Over two years later the censors confronted Trigge yet again, showing him a prescription with his signature on it as evidence of his continued practice. He denied the signature, and upon again being warned not to practise Trigge replied disrespectfully. The college officers determined to resort to trying him in the courts. Tried in king's bench, and despite being defended by John Cooke (who would later argue the army's case against Charles I), Trigge had a judgment entered against him for £115. He apparently continued to practise, however, since the censors ordered him to come before them again on 2 December 1641. With civil war in the offing, however, the college of physicians relaxed its prosecutions.

Yet Trigge was not forgotten. Once a semblance of order returned to London after the imprisonment of the king, on 19 May 1647 Trigge, styling himself 'Doctor of Physic', entered a writ of error in the House of Lords asking their lordships to reverse the decision against him. Although law required that writs of error be signed by the monarch, the lords agreed to allow the solicitor-general to sign the writ. At the same time a petition asking that Trigge be allowed to practise without being a member of the College of Physicians was circulated and signed by 3000 Londoners, Trigge's lawyer Cooke claimed, although someone blocked the actual submission of the petition to the House of Lords. Trigge's case was argued in the house by council from both sides on 30 May 1648, with the result that their lordships asked two judges present (Baron Atkins and Justice Godbolt) to consult with the rest of the judges and report back. On 19 June, having heard from the judges, the lords affirmed the judgment against Trigge. With further turmoil leading up to the execution of the king in 1649, however, it is unclear whether the college was able to profit from the decision against Trigge.

After stability returned under Cromwell, in late March and April 1656 the members of the college resolved to do all they could once more to drive the medical empirics from London. Trigge and several others were tried at Guildhall in 1656, with the outcome decided for the empirics on a technicality: that the king had not signed the parliamentary act granting juridical authority to the college. After almost thirty years of resistance, Trigge had won. Apparently the pill of Trigge's that made him best known was 'The Golden Vatican-Pill'. According to one handbill, after Trigge's death Benjamin Shove purchased the secret of its manufacture and Trigge's own seal from his widow, and sold the pills through up to twenty-seven intermediaries.

Stephen Trigge (*fl.* 1660–1690) followed in his father's footsteps by practising illicitly in London and resisting the college physicians. Anna Sutton, for example, employed Trigge to treat her maid and her daughter with drugs, paying him 40s.; but when her maid died after two venesections performed by Trigge she complained to the college about his practice. Trigge otherwise practised quietly, although apparently at the end of the century he printed a small handbill advertising his practice in Gravel Lane in Southwark, near St George's Field. 'Those that Desire Health, May have the Elixir of Health' at his place. This panacea 'seldom fails, (only it is dear)'. If taken, it would not only keep people in health, but deprive 'many Doctors of getting great Estates', and the public 'of having occasion to take those Mortal Poisons that make a dark Massacre'. It may have been this handbill that provoked the satirical advertisement in *The English Lucian* of 9 February 1698 for a 'Pillulae Morbiferae, or an Antidote against health … ; one of these pills taken at any time of the day or night will infallibly cure you of all diseases.'

William Trigge may also be related to Thomas Trigg, 'Gent. Student in Physic and Astrology', who published an almanac in 1681 with more elaborate rules for medical practice than common.   HAROLD J. COOK

Sources annals, RCP Lond. • 'An advertisement concerning that excellent pill, of the late eminent and worthy Doctor Trigg', BL, 'Medical advertisements' • *The English Lucian, or, Weekly Discoveries of the Witty Intrigues* (1698) • J. Cooke, *Unum necessarium, or, The poore mans case* (1648) • C. Goodall, *The Royal College of Physicians of London founded and established by law* (1684) • C. Merrett, *A collection of acts of parliament* (1660) • CSP dom., *1637* • JHL, 9–10 (1646–8) • A. Clark, *The working life of women in the seventeenth century* (1982), 262–3

Trimble [*married name* Gant], **Joan** (1915–2000), composer and pianist, was born on 18 June 1915 at Orchard Terrace, Enniskillen, co. Fermanagh, the elder of the two daughters of William Egbert Trimble (1882–1967), a newspaper proprietor who owned and edited the *Impartial Reporter* (founded by his grandfather in 1825), and his wife, Marie, *née* Dowse (1887–1968), a Dublin-born violinist and teacher; her father was an amateur bass-baritone and folksong collector. She showed early promise as a violinist, and at the age of four played with the local orchestra. She was educated at Enniskillen Royal School for Girls, whose first head girl she became. Together with her younger sister, Valerie (1917–1980), with whom she was to form a celebrated piano duo, she studied in Dublin, with Annie Lord and Claude Biggs for piano. She also studied composition at the Royal Irish Academy of Music from 1930 with John F. Larchet, and took a BA and MusB at Trinity College, Dublin.

Trimble toured with John McCormack as his solo pianist in 1936 before moving to London to join her sister at the Royal College of Music. There she began writing music with the first of many excellent songs, 'My Grief on the Sea'. She also came under the influence of three composers whose teaching and encouragement gave her career a new impetus: Arthur Benjamin, Herbert Howells, and Ralph Vaughan Williams. From Vaughan Williams, in particular, she gained new discipline and confidence in her idiom, but it was at Benjamin's suggestion that the sisters formed a piano duo. For their début recital in 1938 she wrote three pieces, including her popular reel *Buttermilk Point*, and Benjamin wrote his most famous piece, *Jamaican Rumba*. The success of the concert set the Trimbles on a career that included tours before enthusiastic wartime audiences and broadcasts in the BBC's *Tuesday Serenade*, which from a pilot six-week series was extended to hundreds of programmes over ten years. They also performed at Myra Hess's National Gallery concerts, and gave the first performances of the two-piano concertos of Lennox Berkeley and Arthur Benjamin.

The constraints of wartime touring, together with duties for the Red Cross, limited Trimble's time for composition, but she was still able to write several extended works as well as light pieces and folk-song arrangements. With the *Sonatina for Two Pianos* in 1940 she began to explore a more contemporary style under the influence of Hindemith, but, sensing that this was not her true manner, she followed Vaughan Williams's suggestion that she should enter the 1940 Cobbett competition with a 'Phantasy' trio; it was his more suitable influence that sustained her here, without suppressing her own idiom, and she won the prize. On 27 June 1942 she married John Greenwood Gant (1917–2000), medical practitioner; they had a son and two daughters.

A love of French clarity was expressed in Trimble's two-piano *Pastorale* of 1943, written in homage to Poulenc. Her own voice came fully to the fore again with the song cycle *The County Mayo* (1949). By the 1950s the demands of acting as a doctor's wife and bringing up a young family were added to her performing and teaching. Yet her delightful *Suite for Strings* (1953) came as a reminder of her melodic gift and fine craftsmanship. In 1957 she accepted a BBC commission for a television opera, *Blind Raftery*. It was well received, but various discouragements led her to lose faith in her creative abilities, and she did not compose again for thirty years.

With the advance of her husband's debilitating neurological condition, Joan Trimble moved back to Enniskillen in 1977, also renewing her concern with the *Impartial Reporter*; as its proprietor, she played a pivotal part in Enniskillen's mourning after the poppy day slaughter in 1987. Her day-to-day involvement with the paper, coupled with her care for her husband, meant less time for music. But a commission for *Three Diversions for Wind Quintet* came from the Arts Council of Northern Ireland for her seventy-fifth birthday in 1990 and rekindled her interest in composition. She also returned to the study of Irish folk music, and was gratified to find recognition of her earlier works growing. She received a number of official honours, including the rarely bestowed fellowship of the Royal Irish Academy of Music in 1985, and her music was broadcast more frequently and recorded on CDs. Interviewed at the time, she spoke of the importance to her of 'shape and form, rhythm and clarity, as well as freedom of expression' (*The Times*). She sustained the long burden of her husband's illness with the warmth and good humour that made her widely loved in and beyond the world of music, and in England no less than in Ireland. She died a fortnight after her husband at the Erne Hospital, Enniskillen, on 6 August 2000, of cancer, and was buried at Breandrum, Enniskillen. She was survived by her son Nicholas and her daughters Joanna and Caroline.

JOHN WARRACK

Sources *The Times* (7 Aug 2000) · *The Guardian* (15 Aug 2000) · *The Independent* (25 Oct 2000) · personal knowledge (2004) · private information (2004) [family] · m. cert. · d. cert. **Archives** Royal Irish Academy of Music, Dublin, MSS **Likenesses** photograph, 1994, repro. in *The Times* · T. Carr, oils, priv. coll. · P. Flanagan, bronze head, priv. coll. · C. Graham, oils, priv. coll. · photograph (with Valerie Trimble), repro. in *The Guardian* · photograph, repro. in *The Independent* **Wealth at death** £727,261: probate, 12 Dec 2001, *CGPLA NIre*.

Trimen, Henry (1843–1896), botanist, the fourth and youngest son of Richard and Mary Ann Esther Trimen, was born at 3 Park Place Villas, Paddington, Middlesex, on 26 October 1843. He started a herbarium while still at King's College School, and entered the medical school of King's College in 1860. After spending one winter at Edinburgh University in 1864, he graduated MB with honours at the University of London in 1865. Shortly afterwards, during an epidemic of cholera, he acted as medical officer in the Strand district of London, but his interests were in botany rather than medicine. He joined the Botanical Society of Edinburgh in 1864, took an active part in the Society of Amateur Botanists and the Botanical Exchange Club, and, in 1869, became an assistant in the botanical department of the British Museum. Devoted from the first to the study of critical groups of plants, such as the docks and knotgrasses, he immediately added a minute duckweed, the smallest of flowering plants, to the list of British species. In conjunction with William Thiselton Dyer (later director of the Royal Botanic Gardens, Kew), Trimen published the *Flora of Middlesex* (1869), which was for a long time afterwards regarded as the model for county floras.

Trimen was curator of the anatomical museum of King's College, 1866–7, when he was appointed as lecturer on botany at St Mary's Hospital, a post he held until 1872. After having for some time assisted Dr Berthold Seemann with the *Journal of Botany, British and Foreign*, Trimen became assistant editor in 1870, and on Seemann's death in 1871 succeeded him as editor. In May 1873 Trimen was elected a fellow of the Linnean Society; he soon became an active member of the council, engaging in an acrimonious dispute with George Bentham, the president, and J. D. Hooker, whom he opposed over certain changes to the society's by-laws. From 1875 to 1880 he issued, in conjunction with Professor Robert Bentley, his second important work, *Medicinal Plants*, which appeared in forty-two parts and contains coloured figures of most of the species in the pharmacopoeia.

In 1879 Trimen was appointed to succeed George Henry Kendrick Thwaites as director of the botanical gardens at Peradeniya, Ceylon. Besides rearranging the plants there into scientific order, and much work at economic botany, especially quinology, Trimen diligently explored the island, collecting materials for a flora and publishing *A Systematic Catalogue of the Flowering Plants … in Ceylon* in

1885. In 1888 he was elected fellow of the Royal Society and in 1893 the first volume of his *magnum opus*, *A Handbook to the Flora of Ceylon*, was published. This work was completed after Trimen's death in six volumes (1893–1931) by J. D. Hooker and A. H. G. Alston.

In his last years Trimen's deafness, from which he had suffered for some time, became total. He retired as director on 1 July 1896 and died, unmarried, possibly from apoplexy, at Kandy on 16 October 1896. He was buried on the 18th near his predecessor, Thwaites, in the Mahaiywa cemetery. Trimen's name was given by George King of Calcutta to a magnificent Sinhalese banyan-like species of fig, *Ficus trimeni*. In addition to his three major works, fifty papers by Trimen are enumerated in the Royal Society's *Catalogue of Scientific Papers*.

G. S. BOULGER, *rev.* ANDREW GROUT

Sources *Journal of Botany, British and Foreign*, 34 (1896), 489–94 · *Tropical Agriculturalist*, 20 (1900), 1–6 · R. Desmond, *The European discovery of the Indian flora* (1992), 166–7 · F. A. Stafleu and R. S. Cowan, *Taxonomic literature: a selective guide*, 2nd edn, 6, Regnum Vegetabile, 115 (1986), 489–92 · A. T. Gage and W. T. Stearn, *A bicentenary history of the Linnean Society of London* (1988), 67–73 · E. Nelmes and W. Cuthbertson, eds., *Curtis's Botanical Magazine: dedications, 1827–1927* [1931], 259–60 · *Catalogue of scientific papers*, Royal Society
Archives LPL, corresp. · NHM, corresp. relating to Welwitsch case, papers · RBG Kew, corresp. from Ceylon
Likenesses photograph, *c.*1875, repro. in Desmond, *European discovery*, 167 · Messrs Cameron, photograph, 1887, repro. in *Journal of Botany*, facing p. 489 · photograph, RBG Kew; repro. in Nelmes and Cuthbertson, *Curtis's Botanical Magazine dedications*, 259 · portrait, Hunt Institute for Botanical Documentation, Pittsburgh
Wealth at death £2626 12s. 11d.: probate, 21 Oct 1896, *CGPLA Eng. & Wales*

Trimleston. For this title name *see* Barnewall, John, third Baron Trimleston (1470–1538); Barnewall, Robert, styled twelfth Baron Trimleston (*c.*1704–1779).

Trimmer, Joshua (1795–1857), geologist and agriculturalist, was born at North Cray, Kent, on 11 July 1795, the eldest son of Joshua Kirby Trimmer (1767–1829), and his wife, Eliza Thompson (*d.* in or after 1857). His grandmother was the writer Sarah *Trimmer (1741–1810). About 1800 the family moved to Brentford in Middlesex, where Trimmer's father manufactured bricks and tiles. Trimmer's father and two of his uncles (William Kirby Trimmer and James Rustat Trimmer) were much interested in geology and agriculture and their enthusiasm aroused in the young Joshua an early interest in 'diluvial' deposits. (William Kirby Trimmer supplied fossils from the Brickearth at Brentford to James Parkinson—discussed in the latter's *Organic Remains of a Former World* of 1811.)

In 1814 Trimmer was sent to manage his father's interests in copper mines in north Wales. He returned to Middlesex several years later to take up farming, following the family's interest in agriculture. However, in 1825 his father leased slate quarries at Llanllechid in north Wales; Trimmer was sent to oversee them. His return to north Wales allowed him to study geology in a largely unknown area and in 1831 he started publishing his findings. His first paper, on the diluvial deposits of Caernarvonshire, announced his discovery of marine shells on the summit of Moel Tryfan, 1350 feet above sea level. (The work led to his election as a fellow of the Geological Society in the following year.) Trimmer could not yet reconcile such diluvium as glacial in origin (despite noting striated slates beneath it), and saw instead evidence for a massive flood deposit. Although this interpretation 'was destined to confuse and mislead British geologists for almost half a century' (Davies, 248), Trimmer does deserve credit for being 'the first to recognise the importance of mapping the drifts and other superficial formations' (Geikie, 80); such loose and unconsolidated materials being then considered merely as 'Extraneous Rubbish' (Woodward, 134).

In the 1830s Trimmer lived at Baladeulyn, Caernarfon. He established a museum in the town and became secretary of the Society for Investigating the Natural History and Antiquities of the Counties of Anglesey, Caernarfon, and Merioneth. About 1840 he left Wales and began a new career as a geological writer. His 1841 *Practical Geology and Mineralogy*, a significant attempt to demonstrate the practical aspects of geology, was followed by *Practical Chemistry for Farmers* in 1842. He was mapping drift deposits in Norfolk in 1844–6, helped by the journal committee of the Royal Agricultural Society, which awarded him £50 to investigate the agricultural geology of the county.

In 1846 Trimmer was appointed an assistant geologist to the new Geological Survey of Great Britain at an annual salary of £156. He was initially based in the Cardigan area, but early in 1847 was appointed a government inspector of relief committees in Ireland. Trimmer considered it 'a most laborious and harrowing service' which meant having to 'give geology to the winds' (letter to C. B. Rose, 24 Sept 1847). However, by October of the same year he had returned to England and was busy mapping the Tertiary deposits of the Hampshire basin. In 1850 he issued *Proposals for a Geological Survey, Specially Directed to Agricultural Objects*. He retired from the survey in 1854 and died unmarried in London on 16 September 1857, while engaged in writing a book on the geology of agriculture.

H. S. TORRENS

Sources J. E. Portlock, *Quarterly Journal of the Geological Society*, 14 (1858), xxxii–xxxvi · J. A. Secord, 'The geological survey of Great Britain as a research school', *History of Science*, 24 (1986), 223–75 · J. Lindsay, *A history of the north Wales slate industry* (1974) · W. K. Trimmer, 'An account of some organic remains found near Brentford', *PTRS*, 103 (1813), 131–7 · J. Trimmer, letters to C. B. Rose, 1846–7, RS, Rose MSS · G. L. Davies, *The earth in decay: a history of British geomorphology, 1578 to 1878* [1969] · H. B. Woodward, *The history of the Geological Society of London* (1907) · A. Geikie, *Memoir of Sir Andrew Crombie Ramsay* (1907) · F. J. North, 'Centenary of the glacial theory', *Proceedings of the Geologists' Association*, 54 (1943), 1–28, esp. 10 · letters from and about Trimmer, NMG Wales, De la Beche Archive · J. Trimmer, 'On the geology of Norfolk', *Journal of the Royal Agricultural Society of England*, 7 (1847), 444–85
Archives BGS, maps and notes | ICL, A. C. Ramsay MSS, letters · NL Wales, letters to William Buckland · NMG Wales, H. De la Beche MSS, letters and references · RS, C. B. Rose MSS, letters

Trimmer [*née* Kirby], **Sarah** (1741–1810), author and educationist, was born in Ipswich, Suffolk, on 6 January 1741, the only daughter of the artist Joshua *Kirby (1716–1774) and his wife, Sarah Bull (*c.*1718–1775). She was educated by her father and at Mrs Justiner's School for Young Ladies in

Sarah Trimmer (1741–1810), by Sir Thomas Lawrence, c.1790

Ipswich. In 1755 the family moved to London; acquaintances there included Thomas Gainsborough, Samuel Johnson, Sir Joshua Reynolds, and William Hogarth. Kirby was appointed teacher of perspective drawing to the prince of Wales (afterwards George III) and later held the same appointment to Queen Charlotte. In 1761 he was made clerk of the works for the royal palace at Kew; his family took up residence there.

In September 1762 Sarah Kirby married James Trimmer (1739–1792), a prosperous brick and tile maker of Brentford, Middlesex. They lived in a house at the brickfield in Old Brentford near Kew Bridge, where Trimmer's twelve children were born between 1763 and 1780. Of the six sons and six daughters, nine survived their mother; the best-known to contemporaries was Selina (1764–1829), governess to the Devonshire House nursery.

Trimmer assumed responsibility for the education of her sons and her daughters, sending the boys to a local clergyman for classical languages. Like many other women she became aware of the need for texts for children which would provide interesting as well as proper moral and religious instruction. As a devout evangelical Anglican, Trimmer offered an orthodox answer to these problems. Her earliest publications, *An Easy Introduction to the Knowledge of Nature, and Reading the Holy Scriptures* (1780) and *Sacred History* (6 vols., 1782–5), were the direct result of her domestic teaching.

By the 1780s Trimmer's educational concerns had moved beyond her own family. In 1786 she established a Sunday school in Old Brentford; by 1788 it had over 300 pupils. Many of her publications, such as *The Sunday-School Catechist* (1788), *A Comment on Dr. Watt's Divine Songs* (1789),

and *A Companion to the Book of Common Prayer* (1791), were written for Sunday school use, though they could be equally helpful for training evangelical Anglicans at home.

Trimmer did not limit her educational schemes to religious training. In 1787 she opened a weekday school of industry for girls. The Old Brentford charity school trained orphaned or otherwise distressed middle-class girls as teachers and working-class girls in domestic service or appropriate trades. Trimmer provided several texts for use in these schools, including *The Servant's Friend* (1787), *The Charity School Spelling Book* (1799), reading instruction in *The Ladder of Learning* (1789, 1792), and her simplified versions of scripture. Her charity school work was well known; Queen Charlotte and the dowager Countess Spencer were among those who consulted Trimmer on founding similar institutions. Her views were summarized in *The œconomy of Charity* (1787), one of the most influential works on how and why Sunday and charity schools should be established. She continued to advise in *Reflections upon the Education of Children in Charity Schools* (1792), and *A Friendly Remonstrance* (1792).

In the latter part of her life Trimmer devoted herself primarily to formulating methods, practices, and materials that would be acceptable to evangelical parents educating their children at home and that could be used as well in charity schools. She founded and edited two periodicals, *The Family Magazine* (1788–9) and *The Guardian of Education* (1802–6), which provided both material and methods for teachers. Like most of her female contemporaries, Trimmer was firmly opposed to the educational theories of Jean Jacques Rousseau. In her view, children needed to be taught both necessary skills such as reading and writing and also moral and religious values by properly trained adults. *An Address to Heads of Schools and Families* (1799), *The Teacher's Assistant* (1800), and *An Essay on Christian Education* (1812) were designed to help these instructors keep on the right path. In *A Comparative View of the New Plan of Education Promulgated by Mr. Joseph Lancaster* (1805), Trimmer attacked Lancaster's proposals to use pupil monitors to teach larger numbers of children in charity schools.

Although Trimmer advocated conservative views, later students of educational methods and children's books credit her with two innovations that became commonplace in the nineteenth century. She popularized the use of pictorial material in books for children, a practice first recommended by Mme de Genlis. In 1786 Trimmer published *A Description of a Set of Prints of Scripture History*; it was followed by *A Description of a Set of Prints of Ancient History* (1786), *A Description of a Set of Prints of Roman History* (1789), *A Description of a Set of Prints Taken from the New Testament* (1790), *A Description of a Set of Prints of English History* (1792), *A New Set of Prints … from the Old Testament* (1808), and *A Concise History of England* (1808).

Trimmer's other innovation was the use of animals, birds, and the natural world in stories she called fables. While these tales utilized a certain amount of anthropomorphism, Trimmer also taught careful and kind treatment of animals and all creation. She introduced these views in *Fabulous Histories* (1786). The family of robins in this work so outshone the humans that later editions were retitled to mention them. The story of the robins continued to be published in various, often bowdlerized, forms into the twentieth century. Trimmer produced these fables in part as an alternative to increasingly popular fairy-tales, a popularity that she viewed with alarm, as she disapproved of their lack of any didactic element. Her animals appealed to the imagination of children without resorting to magic, luck, or guile. At the same time they provided moral instruction which fairy-tales lacked.

After her husband's death in 1792 Trimmer continued to live at the brickfields. About 1800 she and her unmarried daughters moved to a house in Windmill Lane, Brentford, owned by her son, the Revd Henry Scott Trimmer. She died there unexpectedly on 15 December 1810 and was buried on 5 January 1811 beside her husband at St Mary's, Ealing. A memorial tablet outlining her achievements was later erected at St George's, Brentford.

Many of Trimmer's works were reprinted during her lifetime and after her death. *Some Account of the Life and Writings of Mrs. Trimmer* (1814), edited by her son, included letters and a selection from her journals. As one of the most prolific and popular writers on education and of children's books, her influence was strong throughout the first part of the nineteenth century. Her most important contribution was in showing how educational material could be made appealing to children.

BARBARA BRANDON SCHNORRENBERG

Sources D. M. Yarde, *The life and works of Sarah Trimmer: a lady of Brentford* (1972) · D. Wills, 'Sarah Trimmer', *British reform writers, 1789–1832*, ed. G. Kelly and E. Applegate, DLitB, 158 (1996), 340–48 · *Some account of the life and writings of Mrs. Trimmer*, 2 vols. (1814) · *DNB*
Archives BL, letters to Caroline Howe
Likenesses T. Lawrence, oils, *c*.1790, NPG [*see illus.*] · W. Bond, stipple, pubd 1799, BM, NPG · T. Chapman, stipple, BM, NPG; repro. in *Ladies Monthly Museum* (1798) · H. Howard, oils, NPG · C. Read, portrait

Trimnell, Charles (1630–1702). *See under* Trimnell, Charles (*bap.* 1663, *d.* 1723).

Trimnell, Charles (*bap.* 1663, *d.* 1723), bishop of Winchester, was baptized on 1 May 1663 at Abbots Ripton, Huntingdonshire, the son of **Charles Trimnell** (1630–1702), Church of England clergyman, who was rector of that parish. His father was the fourth son of Edmund Trimnell of Bremhill, Wiltshire; he was educated at Bremhill School, Wiltshire, and Winchester College, and admitted a scholar of New College, Oxford, in 1647. He was expelled by the parliamentary commissioners in 1648 and subsequently admitted to Queens' College, Cambridge, proceeding BA in 1651/2 and MA in 1655, when he was incorporated at Oxford. He was a fellow of Queens' from 1653 to 1658, becoming rector of Abbots Ripton in 1656. He died in 1702.

The younger Trimnell entered Winchester College in 1674 and matriculated at New College, Oxford, on 26 July 1681, graduating BA in 1685 and MA in 1689 and proceeding BD and DD in 1691, incorporating at Cambridge in

Charles Trimnell (*bap.* 1663, *d.* 1723), attrib. Michael Dahl, *c*.1715–19

1695. Sir John Trevor, master of the rolls, appointed him preacher at the rolls chapel in 1688. On the advice of Thomas Tenison, Trimnell became the second earl of Sunderland's chaplain in 1689, during his exile in the Netherlands, after his resignation from James II's government. Lady Sunderland wrote: 'Dr Tenison has given us a chaplain never enough to be praised, a house is happy where he is' (Kenyon, *Robert Spencer*, 239). Trimnell remained with the Spencers on their return to Althorp, and in 1691 was appointed a prebendary of Norwich Cathedral. In 1694 Sunderland presented him to the rectory of Boddington, Northamptonshire, which he exchanged in 1696 for Brington, which included Althorp, but resigned in 1698, on being collated to the archdeaconry of Norfolk. He married first Henrietta Maria, daughter of William *Talbot, successively bishop of Salisbury and Durham, with whom he had two sons who died in infancy. She died in 1716, and in 1719 he married Elizabeth, daughter of Sir Edmund Wynne, of Nostell Priory, and widow of Joseph Taylor, of the Temple.

Trimnell was a conscientious archdeacon, undertaking a parochial visitation of his archdeaconry in 1699. In the cathedral chapter he was an ally of Humphrey Prideaux, a fellow prebendary and subsequently dean, against Bishop Moore. In 1700 Tenison, now archbishop of Canterbury, sounded out Archbishop John Sharp of York, a former dean of Norwich, whether Prideaux or Trimnell should succeed to the deanery in the event of Dean Fairfax's death. Prideaux was appointed. Trimnell became prominent in the disputes in the lower house of convocation in 1701, opposing the claims of Francis Atterbury and the 'high flying' tories that convocation was on an equal footing with parliament in relation to the crown. He supported the Society for Promoting Christian Knowledge, signing the preamble of the inaugural meeting of the society in 1699 and subscribing to schemes for establishing parochial libraries in the North American plantations, and for catechetical schools and libraries in market towns. He subscribed to the Society for the Propagation of the Gospel and regularly attended its meetings.

Trimnell was appointed a chaplain-in-ordinary to William III in 1701, and to Queen Anne in 1702. In 1703 he was defeated by one vote by Thomas Brathwaite for the wardenship of New College. The queen presented him to the sinecure rectory of Southmere in Norfolk in 1705. He retained the respect of moderate tories, despite his involvement with the convocation controversies, and Archbishop Sharp supported the duchess of Marlborough's application to Queen Anne for Trimnell's appointment as rector of St James's, Piccadilly, in 1706.

In 1707 Archbishop Tenison recommended Trimnell to Godolphin to succeed Sir Jonathan Trelawny as bishop of Exeter, or Nicholas Stratford at Chester, to reinforce the whig representation among the bishops in the House of Lords. Queen Anne resisted this, and promised Exeter to Offspring Blackhall and Chester to Sir William Dawes. Robert Harley, to gain the support of moderate whigs and tories, attempted to resolve the impasse by a compromise, and Anne accepted the duke of Marlborough's advice that to nominate only tory bishops would risk alienating the incipient 'church whig' group. In January 1708 Blackhall was appointed to Exeter, Dawes to Chester, and Trimnell to Norwich.

As archdeacon of Norfolk, and a prebendary of Norwich Cathedral, and with the friendship and support of Humphrey Prideaux, and Charles, Lord Townshend, the high steward of the cathedral, Trimnell already had a strong base in Norfolk, and was on close terms with the whig ascendancy in the county. On Trimnell's arrival in Norwich as bishop Prideaux noted: 'No bishop has been received with better respect since the memory of any alive' (Norfolk RO, dean and chapter of Norwich 115/2, Diarium of Humphrey Prideaux, 225–6). He was permitted to retain the living of St James's, Piccadilly, for a year, to assist with the expenses of his new appointment. A conscientious diocesan bishop, he visited and confirmed in all the major towns in Norfolk and Suffolk during his primary visitation in 1709, and regularly ordained at the canonical seasons, spending the summer months of each year in Norwich. He undertook extensive repairs to the bishop's palace there. He seems to have been tactful in his dealings with his mainly tory clergy.

Trimnell was part of a group of whig senior churchmen, headed by Archbishop Tenison, including bishops William Nicolson and William Wake, deans Francis Blackburne and White Kennett, and Archdeacon Edmund Gibson, closely associated with the earl of Halifax, the duke of Wharton, Lord Somers, and the third earl of Sunderland. He became the object of high-flying tory vilification before and during the trial of Dr Sacheverell. He and

Bishop Wake were accused of monopolizing the debate in the House of Lords on the second article of Sacheverell's impeachment. When Trimnell preached before the House of Lords on 30 January 1712, arguing that resistance to a sovereign was justified in 'extraordinary circumstances' (but not in the case of Charles I), Swift described it as 'a terrible Whig sermon' and the house declined to order it to be printed, but Bishop Nicolson deemed it an 'admirable' sermon (*London Diaries*, 582).

On Archbishop Tenison's death in 1715 gossip spoke of Wake or Trimnell, who had become clerk of the closet in 1714, to succeed him. Although Nicolson thought that the ministry favoured Trimnell, Wake was appointed. Wake failed to establish influence at court, and alienated the ministry by opposing their attempts to reduce the influence of clergy they suspected of Jacobitism. Gibson noted that Trimnell repeated the probably false allegation that 'a general opinion had obtained that there was a great deal of sympathy' between Wake and the actively Jacobite Bishop Atterbury of Rochester, 'so as to make his Grace suspected everywhere by the King's friends' (Sykes, 2.111). Trimnell rather than Wake thus advised Sunderland on ecclesiastical matters. Trimnell may also have been privy to Sunderland and Stanhope's recommendation to the king to prorogue convocation on 10 May 1717, to avoid a furore over the king's order to print a sermon of Bishop Benjamin Hoadly's, ending debates in convocation until 1852. Although Trimnell was implicated in Sunderland and Stanhope's alienation of the moderate church whigs, Bishop Nicolson suggested that Trimnell was prepared to oppose a bill to give the government unlimited power over the universities. On Trelawny's death in 1721 Trimnell was given the better-endowed diocese of Winchester.

Trimnell was reckoned by his contemporaries to have had a kind heart and a cultivated mind. It was claimed that he was 'a very good man whom even the Tories valued, though he preached terrible Whig sermons' (Cassan, 379). Trimnell died on 15 August 1723 at Farnham Castle, Surrey, and was buried in Winchester Cathedral. His second wife survived him. W. M. JACOB

Sources S. H. Cassan, *The lives of the bishops of Winchester*, 2 vols. (1827) · *DNB* · *The London diaries of William Nicolson, bishop of Carlisle, 1702–1718*, ed. C. Jones and G. Holmes (1985) · N. Sykes, *William Wake, archbishop of Canterbury*, 2 vols. (1957) · C. J. Abbey and J. H. Overton, *The English church in the eighteenth century*, 2 vols. (1878) · A. T. Hart, *The life and times of John Sharp, archbishop of York* (1949) · G. V. Bennett, *The tory crisis in church and state: the career of Francis Atterbury, bishop of Rochester* (1975) · G. Holmes, *The trial of Dr Sacheverell* (1973) · E. Carpenter, *Thomas Tenison, archbishop of Canterbury* (1948) · *A chapter in English church history being the minutes of the SPCK, 1698–1704* (1898) · J. P. Kenyon, *Robert Spencer, earl of Sunderland, 1641–1702* (1958) · J. P. Kenyon, *Revolution principles: the politics of party, 1689–1720* (1977) · W. Manross, *SPG papers in the Lambeth Palace Library* (1974) · H. Prideaux, diarium secundum, 1703–13, Norfolk RO, DCN 115/2 · archdeacon of Norfolk's visitation book, 1699, Norfolk RO, ANF/1/13 · BL, Add. MSS · Foster, *Alum. Oxon.* · Venn, *Alum. Cant.*

Archives BL, Add. MS 4043, fols. 304, 318; Add. MS 61443, fols. 54, 73–84b, 88, 94; Sloane MS 4061, fols. 183–93b | BL, Blenheim MSS · BL, corresp. with Lady Sunderland, Add. MS 61640, fols. 199–

202b • Christ Church Oxf., Wake MSS • TCD, corresp. with William King

Likenesses attrib. M. Dahl, oils, *c.*1715–1719, Nostell Priory, Yorkshire [*see illus.*] • J. Faber senior, mezzotint, pubd 1719 (after oil painting at New College, Oxford), BM • oils, bishop's house, Norwich • oils, Wolvesey, Winchester • oils, New College, Oxford

Trinder, Arthur William (1901–1959), bond dealer, was born on 11 August 1901 in Reading, the son of Arthur Trinder, sergeant-major, Royal Berkshire regiment, and his wife, Louisa Jane, *née* Taylor. He was educated at Christ's Hospital from January 1912 until July 1918, having won a place there as a West's scholar in open competition. On leaving school he found employment as a clerk with the Union Discount Company of London Ltd, then the leading house in the discount market.

Trinder took his first step to high office in the 1920s when R. C. Wyse, manager from 1922 to 1940, appointed him as his 'boy' or assistant to the manager. In 1930 he was made assistant manager and when in the following year he was promoted to sub-manager, a contemporary described him as 'the eyes, and ears and often the mouthpiece of the management' (private information). He was deputy manager under E. C. Ellen from 1940 and when Ellen retired in January 1947 Trinder was the natural choice to succeed him.

The sheer size of the Union Discount's operations meant that its managers tended to be the most prominent market experts of their day. This was certainly true of Trinder, who was the acknowledged leader of the discount market in the late 1940s and the 1950s. Between 1953 and 1955 he served as chairman of the London Discount Market Association. Trinder's forte was the bond market: he had an unmatched reputation as an astute and skilful dealer, and from the early days Union Discount had been the market's largest operator. Now it was to bonds rather than bills that the houses had to look for their chief hope of profit; and there was renewed encouragement from the Bank of England for the houses to develop their role, acquired during wartime, of making a market in short-dated government bonds.

Trinder's importance as a bond dealer led to his appearance, in December 1957, before the Parker tribunal, set up to investigate an alleged leakage of information regarding the raising of the bank rate. Trinder argued, in words that lived after him, that prior information would have been of no value, because the size of his bond-holding left no room for manoeuvre: 'I am the market in certain short bonds, so therefore I have to sit tight and do nothing' (*DBB*, 5.555). A few weeks later, in January 1958, he provided further valuable insights into discount market operations, when he gave evidence to the committee on the working of the monetary system (the Radcliffe committee).

'Trin', as he was universally known, was a much loved figure in the discount market, which looked to him as a source of wisdom in all business matters. Trinder with his quick, dry wit would often oblige with an apposite and humorous aphorism known as a 'Trinderism'. He attributed his own success in the bond market, for example, to

the possession of 'a long pocket and strong nerves' (private information). His business style was a successful combination of flamboyance and shrewd calculation. It was not, however, beyond criticism. He had learned management from the autocratic and dictatorial Wyse and he kept too much in his own hands and failed to bring on his management team. His last years were marred by losses in bond dealing, owing to his failure to heed advice; moreover, because Union Discount had a non-executive board he was never made a director of the company.

Little is known about Trinder's private life, including the name of his wife; but they had a daughter and two sons, both of whom followed him into the City. Trinder apparently lived for his work and he was, he always said, 'wedded to Union Discount' (private information). His company's fortunes were at a peak when he retired in 1958, but retirement left him bereft of purpose. Less than eleven months later, he died from gastric haemorrhage and hepatitis at the London Clinic, 20 Devonshire Place, Marylebone, London, on 28 July 1959.

GORDON FLETCHER

Sources G. A. Fletcher and P. J. Lee, 'Trinder, Arthur William', *DBB* • G. Cleaver and P. Cleaver, *The Union Discount: a centenary album* (1985) • private information (2004) • d. cert. • Union PLC Archives, London

Archives Union PLC, 39 Cornhill, London

Likenesses photographs, Union plc, 39 Cornhill, London

Wealth at death £76,835 19s. 6d.: probate, 16 Oct 1959, *CGPLA Eng. & Wales*

Trinder, Thomas Edward [Tommy] (1909–1989), comedian, was born on 24 March 1909 in Streatham, London, the eldest in the family of two sons and one daughter of Thomas Henry Trinder, tram driver and baker, and his wife, Jean Mills. Educated at Queensborough Road School and St Andrew's, Holborn, he left school early to work as an errand boy at Smithfield meat market. Giving up his job at the age of twelve he toured South Africa with a variety company, and then in the following year, 1922, he won a talent competition at Collins's Music Hall, Islington, which led to a week's engagement. He worked in a touring show, Will Murray's Casey's Court, using the name Red Nirt (his own surname backwards) and played the halls for seventeen years before reaching the London Palladium in 1939 in *Band Waggon*. For the next eleven years he played there regularly, first as a supporting act in *Top of the World* (1940), with Bud Flanagan and Chesney Allen, and *Gangway* (1941), with Ben Lyon and Bebe Daniels, and then topping the bill in *Best Bib and Tucker* (1942), *Happy and Glorious* (1944–6), which with 938 performances became the longest running of all Palladium shows, *Here, there and everywhere* (1947), and *Starlight Rendezvous* (1950).

Trinder had a long, thin face, a jutting chin, and a wide smile; he always wore a trilby hat, even with evening dress. Soon after he arrived at the Palladium, he invested £265 a week for two weeks to advertise his chin on twenty-five strategically sited London hoardings. All but one read: 'If it's laughter you're after, Trinder's the name. You lucky people!' The odd one out, opposite Aldgate station, was printed in Hebrew. With his shovel-like jaw, ready grin,

Thomas Edward Trinder (1909–1989), by Baron, 1951

quick-fire topical humour, and 'You lucky people' catchphrase, he became one of the most popular of variety entertainers.

Trinder's film career began in 1939, but it was not until his fifth film, *Sailors Three* (1940), with Claude Hulbert and Michael Wilding, that he made a mark. Of his fifteen films, *The Foreman Went to France* (1941), *The Bells Go Down* (1943), and *Champagne Charlie* (1944), in which he played Victorian music-hall star George Leybourne, are the most notable.

In 1943 Trinder was singled out in the House of Commons for criticism for not having worked overseas for Entertainments National Service Association (ENSA), a criticism which ignored the fact that he had been entertaining troops at home since the outbreak of war. He later became the first major star to visit Italy and in 1946 took the last ENSA party to the Far East. It was Trinder who gave ENSA its sobriquet 'Every Night Something Awful'. Trinder holds a record unlikely to be beaten of playing the most West End theatres in a single night. During the London blitz, when audiences had to remain in their seats during air raids and Trinder was at the Palladium, he drove round the West End and managed to play a ten-minute spot in seventeen theatres before the all-clear sounded.

Known as the Mr Woolworth of show business, Trinder could sometimes be earthy, though never crude, and he hated bad language. When he arrived at Scapa Flow to entertain the Royal Navy he found the padre sitting with his back to the stage watching the audience to see who laughed. He invariably worked alone without the aid of stooges, props, or even a microphone, and frequently without a script, relying on his ready wit. He was noted for his ability to deal with hecklers. When he opened his act at the Embassy Club with his usual 'Trinder's the name', a morose Orson Welles, having that day been divorced from Rita Hayworth, growled 'Well, change it', to which Trinder retorted 'Is that an offer of marriage?'

In 1955 Trinder became the first host of *Sunday Night at the London Palladium*, one of the most successful television variety shows. He fell out with producer Val Parnell and

left the show; his career, although he rarely stopped working, became a series of one-night stands, overseas tours, and pantomimes in the provinces. A firm favourite of the royal family, he appeared before the queen mother at the 1980 royal variety show, in what must have been the oldest chorus line, when thirteen artists, including Arthur Askey, Stanley Holloway, Richard Murdoch, Chesney Allen, and Trinder, with a combined age of 891 years, danced and sang their way through Flanagan and Allen's 'Strollin'.

A lifelong supporter of Fulham Football Club, Trinder was on its board for many years, becoming chairman in 1955, a post he held for twenty-one years despite being forced to apologize publicly for cracking jokes at his players' expense. He was appointed CBE in 1975 for his services to charity (he was thrice chief rat of the show business charity the Water Rats). He married Gwyn (Toni), daughter of Major Gilbert Arthur Lancelyn Green, of the Royal Field Artillery. There was one daughter of the marriage. He died on 10 July 1989 in St Peter's Hospital, Chertsey, Surrey.

RICHARD FAWKES, *rev.*

Sources J. Fisher, *Funny way to be a hero* (1973) · *The Times* (11 July 1989) · *The Independent* (11 July 1989) · *The Independent* (13 July 1989) · private information (1996) · personal knowledge (1996) · CGPLA Eng. & Wales (1989)

Likenesses Baron, photograph, 1951, Hult. Arch. [*see illus.*] · photograph, repro. in *The Independent* (11 July 1989) · photograph, repro. in *The Times* · photographs, Hult. Arch.

Wealth at death under £100,000: administration, 4 Sept 1989, CGPLA Eng. & Wales

Tripe, Linnaeus (1822–1902), photographer and army officer in the East India Company, was born on 14 April 1822 at 4 St Aubyn Street, Plymouth Dock (renamed Devonport in 1824), the ninth of the twelve children of Cornelius Tripe FRCS (1785–1860), surgeon, JP, and alderman of Devonport, and his wife, Mary Fincham (1786–1842), the daughter of James and Martha Fincham of Plymouth Dock. Mary Tripe founded the Royal British Female Orphan Asylum, Devonport, in 1839. Tripe was educated in classics and mathematics at the Devonport classical school, before joining the East India Company's army (which was to become the Indian army) in April 1839. He served with the 12th Madras native infantry, retiring in 1875 as a full colonel. In August 1875 he was granted the honorary rank of major-general, land forces.

Tripe took his earliest surviving photographs in the vicinity of Devonport about 1853, while on furlough in England. In December 1854 he photographed the temples at Halebid and Belur in Mysore during leave from his regiment at Bangalore; the 1855 Madras Exhibition jury recommended purchase of these photographs for the East India Company's court of directors, which had recently declared its interest in the new art of photography. In June 1855, on the recommendation of Lord Dalhousie, governor-general of India, Tripe was appointed photographer to the government of India's mission to Ava in Burma. Bad weather, Tripe's ill health, and ceremonial duties reduced his working time during the four-month mission to thirty-six days, but he made more than 200

Linnaeus Tripe (1822–1902), by unknown photographer

photographs, primarily of temple architecture, at the Burmese capital of Amarapura and sites along the Irrawaddy River, and at Rangoon, capital of British-occupied Pegu. Back in Bangalore, he produced fifty copies of an untitled portfolio containing 120 of the Burma views, his first major photographic work, for the government of India in early 1857.

In March 1857 Tripe became official photographer to the Madras presidency. After completing some minor work, he left Bangalore in December 1857, transporting his photographic equipment in bullock carts, on a 700-mile expedition to photograph temples, palaces, landscapes, and public works in the Salem district, Srirangam, Trichinopoly, Madura, Pudukkottai, and Tanjore. In May and June 1858 at Madras, he photographed the Elliot marbles, sculptures recovered from the ruined Buddhist stupa at Amaravati. On his return to Bangalore in July, he worked unremittingly for twenty months printing his negatives and producing thirty-five to seventy copies of the ten large photographic albums, two stereograph albums, and one photographic scroll ordered by the Madras government. His album *Photographs of the Elliot Marbles, and other Subjects, in the Central Museum, Madras*, produced in 1859, remains a valuable documentary resource. His photographic reputation mainly rests on the images contained in the nine large albums completed in 1860: *Photographic Views in Madura, Parts I to IV*; *Photographic Views in Tanjore and Trivady*; *Photographic Views of Poodoocottah*; *Photographic Views of Ryakotta and other Places, in the Salem District*; *Photographic Views of Seringham*; and *Photographic Views of Trichinopoly*.

While pressing on with this work, Tripe learned in June 1859 that Sir Charles Trevelyan, the new governor of Madras, had ordered the photographic establishment closed as a matter of economy, when the publications in progress were completed. Tripe proposed various alternatives to closure of the establishment, and was strongly supported by the Hon. Walter Elliot, a member of the governor's council, who wrote:

> He is, without question, the ablest Artist in this part of India, and his zeal and love of his art, coupled with his known disinterestedness and modesty, afford ample guarantee that the fullest justice will be done to the prosecution of the experiment, which I have recommended.   (Dewan and Sutnik, 17)

But the governor was unmoved, the army requested Tripe's return to military duty, and the photographic establishment was broken up in April 1860. Tripe's health was broken as well, and he returned to England on sick certificate later that year. In September 1862 he wrote to the secretary of state for India, offering to undertake further photographic work for the Madras government; the offer was curtly declined. His last known series of photographs was taken privately about 1870 at Kasur-do Hill, near the isolated frontier post of Tonghoo, British Burma, where he was stationed with his regiment.

Tripe returned to England in 1873. In later years he collected shells and corals, and two shells which he found in China and the Philippines (*c*.1890) became British Museum holotypes. He died, unmarried, of senile decay and acute prostatitis at his home, 3 Osbourne Villas, Stoke, Devonport, on 2 March 1902 and was buried on 6 March in the Plymouth cemetery.   JANET DEWAN

Sources J. Dewan, 'Linnaeus Tripe, photographer of British India, 1854–1870', in J. Dewan and M. Sutnik, *Linnaeus Tripe, photographer of British India, 1854–1870* (1986), 13–22 [exhibition catalogue, Art Gallery of Ontario, Toronto, 1 Nov 1986 – 11 Jan 1987] · J. Dewan, 'Chronology', in J. Dewan and M. Sutnik, *Linnaeus Tripe, photographer of British India, 1854–1870* (1986), 36–7 [exhibition catalogue, Art Gallery of Ontario, Toronto, 1 Nov 1986 – 11 Jan 1987] · J. Dewan, 'Biography of Linnaeus Tripe', 1985/7, priv. coll. · J. Dewan, '"Near Tonghoo Burmah": Linnaeus Tripe's later photographs', *Photographic Collector*, 5/3 (spring 1986), 271–7 · J. Dewan, 'Linnaeus Tripe: critical assessments and other notes', *Photographic Collector*, 5/1 (autumn 1984), 47–65 · *Western Morning News* (7 March 1902) · *Western Daily Mercury* (7 March 1902) · private information (2004) · d. cert. · d. cert. [Cornelius Tripe] · d. cert. [Mary Tripe] · cadet papers of Linnaeus Tripe, BL OIOC, L/MIL/190/398–401

Archives Art Gallery of Ontario, Toronto · BL OIOC, photographs · BM, Oriental Antiquities · Canadian Centre for Architecture, Montreal · J. Paul Getty Museum, Los Angeles · National Museum of Photography, Film and Television, Bradford, Royal Photographic Society collection, photographs · NL Scot. · V&A

Likenesses Blake Bros Plymouth, carte-de-visite, *c*.1861–1862, priv. coll.; repro. in Dewan and Sutnik, *Linnaeus Tripe* · Wrigglesworth & Binns, Wellington, New Zealand, carte-de-visite, 1890, priv. coll. · photograph, BL OIOC [*see illus.*]

Wealth at death £1295 2*s*. 5*d*.: probate, 8 Sept 1902, *CGPLA Eng. & Wales*

Triplet [Triplett], **Thomas** (1603?–1670), philanthropist, was born in or near Oxford, of unknown parentage, and educated at St Paul's School, London; he matriculated at Christ Church, Oxford, on 16 March 1621, and graduated BA on 27 June 1622 and MA 20 June 1625. At Oxford he became a distinguished Greek scholar, wit, and poet. Bishop Morton presented Triplet in 1630 to Woodhorn vicarage, Northumberland, and in 1631 to Whitburn rectory, co. Durham. On 10 April 1640 he was inducted to Washington rectory, co. Durham, holding three parishes in plurality. He was proctor for the archdeacon of Northumberland in the convocation of 1640, and became prebendary of Fenton in York Cathedral in 1641. In October 1645 he was appointed prebendary of Preston in Salisbury Cathedral; he was collated to the ninth stall in Durham Cathedral on 20 March 1649, but parliament sequestrated his ecclesiastical preferments. Following ejection from Washington on 10 September 1644, he fled to Ireland; in 1649 he was keeping a school in Dublin. He edited the 1651 edition of Lord Falkland's *Infallibility of the Church of Rome*. In 1656 he was resident teacher at the Dutch embassy, and he was mentioned in John Evelyn's diary in May.

At the Restoration, Triplet petitioned for the livings of Whitburn and Washington, regaining Washington rectory in 1660, but resigning in 1662. In April 1661 he proceeded DD by diploma. On 13 March 1662 Triplet established a school at Hayes, Middlesex. Among his pupils was George Ent who, according to Aubrey, was kicked downstairs by Triplet in anger at the boy's cheek. His father, the physician Sir George Ent, took the boy away; 'an accident' that 'did well-nigh breake Dr Triplett's schoole' (*Brief Lives*, 299). The school survives in the form of Dr Triplett's Church of England primary school, Hayes, Middlesex.

By deed dated 18 November 1664 Triplet named ten life trustees, including John Sudbury, William Sancroft, Isaac Basire, and local gentry, to administer his gift of capital to invest in property, first in Ryton, the annual rents to be divided proportionally between his three former parishes for binding out poor children as apprentices. In 1686, after selling the Ryton property, the trustees bought a 42 acre farm at Stockton-on-Tees. As apprenticeship fees died out, much income remained unused. Rents increased, and an acre of land sold to the North Eastern Railway Company yielded £1000. The surplus was invested in 4 per cent navy stock. As new trustees had no local interest, irregularities occurred in applying funds: some parents apprenticed their children to themselves, and others made up the balance of higher premiums for entrants to occupations not intended by the charity. When no children in Woodhorn were eligible in the early nineteenth century, the rector temporarily ceased to participate in the scheme. The trustees refused the charity commissioners' proposal to take advantage of section 30 of the Endaved Schools Act of 1869 to use funds for educational purposes; but in 1895 they were obliged to seek permission to offer grants other than for apprenticeships. From 1898 the charity, like others, was controlled by the charity commissioners. They were then permitted to award scholarships and sums below £10 each to deserving children. In 1943 the charity was re-established in three independent trusts, with new rules for appointing trustees, who were to include local authority representatives.

Triplet died on 18 July 1670. His will bequeaths 20 shillings to buy a ring for each of thirty of his previous scholars, and lists his extensive library, which he disposed of among his friends. He was buried later in July 1670 in Westminster Abbey 'near the Vestry', formerly St Faith's Chapel. In the distant south transept, his wall memorial is surmounted by his uncoloured coat of arms in a circle: a doe statant regardant, transfixed at the neck by an arrow, a chief indented. The tinctures are unrecorded.

MARGOT JOHNSON

Sources E. E. Brown, *The Triplett charity* (1971) • Foster, *Alum. Oxon.*, 1500–1714, vol. 3 • *Aubrey's Brief lives*, ed. O. L. Dick (1949); repr. (1972), 298–9 • P. Mussett, *Deans and major canons of Durham, 1541–1900* (1974) • *Walker rev.*, 68, 84, 144, 377 • Wood, *Ath. Oxon.: Fasti* (1820) • *Fasti Angl.* (Hardy), 3.317 • parish register, Westminster Abbey [burial] • *Diary of John Evelyn*, ed. W. Bray, new edn, ed. H. B. Wheatley, 4 vols. (1879), vol. 2, p. 248 • private information (2004) [Dr Triplett's Church of England primary school, Hayes, Middlesex] • will, PRO, PROB 11/333, sig. 105
Wealth at death see will, PRO, PROB 11/333, sig. 105

Tripp, Henry (1544/5–1612), Church of England clergyman and author, was born in London. He matriculated sizar at Pembroke College, Cambridge, at Easter 1562, graduating BA in early 1566. He was ordained deacon by Edmund Grindal, bishop of London, on 24 February 1570, when he gave his age as twenty-five. Immediately presented to the rectory of North Ockendon, Essex, by Gabriel Poyntz, he was instituted by Grindal three days after ordination.

Tripp commenced MA from Jesus College, Cambridge, in 1571, and was ordained priest by Edwin Sandys on 21 December following. On 10 November 1572 he was instituted rector of St Stephen Walbrook, London, on the presentation of the Grocers' Company. That year he published *The Regiment of the Povertie*, a translation of the Dutch protestant Andreas Gerardus's treatise on the regulation of parish poor relief.

Tripp's first wife, Mary, whom he married probably *c.*1568 and with whom he appears to have had no children, was buried in St Stephen on 20 June 1575. On 9 September 1577 Tripp was granted a diocesan preaching licence by the new bishop of London, John Aylmer. In 1581 he and Robert Crowley confronted Thomas Pownd, a former courtier imprisoned for circulating in manuscript a defence of Edmund Campion. In reply to Pownd's objections to their method of adducing the authority of scripture, Crowley wrote *An Aunswer to Sixe Reasons* (1581) at the behest of the ecclesiastical commissioners. To it was appended a four-page essay by Tripp, 'A breefe aunswer to Maister Pownds six reasons'.

Tripp resigned North Ockendon in or before November 1582, having been collated by the dean and chapter of St Paul's on 14 May 1582 to the rectory of St Faith's, London. The appointment involved a lapse from the crown, and was not confirmed by the lord chancellor until May 1583. At about this time Tripp must have remarried, for a son, William, was baptized and then buried at St Stephen in March 1585. A daughter, Anne, was baptized on 17 July 1587.

The parishes of St Gregory and of St Faith's under St Paul's were the epicentre of London's book trade, and between 1583 and 1596 Tripp regularly preached before the Stationers' Company. He was doubtless the man of those names admitted a freeman of the Stationers on 26 June 1598, 'being put over' from the Goldsmiths (Arber, *Regs. Stationers*, 2.723). He resigned St Stephen Walbrook in or before August 1601 and thereafter seems to have ministered only at St Faith's.

In 1606 Tripp translated, from the Latin of the contemporary German writer Otto Casman, a vade-mecum, *Goe with mee: Deare Pietie and Rare Charitie*. The only book entered in the Stationers' register as printed for him was another translation, *Otho Casmans 'Ethickes and Oeconomykes Philosophicall and Theosophicall'*, on 16 January 1609.

Tripp's association with Crowley, the Grocers' Company, and with the Stationers would suggest that he was a man of wide religious sympathies, but he was never one of London's nonconformist leaders. He died in 1612 and on 22 December that year the Stationers' court granted his widow an annual pension of £4 payable quarterly from that day, as long as she remained unmarried. His successor at St Faith's was collated there on 7 January 1613.

BRETT USHER

Sources Venn, *Alum. Cant.*, 1/4.266 · GL, MS 9535/1, fols. 148r, 151r · GL, MS 9531/13, fols. 153v, 207r · G. Hennessy, *Novum repertorium ecclesiasticum parochiale Londinense, or, London diocesan clergy succession from the earliest time to the year 1898* (1898) · Vicar-General's book, 'Hammond', LMA, DL/C/333, fol. 85v · returns to first-fruits office, James I, PRO, E331/London/D/C/1 and 5 · Arber, *Regs. Stationers*, vol. 1; 2.723; 3.304 · W. B. Bannerman and W. B. Bannerman, jun., eds., *The registers of St Stephen's, Walbrook, and of St Benet Sherehog, London*, 1, Harleian Society, register section, 49 (1919), v, 7, 8, 81, 83 · P. Milward, *Religious controversies of the Elizabethan age* (1977) · W. A. Jackson, ed., *Records of the court of the Stationers' Company, 1602 to 1640* (1957)

Tripp, Kathleen [*née* Kathe Loewenthal; *other married name* Kathe Dampf; *pseud.* Karen Gershon] (1923–1993), poet and writer, was born on 29 August 1923 in Bielefeld, northern Germany, the younger child of Paul Loewenthal, a Jewish architect, and his wife.

Following Hitler's accession to power in 1933 and Nazi persecution of Jews, Kathe became aware of the religious heritage which her Liberal Jewish parents had largely shed. She and her sister also belonged to a Zionist youth club, which prepared them for agricultural life in British-mandated Palestine.

With Jewish life growing ever more precarious, the older daughter left for a kibbutz in Palestine. But Kathe was below the minimum age of seventeen. Her desperate parents put her on a *Kindertransport* train, under the British government approved programme of admitting 10,000 unaccompanied children from Germany.

Kathe arrived in Harwich on the second children's transport on 19 December 1938, aged fifteen, and was sent to Whittingehame Farm School in East Lothian, Scotland, a temporary agricultural training centre on the family estate of the earls of Balfour. An unsettled period followed, including a short-lived marriage to Walter Dampf. Kathe embraced religion, Zionism (expecting to go to Palestine), and educational ambition when she gained a scholarship to Edinburgh University.

In the event, Kathe worked in Leeds, in domestic service and office jobs, then as matron in progressive boarding-schools in Scotland, Kent, and Wales, where she met a gentile humanist art teacher, Cecil Valentine Marshall (Val) Tripp (*b.* 1919). They married on 6 March 1948 at Welton, Lincolnshire, and had two boys and two girls. Her marriage certificate records that she changed her name by deed poll to Kathleen.

In the months following the end of the Second World War Kathleen Tripp learned that her parents had died in a camp in the Latvian capital of Riga. It was a blow from which she never recovered.

In 1950 Kathleen Tripp settled in her husband's home area of Ilminster, Somerset, and started writing in English. Winning a local verse competition in 1950 gave her confidence in her adopted language. Her youthful poems had been published in a German-Jewish magazine, *Die Jüdische Rundschau*, but her despairing mother had asked her how she could 'make poems in the language in which we are being cursed' (Gershon, 'Introduction', *Collected Poems*). Now, in a bleak but piercingly direct style, she wrote about the burden of bereavement, and the guilt of having survived her parents' fate.

Kathleen Tripp was keenly aware of her disjointed background: German which she now rejected, Jewish where her knowledge was too superficial to sustain inner certitude, and English where she felt merely tolerated—'just another bloody Jew' (interview, *Jewish Gazette*, March 1990). The pen-name she chose, Gershon, meaning 'a stranger there', from the name given by Moses to his son born in exile, pinpointed her dilemma. She was forty when her work was published by the left-leaning Victor Gollancz.

In December 1963, twenty-five years after fleeing Germany, Kathleen Tripp revisited Bielefeld. It was a pioneering pilgrimage in that era and an unnerving experience, as she slipped back immediately into feelings of rejection and helplessness. But she was shaken out of paralysis when she saw her father's name erased from the plaque on a building he had designed. Her complaints to the local newspaper led to a lengthy interview and stirred local interest in her, tempered—as she noted—by the townspeople's refusal to accept any responsibility for her family's fate.

Determined to re-examine her formative experiences, Kathleen Tripp appealed in newspaper correspondence columns for others who had arrived similarly in England. From these contacts, she formed a book, *We Came as Children* (1966), a collective autobiography with contributions from 234 anonymous former child refugees. The book opened an aspect of the war people were not yet ready to address and established Karen Gershon as a serious writer.

Gershon's first poetry publication, *Selected Poems*, came out simultaneously. It displayed all her recurrent themes: loss, longing, a sense of incompleteness, and the need to recreate a family. Her grief at the loss of her parents is poignantly expressed in 'I was not there to comfort them', which encapsulates her insatiable thirst in the line 'I must atone because I live.' Revenge was absent.

The two books won Karen Gershon the 1967 Jewish

Chronicle book prize and led to an Arts Council bursary and study grants from Israel and America. In August 1966, following publication, she was invited to Israel for a writers' symposium, and discovered she was not alone either as a Jew or in her psychological scars. The effect was liberating. On her next trip, after visiting Yad Vashem, the Jerusalem memorial museum, the closest she felt she could come to her parents' grave, she came to terms with her background as if she 'had been healed of a sickness' (*Jewish Chronicle*, 21 April 1967).

Her increasing emotional involvement led Kathleen Tripp to move with her family to Israel in 1969. She lectured and researched in Holocaust literature, while her husband taught art. But six years later they returned to England, leaving two married children in Israel. Another child later also married in Israel.

Gershon was a prolific writer: her fifteen volumes included reportage (*Postscript*, 1969), poetry (*My Daughters, my Sisters*, 1975; *Coming back from Babylon*, 1979), semi-autobiography (*Bread of Exile*, 1985), and fiction (*The Fifth Generation*, 1987). She reviewed Holocaust writers, gave poetry readings, including 'dial-a-poem' telephone recordings, and took part in radio and television programmes.

Kathleen Tripp's unremitting focus on grief affected her family. Her husband (who survived her) resented her refusal to let go of the past and felt that his children had been alienated from their English heritage. Her children avoided her work which, in fact, lost some of its edge as her personality grew more integrated. She felt disappointment that her writing did not reach out to a wider audience but stayed confined to fellow sufferers. It was, however, her lifeline. She died in the London Chest Hospital, Bethnal Green, on 24 March 1993, aged sixty-nine. Her final poem, published as *Grace Notes* nearly ten years after her death, showed a coming to terms with ageing and a reconciliation with the passions of youth. Its illustration by her daughter Stella Tripp also testified to easier family relations.   RUTH ROTHENBERG

Sources K. Gershon, 'A journey in exile', *Jewish Chronicle* (6 Dec 1963) · K. Gershon, 'Talking about intermarriage', *Jewish Chronicle* (16 Dec 1966) · K. Gershon, 'A question of pride', *Jewish Chronicle* (21 April 1967) · K. Gershon, 'Israel, my Israel: the voice of the diaspora', *Jewish Chronicle* (7 June 1968) · K. Gershon, 'From tourist to citizen', *Jewish Chronicle* (28 May 1971) · K. Gershon, 'Introduction', *Collected poems* (1990) · K. Gershon, *A Jew's calendar* (1965) · K. Gershon, *Postscript* (1969) · S. Kidron, interview with Karen Gershon, *Jerusalem Post* (8 Dec 1967) · N. Wood, interview, *Jewish Gazette* [Manchester] (30 March 1990) · *A stranger in a strange land*, Channel 4 television programme · R. Grunberger, review, *Jewish Chronicle* (21 Nov 1969) · M. Horowitz, review, *Jewish Chronicle* (23 Feb 1990) · N. Wood, review, *Jewish Chronicle* (23 Feb 1990) · J. Robson, review, *Jewish Chronicle* (20 May 1966) · G. Mayer, review, *AJR Journal* [Association of Jewish Refugees] (Feb 2003) · m. cert. [Cecil Tripp] · d. cert.

Likenesses photographs, *Jewish Chronicle* Library

Tristram, Ernest William (1882–1952), painter and art historian, was born on 27 December 1882 at 36 Richmond Terrace, Carmarthen, the fourth child in a family of five, of Francis William Tristram, engineer (permanent way inspector), and his wife, Sarah Harverson. After some years at the grammar school in Carmarthen, where he early showed much ability in drawing, painting, and design, Tristram obtained an exhibition at the Royal College of Art, South Kensington, as well as an exhibition in chemistry at the Royal College of Science. He elected to take up the College of Art award and studied there mainly in the design school, under the arts and crafts architect and designer W. R. Lethaby, whose fascination with the middle ages he came to share. Tristram was awarded a travelling studentship which enabled him to study early French and Italian painting, as well as examples of English medieval art, especially wall painting and manuscripts, in which he had already taken a particular interest. It proved in the end to be his principal life's work (for the background of which he was particularly well equipped as a practising member of the Roman Catholic church into which he was received in 1914). Since the third edition of C. F. Keyser's *A List of Buildings in Great Britain and Ireland Having Mural and other Painting Decorations* was published in 1883, no publication surveying this field of study had appeared, although many new paintings had been discovered. As his *Times* obituarist commented, Tristram 'was never allowed to have an idle moment' after he embarked on his comprehensive investigation of this neglected subject (*The Times*).

While still a student Tristram had begun making meticulous watercolour copies of medieval wall and panel paintings which were to grow into a very large and important collection, representing almost the only approach to a national record of these art works in Britain. Several hundreds of his sketches, copies, reconstructions, and other records are now held in the Victoria and Albert Museum; a further large collection was bequeathed at his death to Buckfast Abbey, Devon. One of the earliest occasions on which any considerable assembly of Tristram's facsimiles was seen was in the exhibition of British primitives at Burlington House in 1923. The catalogue, published in a limited edition of 150 copies in 1924, reproduced some twenty of these copies, with a general introduction by W. G. Constable, with whom Tristram was also associated.

Tristram combined his work as the chronicler of English medieval wall paintings with an academic career. He returned to the Royal College of Art as a member of the staff in 1906, and after various promotions became professor of design in 1925, a post he held until his retirement in 1948, when he became professor emeritus. A queue of students could always be found in the corridor outside his room waiting to discuss their work; and in his room were generally examples of medieval work or his own copies. Although he was a somewhat unbusinesslike man and not always approachable, he was always generous with his advice to students with interests similar to his own.

In the course of his career Tristram handled and recorded almost every major and many minor wall paintings throughout the country, as well as a number of monuments. Examples included paintings at Westminster Abbey; Canterbury, Exeter, St Albans, and Winchester cathedrals; St George's Chapel at Windsor; Eton

College; and Christ Church, Oxford. In addition to recording their appearance, he also cleaned and conserved many important wall paintings, including the early paintings in the vault of St Gabriel's Chapel and the later *Legend of St Eustace* at Canterbury and the murals in the holy cross and lady chapels at Winchester. At Westminster he was in his element: Lethaby had published his study *Westminster Abbey and the King's Craftsmen* in 1906 and as his pupil Tristram had developed a particular affinity for the artists of Westminster or court school of painting active when the decorated Gothic style was at its height in England. He cleaned and conserved the decoration on the coronation chair, and the then recently discovered wall paintings of the incredulity of St Thomas and St Christopher. Tristram also advised on the cleaning and repainting of the late medieval bosses in the cathedral cloisters at Norwich in 1934, and was concerned with the restoration of the Pre-Raphaelite paintings in the Oxford Union and the cleaning of James Thornhill's murals in the dome of St Paul's Cathedral. Unfortunately his technical methods of preservation were flawed: his use of wax, dissolved in turpentine, as a fixative often proved disastrous, as the impervious and shiny surface thus produced bloomed and collapsed when lime-impregnated damp in the walls could not get out.

In the 1920s Tristram began publishing the results of his labours: a paper, 'English methods of wall painting,' appeared in 1924 and in 1926–7 he published an article jointly with M. R. James in the *Archaeologia*, on the wall paintings in Croughton church, Northamptonshire, which he had investigated with the assistance of three local craftsmen whom he had trained himself. His first important work was *English Medieval Painting*, published in 1927, jointly with Tancred Borenius, in which a high proportion of the plates were reproductions of Tristram's own drawings. Here Tristram, in addition to his now well-developed and sensitive artistic technique as a recorder of English medieval paintings, showed his ability as an art historian, and demonstrated his wide knowledge of medieval art in general. His deductions and interpretations were not always sound or accurate, and his dating was often based more on stylistic grounds, intuition, and experience than on reasoned argument and comparison. But this did not seriously detract from his great knowledge and achievement.

Publications continued to appear in the next decade or so in the journals of almost every county archaeological society where he had done work, notably in Norfolk, Suffolk, Essex, and Buckinghamshire. He frequently contributed reports of preservation work in progress to *The Times* and also wrote for the *Burlington Magazine* and the Walpole Society. But Tristram's greatest works were the monumental volumes published with the aid of the Pilgrim Trust in 1944 and 1950 and entitled *English Medieval Wall Painting*, covering the twelfth and thirteenth century respectively. They offered elaborate discussions of iconography, technique, and subject matter, with indexes and catalogues, and were almost entirely illustrated by his own copies. A third volume, on the fourteenth century,

was posthumously published in 1955, edited by his second wife, Eileen, with a catalogue by Monica Bardswell.

In addition to his sensitive copying of ancient examples, Tristram produced some good original work, such as the paintings to be seen in York Minster, St Elizabeth's Church, Eastbourne, St Fin Barre's Cathedral, Cork, and the reredos in Kedington church, Suffolk, where his second wife was his model for the Virgin Mary. He designed a banner for the Friends of Canterbury Cathedral, which was worked by the Royal School of Needlework.

Tristram was twice married: first, on 24 April 1920, to Mary Esther Hedgecock (*b.* 1892/3), the daughter of the Revd Henry Colburn, vicar of St Barnabas's Church, Gillingham, Kent. This marriage was annulled, and there were no children. On 25 June 1934 he married Eileen Maude (*b.* 1902/3), a student at the Royal College of Art, daughter of Henry Churnside Beaumont Dann, a lieutenant-colonel in the Indian army; they had two daughters. Tristram died at the Melvin Nursing Home, Newton Abbot, on 11 January 1952.

Tristram's work was widely recognized. He received honorary DLitt degrees from Oxford (1931) and Birmingham (1946); he was an honorary ARIBA (1935), and, for a time, a fellow of the Society of Antiquaries. The leading expert in his field by the age of forty, he was invariably consulted every time a wall painting was discovered in a village church: as M. R. James—with whom Tristram collaborated on the Eton College chapel 'frescoes'—put it, 'He is, indeed, the Sherlock Holmes or the Dr Thorndyke of the situation' (*The Times*, 21 Oct 1933). His achievement as the recorder of English wall paintings and the most persistent publicist for their conservation is still unquestioned, and his scholarly publications remain the basis of modern art historical research in his field.

E. C. Rouse, rev. Rosemary Mitchell

Sources *The Times* (12 Jan 1952) · *Antiquaries Journal*, 32 (1952), 267 · *WWW, 1951–60* · J. C. Harvey, 'Tristram, Ernest William', *The dictionary of art*, ed. J. Turner (1996) · R. W. Pfaff, *Montague Rhode James* (1980) · b. cert. · m. cert. · *CGPLA Eng. & Wales* (1952)
Archives Church of England Record Centre, corresp. and papers relating to wall paintings · Derbys. RO, corresp. and papers relating to inspection of wall paintings at All Saints Church, Dale Abbey · V&A NAL, notebooks of him and Monica Bardswell relating to English medieval wall paintings
Wealth at death £13,302 16s. 1d.: probate, 28 March 1952, *CGPLA Eng. & Wales*

Tristram, Henry Baker (1822–1906), geologist and naturalist, born at Eglingham, Northumberland, on 11 May 1822, was the eldest son of Henry Baker Tristram, vicar of Eglingham, and his wife, Charlotte, the daughter of Thomas Smith. His younger brother Thomas Hutchinson Tristram (1825–1912), an ecclesiastical lawyer, became chancellor of London and many other dioceses. Educated first at Durham School, Henry became a scholar of Lincoln College, Oxford, in 1839; he graduated BA with a second class in classics in 1844, and proceeded MA in 1846. He was ordained a deacon in 1845 and priest in 1846, and was curate of Morchard Bishop (1845–6). Because of lung trouble he went to Bermuda, where he was secretary to the governor and naval and military chaplain from 1847 to 1849.

There he took up the study of birds and shells. In 1849 he became rector of Castle Eden, co. Durham, and held the living until 1860. He married in 1850 Eleanor Mary (d. 1903), the daughter of Captain P. Bowlby; they had one son and seven daughters, including the missionary and teacher Katherine Alice Salvin *Tristram.

Because of ill health Tristram journeyed to Algeria for the winters of 1855–6 and 1856–7. He travelled far into the desert, made an ornithological collection, and gathered material for his first book, *The Great Sahara* (1860). In the winter of 1858–9 he visited Palestine and Egypt, and in an article on the fauna of Palestine expressed surprise at the limited knowledge of the plant and animal life of the area, which he attributed to the dangers of travel in the region and the stronger emphasis on history and scripture in its historiography. On his return to England he became master of Greatham Hospital (1860) and vicar of Greatham, co. Durham. After a further visit to Palestine in 1863–4 he published the first of his books on the Holy Land, *The Land of Israel* (1865), produced at the request of the Society for Promoting Christian Knowledge. In 1868 he received from Edinburgh University the honorary degree of LLD, and was elected a fellow of the Royal Society. He was made honorary canon of Durham in 1870 and canon residentiary in 1874, when he left Greatham.

In 1879 Tristram declined Lord Beaconsfield's offer of the Anglican bishopric in Jerusalem, although he visited Palestine again in 1880–01, 1894, and 1897. During 1891 he travelled in Japan, China, and the American north-west. His chief interest lay in work for the Church Missionary Society, and he acted for forty years as its representative in the county of Durham. He was strongly protestant in conviction and associated himself with the moderate evangelicals.

In his travels and work as a naturalist, Tristram was a close observer and an avid and diligent collector. His knowledge of the geology, topography, and natural history of Palestine was very considerable, and he was a pioneer of Palestine zoology. His study of the larks and chats of north Africa, written though not published before the issue of Darwin's *Origin of Species* in 1859, led him to anticipate and subsequently support Darwin and Wallace's communication on evolution to the Linnean Society, though he afterwards modified his views. His collection of 20,000 birds, of which he published a catalogue (1889), he sold to the museum in Liverpool; his collection of birds' eggs ultimately passed to the Natural History Museum. He acted as examiner for the geography prize awarded to public school students by the Royal Geographical Society.

Tristram's scientific competence and easy style made his writings both valuable and popular. In addition to contributions to periodical literature and to Smith's *Dictionary of the Bible*, he published *The Land of Israel: a Journal of Travel with Reference to its Physical History* (1865; 3rd edn, 1876); *The Natural History of the Bible* (1867); *The Topography of the Holy Land* (1872; later entitled *Bible Places, or, The Topography of the Holy Land*, 5th edn, 1897); *The Land of Moab: Travels and Discoveries on the East Side of the Dead Sea and the Jordan* (1873); *Pathways of Palestine: a Descriptive Tour through the Holy Land*

(1881–2); *The Fauna and Flora of Palestine* (1884), a work which laid the foundations of Palestinian biological research and was published as one of the Palestine Exploration Fund's volumes in the monumental survey of western Palestine; *Eastern Customs in Bible Lands* (1894); and *Rambles in Japan* (1895).

Tristram was an enthusiastic freemason, and in 1884 was appointed grand chaplain of England, and in 1885 deputy provincial grand master for Durham. In 1891 he again visited Japan, where one of his daughters was a missionary. In 1893 he presided over the biological section of the British Association at Nottingham. He remained active and alert until his death from heart disease at his residence in The College, Durham, on 8 March 1906.

A. R. BUCKLAND, *rev.* ROBIN A. BUTLIN

Sources A. G., *PRS*, 80B (1908), xlii–xliv · D. Livingstone, *Darwin's forgotten defenders: the encounter between evangelical theology and evolutionary thought* (1987) · Y. Ben-Arieh, *The rediscovery of the Holy Land in the nineteenth century* (1979) · D. W. Freshfield, 'The place of geography in education', *Proceedings* [Royal Geographical Society], new ser., 8 (1886), 698–718 · G. A. Smith, *The historical geography of the Holy Land* (1894) · *The Field* (17 March 1906) · *The Record* (16 March 1906) · *Church Missionary Intelligencer*, 57 (April 1906) · d. cert. · WWW

Archives LPL, corresp. with E. W. Benson · LPL, letters to A. C. Tait relating to Reformed Armenian Church · Palestine Exploration Fund, London, letters to Palestine Exploration Fund

Likenesses Lock & Whitfield, woodburytype photograph, NPG; repro. in T. Cooper, *Men of mark: a gallery of contemporary portraits* (1883)

Wealth at death £9143 3s. 3d.: probate, 31 March 1906, CGPLA Eng. & Wales

Tristram, Katherine Alice Salvin (1858–1948), missionary and teacher in Japan, was born on 29 April 1858 in Castle Eden, co. Durham, as the fifth child of the Revd Henry Baker *Tristram (1822–1906), canon of Durham, and his wife, Eleanor Mary (d. 1903), daughter of Captain P. Bowlby. She was educated at Cheltenham Ladies' College, and in 1882 she was appointed lecturer in mathematics at Westfield College, London, becoming the college's first resident lecturer. She continued her studies while teaching and in 1887 graduated from the University of London less than ten years after women were first admitted to degrees.

In May 1887 Tristram offered her services as a missionary in Japan under a plan for Christian educational institutions which had been put forward by Professor Masakazu Toyama of the University of Tokyo, who was not himself a Christian. The Japanese committee responsible for a newly established institute for women's education in Osaka offered her the principalship, but the missionary societies did not favour the notion of a missionary being employed by a non-Christian committee, so she offered her services instead to the Church Missionary Society and left for Japan on 20 October 1888. She remained in Japan until 1938, seeing her family only during the occasional home leave, apart from the visit of her father to Japan in 1891.

Upon arrival Tristram joined the staff of the Eisei Girls' School, which had been founded in Osaka in 1879 and was taken over by the Church Missionary Society on 1 March

1889. Tristram managed to pass an examination in Japanese in 1889, and in January 1890 she became headmistress of the school. On 10 March 1890 the school was reopened under a new name, the Bishop Poole Memorial Girls' School, after Arthur William Poole, the first English bishop in Japan. At that time there were at the school two other British women apart from Tristram, as well as eight Japanese teachers, including four women, and there were forty-nine pupils, of whom twenty-three were Christians. A year after her arrival she had written, 'Our great hope for the school is that it may be a missionary school, in the sense of the girls themselves who are Christians being missionaries to the others' (*One Hundred and Ten Years of Poole Gakuin in Photographs*, 140), and throughout her fifty years in Japan she remained a keen evangelist. As such, she was responsible not only for the teaching offered in the school but also for spreading the Christian faith among the pupils, in which she met with considerable success at first. Under her guidance as a woman graduate, a rarity among the female missionaries, the school's academic reputation grew; in a report written in 1889 the Revd Charles Frederick Warren, secretary of the Church Missionary Society mission in Japan, noted 'the improvement of the course of study, so as to meet the needs of girls and women of the upper classes' (*Church Missionary Intelligencer*, Sept 1889, 568). It was presumably to meet those needs that, according to her father (Tristram, *Rambles*, 242), flower arrangement and the tea ceremony were included in the curriculum. In 1909 the school finally received government recognition as a high school while retaining the right to preach the gospel, and it was still in existence in 2000 in the form of a private university, Poole Gakuin University.

Tristram was, however, not only seeking to meet the needs of the 'upper classes'. At the time of her father's visit, she was running a Sunday school 'in a poor woman's dwelling-house … in a very poor part of the city' (Tristram, *Rambles*, 230). She was engaged in other work, too, such as nursing the injured following the Osaka earthquake of 1891 and, in 1901–2, running a class for policemen, which consisted of a mixture of English instruction and Bible teaching.

Upon retirement in 1927, Tristram gave much of her time to the Garden Home, a sanatorium established outside Tokyo for sufferers from tuberculosis. In 1931 she was awarded the Ranju Hosho (blue ribbon Distinguished Service Medal) by the emperor in recognition of her work in Japan. In 1937, following the outbreak of war with China and the increasing international isolation of Japan, life became more difficult for the British and American missionaries, and in 1938 she left Japan for good.

Like many other female missionaries, Tristram dedicated her life to her career as a missionary and remained unmarried. She died at Brislington House, Bristol, on 24 August 1948. P. F. KORNICKI

Sources One hundred and ten years of Poole Gakuin in photographs (1990) • E. Stock, *The history of the Church Missionary Society: its environment, its men and its work*, 4 vols. (1899–1916) • Tochio Kubo, 'K. Torisutoramu – Pūru jogakkōchō to shite yonjūnen', *Akashibitotachi – Nihon Seikōkai jinbutsushi* (1974) • H. B. Tristram, *Rambles in Japan* (1895) • WWW, 1951–60 • 'Recollections of Henry Baker Tristram D.D., F.R.S.: an account written by Louisa Hely Hutchinson Tristram, his daughter and secretary, in 1898', ed. L. H. H. Tristram, unpublished typescript, priv. coll. • J. Sondheimer, *Castle Adamant in Hampstead: a history of Westfield College, 1882–1982* (1983) • d. cert.

Archives U. Birm. L., Church Missionary Society archives

Likenesses bust, probably Poole Gakuin Daigaku, Osaka; repro. in *One hundred and ten years of Poole Gakuin*, 93 • photographs, probably Poole Gakuin Daigaku, Osaka; repro. in *One hundred and ten years of Poole Gakuin*

Wealth at death £10,074 6s. 3d.: probate, 7 Dec 1948, CGPLA Eng. & Wales

Tritton, Joseph Herbert (1844–1923), banker, was born on 5 September 1844 at Olney Lodge, Battersea, Surrey, the eldest son of Joseph Tritton (1819–1887), a Quaker banker, and his wife, Amelia, daughter of Joseph Hanson of Brixton. He was educated at Rugby School (c.1855–1862). On 17 June 1867, he married Lucy Jane, the daughter of Henry Abel Smith (1826–1890) of Wilford, Nottingham, a member of a banking family with interests in Lincoln and Nottingham. They had five sons and four daughters. The family house was at Lyons Hall, Great Leighs, Chelmsford, the Essex property inherited by his father and passed on to him.

After leaving Rugby, Tritton joined the bank of Barclay, Bevan, Tritton, Twells & Co. in 1867, and became a junior partner. He was following family tradition, as members of the Tritton family had held partnerships in the firm since 1783, when John Hinton Tritton (his great-grandfather) entered the bank. Through various changes of partnership and the takeover of Ransome, Bouverie & Co. of Pall Mall in 1888 and the Brighton Union Bank in 1894 the name Tritton remained in the title. The bank's name was distinctive and, in the years between 1888 and 1896, Barclay, Bevan, and Tritton, Ransome, Bouverie & Co. was popularly known as 'the long firm' (*DBB*, 558).

The business still operated as a private bank, as a member of the London Clearing House and as clearing bank for a number of country partnerships, many of which had family and Quaker connections with the partners in Barclay, Bevan, Tritton & Co. During the period when Tritton became a full partner it was becoming clear that the days of the private banks were numbered, and that to protect their relationship with the country banks and prevent their absorption into the rapidly growing joint-stock companies it was necessary to form a limited company. The partners in Barclay, Bevan, Tritton & Co. were the key figures in the foundation of Barclay & Co. in 1896. They nevertheless hoped to continue the private character of their existing institutions by restricting shareholdings to the partners of the twenty amalgamating firms (mostly Quaker). The character of the private banker is well illustrated by Tritton's pithy comment that there were 'three cardinal virtues in the banker's character—Incredulity, Affability and the Power to say No' ('President's address to the Institute of Bankers', 1885).

Tritton became a member of the first board of directors,

as well as a local director in the Lombard Street local head office. He remained on the board until his retirement in 1918, and one of his sons followed him into the bank in 1914. Tritton was a progressive banker, and enthusiastic about the establishment of a professional forum for the training of young bankers and the discussion of professional issues. He was a founder member of the Institute of Bankers, serving on the council from the beginning, and served as the institute's third president (1885–1887), after Sir John Lubbock and Richard Biddulph Martin. He also served a second term of office in 1902–4. As president he started the practice of reviewing the previous year in his presidential address. One of the main reasons for establishing the institute was to improve the education of clerks and, in discussions over the type of syllabus to be offered, Tritton supported the Billinghurst scheme, which advocated a practical syllabus for training bankers. In 1902, when he sat on a committee to review the syllabus, he recommended the introduction of commercial history and geography. As chairman in 1886 he announced that his bank would follow the lead of the London and County Bank in offering a gratuity to successful candidates in the institute's exams.

Tritton was active in most of the pressure groups representing bankers in the City. In the institute and other forums he contributed papers and took part in discussions on a variety of practical topics like bills of exchange and the London money market. He was a founder member and treasurer of the Central Association of Bankers formed in 1895 by representatives of the committee of the London Clearing House, the West End banks and the Association of English Country Bankers to 'speak in the name of all the Banks in the Country' (Green, 72). In addition he was a member of the Council of Foreign Bondholders, honorary secretary of the Committee of London Clearing Bankers (1891–1905), and a founder member of the London chamber of commerce, of which he became president.

Tritton was a 'sound money' man and took a prominent position in the defence of the gold standard in the controversy over the remonetization of silver and the establishment of a connected rate for the two metals. Like most City men, Tritton feared it would lead to inflation and undermine Britain's position as a financial centre in the world. He was a chairman of the Gold Standard Defence Association established in 1895, and in the same year gave an address to the London Institution entitled 'The assault on the gold standard'. The assault came from the Bimetallic League, which saw the remonetization of silver as a way of easing trade with the rest of the world and thereby increasing employment at home.

Consistent with his stand on the gold standard and free trade, Tritton argued for free trade saying that 'as a business man, in the centre of the business of the world, and with his hand on the pulse of the trade of the world he looked with dread upon even a suggestion to close our ports whether he considered the home trade or the international trade which brought an enormous profit to this country' (The Times, 4 Jan 1904).

Tritton was a lieutenant for the City of London, chairman of the Indo-European Telegraph Company, and a member of the Company of Shipwrights and of the fellowship of the Russia Company. In his private life he was keenly interested in genealogy and produced a history of his family called Tritton: the Place and the Family in 1907. Like his father, he wrote religious poetry and was involved in charity work, particularly for the Young Men's Christian Association. He received the Persian order of the Lion and the Sun.

In 1918 Tritton retired from the board of Barclays. A fall from his horse restricted his activities in his later years, and he died at his home, Lyons Hall, Great Leighs, Essex on 11 September 1923. He was described in an obituary as 'a link with a generation of business men which has now all but disappeared, and of a time when manners were more stately and life more leisurely' (Journal of the Institute of Bankers, 1923).   JESSIE CAMPBELL

Sources P. E. Smart, 'Tritton, Joseph Herbert', DBB · 'President's address to the Institute of Bankers, 1885', Journal of the Institute of Bankers, 7/pt 8 (Nov 1886) · Journal of the Institute of Bankers (Oct 1923) · E. Green, Debtors to their profession: a history of the Institute of Bankers, 1879–1979 (1979), 72 · The Times (4 Jan 1904) · Y. Cassis, City bankers, 1890–1914, trans. M. Rocque (1994) [Fr. orig., Banquiers de la City à l'époque édouardienne, 1890–1914 (1984)] · J. H. Tritton, Tritton: the place and the family (1907) · J. A. S. L. Leighton-Boyce, Smiths, the bankers, 1658–1958 (1958) · d. cert. · CGPLA Eng. & Wales (1923)
Archives Essex RO | Barclays Bank, Manchester, archives
Likenesses G. Herkomer, portrait, 1905, Barclays Bank, 54 Lombard Street, London · photograph, Barclays Bank, 54 Lombard Street, London
Wealth at death £193,118 13s. 4d.: probate, 25 Oct 1923, CGPLA Eng. & Wales

Tritton, Sir William Ashbee (1875–1946), engineer, was born in Islington on 19 June 1875, the son of William Birch Tritton, a stockbroker, and his wife, Ellen Hannah Ashbee. Tritton was educated at Christ's College, Finchley, and King's College, London. In 1891 he was apprenticed with J. and H. Gwynne of Hammersmith, hydraulic engineers. After completing his apprenticeship and serving with an assay company, he became an inspector of steel rails. He next joined J. I. Thornycroft & Co. at its Chiswick works and was responsible for the building of circulating pumps in torpedo boats. He gained further experience as a shift engineer with the Metropolitan Electric Supply Company and in 1899 entered the toolroom of the Linotype Company. In this post he seems to have visited Germany and gained the experience which enabled him in 1904 to go out on behalf of R. Garrett & Sons Ltd, of Leiston, Suffolk, to clear up difficulties which had arisen in their German works.

In 1905 Tritton accepted the position of general manager of William Foster & Co. Ltd, agricultural engineers, of Lincoln. The firm's affairs were then in a poor condition, but Tritton's energy and ability effected a recovery; in the process he was in touch with agents all over the world, especially in Russia and Argentina. In 1911 he became managing director.

Tritton came into prominence in the First World War through the part he played in the design and production of tanks. At the beginning of the war he was invited to discuss with Rear-Admiral Reginald Bacon, managing director of the Coventry ordnance works, the problem of transporting 15 inch howitzers. Their proposals were laid before Winston Churchill, then first lord of the Admiralty and first sea lord, and an order for tractors was placed with Tritton's company. During the trials, which proved satisfactory, a large ditch was crossed by a tractor, and Churchill asked whether a machine could be constructed which would cross trenches. Tritton designed a tractor which could cross a trench 8 feet wide by laying its own portable bridge. The machine was not used, however, because of its weight, and because in the meantime the whole concept had caught Churchill's imagination; with his customary energy he appointed a 'landships' committee, on 20 February 1915, under the chairmanship of Eustace Tennyson-D'Eyncourt, to investigate the project more fully. Meanwhile, Ernest Swinton was urging similar proposals upon the War Office.

In June 1915 a joint naval and military committee was formed to consider the alternative proposals of a tractor running on large wheels or caterpillar tracks. Tritton, whose firm already made caterpillar tractors, had been involved from the outset and at the end of July he was told more exactly what the landship machine was supposed to do. His first model was ready to move under its own power on 8 September but it required considerable modification before its traction and steering were adjudged satisfactory, on 22 November. This machine was named 'Little Willie'. Tritton continued to modify his design for the body, assisted by Lieutenant (later Major) Walter Gordon Wilson, who was responsible for the engine. Their new version had the now familiar rhomboidal profile, with the tracks running round the periphery and the gun-turret, formerly mounted on top, brought down between the tracks to give greater stability. This machine was named 'Big Willie' or 'Mother'. On comparative trials, Mother demonstrated its superiority as a fighting machine. Swathed in tarpaulins for secrecy, it was taken by rail to Hatfield for trials on 29 January and 2 February 1916, when Lloyd George, Balfour, McKenna, Kitchener, Lieutenant-General Robertson and many other soldiers, and engineers were present. The trials were successful and orders were placed with Fosters and other firms. To preserve secrecy the new machines were described as 'tanks', an inoffensive term which took on a new meaning when the first went into action in France, on 15 September 1916. Although their first appearance was somewhat disappointing, improvements were soon made. Tritton, who was knighted in 1917, was appointed director of construction of the mechanical warfare supply department (tanks) and he devised a modified tank, lighter, smaller, and faster, known as the Whippet, which was used successfully at Cambrai and in the campaigns of 1918 under the command of H. J. Elles.

In 1919 the Royal Commission on Awards to Inventors had the difficult task of assessing the claims of those who had helped in the evolution of the tank. Tritton and Wilson shared £15,000, by far the highest award, and the credit of designing and producing the tank 'in a concrete practical shape'.

In 1927 Tritton formed Gwynnes Pumps Ltd to take over the business of Gwynnes of Hammersmith, and transferred its activities to Lincoln. He took a leading part in the maintenance of essential services during the general strike in 1926 and he became chairman of Fosters in 1939. A cautious and painstaking man, he was a pleasant and hospitable companion and a good employer. He was of even temper, although strong views, strongly expressed, sometimes gave the impression that he was hasty. He took little part in public life, although he gave valuable expert help to the Lincoln County Hospital extension schemes. He became a justice of the peace in 1934 and was for a time chairman of his bench.

In 1916 Tritton married Isabella Johnstone White (d. 1950), daughter of Grahame Gillies, of Perth; there were no children. Tritton died in the Lindum Nursing Home, Lincoln, on 24 September 1946.

J. W. F. HILL, rev. ANITA MCCONNELL

Sources E. H. W. Tennyson-D'Eyncourt, *A shipbuilder's yarn* [1948], 114–38 · A. G. Stern, *Tanks, 1914–18, the log book of a pioneer* (1919) · E. D. Swinton, *Eyewitness* (1932), 169–73, 189–98 · G. Hartcup, *The war of invention: scientific developments, 1914–18* (1988), 80–90
Likenesses photograph, repro. in Stern, *Tanks, 1914–18*
Wealth at death £16,075 7s. 8d.: probate, 11 Dec 1946, CGPLA Eng. & Wales

Trivet, Nicholas. *See* Trevet, Nicholas (b. 1257x65, d. in or after 1334).

Trivet, Sir Thomas. *See* Trevet, Sir Thomas (d. 1388).

Trocchi, Alexander Whitelaw Robertson (1925–1984), writer, was born on 30 July 1925 at 29 Smith Street, Glasgow, the third son of Alfredo Luigi Trocchi (d. 1963) and Annie Jack Langley, *née* Robertson (d. 1942). His father, child of an Italian immigrant, had been a music-hall performer and musician, then turned to managing orchestras and bands. By the time of his youngest son's birth he had partly Anglicized his name to Alfred Louis Trocchi, and mindful of anti-Italian prejudice in Glasgow, his elder sons later dropped his surname in favour of Robertson, their mother's maiden name. Her family were irreproachably middle class. Changing musical tastes and ill health made Alfredo permanently unemployable. The Trocchis moved from the south side to the centre of the city, where Annie ran their premises as a boarding-house. Like his brothers Alexander Trocchi was educated at the very reputable Hillhead primary school and high school, where he did well in his studies and as a sportsman. The school was evacuated to Galloway when the Second World War started, but in January 1942 Alex was called home. His mother had died suddenly, poisoned by a can of pilchards, and was lowered, as he put it, 'into a grave that was my destruction'. He was consciously marked by this blow for the rest of his life.

Trocchi enrolled at Glasgow University later that year, but in February 1943 was called up for war service. He trained as a Fleet Air Arm pilot, partly in Canada, but for reasons not clear was transferred before qualifying into

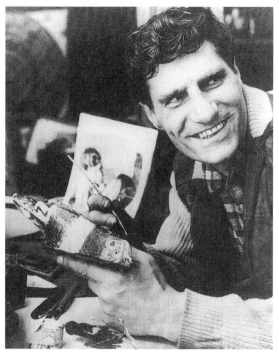

Alexander Whitelaw Robertson Trocchi (1925–1984), by unknown photographer, 1963

the Royal Navy as a seaman. He performed well in escort duties on the icy and perilous Arctic convoy route to Murmansk. Before demobilization in November 1946 he was offered a commission, but chose instead to re-enter Glasgow University as a student of English and philosophy.

Two reputations—for brilliance and for deviance—began at university, where Trocchi displayed his capacity to draw people to him with his charm, and then manipulate them. He lived with a veterinary student, Betty Whyte, in a shepherd's cottage 10 miles out of Glasgow, where he attempted for a time to raise pigs. On 15 January 1947 they were secretly married, and their first daughter, Jacqueline, was born exactly a year later. Betty's studies had lapsed, but in 1950 Alex sat his final exams. Due to a miscalculation in his use of benzedrine Alex fell asleep in a philosophy final, but very good marks in English obtained him second-class honours, and his tutors, who had thought him worthy of a first, secured him the Kemsley travelling scholarship. Alex, however, did not want to become an academic. He had for years been experimenting with creative writing, and with wife and daughter he travelled widely in Europe before settling in a suburb of Paris. In 1951 a long poem by Trocchi appeared in the very prestigious Rome-based journal *Botteghe Oscure*, and launched him as an 'international' writer. A second daughter, Margot, was born in May that year.

In 1952, when Trocchi committed himself to living in Paris, there were thousands of expatriate Americans in the city, many of them aspirant creative writers. Drugs—not only benzedrine, but hashish and cocaine—were part of their culture. Invited by a rich American to edit a new magazine, Trocchi was attracted by Jane Lougee, an American woman with means, from Maine, designated his assistant. He demanded a separation from Betty who eventually, after Trocchi had secured a Mexican divorce in Paris, went to bring up their daughters in New Zealand. In May 1952 the first of eleven issues of *Merlin* appeared. Its 1000 copies were peddled by young avant-gardists in Amsterdam, London, and New York as well as Paris. During its brief existence the journal published work by Sartre, Genet, Eluard, Ionesco, Hikmet, Italo Svevo, Robert Creeley, Pablo Neruda, Henry Miller, and Samuel Beckett. Trocchi and his fellow enthusiasts established Collection Merlin to publish books, and it brought out Beckett's first major English-language publication, *Watt*.

This publishing enterprise came under the control of Maurice Girodias, who backed it on the understanding that Trocchi's circle would supply texts—'dirty books'—for his Olympia Press, founded in 1953 to take advantage of the absence of censorship in France and to tap the local and international markets for English-language pornography. Trocchi himself supplied seven such texts over three years, five under the pseudonym Frances Lengel: *Helen and Desire* (1953); *The Carnal Days of Helen Seferis*, *Young Adam*, *School for Wives* (all 1954); and *White Thighs* (1955). In 1954 he contributed *Frank Harris—my Life and Loves: Volume 5*, a concocted continuation of an existing 'dirty book', and, in 1955, *Thongs*, the 'memoirs' of Carmencita de las Lunas. These books later appeared, with variant titles, in many editions, some pirated, and in numerous languages. They should not be regarded as mere hackwork; Trocchi composed blatant pornography with the skills of a remarkable prose stylist. *Thongs*, for instance, is detached, parodic, and largely hilarious, and involves sharp implicit satire of the Catholic church. *Young Adam* was Trocchi's first 'serious novel', and Trocchi later removed gratuitous sexual episodes on which Girodias had insisted, and published it as his own work. This latter novel was treated respectfully by critics who noted its close relationship with Camus's *L'étranger*. The unlikeable protagonist, Joe, encountered working on a barge on the Forth and Clyde Canal, is and is not responsible for the death of his lover by drowning. Eroticism pervades the book, connected with what may be called Trocchi's major philosophical preoccupation—for the solipsistic narrator the world should exist 'not as a foreign element to be looked at' but as 'an extension of myself'. The proprieties of respectable society prevent us breaking into true continuity of self with others, self with world—'the profoundest experiences are in the ordinary situation locked out from one's arena of experience by the inflexible barrier of good character' (1996 edn, 69, 36).

In August 1954 Jane Lougee went back to America, where she soon afterwards married; Trocchi's already exuberant promiscuity was accentuated. *Merlin* folded in 1955, and Trocchi decided to quit Paris. After some time in London, in April 1956, he followed Jane to the United States, where by the autumn he was a 'scow captain' with the New York Trap Rock Corporation, on a barge shifting heavy cargoes on the city's waterways, a job which gave him much free time for writing. By now his addiction to heroin was confirmed for life, and the country in which he found himself was unsympathetic to drug addicts. From the sphere of high Parisian literary talk Trocchi had descended into a hell of heavily stigmatized criminality. But it was at a literary party in Greenwich Village that he met a respectable 21-year-old, Marilyn Rose Hicks. He left the scows and they drove to Mexico, where Trocchi divorced Betty for a second time and, on 13 August 1957, married Lyn. They wintered in Venice West, Los Angeles, where the new 'beat generation' of writers had one of its epicentres. Trocchi impressed Allen Ginsberg and met Kerouac, Corso, Snyder, and Ken Kesey. They travelled on in April 1958 to Las Vegas, where Lyn made money for heroin through prostitution. Back in New York, their first son, Mark, was born on 2 October.

The following March Trocchi signed a contract with Grove Press for *Cain's Book*, which came out in 1961 and is without doubt Trocchi's major achievement. It had been years in the making, as the book itself explains: it is a book about the writing of a book by another protagonist called Joe who is and is not Trocchi himself, working on a scow in New York and digressing back to experiences in Europe, mostly in Glasgow. It displays Trocchi's range, intellectually evoking existentialism, the beats, surrealism, a species of revolutionary socialism, and a Beckett-like ideology. Stylistically it mixes careful, lucid, naturalistic description with philosophizings which are sometimes pretentious and often opaque, and passages of hilarious or eerie fancifulness. Drug addiction is painfully presented. The solipsism of the book's first-person consciousness, shifting between abjectness, anger, and arrogance, is mitigated by the warmth of unsentimental feeling expressed towards Joe's Scottish-Italian parents. In American and British reprints, and in translations into half a dozen languages, it sold a great many copies. Meanwhile in 1959 Trocchi brought out two more pornographic works with Castle Books of New York, a firm as unscrupulous as Olympia, but less distinguished. Payment for these and other writings was not enough to deter Trocchi from sponging off well-to-do American friends whom he had met in Paris, or from sending Lyn out again to sell her body. The US authorities were cracking down harder than ever on heroin use. Trocchi, sometimes held overnight in police cells, was pusher as well as addict. In April 1961 he was charged with supplying the drug to a minor, and faced a possible death penalty. George Plimpton, a young man of distinguished family, put up bail of $5000, and, wearing two of Plimpton's suits which he had stolen, Trocchi escaped over the Canadian border. The singer–songwriter Leonard Cohen took care of him as he waited for a steamer for the UK.

Britain was a calmer world. The country then had comparatively few heroin addicts and there was as yet little public outcry over drug abuse. Trocchi was still an 'outsider', but merely as an unusual kind of writer, radiating alien influences and uttering heterodox views—though by the end of the decade these would be components,

almost drearily familiar, of the more extreme wing of sixties 'youth culture'. In August 1962 Trocchi clashed at a writers' conference during the Edinburgh Festival with the irascible doyen of Scottish literature, Hugh MacDiarmid, who described him as 'Cosmopolitan scum' and as 'A writer of no consequence whatever'. The two men shortly made a truce, and the controversy increased Trocchi's fame.

Secure in supplies of legally prescribed heroin, Trocchi fitted into the emergent 'sixties' culture of rock music and performance poetry with an ease which perhaps destroyed his talent. Arrogant, paranoid isolation had been his posture. After *Cain's Book* appeared in a British edition from Calder Books (Beckett's London publishers), Sheffield magistrates' court pronounced it obscene but the resulting ban had no effect beyond the city boundaries. Again, the publicity was good for Trocchi. In 1966 the mainstream New English Library republished *Young Adam* in Trocchi's final version. This and his other books continued to sell well, though because of the shaky nature of his contracts with Girodias and other publishers Trocchi never reaped the full benefits of his international fame. Meanwhile, basing himself in London, where Lyn and his son had joined him, he functioned as a guru of the new avant-garde. Thus he compèred an international reading by beat and 'underground' poets at the Albert Hall with an audience of several thousand. In his Paris days he had helped to found the Situationist International, a revolutionary groupuscule which operated with explosive—destructive—effect in the student revolt which hit Europe in 1968–9. In 1964 his essay 'Invisible insurrection of a million minds' announced the formation of 'sigma', a situationist initiative, 'a kind of spontaneous university', designed to link 'thoughtful individuals all over the world' in an assault on capitalist order through such means as privately circulated essays, poetry on toilet rolls, sale of artworks cutting out the middleman, and 'happenings'—bizarre events. A number of significant writers and artists took sigma seriously. Such were the times. Trocchi was fashionable. Dabbling in art now, he was asked to lecture in the sculpture department of the distinguished St Martin's School of Art. The Arts Council gave him a writer's grant of £500 in 1970, though *The Long Book* which Calder had announced for publication in 1966—perhaps, in fact, merely a collection of occasional writings—was never finished. An unsuccessful collection of poems, mostly written in the fifties, *Man at Leisure* (1972), was to be Trocchi's last book.

Lyn had produced a second son, Nicolas, in December 1966. She was worse hit by her addiction than Trocchi, and in November 1972 she died, aged thirty-five, of chronic hepatitis with complications. In May 1977 their promising son Mark died of cancer of the throat. A young New Zealand woman, Sally Child, moved in to console Trocchi. He had lived since the mid-sixties in a penthouse flat in Observatory Gardens, a desirable address in Kensington. Income came from various sources—translations from the French, film rights (a film of *Cain's Book* with major stars came tantalizingly close to realization), and profitable second-hand book stalls. The 'monster' demonized by the press (his pornographic books were still subject to well-publicized seizures and bans) was at last a melancholy, soft-spoken, middle-aged gentleman, to be seen acquiring rare books at Sothebys sales. On 15 April 1984, some time after an operation for lung cancer, Trocchi died at his home of lobal pneumonia. He was cremated at Mortlake crematorium, London, on 25 April. In December of that year fire mysteriously swept through his flat. His son Nicolas shortly afterwards committed suicide by jumping off its roof.

To declare that Trocchi had been unjustly forgotten became at once a favourite posture of those admirers who preferred to think of the man as rejected, misunderstood and, as a result, their private property. In his last twenty-three years he had published no new fiction. Andrew Murray Scott's biography, published in 1991, showed the continuity of academic interest in him in his native Scotland. The biography antedated by two years the wave of Scottish fiction about a new youth 'drug scene' which was launched by Irvine Welsh's immensely successful *Trainspotting* (1993). This provoked further reprints of Trocchi, but, as Welsh's partly dismissive comments about him suggest, the drug scene of the 1950s and 1960s in Britain, when there were few addicts, was very different from that of the 1980s and 1990s, when drugs became a problem affecting a much greater number of people, and engrossing a larger proportion of police time. Trocchi, with his relentless intellectualism and his generally fastidious, often 'poetic' prose, might well strike Welsh as an interesting middle-class antique. And yet, with the publication of *Cain's Book*, Trocchi was established as one of the main Scottish writers of the twentieth century.

ANGUS CALDER

Sources A. M. Scott, *Alexander Trocchi: the making of the monster* (1991) · A. Campbell and T. Niel, eds., *A life in pieces: reflections on Alexander Trocchi* (1997) · J. Calder, T. McGrath, E. Morgan, and C. Logue, 'On Alexander Trocchi', *Edinburgh Review*, 70 (1985), 32–65 [an issue largely devoted to Trocchi and his work] · R. Seaver, 'Introduction', in A. Trocchi, *Cain's book*, repr. (1991) · A. M. Scott, *Invisible insurrection of a million minds: a Trocchi reader* (1991) · b. cert.
Archives priv. coll., estate · Washington University, St Louis, Missouri, corresp., literary MSS, and papers
Likenesses photograph, 1963, priv. coll. [*see illus.*] · S. O'Meara, photograph, c.1975, Hult. Arch. · photographs, repro. in Scott, *Alexander Trocchi*

Trokelowe, John de (*fl.* c.1330). *See under* Rishanger, William (*b.* 1249/50, *d.* after 1312).

Trollope, Sir Andrew (*d.* 1461), soldier, was probably related to the Trollope family of Thornley, co. Durham, some of whom were dyers. From at least the late 1420s he served as a mounted man-at-arms at Tombelaine under Thomas Burgh and at Fresnay-le-Vicomte under Sir John Fastolf, being in the latter's company at the rescue of Caen in 1433. In February 1440 he served under Matthew Gough in the raid that John Beaufort, earl of Somerset, conducted into Picardy, mustering in the following month in the

earl's personal retinue. By 1442 he was lieutenant at Fresnay under Sir Richard Woodville, and held the same post in 1449 under Osbert Mundeford, surrendering the fortress to the French in March 1450. Although the date of his marriage to Elizabeth, sister of Mundeford, is not known, the link with the latter, who became treasurer-general of the duchy of Normandy in September 1448, and with the Beaufort family assisted his rise to prominence (he had been awarded a life grant of the barony of La Ferté Macé in May 1447) and ensured the continuation of his military employment.

By 1455 Trollope was master porter of Calais and was involved in quasi-piratical sorties from the town. Continuing his service there under Richard Neville, earl of Warwick, he was chosen to lead the latter's detachment to England to assist Richard, duke of York, but his links with the Beauforts and his loyalty to the crown persuaded him to defect to the royal camp before the engagement at Ludford Bridge (12 October 1459). This plunged the Yorkists into disarray, not least because Trollope disclosed the intended plan of action, and prompted their early withdrawal from the field. Trollope then accompanied Henry Beaufort, duke of Somerset, in an abortive attempt to seize Calais. His persuasion and reputation were enough to win over the troops at Guînes, and he was entrusted with its defence, being appointed bailiff on 24 March 1460, although subsequent reverses for Somerset at Newham Bridge on 23 April and the interception of Mundeford's reinforcements at Sandwich in June forced the surrender of the fortress.

Trollope gained further kudos in the Lancastrian victory at Wakefield on 31 December 1460, when, according to Waurin, he had, by subterfuge, enticed the Yorkists from their stronghold at Sandal. He was also prominent in the Lancastrian victory at St Albans (17 February 1461): wounded in the foot by a calletrappe, he was the first of those to be dubbed by Prince Edward after the battle. When Edward IV seized London and the throne in the following month, Trollope was among those excepted from the general pardon, having a price put on his head. He met his end at the battle of Towton (29 March 1461), sharing command of the Lancastrian vanguard with the earl of Northumberland. Margaret, his daughter with Elizabeth Mundeford, married Richard Calle of Bacton, bailiff of the Pastons, after the death (c.1479) of his first wife, Margery, the daughter of Sir John Paston (*d.* 1466).

ANNE CURRY

Sources *Recueil des croniques ... par Jehan de Waurin*, ed. W. Hardy and E. L. C. P. Hardy, 5 vols., Rolls Series, 39 (1864–91), vols. 2–4 · Chancery records · Ancient deeds, PRO · French or treaty rolls, PRO, C 76 · Bibliothèque Nationale, Paris, collection Clairambault, manuscrits français · Archives Nationales, Paris, série K, Mi. 204 (Dom Lenoir) · additional charters, BL · *RotP* · J. Gairdner, ed., *The historical collections of a citizen of London in the fifteenth century*, CS, new ser., 17 (1876) · J. Gairdner, ed., *Three fifteenth-century chronicles*, CS, new ser., 28 (1880) · *Hall's chronicle*, ed. H. Ellis (1809) · R. A. Griffiths, *The reign of King Henry VI: the exercise of royal authority, 1422–1461* (1981) · J. Stevenson, ed., *Letters and papers illustrative of the wars of the English in France during the reign of Henry VI, king of England*, 2 vols. in 3 pts, Rolls Series, 22 (1861–4) · J. Stevenson, ed., *Narratives of the expulsion of the English from Normandy, 1444–1450*, Rolls Series, 32

(1863) • N. Davis, ed., *Paston letters and papers of the fifteenth century*, 2 vols. (1971–6) • W. Rye, ed., *The visitacion of Norffolk … 1563 … 1613*, Harleian Society, 32 (1891) • *Itineraries [of] William Worcestre*, ed. J. H. Harvey, OMT (1969) • [J. Raine], ed., *Wills and inventories*, 1, SurtS, 2 (1835)

Trollope, Anthony (1815–1882), novelist, was born on 24 April 1815 at 16 Keppel Street, Russell Square, London, the fourth surviving child of Thomas Anthony *Trollope (1774–1835) and his wife, Frances, *née* Milton (1779–1863) [*see* Trollope, Frances]. Anthony was baptized on 18 May in St George's, Bloomsbury Way.

Childhood and youth Thomas Anthony Trollope was a barrister practising in the chancery court, with chambers at 23 Old Square, Lincoln's Inn. While Anthony was still an infant, the Trollopes migrated to Harrow, where Thomas Anthony had taken a farm to augment his barrister's income and to allow his boys to attend Harrow School free. This scheme to take up farming, Anthony wrote, was 'the grave of all my father's hopes, ambition, and prosperity, the cause of my mother's sufferings, and of those of her children, and perhaps the director of her destiny and of ours' (*Autobiography*, 2).

Thomas Anthony Trollope planned to use Harrow as a preparatory school for his sons while they awaited vacancies at Winchester College, his own old school. Thus Anthony Trollope entered Harrow in 1823 almost as a private pupil, being too young for the school itself. But home boarders or 'village boys' of any age were looked down on and persecuted. Trollope called his Harrow schooldays:

Anthony Trollope (1815–1882), by Julia Margaret Cameron, 1864

> as unhappy as that of a young gentleman could well be, my misfortunes arising from a mixture of poverty and gentle standing on the part of my father, and from an utter want on my own part of that juvenile manhood which enables some boys to hold up their heads even among the distresses which such a position is sure to produce. (*Autobiography*, 2)

After two unsatisfactory years at Harrow School, Anthony Trollope was sent early in 1825 to a private school at Sunbury, where he was also forlorn. Then in 1827 he was admitted to Winchester College, which he found even more painful than Sunbury. His brother Thomas Adolphus *Trollope (1810–1892), as his prefect, beat him daily; the masters heard the pupils 'say' memorized portions of Latin verse and did little else for the boys except 'scourge' them, and, he wrote, 'in the performance of that task only, was my acquaintance with them ripened into intimacy' (A. Trollope, 'Public schools', *Fortnightly Review*, 2, 1 Oct 1865, 478–90). Next, his brother left Winchester, and his mother and sisters went to America, where they remained for four years. His father's finances became perilous as his temper alienated legal clients and his efforts at gentleman farming put him deeper into debt. Anthony Trollope's college bills were not paid: 'My school fellows of course knew that it was so, and I became a Pariah.' Some boys, he noted, do not seem to suffer much from the natural cruelty of other boys, but, as he remembered:

> I suffered horribly! I could make no stand against it. I had no friend to whom I could pour out my sorrows. I was big, and awkward, and ugly, and, I have no doubt, skulked about in a most unattractive manner. Of course I was ill-dressed and dirty. But, ah! how well I remember all the agonies of my young heart; how I considered whether I should always be alone; whether I could not find my way up to the top of that college tower, and from thence put an end to everything? (*Autobiography*, 9)

In summer 1830 Anthony Trollope was withdrawn from Winchester by his father. Back home, where his father had moved to a tumbledown farmhouse at Harrow Weald, and while his mother remained in America, he had to endure his father's rages and depressions. There were times when the man seemed mentally unhinged. Still more painful was Trollope's second attendance at Harrow School:

> [It] was the worst period of my life. I was now over fifteen, and had come to an age at which I could appreciate at its full the misery of expulsion from all social intercourse. I had not only no friends, but was despised by all my companions … What right had a wretched farmer's boy, reeking from a dunghill, to sit next to the sons of peers,—or much worse still, next to the sons of big tradesmen who had made their ten thousand a-year? … As I look back it seems to me that all hands were turned against me—those of masters as well as boys. (*Autobiography*, 11–12)

Frances Trollope arrived home from America in August 1831 and by publishing *Domestic Manners of the Americans* in the following year enabled the family to move back to Julians Hill, their former Harrow farmhouse (the original 'Orley Farm'). But by April 1834 Mr Trollope's affairs had worsened and he fled to the continent to avoid arrest for debt; his family followed and settled at Bruges. Then, in November, through his mother's connection with the Clayton family, which pretty much controlled the Post Office, Trollope was given a clerkship in the secretary's office at London postal headquarters. Anthony's relationship with his mother is difficult to judge. He admired her pluck and courage, her buoyant spirit in the face of financial calamities, the difficult personality of her husband, and the deaths of so many of her children. But at the same time he felt, as *An Autobiography* implies, that she had neglected him; he marvelled at her industry in writing, and later in life certainly followed her example in this regard—although he never rated her books highly.

From the first Trollope failed to do well at the Post Office. He was habitually late and quickly became known for irregularity and unsatisfactory work. Suspensions were threatened, his pay was sometimes docked, dismissal was a possibility. (Some representations of Trollope's clerking days can be found in *The Three Clerks*, *The Small House at Allington*, and *Marion Fay*.) He was unhappy in his social life, and his *Autobiography* hints that he was involved with loose women. He also had constant money problems: living alone in London on £90 a year proved impossible, and he fell into the hands of a moneylender (reincarnated as Jabesh M'Ruen in *The Three Clerks* and as Mr Clarkson in *Phineas Finn*). Trollope insists that during these years he was 'hopelessly in debt'. It is not surprising that money, and especially indebtedness, play so prominent a part in his fiction. 'No other novelist', the *Saturday Review* remarked in 1865, 'has made the various worries about money so prominent a feature of his stories' (Smalley, 216). W. H. Auden wrote, 'Of all novelists in any country, Trollope best understands the role of money' (Auden, 104).

Ireland and authorship Throughout his unhappy London clerking days, Trollope aimed to write. In his journal he wrote that he evidently had not the talent for poetry or drama, nor the erudition for history or biography: 'But I thought it possible I might write a novel'. He continued the day-dreaming he had begun at Winchester, carrying on a story in his mind for months or longer. This 'castle building', which he acknowledged to be a 'dangerous mental practice', none the less taught him how 'to maintain an interest in a fictitious story, to dwell on a work created by my own imagination, and to live in a world altogether outside the world of my material life'. He later believed that had it not been for this day-dreaming he would never have written a novel (*Autobiography*, 43).

In July 1841, after seven years in the London Post Office, dissatisfied with himself and his work, mired in debt, frustrated with his failure to make even an attempt at novel writing, Trollope saw a way out of his London 'miseries'. The post of assistant or clerk to a surveyor in Ireland opened up, and he applied successfully for the transfer. Ireland, he said, changed his life altogether. Not only money problems, but the feeling of uselessness and shame, the failure to be liked and respected, to do something with his life—all these evils disappeared, he said, the moment he set foot in Ireland. He maintained that, from his Irish days onwards, few individuals led more enjoyable lives than he. Among the Irish, among people frequently worse off than he, the 'hobbledehoy' emerged

into a man, flawed certainly, and idiosyncratic in his uncommon forcefulness and pugnacity.

With headquarters at Banagher, in King's county (now co. Offaly), under an indolent superior, Trollope became an active and efficient 'deputy inspector' of country post offices and their books. He took immediately to the physical labour of travelling on horseback. A man of far more than average physical strength and of seemingly indefatigable energies, he found himself at last. With his incessant travel and observant eye he came to know Ireland and her inhabitants as did few Englishmen.

In Ireland Trollope also found his play; he took up hunting to hounds, and it became the great passion of his life. Until age forced him to give it up thirty-five years later, 'neither the writing of books, nor the work for the Post Office, nor other pleasures' were allowed to stand in the way of hunting. It became as much a 'duty' as his work for the Post Office. He loved the sport with 'an affection which I cannot myself fathom or understand', and he frequently 'dragged' hunting scenes into his novels (*Autobiography*, 64).

Trollope had been in Ireland for scarcely a year when he met, at Kingstown (today Dun Laoghaire), Rose (1820–1917), the daughter of Edward John Heseltine, a banker, of Rotherham, Yorkshire. Trollope and Rose were married on 11 June 1844, in the parish church at Rotherham. In *An Autobiography* Trollope is almost entirely silent about Rose: 'My marriage was like the marriage of other people, and of no special interest to any one except my wife and me' (*Autobiography*, 71). Little is known about Rose, who, when she died in 1917, had outlived her husband by thirty-five years; details of her life with Trollope remain a mystery to this day. The Trollopes lived first at Clonmel and then at Mallow. At Clonmel their two sons were born: Henry Merivale Trollope on 13 March 1846 and Frederick James Anthony Trollope on 27 September 1847. Henry eventually took to authorship, without much success; Fred emigrated to Australia, where he was first a sheep farmer, and then, like his father, a civil servant.

While Trollope was engaged to Rose, he had at last, in September 1843, begun his first novel, *The Macdermots of Ballycloran*. It is, perhaps not surprisingly, the story of the ruin of a poor family with former aspirations to gentility, the father overwhelmed by debt and sinking into idiocy while his son, decent but somewhat slow-witted, tries futilely to keep the family afloat. The novel was published by Thomas Cautley Newby, a minor London publisher, in March 1847, when Trollope was almost thirty-two.

The Macdermots of Ballycloran was a very considerable first novel. Though marred by occasionally inflated style, sprawling dialogue, interpolated passages of explanation and commentary, and some melodramatic turns of events, it surpassed many of the novels that followed in rendering private lives emblematic of a whole society; this it did as convincingly as the later *The Way We Live Now* (1875). And although Trollope wrote other tragic or partly tragic novels like *Castle Richmond* (1860), *An Eye for an Eye* (1879), *Orley Farm* (1862), *He Knew He Was Right* (1869), and *Sir Harry Hotspur of Humblethwaite* (1871), *The Macdermots* was unique in its concern for the poor and downtrodden. The novel did not sell; but (Trollope's assertion that it went unnoticed notwithstanding) the book had excellent reviews, more than a dozen of them.

Trollope's second novel, *The Kellys and the O'Kellys*, also set in Ireland, ventured into what became Trollope's more usual métier, comic realism. Henry Colburn published the book in June 1848, but it also failed to sell. Trollope's next effort, *La Vendée* (1850), a tale of the French Revolution, failed even more resoundingly, but deservedly; he had worked up the novel from books, a mistake he never made again.

Barchester After *La Vendée* Trollope's novel-writing career stalled, largely owing to the press of Post Office work. In 1851 he was sent 'on loan' to expand the rural post in the west of England. To establish a regular delivery system throughout Somerset, Wiltshire, Devon, Cornwall, south Wales, and beyond became, he said, 'the ambition of my life'. One assignment took him to the Channel Islands, and, having taken the idea from nearby France, he introduced roadside letter boxes ('pillar boxes'), the first being erected in 1852, at St Helier, whence they spread throughout Great Britain. Then, late in May 1852, at Salisbury,

> whilst wandering there on a midsummer evening through the purlieus of the cathedral I conceived the story of *The Warden*,—from whence came that series of novels of which Barchester, with its bishops, deans, and archdeacon, was the central site. (*Autobiography*, 92)

But Post Office demands increased as Trollope was recalled to Ireland as an acting surveyor; then in October 1854 he was made surveyor for the north of Ireland. The post of surveyor was inferior only to those of secretary and assistant secretary. For the unpromising clerk of twenty years earlier, it was a stunning achievement. Trollope obtained permission to live in Dublin rather than in his district, and he took a house at 5 Seaview Terrace, Donnybrook. Meanwhile *The Warden*, although a short novel, was slow in the making and did not appear until January 1855. It was published under the imprint of William Longman; Trollope changed publishers frequently.

In *The Warden* Trollope dealt with two evils: the misuse of charitable endowments by bishops and clergy of the Church of England, and the 'undeserved severity' with which the press treated those clergymen paid large sums from such endowments. Trollope presented a morally interesting case because he did not make his central figure, Mr Harding, a lazy pluralist doing nothing for the elderly men in his care; rather Mr Harding is a good, almost saintly man, who unwittingly finds himself in the bad position of receiving high pay for little work. *The Warden* netted Trollope less than £10 in 1855 ('Indeed', he wrote, 'as regarded remuneration for the time, stone-breaking would have done better'). But it had fair critical success, and Trollope said that this time he 'could discover that people around me knew that I had written a book' (*Autobiography*, 98). *The Leader* innocently said that *The Warden* 'certainly promises well for the author's future, if he gives us more books' (Smalley, 36).

When Trollope came to write *Barchester Towers*, the sequel to *The Warden*, he adopted two strategies for increased efficiency. First, he began his practice of writing while travelling, and soon found that he could compose as quickly in a railway carriage as at his desk. Years later he had carpenters build writing desks in his cabins on ocean-crossing steamers. Second, he devised ledger-like columned records of his writing, where he would enter exactly how many pages he had produced each day. His aim was forty pages of 250 words each per week. Naturally there were weeks when work, or illness, or hunting interfered, but by and large he managed the forty pages. This diary-regulated writing led to startling results, and with *Barchester Towers*, Trollope's famous productivity took hold.

In *Barchester Towers* Trollope accepted some of the strictures voiced in reviews of *The Warden*. The sequel contained nothing like the parodies of Dickens and Carlyle in the earlier work. On the other hand, Trollope paid no attention to the cautions about facetious names, and until the end he used names like Slow and Bidawhile for lawyers, Fillgrave and Rearchild for physicians (Henry James said of the name Quiverful for a man with fourteen children, 'We can believe in the name and we can believe in the children; but we cannot manage the combination'; James, 12). Trollope, however, was writing comedy, and facetious names were part of a long tradition in comedy. But he did heed the most persistent criticism of *The Warden*, its ambiguity of purpose: reviewers had wanted to know where he stood on ecclesiastical reform. For Trollope the answer was to get away from the novel of 'purpose'. In *Barchester Towers* the wardenship eventually goes to Mr Quiverful (who, with his fourteen children to support, dearly needs the appointment), but the old scandal and the rights and wrongs of the case no longer matter; the issue of reform has been lost to the personalities of the protagonists. And although *Barchester Towers*, like *The Warden*, was again about clergymen, Trollope dealt with his clerics in their social and economic rather than in their religious lives. For the most part, Trollope saw the church as a sort of privileged division of the civil service.

Barchester Towers met with almost unanimous praise from the critics, and now seems the quintessential Trollope novel. He may have written better novels thereafter, but none so sunny, so gloriously comic in tone. It abounds in Trollopian 'personages'—engaging characters, which Trollope regarded as the *sine qua non* of a successful novel. Some were carried over from *The Warden*, including Septimus Harding, the former warden, and Archdeacon Grantly. The newcomers, the henpecked Bishop Proudie, his formidable wife, their hypocritical chaplain, Mr Slope, and the unsettling family of Dr Vesey Stanhope, especially Bertie and his sister Signora Neroni, raise the novel considerably above *The Warden*.

The plot of the next Barchester novel, *Doctor Thorne* (1858), more sensational than those of his other novels, had been suggested to Trollope by his brother Thomas Adolphus Trollope. The public liked the story very much, and it was a critical and commercial success. *Doctor Thorne* introduces the Duke of Omnium, an unmarried 'great debauchee', indifferent to everything but his own pleasure. He remained a constant and important background presence in the remaining Barsetshire novels and gained still more prominence in the first three Palliser novels.

The writing of the next Barsetshire novel, *Framley Parsonage* (1860–61), coincided with Trollope's move back to England as Post Office surveyor of the eastern district. He settled at Waltham Cross, a suburb 12 miles north of London, where he enjoyed his happiest, busiest, most successful years, the decade of the 1860s, a time when he rose to be what one reviewer, in the *National Review*, called 'almost a national institution' (Smalley, 167). At this time he also made regular his practice of early rising, being wakened at 5 a.m. and at his desk by 5.30, where he would spend three hours, the first half hour in rereading the previous day's work, and then, with his watch before him, striving to write 250 words per quarter of an hour. It should be remembered, however, that Trollope considered the real work of novel writing to be his day-dreaming, his 'thinking about' his characters whenever he had a moment free during the day. When putting pen to paper he seemed almost to be dictating the story to a secretary. His manuscripts show, amazingly, almost no revision, little more than a word or two crossed out here and there.

Framley Parsonage came out monthly in the newly launched *Cornhill Magazine*, edited by Thackeray and published by George Smith. This novel brought Trollope enormous popularity. The first issue of the *Cornhill* appeared at Christmas 1859 and was a great success, selling an unheard-of 120,000 copies, much of that success owing to Trollope's story. Mrs Gaskell wrote to George Smith, 'I wish Mr. Trollope would go on writing Framley Parsonage for ever' (*Letters of Mrs Gaskell*, 602). The reviews of the book version of *Framley Parsonage*, even those that were grudging in their praise, testified to the novel's phenomenal popularity. The *Saturday Review* said 'It seems a kind of breach of hospitality to criticize *Framley Parsonage* at all. It has been an intimate of the drawing-room—it has travelled with us in the train—it has lain on the breakfast-table' (Smalley, 121). Trollope himself observed that *Framley Parsonage* 'was received with greater favour than any [book] I had written before or have written since' (A. Trollope, *Thackeray*, 1879, 52). *Framley Parsonage* also turned Trollope into a serial novelist, and for good. The only genius Trollope claimed was a 'mechanical' one, his ability to write his novels to exactly prescribed limits—instalments per novel, chapters per instalment, pages per chapter, words per page.

Trollope's connection with the *Cornhill* also served to introduce him to the literary world that had been denied him by living in Ireland. Of special service was the cordiality and hospitality of the magazine's publisher, George Smith. It was at Smith's celebrated *Cornhill* dinners that Trollope met many of the writers, artists, and politicians who became his associates and friends. George Augustus Sala described him at the very first such dinner; Trollope was forty-five, and, somewhat self-conscious in such company, conducted himself with compensating forcefulness:

> Anthony Trollope was very much to the fore, contradicting everybody; afterwards saying kind things to everybody, and occasionally going to sleep on sofas or chairs; or leaning against the sideboards, and even somnolent while standing erect on the hearthrug. I never knew a man who could take so many spells of 'forty winks' at unexpected moments, and then turn up quite wakeful, alert, and pugnacious, as the author of 'Barchester Towers,' who had nothing of the bear but his skin, but whose ursine envelope was assuredly of the most grisly texture.   (Sala, 30–31)

That evening saw the start of intimate friendships with William Thackeray, whom Trollope had long considered the foremost novelist of his day; Richard Monckton Milnes, writer and politician; G. H. Lewes, critic, philosopher, and consort of George Eliot (Trollope also became good friends with her); William Russell, correspondent for *The Times*; and John Everett Millais, one of the original Pre-Raphaelite painters. Trollope thrived on London life. In 1861 he was elected to the Cosmopolitan Club (the original for the 'Universe Club' in *Phineas Redux*); in the following year he was elected to the Garrick Club and in 1864 to the Athenaeum Club. In 1861 he began his lifelong involvement with the Royal Literary Fund, his favourite charity.

John Everett Millais became not only an intimate but a collaborator. Millais drew six illustrations for *Framley Parsonage* in its *Cornhill* serialization, and, to Trollope's intense delight, eventually provided many more (a total of eighty-seven full-page drawings and nineteen elaborate vignettes). Millais was a 'sixties'-style illustrator, representational and realistic, a style which accorded nicely with that of Trollope, whose writing was often characterized as 'photographic', 'uncompromisingly realistic', and even 'pre-Raphaelite' (Smalley, 171, 318, 333). Millais's most ambitious collaboration with Trollope, forty plates, came in *Orley Farm*. Trollope wrote that he had never known a set of illustrations 'as carefully true … to the conception of the writer of the book illustrated' (Hall, *Trollope*, 214). Millais also illustrated *The Small House at Allington* (1864) and *Phineas Finn* (1869), and supplied frontispieces for *Rachel Ray* (1863) and *Kept in the Dark* (1882). Nine other artists illustrated one novel apiece, with drawings for which Trollope demonstrated for the most part either indifference or contempt.

The penultimate Barsetshire novel, *The Small House at Allington*, features Lily Dale (a 'female prig' Trollope labelled her in *An Autobiography*) and her unsuccessful suitor, Johnny Eames, a partial self-portrait. This story also introduces Plantagenet Palliser and accordingly forms a bridge between the Barsetshire and the Palliser novels. *The Small House at Allington* was another huge success. *The Athenaeum* said that during serialization the question of whether Johnny Eames would marry Lily Dale was as much speculated on as any '"marriage on the tapis" … in any town or village in Great Britain', and demanded that Trollope reopen the story of the leading characters (Smalley, 194–5).

The Last Chronicle of Barset (1867) worthily crowns the series in adding to it a new dimension through the dominating presence of the Revd Mr Crawley, a character from *Framley Parsonage*. Here, although his story is allowed to end happily, Crawley is largely a tragic figure. In him Trollope combined what he had learned from his father's unhappy years of poverty and near madness with his now expert knowledge of the straits to which many poor clergy were reduced.

In the midst of writing *The Last Chronicle*, Trollope, as he told the incident, overheard two clergymen at the Athenaeum Club abusing his practice of introducing reappearing characters, including Mrs Proudie. 'I got up', Trollope said, 'and standing between them, I acknowledged myself to be the culprit. "As to Mrs. Proudie," I said, "I will go home and kill her before the week is over." And so I did'. He occasionally lamented having burnt his bridges to Barsetshire, and said he sometimes regretted killing Mrs Proudie—'so great was my delight in writing about Mrs. Proudie, so thorough was my knowledge of all the little shades of her character' (*Autobiography*, 275, 276). Margaret Oliphant in *Blackwood's Magazine* wrote 'To kill Mrs. Proudie was murder, or manslaughter at the least' (Smalley, 303). The reviews singled out the novel as Trollope's best so far, and Crawley as his highest achievement. R. H. Hutton in *The Spectator* concluded, 'Of its own light kind there has been no better novel ever written than *The Last Chronicle of Barset*' (ibid., 296). Trollope himself thought *The Last Chronicle* his best novel. He was at the pinnacle of his career and of his earning power, selling the copyrights for long novels for some £3000.

Pallisers *Can You Forgive Her?* (1865), nominally the story of the earnest Alice Vavasor and her two suitors, was based on Trollope's old unpublished play 'The Noble Jilt' (written 1850). But what endeared the novel to Trollope and his readers was not the somewhat 'wearying' character of the heroine, but the presentation of the staid Plantagenet Palliser and his unconventional wife, Lady Glencora. These two slight figures from *The Small House at Allington* emerge as fully realized individuals. Palliser and Glencora became his favourite fictional creations, and he used them time after time to express his political, social, and moral convictions: these two, together with their 'belongings', he wrote:

> have been as real to me as free trade was to Mr. Cobden, or the dominion of a party to Mr. Disraeli; and as I have not been able to speak from the benches of the House of Commons, or to thunder from platforms, or to be efficacious as a lecturer, they have served as safety-valves by which to deliver my soul.

Trollope was proud of having created in Palliser 'a very noble gentleman,—such a one as justifies to the nation the seeming anomaly of an hereditary peerage and of primogeniture' (*Autobiography*, 180–81). In Glencora he produced a marvel of quick wit and rebellious spirit, and he treats with sensitivity her continuing love for the handsome, impoverished rogue, Burgo Fitzgerald, after her relatives had forced her into marriage with Palliser. Even after she has been reconciled to marriage and to Palliser,

she retains the mischievousness that is her most charming quality. Although the Pallisers find a *modus vivendi*, in this and in subsequent novels Trollope never blinks at the harsh facts of Glencora's story. The romance of her life is gone with Burgo, and the tale of her difficult marriage to Palliser forms a large part of the six-novel series that begins with this one. Here is a colossal exception to the time-honoured comic tradition Trollope so often followed of ending his stories with wedding bells and happy prospects. The story of Glencora and Palliser begins with their marriage, one of the least 'romantic' in English fiction.

In 1867 Trollope, with some deep regret, resigned from the Post Office. He had always regarded the office as his primary job, but now he had embarked on an additional literary venture, the editorship of a new magazine, *Saint Pauls* (it failed after three years in spite of Trollope's considerable efforts). For its début Trollope had written a political novel, *Phineas Finn*. The book was, of course, only 'semi-political'. For his readers' sake, he explained, he put in love, intrigue, and sport, and peopled the novel with witty, bright, complex women—Lady Laura Standish, Violet Effingham, Lady Glencora, and Madame Max Goesler. The novel is played out against the background of agitation for and passage of the second Reform Bill. Trollope alters history a good deal, but readers and reviewers were quick to identify Conservative leader Daubeny with Disraeli, the Liberal leader Gresham with Gladstone, and the radical Liberal Turnbull with John Bright. Trollope's Liberal Party sympathies remained evident throughout the series. But *Phineas Finn*, though Trollope was pleased with it, did not win the good press that his Barsetshire novels enjoyed.

Phineas Redux (1874), which Trollope regarded as the second half of 'one novel' with *Phineas Finn*, is distinctly more political, more sensational, and more sombre than the earlier story. It is likely that the comparative pessimism of *Phineas Redux* stemmed in part from Trollope's election defeat, which occurred between the writing of the two books. Trollope had long considered a seat in the House of Commons the highest ambition to which an Englishman might aspire. In the general election of 1868, when most of the country returned Liberal candidates, Trollope, standing for parliament as a Liberal for the Yorkshire borough of Beverley, was defeated, evidently because the Conservatives bought votes. Beverley was notorious for dishonest elections, and after this one the borough was disfranchised. The political background of *Phineas Redux* is the disestablishment of the Irish church—something Trollope had vigorously supported from the hustings—but altered in the novel to the more daring plan of Daubeny/Disraeli for disestablishing the Church of England.

The sensationalism of *Phineas Redux* takes the form of Phineas's being shot at by a sexually jealous husband and later being unjustly tried for murdering a member of parliament. His trial occasions the return of Mr Chaffanbrass, Trollope's best-known barrister, famous for his skill in cross-examination (he had appeared in *The Three Clerks* and

Orley Farm). One reviewer labelled Chaffanbrass's 'destruction' of the inept Lord Fawn as one of 'the finest touches' in all Trollope's fiction (Smalley, 381). But more important to Trollope than the politics or the sensationalism of the book was the gradual growth of his characters with the passage of time. Palliser, Glencora, and the duke from earlier novels, along with somewhat newer ones from the first Phineas novel, Finn himself, Lady Laura ('the best character in the two books' in Trollope's view), Violet Effingham, and Madame Max Goesler, kept 'luring' him back:

> So much of my inner life was passed in their company, that I was continually asking myself how this woman would act when this or that event had passed over her head, or how that man would carry himself when his youth had become manhood, or his manhood declined to old age.

Trollope said he knew these characters so thoroughly that the evil or good within them was as 'clear to me as are the stars on a summer night' (*Autobiography*, 319–20). Thus a review in *The Spectator* especially pleased him: 'Indeed, we all of us know those of Mr. Trollope's characters who appear and reappear in the main line of his social tradition, so much better than we know ninety-nine hundredths of our own friends' (Smalley, 378). Virginia Woolf said that readers believe in Trollope's characters 'as we do in the reality of our weekly bills', that they get from his novels 'the same sort of refreshment and delight that we get from seeing something actually happen in the street below' (Woolf, 57, 62).

While Trollope was visiting his son in Australia the third 'Palliser' novel, *The Eustace Diamonds* (1873; published between the two Phineas novels), was appearing serially in the *Fortnightly Review*, a Liberal magazine of which Trollope had been the principal founder in 1865. *The Eustace Diamonds*, which offered Trollope's version of Thackeray's Becky Sharp, was enormously popular and did much to repair the decline in his critical reputation that had set in after the high point achieved with *The Last Chronicle*.

The fifth Palliser novel, *The Prime Minister* (1876), finds Plantagenet Palliser, now the Duke of Omnium, called on to be prime minister of a coalition government. But in spite of his natural timidity he becomes autocratic and peevishly imperious; he grows ill at ease, moody, irritable, unhappy. *The Prime Minister* becomes a chronicle of his weaknesses, many of them the result of his scrupulous honesty and idealism. Trollope thought that in *The Prime Minister* he had another success, but the novel was not well received, and in 1878 he added a footnote to his already completed *Autobiography* saying that the book had been a 'failure' and 'was worse spoken of by the Press than any novel I had written' (*Autobiography*, 360).

In the final Palliser novel, *The Duke's Children* (written 1876, published 1880), the duke is even more at the centre of the book, a spot he had formerly shared with others, most notably with Lady Glencora. A widower now, the trials and sorrows he suffers at the hands of his three children are moving and even sad: his daughter wants to marry a penniless tory commoner; both sons are rusticated from university; both incur gambling debts; the elder wants to marry an American, Isabel Boncassen. This young woman is based in part on Kate Field, the beautiful, witty, clever, lively American woman whom Trollope met in 1860, and for whom he had an innocent but romantic attachment for the rest of his days. Henry James said that Trollope was 'evidently always more or less in love' with all his heroines (James, 16), but this must have been especially the case with Isabel Boncassen. The book received such good reviews in 1880 that Trollope might have been thought as popular as in his heyday two decades before.

Other books Trollope placed the Barsetshire and the Palliser novels at the head of his achievement. But he wrote many other novels, including, to name but a few: *The Three Clerks* (1858), close to its author's heart for the autobiographical picture of a London civil service clerk; *Orley Farm* (1862), largely an analysis of the law; '[Trollope] cannot abide a lawyer' one reviewer in the *London Review*, remarked (Smalley, 156); and of *Miss Mackenzie* (1865) the *Saturday Review* commented 'Nobody but Mr. Trollope would have dared to marry a heroine of some forty years to a widower of fifty with nine children' (ibid., 218). *Nina Balatka* (1867) was a story challenging eastern European antisemitism, and was also the first of his two unsuccessful attempts to establish a second reputation by publishing the novels anonymously. *He Knew He was Right* (1869) represented a lengthy treatment of the Othello theme; and *Lady Anna* (1874) was a novel written entirely aboard ship.

In 1873, after two years of travel to Australia and New Zealand, Trollope settled back into London at 39 Montagu Square. There he wrote his longest and for many readers one of his most important novels, *The Way We Live Now* (1875), a dissection of the greed and dishonesty he saw infecting society. Other novels written during these years include *Is He Popenjoy?* (1878), a book worthily compared to some of the Barsetshire novels; *John Caldigate* (1879), based on his Australian experiences and featuring once again legal trials; *Cousin Henry* (1879), a study of the neurotic, unattractive title character, of whom *The Academy* said, 'No other novelist could have racked through two volumes' such a cowardly figure (Smalley, 465); *Dr. Wortle's School* (1881), a short novel with a Trollope-like title figure; and *Ayala's Angel* (1881), a lightsome comedy of two sisters that has been called Trollope's *Pride and Prejudice*.

In 1880 Trollope, always fond of rural life and thinking that country air would improve his health, moved with Rose to South Harting in Sussex on the Hampshire border. The six books he wrote there include *The Fixed Period* (1882), a futuristic story set in 1980 and centring on a law calling for compulsory euthanasia by age sixty-eight, a novel worthy of mention only as being so much out of Trollope's usual line. The highlight of Trollope's last years is undoubtedly *Mr. Scarborough's Family* (1883), a dark masterpiece of parental intrigue, written a year before his death.

This listing, together with the Barsetshire and Palliser novels, represents only about half of Trollope's fiction. The quantity of his accomplishment remains astonishing: forty-seven novels, five volumes of collected short stories, plus a handful of uncollected stories. He wrote four large travel books: *The West Indies and the Spanish Main* (1859), *North America* (1862), *Australia and New Zealand* (1873), *South Africa* (1878); and a slight book on Iceland. (An indefatigable, unstoppable traveller all his life, Trollope, in James Anthony Froude's words, 'banged about the world' much more than most people, (Escott, 133).) In addition, he produced an autobiography, a biography of Palmerston, the English Men of Letters volume on Thackeray, a translation of Caesar's *Commentaries* (1870), a two-volume *Life of Cicero* (1880; Trollope was a creditable amateur classical scholar), four collections of 'Sketches' (hunting types, clergymen, travellers, tradesmen), a book of social criticism, *The New Zealander* (not published until 1972), and enough essays and reviews to fill three or four more volumes, some seventy books in all. That readers should disagree about the relative merits of his books amid so large a number is only natural. But the degree of difference of opinion about Trollope's novels is extraordinary. There are people who rate, say, *The Belton Estate* (1866) as on a par with anything he ever wrote, while others dismiss it out of hand. With the winnowing of time some agreement might have been expected, but this has not been the case.

Trollope the man A question that puzzled Trollope's contemporaries was how this man could have written these novels. Of course like all writers, Trollope was 'different' from his books. But here the difference was compounded by his elusive and seemingly contradictory personality. W. P. Frith, an intimate of Trollope, said:

> It would be impossible to imagine anything less like his novels than the author of them. The books, full of gentleness, grace, and refinement; the writer of them, bluff, loud, stormy, and contentious, neither a brilliant talker nor a good speaker.

James Bryce, another friend, said that at first 'you were disappointed not to find so clever a writer more original', and even when, on further acquaintance, he appeared more of a piece with his books, one still 'could never quite recognize in him the delineator of Lily Dale'. Frederick Harrison, after describing Trollope's violent passion for hunting, whist, and smoking, his loud talk and 'burly ubiquity and irrepressible energy in everything' as one of the 'marvels' of his generation, was mystified as to how:

> such a colossus of blood and bone [a muscular 5 feet 10, 15 to 16 stone] should spend his mornings, before we were out of bed, in analyzing the hypersensitive conscience of an archdeacon, the secret confidences whispered between a prudent mamma and love-lorn young lady, or the subtle meanderings of Marie Goesler's heart. (Hall, *Trollope*, 507–9)

Although most of Trollope's friends and acquaintances despaired of reconciling the man and the author, they invariably qualified their assessments of Trollope as gruff, outspoken, and boisterous by referring to his proverbial honesty and loyalty: 'a kinder hearted man and truer friend never lived' (Frith); 'Crusty, quarrelsome, wrong-headed, prejudiced, obstinate kind-hearted and thoroughly honest old Tony Trollope' (G. A. Sala); 'as good and staunch a friend as ever lived' (Wilkie Collins). A few friends did insist that they saw the author in the man:

T. H. S. Escott resorted to a simple assertion that style is the man, and that those who did not see the author in the 'unreserved friend' and 'candid, plain-speaking companion' were lacking in perception. Publisher Fred Chapman wrote to a friend that his wife fretted constantly after Trollope's death, saying:

> she never loved any one so much—barring me … He was a very good fellow, very kind … I fancy you met him at our house; if so, and not knowing more of him, your impression would be that he was a rough boisterous man, and too uncouth for the society of ladies—He was the reverse. He was as tender hearted as a girl.   (all quotations found in Hall, *Trollope*, 507–9)

Death and burial On 2 October 1882 Trollope and his son Henry took rooms at Garlant's Hotel, Suffolk Street, London. Trollope had found that the city air was better than country air for the asthma from which he had been suffering for several years.

On Friday 3 November Trollope dined with his brother-in-law John Tilley and Tilley's daughter Edith in St George's Square. After dinner the party retired to the drawing-room where Edith read aloud from a current best-selling comic novel, F. Anstey's *Vice Versa*. For a while 'Uncle Tony roared as usual', and then suddenly Tilley and Edith realized that as they were laughing he was silent. Trollope had had a stroke (J. Tilley, *London to Tokyo*, 1942, 8).

Trollope's seizure paralysed his right side, almost completely impairing his powers of reason and of speech. He was moved to a nursing home at 34 Welbeck Street, and died there at 6 p.m. on 6 December 1882. A relatively small funeral was held on 9 December and Trollope's body was buried the same day in All Souls cemetery, Kensal Green, London.

Reputation Trollope has two distinct reputations, one with critics, another with readers. While he was alive, these two reputations ran together. Critical acclaim in the press, even as it tailed off during the 1870s, matched his popularity with the so-called common reader. Similarly, the prices he could command for his copyrights decreased. He was paid according to volume length: £3200 for the 'five-volume' *He Knew He was Right* in an agreement signed 1867; £2500 for the 'four-volume' *Eustace Diamonds*, 1870; £1600 for the three-volume *Popenjoy*, 1877; £1400 for the three-volume *Duke's Children*, 1878; and £1000 for the three-volume *Mr. Scarborough's Family*, 1881–2 (Sadleir, *Bibliography*, 259ff). Altogether he made more than £75,000 with his writing. Trollope's will, proved in January 1883, gave the gross value of his personal estate, exclusive of copyrights, at £25,892 19s. 3d.

At the time of Trollope's death the two reputations began to divide, and some critics were soon talking of his 'disappearance'. Forty years later Michael Sadleir, who saw himself as an apologist for a neglected writer, made much of this supposed demise. One of his chief arguments was that Trollope's *Autobiography*, published a year after his death, extinguished Trollope's good name (Sadleir, *Commentary*, 363). But Sadleir's speculation does not fit well with the facts. It is true that *An Autobiography*, with its talk about getting up at five o'clock each morning and writing 250 words every fifteen minutes for three hours, with its down-playing of 'inspiration', and with its insistence on comparing novel writing to shoemaking, led a few contemporary critics and many critics after Sadleir to believe that *An Autobiography* demolished Trollope's reputation. But Trollope's working habits were scarcely a secret in 1883, as he had for years gone out of his way to talk to anybody who would listen about the very things thought to be the shocking revelations in the *Autobiography*. He loved to tell people that what a novelist needed most was cobbler's glue on the seat of his pants to keep him at his writing desk. Moreover, reviewers had discussed these sentiments in print. The *Westminster Review*, for example, had said:

> It is told of Mr. Trollope that he considers his own method of art to be purely mechanical, and that he has declared that he could teach easily any one to write as good books as his own in a short space of time. (Smalley, 481)

Furthermore, *An Autobiography* was universally acclaimed on its publication in 1883. It had some fifteen prominent reviews, all of them positive.

A handful of critics did indeed prophesy the disappearance of Trollope: George Saintsbury, Lewis Melville, and Herbert Paul. George Gissing gave the question his own twist, saying that he hoped it were true that 'the great big stupid public' was 'really, somewhere in its secret economy, offended by that revelation of mechanical methods' (Gissing, 213). But when one turns from these few critics to publishers' records, the story is different. For the period of Trollope's 'disappearance', from 1885 to 1915, an incomplete tally of these thirty years shows 25 British publishers issuing more than 180 editions and reprintings of his books, and 22 American publishers producing almost 300 editions and reprintings. While the size of the printings is unknown, these numbers are impressive. It is clear that in regard to readers Trollope never suffered anything resembling total eclipse, even during years when his critical reputation was at its lowest (Hall, 'Disappearance', 6).

After Sadleir's time, there were some further attempts to bring Trollope into mainstream critical acceptance. These included David Cecil's chapter on Trollope in his influential *Early Victorian Novelists* (1934) and the work of Bradford Booth in the 1940s and 1950s, including the founding in 1946 of a scholarly quarterly, *The Trollopian* (subsequently renamed *Nineteenth-Century Fiction*). But for the most part the academy neglected Trollope until the 1970s, when there began an outpouring of work on the novelist, more than thirty-five full-length critical books and four major biographies in five years, by R. H. Super (1988), Richard Mullen (1990), N. John Hall (1991), and Victoria Glendinning (1992).

Trollope's reputation with readers is a very different matter. With writers, who constitute a very special breed of readers, he has always been held in great esteem—from the Brownings and Tolstoy to Virginia Woolf and Max Beerbohm, from Graham Greene and Gore Vidal to Anthony Burgess and P. D. James. George Eliot put it well when she wrote to Trollope congratulating him on his

mastery in organizing 'thoroughly natural everyday incidents', calling this skill 'among the subtleties of art which can hardly be appreciated except by those who have striven after the same result with conscious failure' (*Letters*, 1.238). So did Noel Coward with his laconic 'Thank God for Trollope'. The hundreds of writers who admire Trollope give him a very select place among English novelists.

Trollope's hold on the ordinary adult reader (as opposed to the captive secondary school or college student reader) is also remarkable. Throughout the twentieth century the continuous demand for his works kept his best-known books before the public. After 1920 Oxford University Press World's Classics, which issues so many established works as to be a microcosm of the reprint business, became the foremost publisher of Trollope in both Britain and America. Oxford between 1920 and 1962 (at which latter year the records become spotty) brought out a total of 37 Trollope titles in 185 printings. *Barchester Towers*, the best-selling of his novels, sold during this period some 56,000 copies, keeping pace with the most popular Dickens titles, even outselling *Oliver Twist* by some 12,000 copies (Hall, 'Disappearance', 9). In recent years two British television series have undoubtedly brought Trollope new readers, but it is not a question of his being discovered. A huge, solid base of Trollope readers has existed since his death. Today more than 200 editions of Trollope titles are in print. All the editions and reissues, read round the English-speaking world, add up to an endorsement of a dictum set forth in 1968 by Gordon Ray in one of the most useful essays on its subject: 'Trollope was a great, truthful, varied artist, who wrote better than he or his contemporaries realized, and who left behind him more novels of lasting value that any other writer in English' (Ray, 334).

According to Henry James 'Trollope did not write for posterity; he wrote for the day, the moment; but these are just the writers whom posterity is apt to put into its pocket' (James, 19). That is precisely what has happened: on 25 March 1993 a commemorative stone was laid to Trollope's memory in Poets' Corner, Westminster Abbey.

N. JOHN HALL

Sources A. Trollope, *An autobiography* (1883); ed. F. Page (1950) · *The letters of Anthony Trollope*, ed. N. J. Hall, 2 vols. (1983) · N. J. Hall, *Trollope: a biography* (1991) · T. A. Trollope, *What I remember*, 2 vols. (1887–9) · T. H. S. Escott, *Anthony Trollope: his public services, private friends, and literary originals* (1913) · H. James, 'Anthony Trollope', *Partial portraits* (1888); repr. in *The Trollope critics*, ed. N. J. Hall (1981) · D. Smalley, ed., *Trollope: the critical heritage* (1969) · M. Sadleir, *Trollope: a commentary* (1927); repr. (1961) · M. Sadleir, *Trollope: a bibliography* (1928) · N. J. Hall, 'The truth about Trollope's "disappearance"', *Trollopiana: The Journal of the Trollope Society*, 22 (1993), 4–12 · N. J. Hall, 'A corner of Westminster Abbey that will always be Anthony Trollope', *New York Times Book Review* (21 March 1993), 35 · W. H. Auden, 'A poet of the actual', *New Yorker* (1 April 1972), 104 [review of *Anthony Trollope* by J. P. Hennessy] · *The letters of Mrs Gaskell*, ed. J. A. V. Chapple and A. Pollard (1966) · G. Gissing, *The private papers of Henry Ryecroft* (1903) · G. N. Ray, 'Trollope at full length', *Huntington Library Quarterly*, 31 (1968), 313–40 · G. A. Sala, *Things I have seen and people I have known* (1894) · V. Woolf, 'Phases of fiction', *Collected essays*, 2 (1967) · parish register, London, St George's, Bloomsbury Way, 18 May 1815 [baptism]

Archives BL, autograph MS of autobiography, Add. MS 42856 · Bodl. Oxf., corresp. and publishers' agreements · Boston PL, letters and papers · Harvard U., Houghton L., papers · Hunt. L., letters and literary MSS · Princeton University Library, New Jersey, letters · U. Mich., Harlan Hatcher Graduate Library, letters and papers · University of Illinois, Urbana-Champaign, corresp., literary MSS, and journals · Yale U., Beinecke L., papers | BL, letters to Macmillans, Add. MSS 55253–55255 · BL, letters to Royal Literary Fund, Loan 96 · Bodl. Oxf., letters to George and Elizabeth Smith · Boston PL, letters to Kate Field · LUL, letters to Austin Dobson · NL Scot., corresp. with Blackwoods · NL Scot., letters to Lord Brougham and others · Trinity Cam., letters to Lord Houghton · University of Melbourne, letters incl. to George William Rusden **Likenesses** double portrait, photograph, 1860–64 (with his brother Thomas Adolphus Trollope), Bodl. Oxf.; *see illus. in* Trollope, Thomas Adolphus (1810–1892) · J. M. Cameron, photograph, 1864, NPG [*see illus.*] **Wealth at death** £25,892 19*s.* 3*d.*: probate, 1883, *CGPLA Eng. & Wales*

Trollope, Arthur William (*bap.* **1768**, *d.* **1827**), headmaster, baptized on 30 September 1768, was born in London, the son of Thomas Trollope, a mercer, who was descended from the younger branch of the ancient Lincolnshire family, and his wife, Amelia, daughter of J. Page. He was entered at Christ's Hospital, London in 1775 and received his education there until 1787, when he matriculated as a sizar from Pembroke College, Cambridge. He graduated BA in 1791, MA in 1794, and DD in 1815. He was a classical scholar of no mean reputation. In 1791 he obtained the second chancellor's classical medal, in 1792 he received the second members' prize for middle bachelors, and in 1793 he gained the first members' prize for senior bachelors. In 1795 he was awarded the Seatonian prize for an English poem, the subject being the 'Destruction of Babylon'. He was ordained in 1791, and was appointed in 1796 vicar of Ugley and perpetual curate of Berden in Essex, both of which livings were in the gift of the governors of Christ's Hospital. In 1797 he married Sarah, the daughter of William *Wales, mathematics master at the school.

In 1799, on the resignation of James Boyer, Trollope was elected headmaster of Christ's Hospital. In 1814 he was presented to the rectory of Colne Engaine in Essex by the governors of Christ's Hospital, and resigned his former preferments, Ugley and Berden. As headmaster Trollope showed unwearied assiduity, and was rewarded with unusual success. Bred up under the antiquated discipline of Boyer, he was apt sometimes to display unnecessary severity. But his learning and his faculty for imparting instruction enabled him to train many distinguished scholars. Among his pupils were Thomas Mitchell (1783–1845), Thomas Barnes (1785–1841), the editor of *The Times*, and James Scholefield, regius professor of Greek at Cambridge. At the time of Trollope's resignation all the assistant classical masters and the master of the mathematical school had formerly been his pupils. He resigned his post on 28 November 1826, and was succeeded by the second master, John Greenwood. On the occasion of his retiring he was presented with a silver cup by his former pupils. He died at his home, Colne Engaine rectory on 24 May 1827.

Trollope's eldest son, **William Trollope** (1798–1863), author, was born at Ugley, Essex on 29 August 1798. He was

admitted to Christ's Hospital in September 1809, and proceeded to Pembroke College, Cambridge, in 1817, graduating BA in 1821 and MA in 1824. He was Bell scholar in 1818 and gained the Norrisian and Hulsean prizes in 1821. He was appointed fourth classical master of Christ's Hospital in December 1822, and third classical master in 1827. He resigned his post in 1832 and, having been ordained in 1825, was instituted vicar of Wigston Magna in Leicestershire, a Christ's Hospital living, on 25 September 1834. He retained the vicarage until 1858, when he resigned it and removed to Green Ponds in Tasmania, where he became incumbent of St Mary's Church. Trollope, who was married to Sarah, daughter of William Clarke, of East Bergholt, Suffolk, died at Green Ponds on 23 March 1863.

William Trollope was the author of several exegetical works on the New Testament. In 1828 he published the first volume of his *Analecta theologica, sive, Synopsis criticorum: a critical, philological, and exegetical commentary on the New Testament*; the second volume appeared in 1834 and a new edition of both volumes in 1842. This work was followed in 1837 by an annotated edition of the Greek text of the New Testament, of which new editions were issued in 1850 and 1860. His volumes of questions and answers on the liturgy and the Thirty-Nine Articles of the Church of England (1846 and 1850) went through many editions. In addition to various school editions of classical authors, he produced a history of Christ's Hospital (1833).

E. I. CARLYLE, *rev.* M. C. CURTHOYS

Sources *GM*, 1st ser., 97/1 (1827), 85–7 · Venn, *Alum. Cant.* · Venn, *Alum. Cant.* [William Trollope] · G. A. T. Allan, *Christ's Hospital exhibitioners to the universities of Oxford and Cambridge, 1566–1923* (1924) · Boase, *Mod. Eng. biog.* [William Trollope] · *GM*, 3rd ser., 15 (1863), 108 [William Trollope] **Likenesses** A. Fox, line engraving (after Tannock), NPG · portrait, repro. in W. Trollope, *A history of the royal foundation of Christ's Hospital* (1834)

Trollope, Edward (1817–1893), bishop of Nottingham and antiquary, sixth son of Sir John Trollope, sixth baronet, of Casewick, Lincolnshire, and his wife, Anne, the daughter of Henry Thorold of Cuxwold, Lincolnshire, was born at Uffington, Lincolnshire, on 15 April 1817. His eldest brother, John (1800–1874), after sitting in parliament for Lincolnshire from 1841, was created Baron Kesteven on 15 April 1868.

Edward was educated at Eton College and at Christ Church, Oxford, from where he matriculated on 10 December 1835, but graduated from St Mary Hall in 1839 and proceeded MA in 1859. On 20 December 1840 he was ordained deacon by the bishop of Lincoln, and licensed to the curacy of Rauceby, Lincolnshire, the same day. He was ordained priest on 10 December 1841, and immediately afterwards instituted to the vicarage of Rauceby. In 1843 he was appointed to the rectory of Leasingham, Lincolnshire, by his maternal relative, Sir John Thorold, and held this living for fifty years. On 30 September 1846 he married Grace, the daughter of Sir John Henry Palmer, seventh baronet. On 14 December 1860 he was collated to the prebendal stall of Decem Librarum in Lincoln Cathedral, and in 1866 was elected proctor in convocation. In 1867 he was appointed prebendary of Liddington in Lincoln Cathedral, which he held until 1874. Also in 1867 he was collated to the archdeaconry of Stow. On 21 December 1877 Trollope was consecrated bishop-suffragan of Nottingham, in which capacity he assisted the bishop of Lincoln in the episcopal work of the diocese for sixteen years. On his nomination to the bishopric of Nottingham he was created DD by his university on 11 December 1877 from Christ Church.

The new see of Southwell, established in 1884, in great measure owed its formation to Trollope's exertions and munificence, he himself raising £10,000 towards the fund. He also purchased the ancient palace as the site of a residence for the bishops of Southwell, and at a cost of nearly £4000 restored and furnished the banqueting hall.

It was, however, as an antiquary that Trollope was most widely known. He helped forward the work of church restoration in his diocese, in many instances effectually checking ill-advised alterations. He was for many years general secretary of the Associated Architectural Societies, and ultimately general president; he was also vice-president and chairman of the committee of the Lincolnshire Diocesan Architectural Society. He was elected FSA on 26 May 1853. He contributed fifty-eight papers, chiefly relating to Lincolnshire, to the transactions of the Associated Architectural Societies. Among his other works were a life of Pope Adrian IV (1856), a manual of sepulchral memorials (1858), a work on ancient and medieval labyrinths (1866), a history of Sleaford, Flaxwell, and Aswardhurn (1872), and genealogies of the Thorold and Trollope families (1874 and 1875).

Following the death of his first wife in 1890 Trollope married, in 1892, Louisa Helen, the daughter of the Revd Henry Berners Shelley Harris, master of Lord Leycester's Hospital at Warwick.

Trollope died at his home, Leasingham rectory on 10 December 1893, and was buried at Leasingham on 14 December. His second wife survived him. There were two daughters of his first marriage: Mary Grace, who married Sir Richard Lewis De Capell-Brooke, fourth baronet, and Caroline Julia, who married Wyrley Peregrine Birch.

W. G. D. FLETCHER, rev. TRIONA ADAMS

Sources *The Times* (11 Dec 1893) · *Guardian* (13 Dec 1893) · *Guardian* (20 Dec 1893) · *Lincolnshire, Boston and Spalding Free Press* (12 Dec 1893) · *Lincolnshire, Boston and Spalding Free Press* (19 Dec 1893) · *Lincoln Diocesan Magazine* (Jan 1894) · *Church Portrait Journal*, 3 (1879), 81–2 · Burke, *Peerage* · Boase, *Mod. Eng. biog.*
Likenesses S. A. Walker, photograph, c.1889, NPG · A. E. Fradelle, photograph, repro. in *Church Portrait Journal*, 81 · portrait, repro. in *Daily Graphic* (12 Dec 1893), 14
Wealth at death £57,610 7s. 8d.: probate, 22 Feb 1894, CGPLA Eng. & Wales

Trollope [née Milton], **Frances** (1779–1863), travel writer and novelist, was born at Bristol, possibly at Stapleton, on 10 March 1779, the middle child of William Milton (1743–1824), vicar of Heckfield, Hampshire, and his first wife, Mary (d. 1784x6), the daughter of Francis Gresley of Bristol

Frances Trollope (1779–1863), by Auguste Hervieu, c.1832

and his wife, Cecily. Her maternal grandfather, a respected apothecary who lived in Bristol's fashionable Queen Square, could boast Norman ancestry. Her paternal grandfather, however, was in trade, variously described as a 'distiller' and 'saddler' in Bristol.

Early life, marriage, and motherhood, 1779–1826 The Revd William Milton took up the living of Heckfield in 1774, but after only a year he installed a curate and moved to Bristol, then to the nearby village of Stapleton, and eventually to Clifton, a fashionable spa town overlooking the city. He preferred inventing gadgets to saving souls, and his most important idea was the creation of a tidal bypass to control the water levels of the Avon, allowing ships to sail in and out of Bristol more freely. Of his three children, Frances—or Fanny as she was known to her friends and family—resembled her father most. Like him, she was incapable of sitting still and doing nothing if there was a problem to be solved or a situation to be improved. Without the guidance of her mother, who died when Fanny was only five or six years old, she also learned to be self-reliant. Together these traits—initiative, tenacity, and independence of mind—were to give her the courage, strength, and ability to overcome the many crises which she would have to face in her lifetime; but they also made her sometimes act rashly, without thinking, and thus court disaster.

In 1800 William Milton married Sarah Partington of Clifton, and the following year, after a twenty-seven-year absence, he returned to the quiet Hampshire village of Heckfield with his new wife and family to resume his duties as vicar. The relationship between Fanny and her stepmother was never very close, and within three years of her father's marriage she and her sister Mary, aged twenty-four and twenty-seven respectively, moved to London to keep house for their younger brother Henry, a clerk in the War Office. Fanny had a petite figure, a pleasant face, and 'the neatest foot and ankle' on the dance floor (F. E. Trollope, 2.286), but she was also intelligent, well read and outspoken—in a word, 'blue'—and she was still a spinster when at twenty-nine she met the shy, sober barrister, Thomas Anthony *Trollope (1774–1835), five years her senior. After a year's courtship, on 23 May 1809 they married and settled into conventional domesticity in Keppel Street, near Russell Square. Over the next nine years Fanny gave birth to seven children: Thomas Adolphus *Trollope (1810–1892), Henry, Arthur, Anthony *Trollope (1815–1882), Cecilia, and Emily. The Trollopes' firstborn daughter, another Emily, survived only long enough to be privately baptized.

Fanny adored her children, and her oldest son, Tom, had happy memories of the nursery: 'My mother's disposition … was of the most genial, cheerful, happy, *enjoué* nature imaginable … and to any one of us a *tête-à-tête* with her was preferable to any other disposal of a holiday hour' (T. A. Trollope, 1. chap. 3). Fanny had the knack of making almost anything fun, even learning. By contrast, Thomas Anthony, whose great ambition was that his sons should follow in his footsteps to Winchester College and New College, meted out punishment with a pull of the hair for any blunder made in reciting their lessons. As the years passed Thomas Anthony became ever more argumentative and erratic, almost certainly owing to the effects of calomel, a mercury-based drug which he took for chronic migraine.

The Trollopes' secure world soon began to fall apart. Although he had no experience of farming, Thomas Anthony leased some 160 acres in Harrow from John, Lord Northwick. The Trollopes moved to Julian Hill (Anthony Trollope's model for Orley Farm) and set about improving the property. In 1818 they built a large house, christened Julians after the Hertfordshire estate of his uncle Adolphus Meetkerke, which Thomas Anthony expected to inherit. His prospects were dashed when his elderly uncle married and produced an heir in 1819. The Trollopes' finances went from bad to worse during the agricultural depression of the 1820s, and in 1824 their twelve-year-old son Arthur died of tuberculosis.

Travels in the United States and *Domestic Manners of the Americans* (1832)   When Henry, fun-loving but idle, left Winchester in 1826 before completing his studies, his father was furious: he could not afford to support an indolent son. Within a year Thomas Anthony announced that financial pressures made it necessary to move yet again, this time to a run-down farmhouse. In an almost desperate act Fanny, Henry, and her two young daughters set sail for America on 4 November 1827 to join the charismatic reformer Frances Wright at Nashoba, a community in the backwoods of Tennessee dedicated to the education and emancipation of slaves. Fanny thought it Henry's best chance to find a good prospect in life; she also hoped to ease the family's financial burdens back home while escaping her husband's dreadful temper. She left her two remaining

sons, Tom and Anthony, at home to continue their education. When her friend's utopian dream turned out to be a malaria-ridden swamp, Fanny decamped and headed up the Mississippi to Cincinnati, Ohio, then a booming frontier town dubbed the 'Athens of the West'.

Fanny's life in Cincinnati was a tragicomedy of failed business ventures, scandal, and illness. In an early effort to make money she devised the *Infernal Regions*, a Dantesque spectacle featuring waxworks and electric currents. But Fanny's most ambitious undertaking was what might be called America's first shopping mall, the Cincinnati Bazaar. The townspeople failed to patronize it, and Fanny ended up bankrupt and deathly ill with malaria. Cincinnati society never accepted Fanny. She had arrived in the city penniless, without references and in the company, not of her husband, but of a young French artist, Auguste Hervieu, who, despite the gossip, was in fact nothing more than a devoted friend, without whose help the Trollopes would have starved. After two miserable years in Cincinnati, Fanny admitted defeat and retreated to the east coast, where she travelled for a year before returning to England in August 1831.

Fanny turned her experiences to good effect in her *Domestic Manners of the Americans* (2 vols.), published in March 1832, just three days before the final reading of the first Reform Bill (and nine days after the author's fifty-third birthday). Reformers frequently hailed the United States as a beacon of democracy. Mrs Trollope, who had left England something of a Liberal, had returned home very much a Conservative, and her criticisms were seized upon by the bill's opponents. She set out to expose Americans' boast of 'equality' as a sham. 'You will see them', Fanny wrote:

> with one hand hoisting the cap of liberty, and with the other flogging their slaves. You will see them one hour lecturing their mob on the indefeasible rights of man, and the next driving from their homes the children of the soil, whom they have bound themselves to protect by the most solemn treaties.   (chap. 20)

Domestic Manners of the Americans, which is above all extremely funny and entertaining, created a furore on both sides of the Atlantic and became the touchstone against which subsequent accounts of the United States were judged. It launched Fanny's career as a writer, and it remained in print from the time of its publication to beyond the end of the twentieth century.

Residence in Europe, and family and social circles   The earnings from *Domestic Manners* allowed the Trollopes to move back to their old home Julian Hill and live in relative comfort while Fanny continued to write. Her husband had long since given up his law practice, and Fanny was now the sole breadwinner. However, despite three more books from her pen in two years, the debts incurred by the Harrow farm and Cincinnati Bazaar proved too great, and the Trollopes were forced to flee to Bruges to escape debtors' prison. Within a year both Fanny's beloved 23-year-old son Henry and her husband were dead: the former from tuberculosis, the latter from premature old age. Thomas

Anthony's death came almost as a relief. Anthony later remarked that the touch of his father's hand:

> seemed to create failure … But the worse curse to him of all was a temper so irritable that even those he loved the best could not endure it. We were all estranged from him, and yet I believed he would have given his heart's blood for any of us. His life as I knew it was one long tragedy. (A. Trollope, chap. 2)

Fanny was free to return to England after her husband's death, but she did not settle in any one spot for long. From 1836 she lived in Monken Hadley, a village north of London, until her eldest daughter, Cecilia, announced her engagement to John Tilley, one of Anthony's Post Office colleagues. After a brief period in London at 20 York Street, Portman Square, Fanny undertook to build a house in Penrith, Cumberland, christened Carlton Hill, to be near Cecilia and her husband, who was by this time (1841) surveyor of the northern district. But within a year Fanny had made up her mind to leave Carlton Hill: she found both the neighbours and the weather too dull. In 1843 she fulfilled her lifelong dream of visiting Italy, and there she remained for the rest of her life. From 1850 she shared the Villino Trollope, in the piazza dell'Indipendenza, Florence, with her son Thomas Anthony and his wife, Theodosia *Trollope (1812x19–1865), also writers.

In 1849 Cecilia, thirty-three years old and the mother of five, died from tuberculosis. Consumption had been the family curse: as well as her two sons, Arthur and Henry, Fanny had also lost eighteen-year-old Emily to the disease in 1836. Throughout it all Fanny supported her family through her writing: six travel books and thirty-five novels over a period of twenty-five years. Anthony Trollope recalled that:

> the doctor's vials and the ink-bottle held equal places in my mother's rooms … Her power of dividing herself into two parts, and keeping her intellect by itself clear from the world, and fit for the duty it had to do, I never saw equalled. (A. Trollope, chap. 2)

As her son Tom testified, Fanny had the remarkable ability to 'throw sorrow off when the cause of it had passed' (T. A. Trollope, 1. chap. 14). Fanny loved society, and she seemed to have boundless energy to host at-homes, devise charades, stage amateur theatricals, or organize picnics for family and friends. Yet she was invariably at her desk between four and five the following morning to write the allotted number of pages before breakfast. Anthony's wife Rose said of her:

> there was nothing conventional about her, and yet she was perfectly free from the vice of affectation … She was lavishly generous as regards money; full of impulse; not free from prejudice—but more often in *favour* of people than otherwise,—but once in her good books, she was certain to be true to you. She could say a sarcastic word, but never an ill-natured one. (F. E. Trollope, 2.244)

Over the years her circle of friends encompassed such diverse characters as the actors Edmund Kean and William Charles Macready, the political figures Ugo Foscolo, General Lafayette, and Prince Metternich, the reformer Frances Wright, the artists George Hayter and Hiram Powers, and the authors Mary Russell Mitford, Charles Dickens, and Elizabeth Barrett Browning.

Travel writing and novels Fanny's books, seven of which featured Auguste Hervieu's engravings, were hugely popular in their day. Thackeray once confessed, 'I do not care to read ladies' novels, except those of Mesdames Gore and Trollope' (*Fraser's Magazine*, 18, 1843, 350). 'Certainly no other author has been so much read, so much admired, and so much abused', declared one critic (*New Monthly Magazine*, 55, March 1839, 417). By 1839 Fanny could command £800 per manuscript. She thought of herself primarily as a travel writer: *Paris and the Parisians* (2 vols., 1836) and *Vienna and the Austrians* (2 vols., 1838), a fascinating if uneven portrait of Metternich and *la crème de la crème* of Viennese society, are still worth reading. However, when Fanny calculated that travelling costs outstripped her earnings, she turned to novel writing.

Early on Fanny experimented with several different genres, including the Gothic novel (*The Abbess*, 1833). She also wrote fiction which dealt with social themes, such as the poor law. Like Charles Dickens, Fanny was able to keep to a gruelling schedule, juggling two books at once, published in monthly instalments; for a time in the 1840s Dickens saw her as a serious rival. He even switched the plot midway through *Nicholas Nickleby* away from the Cheeryble brothers' factory when Fanny got in first with a damning exposé of child labour in her novel, *Michael Armstrong, the Factory Boy* (March 1839–February 1840). This tale, published as a three-decker in 1839, elicited a strong response from the critics. *The Athenaeum* (165, 1839, 587–90) claimed that Mrs Trollope was 'scattering firebrands … among an ignorant and excited population to which her shilling numbers are but too accessible'. Her equally powerful anti-slavery novel *Jonathan Jefferson Whitlaw* (1836) preceded *Uncle Tom's Cabin* by more than fifteen years.

Above all, Fanny Trollope excelled in biting satire and broad humour. Two of her best novels are *The Vicar of Wrexhill* (1837), which ridicules evangelicalism, and *The Widow Barnaby* (1839), whose 'heroine' is a female rogue, struggling to make something of herself without the advantages of youth or a large income. Fanny turned her popular *Widow Barnaby* into a fictional series, an innovation in the English novel, with two sequels, *The Widow Married* (May 1839–June 1840), published in three volumes in 1840, and *The Barnabys in America* (April 1842–September 1843), published in three volumes in 1843.

In her later novels, whether set in a cathedral town, a country estate, or London's West End, Fanny combined witty social commentary with strong and often melodramatic plots. At its best, Fanny's writing is subtle and well observed and, even in the most far-fetched romance, she is able to convey with great skill the foibles and follies of human nature—and of English manners in particular. She astutely aimed to hit the somewhat lowbrow taste of the circulating library, and this, as one critic noted, she did 'remarkably well' (*The Spectator*, 6, 1833, 526–7). Nevertheless, her sharp satirical wit, the result of her Georgian upbringing, was increasingly seen as 'coarse' and 'vulgar' as Victoria's reign progressed.

Literary reputation Fanny died in Florence on 6 October 1863, aged eighty-four; she lies buried in the English cemetery there. She had retained her popularity to the end. In its review of her last novel, *Fashionable Life* (1856), *The Critic* deemed Mrs Trollope 'the *doyenne* of English authoresses' (1 Sept 1856, 420). Her books continued to be reprinted until the early 1880s, when they suddenly ceased to appear. A reason for this can be traced to the publication of her son Anthony's *Autobiography* in 1883, the year following his death. Anthony Trollope's ambition to become a novelist had long been overshadowed by his mother's reputation. The chief motivation behind Fanny's writing had been to make enough money to support herself and her family. Anthony, however, was an aspiring man of letters, and his mother's reputation as a 'vulgar' authoress was a continual embarrassment, especially as her books, reprinted and reissued, were displayed alongside his novels in shops and circulating libraries. Anthony used his autobiography as an opportunity publicly to distance himself from his mother. In it he criticizes her politics as merely 'an affair of the heart' and condemns her novels, claiming that 'in her attempts to describe morals, manners, and even facts, [she] was unable to avoid the pitfalls of exaggeration' (A. Trollope, chap. 2). Tom was horrified at his brother's remarks: 'there is hardly a word of this in which Anthony is not more or less mistaken' (T. A. Trollope, 2. chap. 18).

Nevertheless, Anthony Trollope's strictures seem effectively to have buried his mother's literary reputation, and Fanny's books, apart from *Domestic Manners of the Americans*, were largely forgotten for the best part of a century. Only recently have critics and readers rediscovered her writings. Anthony's comments also belie the enormous influence which Fanny had over her son. Anthony drew some of his best-known plots and characters from his mother's novels; he adopted Fanny's innovation of the fictional series for his Barchester and Palliser novels; he even copied her working habits, rising in the early hours to write before breakfast. The much-loved Trollopian world of the cathedral close, middle-class mores and strong-minded women was, in part, a family legacy passed from mother to son. PAMELA NEVILLE-SINGTON

Sources F. E. Trollope, *Frances Trollope: her life and literary work from George III to Victoria*, 2 vols. (1895) · T. A. Trollope, *What I remember*, 2 vols. (1887) · A. Trollope, *An autobiography*, 2 vols. (1883) · P. Neville-Sington, *Fanny Trollope: the life and adventures of a clever woman* (1997) · H. Heineman, *Mrs Trollope: the triumphant feminine in the nineteenth century* (1979) · L. P. Stebbins and R. P. Stebbins, *The Trollopes: the chronicle of a writing family* (1946) · T. Ransom, *Fanny Trollope: a remarkable life* (1995) · 'Memoir of Mrs Trollope', *New Monthly Magazine*, new ser., 55 (1839), 416–17 · W. M. Thackeray, review of *Jerome Paturot*, *Fraser's Magazine*, 28 (1843), 350 · Bristol RO

Archives BL, corresp. and agreements with Richard Bentley, Add. MSS 46612–46613, 46649–46650 · Harvard U., Garnett-Pertz MSS · Princeton University, New Jersey, Morris L. Parrish collection · Princeton University, New Jersey, Robert H. Taylor collection

Likenesses L. Adams, watercolour, 1832, BM · A. Hervieu, miniature, oils, c.1832, NPG [*see illus.*] · engraving, c.1840, NPG · W. Holl, stipple, 1845 (after L. Adams), BM, NPG; repro. in Taylor, *National Portrait Gallery* (1845) · photograph, c.1860, Boston PL · J. Brown, stipple, BM; repro. in 'Memoir of Mrs Trollope' · W. Greatbach, line engraving, NPG; repro. in *Domestic manners of the Americans* (1839)

Wealth at death under £1500: probate, 14 Dec 1863, *CGPLA Eng. & Wales*

Trollope, Frances Eleanor (1835–1913). *See under* Ternan, Ellen Lawless (1839–1914).

Trollope, George Barne (*d.* 1850), naval officer, was born at Huntingdon, the son of the Revd John Trollope, brother of Captain Thomas Trollope of the 40th regiment and half-brother to Sir Henry *Trollope. He entered the navy on 5 May 1790 as a first-class volunteer under Henry Trollope's command in the *Prudente* (38 guns) during the Spanish armament, and followed him to the *Hussar* (28 guns), before serving in her for nearly two years in the channel and the Mediterranean, part of the time as a midshipman.

In August 1792 Trollope was appointed to the *Lion* (64 guns, Captain Erasmus Gower) accompanying Lord Macartney to China. On his return in October 1794 he transferred to the *Argo* (44 guns), but he rejoined Gower three months later in the *Triumph* (74 guns) and thus took part in Admiral William Cornwallis's masterly retreat (16 and 17 June 1795). While still in the *Triumph* he was promoted lieutenant on 13 December 1796, and he remained in her, as part of Admiral Adam Duncan's North Sea Fleet, for the battle of Camperdown, in which he was slightly wounded. From 24 April 1798 he again served with Captain Gower, now in the *Neptune* (98 guns), and he moved to the *Vestal* (28 guns) on 28 January 1799. By January 1801 he was in the *Princess Royal* (98 guns) bearing the flag of Gower (now Sir Erasmus), and he remained in her until she was paid off in April 1802. From 23 October 1803 he was first lieutenant to Captain Lord Cochrane in the *Arab* (22 guns).

Trollope had thus been trained under some of the finest seamen of the day and enjoyed wide-ranging sea experience, so that his promotion to commander, of the sloop *Cerf* at Jamaica (1 May 1804), was well deserved. His career looked promising, but he contracted a severe bout of yellow fever in the West Indies and had to be invalided home in December 1804. It was not until 22 January 1806 that he was appointed to command the bomb-vessel *Hecla* at Sheerness, and this preceded his moving on 1 March to the *Electra* (18 guns), in which he was employed first in the North Sea and then in the Mediterranean. Here he was in charge of the boats which evacuated the garrison of the fortress of Scylla on 17 February 1808, when the British evacuated Sicily, and received the particular thanks of Major-General Sherbrooke for his activity. On 26 March the *Electra* was wrecked at the entrance to Port Augusta, between Syracuse and Messina, and Trollope was without a ship until December. He was then given command of the *Zebra* (16 guns) at Woolwich for two months, after which he was without a command until 22 October 1810, when he was appointed to the cutter *Alert*; and on 1 February 1812 he moved to the *Griffon* (16 guns), serving successively on the Newfoundland and Downs stations.

In the *Griffon*, equipped with fourteen 24-pounder carronades and two 6-pounders, on 27 March 1812 Trollope and the *Rosario* (10 guns), pursued ten French brigs. They drove one heavily armed brig ashore near St Aubin, under heavy fire from the shore batteries, and attacked the remainder, boarding and cutting out one of them. The *Griffon* was considerably disabled, but Trollope's 'prompt attention and gallant conduct' (O'Byrne, *Naval biog. dict.*, 2.1203) was praised in the *Naval Gazette* of 1808.

In 1813 Trollope married Barbara, the daughter of John Goble of Kinsale. He was promoted post captain on 7 June 1814, was made a CB on 8 December 1815, accepted retirement on 1 October 1846, and was promoted rear-admiral on 9 October 1849. He died at Bedford on 31 May 1850.

P. K. CRIMMIN

Sources DNB · O'Byrne, *Naval biog. dict.* · D. Syrett and R. L. DiNardo, *The commissioned sea officers of the Royal Navy, 1660–1815*, rev. edn, Occasional Publications of the Navy RS, 1 (1994) · *GM*, 2nd ser., 34 (1850), 659

Trollope, George Haward (1845–1929), builder and Territorial Army officer, was born at Westminster on 20 January 1845, the elder son of George Francis Trollope (1817–1895), interior decorator and builder, and Constance Haward. His father had been apprenticed to the firm of Haward and Nixon, Constance's family's building business. At the age of fifteen Trollope joined the family building business, George Trollope & Sons, and had only a limited formal education. In the same year he enlisted as a private in the Queen's Westminster rifles, a militia unit. He rose through the ranks to become the commanding officer and, by 1891, a colonel. Thereafter he was commonly known to his peers and employees as 'the Colonel'. Trollope married Jessie, daughter of George Gouldsmith, auctioneer, on 8 April 1869; they had at least two sons, Fabian George Trollope and Howard Woolwright Trollope (who predeceased his father), and a daughter, Sybil L. H. Hickley.

The family firm expanded during the 1850s by undertaking large speculative building projects in Belgravia, but in the later 1860s the economic slump found the building side of George Trollope & Sons dangerously over committed. Fortunately, the firm had been restructured in 1864 to take advantage of limited liability and the assets of its interior decorating, estate agency, and cabinet-making branches were protected. During the 1870s, particularly on the Cadogan estate in Chelsea, the firm re-established itself as builders of residential property. Its reputation was based on the very high quality of craftsmanship and the speed and flexibility with which contracts were executed. The consequent requirement for systematic overtime and disregard for the craft unions' working rules led to repeated outbreaks of industrial strife.

Little is known of Trollope's role in the firm prior to 1891, although he did represent the company on the council of the Institute of Builders. He did not serve a formal apprenticeship in one of the building crafts. By the time that Trollope took control of the business he had acquired

George Haward Trollope (1845–1929), by unknown photographer

his father's hostility to trade unions and the cautious conservatism of his uncle Robert, also a director of the firm. Under his direction, Trollopes remained active in London's West End, building Claridge's Hotel and Alfred Beit's house in Park Lane. The firm also diversified into ship-fitting (making interior woodwork for liners) and the construction of country houses, particularly for South African financiers. Randlord clients included Barnato, Beit, Joel, Phillips, and Wernher. Trollope's imperialistic views and accumulated wealth may have helped to secure these contracts.

In 1894–5 Trollope was at the centre of bitter industrial disputes in London. The trouble began at Beit's house in Park Lane where Trollopes' foreman refused to employ union bricklayers. During the ensuing strike a lurid poster headed 'Trollope's Black List' appeared and Trollope obtained a court injunction prohibiting it. The dispute spilled over onto a Mowlems site where the presence of a 'Trollope blackleg' provoked a strike. In both disputes the Central Association of Master Builders of London played a pivotal role, supporting the firms while moderating their intransigence in negotiations. Trollope served as the association's treasurer, 1892–3, vice-president, 1893–5, and president, in 1895–6. At one point he advocated that it should support the strike-breaking National Free Labour Association, but later changed his mind.

The firm of Trollope and Colls was formed in 1903 and Trollope served as joint chairman until 1910. Although the Trollope family were the majority shareholders, Howard

*Colls appears to have been the driving force of the new firm. Colls had a greater technical understanding of reinforced concrete, structural steel, and other innovations in construction. Following Colls's death in 1910 Trollope became sole chairman of Trollope and Colls, a position he retained until 1924. He recruited Dr Oscar Faber as the firm's first chief engineer, apparently to compensate for the loss of Colls's expertise. During this period the firm undertook very substantial contracts. War work included factories, hospitals, camps, aerodromes, and even an aeroplane factory at Oldham which was the largest in Britain under a single roof (covering 6 acres). After the war large bank contracts were executed, including the construction of the Hongkong and Shanghai Bank building at a cost of £1 million.

During the years 1910 to 1924 Trollope and Colls was transformed into a large public company with family directors and professional management. This change was emphasized by the fact that most of the family directors were on active service, overseas during the war. Despite his age, 'the Colonel' held staff appointments in France, Mesopotamia, and the eastern Mediterranean. He died at his home, Hammershott, Liphook, Hampshire, on 30 May 1929 at the age of eighty-four. His estate was valued at £75,000: this relatively modest sum may be explained by the references to gifts and loans to family members which appear in his will. He was survived by his wife.

ALISTAIR G. TOUGH

Sources G. H. Trollope, letters, *The Times* (12 Sept 1899) · G. H. Trollope, letters, *The Times* (8 June 1919) · G. H. Trollope, letters, *The Times* (25 Feb 1925) · G. H. Trollope, letters, *The Times* (31 July 1928) · G. H. Trollope, letters, *The Times* (15 Oct 1928) · *The Builder*, 136 (1929), 1049 · A. Saint, 'Trollope and Colls: early history' · *City builders for 200 years, 1778–1978*, Trollope and Colls Ltd (1978) · London Master Builders' Association, *London Master Builders' Association seventy-five years on, 1872–1947* (1949) · *An outline history of the National Federation of Building Trades Employers, 1878–1978* (1978) · Trollope and Colls Ltd, *Buildings of today and tomorrow. A review of modern construction* (1924) · A. G. Tough, 'Colls, John Howard', *DBB* · F. H. W. Sheppard, ed., *The Grosvenor estate in Mayfair*, 2: *The buildings*, Survey of London, 40 (1980) · J. N. Summerson, *The London building world of the eighteen-sixties* (1973) · C. G. Powell, *Economic history of British building industry, 1815–1979* (1982) · b. cert. · d. cert. · m. cert.
Archives LMA · Surrey HC
Likenesses photograph, Skanska UK [*see illus.*] · portrait, Trollope and Colls Ltd, London
Wealth at death £75,001 15s. 3d.: resworn probate, 6 July 1929, *CGPLA Eng. & Wales*

Trollope, Sir Henry (1756–1839), naval officer, son of the Revd John Trollope of Bucklebury in Berkshire, was born on 20 April 1756. His grandfather, Henry Trollope, a London merchant, was a younger brother of Sir Thomas Trollope, fourth baronet, of Casewick, Lincolnshire, from whom future baronets and the novelist Anthony Trollope were descended.

Early career, 1771–1779 Henry Trollope entered the navy in April 1771 on the *Captain* (64 guns), ordered to North America under Captain Thomas Symonds and bearing the flag of Rear-Admiral John Montagu. Trollope served in her for

Sir Henry Trollope (1756–1839), by Daniel Orme, pubd 1798

three years and five months, as captain's servant, able seaman, and midshipman. On her return to England in 1774 Trollope went back to North America in the *Asia* (64 guns), serving two years and six months as able seaman and midshipman. He claimed he had been present at the battle of Lexington and at Bunker Hill, presumably in the *Asia*'s boats, sent to cover the retreat from Lexington and the landing of troops to attack Bunker Hill. This taste of action led to his being lent to the sloop *Kingfisher* in Hampton Roads, helping the governor, Lord Dunmore, try to subdue the uprising in Virginia.

Trollope was also at the siege of Boston and in 1777 rejoined the *Asia* to return to England. On 25 April 1777 he was promoted lieutenant and joined the *Bristol* (50 guns) going to North America with troop transports for New York. On arrival Trollope, the *Bristol*'s third lieutenant, was detached to command her boats helping the army up the North River in an attempt to join General Burgoyne. Hearing of Burgoyne's surrender, he returned to New York and the *Bristol* which joined Admiral Howe in the Delaware, and was present at the reduction of Philadelphia. Trollope exchanged into the *Chatham* (50 guns) which, ordered home for repairs, arrived at Sheerness in the spring of 1778. He was appointed first lieutenant of the *Chatham*, but seeing the possibility of rapid advancement upon the alliance of France with the American colonies he applied in February 1778 to command a cutter, the *Kite*, stationed in the Downs and carrying ten 4-pound guns and fifty men. Trollope sailed on 14 March, the day before the French declaration of war, and within eight hours had anchored in the Downs with a French brig, taken under the guns of Calais.

In the following months Trollope was constantly at sea, letting no vessel pass without a strict examination, detaining numbers of neutrals carrying contraband goods, and taking a great number of prizes. On 30 March 1778, cruising off Portland, he engaged and drove off a French frigate of 28 guns which was chasing thirty British merchantmen. The following day he engaged and again drove off an 18-gun French brig, damaging her severely, before retiring to Portsmouth for necessary repairs to his own wounded rigging. As a result of this activity, reported by the port admiral, Sir Thomas Pye, Trollope was promoted commander on 16 April 1779. The promotion gained him the advancement he had desired and with it came recognition as an energetic and fortunate commander.

Gunnery trials and mutiny at the Nore, 1781–1797 In April 1781 Trollope accompanied Vice-Admiral Darby's fleet to the relief of Gibraltar and so pleased was Lord Sandwich, first lord of the Admiralty, with his speed in conveying dispatches between his superior and the Admiralty, that on 4 June 1781 he was promoted post captain and appointed to the *Myrmidon* (20 guns). Trollope joined Admiral Hyde Parker's North Sea squadron at the Nore on 6 August, the day after the battle of the Dogger Bank, and continued on this station under Commodore Stewart. At Stewart's particular request Trollope was appointed on 21 March 1782 to the *Rainbow* (44 guns) then fitting at Chatham and experimentally armed with carronades. These were short light carriage guns firing relatively heavy shot at limited but effective range. There was still a dispute whether such guns could properly form the main armament of a ship. Trollope was known to have paid great attention to training his men in gunnery and was thus selected for the trials. On her passage down channel in late August 1782 the *Rainbow* met heavy weather which caused damage to the shot lockers and had to put in at Plymouth for repairs. Trollope therefore sailed alone to join Commodore Elliot's squadron, looking for a French convoy carrying naval stores and reportedly about to sail from St Malo under the escort of the *Hébé* (38 guns), a new French frigate. Trollope's luck led him to fall in with her off the Isle de Bas (now Île de Batz) at dawn on 4 September 1782. A lucky shot from the *Rainbow* smashed the *Hébé's* wheel as she tried to escape and the French captain, reportedly astonished at the size of the shot, surrendered with little resistance.

Trollope having rejoined Elliot and helped convoy the West Indian fleet past Scilly, now parted from the squadron. Despite taking the *Hébé*, the *Rainbow* had not been able to prove the value of her carronades as armament and Trollope wished to try again against a 74-gun ship. He had no orders to do so, but while cruising off Ferrol he saw a Spanish 74-gun ship, and two French ships of 64 and 40 guns in the harbour. He told his crew he intended to wait until they came out and then engage them, not doubting that he would take the Spaniard and that the French would retreat. Trollope remained off Ferrol until mid-December 1782, when shortage of water forced him to

return to Spithead by the end of the year. The Admiralty demanded the reason for his late return, and though they expressed pleasure at his zeal, they reproved him for remaining so long absent as to be thought lost or captured. Trollope was ordered to place himself under Sir John Jervis for an expedition to the south seas but peace preliminaries were signed in the spring of 1783 and the *Rainbow* was paid off.

Trollope's success in taking prizes during the war was financially rewarding and he now enjoyed the fruits of his success. He retired to a country house in Carmarthenshire for the next eight years and lived in a pleasant, generous manner. At one point his hospitality to the crew of a French merchant ship, locally wrecked, brought official French thanks. In the Spanish armament of 1790 he was appointed to the *Prudente* (38 guns) and on the settlement of the dispute, moved to the *Hussar* (28 guns), in which he went to the Mediterranean to join Admiral Edward Peyton. Once more his speed in delivering dispatches brought rewards, this time a snuffbox from the king of Naples, with the king's portrait set in diamonds and valued at 700 guineas.

Trollope returned to England in the spring of 1792 and since he did not wish to go with the *Hussar* to Halifax, retired to Wales until 1795 when he was appointed to the *Glatton*. She was one of six Indiamen bought into naval service, fitted as warships and armed with carronades. Drawing on his experience Trollope suggested a particular method of fitting carronades in the *Glatton* and persuaded Lord Spencer, first lord of the Admiralty, to allow it, despite objections from the Navy Board. Trollope swore that, if he were allowed a free hand, he would have the *Glatton* ready as soon as the others, and helped by a capable foreman he had her ready and at the Nore almost a month before the other converted Indiamen. The first lord was so pleased he promoted the *Glatton's* first lieutenant to commander. The *Glatton* herself proved an effective warship, while her companions were unserviceable and used only as transports.

For the next two years the *Glatton* was one of the North Sea Fleet under Admiral Adam Duncan. Trollope frequently commanded a small squadron, watching the enemy coast with brief returns to Yarmouth for supplies. On 14 July 1796 he left Yarmouth to rejoin the squadron, and the following afternoon he engaged a Dutch force of six frigates and some smaller ships off Helvoetsluys and drove them into port. The action was short but fierce and the *Glatton's* rigging was very cut up. By this action Trollope saved a large British convoy, homeward bound from the Baltic and escorted by a single sloop. The rewards he received—two pieces of plate (one valued at 100 guineas) from the London merchants, another from the Russia Company, and the freedom of the boroughs of Huntingdon and Yarmouth—reflected the relief felt by the mercantile interest.

Trollope was then sent to cruise off Shetland to intercept Dutch warships and remained there until early November, when he returned to Sheerness for repairs. On leave in London he was suddenly ordered to the Nore to command the *Leopard* (50 guns) and with four frigates, sent to Cuxhaven, which was threatened by a French naval force. Within 48 hours Trollope was in the River Elbe, and he remained there, despite the dangers of ice, until January 1797. On his return to the Nore the Admiralty again expressed its pleasure at his conduct by promoting his first lieutenant to commander, and as *Glatton* was now repaired Trollope returned to her and rejoined Admiral Duncan.

When mutiny broke out at the Nore in May 1797 the men of the *Glatton* mustered on deck and told Trollope that, though they were perfectly satisfied with him and the other officers, they must do as the other ships did, and were resolved to go to the Nore. They permitted Trollope to visit the flagship and Duncan agreed nothing could prevent *Glatton* sailing, but that Trollope must prevent her going to the Nore. While *Glatton* was becalmed off Harwich, on the night of 1 June, Trollope argued with his crew, attempting to bring them back to their duty. With his first lieutenant he determined to retake the ship. Thus 2 June was fraught with danger; some of the crew threatened to fire on the poop and officers if they did not surrender. Trollope replied that he and his officers would die rather than permit the delegates to command. He declared the men should be ashamed of behaviour which was equal to committing piracy, treason, and murder and denounced the oath that every man should go to the Nore.

After some anxious hours these arguments prevailed. When the anchor was weighed Trollope took the *Glatton* to the Downs, where he found the *Overyssel* (64 guns) and the *Beaulieu* (50 guns) in open mutiny. His threats to fire into them returned both ships to their duty and on the following day they sailed to rejoin Duncan at the Texel. Lord Spencer thoroughly approved Trollope's conduct and appointed him to command the *Russell* (74 guns). This was a dubious reward. During the mutiny at Spithead the *Russell* had been notably violent and before he gave him the commission Duncan said he did not wish to put Trollope into a ship in so bad a state of discipline. But Trollope declared himself ready to command her and though there were difficulties at first, within a fortnight there was no further trouble in the ship.

The battle of Camperdown and later career, 1797–1839 For the next four months Trollope was constantly cruising off the Dutch coast, watching the Dutch fleet in the Texel. In Yarmouth at the end of September Trollope found the *Russell* unfit for service. However, following the admiral's reminder of the Dutch threat, Trollope declared himself ready to sail at once and with *Adamant* (50 guns), the frigate *Circe*, and some cutters and was off the Texel just as the Dutch fleet put to sea on 7 October. He immediately sent the news to Duncan and followed the enemy closely, evading their attempts to drive him off. This enabled him to inform Duncan that the Dutch appeared to be steering for England and not further north. On 11 October he joined Duncan's fleet which was hurrying back from Yarmouth where it had been taking on fresh stores. In the battle of Camperdown the following day, Trollope was in Vice-

Admiral Richard Onslow's division which opened the British attack. Trollope opposed the *Delft* (56 guns) and on silencing her went to the assistance of Onslow, in the *Monarch* (74 guns), engaging the *Jupiter* (74 guns), Admiral Reyntjes's flagship, and after she surrendered, passed on to take the *Wassenaar* (64 guns). The *Russell*'s losses were light, but her rigging was badly damaged and Trollope's task of bringing the prizes into Yarmouth was a difficult one. But Trollope performed with his customary skill and efficiency, bringing eleven prizes into Yarmouth and assigning the wounded to the skilful care of Mr M'Grath, the *Russell*'s surgeon who was appointed their superintendent. Lord Spencer congratulated Trollope on his 'steadiness and skill' (Ralfe, 2.333) in shadowing the Dutch and bringing about the juncture between them and Duncan's fleet. In reward he was appointed to command the yacht *Royal Charlotte* in which George III intended to visit the fleet, now returned to the Nore. The king embarked on 30 October, but thanks to a contrary wind had only reached Gravesend two days later. The visit was therefore cancelled, and the king returned to Greenwich where, before landing, he knighted Trollope, who then accompanied the royal procession to St Paul's where the enemy colours were laid up.

During the following two years Trollope continued in command of the *Russell* as one of the Channel Fleet, off Brest, under the command of Lord Bridport. In 1800 he was appointed to command the *Juste* (80 guns) and on 1 January 1801 he was promoted vice-admiral of the white. Unfortunately he became entangled in a dispute with Jervis (now Lord St Vincent), Bridport's successor, who sometimes supplemented his written orders with verbal ones, occasionally contradictory. Upset by this, Trollope accused St Vincent of un-officerlike conduct and since St Vincent would not apologize Trollope declined to serve under him. Shortly afterwards St Vincent became first lord of the Admiralty and did not offer Trollope any appointment, which, on his part, Trollope would probably not have accepted. Although he was promoted rear-admiral of the red on 23 April 1804, he had been incapacitated by a violent attack of gout a year earlier and he seems to have considered his service life at an end. Trollope's request for a royal pension was declined, though he did receive promotion to vice-admiral of the blue on 9 November 1805 followed by further promotion to admiral of the blue (12 August 1812) and admiral of the white seven years later. Although he recovered his health in 1816, peacetime offered no opportunity of service. His wife, formerly a Miss Burt of Surrey, also died in that year at Bath and though he received other appointments and honours—a KCB 19 July 1820, admiral of the red 27 May 1825, and a GCB 8 June 1831—he was childless and from the 1830s gout returned to plague him. This or perhaps loneliness affected his mind. He now lived at Freshford near Bath and became convinced that he would be burgled. He turned his bedroom into an armoury, with a blunderbuss, a big knife, and several brace of pistols. Nobody seems to have thought this anything more than a harmless eccentricity; but on 2 November 1839 he locked himself in his room and blew out his brains. He was buried in St James's Church, Bath.

Trollope's earlier career had been markedly successful. He had risen by merit and zeal, actively pursuing advancement in service in small ships. This made him an expert seaman and proved financially fortunate. The high point of his career was in the months surrounding the battle of Camperdown. The wearing service of watching the Dutch off a dangerous coast in all weathers strained men as well as ships and probably laid the foundations of the gout from which Trollope later suffered. The 1797 mutinies strained the strongest nerves but Trollope's firmness and basic fairness carried him through this testing time. All these qualities won him the approval of his service and civilian superiors. His kindness to the *Hébé*'s crew, when his prisoners in 1782, gained his half-brother Captain Trollope (*d.* 1799) of the 40th regiment equally kind treatment, when he was taken prisoner in 1794 at sea, from his captor who had been a midshipman in the *Hébé*. A month after Captain Trollope's early release, in March 1795, the French captain became a prisoner of war in his turn. Henry Trollope thereupon begged Lord Spencer's influence and the Frenchman was released forthwith.

Trollope's life was almost wholly devoted to the service and he showed no interest in politics. A brother, Lieutenant-Colonel Thomas Trollope, commanded the marines on the *Venerable* (74 guns) at Camperdown. Aside from Captain Trollope, Sir Henry had a second half-brother, George Barne *Trollope, also a naval officer.

P. K. CRIMMIN

Sources *DNB* · J. Ralfe, *The naval biography of Great Britain*, 2 (1828), 311–35 · J. Marshall, *Royal naval biography*, 1 (1823), 145 · *Naval Chronicle*, 18 (1807), 353 · D. Syrett and R. L. DiNardo, *The commissioned sea officers of the Royal Navy, 1660–1815*, rev. edn, Occasional Publications of the Navy RS, 1 (1994), 444–45 · C. Lloyd, *St Vincent and Camperdown* (1963) · lieutenants' passing certificates, PRO, ADM 107/6, 386 · captains' passing certificates, PRO, ADM 6/22
Likenesses D. Orme, stipple, pubd 1798, BM, NPG [*see illus.*] · J. Chapman, stipple, pubd 1801, NPG · G. Noble and J. Parker, group portrait, line engraving, pubd 1803 (*Commemoration of 11th Oct 1797*; after *Naval Victories* by J. Smart), BM, NPG · H. R. Cook, stipple (after R. Bowyer), BM, NPG; repro. in *Naval Chronicle*

Trollope [*née* Garrow], **Theodosia** (1812x19–1865), author, was the only child of Joseph Garrow (*d.* 1857) and his wife, Theodosia Fisher, *née* *Abrams (*c.*1769–1849) [*see under* Abrams, Harriett]. Her date of birth is unknown but her parents married in 1812 and she was included in the will of her aunt Harriett Abrams in 1819. Her father was the son of an army officer of the East India Company and an Indian consort; her mother was a singer, the Jewish widow of a captain in the North Devon militia. Her childhood was spent at Torquay, possibly for reasons connected with her delicate state of health. Small, fragile, precocious, hypersensitive, and, like her mother, very musical, she made her literary début as a poet in 1839. Her verses appeared in *Heath's Book of Beauty* (edited by Lady Blessington), and in *The Keepsake*, and for a while her reputation rivalled that of Elizabeth Barrett. Walter Savage Landor wrote of her early work: 'Sappho was less intense, Pindar less lively' (Artom-Treves, 138)—a verdict that the future Mrs Browning

Theodosia Trollope (1812x19–1865), by unknown photographer

deemed extravagant. Like the Brownings, the Garrows moved to Italy, and settled in Florence in 1844. Here Theodosia practised her skills as a translator, specializing in Italian literature of the modern nationalist school. She produced English versions of the patriotic songs of Dall'Ongaro and Giusti, and in 1846 published her most ambitious work, a verse translation of Giovanni Battista Niccolini's drama *Arnaldo da Brescia*. She contributed to Dickens's *Household Words* and to the *Cornhill Magazine*; but her best-known journalism, a series of letters on the situation in Tuscany in 1859 and 1860, appeared in *The Athenaeum*. Congratulating the Italians on their awakening from 'morbid indifferentism', she took the liberal view and praised the Risorgimento as an exercise in high-minded patriotism and enlightened democracy. Its opponents she denounced as brutal reactionaries and benighted bigots, reserving her severest strictures for the papacy ('a paralyzed heap of malicious dotage'). These articles, which were published separately as a book, *Social Aspects of the Italian Revolution* (1861), did much to turn British public opinion in favour of the liberation and unification of Italy.

In Florence she met and captivated Thomas Adolphus *Trollope (1810–1892), writer on Italy and novelist, elder brother of Anthony Trollope; they were married at the

British legation on 3 April 1848. By now Elizabeth Barrett Browning's fame as a poet had far eclipsed her own, but Theodosia's role as *salonière* made her a much more conspicuous figure in Florentine life than the recluse of Casa Guidi. The Villino Trollope, in the piazza dell' Indipendenza, became the main social focus of Anglo-Florentine society, and a favourite venue for liberal-minded Italian politicians and literati. The young American journalist Kate Field, later a prominent feminist, described it as a scene of exquisite civility, presided over by a hostess who was 'promiscuously talented', but who did 'not go very far in any one thing' (Artom-Treves, 140). The desultory and somewhat febrile nature of Theodosia's literary career was probably linked to her phthisical condition, which the Italian climate failed to repair. She died on 13 April 1865, and was buried in the English cemetery in Florence. She was survived by her husband and their daughter, Beatrice (1853–1881), who married Charles Stuart-*Wortley, Baron Stuart of Wortley (1851–1926) [see under Wortley, James Archibald Stuart-] and died in childbirth.

JOHN PEMBLE

Sources L. P. Stebbins and R. P. Stebbins, *The Trollopes* (1946) • G. Artom-Treves, *The golden ring: the Anglo-Florentines, 1847–1862*, trans. S. Sprigge (1956) • M. Sadleir, *Trollope: a commentary* (1927) • L. Whiting, *Kate Field: a record* (1899) • T. Trollope, 'Giovanni Battista Niccolini', *Cornhill Magazine*, 10 (1864), 683–94 • private information (2004) [O. Baldwin, T. Wilson]

Likenesses photograph, Boston PL, Kate Field MSS [*see illus.*]

Trollope, Thomas Adolphus [Tom] (1810–1892), historian and writer, was born on 29 April 1810 at 16 Keppel Street, Bloomsbury, London, the eldest child of Thomas Anthony *Trollope (1774–1835), barrister, and his wife, Frances *Trollope, *née* Milton (1779–1863), travel writer and novelist. On his father's side, his grandfather, the Revd Anthony Trollope, was the youngest son of a baronet; his paternal grandmother's family, the Meetkerkes, were descendants of the Flemish ambassador to the court of Elizabeth I. At the time of his birth, the Trollopes had only a modest income; but his father expected to inherit the Meetkerkes' Hertfordshire estate, Julians, on the death of his elderly uncle. On family visits to the manor young Tom, as he was known, was 'shown to the tenantry as their future landlord, and all that sort of thing' (T. A. Trollope, 1, chap. 3). Meanwhile, Thomas Anthony, who had pretensions to be a gentleman farmer, leased some land in Harrow and moved his family there. Tom, and eventually his three brothers Henry, Arthur (d. 1824), and the novelist Anthony *Trollope (1815–1882), were able to attend Harrow School as day boys with no fees to pay. In 1817, just before the birth of Emily, their sixth and final child, the Trollopes decided—perversely—to build a spacious dwelling on the rented land, christening it Julians after the Hertfordshire estate. But this merely tempted fate, for all their expectations were dashed when Thomas Anthony's uncle married in 1818 and, a year later, produced a son.

Education and early life Owing to his position as the eldest son and (for a time) heir apparent, Tom developed into a confident, intellectually precocious boy. He had inherited

Thomas Adolphus Trollope (1810–1892), by unknown photographer, early 1860s [left, with his brother Anthony Trollope]

his mother's 'genial, cheerful, happy, *enjoué* nature', as he later put it, along with her ability to 'throw sorrow off' (T. A. Trollope, 1, chaps. 3, 14). His father, on the other hand, brooded over his misfortunes, causing his irascible temper to grow even worse. He had already given up his law practice when the agricultural crisis of the 1820s hit the Harrow farm hard. Thomas Anthony put enormous pressure on his sons to follow in his footsteps to Winchester College and New College, Oxford. Tom was duly elected a scholar at Winchester in 1820. He did well and was popular with his fellow Wykehamists. The fun-loving and idle Henry, however, left Winchester in 1826—before the end of his studies—with no means of earning his keep. Thinking to find a career for Henry while easing the family's financial burdens and escaping her husband's black moods, Fanny Trollope sailed with her son and young daughters to America in 1827. Tom, by this time a school prefect, was left behind, charged by his mother to look after the awkward middle child Anthony, who had recently joined him at Winchester. Tom, it seems, was over-zealous in his duties, thrashing his little brother every day 'with a big stick'. 'In those school-days', Anthony recalled, he 'was, of all my foes, the worst' (A. Trollope, chap. 1).

Tom left Winchester in July 1828 and, while waiting to be offered a place at New College, sailed with his father for the United States to pay a six-month visit to Mrs Trollope and the three children in Cincinnati, Ohio. When Tom learned on his return to England that he was not to have a place at New College after all, his father enrolled him in October 1829 at one of the Oxford halls, which were considered 'a refuge for the destitute' (T. A. Trollope, 1, chap. 9). After two years, owing entirely to an argument over money between his father and the principal, Dr Whately, Tom was forced to leave Alban Hall. He eventually found a place at the academically inferior Magdalen Hall (later Hertford College). During Tom's time at Oxford, his family went through many upheavals. In 1831 his mother returned from the United States, with Henry and the two girls, having failed in all their business ventures. The publication of Fanny's best-selling *Domestic Manners of the Americans* in 1832 relieved the Trollopes from financial embarrassment for a time. However their liabilities were too great, and in spring 1834 Thomas Anthony was forced to flee England to avoid debtors' prison. His family followed him to Bruges—all except Tom who was about to sit his finals. Henry, the companion of Tom's youth, died of tuberculosis while abroad. Not surprisingly, Tom left Oxford in 1835 with a dismal third-class degree.

Towards the end of 1836, after numerous delays, Tom secured a teaching post at King Edward's grammar school in Birmingham which he grew to loathe. He longed to give it up and cultivate a career as a travel writer alongside that of his mother, for, as he confessed, 'I was born a rambler' (T. A. Trollope, 2, chap. 1). Before starting at King Edward's he had accompanied her on her researches to Paris and to Vienna. But Fanny begged him not to give up a salary of £200 per annum; she knew how hard it was for a writer to make ends meet. Although her husband's death in 1835 had allowed the family to return to England free of debt, Fanny still had to provide for her eldest daughter Cecilia. (Anthony had just begun his career at the Post Office; Emily had succumbed to tuberculosis in 1836.) It was not until Cecilia announced her engagement in spring 1838 that Fanny was able to agree with Tom that he should 'become her companion and squire' (T. A. Trollope, 1, chap. 18).

Italy and scholarship Tom became his mother's travel and literary agent, research assistant, and editor. Fanny had extraordinary energy, but she would not have been so prolific—six travel books and thirty-five novels in all—without Tom at her side. For his part, Tom was free at last to pursue his own literary ambitions, which began modestly with periodical articles. His first book, *A Summer in Brittany* (1840), earned him £300 and a commission from the publisher, Colburn, for a second: *A Summer in Western France* (1841). To boost sales, Colburn placed the name of that best-selling author Mrs Trollope on the title-page of both books ('edited by'). Tom and his mother spent the next few years moving about—from London to Cumbria, where they built a house to be near Cecilia—until settling at long last in Italy in 1843.

Italy, Florence in particular, held many charms for both mother and son. Society among the expatriates was easy-going, the climate mild, the cost of living extremely low. Tom was fascinated by the beginning of Italy's bid for freedom from foreign rule. In 1847 he published the *Tuscan Athenaeum*, intended to inform the English-speaking world about matters relating to Italian independence. Also involved in this short-lived enterprise was a young English poet, Theodosia Garrow (1812x19–1865) [see Trollope, Theodosia], who had moved to Florence with her family three years earlier. Although handsome enough at 5 feet 10 inches with blond hair and grey eyes, Tom had always been somewhat shy with women unless they could hold their own in an intellectual conversation. Theodosia was more than equal to the challenge, and they were married at the British minister's chapel on 3 April 1848. Tom and Theodosia collaborated on the volume *Tuscany in 1849*

and 1859 (1859), and both contributed to the London *Athenaeum*. Tom's *Athenaeum* articles were collected and published under the title *Impressions of a Wanderer in Italy, Switzerland, France, and Spain* (1850).

In 1850, with Theodosia's generous inheritance from her half-sister, the couple bought a large three-storey house in piazza dell'Indipendenza, which they shared with Tom's mother and Theodosia's father. In 1853 Theodosia gave birth to a daughter, Beatrice (Bice). The Villino Trollope, as it was called, became a gathering place for English and Italians alike. Tom, who was an avid (not to say, obsessive) collector, filled the villa to overflowing with books and antiquities. Visitors, who included the Brownings, Pasquale Villari, Walter Savage Landor, Harriet Beecher Stowe, George Eliot, and, of course, Anthony Trollope, were treated to talk of Italy's future, séances (all the rage in the 1850s), and theatricals (Tom's stock part was Sir Anthony Absolute, with his mother as Mrs Malaprop, in Sheridan's *The Rivals*).

In 1863 Fanny Trollope died after a long and full life. Two years later when Theodosia died Tom was distraught, believing 'that life and all its sweetness was over for me!' (T. A. Trollope, 2, chap. 19). He sold the Villino Trollope and moved to a villa at Ricorboli, outside the Porta San Niccolo, south of the Arno. The following summer, in 1866, the fiercely intellectual Frances Eleanor Ternan (1835–1913) [see under Ternan, Ellen Lawless] came to Florence to serve as twelve-year-old Bice's governess. Miss Ternan had first met the Trollopes in 1858 when, at twenty-three, she arrived in Florence with a letter of introduction from Tom's close friend Charles Dickens (her sister Ellen was Dickens's mistress at the time). Within a few months of her arrival at the Villa Ricorboli, on 29 October 1866, Frances and Tom, twenty-five years her senior, were married. As in his first marriage, husband and wife helped each other in their writing careers, both contributing to *Household Words* and collaborating on several books, including *The Homes and Haunts of the Italian Poets* (1881).

Trollope liked to think of himself first and foremost as a scholar and historian. *A History of the Commonwealth of Florence* (1865) served, at the time, as a valuable introduction to the subject. For Trollope, the city's past was made all the more vivid through his 'daily and hourly study of living Florentines' (T. A. Trollope, 2, chap. 12), and his historical writing is at its best when dealing, not with broad themes, but with the individuals involved, as in *Filippo Strozzi: a History of the Last Days of the Old Italian Liberty* (1860). The idea of recounting Florence's history through the life, not of a famous man, but of one typical of his age, was unusual for its time. Trollope saw many affinities between contemporary Britain at the height of empire and medieval Florence before its decline under Medici rule, and he wrote with this in mind. He had earlier published *The Girlhood of Catherine de' Medici* (1856), and was also ahead of his time in his attention to women's history. 'The absolute *sine qua non* for the advancement of a civilization', he asserted in his introduction to *A Decade of Italian Women* (1859), must be 'the solidarity, co-operation, and mutual influence of both the sexes'. Trollope also introduced the term 'renaissance' into the English language when referring to the art and architecture of the fourteenth century in *A Summer in Brittany*.

Those qualities which enhance Trollope's scholarship—an interest in people and a keen eye for detail—distinguish his journalism. Fully aware that the English viewed Florence and Rome (if they thought of them at all) simply as museums and not living cities, Trollope sought to interest them in the affairs of contemporary Italy through periodicals and newspapers. (He also contributed to American journals for this reason.) He was not blind to the faults of the country's chief political players, whether the Vatican, Napoleon III, Mazzini, or Garibaldi; and he was even sceptical—though not despairing—of Italians' capacity for self-government. In recognition of his contribution to Italy's cause, the newly crowned King Victor Emmanuel bestowed on Trollope the order of St Maurice and St Lazarus in 1862.

Novels and later life Trollope wrote novels—thirteen in all, both English and Italian stories—but had no pretensions as a novelist. He wrote chiefly to make money: Italian history was not a money-spinner, and his love of antiquities invariably exceeded his income. He thought that his Italian novels were good, and *The Times* (3 September 1862) agreed, praising *Marietta* (1862) for its true and vivid depiction of 'the domestic life of the Italian'. Of *La Beata* (1861), his first work of fiction, G. H. Lewes wrote: 'One feels a breath from the Val d'Arno rustling amid the pages' (T. A. Trollope, 2, chap. 16). Trollope called his English novels, on the other hand, 'unquestionably bad'; he had lived too long as an exile to know much of contemporary English life (ibid., 2, chap. 12). Yet these stories are as interesting today as his Italian ones, for they give a detailed and colourful portrait of the England which Trollope knew intimately, that of his childhood—a virtue shared by his autobiography, *What I Remember* (3 vols., 1887–9). Both Tom and Anthony inherited their mother's industriousness. Tom wrote every day from eight until two standing at a high desk near the window. The two brothers had an ongoing rivalry as to who had written the most—and the fastest. Anthony conceded defeat in the latter category when in 1864 Tom wrote a two-volume novel, *Beppo the Conscript*, in twenty-four days (to raise money to take his then ailing first wife somewhere more conducive to her health).

Although Anthony remarked in his autobiography that he and Tom 'have been fast friends' for forty years (A. Trollope, chap. 1), it is his depiction of Tom as a schoolboy bully which is remembered. This is unfair. By his own admission Tom was not clubbable, but he was good company, always to be found sitting among friends after lunch with a cigar and, somewhat incongruously, a glass of milk. Certainly Tom had a strong sense of right and wrong; Elizabeth Barrett Browning dubbed him 'Aristides, the Just'. During one of the many séances held at Villino Trollope, Tom lost patience and admonished the unearthly visitor: 'Spirit, you know nothing about what you are talking of: you are wrong' (Bosco, 93). G. H. Lewes called him 'a most loveable creature' (Glendinning, 302). He acted as

agent not only for his mother but also for his brother; he even furnished them with plots for their novels *Petticoat Government* and *Doctor Thorne*, respectively. Tom also provided George Eliot with material for her novel *Romola* (1863), set in late fifteenth-century Florence. When she visited Italy in 1860 and 1861 he showed her the city and discussed its history with her. On her return to England she corresponded with him, verifying historical details. Eliot clearly based the character of Tito, *Romola*'s charming but wily husband, on Trollope's portrait of Filippo Strozzi. Although he felt the eponymous heroine was too modern, having 'far too much George Eliot in her', Tom thought 'the pages which describe [Tito] read like a quintessential distillation of the Florentine history of the time' (T. A. Trollope, 2, chap. 15). As he once noted in his wry but good-natured way, 'I declare that a good 25 per cent of my time is occupied in doing the business of other people' (Poston, 1966, 136).

In 1873 Trollope left Florence, where he had been correspondent for the *Daily News* since 1866, and moved to Rome, the newly designated capital, where he lived in the via Nazionale and reported for the London *Standard*. In 1890 Tom and his wife Frances moved back to England, to Budleigh Salterton in Devon. His daughter Bice had in 1880 married the Right Hon. Charles Stuart-*Wortley [see under Wortley, James Archibald Stuart-] but died the next year giving birth to a daughter. During a brief visit to Clifton, where his mother had spent her girlhood, Tom died suddenly in his sleep at 27 Royal York Crescent on 11 November 1892 at eighty-two. He had said to his wife, 'Mind, where I fall let me lie. Make no fuss. Give no trouble.' And so, Frances wrote to a friend, 'I left him on the slope of a pretty cemetery close to Bristol.' After twenty-six years of marriage, she continued in the same letter, 'I never detected in him one base, insincere, or ungenerous thought. Flaws and errors there must have been, because he was human. But of envy, hatred, malice, and all uncharitableness he was incapable' (Neville-Sington, 370).   Pamela Neville-Sington

Sources T. A. Trollope, *What I remember*, 3 vols. (1887–9) · A. Trollope, *An autobiography*, 2 vols. (1883) · F. E. Trollope, *Frances Trollope: her life and literary work from George III to Victoria*, 2 vols. (1895) · P. Neville-Sington, *Fanny Trollope: the life and adventures of a clever woman* (1997) · C. Tomalin, *The invisible woman: the story of Nelly Ternan and Charles Dickens* (1990) · L. Poston, 'Thomas Adolphus Trollope: a Victorian Anglo-Florentine', *Bulletin of the John Rylands Library*, 49 (1966), 133–64 · L. Poston, 'Romola and Thomas Trollope's *Filippo Strozzi*', *Victorian Newsletter*, 25 (1964), 20–22 · G. Artom Treves, *The golden ring: the Anglo-Florentines, 1847–1862*, trans. S. Sprigge (1956) · L. P. Stebbins and R. P. Stebbins, *The Trollopes: the chronicle of a writing family* (1946) · J. L. Mahoney, 'Thomas A. Trollope: Victorian man of letters', *University of Rochester Library Bulletin*, 15 (1960), 25–8 · V. Glendinning, *Trollope* (1992) · R. Mullen, *Anthony Trollope: a Victorian in his world* (1990) · R. A. Bosco, 'The Brownings and Mrs Kinney', *Browning Institute Studies*, 4 (1976), 57–125 · d. cert.

Archives Boston PL, letters and papers | BL, corresp. with Richard Bentley, with related papers, Add. MSS 46619–46624 · DWL, letters to Henry Allon · NL Scot., letters to Blackwoods · Princeton University Library, New Jersey, Morris L. Parrish collection ·

Princeton University Library, New Jersey, Robert H. Taylor collection

Likenesses A. Hervieu, drawing, 1832, NPG · group portrait, photograph, c.1860, priv. coll. · double portrait, photograph, 1860–64, Bodl. Oxf. [see illus.] · double portrait, photograph, 1860–65 (with Anthony Trollope), Princeton University Library, New Jersey, Morris L. Parrish collection · J. M. Cameron, photograph, 1864, NPG · S. Laurence, oils, c.1864, NPG · double portrait, photograph, c.1866 (with Frances Eleanor Trollope), Bodl. Oxf. · H. N. O'Neil, oils, 1873, Garr. Club · Ashford Brothers, carte-de-visite, NPG · Elliott & Fry, carte-de-visite, NPG · Lock & Whitfield, woodburytype, NPG; repro. in T. Cooper, Men of mark: a gallery of contemporary portraits (1878) · London Stereoscopic Co., carte-de-visite, NPG · Naudin, carte-de-visite, NPG · H. N. O'Neil, group portrait, oils (The billiard room of the Garrick Club), Garr. Club · Spy [L. Ward], caricature, watercolour study, NPG; repro. in VF (5 April 1873) · M. Ward, carte-de-visite, NPG · H. Watkins, cartes-de-visite, NPG

Wealth at death £931 14s. 8d.: probate, 23 Jan 1893, CGPLA Eng. & Wales

Trollope, Thomas Anthony (1774–1835), barrister and author, was born on 23 May 1774 at Cottered rectory in Hertfordshire, the only son among the four children of the Revd (Thomas) Anthony Trollope (1735–1806), rector of Cottered and Broadfield, and his wife, Penelope, née Meetkerke (1744–1788). He was educated at Winchester College, and matriculated from St John's College, Cambridge, in 1792, but in 1794 migrated to New College, Oxford, where he was elected fellow in 1796. He was admitted to the Middle Temple in 1801, called to the bar in 1804, and in 1806 he moved to 23 Old Square, Lincoln's Inn. Trollope married Frances Milton (1779–1863), later a successful author [see Trollope, Frances], on 23 May 1809, and they moved into his house at 16 Keppel Street, Bloomsbury. They had seven children: Thomas Adolphus *Trollope (1810–1892), the writer; Henry (1811–1834); Arthur William (1812–1824); Emily (b. 1813), who died in infancy; Anthony *Trollope (1815–1882), the novelist; Cecilia (1816–1849); and Emily (1818–1836). Trollope grew up expecting to inherit his maternal uncle's estate near Royston, Hertfordshire, called Julians, but was disappointed when his uncle, widowed in his sixties, remarried and had a family.

In 1813 Trollope leased Illots Farm on Lord Northwick's Harrow estate and built a new Julians. It was, his son Anthony wrote, 'the grave of all my father's hopes, ambition, and prosperity' (A. Trollope, 2). In 1820, to save money, the family moved into the old farmhouse, which they expanded and named Julian Hill. In 1823 Trollope had published A Treatise on the Mortgage of Ships, as Affected by the Registry Acts, dedicated to the prime minister, the earl of Liverpool, but it did not revive his failing law practice. In 1827 he let Julian Hill and moved to Harrow Weald while Frances Trollope went to America with Emily, Cecilia, and Henry in an effort to help repair the family finances. Trollope followed with Thomas Adolphus, leaving Anthony behind, in 1828. Their planned store in Cincinnati failed, taking the last of Frances's money with it.

As the family finances worsened so did Trollope's health. He had always suffered from severe headaches and a fiery temper, but by the 1830s his temper had grown so bad, reported Thomas Adolphus later, that it was feared

'his reason was, or would become, unhinged'. Thomas Adolphus blamed this on his use of calomel (mercury chloride) for his headaches: 'I believe that he was destroyed mind and body by calomel, habitually used during long years' (T. A. Trollope, 1.295, 297). In December 1830 Trollope petitioned Lord Northwick for reduced rents on behalf of all the tenants because of the agricultural depression—in terms so offensive that all rents but his were reduced.

By 1830 Trollope had given up the practice of law, unable to find or keep clients: he 'never came into contact with a blockhead' his son reported, 'without insisting on irrefutably demonstrating to him that he was such' (T. A. Trollope, 1.56). He retired entirely to Harrow, where he worked on his Encyclopaedia ecclesiastica, or, A Complete History of the Church, a compendium of ecclesiastical terms and practices. It was, as N. John Hall writes, 'a curious undertaking for a man of no particular religious bent' (Hall, 32). The first, and only, volume ('Abaddon' to 'Funeral rites') was published in 1834 by John Murray; in the same year the family fled to the continent to escape creditors.

Trollope died on 23 October 1835 at Château d'Hondt, Bruges, and was buried two days later near his son Henry outside St Catherine's Gate, Bruges.   MICKIE GROVER

Sources N. J. Hall, Trollope: a biography (1991) · V. Glendinning, Anthony Trollope (1992) · A. Trollope, Autobiography (1883) · T. A. Trollope, What I remember, 3 vols. (1887–9) · F. E. Trollope, A memoir of Frances Trollope, 2 vols. (1895) · H. Heineman, Mrs Trollope: the triumphant feminine in the nineteenth century (1979) · R. H. Super, The chronicler of Barsetshire: a life of Anthony Trollope (1988) · Venn, Alum. Cant.

Archives Princeton University Library, New Jersey, Morris L. Parrish collection · Princeton University Library, New Jersey, Robert H. Taylor collection · University of Illinois, Urbana-Champaign

Likenesses G. Hayter, group portrait, oils, 1824 (Trial of William, Lord Russell)

Wealth at death estate seized but declared under £50 so creditor (Geo. Barney) got nothing: Glendinning, Anthony Trollope; Robert H. Taylor collection, Princeton University Library, New Jersey

Trollope, William (1798–1863). See under Trollope, Arthur William (bap. 1768, d. 1827).

Tropnell, Thomas (d. 1487), landowner and administrator, was the son of Harry Tropnell and his wife, Edith Roche. Both families were long established in north-west Wiltshire as minor gentry, but it is unlikely that Harry Tropnell owned land there or elsewhere. Thomas Tropnell was an ambitious pragmatist whose newly acquired wealth from commerce and judicious shifts of political allegiance enabled him to establish and maintain himself, often by dubious means, as a landed gentleman in his native county. The house he rebuilt at Great Chalfield, where the cartulary recording the title deeds of his purchases is still preserved, and chapels constructed for him at Great Chalfield and Corsham, survive as symbols of his success. Tropnell's early career, and presumably the basis of his wealth, was in commerce, and he was a merchant trading through Bristol in the 1450s. He married first in 1431 Agnes (d. before 1453), widow of Thomas Bourton, and second, in

1456, his kinswoman Margaret Ludlow (*d.* by 1479), daughter of William Ludlow (*d.* 1478) and widow of John Erley. With Margaret, Tropnell had two sons, Humphrey (*fl.* 1463–1464), who predeceased him, and Christopher (*d.* 1503), his heir, and two daughters, Anne (*fl.* 1464), and Mary (*fl.* 1464–1487).

As a young man Tropnell became a retainer of the powerful Hungerford family, and, possibly under the patronage of Humphrey Stafford, earl of Stafford, was MP for Great Bedwyn in 1429–30 and for Bath in 1449. His business acumen and legal knowledge were also used by later Hungerfords: Robert, Lord Hungerford (*d.* 1459), probably his contemporary, for whom he acted as receiver-general and feoffee, and who bequeathed to him a silver cup; his son Robert, Lord Hungerford and Moleyns (*d.* 1464); and the younger Robert's sons Sir Thomas (*d.* 1469), and Sir Walter (*d.* 1516). His association with the Hungerfords and Staffords naturally brought him into prominence in the county. In September 1450, with Robert, Lord Hungerford, and his son Robert, Tropnell was appointed a commissioner to find, arrest, and try rebels in Wiltshire. He served on other commissions in 1451 and 1459. His service to the family was uninterrupted and unaffected by the attainder in 1461 and execution in May 1464 of Robert, Lord Hungerford and Moleyns, a Lancastrian in arms.

Tropnell was also prepared to court the Yorkists. In his ultimately successful attempt to resist the claim of a retainer of James Butler, the Lancastrian earl of Wiltshire, on Lyngevers manor in Chicklade, which he acquired in portions between 1453 and 1460, he petitioned the future Edward IV and in August 1464 obtained a general pardon from him. During the readeption of Henry VI he was appointed on 27 October 1470, with George, duke of Clarence, and Richard Neville, earl of Warwick and Salisbury, as a commissioner of oyer and terminer in Wiltshire. He was also a JP for Wiltshire in late 1470. Those services, and acknowledgement of his considerable, though possibly informally acquired, legal ability, may have secured his admission to Lincoln's Inn as an honorary member at Michaelmas 1470. His appointment in August 1473 as a commissioner to inquire into farms paid to the crown from lands in Wiltshire shows that he was trusted by the Yorkists and prepared to serve them with equal diligence. He was pardoned in March 1484 by Richard III, possibly for complicity in Buckingham's rebellion in October 1483. His typical circumspection may have prompted him to obtain a general pardon from Henry VII in 1485.

From 1431 Tropnell lived in a house at Atworth inherited by his first wife and conveyed to him on their marriage, and by 1453 he lived at Neston near Corsham in a house built on land acquired in 1442. From the time of his first marriage he built up by purchase a substantial landed estate in the county. The titles to all the properties were defective, except those to Atworth, Neston, East Harnham manor bought in 1453 from Robert, Lord Hungerford, and the advowson of Great Cheverell bought in 1476 from Margaret, Lady Hungerford and Botreaux. His claim on Great Chalfield manor and advowson, in which he bought an interest in 1437, was not established until 1467. An estate in Maiden Bradley, East Codford, and West Codford was acquired between 1441 and 1447, Lyngevers manor in Chicklade between 1453 and 1460, Hindon manor between 1452 and 1460, and Little Durnford manor with comparatively little trouble in 1474. The legal process, usually tortuous and lengthy, by which most of them were purchased, and a pedigree in which he claimed descent from the Percys of Great Chalfield were entered by Tropnell in a register of deeds which was begun on 2 November 1464 and added to until his death. In 1465 he bought a stone quarry at Hazelbury near Box and, presumably from 1467, began to rebuild the manor house at Great Chalfield in lavish style. He lived on the estate only in his last years.

Richard Page and William King, adversaries of Tropnell in his negotiations for Lyngevers manor in 1453, described him as 'a perillous covetouse man', an assessment with which Tropnell may have concurred since it was transcribed into his cartulary (Tropnell, 2.39). That view of his character is echoed, with an element of caricature, in a wall painting, possibly of Tropnell himself, which survives on the south wall of the dining room at Great Chalfield. To Great Chalfield church, which stood north-east of the manor house and inside its precinct, Tropnell added a south chapel decorated with wall paintings and separated from the nave by a screen embellished with arms depicting his claim to descend from the Percy family and his marriage with Margaret Ludlow. He was said to have died on 31 January 1488 but his death must have occurred between 5 November 1487, when he made his will, and 22 November 1487, when a writ of *diem clausit extremum* was issued. In the south chapel of Corsham church, rebuilt for him as his burial place, he and Margaret were entombed beneath a chest bearing their arms. In his will, proved by his son Christopher on 26 February 1488, he observed fashionable piety and endowed a chantry in the chapel for them both and for certain Hungerfords. Though his career had no national importance, he stands as an exemplar of a particular kind of late medieval gentleman on the make, often a lawyer or expert in the law, who was willing to play fast and loose in local politics and exploit all the opportunities offered by local and national political crises to build up a landed estate. Tropnell also happens to have left a superb memorial of his life, in records and in bricks, mortar, and paint.

JANET H. STEVENSON

Sources T. Tropnell, *The Tropenell cartulary*, ed. J. S. Davies, 2 vols. (1908) · J. C. Wedgwood and A. D. Holt, *History of parliament*, 1: *Biographies of the members of the Commons house, 1439–1509* (1936) · *VCH Wiltshire*, vols. 7, 11, 13, 15 · J. L. Kirby, 'The Hungerford family in the late middle ages', MA diss., U. Lond., 1939 · *Chancery records* · R. Floyd, *Great Chalfield manor* (1990) · J. S. Davies, 'The manor and church of Great Chalfield', *Transactions of the Bristol and Gloucestershire Archaeological Society*, 23 (1900), 193–261 · H. A. Tipping, 'Great Chalfield Manor', *Country Life*, 36 (1914), 230–37 · W. P. Baildon, ed., *The records of the Honorable Society of Lincoln's Inn: admissions*, 1 (1896) · N. H. Nicolas, ed., *Testamenta vetusta: being illustrations from wills*, 2 vols. (1826) · F. W. Weaver, ed., *Somerset medieval wills*, 1, Somerset RS, 16 (1901) · *Select cases concerning the law merchant*, 2, ed. H. Hall, SeldS, 46 (1930) · *CIPM, Henry VII*, 1, no. 351; 2, no. 783 · PRO, PROB 11/8, sig. 7

Likenesses wall painting, Great Chalfield Manor, Wiltshire

Wealth at death manors of Great Chalfield, Chicklade (Lyngevers), Little Durnford, East Harnham, and Hinton; lands at Atworth, Maiden Bradley, East Codford, West Codford, and Corsham; advowson of Great Cheverell; advowson of Great Chalfield: *CIPM, Henry VII*, 1.351; will, PRO, PROB 11/8, fols. 56v–57

Trosse, George (1631–1713), nonconformist minister, was born at Exeter on 25 October 1631, the younger son of Henry Trosse (*d.* 1642), lawyer of Lincoln's Inn, and Rebekah (*d.* after 1671), daughter of Walter Burrow, a prosperous merchant, twice mayor of Exeter. Educated at Exeter grammar school Trosse apparently did well, but with the coming of civil war his uncle Roger Trosse (1595–1674), rector of Rose Ash, Devon, was sequestered and George himself came to hate the puritans, becoming, as he later wrote, 'a zealous and irrational friend to, and contender for, cavaliers, bishops, ceremonies, common-prayer, etc, a great reproacher of strict professors, and a blasphemer of the Spirit' (*Life*, ed. Hallet, 3). Acquiring also 'a roving fancy, a desire to get riches, and to live luxuriously in the world, [he] was bent on merchandize and travelling into foreign parts' (ibid.), so he left school to pursue a career in trade.

The source of this information is Trosse's autobiography, completed in February 1693, one of the most remarkable of the seventeenth century. Its chief interest lies in the outstandingly explicit narrative of youthful sins and folly, of his madness, of failed attempts to live a godly life, and of his relapses into alcoholic excess, in passages cut or omitted by later editors. No other pious autobiographer of the period made admissions as frank as Trosse's recollection of his 'sin, which too many young men are guilty of, and look upon it as harmless, though God struck Onan dead in the place for it' (*Life*, ed. Hallet, 17). In the ports of south Devon, aged fourteen or fifteen, the young Trosse had eagerly sought out bad company, as he awaited his passage for France. At Morlaix, Brittany, he stayed with an English merchant and 'spent much time in tennis courts and taverns' (ibid., 9). Lodging for some months with a clergyman of Pontives to learn the language, he had good success, but during his stay in France his behaviour degenerated, and he almost killed a friend who had slighted him. He drank and squandered money, lying to his mother on his return to Devon about what he had spent it on. Next he stayed with an older brother-in-law in London and exchanged 'amorous glances, words, and actions' with his niece, 'God yet restraining us from grosser enormities' (ibid., 14). By means of his mother's money and his brother-in-law's connection with a Portugal merchant, it was arranged that Trosse should serve in that country as an apprentice of the Woollen Drapers' Company, and should be made free on his return.

Trosse sailed from Gravesend in 1646, and lived in the merchant's household in Oporto. There, he stole, drank, gambled and flirted, although, 'haunted with lascivious speeches, gestures and actions without, and impure fancies within', he was again 'restrained from all gross compleat acts of fornication; though I sometimes did what directly led to it'. This claim was repeated in connection with two later incidents with the rationalization 'that God restrained me ... because he designed me, by his grace' for the ministry, and had willed 'that I might not be rendered unserviceable by a common reproach and infamy' (*Life*, ed. Hallet, 41), but for all the explicitness of the rest of his narrative, the question arises as to whether his later life as a minister precluded the admission of actual sexual immorality. After almost three years in Portugal a dispute over money between Trosse's brother-in-law and the merchant necessitated the young man's return to England, 'under guilt and the divine wrath, fraught with filth and so loathsome to a pure God' (ibid., 23), that he deserved 'God's just vengeance' by drowning on the seas. However, he had been completely oblivious to the danger.

Trosse landed safely about the time of the king's execution. He despised the puritan ministers of Exeter, 'because they would not wear surplices, nor baptize with the sign of the cross etc'; in his family parish of St Kerrian he boycotted services held by Ferdinando Nicolls (*d.* 1662). When he had to escort his mother there, once she was seated he brazenly walked out and 'went to another church, where there was an episcopal minister' (*Life*, ed. Hallet, 29). He was assiduous in spreading lies and damaging gossip about puritans. Reproached by his mother for uncontrolled drunkenness, he became enraged and vowed 'I will go and kill Oliver', apparently with the intention of hurting her by invoking the image of himself upon the gallows (ibid., 37). Soon 'I was forced to sell my interest in an house my father gave me, to defray the charge of my extravagant expenses' (ibid., 42). Beginning to suffer from delirium tremens, he was 'ashamed of this when I appeared before friends and relations' (ibid., 33). Hallucinations set in, with mysterious voices telling him his sins were too grave to be forgiven, and urging him to self-mutilation or suicide. At first convinced that such voices were from God, he later concluded that, like those heard by Quakers, they had come from Satan.

Trosse now descended into insanity, becoming convinced that items of food and drink were all devils or his agents. Eventually friends took him forcibly for treatment by a physician in Glastonbury, where it was often found necessary to restrain his violence with manacles. Convinced that this was the mortification of the flesh commended by scripture, Trosse struggled, deliberately increasing his suffering. After several weeks enforced confinement at Glastonbury he made a partial recovery. Resolving to live as a Christian, he returned to Exeter, but was soon drawn back to his former haunts and activities. Relapsing into insanity, Trosse was returned to Glastonbury, and thought he was 'in Hell again, and that all about me were devils and executioners' (*Life*, ed. Hallet, 71). A second recovery was quickly followed by a second relapse, but finally, through the 'matchless goodness of God ... there was a period put to my rebellious and ungodly courses' (ibid., 77). With this terse statement Trosse ends the sensational story of his first quarter-century, and he provides only a brief and prosaic conspectus of the next.

Together with a friend who had also repented of a misspent youth (probably Timothy Hall, who became bishop of Oxford in 1688), Trosse enrolled at Pembroke College,

Oxford, as a gentleman commoner, matriculating on 6 August 1658. He studied under Thomas Cheeseman, and attended the lectures of John Conant (1608–1694), rector of Exeter College, and Robert Harris (1581–1658), president of Trinity. At Oxford he was thankful for the 'many excellent sermons preached … [by] so many excellent orthodox and practical divines … Then religion was in its glory in the university, and was a qualification for respect and advancement' (*Life*, ed. Hallet, 81). In 1662 he thought at first 'that I should sin if I conformed, and that I should not sin if I forebore it' and therefore resolved to refuse full conformity; later he came to the view that conformity to Anglican worship was permissible, 'as long as I was not active in any thing I scrupled' (ibid., 87). However, Oxford had changed since the Restoration; it was now 'no way suited to a person of my principles, persuasion and inclinations', so Trosse decided to leave without a degree (ibid., 84).

Persuaded by Robert Atkins (1626–1685), in 1666 Trosse was ordained as a presbyterian minister by Joseph Alleine (1633–1668), with the help of Atkins, Thomas Lye, William Ball, and John Kerridge, all ejected ministers. He refused the Oxford oath. Remarkably, Trosse decided to conduct his ministry in Exeter: 'to live as a reformed sinner in the very city where some of his worst outrages had been staged and where his reputation had been notorious' (Brink, 6). For the next two decades, he preached privately and in secret, sometimes as many as eight times a week and usually at considerable length, and for years held meetings 'in the very heart of the city … to a very considerable society, which filled two chambers' (*Life*, ed. Hallet, 91). He 'spent one hour every Monday morning to represent the case of the publick to God' and prayed six or seven times a day, even in great old age (ibid., 27). Three times, in June–July 1673, he was fined £20 by Exeter magistrates for conventicling. In 1680 he married Susanna, daughter of Richard White, a rich merchant of St Kerrian parish and a benefactor to the presbyterians of Exeter. In the wake of Monmouth's rebellion, Trosse and two even older ministers were charged under the Five Mile Act and imprisoned in October 1685 for six months. With the help of wealthy friends they were able to secure decent quarters; on their release the magistrates sought to initiate a new trial on charges of riot but the case was abandoned, according to one life of Trosse, when the magistrates became ashamed of their action.

Though other nonconforming ministers took advantage of James's indulgence to preach publicly Trosse did not, suspecting that the king's intention was 'to weaken the party of the Church of England, whom if he had once brought into contempt, the dissenters would have been easily crushed' (*Life*, ed. Hallet, 92). He regarded the accession of William III as 'a wonder of providence' which 'granted us our liberty' (ibid., 97). Soon after the death of Joseph Hallett on 14 March 1689, Trosse was chosen by the congregation as minister of James's Meeting in Exeter; there he was assisted by the former pastor's son, also Joseph, who in turn succeeded Trosse at his death and prepared his life story for the press. In the Exeter assembly of

ministers, revived after the Toleration Act as the organizing body for the 'United Brethren' of Devon and Cornwall presbyterian and congregational churches, Trosse was a leading figure, often submitting motions for discussion, and acting as moderator. There is much evidence of his charitable giving, to the poor, to beggars, to ministers, and to the refugee Huguenots. His reputation spread far beyond his home county. On 8 August 1691 the dying Richard Baxter wrote to Trosse a warm fraternal letter.

In 1692 Trosse issued *The Lord's Day Vindicated*, against the Saturday sabbath views of Francis Bampfield. During a controversy with the nonconformist John Withers (whom Trosse had ordained in August 1691) an Anglican, John Agate, made insinuations against Trosse, a man 'adored by the Dissenting Party, especially by the female sex', many of whom 'wear his picture among the rest of their lockets', and threatened to write the story of his youthful exploits (quoted in Brink, 12). Trosse aired his own views on separatism in *A Discourse of Schism* (1701), a reply to Robert Burscough. He called for 'understanding and charity towards dissenting Christians, preferring an exercise in peace-making to polemics', arguing that presbyterians should be friends with Anglicans, and become 'of one heart and affection with them, though in all things they cannot be of one head and opinion' (quoted in Brink, 10–11). Those who differed on doctrine might still be 'perfectly cordial friends', as he put it in a private letter (Gilling, 88–9). Before his death Trosse made his wife promise to ensure publication of his autobiography. He died on 13 January 1713, aged eighty-one. His funeral two days later, at St Bartholomew churchyard, Exeter, was attended by 'a very great multitude, among whom were many of the gentry of the city and county' (Gilling, 120–21). He was buried there the same day. STEPHEN WRIGHT

Sources *The life of the Reverend Mr Geo Trosse*, ed. J. Hallet (1714) · A. Brink, *The life of the Reverend George Trosse* (1974) · I. Gilling, *The life of Mr George Trosse, late minister of the gospel in Exon* (1715) · A. Gordon, ed., *Freedom after ejection: a review (1690–1692) of presbyterian and congregational nonconformity in England and Wales* (1917) · Foster, *Alum. Oxon.* · W. P. Baildon, ed., *The records of the Honorable Society of Lincoln's Inn: admissions*, 1 (1896)

Likenesses G. Vertue, line engraving (after J. Mortimer), BM, NPG; repro. in Hallet, ed., *Life*

Trott, Nicholas (1663–1740), jurist and politician in America, was born in London on 19 January 1663, the son of Samuel Trott, merchant. His mother's name is not known. He received his initial education at the Merchant Taylors' School in London and later attended the Inner Temple of the inns of court, being called to the bar in 1695. He was one of the first London-trained lawyers to reside in South Carolina.

Trott's grandfather, Perient Trott, was a director of the Somers Island Company, the colonizers of Bermuda, and his uncle, also Nicholas Trott, was governor of the Bahamas. Probably through his family connections, Nicholas became secretary of the Somers Island Company and attorney-general of Bermuda in 1693. In 1694 he married Jane Willis, of Bermuda.

In 1699 Trott moved to the new proprietary colony of

Carolina and began a long, controversial career as a jurist and politician. In 1699 he was appointed attorney-general and in 1703 became chief justice. Trott was a fierce high-church Anglican and his religious convictions governed many of his political actions. Prior to 1700 nonconformists controlled the Carolina government and the lords proprietors at home in England favoured them. During those years Trott was an acknowledged leader of the local anti-proprietary faction. After 1700 the Church of England conformists gained the upper hand in the colony and on the proprietary council, and they used their political power to defeat their religious opponents. Trott and Governor Nathaniel Johnson led the movement to establish the Church of England in South Carolina and then used the establishment as a political weapon against religious dissenters.

Firmly entrenched in the proprietary party after 1700, Trott expanded his control over South Carolina's legal establishment. In 1714 he attended the proprietors' council in England and secured wide powers. He was given authority to appoint the provincial provost marshal and a *de facto* personal veto over colonial legislation. In addition the proprietors decreed that his attendance was requisite to make a quorum at council meetings in Carolina. Although his veto power was abrogated in 1716, he was appointed vice-admiralty judge. At that point he had a monopoly on all judicial processes in the colony.

By 1719 Trott and William Rhett had alienated many local politicians. Trott had obstructed the popular governorship of Charles Craven and meddled in Commons house of assembly elections. So great was the opposition to Trott that it was a factor in the December 1719 revolution against proprietary rule that ousted Governor Robert Johnson and overthrew the proprietors' government. By the time of the revolution Trott, William Rhett, and Robert Johnson were among a very few who supported the proprietors. After the revolution they were a disruptive political element until Sir Francis Nicholson arrived in 1721 with royal authority to take over the governorship.

With all his political faults, Trott was an eminent jurist. In 1718 he presided in Charles Town at the piracy trial of Stede Bonnet and his crew members. His explication of British piracy laws in the Bonnet case and the trial records were published in London in 1719 and were precedents in subsequent piracy trials. His manuscript 'Eight charges delivered, at so many several general sessions, & gaol deliveries: held at Charles Town', among the collections of the Charleston Library Society, is essentially a series of lectures on British law as practised in Carolina. A compiler of colonial statutes, he published *The laws of the British plantations in America, relating to the church and the clergy, religion and learning* (1721) and in 1736 his most notable work, *The Laws of the Province of South-Carolina*. Another field of scholarly endeavour was biblical exegesis. Trott's *Clavis linguae sanctae*, published in 1719, examined the language of the Psalms.

Nicholas Trott was one of the best educated of Carolina's early settlers. His publications secured for him doctoral degrees in law from the University of Oxford in 1720 and the University of Aberdeen in 1726. He travelled between England and Carolina in the decades after 1720, and in 1729 represented the widow of his uncle, Nicholas Trott, in the chancery court case Danson v. Trott (1729) respecting ownership of proprietary shares. The judgment in this case helped clear the way for the crown to purchase the Carolina charter from its proprietor-owners.

Several years after the death of his first wife, Trott married Sarah (d. 1745), widow of William Rhett who had died in 1723. Trott died on 21 January 1740 in Charles Town and was buried in St Philip's episcopal churchyard there. In his will Trott left all of his possessions to his wife and executor, Sarah. At her death near the end of 1745 she owned Hagan plantation, with lands, slaves, and personalty valued at £7102 11s. 6d. Carolina money. Another inventory placed the value of her personalty, most of which had belonged to her husband, at £4464 10s. She also owned promissory notes to the amount of about £4638. Her assets at the time of her death probably reflect the substantial wealth her second husband had possessed at the time of his death.

ALEXANDER MOORE

Sources L. L. Hogue, 'Trott, Nicholas', *ANB* • L. L. Hogue, 'An edition of "Eight charges delivered … in the years 1703, 1704, 1705, 1706, 1707"', PhD diss., University of Tennessee, 1972 • N. Trott, 'An account of the invasion of South Carolina by the French and Spanish in August 1706', *South Carolina Historical Magazine*, 66 (1965) • L. L. Hogue, 'Nicholas Trott: man of law and letters', *South Carolina Historical Magazine*, 76 (1975) • *South Carolina Gazette* (26 Jan 1740) • will, Charleston county, wills, inventories, and miscellaneous records, works progress administration transcripts, vol. 72B (1740–47), 521–2 [copies at Charleston County Public Library, Charleston SC, and South Carolina department of archives and history, Columbia] • inventories of the estate of Sarah Rhett, Charleston county, wills, inventories and miscellaneous records, works progress administration transcripts, vol. 67B (1732–46), 417–22, 423–5, 426–7 [copies at Charleston county Public Library, Charleston SC, and South Carolina department of archives and history, Columbia]

Archives Federal Record Center, East Point, Georgia, minutes of South Carolina admiralty court, vol. 7

Wealth at death est. £16,205; real estate and personalty: inventories of estate of Sarah Rhett, Charleston county wills, inventories and miscellaneous records, South Carolina Archives and History Center, Columbia, vol. 67B (1732–46), 417–27

Trotter, Alexander Pelham (1857–1947), electrical engineer, was born on 25 June 1857 at Woodford, Essex, the youngest child of Alexander Trotter (d. 1863), a stockbroker, and his second wife, Isabella, the daughter of Sir Thomas Strange. The family were Scottish, related to the earls of Crawford and Balcarres, and included diplomats and academics. As a boy Trotter lived with his mother and four sisters at 40 Montagu Square, London, and attended local schools. He then went to Harrow School but did not enjoy it, although his only complaint was compulsory games and being flogged for evading them. While there he connected an induction coil to the brass candlesticks in his room, giving the servant an electric shock. He also arranged an electric bell between rooms, but his wire was thin and heated up, thus leading him to understand electrical resistance. In school holidays he pursued the early interest in science by reading boys' scientific books and walking to the Royal Polytechnic in Regent Street, where he later recalled demonstrations of engines, a diver, and an induction coil, and dramatic performances which always utilized 'Pepper's ghost'. From 1866 to 1871 he attended the Christmas lectures for young people at the Royal Institution, where he went with his sister Lily. At home he dictated an account of the lectures, which his mother would write out while he drew illustrations. In the summer of 1873 Trotter visited Lord Lindsay, who became earl of Crawford and Balcarres in 1880, at Dunecht, near Aberdeen. Lindsay was keenly interested in scientific matters and the family connection later proved useful.

Trotter spent a year at King's College, London, then a period with a private tutor named Fletcher, preparing for the entrance examination for Trinity College, Cambridge, where his half-brother, the Revd Coutts *Trotter (1837–1887), had lectured in physics and was then vice-master. At King's he gained practical experience of carpentry in the college's excellent workshop. With Fletcher he learned practical photography, making his own glass-plate negatives. Having passed the entrance examination he entered Trinity in 1876, taking the natural sciences tripos, and graduated BA in 1879. He had intended a medical career, but changed to engineering and took an apprenticeship with Easton and Anderson at Erith, Kent. By this time both his parents had died, leaving him about £5000. His brother William, a stockbroker, 'overhauled' his investments and produced the 500 guinea fee for the apprenticeship.

In August 1881 Trotter attended the first International Electrical Exhibition, in Paris, assisting the earl of Crawford and Balcarres, who led the British delegation. He later said that the Paris Exhibition marked the birth of electrical engineering; from that time on, his main professional interest was electric lighting. He made a study of geometrical optics, and sought a solution to the problem of getting uniform illumination from a single light source. The illumination from a simple street lamp, for example, is brightest under the lamp and reduces rapidly as one moves away. Trotter designed a lantern with lenses or prisms arranged to redistribute the light so that the illumination was more uniform. He patented the idea in 1883 (no. 233) but found it difficult to get suitable glassware made. By then he was working in Easton and Anderson's drawing office in Whitehall Place, London, and living in Furnival's Inn, Holborn.

In 1883 Trotter went into partnership with W. T. Goolden, at Halifax, as a manufacturer of electric dynamos. The partnership ended in 1887 when he returned to London. In 1886 he married Alys Fane Keatinge, the daughter of Maurice Keatinge, registrar of the court of Probate in Dublin. They had one son, Nigel, killed in the First World War, and one daughter, Gunda.

Arising from his manufacturing experience, Trotter wrote a paper on regulating generator output, which was published in *The Electrician*, of which he was a regular reader. In 1890 he became editor of *The Electrician*, a post he held until 1896, when he moved to South Africa as electrical adviser to the government of Cape Colony. In 1899 he returned to London and succeeded Philip Cardew as electrical adviser to the Board of Trade, where he played a major part in drafting electricity legislation and regulations, and conducted inquiries for the board. He was held in high regard by the electrical engineering profession, but did not enjoy government bureaucracy; in *Who's Who?* he gave his recreation as 'remembering that he is no longer a Government official'.

On retiring from the Board of Trade in 1917, Trotter joined H. W. Handcock and A. H. Dykes in their consulting engineering practice, but he retired again after two and a half years. He moved to Teffont, near Salisbury, Wiltshire, and continued to be actively involved in electric lighting. He was a founder member of the Illuminating Engineering Society, established in 1909, active in its committees, and president from 1917 to 1920. He gave the second Faraday lecture, on 'Illumination and light', in 1926.

Trotter was 'a very courtly gentleman, tall, distinguished looking and reserved in manner, with a hooked nose, a small beard, and an ear trumpet'. He presented extensive manuscript reminiscences to the Institution of Electrical Engineers. He died of heart failure at his home, Greystones, Teffont, on 23 July 1947.   BRIAN BOWERS

Sources A. P. Trotter, 'Reminiscences', Inst. EE, SC MSS 66 · B. Bowers, 'Alexander Trotter, a well-connected electrician', *IEE Proceedings*, A136 (1989), 337–40 · *Light and Lighting* (Aug 1917), 143 · *WW* · A. P. Trotter, 'Illumination and light', *Journal of the Institution of Electrical Engineers*, 64 (1926), 367–71 · minutes of the Dynamicables, 29 Jan 1919 · *Illuminating Engineer* (Dec 1917), 307–20 · A. P. Trotter, 'The distribution and measurement of illumination', *PICE*, 110 (1891–2), 69–121 · A. P. Trotter, 'On the production of a constant current with varying electromotive force from a dynamo', *The Electrician* (9 Sept 1887), 374–5 · J. W. T. Walsh, 'The early years of illuminating engineering in Great Britain', *Transactions of the Illuminating Engineering Society* (1951), 49–60 · 'Trotter, Coutts', *DNB* · d. cert.

Archives Inst. EE, autobiography and notebook

Likenesses photograph (in uniform of National Guard), repro. in *Illuminating Engineer*, 308

Wealth at death £9785 5s. 10d.: probate, 24 Oct 1947, *CGPLA Eng. & Wales*

Trotter [*married name* Cockburn], **Catharine** (1674?–1749), playwright and philosopher, was born in High Holborn, London, probably on 16 August 1674, the second of the two daughters of David Trotter (d. 1684), naval captain, and his wife, Sarah Bellenden, who was related to Lord Bellenden and the earls of Perth and Lauderdale. Katherine Trotters, the daughter of David and Sarah Trotters, was baptized at St Andrew's, Holborn, on 29 August 1674. This is five years earlier than the date of birth given by Thomas Birch in his life of Trotter, and that recorded on her gravestone, but is probably correct. Her parents were both Scottish. Captain Trotter served under Charles II, but died of the plague while on a voyage to Iskenderun, losing all his effects. His widow was granted a pension by Charles II, which ceased at that king's death, and was not renewed until the accession of Queen Anne in 1702.

Catharine Trotter apparently learned to write and to speak French by her own efforts, but according to the biographical summary, 'The life of Mrs Cockburn', written by Thomas Birch, the editor of *The Works of Mrs. Catharine*

Cockburn, she 'had some assistance in the study of the Latin grammar and Logic' (Birch, 1.v). It is not clear whence that assistance came. Her first published work was an epistolary novella, *The Adventures of a Young Lady*, her anonymous contribution to a collection published by Samuel Briscoe entitled *Letters of Love and Gallantry and Several other Subjects, All Written by Ladies* (2 vols., 1693–4, vol. 1). Although anonymous in this edition, the novella, retitled *Olinda's Adventures, or, The Amours of a Young Lady*, was attributed to Mrs Trotter in a 1718 collection published by Briscoe: *Familiar Letters of Love, Gallantry and Several Occasions*. Her novella is superior in construction and style to the general run of letter fiction in this period.

Trotter wrote five plays, which were all performed on the London stage. About December 1695 her first play, *Agnes de Castro*, was performed at the Theatre Royal, Drury Lane, London. This was followed by *Fatal Friendship*, which was performed at Lincoln's Inn Fields in 1698. Among her contemporaries, the latter was the most acclaimed of her plays. Charles Gildon stated that 'it deserv'd the Applause it met with' (Gildon, 179). George Farquhar wrote to her 'my passions were wrought so high by the representation of *Fatal Friendship*, and since raised so by a sight of the beautiful author' (BL, Birch Add. MS 4264, fol. 102). Her only comedy, *Love at a Loss*, was performed in November 1700 at Drury Lane. This play was later revised and retitled *The Honourable Deceivers*, but was unperformed and no manuscript copies have survived. Her next play, a tragedy, *The Unhappy Penitent*, was staged at Drury Lane in February 1701. After a five-year gap during which she had published her first philosophical work, her last play, also a tragedy, *The Revolution of Sweden*, was produced about February 1706, at the Queen's Theatre at the Haymarket. She had previously shown the manuscript of this play to William Congreve for his suggestions, most of which she did not incorporate in the final version.

Trotter's dramatic work was in many ways in the vanguard of the movement to reform the stage, which gained momentum in the eighteenth century. In the dedication to *Fatal Friendship* she stated that the intention of the play was to 'discourage vice, and recommend a firm unshaken virtue'. Contemporary comment often centred on her ability to entertain and instruct in her drama, as in this anonymous reference to *Fatal Friendship*: 'A celebrated Female in use, has lately convinc'd you, in her *Fatal Friendship*, that 'tis possible to entertain, with all the Judgment, Wit and Beauty of Poetry; without *shocking our senses*, with intollerable prophaness [*sic*] or obscenity' (*A Letter to Mr. Congreve on his Pretended Amendments etc. of Mr. Collier's Short View of the Immorality and Prophaneness of the English Stage*, 1698, 36–7). Acclaim for her writing was often conflated with praise for her beauty. Birch described her as 'small of stature, but had a remarkable liveliness in her eye, and delicacy of complexion' (Birch, 1.xlvi). Gildon praised her for 'two things rarely found together, Wit and Beauty: and with these a Penetration very uncommon in the Sex' (Gildon, 179). Her drama is notable in this period for its unusually rational and politically aware female characters. Although Trotter denied alliance to any political group, she was closely involved with the very politically active Marlborough circle in the early eighteenth century (Kelley, 21), and a close associate of Bishop Burnet and his third wife, Elizabeth, a friend of Sarah Churchill.

In 1702 Trotter published her first, and best-known, philosophical piece, the anonymous *A Defence of the 'Essay of Human Understanding', Written by Mr. Lock*, defending him from the charges of deism and Socinianism which had been levelled at him anonymously in *Remarks* by Dr Thomas Burnet of the Charterhouse in 1697. Elizabeth Burnet, a friend of John Locke, revealed Trotter's authorship to the philosopher, encouraging him to demonstrate his appreciation by gifts of money and books. Subsequently, Trotter published *A Discourse Concerning a Guide in Controversies* (1707), prefaced by remarks by Bishop Gilbert Burnet. This marked her return to the Anglican faith after several years as a practising Roman Catholic.

In 1708 Trotter married the Revd Patrick *Cockburn (1678–1749), eldest son of Dr John Cockburn. After her marriage she moved from London to Nayland, Suffolk, where her husband had a curacy. In February 1713 he became curate of St Dunstan-in-the-West, London, but lost his appointment as he refused to take the oath of abjuration on the accession of George I. In 1726 he was persuaded by his father and Lord Chancellor King to take the oath, and was granted the ministry of the episcopal congregation of St Paul's Chapel in Aberdeen. Subsequently, he was also granted the living of Long Horsley, near Morpeth in Northumberland, although he did not reside there until the bishop of Durham insisted in 1737. He was the incumbent of this parish until his death, on 4 January 1749.

Trotter's later important publications were all concerned with philosophical issues, where she consistently opposed ethical schemes based on voluntarism or moral relativity, in favour of a theistic belief in intrinsic essential moral differences within the law of nature. Her consistent position was that moral principles are not innate, but discoverable by each individual through the use of the faculty of reason endowed by God. She was a lifelong adherent to John Locke's philosophical principles, in 1726 publishing *A Letter to Dr. Holdsworth*, defending Locke against Winch Holdsworth's allegations of heresy. A further vindication of Locke addressed to Holdsworth failed to find a publisher, but was included in her posthumous *Works*. In 1743 her *Remarks upon some writers in the controversy concerning the foundation of moral virtue and moral obligation* was printed, on the recommendation of the Revd Dr Thomas Sharp, archdeacon of Northumberland.

In 1747, despite her age and many years of poor health, Trotter wrote *Remarks upon the principles and reasonings of Dr. Rutherforth's Essay on the nature and obligations of virtue: in vindication of the contrary principles and reasonings, inforced in the writings of the late Dr. Samuel Clarke*, in support of Clarke's ethical principles. This was published by Mr Warburton, prefaced by a very glowing tribute to her powers of reasoning. She has been accused by some critics of not realizing that Clarke's ethical theory is inconsistent with that of Locke, yet there is considerable congruity in their approaches, as she recognized. Both men were concerned with describing a scheme of rational Christian morality; moreover, Locke did not dispute the concept of a fixed law of nature.

Catharine Cockburn died at Long Horsley shortly after her husband on 11 May 1749. Their graves are in the parish churchyard where she was buried on 13 May, together with their daughter Grissel, who had died on 1 November 1742. There were three surviving children, Sarah (Lady Keith), Catharine, and John.

In 1749 Warburton, among others, initiated a project to publish her writings, edited by Thomas Birch. The two-volume *Works* was eventually published by subscription in 1751. It includes all her important philosophical writing, with a few minor pieces, some poetry, many of her letters and one play, *Fatal Friendship*.

Interpretations of Trotter's work have been influenced by changes in the way women writers have been read over the last three hundred years. The early association with the stage quickly gave way to the image of a respectable learned lady, accelerated by the publication of her *Works* in 1751. Nineteenth-century editors substantially reinforced this emphasis on intellect and irreproachable moral standards, and foregrounded her role as wife and mother. It is only in the late twentieth century that the significance of her dramatic and philosophical work has been recognized, and her feminocentric stance as a dramatist and philosopher has been appreciated. Her own life was an argument for female rationality and responsibility, a demonstration that a woman could exercise her intellect in the male-dominated public sphere of philosophical debate.   ANNE KELLEY

Sources T. Birch, 'Life of Mrs. Cockburn', in *The works of Mrs Catharine Cockburn*, ed. T. Birch, 2 vols. (1751); repr. (1992) [repr. 1992] · BL, Birch MSS, Add. MSS 4221–4224, 4244, 4245 · BL, Cockburn MSS, Add. MS 4264, vol. 1 · BL, Cockburn MSS, Add. MS 4265, vol. 2 · A. Kelley, 'Catharine Trotter (1679–1749): a re-evaluation of her literary and philosophical writings, and their interrelationship', PhD diss., University of Hertfordshire, 1998 [incl. the only bibliography of Trotter's works, and works about her] · *The plays of Mary Pix and Catharine Trotter*, ed. E. L. Steeves, 2: *Catharine Trotter* (1982) · J. Pearson, *The prostituted muse: images of women and women dramatists, 1642–1737* (1988), 169–201 · W. Van Lennep and others, eds., *The London stage, 1660–1800*, pt 1: 1660–1700 (1965) · E. L. Avery, ed., *The London stage, 1660–1800*, pt 2: 1700–1729 (1960) · A. Harbage, *Annals of English drama, 975–1700*, 2nd edn, ed. S. Schoenbaum (1964) · parish records, St Andrew, Holborn, 29 Aug 1674 [baptism] · parish records, Long Horsley, 7 Jan 1749 [burial] · parish records, Long Horsley, 13 May 1749 [burial] · wills of Catharine Cockburn and Revd Patrick Cockburn, U. Durham L., archives and special collections · calendar of licences, 1660–1720, GL, MS 21737 · *DNB* · [C. Gildon], *The lives and characters of the English dramatick poets … first begun by Mr Langbain* [1699]

Archives BL, Cockburn corresp. and literary papers, Add. MSS 4264–4267, 4302, 4371 | BL, Birch MS collection, Add. MSS 4221–4224, 4244, 4245

Likenesses etching, NPG, Scot. NPG; repro. in Trotter, *Works*, ed. Birch, frontispiece · line engraving, BM, NPG

Wealth at death see will, U. Durham L.

Trotter, Coutts (1837–1887), college administrator, born on 1 August 1837, was the eldest child of Alexander Trotter (1804–1865) and his first wife, Jacqueline Elizabeth (d.

1849), the daughter of William *Otter, bishop of Chichester. His father was the younger brother of Admiral Henry Dundas Trotter. An acquisition of scientific knowledge began in boyhood, when Trotter attended Faraday's lectures. He was educated at Harrow School, and entered Trinity College, Cambridge, in 1855, graduated BA as thirty-sixth wrangler in 1859, and proceeded MA in 1862. He was elected a fellow of his college in 1861. In 1863 he was ordained to a curacy in Kidderminster, which he served for two years. He next went to Germany to study experimental physics under Helmholtz and Kirchoff, and, after spending some time in Italy, returned to Trinity College, where in 1869 he was appointed lecturer in physical science, a post which he held until 1884. He became junior dean in 1870, and senior dean in 1874. He was tutor of his college from 1872 to 1882, and was appointed its vice-master in 1885. A Liberal in politics, he became an ardent university reformer. From 1874 onwards he was a member of the council of the senate of the university, and at the time of his death was president of the Cambridge Philosophical Society, and vice-president of the council of Newnham College.

Trotter exerted a very remarkable influence in the affairs of his college and of the University of Cambridge, especially in connection with the constitutional changes brought about by the statutes of 1882 and in relation to natural science. This influence had for its basis his very wide and exact knowledge of, and his warm sympathy with, almost every branch of learning studied in the university. Not only with the natural sciences, but with the ancient and modern tongues, with history, philosophy, and art, he had an acquaintance, always real, and in some cases great. Hence in the conflicts taking place in the university between the competing demands of the several branches of learning, the advocates of almost every branch felt that they could appeal to Trotter as to one who could understand and sympathize with their wants. This exceptionally large knowledge was made still further effective by being joined to truthful and straightforward conduct, a patient, sweet temper, and a singular skill in framing academic regulations. Qualities such as these were greatly needed both in preparing for and in carrying out the changes formulated by the statutes of 1882, and especially, perhaps, in adjusting the growing claims of natural science. He played a leading part in the rapid growth of the natural sciences tripos and in the provision of laboratories, and was for many years an influential member of the board of medical studies. The greater part of Trotter's time and energy was devoted to university administration; and to him, very largely, were due the indubitable improvements effected in university matters during his short academic career. 'In fact, what was sometimes called in jest "the Trotterization of the University" was so complete that he had come to be regarded as indispensable' (*Saturday Review*, 1887). Besides pamphlets on university topics, he published little, though his researches were extensive.

After several years of ill health, Trotter died, unmarried, in Trinity College on 4 December 1887 and was buried at

Trumpington on the 8th. He left the most valuable part of his library, together with a large bequest in money, to Trinity College, and the remainder of his library and his entire collection of philosophical instruments to Newnham College.   MICHAEL FOSTER, rev. JOHN D. PICKLES

Sources Cambridge University Almanack and Register (1888) · Saturday Review, 64 (1887), 787–8 · Nature, 37 (1887–8), 153–4 · Cambridge Review (7 Dec 1887) · Cambridge Review (1 Feb 1888) · Cambridge Review (8 Feb 1888) · M. Foster, J. W. Clark, and S. Taylor, Coutts Trotter: in memoriam (1888) · Proceedings of the Physical Society, 9 (1887–8), 14–15 · A. T. Bartholomew, Catalogue of the books and papers ... bequeathed to the university by John Willis Clark (1912) · Catalogue of scientific papers, Royal Society, 8 (1879) · Catalogue of scientific papers, Royal Society, 11 (1896) · Catalogue of scientific papers, Royal Society, 19 (1925) · CGPLA Eng. & Wales (1888) · Burke, Gen. GB · Cambridge Chronicle (9 Dec 1887), 4 · IGI

Likenesses group portrait, photograph, c.1860, Trinity Cam. · T. Woolner, marble bust, 1888, Trinity Cam. · three photographs, Trinity Cam.

Wealth at death £18,704 7s. 6d.: resworn probate, March 1889, CGPLA Eng. & Wales (1888)

Trotter, Eliza H. (fl. 1800–1815). See under Hunter, Robert (d. after 1803).

Trotter, Henry Dundas (1802–1859), naval officer, third son of Alexander Trotter of Dreghorn near Edinburgh, and his wife, Lillias, daughter of Sir John Stuart, baronet, of Allanbank, was born on 19 September 1802. Alexander Trotter served as paymaster of the navy under Henry Dundas, first Viscount Melville. Alexander and his brother John [see below] were wealthy and were active in Edinburgh politics. Henry Trotter entered the Royal Naval College, Portsmouth, on 16 November 1815, and in February 1818 joined the Ister at Leith. In May he was sent to the Eden (26 guns), going to the East Indies and in 1819 taking part in the expedition against the pirates of the Persian Gulf under Captain Francis Augustus Collier. In March 1821 he was moved to the Leander, flagship of Sir Henry Blackwood, and was appointed acting lieutenant; the commission was confirmed from 9 January 1823. He was then appointed to the Hussar, going to the West Indies, and was specially reported by her captain, George Harris, for bravery in the capture of pirates at the Isle of Pines. He served in the Bellette and Rattlesnake and on 20 February 1826 was made commander of the sloop Britomart.

In July 1830 Trotter commissioned the Curlew for service on the west coast of Africa, where he was usually senior officer, the commander-in-chief remaining at the Cape of Good Hope. In May 1833, being at Prince's Island in the Gulf of Guinea, he had intelligence of an act of piracy committed on an American brig in the previous September by the Panda, a Spanish slaver from Havana. On 4 June he seized the Panda in the Nazareth River, but the men escaped ashore. After several months he captured most of them and took possession of the Esperanza, a Portuguese schooner which had been assisting them. The prisoners and the Esperanza he took to England. The prisoners were sent over to Salem, Massachusetts, where most of them were hanged. Trotter received the thanks of the American government. Against the Esperanza there was no legal evidence, and Lord Palmerston, then foreign secretary,

agreed that the schooner should be returned to Lisbon. Consequently Trotter had to fit her out at his own expense. At Plymouth, however, the feeling of the service was so strong that several ships there sent men who completed her refit free of all cost to Trotter; the Admiralty showed its sense of his conduct by specially promoting him captain on 16 September 1835. He married, on 23 November 1835, Charlotte, second daughter of Major-General James Pringle of the East India Company service.

For a few months in 1838 Trotter was flag captain to Sir Philip Durham at Portsmouth. In 1840 he was appointed captain of the steamer Albert and in 1841 returned to west Africa in command of three iron river steamers, built to carry out the ambitious plans of Thomas Fowell Buxton to establish treaties and commercial links with the peoples along the River Niger as a means of ending the slave trade. The little squadron sailed from England in May and entered the Niger on 13 August. In less than three weeks the other two vessels were incapacitated by fever and obliged to return. Trotter in the Albert struggled on as far as Egga, where on 3 October he was prostrated by fever; as the greater part of his ship's company was also down with it he was obliged to turn back. Despite this he established satisfactory treaties with some rulers. The Admiralty, satisfied that everything possible had been done, promoted all the junior officers and offered Trotter the governorship of New Zealand in 1843, the command of an Arctic expedition in 1844, and the command of the Indian navy in 1846. His health, which only slowly and partially recovered from the effects of African fever, compelled him to refuse these offers. It was not until the outbreak of the Crimean War that he was able to accept employment—as commodore at the Cape of Good Hope; he held this office for three years, during which time he established the Cape Town Sailors' Home. On 19 March 1857 he became a rear-admiral on the retired list. He died suddenly at his home, Devonshire Place House, Marylebone Road, London, on 14 July 1859 and was buried in Kensal Green cemetery. Although the initial promise of support contained in his forenames had been destroyed by the events of 1805, when his father's actions led to Lord Melville's impeachment, Trotter still managed to prosper in the navy under the second Lord Melville. His acceptance of the Niger command was brave but, as he had already reached post rank, unnecessary to further his career. The expedition ruined his health and deprived him of the opportunity to exploit his success.

His father's brother, **John Trotter** (1757–1833), army contractor, went to London in 1774. He joined and at an early age became head of a firm of army contractors. After the peace of 1783 he urged on the government the absurdity and extravagance of selling off all the military stores, only to replace them by new purchases on the occasion of any alarm, and offered to warehouse them in his own premises. This was agreed in 1787. On the outbreak of the French war the business increased enormously, and by 1807 he had established 109 depots, containing supplies insured for £600,000. The storekeepers were all appointed and paid by him; there was no government inspection, and apparently no government audit. The agreement was that he was paid the cost of the stores, plus a percentage to cover expenses and profit. In the hands of an honest and capable man the system worked efficiently, but it was felt to be improper to leave the country dependent on one man or to give one man such vast patronage. In 1807 Sir James Pulteney, then secretary for war, established the office of storekeeper-general, giving Trotter the first nomination to the post and taking into service all his employees.

In 1815 Trotter established the Soho bazaar between Soho Square and Oxford Street. Intended at first to enable the distressed widows and daughters of army officers to dispose economically of their home 'work' by renting a few feet of counter, the bazaar eventually proved a source of wealth to its promoter. He was a man of many schemes, some of which led to fortune; others died in their infancy, including one for the establishment of a universal language. He died at Connaught Place, London on 6 September 1833. J. K. LAUGHTON, rev. ANDREW LAMBERT

Sources H. Temperley, *British antislavery, 1833–1870* (1972) · C. Lloyd, *The navy and the slave trade* (1949) · O'Byrne, *Naval biog. dict.* · *CGPLA Eng. & Wales* (1859) · *GM*, 1st ser., 103/2 (1833), 380 [John Trotter] · *GM*, 3rd ser., 7 (1859), 314
Archives Bodl. RH, corresp. with Thomas Buxton · Herts. ALS, letters to E. B. Lytton
Wealth at death under £12,000: probate, 24 Aug 1859, *CGPLA Eng. & Wales*

Trotter, John (1757–1833). *See under* Trotter, Henry Dundas (1802–1859).

Trotter, John Bernard (1775–1818), author, was born on 26 December 1775 in Downpatrick, co. Down, the second son of the Revd Edward Trotter and Mary Dickson. He was the younger brother of Edward Southwell *Ruthven. He was educated at the grammar school at Downpatrick, and entered Trinity College, Dublin, on 1 June 1790, graduating BA in the spring of 1795. He visited London in 1798, entering as a student at the Middle Temple, and during his stay he met Charles James Fox. Like Fox, Trotter opposed the proposed union of Ireland with England, and he sent Fox a pamphlet on the subject. After the peace of Amiens in 1802, Trotter was invited by Fox to accompany him to Paris to assist him in transcribing portions of Barillon's correspondence for his *History of the Early Part of the Reign of James II*. On his return he was called to the Irish bar in Michaelmas term 1802.

Trotter became Fox's private secretary after his appointment as foreign secretary on 7 February 1806 in the administration of 'all the talents'. When Fox died in September 1806 Trotter was at his side. Afterwards he returned to Ireland and later he published a *Letter to Lord Southwell on the Catholic Question* (1808) and *Stories for Calumniators* (1809), in which the characters were drawn from living models and he himself appeared as Fitsmorice. His memoir of Fox's last years, an adulatory record of their friendship, appeared in 1811 and went into three editions within the year. The book was criticized on all sides. Lord Holland wrote that Trotter had misrepresented Fox's religious beliefs, and he resented what he perceived as insinuations

against the family. The *Quarterly Review* thought Trotter unjust to Fox, and held that he had misrepresented the relations between him and Sheridan.

Trotter's later life was passed in poverty and privation, and in his last years he suffered from mental illness. In 1813 he made his last political effort while in the Marshalsea at Wexford, writing a pamphlet on the Irish situation. He died on 29 September 1818, in Hammond's Marsh in Cork, in great poverty, the out-patient of a neighbouring dispensary. His last days were lightened by the devotion of an Irish peasant boy whom he had educated to be his companion, and of his wife, a young woman whom he had married in prison about five years before.

W. F. RAE, rev. MARIE-LOUISE LEGG

Sources J. B. Trotter, *Memoirs of the latter years of the Rt Hon. Charles James Fox* (1811) · S. Ayling, *The life of Charles James Fox* (1991) · L. G. Mitchell, *Charles James Fox* (1992) · Burtchaell & Sadleir, *Alum. Dubl.*, 2nd edn · H. A. C. Sturgess, ed., *Register of admissions to the Honourable Society of the Middle Temple, from the fifteenth century to the year 1944*, 3 vols. (1949) · J. B. Trotter, *Walks through Ireland* (1819) · E. Keane, P. Beryl Phair, and T. U. Sadleir, eds., *King's Inns admission papers, 1607–1867*, IMC (1982)
Archives BL, letters to Lord Liverpool and others

Trotter, (Isabella) Lillias (1853–1928). *See under* Women artists in Ruskin's circle (*act.* 1850s–1900s).

Trotter, Mary Anne (*b.* 1752, *d.* before 1792). *See under* Hunter, Robert (*d.* after 1803).

Trotter, Thomas (*bap.* 1760, *d.* 1832), naval physician, was born in Melrose, Roxburghshire, where he was baptized on 3 August 1760, the second son and third of five children of John Trotter, baker, and his wife, Alison. Trotter was educated at Melrose and Kelso Academy until 1777 when he studied medicine in Edinburgh under Alexander Monro *secundus*. But after two years he left to become a surgeon's mate in the British navy serving on the *Berwick* in the Channel Fleet which sailed for the West Indies in 1780. Trotter later declared that 'it was my fortune, as a medical man to be introduced to the navy early' (Trotter, *Medicina nautica*, 4).

After his exemplary treatment of the wounded at the battle of Dogger Bank in 1781, Trotter received a public accolade from his commodore along with promotion to the rank of surgeon. However, when the American wars ended there was little prospect of work in a much reduced navy, so in 1783 he engaged himself as surgeon on board a Liverpool slave ship called the *Brookes* and had medical charge of a cargo of slaves across to the West Indies, on a voyage of fourteen months. Despite Trotter's recommendations for a fresh and varied diet, the owner, mindful of the extra cost involved, refused to listen to him. This inaction resulted in a violent outbreak of scurvy among the slaves. Trotter was appalled at the suffering caused and became an ardent abolitionist. The Society in Newcastle for the Abolition of the Slave Trade records how he gave evidence to the House of Commons on their behalf in 1791. Trotter's dire firsthand experiences at sea also had demonstrated the importance of the link between prevention of scurvy by the correct diet and led Trotter on a long-term campaign to fight this scourge of the navy. He wrote *Observations on the Scurvy* in 1786 with a second edition in 1792 and can be credited with being the third man, alongside James Lind and Gilbert Blane, responsible for introducing universal distribution of lemon juice throughout the navy in 1795, an action which effectively abolished the problem of scurvy.

In 1784, on his return to England, Trotter settled down in private practice as apothecary and surgeon at Wooler in Northumberland. While on shore Trotter pursued his studies in Edinburgh, where he attended the lectures of William Cullen and in 1788 presented a thesis entitled *De ebrietate ejusque effectibus in corpus humanum*, which he later expanded and published as *An essay, medical, philosophical, and chemical, on drunkenness, and its effects on the human body* (1804). Now armed with his MD, Trotter rejoined the navy. During the Spanish armament of 1790 he was appointed, at the request of Vice-Admiral Robert Roddam, to be surgeon of his flagship, the *Royal William*, and in 1793 was surgeon of the *Vengeance* for a voyage to the West Indies and back. In December Trotter was appointed second physician to the Royal Naval Hospital at Haslar, near Portsmouth, and his courage in voicing strong opinions can be seen during his brief time at Haslar where he soon strove for changes in the provision of health care. He issued reforms in every department under his authority, oversaw the patients' diet, and issued a code of rules for the attending dispensers and nurses; his actions complete with analysis were then published in *Remarks on the Establishment of Naval Hospitals with Hints for their Improvement* (1795). In April 1794 he was nominated by Lord Howe physician to the Channel Fleet. In this capacity he served through the campaigns of 1794 and 1795, was present in the battle of 1 June 1794, appears to have been with Cornwallis on 16–17 June 1795, and to have joined the fleet under Lord Bridport very shortly after the action of 23 June. During the Quiberon expedition at this time, while climbing the side of the *Irresistible* in order to attend the wounds of the captain, Trotter injured himself and suffered a hernia which contributed towards the end of his naval career in 1802, when he retired as the revolutionary wars against France assumed an uneasy peace.

Trotter's latter years of service at sea were characterized by an unrelenting quest for reform in the medical department of the navy, much of which was discussed in his comprehensive three-volume work, *Medicina nautica* (1797, 1799, 1803). Following the example of Gilbert Blane, he called for increased communication from all naval surgeons under his jurisdiction about the treatment of the sick and wounded. He considered not only the patient but also the medical practitioner and advocated a rise in pay after the victory of the 'glorious first of June'—the result being that 200 surgeons were added to the half-pay list. Ironically, while Trotter may have increased the conditions of pay for others, his own pension before deductions was £200 per annum, an amount which failed to reflect his contribution to the British navy; this situation was compounded in 1805 when, although many medical officers received an additional amount of money, Trotter was ignored.

On retiring from the sea service Trotter settled in private practice at Newcastle upon Tyne. His first wife, Elizabeth Juliana (1775–1804), daughter of Captain Michael Everitt, whom he married in 1802, died on 31 April 1804, eleven days after giving birth to their son John Everitt. Six years later he married Isabella Dixon in St John's Church in Newcastle; they had two sons, William Curtis (b. 1812) and Thomas Dixon Marr (b. 1815). From about the age of forty Trotter occupied his time with a diverse range of interests. Besides his professional work, he also belonged to the Literary and Philosophical Society, wrote frequently to newspapers and medical journals, composed a play called *The Noble Foundling of the Hermit of the Tweed: a Tragedy in Five Acts in Verse* (1812) and a book of poems entitled *Sea Weeds* (1829). Both the *Essay on Drunkenness* (1804) and another scholarly work, *View of the Nervous Temperament* (1807), were compiled during this period. An undiminished mission to reform manifested itself in contemporary debates. *A Proposal for Destroying the Fire and Choak Damp of Mines* (1804, and a further discussion in 1806) addressed the issue of coalminers dying underground and assessed ways of improving ventilation. Trotter also suggested ways to alleviate the distress caused by pressganging in *A practical plan for manning the Royal Navy and preserving our maritime ascendancy without impressment* (1819).

Trotter's main residence was at 103 Pilgrim Street, Newcastle, but he also owned a house and a small farm at Easter Housebyres near Melrose until 1830, when he moved to Edinburgh for a short time before returning to Newcastle to live at 15 Leazes Terrace, where he died on 5 September 1832.   J. WALLACE

Sources J. Carmichael, 'Thomas Trotter, 1760–1832, physician to the fleet', *Medicine in Northumbria: essays on the history of medicine in the north-east of England*, ed. D. Gardner-Medwin, A. Hargreaves, and E. Lazenby (1993), 164–92 · A. Cockburn, *Biographical sketch of the late Dr Thomas Trotter as read to the Harveian Society on the 12th April 1845* (1845) · I. A. Porter, 'Thomas Trotter, naval physician', *Medical History*, 7 (1963), 155–64 · R. Porter, 'Addicted to modernity: nervousness in the early consumer society', *Culture in history: production, consumption and values*, ed. J. Melling and J. Barry (1992), 180–94 · T. Trotter, *An essay medical, philosophical, and chemical on drunkenness and its effects on the human body* (1988) [with an introduction by R. Porter] · *GM*, 1st ser., 102/2 (1832), 476 · *The health of seamen: selections from the works of Dr. James Lind, Sir Gilbert Blane and Dr. Thomas Trotter*, ed. C. Lloyd, Navy RS, 107 (1965) · T. Trotter, *Medicina nautica: an essay on the diseases of seamen*, 1 (1797) · J. J. Keevil, J. Coulter, and C. Lloyd, *Medicine and the navy, 1200–1900*, 3–4 (1961–3) · U. Tröhler, 'Quantification in British medicine and surgery, 1750–1830', PhD diss., U. Lond., 1978 · *DNB*

Archives NMM, letters · U. Newcastle, Robinson L. · University of Manchester Library, dissertation for MD and *Medicina Nautica* · Wellcome L.

Likenesses D. Orme?, stipple, 1796, BM, NPG · Lizars, engraving, repro. in T. Trotter, *Sea weeds: poems written on various occasions, chiefly during a naval life* (1829)

Trotter, Wilfred Batten Lewis (1872–1939), surgeon and social psychologist, was born on 3 November 1872 at Coleford, Gloucestershire, the third son of Howard Birt Trotter (1838–1922), a merchant, and his wife, Frances (1840–1895), *née* Lewis. As a result of spinal tuberculosis, Trotter was educated mainly at home until his family moved to London, where he attended University College School

Wilfred Batten Lewis Trotter (1872–1939), by Herbert Olivier, 1940 [replica]

from 1889 to 1891. His medical education was at University College, London, and University College Hospital; he graduated MB with first-class honours in 1896 and MD in 1897. He was made FRCS and BS with gold medal in 1899, and MS in 1901. Of his teachers, he acknowledged the influence of Sir John Rose Bradford, Sir Victor Horsley, and Mr Arthur Barker. Trotter was surgical registrar at UCH from 1901–4, but did not join the consultant staff until 1906.

Trotter spent the interim period partly at University College, where he refined his knowledge of anatomy and carried out research into the regeneration of sensory peripheral nerves. This study was carried out in collaboration with another UCH surgeon, Hugh Morriston Davies, and involved cutting several of the experimenters' own peripheral nerves. Previously, Henry Head and W. H. R. Rivers believed that there were two types of sensory nerve, protopathic (primitive) and epicritic (developed). Trotter and Davies showed that the abnormal sensations felt in the area served by the regenerating nerves were a side-effect of the regeneration process, and not due to regeneration of two types of nerve at different rates.

The same period saw the genesis of Trotter's major contribution to social psychology, one which left a long-lasting legacy in the phrase 'the herd instinct'. Trotter became interested in Freudian psychology after reading a review of *Studies in Hysteria*, and he was to introduce Freud's ideas to Ernest Jones, later to become the doyen of English psychoanalysis (and Trotter's brother-in-law). Trotter first had his studies published in volumes 1 and 2 (1908 and 1909) of the *Sociological Review*. He criticized

Freud for ignoring the social aspects of psychology, and postulated, in addition to instincts for self-preservation, feeding, and sex, one which he called gregariousness.

Trotter was aware that this was not a totally new idea, and he acknowledged Karl Pearson's work in particular. However, he claimed that while the idea that humans were gregarious was familiar, its biological significance was not understood. He argued that 'The cardinal advantage of the herd is homogeneity. It is clear that the great advantage of the social habit is to enable large numbers to act as one' ('Herd Instinct and its Bearing on the Psychology of Civilised Man', *Sociological Review*, 1, 1908, 239), and further, that 'The only medium in which man's mind can function satisfactorily is the herd, which therefore is not only the source of his credulities, his disbeliefs, and his weaknesses, but of his altruism, his charity, his enthusiasms, and his powers' ('Sociological Application of the Psychology of Herd Instinct' *Sociological Review*, 2, 1909, 36).

Trotter's essays of 1908 and 1909 were reprinted with much additional material in 1916 as *The Instincts of the Herd in Peace and War*, perhaps, according to Julian Taylor (*Annals of Royal College of Surgeons*, 4, 1949), at the suggestion of a member of the government as a contribution to national morale in wartime. Trotter identified three varieties of gregariousness, exemplified by the beehive, the sheep flock, and the wolf pack, and he compared England to the beehive and Germany to the wolf pack. Trotter admitted to a degree of prejudice in his 'postscript' to the 1919 edition of *The Instincts*, and much that he called instinct in humankind was later regarded as learned behaviour. But he rejected the inevitability of war and regarded pacifism as a natural development—a remarkable statement for its time.

In 1910 Trotter had married Elizabeth May Jones (1880–1964), daughter of Thomas Jones, colliery owner; they had one son, Wilfred Robert Trotter, who later became a physician. After a few years on the permanent staff of UCH, Trotter himself became one of the greatest surgeons of the day—perhaps of the century—in Britain. His most important work, based on scrupulous technique and a comprehensive knowledge of anatomy, was in surgery of cancer of the head and neck, and he showed that the mutilating operations once in vogue were unnecessary. Trotter was a pioneer in neurosurgery (especially of subdural haematoma—blood clot on the brain), and he made notable contributions to surgery of the overactive thyroid, the bowel, and cancer of the kidney. He was serjeant-surgeon to George V, whose life he saved from empyema (an abscess between the ribs and the lung), in 1928, by applying the same surgical principle (that pus must be let out) for a king as for a commoner. Trotter is said to have travelled by bus to Buckingham Palace to operate on the king, and subsequently to have refused a knighthood.

In 1931 Trotter gave up his private practice to devote himself to his (unpaid) work at UCH, especially the training of young surgeons. The unexpected retirement of Professor C. C. Choyce allowed Trotter to become director of the surgical unit between 1935 and 1938. He was elected fellow of the Royal Society in 1931, and he served on its council and on those of the Medical Research Council and the Royal College of Surgeons, where he was Hunterian professor in 1913 and Hunterian orator in 1922. He delivered a series of addresses, subsequently published in 1941 as *The Collected Papers of Wilfred Trotter*. These contain deep insights into the practice and philosophy of medicine and surgery, and are also masterpieces of English prose.

In adult life, Trotter had a perpetual stoop, making him appear well below average height, and he was never robust, both the aftermath of his childhood illness. Throughout his life he was plagued by kidney stones and consequent urinary infection, which eventually caused his death. His indifferent health makes his achievements the more remarkable. He was modest and retiring (some thought aloof), but a delightful conversationalist among those who knew him well, with a keen yet never unkind wit. He was a lover of the English countryside and rarely travelled in other countries. In his later years he was regarded with adulation at UCH, as reflected in later tributes by his colleagues and pupils. These emphasized his deep kindness and humanity, particularly to his patients; a subsequent director of the surgical unit, Professor Robin Pilcher, described him as 'the perfect example of a good doctor' (*Annals of Royal College of Surgeons*, 53, 1973). Trotter died at his home, Pond End House, Blackmoor, Selborne, Hampshire, on 25 November 1939. He was survived by his wife and son.   DOUGLAS HOLDSTOCK

Sources T. R. Elliot, *Obits. FRS*, 3 (1939-41), 325-44 · J. Taylor, 'Wilfred Trotter', *Annals of the Royal College of Surgeons of England*, 4 (1949), 144-59 · H. C. Greisman, 'Herd instinct and the foundations of biosociology', *Journal of the History of the Behavioral Sciences*, 15 (1979), 357-69 · R. S. Pilcher, 'Wilfred Trotter, FRS, FRCS', *Annals of the Royal College of Surgeons of England*, 53 (1973), 71-83 · D. Holdstock, 'Wilfred Trotter and the biosociology of peace and war', *Medicine and War*, 2 (1986), 43-50 · E. Jones, *Free Associations* (1959) · S. P. W. Black, 'Wilfred Trotter', *Surgical Neurology*, 19 (1983), 1-20 · R. A. Malt, 'Doctors afield: Wilfred Trotter', *New England Journal of Medicine*, 257 (1957), 933-5 · private information (2004) · d. cert. · CGPLA Eng. & Wales (1940) · DNB
Archives Bodl. Oxf., MS Don. d. 81 · Bodl. Oxf., MSS, incl. 'Herd instinct and its bearing upon the psychology of civilised man', MS Don. e. 52
Likenesses M. Ayoub, group portrait, oils, c.1927-1929 (Council of the Royal College of Surgeons, 1926-7), RCS Eng. · W. Stoneman, photograph, 1931, NPG · H. Olivier, oils, 1940, priv. coll. · H. Olivier, oils, replica, 1940, RCS Eng. [see illus.] · M. Ayoub, oils, University College Hospital, London · Paget, silver relief, University College Hospital, London · photographs, priv. coll.
Wealth at death £41,278 11s. 9d.: probate, 23 Jan 1940, CGPLA Eng. & Wales

Troubridge, Sir Edward Thomas, second baronet (*d.* 1852), naval officer, was the only son of Rear-Admiral Sir Thomas *Troubridge, first baronet (*c*.1758-1807), and his wife, Frances, *née* Northall. He entered the navy in January 1797, on the guardship *Cambridge* at Plymouth, and remained on her books until April 1799. In January 1801 he joined the *Achille*, with Captain George Murray, whom he followed to the *Edgar*, in which he was present in the battle of Copenhagen. He was afterwards moved into the *London*, and the following year to the *Leander*. In July 1803 he joined Nelson's flagship *Victory* in the Mediterranean, and in August 1804 was moved from her to the frigate *Narcissus*. On 22 February 1806 he was promoted lieutenant of the *Blenheim* and went out to the East Indies as the flagship of his father, by whom he was appointed to command the brig *Harrier*. In her, in company with the frigate *Greyhound* (32 guns), he assisted in destroying a Dutch brig of war under the fort of Menado on 4 July 1806, and on the 26th in the capture of the frigate *Pallas* (36 guns) and two Indiamen under her convoy. After this Troubridge was appointed captain of the *Greyhound*. His commission as commander was confirmed on 5 September 1806, and that as captain on 28 November 1807. In June 1807, when his letters from the Cape of Good Hope forced the commander-in-chief, Sir Edward Pellew, to fear that the *Blenheim* (commanded by Troubridge's father) and *Java* had been lost, Troubridge, in the *Greyhound*, was ordered to search. Neither at the French islands nor along the coast of Madagascar was anything to be heard of the missing ships, and it was concluded that they had foundered in the hurricane. By the death of his father Troubridge succeeded to the baronetcy. In the following January he was invalided out, and had no further service until 1813. By now a man of independent wealth, he had no further need to serve at sea. He married on 18 October 1810 Anna Maria (*d.* 1873), the daughter of Admiral Sir Alexander Forrester Inglis *Cochrane. They had two sons—Sir Thomas St Vincent Hope Cochrane *Troubridge and Edward Norwich Troubridge, a naval captain who died in China in 1850—and two daughters.

In February 1813 Troubridge commissioned the frigate *Armide* to serve on the North American station under his father-in-law, and he commanded the naval brigade at the battle of New Orleans. From April 1831 to October 1832 he was commander-in-chief at Cork, with a broad pennant on board the *Stag*. From April 1835 to August 1841 he was one of the lords of the Admiralty under Lord Minto. His role at the Admiralty reflected his radical Liberal politics, and he was involved in the selection of officers for posts afloat. His close friends in the service included James W. D. Dundas, Edward Codrington, and Charles Napier. He was nominated a CB on 20 July 1838, and was promoted rear-admiral on 23 November 1841. He was a proprietor of the East India Company, and from 1831 to 1847 he was MP for Sandwich, sitting as a Liberal. He died on 7 October 1852.

J. K. LAUGHTON, *rev.* ANDREW LAMBERT

Sources C. N. Parkinson, *War in the eastern seas, 1793-1815* (1954) · N. Gash, *Politics in the age of Peel* (1953) · M. Lewis, *The navy in transition, 1814-1864: a social history* (1965) · Burke, *Peerage* (1959)
Archives NMM | BL, Napier MSS · NL Scot., Minto MSS · NL Scot., corresp. with Sir Alexander Cochrane

Troubridge, Sir Ernest Charles Thomas (1862-1926), naval officer, was born on 15 July 1862 at Hampstead, London, the third son of Colonel Sir Thomas St Vincent Hope Cochrane *Troubridge, third baronet (1815-1867), and his wife, Louisa Jane (*d.* 1867), daughter of Daniel Gurney of

North Runcton, Norfolk. Troubridge had a formidable family heritage to live up to. His father had lost his left foot and right leg at the battle of Inkerman during the Crimean War and his ancestor, the first baronet, was Rear-Admiral Sir Thomas Troubridge, a friend of Nelson who had distinguished himself at the battle of Cape St Vincent and was widely acknowledged as one of the most talented captains of his time. After attending Wellington College, Troubridge entered the navy in 1875 as a naval cadet at the Royal Naval College, Dartmouth, and was promoted to lieutenant in 1884. In 1888 he won the silver medal of the Royal Humane Society for saving the life of a young seaman who had fallen overboard at night in Suda Bay, Crete.

On 29 December 1891 Troubridge married his first wife, Edith Mary (d. 1900), the younger daughter of William Duffus of Halifax, Nova Scotia. They had one surviving son, later Vice-Admiral Sir Thomas Hope *Troubridge (1895–1949), and two daughters. Several years after the death of his first wife Troubridge married on 10 October 1908 Margot Elena Gertrude (1887–1963), generally known as Una Vincenzo, the daughter of Captain Harry Ashworth Taylor. They had one daughter but separated in 1919. Troubridge's second wife was a sculptor, and about 1915 she had begun a relationship with the novelist Marguerite Radclyffe-Hall.

Troubridge was promoted to commander in 1895 and served in the battleship *Revenge* (1896–8), the flagship of Rear-Admiral Sir Robert Harris and Rear-Admiral Sir Gerald Noel, seconds in command of the Mediterranean Fleet. In 1901 he was promoted to captain and became naval attaché at Vienna, and in 1902 Madrid. He was naval attaché at Tokyo (1902–4) and after the outbreak of the Russo-Japanese War managed to be embarked in Japanese warships and was present at the battle of Chemulpo and the operations off Port Arthur. Troubridge was awarded the Japanese order of the Rising Sun and on his return to England was made CMG and MVO. He was flag captain (1907–8) in the battleship *Queen*, to Admiral Sir Charles Drury, Mediterranean commander-in-chief, and then commodore commanding the royal naval barracks, Chatham (1908–10). In 1910 he became private secretary to the first lord, Reginald McKenna, later Winston Churchill. Troubridge was promoted to rear-admiral in March 1911 and in January 1912 became chief of the newly created war staff.

In January 1913 Troubridge was given command of the cruiser squadron in the Mediterranean Fleet under Admiral Sir Berkeley Milne. The squadron consisted of the armoured cruisers *Defence* (flag), *Black Prince*, *Duke of Edinburgh*, and *Warrior*. On the outbreak of the First World War Troubridge's hitherto promising and successful career was blighted when he was placed in a position where his conduct became a source of controversy. The German battle cruiser *Goeben* and light cruiser *Breslau* had remained in the Mediterranean after the Balkan wars (1912–13) as the *Mittelmeerdivision*, a permanent German naval presence. The British and French suspected that in the event of war they would join the fleets of Germany's triple alliance allies, Austria–Hungary and Italy. The exact role of Italy in war remained doubtful, but Germany's sole reliable ally, Austria–Hungary, had embarked on a naval building programme that included dreadnought-type battleships. The prospect of a triple alliance combination was a very real one—a triple alliance naval convention was actually concluded in 1913—but the Italian decision to remain neutral in August 1914 rendered it harmless. Rear-Admiral Wilhelm Souchon, commander of the *Mittelmeerdivision*,

Sir Ernest Charles Thomas Troubridge (1862–1926), by Bassano, 1912

elected not to be bottled up in the Adriatic with his Austrian allies and after making only a feint towards the Adriatic steamed for the Dardanelles. The French commander-in-chief in the Mediterranean was preoccupied with covering the transport of French troops from north Africa to metropolitan France and also believed Souchon would head for the western Mediterranean. This left Milne with three battle cruisers, four light cruisers and a destroyer flotilla to chase the Germans, but the situation was complicated by the need to respect Italian neutrality and uncertainty over the date of Austria's declaration of war and the possible action of the Austrian fleet. On 7 August Troubridge and his squadron were patrolling off Cephalonia to the south of Corfu at the entrance to the Adriatic. He was in a position to intercept the *Goeben* and actually proceeded to do so only to turn away. Ambiguous Admiralty orders played a major role. The Admiralty had told Milne that his first task was to assist the transport of French troops and if possible bring to action individual German ships. However, the British were to avoid being brought to action against superior forces except in combination with the French as part of a general battle. The Admiralty by 'superior forces' meant the Austrian fleet but in this case Troubridge was apparently persuaded by his flag captain Fawcet Wray that it applied to the *Goeben* and therefore reversed his initial instinct to engage. What would have happened had he done so, and whether the *Goeben* really constituted a 'superior force' that his orders prevented him from engaging, are unanswerable questions. The argument that prevailed was that *Goeben* with her thicker armour and presumed higher speed and 11 inch guns would outrange the British 9.2 inch and 7.5 inch guns and be able to prevent the British cruisers from closing while systematically destroying them. The counter-argument was that there were four British cruisers and the Germans would not have been able to concentrate their fire. Consequently Troubridge might have inflicted at least some damage that would slow the Germans and eventually allow the British battle cruisers to close and destroy them. It is a hypothetical question that can never be answered. The Germans escaped to the shelter of the Dardanelles and there was strong criticism of the actions of both Milne and Troubridge that subsequently grew even stronger when it was widely assumed that the presence of the German ships had been a crucial factor in enabling a faction of the ruling Turkish party to manipulate Turkey's entry into the war on the side of Germany. The Admiralty ordered Troubridge home in September to face a court of inquiry held at the Navigation School, Portsmouth. The court decided to court-martial him on the grounds he had failed to engage the enemy. The court martial, held on board HMS *Bulwark* at Portland, 5–9 November, decided that the charge against Troubridge was not proved and that he was 'fully and honourably acquitted'.

Troubridge's victory was a Pyrrhic one for neither Troubridge nor Milne were ever employed at sea again. There was a widespread feeling he had let the navy down and Churchill eventually found a job for him far from the fleet.

In January 1915 Troubridge was appointed head of the British naval mission in Serbia. He arrived in Belgrade in February to command a small force of seamen and Royal Marines armed with eight 4.7 inch naval guns and later a 45 foot picket boat fitted with torpedo dropping gear. The British were assisting Serbian resistance to the Austrian Danube flotilla of monitors and patrol boats. Serbian ability to keep the Danube blocked grew in importance once the Dardanelles campaign began for it prevented river-borne supplies reaching the Black Sea and Turkey. The effort was finally doomed when Bulgaria entered the war and a combined Austrian-German-Bulgarian offensive in October and November 1915 overran Serbia. Troubridge and the British mission joined the Serbian army in a difficult retreat under appalling winter conditions through the Albanian mountains to the Adriatic coast. Troubridge took command at the primitive Albanian port of San Giovanni di Medua and helped organize the evacuation to Corfu in December and January of the remnants of the Serbian army and thousands of refugees.

Troubridge's conduct had been so impressive that the Serbian Crown Prince Alexander asked for him as a personal adviser and aide. Undoubtedly, with his experience he was now uniquely qualified for the role of liaison officer. Troubridge, promoted to vice-admiral in June 1916, was therefore sent to Salonika where the Serbian army was reformed to fight alongside the allies on the Macedonian front. After the collapse of Bulgaria in September 1918 he was appointed admiral commanding on the Danube by the French commander-in-chief in the Balkans, General Franchet d'Esperey. Troubridge asked for a new naval brigade provided with artillery and special mining and torpedo gear to carry on the war on the Danube. However, the Admiralty preferred to send a flotilla of gunboats and initially tried to prevent Troubridge from having any control over it, rebuking him for accepting an appointment from the French. Troubridge returned to England in early 1919 and was able to restore his position but the situation was complicated after a communist regime was established in Hungary by Béla Kun in March 1919. Troubridge, against orders, attempted to intervene with questionable results.

Troubridge remained out of favour at the Admiralty. He served as president of a provisional inter-allied Danube commission in 1919, but when the permanent international Danube commission was established the Foreign Office, with no objection from the Admiralty, preferred their own representative and Troubridge was removed only to be recalled in June 1920 after both the Foreign Office's and Admiralty's preferred choices departed. He served as president of the commission until March 1924. Troubridge was promoted to admiral in January 1919 and created a KCMG in June of that year. Nevertheless the Admiralty put him on the retired list in 1921, claiming he received his salary from the Danube commission. Troubridge died suddenly in Biarritz on 28 January 1926, and was buried there.   PAUL G. HALPERN

Sources E. W. R. Lumby, ed., *Policy and operations in the Mediterranean, 1912–1914* (1970) · C. E. J. Fryer, *The Royal Navy on the Danube*

(1988) · C. E. J. Fryer, *The destruction of the Serbia in 1915* (1997) · P. J. Kemp, *Die Royal Navy auf der Donau, 1918–1925* (1988) · P. G. Halpern, *The naval war in the Mediterranean, 1914–1918* (1987) · *The Royal Navy list, or, Who's who in the navy* (1915) · G. Miller, *Superior force: the conspiracy behind the escape of Goeben and Breslau* (1996) · A. J. Marder, *From the Dreadnought to Scapa Flow: the Royal Navy in the Fisher era, 1904–1919*, 5 vols. (1961–70), vol. 2 · R. Ormrod, *Una Troubridge: the friend of Radclyffe Hall* (1984) · P. G. Halpern, ed., *The Royal Navy in the Mediterranean, 1915–1918* (1987) · *WW* (1916–28) · Burke, *Peerage* · *The Times* (30 Jan 1926) · *CGPLA Eng. & Wales* (1926)

Archives IWM, diary · NMM, MSS | IWM, Fitch MSS · NA Canada, Lovat Dickson MSS · NMM, Limpus MSS · PRO, 'The British naval mission in Serbia, 1914–1916', ADM 137/1141 **Likenesses** U. Troubridge, sculpture, 1909, priv. coll. · photograph, 1909, IWM · Bassano, photograph, 1912, NPG [*see illus.*] · photograph, 1917, IWM · photograph, *c.*1919, repro. in Lumby, ed., *Policy and operations* · photographs, repro. in Ormrod, *Una Troubridge*

Wealth at death £452 18*s.* 11*d.*: probate, 11 May 1926, *CGPLA Eng. & Wales*

Troubridge, Sir Thomas, first baronet (*c.*1758–1807), naval officer, born in London, was the only son of Richard Troubridge, a baker of Temple Bar and Cavendish Street, and Elizabeth, *née* Squinch, of Marylebone. He was educated at St Paul's School, London (1768 – in or before 1773).

Early career Richard Troubridge became known to Sir Charles Saunders at the Admiralty, who expressed an interest in his son, and while the boy may have made an early merchant voyage to the West Indies, he was certainly entered as able seaman on the *Seahorse* (24 guns) on 8 October 1773. In her he went to the East Indies where he was rated midshipman (21 March 1774) and master's mate (25 July 1776). In 1780 Troubridge was moved into the *Superb* (74 guns), flagship of Sir Edward Hughes, after heroic conduct during the capture of the French frigate *Sartine*. As a result of this activity he was, on 1 January 1781, promoted lieutenant of the *Chaser*, a newly commissioned small vessel which Hughes had bought in 1778 for the navy. Two months later, on 3 March 1781, he was moved to his old ship, the *Seahorse*, and in her he was present at the battle off Sadras on 17 February and the battle off Trincomalee on 12 April 1782. On the following day he returned to the *Superb* as a junior lieutenant, and he was present at Hughes's third and fourth actions against the French. On 10 October 1782 he became first lieutenant of the *Superb* and on the following day he was promoted commander of the sloop *Lizard* (10 guns). Just over two months later, on 1 January 1783, he was made post captain in the frigate *Active* (32 guns), and he took part in Hughes's fifth action off Cuddalore. Hughes appointed him captain of the *Defence* (74 guns) on 23 December 1783 and in the following November captain of the *Sultan*, so that he became flag captain to Hughes, with whom he came home, arriving at Spithead on 16 May 1785.

During the Spanish armament of 1790 Troubridge was appointed to the *Thames* (32 guns) and again went out to the East Indies under Commodore Cornwallis. On his return to England two years later he was appointed to the *Castor* (32 guns). Just over a year later, on 10 May 1794, he was captured with the convoy by part of the French Brest

Sir Thomas Troubridge, first baronet (*c.*1758–1807), by Samuel Drummond

fleet while convoying fourteen merchant vessels from the Channel Islands to Newfoundland. The *Castor* was retaken three weeks later but Troubridge had been moved to the French flagship *Sans Pareil* (80 guns) and in her was present at the battle of 1 June 1794. He had been imprisoned in the bosun's storeroom, 'where he amused himself in pouring forth every invective against the French and the man appointed to guard him', and on hearing the *Sans Pareil*'s mainmast go overboard 'began to jump and caper with all the gestures of a maniac' (Kennedy, 80). When she surrendered Troubridge hauled down her colours and then saw to necessary repairs before taking her into port. Shortly after this he was appointed to the *Culloden* (74 guns) which in February 1795 was part of Lord Howe's command, convoying the East and West India fleets through the channel and then cruising off Brest.

Career under Lord St Vincent Troubridge's activity was given more scope when Sir John Jervis became commander-in-chief in 1796. Jervis had not previously met Troubridge but his letters to Lord Spencer began to record Troubridge's merits. He was employed with an inshore squadron watching Toulon so successfully that for five months no French ship escaped. He and Horatio Nelson, friends since serving together in the *Seahorse*, were the captains on whom Jervis relied for important detached operations. Jervis thought Troubridge capable of commanding the fleet and once declared him 'the best Bayard of the British Navy: the ablest adviser and best executive officer, with honour and courage bright as his sword' (Tucker, 2.402–3).

At the battle of Cape St Vincent (14 February 1797) the *Culloden* led the British line and was the first to open fire on the Spanish ships and to pass through the gap which opened between them. Troubridge anticipated Jervis's signal to tack in succession, which would bring him round to encounter the larger of the two divisions into which the Spanish fleet was now split. He acknowledged the order as the signal for it appeared aboard the *Victory*, swinging his ship on the opposite tack. Jervis was delighted. 'Look at Troubridge there!' he urged the master:

> He tacks his ship in battle as if the eyes of England were upon him; and would to God they were, for they would see him to be, what I know him to be, and, by Heaven, sir, what the Dons will soon feel him to be! (Lloyd, 68)

In July 1797 the *Culloden* formed part of a small squadron—four ships of the line, three frigates, and a cutter—detached under Nelson for an attack on Santa Cruz at Tenerife in the Canary Islands. The plan had been first to take the fort between the landing place and the town, and, once successful, summon the governor to surrender the garrison and town of Santa Cruz. Bad weather prevented the ships arriving before daylight and all surprise was lost, but Nelson determined to press on. Forces under Troubridge were landed to take the heights above the fort, while Nelson with his ships attempted to stand in and bombard the garrison. But the Spaniards occupied the heights, local currents prevented the British ships getting sufficiently close to act, and the attempt was unsuccessful. Nelson faced a similar reversal shortly afterwards during a direct night assault on the town on 25 July.

The Spaniards were well prepared and successfully counter-attacked. Nelson himself was seriously wounded and at daylight Troubridge, who was left on shore in command, found himself in the presence of a numerically overwhelming force which rapidly surrounded his men. In an act of tremendous bluff or impertinent defiance he sent Captain Samuel Hood with a flag of truce to the governor, threatening that if the Spanish forces advanced further he would burn down the town. If the governor would provide them with boats the British would withdraw peacefully, but they must have an answer within five minutes. The governor accepted the terms, inviting Hood and Troubridge to dinner and allowing the detachment to march to the embarkation with drums beating and colours flying. But the expedition was a costly failure while Britain remained excluded from the Mediterranean.

A French expedition from Toulon early in 1798 posed a threat which could not, however, be ignored. On 24 May 1798 Troubridge, in the *Culloden*, was sent as one of a squadron of ten sail of the line by Jervis (now earl of St Vincent) into the Mediterranean to reinforce Nelson, already searching for the French fleet. The French were eventually discovered on the evening of 1 August, moored in Abu Qir Bay at the mouth of the Nile, and the British fleet attacked immediately, forming its line as it entered the bay. Troubridge, who had been some distance astern, was pressing forward to get into station when the *Culloden* struck heavily on the shoal which runs out from Abu Qir Island. All efforts to get her off failed and they were forced to watch the battle without being able to take part in it. This was a bitter disappointment. *Culloden* was got off the next day, though her rudder was torn away and she was making 7 feet of water an hour. But Troubridge was an excellent and resourceful seaman and patched her up sufficiently for her to limp to Naples with the French prizes.

Troubridge's depression at missing the action was increased by news, received *en route* to Naples, of the death of his wife. Troubridge had married Frances Richardson, the widow of 'Governor' Richardson and daughter of Captain John Northall, on 20 December 1787. She died on 13 June 1798 and was buried at St Andrew's Church, Plymouth, leaving two children: Edward Thomas *Troubridge, Troubridge's heir, and a daughter, Charlotte. The weeks that followed, spent in repairing the damage to his own and the other English ships, exacerbated his nerves and his letters are full of complaints and violent diatribes about the neutral American vessels which hid English deserters, the dilatoriness of the Portuguese ships acting as British allies, and the cheating and laziness of the Neapolitans.

Relations with the Neapolitans In October 1798 the king of Naples, with promises of Austrian support, attacked Leghorn. Having conveyed the troops there Nelson returned to Naples, leaving Troubridge in command of a force which was unwilling to act vigorously and whose commanders he suspected of taking bribes. At first Troubridge had longed to be useful to the Neapolitan government, was delighted that King Ferdinand and his troops had taken possession of Rome, and called for 'a war if possible of extermination as long as a Frenchman is left alive' (Troubridge to Sir William Hamilton, November 1798, BL, Egerton MS 2638, fols. 377–8). But when the Neapolitans fled before the French counter-attack and advance on Naples, which forced the court, government, and many refugees to flee to Sicily in December 1798, his opinions changed.

By the time of his arrival at Palermo (1 January 1799) Troubridge was convinced that the Admiralty disapproved of his conduct on 1 August, since he had not received the gold medal awarded to all the captains who had fought at the battle of the Nile. Both Lord St Vincent and Nelson urged Lord Spencer, first lord of the Admiralty, to redress this slight, arguing that, through no fault of his own, Troubridge had been unable to take part in the battle. For Nelson he was 'the most meritorious sea-officer of his standing in the service' (Ralfe, 4.404) while St Vincent considered him 'the greatest man in his walk that the

English navy ever produced' (Corbett, 2.472). This energetic lobbying had the desired effect and Troubridge learnt, while off Alexandria, that he was to have his medal. He returned to Palermo on 17 March 1799 and on 31 March was detached by Nelson, with three ships of the line, to take the islands of Ischia, Procida, and Capri in the Bay of Naples, preventing the French getting supplies and enforcing the allied blockade of Naples. By noon on 3 April he had succeeded. By the beginning of May the French began to evacuate Naples and success seemed in sight.

The arrival of a French fleet under Bruix in the Mediterranean led to Troubridge's recall to Palermo, so that it was not until mid-June that he was able to return to Naples. The Neapolitan rebels had surrendered and the French garrison in St Elmo Castle alone held out. Troubridge, charged with its capture, took the castle in ten days and immediately left with 1000 seamen and marines to take the French garrison left at Capua. When Troubridge returned, successfully, to Naples in July, Nelson appointed him senior officer with a broad pendant and ordered him to reduce the remaining French garrisons at Rome and Civita Vecchia. He did so, warning the commander of the latter that Russian troops under Marshal Suvorov were approaching and that all prisoners taken by them were invariably sent to Siberia. Such savage humour expressed Troubridge's mood. Although he was granted a baronetcy on 23 November 1799 as a reward for retaking Naples and awarded the newly created order of St Ferdinand and Merit by Ferdinand, Troubridge was thoroughly disillusioned with the Neapolitans. No supplies had been forthcoming from them for the virtually starving inhabitants of Procida, Ischia, and Capri, whom Troubridge had supplied at his own expense. He became increasingly embittered by his experiences during the siege of Malta, where he arrived on 15 December 1799, with troops from Messina. In the following months he begged Nelson and Sir William Hamilton to get the Neapolitans to send money and supplies to help the Maltese, without success. Condemnation of the Neapolitan court was mixed with complaints and abuse of fellow officers in terms, and in handwriting, which became increasingly uncontrolled.

In February, when he was ill with jaundice and fever, Troubridge acknowledged he felt too deeply and 'that I hate myself for staying in the country, the more I think of what has pass'd the more I am disgusted' (Troubridge to Hamilton, 7 Feb 1800, BL, Egerton MS 2638, fols. 445–6). He longed to see and confide in Nelson and found the latter's suggestion that he might settle at Bronte inexplicable. But Troubridge, who had been Nelson's most intimate friend and confidant, was vainly struggling against the stronger influence of Lady Hamilton. He remained virtually in command of the blockade at Malta, until *Culloden* was finally ordered home in May 1800. He had hopes that Sir William Hamilton, now replaced as ambassador to Naples, might come to Malta and go home with him, and that Nelson, who had chosen to return home on grounds of ill health, would hoist his flag in the *Culloden* and travel with them. But Troubridge went home alone.

Worsening relations with Nelson and political career Despite expressing his need for a rest, within three weeks Troubridge was appointed flag captain to St Vincent in the Channel Fleet. St Vincent was engaged in introducing the discipline of the Mediterranean Fleet he had so successfully commanded into that of the channel, despite the resistance and resentment of many of its captains. Troubridge, the ideal executive officer, was admirably suited to this task. Believing in the virtue of strict discipline, devoted to the service, and contemptuous of anyone not as devoted and professional as himself, he thoroughly supported St Vincent's measures and his troubled emotions must have been soothed by the approbation of 'the Chief' as he usually referred to St Vincent. Troubridge had been very upset by his differences and misunderstandings with Nelson, so he was deeply grateful when Nelson persuaded the Neapolitan government to pay Troubridge an annual pension of £500. However, on meeting Nelson in London, Troubridge saw enough of the Hamilton–Nelson *ménage* to realize that the relationship was permanent, though he perhaps did not realize its strength.

In February 1801 St Vincent became first lord of the Admiralty in Addington's government. He appointed Troubridge one of the Admiralty commissioners, a position he held from 19 February 1801 to 15 May 1804. His relationship with Nelson now began to cool. Although still a friend, Troubridge, as a commissioner, was technically Nelson's superior. Instead of being allowed to return home after the victory at Copenhagen, Nelson was appointed commander-in-chief in the Baltic. When he finally came home, in June 1801, he was given command of a squadron of frigates and gun boats, defending the south-east coast from a French invasion force at Boulogne. St Vincent, and particularly Troubridge, correctly argued that public fears were calmed by Nelson's presence, but Nelson interpreted these appointments (with some justification) as pretexts to separate him from Lady Hamilton. When his requests for the promotion of protégés were delayed and sometimes rejected, he grew more angry. He dismissed Troubridge's pleas that the Admiralty's problems with promotion were considerable.

Troubridge, who wrote almost daily to Nelson in August and September 1801, made every effort to please. But he was deeply upset by Nelson's accusations of enmity and prejudice, protesting that his gratitude to Nelson was considerable, that his whole study since at the Admiralty had been 'to act in every [way] regular' and pay attention to Nelson's interests. 'I really feel so much hurt and particularly at the latter part [of Nelson's letter] when you say you never had but one real Friend, I know many hundreds who certainly are firm friends to your Lordship' (17 Aug 1801, NMM, CRK/13, T32–86). A further angry letter in which Nelson declared that the Admiralty would envy any success he had, brought a distraught response from Troubridge, accusing unknown enemies of poisoning Nelson's mind against his true friends, and declaring himself 'so unhinged' by this unmerited charge that he was distressed beyond measure. 'I really wish myself out of this', he declared soon after: 'I am ruining my health and losing my friends tho' I feel conscious that I have acted religiously upright' (ibid., 20 Aug and 9 Sept 1801).

Nelson was deaf to these appeals. A cold hostility now informed his view of Troubridge. He wrote most bitterly to Emma Hamilton that Troubridge owed him everything, not merely the gold medal but *'tithes, the colonelcy of marines, diamond boxes* from the King of Naples, 1000 ounces of money for *no* expenses that I know of', plus the Neapolitan pension, and that he now showed his ingratitude (Kennedy, 265). Although Nelson took Troubridge's son, Edward, into the *Victory* as a midshipman in 1803, at his father's request, this was, on his part, the virtual end to a twenty-eight-year friendship.

As an Admiralty commissioner Troubridge entered enthusiastically into the exposure and redress of abuses in the civil departments of the navy, to which St Vincent was committed. With St Vincent and John Markham he formed a triumvirate committed to rooting out corruption (much of it imagined), by force if necessary. His letters reveal his hard work and his almost frenzied contempt for wrongdoers. Once again there were diatribes against 'jobs', and trenchant accusations of bribery against named individuals. His letters sometimes show an unpleasant zest in discovering and exposing such people, reminiscent of his gloating enjoyment over the punishment of rebels and French sympathizers at Naples and Malta. In Troubridge's eyes all were similarly guilty of treachery and undermining the established social order.

To strengthen his political position St Vincent wanted Troubridge in the House of Commons and had undertaken to find him a seat. In October 1801 he sent him, with his nephew Thomas Jervis, to canvass Yarmouth, which he himself had once represented to the satisfaction of the borough and to where Troubridge was returned in 1802, without a contest. During his four years as an MP he never took an active part in the Commons, speaking only once, on 29 February 1804. This was perhaps as well. During the Admiralty's investigation of abuses at Chatham Dockyard, St Vincent was anxious that the disclosures should not provoke a Commons debate in which Troubridge would take too violent and partisan a part.

On 16 March 1803 references were made in the Commons to the fact that Troubridge had been in the City earlier that month and sold out £40,000 of stock. Since he had advance news of an intended press of seamen, which foreshadowed renewed war with France, the inference was of improper use of news for his financial advantage. Admiral Markham refuted the charge on Troubridge's behalf, declaring that the latter's broker had complete authority to deal in his client's stock on any market fall, since Troubridge was engaged in buying an estate. Markham declared Troubridge 'spotless' and moved for a committee of inquiry. Addington, the prime minister, contributed a further explanation and the matter was dropped. But this left lingering suspicions which professional and political enemies were glad to believe and may help to explain Troubridge's references in his letters to Nelson about his pure motives and his claims that his job was ruining both his health and peace of mind.

Troubridge was created rear-admiral of the blue on 23 April 1804, just before Addington's government resigned. He was angry with Addington for supporting William Pitt's succeeding ministry. Because of the bitter political feelings stirred up by St Vincent's reforms, he did not ask for employment from the new Admiralty since he thought it unlikely they would offer it. In August he and St Vincent visited Liverpool and the Lake District. Troubridge, who still tried to keep up a correspondence with Nelson, confessed he was 'still ahankering for Sea', wishing he was with Nelson in the Mediterranean, and promising he had lost neither his zeal nor his health and strength (18 Aug 1804, NMM, CRK/13, T32–86). If this was a hint to be asked to join Nelson it was ignored. In February 1805 he still considered 'lying and scheming … the order of the day … supported openly in the house by ministers' (ibid., Troubridge to Nelson, 12 Feb 1805) and his next appointment seemed to give some credence to this view.

The East India station One of the last acts of Addington's ministry, in April 1804, was the appointment of Sir Edward Pellew as commander-in-chief on the East India station. This was, at least in part, a reward for Pellew's support of St Vincent's naval policy in the Commons debates in March 1804. Such support had made an enemy of Pitt and Lord Melville, first lord of the Admiralty, but Pellew's seat in the Commons saved him from immediate reprisals, and he sailed in July 1804 in the *Culloden*. By January 1805 Addington had joined Pitt's ministry, making a condition that the members of St Vincent's Admiralty board should be 'provided for'. It was unclear to whom this would apply, but Troubridge, though angry and hostile, wished for his son's promotion and was open to offers from the ministry. Hopes of introducing successful reforms on the East India station may also have contributed to his decision. Letters to Admiral Sir C. M. Pole in 1802–3 indicate Troubridge was already concerned with reform there. So when the government, dividing the East India command in two, and reducing Pellew's authority, offered Troubridge one half and his choice of flagship, he accepted, hoisting his flag, in March, in the *Blenheim*, a former three-decked ship, now cut down to carry 74 guns.

He sailed on 27 April 1805 with a convoy of eleven East Indiamen and leaving Madagascar, fell in with the French admiral Linois, in the *Marengo*, on 6 August. Linois at first thought the British ships were an undefended convoy, but on identifying the *Blenheim* he made off. Troubridge arrived at Madras on 22 August. Here he met Pellew who was, as rear-admiral of the white, senior to Troubridge and prepared for confrontation. Troubridge showed Pellew his orders, to take half Pellew's squadron and to command east of a line due south from the Point de Galle on the south-west coast of Ceylon. Such division, as well as causing friction between senior officers, put the whole squadron at risk during the monsoon season, was strategically inept, and was dictated by political malice. Troubridge never imagined that Pellew would disobey Admiralty orders. But he did so, taking Troubridge under his command, despite the latter's violent protests.

After a few days the admirals no longer met but

exchanged notes. Troubridge rejected the first compromise Pellew suggested, but when they came together at Penang (Prince of Wales Island) with their respective convoys, on 25 September 1805, he agreed to consider Pellew's written proposals. These offered Troubridge all the ships assigned to him, except in emergency; suggested that the boundary between the two stations should be modified to bring Madras and Trincomalee, essential harbours for a western squadron during the monsoon, under Pellew's command; and suggested that they share the patronage and emoluments equally between them. Troubridge, whose feelings must have been exacerbated by seeing his former ship, the *Culloden*, now the flagship of his rival, received these decent solutions on 27 September and rejected them the following day. At a final meeting on 30 September Pellew declared he would, nevertheless, act on this basis. The two men never spoke to each other again.

On 1 October 1805 Pellew received secret and incorrect news of a French squadron on its way to India. Without giving the details to Troubridge he informed him that the imminent danger necessitated a concentration of forces and proceeded to Madras, where he wrote to the Admiralty, protesting at the division of his command. Troubridge was given the choice of convoying the China trade in the *Blenheim*, or remaining, without her, at Penang, where he would fly his flag in the only ship left, the sloop *Rattlesnake* (18 guns). He chose the latter option but his emotions can only be imagined and can hardly have been soothed by his promotion to rear-admiral of the white (9 November 1805).

But events in Britain were resolving an impossible situation. Lord Melville fell from office in 1805 and Pitt died in January 1806. A ministry more favourable to both Pellew and Troubridge now took office, to confront the scandal of two senior officers so publicly quarrelling. In a navy all too prone to faction, some were shocked by Pellew's disobedience, notably St Vincent who sided with Troubridge. The government finally decided to restore Pellew to his original, undivided command and to make Troubridge commander-in-chief at the Cape of Good Hope, recently taken from the Dutch. This news was sent on 23 April 1806.

In the meantime Troubridge remained at Penang without news of Pellew. He 'saw nothing to hinder us from Launching 74-Gun Ships, Frigates and Sloops, Admiralty and one or two large Ships for the Company besides' (Parkinson, *Edward Pellew*, 359), though the money sent out to build them would need strict control. Troubridge still anticipated reforming the navy's civil establishment at Madras. He later accused Pellew of keeping him out of the command 'because I would not give him up the *Control of the Civil Departments* which *I thought wanted much correction*' (Troubridge to Admiral Sir Francis Fremantle, 25 June 1806?, Fremantle papers, D/FR/32/4). The rumours of an approaching French force had proved false and Troubridge's squadron returned to him. In August 1806 they took two Dutch prizes, an action in which his son Edward took part. Troubridge made him acting captain

into one of the prizes, writing to friends at the Admiralty to get him confirmed.

News of the Admiralty decision in Pellew's favour arrived in October, though the official confirmation did not come until January 1807 and proved a shattering blow. Troubridge had believed that the new Admiralty would decide in his favour and was mortified by the news. Moreover he was merely notified of his transfer, the Admiralty leaving Pellew to give him his instructions and sailing orders, including the ships assigned him. This would not have included the *Blenheim*, old, worn out, and badly damaged the previous year in the strait of Malacca. In a letter to Fremantle in June 1806 he had declared he would return home if unsupported by the Admiralty, '*marry and live quiet and enjoy my friends*' (Fremantle papers, D/FR/32/4), and Pellew told Admiral Markham in mid-October that Troubridge reportedly talked of going home with his prize money rather than to the Cape. Whatever he intended and despite his captain's protests, Troubridge sailed from Madras on 12 January 1807 in the *Blenheim*, taking with him the *Java* (36 guns), a worn out Dutch prize, and the brig *Harrier* (18 guns). Pellew arrived ten days later.

On 1 February 1807 Troubridge's ships were caught in a cyclone near the south-east end of Madagascar. When last seen by the *Harrier*, both the *Blenheim* and the *Java* had hoisted distress signals and the *Blenheim* was visibly settling in the water, but the *Harrier* herself was in great danger and could do nothing. She lost sight of them in a violent squall and no doubt both of them foundered. When the news reached India in June, Pellew sent Troubridge's son in the *Greyhound* to make inquiries. The French governor of Mauritius gave every help and sent an account of pieces of wreck cast ashore in different places, but nothing could be identified as belonging to either of the missing ships. Rumours that survivors had been seen in Madagascar, and vicious gossip that Pellew had somehow insisted Troubridge take the *Blenheim* and had refused him a better ship, were equally unfounded.

Reputation Though Troubridge lacked the qualities which make a great commander, his professionalism and abilities, as a seaman and an executive officer, were unsurpassed. Nelson, writing to St Vincent in September 1798, urging that Troubridge be allowed to remain with him, confessed 'I know he is my superior: and I so often want his advice and assistance' (*Dispatches and Letters*, 3.133–4). Troubridge's tragedy was that after Naples and the arrival of Lady Hamilton his advice was sought less and less and the assistance eventually rejected. The friendship with Nelson seems the key to Troubridge's emotional and to some degree his professional life. The rupture of that friendship drove him at times to despair. It is apparent that the rigid naval framework of discipline was essential to him and that he regarded the established order as sacrosanct. Threats to them, from mutiny, from inefficiency and indifference, and from corruption made him, as he often wrote, 'mad with rage'. Troubridge's view, common to most naval officers, was that the role of seamen was to obey without offering opinions. When he was asked by

Lord Eldon how he could detect a mutineer, Troubridge replied 'whenever I see a fellow look as if he was thinking, I say that's mutiny' (HoP, *Commons, 1790–1820*, 5.417). This attitude to the lower deck was that of St Vincent rather than of Nelson.

Troubridge had risen by his own merits, with little patronage to help him and from a humbler background than many service contemporaries. Pellew's description, to a confidential friend, of Troubridge as 'un garcon patisser (sic) from St Martin's Lane', and his further comments on Troubridge as 'a weak man—entirely commanded by his passion; who is every week dishonouring himself by striking some of his Midshipmen or anybody else who comes in his way' (Parkinson, *Edward Pellew*, 367), implied that Troubridge's lack of control could be attributed to his humble background. Pellew's remarks certainly describe a man suffering severe stress and present a sadly recognizable picture to those who read Troubridge's letters, though Pellew admitted that even brothers could not have agreed in their situation.

Little is known of Troubridge's early life or family background. Most of his personal and many of his professional papers have not survived. The intemperance of his language and occasionally of his behaviour, and his frequent emphasis on his strong feelings, indicate an emotionalism which make Troubridge more of a Byronic hero than he would have liked. He would have despised such an image. His unnecessary death was largely the result of his impatient desire to escape from an intolerable situation, disregarding professional protests which he knew were well founded. His courage and daring were unquestioned. Writing to Sir William Hamilton on 31 March 1800 he confessed, 'Death does not give me much concern. I meet him cheerfully' (BL, Egerton MS 2638, fol. 459). The finest and happiest period of his career was serving under St Vincent in the Mediterranean, when the latter's victory and the subsequent search for the French fleet, culminating in the battle of the Nile, allowed his active nature full play. United in a common purpose with fellow seamen he respected, faced with difficulties it was a joy to overcome, serving commanders he admired and loved, undistracted by non-professional matters, Troubridge found his true vocation.   P. K. CRIMMIN

Sources *DNB* · J. Ralfe, *The naval biography of Great Britain*, 4 (1828), 397–421 · R. G. Thorne, 'Troubridge, Sir Thomas', HoP, *Commons, 1790–1820* · *Naval Chronicle*, 23 (1810), 1–29 · D. Syrett and R. L. DiNardo, *The commissioned sea officers of the Royal Navy, 1660–1815*, rev. edn, Occasional Publications of the Navy RS, 1 (1994) · Troubridge's corresp. with Nelson, BL, Add. MSS 34902, 34906–34917 · St Vincent's letters, vol. 3, 1799–1801, BL, Add. MS 34940 · corresp. of William Hamilton, 1767–1800, BL, Egerton MS 2638 · T. Troubridge, letters to Nelson, NMM, Croker collection, CRK/13, T32–86, 1801–5 · *The dispatches and letters of Vice-Admiral Lord Viscount Nelson*, ed. N. H. Nicolas, 7 vols. (1844–6) · L. Kennedy, *Nelson's band of brothers* (1951) · C. N. Parkinson, *Edward Pellew, Viscount Exmouth, admiral of the red* (1934) · C. N. Parkinson, *War in the eastern seas, 1793–1815* (1954) · letters, 1806–7, Bucks. RLSS, Fremantle papers, D/FR/32/4 and 5 · GEC, *Baronetage* · J. S. Tucker, *Memoirs of Admiral the Rt Hon. the earl of St Vincent*, 2 vols. (1844) · D. Lyon, *The sailing navy list: all the ships of the Royal Navy, built, purchased and captured, 1688–1860* (1993) · Private papers of George, second Earl Spencer, ed. J. S. Corbett and H. W. Richmond, 2, Navy RS, 48 (1924) · C. Lloyd, *St Vincent and Camperdown* (1963) [British Battles ser.]

Archives BL, corresp. with Sir William Hamilton, Egerton MS 2638 · BL, corresp. with Lord Nelson, Add. MSS 34902–34917, 34940 · BL, letters to General Rainsford, Add. MS 23670 · Bucks. RLSS, corresp. with Admiral Fremantle · NL Scot., letters to Sir Thomas Graham · NMM, letters to Lord Nelson, CRK/13, T32–86 · NMM, papers of Sir C. M. Pole, letters, WYN/103

Likenesses W. Bromley, J. Landseer, and Leney, group portrait, line engraving, pubd 1803 (*Victors of the Nile*; after *Victors of the Nile* by R. Smirke), BM, NPG · Worthington and Parker, group portrait, line engraving, pubd 1803 (*Commemoration of the 14th February 1797*; after *Naval victories* by R. Smirke), BM, NPG · W. Beechey, oils, *c.*1804–1805, NMM · H. R. Cook, stipple (after oils by S. Drummond), BM; repro. in *Naval Chronicle* · S. Drummond, oils, priv. coll. [*see illus.*]

Troubridge, Sir Thomas Hope (1895–1949), naval officer, was born at Southsea, Hampshire, on 1 February 1895, the only son of Lieutenant (later Admiral Sir) Ernest Charles Thomas *Troubridge (1862–1926) and his first wife, Edith Duffus (*d.* 1900). He came of a long line which gave distinguished service to Britain, chiefly in the Royal Navy, and was a direct descendant of Rear-Admiral Sir Thomas Troubridge (*c.*1758–1807) who led the line at the battle of Cape St Vincent. Troubridge entered the Royal Navy as a cadet in 1908, and, passing through the Royal Naval College at Osborne and Dartmouth, was gazetted midshipman in September 1912. In the First World War he saw action off the Dogger Bank and at Jutland, became a lieutenant in 1916, and in the following year was appointed to coastal motor boats in which he remained until the armistice.

Troubridge then served for a time as staff officer to his father who was at Budapest as president of the international Danube commission. There Troubridge learnt German and laid the foundations of a knowledge of foreign countries and of diplomatic usage which became far wider than is usually possessed by a naval officer. On returning to England he took a course in gunnery and then served as a gunnery officer in the *Queen Elizabeth* (1922–4). Specialization in a technical branch was not, perhaps, his true vocation and he soon abandoned a gunnery career to take the naval staff course (1924) after which he served in the Atlantic Fleet as staff officer, operations. In 1925 Troubridge married Lilly, daughter of Herman Greverus Kleinwort, banker, and they had three sons and one daughter. His eldest son entered the Royal Navy and his second son the Royal Marines.

In 1928 Troubridge was appointed to the royal yacht *Victoria and Albert* and was promoted to commander at the end of 1929. He was next selected for the army staff course at Camberley. The friendships which he there made were to stand him in good stead later when, in the Second World War, he came to take a prominent part in combined operations, for many of the senior army officers concerned in them had been at Camberley with him. From the staff college he returned to destroyers with command of the *Voyager* in the Mediterranean Fleet. He remained in destroyers, except for a break for courses, until promoted captain in 1934 at the age of thirty-nine. In that rank his first appointment was in 1936 as naval attaché, Berlin, at a time when it was still hoped that, by the Anglo-German

Sir Thomas Hope Troubridge (1895–1949), by Walter Stoneman, 1946

naval agreement of 1935, a new German challenge to British supremacy at sea might be held off and a *modus vivendi* reached with Hitler. Troubridge remained in Berlin until the end of July 1939.

On 1 January 1940 Troubridge was appointed to command the aircraft-carrier *Furious* in the Home Fleet. The most important operations in which she took part were those off Norway in April and May 1940 when a few dozen naval aircraft working from carriers tried to remedy our lack of air power on land. Their effort, although inevitably unsuccessful, was a glorious chapter in the story of British naval aviation. In June 1941 Troubridge was appointed to command the battleship *Nelson*, then flying the flag of Sir James Somerville in force H at Gibraltar. It was a period of intense activity, chiefly for the supply of the besieged island of Malta. During one of the many convoy operations to carry stores and men to that island the *Nelson* was torpedoed by an aircraft and damaged on 27 September 1941. Troubridge next returned to aircraft-carriers with command of the *Indomitable*, which was serving in the recently reconstituted Eastern Fleet. In her he took part in the assault and capture of the base of Diego Suarez in Madagascar in May 1942. In August of that year Troubridge returned to the task of relieving Malta. The *Indomitable* formed part of a powerful force assembled to fight through a convoy of fourteen ships at a critical time. She

was severely damaged by German dive-bombers in the process and only five of the fourteen merchant ships in the convoy reached their destination. Troubridge was appointed to the DSO for his services in this operation.

The damage to the *Indomitable* released Troubridge at a time when preparations were being made in Britain and the United States for the invasion of north Africa. This was the first major combined operation of the war and marked the resumption by the allies of the strategic offensive. Troubridge was appointed, with the rank of commodore, to command the central task force, the duty of which was to attack and seize the great French naval base at Oran. His force, which consisted of thirty-four transports and seventy warships, struck in the small hours of 8 November 1942. Stiff French resistance had to be overcome, but Oran was captured on 10 November and the first major enemy base in north Africa passed into allied hands. Troubridge received the American DSM and a bar to the DSO. He returned to England early in 1943 and was promoted to rear-admiral. His successful service in the invasion of north Africa made it inevitable that his experience would be used in the other great combined operations now being prepared. With his flag in the headquarters ship *Bulolo* he was next appointed to command, under Sir Bertram Ramsay, one of the four great naval forces organized for the invasion of Sicily.

Troubridge's force, consisting of some seventy-five warships, was responsible for transporting the 5th and 50th divisions and the 231st brigade from ports in the Middle East to the rendezvous off the enemy coast, and thereafter for landing and protecting the troops assigned to the two northern sectors of the assault area on the east coast of Sicily. The landings took place early on 10 July and by 10 a.m. Troubridge was able to report 'all beaches captured'.

The campaign for the liberation of Europe now moved to the mainland of Italy. Troubridge's force did not take part in the landing at Salerno in September, but in January 1944 he was responsible for landing the 1st British division to the north of Anzio. The landings were wholly successful although the operation encountered serious, even critical, difficulties after the troops were ashore.

In July 1944 Troubridge was appointed to command the force of nine British and American escort-carriers organized to give air escort and cover to the forces invading the south of France. The carrier force arrived off the assault area early on 15 August and remained until the 27th, by which time the success of the landings was beyond doubt. For his 'distinguished service and zeal' on this occasion Troubridge was appointed CB. The seven British carriers which he commanded now went back to the eastern Mediterranean. His next duty was to hamper the German withdrawal from Greece, Crete, and the Aegean islands with his carrier aircraft and light surface forces. During the latter part of September many successful minor actions were fought. Early in October Troubridge was relieved and he returned to England shortly afterwards.

On 1 May 1945 Troubridge joined the Board of Admiralty as fifth sea lord, whose particular responsibility was the naval air service. In December he was promoted KCB 'for distinguished service throughout the war in Europe'. In September 1946 he hoisted his flag again, this time ashore, as admiral (air) in command of all naval air stations in Britain. In January 1947 he was promoted vice-admiral and a year later took up his last active appointment—that of flag officer (air) and second in command of the Mediterranean Fleet. He thus returned to the station in which he had served with such distinction during the war. Unhappily his health gave way and he returned home in November 1948. He died suddenly on 29 September 1949 at Hawkley, Hampshire.

Troubridge was an officer of commanding presence, possessed of great gifts of mind and of personality. He played most games and excelled especially at cricket and rackets, for which he won the navy championship. To those who knew him well it was no surprise that war service rapidly proved him one of the outstanding fighting leaders of his service. Although he had no experience of naval aviation until early in the war, he may justly be regarded as one of the pioneers in the use of carrier-borne aircraft, particularly in combined operations. But for his early death he would probably have risen to the highest posts within the Royal Navy.

STEPHEN W. ROSKILL, rev.

Sources The Times (30 Sept 1949) · WWW · S. W. Roskill, The war at sea, 1939–1945, 3 vols. in 4 (1954–61) · CGPLA Eng. & Wales (1950) · 'Troubridge, Sir Ernest Charles Thomas', DNB
Archives IWM · NRA, papers · NRA, priv. coll., diaries kept as naval attaché at Berlin | FILM BFI NFTVA, news footage · IWM FVA, actuality footage · IWM FVA, news footage | SOUND IWM SA, oral history interview
Likenesses W. Stoneman, photograph, 1946, NPG [see illus.] · R. Marientren, portrait, priv. coll.
Wealth at death £964 1s. 7d.: probate, 20 May 1950, CGPLA Eng. & Wales

Troubridge, Sir Thomas St Vincent Hope Cochrane, third baronet (1815–1867), army officer, was born on 25 May 1815, the eldest son of Admiral Sir Edward Thomas *Troubridge, second baronet (d. 1852), and Anna Maria (d. 1873), daughter of Admiral Sir Alexander Forrester Inglis *Cochrane. He was commissioned as ensign in the 73rd foot on 24 January 1834. On 30 December 1836 he was promoted lieutenant and exchanged into the 7th Royal Fusiliers. He served with the regiment at Gibraltar, the West Indies, and Canada, becoming captain on 14 December 1841 and major on 9 August 1850.

Troubridge went with the 7th to the Crimea in 1854, and was in the forefront of the battle at the Alma. He was in command of the right wing of the regiment, which was on the right of the light division, and had to deal with the left wing of the Kazan regiment. On 5 November, at Inkerman, he was field officer of the day, and was posted with the reserve of the light division in the Lancaster battery. This battery was enfiladed by Russian guns to the east of the Careenage Ravine, and Troubridge lost his right leg and left foot. He remained in the battery, however, until the battle was over, with his limbs propped up against a gun carriage. Lord Raglan, in his dispatch of 11 November, said of him that, though desperately wounded, he behaved with the utmost gallantry and composure.

Troubridge returned to England in May 1855, and was present (in a chair) at the distribution of medals by the queen on 18 May. He was made CB, aide-de-camp to the queen, and brevet colonel from that day, having already been made brevet lieutenant-colonel on 12 December 1854. He also received the fourth class of the Mejidiye and the Légion d'honneur. Troubridge married, on 1 November 1855, Louisa Jane, daughter of Daniel *Gurney of North Runcton, Norfolk, and granddaughter of the fifteenth earl of Erroll. She died on 29 August 1867, five weeks before him. They had three sons and four daughters. Their third son was Sir Ernest Charles Thomas *Troubridge (1862–1926).

Troubridge succeeded to the command of his regiment on 9 March 1855, but was unable to serve with it, and was placed on half pay on 14 September. Still capable of official work, he was appointed director-general of army clothing. On 2 February 1857 he exchanged this title for that of deputy adjutant-general (clothing department), and he held this post until his death. Struck by the defects of the regulation knapsack, he designed a valise which was approved by the leading medical officers and was the foundation of later valise equipment. He died at his home, 8 Queen's Gate, Hyde Park, Kensington, on 2 October 1867, and was buried at Kensal Green cemetery.

E. M. LLOYD, rev. JAMES LUNT

Sources GM, 4th ser., 4 (1867), 676 · E. Lodge, Peerage, baronetage, knightage and companionage of the British empire, 81st edn, 3 vols. (1912) · A. W. Kinglake, The invasion of the Crimea, 8 vols. (1863–87) · J. P. Groves, ed., Historical records of the 7th or royal regiment of fusiliers (1903) [compiled from histories of the Royal Fusiliers by the late Mr. Cannon ... and ... G. H. Waller] · Burke, Peerage (1959) · Boase, Mod. Eng. biog. · Dod's Peerage
Archives Bucks. RLSS, corresp. with first Baron Cottesloe
Likenesses engraving, repro. in E. H. Nolan, The illustrated history of the war against Russia, 2 (1857), 296 · wood-engraving, NPG; repro. in ILN (19 Oct 1867)
Wealth at death under £16,000: probate, 5 Nov 1867, CGPLA Eng. & Wales

Troughton, Edward (1753–1835), maker of scientific instruments, was born at Corney, Cumberland, probably in October 1753, the youngest of six children of Francis Troughton, farmer and property owner, and his wife, Mary, née Stable. He worked alongside his father, until the death of a brother in London entirely changed the course of his life. Edward's uncle, John Troughton (c.1716–1788), was the first member of the family to enter the London scientific instrument trade; Edward's brother John (c.1739–1807) was trained by him, and John in his turn took a younger brother as apprentice. The death of this brother resulted in Edward's being sent to replace him, and in December 1773 he was bound apprentice for seven years to John. At this time John Troughton worked for other craftsmen, who brought their sextants and small astronomical quadrants to be divided in his workshop, for he enjoyed a high reputation in this difficult art, which was performed entirely by hand. Between 1775 and 1778 John constructed a dividing engine, on the lines of that recently designed by Jesse Ramsden, by which he was able to increase both his accuracy and his rate of work. Edward took a great interest in this art, and set about building his own engine; he also studied astronomy, resolving, as he later said, 'to aim at the nicer parts of my profession'.

John's profits enabled him to acquire property outside London and, in 1782, to purchase the substantial retail business of Benjamin Cole (1725–1813), at the sign of the Orrery, with its shop at 136 Fleet Street and workrooms to the rear. Around 1788 the brothers entered into partnership, trading as John and Edward Troughton until John's death. Edward became a freeman in the Grocers' Company in 1784 and was able to enrol his own apprentices, his nephew Thomas Suddard being among them. These men, when they came to establish their own businesses, were proud to advertise their years with Edward Troughton.

The Troughtons followed Cole in selling a wide range of articles, many of which were made by craftsmen working for the trade, but from the 1780s orders flowed in for large astronomical apparatus to furnish the many private and government observatories then under construction throughout Britain and Europe. The Troughtons' products were of excellent design and construction, and unrivalled in their accuracy; after Ramsden's death in 1800 the brothers were judged by many to be London's finest instrument makers. After John's death in 1807 Edward furnished the Royal Greenwich Observatory with the major new instruments which supplied observations for definitive star catalogues. At least five standard measures of length were prepared, for home and overseas customers. At the same time, Troughton was improving the designs of the common instruments required by surveyors and navigators and 'Troughton' patterns of barometers, sextants, levels, and surveying circles sold in considerable numbers for many years. The smaller astronomical instruments were tested in an observatory which the Troughtons had constructed on the roof of their house. From this vantage point Edward observed and timed the transit of Mercury across the sun's disc in May 1799 and his report was duly published with others in the astronomical literature. Clocks and clock pendulums also captured his interest and he was one of the experts whose opinion was sought on the rival claims of two London chronometer makers.

In 1809 there were plans to replace the antiquated astronomical instruments at the Greenwich observatory with a new free-standing instrument, similar to Ramsden's circle as recently installed at Palermo observatory. When Troughton was consulted, he set down on paper his thoughts about the construction and performance of the various types of circle then in use, and went on to describe a 'mural circle', a new design that he had been considering for some time. This document demonstrates his thorough grasp of the principles of engineering, and of the materials and design strategies that would best serve his purpose. His well-reasoned argument persuaded his prospective customers and construction of this new apparatus was put in hand. There was one problem: the Troughton workshops gave onto a courtyard whose access to Fleet Street was through a low archway too narrow for the passage of bulky goods. It was resolved by Troughton's friend Bryan Donkin (1768–1855), engineer and amateur astronomer. The larger parts of the circle were cast and turned at Donkin's Bermondsey works, a practice which was to be followed for another apparatus. Charles Hafter's oil painting of Troughton with this circle was exhibited at the Royal Academy in 1808 but has since disappeared.

While the mural circle was taking shape Troughton wrote for Nevil Maskelyne (1732–1811), then astronomer royal, a description of his method of dividing by hand, still the only way to divide large circles, a technique which he had hitherto kept secret. His covering letter made it clear that he regarded this disclosure as a valuable present to young craftsmen, and it was certainly accepted as such. The paper was read to the Royal Society and in gratitude for his generosity Troughton was elected a fellow of the society in 1810 and was awarded its Copley medal. Other honours came his way, election to the Society of Civil Engineers, the American Philosophical Society, the Royal Society of Edinburgh, and the Cambridge Philosophical Society. In 1823 he was presented with the freedom and livery of the Clockmakers' Company. He was among the first members of the Astronomical Society, founded in 1820, serving on its council and as vice-president in 1830–31. He was a member of the Astronomical Dining Club, and was welcomed into the houses of the many eminent astronomers who were his customers. In 1824 he travelled to France to stay with James South (1785–1867) at Passy, then spent three weeks in Paris—'perhaps the last frolic of my life'—meeting there, as he engagingly put it, 'many wise men of the south-east'. He contributed articles to Sir David Brewster's *Edinburgh Encyclopedia* and to other journals. Troughton never married. His friends described him as a modest man, frugal in habit and somewhat careless in dress, who found relaxation in walking and fishing. Reading was the great pleasure of his later years; his library, auctioned by Sothebys after his death, testified to a broad sweep of interests beyond those related to his craft.

By the early 1820s Troughton had come to rely on the support of William Simms (1793–1860) whom he described at that time as one of the best craftsmen known to him. In 1826 he took Simms into partnership; Simms and his wife moved into the Fleet Street house and cared for Troughton in his declining years as he grew more deaf and suffered from rheumatism and lumbago. He nevertheless continued to experiment at his workbench and to converse with customers. As Troughton and Simms the firm undertook the construction of major instruments for George Everest's trigonometrical survey of India and then embarked on Edward Troughton's last project, an equatorial telescope for South. It was an unhappy end to Troughton's distinguished career, for South overruled Troughton on the design and their arguments over this, and the telescope's subsequent disastrous performance, destroyed a long friendship and led to a lengthy court case which was still in progress when Troughton died on 12 June 1835. He was buried at Kensal Green cemetery. Among his bequests were sums to the London Vaccine

Institute and St Bride's parish school. The firm of Troughton and Simms continued in the hands of the Simms family, but with no members of the Troughton family being involved.
ANITA McCONNELL

Sources A. McConnell, *Instrument makers to the world: a history of Cooke, Troughton & Simms* (1992) · A. W. Skempton and J. Brown, 'John and Edward Troughton', *Notes and Records of the Royal Society*, 27 (1972–3), 233–62
Archives CUL, Board of Longitude and Board of Visitors MSS · CUL, Greenwich Royal Observatory MSS · Inst. CE, letters to Thomas Telford
Likenesses C. Hassler, sketch, c.1815 · F. Chantrey, bust, 1822, NMM, Greenwich Observatory · F. Chantrey, three pencil sketches, 1822, NPG · Imbert of New York, lithograph (after C. Hassler) · W. Walker and G. Zobel, group portrait, engraving (after J. F. Skill, J. Gilbert, W. and E. Walker, *Men of science living in 1807–8*), NPG

Troughton, John (c.1637–1681), nonconformist minister and religious controversialist, was born in Coventry, the son of Nathaniel Troughton, a clothier. A severe case of smallpox when he was four resulted in the permanent loss of his sight. Admitted to Merchant Taylors' School in 1642, he was later educated at King Henry VIII Grammar School, Coventry, under Samuel Frankland's tutelage. On 28 March 1655 he matriculated as a scholar from St John's College, Oxford. He graduated BA on 12 February 1659, and afterwards was elected to a fellowship. On 16 May 1662, however, he was deprived by the university visitors on account of his blindness, as well as for refusing to wear a surplice and refusing to attend the college chapel until the services were ended, and because he was suspected of corrupting the younger students with his nonconformity.

Troughton then moved to Bicester, where he lived as 'a moderate nonconformist, read academical learning to young men, and sometimes preached in private whereby he got a comfortable subsistence' (Wood, *Ath. Oxon.*, 4.9). Within a few years he married Rebecca, whose other name is unknown; they had two children, a son, John (1666–1739), and a daughter, Rebecca. Troughton was harassed by the authorities for his nonconformity, and in March 1670 was tried at Oxford assizes for unlawful assembly. Following the Act of Indulgence, on 13 April 1672 Troughton was licensed as a presbyterian both at Caversfield, just north of Bicester, and at his house in the town. He subsequently joined Henry Langley, Thomas Gilbert, and Henry Cornish as ministers to a congregation of nonconformists meeting in Thame Street, Oxford. In spite of his disability, he was considered a worthy preacher. After the indulgence was rescinded Troughton continued to style himself in his publications as a 'Minister of the Gospel' and retained the respect of many in the Church of England because of his learning and moderation.

Troughton became increasingly involved in the theological controversies of his day. As he explained in the first part of *Lutherus Redivivus, or, The Protestant Doctrine of Justification by Faith Onely, Vindicated* (published in two parts, 1677 and 1678), he wrote in direct challenge to certain 'Arminians' like Richard Baxter, who 'took Obedience into the condition of the New Covenant' as 'the best means to oppose the Antinomians' (sig. A2v), that is (as Troughton

saw it), laid too great an emphasis on human works and moral effort in the appropriation of salvation. Troughton singles out Baxter as having 'diffused this Doctrine through all his writings, though he is sometimes various in expressing his mind', and as 'having drest it up in more Scriptural language and made it look, and speak, as if it were very much for holiness', though 'it is no other than the old Popish Doctrine divested of the School-Terms' (p. 6, sig. A2v–3). Troughton also published *The Covenant Interest … of … Infants* (1675), *A Letter to a Friend, Touching on Gods Providence about Sinful Actions* (1678), *Popery the Grand Apostacy* (1680), and *An Apology for the Nonconformists* (1681). Baxter, who could not forget a critic, had harsh words for Troughton and his critique in the preface to his *Scripture Gospel Defended* (1690). Troughton's son, John, himself a dissenting minister, responded with a defence of his father in a letter to Baxter from Clapham, Surrey, on 12 March 1691.

Troughton signed his will on 27 July 1681. He died on 20 August 1681 in the parish of All Saints, Oxford, 'aged 44'. He was buried in Bicester parish church on 22 August. Abraham James, the blind headmaster of Woodstock grammar school, preached the funeral sermon.
J. WILLIAM BLACK

Sources *Calamy rev.*, 494 · Wood, *Ath. Oxon.*, new edn, 4.9–10 · Foster, *Alum. Oxon.* · *DNB* · R. Baxter, *Scripture gospel defended* (1691) · DWL, Baxter letters, MS 59, v, 57

Troughton, William (1613/14–1686×90), clergyman and ejected minister, was the son of William Troughton (b. 1584/5?), rector of Waberthwaite, Cumberland, although he once described Westmorland as his native county. He matriculated from Queen's College, Oxford, on 24 October 1634, aged twenty. There is no record of his having taken a degree, and nothing is known of him for the next thirteen years. In 1647 he was chaplain to Robert Hammond, governor of the Isle of Wight; Anthony Wood recorded that at Carisbrooke, where Charles I was then under arrest, Troughton 'would many times be in the presence chamber when his majesty was at dinner' and would 'argue notably in defence of some tenets he held in opposition to certain ceremonies and discipline in the episcopacy'. The king 'would pleasurably enter into disputation with him' and 'never check'd him' but 'would be very pleasant and merry with him' (Wood, *Ath. Oxon.*, 4.11–12). Edmund Ludlow cast light on the background to these light-hearted exchanges: Charles was 'extremely desirous' that the generals should reconsolidate their grip on the army, persuading Hammond to send 'Mr Traughton his chaplain to the army to persuade them to make use of their success against the Adjutators', and writing to Oliver Cromwell and Henry Ireton urging a speedy agreement. Charles sent his own servant Sir John Berkeley for discussions, but on the way, Berkeley 'met Mr Traughton on his return between Bagshot and Windsor, who acquainted him he had no good news to carry back to the king, the army having taken new resolutions touching his person' (*Memoirs of Edmund Ludlow*, 2.174–5). In June 1648 Troughton issued his *Saints in England under a Cloud*, with a preface to Fairfax, in which he criticized a 'slight spirited' body of men in the army who hold 'many heterodox and unsound opinions', of whom some 'live above ordinances'.

After this foray into politics Troughton returned briefly to obscurity, being admitted on 8 February 1649 as curate of Deerham, Gloucestershire. The following year, on 18 May, the committee of sequestrations ordered that he be paid £140 as rector of St Nicholas, Wanlip, Leicestershire. By this time he had married Sarah, whose other name is unknown; their sons William and John were baptized at Wanlip respectively on 4 November 1650 and 3 April 1652. Here and in nearby villages Troughton became embroiled in controversy with new opponents, the 'general' Baptists, who, however, numbered among their leaders Robert Everard, a former army agitator. On 3 March 1652 at Mountsorrel, Troughton preached a sermon against the Baptists, later published as *Scripture Redemption Restrayned and Limitted* (1652). He attacked the doctrine of general redemption, and his opponents' tendency not only to interrupt services and occupy pulpits, but also to impugn the ministers' right to seek protection from the civil power: thus 'they utterly overthrow the office and power of the magistrate' (preface). *The Declining State under Gospel Administrations* (1652) raised again the alarm sounded in *Saints in England under a Cloud* at the disenchantment with formal ordinances to be found among godly people. Some had been 'cast into a sleepy and languishing condition, and brought to a low ebb in their own sense and feeling'; others acted 'as if you onely did reign, and none were comparable to you, and yet (all this while) you walk proudly, and vainly, and whilst you boast of high attainments, you live much below God' (pp. 1, 20).

On 27 May 1653 Troughton was presented under the great seal to the rectory of St Martin's, Salisbury; Wood reports that he took an active part in suppressing the rebellion led by John Penruddock in that city on 11 March 1655. *The Mystery of the Marriage Song* (1656), signed from Salisbury on 22 April 1656, was dedicated to two pillars of the Cromwellian establishment, Charles Fleetwood and William Steele, and their respective 'virtuous ladies'. Troughton was ejected in 1660 and a successor was instituted on 7 August 1661, though Troughton is reported to have continued at Salisbury, preaching as a congregationalist. He was suspected of involvement in the Tong plot. It was reported from Carlisle that letters from 'William Troughton of Lond' had been intercepted 'bearing postscripts in strange characters' (Greaves, 250). Later that year Troughton moved to Bristol. He was there twelve years later, though his congregation was then described as the smallest and least influential of six then active in the city, comprising 'about twenty, and not fixed to one place … having some honourable women of note amongst them, but few men; they were more obscure' (Hayden, 145).

It may be that the poor state of his congregation was behind Troughton's removal to London, also in 1674. But he seems to have returned to Bristol, for on 26 April 1681 he was presented at the quarter sessions as one of a group of nonconformist preachers there. He was living in London when he signed his will on 13 May 1686, but he bequeathed to his wife property in Bristol valued at £600 in 1695. His widow was granted probate on 8 January 1690. Their three daughters—Sarah Sherwill, Mary Sterne, and Elizabeth Lee—were still living when Sarah Troughton made her will between 25 June 1695 and 27 August 1698; she had died by 9 May 1699, when it was proved.

STEPHEN WRIGHT

Sources *Calamy rev.*, 494 · *The memoirs of Edmund Ludlow*, ed. C. H. Firth, 2 vols. (1894) · Wood, *Ath. Oxon.*, new edn, 4.507 · R. Hayden, ed., *The records of a church in Christ in Bristol, 1640–1687*, Bristol RS, 27 (1974) · will, PRO, PROB 11/398, sig. 12 · PRO, PROB 11/450 [will of Sarah Troughton], sig. 83 · R. L. Greaves, *Deliver us from evil: the radical underground in Britain, 1660–1663* (1986) · W. Troughton, *The mystery of the marriage song* (1656), foreword · IGI [St Nicholas Wanlip parish register]
Wealth at death property in Bristol worth £600: will, PRO, PROB 11/398, sig. 12; PRO, PROB 11/450, sig. 83 [will of Sarah Troughton]

Troup, Sir Charles Edward (1857–1941), civil servant, was born on 27 March 1857 at Bogie Street, Huntly, Aberdeenshire, the eldest son of the Revd Robert Troup, minister of the Independent church, and his wife, Margaret (*née* Macdonald). He was educated at a parish school, at Aberdeen University, whence he graduated MA with a first-class degree in mental philosophy, and at Oxford University, where he matriculated as an exhibitioner at Balliol College in January 1880, and graduated BA in 1883. In his final year at Oxford he won the Cobden prize of £20 and a silver medal for an essay entitled 'In what respects on purely economic grounds is the further application of a free trade policy required in the legislation of this country'. In 1884 this was published as *Future of Free Trade*.

Troup joined the Home Office as a junior clerk in the criminal department in October 1880. He was the first such recruit to be selected through open competition. Though he soon assumed responsibility within the department, his promotion was at first slow. Not until 1886 was he appointed senior clerk, even though he had for some time been performing the duties of a senior clerk. In 1887 he joined the newly created parliamentary branch within the general department, and became responsible for monitoring and evaluating parliamentary bills relating to Home Office business. Troup was called to the bar at the Middle Temple in 1888 and though he never practised law, he developed a 'passion' for the legal work of the Home Office (Petrow, 29). As editor of the judicial statistics of England and Wales between 1893 and 1904, he did much to reform the collation and analysis of Home Office statistics. Under his influence the judicial statistics changed from being among the worst in Europe to among the best. In 1893–4 he chaired a Home Office committee on the identification of habitual criminals, which recommended using photographs, fingerprints, and anthropometric data to assist the identification of convicts and repeat offenders. In 1896 he became principal clerk in the new industrial and parliamentary department. As such, he was responsible for factories and workshops, mines and quarries, and a substantial statistics sub-branch.

Shortly after his promotion Troup married, on 2 January

Sir Charles Edward Troup (1857–1941), by Walter Stoneman, 1920

1897, Winifred Louisa Macdonald, youngest daughter of the poet and novelist Dr George Macdonald and a relative of Troup's mother. They had no children. In 1902 he chaired the departmental committee on cremation that drafted regulations under the Cremation Act. In the following year he was appointed assistant under-secretary, in which position he was responsible for police and criminal work. He took a special interest in these aspects of Home Office business while permanent under-secretary between 1908 and 1922. He played an important part in settling the police strikes of 1918–19; when serious unrest within the metropolitan force developed during August 1918, however, he was absent from the Home Office on a walking holiday in Berkshire. In a display either of the 'ultra-calm' for which he was renowned, or of folly bordering on the negligent, he ignored repeated pleas to return to London to take charge, and returned only on 30 August, by which time the strike was almost solid. As permanent under-secretary he sat on two royal commissions. During the First World War, Troup had important responsibilities on the home front, and was on the departmental committee responsible for enforcing regulations under the Defence of the Realm Act. He was made CB (civil) in 1897, KCB in 1909, and KCVO in 1918. The University of Aberdeen awarded him an honorary LLD in 1912.

Troup, a man of 'rugged Scottish countenance' (Butler, 110), was 'probably the most capable' of those who joined the Home Office with the advent of competitive entry

(Pellew, 42). A contemporary praised him as a 'selfless worker' whose minutes were 'models of exactitude, lucidity, and precision' (Redmayne, 139). Efficient, intellectually able, and personally confident, Troup was a civil servant of 'manifold talents' (Radzinowicz and Hood, 106). As Troup's obituary in *The Times* (26 September 1941) pointed out, he was a civil servant 'of exceptional character and ability, to whom the public of his day owed much and of whom, largely through his own modesty, it knew little'. Given the unrest from suffragettes and militant trade unionism, the Home Office, never an easy department to handle, went through a period of special difficulty while Troup was permanent under-secretary. His influence was crucial in extending Home Office authority over local police authorities and in co-ordinating police powers to cope with industrial unrest. In December 1919 he shrewdly told General McCready that in the next strike special constables would be appointed, so that the military could be held in reserve, commenting that 'the one thing to avoid is the appearance of setting labour and the middle classes against one another' (Morgan, 94). He had scant respect for the idle time-servers who dominated the Home Office clerkships at the time of his appointment. Unlike this older generation of clerks, all too ready to shirk responsibility, he was eager to expand the Home Office's responsibilities and workload and to take on burdensome and complex work. He also recognized the importance of the personal touch, maintaining close contact with his staff and scrupulous in keeping their work up to standard. His one possible flaw as a civil servant was a certain narrowness of vision—related, perhaps, to his inexperience outside the world of bureaucracy.

After he retired from the civil service, Troup published a respected volume on the Home Office in the Whitehall series (1925). He found a new career as treasurer of King's College, London (1922–39), and served on several public bodies, chairing the tribunal on the Royal Irish Constabulary (1922–3), the Safety in Mines Research Board (1923–39), and the Ministry of Pensions' special grants committee (1929–38). He died from arterio-sclerosis at his home, 13 Addison Road, Kensington, London, on 8 July 1941 and was cremated at Golders Green on 10 July. His wife survived him.   P. W. J. BARTRIP

Sources *The Times* (9 July 1941) · *WWW*, 1941–50 · J. Pellew, *The home office, 1848–1914* (1982) · *Aberdeen University Review*, 29 (1941–2), 82–3 · I. Elliott, ed., *The Balliol College register, 1833–1933*, 2nd edn (privately printed, Oxford, 1934) · H. B. Butler, *Confident morning* (1950) · *Oxford historical register, 1220–1900* (1900) · R. E. Squire, *Thirty years in the public service* (1927) · A. S. Redmayne, *Men, mines and memories* (1942) · G. W. Reynolds and A. Judge, *The night the police went on strike* (1968) · L. Radzinowicz and R. Hood, *A history of English criminal law and its administration from 1750*, 5: *The emergence of penal policy in Victorian and Edwardian England* (1986) · S. Petrow, *Policing morals: the Metropolitan Police and the home office, 1870–1914* (1994) · J. Morgan, *Conflict and order: the police and labour disputes in England and Wales, 1900–1939* (1987) · b. cert. · d. cert. · *The Times* (11 July 1941)

Archives HMC, Troup and Ross of Huntly family papers | BL, corresp. with Lord Gladstone, Add. MS 45993 · King's Lond., papers relating to King's College, London · PRO, Home Office papers

Wealth at death £22,902 13s. 11d.: probate, 22 Sept 1941, *CGPLA Eng. & Wales*

Troup, Robert Scott (1874–1939), forestry scientist, was born at Neithrop, near Banbury, Oxfordshire, on 13 December 1874, the second son of James Troup, consul-general at Yokohama, and his wife, Hannah Scott. Educated at the Gymnasium, Grammar School, and University of Aberdeen, he entered the Royal Indian Engineering College at Coopers Hill, Surrey, in 1894 to train for the Indian forest service. Easily top of the course, he was posted to Burma in 1897. As a relatively junior officer he was given charge of the important Tharrawaddy division, where he contributed much towards the technical advance in the raising and management of teak forests.

In 1901, Troup married Elizabeth Campbell, elder daughter of John Mortimer, an Aberdeen merchant. They had two daughters and a son. When the Imperial Forest Research Institute was founded at Dehra Dun, India, in 1906, Troup became a forest economist and spent two fruitful years collecting and publishing information on the utilization of timbers and other forest products. He then changed to the study of Indian silviculture, his special interest, and became the acknowledged leading authority. He travelled extensively in India and Burma. His experiments on many forest problems, particularly on the growth and regeneration of the main tree species, marked the introduction into India of systematic research in these subjects, while his detailed observations, supplemented by his experiments in the provinces and in Dehra, ultimately appeared in 1921 as his most important publication, the three volumes on the *Silviculture of Indian Trees*. Troup did not publish much statistical work, as the measurement plots which he initiated could yield the desired growth data only after a considerable time, but many later studies were in part based on his plots and methods and would have been considerably delayed without them.

In 1915 Troup left Dehra to become assistant inspector-general of forests to the Indian government, serving with George Hart, and in 1917 he was appointed war controller of timber supplies to the Indian munitions board, a post which he held until February 1918. His services to India were recognized in 1920 by his appointment as CIE.

On the retirement of Sir William Schlich from the Oxford chair of forestry in 1920, Troup was elected professor and became a fellow of St John's College. The recruitment of forest officers had ceased during the war and Troup's task was to train new officers quickly in the principles and technical practices of forestry. He took a leading part in successive Empire Forest Conferences in London (1920), Canada (1923), Australia (1928), and South Africa (1935), as well as in the International Forest Congress at Rome (1926) and at Budapest (1936). Largely on account of his representations, the Imperial Forestry Institute was founded at Oxford in 1924 for higher studies and research in forestry. Being professor of forestry, Troup was its first director until a separate post was established

at the beginning of 1936. Even then, he retained administrative control.

Troup was elected FRS in 1926. His specialized knowledge and experience of tropical forestry did not preclude a keen interest in British and temperate forestry. He published *Silvicultural Systems*, a standard text, in 1928 and worked on a more problematic topic, publishing *Forestry and State Control* in 1938. He gave courses to probationers of the colonial administrative service at both Oxford and Cambridge and his lectures were published posthumously in *Colonial Forest Administration* (1940). He visited several colonies to examine the forest position and problems, and his reports on Kenya and Uganda (1922), Cyprus (1930), and Tanganyika (1935) are important historical documents. For this work he was appointed CMG in 1934. He died at his home, 35 St Margaret's Road, Oxford, on 1 October 1939, a few months before he was due to retire as professor of forestry; his wife survived him.

A man of his time, Troup was 'a keen observer of jungle lore and a good big game shot' (*Obits. FRS*, 219). At Oxford, ice skating replaced game hunting as his preferred sport. He is remembered as a pre-eminent silviculturist; the greatest exponent of scientific forestry in his day, whose valued advice and assistance was freely given with quiet and unassuming kindness.

H. G. CHAMPION, *rev.* DAVID E. EVANS

Sources E. P. Stebbing, *Obits. FRS*, 3 (1939–41), 217–19 · *Empire Forestry Journal*, 18 (Dec 1939), 187–9 · *CGPLA Eng. & Wales* (1939)
Likenesses P. A. Hey, oils, 1932, U. Oxf., Forestry Institute · photograph, repro. in Stebbing, *Obits. FRS*
Wealth at death £4951 14s. 7d.: probate, 24 Nov 1939, *CGPLA Eng. & Wales*

Troutbeck, Sir John Monro (1894–1971), diplomatist, was born on 2 November 1894 at 43 Grosvenor Road, Westminster, the younger son and second of the three surviving children of John Troutbeck (1860–1912), coroner for Westminster, and his wife, Harriet Elizabeth, second daughter of Henry Monro, of Craiglockhart, Edinburgh. His grandfather was the Revd Dr John Troutbeck (1832–1899), canon of Westminster Abbey. After attending Westminster School, Troutbeck entered Christ Church, Oxford, as a scholar in 1913, but his studies were interrupted by military service (1914–19) in Queen Victoria's Rifles and the County of London regiment. He was aide-de-camp to his uncle, General Sir Charles Monro, in France, at Gallipoli, and in India. Appointed OBE shortly after demobilization, he returned to Oxford and completed the war-shortened course in modern history, taking his BA in 1922 and MA in 1929. In November 1920 he joined the Foreign Office as a third secretary in the central department, which supervised relations with central Europe from Germany to Greece. His marriage to Katherine Morley, aged twenty-eight, only daughter of William Morley, a London merchant, took place on 4 October 1924. They had two daughters, Mary (1926–1954) and Clare (*b.* 1929).

Jack Troutbeck had seven years' experience of foreign affairs by the time of his first overseas posting, in September 1927, as second secretary at Constantinople. Relations between Turkey and Britain were at last improving after resolution of the Mosul border dispute. Transferred to Addis Ababa in February 1930 with the rank of first secretary from March, he saw the coronation of Emperor Haile Selassie and the start of Ethiopia's modernization. From December 1931 he spent a year at the College of Imperial Defence before serving under Sir William Seeds as first secretary in Rio de Janeiro. Returning to the Foreign Office at the close of 1934, Troutbeck then worked in the American department until sent to the Prague legation in October 1937, again as first secretary. He assisted Basil Newton, the minister, in conveying to the Czechs just how little support they could expect from Great Britain with regard to the Sudetenland. After the Munich agreement he remained in the country as chargé d'affaires until May 1939, witnessing its disintegration and the German invasion. This made him quick to condemn thereafter any policy that might be construed as appeasement. He became a CMG in January 1939 and was promoted to acting counsellor in October that year.

Apart from three months in summer 1940, Troutbeck spent the first four years of the Second World War on secondment from the Foreign Office to the Ministry of Economic Warfare, where he headed a department after attaining the grade of acting principal assistant secretary in January 1942. His emergence as a significant figure in foreign policy making dated from October 1943, when he became the adviser on Germany, co-ordinating planning for the occupation and peace settlement. This in turn led to his appointment as head of the German department of the Foreign Office in spring 1945 and as an assistant under-secretary in June 1946. Hence Troutbeck was much involved in the complex evolution of British thinking on the German question from Draconian early schemes to reduce the birth-rate to later programmes for economic regeneration in the western occupied zones. Though inclined to think that Nazism sprang from deep within German culture, he argued from 1945 that a harsh peace would aid Soviet plans for a communist take-over in Germany.

Troutbeck impressed Ernest Bevin, who chose him to succeed Arnold Overton as head of the British Middle East office (BMEO), located in Cairo, in November 1947. The original purpose of the BMEO, set up in 1945, was to organize economic assistance for lands within the British sphere of influence (on the supposition that material progress would neutralize political unrest). However, the British simply could not afford to finance major development schemes, and Troutbeck in any case thought Arabs too feckless to make the most of economic potential. Essential to stability, in his view, was a settlement of the Palestine problem, so he concentrated on the political function of the BMEO, analysing intelligence and advising on regional strategy. Sir John Troutbeck KCMG—as he became in June 1948—vigorously upheld the justice of the Arab cause in respect of Palestine. The Zionists in his eyes appeared aggressive and unscrupulous; Israel promised to be inherently expansionist and a challenge to British interests. It dismayed him that the USA could be so irresponsible as to back a 'gangster' state. As a realist, however, he accepted that Britain would eventually have to recognize Israel. He joined in secret talks with the United Nations mediator Folke Bernadotte in September 1948, and continued to advocate territorial exchanges and even-handed Anglo-American guarantees of Arab–Israeli borders as the best solution. Britain in the meantime should arm the Arab states and promote Arab unity under its auspices, giving priority to Egypt as the strategic hub of the region. Compared with other British officials, Troutbeck was less hostile to the Arab League and more critical of Jordan.

After leaving the BMEO in November 1950, Troutbeck became ambassador in Baghdad in March 1951. Iraq, though nominally independent since 1932, remained a British client state—all too obviously so. An unimposing man, with thin grey hair and a close-trimmed moustache, Troutbeck attempted to efface himself in public in deference to nationalist opinion. When rioters threatened the embassy in December 1952, he wrily observed, 'Our prestige has become dangerously high again!' (Parsons, 19). Politics in Iraq consisted of palace intrigues, rigged elections, and uprisings. The ruling clique was old-fashioned, corrupt, and embarrassingly pro-British. Troutbeck, alert to the possibility of revolution, tried to accelerate social and economic reforms, but the younger, more progressive politicians were precisely those most likely to resent British interference. Although still committed to British supremacy in the Middle East, he began to perceive the reality of Arab nationalism. Continued reliance on Nuri al-Said, the veteran political 'boss' of Iraq, seemed inescapable if Britain wished to retain its two air bases in the country, yet it offered no long-term assurance.

Troutbeck, who was well-liked by his staff, retired with a GBE in January 1955, vacating the residency by the Tigris for 28 The Causeway, Horsham, Sussex. He served on the Saar referendum commission in 1955 and was chairman of the Save the Children Fund from 1956 to 1962. The Suez crisis (1956) and the Iraqi revolution (1958) distressed him deeply. He died at his home in Horsham of a coronary thrombosis on 28 September 1971, survived by his wife, and younger daughter. As a diplomatist he had never been especially prominent in the public eye. Once the archives were opened, however, his bold and thoughtful contributions to crucial policy debates attracted the attention of historians.

JASON TOMES

Sources W. R. Louis, *The British empire in the Middle East* (1984) · W. K. Wark, 'Development diplomacy: Sir John Troutbeck and the British Middle East office, 1947–50', *British officials and British foreign policy, 1945–50*, ed. J. Zametica (1990), 228–49 · R. Fernea and W. R. Louis, eds., *The Iraqi revolution of 1958* (1991) · P. Kingston, *Britain and the politics of modernization in the Middle East, 1945–1958* (1996) · V. Rothwell, *Britain and the cold war, 1941–1947* (1982) · A. Parsons, *They say the lion* (1986) · 'Sir John Troutbeck', *Iraq*, 34 (1972), 1 · M. Elliot, 'Independent Iraq': the monarchy and British influence, 1941–1958* (1996) · *The Times* (9 Oct 1971) · A. Deighton, *The impossible peace: Britain, the division of Germany, and the origins of the cold war* (1993) · *WWW* · Burke, *Peerage* · *FO List* (–1955) · b. cert. · m. cert. · d. cert.

Archives PRO, general corresp., FO 371 · PRO, British Middle East Office, FO 957

Likenesses photograph, repro. in 'Sir John Troutbeck', *Iraq*, frontispiece

Wealth at death £80,283: probate, 15 Dec 1971, *CGPLA Eng. & Wales*

Trouton, Frederick Thomas (1863–1922), experimental physicist, was born on 24 November 1863 in Dublin, the youngest son of Thomas Trouton. He was educated at Dungannon Royal School, Tyrone, and Trinity College, Dublin, where he studied both physics and engineering. He graduated first senior moderator (equivalent to wrangler) in experimental science, receiving the degrees of MA and DSc; he was awarded the large gold medal in his year, a rare distinction for a science student. Before graduating he undertook surveying for a railway and original research in physical chemistry, formulating Trouton's law; this approximate rule expresses a relation between the molecular latent heats and boiling points of various substances. Following graduation in 1884 he became assistant to the professor of experimental physics, George Francis FitzGerald (*d*. 1901) who became a cherished friend and colleague. On 28 June 1887 he married Anne Maria (*b*. 1864/5), daughter of George Fowler, a Liverpool merchant; they had four sons and three daughters. Their two eldest boys—Eric, a student of physics, and Desmond, an engineering student—were killed in the First World War.

In 1901 Trouton became lecturer in experimental physics, taking over FitzGerald's laboratory, but the following year accepted an appointment as Quain professor of physics at University College, London. He held this post until 1914 when disability compelled him to relinquish it while retaining the title of emeritus professor. Trouton played a leading role in establishing the common electromagnetic nature of light and Hertzian waves. His investigation to test the accuracy of Ohm's law for electrolytes (1886–88) was inspired by FitzGerald with whom he undertook replication of Hertz's work on electromagnetic-wave radiation in 1888. Trouton collaborated with FitzGerald in investigating reflection from substances such as glass and paraffin, and they succeeded in deciding the relation between the direction of vibration in the wave front and the plane of polarization. Trouton also demonstrated a quarter-wave phase change in electromagnetic reflection.

Between 1900 and 1908 Trouton pursued FitzGerald's ideas on the relative motion of the earth and the hypothetical ether. An experiment to discover the mechanical effect of charging a condenser moving in the plane of its plates through the ether gave a negative result. In 1901 Trouton collaborated with Joseph Larmor, who sought experimental evidence against the existence of second order effects of the earth's motion. Trouton's first work at University College was to undertake with H. R. Noble an improved form of the condenser experiment. A later experiment, done in collaboration with A. O. Rankine, was designed to detect the FitzGerald shrinkage, which involved comparing the electrical resistance of a wire when moving in and across the ether stream. The negative result, coupled with earlier disappointments, served as a major setback to his vision of a new source of energy. In fact, Trouton's results accord with the theory of relativity, for which they later offered important evidence.

With E. S. Andrews, Trouton investigated the viscosity of quasi-solids and made a test of Stokes's theory following, by means of X-rays striking a fluorescent screen, the rate of fall (1.8 cm/fortnight) of a ball-bearing through a block of wax. Trouton was the originator of this method for the examination of opaque media. In Dublin he had commenced research on the adsorption of water vapour by various substances in order to construct a recording hygrometer based either on change of weight or of electrical resistance. In London he followed up this work and supervised a long series of investigations on adsorption. In all Trouton published about forty papers—a number of them jointly with collaborators. In 1897 he was elected a fellow of the Royal Society and in 1914 was selected as president of section A for the Australian meeting of the British Association; serious illness however prevented him travelling and delivering his presidential address.

In Ireland, Trouton lived at Killiney, co. Dublin, and in London at Hampstead; in retirement he lived at Tilford in Surrey and later at The Rookery, Downe, Kent. A severe illness suffered in 1912 led to prolonged prostration; an operation in 1914 resulted in paralysis of the lower limbs and total invalidity but he retained his mental faculties unimpaired. He died peacefully at Downe on 21 September 1922; his wife and five children survived him. Integrity, a lively imagination, friendliness, and helpfulness, but also a certain whimsicality were recorded as character traits. In physics he was attributed with particular insight into the provisional character of theory and recognition of the importance of experimental research, especially with a view to utilitarian or engineering benefits.

JAMES G. O'HARA

Sources A. W. P. [A. W. Porter], *PRS*, 110A (1926), iv–ix · *Nature*, 110 (1922), 490–91 · *Men and women of the time* (1899) · H. H. Stephenson, *Who's who in science (international)* (1913) · E. S. Barr, 'Trouton, Friedrick Thomas, 1863–1922', *American Journal of Physics*, 31 (1963), 85–6 · A. Warwick, 'The sturdy protestants of science: Larmor, Trouton, and the earth's motion through the ether', *Scientific practice: theories and stories of doing physics*, ed. J. Z. Buchwald (1995), 300–43 · J. G. O'Hara and W. Pricha, *Hertz and the Maxwellians* (1987) · m. cert. · d. cert. · *CGPLA Eng. & Wales* (1922)

Likenesses engraving, RS; repro. in A. W. P., 'Frederick Thomas Trouton', *PRS*

Wealth at death £3673 16*s*. 3*d*.: probate, 21 Nov 1922, *CGPLA Eng. & Wales*

Trow, Edward (1833–1899), ironworker and trade unionist, was born at Wolverhampton on 29 June 1833, the son of an ironworker. He attended a dame-school in nearby Wednesbury for a few years and at the age of ten entered the iron industry. At thirteen he became an underhand puddler and followed this occupation in a number of places, including Glasgow and Consett, for about fifteen years. By 1863 he had returned to the Black Country and became a lodge secretary in the local puddlers' union which was formed in that year. He held his position until 1867, when he moved to work as a forehand puddler at the Springfield works of Barningham & Co. in Darlington, co. Durham.

The north of England was the preserve of a rival union, the National Association of Ironworkers led by John Kane, but Trow apparently had no qualms about changing his allegiance: perhaps his long absence from the area had softened the local chauvinism characteristic of Black Country people. He joined the northern union's Springfield lodge and was promptly appointed its secretary. When the National Association was reconstituted as the ironworkers' only union in 1868, following the collapse of organization in the Black Country, Trow was elected to the general council. Four years later he became president and assistant secretary and held both offices until 1874. He then relinquished the presidency and took over the combined and paid position of assistant secretary and treasurer.

When Kane died in 1876 Trow succeeded him as general secretary of the union at a salary of £160 per year. He held this post until the National Association was superseded by the Associated Iron and Steel Workers in 1887. He then became general secretary of the new union and remained in this position until his death. Under his leadership the internal friction which had carried over from the regional origins of unionism into the successive national associations was progressively eliminated and his successor, James Cox, took over an organization which was largely free of sectional conflict.

Trow also succeeded Kane as the paid secretary to the workmen's panel of the board of arbitration and conciliation for the manufactured iron trade of the north of England. The success of the board confirmed his belief that industrial relations should be organized on a purely voluntary basis. He said as much in his evidence to the royal commission on labour in 1892, when he dismissed suggestions that the board might consider using statutory arbitration. He was also a member of the commission and his manner of questioning indicated a strong commitment to bringing the two sides of industry closer together. This led him to join Sir David Dale, the chairman of the commission and of the north of England board, in efforts to establish a union of employers and employed. The proposed union was formally constituted in 1895 but it attracted little support and was quickly abandoned.

The political concomitant of these industrial attitudes was 'Lib-Labism' and Trow was vice-president of Darlington Liberal Association for many years. His influence among working men was an important factor in holding Darlington for the Gladstonian candidate in the closely contested elections of 1886 and 1892 but Trow never had any political ambitions himself. He was a trustee of the Sons of Temperance Society and a member of the Darlington school board and served as a magistrate from 1892 but otherwise devoted himself exclusively to his union work. Trow's single-minded dedication to his members' interests was acknowledged by gifts from several groups of ironworkers over the years; he also received tributes from foreign trade union delegations to whom he gave advice and assistance.

Trow died suddenly on 9 February 1899 at his home, 6 Paradise Terrace, Darlington. He was survived by his second wife, Mary, née Batty, and a grown-up family. He was buried in the west cemetery, Darlington, on 14 February 1899, following a service in the cemetery chapel.

ERIC TAYLOR

Sources *Ironworkers' Journal* (1869–99) [esp. March 1899] · *Northern Echo* (10 Feb 1899) · *Darlington and Stockton Times* (11 Feb 1899) · *Sheffield and Rotherham Independent* (11 Feb 1899) · 'Royal commission on labour: group a: mining, iron, engineering, and hardware', *Parl. papers* (1892), 36/1.330–47, C. 6795-IV · J. H. Porter, 'David Dale and conciliation in the northern manufactured iron trade, 1869–1914', *Northern History*, 5 (1970), 157–71 · J. H. Porter, 'Wage bargaining under conciliation agreements, 1860–1914', *Economic History Review*, 2nd ser., 23 (1970), 460–75 · E. Taylor, 'Trow, Edward', *DLB*, vol. 3 · A. J. Odber, 'The origins of industrial peace: the manufactured iron trade of the north of England', *Oxford Economic Papers*, 3 (1951), 202–20 · H. A. Clegg, A. Fox, and A. F. Thompson, *A history of British trade unions since 1889*, 1 (1964) · A. Pugh, *Men of steel, by one of them: a chronicle of eighty-eight years of trade unionism in the British iron and steel industry* (1951) · J. C. Carr and W. Taplin, *History of the British steel industry* (1962) · A. Birch, *The economic history of the British iron and steel industry, 1784–1879* (1967) · W. J. Ashley, *The adjustment of wages* (1903) · d. cert. · *CGPLA Eng. & Wales* (1899)

Wealth at death £819 5s. 0d.: administration with will, 2 March 1899, *CGPLA Eng. & Wales*

Trowbridge Martyr, the. *See* Helliker, Thomas (1783–1803).

Troy, John Thomas (1739–1823), Roman Catholic archbishop of Dublin, was born on 12 July 1739 at Porterstown, near Dublin, the eldest son of James Troy (d. 1791), a merchant in the city, and his wife, Mary Neville. In 1755 he joined the Dominican order and left Dublin to pursue his studies at the convent of San Clemente, Rome. Having been ordained to the priesthood in 1762 he remained in Rome and served as prior of San Clemente from 1772 until his appointment as bishop of Ossory in 1776, in succession to his fellow Dominican Thomas Burke, for whom he had acted as Roman agent.

Following his consecration at Louvain, Troy's return to Ireland marked the real beginning of the revival of Irish Catholicism following the dislocation of the penal era. From the outset he enjoyed the confidence of the Holy See; Valentine Bodkin, Roman agent of the archbishop of Cashel, believed that Troy had been chosen by Congregatio de Propaganda Fide to 'execute the commands of the Sacred Congregation at all times and to give them the requisite information' from Ireland (V. Bodkin to J. Butler, 24 June 1789, correspondence of James Butler II). Troy's adherence to this mandate was absolute, and he immediately accepted an appointment as vicar apostolic to arbitrate in a longstanding dispute between the archbishop of Armagh, Anthony Blake, and his clergy. Never solely a 'Roman hack' Troy was far more than an efficient functionary or bureaucrat. He was above all a conscientious pastor hailed by a suffragan as 'the pattern of the flock and all things to all men' (James Caulfield to *propaganda fide*, December 1786, Peel, 14).

Troy spearheaded the renewal of the Catholic church in Ireland. His priority was the improvement of clerical discipline and religious practice, and this he pursued through regular diocesan visitations and monthly clerical conferences. These efforts intensified on his translation to the archdiocese of Dublin in 1786, following the death of John Carpenter. Comprehensive pastoral instructions were published in November 1787: times of worship were regulated; priests were instructed to preach, promote the Easter duty, and encourage confession, communion, and almsgiving. Never slow to assert his authority, Troy excommunicated Robert McEvoy, a priest of the diocese, in 1792 for taking a wife. In 1814 he took the Dublin grand jury to court in a successful attempt to overturn its appointment of an incompetent chaplain to Newgate prison.

While Troy was confident of the religious enthusiasm of the people he was concerned at its heterodox expression. A perennial anxiety was the popular celebration of festivals and 'patterns' (saints' days), since the religious observances were generally a prelude to more secular, often riotous festivities. In Ossory, Troy attempted to abolish patterns and May balls, and in Dublin one of his first acts was the condemnation of the notorious midsummer festival at Kilmainham. He identified the need for effective catechesis and relied upon the Confraternity of the Christian Doctrine, which he promoted to assist him in this task; by the time of his death, in 1823, there was a confraternity in every parish. He was equally determined to regulate marriages, and in 1789 formally excommunicated 'couple-beggars' (poor clergy who celebrated clandestine marriages) and the contracting parties in illicit marriages.

Politically Troy has been represented as a reactionary at odds with the legitimate ambitions of his people. Though castigated by the United Irishman Theobald Wolfe Tone as a 'great scoundrel' (Keogh, 'The pattern of the flock', 217), Troy was never simply a loyalist. His principal concern was the welfare of the Catholic church in Ireland, and he shared the desire of the laity for repeal of the penal laws. At the Catholic convention in December 1792 he boldly announced his determination to rise or fall with the people of Ireland, declaring that the bishops were 'second to no description of Catholic [in the demand for] their emancipation' (J. Troy to T. Bray, correspondence of Thomas Bray). Throughout Troy followed the advice of Edmund Burke, political mentor of the episcopate who counselled Irish Catholics to show themselves dutiful subjects to the crown and to 'intermeddle as little as possible with the parties that divide the state' (E. Burke to J. Curry, 14 Aug 1779, *Correspondence*, 4.119). Troy believed that successive relief measures, commencing with Gardiner's first act of 1778, had been granted not from any acknowledgement of the natural rights of Catholics but from a combination of expediency and administrative benevolence, and could therefore be repealed in the event of unrest. From this perspective he relentlessly stressed the Christian duties of deference and unwavering obedience to the crown; accordingly he excommunicated a succession of protest groups, beginning with the Whiteboys, in 1779, and the Rightboys in the following decade.

In the 1790s Troy's task proved more formidable and neither his opposition to the radicalism of the Catholic Committee nor his excommunication in turn of Defenders and United Irishmen arrested the advance of the 'French disease'. While he privately communicated his concern at the injustice and persecution suffered by his people to Dublin Castle his repeated public exhortations to loyalty confirmed notions of 'his pious alliance' with the authorities. In 1795, too, his acceptance of an annual endowment of £8000 from the crown towards the establishment of St Patrick's College at Maynooth incensed the laity, who saw it as a cynical sop for the failure of Grattan's Catholic Relief Bill and an attempt by the authorities to detach the clergy from radical politics. Once more, in 1798, the archbishop excommunicated the rebels, thus sending a man 'to the devil for loving his country' (*Irish Magazine*, March 1815).

In the aftermath of the 1798 rising Troy was placed in the invidious position of rescuing the Catholic cause from the débâcle of 1798 and the bitter anti-Catholic onslaught that followed. Compromised by the prominence of clerics among the United Irishmen, he acquiesced in the passage of the Act of Union, accepting Pitt's intimation that a union would open the way to Catholic emancipation, which was barred by the protestant ascendancy in Ireland. Similarly Troy was forced to concede a limited crown veto on episcopal appointments, a decision that dogged the last years of his life.

By the turn of the nineteenth century the archdiocese had been brought firmly into line with Roman practice. In 1809, in consequence of Troy's ill health, Rome appointed Daniel Murray to serve as his coadjutor and chosen successor. This successful partnership produced a more sophisticated development, reflected in increased institutionalization and a flowering of religious life. In education the 'hedge schools' of the penal era increasingly gave way to the parochial schools, which in time would form the basis of the national school system. Chapel building, too, was a feature of the period and Troy's ambitious plan for the erection of a cathedral was realized in April 1815, when he laid the foundation stone for his impressive metropolitan chapel in Marlborough Street; in the style of the Greek revival, it is one of Dublin's most architecturally ambitious buildings. He remained Rome's most trusted adviser in Ireland; his opinion carried sway in the selection of bishops, not only for Ireland but also for England and North America, until his death.

Troy died in Dublin on 11 May 1823 and was interred in Georges Hill Chapel on 15 May; his remains were transferred to St Mary's Pro-Cathedral in Dublin in May 1824. Daniel O'Connell paid fitting tribute:

> in the sentiments of purest religion … he was a charitable man and never known to refuse giving what he could to a person in distress. He governed the Catholic Church in Ireland in a stormy period and was very much loved by his own clergy. (25 May 1823, *Correspondence of Daniel O'Connell*, 2.447)

DÁIRE KEOGH

Sources D. Keogh, *The French disease: the Catholic church and radicalism in Ireland, 1790–1800* (Dublin, 1993) · D. Keogh, 'The pattern of the flock: John Thomas Troy, 1786–1823', *History of the Catholic diocese of Dublin*, ed. D. Keogh and J. Kelly (Dublin, 2000), 215–37 · H. Peel, 'The appointment of Dr Troy to the see of Dublin', *Repertorium Novum*, 4/1 (1965), 5–16 · P. O'Donoghue, 'John Thomas Troy, archbishop of Dublin, 1786–1823: a man of his times', *Dublin and Dubliners*, ed. J. Kelly and U. MacGearailt (Dublin, 1999), 25–35 · M. McCarthy, 'Dublin's Greek pro-cathedral', *History of the Catholic diocese of Dublin*, ed. D. Keogh and J. Kelly (Dublin, 2000), 237–46 · V. J. McNally, *Reform, revolution and reaction: Archbishop John Thomas Troy and the Catholic church in Ireland, 1787–1817* (1995) · *The correspondence of Daniel O'Connell*, ed. M. R. O'Connell, 8 vols., IMC (1972–80) · *The correspondence of Edmund Burke*, ed. T. W. Copeland and others, 10 vols. (1958–78) · corresp. of J. Butler II, Cashel Roman Catholic diocesan archives · corresp. of T. Bray, Cashel Roman Catholic diocesan archives · corresp. and papers of J. T. Troy, Dublin Roman Catholic diocesan archives

Archives Roman Catholic diocesan archives, Dublin, corresp. and papers | Baltimore diocesan archives, corresp. with Carroll · Cashel Roman Catholic diocesan archives, corresp. with Bray · Hunt. L., letters to C. O'Conor · PRO NIre., corresp. with Lord Castlereagh

Likenesses P. Turnerelli, plaster sculpture, 1816, NG Ire. · T. C. Thompson, oils, NG Ire.

Wealth at death under £700: will, 1824, Troy family papers, Dublin Roman Catholic archdiocese archives

Trubleville [Turbeville], **Sir Henry de** (d. 1239), soldier and administrator of Gascony, possibly belonged to a family of Dorset landowners with property around Melcombe, who were probably recent immigrants from Normandy. The surname is derived from Troubleville (Eure) and appears occasionally as Turbeville; one of Henry's brothers, Drogo, was a canon of Rouen; and it was to Normandy that Henry's heart was taken for burial in 1240.

Trubleville's early career was as one of King John's military captains who sustained the Angevin cause between 1215 and 1217. In 1216 he organized payment of royalist troops at Rochester and the following year played a significant part in Hubert de Burgh's victory over the French fleet off Sandwich. Unlike his fellow Norman Falkes de Bréauté or his companion at Sandwich Richard Siward, Trubleville never wavered in his loyalty to Henry III, his efforts being amply rewarded with grants of land, wardships, and offices. His main estates seem to have been in Devon, but other holdings acquired between 1216 and 1233 were spread across Wiltshire, Norfolk, Essex, Warwickshire, Gloucestershire, Somerset, Lincolnshire, Bedfordshire, Oxfordshire, and Suffolk. In 1229, to sustain his activities in Gascony, Trubleville was able to pledge his English lands for two years for £500. On top of these estates Trubleville had property in Gascony and commercial interests, such as Gascon wine and the trading of wool with Normandy. In addition Trubleville received custody of Usk and Glamorgan in 1233; was for some years before his death constable of Corfe Castle at 80 marks a year; and from 1230 was warden of Jersey and Guernsey.

During Henry III's minority Trubleville remained in royal employ; he was a judge at Westminster in 1221; authorized licences to Norman merchants in 1224–5; and negotiated support for the government in the difficult year of 1223. There is evidence that Trubleville worked closely with the justiciar Hubert de Burgh, a connection that stretched back at least to the battle of Sandwich. This association may have been a family matter, since Henry's uncle, Ralph de Trubleville, was a close follower of the justiciar, in 1220 insisting to his patron that 'my sole hope is in God and in you' (Carpenter, 172).

In 1225 Trubleville accompanied the expedition led by Richard, earl of Cornwall, and the earl of Salisbury that recovered Gascony from the French. After the earl's premature departure Trubleville probably assumed field command as the Angevin force tightened its grip on the duchy. The success of the campaign of 1225 led, two years later, to his appointment as seneschal of Gascony. His rule was dogged by factional disputes in Bordeaux, continual rebellion in Bayonne, tension with the vicomte of Béarn, and uneasy relations with France that veered from the truce he negotiated at Nogent in 1228 to the king's ineffectual campaign in Brittany and Poitou of 1230, during which Trubleville was given custody of the strategically vital island of Oléron. Although he was able to convince influential Gascons of the advantages to them of loyalty to the English king, Trubleville was only sporadically able to assert ducal rights, constantly undermined by a chronic lack of adequate funds. By 1234 he was owed 6000 marks arising out of his periods as seneschal.

Between his tours of duty in Gascony Trubleville was closely involved in the political crisis of 1232–4 in England, from which he emerged as one of the king's most important supporters. Initially Trubleville was hounded by the new government of Peter des Roches, probably because of his association with the disgraced Hubert de Burgh. In October 1232 the king repudiated any debts Trubleville had incurred as seneschal in Gascony, claiming with breathtaking disregard for truth that he had been sent adequate funds for his task; in December Trubleville was accused of selling royal lands in the duchy without the king's approval. But the revolt of Richard Marshal forced the king to accept allies wherever he found them and, unlike Richard Siward, Henry de Trubleville, despite his links with Hubert de Burgh, remained loyal. By September 1233 Trubleville was in charge of operations against rebels in the southern Welsh marches. From his base in Bristol in the winter of 1233–4 he conducted a daring naval relief of Carmarthen Castle which was being besieged by an ally of Richard Marshal, Rhys Gryg ('the Hoarse').

In May 1234 Trubleville was reappointed seneschal of Gascony, an office he held, with a short intermission in 1237, until November 1238. The problems of finance and distant but intrusive royal control of his actions continued to restrict his discretion. However, his chief accomplishment was military, both in policing the duchy and campaigning for the duke of Brittany in 1234–5. On visits to England his presence at important political events, such as Henry III's reconciliation with Gilbert Marshal in 1236, point to his stature at court, as does his conduct of an inquiry into the handling of a riot in Oxford against the papal legate and his entourage. None the less, it was as a soldier that Trubleville left his clearest mark. The climax of his career came in 1238 when, with the queen's uncle, William, bishop-elect of Valence, he led English troops who fought for Frederick II in Lombardy, distinguishing themselves at the siege of Milan and in their defeat of the Piacenzans, thereby earning Frederick's warm praise.

On returning to England, where Matthew Paris of St Albans was to laud his martial exploits in a paean of nationalist pride, Trubleville took the cross with Richard of Cornwall on 12 November 1239. He died on 21 December 1239, lamented not only by Paris, but also, it appears, by the king, who, a few days later pardoned one William fitz Richard of debt and restored him to land in Devon 'for God and the soul of our beloved and faithful Henry de Trubleville' (*CClR, 1237–42*, 163), and in early January 1240 he gave Trubleville's brother Drogo 60*s*. 'to buy a cup to place therein the heart of Henry de Trubleville, his brother, for carriage to Normandy' (*CClR, 1237–42*, 165; *CLR, 1226–40*, 444). Trubleville's dynasty died with him, his only child being an illegitimate daughter, Edelina, possibly born in Gascony where she later married Elie de Blénac from the Saintonge. Trubleville himself had married, possibly in 1227, Hawissa, who outlived him. Other relatives, connected by his sisters' marriages, included the Balliols and the Mortimers.

An unswerving loyalist to both King John and Henry III, Trubleville achieved greatest prominence in France, as seneschal of Gascony. His rule was recalled by Gascon critics of Simon de Montfort in 1252 as having been just and peaceful, although in fact it had been largely unsuccessful in solving the political and financial problems of Angevin control of the duchy. Trubleville's reputation rested primarily on his fame as an energetic warrior and skilled general who saw service in the civil war of 1215–17, in Wales, Gascony, and Brittany, and in northern Italy.

C. J. TYERMAN

Sources *Chancery records* · F. Michel, C. Bémont, and Y. Renouard, eds., *Rôles Gascons*, 4 vols. (1882–1962), vol. 1 · Paris, *Chron.* · W. W. Shirley, ed., *Royal and other historical letters illustrative of the reign of Henry III*, 2 vols., Rolls Series, 27 (1862–6) · Rymer, *Foedera* · *Ann. mon.* · J. Williams ab Ithel, ed., *Annales Cambriae*, Rolls Series, 20 (1860) · T. D. Hardy, ed., *Rotuli litterarum clausarum*, 2 vols., RC (1833–4) · C. Roberts, ed., *Excerpta è rotulis finium in Turri Londinensi asservatis, Henrico Tertio rege*, AD 1216–1272, 1, RC, 32 (1835) · D. A. Carpenter, *The minority of Henry III* (1990)
Archives PRO, corresp.

Trübner, Nicholas (1817–1884), publisher and philologist, was born on 17 June 1817 at Heidelberg, Germany, the eldest of four sons of a goldsmith and his wife. His first school was the local *Gymnasium* where he began to study ancient and modern languages. He was apprenticed in 1831 to a university bookseller of Heidelberg, J. C. B. Mohr; during six years in that position he encountered numerous scholars and pursued his further education. Later he worked in bookshops in Göttingen (Vandenhoeck and Ruprecht), Hamburg (Hoffmann and Campe), and Frankfurt am Main (Willmann). While in Frankfurt, Trübner met William Longman, a partner in the English publishing firm, who offered him a position as foreign corresponding clerk. He moved to London in 1843, became fluent in English, travelled frequently to continental Europe

on business, and continued to pursue his scholarly interests. His first publication was a translation, *Sketches of Flemish Life* by Hendrik Conscience (1846).

Having arrived in London without capital, Trübner's first business venture after leaving Longman's employ was with a partner. Beginning in 1851, Trübner and Thomas Delf set up an agency for the sale of American books in Britain, continuing the trade established ten years earlier by Wiley and Putnam. After some initial difficulties they were joined by David Nutt. As well as importing books from the United States, the firm in Ludgate Hill specialized in the literature of India and Asia ('oriental literature') and in philology and philosophy. In 1855 was published the first edition of *Trübner's Bibliographical Guide to American Literature*. His first visit to the United States brought the development of important relationships with American writers and publishers. An early result was an edition of *The Literature of American Aboriginal Languages* (1857), written by Hermann E. Ludewig. For the next three decades, Trübner continued to build a powerful reputation in the two related fields of philological scholarship and international publishing.

Trübner's scholarship was closely related to the business interest. William Heinemann observed:

Nicholas Trübner was the friend and adviser of all who were engaged in the study of oriental literature. His firm during this period has been the intermediary between Europe and the East. His agents are scattered all over the globe, and they send from the remotest parts the literary productions of every people of the world to London. Here they are catalogued and carefully described, and *Trübner's Record* makes them widely known among librarians and scholars. (Mumby, 166–7)

The monthly periodical *Trübner's American and Oriental Literary Record* (1865–91) was widely used by scholars of Asian literatures. In 1878 he launched *Trübner's Oriental Series*, which eventually numbered about fifty volumes. The series was supported by the India Office Library where the editor, E. Reinhold Rost, was employed. Another link to the colonial service was forged when Trübner became the supplier of reference books and periodicals to government bureaux. William R. Greg, controller of the Stationery Office, was also the author of *Enigmas of Life* (1872–9), published in Trübner's series the English and Foreign Philosophical Library. Serving as bookseller, agent, and publisher to nearly fifty government departments and learned societies in England, the United States, Australia, Denmark, and Sweden, as well as holding the agency to supply about thirty libraries around the world, Trübner developed and managed a network of government and scholarly contacts; his role in maintaining the fabric of empire in the mid-nineteenth century would repay further investigation.

In addition to its specialization in imported literature, Trübner's firm operated as a general publisher, publishing (on a commission basis) four of the novels of Charles Read between 1858 and 1861 and *The Breitmann Ballads* (1871) of the American writer Charles Godfrey Leland. It was also Samuel Butler's publisher at an important juncture in the novelist's career, bringing out *Erewhon* in 1871 after it had been rejected by Chapman and Hall. There was a dispute with Butler over the terms for *Life and Habit* (1878), but he later returned to Trübner and remained until the firm's reorganization in 1889. Edwin Arnold's *The Light of Asia* (1879), a book of Indian lore in blank verse, was another enormously popular title for the firm.

Although he had many friends and exerted a remarkable influence in the London literary world, Trübner's international interests set him apart from others in the book trade. John Camden Hotten remarked in 1868 that, although Trübner was 'a capital fellow, brimful of linguistic talent', he nevertheless retained 'an eye reverent to literary journals and powerful critics' (Chatto and Windus letter-book).

Trübner died in London on 30 March 1884, aged sixty-six. Latterly his business partners had been Edward Hanson and Frederick Düffing. With his widow, Marie Cornelia Claire Catherine Trübner (the daughter of Joseph Octave Delepierre, Belgian consul in London), they sold the business in 1889 to the new firm of Kegan Paul, Trench, Trübner & Co. Ltd, which amalgamated Trübner & Co. with two other companies, Kegan Paul, Trench, and George Redway.   LESLIE HOWSAM

Sources F. A. Mumby, *The house of Routledge, 1834–1934, with a history of Kegan Paul, Trench, Trübner and other associated firms* (1934), 162–77 • L. Howsam, *Kegan Paul—a Victorian imprint: publishers, books and cultural history* (1998) • *DNB* • *The Athenaeum* (5 April 1884), 443–4 • 'Karl J. Trübner', *Centralblatt für Bibliothekswesen* (6 June 1884), 240–46 • *Publishers' Circular* (1 April 1884), 323 • Chatto and Windus letter-book, 3, 27 May 1867–26 July 1869, fol. 133, J. C. Hotten to Dr T. Inman, 16 March 1868
Archives UCL, archives with those of Kegan Paul, Trench, and Henry S. King
Likenesses photograph, repro. in Mumby, *The house of Routledge, 1834–1934*, facing p. 162

Trubshaw, James (1777–1853), builder and civil engineer, was born at Colwich Priory in Staffordshire on 13 February 1777, the second son of the seven boys and two girls born to James Trubshaw (*d.* 1808), a stonemason and builder of Colwich, and his second wife, Elizabeth, daughter of John Webb of Levedale. He was educated at a school at Rugeley until the age of eleven, when he was sent each morning to Sandon Hall where his father's workmen were carrying out alterations. He returned only briefly to school, and at sixteen, through the father of the sculptor Sir Richard Westmacott (1775–1856), went to work on the building of Fonthill Abbey, the residence of William Beckford (1759–1844). He subsequently worked at Buckingham Palace and at Windsor Castle. In 1795 he was involved in the construction of Wolseley Bridge, near Colwich, which his father had been commissioned to rebuild. In 1800 he married Mary, youngest daughter of Thomas Bott of Stone; they had three sons and three daughters. Their eldest son, Thomas, born on 4 April 1802, was an architect of considerable ability; he died on 7 June 1842. Their daughter Susanna was a poet and essayist.

After his father's death on 13 April 1808 Trubshaw started in business on his own account at Stone, and attracted the attention of a Mrs Sneyd, a lady residing in the neighbourhood, who commissioned him to rebuild Ashcombe Hall. His success in this commission secured him more offers of work and established his reputation locally.

In 1827 Trubshaw undertook to construct the Grosvenor Bridge over the Dee at Chester, to the design of Thomas Harrison (1744–1829). This consisted of a single arch of 200 feet span, and its construction was pronounced by Thomas Telford and other leading engineers to be impracticable. The first stone was laid in October 1827; the bridge was formally opened in December 1833 but was not available for traffic until 1 January 1834. Models of the bridge, illustrative of the methods of construction employed, were presented by Trubshaw to the Society of Civil Engineers, of which he was a member. Among the buildings he erected were Ilam Hall near Ashbourne, to the design of John Shaw, and Weston House in Warwickshire, designed by Edward Blore. He constructed the Exeter Bridge over the Derwent at Derby, opened in October 1850, a work which presented particular difficulties because of the sudden floods to which the river was prone and the quicksands encountered in the middle of the channel. He was also successful in restoring the church tower of Wybunbury in Cheshire, which had developed a dangerous lean, by using specially designed excavating equipment to remove the earth under the higher side. He was for a time engineer to the Trent and Mersey Canal Company, and their civil engineering works bear many traces of his originality and skill.

Trubshaw died on 28 October 1853 at Haywood, Colwich, and was buried in Colwich churchyard.

E. I. CARLYLE, *rev.* RALPH HARRINGTON

Sources *GM*, 2nd ser., 41 (1854), 97–100 • S. Trubshaw, *Family records* (1876) • *PICE*, 14 (1854–5), 142–6 • A. Bayliss, *The life and work of James Trubshaw, 1777–1853* (1978) • d. cert.
Archives Warks. CRO, vouchers and corresp. concerning building of Weston Hall

Truefitt, George (1824–1902), architect, was born in Manchester and articled in London from 1839 to 1844 to the scholarly Gothic revivalist L. N. Cottingham (1787–1847). He worked briefly in the offices of Sancton Wood (1815–1886) and Harvey Eginton (1809–1849) of Worcester before establishing himself in independent practice in London *c.*1846. After a walking tour in France and Germany he published *Architectural Sketches on the Continent* (1847), which both responded to a growing interest in European Gothic and urged the development of the revival beyond medieval precedents. Shrewdly, it was dedicated to A. J. Beresford Hope (1820–1887), chairman of the Ecclesiological Society, which Truefitt joined in 1848. His Gothic design for London's Army and Navy Club, though unsuccessful in competition, was well publicized and particularly impressed the banker William Cunliffe Brooks (1819–1900), who became his principal patron. Pursuing ecclesiastical Gothic, Truefitt's *Designs for Country Churches* (1850) welcomed the revival's emergence from antiquarian 'copyism' into 'original conception' ('Preface'), and provided twenty imaginary designs, the geometrical simplification and compositional boldness of which—

praised by *The Ecclesiologist* for their 'vigour and spirit' (vol. 11, 1850, 48)—anticipated much of the aesthetic of high Victorian Gothic.

However, Truefitt, an evangelical, was unsympathetic to the high-church arrangements demanded by ecclesiology's leaders, and his career developed on secular rather than ecclesiastical lines. His first major job, the now demolished Newbury Savings Bank (1848–9), was followed by various commissions: Bridgnorth cemetery (1854), a school in Neath (1857), estate buildings for Cunliffe Brooks, and—probably—work on Brooks's Manchester house, Barlow Hall. On 15 January 1856 his son George Haywood Truefitt was baptized at the Old Church, St Pancras, London; his mother's name was there recorded as Mary. When he was elected FRIBA in 1860, Truefitt was engaged in developing the suburban Tufnell Park estate, London, to which he was surveyor from 1865. Here he designed robust, stylistically eclectic villas, including his own house in Middleton Road, and his most important church, St George's (1866–8), where bare Gothic detailing consorts with a circular nave and terracotta-clad iron columns. Its aesthetic toughness recurs in the evangelical citadel of St George's, Worthing (1868), and his later churches at Bromley, Kent (1879), and Davyhulme, Lancashire (1889). Truefitt's stylistic inventiveness and resourceful use of materials are most evident in the three banks he designed in 1869–70 for Cunliffe, Brooks & Co.: a classical and Gothic mix for Manchester, a Romanesque–Renaissance medley at Blackburn, and elaborate timber-framed revival in Altrincham, Cheshire—all strikingly composed and idiosyncratically ornamented. In 1890 Truefitt's London practice was taken over by his son, though he continued as architect to Brooks's Glen Tana estate in Aberdeenshire.

Truefitt's output never rivalled those of the great Victorian architects, but he contributed significantly to high Victorian eclecticism, and his artistic independence resulted in designs of considerable individuality across a wide range of building types. He died at his home, the Old House, Worthing, on 11 August 1902, leaving a widow, Constance, a son, Lieutenant-Colonel Lewis Haywood, and two daughters, Mary Louisa Warleigh and Connie Georgie Truefitt.   CHRIS BROOKS

Sources *Building News*, 59 (1890), 167 · *RIBA Journal*, 9 (1901–2), 461 · *The Builder*, 83 (1902), 153 · *Building News*, 83 (1902), 252 · *Villa and cottage architecture: select examples of country and suburban residences* (1868) · review of *Designs for country churches*, *The Ecclesiologist*, 11 (1850), 47–9 · J. Booker, *Temples of Mammon: the architecture of banking* (1990) · G. Stamp and C. Amery, 'St George's Church, Tufnell Park Rd', *Victorian buildings of London, 1837–1887: an illustrated guide* (1980), 97 · R. H. Harper, *Victorian architectural competitions: an index to British and Irish architectural competitions in The Builder, 1843–1900* (1983) · S. Muthesius, *The high Victorian movement in architecture* (1972) · review of *Architectural sketches on the continent*, *The Ecclesiologist*, 8 (1847–8), 107–8 · review of designs, *The Ecclesiologist*, 17 (1856), 70–71; 18 (1857), 107–8; 19 (1858), 198 · *London: south*, Pevsner (1983) · *London: north*, Pevsner (1998) · *South Lancashire*, Pevsner (1969) · *Sussex*, Pevsner (1965) · *Dir. Brit. archs.* · *CGPLA Eng. & Wales* (1902) · IGI · will of George Truefitt

Likenesses photograph, repro. in *Building News*, 146

Wealth at death £8962 19s. 5d.: probate, 18 Nov 1902, *CGPLA Eng. & Wales*

Trueman, **Sir Arthur Elijah** (1894–1956), geologist and university administrator, was born in Nottingham on 26 April 1894, the son of Elijah Trueman, journeyman lacemaker, and his wife, Thirza Newton, *née* Cottee. He was educated at High Pavement School (1906–11), then taught briefly at a local school before entering University College, Nottingham, in 1912. He graduated BSc (London) in 1914 with first-class honours in geology and, having been rejected on medical grounds for war service, gained an MSc (under H. H. Swinnerton) in 1916 and a DSc in 1918.

In 1917 Trueman was appointed as an assistant lecturer in geology at University College, Cardiff. In 1920 he went as lecturer and head of the geology department to the newly opened University College, Swansea. In the same year he married Florence Kate Offler; they later had one son. In 1930 the name of the Swansea department was changed to geology and geography, and Trueman became professor of geology and head of department. In 1933 he moved to the Chaning Wills chair of geology at Bristol; four years later he was appointed professor of geology at Glasgow. From 1940 onwards, Trueman became increasingly involved in university administration, serving as deputy principal at Glasgow between 1944 and 1946. In the latter year he became deputy chairman of the University Grants Committee; in 1949 he was appointed its chairman. With his experience in the university system, he played a crucial role in the reconstruction of the universities after the war. He resigned in 1953 as a result of ill-health.

Trueman's interests in science spanned geology, palaeontology, and science education. He promoted a popular concern for geology in books—some introductory, others linking geology and scenery—at a time when the subject was not well known but public interest in the conservation of landscape was growing. He was a prominent member of many societies and played a significant role in the introduction of geology to schools and adult education. He also studied the physical and economic geography of south Wales. His main interests, however, were in theoretical palaeontology, in fossil snails, oysters, mussels, and ammonites, and their application to problems in the Lias and the coal measures. This work was extensively reviewed by his Swansea successor, Thomas Neville George, in a volume (edited by T. R. Owen) published in 1974 to celebrate the Swansea department's fiftieth anniversary.

Trueman's work on the ontogeny and phylogeny of fossil forms included studies of recapitulation and a highly original discussion of growth and development in relation to mode of life in ammonites, demonstrating his interest in fossils as once-living organisms actively responsive to their physical environment. His attempts in co-ordinating palaeontological and genetic theory were expressed in his application of taxonomic theory to the study of selected groups of ammonites and gastropods, and of oysters (as in his seminal paper on Gryphaea in 1922). Trueman's interest in ammonites and oysters was directly linked with, and partly prompted by, his interest in Jurassic rocks. It led to the refining of the zonal sequence at a time when there was a divergence of views on the validity of ammonite zones and subzones. It also led to a much more detailed picture of facies variation in the littoral and associated facies from Keuper to Liassic times in the Vale of Glamorgan.

Trueman's interest in the coal measures and its fossils followed his move to Swansea and his acquaintance in 1921 with the local mining geologist J. H. Davies (who subsequently joined his department). Here, accurate correlation of strata was of vital importance to the mining community, but the fossils in the measures (plant remains and non-marine bivalves) were believed to be of little use as a tool because of their long vertical ranges.

Trueman's palaeontology and Davies' intimate knowledge of the coal measures and extensive collection of bivalves resulted in a spectacular breakthrough: it directed research along paths that were both academic and practical. Trueman's experience with oysters, for example, led him to

> analyse the nature of the instruments he was using, and out of it came a concept of fossil populations, of the species as plexus, and of evolutional sequences that for the first time offered a coherent synthesis of earlier studies. (George, 147)

The work provided the basis for an effective zonal sequence and much more accurate correlation than hitherto, and it led to studies of the relation of sequence to environment and the creation of a much more sophisticated palaeogeography.

Trueman's study of the bivalves was sustained until his death by his colleague John Weir, who completed a comprehensive monograph in 1968; Trueman presented the wider stratigraphical syntheses in two presidential addresses to the Geological Society (1946, 1947). He also edited and contributed to an authoritative volume on the coalfields of Great Britain (1954).

Trueman was not physically robust nor temperamentally a field geologist. He was, however, a most effective teacher. His lectures were sometimes formal and impersonal, but his relaxed response to students promoted a warm reaction, devotion, and affection. His friendliness and enthusiasm made him especially successful as a collaborator.

Trueman was president of the Geological Society of London (1945–7) and was awarded its Bigsby (1939) and Wollaston (1955) medals. He was president of section C (geology) of the British Association, a gold medallist of the South Wales Institute of Engineers (1934), and chairman of the Geological Survey Board (1943–54). He was made a fellow of the Royal Society of Edinburgh (1938) and of the Royal Society (1942), received honorary degrees from four universities, and was appointed KBE in 1951. Trueman died at his home, 21 Audley Road, Ealing, on 5 January 1956.

DOUGLAS A. BASSETT

Sources W. J. Pugh, Memoirs FRS, 4 (1958), 291–305 · The Times (7 Jan 1956) · T. N. George, 'Sir Arthur Elijah Trueman', Proceedings of the Geological Society of London, 1541 (1956), 146–9 · T. R. Owen, ed., The Upper Palaeozoic and post-Palaeozoic rocks of Wales: published in memory of Sir Arthur Trueman (1974) · T. N. George, 'Fossil molluscs and molluscs in stratigraphy: the geological work of A. E. Trueman', The Upper Palaeozoic and post-Palaeozoic rocks of Wales: published in memory of Sir Arthur Trueman, ed. T. R. Owen (1974), 1–30 · D. W. Dykes, The University College of Swansea: an illustrated history (1992) · B. Simpson, Department of geology, University College, Swansea: the first fifty years, 1970, University College, Swansea, Department of geology [mimeograph] · CGPLA Eng. & Wales (1956)

Archives Hunterian Museum and Art Gallery, Glasgow, specimens · NHM, specimens · NMG Wales, specimens

Likenesses W. Stoneman, photographs, 1946, RS

Wealth at death £7372 9s. 5d.: probate, 28 April 1956, CGPLA Eng. & Wales

Trueta, Josep Anthony (1897–1977), orthopaedic surgeon, was born in Barcelona, Spain, on 27 October 1897, the elder son and second of three children of Rafel Trueta, physician, and his wife, Mercè Raspall, daughter of a haberdasher. He attended the Barcelona Institute of Secondary Education until 1916 and then began the study of medicine at the University of Barcelona; he graduated in 1921. In 1923 Trueta married Amelia (d. 1975), daughter of Jaume Llacuna, a businessman. They had three daughters and a son (who died at the age of four).

From 1922 Trueta held junior surgical posts at the Hospital de la Santa Creu i de Sant Pau until his appointment as assistant surgeon to Manuel Corachan, professor of surgery at the hospital. In 1929 he became chief surgeon to the Caja de Provision y Socorro, which treated 40,000 accident cases a year, and in 1933 he was appointed assistant professor of surgical pathology at the University of Barcelona. He reached the rank of professor of surgery as chief surgeon to the Hospital de la Santa Creu i de Sant Pau in Barcelona in 1935, just before the outbreak of the Spanish Civil War. Trueta was faced with the mammoth problem of treating casualties from the continuous air raids on the civilian population of Barcelona by nationalist forces, but it was from attending both civilian and battlefield casualties that he perfected the closed-plaster technique, previously pioneered by Winnett Orr but forgotten, of repairing severe compound war wounds, particularly those involving damage to bones. The usual practice had previously been amputation. Trueta was convinced that this should be unnecessary. By the end of the civil war he had personally treated over one thousand casualties, with only six deaths. This experience and the techniques which he had developed were to prove invaluable during the Second World War, particularly in the early days of the blitz.

A man of fervent liberal convictions, Trueta realized that it would be impossible for him to work with the victorious nationalist forces and early in 1939 he emigrated to England with his young family. He was much in demand as a lecturer on air-raid surgery and practical air-raid precautions because of his immense firsthand experience, and he became an adviser to the Ministry of Health.

In September 1939 G. R. Girdlestone, the founder Nuffield professor of orthopaedic surgery, heard Trueta lecture on bombing casualties and invited him to Oxford. This was the start of a long and close friendship which led to the establishment of the Oxford school of orthopaedics.

From 1942 to the end of the war, Trueta was surgeon in charge of the busy accident department at the Radcliffe Infirmary, Oxford. In spite of this heavy clinical load, his research became more experimental, particularly in the field of kidney neurovascular physiology, and he wrote with one of his assistants, M. Agerholm, one of the first papers on the use of penicillin in bone infection (1946).

In 1949 Trueta was elected Nuffield professor of orthopaedic surgery in the University of Oxford and professorial fellow of Worcester College, Oxford. From this position and with remarkable vision he reorganized the Wingfield-Morris Orthopaedic Hospital as the Nuffield Orthopaedic Centre to become the leading centre in the country for treatment, study, and research in orthopaedic surgery. He continued to produce a continuous flow of publications on almost every aspect of orthopaedics. The essence of his scientific philosophy and experimental attack was the primary position of vascularity in health and disease. This concept he researched extensively and with marked originality in renal circulation, in osteogenesis and epiphyseal growth, in the pathology of osteoarthritis, and in the treatment of osteomyelitis, to name but a few examples. Many young assistants from Britain and Europe, particularly from the Iberian peninsula, joined him in these studies and were fired by his enthusiasm and lively imagination, to become scientists as well as surgeons.

The most widely known of Trueta's works are *Treatment of War Wounds and Fractures* (1939) and *The Principles and Practice of War Surgery* (1943). His worldwide reputation as an experimental clinician was established by the publication with colleagues of *Studies of the Renal Circulation* (1947). *The Spirit of Catalonia* (1946) is a work of filial piety containing a unique collection of biographies of Catalan medical practitioners and philosophers and examining their contribution to Western civilization. In 1956, with other colleagues, he published a *Handbook on Poliomyelitis* and he gathered together much of his lifetime's work and philosophy in *Studies of the Development and Decay of the Human Frame* (1968).

Trueta's many honours included an honorary DSc from Oxford (1943), the appointment as chevalier of the French Légion d'honneur, and honorary fellowships of many orthopaedic associations around the world. He was also honoured by the universities of Buenos Aires and of Brazil. He was made FRCS in 1954. In New York he served in 1960 as president of the Société Internationale de Chirurgie Orthopédique et de Traumatologie, and in the same year he was made an honorary fellow of the American College of Surgeons.

Trueta was a handsome, athletic, vivacious man, friendly, particularly to the young, who recognized the colour, warmth, and indeed drama of this Catalan. He adored the society of Oxford, and indeed 'the establishment'. Nevertheless, he retired to Barcelona in 1966 to continue his surgical and scientific work. His was a very close and religious family and the three daughters with their own families were already living permanently in Spain. After a courageous battle against cancer Trueta

died on 19 January 1977 in Barcelona. A few days before his death King Juan Carlos I bestowed upon him the grand cross of Carlos III, the most prestigious award of Spain.

R. B. Duthie, rev.

Sources *The Times* (21 Jan 1977) · *The Times* (27 Jan 1977) · J. A. Trueta, *Trueta, surgeon in war and peace: the memoirs of Josep Trueta*, trans. M. Strubell and M. Strubell (1980) · *Journal of Bone and Joint Surgery*, 59B/2 (May 1977) · private information (1986) · personal knowledge (1986)

Truganini [Trukanini, Trugernanna, Lalla Rookh] (*c.*1812–1876), Australian Aborigine, was born on Bruny Island, south-east Van Diemen's Land, into the Great Swanport tribe. Her father was Manganna (Mangerner; *d.* 1830), a native of the island; her mother, whose name is not known, was killed by sailors soon after Truganini's birth. In 1828 Truganini was carried off by two convict woodcutters, despite the efforts of her fiancé Paraweena, who was killed trying to protect her. She managed to escape to a farm. Late in 1829, now a slim and charming girl, she joined the Bruny Island mission, where she married Wooraddy (*d.* 1842), a local Aborigine. Her father died in January 1830, and in March that year George Augustus *Robinson (1791–1866), whom the government had appointed to try to 'conciliate' the natives, chose Truganini, with a dozen others, to travel with him on the 'friendly missions' to the Aborigines, which he undertook throughout the colony between 1830 and 1834. Truganini allegedly soon became Robinson's lover, and she rescued him from drowning in 1832. He renamed her Lalla Rookh after the title of the poem by Thomas Moore. She helped him to persuade her compatriots to go with him to a government reserve which was finally established on Flinders Island in Bass Strait in 1832. Her hope was to protect her compatriots, but she has sometimes been described as a traitor to her people. In 1835 she settled on the island, where Robinson hoped the Aborigines would be converted to Christianity and Westernized. In 1836–7 she went with Robinson's son to look for her family in Van Diemen's Land but was unsuccessful.

After returning to Flinders Island, Truganini soon became disappointed by its many shortcomings and the heavy death-rate there, and in 1839, with thirteen others, including Wooraddy, she accompanied Robinson to Port Phillip when he was appointed Aboriginal protector there. Although she went with him on one expedition up country, he soon abandoned their association, and in 1841 she took to the bush with the other Tasmanians. In December with four others she was charged with murdering two white people near the south coast. Two men were found guilty and executed; Truganini and the others were acquitted but sent back to Flinders Island. They left in July 1842, with Wooraddy who died on the way, and in 1847 the whole establishment, then only forty-six strong, was moved to Oyster Bay, Swanport, Truganini's original tribal country. Here, contemptuous of Western ways, she more or less went back to her earlier mode of living, fishing and hunting, while the establishment slowly decayed. For a time she had lived with a Big River tribesman, Alphonso (*d.* 1850), and in 1857 she 'married' William Lanney (*d.*

1868), the son of a chief. In 1874 she was taken to Hobart, where she died from bronchial trouble on 8 May 1876, aged about sixty-four, and was buried at the old female penitentiary at the Cascades. In December 1878 the government exhumed her body to prevent a grave robbery, and from 1904 to 1947 her skeleton was displayed in the Tasmanian Museum. Withdrawn then, her remains were cremated on 30 April 1976 and her ashes scattered in D'Entrecasteaux Channel. A. G. L. SHAW

Sources N. J. B. Plomley, ed., *Friendly mission* (1966) · V. Rae-Ellis, *Black Robinson* (1988) · C. Turnbull, *The black war* (1948) · L. Ryan, *The Aboriginal Tasmanians*, 2nd edn (1996) · N. Cato and V. Rae-Ellis, *Queen Trucanini* (1976) · J. Bonwick, *The last of the Tasmanians* (1870) · L. Ryan and W. Smith, 'Trugernanna', *AusDB*, vol. 6 · L. Ryan, 'Tanganini', *Two hundred Australian women*, ed. H. Radi (1988) · L. Ryan, 'The struggle for Trukanini, 1830–1997', *Papers and Proceedings of the Tasmanian Historical Research Association*, 44/3 (Sept 1997), 153–73 · N. J. B. Plomley, *Weep in silence: the Flinders Island Aboriginal settlement, 1835–39* (1987)
Archives Tasmanian Archives, Hobart, corresp.
Likenesses attrib. T. Bock, oils, Tasmanian Museum and Art Gallery

Truman, Sir Benjamin (1699/1700–1780), entrepreneur and brewer, was born in Brick Lane, Spitalfields, London, the younger son in a family of nine children of Joseph Truman, brewer, and his first wife. His father died in 1721 and Truman became a partner in the family firm in 1722 (his elder brother Joseph withdrawing in 1730).

Building up his stake to eleven shares in the partnership out of eighteen by 1743, Truman was the sole partner responsible for management. He was backed by various other investors and took a wealthy sleeping partner, John Baker, with a third share from 1767 to 1771 to help finance prodigious expansion. Production at the Black Eagle Brewery rose from 55,500 barrels in 1750 to 83,000 in 1766, an output surpassed only by the Whitbread and Calvert breweries.

In the 1770s Trumans was one of six 'capital houses' in London. They were virtually single-product businesses, producing porter, a heavy black beer, which was robust enough to stand the hazards of large-scale production, long storage, and distribution. Out of 142 'common brewers' in London in 1776, collectively brewing 1,288,000 barrels, for example, the leading six houses brewed over 40 per cent, an unprecedented example of scale of individual business and industrial concentration. At Benjamin Truman's death the net assets of the firm were £171,900, compared with £23,300 in 1741. His personal estate was worth £180,000 and he had a further £160,000 capital in the business.

This great fortune derived almost exclusively from the profits of the business, which itself grew primarily by internal accumulation from retained profits. Such a high rate of internal investment proved fully compatible with taking enough out of the trade annually to sustain the life of a gentleman consistent with Truman's great fortune. In the 1770s Truman withdrew almost £4000 annually, with large additional sums occasionally to finance the purchase of land and the expenses of his private houses.

These included a country estate, Popes, near Hertingfordbury, Hertfordshire, and a grand city residence by the brewery. Truman was knighted in 1760, on the accession of George III, in recognition of his standing in the London business community and for large loans to the crown. His portrait is one of the largest and most powerful canvases Thomas Gainsborough ever painted (Gainsborough was also commissioned to paint two granddaughters and two great-grandsons).

Unlike Samuel Whitbread, Henry Thrale, and John Calvert, Benjamin Truman never sought a parliamentary seat, which his wealth and city and country position might have suggested. Married to Frances (1702/3–1766), with whom he had a son and a daughter, he was, first and foremost, an entrepreneur and industrialist: his life's priorities may be read in the statement he wrote, as an old man, across the final page of the brewery accounts in 1775, instructing his grandson about the creation of wealth in business: 'there can be no other way of raising a great fortune but by carrying on an extensive trade. I must tell you, young man, this is not to be obtained without spirret and great application' (Mathias, 265). He died on 20 March 1780 in his eighty-first year, and was buried in the churchyard at Hertingfordbury.

Continuity of business at the Black Eagle Brewery was maintained after Truman's death, but not the family dynasty. Truman's son, James, died in 1766 leaving him no male heir. Both his two grandsons by his daughter Frances declined to follow the trade, one of them becoming a general. In his will Truman put his entire estate in trust for his two great-grandsons, appointing as executor his head clerk, James Grant, who was also to continue to run the brewery. Grant became a partner in 1788 but died in July 1789. Sampson Hanbury then bought Grant's share and took over Trumans. Hanbury subsequently brought in Quaker partners, taking the business to greater heights and establishing longer term family dynasties than the Trumans were able to achieve. PETER MATHIAS

Sources P. Mathias, *The brewing industry in England, 1700–1830* (1959), 263–5, 551, 556–8 · *Trumans, the brewers: the story of Truman, Hanbury, Buxton & Co* [1966] · F. H. W. Sheppard, ed., *Spitalfields and Mile End New Town*, Survey of London, 27 (1957), ch. 9, 116–22 · GM, 1st ser., 50 (1780), 155 · tombstone, Hertingfordbury, Hertfordshire
Archives Grand Metropolitan Brewing Ltd, The Brewery, 91 Brick Lane, London, Truman MSS · LMA, Truman MSS
Likenesses T. Gainsborough, oils, probably The Brewery, 91 Brick Lane, London
Wealth at death £160,000, capital in business; approximately £180,000 personal estate; also Hertfordshire estate ('Popes'); town house near brewery: Mathias, *The brewing industry in England*, 274

Truman, Edwin Thomas (1818–1905), dentist and inventor of a gutta-percha preparation process, was born in London on 20 December 1818, the son of Thomas Truman, a descendant of Sir Benjamin Truman, the founder of the firm of brewers Truman, Hanbury, and Buxton. He was educated in London at King's College School and King's College Hospital. In 1845 he married Mary Ann, daughter of Robert Cooper of Eastbourne. He became a member of the Royal College of Surgeons in 1859.

Having established himself as a dentist, Truman was appointed dentist to the royal household on 28 February 1855, and he held this appointment until his death, a period of fifty years. In his practice he acquired a wide reputation for success in correcting cleft palate, and in the course of his work he also studied the varied properties and uses of the natural latex substance known as gutta-percha. He was the inventor of a patent gutta-percha dental stopping, and received a royalty from every dentist making use of his invention. Among his publications were *On the Construction of Artificial Teeth with Gutta-percha* (1848) and *The Strength and Beauty of Mineral Teeth* (1860).

After a decade of experimentation, however, Truman invented an improved method of preparing gutta-percha for an entirely different purpose: to provide the protective covering for telegraph cables. The failure of the first Atlantic cable in 1858 had been due to imperfect insulation, which a committee of inquiry attributed to the improper preparation of the gutta-percha employed. Truman discovered that gutta-percha could be refined by mechanical means, and after his discovery had been satisfactorily tested and the invention patented, on 25 August 1860, the rights were sold to the Gutta-Percha Company; all subsequent Atlantic telegraph cables were covered with gutta-percha prepared by Truman's process. In the same year Truman invented a machine which allowed ever better preparation of crude gutta-percha and he established a processing factory at Vauxhall Cross, London; between 1860 and 1889 he took out many patents for perfecting processes connected with the material. His general purpose was to improve its manufacture and to reduce its porosity and cost; after thirty years of experimentation he succeeded in producing an insulated conductor which, according to Lord Kelvin, had ten times the insulating capacity of the French Atlantic cable. The General Post Office adopted Truman's process for its underground telegraph cables, and until shortly before his death Truman received a minimum annual royalty of £500.

From the age of fifteen Truman was also an enthusiastic collector of books and prints, and a frequenter of Sothebys salerooms. A friend of George Cruikshank, he took a special interest in collecting Cruikshank's satirical prints and caricatures as well as books illustrated by him, eventually forming the largest first-generation collection of his works. Truman's collection, with his general library and historical and other portraits, was sold by Sothebys in 1906 in a sale lasting for twenty-one days and realizing nearly £15,000. Truman also busied himself with religious and social questions, on which he wrote with conviction. He died at his house, Home Field, Putney Hill, London, on 8 April 1905, and was succeeded as dentist to the royal household by his only son, Charles Edwin Truman.

H. W. BRUTON, rev. PATRICK WALLIS

Sources *The Lancet* (22 April 1905) · *The Times* (10 April 1905) · R. L. Patten, *George Cruikshank's life, times, and art*, 2 vols. (1992–6) · *The Times* (18 April 1881), 4 · personal knowledge (1912) · *CGPLA Eng. & Wales* (1905)

Wealth at death £32,762 5s. 4d.: probate, 23 June 1905, *CGPLA Eng. & Wales*

Truman, Joseph (*bap.* 1631, *d.* 1671), clergyman and ejected minister, and religious writer, son of Richard and Mary Truman, was born at Gedling, near Nottingham, and baptized there on 2 February 1631. His father, who was perhaps a curate, was attacked for speaking against the Book of Sports. Joseph was educated first by Laurence Palmer, minister of Gedling, and afterwards at the free school at Nottingham. On 9 June 1647 he was admitted a pensioner at Clare College, Cambridge, and graduated BA in 1650 and MA in 1654. On 27 September 1653 he was ordained as a minister by the Wirksworth classis, as assistant at St Peter's, Nottingham. On 2 June 1654 he was admitted as vicar of Ruddington, Nottinghamshire. On 16 January 1656 Truman took possession of the rectory of Cromwell, near Nottingham, in succession to Henry Trewman, who was buried in the parish on 4 December 1656 and may have been a relation. In the period from 6 January 1658 to 6 June 1660 Truman attended six of the meetings of the Nottinghamshire classis.

After ejection from Cromwell in 1662, Truman moved to Mansfield in order to be near his friend the nonconformist minister Robert Porter. According to Calamy, Truman declined to read the whole of the service in the Book of Common Prayer, because, he told the assize judges, there were 'lies in it', citing as proof the collect for Christmas day (already amended by the Savoy conference), which had stated that Jesus was born both on that day and on the following Sunday (Calamy, *Continuation*, 694). He always attended Church of England services and was well regarded by Stillingfleet and Tillotson, but refused all offers of preferment. A man of 'profound judgement and tenacious memory, very swift in reading books and happy in retaining what he read', Truman was 'often indicted': he was 'once sued to an outlawry, which was very chargeable to him', but pleaded so well in his own cause that he was acquitted (Calamy, *Abridgement*, 2.528). In his work *The Great Propitiation* (1669) Truman sought to explain the apostle Paul's theory of justification by 'faith', a word he understood to include repentance and obedience. In *An Endeavour to Rectify some Prevailing Opinions*, directed against *Harmonia apostolica* by George Bull (1634–1710), bishop of St David's, Truman argued for 'the all-sufficiency of the Mosaic law' which was

> able not only to work true sanctification in man, but, if rightly interpreted, to insure eternal life. Interpreted as a law of grace, it was no type or shadow, but the very gospel itself, to which the sermon on the Mount had added nothing essential, and which remained in force to the present day. (*DNB*)

Further instalments of the dispute with Bull quickly followed. Richard Baxter recommended Truman's work on justification, noting his strong opposition to antinomianism. In 1671 Truman stayed for a day with Baxter at Totteridge, Hertfordshire. On the way back northwards he visited William Stephens, rector of Sutton, Bedfordshire; there he died on 19 July 1671 and was buried in the chancel of the parish church on 21 July. STEPHEN WRIGHT

Sources Calamy rev. · E. Calamy, ed., *An abridgement of Mr. Baxter's history of his life and times, with an account of the ministers, &c., who were ejected after the Restauration of King Charles II*, 2nd edn, 2 vols. (1713) · E. Calamy, *A continuation of the account of the ministers … who were ejected and silenced after the Restoration in 1660*, 2 vols. (1727) · Venn, *Alum. Cant.* · 'The minutes of the Nottingham classis, 1656–1660', *Minutes of the Bury presbyterian classis, 1647–57*, ed. W. A. Shaw, 2, Chetham Society, new ser., 41 (1898), appx 1, 153–74 · *Calendar of the correspondence of Richard Baxter*, ed. N. H. Keeble and G. F. Nuttall, 2 vols. (1991) · *DNB*

Trumbull, Charles (1645/6–1724). *See under* Trumbull, Sir William (1639–1716).

Trumbull, John (1750–1831),

poet and judge in the United States of America, was born on 24 April 1750 in Westbury, Connecticut, the son of the Revd John Trumbull, a Congregational minister, and Sarah Whitman, the daughter of a military officer. Educated by his parents, young John soon revealed prodigious intellectual aptitude; he was admitted to Yale College at the incredible age of seven but sensibly delayed his matriculation for six years until 1763. He graduated in 1767, was a schoolteacher for a time, graduated MA from Yale in 1770, and remained there as a tutor until 1773.

In 1773 and 1774 he read law in Boston with the renowned John Adams, who was soon to be a leading instigator of the American War of Independence and became the second president of the United States. In 1776, the year in which independence was declared, Trumbull married Sarah, the daughter of Colonel Leverot Hubbard; they had four children. During his Connecticut legal career Trumbull served as treasurer of Yale College (1776–82), founded the bar association of Hartford county (1783), served on the Hartford city council (1784–93), was state's attorney (1789–95), was elected to the legislature (1800), and was eventually selected as a judge (1801).

Though an important civic leader throughout his life, Trumbull is remembered mainly for his poetry. Most of this was written with full awareness of the inferiority of what little American literature there was to the formidable accomplishments of his British counterparts. His earliest publications, 'Epithalamion' and 'The Medler', appeared in 1769. In 1770, however, Trumbull's partially versified 'Essay on the uses and advantages of the fine arts' memorably (if optimistically) foresaw a time when the literary accomplishments of the American colonies might vie with those of England. As he then wrote:

This land her Steele and Addison shall view,
The former glories equall'd by the new;
Some future Shakespeare charm the rising age,
And hold in magic charm the listening stage.

But the stylistic flaws disfiguring even this noble utterance demonstrated that he would not be among those to achieve such immortality.

In 1772 and 1773 Trumbull published 'The Progress of Dulness', an amusing three-part burlesque on the foibles of youth. His three defective protagonists are, respectively, Tom Brainless, a dullard ministerial student; Dick Hairbrain, a fop; and Harriet Simper, a modish young belle. Their heavy-handed names obscure the cleverness and deft urbanity with which the poem was written.

Trumbull also published *The Correspondent*, a series of satirical essays, in 1773.

While studying law with John Adams in 1773 and 1774, Trumbull began to compose the long poem for which he is best known. His mock epic *M'Fingal* (1775, 1782) borrowed its title and the name of its protagonist from the supposed ancient Scots poet Ossian (as forged by James MacPherson) and much of its style from the seventeenth-century English versifier Samuel Butler, the author of *Hudibras*. Hudibrastic satire, crude but sometimes effectively epigrammatic, was popular in America at this time as a vehicle for the expression of political grievances. Though Trumbull acceded to this fashion, he believed himself more substantially indebted to the influence of Jonathan Swift and Charles Churchill. He could not conceive of poetry in forms not already established by English predecessors, and as a tutor at Yale had urged his students to study and imitate the styles of Addison, Pope, and Milton.

In politics as in literature, Trumbull was fundamentally conservative. Despite his close association with John Adams, his support for the American patriots was (like that of many) lukewarm at best. In the first two cantos of *M'Fingal* the title character vociferates on behalf of the loyalist position. By 1782, however, Trumbull had yielded to changing events. When, in the concluding portion of the poem, M'Fingal berates the rebellious colonists for erecting a symbolic liberty pole and steadfastly proclaims his trust in 'King George and Providence' (iii. 504), he is tried by an impromptu court and suffers the indignity of being tarred and feathered.

Despite its unskilful versification, *M'Fingal* was hugely successful in the new United States, being republished in more than thirty editions over a hundred years. There were, unusually for an American literary work at that time, London editions also, in 1792 and 1793. The poem owed its unexpected popularity to the evenhandedness with which the excesses of both loyalists and revolutionaries were chided, to the mildness and good nature of its satire, and to the ease with which its unsophisticated humour could be comprehended. As a result of the poem's success Trumbull became the centre of a literary group called the Connecticut (or Hartford) Wits, the first such coterie in the history of the United States. Individually and collectively, the Wits published a number of works during the 1780s, with Trumbull at their head but no longer writing much himself. He was none the less widely regarded as the leading literary figure in the United States at the time.

In 1819 the political patronage system of Connecticut deprived Trumbull of his judgeship, impoverishing him. He moved to Detroit, Michigan, in 1825 to escape from partisan harassments; he lived there with his daughter Juliana Woodbridge, wife of the governor of Michigan. Trumbull died in Detroit on 11 May 1831, largely forgotten.

DENNIS R. DEAN

Sources E. Watts, 'Trumbull, John', *ANB* · V. E. Gimmestad, *John Trumbull* (1974) · A. Cowie, *John Trumbull: Connecticut Wit* (1936) · L. Howard, *The Connecticut Wits* (1943) · J. G. Wilson and J. Fiske, eds., *Appleton's cyclopaedia of American biography*, 6 (1889) · R. E.

Spiller and others, eds., *The literary history of the United States* (1948) · P. B. Briggs, 'English satire and Connecticut wit', *American Quarterly*, 37/1 (1985), 13–29

Archives Detroit Public Library, MSS | Cornell University, Ithaca, New York, Moses Coit Tyler collection

Trumbull, John (1756–1843), painter and diplomat, was born in Lebanon, Connecticut, America, on 6 June 1756. He was the youngest of the six children of Jonathan *Trumbull (1710–1785), a shipowner and later governor of Connecticut, and his wife, Faith Robinson. He attended Harvard College and, while there, visited John Singleton Copley in Boston. After graduating in 1773, he served with the Connecticut 1st regiment in the early months of the American War of Independence, attaining the rank of colonel. He then joined his brother's tea and rum business in 1779.

In 1780, having travelled to Europe to undertake an abortive financial project for family and friends, Trumbull went to London to study under Benjamin West but was arrested, imprisoned as a spy, and forced to leave the country. After negotiating a loan in Amsterdam for the state of Connecticut he returned home, but went back to England in 1784 to continue his strict daily regime in West's studio. He spent evenings attending classes at the Royal Academy and exhibited sixteen paintings there between 1784 and 1818 as well as seven at the British Institution between 1810 and 1813.

In 1785 Trumbull wrote to his father: 'the great object of my wishes … is to take up the History of Our Country' (Cooper, *Trumbull*, 7). He commenced his series of scenes from the American War of Independence, encouraged by Thomas Jefferson, whom he first met in Paris in that year. Paintings such as *The Death of General Warren at the Battle of Bunker's Hill* (1786; Yale University Art Gallery) and *The Death of General Montgomery in the Attack on Quebec* (1786; Yale University Art Gallery) clearly reveal the influence of both West and Copley in their choice of modern subject matter, composition, and use of the sublime. In 1787 he travelled again to Paris to paint Jefferson's portrait for inclusion in *The Sortie Made by the Garrison of Gibraltar* (1787; Corcoran Gallery of Art, Washington, DC).

On his return to America in 1789 Trumbull travelled along the east coast to paint portraits of the participants in the war. However, following the death of his cousin, Harriet Wadsworth, to whom he had proposed, he took up an offer to serve as secretary with the Jay treaty commission in London. There he met and married, in 1800, Sarah Hope Harvey (1774–1824), herself an amateur fruit and flower painter. Their marriage remained childless, but Trumbull accepted responsibility for an illegitimate boy, John Trumbull Ray, born in Connecticut.

Trumbull returned to England for a fourth time in 1808 in search of treatment for his failing eyesight. Because of the tensions between the two countries, which eventually resulted in the Anglo-American War, Americans were not popular, and Trumbull received few commissions, fell into debt, and went back to New York. In 1817 congress passed a resolution to commission Trumbull to decorate the rotunda of the Capitol with four historical murals,

'commemorative of the most important events of the American Revolution' (Cooper, 15). In the same year he was elected president of the American Academy of the Fine Arts, a post he held for nineteen years. However, his financial problems continued and he sold his collection of his own works to Yale College for an annuity in 1831. To house these, he co-designed the Trumbull Gallery with the assistance of Ithiel Town and A. J. Davis. The only other surviving example of his forays into architecture is the neo-classical meeting-house in Lebanon (1804).

Trumbull's autobiography was published in 1841, the first by an American artist. He died in New York on 10 November 1843. He was buried with his wife in the Trumbull Gallery and his memorial tablet is inscribed: 'To his country he gave his sword and his pencil'.

KATE RETFORD

Sources H. A. Cooper, *John Trumbull: the hand and spirit of a painter* (New Haven, 1982) · *The autobiography of Colonel John Trumbull*, ed. T. Sizer (1953) · E. G. Miles and others, *American paintings of the eighteenth century* (1995), 298–9 [catalogue, National Gallery of Art, Washington, DC] · I. B. Jaffe, *Trumbull: the declaration of independence* (1976) · M. Baigell, *Dictionary of American art* (1979), 357–8 · G. C. Croce and D. H. Wallace, *The New York Historical Society's dictionary of artists in America, 1564–1860*, 2nd edn (1964), 637–8 · T. Sizer, *The works of Colonel John Trumbull*, 2nd edn (1967) · I. B. Jaffe, 'Trumbull, John', *ANB* · H. A. Cooper, 'Trumbull, John', *The dictionary of art*, ed. J. Turner (1996) · B. Stewart and M. Cutten, *The dictionary of portrait painters in Britain up to 1920* (1997), 456 · Graves, *RA exhibitors* · Graves, *Brit. Inst.* · Waterhouse, *18c painters*

Archives Connecticut Historical Society, Hartford, family papers · Connecticut State Library, Hartford, family papers · Yale U., MS letters and documents

Likenesses J. Trumbull, self-portrait, 1777 · A. Robertson, miniature on ivory, 1815 · G. Stuart, portrait, 1818, Yale U. Art Gallery; repro. in T. Sizer, ed., *Autobiography of Colonel John Trumbull*, frontispiece · S. Lovett Waldo and W. Jewett, portrait, *c*.1821, Yale U. Art Gallery; repro. in T. Sizer, ed., *Autobiography of Colonel John Trumbull*, 256

Trumbull [*formerly* Trumble], **Jonathan** (1710–1785), revolutionary politician in America, was born Jonathan Trumble on 12 October 1710 in Lebanon, Connecticut, the second of the eight children of Joseph Trumble (1678–1755), farmer and merchant, and his wife, Hannah (1684–1768), daughter of John and Hannah Higley of Simsbury, Connecticut. His father moved to Lebanon between 1704 and 1708, and through hard work became one of the largest landowners and the leading merchant of the small, hilly town in eastern Connecticut. The family prospered sufficiently to send Jonathan in 1723 to Harvard College, where he was ranked thirty-first out of thirty-seven new students on the criterion of social eminence. Trumble's marriage, on 9 December 1735, to Faith (1718–1780), daughter of the Revd John Robinson of Duxbury, Massachusetts, and a descendant of New England's original pilgrim settlers, considerably aided his upward social mobility. He and Faith had six children.

A pious student, Trumble graduated in 1727 at the remarkably young age of sixteen. He went home to Lebanon to prepare for a career in the ministry, but returned to Harvard in 1729 and earned an MA degree in the following year. Shortly after, he was licensed to preach by the association of ministers at Windham, Connecticut. In 1732 Trumble was considering an invitation from the Colchester church, Connecticut, to be its minister when he received news that his elder brother, Joseph, had drowned. Joseph had joined his father's merchant business, and Jonathan now took his place and declined Colchester's offer. For the rest of his life Trumble was enmeshed in a complicated world of trade and finance. Initially successful, he gradually took over the family business from his father in the 1740s, and in 1749 formed a partnership—Trumble, Pitkin, and Williams—with two men born to much greater wealth and prominence, Joseph Pitkin of Hartford and Elisha Williams jun. of Wethersfield. Trumble, Pitkin, and Williams developed a thriving trade with the West Indies, and a lesser but substantial commerce with Britain and the Netherlands. The firm used Norwich, New London, and Haddam, Connecticut, as its trading ports, acted as bankers for several dozen lesser merchants, and specialized within New England in provisioning militia troops on military expeditions. The vast enterprise, which appeared prosperous and powerful on the surface, crashed in bankruptcy in 1762, the victim of over-expansion and excessive ambition. The three partners, however, remained liable for the company's debts. Two years later, in an effort to recoup his fortune, Trumble formed another partnership—Trumble, Fitch, and Trumble—with his eldest son, Joseph, and the merchant Eleazar Fitch of Windham. This also failed, with Trumble's share of the debt amounting to £11,860, a huge sum equal to at least the worth of ten family farms. For the rest of his life he would be mired in debt and forced to scramble to keep his creditors from foreclosing on his property.

In line with his dramatically mixed fortunes as a merchant, Trumble also experienced a number of sharp highs and lows in his political career. Having been elected a deputy to the general assembly in 1733, he was chosen clerk of the assembly in 1736 aged twenty-six, only to be dismissed two weeks later 'upon an extraordinary occasion', as the records cryptically state. Trumble bounced back and was selected speaker of the assembly from 1739 to 1740 and elected to the governor's council from 1740 to 1751. He then failed to be re-elected for three years—an unusual occurrence in Connecticut's legendarily steady politics—but served again from 1754 to 1766, at which date he was elected deputy governor during the Stamp Act crisis, and also changed his name to Trumbull. The freemen failed to reappoint Governor Thomas Fitch, who had reluctantly taken the oath required by Britain to enforce the hated Stamp Act. Deputy Governor William Pitkin was elected governor and Trumbull his deputy governor in Pitkin's place. When Governor Pitkin died three years later in 1769, Trumbull became governor and was re-elected annually until he retired in 1783. Trumbull was the only colonial governor to stay in office in the transition from colony to independent state, and, remarkably, he served throughout the entire revolutionary war.

As a champion of colonial rights in the first half of the

1770s, Trumbull became an early advocate for independence, and in May 1776 began to omit the king's name in official letters, which he signed: 'John Trumbull, Esquire, Captain General and Commander in Chief of the State of Connecticut in America'. On 22 June 1776 he issued a proclamation of independence, two weeks before the famous declaration of the second continental congress. In his role of governor, Trumbull developed a warm, productive relationship with George Washington. His store in Lebanon became the headquarters of Connecticut's revolutionary war effort and the meeting-place of the committee of safety, the body to which the general assembly delegated much of its authority to prosecute the war. In addition, Trumbull drew upon his knowledge as a merchant to make Connecticut the most important supplier of foodstuffs to the continental army during the early stages of the war. His family also played an extraordinary role in the war. His eldest son, Joseph (1737–1778), was the first commissary-general of the continental army; his second son, Jonathan (1740–1809), was General Washington's personal secretary (1778–9); and his youngest son, John *Trumbull (1756–1843), a distinguished artist, painted many of the most famous portraits of revolutionary leaders.

Despite his own and his family's herculean efforts on behalf of the war, Trumbull was not popular with Connecticut's freemen. As deputy governor he lagged significantly behind Governor Pitkin in votes, and in the latter stages of the revolution he faltered badly at the polls. In the elections of 1780, 1781, 1782, and 1783 he received a plurality but not a majority of the freemen's votes, as required by law for election. In cases such as this, which were rare in Connecticut's history, the election was turned over to the general assembly, which did select Trumbull on each of these occasions. He chose not to run in 1784, because he faced certain humiliation at the polls and probable defeat in the assembly. Partly, his financial problems plagued him. False rumours also circulated that Trumbull was making a personal fortune through his provisioning work and through illegal trade with the enemy in New York. More damaging in political terms was the anger of farmers and enlisted soldiers, who, with some justice, perceived that Trumbull's policies favoured the commercial élite. His personal demeanour was also at odds with the spirit of the times. His unquestionable patriotic ardour notwithstanding, he conducted himself more as a puritan magistrate than a republican politician. Instead of courting voters and listening to their opinions, he expected the deference he felt he had earned through a lifetime of service. More dignified and reserved than haughty, Trumbull nevertheless appeared remote and cold to the new type of participatory voter who emerged during the revolutionary era—a great leader of a movement whose inner vitality tragically escaped his knowledge.

Trumbull's wife, Faith, died on 29 May 1780; two of his children also died during the revolution. After stepping down in 1783, Trumbull spent the last two years of his life writing religious sermons and trying unsuccessfully to sort out his tangled finances. He caught a fever and died on 17 August 1785, at Lebanon, after a twelve-day illness. He was buried at Lebanon on 19 August. Much honoured but never beloved in public life, Trumbull was ironically identified by the federalists as a heroic martyr to the cause of nationhood. In the nineteenth century several biographers erroneously claimed that Trumbull was the prototype for 'Brother Jonathan', the name invented by whig historians to describe their ideal of the simple citizen of the fledgeling republic. Few images of Trumbull could be further from the truth.   BRUCE C. DANIELS

Sources G. Weaver, *Jonathan Trumbull: Connecticut's merchant magistrate* (1956) · D. M. Roth, *Connecticut's war governor: Jonathan Trumbull* (1974) · C. K. Shipton, 'Trumbull, Jonathan', *Sibley's Harvard graduates: biographical sketches of those who attended Harvard College*, 8 (1951), 267–300 · I. W. Stuart, *Life of Jonathan Trumbull, sen.* (1859) · J. Trumbull, *Jonathan Trumbull, governor of Connecticut, 1769–1784* (1919) · S. R. Grossbart, 'Trumbull, Jonathan', *ANB*
Archives Connecticut Historical Society, Hartford, papers · Connecticut State Library, Hartford, diaries · Connecticut State Library, Hartford, papers
Likenesses portrait, 1775, Connecticut Historical Society, Hartford; repro. in Roth, *Connecticut's war governor* · J. Bufford, oils, *c.*1777, Museum of Connecticut History, Hartford; repro. in Stuart, *Life of Jonathan Trumbull* · portrait, *c.*1778, Connecticut Historical Society, Hartford; repro. in Stuart, *Life of Jonathan Trumbull* · portrait, Yale U. Art Gallery · portrait, Wadsworth Atheneum, Hartford, Connecticut
Wealth at death see Connecticut State Library, file 3826, probate records, Windham District, 1786

Trumbull, William (1576x80?–1635), diplomat and government official, was the middle son of John Turnebull (*d.* 1603), a tenant farmer at Stirton in the parish of Skipton in Craven, Yorkshire, and his wife, Elizabeth Brogden. By 1594 he was apprenticed to William Dudson, an attorney employed at Hampton Court. He soon came under the favourable notice of the keeper of Hampton Court, the lord high admiral, Lord Howard of Effingham, and began to learn Spanish from two Spanish gentlemen taken by the admiral at sea. He also made many contacts in the Elizabethan civil service, especially among the staff of the privy council, to which he was seconded at busy times. In August 1599 he was transferred permanently from Dudson's service to that of Thomas Edmondes, a clerk of the council and experienced diplomat who was about to be sent on a mission to the Spanish Netherlands.

About this time Trumbull married Deborah (*d.* in or after 1638), daughter of Walter Downe (*d.* 1591), a yeoman of Beltring in East Peckham, Kent, where she had inherited several parcels of land which Trumbull was later to consolidate. She stayed at home while he accompanied Edmondes on several missions to the Spanish Netherlands and France, in 1603 receiving the reversion of a place as post or courier. On the conclusion of hostilities in 1605 Edmondes was appointed to the newly reopened Brussels embassy with Trumbull as his senior secretary. In 1609 Edmondes was transferred to Paris and Trumbull left in charge in Brussels on what was assumed to be a temporary basis. He proved reliable and much cheaper than an ambassador, so was allowed to stay on, sending for his family; he remained the accredited agent of James VI and I

at the court of the archdukes Albert and Isabella (after 1621, Isabella alone) until war broke out again in 1625.

Seen as a safe pair of hands—cautious, discreet, diligent, honest is how the king and his ministers most frequently described him—Trumbull was capable of blistering private exchanges with trusted correspondents, such as Archbishop George Abbot and Sir Ralph Winwood, who shared his antipathies to Rome and Spain. He may indeed have remained so long at his post partly from a sense of obligation to the protestant international whose interests his unrivalled intelligence network did much to serve. He has been called 'a familiar figure in the new age of government by paper: the relatively minor functionary who becomes a major source' (L. J. Reeve, *International History Review*, 12, 1990, 572), and he was valued as such by key contemporary players such as the elector and electress palatine and the duc de Bouillon.

As the king's representative Trumbull conscientiously pressed for British mediation first in the Cleves–Juliers succession crisis and later in the Thirty Years' War, in 1621 undertaking a mission to Germany which resulted in a three months' ceasefire in the Palatinate. He saw to it that no more gunpowder plots were hatched in Flanders, and in 1615 may have helped to bring to light the Overbury murder conspiracy. He was less successful in a protracted attempt to secure the punishment of the author of *Isaaci Casauboni corona regia*, a scurrilous libel on James printed at Louvain in 1615: both he and the king believed it to be the work of Erycius van de Putte—'putidus Puteanus' or putrid Puteanus as Trumbull described him to James—but although the printer testified that Puteanus had corrected the proofs the real author is now thought to have been Cornelius Breda.

Trumbull was the more distressed by his failure because he prided himself on his knowledge of the book trade. Literature, gardening, and music were his three passions and throughout his life he had an extensive acquaintance among their practitioners. He is also a figure of some importance in the history of the fine arts, for much of his time at Brussels was spent procuring paintings and drawings, tapestries and hangings, silver, and jewellery, not only for connoisseurs like the earl of Arundel and Sir Dudley Carleton but also for lesser collectors who could not rise to a Raphael or a Rubens but were still anxious for souvenirs from the art market of Europe. He appears to have taken no commission even for major undertakings such as helping to supply skilled workers and patterns for the tapestry works at Mortlake, but he expected his good offices to be reciprocated.

Trumbull returned to England in October 1625, settled briefly in Thames Ditton, and took up his duties as a clerk of the privy council, for he had bought Edmondes's place for £350 in 1614 and been sworn in while on leave in 1615. However, it brought in only £50 a year, and he began to call in other favours. At a by-election in February 1626 he was returned to parliament for Downton in Wiltshire, a borough in the gift of the earl of Pembroke, whose mother was one of many distinguished visitors to whom he had shown hospitality in Brussels. His parliamentary career lasted only until the dissolution in June, for he did not stand again; he is known to have spoken only once in parliament, and to have sat on only two minor committees. In the autumn, however, he put himself forward to the Levant Company (of which he had been a freeman since 1618) as a candidate for the Constantinople embassy in succession to Sir Thomas Roe, and nearly won election despite the king's expressed preference for Peter Wyche. He was instead appointed keeper of Easthampstead Walk in Windsor Forest, and granted Easthampstead Park, which remained the family seat for over three centuries. He became a JP for Berkshire in 1629 and was also appointed to other royal commissions: in 1629 to examine complaints about Irish causes, in 1632 to investigate smuggling, and in 1634 to inquire into the soap monopoly. In 1632 he was made muster-master-general of England for life. Trumbull's health had never been good, and he fell ill during one of his duty spells in London in the summer of 1635. He made his will on 20 August and died at the beginning of September, probably in his usual lodgings above a barber's shop in the Strand. He was buried on 9 September in the parish church of St Martin-in-the-Fields, survived by his wife and three of their four children.

Trumbull also left an archive which ensured that his memory endured. In 1989 what was then a record price for a private archive was paid by the British Library, with support from the nation, for his papers, together with those of his son, William Trumbull (1603–1678), his grandson, Sir William *Trumbull (1639–1716), and the latter's maternal grandfather, Georg Rudolph *Weckherlin (1584–1653). Trumbull's archive is as bulky as all the rest put together, and is an essential source for an extremely wide range of topics, from the sixteenth-century government of La Rochelle to the Caroline privy council. Above all it is now generally accepted as:

> the basic starting place for any study of Jacobean England … the collection is so rich that, in terms of signal blows to scholarship, Trumbull's recall to London in 1625 must rank with the fire in the Cottonian manuscripts and the destruction of the Irish Record Office. (Cogswell, 324)

SONIA P. ANDERSON

Sources S. P. Anderson, 'The elder William Trumbull: a biographical sketch', *British Library Journal*, 19 (1993), 115–32 · BL, Add. MSS 72242–72480 · PRO, SP 77/9–18 · Berks. RO, D/ED · *Report on the manuscripts of the marquis of Downshire*, 6 vols. in 7, HMC, 75 (1924–95), vols. 2–6 · 'Trumbull, William', HoP, Commons [draft] · will, PROB 11/169, fol. 120 · CSP dom., 1601–36 · D. Howarth, 'William Trumbull and art collecting in Jacobean England', *British Library Journal*, 20 (1994), 140–62 · 'Family and estate papers of the Hill family, marquesses of Downshire', *Annual Review, 1989–1990*, HMC (1990), 23–8 · PRO, SP 105/148 · W. J. Stavert, ed., *The parish register of Skipton-in-Craven, 1592–1680* (1894) · J. V. Kitto, ed., *The register of St Martin-in-the-Fields, London, 1619–1636*, Harleian Society, register section, 66 (1936) · T. Cogswell, *The blessed revolution: English politics and the coming of war, 1621–1624* (1989) · *Principal family and estate collections: family names A–K*, HMC (1996), no. 52 [Hill, marquesses of Downshire] · J. H. Lea, 'Contributions to a Trumbull genealogy', *New England Historical and Genealogical Register*, 49 (1895), 332
Archives BL, Add. MSS 72242–72480 · CUL, his lute book, Add. MS 8844 | Berks. RO, Downshire MSS, estate and family papers, incl. inventories of his estate, D/ED · BL, letters to Sir W. Aston, Add. MSS 36444–36447 · BL, letters to Lord Carlisle, Egerton MSS 2592–2596 · BL, letters to Sir Thomas Edmondes, Stowe MSS 171, 174–176 · PRO, state papers, Flanders, dispatches from Brussels, SP 77/9–18
Likenesses G. Vertue, line engraving, 1724 (after G. Kneller), BM, NPG · G. Vertue, line engraving, 1726 (after O. van Veen, 1617), BM, NPG · S. Gribelin, line engraving, BM, NPG
Wealth at death personal estate valued at £1428; property in the parishes of Easthampstead, Berkshire, East Harlsey, Yorkshire, Wraysbury, Buckinghamshire, and East Peckham, Yalding, Wateringbury, Tudeley, and Brenchley, Kent: inventories, Berks. RO, D/ED/F3; will, PRO, PROB 11/169, fol. 120

Trumbull, Sir William (1639–1716), civil lawyer and government official, was born on 12 or 13 August 1639 at Easthampstead Park, Berkshire, the country residence of his father, William Trumbull (1604/5–1678), politician and minor government official, and his mother, Trumbull's first wife, Elizabeth (1619/20–1652), daughter of the German-born Georg Rudolph *Weckherlin (1584–1653), government official and poet.

Early years and education Trumbull was brought up in the deeply pious household of his father, who supported parliament and then Cromwell in the 1640s and 1650s, but after the Restoration took up a position as clerk of the signet. From an early age he received instruction in Latin and French from his grandfather Weckherlin, and from 1649 until 1655 he attended Wokingham School. He matriculated from St John's, Oxford, on 5 April 1655, and in 1657, the year in which he also enrolled at the Middle Temple, he was chosen a fellow of All Souls and over the next few years progressed through the college offices of dean, bursar, and sub-warden. The bursarship, as he recalled in an unpublished memoir, gave him his first taste of administrative responsibility, but he found public speaking a painful ordeal, an impediment which, with an acutely sober and sensitive temperament, followed him into maturity. He graduated BCL on 12 October 1659.

During 1664–6 Trumbull travelled abroad, chiefly in France and Italy, in the company of Edward Browne, the son of the antiquary Sir Thomas Browne. On returning to Oxford, however, he found that the attractions of college life had faded and prepared for a career in the rarified haven of civil law.

Lawyer and government official, 1667–1685 In 1667, having graduated DCL on 6 July, Trumbull was admitted to the court of arches in October and began practising in the vice-chancellor's court in Oxford. His first cause saw him successfully challenge the vice-chancellor's jurisdiction over All Souls in relation to the fees due from him on taking his doctorate of civil law. This achievement brought him instant recognition and almost all the business of the vice-chancellor's court. He was duly admitted in the following year as an advocate at Doctors' Commons in London, thereby becoming a member of the exclusive fraternity of civil lawyers. Trumbull practised diligently, if unspectacularly, for the next fifteen years in the Admiralty and ecclesiastical courts; his refusal to partake of the easy profits available in his profession ensured that his fee-takings rarely exceeded a modest £500 a year. On 24 November 1670 Trumbull married Katherine (d. 1704),

Sir William Trumbull (**1639–1716**), by George Vertue, 1724 (after Sir Godfrey Kneller, c.1690)

youngest daughter of Sir Charles Cotterell of Westminster and Rousham, Oxfordshire, master of ceremonies at the royal court. The marriage was childless. Through his father-in-law's offices Trumbull was in 1671 appointed chancellor of the diocese of Rochester, whose bishop, John Dolben, the future primate of York, became Trumbull's particular friend and mentor.

From 1683 Trumbull's career began to take a different direction. Early in that year he acquired by reversion the place of clerk of the signet, a post which brought him to the outer fringes of government administration; and in the summer Lord Dartmouth, impressed with Trumbull's ability at the council table, chose him to serve as judge-advocate in his mission to evacuate Tangier. Trumbull was by now regarded as one of the foremost civil lawyers of the day, and Dartmouth (who happened to be a cousin of Trumbull's wife) was anxious to benefit from the best talent available. Reluctantly Trumbull agreed to go, but his bitterness was aroused by the fact that the true object of the mission had been kept from him until after the squadron had set sail. After arriving at Tangier Bay in mid-September, he troubled Dartmouth with incessant complaints on this score and about his loss of fee-takings at home, and made a particular enemy of Samuel Pepys, a fellow commissioner, who was only too glad of the opportunity to demonstrate his own usefulness at the expense of Trumbull's. Quickly tiring of Trumbull's 'ridiculous

melancholy', Dartmouth dispatched him homewards the following month to report on progress.

Despite this friction Dartmouth was careful to commend Trumbull most warmly in the report which Trumbull was to convey to the cabinet council so that he might have no cause to meddle with Dartmouth's reputation at court. Trumbull made an excellent impression on Charles II and his ministers. He returned to business at Doctors' Commons but continued to receive professions of goodwill from Dartmouth, and on Archbishop Dolben's prompting he began to hope that the association might result in some form of preferment. In August 1684 Sidney Godolphin, head of the Treasury, suggested Trumbull for the post of secretary of state, but was refused by the king. A more serious proposition materialized in October when Lord Rochester, lord lieutenant of Ireland, asked Trumbull to serve as secretary at war in the new Irish administration. At first Trumbull accepted, and on 21 November he was knighted by the king. In the weeks that followed, however, he was confirmed in his suspicions that he was in fact being imposed upon Rochester by Lord Sunderland, the secretary of state, whose main purpose was to use Trumbull to monitor Rochester's activities. Realizing he was to be made a tool in Rochester's humiliation, Trumbull declined the post in mid-December.

Early in February 1685 Lord Dartmouth secured for Trumbull the post of clerk of deliveries in the Ordnance office with a salary of £300, and in April he was elected to parliament for the Cornish borough of East Looe. Trumbull recalled in his memoirs that although he had reached a point in his career where 'my reputation stood fair enough with the world', his brief and unsatisfactory experience of the court made him realize that 'my insuperable bashfulness made me very unfit to contend with men of sordid and corrupted tempers' (All Souls College, MS 317, fols. 17–18). However, his contemplation of a life of quiet retirement at the small country house he had lately purchased on the edge of Ealing Common was suddenly interrupted late in August with the news that James II had chosen him as ambassador to France in succession to Lord Preston. Trumbull was filled with misgiving; with King James a declared Catholic and Louis XIV persecuting his protestant subjects, he saw clearly the likelihood of his own staunch protestantism embroiling him in damaging conflict with both the English and the French courts. Once again he suspected he was the victim of some higher political game. In an interview with the king he expressed his preference to succeed the dying Sir Leoline Jenkins as judge of the prerogative court of Canterbury, but James insisted upon his going, assuring him that it would be 'a step to other matters' (ibid., fol. 20).

Ambassador to France and Constantinople, 1685–1692 Finding no way of retreat, Trumbull submitted to what he interpreted as an act of God's providence. Trumbull was not permitted to retain his Ordnance office, but was compensated with a pension of £200. His embassy in France did indeed prove brief and stormy. Upon his arrival at Paris late in November 1685, complaints of ill treatment poured in from English and Scottish residents, Louis XIV having the previous month revoked the edict of Nantes. He openly defended the protestant cause and employed none but protestants in his household. Much of his time was spent in pleading with French officials over occurrences of harshness and persecution against members of the English community, and he issued regular complaints to the French court. He even provided shelter and false passports to several seeking escape from the French authorities. A larger concern was the French annexation of the principality of Orange, for years a haven for Huguenots, and upon the urging of its ruler Prince William he sought the intercession of the prince's father-in-law, James II. Acting on James II's instructions, Trumbull on three occasions presented memorials to the French ministers urging recognition of William's rights to the principality as guaranteed by the treaty of Nijmegen (1678), only to be upbraided by Lord Sunderland, following complaints from the French court, about the abruptness of his tone. Trumbull grew increasingly frustrated at failing to achieve redress from the French on any issue, and was particularly galled that his appeals to King James and the English ministers for positive intervention with the French court had elicited such little concern. The final straw came early in July 1686 when Louis XIV removed diplomatic immunity from protestant servants employed in embassy households. The privy council decided to recall Trumbull for a month, but in a pre-emptive move he asked Sunderland for the vacant embassy at Constantinople, which he was given.

Trumbull returned to London in mid-October, and embarked for the Porte in April 1687. In his memoir he expressed his gratitude that 'providence' had enabled him to maintain his distance from the 'sad catastrophe' that was by then unfolding in England. Trumbull's four years in Constantinople were undoubtedly the happiest of his public career, there enjoying

> the honour of the character, the peace and great plenty of our trade, and (above all) the liberty of my conscience and religion; for the sake of which it was easy to support this banishment with all its attendance and the dwelling in the middle of frequent alarms we received from war, revolutions, tumults, earthquakes and raging plagues among us. (All Souls College, MS 317, fol. 54)

Trumbull's unpublished narrative of events in Turkey during this time was used by Sir Paul Rycaut in his continuation of Richard Knolles's *Turkish History*.

Treasury commissioner, secretary of state, and MP, 1692–1697 Having relinquished his duties in Constantinople in July 1691, Trumbull disembarked at Greenwich in January 1692. Although he disavowed any attachment to party, his professed devotion to the Church of England placed him firmly within the tory fold. Portland and other senior politicians were particularly encouraged by his broad-church views and saw him as a moderate tory who might well serve usefully in the present tory-dominated ministry. Lord Nottingham, lately appointed secretary of state, with whom Trumbull was on friendly terms, saw him as an ideal colleague who, though a most pious Anglican, was 'not for oppressing anybody'; but the earl of Portland, on sounding him in February, found him distinctly non-committal, and the possibility that Trumbull might serve as Nottingham's fellow secretary faded later in the year with the growing need to incorporate more whigs into the government.

In May 1693 Trumbull was offered but declined appointment as one of the lords justices in Ireland, while a judicial post in the prerogative court of Canterbury was denied him. The king and Sunderland, who was acting as the king's political 'broker', were clearly keeping him in reserve and were waiting only for a suitable moment to bring him into high office. In April 1694 the king appointed him a member of the Treasury board. Trumbull was full of apprehension and gloom about re-entering the political world, but his appointment held a twofold significance. The failure of a 'mixed' administration of whigs and tories had led to a refashioning of the ministry on mainly whiggish lines in which it was felt that Trumbull's moderate tory presence would contribute to a smoothing of tension between the parties. More importantly, however, Trumbull was a known 'creature' of Sunderland, and his position on the Treasury board denoted the earl's substantial role in this major shift of power.

A year later, in May 1695, Sunderland engineered Trumbull's appointment as secretary of state in the southern department. Sunderland had been engaged in an intermittent struggle over this vacancy since the beginning of the year with the other secretary of state, the duke of Shrewsbury, who wanted his whig friend Thomas Wharton appointed. Although Trumbull took up his new duties immediately, having been sworn into the privy council on 1 May, he was kept on the Treasury board until November, again largely to avoid the appointment of a junto nominee in his place. However, the underlying conflict between Sunderland and Shrewsbury was to bedevil Trumbull's brief experience of high office and force his early departure from the political arena.

In October 1695 Trumbull was elected MP for Oxford University. He was no parliamentarian, however, finding his duties in the House of Commons intimidating in the extreme. Apart from the formal requirements of his post, he avoided attendance as much as possible. He did, however, at least initially, fulfil his promise as an effective secretary. As early as August intelligence reports began to reach him of a conspiracy to assassinate the king, and Trumbull immersed himself fully in the task of investigation. A highly effective network of informers under his control kept him closely informed about Jacobite activity, and by late February 1696 a full disclosure of the plot was made in council and in parliament. Trumbull's obsessive pursuit of the conspirators sprang from his abiding fears of a Stuart coup and of a Catholic regime bound to France, and he continued to pin down suspects with a zeal that began to cause discomfort in government circles. By the summer, however, near exhaustion had forced him to take several spells of leave, and in consequence the interrogations of Sir John Fenwick and fellow conspirators were handled by Shrewsbury's faithful under-secretary, James Vernon. It was probably just as well, since Fenwick's 'confession' included the revelation that Shrewsbury himself had maintained contact with the exiled court. The king was immediately informed and accepted Shrewsbury's explanation of the circumstances, but Trumbull began to form his own suspicions regarding Shrewsbury.

From this point onwards, Trumbull found himself increasingly ignored in important matters of government, and a mounting sense of grievance began to overwhelm him. Business relating to the Fenwick affair was now managed by Under-Secretary Vernon, Shrewsbury himself pleading ill health and incapacity. The resulting *ad hoc* division of administrative responsibility burdened Trumbull with the heavy, complex tasks, while Vernon's office appropriated much of the more remunerative work. Trumbull brought his catalogue of complaints to the king's attention in mid-October 1696, but he was dissuaded from resigning. Tension between Trumbull and Vernon ran high during the months that followed, not least on account of Trumbull's continuing investigations, which by now had begun to centre upon Shrewsbury. By early 1697, as parliament proceeded with its own inquest into Fenwick's allegations against Shrewsbury and other ministers, Vernon feared that Trumbull had evidence to hand concerning the duke that would corroborate Fenwick and was merely awaiting an appropriate moment. Trumbull, however, was not called upon to testify, though he continued to gather intelligence which incriminated both Shrewsbury and Vernon long after parliamentary interest in the Fenwick plot had subsided. A further attempt to lay down the seals in April 1697 was angrily rebuffed by the king. Neither did he obtain much support from his patron Lord Sunderland, who, after coaxing Trumbull to remain in office, then acquiesced in Shrewsbury's obstruction of several appointments which Trumbull had requested as a condition for staying. Shrewsbury's coldness towards him, Trumbull felt, was a poor return 'for keeping all quiet' (diary, May 1696–Dec 1697, BL, Add. MS 72571). In May his name was omitted from the lords justices appointed to govern in the king's absence, while Vernon's was included. Trumbull was absent from business so often during the summer that he was requested to provide a supply of signed blank warrants, thus prompting his famous complaint that the lords justices treated him more like a footman than a secretary.

Further hostility between Trumbull and Vernon broke out over the ratification of the peace of Ryswick in the autumn. The treaty documents, which were sent to Shrewsbury's office to be handed on to Trumbull, in whose province as northern secretary they properly belonged, were retained by Vernon, who subsequently counter-signed them and pocketed the profits from sealing and publication. Trumbull's hatred of Shrewsbury and Vernon intensified, and by November, in the face of accumulating insults, he was prepared to go on no longer. Sunderland, who still regarded him as a valuable counterweight to the junto politicians, met him on 29 November and entreated him to stay. Reluctantly, Trumbull agreed, but on finding that a prebend at Windsor promised for his

brother Ralph had gone instead to a member of Princess Anne's household, he declared his intention to resign and on 1 December surrendered his seals of office to the king.

Retirement This marked the end of Trumbull's political career. He declined re-election for Oxford University in the following year, having already settled into the retired existence at Easthampstead Park which had often been his ideal when overwhelmed by the iniquities of public office. Although many were impressed by Trumbull's learned and professional skill, his emotions were dominated by a profound sense of pious rectitude which could make him at turns seem stubborn, self-centred, and highly sensitive. As he reflected on his career in later years, he felt justified at having removed himself from a scene of activity which he detested. While he continued to take a detached interest in politics, his own involvement in the public sphere was restricted to a handful of institutions: he was governor of Hudson's Bay Company from 1696 to 1700, and of the Levant Company from 1696 to 1710; a commissioner for the rebuilding of St Paul's Cathedral; and verderer of Windsor Forest in 1703. He was elected FRS in 1692.

Trumbull's wife, Katherine, died in July 1704, and in Scotland in October 1706 he married Lady Judith (*c*.1675–1724), daughter of Henry Alexander, fourth earl of Stirling. They had a son, William (1708–1760), and a daughter who died in infancy. Trumbull's book collecting and literary interests led to friendship with the young Alexander Pope, his near neighbour at Easthampstead, who idolized him in some of his early verse as a paragon of virtuous 'retirement'. The young and aspiring politician Henry St John (later Viscount Bolingbroke) also valued Trumbull as a mentor, and they corresponded for many years. Trumbull died on 14 December 1716 at Easthampstead and was buried at the parish church.

The younger brother of Sir William, **Charles Trumbull** (1645/6–1724), was a nonjuring Church of England clergyman. He matriculated from Christ Church, Oxford, on 1 April 1664, aged eighteen, and graduated BA from Christ Church in 1667 and in 1677 DCL from All Souls, of which college he was a fellow from 1670 to 1680. He was rector of Merstham, Surrey (1678–9), then of Hadleigh, Suffolk, and of Stisted, Essex (1679–91). He was also chaplain to Archbishop Sancroft from 1679, and followed him in resigning his benefices after the revolution. He died on 3 January 1724 and was buried at Hadleigh.   A. A. HANHAM

Sources P. Watson and B. D. Henning, 'Trumbull, William', HoP, *Commons, 1660–90* • 'Trumbull, Sir William', HoP, *Commons, 1690–1715* [draft] • R. Clark, *Sir William Trumbull in Paris* (1938) • *Report on the manuscripts of the marquis of Downshire*, 6 vols. in 7, HMC, 75 (1924–95) • Trumbull diary, 1685–92, BL, Add. MS 52279 • W. Trumbull, autobiography, All Souls Oxf., MS 317 • will, PRO, PROB 11/555, sig. 239 • IGI • DNB • M. Burrows, *Worthies of All Souls* (1874) • G. D. Squibb, *Doctors' Commons: a history of the College of Advocates and Doctors of Law* (1977) • Foster, *Alum. Oxon.* • W. H. Rylands, ed., *The four visitations of Berkshire*, 1, Harleian Society, 56 (1907), 296 • Venn, *Alum. Cant.* • private information (2004) [fellow of All Souls]

Archives Berks. RO, legal papers; incl. papers as chancellor of Rochester diocese • BL, commonplace book, Add. MS 70590 • BL, commonplace books, RP 708 [microfilm] • BL, corresp. and papers,

Dep 8826; further papers Dep 9145 · BL, diary and account of negotiations in Florence, Add. MSS 52279–52280 · BL, legal commonplace book, with inserted letters and papers, Dep 8990 · BL, memorials of embassy in Constantinople, Add. MS 34799 · BL, official account book, Dep 9190 · BL, papers relating to France, Add. MS 61912 · Bodl. Oxf., extracts from letters · CUL, collections and papers relating to Oxford University, his embassy to France, legal career, and Spanish history, Add. MSS 8863–8888 · NRA, admiralty letter-book · NRA, priv. coll., legal commonplace book · NRA, priv. coll., papers relating to embassy to Constantinople · U. Leeds, Brotherton L., diary and travel notes in France · Yale U., papers, incl. letter-book and commonplace books · Yale U., Beinecke L., corresp. and papers | BL, corresp. with Lord Carlisle, Egerton MSS 2592–2596 · BL, corresp. with John Ellis, Add. MS 28895 · BL, corresp. with Lord Lexington, Add. MSS 46525–46526 · BL, letters to Sir J. Williamson and Lord Villiers, Add. MS 28899 · Longleat House, Wiltshire, corresp. with Matthew Prior · PRO, corresp. with George Stepney, SP 105/54, 58–60, 82 · U. Nott. L., letters to the earl of Portland

Likenesses P. Lely, oils, 1670–79, Althorp, Northamptonshire · G. Vertue, line engraving, 1724 (after G. Kneller, c.1690), BM, NPG [see illus.] · H. Cheere, bronze bust, c.1756, All Souls Oxf.

Wealth at death Easthampstead manor; manors in Buckinghamshire, Yorkshire, Kent: will, PRO, PROB 11/555, sig. 239

Trumper, Victor Thomas (1877–1915), cricketer, was probably born on 2 November 1877 in Sydney. He was probably a great-grandson of Charles Trumper, hatter, and his wife, née Samson, who were married in London in 1834 and migrated to Sydney in 1837. His putative parents were Charles Thomas Trumper (1859–1920), a footwear manufacturer, and his wife, Louise Coghlan (1856–1923), who were married at Ultimo, Sydney, on 15 May 1883. Trumper left Crown Street superior public (state) school in 1894 and was a clerk in the New South Wales public service until 1904, when with Hanson Carter, Australia's wicket-keeper, he opened a sports store.

From early boyhood Trumper lived for summer and cricket. Like many first-class Australian players before the 1930s, his gift for the game was nurtured almost daily in the streets of Sydney. He haunted the Sydney cricket ground, near his home, watching the great men at practice, taking every chance to be useful to them, and relishing every important match. Although he was delicate, his enthusiasm and emerging skill made him a schoolboy champion. In 1892 he played for the Carlton Club, and the next year was in the South Sydney first-grade team under Syd Gregory, later captain of the Australian eleven. Selected for the New South Wales junior eighteen against Andrew Stoddart's eleven on 22 December 1894, he scored 67 runs. He played his first game for New South Wales in January 1895, beginning a state career of seventy-three matches, with 5823 runs at an average of 51.08, including fifteen centuries and twenty-nine half-centuries: a fast bowler, he took thirty-three wickets at 34.97. His complete first-class record is 255 matches, 16,939 runs at an average of 44.58 per innings, with forty-two centuries and eighty-seven half-centuries.

By the 1898–9 season Trumper was tall, willowy, and good-looking. He had attracted the first signs of public adulation, which was to run wild as his batting flowered, though it never affected his innate modesty. A late inclusion in the 1899 Australian touring team, he quickly shone, scoring 135 not out in the Lord's test in June, and next month became the first Australian to make 300 in England—against Sussex. Altogether he was to play in 48 test matches (including eight against South Africa) in which he scored 3163 runs at an average of 39.05 per innings, with eight centuries and thirteen half-centuries.

Trumper's luminous role at the federation celebrations in January 1901 in Sydney reflected not only his fame, but also the significance cricket had assumed in Australian culture. Both the personal and the national facets were refined in the 1902 team's tour of England. The Ashes were won and Trumper ignited an inextinguishable beacon in the history of the game. In one of the wettest summers on record he scored 2570 runs at an average of 48.49 per innings, with eleven centuries. He became the first batsman in tests to score a century before lunch—at Old Trafford on 24 July—and the first in first-class cricket to make two centuries in one match (of three days)—against Essex. *Wisden's Cricketers' Almanack* (1903), saluted him as 'the best batsman in the world'. He had set standards of excellence that beckoned young men throughout the British empire.

Although Trumper's achievements of 1902 are impressive on any account, his career record reflects the contemporary manual preparation of pitches and the practice of leaving them uncovered during rain. Bowlers had a decisive advantage, which remained until the 1930s. His fame rests on his artistry rather than on statistics: the primacy of style, the symmetry of grace and timing, which complemented the co-ordination of mind and body that enabled him to judge to perfection the pace, length, flight, and direction of each ball he faced. He played every stroke in the game, and some he invented, with the agility of a ballet dancer. On sticky or otherwise dangerous wickets he improvised with peerless precision. In 1912 Jack Hobbs considered him 'The most perfect batsman … I have ever seen' (Hobbs, 158). Even on his off-days he was good to watch, for his whole approach to cricket was of a piece with his happy-go-lucky personality. Often, in minor games, he sacrificed his wicket to give his team-mates a turn.

On 7 June 1904 in St Patrick's Roman Catholic Cathedral, Melbourne, Trumper married Sarah Ann Briggs (1878–1963). She too was a cricket lover and she persuaded him to improve somewhat his careless dressing, though not to give up his cavalier treatment of bats, or his scorn for batting gloves and rubber grips. She shared his optimistic hopes in business: after much needed restructuring of his enterprises in 1909 and 1912, her venture with E. C. Clifton resulted in £1040 being added to Trumper's debts. Following the great success of his testimonial match in February 1913, the New South Wales Cricket Association wisely placed the proceeds, £2950, in a trust fund. Trumper's backing in 1908 had helped the Rugby League to break away from the Rugby Union, but he did not excel in his brief time as treasurer of the new code.

Trumper's health, never robust, worsened after a bout of scarlet fever in 1908, which caused him to miss the 1908–9 season, and induced a chronic kidney affliction that constricted the rest of his life. Despite that, he starred in the first test series against a South African touring team in 1910–11, scoring 661 runs at an average of 94.93 per innings. In his final tour, of New Zealand, he enlivened Christchurch in February 1914 with 293 runs in 178 minutes.

Trumper died in St Vincent's Hospital, Sydney, on 28 June 1915, survived by his wife, who died on 1 April 1963, and a daughter and son. He was buried on 30 June in the Anglican section of Waverley cemetery, on the western edge of the Pacific Ocean. In 1919 E. C. Clifton was granted administration of Trumper's intestate estate, valued at £5.   BEDE NAIRN

Sources 'Public service list, 1903', *Votes and proceedings*, New South Wales Legislative Assembly (1903), vol. 2, p. 67 · J. B. Hobbs, 'Test-match cricket', *Strand Magazine*, 44 (1912), 154–61 · *Wisden* (1903), lxxxvii–lxxxviii · *Wisden* (1916), 131–2 · P. Sharpham, *Trumper* (1985) · C. B. Fry, *Great batsmen* (1905) · N. Cardus, *The summer game* (1929) · J. H. Fingleton, *The immortal Victor Trumper* (1978) · A. Mallet, *Trumper: the illustrated biography* (1985) · E. Barbour, 'The greatest batsman of all time', *Sydney Mail* (12 Oct 1932), 8–9 · d. cert.
Likenesses photographs, repro. in Mallet, *Trumper*
Wealth at death £5: New South Wales probate office, Sydney, Australia

Truro. For this title name *see* Wilde, Thomas, first Baron Truro (1782–1855).

Truscott, Harold (1914–1992), musicologist and composer, was born on 23 August 1914 at 66 Holmwood Road, Ilford, Essex, the younger son of Ernest Truscott (*c*.1880–*c*.1950) and his wife, Emily Annie Warren (*c*.1890–*c*.1953). His father was a Post Office sorter, later an overseer. He attended Ilford county high school (1925–30), and in 1928, encouraged by an uncle, started composing. His father disapproved strongly, but he continued to compose, and copied out the scores of other composers' works. In 1930, when he was aged almost sixteen, his father took him to a psychiatrist and had him hospitalized in the asylum ward of Oldchurch Hospital, Romford. Ironically, a friendly nurse provided him with manuscript paper and a pencil, which enabled him to continue composing undisturbed during his three-month stay.

On leaving the hospital, Truscott decided to teach himself while working for the Post Office rather than return to school. In 1934 he studied briefly at the Guildhall School, London. Because of a club foot, later successfully operated on, he missed war service. He attended the Royal College of Music in London between May 1943 and 1945, studying the horn with Frank Probin, the piano with Angus Morrison, and composition with Herbert Howells. After returning in April 1947 he gained his performer's ARCM diploma as a pianist.

In 1947–52, with Donald Mitchell (later Britten's publisher), Harry Newstone, Alec Robertson, Robert Simpson, and others, Truscott organized a musical society which met regularly at Crofton Park in south-east London to discuss neglected and new music. Truscott and his fellow composer Simpson had also founded the Exploratory Concert Society in London in 1946 for the performance of neglected music. Truscott's and Simpson's enthusiasm for Nielsen, Havergal Brian, and Bruckner led to a gradual revival of their music worldwide. Truscott performed frequently as a pianist–accompanist, including some of his own early works. He assisted Simpson with the difficult art of piano writing; Simpson's resulting *Variations and Finale on a Theme of Haydn* (1948) was dedicated to Truscott.

On 9 August 1948 Truscott married (Eleanor) Margaret Madge (*b*. 1926) at Central Hill Roman Catholic Church, Norwood, having converted to Catholicism two years earlier. They lived in Croydon, Surrey, and had three children: Hilary, Veronica, and Richard. Truscott taught at the Blackheath Conservatoire of Music (1948–54), then at Sandwich secondary modern school, Kent (1954–6). To compensate for missing his own school certificate he studied at Bretton Hall Teacher Training College near Wakefield in 1956–7. In 1957 he was appointed lecturer in musicianship and history at Huddersfield College of Technology; during the late 1970s he was principal there, retiring in 1979.

Truscott's musical interests were idiosyncratic for his time; liking under-performed composers, he championed, among others, Bantock, Boito, Brian, Busoni, Czerny, Clementi, Dussek, Hummel, Korngold, Mahler, Medtner, Moór, Nielsen, Pfitzner, Reger, Rubbra, Schmidt, Scott, Spohr, and Tovey. Among mainstream composers Truscott loved Bach, Mendelssohn, Schumann, Brahms, Hindemith, Bartók, and Sibelius. His favourite piano performances were Artur Schnabel playing Schubert and Beethoven, each of whose works Truscott knew thoroughly. He completed many of Schubert's unfinished sonatas and, like him, left many of his own movements incomplete, and lost entire works.

Fully half of Truscott's own music is for piano; during his lifetime, his reputation as a composer rested largely on his twenty-one piano sonatas (another was unfinished), ten of which were recorded. Truscott's other works included three sonatas for violin and piano, and also individual sonatas for solo violin, oboe, and horn; and three sonatas for the clarinet. His larger works consisted of a symphony as well as movements for projected second and third symphonies, a suite for orchestra, and a fantasy for strings. There are few songs: he liked a challenge, and he found that the presence of words made the task too easy, besides which he preferred absolute music. Closest to Nielsen and later Schmidt in style, unashamedly tonal, and with little interest in originality for its own sake, his finest music combines tremendous vigour with economy and mastery of form, developing in a Beethovenian way. He liked the lower register, which makes the trio for flute, violin, and viola of special interest as it has uncharacteristically little bass. This was one of his first broadcast works (1955). Owing to a total breakdown in relations with William Glock at the BBC, little of Truscott's music was subsequently broadcast.

As a writer Truscott published widely in journals and magazines. His first volume on Franz Schmidt was well received; two further volumes were incomplete as he was denied access to primary sources. He wrote numerous articles, and gave many valuable radio talks. He was also an avid reader. After finishing all Henry James's novels he would reread them. Other favourite writers were J. B. Priestley, especially for *The Good Companions*, George Eliot, E. M. Forster, Aldous Huxley, Jerome K. Jerome, Thomas Mann, and Marcel Proust. He worked long hours, and could be seen reading or correcting proofs in concert intervals, and while eating: he said that 'to eat without a book is time wasted'. His enjoyment of silent films— Buster Keaton, the Keystone Cops, Laurel and Hardy—was more than just a pastime.

Harold Truscott died of coronary artery atherosclerosis, chronic bronchitis, and emphysema at the William Harvey Hospital, near Ashford, Kent, on 7 October 1992. The funeral took place on 13 October 1992 at Barham crematorium, Kent. His wife, Margaret, survived him.

Utterly neglected as a composer for most of his life, Truscott used his even temper to balance a strong sense of humour with an extremely serious disposition; these— together with his kind, courteous nature—preserved his sanity following the early traumas and later frustrations. Blunt, honest, and without affectation or social graces, he could be aloof. His head was broad, his straight hair brushed back unparted; he wore thick tweedy suits, checked shirts, and ties, and was small in stature. His short sight made him accident-prone. Curiously, in character, looks, and achievement he was an amalgam of Schubert, Beethoven, and Bruckner, three composers he revered. As a 'complete' musician he ranks alongside Nadia Boulanger, Benjamin Britten, Arnold Schoenberg, Sir Donald Tovey, and Alexander Zemlinsky. No half measures for Harold Truscott: the man simply lived, loved, and breathed music.   RICHARD STOKER

Sources G. Rickards, *Contemporary composers* (1990) · R. Stoker, *Open window—open door* (1985) · *The Oxford dictionary of music*, 2nd edn (1997) · A. Jacobs, ed., *The music yearbook 1972–3* (1972) · *Donald Mitchell on Benjamin Britten* (1978) · *HT: 75th birthday celebration* (1989) · *Havergal Brian Society Newsletter*, 87 (1990) · personal knowledge (2004) · private information (2004) [Margaret Truscott, widow; P. Horton, Royal College of Music, London, library and archive; Donald Mitchell] · *The Independent* (15 Oct 1992) · *The Independent* (28 Dec 1992)
Archives SOUND BBC WAC, BBC Gram Library · BL NSA, performance recordings · British Music Information Centre, London W1, recordings of Truscott's music · British Music Society, cassette recordings, BMS410 (MC) · priv. coll., privately recorded LP
Likenesses portrait, priv. coll. · portrait, priv. coll. · portrait, University of Huddersfield, music faculty · portrait, priv. coll.

Trusler, John (1735–1820), Church of England clergyman and author, was born in Hanover Square, London, in July 1735, the elder and only surviving son of John Trusler. His mother came from a family of Wiltshire clothiers named Webb and was related to Philip Carteret Webb. His father was proprietor of the Rose tavern and tearooms at Marylebone Gardens, and though not a wealthy man he took care to educate his son as a gentleman. Trusler accordingly was sent, in his tenth year, to Westminster School, and

remained there until he was fifteen, when he was transferred to the fashionable seminary in Marylebone run by Mr Fountaine. On 16 May 1753 he entered Emmanuel College, Cambridge, as a sizar. After graduating BA in 1757 he returned to Marylebone, where he assisted his future brother-in-law Stefano (Stephen) Storace in translating into English the popular Italian burletta *La serva padrona*, by Giovanni Battista Pergolesi; it was performed in Marylebone Gardens in June 1758.

After some difficulties Trusler was ordained deacon in London, on 23 September 1759, by the bishop of Salisbury. He was curate briefly of Enford in Wiltshire, before moving to Hertford, where he officiated at Sunday services. He then served as curate at Hythe church in Colchester. In 1759 he took priests' orders, married (his first wife's name is unknown), and took up curatorial duties at Ockley, Surrey. He soon exchanged this church for St Clement Danes in the Strand, London, where he was kept busy ministering to a large congregation while enjoying a salary of £100 p.a. In 1761 he became chaplain to the Poultry Compter through the influence of Dr Bruce, the king's chaplain at Somerset House, who made him his assistant in the same year. During this time he and his wife and their son lived in Rotherhithe on an income of £70 p.a. His lighter workload allowed him to hold lectureships at St George's, Botolph Lane, and at St Botolph, Billingsgate. Following the death of his wife in December 1762, Trusler apparently exchanged duty with a clergyman in Solihull, Warwickshire. He returned to London, where he married Elizabeth (d. 1780), daughter of James Burns of St Paul's, Covent Garden, on 10 October 1764 at St Margaret's, Westminster. They had five daughters. In his will (dated 6 June 1818) Trusler names another wife, Mary, who survived him, but nothing further is known of her.

Trusler's interests were diverse. In 1762, when he was living in Somerset House, he established an academy for teaching oratory mechanically, but this did not prove a success. Wishing to offer medical advice to his parishioners, he then turned his attention to medicine, and admitted himself as a perpetual pupil of Dr William Hunter and Dr George Fordyce; he apparently took the degree of MD from Leiden University, but he is not included in its list of graduates. Nevertheless he acquired or assumed the title of doctor and described himself as 'a medical gentleman' in his *An easy way to prolong life, by a little attention to what we eat and drink … collected from the authorities of some of the ablest physicians* (1773).

In 1765 Trusler published a circular announcing the formation of 'the Literary Society', created to fill the gap left by the Royal Society for the Encouragement of Arts, Manufactures, and Commerce, which Trusler felt did not promote literary merit sufficiently. According to Trusler's *Plan of the Literary Society* the society would express its patriotism through supporting authors and encouraging literary talent by offering assistance with the publication of works. It was announced also that an academy would be established for the study of eloquence, and a quarterly review would be published. The society had its own printing house—the Literary Press—which was first at 14 Red

Lion Street, Clerkenwell, London, and then at 62 Wardour Street, Soho; it seems to have been run by Trusler at both addresses. A committee of members was to approve manuscripts sent in by prospective authors and, if approved, the work could be published by the Literary Society. The society would be responsible for the risks and costs of publication, and the author would receive all the profit after the society's expenses had been paid. Subscriptions were invited from the general public but the society's publicity noted that booksellers and printers could not join. A number of Trusler's own works printed at the Literary Press were listed in a printed handbill of 1793 but only a few by other authors, such as Elizabeth Ryves and Mrs. A. Gomersall. The publication by the Literary Press of the sensational work by Elizabeth Steele, *Memoirs of the Late Mrs Sophia Baddeley*, in 1787 led to a row between Trusler and the author after Trusler publicly accused Steele of pirating the work. She defended herself in a handbill dated 23 July 1787, accusing Trusler of possessing 'an effrontery peculiar to himself'.

Trusler published a prodigious range of works on topics as diverse as medicine, farming, history, politeness, law, theology, travel, and gardening. In 1766 Jane Hogarth, widow of the artist, employed Trusler to supply explanatory commentaries of the prints, and she herself sold the resulting *Hogarth Moralized* (1768). Trusler was an enthusiastic and fearless compiler of others' works, the most popular of which was his 'methodised and digested' version of Lord Chesterfield's *Letters to his Son* (1774), published as *Principles of Politeness* in 1775. In the same year he published a second volume, aimed at young ladies, which was written by himself. He also abridged William Blackstone's *Commentaries* in 1788 and Thomas Stackhouse's biblical history for the use of schools, entitled *A Compendium of Sacred History* (1797).

Trusler wrote several books on conduct as well as self-help manuals, including the popular and practical *The Way to be Rich and Respectable, Addressed to Men of Small Fortune* (1775), which explains how a country gentleman may 'live as well as, and make an appearance in life equal to, a man of £1000 a year and not expend £400' (title-page). Equally popular was his compendium of dates and historical tables—*Chronology, or, The Historian's Vade-Mecum* (1769)—and his range of almanacs, guidebooks, and manuals authored by himself and others. He is credited with publishing the first thesaurus to the English language; entitled *The Distinction between Words Esteemed Synonymous* (1766), this was one of a number of educational works produced by Trusler. Many of his publications are advertised as being beautifully illustrated or of a small and convenient size; John Bewick illustrated two, *Proverbs Exemplified* (1790) and *The Progress of Man and Society* (1791).

One of Trusler's enterprises was to publish sermons in cursive script for clergymen who did not want to write their own sermons but wished to appear as though they did. He assured prospective buyers that 'only 400 copies of any one sermon, are, at any time vended; that they do not pass through the hands of the booksellers, of course, the Clergy may rest satisfied that they never can be too

general' (*List of Books*, 10). The list noted that 150 sermons were then available and offered a discount for bulk: purchasers might have any at 1*s*. each or 9*d*. each if they bought 100.

Trusler's publishing enterprises proved profitable, and he moved to Bath on the proceeds. There he published the first part of his rambling and anecdotal *Memoirs of the Life of the Rev. Dr. Trusler* (1806), but according to Lowndes he regretted its publication and tried to suppress it by destroying all the copies that he could find. The manuscript of the second part of his memoirs is now in the Lewis Walpole Library, Yale University. Trusler may have owned an estate at Englefield Green, Middlesex, where he lived for some time, but by 1819 he was less affluent and was living at Villa House, Bathwick, Somerset, where he died in June 1820.

Trusler's will shows him to have been far from wealthy on his death. The first section betrays his fear of being buried alive: he stipulated that he was not to be buried until his body showed signs of decay and that he should not be put in a sealed coffin. He directed that there should be no funeral pomp and requested that his burial should be attended by two poor men in black cloaks with 'round felt hats worth 3 s'. At his request he was buried in Bathwick burial-ground, on 23 June 1820. Trusler left no real estate and distributed his books, furniture, and jewellery between his wife, daughter, and son, who were also his executors; he left only £12 in money bequests and directed that the cost of his funeral should not exceed £10. Special mention is made of three portraits of Trusler: a miniature, a large portrait, and a wax portrait at that time in the possession of his sister Sarah.

EMMA MAJOR

Sources *Memoirs of the life of the Rev. Dr. Trusler … written by himself* (1806) • Venn, *Alum. Cant.*, 1/4 • ESTC • will, PRO, PROB 11/183, fol. 66r–v • DNB • *A list of books, published by the Rev. Dr. Trusler* (1790) • *N&Q*, 3 (1851), 110; 4th ser., 3 (1869), 421–2 • W. T. Lowndes, *The bibliographer's manual of English literature*, ed. H. G. Bohn, [new edn], 4 (1864), 2715 • R. Paulson, *Hogarth*, vol. 3 (1993), 438 • *GM*, 1st ser., 90/2 (1820), 89, 120 • Watt, *Bibl. Brit.*, 2.917
Archives Bath Central Library, autobiography • Yale U., Farmington, Lewis Walpole Library, MS of part two of his memoirs
Likenesses L. Legoux, line engraving, pubd 1807 (after Bonmaison), BM • Dent, line engraving, BM; repro. in J. Trusler, *Hogarth memorialized* (1768) • silhouette portrait, repro. in *Memoirs of … Rev. Dr. Trusler*, frontispiece
Wealth at death see will, PRO, PROB 11/183, fol. 66r–v

Trussell, Sir John (1349–1424). *See under* Lollard knights (*act. c.*1380–*c.*1414).

Trussell, John (*bap.* 1575, *d.* 1648), antiquary and historian, was baptized on 19 January 1575 at St Dunstan-in-the-West, London, the third child and elder son of Henry Trussell (*c.*1545–1612/13), attorney, and his wife, Sarah (*bap.* 1550, *d.* 1613), daughter of John Kettlewood, citizen and goldsmith of St Mary Woolnoth, London. Trussell's grandfather John (*c.*1515–1571/2) was the younger son of a gentry family of Billesley, Warwickshire, who entered the service of the Willoughby family of Nottinghamshire as steward of their coalpits at Wollaton. His elder son Henry moved first to London where he married and practised as an attorney. John Trussell was born in London, and his description of William Camden as 'my ever to bee reverenced and remembred Schoolmaster' ('Touchstone of tradition', fol. 29) suggests that he attended Westminster School. No evidence of either university or legal education survives although Trussell, like his father, later earned his living in the law.

Three literary works published in the mid-1590s, apparently written by a young man, have been attributed to Trussell (Shaaber, 407–48). *Raptus I. Helenae: the First Rape of Faire Hellen, done into Poeme by J.T.* (1595) shows the author's name amplified to 'JOHN TRUSSEL', and refers to it as his 'first fruits'. The work is prefaced by three commendatory poems, all emphasizing the writer's youth. This may create a problem in accepting Trussell's authorship of a second poem published a year earlier, *An Ould Facioned Love* (1594), by 'J.T. gent.', which has also been tentatively attributed to him, unless *Faire Hellen* had been written earlier (Eccles, 169–70). The third work consists of three dedicatory verses signed 'John Trussell' prefixed to *Triumphs over Death*, a poem written by the Jesuit Robert Southwell and published after his execution in 1595. The verses dedicate the work to the children of Robert Sackville, later second earl of Dorset, the death of whose wife, Margaret, in 1591 had occasioned the composition of Southwell's poem, and it is possible that Trussell was the children's tutor (Shaaber, 413). Clearly there was a young poet in London named John Trussell publishing in the 1590s, and he could plausibly be identified with the antiquary. The theory that 'John Trussell' was a pseudonym for William Shakespeare deserves rather less credence (R. Southwell, *Triumphs over Death*, ed. J. W. Trotman, 1914, 110–36).

After a period of service with the Willoughby family, Henry Trussell followed his sister Elizabeth to Winchester in 1596 when her husband, John Harmar, became warden of Winchester College and appointed his brother-in-law as steward of the college manors. By 1606 John Trussell too had settled in Winchester and in that year was elected a freeman of the city. His first marriage, between 1603 and 1609, was to Elizabeth (*bap.* 1574), daughter of Thomas Colly, a Winchester clothier; she was the widow of Gracian Patten, whose father, William, had been a member of the Elizabethan Society of Antiquaries. Three daughters were born to the marriage by 1622, although only two children were mentioned in 1631. Trussell's second wife, whom he married on 10 August 1634, was Margaret, daughter of Christopher Smith, woollen draper, and widow of William Luke, a pewterer and former mayor. She survived him and died in 1677.

Once established in Winchester, Trussell pursued an active career as a provincial attorney, appearing in the city court, quarter sessions, and assizes. He was frequently employed by the city to transact business in London and represented the corporation and other clients before the Westminster courts. The dean and chapter appointed him as bailiff of their liberties in Hampshire 1613–16; however the assertion that Trussell was steward to the bishop of Winchester, first made in the anonymous *History and Antiquities of Winchester* (1773) and repeated by most subsequent writers, appears to be incorrect. Office-holding

within the corporation accompanied his legal career and he served as bailiff of the twenty-four (the senior of the two city bailiffs) in 1616–17, an alderman, and mayor of Winchester in 1624–5 and 1633–4.

Trussell's real love, however, was history, and in his usual alliterative style he confessed to leaving 'no chronicle of this land, that purse, or prayer could purchase or procure, unperused' (*Continuation*, epistle to reader). In 1636 John Trussell published *A continuation of the collection of the history of England, beginning where Samuel Daniell esquire ended, with the raigne of Edward the Third, and ending where the honourable Vicount Saint Albones began, with the life of Henry the Seventh, being a compleat history of the beginning and end of the dissention betwixt the two houses of Yorke and Lancaster*. Defining history as 'a perfect register of things formerly done', he promised to eschew 'superfluous exuberances' such as accounts of coronations, pageants, and miraculous events. Trussell corresponded with other historians and based his narrative on wide reading of printed sources, but his continuation was pedestrian in comparison with Daniel's work. With Michael Drayton and others, Trussell also contributed two poems in 1636 to the *Annalia Dubrensia*, collected for Captain Robert Dover.

Trussell also turned his attention to the history of Winchester, and his unpublished antiquarian writings offer more sophistication and originality. His main work, the 'Touchstone of tradition' (referred to by Wood and others who had not seen it as 'A description of the city of Winchester'), started with the earliest origins of urban society which Trussell attributed to the human need for the preservation of property and social distinction. Tracing Winchester's foundation back to the legendary Lud Hudibras, Trussell acknowledged the difficulty of writing about the distant past, but argued that 'to beleive nothing of Antiquitie, but what is perspicuous and unquestionablie proved, is but the bare refuge of dulpated ignoraunt droanes, or meachanicke precise plebeyans' ('Touchstone', fol. 10). Nevertheless he made careful and critical use of his sources, which were for the most part printed chronicles and legal records, augmented by the city records and manuscripts in the cathedral library. Acutely aware of the contrast between Winchester's proud medieval past and its contemporary 'dotage', Trussell saw the recording of its history as a service which he hoped would suggest solutions to the city's current ills. The 'Touchstone of tradition' was the last of his writings, completed in 1647; the manuscript was in Lord Mostyn's library by 1744, and remained there until it was acquired by the city council in 1974.

The 'Origin of cities', written *c.*1636, was an earlier draft of the first three of the four books of the 'Touchstone of tradition'. According to a note on the flyleaf the manuscript was lent to Sir John Oglander while in prison in 1644. It was owned by John Duthy (*d.* 1784), clerk of the peace for Hampshire, and his son John (*d.* 1839), and was known to local historians including the Revd John Milner who used it in writing *The History and Survey of the Antiquities of Winchester* (1798). In 1937 the manuscript was bequeathed to the city.

Another section of the 'Touchstone of tradition' was Trussell's 'Epitome of the forest law', also found in two other copies, one of which also contains a 'Collection of cases concerning tithes'. Trussell appealed unsuccessfully to Sir John Finch in 1639 for permission to publish his exposition of forest law, which was intended to inform readers whose ignorance had recently brought them before the revived forest courts at Winchester and elsewhere. Many of his writings were dedicated to prominent judges and leading Hampshire gentry, a reflection of his legal career. A history by Trussell of the bishops of Winchester, mentioned by Wood and dismissed unseen by White Kennett (W. Kennett, *Life of Mr Somner*, 1693, 20–21), probably never existed as a separate work but was yet another section of the 'Touchstone of tradition'.

John Trussell's other manuscript work, a miscellaneous volume known as the 'Benefactors to Winchester', was compiled piecemeal from the 1620s to 1647. Its lists of city documents, benefactors, and mayors and bailiffs were the conventional stuff of urban annals, but Trussell also aimed to instruct the city's governors. Referring to disputes within the corporation in 1622, he denounced those 'troubled with a pruriticall itch of scratching against authority' and extolled the benefits of order. His fellow aldermen were castigated for failing to enforce the city ordinances and their shortcomings were described in verse; not surprisingly, Trussell complained that he was unpopular and felt his intentions were misunderstood. The last section of his 'Benefactors' is a history of Winchester in verse, 'The declaration of Caerguent's lament', ending with a vivid description of the social dislocation brought about by the civil war and Trussell's fervent wish for a royalist victory. The manuscript was later owned by the book collectors Richard Heber (*d.* 1833), Sir Thomas Phillipps (*d.* 1872), and James Osborn (*d.* 1976) who presented it to the Bodleian Library in 1964.

Since the early 1640s Trussell had been complaining that the ailments of old age made writing increasingly difficult, and in September 1646 he was exempted from standing for election as mayor 'in respect of his impotency and infirmity' (Hants. RO, W/B1/4, fol. 161). He died between 7 August and 18 September 1648.

ADRIENNE ROSEN

Sources T. Atkinson, 'The Trussell manuscripts', *Proceedings of the Hampshire Field Club*, 19 (1955–7), 290–98 · G. W. Marshall, ed., *The visitations of the county of Nottingham in the years 1569 and 1614*, Harleian Society, 4 (1871), 4.28 · W. H. Rylands, ed., *Pedigrees from the visitation of Hampshire … 1530 … 1575 … 1622 … 1634*, Harleian Society, 64 (1913), 223 · *Report on the manuscripts of Lord Middleton*, HMC, 69 (1911), 315–16, 388, 396, 474, 524, 551, 553 [service with Willoughby family] · will, 1571, Borth. Inst., Prob. Reg. 19 [John Trussell], fol. 399 · M. A. Shaaber, 'The *first rape of faire Hellen* by John Trussell', *Shakespeare Quarterly*, 8 (1957), 407–48 · M. Eccles, *Christopher Marlowe in London* (1934), 169–70 · S. Himsworth, ed., *Winchester College muniments: a descriptive list*, 3 vols. (1976–84) · Hants. RO, W/B1/1–5 · lease to John and Elizabeth Trussell, 1616, Hants. RO, W/F2/3 · Hants. RO, W/E6/1–2 · will of Gracian Patten, PRO, PROB 11/102, sig. 88 · Hants. RO, 1M82W/PR1–3 · will, 1609, Hants. RO, A21 [Thomas Colly] · D. R. Woolf, *The idea of history in early Stuart England* (1990), 241–2 · parish register, London, St Dunstan-in-the-West, 19 Jan 1575, GL [baptism] · Winchester Cathedral, dean and chapter reg. 11, fol. 16*v* · Shakespeare Birthplace Trust RO, Stratford upon Avon, DR 37/88/68

Trussell, Thomas (*b.* in or before **1564**, *d.* **1640**), army officer and military writer, was the eldest son of John Trussell, esquire (*c.*1540–1581/2), of Billesley, Warwickshire, and his wife, Mary, *née* Grimston. The family had held Billesley, near Stratford upon Avon, since the twelfth century and had long since converted the parish to sheep pasture. Thomas presumably grew up there, and attended school locally. In 1581 he was old enough to write and witness his father's will, and when John Trussell died Thomas inherited both his father's financial problems and responsibility for his three brothers and five sisters.

In August 1585, 'newly come of full years and altogether unexperienced in worldly affairs' (PRO, STAC5/O.4/25), Trussell was persuaded by his brother-in-law and an old schoolfriend to commit a highway robbery at Bromley, Kent, apparently in an attempt to defraud him of lands and money. On the advice of his mother's second husband, Henry Fenton, and his brother Geoffrey *Fenton, principal secretary of state in Ireland, Trussell petitioned the privy council and was not prosecuted for the offence, but his financial affairs became ever more tangled. Billesley was either sold or mortgaged; desperate to recover his lands, Trussell in July 1588 apparently procured his own arrest in Kent for the earlier robbery, in the hope that upon conviction his lands would escheat to the earl of Warwick who might be persuaded to regrant them for the use of the family. Trussell was indeed convicted and sentenced to hang, but a letter from the earl of Leicester and Sir Francis Walsingham ordered his reprieve and transfer to a London prison 'for some causes of special service of her majesty' (Cockburn, 279), and in April 1589 he was a prisoner in the Compter in Wood Street. Billesley, however, was forfeited to the crown and lost.

The nature of Trussell's 'special service' is unknown, and there is no evidence as to his movements during the 1590s apart from a deed of 1598 which shows him resident in London. However, the later description of him in the herald's visitation of Warwickshire in 1619 as a soldier and his authorship of a drill manual imply extensive military experience, presumably while he was a young man. Trussell's book *The souldier pleading his owne cause: furnished with argument to encourage, and skill to instruct, with an epitome of the qualities required in the severall officers of a privat company* was published in a second edition 'much enlarged with military instructions' in 1619, and a third edition appeared in 1626. The date of its first edition is not known. After a preface defending the honour of 'soldier-ship' against those who 'despise the profession as base and vile', the book lists the qualities of a good soldier and the duties of each rank and sets out 'certain military instructions for young soldiers, agreeable to the discipline practised in the Netherlands', including drill used by the prince of Orange's guard. The volume is small enough to be carried in a pocket, and it has been posited that the book's portability accounts for its success (M. J. D. Cockle, *A Bibliography of English Military Books up to 1642*, 1900, 77–8).

On 9 October 1603 Thomas Trussell married Margaret

Boughton (*bap.* 1581, *d.* 1622), the youngest daughter of Edward Boughton (*d.* 1589) of Cawston, near Rugby. Boughton had been a gentleman of substance, favoured by the earl of Leicester, and had served as sheriff of Warwickshire (1579–80) and MP for Coventry in 1584. His estate and newly built mansion house had been settled on his widow, Susanna, for life, and the baptism nearby at Dunchurch of several children born to Thomas and Margaret Trussell between 1605 and 1616 suggests that they too were living at Cawston. Susanna Boughton had opposed her daughter's marriage to Trussell, whom she described as 'a man both needy and shifty, having for many years … very little wherewithal to maintain himself, his wife, children and family, more than what [she] did give and allow him' (PRO, STAC8/38/8). Trussell was permitted to live in the mansion house as bailiff to its lessees, but when he failed to pay his rent and installed his own cattle on her pastures his mother-in-law sued, and tried unsuccessfully to evict him. Finally in September 1617 her relatives entered the house by force and drove the Trussells out. Their home thereafter was another Trussell family estate (not forfeited in 1588) at Nuthurst, near Lapworth, Warwickshire. Margaret Trussell was buried at Lapworth on 22 March 1622.

Trussell had in 1610 written to the earl of Salisbury offering a 'small labour' dedicated to him for 'the supply of his majesty's private state, the general blessed peace, enriching of the common weal' (PRO, SP 14/54/75), but apparently without response. He enjoyed a closer relationship with Lord Conway, who was his countryman and contemporary and like Trussell a former soldier. A letter written from Nuthurst in January 1624 offered Conway advice on the calling of a new parliament, though Trussell lamented that he was 'to the world forgotten and buried alive' (PRO, SP 14/158/6), and he dedicated the third edition of his book to Conway in 1626. Possibly it was Conway who secured employment for Trussell at court as a messenger of the privy chamber from 1620 to 1627.

After Conway's death in 1631 Trussell appears to have retired to his estate at Nuthurst. Always short of money, he and his son Edward leased Nuthurst in 1639 to their neighbour Edward Ferrers of Baddesley Clinton; the whole estate was sold within months after his death to William Jesson the elder, alderman and dyer of Coventry, for £1326. Thomas Trussell's will, made in January 1640, left his gilt sword and hanger to his son and emerald and diamond rings to his three daughters. He died in the parish of St Dunstan-in-the-West, Fleet Street, London, and was buried there on 26 February 1640.

ADRIENNE ROSEN

Sources VCH Warwickshire, 3.60 · W. Dugdale, *The antiquities of Warwickshire illustrated*, rev. W. Thomas, 2nd edn, 1 (1730), 287; 2 (1730), 714–19, 958 · W. Camden, *The visitation of the county of Warwick in the year 1619*, ed. J. Fetherston, Harleian Society, 12 (1877), 93 · J. S. Cockburn, ed., *Calendar of assize records: Kent indictments, Elizabeth I* (1979), nos. 1677–80 · *CSP dom.*, 1625–6, 286, 321 · *APC*, 1619–27 · will of John Trussell of Billesley, 1582, PRO, PROB 11/64, sig. 45 · will, 1640, PRO, PROB 11/182, sig. 41 · will of Edward Boughton, 1589, PRO, PROB 11/74, sig. 90 · PRO, E178/2344 · PRO, C2/Jas.I/ C.1/75 · PRO, star chamber proceedings, STAC8/38/8; STAC5/ O.4/25; STAC5/O.8/39; STAC5/O.9/19; STAC5/U.2/25 · PRO, state papers, James I, SP14/54 no. 75; SP14/56 no. 8; SP14/158 no. 6 · parish registers, Dunchurch and Lapworth, Warks. CRO · Shakespeare Birthplace Trust RO, Stratford upon Avon, DR 37/2285a/113, 119–21; DR 3/480, 607 · parish register of St Dunstan-in-the-West, GL, MS 10345 · J. J. Belton, *The story of Nuthurst-cum-Hockley Heath, Warwickshire* (1948), 13, 35–6 · C. J. Bond, 'The deserted village of Billesley Trussell', *Warwickshire History*, 1 (1969), 15–24 **Wealth at death** see will, PRO, PROB 11/182, sig. 41

Trussell, Sir William (*fl.* 1307–1346/7), administrator and landowner, is sometimes difficult to distinguish from a number of namesakes. An elder William Trussell received a summons to parliament in 1294 and was sheriff of Kent in 1297–8. A younger namesake held the manor of Kibblestone, Staffordshire, was receiver of the king's chamber in 1333–5, and hereditary sheriff of Anglesey. This William Trussell founded a chantry college at Shottesbrooke, Berkshire, in 1337, and may have been the Trussell appointed admiral of the western fleet in 1339 and of the northern fleet in 1342. He died in 1363. A third namesake was the son of the man who is the subject of this article.

William Trussell held land in Peatling Magna, Leicestershire, and from 1307 for at least thirty years occurs as a Lancastrian retainer. When Thomas, earl of Lancaster, declined to perform service in person against the Scots in 1310 Trussell was one of the knights sent in his stead. In both 1313 and 1318—at the time of the treaty of Leake—he received pardon as one of Lancaster's men. In 1314 he was returned to parliament as knight of the shire for Leicester and in 1316 for Leicester and Warwick. He was in receipt of a fee of £10 from Lancaster's estate at Higham Ferrers in Northamptonshire in 1314, and in the following year the earl asked Chancellor John Sandale (*d.* 1319) to appoint Trussell and others to inquire into the death of his valet, John Swinnerton. Trussell is described at that time and in a commission of oyer and terminer of 1321 as 'of Nuthurst' (Warwickshire).

Trussell participated in Lancaster's rebellion of 1321–2 and following the débâcle at Boroughbridge fled abroad, though apparently not until after March 1323, when he was said to have taken part in an attack on the properties of Hugh Despenser the elder in the midlands. He then joined other exiles in France and returned with Queen Isabella in September 1326. After the fall of Bristol he acted as judge at the trial of the elder Despenser, earl of Winchester, and at that of the younger Despenser at Hereford, but his principal claim to fame arises from his part in Edward II's deposition. The most circumstantial account is in Baker's *Chronicon*. After the Ephiphany (6 January 1327), Baker writes, it was decided to send a deputation from parliament to the king at Kenilworth. He then gives Thomas de la More's eyewitness account of how Edward II reluctantly assented to abdication. On the following day (given elsewhere as 20 January) Trussell, according to the *Rolls of Parliament* speaking as 'proctor of the prelates, earls and barons and of other persons (*gentz*) named in my proxy', renounced fealty and allegiance. On the deputation's return to Westminster the young Prince Edward was acknowledged as king instead.

On 28 February 1327 Trussell was deputed with others to seek Thomas of Lancaster's canonization and was appointed southern escheator. In March 1328 he was sent on another mission, but at the Salisbury parliament in October armed conflict threatened to erupt between the Mortimer and Lancaster factions. Trussell was present on 21 December at the London Guildhall when a *pièce justificative* was read out on behalf of the government in an attempt to dissuade the Londoners from assisting the Lancastrians, who thereupon dispatched a riposte to the court at Worcester. The Lancastrians assembled at St Paul's on 2 January 1329 and bound themselves together by oath. The government of Mortimer and Isabella demanded their surrender and promised an amnesty, from which Trussell was excepted. The rising collapsed at Bedford, but at the Winchester parliament of March 1330 Trussell was reconciled to Mortimer and pardoned, although the pardon is annotated *vacatur quia non habuit cartam* ('void because he had no charter'). In May he was appointed to secure an alliance with the kings of Aragon, Portugal, and Majorca, and to arrange a marriage between Pedro, the infante of Aragon, and Edward III's sister, Eleanor, but this did not materialize.

Mortimer was arrested and subsequently condemned in the parliament of November 1330. In the following January Trussell was one of the jury of knights that exonerated Thomas Berkeley from culpability in Edward II's death. He also resumed his escheatorship. He received 100 marks in the summer for expenses on royal business and he and John Darcy were sent to France to negotiate a marriage between the infant Edward of Woodstock (*d.* 1376) and Jeanne, daughter of the king of France. For his services he was granted the lordship of Bergues in Flanders, and in 1332 both he and his son William were sent to the Avignon curia.

Between 1333 and 1345 a William Trussell, who could equally have been the son, was engaged in numerous diplomatic missions: to the papal court several times, to France, to the Low Countries, and to Austria. In 1340 a William Trussell sailed with the king and was sent back to announce to parliament the naval victory of Sluys. The same man in April 1343 in the White Chamber at Westminster Palace gave assent to the truce with France on behalf of the knights and commons (*les Chivalers des Counteez et les Communes*). Whether he is to be identified as the judge of the earls of Monteith and Fife after the battle of Nevilles Cross (1346) is unclear. Because of an individual summons in 1342 to a council—not a parliament—William Trussell has sometimes been styled Baron Trussell. With equal lack of justification his role in the events of 1327 led to his being regarded as the first speaker of the Commons. Baker's questionable claim that he acted as 'spokesman for the community of the whole realm' is insufficient to rule out such a view; more significant is the fact that Trussell had no clearly defined place in the 1327 parliament. The elder William Trussell would appear to have died in either 1346 or 1347, since during the 1346–7 financial year the sacrist of Westminster Abbey received a legacy from his executors. He is believed to have been buried in the east aisle of the abbey's north transept—the later St Michael's Chapel.   ROY MARTIN HAINES

Sources PRO, Anc. Corr. SC 1 · *Chronicon Galfridi le Baker de Swynebroke*, ed. E. M. Thompson (1889) · W. Stubbs, ed., *Chronicles of the reigns of Edward I and Edward II*, 2 vols., Rolls Series, 76 (1882–3) · *Chronicon Henrici Knighton, vel Cnitthon, monachi Leycestrensis*, ed. J. R. Lumby, 2 vols., Rolls Series, 92 (1889–95) · G. J. Aungier, ed., *Chroniques de London*, CS, 28 (1844) · J. B. Sheppard, ed., *Literae Cantuarienses: the letter books of the monastery of Christ Church, Canterbury*, 3 vols., Rolls Series, 85 (1887–9) · A. H. Thomas and P. E. Jones, eds., *Calendar of plea and memoranda rolls preserved among the archives of the corporation of the City of London at the Guildhall*, 6 vols. (1926–61) · *List of various accounts and documents connected therewith, formerly preserved in the Exchequer*, 35 (1912); repr. (1963) [Nuncii's accounts] · Chancery records · Rymer, *Foedera* · RotP · W. Dugdale, *The baronage of England*, 2 vols. (1675–6) · J. Bree, *The cursory sketch of the naval, military and civil establishment … Edward III* (1791) · T. Madox, *The history and antiquities of the exchequer of the kings of England*, 2nd edn, 2 vols. (1769); repr. (1969) · Tout, *Admin. hist.* · M. V. Clarke, *Medieval representation and consent: a study of early parliaments in England and Ireland* (1936); repr. (1964) · J. Stow, *A survey of the cities of London and Westminster and the borough of Southwark*, ed. J. Strype, new edn, 2 vols. (1720); rev. edn (1754) · A. P. Stanley, *Historical memorials of Westminster Abbey*, 6th edn (1886) · J. R. Maddicott, *Thomas of Lancaster, 1307–1322: a study in the reign of Edward II* (1970) · N. Fryde, *The tyranny and fall of Edward II, 1321–1326* (1979) · J. S. Roskell, *The Commons and their speakers in English parliaments, 1376–1523* (1965) · B. Harvey, *Westminster Abbey and its estates in the middle ages* (1977), 377

Trye, Charles Brandon (1757–1811), surgeon, the elder son of John Trye (1717–1766), rector of Leckhampton, near Cheltenham, and his wife, Mary, daughter of the Revd John Longford of Haresfield, near Stroud, was born on 21 August 1757. Both his parents died while he was at the grammar school in Cirencester. He was apprenticed in March 1773 to Thomas Hallward, an apothecary in Worcester, and in 1778 he became a pupil of William Russell, then senior surgeon to the Worcester Infirmary. At the expiration of his indentures in January 1780 he went to London to study under John Hunter and was appointed house apothecary or house surgeon to the Westminster Hospital, acting more particularly under the influence of Henry Watson, the surgeon and professor of anatomy at the Royal Academy. He acted as house surgeon for nearly eighteen months, and his skill as a dissector appears to have attracted the notice of John Sheldon, who engaged him to assist at his private anatomical school in Great Queen Street. Sheldon's illness and his enforced retirement from London led to the end of this arrangement, and Trye returned to Gloucester, where he was appointed house apothecary to the infirmary on 27 January 1783, and shortly after quitting this post he was elected in July 1784 surgeon to the charity, a position he held until 1810. He was admitted a member of the Company of Surgeons on 4 March 1784. Trye married, in May 1792, Mary (*d.* 1848), the elder daughter of Samuel Lysons, rector of Rodmarton, near Cirencester, and sister of Daniel Lysons (1762–1834); the couple had ten children. In 1793 Trye established, in conjunction with the Revd Thomas Stock, a lying-in charity in Gloucester, which, for seven years, they supported almost entirely at their own expense. In 1797 Trye succeeded under the will of his cousin, Henry Norwood, to a considerable estate in the parish of Leckhampton, near Cheltenham, but he still continued to practise medicine, for he devoted his rents to the payment of his cousin's debts. Trye opened up the stone quarries at Leckhampton Hill, and constructed a branch tramway, opened on 10 July 1810, to bring the stone from the quarries to within reach of the Severn at Gloucester. He was admitted a fellow of the Royal Society on 17 December 1807, and at the time of his death he was a member of the Royal Medical Society of Edinburgh. Trye was a man of considerable local importance. As a surgeon he acquired unusual skill in performing some of the most difficult operations. He was the steady friend and promoter of vaccination, and Jenner had a high opinion of his abilities.

Trye published *Remarks on Morbid Retentions of the Urine* (1774), *Review of Jesse Foote's Observations on the Opinions of John Hunter on the Venereal Disease* (1787), *An Essay on the Swelling of the Lower Extremities Incident to Lying-in Women* (1792), *Illustrations of some of the Injuries to which the Lower Limbs are Exposed* (1802), and *Essay on some of the Stages of the Operation of Cutting for Stone* (1811).

Trye died in Gloucester on 7 October 1811, and was buried in the churchyard of St Mary de Crypt at Gloucester. A plain tablet, with an inscription prepared by himself, was put up in the church at Leckhampton, and a public memorial to perpetuate his memory was placed in Gloucester Cathedral. He was survived by his wife, three sons, and five daughters.

D'A. POWER, rev. MICHAEL BEVAN

Sources D. Lysons, *A sketch of the life and character of the late Charles Brandon Trye* (1848) · private information (1898) · *GM*, 1st ser., 81/2 (1811), 487 · Foster, *Alum. Oxon.*, 1715–1886 [John Trye] · *GM*, 1st ser., 36 (1766), 551 [John Trye]
Archives Glos. RO, papers
Likenesses J. Neagle, line engraving (after R. Smirke; after C. Rossi), Wellcome L. · C. Rossi, medallion bust, Gloucester Cathedral

Trye [née O'Dowde], **Mary** (*fl.* 1675), medical practitioner, daughter of the physician Thomas *O'Dowde (*d.* 1665), took up her pen in 1674 to defend the reputation of her father, and so was one of the few early modern women medical practitioners to publish a book. The dedication of her *Medicatrix, or, The Woman-Physician* (1675), written to Lady Fisher of Packington Hall in Warwickshire, is dated 1 December 1674, and gives Trye's address as 'the Feathers' in 'Old Pell-Mell' near St James's. In it she says that she had moved to London from Warwick 'October last', where she became aware of the published attacks of Henry Stubbe on her father. Trye, like Stubbe, had practised in and around Warwick before moving to London, and she not only felt compelled to defend her father's reputation but to lambast Stubbe. Her father was not only a medical chemist but a well-born and loyal royalist who had lost his fortune during the troubles in Ireland of the 1640s, and who died during the plague of 1665. Trained by her father in medicine and medical chemistry she had continued to sell his medicines to the poor in Warwick 'more out of Charity then my private Interest'. While she says little about herself, she does claim in the introduction to her book to be 'satisfied there is Ability enough in my Sex, both to discourse [Stubbe's] envy, and equal the Arguments of his Pen in those things that are proper for a woman to engage'.

Apart from defending her father and attacking Stubbe, Trye mounts a defence of her medical views and remedies. Like most other medical chemists, she attacks the practice of phlebotomy. Like many of them, too, she declares that she esteems 'real Learning, and the Foundation, Promoters, and Doctors thereof', but that academic dress had too often become a shield for laziness and arrogance. Only in conjunction with the humility that comes from both practising among ordinary people and wrestling with nature in the laboratory could medical learning be perfected, she claims. Trye does quote from French sources, but has no citations from Latin or Greek, suggesting that she was no more academically educated than her father. It is clear, however, that Trye's book was in part intended to advance her own interests, for (like so many other medical tracts of the day) it concludes with an eight-page 'Advertisement of Dr. O'Dowdes Medicines, and the Authors'.

HAROLD J. COOK

Sources H. J. Cook, 'The Society of Chemical Physicians, the new philosophy, and the Restoration court', *Bulletin of the History of Medicine*, 61 (1987), 61–77 · M. Trye, *Medicatrix, or, The woman-physician* (1675)

Tryon, Sir George (1832–1893), naval officer, third son of Thomas Tryon (*d.* 1872) of Bulwick Park, Northamptonshire, and his wife, Anne (*d.* 1877), daughter of Sir John Trollope, sixth baronet, was born on 4 January 1832. The Tryons are believed to have been of Dutch origin, but had resided at Bulwick since the reign of James I. After some years at Eton College he entered the navy in the spring of 1848, as a naval cadet on board the *Wellesley*, then fitting for the flag of Lord Dundonald as commander-in-chief of the North American station. He was somewhat older than was usual, and bigger. When he passed for midshipman he was over eighteen, and was more than 6 feet tall. His size helped to give him authority, and his age gave him steadiness and application; zeal and force of character were natural gifts, and when the *Wellesley* was paid off in June 1851 he had won the very high opinion of his commanding officer. A few weeks later he was appointed to the *Vengeance* (Captain Lord Edward Russell) for the Mediterranean station, where he still was at the outbreak of the Crimean War. On 15 March 1854 he passed his examination in seamanship, but continuing in the *Vengeance*, from her maintop he watched the battle of the Alma, in which his two elder brothers fought. Shortly after the battle of Inkerman he was landed for service with the naval brigade, and a few days later was made a lieutenant in a death vacancy of 21 October; the admiral wrote to him, 'You owe it to the conduct and character which you bear in the service'. In January 1855 Tryon was re-embarked and returned to Britain in the *Vengeance*; but when he had passed his examination at Portsmouth, he was again sent

Sir George Tryon (1832–1893), by unknown engraver (after C. W. Walton, in or after 1891)

out to the Black Sea as a lieutenant of the *Royal Albert*, flagship of Sir Edmund Lyons, whose captain, William Mends, had been the commander of the *Vengeance*. The *Royal Albert* returned to Spithead in the summer of 1858, formed part of Queen Victoria's escort to Cherbourg in July, and was paid off in August. In November Tryon was appointed to the royal yacht, at the request of his father's friend Lord Derby, the prime minister. This ensured his promotion to commander on 25 October 1860.

In June 1861 Tryon was selected to be the commander of the *Warrior*, the first British seagoing ironclad, then preparing for her first commission. This was a prestigious appointment and Tryon made the most of it; he also came into contact with John Fisher, the ship's gunnery lieutenant. Tryon remained in the *Warrior*, attached to the Channel Fleet, until July 1864, when he was appointed to an independent command in the Mediterranean, the gunvessel *Surprise*, which he brought home and paid off in April 1866. He was then (11 April) promoted captain. During the next year he went through a course of theoretical study at the Royal Naval College, Portsmouth, and in August 1867 was away fishing in Norway, when he was recalled to go out as director of transports in Annesley Bay, where the troops and stores were landed for the Abyssinian expedition to rescue the hostages at Magdala. The work, neither interesting nor exciting, was extremely hard in a sweltering and unhealthy climate. Tryon's talent for organization, his foresight and clear-headedness, his care and his intimate knowledge of details impressed other officers, naval and military. He also won the esteem and regard of the masters of the transports—who were not always very amenable to discipline—and after his

return to Britain they presented him with a handsome service of plate in commemoration of their gratitude. His health, however, was severely tried, and for some months after his return to Britain he was very much of an invalid. On 5 April 1869 he married Clementina Charlotte, daughter of Gilbert John Heathcote, first Lord Aveland, and then went for a tour in Italy and central Europe, before settling down in the autumn near Doncaster.

In April 1871 Tryon was appointed private secretary to George Joachim Goschen, then first lord of the Admiralty; and, though his want of time and service as a captain might easily have caused some jealousy or friction, his good-humoured tact and ready wit overcame all difficulties, and won for him the confidence of the navy as well as of Goschen. In January 1874 he was appointed to the large frigate *Raleigh*; he commanded her for more than three years in the flying squadron, in attendance on the prince of Wales during his tour in India, and in the Mediterranean. In June 1877 he was appointed one of a committee for the revision of the signal-book and the manual of fleet evolutions, and in October 1878 took command of the *Monarch*, in the Mediterranean, one of the fleet with Sir Geoffrey Hornby in the Sea of Marmora, and in the autumn of 1880 with Sir Frederick Beauchamp Paget Seymour (afterwards Lord Alcester) in the international demonstration against the Turks in the Adriatic. During the summer and autumn of 1881 Tryon was specially employed as senior officer on the coast of Tunis, and by his 'sound judgment and discretion' gained the approval of the foreign secretary and the lords of the Admiralty. In January 1882 the *Monarch* was paid off at Malta, and shortly after his return to Britain Tryon was appointed secretary of the Admiralty, an office he held until April 1884, and in the autumn of 1882 he was largely responsible for the establishment of what became the naval intelligence division.

On 1 April 1884 Tryon was promoted rear-admiral, and in December he left Britain to take the command-in-chief of the Australian station, where, during the Russian war 'scare' of 1885 and afterwards, he formulated the scheme of colonial defence which was subsequently implemented. In June 1887 he returned to Britain; on the 21st he was nominated a KCB (a jubilee promotion). That September he stood as a Conservative candidate for the constituency of Spalding, without success. After a few months' holiday, including a season's shooting, he was appointed in April 1888 superintendent of reserves, which carried with it also the duty of commanding one of the opposing fleets in the summer manoeuvres. This Tryon performed for three years, bringing into the contest a degree of vigour which, especially in 1889, went far to solve some of the strategic questions then discussed in naval circles. He also at this time wrote an article on 'National insurance' (*United Service Magazine*, May 1890), in which he put forward a scheme for the protection of commerce, and especially of the supply of food in time of war. This scheme was not favourably received by shipowners and merchants, and, indeed, Tryon's principal object was probably rather to lift the discussion out of the academic or abstract groove into which it had fallen, and to force people to consider the question as one of the gravest practical importance. The subsequent introduction of such a scheme in time for the First World War indicated his concept.

On 15 August 1889 Tryon became a vice-admiral, and in August 1891 he was appointed to command the Mediterranean Fleet, where, as often as circumstances permitted, he collected his force to practise the naval drill in shiphandling and squadron cohesion, commonly termed evolutions, on a grand scale. There was subsequently much discussion about his methods, and especially about one—manoeuvring without signals—which was widely denounced as most dangerous, and, in fact, suicidal. But Tryon conceived it to be the best and most fitting training for the manoeuvres of battle. It was repeatedly practised by the fleet without any untoward incident, and it had nothing to do with the dreadful accident which closed Tryon's career. The manoeuvre which resulted in that calamity was ordered deliberately, by signal.

On the morning of 22 June 1893 the fleet weighed from Beirut, and a little after 2 p.m. was off Tripoli, where it was intended to anchor. Battleships then had pointed ram bows, designed to slice open and sink an opponent's hull. The ships were formed in two columns 1200 yards apart; and about half-past three the signal was made to invert the course in succession, turning inwards, the leading ships first. The two leading ships were the battleship *Victoria*, Tryon's flagship, and the battleship *Camperdown*, with his second in command, Rear-Admiral Albert Hastings Markham. It was clear to everyone, except Tryon, that the distance between the columns was too small to permit the ships to turn together in the manner prescribed, and by some, at least, of the captains, it was supposed that Tryon's intention was for the *Victoria* and the ships astern of her to turn on a large circle, so as to pass outside the *Camperdown* and the ships of the 2nd division. That this was not so was only realized when it was seen that the two ships, turning at the same time, both inwards, must necessarily come in collision. They did so. It was a question of but two or three seconds as to which should give, which should receive the blow. The *Victoria* happened to be by this time ahead of the *Camperdown*; she received the blow from the ram bow on her starboard bow, which was cut open. She rapidly flooded, as her watertight doors had not been secured, and then turned over and plunged head first to the bottom. The boats of the other ships were immediately sent to render assistance but the loss of life was very great. Tryon went down with the ship, and was never seen again. The most probable explanation of the disaster seems to be a simple miscalculation by Tryon, a momentary forgetfulness that two ships turning inwards needed twice the space that one did. As the two ships were approaching each other and the collision was seen to be inevitable, Tryon was heard to say 'It is entirely my fault'. His wife survived him.

Tryon's powerful political connections quickly compensated for his late entry into the service, although his merit was always obvious. Tryon was a man of immense stature. Physically imposing, unusually tall and very stout, he was equally impressive in debate, his intellect being quick and incisive. Throughout his career he had taken on the most difficult tasks, and excelled in them. Had he avoided the disastrous error that ended his life, he would surely have taken up the post of first sea lord and contributed much more to the revitalization of the Royal Navy, ensuring that it adopted a modern tactical system.

J. K. LAUGHTON, *rev.* ANDREW LAMBERT

Sources C. C. P. Fitzgerald, *Sir George Tryon KCB* (1897) · A. Gordon, *The rules of the game: Jutland and British naval command* (1996) · A. J. Marder, *The anatomy of British sea power*, American edn (1940) · R. F. MacKay, *Fisher of Kilverstone* (1973) · *The Red Earl: the papers of the fifth Earl Spencer, 1835–1910*, ed. P. Gordon, 2 vols., Northamptonshire RS, 31, 34 (1981–6) · J. F. Beeler, *British naval policy in the Gladstone–Disraeli era, 1866–1880* (1997) · CGPLA Eng. & Wales (1893)

Archives BL, Spencer (Althorp) MSS · NA Scot., letters to Sir H. B. Loch

Likenesses Easton, miniature, 1857, repro. in Fitzgerald, *Sir George Tryon*, p. 72 · F. S. Baden-Powell, silhouette, 1892, NPG · engraving (after drawing by C. W. Walton, in or after 1891), NPG [*see illus.*] · portrait (after drawing by C. W. Walton), repro. in Fitzgerald, *Sir George Tryon*

Wealth at death £34,794 17s. 2d.: probate, 14 Sept 1893, CGPLA Eng. & Wales

Tryon, Thomas (1634–1703), vegetarian and author, was born in Bibury near Cirencester, Gloucestershire, on 6 September 1634, the son of an 'honest and sober' tiler and plasterer William Tryon, and his wife, Rebeccah. Tryon went briefly to the village school, and had his first mystic experience at the age of six, a dream of God appearing face to face with him, which, as he later recorded, 'made so firm an impression on me as neither Time nor the Cares and Business of the World, could obliterate' (*Some Memoirs*, 9). Being one of a large family he was set to work spinning and carding, at which he became expert, producing 4 lb of wool a day and earning 2s. a week. But every Sunday and on all holidays he would take to the hills and mind sheep. At the age of thirteen he finally persuaded his father to buy him a small flock 'to which the keeping and management whereof I betook myself with much satisfaction and delight as well as care' (ibid., 13). The following year he taught himself to read and write. Tryon managed his flock so well that when at the age of eighteen he 'grew weary of shepherdizing, and had a earnest desire to travel' (ibid.), he was able to sell it at a profit of £3. With this he went in 1652:

> directly to London and with the Money bound my self Apprentice to a Castor-maker [hatter] at Bridewell-Dock near Fleet St; and I informed my father what I had done and he was well pleased. My master was an honest sober man, one of those called Anabaptists … After I had been with him about two years I enclined to that Opinion and was … admitted into a Congregation. (*Some Memoirs*, 17–18)

Whether or not there were any family connections is unknown, but it was at this point that Tryon entered the tumultuous sectarian world of east London, part of the dissenting 'golden triangle' stretching up from the City through Hackney into Essex. Tryon again worked tirelessly (as he was to do throughout his life, disdaining all pleasure and leisure hours), earning the extra wages with which to provide himself with books and tutors. The key

Thomas Tryon (1634–1703), by Robert White, pubd 1703

element in his thought, developed at this time, was his belief in God's government through natural physical forces, as outlined in Greek cosmology and the science of astrology:

> a Science too rashly decried by some, who consider not the Subordinate Administration of the Almighty, by the Illuminated Powers of the Coelestial Region, nor discern their Operations in Nature, and Influences on the Animal Life, in the complexions of Men and Things, and in the Generation and Prevention thereof. (*Some Memoirs*, 21)

This belief led Tryon to study 'Physick', the science which pertained to 'the whole study of Nature', and 'several other Natural Sciences and Arts' (ibid., 25). About 1657 these beliefs were strengthened by reading the mystical works of Jakob Boehme, after which Tryon underwent a spiritual revelation which led him to break with the Baptists:

> The blessed day-star of the Lord began to arise and shine in my heart and soul, and the Voice of Wisdom … called upon me for seperation and self-denial … retrenching vanities and flying all intemperance … I … forbore eating any kind of flesh or fish, confining myself to an abstemious self-denying life. My drink was only water, and food only bread and some fruit. But afterwards I had more liberty given me by my guide, Wisdom, viz. to eat butter and cheese. My clothing was mean and thin, for in all things self-denial was now become my main business. (*Some Memoirs*, 26–7)

After several relapses over the two succeeding years Tryon settled into his reformed life and regimen, which he practised strictly until his death.

In 1661 Tryon married a 'sober young woman', Susannah, whom he did not succeed in converting to his own 'innocent way of living', but who seemingly tolerated the constant criticism by neighbours and the unconverted, since the marriage survived and she bore five children, two sons and three daughters. Two years after the marriage Tryon went to Barbados for a year, to the Netherlands briefly, and then back to Barbados for four years, 'making Beavers to Success'. He then returned to England, where he 'settled for altogether with my wife' and prospered as a hatter, living with his young family in the leafy suburbs of Hackney, and taking up music (the bass viol). In these peaceful surroundings he became conscious of an urge to 'Write and Publish something to the World', and thus at the age of forty-eight started a new career as a popular author of some fame and influence, publishing approximately nineteen titles in eighteen years, all of them in the notably direct and forceful style that derived from his convictions and his knowledge in many fields. In a comment written by Sir John Sinclair in 1805, a century after Tryon's death, he was described as 'one of the most extraordinary self-taught geniuses, and original writers that ever existed in this country, particularly on the subject of health and Temperance, to which all his writings allude' (Sinclair, 2.297).

Tryon became a polymath in the popular advice-book tradition, producing works on health regimen and housewifery; brewing, farriery, and cookery; education and manners; he wrote also a budget book and advice on business, and at least two treatises on mystic philosophy. The full range of his output is yet to be established, since Sinclair cites three additional works not yet found: *Auerroena, or, Letters from Auerraes, an Arabian Philosopher, to Metrodones* (1695); *A Brief History of Trade in England, and on the Management of the Poor* (1702); and *The countyman's companion, or, New method for ordering horses and sheep, so as to prevent them from diseases and casualties* (n.d.) (Sinclair, 2.298).

The title of Tryon's first work set out his vegetarian beliefs in a typically practical manner: *A treatise on cleanness in meats, and drinks, of the preparation of food … and the benefits of clean sweet beds; also of the generation of bugs and their cure … to which is added a short discourse of pain in the teeth* (1682). He never deviated from this moral message, and ten years later was still urging godly readers to:

> avoid all excesses in foods and drinks, either in quality or quantity, to eschew things derived from violence, and therefore be considerate in eating Flesh and Fish, or any thing not procured but by the death of some of our fellow creatures; rather let them content themselves with the Delicacy of Vegetables, which are full as nourishing, much more wholesome, and indisputably innocent. (*Pythagoras his Mystick Philosophy Reviv'd*, 246–7)

Meat-eaters were 'digging their *Graves* with their own *Teeth*' (Gibbons, 115). As well as 'clean' vegetable food, Tryon constantly recommended an ascetic, hygienic, 'cold' regimen—'labour hard, cloathing thin, open Air, cold houses, small fires, hard beds'—without tobacco, alcohol, or any 'hot' luxuries (*Health's Grand Preservative*, 7).

This physical privation was, in the ancient ascetic tradition, truly the way to God: 'for by thoroughly cleansing the outward court of terrestrial nature, it opens the windows of the inward senses of the soul' (*Some Memoirs*, 29–30). In the same year he published his most famous work, *Health's Grand Preservative* (1682), reprinted as *The Way to Health* (1683), and reached a wider audience. The poet Aphra Behn wrote an ode to Tryon and his primeval visions in the flyleaf of her own copy of the second edition (now in the Wellcome collection). During the 1690s most of Tryon's works went into two or three editions, and seem to have been widely read by sectarians of various schools, both in Britain and in North America, one being Benjamin Franklin, who read and absorbed *The Way to Health* in his youth. The number of Tryon's works in collections in the United States shows the extent of his influence on protestant emigrants; including, for example, the only known copy of *A discourse of waters, shewing the particular virtues, wonderful operations, and various uses, both in food and physic* (1689).

In his horror of war and the killing of animals, and his advocacy of silent meditation, Tryon forms an interesting link between the Behmenists and the early Quakers. There seem also to be hints of eastern Zoroastrianism, with its strong philosophic dualism and purifying rituals, while later vegetarians described Tryon in their own terms as a 'Pythagorean'. Tryon himself did not admit allegiance to any sect or school after abandoning the Baptists. His works in the last decade of his life included his acclaimed *Letters Domestick and Foreign* (1700), and the final summary of all his philosophy, *The knowledge of a man's self the surest guide to the true worship of God and good government of the mind and body* (1703). Tryon died at Hackney after a short illness from 'strangury' on 21 August 1703, at the age of sixty-eight, leaving property to his surviving daughters, Rebeccah, married to John Owen, and Elizabeth, married to Richard Wilkinson, with bequests to charity and to his native Bibury.

Tryon's final work, published posthumously, was *Some Memoirs of the Life of Mr. Thomas Tryon, Late of London, Merchant* (1705), an edited version of papers found by his Quaker friends and publishers after his death; it had a frontispiece portrait of Tryon, with a severe face and a square-shaped, massive head. In this work Tryon laid down extensive disciplinary rules for a pure and chaste 'Tryonite' sect; no such sect is believed to have actually existed, and with his death his personal influence waned. But some thirty years later the fasting, vegetable-based diet became a medical fad and a therapy through the popular works of George Cheyne; and the vegetarian argument found new adherents at the end of the eighteenth century, notably the poet Shelley, the physician William Lambe, and the surgeon John Abernethy. In 1802 Tryon's position on vegetarianism was cited in Joseph Ritson's *Essay on Abstinence from Animal Food*—Ritson referred to him as 'Old Tryon'. Mystical views somewhat similar to Tryon's were held in the 1830s by Lewis Gompertz, the founder of the Society for the Prevention of Cruelty to Animals, and the American wholefood propagandist Sylvester Graham paid tribute to Tryon in the 1850s. In 1883 Howard Williams, a proponent of the British mass-movement vegetarianism of the later nineteenth century, praised Tryon as 'one of the best known of the seventeenth century humane Hygeists … his humane arguments indeed are worthy of the most advanced thinkers of the present day'. Echoing the controversy which undoubtedly faced Tryon in his own life, and paying tribute to the enduring quality of his work, Williams added:

> those who are raised in the anti-kreophagist literature of the last twenty years—in the controversy in the press, and on the platform—will, perhaps, be surprised to find that the ordinary prejudices or subterfuges of this year 'of Grace' are identical with those current in the year 1683 … His chapters, in which he deals with the relations between the sexes and the married state, shows him to have been as much in advance of his time, in a sound knowledge and apprehension of Physiology, and of the laws of Health, in that important part of hygienic science, as he was in the special branch of Diet. (Williams, *Ethics of Diet*, 309–14)

But twentieth-century vegetarians were forced to shift their scientific ground, and Tryon's place in the annals of British neo-classical hygiene and vegetarianism disappeared with the final eclipse of the holistic models of science and physiology during the microbiological revolution of the early twentieth century. VIRGINIA SMITH

Sources *Some memoirs of the life of Mr. Thomas Tryon, late of London, merchant* (1705) · *DNB* · T. Tryon, *Health's grand preservative, or, The women's best doctor* (1682) · T. Tryon, *Pythagoras his mystick philosophy reviv'd, or, The mystery of dreams unfolded* (1691) · A. Gordon, *A Pythagorean of the seventeenth century*, Liverpool Literary and Philosophical Society (1871) · G. Smith, 'Thomas Tryon's regimen for women: sectarian health in the seventeenth century', *The sexual dynamics of history*, ed. London Feminist History Group (1983), 47–65 · V. Smith, 'Cleanliness: the development of idea and practice in Britain, 1770–1850', PhD diss., U. Lond., 1985 · J. Sinclair, *Code of health and longevity*, 2 (1807) · H. Williams, *The ethics of diet: a catena of authorities deprecating the practice of flesh-eating* (1883) · C. G. [C. Gildon], *The post-boy robbed of his mail, or, The pacquet broke open*, 2 (1693) [letter lxvi] · *Monthly Repository*, 9 (1814), 170–74 · B. Franklin, *Autobiography of Benjamin Franklin*, ed. J. Bigelow (1868) · R. Springer, *Wegweiser in der vegetarianischen Literatur* (Nordhausen, 1878); repr. (1880) · H. Williams, *The pioneers of humanity* (1907) · S. Graham, *The science of human life* (1849) · J. Caulfield, *Collection of four hundred portraits*, 1 (1880) · B. J. Gibbons, *Gender in mystical and occult thought* (1996), 115–16

Archives BL · NL Scot. · Wellcome L.

Likenesses T. Tryon, engraving (after R. White, c.1690), repro. in J. Caulfield, *Portraits, memoirs, and characters, of remarkable persons*, 4 vols. (1819–20), vol. 1, pp. 54–6 · R. White, line engraving, BM, NPG; repro. in T. Tryon, *The knowledge of a man's self* (1703) [*see illus.*]

Tryon, William (1729–1788), army officer and colonial governor, was born on 8 June 1729 at his family's seat, Norbury Park, Surrey, the fourth of the seven children of Charles Tryon (1702–1768), landowner, and Lady Mary Shirley (d. 1771), daughter of Robert Shirley, first Earl Ferrers. Well born and in an excellent position to use highly placed relatives for advancement, he grew up at Norbury Park (which he later inherited and referred to as his 'Hobby Horse'), where he received some tuition, though Councillor William Smith of New York declared in 1773 that Tryon 'had not even a Grammar School Education' (*Historical Memoirs from 16 March 1763*, 1.147). In 1751 he became a soldier, and was commissioned a lieutenant in the 1st regiment of foot. That same year he was promoted to a captaincy in the 1st foot, and in 1758 he achieved the army rank of lieutenant-colonel. As a young officer he had an affair with one Mary Stanton, with whom he had a child, Elizabeth. He supported both the mother and daughter for the remainder of his life and provided for them in his will.

On 26 December 1757 Tryon married Margaret Wake, daughter of William Wake, a wealthy merchant with the East India Company. This union brought him control of an estate of £30,000 and connections with an influential family friend, Wills Hill, earl of Hillsborough, president of the Board of Trade and Plantations from 1763 to 1769 and secretary of state for the colonies between 1768 and 1772. In 1758 he accompanied the 1st foot guards on an expedition against Cherbourg and St Malo, where he was almost killed in action. Three years later the Tryons produced their only child, a daughter, who was also named Margaret. In 1764, using Hillsborough's influence, he was appointed lieutenant-governor of North Carolina and began his long tenure of service in America by removing with his family to Brunswick, on the Cape Fear River. A year later, when Governor Arthur Dobbs died, he was appointed governor of the province. Faced with a host of problems, he was to acquit himself well. In 1770 the governor of Virginia, Norbonne Berkeley, Baron de Botetourt, declared to Hillsborough that Tryon was one of the two best governors in the colonies (the other being Guy Carleton in Canada).

As he assumed office, Tryon was scandalized by the laxness that he saw around him and immediately set about to rectify problems. He systematized collection of quit rents, established a postal service, and co-operated with General Thomas Gage in improving the defences of North Carolina. Working well with the assembly, he managed the establishment of the Anglican church in the province and gave assistance to local parishes and priests. He also got the legislators to appropriate £15,000 for the erection of a new governor's mansion, 'Tryon Palace', at New Bern. He supported the assembly's unsuccessful attempts to get approval from London for the printing of paper money, and he had a boundary line drawn between North and South Carolina. In 1765, confronted by the Stamp Act crisis, he strove to convince the Carolinians that he favoured them in their protests against the measure. For his pains, he was resisted by the people and was extricated from a difficult position only by parliament's repeal of the law. He was aggrieved in 1769 when the assembly voted for a non-importation scheme to resist the Townshend duties. However, he was aided by the legislators two years later in organizing an army to suppress the regulator movement in western North Carolina, after he had attempted for a number of years to redress many of the regulators' demands for greater representation in the colonial assemblies. At the battle of the Alamance on 16 May he defeated a regulator army, in one of his last acts as governor of North Carolina.

In 1771 Tryon moved to the governorship of New York, where he also had to contend with unruly frontiersmen. He quarrelled with the citizens of New Hampshire over control of the territory now encompassed by the state of Vermont, and he got into difficulties with the ministry in England when he granted huge tracts of land to colonial aristocrats—and to himself. His purpose, as he told London, was to counteract democratic tendencies in America. He also fostered hierarchy by establishing a militia for the province and commissioning only well-born gentlemen as officers. Confronted with resistance to the Tea Act in the mid-1770s, he attempted to isolate radical leaders from the rest of the colonists while imploring the ministry in England to cease taxing Americans. Having failed on both counts, he fled to a British ship in October 1775 and adopted a military role for the remainder of his service in the colonies. He was promoted major-general in America and in 1778 was made colonel of the 70th regiment. Commanding a force of loyalists, he assaulted Danbury, Connecticut, in April 1777 and two years later conducted a series of attacks on the Connecticut coast. In these raids he practised what he called 'desolation warfare', insisting that Americans would never submit without merciless coercion. Convinced by 1780 that the war was not winnable, he abandoned this policy, resigned his civil and military positions, and returned to England. He lived quietly with his family on Upper Grosvenor Street in the fashionable Mayfair district of London.

As a crown servant Tryon impressed some of his contemporaries as being vain, overprotective of his dignity, cruel, and vindictive. Others, however, he impressed with his generosity, politeness, and tact. A strong advocate of social hierarchy, he believed Americans were too democratic for their own good. Popular with both his superiors in London and colonists until 1775, he was overwhelmed by the American rebellion: he was an intelligent and humane man who fell prey to forces over which he could exert little control. He died at Upper Grosvenor Street on 27 January 1788, and was buried at St Mary's Church, Twickenham, Middlesex.   PAUL DAVID NELSON

Sources *The correspondence of William Tryon and other selected papers*, ed. W. S. Powell, 2 vols. (Raleigh, NC, 1980–81) · E. B. O'Callaghan and B. Fernow, eds. and trans., *Documents relative to the colonial history of the state of New York*, 15 vols. (1853–87) · W. L. Saunders and W. Clark, eds., *The colonial records of North Carolina*, 30 vols. (1886–1907) · *Historical memoirs from 16 March 1763 to 25 July 1778 of William Smith*, ed. W. H. W. Sabine, 2 vols. (1956–8) · *Historical memoirs from 26 August 1778 to 12 November 1783 of William Smith*, ed. W. H. W. Sabine (1971) · *The diary and selected papers of Chief Justice William Smith, 1784–1793*, ed. L. F. S. Upton, 2 vols. (1963–5) · P. D. Nelson, *William Tryon and the course of empire: a life in British imperial service* (1990) · M. D. Haywood, *Governor William Tryon and his administration in the province of North Carolina, 1765–1771* (1903) · S. Henner, 'The career of William Tryon as governor of the province of New York, 1771–1780', PhD diss., New York University, 1968 · A. T. Dill, *Governor Tryon and his palace* (1955) · A. R. Ekirch, 'Poor Carolina': politics and society in colonial North Carolina, 1729–1776* (1981)
Archives Harvard U., Houghton L., letter-book · PRO, corresp., PRO 30/55 | NRA, letters to Lord Dartmouth

Likenesses J. Wollaston, oils, 1767, North Carolina Division of Archives and History, Raleigh
Wealth at death over £30,000: Nelson, *William Tryon*, 8; will, 21 Nov 1787; *Correspondence of William Tryon*, ed. Powell, 2.888–92

Tschichold, Jan [*formerly* Johannes Tzschichhold] (1902–1974), typographer and writer, was born on 2 April 1902 at Leipzig, the eldest son of the sign-painter Franz Tzschichhold (1878–1947) and his wife, Maria, *née* Zapff (1874–1947). He was educated successively between 1916 and 1923 at the teacher-training college at Grimma, near Leipzig, and in Leipzig at various graphic arts academies. He married on 31 March 1926 Edith Kramer (1905–1986), a journalist; their son Peter was born in 1929. They lived mainly in Basel from 1933 to 1968, when they moved to Berzona, Ticino, Italy. He died in hospital in Locarno, Italy, on 11 August 1974, and was buried on 13 August.

Tschichold lectured on typography and lettering at Leipzig and later at the school for German master printers at Munich. After the Nazi government terminated this appointment and placed Tschichold and his family in 'protective custody' in 1933, he moved to Basel to write and practise as a freelance typographer. Although never connected with the Bauhaus, he was an early exponent of asymmetrical design and the use of sans-serif types, exemplified in his first book, the didactic *Die neue Typographie* ('The new typography', 1928), and in the less dogmatic *Typographische Gestaltung* ('Typographic design', 1935). Later work for Swiss publishers employed traditional centred designs and seriffed types.

Tschichold was a masterly typographer in many media, particularly books, posters, and commercial jobbing printing, where his constant search for transparent clarity and fashionable predilection for asymmetric design ensured a steady demand for his services. By middle age, however, he was a leading advocate of traditional centred design for books and acknowledged as a leader in this craft. He is best known in Britain for his subtle and magisterial typographical redesign of Penguin books between 1947 and 1949, when he was living in Nottinghamshire. Without obtrusively disturbing the familiar format and livery of the various series, he imposed on Penguin's printers the highest standards of design, composition, and page make-up consistent with mass production. These standards, similar to those already employed by discerning publishers and printers such as the Oxford and Cambridge university presses, were taken up enthusiastically by many others who wished to produce books of a quality to match the Penguins, which had achieved a commanding position in both popular and accessibly scholarly publishing during the Second World War. The Penguin composition rules written by Tschichold to codify his requirements showed the way to a more professional attitude to book production among emerging British book designers.

Tschichold was an accomplished designer of types. Sabon, designed between 1964 and 1967, is a masterpiece. It was the first typeface to be designed for hand composition and hot-metal setting on the Monotype (single-character) and Linotype (line of type) composition systems, has triumphantly survived adaptation to photocomposition, and is today one of the most popular typefaces for bookwork.

Like his English counterpart Stanley Morison, Tschichold was a fluent and assertive writer on typographic design and widely read in the history of printing. He had a particular interest in Chinese and Japanese calligraphy and Chinese colour printing, on which he published six works between 1940 and 1970.   JOHN TREVITT

Sources R. McLean, *Jan Tschichold: typographer* (1975) • R. McLean, *Jan Tschichold: a life in typography* (1997) • H. Schmoller, *Two titans: Mardersteig and Tschichold* (1990) • J. Hochuli, ed., *Jan Tschichold: typographer and type designer* (1982) • private information (2004) • S. Carter, *Twentieth-century type designers* (1987)
Likenesses Havemeister, photograph, 1920, repro. in Schmoller, *Two titans* • F. Bolliger, photograph, 1962, repro. in Schmoller, *Two titans* • R. McLean, two photographs, 1971, repro. in R. McLean, *Jan Tschichold: a life in typography* • S. Huth, photograph, 1973, repro. in Hochuli, *Jan Tschichold*

Tschudi, Burkat. *See* Shudi, Burkat (1702–1773).

T'Serclaes, Baroness Elizabeth Blackall de [*née* Elizabeth Blackall Shapter; *other married name* Elizabeth Blackall Knocker] (1884–1978), ambulance driver and first aider, one of the two Women of Pervyse, was born on 29 July 1884 at 1 Barnfield Crescent, Exeter, Devon, the fifth child of Lewis Shapter, physician, and his wife, Charlotte Bayly. Orphaned at an early age, Elsie, as she was known, was cared for by a maternal uncle. Privately educated, she attended finishing school at Lausanne, Switzerland, and a cookery school at Trowbridge, Wiltshire. On 5 April 1906 in Wiltshire she married Leslie Duke Knocker (*b.* 1874/5), an accountant, and went out to Singapore; she returned to England for the birth in 1907 of her only child, Kenneth Duke Knocker.

After parting from her husband, she trained as a nurse at the Children's Hip Hospital, Sevenoaks, Kent, and worked for a time in Java and Australia. She then trained in midwifery at Queen Charlotte's Hospital, London. About 1913 she went as housekeeper to a brother at Fordingbridge, Hampshire. With a legacy she purchased a Chater Lea motorcycle, and, nicknamed Gypsy after the club she founded, she became a leading light in the motorcycling fraternity. It was through this shared interest that she met Mairi Lambert Gooden *Chisholm of Chisholm (1896–1981), with whom she was to work in Belgium.

In August 1914 Elsie Knocker went to London as a dispatch rider with the Women's Emergency Corps, where she was noticed by Dr Hector Munro, founder of the Flying Ambulance Column, who invited her to join. The Flying Ambulance Column left for Belgium on 25 September. Unlike the British military authorities, the Belgians welcomed the volunteers who were based at the Belgian headquarters at La Panne. Equipped with a Wolseley ambulance, donated by the people of Sutton Coldfield, Elsie Knocker, followed shortly by Mairi Chisholm, went up to the Belgian front line at Pervyse.

Elsie Knocker early realized that many of the wounded

Baroness Elizabeth Blackall de T'Serclaes (1884–1978), by S. A. Chandler & Co., pubd 1916 [left, with Mairi Chisholm]

being transported were dying unnecessarily because the effects of clinical shock were not treated quickly. She was one of the first volunteers to recognize that giving the wounded basic first aid before moving them increased their chances of survival ('Mairi Chisholm', *Yesterday's Witness*). With Dr Munro's support, she got Belgian agreement to set up a forward first-aid post in the partly ruined Cellar House of Pervyse on the front line. She left a graphic account of her work in the diaries she kept at the time (later deposited in the Imperial War Museum).

The work of the Cellar House attracted considerable publicity. The enterprise was accorded celebrity status, which Elsie Knocker rather enjoyed, and this contributed to the rapid breakdown in relations with Dr Munro. Not a woman to mince her words, Knocker described him as an 'idiot', adding, for good measure, 'I simply loathe him' (diaries, 1 Nov 1914). Disgusted and disturbed by what she regarded as major failings of leadership and organization, she increasingly sought support from the Belgian authorities and from friends among senior British and Belgian officers. After spending Christmas 1914 in England, she returned to the Cellar House and on 31 January 1915 was appointed chevalier of the order of Leopold by King Albert of the Belgians. This award brought to a head the personality clash between Mrs Knocker and Dr Munro and effectively ended their association. Thereafter, the Cellar House distanced itself from the Flying Ambulance Column (ibid., 31 Jan 1915).

In April 1916 Elsie Knocker married a Belgian pilot, Baron Harold de T'Serclaes (*d.* 1919). The baroness continued her work until early 1918, when a gas attack during

the final German offensive forced the evacuation of the Cellar House and her return to England. Contemporary photographs show her in the uniform of veil, long coat, breeches, and knee-length boots that she designed; she was a striking woman of above average height, with dark hair and strong, well-defined features. The two Women of Pervyse treated some 23,000 casualties in nearly four years at the front. The baroness finished the war as an officer in the newly formed Women's Royal Air Force.

With the war ended, the baroness's life seemed to lose direction. Widowed in 1919, she tried several jobs, charity work with former servicemen, setting up a small business, driving, and housekeeping on country estates. During the general strike of 1926 she ran a medical post in Poplar in the East End of London. When war broke out in September 1939 she joined the reformed Women's Auxiliary Air Force, as an assistant section officer, but resigned shortly after her son, an RAF wing commander, was killed in action over Holland on 3 July 1942. She later worked for the RAF Association in Epsom, Surrey, and from 1949 to 1959 for the RAF Benevolent Fund.

In 1964 Baroness de T'Serclaes emerged from obscurity with the publication of her memoirs, *Flanders and Other Fields*. The book reveals little of her life before 1914 and is less than generous in its mention of the enormous contribution made by Mairi Chisholm at Pervyse. Ironically, given her strength of character and flair for publicity, T'Serclaes remains an enigma. Hers was a character brought sharply into focus in time of war, yet one that seems curiously diminished and lacking focus in time of peace. That she herself was aware of this contradiction is clear in her summing up of her life:

> I have always had to make my own way, I have been lonely, and I still am. But for all my feeling of deprivation, I do not despair. This life of mine has been a bungled affair. Only in time of war have I found any real sense of purpose and happiness. (T'Serclaes, 213)

In 1977 the baroness was featured in the Imperial War Museum's exhibition 'Women at War, 1914–1918', where her diaries and medals, including the Military Medal awarded on 10 October 1917, were shown. She also featured in an episode of the BBC television series *Yesterday's Witness*, broadcast that same year. She died aged ninety-four in a nursing home at 1 West Park Road, Epsom, from bronchopneumonia on 26 April 1978 and was cremated at Randalls Park crematorium, Leatherhead, Surrey, on 4 May.   DIANA CONDELL and JEAN LIDDIARD

Sources E. de T'Serclaes, *Flanders and other fields* (1964) · E. Knocker, diaries, 1914–18, IWM · *The Times* (6 May 1978) · D. Condell and J. Liddiard, *Working for victory: images of women in the First World War, 1914–18* (1987) · 'Mairi Chisholm', *Yesterday's witness*, BBC, 1977, IWM FVA [television programme] · b. cert. · m. certs. · d. cert.

Archives IWM, MSS | IWM, Chisholm MSS; Women's Work collection | FILM IWM, film archive | SOUND IWM SA, interview Miss M. Chisholm of Chisholm MM

Likenesses H. Nicholls, photograph, *c*.1915, IWM · S. A. Chandler & Co., photograph, pubd 1916, NPG [*see illus.*] · photograph, *c*.1917, IWM

Tsuda, Umeko [Ume] (1864–1929), teacher in Japan and expert on women's education, was born on 31 December 1864 in Ushigome-Minami-cho, Edo, Japan, the second of eight children and the second daughter of Sen Tsuda and his wife, Hatsuko. Her father, a progressive Samurai, was a horticulturalist and educator who advocated the adoption of Western ways. At the age of six, Tsuda was sent by the government (with four other girls) for education in America; it was intended that the girls would, on their return, transmit to Japanese women those qualities which enabled American women to contribute to America's success as a modern society. In Washington, DC, Tsuda became the foster daughter of Adeline and Charles Lanman; she attended the Georgetown Collegiate Institute (1872–8) and the Archer Institute (1878–82) in Washington. In 1873 she became a Christian. Tsuda returned to Japan in 1882, having forgotten the Japanese language, with an experience of happy protestant middle-class family life and an appreciation of individual freedom that formed the framework of her subsequent life and work.

During Tsuda's absence from Japan, policy on women's education had reverted to an emphasis on obedience to a husband and sacrifice to the family, so that more than two years elapsed before Tsuda was given a government teaching post. In the interim she taught briefly in a mission school before being appointed as English teacher in Toyo Jo Juku, a private finishing school for the wives and daughters from high-ranking families. When, in 1885, this school was absorbed into a new government school Kazoku Jogakko (the 'peeresses' school'), Tsuda continued as an English teacher with, in addition, a high rank in the civil service.

From 1889 Tsuda was given paid leave for three years to study biology at Bryn Mawr College, Philadelphia, and to observe American education. During her stay, with Bryn Mawr friends, she raised money for a scholarship to enable Japanese women to study in America. On her return to the Peeresses' School she was an acknowledged national expert and spokeswoman on women's education. In 1898 she was sent to England at the invitation of eighteen Anglican women; while there she consulted Dorothea Beale, Elizabeth Phillipps Hughes, and the archbishop of York (W. D. Maclagan), and met Florence Nightingale. She visited Newnham and Girton colleges at Cambridge and several girls' schools (spending ten days at Cheltenham Ladies' College). For a term she studied at St Hilda's Hall, Oxford.

A year after her visit to England, Tsuda resigned (not without difficulty) from the Peeresses' School in order to found (on borrowed money) Joshi Eigaku Juku (the 'women's institute of English studies'), the first private school of higher education for women in Japan. She provided an education which, she believed, would equip the school's graduates to pursue independent careers and also to carry family responsibilities; she expected these women, by their example and actions, to lead the process of raising the status of all Japanese women. The school's academic standards were high; students were selected through an entrance examination, they were required to

work hard, and were expected to graduate with a national qualification in English. Under Tsuda's adroit leadership the number of students grew rapidly from the original ten and, in 1904, the government recognized the school as a vocational college, the highest level that could then be achieved by a women's private school. Many of the school's graduates became teachers. A large part of the money for land and school buildings was raised or given by American women; American women (notably Alice Bacon and Anna Hartshorne) joined the school as teachers and administrators and were Tsuda's personal friends.

After 1915 encroaching illness prevented Tsuda taking part in the running of the college but she continued to write textbooks for the teaching of English. She died at Kamakura on 16 August 1929, and her ashes were interred at the college, which was renamed Tsuda Eigaku Juku ('Tsuda College') in her memory; in 1948 it became a university.   MARGARET E. RAYNER

Sources Y. Furuki, *The white plum: a biography of Ume Tsuda, pioneer in the higher education of Japanese women* (1991) · B. Rose, *Tsuda Umeko and women's education in Japan* (1992) · *The attic letters: Ume Tsuda's correspondence to her American mother*, ed. Y. Furuki and others (1991) · *The writings of Umeko Tsuda*, ed. Y. Furuki and others, rev. edn (1984) · G. Itasaka, ed., *Kodansha encyclopedia of Japan* (1983) · private information (2004)
Archives Tsuda College, 2-1-1 Tsuda-Machi, Kodaira-shi, Tokyo, Japan
Likenesses T. Moriya, portrait (*Umeko Tsuda: study abroad*), Tsuda College, 2-1-1 Tsuda-Machi, Kodaira-shi, Tokyo, Japan · H. Yamaguchi, portrait? (*The dispatch of Iwakura's mission to Europe and America*), Meiji Shrine, Shotoku Kinen Kaigakan (Memorial Picture Gallery) · photographs, Tsuda College, 2-1-1 Tsuda-Machi, Kodaira-shi, Tokyo, Japan

Tuathal Máelgarb mac Cormaic (*fl.* 535–539), high-king of Ireland, was the only recognized king of Tara (the title of the high-kings of Ireland) from among the descendants of Coirpre, one of the sons of *Níall Noígíallach (Niall of the Nine Hostages). Entries in the annals recording Coirpre mac Néill's victories, together with the imperative need felt as late as the end of the seventh century to deflate his reputation, suggest that he played a key role in the conquest of the midlands by the sons of Níall. Tuathal Máelgarb's victory over the Ciannacht Breg at 'Luachair between the two estuaries', placed both under 535 and under 539 in the annals of Ulster, may be seen as the culmination of this conquest. It established the power of the sons of Níall over the principal people of the eastern seaboard immediately north of the River Liffey. Its precise date is evidently uncertain, but the form in which it is recorded under 535 suggests that the original annal was written in the late sixth century, before the deflation of Cenél Coirpri was complete. Otherwise, Tuathal Máelgarb was a figure of legend, aided by the monopoly of power in the midlands enjoyed by the descendants of his successor as king of Tara, Diarmait mac Cerbaill. The monastery of Clonmacnoise advanced the claims of St Ciarán as the saviour of Diarmait, the prince pursued by his malevolent kinsman Tuathal. The seventh-century bishop Tírechán replied on behalf of St Patrick, asserting Patrick's role as the prophet who cursed Coirpre, so excluding his descendants from the kingship of Tara; all except, as the tripartite life of Patrick was compelled to admit, Tuathal Máelgarb.   T. M. CHARLES-EDWARDS

Sources *Adomnán's Life of Columba*, ed. and trans. A. O. Anderson and M. O. Anderson, rev. edn, rev. M. O. Anderson, OMT (1991) · W. Stokes, ed., 'The annals of Tigernach [8 pts]', *Revue Celtique*, 16 (1895), 374–419; 17 (1896), 6–33, 119–263, 337–420; 18 (1897), 9–59, 150–97, 267–303, 374–91; pubd sep. (1993) · *Ann. Ulster* · G. Murphy, 'On the dates of two sources used in Thurneysen's *Heldensage*: 1. *Baile Chuind* and the date of *Cin Dromma Snechtai*', *Ériu*, 16 (1952), 145–56, esp. 145–51 · M. C. Dobbs, ed. and trans., 'The Banshenchus [3 pts]', *Revue Celtique*, 47 (1930), 283–339; 48 (1931), 163–234; 49 (1932), 437–89 · W. M. Hennessy, ed. and trans., *Chronicum Scotorum: a chronicle of Irish affairs*, Rolls Series, 46 (1866) · M. A. O'Brien, ed., *Corpus genealogiarum Hiberniae* (Dublin, 1962) · K. Meyer, ed., 'The Laud genealogies and tribal histories', *Zeitschrift für Celtische Philologie*, 8 (1910–12), 291–338 · Tírechán, 'Collectanea de Sancto Patricio', *The Patrician texts in the Book of Armagh*, ed. and trans. L. Bieler, Scriptores Latini Hiberniae, 10 (1979), 122–67, esp. 132 · K. Mulchrone, ed. and trans., *Bethu Phátraig: the tripartite life of Patrick* (1939) · F. J. Byrne, *Irish kings and high-kings* (1973)

Tuchet, James, seventh Baron Audley (*c.*1463–1497), rebel leader, was the second son, and heir, of John Tuchet, sixth Baron Audley (*d.* 1490), and Anne Echingham. James Tuchet's first wife was Margaret Dayrell and his second, by 1488, was Joan Bourchier (*d.* 1532), daughter of Fulk, Lord Fitzwarine, and Elizabeth, Lady Dinham. In the 1470s and 1480s the Audley family was part of the Yorkist political connection. Tuchet's elder brother, Edward (*d.* 1478), was a godson of Edward IV and henchman to Edward, prince of Wales, while John, his younger brother, was married to an illegitimate daughter of Edward IV. Tuchet himself was created a knight of the Bath at the investiture of Edward as prince of Wales in 1475. His father became lord treasurer of England in 1484.

The first mention of James Tuchet in Henry VII's reign is at the baptism of Prince Arthur in 1486, when he helped to bear the infant's train. Tuchet fought at East Stoke on 16 June 1487. In 1490 he inherited his title. The Audleys were a north Staffordshire family, but they had residences at Shere, Surrey, and at Nether Stowey, Somerset. Tuchet lived there having, to all intents and purposes, severed any connection with Staffordshire. He was a justice of the peace in the early 1490s, and attended parliaments in 1491, 1495, and 1497. In 1492 he took a small retinue— three men-at-arms, twenty half-lances, twenty foot and twenty mounted archers—to France. Here he set his name to a petition by which the Lords requested Henry VII to settle his differences with Charles VIII. It is possible, though unlikely, that this action gave rise to the story that Audley lost his fortune in France, became bitter, and therefore rebelled in 1497. His last recorded public act, before rebellion, was in August 1496. As one of a group of important westerners he stood bail for Thomas Grey, marquess of Dorset, to ensure his loyalty during the forthcoming campaign against James IV of Scotland. Audley himself was appointed to serve in the royal vanguard in June 1497.

Rebellion broke out in Cornwall in May 1497 when taxes were levied to pay for the war with Scotland. The rebels marched to Somerset and established headquarters at Wells. Here Lord Audley became one of the leaders with Michael Joseph the Blacksmith and Thomas Flamank. The commanders attempted to secure Bristol for their cause, but failed, and may have sent letters inviting Perkin Warbeck to invade England. From Wells they marched on London, via Salisbury, Winchester, Farnham, and Guildford. It is possible that some opposition was encountered in Hampshire, but no important fighting occurred until the rebels reached Guildford. None the less, a force of between 8000 and 10,000 men arrived at Blackheath on 16 June 1497. On the next day the rebels were defeated in battle and Lord Audley was captured. Along with Michael Joseph and Thomas Flamank, Audley was examined by Henry VII and his council. On 27 June he was tried at Whitehall. Found guilty of treason, he was taken to Newgate prison. The next day he was marched through London in a surcoat of paper bearing his coat of arms cut to shreds—a slight on his treacherous nobility. He was beheaded on Tower Hill and his mortal remains were buried at Blackfriars, Ludgate.

Lord Audley's reasons for joining the rebellion have always been obscure. A context for his involvement is provided by the knowledge that more than twenty-four Somerset gentlemen were also involved. The normal suggestion—that Audley was poor—must be dismissed as speculation since the value of his lands at his death was reckoned at £1200. Political alienation at displacement from power by Sir John Cheyne, a mid-western favourite of Henry VII, is a possible explanation. Audley's action is placed in a wider context by the wavering allegiance of George Neville, Lord Bergavenny, and the welcome given by some of Audley's servants to Perkin Warbeck when he arrived to begin a second, autumn, rebellion. Audley's background—his father's intimacy with Edward IV and his brother John's marriage to one of Edward's bastard daughters—might argue overtly political motives. If by John Audley's marriage to Edward's daughter the Audleys are considered within the extended Yorkist royal family then James, Lord Audley, was brother-in-law to the putative Richard, duke of York, Perkin Warbeck. An invitation to Warbeck to enter England, and the June rebellion, might in this light be seen as an attempt to engineer a coup either for Warbeck or for the Yorkist heir to the throne, Edward, earl of Warwick.

In the event Audley's action was a disastrous miscalculation of the political will of the realm. He was attainted in 1504, but the breakup of the family estates began even before his execution. His heir John was restored to the blood in 1512, but the price of his restoration was so high that he was plunged into a humiliating cycle of debt, terminated only by sales of the family lands in 1535. James Audley's widow fared even worse. By 1510 she was described as prostrated and in the care of her mother-in-law. In 1515 her prostration was termed insanity. Her death in 1532 allowed James's son John to recoup some of the family fortune, but not before his uncle, another John, who had accompanied his father in rebellion, and supported Warbeck in 1498 and 1499, contested his right. The ruination of the Audleys was the direct result of James's wild misjudgement of 1497. IAN ARTHURSON

Sources Chancery records · CPR, 1461–1509 · RotP, vol. 6 · C. L. Kingsford, ed., Chronicles of London (1905) · A. H. Thomas and I. D. Thornley, eds., The great chronicle of London (1938) · J. Collinson, The history and antiquities of the county of Somerset, 3 vols. (1791) · Joannis Lelandi antiquarii de rebus Britannicis collectanea, ed. T. Hearne, 6 vols. (1715) · Rymer, Foedera · LP Henry VIII · GEC, Peerage · PRO, SC 11/828 · exchequer of receipt, tellers' rolls, PRO, E405 · court of king's bench, ancient indictments, PRO, KB9 · special collections, ancient correspondence, PRO, SC1 · special collections, rentals and surveys (general series), PRO, SC11
Archives Shrewsbury Public Library, MS letter on his wife's health, c.1510
Wealth at death approx. £1200: PRO, SC 11/828

Tuck, Friar (fl. 15th cent.), legendary outlaw, may have originated in a real individual, but his mythic qualities as a member of Robin Hood's band are his own, and have become indelibly established in the popular mind. In the developed stories he enters the band, like other recruits, by a personal encounter with Robin Hood in which a contest of wits and physical prowess brings each to respect the other. Once in the greenwood, he dispenses joviality and brings a sly wisdom to the outlaws' councils. His clericity, ordinarily not much in evidence, gives him a status that strengthens rather than disturbs the structure of the band.

Like Sherwood itself, Friar Tuck does not appear in the verses that are the earliest surviving manifestations of the legend, though he is named with other members of the company in a dramatic fragment of c.1475. He is probably prefigured in the tale of a curtal or kirtled friar—a friar wearing a travelling habit—whom Robin finds at Fountains Abbey, an unusual lodging for a friar even when in a travelling mode. In the late fifteenth century, when there are explicit references to the themes of the May day games, their characters include Maid Marian, who was subsequently assimilated to the outlaws in Sherwood, and a friar, who is unnamed but may by that time have already made the same transition.

The earliest known use of the name Friar Tuck attributes it to a disturber of the peace in Surrey and Sussex, in Henry V's reign. A parliamentary petition of 1417 complains of armed gangs at large, said to contain Lollards, heretics, and rebels who defied capture. The Lollards and rebels are probably echoes of Oldcastle's rising in 1414, but violent disturbances were endemic. In February 1416 a commission was issued for the apprehension of one assuming the name of Friar Tuk, marauding in Sussex and Surrey with his followers. It was repeated in May 1417, with a pained reference to the miscreant's unusual name and a list of his depredations in parks and forests, including the theft of game and the burning of foresters' lodges and houses. Nobody was arrested, and the chase was abandoned in 1429, when the offender was pardoned and his identity revealed as Richard Stafford, a Sussex chaplain.

The commissions can be read in two ways. The name is explicitly an alias, so it is either Stafford's own invention, or a familiar invocation to which others would respond. If Stafford was the first man to call himself Friar Tuck he secured both local anonymity and an enduring vicarious fame. On the other hand he may have had the friar in mind as a popular hero who harassed officials and dined on venison, and borrowed his name to his own greater glory. In 1422 there was a reference in king's bench to Richard Herring, alias Juliana wife of Friar Tuck. Who was concealing what from whom on that occasion is uncertain, but either Stafford's fame had spread rapidly or the name of Tuck was known as a present help. The appearance of Juliana weakens rather than strengthens the argument that Stafford was the original Friar Tuck, but the fact remains that the earliest use of the name is, by a narrow margin, attached to a historical individual who was also a runagate cleric.

The indeterminate factor is the early currency of the Robin Hood tales, which were recited before, and probably very long before, they were written down. The earliest known reference to them occurs in Langland's *Piers Plowman* of about 1377, where Sloth, who can be bothered with little else, claims to know their rhymes. Friar Tuck may therefore have been at large well before 1416, but it is not known that he was. As a friar, he could hardly predate the appearance of the mendicant orders in England in the early thirteenth century, though that would still give him time to have made his mark.

Given the great cultural change of the Reformation, after which English perceptions of the medieval church rapidly blurred, what is most important is that Tuck was established as one of Robin Hood's companions before the end of the fifteenth century. He can therefore be assessed in a medieval context beyond the riotous anachronisms of his later adventures. His role in the greenwood is that of a chaplain: not such a hedge-priest as Richard Stafford might be presumed to be, but a confessor and counsellor to Robin Hood and his quasi-royal household. Without disparagement to any order he is more probably a Franciscan than a Dominican, Carmelite, or Augustinian. Friars were resolute champions of orthodoxy, but they set out to redress the pastoral deficiencies of the medieval church, and they were often inclined to radicalism. Friar Tuck is not evidently learned, but he is resourceful and resilient, and undeniably radical. He is also some 600 years old, and shows no sign of flagging, on or off the screen.

G. H. MARTIN

Sources J. C. Holt, Robin Hood, 2nd edn (1989) · B. Dobson and J. Taylor, Rymes of Robin Hood, 2nd edn (1997) · M. Keen, The outlaws of medieval legend, 2nd edn (1977) · E. Powell, Kingship, law, and society: criminal justice in the reign of Henry V (1989) · CPR, 1416–22 · I. Fennessy, 'Friar Tuck, no Franciscan', Newsletter of the Irish Franciscan Province, 189 (March–April 1995), 6–7

Tuck [née McDermott], **Mary** (1928–1996), social scientist and civil servant, was born on 5 May 1928 in St Helens, Lancashire, the daughter of Stephen McDermott (1883–1929) and his wife, Theresa, née Taylor (1896–1982), both schoolteachers. Her father had been born in Ireland and Ireland's situation and history were often in her thoughts. The family were devout Roman Catholics. She attended

Mary Tuck (1928–1996), by unknown photographer

Notre Dame High School in St Helens (where she became head girl) before spending a year at Liverpool University. In 1946 she went as a scholar to St Anne's College, Oxford, where she read English, graduating with a second-class degree in 1949. From Oxford she won a Fulbright scholarship and spent a year at Pittsburgh University in the United States. On returning to England she worked for some time on codes and ciphers at the still highly secret government communications headquarters. Her career then changed direction and she worked for several years in journalism and market research. She married Robin Tuck (b. 1930), a businessman, on 23 February 1955; they had two daughters and two sons. She took an MSc in social psychology at the London School of Economics in 1969.

The part of her career for which Tuck is best remembered began when she joined the Home Office as a direct entry principal in 1972. After a period in the broadcasting department she joined the Home Office research unit (later the research and planning unit) as a principal research officer in 1975. She worked first with John Croft and then with Roger Clarke as head of the unit before herself being appointed as head of the unit in 1985. During the time since its formation in 1957 the unit had established a powerful reputation in the academic community, and had influenced successive governments towards a more scientific, evidence based approach towards crime and criminal justice. In doing so, and especially by challenging some of the common sense views of the effectiveness of law enforcement and punishment as a means of controlling crime, it had gained a reputation for liberal thinking which did not correspond with the political outlook of the government which was by then in office. It was also a period when the disciplines of economics and accounting were coming to be valued more than those of

social science, and when all parts of the public service, but especially those concerned with research, were being increasingly required to demonstrate their effectiveness and value for money. The situation which Tuck faced as head of the unit in 1985 needed exceptionally skilful handling, scientifically, administratively, and politically.

In the event, the following four years were among the most productive and influential in the unit's history. Tuck quickly gained the confidence of ministers, especially Douglas Hurd as home secretary and John Patten as minister of state; her experience in market research gave her a ready understanding of customers' expectations and how to meet them, and of how research could be applied to the demands of the moment. But she also had a vision of the longer term direction of policy and research, and work undertaken under her leadership, on such subjects as victims' experiences of crime, community safety, disorderly behaviour, and patterns of criminal behaviour, laid the foundations for policies which were still being developed (by a different government) ten years later. She would not allow herself to be described as a feminist, nor a campaigner for minority rights, but her influence and example had an important effect on the department's policies on issues of gender and race, and also on its own internal practice. She was appointed CBE in 1989, the year in which she retired from the Home Office.

Tuck was active throughout the period after her retirement. She was a visiting professor at Cranfield University, a member of the Economic and Social Research Council, a member of the Parole Board for England and Wales, a member of the lord chancellor's commission on legal education and training, and chair of Victim Support, for whom she chaired an authoritative committee on domestic violence. As one of its assessors she had an important influence on Lord Woolf's inquiry into the disturbances in Strangeways and other prisons in April 1990. She was in constant demand as a lecturer and broadcaster, and wrote regular reviews for the Roman Catholic weekly, *The Tablet*.

Tuck's main published works were *How Do We Choose* (1976), a psychology textbook written before her appointment to the Home Office, and Home Office research studies on *Alcoholism and Social Policy* (1980), *Ethnic Minorities and Policing* (with Peter Southgate, 1981), and *Drinking and Disorder* (1989). These titles do not, however, begin to reflect the volume or character of her output, most of which was in the form of unpublished lectures and papers, including most significantly her lecture on the dangers of a carceral society, delivered in Australia at a congress on corrective services in January 1988 to mark the 200th anniversary of the beginning of transportation. She also had a powerful influence on a range of other Home Office scientific papers, policy documents (including the green and white papers preceding the Criminal Justice Act, 1991), and reports (especially the report of Lord Woolf's inquiry).

Tuck was an active member of her local community in North Kensington, and made an important contribution to community relations in that area. She died while preparing to chair a session of the lord chancellor's advisory committee on legal education and training, at Ettington Park Hotel, Stratford upon Avon, on 20 October 1996. She was buried at Kensal Green cemetery ten days later. She was survived by her husband and four children.

DAVID FAULKNER

Sources personal knowledge (2004) · private information (2004) · *The Times* (28 Oct 1996) · *The Independent* (28 Oct 1996) · *Daily Telegraph* (30 Oct 1996)
Archives ESRC · European Society of Marketing and Research · Home Office · NACRO · priv. coll., personal papers · St Anne's College, Oxford · U. Oxf., Centre for Criminological Research · Victim Support
Likenesses photograph, News International Syndication, London [*see illus.*] · photograph, repro. in *Daily Telegraph* · photograph, repro. in *The Independent*
Wealth at death £495,372: probate, 22 Aug 1997, CGPLA Eng. & Wales

Tuck, Raphael (1821–1900), art publisher, was born into a Jewish family in Germany. He came to England as a young man at a time when both Jews and gentiles from Germany were settling abroad, bringing with him his German wife, Ernestine, three years his junior, and his children, including four sons, Hermann, Adolph, Gustave, and Hugo, and three daughters, Julia, Rose, and Minnie.

The family settled in London, and there in 1866 Tuck established himself in a new building in Union Street, Spitalfields, his business being the production of chromos, oleographs, and black and white lithographs. His speciality from the start was the printing of coloured reproductions. In 1871 Tuck turned his attention to the printing of Christmas cards, entrusting the venture to his son Adolph, who had joined the business the previous year at the young age of sixteen. His brothers Hermann and Gustave subsequently joined him. Four years later, on 30 January 1875, Raphael Tuck was naturalized as a British citizen.

The large editions produced by Tuck's firm every season enabled them to provide cards of quality even in the cheapest ranges. Special attention was paid to design and finish. A close watch was also kept on changing tastes over the years, and Tuck aimed to meet the popular demand, however ephemeral, for a particular theme or design. In 1880 the firm held its first Christmas cards competition and exhibition, with prizes of 500 guineas awarded for the best designs submitted. Moreover, as well as offering prize money of this kind, the firm bought designs to the value of over £2500 from competitors. The exhibition itself was held in the Dudley Galleries in London, and together with the competition gave considerable impetus to the Christmas card trade.

Tuck was equally ambitious in his commissions. Such well-known painters as Sir Edward Poynter, Marcus Stone, William Dobson, John Horsely, George Storey, and James Sant were engaged to paint a series of appropriate designs. Nor was the literary merit of the cards overlooked, and Tuck offered 1000 guineas to Tennyson to compose verses of eight lines each for cards of different types. It is doubtful whether the poet laureate ever had a more generous offer for such a small commission. The firm also organized a competition for amateur artists,

again with handsome prizes for work accepted. The submissions were judged by a panel of eminent academicians, including Millais, Marcus Stone, G. H. Boughton, and Solomon J. Solomon. Tuck is cited by Boase (711) as being for many years 'publisher to the Queen and Prince of Wales'.

Tuck remained in active touch with all operations of the thriving business until his retirement at the age of sixty in 1881, when the increasingly cramped quarters of the Union Street premises necessitated a move to Coleman Street, in the City. Further branches of the business opened in separate buildings elsewhere, specializing in the publication of cards, calendars, and educational books, until it was realized that new, unified premises were needed. A search was made for a suitable site, and one was found in Moorfields. Construction of the new Raphael House, as it was to be called, began in September 1897, by which time publication of the familiar pictorial postcards had begun. On 5 April 1898 Tuck laid the foundation stone of the new premises, and in July the following year personally opened the building. He died of influenza at his family home, 19 Balfour Road, Highbury, London, on 16 March 1900.

ADRIAN ROOM

Sources *Raphael house*, private publication (1899) · *The Times* (19 March 1900) · Boase, *Mod. Eng. biog.* · census returns for Islington, 1891, Islington Central Reference Library · d. cert.
Wealth at death £2686 18s. 5d.: probate, 21 June 1900, CGPLA Eng. & Wales

Tucke, John (b. c.1482, d. in or after 1540), schoolmaster and musician, was born probably in Burford, Oxfordshire. He was admitted as a scholar to Winchester College in 1495 and took the oath on 7 August 1497. His education continued at New College, Oxford, which he entered as probationary fellow on 20 March 1501; he gained full fellowship on 24 March 1502, and was paid 12d. in 1505–6 'for writing out and notating a mass' (New College, Oxford, bursars' rolls, 1505–6, 'custus capelle'). About Easter 1504 Tucke was admitted to the degree of BA. Thereafter he began studies for the master's degree, but although he supplicated successfully for his MA on 30 March 1507, he appears never to have incepted, instead resigning his fellowship before June of that year to take up a teaching post (in either music or grammar) at Higham Ferrers College, Northamptonshire, where Archbishop Henry Chichele's 1422 statutes provided for a choir of eight chaplains, four clerks, and six choristers.

On 16 April 1515 Tucke was appointed lay master of grammar, master of the boys of the lady chapel, and organist at the Benedictine abbey of St Peter, Gloucester. His duties included teaching grammar to some of the junior monks and to thirteen boys; he was also to teach plainsong, polyphony (*cantus divisus* or *fractus*), and descant to five or six boys, and to participate as either singer or organist at high mass and both vespers on feast days. He remained until the dissolution and surrender of the abbey to the crown in 1540, and his services as 'master of the children' were subsequently retained by the king's commissioners during the interim before the secular foundation of Gloucester Cathedral, of which it is possible that he became the inaugural organist and master of the choristers.

Tucke was married, perhaps twice. Anne, who may have been his second wife, was cited in various property leases in Gloucester, along with a daughter, Joan, and a son, John. His exact date of death is not known; it is likely that he died in Gloucester and was buried within the cathedral precincts.

Tucke's contribution to the history of music rests largely on the survival of his notebook (BL, Add. MS 10336), which contains important though often enigmatic theoretical material relating to the notation of early Tudor polyphonic music. The notebook was compiled, mostly in his own hand, over a long period, from his student days at Winchester through to his last years at Gloucester. Part of its contents transmits a number of traditional theoretical texts, including an abbreviated version of the *Libellus cantus mensurabilis* attributed to Johannes de Muris, a treatise on musical proportion by John Otteby (Hothby), and notes on Boethian number theory. Much more interesting, however, are the texts (some in English) relating to polyphonic composition, which discuss the notation of rhythmic proportion through complex coloration schemes (blue, green, and yellow in addition to the usual red) and use rare Latin terminology that tries to articulate the manipulation of musical material during the compositional process. Although no compositions by Tucke himself have survived, the practical relevance of this sometimes recondite theoretical work can be traced in the repertories of some of his most notable contemporaries, such as Fayrfax, Taverner, and Ashwell; and even if certain elements of these texts cannot be claimed as wholly original, Tucke's notebook nevertheless remains the fullest exposition of polyphonic music theory surviving in Britain between the 1460s and 1580s. Substantial portions of Tucke's work were further copied and slightly recast by William *Chelle of Hereford, apparently directly from Add. 10336, indicating a personal acquaintance with Tucke, presumably during their time in the west country.   RONALD WOODLEY

Sources R. Woodley, *John Tucke: a case study in early Tudor music theory* (1993) · J. A. Caldwell, 'Music in the faculty of arts', *Hist. U. Oxf.* 3: *Colleg. univ.*, 201–12 · F. L. Harrison, *Music in medieval Britain*, 2nd edn [1963] · R. Bray, 'Editing and performing *musica speculativa*', *English choral practice, 1400–1650*, ed. J. Morehen (1995), 48–73 · R. Bray, 'Music and musicians in Tudor England: sources, composition theory and performance', *The sixteenth century*, ed. R. Bray, Blackwell History of Music in Britain, 2 (1995), 1–45 · R. Bray, 'Music and the *quadrivium* in early Tudor England', *Music and Letters*, 76 (1995), 1–18 · BL, Add. MS 10336

Archives BL, notebook, Add. MS 10336

Tucker, Abraham (1705–1774), philosopher, was born on 2 September 1705 in London, the son of James Tucker, an eminent London merchant from a Somerset family, and his wife, Judith, daughter of Abraham Tillard. His father died when he was a child, and he was placed under the guardianship of his uncle, Sir Isaac Tillard. He attended school at Bishop's Stortford, and entered Merton College, Oxford, as a gentleman commoner in 1721, where he

devoted the greater part of his time to philosophical and mathematical studies. At Oxford he also pursued an interest in music, for which he possessed a natural talent, and he studied French and Italian. In 1724 he entered chambers at the Inner Temple, but was never called to the bar since he did not need to practise, so comfortable were his circumstances. He travelled extensively in England, Scotland, France, and Flanders. In 1727 he bought Betchworth Castle near Dorking, where he applied himself to the study of rural economy. On 3 February 1736 he married Dorothy, the daughter of a neighbour, Edward Barker of East Betchworth, cursitor baron of the exchequer and receiver of the tenths. She died on 7 May 1754. They had two daughters, Judith, his heir, who died unmarried on 26 November 1794, and Dorothea Maria, who married on 27 October 1763 Sir Henry Paulet St John, baronet, of Dogmersfield Park, Hampshire; she died on 5 May 1768, and her son, Sir H. P. St John Mildmay, later provided a life of Tucker which was prefaced to the 1805 edition of *The Light of Nature Pursued*. Tucker was severely affected by the death of his wife, and he collected their letters as 'The picture of artless love', one copy of which he sent to his father-in-law, the other of which he kept and read to his daughters, whose education he undertook.

Tucker had no interest in party politics, and refused to stand for the county of Surrey. He was ridiculed by the whigs in a ballad after attending a meeting in Epsom; Tucker set their work to music. He quietly satirized the ways of local partisan politics in a pamphlet, *The Country Gentleman's Advice to his Son on the Subject of Party Clubs*, which he published anonymously in 1755. In 1756 he began work on his most important book, *The Light of Nature Pursued*, which he twice transcribed in his own hand. He published a specimen of the work, *Freewill, Foreknowledge and Fate* in 1763, using the pseudonym Edward Search. His grandson assumed that the use of a feigned name indicated his disinclination to attract public notice. The 1763 fragment was strongly criticized in the *Monthly Review*, to which Tucker provided a humorous reply, *Man in Quest of Himself*, under the new pseudonym Cuthbert Comment. In 1768, again using the pseudonym Edward Search, he published the first four volumes of his book; the last three volumes were posthumously published under the editorship of his daughter Judith in 1778. He was of a very abstemious nature, and physically very active, taking a keen interest in walking. He kept a house in Great James Street in London, where he spent some months every year, holding gatherings in which he specialized in conducting disputations in the Socratic manner. He was close to a young relative, James Tillard, who had taken it upon himself to defend the ancients from William Warburton's representation of their arguments in *The Divine Legation of Moses Demonstrated* (1738–41). Tucker's opinion of Warburton's work has not come down to us, although his grandson noted a sarcastic response in one of his private letters to a passage in *The Divine Legation*. He made some use as a JP of his legal knowledge and training. He developed cataracts in later life and, following a fever in 1771, he went blind, building himself a machine for writing and making use of an amanuensis in compensation. His daughter Judith transcribed what remained to be written of *The Light of Nature Pursued*, learning Greek in order to do so, 'like Milton's daughter' (Mildmay, xxii). A highly technical and rather eccentric text devoted to the relationship between sounds and letters, *Vocal Sounds*, was published as the work of Edward Search in 1773. This work emphasized the important differences between spoken and written language, and is of some importance in the history of language theory.

Although Theophilus Lindsey claimed Tucker to be a Unitarian, on the evidence of a suppressed chapter on the opening verses of St John's gospel in *The Light of Nature Pursued*, Judith Tucker insisted that she had kept it back because of her conviction that her father was strictly and conscientiously attached to the Church of England. The suppressed chapter was restored in the edition overseen by St John Mildmay in 1805. Although an occasionally eccentric and digressive text, *The Light of Nature Pursued* enjoyed a high reputation from its first appearance. In the introduction to his *Moral and Political Philosophy* (1785) William Paley emphasized his deep indebtedness to Tucker in expounding his ethical theory. Paley considered Tucker to be a very original thinker. His work was also highly praised by Sir James MacIntosh, who had used his ideas in his lectures on ethics. Mildmay had looked to MacIntosh to provide an introduction to his edition of the work, but MacIntosh had been too busy to oblige. Hazlitt produced an abridged edition in 1807. Tucker's speculations also had some influence on Malthus, whose family were resident in Surrey.

Tucker's style is direct, conversational, and full of deliberately familiar metaphors and analogies. He was very much an amateur metaphysician, and *The Light of Nature Pursued* is noticeably unsystematic and occasionally rambling in tone. His theory of consciousness and knowledge owes a great deal to John Locke, though his speculations about the nervous system and the brain are closer to those of David Hartley, whom he nevertheless disliked and whose theories he criticized, and this despite the proximity of his own ideas on the relationship between the body and our knowledge of the outside world to those of his opponent. A good deal of his argument takes the form of lauding Locke, of whom he was also occasionally critical, and of distancing himself from such contemporaries as Hartley. This Lockian inheritance takes a surreal form in an extended fantasy sequence, the 'Vision', in which Tucker imagines the separation of what he calls the 'vehicular soul' from a sleeping body into an intermediate state populated by such souls, where the soul's guide is a disembodied John Locke. Rewards and punishments are meted out in this intermediate state, to which Locke and his newly acquired pupil act as witnesses. It is notable that these punishments are seen as being limited in duration; Tucker questioned the reality of eternal damnation. This sequence displays Tucker's humorous gifts to the full, as well as demonstrating the tentative nature of his eschatological theories.

Ethics predominated over metaphysics in *The Light of Nature Pursued*, and Tucker laid out the grounds for living a fairly conventional moral life in Christian terms in a way which strongly influenced Paley, Malthus, and other Christian utilitarians. The link between his metaphysical ideas and his ethical theory is to be found in his psychological hypotheses, which owe a good deal to Hartley. Tucker noted that belief in an afterlife was the only guarantee of good behaviour in this life, and he therefore sought to justify the likelihood (and nature) of post-mortem existence. He was also very much aware of the problem of evil, which he attempted to demonstrate as being vital to the evolution of mind, since the struggle with a fallen world ensured that humanity sought to make progress in its understanding and control of the world if it was not merely to be overwhelmed by it. Evil was a stimulus to the exercise and improvement of necessary mental energy. It was this ethical engagement, combined with his sometimes eccentric if optimistic theology, which made his an authoritative text in the closing decades of the eighteenth century. Hazlitt's abridgement of *The Light of Nature Pursued* was designed to present the core of a work which was otherwise repetitive and often irritatingly digressive, though also frequently entertaining. Tucker died, 'as he had lived, with perfect calmness and resignation' (Mildmay, xxiii) on 20 November 1774, having completed his major work earlier that year. A tablet to his memory was placed in Dorking church.   B. W. YOUNG

Sources H. P. St J. Mildmay, 'Some account of the life of Abraham Tucker', in A. Tucker, *The light of nature pursued* (1805) · W. Paley, *The principles of moral and political philosophy* (1825) · A. Tucker, *The light of nature pursued*, ed. W. Hazlitt (1807) · N. Hudson, *Writing and European thought, 1600–1830* (1994) · A. M. C. Waterman, *Revolution, economics and religion: Christian political economy, 1798–1833* (1991) · *DNB · IGI*

Archives Hants. RO, MS writings incl. *The light of nature pursued*

Likenesses E. Seeman, oils, 1739, NPG · W. Say, mezzotint, pubd 1803 (after E. Seeman), BM

Tucker, Alfred Robert (1849–1914), bishop of Uganda and missionary, was born at Woolwich on 1 April 1849, the second son of Edward Tucker (*c*.1830–1909) and his wife, Julia Mary, *née* Maile, both artists. His father was a landscape and coastal painter who exhibited at the Royal Academy and the Society (later Royal Society) of British Artists, Suffolk Street, London. Tucker left school aged thirteen, and, together with his brothers, worked in his father's studio. In 1865 the family settled in Langdale, Westmorland. From 1874 he exhibited at the Royal Academy under the pseudonym A. Maile—other exhibitions were to follow. Physically robust, he played football and cricket for local teams, and reportedly in June 1877 he and his brothers walked more than 60 miles, including ascents of Scafell, Bow Fell, Skiddaw, and Helvellyn, in under twenty hours. Despite family opposition he went to Oxford in 1879 as a non-collegiate student (he matriculated 11 October 1879, aged thirty), and he sold paintings to help pay his way. He transferred to Christ Church in 1881, and graduated with a pass degree (BA, 1882; MA, 1886; honorary DD 1891). He was ordained deacon (1882), priest (1883), and was appointed to a curacy at St Andrew-the-Less, Clifton, in 1882. That year he married Hannah Josephine (*d.* 1936), second of

Alfred Robert Tucker (1849–1914), by Samuel Alexander Walker, pubd 1890

seven daughters of William Fisher Sim, of Southport, Lancashire, a Quaker merchant who had retired to Elterwater Hall, Langdale: they had one son. Tucker moved to Durham as curate of St Nicholas in 1885. The parishes he served in were strong supporters of the Church Missionary Society (CMS).

In 1890 Tucker wrote to the CMS offering to serve as a missionary in Africa. The archbishop of Canterbury, Edward White Benson, invited him to become bishop of eastern equatorial Africa, an ill-defined area of what was to become Kenya, Uganda, and western Tanganyika, the two previous bishops—James Hannington (d. 1885) and Henry Perrot Parker (d. 1888)—having died before reaching Buganda. Tucker's promotion from curate to bishop was extraordinary—he was amazed at it—and presumably indicative of the perceived danger. He was consecrated in Lambeth parish church on 25 April 1890 and embarked for east Africa the same day, leaving his wife and baby son in England. They never joined him in Africa. After visiting the CMS missionaries around Mombasa, he and his party arrived in Uganda on 27 December after a four-month journey on foot—travelling with the caravan of Charles Stokes, the gun-runner, and suffering from fever and ophthalmia—his fell-walking standing him in good stead on this and other African journeys.

What later became Uganda was then separate states: most important was the kingdom of Buganda, whose kabaka (king) was Mwanga. In Buganda since the 1870s there had been rival CMS and French White Father missionaries. Uganda was within the British sphere but was not effectively occupied or controlled by the underfinanced and unprofitable Imperial British East Africa Company (IBEAC) whose chairman was Sir William Mackinnon; and rival Ganda Catholic, protestant, and Muslim factions were competing for power. Following the martyrdoms of 1884–7 there was a vibrant Christianity there. The rival factions were virtually at war: Tucker described the situation in December 1890 as 'like a volcano on the verge of an eruption' (Tucker, *Eighteen Years in Uganda*, 1.100). Captain Frederick Lugard, the new IBEAC representative, who reached Kampala shortly before Tucker, was in a difficult and dangerous position. Tucker was impressed by the demand for Christian instruction and baptism, and the size of congregations, but initially surprised that they brought their guns to church. In 1891, ill, he returned to the coast and to England, to recruit more missionaries. The IBEAC lacked the resources to continue in Uganda and intended to withdraw. Tucker, fearing British withdrawal could result in Catholic and French or Muslim domination and possibly the massacre and enslavement of the Buganda protestants, believed British retention of Uganda essential and tried to ensure it. Mackinnon told Tucker that if he could raise £15,000 the company would continue in Uganda for at least another year, pending the hoped-for British protectorate. On 30 October 1891 Tucker, about to return to Africa, made an impassioned appeal at the CMS Gleaners' Union anniversary meeting at Exeter Hall, London, and raised more than £8000—some people even gave their watches and brooches—and within a few days the required £15,000 had been passed. The IBEAC continued in Uganda. In early 1892 Lugard and the protestants defeated the Catholics. Later in 1892, following allegations against Lugard by the French missionaries and his enemy Captain J. R. L. Macdonald, Tucker defended Lugard. Tucker's evidence influenced the cabinet, because of his reputation for high character and moderation: in 1890 Sir Charles Euan-Smith had described him to Salisbury as 'a very fine fellow, a muscular Christian in the best sense of the word, and a man of striking energy and lovable character' (Perham, 364). Following a vigorous retention campaign in Britain in 1892 by Lugard, the CMS, and anti-slavery supporters, finally Rosebery's government in April 1893 established a provisional British protectorate over Uganda, made permanent in 1894.

Tucker and the other missionaries played an important role in drafting preliminary agreements between Britain and the Ganda, and in the 1900 Buganda agreement, negotiated by Sir Harry Johnston. These treaties were not mere impositions: the Ganda were still armed, and with missionary help the interests of the new Christian élites were strongly represented, the protestants gaining an ascendancy over the Catholics, which bred resentment.

Tucker was impressed by the quality of Christian leadership in Uganda, and imbued with a vision of a local church which would be self-sustaining on the principles laid down by Henry Venn (CMS secretary, 1841–73). He moved quickly to train and ordain Africans who had proved themselves as Christian leaders, and to strengthen the embryonic Church Council, which dated from the 1880s when Christianity had been endangered. He encouraged the spontaneous expansion of the church from Buganda into the neighbouring kingdoms and chieftaincies, where African evangelists pioneered the way. He encouraged the building and rebuilding of Namirembe Cathedral, near Kampala, and travelled much, carrying out confirmations and considering the establishment of new missions. He delighted in the Ugandan countryside, which he frequently sketched, and kept a journal of his travels. Not wanting to 'Europeanize' Africans, he ruled that evangelists and pastors studying divinity should wear the kanzu (long robe). He wrote that the CMS missionaries did not want 'to denationalise the Baganda … to turn them into black Englishmen (if such a thing were possible) but rather to strengthen their own national characteristics' (Tucker, *Eighteen Years in Uganda*, 2.366).

In Mombasa, at the other end of Tucker's immense diocese, Christianity made much slower progress in a predominantly Muslim area. Here his predecessor, Hannington, had already ordained two deacons at Freretown, the freed slave community, but not until 1895 did Tucker ordain anyone to the priesthood in spite of their long record of faithful service. This work and its personnel lacked the *élan* of the Uganda mission. The CMS and missionaries wanted slavery abolished, but in Mombasa it was still legal. In late 1897 when Tucker was visiting there, a fleeing slave woman, Heri Karibu, a Kamba, implored him to save her. He sheltered her and pleaded her case in the Mombasa court. Although the judge was British, with local assessors, the law was Zanzibari. Tucker, on a point of law (illegal importation), secured her freedom. In 1899 his diocese was divided, the eastern part becoming the diocese of Mombasa; he became bishop of Uganda (including Nyanza province).

Enthusiastically supported by the katikiro (chief minister), Apolo Kagwa, and other leading Ganda, under Tucker educational and medical work in Uganda progressed rapidly. As well as bush schools to teach basic literacy so converts could read the Bible, élite schools were established, for most of the rulers and chiefs were protestants—notably the prestigious CMS foundations, King's College, Budo (1906), and Gayaza High School for Girls (1905). The CMS Mengo Hospital (1897) was the first hospital in Uganda, and pioneered Western medicine there. The sleeping sickness epidemic of 1901 onwards which led to the evacuation of large areas around Lake Victoria and elsewhere emphasized the importance of medical work, and the achievement of Dr Albert Cook and his colleagues at Mengo set a high standard. Tucker encouraged the development of this professionalism against those missionaries who saw it as a diversion from the primary task of evangelism, supporting the recruitment and appointment of suitable personnel. He opposed the proposal by Sir Hesketh Bell (governor, 1906–9), following depopulation by sleeping sickness, to settle Indian immigrants on African land in Busogo. It was not implemented.

By 1897 Tucker had become convinced that the church in Uganda had developed to the point where it should have its own constitution and move away from mission dependence, though he did not follow Venn's principles through fully: he wanted the missionaries to be fully integrated into the church; Venn envisaged them moving on to evangelize new fields, but as colonialism became bedded down, that became unthinkable. Initial discussions had taken place with the CMS in 1897, when Tucker was in Britain for the Lambeth conference. His proposals were put to the missionaries in 1898, but they would not accept being subjected to a synod on which Africans would predominate. Missionaries who had previously written in praise of the maturity and vigour of the church now began to talk of the intellectual immaturity of the Ugandan Christians. The west African tragedy in which Bishop Samuel Adjai Crowther was undermined and driven to resignation by young and over-zealous missionaries was understood to mean that Africans were not yet ready to take responsibility. The dispute also showed up weaknesses in the authority structure of the mission: those who disagreed with the bishop could appeal both to local governing committees and to the mission's home committees, and each put forward his or her own views on the proposals, united only in rejecting any suggestion that they would work under Africans. The matter dragged on until 1908, hampering the church, until Tucker gave way on this fundamental point of principle and agreed that the missionaries should be exempted. In 1908 he published *Eighteen Years in Uganda and East Africa* (2 vols.), based on his journals and illustrated with his paintings, describing the progress of the church in Uganda and praising the Pax Britannica.

Ill health led Tucker to resign from the Uganda mission in 1910. In 1911 he accepted a canonry at Durham Cathedral, but suffered from culture shock and cold, and found aspects of English church life—such as clerical concern with 'millinery'—irritatingly petty. He preached tirelessly on behalf of the Uganda church, attended CMS committees and the ecumenical missionary conference held in Edinburgh in 1910 which was one of the precursors of the World Council of Churches, and energetically raised funds for the rebuilding of Namirembe Cathedral, struck by lightning and burnt down in September 1910: £10,000 was raised in England and £20,000 in Uganda. When support for the Uganda mission was threatened by retrenchment in 1913 he campaigned against the planned reduction. He also continued to paint, and had works hung at the Royal Academy in 1913 and 1914. On 15 June 1914 he was attending an interdenominational 'faith and order' conference at Westminster when he suffered a sudden heart attack, and died soon after in the deanery, Westminster Abbey. He was buried probably on 19 June, in the cathedral precincts at Durham. His wife survived him. Bishop Tucker Theological College in Uganda is a fitting memorial to him. M. LOUISE PIROUET

Sources A. R. Tucker, *Eighteen years in Uganda and east Africa*, 2 vols. (1908) • A. R. Tucker, *Toro: visits to Ruwenzori* (1899) • U. Birm. L., special collections department, Church Missionary Society archive • E. Stock, *The history of the Church Missionary Society: its environment, its men and its work*, 3 (1899); 4 (1916) • A. P. Shepherd, *Tucker of Uganda: artist and apostle, 1849–1914* (1929) • H. B. Hansen, *Mission, church and state in a colonial setting: Uganda, 1890–1925* (1984) • *Church Missionary Intelligencer*, 41–57 (1890–1906) • *Church Missionary Intelligencer*, 57–65 (1906–14) • *Mengo Notes* (1900–Jan 02) • *Uganda Notes* (1902–13) • *Register of missionaries … from 1804 to 1904*, Church Missionary Society (privately printed, c.1905) • D. A. Low, 'The making and implementation of the Uganda agreement of 1900', *Buganda and British overrule, 1900–1955: two studies*, ed. D. A. Low and R. C. Pratt (1960), 3–159 • D. A. Low, *Buganda in modern history* (1971) • H. B. Hansen, 'European ideas, colonial attitudes and African realities: the introduction of a church constitution in Uganda, 1898–1908', *International Journal of African Historical Studies*, 13 (1980), 240–80 • M. Perham, *Lugard*, 1: *The years of adventure, 1858–1898* (1956) • Makerere University archives, Kampala, Uganda • Foster, *Alum. Oxon.* • Crockford • Wood, *Vic. painters*, 2nd edn • Durham Cathedral archives • *CGPLA Eng. & Wales* (1914)
Archives Durham Cath. CL, papers • Durham Cathedral • LPL | Entebbe Secretariat, Entebbe, Uganda, archives • Foreign Office, London • Makerere University, Uganda, archives • U. Birm. L., Church Missionary Society archive
Likenesses S. A. Walker, photograph, pubd 1890, NPG [*see illus.*] • L. G. Fawkes, drawing, repro. in A. R. Tucker, *Eighteen years in Uganda and east Africa*, 1 vol. edn (1911), frontispiece • C. W. Hattersley, photograph, repro. in C. W. Hattersley, *Uganda by pen and camera* (1908) • R. T., wood-engraving (after photograph by S. A. Walker), NPG; repro. in *ILN* (17 May 1890) • group portrait, photograph, NPG • photograph, repro. in Shepherd, *Tucker of Uganda*, frontispiece • print (after photograph by S. A. Walker), NPG
Wealth at death £3603 14s. 7d.: probate, 20 July 1914, *CGPLA Eng. & Wales*

Tucker, Benjamin (1762–1829), Admiralty official, was born on 18 January 1762, the son of Benjamin Tucker (d. Crediton, 1817), a warrant officer in the navy, and Rachel, daughter of John Lyne of Liskeard. Brought up in the navy, between 1792 and 1798 he was purser of the *Assistance*, the *Pompée*, and the *London*, being discharged from the last ship in July 1798 as secretary to the earl of St Vincent. He was closely connected with St Vincent for the next decade, remaining with him during his commands in the Mediterranean and off Brest. On 17 April 1801, after St Vincent had been appointed first lord of the Admiralty, he became his official private secretary until 5 January 1802; and from the 21st of that month until 21 May 1804 he was second secretary of the Admiralty, an office he left when St Vincent resigned in May 1804. During this Admiralty office administration he assisted his patron in exposing incidents of apparent mismanagement, many of which were investigated by the parliamentary commission to inquire into irregularities, frauds, and abuses practised in the naval departments. He was again second secretary at the Admiralty between 10 February 1806 and 5 April 1807, and from 28 June 1808 was surveyor-general of the duchy of Cornwall. In this capacity he drew up in 1810 and presented to the prince regent a report as to the feasibility of forming a roadstead for the Isles of Scilly.

Tucker obtained a long lease of Trematon Castle, near Saltash, Cornwall, and built a new house. Using information derived from his brother Joseph, a surveyor of the navy, he continued to criticize the management of the navy until his death. He was twice married and had four sons and three daughters. His first wife was Jane, daughter of the Revd John Lyne (possibly the John Lyne who was rector of St Ives and died in 1791). Tucker died at the house of his brother Joseph in John Street, Bedford Row, London, on 11 December 1829. His eldest son, Jedediah Stephens Tucker (*b.* 12 June 1800), published in 1844 *Memoirs of the Earl of St Vincent* (2 vols.), mainly written from his father's notes, put together for the express purpose, and with St Vincent's knowledge. His second son, John Jervis Tucker (1802–1886), born on 25 March 1802, entered the Royal Navy in August 1815 and after a varied career was promoted vice-admiral in February 1864 and admiral (on half pay) in September 1869. He died at Trematon Castle on 14 March 1886.　　J. K. LAUGHTON, *rev.* ROGER MORRISS

Sources J. S. Tucker, *Memoirs of Admiral the Rt Hon. the earl of St Vincent*, 2 vols. (1844) • B. Tucker, *A key to the papers presented to the House of Commons upon the subject of the charges preferred against the earl of St Vincent by Mr Jeffrey, MP for Poole* (1806) • *GM*, 1st ser., 82/1 (1812), 286 • *GM*, 1st ser., 100/1 (1830), 88 • *Naval Chronicle*, 13 (1805), 368 • Boase & Courtney, *Bibl. Corn.*, 2.808; 3.1353 • E. P. Brenton, *Life and correspondence of John, earl of St Vincent*, 2 vols. (1838) • H. Raikes, ed., *Memoir of the life and services of Vice Admiral Sir Jahleel Brenton* (1846), 421 • Burke, *Gen. GB* (1858) • Boase, *Mod. Eng. biog.* • Foster, *Alum. Oxon.* • O'Byrne, *Naval biog. dict.*
Archives BL, corresp. and papers, Add. MS 41402 [copies] • NA Scot., letters • NMM, papers • PRO, Admiralty MSS | BL, letters to Thomas Grenville, Add. MS 41857 • BL, letters to Lord Nelson, Add. MSS 34908–34936, *passim* • Hunt. L., letters to Grenville family • NRA, priv. coll., letters to William Adam • U. Durham L., letters to Earl Grey

Tucker, Sir Charles (1838–1935), army officer, was born on 6 December 1838 at Ashburton, Devon, the younger son of Robert Tucker of The Hall, Ashburton, and his wife, Livinia, daughter of William Hancock, banker, of Wiveliscombe, Somerset. After education at Marlborough College, when barely seventeen he was commissioned in 1855 an ensign in the 22nd (later the Cheshire) regiment. In May 1860 he was promoted captain and in November transferred to the 80th Staffordshire volunteers (later the 2nd South Staffordshire regiment). In 1865 he married Matilda Frederica (d. 1897), daughter of John Hayter, younger brother of Sir George Hayter, the painter, and had two sons and a daughter.

Also in 1865 Tucker served with his battalion in the Bhutan expedition. Ten years later the battalion was stationed in the Straits Settlements, and during the operations at Perak in 1875 he was brigade major. He was promoted brevet major in 1872 and major in 1877. In 1878 he was second-in-command of his battalion in South Africa during the early operations against Sekukini. Later that year he commanded the 80th regiment in the valley of the Pongola when the full-scale operations against the Zulu began. He was among the first on the spot after the disaster to one of his companies at the Intombi river drift. Later the 80th was on the front face of the square at the battle of Ulundi (4 July 1879).

Tucker was promoted lieutenant-colonel and, with two mentions in dispatches to his credit, was appointed CB in

1879. After some seven months on half pay as brevet colonel he was appointed commander, Middlesex regimental district, Hounslow, in February 1885, and in 1891, after another year on half pay, he was first colonel on the staff and later brigadier-general with the troops in Natal. He was promoted major-general in 1893 and in 1895 left Natal for India, where he commanded the Secunderabad district.

In December 1899 Tucker was sent to command the 7th division under Lord Roberts in South Africa. His division fought with distinction during the operations for the relief of Kimberley, the rounding up of General Piet Cronje, and particularly at Poplar Grove (7 March 1900) during the advance on Bloemfontein. After the fall of Pretoria he commanded a mixed force which, based on Bloemfontein, occupied a section of the lines of communication, and he was also in charge of a group of mobile columns. He gained Roberts's praise, and a KCB in 1901. In 1902 he married Ellen Mary (d. 1945), only daughter of Sir Maurice James O'Connell, second baronet.

Also in 1902 he was promoted lieutenant-general and 1903 was appointed commander-in-chief, Scottish district. He retired in 1905 and, a friend of Edward VII, was appointed GCVO in that year. He spent many years of his retirement at Biarritz: but soon military duties brought him home every year, for he was colonel of the Cheshire regiment from 1909 to 1911, then of the South Staffordshire regiment, an honour of which he was extremely proud. He was appointed GCB in 1912. Tucker was known for his forcefulness of expression and his hatred of red tape. He died at his home at Chalet St Pierre, Biarritz, on 22 December 1935, and was buried at his Devon home, Ashburton.   G. DAWES, rev. JAMES LUNT

Sources J. P. Jones, *History of the South Staffordshire Regiment* (1923) · J. P. C. Laband, ed., *Lord Chelmsford's Zululand campaign, 1878–1879* (1994) · D. R. Morris, *The washing of the spears* (1966) · *The Times* (24 Dec 1935) · W. L. Vale, *History of the South Staffordshire Regiment* (1869) · private information (1949)
Archives Museum of the Staffordshire Regiment, Lichfield, Staffordshire, papers
Likenesses H. A. Olivier, two oil paintings, Museum of the Staffordshire Regiment, Lichfield
Wealth at death £6749 8s. 10d.: probate, 4 April 1936, *CGPLA Eng. & Wales*

Tucker, Charlotte Maria [*pseud.* A. L. O. E.] (1821–1893), children's writer and missionary, was born at Friern Hatch, Barnet, Hertfordshire, on 8 May 1821, the sixth child and third daughter of the ten children of Henry St George *Tucker (1771/2–1851), chairman of the East India Company, and his wife, Jane Boswell (d. 1869) of Edinburgh, a distant relative of Johnson's biographer. In 1822 the family moved to London, and until her mother's death in 1869 Charlotte lived at 3 Upper Portland Place.

The Tuckers were wealthy and well connected; Charlotte was unusual among evangelical women writers in that, prior to her conversion in the late 1840s, she had a largely secular upbringing and served her apprenticeship as a writer producing poems and plays (including farces) which were performed by her family. A legacy of this early phase is the well-observed dialogue which characterizes her later stories and novels, written under the pseudonym A. L. O. E. (that is, A Lady of England). Another trait of her writing is its accurate portrayal of children, perhaps because in 1847 she took on the responsibility of teaching her brother Robert's three children. Certainly, she said her first manuscript, *The Claremont Tales* (1852), was 'originally composed for young children under my charge' (Bratton, 71).

Henry Tucker did not approve of women working; after his death in 1851 Charlotte began a new phase of her life in which work figured prominently, although she did not need to earn her living. As she explained to her publisher in a letter of 1851, 'my position in life renders me independent of any exertions of my own; I pray but for God's blessing upon my attempts to instruct His lambs in the things which concern their everlasting welfare' (Avery, 101). It is difficult to calculate exactly how many books and stories were written by A. L. O. E., because her stories frequently appeared first in magazines and were subsequently collected to make Sunday school prizes and other books. Cutt credits her with 150 titles; the proceeds from all her writing were given to support charity and mission work.

Described as 'hard-featured, gingery-haired, tall, thin and awkward … fidgety, untidy and loquacious', according to Charlotte Tucker's biographer Agnes Giberne, 'Directness to a fault was … a leading characteristic of Charlotte all through her life' (Cutt, 81). She was an energetic and effective organizer, a dutiful daughter, and a tireless campaigner. Her books were written with the idea of teaching her readers practical, moral, and religious lessons—particularly the value of work. Although fervently evangelical, she placed emphasis not on original sin but on the possibility of improvement for people of all classes and races.

Contemporaries criticized Charlotte Tucker's strenuous didacticism, evident in books such as *The Children's Tabernacle* (1871), a dour tale preoccupied with conscience-searching and religious prohibitions. However, the range of her writing, which encompassed adventure, romance, and oriental tales as well as more conventional stories about domestic life, belies this characterization, as does her even-handed justice. Rich and poor alike are ruined and saved in her stories according to their behaviour and moral precepts. Her portrayal of the lives of the poor is realistic, having some basis in first-hand observation, gained during her time as a workhouse visitor at Marylebone workhouse (another occupation which her father deplored and which she began upon his death). Better are more imaginative works such as *Rambles of a Rat* (1857), in which anthropomorphized rats tell the tale of their lives and travels, and *The History of a Needle* (1858), narrated by the needle, which provide less overtly didactic lessons.

Particularly interesting are Charlotte Tucker's tales of India (often translated into various Indian dialects), many of them in the form of allegory, which, taking her cue from *Pilgrim's Progress*, A. L. O. E. used often and effectively. They reveal her lifelong concern to bring together the two countries she loved: much of her charitable work for the first twenty-five years following her father's death went to supporting missions in India. At the age of fifty-four, having taught herself Hindustani, she travelled as a self-supporting volunteer missionary to Amritsar, Punjab, to work with the Indian Female Normal School and Instruction Society. Three years later she moved to Batala, near Amritsar, where she worked in the high school for Christian boys and as the zenana visitor (a female missionary who explained Christian beliefs to native women) for the rest of her life. By all accounts she delighted in her work and was loved by the native women and boys; on her death she endowed the school which was later renamed in her honour.

Charlotte Maria Tucker died in Amritsar on 2 December 1893. She was buried at Batala on 5 December, without a coffin and at a cost not exceeding 5 rupees, in accordance with her instructions. An inscription to her memory in the Uran dialect was placed in the local church, and a memorial brass in Lahore Cathedral.

KIMBERLEY REYNOLDS

Sources M. N. Cutt, *Ministering angels: a study of nineteenth-century evangelical writing for children* (1979) · J. S. Bratton, *The impact of Victorian children's fiction* (1981) · G. Avery, *Nineteenth-century children* (1965) · *The Times* (29 Dec 1893) · *DNB* · A. Giberne, *A Lady of England: the life & letters of Charlotte Maria Tucker* (1895) · Allibone, *Dict.*
Likenesses photograph, 1875, repro. in A. Giberne, *A Lady of England* (1895) · photograph, 1882, repro. in A. Giberne, *A Lady of England* (1895)
Wealth at death £9098 11s. 4d.: probate, 7 Feb 1894, *CGPLA Eng. & Wales*

Tucker, Henry St George (1771/2–1851), East India Company servant, eldest son of Henry Tucker (1742–1802), president of the council of the Bermudas, and his wife, Frances (d. 1813), daughter of George Bruere, governor of Bermuda, was born on St George's Island on 15 February 1772 (some sources give 1771). Thomas Tudor *Tucker was a younger brother. In 1781 Henry was sent to England and until January 1786 attended Dr Alexander's school at Hampstead.

In 1786 Tucker sailed to Calcutta as a midshipman on an East Indiaman and upon arrival took up various clerical appointments, including that of private secretary to Sir William Jones. In 1792 he joined the Bengal civil service and was much impressed by Cornwallis's vision of modest and prudent government. In 1794 he was appointed deputy registrar of the *sadr diwani* and *nizamat adalat*. Financially acute, in the 1790s he drafted plans for establishing a bank, partly under government control, which were afterwards realized in the Bank of Bengal. In 1799 he was appointed judicial and revenue secretary and then in 1801 took a large cut in salary to become accountant-general, a position he held until 1806, except for an eighteen-month interlude in 1804–5 given over to managing the firm of Cockerell, Traill, Palmer & Co. In the wake of Wellesley's extravagance it fell to Tucker to recoup the company's finances and his measures of economy aroused considerable local resentment. The directors, however, were delighted.

In December 1806 he was convicted of the attempted rape of Dorothea Simpson, wife of a junior partner in his former firm, and was imprisoned for six months and fined Rs 4000. Tucker's defence was one of misunderstanding, saying that he had believed Mrs Simpson to reciprocate his affections. Remarkably, the affair did not adversely affect his career, presumably because his acquaintances were happy to dismiss it as an act of folly, and what had been a *cause célèbre* in Calcutta was soon resolutely forgotten. In memoirs of Tucker's life, most notably J. W. Kaye's biography but also the obituary in *The Times*, there is no mention of the incident, merely a defensive insistence on Tucker's integrity and probity.

Upon his release from gaol in June 1807 Tucker was appointed to the commission for superintending the settlement of the Ceded and Conquered Provinces. Although an advocate of permanent settlement, he accepted that the state of cultivation in the territories was as yet too unsettled to admit permanent revenue contracts; he did expect, however, that they would be introduced in the future. In 1808 he resigned from the commission and in 1809 was appointed secretary to government in the public department. In 1811 he returned to England and was voted a gratuity of Rs 50,000 by the directors in recompense for having undertaken the poorly paid job of accountant-general. On 30 September 1811 he married Jane (d. 1869), daughter of Robert Boswell of Edinburgh, writer to the signet. Their third daughter was Charlotte Maria *Tucker; a son, Henry Carre, followed his father into the Bengal civil service. Tucker returned to India in mid-1812 and became secretary in the colonial and financial department and then acting chief secretary. He left India permanently in June 1815.

In 1826 Tucker was elected a director of the East India Company and, apart from the obligatory years of exclusion, remained on the court until his death in 1851, devoting great energy to issues of Indian administration. As a tory who had first served under the paternalistic reigns of Cornwallis and Wellesley, he spearheaded the conservative reaction to the radical anti-landlord revenue settlements of the 1830s and rallied support against the prolonged assault of missionaries and free-traders on the company's privileges. He also led the company's opposition to the annexation of Sind and the First Afghan War. In recognition of his application and remarkably broad experience, he was elected chairman of the company in 1834 and again in 1847.

He died at his London home, 3 Upper Portland Place, on 14 June 1851 and was buried at Kensal Green cemetery. Tucker was a literary man and, in addition to his voluminous minutes on Indian affairs, wrote *Tragedies: 'Harold' and 'Camoens'*, published in London in 1835.

KATHERINE PRIOR

Sources J. W. Kaye, *Life and correspondence of Henry St. George Tucker* (1854) · J. W. Kaye, ed., *Memorials of Indian government* (1853) · *The trial of H. St. G. Tucker, esq., for an assault, with intent to commit a rape, on the person of Mrs. D. Simpson* (1810) · *The Times* (21 June 1858), 8 · BL OIOC, Haileybury MSS · H. T. Prinsep and R. Doss, eds., *A general register of the Hon'ble East India Company's civil servants of the Bengal establishment from 1790 to 1842* (1844) · *East-India Register and Directory* (1825–51)

Archives BL OIOC, corresp. and family papers, incl. deeds, journals, and printed material, MS Eur. F 238 • Hants. RO, letters | BL, Broughton MSS • BL, corresp. with Sir John Cam Hobhouse, Add. MS 36679 • BL, corresp. with Sir Robert Peel, Add. MSS 40487–40536 • BL OIOC, corresp. with Sir John Cam Hobhouse, MS Eur. F 213 • NL Scot., corresp. with Lord Minto • U. Nott. L., corresp. with Lord William Bentinck • U. Southampton L., letters to duke of Wellington

Tucker, Henry William (1830–1902), Church of England clergyman and missionary society administrator, born at Exeter, Devon, on 17 August 1830, was the only son of William Tucker of Exeter, barrister, and his wife, Sophia, daughter of Colonel Cole of Pedmore, Worcestershire. He entered Exeter grammar school on 1 February 1841, and matriculated at Magdalen Hall, Oxford, in December 1850. He graduated BA in 1854 and MA in 1859. Ordained deacon in 1854 and priest in 1855, he was successively curate of Chantry, Somerset (1854–6); West Buckland, Devonshire (1856–60); and Devoran, Cornwall (1860–65). At Chantry he came to the notice of Richard William Church, then rector of Whatley, Somerset, and afterwards, in London, dean of St Paul's Cathedral. He married in 1860 his second cousin, Jeannetta, daughter of William Tucker of Exeter.

In 1865 Tucker was appointed an assistant secretary of the principal high-church Anglican foreign missionary society, the Society for the Propagation of the Gospel (SPG). In 1875 he undertook additional work in the secretaryship to the associates of Dr Bray, an organization allied in origin to the SPG. In 1879 he succeeded W. T. Bullock as principal secretary of the SPG, becoming also honorary secretary of the colonial bishoprics fund. In 1881 the bishop of London made him a prebendary of St Paul's.

Tucker served the SPG for thirty-six years, as chief correspondent for the colonial and missionary work of the society. During his career colonial and missionary sees increased from 47 to 103, and he was consulted by successive primates as to the church's work abroad. Contemporaries praised Tucker for his knowledge, thoroughness, and devotion to duty. But his methods, often autocratic, created resentment.

Tucker published biographies of bishops Field of Newfoundland and Selwyn of New Zealand; two missionary histories, *Under his Banner* (1872) and *The English Church in other Lands* (1886), and numerous SPG pamphlets. Despite Tucker's sympathy with ritualism, opposition arose to his secretariat, led by Anglo-Catholics at home and abroad, because of his defence of Erastianism, suspicion of enthusiasm, and insistence on the autonomy of the SPG. Critics persistently contrasted the SPG with its more successful evangelical rival, the Church Missionary Society, but Tucker resisted pressures to resign until July 1901, when the society acknowledged his 'invaluable assistance and unexampled services'. He declined the deanery of Salisbury, and died in Italy at the Hotel Bellini, Florence, on 3 January 1902, being buried in the English cemetery there. He left one daughter.

A. R. BUCKLAND, *rev.* STEVEN S. MAUGHAN

Sources 'Prebendary Tucker', *The Times* (7 Jan 1902) • S. Maughan, 'Regions beyond and the national church: domestic support for the foreign missions of the Church of England in the high imperial age, 1870–1914', PhD diss., Harvard U., 1995 • H. P. Thompson, *Into all lands* (1951) • Foster, *Alum. Oxon.* • private information (1912) • *CGPLA Eng. & Wales* (1902)

Archives BL, letters to W. E. Gladstone, Add. MSS 44451–44514, *passim* • Bodl. RH, United Society for the Propagation of the Gospel MSS • LPL, corresp. with E. W. Benson • LPL, Davidson MSS • LPL, corresp. with A. C. Tait • LPL, Temple MSS

Likenesses three photographs, Bodl. RH

Wealth at death £8570 16s. 9d.: probate, 11 March 1902, *CGPLA Eng. & Wales*

Tucker, (Frederick) James, Baron Tucker (1888–1975), judge, was born at Pietermaritzburg, Natal, on 22 May 1888, the only child of Frederick Nugent Tucker (1847–1924), member of the legislative assembly, Natal, and later of the Grey House, Epsom, and his wife, (Eliza) Alice Sophia (d. 1889), daughter of the Very Revd James Green DD, of Pietermaritzburg, Natal. His mother died in childbirth fifteen months after he was born. He was educated at Winchester College and at New College, Oxford, where he obtained a third class in classical honour moderations in 1909 and a second in jurisprudence in 1911. He was called to the bar by the Inner Temple in 1914, but he thereafter immediately joined the army on the outbreak of the First World War, becoming a lieutenant (general list) in 1917. On 19 March 1918 he married (Elisabeth) Benedicta Palmer, daughter of the Revd Charles Powell Berryman, vicar of Camberley, Surrey; there were no children of the marriage.

After the armistice Tucker returned to the Temple to commence his career as a barrister and he became the pupil of Rayner (later Lord) Goddard with whom he formed a lifelong friendship, remaining in Goddard's chambers after completing his pupillage. He also joined Goddard's circuit, the western, where he soon acquired a busy criminal practice at the Wiltshire sessions, as well as some civil work in London. His physical presence and his ease of manner attracted clients and tribunals alike, and he was early marked for distinction in his profession. He was always a 'clubbable' man. He enjoyed circuit life, and he had a fund of good stories. He was excellent company in the bar messes at the circuit towns. Although success came early and easily, he was wholly free from side or conceit, while he won immediate pre-eminence among his contemporaries.

When Goddard took silk in 1923 Tucker inherited some of the former's junior banking work so that he thereafter graduated into a substantial civil practice in London. From 1930 to 1937 he was a member of the bar council. He took silk in 1933 and subsequently was a leading barrister in London, although on occasions and in important cases he still went on circuit. In 1936 he was appointed recorder of Southampton. The following year Viscount Hailsham nominated him, at the early age of forty-nine, as a judge of the High Court attached to the King's Bench Division, an appointment which proved as successful as it was popular. At the same time he received the customary knighthood. In 1945 he presided over the trial at the central criminal court of William Joyce (Lord Haw Haw) for treason.

Later in 1945 he was promoted to the Court of Appeal and sworn of the privy council.

It was at this time that Tucker was an obvious candidate for appointment as lord chief justice on the retirement of Chief Justice Inskip, Viscount Caldecote. But Goddard was preferred, and Tucker remained in the Court of Appeal until he went to the House of Lords in 1950 as a life peer and lord of appeal in ordinary.

On the bench Tucker reflected the qualities which he had shown at the bar. He was civil, courteous, and humane, doing his judicial work with skill and celerity although he was never brusque and always appeared open to argument and attentive to pleas in mitigation.

In June 1954, as chairman of a departmental committee on new trials in criminal cases, Tucker recommended that the court of criminal appeal and the House of Lords should be empowered to order a new trial where the appeal was based on the ground of fresh evidence but (by a majority of five to three) not in other cases. It was not, however, until 1964 (three years after he had retired at the age of seventy-three) that power was given under the Criminal Appeal Act to order a new trial in certain cases.

Wykehamist, with the legendary manners, Oxonian, with the legendary graces, barrister, with the legendary style, judge, with the legendary *gravitas*, Tucker followed and enhanced the tradition of the English barrister and judge. His career at the bar and on the bench exhibited high standards of courteous and attractive address and of fair and reasonable judgment. A fine Latin scholar, a sound common lawyer, and above all a man of sense and personal grace, he was only unfortunate in the sense that when the time came in 1945 for the selection of a new lord chief justice there was already in the lists his former pupil-master, the formidable Rayner Goddard. Tucker's talents lay in the cultivated and lucid exposition of the law, delivered always with style and polish, often with wit, and without the trenchant and sometimes abrasive language of his rival. It is improbable, however, that Tucker regretted (as most certainly he never resented) the preferment of his friend. He went on to serve as a distinguished member of the judicial committee, retaining the high regard and affection of his colleagues and of the bar which accompanied his whole progress through his career. He was made an honorary fellow of New College in 1946. He became a bencher of his inn in 1937 and treasurer in 1960. In 1973 his wife predeceased him. Tucker passed fourteen years in retirement in Great Bookham, in Surrey, where he died at home, Fairfield House, on 17 November 1975.   PETER RAWLINSON, *rev.*

Sources personal knowledge (1986) · *The Times* (18 Nov 1975) · Burke, *Peerage* (1967)

Wealth at death £287,065: probate, 2 Jan 1976, *CGPLA Eng. & Wales*

Tucker, Josiah (1713–1799), economist and political writer, was born at Laugharne, Carmarthenshire, in December 1713. His reluctance to discuss his antecedents left few details regarding his family and later gave rise to many apocryphal stories regarding his Welsh peasant stock, long life, and physical strength. His father, however, was probably Josiah Tucker, a member of the salt office at Nevern, Pembrokeshire, who, after his marriage to Eliza Bradshaw at Laugharne in October 1711, inherited a small estate in Aberystwyth. A certain amount of mystery also surrounds Tucker's two marriages. His first wife was Elizabeth Woodward (1696–1771), a widow seventeen years his senior. Although the couple lived apart Tucker educated her sons, one of whom, Richard *Woodward, later became bishop of Cloyne, Ireland. In 1781 Tucker married his housekeeper, a Miss Crow, the daughter of a local schoolmaster. This second marriage, which seems to have been one of genuine affection, produced no children. Tucker's later correspondence indicates that he had a sister whose eight children he helped to provide for.

Early career Whatever his background, Tucker received an excellent education. Following his attendance at the endowed Elizabethan grammar school at Ruthin, Denbighshire, he went up as an exhibitioner to St John's College, Oxford, in January 1733. Having graduated BA in 1736 he took holy orders; he graduated MA in 1739, and DD in 1755. He was appointed curate of St Stephen's, Bristol, in 1737 and made rector of All Saints', in the same city, two years later. In 1750 he was appointed vicar of St Stephen's, a large and wealthy parish, and his long residence in Bristol, England's second city and an important commercial centre, was crucial to the development of his religious, political, and economic viewpoints. It also brought him into contact with the bishop, Joseph Butler (1692–1752).

One of the most celebrated theologians of his day, Butler greatly influenced Tucker's outlook regarding human motivation, as well as the role that private virtue and enlightened self-interest could play in public life. Tucker considered Butler's *Analogy of Religion* (1736) a masterpiece. Their close friendship led to Tucker's advancement: Butler appointed Tucker his private chaplain in 1738 and a minor canon in Bristol Cathedral in 1742. A decade later Tucker acted as one of the executors of Butler's will. Butler's scepticism regarding religious freethinkers, deists, and the growing movement of religious enthusiasm also influenced Tucker's views and involved him in local controversy regarding Methodist beliefs then taking root under George Whitefield and John Wesley in Bristol.

In 1739 Tucker's first published work, attacking Methodism, led to a heated newspaper exchange, a lengthy rebuttal of his attacks in *An Answer to Mr. Tucker's Defence of his Queries*, possibly written by Wesley, and to Tucker being physically assaulted in the streets of Bristol. Ignoring his local unpopularity, Tucker went on to publish, at the request of the archbishop of Armagh, *A Brief History of the Principles of Methodism* (1742). One of his twelve published works on religious topics, all of which displayed great learning, this work attacked Methodism as little more than a medley of older, conflicting religious ideas artificially thrown together by the personal whim of Whitefield himself. Wesley, who admired Tucker as a preacher, published a sincere reply, *Principles of Methodism* (1746), which brought an end to this particular controversy but not to Tucker's development as something of a born controversialist. In a long career he published over forty-four works, many of which considered the pressing problems of the day. His published works consistently interwove moral, religious, political, and—above all—economic ideas into a general outlook that many interpreted as toryism, although he considered himself a true whig and an upholder of the revolution settlement of 1689.

Tucker's first major work on economics, *A Brief Essay on the Advantages and Disadvantages, which Respectively Attend France and Great Britain*, which was published in 1749 and thereafter went through numerous editions, made his name in the new discipline of economic theory; it was later translated into French by Plumart d'Angeul and influenced the later French physiocrats. Dedicated to the earl of Halifax, president of the Board of Trade from 1748, *A Brief Essay* attacked unnatural restrictions on national trade as well as the continuing monopolistic vested interests that hampered its growth. Rejecting the older notion of bullionism—which maintained that commercial success could be measured by the national acquisition of gold—Tucker argued that commerce was really an artificial exchange motivated by both individual and national wants, and that the wealth of a nation could only be truly measured by the useful and profitable employment of its people. Tucker did not, and never did, advocate a truly *laissez-faire* system, one which favoured the abolition of all governmental control of commerce, for he believed that the true role of government was to consider economic self-interest by passing judicious laws necessary for directing commerce into its proper and profitable channels. This work also considered other themes evident in Tucker's later publications, including the need to create a true national and constitutional union with Ireland as well as the necessity of restructuring the questionable liberties afforded by the British constitution itself. While Tucker attacked the autocracy of the French government he none the less believed that British liberties encouraged the pursuit of pleasure in the lower orders at the expense of industry. His *Brief Essay* therefore recommended the increase in taxes on spirituous liquor, government action over increasing smuggling, and changes in the ballot by restricting it to £20 for freeholders in the counties and to £200 in stock for tradesmen in the boroughs. Adam Smith is known to have owned a copy of *A Brief Essay*, though Tucker's influence on Smith's later writings remains debatable.

In the third edition of the work (1753) Tucker added new proposals for the encouragement of the American colonial trade. Before 1754 he was hardly opposed to the colonies and, in echoing the work of earlier economic theorists such as Charles Davenant, Sir Josiah Child, and Joshua Gee, he stressed the need to strengthen a mutually beneficial trade with America. This, he thought, could best be encouraged by government action: by granting bounties upon required raw materials and by the reduction of customs duties to discourage colonial smuggling. Smuggling, he believed, damaged not only the economic but also the political connection, as it bred economic independence, debauched its participants, and tutored the colonials in vice and perjury. Such viewpoints were also evident in Tucker's letters to the press and in his *Case of the Importation of Bar Iron from our Colonies in North America* (1756).

Jewish naturalization In 1752, at the request of Thomas Hayter, bishop of Norwich and tutor to the future George III, Tucker began work on his most systematic book on commerce, a work that remained unfinished. Part of this major work was privately printed and circulated among friends as *The Elements of Commerce and Theory of Taxes* (1755), and fragments of it appeared as *Instructions for Travellers* (1758) and *The Case of Going to War for the Sake of Procuring, Enlarging or Securing of Trade, Considered in a New Light* (1763). The latter work was Tucker's first publication critical of Britain's American colonies, expressing a viewpoint developed by his opposition to the Seven Years' War (1756–63). He did not publish the whole work, he informed Lord Kames in October 1761, because his ideas remained out of step with public opinion.

In 1747 Robert Nugent, later Viscount Clare and Earl Nugent (1702–1788), introduced into the Commons a bill to relax the British naturalization laws against resident foreign protestants. The bill had a stormy passage, its third reading being delayed until April 1751. To support the bill Tucker published a history of Britain's lamentable treatment of industrious foreign residents, *Reflections on the Expediency of a Law for the Naturalization of Foreign Protestants* (1751). Following the bill's failure he published a review of its history in a second part, published in the following year. It was in this work that he developed the established theory that a concentrated, industrious population generated economic success. The opposition to the naturalization bill was generated, he believed, by both bigotry and entrenched, monopolistic vested self-interest. His strong views received support from Charles Townshend, third Viscount Townshend, who anonymously published a work on the subject, *National Thoughts Recommended to the Serious Attention of the Public by a Landowner* (1751).

The failure of Nugent's bill was not the end of the naturalization question. In 1753 the Portuguese and Spanish Jewish residents in Britain petitioned parliament for the removal of similar restrictions that prevented them from gaining citizenship, a petition supported by Nugent and other whig politicians such as Henry Pelham, the earl of Hardwicke, and the earl of Halifax. In the face of great opposition the Jewish Naturalization Act was passed in 1753, and Tucker again involved himself in controversy. In *A Letter to a Friend Concerning Naturalization* (1753) he attacked the religious bigotry that he believed lay behind the opposition of such groups as the common council of the City of London. In that same year he published another work in which the historical treatment of Jews in Britain was reviewed, *A Second Letter to a Friend Concerning Naturalization*. His efforts failed to prevent the repeal of the Jewish Naturalization Act later in the same year. Tucker also supported Nugent's attempt to relax the restrictive membership policies of the Levant Company, which controlled British commerce with the eastern

Mediterranean, in *Reflections on the Expediency of Opening the Trade to Turkey* (1753). He believed that the company's monopolistic policies had transformed this once important trade into a losing concern, and for his efforts in support of these unpopular policies he was burnt in effigy in Bristol and ridiculed as 'Josiah ben Judas Iscariot'.

Tucker's important political influence in Bristol and his interest in commercial reform forged a strong political alliance with Nugent, a politician whom he helped to have elected for Bristol in the general election of 1754. In turn Nugent, who was appointed a member of the Treasury board that same year, further advanced Tucker's career. Owing to both his and Lord Hardwicke's influence Tucker was appointed in 1756 to the third prebendal stall in Bristol Cathedral, and two years later he was made dean of Gloucester. He retained the vicarage at St Stephen's until 1793, dividing his time between the two cities. An apparently hard-working dean, he did much to restore the fabric of Gloucester Cathedral. He also remained a firm political ally of Nugent, who, following his resignation from his seat in Bristol in 1774 (owing to his firm stand regarding the American colonies), received praise for his political career in Tucker's *A Review of Lord Viscount Clare's Conduct as Representative of Bristol* (1775).

Attitudes to America On 22 March 1775 Tucker's view of America was attacked in a speech by Edmund Burke, the recently elected MP for Bristol. Tucker was, Burke argued, little more than a court reporter, a vermin whose outlook was motivated by his wish for a bishopric. In turn Tucker attacked as ridiculous Burke's plan to allow the colonies to regulate themselves within the empire. His *Letter to Edmund Burke* (1775) was the beginning of a systematic attack on the opinions of the friends of the American revolutionaries and the radical element within British politics. In his correspondence with the historian and biographer Thomas Birch, Tucker had expressed the beginnings of his critical views of the American colonies as early as 1754, opinions which he also published in the press. Opposing the outbreak of hostilities in the Ohio region that led to the Seven Years' War he warned that Britain already owned more territory in America than it could populate in 500 years. Dismissing notions of a French threat to British commercial interests in America he warned that an extension of British colonial territory west of the Appalachian mountains could lead only to colonial manufacturing, colonial economic independence, additional and unnecessary British expense, and conditions that would create a future harvest of colonial complaints.

Already unpopular, Tucker remained surprisingly quiet during the Seven Years' War but he became increasingly vocal after the peace of Paris in 1763. The developing American crisis over taxation touched upon all Tucker's major interests: the need to maintain a mutually self-interested and beneficial trade between Britain and her colonies, his dislike of war and mock patriotism, and his distrust of political radicalism. His *Case of Going to War*

(1763) argued that a nation would never improve its commerce by bankrupting its neighbours, and he drew comparisons between Britain's own growing imperial concerns with those conditions that had led to the decline of Rome. His warnings went largely unnoticed before the Stamp Act crisis (1765–6) and he came to view himself as something of a Cassandra, a pen-name that he frequently employed in his letters to the press.

Tucker's developing attitude to the American colonies was motivated neither by a belief in free trade nor by any sympathy for the Americans themselves, a people he came to see as grasping and ungrateful. Their rapid economic growth and dislike of regulation would, he believed, eventually lead them to separate from Britain through self-interest. He argued that all colonies historically had their date of independence and, concerned that their radical political ideas would eventually infect Britain, he advocated as early as 1766 the separation of Britain and her American colonies. In *A Letter from a Merchant in London to his Nephew in North America* he dismissed objections to British taxation as political cant masking the American desire for independence. In rejecting calls for colonial representation at Westminster as both impracticable and unwise he upheld the notions of parliamentary sovereignty and virtual representation, yet also rejected the forcible coercion of the colonies. A shopkeeper, he advised, would never increase his custom by beating his customers and, consequently, what was true for a shopkeeper was true for a shopkeeping nation.

Tucker returned again and again to the need for a political separation in a series of tracts and sermons that he had republished on the eve of the final crisis as *Four Tracts with Two Sermons* (1774). Responding to the decisions of the first continental congress he published *The Respective Pleas and Arguments of the Mother Country and her Colonies* (1775), in which he argued that any compromise was now impossible and took the opportunity to berate the Americans over their treatment of their slaves and the Native Americans. This work too was republished, together with the other four tracts, in the year of the Declaration of Independence (1776). In *A Series of Answers to Certain Popular Objections Against Separating from the Rebellious Colonies* (1776) Tucker praised the wisdom of Thomas Paine's *Common Sense*, concluding that although separation was not a popular idea in Britain, to achieve this voluntarily would be in Britain's long-term economic interest. Britain and America, he believed, belonged to two distinct political systems, and he warned France that its increasing involvement in the conflict could only bring about its destruction.

The escalation of the war prompted Tucker to undertake a systematic analysis of the possible results of the war as well as the effects it had on generating radicalism within Britain itself. As early as 1778 he had attacked the friends of America, including John Cartwright, Joseph Priestley, and especially John Wilkes, whom he personally detested, in a privately printed work, *The Notions of Mr. Locke and his Followers*. Most of his themes found a place in two later wartime works, *Cui bono?* and *A Treatise Concerning Civil Government*, both published in 1781. Addressed to the late French minister Jacques Necker, *Cui bono?* predicted a Franco-American victory but also the dissolution of the American union and the post-war resumption, to Britain's vast benefit, of the American trade. While a number of the states, especially those in the southern part of America, would probably petition to rejoin the empire, France's involvement in the war would ultimately lead to her destruction, owing to her alliance with republics founded upon the dangerous Lockean notion of natural liberty. Tucker considered the Lockean concept that government could be based only upon the consent of the governed as the new intolerant enthusiasm of the age. It was, he argued, becoming as much of a religion as the divine right of kings had been in the previous century. Its religious devotees, the friends of America, were involved in little more than a conspiracy to extend republicanism to Britain, a political catastrophe that would increase the power of the people to the destruction of the established institutions of the country. Tucker's own experience of the ordinary people of England reinforced his misgivings, and in one of his earliest published sermons, *Hospitals and Infirmaries, Considered as Schools of Christian Education* (1746), he had dismissed the common people of England as 'the most depraved and licentious wretches upon the earth' who had already drunk too deep of the 'cup of liberty' (pp. 8–9). In view of his belief that the origin of government was not to be found in a state of nature but in the divine purpose of God it is not surprising that he resisted any extension of the franchise or weakening of the established relations between church and state. Unlike many of the dissenting ministers who came to support the radical reform of the constitution he firmly adhered to what he saw as a balanced constitution and the subscription to the Thirty-Nine Articles of the Church of England.

In the last two decades of his life Tucker was viewed in some circles as something of a sage. His writings declined as he aged, although he continued to champion schemes he had long supported, especially the need for a union between Britain and Ireland. Following the gradual decay in his health he resigned his position at St Stephen's in November 1793; he suffered a paralytic stroke in his deanery, and died on 4 November 1799, survived by his wife. His death was noted in the British press and caused lengthy comments in both the *Gentleman's Magazine* and the *European Magazine*. He was buried in the south transept of Gloucester Cathedral, where a monument was later erected to his memory. A controversial figure during his lifetime, he has been increasingly recognized as an important and original eighteenth-century theorist. If his influence upon the later economic ideas of Adam Smith remains debatable, he was, as Karl Marx thought, a competent political economist. RORY T. CORNISH

Sources DNB · *Josiah Tucker: a selection from his economic and political writings*, ed. R. L. Schuyler (New York, 1931) · G. Shelton, *Dean Tucker and 18th-century economics and political thought* (New York, 1981) · B. Semmes, *The rise of free trade imperialism* (1970) · W. E. Clark, *Josiah Tucker, economist: a study in the history of economics* (New York, 1903) · K. Knorr, *British colonial theories, 1570–1850* (Toronto, 1968) · J. Stern, introduction, in *Collected works of Josiah Tucker*, ed. J. Stern, 6 vols. (1993)

Archives Gloucester Public Library, letters · St John's College, Oxford, letters and papers | BL, corresp. with Thomas Birch, Add. MSS 4291, 4308, 4319, 4326B · BL, letters to Nugent, Add. MS 32867 · NA Scot., letters to Lord Kames

Likenesses R. Clamp, stipple, BM, NPG; repro. in S. Harding, *Biographical mirrour* (1793) · engraving (after portrait by G. Russell), repro. in Schuyler, ed., *Josiah Tucker* · line engraving (after unknown portrait), BM, NPG; repro. in *European Magazine* (1799) · portrait, priv. coll. · portrait, BM, Add. MS 40122, fol. 45

Tucker, St George (1752–1827), jurist and poet in the United States of America, was born on 29 June 1752 at Port Royal, Bermuda, the son of Henry Tucker, merchant, and Anne Butterfield. After receiving some education at home, he emigrated to Virginia in 1771 and enrolled as a student at the College of William and Mary. Having graduated a year later, he entered into the study of law with George Wythe. He was admitted to the bar in 1774, and was appointed clerk of the court of Dinwiddie county. His career as a lawyer was immediately interrupted by the outbreak of conflict between Britain and the American colonies, for in 1774 the courts were closed by Lord Dunmore, the royal governor. Taking the side of the colonies, he returned to Bermuda and joined with his near relatives in illicit trade with the American rebels. In 1776 he came back to Virginia and continued to work for the revolutionaries, at the same time forwarding the interests of his family's business. On 23 September 1778 he married Frances Bland Randolph, widow of John Randolph of Matoax in Chesterfield county and mother of John Randolph of Roanoke. They had five children before she died in 1788. On 8 October 1791 Tucker married another widow, Lelia Skipworth Carter. They had three children, all of whom died before reaching maturity. Having settled at Matoax in 1778, Tucker spent the next three years in the peaceful pursuits of the law, agriculture, and family life. When the British invaded the south in 1781, he was commissioned a colonel of Chesterfield county militia and fought bravely at the battle of Guilford court house on 15 March. Later, while serving as lieutenant-colonel of a troop of cavalry, he took part in the siege of Yorktown and was slightly wounded.

At the conclusion of the American War of Independence, Tucker returned to public service and the practice of law. In 1783 he was appointed commonwealth's attorney for Chesterfield county, and he served for a short time on the council of state. Alarmed about growing barriers to interstate commerce under the articles of confederation, he served as a commissioner at the Annapolis convention in 1786. When the constitution of 1787 was proposed, he opposed its ratification in Virginia. By now he had become more involved in pleading cases before courts in Richmond, and in 1786 he resigned as commonwealth's attorney. His distinguished career as a judge began in 1788, when he was appointed to the bench of the Virginia general court, and a year later he joined a committee to revise the laws of Virginia. Throughout the 1780s he

St George Tucker (1752–1827), by Charles Balthazar Julien Févret de Saint-Mémin, 1807–8

served on the board of visitors of the College of William and Mary. In 1790 he was appointed professor of law to replace his old mentor, George Wythe, who had just resigned the post. Taking advantage of his excellent home library of 500 volumes, he and his students began to hold classes there rather than at the college. Troubles developed between him and the board of visitors over this practice, and in 1803, when he was elected to the court of appeals of Virginia, he resigned his chair in law.

As a judge on both the general court and the court of appeals, Tucker strongly advocated the independence of the judiciary, particularly in the matter of judicial review. He argued in *Kamper* v. *Hawkins* (1793) that the Virginia constitution was the supreme law of the commonwealth, taking precedence over any state law that might violate its writ. In a dissenting opinion in *Woodson* v. *Randolph* (1799) he maintained that the United States congress had violated the federal constitution by changing rules of evidence that applied to state courts. Finally, he held in *Turpin* v. *Locket* (1804) that a law which applied the glebes of the Episcopal church to poor relief was constitutional. He also asserted himself on judicial and political matters in a number of pamphlets and essays. A strongly Jeffersonian republican, he was a classical liberal who believed in states' rights. In 1788 he satirized federalist politicians and programmes in the *National Gazette*, and in *Letter to a Member of Congress* (1799) he vehemently protested against the Alien and Sedition Acts. To support President Thomas Jefferson's purchase of the Louisiana Territory in 1803, he wrote *Reflections on the Cession of Louisiana to the United States*.

In a widely disseminated essay, *Dissertation on Slavery: with a Proposal for its Gradual Abolition in Virginia* (1796), Tucker manifested his disgust with the institution of human bondage, asserting that it was a threat to republican government and a violation of natural law. To eliminate the institution in Virginia, he advocated that slave women and their children be gradually manumitted, that slave owners be compensated for the loss of their property, and that all freed black people be removed to the west. He spent much time in the late 1790s and early 1800s working on an annotated edition of Sir William Blackstone's *Commentaries on the Laws of England*, which he published in five volumes in 1803. Applying Blackstone's principles to the operations of republican government, he also added a number of appendixes on topics such as judicial interpretation of the federal constitution, slavery, and civil liberties. These volumes were popular with American law students and lawyers for a number of years. In 1811 he resigned from the court of appeals because of friction with a fellow judge, Spencer Roane. Two years later he was appointed by President James Madison judge for the district court of the district of Virginia. On the federal bench he continued to support states' rights and complained about encroachments of federal power. He retired in 1825 because of failing health.

Tucker was a man of many parts, a well-rounded intellectual in the age of Jefferson. He possessed one of the best minds of his generation, fully aware that Virginia could not become 'a great nation' until its spiritual and aesthetic life equalled its political accomplishments. A deist in religion, he shared the philosophical optimism of men like Jefferson and Benjamin Franklin, and was strongly influenced by John Locke to believe that man could perfect himself by the application of reason. His stepson, John Randolph of Roanoke, a devout and orthodox Christian, accused Tucker of exercising an altogether deleterious influence upon him in his youth. Tucker was a poet of some note, leaving behind more than two hundred poems. Besides verses with religious themes, such as 'Written on Christmas Day, 1820', he wrote poems for his friends, for public occasions, to celebrate patriotism, and to satirize various opponents. He also wrote satirical and propagandist dramas, such as *The Wheel of Fortune* (c.1796) and *The Times* (1811). Critics suggest that he may deserve to be ranked among the first of literary men in his generation. He also dabbled in architecture and music, and in science he was interested in both theoretical and practical knowledge. In 1773 he helped found the Virginia Society for Promoting Useful Knowledge, 'a sort of colonial Royal Society' (R. B. Davis, 178), and was elected the society's assistant secretary. He studied astronomy, and in his commonplace books and letters described a number of inventions, such as an 'earth closet' that emptied from the outside and a steam engine for drawing water. In old age he retired to the home of Joseph C. Cabell in Warminster, Nelson county. There he died, on 10 November 1827; his wife survived him.   PAUL DAVID NELSON

Sources C. T. Cullen, *St George Tucker and law in Virginia, 1772–1804* (1987) · C. T. Cullen, 'St George Tucker', *Legal education in Virginia, 1779–1979: a biographical approach*, ed. W. H. Bryson (1982) · C. T. Cullen, 'St George Tucker', *The Virginia law reporters before 1800*, ed.

W. H. Bryson (1977) · C. R. Dolmetsch, 'St George Tucker', *Fifty southern writers before 1900*, ed. R. Bain and J. M. Flora (1987) · R. B. Davis, *Intellectual life in Jefferson's Virginia, 1790–1830* (1964) · *The poems of St George Tucker of Williamsburg, Virginia, 1752–1827*, ed. W. S. Prince (1977) · B. Davis, *A Williamsburg galaxy* (1968) · M. H. B. Coleman, *St George Tucker, citizen of no mean city* (1938) · E. L. Shepard, 'Tucker, St George', *ANB* · A. M. Dobie, 'Tucker, St George', *DAB*, 19.38–9
Archives College of William and Mary, Williamsburg, Virginia, Earl Gregg Swem Library, Tucker–Coleman collection
Likenesses C. B. J. F. de Saint-Mémin, engraving, 1807–8, Corcoran Gallery of Art, Washington, DC [*see illus.*] · B. Moore, oils (after engraving by Saint-Mémin), College of William and Mary, Williamsburg, Virginia

Tucker, Thomas Tudor (1775–1852), naval officer, the son of Henry Tucker, secretary of the council of the Bermudas, and his wife, Frances, the eldest daughter of George Bruere, governor of the Bermudas, was born on 29 June 1775. He was the third of eight sons, all of whom went into public service: Henry St George *Tucker was his eldest brother. After two voyages in the service of the East India Company he entered the navy in 1793 as master's mate of the *Argo*, with Captain William Clark, whom he followed to the *Sampson* and the *Victorious*; he was present in the latter at the capture of the Cape of Good Hope. On 21 March 1796 he was appointed acting lieutenant of the *Suffolk* on the East India station, in which, and afterwards in the sloop *Swift*, again in the *Victorious*, and in the *Sceptre*, he served as acting lieutenant for nearly four years. On her way homewards the *Sceptre* was lost in Table Bay, on 5 November 1799. Many of her crew drowned, and Tucker had to find his own passage to England. On arriving in London in May 1800 he learned that the Admiralty refused to confirm his irregular promotion. After passing a second examination, however, he was made lieutenant on 20 May 1800, on the *Prince George*, in which, and afterwards in the *Prince*, he served in the Channel Fleet until the peace.

In June 1803 Tucker was appointed to the *Northumberland* (74 guns), the flagship of Rear-Admiral Cochrane, off Ferrol, and later in the West Indies, where, on 6 February 1806, he was present in the battle of San Domingo. He was then appointed by the admiral acting commander of the *Dolphin* (44 guns) and, in succession, of several other ships, but the rank was not confirmed until 15 February 1808. In April of that year he was moved into the *Epervier* (16 guns), in which, and afterwards in the *Cherub* (18 guns), he repeatedly distinguished himself in the capture of enemy vessels even when protected by batteries. In February 1810 he assisted in the capture of Guadeloupe. On the special recommendation of the commander-in-chief, Sir Francis Laforey, he was promoted to post rank on 1 August 1811, but was continued in the *Cherub*, which he took to England in September 1812 in charge of a large convoy. On 23 January 1811 he married Anne Byam Wyke, the eldest daughter of Daniel Hill of Antigua; they had two sons and three daughters.

Tucker was immediately ordered to refit the *Cherub* for foreign service, and the crew were permitted leave: exceptionally, all returned, a tribute to his command. Early in December 1812 he sailed for South America and on to the Pacific. At Juan Fernandez he joined Captain James Hillyar

of the *Phoebe*, with whom he continued, and assisted in the capture of the US frigate *Essex*, near Valparaiso, on 28 March 1814, when he was severely wounded. The small force of the *Cherub* had, necessarily, little influence on the action, but in the previous blockade she had rendered important service in helping to frustrate the enemy's attempts to escape. In August 1815 she returned to England, and was paid off. Tucker afterwards commanded the *Andromeda* (22 guns) and the *Comus* (22 guns) for a few months, but after May 1816 had no employment. On 4 July 1840 he was made a CB, and on 31 October 1846 was put on the retired list with the rank of rear-admiral. He died at Portman Square, London, on 20 July 1852. The place where he was buried is unknown

J. K. LAUGHTON, rev. ANDREW LAMBERT

Sources D. F. Long, *Nothing too daring: Commodore David Dixon Porter USN* (1970) · D. Syrett and R. L. DiNardo, *The commissioned sea officers of the Royal Navy, 1660–1815*, rev. edn, Occasional Publications of the Navy RS, 1 (1994) · O'Byrne, *Naval biog. dict.* · *GM*, 2nd ser., 38 (1852), 539 · J. Marshall, *Royal naval biography*, suppl. 2 (1828) · Boase, *Mod. Eng. biog.*
Likenesses oils, *c*.1790, Bermuda Historical Monuments Trust

Tucker, William (*b.* *c*.**1589**, *d.* before **1640**?), colonist in America, was born in England. Little is known of his early life. He married, before 1618, Mary, daughter of Robert Thompson of Watton, Hertfordshire; she was aunt to the first Baron Haversham. He was one of the first subscribers to the Virginia Company, and in 1617 sent over two men in his service to the colony, himself following in 1618. He apparently devoted himself to trading voyages as well as to planting, and probably from this obtained the title Captain by which reference is generally made to him. To judge from instructions which he left on one of his visits to England, he was a shrewd and hard man of business (*CSP col.*, 1.151). He resided at Kiccowtan (afterwards Elizabeth Town), where he had an estate of 800 acres and a large establishment, and on 30 July 1619 he was elected member for that town to the first assembly of Virginia. He took a leading role in the defence of the colony from the Algonquian Indians led by Opechancanough. Before 1623 he had become a member of the council of Virginia, and apparently was reappointed in subsequent years until his death. In 1630, and again in 1632 and 1633, he made voyages to England. On the last of these occasions he made an application to the privy council for a renewal of the ancient charter of Virginia, and for restraint of the Dutch from the trade. He seems to have died in England, probably before 1640.

TROY O. BICKHAM

Sources *DNB* · *CSP col.*, vol. 1 · A. Brown, ed., *The genesis of the United States*, 2 vols. (1890) · E. D. Neill, *Virginia Carolorum: the colony under the rule of Charles I and II* (1886) · W. F. Craven, *The Virginia Company of London, 1606–1624* (1957)

Tucker, William (*bap.* **1622**?, *d.* **1679**), musician and composer, may have been the son of Edmund Tucker, organist of Salisbury Cathedral, baptized there on 24 June 1622. Details of his education are unknown, although it is possible he may have been a chorister. After the Restoration William Tucker became a minor canon at Westminster Abbey, receiving instructions on 11 December 1660 to 'take the order of Priesthood the next ordination day being the 23rd of December' so that he was eligible for the post (chapter act book 3, fol. 27v). By April 1661 he was also a gentleman of the Chapel Royal. As a minor canon of Westminster he was entitled to a house in the abbey precincts: his wife was named Elizabeth, and four children were baptized or buried at the abbey between 1662 and 1670.

Tucker's surviving compositions, consisting of three services and a number of full and verse anthems, are competently written, straightforward works which circulated beyond London and Westminster to provincial cathedrals, but he is most important for the light his music copying casts on the wider history of Restoration sacred music, in particular the development of the major composers John Blow and Henry Purcell. In the year ending at Michaelmas 1677 he received £20 'for Coppying out some Musick bookes' at Westminster Abbey (Westminster Abbey muniments, 33712, fol. 5v) and on 15 February 1685 his widow Elizabeth was belatedly paid £15 'for her husband's writing in 15 Books the Anthems wth Symphonies for King Charles 2nds use in his Chappell Royall' (Ashbee, 5.272). Comparison of the ascriptions of Tucker's own works with his signature in the abbey precentor's book allows identification of his copying, in which he was sometimes assisted by two other scribes who wrote only words. The abbey payment was almost certainly for his contribution to the partbooks of the now incomplete Triforium set I; that at the Chapel Royal was for a set represented by two extant bass partbooks (BL, Add. MS 50860; Nanki Library, Tokyo, N-5/10). Further examples of Tucker's hand appear in the earliest layers of the Chapel Royal partbooks (BL, Royal Music 27.a.1–8) and a Chapel Royal organ book (Fitzwilliam Museum, Cambridge, MU MS 152): he is also known to have made copies for Peterborough Cathedral in 1669–70.

Tucker's death on 28 February 1679 provides a latest possible date for music in his hand, often limited still further by attributions to 'Mr' John Blow, which must precede his doctorate, conferred on 10 December 1677, or by the probable completion of Tucker's work in Triforium set I by Michaelmas 1677. Several anthems by Purcell are thereby shown to be products of the composer's teenage years, most notably the symphony anthem 'My beloved spake'. Tucker was buried in the cloisters of Westminster Abbey on 1 March 1679, and administration of his estate was granted to Elizabeth by the court of the dean and chapter on 29 May.   ROBERT THOMPSON

Sources chapter act book 3, 1660–62; precentor's book, 1660–72; Westminster Abbey muniments 61228A; treasurers' books, 1660–79; Westminster Abbey muniments 33694–33710; 33712–33714, Westminster Abbey · I. Spink, *Restoration cathedral music, 1660–1714* (1995) · H. W. Shaw, *The succession of organists of the Chapel Royal and the cathedrals of England and Wales from c.1538* (1991) · E. F. Rimbault, ed., *The old cheque book, or book of remembrance of the Chapel Royal, from 1561 to 1744*, CS, 3rd ser., 3 (1872); 2nd repr. (New York, 1966) · A. Ashbee, ed., *Records of English court music*, 1 (1986) · A. Ashbee, ed., *Records of English court music*, 5 (1991) · A. M. Burke, ed., *Indexes to ancient testamentary records of Westminster* (1913) · administration, prerogative court of the dean and chapter of Westminster, City

Westm. AC, act book 6, fol. 140v · H. W. Shaw, 'A Cambridge manuscript from the English Chapel Royal', *Music and Letters*, 42 (1961), 263–7 · J. L. Chester, ed., *The marriage, baptismal, and burial registers of the collegiate church or abbey of St Peter, Westminster*, Harleian Society, 10 (1876) · M. Laurie, 'The Chapel Royal part-books', *Music and bibliography: essays in honour of Alec Hyatt King*, ed. O. Neighbour (1980), 28–50 · register (baptism), Salisbury Cathedral

Archives BL, Chapel Royal bass partbook, Add. MS 50860 · BL, Chapel Royal partbooks, Royal Music 27.a.1–8 · FM Cam., Chapel Royal organ book · Nanki Library, Tokyo, Chapel Royal bass partbook · Westminster Abbey, two partbooks · Westminster Abbey, chapter act book 3 · Westminster Abbey muniments 33694–33710, 33712–33714 · Westminster Abbey, Westminster Abbey muniments 61228A · Westminster Abbey, precentor's book · Westminster Abbey, treasurers' books

Tuckey, James Kingston (1776–1816), naval officer and explorer, the youngest son of Thomas Tuckey of Greenhill, near Mallow, co. Cork, Ireland, and his wife, Elizabeth, the daughter of the Revd James Kingston of Donoughmore, was born in August 1776. His parents died in his infancy, and he was brought up by his maternal grandmother. After a voyage to the West Indies in a merchant ship, he was in 1793, through the influence of a relative, Captain Francis John Hartwell, afterwards commissioner of the navy, placed on the *Suffolk*, going out to the East Indies with the broad pennant of Commodore Peter Rainier. In her he was present at the capture of Trincomalee in August 1795 and of Amboyna, where he was wounded in the left arm by a shell fragment. He was afterwards put in command of a prize brig and ordered to cruise off the island to prevent a threatened native insurrection. When his right arm was broken by the bursting of a gun Tuckey had to set it himself; it had to be broken again by the surgeon of the *Suffolk*, and he never quite recovered its use. In January 1798 he assisted in suppressing a serious mutiny on the *Suffolk*, and Rainier, in approving his conduct, gave him an acting order as lieutenant and appointed him to the frigate *Fox*. At Madras in February 1799, when the *Sibylle* was sailing to search for the French frigate *Forte*, Tuckey, with a party of seamen from the *Fox*, volunteered to serve in her, and took part in capturing the *Forte* a few days later. He was confirmed lieutenant on 6 October 1800. He rejoined the *Fox* in the Red Sea, and, after returning to Bombay, was again in the Red Sea at the end of 1800. He suffered much from the heat, and the foundations were laid of 'a hepatic derangement', from which he suffered for the rest of his life. He was invalided to India, and was sent home with dispatches.

In 1802 Tuckey was appointed first lieutenant of the *Calcutta* (54 guns), going out to New South Wales to establish a colony at Port Phillip. He made a complete survey of the harbour of Port Phillip and a careful examination of the adjacent coast and country. On his return to England in the autumn of 1804 he published *The Account of a Voyage to Establish a Colony at Port Phillip* (1805). The *Calcutta* was then sent out to St Helena to convoy the homeward-bound East Indiaman. While she was returning she met the Rochefort squadron and was captured. Her captain, Woodriff, was exchanged some eighteen months later, but for Tuckey no exchange was permitted, and he was detained a prisoner in France, mostly at Verdun, until the peace of 1814. While at Verdun, in 1806 Tuckey married Margaret Stuart, the daughter of the captain of an Indiaman and a fellow prisoner; they had children. Also during this time he wrote the comprehensive *Maritime Geography and Statistics*, which was published on his return to England (4 vols., 1815). He was promoted commander on 27 August 1814.

After the peace of 1815 the government decided to send an expedition to explore the River Congo. Despite his uncertain health, Tuckey was put in charge of this. He sailed early in 1816 in a specially built survey schooner, the *Congo*, which had briefly been equipped with a steam engine, and was accompanied by the storeship *Dorothy*. The *Dorothy* remained in the lower river, while the *Congo* pushed up as far as the cataracts. Tuckey then undertook a journey by land to see what was above the cataracts, but his health completely broke down, and he was obliged to return. Worn out, he arrived back at the *Congo* on 17 September; on the following day he was sent down to the *Dorothy*, and he died on board her on 4 October, 'of exhaustion rather than of disease'. The surgeon reported that, 'since leaving England he never enjoyed good health, the hepatic functions being generally in a deranged state'. Tuckey's journal, as he wrote it, was published, by permission of the Admiralty, as *Narrative of an Expedition to Explore the River Zaire, Usually called the Congo* (1818).

J. K. LAUGHTON, rev. ANDREW LAMBERT

Sources G. S. Ritchie, *The Admiralty chart: British naval hydrography in the nineteenth century* (1967) · H. B. Carter, *Sir Joseph Banks, 1743–1820* (1988) · C. N. Parkinson, *War in the eastern seas, 1793–1815* (1954) · J. K. Tuckey, *Narrative of an expedition to explore the River Zaire* (1818) · *GM*, 1st ser., 87/1 (1817)

Tuckney, Anthony (1599–1670), Church of England clergyman and college head, was born on 22 September 1599 at Kirton in Holland, Lincolnshire, the son of William Tuckney, the vicar there. He entered Emmanuel College, Cambridge, as a scholar in 1613, graduated BA in 1617, was elected a fellow in 1619, and proceeded MA in 1620 and BD in 1627.

Emmanuel and Lincolnshire connections made Tuckney's life and career, and he continuously identified with 'that good old Doctrine according unto godliness' of the Church of England preached by 'those Worthies of God' under whom he had been trained (Tuckney, *Death Disarmed*, epistle). Before taking up his tutorial functions he had served as household chaplain to Theophilus Clinton, fourth earl of Lincoln, which was the beginning of his sympathetic connection with New England, since the earl's sister married Tuckney's contemporary Isaac Johnson, who embarked with his wife in the first fleet for Massachusetts. Tuckney maintained a lifelong correspondence with another contemporary, Samuel Whiting, his schoolfriend and chamber fellow, who was to minister at Lynn in Massachusetts from 1636 until 1679. In later years, Tuckney was said to have been 'very zealous for the conversion of the Indians and propagating the gospel in America' (Baker, 230). In the 1620s, which saw the Emmanuel mastership of John Preston, Tuckney was one of those sent off to what became known as Preston's 'seasoning vessel', the family of his cousin John Cotton at Boston in

his native Lincolnshire, a kind of laboratory for that other Boston for ever associated with Cotton. Tuckney later remembered that his fellow lodger Thomas *Hill (later, and briefly, master of Emmanuel) had been 'much improved and furthered … heaven-way' by his time with Cotton, but John Angier thought Tuckney himself 'a serious, settled, good man' even before he left Cambridge (*Heywood's Life of John Angier*, 52).

When Cotton left for New England, Tuckney succeeded him as preacher and then vicar of Boston. He may be regarded, even in the years of Archbishop Laud's dominance, as an establishment puritan. He was occasionally in trouble with the church courts, but his *Forty Sermons* (1676) include assize and visitation sermons, among them a sermon preached in 1634 'before Sir Nathaniel Brent, visitor for the archbishop of Canterbury'. In 1635 he founded a parish library in Boston, to which he contributed many of his own books. At an unknown date, but presumably after his move to Boston, Tuckney married his first wife, Mary, who was the mother of his only surviving son, Jonathan. She died on 26 October 1633, and was buried there. Some time after, Tuckney married Elizabeth, of whom nothing is known.

Tuckney began to be a national figure with his election in November 1640 to the lower house of convocation as a clerk for Lincoln diocese. On 30 August 1643 he preached one of the regular fast sermons before the House of Commons. This was at a dark moment in the civil war, and Tuckney's sermon, published as *The Balm of Gilead for the Wounds of England* (1654), was notable for its sombre and judgemental tone. It was a time for 'mourning Suits' rather than 'Fidling Jigges' (sig. A2). All the blood which had been shed would be amply repaid if God's worship and truth were purged, church and state reformed, and a righteous peace settled. On 12 June of the same year he had been made a member of the Westminster assembly of divines, again representing Lincoln. At this point he moved to London, was given the sequestered rectory of St Michael-le-Querne, Paternoster Row, and left a curate in charge at Boston. Tuckney played a major role in the assembly as an architect of its doctrinal formulations. He made significant contributions to both the catechism and the shorter catechism, and he drafted the articles on free will and 'perseverance and certainty of salvation' for the confession of faith, reporting from his committee on such other matters as worship, the sabbath, and marriage and divorce. By this time he might legitimately be described not only as a Calvinist but also as a presbyterian, although in the assembly he voted that while public criticism of the confession of faith should not be allowed, the confession should never be imposed by subscription, 'we having bin burnt in the hand in that kind before' (*DNB*).

In 1645 Richard Holdsworth, who was *persona non grata* with parliament, was removed from the mastership of Emmanuel. He was replaced by Thomas Hill, but Hill was almost immediately translated to Trinity, and on 11 April 1645 Tuckney was thought 'fit and worthy' by the assembly to be master of Emmanuel (*Minutes of the Westminster Assembly*, 79). Whether all members of that society thought him fit and worthy was another matter, and the future Archbishop William Sancroft found it impossible even to speak to this usurper face to face. Writing to his father, Sancroft called Tuckney his 'continuing inconvenience' (Bendall, Brooke, and Collinson, 253). Tuckney himself showed some diffidence in intruding into a master's lodge still full of Holdsworth's things, and especially his enormous library. More than three years after his appointment, he visited Holdsworth and asked if he could have the use of his household goods 'and to look somewhat into my study', which Holdsworth granted, on conditions. The reason for this was that the Westminster assembly, which had earlier excused Tuckney from residence in Cambridge on account of 'the special employment' it had imposed upon him, had completed its doctrinal work, so that in 1648 Tuckney moved his family to Cambridge and was soon serving as vice-chancellor. In 1649 he proceeded DD. About this time he was named to the Lady Margaret chair of divinity, but seems never to have taken up the appointment. In June 1653 he became master of St John's. When his old friend Hill died in December of that year, Tuckney preached the funeral sermon; later he married, as his third wife, Hill's widow, Mary Willford, who 'made it her business to make him merry; and she had a fine way of doing it' (Baker, 642).

With Cromwell in power and presbyterianism generally in eclipse, Tuckney's promotions were on the face of it surprising, although testament to his lingering influence at Cambridge. The Anglican and royalist Johnian Henry Paman told his old tutor Sancroft that 'I may no more speak against a Presbyterian in the college than an Independent in the state' (Bodl. Oxf., MS Tanner 54, fol. 96). Paman reported that Tuckney's elevation to the regius chair of divinity in 1656 was owing to the 'importunities' of the leading presbyterians Edmund Calamy, Simeon Ash, and Stephen Marshall, who had declared on his deathbed that he would die happy if that place were to be so 'carefully and safely bestowed', whereas Cromwell was certain to be angry (Bodl. Oxf., MS Tanner 52, fol. 70).

There is no reason to suppose, however, that Tuckney was anything but an effective and considerate head of house. Thomas Baker, the historian of St John's and anything but a coreligionist, thought him 'as much esteemed and revered as any master ever was' (Baker, 229). Years earlier, in 1635, Tuckney had written to the then master of Emmanuel, Sancroft's uncle William Sancroft, begging him to 'study the college's peace', and to maintain the lawful privileges of the fellows even when they were opposed to him, offering to act as a mediator and recalling John Preston's 'clashes' with the fellowship, 'jars' which had threatened the ruin of the college (Bendall, Brooke, and Collinson, 220). Yet Tuckney was a stern disciplinarian. When he arrived at St John's, Henry Paman was warned to expect 'a very severe schoolmaster', and reported that on leaving Emmanuel, Tuckney had asked the college to forgive him for his severity. At St John's he was in chapel every morning, upbraiding the laxity of 'the lazy seniors' (Bodl. Oxf., MS Tanner 52, fol. 70). During these years of the Commonwealth and protectorate, Tuckney was an indefatigable preacher, regularly repeating his Great St Mary's sermons at St Paul's in London.

Even by the early 1650s, however, Tuckney was something of a theological dinosaur, defending what he called 'that good old doctrine', 'God's sovraignty in his decrees', 'his inconditionate most free electing love', 'perseverance in grace' rather than the pernicious doctrine of 'the perfection of inherent righteousness now attainable by us in this life'. This was no sectarian 'presbyterian' doctrine but 'of the life-blood of Faith' (Tuckney, *Death Disarmed*, epistle and 45). Tuckney's old-fashioned convictions were at odds not only with the avant-garde high-churchmanship of the likes of Sancroft and Paman but with the more alarming modernizing tendencies known to history as Cambridge Platonism, an intellectual fashion which had been bred in the very womb of Tuckney's own alma mater of Emmanuel, among its leaders his own prize pupil Benjamin Whichcote, whose impact as the lecturer from 1636 to 1656 at Holy Trinity Church, and personally, was very great, and another Emmanuel man, Ralph Cudworth, whose religion has been defined as the common faith of all who fell under the influence of Benjamin Whichcote. Christianity was sent 'both to elevate and sweeten human nature'. Man was a reasonable creature, and 'to go against Reason is to go against God' (Bendall, Brooke, and Collinson, 260).

In 1651 a kind of theological San Andreas fault opened up in a famous exchange of letters between Tuckney and Whichcote, now provost of King's and vice-chancellor, which was provoked by a commencement address which Tuckney interpreted as a personal attack on his own address of a year before. Tuckney realized that while he had admired his pupil's dutiful studiousness, he should have been more alert to his 'somewhat cloudy and obscure expressions'. Whichcote's doctrine that Christ saves us not without us but within us was a divinity which, Tuckney said, 'my heart riseth against'. It was a fatal departure from the 'spiritual, plain, powerful' tradition for which Cambridge had been famous, 'a kind of Moral Divinitie' with only a little tincture of Christ added, 'nay a Platonique faith' (Bendall, Brooke, and Collinson, 261). When Tuckney attacked Whichcote's critical use of reason and defence of toleration and Whichcote asked what else universities were for, a curtain was drawn back on the future. But the two old friends agreed to differ, and both Whichcote and Cudworth supported Tuckney's election as regius professor, as did the royalist James Duport.

With the Restoration, Tuckney, who had recently celebrated his sixtieth birthday, was redundant and the story of his last decade is soon told. It was not until August 1660 that he resigned Boston vicarage, which he did in favour of Obadiah Howe, who seems to have been his preferred successor. As royalist fervour gripped St John's the younger fellows, many of whom owed their places to him, complained that since the reintroduction of the prayer book the master had absented himself from chapel. In June 1661 a letter from Charles II prevailed upon him to resign, ostensibly on account of 'some infirmitie of body'

(*Calamy rev.*, 496), and he retired on a pension of £100 payable from the Cambridgeshire living of Somersham which was attached to the regius chair. He withdrew to London, living in the parish of St Mary Axe and occasionally preaching in private. He had been appointed to the Savoy conference for the reform of the prayer book but took no part in it, according to Richard Baxter 'alledging his backwardness to speak' (ibid.). In the plague year (1665) he moved to the midlands, making use of Emmanuel connections, among them the Pierrepoint family of Colwick Hall, Nottinghamshire, and Oundle, Northamptonshire, where his successor as master of Emmanuel, William Dillingham, was living after sharing Tuckney's fate. In Tuckney's absence the great fire of 1666 destroyed his library, which he had deposited in Scriveners' Hall. He was in trouble for nonconformity, and even imprisoned for a time, although on 30 September 1668 he married his fourth wife, Sarah, widow of yet another Emmanuel contemporary, presbyterian, and assembly man, William Spurstowe, rector of Hackney. Tuckney returned to London in poor health in 1669 and died of scurvy and jaundice in Spital Yard in February 1670. He was buried on 1 March at St Andrew Undershaft. His son Jonathan, who had graduated from Emmanuel and been ejected from a St John's fellowship in 1662, a man of good learning 'render'd useless by melancholy' (*Calamy rev.*, 496), edited his father's *Forty Sermons* (1676) and his *Praelectiones theologicae* (1679).   PATRICK COLLINSON

Sources W. D[illingham], 'Account', in *Praelectiones theologicae*, ed. J. Tuckney (1679) · will, PRO, PROB 11/332, fol. 330 · *DNB* · S. Bendall, C. Brooke, and P. Collinson, *A history of Emmanuel College, Cambridge* (1999) · J. Twigg, *The University of Cambridge and the English Revolution, 1625–1688* (1990) · S. Salter, ed., *Moral and religious aphorisms … to which are added, eight letters which passed between Dr Whichcote, provost of King's College and Dr Tuckney, master of Emmanuel College in Cambridge* (1753) · *Calamy rev.* · A. Tuckney, *Death disarmed and the grave swallowed up in victory: a sermon preached … at the publick funeral or Dr Hill* (1654) · Bodl. Oxf., MSS Tanner 47, 52, 57 · CUL, MS Mm.1.45 (Baker 34) · *Oliver Heywood's life of John Angier of Denton*, ed. E. Axon, Chetham Society, new ser., 97 (1937) · A. F. Mitchell and J. Struthers, eds., *Minutes of the sessions of the Westminster assembly of divines* (1874) · T. Baker, *History of the college of St John the Evangelist, Cambridge*, ed. J. E. B. Mayor, 2 vols. (1869)
Archives BL, corresp. with Benjamin Whichcote, Sloane MSS 1710, fols. 309–53; 2903, fols. 88–101 [copies made 1685]
Likenesses R. White, line engraving, BM, NPG; repro. in T. Tuckney, *Forty sermons* (1676)

Tuckwell, Gertrude Mary (1861–1951), trade unionist and social reformer, was born on 25 April 1861 in Oxford, the second daughter of the Revd William Tuckwell and his wife, Rosa, daughter of Captain Henry Strong of the East India Company. Her father was master of New College School and a chaplain of New College. He espoused Christian socialist beliefs, advocated tax and land reform, and his autobiography, dedicated to his daughter Gertrude, was entitled *Reminiscences of a Radical Parson* (1905).

Gertrude Tuckwell spent her childhood in Somerset and Warwickshire parsonages. Although her father's beliefs influenced her throughout her life, it was her maternal aunt Emilia Strong (later Emilia *Dilke, Lady Dilke),

Gertrude Mary Tuckwell (1861–1951), by Lafayette, 1930

whose first husband, Mark Pattison (1813–1884), was rector of Lincoln College, Oxford, who made the deepest impression on her. In her unpublished autobiography, 'Reminiscences', she described Mrs Pattison, an accomplished art historian and critic, as 'the greatest person I have ever known'.

While staying in Oxford with her aunt in 1878 Gertrude Tuckwell met two women members of the London school board and decided on a teaching career. She enrolled as a pupil teacher at a Liverpool training college, doing teaching practice in the slums. In 1882, after a year there, she moved to Bishop Otter College, Chichester, for a further two years. Her first post was at an elementary school in Park Walk, Chelsea, and she spent six years teaching working-class infants until forced to resign on account of ill health. In 1893 she succeeded May Abraham [see Tennant, Margery (1869–1946)] as labour secretary to her aunt Emilia, who was now living in London with her second husband, Sir Charles Dilke MP (1843–1911). During this time Gertrude Tuckwell wrote *The State and its Children* (1894) in which she advocated the prohibition of half-time child labour. She found the intellectual and political milieu of the Dilke household a stimulating experience— 'a lesson in the art of living' (Tuckwell) though a lesson which stressed work as paramount.

Gertrude Tuckwell also became honorary secretary of the Women's Trade Union League which had grown out of the Women's Protective and Provident League founded in 1874, and she edited the league's journal. After her aunt's death she succeeded Lady Dilke as president of the league in 1905. Three years later she became president of the National Federation of Women Workers. She played a key role in the formation of the Industrial Law Committee and actively campaigned to protect women workers from industrial injuries, notably lead poisoning and 'phossy jaw'. The latter was the workers' name for phosphorus necrosis, a disease contracted by large numbers of match workers who inhaled phosphorus fumes. She personally investigated hazardous white lead mills and sat on the departmental committee on the dangers attendant on the use of lead. She helped to form the National Anti-Sweating League and was a keen advocate of the statutory minimum wage. She gave evidence to the 1907 select committee on home work and also sat on the executive committee of the International Association for Labour Legislation from 1906, founding a British section with Sidney Webb as chairman. Her advocacy of women's trade unionism was predicated upon a belief in improving conditions at the workplace and in educating women to their own needs.

Although she formally retired from women's trade union work in 1918, Gertrude Tuckwell remained extremely active in public life, especially in legal and health-related matters. She became one of the first women justices of the peace and served on an advisory committee to assist the lord chancellor in appointing women justices. She was a founder of the Magistrates' Association, sitting on its council between 1921 and 1940, and she chaired the National Association of Probation Officers from 1933 to 1941. She also served on the advisory committee to the Ministry of Health (1905–23), on the Central Committee on Women's Training and Employment, and on the royal commission on national health insurance (1924–6). Concerned about the alarmingly high maternal mortality rate, she and her friend May Tennant formed the Maternal Mortality Committee. Between 1922 and 1929 she was president of the Women Sanitary Inspectors and Health Visitors' Association. She was also president of the Women Public Health Officers' Association and a member of the Women's Health Inquiry Committee which in 1939 investigated the health of married women.

The Dilkes' concern about the conditions of women workers had always been a great stimulus to Gertrude Tuckwell's own efforts. When Sir Charles Dilke died in 1911 she became his literary executor and, with Stephen Gwynne, produced in 1917 a two-volume biography based on his memoirs and correspondence. Since her days as an elementary schoolteacher Gertrude Tuckwell's close friends had tended to be those women with whom she also shared a commitment to improve labour conditions. When her colleague Mary Macarthur died prematurely in 1921, she chaired her memorial which provided scholarships to women in the trade union and labour movement. Violet Markham, whom she called 'my constant friend' (Tuckwell), recalled Gertrude Tuckwell as 'Tall and beautiful', adding that she was 'not only a highly cultured and distinguished woman but she had a rare and tender

nature, unswerving in its affection and loyalty' (*DNB*). She was guided by lifelong Christian socialist principles, and from 1898 to 1911 was secretary of the Christian Social Union Research Committee. Her Labour sympathies led Gertrude Tuckwell to support adult suffrage, and she was a firm advocate of equal pay.

Gertrude Tuckwell was appointed CH in 1930. She spent her last twenty years at Little Woodlands, Wormley, near Godalming, Surrey. She died aged ninety on 5 August 1951 in the Royal Surrey County Hospital, Guildford, after an accident. During her long life she played a seminal role in the development of women's trade unionism and the labour movement. In the inter-war period she actively embraced the more public and official roles that became available to able women, most notably in the areas of the law and public health.　　　　　　ANGELA V. JOHN

Sources G. Tuckwell, 'Reminiscences', Trade Union Congress Library, London, Gertrude Tuckwell MSS · M. Kozak, 'Tuckwell, Gertrude Mary', *DLB*, vol. 6 · *The Times* (6 Aug 1951) · J. Morris, 'The Gertrude Tuckwell collection', *History Workshop Journal*, 5 (1978), 155–62 · B. Drake, *Women in trade unions* (1920) · K. Israel, 'Drawing from life: art, work and feminism in the life of Emilia Dilke, 1840–1904', PhD diss., Rutgers University, 1992 · J. Lewis, *The politics of motherhood* (1980) · J. E. Courtney, *The women of my time* (1934) · d. cert.
Archives BL, corresp. and papers relating to the life of Sir Charles Dilke, Add. MSS 43967, 49612 · London Metropolitan University, corresp. and papers | BLPES, corresp. with V. R. Markham and papers relating to May Tennant
Likenesses Lafayette, photograph, 1930, NPG [*see illus.*] · photograph (probably in her thirties), Labour History Archive and Study Centre, Manchester, labour party archives
Wealth at death £12,685 17*s.* 10*d.*: probate, 30 Oct 1951, *CGPLA Eng. & Wales*

Tuddenham, Sir Thomas (1401–1462), landowner, was born at Eriswell, Suffolk, the younger son of Sir Robert Tuddenham of Eriswell (1366–1405) and his wife, Margaret, daughter of John Harling, esquire. Thomas inherited the Tuddenham estates on the death of his elder brother, Robert, in 1415. His wardship and marriage were granted to Sir John Rodenhale and John Wodehous, esquire, in July 1417. It was probably in the following year that Tuddenham married Wodehous's daughter Alice. The couple lived together until about 1425, and during that time Alice gave birth to a short-lived son. The marriage did not last; both later stated that it had never been consummated, and Alice acknowledged that her child had been the result of a liaison with her father's chamberlain. They separated formally by 1429, when Alice entered the Augustinian nunnery of Crabhouse, Norfolk. She seems still to have been living there in 1475. Although the marriage was annulled in 1436, Tuddenham never remarried.

Tuddenham received livery of his estates in March 1423. His association with his father-in-law, Wodehous (which does not seem to have been compromised by the failure of his marriage), involved him with a powerful political network in Norfolk which had developed since 1399 around those local men who were associated with the management of the king's duchy of Lancaster estates in the north of the shire. Wodehous had held the duchy of Lancaster stewardship in East Anglia since 1415, but on 30 June 1425 he surrendered the office so that it could be granted for life to Tuddenham, who seems also to have been knighted about this time. It was probably through Wodehous's influence that Tuddenham became a member of the household of Thomas Beaufort, duke of Exeter, the most powerful nobleman in Norfolk until his death in 1426. Tuddenham's involvement in Norfolk politics was reinforced in 1434 when he inherited the manor of Oxburgh, which was to become his principal residence, from a distant cousin.

By the later 1430s William de la Pole, earl (later duke) of Suffolk (1396–1450), succeeded in establishing himself as Exeter's successor at the head of the Norfolk network of which Tuddenham was a part. Suffolk was also by this time in the ascendant at court. Tuddenham's position as one of Suffolk's most influential supporters was reflected in his many appointments and grants in East Anglia and in the king's household. Tuddenham was appointed sheriff of Norfolk and Suffolk in 1432; he was MP for Suffolk in 1431, and for Norfolk in 1432, 1435, and 1442. He was named to every peace commission in Norfolk between 1434 and 1450. On 29 September 1443 he was appointed chief steward of the north parts of the duchy of Lancaster jointly with Suffolk, and on 26 October 1446, as a king's knight, he was made keeper of the great wardrobe.

The degree of influence wielded in East Anglia by Tuddenham and associates such as John Heydon of Baconsthorpe during the 1440s is usually described as the temporary hijacking of regional power structures by Suffolk's henchmen, a view reinforced by the hostility with which they were portrayed in the Paston letters, but the local influence of Tuddenham's broad circle had much deeper roots than their identification as a court clique allows. Their regional dominance both predated Suffolk's rise to power, and survived his fall in 1450. In that year and the next Tuddenham lost his position on the Norfolk peace commission, his keepership of the great wardrobe, and his stewardship of the north parts of the duchy, and charges were brought against Tuddenham and Heydon by their local opponents, prominent among whom were the Pastons. However, the influence of Tuddenham and his associates was quickly reasserted under the leadership of the dowager duchess of Suffolk and Thomas, Lord Scales. By 1452 Tuddenham and Heydon were again being appointed to special commissions, and in 1455 both were reinstated as JPs in Norfolk.

The connections between Tuddenham's circle and the court meant that during the 1450s they aligned themselves with Queen Margaret against Richard, duke of York. Under the financial resettlement initiated by the queen at the end of 1458 Tuddenham became treasurer of the royal household. After the Yorkist victory in 1461 a commission for Tuddenham's arrest was issued, and he was executed on 23 February 1462 as a rebel and traitor. His lands passed to his sister Margaret, wife of Sir Edmund Bedingfield. Tuddenham was buried in the church of the Austin Friars in London.   HELEN CASTOR

Sources *The Paston letters, AD 1422–1509*, ed. J. Gairdner, new edn, 6 vols. (1904) · *Chancery records* · R. Virgoe, 'The divorce of Sir Thomas Tuddenham', *Norfolk Archaeology*, 34 (1966–9), 406–18 · R. Somerville, *History of the duchy of Lancaster, 1265–1603* (1953) · PRO · Norfolk RO · H. Castor, 'The duchy of Lancaster and the rule of East Anglia, 1399–1440: a prologue to the Paston letters', *Crown, government, and people in the fifteenth century*, ed. R. E. Archer (1995), 53–78 · F. Blomefield and C. Parkin, *An essay towards a topographical history of the county of Norfolk*, [2nd edn], 11 vols. (1805–10) · *Itineraries [of] William Worcestre*, ed. J. H. Harvey, OMT (1969) · J. Gairdner, ed., *Three fifteenth-century chronicles*, CS, new ser., 28 (1880) · N. H. Nicolas, ed., *Testamenta vetusta: being illustrations from wills*, 2 vols. (1826) **Wealth at death** see will, Nicolas, ed., *Testamenta*, vol. 1, pp. 297–8

Tudor family, forebears of (*per. c.*1215–1404), administrators and landholders, were prominent in Wales from at least the thirteenth century. **Ednyfed Fychan** (*d.* 1246), dynast and administrator, was the son of Cynwrig ab Iorwerth ap Gwrgant; the family came from the cantref of Rhos in north-east Wales and still had lands there in the fourteenth century.

Princely service and rewards Ednyfed (whose epithet means 'little') is said to have become the steward or *distain* of *Llywelyn ab Iorwerth (*d.* 1240), prince of north Wales, about 1215, when he first appeared as witness to a charter, although the earliest reference to him as holder of that office was when he witnessed a grant by Llywelyn in 1225. He appeared on a number of occasions as witness, arbitrator, and diplomatic representative of the prince; his last appearance was in 1245, when he led a delegation sent by Llywelyn's son and successor *Dafydd ap Llywelyn (*d.* 1246) to meet Henry III and his council at Deganwy. In 1235 he had been granted a safe conduct by the king to travel through England on his way to the Holy Land and Henry gave instructions for a silver cup to be presented to him during his stay in London, although the gift does not seem to have been made. At his death, almost certainly in 1246, he was described by the Chester annals as justiciar of Wales, although one of his sons, Tudur, may already have taken over the post of steward from him in 1241. Ednyfed's elegy was sung by the poet Elidir Sais.

Ednyfed was the leading servant and adviser of Llywelyn ab Iorwerth and Dafydd ap Llywelyn. The *distain* had originally been responsible for the domestic organization and economy of the royal court, but by the thirteenth century he had come to be the prince's chief counsellor. The value of Ednyfed's service was reflected in the lands and privileges granted to him by Llywelyn. His descendants held these lands by a tenure described as that of *wyrion Eden* ('the grandsons of Ednyfed'), which involved exemption from all rents and obligations except suit to the prince's court and military service. In the cantrefs of Rhos and Rhufoniog these privileges were enjoyed by all the descendants of his grandfather; it has been suggested that here the tenure was connected with the defence of one of the main routes into Snowdonia. Lands, including Penmynydd in Anglesey, which came to be regarded as the traditional seat of the family, were also granted to him in other parts of Gwynedd.

Founder of a dynasty According to the pedigrees Ednyfed was twice married, his first wife being a daughter of the Anglesey nobleman Llywarch ap Bran and his second Gwenllian, a daughter of *Rhys ap Gruffudd (*d.* 1197), the ruler of Deheubarth; she died in 1236. Through Gwenllian the family acquired some small lordships in the later counties of Cardigan and Carmarthen. He had several sons and daughters; one son, Iorwerth, is said to have been a leper, one may have been one of the Welsh prisoners killed by Henry III's invading army in 1245, and one, Hywel, was bishop of St Asaph from 1240 to 1247. Three other sons, Tudur, Gruffudd, and Goronwy, and their descendants, continued the tradition of service, both before and after the conquest of 1282, while his nephew Goronwy ap Heilin served both the crown and Llywelyn ap Gruffudd (d. 1282) at different times and died in action in 1283 as the steward of the last native prince, Dafydd ap Gruffudd (d. 1283).

Tudur ab Ednyfed and his descendants, 1241–1431 Tudur ab Ednyfed

(d. 1278), administrator, was described as Dafydd ap Llywelyn's steward in 1241. In 1245–6 he was a prisoner in England and on his release he had to hand over two sons as hostages. For several years he seems to have been in the service of Henry III and in 1259 and 1260 he represented the king in negotiations with Llywelyn ap Gruffudd about a truce. It has been suggested that it was after the release of his son Heilin by the king in 1263 that he joined Llywelyn; he appeared subsequently as witness and arbitrator and he was one of the prince's sureties under the treaty of Montgomery in 1267. In 1268 he succeeded his brother Goronwy as steward and he is described on a number of occasions as steward or justiciar. In November 1277 he and his cousin Goronwy ap Heilin were Llywelyn's plenipotentiaries in the negotiations that led to the treaty of Aberconwy. He died in the following year. Tudur's descendants had lands at Nant near Prestatyn in Flintshire; his great-great-grandson Gruffudd ap Gwilym ap Gruffudd ap Heilin (d. 1405) married a descendant of Goronwy ab Ednyfed and inherited extensive lands in Anglesey and Caernarvonshire from his maternal uncle. Two of Gruffudd's sons, Gwilym and Robin, were the ancestors of the Caernarvonshire families of Penrhyn and Cochwillan. The well-timed submission of **Gwilym ap Gruffudd** (d. 1431), landholder, during the Glyn Dŵr revolt enabled him to add substantially to his lands at the expense of some of his kinsmen and to become the most powerful figure in the principality of north Wales, where his family, the Griffiths of Penrhyn, were to dominate until 1540.

Gruffudd ab Ednyfed and sons, 1246–1284 Gruffudd ab Ednyfed

(fl. 1246–1256), administrator, is traditionally said to have been obliged to seek temporary refuge in Ireland because of a slander about Joan, the wife of Llywelyn ab Iorwerth. He may have been the steward of Llywelyn ap Gruffudd, probably between 1246 and 1255, when Gwynedd west of the Conwy was divided between Llywelyn and his brother Owain; he appeared for the last time in 1256, when he led a delegation to England for talks with Henry III. The date of his death is unknown; his elegy was sung by Dafydd Benfras. It is possible that his relations with Llywelyn had deteriorated; certainly the loyalty of two of his sons, Rhys ap Gruffudd and Hywel ap Gruffudd [see below], was less than wholehearted, and they fought for Edward I

in the war of 1282. **Rhys ap Gruffudd ab Ednyfed** (d. 1284), landholder, had been in the service of the prince but in May 1277, during the first Anglo-Welsh war, he and Hywel came into the king's peace and a third brother, Llywelyn, the prior of the Dominican friary at Bangor, acted as an intermediary. The treaty of Aberconwy stipulated that Llywelyn should restore Rhys to the position he had occupied before his submission, and in 1281 he undertook to pay the prince £100 because of his disobedience and contempt to him. The fact that Rhys was married to Margaret Lestrange, whose sister was the wife of Llywelyn's opponent Gruffudd ap Gwenwynwyn (d. 1286) of Powys, may have contributed to the breakdown of relations. In 1278 he had been a member of the mixed Anglo-Welsh commission appointed by Edward to deal with pleas in Wales and the marches.

Leaders of native Wales: Sir Gruffudd Llwyd and Sir Rhys ap Gruffudd

The English conquest of Wales made no difference to the influence and authority of the descendants of Ednyfed Fychan. Rhys's son Gruffudd, known as Sir *Gruffudd Llwyd (d. 1335), spent many years in the service of the crown. By 1301 he had been knighted and between 1302 and 1317 he was, at different times, sheriff of Caernarvonshire, Anglesey, and Merioneth. During the troubles of Edward II's reign he was the leader of the royalist party in north Wales; after Edward's deposition in 1327 he was one of several prominent Welshmen imprisoned for a time. But his loyalty was not unquestioned; during Edward Bruce's invasion of Ireland, which began in 1315, he was in correspondence with the Scottish leader, promising him support in the event of a landing in Wales. It may have been a memory of his dealings with Bruce that gave rise to the story that he had led an unsuccessful revolt and had been executed. He died in 1335, leaving several daughters and one surviving son, Ieuan (d. c.1352), who became archdeacon of Anglesey.

Hywel ap Gruffudd ab Ednyfed (d. 1282), landholder, was killed at the abortive crossing of the Menai Strait on 6 November 1282. His son Gruffudd (d. 1308) had two sons, Rhys and Robert. Like his kinsman Sir Gruffudd Llwyd, Sir *Rhys ap Gruffudd (d. 1356) had a long career in royal service. His first appointment was as steward of Cardiganshire in 1308 and this was followed by a succession of offices, culminating in two terms as deputy justiciar of south Wales. He also built up a substantial estate in Cardiganshire and Carmarthenshire. Rhys was frequently summoned for military service; in 1315 he was leading troops against the Glamorgan rebel Llywelyn Bren (d. 1317) and he led Welsh troops to Scotland and France, serving at Crécy in 1346. Like Sir Gruffudd Llwyd he remained loyal to Edward II until the end. The failure of his attempt to rescue Edward from captivity in 1327 forced him to flee for a time to Scotland and in 1330 he fled abroad after the failure of the earl of Kent's plot against Mortimer. The fall of Mortimer later the same year restored him to favour and for the rest of his life he was the effective ruler of the principality of south Wales. He had been knighted by 1330. He married an English heiress, Joan Somerville, and through her acquired lands in five English counties; he died on 17

May 1356. An elegy, according to which he was buried at Carmarthen, was composed by Iolo Goch (*fl.* 1345–1397); he was related, through his mother, to the leading poet of the time, Dafydd ap Gwilym (*fl.* 1330–1350). Not long before his death he inherited the lands in south Wales of Sir Gruffudd Llwyd; most of his lands and those of his wife passed to his eldest son, Sir Rhys the younger (*d.* 1380), but those held by Welsh tenure passed to a younger son, Henry.

Alleged oppression and opposition to the English king The activities of Sir Rhys's brother Robert and Robert's son Rhys were mainly in the north-east. **Rhys ap Roppert** (*d.* 1377), administrator, held various local offices and from 1349 to 1351 he was joint sheriff of Flintshire. From 1357 to 1360 he was sole sheriff; his term of office was marked by complaints about his oppressive behaviour and in September 1358 the men of the cantref of Tegeingl submitted a massive and detailed petition complaining about the extortionate and oppressive activities of Rhys and his former colleague in the shrievalty, Ithel ap Cynwrig Sais. This misrule was the result of the widespread practice of farming offices to the highest bidder. There were also more serious accusations. On 20 January 1372 a jury at Flint stated that Rhys's son Ieuan was a traitor and that he was in the company of Owain ap Thomas ap Rhodri (Owen of Wales, *d.* 1378) in the service of the king of France. Rhys knew this and had sent him substantial sums of money. A further inquisition on 25 September 1374 stated that Rhys and his son Madog were adherents of Owain Lawgoch (Owen of Wales) and Ieuan ap Rhys ap Roppert, traitors, that they had received treasonable letters from them, and that Rhys had sent them gold and silver on various occasions. Madog had subsequently gone to France to join Owain and Ieuan. Although no further action was taken against Rhys, these indictments are particularly interesting because they suggest that Owen of Wales could have depended on influential support had either of his two abortive expeditions been successful. The sons were certainly in French service; Ieuan was probably the Ieuan Wyn who was Owen's lieutenant and who took over his company after his assassination in 1378, while Madog was still serving the French crown in 1392. Rhys married Gwladus, the daughter of Madog Llwyd ab Iorwerth Foel of Nanheudwy. He died in 1377.

The line of Tudur Hen ap Goronwy ab Ednyfed, 1258–1411 Goronwy ab Ednyfed (*d.* 1268), administrator, like his brothers, was in the service of Llywelyn ap Gruffudd. He may have become steward about 1258 and he appears on various occasions as an arbitrator and a witness. In 1258 he was one of the Welsh leaders who made an agreement with a faction of Scottish lords and in 1263 he led a military campaign in Gwent. He died in 1268 and his elegy was sung by Bleddyn Fardd (*fl.* 1268–1284) and Y Prydydd Bychan (*fl.* 1222–1268). He had at least three sons, Tudur, known as Tudur Hen (Tudur the Old), Hywel, and Goronwy Fychan. **Tudur Hen ap Goronwy ab Ednyfed** (*d.* 1311), administrator, was probably in the service of Llywelyn before 1282; in 1294–5 he and Goronwy Fychan were

involved in the revolt of Madog ap Llywelyn and in one document he is described as Madog's steward. But he was soon back in favour and in 1296 he was a member of a deputation from north Wales which expressed the community's concern to Edward I about rumours that the Welsh were disloyal. In 1301 he did homage to the new Prince Edward of Caernarfon and in 1305 he submitted several petitions to that prince. He died in 1311 and was buried in the Dominican friary at Bangor, a house with which the family had a close relationship.

Tudur's son **Goronwy ap Tudur** (*d.* 1331), administrator, held local offices in Anglesey and served in Scotland; he may have fought at Bannockburn in 1314. In 1318 he followed Sir Gruffudd Llwyd as forester of Snowdon and like him he stood by Edward II at the end of his reign. When an action was brought in 1331 against the former deputy justiciar of north Wales, William Shalford, accusing him of having encompassed the king's murder, Goronwy and Sir Gruffudd were among the sureties. He died in 1331 and was buried at Bangor; he had three sons, Hywel, Tudur, and Gruffudd (*d. c.*1344).

Hywel ap Goronwy (*d.* 1366?), cleric, and **Tudur ap Goronwy** (*d.* 1367?), landholder, were among the leading figures in the principality of north Wales in the mid-fourteenth century. Hywel became archdeacon of Anglesey. An apocryphal story related how Tudur called himself Sir Tudur; on being summoned by Edward III to explain himself, he answered with such spirit that the king immediately knighted him. The story, attributed to the antiquary Robert Vaughan (1592–1667), may have originated in the sixteenth century, the implication being that Tudur foresaw that his descendants would have the power to confer knighthood. Hywel and Tudur were involved in an episode in 1345 which probably reflected contemporary unrest among the leaders of the community. On 14 February Henry Shalford, the prince's newly appointed attorney, was travelling from Denbigh to Caernarfon when he was attacked and killed near the house of Hywel in Bangor by a band of men led by Tudur. The result was panic among the English burgesses in north Wales, the more so since many leading Welshmen appear to have been implicated, and it was suggested that Shalford had died because 'he had more knowledge than any other man of those who have disinherited my lord' (J. G. Edwards, ed., *Calendar of Ancient Correspondence Concerning Wales*, 1935, 233). Hywel was imprisoned for a time at Launceston in Cornwall, and Tudur in Chester, but they do not seem to have suffered any further punishment; in 1352 they were both in possession of their ancestral lands in Anglesey.

Hywel probably died in 1366 and Tudur probably in 1367. Tudur's wife and Owain *Glyn Dŵr's mother were sisters; this relationship was to prove significant during the revolt. Tudur had five sons, Goronwy, Ednyfed, Gwilym, Rhys, and Maredudd. **Goronwy ap Tudur** (*d.* 1382), soldier and administrator, lived at Penmynydd, the traditional seat of the Tudors, as they can now be called; he served in France with Edward, the Black Prince, and in 1368–9 he was at Northampton in the prince's retinue. He was forester of Snowdon and steward of the bishop of Bangor's Anglesey lands and in 1382 he was appointed constable of Beaumaris Castle, one of the very few occasions on which a Welshman was appointed to such an office; four days later he died, apparently by drowning, in Kent. His death was mourned by several poets and he was buried in the Franciscan friary at Llanfaes in Anglesey; his impressive alabaster tomb was moved to Penmynydd church at the dissolution of that house. His wife was Myfanwy, the daughter of Iorwerth Ddu of Pengwern, near Llangollen. His son Tudur was dead by 1400; his daughter Morfudd married Gwilym ap Gruffudd and his lands therefore passed to the Penrhyn family, although they were eventually to be recovered by Morfudd's descendants, the Owen Tudors of Penmynydd.

Ednyfed ap Tudur died around the same time as Goronwy; **Gwilym ap Tudur** (d. after 1401) and **Rhys ap Tudur** (d. 1411), administrators, were both in the service of Richard II; the latter held the offices of sheriff and escheator of Anglesey and forester of Snowdon. Both brothers were involved in the revolt of their cousin Owain Glyn Dŵr, possibly from the beginning; their exclusion from the pardon granted at the end of the first phase of the revolt may have led to their capture of Conwy Castle on Good Friday 1401, when the garrison was in church. They withdrew after negotiations and were pardoned, but they seem to have continued in rebellion until the end and Rhys was eventually captured and executed in Chester in 1411. Their lands passed to their kinsman Gwilym ap Gruffudd.

The Tudor dynasty and its Welsh ancestors Maredudd ap Tudur (fl. 1388–1404), administrator, was escheator of Anglesey between 1388 and 1391 and was a burgess of the town of Newborough in the same county. He took part in the Glyn Dŵr revolt, but nothing is known of his fate. Maredudd, however, was the ancestor of the Tudor dynasty; his son Owen *Tudor (c.1400–1461) married *Catherine of Valois (d. 1437), the widow of Henry V, and was the grandfather of *Henry VII.

The descendants of Ednyfed Fychan were, without a doubt, the most powerful family in thirteenth- and fourteenth-century Wales. They were the leading servants of the princes of Gwynedd and played a key part in the attempt of those princes to create a single Welsh principality. Some were prescient enough to transfer their allegiance to Edward I before 1282; the rest made their peace very soon after and continued to enjoy a significant role in all the royal lands in Wales; at the local level they were often the ones who exercised effective power in the name of the king of England. But there remained an awareness of their Welshness, with its concomitant loyalties, which surfaced from time to time in the fourteenth century and which led them to the side of Owain Glyn Dŵr and to the end of that predominance which had lasted since the early thirteenth century. And it was a descendant of one of those rebels against the English crown who won that crown in 1485.   A. D. CARR

Sources G. Roberts, '"Wyrion Eden": the Anglesey descendants of Ednyfed Fychan in the fourteenth century', Transactions of the Anglesey Antiquarian Society and Field Club (1951), 34–72; repr. in

G. Roberts, Aspects of Welsh history (1969), 179–214 · R. R. Davies, The revolt of Owain Glyn Dŵr (1995) · G. Roberts, 'Teulu Penmynydd', Transactions of the Honourable Society of Cymmrodorion (1959), 9–37; repr. in G. Roberts, Aspects of Welsh history (1969), 240–74 · R. A. Griffiths and R. S. Thomas, The making of the Tudor dynasty (1985) · A. D. Carr, Medieval Anglesey (1982) · D. Stephenson, The governance of Gwynedd (1984) · A. D. Carr, 'Gwilym ap Gruffydd and the rise of the Penrhyn estate', Welsh History Review / Cylchgrawn Hanes Cymru, 15 (1990–91), 1–20 · J. G. Edwards, 'Sir Gruffydd Llwyd', EngHR, 30 (1915), 589–601 · J. B. Smith, 'Gruffydd Llwyd and the Celtic alliance, 1315–1318', BBCS, 26 (1974–6), 463–78
Archives U. Wales, Bangor, Penrhyn MSS; Penrhyn further additional MSS

Tudor, Antony [formerly William John Cook] (1908–1987), choreographer and ballet teacher, was born on 4 April 1908 at 105 Central Street, Finsbury, London, the second among the two sons of Alfred Robert Cook (d. early 1940s), a butcher, and his wife, Florence Ann Cook, née Summers (d. 1953?), who had French forebears. Alfred Cook came from a line of hard-working butchers.

Already captivated by the theatre at four via the popular music-hall, Cook learned to play the piano, produced 'shows' with his friends, read voraciously, and thanks to the generosity of an uncle had a better than average schooling at the Alice Owens School for Boys. On leaving school at sixteen, two years beyond the legal requirement, he became a clerk at the Smithfield meat market. While still at school Cook discovered dance classes, attending the Susie Boyle school; he later recalled that the classes were dreadful. His evenings were mostly spent acting in amateur dramatic societies.

At nineteen Cook saw the Diaghilev Ballet performing the Balanchine/Stravinsky Apollon musagète. Struck by its beauty, he decided to pursue a career in dance and, on the advice of the ballet critic Cyril Beaumont, enrolled to study with Marie Rambert. She was impressed not only by his coming to class after working from 5 a.m. in the market, but also by his 'poetic eyes' (Clarke). Thus began the English decade of his professional life.

In 1929 Tudor made his début, dancing with the English Opera Company, opting to change his name from the humdrum William Cook to the more elegant Anthony Tudor, later permanently dropping the h to become Antony. In 1930 the tiny Mercury Theatre was established by Rambert in London near Notting Hill Gate, and the Ballet Club was subsequently formed. Tudor's employment as secretary and general factotum for the club allowed him to leave Smithfield market forever. Soon he decided that his real aim was to create ballets, not to dance in them. That year he produced his first work, Cross Garter'd, which critics described as promising and which attracted praise from Léonide Massine.

From 1931 to 1937 Tudor went on to produce many works for the Ballet Rambert, among them several dances considered today to be masterpieces. In 1932 two notable works were performed. Lysistrata, with music by Prokofiev, was a wonderfully comic retelling of Aristophanes, with several innovative choreographic touches. Another, Adam and Eve, to music by Constant Lambert, was a wicked commentary on the first book of Genesis. In Atalanta of the

East (1933) Tudor shifted the Greek legend to an Asian setting. This was his first foray into orientalism, something which preoccupied him for much of his life. In 1934 *The Planets*, a lovely ballet in which Tudor illustrated the music of Gustav Holst, experimented with both movement and musicality outside the classical canon.

One of Tudor's finest early works was *Jardin aux lilas* (1936) to music by Ernest Chausson. This showed 'a formal engagement party in a garden of lilacs, in which the heroine, about to be married to a man she does not love, tries to take a last farewell of her former lover' (Clarke). Tudor conceived for himself the role of the Man She Must Marry. His next major work, *Dark Elegies* (1937), to music from Gustav Mahler's *Kindertotenlieder*, was a poignant outburst of grief and despair over a group of lost children. The dance finally resolves itself in a renewal of faith and trust in those still left after the visitation of death. The ballet is one of the most moving ever created.

In addition, during the Rambert years Tudor choreographed for theatre, opera, and the brand-new medium, television, where his work was particularly innovative. His *Fugue for Four Cameras* is regularly cited as among the earliest experimental uses of the medium.

In 1931 Hugh Laing (1911–1988), born Hugh Skinner, had appeared at the Rambert studios and was at once co-opted into the school and emerging company. He and Tudor were immediately attracted to one another and began a lifelong companionship. They became lovers and lived together from that early time except for a brief period in the late 1940s when Laing was married to the dancer Diana Adams. Laing created many leading roles in Tudor's ballets. He was Tudor's harshest critic and most loyal friend. In turn, Tudor taught Laing about dance technique and looked after him both bodily and financially. Their relationship was always stormy, but their mutual devotion unquestioned.

In 1938 Tudor left Rambert and teamed up with his friend Agnes de Mille to form the short-lived Dance Theatre. When first they met at Rambert, de Mille described Tudor as slow, gentle, diffident, humorous, courteous, and much abused. He watched everything observantly, wrapped in dreams of world renown. Tudor was very attractive, tall and handsome with a piercing gaze and an aristocratic carriage. Dance Theatre played only for one week at Oxford University and had a short run at the Westminster Theatre; however, for the engagement Tudor created another of his enduring works, *Judgment of Paris*, as well as the ribald *Gallant Assembly*.

Having tasted freedom from Rambert, Tudor went on to found his own company, the London Ballet. From 5 December 1938 to 26 April 1939 the company gave fortnightly Monday evening performances, Tudor being responsible for virtually all the choreography. In the repertory were *Dark Elegies*, *Descent of Hebe* (1935), *The Planets*, and two new works, *Soirée Musicale* and the much-hailed comedic, *Gala Performance*.

In 1940 Tudor participated in founding American Ballet Theatre. His trip to the USA was intended to last only ten weeks, in order to stage three ballets: *Jardin aux lilas*, *Dark Elegies*, and *Gallant Assembly* (for which *Judgment of Paris* was eventually substituted). However, with the progress of the Second World War civilian transport across the Atlantic ceased; thus Tudor was forced to remain in the United States. His collaboration with American Ballet Theatre continued on and off for the rest of his life except for brief interludes with the New York City Ballet and the Royal Swedish Ballet in the 1950s.

Among the many ballets Tudor created for American Ballet Theatre, *Pillar of Fire* (1942) was his first and most lasting success. It was followed in 1943 by the remarkable *Romeo and Juliet*, the Proustian *Dim Lustre* (1943), and the audacious *Undertow* (1945). Other lesser known but perhaps equally fascinating ballets included *Shadow of the Wind* (1948) and *Nimbus* (1950).

For the New York City Ballet Tudor choreographed *Lady of the Camellias* (1951) and *La gloire* (1952); for the Jacob's Pillow dance centre, *Dear Departed* (1949), *Les mains gauches* (1951), *Ronde du printemps* (1951), and *Little Improvisations* (1953). And, after a long choreographic silence, for the Royal Swedish Ballet—which he considered his second home and to which he returned several times—Tudor choreographed his moving anti-war ballet *Echoing of Trumpets* (1963).

In the 1960s Tudor devoted himself mostly to teaching, at the Juilliard School in New York, in Philadelphia, and at the Metropolitan Opera Ballet School, which he founded. During those years he restricted his choreographic output mostly to works for the students. Most notable were: for Philadelphia, *Offenbach in the Underworld* (1954) and for Juilliard, *A Choreographer Comments* (1960) and *Dance Studies Less Orthodox* (1962). For the Metropolitan Opera Ballet he created two substantial works: *Hail and Farewell* (1959) and *Concerning Oracles* (1966), as well as a chamber ballet, *Fandango* (1963).

Throughout his career Tudor travelled widely and staged his works all over the world. New ballets were created in Argentina (*La leyenda de José*, 1958), and in Australia (*The Divine Horseman*, 1969). In 1967 he finally returned to England to choreograph for the Royal Ballet, 'having became estranged from the company when Valois appointed Ashton as her resident choreographer in 1935' (Clarke). Inspired by Kipling's *Jungle Books* and by his practice of Zen Buddhism, Tudor created *Shadowplay* for the Royal Ballet; and for its touring company, *Knight Errant* (1968). In 1971 the National Endowment for the Arts in the United States commissioned Tudor. For the commission he decided to create three chamber ballets which could be suitably staged by small and pre-professional companies. Employing graduating Juilliard students with the funds provided by his grant, Tudor created *Cereus*, *Sunflowers*, and *Continuo*.

In the 1960s Tudor officially adopted Zen Buddhism as his religion, moving into the First Zen Institute in New York, and becoming its president. There he arose every morning in time to sound the wakening gongs, and there he spent the weekends in meditation. As his preoccupation with Zen grew his choreographic activity waned.

Not until 1975 did Tudor choreograph another work. It was worth waiting for: he produced one of his most beautiful ballets, *The Leaves are Fading*. It was his penultimate contribution; his final work was the less successful *Tiller in the Fields* (1978). His advanced age did not prevent him from shocking; one feature of the ballet is the appearance of a very pregnant ballerina.

In 1979—during one of his annual visits to Laguna Beach, California, to relax and teach at the University of California at Irvine—Tudor suffered a massive heart attack. Even though he made a rapid recovery, he never returned to his former vigour. He ceased all teaching and became increasingly undernourished and weak; his gait became a shuffle and he ceased to enjoy his work with Ballet Theatre dancers. In his final years, the accolades he so richly deserved finally came his way: the Queen Elizabeth II coronation award of the Royal Academy of Dancing (1985); and in 1986 the Capezio award; a Dance USA award; New York city's Handel medallion; and, in December, the Kennedy Center honours. On 4 April 1987 he died of a heart attack at the Zen Institute, 113 East 30th Street, New York, and was cremated according to Zen custom. His ashes were buried at Woodlawn cemetery, New York.

While Tudor's many years in America had high and low points, moments of triumph and moments of tension, his contribution to Ballet Theatre and to dance in America has not been adequately recognized. He is one of a very few major talents of our time, and his choreography outlives him as only work of genius can.   MURIEL TOPAZ

Sources M. Topaz, *Undimmed lustre: the life of Antony Tudor* [forthcoming] • C. Payne, *American ballet theatre* (1978) • J. Chazin-Bennahum, *The ballets of Antony Tudor* (1994) • A. Tudor and H. Laing, letters and papers, NYPL for the Performing Arts • private information (2004) [G. Andersson, S. Brayley Bliss, I. Brown, M. Lloyd, D. Mahler, C. Palmer, D. Saddler, E. Schooling, S. Wilson, N. Zeckendorf] • M. Rambert, *Quicksilver* (1972) • *The Times* (21 April 1987) • M. Clarke, *The Guardian* (22 April 1987)
Archives American Ballet Theatre archive • Boston University • English National Ballet, London • Juilliard School, Lincoln Center, New York • Metropolitan Opera, New York • NYPL, Library for the Performing Arts • Rambert Dance Company, Chiswick, London • U. Cal., Irvine • V&A | FILM Juilliard School, Lincoln Center, New York • NYPL for the Performing Arts
Likenesses F. Fehl, photograph (with Nora Kaye in *Jardin aux lilas*), NYPL for the Performing Arts, Lincoln Center Plaza, New York, Dance Collection • E. Sawyer, photograph, NYPL for the Performing Arts, Lincoln Center Plaza, New York, Dance Collection • portrait, NYPL for the Performing Arts, Lincoln Center Plaza, New York, Dance Collection
Wealth at death approx. $250,000

Tudor, Edmund [Edmund of Hadham], **first earl of Richmond** (c.1430–1456), magnate, was the eldest son of Owen *Tudor (c.1400–1461) and *Catherine of Valois (1401–1437), widow of Henry V. He is sometimes referred to as Edmund of Hadham, presumably from his having been born at Much Hadham, Hertfordshire. As the father of *Henry VII he gave his name to a new royal dynasty.

Fearful that Queen Catherine might contract an undesirable second marriage (possibly with Edmund Beaufort, count of Mortain), the parliament of 1427–8 enacted a statute which forbade any man to marry a dowager queen without first obtaining the king's assent (provided the king had reached years of discretion), on pain of losing all his goods and lands. Impatient of this constraint, by about 1428–9 the dowager queen had secretly married an obscure Welsh squire, Owen Tudor, quite possibly a member of her household. With him she probably had three children, of whom the sons, Edmund and Jasper, both became prominent. Queen Catherine died on 3 January 1437 and by July of that year Edmund and Jasper had been placed in the keeping of Katherine de la Pole, abbess of Barking, where they remained until at least 1442. In the meantime their father was punished for marrying the dowager queen, although he was pardoned in 1439. In their boyhood and youth the Tudors' half-brother, *Henry VI, put them under the care of 'virtuous and worthy priests' (Blakman, 30–31). Neither at the time of Queen Catherine's remarriage nor later in the fifteenth century was it suggested that her union with Owen Tudor was void and their children illegitimate. Despite the speculations of some modern historians, there is no firm evidence that Edmund Tudor was the illegitimate son of Edmund Beaufort (or possibly his godson), and that, following Edmund Tudor's later marriage to Margaret *Beaufort (1443–1509), the 'Tudor' dynasty sprang from Beaufort lines on both sides.

Almost certainly for personal and dynastic reasons, Henry VI ennobled his stepbrothers on 23 November 1452 as premier earls, Edmund as earl of Richmond, and Jasper *Tudor as earl of Pembroke. They were knighted at the Tower of London on 5 January 1453 and belted the following day. At the Reading parliament in March 1453 they were formally recognized as the king's legitimate uterine brothers. In the meantime (February 1453) the dowager duchess of Somerset had been summoned to London, no doubt bringing with her her ten-year-old daughter, Margaret Beaufort, a direct descendant of *John of Gaunt, duke of Lancaster, and one of England's wealthiest heiresses. On 24 March the king granted the wardship and marriage of Lady Margaret to his half-brothers, having already richly endowed them with land. (It is possible to surmise that in the early months of 1453, lacking an heir and unaware of his wife's pregnancy—Prince Edward was not born until 13 October—Henry VI may even have had it in mind to nominate Edmund Tudor as his heir in the right of Margaret Beaufort.)

Despite their royal kinship and elevation, Edmund and Jasper Tudor, in common with many other lords, tried to keep out of the disputes between the dukes of York and Somerset that developed in the early 1450s. They might have been expected to side with Somerset, the uncle of Margaret Beaufort, yet in January 1454 it was rumoured that, should they come to London with York, they could expect to be arrested. Later in the year they supported York's attempts as protector to reform the royal household, but they remained firmly loyal to Henry VI. By the time York was appointed protector for a second time in November 1455, Earl Edmund had almost certainly married his twelve-year-old ward and moved to south-west

Wales to assert the king's authority: he was staying at the bishop of St David's palace at Lamphey, Pembrokeshire, by 30 November, and may even have been there since September. His presence was a threat to the long-standing hegemony of the local political magnate, Gruffudd ap Nicholas, and the two came into conflict. By June 1456 both men were said to be 'at werre gretely in Wales' (*Paston Letters*, 3.92), a conflict that seriously disrupted the day-to-day administration of the principality of south Wales. By August 1456 Earl Edmund had emerged victorious, having wrested control of Carmarthen Castle from Gruffudd and thereby captured the centre of royal government in the region.

Edmund Tudor's success proved too much for York's supporters: a force of 2000 men from Herefordshire and the neighbouring marches set out for west Wales, led by Sir William Herbert and Sir Walter Devereux, two of the duke's leading retainers. They made straight for Carmarthen, seized its castle, and imprisoned Edmund Tudor. He was released from custody soon afterwards, but died of plague at Carmarthen on 1 November 1456. The Welsh poet Lewys Glyn Cothi wrote his elegy. Richmond's widow, now some six months pregnant, took refuge in her brother-in-law's castle at Pembroke and it was there, on 28 January 1457, that Henry Tudor was born. Edmund Tudor was buried at the church of the Greyfriars in Carmarthen. In her first will of 1472 Margaret Beaufort made provision for Edmund's remains to be moved from Carmarthen to a tomb beside her at Bourne, Lincolnshire. In the event, he was left undisturbed until the Reformation, when his tomb was removed to the choir of St David's Cathedral, where it remains.   R. S. THOMAS

Sources R. S. Thomas, 'The political career, estates and "connection" of Jasper Tudor, earl of Pembroke and duke of Bedford (d. 1495)', PhD diss., U. Wales, Swansea, 1971 • R. A. Griffiths and R. S. Thomas, *The making of the House of Tudor* (1993) • M. K. Jones and M. G. Underwood, *The king's mother: Lady Margaret Beaufort, countess of Richmond and Derby* (1992) • R. A. Griffiths, *King and country: England and Wales in the fifteenth century* (1991) • R. A. Griffiths, *The reign of King Henry VI: the exercise of royal authority, 1422–1461* (1981) • R. A. Griffiths, introduction, in H. T. Evans, *Wales and the Wars of the Roses*, new edn (1995) • *Gwaith Lewis Glyn Cothi*, ed. D. Johnston (1995) • *Chancery records* • duchy of Lancaster ministers' accounts, PRO, DL 29 • exchequer, exchequer of receipt, warrants for issues, PRO, E 404 • court of king's bench, ancient indictments, PRO, KB 9 • J. Blakman, *Henry the Sixth*, ed. M. R. James (1919) • *Polychronicon Ranulphi Higden monachi Cestrensis*, ed. C. Babington and J. R. Lumby, 9 vols., Rolls Series, 41 (1865–86), vol. 8 • *Collectanea Topographica et Genealogica*, 1 (1834) • A. H. Thomas and I. D. Thornley, eds., *The great chronicle of London* (1938) • J. Lewis, *The life of Dr John Fisher, bishop of Rochester*, 2 vols. (1855) • B. Willis, *A survey of the cathedral church of St David's* (1717) • *The Paston letters, AD 1422–1509*, ed. J. Gairdner, new edn, 6 vols. (1904)

Tudor, Jasper [Jasper of Hatfield], **duke of Bedford** (*c.*1431–1495), magnate, was probably born at Hatfield, the second son of Owen *Tudor and *Catherine of Valois (1401–1437), widow of Henry V. Jasper and his elder brother Edmund *Tudor, half-brothers of Henry VI, were raised by nuns and, later, by priests in some privacy. On 23 November 1452 both were ennobled as premier earls and summoned to the Reading parliament on 6 March 1453 as

earls of Richmond and Pembroke. Richly endowed with land, they were jointly granted the wardship and marriage of Lady Margaret Beaufort, only daughter of John, duke of Somerset, and one of England's wealthiest heiresses.

Despite their royal kinship both brothers took an independent line in the faction-ridden court of Henry VI. Jasper was present with the king at the first battle of St Albans on 22 May 1455, but afterwards continued to associate with York. Edmund restored royal authority in south-west Wales, but he was imprisoned by York's supporters in August 1456, and, though released soon afterwards, he died of plague at Carmarthen on 1 November. His son, Henry Tudor (afterwards *Henry VII), was born posthumously at Jasper's castle of Pembroke on 28 January 1457; thereafter Jasper Tudor was the main champion of Henry VI's cause in Wales. He replaced York as constable of the castles of Aberystwyth, Carmarthen, and Carreg Cennen in April 1457, and strengthened the walls of Tenby later in the year. He was elected knight of the Garter by April 1459. Following the outbreak of hostilities between York and the king's forces Jasper Tudor arrived at the Coventry parliament in December 1459 with 'a good fellowship', and he and his father profited from grants of confiscated Yorkist lands. Early in 1460 he subdued York's castle of Denbigh, but in the following year (2 February 1461) he was defeated by York's son, Edward, earl of March, at Mortimer's Cross. Owen Tudor was captured and executed at Hereford.

Fleeing west to Tenby, on 25 February Jasper Tudor wrote bitterly of his defeat and his father's death; for the best part of the next twenty-five years he led the life of a fugitive. He lost his lands and power in Wales during 1461; attainted on 29 December, he probably fled to Scotland. The exiled Lancastrians tried to drum up diplomatic and military support in Scotland, Flanders, France, and Brittany. To that end Tudor arrived in Brittany by 25 March 1462 and then travelled to the Loire valley in June for negotiations between Louis XI and Margaret of Anjou. Later in the year the Lancastrians invaded Northumberland but, although they captured Bamburgh Castle, Jasper Tudor and his allies surrendered on 24 December 1462. He accepted a safe conduct and returned to Scotland. In the spring of 1463 he was in France again to meet Louis XI and returned to Scotland by December, probably to join Henry VI at Bamburgh. By spring 1464 he was in Brittany, where Duke François (II) provided a fleet to return to England; there is no evidence that it set sail, perhaps because Louis XI objected to Duke François's support of the Lancastrians. Tudor certainly remained on excellent terms with King Louis: by December 1464 he had been recognized as a cousin-german and was a member of Louis's household. The tides of European diplomacy eventually turned in the Lancastrians' favour in 1468. In June Louis provided Tudor with a small force which landed near Harlech (24 June) and marched across north Wales, retaking Denbigh Castle and holding courts in Henry VI's name. But the invasion failed: Harlech Castle fell to Lord Herbert on 14 August 1468 and Tudor fled back to the French court.

A new invasion plan involving Margaret of Anjou and

her son, Prince Edward, and also dissident Yorkists led by Warwick and the duke of Clarence, was hatched with Louis in 1470, and on 13 September Jasper Tudor, Warwick, and Clarence landed at Dartmouth; Jasper made for Wales, pausing at Hereford to be reunited with his young nephew Henry Tudor. Jasper brought the boy to London where he was presented to the newly restored Henry VI and reunited with his mother. Indeed Jasper played a significant role in the restored Lancastrian regime. Uncle and nephew returned to Wales at the end of November, no doubt to secure it for the crown; this was facilitated by substantial land grants and the restoration of Jasper's earldom of Pembroke (by February 1471). But Henry VI's readeption was short-lived; at the battle of Tewkesbury on 4 May 1471 Margaret of Anjou was captured and her son killed. Jasper heard the news at Chepstow where he intercepted Roger Vaughan, sent by Edward IV to capture him. Holding Vaughan responsible for Owen Tudor's execution after Mortimer's Cross, Jasper took his revenge and executed Vaughan. He and his nephew sped to Pembroke and made good their escape from Tenby to Brittany. They were detained for thirteen years, in honourable confinement, by Duke François. If anyone can be considered the mentor of the young Henry Tudor in these years, it was his uncle Jasper. In the autumn of 1483 the duke provided them with a small fleet and they embarked on another invasion of England to coincide with the duke of Buckingham's rebellion. Blown off course they returned to Brittany but fled to France in September 1484 in a more threatening political climate in which Richard III was intriguing to have the Tudors handed over to him.

At the court of Charles VIII, Henry Tudor (now twenty-eight years old), accompanied by his uncle and several hundred Lancastrian and Yorkist sympathizers, plotted the overthrow of Richard III in concert with supporters in England and Wales. On 1 August 1485 their invasion fleet left the Seine estuary and on 7 August landed in Milford Haven, in Jasper's lordship of Pembroke. Marching cautiously north and then east their forces defeated King Richard at Bosworth Field on 22 August. It is not known whether Jasper actually fought in the battle, but his nephew, now Henry VII, was deeply in debt to him and rewarded him handsomely. On 28 October 1485 Jasper was created duke of Bedford (the only other new dukes created by Henry VII were the king's own sons). He was also restored to his estates and the earldom of Pembroke, and at the same time was granted extensive new lands: the lordships of Glamorgan and Abergavenny, and Sudeley, Gloucestershire, in March 1486; the lordship of Haverford in 1488 and the lordship of Builth in 1491. By 7 November 1485 he had married Katherine Stafford, widow of the duke of Buckingham and sister of Edward IV's widow, *Elizabeth Woodville. Like the king's own marriage this was a union of Lancaster and York. Katherine brought her husband very extensive Stafford estates, so that he now enjoyed territorial authority over, and income from, a great triangle of land, from Milford Haven in the west to Essex in the east, with its apex in Derbyshire. Jasper Tudor was prominent at Henry VII's coronation on 30 October

1485 and was one of the king's councillors. His main contribution to the establishment of the new dynasty was in the political and military fields. In December he was appointed to several important offices in south Wales and the marches, chief among them the justiciarship of south Wales for life. In the spring of 1486 he was also given wide-ranging powers to improve the fiscal and judicial administration of the area. In March 1486 he was appointed lieutenant of Ireland, though he seems never to have visited it. He played a prominent part in the suppression of the Lovell and Stafford rebellion in 1486, and he was in joint command of the royal army that defeated Lambert Simnel's rebellion at Stoke on 16 June 1487. In July 1488 he was nominated one of the conservators of the truce with France and, for the time being, became lieutenant of Calais. Anglo-French relations deteriorated and in October 1492 he was named joint commander of the expeditionary force assembled by Henry VII against France. In Wales Tudor continued to suppress rebellion and seek to improve order. The king's indenture for the marches concluded with him and other marcher lords on 1 March 1490 was but part of the crown's attempt to improve government in this region. By now Tudor was about sixty years of age and from 1492 played a decreasing role in public life. He spent much of his last years at his castles of Thornbury and Sudeley in Gloucestershire and at Minster Lovell, Oxfordshire. He made his will on 15 December 1494 at Thornbury, where he died on 21 December 1495. Henry VII and his queen attended his funeral, held before the end of the year at Keynsham Abbey, near Bristol. He seems to have fathered no children, and the king was his heir.

R. S. Thomas

Sources R. A. Griffiths and R. S. Thomas, *The making of the house of Tudor* (1993) · R. S. Thomas, 'The political career, estates and "connection" of Jasper Tudor, earl of Pembroke and duke of Bedford (d. 1495)', PhD diss., U. Wales, Swansea, 1971 · R. A. Griffiths, *King and country: England and Wales in the fifteenth century* (1991) · R. A. Griffiths, *The reign of King Henry VI: the exercise of royal authority, 1422–1461* (1981) · C. Rawcliffe, *The Staffords, earls of Stafford and dukes of Buckingham, 1394–1521*, Cambridge Studies in Medieval Life and Thought, 3rd ser., 11 (1978) · M. K. Jones and M. G. Underwood, *The king's mother: Lady Margaret Beaufort, countess of Richmond and Derby* (1992) · H. T. Evans, *Wales and the Wars of the Roses*, new edn (1995) · R. A. Griffiths, *Sir Rhys ap Thomas and his family: a study in the Wars of the Roses and early Tudor politics* (1993) · *Polychronicon Ranulphi Higden monachi Cestrensis*, ed. C. Babington and J. R. Lumby, 9 vols., Rolls Series, 41 (1865–86), vol. 8, p. 565 · F. W. D. Brie, ed., *The Brut, or, The chronicles of England*, 2 vols., EETS, 131, 136 (1906–8), vol. 2, p. 11 · *Hall's chronicle*, ed. H. Ellis (1809), 184–5 · GEC, *Peerage*, new edn, 2.73 · *CIPM, Henry VII*, 3, no. 396 · *The maire of Bristowe is kalendar, by Robert Ricart*, ed. L. Toulmin Smith, CS, new ser., 5 (1872), 48

Tudor, Owen [Owain ap Maredudd ap Tudur] (*c.*1400–1461), courtier, the second husband of *Catherine of Valois (1401–1437), Henry V's widow, was the son of *Maredudd ap Tudur ap Goronwy (*fl.* 1388–1404) [*see under* Tudor family, forebears of] and Margaret, daughter of Dafydd Fychan. His father's line, descended from Ednyfed Fychan (*d.* 1246), settled at Penmynydd in Anglesey, where it was prominent. His grandfather Tudur ap Goronwy (*d.* 1367?) married Margaret, daughter of Thomas ap Llywelyn ab Owain of Cardiganshire, the last male of the princely house of Deheubarth; her elder sister married Gruffudd Fychan of Glyndyfrdwy, whose son was Owain Glyn Dŵr. Maredudd ap Tudur and his older brothers were prominent in the rebellion of Glyn Dŵr, their kinsman. Owen Tudor was born *c*.1400; William Worcester's comment that he was about fifty when he died in 1461 is not reliable.

Owen Tudor's marriage and his family's rebellion explain why he became the subject of myth and storytelling in Wales, England, and abroad. In sixteenth-century France and Italy he was said to be the bastard son of an alehouse keeper, and two of his sons, Edmund and Jasper, were also described as bastards. In eighteenth-century Wales it was believed that his father was a fugitive murderer at the time Tudor was born. The story that he fought at Agincourt and became an esquire of Henry V's body is equally unsupported. Yet he met Queen Catherine. Like several Welshmen after Glyn Dŵr's rebellion, he may have secured a position at court, and in May 1421 'Owen Meredith' joined the retinue of Sir Walter Hungerford, steward of the king's household (1415–21), to serve in France. Antiquarians say that he was keeper of Queen Catherine's household (or of her wardrobe); although there is no evidence for this (still less for later French claims that he was her tailor), the sixteenth-century Welsh chronicler Elis Gruffudd noted that he was her sewer and servant. The circumstances of their first meeting have engaged the interest of poets and romanticists ever since. According to one story, their relationship began when Tudor fell into the queen's lap while dancing; according to another he caught the queen's eye when swimming.

Mystery also surrounds Owen Tudor's marriage, but there is no question as to its validity or the legitimacy of his offspring. Richard III's proclamations described Tudor as a bastard; his marriage, however, was not disputed. No dowager queen of England had married in England since the 1130s. One chronicler, who may have had special knowledge of Catherine, said that she was 'unable fully to curb her carnal passions' (Giles, 4.17); and any proposal for marriage was bound to concern the council of her son, Henry VI. The chronicler claimed that she wished to marry Edmund Beaufort (*d*. 1455), nephew of Bishop Henry Beaufort (*d*. 1447), which was opposed by Humphrey, duke of Gloucester (*d*. 1447), and other lords. The council introduced a bill in the parliament of 1427–8 requiring the consent of an adult king before a dowager queen could marry, and decreeing forfeiture of goods and possessions by anyone who disobeyed. This bill (and the statute based on it) was probably introduced in response to the Beaufort liaison, before the marriage with Tudor. Catherine was in Henry VI's household until at least 1430, after which the marriage may have taken place. The sixteenth-century story that she presented Tudor's pedigree to the lords in parliament may refer to the assembly of 1431, in which case it could have been a prelude to Owen's letters of denizenship (1432).

The marriage was not common knowledge before the queen died (3 January 1437). She and Tudor had four children, three sons (Edmund *Tudor, Jasper *Tudor, and Owen) and a daughter who may have become a nun and died young. Edmund and Jasper were born in Hertfordshire, where the queen had estates, and in residences—Much Hadham and Bishop's Hatfield respectively—belonging to two bishops close to Henry V. The intriguing suggestion (Harriss, 178) that Edmund was Edmund Beaufort's son is unprovable. Owen (who is also referred to as Edward) became a Benedictine monk at Westminster Abbey. After Catherine died, Gloucester summoned Tudor before the council under a safe conduct; he sought sanctuary at Westminster. He maintained his innocence of any charge and was released, but on his way to Wales was arrested. His goods, worth £137 10*s*. 4*d*., were seized and he was consigned to Newgate prison, whence he escaped in January or early February 1438. After his recapture by John, Lord Beaumont (*d*. 1460), he returned to Newgate, and was then transferred to Windsor Castle (14 July) in the charge, soon afterwards, of Edmund Beaufort. Released in July 1439 on a £2000 recognizance, he was pardoned all offences on 12 November. Thereafter he was a member of the king's household; his two sons were in the care (1437–42) of the earl of Suffolk's sister, Katherine de la Pole, abbess of Barking, at the king's expense.

In November 1452 Edmund and Jasper Tudor were created earls of Richmond and Pembroke and acknowledged to be the king's uterine brothers. Owen Tudor may have accompanied Earl Edmund to south Wales in autumn 1455, and after Edmund died (3 November 1456) he may have joined Earl Jasper there. In 1459 the earl and his father were commissioned to arrest a servant of John Dwnn of Kidwelly, a Yorkist, and later in the year Owen Tudor acquired an interest in the forfeited estates of another Yorkist, John, Lord Clinton. On 5 February 1460 he and Jasper were granted for life offices in the duke of York's lordship of Denbigh, as a prelude to seizing the lordship. Tudor joined Jasper's army in Wales in January 1461; at Mortimer's Cross (2 or 3 February) it was defeated by Edward, earl of March. Owen Tudor was captured and beheaded at Hereford, where his head was placed on the market cross, 'and a madde woman kembyd hys here and wysche a way the blode of hys face' and set 100 candles about him. Moments before his execution he realized that he was to die and murmured 'that hede shalle ly on the stocke that wass wonte to ly on Quene Katheryns lappe' (Gairdner, 211). His body was buried in a chapel on the north side of the Greyfriars' Church, Hereford. It had no memorial until his bastard, David (*d. c.*1542), born in Pembroke Castle in 1459 of an unknown liaison, paid for a tomb before the friary was dissolved. Several Welsh poets wrote eulogies after his death.   R. A. GRIFFITHS

Sources R. S. Thomas, 'The political career, estates and "connection" of Jasper Tudor, earl of Pembroke and duke of Bedford (d. 1495)', PhD diss., U. Wales, Swansea, 1971 · R. A. Griffiths, 'Queen Katherine of Valois and a missing statute of the realm', *Law Quarterly Review*, 93 (1977), 248–58 · G. O. Sayles, 'The Royal Marriages Act, 1428', *Law Quarterly Review*, 94 (1978), 188–92 · N. H. Nicolas, ed., *Proceedings and ordinances of the privy council of England*, 7 vols., RC, 26 (1834–7), vol. 5 · J. A. Giles, ed., *Incerti scriptoris chronicon Angliae de* *regnis trium regum Lancastrensium*, pt 4 (1848) • J. Gairdner, ed., *The historical collections of a citizen of London in the fifteenth century*, CS, new ser., 17 (1876) • G. L. Harriss, *Cardinal Beaufort: a study of Lancastrian ascendancy and decline* (1988), ch. 9 • F. Palgrave, ed., *The antient kalendars and inventories of the treasury of his majesty's exchequer*, 3 vols., RC (1836) • *Chancery records* • PRO • *Itineraries [of] William Worcestre*, ed. J. H. Harvey, OMT (1969) • *The itinerary of John Leland in or about the years 1535–1543*, ed. L. Toulmin Smith, 11 pts in 5 vols. (1906–10), vols. 1–2

Tudur ab Ednyfed (d. **1278**). *See under* Tudor family, forebears of (*per. c.*1215–1404).

Tudur Aled (*c.*1465–1525×?), Welsh poet, was of noble stock; he was the son of Robert ab Ithel ap Llywelyn Chwith and descended from Hedd Molwynog, chieftain of one of Gwynedd's fifteen tribes. His great-grandfather lived in Chwibren in the parish of Llansannan in the commote of Is Aled, but although a memorial in Llansannan claims Tudur as a native, in keeping with a tradition propagated in the second half of the nineteenth century, and repeated as late as 1998 in *The New Companion to the Literature of Wales* (1998), and although it is logical to identify Tudur with the River Aled, which flows through the parish, the poet's link with Llansannan cannot be substantiated. In adopting the name Aled, it is possible that Tudur was simply following the example of Lewys Aled, his father's cousin, who is also described as a poet. Many of Llywelyn Chwith's descendants took up residence in other parts of north Wales, and three of Tudur's sons are known to have settled in towns close to the border: Robert at Oswestry, Rhosier at Ruthin, and Ffowc at Wrexham. A fourth son, Syr Siôn Aled, served as vicar in Llansannan during the years 1522–36, the possible source of subsequent erroneous traditions concerning his renowned father. Tudur himself implies in one of his poems that he was a native not of Llansannan but of Iâl.

An outline of Tudur's bardic instruction can be gleaned from his extant poems and from the tributes of his elegists. He acknowledges his debt to Dafydd ab Edmwnd, to whom he was related, and to Ieuan ap Llywelyn ab Ieuan. He also states that his early learning was rewarded at the wedding feast of Ieuan ap Dafydd ab Ithel Fychan, a near neighbour of Dafydd ab Edmwnd in Tegeingl. The latter had gained pre-eminence at the bardic congress, or eisteddfod, held at Carmarthen about 1450. Tudur, likewise, played a central role at the Caerwys eisteddfod of July 1523. Together with Gruffudd, son of Ieuan ap Llywelyn, he directed events, and contributed to the efforts to organize the bardic order. In winning the silver chair, his status as chief master craftsman and teacher was confirmed, and his nine elegists pay equal tribute to his extensive learning and mastery of the secrets associated with *cerdd dafod* (literally, the craft of the tongue).

Nine of Tudur's poems appeared in print in Rhys Jones's *Gorchestion beirdd Cymru* (1773), and two volumes of his poems, collected and edited by T. Gwynn Jones, were published in 1926 (*Gwaith Tudur Aled*, 1926). Unfortunately, the editor failed to curb his own poetic genius; as a result, many lines bear T. Gwynn Jones's hallmark, and in certain cases manuscript and printed versions differ substantially. Nevertheless, in the absence of a modern critical edition, *Gwaith Tudur Aled* offers a valuable introduction to Tudur's work and facilitates a general assessment of his characteristics as a poet.

In keeping with the traditional role of the professional poet in medieval Wales, Tudur sang the praises of his patrons in both *cywydd* and *awdl* metres [*see* Cywyddwyr (*act. c.*1330–*c.*1650)]. Eulogies account for approximately half the 120 or so formal pieces in *Gwaith Tudur Aled*; elegies and request poems make up the remainder. Although hitherto unknown pieces have come to light since the publication of the 1926 edition, the overall picture remains unchanged, and shows that Tudur chose to remain in the vicinity of Iâl, where there was no lack of patrons for a poet of his calibre. Indeed, the excellence of its poets and the abundance of cultured patrons made north-east Wales a powerhouse of the poetic tradition at the turn of the sixteenth century. Tudur occasionally ventured towards the two western counties of Anglesey and Caernarvonshire; it is somewhat ironic, in view of the scarcity of his visits to south Wales, that he should end his days in Carmarthen. With the exception of Sir Rhys ap Thomas and son, the only south Walian recipient of a praise poem by Tudur was Edward Llwyd of Carmarthen, who was a native of the Vale of Clwyd. Edward served as archdeacon of Carmarthen, and Tudur had clearly fostered a fruitful relationship with those in religious calling. A quarter of Tudur's formal pieces (including five of the eleven extant *awdlau*) were composed to representatives of the church and the monastic houses which included Valle Crucis, Basingwerk, Ystrad Marchell, and Maenan. The number of praise and request poems (the elegies, not unexpectedly, are few and far between) indicate the material wealth of these institutions and the cultural inclinations of their representatives, many being members of indigenous Welsh families. Tudur followed well-trodden routes to Nannau and Y Penrhyn, homes with an honourable history of patronage, but his principal patrons were undoubtedly the Salesbury family of Lleweni together with cadet branches; other families addressed, originally of English descent, but by the sixteenth century thoroughly immersed in the Welsh way of life, included the Conways, Pulestons, and Eytons.

In spite of his association with the spiritual leaders of his day, Tudur is not renowned for his religious verse (although further research might change this view). His *cywydd* to Gwenfrewi, commissioned by Thomas Pennant, abbot of Basingwerk, attests to the miracles performed by the most popular saint of the day, but reveals little of the poet's own spiritual disposition. Several love poems are attributed to him (these include the familiar themes of the jealous husband and the spurning of the lover's advances) and numerous *englynion*. The latter show Tudur's involvement in the humorous and satirical diatribes—his own contributions are surprisingly tame in view of the crude tone associated with the genre—which would have characterized wedding feasts and the three festivals Christmas, Easter, and Whitsun, when poets together with patrons and their entourages would assemble in the great hall. Lewys Môn seems to have been a regular companion and adversary in dispute. Other poets mentioned include Gutun Owain, Rhys Nanmor, Rhys Pennardd, and Siôn ap Hywel.

The light-hearted note in his love poems and *englynion* should not undermine the serious vein in Tudur's poetry. In his formal verse he commends generosity, lineage, learning, military prowess, authority, and fair judgement. He also comments on, and apparently approves, the social changes evident in the early decades of the Tudor era: appointments to public posts and service at the royal court, the buying of land, and the accumulation of wealth. But he was also aware of the social dangers as the ambitious followed the route of self-advancement. In his best-known poem, a poignant effort to reconcile family members embroiled in a long-lasting land dispute, he pleads for unity and harmony, the prerequisites of a stable and successful society.

Tudur's work represents the pinnacle in the development of the strict metre poetry and the *cywydd* in particular (although he shares many features with his contemporaries). The compact diction demanded by the seven-syllable *cywydd* metre, the majestic movement from couplet to couplet, the profusion of metaphors, embellished by the rich alliteration of *cynghanedd*, all create a dramatic effect which cannot fail to impress, although nigh impossible to convey in a different tongue. There is, however, an underside to Tudur's tenacious loyalty to *cynghanedd groes*, regarded as supreme among all *cynganeddion*. His poems lack the rhythmic diversity found in the works of the fifteenth-century grand masters Guto'r Glyn and Lewys Glyn Cothi. 'His cynghanedd is often monotonous', claimed John Morris Jones (J. M. Jones, 47), and R. Williams Parry for his part was unimpressed by 'awen galed Reolaidd Tudur Aled' ('Tudur Aled's harsh and orderly muse'; R. Williams Parry, *Cerddi'r gaeaf*, 1971, 20). The poet's nine elegists would have disagreed. Tudur would never be surpassed, according to Huw ap Dafydd: 'A diobaith ei debyg' ('There is no hope of an equal'; *Gwaith Huw ap Dafydd*, ed. A. C. Lake, 1995, 48).

Tudur ended his days, and was buried, in the Franciscan friary at Carmarthen, where Sir Rhys ap Thomas was laid to rest in the summer of 1525. The absence of an elegy by Tudur upon Sir Rhys's death has prompted the assumption that Tudur was the first to die, but Lewys Daron and Lewys Morgannwg, two of Tudur's elegists, confirm that Tudur survived Sir Rhys. Another elegist, Lewys Môn, died in 1527. One concludes, therefore, that Tudur died between 1525 and 1527.　　　　A. Cynfael Lake

Sources P. C. Bartrum, ed., *Welsh genealogies, AD 1400–1500*, 18 vols. (1983) · C. Fychan, 'Tudur Aled: ailystyried ei gynefin', *National Library of Wales Journal*, 23 (1983–4), 45–74 · C. Fychan, 'Dau o feibion Tudur Aled', *National Library of Wales Journal*, 20 (1977–8), 204–6 · C. Fychan, 'Y canu i wŷr eglwysig gorllewin Sir Ddinbych', *Transactions of the Denbighshire Historical Society*, 28 (1979), 115–82 · M. Richards, 'Mab Tudur Aled', *National Library of Wales Journal*, 13 (1963–4), 196 · *Gwaith Tudur Aled*, ed. J. G. Jones, 2 vols. (1926) · M. Stephens, ed., *The new companion to the literature of Wales* (1998) · *DWB* · E. Rowlands, 'Tudur Aled', *A guide to Welsh literature*, ed.

A. O. H. Jarman and G. R. Hughes, 2: *1282–c.1550* (1979), 322–37 · S. Lewis, 'Tudur Aled', *Meistri'r Canrifoedd*, ed. R. G. Gruffydd (1973), 98–115 · J. M. Jones, 'Tudor, Aled', *Transactions of the Honourable Society of Cymmrodorion* (1908–9), 21–52 · E. Roberts, 'Cywydd Cymod Hwmffre ap Hywel ap Siencyn a'i Geraint', *Journal of the Merioneth Historical and Record Society*, 4 (1961–4), 302–17

Tudur ap Goronwy (d. 1367?). *See under* Tudor family, forebears of (*per. c.*1215–1404).

Tudur ap Goronwy ab Ednyfed (d. 1311). *See under* Tudor family, forebears of (*per. c.*1215–1404).

Tudway, Thomas (c.1650–1726), organist and composer, was the second son of Thomas (d. 1671) and Anne Tudway of Windsor. His father was a lay clerk of St George's Chapel, and he himself may have been a chorister there for a time. Possibly he was one of two Windsor choristers impressed into the Chapel Royal in 1664. He sang in the chapel until his voice broke in 1668 and received maintenance from Michaelmas until his appointment as organist of King's College, Cambridge, two years later. Between 1671 and 1680 he also served as master of the choristers. He graduated MusB in 1681, his exercise comprising settings of 'The Lord hear thee' and *Quare fremuerunt gentes*. Subsequently he added the organistships of Great St Mary's, Peterhouse, and Pembroke College to his sources of income. In 1702 he unsuccessfully petitioned for one of the organists' places in the Chapel Royal, which he said Charles II had promised him in 1682 and was now vacant. He became doctor of music at Cambridge in January 1705 and was made professor of music at the same time.

An ardent tory, Tudway was deprived of his university and college appointments in July 1706 and 'degraded from all degrees, taken and to be taken' ostensibly for speaking slightingly of the queen, though after a public recantation he was restored to his posts in March the following year. In practical terms, however, while officially remaining organist, he ceased to perform his duties from Christmas 1706, a deputy being paid during the remainder of his tenure. This was probably the period (1706–10) he referred to in a letter of 9 August 1714 to Robert Harley, earl of Oxford, claiming to have been:

> barbarously used by the late Ministry for several years ... all my subsistence taken from me, turned out of my house where I had lived with my family almost twenty years, a livelihood to seek at near threescore years of age.

A few weeks later he wrote again asking Harley for support in connection with a place in the new Chapel Royal, but to no avail. However, he was soon to enjoy the patronage of Harley's son Edward, Lord Harley, for whom, between 1714 and 1720, he compiled his comprehensive six-volume manuscript collection of English church music from the Reformation to the death of Queen Anne, and for which he is best known. It represents the work of 85 composers and contains 70 services and 244 anthems; he received 30 guineas a volume for it. He also styled himself 'Master of the Music' to Harley's chapel at Wimpole (emulating Handel at Cannons under the duke of Chandos) and wrote music for its intended consecration in 1721—though in fact the chapel was never consecrated. At some stage in his career he may have received ordination, for he appears as 'Reverend Thomas Tudway, Cambridge, Doctor of Music' in the subscription lists to Richard Neale's *A Pocket Companion for Gentlemen and Ladies* (1724–5). He died on 23 November 1726.

Most of Tudway's compositions are for the church; three services, twenty-four anthems, and a burial service can be traced. His early work is restrained but those written after the turn of the century, being mainly celebratory occasional pieces, are more extravagant—even though he strongly disapproved of the 'theatrical style' for church music. They include 'The Lord hath declared' ('Thanksgiving for the discovery of the Rye House Conspiracy … 1682'), 'Behold how good and joyful' for the Act of Union (1707), and various anthems to mark Marlborough's victories: 'I will sing unto the Lord' for Blenheim (1704), 'O praise the Lord, for it is a good thing' for Oudenarde (1708), and 'Give the Lord the honour due' and 'My heart rejoiceth' for the peace of Utrecht (1713). Among the works expressly written for King's College are 'Thou, O Lord, hast heard our desire' for the visit of Queen Anne to the college on 16 April 1705 (this was also his MusD exercise) and 'Hearken unto me' for the laying of the foundation stone of Gibbs's new building on 25 March 1724. He also wrote a burial service for the funeral of the marquess of Blandford, the duke of Marlborough's only surviving son, who was a student of King's (24 February 1703).

While rarely approaching Purcell's standard, Tudway's music is by no means devoid of merit, either technically or expressively. A dozen or more songs came out in the popular miscellanies of the 1680s, but his only large-scale secular piece is a birthday ode in honour of Queen Anne, *Hail Happy Day, Auspicious Light*, the date of which is unknown, though in the absence of other contenders 1706 has been suggested.

Tudway married Margaret, daughter of Samuel Rix of Canterbury; they had at least one son. Hawkins quotes from a letter to him (no longer traceable) in which the father recalls his early days as a musician, and especially his admiration for Henry Purcell, his fellow chorister in the Chapel Royal. He seems to have been a sociable man, though one of forceful opinions. At Cambridge he had a reputation as a punster. (The one about the chancellor, the duke of Somerset, niggardly with the patronage at his disposal, riding them all 'without a bit in our mouths', is an example.) His correspondence with Humfrey Wanley, Harley's librarian, over the progress of his great collection is of particular interest, as are the prefaces to some of its volumes—especially the much-quoted reminiscences of his time as a boy in Charles II's chapel in volume two. Also, according to Hawkins, he was a member of a circle that met weekly at Harley's house, members of which included Matthew Prior, Sir James Thornhill, 'and other ingenious artists'. Apparently Thornhill made sketches of them all, that of Tudway showed him playing the harpsichord. There is also a portrait of him in full academicals, by Thomas Hill in the faculty of music at Oxford, holding his doctoral exercise 'on the occasion of her majesty's presence in King's Coll. Chapel, Cambridge, April the 16, 1705'.

IAN SPINK

Sources A. Ashbee and D. Lasocki, eds., *A biographical dictionary of English court musicians, 1485–1714*, 2 (1998), 1100–02 · H. W. Shaw, *The succession of organists of the Chapel Royal and the cathedrals of England and Wales from c.1538* (1991), 357–8 · J. Hawkins, *A general history of the science and practice of music*, new edn, 3 vols. (1875), 794–5 · E. Turnbull, 'Thomas Tudway and the Harleian collection', *Journal of the American Musicological Society*, 8 (1955), 203–7 · I. Spink, *Restoration cathedral music, 1660–1714* (1995), 196–201 · *The manuscripts of his grace the duke of Portland*, 10 vols., HMC, 29 (1891–1931), vol. 6, p. 485

Archives BL, music collections, Harley MSS 4142, 7337–7341 · BL, music MSS and papers, Add. MSS 17835, 30932, 31444–31445, 31459, 36268 | BL, corresp. with Humfrey Wanley, Harley MS 3779

Likenesses T. Hill, oils, 1705, faculty of music, U. Oxf.

Tuer, Andrew White (1838–1900), printer, publisher, and author, was born in Sunderland on 24 December 1838, the son of Joseph Robertson Tuer and his wife, Jane Taft. According to the recollections of one contemporary, his parents died when he was a child and he was brought up by his great-uncle, Andrew White, who was MP for Sunderland and whose name he adopted. He was educated in Newcastle upon Tyne before moving to Dr Bruce's school at York. Though details remain unclear, it seems that he was expected to take holy orders but instead he pursued a medical training and worked for a short while at a London hospital. Tuer showed little enthusiasm for the doctor's life and, having 'already, as an amateur, made experiments in printing' (*The Athenaeum*), he decided to turn to publishing.

About 1862 Tuer set up the company of Field and Tuer, in partnership with a Mr Field who already had an established business as a stationer and printer. Under Tuer's influence, Field and Tuer specialized in producing books of high quality 'ornamental and ancient' (*Literature*) printing and typography. Over the next thirty-eight years Tuer's company, operating from 50 Leadenhall Street, London, under the imprint Yᵉ Leadenhall Presse, was renowned for its facsimile publications of popular and decorative eighteenth-century texts, especially chapbooks and children's literature. In this regard, Tuer was motivated by his antiquarian interests and his own fascination with the history of printing and book production. However, he was also forward-looking and willing to take commercial risks; Field and Tuer were the first publishers to recognize the potential of the young Jerome K. Jerome, and many of his earliest works were issued by them. Tuer was also committed to raising the standards and status of modern commercial printing and with this intention, in 1877, he instigated and edited the quarterly *Paper and Printing Trades Journal*. Following the success of this professional journal, in 1880, Tuer launched the *Printers' International Specimen Exchange*, which circulated a selection of various printers' best designs and typography as technical models and inspiration for its subscribers. As each copy consisted of 200 hand-mounted examples, this project was no doubt made viable by Tuer's 'Stickphast' glue, which he had invented at the end of the 1860s. Between 1868 and 1890 Tuer and other members of his firm patented various devices and mechanisms, many of which were expressly tailored to the book trades. Until the end of the century, the Leadenhall Press went from strength to strength, opening a number of international offices and, following Field's death, it became a limited company in February 1892.

From about 1870 Tuer had been a regular correspondent to *The Times*, *The Athenaeum*, and *Notes and Queries*, writing letters on diverse subjects including copyright legislation, London's sanitation, and book collecting. After such modest beginnings, in 1879 Tuer began a complementary career as an author with his illustrated book *Luxurious Bathing*. Over the next twenty years, he combined his passion for prints, rare books, and eighteenth-century popular culture with his love of writing. Two of his most famous books were *Bartolozzi and his Works* (1882) and *History of the Horn Book* (1896), both of which were informed, discursive, and highly illustrated accounts containing practical advice for collectors. Indeed, his catalogue of the work of Bartolozzi was a landmark achievement which reveals his thorough knowledge of all the figures surrounding this eighteenth-century engraver.

In both business and private life Tuer was described as 'ingenious and resourceful' and 'one of the kindliest and most hospitable of men' (*The Athenaeum*). He was also an ardent antiquarian and a voracious collector. Although his extensive collection of Bartolozzi's prints was dispersed at Christies on 12 April 1881 and 22 April 1884, he continued to collect samplers, old clocks, children's books, and lottery tickets. Tuer died on 24 February 1900 at his home, 18 Campden Hill Square, London. He was survived by his wife, Thomasine Louisa (*née* Louttit), whom he had married on 10 October 1867. Following his death, his wife raised £600 through the sale of his library at Sotheby, Wilkinson, and Hodge in July 1900. LUCY PELTZ

Sources *DNB* · H. Carpenter and M. Prichard, *The Oxford companion to children's literature* (1984) · W. Y. Fletcher, *English book collectors* (1902) · A. W. Tuer to W. E. Gladstone, 15 March 1882, BL, Add. MS 444754, fol. 254 · *CGPLA Eng. & Wales* (1900) · *The Athenaeum* (3 March 1900), 276 · *Literature* (3 March 1900), 179 · *The Times* (27 Feb 1900), 6 · *Printers' International Specimen Exchange*, 1 (1880) · A. W. Tuer, 'Authors, publishers, and booksellers', *The Times* (19 Nov 1897), 7 · A. W. Tuer, letters, *The Times* (14 Oct 1867) · A. W. Tuer, letters, *The Times* (2 Aug 1871), 2 · A. W. Tuer, letters, *The Times* (27 Dec 1886), 10 · *WWW*

Archives BL, letters to W. E. Gladstone, Add. MS 444474, fol. 254 · BL, letters to W. C. Hazlitt, Add. MS 3890, fols. 37 and 107

Wealth at death £72,176 9s. 5d.: probate, 20 April 1900, *CGPLA Eng. & Wales*

Tufnell, Edward Carleton (1806–1886), civil servant and educationist, was born on 27 October 1806 at Marylebone, Middlesex, the younger son in the family of two sons and one daughter of William Tufnell (1769–1809) and his wife, Mary (*d.* 1829), daughter of Thomas Carleton. His father, a barrister, MP for Colchester 1806–7, and lord of the manor of Barnsbury, was an estate developer after whom Tufnell Park in north London was named. His mother was heir to estates in Cumberland. His elder brother was Henry *Tufnell, a whig MP. He was educated at Eton and at Balliol College, Oxford, where he obtained first-class honours in mathematics and graduated BA in 1828. He was admitted a student of Lincoln's Inn in 1827, but was never called to the bar.

Appointed an assistant commissioner by the royal commission on the poor laws in July 1832 to conduct local investigations into the working of the poor law, Tufnell visited Edinburgh to obtain Thomas Chalmers's views on poor relief. In the following year he was a member of the royal commission on children's employment in factories. He published in 1834 *Character, Objects, and Effects of Trades Unions*, which restated many of the contemporary objections to trade unions. From May 1834 until 1835 he was honorary secretary of the newly founded Statistical Society of London. In July 1835 he had official employment as one of the assistant commissioners to administer the poor law, and held this position until the dissolution of the commission in 1846. In that year he married Honoria Mary (1824–1877), only daughter of Colonel William Macadam, knight of Hanover, through whom he inherited the Dollars estate, Kilmarnock, Ayrshire.

During the controversies which surrounded the work of the poor-law commission Tufnell was a supporter of Edwin Chadwick, to whose constabulary commission he gave evidence in 1838. His district responsibility was for Kent, and his publication *On the Dwellings and General Economy of the Labouring Classes in Kent and Sussex* (1841) was based on this experience. He took a particular interest in workhouse schools. He collaborated with J. P. Kay, whom he had met in connection with his Statistical Society work. They visited Scotland to see David Stow's model school in 1837 and travelled to France, Switzerland, Holland, and Germany in 1839 to investigate education on the continent. In 1839 they jointly published *Reports on the Training of Pauper Children*. Together they founded and financed in 1840 the Battersea Normal College for the training of teachers of pauper children, which was important in the development of the pupil-teacher system.

From the establishment of the poor-law board in 1847 until his retirement in June 1874 Tufnell was an inspector of the administration of government grants to workhouse schools in the London area. His advocacy of state provision of industrial training for workhouse children, stated in his evidence to the Newcastle commission on popular education (1861), brought him into conflict with the supporters of ragged schools run by voluntary effort. A member of the Society of Arts from 1853, he was on its council from 1869 to 1873 when, with Edwin Chadwick, he developed schemes for the introduction of drill into elementary schools. From 1862 until 1867 he was a member of the children's employment commission, producing with H. S. Tremenheere a report on the legislation affecting printworks and bleaching and dyeing works. Between 1867 and 1871 he and Tremenheere were appointed commissioners to investigate the employment of women and children in agriculture.

Tufnell died on 3 July 1886 at his home, 26 Lowndes Square, London, leaving three sons and a daughter: Carleton (1847–1893), commander RN; Edward (1848–1909), Conservative MP for South-East Essex, 1900–06; Mary (1850–1928); and Frederick (1860–1920), a Church of England priest.   P. R. D. CORRIGAN

Sources *Journal of the Society of Arts*, 34 (1885–6), 898 · E. B. Tufnell, *The family of Tufnell* (1924) · J. M. Collinge, *Officials of royal commissions of enquiry, 1815–70* (1984) · R. J. Phillips, 'E. C. Tufnell: inspector of poor law schools, 1847–1874', *History of Education*, 5 (1976), 227–40 · D. G. Paz, *The politics of working-class education in Britain, 1830–50* (1980) · S. E. Finer, *The life and times of Sir Edwin Chadwick* (1952) · R. J. W. Selleck, *James Kay Shuttleworth* (1994) · R. J. Phillips, 'E. C. Tufnell', PhD diss., Sheffield University, 1973
Archives NL Wales, corresp. with Sir George Cornewall Lewis · PRO, MH 12; MH 32 · UCL, Brougham papers · UCL, corresp. with Sir Edwin Chadwick
Wealth at death £65,709 2s. 11d.: probate, 23 Aug 1886, CGPLA Eng. & Wales

Tufnell, Henry (1805–1854), politician, born at Chichester, was the elder son of William Tufnell of Chichester (1769–1809), and his wife, Mary (d. 1829), daughter and coheir of Lough Carleton. His younger brother was Edward Carleton *Tufnell. He was educated at Eton College, and at Christ Church, Oxford, matriculating on 21 May 1825; he graduated BA in 1829. On 27 April 1827 he became a student at Lincoln's Inn. In 1830 he married Anne Augusta (d. 1843), daughter of Sir Robert John Wilmot-Horton; in the same year he translated, with Sir George Cornewall Lewis, a work by K. O. Müller as *History of the Antiquities of the Doric Race*.

In 1831, when his father-in-law was appointed governor of Ceylon, Tufnell accompanied him as his private secretary, and, after returning home about 1835, he became private secretary to Gilbert Elliot, second earl of Minto, first lord of the Admiralty. From April 1835 to September 1840 he was one of the lords of the Treasury under Lord Melbourne's administration, and on 27 July 1837 he was returned for Ipswich as a whig, but was unseated on petition on 26 February 1838. On 24 January 1840 he was returned for Devonport, and retained his seat to within a few months of his death. On the return of the whigs in July 1846, Tufnell became secretary to the Treasury; but in July 1850 ill health compelled him to resign office.

After the death of his first wife, Tufnell married, in 1844, Frances (d. 1846), second daughter of John *Byng, first earl of Strafford, with whom he had a daughter. In 1848 he married, as his third wife, Anne, second daughter of Archibald John *Primrose, fourth earl of Rosebery; they had a son Henry. Tufnell died on 15 June 1854 at Catton Hall, Derbyshire.

                                    E. I. CARLYLE, rev. H. C. G. MATTHEW

Sources GM, 2nd ser., 42 (1854), 299–300 · *The Times* (17 June 1854)
Archives BL, corresp. with Sir John Hobhouse, Add. MS 36471 · Borth. Inst., letters to Sir Charles Wood · Derbys. RO, letters to Sir R. J. Wilmot-Horton · NL Scot., letters to Andrew Rutherford · NMM, letters to Lord Minto · PRO, corresp. with Lord John Russell, PRO 30/22
Likenesses W. Holl, stipple (after G. Richmond), BM, NPG

Tufnell, Thomas Jolliffe (1819–1885), military surgeon, fifth son of John Charles Tufnell (d. 1841), lieutenant-colonel of the Middlesex militia, and his wife, Uliana Ivaniona, only daughter of John Fowell, rector of Bishopsbourne, Kent, was born at Lackham House, near Chippenham, Wiltshire, on 23 May 1819. He was educated at Dr Radcliffe's school at Salisbury, and was apprenticed in 1836 to Samuel Luscombe of Exeter, then senior surgeon to the Devon and Exeter Hospital. After studying at Exeter for three years, Tufnell went to London and entered at St George's Hospital, where he trained under Sir Benjamin Collins Brodie and Caesar Hawkins. Tufnell was admitted a member of the Royal College of Surgeons in May 1841, and on 11 June in the same year he entered the army as assistant surgeon to the 44th regiment, then serving in India. He travelled to Calcutta, where he took medical charge of all the troops as they arrived from England, and he remained at Chinsura until the last detachment had landed at Christmas.

Tufnell returned to England in October 1842 and was posted to the 3rd dragoon guards, with whom he served at Dundalk, Dublin, and Cork. In 1844 he married Henrietta, daughter of Croasdaile Molony of Granahan, and widow of Robert Fannin. The marriage produced two daughters: Iva, who married Peter Leslie Peacocke, and Florence, who married Thomas Turbitt of Owenston.

On 14 April 1846 Tufnell was transferred to the army medical staff at Dublin, and shortly afterwards he became surgeon to the Dublin district military prison. He was admitted in 1845 the first fellow by examination of the Royal College of Surgeons in Ireland, and in 1846 he began lecturing on military hygiene. He also lectured on this subject at the St Vincent and Baggot Street hospitals until his appointment as regius professor of military surgery at the college in 1851. He lectured in this capacity until 1860, when the chair was abolished by the government as a result of the foundation of the Netley military school.

Tufnell again saw service; in the war between Russia and Turkey he went to the Crimea with a Scottish regiment. He acted as an examiner in surgery at the Royal College of Surgeons in Ireland, but he resigned the post on becoming a candidate for the office of vice-president in 1873. He served the college as president in 1874–5, and he was surgeon to the City of Dublin Hospital for more than twenty years. He published extensive works on the treatment of aneurysm. Tufnell died on 27 November 1885, and was buried in Mount Jerome cemetery, Dublin.

                                    D'A. POWER, rev. JAMES MILLS

Sources C. A. Cameron, *History of the Royal College of Surgeons in Ireland* (1886), 442 · *BMJ* (5 Dec 1885), 1088–9 · *Medico-Chirurgical Transactions*, 69 (1886), 18–21 · Burke, *Gen. GB* (1898)
Likenesses T. A. Jones, oils, exh. 1875, Royal College of Surgeons in Ireland, Dublin

Tufton, Sackville, ninth earl of Thanet (1769–1825), aristocrat, was born at Hothfield House in Kent on 30 June 1769, the eldest son of Sackville Tufton, eighth earl (1733–1786), and Mary Sackville (1746–1778), daughter of Lord John Philip Sackville. His maternal uncle, John Frederick

Sackville, third duke of Dorset, acted as his guardian during his minority.

In early life Thanet spent much time abroad, especially in Vienna, where he formed an alliance with a Hungarian lady, Anne Charlotte de Bojanowitz, to whom he was married, under the Anglican rite, at St George's, Hanover Square, London, on 28 February 1811. Some light would appear to be thrown upon their intimacy in a letter from William Windham, dated Paris, 15 September 1791: 'Thanet has arrived here with a Hungarian lady whom as a brilliant achievement he carried off from her husband at Vienna' (*Diary of William Windham*, 237). Lady Thanet died on 15 February 1819, having had no children.

Thanet took no prominent part in politics, but consistently supported Fox. In May 1798 he was present with Fox, Sheridan, Erskine, and other whig sympathizers at the trial of the United Irishman, Arthur O'Connor, at Maidstone. O'Connor was found not guilty, but was immediately rearrested on another charge. Thanet and others were charged with having created a riot in the court and put out the lights in an attempt to rescue the prisoner, or at least to facilitate his escape. The case was tried before Lord Kenyon at the king's bench on 25 April 1799. Sir John Scott (afterwards Lord Eldon) and Edward Law (later Lord Ellenborough) prosecuted, and Thomas Erskine conducted the defence. Thanet was convicted of riot and assault, and on 10 June 1799 he was sentenced to a year's imprisonment in the Tower and a fine of £1000, and on his release he was ordered to give security for his good behaviour for seven years in sureties to the amount of £20,000. The sentence was excessively severe; it was subsequently believed that Thanet had not, in fact, committed the assault.

After his release the earl lived at Hothfield, and became a popular agriculturist, regularly visiting the stock market at Ashford, and conversing with the graziers. He was a supporter of Queen Caroline during the trial of 1820; with Lord Sefton he advanced her the money to purchase a house in South Audley Street, and on 17 August 1820 voted in the minority in favour of the duke of Leinster's motion to reject the bill of pains and penalties without debate.

Thanet was famous as a gambler, reported as winning £40,000 in one evening, and losing £120,000 at the Salon des Étrangers, Paris, in one night. Towards the end of his life he lived chiefly in France, where he died at Chalons, near Paris on 24 January 1825, having suffered from numerous disorders, including erysipelas, cholera, and gout. He was buried with his ancestors in the Tufton chapel in Rainham church, Kent, on 7 February 1825. He was succeeded in turn by his brothers Charles (1770–1832) and Henry Tufton, eleventh and last earl of Thanet (1775–1849). THOMAS SECCOMBE, rev. K. D. REYNOLDS

Sources GEC, *Peerage* · R. C. Fergusson, *The whole proceedings… against… Sackville earl of Thanet* (1799) · R. Pocock, *Memorials of the family of Tufton, earls of Thanet* (1800) · *Diary of William Windham, 1784–1810*, ed. H. Baring (1866) · *The Farington diary*, ed. J. Greig, 4 (1924), 214; 7 (1927) · *The Creevey papers*, ed. H. Maxwell, 2 vols. (1903) · A. M. W. Stirling, *The letter-bag of Lady Elizabeth Spencer-Stanhope*, 2 vols. (1913) · E. A. Smith, *A queen on trial: the affair of Queen Caroline* (1993)

Archives Skipton Castle, Veteripont Ltd MSS · W. Yorks. AS, Leeds, Yorkshire Archaeological Society, corresp. and papers | BL, corresp. with Lord Holland, Add. MS 51571 · Oxf. U. Mus. NH, corresp. with William Smith · U. Durham L., letters to Lord Grey · UCL, letters to James Brougham
Likenesses J. Reynolds, double portrait, oils, 1777, Petworth House, West Sussex · G. Hayter, group portrait, oils (*The trial of Queen Caroline*, 1820), NPG

Tuke, Anthony William (1897–1975), banker, was born on 24 February 1897 at Saffron Walden, Essex, the son of William Favill Tuke, a banker, and his wife, Eva Marian, *née* Nockolds. The Tukes were a Quaker family, originally from York, where they were prominent tea and cocoa merchants. Anthony's grandfather William Murray Tuke left this family business and joined his brother-in-law as a partner in the Saffron Walden and North Essex Bank, one of the banks that in 1896 formed Barclay & Co. Ltd, for which William Murray Tuke served as a local director.

Tuke attended Winchester College, and throughout his life always valued the classical education he received there. During the First World War he served with the Cameronians (Scottish Rifles). In 1919 he married (Agnes) Edna Gannaway (d. 1966), with whom he shared a love of gardening and the arts, especially the theatre; they had three sons, two of whom predeceased him. He joined Barclays in the same year and rose rapidly through the senior positions, being appointed a local director at Luton in 1923, and a London-based general manager in 1931, working with successive chairmen, including his own father. In 1946 he was elected a vice-chairman, and in 1947 he was deputy chairman. In that capacity he worked with the chairman, Sir William Goodenough, whose manifold activities led to his death in 1951. Tuke succeeded him as chairman, a position he held until 1962.

Although shy and somewhat reserved, Tuke was dubbed the Iron Tuke by a financial journalist and the nickname reflected his high standards. 'His directives were unambiguous and urgent, his memory infallible, and woe betide the careless or the dilatory in executing his instructions' (Lambert). He was the product of Barclays' decentralized structure, with the principal office-holders appointed largely from family members. He saw nothing wrong in this, provided that family entrants who did not prove satisfactory were quietly eased out of the bank, and that talented outsiders were not barred from promotion.

During Tuke's ten years as chairman bank lending was restricted by government and Bank of England pressures. Nevertheless by the time he retired Barclays had become the largest of the clearing banks. He presided over the beginnings of computerization, and in spite of restrictions the bank's deposits increased from just over £300 million to £3000 million. However, as he grew older he became more wary of innovation, being careful, for instance, to distance Barclays from the moral hazards of hire purchase, even while acquiring a quarter of United Dominions Trust, a major hire-purchase company. He saw Barclays as trustees of the national good and was ready to conform with Bank of England restrictions on lending, though very willing also to forge ahead with export guarantee loans when the signal was given.

Anthony William Tuke (1897–1975), by Olive Edis, 1931

In Tuke's view, as custodians of other people's money and providers of credit, and a formative influence in the economy, bankers had wide obligations, not only to their shareholders but also to society. Thus, in addition to committee membership and office-holding for the British Bankers' Association and the Bank Clerks Orphans fund, he served on the committee of the Historic Churches Preservation Trust. He was also a director of Yorkshire Insurance and of the Reinsurance Corporation, and was twice a fellow of Winchester College and in 1962 its warden.

Within Barclays, Tuke resigned his directorships of subsidiaries on becoming chairman, being advised by the board of Barclays not to take on as much as his predecessor had done. He wanted to see Barclays advance overseas, particularly in the Commonwealth, and as its chairman was rather surprised when his strategy of buying into Commonwealth banks was viewed with some suspicion, even hostility, by those increasingly nationalistic bodies. He had naïvely thought that he was doing them a favour: putting Barclays' name behind them. His pride in Barclays was also shown in his joint authorship of two histories of the bank: the *History of Barclays Bank Limited* (1926) and *Barclays Bank Limited, 1926–1969* (1972), written after his retirement as chairman. The first is an invaluable (though not entirely accurate) record of the constituent partnerships from which Barclays was formed, and of its early years; the second, a briefer but more analytical account. After retirement as chairman, Tuke became a local director (in Southampton) again, for ten years. He also remained a main board director, his presence accepted with equanimity by John Thomson, his successor. Tuke died peacefully at his home, Freelands, Wherwell, near Andover, Hampshire, on 12 June 1975. His son, Sir Anthony Favill Tuke (*b.* 1920), also made a career with Barclays, serving as chairman from 1973 to 1981.   MARGARET ACKRILL

Sources P. W. Matthews, *History of Barclays Bank Limited*, ed. A. W. Tuke (1926) · A. W. Tuke and R. J. H. Gillman, *Barclays Bank Limited, 1926–1969: some recollections* (1972) · P. E. Smart, 'Tuke, Anthony William', *DBB* · *Spread Eagle*, 26 (1951), 133 · *Spread Eagle*, 37 (1962), 77 · *Spread Eagle*, 50 (1975), 272–3 · H. U. A. Lambert, *The Wykehamist* · 'A. W. T.', *Essay* [Barclays Bank Staff Association] (summer 1962) · E. Smart, 'Tuke of Barclays: a personal history', *The Banker*, 122 (1972), 1585–90 · Barclays Records Services, group archives · personal knowledge (2004) · d. cert. · *CGPLA Eng. & Wales* (1975)
Likenesses O. Edis, photograph, 1931, NPG [*see illus.*] · photographs, Barclays Group, London archives, vol. 37, March 1962
Wealth at death £167,369: probate, 8 July 1975, *CGPLA Eng. & Wales*

Tuke, Sir Brian (*d.* 1545), administrator, was the son of Richard Tuke (*d.* 1498?), of Kent, and his wife, Agnes Bland of Nottinghamshire. His father may have been a member of the household of Thomas Howard, second duke of Norfolk. By 1518 Tuke had married Grisilde Boughton (*d.* 1538) of Woolwich, and together they had four daughters and three sons.

Tuke entered the household of Henry VII as a clerk of the spicery some time before 1506, when he was appointed feodary of Wallingford. Two years later, now a signet clerk, he received the post of bailiff of Sandwich (which he held until 1524). Following Henry VIII's accession he continued as a signet clerk, and his responsibilities multiplied rapidly. In October 1510 he was named clerk of the council at Calais, and was soon master of the posts, in charge of the system of diplomatic couriers. In his secretarial work he drafted letters on behalf of the busy Cardinal Wolsey, served as a messenger between king and minister, and handled correspondence with ambassadors abroad. In September 1513 he was present at the English capture of Tournai, and he was knighted three years later.

Owing to the demands of attendance upon king and cardinal, Tuke surrendered his Calais clerkship in 1520. In March 1523 he was promoted to the post of French secretary, and the following month succeeded John Taylor as clerk of parliaments. As a councillor and French secretary he assisted in negotiating the treaty of the More with France (August 1525), and was among those subsequently rewarded with a pension by François I. By early 1528 he was busier than ever, for in addition to his own work he was filling in for Wolsey's absent secretary Stephen Gardiner. It was about this time that he sat for the painter Hans Holbein (whose portrait of Tuke now hangs in the National Gallery, Washington). In June 1528 he joined Bishop Cuthbert Tunstal in negotiating a truce with France and Flanders at Hampton Court, and defended its terms before a dissatisfied Henry VIII. That same month the king made his secretary privy to 'the other secret matter of his will' (the divorce), and set him to work drafting a book on the subject.

Sir Brian Tuke (*d.* 1545), by Hans Holbein the younger

On 13 April 1528 Tuke attained his highest office, with his appointment as treasurer of the chamber. Since its heyday under Sir John Heron (*d.* 1522), however, the chamber's central role in royal finances had steadily been eroded, and the allocation of much of its former revenue to other financial departments left its new treasurer chronically short of funds. During the 1530s Tuke repeatedly petitioned Thomas Cromwell (in vain) to restore subsidy and other revenues to the chamber, while at the same time peppering him with memoranda advocating reforms of chamber administration. Despite this new responsibility he continued his work as royal secretary and councillor; for example, during the uprisings of 1536 he was a member of the London council and organized the vital posts between the capital and the north. Nevertheless, by the end of the decade there were growing complaints that he was neglecting his many duties. In response to these concerns (and his advanced age) he surrendered his parliamentary clerkship in 1539, and a successor as French secretary was appointed three years later. On 1 May 1542, however, Tuke (as treasurer of the chamber) was named treasurer of the new court of general surveyors, responsible for the administration of crown lands.

In addition to his administrative work, Tuke found occasion to pursue scholarly interests. At the request of William Thynne (a colleague in the royal household), he wrote the preface to his 1532 edition of Chaucer's works, arguing for the poet's pivotal role in the development of the English language. John Bale records that he completed a (lost) treatise attacking Polydore Vergil. He supplied the antiquary John Leland with medieval manuscripts; Leland in turn included a total of nine poems in his *Encomia* praising the virtues of his friend, the 'Gazophylax camerae': 'Quanto privatus minor extat principe, tanto / Maior Romano, Tucca Britannus erit' (Leland, 23).

Sir Brian Tuke owned a house in St Margaret Lothbury, London, as well as properties at Stepney, and at Pyrgo in the royal manor of Havering, Essex, of which he was briefly steward (1536–7). Following the dissolution of Waltham Abbey he purchased the manor of South Weald, Essex, in 1541, and the next year acquired a fine dwelling at nearby Layer Marney, which became his principal residence. He served as an Essex JP (1515–45), as well as on the Middlesex (1528–45) and Surrey (1528–32) commissions of the peace. In November 1533 he was pricked as sheriff of Essex and Hertfordshire, and was included in the 1535 commission compiling the *valor ecclesiasticus* for Essex.

From the mid-1520s onwards Tuke was afflicted with a succession of illnesses which incapacitated him for months at a time and placed him regularly in the care of physicians (who on one occasion included Henry VIII himself). His difficulties as treasurer of the chamber and the constant demands of royal creditors added to his woes, and in the summer of 1545 secretary Wriothesley reported that Tuke was 'run out of town [to Essex] … because he hath no money' (*LP Henry VIII*, 20/2, no. 453). Ill and weary, on 26 September 1545 he drafted his will, which opens with a lengthy meditation on man's mortality (presumably penned by Tuke himself). He died at Layer Marney one month later, on 26 October 1545, and was buried beside his wife in the London church of St Margaret, Lothbury. P. R. N. CARTER

Sources *LP Henry VIII* · G. R. Elton, *The Tudor revolution in government* (1953) · W. C. Richardson, *Tudor chamber administration, 1485–1547* (1952) · J. Leland, *Principum, ac illustrium aliquot et eruditorum in Anglia virorum* (1589) · *CPR, 1494–1509* · *VCH Essex*, vol. 8 · G. R. Elton, 'The materials of parliamentary history', *Studies in Tudor and Stuart politics and government*, 3 (1983), 58–155 · M. K. McIntosh, *A community transformed: the manor and liberty of Havering, 1500–1620* (1991) · D. S. Chambers, ed., *Faculty office registers, 1534–1549* (1966) · R. G. Lang, ed., *Two Tudor subsidy assessment rolls for the city of London, 1541 and 1581*, London RS, 29 (1993) · M. McKisack, *Medieval history in the Tudor age* (1971) · will, PRO, PROB 11/31, sig. 1 · J. Stow, *The survey of London* (1912) [with introduction by H. B. Wheatley] · P. Ganz, *The paintings of Hans Holbein* (1950) · R. R. Tatlock, 'Sir Bryan Tuke, by Holbein', *Burlington Magazine*, 42 (1923), 246–51 · Nichols, *Lit. anecdotes*, vol. 9

Archives BL, Arundel MS 97 · BL, Cotton MSS · BL, Stowe MS 554 · PRO, Exchequer accounts, E 101 · PRO, state papers, Henry VIII, SP 1

Likenesses H. Holbein the younger, oils, National Gallery of Art, Washington, DC [*see illus.*] · H. Holbein the younger, oils, Cleveland Museum of Arts, Ohio · portrait (after H. Holbein the younger), Alte Pinakothek, Munich

Tuke, Daniel Hack (1827–1895), physician and writer on psychological medicine, was born on 19 April 1827 at St Lawrence Street, York, the youngest of the thirteen children of Samuel *Tuke (1784–1857), asylum reformer and Quaker philanthropist, and his wife, Priscilla (1784–1827), daughter of James Hack, banker, of Chichester and Hannah Jeffreys, of London. James Hack *Tuke (1819–1896)

Daniel Hack Tuke (1827–1895), by Charles Callet, c.1888

was his elder brother. Daniel Hack Tuke was a delicate child (whose twin brother died at birth, and his mother during his infancy), and this physique limited his education. Ill health also influenced his career, putting a premature end to an uncongenial period spent in legal articles to a Bradford solicitor in 1845, while less strenuous forms of activity in his preferred choice of a medical vocation were dictated by a diagnosis of tuberculosis in 1853. Also in 1853 came marriage to Esther Maria Stickney (1826–1917), of Holderness, Yorkshire. They had three children, the second son being Henry Scott *Tuke RA (1858–1929).

Daniel Hack Tuke was profoundly influenced by being brought up in close proximity to the private asylum of the Society of Friends, the York Retreat, which had been founded by his great-grandfather William Tuke. In 1847 Daniel was appointed Retreat secretary and house steward, and was thereby enabled to study patients and their illnesses, and read widely about insanity. After three years he began medical studies at St Bartholomew's Hospital, London, qualifying MRCS in 1852, followed in 1853 by the degree of MD (Heidelberg). In later life he became LRCP then FRCP (1875) as well as an honorary LLD (Glasgow). In 1853 he returned to The Retreat as assistant medical officer, making a distinctive contribution through constructing detailed patient histories and case notes. He also devised a new course on psychological medicine at York medical school, bringing his students to the retreat to observe patients.

In 1854 Tuke began a distinguished career as author and

medical publicist. His study of the moral management of the insane gained the award of prize essay from the Society for Improving the Condition of the Insane. Here he sought to write dispassionately but showed a progressive trend in which The Retreat's 'great experiment' in championing humane methods had culminated in a campaign to end mechanical restraint. It was mainly at The Retreat that Tuke, together with J. C. Bucknill, wrote *A Manual of Psychological Medicine* (1858). Tuke wrote on history, nosology, and statistics leaving the sections on diagnosis, pathology, and treatment to Bucknill. In becoming the standard text on insanity (going through four editions by 1879), the volume created a national reputation for Tuke.

Before its publication Tuke's illness forced him to move to the milder climate of Falmouth, where he remained for fifteen years. His precarious health only permitted consultancy and he became visiting physician to the retreat. He became a general consultant in lunacy during the mid-1870s when better health made it feasible to move to London. In the capital he became a lecturer at Charing Cross Hospital medical school, an examiner in mental physiology in the University of London, a governor of Bethlem Hospital, and a founder of the After-Care Association. In 1880 he was made joint editor of the *Journal of Mental Science* and in the following year was elected president of the Medico-Psychological Association. The professional pinnacle of a commissionership in lunacy eluded him, probably because he never held a leading asylum post. Indeed, Tuke's contribution to the developing field of mental science lay less in the practical world of asylums than in his influential studies of the comparative, historical, and medical aspects of psychological medicine.

A central theme in Tuke's medical writing was the complex interaction of the mental and the physical: his studies of psycho-physical phenomena included hallucination, somnambulism, and hypnosis. Like his father, Samuel Tuke, Daniel showed a pronounced interest in the comparative treatment of insanity and with a similar reforming purpose. He visited, and published critical observations on, asylums in the Netherlands, France, and North America. Tuke also found it useful to set insanity in its historical and geographical contexts, notably in *Chapters in the History of the Insane in the British Isles* (1882) a historical work (based on careful research that included the study of archival material) which ranged from classical to modern times. Here an almost filial piety to The Retreat led him to highlight its significance as the cradle of reform for the humane treatment of the insane. It was significant that Tuke presented the first copy of his most substantial academic work to the superintendent of The Retreat on the occasion of its centenary in 1892. This was the notable two-volume *Dictionary of Psychological Medicine* (1892), in which he contributed sixty-eight original entries and edited the remainder. Like the earlier *Manual of Psychological Medicine* (1858) this was directed solely at practitioners of mental medicine, whereas elsewhere his breadth of vision enabled him also to popularize psychological medicine to a lay readership.

A gentle and sociable man, Daniel Hack Tuke enjoyed

the company of his family and friends. In his *Illustrations of the Influence of the Mind upon the Body* (1872) he had noted that the power of the will in resisting disease was unquestionable. His wide-ranging activities suggest that this was a personal belief since it was the pattern, rather than the power, of his professional dedication that was influenced by persistent ill health. Tuke died on 5 March 1895 at his address at 63 Welbeck Street, London, three days after an attack of apoplexy. Although he had departed from formal adherence to its religious tenets, he was interred in the burial-ground of the Society of Friends, Saffron Walden, Essex. ANNE DIGBY

Sources *Journal of Mental Science*, 41 (1895), 377–86 · retreat archives, Borth. Inst. · Munk, *Roll* · *CGPLA Eng. & Wales* (1895) · A. Digby, *Madness, morality and medicine: a study of the York Retreat, 1796–1914* (1985) · *DNB*
Archives Borth. Inst. · RS Friends, Lond.
Likenesses C. Callet, etching, *c*.1888, Wellcome L. [*see illus.*] · double portrait (with William Murray), repro. in W. K. Sessions and E. M. Sessions, *The Tukes of York* (1971) · photograph (in later years), repro. in *Journal of Mental Science* · photograph (as a young man), repro. in W. K. Sessions and E. M. Sessions, *The Tukes of York* (1971)
Wealth at death £29,459 17*s*. 8*d*. effects in England: probate, 9 April 1895, *CGPLA Eng. & Wales*

Tuke, Henry (1755–1814), Quaker minister and writer, was born at York on 24 January 1755, the son of William *Tuke (1732–1822) and his first wife, Elizabeth (1729–1760), daughter of John Hoyland of Woodhouse, Yorkshire. After his wife's death Tuke's father remarried. Esther Tuke (1727–1794) was an affectionate stepmother who became a major influence on her stepson's subsequent career.

Tuke was educated at a Quaker boarding-school at Sowerby, Yorkshire, and became interested in a medical career. However, he deferred to his father's wishes and in 1770 he entered the family grocery and tea business at York, of which he became a partner in 1785. He proved a shrewd and careful businessman; he added cocoa and chocolate making to the business and he enabled his parents to pursue their interests in the foundation of a Quaker school for girls (1784; later the Mount School, York) and in the establishment of the city's Retreat, in 1796, for the care of the mentally ill. On 20 September 1781 Tuke married Mary Maria Scott (1748–1815), the daughter of a Norwich lawyer, who had become a Quaker in 1780 after two years' stay with Tuke's parents; they had six children, three of whom survived into adulthood. Their second child was the asylum reformer Samuel *Tuke.

In 1780 Tuke became a Quaker minister and undertook some ministerial visits to all parts of the British Isles. With other members of the Tuke family he played a major role in moving York Quakers away from the deadening effects of quietism to a more active and informed faith. He held parochial appointments in the parish of St Mary's, Castlegate, as an overseer of the poor in 1782 and as auditor of the poor rate accounts between 1793 and 1795. Having secured his freedom of the city in 1782 he served as a chamberlain for York corporation in 1787, and kept and audited the corporation accounts. He supported, with other Quakers, evangelical Anglican and other philanthropic activity in York, including the York Dispensary,

founded in 1788, the anti-slavery campaign, and the British School for the education of non-Quaker girls, founded in 1812. He was a founder member, in 1813, of the York Auxiliary Bible Society, which gave opportunity for interdenominational discussion as well as making scripture available to a wider audience. He disapproved of Quakers voting but recognized that decisive action was needed when, with other Quakers, he assisted William Wilberforce in his successful re-election for Yorkshire in 1807 on the grounds of his anti-slavery stand.

Since 1770 Tuke had continued his religious and classical studies. His thirty-year friendship with the American Quaker Lindley Murray, who settled in York in 1784, proved a great stimulus to him as a writer. From 1803 Tuke became a regular contributor to the *Monthly Review*, the *Eclectic Review*, and the *Christian Observer* with articles on Quakerism, theology, and biblical translation. Between 1801 and 1815 five works appeared under his name, of which the most important was *The Principles of Religion as Professed by the Society of Christians Usually called Quakers* (1805), which had run to twelve editions by 1852. Written for Quaker youth and widely read by British and American Quakers it was also intended for an interdenominational readership; translations had appeared in German, French, and Danish by 1855. Tuke's other works included selections from Quaker writings (1801) and the scriptures (1809), two volumes of *Biographical Notices* of Quakers (1813 and 1815), and *The Duties of Religion and Morality as Inculcated in the Holy Scriptures* (1807). From 1805 a growing evangelical emphasis had appeared in Tuke's writings—in his attitude to the primacy of scripture and in his discussion of Quaker doctrine. His writings proved a significant foundation in the movement of British Quakers towards evangelicalism, completed by Joseph John Gurney and others in the 1830s.

After a painful illness Tuke died at St Saviourgate, York, on 11 August 1814 and was buried five days later at the Quaker burial-ground, having been much respected in that city. Through his son Samuel, Tuke was the grandfather of Daniel Hack Tuke and of James Hack Tuke.

H. F. GREGG

Sources S. Wright, *Friends in York: the dynamics of Quaker revival, 1780–1860* (1995) · S. Tuke, *Memoirs of Samuel Tuke*, 2 vols. (1857) · W. K. Sessions and M. Sessions, *The Tukes of York in the seventeenth, eighteenth and nineteenth centuries* (1971) · digest registers of births, marriages, and burials, RS Friends, Lond. [Yorkshire; microfilm, reels 21–5] · L. Murray, *A biographical sketch of Henry Tuke* (1815) · R. M. Jones, *The later periods of Quakerism*, 2 vols. (1921) · *Biographical catalogue: being an account of the lives of Friends and others whose portraits are in the London Friends' Institute*, Society of Friends (1888) · J. Smith, ed., *A descriptive catalogue of Friends' books*, 2 vols. (1867); suppl. (1893) · *DNB*
Archives Borth. Inst., corresp. and papers; family MSS
Likenesses silhouette, 1809, RS Friends, Lond. · C. Wilkinson, portrait (after drawing, 1889), RS Friends, Lond.
Wealth at death £7500: Wright, *Friends in York*, 147

Tuke, Henry Scott [Harry] (1858–1929), landscape and figure painter, was born at Lawrence House, St Lawrence, York, on 12 June 1858, the second son of Daniel Hack *Tuke (1827–1895), a physician, and his wife, Esther Maria

Henry Scott Tuke (1858–1929), self-portrait, 1920

Stickney (1826–1917), of Ridgmont, Holderness. His great-grandfather William *Tuke (1732–1822) had founded the Friends' Retreat in York in 1792 for the care of the mentally ill. Daniel Tuke continued in the profession of caring for psychiatric patients and wrote about insanity. Owing to his father's ill health the family moved to Falmouth, Cornwall, and at the age of six Tuke was sent to a Quaker school at Weston-super-Mare. Unlike his brother William, who went into the medical profession, Harry Tuke had shown artistic promise from an early age. His sister Maria was also artistically gifted. In 1875 Tuke entered the Slade School of Fine Art, London, where he studied under Alphonse Legros. While at the Slade he made friends with Thomas Cooper Gotch. Tuke produced some fine etchings as a student, including one of his brother William. He had his first oil painting, *The Good Samaritan*, accepted for exhibition at the Royal Academy in 1879. A group portrait of his Slade friends, the Stantlet sisters and Caroline Yates (the future Mrs Gotch) (York City Art Gallery), was exhibited at the academy in 1880. For the rest of his professional career, from 1879 onwards, Tuke kept a register of paintings listing most of his major works as well as studies.

From November 1880 to July 1881 Tuke studied art in Florence, Italy. There he met the artist Arthur Lemon, who took him to stay with Charles Heath Wilson at Forte dei Marmi, where they spent a month painting the male nude outdoors. This was the style of painting and a way of life

that suited Tuke, and it became his métier. In October 1881 Tuke travelled to Paris to study at the atelier of Jean Paul Laurens. He was in the company of many of his Slade friends, including (Albert) Chevallier Tayler, Fred Millard, and William Strang. They all went to admire the French painter Jules Bastein Lepage, but it was the American artist Alexander Harrison who had the biggest influence on Tuke, as he too painted the nude outdoors. While studying in Paris, Tuke made regular trips home to Bournemouth, where his parents and brother William were living. Towards the end of his studies in Paris, William died of tuberculosis, and his family decided to move to Hanwell in Middlesex. It was a watershed in Tuke's life. He decided to return to Cornwall and went first, in 1883, to Newlyn, where many of his friends from the Slade were based. Here in 1884 he painted *Summertime*, the subject of which was boys in boats, a theme that was to prove enduring in Tuke's work. On 5 June 1885 Tuke moved back to Falmouth, renting rooms in a cottage at Pennance Point outside the town where he could paint male nudes on the local beaches in privacy. He also painted several pictures featuring his housekeeper, Mrs Fouracre, such as *The Message* (1890; Falmouth Art Gallery). Later he built a studio at Pennance which was his base for the next forty years, and he purchased an old French brigantine, the *Julie of Nantes*, which became his floating studio. Tuke used local lads and fishermen in his paintings executed on board the *Julie*, including *All Hands to the Pump* (Tate collection), shown at the Royal Academy in 1889 and bought for the nation by the Chantrey Bequest.

Tuke's earlier nudes are somewhat over-worked; it is in his studies that his fresh, unique ability to paint skin tones reflected in water is visible. The evident homoerotic element in his paintings has given rise to speculation that Tuke was homosexual. The male nude was certainly his muse, but it was not an unusual subject and showed in his *plein air* painting 'alertness to tensions and movements in the human body and his ability to combine classical compositional principles with naturalistic detail, while giving coherence by sensitive rendering of atmosphere' (Hopkins, 418). Apart from his works, there is little evidence to support this view of Tuke's sexuality, although it is possible that evidence was destroyed by his sister after his death. *August Blue* (1893–4; Tate collection) was his turning point. It freed him from the Newlyn group association, as the picture had no narrative. The title was made up from the principal colours in the painting rather than the subject, an idea initiated by Whistler. The title was taken from Swinburne's poem 'Sundew':

> Thou wast not worth green midsummer,
> Nor fit to live to August Blue,
> My Sundew, not remembering her.

It reflected the growing influence of the aesthetic movement and impressionism on his work. The turn of the century saw a broadening of Tuke's style: he became freer in his handling of the paint in works such as *To the Morning Sun* (1904; Hugh Lane Municipal Gallery of Modern Art,

Dublin). In 1886 Tuke was a founder member of the New English Art Club; he was elected to the Royal Academy firstly as an associate member in 1900 and then as a Royal Academician in 1914. His diploma work, *A Bathing Group*, was of male nudes on the rocks in Falmouth.

By 1914 Tuke was also a highly-sought after portrait painter. Among others, he depicted Sir George Armytage and Mrs Stanley Boyd MD, as well as local people and sporting heroes such as the cricketers Ranjitsinjhi and W. G. Grace (Middlesex County Cricket Club, London). Alfred De Pass, a South African, became a great friend and benefactor to Tuke and was an important art collector who donated several works by the artist to Falmouth Art Gallery as well as the National Gallery of South Africa.

Tuke's involvement with ships and boats was a lifelong passion. He painted every kind of sailing ship, but his greatest love was the square-rigger. He painted the *Cutty Sark*, which was moored in Falmouth from 1923 to 1938, several times. Tuke went on occasional trips on square-riggers, including in 1908 the *Grace Har'var*, from Falmouth to Bremerhaven. He also visited St Tropez and Genoa and painted boats there. He used mainly watercolours on his travels and developed great skill in this medium, which was recognized in 1911 by his full membership of the Royal Watercolour Society. He had numerous racing yachts and helped found the Falmouth Sailing Club in 1894, becoming its commodore in 1898. It was his love of sailing which was to take him on his final ill-fated trip to the West Indies in November 1923 with the explorer F. A. Mitchell Hedges. Tuke contracted malaria and was seriously ill. The disease seriously weakened his heart and eventually led to his death, at Pennance Budock, Cornwall, four years later, on 13 March 1929. He was buried in Falmouth cemetery. He did not marry. Tuke was a handsome man with classically proportioned features, 'Well built, about medium height with black hair and a strong, manly face absolutely bronzed with the sun, he looked every inch an athlete—certainly anything but a typical artist' (Kickmann, 606).

CATHERINE S. WALLACE

Sources D. Wainwright and K. Dinn, *Henry Scott Tuke, 1858–1929, under canvas* (1989) · M. T. Sainsbury, *Henry Scott Tuke: a memoir* (1933) · *The registers of Henry Scott Tuke*, ed. B. D. Price, 2nd edn (1983) · F. Kickmann, 'The life story of a famous painter', *Windsor Magazine* (1895), 606 [interview] · M. Postle and W. Vaughan, *The artist's model from Etty to Spencer* (1999), 124 · C. Wallace, *Before the mast* (1998) [exhibition catalogue, Falmouth Art Gallery, July 1998] · b. cert. · d. cert. · *CGPLA Eng. & Wales* (1929) · J. Hopkins, 'Tuke, Henry Scott', *The dictionary of art*, ed. J. Turner (1996)
Archives priv. coll., register of paintings
Likenesses H. S. Tuke, self-portrait, 1920, Royal Institution of Cornwall, Truro [*see illus.*] · Elliott & Fry, cabinet photograph, NPG
Wealth at death £35,840 2s. 5d.: probate, 26 April 1929, *CGPLA Eng. & Wales*

Tuke, James Hack (1819–1896), philanthropist, was born in York on 13 September 1819. He was the seventh child of Samuel *Tuke (1784–1857) and his wife, Priscilla, *née* Hack (1784–1827). The Tukes were a leading Quaker family in York, much involved in local charitable activity. Daniel

James Hack Tuke (1819–1896), by Charles Napier Kennedy, 1877

Hack *Tuke, mental specialist, was James's younger brother.

James was educated at the Friends' school in York, and in 1835 entered his father's wholesale tea and coffee business in the city. On 3 August 1848 he married his father's ward, Elizabeth (*d.* 1869), the daughter of Edward and Elizabeth Janson of Tottenham. The youngest of their five children was Dame Margaret Janson *Tuke. In 1852 Tuke became a partner in the banking firm of Sharples & Co. of Hitchin, Hertfordshire, which from that time became his home. During his early years in York he devoted constant thought to educational subjects, as well as to the management of the Friends' asylum known as The Retreat, which his great-grandfather had been largely instrumental in establishing. In the autumn of 1845 Tuke accompanied William Forster (1784–1854) and Joseph Crosfield on a tour of the United States and Canada. During this journey he visited all the asylums for the insane that came within his reach, and noted his observations on them for the benefit of his father and others interested in The Retreat. He also, in 1846 and 1853, read papers to the Friends' Educational Society on the free schools and educational institutions of the United States. It was on this American tour that he first developed an interest in the emigration question.

Throughout his life Tuke devoted whatever leisure he had from business to public projects and charitable concerns. He worked on nearly all the important committees of Friends' associations, assisted in founding others, was treasurer for eighteen years of the Friends' Foreign Mission Association, and chairman for eight years of the Friends' Central Education Board. He was involved in the National Freedman's Aid Union of Great Britain, which assisted freed slaves in the aftermath of the American Civil War, and in 1869 collaborated with Emily Davies in establishing at Hitchin the first British University College for Women (later to become Girton College, Cambridge).

Tuke was one of the first to enter Paris after its evacuation by the Germans in March 1871. As a commissioner of the Friends' War Victims Fund he undertook to distribute £20,000 subscribed by English Quakers for the relief of those whose property around the city had been destroyed during the siege. Their work was nearly completed when the revolution of the commune broke out. Tuke was strongly hostile towards the insurgents, and published an account of his experiences as *A Visit to Paris in the Spring of 1871* (1871). In 1879 he published *A Sketch of the Life of John Fothergill, MD, FRS*, the founder of Ackworth School. His first wife having died in 1869, Tuke married Georgina Mary, daughter of Evory Kennedy, on 9 November 1882. An Anglican in religion, Georgina became an active participant in Tuke's charitable activities.

It is by his philanthropic work in Ireland that Tuke is best remembered. His interest in Ireland was first aroused during the great famine of 1845–50. In December 1846 Tuke joined William Forster and the Irish Quaker Marcus Goodbody on their tour of the distressed counties of north-western Ireland. Tuke's narrative of the visit, exposing the scale of the catastrophe and the inadequacy of the government's response, and recounting the group's efforts to establish soup kitchens in the localities, was published in January 1847 and was widely distributed by Quaker relief bodies in Ireland and England. He returned to Ireland for a second tour in September 1847. His observations, published as *A Visit to Connaught in the Autumn of 1847* (1847), warned of the impending collapse of the poor-law system in the west, advocated the provision of public works on waste-land reclamation, fishery development, and railway construction, and urged the passage of an encumbered estates act to free the land for investment. His criticism of individual landlords by name caused some controversy in parliament and the press. Despite the threat of a horsewhipping, he returned to Erris in February 1848 to substantiate his exposure of J. Walshe's clearances. However, the Dublin Central Relief Committee expressed embarrassment over Tuke's account of evictions on Sir R. O'Donnell's Achill Island estate (they were at the time co-operating with O'Donnell in promoting flax cultivation in Mayo), and Tuke was persuaded to amend these references in a second edition of his book. In 1848 Tuke suffered from a dangerous attack of cholera, contracted when visiting the hospital sheds provided by his father for the starving Irish who had sought refuge in York.

The impression produced upon Tuke's mind by the scenes he had witnessed in Ireland in 1847 was never effaced. He remained active in Irish charity work in the 1850s, and became increasingly convinced that emigration held out the best hope for the Irish west. Early in 1880, when the threatened acute distress in the west of Ireland was absorbing public attention, Tuke, urged by his old friend W. E. Forster (chief secretary, 1880–82), spent two months in the distressed or 'congested' districts, distributing in relief £1200 privately subscribed by Quakers. His observations were recorded in letters printed for circulation among his friends, in letters to *The Times*, in an article in the *Nineteenth Century* (August 1880), and more fully in his pamphlet *Irish Distress and its Remedies* (1880). The pamphlet was immediately recognized by the members of all political parties as an authoritative statement of the economic position, and ran rapidly through six editions. Holding that Irish distress was due to economic and not to political causes, he advocated state-aided land purchase, the gradual establishment of peasant proprietorship, the construction of light railways in remote districts, and the fostering by government of fishing and other local industries. For the smallest and poorest tenants, whom no legislation could immediately benefit, he urged 'family emigration'. He proposed a scheme of government-aided emigration to Manitoba, and toured Canada and the USA, afterwards publishing his observations (*Nineteenth Century*, Feb 1881). As a result, Forster inserted a clause in the Irish Land Act, 1881, to facilitate state-aided family emigration by means of loans, although this proved unworkable.

Twice during 1881, and in February 1882, Tuke visited Ireland, again publishing his views (*Contemporary Review*, April 1882), with the result that at a meeting held at the house of the duke of Bedford on 31 March an influential committee was formed to administer 'Mr Tuke's Fund', and £9000 was subscribed to carry out a comprehensive scheme of family emigration. By 4 April 1882 Tuke was again in Ireland, and within a few weeks 1200 emigrants had been sent to America at a cost of nearly £9000. On his return to England he described the vehement desire of the Irish for further assistance (*Nineteenth Century*, July 1882). His committee then prevailed on the government to insert a clause in the Arrears of Rent (Ireland) Act granting £100,000 to further assist family emigration from Ireland. Part of this sum was spent by government, and the rest was entrusted to Tuke's committee for use in Mayo and Galway. In 1883 the number of emigrants was 5380. Owing to the continued demand for emigration, the Tuke committee next obtained a further grant under the Tramways (Ireland) Act of 1883, by means of which 2800 persons emigrated in 1884, making about 9500 in all. The labour involved in this work was enormous, and it was largely carried out during severe winter weather, in districts which lacked railway communications. Tuke personally superintended most of the work, which included the selection of suitable families, arrangements for their clothing, their conveyance to the port of embarkation (often a distance of 50 miles by road or boat), as well as their reception on landing in the United States or Canada, and their conveyance to their final destinations. The total expenditure of the Tuke Fund amounted to £70,000, nearly one-third of which was raised by private subscription. Tuke responded to clerical and nationalist criticism of this work in two articles in the *Nineteenth Century* (February 1885 and March 1889).

In the winter of 1885–6 distress again became acute in some of the western districts because of another failure of the potato crop. The government made a relief grant, but appealed to Tuke to avert famine by supplying seed potatoes. Tuke raised by private subscription a sum of £5000, with which seed potatoes were purchased and distributed under his personal supervision on Achill Island and the Mayo coast. In *Achill and the West of Ireland* (1886) and *The Condition of Donegal* (1889)—a collection of letters to *The Times* written during the distress of 1889—Tuke again pointed out the measures he deemed necessary for the permanent improvement of the congested districts. His recommendations bore fruit in 1889, when the government passed a bill for promoting the construction of light railways, and again when the 1891 Irish Land Act established the congested districts board, with an income of £40,000 a year, for the development of these districts. Tuke was closely associated with the planning of both these measures, which realized nearly all that he had advocated. Until 1894, when his health failed, he was an active member of the board, and he visited Ireland every month to attend its meetings.

Like his close friend W. E. Forster, Tuke was appalled by the violence of the land war (1879–82), and was convinced that the Irish were incapable of self-government. He vigorously opposed Gladstone's 1886 Home Rule Bill, fearing it would open the door to 'Socialism' in Ireland and deliver policing into the hands of the 'Dictator Parnell'. He presided at joint meetings of Irish and British Quakers called to protest against home rule in 1886 and 1893, and was fully supportive of the 'constructive unionist' policy pursued by Arthur Balfour from 1887. In 1884 the committees of both the Athenaeum and Reform clubs elected Tuke an honorary member. It was largely through his efforts that the emigrants' information office was established in 1886 as a department of the Colonial Office. He was invited to stand as an MP for York several times but, like his father before him, declined to do so since it would, from a traditional Quaker perspective, have appeared too worldly to be involved in parliamentary politics.

Of slight, erect figure and of medium height, Tuke possessed an unusual grace and courtesy of manner and an almost magnetic influence over others. The unique position which he held may be inferred from the fact that, for the last sixteen years of his life, his advice on nearly all Irish questions was sought by the chief secretaries of both political parties. He died on 13 January 1896, and was buried four days later at the Quaker burial-ground, Hitchin.

MILLER CHRISTY, *rev.* PETER GRAY

Sources E. Fry, *James Hack Tuke: a memoir* (1899) · H. E. Hatton, *The largest amount of good: Quaker relief in Ireland 1654–1921* (1993) · H. F. Gregg, 'English and Irish Quakers and Irish home rule', *A Quaker miscellany for Edward H. Milligan*, ed. D. Blamires, J. Greenwood, and A. Kerr (1985) · Boase, *Mod. Eng. biog.*

Archives Borth. Inst., papers · RS Friends, Lond., letters | BL, corresp. with Arthur James Balfour, Add. MS 49817, *passim* · Wellcome L., letters to John Hodgkin

Likenesses C. N. Kennedy, portrait, 1877, NPG [*see illus.*] · photograph, repro. in Fry, *James Hack Tuke*

Wealth at death £92,067 11s. 2d.: probate, 8 May 1896, *CGPLA Eng. & Wales*

Tuke [*née* Lear], **Mabel Kate** (1871–1962), suffragette, was born on 19 May 1871 at 40 Crescent Road, Plumstead, Kent, the eldest of the four children of Richard Lear (1834–1894), clerk of works in the Royal Engineers department at Woolwich arsenal, and his wife, Emma Margaret, *née* Lear (*b.* 1836). Both her parents had been born in Alverstoke in Hampshire and were probably cousins. Nothing is known of the type of education Mabel Lear enjoyed; after it ended she does not appear to have had any paid occupation.

The Lear family lived for some of the years of Mabel's youth in Lichfield, Staffordshire, but by 1891 had returned to Plumstead, where on 25 February 1895, two months after the death of her father, she married James Quarton Braidwood, a gas engineer. Nothing can be traced of the fate of this marriage; it was presumably ended, possibly in South Africa, by the death of her husband. In 1901 she married, probably in South Africa, George Moxley Tuke, a captain in the South African constabulary. He, too, died young, however, and in 1905 Mabel Tuke returned to England. In the course of this voyage she got to know of Frederick and Emmeline Pethick-Lawrence. It was through a growing friendship with the latter, who held her interest with a description of her work with the Espérance Girls' Club in Somers Town, that she was introduced to the embryonic London branch of the Women's Social and Political Union, the organization that had been formed in Manchester in 1903 by Emmeline Pankhurst to lobby for women's enfranchisement. From 1906 until the outbreak of war in 1914 Mabel Tuke was the honorary secretary of the WSPU, in titular charge of its head office in Clement's Inn. She was particularly close to Christabel and Emmeline Pankhurst, to whom she was affectionately known as Pansy, a nickname obviously inspired by her luminous dark eyes. Beautiful, soft, and appealing, she represented the 'womanly' image that the Pankhursts were keen to promote in order to counteract the popular conception of the suffragettes. She was not involved in any of the WSPU's militant activities until, on 1 March 1912, with Emmeline Pankhurst, she went to Downing Street and threw a stone through the window of no. 10. For this she received a sentence of three weeks' imprisonment and while in Holloway was charged with conspiracy, along with Christabel and Emmeline Pankhurst and the Pethick-Lawrences. She was, however, dismissed from the case on 4 April.

On 15 June, with the leaders of the WSPU in prison or, in the case of Christabel Pankhurst, in Paris, Mabel Tuke took the chair at a triumphant WSPU fund-raising meeting in the Albert Hall. From prison Emmeline Pethick-Lawrence wrote to her that Mr Marshall, the WSPU's solicitor, had told her that he 'could not believe that you were not a practised orator and chairman. Said he had

Mabel Kate Tuke (1871–1962), by Mrs Albert Broom

never been at a meeting more brilliantly conducted' (BL, Add. MS 58226, fol. 2). Tuke had never been strong, however, and after this experience her health deteriorated and in the autumn, after the Pethick-Lawrences had been expelled from the WSPU, she embarked on a recuperative sea journey to South Africa. On her return she frequently visited Christabel Pankhurst in Paris, and remained a loyal friend to the Pankhursts after they had ceased their involvement with the suffrage cause. In 1925 she took part, with Emmeline and Christabel Pankhurst, in an ill-fated scheme to run a tea-shop (the English Tea-Shop of Good Hope) at Juan-les-Pins on the French riviera. Mrs Tuke provided most of the capital and did the baking. In later life she lived in the care of her nephew the Revd Alban Prentice at Shadforth in co. Durham. She died of cerebral thrombosis in Ashbrooke Nursing Home, 12 St John's Road, Nevilles Cross, Durham, on 22 November 1962.   ELIZABETH CRAWFORD

Sources BL, H. D. Harben corresp., Add. MS 58226, fols. 1, 2, 7, 175 · D. Mitchell, *Queen Christabel: a biography of Christabel Pankhurst* (1977) · b. cert. · m. cert. · d. cert. · E. Crawford, *The women's suffrage movement: a reference guide, 1866–1928* (1999) · CGPLA Eng. & Wales (1963)
Likenesses photograph, c.1908, Museum of London · Mrs A. Broom, photograph, priv. coll. [*see illus.*]
Wealth at death £1860 5s. 10d.: probate, 4 Feb 1963, CGPLA Eng. & Wales

Tuke, Dame Margaret Janson (1862–1947), educationist and college head, was born in Hitchin, Hertfordshire, on 13 March 1862, the youngest of five children of James Hack *Tuke (1819–1896), banker and philanthropist, and his first wife, Elizabeth Janson (d. 1869). In unpublished autobiographical notes written in 1942, she recorded that her Quaker upbringing gave her a lifelong dislike of 'any ill feeling, clique or schism', but while she dutifully attended Bible meetings 'it was in a cold, unreceptive spirit', and she joined the Church of England in 1946. Her childhood was marred by the death of her mother and two of her sisters.

Margaret was educated at home until the age of fifteen mainly by a succession of, she believed, woefully inadequate governesses. She spent the next two years at St John's School in Withdean, Brighton, where she was similarly unimpressed by the standard of teaching. At seventeen she returned to Hitchin from where she travelled to Bedford College, London, one day a week during the Michaelmas term of 1879. She explained in her autobiographical notes that she entered Newnham College, Cambridge, in 1885 not as 'an enthusiast or firm believer in the new Women's Movement, but as an enquirer'; none the less she quickly became 'a devotee of the Higher Education of Women'. In 1888 she gained a first in the medieval and modern languages tripos. Her BA and MA were conferred upon her by Trinity College, Dublin, in 1905.

Margaret Tuke went on to hold a number of positions at Newnham including secretary to Helen Gladstone, the vice-principal, and staff lecturer in modern languages. Her association with Newnham continued long after she had left the college: she served on the governing body, on the college council, and she was an associate fellow. It was her love of change, but also her commitment to spreading the Newnham ethos, which led her to accept the post of tutor to women students at Bristol University College in 1905. She enjoyed this short period in her life, and viewed it as an oasis between the more demanding times at Newnham and Bedford. She took up her appointment as principal of Bedford College, London, in 1907, and in the next twenty-two years the college was so completely transformed that she came to be regarded as its second founder. The college moved to purpose-built premises in Regent's Park, student numbers nearly doubled, and academic standards were raised. She served on the senate of London University from 1911 to 1929. As principal of Bedford College, she aimed to attract staff who were highly regarded in their field, regarding it as particularly important for a women's college to develop a high academic reputation. She promoted the move to establish London University professorships and readerships at the college, and was also keen that there should be a balance in the numbers of women and men holding these titles.

Margaret Tuke retired in 1929 and subsequently received a number of honours in recognition of her work in education. She became fellow of Bedford College in 1930; the following year the college paid tribute to her when the Tuke Building was opened in Regent's Park, and the college commissioned Francis Dodd to paint her portrait. She was appointed DBE in 1932, and was awarded an honorary doctorate by Reading University in 1937. During

Dame Margaret Janson Tuke (1862–1947), by unknown photographer

for women who, like herself, never married. In 1928 she was appointed by the senate of London University to join the committee investigating the ban on women medical students at various London teaching hospitals.

Nora Cooke-Hurle described in the *Newnham College Roll* how Margaret Tuke's 'small and slight body and wonderful eyes … struck one at first sight' (Cooke-Hurle, 1948). She impressed colleagues, friends, and family with her impartiality, her quiet determination to achieve her goals, and her deep humanity. Margaret Tuke died at her home, Rectory Manor, Pirton, near Hitchin, Hertfordshire, on 21 February 1947. SOPHIE BADHAM

Sources M. Tuke, 'Autobiographical notes', 1942, Newnham College Library, Cambridge [second copy in Royal Holloway College Library] · G. Jebb, *The Fawcett lecture, 1952–1953, on the life of Dame Margaret Tuke* (1952) · N. Cooke-Hurle, 'Dame Margaret Janson Tuke', *Newnham College Roll Letter* (1948) · G. Jebb, 'Margaret Tuke as principal of Bedford College, 1907–1929', *Newnham College Roll Letter* (1948) · M. J. Tuke, *A history of Bedford College for Women, 1849–1937* (1939) · C. Dyhouse, *No distinction of sex? Women in British universities, 1870–1939* (1995) · [A. B. White and others], eds., *Newnham College register, 1871–1971*, 2nd edn, 1 (1979)

Archives Newnham College, Cambridge, Newnham College papers · Royal Holloway College, London, Bedford College papers, personal file; autobiographical notes, corresp., and papers for her history of Bedford College, AR 150/D 203; RF 130

Likenesses F. Dodd, oils, 1934, Royal Holloway College, Egham, Surrey, Founder's Building · eleven photographs, U. Lond., Royal Holloway archives · photograph, repro. in Tuke, *A history of Bedford College* [*see illus.*] · two portraits, Royal Holloway College, Egham, Surrey, Founder's Building

Wealth at death £24,861 5s. 7d.: probate, 16 June 1947, *CGPLA Eng. & Wales*

her retirement, as well as indulging her love of travel she served on the governing body of Hitchin Girls' Grammar School; she was a member of the international fellowship committee of the British Federation of University Women (she had previously been vice-president and president of the federation, and was also involved in the International Federation of University Women). She was asked to write a history of Bedford College, and her *History of Bedford College for Women, 1849–1937* is characteristically modest in that it makes scant reference to her role in shaping developments in the college.

Politics interested Margaret Tuke throughout her life. She was the leader of the Conservatives in the Political Society at Newnham. She belonged to the Women's Local Government Society and later became an active member of the National Union of Women's Suffrage Societies. She was one of the original members of the Conservative and Unionist Women's Franchise Association. Her most passionate concern was, however, for women's education. She was a member of the Association of University Women Teachers and was, for a time, its president. She regretted the fact that few women seemed to see a university education as an end in itself, and wanted more women of the leisured classes to study for degrees (see her article 'Women students in the universities', *Contemporary Review*, 1928, 71–7). She also wanted women to be able to enter a greater variety of professions. She showed great concern for women who needed to earn their living, and

Tuke, Sir Samuel, first baronet (*c*.1615–1674), royalist army officer and playwright, was the third son of George Tuke of Frayling, Essex, and his wife Elizabeth Wase. He was admitted to Gray's Inn on 14 August 1635, at the same time as his eldest brother, George Tuke. Tuke acquired military experience on the continent prior to the outbreak of the civil war. He sided with the royalists and by late 1642 held a major's commission in the duke of York's regiment. He served in the earl of Newcastle's northern army, and on 28 March 1644, at Lincoln, he wrote a sharp letter to George Porter, Newcastle's major-general of foot, at Newark. He fought at Marston Moor on 2 July 1644 and subsequently served intermittently with the Northern horse who escaped from the battle. He wrote six letters to Prince Rupert from the Welsh marches in September 1644.

In 1645 Tuke served in the west of England under George Goring and, being the eldest colonel of horse in that army, expected to be made major-general of horse, but was disappointed by the double-dealing of George Porter, Goring's brother-in-law, who received the rank. Tuke resigned his commission and endeavoured to force Porter to a duel, but was obliged by the council of war to apologize for his conduct. In 1648 Tuke was one of the defenders of Colchester, and acted as one of the commissioners for the besieged when it surrendered. He never compounded and went into exile in France.

In 1649 John Evelyn mentioned meeting 'my cousin

Tuke' at Paris (*Diary of John Evelyn*, 2.8). Tuke remained abroad during the protectorate, gaining in exile the reputation of a court wit and formidable duellist, 'soe deadly it seems is that Collonels hand' (*Nicholas Papers*, 2.39). Secretary Nicholas commented on Tuke, 'whom some think an atheist but a great oracle in this little Court' (ibid., 2.10). Tuke attended Henry, duke of Gloucester, and had hopes of becoming his governor. 'I will undertake for him if he can get that charge', Nicholas wrote, '[that] he shall not stick to conform to any profession of religion' (ibid., 2.11). On 20 September 1657 Queen Henrietta Maria recommended Tuke to Charles II as secretary to the duke of York, to which the king, at Sir Edward Hyde's instigation, replied that he was unfit for that office. By 1659, if not earlier, Tuke had become a Roman Catholic.

After the Restoration, Tuke was treated with great favour by Charles II, who sent him to the French court on 1 March 1661 to condole on the death of Cardinal Mazarin. He was knighted on 3 March 1664 and created baronet on the 28th. He married his first wife, Mary (d. 1666), daughter of Edward Guldeford of Hamstead, Kent, and a kinswoman to Lord Arundell of Wardour, in 1664. His second wife, whom he married in 1668, was Mary (d. 1705), daughter of Edward Sheldon of Ditchford, Warwickshire, a dresser in the service of Queen Catherine of Braganza. Letters from her to Mary Evelyn, wife of John Evelyn, were printed in the appendix to Wheatley's nineteenth-century edition of Evelyn's diary (*Diary of John Evelyn*, 4.59, 62). In 1679 she was accused of tampering with one of the witnesses to the Popish Plot. In 1692 she accompanied Catherine, by then queen dowager, to Portugal, where she died in 1705.

Tuke was the author of a play, *The Adventures of Five Hours*, the first edition of which appeared in 1661 and a third and revised edition in 1671. The comedy (or, as Tuke called it, tragi-comedy) was adapted from *Los empeños de seis horas*, attributed by Tuke to Calderón (but probably not by him), which the king had suggested Tuke produce for the English stage. Pepys attended the first public performance of the play at Lincoln's Inn Fields on 8 January 1663, finding it, 'in one word … the best, for the variety and the most excellent continuance of the plot to the very end, that ever I saw or think ever shall' (Pepys, *Diary*, 4.8), and going on to see the play again nine days later. Three years later he reflected that it was still 'the best play that ever I read in my life' (*Diary of Samuel Pepys*, ed. Wheatley, 5.403). The comedy was a major success. The plot-laden structure of the play and its tone—'very admittible and not one word of ribaldry' (Pepys, *Diary*, 4.8)—which Pepys admired so much has been described as starting 'a vogue for cape and sword plays that lasted for several years, a vogue for plays with action-filled plots, exemplary characters, and a high-toned purity that did not survive the decade' (Corman, 55–6). Complimentary verses by Evelyn, Abraham Cowley, and others are prefixed to the second edition of the play. In *The Session of the Poets* (1696) Cowley is charged that he 'writ verses unjustly in praise of Sam Tuke' and Tuke's poetical pretensions are mocked. Tuke is mentioned

among the authors of *Pompey the Great* in 1664 in a catalogue of publications of Henry Herringman in 1684. He also contributed to the *Transactions* of the Royal Society (of which he was one of the first members) a history of the ordering and generation of green Colchester oysters (reprinted in T. Sprat, *History of the Royal Society*, ed. J. I. Cope and H. Whitmore, 1966, 307–19). A pamphlet on the character of Charles II has been attributed to him (and is reprinted in E. M. Thompson, ed., *Correspondence of the Family of Hatton*, 2 vols., CS, new ser., 22–23, 1878, 1.20).

Tuke was prominent as an advocate of the claims of loyal Catholics to a remission of the penal laws, and was heard on their behalf before the House of Lords on 21 June 1661 and, according to John Evelyn, also on 4 July 1660 and 15 March 1673. Anthony Wood described him as 'a person of complete honour and ingenuity' (Wood, *Ath. Oxon.*, 2.802) and Evelyn frequently mentions him with high praise. 'I do find him, I think', wrote Pepys, describing an accidental meeting at his bookseller's where they chatted about John Evelyn's garden, 'a little conceited but of very fine discourse as any I ever heard almost' (Pepys, *Diary*, 9.449). Tuke died at Somerset House on the Strand on 26 January 1674 and was buried in the chapel there. His eldest son, Charles (1671–1690), fought for James II in Ireland as a captain in Tyrconnell's horse and died of the wounds he received at the battle of the Boyne.

C. H. FIRTH, *rev.* ANDREW J. HOPPER

Sources GEC, *Baronetage*, vol. 3 · *Diary of John Evelyn*, ed. W. Bray, new edn, 2–3, ed. H. B. Wheatley (1879) · *The Nicholas papers*, ed. G. F. Warner, 4 vols., CS, new ser., 40, 50, 57, 3rd ser., 31 (1886–1920) · P. R. Newman, *Royalist officers in England and Wales, 1642–1660: a biographical dictionary* (1981) · P. R. Newman, *The old service: royalist regimental colonels and the civil war, 1642–1646* (1993) · *Memoirs of Prince Rupert and the cavaliers including their private correspondence*, ed. E. Warburton, 3 vols. (1849), vol. 1 · W. Ansell Day, ed., *The Pythouse papers* (1879) · *CSP dom., 1660–61* · *The manuscripts of the duke of Beaufort … the earl of Donoughmore*, HMC, 27 (1891) · Wood, *Ath. Oxon.*, 2nd edn, vol. 2 · J. Foster, *The register of admissions to Gray's Inn, 1521–1889, together with the register of marriages in Gray's Inn chapel, 1695–1754* (privately printed, London, 1889) · *The diary of Samuel Pepys*, ed. H. B. Wheatley and others, 10 vols. (1893–9), vols. 3, 5, 8 · Pepys, *Diary*, vols. 4–5, 9 · B. Corman, 'Comedy', *The Cambridge companion to English Restoration theatre*, ed. D. P. Fisk (2000), 52–69 · W. C. Hazlitt, ed., *A select collection of old English plays, originally published by Robert Dodsley in the year 1744*, 15 vols. (1874–6), vol. 15 · BL, Rupert corresp., Add. MS 18981, fols. 255, 257, 268, 274, 285 · will, PRO, PROB 11/345, sig. 78 · IGI · W. C. Metcalfe, ed., *The visitations of Essex*, 2 vols., Harleian Society, 13–14 (1878–9)

Archives BL, Add. MS 18981, fols. 255, 257, 268, 274, 285

Wealth at death see will, 1674, PRO, PROB 11/345, sig. 78

Tuke, Samuel (1784–1857), asylum reformer and philanthropist, was born on 31 July 1784 at York, the second of the six children of Henry *Tuke (1755–1814), tea dealer and Quaker writer, and Mary Maria Scott (1748–1815). In 1810 he married Priscilla Hack (1784–1827), daughter of James Hack of Chichester and Hannah Jeffreys of London, and they had thirteen children, including James Hack *Tuke and Daniel Hack *Tuke. Samuel had wished to become a doctor, but economic reasons dictated an entry to the family tea business in York at the age of thirteen, after education at Ackworth School, Yorkshire, and Blaxland's School, Hitchin.

Samuel Tuke's portrait shows a melancholic cast of feature which reflected humility in relation to the doctrine of perfection, and perhaps a pessimism about his own salvation. This was a driving motivation in his resolve 'to be never idle', and thus in his unceasing promotion of the public good. Much of his activity was associated with The Retreat, a Quaker asylum founded in 1796 by his grandfather, William *Tuke, and where Tuke acted as treasurer from 1822 to 1853. This establishment rejected traditional methods of treating the insane as akin to animals in favour of a moral treatment that emphasized similarity, not difference, between the mentally ill and the sane. A request from his father to write about The Retreat's methods led in the following year to a short article in *The Philanthropist* (1811), which was extended and published as *Description of The Retreat* (1813). This was the first detailed account of reformed methods of treating the insane, and was significant in the wider diffusion of moral treatment, particularly in British and American asylums. Tuke thus exceeded his hope in writing the *Description* that 'by the weight and importance of ... facts' one can 'almost force the general introduction of a better system'.

The *Description* also provided the trigger for reform of the York Lunatic Asylum, which had betrayed the humane ideals of its foundation in 1777. Its physician took public exception to the *Description*, thus enabling Tuke (and others) to create publicity by writing pseudonymous letters to the press, recruiting new reforming governors, and providing evidence of abuse to the reforming magistrate, Godfrey Higgins, during local reform of the institution during 1813–14 and later, when there was discussion over the need for a national reform of asylums, at hearings of the select committee on madhouses (1814–16). Higgins initiated a new pauper lunatic asylum at Wakefield and asked Tuke to advise the architects. Conscious that the central issue of the York scandal had been 'who keeps the keepers', Tuke emphasized that asylum architecture should provide 'the facility of inspection' for patients and attendants in his *Practical Hints on the Construction and Economy of Pauper Lunatic Asylums* (1815), as well as in his 'Instructions' to the architects Watson and Pritchett in *Plans, elevations, sections and descriptions of the pauper lunatic asylum lately erected at Wakefield* (1819). His later introductory observations to M. Jacobi's *Constitution and Management of Hospitals for the Insane* (1841) and his *Review of the Early History of The Retreat* (1846) indicated his continuing belief in the overriding importance of 'moral agency' in the treatment of insanity.

Tuke was recognized as a Quaker minister in 1825, and was a leader at both local and national levels in the Society of Friends. He was prominent in new initiatives, including the Friends Provident Institution in 1832, as well as many of an educational character, helping to found the Friends Educational Society in 1837, serving on the Ackworth management committee, acting as a York Adult School teacher, being a founder member of the Bootham School committee, and acting as treasurer to the Mount School. He held the office of treasurer to the York quarterly meeting, while national recognition of his ability came with

service as clerk of the yearly meeting from 1832 to 1837. This was the period of the Beaconite controversy over the relative importance of inherited Quaker faith, the inner light, and the scriptures, which resulted in a schism of evangelical Friends and in 1836 to Tuke writing *A Letter to John Wilkinson*, one of the secessionists. In this he represented not only his own views but those of prominent members of the yearly meeting in arguing against what he perceived to be an evangelical narrowing of the basis of divine truth. His interest in notable early Quakers had resulted in his *Memoirs of the Life of Stephen Crisp* (1824), *Selections from the Epistles of George Fox* (1825), and *Introductory Observations to Memoirs of George Whitehead* (1830). Now the crisis in Quakerism, and his view that 'few are imbued with the spirit of the early Friends', led to the *Plea on Behalf of George Fox, and the Early Friends* (1837). He also acted as editor of the *Annual Monitor*.

Deep moral seriousness led Tuke to shoulder an extraordinary range of responsibilities, although refusing to stand in 1833 as a Liberal parliamentary candidate for York because of his position as clerk to the Society of Friends. He served as a very active member of the city council, the local board of health, the board of poor-law guardians, and the York Asylum committee of management, as well as doing good works within the prison and the penitentiary. In addition, his financial and business expertise benefited a number of organizations, including the York Savings Bank, the committee of management of the York Gas Light Company, and the board of the Yorkshire Fire and Life Insurance Company.

Despite a slight stroke in 1848 Tuke continued to be actively engaged with philanthropic and public concerns until a more serious paralytic stroke forced him to retire in 1854. He died in York, aged seventy-three, on 14 October 1857 and was buried in the Quaker burial-ground, Heslington Road, York.   ANNE DIGBY

Sources S. Tuke, *Memoirs*, 2 vols. (1860) • C. Tylor, *Samuel Tuke: his life, work and thoughts* (1900) • A. Digby, *Madness, morality and medicine: a study of the York Retreat, 1796–1914* (1985) • A. Digby, 'Changes in the asylum: the case of York', *Economic History Review*, 2nd ser., 36 (1983), 218–39 • A. Digby, *From York Lunatic Asylum to Bootham Park Hospital*, Borthwick Papers, 69 (1986) • D. H. Tuke, *Chapters in the history of the insane in the British Isles* (1882) • R. M. Jones, *The later periods of Quakerism*, 2 vols. (1921) • J. S. Rowntree, *Quakerism, past and present* (1859) • H. C. Hunt, *A retired habitation: a history of The Retreat* (1932) • *Annual Monitor* (1858)

Archives Borth. Inst., corresp. and papers | U. Leeds, Brotherton L., papers relating to Retreat • York Health Archives

Likenesses H. S. Tuke, pastels, The Retreat, York; repro. in Hunt, *A retired habitation*, facing p. 8 • pencil sketch, repro. in Digby, *Madness, morality and medicine*, p. 19

Tuke, Thomas (1580/81–1657), Church of England clergyman, was educated at Christ's College, Cambridge, from where he graduated BA in 1600 and proceeded MA in 1603. It seems likely that Tuke came under the influence of William Perkins during this time, given that his first publication was a joint translation with Francis Cacot of a treatise on predestination by Perkins, issued as *A Christian and Plaine Treatise of ... Predestination* (1606). After university Tuke may initially have sought preferment in Kent; the preface to three sermons delivered at Faversham, *The True Trial and Turning of a Sinner*, was dated from Cuxton, Kent, in 1607. In the next few years he published a number of works, many of which make clear his own moderate puritan sympathies, including *A Discourse of Death* (1613) and another on justification (1609), which was translated into Dutch by Henry Hexham and published in Dort in 1611. A work such as *A Treatise Against Painting and Tincturing of Men and Women: Against Murther and Poysoning: Against Pride and Ambition: Against Adulterie and Witchcraft, and the Roote of these, Disobedience to the Ministrie of the Word* (1616), published in the aftermath of the murder of Sir Thomas Overbury, is noteworthy as a sustained, biblically inspired attack on cosmetics. Some of Tuke's works theoretically sought a broad readership, but he seems to have found it difficult to break free from his usual, painfully learned style.

By at least 1612 Tuke was curate at St Clement Danes in London, where he was later said to have defaced the existing table of church fees, perhaps when the rates of payment were raised—a change which would have impinged directly on his financial situation. In 1614, described as a widower aged thirty-three and curate at St Giles-in-the-Fields, he married Mary, daughter of William Stampe of Wallingford, Berkshire. It was in 'my study in Saint Giles in the Fields' that Tuke penned a number of works, describing his position there in his *New Essays* (1614) and *The Christians Looking Glasse* (1615) as 'minister of Gods Word' (*New Essays*, epistle dedicatory).

On 19 July 1617 Tuke was presented by the crown to the living of St Olave Jewry. After this his literary output virtually ceased, although in 1618 he did publish *Improbus foeneratorum spiritus variis tormentis exercitatus, sive, Tractatus de usurariorum statu calamitoso*, a little known anti-usury tract dedicated to the lord chancellor, Francis Bacon, which was published in Frankfurt. As minister at St Olave Jewry, Tuke's relations with his parishioners were not always harmonious, a fact possibly related to the composition of the vestry, which included such wealthy puritan laymen as Alderman Rowland Heylyn, one of the feoffees for impropriations. In 1624 Tuke appears to have intervened during the appointment of a parish lecturer funded by the enormous bequest of Mary, Lady Weld, who had been a parishioner at St Olave's. Ultimately Tuke agreed not to interfere with the parishioners' election in consideration of a payment of £12 to pay off his debts and meet his other necessary expenses. The vestry thereupon selected as lecturer Theodore Herring, curate at St Anne Blackfriars under the noted puritan William Gouge and possibly a relative of the radical puritan Julines Herring, who enjoyed the patronage of Rowland Heylyn.

During the civil war Tuke's anti-parliamentary stance is well documented and he apparently refused to read parliamentary declarations from the pulpit: 'when he had read out one he held up his hand & cried out "the Devil confound all Traitors, Rebels and turbulent Spirits"' (*Walker rev.*, 60). He was also accused of preaching against those who gave money to parliament. In March 1643 Tuke was imprisoned and sequestered, but shortly thereafter the mayor, Isaac Penington, wrote to the speaker that Tuke and another minister, Matthew Griffith, were now bailed from Newgate and more insolent than ever. Accusations of ceremonialism and not observing the sabbath made against Tuke may not be straightforward. In works such as *A Discourse of Death*, Tuke had himself written very strongly against sabbath breaking, although it is possible that his religious views had altered over time, perhaps in response to more radical and activist puritan parishioners. Tuke's wife, Mary, was allowed to compound for her husband on 6 August 1646, and it appears that he retired to the country. In 1651 Tuke published *The Israelites Promise or Profession Made to Joshua*, a sermon delivered at Tattershall, Lincolnshire, and dedicated to Elizabeth Clinton, countess of Lincoln, in which he lamented that 'Religion in these irreligious, yet religious seeming dayes, is to be found in mens lips rather then lives' and reminded listeners that 'there is no safety but in the service of God' (sig. A2v, 25).

Mary Tuke died in 1654 and was buried on 17 June at St Olave Jewry. Tuke himself died in 1657 and was buried on 13 September at the new chapel in Lincoln's Inn Fields.

J. F. MERRITT

Sources *Walker rev.*, 60 · GL, MS 4415/1, fols. 10v, 15v, 16 · 'epistle dedicatory', T. Tuke, *A discourse of death* (1613), 89 · P. S. Seaver, *The puritan lectureships: the politics of religious dissent, 1560–1662* (1970), 139, 233 · PRO, E 178/5482 · Venn, *Alum. Cant.*
Archives Som. ARS, newsletters to Sir William Armyne

Tuke, William (1732–1822), philanthropist and founder of the York Retreat, was born in York on 24 March 1732, the son of Samuel Tuke (1703–1748), stuff weaver and hosier, and his wife, Ann (d. 1755), daughter of John Ward of Dronfield, Derbyshire. The Tukes were a long-standing York family, which had been among the earliest converts to the Society of Friends. Tuke was educated at day school and boarding-school, and received tuition from a clergyman. At the age of nineteen he was apprenticed to an aunt, Mary Frankland, in the wholesale tea and coffee trade, taking over the business the following year, and further developing it to include cocoa. He remained in the business until the age of eighty-six. Equivalent energy and application were displayed in his philanthropic activities. He was a patron of the Bible Society and thus supported the spread of the scriptures at home and abroad, and he was a campaigner for the abolition of the slave trade where, notably, he gave public support to the election of the abolitionist, William Wilberforce, in the Yorkshire parliamentary election of 1806. In 1754 Tuke married Elizabeth (b. 1729), daughter of John Hoyland of Woodhouse, Yorkshire; they had five children, their eldest son being Henry *Tuke (1755–1814) and the eldest daughter the religious writer Sarah *Grubb (1756–1790). Elizabeth died in 1760, and in 1765 he married Esther (1727–1794), daughter of Timothy Maud of Bingley; they had three children.

From the mid-1760s Tuke became a staunch activist in the Society of Friends. He attended regularly at York meeting and acted as its treasurer for twenty years. For half a century he was a habitual attender at the yearly meeting in London, and in 1783 he also acted as its clerk—an onerous duty. He was committed to the revival of stricter discipline in the Society of Friends, and reprimanded those who fell short of his own high standards of conduct. Tuke showed great energy in founding and developing institutions: he was a member of the country committee of Friends which helped establish Ackworth School in 1779; in 1818 he put forward the first proposal for the educational establishment which in 1829 became Bootham School; and he acted as helpmeet to his second wife Esther, when she founded the Trinity Lane Quaker Girls' School, a precursor of the Mount School.

It is in the field of mental asylums and reform in the treatment of lunatics, however, that Tuke's historical reputation is based. His interest in the subject was first aroused in 1790 when a fellow member of the Society of Friends, Hannah Mills, died in the York Asylum. Friends had been prevented from visiting to offer her religious consolation, and there were suspicions that she had not received good care and treatment. His conscience stirred, Tuke decided in 1792 to create a mental establishment run by Friends for Friends. He drove the project through against the cautious conservatism of fellow Quakers, taking key responsibilities in fund-raising, gaining useful information through corresponding with those working in the field of mental illness, and visiting existing asylums in order to see how to achieve a functional architectural design. At St Luke's Hospital his compassion was further fuelled when he saw a naked female patient in dirty surroundings and realized that older ideas on the insensibility of the mad to their surroundings were still prevalent. When it opened in 1796 The Retreat offered very different, humane conditions. This mild regime, with discriminating medical treatment and only a limited use of physical restraint, was termed moral treatment. At The Retreat this was a lay therapy which was distinctive not least because those administering treatment saw themselves as mere instruments of God's will in offering a divine art of healing.

Tuke's judgement and disciplined activity were particularly conspicuous during the first year of The Retreat's operation when, having to act as *de facto* superintendent he displayed a thoughtful thoroughness in making appropriate appointments, and an affectionate concern with individual patients' needs, despite carrying a great weight of administrative responsibilities. Although its treatment was largely determined pragmatically, The Retreat was part of a wider European reform movement. However, The Retreat's moral treatment was unique both in perceiving the desirability of patients participating in religious activity, and in emphasizing humanity to the weak alongside disciplined living to encourage the weak to become strong—so assuming responsibility for their lives. This reflected the beliefs of the founder, William Tuke, in his adherence to the tenets of the Society of Friends which linked humane sentiments to stern self-discipline.

The same vigilance and earnest sense of moral purpose was shown during 1813–14 when neglect and ill treatment of patients behind the closed doors of the York Asylum recurred, and William Tuke wrote forcibly to the local press to remind the asylum's governors of their need to effect radical reform in order to safeguard the interests of patients. When this 'war of the asylums' was translated to the national stage with the select committee on madhouses of 1814–15, Tuke gave evidence in May 1815. Here his unrivalled stature as the founder of The Retreat gave his evidence considerable weight, and thus contributed to the impact of the inquiry's report in discrediting older brutish methods of treating the insane, and thereby to the growing predominance of the new reforming ideology of moral treatment of which The Retreat had been a pioneer.

Tuke had a long, active, and useful career. What were the sources of this self-confident activism? It was aptly said of Tuke that he had 'an iron will as well as a kind heart' (Tuke, *Chapters*, 113–14). His steadfast single-mindedness, his determined (some said obstinate) inner conviction gave great strength to his practical idealism. In a letter to his future second wife, Esther Maud, he remarked that 'I never could find that there's more required than there's ability given to perform' (Sessions and Sessions, 93). An important application of this philosophy was his lifetime's interest in The Retreat so that it was not until 1820, when he became blind at the age of eighty-eight that William Tuke gave up the treasurership of The Retreat—an office he had first taken up in 1792. His grandson Samuel *Tuke (1784–1857) succeeded to this position and he, together with his son, Daniel Hack *Tuke (1827–1895), did much to publicize William Tuke's achievements through their extensive writings.

In extreme old age William Tuke's view was that 'A man's *life* is his Testimony' (Hunt, 18). York monthly meeting took the same view in very unusually recording Friends' views on Tuke's life. They spoke of a 'great respect for his memory', recollected the 'strict integrity of his mind, joined to the soundness of his judgement', and remembered his 'uncommon firmness of mind … sympathetic regard to others, joined to a tenderness of spirit' (*A Memorial*, 1823). Indeed, it was these qualities that had enabled Tuke to create an asylum which acted as a highly influential model in nineteenth-century psychiatric reform. John Conolly aptly referred to him as 'the great founder of the new asylum' (*Daily News*, 1 April 1852). And at the centenary meeting of the foundation of The Retreat in 1892 the Medico-Psychological Association acknowledged its debt to William Tuke and recorded 'its admiration of the spirit which animated William Tuke and his fellow workers' (Digby, *Madness*, 256). Tuke died on 6 December 1822 following a paralytic attack and was buried in the Friends' Bishophill burial-ground, York.

ANNE DIGBY

Sources *A memorial of York monthly meeting held 14th of 5th month 1823 concerning William Tuke* (1823) • D. H. Tuke, *The moral management of the insane* (1854) • D. H. Tuke, 'William Tuke: the founder of The Retreat', *Journal of Psychological Medicine and Mental Pathology*, 8 (1855) • J. C. Bucknill and D. H. Tuke, *A manual of psychological medicine* (1858) • S. Tuke, *Memoirs*, 2 vols. (1860) • D. H. Tuke, *Chapters in the history of the insane in the British Isles* (1882) • D. H. Tuke, *Reform in* the treatment of the insane: early history of The Retreat, York, its objects, and influence (1892) · 'The centenary of non-restraint', BMJ (6 Aug 1892), 318–19 · R. M. Jones, The later periods of Quakerism, 2 vols. (1921) · H. C. Hunt, 'The life of William Tuke, 1732–1822', Journal of the Friends' Historical Society, 34 (1937), 18 · W. K. Sessions and M. Sessions, The Tukes of York in the seventeenth, eighteenth and nineteenth centuries (1971) · A. Digby, Madness, morality and medicine: a history of the York Retreat, 1792–1914 (1985) · A. Digby, From York Lunatic Asylum to Bootham Park Hospital, Borthwick Papers, 69 (1986) · IGI

Archives Borth. Inst., corresp. on reform of York lunatic asylum; corresp. and papers, L/3/1–2 · Borth. Inst., early corresp., Retreat collection H2 · Borth. Inst., Retreat corresp., C/1 · Herts. ALS, corresp. and papers, D/ESe

Likenesses portrait, 1892, repro. in Tuke, Reform, frontispiece · C. Callet, etching, Wellcome L. · Danielsson, photogravure (after N. Dawson) · H. S. Tuke, portrait (posthumous) · pencil sketch, repro. in Digby, Madness, morality and medicine, p. 19 · photograph, Wellcome L.

Tuker [formerly Tucker], **Sir Francis Ivan Simms** (1894–1967), army officer and military historian, was born at 22 College Road, Brighton, on 14 July 1894, one of three sons of William John Sanger Tucker, who cultivated coffee in the West Indies and later grew fruit in Essex, and his wife, Katharine Louisa Simms. Tucker was educated at Brighton College and the Royal Military College, Sandhurst (1912–13), and during this period he changed his surname to Tuker. He was commissioned a second lieutenant on 14 January 1914, and was briefly attached to the Royal Sussex regiment, with which he maintained close contact throughout his career.

In March 1914 Tuker arrived in India and joined the 2nd (King Edward VII's Own) Gurkha rifles (the Sirmur Rifles). He served with this regiment throughout the First World War and on 13 April 1916 was wounded in Mesopotamia. Tuker saw further active service as a column commander during the 1918 Kuki punitive expedition on the north-east frontier of India and again in 1920 against the Bolsheviks in north-west Persia.

Tuker returned with the 1st battalion 2nd Gurkha rifles to India in June 1921 where he was appointed adjutant. During the prince of Wales' visit to India in 1922 he commanded the ceremonial regimental truncheon party which participated in the official state entry into New Delhi. On 26 April 1923 he married Catherine Isabella (d. 1947), daughter of William St Vincent Bucknall of Horsham; they had three daughters. Tuker attended the Staff College at Camberley in 1925–6, following which he served in a series of alternating regimental and staff appointments for the next ten years. In early 1932 he returned to his regiment and on 14 January 1933 he was promoted major. During the early 1930s he combined a passion for polo with a questioning interest in military affairs. In July 1933 he was promoted brevet lieutenant-colonel and was made second in command. Tuker was appointed officiating commandant of the 1st battalion 2nd Gurkhas in October 1936 (confirmed four months later) and during his tenure of command introduced innovative new infantry training methods. When the battalion was employed during the 1936–7 Waziristan campaign on the north-west frontier of India, Tuker was given an opportunity to test his system of training in practice.

During operations on the Razani sector of the lines of communications of 'Wazirforce', his aggressive new mountain warfare tactics attracted the attention of the military authorities. For his services Tuker was appointed OBE and mentioned in dispatches. At the direct request of the deputy chief of the general staff he wrote a series of articles on mountain warfare, and his individual training methods were later adopted throughout the Indian army.

Tuker was appointed director of military training at general headquarters, India, on 17 September 1940, with the rank of brigadier. Despite the scepticism of many senior officers about this appointment, Tuker was instrumental in modernizing the system of training in India. In October 1941 he was promoted acting major-general and given command of the newly raised 34th Indian division. Early in 1942 he took command of the 4th Indian division, serving in the western desert in north Africa. Under his command this formation distinguished itself during the difficult long retreat to El Alamein.

Tuker led the 4th Indian division during the battle of El Alamein and the subsequent advance into Tunisia. Following the Eighth Army's turning of the Mareth line, Tuker achieved his most striking success when he prepared a bold and imaginative plan to break into the left flank of a strong axis defensive position at Fatnassa on the Tunisian massif. A surprise attack carried out by the 2nd and 9th Gurkhas, without artillery support, on the night of 5/6 April 1943 suffered only light casualties and was completely successful. This decisive action opened the way to Wadi Akarit and destroyed the remaining obstacles preventing the junction of the Eighth and First armies. Tuker was made a substantive major-general in May 1943, awarded the DSO in June 1943, appointed a CB in August for his services in Tunisia, and twice mentioned in dispatches.

The 4th Indian division later took part in the Italian campaign. Shortly before it saw action at Monte Cassino, however, Tuker fell seriously ill, probably with rheumatoid arthritis, and he relinquished command in February 1944. Following a partial recovery, Tuker was recalled to India and briefly served as general officer commanding (GOC) Ceylon, before being made (in September 1944) chairman of a committee appointed to recommend improvements in the system employed to maintain order among the independent Pathan tribes on the north-west frontier. On 14 July 1945 he temporarily replaced Sir Frank Messervy as GOC, 4th Indian corps, in Burma. Under his leadership this formation inflicted heavy casualties during the monsoon on the Japanese Twenty-Eighth Army as it attempted to rejoin the remnants of Burma Area Army on the Burma–Thailand border, for which he was mentioned in dispatches. Following his return from Burma, Tuker commanded Lucknow district, was appointed commander-in-chief of eastern command in 1946–7, and was promoted lieutenant-general in April 1947. During the last days of the British raj Tuker played a key role in maintaining order within this command, stretching from Delhi to Assam, that was affected by widespread rioting and communal disorder. Tuker was appointed a KCIE in

1946 and later that year became colonel of the Sirmur Rifles.

Tuker retired from the army in 1948 and settled at Mawnan Smith, Cornwall. His wife had died on 2 October 1947, and on 29 May 1948 he married Cynthia Helen, daughter of Ronald Gale of Sevenoaks, and widow of Lieutenant-Colonel R. B. Fawcett. In retirement Tuker occupied himself with sailing, running a thriving fruit and flower farm, and writing, principally on military affairs. For his book *Gorkha: the Story of the Gurkhas of Nepal* (1957) he was awarded the Sykes memorial medal by the Royal Central Asian Society. His other publications included a life of Major-General Sir William Henry Sleeman; a commentary on the battles of the Eighth Army (1941–3); *Does Stalin Mean War?* (1952); and *While Memory Serves* (1950), an account of the last two years of British rule in India. He also wrote a volume of verse, and an unpublished, and unperformed, operetta, *May I Call you Julie?* Tuker fought against increasing illness, but finally died at his home, Bosilliac, Mawnan Smith, Cornwall, on 7 October 1967. T. R. MOREMAN

Sources IWM, Tuker papers · G. R. Stevens, *History of the 2nd King Edward VII's own Goorkha rifles (the Sirmoor rifles)*, 3 (1952) · G. R. Stevens, *Fourth Indian division* (1948) · F. I. S. Tuker, *While memory serves* (1950) · T. R. Moreman, *The army in India and the development of frontier warfare, 1849–1947* (1998) · *Official history of operations on the north west frontier of India, 1936–37* (1943) · *Frontier committee of 1945* (1945) · *Dispatch on operations against the Kuki tribes of Assam and Burma, November 1917 to March 1919* (1919) · DNB · *Army List* · b. cert. · d. cert. · m. cert. [1948] · *The Times* (9 Oct 1967) · CGPLA Eng. & Wales (1968)

Archives IWM, Tuker MSS | JRL, letters to the *Manchester Guardian* | FILM IWM FVA, actuality footage | SOUND IWM SA, recorded talk

Likenesses photograph, repro. in Stevens, *History of the 2nd King Edward VII's own Goorkha rifles*, vol. 3, frontispiece

Wealth at death £3845: probate, 2 Jan 1968, CGPLA Eng. & Wales

Tulk, Charles Augustus (1786–1849), Swedenborgian writer and politician, was born at Richmond, Surrey, on 2 June 1786. He was the eldest son of John Augustus Tulk, a man of independent fortune and an original member of the Theosophical Society formed (December 1783) by Robert Hindmarsh for the study of Swedenborg's writings. Charles was educated at Westminster School, of which he became captain, and was famed for his excellent voice in the abbey choir. He was elected a king's scholar in 1801, and matriculated as a scholar from Trinity College, Cambridge, in 1805. On leaving the university he began to read for the bar, but, having ample means, he followed no profession. He married, in September 1807, Susannah Hart (d. 1824), the daughter of a London merchant. In 1810 he assisted John Flaxman in founding the London society for publishing Swedenborg's works; he served on its committee until 1843, and often presided at its annual dinners, though after some controversy with Samuel Noble he was excluded from the society. He never joined the New Church or had any connection with its conference. After leaving Cambridge he rarely attended public worship, but conducted a service in his own family, using no prayer but the paternoster. He became connected with the Hawkstone meeting, projected by George Harrison, translator

of many of Swedenborg's Latin treatises, fostered by John Clowes, and held annually in July for over fifty years from 1806 in an inn at Hawkstone Park, Shropshire. Tulk presided in 1814, and at intervals until 1830. In social matters he early took part in efforts for bettering the condition of factory workers, aiding the movement by newspaper articles. He was returned to parliament for Sudbury on 7 March 1820, and retained his seat until 1826. A widower since October 1824, he was returned to parliament as member for Poole on 7 January 1835, but retired at the dissolution in 1837. His radical political views brought him into close friendship with Joseph Hume. He was an active county magistrate for Middlesex (1836–47), and took special interest in the management of prisons and asylums, acting (1839–47) as chairman of committee of the Hanwell asylum. He was strongly opposed to capital punishment.

Tulk turned to physical science, particularly to chemistry and physiology, partly in order to combat materialism on its own ground. He corresponded with Spurzheim, and was intimate with Coleridge. He devoted much time to the elaboration of a rational mysticism, which he found below the surface of Swedenborg's writings, as their underlying religious philosophy. He contributed for some years to the *Intellectual Repository*, started in 1812 under the editorship of Samuel Noble. He formulated some of his religious views in a few publications, but more importantly in a series of papers in the *New Church Advocate* (1846), which were much controverted. He began the serial publication of a *magnum opus*, *Spiritual Christianity* (1846–7), but did not live to finish it. In 1847 he went to Italy, returning in the autumn of 1848. He died at his home, 25 Craven Street, London, on 16 January 1849, and was buried in Brompton cemetery. Of his twelve children, five sons and two daughters survived him.

ALEXANDER GORDON, rev. TIMOTHY C. F. STUNT

Sources M. C. Hume, *A brief sketch of the life, character and religious opinions of Charles Augustus Tulk*, ed. C. Pooley, 2nd edn (1890) · W. White, *Swedenborg, his life and writings*, 2 (1867), 599, 616ff. · T. Compton, *Life and correspondence of J. Clowes* (1874), 84, 144ff. · *Old Westminsters*, vols. 1–2 · Venn, *Alum. Cant.*

Tull, Ebenezer (1732/3–1761/2), landscape painter and schoolmaster, was born probably in Southwark, London, though there is no record of his place of birth or of his parentage. As a youth he was successively assistant in the writing- and reading-schools (elected 1745) and upper usher of the reading-school (elected 1748) at St Olave's Grammar School, Southwark, where he later became master of the reading-school, the post in which he died. On 1 January 1755 he married, at St James's, Piccadilly, London, Ann Ravener, then a minor aged nineteen, daughter of James Ravener. The couple had four children, including a son, Ebenezer, who was baptized at St Olave's, Southwark, on 12 April 1758.

Tull was an amateur landscape painter of sufficient merit for J. H. Pott to include him in the second rank, with John Wootton, Francis Wheatley, and others, of 'the most eminent landscape painters of this country' (J. H. Pott, *An Essay on Landscape Painting: with Remarks General and Critical on the Different Schools and Masters, Ancient and Modern*, 1782).

Tull, like Gainsborough, used the silversmith and picture dealer Panton Betew of Old Compton Street, Soho, as an outlet for his landscapes, and Betew had six of them engraved as a set by Thomas Vivares and William Elliott. (The original of one of these is in Leeds City Art Gallery and is the only certainly identifiable landscape painting by Tull.) He exhibited two small landscapes at the first exhibition of the Society of Artists in 1761. William Hamilton was among those who owned a landscape by him (he sold it in 1765), but the inclusion of upwards of eighty of his landscapes (some of them admittedly sketches) in the auction sale held after his death does not suggest that his pictures sold well. Tull was described as the British Ruisdael, and the engraved landscapes demonstrate the influence of Jan van Goyen, Meindert Hobbema, and Jacob van Ruisdael. The Leeds picture gives some indication of his rhythmical rococo style and his sensitivity to effects of light. He also painted topographical views, chiefly around London, and a few sea pieces. He himself collected pictures, mainly landscapes and seascapes by Dutch and contemporary British artists; these included five works by Gainsborough.

Tull probably died in Southwark and was buried at St Olave's, Southwark, on 8 January 1762; he was survived by his wife. His paintings and his collection were sold at auction by Prestage and Hobbs, Savile Row, London, on 30 April and 1 May 1762. Horace Walpole wrote that his prints were auctioned in March 1763, but no sale catalogue has been discovered.   JOHN HAYES

Sources J. Hayes, 'Ebenezer Tull, "the British Ruysdale": an identification and an attribution', *Burlington Magazine*, 120 (1978), 230–33 · 'Mr. Tull sale', Prestage and Hobbs, 30 April–1 May 1762 [LUGT 1223, unique copy in Rijksprentenkabinet, Amsterdam] · private information (2004) [J. Hawkins, St Olave's and St Saviour's Grammar School Foundation] · IGI

Tull, Jethro (*bap.* 1674, *d.* 1741), agricultural innovator and writer, was born at Bradfield, near Basildon in Berkshire and baptized on 30 March 1674, 'the sonne of Jethro and Dorothy Tull'. The family was frequently stated to have been of Yorkshire origin, but the branch of it to which Tull belonged had long been settled on the borders of Oxfordshire and Berkshire. He matriculated from St John's College, Oxford, on 7 July 1691. On 11 December 1693 he was admitted a student of Gray's Inn, and on 19 May 1699 he was called to the bar. Apparently he had no intention of practising, but studied law as a preparation for political life. On 5 May 1724 he was nominated a bencher of Gray's Inn, but he did not sit.

Almost immediately after his marriage on 26 October 1699 to Susannah Smith, of Burton Dassett, Warwickshire, Tull commenced farming on his father's land at Howberry, Crowmarsh, near Wallingford, Berkshire. He had a number of health problems including, possibly, tuberculosis, which together perhaps with his father's debts and lawsuits prevented him from following up his political ambitions. It was on the farm at Howberry that Tull invented and perfected his seed drill, probably in 1701. In his preface to his *Horse-Hoeing Husbandry*, published in 1731, Tull gave an account of the stages by which

Jethro Tull (*bap.* 1674, *d.* 1741), by unknown artist

he arrived at this invention. Finding his plans for sowing his farm with sainfoin in a new manner hindered by the opposition of his labourers, he resolved:

> [to] contrive an engine to plant St Foin more faithfully than such hands would do. For that purpose I examined and compared all the mechanical ideas that ever had entered my imagination, and at last pitched upon a groove, tongue, and spring in the soundboard of the organ. With these a little altered and some parts of two other instruments, as foreign to the field as the organ is, added to them, I composed my machine. It was named a drill, because when farmers used to sow their beans and peas into channels or furrows by hand, they called that action drilling   (Tull, 1829, 454.)

Tull was not the first to design a drill, having been anticipated by John Worlidge in 1699. But he was almost certainly the first to produce a working machine, there being no evidence that Worlidge's design was ever made successfully.

Tull farmed part of his Oxfordshire estate for nine years with considerable success, as he himself claims, after which he moved about 1709 to Prosperous Farm at Shalbourne, near Hungerford in Berkshire. Possibly his leaving Howberry was due to bad health, the situation and climate of his new farm suiting him better, but in April 1711 Tull was forced to travel further afield for the sake of his health. He journeyed through France and Italy, carefully noticing on the way the agricultural practices of both countries; he made a stay at Montpellier, and returned home in 1714. (Alternative dates of 1713 to 1715 have been suggested for this visit abroad.) Recommencing his interrupted drill husbandry at his Berkshire farm, he added improvements founded upon his observations during his travels. He had noticed the ploughed vineyards near Frontignan in Languedoc, where the pulverization of the earth between the rows of vines was standard practice. From this Tull concluded that finely tilled soil helped plants to receive air, water, and nutrients, and on his return home he tried this method at Prosperous Farm, first on turnips and potatoes, and then on wheat. Contrary to what his critics alleged, Prosperous Farm was hilly and its soils were partly chalk and partly heath ground. It was, in Tull's words, 'noted for the poorest and shallowest soils in the neighbourhood' (Tull, 1829, 213–14). It was there that he invented his horse-hoe and his four-coultered plough, both being necessary, with the drill, to his new system of grain cultivation. As he noted, 'I owe my principles and my practice originally to my travels, as I owe my drill to the organ' (ibid., 455). By contour ploughing, drilling his seed at wide intervals, and using his horse-hoe to destroy weeds, Tull was able to grow wheat on the same fields for thirteen years continuously without manuring. His distrust of manure was partly due to his belief that it encouraged the spread of weeds.

It was not until the last decade of his career that at the request of many distinguished visitors to his farm Tull published a 'specimen' of his *Horse-Hoeing Husbandry* (1731), which was at once pirated in Dublin. Hearing of this Tull determined to print no more, but he was dissuaded by his admirers, and accordingly *The Horse-Hoeing Husbandry, or, An Essay on the Principles of Tillage and Vegetation, by J. T.*, appeared in 1733. It was at once attacked by the Private Society of Husbandmen and Planters, headed by Stephen Switzer, in its monthly publication, *The Practical Husbandman and Planter*. Tull was accused of having plagiarized from Fitzherbert, Sir Hugh Plat, Gabriel Plattes (who is confused with Sir Hugh), and John Worlidge, and several of his theories about the value of manure and the practice of pulverizing the earth were contested. The credit undoubtedly due to his forerunners need not detract from Tull, for there is no reason to think that Worlidge's drill materially aided Tull in the conception of his device, and it is unlikely that Tull had ever read Sir Hugh Plat's 'New and admirable Arte of setting of Corn'. Tull was morbidly sensitive to these attacks, and he defended himself in various subsequent writings, mostly taking the form of notes on his longer work. His troubles were increased by the hostility of his labourers towards his methods. He was also harassed by the speculations of his spendthrift son, John. Tull published *A Supplement to the Essay on Horse-Hoeing Husbandry* in 1735, *Addenda to the Essay* in 1738, and his *Conclusion* in 1739.

Tull died on 21 February 1741 at Prosperous Farm and was buried at his birthplace, Basildon, on 9 March. A memorial to him was built in the church there. By his will, dated 24 October 1739, he left his property to his sister-in-law and his four daughters. His only son John received the sum of 1*s*.; he died in the Fleet prison, twenty-three years later.

After Tull's death a second edition of *Horse-Hoeing Husbandry* appeared in 1743, in which his later publications were also reprinted. In 1822 the book was edited and published, with some alterations, by William Cobbett. Meanwhile in 1753 a French translation had appeared, the history of which shows the importance attached abroad to the 'new husbandry'. The Maréchal de Noailles employed M. Otter to translate Tull's work; the translator's lack of technical knowledge was rectified by submitting the version to the revision of Buffon. At the same time a second independent translation, made also under high patronage by M. Gottfort, was in a similar way submitted to Duhamel du Monceau, the famous French agriculturist. The work of translation was finally concentrated in Duhamel's hands, and between 1753 and 1757 he issued a free translation of Tull's work, followed by several volumes of commentary, giving an account of his own elaborations of the Tullian system and of the experiments made in the new style of husbandry by many French gentlemen, chief among whom was M. de Châteauvieux. Voltaire was a disciple of Tull, and cultivated land at Ferney according to the precepts of the new husbandry. Boswell records how Dr Johnson discussed the Tullian system with a Dr Campbell in the course of his tour in the Hebrides (1773). However, owing to practical difficulties in making and improving the design of the seed drill, it was not widely used in England before factory-made machines became available in the nineteenth century; and Tull's system generally, though economical in seed and manure, was wasteful of land, and was not always successful with wheat, both of these factors working against its widespread adoption.

ERNEST CLARKE, rev. G. E. MINGAY

Sources N. Hidden, 'Jethro Tull I, II, and III', *Agricultural History Review*, 37 (1989), 26–35 · G. E. Fussell, *Jethro Tull: his influence on mechanized agriculture* (1973) · J. Tull, *The horse-hoeing husbandry*, ed. W. Cobbett, new edn (1829) · E. Cathcart, 'Jethro Tull, his life, times and teaching', *Journal of the Royal Agricultural Society of England*, 3rd ser., 2 (1891), 1–40 · R. E. Prothero, *English farming past and present*, ed. D. Hall, 6th edn (1961), 170–2 · R. Trow-Smith, *English husbandry* (1951), 138 · E. R. Wicker, 'A note on Jethro Tull: innovator or crank?', *Agricultural History* (1957), 47–8 · A. Young, *Rural Oeconomy: or, essays on the practical parts of husbandry* (1770), 314–34 · W. Marshall, *Rural economy of Norfolk* (1787), 1, 59
Likenesses oils, Royal Agricultural Society of England, Stoneleigh Park, Warwickshire [*see illus.*]

Tull, Walter Daniel John (1888–1918), footballer and army officer, was born on 28 April 1888 at 57 Walton Road, Folkestone, Kent, the fifth child of Daniel Tull (*c*.1856–1897) and his wife, Alice Elizabeth Palmer (*c*.1853–1895). Daniel, a carpenter, was born in Barbados and in 1876 settled in Folkestone. Through attendance at the Grace Hill Wesleyan Methodist Chapel he met Alice, born in Hougham, Kent. She gave birth to six children. In 1896, a year after the death of Alice from cancer, Daniel married her cousin Clara Alice Susannah Palmer. They produced a daughter Miriam, born on 11 September 1897. Three months later Daniel died from heart disease. Unable to cope with five stepchildren and an infant child of her own, Clara placed the youngest boys—Edward, eleven, and Walter, nine—in the children's home and orphanage in Bonner Road, Bethnal Green, on 24 February 1898. Edward was adopted in 1900 by the Warnock family of

Walter Daniel John Tull (1888–1918), by unknown photographer, c.1910

Glasgow, where he qualified as a dentist in 1912 and practised, probably as the first black dentist in Britain, at 419 St Vincent Street (as Edward James Alexander Tull-Warnock) until his death in 1950.

Walter Tull served an apprenticeship as a printer but made his name as a footballer. In 1908–9, his first season in senior competitive football, he was described as the 'catch of the season' for his team (*Football Star*). Clapton won the amateur cup, the London county amateur cup, and London senior cup. Tottenham Hotspur, impressed by his coolness, skilled technique, and robust tackling invited him on their summer tour of Argentina and Uruguay. On return he was invited to sign professionally, and made his first team début in Tottenham's inaugural game in the first division, away at Sunderland. His home début was against FA cup holders Manchester United in front of a crowd of 32,000:

> [Tull's] display on Saturday must have astounded everyone who saw it. Such perfect coolness, such judicious waiting for a fraction of a second in order to get a pass in not before a defender has worked to a false position, and such accuracy of strength in passing, I have not seen for a long time ... Tull is very good indeed. (*Daily Chronicle*, 13 Sept 1909)

He had 'much to contend against on account of his colour', commented one contemporary (but anonymous) journalist. During a match at Bristol in October 1909 the same reporter notes he received 'a cowardly attack on him in language lower than Billingsgate'. Yet, 'Tull is so clean in mind and method as to be a model for all white men who play football ... [He] was the best forward on the field' (undated press cutting, Finlayson collection). Mysteriously, by the end of the month, he had been dropped.

At the end of the following season (1910–11) Tull was transferred to Herbert Chapman's Northampton Town, for whom he played over 110 matches, mostly as an inside forward. In December 1914, after the outbreak of the First World War, he enlisted in the British army—the first among his colleagues to do so—and was appointed lance-corporal in the 17th (1st football) battalion, the Middlesex regiment. He was promoted to corporal then lance-sergeant before he had seen any action. In April 1916, after six months in France, he was hospitalized, suffering from shell shock. In September 1916 he returned to action with the 23rd (2nd football) battalion, which suffered heavy losses in the battle of the Somme. He then returned to Britain for officer training at Gailes in Ayrshire and on 10 May 1917 he was appointed to a commission in the special reserve of officers, before rejoining the 23rd battalion of the Middlesex regiment as a second lieutenant.

Not only was it virtually impossible for a man of colour to be commissioned an officer, but the *Manual of Military Law, 1914* stated that 'aliens [including blacks must] ... not ... exercise any actual command or power' (p. 471). He came to hate the conflict but was decorated with the 1914–15 star and British war and victory medals. Yet Tull led his men and was mentioned in dispatches for his 'gallantry and coolness' at the battle of Piave in Italy in January 1918. He died, unmarried, on 25 March 1918, shot through the head in no man's land near Favreuil, France, during the second battle of the Somme. Subsequently the commanding officer of the 23rd battalion recommended him for a Military Cross. Tull, through his actions, ridiculed those barriers that tried to deny people of colour equality with their contemporaries, revealing the shallow substance of these obstacles by the strength of his integrity. A garden of remembrance for all those connected with Northampton Town Football Club who died in the two world wars, with a sculpture to commemorate Tull forming its centrepiece, was dedicated on 11 July 1999.　PHIL VASILI

Sources priv. coll., Finlayson collection · 'form for application for admission of a child', NCH, Action for Children Archives, London, Tull file · *Football Star* (20 March 1909) · *Daily Chronicle* [London] (13 Sept 1909) · *Northampton Daily Chronicle* (22 Dec 1914) · P. Vasili, 'Walter Daniel Tull: soldier, footballer, black', *Race and Class*, 38/2 (1996) · *Dentists Register* (1913) · *Dentists Register* (1950)
Archives NCH, Action for Children, 85 Highbury Park, London, file · PRO, military service record, WO 339/9023 file 175446 | priv. coll., Finlayson collection · PRO, war diaries of the 17th (1st Football) Middlesex Regiment, WO 95/1361
Likenesses photograph, c.1910, unknown collection; copyprint, priv. coll. [*see illus.*] · photographs, priv. coll. · photographs, History of Black Footballers Exhibition, 150 Peverel Road, Cambridge
Wealth at death £229 0s. 6d.: PRO, W. D. Tull WO 339/90293 file 175446

Tullibardine. For this title name *see* Murray, William, styled second duke of Atholl and marquess of Tullibardine (1689–1746).

Tullidelph, Thomas (d. 1777), a founder and first principal of United College, St Andrews University, was the son of

John Tullidelph (d. 1714), minister of Dunbarney, Perthshire, and his second wife, Katherine Rankine. He probably attended St Andrews University, and his commonplace book from 1717, with later additions, is now deposited in the University of St Andrews Library. The usually reliable historian of that university says that 'Tullidelph had been a merchant in Edinburgh and was also thought to have served as an officer in the Swedish army' (Cant, 90, note 2), but it is difficult to square this assertion with Tullidelph's half-century clerical and academic career in Perthshire and Fife. Ordained to the parish of Dron, near Perth, on 2 November 1727, he was translated to Markinch, in Fife, four years later. He was appointed to the divinity chair in St Mary's College, St Andrews, on 17 October 1734, and on 13 September 1739 was translated to St Leonard's Church, St Andrews, in conjunction with the principalship of St Leonard's College—positions that had also been held jointly by his grandfather, William Tullidelph, from 1691 to 1695.

Tullidelph was elected moderator of the general assembly of the Church of Scotland on 6 May 1742 and was appointed one of his majesty's chaplains in ordinary in June 1744. From the late 1730s he was a major force in the negotiations that resulted in a parliamentary act of 1747, establishing the United College of Saint Salvator and Saint Leonard in the University of St Andrews, and on 24 June of that year he was appointed the first principal of the newly amalgamated college. The institutional reorganization was accompanied by curricular reform, as the old regenting system gave way to eight specialized chairs in the arts and sciences. Although these developments marked a turning point in the academic revitalization of St Andrews, for which Tullidelph deserves much of the credit, John Ramsay states that he was personally unpopular with students on account of his pride, selfishness, aloofness, and susceptibility to flattery (Scotland and Scotsmen, 1.265–6). In late March 1768 he expelled from the university Robert Fergusson, the future poet, on account of a prank, though he was reinstated several days later at a meeting of the professors.

Tall and thin, Tullidelph was a fine preacher and religious lecturer, and an extraordinary ecclesiastical orator. Alexander Carlyle considered him 'the most powerful speaker ever I heard', William Pitt not excepted (Autobiography, ed. Burton, 265). During the 1760s, when long past his prime, Tullidelph was the representative of his university in the general assembly on six occasions, and what Thomas Somerville termed his 'ardent and vehement eloquence' (sometimes too vehement, according to Ramsay) was still in evidence during important debates like the one on the schism overture affair in 1766, when his eloquence helped the moderate party carry the day (Somerville, 96).

On 31 October 1722 Tullidelph married Alison Richardson (d. 1758). All five of their surviving daughters married Church of Scotland ministers. Tullidelph is not known to have published anything but, after his death on 14 November 1777, his son-in-law, the Revd Thomas Bisset of Logierait, was said to possess 'some valuable manuscripts ready for publication' (Scotland and Scotsmen, 1.266), including a paraphrase and notes on the New Testament. On 18 October 1781 the London publisher William Strahan replied to a query by his Edinburgh associate William Creech: 'As for Mr. Tullidelph's Papers, I am clearly of Opinion we ought to have nothing to do with them' (NA Scot., RH4/26/3). Two Tullidelph manuscripts in the University of St Andrews Library, 'An enquiry concerning the intention of the evangelists' and 'Oratio proemialis', were presumably among the papers in Bisset's possession. RICHARD B. SHER

Sources R. G. Cant, The University of St Andrews: a short history, rev. edn (1970) · The autobiography of Dr Alexander Carlyle of Inveresk, 1722–1805, ed. J. H. Burton (1910) · D. Daiches, Robert Fergusson (1982) · Scotland and Scotsmen in the eighteenth century: from the MSS of John Ramsay, esq., of Ochtertyre, ed. A. Allardyce, 2 vols. (1888) · Fasti Scot., new edn, 7.414 · R. B. Sher, Church and university in the Scottish Enlightenment: the moderate literati of Edinburgh (1985) · T. Somerville, My own life and times, 1741–1814, ed. W. Lee (1861) · M. Simpson, 'Robert Fergusson and St Andrews student culture', Heaven-taught Fergusson: Robert Burns's favourite Scottish poet, ed. R. Crawford (2003), 21–39
Archives U. St Andr., commonplace book, MSLF1109.T8C6

Tullie, George (bap. 1654, d. 1695). See under Tully, Thomas (1620–1676).

Tullis [née Palau], **Julia Elissa May** [Julie] (1939–1986), mountaineer and climbing instructor, was born at 3 Kingsdown Avenue, Croydon, on 15 March 1939, the daughter of Francisco Juan Palau (b. 1896), who came from Spain, and his wife, Erica Julia Augusta, née Saucerotte, who was born in Germany. The couple had met and married while working in a hotel near Croydon, and went on to run a Basque restaurant in Knightsbridge, London. Julie (as she was always known) was their second daughter. Like other British children during the war, Julie and her sister, Zita, were evacuated out of the capital to escape the bombing. They stayed on a farm in Norfolk and adored the country life. Once the war was over, their mother took the girls abroad during most summers to see relatives scattered throughout Europe. Julie always said that driving in old cars (bought each year for the purpose) and camping along the way were what encouraged her lifelong wanderlust.

Tullis, who attended Godolphin and Latymer School, Hammersmith, until she was seventeen, discovered rock-climbing as a teenager and spent most of her weekends either in the mountains of north Wales or on the sandstone outcrops of the Kent and Sussex border, a popular training ground for London climbers. In 1956, at High Rocks near Tunbridge Wells, she met Terence Michael (Terry) Tullis (b. 1935), the son of Frank Charles Tullis, originally from Fife. They married at Streatham on 7 November 1959 and had a son, born in 1962, and a daughter two years later; by then the Tullises were living in Groombridge, Sussex, where they ran the village shop and climbing café.

Both Julie and Terry Tullis also worked as climbing instructors, mostly with school groups. Their students included young people with physical and mental disabilities, work for which Julie's patience and natural warmth made her particularly suited. She encouraged many able-

Julia Elissa May Tullis (1939–1986), by Terry Tullis

bodied and disabled youngsters to widen their horizons, while at the same time her own confidence and horizons were widening with the discovery of budo. This combination of various martial art disciplines, including karate and aikido, transformed her attitude to life. The flexibility and mental strength she derived from it infused her climbing. It was not simply that practising slow, controlled movements improved balance and co-ordination, she wrote in her autobiography, *Clouds from Both Sides*; with budo came an understanding that tiredness and pain do not mean that one has to give up. The body can go on. This truth subsequently saved her life on several occasions.

In 1978, with their children in their mid-teens, the Tullises went on their first major climbing expedition, to Peru. Terry by this time was limited in what he could achieve, having suffered a horrific leg injury some years before, but Julie climbed two Andean peaks, Pisco (18,898 feet) and Huascaran Norte (21,800 feet), and her passion for high places was ignited. Forming a climbing partnership with the well-respected Austrian mountaineer Kurt Diemberger, a family friend, she turned her sights to the Himalayas. Diemberger, in a climbing career spanning thirty years, had already trodden the summits of five 'eight-thousanders' (the fourteen highest mountains in the world), two of them as first ascents. He was also a film-maker, and in need of an assistant. Julie set herself to become a sound recordist to be able to complement his camera work. It delighted them both how well they worked and climbed together, and in time, as they went from one Himalayan giant to the next, they came to be known as 'the highest film team in the world'.

Their first joint assignment, to Nanga Parbat with a French expedition, was in many ways disappointing, as the leader—having convinced himself Tullis must have lied about her altitude experience—would not countenance her climbing above camp 1. Nevertheless, she found the mountain enchanting, and hoped to return. Their film picked up many awards. In 1983 they went to the Chinese (northern) side of K2 (28,250 feet) with an Italian party, and this time climbed together to 26,248 feet, the magic 8000 metre line. In addition they tramped many extra glacier miles exploring the empty valleys of this rarely visited side of the Karakoram and Aghil ranges. Within a year they were back on K2 with an international team, attempting the more frequented Abruzzi Ridge in Pakistan. This time their high point was 24,115 feet. Nearby Broad Peak beckoned. This was one of the eight-thousanders already climbed by Diemberger twenty-seven years before. He could not resist trying it again. When they came down from K2, he and Tullis decided to make a lightweight raid on its summit. They were, as Diemberger later wrote in his book *The Endless Knot: Triumph and Tragedy on K2* (1991), 'probably the oldest couple climbing in the Himalayas', but after two months in the Karakoram they were at a peak of condition and acclimatization. They made it to the summit, only to be faced with a nightmare descent through unstable, new snow. They survived one avalanche and dodged others before getting down safely.

The busiest year for Tullis and Diemberger was 1985, with attempts on Everest and Nanga Parbat. They made films of both trips, and also shot a delightful documentary of a remote Himalayan village tucked under the great peaks of Makalu and Everest. *Tashigang: Tibetan Village between the Worlds of Gods and Men* went on to take a first prize at the annual Trento mountain film festival. When the opportunity came to return to K2 the following year, they jumped at it. Of all the high peaks they had come to know, the second highest mountain in the world was their 'mountain of mountains', and they welcomed another chance to climb it.

The summer of 1986 proved a disastrous one for the eleven expeditions booked to attempt K2. Though some climbers reached the top, by the end of July six had died on the mountain. Two more perished in the first week of August. Meanwhile, those who still entertained summit hopes—representatives from four separate expeditions—were attempting the mountain simultaneously, Diemberger and Tullis among them. On 4 August they stood on top of K2, as did several of the others, including another Briton, Alan Rouse. Tullis's was the second British ascent of K2; no British woman had ever climbed so high.

But it was late in the day, and disastrously late in the season. Five climbers made it back that night to camp 4 (still above 8000 metres), only to be trapped there by fierce storms. Diemberger and Tullis did not join them there until the following day, having survived a fall and been forced to bivouac on their way down. The storms raged on for days. Julie Tullis succumbed to high altitude during the night of 6–7 August 1986. She was buried in a crevasse at camp 4, with a memorial on the Gilkey Cairn below. Of the seven people marooned in that camp only two got down alive, Kurt Diemberger and Willi Bauer, on 11 August.

Although Julie Tullis was undoubtedly Britain's most experienced female high-altitude mountaineer up to the time of her death, her achievements received little recognition in a climbing establishment that was all too ready to mark her down as a star-struck appendage of Kurt Diemberger. Yet her resilience and calm brought much to that partnership. For the style of mountaineering they preferred, they complemented each other perfectly, with Tullis providing a steadying foil for Diemberger's volatility. It is hard to believe that six major expeditions to the world's highest mountains and a lifetime's dedication to climbing would have been so lightly dismissed had she been a male mountaineer. Tullis's career as a high alpinist is the more remarkable for not having begun until her fortieth year. She was once asked if she felt it had all happened too late. 'Not at all', she responded. 'I think I am enjoying it more now than ever I would have done earlier' (personal knowledge). Most of her climbing partners were older than she was: Diemberger was seven years older. He was so full of vitality, she observed, that he would go on enjoying mountains and exploration for a long time. 'Age doesn't frighten me', she said, 'I just take each year as it comes' (ibid.). A commemorative campsite in memory of Julie Tullis was opened at Harrisons Rocks, Groombridge, near the home she shared with Terry, who survived her.

AUDREY SALKELD

Sources J. Tullis, *Clouds from both sides*, paperback edn (1987) [with additional chapter by P. Gillman] · K. Diemberger, *The endless knot: triumph and tragedy on K2* (1991) · private information (2004) [Terry Tullis, husband; K. Diemberger] · personal knowledge (2004) · b. cert. · m. cert. · d. cert.
Likenesses T. Tullis, photograph, Alpine Club, London [*see illus.*] · photographs, priv. coll. · photographs, priv. coll.
Wealth at death £22,891: administration, 5 Nov 1987, *CGPLA Eng. & Wales*

Tulloch, Sir Alexander Murray (1803–1864), army officer, eldest son of John Tulloch and his wife, Anne, daughter of Thomas Gregorie of Perth, was born in Newry, Ireland. Tulloch's father, who possibly served in the British army as a captain, descended from a thirteenth-century Scottish family, which five centuries later lost property and status for supporting the Jacobites. After briefly working in a legal office in Edinburgh, Tulloch forsook the law, purchased a commission as ensign in the 45th foot on 9 April 1826, joined the regiment after the close of the First Anglo-Burmese War at Rangoon, and advanced to lieutenant on 30 November 1827. Concerned for the troops' welfare, he was instrumental in securing better provision of meat, bread, and vegetables for the 45th and other troops in Burma. Tulloch exposed the practice of corrupt officials acting for the East India Company, who paid the men in debased silver, and the fact that privates using the company's canteens were charged five times the real value of liquor, highlighting these and other abuses in letters to

Indian journals signed Dugald Dalgetty. When the regiment moved up-country in November 1826 it undertook non-military construction work but also saw 'a certain amount of active service in checking the lawlessness ... of marauders' (Wylly, 1.289), tasks in which, presumably, Tulloch was involved. He returned to England on sick leave in 1831 (though he attended the Royal Military College's senior department from 1 August 1831 until 7 November 1832), taking with him examples of the debased coinage, the flawed nature of which was confirmed by the Royal Mint. Presented with this evidence the secretary at war, Sir John Cam Hobhouse, demanded an explanation, but the East India Company denied wrongdoing. In 1836, prompted by Tulloch, another secretary at war, Lord Howick, instituted further wide-ranging inquiries. It emerged that a fraud of about £1 million had been perpetrated, and the East India Company agreed over a period of time to supply coffee, tea, sugar, and rice to army units in reparation.

While in Burma, Tulloch had noted the high rate of sickness among troops, with his own regiment suffering badly. In England, using obituaries from the *Monthly Army List* and information from regiments where he had personal contacts (the 45th lost 109 through cholera in 1832), he compiled tables showing the approximate death rates at selected stations over twenty years. After these were published in the *United Service Journal* in 1835 Howick appointed Henry Marshall, a half-pay deputy inspector-general in the army medical department, Dr Balfour, and Tulloch to produce a comprehensive report for parliament. The study lasted until 1840 and resulted in four volumes of data. During this work Tulloch became aware of the surprising longevity of army pensioners, and it soon became clear that many relatives continued to draw the pension after a man died. Tulloch, therefore, recommended organization of out-pensioners into a corps with its own officers and recognized rank structure, which would make such deceit impossible, at the same time establishing a 20,000-strong body to aid the civil power in times of emergency. Tulloch used an analysis of sickness among troops to recommend improvements in the sanitary condition of barracks in Jamaica, and he devised a more equitable system of relief for regiments serving overseas (the 45th had been continuously abroad from 1819 to 1838). In 1851 he prepared a 'summary of arrangements relative to the emigration of pensioners and their families as convict guards' for penal settlements in the colonies.

Tulloch obtained a captaincy (12 March 1838), went on half pay (1 June 1838), and became an unattached major (12 April 1839) before once more going on half pay (6 August 1841). He returned to the active list as lieutenant-colonel on 31 May 1844, on appointment to be military superintendent of out-pensioners, reverting to half pay on 10 February 1852. He became closely involved in preparations to deal with anticipated trouble connected with presentation of the third Chartist petition to parliament during April 1848. At first offering 800 pensioners to guard important buildings like the Tower of London and Bank of

England, he was required by the home secretary to extend coverage to other locations, including the Mansion House and British Museum. He took three companies to Blackfriars Bridge on 10 April, placing himself and them under the command of Major-General T. W. Brotherton. However, no armed action was necessary. Meanwhile in London, on 16 May 1844, he had married Emma Louisa, youngest daughter of Sir William Hyde Pearson MD.

Tulloch advanced to colonel on 20 June 1854. Widespread criticism of the provision of food and forage to troops in the Crimea led to Tulloch and Sir John McNeill being instructed on 19 February 1855 to 'proceed to the Crimea in order to inquire into the whole arrangement and management of the Commissariat Department'. Three days later they were directed to look into 'what may have been the sources of supply … [and] the alleged delay in unshipping and distributing the clothing and other stores', which would involve examining the work, as well, of the quartermaster-general's department. In the House of Commons the prime minister, Lord Palmerston, explained that 'they would have authority to carry into execution immediately any change or arrangement they might think essential to the public service', though he declined to confirm whether or not McNeill and Tulloch could exercise powers of 'appointment and dismissal' (Sweetman, *War and Administration*, 51). Two reports were produced, from Constantinople on 10 June 1855 and London on 20 January 1856. They severely criticized the military staff of the British commander, Lord Raglan, and commissary-general William Filder. Raglan defended his staff and rejected the suggestion of Lord Panmure, secretary of state for war, that Filder be replaced by Tulloch. The military demanded an opportunity personally to defend themselves, and a board of general officers under Lord Seaton therefore convened at the Royal Hospital, Chelsea, in 1856. McNeill refused to take part in the proceedings, but Tulloch attended to combat charges of bias and incompetence, not least those vehemently aired by Lord Lucan. The board's report rejected the findings of McNeill and Tulloch, shifting responsibility for supply difficulties from the Crimea to civilian departments in Whitehall. In 1857 Tulloch published a detailed justification of his actions in *The Crimean Commission and the Chelsea Board*, which drew further criticism from Filder but secured parliamentary approval; he was appointed KCB in April 1857.

In 1857 Tulloch gave evidence to a commission inquiring into the state of the army medical department. In 1860–61 he chaired a committee examining payments made in England on account of troops serving in India and also drafted a report comparing losses (through action and sickness) among soldiers in India prior to the mutiny and those who arrived for service during the mutiny. On 9 September 1859 Tulloch advanced to major-general. Owing to failing health, which had deteriorated sharply since the Chelsea board, he resigned from his staff appointment with the out-pensioners in 1862. He died in Winchester on 16 May 1864, survived by his wife; there were no children of the marriage. He was buried four days later at Welton, near Daventry, Northamptonshire, in a private ceremony.

Tulloch was essentially a reserved man, who devoted long hours to office work and concerned himself constantly with welfare matters, even after retirement writing in the *Journal of the Statistical Society of London* (1863) to compare unfavourably the income of soldiers with that of agricultural workers. A long-standing friend observed:

> He was plain and unassuming in appearance, but was possessed of extraordinary talents; and he had a fund of dry humour which would have been caustic had it not been tempered by his natural kindness of heart and never-tiring benevolence. (*Colburn's United Service Magazine*, 1864, pt 2, 407)

E. I. CARLYLE, rev. JOHN SWEETMAN

Sources *Army List* · *United Service Journal*, 2 (1835) · *Colburn's United Service Magazine*, 2 (1864) · J. Sweetman, *War and administration: the significance of the Crimean War for the British army* (1984) · J. Sweetman, *Raglan: from the Peninsula to the Crimea* (1993) · H. C. Wylly, *History of the 1st and 2nd battalions, the Sherwood Foresters, Nottinghamshire and Derbyshire regiment, 1740–1914*, 1 (1929) · Boase, *Mod. Eng. biog.* · *Dod's Peerage* (1858) · *DNB* · Staff College archives, Camberley
Archives Gwent RO, Cwmbrân, corresp. and papers | NA Scot., corresp. with Sir John McNeill · U. Durham L., letters to third Earl Grey, incl. memoranda
Likenesses wood-engraving, NPG; repro. in *ILN* (2 July 1864), 17
Wealth at death under £25,000: resworn probate, Aug 1867, *CGPLA Eng. & Wales* (1864)

Tulloch, John (1823–1886), Church of Scotland minister and university principal, was born, one of twin sons, on 1 June 1823 at his maternal grandfather's farm at Dron, Perthshire. His mother was Elizabeth, the daughter of a Perthshire farmer named Maclaren. His father, William Weir Tulloch, was parish minister of Tibbermore, near Perth. Until about his sixth year Tulloch was boarded at Aberargie, in the neighbourhood, with a family named Willison. After some time at Perth grammar school he spent two years at Madras College, St Andrews, and in 1837 entered the University of St Andrews, carrying a bursary in the gift of Perth presbytery. Adding private teaching to this means of support, he completed his curriculum without straining home resources. As a student he gained distinction by his translation from Greek authors and his knowledge of Greek literature, by his mathematical accomplishment, and by his essays in mental philosophy. He won the Gray prize for history. Beginning his theological studies at St Mary's College, St Andrews, he completed them at Edinburgh, where he formed a lasting friendship with William Smith, afterwards minister of North Leith.

Licensed as a preacher by Perth presbytery in June 1844, Tulloch was almost immediately appointed assistant to the senior collegiate minister of Dundee parish church. On 5 February 1845 he was ordained minister of St Paul's, Dundee, an offshoot of the parish church. In July 1845 he married, at St Laurens, Jersey, Jane Anne Hindmarsh, daughter of a professor of elocution who had taught at Perth and St Andrews. They had many children. After an attack of influenza in the spring of 1847, Tulloch spent three months in Germany, studying at Hamburg and visiting Berlin, Wittenberg, and other centres of interest (an

John Tulloch (1823–1886), by Sir George Reid, 1880

important and formative experience, familiarizing him with German biblical criticism). In 1848 he began literary work, contributing memorial notices to Dundee newspapers, and writing for Kitto's *Sacred Journal* and other periodicals. On 20 September 1849 he was appointed parish minister of Kettins, Forfarshire, where he remained until 1854, making in the interval steady progress as a man of letters. A review in the *Dundee Advertiser* of Sir James Stephen's *Essays in Ecclesiastical Biography* brought him an appreciative letter from the author, while an article on the 'Hippolytus' in the *North British Review* of 1853 won for him the acquaintance of Baron von Bunsen. Throughout 1852–3 he was preparing an essay on theism in competition for the open Burnett prize at Aberdeen.

In May 1854 Tulloch was presented by the crown to the post of principal and primarius professor of theology in St Mary's College, St Andrews, his appointment owing something to the strong commendation of Bunsen. His inaugural address at the beginning of the winter session, 'Theological tendencies of the age' (thus early identifying his abiding interest), discussed the issue with freshness, breadth, and freedom. In January 1855 Tulloch came second in the Burnett prize, winning £600. Although his college work was exacting at the outset, Tulloch's energetic habits speedily engaged him on various related issues one of which was university reform, a subject with which he was concerned throughout his career. In July 1858 he went to Paris, by appointment of the general assembly, to establish a presbyterian church for the Scottish residents. In the autumn, prompted by his interest in German literature and speculation, he visited Heidelberg and Cologne,

returning in December by way of Paris. In 1859 the university commissioners increased his modest income of £300 to £490. At this time Scottish audiences appreciated lectures on great themes, and at the Edinburgh Philosophical Institution in 1859 Tulloch delivered a course on Luther and other leaders of the Reformation. In the same year he was appointed one of her majesty's chaplains for Scotland. In 1861 he visited remote highland churches, writing graphic letters on his experience (Oliphant, 150). In 1862 he was appointed depute-clerk of the general assembly, and about the same time he became editor of the *Church of Scotland Missionary Record*. Persistent illness in 1863 led Tulloch to spend the greater part of that and the next year in foreign travel in eastern Europe and in Germany.

In the following years Tulloch was actively interested in controversies concerning sabbath observance and 'innovations' in the church service, and in educational questions affecting Scotland. When the Scottish education bill passed at the close of the session of 1872 he was made a Scottish commissioner. In 1874 he visited London to urge the appointment of a professor of education at St Andrews, and in the long vacation he went for change to the United States and Canada. The letters he wrote there are marked by keen observation and good-natured criticism. In 1875 Tulloch was appointed chief clerk of the general assembly, and from that time onward—Dr Norman Macleod having died in 1872—he was the most prominent churchman in Scotland. His stately presence, natural eloquence, genial demeanour, and resonant voice secured attention for his strong common sense and his enlightened opinions. Two questions that now absorbed much of his time and strength were the proposal to disestablish the Church of Scotland, which he stoutly opposed, and the affiliation of a college in Dundee to the University of St Andrews. He was moderator of the general assembly of the Church of Scotland in 1878 and conducted the business with dignity and skill; his closing address—a plea for lofty Christian aims and ideals—was published, and ran through four editions in the year. Combating disestablishment, he prepared a statement of a proposed Scottish Association for the Maintenance of National Religion. On 30 November 1878, under the auspices of Dean Stanley, he conducted services in Westminster Abbey. In 1879 Glasgow University conferred on Tulloch the honorary degree of LLD, and in the summer of the same year he undertook the editorship of *Fraser's Magazine*, holding the post for a year and a half. From December 1880 to April 1881 he was seriously ill (Oliphant, 369–73), but a visit to Torquay restored his health.

In May 1882 Tulloch delivered to the general assembly a great speech on church defence, which was widely circulated as a pamphlet. On 4 June he became dean of the Chapel Royal and dean of the Thistle. In the general assembly of 1883 he delivered an admirable speech on the report of the church interests committee. In the same year he gave a course of lectures in Inverness entitled 'The literary and intellectual revival of Scotland in the eighteenth century', the subject being one which engaged his leisure for years in preparation for a history of modern

Scotland, which was never completed. On 28 March 1884 he opened in Pont Street, London, a new church connected with the Church of Scotland. Immediately afterwards he attended the tercentenary celebration at Edinburgh University, when he received the honorary degree of LLD. In 1884–5, besides his professorial work, he delivered a course of lectures in the church of St Giles, Edinburgh, published in 1885 as *Movements of Religious Thought in the Nineteenth Century*, a remarkable synthesis which is both a classic text of its period and a still reliable analysis of it. It exemplifies Tulloch's broad-church view that, given humanity's necessarily partial and fallible understanding of theology, ideas must be understood in the historical context in which they are expressed. In the general assembly of 1885 he spoke once more with impressive power on church defence. But his health was failing, and he died at Duncan House, Torquay, on 13 February 1886, his wife surviving him. He was interred in the cathedral burial-ground, St Andrews, where there is a monument to his memory.

In his intellectual, theological, and political position Tulloch linked theological liberalism and a staunchly conservative establishmentarianism. He believed that theological comprehension and integration would strengthen the established Church of Scotland. In addition to *Movements of Religious Thought*, he published widely on historical subjects, his works including *Leaders of the Reformation* (1859) and *English Puritanism and its Leaders* (1861), and also on theology, especially *Theism* (1855), *The Christ of the Gospels* (1864) (an attack on Renan), and *Rational Theology and Christian Philosophy in England in the Seventeenth Century* (2 vols., 1872), a still valuable analysis. He wrote frequently for the newspapers, including *The Scotsman*, for the *Encyclopaedia Britannica* (ninth edition), and for the main English periodicals of the day, such as the *Contemporary Review*, the *Nineteenth Century*, *Blackwood's Magazine*, and *Fraser's Magazine*. What Tulloch said of Chillingworth (*Rational Theology*, 1, 1872, 168) applied with singular exactness to himself: 'It seemed to him, as it has seemed to many since, possible to make room within the national church for wide differences of dogmatic opinion, or, in other words, for the free rights of the Christian reason incessantly pursuing its inquest after truth.' At first regarded in some quarters as an advocate of too broad and lax theological tenets, Tulloch was ultimately recognized as an enlightened interpreter of dogma and a champion of orthodoxy. He was consistent in the manifold application of his energies—in his college lectures, and in his position as churchman, preacher, educational reformer, and author—and his strong personality, independence of attitude, and keen and energetic liberal instincts prompted his welcome of the historical and comparative method into scriptural and theological domains. From his influence, more than that of any other man or any party, sprang the intelligent liberalism characteristic of the Church of Scotland in the last quarter of the nineteenth century.

T. W. BAYNE, *rev.* H. C. G. MATTHEW

Sources Mrs Oliphant, *A memoir of the life of John Tulloch* (1888) • *The Scotsman* (15 Feb 1886) • J. Tulloch, *Movements of religious thought in Britain during the nineteenth century* (1885); repr. with introduction by A. C. Cheyne (1971) • A. C. Cheyne, 'Church reform and church defence: the contribution of Principal Tulloch', *Records of the Scottish Church History Society*, 23 (1987–9), 397–416 • [A. K. H. Boyd], *Twenty-five years of St Andrews*, 2 vols. (1892)

Archives NRA, priv. coll., letters relating to disestablishment • U. St Andr. | ICL, letters to Lord Playfair • NL Scot., corresp. with Blackwoods; letters to J. S. Blackie; letters to Alexander Campbell-Fraser • U. St Andr. L., corresp. with James Daniel Forbes

Likenesses R. Herdman, oils, 1879, U. St Andr.; replica, 1880, Scot. NPG • G. Reid, oils, 1880, Royal Collection [*see illus.*] • A. E. Emslie, group portrait, oils (*Dinner at Haddo House*), NPG • J. Moffat, photograph, NPG • T. Rodger, carte-de-visite, NPG

Wealth at death £6745 17s. 8d.: probate, 25 May 1886, *CGPLA Eng. & Wales*

Tulloch, William John (1887–1966), bacteriologist, was born on 12 November 1887 at Dundee, the youngest of two sons and three daughters of Henry Tulloch, hatter, and his wife, Coralie van Wasserhove of Waerschoot in Belgium. Educated at Dundee high school, he studied medicine at the University of St Andrews and graduated MB, ChB, with distinction in 1909. He became a house physician at the Royal Infirmary of Hull but within months the University of St Andrews claimed him to become assistant to Professor L. R. Sutherland in the department of pathology in Dundee. In 1911 he went to Newcastle as assistant in comparative pathology in the Durham College of Medicine, and during his time there he investigated and diagnosed a fatal case of septicaemic plague, a notable feat for a young bacteriologist.

Tulloch returned to Dundee in October 1914 as lecturer in bacteriology, and in the same year he was awarded the degree of MD at St Andrews, with honours for a thesis entitled 'The influence of electrolytes on agglutination'. In the January of the following year he married Florence Sheridan (d. 1975); they had one son and two daughters. In March 1916 he entered the Royal Army Medical College, at Millbank, London, where he remained until 1919. He was allotted to bacteriological work and was in contact with Sir David Bruce. He was engaged on two problems of great consequence: wound infections—especially the incidence of tetanus—and outbreaks of cerebrospinal fever in young soldiers in crowded barracks. His work was well appreciated and he was mentioned in dispatches, promoted major, RAMC, and appointed OBE (military division) in May 1919. His work in the war years was recorded in the Medical Research Council's Special Reports, and also in the *Proceedings of the Royal Society*, series B, 1918 and 1919. He was one of the authors of *Cerebrospinal Fever* (1920).

On his discharge from war service Tulloch returned to Dundee to resume his duties as lecturer. He set up the bacteriology department and also organized public health bacteriology in Dundee. He was appointed the first professor of bacteriology at St Andrews in October 1921. In addition to his teaching commitments, he was bacteriologist to Dundee Royal Infirmary and responsible for public health bacteriology not only in Dundee but also in the counties of Angus (Forfarshire), Fife, and Perthshire. His research activities continued and he made important contributions to the subject of gonorrhoea and to the serological diagnosis of smallpox. Of all his various duties, the one which he loved best and which was his first priority was the teaching of medical students. He was a dynamic and conscientious teacher with a well-developed personal approach, as generations of graduates testified. He set out to teach his pupils not a dry technical discipline but a living practical subject, and he used his gift for acting to make the subject come alive. He educated his students in the widest sense and had no time for lists of facts. He was also a man of strong religious beliefs, which coloured his life and produced compassionate relationships with students, colleagues, and others.

Tulloch was a member of the General Medical Council from 1949 to 1962 and of the General Dental Council from 1956 to 1959. He was dean of the faculty of medicine at St Andrews from 1945 to 1956 during a time of expansion in the university. One of the last professors appointed *ad vitam et culpam* he retired voluntarily in September 1962 when he was honoured by the university with the degree of DSc, the first occasion that this honorary degree had been awarded. Outside his professional life he was interested in the history of the Dutch Republic, and he was also a sprinter, a yachtsman, and a figure-skater. On his retirement Tulloch went to live in Hampshire to be near one of his daughters and her family. He died in Cosham, Hampshire, on 26 August 1966, survived by his wife.

D. M. GREEN, rev.

Sources *The College*, 19 (Dec 1921), 3–5 · J. Macleod, *Journal of Pathology and Bacteriology*, 95 (1968), 336–48 · personal knowledge (1981) · private information (1981)
Likenesses A. Ross, oils; known to be at Ninewells Hospital, Dundee, 1981
Wealth at death £26,212 9s.: confirmation, 6 Feb 1967, CCI

Tully, Thomas (1620–1676), college head and religious controversialist, was born, the son of George Tully, in St Mary's parish, Carlisle, on 22 July 1620. He may have been born or brought up in Abbey Street, to whose poor he was especially generous in his will. He was educated at the parish free school and the school at Barton Kirk in Westmorland. On 17 October 1634, at the tender age of fourteen, he matriculated from Queen's College, Oxford; he graduated BA on 4 July 1639 and proceeded MA on 1 November 1642. He was elected a fellow on 23 November 1643.

On the purging of the college at the parliamentary occupation Tully left Oxford (though he was not one of those expelled by the visitors) and worked as a schoolmaster at the grammar school at Tetbury. He was also the incumbent of a living which 'he did not find very grateful to him' and was troubled by 'some turbulent Anabaptists in the Parish' (MS letters of Edward Heath).

After returning to Oxford and his fellowship, Tully was admitted BD on 23 July 1657 and devoted himself to his college duties. Provost Langbaine commended his work when 'after the surrender of Oxford, he returned home, and repeopled the College with a new Colony of Commoners to whom he is Tutor and Reader of Hebrew in the House' (Queen's College, Oxford, Pyx.2.v).

Tully's enthusiasm for college life and work persuaded Queen's to appoint him principal of St Edmund Hall (a surviving medieval academic hall in the possession and governance of Queen's) on 22 December 1658, a post he held until his death and in which he made an outstanding contribution to the life and buildings of that ancient establishment. He found the old refectory in a ruinous state and in its place built a new hall with many rooms above, one of the few Oxford buildings erected during the Commonwealth. He himself contributed the large sum of £200 and proved an efficient fundraiser as a list of his benefactors shows (MS Wood F.28, fol. 306). Under his guidance the hall prospered and the number of undergraduates increased from twenty in 1662 to sixty-five in 1668. A succeeding vice-principal claimed that the hall 'flourished in proportion to its bigness equal with any other in the University' (MS Tanner 454, fol. 142r–v). Tully cared for his undergraduates in a fatherly way unusual in the century. It was his custom to visit 'the schollers chambers … almost everyday to observe whether they followed their studyes' and to encourage and cheer them (MS top. Oxon. f.31, 18–19).

Throughout these years Tully was rector of Grittleton in Wiltshire, where life was not always tranquil. He writes that 'we have been lately troubled in my parish and the neighboured parts with two women preachers. What doctrine one of them brought forth I know not, only she has in her time brought forth two bastards' (*CSP dom.*, 1672, 457). In his extensive writings which occupied these same years he endeavoured from a Calvinist standpoint to defend, in his own opinion, the Church of England from false doctrines. Wood remarks that Tully 'was characterized by some churchmen and phanaticks to have been a main pillar of the church in defence of her true doctrine' (MS Tanner 102, the year 1666). Only two years before his death Tully entered into controversy over George Bull's *Harmonia apostolica*, an attempted reconciliation of the teachings of St Paul and St James on justification by faith and works. Tully's *Justificatio Paulina*, published in 1674, reasserted the doctrine of justification by faith alone. Had his death not intervened, it was planned that Tully should have succeeded Thomas Barlow as Lady Margaret professor of divinity to reinforce the defence of Calvinism at Oxford.

Tully was not without powerful friends, especially Sir Joseph Williamson, secretary of state from 1674, and Lord Crewe, bishop of Durham. At the Restoration he was created DD, was made one of the royal chaplains in ordinary, and preached before the king and Prince Rupert at Harwich.

Increasing infirmity dogged his later years and when his greatest preferment came, it was too late. We read that:

one day at dinner the Bishop [of Durham] waiting … upon King Charles, recommended Dr. Tully who had been long a Chaplain, & was a very learned Man, to the Deanery of Rippon; the King immediately granted the Bishop's request. (*Memoirs of Lord Crewe*, 20)

Tully was now too ill and weak to leave Grittleton. He died in his rectory on 14 January 1676, a dean of Ripon who had never seen his minster. He was buried in the chancel of his church.

Tully's will is marked by an intense Calvinist piety:

> Rendering all praise and glory to Almighty God Father Sonn and Holy Ghost for all the Rich Treasures of his Grace vouchsafed unto me, and for all the great mercyes wherewith he hath followed me all my dayes above Thousands who are as good by nature though I am infinitely lesse then them all and have not returned to him according to what I have received, God be mercifull to me a sinner. (PROB 11/350, fol. 346v)

Among his bequests the bachelor Tully remembered his brother Timothy, his nieces and nephews, 'that beloved City' of Carlisle, and the poor of Grittleton (ibid.). His books he divided between his nephews George and Thomas, St Edmund Hall, and Queen's College (the last also received his brass sphere and great brass quadrant). St Edmund Hall was also remembered in the donation of 20s. apiece to each MA resident there at the time of his death and 50s. to 'Goodwife Smith my Bedmaker' (PROB 11/350, fol. 347r).

George Tullie (bap. 1654, d. 1695), Church of England clergyman, nephew of Thomas Tully and son of Isaac Tully of Carlisle, was baptized in St Mary's Church there on 5 September 1654. He entered Queen's College, Oxford, on 17 May 1670, graduated BA on 6 February 1675 and MA on 1 July 1678. He was elected a fellow on 15 March 1679. After becoming chaplain to Richard Sterne, archbishop of York, he was appointed subdean in 1680 and a prebendary in 1681. For a time a preacher of St Nicholas's Church in Newcastle upon Tyne, he was presented to the rectory of Gateshead, where he died on 24 April 1695, leaving a wife and two children, and was buried in the church. He published anti-Roman Catholic books against infallibility and clerical celibacy, as well as a translation of Plutarch's *Morals*.

GRAHAM MIDGLEY

Sources Wood, *Ath. Oxon.*, new edn, 3.1055–9 · Foster, *Alum. Oxon.* · J. N. D. Kelly, *Almost seventeen hundred years* (1989), 41–4 · letters of Edward Heath, St Edmund Hall, Oxford · Queen's College, Oxford, Pyx.2.v · Bodl. Oxf., MS Tanner 454, fol. 142 · memorials and remains by Nathaniel Freind, Bodl. Oxf., MS Top. Oxon. f.31 · *CSP dom.*, 1672, 457; 1668–9, 9 · Bodl. Oxf., MS Tanner 102 · [J. Smith], 'Memoirs of Nathaniel, Lord Crewe', ed. A. Clark, *Camden miscellany*, IX, CS, new ser., 53 (1895), 20 · Bodl. Oxf., MS Bodley F. 28, fol. 306 · PRO, PROB 11/350, fols. 346v–347v [T. Tully] · *Hist. U. Oxf.* 4: *17th-cent. Oxf.* · *Walker rev.* · *IGI*

Archives Queen's College, Oxford

Likenesses portrait, St Edmund Hall, Oxford

Tunnard, John Samuel (1900–1971), painter, was born on 7 May 1900 at Caesar's Camp, Sandy, Bedfordshire, the son of John Charles Tunnard (1873–1960), landowner and sporting artist, and Nina Isabel Christian, *née* Long (d. 1950). He was educated at Horton School, Ickwellbury, Bedfordshire, and then at Charterhouse, Surrey (1913–18), where he won the Struan Robertson prize two summers in succession. From 1919 he attended the Royal College of Art in London, where he studied design until 1923. As a student he was the drummer in a four-piece dance band, and his enthusiasm for jazz and dance music lasted all his life. In 1924 he became a textile designer for Tootal, Broadhurst, Lee & Co., and left in 1927 to be art adviser to H. and

M. Southwell, carpet manufacturers; in 1929–30 he was a selector for the John Lewis partnership. On 11 September 1926 he married a fellow student at the Royal College of Art, Mary May (Bob) Robertson (1901/2–1970), daughter of Peter Robertson; they had no children. In 1929 he taught design at the Central School of Arts and Crafts in London, having begun to paint seriously in the previous year.

Tunnard showed three pictures at the Royal Academy for the first time in 1931, and one with the London group, which he joined in 1934 and where he exhibited regularly. In 1932 he had his first major exhibition (shared with Vere Temple) of landscapes, marines, and still lifes at the Redfern Gallery. In 1933 the Tunnards moved to Cadgwith, Cornwall, at first living in a Gypsy caravan and then in a cottage, where they started making hand-blocked printed silks. They also travelled abroad for the first time that year, visiting the Balearic Islands, and from this period date Tunnard's first abstractions and works influenced by the art of Miró and Klee; in 1936 his wife gave him a copy of Herbert Read's *Surrealism*, and he became on friendly terms with Julian Trevelyan and Henry Moore. Other close friendships were with John Betjeman and Humphrey Spender. From that time on Tunnard's work responded to the joint impulses of surrealism and constructivism, his strongly textured compositions, even when highly abstracted, usually evoking natural forms, space, and the sea. They are distinguished by strong, swinging, rhythmical lines and by curved elements which interpenetrate and melt into one another. In some respects his work has affinities with the engravings of his contemporaries Stanley Hayter and John Buckland-Wright. His colours are usually close in tone and harmonious. Later in life he was in part inspired by the exploration of outer space. He exhibited frequently all his life, and had a notable one-man show at Guggenheim Jeune in London in 1939. In the 1950s and 1960s he exhibited at the McRoberts and Tunnard Gallery, London, run in partnership by his cousin Peter. Many museums in Britain and abroad possess examples of his work: Leeds City Art Gallery, for example, has his superb *Davy Jones' Locker* (1940), with its evocation of a sea bed populated with fantastic shapes; the collection of the Museum of Modern Art in New York includes *Fugue* (1938), which has characteristically clear, sharp, geometric lines and a perfect circle inscribed on a field of floating organic shapes, some flatly painted, some textured; the Tate collection holds six works and an example of *Holiday* (1947), a lithograph he executed for the School Prints scheme.

In Cornwall, Tunnard became an auxiliary coastguard and, for a period in 1939, a fisherman, making crab pots. Although he caught fish, he detested hunting, and his relationship with his father broke down over his opposition to blood sports. As a conscientious objector he avoided directly helping the war effort during the Second World War (though he wrote an article for *Picture Post*, published in December 1940, about his life and look-out duties as a coastguard) but continued to paint prolifically. Often short of money at this period, from 1945 until 1965 he taught at the Penzance School of Art. He was commissioned by the Arts Council in 1951 to contribute a major painting, *The Return*, to the exhibition 'Sixty paintings for 51', and he also painted a large mural for the Regatta restaurant at the Festival of Britain. He inherited some money at the death of his mother in 1950 and bought a fair-sized house, Trethinick, in Lamorna, Cornwall, where at lively, alcoholic parties he would perform a top hat and cane routine for his guests. He was remembered by his friends as a buoyant, easy-going person, though to some people he could be reclusive and unwilling to be friendly, however; he ignored invitations to join the Penwith Society, but joined and supported the Newlyn Society of Artists.

Tunnard began to exhibit at the Royal Academy again in 1960, and in 1967 was elected an ARA. He loved birdwatching, and his interest in entomology led him to collect rare specimens of seaweed and insects for the British Museum. As can be seen in his *Self-Portrait* (1959, National Portrait Gallery, London), he wore spectacles, and he had a long face with deeply grooved cheeks, a thin nose and mouth, and receding hair. John Tunnard died on 18 December 1971 in Penzance and was buried alongside his wife in the churchyard in Zennor.   ALAN WINDSOR

Sources A. Peat and B. A. Whitton, *John Tunnard: a life and catalogue of the work* (1996) • *The Times* (20 Dec 1971) • b. cert. • m. cert. • private information (2004)
Archives Tate collection, corresp. with Curt Valentin
Likenesses J. Tunnard, self-portrait, oils, 1959, NPG • portrait, repro. in Peat and Whitton, *John Tunnard*, fig. 22
Wealth at death £132,765: probate, 25 Jan 1972, *CGPLA Eng. & Wales*

Tunnicliffe, Charles Frederick (1901–1979), artist and illustrator, was born on 1 December 1901 at Langley, east Cheshire, the only son in the family of five children of William Tunnicliffe, shoemaker, of Langley, and Margaret, daughter of George Mitchell, a farmer. He was raised on a 20 acre farm in the nearby village of Sutton, to which his father had moved in 1902, and was educated at the local St James's church school. In 1915 he entered Macclesfield School of Art, Cheshire, and soon afterwards Manchester School of Art. In 1921 he was awarded a royal exhibition to the Royal College of Art in London and he stayed there, perfecting his skill as an engraver, until he left in 1925 to join the staff of Woolwich Polytechnic.

Tunnicliffe's prodigious industry and rapidly developing skill as an etcher soon became known to the public and he found that there was a market for his work. He first exhibited at the Royal Academy in 1934 and from that date his work was to be seen in every summer exhibition until 1978. Also in 1934 he was elected a fellow of the Royal Society of Painter–Etchers and Engravers.

In 1929 Tunnicliffe had married Winifred (d. 1969), daughter of Frederick Wonnacott, a sewing machine salesman in Belfast; the couple had no children. Winifred had been a fellow student at the Royal College of Art and shared her husband's passion for natural history. After their marriage they settled in Macclesfield, where the artist began his record of the birds of Britain. These drawings, accurate to within 1 millimetre, were made from dead specimens and carried out in watercolour, gouache,

and ink, accompanied by informative handwritten notes. His sketchbooks date from this period.

As Tunnicliffe had become a master craftsman as well as an artist he was able to carry out commissions covering a very wide field. Commercial firms became aware that his work was accurate and well executed; furthermore they knew that the artist was reliable. In 1932 he illustrated *Tarka the Otter* by Henry Williamson, and consequently he was seldom without work as an illustrator. He held his first one-man show in 1938 at the Arthur Greatorex Galleries in London.

From 1939 to 1945 Tunnicliffe worked as an assistant art-master at Manchester grammar school and in 1942 his first book, *My Country Book*, was published. He was an able writer and his best-known book was *Shorelands Summer Diary*, published in 1952, in which he described and illustrated the land and life around his home in Anglesey. In 1944 he was elected an associate of the Royal Academy as an engraver and in 1947, with the security of an established reputation, he bought Shorelands, a house on the Cefni estuary at Malltraeth, near Bodorgan, in Anglesey. This was to be the Tunnicliffes' home for the rest of their lives.

In 1954 Tunnicliffe was elected Royal Academician and also vice-president of the Royal Society for the Protection of Birds. In 1968 he was made a vice-president of the Society of Wild Life Artists. In 1974 the Royal Academy mounted a major exhibition of his measured drawings and sketchbooks and for the first time the art world and the public were able to see the importance of his work. In 1975 he was awarded the gold medal of the Royal Society for the Protection of Birds and in 1978 was appointed OBE.

Tunnicliffe seemed to be more at ease in the countryside than with people, avoiding society in general and contenting himself with a few good friends who benefited from his generosity and cheerful company. Physically he was a large ruddy-faced man with a ready laugh, but this compensated for a natural reticence which allowed the development of the dedication and obsession that resulted in his extraordinary output. He was admired internationally for his watercolours of birds and animals and nationally for his wood-engravings and etchings. These works were a very great influence on younger wildlife artists. His illustrations to some of the Ladybird books for children in the 1960s also introduced a generation of younger readers to the British countryside. Nevertheless it became apparent in the last decade of his life that his greatest contribution to art lay in his measured drawings and sketchbooks. He never truly mastered the handling of oil paint.

Charles Tunnicliffe died at his home at Malltraeth on 7 February 1979. In May 1981 his measured drawings and sketchbooks were purchased by Anglesey borough council.   KYFFIN WILLIAMS, *rev.*

Sources personal knowledge (1986) • private information (1986) • *CGPLA Eng. & Wales* (1979) • I. Niall, *Portrait of a country artist: Charles Tunnicliffe R.A., 1901–1979* (1980) • *Bird drawings by C. F. Tunnicliffe* (1974) [exhibition catalogue, RA] • *Wild lives: the art of Charles F. Tunnicliffe / Bywydau gwyllt: celfyddyd Charles F. Tunnicliffe*, Welsh Arts

Council (1980) [exhibition catalogue, Mostyn Art Gallery, Llandudno, 9 Aug – 20 Sept 1980]
Archives Oriel Ynys Môn, Llangefni, papers, sketchbooks, drawings | JRL, letters to Alison Uttley
Wealth at death £200,712: probate, 27 April 1979, *CGPLA Eng. & Wales*

Tunstal [Tunstall], **Cuthbert** (1474–1559), bishop of Durham and diplomat, was born near Hornby Castle in Hackforth, Yorkshire, the son of Thomas Tunstal, later a squire of the body to Richard III, and of his future second wife, a daughter of Sir John *Conyers of Hornby Castle [*see under* Conyers family]. The circumstances of his birth were never held against him as his parents' subsequent marriage legitimated him under canon and civil law, if not under common law. He had three brothers and three sisters, some of whom may have been the children of his father's first wife, Alice Neville. One brother was Brian Tunstal, the so-called 'stainless knight', killed at the battle of Flodden in 1513; Cuthbert became supervisor of his will and guardian of his son Marmaduke.

Education and early career Nothing is known of Tunstal's childhood except that (apparently on his own relation) he spent two years as a kitchen boy in the household of Sir Thomas Holland, possibly at Lynn, Norfolk, before 'being knowne, he was sent home to Sir Richard [*sic*] Tunstall his father' (Blomefield, 1.232). Perhaps he returned to his father's household on his parents' marriage. In any case his father appears to have provided for his education, though the suggestion that he was at St Anthony's School in Threadneedle Street, London, and first met Thomas More there, is entirely speculative.

About 1491 Tunstal was admitted to Balliol College, Oxford. While there he became a friend of Thomas More, John Colet, Thomas Linacre, and William Grocyn. Some years later he left the university, according to Anthony Wood because of an outbreak of plague; if so, this must have been in 1493, but that would leave about three years unaccounted for. In 1496 he became a scholar of the King's Hall, Cambridge, for which he seems to have retained greater long-term affection, but again he left without a degree.

From 1499 Tunstal spent six years at the University of Padua, where before his departure he received the degrees of DCnL and DCL. He studied under Leonico Tomeo and Pietro Pomponazzi, two of the leading humanists of the day, and established a reputation for outstanding scholarship, excelling in Greek, Latin, and mathematics. Among his friends were his fellow English students William Latimer and Richard Pace, and Jerome Busleiden (later the Flemish diplomat), Antonio Surian (later the Venetian diplomat), and Aldus Mantus (the printer). At or near the end of his studies, in 1505 Tunstal visited Rome. In a Palm Sunday sermon in 1539 he claimed that it was at this time that he lost respect for the papacy when he witnessed the arrogant behaviour of Pope Julius II forcing a nobleman to kiss his foot. However in the intervening years much had changed in the Church of England and Tunstal had discarded his natural orthodoxy and buckled

Cuthbert Tunstal (1474–1559), by unknown artist

under the pressure applied by the king on the royal supremacy, so this 'memory' is difficult to evaluate.

After his return to England later in 1505, Tunstal began a long and distinguished career in the church. Although not yet ordained, he was admitted on 25 September 1506 to the rectory of Barmston, Yorkshire, on the presentation of his brother Brian's mother-in-law, Margaret, Lady Boynton, but he held it for less than six months. He was made rector of Stanhope, Durham, in 1508 and rector of Aldridge, Staffordshire (vacated by July 1509). His talents were recognized by Archbishop William Warham, who appointed him as his chancellor and auditor of causes about 1508. Finally ordained subdeacon on 25 March 1509 and deacon on 7 April, he was rector of Sutton Veny, Wiltshire, from November 1509 to February 1510, of Steeple Langford, Wiltshire, from February 1510 to early 1511, and of East Peckham, Kent (vacated December 1511); it is unlikely that he resided in any of these benefices. Ordained priest in April 1511, he continued to serve Warham in several capacities, including those of commissary-general of the prerogative court of Canterbury (he was appointed on 25 August 1511) and visitor for the archbishop during that year's visitation of the Canterbury diocese. Collated to the rectory of Harrow on the Hill, Middlesex, on 16 December, he retained it until 1522 and seems to have resided in this conveniently placed cure. His association with Warham had brought him to the attention of the court early in the reign of Henry VIII, and in 1514 he gave an oration at the ceremonial presentation of papal gifts to the king. It also brought promotion: that year Tunstal succeeded Thomas Wolsey as canon of Lincoln and prebendary of Stow Longa, and in 1515 he became archdeacon of Chester following the elevation of John Veysey to the bishopric of Exeter.

Diplomacy, 1515–1522 In 1515 Wolsey called upon Tunstal to serve as a diplomat. Sent as an envoy to the young Charles, duke of Burgundy, Tunstal joined Thomas More and several others in the negotiations to maintain the trade treaties that had been agreed during the reign of Henry VII in 1495 and 1506. The negotiations were long and difficult but Tunstal's conduct established him as an invaluable representative of the government. He proved a keen observer, with valuable insights into the diplomatic situation, and an astute judge of Flemish and imperial strategy. He was also shrewd enough to recognize both the skill of Charles's main adviser, Chièvres, and the duplicity of the ageing Emperor Maximilian when the latter suggested that he might be inclined to resign the empire in favour of Henry VIII. Tunstal's comment to Henry that such an election would not happen, and that the offer was made to squeeze yet more money out of the English, was directly to the point. What is more, Tunstal had the courage to take independent action where he thought it necessary, even if the consequences might be dire. Although in later life he might be accused of timidity, he seems never to have been afraid to speak his mind, and on several occasions he withheld letters from the king and from Wolsey that he considered too intemperate to deliver during his negotiations.

Tunstal's stay in Burgundy was extended after the renegotiation of the trade treaties. His new instructions were to conclude an alliance with Charles and the emperor against the French. The French victory at Marignano (13–14 September 1515) and the succession of Charles to the crown of Spain after the death of Ferdinand of Aragon (1 February 1516) made aggressive action against the French in Italy desirable in English policy but unlikely from an imperial standpoint. Tunstal's stubborn expression of doubt about this policy earned him a mild rebuke from the king, but he followed his instructions. In May 1516 he was rewarded for his efforts by being appointed master of the rolls and vice-chancellor. Although he was in no position to take up the duties of his appointment, he found the supplement to his income useful as he was always short of money. Aware of the impending treaty of Noyon before it was signed in August 1516, he did not seem too concerned about it once it occurred. Always more friendly to the empire than to France, and fearing an alliance against England between them, Tunstal was sanguine about the agreement and recognized that the impending fall of Verona would not alter the English position in the slightest—he certainly did not feel that the English crown should pour more money into Maximilian's pocket. The negotiations with Maximilian and Charles continued in spite of the treaty of Noyon. When, in September 1517, Charles finally set sail for Spain to assume his crown, the English had managed to maintain friendly relations in large part because of Tunstal's patience and wisdom. Tunstal returned to England in October 1517.

While in the Netherlands in 1516 Tunstal had the opportunity to establish a close and lasting friendship with Erasmus. Although they had known each other at least from 1507, it was not until 1516 that they became intimate friends. Throughout 1516 they were almost constant companions, and Erasmus had rooms near Tunstal while in Brussels. From this point onwards Tunstal figured in much of Erasmus's correspondence. It is clear that he held Tunstal in high esteem:

> besides a knowledge of Latin and Greek second to none among his countrymen, he has also a seasoned judgment and exquisite taste and, more than that, unheard-of modesty and, last but not least, a lively manner which is amusing with no loss of serious worth. (*Correspondence*, 4.103)

Certainly Tunstal's judgement and scholarship were trusted by Erasmus and by Thomas More. While in Brussels, Tunstal assisted Erasmus in the production of the second edition of his Greek New Testament and also cast a critical eye over More's *Utopia*. He was also one of Erasmus's greatest patrons.

Neither the failure to prevent a Franco-imperial treaty nor the replacement of Warham with Wolsey as chancellor affected Tunstal's career. He was, in fact, becoming known as a safe pair of hands in diplomatic circles. Little is known of him after his return to England until 5 October 1518, when he delivered the benign but banal oration 'In praise of matrimony' at the betrothal of the two-year-old Princess Mary to the infant dauphin of France at Greenwich. However, this event was entirely for show as Wolsey was already planning to arrange the marriage of Mary to Charles V.

Whether Tunstal was present at the meeting of Henry VIII and Charles V on Whitsunday 1520, or had anything to do with the discussions that took place at that time, is unknown. He does appear to have been present as one of the king's chaplains at the meeting between the king and François I at the Field of Cloth of Gold. He took a more active role in the discussions with Charles that took place immediately afterwards at Calais and Gravelines, and was subsequently commissioned as ambassador to Charles's court. From the middle of September 1520 until April 1521 Tunstal was with the emperor, accompanying him to Aachen, where Charles was to be crowned king of the Romans, although he was prevented from attending the coronation by a dispute over ambassadorial precedence. Tunstal then travelled to Worms, where the imperial diet was scheduled to begin in January 1521. His purposes were to persuade the emperor to commit himself to an alliance with England, to prevent the amity with France that was being urged on the emperor by Chièvres, and to finalize the plan to marry Charles to Princess Mary, but he encountered delay on all of these points. Recalled by a frustrated king, he was present at the diet until 11 April but missed the appearance of Martin Luther on 17 and 18 April, although he sent to the king the copy of Luther's *Babylonian Captivity of the Church*, which Henry subsequently refuted. However, Tunstal played a large part in subsequent negotiations until August 1521, serving as Wolsey's deputy both at Calais and, later, at Bruges.

Bishop of London Promotion continued to come Tunstal's way. In 1519 he succeeded John Colet as canon of York and prebendary of Botevant. Two years later he became dean of Salisbury and prebendary of Combe and Hornham. After the death of Richard Fitzjames in January 1522, Tunstal was made bishop of London; he was consecrated by Warham, Thomas Ruthall, and John Fisher on 19 October 1522. At the same time, Tunstal published his most famous work, *De arte supputandi*, on arithmetic. The book was received exceptionally well, and Tunstal began to acquire the reputation among his friends of being a polymath and an example to other bishops. He continued to be vigilant about heretical books, bringing to Fisher's attention Ulrich Velenus's *Libellus* against the papacy and lending him a Greek text of the liturgy of Basil and Chrysostom for reference in a refutation of Oecolampadius. Fisher acknowledged Tunstal's assistance with his *Assertionis Lutheranae confutatio* (1523) and dedicated to him his *Sacro sacerdotii defensio* (1525). With Fisher, Tunstal was chiefly responsible for censoring the book trade, and he licensed More to read heretical books in order to refute them.

Tunstal's position as bishop of London threw him into the middle of the preparations for war begun in June 1522. He opened, with a long speech, the parliament of April of 1523, in which the government's efforts to raise funds by a forced loan failed. On 25 May 1523 he was appointed keeper of the privy seal, an office he held until January 1530, but after the battle of Pavia in February 1525 Tunstal was again called upon to serve as ambassador to Charles V. Both the king and Wolsey saw this as an excellent opportunity to make gains at the expense of the defeated French. Tunstal and Richard Wingfield bore the English plan to Spain, arriving at Toledo in May. The embassy was never likely to succeed and was only made more difficult by the fact that both Wingfield and Tunstal fell ill with dysentery, Wingfield dying of it very soon, on 22 July. It soon became clear that Henry VIII was negotiating a separate peace with the French. Tunstal, aware of this only at second hand, urged the king and Wolsey to be more transparent with the emperor, but he himself heard of the treaty of the More only after the event. He returned to England in January 1526, travelling overland through France. In 1527 Tunstal again accompanied Wolsey, this time on an embassy to France, and was involved in the negotiations that led to the treaty of Cambrai in 1529.

Despite his various diplomatic commitments, Tunstal attempted to be an active presence within the diocese of London, where he determinedly preferred his relatives, including Robert Ridley (who became his secretary) and Walter Preston. According to Polydore Vergil, 'Cuthbert Tunstal was elevated to the great joy and pleasure of the citizens, for the city was anxious to have him on account of his splendid reputation for virtue' (*Anglica historia*, 305). He was no friend of heresy and had written against the doctrine of Luther despite his sympathy with many of the criticisms of the abuses within the church. In his own diocese he prohibited Tyndale's New Testament and Simon Fish's 'Supplication for the beggars'. Yet he took no lethal action against those accused of heresy, and his leniency and willingness to encourage recantation became renowned. Tunstal presided at the trial of Thomas Bilney, and it was largely because of his patience that Bilney was persuaded to recant. This established Tunstal's reputation for being both even-handed and reluctant to execute people for their beliefs. John Foxe, writing of Tunstal's conduct during the Marian persecutions, referred to him as 'no great bloody persecutor' (Foxe, 2.2102).

The divorce and the bishopric of Durham The advent of Henry's scruples about his marriage in 1527 proved awkward for Tunstal. Initially, he seems to have adopted a position close to that of More and Fisher and was convinced of the injustice of the king's desires. He was chosen by Queen Katherine as one of her defence counsel and was apparently active in that role. However, he was not present at Cambrai during the summer of 1529 when Cardinal Campeggi presided over the court of inquiry at Blackfriars. It may be that Tunstal and More were both commissioned to go to Calais in order to remove them from the proceedings. Soon after his return, he was translated to the see of Durham on 25 March 1530 and appointed president of the council of the north in June. It is possible that this too was a move designed not only to strengthen government there but also to keep him out of the way.

Tunstal was never inclined to protestant doctrine, and he opposed most of the changes in religion that occurred during the next few years. However, he was prepared to acquiesce once those changes became law. His attitude appears to have been to remain obedient to the king, and though he might be vocal in his opposition during the debate, he was prepared to comply with the judgment of the king and parliament. On the royal supremacy, Tunstal was prepared to argue strongly against it from the beginning, but once it had become law he became an equally strong advocate. He was even prepared to go so far as to preach before the Carthusian monks who had been condemned for refusing to swear the oath of supremacy, an action that must surely have surprised and upset More as much as Tunstal's volte-face disillusioned Reginald Pole. Even so, the thought that Tunstal might oppose the crown's plans to dissolve the lesser monasteries in 1536 led the king and Cromwell to order him not to attend parliament.

Tunstal's position on the matter of the annulment of the king's first marriage was slightly more complex. Although he was prepared to defend Katherine to the best of his ability, it was clear to him by 1533 that the matter had been decided. He argued energetically in her favour during the northern convocation in January 1533, but he still attended the coronation of the new queen in June. By May 1534 Tunstal openly accepted that Katherine's marriage to Henry was invalid and was prepared to visit her and ask her to renounce her title. There is some evidence to suggest that Tunstal's position altered under some duress: he was aware that Fisher and More were in prison and that his houses in Durham, Auckland, and Stockton had been searched; his secretary Ridley was imprisoned after compromising material was found in his possession. Whatever the reasons he gave for his defection away from

Katherine and her supporters, Tunstal appears to have succumbed to the king's pressure.

At Durham, Tunstal oversaw the sharp restriction of the traditional privileges of the bishop palatine undertaken by Thomas Cromwell, including the closing of the ecclesiastical mint. He took up the presidency of the council of the north in June 1530. Limited as its jurisdiction was to the county and city of York and the city of Hull, he seems to have been occupied with mainly judicial matters, especially after the 1533 appointment of the earl of Northumberland as the king's lieutenant. There is some question as to how competently Tunstal was able to conduct his business in the north, and Northumberland's appointment has sometimes been seen as indicative of his inability to maintain his authority. The position was fraught with difficulty, but Tunstal apparently continued in the post until it collapsed during the Pilgrimage of Grace.

Tunstal's own behaviour during the pilgrimage has always been suspect. When he became aware that the pilgrims were advancing on Auckland, he fled to his castle in Norham-on-Tweed. He remained there until the troubles were ended, refusing to leave even when summoned by the king. At the very least, keeping such a low profile prevented him from having to declare his position; and, unlike some other members of the council of the north who threw in their lot with the rebels, Tunstal sat on the council again when it was reconstituted in 1537. Although it was clear that the duke of Norfolk was in charge, Tunstal still retained the title of president, even though he himself was not convinced that he was the right man for the job. He remained in the post until June 1538, when he was replaced by Bishop Robert Holgate of Llandaff (later archbishop of York). Tunstal's experience remained invaluable to the crown in the north as he was subsequently and often used in negotiations with the Scots.

For the remainder of Henry's reign Tunstal was employed in a number of different capacities. He had a small hand in the production of the ten articles in 1536 and a more significant role in producing the *Institution of a Christian Man*. During the debates on the Act of Six Articles, Tunstal championed auricular confession and was seen as a more dangerous opponent to religious reform than Gardiner; it has been argued that he played an important part at this point in slowing its tide. In 1538 he was in Henry's entourage during his summer progress, and that year he was involved in the heresy trial of John Lambert. Yet in a letter to Reginald Pole, co-written with John Stokesley probably in 1537, Tunstal deployed arguments against papal authority akin to those used in his Palm Sunday sermon of 1539. After 1542 most of Tunstal's time was spent in the north, where he was involved in diplomatic business arising as a result of the war with the Scots. However, in 1545 he was sent to Calais to negotiate peace with the French, and he was present at Fontainebleau in August 1546 for the ratification of the treaty of Camp. In 1546 he participated in the examination of Hugh Latimer's involvement with the preacher Edward Crome.

Under Edward VI and Mary The accession of Edward VI in January 1547 ushered in a period of religious change. With characteristic moderation and a good relationship with the duke of Somerset, Tunstal managed to navigate a safe course through the first half of the reign despite his obvious theological misgivings. His experience and expertise in the north were still much valued, and he was employed usefully there making preparations for defence and invasion. He was one of sixteen executors of Henry's will and served as an active member of the council during the transition to a new government. He officiated at the coronation of Edward VI in February and was an important figure in parliament. His participation in council affairs was patchy through this period because he was either in the north or ill. Despite his reluctance to break openly with the government in matters of religion, Tunstal's position became increasingly difficult. He opposed bills abolishing the chantries and clerical celibacy, and introducing the Act of Uniformity, and he argued strongly from the conservative point of view on the matter of the sacrament of the altar and the Book of Common Prayer, despite having been a member of the Windsor commission, which helped to prepare it. However, once these bills became law, he enforced them.

Tunstal was able to maintain his position until 1550. Somerset's fall and the rise of the duke of Northumberland, while initially providing some hope among conservatives for a reversal of religious policy, led to disappointment. Tunstal stood in the way of Northumberland's strategy to acquire power in the north, and their relationship deteriorated. Accused of misprision of treason for his alleged involvement in a conspiracy to rebel in the north, he was arrested, confined to his house in London, and finally imprisoned in the Tower. Proceedings against him in parliament failed when the Commons resolved that Tunstal should have an opportunity to defend himself in public—an eventuality that Northumberland was hoping to avoid. Instead, Tunstal was convicted by a special commission, not of treason but of felony. He was deprived of his bishopric on 14 October 1552, and the see itself was dismembered. He remained in prison, first in the Tower and then in the king's bench, until the end of the reign and used the time to write his treatise on the eucharist, *De veritate corporis et sanguinis domini nostri Jesu Christi in eucharistia*. He also produced an edition of his cousin John Redman's *De justificatione*.

After the accession of Mary, Tunstal was released from prison on 6 August 1553. The see was restored in April 1554 and Tunstal was restored as its bishop. He subsequently participated to some degree in the trials of notable protestants, including John Hooper, Robert Ferrar, and Rowland Taylor. He condemned no one to death and seems to have been on the whole unconvinced by the policy of persecution.

Last months and reputation On the accession of Elizabeth, Tunstal, now eighty-four, was not required to attend either parliament or the coronation of the new queen. His refusal to change once again and take the oath of supremacy under Elizabeth led to his deprivation. He remained in London in the kind custody of Archbishop Matthew

Parker until his death on 18 November 1559. He was buried at Lambeth.

There was nothing of the martyr in Tunstal. His survival through four Tudor reigns and into a fifth testifies to the flexibility of his mind and the moderation of his temperament. Although strong in his opinions and not backward in arguing them, once policy was made he was content to carry it out. Uncomfortable persecuting heretics, he managed to avoid condemning them to death and had a reputation for honesty second to none: as Thomas Bilney noted, 'how can I think in Tonstal any craft or doublenes to dwell' (Foxe, 2.1006). His desire to avoid persecutions led him to go so far as to buy copies of William Tyndale's New Testament in order to burn them, rather than burn or prosecute those who bought them (Hall's chron., 762). A gentle man given to collecting coins and gardening, he was probably the most widely respected bishop and scholar in sixteenth-century England.

Tunstal was never a prolific writer: his most important works were *De arte supputandi* (1522) and *De veritate corporis et sanguinis domini*. While bishop of Durham, he made many important improvements to Durham Castle, reshaping the gatehouse and providing a new chapel and gallery. He also improved the episcopal residence at Auckland.   D. G. NEWCOMBE

Sources APC · W. W. Rouse Ball and J. A. Venn, eds., *Admissions to Trinity College, Cambridge*, 5 vols. (1911–16) · F. Blomefield and C. Parkin, *An essay towards a topographical history of the county of Norfolk*, 5 vols. (1739–75) · *The diary of Henry Machyn, citizen and merchant-taylor of London, from AD 1550 to AD 1563*, ed. J. G. Nichols, CS, 42 (1848) · Emden, *Cam.* · J. Foxe, *Acts and monuments* (1583) [edition used: D. G. Newcombe, ed., *A facsimile of John Foxe's Book of martyrs, 1583* (2001); version 1.0 on CD-Rom] · *LP Henry VIII* · *Hall's chronicle*, ed. H. Ellis (1809) · J. Leland, *Itinerary* (1745) · *The correspondence of Erasmus*, ed. and trans. R. A. B. Mynors and D. F. S. Thomson (Toronto, 1975) · J. G. Nichols, ed., *Narratives of the days of the Reformation* (1859) · M. Noble, *Two dissertations upon the mint and coins of the episcopal-palatines of Durham* (1780) · R. R. Reid, *The king's council in the north* (1921) · C. Sturge, *Cuthbert Tunstal* (1938) · *The Anglica historia of Polydore Vergil*, ed. D. Hay (1950) · T. D. Whitaker, *A history of Richmondshire*, 2 vols. (1823) · C. Wriothesley, *A chronicle of England*, ed. W. D. Hamilton, 2 vols. (1875–7)
Archives BL, Cotton MSS, misc. corresp. · BL, corresp., Add. MSS 32647–32655 · U. Durham L., register as bishop of Durham
Likenesses group portrait, oils, *c.*1570 (*Edward VI and the pope*), NPG · oils, Burton Constable, Yorkshire [*see illus.*]

Tunstall, James (*c.*1708–1762), Church of England clergyman and classical scholar, was born at Aysgarth, in the North Riding of Yorkshire, the son of James Tunstall, an attorney of Richmondshire. He was educated at the recently endowed Slaidburn grammar school, and was admitted a sizar at St John's College, Cambridge, on 29 July 1724, aged about sixteen, where he was partly maintained by an uncle. He graduated BA in 1727, MA in 1731, BD in 1738, and DD on 13 July 1744 (incorporated at Oxford, 1742). He contributed a set of Greek verses to the university collection of poems for the accession of George II. Having previously been ordained deacon (he was not priested until 5 March 1732), he was elected to a college fellowship on 24 March 1729; eventually he became senior

dean, and in 1743–4 he was one of the two principal tutors of the college. His classical knowledge and kindness of manner made him popular among undergraduates; it was reported of him that 'As a Pupil Monger, no one took more pains for the improvment of such as were placed under his care' (Masters, 114).

It was while Tunstall was at St John's that he became caught up in a learned dispute with his Cambridge colleague Conyers Middleton that lasted from 1741 to 1745. Debate centred on Tunstall's doubts over whether Cicero's letters to Brutus could be accepted as genuine, as Middleton had done in his *Life of Cicero*. Tunstall's interest in Cicero was enduring. He advertised a new edition of Cicero's letters to Pomponius Atticus and to his brother Quintus, and he took with him to London in 1762 his annotations on the first three books of the letters. They were offered to William Bowyer, who refused to take them until the whole copy was complete. Tunstall died before he could comply.

After ordination Tunstall, on the presentation of Edward Harley, second earl of Oxford, was instituted to the rectory of Sturmer, in Essex, which he held until 1746. In October 1741 he was elected public orator at Cambridge University, polling 160 votes against the 137 recorded for Philip Yonge, later bishop of Norwich. Though absent from the university he retained the office until 1746, when his grace for the continuance of the permission was refused. This absence was caused by his appointment in summer 1744 as junior domestic chaplain to John Potter, archbishop of Canterbury. It was Potter who in 1744 offered Tunstall the rectory of Saltwood, Kent, which he declined. Instead he accepted the vicarage of Minster, on the Isle of Thanet (collated 12 February 1747) and, by dispensation, the rectory of Great Chart, near Ashford, Kent (collated 6 March 1747), each of which was worth about £200 annually. From 1746 until his death he was treasurer and canon residentiary of St David's Cathedral. As a result of these preferments he vacated his fellowship of St John's in February 1747. He was also free to marry, which he did on 6 September 1750. His bride was Elizabeth (1723/4–1772), daughter of John Dodsworth and Henrietta Hutton of Thornton Watlass, Yorkshire. Tunstall's mother-in-law was sister of Matthew Hutton, successively archbishop of York and of Canterbury. Tunstall naturally hoped that the match would bring him further advancement. Waiting in vain for a prebendal stall at Canterbury, and unhappy at the income generated by his Kent livings, he was finally, on Hutton's nomination, collated on 11 November 1757 to the vicarage of Rochdale, in Lancashire, which, though reputed to be worth about £800 p.a., fell well short of that amount. Tunstall had expectations of Charles Yorke as a patron, but their amicable correspondence yielded no material gains.

Tunstall was well-known in literary circles. His correspondents included the second earl of Oxford, Thomas Birch, and Zachary Grey, while William Warburton, Thomas Baker, and John Byrom, the poet and nonjuror, were among his friends. He published not only on Cicero.

He became involved in the controversy surrounding Lord Hardwicke's Marriage Act of 1753 and, in answer to treatises of Henry Stebbing, wrote a *Vindication of Power of States to Prohibit Clandestine Marriages* (1755) and *Marriage in Society Stated* (1755). In theology he produced *Academica: part the first. Discourses on the certainty, distinction, and connection of natural and revealed religion* (1759); his *Lectures on Natural and Revealed Religion Read in the Chapel of St. John's College, Cambridge* (1765) were posthumously published by subscription for the benefit of his widow and children, and were edited by his brother-in-law. These lectures (twenty-seven were delivered) had been commenced while he was a tutor at St John's but progress faltered after he had been appointed chaplain to Potter. They proclaim Tunstall's moderate churchmanship and his emphasis on practical morality. Arguing that all societies are founded on restraint of liberty he emphasized the need for church authority to be enforced by law, although a degree of dissent from her doctrines was permissible. He took comfort from knowing that 'our ecclesiastical constitution is erected on the foundation of natural religion and the Christian revelation together' (lectures 17, 21). The lectures tried to establish the necessity of revealed religion; natural religion was defined as 'a system of principles and rules only, which our reason can collect from the nature and revelation of things' (p. 41).

Tunstall died, in reduced circumstances, at his brother's house in Mark Lane, London, on 28 March 1762 and was buried in the chancel of St Peter Cornhill on 2 April. His widow moved to Hadleigh, Suffolk, whose rector, Dr Thomas Tanner, was the husband of Archbishop Potter's daughter, and died there, on 5 December 1772, in her forty-ninth year. Her brother Dr Frederick Dodsworth, later canon of Windsor, had helped her to bring up the children; three daughters were living in 1772. Tunstall's library was sold in 1764. He had made critical annotations to the first edition of John Duncombe's translation of Horace, and bequeathed 152 manuscript sermons to his son-in-law, Sir Everard Home.   NIGEL ASTON

Sources *GM*, 1st ser., 32 (1762), 194 · Venn, *Alum. Cant.*, 1/2.272 · J. E. B. Mayor and R. F. Scott, eds., *Admissions to the College of St John the Evangelist in the University of Cambridge*, 3 vols. in 4 pts (1882–1931), 2.110–13, 372–4 · R. Masters, *Memoirs of the life and writings of the late Rev. Thomas Baker, B.D.* (1784), 83, 114–15 · *Fasti Angl.* (Hardy), 1.318; 3.614; 4.372–4 · P. Morant, *The history and antiquities of the county of Essex*, 2 (1768), 347 · E. Hasted, *The history and topographical survey of the county of Kent*, 2nd edn, 10 (1800), 294 · parish registers, Thornton Watlass, N. Yorks. CRO · H. Fishwick, *The history of the parish of Rochdale in the county of Lancaster* (1889), 237–8 · T. D. Whitaker, *An history of the original parish of Whalley*, 3rd edn (1818), 447 · H. Pigot, *A guide to Hadleigh*, 2nd edn (1874), 211–12 · [S. Pegge], *Anonymiana, or, Ten centuries of observations on various authors and subjects* (1809), 177–8 · Nichols, *Lit. anecdotes*, 2.166–70; 3.668; 5.412–13 · Nichols, *Illustrations*, 2.106, 124–5; 3.703–5; 4.372–4 · *The private journal and literary remains of John Byrom*, ed. R. Parkinson, 2 vols. in 4 pts, Chetham Society, 32, 34, 40, 44 (1854–7), vol. 2, pt 1, p. 42; vol. 2, pt 2, pp. 336, 421 · *N&Q*, 8th ser., 11 (1897), 85, 131 · *DNB* · parish register, St Peter Cornhill, 2 April 1762 [burial]

Archives BL, letters to Dr Grey, Add. MS 23990, fols. 2, 3 · BL, letters to Lord Harley, Add. MS 4253, fols. 86–97 · BL, letters to C. Yorke, Add. MSS 35603, 35633–35635, *passim*

Tunstall, Marmaduke (1743–1790), naturalist, was baptized Marmaduke Cuthbert Constable on 22 July 1743 (the day of his birth), at Swine, Yorkshire, the second son of the antiquary Cuthbert *Constable (*c.*1680–1747), of Burton Constable, Holderness, Yorkshire, and his second wife, Elizabeth (1709–1765), daughter of George Heneage, of Hainton, Lincolnshire, and his wife, Elizabeth. His father had changed his surname in 1718, from Tunstall on inheriting the Burton Constable estate from his brother-in-law, William Constable, fourth Viscount Dunbar.

Marmaduke Constable (called Duke or Dukey by his family) spent the winters between 1754 and 1756 in London. At about this time he was sent to France, to be educated at Douai College and, later, under a tutor in Paris. In 1760, on the death of his uncle, Marmaduke Tunstall, he succeeded to the estates of Scargill, Hutton, Long Villiers, and Wycliffe, Yorkshire, and re-adopted the name of Tunstall. In 1764 he started construction of a hall at Wycliffe.

Tunstall devoted himself to literature and science. During the 1760s and 1770s, while residing at his London town house in Welbeck Street, he began the formation of a natural history museum. His museum contained both living and preserved specimens, and was a source of information for many artists and authors, including the engraver Thomas Bewick and the naturalist Thomas Pennant. Tunstall's ornithological collection was particularly impressive, not least because of its systematic arrangement. His collections included ornithological specimens brought back by Sir Joseph Banks from Cook's first voyage to the south seas, and entomological specimens from the second voyage, in addition to shells, fossils, minerals, and human artefacts.

Tunstall corresponded with a number of the leading naturalists of his day, including Daniel Solander and the ornithologist John Latham. He was elected a fellow of the Royal Society on 11 April 1771, and in the same year published privately his *Ornithologia Britannica*, a rare work which was reprinted by the Willughby Society in 1880. In 1774 Tunstall was elected a fellow of the Society of Antiquaries. He also published 'An account of several lunar iris (or rainbow)' for the *Philosophical Transactions of the Royal Society*, in 1783.

In 1776 Tunstall married Mary, the daughter and coheir of George Markham of either Hoxly, Lincolnshire or Ollerton, Nottinghamshire, and his wife, Mary. The couple (who had no children) moved to Tunstall's house at Wycliffe. His collections were not transferred until some seven years later to Wycliffe, where a special museum room had been constructed. At Wycliffe, Tunstall became acquainted with a fellow naturalist, Thomas Zouch (1737–1815), the rector of Wycliffe. The two became friendly, despite the fact that Tunstall (a Roman Catholic) had opposed Zouch's presentation to the benefice, of which Tunstall was the patron. Following Tunstall's death, Zouch described his amiable neighbour as 'the poor man's friend', whose 'deeds of charity were many' (Boyd and Jessop, 230). Tunstall died suddenly (possibly from pneumonia), at Wycliffe Hall on 11 October 1790, and was buried a week later in the chancel of the church at Wycliffe.

He was survived by his wife, Mary, who died in October 1825, at Sales House near Shepton Mallet, Somerset (or at Hammersmith).

Tunstall's splendid museum (and most of his estate) was bequeathed to his elder half-brother William Constable, who died a few months later, on 18 May 1791. In turn, the estates of Wycliffe and Burton Constable passed to Edward Sheldon (1750–1803), William Constable's nephew. A large part of Tunstall's museum was purchased by his friend, the lawyer and antiquary George Allen (1736–1800) of Blackwell Grange, Darlington, where he opened up Tunstall's collection to the public in June 1792. Allen also extended and improved the collection which later formed the basis of the Hancock Museum, Newcastle upon Tyne.   B. B. WOODWARD, *rev.* YOLANDA FOOTE

Sources G. T. Fox, *Synopsis of the Newcastle Museum* (1827) · *GM*, 1st ser., 60 (1790), 959 · *Ornithologia Britannica*, ed. A. Newton (1880), prefix · C. E. Jackson, *Bird etchings: the illustrators and their books, 1655–1855* (1985) · G. T. Fox, *Memoirs of Marmaduke Tunstall esq, and George Allen esq, together with notices of the works of Thomas Bewick* (1827) · I. Hall and E. Hall, *Burton Constable Hall* (1991) · J. Kirk, *Biographies of English Catholics in the eighteenth century*, ed. J. H. Pollen and E. Burton (1909) · M. J. Boyd and L. Jessop, 'A "truly amiable gentleman": new light on the life and work of Marmaduke Tunstall (1743–1790)', *Archives of Natural History*, 25 (1998), 221–36 · IGI

Archives BL, notebook written as student at Douai, Add. MS 57340 · Burton Constable Hall, MSS · U. Newcastle, Hancock Museum | Bodl. Oxf., corresp. with John Charles Brooke · Bodl. Oxf., corresp. with his brother William Constable, etc.

Likenesses Lambert, line engraving, BM, RS · H. Walton, oils, Leeds Museums and Galleries

Tunstall, Thomas (*d.* 1616), Roman Catholic priest and martyr, was born in Whinfell, Kendal, Westmorland. Nothing is known of his parents, nor is the date of his birth known. He was collaterally descended from the Tunstalls of Thurland Castle, Tunstall, Lancashire, who had held the barony of Kendal, and who subsequently moved to Scargill, Hutton, and Wycliffe, in Yorkshire. A prominent member of this family was Cuthbert Tunstal, bishop of Durham, deprived under Elizabeth I. The register of the English College, Douai, describes Thomas Tunstall as 'Carliolensis' and 'Kendallensis'. He matriculated under the alias Helmes at the college on 7 October 1607. The name Helmes is found in the Kendal church registers; it is possible that Thomas's mother was of this family. Nine recusants from Kendal, including three of the Helmes family of Whinfell, are recorded.

Thomas Tunstall was ordained priest on the continent in 1609 and sent to England in 1610. Shortly after his arrival in England he was apprehended and imprisoned under the alias of Richard Dyer. He spent the next four or five years in Newgate and other prisons, latterly in Wisbech Castle. He escaped from Wisbech Castle by rope, but cut his hands so severely that he went to a charitable protestant lady, the wife of a magistrate, Sir Hammond L'Estrange, for his wounds to be dressed. When L'Estrange discovered this, despite his wife's entreaties, he had Tunstall committed to Norwich Castle. Tunstall was tried at the next assizes and condemned to death. At the trial '[l]aw … and procedure regarding evidence were all utterly disregarded. The prisoner was convicted upon the evidence of

one single witness, though, in cases of high treason, two were required' (Foley, 5.691). That one witness gave perjured evidence. On 13 July 1616 Thomas Tunstall was hanged, drawn, and quartered outside Magdalen gates, Norwich, and his head was placed over St Bennet's gate.

Recusancy in the Tunstall family continued. Two of Tunstall's nephews were Jesuit priests: Thomas (*c.*1611–1640) and another Thomas (*b.* 1614). There were also six Tunstalls at St Omer and Bruges English colleges after Thomas Tunstall's death. Following the sale of the Tunstall family effects in 1700 a portrait of Thomas Tunstall the martyr ultimately came into the hands of Canon Raine of York. He gave the portrait to Stonyhurst College, saying: 'I possess a small portrait on panel of a Yorkshire gentleman who was a missionary priest and died for his religion upon the scaffold—Thomas Tunstall of Scargill' (Raine, 44). Tunstall was one of the 136 martyrs beatified by the pope in 1929.   ANTONY CHARLES RYAN

Sources H. Foley, ed., *Records of the English province of the Society of Jesus*, 5 (1879), 690–92; 7 (1882–3), 784–5 · G. Anstruther, *The seminary priests*, 2 (1975), 324 · R. Challoner, *Memoirs of missionary priests*, ed. J. H. Pollen, rev. edn (1924) · J. Raine, ed., *Depositions from the castle of York relating to offences committed in the northern counties in the seventeenth century*, SurtS, 40 (1861) · F. Blomefield and C. Parkin, *An essay towards a topographical history of the county of Norfolk*, [2nd edn], 11 vols. (1805–10), vol. 3, p. 366 · D. A. Bellenger, ed., *English and Welsh priests, 1558–1800* (1984) · T. M. McCoog, *English and Welsh Jesuits, 1555–1650*, 2, Catholic RS, 75 (1995) · F. Nicholson and E. Axon, *The older nonconformity in Kendal* (1915), 207 · Gillow, *Lit. biog. hist.* · parish register, Kendal, 1558–March 1587, 1591–, Cumbria AS, Kendal · E. Peacock, *A list of the Roman Catholics in the county of York in 1604* (1872) · P. R. Harris, ed., *Douai College documents, 1639–1794*, Catholic RS, 63 (1972)

Likenesses portrait on panel, Stonyhurst College, Lancashire

Tunsted, Simon (*d.* 1369), Franciscan schoolman, was born in Norwich of a Norfolk family. His surname derives from the village of Tunsted to the north-east of Norwich. The custom in the English Franciscan province was initially for friars to take the name of their home town, and it is this name that is given where friars appear in episcopal registers. Simon Tunsted became, according to Francis Blomefield (*d.* 1752), warden of the Franciscan house at Norwich. He gained a doctorate in theology at Oxford, and in 1351 was regent master of the Franciscans there. In 1360 he became the twenty-third minister-provincial of the English province. According to a list of English ministers-provincial, after his death in 1369 he was buried in the nunnery of Bruisyard in Suffolk.

A colophon, dated 1351, to the treatise *Quatuor principalia musicae*, attests Tunsted's tenure of office as regent master in Oxford, and also his proficiency in music: 'In that year the regent among the Minors at Oxford was Friar Simon of Tunstede, DST, who excelled in music and in the seven liberal arts' (Little, 60). On these grounds the treatise was from the time of John Bale (*d.* 1563) attributed to Tunsted; more recent scholarship, however, has established that there is insufficient evidence for such an attribution. A further note in one of the manuscripts (Bodl. Oxf., MS Digby 90, fol. 1) records the presentation of the treatise to the Oxford Franciscans by John Tewkesbury in 1388, with the assent of the minister-provincial. This gave rise to the theory among early musicologists, notably Edward Bernard and Anthony Wood in the late seventeenth century, that John (or Thomas) Tewkesbury must have edited the treatise, and on the strength of this an anonymous work in Oxford (Bodl. Oxf., MS Digby 17) was attributed to him. F. L. Harrison has argued that the treatise *Quatuor principalia musicae* was indeed written in Oxford by an Oxford Franciscan, but certainly not by Tunsted, and suggests John Tewkesbury as a more plausible candidate, noting the similarity of the hand of MS Digby 90 with that of a known work of Tewkesbury's *De situ universorum*. The importance of the *Quatuor principalia musicae* lies in its introduction of melodic 'coloration', in which melodic strength replaces rhythmical intensity. This development appears to have been of English origin, and was perhaps first articulated in Oxford during Tunsted's term as regent master.

Tunsted's interest in the subjects forming the quadrivium in the arts faculty is further shown by the commentary on Aristotle's *Meteorics* ascribed to him by Leland, a work that may survive in a collection edited in 1639 by the Franciscan Luke Wadding; the attribution has, however, been disputed. He applied his expertise to practical matters as well, making improvements in the clock that Richard Wallingford, abbot of St Albans, had constructed in 1326, and also (rather superficially) to the book Wallingford wrote about his invention.   ANDREW JOTISCHKY

Sources S. Rankin and D. Hiley, eds., *Music in the Medieval English liturgy* (1993) · C. E. H. de Coussemaker, ed., 'Quatuor principalia musicae', *Scriptorum de musica medii aevi*, 4 (Paris, 1876), 200–98 · D. A. Hughes and G. Abraham, eds., *Ars nova and the Renaissance, 1300–1549* (1960), vol. 3 of *New Oxford history of music* (1954–68) · J. North, 'Natural philosophy in late medieval Oxford', *Hist. U. Oxf.* 2: *Late med. Oxf.*, 65–102, esp. 100 · A. G. Little, *The Grey friars in Oxford*, OHS, 20 (1892) · R. P. F. Ioannis Duns Scoti … *opera omnia*, ed. L. Wadding and others, 3 (Lyons, 1639) [incl. *Quaestiarum meteorologicarum* attributed to Tunsted] · J. S. Brewer, ed., *Monumenta Franciscana*, 1, Rolls Series, 4 (1858) · Emden, *Oxf.* · F. Blomefield and C. Parkin, *An essay towards a topographical history of the county of Norfolk*, 5 vols. (1739–75), vol. 4

Tuohy, John Francis [Frank] (1925–1999), writer and university teacher, was born on 2 May 1925 at Uckfield, Sussex, the only son and the younger of the two children of Dr Patrick Gerald Tuohy (1888–1958), general practitioner, and his wife, Dorothy Marion (1884–1964), daughter of James Annadale of Polton, Edinburgh, and his wife, Muriel. His father was Irish and his mother Scottish.

Frank Tuohy was born with a hole in his heart and it seemed likely that his life would be short. His parents were determined that he should none the less lead as normal a life as possible. He was an exceptionally bright child with a passion for reading, and his governess inspired in him a lifelong interest in the natural history of the surrounding Sussex countryside. He survived two years at a local boarding-school where, forbidden any form of strenuous exercise, he escaped the compulsory games (then considered so good for the character) and in 1938 he won a scholarship to Stowe School. There he benefited from the liberal regime of the school's founding headmaster, J. F. Roxburgh, and from having the run of its famous

grounds and lakes. His chilling story *The Palladian Bridge*, published many years later, is set there.

Nearly all Tuohy's friends and contemporaries were called up at the statutory age of eighteen and, although his heart condition had not deteriorated and he had grown into a good-looking black-haired young man, he was inevitably turned down for military service. Instead he was encouraged to take up the scholarship to King's College, Cambridge, which he had won the year before. There he read English and philosophy and duly got his first in 1946. In the cheerless atmosphere of post-war England he decided to look for work abroad and was pleased to be offered a place on the permanent staff of the British Council. The offer was no sooner accepted than it was abruptly withdrawn after he failed yet another medical examination. A few months later the British Council relented to the extent of nominating him for a temporary job as a lecturer at Turku University in Finland.

Post-war Finland was no more cheerful than England, but the year Tuohy spent there (1947–8) proved to be extremely useful. He discovered and nurtured a talent for lecturing to students for whom English was at best a third language and, equally important to him, he had the time to work on his own writing. So the appointment was a success all round, and he came home with a viable design for living for as long as he was spared.

Tuohy heard of several possible academic jobs in South America and he set off to Brazil to try his luck there. He taught for a few months in an English school before being appointed professor of English language and literature in 1950 at São Paulo University, where he remained for six enjoyable and productive years. He was fluent in Portuguese and had many Brazilian friends with whom he kept in touch when he moved back to England in 1956. He took Brazil as the setting for his first two novels, *The Animal Game* (1957) and *The Warm Nights of January* (1960), both acclaimed by the critics; his wonderful long story, also set in Brazil, 'The Admiral and the Nuns', won him the Katherine Mansfield-Menton short story prize in 1960. Perhaps it was those solitary hours as a child devoted to watching the private lives of birds and small animals that led to his equally devoted study of the foibles and failings of his fellow beings and thence to the writing of his stories. Each, whether long or short, is complete in itself, a novel in miniature. The settings range from Tunbridge Wells to Tokyo, and his characters, whatever their nationality and whatever their station in life, suffer the social embarrassments so craftily devised for them. There are no winners in a Tuohy story. His matter-of-fact style and focus on everyday experience has been likened to Chekhov, while others find de Maupassant a more apt comparison: 'each story, mordant, concise and a small miracle of construction, represents, as he himself put it, "a painful bite down on the rotten tooth of fact"' (*The Independent*).

Dr Christiaan Barnard's researches into the possibilities of heart transplants had opened up the whole field of heart surgery, and Tuohy had been advised that he could be a candidate for an operation in a year or two. With this in mind he accepted an invitation to join the academic staff of the Jagiellonian University of Krakow in Poland for a period of two years. It was a fascinating if sometimes harrowing experience matched only by the one awaiting him in St Bartholomew's Hospital on his return to London. But all went well and within a few months he started work on his third and best novel, *The Ice Saints*. Set in the uneasy post-Stalin period of the Poland which he had just left, the book had an immediate success and won both the James Tait Black and the Geoffrey Faber prizes for the best novel of the year (1964). C. P. Snow, reviewing all three novels, wrote that they established Tuohy in the first flight of English novelists. In 1965 Tuohy was elected a fellow of the Royal Society of Literature. 'Although his creative output was relatively small in volume—as a novelist he was even more reticent than his admired E. M. Forster—Frank Tuohy came to occupy a position in contemporary English fiction which he made completely his own' (*The Times*).

After triumphs, both literary and cardiac, Tuohy turned to the Far East and was a visiting professor at Waseda University from 1964 to 1967. There were no more novels but he continued to write short stories—often first published in the *London Magazine*. His volume of stories *Fingers in the Door* (1970) won the E. M. Forster memorial prize, while another, *Live Bait* (1972), earned him the Heinemann award. He also published a travel book on Portugal (1970) and a masterly short biographical study of W. B. Yeats (1976).

Tuohy travelled widely in the United States and acted as writer in residence and visiting professor at Purdue University, Lafayette, Indiana, which later awarded him an honorary DLitt. In 1983 he returned to Japan as visiting professor at Tokyo's Rikkyo University, a post he held for six years.

Tuohy retired in 1989 to a converted barn in Somerset; country life suited him and he drove a small, elderly car with hair-raising confidence. He loved food and drink, and was a host for all seasons and an inspired cook. He was a loyal and affectionate friend and, surprisingly for a writer whose work was not exactly cheerful, had a wonderful sense of humour. Although he never married, his extended family, including his older sister and her brood and a large number of cousins, were central to his life.

Frank Tuohy died on 11 April 1999 in hospital at Shepton Mallet, Somerset, and after cremation his ashes were scattered eight days later in his garden at Shatwell Cottage, Yarlington, Somerset.   ALAN MACLEAN

Sources personal knowledge (2004) · private information (2004) [Mrs David Driver, sister; James Macaskie; Francis King] · *The Times* (15 April 1999) · *The Independent* (15 April 1999)
Archives Boston University, Massachusetts · NRA, papers

Tupper, Sir Charles, first baronet (1821–1915), doctor and prime minister of Canada, was born on 2 July 1821 just outside Amherst, Nova Scotia, the elder of the two sons of Revd Charles Tupper and his first wife, Miriam, *née* Lockhart, the widow of John Lowe. Tupper's great-grandfather had emigrated from Connecticut to Nova Scotia in 1763 and his father was a leading figure in the Baptist church and a formidable scholar. Tupper's early education took

Sir Charles Tupper, first baronet (1821–1915), by Barraud, pubd 1891

place within the family home and at local grammar schools, but in 1837–9 he attended Horton Academy (later Acadia University), Nova Scotia, and in 1840 entered the University of Edinburgh. He received a diploma from the Royal College of Surgeons on 20 April 1843 and became an MD on 17 August that year. On 8 October 1846 he married Frances Amelia (*d*. 1912), the daughter of Silas H. Morse of Amherst. They had three daughters, two of whom died in infancy, and three sons.

Tupper established a medical practice and opened a drug store in Amherst. As a country doctor he journeyed on horseback to see patients and turned his hand to everything from surgery to pulling teeth. After moving to Halifax in 1859 he became city medical officer, served on the surgical staff of the City and Provincial Hospital, and was chairman of the committee responsible for establishing a medical school. In 1863 he was president of the Nova Scotia Medical Society and from 1867 to 1870 first president of the Canadian Medical Association. After 1868 he practised in Ottawa and Toronto, but medicine occupied less and less of his time.

Nova Scotian politician In 1855 Tupper entered the Nova Scotia assembly as a Conservative and at the first caucus advocated appealing for the votes of the Roman Catholic minority and abandoning the party's opposition to the government construction of railways. James William Johnston effectively surrendered the leadership of the party to Tupper during the 1856 session, and early in 1857

Tupper persuaded a bloc of Catholic members of the legislative assembly to defect to the Conservatives, who took office on 23 February 1857 with Tupper as provincial secretary. That June he opened discussions with the governments of New Brunswick and Canada to secure an intercolonial railway, and in September 1858 he went to London seeking imperial support. Tupper blamed the failure of the negotiations on the short-sightedness of the British cabinet, and he returned convinced of the need to restructure the imperial relationship and to seek closer ties with the other British North American colonies.

In the election of 1859 Tupper barely retained his seat, and in February 1860 the Conservatives were forced to resign. For the next three years Tupper ferociously attacked the Liberal government in the assembly and through the Conservative Party's organ, the British *Colonist*, and in 1863 the Conservatives were returned with the largest majority in a decade. Johnston again became prime minister and Tupper provincial secretary on 11 June 1863, but on 24 May 1864 Johnston went to the bench and Tupper succeeded him as prime minister. During the election campaign Tupper had committed his party to extending the provincial railway to Pictou on the northern coast, and he awarded the contract to Sandford Fleming, the chief engineer, without public tendering. In later years Tupper would be haunted by the charge that he and Fleming had conspired for personal profit, but judged by its results the contract was a good one, for the line was completed ahead of schedule and on budget. In 1864 Tupper introduced his most controversial measure, a Free School Act establishing a system of state-subsidized schools. The act encouraged school districts voluntarily to impose compulsory assessment, but Tupper aroused a public outcry by imposing compulsory taxation in 1865. When one of his own Catholic supporters moved to amend the 1865 bill to allow Catholics to have state-supported separate schools, Tupper opposed the amendment but agreed that Catholic-run schools could offer religious instruction after hours and still receive public grants.

Father of Canadian confederation In a speech in 1860 Tupper committed himself to British North American union. The speech reflected his anger at imperial policies which did not recognize the potential value of the British colonies overseas, and his belief that Nova Scotia could never occupy a position of importance within the empire except in alliance with Canada. In 1861 Tupper supported a resolution in favour of union and in 1864 he called for a conference to discuss union of the maritime provinces as a preliminary step towards the creation of a British North American union. At the conference in Charlottetown, Tupper and Samuel Leonard Tilley, the prime minister of New Brunswick, acted as the joint secretaries, but a delegation from the united province of Canada persuaded the conference to endorse a plan for confederation and to meet at Quebec City to work out the details.

At Quebec, Tupper again headed the Nova Scotian delegation. Although his own preference was for a legislative union, he knew this was unacceptable and so supported the Canadian proposals for a highly centralized federal union. He was, however, concerned to offset the preponderance Canada would have in the elected House of Commons by ensuring equal representation for the maritime provinces in the appointed senate. Another crucial issue was the value of the customs duties to be surrendered to the new federal authority. To reach an agreement Tupper deliberately underestimated the potential shortfall in provincial revenues for Nova Scotia and agreed to the wholly inadequate annual subsidy of 80 cents per capita. Opposition to the resolutions adopted at Quebec quickly mounted across Nova Scotia, and, after the defeat of Tilley and the pro-confederate forces in New Brunswick in 1865, Tupper marked time until Tilley regained power. Then, promising changes in the Quebec Resolutions, he persuaded the assembly on 23 April 1866 to endorse a motion in favour of union. In fact, the only really significant change made at the London conference in 1866 was to give protection to separate schools where they had been legally established before confederation, and Tupper opposed an attempt to extend similar guarantees to the maritime provinces. He pushed for a revision of the subsidy formula, but only minor changes were made in it.

Federal politician On 1 July 1867 Tupper handed over power to a revamped provincial administration. When John A. Macdonald had difficulties in constructing the first federal cabinet Tupper persuaded Thomas D'Arcy McGee that they should both step aside to allow the appointment of an Irish Catholic from Nova Scotia, Edward Kenny. In the first federal elections Tupper was the only pro-confederate elected in Nova Scotia, and then by a very narrow margin. When Joseph Howe, the leader of the anti-confederates, went to London in 1868 to push for repeal of the union, Tupper effectively presented the case against repeal and helped to persuade Howe to enter the cabinet. On 21 June 1870 Tupper became president of the privy council and on 2 July 1872 minister of inland revenue. His influence was soon felt. Convinced that the United States would never compromise over the Atlantic fisheries dispute, he pushed strongly for an end to the system of giving fishing licences to Americans. This action precipitated the negotiations which culminated in the treaty of Washington in 1871. Although not entirely happy with the treaty, which allowed Americans access to the fisheries, Tupper defended it in the House of Commons. In the election of 1872 he organized the campaign in Nova Scotia, and only one of the twenty-one members was elected as an opponent of the government.

On 22 February 1873 Tupper became minister of customs and, although he held office only until 6 November, when Macdonald resigned because of scandal over loans to the Canadian Pacific Railway Company, he established the British system of weights and measures as a uniform standard across Canada. In 1874 Tupper and only one other Conservative were elected in Nova Scotia. None the less, a vacuum existed at the very heart of the Conservative Party and Tupper moved to fill it. He loyally stood by Macdonald and over the next four years campaigned in virtually every by-election in Canada. In the House of Commons, Tupper gained a reputation for making long-winded and highly partisan speeches, but his command of detail and his memory were outstanding and there were few speakers who could match him at a public meeting. Indeed, he was generally seen as Macdonald's heir-apparent.

Tupper's influence in the formulation of Conservative policy during this period was critical. The growth of protectionist sentiment was an inevitable reaction to the American refusal to renegotiate reciprocity, but Tupper was an early convert, arguing for a 'national policy' to protect Canadian industry. As the recession of the 1870s deepened, Tupper focused increasingly on the issue of protection. There is an apocryphal story that he arrived at the budget debate of 1876 prepared to advocate free trade in the event that the Liberals adopted protectionist policies. Certainly Tupper was prepared to attack across-the-board tariff increases, but he knew the Liberals would never introduce the kind of selective increases to protect Canadian industries to which he was deeply committed, more deeply indeed than Macdonald. Similarly, it was more than political opportunism which led Tupper to attack the government's railway policies. He was particularly critical of the Liberals for not giving greater priority to the completion of a railway to British Columbia over an all-Canadian route. Tupper placed these policies at the centre of the Conservative platform. His speeches in their defence were distributed to party organizers across the country, the Nova Scotia Liberal–Conservative Association which he established in 1874 was used as a model in other parts of the country, and he actively campaigned in both the maritime provinces and Ontario during the election of 1878, which saw the Conservatives returned with a healthy majority.

Tupper was appointed minister of public works and railways on 17 October 1878, but on 20 May 1879 railways and canals were hived off as a separate department with Tupper as minister. His greatest challenge was the completion of the Pacific Railway. Signs of interest from a syndicate headed by George Stephen persuaded him that the construction and operation of the railway could be given to private enterprise, and he and Macdonald negotiated an agreement with the Canadian Pacific Railway (CPR) Company, which Tupper signed on 21 October 1880. With hindsight the terms appear unnecessarily generous, but they were lower than Tupper had originally forecast as essential. Tupper believed it was in the national interest for the company to succeed, and his commitment to the CPR was virtually limitless. When the CPR required additional financial support in December 1884 he worked out a rescue plan for the company, and in February 1885 he pleaded with Macdonald for yet another loan.

During the latter part of 1879 the relations between Tupper and Macdonald deteriorated and, although seated side by side in the House of Commons, they did not communicate except on public business. Although the breach was eventually healed, Tupper was no longer clearly the heir-apparent; his health was not good and in the election of 1882 he campaigned only in Nova Scotia. On 30 May 1883, without surrendering his cabinet post, he became unpaid acting Canadian high commissioner in London, but there was increasing criticism of his holding two incompatible offices, and in May 1884 he resigned from the cabinet and abandoned his seat in parliament. Partly to deal with the secessionist cry raised by W. S. Fielding in Nova Scotia, on 27 January 1887 Tupper returned to the cabinet as minister of finance, while remaining high commissioner, and in 1887 he campaigned vigorously in Nova Scotia, carrying fourteen of the twenty-one seats and undermining Fielding's campaign for repeal. Tupper not only defended protection during the election, but, in a bold move, extended it to the iron and steel industry in his 1887 budget.

Canadian high commissioner in London In 1886 the American government abrogated the fisheries clauses of the treaty of Washington, precipitating a crisis in American–Canadian relations. In May 1887 Tupper had informal conversations with the American secretary of state, T. F. Bayard, which resulted in the appointment of a joint commission. Tupper helped draft the British terms of reference, and as one of the three British commissioners in 1887–8 he secured a treaty which included significant concessions to Canada, so significant that the treaty was rejected by the American senate. In 1888 Tupper, who had been created a CB in 1867, a KCMG in 1879, and a GCMG in 1886, was made a baronet of the United Kingdom. The same year he resigned from the cabinet, but in 1891 he returned to campaign in defence of the 'national policy', criss-crossing Ontario with Macdonald and twice going to Washington in abortive attempts to negotiate a limited reciprocity agreement. So flagrant was his partisanship that a resolution condemning his conduct as high commissioner was narrowly defeated in the commons.

In London, Tupper extended his duties to include an ever wider range of activities. He promoted immigration and served on the commission appointed in 1889 to examine crofter emigration. He made an important contribution to the Canadian cattle industry by demonstrating that Canadian cattle were free from disease, he negotiated loans for the Canadian government and the Canadian Pacific Railway, he helped to organize the Indian and Colonial Exhibition in London in 1886, and he arranged for a mail subsidy for a steamship service from Vancouver to the Orient. Tupper moved in high social circles, meeting British statesmen and members of the royal family on intimate terms, and he even assisted in drafting British commercial legislation affecting Canada. In October 1883 he represented Canada at an international conference on submarine cables and disagreed openly with the British delegation. He also established that Canada might make commercial arrangements with other countries without extending them to the United Kingdom and in 1884 opened abortive commercial negotiations with Spain. In 1889 he returned to Washington to help negotiate a treaty on seal fishing in the Bering Sea, antagonizing the British government by his uncompromising defence of Canada's rights. In November 1892 he successfully negotiated a commercial agreement with France. Largely because of

Tupper, by the 1890s the colonial representatives in London had come to be treated as diplomatic agents.

Although Tupper believed that the attempt to turn the empire into a federal union was impracticable, he served on the executive committee of the Imperial Federation League. During the Sudan crisis of 1885 he rashly suggested that Canada demonstrate its loyalty by sending troops to assist in the campaign, a suggestion vetoed by Macdonald. Tupper had intended only that Canada make a gesture, and he was opposed to regular contributions for imperial defence. After 1887 the Imperial Federation League was racked by internal dissent over this issue and Tupper was blamed by some imperial federationists for the league's collapse in 1893, but he believed that the best way to strengthen the imperial connection would be through a mutual preferential trading agreement, as he indicated in a series of articles in the *Nineteenth Century* in 1891–2.

Prime minister from 1896, death, and burial The death of Macdonald in 1891 offered Tupper an opportunity to become prime minister, but for the next four years he did not actively seek the leadership. With Sir John Thompson's sudden demise in December 1894, Tupper was the logical candidate, but his health was not good and the governor-general, Lord Aberdeen, asked Sir Mackenzie Bowell to form a government. As it became clear that Bowell was incapable of resolving the conflict within the Conservative Party over the Manitoba schools question, in January 1896 seven members of the cabinet resigned and compelled Bowell to agree that Tupper would enter the cabinet as secretary of state and become prime minister on dissolution. On 15 January Tupper took charge of the government and on 4 February he was elected in a by-election in Cape Breton county. Although personally opposed to separate schools, Tupper believed a promise had been made to the Catholic minority in Manitoba, and in March he introduced a bill restoring separate schools. Although he was forced to abandon the bill, he insisted that the party would honour its commitment after an election. On 1 May 1896 Tupper became prime minister. In the election he sought to focus on the issue of protection, but the Conservative Party remained bitterly divided over the schools issue. In the end Tupper did win more votes than the Liberals, carrying about half the seats outside of Quebec, but, without a strong Quebec lieutenant, the Conservatives were routed in Quebec and on 8 July Tupper resigned.

For the next four years Tupper worked to woo back those Conservatives who had deserted the party in 1896 by questioning the loyalty of the Liberals to the empire. Tupper strongly supported Canada's participation in the Second South African War, but Sir Wilfrid Laurier managed to defuse the issue, and in 1900, while Tupper gained seventeen seats in Ontario, Laurier carried the rest of Canada. Tupper went down to defeat in Cape Breton and two days after the election he resigned, selecting as his successor his fellow Nova Scotian, Robert Borden. For the next

fifteen years he resided mainly in England, at the home of his daughter, although with frequent trips to visit his sons in Winnipeg and Vancouver. On 21 December 1907 he was made a member of the British privy council. He served on the executive committee of the British Empire League and wrote articles and public letters promoting closer economic ties. Gradually his health declined, and on 30 October 1915 the last of the original fathers of confederation died at Bexleyheath, Kent. His body was returned to Halifax, where after a state funeral he was buried in St John's cemetery beside his wife.

Progeny All three of Tupper's sons benefited from their father's political and corporate connections. James Stewart and William became partners in a Winnipeg firm, whose clients included the CPR, but Tupper was closest to his second son, **Sir Charles Hibbert Tupper** (1855–1927). Born in Amherst on 3 August 1855 and educated at McGill and Harvard universities, the younger Tupper practised law in Halifax. In 1879 he married Janet McDonald, and from 1882 to 1904 he served as the MP for Pictou county. In 1888 he became minister of marine and fisheries, the youngest person to enter the federal cabinet at that date, and he was knighted in 1893 for his work as the British agent in the Bering Sea dispute with the United States. In 1894 he was appointed minister of justice in Bowell's government, but he was one of the leaders in the cabinet revolt, and became solicitor-general from May to July 1896 in his father's short-lived administration. He followed his father into retirement in 1904 and established a law practice in Vancouver, where he died on 30 March 1927.

Assessment Throughout his political career Tupper was variously described as 'the Boodle Knight', the 'Great Stretcher' (of the truth), 'the old tramp', the 'Arch-Corruptionist', and 'the old wretch'. Much of this abuse Tupper brought upon himself by his combativeness, his partisanship, and his pomposity. None the less, his faults were blown out of proportion by his political foes. Since patronage was the way in which local loyalties were harnessed to the national interest, there was nothing unusual about Tupper's concern to reward his supporters. In the interests of holding power he could be ruthless and his standards of political morality were low, but so were those of his contemporaries.

Tupper became a very wealthy man. Initially his income was derived from professional fees, but he was soon loaning out money for mortgages and making speculative investments in the Spring Hill coal mines, the interests of which he assiduously promoted. As his political influence increased so did the opportunities for corporate directorships. Tupper served on the board of the Crown Life Insurance Company, the Bank of British Columbia, a cable company located in Brazil, the General Mining Association, and the British Empire Finance Corporation, and as chairman of the New Goldfields and the Klondyke Mining, Trading, and Transportation companies, two highly speculative gold-mining ventures. The salaries which he received for such activities were not large, but insider knowledge provided opportunities for windfall profits from stock investments.

In an age with only the haziest notion of conflict of interest, Tupper operated on the fringes of what was acceptable, and in retirement he went to great lengths to set the record straight. He gave a series of public interviews to a Vancouver journalist, W. A. Harkin, which were published in 1914, as were Tupper's own *Recollections of Sixty Years*. Longevity brings many rewards, and by the time of his death Nova Scotians had become reconciled to confederation and had come to see Tupper as one of their most distinguished native sons. At the national level, too, respect for Tupper grew over time. Modern Canadian historiography has been less generous. Tupper is praised for his essential role in bringing about confederation but thereafter is relegated to a mere appendage of Macdonald. Yet he was at least as responsible as Macdonald for rebuilding the Conservative Party after 1874 and for designing and implementing the 'national' policies with which the party became identified. Tupper was also responsible for turning the office of high commissioner into one of real importance. In every position which he held he added important measures to the statute book. There is much not to admire about Tupper: his racial chauvinism, his relentless pursuit of power and fortune, his partisanship, his social conservatism, and his boastfulness. But as the Toronto *News*, a Liberal paper, declared on 16 February 1903: 'With all his faults he was essentially a policy-maker and a constructive statesman.'   PHILLIP BUCKNER

Sources P. Buckner, 'Tupper, Sir Charles', *DCB*, vol. 14 · E. M. Saunders, *Life and letters of the Right Hon. Sir Charles Tupper*, 2 vols. (1916) · C. H. Tupper, *Supplement to the life and letters of the Right Hon. Sir Charles Tupper* (1926) · C. Tupper, *Recollections of sixty years* (1914) · A. W. MacIntosh, 'The career of Sir Charles Tupper in Canada, 1864–1900', Ph.D. diss., University of Toronto, 1960 · J. W. Longley, *Sir Charles Tupper* (1916) · K. G. Pryke, *Nova Scotia and confederation, 1864–1874* (1979) · D. A. Muise, 'Elections and constituencies: federal politics in Nova Scotia, 1867–1878', Ph.D. diss., University of Western Ontario, 1971 · P. A. Buckner, 'The 1860s: an end and a beginning', *The Atlantic region to confederation: a history*, ed. P. A. Buckner and J. G. Reid (1994), 360–86 · P. B. Waite, *The life and times of confederation, 1864–1867* (1962) · A. Wilson, 'Fleming and Tupper: the fall of the Siamese twins', *Character and circumstance: essays in honour of Donald Grant Creighton*, ed. J. S. Moir (1970), 99–127 · J. M. Robinson, 'A Canadian at the court of Queen Victoria: the high commissionership, 1880–1895', MA diss., University of Calgary, 1967 · W. A. Harkin, *Political reminiscences of the Right Honourable Sir Charles Tupper* (1914) · H. Charlesworth, *Candid chronicles* (1925) · R. Page, 'Tupper's last hurrah: the years as opposition leader, 1896–1900', *The west and the nation*, ed. C. Berger and R. Cook (1976) · L. C. Clark, 'A history of the Conservative administrations, 1891–1896', Ph.D. diss., University of Toronto, 1968 · W. K. Lamb, *History of the Canadian Pacific Railway* (1977) · R. C. Brown, *Canada's national policy, 1883–1900* (1964) · E. R. Forbes and D. A. Muise, eds., *The Atlantic provinces in confederation* (1993) · D. G. Creighton, *John A. Macdonald*, 2 vols. (Toronto, 1952–5) · W. S. Wallace, ed., *The Macmillan dictionary of Canadian biography*, 3rd edn (1963) · *New Canadian Encyclopedia* · H. J. Morgan, ed., *The Canadian men and women of the time*, 2nd edn (1912) · *Morning Chronicle* [Halifax, Nova Scotia]

Archives NA Canada · Public Archives of Nova Scotia, Halifax | CCC Cam., letters to sixteenth earl of Derby · NA Canada, John A. Macdonald MSS · U. Lond., Institute of Commonwealth Studies, corresp. with Richard Jebb · University of British Columbia, Sir Charles Hibbert Tupper MSS

Likenesses Barraud, photograph, NPG; repro. in *Men and Women of the Day*, 4 (1891) [*see illus.*] · W. & D. Downey, woodburytype photograph, NPG; repro. in W. Downey and D. Downey, *The cabinet portrait gallery*, 2 (1891) · Owl, caricature, mechanical reproduction, NPG; repro. in *VF* (30 July 1913) · R. T., wood-engraving, NPG; repro. in *ILN* (31 July 1886) · portrait, NA Canada

Tupper, Sir Charles Hibbert (1855–1927). *See under* Tupper, Sir Charles, first baronet (1821–1915).

Tupper, Sir (Charles) Lewis (1848–1910), administrator in India and legal historian, was born in London on 16 May 1848, the elder son of Captain Charles William Tupper (d. 1881) of the 7th Royal Fusiliers, and his wife, Frances Letitia (d. 1908), sister of Sir Charles F. D. Wheeler-Cuffe, second baronet. Rear-Admiral Reginald Tupper was his younger brother. Tupper, known throughout his life as Lewis, was educated at Harrow School and at Corpus Christi College, Oxford, where he graduated BA in 1870. He came fourth in the Indian Civil Service examination of 1869, and arrived in India in November 1871.

Tupper spent most of his official life in the Punjab. Initially appointed assistant commissioner at Lahore, in 1873 he became assistant settlement officer at Dera Ghazi Khan. On 2 October 1875 he married Jessie Catherine, daughter of Major-General Henry Campbell Johnstone, with whom he had two sons and a daughter. Dera Ghazi Khan was virtually the last of Tupper's district postings. Early in his career, his aptitude for detailed research and legalistic argument marked him out for secretariat duties and from January 1877 to May 1898, when he was appointed commissioner of Rawalpindi, he worked in the secretariat of either the local government or the government of India. He was secretary to the Punjab government from November 1888 and chief secretary from March 1890.

An admirer of Henry Maine, Tupper was a traditionalist, but one who was prepared to use modern methods to uphold age-old institutions. As a settlement officer in Dera Ghazi Khan he had become convinced of the need for legislative intervention to preserve traditional village communities from the inroads of the trading castes, a view which hardened in the subsequent years of official debate about the desirability of limiting land transfer in the Punjab. He also brought legal innovation to his studies of customary law and paramountcy. In 1880, under official authority, he produced *The Customary Law of the Punjab*, a minutely detailed attempt to codify local unwritten law. In 1893 he published independently *Our Indian Protectorate*, in which he argued that the relationship between the British and India's princely states was essentially a feudal one, based on Indian precedent. Following the publication of this work, and at the expense of his Bombay contemporary William Lee-Warner, Tupper was chosen by the foreign department to revise Mortimer Durand's *Leading Cases*, the first official textbook of Indian political law. Tupper's version, *Political Law and Policy*, although acknowledged as a brilliant piece of legal theorizing by his colleagues, was reckoned insufficiently practical for the men in the field, so his secondment to the government of India was extended to enable him to produce what was in effect a manual of case law: *Indian Political Practice* (3 vols.) was printed confidentially in 1895. Ironically, however, almost as soon as Tupper had finished his mammoth task of codifying customary relations with the princes, the government realized that the long-standing practice of not writing things down had afforded them much greater flexibility. By 1908 Tupper's approach had been eclipsed by Lee-Warner's new readiness to accept that paramountcy was based solely on Britain's power, and that it was best not to inquire too deeply into its origins.

In November 1899 Tupper was appointed financial commissioner of the Punjab, in which post he saw the Punjab Alienation of Land Act of 1900 through the legislative council. In 1900 he served on both the provincial and supreme legislatures, and for a session in 1905, and again in 1906, acted as a member of the executive council.

In October 1882 Tupper helped to create the Punjab University, and was its vice-chancellor in 1900–01. He was also one of the founders of the Punjab Law Society in 1903. He was made a CSI in 1897 and a KCIE in 1903. He left India in 1907 and settled in East Molesey, Surrey. In retirement he served on Surrey county council and was president of the local branch of the National Service League. He died at his home, Glenlyn, East Molesey, on 20 July 1910 and was buried three days later in West Molesey cemetery. His wife and three children survived him.   KATHERINE PRIOR

Sources I. Copland, *The British raj and the Indian princes* (1982) · P. H. M. van den Dungen, *The Punjab tradition: influence and authority in nineteenth-century India* (1972) · *WWW*, 1897–1915 · *History of services of gazetted officers employed in the Punjab* (1906) · M. G. Dauglish and P. K. Stephenson, eds., *The Harrow School register, 1800–1911*, 3rd edn (1911) · *DNB* · *The Times* (22 July 1910), 1, 13 · Burke, *Peerage* (1939) · *CGPLA Eng. & Wales* (1910)

Archives BL OIOC, papers [copies]

Wealth at death £1866 7s. 7d.: probate, 9 Sept 1910, *CGPLA Eng. & Wales*

Tupper, Martin Farquhar (1810–1889), poet and writer, was born at 20 Devonshire Place, Marylebone, Middlesex, on 17 July 1810, the eldest of five sons of Dr Martin Tupper FRS (1780–1844), a successful London physician, and his wife, Ellin Devis Marris (d. 1847), daughter of the Lincolnshire landscape painter Robert Marris. At the age of seven Tupper was sent to school at Egglesfield House, Brentford Butts, but he was removed after less than a year and transferred to Eagle House, Brook Green, where he remained until 1821, when he entered Charterhouse. Already afflicted with a bad stammer (the result, perhaps, of mistreatment at Egglesfield House), he was ill-suited for life at a large public school and at about the age of sixteen he was withdrawn from Charterhouse and sent to a succession of private tutors until his matriculation from Christ Church, Oxford on 21 May 1828. At Oxford, although his stammer precluded him from honours, Tupper read assiduously and formed what became a lifelong, if sometimes strained, friendship with W. E. Gladstone, whom in 1830 he beat for a theological prize offered by the regius professor of divinity. Following his graduation in 1832 (he proceeded MA in 1835 and DCL in 1847), Tupper's preference would have been to take orders (he had been a fervent evangelical since childhood), but his halting speech once again proved an impediment and he decided instead to

Martin Farquhar Tupper (1810–1889), by Ernest Edwards, pubd 1865

enter Lincoln's Inn. On 26 November 1835, the day after he was called to the bar, Tupper married his cousin Isabelle Devis (1811–1885), the younger of two daughters of the historical painter Arthur William *Devis (1762–1822).

Although he shared chambers with a friend for some years, Tupper never practised, depending instead on his father's generosity and passing his time in desultory and initially unremunerative authorship. His first book, *Sacra poesis* (1832), had attracted little notice, but in 1837, at the urging of Henry Stebbing, Tupper polished up and extended a series of loosely rhythmical aphorisms on such subjects as marriage, friendship, and humility, which he had presented to his fiancée some years before, and offered them to the publisher Joseph Rickerby. The volume appeared in January 1838 with the title *Proverbial Philosophy: a Book of Thoughts and Arguments* and elicited generally positive reviews. A second edition was immediately undertaken and the book embarked on a quarter of a century of phenomenal popular success. A second series followed in 1842 and by 1860 there had been thirty-eight editions. Translations appeared in most European languages and, for many years, the poet's annual income from the book fluctuated between £500 and £800.

Literary earnings, together with the patrimony he inherited in 1844, enabled Tupper to lead the life of a country gentleman at Albury House in Surrey (which had come to him through his mother's Devis connection) and to support a steadily increasing family. Three daughters—Ellin Isabelle (1836–1924), Mary Frances (1838–1920), and Margaret Eleonora (1840–1894)—were followed by four sons—Martin Charles Selwyn (1841–1879), William Knighton (1844–1930), Henry de Beauvoir (1847–1871), and Walter Farquhar (1848–1905); an eighth child, Alice, was born in 1851 but died in 1853.

The responsibilities of family and social life, however, did nothing to check Tupper's literary productivity. Shortly after the appearance of *Proverbial Philosophy* he published *Geraldine* (1838), a continuation of Coleridge's unfinished *Christabel*, for which he was excoriated by John Wilson in *Blackwood's*. *A Modern Pyramid* appeared in 1839 and in 1841 Tupper produced *An Author's Mind*, consisting of outlines for thirty-four projected books (among them a tragedy on Nero and an epic poem to be entitled 'Home'). This was followed by three novels, one of which, *The Crock of Gold* (1844), went through five editions; *A Thousand Lines* (1845), which included the popular and inspiriting 'Never Give Up'; *Probabilities* (1847), in which Tupper tackled religious doubt with more conviction than subtlety; and by more than thirty later publications of widely various length and content. Public events, especially those involving royalty, seldom took place without eliciting at least one metrical effusion, and even the most fugitive of Tupper's enthusiasms generally found expression in print. His interest in excavation issued in a report (1850) on the Roman remains at Farley Heath (it was, indeed, for services to archaeology that he was elected to the Royal Society in 1845); his veneration for Alfred the Great led him not only to organize an Alfred jubilee at Wantage in 1849, but to translate Alfred's poems (1850); his suspicion of the French resulted in fervent championship of the volunteer rifle corps, whom he encouraged with a sheaf of verses and articles (1859).

Despite this prolific output, Tupper's international celebrity continued to rest chiefly on *Proverbial Philosophy*, which, by the mid-1840s, had achieved the status of a runaway best-seller in the United States. In 1851 Tupper, who had long been interested in Anglo-American relations (*A Loving Ballad to Brother Jonathan* appeared in 1848), embarked on a wildly successful tour of the eastern States and eastern Canada, fêted wherever he went and dining informally at the White House with President Fillmore. The extent of his prestige can be gauged from the appearance in Philadelphia of a compilation by James Orton entitled *The Proverbialist and Poet* (1852), which consisted almost exclusively of elevating quotations from Tupper, Solomon, and Shakespeare.

Although the first American tour perhaps marked the high point of his reputation, Tupper's popularity remained largely intact until the early 1860s, when his buoyant optimism about things in general began to seem both naïve and outdated. Increasingly he became the butt, not only of serious critics, but also of the comic press: his stately platitudes were remorselessly parodied and his name became a byword for banality. *Proverbial Philosophy* still found a market (in 1867 and 1869 Tupper produced two new series), but editions grew smaller and less frequent. In addition to declining popularity, moreover, Tupper began to experience domestic and financial misfortune. His surviving daughters were a source of comfort

(in 1864 they published *Poems by Three Sisters*), but his eldest son became a chronic gambler and an alcoholic, whose large debts imposed a serious drain on Tupper's income, already diminished by a series of poor investments. Attempts to recoup his position by writing plays failed dismally (*Alfred* was briefly staged at Manchester in 1861, but *Raleigh* and *Washington* found no backers); public readings (the stammer had been overcome long since) produced only marginal profits; and even a second American tour in 1876–7 proved a pale shadow of the first. The civil-list pension of £120 which Gladstone procured for him in 1873 (and which he had first urged on Queen Victoria in 1869) was not only welcome but essential. Albury House was heavily mortgaged and permanently let, and in 1880 the Tuppers moved to a modest semi-detached house at 13 Cintra Park, Upper Norwood, London. Here Tupper passed his final years, still turning out verses on topical subjects which were either guyed or ignored, and working on his rambling, self-congratulatory autobiography, which appeared in 1886, shortly before he suffered a disabling stroke. He lingered on for three more years and died peacefully at his home at Cintra Park on 29 November 1889. He was buried in Albury church, Surrey.

For all his vanity, Tupper emerges as a likeable figure, courageous in adversity, generous, firm in his Christian faith, and industriously dedicated to the pursuit of literary immortality. Of the myriad works on which he based his hope of enduring fame, however, only *Proverbial Philosophy* still occupies even a marginal place in cultural history. Tupper's *magnum opus* enshrined the moral commonplaces of early Victorian bourgeois ideology in a sonorous, pseudo-scriptural language which enhanced their dignity and seemed to guarantee their permanence. He presented as vatic wisdom the established convictions of his readership, which responded by venerating him as a sage. But as those convictions themselves began to crumble in the 1860s, under the pressure of scientific advance and social change, so Tupper's status declined and he came to seem an embarrassing survival from a superseded past, a victim of the progress he had so earnestly celebrated.

ROBERT DINGLEY

Sources D. Hudson, *Martin Tupper: his rise and fall* (1949) · M. F. Tupper, *My life as an author* (1886) · P. Scott, 'Martin F. Tupper', *Victorian poets before 1850*, ed. W. E. Fredeman and I. B. Nadel, DLitB, 32 (1984), 288–98 · R. Buchmann, *Martin F. Tupper and the Victorian middle-class mind* (1941) · DNB · Gladstone, *Diaries*

Archives Christ Church Oxf. · Hunt. L. · University of Illinois, Urbana-Champaign | BL, Gladstone MSS, MS 44336

Likenesses F. T. Rochard, drawing, 1846, NPG · J. Baker, stipple, NPG · Duthie, carte-de-visite, NPG · E. Edwards, photograph, NPG; repro. in *Portraits of men of eminence*, 3 (1865) [*see illus.*] · D. J. Pound, stipple and line engraving, NPG · Southwell Bros, carte-de-visite, NPG · W. Walker, stipple (after H. W. Pickersgill), NPG

Turbervile [Turbervile], **George** (*b.* 1543/4, *d.* in or after 1597), poet and translator, was born in Whitchurch, Dorset, the fifth son of Henry Turbervile (*d.* 1549) and Jane Bampfield, daughter of Thomas Bampfield.

Family and early years Turbervile's ancient family had strong roots in Dorset; they are the subject of Thomas

Hardy's novel *Tess of the D'Urbervilles*, where their genealogy, arms, and monuments are faithfully reflected. His grandfather John Turbervile had been a favourite of Henry VII and had acquired the family's riches: the poet's father was the fifth son, who inherited the family's farm at Winterborne Whitchurch.

Turbervile's birth date is best calculated from his poem 'The Lover to *Cupid* for Mercie', which says that:

In greene and tender age
(my Lorde) till .xviii. yeares,
I spent my time as fitted youth
in Schole among my Feeares.

Wood (from lost records) states that he left New College, Oxford, in 1562. Before going to university he had been to Winchester College, and afterwards he attended the inns of court: probably one of the minor inns of chancery for which no records survive. There he met lasting literary friends: Arthur Broke, Richard Edwards, Thomas Twyne, Barnabe Googe, and George Gascoigne. It seems likely that he is the 'G.T.' credited with compiling the latter's *Hundreth Sundrie Flowres*.

There is little other evidence of his early years. After Henry Turbervile's death in 1549 the family property was held in trust for the eldest son, Nicholas, until his coming of age. From this he was to pay an annuity of 20 marks to his brother. Turbervile's uncle James *Turberville was bishop of Exeter under Mary, and was deposed by Elizabeth in 1560. His second cousin Thomas Turberville was the most persistent among several members of his family who encountered trouble for their recusancy; doubtless the poet had some sympathy with them. Some Catholic friends are mentioned in his work: Roger Baynes is asked to supervise the publication of *Tragicall Tales*, and writes commendatory poems; Nicholas Roscarrock is mentioned twice, once in a poem encouraging him to marry. However, Turbervile's friendship with the passionate protestant Googe, for example, suggests that he was not a strong or consistent espouser of the Catholic cause.

In his poem 'To his Friende: P: of Courting, Travailing, Dysing, and Tenys' Turbervile depicts himself resisting the leisure pursuits of most young men. His bookishness is affirmed by another source: there is a letter from the privy council to the justices of the peace in Dorset, saying that they have made poor choices for captains of the army, namely 'one Hugh Bampfield, an old man, and George Turbervile, who hath ben alwaies from his youth, and still is, gyven to his boke and studie and never exercised in matters of warre' (*APC*, 1571–5). During his time at the inns of court Turbervile's reputation as a writer developed; it was greatly enhanced by the publication of three major works in 1567.

Literary career Their chronology is difficult to determine with complete certainty, but it seems that Turbervile's *Heroycall Epistles*, a translation of Ovid's *Heroides* including the much later replies of Angelus Sabinus, came first, dated 19 March. Second was a collection of his own verse, his *Epitaphes, Epigrams, Songs and Sonets*, and third was a translation of Mantuan's *Eglogs*. The Stationers' register

actually includes entries for parts of the Ovid and the Mantuan before their wholes, for two printers (Denham and Bynneman respectively), but these were probably not published. Turbervile, then, was writing or finishing multiple projects for different printers at the same time. The title-page of *Epitaphes* also indicates possible earlier publication, saying it is 'newly corrected with additions'.

Epitaphes, Epigrams, Songs and Sonets contains no true sonnets in the modern sense, grouping various verse forms under that title. Its particular novelty is that most of the love poems in the book are written in honour of Anne Russell, daughter of the second earl of Bedford, under the name of Pandora or Pyndara, with the poet dubbing himself Tymetes. Turbervile's speaker tells the story of her marriage to another (Ambrose Dudley, earl of Warwick, on 11 September 1565), and renounces love as a result. In his preface to the reader, he actually writes of the 'meere fiction of these Fantasies'. Hankins, however, believes that there may have been something more substantial given the fact that numerous poems in the collection were written before 1565, and the journey of Pyndara to London at one point 'bears all the hallmarks of an actual incident' (Hankins, 11). However, Turbervile is clearly exploiting a convention, as there was apparently no scandal as a result of his devotion: links with the family continue and later works are dedicated to family members.

Turbervile's translation of Ovid includes six poems in blank verse, a significant early use of that metre. It was a success, but was overtaken by the Mantuan translation, which went through four editions before 1597. The next year, 1568, saw the publication of another translation, *A Plaine Path to Perfect Vertue*, featuring the prolonged moralizations of Dominicus Mancinus. This was relatively unsuccessful but adds to the substance of Turbervile's career as a translator of major works in an important period of translation. Nevertheless, his early poetic career did not bring him financial security. In his poem 'Farewell to a Mother Cosin, at his Going Towardes Moscovia', he says that his journey is to improve his finances after much time 'in studies fond applide'.

Turbervile became secretary to Thomas Randolph on his mission to visit Ivan the Terrible, emperor of Russia, between June 1568 and September 1569. According to Wood (*Ath. Oxon.*, 1.627) this resulted in *Poems Describing the Places and Manners of the Country and People of Russia*. There is no other evidence of this, though some related material appears in the later collection *Tragicall Tales*. 'The Author being in Moscovia Wrytes to Certaine his Frendes in Englande', a poem by Turbervile describing the state of Russia, is included in Richard Hakluyt's *Voyages*. There are also three epistles—to 'Master Edward Dancie', 'Parker', and 'Spencer'. Edmund Spenser is surely too young to have been the 'Spencer' of this poem, but it does seem likely that Harpalus ('nowe woxen aged / In faithfull service of faire Cynthia') in Spenser's *Colin Clouts Come Home Againe* may well be Turbervile, as he uses the name of himself in 'He sorrowes other to have the fruites of his service'. As well as Turbervile's own writings on the subject, details of his journey can be found in the account of Thomas Randolph's journey in Hakluyt, and a confidential letter from Randolph to William Cecil, dated 12 August 1568 (*CSP for.*, *1566–8*, 517). The expedition was to negotiate special privileges for an English trading company in Russia, and it was a success. Both Turbervile and Randolph record adverse impressions of Russian monks and religion (in Turbervile's words, 'vile and vaine'), and of the plight of the Russian peasants.

Nevertheless, Turbervile's fortunes were not improved by the Russian expedition and he continued writing. He published two technical works with an eye on illustrious patronage, *The Booke of Faulconrie, or Hauking* (1575) and *The Noble Arte of Venerie or Hunting* (n.d., but an epistle to the reader is dated 16 June 1575). The latter was published anonymously and has been attributed to George Gascoigne because of his commendatory verses, but the argument from association makes Turbervile a stronger candidate. *The Booke of Faulconrie*, dedicated to the earl of Warwick, is a practical manual 'collected out of the best authors, as well Italian as Frenchmen, and some English practices withall'. *The Noble Arte* is a translation of an unidentified French work, but there are numerous new insertions, such as anecdotes of the animals hunted and the festivities surrounding hunting. In *The Booke of Faulconrie* Turbervile writes how sickness following his troubles has delayed the work and his planned translation of Lucan. In the second edition of the *Myrroure for Magistrates* (1578) Thomas Blenerhasset quips that 'he was inforced to unyoke his Steeres and make holy day'.

A collection of *Tragicall Tales* is Turbervile's achievement during the 1570s. Seven of the stories are from Boccaccio's *Decameron*, two appear in Bandello's *Novelle*, and the last originally in Plutarch's *De mulierum virtutibus*. It seems likely that these last three are in fact taken from Mambrino da Fabriana's 1556 *La selva*. The only surviving *Tragicall Tales* copy dates from 1587, but there is much evidence of an earlier edition, probably 1574. As well as the tales themselves, there are sonnets (as in his earlier volume not restricted to any one metre or length), and epitaphs for William Herbert, earl of Pembroke, Henry Sydenham, Gyles Bampfield, and 'Maister Edwards, sometime Maister of the Children of the Chappell' (that is, Richard Edwards).

Turbervile's troubles and final years In his works of the 1570s Turbervile makes reference to his 'troubles', as on the title-page, introduction, and dedication (to brother Nicholas) of *Tragicall Tales*. Turbervile does not specify their nature, but there is a record of a pardon awarded on 24 October 1573 to George Turbervile, gentleman, for acting in self-defence when killing an assailant (patent roll (chancery) 15 Eliz., part 12, m. 38, discovered by Ward). This document records that on 26 September 1573 Turbervile was walking between Blandford and Strickland, near his home. Early in the afternoon one Robert Jones rode after him and attempted to kill him at Brienston. Turbervile was wounded in the abdomen, tried to flee, but then retaliated twice with a sword and killed his attacker. Ward suggested that Jones may have been a puritan fanatic attacking a Catholic sympathizer, but a quarrel with a neighbour is a much more likely cause of the fracas, and tensions in the Dorset countryside probably lie behind Turbervile's 'troubles'.

There is evidence of considerable problems relating to property in Dorset. In 1572 he was involved in a lawsuit against his brother, from whom he aimed to recover lands at the manor of Winterborne Musterton. On 11 August 1577 the privy council instructed the marquess of Winchester and the justices of the assizes in Dorset to sort out a quarrel between him and Sir Henry Ashley. The worst and most public incident came on 23 January 1580, when his brother Nicholas Turbervile was killed by his brother-in-law John Morgan at Cavit Wollent, Somerset. This murder was notorious in England at the time, and Morgan was tried and hanged.

Some time before the publication of *Tragicall Tales* (*c.*1574) Turbervile was married. His poem to Roscarrock on the subject is a little ambiguous, praising the state at one point, but later saying he should seek a maid 'with wealth and coyne enough'. About this time he established a home at Shapwick, near Winterborne Whitchurch, and the timing suggests that his wife's dowry may have been a factor. Turbervile's literary career comes to a more or less complete halt, though he does have dedicatory verses in Sir Geoffrey Fenton's *Tragicall Discourses* (1579) and at the end of Rowlands's *Pleasant Historie of Lazarillo de Tormes* (1596). He had achieved a degree of wealth that removed the need for gainful employment in writing. Residence at the inns of court doubtless spurred his early writings, while married life in Dorset, due to problems and distractions as well as wealth and contentment, was less conducive. In addition, the fervour among patrons for translation projects had its heyday during the brief period of Turbervile's writing career. He always viewed his translations as the substantial part of his *œuvre*, in comparison with his occasional poems, so a change in the literary climate is also a possible cause of his cessation.

The last reference certainly to Turbervile is made on 26 August 1580, when commissioners for musters in Dorset told the privy council they had appointed a new captain in Ireland, instead of 'Mr. George Turberville, who was a great spurner of their authority' (*CSP dom.*, *1547–80*, 673). John Payne Collier noted an example of Turbervile's signature on the title-page of a 1557 folio of Thomas More's works, dated 14 November 1584. The book was apparently sold as part of Collier's library and is now untraceable. A later reference is more doubtful: a letter from the council to the lord treasurer, 12 April 1588, has one 'George Turvyle' appointed by the earl of Warwick to be muster master in Warwickshire. The family connection makes the poet a possible candidate, but the name is spelt unusually for the poet, and there are other Turvyles.

The first notice that Turbervile is probably dead comes in the 1611 edition of the *Book of Faulconrie*. The work is described as 'Heretofore published by George Turbervile, gentleman', so it is possible to assume that he was dead before that year. There is also a reference to Turbervile's death in the first edition of Sir John Harington's *Epigrams*.

Although this was not printed until 1618, most of the poems which can be dated seem attributable to the late 1590s, with the latest datable being to the execution of Essex in 1601. Another piece of evidence—a lease of property in Shapwick to Troilus Turbervile (the poet's nephew) on 23 April 1597 (quite possibly George Turbervile's lands, or some part of them)—makes early 1597 the most likely date for his death.

Rollins (p. 538) prints a manuscript elegy for the poet (from BL, Sloane MS 1709, fol. 270v). It is a burlesque of Turbervile's own style of epitaph, and does not display much esteem for the poet's abilities. Like many others Turbervile falls short of C. S. Lewis's standards: he placed him squarely in the Drab Age and depicted him 'ruthlessly on the march along the hard shadeless road of poulter's and fourteeners' (Lewis, 260). Thomas Nashe, in his preface to Greene's *Menaphon*, prefigures this by saying 'neither was Master *Turbervile* the worst of his time, though in translating he attributed too much to the necessitie of rime'. Both emphasize a certain formal rigidness, though his positive influence in regularizing English metres could be asserted. Despite the predictable mentions by William Webbe, George Puttenham, and Francis Meres, Turbervile is not a major literary figure of his age. However, his career is unusual for its success, and Rollins is justified in dubbing him 'the most important professional poet in London' in 1567. On becoming a country landowner, however, he seems to have abandoned (with no recorded regret) the difficult life of a poet.

RAPHAEL LYNE

Sources J. E. Hankins, *The life and works of George Turbervile*, University of Kansas Humanistic Studies, 25 (1940) · H. E. Rollins, 'New facts about George Turbervile', *Modern Philology*, 15 (1918), 513–38 · W. E. Sheidley, 'The poetry of Barnabe Googe and George Turbervile: a study', PhD diss., Stanford University, 1968 · B. M. Ward, 'Further research on *A hundreth sundrie flowres*', *Review of English Studies*, 4 (1928), 35–48 · Wood, *Ath. Oxon.*, new edn · N. H. Hodgson, 'The murder of Nicholas Turberville', *Modern Language Review*, 33 (1938), 520–27 · R. Pruvost, 'The source of George Turbervile's *Tragical tales*, nos. 2, 5, and 8', *Review of English Studies*, 10 (1934), 29–45 · J. Payne Collier, *A bibliographical and critical account of the rarest books in the English language* (1865) · C. H. Conley, *The first English translators of the classics* (New Haven, 1927) · C. S. Lewis, *English literature in the sixteenth century excluding drama* (1954) · G. G. Smith, ed., *Elizabethan critical essays*, 2 vols. (1904)

Turbervill, Edith Picton- (1872–1960), social reformer, was born on 13 June 1872 at Lower House, Fownhope, Herefordshire, the daughter of Captain John Picton-Warlow (*b.* 1838), an officer in the Indian army, and his second wife, Eleanor Temple (*d.* 1887). She and her twin Beatrice were the third and fourth children of the eight sons and three daughters (including three sets of twins) born of this marriage; her father had also had two children from a previous marriage. Edith and several siblings spent their early years in Brighton in the care of a maiden aunt, but in 1883 her parents returned from India and after a brief spell in Bruges moved the family to the Vale of Glamorgan in Wales. There Edith passed a happy and vigorous country childhood, seemingly little marred by the death of her mother in 1887 and her father's remarriage two years

Edith Picton-Turbervill (1872–1960), by Sir Cedric Morris, 1935

later. Initially educated by governesses, she was sent to the Royal School in Bath in her late teens.

In 1892 John Picton-Warlow inherited the Ewenni Priory estate and took the name Picton-Turbervill. The family now entered a period of real affluence, and Edith led the life of a country squire's daughter, attending house parties and balls, and teaching Sunday school at the local church. On 13 June 1895, however, in the unlikely venue of an express train from London to Bridgend, she had a conversion experience, and from that date entered on a life of religious activism. She began by proselytizing to the navvies building the Vale of Glamorgan Railway, and then secured her father's consent to train for a year in mission work at a Mildmay school in London (a training that included 'practical work' in the Shoreditch slums) and then to take a post with the Young Women's Christian Association (YWCA) in India. With the exception of a year's return to England following a bout of typhoid in 1905, Picton-Turbervill remained in India from 1900 until 1908, where she in turn lectured on English literature at a women's college in Calcutta, founded (with Mary Dobson) a settlement for university women in Kamballa, opened a holiday home for Indian girls in Simla, and (with Marjorie Hobbs) co-ordinated YWCA work in Bangalore. Picton-Turbervill enjoyed this mix of social service and evangelism, and left India only after a severe attack of malaria.

She returned to a country and to friends much preoccupied by questions of social reform, and in that atmosphere her own concerns widened. She continued to work for the YWCA, as the chairman of its foreign department in 1909 (and hence responsible for the training of workers sent all over the world) and its national vice-president from 1914 to 1920 and from 1922 to 1928, but she found her theological convictions changing. Believing that women could bring a new spirit of devotion and service to both religious and public life, she joined with Maude Royden to call on the Church of England to open the ministry to women, and published several essays and books—including *Christ and Woman's Power* (1919), *Musings of a Lay Woman* (1919), and, with Canon Streeter, *Women and the Church* (1917)—calling for a return to Christ-centred doctrine and for wider lay involvement within the church. She also became active in the non-militant wing of the women's suffrage movement, and while she worked to set up hostels, canteens, and clubs for women workers during the war (for which she was made an OBE in 1917), she was troubled by the government's bellicose attitude and in 1915 was one of the women who sought unsuccessfully to attend the International Women's Peace Conference at The Hague.

In January of 1919, having concluded that its programme was most in keeping with Christian ethics, Picton-Turbervill joined the Labour Party. Well known in reform-minded circles, she unsuccessfully contested North Islington in November 1922 and Stroud in October 1924, before being returned for The Wrekin in Shropshire in the general election of June 1929. One of only fourteen women MPs (nine of them Labour members) in the 1929–31 parliament, Picton-Turbervill's influence as a backbencher was limited, but she successfully sponsored a private member's bill outlawing the pronunciation of a sentence of death on a pregnant woman, served on the ecclesiastic committee of the Commons and the Lords and, perhaps equally important, insisted that women MPs (like their male colleagues) be provided with bathing facilities in the Commons. On friendly terms with Ramsay MacDonald, Picton-Turbervill abstained from the 'no confidence' motion supported by Labour MPs on the formation of the National Government but declined to join the 'National Labour' camp. Remaining in the party, she was defeated in a straight fight against a 'national' candidate in October 1931.

In the thirties Picton-Turbervill withdrew from some of her earlier philanthropic involvements but remained active in women's international organizations, leading the British delegation at the International Alliance of Women congresses in Istanbul in 1935 and Copenhagen in 1939. In 1936 she was appointed by J. H. Thomas, then colonial secretary, to a three-member commission to investigate the much-discussed problem of indentured girl servants, known as *mui tsai*, in Hong Kong and Malaya. Fears that the *mui tsai* were essentially slaves had been expressed in the Commons on several occasions (including by Picton-Turbervill), and the testimony she heard in Hong Kong and Malaya did not allay them. Breaking with her malleable co-members, she wrote a minority report calling for the registration and inspection of all transferred children; more remarkably, she was able to bring the governor of Malaya, and ultimately the Colonial Office, around to her position, resulting in an expansion of child welfare services in both colonies. During the Second World War she worked for a time for the Ministry of Information.

Picton-Turbervill's life resists easy summary, for she was active in many arenas. Yet all of her commitments—from feminism to labour politics—stemmed from her religious beliefs. Espousing a 'Christ-centred' faith, she remained critical of the church, calling for liturgical reform and for the ordination of women long before such positions had much support. And while her religiosity, her philanthropic concerns, her support for sexual purity campaigns, and even her singleness might appear to mark her out as a rather Victorian figure, she was in many respects forthright, pragmatic, and modern. Vigorous, tall (5 feet 10 inches), and physically active, she was very close to her twin sister, Beatrice (who for many years ran a girls' hostel), and maintained a wide circle of women friends, among them Frances Balfour, Chrystal Macmillan, Lilian Baylis, Cicely Hamilton, and Emily Kinnaird, with whom she for a time lived. Distressed by the propensity in the twenties and thirties to label such friendships as 'unwholesome' or perverse, in her autobiography published in 1939 Picton-Turbervill insisted 'with a ring of challenge' that women's loving friendships could be 'as deep, as beautiful, and as exhilarating as any human relationship' (*Life is Good*, 94). Having spent the last years of her life living near Cheltenham, Edith Picton-Turbervill died at Barnwood House Hospital, Barnwood, Gloucestershire, on 31 August 1960.   SUSAN PEDERSEN

Sources E. Picton-Turbervill, *Life is good: an autobiography* (1939) • E. Picton-Turbervill, *Musings of a lay woman* (1919) • E. Picton-Turbervill, *Christ and woman's power* (1919) • O. Banks, *The biographical dictionary of British feminists*, 2 (1990) • P. Brookes, *Women at Westminster: an account of women in the British parliament, 1918–1966* (1967) • WWBMP, vol. 3 • E. Picton-Turbervill, 'Edith Picton-Turbervill … childhood in Brighton and Bruges', *Myself when young, by famous women of to-day*, ed. Countess of Oxford and Asquith (1938), 313–60 • B. H. Streeter and E. Picton-Turbervill, *Women and the church* (1917) • E. Picton-Turbervill, *Christ and international life* (1921) • *The Times* (3 Sept 1960) • b. cert. • d. cert. • CGPLA Eng. & Wales (1960)

Archives NRA, priv. coll., letters, scrapbooks, etc.

Likenesses C. Morris, portrait, 1935; Sothebys, 21 Oct 1996, lot 47 [*see illus.*] • photograph, repro. in Countess of Oxford and Asquith, ed., *Myself when young, by famous women of today*

Wealth at death £25,555 11s. 1d.: probate, 18 Oct 1960, CGPLA Eng. & Wales

Turbervill [Turberville], **Edward** (1653/4–1681), informer, was born at Y Sger, Glamorgan, a younger son of an 'ancient' family. His parents, whose names are unknown, were Roman Catholics and he 'was brought up in all the most exact precepts and doctrine of the Church of Rome' (*The Full Narrative*, 2). Aged eighteen in 1672, he entered the service of Lady Molyneux, a daughter of William Herbert, fourth earl and later first marquess of Powis. According to Turbervill's account, after three years' service he was encouraged by Lady Powis and William Morgan, a Jesuit, to travel to Douai to become a friar. Finding the discipline of his new vocation too irksome, he soon returned to England. However, his reception from the earl of Powis and his wife was such as to convince Turbervill that they had 'become my utter enemies' (ibid., 8). He then left for Paris, where his brother was a Benedictine monk. There he met William Howard, Lord Stafford, who recruited him to a plot to kill Charles II. Instead of returning to England, Turbervill joined the duke of Monmouth's regiment in the French army, serving as a trooper before being discharged at Aire in 1676. He then spent some time at Neath Abbey before again contacting Powis in the hope of a recommendation for a commission in the troops being raised for service in Flanders. Rebuffed again he seems to have attached himself to William Lloyd, rector of St Martin-in-the-Fields, and future bishop of St Asaph, and contemplated changing his religion. However, he always denied to Lloyd that he knew anything of plots. Turbervill then disappeared from view only to resurface in 1680.

Turbervill made his entrance in the Popish Plot on 9 November 1680 when he recounted his evidence before the House of Commons. Crucially, he provided evidence against Lord Stafford at the time when the case against the five popish lords had been weakened by the death of the informer William Bedloe. His information probably ensured that Stafford was tried first, as Turbervill convinced many that the peer had indeed offered him money to kill the king. At the trial, which began in the House of Lords on 30 November, Turbervill proved an effective witness, despite getting the year wrong in which Stafford supposedly recruited him to the plot. His detailed knowledge of Paris helped him describe the house in which the events took place, and other witnesses corroborated incidental details of his story. Stafford was duly found guilty and executed; Turbervill meanwhile was granted a pardon and, following an application by the Commons, received subsistence of 20 s. per week.

Turbervill's main reason for becoming an informer may well have been financial, and he was reported as saying that 'he would set up for a witness, for none lived so well as witnesses' (*Bishop Burnet's History*, 267). He also had an astute sense of the prevailing wind, for soon after the trial of Edward Fitzharris in May 1681, he switched sides and provided the government with evidence of whig plotting during the Oxford parliament of March 1681. By June he was reported to be ready to divulge his evidence and his allowance from the government, which may have been stopped in mid-April, was raised to 30 s. per week about the beginning of July. Turbervill was a government witness against Stephen College at his trial in Oxford for high treason in August. He was then a witness at the Old Bailey in November when the earl of Shaftesbury was tried and acquitted on treason charges.

Shortly after the Shaftesbury trial Turbervill was taken ill. Initial reports of poisoning proved unfounded, and he died in London from smallpox on 18 December 1681. Accounts of his deathbed pronouncements differ, but it seems that he maintained the guilt of both Stafford and Shaftesbury, and that he died a protestant.

STUART HANDLEY

Sources *The full narrative and further discovery of Edward Turbervill of Skerr* (1681) · *The information of Edward Turbervill of Skerr* (1680) · J. Kenyon, *The Popish Plot* (1972) · N. Luttrell, *A brief historical relation of state affairs from September 1678 to April 1714*, 6 vols. (1857), vol. 1 · K. H. D. Haley, *The first earl of Shaftesbury* (1968) · *Bishop Burnet's History*, vol. 2 · *CSP dom.*, 1681–2 · J. Y. Akerman, ed., *Moneys received and paid for secret services of Charles II and James II from 30th March 1679 to 25th December 1688*, CS, 52 (1851) · *Calendar of the manuscripts of the marquess of Ormonde*, new ser., 8 vols., HMC, 36 (1902–20), vol. 5 · *The manuscripts of the earl of Westmorland*, HMC, 13 (1885); repr. (1906), 172–4 [Morton] · *JHC*, 9 (1667–87), 649 · *DNB*

Turberville [de Turberville] **family** (*per. c.*1125–*c.*1370), gentry, would seem from their name to have derived ultimately from Touberville (Eure). The first known member of the family in Glamorgan is **Payn** [i] **de Turberville** (*fl.* 1126–1130) whom Neath Abbey sources and the Book of Llandaff mention as a follower of Earl Robert of Gloucester. He married one Sibyl, who was doubtless a member of the Londres family, lords of Ogmore, for by her came to Payn's sons the manor of 'Siblewick' on the River Alun in the lordship of Ogmore (with other lands at Corntown and Heronston near Ogmore). However, the core of the family's endowment in Glamorgan was the lordship of Coety, north of Ogmore, and it would seem most likely that Payn [i] already held this endowment in the 1120s (perhaps part of the fruits of Earl Robert's campaigning in western Glamorgan). Payn would seem to have divided his lands between his sons. The elder, **Gilbert** [i] **de Turberville** (*d.* before 1183), seems to have taken Coety while the younger, Simon, took his mother's inheritance. Both were clearly active and important in Glamorgan until after 1148. Gilbert [i] inherited Simon's lands in the Ogmore lordship before 1166, confirming his grants to Ewenni Priory and Neath Abbey. Gilbert married one Agnes and died before 1183, being buried in Ewenni Priory.

Gilbert was succeeded by his son **Payn** [ii] **de Turberville** (*d.* in or before 1208) who appears both alone and with his father in several acts of Earl William of Gloucester. Payn was one of the leaders of Henry II's forces resisting Welsh incursions in Glamorgan in 1185. A series of lawsuits dating between 1199 and 1201 reveal that he then controlled the lordship and castle of Coety with other manors at Nolton, Newton, and Coychurch. He was resisting the claim of Walter de Sully to a knight's fee at Newton and Coychurch (a dispute that would of itself date back the Turberville possession of Coety at least one generation). The dispute was eventually settled by the grant of an annuity of a half-mark from Coychurch to the Sully family. Payn [ii] had been succeeded by **Gilbert** [ii] **de Turberville** (*d. c.*1238), his son, by 1208. This Gilbert married Mathilda daughter of Morgan Gam, lord of Afan, who brought him as marriage portion Landimore and both Rhossilis (the contract was once to be seen in the lost Neath cartulary). This Welsh match would seem to have been his second marriage, for he appears between 1210 and 1219 as married to a woman called Agnes who had as dower his manor of Corntown. It appears to have been this Gilbert's son, **Gilbert** [iii] **de Turberville** (*fl.* 1242) who fell out with the lord of Glamorgan, Earl Richard de Clare, over warfare waged against the Welsh lords of Meisgyn and Senghennydd to the north of Coety in the summer of 1242. However later sources reveal that he had a grant from the same earl of the manor and castle of New-castle, next to Bridgend, by charter, in return for service of a tenth of a fee. It was also this Gilbert who between 1238 and 1246 granted the family's manor of South Molton in Devon, held of the earls of Gloucester since about the middle of the twelfth century, to Nicholas fitz Martin, in exchange for Nicholas's manor of 'Treguz' in Glamorgan. Gilbert [iii] was followed by his son, **Richard** [i] **de Turberville** (*d.* in or before 1303), who also experienced the disfavour of the earl of Gloucester, losing tenants to the earl in the detached manor north of Llanhari, which had perhaps come into the Turberville family's possession as a result of patronage from the Londres family (which held the lordship of upland Glynogwr).

Richard was succeeded by his son **Payn** [iii] **Turberville** (*d.* in or before 1327) by 1303, when in deeds dated at Coety he confirmed his family's grants to Ogmore Priory, and added a peasant at Heronston. This Payn was keeper of Glamorgan after the death of Earl Gilbert de Clare in 1314, until 1316. In 1314 he was recorded as holding Coety Castle and manor with 'regalian liberty', by service of acting as master hunter of the earl's forest of Newcastle, without answering for anything other than wardship and marriage to the lord of Cardiff. He also held a half-fee at Llanhari and a tenth of a fee at Newcastle. The Despenser survey of 1320 also records a fee at Coychurch. Payn [iii] married Gwenllian, daughter of Sir Richard Talbot. He was succeeded before 1327 by his eldest son Gilbert [iv] who was alive in 1341 but was then succeeded by his son Gilbert [v], who died in 1350. The inquisition on his death confirms what is known of the Turberville landed interests and reveals moreover that Payn [iii] had settled a one-third interest in the family lands on his younger son **Richard** [ii] **Turberville** (*c.*1320–*c.*1367) who succeeded his childless nephew Gilbert [v], being then about thirty years old. This Richard had an active career as a retainer of the later Despenser lords of Glamorgan. Richard [ii] died soon after 1366 and was probably buried in Margam Abbey, where he founded a perpetual chantry for the souls of himself and his ancestors at the altar of St Mary Magdalene, with an anniversary mass to be celebrated by the full community. Before his death he entailed his lands on the consecutive male issue of his five sisters. The lordship of Coety came first to Sir Lawrence Berkerolles, the younger son of Katherine, the second sister, and after Lawrence's death without male issue in 1411, it remained with William [ii] Gamage, the great-grandson of Sarah, the youngest.

The Turbervilles are an interesting example of a long-lived dynasty of greater marcher gentry. The attendance of successive heads of the family on their territorial lord lasted for over 250 years. The family conserved its original endowment with great tenacity over the centuries. Richard [ii] enjoyed the same handsome endowment as his twelfth-century predecessors, but much augmented by several good marriages. Cadets of the family survived into the sixteenth century, but none had established themselves on the patrimony, and indeed the Turberville manor of Llanhari, which was endowed on a thirteenth-century cadet line, returned to the main line. Testimony to the wealth and pretensions of the Turbervilles is their magnificent castle of Coety, of which there are considerable remains, including a well-proportioned and ambitious square keep. To this catalogue of architectural patronage might perhaps be added the handsome, and still surviving, fourteenth-century parish churches of Coety and Coychurch.   DAVID CROUCH

Sources G. T. Clark, ed., *Cartae et alia munimenta quae ad dominium de Glamorgancia pertinent*, ed. G. L. Clark, 6 vols. (1910) · B. L. James, ed., *Morganiae archaiographia*, South Wales and Monmouth RS, 1 (1983) · R. B. Patterson, ed., *Earldom of Gloucester charters* (1973) · muniments of the dean and chapter of Hereford, charters 2292–5, 2298, 2301, 2305–6 · muniments of the dean and chapter of Gloucester, deeds, vol. 5 · Penrice and Margam charters, NL Wales, 7, 156, 2306 · F. Palgrave, ed., *Rotuli curiae regis: rolls and records of the court held before the king's justiciars or justices*, 2 vols., RC, 27 (1835) · *Curia regis rolls preserved in the Public Record Office* (1922–) · *Chancery records* · CIPM, vols. 2, 9, 19 · *An inventory of the ancient monuments in Glamorgan*, 3/1a: *The early castles, from the Norman conquest to 1217*, Royal Commission on Ancient and Historical Monuments in Wales and Monmouthshire (1991), 218–88 · H. Summerson, ed., *Crown pleas of the Devon eyre of 1238*, Devon and Cornwall RS, new ser., 28 (1985), 54

Turberville, Daubeney (1612–1696), physician and oculist, was born in Wayford, Somerset, the son of George Turberville of Wayford and his wife, who was a member of the Daubeney family. That family was prominent in Somerset, several forebears having served as sheriff in the county. Daubeney Turberville matriculated from Oriel College, Oxford, on 7 November 1634. He received his BA on 15 October 1635, and his MA on 17 July 1640. At the outbreak of the civil war he joined the king's cause and took part in the defence of Exeter when it was besieged in 1645. When the city was captured by Fairfax he abandoned the military life and settled at Wayford, where in 1646 he married Anne (*d.* 1694), daughter of the Revd James Ford of Hawkchurch, Dorset. There were no children from this marriage. Turberville began practising medicine at Wayford and at the neighbouring town of Crookhorn, before moving to Salisbury, Wiltshire. At the Restoration, on 7 August 1660, he took the degree of MD at Oxford. Apparently at the urging of his mother, Turberville took up the special study of diseases of the eye. He gained considerable fame in the treatment of eye disorders; and when his practice had become sufficiently successful, he moved for a time to London. However, the city air affected his health, and he returned to Salisbury, occupying a house near the St Anne Street Gate.

Turberville's medical prowess brought him to the attention of the royal court. When as a child Queen Anne suffered a dangerous eye inflammation that the court physicians were unable to cure, Turberville was sent for and was asked to treat her. This he did successfully, much to the shock of the court physicians, who thereafter detested him. Turberville's skills also captured the attention of Robert Boyle, who communicated with him frequently until the end of his life about his own persistent eye disorders, and recommended him, in turn, to Samuel Pepys, who wrote about his own consultation with Turberville in his diary entry for 22 June 1668. Boyle encouraged Turberville to return to London to practise, to no avail; he was, however, able to persuade Turberville to make one or two regular, extended trips to London each year, so that those in that city wishing to consult him could do so. Turberville continued to treat patients in Salisbury, accepting payment on the basis of what each could afford, and he often treated the poor for free. He received patients from all over the country and occasionally from abroad.

Two letters from Turberville to William Musgrave, of Oxford, were published in the *Philosophical Transactions of the Royal Society*. The first letter, dated London, 4 August 1684, discusses a case of an unusual eye inflammation which he brought to Boyle's attention 'as a fit subject for so great a philosopher to make his remarks on'. The second letter, dated Sarum, 5 October 1684, gives an account of several cases Turberville cured, including one in which he used a magnet to remove a piece of steel embedded in the 'iris' (evidently meaning the cornea at the limbus). He corresponded with Boyle on a variety of topics. For example, in 1664 he sent Boyle an account of a 'monstrous birth' in Salisbury, including a drawing of what are clearly conjoined twins. Boyle, in turn, sent the information to Henry Oldenburg, then secretary of the Royal Society.

Turberville died at Salisbury on 21 April 1696 and was buried in Salisbury Cathedral, where there is an inscription on a mural tablet on the west wall. His epitaph was written by the astronomer Walter Pope, a grateful former patient. Turberville divided his estate between a niece of his wife and his sister Mary Turberville, who had become very familiar with Turberville's techniques and recipes, and set up practice in London, where she acquired a good reputation as an oculist in her own right.

BARBARA BEIGUN KAPLAN

Sources Foster, *Alum. Oxon.* · *The correspondence of Henry Oldenburg*, ed. and trans. A. R. Hall and M. B. Hall, 2 (1965), 212–14, 277–8 · R. R. James, ed., *Studies in the history of ophthalmology in England prior to the year 1800* (1933), 63–74 · L. T. More, ed., *The life and works of the Honourable Robert Boyle* (1944), 107–9 · W. Pope, *The life of the right reverend father in God, Seth, lord bishop of Salisbury* (1697), 98–109 · A. Sorsby, *A short history of ophthalmology* (1948), 86

Archives RS

Wealth at death estate divided between sister and niece

Turberville, Edward. *See* Turbervill, Edward (1653/4–1681).

Turberville, George. *See* Turbervile, George (b. 1543/4, d. in or after 1597).

Turberville, Gilbert de (d. before 1183). *See under* Turberville family (*per. c.*1125–*c.*1370).

Turberville, Gilbert de (d. *c.*1238). *See under* Turberville family (*per. c.*1125–*c.*1370).

Turberville, Gilbert de (fl. 1242). *See under* Turberville family (*per. c.*1125–*c.*1370).

Turberville, Henry (*c.*1607–1678), Roman Catholic priest, was born in Staffordshire, the son of Troilus Turberville (d. 1609?) of Dorset and his wife, Anne. He entered the English College at Douai on 23 January 1629 and was ordained there at a date unknown. Sent back to England, he became chaplain to Henry Somerset, first marquess of Somerset,

during the civil war, and later lived with Sir George Blount of Sodington as his chaplain. He occupied several responsible posts in the church, including membership of the secular chapter from 1644, and service as archdeacon of Worcestershire and of Oxfordshire. He was, however, to be best known subsequently for his *Abridgement of Christian Doctrine*, which was published at Douai in 1649 and soon became known as the 'Doway catechism'. Catechisms of Christian doctrine were commonplace in the Reformed churches in the sixteenth century. For Roman Catholics, the Jesuit Peter Canisius had produced his catechism in 1555, which dealt with faith (the creed), hope (the Lord's prayer and Hail Mary), charity (the decalogue and precepts of the church) and the sacraments; its second part considered the seven capital sins, and part three good works, the beatitudes, evangelical counsels, and the four last things. This order was followed by Robert Bellarmine, also a Jesuit, in his even more popular work of 1597 despite the adoption of a radically different approach in the catechism of the Council of Trent, published in 1566. Turberville's catechism followed the Jesuit arrangement of material and has been considered to have had an enormous impact. It ran into several editions, the last being a revision by James Doyle, published in Dublin in 1828. It has, however, been deemed 'large, complex and expensive' (Bossy, 272), and a shorter version, published a year or two after Turberville's death, and known as 'An abstract of the Doway catechism', proved even more influential. Richard Challoner apparently took it as a basis for his eighteenth-century catechism, while the 1859 *Catechism of Christian Doctrine*, popularly known as the 'Penny catechism', which became, in its various revisions, required learning for Catholic schoolchildren and students for over a hundred years, derived, it has been argued, from Turberville's work at Douai by way of Challoner.

In his own lifetime Turberville was better known as a controversialist. His *Manual of Controversies* (1654) elicited replies from the leading Baptist John Tombes, from Henry Hammond, and from William Thomas, bishop of Worcester. Dodd reports that the clergy 'had a great esteem for him, and consulted him in all matters of moment' (Dodd, 3.302). By 1668 he was nearly blind, and died in Holborn, London, on 20 February 1678.

THOMPSON COOPER, rev. D. MILBURN

Sources G. Anstruther, *The seminary priests*, 2 (1975), 325 · E. H. Burton and T. L. Williams, eds., *The Douay College diaries, third, fourth and fifth, 1598–1654*, 1, Catholic RS, 10 (1911), 274, 276, 285; 2, Catholic RS, 11 (1911), 534 · C. Dodd [H. Tootell], *The church history of England, from the year 1500, to the year 1688*, 3 (1742), 302 · Gillow, *Lit. biog. hist.*, 5.559 · B. Pickering, 'Bishop Challoner and his catechism', *Clergy Review* (Jan 1980), 7–14 · B. L. Marthaler, *The catechism yesterday and today: the evolution of a genre* (1995) · J. Crichton, 'Challoner and the *Penny catechism*', *Recusant History*, 15 (1979–81), 425–32 · J. P. Marmion, 'The Penny catechism as a text book', 1998 [unpubd article] · PRO, PROB 11/356, fol. 220r–v · J. Bossy, *The English Catholic community, 1570–1850* (1975)

Archives Westminster Archdiocesan Archives, London, Old Brotherhood MSS

Wealth at death money to Douai and Lisbon colleges, and to many priests; mostly small cash sums to nephews, nieces, etc., incl. £240 p.a. to niece/god-daughter: will, proved 1 March 1678, PRO, PROB 11/356, sig. 28, cited Anstruther, *Seminary Priests*

Turberville, James (1494–1570?), bishop of Exeter, was born at or before Christmas 1494, the second surviving son of John Turberville, esquire (d. 1536), of Bere Regis, Dorset, and his wife, Isabel, daughter of John Cheverell. The Turbervilles were an old-established family of gentry, and John served as sheriff of Somerset and Dorset. James was admitted as a scholar of Winchester College in 1507, aged twelve, became a scholar of New College, Oxford, on 5 April 1512, and was promoted to be a full fellow two years later. He graduated BA in 1516 and MA in 1520. From 1521 to 1524 he was employed as a scribe of the university and acted as a notary public. He was ordained priest in 1525 and later studied theology abroad, gaining a doctorate of theology by 1531 and being incorporated in the same degree at Oxford in 1532. He resigned his fellowship in 1529, shortly after acquiring his first benefice, the rectory of Woodmancote, Sussex, and was subsequently admitted to the rectories of Over Moigne in 1532 and Lytchett Matravers in 1536, both in Dorset, and to a canonry of Chichester Cathedral with the prebend of Wittering in 1538, a post traditionally charged with delivering theological lectures. He also became rector of Hartfield, Sussex, in 1541, and a canon and prebendary of Winchester Cathedral in 1549. Apart from Woodmancote, which he resigned by 1535, he occupied all his benefices in plurality until his promotion as bishop.

Turberville does not appear to have taken a prominent part in church affairs under Henry VIII or Edward VI, a fact that may have recommended him when Mary I became queen in 1553. He was nominated as bishop of Exeter by the crown on 11 March 1555, given custody of the temporalities of the see on 6 May, provided by the pope in September, consecrated on or about the 8th of that month, and granted the temporalities on the 21st. As a church leader charged with re-establishing Catholicism, he was fortunate in ruling a conservative diocese which had only recently witnessed the western rebellion of 1549 against the introduction of the Book of Common Prayer. Even the ejection of married clergy in the diocese had been largely completed under his predecessor, John Veysey. Little is known, however, about Turberville's own initiatives as bishop. His ordinations of clergy, the only evidence for his movements, were all carried out at Exeter, save once at Crediton in 1558. Crediton, a valuable episcopal estate, had been lost to the see by Bishop Veysey under Henry VIII, but was leased back to Turberville by the crown in 1556. He subsequently rented part of the property to his nephew Nicholas. Turberville's Exeter contemporary, John Hooker, a man of protestant convictions, describes him as a 'gentleman borne …, verie gentle and courteous …, but most zelous in the Romish religion' (Hooker, *Catalog*, sig. I.iiv). Hooker concedes that he was not personally 'cruell nor bloodie', but blames him (possibly unfairly) for supporting the prosecution for heresy of Agnes Priest of Boyton, Cornwall, who was burnt at Exeter in August 1558—the only such casualty of his episcopate.

After the accession of Elizabeth I, Turberville joined the rest of Mary's bishops in voting in the House of Lords against the Bill of Supremacy and other Reformation legislation during the spring of 1559. In due course he refused to take the oath of supremacy to the queen as supreme governor of all spiritual matters, and was deprived of his bishopric in August. The fact that no successor was appointed until William Alley was nominated in March 1560 suggests that the crown still hoped for Turberville's compliance, but when this hope expired he was sent to the Tower of London on 18 June 1560, along with most of his colleagues. At first they were apparently kept apart but in September were allowed to eat together. Turberville was released from the Tower on 6 September 1563, after intercessions by the emperor Ferdinand, and transferred to the custody of Edmund Grindal, bishop of London. On 30 January 1565 the privy council approved a request from Grindal that Turberville might be freed, on condition of remaining in London and making himself available when required. He probably stayed there until his death, said to have taken place in 1570.

NICHOLAS ORME

Sources Emden, *Oxf.*, 4.579 · J. Hutchins, *The history and antiquities of the county of Dorset*, 3rd edn, ed. W. Shipp and J. W. Hodson, 1 (1861), 136–40, 159 · J. Hooker [J. Vowell], *A catalog of the bishops of Excester* (1584), sig. 1.iiv · J. Hooker, commonplace book, Devon RO, book 51, fol. 352v · episcopal register of Bishop Turberville, Devon RO, Chanter XVIII–IX · H. Gee, *The Elizabethan clergy and the settlement of religion, 1558–1564* (1898) · registrum primum, Winchester College, p. 52 · *JHL*, 1 (1509–77) · *CPR, 1553–66* · *APC, 1552–70*
Archives Devon RO, episcopal register, Chanter XVIII–XIX

Turberville, Payn de (*fl.* 1126–1130). *See under* Turberville family (*per. c.*1125–*c.*1370).

Turberville, Payn de (d. in or before **1208**). *See under* Turberville family (*per. c.*1125–*c.*1370).

Turberville, Payn (d. in or before **1327**). *See under* Turberville family (*per. c.*1125–*c.*1370).

Turberville, Richard de (d. in or before **1303**). *See under* Turberville family (*per. c.*1125–*c.*1370).

Turberville, Richard (*c.*1320–*c.*1367). *See under* Turberville family (*per. c.*1125–*c.*1370).

Turberville, Sir Thomas de (d. 1295), soldier and traitor, is of uncertain origins, but his father was probably Sir Hugh de Turberville (d. 1293). It was probably Sir Thomas, not a namesake, who was a follower of John Giffard (d. 1299) in the civil wars of the late 1260s, and who was rewarded for his loyalty to the crown with a grant of land in Northamptonshire. He was probably also the man of that name charged at the Wiltshire eyre of 1280/81 with robbery and homicide. Cleared of the former charge, he refused to plead to the latter, but was eventually cleared when it was found that the killing had been committed during the civil war. There was a strong tradition of royal service in the Turberville family: Hugh de Turberville had served Edward I with distinction since before his accession. Thomas de Turberville was certainly a royal household knight in 1282, when he took part in the Welsh war. In 1286 he accompanied Edward to Paris and on to Gascony.

When war broke out between England and France in 1294 he served with a retinue of at least nine knights in John of Brittany's expedition to Gascony. Initial successes were considerable. Turberville was part of the force that occupied Rioms. In April 1295, however, the French seized the town after a riot among the English troops. John of Brittany and much of the garrison fled by ship, but Turberville was captured along with a dozen other knights.

In August, Turberville returned to England, claiming that he had escaped from prison. It was soon discovered that he was in fact spying for the French. A messenger he had employed to take a letter to France revealed its contents to the king. In it Turberville informed the provost of Paris that Wales was now at peace. He reported that the Isle of Wight was not guarded, and that the king was to send a powerful embassy to the German king. Twenty ships were to be sent with grain supplies to Gascony, and an expedition there was to be headed by the earls of Lancaster, Lincoln, and Warwick, along with Hugh Despenser, later earl of Winchester (d. 1326). Turberville claimed to have reached agreement with the recently defeated Morgan ap Maredudd that the latter should rebel again if the Scots would follow suit. He advised the French to send a powerful embassy to Scotland. The letter reveals that Turberville's sons had been kept in Paris as hostages, and that he had been promised £100 worth of land as his reward for treachery.

The letter seems genuine. It is reasonably circumstantial, and the description of English plans is very plausible, even though Warwick and Despenser did not sail for Gascony, and no embassy as described went to Germany in 1295. It is inconceivable that Edward would, for propaganda purposes, have falsely implicated one of his own household knights in treason, and in any case he had set a spy upon Turberville, who appears to have tried to flee to Wales.

Turberville was arrested on 24 September 1295, and was tried promptly, on 8 October. The chief justice of the king's bench pronounced the verdict. The guilty man, who was probably the first man in England to be executed for spying, was to be drawn on an oxhide to the gallows, where he was to be hanged; the sentence was executed the same day. News of the event was widely circulated, as a form of war propaganda, and it was also commemorated in a popular song or poem.   MICHAEL PRESTWICH, *rev.*

Sources *Bartholomaei de Cotton … Historia Anglicana*, ed. H. R. Luard, Rolls Series, 16 (1859), 304–6 · *The chronicle of Walter of Guisborough*, ed. H. Rothwell, CS, 3rd ser., 89 (1957), 252–4 · J. G. Edwards, 'The treason of Thomas Turberville', *Studies in medieval history presented to Frederick Maurice Powicke*, ed. R. W. Hunt and others (1948), 296–309 · *Thomas Wright's 'Political songs of England'*, ed. P. R. Coss (1996), 278–81 · M. Prestwich, *War, politics, and finance under Edward I* (1972) · M. Prestwich, *Edward I* (1988)

Turbeville, Henry de. *See* Trubleville, Sir Henry de (d. 1239).

Turé, Fodé Ibrahim [*known as* Fodé Kombo Sillah] (*c.*1825–1894), political leader in the Gambia, was born in Konoto, the Turé family compound in the town of Gunjur, Kombo kingdom, Gambia, west Africa. Konoto had been built by his great-grandfather Amatora Turé, a famous Muslim scholar, during the first half of the eighteenth century. Fodé Ibrahim's father was Maley Burama Turé and his mother was Mbesine Njai from Sine in Senegal. The Turé clan produced notable Muslim teachers and helped to establish Islamic institutions and ideas in many west African territories. Ibrahim Turé followed a typical path for a talented male member of his clan. He studied the Koran and fundamental Islamic doctrines at the school run by his father and his uncle Fodé Kang Kaba Turé, until about the age of twelve, when his father died. His uncle then sent him to study advanced Islamic texts with Fodé Ibrahim Sillah Ba, a famous scholar, in Darsilami, Pakao (Casamance, Senegal). There he became known as Fodé Kombo Sillah, and after he had mastered law and theology he returned to Gunjur about 1850 as a teacher and missionary in Kombo. His knowledge and spirituality became well recognized among the Muslim community in the kingdom.

Fodé Kombo Sillah's uncle Fodé Kang Kaba Turé, and other Muslim leaders had been engaged in a series of wars against the non-Muslim rulers of Kombo since about 1849 but had not managed to establish an Islamic state. These wars were perceived by British officials as a threat to the settlements at Bathurst and in British Kombo. Some time after 1865 Fodé Kombo Sillah began a series of spiritual meditations to learn from Allah about his role in the struggle, and about 1870 he made a spiritual retreat (*khalwa*) to a small island where he prayed for the title of *waliyu Allah* (delegate of Allah) and for a sign to call for jihad. During 1872 the Muslims launched new attacks against the Kombo rulers. In 1873 Fodé Sillah agreed to lead the Muslims, proclaimed the jihad and assumed the title of amir (commander).

On 29 September 1875 the king of Kombo surrendered to Fodé Sillah and agreed to become a Muslim. Treaties of 24 March 1873 (PRO, CO 87/104, dispatch 49) and 29 September 1875 (PRO, CO 87/108, dispatch 71) between the British and Muslim leaders recognized Kombo with Fodé Sillah as its ruler. He established Islamic courts wherein the shariʿa (Islamic law) was applied. The requirements for forced labour and taxes on produce were abolished, and the consumption of alcohol was forbidden. The Muslim community built new mosques and schools throughout Kombo, and conversion to Islam was promoted.

Fodé Sillah spent the next nineteen years trying to extend his territory and putting down rebellions by non-Muslim and Muslim dissidents. His military actions, like his Islamic programmes, were ultimately successful, but he became increasingly worried about British and French encroachment on his state. On the other hand, British colonial officials became alarmed about the growing threat of Islamic expansion, especially after 1885 when the British took action to create a protectorate over the south bank of the Gambia River. During 1887 Fodé Sillah negotiated with British and French officials for protectorate status, but he vacillated. Ultimately, at a meeting in July 1887 with Governor Samuel Rowe, he threatened to use force against the British to preserve his power in

Kombo. Governor Rowe recommended military action in a letter to the Colonial Office (PRO, CO 879/27/348). Also, in 1888 Fodé Sillah's opponents in northern Kombo sought British protection, so new bases for conflict were emerging.

In 1889 the French and British created a joint boundary commission to settle their territorial disputes. Fodé Sillah rejected their right to create boundaries in Kombo, and he interfered with the commission's work. A meeting with British military officials in 1890 did not resolve the dispute, and between 1891 and 1894 Fodé Sillah's relations with the French and British deteriorated further as he asserted his position through military actions. British administrators described Fodé Sillah as a 'marauding slave dealer' and an 'excitable fanatic' who would have to be forcefully opposed. He refused to negotiate with the British and rejected an offer to disband his army, resettle in British Kombo and receive a stipend of £100. The British responded with military action. After a battle in which the British were routed, a major military expedition was mobilized in February 1894. On 9 March, British forces found Fodé Sillah's capital abandoned, and the British took control of the Kombo region. Fodé Sillah and his family surrendered to the French on 11 March, and they were resettled in Sakha, 2 kilometres from Ngaimékhé in Cayor, Senegal. Fodé Sillah died there on the night of 19–20 September 1894 and was buried on 21 September. In the century following his death he came to be revered as a *waliyu Allah* and honoured as a leader of African resistance to colonialism, and his tomb at Sakha became a site for annual pilgrimage organized by the Ebrima Foday Kombo Sillah Touray Association.   DAVID E. SKINNER

Sources D. Skinner and M. Stevens, 'Islam in Kombo: the spiritual and militant jihad of Fodé Ibrahim Turé', 1990, History of Kombo Collection, Banjul, The Gambia, oral history division [paper presented to African Studies Association, Baltimore] • K. Alhaji Bai, 'A history of Kombo', ed. W. Galloway (1980) [History of Kombo Collection, Banjul, The Gambia, oral history division] • Touray Nyonko Amaddu, 'The history of Ebrima Fodé Kombo Sillah Touray, the emir who caused the Islam in Kombo in 1873', ed. D. Skinner (1988) [History of Kombo Collection, Banjul, The Gambia, oral history division] • C. Roche, *Histoire de la Casamance: conquête et résistance, 1850–1920* (Paris, 1985) • B. Barry, *Le Sénégambie du XVe au XIXe siècle* (Paris, 1988) • N. Baro, 'History of Gunjur', 1973, History of Kombo Collection, Banjul, The Gambia, oral history division, file 212c • *Journal officiel du Sénégal* (1894)
Archives History of Kombo Collection, Banjul, The Gambia, oral history division | PRO, CO 87, 879

Turford, Hugh (d. 1713), religious writer, was a schoolteacher in Bristol and a Quaker. Virtually nothing is known of his life: his name does not appear, for instance, in the minutes of the men's meetings of the Bristol Friends between 1667 and 1704. A relative, Elizabeth Turford, was among 104 Friends gaoled by the mayor of Bristol in 1664 for violating the Conventicle Act. Hugh's wife, Jane, and a son and daughter had died by 1674, and he himself was buried at Bristol on 5 March 1713.

In 1702 he published in London *The grounds of a holy life, or, The way by which many heathens came to be renowned Christians … to which is added Paul's speech to the bishop of Cretia; as also 'A true touchstone, or, Tryal of Christianity'*. This small devotional classic (123 or 146 duodecimo, or 56 octavo pages) was reprinted by Quaker publishers in 1723 and kept in print through twenty-one London editions from 1747 to 1843, besides others from Bristol, Newcastle, Philadelphia, and four from Manchester. It was translated into German (n.d.), French (Nîmes, 1824, but Sarah Grubb on page 197 reports carrying to France an earlier version in 1790), Spanish (London, 1844), Italian (London, 1823, 1846), and Danish (Stavanger, 1856). The three sections are based on Galatians 5: 16, Titus 2: 11–13, and the sermon on the mount. The second and third parts were often reprinted separately from 1785 to 1814 in Leeds, Waterford, Bristol, Whitby, York, or London.

Turford's book presents without a sectarian label the challenge provided by quietism which increasingly dominated the Society of Friends in the eighteenth century, a truly 'innerworldly asceticism' (in Max Weber's phrase) which denied self-will so that the divine Spirit might lead and work. Luxury and social pride must be set aside, not as evil but because to care about them distracts any person from obedience to the leadings of the light within, which shows men evil. 'The more light any of us have, the greater discovery it makes of what is amiss in ourselves and others' (Turford, 56). Rejecting Calvinist predestination, Turford assumes that each person 'bears two seeds' (ibid., 40), the ego and the conscience, one or other of which will grow each time the inner monitor is followed or ignored. Once thoughts have led to actions 'after the flesh' or 'the Spirit', 'sinful actions are past recall' (ibid., 50), but in people 'where the righteous seed is risen … they cannot be unjust in their dealings, nor unfaithful in their promises; they cannot tell an untruth, … oppress the poor, … nor take by violence that which they have no right to' (ibid., 64). Turford warns against underpaying workmen and deceit in trading, but ignores cruelty within families. He does not claim people can achieve moral perfection by their own efforts, without divine grace and power, nor gives any credit to clergy or rituals apart from silently shared worship. Yet the Quaker quietists' inner sensitivity to moral issues made them pioneers throughout the century in educating the poor and in rejecting slavery, capital punishment, and brutality to the insane.

Turford's was the only Quaker book found in the library of the major devotional writer William Law at King's Cliffe; Law's was the 1758 edition, but he may also have read an earlier edition, along with works by Isaac Penington and Robert Barclay. In Law's later works, *The Spirit of Love* (1752, e.g. pp. 404, 430–34), and *An Address to the Clergy* (1761), he followed these Friends and Jakob Boehme in emphasizing the Spirit's leadings and rejecting merely substitutionary atonement, rather more than in his *Serious Call to a Devout and Holy Life* (1728), with its stress on 'dying to self' (pp. 31, 365) and the discipline of fixed daily hours of prayer. Turford's and Law's call to inner self-purification responded directly to the perceived libertinism of the 'Augustan age' in England.

HUGH BARBOUR

Sources H. Turford, *The grounds of a holy life, or, The way in which many who were heathens came to be Christians, … to which is added Paul's*

speech to the bishop of Crete; as also 'A true touchstone, or, Trial of Christianity', 19th edn (1823) • *Some account of the life and religious labours of Sarah Grubb* (1795) • J. Smith, ed., *A descriptive catalogue of Friends' books,* 2 vols. (1867); suppl. (1893), vol. 2, pp. 832–5; suppl., pp. 343–4 • R. M. Jones, *The later periods of Quakerism,* 2 vols. (1921) • S. Hobhouse, *William Law and eighteenth-century Quakerism* (1927) • *Selected mystical writings of William Law,* ed. S. Hobhouse (1948) • A. K. Walker, *William Law, his life and thought* (1973) • W. Law, 'A call to a devout and holy life' and 'The Spirit of Love' (1978) • *DNB*

Turgeon, Pierre Flavien (1787–1867), Roman Catholic archbishop of Quebec, was born in Quebec on 12 November 1787. He was ordained priest in 1810, appointed to the chair of theology in the Quebec seminary in 1814, and made director in 1821. From 1808 he was secretary to Mgr Plessis, whom he accompanied to England and Rome in 1819–20, and had much to do in settling the status of the Roman Catholic church in Canada and in obtaining recognition for the episcopate. The French ambassador at Rome fruitlessly opposed a bull (28 February 1834) appointing him bishop of Sidyme *in partibus* and coadjutor to Mgr Signay, the Roman Catholic bishop of Quebec 'cum futura successione', on the ground, it was said, of his pro-English leanings, which had been shown in the Anglo-American War of 1812–14. They were seen later in the rebellion of 1837 and in his support of the union of 1841.

Turgeon instituted the ecclesiastical structure of the province and is credited with a principal share in the ecclesiastical legislation passed by the special council of 1839, preliminary to the union of 1841. This legislation included ordinances recognizing the Montreal episcopate, confirming the ecclesiastical title to Montreal Island Saint Sulpice and to Lake of the Two Mountains, and repealing the Mortmain Act (1830), thus allowing religious bodies to hold immovable property in the name of trustees as civil corporations. He became administrator of the archdiocese in November 1849 and succeeded as the second titular archbishop of Quebec in October 1850. The first (1851) and second (1854) councils of Quebec, both of which were attended by all Roman Catholic bishops of British North America, were held under him. He founded Laval University, which was granted a royal charter on 8 December 1852 and, after canonical sanction had been obtained, was opened by him on 1 September 1854. La Maison du Bon Pasteur was also instituted by him. In 1855 he was struck by paralysis and resigned the administration to his coadjutor and successor, Mgr Baillargeon. He died on 25 August 1867.

T. B. BROWNING, rev. LEO GOOCH

Sources C. Tanguay, *Répertoire général du clergé canadien,* 2nd edn (1893), 9 • M. Bibaud, *Le panthéon canadien,* rev. A. Bibaud and V. Bibaud, new edn (Montreal, 1891), 288 • L. P. Turcotte, *Le Canada sous l'union, 1841–1867,* 2 vols. (1882), vol. 1, 92–6; vol. 2, 148, 278–82 • F. X. Garneau, *Histoire du Canada,* 2nd edn, 3 vols. (1852), 3, 226 • E. Lareau, *Histoire du droit canadien,* 2 vols. (1888–9), vol. 2, pp. 443–6, 454–7

Turges [Thorgest, Thorgils, Thurkill] (d. 845), viking leader, led raids into Ireland in the early ninth century and for a time was successful in the north-east. The name Turges given to him in the Irish records suggests that his real name was Thorgest (þorgestr) or Thorgils (þorgils). Nothing is known of his ancestry, although the Icelandic historian Snorri Sturluson, in his *Heimskringla,* seems to have confused Turges with a son of the Norwegian king Harald Hárfagri (Harald Finehair). The most complete account of his career in Ireland is found in the tract *Cogad Gáedel re Gallaib* ('The war of the Irish and the Foreigners') in the Book of Leinster.

Although vikings had been raiding Ireland and Britain since the late eighth century, in the second quarter of the ninth century the raiders began to use systematically the interior waterways of Ireland, and they began the establishment of permanent bases that would lead eventually to the Hiberno-Scandinavian towns. In 832 vikings plundered the monastery of Armagh three times in one month. *Cogad Gáedel re Gallaib* claims that Turges led the raids; and at some point the abbot, named Forindán, was replaced as abbot by Turges, who assumed the office for a period of time. Those actions need not have been anti-Christian, but rather an indication of an awareness of the important connection between ecclesiastical support and political power in Ireland. He took control of the viking companies in Ireland and maintained fleets on Lough Neagh and in Louth. He also established a fleet on Lough Ree in 845, whence his troops plundered Meath and Connacht, with destruction of the monasteries of Clonmacnoise, Clonfert, Lough Derg, Terryglass, and Lorrha (Tipperary). This campaign seems to have given Turges control of the monastery of Clonmacnoise, the important midland ecclesiastical centre. His wife, Ota, put it to her own uses by giving audiences while seated on the altar of the church. This seems to have been a ceremony of divination. Also in 845 a viking force, possibly led by Turges, was defeated by the high-king Niall Caille mac Áeda at Mag Itha. Turges's supremacy ended in that year when he was captured by the king of Clann Cholmáin and future high-king, Máel Sechnaill mac Máele Ruanaid, and drowned in Lough Owel (Westmeath).

The career and death of Turges became part of Irish literature. In the eleventh century the Irish historian Gilla Coemáin mac Gilla Samthainne included his drowning as a chronological marker in the versified chronicle *Annalad anall uile.* By the twelfth century Gerald of Wales was claiming that Turges was responsible for leading the vikings into Ireland, and he gives an interesting, and apparently fictitious, story of the circumstances of his death. In that tale Turges asked for the hand of the daughter of Máel Sechnaill, who publicly agreed to the union, but secretly disguised fifteen warriors as his daughter and her retinue. When the viking came to claim his bride, Turges and his company were slain by the decoys.

BENJAMIN T. HUDSON

Sources *Ann. Ulster* • J. H. Todd, ed. and trans., *Cogadh Gaedhel re Gallaibh / The war of the Gaedhil with the Gaill,* Rolls Series, 48 (1867) • R. I. Best and others, eds., *The Book of Leinster, formerly Lebar na Núachongbála,* 6 vols. (1954–83) • *Gir. Camb. opera*

Turges [Sturges], **Edmund** (b. c.1445), composer, is of obscure origins. Nothing is known about his parentage or the circumstances of his birth or death; his surviving music is found in manuscript sources of *c*.1500–1520. In 1469 he was established in the London area and was admitted to membership of the fraternity of St Nicholas, a guild of parish clerks and professional musicians working in the collegiate and parish churches of London and its immediate environs. From this a birth date of about 1445 may be inferred. It is just possible that he may be identified with one Sturges who was a chaplain of the choir of New College, Oxford, during 1507–8. Since he composed secular as well as sacred music, it is equally possible that he spent much or most of his career in the employment of aristocratic families whose records have perished, composing sacred music for the chapel and secular music for entertainment.

Turges is not known to have served in the Chapel Royal, but the texts of two of the four songs attributed to him in the Fayrfax book suggest contact with the royal family. In 'Enforce yourselfe as Goddis Knyght' an unnamed king (almost certainly Henry VII) is urged to uphold the rights of the commons against 'all mysdone thinges'. The carol 'From stormy wyndis and grevous wethir' prays for the protection of 'Arthur oure prynce', perhaps on a sea voyage or other hazardous journey. Composition may have been prompted by the departure of Arthur and Katherine of Aragon for their court at Ludlow as prince and princess of Wales in December 1501. The prayer is, however, for Arthur exclusively, and possibly the 'stormy wyndis and grevous wethir' are to be understood metaphorically. This carol was apparently sufficiently admired for John Browne to use melodic material from it in his fine votive antiphon *Stabat iuxta Christi crucem*, composed about 1502.

Turges has never enjoyed the reputation of, for example, Robert Fayrfax (*d.* 1521) or John Taverner (*d.* 1545); nevertheless, his work is accomplished, and sometimes striking. The five-voice Magnificat in the Caius choirbook is exceptionally extended and contains passages that are extremely busy rhythmically, even in terms of the florid style of much contemporary English music. The five-voice setting of the Marian antiphon *Gaude flore virginali* (in the Eton choirbook) gives unusual prominence to boys' voices; if the composer was indeed ever a chaplain of New College, he may have designed it specifically for its chapel choir, with its many boys and few men. The work contains several phrases that seem to recall melodic material from 'From stormy wyndis'. It may have been intended to compliment Prince Arthur if it belongs to the short period between the writing of 'From stormy wyndis' and Arthur's death in April 1502, or to commemorate him if it dates, for example, from Turges's possible stay at New College. A four-voice setting of *Gaude flore virginali* also exists; this can be sung by men only, as can a three-voice Kyrie and Gloria by 'Edmund Sturges' in the Ritson manuscript.

Much music by Turges has been lost. The Eton choirbook once contained three four-voice settings of the Magnificat. 'Turges massys and antems' appeared in partbooks belonging to King's College, Cambridge, in 1529; as six-voice works they must have been among the composer's most ambitious. While it is possible that these were by Edmund Turges (*b.* 1506), fellow of King's from 1526 to 1535, this is unlikely, not least because the repertory of the partbooks generally suggests composition before the 1520s. HUGH BENHAM

Sources R. Bowers, 'The vocal scoring, choral balance and performing pitch of Latin church polyphony in England, *c*.1500–58', *Journal of the Royal Musical Association*, 112 (1987), 38–76 • H. Benham, 'Prince Arthur (1486–1502), a carol and a *cantus firmus*', *Early Music*, 15 (1987), 463–7 • R. Bowers, 'Early Tudor courtly song: an evaluation of the Fayrfax Book (BL, Additional MS 5465)', *The reign of Henry VII* [Harlaxton 1993], ed. B. Thompson (1995), 188–212 • H. Baillie, 'A London gild of musicians, 1460–1530', *Proceedings of the Royal Musical Association*, 83 (1956–7), 15–28 • Venn, *Alum. Cant.*, 1/4.272 • H. Benham, 'All about Edmund', *MT*, 140 (1999), 44–55 • D. Greer, 'Turges, Edmund', *New Grove* • J. Stevens, *Music and poetry at the early Tudor court* (1961); repr. with corrections (1979) • F. L. Harrison, ed., *The Eton choirbook*, 3, Musica Britannica, 12 (1961) • J. Stevens, ed., *Early Tudor songs and carols*, Musica Britannica, 36 (1975) • P. Doe, ed., *Early Tudor magnificats*, 1 (1964) • C. K. Miller, 'A fifteenth-century record of English choir repertory: BM Add MS 5665: a transcription and commentary', 2 vols., PhD diss., Yale U., 1948 • 'An inventarye of the pryke songys longynge to the Kyngys College in Cambryge', King's Cam., KCA 22, fol. 46*r* [repr. in F. Ll. Harrison, *Music in medieval Britain*, 2nd edn (1965), 432–3]

Archives BL, Fayrfax Book, Add. MS 5465 • BL, Ritson MS, Add. MS 5665 • Bodl. Oxf., MS New College 368/1, Bowers 38 • Eton, Eton Choirbook, MS 178 • Gon. & Caius Cam., Caius Choirbook, MS 667

Turgot (*c*.1050–1115), author and bishop of St Andrews, was, according to Symeon of Durham (the source for almost all that is known of Turgot's early life), born of a 'not undistinguished' English family from Lindsey, Lincolnshire. He was evidently a clerk. After the Norman conquest Turgot was held as a hostage by the Normans in Lincoln Castle, but bribed his way out of captivity and escaped on a Norwegian merchant ship from Grimsby. In Norway he was well received by King Olaf III (*d.* 1093), became a teacher of psalmody, and was patronized by the king and the Norwegian nobles. Although he felt leanings to a monastic vocation, the wealth and comfort of his life meant that he did not act on them at this time; but he again began to consider entering the religious life after losing all his property in a shipwreck while returning to England. At the suggestion of Walcher, bishop of Durham (*d.* 1080), he went to live in the newly refounded monastery of Jarrow under Prior Aldwin, though he still remained a clerk rather than a monk (*c*.1074). He subsequently went with Aldwin to Melrose and attempted to establish an ecclesiastical community there, but the pair were faced with threats from Malcolm III, king of Scots (*d.* 1093), since 'they were unwilling to swear fealty to him' (Symeon of Durham, *Opera*, 1.112). On their return south, Turgot became a monk at the new foundation of Wearmouth (*c*.1075). It is probable that he was one of the monks who went from Wearmouth to help found the monastic community at Durham in 1083, and he was appointed prior there in 1087. From 1093 this was a post that he combined (unusually) with the archdeaconry of Durham.

As prior, Turgot played an active role in the transformation of Norman Durham. He administered the diocese during the exile of Bishop William of St Calais (*d.* 1096) between 1088 and 1091. Along with the bishop he laid the foundation stone of the new cathedral in 1093 and he was the prime organizer of the translation of the relics of St Cuthbert to the new east end in 1104. His earlier difficulties with King Malcolm seem not to have prevented close relations with the Scottish royal family. Malcolm himself was among those at the foundation ceremony of 1093, and the king and his wife, Margaret (*d.* 1093), together with their children, were admitted to religious confraternity with the monks and had special commemoration at Durham, while their son Alexander (later king—*d.* 1124) was present at the translation of 1104. The Scottish kings were also generous in their endowments. The grant by Edgar (*d.* 1107) in 1095 included Coldingham and its shire, the nucleus of the later priory of Coldingham, a dependency of Durham. Turgot's period of office also witnessed losses for Durham, however. He was unable to recover the priory of Tynemouth, which Earl Robert de Mowbray had taken from the monks of Durham and granted to the abbey of St Albans. And the claim to archidiaconal rights over Carlisle and Teviotdale had to be abandoned in 1101, though the real exercise of such authority earlier, at least in Teviotdale, is shown by the fact that Turgot was able to have the body of Bishop Walcher's killer expelled from the church of Jedburgh—an act that also avenged his earlier patron.

Glimpses of Turgot's life as prior can also be obtained from a contemporary account of Cuthbert's miracles. He is seen on a journey to the south of England, seeking hospitality for the night and, later, entertaining the royal court with the story of a miracle; on Lindisfarne, helping some storm-driven sailors, who turn out to be pirates, and then exercising mercy toward them; in Durham Cathedral, advising the victim of a punitive miracle that no further penance will be demanded of him. Vigour and mercifulness are the characteristics that emerge. In June 1107 Turgot was elected bishop of St Andrews, at the wish of the Scottish king, Alexander I. Consecration was delayed by ecclesiastical disputes between York and St Andrews, with York claiming authority over St Andrews. Eventually Turgot was consecrated by Thomas, archbishop of York, on 1 August 1109, but with mutual reservation of rights. He found, according to Symeon of Durham, that he could not exercise his episcopal office in Scotland 'worthily' and resolved to go to Rome, but was prevented by the king. He subsequently became ill and was allowed to return to Durham, where he died on 31 August 1115 and was buried in the chapter house.

The only extant writing by Turgot is his life of Margaret, queen of Scots, of which there are two manuscripts, one in the British Library (Cotton MS Tiberius D.iii) and one in the library of the royal palace in Madrid (Palacio Real, MS II 2097), in addition to the late medieval abbreviated version of John of Tynemouth. (Doubts about the attribution of the work and the hypothesis of the existence of two early versions are groundless.) The life was composed between 1100 and 1107 and dedicated to Margaret's daughter Matilda, queen of Henry I of England. Turgot explains in the preface that Matilda had urged him to write the work since she knew that he had been 'well informed

about the queen's private life because of the great friendship between them' (Turgot, 234). When exactly Turgot established this close contact with Margaret is not clear, although it was obviously some time between his return to England *c.*1074 and her death in 1093. He mentions the 'long period' he served in the church at Dunfermline and his frequent private conversation with her about religious matters. He 'returned home', as he himself puts it, at least six months before her death. This evidence might suggest either a long period at the Scottish court or shorter frequent visits.

Turgot portrays Margaret in the work as a grave and devout reforming queen. Her descent from the Wessex line of kings is stressed, as is the way she made court ceremonial in Scotland more seemly and ostentatious. Focus is placed on her knowledge of scripture, austerities, constant prayer, and generosity to the church and the poor. In particular, Turgot speaks of the reforming councils she held, and it has been noticed that the programme of reform undertaken by these councils bears a strong resemblance to that outlined in two papal letters sent to Turgot and the Scottish church by Pope Paschal II, probably in 1114 and presumably in response to information sent by Turgot himself. It may thus be assumed that these issues were important to him. They include proper observance of days of feast and fast, confession, communion, and marriage law. This combination of ritual and pastoral concerns reflects very well both the clerk and the monk in Turgot. A well-born Anglo-Saxon cleric of the Danelaw who looked naturally to Scandinavia, Turgot also worked effectively in the world of post-conquest England, furthering the beauty and the interests of his church of Durham and playing an important part in the process of Anglicization and ecclesiastical reform in Scotland that is linked with the name of the Anglo-Saxon princess Margaret.

ROBERT BARTLETT

Sources Symeon of Durham, *Opera* · Turgot of Durham, 'Vita sanctae Margaritae Scotorum reginae', in *Symeonis Dunelmensis opera et collectanea*, ed. [J. Hodgson Hinde], SurtS, 51 (1868), 234–54 · D. E. R. Watt, *Ecclesia Scoticana* (Stuttgart, 1991), 81–2 · D. Bethell, 'Two letters of Pope Paschal II to Scotland', *SHR*, 49 (1970), 33–45 · D. W. Rollason, M. Harvey, and M. Prestwich, eds., *Anglo-Norman Durham* (1994) · A. A. M. Duncan, 'The earliest Scottish charters', *SHR*, 37 (1958), 103–35 · L. L. Huneycutt, 'The idea of a perfect princess: the *Life of St Margaret* in the reign of Matilda II (1100–1118)', *Anglo-Norman Studies*, 12 (1989), 81–97 · D. Baker, 'A nursery of saints: St Margaret of Scotland reconsidered', *Medieval women*, ed. D. Baker, SCH, Subsidia, 1 (1978)

Archives BL, Cotton MS Tiberius D.iii · Palacio Real, Madrid, MS II 2097

Turing, Alan Mathison (1912–1954), mathematician and computer scientist, was born on 23 June 1912 at Warrington Lodge, Warrington Avenue, London, the younger child (after his brother, John) of Julius Mathison Turing, of the Indian Civil Service, and Ethel Sara Stoney (1881–1976), daughter of Edward Waller Stoney, chief engineer of the Madras Railways. The unusual name of Turing was best known for the work of H. D. Turing on fly-fishing; more scientific connections could be found in the Stoneys

Alan Mathison Turing (1912–1954), by Elliott & Fry, 1951

(notably in a remote relative, the Irish physicist G. J. Stoney).

Education and early scientific interests Until his father's retirement in 1926 the sons were fostered in various English homes, and Turing attended Hazelhurst preparatory school in 1922–6; during those years he found his extra-curricular passion for chemistry experiments. At twelve he expressed conscious fascination with using 'the thing that is commonest in nature and with the least waste of energy' (letter from Turing to his mother, 1925, cited in Hodges, *Enigma*, 19), presentiment of a life seeking fresh answers to fundamental questions. Despite this, he was successfully entered for Sherborne School. The headmaster soon reported, almost correctly: 'If he is to be solely a scientific specialist, he is wasting his time at a Public School' (Hodges, 26).

Turing's private notes on the theory of relativity showed a degree-level appreciation, yet he was almost prevented from taking the school certificate lest he shame the school. The stimulus for communication and competition came only from another very able pupil at Sherborne, Christopher Morcom, to whom he found himself powerfully attracted. Morcom gave Turing a vital period of intellectual companionship, which ended with the former's sudden death in 1930.

Turing's conviction that he must now do what Morcom could not apparently sustained him through a long crisis. His thoughts turned to the question of how the human mind was embodied in matter, and whether, accordingly,

it could be released from matter by death. This led him to wonder whether quantum mechanical theory affected the traditional questions of mind and matter. As an undergraduate at King's College, Cambridge, from 1931, he entered a world more encouraging to free-ranging thought. His reading of J. von Neumann's new work on the logical foundations of quantum mechanics helped a transition from emotion to intellectual enquiry.

Turing's homosexuality became a definitive part of his identity, and the special ambience of King's College gave him a first real home. His association with the anti-war movement of 1933 did not develop into Marxism, nor into the pacifism of his occasional lover James Atkins, a fellow mathematician. He was closer in thought to the liberal-left economists J. M. Keynes and A. C. Pigou. His relaxations were not found in the literary circles generally associated with the King's College homosexual milieu, but in rowing, running, and later in sailing a small boat.

The universal Turing machine Turing's progress seemed assured: a distinguished degree in 1934 was followed by a fellowship of King's in 1935 and a Smith's prize in 1936 for work on probability theory, and he might then have seemed on course for a successful career as a mildly eccentric King's don engaged in pure mathematics; but his uniqueness of mind drove him in a direction none could have foreseen. By 1933 he had introduced himself to Russell and Whitehead's *Principia mathematica* and so to the arcane area of mathematical logic. However, many questions had by then been raised about how truth could be captured by formalism. K. Gödel had shattered Russell's picture by showing the existence of true statements about numbers which could not be proved by the formal application of rules of deduction. In 1935 the topologist M. H. A. Newman introduced Turing to a question which still lay open: the question of decidability, the *Entscheidungsproblem*. Did there exist a definite method or process by which all mathematical questions could be decided?

To answer such a question needed a definition of 'method' both precise and compelling, and this Turing supplied. He analysed what could be achieved by a person performing a methodical process, and, seizing on the idea of something done 'mechanically', expressed the analysis in terms of a theoretical machine able to perform certain precisely defined elementary operations on symbols. He presented convincing arguments that the scope of such a machine was sufficient to encompass everything that would count as a 'definite method'. Daringly he included an argument based on 'states of mind' of a human being performing a mental process. Having made this novel definition of what should count as a 'definite method' it was possible to answer this question in the negative: no such method exists.

In April 1936 Turing showed his result to Newman, but at the same moment the parallel conclusion of the American logician A. Church became known, and Turing was robbed of his full reward. His paper, 'On computable numbers with an application to the *Entscheidungsproblem*' (*Proceedings of the London Mathematical Society*, 42, 1936, 230–65; 43, 1937, 544–6) was delayed. However the originality of his concept—the 'Turing machine'—was recognized and has become the foundation of the theory of computation.

The 'universal Turing machine' was an idea of immense practical significance: there is an infinity of possible Turing machines, each corresponding to a different 'definite method' or algorithm. But imagine, as Turing did, each particular algorithm written as a set of instructions. Then the work of interpreting and obeying these instructions is itself a mechanical process, and so can itself be embodied in a particular Turing machine, namely the universal Turing machine.

The Turing machine can now be thought of as a computer program, and the mechanical task of interpreting and obeying the program as what the computer itself does. So the universal Turing machine is now seen to embody the principle of the modern computer: a single machine which can be turned to any task by an appropriate program. The universal Turing machine also exploits the fact that symbols representing instructions are no different in kind from symbols representing data—the 'stored program' concept of the digital computer. However, no such computer existed in 1936, except in Turing's imagination.

Turing spent two years at Princeton University enrolled as a graduate student. He did not shoot to fame, but worked on showing that his definition of computability coincided with that of Church, and on an extension of these logical ideas for a PhD. This, his deepest and most difficult work, investigated the structure of uncomputable functions, with a suggestion that these were related to human intuition. He also published new theorems in algebra and number theory. Yet he found time to make an electromagnetic cipher machine, a link from 'useless' logic to what Turing saw as the prospect of war with Germany.

Code-breaking, 1938–1945 In 1938 Turing was offered a temporary post at Princeton by von Neumann, who was by then acquainted with his ideas, but he preferred to return to Cambridge, even though without a lectureship. Unusually for a mathematician, he joined in Wittgenstein's classes; unusually again, he engineered a cogwheel machine to calculate the Riemann Zeta-function. Publicly he sponsored the entry of a young German refugee. Secretly, he worked part-time for the government cryptanalytic department. Pre-scientific methods had failed to penetrate the mechanical Enigma cipher used by Germany. No significant progress was made, however, until the gift of information and ideas from Poland, where mathematicians had long been employed on the problem.

When war was declared Turing moved to the Government Code and Cypher School at Bletchley Park. One Polish idea, embodied in a machine called a Bombe, was developed by Turing into a far more powerful device. Another Cambridge mathematician, W. G. Welchman, made an important contribution, but the critical factor was Turing's brilliant mechanization of subtle logical deductions. From late 1940, the Turing–Welchman Bombe

made reading of Luftwaffe signals routine. In contrast, the more complex Enigma methods used in German naval communications were generally regarded as unbreakable. Happy to work alone on a problem that defeated others, Turing cracked the system at the end of 1939, but it required the capture of further material by the navy, and the development of sophisticated statistical processes, before regular decryption could begin in mid-1941. Turing's section, Hut 8, which deciphered naval and in particular U-boat messages, then became a key unit at Bletchley Park. The battle of the Atlantic turned towards allied advantage, but in February 1942 the Atlantic U-boat Enigma was changed and this advantage annihilated.

Electronics then made its first appearance at Bletchley as telephone engineers were pressed into an effort to enable the machines to work at ever higher speeds, and thus Turing was introduced to the potential of this new and untried technology. As it turned out, however, the electronic engineers found themselves called upon to mechanize the breaking of the 'Fish' material: messages enciphered on the quite different system used for Hitler's strategic communications. Here again Turing's statistical ideas underlay the methods employed, though it was M. H. A. Newman who played the organizing role.

By this time Turing was the *genius loci* at Bletchley Park, famous as 'Prof', shabby, nail-bitten, tieless, sometimes halting in speech and awkward of manner, the source of many hilarious anecdotes about bicycles, gas masks, and the Home Guard, the foe of charlatans and status-seekers, relentless in long shift work with his colleagues, mostly of student age. To one of these, Joan Clarke, he proposed marriage and was gladly accepted, but he then retracted, telling her of his homosexuality.

Turing crossed the Atlantic in November 1942, for liaison not only on the U-boat Enigma crisis, but on the electronic encipherment of top-level speech signals. Before his return in March 1943 logical weaknesses in the changed U-boat system had been brilliantly detected, and U-boat Enigma decryption restored. With the battle of the Atlantic regained for the allies, chess champion C. H. O'D. Alexander took charge of Hut 8, and Turing became the chief consultant to the vast cryptanalytic operation. As such he saw the Fish material cracked by the Colossus machines in June 1944, demonstrating the feasibility of large-scale digital electronic technology. He himself devoted much time to learning electronics, ostensibly for his own, elegant, speech secrecy system, effected with one assistant, Donald Bayley, at nearby Hanslope Park. However, he had a more ambitious end in view: in the last stage of the war (for his part in which he was appointed OBE), he planned the embodiment of the universal Turing machine in electronic form, or, in effect, invented the digital computer.

The electronic digital computer In 1944 Turing knew his own concept of the universal machine; the speed and reliability of electronics; and the inefficiency of building new machines for new logical processes. These provided the principle, the means, and the motivation for the modern computer, a single machine capable of any programmed task. He was spurred by a fourth idea that the universal machine should be able to acquire the faculties of the brain. Turing was captivated by the potential of the computer he had conceived. His earlier work had shown the absolute limitations on what any Turing machine could do, but his fascination now lay in seeing how much such machines could do, rather than in what they could not, and in the power of the concept of the universal machine. Indeed from now on he argued that uncomputable functions were irrelevant to the problem of understanding the action of the mind. His thought became strongly determinist and atheistic in character, holding that the computer would offer unlimited scope for practical progress towards embodying intelligence in an artificial form.

For a second time Turing was pre-empted by an American publication, in this case the 1945 EDVAC plan for an electronic computer, written in von Neumann's name, but this competition stimulated the National Physical Laboratory (NPL) to appoint him to plan a rival project. He despised his nominal superior J. Womersley, but this applied mathematician showed an appreciation of Turing's ideas, and steered his completely original design to approval in early 1946 as the Automatic Computing Engine, or ACE. The details of the design were short-term, but Turing's prospectus for the use of the computer was visionary. He projected a computer able to switch at will from numerical work to algebra, code-breaking, file handling, or chess-playing. Methods for handling subroutines included a suggestion that the machine could expand its own programs from an abbreviated form, an idea well ahead of contemporary American plans. He depicted a computer centre with remote terminals, and the prospect of the machine progressively taking over more advanced levels of programming work. However, nothing of the ACE was assembled, and Turing remained without influence in its engineering. The lack of co-operation, so unlike the wartime spirit, he found deeply frustrating.

From October 1947 the NPL allowed, or preferred, that Turing should spend a year at Cambridge. After study in neurology and physiology, he wrote a paper exploring the properties of what would now be called neural nets, amplifying his earlier suggestions that a mechanical system could exhibit learning ability. This was submitted to the NPL but never published in his lifetime. No advance was made with the construction of the ACE, and other computer projects took the lead. Indeed it was Newman, who had been the first reader of 'On computable numbers', and in charge of the electronic breaking of the 'Fish' ciphers, who was partly responsible for this. On his 1945 appointment to the chair of pure mathematics at Manchester University, he had negotiated a large Royal Society grant for the construction of a computer. Newman strongly promoted Turing's principle of the stored-program computer, but unlike Turing, intended no personal involvement with engineering. He conveyed the basic ideas to the leading radar engineer F. C. Williams, who had been attracted to Manchester, and the latter's

brilliant innovation made possible a rapid success: Manchester in June 1948 had the world's first demonstration of Turing's computer principle in working electronics.

Although losing in this race, Turing ran very competitively in a literal sense. He developed his strength with frequent long-distance training, and top-rank competition in amateur athletics. Return to Cambridge gave him a circle of lasting friendships, particularly with Robin Gandy, who later inherited Turing's mantle as a leading mathematical logician. Although never secretive about his sexuality, he now became more outspoken and exuberant, and all conformity was abandoned. A mathematics student at King's College, Neville Johnson, became a lover.

Newman offered Turing the post of deputy director of the Manchester Computing Laboratory. Turing accepted, resigned from the NPL, and moved in October 1948. The meaningless title reflected an uncertain status. He had no control over the project, whose government funding was determined by its sudden necessity for the British atomic bomb, but he had a clear role as the organizer of programming for the engineers' electronics. Having lost the chance to put his name to the first working computer hardware, he now had the opportunity to shape the nascent world of programming, but although exploring advanced ideas, such as the use of mathematical logic for program checking, he largely missed this opportunity. His work on programming at Manchester, produced only as a working manual on machine-code writing, was limited in scope.

Turing hovered in 1949 between many other topics new and old. Out of this confused era arose, however, the most lucid and far-reaching expression of his philosophy in the paper 'Computing machinery and intelligence' (*Mind*, 59, 1950, 433–60). This, besides summarizing his view that the operation of the brain could be captured by a Turing machine and hence by a computer, also absorbed his first-hand experience with machinery. The wit and drama of the 'Turing test' has proved a lasting stimulus to later thinkers, and a classic contribution to the philosophy and practice of artificial intelligence. At the same time, in 1950, there emerged a clear direction for new thought: as Turing settled in Manchester, with a house at outlying Wilmslow, he had a fresh field in view—the mathematical theory of morphogenesis, the theory of growth and form in biology.

Outwardly an extraordinary change of direction, for Turing this was a return to a fundamental problem; even in childhood he had been observed 'watching the daisies grow' (caption, by Turing's mother, to a pencil sketch of him playing hockey, 1923, cited in Hodges, *Enigma*, 28). He fixed on the emergence of asymmetry out of initially symmetric conditions as the first thing requiring explanation, and answered that it could arise from the non-linearity of reaction and diffusion. He modelled hypothetical chemical reactions, and became the pioneer user of a computer in testing them numerically. He was elected to a fellowship of the Royal Society in 1951 for the work done fifteen years before, but equal originality was soon to appear: his paper 'The chemical basis of morphogenesis' (*PTRS*, 237, 1952, 37–72) was submitted that November. Long overlooked, it was a founding paper of modern non-linear dynamical theory.

Trial and death Turing was brought to trial on 31 March 1952 for his sexual relationship with a young Manchester man. He made no serious denial or defence, instead telling everyone that he saw no wrong in his actions. He was concerned to be open about his sexuality even in the hard atmosphere of Manchester engineering. To avoid prison he accepted, for a year, injections of oestrogen. His work on the morphogenetic theory continued. He developed his theory of pattern formation into the realm of spherical micro-organisms and plant stems, setting as a particular goal the explanation for the appearance of the Fibonacci numbers in the leaf patterns of plants. He also refreshed his early interest in quantum physics and relativity, with a hint of considering a non-linear mechanism for wave-function reduction.

Turing had also continued to be consulted by GCHQ, the successor to Bletchley Park, but homosexuals had become ineligible for security clearance, and he was now excluded. His personal life was now subject to intense surveillance by the authorities, who regarded his sexuality as a security risk. State security personnel also seem to have been responsible for what he described as another intense crisis, as police searched for a visiting Norwegian youth, and a holiday in Greece taken by Turing was unlikely to calm the nerves of intelligence officers. Though silent with his friends on questions of official secrecy, in other ways he sought greater intimacy with them and with a Jungian analyst. Eccentric, solitary, gloomy, vivacious, resigned, angry, eager—these were Turing's ever-mercurial characteristics, and despite his strength in defying outrageous fortune, no one could safely have predicted his future course.

Turing was found dead by his cleaner, at his home, Hollymeade, Adlington Road, Wilmslow, on the morning of 8 June 1954. He had died the day before of cyanide poisoning, a half-eaten apple beside his bed. His mother held that he had accidentally ingested cyanide from his fingers after an amateur chemistry experiment, but it is more credible that he had successfully contrived the manner of his death to allow her to believe this. At his inquest the verdict was suicide. His remains were cremated at Woking crematorium on 12 June 1954.   ANDREW HODGES

Sources A. Hodges, *Alan Turing: the enigma* (1983); repr. (1992) · E. S. Turing, *Alan M. Turing* (1959) · R. Herken, ed., *The universal Turing machine* (1988) · *Collected works of A. M. Turing*, ed. J. L. Britton, D. C. Ince, and P. T. Saunders (1992) · M. H. A. Newman, *Memoirs FRS*, 1 (1955), 253–63 · A. Hodges, *Turing: a natural philosopher* (1997) · inquest documents, King's Cam. · records of Woking crematorium
Archives King's AC Cam., corresp. and papers · University of Manchester, National Archive for the History of Computing, working papers | Trinity Cam., corresp. with A. E. Ingham
Likenesses Elliott & Fry, photograph, 1951, NPG [*see illus.*] · Elliott & Fry, photograph, RS; repro. in Newman, *Memoirs FRS* · W. Stoneman, photograph, RS · photographs, King's Cam.
Wealth at death £4603 5s. 4d.: probate, 20 Sept 1954, CGPLA Eng. & Wales

Turle, Henry Frederic (1835–1883), journal editor, the fourth son of James *Turle (1802–1882), organist of Westminster Abbey, and his wife, Mary Honey (d. 1869), was born in York Road, Lambeth, on 23 July 1835. In September 1841 the family went to live in the cloisters of Westminster Abbey; on 31 March 1845 Henry Turle was admitted as a chorister at Westminster School. Here he was educated under Dr Williamson and Dr Lidell. Because of delicate health, he attended the school of George Roberts (d. 1860) at Lyme Regis from 1848 to 1850. He was readmitted at Westminster on 3 October 1850. He remained closely associated with the school for the rest of his life and was an expert on the history of the abbey, which formed a focus for his interests in archaeology and church architecture.

From 1856 to 1863 Turle was a temporary clerk in a branch of the War Office, which was stationed at the Tower of London. Finding the work uncongenial, in 1870 he became assistant to William John Thoms (1803–1885), the founder and editor of *Notes and Queries*. In 1872, when John Doran (1807–1878) succeeded Thoms, Turle was promoted to sub-editor, and on Doran's death in 1878 he became editor. Under his editorship *Notes and Queries* preserved its reputation for accurate information and varied interest. Turle was busy at work when he died suddenly from heart disease on 28 June 1883 in his rooms at Lancaster House, The Savoy, London. After a funeral service at the Chapel Royal, Savoy, he was buried on 3 July in the family grave in Norwood cemetery. He was commemorated on the tablet which was placed to the memory of his parents on the wall of the west cloister of Westminster Abbey.   W. P. COURTNEY, rev. VICTORIA MILLAR

Sources *N&Q*, 6th ser., 8 (1883), 1 · *The Athenaeum* (7 July 1883), 18 · W. P. Courtney, *The Academy* (7 July 1883), 9 · *Men of the time* (1856) · Boase, *Mod. Eng. biog.* · *The Times* (3 July 1883) · G. F. R. Barker and A. H. Stenning, eds., *The Westminster School register from 1764 to 1883* (1892), 232 · private information (1898)
Wealth at death £5202 11s. 6d.: administration, 17 Nov 1883, CGPLA Eng. & Wales

Turle, James (1802–1882), organist, son of James Turle, an amateur cellist, was born at Taunton, Somerset, on 5 March 1802. From July 1810 to December 1813 he was a chorister at Wells Cathedral under Dodd Perkins, the organist. At the age of eleven he went to London, and was articled to John Jeremiah Goss, but in fact he was largely self-taught. He had an excellent voice and frequently sang in public. John Goss, his master's nephew, was his fellow student, and thus the future organists of St Paul's Cathedral and Westminster Abbey were pupils together. Turle was organist of Christ Church, Southwark, from 1819 to 1829, and of St James's, Bermondsey, from 1829 to 1831, and also acted as music master to the School for the Indigent Blind from 1829 to 1856. In 1823 he married Mary Honey, the daughter of Andrew Honey, of the exchequer office. She died in 1869, leaving nine children. Henry Frederic *Turle was their fourth son.

Turle's connection with Westminster Abbey began in 1817, when he was only fifteen. He was at first pupil of and assistant to G. E. Williams, and subsequently deputy to

Thomas Greatorex, Williams's successor as organist of the abbey. On the death of Greatorex on 18 July 1831, Turle was appointed organist and master of the choristers, an office which he held for a period of fifty-one years. He played at several of the great musical festivals, for example Birmingham and Norwich, under Mendelssohn and Spohr, but all his interests were centred on Westminster Abbey. His playing at the Handel festival in 1834 attracted special attention. At his own request the dean and chapter relieved him of the active duties of his post on 26 September 1875, when Sir John Frederick Bridge became permanent deputy organist. Turle continued to hold the titular appointment until his death, which took place at his house in the cloisters at Westminster on 28 June 1882. The dean offered a burial-place within the precincts of the abbey, but Turle was interred at his own express wish beside his wife in Norwood cemetery. A memorial window displaying portraits of Turle and his wife was placed in the north aisle of the abbey by one of his sons, and a memorial tablet was affixed to the wall of the west cloister.

Turle was an able organist of the old school, which treated the organ as essentially a legato instrument. He favoured full 'rolling' chords, which were given a remarkable effect by the vast reverberating space of the abbey. He had a large hand, and his 'peculiar grip' of the instrument was a noticeable feature of his playing. His accompaniments were largely traditional, comprising all that was best in his distinguished predecessors, and he greatly excelled in his extemporaneous introductions to the anthems. Like Goss, he possessed great facility in reading from a figured bass. His compositions included services, anthems, chants, and hymn tunes, and several glees remained in manuscript in the early twentieth century. In conjunction with Edward Taylor he edited *The People's Music Book* (1844), *The Art of Singing at Sight* (1846), and *Psalms and Hymns* (1862). His hymn tunes were collected by his daughter S. A. Turle and published in one volume in 1885.

F. G. EDWARDS, *rev.* NILANJANA BANERJI

Sources *New Grove* · Grove, *Dict. mus.* (1954) · J. E. West, *Cathedral organists past and present* (1899) · Brown & Stratton, *Brit. mus.* · *MT*, 23 (1882), 425–6 · R. Edgcumbe, *Musical reminiscences, containing an account of the Italian opera in England from 1773*, 4th edn (1834) · C. E. Stephens, ed., *Bemrose's choir chant book* (1882)
Wealth at death £24,147 16s. od.: probate, 2 Aug 1882, *CGPLA Eng. & Wales*

Turmeau, John (*bap.* 1756). *See under* Turmeau, John (1776–1846).

Turmeau, John (1776–1846), miniature and portrait painter, was born on 11 November 1776, and baptized on 5 December 1776 at St Anne's, Soho, London, the son of **John Turmeau** (*bap.* 1756), jeweller and painter, of London, and of Elizabeth Sandry of Cornwall. John Turmeau senior was baptized on 25 July 1756 at the French Huguenot church, Glasshouse Street, Leicester Fields, London, the son of Allen Turmeau, an artist of Huguenot descent,

and his wife, Charlotte Buxton. He specialized in the production of pictures created with human hair and exhibited two landscapes made of hair at the Free Society of Artists in 1772, when his address was given as Great Earl Street, Seven Dials, London, and in 1773. About 1775 he married Elizabeth Sandry. John Turmeau junior may have received instruction in painting from his father or grandfather but no record exists of any formal training or apprenticeship after his attendance as a boy at Frampton's School in Putney. He appears to have become established as a painter by the age of seventeen, when he first exhibited two miniatures at the Royal Academy. He exhibited seven miniatures at the academy between 1793 and 1796, practising from an address at 23 Villiers Street, London, from 1793 to 1795 and from 44 Sackville Street, London, from 1796 to 1798. By 1799 he had moved to Liverpool, where he worked as a miniaturist and portrait painter in watercolour and oil as well as running a printseller's shop and dealing in watercolours. He was one of the founder members of the Liverpool Academy in 1810 and was president from 1812 to 1814. No exhibitions were staged by the academy from 1814 to 1822 but when it developed into the Academy of the Royal Institution in 1822 Turmeau was made treasurer. He exhibited there until 1838, and again in 1842, lending in all about 100 miniatures, drawings, and oil paintings. Turmeau and his wife, Sarah Wheeler (*b.* 1780/81), a tobacconist, whom he married in 1807, had eight or nine children. One of his sons, **John Caspar Turmeau** (1809–1834), architect, also became a painter, training under his father and exhibiting at the Liverpool Academy from 1827 to 1832. In 1832 he exhibited eight Italian subjects, which made manifest his intention of becoming a landscape painter. He had visited Rome in the company of the sculptor John Gibson (1790–1866), an acquaintance of his father, perhaps because of his failing health. After his return from Italy J. C. Turmeau practised as an architect in Liverpool, working from his father's house in Castle Street, where he died, unmarried, in 1834. John Turmeau also died there, on 10 September 1846, and was buried in Edge Hill churchyard. His self-portrait miniature, probably the one exhibited at the Liverpool Academy in 1822, is in the Walker Art Gallery, Liverpool; other examples of his work are in the Victoria and Albert Museum, London, and in the Glynn Vivian Art Gallery, Swansea (Gordon Pye collection).   V. REMINGTON

Sources E. R. Dibdin, 'John Turmeau: miniaturist', *The Connoisseur*, 61 (1921), 20–24 · H. C. Marillier, *The Liverpool school of painters: an account of the Liverpool Academy from 1810 to 1867, with memoirs of the principal artists* (1904), 224–5 · D. Foskett, *Miniatures: dictionary and guide* (1987), 274–5, 666 · B. S. Long, *British miniaturists* (1929), 442–3 · L. R. Schidlof, *The miniature in Europe in the 16th, 17th, 18th, and 19th centuries*, 2 (1964), 832 · B. Stewart and M. Cutten, *The dictionary of portrait painters in Britain up to 1920* (1997) · Graves, *RA exhibitors* · *DNB*
Likenesses J. Turmeau, self-portrait, watercolour on ivory, c.1810–1820, Walker Art Gallery, Liverpool; repro. in Dibdin, 'John Turmeau: miniaturist', 20

Turmeau, John Caspar (1809–1834). *See under* Turmeau, John (1776–1846).

Turnbull, Sir **Alexander Cuthbert** (1925–1990), obstetrician and gynaecologist, was born in Aberdeen on 18 January 1925, the elder son (there were no daughters) of George Harley Turnbull, sales manager, and his wife, Anne Whyte Cuthbert. He was educated at Robert Gordon's College in Aberdeen, Merchant Taylors' School in Liverpool, and Aberdeen grammar school, where he was modern dux in 1942. He entered the University of Aberdeen in the same year to read medicine and graduated MB ChB in 1947. He then did his national service in the army, spending part of the time in India. His early general medical and specialist training took place in Aberdeen. He was awarded a Medical Research Council scholarship in 1951.

Turnbull had by then come under the influence of Dugald Baird, who made him his lecturer at Aberdeen in 1955. In 1953 he married Elizabeth Paterson Nicol (Elsie), daughter of Alexander Bell, farmer. Herself a doctor, she collaborated in his early research work. They had one daughter (a doctor) and one son.

In 1957 Turnbull became senior lecturer in the University of Dundee and an honorary consultant obstetrician and gynaecologist to the Dundee teaching hospitals, only to return to a similar position in the University of Aberdeen in 1961. In 1966 he graduated MD with honours from the same university and gained the Thursfield award for the best thesis of the year.

Turnbull was appointed to the chair of obstetrics and gynaecology in the Welsh National School of Medicine in Cardiff in 1966. In 1973 he was invited to become Nuffield professor of obstetrics and gynaecology in the University of Oxford, to work within the new John Radcliffe Maternity Hospital. He was elected a fellow of Oriel College, Oxford, in the same year.

Early in his career Turnbull developed a scientific and clinical interest in the physiology and pathology of labour. During his time as senior lecturer in Aberdeen he formed a highly productive professional association with Anne Anderson, which lasted until her death in 1983. In this synergistic scientific collaboration it was frequently she who translated his exciting and novel ideas into successful projects. Basic observations on the mechanisms of labour were matched by important clinical studies on 'premature' (pre-term) labour, and safer pharmacological interventions to induce and stimulate labour. Turnbull developed an infusion pump designed to give sufficient oxytocin to cause the uterus to contract. The decade of the 1970s had been associated with an increasingly uncritical trend towards induction and acceleration of labour by uterine stimulants, and Turnbull participated in an interview for the BBC television programme *Horizon* on the induction of labour. He was portrayed as an arch-interventionist—a gross misrepresentation of his caring and conservative nature. Deeply hurt by this, and using data collected at his instigation in Cardiff between 1964 and 1973, he undertook a critical review of his research and clinical approach, and decided that the scientific evidence indeed showed no real benefit to women or babies from induction. In the years that followed, an increasing amount of research from his team reinforced this conservative view. From 1973 to 1984 Turnbull played a major role in the influential triennial confidential enquiry into maternal mortality. He was a prolific author of original scientific papers and books.

Turnbull influenced a generation of young doctors and scientists, many of whom later held eminent positions at home and abroad; they felt great esteem and affection for him. He travelled widely and had friends in every part of the world. He became a member of the Royal College of Obstetricians and Gynaecologists in 1954, a fellow in 1966, and was vice-president from 1983 to 1986. In 1981 he was awarded the Semmelweiss medal of the Hungarian Society for Gynaecology. In 1990, not long before his untimely death, he received the Sir Eardley Holland medal of the royal college and the rarely conferred honorary fellowship, in recognition of his outstanding lifelong contribution to obstetrics and gynaecology. Turnbull was appointed CBE in 1982 and knighted in 1988. He was awarded an honorary DSc degree of the University of Leicester in 1989.

Turnbull was strikingly handsome, with his aquiline nose, warm but penetrating blue eyes, and, in his later years, a profusion of white hair. His athletic build was rounded by middle age before being ravaged by his illness. Despite his talents and achievements, he had an underlying feeling of insecurity and always needed to drive himself a bit harder. As a result of not wanting to hurt anybody, he found it difficult to say 'no'. His innate drive helped greatly in his courageous ten-year fight with cancer. Turnbull died on 18 August 1990 in Oxford from the late consequences of oesophageal cancer. His wife survived him.   GORDON STIRRAT, *rev.*

Sources   *The Independent* (25 Aug 1990) · *The Times* (22 Aug 1990) · personal knowledge (1996) · private information (1996) · *CGPLA Eng. & Wales* (1990)
Likenesses   photograph, repro. in *The Independent*
Wealth at death   £3669: probate, 20 Oct 1990, *CGPLA Eng. & Wales*

Turnbull, **Alexander Horsburgh** (1868–1918), book collector, was born on 14 September 1868 at Dixon Street, Wellington, New Zealand, the sixth of seven children of Walter Turnbull, merchant, and his wife, Alexandrina Horsburgh. In 1857 his parents had migrated from Scotland to Wellington, where his father established a successful general merchandising business, W. and G. Turnbull, later expanding into shipping and insurance. Turnbull had two years' schooling in Wellington before the family moved to London in 1875. In 1881 he entered Dulwich College, where his scholastic career was undistinguished. Although he grew up in a bookish household, the origins of his vocation as a collector are rather to be found in his response to the colonial experience.

On leaving school in 1884 Turnbull joined the London office of the family drapery firm, Turnbull, Smith & Co. Over the next few years he returned to his native country twice, the second time for a tour of its exotic sites: on the journey out he read J. H. Kerry-Nicholls's *The King Country, or, Explorations in New Zealand* (1884), on the flyleaf of which he later inscribed, 'This was the first book of my collection'. By the late 1880s he was an ardent acquirer of anything published in or about the colony. He was also buying English literature, especially John Ruskin. Voyage literature, particularly the discovery and exploration of the Pacific, was an early and enduring interest; the life of Napoleon was another youthful enthusiasm. He was indulging in a pursuit common to members of his class, and in his search for New Zealand in literature was entering an expanding market.

The sale of the firm in 1888 left Turnbull with leisure to act the young man about town, and to travel in Europe and Africa. But books were becoming his consuming passion. In 1889 he began compiling a bibliography, and in 1891 commissioned the first of several bookplates. His collection was then valued at £1500. He developed discerning tastes, instructing his agents to seek out first editions and mint specimens, and extended his search beyond the metropolitan booksellers to provincial dealers.

In 1892 Turnbull returned, with some reluctance, to Wellington to assume his responsibility in the family business. Within a year he made two important decisions: to form a Milton collection and to make his New Zealand one comprehensive. Why he chose Milton is unclear. However, for a private collector aspiring to completeness in a literary subject, but with insufficient resources to embark on Shakespeare, this smaller and as yet uncrowded field was a wise choice. By the time of his death he had amassed a Milton collection of world standing, especially strong in seventeenth-century first editions and poetry, and a New Zealand collection without peer. 'Anything whatever relating to this Colony,' he had stated in 1893, 'on its history, flora, fauna, geology & inhabitants, will be fish for my net.'

By the end of the 1890s virtually all the areas of Turnbull's collecting were established: voyages and naval literature, James Cook, New Zealand, Scottish history, English literature, and the art and history of the book. His interest in New Zealand now extended to the Pacific and Australia. In 1893 he had become a member of the newly established Polynesian Society, centre of the colony's developing indigenous intellectual life. Its co-founder S. Percy Smith and others active in the emerging field of Maori ethnology became voluntary agents in his ancillary search for Maori and Pacific artefacts, of which he acquired several hundred.

Turnbull had also become a fellow of the Linnean Society before leaving London. However, he took little part in public life. His greatest enthusiasm after his library was yachting. Increasingly he neglected his business affairs, and he never married. After about 1907 he led a solitary, increasingly reclusive life at Elibank, the family home, devoted to what he described as 'one of the most fa[s]cinating of human follies', bibliomania.

While in one respect Turnbull's life contracted, in another it expanded. His collection became well known to local scholars and collectors, serving as a *de facto* national reference library. He continued to buy extensively in the field of English literature, and to purchase most of his books (along with his suits and cigars) from London, although his international network now extended to Australia, America, and Europe. New Zealand material was procured from an increasing array of local and overseas sources, as he searched out printed matter of all kinds. Turnbull differed from his fellow collectors (such as Dr T. M. Hocken of Dunedin, his only serious rival as New Zealand's pre-eminent collector) in that he was neither a scholar nor a writer. He corresponded and debated keenly about the provenance of his New Zealand material and the history it recorded, but left few explicit statements about why he collected it.

The last two years of his life were devoted wholly to this purpose. Elibank had been sold in 1914 and the business in 1916, and that year Turnbull moved into a new, purpose-built home and library. He began collecting books relating to English theatre. His health, however, was deteriorating. It was widely known to his contemporaries that he had inherited the family weakness for drink. He was also using cocaine, which had probably begun to affect his bibliophilic judgement. He died at Bowen Street Hospital in Wellington on 28 June 1918 after a sinus operation, and was buried two days later at Bolton Street cemetery.

Turnbull had already given his Maori artefacts to the Colonial Museum. In his first will, made in 1907, he left his printed collection to Wellington's Victoria University College, but in a codicil of March 1918 he instead bequeathed his library, now numbering some 55,000 books, along with drawings, prints, paintings, maps, and manuscripts, to the crown, with instructions that it be kept together in Wellington to form 'the nucleus of a New Zealand National Collection'. Housed until 1973 in the home he had built for it, the Alexander Turnbull Library, New Zealand's premier historical research library, continues to serve its founder's vision: that 'My books & MSS. I hope will assist future searchers after the truth'.

RACHEL BARROWMAN

Sources E. H. McCormick, *Alexander Turnbull: his life, his circle, his collections* (Wellington, 1974) · R. E. Barrowman, *The Turnbull: a library and its world* (1995) · E. H. McCormick, *The fascinating folly: Dr Hocken and his fellow collectors* (1961) · K. A. Coleridge, *A descriptive catalogue of the Milton collection in the Alexander Turnbull Library, Wellington, New Zealand* (1980) · J. Rumrich, 'Paradise reinterpreted in the Alexander Turnbull Library', *Turnbull Library Record*, 25/1–2 (1992), 51–7 · d. cert.
Archives NL NZ, Turnbull L.
Likenesses Van der Weyde, photograph, 1891, NL NZ, Turnbull L. · R. S. Clouston, oils, 1909, NL NZ, Turnbull L.
Wealth at death approx. £61,700–£109,700; house, library, and fittings valued at £9700

Turnbull, Colin Macmillan (1924–1994), anthropologist, was born on 23 November 1924 at Highfield, Northwick Avenue, Wembley, Middlesex, one of two sons of John Rutherford Turnbull, chartered accountant, and his wife, Dorothy Helena Wellesley, daughter of the Revd Arthur Wellesley Chapman of Toronto. His father was Scottish, and his mother Irish-Canadian. He was educated at Cumnor House, Purley, and Westminster School, where he became a renowned organist. After two years at Magdalen College, Oxford, he joined the Royal Naval Volunteer Reserve, being commissioned a sub-lieutenant in November 1944, and serving on motor launches searching for torpedos and recovering dog tags from soldiers killed at sea. His only sibling, Ian, an RAF pilot, was killed in action during the war. Following demobilization Turnbull completed a degree under war regulations at Oxford, graduating BA in 1947. In 1948 he obtained a diploma in education from London University. He then enrolled at Banaras Hindu University, Varanasi, India, where he earned a master's degree in Indian religions and philosophy. Between 1949 and 1951 he was one of only a handful of Europeans allowed to reside at the exclusively Brahman ashram of one of the most illustrious female gurus in contemporary Indian history, Sri Anandamayi Ma.

With an American friend, a music teacher from Ohio named Newton Beal, Turnbull then went to Kenya to stay with a wealthy entrepreneur, Sir Charles Markham, who recommended that Turnbull and Beal visit his friend Patrick Putnam, a former PhD candidate in anthropology from Harvard University. Putnam, who was living among the pygmies and managing a small tourist hotel, received Turnbull warmly, but when Turnbull ran out of money Putnam could not honour his request for paid work. He found work instead with the famed Hollywood producer Sam Spiegel, for whom he constructed and transported the boat *The African Queen*, for the film of the same name, starring Humphrey Bogart and Katharine Hepburn. Filthy and unshaven, Turnbull and Beal travelled home overland, but unfortunately carried their things in a trunk Turnbull's father had borrowed from his friend Sir Donald Maclean, whose name was written in large letters on the side. They were immediately arrested by British authorities in Sudan and detained for two weeks, on suspicion of being the famous spies Guy Burgess and Donald Maclean.

After a brief position as secretary of the Racial Unity movement, founded by Mary Attlee (the sister of Clement Attlee), Turnbull returned to central Africa in 1953 and again in 1957, where he gathered enough data to earn a diploma with distinction in social anthropology (in 1956) and to complete a BLitt (in 1957) and a DPhil (in 1964) at Oxford University, where he studied under Edward Evans-Pritchard. In 1959 he was appointed assistant curator (later curator) of African ethnology at the American Museum of Natural History, New York. In 1961 he published his first book, the best-selling *The Forest People*, a study of the Mbuti pygmy hunter–gatherers in the Ituri rain forest. The book idealized the egalitarian pygmies as the exemplars of the best of humanity, and criticized western civilization's emphasis on individualism and social status.

If *The Forest People* made his reputation, Turnbull's next major publication, *The Mountain People* (1973), made him controversial. His story of the starving Ik of Uganda, a people on the brink of extinction whose depravity Turnbull described in stark detail, illustrated the other end of the spectrum. In *The Forest People*, Turnbull had thanked his Indian guru, Sri Anandamayi Ma, for giving him his mantra, 'Satyam, sivam, sundarm' ('truth, goodness, beauty'), and for convincing him that those qualities could be found if he looked hard enough; they were the same qualities he had found among the pygmies and which he believed the Ik had cast aside. The Ik were materially and morally impoverished, having abandoned the values of family, love, and altruism for a cut-throat individualism matched only by western civilization. He watched with horror as Ik men and women attacked each other, even within their own families, to induce vomiting and then eat the vomit; people defecated on each other's doorsteps, expressed joy at the tragedies of others, and, having abandoned any effort to co-operate or share, the stronger left the weaker, usually children and the elderly, to die of starvation. 'That is the point', he wrote in *The Mountain People*, 'at which there is an end to truth, to goodness, and to beauty … The Ik have relinquished all luxury in the name of individual survival, and the result is that they live on as a people without life, without passion, beyond humanity' (C. Turnbull, *The Mountain People*, 1972, 294–5). He proposed to the Ugandan government that the Ik society should be eliminated, that individuals should be rounded up and dispersed over an area wide enough to make sure they never found each other again. The Ugandan government and the anthropological community were outraged. Angered by the proposal, and by what he saw as a complete lack of objectivity, the anthropologist who led the international attack against Turnbull, Fredrik Barth, wrote that *The Mountain People* 'deserves both to be sanctioned and to be held up as a warning to us all', and that the book was 'dishonest', 'grossly irresponsible and harmful', and threatening to the 'hygiene' of the discipline (Barth, 99–102). Turnbull was unmoved by the academic criticisms because he did not want to write for academics. For him, the truth of the central African rain forest or the tragedy of the Ugandan mountains could not be conveyed in an academic publication to be read by a few hundred scholars. It had to reach millions of people and to come from the heart—not through science, but through the emotional and spiritual paths for which his anthropology was a continuing quest.

Turnbull resigned from the American Museum of Natural History in 1969, amid charges that the museum had discriminated against him and his partner, Joseph A. Towles, an African-American anthropologist he had met in 1959. But he left his mark on the museum in the permanent exhibition in the hall of Man in Africa, which he had conceived and executed and which remained on display at the end of the twentieth century. He subsequently taught at Vassar College, Hofstra, Virginia Commonwealth, West Virginia, George Washington, and New York universities. From 1975 to 1977 he devoted most of his energies to producing the play *The Ik*, with Peter Brook, the former director of the Royal Shakespeare Company. In 1983 he published a partly autobiographical comparative study of rites of passage which he entitled *The Human Cycle* after a book of the same title written by one of his Indian heroes, Sri Aurobindo.

Between 1970 and 1988 Turnbull and Towles lived

openly as a gay, interracial couple in Lancaster, one of the smallest and most conservative rural towns in Virginia. In 1983 Turnbull rejected tenure when it was offered to him at George Washington University and devoted himself to the care of Towles, who began to suffer from AIDS. When Towles died in 1988 Turnbull buried two coffins, one for Towles and one for himself, and then virtually disappeared. He severed all family ties and donated his entire savings and real estate (worth about $1 million in 1988) as well as all future royalties, to the United Negro College Fund. His tombstone, soon overgrown with weeds on his former Virginia estate, says that both he and Towles died on 19 December 1988. Turnbull in fact outlived Towles by nearly six years. In 1989 he travelled to American Samoa and India, and then to Bloomington, Indiana. In Bloomington he helped his former museum colleague, Thubten Norbu (the eldest brother of the Dalai Lama), to build the Tibetan Cultural Center, and Norbu arranged for Turnbull to be trained as a Buddhist monk. In 1993, at the Nechung monastery in Dharmsala, India, he was ordained a Gelong monk by the Dalai Lama and given the new name of Lobsong Rigdol. He returned to Kilmarnock, Virginia, shortly before his death there, of AIDS-related pneumonia, on 24 July 1994. He was buried next to Towles on their former Virginia estate. At Turnbull's request there were no formal services. However, on 21 January 1995, in Epulu, Democratic Republic of Central Africa, the Mbuti pygmies performed a funeral ceremony for both Turnbull and Towles.　　　　ROY RICHARD GRINKER

Sources *The Times* (1 Aug 1994) · C. Turnbull, *The human cycle* (1983) · R. Grinker, *In the arms of Africa: the life of Colin M. Turnbull* (2000) · F. Barth, 'On responsibility and humanity: calling a colleague to account', *Current Anthropology*, 15/1 (1974), 99–102 · b. cert. · *Old Westminsters*, vol. 3
Archives SOUND BL NSA, sound recordings (Mbuti pygmies of Ituri rainforest recorded by Colin Turnbull)

Turnbull, Gavin (*b. c.*1765, *d.* in or after **1808**), poet and actor, was born in south-west Scotland, the son of Thomas Turnbull of Hawick and Kilmarnock, a wool dyer. He told an anonymous acquaintance 'that he was born in one of the border counties washed by the Tweed; that in early life he had received the rudiments of a classical education, and that his parents had at one time been in decent circumstances' (*Contemporaries of Burns*, appendix, 23). In the preface to his *Poetical Essays* Turnbull speaks bitterly of being removed from school before he could complete a liberal education. As a young man he encountered vernacular poetry in the ale house where his father, known as 'Tammy Turnbull', had a reputation as a carouser.

After his brief schooling Turnbull was set to weaving carpets for the firm of Gregory and Thomson in Kilmarnock; he slept on straw in an unfurnished garret while composing songs and studying the English poets. David Sillar and Robert Burns were among his early acquaintances. Turnbull afterwards moved with his father's family to Glasgow, where *Poetical Essays* was published in 1788. Burns sold six copies in Kilmarnock; in two surviving letters Burns attempts to locate the author in order to return the small remittance. Turnbull is next heard of in the early 1790s performing as a comedian in Dumfries, where he renewed his acquaintance with Burns and married an actress. During this period he befriended another weaver-poet, Alexander Wilson, later famous as an American ornithologist. In 1793 Burns tried unsuccessfully to assist Turnbull by placing some of his songs with the publisher George Thomson. In the following year *Poems, by Gavin Turnbull, Comedian* was published. Turnbull probably emigrated to America shortly afterwards, certainly before 1798, when he was mentioned in Alexander Campbell's *Introduction to the History of Poetry in Scotland*. Nothing is recorded about his later life, though two poems by Turnbull were published in the *Port Folio*, a Philadelphia literary magazine (3, 11 April 1807, 237–8; 6, 20 August 1808, 127–8). The first, an ode in imitation of William Collins, was reprinted from the *Charleston Courier* in 1807; the second, a comic 'Elegy on my Auld Fiddle', appeared in 1808. Since Alexander Wilson (who had emigrated in 1794) was a leading contributor to the *Port Folio*, it would appear that the two former weavers were still communicating. Turnbull wrote poetry in both Scots and English. In *Poetical Essays* he is at pains to display his grammar-school acquirements in hapless imitations of Pope's pastorals, Shenstone's elegies, and 'Silvanus', a blank-verse fragment after James Beattie's *Minstrel*. In 'The Cottage' and 'The Bard' he attempts to outdo Burns as an imitator of Fergusson and Shenstone. His second volume seems to have sunk without trace, unremarked by his contemporaries and unseen by his few biographers. Turnbull was described as short and dark, a boon companion admired for his love of the muses and refusal to accept the hard lot imposed on him. Offering his songs to Thomson, Burns wrote 'Possibly, as he is an old friend of mine, I may be prejudiced in his favour: but I like some of his pieces very much' (*Letters*, 2.257).　　　　DAVID HILL RADCLIFFE

Sources G. Turnbull, *Poetical essays* (1788) · A. Campbell, *An introduction to the history of poetry in Scotland*, 2 pts in 1 (1798–9) · J. Paterson, *The contemporaries of Burns and the more recent poets of Ayrshire* (1840) · R. Inglis, *The dramatic writers of Scotland* (1868) · G. Eyre-Todd, ed., *Scottish poetry of the eighteenth century*, 2 vols. (1896) · M. Lindsay, *The Burns encyclopedia*, 2nd edn (1970) · *The letters of Robert Burns*, ed. J. de Lancey Ferguson, 2nd edn, ed. G. Ross Roy, 2 vols. (1985)

Turnbull, George (1569–1633), Jesuit and theologian, was born on 13 January 1569 at Tranent, Haddingtonshire, the son of Catholic parents, Thomas Turnbull and his wife, Martha Spreule. He entered the Scots College at Pont-à-Mousson in Lorraine (later at Douai) in 1583. Having graduated in arts and philosophy in 1589 he entered the Jesuit noviciate at Tournai in September 1591 and was ordained priest at Rome in 1596. His theological studies were undertaken at Louvain and Rome and thereafter his career was an academic one. He taught philosophy, and perhaps theology also, at Avignon 1598–1600 and scholastic theology at Pont-à-Mousson 1606–13. In January 1610 he was professed of the four Jesuit vows. He was at Rouen in 1614, where he was in charge of moral theology, then in 1614–17 was at the Scots College, Douai, being superior in 1615. He was again at Pont-à-Mousson 1620–27 and at Rheims 1628–

33, teaching and writing. It can be presumed that, of his unrecorded years, he was at Pont-à-Mousson in 1601–05 and either there or at Douai 1618–19.

In 1627 a minister in Aberdeen, Robert Baron, published a thesis on scripture as the formal object of faith, reportedly saying that no Jesuit could refute it. Turnbull's reply was *Imaginarii circuli quadratura catholica* ('Catholic squaring of an imaginary circle', Rheims, 1628). Baron's rejoinder in 1631 elicited Turnbull's further work, *In sacrae scholae calumniatorem* ('Against the calumniator of a sacred school', Rheims, 1632). Turnbull also left in manuscript two theological treatises. He died at Rheims on 11 May 1633.   T. F. HENDERSON, *rev.* MARK DILWORTH

Sources biographical data, Jesuit Archives, London · H. Foley, ed., *Records of the English province of the Society of Jesus*, 7 (1882–3), 785–6 · J. F. S. Gordon, ed., *The Catholic church in Scotland* (1874), 621 · J. F. Kellas Johnstone and A. W. Robertson, *Bibliographia Aberdonensis*, ed. W. D. Simpson, Third Spalding Club, 1 (1929), 232–58 · P. J. Anderson, ed., *Records of the Scots colleges at Douai, Rome, Madrid, Valladolid and Ratisbon*, New Spalding Club, 30 (1906)
Archives Metz, Catalogue des MSS

Turnbull, George (1698–1748), theologian and teacher, was born on 11 July 1698 in Alloa, Clackmannanshire, the third of nine children of the minister George Turnbull the elder (1657–1744) and his wife, Elizabeth, daughter of Alexander Glass of Sauchie. He entered the University of Edinburgh in the autumn of 1711 and began to study for divinity in 1717, but did not graduate MA until May 1721. While in Edinburgh Turnbull became a member of the Rankenian Club, founded in 1716 or 1717 by a circle of iconoclastic students and their friends, which included two of his closest associates, the preacher William Wishart (*c*.1692–1753) and the surgeon George Young (1692–1757). Turnbull was then apparently preoccupied with fashioning a rational form of Christianity, which prompted him to attempt to initiate a correspondence with John Toland (1670–1722) in November 1718, and to write a passionate defence of religious toleration which he later claimed had remained unpublished because booksellers had baulked at its advocacy of freethinking in religion.

Turnbull was elected a regent at Marischal College, Aberdeen, on 14 April 1721. His two published graduation theses, *De scientiae naturalis cum philosophia morali conjunctione* (1723) and *De pulcherrima mundi cum materialis tum rationalis constitutione* (1726), show that he was the first Scottish academic to advocate in print the use of the Newtonian method in moral philosophy, and that he continued to engage with the ideas of heterodox thinkers like Toland. Along with his colleague David Verner (1688–1752), Turnbull expounded the ideas of Lord Shaftesbury (1671–1713) and promoted instruction in natural jurisprudence and history. Additionally, he seems to have championed the ideology of 'old whigs' such as Lord Molesworth (1656–1725), with whom he corresponded in 1722–3. Yet he also dwelt on the moralists of classical antiquity, whose writings he regarded as an antidote to the pedantry of scholasticism. Through this intellectual diet, Turnbull aspired to produce virtuous citizens and rational Christians who were schooled in polite and useful knowledge.

Despite his success in the classroom and his influence on pupils such as Thomas Reid (1710–1796), Turnbull rapidly became disillusioned with Marischal. As early as May 1723 he was seeking a position elsewhere through the patronage of Molesworth and, in March 1725, Turnbull and his friend, the professor of mathematics Colin Maclaurin (1698–1746), quarrelled with the principal, Thomas Blackwell the elder (1660?–1728). Maclaurin resigned, and Turnbull left without permission to serve as tutor to the Udney family. He was summoned back from the continent, and resumed teaching in January 1726. In the spring of 1727 he finally resigned, and was awarded an honorary degree of LLD from the college.

Turnbull now became tutor to Andrew Wauchope of Niddry, and during the next five years travelled to Edinburgh, Groningen, Utrecht, and various stops in the Low Countries, Germany, and France. He was back in London by May 1732 looking for further employment, and received a second LLD degree, from the University of Edinburgh, on 13 June. Letters to a friend, the Edinburgh professor of universal history Charles Mackie (1688–1767?), show that Turnbull was cultivating the patronage of the Jacobite Lord Cornbury (1710–1753), among others, but he temporarily failed to secure another suitable position. Turnbull evidently decided at this juncture that he might seek preferment in the Anglican church, for he matriculated at Exeter College, Oxford, in the Michaelmas term of 1733 and was granted a BCL degree.

Despite serious misgivings about leaving England to act as a tutor, Turnbull's precarious finances forced him to travel to Italy in 1735 with the son of Lord Rockingham, Thomas Watson (1715–1746), where they remained until 1737. On his return Turnbull again sought gainful employment in London and, after an unsuccessful bid in early 1739 to become the secretary of the Society for the Encouragement of Learning (to which he had belonged since its foundation in 1735), he used his connections with Thomas Birch (1705–1766) and the latitudinarian divine Arthur Ashley Sykes (1684?–1756) to secure ordination by the bishop of Winchester, Benjamin Hoadly (1676–1761). He also began to move in court circles, and in 1741 was appointed as a chaplain to the prince of Wales, while continuing to ply his trade as a tutor at Kew. The following year Turnbull was made rector of Drumachose, co. Derry, by the bishop of Derry, Thomas Rundle (1688?–1743). Presumably through connections at court, Turnbull became tutor to Horace Walpole, and embarked on another tour of Italy in 1744. After stops in Milan and Turin, Turnbull and his pupil resided in Florence in 1745–6 and then left for Rome, partly because the duke of Newcastle wanted Turnbull to obtain intelligence about the Jacobites.

During the 1730s and early 1740s Turnbull issued a series of pamphlets and books which owed much to his Marischal College lectures and to his earlier theological concerns. In 1731 he published a small tract written in 1726 and inspired by a passage in Shaftesbury, *A philosophical enquiry concerning the connexion betwixt the doctrines and miracles of Jesus Christ*, in which he argued that just as experiments prove the validity of scientific propositions,

Christ's miracles prove the truth of the Christian doctrine of the afterlife. This tract was intended to counteract the views of Anthony Collins (1676–1729) and Matthew Tindal (1657–1733), and Turnbull again attacked Tindal in *Christianity neither False nor Useless, Tho' not as Old as the Creation* (1732), which took up the question of miracles as part of a defence of Samuel Clarke's account of the relation between natural and revealed religion.

While he was in Italy in the mid-1730s Turnbull seems to have conceived the idea for a work on the art of classical antiquity, and back in London he was able to secure a fine set of illustrations by Camillo Paderni through his fellow Scot, the painter Allan Ramsay the younger (1713–1784), who was then in Rome. After delays caused by money problems, which were exacerbated by his failure to secure the sponsorship of the Society for the Encouragement of Learning, Turnbull's *A Treatise on Ancient Painting* finally appeared in 1740. Although the book was satirized a decade later in William Hogarth's print *Beer Street*, Turnbull developed an innovative case for the educational purposes of the fine arts based on his theory that painting is a language which conveys truths about nature or morality, and in so doing challenged the common assumption that history painting was superior to other genres such as portraiture and landscapes.

The year 1740 also saw the publication of another brief religious work, *An Impartial Enquiry into the Moral Character of Jesus Christ*, wherein Turnbull claimed that Christ was the greatest of all moral philosophers and that the purity of his morals demonstrated the truth of his teachings, along with the most comprehensive statement of his philosophical ideas, *The Principles of Moral and Christian Philosophy*. Drawing on his Aberdeen lectures as well as his contacts with professors of natural jurisprudence in the Netherlands, Turnbull produced in 1741 an annotated translation of a Latin text by J. G. Heineccius, *A Methodical System of Universal Law*, which contains an important appendix in which he affirms that the study of natural law is an empirical science grounded on the anatomy of human nature. His last major work, *Observations upon Liberal Education*, appeared in 1742 and advanced a novel view of the interconnections between the various branches of human knowledge; it had a profound impact on curriculum reforms undertaken at Marischal and King's College in Aberdeen in 1753. In addition, Turnbull issued three minor translations, of which *Justin's 'History of the World'* (1742) is the most noteworthy for its lengthy preface, which amplifies his remarks in the *Observations* regarding the value of historical knowledge. Following his appointment as rector at Drumachose in 1742 Turnbull lived in obscurity. He died from unknown causes in The Hague on 31 January 1748 while gathering information on the Jacobites for Lord Newcastle.   PAUL WOOD

Sources M. A. Stewart, 'George Turnbull and educational reform', *Aberdeen and the Enlightenment*, ed. J. J. Carter and J. H. Pittock (1987), 95–103 · P. B. Wood, *The Aberdeen Enlightenment: the arts curriculum in the eighteenth century* (1993) · J. McCosh, *The Scottish philosophy: biographical, expository, critical, from Hutcheson to Hamilton* (1875) · C. Gibson-Wood, 'Painting as philosophy: George Turnbull's "Treatise on ancient painting"', *Aberdeen and the Enlightenment*, ed. J. J. Carter and J. H. Pittock (1987), 189–98 · *The diary of the Rev. George Turnbull*, ed. R. Paul (1893) · P. J. Anderson and J. F. K. Johnstone, eds., *Fasti academiae Mariscallanae Aberdonensis: selections from the records of the Marischal College and University, MDXCIII–MDCCCLX*, 3 vols., New Spalding Club, 4, 18–19 (1889–98) · A. Smart, *Allan Ramsay: painter, essayist, and man of the Enlightenment* (1992) · Walpole, *Corr.* · J. Ingamells, ed., *A dictionary of British and Irish travellers in Italy, 1701–1800* (1997)

Archives BL, letters to Thomas Birch, Add. MS 4319, fols. 279–89, 293–5 · NL Ire., corresp. with Robert Molesworth [microfilm] · U. Edin. L., corresp. with Charles Mackie, MS La.II.91

Turnbull, Sir George Henry (1926–1992), car manufacturer, was born on 17 October 1926 at 25 Prince George's Avenue, Merton, London, the younger son and second child in the family of two sons and one daughter of Bartholomew Turnbull (1892–1962), an employee of the Standard Motor Company in Coventry, and his wife, Pauline Anne (d. 1964), *née* Konrath. He was educated at the King Henry VIII School, Coventry, and with the help of his father, who was apprentice supervisor at the time, became the first apprentice engineer at Standard in 1941. His father also persuaded the managing director of Standard to found a scholarship, and Turnbull was the first holder of the Sir John Black scholarship, at Birmingham University, from where he graduated with a degree in mechanical engineering in 1950. On 21 March 1950, at St Peter's Catholic Church, Leamington Spa, he married Marion (b. 1924/5), daughter of Henry George Wing of Leamington Spa, a Standard Motor Company executive. They had one son and two daughters.

Turnbull returned to Standard-Triumph (Standard had bought Triumph in 1944) in 1950, when he was appointed personal assistant to the technical director, Edward Grinham. In 1951 he became liaison officer between Standard-Triumph and Rolls-Royce, with whom Standard-Triumph were developing a gas turbine engine. He was in charge of the experimental department from 1954 to 1955, but in the latter years he felt he needed experience in production, and went to Petters Ltd, the diesel engine manufacturer, as works manager. In 1956 he was enticed back to Standard-Triumph to be manager of the car section, and in 1959 he became general manager, a position he retained after the merger of Standard-Triumph and Leyland Motors in 1961.

When the government persuaded the two large conglomerates, Leyland Motors and British Motor Holdings (the former BMC, which had taken over Jaguar in 1966), to merge in 1968 to form British Leyland Motor Corporation (BLMC), under the chairmanship of Sir Donald Stokes, Turnbull became managing director of the Austin-Morris division, at Longbridge, Coventry, the largest division within BLMC. Although Turnbull inherited the Austin 1100/1300 series, Britain's best-selling car throughout the 1960s, it was decided that a replacement was needed, and work began in 1968 on what was to become the Austin Allegro. Turnbull approved the design, and was himself responsible for the eccentric 'quartic' steering-wheel, shaped like a television screen, but when it was launched in 1973 it had a lukewarm reception, and sales were poor. After Stokes appointed John Barber, the former finance director, as deputy chairman, with Turnbull as managing director but responsible to Barber, Turnbull realized that he would never succeed Stokes as chairman of BLMC, and he resigned in September 1973. He was unhappy with the direction in which BLMC was going. Lord Stokes wanted all major decisions to be taken centrally, whereas Turnbull believed the divisions should remain autonomous. Moreover, Turnbull felt that the future of British Leyland lay as a mass producer of popular cars, whereas Barber wanted to concentrate on up-market specialist cars, and at the time of the latter's appointment a major shift of investment from Austin-Morris into the Jaguar and Rover-Triumph divisions was announced. While running Longbridge Turnbull had had to contend with almost continuous industrial unrest, and he later described his time there as 'five years of extremely hard work … I will never work so hard again, nor wish to' (Taylor, 70).

Turnbull was asked to go to South Korea in 1974 as vice-president and director of Hyundai Motors. Hyundai had been assembling Ford Cortinas from British-made components since 1967, but in 1973 the Korean government announced plans to set up a car manufacturing industry. With the help of a team of British engineers Turnbull built a large car plant, and began production of the 'Pony', the first Korean car, based on the old Austin-Morris cars. In 1977 he went on to spend two years in Iran, as adviser and later as deputy managing director of the Iran National Motor Company.

At the end of 1978 Turnbull returned to England, and in January 1979 was appointed chairman and managing director of Chrysler UK, recently acquired by Peugeot, and renamed Talbot UK later that year. He was given the task of returning the company to profitability within five years. With the rise in oil prices biting, it was a difficult time in the motor industry, and between 1978 and 1982 Talbot's share of the British market fell from 8 to 4 per cent. After Talbot lost £61.9 million in 1981, Turnbull had to close the Linwood factory in Scotland, but in 1983 Talbot made a net profit of £3.1 million, largely because of a contract to supply the Iran National Motor Company with components for the Paykan car. Before he left, Turnbull was able to announce that Peugeot was to invest £20 million in building a new range of cars at the Ryton assembly plant in Coventry.

The final chapter in Turnbull's career was with the Inchcape Group, which had extensive interests in car distribution in Britain and overseas. He was managing director from 1984 to 1986, and chairman and chief executive from 1986 until his resignation because of ill health in 1991. Turnbull was responsible for Inchcape becoming the sole distributor for Toyota cars in ten countries, including Britain, and he also played a key role in persuading Toyota to establish a factory at Burnaston, Derbyshire.

Turnbull was knighted in 1990 for his services to the motor industry. He was president of the Society of Motor Manufacturers and Traders from 1982 to 1984, and chairman of the Industrial Society from 1987 to 1990. He died on 22 December 1992 at his home, Morrell House, Moreton Morrell, Warwickshire, and was buried in the village at Holy Cross Church. ANNE PIMLOTT BAKER

Sources N. Georgano, ed., *Britain's motor industry: the first hundred years* (1995) · M. Taylor, 'Troubled times', *Classic Car* (May 1987), 67–70 · D. Thoms and T. Donnelly, *The motor car industry in Coventry since the 1890s* (1985) · J. Daniels, *British Leyland: the truth about the cars* (1980), 118–27 · *WW* · *The Times* (24 Dec 1992) · *The Independent* (24 Dec 1992) · *The Times* (7 Sept 1954) · *The Times* (15 May 1973) · *The Times* (17 May 1973) · *The Times* (28 Feb 1974) · *The Times* (7 Jan 1984) · *The Times* (7 March 1984) · *The Times* (21 March 1984) · private information (2004)
Likenesses photograph, repro. in *The Times* (24 Dec 1992) · photograph, repro. in *The Independent* · photograph, repro. in Taylor, 'Troubled times', 66
Wealth at death £1,021,512: probate, 9 March 1993, *CGPLA Eng. & Wales*

Turnbull, Hubert Maitland (1875–1955), pathologist, was born in Glasgow on 3 March 1875, the fifth of the six children of Andrew Hugh Turnbull, actuary, and his wife, Margaret Lothian, daughter of Adam *Black, the publisher and Liberal politician. He was educated at St Ninian's, Moffat, Charterhouse School, and at Magdalen College, Oxford, where he played association football for the university (1897), obtained a second-class degree in physiology (1898), and was awarded the Welsh memorial prize in anatomy (1899). In 1900, with the Price university entrance scholarship, he began his clinical studies at the London Hospital; he became MRCS, LRCP, and qualified BM, BCh, and MA (Oxon.) in 1902. His long career, until his retirement in 1946, was spent at the London Hospital, with a brief interlude of study at Copenhagen and Dresden as Radcliffe travelling fellow from 1904 to 1906. His experiences as voluntary assistant to Professor Georg Schmorl at Dresden determined his choice of pathology as his career. Schmorl was an inspiring teacher and a leading exponent of bone pathology. His pupil carried his methods back to London where he developed that as a specialism.

In 1906 Turnbull accepted the appointment of director of the Bernhard Baron Institute of Pathology at the London Hospital; he held this position until 1946, receiving the title of reader in morbid anatomy in London University in 1915 and professor in 1919. He became professor emeritus in 1947. In 1906 he proceeded to the degree of DM (Oxon.), and in 1945 he was created an honorary DSc. He was elected a fellow of the Royal College of Physicians in 1929 and of the Royal Society in 1939. He was a founder member of the Pathological Society of Great Britain and Ireland and was elected an honorary member in 1948. In 1916 Turnbull married Catherine Nairne Arnold (d. 1933), daughter of Frederick Arnold Baker, solicitor; they had one daughter and three sons.

Turnbull's principal aim in pathology was to raise the study of morbid anatomy to a more scientific level. To this end he introduced meticulous methods of observation and recording of biopsies and necropsies, building up a body of data unrivalled in this country as a source for research. His teaching was based mainly upon his own experience and dictated by a passion for truth; it was often in advance of the current textbooks. Thus his reputation grew, and a steady stream of postgraduates, from home and abroad, came to study in the institute. Inspired by their experience, they implanted Turnbull's methods widely in other centres.

Long hours spent in supervising his pupils meant that many of Turnbull's original observations were published under the names of others. His own reluctance to publish was attributable to his extreme caution over controlled observation and to the level of his self-criticism. But he could speak and write with authority upon any tissue of the body and, especially, on the skeleton. He is perhaps best known as the first to identify post-vaccinal encephalomyelitis in 1922–3.

In person Turnbull was tall and thin, with scholarly ascetic features. Lifelong suffering from migraine made him somewhat of a recluse. Within his department he was an exacting master, but his severity masked great depths of altruism and understanding. His hobbies included bird-watching, the cultivation of rhododendrons, and golf. Turnbull died in the London Hospital on 29 September 1955.   D. S. RUSSELL, *rev.*

Sources election certificate, RS · autobiographical notes, RS · personal knowledge (1971) · *WWW*
Archives Royal College of Pathologists, London, papers · U. Oxf., Edward Grey Institute of Field Ornithology, ornithological notes
Likenesses W. Kaufmann, oils, Middlesex Hospital, London, Bernard Baron Institute of Pathology · E. Nelson, oils, London Hospital · W. Stoneman, photograph, RS
Wealth at death £68,727 6s. 6d.: probate, 23 Jan 1956, *CGPLA Eng. & Wales*

Turnbull, Hugh (*b.* **1517**, *d.* in or before **1566**), dean of Chichester and administrator, was from Lincolnshire, born to an unknown family. He was admitted *discipulus* of Corpus Christi College, Oxford, on 27 April 1532, probationary fellow on 10 January 1536, and fellow in 1538; he remained a fellow until 1543. His logic lectures, begun in 1535, attracted complaints to Archbishop Cranmer. Turnbull took the degrees of BA in 1536 and MA on 31 March 1539. Ordained subdeacon on 18 December 1540 and deacon on 12 March 1541, he took priest's orders on 2 April 1541 to the title of his fellowship. He was admitted BTh in 1545 and matriculated at Louvain on 12 July 1547. In 1551 he received his DTh degree from the University of Padua by grant from the count palatine Transalgardo Capoditista, using an imperial privilege; this allowed him to avoid swearing an oath to the pope.

Turnbull tutored at Padua in both humanities and civil law, although he never took a degree in law. The civilians John Tregonwell and Anthony Hussey were his patrons, and he may have studied under or at least known the eminent legist Marco Mantova Benavides, since he wrote to Cardinal Pole the day after Mantova did in March 1555 congratulating him on the reconciliation of England and sending some lost questions on scripture, judged 'papistical' by the Stuart antiquary Brian Twyne. Turnbull had long been a successful pluralist by this time. He was rector of Acton, Middlesex, from 7 May 1542 (vacated by 1563) and of Batcombe, Somerset, from 6 April 1547 (vacated by

December 1564); canon of Canterbury and ninth prebendary by royal nomination (30 March 1554; admitted 6 April until death); dean of Chichester from 27 April 1558 (until death); and canon of Salisbury and prebendary of South Grantham from 14 July 1562 (until death) by the patronage of Thomas Lodge and Benjamin Jonson, executors of Hussey's will.

Turnbull's appointment to Chichester may well have been an effort to resolve persistent difficulties in the finances of the see, drawing on experience gained as treasurer and prebendary of Christ Church Cathedral (by 1557). He was first dispensed to hold an additional benefice on 25 February 1547, and by the pope for non-residence at an unknown date and on 5 July 1555 to hold incompatible benefices. Cardinal Pole named him a commissioner against heresy in the diocese of Canterbury on 28 March 1558 and occasionally used him as his proctor at Canterbury. Archbishop Parker had him excommunicated for contumacy at his visitation on 17 September 1560, but he was absolved on 9 October.

Turnbull was dead by 21 November 1566, when his will was proved, although records at Chichester give the date of his death as 23 November. By it he left bedding to a large number of servants: William Fells, Richard Lane, John Brewer, Thomas Bowser, John Milles (perhaps a relative of Turnbull's fellow canon of Canterbury of the same name), and Thomas Raddish. 40 marks went to his nephew George Turnbull, and the residue of his estate to other nephews at Canterbury and Oxford; his sister was to have a similar portion. Lawrence Hussey (probably the son of Anthony Hussey the civilian), Turnbull's brother William, and William Cauthant, the husband of his sister's daughter, were named executors. He also gave a copy of Basil's *Opera* (Venice, 1535) to Corpus Christi College, the edition in which Pole's household had been involved.

T. F. MAYER

Sources Emden, *Oxf.* · Bodl. Oxf., MS Rawl. D. 400, fols. 171v–172r · Bodl. Oxf., Bodl. Rolls 13 · Bodl. Oxf., MS Tanner 106, fol. 42 · dean and chapter, register VI, Canterbury Cathedral archives, fols. 30v, 32r, 33r · Pole's register, LPL, fols. 29v–30r · PRO, PROB 11/48/31, fol. 473 · *Fasti Angl., 1541–1857,* [Salisbury], 45 · *CSP for., 1547–53,* 148 · Biblioteca Nazionale Marciana, Venice MS Ital. 6606, fol. 34 · J. Woolfson, *Padua and the Tudors: English students in Italy, 1485–1603* (1998) · W. D. Peckham, ed., *The acts of the dean and chapter of the cathedral church of Chichester, 1545–1642,* Sussex RS, 58 (1959), no. 694
Archives Bodl. Oxf., MS Rawl. D. 400, fols. 171v–172r
Wealth at death over 40 marks: PRO, PROB 11/48, fol. 473

Turnbull, John (*fl.* **1799–1813**), traveller, was a sailor in the merchant service. While second mate of the *Barwell* in 1799 he visited China, and came to the conclusion that the Americans were carrying on a lucrative trade in northwest Asia. On his return home he induced an enterprising merchant to fit out a vessel to visit those parts. Sailing from Portsmouth in May 1800 in the *Margaret*, a ship of ten guns, he touched at Madeira and at Cape Colony, which had recently passed into British hands. On 5 January 1801 he arrived at Botany Bay. The north-west speculation turned out to be a failure and Turnbull resolved to visit the islands of the Pacific. He devoted the next three years to exploring New Zealand, the Society Islands, the Sandwich Islands, and many parts of the south seas. At Tahiti he encountered the agents of the London Missionary Society, to whose zeal he bore testimony while suggesting they change their methods. After visiting the Friendly Islands he returned home by Cape Horn in the *Calcutta*, arriving in England in June 1804. In the following year he published the notes of his travels, under the title *A Voyage Round the World*. An abridged version of the work appeared in 1806, and a second, enlarged, edition in 1813. Although of interest at the time of their publication, when little was known of Australia and the south seas, his books have no lasting merit. Punctuated by such sentences as 'the sloth is an animal more disgusting than mischievous' (Turnbull, 47–8), they serve mainly to reveal Turnbull's disdain for cultures and landscapes other than his own.

E. I. CARLYLE, *rev.* ELIZABETH BAIGENT

Sources *GM*, 1st ser., 83/1 (1813), 547–9 • J. Turnbull, *A voyage round the world*, 2nd edn (1813) • *EdinR*, 9 (1806–7), 332–47

Turnbull, John Arthur (1851/2–1895). *See under* Asser, Ernest (1863–1931).

Turnbull, Percy Purvis (1902–1976), composer and pianist, was born on 14 July 1902 at 51 Denton Gardens, Old Benwell, Newcastle upon Tyne, the younger of the two sons of James Barton Turnbull (d. 1935), joiner and later master builder, and his Scottish wife, Elizabeth Ann Purvis (d. 1951). He was educated locally, learning the piano with Sigmund Oppenheimer and singing in the choir of the cathedral church of St Nicholas in Newcastle. Both his parents were musical. His father played the organ in the local parish church, and with his sons played symphonies and chamber works by classical composers including Haydn, Mozart, and Beethoven, arranged for two pianos. Percy Turnbull spent much of his childhood reading in the library of the Newcastle Literary and Philosophical Society, where his father was a member. He left school in 1916, but when his father was conscripted into the army Turnbull was unable to take up a scholarship to study jewellery design at Armstrong College of Art, and went to work in the office of the Tyne Improvement Commission.

In his spare time, Turnbull began to write music, and formed a friendship with William Gillies Whittaker, founder and conductor of the Newcastle upon Tyne Bach Choir Society, which performed the works of Bach as well as contemporary music by British and French composers. In 1923 Turnbull won a foundation scholarship to the Royal College of Music (RCM), where he studied composition with Gustav Holst, Ralph Vaughan Williams, and John Ireland, who became a lifelong friend. At the RCM his contemporaries included the composers Michael Tippett, Edmund Rubbra, and Elizabeth Maconchy and the pianist Kendall Taylor. As well as winning the Mendelssohn scholarship and the Arthur Sullivan prize for his compositions, he became known as a pianist, and picked up work with 2LO, the first broadcasting company, accompanying singers and violinists.

Turnbull left the RCM in 1927, and took a job under Percy Scholes with the Aeolian Piano Player Company, editing piano rolls. On 16 December 1930 Turnbull married Ivy Ramsay Hobday Griffiths (b. 1906/7); the couple moved to Swansea, where he played the piano at the Empire Theatre in the evenings and taught piano pupils during the day. At the same time he did some accompanying for the BBC, and copied parts and scores for Hubert Foss, head of the music department of Oxford University Press: it was Turnbull who made the first copies of Vaughan Williams's fourth symphony and *Job*, and William Walton's viola concerto. In the mid-1930s he moved to Chalfont St Giles in Buckinghamshire, where his friend John Longmire lived; after Longmire moved to Guernsey with John Ireland, Turnbull visited them in May 1940, shortly before the German invasion of the Channel Islands, from which they managed to escape only days before the occupation. Turnbull was conscripted into the army in 1941, and spent the war in the Royal Artillery as a member of an anti-aircraft battery on the north-east coast. After demobilization in 1946 he moved to Ewell, Surrey, and was principal piano teacher at the Surrey College of Music at Fitznells until it closed in 1956; he also did some extramural lecturing for the University of London. His first marriage had ended in divorce, and on 20 July 1956 he remarried; his second wife was Mary Elizabeth Parnell (b. 1918/19), daughter of John Brooke Molesworth Parnell, the sixth Baron Congleton. In the same year he moved to Pulborough in Sussex.

Turnbull began composing as a very young man, before he entered the RCM, but much of his work remained unpublished in his lifetime. He wrote a number of songs, mainly in the 1920s, beginning with 'Chloris in the snow', a setting of a poem by William Strode composed about 1920 but not published until 1950, and his partsongs include a setting of Shakespeare's 'You spotted snakes with double tongue' (1928). While still at the RCM he wrote some orchestral and chamber music, including *Variations on an Original Theme* (1923) for string quartet, a violin sonata (1925), regarded by many as the most outstanding of his compositions, and *Northumbrian Rhapsody* (c.1927), for orchestra. But most of his output was for the piano, consisting mainly of short pieces, such as *Seven Character Sketches* (1923–7), *Eight Short Piano Pieces* (published under the pseudonym Peter Thrale) (1931), *Six Pastoral Miniatures* (1938), and *Three Winter Pieces* (1956–7). His longer piano works include a sonatina (1948) and *Pasticcio on a Theme of Mozart* (1957). John Ireland was an important influence on his style, which also owed a lot to other early twentieth-century British and French composers, including Frederick Delius, Gabriel Fauré, and Maurice Ravel. After he left the RCM, Turnbull wrote almost exclusively for the piano; he stopped composing in 1960.

By then Turnbull was spending most of his time drawing and painting in watercolour. His love of John Constable and the Norwich school of landscape painters influenced his choice of subjects, which tended to be old farm buildings, scenes on river banks, and cloud-filled skies. He also taught himself to play the violin. A good conversationalist, with a great sense of humour and a gift for mimicry, Turnbull continued to read English and French literature (in translation); in the 1930s he learned the craft of bookbinding and began to bind his collection of books and sheet music in ornate leather covers.

Percy Turnbull died on 9 December 1976 at his home, West Broomers, Broomers Hill, Pulborough, Sussex. He had no children. In 1979 his widow helped to set up the Turnbull Memorial Trust with the aim of publishing and broadcasting his work. A collected edition of his songs appeared in 1988, and selections from his piano music were edited by Jeremy Dibble and published in eleven volumes between 1992 and 1997. Two recordings were issued: *The Piano Music of Percy Turnbull* (2000) and *Percy Turnbull: the Songs and Part-Songs* (2001).   ANNE PIMLOTT BAKER

Sources M. Turnbull, 'A profile of Percy Turnbull', *British Music Society Journal*, 1 (1980), 47–52 • J. Dibble, disc notes, *The piano music of Percy Turnbull* (2000) [CD] • R. Bowman, disc notes, *Percy Turnbull: the songs and part-songs* (2001) [CD] • *New Grove*, 2nd edn • private information (2004) [Mary Turnbull, widow] • b. cert. • m. certs. • d. cert.
Archives Turnbull Memorial Trust, MSS
Likenesses photograph, 1969, repro. in Turnbull, 'A profile of Percy Turnbull'
Wealth at death £51,682: probate, 16 June 1977, *CGPLA Eng. & Wales*

Turnbull, **Sir Richard Gordon** (1909–1998), colonial governor, was born on 7 July 1909, at 18 Blandford Road, St Albans, the son of Richard Francis Turnbull (1878–1963), chartered accountant, and his wife, Harriet Livia, *née* Causley (1877–1949). His father was originally from the Scottish borders, but had moved south to Laleham in the Thames valley. Turnbull was educated at University College School, London, and then University College, London, where he took a degree in physical chemistry (a rare discipline among his future colonial service colleagues) and rowed in the university eight. Abandoning the idea of a career in industry, he applied for the colonial administrative service in 1930 and was sent to Magdalene College, Cambridge, to attend the probationers' course.

In 1931 Turnbull was posted to Kenya, where he quickly made his mark in the provincial administration. On 25 March 1939 he married Beatrice Gunn Wilson (1908–1986), daughter of John Wilson, of Doonfoot, Ayr. She was an Edinburgh graduate who had been Lord Reith's secretary at the BBC, and was to be a sheet anchor in Turnbull's career. They had a twin son and daughter and a second son. In 1948 Turnbull became one of the youngest provincial commissioners. It was during his time as a district and then provincial commissioner in the exhilarating and often turbulent northern frontier district (later province) that he found his soul and was able to give full rein to his reputation as a memorable character. By the time he left the northern frontier district, he had earned a place in the pantheon of his legendary predecessors. The Turnbull legend, in the words of one of his devoted juniors, 'developed spontaneously, requiring neither attention nor nourishment' (Chenevix Trench, *The Desert's Dusty Face*, 2).

An awesome walker, he was reputed to have once undertaken a 300 mile safari on foot just to take breakfast with his neighbours at Wajir. Witty and widely read, he had an impish sense of fun (reflected in what he taught his parrot to recite) and was a sparkling raconteur; in the Kenyan service his *bons mots* were enthusiastically collected as 'Turnbulliana'.

Turnbull's adventurous years among the individualistic and independent-minded peoples in the harsh scrubland of the northern frontier district came to a close in 1953, the year in which he was appointed CMG, when he was transferred to cosmopolitan Nairobi and given the political task, as minister for internal security and defence, of suppressing the Mau Mau uprising which had brought Kenya to a state of emergency. So successful was he in the planning of operation Anvil, the dawn sweep of Nairobi which rounded up 30,000 Mau Mau suspects, that a year later he was promoted chief secretary.

By 1958 the Colonial Office felt that in neighbouring Tanganyika the paternalistic governorship of Sir Edward Twining had alienated the nationalists, and Turnbull was offered the post. This decision was unexpected at two levels: uncertainty about how the man who had defeated Mau Mau might be received in the constitutionally advancing United Nations trust territory of Tanganyika, and surprise that one whose career had pointed ineluctably to the next governorship of British Somaliland should now be diverted. Indeed, Ronald Hyam has implied that Turnbull (the most junior on the shortlist) was Alan Lennox-Boyd's personal nomination in his capacity as secretary of state for the colonies rather than being the first choice of the Colonial Office, anxious about some of Turnbull's skills. In the event lesser Somaliland's loss was Tanganyika's gain. It instantly became clear that Turnbull (who was advanced to KCMG on his appointment) intended to co-operate with the Tanganyikan African national union, and his reputed initial greeting of its leader, 'You and I have important work to do together, Mr Nyerere', became an instant part of the continuing Turnbull legend (*Daily Telegraph*). So, too, did his habit of cycling round Dar es Salaam at dawn, along with Government House's new reputation for Scottish dancing parties into the wee hours. Turnbull was committed to ensuring a smooth and swift transfer of power, a process which in retrospect has been hailed as exemplary in the history of decolonization. His warm personal relations with Julius Nyerere continued long after he left Tanganyika, where he stayed on at Nyerere's request for a year beyond independence as governor-general.

Turnbull left the colonial service in 1962, and was promoted GCMG. Too restless for retirement, within a year he was back in Kenya, responsible for the central land board in its delicate procedures for buying land from European settlers for African resettlement. Another year on and he was back in government service, this time to succeed Sir Kennedy Trevaskis as high commissioner for Aden. British policy was that, following a merger of the colony of Aden with the feudal sheikhdoms of the protectorate, the new federation should become independent in 1968. But the political parties, buoyed by militant anti-British sentiment in the Arab world, set about disrupting the constitution through a campaign of violence and intimidation. Turnbull, himself a target for assassination, concluded that the only way to halt the crisis was to suspend the constitution. Subsequently he was to feel let down by the Foreign Office, who appeared to him more concerned with how the UN might react to the imposition of direct rule. The visiting UN mission in April 1967 did indeed accuse Turnbull of being consistently unco-operative, and after several rows in Aden they stormed out in fury. It was with relief that Turnbull left Aden in May 1967, to be replaced by Sir Humphrey Trevelyan, though his integrity prevented him from expressing his deep sense of betrayal, particularly by the foreign secretary, George Brown, and his abrupt sacking of Turnbull.

Retiring to the Thames valley of his youth, Turnbull acted for a while as consultant on graduate recruitment to a mining consortium. He also assisted with the resettlement of Asians expelled from Uganda. He and his wife bought a riverside house at Henley-on-Thames. There he could indulge his love of gardening and poetry, erudite and witty conversation, fine wine, and music—in Kenya he had been one of the first owners of a long-horned gramophone. He could, too, revive his interest in rowing (not a pastime one could practise in the northern frontier district, despite the whimsical existence of the jokingly titled Royal Wajir Yacht Club), making him a well-known figure at the Henley regattas and an enthusiastic coach of the Sandhurst eight. He was a fellow of University College, London, and an honorary fellow of Magdalene College, Cambridge.

In 1979 Turnbull moved back to the borders, finally settling in Jedburgh. Following his wife's death in 1986 his health slowly deteriorated, and after two years in nursing homes he died on 21 December 1998 at Hunters Care Centre, Cirencester, Gloucestershire. He was buried on 30 December at Bedrule church, Roxburghshire, and was survived by his two sons and one daughter.

Turnbull's career reflected the fundamental colonial service paradox expected of its latter-day administrators: a capacity to negotiate diplomatically yet to act decisively. To exercise the dualism of authority and accommodation constituted the ultimate skill in the art of decolonization. Although it is by his adroit governorship of Tanganyika and his tempestuous years in Aden that Dick Turnbull is likely to be remembered by historians, his own affection and reputation lay in Kenya, above all in the scrubland and deserts of the northern frontier district. It was, as he once told Elspeth Huxley, 'the romance' that attracted him.

A. H. M. KIRK-GREENE

Sources The Times (26 Dec 1998) · Daily Telegraph (25 Dec 1998) · C. Chenevix Trench, Men who ruled Kenya (1993) · C. Chenevix Trench, The desert's dusty face (1964) · R. Neillands, A fighting retreat: the British empire, 1947–97 (1996) · D. A. Low and A. Smith, eds., History of East Africa, 3 (1976) · J. Listowel, The making of Tanganyika (1965) · private information (2004) [G. Hector, M. Irving, M. Maciel] · 'Gain and loss', Daily Telegraph (9 Jan 1958) · C. Allen, Tales from the dark continent (1979) · R. Hyam, Magdalene College Magazine and Record, new ser., 43 (1998–9), 2–5 · C. Pratt, The critical phase in Tanzania, 1945–1968: Nyerere and the emergence of a socialist strategy (1976) · WWW · Burke, Peerage · personal knowledge (2004) · b. cert.

Archives Bodl. RH, papers relating to service in Kenya · Bodl. RH, interview · IWM, interview · priv. coll., papers

Likenesses photograph, repro. in The Times · photograph, repro. in Daily Telegraph (19 Dec 1962) · photograph, repro. in Daily Telegraph (9 June 1958) · photographs, repro. in Allen, Tales from the dark continent · portrait, repro. in K. Ingham, A history of east Africa (1962), 338

Turnbull, William (c.1400–1454), bishop of Glasgow, was born at Bedrule, Roxburghshire. He described himself as 'of noble race by both parents'; his mother was presumably a Stewart, since he was related to the king. He passed to the new University of St Andrews, taking his MA there in 1420. It was determined by statute that a student had to be twenty to graduate MA, so he was probably born c.1400. In 1431 he enrolled at the University of Louvain as a canon law student and by January 1434 was bachelor of canon law, although on becoming dean of the arts faculty at St Andrews in February 1430 he was already described as rector of Hawick and licentiate in canon law. When Andrew Stewart, dean of Moray, died (before January 1434), James I presented Turnbull to Stewart's vacant benefices, including his deanery and canonries of Glasgow (Provan) and Aberdeen (Belhelvie). Turnbull was forced to litigate about Stewart's livings, however, and in spite of papal support lost them all except the lordship of Provan. The Roman curia was at Florence during the council there from 1439 to 1443 and presumably Turnbull, who had registered his presence at the Council of Basel in March 1435, attended the sessions when he was resident in Florence. In 1439 he was at the University of Pavia, where he became doctor of canon law. Described as papal chamberlain in 1433 and papal cubicular in 1443, he found Pope Eugenius IV anxious to lavish privileges on him. When the pope provided him to the see of Dunkeld on 10 February 1447, Turnbull was archdeacon of Lothian (a benefice of his often overlooked). As yet unconsecrated, he was translated to the see of Glasgow on 27 October and was consecrated between December 1447 and May 1448, the first bishop of Glasgow to style himself 'bishop by the grace of God and the apostolic see'.

Besides being a papalist, Turnbull was also a king's man. Before the death of James I in 1437 he had already acted as royal procurator in Rome. On 28 February 1433 he was dispatched from Rome to King James with William Croyser. Croyser later adhered to the Council of Basel when it withdrew its support from Pope Eugenius, and Turnbull succeeded to Croyser's lapsed benefice, the archdeaconry of Lothian. Croyser was never reconciled to James I, and the king's murder in 1437 had profound consequences for Scottish–papal relations, especially after the pope transferred the council to Ferrara and then to Florence. By late 1437 Turnbull was free to return to Scotland, where by August 1440 he was keeper of the privy seal and in royal councils upheld the pope's authority. He was evidently a man of consequence at the king's council table, remaining there until his death. By royal appointment he became vicar of Edinburgh before March 1446. Following his translation to the see of Glasgow he continued as keeper of the privy seal until 1448 and was a regular witness to deeds of James II. On the king's behalf he corresponded with the lord and lady of Veere about the loss sustained by Scots merchants as a result of the plundering of goods from a wrecked ship. He wrote to Charles VII of France offering his help through the latter's chamberlain, Sir William Monypenny. When Turnbull became bishop of Dunkeld, Edinburgh merchants found part of his costs at Rome. As bishop of Glasgow he arranged via his agent in Rome that the 1450 papal jubilee should be celebrated in his cathedral, where pilgrims could share in the jubilee indulgence. He also set about completing the upper chapter house of the cathedral, which had suffered from fire.

The work for which Turnbull is best known, the foundation of Scotland's second university at Glasgow, was assured by a bull of Nicholas V of 7 January 1451. Its model was to be not Paris, as in the case of St Andrews, but Bologna, 'freest of universities'. Turnbull initially envisaged mature students taking theology and law (a fragment of the statutes of law still survives). The bishop's early death precluded this, and a new arts foundation was subsequently established. His first arts principal and his first theologian were both Cologne graduates, and the philosophy taught was that of Albert the Great, far removed from the nominalism characteristic of early St Andrews. In the meantime, Turnbull had continued to be closely involved in national politics, as one of James II's main advisers. According to John Law, a canon of St Andrews but originally a schoolmaster at Ayr (which had also planned a university), writing in a chronicle at least seventy years later, the bishop was among those who plotted the downfall and death of William, earl of Douglas, killed by James on 22 February 1452; Turnbull probably played a part in Douglas's downfall, but his death was solely the king's responsibility. Before it an uneasy peace reigned, for which Turnbull must take some credit. The ensuing campaign against Douglas supporters drew heavily on Turnbull's jubilee pardon funds, providing James with a loan of 800 merks. The king showered Glasgow with favours: neighbouring burghs might not disturb merchants on their way to its markets; its bishop was granted a house in Stirling; its barony became a regality. Turnbull, on his fellow bishops' behalf, obtained freedom to dispose of their goods on their deathbeds. His chapter granted him a chaplaincy of St Catherine in their cathedral. His arms on a nave pillar at Dunfermline Abbey testify to his friendship with Abbot Richard Bothwell, while his arms on the west-facing wall of the chapter house of Glasgow Cathedral testify to his building there. The jubilee funds were applied to other purposes by James II, and the university lost these resources. Turnbull died, probably at Glasgow, on 3 September 1454.   JOHN DURKAN

Sources J. Durkan, *William Turnbull, bishop of Glasgow* (1951) · J. Durkan and J. Kirk, *Glasgow University, 1451–1577* (1977) · C. McGladdery, *James II* (1990) · J. H. Burns, *Scottish churchmen and the Council of Basle* (1962) · A. I. Dunlop, ed., *Calendar of Scottish supplications to Rome*, 4: *1433–1447*, ed. D. MacLauchlan (1983) · C. Innes, ed., *Registrum episcopatus Glasguensis*, 2 vols., Maitland Club, 61 (1843)

Turnbull, William (1729?–1796), physician, was born at Hawick, Roxburghshire, into the family of Turnbull of Bedrule, dissenters. He attended school at Hawick and studied medicine at Edinburgh, where he obtained his MD, and afterwards at Glasgow. About 1752 he settled at Wooler, Northumberland, where many patients were sent to him from Edinburgh. He was noted for his care of the poor, and was appointed as physician of the Bamburgh Infirmary.

During his twenty-five years at Wooler, Turnbull and his wife, whose name is not known and who predeceased him, raised at least two sons and a daughter. The eldest son died in the prime of life; another son, William, and a married daughter survived him. His publications on the diseases of women and children took the form of letters to the *Ladies' Magazine*, and his essay on the croup appeared in the *Scots' Magazine* in 1756. He was also editor of the medical part of *Middleton's Universal Magazine*.

In 1777 Turnbull settled at Well Close Square, Whitechapel, on the eastern outskirts of London, where he was appointed physician to the Eastern Medical Dispensary in Great Alie Street. He contributed articles on medicine, chemistry, and anatomy to the second edition of the *New and Complete Dictionary of Arts and Sciences* (1778). Turnbull suffered a short severe illness and died in London on 2 May 1796, leaving papers for a nearly completed practical system of medicine. In 1805 his son William Turnbull, who was surgeon to the Eastern Medical Dispensary, published volume 1 of *The Medical Works … Containing a Popular Treatise on Health and the Means of Preserving it*, with a memoir of his father's life. No further volume was published.

E. I. CARLYLE, *rev.* ANITA McCONNELL

Sources A. Jeffrey, *The history and antiquities of Roxburghshire and adjacent districts*, 4 vols. (1864) · J. Wilson, *Hawick and its old memories* (1858) · *N&Q*, 2nd ser., 5 (1858), 276 · *GM*, 1st ser., 66 (1796), 444 · PRO, PROB 11/1275, sig. 279

Turnbull, William Barclay David Donald (1811–1863), archivist and antiquary, was born on 6 February 1811 in St James's Square, Edinburgh, the only child of Walter Turnbull (d. 1819), armiger, from Hanover in Jamaica and later of Leven Lodge, near Edinburgh, and Torryburn, Fife. His mother was Robina (d. 1842), daughter of William Barclay, a merchant of Edinburgh. He first studied law as an apprentice to a writer to the signet, but soon after his majority was admitted an advocate in 1832. He was

> a fine linguist, forcible and animated in conversation, and in person [a] splendid specimen of a sturdy, manly, towering Scotchman … No one could … mistake his strong nationality, as evidenced not only in his Mid Lothian [*sic*] dialect but in that warmth and geniality of manner … [notable in] the gentry and learned men of Scotland. (*The Tablet*, 9 May 1863, 301)

On 20 March 1833 he founded the Abbotsford Club, named in honour of Sir Walter Scott, the aim of which was to publish original works and reissues relevant to Scottish history. Turnbull was its secretary until November 1841. He married on 17 December 1838 Grace, second daughter of James Dunsmore of Edinburgh. A son was born on 9 October 1839, but lived only a day. A daughter, Susan Grace,

William Barclay David Donald Turnbull (1811–1863), by James Archer

born on 26 April 1841, died on 9 September 1845. There is no record of other children.

Turnbull's parents belonged to the kirk but he became an Episcopalian, contributing liberally to the erection of the Dean Chapel in Edinburgh. In 1843 he took the longer step in becoming a Roman Catholic, apparently influenced by his extensive medieval studies, including the crusades.

His works published from 1835 until 1843 reflect his interest in Scottish history and genealogy: *Extracta e variis chronicis Scocie* [sic] (1842) and *The Blame of Kirk-Buriall* (1836) are particularly noteworthy. After 1843 his works show the influence of his conversion: translations of letters from the Labanoff collection of the letters of Mary, queen of Scots (1845); More's *Dialogue of Comfort* (1847); and later the poems of Richard Crashaw, Robert Southwell, and William Drummond. He also produced two volumes translated from Ardin's life, writings, and doctrines of Martin Luther (1854). An ardent and discerning bibliophile, the sale of Turnbull's library in November 1851, before he moved to London in 1852, took two weeks. He built up another significant library in London, where he studied for the English bar, to which he was called as a member of Lincoln's Inn on 26 January 1856. He had time over from the law to publish in 1858 *The buik of the chronicles of Scotland, or, A metrical version of the history of Hector Boece, by William Stewart*, in three volumes.

A learned, industrious, and careful scholar, Turnbull's scholarly caution did not extend beyond the pages of his works; his biographer, Eyton, ascribed to him 'an ardent temperament, cherishing strong prejudices, which impelled him to the expression of his opinions in unmitigated terms, and on several important occasions to a hasty and incautious course of action' (Eyton, 5). Nevertheless his life so far had been tranquil enough; but in August 1859 he embarked on a new phase of his career which was to bring him into the unwelcome and unexpected glare of a brief notoriety. On the recommendation of Duffus Hardy, Sir John Romilly, master of the rolls, took him on as a calendarer for the record commission. His correspondence with Hardy reveals a pawkily humorous side. In dealing with an office problem he suggested suspending 'a good sized bladder (old Palgrave's if you can get it!)' in a flue to prevent smoke blowing down (Cantwell, 192). But the scholar produced in 1860 a useful calendar of the state papers foreign for the reign of Edward VI and a companion volume for Mary I in 1861.

Although Roman Catholics had been legally emancipated in 1829, for many protestants the smell of sulphur and gunpowder still clung to them. In the summer of 1860 the Protestant Alliance, the Religious Tract Society, and the Scottish Reformation Society sent up a rocket to warn the nation of the presence of a papist in a national sanctum. A memorial signed 'very numerously ... praying for his dismissal' was submitted to authority (Eyton, 11). Romilly knew him well enough to support him, but Turnbull, shaken by the clamour, resigned on 28 January 1861. He attempted a libel action against the secretary of the Protestant Alliance in July 1861, but without success. Nevertheless, he had much support from scholarly and professional circles. C. H. Pearson, history professor at King's College, London, and Henry Folkard, an eminent barrister, urged Romilly not to accept the resignation. A counter-memorial was addressed to the lords of the Treasury signed by Lord Lindsay, Sir Francis Palgrave, Dean Stanley of Westminster, James Anthony Froude, Benjamin Jowett, and several hundred other professional figures. The marquess of Normanby presented it to Lord Palmerston on 19 February 1861. Palmerston, with a keen instinct for the popular mood, responded pragmatically: he had 'no doubt that ... Romilly's opinion of Mr Turnbull's faithfulness [was] perfectly well founded' (Eyton, 11), and no reflection on Turnbull was intended in accepting his resignation, but a select committee on the issue was refused. Palmerston expressed himself even more clearly when the subject came up in the Commons, not for the first time, on March 15, describing the appointment as inexpedient and commending Turnbull for honourably resigning.

The Alliance, not satisfied with this success, continued to harry its wounded prey. Its *Monthly Letter* of 16 March 1863 published a list of documents which had disappeared from the state papers, with the implication that Turnbull was responsible. A letter from Romilly to the home secretary denied the charge and enabled the government to lay the correspondence before parliament. The voice of the extremists was muted for a time but not their influence: the whole affair persuaded Romilly he could not in future employ a Roman Catholic for editing tasks without recourse to the lords commissioners, who could be trusted to refuse permission. A contemporary comment in the Roman Catholic press indicated the ironies of Turnbull's persecution, perceiving a general dilemma in his situation:

> A person of strong religious convictions is not to be trusted to write history—a conclusion which … may be very true, but it is a very awkward one to come from the Protestant Alliance … It rather disposes of Foxe and Strype … The same admirable argument that relieves us from Dr Lingard settles Burnet … (*The Tablet*, 20 July 1861, 455)

Turnbull was, however, particularly unlucky. The anti-Catholic prejudices of his opponents had hitherto been supported by a traditional protestant interpretation of English history. This interpretation was becoming increasingly less credible with the late nineteenth-century publication of state papers and documents, thus making his role in editing controversial sixteenth-century papers seem particularly dangerous to radical protestants.

It may well be that the moral support he received in many quarters was not enough to save Turnbull from the physical consequences of this crisis. By the time of his early death he belonged to several learned bodies including the Society of Antiquaries of Scotland, the Newcastle Society of Antiquaries, and the Royal Society of Antiquities of Copenhagen, and he was a correspondent of the Comité Impérial des Travaux Historiques et des Sociétés Savants de France. He died at 6 Lower Brunswick Terrace, Barnsbury, his London home, on 22 April 1863; his body was interred in the more congenial soil of his native Scotland, in the grounds of the Episcopal church of Dean Bridge, Edinburgh. His wife survived him, and died in London on 27 May 1884, aged seventy-two.

FRANCIS EDWARDS

Sources J. W. K. Eyton, *Herald and Genealogist*, 2 (1865), 170–79 · Gillow, *Lit. biog. hist.* · Boase, *Mod. Eng. biog.* · J. D. Cantwell, *The Public Record Office, 1838–1958* (1991) · *The Tablet* (8 Oct 1859), 651 · *The Tablet* (3 Dec 1859), 780 · *The Tablet* (23 Feb 1861), 119 · *The Tablet* (23 Feb 1861), 123 · *The Tablet* (20 July 1861), 454–5 · *The Tablet* (9 May 1863), 301 · BL, Add. MS 37967, fol. 164r/v · BL, Add. MS 24876, fol. 102 · *DNB*
Archives NL Scot., biographical, genealogical, and other notes · NL Scot., papers | BL, Add. MSS 37965, 37967, 40856, 40545, 24876, 34573, 34578 · BL, Egerton MSS · NL Scot., letters to David Laing and James Maidment · PRO, 1/129: T 1/6323 A/16560/1861 · U. Edin. L., letters to David Laing
Likenesses J. Archer, lithograph, AM Oxf., BM [*see illus.*]
Wealth at death under £1500: probate, 21 Oct 1863, *CGPLA Eng. & Wales*

Turnemire, William de (*fl.* 1279–1284). *See under* Moneyers (*act. c.*1180–*c.*1500).

Turner. For this title name *see* Robertson, Eileen Arbuthnot [Eileen Arbuthnot Turner, Lady Turner] (1903–1961).

Turner [*née* Norton], **Anne** (1576–1615), accessory to the murder of Sir Thomas Overbury, of whose origins little is known, was born on 5 January 1576 of humble parentage, and had at least one sister and one brother living at the time of her death. She entered the glittering orbit of court

Anne Turner (1576–1615), by unknown engraver

society in the company of her husband, George *Turner, a physician so fashionable that Queen Elizabeth herself supported his promotion within the College of Physicians when his Catholicism threatened to stall it. Anne too was a Catholic: she took what she admitted was her first protestant communion only days before her execution. George Turner died in 1610, leaving his widow to care for their children. By then, however, Anne had acquired a powerful friend and confidante, Frances Howard, daughter of Thomas Howard, earl of Suffolk, and wife of the third earl of Essex, a woman, Anne later claimed, 'as deere unto me as my owne soule' (PRO, SP 14/83/19). Following her husband's death Anne lived in London on Paternoster Row, but after the Essex marriage was annulled in September 1613, allowing Frances to marry the royal favourite, Robert Carr, earl of Somerset, the following December, Anne moved into the countess's household—though not, she later insisted, as a servant.

This friendship drew Anne into the plot to murder Sir Thomas Overbury, then a prisoner in the Tower of London, during the summer of 1613. Overbury died in September 1613, and at the time his death was attributed to natural causes. Two years later, however, Sir Gervase Elwes, lieutenant of the Tower, confessed that in 1613 he had discovered and, he had believed at the time, thwarted an attempt to poison Overbury. Elwes's statement triggered further investigation. He named Overbury's keeper, Richard Weston, as the attempted poisoner, and under questioning Weston confessed a series of attempts to poison Overbury, implicating Frances Howard and Anne Turner in the plot. During repeated examinations and at her trial Anne Turner denied poisoning Overbury, and the case against her rested almost entirely on Weston's confessions. She was tried on 7 November 1615. Prosecutors contended that Anne and her friend had poisoned Overbury to ensure his silence and to exact revenge: Overbury had opposed his friend Carr's growing intimacy with Frances Howard, whom he brazenly insulted, and had threatened to expose their adulterous liaison. In May 1613, the prosecution argued, Anne recruited Weston from among her servants and the countess recommended him to be Overbury's keeper in the Tower. According to prosecutors, Anne, at her friend's behest, gave Weston instructions for poisoning Overbury, supplied him with potions and powders, arranged for the poisoned enema that finished Overbury off, and then paid Weston his £180 reward. The basic outline of the charge was embellished with electrifying details. The prosecutors alleged that the two women had bought from the astrologer Simon Forman charms and images to help Frances seduce Carr and Anne to seduce Sir Arthur Mainwaring, with whom, it was asserted, she had three illegitimate children. Prosecutors read aloud salacious letters from Frances to Anne and Forman, and displayed a variety of sexually explicit magical images. They also charged that Anne had helped pass letters from the countess to Carr, and on at least one occasion had lent her house for an illicit meeting. At Anne's trial Sir Edward Coke declared her 'a whore, a bawd, a sorcerer, a witch, a papist, a felon, and a murderer, the daughter of the devil Forman' (*State trials*, 2.935). Others added another crime to Coke's tally: the introduction into fashionable society of the morally noxious craze for starched yellow ruffs. Contemporaries found in this yoking of murder to sexual transgression, witchcraft, and sartorial excess a compelling explanation of Anne Turner's life and crimes as well as an unnerving embodiment of their dread of female decadence. Her perverted religious loyalties made her transgressions all the more comprehensible and chilling.

Anne Turner was convicted and sentenced to hang. Under the guidance of the cleric sent to prepare her for death Anne admitted that she had known of the poisoning and had kept it secret to protect her friend. At her hanging at Tyburn on 14 November she made what contemporaries considered an exemplary end: she admitted her conviction was just; urged others to amend their lives; and railed against pride, wantonness, and sartorial excess. Declaring herself a protestant she led the audience in prayer, and threw her repentant soul on Christ's mercy. Her final performance left a lasting impression, transforming Anne Turner from the epitome of female criminality into a moral exemplar whose warnings later writers used to support their diatribes against sartorial excess and other female transgressions. She was buried in St Martin's churchyard the same day.   ALASTAIR BELLANY

Sources *State trials*, 2.911–36 • PRO, SP 14/81/86, SP 14/82/1, 21, 45, SP 14/83/19, 21, 32–4 • Munk, *Roll*, 2.89–91 • *The bloody downfall of adultery, murder, ambition* (1615) • R. Niccols, *Sir Thomas Overburies vision* (1616) • *Mistris Turners farewell to all women* (1615) • *Mistres Turners repentance* (1615) • B. Rich, *The Irish hubbub, or, The English hue and crie* (1619), 40 • A. Bellany, 'Mistress Turner's deadly sins: sartorial transgression, court scandal, and politics in early Stuart England', *Huntington Library Quarterly*, 58 (1996–7), 179–210 • A. Somerset, *Unnatural murder: poison in the court of James I*, pbk edn (1998), 86–8
Archives NRA, priv. coll., report on her trial for poisoning Sir Thomas Overbury in the Tower of London
Likenesses line engraving (after unknown artist), BM, NPG [*see illus.*]

Turner, Sir Ben (1863–1942), trade unionist and politician, was born at Boothhouse, Austonley, a hamlet 2 miles from Holmfirth, Yorkshire, on 25 August 1863, the second son of Jonathan Turner and his wife, Emma (*née* Moorhouse). His father worked in mills, operating a woollen powerloom, and his mother had been a hand-loom worker (she was illiterate at the time of Turner's birth). Both sides of Ben's family were chapel folk and both parents were radicals in politics. His father, who read radical newspapers at the village cobbler's shop, was a great admirer of Ernest Jones and the Chartists and an active trade unionist, who was on the local committee at the time of the great weavers' strike in Holmfirth in 1872 and later a member of the Power-loom Weavers' Union. Turner was greatly influenced by his father, in his politics, his trade unionism, and in a taste for homely dialect verse.

Turner went to a dame-school then to a national school. As a member of a large family (three boys, four girls), he began to contribute to the family income six months before he was ten, working as an assistant in hand-loom weaving to both his aunt and an elderly man. At ten he became a half-timer, attending school only half the day and working the rest in a mill, a practice which he later campaigned against as a trade union official. At Easter 1877 the family moved to Huddersfield, the second time that Ben had left the vicinity of his village.

In Huddersfield Turner attended the secular Sunday school, becoming its secretary at eighteen. There he heard addresses by Annie Besant, G. J. Holyoake, Harriet Law, Dr Aveling, and others. He went to the mechanics' institute night school, read widely, and wrote labour notes for a local radical newspaper. On 5 October 1884 Turner married Elizabeth (1857/8–1939), daughter of Joash Hopkinson, a cotton spinner. A piecer in a spinning mill, she subsequently became an active suffragette. Turner and his wife had five daughters; they were both anti-vaccination campaigners and were taken to court for refusing to have their daughters vaccinated.

In 1882 Turner joined the Weavers' Union, established in 1881 in Huddersfield, and became actively involved in its committees and as a speaker from 1885. Historically, trade union organization was weaker in wool than in cotton: wool spinning was traditionally carried out in small and scattered units, and power-looms had spread more slowly. Turner was therefore faced with a surplus of labour (with male wages tending to drift down towards women's rates).

Sir Ben Turner (1863–1942), by unknown photographer, 1928

In 1887 Turner was victimized for his trade union work, spending a period unemployed before working as a clothing salesman and then an insurance agent. By this time he was a member of the Social Democratic Federation (SDF), joining in late 1886 after witnessing the suppression of a banned SDF unemployed demonstration in Trafalgar Square on 9 November 1886. Turner was strong in his commitment to the labour movement, but his socialist views were conciliatory not revolutionary. He was a believer in joint conciliation schemes with employers, publicly praising such systems of 'cosy co-operation' (Wrigley, 7).

In August 1889 Turner moved to Leeds after being offered work there writing for the *Yorkshire Factory Times*. He combined writing for this and the *Workman's Times*, started in 1890, with trade union work. He spoke across the midlands and north, and was actively involved in major strikes such as that at the Manningham mills in 1890–1. In 1889 he joined the Leeds Trades Council, which sent him as a delegate to the 1890 Trades Union Congress, and the Leeds Socialist Society.

With his move to Batley in July 1891 Turner returned to a smaller urban area, one which was central to the heavy woollen district for his trade union work and one in which he was to be the major Labour figure. He was elected to the school board in 1892 and served until it was abolished in 1902. He was elected to Batley council in 1893 and, before he died, was an alderman and four times mayor (1914–16 and 1934–5). He was made a freeman in 1919. He also served as a councillor and alderman on West Riding county council from 1910 to 1942. He was appointed OBE (1917), CBE (1930), and knighted in 1931.

Turner was a member of the Fabian Society for a few years, and was foundation secretary of the Batley branch in 1891 and treasurer of the Yorkshire society. However, the main focus of his activities was the Independent Labour Party (ILP), of which he was a founder member in 1893. He was a delegate from the Batley Labour Party which held its meetings in his house. The ILP provided a congenial home for Turner and his moralistic, pacifist, and moderate socialism. Turner also increasingly played a role in national Labour politics. He was elected to the national executive committee of the Labour Representation Committee and the Labour Party for 1903–4 and then 1905–21, when he retired in favour of serving on the general council of the TUC. He chaired the 1912 Labour Party conference. He stood for parliament in 1906, 1908 (by-election), December 1910, and 1918 before being elected for Batley and Morley in 1922 and in 1923. After defeat in 1924, he won again in 1929, but lost in 1931. He held office as secretary for the mines from June 1929 to September 1930.

Turner attended pre-war congresses of the Second International, including those in London in 1896 and Basel in 1912. He was a founder in 1894 of the International Textile Workers' Federation. In 1910 he went to St Louis as a TUC fraternal delegate to the American Federation of Labor conference. In 1920 he was chairman of the British Labour delegation to Russia, which went at the time the labour movement was campaigning against allied intervention in Russia. Turner was impressed by Lenin but not by his revolutionary politics.

Turner's greater role was as a trade union leader. With Allen Gee (1852–1939), he became a leading figure of Yorkshire woollen trade unionism. After part-time union work, in 1892 he became secretary of the Heavy Woollen district branch of the West Yorkshire Power-loom Weavers' Association. He worked to bring all textile workers into the union (which became the General Union of Weavers and Textile Workers in 1900 and the General Union of Textile Workers in 1912). By 1919 his union had taken over the *Yorkshire Factory Times*, now named *Labour Pioneer*, and Turner edited it until it ended with the general strike, in 1926. He was the first president of the National Union of Textile Workers (1922–33). From 1917 to 1929 he was also president of the National Association of Unions in the Textile Trade. He was a member of the general council of the TUC from 1921 until 1928.

As president of the TUC in 1927–8 Turner took part in the discussions with a group of major industrialists led by Sir Alfred Mond, known as the Mond–Turner talks. These talks explored possibilities for substituting joint consultation and co-operation for conflict in British industry. This was a reaction against the bitter confrontations in British industrial relations of the post-war years that had led to the general strike in 1926. Nevertheless the talks built on a strong strand of labour movement sentiment in favour of conciliation committees, which had been evident even in 1919–26 and was embodied by Turner as well as by figures such as Arthur Henderson and J. R. Clynes.

Turner was very proud of being a Yorkshireman. He missed few opportunities to publish his dialect verse in a range of local and Labour newspapers. In 1934 his collected *Rhymes, Verses and Poems from a Yorkshire Loom* were published, with a foreword by Philip Snowden. Turner was generally a good-natured man whom most found to be agreeable company. In his later years he was teetotal.

He deplored bringing issues such as birth control into politics, observing that 'sex complexities' were 'extraneous' to socialism. For him, 'Labour stands for cleanliness of mind, body and soul' (*About Myself*, 162 and 169).

As a tireless campaigner for trade unionism and a pioneer socialist, Turner was widely respected in the labour movement. In national politics, however, he was a worthy rather than a front-rank figure. Turner died at his home, The Homestead, 25 Carlton Avenue, Batley, Yorkshire, on 30 September 1942, and his ashes were scattered over the family grave at Batley cemetery. His wife predeceased him in 1939.   CHRIS WRIGLEY

Sources B. Turner, *About myself, 1863–1930* (1930) · B. Turner, *Short history of the General Union of Textile Workers* (1920) · B. Turner, *Rhymes, verses and poems from a Yorkshire loom* (1934) · D. E. Martin and B. Turner, 'Turner, Sir Ben', *DLB*, vol. 8 · K. Laybourn and J. Reynolds, *Liberalism and the rise of labour, 1890–1918* (1984) · K. Laybourn and D. James, eds., *"The rising sun of socialism": the independent labour party in the textile district of the West Riding of Yorkshire between 1890 and 1914* (1991) · M. Crick, *The history of the Social Democratic Federation* (1994) · C. Wrigley, *Cosy co-operation under strain: industrial relations in the Yorkshire woollen industry, 1919–1930* (1987) · K. E. Smith, 'Ben Turner', *West Yorkshire dialect poets* (1982), chap. 4 · G. W. McDonald and H. F. Gospel, 'The Mond–Turner talks, 1927–33', *Business History*, 21 (1979), 180–97 · *DNB* · S. V. Bracher, 'Mr Ben Turner', *The Herald book of labour members* (1923) · *CGPLA Eng. & Wales* (1942) · b. cert. · m. cert. · d. cert.

Archives JRL, Labour History Archive and Study Centre, papers · W. Yorks. AS, Kirklees, scrapbook incl. letters, papers | JRL, Labour History Archive and Study Centre, corresp. relating to his candidature · JRL, Labour History Archive and Study Centre, corresp. relating to joint board matters · JRL, Labour History Archive and Study Centre, papers relating to war emergency workers national committee · W. Yorks. AS

Likenesses R. H. Blackham, oils, 1917, Batley council chambers, Yorkshire · photograph, 1928, People's History Museum, Manchester [*see illus.*] · D. Low, pencil caricature, NPG · photographs, Trades Union Congress, London

Wealth at death £399 16s. 9d.: probate, 9 Nov 1942, *CGPLA Eng. & Wales*

Turner, Benjamin Brecknell (1815–1894), photographer, was born on 12 May 1815 at 31–2 Haymarket, London, the eldest son of Samuel Turner (1784–1841) and Lucy Jane Fownes (1786–1870). He was apprenticed to his father at the age of sixteen as a tallow chandler and later ran the family firm of Brecknell, Turner Ltd, which made candles, soap, and saddle soap. The factory and shop were at 31–2 Haymarket. However, Turner is best-known as a pioneering amateur photographer of the 1850s. According to family tradition, he took up William Henry Fox Talbot's calotype process in 1849—but it was probably seeing the display of photographs at the Great Exhibition of 1851 that sharpened his ambition. Turner assembled a majestic album of his photographs from the years 1852–4 and opened the sequence with two remarkable views of the interior of the Crystal Palace in Hyde Park taken in March 1852—when Paxton's iron and glass structure had been emptied of exhibits before being dismantled and rebuilt at Sydenham. Turner's photographs capture the light-filled interior's revolutionary scale and elegance of engineering. His finesse in composing subjects, and adroit handling of a large camera, is witnessed by the other

Benjamin Brecknell Turner (1815–1894), self-portrait, *c*.1850

photographs in the album, now in the Victoria and Albert Museum. His characteristic subjects were English abbeys, castles, cottages, and farms. Many of his finest photographs were made in or around the Worcestershire village of Bredicot, where he married Agnes Chamberlain (1828–1887) on 17 August 1847. They and their eight children spent many summers at Bredicot Court, the Chamberlain family home.

Unlike nearly all other British photographers, Turner remained faithful to Talbot's calotype process for most of his career. However, after beginning with small negatives at the start of his career (1849–51) Turner's later paper negatives were on a heroic scale—usually about 26 by 38 cm. Turner exhibited regularly and with critical success from 1852 onwards, when six of his photographs appeared in the world's first ever purely photographic exhibition, organized by the Society of Arts in London. His paper (rather than glass) negatives—almost always printed on albumen-coated papers—gave a broad, textured handsomeness to his photographs of the canonical picturesque subjects—vernacular architecture, farm carts and implements, rick yards, and ivy-clad ruins. The collection of some 250 paper negatives by Turner preserved by the Royal Photographic Society (and now in the National Museum of Photography, Film and Television, Bradford) demonstrates that he was not merely a 'straight' photographer: he compensated for the shortcomings of his negatives by adding pencilled foliage details, for example, or blacking out skies with Indian ink. About 1855 he built a glasshouse above the family home and business premises in the Haymarket and made portraits of friends, relatives, business associates, and fellow photographers. For these he used the wet collodion on glass process introduced in 1852. He also experimented with collodion negatives for landscape subjects in 1856 but the results lacked the charm of his works from paper, to which he immediately returned.

Turner had a high reputation among critics, connoisseurs, and collectors in the 1850s. His work was constantly praised by reviewers of the time. He exhibited at the Universal Exhibition held in Paris in 1855—a major milestone for photography in France—and was awarded a bronze medal. Turner was a founder member and later a vice-president of the Photographic Society of London (founded 1853). He was also an honorary secretary and treasurer of the Photographic Club, within the society, which produced large and beautiful albums of photographs in 1855 and 1857. Members used the albums as a means of exchanging their works. Turner organized the 1857 album. These albums are now treasured by students of photography, as are Turner's own prints and negatives; they are to be found in the great museums around the world. Turner died at 133 Tulse Hill, Brixton, London, on 29 April 1894. The first exhibition devoted to his work took place in April 2001 at the Victoria and Albert Museum, London.

MARK HAWORTH-BOOTH

Sources family history, compiled by Muriel Arber (great-granddaughter), V&A · family history, compiled by Philip Dymock Turner (son), V&A · memoir by Agnes Turner, V&A · *Photographic Journal*, 1-new ser., 18 (1853–94) · M. Barnes, M. Daniel, and M. Haworth-Booth, *Benjamin Brecknell Turner: rural England through a Victorian lens* (2001)
Archives V&A, photography collection files, family histories and other documents accumulated over 25 years
Likenesses self-portrait, photograph, c.1850, priv. coll.; on loan to V&A [see illus.]

Turner, Charles (1774–1857), engraver, was born on 31 July 1774 in Woodstock, Oxfordshire, the son of Charles Turner (1741–c.1793) and his wife, Jane, née Davies. His father was an excise officer, whose career and health were ruined when he temporarily mislaid some official documents, and after his death Jane Turner re-entered the duchess of Marlborough's household at Blenheim Palace, where she had worked before her marriage. Turner came to London around 1789 and on 21 September of that year was apprenticed to the engraver John Jones for seven years. He also studied at the Royal Academy schools. He worked primarily in mezzotint, but also in aquatint and stipple, and began to publish his own prints in 1796 as well as working for publishers in London and Scotland. He hired James Easling as his apprentice on 14 January 1800. On 27 February 1802 Turner married Ann Maria Blake (d. 1836); they had three children, Charles (1803–1826), Ann Maria (b. 1805), and Jane (1806–1881).

Skilful and industrious, and an able businessman, Turner became the most important mezzotint engraver of his day, and in 1812 he was appointed engraver-in-ordinary to the king. He was elected associate engraver at the Royal Academy in 1828, and exhibited there until the year he died. Turner's speed and facility enabled him to

Charles Turner (1774–1857), self-portrait, 1850

produce engravings of topical interest, and among his early successes in this vein were his mezzotints of *Bonaparte Reviewing the Consular Guards* after John James Masquerier of 1802 (original painting untraced), and *Lord Nelson* after John Hoppner (original painting, 1800, the Royal Collection) published on 9 January 1806, the day of Nelson's funeral. Turner was an innovative engraver (his 'Time Book' for 1798 records an attempt to make 'a Machine to Lay the grounds'; Turner, 'Time Book') and began using steel plates from 1821. His considerable output numbered 638 portraits and more than 300 subject engravings, mainly after contemporary artists including Sir Henry Raeburn, William Beechey, James Northcote, and Sir Thomas Lawrence, and he also engraved his own compositions.

Turner is well known for his engravings after his namesake J. M. W. Turner (no relation), with whom he had a long and sometimes fraught friendship. The two initially collaborated on a scheme to publish a large single-plate mezzotint of the latter's picture of *The Shipwreck* (1805; Tate collection, Turner bequest; engraving published 1807), and around the same time they began to work together on the *Liber Studiorum*, a series of engravings after J. M. W. Turner's designs. Charles Turner engraved the first twenty published plates and acted as publisher, but the arrangement was discontinued around 1810 when the two Turners, both irascible men, quarrelled. In later life Charles Turner claimed that the rift had lasted for nineteen years, but the publication of his engraving after J. M. W. Turner's *Eruption of the Souffrier Mountain* (exhibited 1815; University of Liverpool) in November 1815 indicates that the dispute was relatively short-lived. J. M. W. Turner appointed him a trustee of his proposed charitable institution and an executor of his will in 1831, and the two men remained friends until the painter's death in 1851.

Charles Turner died on 1 August 1857 at 50 Warren Street, Fitzroy Square, London, where he had lived since 11 April 1803, and was buried in Highgate cemetery.

GILLIAN FORRESTER

Sources A. Whitman, *Charles Turner* (1907) · C. Turner, 'Time Book, 1798–1804', BL, Add. MS 37525 · C. Turner, diary, 1851–7, Yale U., Beinecke L., d.62 · D. Alexander, 'Turner, Charles', *The dictionary of art*, ed. J. Turner (1996) · *DNB* · R. K. Engen, *Dictionary of Victorian engravers, print publishers and their works* (1979), 202–3 · *Collected correspondence of J. M. W. Turner*, ed. J. Gage (1980), 290–91 · G. Forrester, *Turner's 'drawing book': the Liber Studiorum* (1996) [exhibition catalogue, Tate Gallery, 20 Feb – 2 June, 1996] · J. Pye and J. L. Roget, *Notes and memoranda respecting the 'Liber Studiorum' of J. M. W. Turner, R.A.* (1879) · B. Hunnisett, *Engraved on steel: the history of picture production using steel plates* (1998), 64, 68, 69, 82 · R. J. B. Walker, 'The portraits of J. M. W. Turner: a checklist', *Turner Studies*, 3/1 (1983), 23–4, 28 · R. Ormond, *Early Victorian portraits*, 2 vols. (1973) · private information (2004) [D. Alexander]
Archives BL, time book, Add. MS 37525 · Yale U., Beinecke L., diary, incl. details of household expenses, d.62
Likenesses W. Brockedon, chalk and pencil drawing, 1832, NPG · C. Turner, self-portrait, chalk drawing, 1850, NPG [*see illus.*] · J. Boaden, oils · C. Turner, mezzotint (after J. Lonsdale), NPG

Turner [*formerly* Tennyson], **Charles** (1808–1879), poet, was born on 4 July 1808 at Somersby rectory, Lincolnshire, the second surviving son of the Revd Dr George Clayton Tennyson (*bap.* 1778, *d.* 1831) and his wife, Elizabeth (*bap.* 1780, *d.* 1865), daughter of the Revd Stephen Fytche, formerly vicar of Louth, and his wife, Martha. He was educated at Louth grammar school from 1815 to 1821 and then with his next youngest brother, Alfred *Tennyson, under their father who gave them rigorous tuition in preparation for admission to Cambridge. Tennyson was admitted to Trinity College, Cambridge, in October 1827, the year in which, with Alfred and his elder brother, Frederick *Tennyson, he published *Poems by Two Brothers*. While at Cambridge he produced his first independent volume, *Sonnets and Fugitive Pieces* (1830), a collection of delicate verse expressive of a gentle disposition much admired by Coleridge. He graduated in 1832 and was ordained deacon in 1832 and priest in 1833. On the death in 1835 of his great-uncle, the Revd Samuel Turner, Tennyson inherited property in Caistor, Lincolnshire, and the lordship of the manor of Grasby nearby. In the same year, in deference to the terms of his great-uncle's will, he changed his name by royal licence from Tennyson to Turner and it was under the name Charles Turner that he published his subsequent volumes, though the sobriquet Tennyson Turner became established in his lifetime.

On 24 May 1836 Turner married Louisa Sellwood (1816–1879), the youngest daughter of a Horncastle attorney and sister of Emily who was to marry Alfred in 1850. Also in 1836, on the death of the incumbent vicar, he was instituted into the living of Grasby, which was in his own gift. This was to remain his parish until his death. Soon after their marriage his wife's mental powers became impaired and this distressing situation, exacerbated by his resorting to opium, led to their separation in 1839. Largely residing in Cheltenham, he was an absentee priest from 1843 to 1849 when he was reunited with his wife. Despite her continued mental illness, they resumed their marital life in Grasby vicarage, newly built in 1850. They remained childless.

After not writing poetry for some years, Turner suddenly produced an elegiac sonnet on the death of a relative in 1854. It was the first of a number of contributions to periodicals and was published in 1860 in the new *Macmillan's Magazine*. In 1864 he published *Sonnets*, a volume which reveals the influence of the sacramentalist idiom of Keble, a pronounced antipathy to current neologistic thinking, and a sensitive delicacy in its descriptions of natural forms. This was followed in 1868 by *Small Tableaux* and in 1873 by *Sonnets, Lyrics and Translations*, which betrays a preoccupation with human relationships in the context of love and marriage.

Illness forced Turner to withdraw from the offices of the church in 1866, although he never resigned the living. He nevertheless maintained the pastoral care of his parishioners and in 1869 at his own expense rebuilt the church, employing an architect of high-church persuasion, Charles Buckeridge.

Turner died at 6 Imperial Square, Cheltenham, from a bladder complaint on 25 April 1879. His wife, who had been confined in an asylum for the insane near Salisbury since October 1878, survived him by less than a month. They were buried (Turner on 1 May) in the same plot in Bouncers Lane cemetery, Cheltenham. Some fifty unpublished sonnets found among Turner's papers were added to his collected poems in a memorial volume edited jointly in 1880 by Hallam Tennyson and James Spedding with Alfred Tennyson taking overall control in its early stages and contributing a moving prefatory poem. The best of the 343 sonnets and the handful of lyrics which constitute the corpus of his work are notable for their compassion and for their quite individual perception of flux in diurnal and seasonal conditions in the Lincolnshire landscape he loved.

ROGER EVANS

Sources Tennyson family letters, diaries and notebooks, Tennyson Research Centre, Lincoln · Lincs. Arch., Tennyson family papers · Lincs. Arch., Turner family papers · Lincs. Arch., Bishop Kaye papers · R. Evans, 'Secret rooms: the life and work of Charles Tennyson Turner', PhD diss., U. Hull, 1993 · R. W. Goulding, ed., *Louth old corporation records* (1891) · *LondG* (4 Sept 1835), 1677 · E. F. Shannon, 'Alfred Tennyson's admission to Cambridge', *TLS* (6 March 1959), 136 · S. T. Coleridge, MS marginalia in copy of *Sonnets and fugitive pieces*, 1830, Tennyson Research Centre, Lincoln · d. cert. · parish register (marriages), St Mary's Church, Horncastle
Archives Lincoln Central Library, Tennyson Research Centre, corresp., diaries, and papers · Lincs. Arch., family corresp. | BL, letters to Macmillans, Add. MSS 55252–55254 · Lincs. Arch., Dixon archive · Lincs. Arch., Kaye archive · Wilts. & Swindon RO, register of Laverstock House lunatic asylum
Likenesses J. J. E. Mayall, photograph, 1864, Tennyson Research Centre, Lincoln · T. J. M. Townsend, oils, 1868, Tennyson Research Centre, Lincoln
Wealth at death under £1500: administration with will, 16 Aug 1879, *CGPLA Eng. & Wales*

Turner, Charles Edward (1831–1903), Russian scholar, was born at King's Lynn on 21 September 1831, the second son of John Alderson Turner of the legacy office. He entered St Paul's School on 9 February 1843, and remained until August 1850. On 29 March 1854 he was admitted commoner at Lincoln College, Oxford. Although shy and reserved until he was drawn out in congenial company, he took a prominent part in his college debating society, where he showed an exceptional knowledge of European politics. On leaving Oxford without graduating he worked for three years as a schoolmaster. In 1859 he went to Russia, and in 1862 was elected, after competitive examination, professor of English literature at the Imperial Alexander Lyceum in St Petersburg. In 1864 he was, again by competitive examination, appointed lector of the English language in the Imperial University of St Petersburg, a post he held for life. On occasional visits to England he frequently lectured on Russian literature.

Turner became intimately acquainted with Russian culture, and in his writings on Russian literature showed sound critical judgement and a grasp of its history. He gave lecture series at the Royal Institution in London—in 1881 'Famous Russian authors' (published in 1882 in amplified form as *Studies in Russian Literature*); in 1883 'Russian life'; and in 1888 'Count Tolstoi as novelist and thinker' (published in amplified form in the same year). In 1889 he lectured at the Taylor Institution in Oxford on the modern novelists of Russia; the subject matter was amplified for publication in 1890. In 1893 came a translation of C. A. Behrs's *Recollections of Count Leo Tolstoy*, and in 1899 *Translations from Pushkin in Memory of the Hundredth Anniversary of the Poet's Birthday* (London and St Petersburg). Other works published in St Petersburg include *Our Great Writers, a Course of Lectures on English Literature* (2 vols., 1865) and *Lessons in English Literature* (2 parts, 1870). He also published an English grammar (1879) and an English reader (1891). Other works, on Burns, on the Romantic poets, and *Robert Browning's 'Sordello'* (1897), appeared only in Russian translations from Turner's English manuscripts. *On the Eve*, a translation of Turgenev, appeared in 1871.

Turner was highly respected both by the British colony in St Petersburg and by Russian friends and colleagues. He died at St Petersburg on 14 August 1903, and was buried there in the Smolensk cemetery. A monument to his memory, raised by public subscription, was unveiled by his successor, William Sharpe Wilson, in 1905. He was married, but had no children.

NEVILL FORBES, rev. JOHN D. HAIGH

Sources *The Athenaeum* (29 Aug 1903), 291–2 · private information (1912) · Foster, *Alum. Oxon.* · register, Lincoln College, Oxford · *BL cat.*

Turner, Cuthbert Hamilton (1860–1930), ecclesiastical historian and New Testament scholar, was born in Paddington, London, on 7 July 1860, the eldest son of Edwin Goldwin Turner, solicitor, and his wife, Catharine (*d.* 1914), daughter of Cuthbert Finch. In 1872 he was elected, at the same time as the historian Charles Oman, his lifelong friend, and D. S. Margoliouth, to a scholarship at Winchester College. There he laid the foundations of his accurate scholarship, acquired a beautiful handwriting, discussed theology—he was even then an earnest high-

Cuthbert Hamilton Turner (1860–1930), by Lafayette, 1928

churchman—and maintained in debate the cause of Gladstonian Liberalism.

In 1879 Turner proceeded, as a scholar, to New College, Oxford; and in Oxford the whole of his mature life was spent. He did brilliantly in classical honour moderations, obtaining in 1881 one of the best first classes of the year, and in 1883 a second class in *literae humaniores*.

After taking his degree, Turner stayed on in Oxford, writing reviews for *The Guardian* and political articles for the *Oxford Review*; he was keenly studying theology, but no college work came his way until 1885, when he was appointed theological lecturer at St John's College. In the following year he won the Denyer and Johnson scholarship; by that time he had acquired a deep knowledge of the methods and problems of chronology in their bearing on the history of the early church. This knowledge enabled him in 1887 to complete a first-rate piece of research, and to establish conclusively the correct date (Saturday, 22 February 156) of the martyrdom of St Polycarp (published in *Studia Biblica*, 1890).

In 1888 William Bright, the regius professor of ecclesiastical history at Oxford, appointed Turner as his assistant lecturer. He continued to work for Bright until the latter's death in 1901, after which he repaid his debt of gratitude by preparing for publication the professor's lectures on *The Age of the Fathers* (1903). In 1889 Turner became a fellow of Magdalen College. The prize fellowship to which he was then elected was renewed as a research fellowship in 1896, and he remained a fellow until his death.

As well as taking tutorials and lecturing for the theological school, Turner wished to make a contribution to the study of Christian antiquity. Keenly interested in textual criticism, he chose to concentrate primarily upon the textual material of early Western canon law. He had it in mind to work at the same time upon a book which would have been similar in scale to Louis Duchesne's *Histoire ancienne de l'église chrétienne* (1906–10). However, his studies in canon law involved complex investigations into the history of manuscripts and manuscript tradition; he became increasingly interested in New Testament studies; and in the end he left behind him no such church history as he had planned to write, but one *magnum opus* carried a long way towards completion, and a large number of *opuscula* which ranged in subject over many fields of research.

Turner's position down to 1920 was that of a research fellow. He was also the first holder of the speaker's lectureship in biblical studies from 1906 to 1910, and a university lecturer in early Christian history and literature from 1914 to 1920. During this period he was an active member of the board of the faculty of theology. In 1920, when Walter Lock succeeded William Sanday in the Lady Margaret chair of divinity, Turner succeeded Lock in Dean Ireland's professorship of exegesis, a position which he held for the remainder of his life. In 1909 he was elected a fellow of the British Academy.

Turner's main vocation as a scholar was to edit the successive *fasciculi* of his great work, *Ecclesiae occidentalis monumenta juris antiquissima*. A general sketch of the development of early canon law, in a chapter contributed by Turner to the *Cambridge Medieval History*, volume 1 (1911), 'The organization of the church', and a course of Birkbeck lectures given at Trinity College, Cambridge, in 1921 and 1922 (but never published) were the only elucidations which he ever supplied of the documents published in his *Monumenta*. The nucleus of early Western canon law was formed by what was believed in the West to be Nicene material; but the word 'Nicene' did not cover the whole Nicene code and was allowed to include much that was not Nicene at all; other Eastern councils, such as those of Ancyra, Neo-Caesarea, Gangra, and Antioch, were appended to it, and the canons of Sardica were commonly joined without a break to those of Nicaea. In the early collections of canon law, its three elements—the 'Nicene', the Latin, and the papal decretals—were combined with bewildering diversity. Turner set himself to edit all these collections, beginning with the Latin versions of the canons of the apostles, going on to Nicaea and beyond that as far as Ephesus and Chalcedon, and including also the fourth- and fifth-century councils of Africa, Gaul, and Spain. Six sections of this work were published (vol. 1, four parts, 1899–1930; vol. 2, two parts, 1907–13); they contain the canons of the apostles, the Nicene Council, and those of Ancyra, Neo-Caesarea, Gangra, and Antioch; two *fasciculi* also include matter supplementary to Nicaea, a fine piece of work upon the council of Sardica, and the *Gesta de nomine Apiarii*, the record of a crucial dispute between the churches of Rome and Carthage. Two more sections, containing the first and second councils of Arles, with that of

Valence, and the councils of Laodicea and Constantinople respectively, were all but finished at the time of Turner's death. The editing of this material involved the collation of a large number of manuscripts and many visits to foreign libraries. In his yearly journeys abroad for this purpose Turner, who never married, enjoyed, for twenty-two years, the companionship of his mother, whose aid and sympathy are acknowledged in the touching dedication prefixed to a section published in 1930.

Of Turner's minor works the best-known is his article 'Chronology of the New Testament' in the first volume of J. Hastings's *Dictionary of the Bible* (1898). He also contributed an essay, 'Text of the New Testament', to *Murray's Illustrated Bible Dictionary* (1908), and an elaborate treatise on *Greek Patristic Commentaries on the Pauline Epistles* to the supplementary volume of the larger work (1904). The 'Chronology' was particularly noteworthy. Turner did the major part of the work needed to complete an enterprise begun by Sanday—the editing of the New Testament quotations in Irenaeus, a labour begun as early as 1884, and not completed until 1923, when the *Novum Testamentum S. Irenaei* appeared as no. 7 in the series Old Latin Biblical Texts. For the dean and chapter of Worcester Cathedral he devoted great pains and palaeographical skill to the editing of early manuscript fragments preserved as guard-leaves to books in the chapter library; a stately volume, *Early Worcester MSS*, published by the Clarendon Press in 1916, was the fruit of this research. In 1912 Turner collected some of his earlier work into a volume of essays with the title *Studies in Early Church History*; this included a valuable paper, 'Letters of St Cyprian', but an essay, *The History and Use of Creeds and Anathemas in the Early Centuries of the Church*, which had been published for the Church Historical Society in 1906, was too long for inclusion.

From 1910 onwards Turner was greatly interested in the preparation of the volume planned by Henry Barclay Swete, *Essays on the Early History of the Church and the Ministry* (1918), and after Swete's death in 1917 he took over the editorial supervision of the volume. His own contribution, an essay, 'Apostolic succession', was a fully documented study of the word *diadochē* in the earliest centuries and of the problem of non-Catholic orders in the time of St Augustine. Turner's exposition of 'succession language' in the early fathers, and of the controversy about Donatist ordinations, attracted a considerable measure of attention.

Before he was elected professor, Turner undertook for Bishop Gore the revision (1919) of the latter's work *The Church and the Ministry*, a revision so thorough as to give the book, in its author's opinion, an entirely new value. As professor, he inaugurated his work with a lecture published as *The Study of the New Testament, 1883 and 1920*, particularly valuable for its full and just estimate of Sanday's place in the history of scholarship. Another lecture, delivered and published in 1924, *The Early Printed Editions of the Greek Testament*, had an interesting context, for it was based upon an all but complete collection of sixteenth-century Greek testaments (including the Complutensian polyglot) which he had made himself in order to give it to his old school. He was happy to be able to transfer the collection to Winchester in the summer before his death. As professor also, Turner made an intensive study of St Mark's gospel, and this study bore fruit in the luminous exposition which he contributed to the one-volume *New Commentary on Holy Scripture* issued by the Society for Promoting Christian Knowledge in 1928.

Among the minor interests which absorbed so much of Turner's working time, mention should be made of the *Lexicon of Patristic Greek*, for which he schemed and planned harder than anyone, and above all, of the *Journal of Theological Studies*, of which he was first editor, 1899–1902. His work for the *Journal* ended only with a paper on the *Actus Petri* which appeared after his death. It was a continuous flood of articles, documents, notes, and reviews; there are studies in the textual history of St Cyprian, and of his own *Monumenta*, texts of Niceta of Remesiana, a re-collation of Codex Bobiensis (*k*), and documents from the chapter library of Verona; and in volumes 25–9 there was a notable series, 'Notes on Marcan usage'.

Part of the material for a second volume of papers was collected by Turner about 1926; this was put into shape in 1931 at the desire of his literary executors under the title of *Catholic and Apostolic*, with a memoir by his friend and former colleague, H. N. Bate. Some of Turner's projects of work were carried so far by him as to justify their being completed after his death. A study of the St Gallen palimpsest fragments (St Gallen 1395) had been in type since 1909: it was finished and published in 1931, with the title *The Oldest Manuscript of the Vulgate Gospels*, by Professor Alexander Souter, of Aberdeen University.

Turner's journeys in pursuit of learning brought him into contact with many eminent scholars. He was a welcome guest at the great libraries in Rome, Milan, Paris, Verona, and elsewhere; and interchanged letters with Pope Pius XI when he was prefect of the Ambrosian Library at Milan. He cherished an especial affection for Verona and its librarian, but the Belgian hagiographer Père Delehaye was perhaps his most intimate foreign friend.

Although his reverence for such German scholars as Ludwig Traube was very deep, Turner found French and Italian erudition more congenial than that of the Germans, whose language he never fully mastered. His own mind was of the Latin order: it was accurate, clear, logical, and not given to the pursuit of abstractions. It was at this point that he diverged from William Sanday; united with him in all his interests as a palaeographer, as a critic, as a student of documentary history, although more conservative in his adhesion to the verdicts of tradition, he was not able, like Sanday, to absorb and appraise the mass of German work in those fields. But he knew—and perhaps enjoyed—his own limitations. The history of doctrine and the systematizing of theology did not attract him; the study of texts, their origin, their critical history, was his métier, and in that area his work was consistently first-rate. Sanday paid him a tribute which Turner would have valued above all others, in comparing his work with that of F. J. Hort. 'At the present time', he wrote in 1910, 'and

taking the whole world over, there is no one who occupies so nearly the position that Hort had in the last generation—with an added effectiveness and force to which Hort did not attain' (Bate, 13).

Turner was never robust, though his alertness and vivacity made him seem stronger than he was, and led his friends to think him too minutely careful of his health. Some years after his mother's death in 1914 he moved out of college to a house in north Oxford, where he was always accessible to his old friends, to the younger scholars who attended his seminar on St Mark, and to a group of promising undergraduates from Eton and Winchester whose friendship gave him the keenest pleasure. In the autumn of 1930 he had a sudden seizure and died at his home, 21 Norham Road, Oxford, on 10 October. He was buried, as he had desired, in his mother's grave at Abingdon.

H. N. BATE, *rev.* ROBERT BROWN

Sources H. N. Bate, 'Cuthbert Hamilton Turner: a memoir', *Catholic and apostolic: collected papers by the late Cuthbert Hamilton Turner*, ed. H. N. Bate (1931), 1–65 • *The Times* (11 Oct 1931) • personal knowledge (1937) • *WWW* • F. L. Cross, ed., *Oxford dictionary of the Christian church*, 3rd edn, ed. E. A. Livingstone (1997) • *CGPLA Eng. & Wales* (1930)

Archives Bodl. Oxf., corresp. • Pusey Oxf., theological papers | Bodl. Oxf., letters to J. E. A. Fenwick and T. F. Fenwick

Likenesses Lafayette, photograph, 1928, NPG [*see illus.*]

Wealth at death £6387 11s. 0d.: probate, 27 Nov 1930, *CGPLA Eng. & Wales*

Turner, Daniel (1667–1741), surgeon and physician, was born, probably in London, on 18 September 1667, the third son of John Turner (*d.* 1697), a freeman of London's Tallow-Chandlers' Company, and his wife, Rebecca. Turner was admitted into the freedom on the surgeons' side of the Barber–Surgeons' Company of London in 1691, after completing two years of apprenticeship under the London surgeon Charles Bateman, and five years under the surgeon Thomas Lichfield. While apprenticed to Lichfield, Turner began to assist in private human dissections: the reports of four dissections were published in the Royal Society's *Philosophical Transactions* (1693–4). In 1695 Turner wrote a pamphlet, *Apologia chyrurgica: a Vindication of the Noble Art of Surgery*, directed to the Barber–Surgeons' Company, explaining his plan to reform the 'shameful' state of surgical practice; he reiterated his view of reforming 'vulgar' surgical practice in *The Present State of Chyrurgery* (1703).

After practising surgery in London for twenty years, Turner relinquished his Barber–Surgeons' Company position in 1711 and was admitted as a licentiate to the Royal College of Physicians. He married Elizabeth Altham, daughter of James Altham of Latton, Essex, on 6 January 1712, in the parish church of St Helen's Bishopsgate, London. They had three children: Daniel (1715–1723), Susanna Lee (married 1736), and Mary.

Little is known of Turner's medical practice: he claimed that his new medical career offered him more 'leisure' than did his 'toilsome' surgical practice. Most of the thirty-four texts and treatises published before his death describe aspects of either his own surgical practice or his further attempts to reform the surgical art. Turner's two-

Daniel Turner (1667–1741), by John Faber junior, 1734

volume *Art of Surgery* (1722) provided 110 detailed case histories, exemplifying the treatments of conditions which contemporary surgeons were likely to encounter. In *De morbis cutaneis: a Treatise of Diseases Incident to the Skin* (1714), the first book in English devoted to a study of skin disease, Turner used case histories to demonstrate ways in which the pores of the skin allowed externally applied medicines to enter. He also argued that surgeons, who for centuries had been relegated by physicians to treating external diseases, should be given the right to administer internal medicines as well, since the medicines they were applying externally were also producing internal effects. In this work, Turner also expressed his view that a pregnant woman's imagination could be transferred to her unborn child, imprinting the foetus with various skin markings and physical deformities. James Blondel sought to refute this view in 1727, and Turner and Blondel began a pamphlet war that ultimately raised the phenomenon of the maternal imagination from an issue of folk belief to a concern of eighteenth-century medicine. Turner's two additional works on this subject were *An Answer to a Pamphlet on the Powers of Imagination in Pregnant Women* (1729), and *The Force of the Mother's Imagination upon the Foetus in Utero Still Further Considered* (1730).

Turner also engaged in publishing wars regarding the recognition and treatment of syphilis. His writings on the treatment of syphilis include *Syphilis: a Practical Dissertation on the Venereal Disease* (1717), *Remarks upon Dr. Willoughby's Translation of Monsieur Chicoyneau's Method of Cure* (1727), *Discourse Concerning Gleets* (1729), *The Ancient Physician's Legacy Impartially Survey'd* (1733), *The Drop and Pill of Mr. Ward Consider'd* (1735), and *Syphilis: the Second Part* (1739). He also wrote an elaborate preface for Aloysius Luisini's

Aphrodisiacus, Containing a Summary of the Ancient Writers on the Venereal Disease (1736), and a revision of the English translation of Ulrich von Hutten's *De morbo Gallico* (1730). Turner chiefly opposed the excessive quantities of mercurial remedies administered orally or in an unregulated manner, and despised the promotion of 'secret' remedies.

Turner, a high-church tory, and his family resided in Devonshire Square, in the parish of St Botolph without Bishopsgate. In September 1722 he forwarded a collection of twenty-five books from his own extensive library to the 'Academy of Yale'; in the postscript of the letter accompanying this contribution, Turner noted that in return for these books, he would be most grateful to receive a doctoral degree from the Yale Academy. On 11 September 1723 Turner was awarded an honorary degree of doctor of medicine, the first medical degree issued from colonial America.

As early as 1714 Turner began displaying frontispiece portraits in his major writings. Some of these included the motto *nullius in verba* beneath his portrait, whereas others included the Turner coat of arms. This decoration of his portraits substantiates his desire to display the trappings of gentility. However, his precise reasons for displaying this motto of London's Royal Society, of which he was not a member, and a coat of arms which was not his by right of descent, remain unknown, although they may be connected to issues surrounding the pedigree of his wife's family [*see* Altham, Sir James]. A 1734 mezzotint of Turner, quill in hand, seated at a writing-desk, surrounded by shelves of leather-bound books, unmistakably introduces him as a man of letters. Turner died at his home in Devonshire Square, London, on 13 March 1741, and was interred in the graveyard of the Watton-at-Stone parish church, Hertfordshire, near the home of his sister, Mary Miles.

PHILIP K. WILSON

Sources P. K. Wilson, '"Out of sight, out of mind?": the Turner–James Blondel dispute over the power of the maternal imagination', *Annals of Science*, 49 (1992), 63–85 • P. K. Wilson, 'Daniel Turner and the *Art of Surgery* in early eighteenth-century London', *Journal of the Royal Society of Medicine*, 87 (1994), 781–5 • P. K. Wilson, 'Reading a man through his gifts: Daniel Turner's 1722 book donation to Yale College', *Yale University Library Gazette*, 69 (1995), 129–48 • P. K. Wilson, 'Surgeon "turned" physician: the career and writings of Daniel Turner', PhD diss., U. Lond., 1992 • will, PRO, PROB 11/709 • D. Turner, 'Religio medici reformata', BL, Add. MS 14404, fol. 23 • *DNB*

Archives Yale U.

Likenesses G. Vertue, two line engravings, *c.*1712–1714 (after J. Richardson), BM, Wellcome L. • J. Faber junior, mezzotint, 1734, BM, NPG [*see illus.*] • G. Vertue, engraving (after John Faber junior, 1734), Yale U.

Wealth at death see will, PRO, PROB 11/709

Turner, Daniel (1710–1798), hymn writer, was born at Blackwater Farm, near St Albans, on 1 March 1710. He was educated for the ministry by Philip James of Hemel Hempstead and then kept a boarding-school in that town, but at the same time made a reputation as an occasional preacher in Baptist chapels. In 1741 he was called to be pastor of the Baptist church in Reading. He moved in 1748 to Abingdon, and held the pastorate there until his death. He received the honorary degree of MA from the Baptist college, Providence, Rhode Island, USA. He was a friend and correspondent of Robert Robinson, John Rippon, Dr Watts, and other ministers. On 8 April 1729 he married Ann Fanch (*d.* 1744) of Hemel Hempstead and they had two sons, both of whom predeceased him. One of their sons, Daniel Turner, was educated by Dr Richard Price in London in the 1750s. Following his wife's death Turner married Mrs Lucas, a widow, of Reading; they had no children.

An early supporter of open communion, in 1772 Turner advocated the practice in *A Compendium of Social Religion.* Writing under the *nom de plume* of Candidus, he also published in 1772 *A Modest Plea for Free Communion,* and in 1780 he was instrumental in reconstituting the Baptist cause in Oxford, on a covenant which granted membership to both Baptists and paedobaptists. In 1781 he entertained the idea of setting up an academy in the neighbourhood of Oxford for the children of dissenters.

Turner was well known for his hymns, four of which appeared in the Bristol *Baptist Collection* (1769) and eight in Rippon's *Collection* of 1787. One, 'Beyond the glittering starry skies', was published by his brother-in-law, James Fanch, Baptist minister of Romsey, Hampshire, in the *Gospel Magazine* (June 1776). Turner later expanded it by twenty-one stanzas and included it in his *Poems Devotional and Moral* of 1794. He also published other poems and essays, sermons, and works on English grammar. He died in Abingdon on 5 September 1798 and was buried in the Baptist graveyard in the town.   S. L. COPSON

Sources J. Ivimey, *A history of the English Baptists,* 4 vols. (1811–30), vol. 4, pp. 35, 42 · J. Julian, ed., *A dictionary of hymnology* (1892) · *Protestant Dissenter's Magazine,* 6 (1799), 41 · DNB · IGI
Archives Regent's Park College, Oxford, Angus Library, corresp.

Turner, Dawson (1775–1858), banker, botanist, and antiquary, was born on 18 October 1775 at 40 Middlegate Street, Great Yarmouth, the eldest of the three surviving children of James Turner (1743–1794), merchant and banker, and his wife, Elizabeth (1742–1819), only daughter of John Cotman, merchant and former mayor of Yarmouth. He was educated at North Walsham grammar school and then at Barton Bendish, Norfolk, as a pupil of Robert Forby, who fostered his taste for botany. In 1792, intended for the church, Turner was admitted to Pembroke College, Cambridge (where his uncle, Joseph Turner, was master), but left shortly before his father's death in 1794. In 1796 he joined Gurney and Turner's Bank in Yarmouth and in the same year, on 14 March, married Mary (1774–1850), second daughter of William Palgrave of Yarmouth and Coltishall, Norfolk. Over the next twenty years the couple had eleven children, of whom six daughters and two sons survived infancy.

The key elements in Turner's subsequent life—banking, family, and a studious disposition—were now in place. He devoted his days to business downstairs in Bank House and the evenings to his scholarly interests upstairs, financed by an ample inheritance and shrewd management of the bank, and assisted by a talented family. Initially his main passion was botany, especially mosses,

lichens, and algae. From 1800 to 1808 he published nine papers in the *Transactions of the Linnean Society of London* and in *Annals of Botany.* His reputation as a botanist won him election as FRS in 1802, the year in which his first book, *A Synopsis of British Fuci* (2 vols.), appeared. Then followed his *Muscologiae Hibernicæ spicilegium,* in Latin (1804), and *The Botanist's Guide through England and Wales* (2 vols., 1805), written with Lewis Weston Dillwyn. The four volumes of his *Fuci* (1808–19), magnificently illustrated, proved to be his last botanical work, apart from *Specimen of a Lichenographia Britannica* (1839), produced from sheets that he and William Borrer had collaborated on decades before.

Over the years other interests progressively supplanted botany—antiquities, pictures, and his library of books and manuscripts. Turner marshalled a band of helpers, starting with his wife and daughters. Mrs Turner became a skilled draughtswoman under the tutelage of John Crome, whose tuition gradually extended to the older daughters. When Crome gave up his teaching practice, Turner prevailed upon John Sell Cotman to act as drawing master to the household, and from 1812 to 1823 Cotman submitted his gifts to his patron's forceful personality. Several guests who stayed under Turner's hospitable roof left impressions of the regime in his library. In 1817 the painter Benjamin Robert Haydon (1786–1846) recorded that it was run like a school: 'One seized a drawing, another a French grammar, a third her spelling book, a fourth her etching needle'. Turner's life he described as 'one incessant scene of fact collecting … He was an immense, living Index' (*Diary,* ed. Pope, 2.127–8). Only a month before, Charles Lyell had reported: 'What I see going on every hour in this family makes me ashamed of the most active day I ever spent even at Midhurst', his former school (*Life, Letters, and Journals,* 1.42). The daughters tackled their assignments with every appearance of enjoyment. The prodigious output of drawings, paintings, etchings, and lithographs, together with their work on transcribing, cataloguing, and indexing, fed Turner's publications and extra-illustration of books. His *Account of a Tour in Normandy* (2 vols., 1820) relied heavily on letters, drawings, and etchings from Cotman, Mrs Turner, and two of his daughters. He produced at his own expense Cotman's *Architectural Antiquities of Normandy* (2 vols., 1822), for which he wrote a commentary. He also provided descriptive notes for *Specimens of Architectural Remains in Various Counties* (2 vols., 1838), a vehicle for etchings by Cotman, with architectural observations by Thomas Rickman.

Bank House was adorned with Turner's collection of paintings by Dutch, Flemish, Italian, and Norwich school artists, catalogued in his *Outlines in Lithography* (1840). His literary, scientific, and antiquarian tastes were reflected in a library of 8000 volumes, often extra-illustrated. His major achievement of this kind was to expand Blomefield's *History of Norfolk* to fifty-six volumes by the addition of some 7000 engravings, lithographs, and original drawings. His manuscript collection grew to 34,000 manuscripts and letters, including historical documents, travel journals, and literary and scientific correspondence of many eminent people. From this activity emerged his *Guide … towards the Verification of Manuscripts by Reference to Engraved Facsimiles* (1848), editions of the correspondence of John Pinkerton (2 vols., 1830), of letters from Isaac Newton to John Covel (1848), and of the (borrowed) letters of Richard Richardson (1835). His antiquarianism prompted a considerable number of articles, pamphlets, and volumes, among the more substantial of which were his *Sketch of the History of Caister Castle* (1842), his *List of Norfolk Benefices* (1847), and, on Yarmouth, *Sepulchral Reminiscences of a Market Town* (1848).

Several of Turner's daughters married men of note. Maria, the eldest, married William Jackson Hooker, one of the foremost botanists of his day; Elizabeth married Francis Palgrave, subsequently deputy keeper of public records; Harriet married John Gunn, a well-known Norfolk antiquary and geologist; and Eleanor Jane, the youngest, married William Jacobson, later bishop of Chester. When, in 1839, Hanna Sarah married a banker, the extended family's symmetry with Turner's range of interests was complete.

The family harmony was shattered when Mrs Turner died in 1850 and her husband, a year later, on 20 September carried off to Gretna Green a widow many years his junior and of markedly humbler background. His new bride was Rosamund Matilda Duff (1810–1863), *née* Neave. The consequence was estrangement from his family, disagreements with banking partners, and loss of many friends. Turner quit Yarmouth and moved to the London area, setting up house first at Barnes and then, in June 1853, in Old Brompton. There was no question now of surrounding himself with his collections. He auctioned off most of his pictures and over half his library and sold five volumes of manuscripts to the British Museum. Much of the rest was stored in an empty house at Yarmouth. Turner's health began to fail, and Francis Palgrave effected a reconciliation for the family. When Turner suffered a stroke, his wife nursed him affectionately, but his recovery was only partial. The end came, at his home, Lee Cottage, Old Brompton, on 20 June 1858 from another stroke. He was buried in Brompton cemetery. What remained of his library and manuscripts was sold in 1859. Much of the material from Turner's collections is now in the British Library, Royal Botanic Gardens, Kew, and Trinity College, Cambridge.

Turner's only son to reach maturity, **Dawson William Turner** (1815–1885), historian and headmaster, born on 24 December 1815 at Great Yarmouth, was educated at Rugby School and graduated BA from Magdalen College, Oxford, in 1838. He was ordained deacon in 1840. On 30 June 1846 he married Ophelia Dixon (1828–1896), with whom he had two daughters and a son. He was the author of a range of educational books, and from 1851 was headmaster of the Royal Institution School, Liverpool. In a series of synoptic works he covered the histories of England and France (1845), Rome (1853), Greece (1853), and Germany (1866). He produced *Notes on Herodotus* (1848), translated Pindar's *Odes* (1852), and edited three plays of Aristophanes (1861–65).

His *Rules of Simple Hygiene* (1869) ran to seven editions. During his final decade he lived in central London, and his untidy figure became familiar to the needy in hospitals and on the streets, whom he assisted with dedicated benevolence. He died in Charing Cross Hospital, London, on 29 January 1885, and was buried at Brompton cemetery. ANGUS FRASER

Sources A. N. L. Munby, *The cult of the autograph letter in England* (1962) · W. R. Dawson, 'Dawson Turner (1775–1858)', *Journal of the Society of the Bibliography of Natural History*, 3 (1958), 303–10 · W. R. Dawson, 'A bibliography of the printed works of Dawson Turner', *Transactions of the Cambridge Bibliographical Society*, 3 (1959–63), 232–56 · H. Turner and F. Johnson, *The Turner family of Mulbarton and Great Yarmouth*, new edn (1907) · S. D. Kitson, *The life of John Sell Cotman* (1937) · *The Times* (31 Jan 1885) · *The Times* (5 Feb 1885) · *The diary of Benjamin Robert Haydon*, ed. W. B. Pope, 5 vols. (1960–63) · *Life, letters, and journals of Sir Charles Lyell*, ed. Mrs Lyell, 2 vols. (1881) · CGPLA *Eng. & Wales* (1885) · d. cert. · d. cert. [Dawson William Turner]

Archives BL, annotated copies of publications · BL, letters and papers, Add. MSS 23013–23067, 23106–23107, 27967, 28652, 28655–28657, 47458, 29738, 50484–50489 · Bodl. Oxf., corresp. · NHM, letters of botanists; papers · Norfolk RO, corresp. and papers · Norwich Castle Museum, travel journals · NRA, priv. coll., corresp. and papers · RBG Kew, memoranda of botanical corresp. · Saffron Walden Library, collection of booksellers' bills · Trinity Cam., corresp.; family corresp. and papers related to him · U. Edin. L., corresp. · Virginia Historical Society, Richmond, botanical and literary notes | BL, letters to T. Sharp, Add. MS 43645 · Bodl. Oxf., letters to Isaac D'Israeli; letters to T. J. Pettigrew; corresp. with Sir Thomas Phillipps · Linn. Soc., letters to Sir James Smith · NHM, letters to James de Carle Sowerby and James de Carle Sowerby · Norwich Castle Museum, corresp. with Samuel Woodward · RBG Kew, letters to William Borrer; corresp. with Sir William Hooker; letters to Ellen Hutchins · Trinity Cam., letters to William Whewell · Yale U., Beinecke L., Osborn collections

Likenesses W. Drummond, lithograph (after portrait, *c.*1827), repro. in Dawson, 'Dawson Turner' · W. Drummond, lithograph, BM; repro. in *Athenaeum Portraits* (1837) · A. Fox, line engraving (after M. W. Sharp), BM, NPG · T. Phillips, group portrait, oils, priv. coll.; repro. in A. Moore, *Family and friends* (1992) · M. Turner, engraving (after portrait by T. Phillips, 1816), repro. in Turner and Johnson, *The Turner family* · Miss Turner, lithograph (after J. P. Davis), BM

Wealth at death under £70,000: probate, 30 July 1858, CGPLA *Eng. & Wales* · £6437 3s.—Dawson William Turner: will, 22 May 1885, CGPLA *Eng. & Wales*

Turner, Dawson William (1815–1885). *See under* Turner, Dawson (1775–1858).

Turner, Edward (1796–1837), chemist, was born in Kingston, Jamaica, in July 1796, the second son of a Scottish sugar planter, Dutton Smith Turner (d. 1816), and his Creole wife, Mary Gale Redwar. He was sent at an early age to Bath, where he received his schooling at the grammar school until 1811. After serving a medical apprenticeship and graduating MD at Edinburgh in 1819 he practised medicine in Bath for some time before he joined his Edinburgh friend, Robert Christison, in chemical and pharmaceutical studies in Paris. From 1821 to 1823 he studied mineral analysis under Friedrich Stromeyer, one of the German pioneers of practical chemistry teaching, at the University of Göttingen. In 1824 he established himself as an extramural lecturer in chemistry at Edinburgh, where he also held practical classes and published a students' guide to Dalton's atomic theory and Berzelius's views on chemical composition. In November 1827, despite strong evangelical convictions, he accepted the chair of chemistry and a lecturership in geology on the opening of the secular University of London, posts he occupied, despite serious ill health, for the rest of his life.

Edward Turner wrote one of the best of all nineteenth-century textbooks of chemistry, *Elements of Chemistry* (1827), which went through eight editions, being revised and enlarged after his death by his brother, W. G. Turner [*see below*], in conjunction with Justus Liebig and William Gregory, who modernized organic chemistry. In 1834 Turner persuaded a British Association committee of the value of Berzelius's chemical symbols, the fourth (1833) edition of his textbook being the first to deploy them consistently. Most of his forty published papers and memoirs dealt with the analysis of minerals and salts, but only his elucidation of the ores and oxides of manganese was important. Of greater long-standing significance was his work on atomic weights. Stimulated by the hypothesis proposed by William Prout, and by the experimental work by which Thomas Thomson in 1825 sought to confirm it, Turner examined the question for himself. In two important review papers published in the Royal Society's *Philosophical Transactions* (1829 and 1833) he pointed out many sources of errors in Thomson's work, and obtained accurate results that agreed with those of Berzelius. He concluded that Prout's hypothesis that 'all atomic weights are simple multiples of that of hydrogen—can no longer be maintained' (*PTRS*, 1833, 544). Nevertheless, he did not deny that a simple relationship between atomic weights might one day be discovered.

Turner was elected a fellow of the Royal Society in March 1830 and was also a fellow of the Royal Society of Edinburgh. His strong interests in geology and mineralogy led to his appointment as secretary of the Geological Society from 1830 to 1835, when he became a vice-president. He died in London, at his home, Hampstead, 38 Upper Gower Street, from stomach cancer and influenza on 12 February 1837. He was buried in Kensal Green cemetery on 18 February. He remained unmarried, being cared for by sisters.

Turner's younger brother, **Wilton George Turner** (1811–1855), was born in Jamaica on 9 June 1811. He was a student at the Edinburgh Academy before joining his brother in London and attending mathematics and chemistry classes at University College, London (UCL). Following his rejection for the chairs of mathematics at UCL and for another in mineralogy in 1834, he taught mathematics at University College School from 1832 to 1839. After teaching chemistry at Sydenham College he became a partner of Christian Allhusen (1806–1890) at Newcastle upon Tyne in the manufacture of alkali. Following research on the use of guano as a feedstock for chemical manufacturers, he emigrated to Demerara, British Guiana, to run a sugar plantation and zinc refinery. He married a sister of the Berlin chemist Gustav Rose. He died at Salt Cay, Turks Island, West Indies, on 23 October 1855.

W. H. BROCK

Sources R. Christison, *Biographical sketch of the late Edward Turner* (1837) • T. Dale, *The philosopher entering the kingdom of heaven* (1837) • H. Terrey, 'Edward Turner', *Annals of Science*, 2 (1937), 137–52 • W. H. Brock, *From protyle to proton: William Prout and the nature of matter, 1785–1985* (1985) • W. H. Brock, 'British Association Committee on chemical symbols, 1834', *Ambix*, 33 (1986), 33–42 • *DSB* • J. C. Poggendorff and others, eds., *Biographisch-literarisches Handwörterbuch zur Geschichte der exacten Wissenschaften*, 2 (Leipzig, 1863) • J. Fenwick Allen, *Some founders of the chemical industry: men to be remembered*, 2nd edn (1907) • *The life of Sir Robert Christison*, 2 vols. (1885–6) • H. J. K. Usher and others, *An angel without wings: the history of University College School, 1830–1980* (1981) • *DNB* • [T. Henderson and P. F. Hamilton-Grierson], eds., *The Edinburgh Academy register* (1914), 14
Archives UCL, letters
Likenesses Butler, marble bust, UCL

Turner, Edward (1901–1973), motor cycle designer and manufacturer, was born on 24 January 1901 at 32 Bronti Place, Walworth, Surrey, one of seven surviving children of William Turner, mechanical engineer, and his wife, Fanny, *née* Hillman. Edward Turner gained an early familiarity with metal working and tool making in his father's light engineering works. After some time at the Marconi School and a spell as wireless operator in the merchant navy during the First World War, he opened his own motor cycle shop in Peckham Road, Dulwich. In 1927 he designed and made his own 350 cc motor cycle, the Turner Special. While trying to find someone to manufacture this model, he met John Young (Jack) Sangster, the managing director of the Ariel Cycle Company, and was persuaded to become chief development engineer at the Ariel works in Birmingham in 1927. Turner spent the rest of his working life with Ariel, Triumph, and BSA, and, in collaboration with Val Page and Herbert (Bert) Hopwood, his senior and junior colleagues respectively, was responsible for the creation of many of the principal motor cycle models produced in Britain up to the 1960s.

Turner became chief designer at Ariel in 1932. He designed the four-cylinder Square Four power unit, which sold well from 1932 to 1959 and was scaled up to 500 and 1000 cc. In 1936 he moved to Triumph in Coventry after it was purchased by Sangster. There, in 1937, he designed the Speed Twin that 'changed the whole concept of motor cycle design … A determined and ambitious man who had no time for fools, he was to bring a kind of engineering dictatorship to Triumph … Above all, Edward Turner had a flair for styling' (Louis and Currie, 114). He rationalized the eighteen existing models and generated new ideas that earned good profits. He was also an enthusiastic rider.

These were Turner's best years. He became a substantial shareholder in Triumph. Then, in July 1939, his first wife, Edith Marion, was killed in a car accident. He took the loss hard. A therapeutic visit to the United States was the first of many. He was also badly affected by the bombing of Coventry, which destroyed the Triumph factory in 1940, and he may also have begun to suffer from the diabetes that later affected him. It is said that, thereafter, he became a different man, less dynamic, more cantankerous. He was managing director of Triumph from 1944 to 1956 and of the motor cycle division at BSA from September 1956, under Sangster's chairmanship, until January 1964; he remained on the board until 1967. Although in charge at Small Heath, Birmingham, he preferred Triumph's Meriden factory, but did nothing to eliminate tension between the two works and their staff and styles. Triumph with its annual output of 5000 machines was much smaller than Small Heath, where 50,000 motor cycles and other products were made in 1951.

Turner's responsibilities in the late 1950s covered Ariel, Triumph, BSA, and Sunbeam, and the Redditch works where scooter engines and small motor cycles were made. He had a brief design interest in luxury cars before Daimler was sold to Jaguar in 1960. In 1955, a Triumph reached 193 m.p.h on the Bonneville track in the USA. Outstanding successes were the BSA Rocket and Triumph Trident Three in the 1960s. At this time, Triumphs in particular were selling well in the USA and the group commanded the British market, though rivalled by Norton in both markets. But there were also failures—no successful scooters, no sharing of components and tools across marques, and no drive for a full-size range to meet Japanese competition arriving in the early 1960s and dominant in all except the largest machines by the end of the 1960s. Suggested plans to combat the threat in these ways were called 'potty' or 'irrelevant' by Turner (Hopwood, 193, 197, 201). The bad management that finally broke the group and the British motor cycle industry in 1969 and in the 1970s began under Turner and Sangster. One element was Turner's bad temper and jealous attitude to his designers and engineers. Another was his regular absence from the group in California, where he spent several months each year. Writing in 1981, Bert Hopwood, a senior designer in the group, was sharply critical of Turner, giving evidence of his waywardness. Davies (86) described his temper as 'ferocious', one designer actually being kicked. Others, including Ryerson, offered a more favourable picture.

Turner became a rich man, living in some style near Kenilworth until moving on his retirement to Rutland Gate in London and later to Capel, a few miles from Dorking in Surrey. He was a member of the Institution of Mechanical Engineers and of the Institute of Directors and a liveryman of the Worshipful Company of Coachmakers. He married for a second time on 19 July 1952. His second wife, Shirley Joan, *née* Watts, from Sydney, was a teenage Australian for whom he seems to have felt an 'uncharacteristic tenderness' (*DBB*, 5.569). They had three children before divorcing about 1968. Turner died on 15 August 1973, aged seventy-two, at his home, Newlands, Weare Street, Capel. BARBARA M. D. SMITH

Sources B. M. D. Smith, 'Turner, Edward', *DBB* · B. M. D. Smith, *The history of the British motorcycle industry, 1945–75* (1981) · I. Davies, *It's a Triumph* (1980) · B. Holliday, *The story of BSA motor cycles* (1978) · B. Hopwood, *Whatever happened to the British motorcycle industry?* (1981) · P. Hartley, *The Ariel story* (1980) · H. Louis and B. Currie, *The story of Triumph motorcycles*, 2nd edn (1978) · B. Ryerson, *The giants of Small Heath: the history of BSA* (1980) · *The Times* (16 Jan 1967) · *The Times* (19 Dec 1967) · *Who's who in the motor industry*, 4th edn (1959) · *BSA Group News* (Jan 1964) · *BSA Group News* (Dec 1965) · *Birmingham Post Year Book* (1963–4) [and other issues] · b. cert. · m. cert. · d. cert.
Archives Birm. CL, BSA MSS · priv. coll., unpublished material on the British motor cycle industry · U. Warwick Mod. RC, Triumph archive

Likenesses portrait?, repro. in Smith, 'Turner, Eduard' · portrait?, repro. in Ryerson, *Giants of Small Heath*
Wealth at death £316,239: probate, 7 Dec 1973, *CGPLA Eng. & Wales*

Turner, Eric (1918–1980), motor cycle manufacturer, was born on 18 July 1918 at Burton upon Trent, Staffordshire, the son of William Edmund Turner, headmaster, and his wife, Elsie Emma, *née* Hartwell. He was educated at Chesterfield School, 5 miles from Staveley. Nothing else is known about the years prior to 1940, when he qualified as an accountant just after the outbreak of war. He was an associate and later a fellow of the Institute of Chartered Accountants. Turner left accounting to join the Royal Army Service Corps as a driver. He served in France, and was briefly a staff sergeant, just before Dunkirk. By the age of twenty-six he was a lieutenant-colonel in command of 100 Dakotas and 3000 men airlifting troops into Burma to fight the Japanese in 1943–4. In 1943 he married Zena Doreen Schellenberg, who died about 1973; they had a son and a daughter.

On demobilization, Turner reverted to accountancy, joining the Blackburn aircraft company at Brough in Yorkshire as chief accountant despite his total lack of relevant experience. He became company secretary two years later and a director in 1950. He was made managing director at thirty-two, the youngest head of an aircraft company in the country. Although lacking in executive experience, he tried to get to know his staff and to weld them into a team. 'I am expert in nothing', he said (Rae, 74–7).

In 1959 Turner agreed to join the board of Birmingham Small Arms (BSA) and he became chief executive and deputy chairman on 1 January 1960. He absorbed the chairmanship in June 1961 when Jack Sangster retired. Shortly afterwards he served as president of the British Cycle and Motor Cycle Association, for the year 1962–3. This was the time when a trade treaty was signed with Japan giving Japanese-made goods, including motor cycles, most favoured nation treatment in Britain without corresponding entry to the Japanese market. The industry protested fruitlessly but BSA, despite the managing director Edward Turner's visit to Japan in 1960, failed to act to meet the new threat.

Turner was the first chief executive of the BSA group following the reorganization associated with the dismissal of Sir Bernard Docker as chairman in 1956. He was picked specifically for his accountancy expertise, but as a man with no experience of the industry he was a remarkable choice, and he may have been headhunted at the suggestion of consultants Lazards and Deloitte, Plender; his appointment turned out to be a disastrous misjudgement. The group, with its head office in Small Heath, Birmingham, and 20,000 employees in factories around Britain, had 34 per cent of its sales in motor cycles, 15 per cent in Daimler cars and buses, 13 per cent in steel and titanium, and 21 per cent in small arms and engineering; Turner switched products, appointed new directors and executives, and introduced new functions such as research and personnel, but the changes upset rather than developed the organization's strengths.

Turner may have sought teamwork, 'a long broad view' (Ryerson, 171), and a 'consistent profitability' (Hopwood, 240, 243) but he was hardly successful. New men were brought in, many from the aircraft industry then in recession, rather than existing ones promoted, notably on the motor cycle side; one such was Lionel Jofeh. These newcomers were 'ignorant and unsympathetic to the problems of motorcycle design and production' (Smith, DBB) and the outcome was a series of unsuccessful models that reached the market too late in the season and were unacceptable. 'The decision that change was needed was right; the method of introducing it questionable; the outcome disastrous' (ibid.). Over £1 million was lost in orders and returned motor cycles in 1967–8, £8 million in 1970–71, and £3 million in the following two years. Turner, after sacking Jofeh, resigned himself and BSA was forced to its knees, never to rise fully again.

To a degree the tension lay between the accountant and the engineer, the new thinking on value engineering, computerization, and research versus traditional, well-tried methods used by men who knew and loved motor cycles. For example, 300 newcomers were taken on in the research unit established at Umberslade Hall, with virtually no communication with the experienced staff at Small Heath 20 miles away. Ryerson described 'the management at BSA (as) very highly skilled, and … very bad' (Ryerson, 137–40), concerned with making money but not with the means to do so. Ryerson saw BSA's collapse as the result of a 'quiet, steady merciless erosion of the company due to lack of true, deepseated commitment and sense of purpose in the manufacture of motorcycles' (ibid., 167).

Turner left BSA in 1971 aged fifty-two. He was already a director of English and Scottish Investors, and had been, until 1967, of Associated Electrical Industries. He was on the advisory council attached to the export credits guarantee department (1965–70), on the Malta Industrial Development Board (1959–65), and chairman of the finance committee of the University of Aston in Birmingham (1968–76); Aston awarded him an honorary DSc when he left office. He was also chairman of the right-wing Economic League (1967–72) and president of the Birmingham chamber of commerce (1971–2), being concerned with the integration of midlands industry into the Common Market. He moved into the insurance brokerage business and became an underwriting member of Lloyds.

In 1974, shortly after the death of his first wife, Turner married Eileen Laura Svrljuga. Prior to leaving BSA, he had become a founder director of what is now the National Exhibition Centre, which opened just outside Birmingham in 1976. He served for ten years to 1979. In that year, Turner moved from Dale Cross Grange, Barnt Green, near Birmingham, where he had lived for many years, to live with his daughter at Windlesham in Surrey. Ill health may have caused the move, for he died of lung cancer at the age of sixty-two on 21 September 1980, at his daughter's house, at Lennoxwood, Westwood Road, Windlesham. The business career that had started so well when he was young terminated early and blighted.

BARBARA M. D. SMITH

Sources B. M. D. Smith, 'Turner, Eric', *DBB* • B. M. D. Smith, *The history of the British motorcycle industry, 1945–75* (1981) • B. Hopwood, *Whatever happened to the British motorcycle industry?* (1981) • B. Ryerson, *The giants of Small Heath: the history of BSA* (1980) • G. T. Rae, 'BSA gets the Turner treatment', *Business* (June 1960) • I. Davies, *It's a Triumph* (1980) • *Birmingham Evening Mail* (23 Sept 1980) • *Birmingham Post* (24 Sept 1980) • *Birmingham Post Year Book* (1969–70) • *Birmingham Post Year Book* (1974–5) • *BSA Group News* (Dec 1959) • *BSA Group News* (7 June 1961) • *BSA Group News* (July 1961) • *The Times* (26 Sept 1980) • *The Times* (16 Dec 1980) • *Directory of Directors* (1961–4) • *Directory of Directors* (1980) • BSA annual report to shareholders, 1959 • BSA annual reports to shareholders [etc.] • d. cert.
Archives Birm. CL, BSA MSS
Likenesses portrait, repro. in Smith, 'Turner, Eric'
Wealth at death £297,563: probate, 4 Dec 1980, CGPLA Eng. & Wales

Turner, Sir Eric Gardner (1911–1983), classical scholar, was born at 437 Glossop Road, Sheffield, on 26 February 1911, the son of William Ernest Stephen *Turner (1881–1963), professor of glass technology at the University of Sheffield, and his first wife, Mary Isobel Marshall (d. 1939). After dame-school and preparatory school, he attended King Edward VII Grammar School, Sheffield, and in 1930 went up to Magdalen College, Oxford, where he took firsts in classical moderations (1932) and *literae humaniores* (1934). After graduating he turned his attention immediately to the texts, both literary and documentary, preserved on papyrus in the dry climate of Egypt. In the only surviving account Turner gave of his career, when elected to a corresponding fellowship of the Austrian Academy in 1975, he attributed his choice to the influence of Hugh Last. It is clear that for his European audience he spoke of his teachers as professors, without attempting to explain the institution of tutorial fellows, for Turner mentioned Gilbert Murray, professor of Greek, along with Last. He was perhaps influenced by the fact that Last became professor of Roman history at Oxford from 1936 to 1948, whereas in 1934 he was tutorial fellow at St John's College. A near contemporary of Turner who graduated in 1939 recalls the brilliance of Last's lectures, and it may be that, even before his appointment as professor, Last was a natural source of advice to those interested in Roman history. Turner's tutor in papyrology was Colin Roberts, but it was Last who introduced Turner to Sir Idris Bell.

Turner taught classics at the University of Aberdeen from 1936 to 1948, apart from service at Bletchley Park from 1941 to 1945, working in naval intelligence: he later remarked that he had known before Hitler that the *Bismarck* had been sunk. On 3 October 1940 he had married Louise Barbara Taylor, a modern historian; their children Hilary and Nicholas were born in 1942 and 1944. In 1948 Turner was appointed to a newly created readership in papyrology at University College, London, becoming professor *ad hominem* in 1950 and remaining there until his retirement in 1978. He was elected a fellow of the British Academy in 1956, became CBE in 1975, and was knighted in 1981.

In addition to research and the normal run of teaching and administration, Turner undertook a series of tasks which changed the face of classical and papyrological studies in the United Kingdom and overseas. First, he helped to create the Institute of Classical Studies in 1953, and became its first director. In that context he demonstrated by his example the importance of a commitment to research seminars, setting high standards by his contributions to discussion. (He also for many years chaired the committee of the Warburg Institute.) Despite recurring illness, from 1956 to 1978 he chaired the Egypt Exploration Society, rebuilding relations with Egypt after the Suez crisis. In the context of the British Academy, he was a member of the organizing committee of the Corpus Vitrearum Medii Aevi, picking up the work of his father, who in 1915 had created at Sheffield a department of glass technology. One of Turner's last major articles, in *Antike Kunst* 24 (1981), set out to identify as deriving from a comedy a scene portrayed on a Hellenistic glass beaker. Turner also played a major part in the work of the overseas policy committee and through it in that of the Union Académique Internationale. For much of the scholarly world in Europe, America, and elsewhere he *was* papyrology, and many of the leading papyrologists of the next generation were his pupils.

Turner's greatest achievement was to revitalize publication of the collection of papyri from Oxyrhynchus owned by the Egypt Exploration Society. These had been entrusted to Edgar Lobel, whose interest was limited to Greek poetry. With humour, tact, and firmness Turner persuaded Lobel to release texts in which he was not interested, initially for presentation and discussion at seminars, and got the enterprise as a whole moving. He signed his first preface as general editor of the series in 1954 and by 1961 had achieved an annual rhythm for the appearance of the volumes.

Apart from publishing, with scholarly annotation, hundreds of new texts, Turner wrote three major books on his work, two of which are indispensable handbooks for anyone who cares about the transmission of knowledge in and about antiquity: *Greek Papyri: an Introduction* (1968; 2nd edn, 1980), *Greek Manuscripts of the Ancient World* (1970; 2nd edn, 1987, published after Turner's death but following his design and incorporating his material), and an exploration of the origin of the form of the book with which we are familiar today, *The Typology of the Early Codex* (1977). A characteristic piece of work is the publication, in *Museum Helveticum*, volume 33 (1976), of a papyrus of part of a satyr-play, the fourth element in the complex of plays presented by the Athenian tragedians at the annual dramatic festivals. Turner was able to show that the play had been rewritten so as to exclude the letter sigma, thus providing an example of one of the more bizarre byways of Greek literature. His work also appeared in major contributions to, and encouragement of the contributions of others to, the understanding of the Athenian comic playwright Menander.

In retirement Turner settled in Fortrose, Ross-shire. He died on 20 April 1983. His obituarist for the British Academy, Peter Parsons, placed him below the greatest in the two fields of literary and documentary papyri, but few have done as much as he in both. The range over which, and the care with which, he worked, evident also for

instance in his British Academy obituary of the numismatist Derek Allen, gave him both an astonishing sense of the overall shape of the material of which time has left us a rather erratic selection (see in particular his chapter on the nature of papyrological evidence in *Cambridge Ancient History*, 7, pt 1, 1984) and an outstanding ability to transmit his understanding to others. His enjoyment of great music, as performer on the violin and listener, and of good food, good wine, and congenial company, was simply the other side of his urge to share with others what he found good.   MICHAEL H. CRAWFORD

Sources P. J. Parsons, *PBA*, 73 (1987), 685–704 · E. W. Handley, 'Memorial address for Eric Gardner Turner', *Annual Report* [Institute of Classical Studies], 13 (1982–3), 27–9 · E. G. Turner, 'Edgar Lobel', *Gnomon*, 55 (1983), 275–80 · personal knowledge (2004) · private information (2004) [P. A. Brunt, M. S. Drower, P. M. Fraser, A. H. Griffiths, E. W. Handley, J. A. North, P. J. Parsons] · b. cert.
Archives BL, corresp. with Sir Idris Bell, Add. MSS 59521, 71110
Likenesses portrait, repro. in Parsons, *PBA*, pl. XLI

Turner, Eustace Ebenezer (1893–1966), organic chemist, was born in Bromley, Kent, on 22 May 1893, the youngest in the family of one daughter and two sons of John Turner, salesman, and later piano merchant, whose family came from Finchingfield, Essex, and his wife, Annie Elizabeth Coates, from Windermere.

Turner's interest in organic chemistry began at an early age, and while a schoolboy at the Coopers' Company's School (1906–1910) he practised organic chemistry in a room at his home. He entered East London (later Queen Mary) College, London, with an exhibition in 1910 to study chemistry, and graduated BSc with first-class honours in chemistry in 1913. He obtained a London DSc in 1920.

Following graduation Turner undertook research into the preparation of biaryls with G. M. Bennett, the results from which were published in the *Journal of the Chemical Society* (105, 1914). Turner's interest in biaryls continued during his time as lecturer at Goldsmiths' College in 1914–15. During this period he published a paper questioning the validity of the then accepted structure for biphenyl, the Kaufler formula, citing as experimental evidence the non-formation of several derivative compounds expected on the basis of that formula. Turner was correct and, together with R. J. W. Le Fèvre, conclusively disproved the Kaufler formula during the 1920s.

From 1916 to 1919 Turner was engaged in work on organo-arsenic compounds as chemical warfare agents under W. J. Pope at Cambridge. The interest he acquired there in the organic chemistry of arsenic was sustained during 1919–20, when he lectured in organic chemistry at the University of Sydney. In collaboration with G. J. Burrows he was able to demonstrate optical activity in a quaternary arsonium salt, and developed an arsenic analogue of indole which an astute journal editor renamed arsinole from a rather more vulgar original. While at Sydney, Turner married, in 1921, Beryl Osborne, daughter of Reginald Wyndham of New South Wales. They had a daughter, Patricia Wyndham (b. 1921).

In 1921 Turner returned to England and worked at the

Royal Arsenal, Woolwich, until 1923, when he was appointed senior lecturer at East London College. In 1928 he became reader at Bedford College in Regent's Park, where he spent the rest of his academic career. The title of professor was conferred upon him in 1944, and in 1946, on the retirement of J. F. Spencer, he became head of the chemistry department. On his retirement in 1960 he was made professor emeritus, and continued to work in the organic chemical field as research director of Biorex Laboratories for several years.

Turner's contributions to modern organic chemistry were inspired largely by his lifelong interests in stereochemistry and biaryls. With Le Fèvre he contributed greatly to the establishment of the correct 'linear' structure of the biaryl system, and explained the occurrence of optical isomerism in biphenyl derivatives substituted in 2-, 2′-, 6-, and 6′-positions as being due to restricted rotation about the internuclear bond. In the course of this work many fundamental stereochemical concepts (such as that of 'asymmetric transformation') were established.

Turner was elected in 1939 to the fellowship of the Royal Society. He was also a fellow of the Royal Institute of Chemistry, and served on the council of the Chemical Society. He was a fellow of Queen Mary College, a freeman of the City of London, and a liveryman of the Coopers' Company. He gave distinguished service on many Bedford College and University of London bodies, and was for many years assistant editor of *British Chemical Abstracts*. Together with Margaret M. Harris he wrote a classic textbook, *Organic Chemistry*, 1952.

Turner was essentially an experimentalist, and the practice of organic chemistry was his abiding interest in life. However, he still took an intense personal interest in all his assistants and collaborators. He was an amusing raconteur and mimic with a sometimes disconcerting knack of puncturing the pompous. Turner greatly enjoyed his own pleasant garden, as well as the wider countryside; he was a particularly enthusiastic motorist. He died at his home, Ridge End, 30 The Ridgeway, Tonbridge, on 8 September 1966, survived by his wife and daughter.

G. H. WILLIAMS, *rev.*

Sources C. Ingold, *Memoirs FRS*, 14 (1968), 449–67 · D. M. Hall, 'Eustace Ebenezer Turner, 1893–1966', *Chemistry in Britain*, 3 (1967), 74–5 · M. M. Harris, *Chemistry and Industry* (19 Nov 1966) · personal knowledge (1981)
Likenesses Stoneman, photograph, *c*.1955, RS
Wealth at death £6372: probate, 13 April 1967, *CGPLA Eng. & Wales*

Turner, Dame Eva (1892–1990), singer, was born on 10 March 1892 in Oldham, Lancashire, the elder child and only daughter of Charles Turner, chief engineer of a cotton mill, and his wife, Elizabeth Park. She was educated at Werneth council school, Oldham, until she was ten, when her father moved to Bristol to take up an appointment as manager of another mill in the south-west of England. There she heard her first opera, performed by the Royal Carl Rosa Opera Company, and so struck was she by this that she was determined to become a singer herself. Her

Dame Eva Turner (1892–1990), by Maurice Seymour, 1947 [as Turandot]

parents were musical and gave her every encouragement, sending her for lessons to Daniel Rootham, who taught Clara Butt. Her studies were continued at the Royal Academy of Music in London from 1911 to 1915, during which time she was briefly betrothed. In 1915 she joined the chorus of the Royal Carl Rosa Opera Company: she entered her new life with enthusiasm and with the serious determination and commitment that were to characterize her life. When not singing in the chorus she never lost an opportunity to observe other performers from the wings, studying the action and learning the soprano repertory. Anxious for progress, she badgered the management to find her roles and she soon made her solo début as the page in *Tannhäuser*.

But Turner was still not satisfied, and on the advice of the company's principal tenor she began to work with an Australian singer, Richard Broad, who had recently joined the management of the Carl Rosa. He had sung as a bass under Hans Richter at Covent Garden, but it was as an authority on voice production that he was better known. This proved to be a most successful relationship, and Broad continued as her coach, adviser, and friend until his death some twenty-five years later.

The small parts became larger and by 1920 Eva Turner was assuming dramatic roles as her voice increased in power and weight. In that year the company gave a four-week season at Covent Garden, in which she sang Santuzza (*Cavalleria rusticana*), Musetta (*La Bohème*), Leonora (*Il trovatore*), Butterfly (*Madama Butterfly*), Antonia (*The Tales of Hoffmann*), and Venus (*Tannhäuser*). The *Times* critic described her Leonora as promising. Another Covent Garden season followed a provincial tour in 1921. *Tosca* and *Lohengrin* were two operas added to her repertory that year. In 1922 she appeared as Eva in *The Mastersingers* with the Carl Rosa at Covent Garden, and won a favourable review from *The Times*.

In 1924 the Carl Rosa was at the Scala Theatre, London, for a four-week season, which was to be a turning point in Turner's career. Among other roles she sang Butterfly on 3 June, a performance with which *The Times* did not find entire favour but which so impressed Ettore Panizza, Arturo Toscanini's assistant at La Scala, Milan, that he asked her to sing to the maestro. She auditioned successfully and was offered Freia and Sieglinde in the 1924/5 La Scala season. Her characteristic loyalty persuaded her to tell La Scala that she was not free to accept because of her Carl Rosa contract. However, she was released from that and she spent the intervening period learning Italian and her roles in that language in preparation for her début, as Freia in *Das Rheingold*, conducted by Vittorio Gui.

Thus began the most important part of Turner's career and a love affair with Italy, one of the outcomes of which was the Italianate colouring, with strongly enunciated consonants, that she applied to her speaking voice. She was then to sing in many Italian cities, including Brescia, where she first sang Turandot with conspicuous success. This became the role with which she was most identified, though from all accounts her portrayal of Aida was equally outstanding. She built and settled in a villa on Lake Lugano.

By now Eva Turner's international career was developing rapidly, with appearances in Europe and in North and South America. She returned to Covent Garden in 1928 in a season managed by the Covent Garden Syndicate, and scored a major triumph with the press and public with Turandot. Nobody was prepared for such a magnificent performance. Nothing could then hold her back, and with her glorious voice she took a leading place in the seasons at Covent Garden and abroad until the outbreak of war in 1939. Small of stature, Eva Turner had a vocal command that was astonishing, with a voice of extraordinary sumptuousness and steadiness that could project through the loudest orchestral sound without any loss of quality. She surmounted all the technical challenges of the German and Italian repertoire and left her audiences spellbound. Turner's colossal success did much to encourage British opera singers, who at that time were probably more noted for dependability than brilliance and rarely given chances to prove anything else. An English name was a handicap and Eva Turner was urged to change hers. Proud of her Lancastrian roots, she refused.

Undoubtedly the war deprived Turner of the final climax to her career, including the conquering of audiences at the Metropolitan in New York. After a performance of Turandot in Brescia in 1940 she returned to England, where she spent the war singing in concerts for the armed forces and the radio, and in the Proms. A staunch patriot, this was what she believed she needed to do and she declined invitations to work in America.

In the 1947 and the 1948/9 seasons at Covent Garden Turner joined the newly formed company for Turandot, in which once again she astonished and thrilled the public and press. Then, in 1949, she accepted an invitation to teach at the University of Oklahoma for one year, and stayed for ten. After that she returned to London to teach at the Royal Academy of Music. Teaching occupied her for several more years and she passed on to many singers, established and young alike, her wealth of experience, with her inimitable generosity but also with a ferocious expectation of hard work and high standards in return. For her it was serious work that produced the results, however talented the individual. President of the Wagner Society from 1971 to 1985, she was appointed DBE in 1962. She was FRAM (1928), FRCM (1974), an honorary citizen of the state of Oklahoma (1982), and a first freeman of Oldham (1982). She was awarded honorary DMus degrees from Manchester (1979) and Oxford (1984) and became an honorary fellow of St Hilda's College, Oxford (1984).

Well into her nineties and still immaculately groomed and handsome, Turner maintained her enthusiasm and capacity for work, serving on committees and lecturing endlessly to music clubs and societies. She was constantly to be seen at opera performances and concerts, travelling and coaching with an eagerness and display of energy that left many breathless. She never married, probably because she believed she could not find the time for the kind of relationship that marriage demanded. She led an intensely busy life, ably assisted by Ann Ridyard, her companion and secretary for thirty-five years, whose descent into senile dementia caused Eva Turner's last years to be burdensome. Eva Turner died on 16 June 1990 in the Devonshire Hospital, Marylebone, London. A memorial service was held in Westminster Abbey on 5 February 1991.

JOHN TOOLEY, rev.

Sources *Record Collector*, 11/2 (Feb–March 1957) · J. Steane, *The grand tradition* (1974) · H. Rosenthal, Royal Opera House programme note for concert celebrating Eva Turner's ninetieth birthday, 14 March 1982 · personal knowledge (1996) · private information (1996) · *The Independent* (18 June 1990) · *The Times* (18 June 1990) · *The Times* (5 Feb 1991) · *CGPLA Eng. & Wales* (1991)

Likenesses photograph, 1939, Hult. Arch. · F. Mann, photograph, 1943, Hult. Arch. · M. Seymour, photograph, 1947, Royal Opera House, London [see illus.] · photograph, repro. in *The Independent* · photograph, repro. in *The Times* (18 June 1990)

Wealth at death £595,136: probate, 1 Feb 1991, *CGPLA Eng. & Wales*

Turner, Dame Evelyn Marguerite [Margot] (1910–1993), military nurse, was born on 10 May 1910 in Finchley, Middlesex, the only daughter and one of four children of Thomas Frederick Turner, an employee in a solicitor's office, and his wife, Molly Cecilia (née Bryan). Her father died when she was thirteen, and her mother remarried; nevertheless Turner enjoyed a happy childhood. She was educated at Finchley county school and trained as a nurse at St Bartholomew's Hospital, London, from 1931 to 1935. In 1937 she joined Queen Alexandra's Imperial Military Nursing Service, which in 1949 became Queen Alexandra's Royal Army Nursing Corps (QARANC). After training in the United Kingdom she was posted to India, then back to Europe, and after war broke out in 1939 to Malaya, where she served as a theatre sister. When the Japanese invaded Malaya in December 1941, with air and naval superiority, she was moved down the peninsula, eventually working in Singapore under bombardment.

When the fall of Singapore was seen to be inevitable, Turner, with British and Australian nurses and some civilian women and their children, was ordered to be evacuated on a crowded ship. Her ship was ambushed and sunk by Japanese warships and aircraft off Sumatra, and as the survivors struggled in the water they were machine-gunned by the aircraft. However, some of the survivors struggled ashore to a small, uninhabited island, from which they were picked up three days later by another ship full of women and children. This ship was then sunk by a Japanese warship, but Turner swam to a raft onto which she managed to rescue sixteen others, of whom six were children. With no water or shelter from the burning sun all the survivors except Turner died during the next three days, some going mad first. On the third night it rained for a short time and she managed to collect a few drops; she also ate some seaweed. On the fourth day she was picked up by a Japanese cruiser. By this time her eyes were so sunken and her skin burnt so black by the sun that the Japanese were not at first able to tell what nationality she was. Once this was established she was interned in a women's prison camp on Bangka Island, off Sumatra. Her height, fair skin, and bearing made her an object of special dislike to the Japanese. On one roll-call (tenko), she was hit in the face by a blow which knocked out a tooth, but worse was in store when the Japanese secret police, the dreaded Kempei Tai, arrived and removed her, with three others, for special investigation into alleged spying activities. It is extremely unlikely that the Kempei believed their wild accusations, although they were always on the lookout for concealed radios, the possessors of which, if found, would suffer an appalling fate, but they probably saw her as a natural leader who might make the other captives less docile. She was taken to Palembang and incarcerated in a small cell with local criminals. Although these included murderers, thieves, and perpetrators of horrible crimes, and were themselves thinned out by daily executions, they were extremely kind to her and made her six months in the squalid surroundings slightly more endurable. Eventually she was transferred to spend the rest of her three and a half years' captivity in a more normal camp, where she had to perform manual labour, including digging graves for the steady stream of dying inmates. By the time release came, half of her fellow inmates had died of diseases such as dysentery, or of starvation.

Subsequently Turner was very reluctant to talk about her experiences and when, in 1968, she learned that Thames Television was planning to make her the subject of a *This Is Your Life* programme, she requested the company firmly not to do so. However, many of her friends and colleagues considered that the story of her life might prove an inspiration to others, and persuaded Eamonn Andrews to revive the project. It was sprung upon her in 1978 and produced remarkable dramatic moments, in which she showed composure and humour, when she was confronted with fellow prisoners and others whom she had not seen since 1945. The interview was seen by a woman television producer who decided that the experiences of women in Japanese prisoner-of-war camps were scarcely known, and devised the series *Tenko*, in which their sufferings and fortitude were clearly shown. The series proved enormously popular and ran from 1981 to 1984.

After her release and recovery Turner returned to nursing and served in Hong Kong, Bermuda, Germany, Malta, Cyprus, Libya, Egypt, and Eritrea, in the course of which she rose steadily in the corps. From 1964 to 1968 she was matron-in-chief and director of army nursing services. She had been made MBE in 1946 and awarded the Royal Red Cross in 1956, and was appointed DBE in 1965. She was colonel commandant of QARANC from 1969 to 1974, during which time she fostered close links with the QARANC association and was an active supporter of the museum.

Turner, a tall, good-looking woman, was a natural leader who would have made her mark in any profession. She was kind, canny, and courageous, and exercised authority with a ready smile. Undoubtedly she inspired many of her fellow prisoners with a will to live when all they hoped for was a quick end to their suffering. In younger days she had been an excellent swimmer, golfer, and tennis player. Although extremely attractive to men, she never married. She died in Brighton on 24 September 1993, and was survived by one brother. A memorial service was held in the royal garrison church of All Saints, Aldershot, on 8 December 1993.   PHILIP WARNER

Sources *WWW*, 1991–5 · QARANC records, QARANC Museum, Keogh Barracks, Aldershot · *The Times* (2 Oct 1993) · *The Independent* (12 Oct 1993) · J. Smyth, *Will to live: the story of Dame Margot Turner* (1970) · Burke, *Peerage*
Archives FILM BFI NFTVA, *This is your life*, BBC, 1978
Likenesses photograph, repro. in *The Times* · photograph, repro. in *The Independent*

Turner, Francis (1637–1700), bishop of Ely, nonjuror, and Jacobite conspirator, was born on 23 August 1637, the eldest son of Thomas *Turner (*bap.* 1592, *d.* 1672), chaplain to Charles I and dean of Canterbury, and his wife, Margaret (1607/8–1692), daughter of Charles's secretary of state, Sir Francis *Windebank. Thomas *Turner, president of Corpus Christi College, Oxford, and William Turner, archdeacon of Durham, were younger brothers.

Education and early career During the civil war and interregnum the family suffered losses and disruptions for royalism and Anglicanism. Turner was elected scholar of Winchester College in 1650 as of Hurst, Wiltshire. At Winchester he befriended his future colleague Thomas Ken. He proceeded to New College, Oxford, where he was admitted probationer fellow on 7 November 1655, and graduated BA on 14 April 1659 and MA on 14 January 1663. He had taken the engagement, expressing his loyalty to

Francis Turner (1637–1700), by unknown artist, c.1670

the Commonwealth. None the less, following the Restoration Turner accepted a court post as a chaplain to Anne, duchess of York, wife of the future James II. On 30 December 1664 he became rector of Therfield, Hertfordshire, succeeding John Barwick. On 17 February 1665 he was incorporated at nearby Cambridge, and on 8 May 1666 he was admitted fellow-commoner in St John's College, Cambridge, attracted by the prospect of patronage from the master, Peter Gunning. He compounded BD and DD at Oxford on 6 July 1669. That 7 December he received the prebend of Sneating in St Paul's Cathedral, of which William Sancroft was then dean. On 11 April 1670 he succeeded Gunning as master of St John's College, Cambridge. Under Turner the college's third court was completed in 1671. Benefactions at St John's and rebuilding the chancel at Therfield, where he lived alternately with St John's, cost him £1000. This was one reason he gave his bachelor patrons when he was married on 18 October 1676, at Ely House Chapel, London, by Gunning, now bishop of Ely, to Anna (1651/2–1678), daughter of Walter Horton of Catton, Derbyshire. She had lived at court and was studious. She died in childbirth at Therfield on 28 January 1678. Their daughter, Margaret, survived.

In 1676 Turner published, probably at Gunning's instance, some clumsily sarcastic *Animadversions* on Bishop Herbert Croft's pamphlet *The Naked Truth*, which had opposed the enforcement of uniformity on protestants. Turner was lampooned for it by Andrew Marvell in *Mr Smirke, or, The Divine in Mode*, as 'this close youth who treads always upon the hem of Ecclesiastical Preferment … It is not every man that is qualified to sustain the Dignity of the Churches Jester' (Marvell, 3–4). In 1678 Turner was university vice-chancellor.

Ally of James In late 1679 came the turning point in Turner's career. His courtier's zeal was magnified by the Popish Plot, and James, duke of York, exiled to Scotland, selected him to be chaplain to the Anglicans in his household. He resigned his mastership that Christmas, once a suitable successor was ready.

James upheld the established episcopal church during his government of Scotland, which appeared to justify tory trust in his reliability. Turner acted as an intermediary between James and the English hierarchy, and between them and the Scottish hierarchy—in, for instance, preventing a proposed appeal to James for toleration from Scottish Catholics and presbyterians. After Charles II in 1681 established a commission for ecclesiastical promotions to recommend the ablest and reject scandalous clerics, which was dominated in practice by James's brothers-in-law Henry Hyde, second earl of Clarendon, and Laurence Hyde, first earl of Rochester, and William Sancroft, archbishop of Canterbury, Turner became an intermediary also between James and the commission—and one of its main beneficiaries. On 20 July 1683, as had been planned since 1681, he was installed as dean of Windsor, also becoming rector of Great Haseley, Oxfordshire, though he had to resign Therfield. On 11 November 1683 he was consecrated bishop of Rochester. He retained the deanery, needed to subsidize the impoverished see of Rochester, and was also made lord almoner, despite his protests that such rapid preferment would provoke envy. Finally, on 21 July 1684 (confirmed on 23 August) he was translated to Ely, again in succession to Gunning, whose literary executor he was. R. A. Beddard concludes that Sancroft was advancing him not only as the church's agent at court, using the political skills and *savoir-faire* which Sancroft himself lacked, but as his own eventual successor at Canterbury. James also, still committed to the Anglican alliance, was believed to have the same intentions. Turner preached the sermon at James's coronation on 23 April 1685, and in July he and Ken vainly tried to make James Scott, duke of Monmouth, eldest illegitimate son of Charles II, repent his rebellion.

The warm relationship between Turner and his king cooled as James's religious policy took shape. On 5 November 1685 Turner preached an anti-Catholic sermon before James. By January 1686 rumour was bracketing him with James's *bête noire*, Henry Compton, bishop of London. Catholics began to call him a seditious preacher. However, James's direct attacks on the Church of England did not at first involve him. When James barred Sancroft from court Turner, who had recently gone there mainly in Sancroft's company, had his remaining links with the court further reduced.

The crises of 1688–1689 In May 1688 James confronted the Anglican clergy with the order to read the declaration of indulgence from their pulpits, granting freedom of worship to Catholics and dissenters, thereby undermining the established church and discrediting Anglican churchmen by presenting them as subservient to the king's will. Turner was a leading figure in organizing the consultations which established the opposition of the London parochial clergy to the declaration, without which the bishops would not have risked petitioning. He was one of the seven bishops who signed the petition, requesting that they should not be required to distribute or proclaim the declaration. He was also one of the six bishops who delivered the petition to James. The king looked at Turner when he told the bishops: 'Here are some I did not expect to see on such an occasion' (*Works of Symon Patrick*, 9.511–12). When James decided to prosecute, Turner obtained from lawyers arguments justifying their refusal to give recognizances, which led to their brief imprisonment in the Tower. This was a propaganda triumph for them, but permanently damaged James, as Turner afterwards recalled with regret. George Legge, first Baron Dartmouth, an old friend from James's household, made a special appeal to Turner to submit just before the bishops' trial, unsuccessfully. As the country erupted in rejoicing at the acquittal, he claimed, his heart bled for his master. Yet he told well-wishers privately: 'Wait patiently a while, and we shall all be delivered' (ibid., 514). Arthur Maynwaring's 1713 biography of John Churchill, duke of Marlborough, claimed that Churchill, formerly one of Turner's flock in James's household, consulted him over his conflicting obligations. Turner told him that 'to side with those that attempted to destroy our Civil and Religious Rights, was to be in a down-right Rebellion against God', and that even neutrality towards 'such as come to the help of the Lord against the Mighty' would incur a curse (Maynwaring, 22–3). This confirmed Churchill's intention to desert with the army to William, who, both men naïvely believed, would act altruistically and leave James as at least king in name.

When the first realization of William's coming invasion made James at length offer reconciliation to the Church of England, Turner was the first bishop whom he consulted, on 26 September. Turner's heart and head were necessarily at odds. He expressed joy extravagantly at this favour, 'having so long time (for I thought four months very long) languished under his Maj[es]ty's displeasure' (memoir, BL, Add. MS 32096, fol. 331). He hoped that the bishops could use their new popularity to help the king, but knew that rousing public suspicions could immediately lose them their advantage. He therefore offended James again by raising constant detailed objections to his offers. When James issued a general pardon Turner imagined that the wording might covertly except the clergy. He signed the bishops' advice of 3 October urging the reversal of most of James's policies. He apparently did not modify his advice to Churchill. In November Turner probably drafted a tract justifying the evasion by Sancroft and other bishops of James's request that they publish their abhorrence of William's proposed invasion. In mid-November, after William had landed, he with other bishops petitioned James for a free parliament. James consented, but shocked Turner by recalling how Richard II's last parliament treated him.

Turner became more active in early December. James seemed likely to flee leaving no central authority. Turner and the earl of Rochester prepared letters summoning the peers to the Guildhall, and a declaration for recalling James with honour and safety. This would give them a basis for more authoritative negotiations with William, and a restored James would owe too much to his saviours to defy their advice. Following James's flight on 10–11 December Turner and Rochester assembled the provisional government of twenty-nine peers at the Guildhall. James's enemies among the peers cut the draft declaration's provisions in the king's favour; but the Guildhall declaration was still lukewarm enough towards William to exasperate the prince when Turner and others presented it. On 17 December Turner headed a group of bishops who discussed with the recaptured James the major concessions he would have to grant; he informed a Williamite that James would even make William regent for life. After James's flight to Rochester, Turner sent the historian Dr Robert Brady to follow him and to urge him not to leave for France, and later demanded an inquiry into whether he had not been forced away.

In the 1689 convention that met to settle the constitution following James's flight Turner was one of the strongest opponents of the campaign for William's assumption of the throne. Though privately hostile, he supported a regency for life as the most they could then obtain. He argued on 5 February 1689 that James II could not rule England as he was a Roman Catholic, a status he compared to 'sickness, lunacy, doating old age, or an incurable disease rendering the party unfit for human society, as leprosy, or the like' (Cobbett, *Parl. hist.*, 5, 1688–1702, 73), but that the succession still rightly belonged to him: he had not renounced that right, as his departing the country did not amount to an abdication. Defeated, Turner last attended the Lords on 28 February; observing the promise in the seven bishops' petition, he voted for the new Toleration Bill.

Deprivation Turner would not take the oaths to William and Mary and was suspended with other nonjuring bishops on 1 August 1689. A commission of bishops Compton of London and Turner's old friend William Lloyd of St Asaph administered his diocese. Yet he was extremely reluctant to see a schism develop, and would apparently have endorsed a settlement where the oaths were put to new clerics but not established ones, who could pray for the monarchs without naming them. However, he, Sancroft, and William Lloyd, bishop of Norwich, replied to advances in December 1689 that they would make no concessions. In particular Turner opposed a government plan to spare the most esteemed nonjurors in return for Anglican support for comprehension, 'to barter & breake the Church to save a few Churchmen' (Bodl. Oxf., Rawl. MS letters 98, fol. 93v). On 1 February 1690 the nonjuring bishops were formally deprived, but were left in physical possession of their palaces. Turner continued to conduct services in Ely House Chapel, London, until twice warned to desist. Sancroft's conduct throughout the proceedings restored Turner's admiration and he urged the young Jonathan Swift to write an ode praising the archbishop.

When French invasion threatened in June 1690, the nonjuring bishops' enemies circulated a forged address from them to Louis XIV and a forged liturgy praying for the invaders' success. Turner drafted a proposed defence of the bishops, and signed the shorter *Vindication* published in July, in which they denied, on the whole truthfully, any involvement in Jacobite plotting. It was received with widespread scepticism. Turner's own conduct that winter would make this seem justified.

Turner helped Richard Graham, Viscount Preston, James's secretary of state, and Clarendon revise a conciliatory declaration which the latter had drafted for James to issue, recognizing the Anglican character of English society, as part of a major plot for his restoration. He also wrote two letters for Preston to carry to James and his queen, 'Mr and Mrs Redding', with assurances of loyalty and Jacobite zeal on behalf of himself, Sancroft, and the four other deprived bishops, although he admitted to Preston that he had consulted only Sancroft.

In hiding Following Preston's arrest, with his letters and documents intact, while attempting to cross to France on new year's day 1691, the government sought Turner too. On 10 January it was reported that he had absconded from his home in Putney. On 20 January a messenger was within an hour of catching him near Newbury—the last public sighting of him for nearly six years. He wrote that he was not staying because he would not submit to government and feared an unfair trial. On 5 February a proclamation was issued for his arrest. It was generally assumed that Turner had fled to St Germain. In reality the public exposure of the plotters' schemes had discredited them there, and Turner would not have risked forfeiture by going to St Germain without strong reasons for believing in the likelihood of James's restoration; he had restrained Jeremy Collier from doing so. He fled heavily disguised; his private letters (intended to deceive if intercepted) suggest that he headed for Germany, but halted in the Netherlands. He apparently returned to England before August 1691.

Turner's letter of 19 January 1691 to Sancroft expresses regret for having brought trouble on his fellow suspended bishops through Preston's failure to destroy the letters, but no remorse for having misrepresented them. He suggested that they could declare their innocence, but recalled discouragingly how their last *Vindication* had been received. This memory, and their reluctance to prejudice Turner's trial, if he should be captured, by recognizing the letter as genuine, prevented the nonjuring bishops from publishing an abhorrence. Their refusal to distance themselves ensured that they were physically ejected in May, and new bishops named. The former court circle with whom Turner had conspired had been shattered, and following Sancroft's retirement it was William Lloyd of Norwich, not Turner, who became the leading nonjuring bishop and an active Jacobite plotter.

Sancroft heard that Turner had ventured to London in early 1692. Sometimes his brother Thomas Turner hid him at Oxford, but otherwise his concealment in England, while spreading rumours that he was overseas, was for years too good: his own closest allies often could not find him. The one major action in which he was involved

throughout was the consecration of nonjuring suffragan bishops. In 1691 he recalled that an interregnum precedent existed, and obtained copies of documents from St John's College, Cambridge, and a testimony by Clarendon, making it possible to proceed. He maintained pressure on the reluctant George Hickes to cross to St Germain to obtain permission from James II for the appointment of the bishops, and was one of the three deprived bishops who on 24 February 1694 consecrated Hickes and Thomas Wagstaffe at Southgate, Middlesex.

Turner himself was never at St Germain; but the testimony of false witnesses and incompetent spies probably convinced the government, like the public, that he had crossed several times. This, rather than his real actions, would probably have been the basis for a trial or harassment had he reappeared. In August 1694 various Jacobites urged James to summon Turner, who could support himself financially, to live at St Germain. However, his presence would only have emphasized Louis XIV's prohibition on all protestant services. In May 1695, pardoned his actual crimes under the general Act of Grace, Turner applied to William to be free from harassment if he emerged from hiding, and in May 1696, after the constant searches and arrests in the wake of the assassination plot, for a pass to some foreign country, which the king agreed to grant. In December 1696 messengers hunting the Jacobite pamphleteer Samuel Grascome finally arrested Turner under the alias Harris. He was freed on condition of leaving the country, but was rearrested late that month. He apparently did not have to leave England, and the treaty of Ryswick in 1697 ended his problems.

Death On 4 June 1698 Turner was a pallbearer at the funeral of his fellow deprived bishop Thomas White at St Gregory by Paul's, London, having been forbidden by the turncoat dean, William Sherlock, from conducting the service. He lived at Leytonstone and then at Putney. After a painful illness Turner died at London on 2 November 1700. He was buried on 5 November in the chancel at Therfield beside his wife. His intestacy gave all his effects to his daughter, Margaret (1678–1724), wife of Richard Goulston of Widdihill, Hertfordshire, though St John's College, whose strongly Jacobite tone was sometimes attributed to his selections when master, had hoped for further benefactions.

Turner was tall and long-faced and, until driven to disguise, wore his own long black hair; his great Roman nose, Sancroft feared, was unmistakable.

Turner's promotion reflected the special political needs of the Restoration church and court: the revolution made him obsolete. He was an old style supporter of church hierarchy, seeing both popery and presbyterianism as undermining bishops' rights, and believing that, as he wrote in his wife's epitaph, priests should lead. He was probably, as Bishop Burnet claimed, no deep scholar, but his abilities were not done justice by the items he published. He researched and wrote a life of Nicholas Ferrar of Little Gidding, marking the path of retired contemplation which he had not taken. Many other works, including memoirs on the revolution, survive only in fragments, some copied by his former chaplain George Harbin, who refused the oaths with him and became a major nonjuring historical scholar. PAUL HOPKINS

Sources A. Strickland, *The lives of the seven bishops committed to the Tower in 1688* (1866) · J. H. Overton, *The nonjurors: their lives, principles, and writings* (1902) · Turner correspondence, Bodl. Oxf., MS Rawl. letters 98–99 · Sancroft papers, Bodl. Oxf., MSS Tanner · R. A. Beddard, 'The loyalist opposition in the interregnum: a letter of Dr Francis Turner, bishop of Ely, on the revolution of 1688', *BIHR*, 40 (1967), 101–9 · R. Beddard, ed., *A kingdom without a king: the journal of the provisional government in the revolution of 1688* (1988) · R. A. Beddard, 'The commission for ecclesiastical promotions, 1681–4: an instrument of tory reaction', *HJ*, 10 (1967), 11–40 · R. A. Beddard, 'The Guildhall declaration of 11 December 1688 and the counter-revolution of the loyalists', *HJ*, 11 (1968), 403–20 · *The correspondence of Henry Hyde, earl of Clarendon, and of his brother Laurence Hyde, earl of Rochester*, ed. S. W. Singer, 2 vols. (1828) · excerpts from Turner's memoirs, BL, Add. MS 32096, fols. 301–4 · T. Baker, *History of the college of St John the Evangelist, Cambridge*, ed. J. E. B. Mayor, 2 vols. (1869) · *State trials*, vol. 12 · R. A. Beddard, ed., *The revolutions of 1688: the Andrew Browning lectures, 1988* (1991) · [A. Maynwaring], *The lives of the two illustrious generals: John, duke of Marlborough, and Francis Eugene, prince of Savoy* (1713) · U. Glas. L., Hunterian MS 73 · *The works of Symon Patrick, D.D., sometime bishop of Ely*, ed. A. Taylor, 9 vols. (1858), vol. 9 · A. Marvell, *Mr Smirke, or, The divine in mode … together with a short historical essay concerning general councils, creeds, and impositions, in matters of religion* (1676) · Bishop Lloyd of Norwich papers, LPL, MSS 3894–3900 · E. H. Plumptre, *The life of Thomas Ken*, 2nd edn (1890) · J. Macpherson, ed., *Original papers, containing the secret history of Great Britain*, vols. (1775) · *Report on the manuscripts of Allan George Finch*, 5 vols., HMC, 71 (1913–2003), vol. 3 · *Report on the manuscripts of the marquis of Downshire*, 6 vols. in 7, HMC, 75 (1924–95), vol. 1 · *Bishop Burnet's History of his own time: with the suppressed passages of the first volume*, ed. M. J. Routh, 6 vols. (1823) · *A hue and cry after the abdicated B— of E—* (1691) · *The life and times of Anthony Wood*, ed. A. Clark, 5 vols., OHS, 19, 21, 26, 30, 40 (1891–1900) · J. E. Cussons, *History of Hertfordshire*, 3 vols. (1870–81); facs. repr. (1972) · *DNB* · G. H. Jones, *Convergent forces: immediate causes of the revolution of 1688 in England* (1990) · Cobbett, *Parl. hist.*, 5.72–74 · Foster, *Alum. Oxon.* · J. L. Chester and J. Foster, eds., *London marriage licences, 1521–1869* (1887)
Archives Bodl. Oxf., corresp. and papers, MS Rawl., letters 98–99 | Bodl. Oxf., Tanner MSS, corresp.
Likenesses oils, *c*.1670, St John Cam. [*see illus.*] · attrib M. Beale, oils, *c*.1683–1688, NPG · G. Bower, silver medal, 1688, NPG · R. White, line engraving, pubd 1689 (after unknown artist), NPG · W. Vincent, mezzotint, repro. in R. Sharp, *The engraved record of the Jacobite movement* (1996), no. 654 · group portrait, oils (*The seven bishops committed to the Tower in 1688*), NPG; on display at Beningbrough Hall and Gardens, Yorkshire · mezzotint (after P. Schenck), NPG · oil paintings, repro. in T. B. Macaulay, *The history of England*, ed. C. H. Firth, 6 vols. (1913–15), vol. 1, p. 471; vol. 2, p. 1005 · oils, CCC Cam.
Wealth at death wealthy, incl. landed estate, but died intestate leaving no record

Turner, George (*d.* 1610), physician, was born in Suffolk. He may have been the George Turner who entered St John's College, Cambridge, as a sizar in November 1569, became a Beresford scholar there on 9 November 1570, and graduated BA in 1573, and MA in 1576. He took the degree of MD at the University of Venice. Alternatively he may have been the George Turner of Balliol College, Oxford, who took his BA on 27 March 1572 and was elected a probationer fellow of Balliol on 29 November 1572. This Turner was abroad in the company of a physician in mid-1583 and was practising in Fetter Lane, London in 1602.

Turner became a candidate at the College of Physicians of London on 4 September 1584, was elected a fellow on 29 February 1588, and was censor in 1591, 1592, 1597, 1606, and 1607. He was a friend of Simon Forman, and seems himself to have dabbled in alchemy (see MS Ashmole 174, fols. 370, 1477, iv. 24, 1491, fol. 61 *b*). He attained considerable practice, and Queen Elizabeth favoured him, so that when his theological opinions as a Roman Catholic were in 1602 urged against his election as an elect in the college, Sir John Stanhope and Robert Cecil wrote a letter saying that his appointment would be pleasing to the queen since there was no objection to him but his 'backwardness in religion, in which he is in no way tainted for malice or practice against the state' (Munk, *Roll*). He was chosen an elect the day after this letter, 12 August 1602. He was appointed treasurer in 1609. His wife, Anne *Turner, *née* Norton (1576–1615), was involved in the Overbury poisoning plot. Turner died on 1 March 1610. In his will he left bequests to his wife, his daughters Barbara, Mary, and Katherine, and his sons Henry, John, and Thomas.

NORMAN MOORE, *rev.* ROGER HUTCHINS

Sources Cooper, *Ath. Cantab.*, 2.526–7 · Munk, *Roll*, 1.89–90 · A. Somerset, *Unnatural murder: poison in the court of James I*, pbk edn (1998) · Foster, *Alum. Oxon.* · private information (2004) [Dr John Jones, Balliol Oxf.] · Bodl. Oxf., MSS Ashmole 174, fols. 370, 1477, lv.24, 1491, fol. 61b · annals, RCP Lond. · will, 1610, PRO, PROB 11/115, sig. 37
Wealth at death number of bequests; owned property in Bedfordshire: will, PRO, PROB 11/115, sig. 37

Turner, Sir George (1851–1916), politician in Australia, was born in Melbourne, Australia, on 8 August 1851, the only child of English parents Alfred Turner, a cabinet-maker, and his wife, Ruth Dick. He was educated at the National Model School, Melbourne, but left at the age of fourteen to work in the office of John Edwards, a solicitor. On 10 August 1872 he married 21-year-old Rosa, the daughter of John Morgan, a potter from Devon; they had a son and a daughter. Turner matriculated in 1874, took the articled clerk's course, and was admitted to practice in 1881, when he went into partnership with Samuel Lyons to form the legal firm of Lyons and Turner. He was involved in various lodges and friendly societies, notably the Australian Natives' Association, an organization of people born in Australia which became politically very important in this period.

Turner was an elected member of the St Kilda local government council (1886–1900), and was mayor in 1897. In 1889 he entered the legislative assembly of the Victorian parliament as member for St Kilda, having campaigned as a Liberal Protectionist. In what were politically unstable times he served as minister for customs and commissioner for trade in the Munro government (1890), posts he retained in the Shiels government (1892). With the defeat of the Shiels government by James Patterson in 1893, Turner reluctantly became leader of the opposition Liberal Party when the leading Liberal, Alfred Deakin, a trusted colleague of Turner, refused the position. On the defeat of the government in September 1894, at a time of severe economic depression, Turner became the first Australian-born premier of Victoria. This dour, steady plodder, who lacked the oratorical skills of some of his contemporaries, was an unlikely leader. However, to a public shocked by the boom and the consequent depression, his down-to-earth, businesslike approach, retrenching and cutting expenditure, was appealing. Beatrice Webb, on meeting Turner in 1898, described him in her diary as 'a modest unassuming businessman, a solicitor by profession, who has gained the approbation of the majority of the people and of the House by his cautious administration, his plain business ways and his indomitable industry' (Webb and Webb, 66). Mindful of public opinion, Turner was pragmatic in gaining political support and tenacious in resolving issues, and was beholden to Deakin and to David Syme, the proprietor of *The Age* newspaper. He gained the respect and confidence of the state and was re-elected in 1897. While restoration of fiscal confidence was his main contribution, during his premiership some notable legislation was passed, including, in 1896, the Factories and Shops Act, which reduced 'sweated labour', and savings bank legislation, and, three years later, the abolition of plural voting. While by temperament cautious, as the Melbourne *Age* wrote in its obituary (14 August 1916), 'his liberalism led him often to the left wing of his party', and his willingness to accommodate Labor Party members and his support for old-age pensions are indicative of this.

In June 1897 Turner went with other colonial premiers to Britain for Queen Victoria's diamond jubilee celebration, and was appointed privy councillor and KCMG and received an honorary LLD from both Oxford and Cambridge universities. He also became an important figure in the federation movement, attending the federal councils of 1895 and 1897. In 1898 he was elected (topping the poll) to represent Victoria in the national convention to frame a federal constitution, and the following year he became president of the council. He worked with Deakin, Isaacs, and Peacock and leaders from other states in the difficult and tortuous negotiations leading to federation, and was often an important 'solvent' and behind-the-scenes negotiator. His contribution to the federal movement has often been underestimated, and, as Deakin wrote in his *Federal Story* (1944), his 'sterling qualities of fairness, thoroughness, sincerity and reliability shone' (Deakin, 85), especially in contrast to others such as the flamboyant Reid.

In Victoria in October 1899 Turner was temporarily dislodged by disaffected rural Conservatives led by McLean, but was restored to office in November 1900. When he resigned in 1901 to stand for the federal seat of Balaclava he was the longest-serving Victorian premier. He declined to work with Lyne, who tried to form the first federal ministry (the Hopetoun blunder), but became the first commonwealth treasurer in the Barton ministry (1901–3); he also served in the Deakin ministry and later in the Reid ministry. Sound in finance and an able administrator, he was a successful treasurer and, as mentioned in *The Age* obituary, established a 'tradition of economy, laid the

foundations of honest book keeping and gave clear full official statements of expenditure'. He brought in the first four federal budgets. He became an influential and trusted member, and it surprised nobody when the Watson Labor ministry invited him to continue as treasurer, though he refused.

In declining health, Turner retired at the election of 1906. He resumed his law practice and became chairman of commissioners of the State Savings Bank of Victoria. His son was killed in a train accident in 1908. Turner himself died from heart disease on 13 August 1916 at his Hawthorn home, Summerlea, 78 Riversdale Road (he had moved from St Kilda in 1904), survived by his wife and daughter. He was buried with Church of England rites at the St Kilda cemetery on 15 August.

Dull and prosaic in manner, Turner had a high-pitched, almost falsetto voice, and his speeches were devoid of ornament. Deakin described him as

> the ideal bourgeois, who married early and who was in dress, manner and habits, exactly on the same level as the shopkeepers and prosperous artisans who were his ratepayers and constituents. He was also bourgeois in his uprightness, straightforwardness, domestic happiness and regularity of habits. His facility of work was enormous, his love of detail great. (Deakin, 66)

Physically Turner was a big man, bespectacled, with a large head and a bristling moustache. An able yet underrated politician, administratively and financially competent, he was an important figure in achieving federation and in establishing the commonwealth government.

ALAN GREGORY

Sources G. Serle, 'Turner, George', *AusDB*, vol. 12 • J. Smith, ed., *The cyclopedia of Victoria*, 1 (1903), 176–8 • *The Leader* (4 Feb 1899) • *The Leader* (5 Oct 1901) • *The Leader* (19 Aug 1916) • *The Age* [Melbourne] (14 Aug 1916) • A. Deakin, *The federal story: the inner history of the federal cause*, ed. H. Brookes (1944) • C. E. Sayers, *David Syme: a life* (1965) • *The Webbs' Australian diary, 1898*, ed. A. G. Austin (1965) • L. F. Crisp, *Federation fathers*, ed. J. Hart (1990) • R. Norris, *The emergent commonwealth* (1975) • b. cert. • d. cert.
Archives NL Aus. | NL Aus., Deakin MSS • State Library of Victoria, Melbourne, Crouch MSS, La Trobe manuscript collection
Likenesses H. F. Allkins, oils, 1889, St Kilda town hall, Melbourne • B. MacKennal, bust, Parliament House, Canberra • photograph, St Kilda town hall, Melbourne • photograph, Parliament House, Melbourne
Wealth at death £3789: probate, *CGPLA Eng. & Wales*

Turner, George Charlewood (1891–1967), headmaster and university principal, was born at the rectory, Cannon Street Road, London, on 27 March 1891, the fourth son in the family of four sons and five daughters of the Revd Charles Henry Turner (1842–1923), later bishop of Islington, and his wife, Edith Emma, daughter of the Revd Alfred Earle MacDougall, who later became a bishop. A large, intelligent, and self-sufficient family, centring on his able and charming mother, set the tone of Turner's character, of the incisive confidence of his judgements, and of his instinctive ease and elegance. He was educated at Marlborough College and at Magdalen College, Oxford, where from 1910 to 1914 he was a classical demy. At Marlborough he was deeply influenced by the master, Frank Fletcher, whose scholarship and force he admired, and at

Magdalen he absorbed the traditional values of classical Oxford, though his second class in classical moderations (1912) and second class in *literae humaniores* (1914) hardly represented the outstanding abilities he afterwards displayed.

Commissioned in 1914 in the 23rd London regiment, from 1914 to 1919 Turner served on the general staff 47th (London) division, being twice mentioned in dispatches, reaching the rank of major, and in 1918 being awarded the MC. This decoration, according to his own account, he obtained simply by presence of mind: when, armed only with a walking stick, he chanced on some Germans in a dug-out, he at once put up his stick and ordered them in their own language: 'Follow me!' This they promptly did.

In 1919, matured and hardened by the war, Turner returned as an assistant master to Marlborough, where since 1916 Cyril Norwood had been master. Here, besides working under a great headmaster, Turner found congenial colleagues, particularly C. B. Canning, afterwards headmaster of Canford. Norwood had reorganized Marlborough with outstanding success, and Turner contributed to this phase of all-round achievement; but it was flawed by a rift between the 'aesthetes' or 'intellectuals' and the 'hearties', who, not least on the staff, made a philistine and exclusive cult of games; and when in 1925 Norwood had left for Harrow School and Turner succeeded him as master, he proved just the person to assuage the conflict without friction.

Turner accomplished this civilizing mission more by example than by precept. He had been a boy at Marlborough, a young master, and a housemaster; he knew what every stratum needed to attain this humane objective, which he summed up in his advice: 'Remember, we are teaching boys, not subjects.' As one boy later put it: 'He didn't do anything; he just was, and that was enough.' In fact he 'did' a good deal, consolidating and rounding off Norwood's reforms, abolishing beating by house captains, and entertaining with elegant hospitality at the lodge, run for him first by his mother, then by his sister Ruth. Though he could wield easy authority, he was not aloof, and would often of an evening visit colleagues for a talk. He encouraged the arts and drama, and, himself a good actor, would sing tunefully at school concerts.

Though happy at Marlborough, when in 1939 he was invited to become principal of Makerere University College, Kampala, Uganda, Turner welcomed the exotic adventure, remarking with typical understatement, 'One can't do the same thing all one's life.' His influence at Makerere proved pervasive and important, since many of his students who had studied the humanities and the arts as well as agriculture, science, and technology, took up key positions in east Africa. As at Marlborough he made his high standards catching by example, and when in 1963 the college became part of the University of East Africa and in 1970 a university in its own right, Turner's influence was further developed. In 1944 he was appointed an honorary fellow of Makerere and in 1945 he was appointed CMG.

In 1947 Turner was appointed headmaster of Charterhouse School. Here, after wartime difficulties, his mild but firm regime gave needed time for recovery. Within clearly defined limits, he had always been tolerant; now he remarked: 'At my age I can no longer take too seriously the peccadilloes of the young.' He was particularly helpful and considerate to colleagues, and the big chapel at Charterhouse made a setting for the clarity and wisdom of sermons well adapted to his congregation.

In 1950 Turner was chairman of the Headmasters' Conference; he also made a tour of schools in Australia and helped to establish Kurt Hahn, the founder of Salem in Germany, at Gordonstoun, of which Turner became a governor. He never married, and in 1952 retired to a spacious house in Chichester, which he made a headquarters for his surviving brothers and sisters. He died on 11 April 1967 at Watersmeet Hotel, Woolacombe, Devon.

Turner was small, neat, and handsome, with fine dark eyes and a mellifluous voice. With a successful headmaster's sense of occasion and power of command, he was dignified but never pompous, and, with a singular flair for essentials, made memorable remarks in a polite and sometimes quaintly academic manner. His competence, insight, and kindness made him widely admired and beloved. He was a salutary and civilizing influence in the public school life of his time.　　　　JOHN BOWLE, *rev.*

Sources private information (1981) · personal knowledge (1981) · *The Times* (13 April 1967) · *The Times* (14 April 1967) · *The Times* (16 April 1967) · *The Times* (22 April 1967) · WWW · b. cert. · d. cert. · *CGPLA Eng. & Wales* (1967)

Archives Bodl. RH, corresp., MS Afr. s. 643

Likenesses R. G. Eves, portrait, 1937, Marlborough College, Wiltshire · P. Greenham, portrait, 1952, Charterhouse, Godalming, Surrey

Wealth at death £34,159: probate, 13 June 1967, *CGPLA Eng. & Wales*

Turner, George Grey (1877–1951), surgeon, was born on 8 September 1877 at 2 Widdrington Place, North Shields, Northumberland, the second son in the family of five sons and one daughter of James Grey Turner, a bank clerk, and his wife, Evelyn, *née* Grey. He was educated at a private school in North Shields, then at Rutherford Technical College, Newcastle, followed by a short period as a dresser at the Old Infirmary, before entering the Newcastle medical school of Durham University as a Heath scholar, where he graduated MB BS with first-class honours (1898), and MS (1901). He obtained his MRCS in 1899 and his FRCS in 1903. After holding resident surgical posts at Newcastle, Turner went to London and continued his postgraduate studies at King's College Hospital, from where he made the first of several visits to hospitals in Vienna. Returning to Newcastle, Grey Turner, as he was always known, soon became an able clinical teacher and was appointed to the staff of the Royal Victoria Infirmary. He greatly admired Rutherford Morison, who was professor of surgery at Newcastle, and was delighted when Morison asked him to become his assistant.

In 1908 Grey Turner married Alice (Elsie) Grey (d. 1962), daughter of Frederick E. Schofield, pharmacist, of Morpeth. There were three daughters, and one son, Elston

George Grey Turner (1877–1951), by Harry Lister, 1947

Grey Turner MRCS, who won the MC in Italy in 1944, and who became secretary of the British Medical Association.

In his early years as a surgeon Grey Turner operated not only at the infirmary but in nursing homes, houses, and cottages in the surrounding district. He was to be seen at his best operating on an improvised kitchen operating table, with an oil lamp as a source of light, and the assistance of a country practitioner. (Anaesthesia in those days was either ether or chloroform or a mixture of both.) He thoroughly enjoyed these all too common occurrences and the more difficult and urgent the operation the better he became. He was a sound, experienced surgeon and his methods and techniques soon became familiar to surgeons both at home and abroad. The Newcastle school of surgery owes much to such men as Morison and Grey Turner.

On the outbreak of war in 1914 Grey Turner was called up for service in the Royal Army Medical Corps which he had joined when the Territorial Force was formed, and after two years as consulting surgeon in the Middle East with the rank of colonel became consulting surgeon and specialist in chest surgery to the northern command in England. After the war he returned to his duties at the Royal Infirmary, Newcastle, and to the Tynemouth Infirmary, and was professor of surgery at Newcastle from 1927 until 1934. He then became the first director of surgery at the new Royal Postgraduate Medical School at Hammersmith where he remained until 1946, to be succeeded by Ian Aird. There he gathered around him postgraduate students from all over the world to hear his lectures and attend his operation sessions. He had always shown a great interest in cancer and devised many new techniques for the removal of cancer in different parts of the body, especially the gullet. His outstanding work on the surgical treatment of cancer of the oesophagus was developed further by his pupil R. H. Franklin, who became the leading London surgeon in this field. Grey Turner was also one of the first to succeed in transplanting ureters into the colon, used in the treatment of bladder disorders.

Besides his active academic duties Grey Turner's other interest was the Royal College of Surgeons of England. He was elected to the council in 1926, and served three terms of eight years, retiring in 1950. He was Hunterian professor (1928 and 1944), Bradshaw lecturer (1935), and Hunterian orator (1945), and was elected trustee of the Hunterian Collection in 1951. He was particularly interested in the museum and the library and he had a very extensive knowledge of John Hunter and his writings and his museum which the government of the day in 1799 gave to the college. Turner's Hunterian oration—'The Hunterian Museum: yesterday and tomorrow'—formed the basis for the replanning of the museum after the war. Grey Turner was also active at the Royal Society of Medicine and took part in many discussions at its meetings. He was president of the sections of surgery and proctology and was president-elect of the clinical section at the time of his death.

Grey Turner travelled widely and visited North America, Australia, Africa, and the main cities of Europe; he was a prodigious writer and many hundreds of his papers were published in English and American surgical journals. He was an honorary fellow of the American (1918) and Royal Australasian (1937) colleges of surgeons and received the honorary degrees of LLD from Glasgow (1939) and DCh from Durham (1935).

Grey Turner was a short man who dressed shabbily and wore a very old bowler hat on the back of his large head, which he had a habit of placing over his teacup to keep it warm. He wore heavy boots with thick soles; and, in the winter months, his hands were encased in knitted mittens. His friends were apt to chaff him on his appearance, and although he took this in good part, it was like water off a duck's back for he never altered. His kindness and courtesy were appreciated by all who knew him and he was dearly loved by his colleagues and students.

On moving to London in 1934 Grey Turner settled at Huntercombe Manor, near Taplow, Buckinghamshire, a historic house with a beautiful garden and fine topiary hedges. He died on 24 August 1951 at King Edward VII Hospital, Windsor. He was survived by his wife.

CECIL WAKELEY, *rev.* CHRISTOPHER C. BOOTH

Sources *BMJ* (1 Sept 1951), 550–53 · N. Hodgson, *BMJ* (15 Sept 1951), 679–81 · *George Grey Turner* (1986) · E. G. Turner, *The casting of a pebble* (1934) · *The Lancet* (1–8 Sept 1951), 406–7, 455 · *The Times* (28 Aug 1951), 6e · G. G.-T. and C. L. R., *British Journal of Surgery*, 39 (1951), 193–4 · *Newcastle Medical Journal*, 24 (Dec 1951), 87–91 · 'George Grey Turner, 1877–1951; centenary celebrations at the Royal Postgraduate Medical School', *Annals of the Royal College of Surgeons of England*, 60 (1978), 298–316 · personal knowledge (1971) [Cecil Wakeley] · private information (1971) · *WWW*

Archives U. Leeds, Brotherton L., account of visit to Viennese hospitals · Wellcome L., corresp. and papers
Likenesses M. Ayoub, group portrait, oils, c.1926–1929 (Council of the Royal College of Surgeons, 1926–7), RCS Eng. · H. Carr, group portrait, oils, 1946–7 (Council of the Royal College of Surgeons of England), RCS Eng. · H. Lister, photograph, 1947, Wellcome L. [see illus.] · photograph, repro. in Newcastle Medical Journal, facing p. 87
Wealth at death £91,025 7s. 8d.: probate, 18 Dec 1951, CGPLA Eng. & Wales

Turner, Sir George James (1798–1867), judge, was born on 5 February 1798 at Yarmouth, the ninth son of the Revd Richard Turner (1751–1835), incumbent of Yarmouth, and his second wife, Elizabeth (1761–1805), daughter of Thomas Rede. William *Turner (1792–1867) was his brother. He attended Charterhouse School and Pembroke College, Cambridge, and graduated BA as ninth wrangler in 1819; he gained a fellowship in 1820, which he held until his marriage, and proceeded MA in 1822. A pupil under Charles Pepys (1781–1851), later Lord Cottenham, Turner was called to the bar of Lincoln's Inn in July 1821. In 1823 he married Louisa, youngest daughter of Edward Jones of Brackley, Northamptonshire. They had six sons and three daughters.

In 1832 Turner was co-editor, with James Russell QC (1790–1861), of chancery reports from Eldon's time, covering the period 1882–4. In May 1840 Turner became a QC, and his extensive practice, while focused on the rolls court, included much work before the privy council and House of Lords. Most famously, he was counsel for the canal company in Dimes v. Grand Junction Canal Company (1849) and for George Gorham in the Gorham case of 1850. He was bencher of Lincoln's Inn from 1840, and treasurer in 1858.

In July 1847 Turner was returned as MP for Coventry, a seat which he held until elevated to the bench in 1851. A liberal conservative, he spoke mainly on legal questions. He promoted an act (13 & 14 Vict. c. 35, Turner's Act) which made minor procedural improvements in the running of the equity courts; he was subsequently made a member of the chancery commission, the report of which led to the more searching reforms in the Court of Chancery Act 1852.

On 2 April 1851 Turner was appointed vice-chancellor, and subsequently knighted. On 10 January 1853 he was promoted to lord justice of the Court of Appeal in Chancery, and in 1857 he was sworn of the privy council. As a judge, he was reputed to be grave, painstaking, and legally erudite; he was often contrasted with the more loquacious Sir James Knight-Bruce (1791–1866), with whom he frequently shared the chancery bench and whose talents were generally agreed to complement Turner's nicely. Turner was said to be 'on all occasions jealous to repel any attempt to narrow the limits of the jurisdiction of the court, and courageous in expanding its remedial powers to meet modern developments' (DNB). He was much in demand for the equity work of the privy council. Of his judgments, the most famous are Attorney-General v. Bishop of Worcester (1851) on the right of Kidderminster School to take boarders; Burgess v. Burgess (1853) on trade names; Jenner v. Morris (1861) on married women's property; Milroy v.

Lord (1862) on the constitution of trusts; and Re Gregson's estate (1864) on wills.

Turner died from congestion of the lungs on 9 July 1867 at his home, 23 Park Crescent, Portland Place, London, only ten days after last sitting at court. His widow survived him. He was buried at Kelshall, near Royston, Hertfordshire. His eldest son, George Richard Turner (d. 1875), was rector of Kelshall, Hertfordshire; his second son, Edmond Robert Turner (1826–1899), was county court judge for Yorkshire; another son, James Francis Turner (1829–1893), was bishop of Grafton and Armidale, New South Wales.

STEVE HEDLEY

Sources Solicitors' Journal, 11 (1866–7), 1865 · Law Times (20 July 1867) · E. Foss, Biographia juridica: a biographical dictionary of the judges of England … 1066–1870 (1870) · R. E. Megarry, 'The vice-chancellors', Law Quarterly Review, 98 (1982), 370–405
Likenesses W. Holl, stipple (after G. Richmond), BM, NPG
Wealth at death under £35,000: probate, 6 Aug 1867, CGPLA Eng. & Wales

Turner, Harold (1909–1962), ballet dancer, was born in Manchester on 2 December 1909, the son of Edward Harold Turner, viola player with the Hallé Orchestra and the London Symphony Orchestra, and his wife, Laura Greenwood. He studied dancing with Alfred Haines in Manchester, making his stage début at a pupil show in 1927. Shortly afterwards he went to London and started work first with Léonide Massine and then with Marie Rambert, making one of a talented group with such dancers as Pearl Argyle, Diana Gould, and Prudence Hyman, and the choreographers Frederick W. M. Ashton and Andrée Howard. He soon established himself as a strong classical dancer, creating two roles in Ashton ballets, Les petits riens in 1928 and Capriol Suite in 1930. In the same year he partnered Tamara Karsavina in Les sylphides and Le spectre de la rose. He appeared in Camargo Society performances, as guest artist in 1929–30 at the Vic-Wells Ballet (which later became the Sadler's Wells Ballet and subsequently the Royal Ballet). In 1935 he became a permanent member of the company, taking leads in the classical ballets and creating the red knight (Checkmate), the blue skater (Les patineurs), and the dancing master (The Rake's Progress).

Turner remained with the company except for a brief interval with the International Ballet and the Arts Theatre Ballet and for war service in the Royal Air Force, retiring in 1955 save for an occasional guest appearance. He then taught at the Royal Ballet School and became a director of the Covent Garden Opera Ballet.

Harold Turner's contribution to British ballet was a major one. He was the first outstanding male dancer to win acclaim under his own English name. He was virile, a brilliant technician who shone in such dances as the blue bird in The Sleeping Beauty and the peasant's pas de deux in Giselle. The blue skater in Les patineurs was an astonishing piece of brio. He was a considerable partner, a danseur noble, who always showed his ballerina to advantage, yet he was versatile enough to dance such character roles as the miller in The Three-Cornered Hat and the cancan dancer in La boutique fantasque and to make an impact in a small character role, the chief coachman in Petrushka, which was in fact his last appearance. In addition to the handicap of an English name, he had to overcome the additional handicap, a severe one until recently, of the prejudice against male dancers. His athleticism did much to dispel this prejudice, to make the path of his successors an easier one, and to help in the recruitment of male dancers.

On 9 July 1938 Turner married Mary Honer (*b*. 1913/14), a dancer, at St Andrew's Presbyterian Church, Hampstead, London. The marriage was dissolved and in 1944 he married Gerd Elly, daughter of Leonard Larsen, civil servant with the Norwegian government, of Oslo. She was herself a dancer and became the senior teacher at the Royal Ballet. There was one daughter of the second marriage.

In 1962 Turner was returning to play the role of the elderly marquess in a revival of the Massine ballet *The Good-Humoured Ladies* with a distinguished cast which included Lydia Sokolova. After a rehearsal at Covent Garden he died at the Middlesex Hospital, London, on 2 July 1962.

ARNOLD HASKELL, *rev.*

Sources *The Times* (3 July 1962) · *Dancing Times* (Aug 1971) · private information (1981, 2004) · *CGPLA Eng. & Wales* (1962)
Likenesses photographs, 1942–9, Hult. Arch. · T. H. Elliot, two drawings, priv. coll.
Wealth at death £3046 14*s*. 1*d*.: administration, 26 Oct 1962, *CGPLA Eng. & Wales*

Turner, Henry (1656/7–1724), lawyer, was the eldest son of John Turner (*d*. 1669), a merchant of Fulham, London, and his wife, Martha Pettiward (*d*. 1681) of Putney, Surrey. Turner's parents married in December 1655, John Turner receiving a marriage portion of £2500. With some of this money, in 1658 John Turner purchased some land from the St John family in Leicestershire, and acquired a mortgage on Cold Overton Hall, where he made his seat. Henry Turner was admitted to Lincoln's Inn on 6 February 1672, and he may have entered Oriel College, Oxford, on 28 April 1672. The law was his chosen career, and he was called to the bar on 9 July 1679. In 1681 Turner had to ward off a challenge to his right to present to Sapcote, Leicestershire, from the earl of Huntingdon.

Turner married on 9 February 1688 at St Martin Outwich, London, Mary (1671/2–1735), daughter of Thomas Frewen MP of Brickwell House, Northiam, Sussex, and his second wife, Bridget Layton. They had one son and one daughter. In June 1691 Turner and his fellow barrister Edward Strode challenged the right of the masters of the bench of Lincoln's Inn to appoint a preacher in succession to John Tillotson, the new archbishop of Canterbury, but without success. Turner was made a serjeant-at-law in November 1700, being sponsored by his father-in-law, Frewen, and the tory politician Anthony Hammond.

Turner was presumably a very active barrister, for in December 1717 he was sufficiently wealthy to invest £600 in East India Company stock. He served as treasurer of Serjeants' Inn from 1721 to 1724. Turner died on 29 March 1724, aged sixty-seven, while attending the assizes at Coventry, and was buried at Sapcote on 4 April. His will, made in December 1718, made reference to the fact that most of his landed estate had been settled previously. The remainder of his real and personal estate was left to his son, John

(1691–1753), also a barrister. In 1727 John married Selina Frewen, the daughter of Sir Edward Frewen and a granddaughter of Thomas Frewen and his first wife, Judith Woolverstone. Turner's daughter, Martha (1695–1752), had married in 1713 Selina's brother, Thomas Frewen. Turner's wife survived him, dying on 13 October 1735.

STUART HANDLEY

Sources Baker, *Serjeants* · W. P. Baildon, ed., *The records of the Honorable Society of Lincoln's Inn: admissions*, 1 (1896), 312 · W. P. Baildon, ed., *The records of the Honorable Society of Lincoln's Inn: the black books*, 3 (1899), 126, 178 · Foster, *Alum. Oxon.* · H. M. Warne, *A catalogue of the Frewen archives* (1972) · IGI · will, PRO, PROB 11/597, sig. 101 · H. Whitley, *History of the parish of Sapcote, in the county of Leicester* (1853), 1–69 · D. Lemmings, *Gentlemen and barristers: the inns of court and the English bar, 1680–1730* (1990), 158
Archives E. Sussex RO, Frewen MSS

Turner, Herbert Hall (1861–1930), astronomer and seismologist, was born at Leeds on 13 August 1861, the eldest son of John Turner, an artist, and his wife, Isabella Hall, of Hexham. He was educated at Leeds modern school, then from 1874 at Clifton College, Bristol, and gained a scholarship to Trinity College, Cambridge, in 1879. He graduated in 1882 as second wrangler, and was second Smith's prizeman in 1883. In 1884 he became chief assistant at the Royal Greenwich Observatory. He was elected fellow of the Royal Astronomical Society (RAS) in 1885 and FRS in 1896. A general secretary of the British Association for the Advancement of Science (BAAS) from 1913 to 1922, he received honorary degrees from various universities.

At Greenwich Turner worked on the international *Carte du ciel* photographic survey and catalogue originated in 1887 and jointly undertaken by eighteen observatories. He devised two essential means for expediting progress. One was explained in his classic paper proposing a rectilinear co-ordinate system to convert any star's apparent to true position. The laborious corrections for the earth's motion and atmosphere were combined with those for adjustment of the photographic plates in one operation by applying simple linear equations. This enabled photographic surveys to replace much meridian circle work, and was emphasized when Turner was awarded the Bruce gold medal of the Astronomical Society of the Pacific in 1927.

Turner's second invention was an eyepiece scale for plate measurements which enabled observatories to employ affordable semi-skilled labour for reduction and publication. At Clifton he had learned to value the collection of precise measurements, so that 'no good honest work is thrown away' and 'the record is sacred and must not be broken' (H. H. Turner, *Report of the British Association for the Advancement of Science*, 1911, 331). This conviction was a major influence on his career. He brought the work of four British variable star observers to publication, subjected the data from different catalogue zones to statistical analyses, and in the 1920s was the first to suggest star-streaming. His term 'parsec' denotes one of the astronomical units of distance. He devised a new method of deducing stellar magnitudes from measured diameters of their images and thereby made available a standardized mass of valuable material to stellar statisticians.

In 1893 Turner succeeded Charles Pritchard as Savilian professor of astronomy at Oxford, with the associate fellowship of New College. Since 1839 there had been complete disconnection between the privately owned Radcliffe Observatory and the university. Several attempts made by Turner to have a house built at his observatory in the 'Parks' so that he could work more efficiently were thwarted by Sir William Anson, warden of All Souls College and a Radcliffe trustee, in a *cause célèbre* of 1907. In contrast to his successes with astronomical committees, Turner was impatient with and neglected essential lobbying in the university in advance of initiatives he claimed were crucial. The fracas proved that the nearby Radcliffe Observatory, expensively re-equipped in 1902, had become a blight upon the development of the university's observatory. Unable to renew instruments or to increase the specialized staff, Turner had little opportunity to compete internationally in observational astronomy after 1914.

Turner fostered international organizations and reached the public through his lectures and his four books. He had great influence and was an outstanding figure in the affairs of the RAS as a council member for forty-three years; he was secretary (1892–9), president (1903–5), foreign secretary (1919–30), and president of its club (1921–30). In 1919 he had much to do with the RAS forming a geophysical committee, and the following year he became its secretary because he believed that astronomy and geophysics needed each other. When the new International Astronomical Union was established in 1919, Turner became president of the commission for the catalogue, and served until his death. He was also elected first president of the commission on seismology in the International Union for Geodesy and Geophysics. When his seismologist friend John Milne died in 1913, Turner took 'temporary' care of the worldwide organization, after 1917 wholly at Oxford. Seismology increasingly overtaxed the observatory's resources as the number of stations grew from seventy-four to 259 in 1929. Routine reduction and then analysis deflected Turner for his last twelve years. But by 1922 he had developed a unique resource, and he wrung from it two discoveries.

In 1929 Turner warmly supported the Radcliffe observer's plan to move the trustees' observatory to a fine climate and southern site in South Africa because it was in the best interests of astronomy. He agreed a co-operation including an all-important Radcliffe studentship to support graduate research and access to the new observations—the proven American recipe for success. The windfall of £100,000 offered for the trustees' site and to finance the move was also the only source for renewing science at Oxford. Struggling to rejuvenate his Clarendon Laboratory, Professor Frederick A. Lindemann (1886–1957) aggressively lobbied the senior figures. In *The Times* he made a wounding attack on Turner, questioned his health, and derided him as 'subterranean' (*The Times*, 23 April 1930, 8).

Turner defended his positional astronomy, and characterized Lindemann as 'depressingly parochial' (*The Times*, 26 April 1930).

Turner entered fully into the life of New College, but was blind to the necessity of making his case carefully in the university. Despite the fracas of 1907, he was no better prepared when confronted in 1930. The combination of overwork, vituperative personal attacks by Lindemann, his budget in the red, and his observatory once more a pawn in university politics overwhelmed him, and may have contributed to the stroke he suffered shortly afterwards.

Turner's achievements lay within the balance he struck between astronomy and seismology throughout his tenure of thirty-six years. In astronomy his two inventions were crucial breakthroughs. He used his observatory's resources to bring nearly a quarter of the entire catalogue project to completion at Oxford.

In seismology Turner's reputation is based principally on two theoretical and two administrative achievements. He kept Milne's international organization for reporting earthquakes in being, and he made the crucial reorganization of changing the data from collation by reporting station to that of seismic events. He developed the Zoppritz–Turner tables for the better location of earthquakes. Using these resources, and against current consensus, his discovery in 1922 of deep focus earthquakes was a great step forward. Between 1918 and 1922 he founded the International Seismological Survey (ISS) at the observatory, and had it adopted as the international publication of seismic events. Between 1919 and 1924 he promoted the broadcasting of a world time service so that earthquake reports could be accurately correlated. He was one of the first to suggest that the earth had a liquid core and solid mantle; the tables he prepared were the basis for the work of Sir Harold Jeffreys and David Bullen which proved that hypothesis. In 1930 Turner's second discovery was to map volcanic and earthquake events as the 'ring of fire' around the Pacific rim. He changed the way that seismology is undertaken, and the ISS and his discovery of deep earthquakes are a lasting legacy. By these works, his offices, and his tireless committee work, he kept his obsolete observatory in the front rank.

A big and extrovert man, a keen cricketer and choir member, Turner was loyal to his friends and encouraged young talent and volunteers in his observatory. He inspired devotion in his overworked staff and respect and affection among British and American astronomers. Decisive, and obstinate, he was a man of unswerving commitment; when he failed to persuade, he filled the gap with his own exertion. Before 1914 he lectured frequently to the Workers' Educational Association. He had no love of observing stars for the sake of it, but was a mathematician and manager. He died on 20 August 1930 in Sabbatsberg Hospital, Stockholm, four days after a stroke suffered while presiding at a meeting of the international commission on seismology. He was survived by his wife, Agnes Margaret, *née* Whyte, whom he had married in 1899, and their only child, a daughter.   ROGER HUTCHINS

Sources *Monthly Notices of the Royal Astronomical Society*, 91 (1930–31), 321–34 · *Publications of the Astronomical Society of the Pacific*, 39 (1927), 2–8 · historical file, International Seismology Centre, Newbury, Berkshire · *History of the Royal Astronomical Society*, 2: *1920–1980*, ed. R. J. Tayler (1987), 7, 16, 19 · I. Guest, *Dr John Radcliffe and his trust* (1991) · Sir William Anson correspondence, Bodl. Oxf., MS Top. Oxon. d. 310 · Bodl. Oxf., MSS Radcliffe Trust · Bodl. Oxf., U. Oxf. Observatory, GA Oxon b 140 · F. A. Bellamy and E. F. B. Bellamy, *Herbert Hall Turner: a notice of his seismological work* (1931) · K. E. Bullen, 'Turner, Herbert Hall', *DSB* · private information (2004)
Archives MHS Oxf., corresp. and papers | Bodl. Oxf., Sir William Anson corresp. · Bodl. Oxf., letters to Gilbert Murray · CUL, letters to Sir George Stokes · International Seismology Centre, Newbury, Berkshire, historical file · Nuffield Oxf., corresp. with Lord Cherwell · RAS, letters to Royal Astronomical Society of London · RGS, letters to Sir David Gill · UCL, letters to Karl Pearson
Likenesses W. Rothenstein, pencil drawing, 1916, Trinity Cam. · W. Stoneman, photograph, 1918, NPG · portrait, 1921, Bodl. Oxf. · portrait, 1923–7, MHS Oxf. · C. Dodgson, chalk drawing, RAS · portrait, MHS Oxf.
Wealth at death £5914 17s. 1d.: probate, 15 Oct 1930, *CGPLA Eng. & Wales*

Turner, Jacob (1643–1709), merchant, was born in July 1643 in Smarden, Kent, the younger son of Jacob Turner (1613–1672), clothier, and his wife, Anne, *née* Tray, of Bredhurst, Kent. On 19 March 1657 he was apprenticed for a period of seven years to Richard Baker, an assistant in the Levant Company. However, when Baker was appointed consul at Smyrna, the apprenticeship was transferred to Daniel Morse.

Turner went to Smyrna in 1663 and was granted liberty of trade in December 1664. While home on leave, he was admitted to the freedom of the Levant Company and on 18 July 1668 to the Mercers' Company. Although recorded in the 1660s as being 'of St Botolph without Bishopsgate, London' (Armytage), he remained in Smyrna for a further seven years, initially in partnership with John Sayer and Thomas Thynne, then with Thynne alone. Currants formed the staple of the Levant trade, but Turner's meticulous account books are also dotted with references to raw silk, 'goats haires' (mohair), 'Angora yarne', and 'mastick', among other items (PRO, C 104/44). Apart from Smyrna, the main centres of the Levant Company were Aleppo and Constantinople, all then under Ottoman rule.

On 6 September 1675 Turner and four other English merchants left Smyrna on the *Bristol Merchant*, but were captured by Tripoline privateers on 20 September. The entire ship's company was forced to walk from Darnah through the Libyan desert to Tripoli—a distance of some 800 miles—in thirty-four arduous days. They were kept in the consul's house in plague-stricken Tripoli. On 13 January 1676 Turner delivered the local ruler's ultimatum to the flagship of the blockading British fleet: the hostages would be put to work in the stone quarries if Tripoline peace terms were not met. But Vice-Admiral Sir John Narbrough stood firm, and the merchants were indeed sent to the quarries in chains for a few days. Following the British bombardment of the city, however, in March 1676 the Tripolines capitulated and the captives were released.

Once installed back in London, Turner married Mary, daughter of the Hamburg merchant Lucy Knightley, at St Mary-le-Bow on 22 November 1676; they had eight children, six of whom predeceased him. Like many Levant merchants, Turner invested in the East India trade as well as in shipping and insurance. He also acted as an agent for Sir Paul Rycaut, the Levant Company's consul in Smyrna from 1667 to 1678, while continuing to operate from London as the senior partner of Turner and Thynne until the partnership was dissolved in July 1678. Even after that date he collaborated with Thynne and a succession of new partners. When the firm's books were destroyed in the Smyrna earthquake of 1688, his kinsman William Becher managed to salvage Turner's goods but was subsequently incapacitated by illness. In 1690, therefore, Turner returned to Smyrna to sort out the business and stayed there until 1695, establishing the new partnership of Turner, Hill, and Jones. One of his sons, John, became a factor at Smyrna, but died young.

Jacob Turner died in Hackney in 1709 and was buried at Smarden, where in 1686 he had donated money for church repairs and set up a trust 'for the benefit of the superannuated poor'; a monument was erected in the chancel (Hasted, 7.482–3). Fittingly, he left £200 'for Redemption of English Slaves out of Turkish Captivity to be disposed of to that end by the Levant Company' (PRO, PROB 11/510, fol. 182). JENNY MARSH

Sources S. P. Anderson, *An English consul in Turkey: Paul Rycaut at Smyrna, 1667–1678* (1989), esp. 76–81 · J. A. Elin, 'A seventeenth-century Levant merchant: the life and letters of Jacob Turner', PhD diss., University of New York, 1975 · E. Hasted, *The history and topographical survey of the county of Kent*, 2nd edn, 7 (1798) · A. C. Wood, *A history of the Levant Company* (1935) · R. Knolles and P. Rycaut, *The history of the Turks*, 6th edn, 3 vols. (1687–1700) · *Index to apprentices, 1619–1899*, Mercers' Hall, London · G. J. Armytage, ed., *A visitation of the county of Kent, begun … 1663, finished … 1668*, Harleian Society, 54 (1906), 170–71
Archives PRO, C 104/44, 45
Wealth at death see will, PRO, PROB 11/510, fol. 182

Turner, James (d. 1664), thief, was born at Hadley, near Barnet, Hertfordshire, the son of 'an ancient, reverend divine' (*State trials*, 6.621). Apprenticed to a lace merchant in Cheapside he became a goldsmith. He claimed to have served in the civil war as a captain of horse under the royalist marquess of Newcastle for four years. Later he became a lieutenant-colonel in the City of London militia.

Turner later achieved notoriety as a 'mad swearing confident fellow, well known by all, and by me' (Pepys, 5.10), alleged to be involved in many criminal activities. Arrested for robbing a 'rich usurer and jeweller', he was sentenced to death at the Old Bailey on 19 January 1664. 'This famous more properly infamous bravo hath attracted upon him the odium of all sorts of people to a strange degree; and yet he is insufferably insolent upon hopes of a reprieve' (*Hastings MSS*, 2.144–5). Pepys watched his execution two days later; 'A comely-looked man he was, and kept his countenance to the end—I was sorry to see him'—a rather hypocritical sentiment as Pepys had paid a shilling to get a good view and waited an hour (Pepys, 5.23). Turner was hanged at Lime Street, London, near the site of his crime, and was buried nearby.

Turner's fame was reflected by the publication of at least five pamphlets on his trial and execution. He said that he had had twenty-seven children with his wife, Mary, which, according to one observer, 'equals not his bastards' (*Hastings MSS*, 2.145).   DAVID STEVENSON

Sources *State trials*, 6.566–630 • Pepys, *Diary* (1970–83), vol. 5 • *Report on the manuscripts of the late Reginald Rawdon Hastings*, 4 vols., HMC, 78 (1928–47), vol. 2, pp. 144–5 • *The triumph of truth: in an exact and impartial relation of the life and conversation of Col. James Turner* (1663) [1664] • *The speech and deportment of Col James Turner at his execution in Leaden-Hall-street, January 21. 1663* (1663) [1664] • *The life and death of James commonly called Collonel Turner* (1663) [1664] • *The several examinations and tryal of Colonel James Turner, Mary Turner his wife, John Turner, Ely Turner his sons, and William Turner his brother* (1664) • *A true and impartiall account of the arraignment, tryal, examination, confession and condemnation of Col. James Turner for breaking open the house of Francis Tryon, merchant, in Limestreet, London* (1664)
Likenesses line engraving (copy from *Life and death*, 1664), BM, NPG; repro. in Caulfield, *Remarkable persons* (1793)

Turner, Sir James (*b. c.*1615, *d.* in or after **1689**), army officer and author, was the eldest son of Patrick Turner (1575–1634), minister of Borthwick (later Dalkeith), and his second wife, Margaret Law, daughter of James *Law, archbishop of Glasgow. Turner graduated master of arts from Glasgow University in 1631 'much against my will' as he had no intention of becoming a minister as his father wished (Turner, 1). He spent a year at home in Dalkeith studying history, literature, and religious controversy before joining (as an ensign) levies being raised for the Swedish service by Sir James Lumsden. Landed at Rostock, he was sent to 'reduce some obstinate countries to order, and force them to submit to the Suedish yoake' (ibid., 4). In 1633 he served under the duke of Brunswick in the siege of Hameln, and fought in the battle on 28 June that defeated the imperial army sent to relieve the city. Service at other sieges followed before he visited Scotland late in 1634 in order to see his mother after his father's death. Returning to Germany in 1635 he sought to rejoin Lumsden's regiment at Osnabrück. He found that his position had been filled, but when the city was blockaded by imperial forces he was employed in its defence.

Further service under Swedish command followed, but in 1639 Turner (now a captain) quarrelled with his colonel and came to Scotland, hoping to take part in a scheme to raise levies to fight for the elector palatine, but the plan was thwarted by the first bishops' war. He therefore rejoined the Swedish service, but again he fell out with a superior officer, and he resolved instead to find service in Britain in the second bishops' war. By his own account (written much later, when he was a royalist and trying to explain his covenanting past), he was indifferent as to which side he fought on, and justified this by the honour code of the mercenary: 'I had swallowed without chewing, in Germanie, a very dangerous maxime, which militarie men there too muche follow, which was, that so we serve our master honestlie, it is no matter what master we serve' (Turner, 14). As, Turner claims, the first available ship was bound for Scotland, he joined the covenanters. By the time he landed in September 1640 their army had already invaded England, and he was appointed major of a

Sir James Turner (*b. c.*1615, *d.* in or after **1689**), by Robert White, pubd 1683

regiment stationed in Newcastle. He was never pressed to swear the national covenant, but admitted that he would have done so if necessary, believing at that time that nothing he did in accordance with orders was a matter for his conscience.

The Scots army withdrew from England and disbanded in August 1641, but when a new army was raised to help protestant settlers in Ulster resist the Irish rising of October 1641 Turner was appointed major of Lord Sinclair's regiment. The army landed in May, and from April 1642 to February 1644 Turner served in the garrison of Newry. During this period discontent grew as lack of pay and supplies caused hardship and made it impossible to prosecute the war effectively. In addition political complications emerged, with alliance between the covenanters and the English parliament leading to plans to withdraw the Scottish army from Ireland and send it to fight the king in England. It was at this point that concern about political principles first troubled Turner, and in 1643 he first drafted 'Buchanan revised', a treatise questioning the ideas of George Buchanan which were central to the covenanters' justification of resistance to the king.

In February 1644 Sinclair's regiment abandoned Newry and returned to Scotland amid a fog of contradictory orders. Unhappy with the solemn league and covenant and embittered by neglect in Ireland, many officers were willing to contemplate switching to the king's service, but they were deterred by the absence at this point of any credible royalist leader in arms in Scotland, and by the assurances of the earl of Callendar (whom the covenanters had appointed to raise a new army in Scotland) that he was himself at heart a royalist, so they should obey his orders. This was agreed, and Turner thus came to serve with reinforcements sent to the Scottish army which had entered England in January 1644. He and his fellow officers 'made a fashion [pretence]' of swearing the solemn league and covenant so that 'we might ruine the Covenanters' (Turner, 37–8)—or so he subsequently claimed. However, he took part in the storming of Newcastle by the Scots on 19 September 1644, and served at the siege of Newark-on-Trent the following winter. When in 1646 the defeated Charles I joined the Scottish army rather than risk falling into the hands of the English parliament, and became in effect a prisoner, Turner urged him to try to escape. Fearing the discovery of his intrigues with royalists Turner himself contemplated flight abroad, but then turned his mind to domestic matters. While serving in Newry he had fallen in love with Mary White. She was thought 'by others, much more by me, to be of a good beautie' but he had not been able to marry her because of his lack of the means to support her and because 'at that time she was tenacious' in her Roman Catholic faith (ibid., 34). She now joined him in England, finding him disabled by wounds incurred in a drunken duel. 'This was ane effect of drinking, whiche I confesse, beside the sine against God, hath brought me in many inconveniencies' (ibid., 42–3). They were married in Hexham on 10 November 1646.

After the Scottish army withdrew from England in 1647 Turner accepted employment as adjutant-general of the 'new model' army raised to suppress Alasdair MacColla, the marquess of Montrose's former major-general, in the western highlands, later excusing this further service to the covenanters by claiming indignation at MacColla's desertion of Montrose. He was present when the garrison of Dunaverty in Kintyre surrendered in June 1647, and argued against the massacre of prisoners that followed—though accepting that it was not a breach of the customs and laws of war.

In 1648 there at last came an opportunity to fight for the king, when the engagement allied moderate covenanters and royalists. Turner was given command of a regiment on his superior officers' refusing to serve the engagers, and was sent to Glasgow to force it into obedience to the new regime. There he demonstrated that heavy military quarterings would make 'the hardest headed Covenanter in the toune to forsake the kirk' (Turner, 54). He was involved in suppressing the 'slashing communicants' who attempted resistance at Mauchline Moor on 12 June, but he also shared in the disaster that overwhelmed the engagers' army at and after the battle of Preston (17 July). His contribution to the defeat included a shameful incident in which during the chaos of night-fighting he was attacked and wounded by his own pikemen, they 'being demented (as I thinke we were all)'. 'This made me forget all rules of modestie, prudence and discretion' and in fury he forced Scots cavalry to charge and scatter the offending formation of infantry (ibid., 66–7). He surrendered at Uttoxeter on 25 July 1648. Imprisoned in Hull until November 1649 he mused sadly that 'What was intended for the Kinge's reliefe and restoration, posted him to his grave' (ibid., 77), and indulged his literary tastes by writing essays on political, historical, and literary topics. When freed he took ship to Hamburg and spent the winter of 1649–50 in the Netherlands. A visit to Sweden to procure arrears of pay dating from the 1630s proving abortive, Turner returned to Scotland in September 1650, but not until April 1651 was his repentance for his part in the engagement accepted. He was then appointed adjutant-general of the foot and colonel of a regiment in the army resisting the Cromwellian invasion. After taking part in Charles II's invasion of England he was captured at the battle of Worcester (3 September), but escaped and joined the king in Paris. He lived mainly in Bremen and Amsterdam for two years, and ventured to land in Fife in June 1654 to see if there was any hope of a royalist rising there. Following a hasty withdrawal he spent a few years in a mixture of royalist intrigue and the search for employment, offering his services against the Swedes to the Poles and the Danes. On the outbreak of peace he settled at Breda with the exiled court of Charles II in 1659–60.

Restoration of the monarchy brought Turner a knighthood, and in August 1662 he was appointed major of the king's footguards in Scotland. In July 1666 he was promoted lieutenant-colonel, and took command of the forces employed in suppressing presbyterian dissidents in south-west Scotland. His harsh quarterings and finings designed to enforce obedience instead helped to provoke the Pentland rising. On 15 November Turner was captured in Dumfries. He was spared from death, he claimed, because the rebels, on reading the orders captured with him, accepted that however harsh he had been, he had not acted with the full severity that had been authorized. Humiliated, he was paraded around by the rebels as they sought to gather an army and march on Edinburgh, but when they were defeated at the battle of Rullion Green (28 November) his guards fled. Turner was made the scapegoat for the failed policies of severe repression, and as 'a man of spirit' he refused to co-operate with the 1667 inquiry into his actions and who had authorized them (*Burnet's History*, 1.427). On 10 March 1668 he was deprived of his commissions.

In retirement Turner occupied himself with writing, at Glasgow or in his house at Craig, Ayrshire. All his earlier literary efforts had been destroyed in Dundee, where he had left his papers, when the town was stormed by the English in September 1651. In Bremen in 1655 and The Hague in 1659 he had rewritten 'Buchanan revised', and he rewrote the tract again in 1669, adding an introduction to it in 1679. The memoirs which he also composed are an attempt to justify his chequered career, and particularly his services to the covenanters, but they are also remarkably frank about the life and morality of a mercenary soldier, and about his personal faults such as drunkenness and rage. The memoirs are interspersed with political and literary essays, and Turner also compiled notes denouncing inaccuracies in Bishop Henry Guthry's manuscript history of the civil wars in Scotland. In 1670–1 he wrote *Pallas armata: Military Essayes of the Ancient Grecian, Roman, and Modern Art of War*, and this probably helped in his rehabilitation after the disgrace of 1666. In 1681 he was granted copyright of the book for seven years and it was published in 1683. The 'modern' section of the book thoroughly discusses most aspects of warfare, with copious examples, looking backwards rather than forwards—as in lamenting neglect of the pike and arguing in favour of reviving bowmen. His final chapter discusses whether it is lawful to serve as a soldier for pay, rather than through conviction or obedience to superiors, and concludes that men 'may serve for wages, though they neither know nor examine whether the cause be just or not' (Turner, *Pallas armata*, 372). Thus he remained loyal to the mercenary's creed.

Turner also returned briefly to military practice as well as theory, for he was appointed major of the King's regiment of dragoons in November 1681, and he took an active part in operations against Scottish dissidents in the years that followed. He resigned his commission in 1686, and was granted a pension of £100 sterling per annum. He was still alive in 1689 (his manuscript life of Queen Kristina of Sweden mentions her death in that year), and his widow, Mary, died about 1716. In popular memory in Scotland he long survived as the brutal persecutor of 1666, but it was his memoirs, along with those of Major-General Robert Monro, that helped to inspire Sir Walter Scott's Dugald Dalgetty in *A Legend of the Wars of Montrose* (1819). Turner would probably have accepted Gilbert Burnet's judgement that he was a man 'naturally fierce, but was mad when he was drunk, and that was very often … He was a learned man, but had been always in armies, and knew no other rule but to obey orders' (*Burnet's History*, 1.364–5).

DAVID STEVENSON

Sources DNB · J. Turner, *Memoirs of his own life and times, 1632–1670*, ed. T. Thomson, Bannatyne Club, 28 (1829) · *Fasti Scot.* · *Bishop Burnet's History of his own time: with the suppressed passages of the first volume*, ed. M. J. Routh, 6 vols. (1823) · R. Wodrow, *The history of the sufferings of the Church of Scotland from the Restoration to the revolution*, ed. R. Burns, 4 vols. (1828–30) · *Reg. PCS*, 2nd ser. · *Reg. PCS*, 3rd ser. · S. Murdoch and A. Grosjean, 'Scotland, Scandinavia and Northern Europe, 1580–1707', www.abdn.ac.uk/ssne/
Archives BL, corresp. and memoirs, Add. MSS 12076–12078
Likenesses R. White, line engraving, BM, NPG; repro. in J. Turner, *Pallas armata* (1683), frontispiece [*see illus.*] · medal, Scot. NPG

Turner, James Smith (1832–1904), dentist, was born at Edinburgh on 27 May 1832, the son of Joseph Turner and his wife, Catherine Smith. His father, a hatter, was well known as a political speaker against the corn laws. At the age of fourteen Turner was apprenticed as a mechanic to an Edinburgh dentist named Mien. Turner arrived in London in 1853, just after the failure of an appeal to the Royal College of Surgeons to give dentists a professional status. At first he supported himself by carrying out mechanical work for other dentists; he then entered into a partnership with a Mr Bell. In 1857 Turner became a member of the College of Dentists, and in August 1863, after a period studying at the Middlesex Hospital, London, he was admitted MRCS and a licentiate in dental surgery of this body, the first examination for the LDS having been held in May 1860.

Turner was appointed assistant dental surgeon to the Middlesex Hospital on 19 July 1864; dental surgeon on 16 April 1874; lecturer on dental surgery on 2 February 1881; and consulting dental surgeon on 22 February 1883. In succession to Robert Hepburn he was lecturer on dental surgery mechanics at the Royal Dental Hospital, London, from 1871 until 1880, and served on its management committee; he became consulting dental surgeon in 1896 and was an examiner on the dental board of the Royal College of Surgeons in 1886–8.

In association with John Tomes and a few others Turner was one of the leading campaigners for the professionalization of dentistry. In 1872 he visited the United States to study the conditions of dental practice there, and in 1875 he began work as secretary of the executive council of the dental reform committee. Its aim was to obtain an act of parliament to regulate dental practice and to provide for a dentists' register supervised by the General Medical Council. Opposition from the medical profession was overcome largely by Turner's untiring energy. The Dentists Act was passed with the help of Sir John Lubbock (Lord Avebury) and received royal assent on 22 July 1878; and on 15 August the dental register was opened. The British Dental Association was founded early in 1879, and Turner was its first honorary secretary and also for many years the president of its representative board. Through this he became deeply involved with the *Monthly Review of Dental Surgery*. He also held office at the Odontological Society of Great Britain from 1873 until 1884, when he was chosen president.

Turner married first, in November 1866, Annie, daughter of Richard Whitbourn of Godalming, with whom he had five sons and three daughters; second, he married Agnes Jane, daughter of the Revd Henry Ward, in December 1900. Turner died at his home, 79 Gordon Road, Ealing, Middlesex, on 22 February 1904, and was buried on 25 February at St George's cemetery, Ealing. His wife survived him. A scholarship in practical dental mechanics, awarded by the British Dental Association, was established in his memory.

D'A. POWER, rev. PATRICK WALLIS

Sources *BMJ* (27 Feb 1904), 523 · *The Lancet* (27 Feb 1904) · *British Dental Journal*, 25 (1904), 153–81 · *The advance of the dental profession: a centenary history, 1880–1980*, British Dental Association (privately printed, London, 1979) · private information (1904) · *CGPLA Eng. & Wales* (1904)
Likenesses S. Hodges, oils, 1890; at British Dental Association, London, in 1912
Wealth at death £13,533 17s. 2d.: resworn probate, 26 March 1904, *CGPLA Eng. & Wales*

Turner [*née* Cook], **Joanna** (1732–1784), evangelist, was born probably in Trowbridge, Wiltshire, where she was baptized on 26 July 1732, the daughter of John Cook (*d. c.*1749), clothier, and Honour Coles (*d. c.*1741), who had married in Trowbridge on 4 January 1724. Especially after the death of her mother, when she was eight or nine, Joanna thought much about death and judgement, and struggled to be a good Christian. At twelve or thirteen she was sent to what she described as 'a very genteel boarding school; indeed, one too high for my fortune' but one where a first cousin was being educated (Wells, *Memoir*, 8). There she acquired more worldly tastes, including an interest in fashion and reading romances, novels, and plays. There too she committed what she regarded as the great crime of her life: the theft of a shilling. That she had stolen was not discovered, but especially after her father's death, when she was about seventeen, her conscience tormented her with her sinfulness. In her late teens she struggled with her soul, burnt her romances, and finally became convinced that Jesus Christ had died to save her from her sins. She had returned home from school after her father's remarriage but she was unhappy because of her stepmother's dislike and harsh treatment of her.

Joanna Cook began life as a member of the Church of England, and may never have formally left it, yet in the 1750s she sought out evangelical preachers of various denominations. In London she heard William Romaine, a Church of England clergyman who made St Dunstan-in-the-West in Fleet Street a London centre of Christian evangelicalism. From the perspective of evangelicals like George Whitefield, whom she also heard preach and whose writings she read, the faithful were called to eschew the idle amusements of the world in order to devote themselves to strenuous lives of prayer, evangelizing, and charitable works. In her twenties, when she was still enjoying balls, romances, and 'the praise of men', Cook again became convinced that she was a sinner beyond hope of redemption, and lived for two years 'under continual terror' of damnation (Wells, *Memoir*, 36–7). She frequently visited relatives in Bristol, which was one of the centres of emerging Methodism, and was encouraged by her cousin Elizabeth Johnson and other 'respectable persons belonging to Mr. Whitefield's and Mr. Wesley's society' (ibid., 41); she again found conviction of salvation and finally abandoned 'the world' for a life devoted to evangelical faith and work.

As an evangelical Christian in Trowbridge Joanna Cook boldly rejected some of the conventional conduct thought appropriate to her gender and her class, and found opportunities for religious activism. She ventured to write letters of reproof to ministers whom she discovered attending balls or horse races. She distressed her family by walking considerable distances with very poor people to hear preachers and by establishing a local society which met every Thursday to read the Bible, hear and read sermons, sing hymns, and pray. Told to abandon the Methodists or move out of the family house, she elected to rent lodgings, where she continued her meetings. Though she had only the income from £500 and what she could earn from sewing, she assisted the sick and the poor, and, as the numbers at meetings grew, spent £60 to build a tabernacle.

On 9 February 1766 Joanna Cook married Thomas Turner, a Trowbridge grocer and fellow evangelical Christian. She worked in his shop for ten years, helped to keep the books, and dispensed religious advice along with the groceries. From the profits of their shop Thomas and Joanna contributed most of the money required to build a new chapel, opened on 20 November 1771. In the 1780s Thomas allowed Joanna temporarily to move to the neighbouring village of Tisbury, where he had been born, to spread the gospel there. She bought a house in Tisbury, taught religion to children, distributed bibles, entertained preachers, and established a small congregation. On 22 May 1782 the Turners opened a chapel in Tisbury to which 'Christians of all denominations came, with their respective ministers' (Wells, *Memoir*, 157).

Throughout her life Joanna Turner yearned for a comprehensive, evangelical protestant church not divided by theological differences. In 1772, at a time of dissension among Calvinist and Arminian Methodists, she wrote to John Wesley describing herself as 'not … one of your Society' but one who sought to 'pour out' her soul to him 'as to a Father in Christ'. She declared herself anguished that 'the redeemed of the LORD' should 'speak and write against each other' (*Methodist Magazine*). Wesley, whose movement depended significantly on the activism and contributions of women, replied politely, justifying his own controversial writings but agreeing that the kingdom of God was not dependent upon opinions.

Joanna Turner died of breast cancer, on 24 December 1784 in Trowbridge, where she was almost certainly buried on 5 January 1785. Her funeral sermon was preached by her minister, John Clark (1746–1809), on a text chosen by herself: 'I am nothing'; 'not less than 40 ministers of different denominations' were present (*Memoirs*, 60). She was survived by her husband but much of our knowledge of her life comes from a memoir compiled and written by her friend Mary Wells: *The triumph of faith … exemplified in the life, death, and spiritual experience of that burning and shining light, Mrs. Joanna Turner*. The book includes Turner's account of her early life, extracts from her later diaries, a number of her letters, and several of her poems. Wells adds biographical narrative and shapes her material into the conventional form of evangelical protestant hagiography of the period.

SUSAN STAVES

Sources M. Wells, *The triumph of faith, over the world, the flesh, and the devil: exemplified in the life … Mrs. Joanna Turner* (1796) • M. Wells, *Memoir of Mrs. Joanna Turner as exemplified in her life, death, and spiritual experience* (New York, 1827) • J. B. Gillespie, 'Grasping for larger measures: Joanna Turner, eighteenth-century activist', *Journal of Feminist Studies in Religion*, 3 (1987), 31–55 • Joanna Turner, letter to John Wesley, *Methodist Magazine*, 21 (1798), 46–7 • S. J. Rogal, *A biographical dictionary of 18th century Methodism*, 10 vols. (1997–9) • *The letters of the Rev. John Wesley*, ed. J. Telford, 5 (1931), 338–40 • [E. Ritchie], *An account of Mrs. Elizabeth Johnson, well known in the city of Bristol for more than half a century, for her eminent piety and benevolence. To which is added an extract from her diary* (1799) • *The works of John Wesley*, [another edn], 23, ed. F. Baker and others (1995), 186 • Miss C—, 'On the *death* of Mrs Joanna Turner', *Arminian Magazine*, 13 (1790),

223–4 · J. H. Chandler, ed., *Wiltshire dissenters' meeting house certificates and registrations, 1689–1852*, Wilts RS, 40 (1985) · T. Bridges, *Proceedings of the Wesley Historical Society*, 4 (1903), 51–9 · M. Ransome, ed., *Wiltshire returns to the bishop's visitation queries, 1783*, Wilts RS, 27 (1972) · H. D. Rack, *Reasonable enthusiasm: John Wesley and the rise of Methodism*, 2nd edn (1992) · R. Southy, *The life of Wesley and the rise and progress of Methodism*, 2 vols. (1925) · T. Mann, *A brief history of the Tabernacle Church, Trowbridge* (1884) · IGI · *Memoirs of the late Revd John Clark, written by himself*, ed. W. Jay (1810)

Turner, John Doman (1872/3–1938). *See under* Camden Town Group (*act.* 1911–1913).

Turner, Joseph (1745–1828), college head and dean of Norwich, was born at Great Yarmouth, Norfolk, on 3 October 1745 into a family long associated with the town. He was the third of four sons of the Revd Francis Turner (1716–1790), minister of St George's Chapel, Great Yarmouth (1742–90), and rector of South Elmham (1743–90), and his wife, Sarah, *née* Dawson, also from Great Yarmouth. Turner began a lifelong connection with Pembroke College, Cambridge, when he was admitted as a sizar on 26 January 1763 and matriculated at Lent the same year. He graduated BA (senior wrangler) in 1767, MA in 1770, and DD in 1785.

In October 1773 Turner was elected lecturer in Greek and Hebrew at Pembroke, serving as tutor in mathematics from 1776 alongside George Pretyman, both men including William Pitt the younger among their charges. Turner took a genuine interest in the progress of all the undergraduates, as one of them, Henry Ainslie, reported on 3 November 1777, after completing his examinations, 'when he [Turner] heard I was first he shook my hand for 10 minutes & paid me a thousand compliments' (*Gazette*, 15). Turner's teaching and administrative services to Pembroke were recognized by his nomination as master in 1784 in succession to James Brown, a post he held until his death. It was fortunate that Turner's appointment roughly coincided with Pitt's assumption of the premiership. This ensured that Pembroke's welfare (and Turner's own) were not overlooked at the highest levels of government. Turner's quiet efficiency as master contributed to the continuing academic distinction enjoyed by the college in the late eighteenth century. This scholarly revival continued until at least the halfway point in his mastership. Thereafter Turner's increasing age, residence for three or four months yearly in Norwich, and differences of opinion with some of the fellows (he failed in legal proceedings to obtain the use of a property bequest to Pembroke) may have adversely affected the college.

Turner's administrative abilities were also called upon when he twice served as vice-chancellor of the university (in 1785–6 and 1805–6). During both terms he presented addresses to George III on behalf of the university: the first, attended by William Pitt, Edward Eliot (Pitt's brother-in-law), and George Pretyman, congratulating the king on the preservation of his life after Margaret Nicholson's assassination attempt; the second offering a loyal expression of thanks for Nelson's victory at Trafalgar. Turner undoubtedly benefited from Pretyman's role as secretary to William Pitt and subsequently from his promotion to the bishopric of Lincoln in 1787. Pitt secured his former teacher a second major post in 1790 when Turner was named dean of Norwich, being installed and inducted on 24 June. Thereafter he resided for part of the year in Norwich, attended the twice-yearly meeting of the general chapter, and was conscientious in his discharge of chapter business. He married on 5 January 1793, at Lambeth Palace, Mary (*b.* 15 Jan 1764), the eldest daughter of Philip Derbyshire. She died on 10 March 1804, and was buried in Norwich Cathedral on 17 March. Six years later, on 3 January 1810, he married Mary, daughter of John Taylor of Great Yarmouth. During these Norwich years a restoration of the cathedral took place which showed a sensitivity to fittings not always evidenced by late Georgian chapters. Turner oversaw the major repairs to the cathedral fabric undertaken in 1806. These included the provision of a new pulpit and extra seats in the choir. However, failing health in the 1820s curtailed the extent of his appearances in Norwich, and by that date chapter records suggest a perceptible decline in organizational efficiency.

First and foremost an administrator Turner published nothing, but became a fellow of the Society of Antiquaries in 1801. In addition to his mastership and deanery he was also awarded by the crown the wealthy rectories of Sudbourne and Orford in Suffolk in 1787, and held them until his death at the deanery, Norwich, on 2 August 1828. He was buried in the choir of Norwich Cathedral on 12 August, where a brass recalls that: 'The general uprightness and integrity of his character were invariably acknowledged by all with whom the duties of his public situations brought him in connection'. Turner was survived by one son from his first marriage, William Hamilton (*b.* 1803), who became a country clergyman. His second wife died on 25 February 1842 and was buried at St Peter Mancroft, Norwich.   NIGEL ASTON

Sources GM, 1st ser., 98/2 (1828), 648 · H. Turner and F. Johnson, *The Turner family of Mulbarton and Great Yarmouth*, new edn (1907) · D. Turner, *Sepulchral reminiscences of a small town* (1848) · A. L. Attwater, *Pembroke College, Cambridge: a short history*, ed. S. C. Roberts (1936) · *Gazette* [Pembroke College Cambridge Society], 11 (1937), 13–19 · H. Gunning, *Reminiscences of the university, town, and county of Cambridge, from the year 1780*, 2 vols. (1854) · *Fasti Angl., 1541–1857*, [Ely] · J. Gascoigne, *Cambridge in the age of the Enlightenment* (1989) · I. Atherton and others, eds., *Norwich Cathedral: church, city and diocese, 1096–1996* (1996) · Great Yarmouth church registers · *Register of burials in the cathedral church of Norwich, 1813–*
Archives CUL · Norfolk RO, corresp. and papers relating to estate business · Pembroke Cam. | BL, corresp. with Lord Hardwicke and others, Add. MSS 23947, 35649, 35658, 35682–35687
Likenesses Schipper, portrait, 1817 · H. E. Dawe, portrait, 1828, Pembroke Cam.

Turner, Joseph Egbert (1853–1897), Benedictine monk and composer, was born on 10 January 1853 at 4 Fishergate, Preston, Lancashire, the seventh of the ten children of James Turner, a master tailor and draper, and his wife, Martha, the daughter of Robert Railton of Blackburn. After receiving an education from the Benedictine monks at Ampleforth, Yorkshire, he joined that community and was sent to Belmont Priory, Hereford, which was then the common novitiate for all English Benedictines, but he returned to Ampleforth for solemn profession on 8 December 1876. At that time a new foundation was being established at Fort Augustus on Loch Ness. Turner joined it and was ordained priest there on 22 May 1880. In 1883 he was recalled to Ampleforth as organist and choirmaster.

Little or nothing is known about Turner's musical education. Dom Cuthbert Hedley, his superior at Belmont, was an accomplished organist, and there is some tradition that R. W. Oberhoffer, of York, gave him some tuition. Much of the appeal in Turner's music lies in its quaintly honest structure. Almost self-taught, he attained a standard of craftsmanship always scrupulously correct; he had a special gift of melody, and he was careful never to violate the academic rules of harmonic progression. His work may be described as highly polished if not brilliant. Only in the latter years of his life, years spent in Benedictine parishes, did he achieve fame as a composer and the reputation of one whose church music was without rival in popularity among Roman Catholic choirs, large or small. He was curate at St David's, Swansea (1885–9), St Michael's, Workington (1889–91), St Mary's, Warrington (1891–3), and St Anne's, Edge Hill, Liverpool (1893–7). In Liverpool, Turner was the musical correspondent of the *Catholic Times* and a close friend of Sir Charles Santley and the first Eugene Goossens.

Turner's publications consist of seven motets, six litanies, four masses, three benediction services, a *Festival Litany of Loreto*, and a few arrangements of other pieces. It was said at his funeral that he also had plans for a grand oratorio. But it was as a composer of settings of the Latin mass that his name became renowned. His first mass ('St John the Baptist') has a ring of joyous solemnity and a pleasing, often noble, melodic line. Its Sanctus might owe something to Mozart's Requiem but its Gloria is pure Turner. His second mass ('St Cecilia') was the most popular of its type ever written. Though it is capricious in places, the celestial-sounding opening of its Gloria and its copious solo passages led to the publication of eleven editions between 1892 and 1973. His third mass ('St Mary Magdalen') is a work of splendid fervour, having a magnificent Kyrie and Gloria and a Benedictus of angelic simplicity. His fourth mass ('The Good Shepherd') was, in the opinion of his publisher, Alphonse Cary, his best work. There is a Kyrie of elegiac beauty and a Gloria and Credo containing true polyphony, while the 'Dona nobis pacem' of the Agnus Dei culminates in a mighty fugue. The seven motets—*Adoro te devote* (two settings), *Ascendit Deus*, *Ave Pater sanctissimae*, *Ave verum*, *O sacrum convivium*, and *O quam suavis*—all exhibit similar characteristics.

In September 1897 the 1300th anniversary of the arrival of St Augustine and his companions was celebrated on the shores of Kent, with magnificent ceremonial. A choir of forty Benedictine monks was to take part, but, when summoned to take his place in procession, Turner was found to be stricken with pleurisy and unable to move. Pneumonia developed, and on Sunday 19 September 1897 he died,

at 45 Grange Road, Ramsgate, Kent. His grave, with the epitaph 'Now I will sing of Thy great mercy', is in the cemetery attached to St Augustine's Abbey, Ramsgate.

BRIAN PLUMB

Sources B. Plumb, 'A Victorian monk–musician', *Ampleforth Journal*, 79 (1974), 61–4 · T. B. Snow, *Obit book of the English Benedictines from 1600 to 1912*, rev. H. N. Birt (privately printed, Edinburgh, 1913) · M. Purcell, *Census of the Catholic congregation of Preston* (1993) · b. cert. · d. cert. · census returns, 1871 · M. Conlon, *St Alban's, Blackburn, 1773–1973* (1973) · baptismal register, St Wilfrid's R.C. church, Preston

Turner, Joseph Mallord William (1775–1851), landscape and history painter, was born in 1775 (according to his own reminiscence on 23 April), the son of William Turner (1745–1829), barber and wig-maker, of 21 Maiden Lane, in the parish of St Paul's, Covent Garden, London, and his wife, Mary Marshall (1739–1804), whom he had married at St Paul's on 29 August 1773. The baby was baptized at St Paul's on 14 May (in the register Mallord was spelt Mallad). William Turner was of a Devonshire family, and was born in South Molton, where his father was a saddler, on 29 June 1745. Mary Marshall was six years older than her husband and came from a family of artisans and tradesmen living in the outskirts of London. She named her son after one of her brothers, Joseph Mallord William Marshall, who was a butcher in Brentford, Middlesex, and with whom Turner was sent to stay in 1785. Turner was known in his early years as William Turner. An elder sister married a curate at Islington, Henry Harpur, whose grandson, another Henry, was one of Turner's executors. Another Marshall relative, perhaps also a brother, was a fishmonger at Margate, Kent, with whom Turner was sent to stay in 1786. These absences from home were probably because of the ill health and instability of his mother, who became insane at the end of her life and died in an asylum on 15 April 1804. Turner's only surviving sibling, Mary Ann, was baptized at St Paul's, Covent Garden, on 6 September 1778, and was buried there on 8 August 1783.

Education and training There is little firm information about Turner's education and training. When staying at Brentford in 1785 he attended John White's school, and while in Margate in the following year he was at the school of Thomas Coleman, an active Methodist preacher. At Brentford the ten- or eleven-year-old Turner is said to have coloured some of the engravings in a copy of Henry Boswell's *Antiquities of England and Wales* for John Lees, foreman of a distillery, who paid him 2*d*. for each plate. Turner's earliest surviving watercolour drawings are of subjects in and near Margate (W 1–4, all priv. coll.) and were probably made during the 1786 visit. The earliest drawings in the Turner Bequest in Tate Britain are copies from engravings dated 1787 (W 5–6). Tradition has it that Turner's father encouraged his son's artistic talents, and displayed some of his drawings for sale in his shop window and doorway—the family had by now moved to 26 Maiden Lane—at prices ranging from 1 to 3*s*. Another longstanding tradition is that he was employed to hand-colour prints by the leading mezzotint engraver John Raphael

Joseph Mallord William Turner (1775–1851), self-portrait, *c.*1798

Smith, one of the many printmakers working in the Covent Garden area.

There are also claims that the young Turner was apprenticed to or employed as a draughtsman by a number of architects, among them Thomas Hardwick, William Porden, and Joseph Bonomi; the strongest evidence for such employment is with Thomas Hardwick, who was from 1787 to 1790 in charge of rebuilding the church of St Mary in Wanstead, Essex, of which there is a drawing by Turner in the Turner Bequest (TB IV A). In the summer of 1789 the young artist stayed at Sunningwell, near Oxford, with his maternal uncle Joseph Marshall, and he filled a sketchbook (TB II) with pencil drawings of buildings and views in and around Oxford, from some of which he completed finished watercolours. By the end of 1789 Turner was definitely working with the architectural draughtsman Thomas Malton the younger, and on 11 December he was admitted as a student at the Royal Academy Schools, which he attended for several years. In the Turner Bequest there is a group of drawings from the antique (TB V), most of which were probably the result of his early studies in the plaster academy at the Royal Academy Schools. He began to work in the life academy in June 1792, and last signed its register in November 1799.

However, landscape and topographical drawing and painting were not taught at the Royal Academy, and in this vital area Turner was in many ways his own teacher, except for the encouragement and help provided by Dr Thomas Monro and his so-called academy. Monro, a physician who specialized in mental disorders, was a collector and amateur artist who from about 1794 assembled young artists at his house in the Adelphi to copy from drawings in his collection, many of them by J. R. Cozens, who spent the last years of his life in the doctor's care. Turner's close contemporary and friend Thomas Girtin was among his fellow students at the Adelphi, and it is often difficult to be certain which of them was responsible for specific 'Monro school' drawings. Our most detailed information about the Monro academy comes from the diary of Joseph Farington, who first mentioned it in December 1794 and then recorded on 12 November 1798 that:

> Turner & Girtin told us that they had been employed by Dr. Monro 3 years to draw at his house in the evenings. They went at 6 and staid till Ten. Girtin drew in outlines and Turner washed in the effects. Turner afterwards told me that Dr. Munro had been a material friend to him, as well as to Girtin. (Farington, *Diary*, 3.1090)

First tours and exhibits, 1790–1798 Turner's first exhibit at a Royal Academy summer exhibition was no. 644 in 1790, a watercolour of the archbishop's palace, Lambeth (W 10; Indianapolis Museum of Art), an exercise in perspective drawing in which the influences of Malton and of Paul Sandby can be seen. The drawing was not sold, and after the exhibition Turner gave it to his father's friend John Narraway of Bristol, with whose family he stayed for several weeks in 1791 during his second sketching tour, which resulted in the 'Bristol and Malmesbury sketchbook' (TB VI), which contains several drawings of the Avon Gorge and of Malmesbury Abbey, some of which he again developed into exhibition and other finished watercolours. These annual sketching tours, during which he gathered material for his finished work, became a regular feature of Turner's working life, as they were for most British topographical artists of this period. Turner can rarely have been without a sketchbook and pencil to hand, and must have been drawing continuously during his travels, as the close on 300 sketchbooks in the Turner Bequest reveal. These sketchbooks, which he himself labelled carefully, became the artist's reference library, the contents of which were regularly used as the basis of finished drawings, including those for engraving, and paintings. As well as providing evidence of Turner's progress and development as an artist, the sketchbooks also contain much precious information to boost the scant biographical material otherwise available.

Turner exhibited two watercolours at the Royal Academy in 1791 and another two in 1792. Of these, *The Pantheon, the morning after the fire* (TB IXA, W 27) was one of several depictions of the disaster on 14 January 1792 when the theatre in which Turner was currently employed by William Hodges as an assistant scene painter was gutted. A second visit to the Narraways at Bristol in the summer of 1792, on his way to his first sketching tour in Wales, resulted in two River Avon subjects among the three drawings shown in 1793, while in 1794 his five exhibited watercolours included two Welsh scenes. Another, *St Anselm's Chapel, Canterbury Cathedral* (W 55; Whitworth Art Gallery, University of Manchester), was bought by Dr Monro, and in 1794 Turner's exhibits were noticed for the first time in the press—briefly but favourably. That year also saw the publication of the first two of a series of small topographical engravings after drawings by Turner, in the *Copper-Plate Magazine* (R 1–15) which continued to 1798, while a similar series was published in 1795–6 in the *Pocket Magazine* (R 16–31). The artist collected material for these prints on tours in the midlands and Wales in 1794, and in the north, including the Lake District, Yorkshire, and the Northumberland coast, in 1797.

The 1794 tour also provided material for the eight watercolours that Turner showed at the Royal Academy in 1795, which again did much to enhance the young artist's reputation, and attracted patronage from some of the leading collectors of the day, among them Sir Richard Colt Hoare, of Stourhead, Wiltshire, where Turner was probably a visitor that year. Sir Richard commissioned a series of drawings of the cathedral and other buildings in Salisbury, hoping to use them to illustrate a history of Wiltshire which was never completed, as well as two of Hampton Court in Herefordshire, the seat of Viscount Malden, later fifth earl of Essex, who also ordered views of his house. These and other commissions, including one from the engraver John Landseer, were listed by Turner in the 'South Wales' sketchbook used in 1795 (TB XXVI). Turner was kept busy by all this work as well as by his preparations for the 1796 summer exhibition, at which he showed ten watercolours and his first oil painting, *Fishermen at Sea* (BJ 1; Tate collection), a competent atmospheric moonlit scene off the Isle of Wight, which Turner had visited the previous summer. In the tradition of Joseph Vernet, Joseph Wright of Derby, and others, the painting received favourable notices, while Farington described the drawings as 'very ingenious, but it is a manner'd harmony which He obtains' (Farington, *Diary*, 2.518, 2 April 1796). Two of the watercolours are impressive interior views in Westminster Abbey and Ely Cathedral, in which Turner's mastery of architectural detail and of the depiction of space, light, and shade is breathtaking. The Westminster Abbey drawing, of Bishop Islip's chapel, was the first work by Turner bought by Edward Lascelles the younger, friend of Viscount Malden and son and heir of the first earl of Harewood, who died before his father. Between 1796 and 1808 Lascelles was a major collector of contemporary British artists, Girtin and Turner foremost among them, and in 1797 Turner visited Harewood to gather material for a series of views of the great Yorkshire house and its park, some of which remain at Harewood today.

In 1797 Turner's contribution to the Royal Academy was two oil paintings and four watercolours, including two of Salisbury Cathedral, and in the following year there were four paintings and four watercolours, all but one of them of Lake District, Yorkshire, and Northumberland subjects. The 1797 oils were another, but quite small, moonlit scene and the very well-received but now lost 'Mildmay Seapiece', *Fishermen coming ashore at Sun Set, previous to a Gale* (BJ 3), Turner's first seascape in the Dutch tradition. In November 1798 Turner, supported by Joseph Farington, who recorded full details of the election, stood as one of twenty-four candidates for two vacancies for associate membership of the Royal Academy, and came third. Soon after the election, on 28 November, Turner told Farington, 'He was determined not to give any more lessons in drawing. He has had only five Shillings a lesson' (Farington, *Diary*, 3.1098). The 23-year-old Turner was himself still learning by emulating the work of his predecessors, and at this time he was working on *Aeneas and the Sibyl, Lake Avernus* (BJ 34; Tate collection), his first effort in the classical tradition of historical landscape, painted for Colt Hoare in the manner of Richard Wilson.

From ARA to RA, 1799–1802 1799 was an auspicious year for Turner, who was able to report to Farington on 6 July that 'He had 60 drawings now bespoke by different persons' (Farington, *Diary*, 4.1249). Earlier that day the diarist had told Turner that 'He might be assured of being elected [to the Royal Academy], to remove his anxiety' (ibid.). Among his new patrons were the earl of Yarborough, who commissioned drawings (destroyed by fire) of the mausoleum built on his Lincolnshire estate by James Wyatt, and William Beckford, who ordered watercolours of his great Gothic abbey at Fonthill in Wiltshire, also designed by James Wyatt (W 335–42, various locations), for which he was to receive 35 guineas each. It is not surprising that in April of this year Turner, who had been recommended by Benjamin West, did not reach an agreement with Lord Elgin to accompany him as draughtsman on his projected expedition to Athens; it seems that Turner demanded the very high salary of £400 per annum, while the earl expected to keep all the artist's work. However, later in the year Turner did accept the low fee of 10 guineas per drawing from the Oxford University Press for the prestigious commission to provide ten watercolours for engraving as the headpieces of the annual *Oxford Almanack*, which were published between 1799 and 1811 (W 295–304; Ashmolean Museum, Oxford; engravings R 38–47).

At the summer exhibition of 1799 Turner was represented by four oil paintings (BJ 8–11) and seven watercolours, and in both media the artist amply demonstrated the strengths and variety of his work at this crucial time. One of the watercolours, a glowing sunset view, reminiscent of a Claude harbour scene, of Caernarfon Castle (W 254; priv. coll.), was purchased by the great collector John Julius Angerstein, who paid 40 guineas for it, a price, as reported by Farington, fixed by the purchaser and 'much greater than Turner wd. have asked' (Farington, *Diary*, 4.1229, 27 May 1799). Turner's mastery of watercolour was now widely admired, though in technique and style the impressive compositions of his exhibition pieces remained varied and unpredictable. On 21 July 1799 Farington recorded that Turner told him, 'He has no systematic process for making Drawings—He avoids any particular mode that He may not fall into manner' (ibid., 4.1255), and later in the year (17 November) the diarist reported, 'Turner has no settled process but drives the colours abt. till He has expressed the idea in his mind' (ibid., 4.1303). Earlier that month Turner, who had only that year reached the lower age limit of twenty-four, had easily come top of the ballot for the election of two associate members of the Royal Academy. Soon after his election the artist left home and took rooms at 64 Harley Street, installing his mistress, Sarah Danby, not far away.

In the months between the two diary entries Turner had made two important visits. In August–September he stayed for three weeks with William Beckford at Fonthill Abbey, which was still in the hands of the builders, making many drawings in two large sketchbooks (TB XLVII and XLVIII) in preparation for the finished drawings of the abbey, seen only in the distance, and its surrounding landscape (W 335–9). From Fonthill Turner travelled north via London for an extended tour in Lancashire, Yorkshire, and north Wales. This tour centred round the commission, initiated by the great collector of antique sculpture Charles Townley, to make drawings to illustrate Dr Whitaker's antiquarian *History of the Parish of Whalley*, published with ten very old-fashioned engravings after Turner in 1801 (R 52–61). During this tour the artist met several future patrons, Walter Fawkes of Farnley Hall among them.

At the 1800 Royal Academy exhibition Turner showed two oil paintings and six watercolours, five of which were his finished Fonthill drawings. One of the oils, *The Fifth Plague of Egypt* (BJ 13; Indianapolis Museum of Art), which in fact represents the seventh plague, was Turner's first historical picture and displays the strong influence of Poussin. It was purchased for 150 guineas by William Beckford, and was very warmly received by the critics. That summer Turner was again at Fonthill, but did little other travelling. He had been commissioned by the eighth earl of Bridgewater to paint, for 250 guineas, a pendant to his large Van de Velde seascape, *A Rising Gale*. 'The Bridgewater Seapiece', as it is generally known (*Dutch Boats in a Gale*, BJ 14; priv. coll.), was Turner's major Royal Academy exhibit in 1801, with one other oil and four watercolours, and it became the picture of the year. Much admired by Benjamin West and other fellow artists, it was also attacked by some critics for its 'lack of finish'. In the summer Turner, helped with his itinerary by Joseph Farington, made his first Scottish tour, visiting Edinburgh, travelling extensively in the highlands, where the mountains made a strong impact on him, and returning via the Lake District. A few months later, on 12 February 1802 Turner was elected a Royal Academician. The cockney barber's son had reached the summit of his ambitions at the age of twenty-six, and was entitled to the coveted and then meaningful title of 'esquire'; though now a 'gentleman' he apparently never lost his cockney accent.

Some two months later the summer exhibition included eight works by Turner. There were three powerful watercolours of Scottish subjects, two imposing canvases of marine subjects, one of them, the so-called 'Egremont Seapiece' (BJ 18), the first Turner bought by the third earl of Egremont and still at Petworth, and two historical subjects, which were not sold in Turner's lifetime. The reception of this varied group was mixed, but on the whole favourable.

First foreign tour, 1802 A treaty signed on 25 March 1802 established the peace of Amiens and began a fourteen-month breathing-space in the war between Britain and France. For the first time in some nine years ordinary travellers were again able to cross the channel, and Turner was among the many British artists who flocked to Paris and beyond. He was on the continent from 15 July to mid-October, travelling in some style, accompanied by a Durham country gentleman and amateur artist, Newbey Lowson, through France and Switzerland, but not quite reaching Italy. On the return journey he spent some three weeks in Paris, during which he filled the small 'Studies in the Louvre' sketchbook (TB LXXII) with numerous heavily annotated copies after Titian, Poussin, Rubens, and others. On this journey he used eleven sketchbooks in all, some of them quite large, with a total of over 400 drawings. Not long after his return to London Turner attended Thomas Girtin's funeral at St Paul's, Covent Garden; he had lost a friend and a potential rival, as Turner himself was the first to recognize.

The Royal Academy exhibition of 1803, for which Turner was on the hanging committee for the first time, presented the new academician at full strength with five oil paintings and two watercolours, all derived from the experiences of his 1802 tour. Four of the paintings reflected the powerful impact of his study of Poussin, Claude, and Titian in the Louvre; the fifth—*Calais Pier, with French Poissards preparing for Sea: an English Packet arriving* (BJ 48; National Gallery, London)—is a vivid record of his stormy crossing of the channel that July. Like the two imposing watercolours of Swiss scenes, this dramatic composition was very much in Turner's 'own manner', an early example of his ability to create a type of 'history painting' from an ordinary everyday event. That May Farington recorded many varied comments among fellow artists about Turner and his work; on 13 May he himself summed up Turner as 'confident, presumptuous,—with talent' (Farington, *Diary*, 6.2030).

Wealth and fame, 1803–1811 Turner undertook no tours in 1803, which was a turbulent year for members of the Royal Academy as several controversies and numerous meetings took up much of their time. Turner was a member of the academy council that year, and he was also busy in building a large gallery of his own—70 feet long and 20 wide—attached to his house in Harley Street, in which the first exhibition, of which no details are known, opened in April 1804, shortly before the Royal Academy exhibition at which Turner showed only two paintings and one watercolour. At the end of the year or early in 1805 Turner became the tenant of Sion Ferry House, on the Thames at Isleworth, and from late 1806 until 1811 he rented a house at Upper Mall, Hammersmith. It is probable that he had a boat on the river, and in the years around 1806–7 he painted a series of large (BJ 160–76) and small (BJ 177–94) Thames sketches which are all in the Turner Bequest. The latter are painted on mahogany panels and it is likely that many of these rapid and effective studies were painted out of doors, some of them while in the boat. They combine disciplined compositions with the direct and fluent depiction of the river scenery to achieve the most 'modern' element in Turner's work so far. In painting these series Turner was, however, not alone, for during this decade a number of fellow artists, outstanding among them John Constable, were likewise working in oils from nature, several of them also in the area of the Thames.

For the first time since 1790 Turner was not represented in the Royal Academy exhibition in 1805. There was an exhibition in his own gallery, to which, according to Farington, Turner invited all his fellow academicians. It included *The Shipwreck* (BJ 54; Tate collection), which was bought for £315 by Sir John Leicester, and was the subject of the first major individual print after Turner, engraved in mezzotint by Charles Turner, and published on 1 January 1807 (R 751). The success of this large plate was one of several factors that led Turner, encouraged by his great friend William Wells, a minor watercolour artist and a founder of the Society of Painters in Water Colours in 1804, to devise and launch his great series of mezzotint engravings, the *Liber Studiorum*. Owing much to the example of Claude Lorrain's famous *Liber Veritatis*, which was a personal record of that artist's works, the *Liber Studiorum* was at once a work of instruction and a manifestation of Turner's own very varied achievements as a painter so far. The plan was for 100 plates in twenty parts and two volumes, without any text but arranged in didactic groups to demonstrate the various categories of landscape art. Turner himself was the publisher of most of the series, of which the first part appeared in 1807. In the end only seventy-one plates were published, the last ten in 1819. Turner produced the monochrome wash drawings, many of them versions of earlier paintings, and also made the majority of the outline etchings for the mezzotinting, which he himself undertook for ten of the published plates. The *Liber Studiorum* was central to Turner's career as the most personal and carefully conceived series of prints in his entire *œuvre*. The mezzotints and etchings were eagerly collected in the second half of the nineteenth and the early years of the twentieth century.

In the meantime Turner continued to exhibit some oil paintings and a few watercolours at the Royal Academy, the newly formed British Institution, and rather more in his own gallery. In 1807 he was elected professor of perspective at the Royal Academy, though he did not deliver his first lectures until 1811. The lectures were beautifully illustrated with specially made large-scale diagrams and drawings, but were difficult to hear and understand. The notes survive, but are also difficult to decipher; what has been published so far indicates that these lectures provide considerable insight into Turner's deep knowledge of the history of landscape painting and of his own theories on the subject. Our first detailed information about one of the exhibitions in Turner's own gallery is for that in 1808, and comes from the long review by the engraver John Landseer in the second issue of his own short-lived journal, the *Review of Publications of Art*. This discusses eleven paintings (BJ 70–80) of which 'the greater number … are views on the Thames, whose course Mr. Turner has now studiously followed, with the eye and hand at once of a painter and a poet' (*Turner Studies*, 7/1, 1987, 28). In his text and in a footnote Landseer referred to Turner's *Liber*

Studiorum 'classification of the various styles of landscape', and a large group of the *Liber* sepia drawings was shown in the exhibition. Catalogues have survived for the 1809 and 1810 Turner's gallery exhibitions, listing sixteen oil paintings and two watercolours in 1809 and seventeen exhibits in 1810, several of which had already been shown before. Turner's gallery was closed in 1811, pending alterations, and that summer he again showed more work at the Royal Academy. Turner had been irregular in his attendance of Royal Academy meetings in the last few years, but he was elected to the council for 1811, and he attended regularly during that year and also in 1812.

During this busy period Turner undertook no specific sketching tours, but most summers he stayed with one or other of his patrons, including in 1808 his first stay at Farnley Hall, the Yorkshire seat of Walter Fawkes, and in 1809 what was probably his first visit to Lord Egremont at Petworth, to make views of the great Sussex house and other Egremont property. Fawkes was to become a close friend and an important patron, as was Lord Egremont, though the friendship between the eccentric peer and the eccentric artist only really blossomed after the death of Walter Fawkes in 1824. However in the summer of 1811 Turner did undertake another lengthy sketching tour, in Dorset, Devon, and Cornwall, in order to begin work on an important commission from the engraver brothers George and William Bernard Cooke to provide the drawings for a major topographical publication, *Picturesque Views on the Southern Coast of England* (R 88–127) of which the first plates appeared in 1814. This ambitious series was never completed, and only thirty-nine of the projected forty-eight plates were published, the last four in 1826. The project was marred and delayed by squabbles between Turner and the Cookes, and between the engravers and the publisher, John Murray. On the other hand Turner provided some of the best watercolours he had yet made, and also took immense pains in supervising the work of the engravers. This series produced the first of the high-quality copper-engravings after Turner, and was a watershed in the standard of the prints based on his work, and of such prints in Britain as a whole.

In 1810 Turner had shown three oils at the Royal Academy, all views of two of his patrons' great houses—one of Petworth (BJ 113) and two of Lowther Castle, the Westmorland seat of the earl of Lonsdale (BJ 111–12). One of the four paintings shown in 1811, when he also exhibited five watercolours, was the lovely *Somer-Hill Near Tunbridge, the seat of W.F. Woodgate, Esq.* (BJ 116), now in the National Gallery of Scotland, Edinburgh. These and other paintings of country houses certainly brought Turner considerable sums, and his growing number of drawings for engraving must also have been profitable. In 1812 Turner felt able to begin building his own country house, or rather Thames-side villa, for which he had bought the plot at Twickenham for £400 late in 1807.

Consolidation, 1812–1819 There are nearly fifty drawings connected with the design of Sandycombe Lodge (initially named Solus Lodge) in various sketchbooks used by Turner between 1807 and 1812, and it is certain that Turner himself designed the essentially modest house, which still survives today. The plan is symmetrical, the rooms are small and the ornamentation is restrained, showing the influence of Turner's architect friend and fellow academician John Soane. Turner started paying rates in 1813, but little is known about his actual use of the house, though he did entertain there and the garden provided happy occupation for the artist's father, who lived with his son. One reason given for the sale of the house in 1826 is that William Turner senior, now in his eighties, was no longer able to enjoy working in the garden.

Turner's supervision of the building of Sandycombe Lodge ruled out travel in 1812, but his altered gallery, now approached from Queen Anne Street West, reopened in May with an exhibition that included several paintings of west country scenes. At the Royal Academy he exhibited four paintings, including the two views of Oxford (BJ 102 and 125) commissioned by the Oxford picture dealer and framemaker James Wyatt to be engraved. Turner was ill at the end of the year, and postponed his third series of perspective lectures, due early in 1813. For the next few years Turner did give his lectures fairly regularly, for the last time in 1828, though he did not resign the chair until 1837.

Turner's lectures were, on the whole, coolly received, and though there was generally praise for his paintings during these years there was also some strong criticism. Much of this came from Sir George Beaumont, great collector, patron, amateur landscape artist, and leader of taste, and from some of his associates. Turner was certainly upset by this, and it was perhaps in an attempt to show his displeasure that he made a late and inappropriate submission in February 1814 for one of the annual premiums, designed for young and unestablished artists, offered by the British Institution, of which Sir George was one of the most active directors. The prize was for a landscape which in previous years had been expected to be in the classical tradition, and Turner submitted *Apullia in Search of Appulus vide Ovid* (BJ 128; Tate collection), a large canvas closely modelled on Lord Egremont's great Claude *Landscape with Jacob and Laban*. The premium was awarded to T. C. Hofland, who was actually only two years younger than Turner and until winning this prize was best-known as a copyist. Turner's only work at the Royal Academy that summer was another vast historical landscape, *Dido and Aeneas* (BJ 129; Tate collection), which, like much of his work at this time, remained unsold. There is no information about that year's exhibition in his own gallery, which was announced as 'the last Season but two', an indication of plans for yet another enlargement, which was finally begun in 1819.

1815 was a difficult year for Turner, as his Royal Academy exhibits that summer brought to a head the severe and hurtful criticism of Sir George Beaumont and his circle. Turner's four paintings and four watercolours (all very large and powerful Swiss scenes, three of which had been painted for Walter Fawkes some ten years earlier) were a very mixed group, of which the two great Claudian compositions, *Crossing the Brook* (BJ 130; Tate collection) and *Dido building Carthage* (BJ 131; National Gallery, London), were much praised by fellow artists and several critics, and have become two of Turner's best-known earlier works. However, these were also the two paintings which most annoyed Beaumont, who is reported by Farington to have commented that *Crossing the Brook* 'appeared to Him weak and like the work of an Old man … it was all of peagreen insipidity', while the *Dido* was 'painted in a false taste, not true to nature; the colouring discordant, out of harmony' (Farington, *Diary*, 13.4638, 5 June 1815). Beaumont's opinions were widely known, and he was one of the principal targets in an anonymous pamphlet entitled *A Catalogue Raisonné of the Pictures now Exhibiting at the British Institution*, which was a forceful attack on the directors of the institution, ostensibly for staging their loan exhibitions of old master paintings, which were unpopular with living artists, but it also defended Turner against the abusive criticism of his work.

During August Turner escaped from all the controversy and went to Farnley Hall, where he was now a frequent summer visitor treated almost as a member of the Fawkes family. He arrived in time for the grouse shooting, and also found relaxation in making some of his series of watercolour drawings to record Walter Fawkes's collection of 'Fairfaxiana' and some of the twenty beautiful studies of birds for the family's ornithological collection. He was at Farnley again the following summer, which was very wet. After a short tour with Fawkes and his family, he continued on his own, touring Yorkshire and Lancashire in pursuit of material for Dr Whitaker's proposed *History of Yorkshire*. The antiquarian had commissioned Turner to make 120 drawings for this ambitious project, of which, however, only the *History of Richmondshire* was completed, published between 1818 and 1822 with twenty plates after some of Turner's most attractive watercolours (R 169–88; W 559–81).

Before this Yorkshire visit Turner had again opened an exhibition in his gallery and sent a pair of very large and imposing classical scenes to the Royal Academy exhibition (BJ 133 and 134). Both featured the temple of 'Jupiter Panellenius' on the island of Aegina, and presented an audacious and carefully orchestrated challenge, indicating his sympathy with the cause of Greek liberation and his knowledge of current archaeological activities in Greece, to the critics of his two Claudian compositions the year before. Turner continued his campaign in 1817, when his only Royal Academy exhibit was the even larger *Decline of the Carthaginian Empire* (BJ 135; Tate collection), a companion to the 1815 *Dido building Carthage*, and again highly praised by most of the critics. This pair has been interpreted as Turner's telling commentary on the rise and fall of the Napoleonic empire. Visits to the continent were again a possibility, but Turner's own second crossing of the channel was delayed until the summer of 1817. He sailed from Margate to Ostend on 10 August, and after visiting the battlefield of Waterloo travelled up the Rhine from Cologne to Mainz, returning in mid-September via Belgium and the Netherlands. Soon after his return to

England Turner visited Raby Castle, seat of the earl of Darlington, to collect material for his fine painting of the house in its landscape (BJ 136; Walters Art Gallery, Baltimore). After more sketching in co. Durham, Turner ended his tour at Farnley, where he spent about three weeks.

It was during this visit that Walter Fawkes purchased the famous series of fifty watercolour views of the Rhine based on drawings in the sketchbooks used during the Rhine tour (W 636–86). These represent a new development in Turner's work in watercolours and gouache, for they were clearly quite rapidly and spontaneously executed, using a limited range of colours, though appearing 'finished', and were long considered to have been painted on the spot. When they were completed is not known, and it is probable that Turner was working on the series during the evenings in Germany and then while at Raby. He was back in London in December, and must have begun working on his three large and important canvases for the next Royal Academy exhibition.

As well as the *Raby Castle* these were the luminous *Dort, or Dordrecht* (BJ 137; Yale U. CBA), Turner's most important homage to Albrecht Cuyp, who was born in Dordrecht, and the dramatic and Rembrandtesque *Field of Waterloo* (BJ 138; Tate collection), both resulting from the scenery as well as the paintings he had seen on his 1817 continental tour. Turner's fourth Royal Academy exhibit that year was a large watercolour of an Italian scene, *Composition of Tivoli* (W 495; priv. coll.). He had yet to visit Italy, but at this time he was working on the commission from the architect James Hakewill, who had toured and sketched in Italy in 1816 and 1817, to make twenty watercolours after his own drawings, of which eighteen were engraved for Hakewill's *Picturesque Tour in Italy* and published by John Murray between 1818 and 1820 (R 144–61). Many years later Ruskin thought that Turner's Hakewill drawings were done *after* the artist's first Italian tour, which took place in 1819. Turner did travel again in the autumn of 1818, to Scotland to collect material for Walter Scott's *Provincial Antiquities and Picturesque Scenery of Scotland* to be published as a speculative venture in Edinburgh. The distinguished author had insisted that Turner should be one of the illustrators of this work, believing that his inclusion would ensure the success of the publication. Ten plates and two vignettes after his drawings were engraved for the two volumes between 1819 and 1826 (R 189–200), but the venture was a commercial failure.

In the remarkably varied small group of 1818 exhibits Turner had proved yet again his versatile mastery of several styles and traditions, as he was also continuing to do in the last four parts of the *Liber Studiorum*, published in 1816 and 1819. At the 1819 summer exhibition Turner showed two contrasting canvases, the *Entrance of the Meuse* in the Dutch marine tradition, and the very large *England: Richmond Hill, on the Prince Regent's Birthday* (BJ 139 and 140; both Tate collection), a Claudian composition of one of the most painted distant views of the Thames. Neither of these ambitious works sold, but two other exhibitions in London that season demonstrated Turner's successes with major patrons. In March Sir John Leicester opened his collection of modern British pictures, including eight paintings by Turner, to the public in the recently completed gallery at his house in Hill Street, Mayfair. A month later Walter Fawkes showed his great collection of watercolours, which included some seventy works by Turner, at his London residence, 45 Grosvenor Place. These two exhibitions were well attended and did much to confirm Turner's place as the leading landscape artist of the day. On 2 July Thomas Lawrence, who was in Rome, wrote to Joseph Farington, 'Turner should come to Rome. His Genius would here be supplied with new materials, and entirely congenial with it' (Lawrence MSS, RA, LAW/3/52).

First visit to Italy, 1819–1820 Turner, well provided with detailed advice from Hakewill and with guidebooks, set off for Rome on 31 July 1819, crossing the channel from Dover to Calais, and travelling rapidly through France for some two to three weeks before crossing the Mont Cenis pass to Turin and Milan. He then explored some of the Italian lakes, before reaching Venice, where he spent only a few days. He finally arrived in Rome early in October, and stayed there for about two months, during which he visited Tivoli and also undertook a journey south, to Naples, Pompeii, and Paestum. During his travels and in Rome itself he was continuously drawing, and filled over twenty, mostly small, sketchbooks, with quick pencil drawings which became noticeably less detailed as his journey proceeded. Turner also completed some fifty watercolour studies, many of them drawn on the spot, which reveal his excited reaction to the clear Italian light. He left Rome, where he had mixed with some of the many artists and British visitors then in the city, and was elected an honorary member of the Academy of St Luke, in time to spend Christmas in Florence, before crossing the Alps in severe winter weather to arrive back in London on 1 February 1820.

During his relatively rapid journey Turner managed to see and record most of what the much more leisurely grand tourist usually saw, and he also absorbed the atmosphere and aura of ancient and modern Italy, so that the whole classical tradition centred on Italy, which had long been a vital second-hand element of his art, became an even more integral part of his creative and imaginative genius. It took Turner several years to assimilate all this, and his attempt to encapsulate it all immediately in a great public statement was over-ambitious. On his return he set to work on the huge canvas which was his only exhibit at the 1820 Royal Academy exhibition, entitled *Rome from the Vatican: Rafaelle accompanied by La Fornarina, preparing his Pictures for the Decoration of the Loggia* (BJ 228; Tate collection). At once topographical, historical, and imaginary, this brightly coloured and theatrical composition, with its puzzling perspective, made full use of a considerable number of the sketchbook drawings.

Having not exhibited at the Royal Academy in 1821 (for the first time since 1805) and having exhibited only one small and uncharacteristic canvas, *What You Will!* (BJ 229; priv. coll.) in 1822, Turner again exhibited a single Italian work in 1823. *The Bay of Baiae, with Apollo and the Sibyl* (BJ

230; Tate collection) is somewhat smaller and even more colourful than *Rome from the Vatican*, and is a poetical and fluent Claudian composition based on drawings done during Turner's visit to Baiae from Naples in 1819. Rome again provided the subject matter for the third of Turner's large-scale Italian subjects shown at the Royal Academy. This was the *Forum Romanum, for Soane's Museum* exhibited in 1826 (BJ 233; Tate collection), which Turner painted for Soane but which 'did not suit the place or the place the picture' in the museum that the architect was creating in Lincoln's Inn Fields (MS note attached to letter from Turner dated 8 July 1826; Gage, *Collected Correspondence*, 101). In these three imposing Italian canvases Turner had depicted ancient, Roman, and Renaissance Italy; all these three aspects, as well as on one or two occasions modern Italy, continued to be an essential feature of Turner's inspiration, which was to be reinforced by his second visit to Italy in 1828.

Travels at home and abroad and topographical work, 1820–1830 Soon after his return to London Turner's life was disrupted by major rebuilding work in his house and gallery, which was probably the reason for his not exhibiting at the Royal Academy in 1821. However, he did complete a small series of quite large finished watercolours of Italian scenes, which was acquired by Walter Fawkes (W 718–24). In September Turner was able to get away for a brief journey in France, visiting Paris and exploring the River Seine, perhaps already with a series of engravings in mind. On the whole the first four or five years of the 1820s were a period of relative lull for Turner, who was then in his later forties. There were few exhibits at the Royal Academy, but in April 1822 Turner opened his new gallery in Queen Anne Street showing unsold earlier work, and that spring a notable group of his watercolours was included in the Cooke brothers' exhibition 'Drawings by English Artists'. It seems that at this time Turner, having stopped publication of the *Liber Studiorum* in 1819, was eager to initiate new schemes for engravings after his work. His proposal that summer to Messrs Hurst and Robinson to produce four paintings of subjects of classical mythology for engraving as single plates came to nothing. In early August Turner sailed to Edinburgh to be present at George IV's ceremonial visit, the first to Scotland of a Hanoverian king. Material in the sketchbooks which he used suggests that he had in mind a series of commemorative canvases or, more probably, a set of engravings of the occasion, but neither scheme was carried out, though there are four unfinished oil studies on panel (BJ 247, 248, 277, and 278) in the Turner Bequest as further evidence of his plans.

Two new projects for engravings were, however, initiated at this time; first was the Cookes' *The Rivers of England*, a series of thirty-six mezzotints to be engraved on the recently introduced steel plates. The uncompleted series included sixteen plates after Turner (R 752–67), published between 1823 and 1827 and based on some of the most attractive watercolours he had yet produced. One of the engravers for the *Rivers* was Thomas Lupton who launched a similar scheme, *The Ports of England*, in 1826, but this

again was not completed, though republished as *The Harbours of England* in 1856 (R 778–90). During his work on these two series Turner was involved in disagreements with both W. B. Cooke and Thomas Lupton, and there is ample evidence that the artist was not an easy man to deal with. However, this did not stop the print publisher and engraver Charles Heath from launching the most ambitious project for the publication of engravings after Turner, the *Picturesque Views in England and Wales*, a series of 120 copper-engravings all after drawings by Turner, of which, in the end, only ninety-six plates in twenty-four parts were published between 1827 and 1838 (R 209–304). Though a commercial failure, the *England and Wales* was a triumph from the artistic point of view, including some of the finest British topographical engravings of the nineteenth century based on some of Turner's most memorable watercolours. The artist was closely involved in supervising the engraving of these drawings and this publication marks a high point in the development of what has come to be known as the Turner school of engravers.

In 1825 Turner showed only one watercolour and one oil at the Royal Academy, but the latter was the magnificent *Harbour of Dieppe* (BJ 231; Frick Collection, New York), which initiated a more fluent and colourful sequence of topographical compositions. The next, *Cologne, the Arrival of a Packet Boat* (BJ 232), is also in the Frick Collection and was one of four oil paintings shown at the Royal Academy in 1826. This was partially based on drawings made during Turner's tour of the Low Countries in the summer of 1825. He had not been abroad since 1821, though he had made several sketching tours in England to collect material for the various topographical series. In the winter of 1824 he paid what was to be his last visit to Farnley, for Walter Fawkes died in October 1825. Within a year or two Farnley was replaced as Turner's country retreat by Petworth, where he was a regular and welcome guest of his longtime patron Lord Egremont until the eccentric earl's death in 1837. Turner clearly felt very much at home at Petworth, as he had done at Farnley. During his visits of earlier years he had drawn considerable inspiration from the great collection of old master paintings in the house; now the house itself, with its magnificent interiors and surrounding parkland, inspired Turner to produce the series of over one hundred rapid gouache drawings on blue paper, probably all dating from his visit in the late summer of 1827. Between 1828 and 1837 Turner also executed some fifteen oil paintings depicting the landscape and interior of Petworth, of which the landscapes were commissioned by the earl. None of these drawings or paintings was engraved or exhibited during the artist's lifetime, indicating that for Turner his visits to the great aristocratic house were a personal and private experience.

After his 1827 stay at Petworth, Turner was the guest of the architect John Nash at East Cowes Castle on the Isle of Wight at the time of Cowes regatta of which he painted two pictures for his host, which were among the four paintings shown at the 1828 summer exhibition (BJ 242 and 243; Indianapolis Museum of Art and V&A). They were based on a group of nine small oil sketches of the regatta, painted on two rolls of canvas (BJ 260–68; all Tate collection). Some of these may have been painted when aboard a man-of-war. Turner also made numerous drawings of the castle and its surroundings, some of them on blue paper.

Turner's work on his Petworth landscapes was interrupted by the artist's second visit to Italy, which he may have been encouraged to undertake at this time by his recent work on the twenty-five watercolour vignettes (W 1152–76) engraved on steel for the 1830 illustrated edition of Samuel Rogers's poem *Italy* (R 348–72). He set out in early August 1828, reaching Rome in early October, and stayed there for three months. On this visit Turner was determined to complete some finished paintings, especially one, *Palestrina* (BJ 295; Tate collection), as a companion for Lord Egremont's great Claude. His studio was at 12 piazza Mignanelli, the house in which his fellow artist Charles Lock Eastlake, who had recently been elected an associate of the Royal Academy, was living. In the second half of December Turner showed three completed canvases, framed in yellow-painted rope, in the rooms to which he had moved near the Quattro Fontane. These were *Regulus*, *View of Orvieto*, and *Vision of Medea* (BJ 294, 292, and 293; all Tate collection), of which the last two were shown again at the Royal Academy in 1830 and 1831 respectively, and the first in 1837. The Rome exhibition was seen by more than a thousand visitors and caused considerable controversy and adverse criticism. The *Palestrina* was not shown in Rome but was at the 1830 academy; it was not bought by Lord Egremont. Turner left Rome in January and was back in London in time for the academy council meeting on 10 February 1829, at which Constable was at last elected a Royal Academician.

Much to Turner's dismay his completed Rome paintings had not reached London in time for the academy exhibition of 1829, though some of the oil sketches made in Rome must have travelled with him, for he used two of them in composing *Ulysses deriding Polyphemus—Homer's Odyssey* (BJ 330; National Gallery, London), which he painted in London in time for the exhibition. This *'central picture* in Turner's career', to quote John Ruskin, heralded Turner's mature manner as the painter of colour and light—a manner which had already been seen on occasions in earlier work, such as the Petworth landscapes, but which from now on was to be the norm (E. T. Cook and A. Wedderburn, eds., *The Works of John Ruskin*, 13, 1904, 136).

Turner had planned to return to Rome in the summer of 1829, but his father's poor health prevented this. He did visit Paris in August, and toured down the Seine and along the Normandy coast, returning early in September. William Turner senior died on 21 September, and this blow was followed in January by the death of Sir Thomas Lawrence, whose funeral at St Paul's Cathedral Turner recorded in a large watercolour exhibited at the academy at its next exhibition.

Exhibits in the 1830s   At the 1830 summer exhibition Turner showed six oil paintings, including two of those

painted in Rome. Two of the others—*Jessica* and *Pilate washing his Hands* (BJ 332–3; Tate collection and Petworth House, Sussex)—both displayed the influence of Rembrandt and received virulent criticism. On the other hand the eloquent *Calais Sands* (BJ 334; Bury Art Gallery and Museum), a luminous composition reminiscent of the coast scenes of the recently deceased young landscape artist R. P. Bonington and probably conceived as an act of homage to him, was generally well received.

There were seven exhibits in 1831, all of them oils and including another of the paintings shown in Rome in 1828, the *Vision of Medea* (BJ 293; Tate collection), which was given a mixed, but generally critical, reception. There was, however, praise for the two coast scenes, *Life-Boat and Manby Apparatus* (BJ 336; V&A) and *Fort Vimieux* (BJ 341; priv. coll., England), in both of which Turner achieved wonderful effects of light and weather, in contrast to the calm classical atmosphere of the Claudian *Caligula's Palace and Bridge* (BJ 337; Tate collection). The single marine, *Admiral Van Tromp's Barge at the Entrance of the Texel, 1645* (BJ 339; Sir John Soane's Museum, London), was also reminiscent of Turner's earlier 'old master' work, while the remaining two paintings—*Lord Percy under Attainder* and *Watteau Study by Fresnoy's Rules* (BJ 338 and 340; both Tate collection)—both small and on panel, introduced a new type of subject picture based on Turner's close study of the interior of Petworth House and demonstrating in a didactic way his theories on the painting of light and colour. The variety and challenge of these seven 1831 exhibits set the pattern for Turner's public work in the last two decades of his career. Up to 1841, when all six exhibited works were sold, the majority of these exhibited paintings found buyers, and on the whole the critics admired, or at least tolerated, nearly all of them.

The six paintings shown at the Royal Academy in 1832 again included a very large classical composition, *Childe Harold's Pilgrimage—Italy* (BJ 342; Tate collection), which was exhibited with seven lines from canto 4 of Lord Byron's epic poem. There were three historical 'Dutch' marines, one another Van Tromp subject, the second illustrating William III's stormy landing at Torbay in 1688, and the third a calm scene of shipping off the Dutch coast. Turner's fourth 1832 marine is very different and features a steam boat. The dramatic *Staffa, Fingal's Cave* (BJ 347; Yale U. CBA) records the artist's own turbulent experiences in August 1831 when visiting Staffa and Iona; it was the first painting by Turner to reach America when purchased in 1845 by Colonel James Lenox of New York. The final 1832 exhibit was the most controversial and is a confusing but colourful biblical scene, *Shadrach, Meshech and Abednego in the Burning Fiery Furnace* (BJ 346; Tate collection), painted in light-hearted competition with his friend and fellow academician George Jones.

The pattern of a varied selection of six exhibits continued for another year, and in 1833 it included Turner's first two exhibited Venetian subjects, one now lost and the other *Bridge of Sighs, Ducal Palace and Custom-House, Venice: Canaletti Painting* (BJ 349; Tate collection). This small but powerful composition, which was bought by the major collector of contemporary British painting Robert Vernon, is said to have been very largely painted when already hanging at the academy on the varnishing days, a feat that Turner repeated on numerous later occasions, perhaps, it has been suggested, to give his fellow artists some idea of his revolutionary working methods. The Venetian compositions must have been based on Turner's 1819 drawings, for his second visit to the city did not take place until the autumn of 1833. The other four 1833 paintings were all seascapes, three of them quite conventional but atmospheric 'Dutch' marines, and the fourth the dramatic *Mouth of the Seine, Quille-Boeuf* (BJ 353; Gulbenkian Foundation, Lisbon). This is based on the composition of one of Turner's Seine subjects, of which the engraving was published in his *Rivers of France* series in the following year, and it was probably exhibited to draw attention to that publication.

None of the five 1834 Royal Academy exhibits forms part of the Turner Bequest as all were sold or commissioned. *Venice* (BJ 356), now in the National Gallery of Art, Washington, was painted for Henry McConnell, while Robert Vernon purchased *The Golden Bough* (BJ 355; Tate collection) before the exhibition. This was certainly conceived as a pair to the equally Claudian *The Fountain of Indolence* (BJ 354; Beaverbrook Foundation). Perhaps also commissioned, this time by Vernon's rival collector John Sheepshanks, was the small *St. Michael's Mount, Cornwall* (BJ 361; V&A), a relatively calm scene when compared to the larger *Wreckers—Coast of Northumberland* (BJ 357; Yale U. CBA), with its wild waves in the foreground.

On 16 October 1834 Turner was an onlooker as fire destroyed a large part of the houses of parliament in London. He recorded the scene in a series of nine very rapid on-the-spot watercolour studies, and in 1835 he exhibited two spectacular oil paintings of the subject, both of which he sold (BJ 359 and 364; Philadelphia Museum of Art and Cleveland Museum of Art, Ohio). The first was shown at the British Institution, where Turner had not exhibited since 1816, and was painted almost entirely on the walls of the gallery during varnishing days, as famously recounted some years later by the Norfolk artist E. V. Rippingille. The second, almost identical in size but a distant view and totally different in composition, was one of Turner's five Royal Academy exhibits that summer. Also in America today, in the National Gallery of Art, Washington, is the sombre *Keelmen heaving Coals by Night* (BJ 360), a scene on the River Tyne painted for Henry McConnell as a companion for his 1834 *Venice*. The only Venetian exhibit this year, *Venice, from the Porch of Madonna della Salute* (BJ 362; Metropolitan Museum of Art, New York), was bought by H. A. J. Munro of Novar, while *The Bright Stone of Honour (Ehrenbreitstein)* (BJ 361; priv. coll., London) was painted for the engraver John Pye, whose engraving of it was published ten years later. The fifth painting, *Line-Fishing, off Hastings* (BJ 363; V&A), was also sold, to John Sheepshanks.

The three paintings at the Royal Academy in 1836 were also all sold, two of them, both Italian subjects, from the exhibition to Munro of Novar, who accompanied Turner

on his continental tour later that year. These were the spectacular *Juliet and her Nurse* (BJ 365; priv. coll., Argentina) and *Rome from Mount Aventine* (BJ 366; priv. coll.). *Juliet* was the particular target of the Revd John Eagles in a scathing review in *Blackwood's Edinburgh Magazine*, as was *Mercury and Argus* (BJ 367; National Gallery of Canada, Ottawa), a loosely painted classical composition, purchased by Joseph Gillott, another of Turner's major patrons at this time. It was the *Blackwood's* review that moved the young John Ruskin to write a powerful letter in support of Turner, and though this was not published it sowed the seed that led to Ruskin's famous defence of Turner in his *Modern Painters*, of which the first volume was published anonymously in 1843. In 1837 the Royal Academy held its first exhibition in its new premises in Trafalgar Square, and Turner was on the hanging committee. He himself showed four paintings, which were again attacked by Eagles, who described them as 'a bold attempt to insult the public taste' (*Blackwood's Edinburgh Magazine*, 42, July–Dec 1837, 335). Only two were sold, *The Grand Canal, Venice* (BJ 368; Henry E. Huntington Art Gallery, San Marino, California), with its reference to Shakespeare's *Merchant of Venice*, and the sensational mountain scene *Snow-storm, Avalanche and Inundation—a Scene in the Upper Part of Val d'Aouste* (BJ 371; Art Institute of Chicago), both bought by Gillott. The two great classical compositions, the Claudian *Story of Apollo and Daphne* and the powerful Poussinesque *The Parting of Hero and Leander* (BJ 369 and 370), both remained in Turner's studio to form part of the bequest.

In 1838 Turner again exhibited an earlier work, retouched on varnishing day, *Fishing Boats with Hucksters bargaining for Fish* (BJ 372; Art Institute of Chicago), at the British Institution, where he had shown his much repainted 1828 *Regulus* the year before. At the Royal Academy there were three paintings, the unsold *Phryne going to the Public Baths as Venus* (BJ 373; Tate collection) and the pair *Modern Italy—the Pifferari* and *Ancient Italy—Ovid banished from Rome* (BJ 374 and 375; Glasgow Art Gallery and priv. coll.), both bought by Munro of Novar.

What has become Turner's most famous painting was one of the five which he showed at the Royal Academy in 1839. Described by W. M. Thackeray (writing as Michael Angelo Titmarch in *Fraser's Magazine*, 10, June 1844, 712–13) as 'as grand a painting as ever figured on the walls of any academy, or came from the easel of any painter', *The Fighting 'Temeraire', tugged to her Last Berth to be broken up, 1838* (BJ 377; National Gallery, London) was acclaimed by the critics of the day and has been admired and idolized ever since. This masterpiece overshadowed Turner's other exhibits this year, all of them with classical or Italian subject matter, including another pair featuring ancient and modern Rome (BJ 378 and 379). Munro bought *Modern Rome* (priv. coll.) and Gillott acquired *Cicero at his Villa* (BJ 381; priv. coll.). In contrast to his praise for *The Fighting 'Temeraire'* Thackeray condemned *Pluto carrying off Proserpine* (BJ 380; National Gallery of Art, Washington, DC), which he found incomprehensible. As at the beginning of the decade, Turner's exhibits provided challenging variety at its end, as they were to do also throughout the 1840s.

Watercolours and engravings in the 1830s Some seventy engravings on copper and over 300 on steel after drawings by Turner were published in the 1830s. Most of his travels in this decade, during which he reached his sixties, were undertaken to collect topographical material for these engravings, and it was largely through them that the artist's fame spread in Europe and America. The sixth and seventh parts of the *England and Wales* series were published in 1829, and a further seventeen parts with sixty-eight copper-engravings in the 1830s, the twenty-fourth and final part in 1838. In June and July 1829 the publisher Charles Heath held an exhibition including some forty of Turner's *England and Wales* watercolours in the Egyptian Hall in London, but Turner drew many of the later *England and Wales* watercolours, some of them based on studies made on recent travels, not long before they were sent to the engravers. Throughout the publication of this ambitious but unprofitable series he maintained close control over the actual engraving, as is shown by the large number of surviving touched proofs.

One of the reasons for the commercial problems of the *England and Wales* series was that steel, introduced in the mid-1820s, very quickly ousted the traditional copper as the prime material from which engravers' plates were made. Turner rapidly acclimatized himself to the new method, which resulted in more precise images which could be printed in much larger numbers, and produced some thirty drawings for a number of the popular annuals from 1826 onwards. His first outstanding success with steel were the twenty-five small vignettes (R 348–72) commissioned by the banker–poet Samuel Rogers to illustrate a luxury edition of his poem *Italy* published in 1830, and still regarded as one of the outstanding examples of the illustrated book in the first half of the nineteenth century. As always Turner carefully guided and supervised the engravers and there are again many touched proofs. In these tiny compositions artist and engraver succeeded in combining a wealth of detail with telling effects of light and atmosphere. The success of *Italy* persuaded Rogers to undertake a similar costly edition of his *Poems* which was published in 1834 with thirty-three vignettes after Turner (R 373–405). Turner—himself a writer of poetry and clearly very sympathetic to that of Samuel Rogers—created some of his most telling images for these two beautiful books, which established him as the leading illustrator of the day, and produced numerous demands for illustrative drawings for engraving, for during these years Turner's involvement greatly enhanced the sales of a book.

While in Rogers's *Italy* and *Poems* Turner provided illustrations for an existing text, in the famous *Rivers of France* series, published in three volumes in 1833–5, the text was written, by the popular hack author Leitch Ritchie, to accompany Turner's plates. Published for Charles Heath by Longman's as *Turner's Annual Tour*, the first volume with a vignette and twenty plates was devoted to the River Loire (R 432–52), and the second and third, each with a vignette

and nineteen plates, to the Seine (R 453–92). The beautiful engravings were based on Turner's relatively broad gouache and watercolour drawings on blue paper, which in their turn were based on the artist's numerous drawings and studies in pencil, pen and ink, watercolours, and gouache, executed during several sketching tours along the rivers in 1821, 1826, possibly 1827, 1829, and 1832, when he was travelling for ten weeks. Turner put a great deal of preparatory work into his drawings for these volumes, perhaps realizing that much would be expected of him in an annual series which, almost uniquely, was published under the artist's name. The *Rivers of France* plates became the best-known prints after Turner, but none the less plans to continue the series as *Rivers of Europe* were stillborn.

From now on Turner's work for engraving was largely to illustrate existing texts—prose, poetry, and even the Bible. The first major author for whose writings he was commissioned to provide illustrations was Lord Byron, whose poetry had inspired his 1818 painting *The Field of Waterloo*, and who was to inspire several more in the 1830s and 1840s, especially the fine *Childe Harold's Pilgrimage—Italy* exhibited in 1832. In 1830 Turner was commissioned by the engraver William Finden to provide drawings for a publication of landscape engravings illustrating Byron's travels and writings. After much complex negotiation between artist, engraver, author, and publisher, one of whom was John Murray, nine subjects after Turner finally appeared in Finden's *Landscape Illustrations* to Byron published in fourteen monthly parts of five plates from January 1832. Some of the same Turner compositions were used in the much more important and successful edition of *The Works of Lord Byron: with his Letters and Journals, and his Life, by Thomas Moore*, published by John Murray in 1832–4 in seventeen volumes, with illustrations by a number of artists, including twenty-six landscape vignettes after Turner, most of which appeared at the start of each volume; they also appeared in several further publications and editions (R 406–31). Many of Turner's Byron subjects were of places he had not visited, including, of course, Greece, and were based on the drawings of others. Most of the watercolours are very tight and precise, and these illustrations largely lack the harmony and fellow feeling of his illustrations to Samuel Rogers's work.

There was, however, again much greater affinity with the author in Turner's numerous illustrations to the writings of Sir Walter Scott, the first of which he had provided for the unsuccessful *Provincial Antiquities of Scotland* between 1818 and the mid-1820s. Though Scott was apparently not impressed by the man, he was an admirer of Turner's art, and after seeing the 1830 edition of Rogers's *Italy* he agreed that Turner should be invited to provide illustrations for a new edition of his *Poetical Works* planned by the Edinburgh publisher Robert Cadell. In persuading Scott to accept Turner as the sole illustrator Cadell wrote, 'with his pencil I shall insure the subscription of 8000—without, not 3000' (W. Partington, *The Private Letter-Books of Sir Walter Scott*, 1930, 252, n. 1). On about 20 July 1831 Turner left London by coach on what was his fourth visit to Scotland, which lasted some six weeks. In early August he spent five days as Scott's guest at Abbotsford, on each of which sketching trips were organized, several of them joined by Scott, who was already a sick man and died a year later, and all in the company of Cadell, who then went with Turner to Edinburgh but did not join the rest of the artist's sketching tour of the highlands and the Western Isles. The twelve volumes of Scott's *Poetical Works* were published in 1834, each with a topographical frontispiece and a vignette after Turner (R 493–516). Many of the vignettes are full of personal detail, reflecting the artist's close contacts with author and publisher, which resulted in designs of the highest quality.

Turner was then also employed by Cadell to provide illustrations for a new edition of Scott's *Prose Works*, ultimately published in twenty-eight volumes. He completed his designs for forty prints (R 517–56), half of them vignettes, between 1833 and 1835, making another tour to collect material in Scotland in September 1834. Sixteen of these prints illustrated the nine volumes devoted to Scott's *Life of Napoleon Buonaparte*, and here again Turner's admiration for the subject resulted in some of his most telling compositions, in which the drama of particular events in the emperor's career was brought to life with telling details on the tiny scale of a vignette.

Large groups of Turner's watercolours for the *England and Wales* series and for several of the illustrated books were exhibited in London in 1832, 1833, and 1834 at the Pall Mall gallery of Moon, Boys, and Graves, who had taken over the *England and Wales* in 1831 and were Cadell's partners in the publication of the Scott series. However, Cadell's plans to continue Turner's involvement in illustrating the work of Walter Scott in a luxurious new edition of the Waverley novels came to nothing, though the artist did provide a few drawings for two further Scott publications (R 560–68).

Amazingly Turner was able to work for yet more publications in the mid-1830s. He was one of eleven artists employed by the Finden brothers to provide drawings for engraving on steel for a large series, *Landscape Illustrations of the Bible*, first issued in monthly parts in 1834 and 1835, and then published in two volumes in 1836 (R 572–97). Turner's contribution was twenty-six small watercolours based, as he himself had not visited the Holy Land, on the drawings of a number of other artists, including the young architects Charles Barry and C. R. Cockerell. A second commission for designs based on the work of another artist resulted in seven somewhat mechanical and larger engravings after the author's drawings for Lieutenant G. F. White's *Views in India*, first published in 1836 (R 606–12).

During the same period Turner drew seven lively and imaginative vignettes for John Macrone's edition of the *Poetical Works of John Milton* published in seven volumes in 1835 (R 598–604). Intricate and often crowded figure compositions here replace topography, which is again more in evidence in some of Turner's twenty vignette illustrations for Edward Moxon's edition of Thomas Campbell's *Poetical Works*, published in 1837 (R 613–33), for some of which he

made studies during his tour in Germany and Austria in 1835. Most of the Campbell vignettes were engraved by Edward Goodall who had made his first engraving after Turner in 1822, and became one of the most prolific engravers of his work. Goodall was also responsible for engraving the four theatrical compositions drawn by Turner, using his powers of descriptive illustration to the full, to illustrate the vivid prose of Thomas Moore's popular novel *The Epicurean*, published by John Macrone in 1839 (R 634–7). Except for six fine compositions with striking light effects engraved to illustrate the mysterious private edition of *Dr. Broadley's Poems* (R 638–43), published in the early 1840s, Turner, who was now well into his sixties, produced no further drawings for publishers.

The modern master in the 1840s The Turner Bequest includes some 200 late 'unfinished' oils, and there are a few more in other collections. Dating from the last twenty years of Turner's career and mostly painted in his studio, they represent his instinctive reactions to land and seascape and the total freedom and painterliness of his 'private' art, and were not intended for exhibition. Largely ignored until the 1930s, this considerable body of work has gradually come to be appreciated as a significant element of Turner's *œuvre*, showing him at his most natural and painterly, and sealing his place as one of the first 'modern' masters. This phase of appreciation came to a head with the notable exhibition 'Turner: Imagination and Reality' at New York's Museum of Modern Art in 1966, and was revived by another New York exhibition, 'Exploring Late Turner' (Salander-O'Reilly Galleries, 1999). These rapid paintings on canvas, panel, or board are different from the usual oil studies or sketches, and are matched by hundreds of equally compelling watercolour 'colour beginnings' in the Turner Bequest. Together these formed the basis of much of the artist's late 'finished' work in all media, some of which is almost as fluent and fluid as are the 'beginnings'. Turner frequently submitted some of his canvas oil 'beginnings' to the annual summer exhibition at the Royal Academy, and then completed his 'finished' picture on the walls of the gallery on the varnishing days. It may well be that in adopting this method of working Turner was looking back to his earliest days, when watercolour drawings were traditionally laid in in monochrome over which the colour was applied.

In 1840 Turner was represented by seven paintings at the Royal Academy, including another of his most famous works, *Slavers throwing overboard the Dead and Dying—Typhon coming on* (BJ 385; Museum of Fine Arts, Boston, Massachusetts), which is better known as 'The Slave Ship'. This great icon of the anti-slavery campaign was given by his father as a new year gift in 1844 to John Ruskin, who wrote some of his most stirring passages in its praise, before finding it 'too painful to live with' and sending it to auction in 1869. The critics were almost unanimous in reviling 'The Slave Ship', and most of Turner's other 1840 exhibits, which included two broadly painted Venetian scenes (BJ 383 and 384), one of which was painted for John Sheepshanks. The sparkling *Neapolitan Fisher-Girls* (BJ 388) was bought by Robert Vernon, though he sold it two years later at Christies, where it fetched only 55 guineas. The powerful *Rockets and Blue Lights* (BJ 387; Sterling and Francine Clark Institute, Williamstown, Massachusetts) was shown again in 1841, at the British Institution, and then remained with Turner's dealer, Thomas Griffith, until sold in about 1843, and only two of the remarkable and challenging 1840 group remained unsold and are in the Turner Bequest (BJ 382 and 386).

In the summer of 1840 Turner paid his third and last visit to Venice, staying there for two weeks. He must have spent much of his time drawing and sketching in pencil and watercolours, using larger roll sketchbooks (which could be rolled up and kept in a pocket) for the latter. These marvellously observed and rapidly executed—perhaps often on the spot—Venetian watercolours herald Turner's late work in this favourite medium. From now on there are few 'finished' watercolours for engraving or display, and the artist again and again seems to wish the watercolour onto the paper to produce telling visions of light and colour, which are among Turner's most 'modern' works, and which strongly influenced some of the impressionists and other later artists. As well as Venetian scenes, his subject matter ranged from individual fish to Swiss mountains, and today the later watercolours which have been sold are among the most prized of Turner's works.

Three of Turner's six 1841 Royal Academy exhibits were of Venetian subjects, one of which, *Ducal Palace, Dogano, with part of San Giorgio, Venice* (BJ 390; Allen Memorial Museum, Oberlin College, Ohio), was painted for Turner's friend the sculptor Sir Francis Chantrey. The second, *Giudecca, la Donna della Salute and San Giorgio* (BJ 391; Art Institute of Chicago), was priced by Turner at 250 guineas and was the first of his oils bought by Elhanan Bicknell, one of his major patrons in these late years. The third, the imaginary 'historical' scene *Depositing of John Bellini's Three Pictures in la Chiesa Redentore* (BJ 393; priv. coll.), was priced at 350 guineas and acquired by Charles Birch, another important collector of the late paintings. Though not bought by the royal couple and apparently not even noticed by Queen Victoria, *Schloss Rosenau, Seat of H.R.H. Prince Albert of Coburg, Near Coburg, Germany* (BJ 392; Walker Art Gallery, Liverpool) was eventually sold, to another leading Turner collector, Joseph Gillott. The two remaining exhibits, the circular *The Dawn of Christianity* (BJ 394; Ulster Museum, Belfast) and the square *Glaucus and Scylla* (BJ 395; Kimbell Art Museum, Fort Worth, Texas), were both bought by B. G. Windus, already one of the principal collectors of Turner's watercolours.

In the summer of 1841 Turner undertook the first of four annual visits to Switzerland, during each of which he spent much time at Lucerne. As usual he was constantly drawing, using numerous sketchbooks, including again roll sketchbooks in which he made rapid and fluent on-the-spot watercolour studies, often with spectacular light and weather effects. In these late visits Turner was recording the Swiss landscape, and especially the lakes, at ground level, usually seeing the mountains in the distance rather than close up as in his younger years. When in Lucerne he stayed at the Swan Hotel, overlooking the lake, from which he could observe the spectacular isolated Mount Rigi on its northern shore, at different times of day and in a variety of weathers, achieving a series of outstanding watercolour studies similar to those he had made in Venice. On his return to London, Turner chose fifteen 'samples' from his Swiss watercolours and provided four finished specimens for Thomas Griffith to obtain commissions for ten quite large watercolours, including three featuring Rigi, to be sold for 80 guineas each (W 1523-32). In the event the agent achieved only nine orders, five of them from Munro of Novar and two each from Bicknell and Ruskin. In 1843 a similar project had less success, and only six watercolours were completed and sold (W 1534-9). Ruskin again bought two of them, including the spectacular *Goldau* (W 1537; priv. coll., USA). Another set of ten was made and sold in 1845 (W 1540-49), and a few similar drawings date from the later 1840s. For the young John Ruskin, who was very much involved at the time, some of these Swiss watercolours ranked as Turner's greatest achievements in that medium, and they are still regarded as among the outstanding English watercolours of the nineteenth century.

Despite his work on the Swiss watercolours, Turner showed five oil paintings at the Royal Academy in 1842, of which only the two Venetian scenes were sold, both at the exhibition. Bicknell bought the lovely *Campo Santo, Venice* (BJ 397; Toledo Museum of Art, Toledo, Ohio) and Robert Vernon *The Dogano, San Giorgio, Citella, from the Steps of the Europa* (BJ 396; Tate collection). The other three paintings (BJ 398-400; all Tate collection) were more challenging, especially *Snow storm—Steam-Boat off a Harbour's Mouth making Signals in Shallow Water, and going by the Lead. The Author was in this Storm on the Night the Ariel left Harwich.* Turner's claim that this dramatic seascape was based on an actual experience was probably apocryphal, but there is no doubt that it was his own grief at the loss of his much younger friend that helped Turner to achieve the powerful effect of mourning in *Peace—Burial at Sea*. This was painted to commemorate the death the previous summer of Sir David Wilkie on his return journey from the Middle East and his burial at sea off Gibraltar. Its pair, *War: The Exile and the Rock Limpet*, is a poignant reflection on the fate of Turner's hero, Napoleon, whose ashes had recently been brought back from St Helena for a state burial at Les Invalides in Paris.

1843 was another vintage year at the Royal Academy, with three Venetian pictures among Turner's six exhibits. Foremost was the pessimistic *Sun of Venice going to Sea* (BJ 402; Tate collection), which became one of Ruskin's favourites. The first volume of his *Modern Painters*, with its renowned and influential defence of the later work of Turner, was published anonymously that May, and the first small edition was quite quickly sold out. *The Opening of the Wallhalla* (BJ 401; Tate collection) was generally well received by the British press, but not in Germany when exhibited in Munich in 1845. The term 'daub' was now being frequently used by critics of Turner's paintings, as in several discussions of the pair of puzzling didactic compositions shown in 1843, *Shade and Darkness—the evening of the Deluge* and *Light and Colour (Goethe's Theory)—the Morning after the Deluge* (BJ 404–5; Tate collection).

The seven works he exhibited at the Royal Academy in 1844 included another of Turner's most renowned and influential paintings, *Rain, Steam and Speed—the Great Western Railway* (BJ 409; National Gallery, London). There were also three vivid marines (BJ 407–8 and 410), of which the first, *Ostend* (Neue Pinakothek, Munich), was bought by Munro of Novar. The three Venetian scenes were again all very loosely painted, and only one was sold. In 1845, a year in which the seventy-year-old Turner served as acting president of the Royal Academy during the president's illness, and was also on the hanging committee, only one of his six exhibited works found a buyer. This was one of the two paintings entitled *Whalers* (BJ 414–15), depicting stormy scenes of whale fishing, which may actually have been painted for the whaling entrepreneur Elhanan Bicknell, who found fault with it and very quickly sold it, perhaps to Munro of Novar. There were four Venetian scenes, even more diffuse and gloomy than before. In 1846 Turner again showed a painting at the British Institution, a rare Shakespearian subject, *Queen Mab's Cave* (BJ 420; Tate collection), which was very thickly painted and which the critic of the *Art-Union* described as being 'a daylight dream in all the wantoness of gorgeous, bright, and positive colour, not painted but apparently flung upon the canvas in kaleidoscopic confusion' (*Art-Union*, 8, 1846, 76). The six oils at the Royal Academy included two whaling subjects (BJ 423 and 426) and a pair of square canvases with remarkable visionary subjects, *Undine giving the Ring to Massaniello* and *The Angel standing in the Sun* (BJ 424–5), all of which were unsold. Surprisingly another pair—exotic Venetian subjects entitled *Going to the Ball (San Martino)* and *Returning from the Ball (St. Martha)* (BJ 421–2; priv. coll.)—did find a buyer, and was soon in W. G. Windus's collection.

Turner's failing health is reflected in his Royal Academy exhibits in his final years. In 1847 there was only one work, *The Hero of a Hundred Fights* (BJ 427; Tate collection), a reworked canvas of about 1800. There was nothing in 1848, and in 1849 he showed two much earlier works, one borrowed from Munro of Novar (BJ 428; Walker Art Gallery, Liverpool). In 1850 Turner exhibited at his beloved academy for the last time, submitting a series of four dark compositions depicting subjects from the *Aeneid* in a remarkable distillation of his Claudian manner (BJ 429–32; Tate collection). It was recorded by a fellow artist, J. W. Archer, that Turner painted these while in Chelsea, and that 'they were set in a row and he went from one to the other, first painting upon one, touching on the next, and so on, in rotation' ('Reminiscences', *Once a Week*, 1 Feb 1862, 162–6). This report lends weight to considering Turner as a 'modern master'.

Turner's appearance, character, and private life The facts of Turner's private life and a valid picture of his character are just as enigmatic as much of his late painting. We know from numerous verbal descriptions that he was short and became corpulent, that in later life he dressed badly, and

that he usually talked hesitantly and with a strong cockney accent. This image is confirmed by several of the sketches and drawings of him, some of them showing Turner at work. Surprisingly for such an eminent artist there exists no major formal painted portrait or bust of Turner, and the best image we have is his well-known youthful self-portrait of about 1798 (BJ 25; Tate collection).

There are also many accounts of Turner's character and behaviour, some of them contradictory but most of them giving the impression of a difficult and very private person, though not, apparently, when with his closer friends. He could be both gruff and very friendly, miserly and very generous. He is often described as restless, but his chief relaxation was river and lake fishing, and he composed much of his poetry on river banks, where he was also, of course, able to study such vital elements of his art as light, water, sky, landscape, and weather. Turner was a great reader of poetry, and was himself a frequent versifier, as seen in numerous jottings in his sketchbooks, including the so-called 'Verse Book' (priv. coll.) used from about 1805 to 1810. The titles of many of his Royal Academy exhibits were accompanied in the catalogues by poetic quotations of his own writing, most of them from 1812 onwards designated as from the manuscript poem 'The Fallacies of Hope'. The titles of some forty of Turner's paintings have references to music, indicating the artist's lifelong interest in music and opera, and he also maintained his love of the theatre initiated in his early days as a scene painter.

John Constable, in a letter written in 1813 soon after sitting next to Turner at a Royal Academy dinner, summed him up as follows: 'he is uncouth but has a wonderful range of mind' (*John Constable's Correspondence*, 2, 1964, 110). The two never became friends, but Turner had numerous other artist friends most of whom have already been mentioned. Especially to be remembered is W. F. Wells (1762–1836) who was probably his closest friend, and whose daughters, Clara and Emma, were among his favourite younger people. Turner was also very popular with the Fawkes children at Farnley in Yorkshire, the home of a fellow spirit, Walter Fawkes, another of the artist's close friends. On a different level were the artist's friendship with Lord Egremont, and his warm welcome at Petworth. Other long-term friends included two clergymen, H. S. Trimmer, a frequent fishing companion, and E. T. Daniell, who both probably helped the artist to acquire his considerable knowledge of the Bible and of classical languages and literature.

Turner, who never married, was very close to his father, who, until he died in 1829, was his studio assistant and often cook in Queen Anne Street, and also did the gardening at Sandycombe Lodge. Sarah Danby, *née* Goose, widow of the composer John Danby (1756/7–1798), who was somewhat older than Turner, became his mistress and housekeeper, and was the mother of his two daughters, Evelina, born in 1800/01, and Georgiana, born some ten years later. Sarah's relationship with Turner ended about 1813. Her late husband's niece Hannah had joined the Turner household as a servant in 1809, becoming housekeeper a few years later. It is clear from several sketchbooks and passages of his poetry that Turner was something of a womanizer, but the facts of his liaisons and fatherhood remain uncertain. Later in his life, in the early 1830s, Turner developed a relationship with his Margate landlady, the twice-widowed Sophia Booth, whose first husband, drowned in 1821, was Henry Pound. In 1846 Turner acquired a small house by the Thames in Chelsea—6 Davis Place, Cremorne New Road, an extension of Cheyne Walk. He moved in with Mrs Booth in October, and spent most of his final years there, well looked after by Mrs Booth, trying to remain incognito, and known locally as Admiral Booth.

Turner's legacies Turner died at 6 Davis Place on 19 December 1851, lay in state in his gallery in Queen Anne Street, and was buried in the crypt of St Paul's Cathedral on 30 December. A statue of Turner by Patrick MacDowell, provided for in the artist's will, was erected in St Paul's in 1862.

Immediately after the funeral the will was read to five of Turner's executors, initiating controversy which lasted many years. His first will was executed on 30 September 1829, leaving various modest legacies and annuities to relatives and members of the Danby family, and a fund for a professorship of landscape painting and a Turner gold medal at the Royal Academy. The residue was to finance a charity for 'decayed English artists (Landscape painters only) and single men' to be built on Turner's land at Twickenham and to include a gallery for Turner's paintings. Two paintings—*Dido building Carthage* (BJ 131) and *The Decline of the Carthaginian Empire* (BJ 135)—were specifically bequeathed to the recently founded National Gallery to hang with two of the Angerstein Claudes. In June 1831 a more carefully prepared will was drawn up, which replaced the *Dido* painting with *Sun rising through Vapour* (BJ 69) and made other changes. Amended by four codicils (1831, 1832, 1848, and 1849) the 1831 will was granted probate on 6 September 1852.

Turner's cousins, who had already unsuccessfully challenged the validity of his will immediately after his death, resumed their litigation after probate, on the grounds that the charity provisions were void because they had not been properly registered in the court of chancery. After three years a compromise was reached by a court decree of 19 March 1856; the charity was abandoned and his relatives were granted much of Turner's considerable property, and all his engraved works. The relatively modest bequest to the Royal Academy was increased to £20,000, and 'all the Pictures, Drawings and Sketches by the Testator's hands without any distinction of finished or unfinished' were assigned to the National Gallery, whose trustees took legal possession on 25 September 1856. Consisting of some 300 oil paintings (100 of them designated as 'finished') and some 19,000 watercolours and drawings, this great collection, usually known as the Turner Bequest, has had a chequered and often controversial career for over a century. It was not until the opening of the Clore Gallery at the Tate Gallery in 1987 that the bulk of the bequest has been preserved and partially displayed under one roof, fulfilling to a large extent Turner's desire that his work should be seen 'all together'.

Turner's reputation Turner was recognized as an artist prodigy and his reputation, especially among his fellow artists, was established rapidly as shown by his very early election to the Royal Academy. He retained and enhanced that reputation throughout his long career, though, as recorded above, there was always a degree of adverse criticism and hostility for the increasingly personal and advanced manner and technique of his work. The eccentricity of his behaviour and appearance meant that Turner was never wholly accepted by society, though he was a valued member of his small circle of friends and colleagues. All this was summed up in one of his obituaries:

> Whatever hesitation might have been felt by the mass of those who gazed on the later efforts of his brush in believing that he was entitled to the highest rank in his profession, none of his bretheren seems to have any doubt of his decided excellence, and the best of them all have ever admitted to his superiority in poetry, feeling, fancy and genius. Long ere his death he had the felicity of knowing that his name and his works were regarded with that reverential respect and estimation which is given to other artists by posterity alone. (*The Times*, 31 Dec 1851)

'Posterity' has never lessened its admiration for Turner's work, though from time to time it has changed the areas of his work which are most admired. In the second half of the nineteenth century the writings of John Ruskin and his disciples kept Turner's reputation very much alive, and during this period it was the *Liber Studiorum* that became especially esteemed by scholars, students, and collectors. The first half of the twentieth century saw a relative lull in Turner's reputation, though there was increased appreciation of his unfinished and 'impressionistic' oils in the Turner Bequest. A new period of celebrity and eager collecting was launched by the two great bicentenary exhibitions in London in 1975—a superb overall survey at the Royal Academy and a selection of watercolours and drawings, largely from the Turner Bequest, at the British Museum. 1975 saw the creation of the Turner Society and the start of an extensive series of Turner exhibitions at home and abroad, which has been enhanced by the many scholarly exhibitions held regularly in the Clore Gallery since its opening in 1987. As the last section of this article will show Turner scholarship blossomed during these years with a vast number of books, catalogues, and articles, and a learned journal, *Turner Studies*, devoted almost exclusively to him, published twice a year from 1981 to 1991. The last decades of the twentieth century also saw huge rises in the value of paintings and drawings by Turner, as shown by the sale in New York in May 1980 of the notorious 1836 *Juliet and her Nurse* (BJ 365) for $6,400,000, then a record price for any painting sold at auction.

The Turner literature Turner was not well served by his first biographer, Walter Thornbury, whose *Life of J. M. W. Turner, R.A.* (1862; 2nd edn, 1877) was often inaccurate and misleading. However, at this period readers were able to consult the brilliant writings on Turner of John Ruskin in *Modern Painters* (1843–60) and elsewhere, which are still considered to include some of the most perceptive and compelling passages written about the artist. There were other short accounts of Turner in the two decades after his death, and P. G. Hamerton's fuller and sensitive biography was published in 1879. One of the leading later nineteenth-century Turner scholars, W. G. Rawlinson, published his catalogue of the *Liber Studiorum* in 1878 (2nd edn, 1906), and the two volumes of his invaluable *Engraved Work of J. M. W. Turner, R.A.* in 1908 and 1913. In 1902 Sir Walter Armstrong's *Turner* appeared, a massive and luxurious volume ending with two informative lists of paintings and watercolours. A. J. Finberg's major contributions to Turner scholarship began in 1909 with his two-volume *Inventory of the Drawings in the Turner Bequest*. His updated catalogue and history of the *Liber Studiorum* was published in 1924, followed in 1939 by *The Life of J. M. W. Turner, R.A.* (2nd edn, 1961), which remains the most comprehensive and informative biography.

In the 1960s a considerable number of picture books devoted to Turner were produced, as well as Jack Lindsay's *Critical Biography* (1966) and Graham Reynolds's readable and well-illustrated *Turner* in 1969. John Gage's *Colour in Turner: Poetry and Truth*, a pioneering and challenging analysis of the artist, was also published in 1969. The first catalogue raisonné of the Turners in a public collection was Luke Herrmann's *Ruskin and Turner*, giving full details of the collection of watercolours and drawings in the Ashmolean Museum, Oxford. Other catalogues of Turner's works in British public collections are: Fitzwilliam Museum, Cambridge (1975), City Art Gallery, Manchester (1982), Whitworth Art Gallery, Manchester (1984), National Gallery of Ireland, Dublin (1988), Merseyside Collections (1990), and National Gallery of Scotland, Edinburgh (1993).

The number of books, exhibition catalogues, and articles devoted to Turner in the last quarter of the twentieth century is enormous. Outstanding among them are *The Paintings of J. M. W. Turner* by Martin Butlin and Evelyn Joll (1977; revised edn, 1984) and Andrew Wilton's *The Life and Work of J. M. W. Turner* (1979) which includes a catalogue of the finished watercolours. Wilton's *Turner in his Time* (1979) and Gage's *J. M. W. Turner: 'A Wonderful Range of Mind'* (1987) both provide stimulating surveys, while Cecilia Powell's *Turner in the South* (1987) gives the fullest information about Turner's travels in Italy. Another valuable contribution from John Gage is the skilfully edited *Collected Correspondence of J. M. W. Turner* (1980). Eric Shanes, editor of the journal *Turner Studies*, published his useful and well-illustrated *Turner's Picturesque Views in England and Wales* in 1979, followed by the similar *Turner's Rivers, Harbours and Coasts* in 1981. In both these Shanes examined the symbolism and political meaning of Turner's compositions, and he enlarged on these themes in his *Turner's Human Landscape* (1990). Similarly didactic is Kathleen Nicholson's *Turner's Classical Landscapes: Myth and Meaning*, also published in 1990. A revival of interest in Turner's work for engraving was marked by Luke Herrmann's *Turner Prints*, another publication of 1990.

Throughout the 1980s and 1990s the results of much of the research devoted to Turner appeared in exhibition catalogues and in articles in *Turner Studies* and other journals in Britain and America. Regional exhibitions, such as Andrew Wilton's *Turner in Wales* (1984), were followed by David Hill's books devoted to Turner's travels and work in specific areas, such as *In Turner's Footsteps* (1984) which follows him in northern England. Lindsay Stainton's *Turner's Venice* (1985) provides, with beautiful illustrations, full guidance on that fascinating theme, as the multi-author volume *Turner at Petworth*, published by the Tate Gallery in 1989, does for Petworth. Two new biographies of Turner, by Anthony Bailey and James Hamilton, both published in 1997, reflect the enormous quantity of new material available but still fall short of being convincing portraits of the elusive artist, whose life and work will continue to exercise scholars and students. A pioneering reference book, *The Oxford Companion to J. M. W. Turner* (2001), edited by Evelyn Joll, Martin Butlin, and Luke Herrmann, provides a compendium of the artist's life, work, and environment.

LUKE HERRMANN

Sources Farington, *Diary* · J. Ruskin, *Modern painters*, 5 vols. (1843–60) · A. A. Watts, 'Biographical sketch of J. M. W. Turner', in L. Ritchie, *Liber fluviorum, or, River scenery of France* (1853), vii–xlviii · W. Thornbury, *The life of J. M. W. Turner*, 2 vols. (1862); new edn (1877) · P. G. Hamerton, *The life of J. M. W. Turner* (1879) · W. G. Rawlinson, *The engraved work of J. M. W. Turner*, 2 vols. (1908–13) [cited as R] · A. J. Finberg, *A complete inventory of the drawings in the Turner Bequest*, 2 vols. (1909) [cited as TB] · A. J. Finberg, *The history of Turner's Liber Studiorum, with a new catalogue raisonné* (1924) · A. J. Finberg, *The life of J. M. W. Turner* (1939); 2nd edn (1961) · L. Gowing, *Turner: imagination and reality* (1966) [exhibition catalogue, Museum of Modern Art, New York] · *The sunset ship: the poems of J. M. W. Turner*, ed. J. Lindsay (1966) · J. Gage, *Colour in Turner: poetry and truth* (1969) · J. Russell and A. Wilton, *Turner in Switzerland*, ed. W. Amstutz (1976) · M. Butlin and E. Joll, *The paintings of J. M. W. Turner*, 2 vols. (1977); rev. edn (1984) [catalogue of all oil paintings; cited as BJ] · A. Wilton, *The life and work of J. M. W. Turner* (1979) [incl. catalogue of finished watercolours; cited as W] · E. Shanes, *Turner's Picturesque views in England and Wales* (1979) · G. Finley, *Landscapes of memory: Turner as illustrator to Scott* (1980) · *Collected correspondence of J. M. W. Turner*, ed. J. Gage (1980) · D. Hill, *In Turner's footsteps: through the hills and dales of northern England* (1984) · L. Stainton, *Turner's Venice* (1985) · J. Gage, *J. M. W. Turner: 'a wonderful range of mind'* (1987) · C. Powell, *Turner in the south: Rome, Naples, Florence* (1987) · A. Wilton, *Turner in his time* (1987) · M. Butlin, M. Luther, and I. Warrell, *Turner at Petworth: painter and patron* (1989) · L. Herrmann, *Turner prints: the engraved work of J. M. W. Turner* (1990) · A. Bailey, *Standing in the sun: a life of J. M. W. Turner* (1997) · J. Hamilton, *Turner: a life* (1997) · E. Joll, M. Butlin, and L. Herrmann, eds., *The Oxford companion to J. M. W. Turner* (2001) · *Turner, 1775–1851* (1974) [exhibition catalogue, Tate Gallery and RA, 16 Nov 1974 – 2 Mar 1975] · A. Wilton, *Turner in the British Museum: drawings and watercolours* (1975) [exhibition catalogue, British Museum, London] · [F. Baumann and K. Seltmann], eds., *Turner und die Schweiz* (Zürich, 1976) [exhibition catalogue, Kunsthaus, Zürich, 7 Oct 1976 – 2 Jan 1977] · M. Omer, *Turner and the Bible* (1979) [exhibition catalogue, Israel Museum, Jerusalem, 1979; AM Oxf., Jan–March 1981] · A. Wilton, *Turner and the sublime* (1980) [exhibition catalogue, Toronto, New Haven, and London, 1 Nov 1980 – 20 Sept 1981] · J. Guillaud and M. Guillaud, *Turner en France* (Paris, 1981) [exhibition catalogue, Centre Culturel du Marais, Paris, 7 Oct 1981 – 10 Jan 1982] · C. Powell, *Turner's rivers of Europe: the Rhine, Meuse, and Mosel* (1991) [exhibition catalogue, Tate Gallery, 11 Sept 1991 – 26 Jan 1992; Musée d'Ixelles, Brussels, Feb–April 1992] · D. B. Brown, *Turner and Byron* (1992) [exhibition catalogue,

Tate Gallery, London, 3 June – 20 Sept, 1992] · J. Piggott, *Turner's vignettes* (1993) [exhibition catalogue, Tate Gallery, 29 Sept 1993 – 13 Feb 1994] · C. Powell, *Turner in Germany* (1995) [exhibition catalogue, Tate Gallery, 23 May – 10 Sept 1995] · G. Forrester, *Turner's 'drawing book': the Liber Studiorum* (1996) [exhibition catalogue, Tate Gallery, 20 Feb – 2 June, 1996] · I. Warrell, *Turner on the Loire* (1997) [exhibition catalogue, Tate Gallery, 30 Sept 1997 – 15 Feb 1998] · I. Warrell, *Turner on the Seine* (1999) [exhibition catalogue, Tate Gallery, 29 June – 3 Oct 1999] · L. Parris, ed., *Exploring late Turner* (1999) [exhibition catalogue, Salander-O'Reilly Galleries, New York, 1 April – 5 June 1999] · R. J. B. Walker, 'The portraits of J. M. W. Turner: a checklist', *Turner Studies*, 3/1 (1983) · E. Shanes, ed., *Turner Studies*, 11 vols. (1981–93) · d. cert.

Archives BL, lecture notes, Add. MS 46151 · FM Cam., letters · Tate collection, album of engravings, corresp., and press cuttings | Bodl. Oxf., corresp. and papers relating to Turner Bequest · Ches. & Chester ALSS, letters to Sir John Leicester and related papers · RA, corresp. with Thomas Lawrence · University of Lancaster, Ruskin Library, MSS relating to Ruskin Library

Likenesses J. M. W. Turner, self-portrait, watercolour drawing, 1792, NPG · J. M. W. Turner, self-portrait, oils, *c*.1793, Indianapolis Museum of Art · J. M. W. Turner, self-portrait, oils, *c*.1798, Tate collection [*see illus.*] · G. Dance, pencil and chalk drawing, 1800, RA · E. Bird, pencil drawing, 1815, BM · C. R. Leslie, pencil drawing, 1816, NPG · E. Bell, sketch, 1828, BM · J. T. Smith, watercolour drawing, 1830–32, BM · pencil, *c*.1837 (after J. Gilbert), NPG · J. Linnell, oils, 1838, NPG · C. Turner, chalk and watercolour drawing, 1841, BM · C. Turner, chalk drawing, 1842 (after his earlier work), NPG · C. Martin, pencil drawing, 1844, NPG · watercolour with bodycolour over pencil, 1844 (after C. Martin), NPG · R. Doyle, woodcut, 1846, NPG · J. Gilbert, drawing, 1846, Courtauld Inst. · W. Parrott, oils, *c*.1846, U. Reading · P. MacDowell, statue, 1851, St Paul's Cathedral, London · attrib. T. Woolner, plaster cast of death mask, 1851, NPG · C. Turner, stipple, pubd 1852 (after Count D'Orsay), BM, NPG · J. B. Hunt, stipple, pubd 1852 (after unknown artist), BM, NPG · L. C. Wyon, medal, 1876, NPG · S. Haydon, drypoint etching (after D. Maclise), NPG · W. B. Richmond, pencil drawing, NPG · attrib. J. T. Smith, oils, Tate collection

Wealth at death approx. £140,000 estate

Turner, Sir (Ronald) Mark Cunliffe (1906–1980),

merchant banker, was born on 29 March 1906 at 41 Cheyne Court, Chelsea, the only son and younger child of Christopher Rede Turner (1877–1967), clerk in the House of Commons, and his wife, Jill Helen, daughter of Harry Pickersgill Cunliffe (1858–1919), of Staughton Manor, Huntingdonshire. He was grandson of Major-General Sir Alfred Turner (1842–1918), military policeman, alpinist, polyglot, and chairman of the North Borneo State Rubber Company. After schooling at Wellington College, Mark Turner at the age of eighteen became a messenger at the merchant bank of M. Samuel in 1924. He came to specialize in corporate finance, but after the rejection of his proposals for the bank to fund capital-starved businesses with good growth prospects he transferred in 1934 to the smaller merchant banking house of Robert Benson & Co.

Bensons had recently formed the Kenterne Trust to operate in the new issues business. Turner's energy and ingenuity in ensuring successful share issues in textiles, steel, paper, and catering propelled Bensons to a higher ranking among City merchant banks. Turner was firm, tactful, and decisive, with superb powers of assimilation and analysis enabling him to form clear views and reliable recommendations on diverse business propositions. Both

then and in later life he worked intensely hard and marshalled his time and energy with remarkable effectiveness. He had much charm, and an eager smile. When young he was active in the Peckham Health Centre, a pioneering institution promoting family health, and he maintained progressive sympathies throughout his life.

In 1931 Turner married Elizabeth Mary (*b*. 1910), daughter of Major-General Hugh Clement Sutton, and granddaughter of Charles Lindley Wood, second Viscount Halifax. They had one daughter. This marriage was dissolved in 1936 and in 1939 he married Margaret (1913–1997), daughter of Major-General Sir Hereward Wake, thirteenth baronet, and granddaughter of the founder of Robert Benson. 'Peggy' Turner was a delightful woman, with an attractively deep voice, a slightly scatterbrained manner, a wry, shrewd humour, and an infectious capacity for enjoyment. They had three sons and two daughters.

Between 1939 and 1944 Turner was an official at the Ministry of Economic Warfare. He was responsible for devising and operating a blockade of petroleum oil supplies to Spain in 1940–42. This deterred the Spanish from joining the axis powers, and turned Generalissimo Franco's regime from a stance of non-belligerency in 1940 to neutrality by 1942. He also advised on the destruction of Romanian oilfields and on oil policy generally. Turner was recruited to the Foreign Office in 1944 as head of a new department charged with preparing the post-war allied administration of Germany and Austria. At the request of Ernest Bevin he postponed his return to banking, and served in 1945–7 as under-secretary for economic affairs at the Control Office for Germany and Austria. He was knighted in 1946.

Turner resumed his banking career in 1947 and became joint managing director of the newly expanded Robert Benson, Lonsdale & Co.; during the early 1950s he emerged as the leading figure in the bank. He instigated the merger of Robert Benson Lonsdale with the accepting house, Kleinwort, to form the highly successful merchant bank of Kleinwort Benson in 1961. He was a director of Kleinwort Benson from its formation until 1977, and acted as senior executive (1961–71) and deputy chairman (1966–71). As a merchant banker with great mental gifts his expertise was sought by many businesses. He joined the boards of such companies as Rio Tinto (1947), Commercial Union Assurance (1948), Calico Printers (1952), Tanganyika Concessions, Tunnel Portland Cement, Nuclear Developments, Transport Holdings (1962), Toronto-Dominion Bank (1963), Midland and International Banks (1966), National Cash Register (1968), Whitbread Investment (1969), Bank of America Limited (1971), and the Sotheby Park Bernet art auctioneers (1977). As one example of the facilitating role he filled as a non-executive director, Turner was still on the board of Commercial Union, and Kleinwort Benson was its financial adviser, when Commercial Union took over Northern and Employers in what was then the largest ever insurance merger (1968). Turner was also chairman of the Mercantile Credit Company (1957–72) during a period of strategic reform and dynamic expansion; later he was chairman of British Home Stores (1968–76).

The most important of Turner's outside interests was Rio Tinto. Acting as part-time managing director in 1948–50, Turner laid the strategy which transformed a vulnerable business, with only a pyrites mine in Spain and investments in the Rhodesian copperbelt, into one of Britain's most powerful multinationals. He determined that the company must expand into metal mining in politically stable nations, and selected many key personnel to implement this strategy. His recruitment of J. N. V. Duncan, and their subsequent co-operation, was decisive in Rio Tinto's regeneration. Turner was crucial in its merger with the Zinc Corporation to form Rio Tinto Zinc (1961) and in raising large funds for mining development with little security other than long-term supply agreements. His diplomatic skills were valuable in negotiations with foreign governments. Following Duncan's sudden death Turner became chief executive (1975–8) and chairman of RTZ from 1975 until his death. During this period he had to justify the company's plans to its environmentalist critics, and he was involved in other delicate issues: he pleaded the fifth amendment in litigation pursued by Westinghouse Electric, alleging an international uranium cartel (1977). Lord Charteris of Amisfield, who was Turner's co-director at RTZ, admired 'his imagination, his humour, his infectious sense of fun, his care for others and his determination always to hold to what was true' (The Times, 17 Dec 1980).

Although Tony Benn in 1975 claimed that Turner was an archetype 'of the international capitalist and British tory establishment' (Benn, 403), Turner had an active social sense and considerable moral courage. When he joined the Observer Trust in 1959, that reformist Sunday newspaper was still anathema in the City, owing to its opposition to the Anglo-French expedition at Suez in 1956. Friends and colleagues were angered by Turner's decision but, according to the editor of The Observer, David Astor, 'for the next seventeen years [Turner] supported the paper's position of independence with vigour, and devoted long, unremunerated hours to steering its financial course' (The Observer, 21 Dec 1980). Turner retired as trustee in 1976.

Turner had discriminating cultural tastes, and in 1944 was involved in negotiations with the Pilgrim Trust and the National Trust to secure the future of Audley End after Lord Braybrooke's death in action. Later he was a governor of Brunel University, and a trustee of the Glyndebourne Arts Trust. He died of abdominal cancer on 13 December 1980 at his home, 3 The Grove, Highgate, London, survived by his second wife, who died on 21 April 1997.

RICHARD DAVENPORT-HINES

Sources The Times (15 Dec 1980) · The Times (17 Dec 1980) · The Times (30 Dec 1980) · Financial Times (15 Dec 1980) · The Observer (21 Dec 1980) · personal knowledge (2004) · private information (2004) · D. Avery, Not on Queen Victoria's birthday: the story of the Rio Tinto mines (1974) · C. E. Harvey, The Rio Tinto Company: an economic history of a leading international mining concern, 1873–1954 (1981) · J. Wake, Kleinwort Benson: a history of two families in banking (1997) · T. Benn, Against the tide: diaries, 1973–1976 (1989) · J. Lees-Milne, Prophesying peace (1977), 127, 136, 144 · b. cert. · d. cert. · m. cert. · Debrett's Peerage

Archives City Westm. AC, corresp. relating to Allied Circle · London, Kleinwort Benson papers · London, Rio Tinto Zinc Corporation papers

Likenesses photograph, c.1960, repro. in Avery, Not on Queen Victoria's birthday, 393 · photograph, 1968, repro. in The Times (13 March 1968), 19 · photograph, 1968, repro. in The Times (27 June 1968), 23 · photograph, 1978, repro. in The Times (31 Jan 1978), 27b · photograph, 1978, repro. in The Times (12 April 1978), 26 · photograph, 1978, repro. in The Times (15 May 1978), 23e · photograph, 1978, repro. in The Times (25 May 1978), 24c

Wealth at death £434,403: DBB

Turner, Matthew (d. 1789?), chemist and radical theologian, was an established surgeon and teacher by 1760; little is known of his life before then. During his most productive years he worked and socialized in the non-Anglican milieu of England's north-western counties, his friends and colleagues including Josiah Wedgwood, Thomas Bentley, John Wyke, Joseph Priestley, and Joseph Wright. His activities and accomplishments were numerous and diverse, though he is best remembered for his relationship with Wedgwood and his theological dispute with Priestley.

As a surgeon and chemist, Turner based his activities at his home at 7 John Street in Liverpool. It was here that Josiah Wedgwood came in 1762 to be treated for an injured knee. A friendship developed, and, besides introducing Thomas Bentley to Wedgwood, Turner devised a number of new chemical techniques that proved very useful in the potter's manufactures. These included varnishes, bronze powders, and a variety of brilliant colouring agents. In addition to these innovations, it is claimed that Turner 'invented, or at least brought to tolerable perfection, the art of copying prints upon glass' (Memoirs of Dr Joseph Priestley, 61–2). During the 1760s he also devised new treatments for several maladies. In 1761 he published An Account of the Extraordinary Medicinal Fluid, called Aether, in which he contended that vitriolic aether, a solvent that he manufactured and sold, could be employed to remedy numerous medical problems, ranging from vertigo and rheumatism to asthma and windy disorders of the stomach. The following year, in a paper entitled 'The cure of Ascarides', he proposed that intestinal worms could be treated by the use of an enema derived from tobacco smoke.

Turner was a proficient and witty teacher. From 1762 to 1765, he delivered lectures on chemistry and pneumatics at the dissenting Warrington Academy. It was at these lectures that Priestley came into contact with 'a very useful Apparatus for Experimental Philosophy consisting of the most capital instruments' (Memoirs of Dr Joseph Priestley, 61). In later years, Turner lectured on anatomy and the theory of forms at the Liverpool Academy of Arts, an institution of which he was among the founding members.

Turner's contemporaries also remembered his radical political and theological commitments. As a republican, he supported the revolutionaries during the American War of Independence, and quipped that the loss of the terra firma of the thirteen colonies would be replaced by Herschel's recent discovery of the extensive terra incognita of Uranus (*Memoirs of Dr Joseph Priestley*, 61–2). In religion he was raised as a theist, but in 1782, in an *Answer to Dr. Priestley, on the Existence of God*, a response to Priestley's *Letters to a Philosophical Unbeliever*, he described himself as a freethinker (p. 5). This work, first published under the pseudonym William Hammon, was subsequently republished by Richard Carlile in 1826. In the pamphlet Turner declared that he was an atheist, though he did admit that the 'vis naturae', gravity, and matter's elasticity and repulsive powers demonstrated that the universe was permeated by 'a principle of intelligence and design' (ibid., 17). Despite the 'perpetual industry' of nature, he denied that this intelligence entailed that philosophers needed to posit the existence of a deity extraneous to the material world. In his counter-attack, Priestley contended that Turner's 'ingenuousness and courage' were a façade, and reiterated the central principles of his argument from design (Priestley, *Additional Letters*). However, the polite dispute did not persist. Turner died a few years later, probably in Liverpool.   E. I. CARLYLE, *rev.* KEVIN C. KNOX

Sources E. Meteyard, *The life of Josiah Wedgwood, from his private correspondence and family papers*, 2 vols. (1865–6) • M. Turner, *Answer to Dr. Priestley on the existence of God*, 3rd edn (1833) • *Memoirs of Dr Joseph Priestley*, ed. J. Priestley, T. Cooper, and W. Christie, 2 vols. (1806) • J. Priestley, *Additional letters to a philosophical unbeliever* (1782) • J. Posner, 'Josiah Wedgwood's doctors', *Pharmaceutical History*, 1/3 (1973), 6–8 • J. Posner, 'Josiah Wedgwood's doctors', *Pharmaceutical History*, 2/3 (1973), 2–5 • *Proceedings and Papers of the Historic Society of Lancashire and Cheshire*, 5 (1852–3), 147; 6 (1853–5), 72, 75 • H. McLachlan, *Warrington Academy: its history and influence*, Chetham Society, 107, new ser. (1943) • *The Liverpool Directory* (1766–90) • P. J. Wallis and R. V. Wallis, *Eighteenth century medics*, 2nd edn (1988) • R. Reilly, *Josiah Wedgwood, 1730–1795* (1992)
Archives Wedgwood Museum, Stoke-on-Trent, Wedgwood correspondence • Staffordshire, Etruria collection, Wedgwood correspondence

Turner, Merfyn Lloyd (1915–1991), penal reformer and author, was born on 20 October 1915 in Pen-y-graig, Rhondda, Glamorgan, the third of four children of Edward Godfrey Turner (1873–1954) and his wife, Lizzie Violet, *née* Lloyd (1889–1979). The family's first language was Welsh. Turner's father, a Wesleyan minister, moved his ministry every three years and the children went from manse to manse throughout Wales, attending local schools. Turner took an arts degree at the University College of Wales, Aberystwyth (1935–8), where he won the Gladstone prize for history, and he gained a teaching certificate at Westminster College, London (1938–9).

In 1940 Turner, a lifelong pacifist, was rejected as a conscientious objector and sentenced to three months' hard labour in Swansea gaol. This experience was seminal, and nurtured in Turner a passionate commitment to those on the margins of 'normal' society, especially those in prison. He said of his own prison experience, 'I felt as if all the world had abandoned me' and he never forgot how 'prison degraded the man' (*In Prison*). On release he was active in social work in Cardiff, establishing a youth club in Tiger Bay, working with the pacifist service unit, and playing football as an amateur for Cardiff City. In 1944 he moved to Oxford House, the settlement in Bethnal Green,

London, and the seedbed for many social work pioneers, whom Turner viewed as kindred revolutionaries, 'comradeship in practice'. He lived and worked in London for the rest of his life, though maintaining a Welsh base. He was appointed warden of the Webbe Boys' Club in Bethnal Green but characteristically became drawn to those boys who would not join that or any other club, the 'unclubbables'. Encouraged in that interest by a committee of like-minded individuals, some of whom remained closely associated with Turner's work for over forty years, funding was obtained from the London Parochial Charities (now the City Parochial Foundation) to acquire a barge moored at Wapping. In 1949 the Barge Club experiment for 'unclubbable' boys began, with Turner as the worker until 1952. It was his first innovative success.

All his life Turner kept notes on his work (in Welsh or English). In both languages he wrote numerous articles, and gave countless talks, including memorable ones on the BBC in the 1950s and 1960s. He wrote very little about himself, but in an early Barge Club report described himself as 'unclubbable'. He was a left-handed nonconformist who essentially worked on his own initiatives, not fitting easily into existing structures. He was not conventionally charismatic but he inspired others. Angular and lean, he had a quiet presence, unnoticed in many gatherings. Yet whenever he spoke, be it to one or a hundred, he was clear, persistent, and persuasive. He rooted his arguments in the real experience of men he knew in prison or in lodging-houses. Few conversations with him progressed far without him saying, 'I was talking to a man in prison last night'. His vision was of practical compassion because, as he concluded in his BBC Wales lecture for 1971, 'Who cares?', 'we know that if we exclude the undeserving from our society, we ourselves will also be diminished by their absence and by their loss' (Cook, 205). His own prison experience led him in 1946 to become a voluntary prison visitor at Pentonville prison, where he visited regularly until March 1991. He saw men leaving prison homeless, isolated, and unrecognized by society. Turner spent three months living in a common lodging-house, the usual bleak destination of 'inadequate' ex-prisoners. By 1953 he had developed his scheme to establish Norman House, a family home for twelve homeless former prisoners. It was funded by the London Parochial Charities, and opened in 1955 with Turner as the worker. He believed that to give former prisoners a chance was 'not an act of charity but a matter of right' (ibid., 67). The experience of the house was to be one of 'great difficulty, crisis and ultimate success' (ibid., 79). It changed forever the penal system's, and society's, thinking about prison aftercare. This, the original 'half-way house', was the second and greater of Turner's pioneering initiatives, and it stimulated a national and international network.

The Norman House truly became a family home when on 12 August 1955 Turner married Shirley Elizabeth Davis (*b.* 1932), a young barrister who had applied to become a befriender to the residents. They lived there until 1960, and Turner also undertook in 1959 a detailed study of lodging-houses. They had five children. From 1960 to 1980 Turner—funded by the City Parochial Foundation, the Gulbenkian Foundation, and others—worked tirelessly to spread the idea of aftercare hostels at home and abroad and to advocate effective alternatives to prison. He also visited patients in Broadmoor and extended aftercare opportunities to them. After retiring in 1980 he continued as before, and developed a particular interest in men in the deportation wing in Pentonville as well as visiting Western prisoners in Turkish prisons.

Turner was a modest and humorous man with a passion for all things Welsh, from poetry to rugby, and was especially proud of the honorary doctorate conferred on him by the University of Wales in 1982. His writings, including correspondence with men in prison, continued until just before his death. He published four major books, which described particular aspects of his work and distinctive approach in detail. *Ships without Sails* appeared in 1953, followed by *Forgotten Men* (1960), *Safe Lodging* (1961), and *A Pretty Sort of Prison* (1964). Unpublished material was subsequently deposited at the Institute of Criminology, Cambridge. He died of cancer on 6 August 1991 in the Royal Free Hospital, London, and was cremated at St Marylebone crematorium six days later. His wife survived him.

TIM COOK

Sources T. Cook, ed., *Practical compassion: an anthology—Merfyn Turner, 1915–1991* • *In prison*, 1960 [BBC Wales; transcript at Institute of Criminology, Cambridge] • *CGPLA Eng. & Wales* (1991) • private information (2004) [S. E. Turner, widow]
Archives U. Cam., MSS
Wealth at death £153,902: probate, 6 Nov 1991, *CGPLA Eng. & Wales*

Turner, Sir **Michael William** (1905–1980), banker, was born on 25 April 1905 at 7 Kingsgate Street, Winchester, the only son of the two children of Sir Skinner Turner (1868–1935), a high-court judge in Bangkok, and his wife, Millicent, daughter of the Revd W. H. Hewett. Educated at Marlborough College and at University College, Oxford (where he played varsity hockey), he joined the Hongkong and Shanghai Banking Corporation in 1926; he served an apprenticeship in London, and was sent East in 1930. On 26 November 1938 he married Wendy Spencer Stranack (*b.* 1918), second daughter of Morris William Stranack (*d.* 1940), of Durban, South Africa, and Lucy Magdalene Poynton (*d.* 1945), in the Anglican cathedral, Shanghai. They had three sons.

Turner's first Eastern assignment was in Hong Kong, where he was to be closely associated with the future chief manager, Sir Arthur Morse. In 1936 he was transferred to Shanghai, in charge of 'books', thus providing an opportunity to view this key branch's overall operation. Turner's willingness to act decisively was demonstrated when, on behalf of his fellow juniors and over the local management's objections, he appealed to head office to set a more realistic rate of exchange for the calculation of salaries. He had his facts right; his request was not only accepted but backdated.

Turner joined the bank's Singapore branch in early 1942, where he was almost immediately confined in the notorious Changi internment camp; his wife barely escaped to South Africa. His survival was due in part to the faith encouraged by a leader of the Salvation Army; indeed, Turner briefly considered abandoning banking for the church. He returned to England a virtual skeleton. With his rehabilitation bonus of £2000, however, he and his wife spent a month in the Savoy Hotel. While others returned to the East fully equipped, the Turners returned to the bank in Hong Kong in 1946 with nothing but happy memories; perhaps that made the difference. Turner was appointed chief accountant (1949), manager, Hong Kong (1951), and chief manager (1953), in succession to Sir Arthur Morse.

Turner instituted changes which began to transform the bank into a modern multinational. Having made a final settlement with China—leaving only a presence in Shanghai—Turner shifted the bank's operating focus from politically unfriendly or high-tax areas to British Borneo, Singapore, Malaya, and Thailand. The need to develop operations in the United States forced the establishment of a separate, wholly-owned banking subsidiary, the Hongkong and Shanghai Banking Corporation of California.

Traditionally, bank staff had been organized in three tiers: foreign staff as executives, Portuguese as clerks, and Chinese as 'shroffs' (employees responsible for handling cash). However, the emigration of the Portuguese from Hong Kong and the China coast, and the cost of even junior expatriate staff, forced Turner to break with the past: selected senior Portuguese personnel who remained would be appointed local officers authorized to initial routine documents. Further reforms followed slowly, but the notice, typical of foreign firms in the East, 'Not valid unless signed by a member of the European Staff', no longer applied.

The compradoric system whereby Chinese staff were employed and guaranteed by a single Chinese manager, the compradore, was proving an impediment to expansion; local and regional Chinese officers were accordingly created from both within the staff and by recruitment. By the end of Turner's administration the bank was in direct contact not only with a few major Chinese customers but also with members of the expanding professional classes and with the new generation of local entrepreneurs.

Turner was drawn inevitably into the important question of the fate of those British-owned colonial banks whose principal areas of business had, unlike Hong Kong, proved a difficult base from which to operate profitably. He grasped the crucial fact that his own bank had either to take over or, eventually, be taken over. That Turner made the former choice and initiated the organizational changes to make it effective is a measure of his character and of his contribution to British post-war banking. The first such acquisition was the Mercantile Bank (of India). When, at almost the same time, the future of the British Bank of the Middle East (formerly the Imperial Bank of

Persia) was in question, Turner acted decisively: he bought it.

As a result of these acquisitions during 1959 and 1960, Turner had to direct two further sets of 'European' staff, traditionally loyal but to their own company procedures and traditions. Turner developed a less personal form of control; he reviewed and partially restricted the authority of independently minded branch managers and created a separate 'head office', thereby differentiating corporation-wide affairs from local Hong Kong concerns. This, *inter alia*, permitted the reception of technical specialists, who could now serve as permanent staff and would be integrated as such. Developments in transportation and communication facilitated Turner's task by enabling him to make extensive tours of the bank's offices outside Hong Kong. With him went Wendy Turner, whose reports on staff housing and other personnel matters were, though unofficial, the basis for action; she bridged the gap between local branch control and the creation of formal personnel services.

Meanwhile, in Hong Kong, Turner was presiding over the bank's participation in the territory's 'economic miracle', not through an overall plan but rather by innovative adjustment of British banking practice to meet extraordinary circumstances as they arose. He established an industrial banking department, developed contacts with former Shanghai customers who were now immigrants in Hong Kong, and extended operations in Mongkok, then a centre of industrial growth, and in the growing urban centres of the New Territories. At the same time his policies were beginning to meet the needs of ordinary residents through more accessible savings' facilities and innovations in consumer credit. The positive overall impact of Turner's policies can be seen from the bank's changing balance sheet. Its total assets during the period 1954–62 increased from HK\$3.6 to HK\$9.6 million.

An active figure in the Hong Kong community, Turner received the colonial police medal (1956) and was appointed CBE (1957). He served on Hong Kong's executive council (1954–62), and was knighted in 1961. On his retirement and return to London in 1962 Turner became a member of the London bank's consultative committee. He joined the boards of the British Bank of the Middle East and the Westminster Bank. A freeman of the City of London, he also served as master of the Skinners' Company (1967–8). Sir Michael Turner died at his London home, 6/39 Egerton Gardens, on 27 September 1980, and was buried at Holy Trinity Church, Cookham, Berkshire. He was survived by his wife.   FRANK H. H. KING

Sources F. H. H. King, *The history of the Hongkong and Shanghai Banking Corporation*, 3–4 (1988–91) · F. H. King, ed., *Eastern banking: essays in the history of the Hongkong and Shanghai Banking Corporation* (1983) · G. Jones, *The history of the British Bank of the Middle East*, 2: *Banking and oil* (1987) · *WWW* · b. cert. · Burke, *Peerage* · private information (2004) · d. cert.
Archives HSBC Group Archives, London, Midland Bank archives | SOUND HSBC Group Archives, London, Midland Bank archives, Hongkong Bank Group collection, oral histories of Sir Michael Turner by Christopher Cook and of Lady Turner by Catherine E. King

Likenesses N. Hepple, portrait, Hongkong Bank, 1 Queen's Road, Central, Hong Kong · photographs, HSBC Group Archives, London, Midland Bank archives, PHST 63.1, 2, 7, 8; repro. in King, *History of the Hongkong and Shanghai Banking Corporation*, vol. 4, facing p. 496
Wealth at death £17,873—gross: probate, 30 Oct 1980, CGPLA Eng. & Wales · £3674—net

Turner, Peter (1542–1614), physician, the only son (there were two daughters) of William *Turner (1509/10–1568), clergyman, and his wife, Jane, daughter of George Alder, alderman of Cambridge, spent most of his childhood and adolescence in Germany. He matriculated at St John's College, Cambridge, in 1564, and at Heidelberg in 1566, became MD Heidelberg in 1571, was incorporated MD Cambridge in 1575 and DN Oxford in 1599. He held the post of physician at St Bartholomew's Hospital, London, from 1582 and throughout the plague year 1583, but relinquished it in 1584. In December 1582 he was made a licentiate of the College of Physicians, despite being censured for practising medicine in London without having obtained the college's licence in advance. He never became a fellow. The reason for this is not clear. It may be that he excited hostility as an immoderate advocate of the teachings of Paracelsus; however, equally outspoken defenders of chemical medicine, including Turner's friends Thomas Penny and Thomas Mouffet, did become fellows. In the parliament of 1584–5, where he sat as member for Bridport, Turner proposed a 'book and a bill' which, if enacted, would have replaced the Book of Common Prayer with an officially enforceable Genevan style of worship, and Elizabethan church government with a thoroughgoing Presbyterian discipline. In making these proposals he was almost certainly acting as a spokesman for John Field and the London conference.

During his studies at Heidelberg in the 1560s Turner had accompanied the entomologist and botanist Thomas Penny on field trips. He sent Penny a dried specimen of a rare variety of cranesbill (*Geranium bohemicum*) which he had found near Copenhagen. Turner was thanked by the naturalist and chemical physician Thomas Mouffet in his *Theatrum insectorum* (1634) for his help in the task of bringing order to the great mass of Penny's notes on entomology.

Despite his introduction in his youth to botany and to natural history, there is little evidence that Turner kept up these studies in any serious way. Nor did he publish anything in this field. He contributed some Latin verses to Mouffet's *Nosomantica* (1588). His 'godlie hymne' or 'spirituall song to the praise of Almightie God for delivering England from the Spaniards', printed with Oliver Pygge's *Meditations* (1588), is a rousing set of stanzas on the defeat of the armada. In his *The opinion of Peter Turner doctor in physick, concerning amulets or plague cakes, whereof perhaps some holde too much, and some too little* (1603), a pamphlet defending the use of arsenic wrapped in cloth and hung round the neck as a prophylactic against plague, Turner claims that such amulets work to 'draw out the poison of the plague' by virtue of the 'spirits of gold' the arsenic contains. To regard the efficacy of the amulets as 'magicall' is to be guilty of 'idolatrie and superstition'; the effect is entirely natural. He calls in aid 'Theophrastus Paracelsus, who was absolutely the most learned chimicall writer and worker that ever wrote', and dismisses as ignorant the censures of 'such Phisitians or Philosophers which are not acquainted neither with the chymicall theory nor practise' (*The Opinion of Peter Turner*, 8–9). He concludes on a pious and cautionary note: it is reprehensible, indeed 'accursed', to put one's 'whole confidence in secondary means', 'for it is neither herbe nor salve nor any thing els that healeth, but only the blessing of the Head Physitian'. In *A Modest Defence of the Caveat Given to the Wearers of Impoisoned Amulets, as Preseruatiues from the Plague, wherein that Point is Somewhat More Largely Reasoned and Debated with an Ancient Physician, who Hath Mainteined them by Publicke Writing* (1604), Francis Herring, a fellow of the College of Physicians and an opponent of Paracelsan medicine, scathingly dismissed Turner's claim that arsenic contains 'spirits of Gold'. Wilfully ignoring the alchemical vocabulary which this statement employs, Herring chooses ridicule as a weapon and scoffs that even unlettered refiners of metal know for a fact that 'there is as much Golde in Arsenicke as in a Rat'.

In 1606 Turner attended Sir Walter Ralegh in the Tower. Turner married Pascha, daughter of Henry *Parry, bishop of Worcester; Peter *Turner (1586–1652) and Samuel *Turner (d. 1647?) were their sons. Turner died in London on 27 May 1614. He was buried near his father in the church of St Olave, Hart Street, London, in a coloured tomb on which his effigy kneels in a scarlet gown.

G. LEWIS

Sources Venn, *Alum. Cant.* · G. Toepke, ed., *Die Matrikel der Universität Heidelberg*, 7 (Heidelberg, 1916), 39, 464 · N. Moore, *The history of St Bartholomew's Hospital*, 2 (1918), 429–33 · Munk, *Roll*, 1.84 · G. Clark and A. M. Cooke, *A history of the Royal College of Physicians of London*, 1 (1964), 142 · W. H. Frere and C. E. Douglas, eds., *Puritan manifestoes: a study of the origin of the puritan revolt, with a reprint of the 'Admonition to the parliament', and kindred documents, 1572* (1907); repr. (1954) · P. Collinson, *The Elizabethan puritan movement* (1967), 286–8 · C. E. Raven, *English naturalists from Neckam to Ray: a study of the making of the modern world* (1947), 169 · J. Ward, *The lives of the professors of Gresham College* (1740), 131 · annals, RCP Lond., 2.19 · *CSP dom.*, 1603–10, p. 307 · *DNB* · T. Mouffet, *Theatrum insectorum* (1634), 16
Likenesses effigy on tomb, St Olave, Hart Street, London

Turner, Peter (1586–1652), mathematician, was born in Middlesex, the son of Peter *Turner (1542–1614) and Pascha Parry, and brother of Samuel *Turner. He matriculated at St Mary Hall, Oxford, on 31 October 1600, graduated BA from Christ Church on 27 June 1605, was elected a fellow of Merton in 1607, and graduated MA on 9 March 1612. On 25 July 1620 he became professor of geometry in Gresham College in London, following Henry Briggs. In 1629, at Archbishop Laud's request, he drew up the Caroline cycle to regulate the election of proctors from the various colleges. About the same date he also served on a committee established to revise the university statutes. He succeeded Henry Briggs as Savilian professor of geometry at Oxford, resigning the Gresham professorship on 20 February 1631.

On his appointment as chancellor of the university in 1631, Laud urged on the work of revising the statutes. The task was supervised by Brian Twyne but the work of final revision was entrusted to Turner. The statutes were published in 1634.

On 31 August 1636, during a royal visit, Turner received the degree of MD. This mark of the king's favour was either purchased or repaid by an ardent loyalty. In 1641 Turner was one of the first from Oxford to enlist under Sir John Byron. He was taken prisoner in a skirmish near Stow on the Wold on 10 September and imprisoned first in Banbury and later in Northampton, his belongings at Oxford being seized when the town surrendered. In 1642 he was taken to London and imprisoned in Southwark, and in July 1643 he was exchanged for some parliamentary prisoners at Oxford.

On 9 November 1648 Turner was ejected by the parliamentary visitors from his fellowship at Merton and from the Savilian professorship, in which he was succeeded by John Wallis. Being reduced to great poverty, he retired to Southwark to live with his sister, the widow of a brewer named Wats. At her house near the debtors' prison he died, unmarried, in January 1652, and was buried that month in the church of St Saviour.

Despite a good reputation as a classicist and mathematician Turner left almost no written work. Nevertheless he rejected Laud's offers of promotion to high office, preferring a scholar's life. He has recently been described by Adamson as 'more obviously a Royalist and an Anglican than an academic of any sort' (Adamson, 134).

E. I. CARLYLE, *rev.* H. K. HIGTON

Sources J. B. Easton, 'Turner, Peter', *DSB* · I. R. Adamson, 'The foundation and early history of Gresham College, London, 1596–1704', PhD diss., U. Cam., 1976 · J. Ward, *The lives of the professors of Gresham College* (1740) · Foster, *Alum. Oxon.* · G. C. Brodrick, *Memorials of Merton College*, OHS, 4 (1885) · Wood, *Ath. Oxon.*

Turner, Sir Ralph Lilley (1888–1983), orientalist and academic administrator, was born on 5 October 1888 in Charlton, London, the second of the three sons and third of the four children of George Turner (1852–1929), schoolmaster, of Cambridge, and his wife, Bertha (1857–1952), daughter of William Eaden Lilley. He was educated at the Perse School under W. H. D. Rouse, who introduced him to Sanskrit, and at Christ's College, Cambridge (senior scholar). He obtained first classes in the classical tripos (parts one and two, 1909 and 1911) and the oriental languages tripos (1910); was awarded the Brotherton memorial Sanskrit prize; and was elected a fellow of Christ's (1912). In 1913 he entered the Indian educational service as lecturer at Queen's College, Benares. From 1915 to 1919 he served in Palestine and India with the 2nd/3rd Queen Alexandra's Own Gurkha rifles; he was wounded, awarded the MC, and twice mentioned in dispatches. From 1920 to 1922 he was professor of Indian linguistics at Benares Hindu University. On 3 November 1920 he married Dorothy Rivers (1892–1972), daughter of William Howard Goulty, solicitor; they had one son and three daughters.

In 1922 Turner was elected to the chair of Sanskrit in the University of London (at the School of Oriental Studies), which he occupied until the age of retirement in 1954. He wrote many important articles (later republished as *Collected Papers, 1912–1973*, 1975) and *A Comparative and Etymological Dictionary of the Nepali Language* (1931), meanwhile steadily accumulating the vast collection of word slips on which his later lexicographical work was based. In 1942 he was elected a fellow of the British Academy.

These achievements were the more remarkable because from 1937 to 1957 Turner was also director of the School of Oriental and African Studies (as it became in 1938) with heavy administrative responsibilities. The early years of his tenure saw the creation under Ida Ward of the first department of the languages and cultures of Africa in a British university, and the successful negotiation of the school's removal from the City of London to Bloomsbury. After the outbreak of war his frequent warnings that the forces were seriously under-provided with personnel trained in key Asian languages went unheeded until Japan attacked, when the school was called upon to train many hundreds of young servicemen (including some Americans) in Chinese and Japanese for intelligence work in eastern theatres of war.

Meanwhile Turner was looking ahead to the post-war period. Largely through his patient, persistent advocacy, the government of Winston Churchill appointed in 1944 the Scarbrough commission, which, on the basis of evidence he submitted and marshalled, recommended a great expansion of the provision in British universities for the study of the languages, history, and cultures of Asia and Africa, and development of the school as the main centre. The government of C. R. Attlee accepted the recommendations; Turner's second decade as director was devoted primarily to implementing them, recruiting and training young scholars, including many whose interest had been aroused during war service in Asia or Africa, and building up strong academic departments. Self-effacing and reserved, he was nevertheless a resolute, wise, and far-sighted leader, universally respected and trusted. By 1957 the school was the pre-eminent institution in Europe in its fields of study. It had been a great directorship.

Thereafter Turner began to write *A Comparative Dictionary of the Indo-Aryan Languages* (1966), followed (1969) by indexes (by Lady Turner) and a phonetic analysis (1971). As an outstanding event in the history of Indian linguistic studies, it placed Turner alongside Sir William Jones and Sir George Grierson. He continued working until a week before his death and left virtually complete a large volume of addenda (published posthumously in 1985).

Turner was knighted in 1950. His many honours included the Nepalese order of Gorkha Dakshina Bahu, honorary doctorates of the universities of London, Benares, Santiniketan, Katmandu, and Ceylon; and honorary fellowships of Christ's College, Cambridge, the School of Oriental and African Studies, and Deccan College, Poona. He rendered great services to the Royal Asiatic Society

(president, 1952–5; gold medallist, 1953) and the Philological Society (treasurer, 1931–62; president, 1939–43). He died at his home, Haverbrack, Barrells Down Road, Bishop's Stortford, Hertfordshire, on 22 April 1983.

J. R. BRACKEN, rev.

Sources archives and annual reports, SOAS · J. C. Wright and C. D. Cowan, *Bulletin of the School of Oriental and African Studies*, 47 (1984), 540–48 · personal knowledge (1993) · private information (1993) [friends, family, and colleagues] · R. H. Robins, 'Ralph Lilley Turner, 1888–1983', *PBA*, 90 (1996), 543–53 · *CGPLA Eng. & Wales* (1983)

Archives BL OIOC, papers, MS Eur. D 1166 · SOAS, academic research notes, First World War diaries, corresp. and plans relating to SOAS building

Likenesses W. Stoneman, photograph, 1945, NPG · W. Stoneman, photograph, 1953, NPG · L. Boden, oils, 1957, BL OIOC, SOAS

Wealth at death £220,599: probate, 1 June 1983, *CGPLA Eng. & Wales*

Turner, Richard (*d.* in or before **1565**), Church of England clergyman, was born in Staffordshire and became a fellow of Magdalen College, Oxford, in 1523. He took his BA the following year and his MA in 1529, and was ordained deacon in 1531. In 1536 he was admitted BTh, but in the same year resigned his fellowship, having been elected to the Edward IV chantry at St George's Chapel, Windsor.

The first evidence for Turner's radical religious views comes from this time in Windsor. By October 1537 Thomas Cromwell had Turner marked as a man suitable for promotion. While in Windsor, Turner met the evangelical musician John Marbeck, who was busy transcribing the entire English Bible. Turner suggested that if Marbeck had a taste for pious and monotonous labour, it would be more useful to compile a concordance; advice which Marbeck duly followed. During this period Turner also allegedly preached against prayer for the dead, purgatory, and pilgrimages, and prepared and used an English translation of the mass.

In the early 1540s Archbishop Cranmer's secretary Ralph Morice picked Turner to be rector of the wealthy Kent benefice of Chartham. Under the benevolent eye of Cranmer's administration, Turner implemented a vigorous reformation. He stopped the use of anointing in baptism, of holy water, of incense, and of holy candles. He met with other radicals in Canterbury, and taught an expurgated version of the Ave Maria to children in Canterbury's most evangelical parish, St Mary Northgate. His sermons at Chartham drew substantial crowds, filling the parish church to overflowing.

Turner's conservative clerical neighbours were alarmed. After he preached against the sacrifice of the mass on 11 March 1543, he was denounced as a heretic. He was a strategically important target for conservatives plotting against Archbishop Cranmer, as he could be used to link the evangelical undergrounds in Windsor and in Kent, and to tie both to Cranmer. After this first arrest, however, Cranmer himself headed the commission to investigate the charges, and predictably, Turner was cleared by the end of April. However, according to his enemies, his return to Chartham was provocatively triumphal, with five hundred people laying on a banquet to greet him. The charge reached the ears of Henry VIII, who was infuriated, and despite his denials Turner was rearrested. Prompted by Morice, however, Cranmer pacified the king and Turner was again released. He was arrested for a third time in July 1543, this time on the privy council's orders and on fresh charges which predated his arrival in Chartham. In September he was indicted under the Act of Six Articles and ordered to recant. Morice again intervened, asking the court evangelicals William Butts and Sir Anthony Denny to intercede with the king; a request which seems to have succeeded.

By April 1545 Turner had relinquished Chartham, but on 1 July 1545 he was instituted vicar of St Stephen's by Saltash, Cornwall. He was again imprisoned in May 1546 during a general purge of evangelicals, and suffered from a quartan fever while in prison. However, he was soon released and in October he was licensed to hold an additional benefice. After Edward VI's accession he returned to Kent, becoming vicar of Dartford in 1547 and one of the six preachers of Canterbury Cathedral about the same time. He twice preached at the rebel encampments in Kent in July 1549, 'for the which', Cranmer wrote, 'the rebels would have hanged him' (*Miscellaneous Writings*, 439); however, he survived, with his political credibility much enhanced. In 1552 Cranmer recommended him for the archbishopric of Armagh, praising his preaching and claiming that 'besides that he is merry and witty withal, *nihil appetit, nihil ardet, nihil somniat, nisi Jesum Christum*' (Strype, *Cranmer*, 2.670). Turner, however, refused the post, despite considerable pressure, on the (perhaps disingenuous) grounds that he spoke no Irish.

When Catholicism was restored under Queen Mary Turner fled abroad. He spent much of his exile at Basel, where he lectured on scripture; he also opposed John Knox's radical view of civil government at Frankfurt. After Elizabeth's accession he was restored to Dartford and was reappointed one of the six preachers. He preached at Paul's Cross on 10 September 1559, Archbishop Parker appointed him as a visitor to reform abuses in Kent in 1560, and he preached one of the Spital sermons on 1 March 1561. The date of his death is unknown, but the vicarage of Dartford was vacant by 1565. No details of his family are known, although his deprivation in 1554 was most likely in consequence of marriage.   ALEC RYRIE

Sources *The acts and monuments of John Foxe*, ed. S. R. Cattley, 8 vols. (1837–41), vol. 5, pp. 482–3; vol. 8, pp. 31–4 · Emden, *Oxf.*, 4.580–81 · CCC Cam., MS 128, pp. 33–4, 62, 72, 75 · D. MacCulloch, *Thomas Cranmer: a life* (1996) · J. Strype, *Memorials of the most reverend father in God Thomas Cranmer*, 2 vols. (1848), vol. 2 · *Miscellaneous writings and letters of Thomas Cranmer*, ed. J. E. Cox, Parker Society, [18] (1846) · APC · LP Henry VIII, 12/2, no. 809 · exchequer, first fruits and tenths office, composition books, PRO, E 334/3, fol. 51v · CSP dom., rev. edn, 1547–53, no. 549 · J. Strype, *Ecclesiastical memorials*, 3/1 (1822), 232 · *Registrum Matthei Parker, diocesis Cantuariensis, AD 1559–1575*, ed. W. H. Frere and E. M. Thompson, 3 vols., CYS, 35–6, 39 (1928–33)

Turner, Richard (*bap.* 1720, *d.* 1791), Church of England clergyman and educational writer, was baptized on 18 April 1720 at Great Witley, Worcestershire, the son of Thomas Turner of Great Witley. He matriculated from Magdalen Hall, Oxford, on 14 July 1748; his age was then

given as twenty-four. He became chaplain to the countess dowager of Wigton, and on 11 June 1754 was instituted vicar of Elmley Castle in Worcestershire. On 19 June of the same year he was appointed rector of Little Comberton. In 1785 he received the honorary degree of LLD from Glasgow University. Turner married Sarah, only sister of James Greene, a barrister, of Burford, Shropshire. She died in 1800. They had two daughters and three sons: Thomas *Turner (*bap.* 1747, *d.* 1809), a potter, Richard *Turner (*bap.* 1753, *d.* 1788), an author, and Edward, a general in the Indian army.

Turner was the author of a number of educational texts. *The Young Gauger's Best Instructor* appeared in 1762, as did *A View of the Earth: a Short but Comprehensive System of Modern Geography*. He wrote an introduction to trigonometry which was published in 1765, with a new edition in 1778. *A View of the Heavens* (1783) was followed by a young person's guide to geometry (1787) and an account of a system of education (1791). Turner died on 12 April 1791 and was buried at Norton-juxta-Kempsey in Worcestershire.

E. I. CARLYLE, *rev.* ROBERT BROWN

Sources Foster, *Alum. Oxon.* · H. Smith, *Pedigree of the Turner family, and its representatives in 1871* (1871) · W. I. Addison, *A roll of graduates of the University of Glasgow from 31st December 1727 to 31st December 1897* (1898) · Watt, *Bibl. Brit.* · J. Shearman and N. Shearman, 'Thomas Turner revisited', *Northern Ceramic Society Journal*, 14 (1997), 71–9 · parish register, Worcester, 18 April 1720 [baptism]
Likenesses Stainier, engraving, 1787 (after portrait by Albert?)

Turner, Richard (*bap.* 1753, *d.* 1788), educational writer and schoolmaster, was baptized on 26 December 1753 at St Helen's, Worcester, the second surviving son of Richard *Turner (*bap.* 1720, *d.* 1791), Church of England clergyman and educational writer, and his wife, Sarah Greene (*d.* 1800). Thomas *Turner (*bap.* 1747, *d.* 1809), a porcelain manufacturer, was his elder brother.

Turner matriculated from Magdalen Hall, Oxford, on 9 February 1773. His six extant published works were written primarily for the education of young people. The first, *An heretical history, collected from original authors, in which is shewn the origin, doctrine, and changes of the several religious systems of the earlier Christian world*, appeared in 1778. This was followed in 1779 by *A view of the earth as it was known to the ancients, being a short but comprehensive system of classical geography*. Subsequent general introductions to the arts and sciences, geography, and history were all either written 'in series of letters to a youth at school' or described as 'adapted to the use of schools and academies'.

During the 1780s Turner was a partner in Loughborough House School, in Brixton, Surrey, probably with his father and certainly with his brother-in-law William Hancock Roberts, husband of his sister Sarah. In 1783 he published *The young orator, containing a collection of lessons in elocution, taken from the best English and French writers, selected for the use of Loughborough House School*.

In 1784 Turner was nominated honorary burgess of Much Wenlock in Shropshire by his brother Thomas, bailiff of the town in that year. By then he was styled 'Reverend Doctor', for he was said to have gained the degree of LLD. On 2 November 1786, at St George's, Hanover Square,

London, he married Ann Farrer, *née* Greening, the widow of Colonel Joseph Liddell Farrer. There were no children of that marriage but four from Ann's previous marriage, of whom at least one, also Joseph Liddell, had been born in India.

Richard Turner died at Margate on 22 August 1788. In his will, written only a few weeks earlier, he left his house in Great George Street, Westminster, and its contents to his widow, and his library of books and all his globes and manuscripts to his stepson Joseph Liddell Farrer. He also made provision for his mother, his sister Eliza Wyke, and his stepchildren.

Turner's most successful works went through many further editions after his death. In 1795 his *Universal History, Ancient and Modern* (1787) was published in an Italian translation. The fourteenth edition of *A New and Easy Introduction to Universal Geography* (1780) appeared in 1810 and was followed by at least one more. *An Easy Introduction to the Arts and Sciences* (1783) reached its nineteenth edition in 1825, and as late as 1832 it reappeared 'altered and improved' by another hand but still described as 'originally compiled by R. Turner'. J. SHEARMAN and N. SHEARMAN

Sources *DNB* • H. Smith, *Pedigree of the Turner family* (1871) • Foster, *Alum. Oxon.* • G. H. Cameron, *John Cameron, non-juror* (1919) • E. Brayley, *History of Surrey* (1841) • parish register, Worcester, St Helen's, 26 Dec 1753 [baptism] • parish register, Worcester, Great Witley, 18 April 1720 [baptism: R. Turner, father] • parish register, St George's, Hanover Square, 2 Nov 1786 [marriage] • parish register, Shropshire, Burford, 7 May 1742 [marriage: R. Turner and S. Greene] • *The Times* (30 Aug 1788) • will, proved, 4 Sept 1788, PRO, PROB 11/1170, sig. 461 • *GM*, 1st ser., 61 (1791) • parish register, 30 Dec 1800 [burial: S. Turner]

Likenesses portrait, repro. in *Connoisseur Magazine* (1919)

Wealth at death see will, signed 1 July 1788; proved 4 Sept 1788

Turner, Richard (1790–1846), temperance activist, was born on 25 July 1790 in Bilsborough, the youngest of five children. He had poor sight following a childhood attack of measles. He became a spinner in a Preston cotton mill, but disliked the restricted life and left at the age of seventeen. On 25 November 1817 in Preston he married Betty Cook of Preston; the couple were unable to sign the register. Betty bore him two daughters. He became a plasterer, but left his wife in 1825 and became a fish hawker—hence his nickname Cockle Dick.

Early in the 1830s an alliance between progressive provincial middle-class reformers and respectable working men was seizing control of the London-based anti-spirits movement from its well-to-do leaders and converting it into a broader-based total abstinence crusade against all alcoholic drinks. Not entirely sober one evening in 1832, Turner entered a Preston temperance meeting for a joke but came out converted. He was among the pioneering 'seven men' of Preston who signed the pledge of total abstinence in that year. He became a Wesleyan Sunday school teacher and an enthusiastic if unsophisticated temperance advocate—the sort of convert to respectability whose transformed life the new movement liked to advertise. His strong dialect and ungrammatical turns of phrase often made him unintentionally amusing, but his dark and ruddy complexion, coarse features, and shabby

clothes gave him a hold over the type of working man the total abstainers sought to reach.

It was on the teetotal platform in September 1833 that Dicky, as temperance reformers affectionately called him, won his modest place in British history. Dismissing the anti-spirits movement's idea of imposing a pledge only to moderation in wine and beer, he announced amid cheers that 'nothing but the tee-total would do' or, according to some accounts, 'I'll be reet down out-and-out t-t-total for ever and ever'. This gave the total abstinence movement the eye-catching label it needed. There was much subsequent controversy about who invented the word and how to spell its derivatives. Irishmen had long used it to denote 'complete' or 'permanent', and Irish labourers brought it to Lancashire; Turner did not invent the term, but merely gave it a new and more specialist application. Like many titles embraced by new reforming movements, it was at first thought rather vulgar.

Turner suffered from asthma for many years, but persisted with his rather eccentric temperance lecturing. In later life he had to be subsidized by the teetotal movement and lived with his eldest sister. In August 1846 he walked from Preston to the World's Temperance Convention in London, preaching teetotalism on the way. On 27 October 1846 he died in Preston when he burst a blood vessel during a fit of coughing, and was buried in St Peter's churchyard, Preston. BRIAN HARRISON, *rev.*

Sources P. T. Winskill, *Temperance standard bearers of the nineteenth century: a biographical and statistical temperance dictionary*, 1 (1897) • B. H. Harrison, *Drink and the Victorians*, 2nd edn (1994)

Turner, Richard (*c*.1798–1881), iron manufacturer and engineer, was the third son of Timothy Turner (*d*. 1822) and his wife, Catherine Sisson. The Turners had long been associated with the ironmongery trade in Dublin. His great-grandfather was 'iron smith' to the Irish House of Commons and Trinity College in the mid-eighteenth century. Turner inherited from his uncle the family ironmongery business which was located at 4 St Stephen's Green.

About 1816 he married Jane, daughter of Thomas Goodshaw of Collams Well, Leixlip. They had four sons and four daughters, as well as three children who died in infancy. Two of his sons, Thomas and William, were later to work with him.

In 1833 Turner erected large premises called the Hammersmith Iron Works, south of Dublin in Ballsbridge. During this time he expanded the ironmongery business to include the manufacture of wrought-iron conservatories like those advocated by John Claudius Loudon, who invented the first wrought-iron glazing bar in 1816 (manufactured and later patented in 1818 by W. and D. Bailey of Holborn in London). Turner's earliest glasshouses closely followed the curvilinear designs illustrated in Loudon's *An Encyclopedia of Gardening* (1822). One of Turner's earliest known wrought-iron conservatories was the range erected in 1836–7 at the vice-regal lodge in Phoenix Park, Dublin. Over the following four decades, his firm specialized in the manufacture of these buildings and erected many examples throughout Britain, including those at Marlfield, co. Tipperary; the wings of the palm house at

Belfast Botanic Gardens (1839–40); the range at Killakee, co. Dublin; the curvilinear range in the Botanic Gardens (now the National Botanic Gardens), Dublin (1843–8 and 1868–9); the winter garden in the Inner Circle, Regent's Park, London (1845–6, 1870–71, and 1875–6, demolished 1932); the range at Haddo House, Aberdeenshire (1844–5); the Victoria Regia House, Royal Botanic Gardens, Kew (1852), and Woodstock, co. Kilkenny.

The palm house at the Royal Botanic Gardens, Kew, 1844–8, was Turner's greatest achievement. Designed in collaboration with Decimus Burton, it was based on Loudon's ideas for the best form and construction of a glasshouse. Its scale surpassed all other iron and glass structures at that time and it is famous as the finest example of a curvilinear wrought-iron and glass conservatory. Turner's significant contribution was the use of wrought iron, and in particular the adoption of a single rolled wrought-iron 'I' section of 'deck beam' as the primary structural member; the palm house was the first building to be erected in England with this type of section. The deck beam had been developed for use in shipbuilding and was patented in 1844 by James Kennedy and Thomas Vernon of Liverpool. In 1846 Turner patented its use in buildings and later incorporated different depths of deck beam in other buildings.

The largest structure designed and erected by Turner was the station roof at Liverpool's Lime Street Station, 1849–50. It was the largest iron roof-span erected at that time, with arches composed of wrought-iron deck-beam spanning 153 feet 6 inches. Turner also utilized deck-beam sections in the roofs of Broadstone Station, Dublin (1847), York Road Station, Belfast (1848), and Galway Station (1851). With his architect son, Thomas, he entered the competition for the building for the Great Exhibition of 1851, receiving an honourable mention along with Hector Horeau.

In the 1830s Turner had been in partnership with William Walker, and in the early 1860s the firm was known as Turner and Gibson. Turner's third son, William, worked with him from the 1840s and in 1863 assumed control of the Hammersmith Iron Works. Turner remained involved in the business until 1880, in particular over the additions to the winter garden at Regent's Park and those to the curvilinear range at the Botanic Gardens, Dublin. In 1872 Hammersmith Iron Works was closed and William Turner continued the business from the Oxmantown foundry on the north side of Dublin, until 1888 when it closed. Turner died in Dublin on 31 October 1881.

EDWARD DIESTELKAMP, rev. MIKE CHRIMES

Sources E. J. Diestelkamp, 'Richard Turner and the palm house at Kew Gardens', *Transactions of the Newcomen Society*, 54 (1982–3), 1–26 · E. J. Diestelkamp, 'The design and building of the palm house, Royal Botanic Gardens, Kew', *Journal of Garden History*, 2/3, 233–72 · E. J. Diestelkamp, 'The curvilinear range at the National Botanic Gardens, Glasnevin', *Journal of the Irish Garden Plant Society*, 9 (Dec 1990) · E. J. Diestelkamp, 'Richard Turner (c. 1798–1881) and his glasshouses', *GLASRA*, 5 (1981), 51–3 · J. Hix, 'Richard Turner: glass master', *ArchR*, 152 (1972), 287–93 · H. Dixon and A. Rowan, 'The architecture of Thomas Turner', *Country Life* (24 May 1973)

Archives PRO, records · RBG Kew · TCD | Inst. CE, membership records, etc.
Likenesses oils, 1865, Glasnevin Gardens, Dublin; repro. in Diestelkamp, 'Richard Turner and the palm house', 3

Turner, Robert (*d.* 1599), Roman Catholic priest, was born at Barnstaple, Devon. His family were of Scottish origin, but the identity of his parents is unknown. He spent time studying at Exeter College, Oxford, and at Christ's College, Cambridge. Although he matriculated at Cambridge in 1567 there is no record of his being awarded a degree at either university. His first association with Edmund Campion, who was at St John's College, Oxford, from 1558 to 1564, may date from this time. He stated that Campion taught him.

Following the example of many Catholics at the time, Turner left England and is recorded as being at the English College, Douai, in 1572, when Campion also first arrived there. He was appointed professor of rhetoric there and was probably ordained to the priesthood in 1574. In 1576 he moved to Rome and spent some years teaching classics at the German College there. Although he was associated with the Society of Jesus, there is no record of his becoming a Jesuit.

After a time in Rome he was appointed prefect of studies at the college of Eichstätt in Bavaria. It seems that he was very active in the Roman Catholic cause and travelled on various missions. On the recommendation of Cardinal William Allen, founder of the English seminary colleges of Douai and Rheims, he was appointed professor of eloquence and ethics at the University of Ingolstadt and received the degree of DTh in 1586. He later became rector of the university. He was a member of the privy council of William Wittelsbach, duke of Bavaria, but fell out of favour and moved to Paris. He returned to Germany about two years later and was made a canon of the diocese of Breslau in Silesia. Later he was appointed Latin secretary to Ferdinand Habsburg, archduke of Austria, by whom he was held in some esteem. He died at Graz in Styria on 28 November 1599.

Turner wrote and dedicated numerous Latin volumes, some of which were connected with Campion. He seems to have been a devoted follower of Campion who was concerned with the promulgation of the latter's work in order to preserve his memory during the Counter-Reformation. He may have initially been attracted to Campion's ideas because both men were interested in rhetoric. Turner's works include *Sermo panegyricus de divi Gregorii Nazianzeni corpore … translato* and *Epistolae aliquot* (dedicated to Allen), which were both published in Ingolstadt in 1584. Several posthumously published collections culminated in the printing of *Roberti Turneri Devonii oratoris et philosophi Ingoldstadiensis panegyrici duo* in Ingolstadt in 1609 and the more complete edition published in Cologne in 1615.

PETER E. B. HARRIS

Sources *DNB* · G. Anstruther, *The seminary priests*, 1 (1969) · A. F. Allison and D. M. Rogers, eds., *The contemporary printed literature of the English Counter-Reformation between 1558 and 1640*, 2 vols. (1989–94) · A. Sternhuber, *Geschichte des Kollegium Germanikum Hungarikum in Rom*, 2 vols. (Freiburg-im-Breisgau, 1906) · Wood, *Ath. Oxon.*, new edn · J. Strype, *Annals of the Reformation and establishment of religion … during Queen Elizabeth's happy reign*, 3rd edn, 4 vols. (1731–5)

Turner, Robert (*b.* 1619/20, *d.* in or after 1664), writer and translator of occult and medical works, was born at Holshot, near Saffron Walden, Essex, the third son of Edmund Turner and his wife, Elizabeth, daughter of Henry Marsh, of Barnard's Inn. He was admitted pensioner to Christ's College, Cambridge, on 17 June 1636, and received his BA in 1639; he was admitted to the Middle Temple on 9 October 1637 and to Lincoln's Inn on 2 November 1639.

Turner was the author of two books, *Mikrokosmos: a Description of the Little-World* (1654) and *Botanologia: the Brittish Physician* (1664), but is chiefly known for at least ten translations of medical and astrological works published between 1655 and 1658. He usually identifies himself as Philomathus in his title pages and prefaces, and his books generally include dedications to friends, doctors, and local dignitaries as well as commendatory poems. *Mikrokosmos*, his earliest authored work, applies astrological principles to the art of healing. In 1655 he published a translation of works by Johannes Regiomontanus and Johannes Angelus, entitled *Esoptron Astrologikon: astrologicall opticks: wherein are represented the faces of every signe, with the images of each degree in the zodiack*, which contains a commendatory note by William Lilly the astrologer. His supposed translation of Henry Cornelius Agrippa's *Fourth Book of Occult Philosophy* (also 1655), is prefaced by a short defence of magic (dated August 1654) and six commendatory poems, five by writers affiliated to Cambridge University. Of the two translations published in 1655 and 1656, *Paracelsus, Of the Supreme Mysteries of Nature* clearly points the iatrochemical direction that Turner was to follow, and *The compleat bone-setter … whereunto is added the perfect oculist, and the mirrour of health … written originally by Friar Moulton* prescribes treatments for a broad range of illnesses and injuries. From his prefaces and dedications it is clear that he lived in London from about 1655 until at least 1664.

In 1657, his most productive year, Turner published no fewer than five translations. *Paracelsus of the chymical transmutation … whereunto is added, the philosophical and chymical experiments of R. Lully* is dedicated to William Bakehouse or Backhouse of Swallowfield, friend and alchemical master of Elias Ashmole, and the address 'To the reader' announces Turner's intention to 'revive the everlasting fame of Paracelsus … that the English Tyroes may hereafter reap the benefit of his admired and experienced labours'. *Sal, lumen, & spiritus mundi philosophici, or, The Dawning of the Day*, a treatise on mystical alchemy, is Turner's English version of a Latin translation of a French original by Clovis Hesteau, Sieur de Nuysement. The dedication is signed 'Robert Turner of Holshot' and, as is typical of his prefaces, he severely disparages those ignorant of the hermetic art. Also in 1657, he translated out of Alexander Massaria a work on female illnesses entitled *De morbis foemineis, the Womans Counsellour*; from Latin, the *Ars notoria: the Notory Art of Solomon … whereunto is Added an Astrological Catechism*; and, finally, the *Enchiridion medicum*,

from the Latin original of his contemporary, John Sadler, 'Dr. in Physick' and probable author of *The Sicke Womans Private Looking-Glasse* (1636).

The compiler of *Astrological Institutions, being a Perfect Isagoge to the Whole Astral Science* (1658) identifies himself only as 'a student in physick and astrologie', but there is sufficient evidence to attribute the work to Turner. According to its preface, the work seeks to initiate the reader into 'the perfect and exact Rudiments of Astrologie', a task for which there are few suitable English books in print, though many in Latin. In the political controversy surrounding the theory and practice of medicine in the mid-seventeenth century, Turner clearly positions himself as an outspoken defender of Paracelsus, astrology, magic, and 'curing diseases by sigils and characters, made and applyed in fit elected times and seasons'; opposing him were the 'common Collegians, who ground the greatest reason of their Recipes from a Galen's or a Pliny's Probatum' (*Paracelsus, Of the Supreme Mysteries of Nature*, 1655, dedication and preface). Along with John Hester, John Harding, John French, Richard Russell, William Cooper, William Dugard, and Henry Pinnell, he was one of an important group of translators who supplied English audiences with a wide range of occult and medical treatises and particularly with the writings of Paracelsus.

Turner's final and most important work is *Botanologia: the Brittish Physician, or, The Nature and Vertues of English Plants*, originally published in 1664, with another edition of 1687 which includes a frontispiece portrait of Turner above a gardening setting. This book is a guide to the 'compleat body of Medicinal Vegitables … whether naturally growing in England, or common to be had at our Druggists and Apothecaries Shops'. Scientific nomenclature and information on the habitats, appearances, and uses of medicinal plants are included to enable readers to become their own physicians, and in keeping with his abiding interests, Turner also sets forth the astral influences and divine signatures assigned to various species. Because of this combining of astrology with botany and medicine, Turner was occasionally disparaged for his credulity and superstition during the Enlightenment; none the less, through his herbal, he continued to be known to historians of science into the early nineteenth century.

While his earlier prefaces and dedications might suggest that Turner's political position was republican and nonconformist, in the post-Restoration *Botanologia* his sympathies were plainly royalist. Allegorizing two of the species of flowers included in his book, he notes:

> In the *Heliotrope* and *Marigold*, subjects may learn their duty to their Sovereign; which his Sacred Majesty King *Charles* the First mentions in his Princely Meditations, walking in a Garden in the *Isle of Wight*, in the following words, viz.
>
> *The Marigold observes the Sun*
> *More then my Subjects me have done.*

The date of Turner's death is unknown, and it is also not clear if the 1687 edition of *Botanologia* was posthumous. In any event he published no new works after 1664.

STANTON J. LINDEN

Sources Venn, *Alum. Cant.* · J. Peile, *Biographical register of Christ's College, 1505–1905, and of the earlier foundation, God's House, 1448–1505*, ed. [J. A. Venn], 1 (1910) · R. Pulteney, *Historical and biographical sketches of the progress of botany in England*, 2 vols. (1790)
Archives Wellcome L., medical papers
Likenesses engraving, repro. in R. Turner, *Botanologia: the Brittish physician* (1687) · line engraving, BM, NPG; repro. in R. Turner, *Botanologia: the Brittish physician* (1664) · line engraving (aged thirty-nine), NPG; repro. in T. Moulton, *The compleat bone-setter*, rev. edn, rev. R. Turner (1656)

Turner, Samuel (*d.* 1647?), physician and politician, was the son of Peter *Turner (1542–1614), physician and politician, and his wife, Pascha, daughter of Henry Parry, chancellor of Salisbury Cathedral, and the brother of Peter *Turner (1586–1652), mathematician. He is known to have fathered a son, also Samuel, outside marriage, for whom he provided until his majority. Turner graduated BA from St Mary Hall, Oxford, on 11 February 1602 and was licensed to proceed MA from St Alban Hall on 22 October 1604. In 1633 he claimed a family interest in Pembroke College, Cambridge, where his grandmother had made provision for a fellowship. His medical degree was gained from the University of Padua in 1611. Little seems to be known about his medical career in England. He was described by Sir Philip Warwick as an 'inconsiderate as well as inconsiderable courtier-dependant' and by Sir Henry Wotton as 'a travelled doctor of physic, of bold spirit and able elocution' (Johnson, 1.39n.). The undated paper in the duke of Manchester's collection entitled 'Dr. Turnor's directions for my "Lady at Bath"', wherein 'The mode of bathing' is described and some prescriptions are appended, is no doubt attributable to Samuel (*Eighth Report*, HMC, 2.29a). His reputation was such in 1619 that he was called to attend Queen Anne at the time of her death. He may have accompanied the earl of Arundel to Vienna in 1636, and apparently throughout the 1630s had a connection with the earls of Pembroke. No reference to income from a private practice was referred to when he later compounded for royalism. He declared his estate then as a house in Whitehall and an income of £250 from professional services at court.

Like his father Turner was to sit in parliament. He was returned for Shaftesbury, Dorset, in 1626, and made a reputation for himself in the proceedings against George Villiers, duke of Buckingham. In an effort to bring focus to an ongoing debate, on 11 March he raised six general questions regarding Buckingham's activities. The questions were seized upon as critical of the king's favourite and were instantly copied and circulated as 'Doctor Turner's Queries'. The previous day Clement Coke, speaking of the state of the kingdom, had declared that 'it is better to suffer by a foreign hand than at home' (Bidwell and Jansson, 2.250). On hearing reports of the two speeches the king was irate. Turner's 'Queries' raised the question of accusations by 'rumour' and 'common fame'; Coke's remarks touched on treason. On 14 March the king requested that the Commons censure the two members. In notifying the house on that day that he could 'no ways suffer that the meanest of his servants should be questioned without his leave, much less one so near him' (ibid., 2.285) the king

addressed the issue of royal authority that would cause him to dissolve the parliament. Heated debate on the matter lasted a week. Turner said he had spoken 'out of loyalty and sincerity for the good of his country'. He would not, he said, have called one of the king's servants in question if he had thought it should offend (ibid., 2.299). In the midst of the crisis he was taken ill and could not attend the house. On 18 March he explained in a letter to the speaker that he had raised the six questions in an effort to direct the debate 'to the finding out of the first griever, or the first cause'; he said he thought 'it was then full time to agree the agent and the actions' and to end the discussion of grievances in the abstraction (ibid., 2.317). The case resulted in a remonstrance to the king defending Coke and Turner and supporting the Commons' right to continue in their proceedings against Buckingham. Turner recovered from his illness, returned to the Commons, and is recorded as speaking on 6 June, nine days before the dissolution.

In spring 1640 Turner was returned for Shaftesbury in a by-election to the Short Parliament, to sit in the place of Edward Hyde who, doubly returned, chose to represent Wootton Bassett, Wiltshire. Turner apparently never went to London; the indenture is dated 4 May, one day before the parliament's dissolution. He was returned again for Shaftesbury in the Long Parliament, perhaps owing his seat to the Herberts. He spoke rarely in the first session but voted against the attainder of Thomas Wentworth, earl of Strafford—as did John Selden, a friend of Turner and later one of his executors, and George Parry, a first cousin. He had not lent money to support the king's journey to the north in 1639, nor did he contribute to any of the levies organized through parliament in 1640 and 1641 to aid the northern armies. He rarely attended the house after 1642. On 24 January 1644 he was disabled from sitting in the Long Parliament and took a seat for Shaftesbury in the king's parliament in Oxford, which he kept until its dispersal. The day of his death is not known but he probably died in 1647 in London; his will was probated on 1 December 1647. MAIJA JANSSON

Sources Foster, *Alum. Oxon.* · CSP dom., 1619–23, 66; 1623–34, 223 · G. W. Johnson, ed., *The Fairfax correspondence: memoirs of the reign of Charles the First*, 1 (1848), 39n. · Keeler, *Long Parliament*, 367–8 · *Eighth report*, 2, HMC, 2 (1910), 29a · W. B. Bidwell and M. Jansson, eds., *Proceedings in parliament, 1626*, 2: *House of Commons* (1992), 250, 282, 299, 317 · 4 May 1640, HLRO, main papers collection · Cobbett, *Parl. hist.*, 2.756–7 · PRO, PROB 11/202, fols. 330–31

Turner, Samuel (1759–1802), army officer in the East India Company and diplomatist, was born on 19 April 1759 and baptized on 17 May at St John's Church, Gloucester. His father, John Turner, was a prosperous local grocer and his mother was Ann Warren; the couple also had at least two daughters. Ann's sister, Hester, married Penyston Hastings and was the mother of the Bengal governor-general, Warren Hastings, Turner's cousin and later patron. He was given an East India cadetship in 1780, appointed ensign in the same year, lieutenant on 8 August 1781, captain on 8 June 1796, and regimental captain on 18 March 1799. His military career was spent entirely in India except for the period 1783–4 when he led Hastings's second mission to Tibet and fourth to Bhutan. Turner's *Account of an Embassy to the Court of the Teshoo Lama in Tibet* (1800) was the first eyewitness report on Tibet and Bhutan to be published in English. The book remained the only account of those countries available to English readers until the publication in 1876 of the journals of George Bogle and Thomas Manning. Through the editions that quickly followed in French (1800), German (1801), and Italian (1817), the book had a considerable impact on the European imagination.

The purpose of the 1783–4 mission, like that led by Bogle in 1774–5, was to further Hastings's ambitions of promoting British-Indian trade across the Himalayas, and to satisfy his scientific and scholarly interests through Asian exploration. Although Tibet's capital at Lhasa remained firmly closed to European travellers because of Chinese opposition, the quasi-autonomous principality of the Panchen Lama, centred on Shigatse, responded more willingly to foreign overtures. The death in Peking (Beijing) of the third Panchen Lama, Lobsang Palden Yeshé (1738–1780), who had served as Bogle's most hospitable host, gave Hastings the opportunity to send a complimentary mission to the child who was recognized as the lama's incarnation, Lobsang Tenpé Nyima (1782–1853). Turner's lyrical description of his audience on 4 December 1783 with this child later created much interest. It was the source for George Moore's humorous poem 'The Little Grand Lama' (1823). From the lama's own biography in Tibetan it is clear that Turner's sensitivity, tolerance, and good manners were warmly welcomed at the lama's court. While the political and commercial results of the mission were negligible, and it was not until very late in the nineteenth century that direct relations with Tibet were re-established, Turner's sober account of carefully observed conditions in Tibet and Bhutan, their forms of government, religious customs, trade, and topography, has stood the test of time and remained a source of great value. Tibetan relations with China in this period are well described, so also is an attempted insurrection against the Bhutanese ruler, Jigme Senge (r. 1776–88). Turner's testimony is supplemented by those of his subordinates on this mission, the botanist and surgeon Robert Saunders and the surveyor and amateur artist Samuel Davis. That he was himself a competent artist is clear from the reworkings by others of two of his views of Tashilhunpo, main seat of the Panchen Lama. The other pictorial legacy of the mission consists of two paintings by George Stubbs of a Bhutanese yak which Turner succeeded in sending alive by ship to his patron Warren Hastings in England.

Turner was among the officers with Lord Cornwallis, the governor-general, on 6 February 1792 at the siege of Seringapatam in command of a troop of the governor-general's bodyguard of cavalry. He later acted as envoy to Tipu Sultan, with whom he concluded successful negotiations. While serving in the East India Company's 3rd European regiment, he went home on leave to England in 1798 and purchased an estate in Gloucestershire. Cornwallis recommended him for a pension in 1800. After publishing in that year the account of his 1783 mission, on 7 July

he was made an honorary doctor of law at Oxford University, and on 15 January 1801 was elected a fellow of the Royal Society. However, he was not to enjoy for long the benefits of honour and retirement. On 21 December 1801 he was taken seriously ill while walking at night in the neighbourhood of Fetter Lane and brought to the workhouse in Shoe Lane. His name and address in St James's Place were found on his person but he was too ill to be moved, and he died at the workhouse on 2 January 1802. He was buried at St James's Church, Piccadilly, where the Latin inscription on his memorial tablet records how he 'after great labour in far away regions beyond the sea and having safely undertaken journeys in the remotest lands, here at last rested in death'. His property in Gloucestershire went to his sisters, one of whom, Mary (d. 1811), married Joseph White, regius professor of Hebrew at Oxford. The Bodleian Library preserves his papers and correspondence in Tibetan and Bengali relating to the mission to Bhutan and Tibet.   MICHAEL ARIS

Sources S. Turner, *An account of an embassy to the court of the Teshoo Lama in Tibet* (1800) · H. Richardson, introduction, in S. Turner, *An account of an embassy to the court of the Teshoo Lama in Tibet* (1971), i–ii · L. Petech, 'The missions of Bogle and Turner according to the Tibetan texts', *T'oung Pao*, 34 (1950), 330–46 · M. Aris, 'Introduction', in *Views of medieval Bhutan: the diary and drawings of Samuel Davis, 1783*, ed. M. Aris (1982), 10–39 · P. Bishop, 'Tibet discovered, 1773–92', *The myth of Shangri-la: Tibet, travel writing, and the Western creation of sacred landscape* (1989), 25–64 · A. Disom, *A narrative of the campaign in India which terminated the war with Tippoo Sultan in 1792* (1793) · *DNB* · memorial tablet, St James's Church, Piccadilly, London

Archives Bodl. Oxf., MS Asiat. misc. a.4 · Bodl. Oxf., corresp., MS Tibet a.7–8 · Bodl. Oxf., MSS | BL, letters to W. Hastings and others, Add. MSS 29162, 29168–29176, 39892, fol. 14, 39871, fol. 51, 29204, fols. 339, 344

Turner [*alias* Richardson], **Samuel** (1765–1810?), informer, born in co. Armagh, was the son of Jacob Turner (d. 1803) of Turner's Glen, near Newry, a man of property. He was educated at Trinity College, Dublin, where he entered on 2 July 1780, and graduated BA in 1784, and LLD in 1787. Turner was called to the Irish bar in 1788, but does not seem to have practised, and became involved in the United Irish movement in Ulster.

Among the more militant wing of United Irish activists who advocated a rising in Ulster early in 1797, Turner was forced to flee the north when a warrant was issued for his arrest. After a brief time in Manchester, where he assisted Father James Coigley in organizing the underground republican movement, he escaped to Hamburg and participated in the growing network of United Irish agents negotiating for a French invasion. He was included in the act of attainder in 1798 as one concerned in the rising of that year; but in 1803, on the death of his father, he returned to Ireland, and the attainder was reversed on proof of Turner's absence from Ireland for more than a year before the outbreak of the insurrection. He lived in Dublin until his death, preserving to the end the reputation of a patriot among the Irish nationalists, and enjoying the friendship of Daniel O'Connell.

W. J. Fitzpatrick, however, conclusively established the treachery of Turner to the cause he espoused. By October

1797 Turner had approached Lord Downshire and offered to serve the government in securing information on the United Irishmen. His alienation was caused by his perception that the Catholics, intent on establishing their own religious supremacy, were betraying the secular republicanism of the movement. His correspondence to Downshire (usually under the alias of Richardson) provided extensive and accurate information on the leadership of the United Irish movement in Ireland and their activities on the continent. Turner refused, however, to offer his evidence in open court against his colleagues. For his services as an informer Turner was awarded by the government a secret pension of £300 a year, which was subsequently increased to £500. According to Fitzpatrick, Turner was killed in the Isle of Man in a duel with a man named Boyce (Fitzpatrick, 104). The exact date of his death is unknown but is believed to have been 1810.

C. L. FALKINER, *rev.* NANCY J. CURTIN

Sources R. R. Madden, *The United Irishmen: their lives and times*, 3rd ser., 7 vols. (1842–6) · W. J. Fitzpatrick, *Secret service under Pitt* (1892) · M. Elliott, *Partners in revolution: the United Irishmen and France* (1982) · Burtchaell & Sadleir, *Alum. Dubl.*
Archives PRO, HO. 100 | PRO NIre., Downshire MSS

Turner, Sharon (1768–1847), historian, was born in Pentonville on 24 September 1768, the eldest son of William and Ann Turner. His parents were of Yorkshire origins but had emigrated to London on their marriage. Turner, who lived in the London area throughout his long life, was educated at the academy of Dr James Davis, rector of St James's, Clerkenwell, where he acquired a sound foundation in the classics. He left school at the age of fifteen to be articled to an attorney in the Temple. Six years later the attorney died, but in spite of his youth, Turner was able to carry on the practice, as he enjoyed the confidence of many of the leading clients, including an element active in the publishing world. He married Mary Watts (*bap.* 1768, *d.* 1843) on 18 January 1795, with whom he had at least six children, and set up office in Red Lion Square, conveniently close to the British Museum, where he became an energetic member of a group of gentleman scholars involved in the study of letters and antiquity. Turner himself had been early attracted to old Norse literature, initially through Thomas Percy's translations, notably of the 'Dying Ode of Regner Lodbrog', referred to later and more accurately as 'The Death-Song of Ragnar Lothbrok', published in *Five Pieces of Runic Poetry Translated from the Islandic Language* (1763). He was surprised at the way historians, including even Joseph Hume, had neglected the valuable social and philological wealth hidden in these sources. In 1799 he published the first volume of his *History of the Anglo-Saxons* (4 vols., 1799–1805), a work which was to have a powerful influence on historical thought for the succeeding half-century. It brought him an immediate and substantial scholarly reputation. In February 1800, at a meeting of the Society of Antiquaries of London, a testimonial was presented, recommending him as a 'gentleman eminently versed in the History of Antiquities of this country, and author of the History of

Sharon Turner (1768–1847), by Sir Martin Archer Shee, *c.*1817

the Anglo-Saxons'. He was duly elected a fellow of the society on 13 March 1800, at the age of thirty-one.

The timing of Turner's work was propitious. The notion of Anglo-Saxon liberty as opposed to Norman tyranny had been strong since the seventeenth century, and had been both exaggerated and clouded by the French Revolution. With the emergence of the consulate and subsequently the Napoleonic empire the issue was simplified again: the English freeman was still capable of fighting against the Norman yoke. Patriotic Englishmen of a conservative nature could read their heritage as happily uniting the principles of order and liberty. Edmund Burke had looked behind Magna Carta to the coronation charter of Henry I, and had hinted at yet more ancient liberties (*Reflections on the Revolution in France*, ed. A. J. Grieve, 1910; repr. 1967, 29–30). Turner gave copious illustrations of those liberties in the shape of a good constitution, temperate kingship, the witenagemot, and general principles of freedom. Veneration of King Alfred was taken to extremes, though not always without criticism of Alfred's actions in detail. The main thrust of Turner's picture of the Anglo-Saxon heritage was summed up, firmly if awkwardly, in the preface to his sixth edition of the *History of the Anglo-Saxons* (1836) when he wrote:

> The Anglo-Saxons were deficient in the surprising improvements which their present descendants have attained; but unless they had acquired and exercised the valuable qualities, both moral and intellectual, which they had progressively advanced to before their dynasty ceased, England would not have become that distinguished nation which, after the Norman graft on the original Saxon stock, it has since gradually led to be.

The merit and enduring quality of Turner's work did not

rest on his style: he was no Gibbon. His outstanding attributes were a formidable intellectual curiosity and a practical desire to bring to general notice historical evidence that had long been neglected or ignored. With only mild exaggeration he reflected in 1820 that when his first volume had been published in 1799 Anglo-Saxon antiquities had been nearly forgotten by the British public, that many major manuscripts were unexamined, and that neither their content nor important facts were part of general British history. He laboured at the British Museum to open up these treasures, acquiring a good knowledge of Anglo-Saxon in the process, and working hard on the Cottonian collection of manuscripts. Many critics recognized his achievement: Robert Southey praised his Anglo-Saxon works, stating that 'so much information was probably never laid before the public in one historical publication' (*Life and Correspondence*, 1849–50, chap. 11). The *Edinburgh Review* (1804, 360ff.) was not so kind. It praised his diligence but noted a lack of discrimination, a predilection for romance, and an inflated diction. In response to critics who objected to his handling of Celtic material, Turner sprang to his own defence, publishing in 1803 *A vindication of the genuineness of the antient British poems of Aneurin, Taliesin, Llywarch Hen and Merdhin with specimens of their poems*. He ranged widely over many new scientific and anthropological fields, studying geology, the time-scale of human development, and migration, fields which promoted many contemporaries to reject orthodox religious belief. Turner, however, remained solidly loyal to the Anglican church throughout his career.

Turner's Anglo-Saxon books established his reputation and confirmed his standing within the literary and antiquarian circles of London. His advocate's practice flourished as he developed into a recognized authority on one of the contentious issues of the day, the law of copyright and, closely associated with it, the obligation on the part of publishers to deposit copies of new works in stated learned libraries, of which no fewer than eleven existed in the United Kingdom by 1801, including five in Scotland and two in Ireland. Turner's standing was such that he was empowered to state the publishing trade's proposed solution to the problems before a select committee of the House of Commons in 1813. He continued in practice until after his sixtieth birthday, into 1829. There are some references to anxiety over health, a nervous asthma in 1815–18, and some debility later. Considering the way in which he drove himself in his literary work, this is not surprising. His circle of friends in London remained constant, most prominent among them being Isaac D'Israeli and the publisher John Murray (1778–1843). It was Turner who advised D'Israeli to have his children baptized on the grounds that, even if perfunctory, this would give them a better chance in life. Turner acted as sponsor for Benjamin Disraeli in August 1817, and remained in touch, acting as intermediary with John Murray in 1829 when Benjamin was involved in a publishing dispute.

In the post-Napoleonic war years Turner's writing energies never flagged. He kept his Anglo-Saxon volumes up to date. In 1820 he mentioned, among other additions to his text, the use of *Beowulf* (virtually unknown when he started to write) and a detailed analysis of the English population at the time of Domesday Book. He further extended his history of England, producing volumes (1813–24) on English history from the Norman conquest to the end of the middle ages. In 1826 he published a rather poor history of the reign of Henry VIII, partly to oppose what he considered the papalist views of John Lingard; and in 1829 continued the story down to 1603. He was elected a member of the Athenaeum in 1831, and in 1835 was awarded a civil-list pension of £300 a year. His publishers co-operated resolutely, keeping his historical work in print through many editions, and issuing it in a uniform complete set of twelve volumes in 1837. A seventh edition of the Anglo-Saxon volumes, edited by Turner's son Sydney, appeared in 1852. His later work did not have the quality of his pioneering efforts on the Anglo-Saxons: critics complained of its wearisome length. Academic opinion was summed up by W. Smyth, regius professor at Cambridge, who condescendingly dismissed Turner as 'an amiable man rather than one of a very superior understanding' (*Lectures on Modern History*, 1840, 1.118). Nevertheless he continued to be read. It was not until Benjamin Thorpe's translation of Johann Lappenberg's work in 1845 and the appearance of John Kemble's volumes on *The Saxons in England* in 1849 that serious rivals to Turner's work on the Anglo-Saxons appeared, and his judgments on the Normans also continued to be enormously influential. Sir Walter Scott paid full tribute to the debt he owed to Sharon Turner in his dedicatory epistle to *Ivanhoe* in 1819, a tribute echoed strongly by readers in the following generation.

It is as a historian of the Anglo-Saxons that Turner deserves to be remembered. He was also a true son of the Enlightenment, who took other disciplines—theology, philosophy, and poetry—in his stride. He wrote a note in 1802 on the use of rhyme, a short poetic tract on *Prolusions on the Present Greatness of Britain* in 1819, and was even interested in Maori poetry, which he saw in 1827 as reflecting the same 'spirit of active mind, high spirit, fearless boldness, unfeeling cruelty, and barbarous ignorance which distinguishes our ancestors' (*History of the Anglo-Saxons*, 1840, 3.154, n.1). His avowed masterpiece, over which he brooded for fifty-three years (1792–1845), was a very long epic poem on Richard III. Anticipating later scholarly thought, he argued that Richard could not have been the monster described by the Lancastrian victors. Turner's poetic sense was not up to his historian's judgement, and the poem limps on for some 300 tedious pages. He sent a copy of it to John Lingard, who commented somewhat unkindly in a letter to John Coulson on 10 June 1845:

> You probably know little of Sharon Turner, an old opponent, I mean literary opponent of mine. To my surprise he has written me a congratulary letter, though he never wrote to me before, though often against me, and has sent me a poem which he has just published. Unfortunately that detracts from the compliment, for he is 77, and a man who publishes a poem in his 77th year must be on the high road to a second childhood. (P. Phillips, *Recusant History*, 23/2, 1996, 187)

His theological opinions, ultimately orthodox, found

expression in his *Sacred History of the World … Considered in a Series of Letters to a Son* (3 vols., 1832; 8th edn, 1848). Solidly protestant, he contrasted monkish and papal Christianity with its purest apostolic form.

After 1815 Turner's patriotism and conservatism grew more pronounced. Pondering on Thorkelin's transcript of *Beowulf*, he was worried that the English should have left 'this common relict of our ancestors' to be printed by a Dane. A firm belief in progress informs his thought. Patriotism shines through his account of the British, who from a barbarous ancestry had created in the course of twelve centuries a nation 'inferior to none in every moral and intellectual merit, [and] superior to every other in the love and possession of useful liberty'. The nation was said to cultivate with equal success 'the elegancies of art, the ingenious labours of industry, the researches of science and the richest productions of genius' (S. Turner, *History of the Anglo-Saxons*, 1840, 3.1). It is no wonder his books sold well. He gave his English readers a good conceit of themselves.

Turner's domestic life appears to have been happy and stable. His wife, described as beautiful, accomplished, and agreeable, died in 1843 and Turner himself moved into his son's house at Red Lion Square, where he died on 13 February 1847. His youngest son, Sydney *Turner (1814–1879), became inspector of reformatory schools (1855–73) and was nominated dean of Ripon (1875–6), but retired to the rectory of Hempsted in Gloucestershire. A daughter, Mary (*d.* 1870), was married to William *Ellis (1800–1881).

H. R. LOYN

Sources BL cat. · *GM*, 2nd ser., 27 (1847), 434–6 · *Annual Register* (1847), 208–10 · *EdinR*, 3 (1803–4), 360–74 · *EdinR*, 4 (1804), 198–206 · *The life and correspondence of Robert Southey*, ed. C. C. Southey, 6 vols. (1849–50) · W. H. Prescott, *Biographical and critical essays* (1855) · Allibone, *Dict.* · S. Smiles, *A publisher and his friends: memoir and correspondence of the late John Murray*, condensed edn, ed. T. Mackay (1911) · J. Ogdon, *Isaac D'Israeli* (1969) · J. V. Lee, 'Political antiquarianism unmasked: the conservative attack on the myth of the ancient constitution', *BIHR*, 55 (1982), 166–79 · J. Feather, 'Publishers and politicians: the remaking of the law of copyright in Britain, 1775–1842, part I: legal deposit and the battle of the library tax', *Publishing History*, 24 (1998), 49–76 · J. W. Burrow, *A liberal descent: Victorian historians and the English past* (1981) · P. Phillips, 'John Lingard and *The Anglo-Saxon church*', *Recusant History*, 23 (1996–7), 178–89 · *DNB* · *IGI*

Archives BL, diary extracts, 1838, Add. MS 51055 | BL, corresp. with Sir Robert Peel, Add. MSS 40419–40595 · Bodl. Oxf., Disraeli MSS, corresp. with Isaac D'Israeli · NL Wales, letters to Johnes family

Likenesses M. A. Shee, oils, *c.*1817, NPG [*see illus.*]

Turner, Sydney (1814–1879), Church of England clergyman and school inspector, was born on 2 April 1814, the youngest son of Sharon *Turner (1768–1847), historian of Anglo-Saxon and medieval England, and his wife Mary Watts (*bap.* 1768, *d.* 1843). Sydney Turner edited and prepared the index to his father's *Sacred History of the World* (3 vols., 1848). He matriculated at Trinity College, Cambridge, in 1832, took his BA degree as eighteenth wrangler in 1836, and proceeded to MA in 1839. He was ordained by the bishop of Winchester in 1838 and held for some years the curacy of Christ Church, Southwark. He married Mary Ann Rippon on 6 June 1839.

For most of his adult life, Turner was involved in the movement to create reformatory schools in which juvenile offenders could be re-educated into respectability. In 1841 he became the resident chaplain to the institution of the Philanthropic Society for the Reformation of Juvenile Offenders, which placed him at the head of a large reformatory school for convicted boys. He used this position to campaign for the introduction of government-sanctioned institutions to reform and rescue wayward children. Matthew Davenport Hill, the recorder of Birmingham, described Turner as 'a gifted philanthropist' (*Reformatory and Refuge Journal*, 90, August 1879, 70). Turner was the author of many articles and pamphlets on the reformatory movement, including *Mettray*, written in 1846 with the police magistrate Thomas Paynter.

In 1857 Turner was appointed the first government inspector of reformatory and industrial schools. Until 1862 he had no help with visiting the rapidly growing number of institutions, all of which needed at least annual inspection. In that year, on Turner's recommendation, Henry Rogers, a former colleague at the Philanthropic Society's reformatory, was appointed assistant inspector.

Inspector Turner's annual reports could be fairly critical of individual schools, though he tended to communicate his most serious points to school managers privately. His generalizations about the reformatory system were invariably positive. An article in *The Month* noted his 'tendency to look at the brighter side of affairs, to notice defects as lightly as possible' (W. G. Todd, 'English reformatories and industrial schools', *The Month*, 2, 1870). Turner firmly believed that reformatory schools could be effective only if they were arranged in small units with a family atmosphere, dealing with children who were neither too hardened in criminality nor too old. He was also suspicious of large emigration societies which treated children as a mass instead of individuals, though he was not against child emigration in principle.

The majority of Turner's fellow workers in the reformatory movement shared his beliefs that reformatory inmates needed education in industrial rather than 'literary' skills. However, Turner and his colleagues were not always of one mind. Most notably, his belief that children convicted of a crime should be imprisoned before being placed in a reformatory greatly irritated Mary Carpenter, who sought to end the imprisonment of children. In general, Turner's relationship with Carpenter was uneasy. In 1860 she had threatened to resign the certificate of Red Lodge reformatory because he had taken the side of her staff against her and, as she put it in her diary, 'spoken to me in an overbearing way which I am sure he would not have done to a gentleman'. Turner eventually apologized.

As an Anglican clergyman, Turner was in a difficult position with regard to Roman Catholic schools. The troubles which dogged the Roman Catholic Mount St Bernard reformatory were, Turner believed, due entirely to the weakness of the religious brothers in charge. Turner had more respect for religious sisters, though he was insistent that no foreign nuns should be placed in charge of schools. Attitudes towards Turner in the Roman Catholic community were mixed. Occasionally the Catholic press carried letters and articles of great hostility, accusing him of bigotry and bias against the Catholic schools. However, at least one Catholic correspondent, William Harper of Bury, thought him 'gentlemanly, kind, tolerant, and for-bearing … and anything but a bigot' (Sheffield Archives, MD 7138/12/168).

Suffering from poor health, Turner retired as reforma-tory inspector in 1876 and was succeeded by William Inglis. Disraeli rewarded his public service by promoting him to the deanery of Ripon; he was installed as dean on 26 January 1876, but never went into residence. His worsening health compelled him to resign the position in March 1876 and retire to the rectory at Hempsted in the diocese of Gloucester and Bristol, where he was often con-fined to bed by his 'internal troubles'.

Turner died at Hempsted rectory on 26 June 1879. The first part of his funeral service was conducted on 2 July at Hempsted before a large number of local magistrates, leading clergymen, and notables. His body was then trans-ported to Redhill, where the service continued before a gathering of reformatory school staff and managers, led by Turner's three sons and two daughters. His body was finally laid to rest in Reigate cemetery on 4 July 1879. The following year his daughter Mary Ann Turner was granted a civil-list pension of £75.   MICHELLE CALE

Thomas Turner (*bap.* 1592, *d.* 1672), by unknown artist

Sources *Reformatory and Refuge Journal* (1861–79) · *The Times* (2 July 1879) · W. W. Rouse Ball and J. A. Venn, eds., *Admissions to Trinity College, Cambridge*, 4 (1911) · Crockford (1878), 955 · 'Reformatory schools', *Dublin Review*, new ser., 3 (1864), 455–82 · PRO, Red Lodge & St Joseph's Reformatories, Gem St Industrial School, esp. HO45 and HO144 · Boase, *Mod. Eng. biog.* · 'Inspector of reformatory schools of Great Britain', *Parl. papers* (1857–76) [reports 1–19] · d. cert. · m. cert.
Archives BL, corresp. with Sir Stafford Northcote relating to reformatories · Surrey HC, Royal Philanthropic Society MSS · W. Sussex RO, letters to duke of Richmond
Wealth at death under £4000: probate, 29 July 1879, *CGPLA Eng. & Wales*

Turner, Thomas (*bap.* 1592, *d.* 1672), dean of Canterbury, was baptized at St Giles, Reading, Berkshire, on 16 January 1592, a son, probably the third, of Thomas Turnor (*bap.* 1564?, *d.* in or after 1643), alderman and mayor of Reading, and also of Heckfield, Hampshire, and his wife, Mary, *née* Bye. He was educated at Reading grammar school, and proceeded on a Reading scholarship to St John's College, Oxford, matriculating on 26 June 1610. The fellows there were to have a decisive influence on his future life. William Juxon was his tutor, and William Laud became presi-dent of the college during his sojourn there. Turner gradu-ated BA on 6 June 1614, and became college lecturer in dia-lectic in 1617, proceeding MA on 9 May 1618. In 1621 he became library keeper, and in the same year was made deacon on 27 May and priest on 27 September. He held St Giles', Oxford, a college benefice, from 1624, proceeded BD on 20 July that year, and became lecturer in Greek in 1626. In the mid-1620s he seems to have acted as eyes and

ears in Oxford for Laud, absent in St David's and then Bath and Wells. Probably through Laud's patronage he became a member of the ecclesiastical commission on 7 January 1628.

In 1629 Turner resigned his fellowship and St Giles when Laud, as bishop of London, preferred him to the Newing-ton prebend of St Paul's Cathedral, and the diocesan chan-cellorship, also making him his chaplain and licenser. Laud esteemed him so highly that on his death sixteen years later he left him his diamond ring surrounded by the Garter. Before long Turner became chaplain-in-ordinary to Charles I, and on 1 April 1633 was created DD. He became rector of St Augustine by St Paul, London, in May 1631, but resigned it when presented by the king in November that year to St Olave, Southwark, London. In 1633 Charles I commanded him to accompany him on his coronation visit to Scotland, and on 11 November 1634 he was presented in plurality to Fetcham rectory, Surrey, by Sir Francis Vincent. Turner became a client of Sir Francis Windebank (1582–1646), secretary of state, in this period, and by 1637 had married his daughter Margaret (1607/8–1692). They had three known children, Francis *Turner (1637–1700), later nonjuring bishop of Ely, Thomas *Turner (1645–1714), later president of Corpus Christi Col-lege, Oxford, and William, archdeacon of Northumber-land.

Turner preached quite moderately in the controversies of the 1630s, contending in *A Sermon Preached before the King* (1635) that works of love and mercy were more important than outward religious observances, and Sunday sports merciful to servants, while ceaseless sermon going was harmful to domestic life. At St Olave's the communion table was railed in during his incumbency, and Turner took no action when hundreds reportedly refused to communicate as a result. On the churchwardens removing the rails, allegedly to avoid disorder, they were presented at the ecclesiastical court. On 31 December 1638 the king granted Turner and John Juxon, as trustees, leases of the prebend and rectory of Aylesbury, Buckinghamshire, and the rectory of Presteigne, in the shires of Hereford and Radnor, disingenuously stating that they should fulfil the intentions of the feoffees for impropriations, recently dissolved, when in fact they were to use the money to augment benefice income, rather than creating lectureships as the feoffees had done.

On the meeting of the Long Parliament these views and actions resulted in St Olave's congregation petitioning the House of Lords against Turner on 15 June 1641. He was subsequently sequestrated from the parish and was in the custody of the serjeant-at-arms until he paid £100 for his release, and an equal amount as security, on 20 May 1643. Nevertheless, on 16 February 1642 Charles I nominated him dean of Rochester. On 26 May 1643 the committee for sequestrations ordered that £80 worth of his goods be seized because he had sent money and plate to the royalist forces at Reading, and in the same year he was seized from Fetcham for sending £120 to the king. Soldiers reportedly trod the prayer book in the mud, and put his surplice on a trooper before imprisoning him at the White Lion, Southwark. His successor supposedly evicted Turner's wife from the rectory despite advanced pregnancy. Later his London goods were seized. On 3 January 1644 the king named Turner as dean of Canterbury, though this was nominal since parliament controlled Kent, and he lost both deaneries on the abolition of deans and chapters.

Turner attended Charles I at Hampton Court in 1648, and when the king was removed from Carisbrooke Castle in the Isle of Wight to Newport for negotiations with parliament in September that year Turner was one of the six chaplains whom the king requested, and was allowed. They stood behind his chair during the negotiations. Thence he retired to Hertfordshire, but was convicted of malignancy by the county committee for attending and praying for the king. However, in October 1651 the committee for compounding ratified his discharge on his taking the oath of abjuration, and producing a certificate that he was attending church and receiving the sacrament. He was then living at Ashendon, near Aylesbury, Buckinghamshire.

At the Restoration Turner was instituted as dean of Canterbury and restored to his Surrey rectories, reportedly refusing a bishopric 'preferring to set out with too little than too much sail' (*DNB*). At Canterbury the cathedral had been devastated by parliamentary troops in 1642. They had overthrown the communion table, defaced the sanctuary ornaments, broken the font and much statuary, spoilt the organs, music, and prayer books, and destroyed robes and some stained glass. By the Restoration the lead was largely stripped and the roof ruined. Turner worked

zealously at restoration: by 1662 the chapter, encouraged by him, had spent £5248 on the fabric. Much was also spent on communion vessels, furnishings, hangings, and a new lectern. Turner donated an altar bible with beaten silver covers and double gilt. With the help of the minor canons he also endeavoured to restore choral music.

Under Turner the chapter gave the Canterbury corporation a large sum to ease famine in the bad harvests of the 1660s, augmented vicarages, raised low salaries, and negotiated abatements with royalist tenants who had suffered in the civil war. Turner was also generous with time and money elsewhere. He befriended Dr John Barwick when he moved from the deanery of Durham to St Paul's and spent £1000 on building a canon's house for his successors there, as well as giving £500 to rebuild St Paul's Cathedral and £40 each to Trinity and Corpus Christi colleges, Oxford.

Turner continued to preach at court, where John Evelyn heard him in 1665, and elsewhere until he was eighty. Peter Barwick described him as 'a practical useful Preacher, much followed by all the Orthodox' (Barwick, 308). In the last few months of his life he suffered from gallstones; complications from these led to his death on 8 October 1672. He was buried in the deans' chapel, Canterbury Cathedral.   ELIZABETH ALLEN

Sources DNB · J. Gregory, 'Canterbury and the ancien régime: the dean and chapter, 1660–1828', *A history of Canterbury Cathedral, 598–1982*, ed. P. Collinson and others (1995), 204–55, esp. 205, 212–14, 228–9 · *Walker rev.*, 60 · W. C. Costin, *The history of St John's College, Oxford, 1598–1860*, OHS, new ser., 12 (1958), 47–8, 73 · J. W. Legg and W. H. St J. Hope, *Inventories of Christ Church, Canterbury* (1902), 267–74, 277 · *CSP dom.*, 1625–6; 1638–9, 191; 1640, 11; 1640–41, 562–3 · M. A. E. Green, ed., *Calendar of the proceedings of the committee for compounding … 1643–1660*, 4, PRO (1892), 2877 · T. Herbert, 'Threnodia Carolina', *Memoirs of the martyr king*, ed. A. Fea (1905), 74–153, esp. 109–10 · E. Hasted, *The history and topographical survey of the county of Kent*, 2nd edn, 12 (1801), 24–5 · A. Paske, *The copy of a letter* (1642), 4 · P. Barwick, *The life of … Dr John Barwick*, ed. and trans. H. Bedford (1724), 307–8 · G. J. Armytage, ed., *A visitation of the county of Kent, begun … 1663, finished … 1668*, Harleian Society, 54 (1906), 169 · Oxon. RO, Oxford diocesan papers, c.264, fols. 100v, 102 · J. Walker, *An attempt towards recovering an account of the numbers and sufferings of the clergy of the Church of England*, pt 2 (1714), 6 · Evelyn, *Diary*, 3.415 · gravestone, St Giles Church, Oxford, south chapel [Margaret Turner and a son] · J. Hacket, *Select and remarkable epitaphs*, 1 (1757), 264 · J. M. Guilding, ed., *Reading records: diary of the corporation*, 1 (1892), 387, 451 · J. M. Guilding, ed., *Reading records: diary of the corporation*, 4 (1896), 92 · O. Manning, *History of Surrey* (1797–1801), 1.486–7; 3.606 · *Fasti Angl.* (Hardy), 2.577; 3.308 · parish register, Oxford, St Giles, Oxon. RO, 1692 [burials] · parish register, Reading, St Giles, 16 Jan 1592, Berks. RO [baptism] · parish register, Bradfield, Berks., 29 June 1564, Berks. RO [baptism; Thomas Turnor] · parish register, Reading, St Giles, 1585, Berks. RO [marriage; Thomas Turnor]
Likenesses oils, deanery, Canterbury [*see illus.*]
Wealth at death substantial: Hasted, *History of Kent*, 25

Turner, Thomas (1645–1714), college head, was born in Bristol on 19 or 20 September 1645, the second of three sons of Thomas *Turner (*bap.* 1592, *d.* 1672), dean of Canterbury, and his wife, Margaret (1607/8–1692), daughter of Sir Francis *Windebank. Having matriculated in 1662 from Hart Hall, Oxford, he was admitted on 6 October

1663 to a Gloucestershire scholarship at Corpus Christi College. He graduated BA in March 1666, proceeded MA in 1669, became a fellow of Corpus in 1672, and proceeded BD in 1677 and DD in 1683. During his career he held a number of livings, being vicar of Milton-next-Sittingbourne, Kent (1672–95), rector of Thorley, Hertfordshire (1680–89), and rector of Fulham, Middlesex (1688–1714); he was also made archdeacon of Essex (1680), a canon of Ely (where his elder brother, Francis *Turner (1637–1700), was by that time bishop) in 1686, and a canon and precentor of St Paul's Cathedral, London. However, he seems to have preferred to remain in Oxford. Others preached for him at St Paul's and a letter from Ely of 12 August 1704, which requested him to come 'once in two or three year' (Bodl. Oxf., MS Rawl. 92, fol. 249), complained of his being 'wholly absent when you are in good health'. He was, however, a chaplain to James II, and in that capacity preached at Whitehall on 29 May 1685 a sermon on Isaiah 1: 26, which dwelt on restoration and the blessings of the past and which was published that year.

On 13 March 1688 Turner was elected president of Corpus. Modern historians see Turner as important for creating 'a college which earned the reputation of being the home of the most assertive high tories in the university' (Bennett, 43). Although he may have taken the oaths in 1689 'he remained deeply hostile to the new order', avoiding confrontation, but exercising covert influence. His correspondents reveal that he was in close touch with men of affairs: nonjuring bishops and clergy, government ministers, members of both houses of parliament, including Clarendon and Weymouth, and friends all sought his help and advice, knowing that enquiries would be made 'without noise' (1 Oct 1701, Bodl. Oxf., MS Rawl. 92, fol. 67) and that financial help would be forthcoming; his nonjuring brother Francis trusted him throughout his troubles. However, the college, to which he was so munificent a benefactor, took up most of his attention.

Shortly after he took office, Turner set about rebuilding and repairing the president's lodgings. New wings were added to the south and to the east of the old Jacobean house, which was itself remodelled. A feature which subsequently disappeared was a small tower with a cupola, clearly visible in depictions in the *Oxford Almanack* of 1726. The college accounts for internal expenses rose dramatically over the decade from 1689 to 1699, but separate large sums were paid by the president for the work done in the hall and the chapel, especially for the woodwork and carving. As he wrote to his agent in London on 13 November 1699: 'I doubt I can not well spare this just now; but I can not deny the college' (Bodl. Oxf., MS Rawl. 98, fol. 190). The following decade saw the erection of the building which for many years bore his name and for which he bore the cost, including £1223 for the mason's bill alone.

Turner's second great benefaction to the college was his collection of books, the list of which (Corpus Christi College archives, D/2/6) covers 112 folios. There are a few rare works, but the greater part consists of contemporary writing, with a heavy bias toward theological treatises and polemics. Little survives of Turner's own writing except sermon notes, some of them in shorthand. They have a strong emphasis on legality, justice, and righteousness and develop themes into a practical morality, but they also acknowledge humbly the duty of prayer. As the nineteenth-century historian of the college, Thomas Fowler, observed, *A defence of the doctrine and practice of the Church of England, against some modern innovations* (1712), once attributed to him, is not his work.

Turner died at Corpus on 29 April 1714. He was buried in college on 2 May, after a service in which William Tilly delivered the panegyric, later published as *Oratio funebris* (1714). In his will Turner was sensitive to his 'private obligations' and left substantial sums to his niece, nephews, kinsfolk, and servants, being particularly sensible to the position of women. Considering his public obligations he thought first of his college, 'The place where I have had my education and spent the greatest and best part of my life', and made provision for the completion of his cherished projects, the fellows' building and the library; he also left a contingency sum in case he had unwarily wronged the college (by spending more than the founder allowed) when he had held the office of bursar or dean (he only had a year in each office), and in a codicil earmarked income from land at Brill to pay a librarian chosen 'into that office from year to year by the President'. Acknowledging that: "I have received very considerable sums of money and tis fit that I should sow as well as reap" Thomas Turner left money to the parishes where he had held office (Fulham and Thorley) and owned land (Bishop's Stortford), making a provision that the benefit should be reaped by the young through endowed apprenticeships. It was for the benefit of the poor lay singing men (and not the minor canons or choristers) that the dean and canons of Ely were to disburse the income from land bought to endow a trust in perpetuity. Two particularly strong attachments, his long-standing friend (and tireless correspondent on all manner of affairs in Cambridge) Francis Roper, and Thomas Gilbert, his agent ('I owe indeed almost all that I am worth to his great kindness and good management') were duly recognized. The residue of his considerable estate was used to buy land at Stowe Nine Churches, the income from which was to settle on the trustees of the corporation for the relief of poor clergymen's widows and orphans. An account of 'the particulars of Dr Turner's will' was attached to *The Excellency of Proper, Charitable Relief*, a sermon to the clergy published in 1714.   CHRISTINE BUTLER

Sources T. Fowler, *The history of Corpus Christi College*, OHS, 25 (1893) · Foster, *Alum. Oxon.* · G. V. Bennett, 'Against the tide: Oxford under William III', *Hist. U. Oxf.* 5: *18th-cent. Oxf.*, 31–60 · Bodl. Oxf., MSS Rawl. letters 91–92, 98 · Bodl. Oxf., MSS Rawl. E. 186–190 · admissions, CCC Oxf., B/1/1/2 · benefactions and wills, CCC Oxf., B/11/1/2 · accounts, CCC Oxf., C/1/1/14–C/1/1/15 · tower book, CCC Oxf., C/7/2 · building accounts, CCC Oxf., H/4/1/3, H/1/3/1 · Dr Turner's benefaction, CCC Oxf., D/2/6 · bindings, CCC Oxf., Add 051/1 · CCC Oxf., B/1/3/4

Archives Bodl. Oxf., Rawl. MSS · U. Birm. L., sermons, 1957/ i/22–3

Likenesses T. Stayner, sculpture, 1714, St Michael's Church, Stowe-Nine-Churches, Northamptonshire · bas-relief bust, marble?, CCC Oxf.

Turner, Thomas (1729–1793), diarist and shopkeeper, was born on 9 June 1729 at Groombridge in the parish of Speldhurst, Kent, the eldest of the four children of John Turner (1689–1752), a shopkeeper, and his second wife, Elizabeth Ovenden (1697–1759), of Rotherfield, Sussex. In 1735 the family moved to Framfield, Sussex, where John Turner took a shop and from where Thomas's two brothers, Moses and Richard, were apprenticed to their father's trade. Nothing is known of Thomas's schooling and apprenticeship, but by the time that he was twenty-one (in 1750) he had leased a shop in East Hoathly, Sussex, and had acquired the ability to reckon and cast accounts and to write a bold, clear hand.

On 15 October 1753 Turner married Margaret (Peggy) Slater (1733–1761) in Lewes. She was the daughter of a Hartfield farming couple, Samuel and Ann Slater. The marriage was not always happy; Margaret's health was not good, she was frequently not as helpful in the shop as Turner would have liked, and her mother proved a thorn in Turner's side. Their only child, Peter, who was born on 19 August 1754, lived for less than five months, and Margaret herself died, after a long illness, on 23 June 1761.

Early in his married life Turner began keeping a diary, the first surviving entry in which is dated 21 February 1754. The diary chronicles in detail the next eleven years not only of the life of a busy, worried, and frequently unhappy supplier of virtually every retail commodity to a rural community, but also of the life of the community itself. East Hoathly, on the edge of the Sussex Weald, was an agricultural village with a population of some 350 people. Turner recorded its activities at a time when the Seven Years' War brought constant rumours of a threat to invade from across the channel, and when, within the parish's western boundary, stood Halland House (since demolished), the Sussex mansion of the duke of Newcastle, first lord of the Treasury for almost eight of the diary years.

Within this community Turner played an essential role. His shop was a centre for the gathering and dissemination of information, he was the local expert in money matters, he was the village undertaker, he wrote wills, kept accounts, collected taxes, served in one parish office after another, aided successive excisemen, surveyed fields, conducted auctions, and at one stage kept the village school. All these activities he chronicled in detail, embellishing his narrative with vivid thumbnail word sketches of his contemporaries, whether friends or enemies. In addition the diary gives details of his extensive reading and of his activities as drinking companion, party-goer, and cricketer.

The diary has never been published in full and until 1984 the only publicly available extracts were those first given in the article in the *Sussex Archaeological Collections* for 1859 by R. W. Blencowe and M. A. Lower, whose purpose was to contrast fashionable mid-nineteenth-century Sussex with the 'secluded and uncivilized' county of one hundred years before. These extracts, re-edited by F. M. Turner in 1925 and again by G. H. Jennings in 1979, did Turner no service, and it was as something of a figure of fun that he was noted by subsequent writers on diarists from Charles Dickens (*All the Year Round*, 13 April 1861) onwards. Vaisey's edition of 1984 reproduces about one third of the whole and shows Turner to have been an important observer of eighteenth-century life.

The surviving 111 volumes of the diary end with an entry written on 31 July 1765 recording Turner's marriage on 19 June to Mary (Molly) Hicks (1735–1807), daughter of Thomas and Mary Hicks of Chiddingly, Sussex. Turner lived on in East Hoathly for twenty-eight years after he stopped writing his diary, and during those years he prospered. He acquired land, and bought both his shop and the principal public house in the village. Seven children (two of whom died in infancy) were born of his second marriage, and at least two of his sons carried on the trade. He died on 6 February 1793 at East Hoathly and was buried in the churchyard there on 11 February. A table-tomb marks his grave. His house in the village bears a plaque recording his residence. His widow survived him by fourteen years and was buried at East Hoathly on 1 December 1807.

DAVID VAISEY

Sources *The diary of Thomas Turner, 1754–1765*, ed. D. Vaisey (1984); pbk edn (1994) · D. K. Worcester, *The life and times of Thomas Turner of East Hoathly* (1948) · *The diary of Thomas Turner of East Hoathly, 1754–1765*, ed. F. M. Turner (1925) · T. Turner, *The diary of a Georgian shopkeeper / Thomas Turner*, 2nd edn, ed. G. H. Jennings, R. W. Blencowe, and M. A. Lower (1979) · R. W. Blencowe and M. A. Lower, 'Extracts from the diary of a Sussex tradesman, a hundred years ago', *Sussex Archaeological Collections*, 11 (1859), 179–220 · Bishop's transcripts, CKS · parish register, 1793, East Hoathly, Sussex [burial]
Archives E. Sussex RO, diaries, AMS 5841 [transcript] · Yale U., Sterling Memorial Library | E. Sussex RO, East Hoathly parish records, PAR 378
Wealth at death see will, 28 Sept 1793, E. Sussex RO, Lewes archdeaconry wills register A 66, 728

Turner, Thomas (*bap.* 1747, *d.* 1809), porcelain manufacturer, was baptized on 9 November 1747 at St Swithun's, Worcester, the eldest son of Richard *Turner (*bap.* 1720, *d.* 1791), a Church of England clergyman and educational writer, and his wife, Sarah Greene (*d.* 1800). The author Richard *Turner (*bap.* 1753, *d.* 1788) was his younger brother.

Turner very probably had some early connection with the china trade in Worcester, but his formal apprenticeship (1761) was to his father, who was also a writing master. He thereby gained the right to trade in the city by becoming a freeman (1771). Most likely in 1772, while still trading in china in Worcester, he moved to Caughley, in the parish of Barrow, Shropshire. There he expanded a pottery managed by Ambrose Gallimore, on land leased since 1754 from the Brownes of Caughley Hall. He completed the first stage of his improvements by 1775 and was then producing soft-paste porcelain on a commercial scale, for the first time in Shropshire.

Some association with Gallimore lasted until at least 1787, but Turner was evidently the dominant partner. The works, known as the Salopian China Manufactory, was very successful during its short life. In 1775 the draughtsman and engraver Robert Hancock, with whom Turner may have worked in Worcester, opened a warehouse in Bridgnorth, and there was another in London, in Portugal Street. Some 80 per cent of Caughley wares were in underglaze blue. Designs included copies of Worcester patterns, and many in the then very popular Chinese style. There were some original features, including European landscapes and ornamentation of the underglaze blue in burnished gold. White pieces, known as 'blanks', were decorated by Robert Chamberlain of Worcester.

Turner visited France, certainly in 1787 and perhaps as early as 1780. He may well have returned with both ideas and workmen, which influenced the design both of his pottery and of Caughley Place, the fine residence he built nearby. A nineteenth-century authority described him thus: 'he was an excellent chemist, had thoroughly studied the various processes connected with porcelain manufacture, was a skilful draughtsman, designer, and engraver, and was also a clever musician' (Jewitt, 159).

Turner became a burgess of Much Wenlock (1784) and Bridgnorth (1795). He was bailiff of Wenlock and justice for the borough on five occasions between 1784 and 1804, and briefly captain of the Wenlock loyal Volunteers. On 3 October 1783 he married Dorothy Gallimore, niece of Ambrose. She died without surviving children and was buried at Barrow on 28 July 1794. On 21 September 1796 Turner married Mary Alsop, née Milner (bap. 1758, d. 1815). They had two children, a son and a daughter.

In October 1799 Turner gave up the business through ill health. It was sold to, among others, John Rose, a former employee, who carried it on with his own works at Coalport until finally abandoning the Caughley site almost twenty years later. Turner died intestate, probably at Caughley Place, and was buried on 27 February 1809 in the family vault at Barrow. The will of his widow, Mary, who was buried at Bridgnorth on 23 November 1815, reveals that he left 'considerable real estate but a very small personal estate'. Examples of Caughley wares are in the Victoria and Albert Museum, London, and the Coalport China Museum, Telford.   J. SHEARMAN and N. SHEARMAN

Sources J. Shearman and N. Shearman, 'Thomas Turner revisited', *Northern Ceramic Society Journal*, 14 (1997), 71–9 · G. Godden, *Caughley and Worcester porcelains, 1775–1800* (1969) · G. B. Roberts, 'Serendipity: a new look at Thomas Turner', *Ars Ceramica*, 7 (1990), 40–42 · L. Jewitt, *Ceramic art of Great Britain* (1883) · B. Watney, *English blue and white porcelain of the eighteenth century* (1973) · H. Smith, 'A pedigree of the Turner family', *Miscellanea Genealogica et Heraldica*, new ser., 1 (1874), 158–60 · *DNB*
Likenesses L. F. Abbott, oils, Ironbridge Gorge Museum Trust
Wealth at death 'considerable real estate but a very small personal estate': will of widow, Mary, 1815

Turner, Thomas (1793–1873), surgeon and founder of Pine Street School of Medicine, was born on 13 August 1793 in Truro, the fifth and youngest child of Edmund Turner (d. 1821), banker, and his wife, Joanna (d. 1814), daughter of Richard Ferris. Turner was educated privately before entering Truro grammar school. His father wanted him to enter the church but Thomas was determined to pursue a medical career and became apprenticed to Nehemiah

Duck, a surgeon at St Peter's Hospital, Bristol. In the autumn of 1815 he left Bristol for London, joining the united borough hospitals of Guy's and St Thomas's as a student. There he became a pupil of the great surgeon, Sir Astley Cooper. The following year he qualified with the licence of the Society of Apothecaries and the membership diploma of the Royal College of Surgeons. That summer he travelled to Paris, then renowned for progressive medical teaching, to complete his education. He remained there until the spring of 1817.

Turner then moved to Manchester where his youngest sister was married to a Richard Smith. He was appointed house surgeon to the Manchester poorhouse, succeeding William Whatton. In September 1820 he resigned this post because of illness and, after a brief period studying in Edinburgh and Glasgow, established himself in private practice. Shortly after, he joined the Manchester Literary and Philosophical Society and the Natural History Society, where the young doctor met many influential individuals, including John Dalton.

In 1817, while in Paris, Turner had written an essay on medical education, outlining a scheme which would integrate lecture courses more closely with practical training which then took the form of apprenticeship. Two years previously, the Apothecaries' Act had come into force, establishing the licence of the Society of Apothecaries, the LSA, as a legal requirement for general practitioners in England and Wales. The regulations for the LSA included five years' apprenticeship to a qualified practitioner and attendance at a prescribed list of lecture courses. The act proved an important milestone for medical education. The Royal College of Surgeons revised its regulations, setting up an examination for its membership diploma which was very similar to the LSA.

In 1822 Turner began lecturing on anatomy and physiology using the rooms of the Literary and Philosophical Society. In 1824 he outlined his ideas on professional training to the society and the address was subsequently published. His ideas were received so positively that Turner transferred his lecture course to a house in Pine Street and set about organizing a school of medicine where students could gain experience of dissection as well as attend a range of lecture courses. This school is regarded as the first complete provincial school of medicine. Certificates of attendance at lecture courses at the Pine Street School were very soon recognized by the Society of Apothecaries and the Royal College of Surgeons of Edinburgh. The Royal College of Surgeons in London recognized the school in 1827. In 1826 Turner married Anna Clarke (d. 1861), daughter of James Clarke, a wealthy gentleman from Medham, Isle of Wight. The couple had two sons and three daughters.

Initially Turner had been able to persuade John Dalton to support the Pine Street School and to lecture on chemistry there. Soon many of the leading medical practitioners of the town, including honorary physicians and surgeons of the infirmary, were also giving courses. These associations with distinguished colleagues assisted Turner in establishing himself as a leading practitioner within the town. In 1825 he was elected surgeon to the deaf and dumb institution. Five years later, he was elected honorary surgeon to the Manchester Infirmary.

Turner was not the first medical teacher in Manchester to establish a school. In 1814 Joseph Jordan had opened a school of anatomy in Bridge Street. The Society of Apothecaries had recognized its lecture courses in 1817. In 1826, two years after Turner opened the Pine Street School, Jordan expanded his school and moved into purpose-built premises in Mount Street. There was intense rivalry between the two institutions both for teachers and for students. In 1834 Turner and Jordan reached agreement that students from Mount Street would be transferred to Pine Street if the Pine Street staff would publicly support Jordan's attempt to be elected to the honorary staff of the Manchester Infirmary. Two years later the combined school became the Royal School of Medicine, and this institution enjoyed a monopoly until 1850 when George Southam established a school in Chatham Street. In 1856 these two schools merged, following an unsuccessful attempt to unite with Owens College, the recently founded university college. Ten years later negotiations with Owens College were reopened, and the Royal School of Medicine became the faculty of medicine of the college in 1872. Although no longer actively involved in teaching, Turner delivered the inaugural address of the new medical faculty in recognition of his role in founding the original school.

In 1843 Turner became honorary professor of physiology at the Manchester Royal Institution. Although the post was unpaid it brought with it prestige. Turner continued to give his annual lecture until the year before his death. He became a fellow of the Royal College of Surgeons in 1843 and served on the college council from 1865 until 1873. In 1843 he published a short study, concerning dislocations of the toes, which had previously been presented as a paper to the Royal College of Surgeons. The study became a standard work.

Turner was an active and committed member of the Anglican church. In 1852 he set up the Manchester and Salford Sanitary Association with Canon Richeson of the collegiate church. The association took the message of cleanliness to the working classes through its programme of lectures, home visits, and publications. Turner was president of the association from 1858 until his death. Turner died after a short illness at his house, 77 Mosley Street, Manchester, on 17 December 1873. He was buried later in the same month with his wife and eldest daughter at Marton near Skipton in Craven, Yorkshire, where his son-in-law was vicar.   STELLA BUTLER

Sources *Memoir of Thomas Turner, FRCS, FLS, by a relative* (1875) · *Proceedings of the Manchester Literary and Philosophical Society*, 13 (1874), 151–3 · E. M. Brockbank, *Sketches of the lives and work of the honorary medical staff of the Manchester Infirmary: from its foundation in 1752 to 1830* (1904), 275–80
Likenesses photograph, repro. in *Memoir of Thomas Turner*, frontispiece · photograph, Wellcome L.
Wealth at death under £12,000: resworn probate, Feb 1877, *CGPLA Eng. & Wales* (1874)

Turner, Thomas Hudson (1815–1852), antiquary, born in London, was the eldest son of Thomas Turner of Pall Mall, London, a printer employed by William Bulmer. The elder Turner was a cultured man, with considerable knowledge of English literature. He assisted William Gifford (1756–1826) in his edition of Ben Jonson (1816).

The younger Turner lost his father at an early age. He was left in poverty and received assistance from Bulmer and from Bulmer's nephew William Nicol. He was educated at a school in Chelsea, where he was distinguished by his literary and antiquarian enthusiasms. In 1830 he entered Nicol's Pall Mall printing office. He spent his free time studying and soon obtained a post at the record office in the Tower of London, where he read and translated records. Taking advantage of his new opportunities for research, he undertook a history of England during the reigns of John and Henry III, which he did not complete. The work was abandoned when he left the record office to collect materials for a history of London for Edward Tyrrell, the city remembrancer. In 1841 he edited for the Roxburghe Club *The Manners and Household Expenses of England in the Thirteenth and Fifteenth Centuries*, to which he wrote a well-informed introduction (this edition has, however, also been attributed to Beriah Botfield). Subsequently for a short time he was resident secretary of the Archaeological Institute. His principal work was entitled *Some account of domestic architecture in England from the conquest to the end of the thirteenth century* (1851–9). The last section, continuing the history from Edward I to Henry VIII, was by John Henry Parker. The book, an enterprising work for its time, covers a wide range of subjects, including furniture and household implements. Turner died in Stanhope Terrace, Camden Town, London, on 17 January 1852. He contributed papers to the *Archaeological Journal*, and made several communications to the Society of Antiquaries of Newcastle, printed in the third volume of *Archaeologia Aeliana*; he also edited an introduction to John Lewis's *Life of Dr John Fisher, Bishop of Rochester* (1855).

E. I. CARLYLE, *rev.* G. H. MARTIN

Sources *GM*, 2nd ser., 37 (1852), 206 · C. Knight, ed., *The English cyclopaedia: biography*, 6 (1858) · Boase, *Mod. Eng. biog.*

Turner, Sir Timothy (1585–1677), serjeant-at-law and judge, was born on 11 July 1585, the first son of Thomas Turner, esquire, a barrister of Gray's Inn and Astley, Shropshire, and his wife, Susanna, the daughter and heir of John Farmer, a member of the Grocers' Company in London. Having migrated from Staple Inn to Gray's Inn on 8 March 1607 he was called to the bar on 30 October 1611. While a junior barrister in the mid-1610s Turner was apparently strongly affected by the heated controversies then taking place between Sir Edward Coke and Lord Chancellor Ellesmere about the jurisdictional relationship between the common law on the one side and the court of chancery and the ecclesiastical courts on the other. Private comments in his manuscript notebooks accuse Ellesmere of attempting to discredit Coke, and contain a list of sixteen 'dangerous' and 'absurd' (Ogden MS 29, fol. 568v) positions that the chancellor was trying to put forward to the king. Turner thought that Ellesmere's claim that the prerogative was 'transcendent to the common law' (BL, Add. MS 35957, fol. 56v) created a situation where the liberties of the subject would be taken away, where the only law would be prerogative law, and where the government of the country would slip into the hands of a few favourites.

Over the next decade Turner concentrated on a private practice centred on the administrative and legal capital of the Welsh marches, Ludlow, though his official and professional progress was not particularly notable until 1626, when he was made a justice of the peace for Shropshire. Turner himself attributed this breakthrough to the favour of Lord Keeper Sir Thomas Coventry, but ironically it may also have owed something to his connections with John Egerton, the first earl of Bridgewater, the son and heir of Ellesmere, who was at about the same time rising to greater political prominence in London and on the Welsh borders. Turner was a legal adviser to Bridgewater, and the relationship also had a personal dimension. After the death of his first wife, Jane, the daughter of Francis Newton of Highley, Shropshire, Turner married Ann, the widow of Thomas Johnston, who was Bridgewater's solicitor.

Turner acted as a commissioner in Shropshire and at Ludlow for the forced loan of 1626. He held the post of king's solicitor before the council of the marches in Wales for a decade from 1627, and obtained a patent as a master in chancery extraordinary in 1630. In 1632 he gave the Lent reading at Gray's Inn and became a bencher. Appointed puisne judge for the northern circuit of the court of great sessions in Wales in 1634 he was promoted to chief justice for south Wales three years later. Still an active JP in Shropshire, in April 1635 he became involved in a notable incident at quarter sessions when grand jurors presented as a grievance the fee raised on the county to pay the muster master of the militia. Telling the grand jurors that they were 'too busie' (Ellesmere MS 7632) in making their presentment, Turner also criticized another JP, Sir John Corbet, who had challenged Turner's intervention by asking the clerk of the peace to read out the petition of right.

Having been imprisoned for several years as a result of a privy council investigation of the incident that had been initiated by Bridgewater, Corbet petitioned the House of Commons about it in 1640, and articles of impeachment were eventually brought against the earl. Although Turner was not directly named in the case he feared that he might be and was obliged to give evidence. In August 1642 there was a report to the House of Commons that Turner, who had been made recorder of Shrewsbury in 1638, and the town's mayor, had put a declaration before the grand jury that acknowledged the legitimacy of the commissions of array and contained a promise to defend the king's person as well as the laws and just privileges of parliament. Turner later claimed that he had been forced to take up this position owing to the strength of the royalists in Shropshire rather than because of personal conviction, and several members of his household, including his

own son, who was killed in battle, served the parliamentary cause. Nevertheless, by the end of 1645 parliament stripped him of all of his offices and he was subsequently forced to compound for his delinquency.

Looking back in 1658 at his earlier observations on the conflict between Coke and Ellesmere, Turner noted that 'This overthrew all at Last *and* brought the whole nation under a fewe into that slavery under which it now Labours' (BL, Add. MS 35957, fol. 56v). But having kept his head down during the interregnum Turner prospered with the return of the Stuarts in 1660. He was made chief justice for mid-Wales in August 1660, and served as recorder of Shrewsbury from the same date until 1670. He was reappointed as an alderman of the town in the charter issued in 1664, and also resumed an active role on the commission of the peace. In 1669 he became one of the oldest men ever to have been made a serjeant-at-law, and he was knighted a year later. He died in January 1677 and was buried at St Mary's, Shrewsbury. A rich man, he left considerable sums to the poor of both Shrewsbury and Ludlow.

CHRISTOPHER W. BROOKS

Sources J. H. Baker, *The legal profession and the common law: historical essays* (1986), ch. 13 · W. R. Williams, *The history of the great sessions in Wales, 1542–1830* (privately printed, Brecon, 1899) · W. R. Prest, *The rise of the barristers: a social history of the English bar, 1590–1640* (1986) · Baker, *Serjeants* · BL, Add. MS 35957 · UCL, Ogden MS 29 · Hunt. L., Bridgewater Collection, Ellesmere MS 7632 · BL, Harley MS 163 · *VCH Shropshire*, vol. 3 · *CSP dom.*, 1660 · will, PRO, PROB 11/353, sig. 25

Archives BL, Add. MS 35957 · UCL, Ogden MS 29 | Hunt. L., Bridgewater collection, Ellesmere MSS, letters

Wealth at death income £300–£430 in 1640; manor of Winsley, Ford, Shropshire, also house in Shrewbury: will, PRO, PROB 11/353, sig. 25; Prest, *Rise of barristers*, 398

Turner, Sir Tomkyns Hilgrove (*c.*1766–1843), army officer and courtier, was commissioned an ensign in the 3rd foot guards on 20 February 1782, and was promoted to lieutenant and captain on 13 October 1789. He went to the Netherlands in February 1793 with the brigade of guards under the duke of York. After landing at Helvoetsluys on 5 March, Turner marched to Tournai, encamped at Maulde in May, and took part in the battle of St Amand (8 May) and the action of Famars (23 May). He participated in the siege of Valenciennes in June and July, which culminated in the successful assault of 25–28 July. On 18 August he was present at the brilliant affair of Lincelles, a village the French had recently captured from the Dutch. The outnumbered guards succeeded in driving the French out of their entrenched position.

During the British siege of Dunkirk in September, Turner was involved in repulsing the garrison's attempted sorties of 6 and 8 September. However, the covering army withdrew to Furnes under pressure from Houchard, and this forced the duke of York to raise the siege. Turner next marched with the guards to Cysoing situated between Lille and Orchies. On 5 October the guards joined the Austrians across the River Sambre to surround Landrecy. However, the siege was not prosecuted, and Turner re-crossed the river with his regiment *en route* for Ghent.

On 17 April 1794 Turner took part in the successful

attack on the French forces posted at Vaux, between Landrecy and Guise. The enemy were driven behind the Oise and Landrecy was besieged. Turner was present during this siege, and was also at the action of Cateau, near Troixville, on 26 April. He then went with the duke of York's army to Tournai and participated in the repulse of the French attack on 23 May. He accompanied the army in its retreat towards the Netherlands in July and behind the Aar in September, took part in the action at Boxtel on 15 September, and then in the retreat behind the Meuse to Nijmegen. He greatly distinguished himself during Abercromby's capture of Fort St André on 11 October prior to the army's retreat behind the Waal.

Turner was promoted captain of the 3rd foot guards and lieutenant-colonel on 12 November 1794, when he returned to England. He was promoted brevet colonel on 1 January 1801, the year in which he went with his regiment to Egypt, landing at Abu Qir Bay on 8 March. He participated in the battle of Alexandria on 21 March. He was also involved in the action in the western part of Alexandria with the guards brigade under Lord Cavan on 22 August, and witnessed the surrender of the city on 2 September. For his services in Egypt Turner received the medal, and was made a knight of the order of the Crescent of Turkey by the sultan, and a knight of the order of St Anne of Russia by the tsar.

Under the terms of article 6 governing the surrender of Alexandria, all the man-made and natural wonders collected by the Institut de France were to be handed over to the allies. The French attempted to evade the agreement on the ground that the collections were all private property. For example, General Menou claimed that the Rosetta stone, discovered by the French in 1798 when repairing the ruined Fort St Julien, and now in his house in Alexandria was his. Turner, who was a fine antiquary, was ordered by Lord Hutchinson to negotiate on the subject. After much correspondence and several meetings with Menou it was decided that, owing to the manner in which the French had cared for the collection of insects and animals, these should be retained by their present owners. However, Lord Hutchinson, 'with his usual zeal for science', in Turner's words, insisted that the French hand over all antiquities and Arabian manuscripts. This decision provoked the French into breaking the cases and removing the protecting coverings of many of their precious artefacts. Turner went with a party of gunners, the first British soldiers to enter Alexandria, and a 'devil' cart to transport the Rosetta stone from Menou's house amid the jeers of the French officers and men. Having seen the remains of more ancient Egyptian sculpture being taken aboard the *Madras*, Admiral Sir Richard Bickerton's ship, Turner embarked with the Rosetta stone, determined to share its fate, aboard an Egyptian frigate that had been captured in Alexandria harbour. In February 1802 Turner landed at Portsmouth and persuaded the secretary of state for war and the colonies, Lord Hobart, the future earl of Buckinghamshire, that the stone should initially be sent to the Society of Antiquaries. It resided there for much of the year before being deposited in the British Museum. In January 1803 Turner sent the Society of Antiquaries a version of the inscription on Pompey's Pillar, taken by Captain Dundas, Royal Engineers. He later contributed several more articles to the society's journal *Archaeologia*.

In July 1803 Turner was appointed assistant quartermaster-general to the forces at home and on 25 June 1804 he was made a brigadier-general on the home staff. In April 1807 he was transferred as a brigadier-general to the staff in South America; he embarked on 24 June and returned home the following spring. Turner was promoted to major-general on 25 April 1808, and commanded a brigade in London until 1813. He was deputy secretary at Carlton House under Colonel Sir John McMahon for several years. He was appointed colonel of the 19th foot or 1st Yorkshire (North Riding) regiment on 27 April 1811 after a transfer from the colonelcy of the Cape regiment, which he had recently held. He was promoted to lieutenant-general on 4 June 1813. On 4 May 1814 he was made a DCL of Oxford while attending to the Archduchess Catherine of Russia. On 28 July, having attended to the duchess of Oldenburg during her visit to England, he was knighted by the prince regent. On 12 June he had been appointed lieutenant-governor of Jersey and commander of the troops there, a post he held until March 1816. In 1820 Turner was made a KCH and in 1827 a GCH.

In 1825 Turner was appointed governor of Bermuda, a post in which he remained for six years. On 22 July 1830 he was promoted general, and on his return from Bermuda he was appointed a groom of the bedchamber in the royal household. He died on 7 May 1843 at his home, Gowray, Jersey.

R. H. VETCH, *rev.* S. KINROSS

Sources J. Haydn, *The book of dignities: containing rolls of the official personages of the British empire* (1851) · R. E. Dupuy and T. N. Dupuy, *The Collins encyclopedia of military history*, 4th edn (1993) · J. S. Watson, *The reign of George III* (1960) · *GM*, 2nd ser., 19 (1843), 653 · *Military Annual* (1846) · J. Philippart, ed., *The royal military calendar*, 3rd edn, 5 vols. (1820) · PRO, War Office records · A. B. Rodger, *The war of the second coalition: 1798–1801, a strategic commentary* (1964) · R. Muir, *Britain and the defeat of Napoleon, 1807–1815* (1996)

Turner, Victor Witter (1920–1983), social anthropologist, was born on 28 May 1920 at 13 Riverside Road, Cathcart, Glasgow, the only child of Captain Norman Turner (1895–1975), electrical engineer and officer in the Royal Flying Corps during the First World War, and Violet, *née* Witter (1889–1966), repertory actress and a founder of the Scottish National Players. Turner was baptized into the Congregational church and received his earliest education at the Montessori School, Belmont Crescent, Glasgow (1925–6), before going to the Glasgow Academy (1926–31). When his parents divorced, the eleven-year-old Turner accompanied his mother to live with her parents, who had retired from Glasgow to Bournemouth: Arthur Witter (d. 1935) was English; his wife, Jeanie Witter (*née* Johnston), Scottish. Turner's estrangement from his father was to be lifelong. While attending Bournemouth grammar school (1931–8) Turner developed interests in Latin and Greek classical literatures and in poetry writing, which were reflected in his initial choice of degree subject.

Turner studied English language and literature at University College, London, from 1939 until drafted for war service in 1941. As a conscientious objector and noncombatant, he volunteered between 1941 and 1946 to serve in 104 bomb disposal squad, 8 company, Royal Engineers. On 30 January 1943 he married Edith Lucy Brocklesby (Edie) Davis (b. 1921), with whom he had four sons and one surviving daughter. They established their first home in a Gypsy caravan outside Rugby, where he was based. Turner's earliest publications (1943–4) were poems published in the magazine *Oasis*, which he helped to start with a wartime friend, John Bate (E. Turner, *Bibliography*; private information).

By the time he returned to University College in 1946 Turner had resolved to become an anthropologist and transferred into the department of anthropology which had been established in the previous year by Daryll Forde. After graduating in 1949, he moved that year, initially as a research assistant, to the University of Manchester, where Max Gluckman was establishing an outstanding centre of anthropological research with particular interests in central and southern Africa. The left-leaning ethos of the place would have been conducive to Turner's communist beliefs. Between 1950 and 1954 Turner was a research officer of the Rhodes–Livingstone Institute—an appointment arranged by Gluckman, who encouraged him to research among the Ndembu, a branch of the Lunda people of Zambia (then Northern Rhodesia), on account of their complex ritual life. Research carried out between December 1950 and February 1952 and between May 1953 and June 1954 was written up in a series of publications about the Ndembu that established Turner's early reputation as an outstanding fieldworker and ethnographer.

In 1955 Turner completed the doctorate subsequently published as *Schism and Continuity in an African Society: a Study of Ndembu Village Life* (1957). The book's extended 'social dramas'—units of disharmonic social process—illustrated and explained the recurrent processes, to do with matrilineal descent and choice of residence, that lay behind the splitting of Ndembu village communities. By systematically exploring the phases of social drama (norms breached, mounting crisis, redress to limit that crisis, and recognition of the new outcome) Turner reinvigorated the Manchester school's existing concern with disputes and their resolution by embedding these processes in extended and lively case studies. Having resigned from the British Communist Party in 1957 (Deflem, 4), in May 1958 Turner was received into the Catholic church:

> After many years as an agnostic and monistic materialist I learnt from the Ndembu that ritual and its symbolism are not merely epiphenomena or disguises of deeper social and psychological processes, but have ontological value, in some way related to man's condition as an evolving species, whose evolution takes place principally through its cultural innovations. (*Revelation and Divination*, 31)

Studies of ritual processes predominated in Turner's ensuing publications. His interest in local exegesis was evident in his celebrated portrait of a key informant: 'Muchona

the Hornet' (1959). However, Turner's unwillingness to restrict symbolic analysis to the terms of conscious local models was apparent from the essays on the symbolism of Ndembu rituals of initiation and affliction written between 1958 and 1966 that were collected, together with 'Muchona', in *The Forest of Symbols: Aspects of Ndembu Ritual* (1967). Among the most influential ethnographies written by the outstanding generation of social anthropologists trained immediately after the Second World War, *The Forest of Symbols* renewed symbolic analysis in anthropology and provided an important step towards Turner's own later work. Turner (who described himself as a 'comparative symbologist') argued that dominant symbols condense diverse meanings that cluster around two poles: the physiological and the normative. For instance, the white sap of a tree may evoke both maternal nurturance and the more abstract ideas of matrilineal solidarity and dispute. Turner's discussion of the 'liminal' period in rites of passage that had been famously analysed by Arnold van Gennep (1909)—whom Turner read in 1961, and again in 1963 (E. Turner, 'From Ndembu to Broadway', 7–8)—as an extended period 'betwixt and between' formal statuses, highlighted the ambiguities, paradoxes, and confusion of customary categories universally typical of liminal status. Turner noted that there existed an authoritative relation between neophytes and their instructors, but among neophytes relations were commonly egalitarian.

Composition of the essays in *The Forest of Symbols* straddled Turner's move from the UK to the USA. After appointment as a fellow of the Center for Advanced Behavioral Sciences at Palo Alto in California 1961–2, while he was working on *The Drums of Affliction* (1968), Turner left the University of Manchester (where since gaining his doctorate he had been successively Simon research fellow 1957–9, lecturer, 1959–61, and senior lecturer, 1962–3) to join the anthropology department of Cornell University as professor (1964–8). This was a particularly productive period, recognized by the award of the Rivers memorial medal of the Royal Anthropological Institute in 1965: aside from completing *The Forest of Symbols* and *The Drums of Affliction*, Turner accepted an invitation to deliver the Lewis Henry Morgan lectures at the University of Rochester in April 1966. The ensuing publication, *The Ritual Process: Structure and Anti-Structure* (1969), demonstrated his use of Ndembu analysis as a springboard to universal concerns. The first half of the book, roughly corresponding to the lectures delivered, begins with an intensive analysis of an Ndembu women's fertility ritual; initially through other Ndembu case studies, next in comparative sub-Saharan terms, Turner proceeds to argue the co-presence in African societies of two forms of sociality corresponding to the dictates of social structure and to those of 'communitas'—an egalitarian repudiation of structure. In pre-industrial societies communitas is particularly—but not solely—associated with liminal states. The remainder of *The Ritual Process* explores forms of communitas in more complex societies: 'Together [structure and communitas] make up one stream of life; the one affluent supplying power, the other alluvial fertility' (*Ritual Process*, 128, Penguin [Pelican] edition, 1974).

The linked concepts of communitas (based in shared humanity) and the 'liminoid' (times and spaces outside normal social process) energized Turner's later works. Between 1968 and 1977, when professor of social thought and anthropology on the University of Chicago's 'Committee on Social Thought', Turner researched for and collected the essays published as *Dramas, Fields, and Metaphors: Symbolic Action in Human Society* (1974). His interests ranged widely from pilgrimage sites in Mexico, Ireland, and England—presented as functional equivalents of rites of passage in less complex societies—to the historical production of myth and symbol in medieval England and during the Mexican Revolutionary War.

From 1977 until his death in Charlottesville, Virginia, on 18 December 1983, following a second heart attack, Turner was William R. Kenan professor of anthropology and religion at the University of Virginia. Travelling widely, he pursued his interests in theatre and performance studies, in pilgrimage, and in the 'liminoid' in complex, postindustrial societies—for which he sought a neurological as well as social basis. Some of these later works were written jointly with his wife, Edith L. Turner, whom Turner had never failed to acknowledge as an influence and co-worker in earlier writings. After a requiem mass at Holy Comforter Church, Charlottesville, on 21 December, Victor Turner was cremated at Harrisonburg, Virginia. At home, family and friends re-enacted a 'full-scale Ndembu funeral for a tribal chief … with drums, masked dancers, ritual, and large quantities of beer and spirits' (Turner and Turner, 16; Willis). Turner's ashes were placed on the peak of the island of Barra, Scotland, the home of his mother's McNeil ancestors. His wife survived him.

RICHARD FARDON

Sources H. G. Barnard, 'Victor Witter Turner: a bibliography (1952–1975)', *Anthropologica*, new ser., 27/1–2 (1985), 207–33 · M. Deflem, 'Ritual, anti-structure, and religion: a study of Victor Turner's processual symbolic analysis', *Journal for the Scientific Study of Religion*, 30/1 (1991), 1–25 · M. Douglas, *Royal Anthropological Institute News*, 61 (1984), 11 · A. Edwards, 'V. W. Turner: a pathbreaker in the forest of symbols', *Clergy Review*, 57 (Jan–June 1972), 410–18 · P. L. McLaren, 'A tribute to Victor Turner (1920–83)', *Anthropologica*, new ser., 27/1–2 (1985), 17–22 · F. E. Manning, 'Victor Witter Turner: a bibliography (1975–1986)', *Anthropologica*, new ser., 27/1–2 (1985), 235–9 · R. Schechner, 'Victor Turner's last adventure', *Anthropologica*, new ser., 27/1–2 (1985), 190–206 · L. E. Sullivan, 'Victor W. Turner (1920–83)', *History of Religions*, 24/2 (1984), 160–63 · E. L. Turner, 'Bibliography of the works of Victor Turner', unpublished typescript · E. L. Turner, 'Vic Turner: biography, influences, interests', unpublished typescript, 1983–4; rev. 1998 · E. L. Turner, 'Prologue: from Ndembu to Broadway', in V. Turner, *On the edge of the bush: anthropology as experience*, ed. E. L. B. Turner (Tucson, 1985), 1–15 · E. L. Turner, 'Prologue: exploring the trail', in V. Turner, *Blazing the trail: way marks in the exploration of symbols* (Tucson, 1992), ix–xxi · E. Turner and F. Turner, 'Victor Turner as we remember him', *Anthropologica*, new ser., 27/1–2 (1985), 11–16 · V. W. Turner, *Schism and continuity in an African society: a study of Ndembu village life* (1957) · A. van Gennep, *The rites of passage* (1960) · R. Willis, 'Victor Witter Turner (1920–83)', *Africa*, 54/4 (1984), 73–5 · private information (2004) [Matthew Engelke] · M. Engelke, 'An interview with Edith Turner', *Current Anthropology*, 41/5 (2000), 843–52 · b. cert.

Turner, Walter James Redfern (1889–1946), poet and literary critic, was born on 13 October 1889 at Melbourne, Victoria, Australia, where his father, Walter James Turner (1857–1900), was a well-known figure and served as organist of the pro-cathedral. His mother, Alice May Watson, was also a capable musician; and Noel Mewton-Wood, the pianist, was his nephew. The death of Turner's younger brother on 23 October 1899 caused a violent shock which afterwards gave rise to a personal mythology which emerges in several of his books and poems, including the famous 'Romance'. He was educated at Carlton state school and Scotch College, Melbourne; afterwards, he had a single year at the School of Mines and then joined the Melbourne office of an export–import firm. He left Australia in March 1907, determined to create a career for himself as a writer in London. He worked in Dresden, Germany, from 1908; during this period he travelled in France, Italy, Austria, and South Africa. He returned to England in July 1914 and began writing reviews for the *Musical Standard* and, from 1915, for the *New Statesman*.

Turner enlisted in 1916 and served with the Royal Garrison Artillery, where, to his lasting surprise, he rose to the rank of captain. But he never saw fighting in France and continued to write poetry. *The Hunter and other Poems* was published in 1916 and Edward Marsh included his poems in *Georgian Poetry, 1916–17*. He emerged from the war a recognized poet and member of the Georgian group. Among his closest friends at this time were Siegfried Sassoon and Ralph Hodgson. On 5 April 1918 he married Delphine Marguerite (d. 1951), daughter of Gabriel Dubuis, a scientific and medical inventor. They had no children. Turner was to have several extramarital relationships, the most important of which was with Cynthia Saxon Noble, for whom he contemplated divorcing his wife.

After the war Turner resumed his journalistic career. He was an influential music critic of the *New Statesman* until 1940 and theatre critic of the *London Mercury* from 1919 to 1923; he served as literary editor of the *Daily Herald* from 1920 to 1923 when it was under the idealistic management of George Lansbury, and was literary editor of *The Spectator* from 1942 until his death in 1946. He led the onslaught against what he perceived as sterile theatrical conventions and sought a new movement in theatre. This attitude influenced his own satiric comedy *The Man who Ate the Popomack* (1922). Only three of his plays were publicly performed, but fourteen others survive in manuscript and testify to his devotion to the theatre. His forthrightness made him some enemies, including Lady Ottoline Morrell, who never forgave him for his representation of her in *The Aesthetes* (1927).

All through the inter-war years Turner was immensely prolific, publishing a volume of poems every two or three years, several minor works of musical criticism, and studies of Beethoven, Mozart, Wagner, and Berlioz. He was one of a group of friends, which included Mark Gertler and Professor John Nicolas Mavrogordato, much addicted to conversation. During the thirties his friendship with W. B. Yeats also ripened. Yeats, who delighted in his poetry, included a large selection in the *Oxford Book of Modern Verse*, though it was often considered unfashionable; despite his experiments with free metrical form and colloquial idiom, his poetry was too lyrical and unintellectual for prevailing tastes. Through Yeats, Turner met the poet Dorothy Wellesley and with her was associated in the wartime launching of the successful Britain in Pictures series of which he was the general editor. The autobiographical *Blow for Balloons* and *Henry Airbubble* appeared in 1935 and 1936: with their wit, poetic penetration, fantasy, and occasional cussedness they perfectly reflect the author's own nature.

The last years of Turner's life, from 1939 to 1946, proved busy, as he engaged in a remarkable diversity of activities. He wrote a large number of poems, most of which appeared in his last volume, *Fossils of a Future Time?* (1946), wrote short stories for *Fables, Parables and Plots* (1943), translated French and German poetry, wrote numerous reviews, and was very active in radio broadcasting. He died, after a cerebral haemorrhage, on 18 November 1946 at his home in Hammersmith Terrace, Chiswick, Middlesex.   JACQUETTA HAWKES, *rev.* SAYONI BASU

Sources W. McKenna, *W. J. Turner: poet and music critic* (1990) · *The Times* (20 Nov 1946) · A. M. Holcomb, 'Scott and Turner', *Scott bicentenary essays* [Edinburgh 1971], ed. A. Bell (1973), 199–212 · W. H. Wilde, J. Hooton, and B. Andrews, *The Oxford companion to Australian literature*, 2nd edn (1994) · C. W. F. McKenna, 'Turner, Walter James Redfern', *AusDB*, vol. 12

Archives NRA, corresp. and literary papers · Temple University, Philadelphia, Paley Library, corresp. and papers | BL, letters to S. S. Koteliansky, Add. MS 48974 · BL, corresp. with League of Dramatists, Add. MS 63455 · BL, corresp. with Society of Authors, Add. MS 63339 · U. Reading L., letters to George Bell & sons

Likenesses H. Coster, photographs, 1930–39, NPG · E. Kennington, drawing, priv. coll. · W. Nicholson, portrait, priv. coll. · W. Rothenstein, drawing, repro. in W. Rothenstein, *Twenty-four portraits*, 2nd ser. (1923) · G. Spenser, portrait, priv. coll.

Turner, William (1509/10–1568), naturalist and religious controversialist, was born at Morpeth in Northumberland, the son of a tanner of the same name.

Education and early travels In 1526 Turner became a student of Pembroke College, Cambridge, assisted by a 'yearly exhibition' from Thomas, Baron Wentworth. He proceeded BA in 1529–30, was elected a fellow of Pembroke in 1531 and made junior treasurer in 1532; he commenced MA in 1533, before becoming Pembroke's senior treasurer in 1538. A friend of Ridley, and deeply influenced by Latimer, Turner's prominence in Cambridge protestant circles became increasingly risky—the first martyrdoms had already occurred. In 1536 he took deacon's orders, and reputedly commenced itinerant preaching. Yet, in clear contravention of his diaconal vow of chastity, in November 1540 Turner married Jane Alder, daughter of George Alder, a Cambridge alderman. In February 1541 he did not appear to face ecclesiastical court action but fled abroad—accompanied, or soon joined, by his wife.

Receipt of a benevolence from Pembroke College in 1542 suggests that furtherance of his medical studies was one reason for Turner's departure. He travelled up the Rhine and reached north Italy, an acknowledged centre of medical excellence, settling at Ferrara, where there existed a pocket of refugee protestants. Yet it was almost certainly at nearby Bologna that he secured his MD degree, while simultaneously pursuing botanical studies. After about a year at the Italian universities Turner left, travelling via Milan, Como, and Chiavenna, then over the Splügen Pass to Chur in Switzerland.

In terms of plant locations and bird sightings, the journey is meticulously recorded, but the virtual absence of marital references supports the contention that his wife had remained in the Rhineland. On reaching Zürich, Turner met Conrad Gesner, the greatest of mid-sixteenth-century naturalists, with whom he established a lifelong rapport. His sojourn in Zürich may well be doctrinally significant, for this had been the city of Zwingli, the continental reformer whose views, together with those of Bucer, Turner found most congenial. Two decades later it was to Zwingli's successor, Heinrich Bullinger, that Turner and his kindred spirits in the vestiarian controversy were to appeal. Turner's return to the Rhineland, to spend time in Basel, Bonn, and Cologne, was followed by the arrival of sisters to his son Peter *Turner (1542–1614). These years saw the publication of Turner's first religious polemic, *The Huntyng & Fyndyng out of the Romishe Foxe* (1543). Its principal target, Stephen Gardiner, bishop of Winchester, was to Turner and his fellow protestants the hated focus of their belief that English papists had halted, or even reversed, any trend towards genuine doctrinal reform within the Henrician reformation. In the same year he also published a tract on birds. Despite indifferent health, he earned his living as a practising physician, and it was very probably the wish for a steady income that took him to East Friesland to serve the duke of Emden for 'four full years' (Jones, 16–18). Alongside a naturalist's eager observation of a marshy, seaside ecology, went congenial contact with a fellow exile of Zwinglian persuasions: the Pole John à Lasco. Publication of another anti-Gardiner religious polemic in 1545, and inclusion of Turner's name in a condemnatory royal proclamation of July 1546, explain his cautious delay in returning to England after the death of Henry VIII.

Protestant reformer and churchman Later in 1547 (his growing medical and religious repute being augmented by a Wentworth family connection) Turner became physician and auxiliary chaplain to Protector Somerset, residing at Kew, as well as being MP for Ludgershall in the parliament of 1547–52. In 1549 he published his *Names of Herbes*; yet he complained of lack of time for his botanical studies, and his letters to William Cecil, the protector's secretary, sought preferment in increasingly querulous terms. On 12 February 1550 Turner was collated to the prebend of Botevant at York, but attempts to become provost of Oriel College, Oxford, and president of Magdalen, as part of a struggle to get protestant evangelicals into positions of influence in the university, both went astray. More successful, and, in the eyes of both contemporaries and historians a catalyst for developments of very great doctrinal significance in the early stages of the Edwardian reformation, was Turner's persuasive urging, most notably to Cranmer himself, that the help of continental protestants be secured. He certainly exercised some influence in bringing to England the Zwinglian John à Lasco, but by now suspicions that residual papist interests were blocking his advancement brought Turner near to paranoia. Increasing disillusion accompanied the fall of Somerset and an unedifying contemporary account of his participation in a sharing out of ducal household goods. But Cecil had remained principal secretary to the council, and on 24 March 1551 Turner was presented by the king to the deanery of Wells. Perhaps predictably he found it difficult to eject the former incumbent, John Goodman, from his house and to gain control of the landed property. The Wells chapter perhaps placated him by granting a dispensation to go on preaching (and also perhaps botanical) tours, and the first part of his great *Herball* appeared in 1551. The new dean now engaged once more in religious controversy, but it was as late as 21 December 1552 that Bishop Ridley ordained him priest. However, Queen Mary's accession in July 1553 led to a second period of exile.

Those protestant leaders who remained in England, some marked for martyrdom, did not reproach those who chose exile; Turner himself acknowledged receipt of help from the imprisoned Ridley. This second exile was spent at Cologne, Worms, and Weissenburg. Turner continued on the second part of his *Herbal* as well as on an extended essay on fishes (printed by Gesner in his *Historia animalium*) and one on medicinal baths. But his principal publications during this era were *The Huntyng of the Romyshe Wolfe* and *A New Booke of Spirituall Physik*: the first another anti-Gardiner diatribe, the second by far the fullest exposition of Turner's chagrin at England's failure to establish the social values and ideals of a Christian commonwealth. After the death of Mary Tudor, Turner's reoccupation of his deanery was neither smooth nor rapid. In September 1559 he preached at the prestigious location of Paul's Cross, but not until June 1560 do the Wells Cathedral records note his restoration—without the acquiescence of the sitting occupant. The proceedings of a commission held up formal confirmation for a year or so, though Queen Elizabeth had already sanctioned permission to preach elsewhere.

Turner's remaining years were productive of scholarly publication, notably parts 2 and 3 of his *Herball* and his very much shorter books on wines, baths, and 'triacles'. But the religious controversialist was not yet done. Forthright expression of his distaste for what he deemed the rags and trappings of a papist prelacy involved him in the vestiarian controversy. His commonplace book (rediscovered in 1988 by George Chapman) includes a copy of a letter to Lawrence Humphrey with greetings to Thomas Sampson, like himself, a leading opponent of 'papist' vestments. This issue became a running dispute with Turner's own bishop, Gilbert Berkeley, while Archbishop Parker was not pleased by a report 'that Turner of Wells hath enjoined a common adulterer to do his penance in a square priest's cap' (BL, Lansdowne MS 8, fols. 140–41).

Meanwhile, sniping protests from those within the diocese who saw him not as scholar but as carpet-bagger persisted until Turner's death. In 1566 he was among those who remained obdurate on the issue of ritual uniformity after examination by ecclesiastical commissioners; Berkeley complained of him both to Cecil and to Parker himself. Turner's last years were in fact spent at his home in Crutched Friars, London, where he died on 7 July 1568. He was buried in St Olave's, Hart Street, on the 9th.

Naturalist and physician Turner probably saw himself as a herbalist rather than as a botanist in any modern sense. Yet identification as 'the father of English botany and of ornithology' (Hoeniger and Hoeniger, 21) constitutes his greatest claim to real eminence. His childhood faculty for acute observation continued and developed at Cambridge. His *Libellus de re herbaria novus* (1538), purportedly 'a book on herbalism' (title-page, 42), is undoubtedly significant in the emergence of botanical studies. Habitats identified therein are all English, but his much longer *Names of Herbes* (1549), recognized as a classic in the history of English botany, reflects the unremitting application of a questing and perceptive intelligence throughout the years of exile, with many entries for Germany, Italy, East Friesland, and the Low Countries. Notably, Turner's suggestions of English names include some which—like yellow loosestrife and goat's-beard—were destined to endure.

Parts 1 (1551) and 2 (1562) of the massive *Herball*, Turner's lasting memorial, were in concept one book, with part 3 an addendum (1568). Plant descriptions were now embellished by many high-quality woodcut illustrations, some four hundred of those used being by Leonhard Fuchs. Locations identified extended from Portland in Dorset to Venice, Lake Como, the Alps, East Friesland, and the Rhine. Turner's detailed descriptions (as of the way in which the roots of orobanche may strangle clover) are again accompanied by English names. These range in felicity from the inspired suggestion that *Amara dulcis* 'may be called Bitter Sweet' to the unattractive proffering of 'Calf's Snout' for antirrhinum (part 3, 2; part 1, 49). Once more, social and culinary comments enliven his writing: near Bonn, when 'the Fieldfares feed only of Junipers' berries, the people eat the Fieldfares undrawn with guts and all because they are full of the berries' (part 2, 25). Old wives' tales are not always denounced: the legend that mandrake 'doth … rise of the seed of man that falleth from him that is hanged' gets short shrift, but the notion of *Nepeta cataria* as a feline aphrodisiac 'about the time of their catterwauling' is cautiously recorded (part 2, 45–6; part 1, 102–3). Yet although the *Herball* was a major landmark in the development of English botany, with a range and accuracy of enquiry far outstripping Turner's predecessors, it was also primarily a physician's guide to herbs. Its author made no attempt to consider the relationship or classification of plants in any scientific way.

A similar reservation applies to *Turner on Birds* (1544), which does not demonstrate the modern zoologist's technique. Yet present-day specialists are virtually unanimous in their recognition that it is as a pioneer also of ornithology that Turner stands alone in sixteenth-century England. His work in identification and nomenclature produced several dozen 'firsts'. His striking and evocative imagery ranges from the nest building of the robin in his Northumberland youth to the spectacle of storks nesting on chimney tops in Germany, the detailed description of the savage activities of the shrike (amply justifying the sobriquet 'butcher bird'), the vehemence of the hedge sparrow's late evensong, and the remarkable rapacity of the red kite—then still abundant and 'wont to snatch food out of children's hands, in our cities and towns' (*Turner on Birds*, 157, 55, 119–21, 137, 117). Finally, brief mention must be made of 'Turner on fishes', printed verbatim in his friend Conrad Gesner's *Historia animalium* (1558). Once more, his observations extend from his native Northumbria to the Portland peninsula, the Thames above London, Lower Germany, and East Friesland.

With his prestigious Italian qualification augmented further by an Oxford DM, Turner once described himself as 'a physician delighting in the study of sacred literature' (Robinson, 2.126). His double role in Somerset's household was typical of his era. While he published nothing by way of general medical exposition, the herbalism of his major works was in mid-Tudor England a study subordinate to that of medicine. The therapeutic qualities of certain plants commended sometimes anticipate the modern herbalist's identification of such as feverfew or eyebright, but caution is urged in using 'the juice of the Black Poppy, called opium' (*Names of Herbes*, 158; Turner, *Herball*, part 2, 29–30, 77v). Turner also penned three lesser works of some medical relevance. Most notable was his *New Boke of the Natures and Properties of All Wines* (1568), written as an appreciative consumer as well as medical adviser. In this work Turner, a long-term sufferer from the stone, assesses the properties of Rhenish wines in this connection, but also considers other vintages. Jointly published was a purportedly corrected version of his *Booke of the Natures and Vertues of Triacles* (or ointments), complete with professional warnings not to make use of any such 'rashly and unadvisedly' on the advice of some 'prating runagate peddler' (F.viii–G.i). Published earlier, in 1562, was Turner's survey *Of the natures and properties aswell of the bathes in England as of other bathes in Germany and Italy*. The many citations of Turner's personal experiences as a physician range from statistics of the frightening efficacy of some purgatives to the case of the sick beggars who spurned his curative offers—'for they had much liever be sick still with ease and idleness, than to be whole … to earn honestly their living' (*Spirituall Physik*, I.b–2).

Religious writings Turner's achievement in translations did not match Tyndale's, nor his doctrinal impact that of Cranmer, nor his preaching that of Latimer, yet all these, together with his anti-Gardiner polemics and his participation in the vestiarian controversy, make him a significant figure. Most crucially, Turner commended scriptural authority as the sole touchstone of faith. His translations, of Joachim von Watt, entitled *Of ye Olde God & the Newe*

(1534), and *The Olde Learnyng & the Newe* from Urbanus Rhegius (1537), exemplify his identification of the Roman church as guilty of doctrinal innovation. Their Swiss and German provenance establish (alongside residual Wycliffite Lollardy) the Lutheran, and above all Zwinglian, influences on Turner's doctrinal development. The first of his polemics, *The Huntynge & Fyndyng out of the Romishe Fox* (1543), excoriates such as enjoin creeping to the cross, image-worship, the retention of 'vestments and copes, incense, and altars', and who condemn the marriage of priests while condoning their resorting to concubines. Lamentably, monastic spoil has not been directed to aiding poor Christian folk or 'preachers of the Word of God'—who are in fact sometimes put to death (A.vi–B.viii.b). Oh that Henry VIII, 'supreme governor', would root out the Romish beasts still within the church in England (title-page, S.ii–iiii). Turner's exposition of protestant teachings alternates with sometimes scurrilous sexual imagery and coarsely textured abuse—the fact that the diocese of Winchester extended into Southwark enabled him to present his *bête noire* as 'Steven, master steward of the stews' (F.i–iv). Alas, two years later, *The Rescuynge of the Romishe Fox* depicts 'the banished fox of Rome' declaring that, although a weeping Gardiner has cropped his ears, his body and in particular 'his gorgeous and fair tail' remain; even his ears will grow once again 'when all the gospellers are once slain' (title-page, A.ii–iv).

In Turner's *Examination of the Masse and of that Kind of Priesthood* this rite implies (1548), 'Mistress Mass' derides 'the Supper that these fellows speak of [as] but a memorial of Christ's death', but is in turn reproved that 'your chaplains are bloody sacrificers [who] kill Christ a thousand times in one year'. Surely Edward VI, the young Josiah, will now purge the church 'and try with the touchstone of God's word' (A.v–vi). Edward's death cut short such hopes. In 1555 *The Huntynge of the Romyshe Wolfe* relates how:

> Gardiner my Son which with weeping tears,
> Cut once away quite the tops of mine ears,
> Hath taken for me of late such pain,
> That they are grown and healed again.

A folding print depicts the savage slaughter of Hooper, Cranmer, Ridley, and Latimer, by 'the Wolf of Winchester [and] his fellow bloody Bonner' (A.iii, A.viii–B.i, D.ii, E.i). Yet alongside this are Turner's detailed proposals for changes in church government and administration, including near-democratic lay participation, and for more laudable use of church wealth, which anticipate much of Elizabethan controversy (E.viii–F.iv).

Yet Turner was no congregationalist. Indeed, *Agaynst the poyson of Pelagius, lately renued, and styrred up agayn, by the furious secte of the Annabaptists*, written in 1552 when he was briefly and precariously in favour with the establishment, exemplifies the dread inspired therein by extremists. Nevertheless, he was personally reluctant to invoke the punishment enacted by the civil power. He had exerted indirect doctrinal influence in persuading Cranmer to bring John à Lasco to England. Later, ill health and death prevented Turner from contributing more to one last action in the 1560s against what to him was residual popery. The title of *Poyson of Pelagius* and several passages therein exemplify his transference of medical imagery to religious issues. Turner's *New Booke of Spirituall Physik* (1555) extends the device to social and economic as well as religious problems, by way of a protracted analogy between the ills of the human body and those of the body politic. Enjoining morality in all social relationships, it demonstrates his sympathy with commonwealth ideals, combined with a traditional approach to a hierarchical society, but also his bitter realization that the expected fruits of the crown's appropriation of church wealth had turned sour.

The man and his achievement Alongside Turner's considerable academic endowments went an idiosyncratic personality. At Wells, he trained his little dog to leap up and snatch off the corner-cap of a bishop at table. A handsome and witty man, he did not suffer fools gladly. Eager for preferment, he scorned the diplomatic niceties required for its attainment, then became querulous with disappointment. The interplay of his diverse—perhaps distracting—interests gives an added dimension to much of Turner's writing. But his often picturesquely evocative botanical descriptions contrast ill with such scurrility as the identification of Gardiner as one who 'was long with the whore of Babylon and brought the Romish pox into England again' (*Spirituall Physik*, 76–7). By profession a medical practitioner, his herbalist interests expanded into making him a naturalist of the first rank, yet his most combative endeavours came in the field of religion, where his permanent mark was not so great. None the less, while his role of priest–physician was then quite usual, his achievement of considerable eminence alike as man of medicine, botanist, ornithologist, and religious controversialist assuredly was not. He died, aged fifty-eight, disappointed in lack of progress toward a church which should be 'a Commonwealth of Christians'; but his stature in laying the foundations both of botany and of ornithology remains undisputed.   WHITNEY R. D. JONES

Sources W. Turner, *The first and seconde partes of the herbal of William Turner doctor in phisick ... with the third parte* (1568) · W. Turner, *The names of herbes*, facsimile reprint, 1965 (1549) · *Turner on birds* (1544); A. H. Evans, ed. and trans. (1903) · W. Turner, *The huntyng & fyndyng out of the Romishe foxe* (1543) · W. Turner, *The rescuynge of the Romishe fox* (1545) · W. Turner, *The huntyng of the Romyshe wolfe* (1555) · W. Turner, *The examination of the masse* (1548–9) · W. Turner, *A new booke of spirituall physik for dyverse diseases of the nobilite and gentlemen of Englande* (1555) · W. Turner, *Agaynst the poyson of Pelagius* (1552) · W. R. D. Jones, *William Turner: Tudor naturalist, physician and divine* (1988) · C. E. Raven, *English naturalists from Neckam to Ray* (1947) · E. J. Carlson, 'The marriage of William Turner', *Historical Research*, 65 (1992), 336–9 · R. Morrice, 'The Puritan Controversy', DWL, A, B, and C · MSS, Cathedral Library, Wells, Ledger E · W. Turner, 'Commonplace book', 2 vols., Central Library, Bath · PRO, PROB 11/50, Section 14 (p. 105, lower) · G. T. L. Chapman, 'William Turner of Morpeth', in W. Turner, *A new herball*, ed. G. T. L. Chapman and M. N. Tweddle (1989) · B. D. Jackson, *A life of William Turner*, reprint (1965) · C. Hughes, 'John Bradford and William Turner', *Bulletin of the John Rylands University Library*, 66 (1983–4), 104–38 · J. Bale, *Illustrium Maioris Britannie scriptorum ... summarium* (1548) · Bale, *Cat.* · *The acts and monuments of John Foxe*, ed. S. R. Cattley, 8 vols. (1837–41) · *DNB* · Cooper, *Ath. Cantab.*, vol. 1 · *Calendar of the manuscripts of the dean and chapter of Wells*, 2 vols., HMC, 12 (1907–14) · J. Vadianus [J. von Watt], *A worke entytled of ye olde god [and] the newe*, trans. W. Turner (1534) · Urbanus Rhegius, *The olde learnyng & the newe*, trans. W. Turner (1537/48) · W. Turner, *Libellus de re herbaria novus*, Ray facsimile, 1965 (1538) · W. Turner, *The natures and properties as well as of the bathes in England as of other bathes in Germany and Italy* (1562) · W. Turner, *A new boke of the natures and properties of all wines ... whereunto is annexed the booke of the natures and vertues of triacles* (1568); repr. as *A book of wines ... together with a modern English version of the text*, ed. S. V. Larkey (1941) · Wood, *Ath. Oxon.*, new edn, 1.361–4 · BL, Lansdowne MS 8 · *The diary of Henry Machyn, citizen and merchant-taylor of London, from AD 1550 to AD 1563*, ed. J. G. Nichols, CS, 42 (1848) · *The works of Nicholas Ridley*, ed. H. Christmas, Parker Society, 1 (1841) · H. Robinson, ed. and trans., *The Zurich letters, comprising the correspondence of several English bishops and others with some of the Helvetian reformers, during the early part of the reign of Queen Elizabeth*, 2 vols., Parker Society, 7–8 (1842–5) · C. Gesner, *De raris & admirandis herbis* (1669) · C. Gesner, *Historia animalium* (1558), 4.1294–7 · *The Marprelate tracts, 1588, 1589*, facs. edn (1967) · F. D. Hoeniger and J. F. M. Hoeniger, *The development of natural history in Tudor England* (Charlottesville, VA, [1969]); repr. (1973) · A. Pettegree, *Marian protestantism: six studies* (1996)

Archives Bath Central Library, commonplace book · Wells Cathedral, MSS, ledger E | BL, Lansdowne MSS 2 (42, 63, 75), 3 (4), 7 (78), 8 (3, 47), 10 (10), 107 (1) · PRO, SP Dom. Edw. VI, 5 (12); 7 (32); 8 (56); 9 (52); 10 (20, 34); 11 (14); 13 (1, 4, 19)

Wealth at death see PRO, PROB 11/50, Section 14 (p. 105 lower)

Turner, William (1651/2–1740), singer and composer, is thought to have been born in Oxford, the son of Charles Turner, cook of Pembroke College, Oxford. The cathedral disbursement books do not support Anthony Wood's claim that at the Restoration Turner became a chorister at Christ Church, Oxford. Instead, he was admitted to a similar position at the Chapel Royal, and at some time before January 1664 collaborated with his fellow choristers Pelham Humfrey and John Blow in the composition of the so-called 'Club' anthem, 'I will alway give thanks' (Turner contributed the middle section, a bass solo).

Turner's voice had broken by Lady day 1666, when he was discharged into the care of Henry Cooke, the master of the Chapel Royal choristers. On 28 November 1667 he became master of the choristers at Lincoln Cathedral, a post which he held (at least nominally) until 7 June 1670. He quickly developed a fine high countertenor voice, and on 11 October 1669 returned to the Chapel Royal as a gentleman of the chapel (succeeding Edward Coleman). A further court appointment—to the lutes and voices of the King's private musick—followed on 15 July 1672.

For much of the 1670s Turner combined his court duties with work as a theatre singer and composer. In the summer of 1674 he was excused from weekday services in the Chapel Royal (then resident at Windsor Castle) so that he could perform in Thomas Shadwell's *The Tempest*, and in 1675 he sang the leading roles in John Crowne's masque *Calisto*. Turner provided incidental music and songs for four productions by Shadwell and Thomas D'Urfey between 1675 and 1677. Several other songs and catches by Turner were published in anthologies during the 1670s and 1680s. He joined the Corporation of Musick of Westminster at some time before July 1676, and served as warden between June 1677 and June 1678.

By 1685 Turner had established his position as one of the leading court musicians: he contributed two anthems to

James II's coronation service, and also composed the 1685 St Cecilia's day ode ('Tune the viol, touch the lute', to a text by Nahum Tate); none of these is now extant. Throughout the next decade he was a regular countertenor soloist in court odes by John Blow, Giovanni Draghi, and Henry Purcell. Outside the court, Turner now abandoned theatre work in favour of additional church appointments: he became a vicar-choral at St Paul's Cathedral on 7 February 1687 and a lay vicar at Westminster Abbey in 1699, and retained these posts, and his Chapel Royal position, until his death.

In July 1696 Turner received the Cambridge degree of MusD, and a Latin poem written in celebration of the occasion declared that only Purcell was more learned. This event heralded a final creative outburst. Turner provided music for the annual St Cecilia's day celebrations in 1696 (a Te Deum and Jubilate) and 1697 (an anthem, 'The king shall rejoice', which was also performed at an elaborate charity concert staged by Weedon in Stationers' Hall on 31 January 1702). In 1698 Turner composed the birthday ode for Princess Anne, which received a second performance—with other 'New Vocal and Instrumental Musick' by Turner—at a concert in York Buildings in May of that year.

The date of Turner's marriage is unknown, but was probably during the early 1670s. His will (dated 4 January 1728) lists five surviving children born to him and his wife, Elizabeth (b. 1654/5). The youngest, Ann Turner *Robinson [see under Robinson, John], was a soprano soloist in several of Handel's productions and married John *Robinson (organist of Westminster Abbey from 1727). Elizabeth died on 9 January 1740, aged eighty-five. Turner himself died aged eighty-eight on 13 January 1740 at King Street, Westminster, and was buried three days later together with his wife in the west cloister of Westminster Abbey.

Turner was an accomplished composer, particularly of sacred music: three services and over forty anthems are extant (the latest dating from c.1705). Two anthems from the period 1670–76 enjoyed widespread popularity (one, 'Lord, thou hast been our refuge', was included in William Boyce's *Cathedral Music*). But most of his church music survives only in manuscripts directly associated with institutions where he worked and in anthologies compiled by colleagues such as Stephen Bing (York Minster, 1/1–8), John Gostling (Bodl. Oxf., T 797–803, 1176–1182; and University of Austin, Texas, Pre-1700 85), and Thomas Tudway (BL, Harley MSS 7339–7341).

Turner's early verse anthems (c.1668–76) display the influence of Matthew Locke, while his later symphony anthems are written in a more overtly Italianate style. His final works were written soon after the opening of the new St Paul's Cathedral, in 1697; their increased scale and rich choral texture were almost certainly a response to the sumptuous acoustic of Wren's new cathedral. Turner was also an important figure in the early development of Anglican (as opposed to metrical) psalmody: five of his chants were published in John Playford's *An Introduction to the Skill of Musick* (1674).

A theoretical treatise, *Sound Anatomiz'd … to which is Added a Discourse Concerning the Abuse of Musick*, by 'William Turner', was published in 1724. It is highly conservative, even arguing against the use of key signatures. However, it is not certain that it was written by the subject of this article. The author, if it is a different William Turner, also composed songs and incidental music for various stage productions (c.1715–18), and may also have edited a 1728 version of Thomas Ravenscroft's *The Whole Book of Psalm-Tunes in Four Parts*.

KERI DEXTER

Sources A. Ashbee and D. Lasocki, eds., *A biographical dictionary of English court musicians, 1485–1714*, 2 (1998), 1103–5 · D. Franklin, 'Turner, William (ii)', *New Grove*, 2nd edn · cathedral disbursement books, Christ Church Oxf., MSS D&C xii.b. 103–107 · M. Tilmouth and R. Ford, 'Turner, William (iii)', *New Grove*, 2nd edn · I. Spink, *Restoration cathedral music, 1660–1714* (1995), 137–45 · D. Burrows, *Handel* (1994), 453 · S. Boyer, 'The cathedral, the city and the crown: a study of the music and musicians of St Paul's Cathedral, 1660 to 1697', PhD diss., University of Manchester, 1999, 425 · *DNB*
Archives York Minster, MS M1 (s)
Wealth at death see will, 4 Jan 1728, PRO, PROB 11/700, sig. 53

Turner, William (1652/3–1701), Church of England clergyman and author, was the son of William Turner of Marbury, Cheshire, where he was born. He received his early education from a private tutor and in 1668 went to live in the house of the eminent nonconformist divine Philip Henry at Broad Oak, Flintshire. There he benefited from Henry's instruction, and acted as tutor to the latter's children, Matthew and Sarah. Turner and Henry forged a 'most entire and affectionate friendship' that was nurtured throughout their lives by means of a 'constant and endearing correspondence' (Henry, 122–3). Turner matriculated at St Edmund Hall, Oxford, on 26 March 1669, aged sixteen. He graduated BA in 1672 and MA in 1675. He later took holy orders, becoming vicar of Walberton, Sussex, in 1680, and rector of Binstead in 1697. He died at Walberton, and was buried there on 6 February 1701, leaving a widow, Magdalen, and a son, William, born on 6 June 1693.

Turner is chiefly known as the author of two works. The first of these, *The History of All Religions in the World*, was a great compendium of all known faiths and was published by John Dunton in octavo in 1695. The book was written with missionary zeal, and was intended to counter the influence of 'Scepticism *and* Atheism *and* Impiety *in the* World' (Turner, *History*, preface). A folio edition of Turner's second well-known work, *A Compleat History of the most Remarkable Providences*, dedicated to John Hall, bishop of Chichester, was printed by Dunton in 1697. This compilation of providential stories that had been sent to Turner 'from divers Parts of the Three Kingdoms' was 'Recommended as useful to *Ministers* in Furnishing *Topicks of Reproof* and *Exhortation*', as well as to laypersons for their own private edification (Turner, *Compleat History*, preface). Turner was described by his publisher as 'a Man of wonderful Moderation and of great Piety' (Dunton, 225). As a preacher, he was 'very serious, laborious and useful' (Tong, 21–2). His unusual generosity regarding the publication of his books was also commendable in an age of hack writers: he 'wou'd not receive a Farthing for his Copy till the Success was known' (Dunton, 225). He was described posthumously by Matthew Henry as a 'very worthy conformist' (Henry, 231–2).   HELEN BERRY

Sources J. Dunton, *The life and errors of John Dunton … written by himself* (1705) · *An account of the life and death of the late Reverend Mr. Matthew Henry*, ed. W. Tong (1716) · J. B. Williams, *Memoirs of the life and character of Mrs Sarah Savage* (1818) · W. Turner, *The history of all religions in the world* (1695) · W. Turner, *A compleat history of the most remarkable providences* (1697) · M. Henry, *The life of the Rev. Philip Henry, A.M.*, ed. J. B. Williams (1825) · Foster, *Alum. Oxon.* · DNB

Turner, William (1714–1794), dissenting minister, was born at Preston, Lancashire, on 5 December 1714, the son of John Turner (1689–1737), dissenting minister, and Hannah (*d.* 1747), daughter of William Chorley of Preston. His father held several ministries successively at Preston, Rivington, Northwich, Wirksworth, and Knutsford, and was active in support of the Hanoverian cause in 1715. Turner was educated at the Findern Academy (1732–6) under Ebenezer Latham and at Glasgow University (1736–7). He served as minister at Allostock, Cheshire, from 1737 to 1746 and was ordained on 7 August 1739. Ill health caused him to discontinue his ministry and to keep a school for eight years, but he returned to the ministry at Congleton, Cheshire, in 1754. On 15 August 1758 he married Mary (1724/5–1784), daughter of John Holland of Mobberley, Cheshire; they had two sons, the elder of whom was William *Turner (1761–1859), Unitarian minister. In April 1761 Turner moved to Wakefield, where he continued as minister to the Westgate Chapel until July 1792. His income was £60 a year, together with a good house, and from 1773 he received an additional annual present or payment of £60. He was provided with an assistant minister in 1790 and an income of £63 p.a. until his retirement in 1792, when he received £50 p.a. and the use of the house for life; Thomas Johnstone, his assistant, was appointed minister on an income of £120 p.a. Turner's Wakefield ministry brought him into close contact with a wealthy and influential congregation that included one MP and several JPs, and possibly Thomas Amory, author of *The Life of John Buncle* and an anti-trinitarian, though Amory's name is not listed among the pew-rent payers at Westgate Chapel. Turner became the intimate friend of Joseph Priestley, minister at Leeds from 1767 to 1773, and Theophilus Lindsey, whom he advised to take a dissenting pulpit upon resigning the Anglican living at Catterick. Lindsey and his wife stayed with the Turners at Wakefield in 1774 on their journey from Catterick to found an avowedly Unitarian congregation in London.

By the 1760s Turner's theological stance had moved from orthodoxy to the unitarianism adopted by Priestley and Lindsey. The chapel at Wakefield, for a congregation founded before 1662, had been opened in 1752 by a minister known to be heterodox, and Turner's congregation there, many of whom were well educated and worldly-wise, were well read in heterodox theology. Turner and his congregation supported the later eighteenth-century movements for ecclesiastical, social, and political reform. He participated in dissenting ordinations in the West Riding and opened the Unitarian Mosley Street Chapel in

Manchester in 1789. He took a leading part in establishing a public library in Wakefield in 1786 and a dispensary in 1787. Turner's manuscript criticisms suggested to Priestley the project of his *Theological Repository*, to which Turner contributed from 1768 to 1771 under the signature 'Virgilius'; Priestley's journal circulated in the book society of Turner's Wakefield congregation. Turner contributed notes, signed 'T', to Priestley's *Harmony of the Evangelists* (2nd edn, 1780), and several of his sermons were published, some posthumously. He subscribed to various theological works, including two copies of Joshua Toulmin's *Memoirs of Faustus Socinus* (1778).

Described by Thomas Belsham as 'learned, liberal and pious' (Belsham, 24), Turner died at his home on 28 August 1794, aged seventy-nine. On his death his house had to be fumigated, and he was buried in the Old Chapel Yard, Westgate End, Wakefield, where his tombstone survives.

ALEXANDER GORDON, *rev.* JOHN GOODCHILD

Sources W. Wood, *A sermon preached on occasion of the death of the Rev. William Turner … To which are added, memoirs of Mr Turner's life and writings* [W. Turner] (1794) · W. Turner, *Lives of eminent Unitarians*, 2 (1843), 336–81 · papers of Westgate Chapel, Wakefield, Local History Study Centre, Wakefield [sermons; publications listing W. Turner as a subscriber; papers relating to libraries, dispensary, etc.] · G. E. Evans, *Vestiges of protestant dissent* (1897), 245–6 · T. Belsham, *Memoirs of the late Reverend Theophilus Lindsey*, 2nd edn (1820), 24 · J. Toulmin, *Memoirs of Faustus Socinus* (1778), 10 · *Protestant Dissenter's Magazine*, 2 (1795), 123–4 · A. Gordon, ed., *Cheshire classis: minutes, 1691–1745* (1919), 84–92, 107–9, 209–10 · J. Hunter, *Familiae minorum gentium*, ed. J. W. Clay, 1, Harleian Society, 37 (1894), 175 · JRL, Turner MSS
Archives JRL, MSS · Local History Study Centre, Wakefield, papers
Likenesses W. Collard, engraving, Local History Study Centre, Wakefield · silhouette, repro. in W. Turner, *Three discourses* (1803)

Turner, William (1761–1859), Unitarian minister, was born on 20 September 1761 at Wakefield, the eldest son of William *Turner (1714–1794), minister at Wakefield, and Mary (1724/5–1784), daughter of John Holland (1690–1770), gentleman, of Mobberley, Cheshire. He was educated first by the Revd Joseph Dawson (1740–1813) of Idle, and then in the well-known school of his uncle, the Revd Philip Holland (1721–1789) of Bolton, Lancashire. In 1777 he entered Warrington Academy, where his principal teachers were John Aikin (1713–1780) and William Enfield (1741–1797). Having left Warrington after Aikin's death, in 1781 he enrolled in the University of Glasgow. The next year he accepted the pulpit of Hanover Square Chapel in Newcastle upon Tyne at a salary of £100, and on 25 September was ordained at a meeting of West Riding ministers at Pudsey.

On 24 July 1784 Turner married his cousin Mary (1759–1797), daughter of Thomas Holland, a Manchester merchant. They had two daughters and five sons, of whom two survived to adulthood: the eldest son, also named William (1788–1853), is noticed below, and Henry Turner (1792–1822), their fourth son, was minister at High Pavement Chapel, Nottingham. After Mary Turner's death, in 1799 Turner married Jane, the youngest daughter of the Revd William Willets (1697–1779), minister at Newcastle under Lyme, Staffordshire; they had no children, and she died on 25 December 1826.

In answering the questions put to him at his ordination, Turner stated beliefs generally consonant with the advanced Unitarianism of his time: the unity of God, the humanity of Jesus, the certainty of the resurrection, the authority of the Bible, and the metaphysical views associated with Joseph Priestley (1733–1804), his father's friend. But, as Turner's principal obituarist (probably John Kenrick) put it, 'the bent of his mind was altogether to the practical and tangible, rather than to the speculative or mysterious' (*Christian Reformer*, new ser., 15, 1859, 455). In some respects he was quite other-worldly, and his susceptibility late in life to pleas for help from persons he did not know, sometimes involving him in considerable financial loss, was a matter of concern to his family. But the uncontroversial doctrinal exposition and sound ethical counsel of his sermons helped to bind his congregation together over sixty years and to ensure the admiration in which he was held throughout the denomination and beyond.

Turner's separately published works were largely devotional aids, occasional pieces, and sermons; in addition, he contributed extensively to periodicals (see provisional list in Harbottle, appx B). When a volume of collected sermons appeared in 1839, Edward Maltby (1770–1859), bishop of Durham, was among the subscribers; responding to criticism for the gesture and stressing his disagreement with Unitarian doctrine, Maltby emphasized co-operation with other denominations in good works, a possibility that Turner admirably exemplified. In 1809 he had helped to found the Auxiliary Bible Society, associated with the British and Foreign Bible Society, and, despite a complaint from the 'high-and-dry' Anglican Henry Handley Norris (1771–1850), he continued as joint secretary until 1831. Deeply committed to the anti-slavery cause, he served as secretary of the short-lived Newcastle Society for the Abolition of the Slave Trade from 1791 to 1793 and was actively involved thirty years later in the Society for Promoting the Gradual Abolition of Slavery.

At Hanover Square, Turner established a vestry library and a Sunday school. From 1785 to 1803, and again in 1813–24, he conducted a school, educating upward of 200 boys. He was a founder of the Newcastle Mechanics' Institute and of the Royal Jubilee School established in 1810 to commemorate the fiftieth anniversary of the accession of George III. Turner had declined an offer to become theological and resident tutor at Manchester College in 1797, but in 1808 became visitor to the college, delivering an address every year at the close of session until the college's return from York to Manchester in 1840.

To the demands of a large congregation and an astonishing round of denominational, civic, and charitable activity, Turner added a noteworthy intellectual life. While hardly a scholar, he was certainly a polymath, which led one evangelical to dismiss him as knowing '*everything* but Christ' (*Christian Reformer*, new ser., 15, 1859, 454). The Newcastle Literary and Philosophical Society was founded on his direct initiative in 1793, and he served as its secretary until 1837. When the 'Lit and Phil' became primarily a library, Turner took the lead in organizing societies to cater to more specialized interests: the 'New Institution' for public lectures on natural philosophy of 1802, to which he lectured for thirty years on various scientific subjects (listed in Harbottle, appx A); the Society of Antiquaries of Newcastle-upon-Tyne in 1813; and the Natural History Society in 1829. Newcastle offers remarkable testimony to the vigour and tolerance of provincial culture, to a surviving if threatened unity of knowledge, and to the manifold accomplishment then still possible for a single individual who embodied the ideals of eighteenth-century rational religion.

Turner retired on 20 September 1841 and moved to Manchester, where he lived with his daughter Mary (1786–1869), who had married the Revd John Gooch Robberds (1789–1854), minister of Cross Street Chapel. Turner died at his Manchester residence, in Loyd Street, Chorlton upon Medlock, on 24 April 1859. On 28 April he was buried at Upper Brook Street Chapel, Manchester.

His eldest son, **William Turner** (1788–1853), Unitarian minister, was born at Newcastle on 13 January 1788. He was educated first by the Revd Edward Prowitt (1760–1802), his father's assistant, then by his uncle, the Revd John Holland of Bolton (1766–1826), and finally in his father's school. He matriculated in the University of Glasgow in 1803, with an exhibition from Dr Williams's Trust, and graduated MA in 1806, having been especially impressed by James Mylne (1757?–1839), professor of moral philosophy. In 1806–8 he was at Manchester College, York, and then, on his father's advice, declined an offer from the Unitarian chapel in Chester and enrolled in the University of Edinburgh to remedy defects in his Glasgow education.

In 1809, when a third tutorship was established at Manchester College in mathematics, physics, and mental and moral philosophy, Turner was chosen to fill it, thus becoming a colleague of the principal Charles Wellbeloved (1769–1858) and John Kenrick (1788–1877). Although he had the potential to be an excellent mathematician, his training and sympathy inclined him to the philosophical side of his duties. The funeral sermon by his pupil Edward Higginson (1807–1880) *Eternal Life, the Gift of God in Jesus Christ* (1854) includes an extensive discussion of the content and method of Turner's teaching, passages that John Kenrick extracted for his obituary in the *Christian Reformer* (new ser., 10, 1854, 132–7). Turner became resident tutor as well, following his marriage in 1817 to Mercy Benton (*d.* 1862), daughter of John Benton, a Birmingham hardware manufacturer, and niece of the Revd Newcome Cappe (1733–1800), minister at York. There were no children.

In 1827 Turner left Manchester College and became minister of Northgate End Chapel in Halifax. There, emulating his father, he founded a mechanics' institute and a literary and philosophical society, and was closely involved with the working of the local British and foreign schools. He wrote for Unitarian periodicals and published a few sermons and theological essays, but was best-known for *Lives of Eminent Unitarians* (1840–43); the projected third volume, on foreign Unitarians, he was unable to complete. He died of heart disease and bronchitis at New Road, Halifax, on 30 December 1853 and was buried in Halifax on 5 January 1854. R. K. WEBB

Sources S. Harbottle, *The Reverend William Turner: dissent and reform in Georgian Newcastle upon Tyne* (1997) · *Christian Reformer, or, Unitarian Magazine and Review*, new ser., 15 (1859), 351–66, 410–24, 454–61 · J. Kenrick, 'Memoir of the late Rev. William Turner', *Christian Reformer, or, Unitarian Magazine and Review*, new ser., 10 (1854), 129–43 · D. Orange, 'Rational dissent and provincial science: William Turner and the Newcastle Literary and Philosophical Society', *Metropolis and province: science in British culture, 1780–1850*, ed. I. Inkster and J. Morrell (1983), 205–30 · R. S. Watson, *The history of the Literary and Philosophical Society of Newcastle-upon-Tyne, 1793–1896* (1897) · P. Holland and others, *Sermons delivered at Pudsey* (1782) · J. Hunter, *Familiae minorum gentium*, ed. J. W. Clay, 1, Harleian Society, 37 (1894) · William Turner (II) letters, Literary and Philosophical Society of Newcastle-upon-Tyne · Hanover Square Chapel records, Tyne and Wear RO · J. Chapple, *Elizabeth Gaskell: the early years* (1997) · J. Raymond and J. V. Pickstone, 'The natural sciences and the learning of the English Unitarians', *Truth, liberty, religion: essays celebrating two hundred years of Manchester College*, ed. B. Smith (1986), 127–64 · E. Higginson, *Eternal life, the gift of God in Jesus Christ* (1854) · *CGPLA Eng. & Wales* (1859) · d. cert. [W. Turner III, 1853]
Archives Literary and Philosophical Society of Newcastle-upon-Tyne, letters | Harris Man. Oxf., Lant Carpenter MSS · Harris Man. Oxf., G. W. Wood MSS · Keele University, Wedgwood MSS · Tyne and Wear RO, Hanover Square Chapel records
Likenesses oils, 1805–10, Literary and Philosophical Society of Newcastle-upon-Tyne · A. Morton, oils, *c.*1823, Church of the Divine Unity, Newcastle · A. Morton, oils, 1829, Literary and Philosophical Society of Newcastle-upon-Tyne · E. H. Baily, marble bust, 1829–30, Literary and Philosophical Society of Newcastle-upon-Tyne · T. H. Carrick, oils?, 1837 · W. J. Ward, mezzotint, pubd 1838 (after T. Carrick), BM · J. H. Mole, watercolour, 1840, Newcastle City Library · S. Humble, oils, 1843, Literary and Philosophical Society of Newcastle-upon-Tyne · W. Collard, line engraving (after A. Morton), NPG · W. Nicholson, oils · T. Ronson, line engraving (after W. Nicholson), NPG · engraving (after W. Nicholson), Literary and Philosophical Society of Newcastle-upon-Tyne · engraving (after A. Morton, *c.*1823), Literary and Philosophical Society of Newcastle-upon-Tyne · engraving (after T. H. Carrick, 1837), Literary and Philosophical Society of Newcastle-upon-Tyne
Wealth at death under £2000: probate, 2 Aug 1859, *CGPLA Eng. & Wales*

Turner, William (1788–1853). *See under* Turner, William (1761–1859).

Turner, William [*known as* William Turner of Oxford] (**1789–1862**), landscape painter, was born on 12 November 1789 at Black Bourton, near Bampton, Oxfordshire, the eldest child of Robert Turner (*d.* 1791) and his wife, Mary Cox (*bap.* 1767, *d. c.*1803?). Following his father's early death William and his two sisters, Anne (*b.* 1791) and Margaret (*b.* 1792), were brought up by their mother. The children were probably provided for by William Turner, a wealthy uncle after whom the future artist was named. In 1803 the uncle acquired the manor of Shipton-on-Cherwell near Woodstock; the younger William went to live with him there and may then have received his first formal instruction in drawing from William Delamotte (1775–1863) in Oxford. The following year Turner was sent to London to study with John Varley. He there encountered William Mulready, William Henry Hunt, and John Linnell, and all, at Varley's insistence, worked regularly

William Turner [of Oxford] (**1789–1862**), self-portrait

out of doors, making closely focused landscape studies, either in chalks on paper or in oil, though none of the latter by Turner has survived from this period.

Turner first exhibited at the Royal Academy in 1807; of the three landscapes, two were Oxfordshire subjects. In January 1808 he became the youngest associate of the Society of Painters in Water Colours and in November a full member. His precocity was further recognized when he was chosen to preside at the inaugural meeting of the Society for Epic and Pastoral Design, a reincarnation of the Sketching Society which earlier included Thomas Girtin and John Sell Cotman as well as Varley among its members. This was the moment when Varley, 'at Millar, the Booksellers evening Converzatione', at which leading artists were gathered, 'spoke violently of the merit of a young man who had been his pupil in learning to draw in watercolour and Reinagle said "He had never before seen drawings equal to them". His name Turner' (Farington, *Diary*, 9.3209). In 1810 one critic voiced the opinion, 'it is not flattery to say that he has outstripped his master' ('Watercolour exhibitions', *Ackermann's Repository of the Arts, Literature and Commerce*, 3, July 1810, 432). *Whichwood Forest, Oxfordshire* (exh. Society of Painters in Water Colours, 1809; V&A) is the climax of these early years, and shows a dense yet animated forest interior in which a confined encounter with nature in an apparent state of tumult is contrasted with a distant glimpse of tranquillity. The technical and imaginative resources of this work are the fruit of Turner's study of both old and modern masters, from Titian to Gainsborough and Girtin, evident in the compilations of early sketches now preserved in the Huntington Library, San Marino, California.

About 1812 (the date when the Watercolour Society collapsed, then reformed in less exclusive guise, admitting oil paintings) Turner returned to Oxfordshire, probably living initially at Shipton, and depending for his income on giving lessons, both in the University of Oxford and around the county. Teaching was to provide the basis of his income for the rest of his life. His subject matter expanded beyond his home territory with his regular summer sketching tours. He made a point of familiarizing himself with all the prime sites of the picturesque and made visits to the Lake District in 1814, Wales in 1817, and the Peak District in 1818. These followed a brief trip to Clifton Gorge and the Wye in 1808 or 1809.

On 5 July 1824 Turner married Elizabeth Ilott (*bap.* 1782, *d.* 1851); there were no children. About this date a cousin acquired a farm in the New Forest and Turner was a regular visitor. He exhibited scenes of that ancient woodland from 1827 and also began to explore the south downs, which he depicted in sparse panoramic vistas overlooking Portsmouth harbour or Bowhill near Chichester. In keeping with the times, these could be monumental in scale. One of the occasional oils Turner continued to paint from time to time throughout his career, *View of Portsmouth Harbour from Portsdown Hill*, exhibited at the British Institution in 1841, measured 6 feet 7 inches wide, including the frame.

In the summer of 1838 Turner undertook his longest tour, to the very north of Scotland and the Western Isles. For the next twenty-five years he continued to portray this remote scenery as the epitome of an untouched, primeval landscape. He distanced himself from the modern age in time as well as space: his watercolours of Stonehenge or the Nine Maidens at Penwith in Cornwall (all Ashmolean Museum, Oxford) evoke a human interaction with the land far removed from modern agriculture. Nearer home, the lush series of views of water-lilies on the Cherwell at Shipton show the river returning to a state of nature after being bypassed by a recent canal. Such political undercurrents went apparently undetected by critics, and Turner appears to have been content with his reputation as a provincial painter. Thanking the secretary of the Old Watercolour Society for an invitation in 1857, he wrote, 'for some years past I have gone very little from home, and dinner parties have been entirely declined' (Royal Watercolour Society archives). Not that he was entirely as isolated as he imagined: the intense colour and rich stippled effects of his large, late set pieces have a good deal in common with a much younger generation exemplified by George Price Boyce (1826–1897) or Birket Foster (1825–1899), though Turner's dreamy mood is more in tune with contemporary work by Samuel Palmer (1805–1881).

At the outset of his career Turner sold watercolours to leading collectors such as Lord Essex and the marquess of Stafford. His later work found its way largely into the homes of Oxford-educated clergymen and was acquired regularly by the Oxford printseller James Wyatt and the university solicitor Baker Morrell. Ruskin, having earlier passed his work without comment, in 1851 praised his 'quiet and simple earnestness, and tender feeling' (*Modern Painters*, 5th edn, 1851, pt 2, section 4, chap. 3, para. 28; *Works*, 3.472). Turner's death at his home, 16 St John Street, Oxford, on 7 August 1862 passed unnoticed in the wider world. He was buried on 14 August at Shipton-on-Cherwell, where in 1831 he had taken a leading role in providing plans for the restoration of the church. The contents of his studio were auctioned at Christies on 9 March 1863. About 100 of Turner's works including drawings, oils, and watercolours are in the Ashmolean Museum, Oxford. TIMOTHY WILCOX

Sources T. Wilcox and C. Titterington, *William Turner of Oxford (1789–1862)* (1984) [exhibition catalogue, Oxfordshire County Museum, Woodstock] · M. Hardie, 'William Turner of Oxford (1789–1862)', *Old Water-Colour Society's Club*, 9 (1931–2), 1–22 · L. Herrmann, '"This patient and unassuming master": William Turner of Oxford', *The Connoisseur*, 162 (1966), 242–7 · T. Wilcox, 'Beauty of association: William Turner of Oxford', *Country Life*, 176 (1984), 760–61 · J. Hamilton, *The Sketching Society, 1799–1851* (1971) [exhibition catalogue, V&A] · A. L. Baldry, 'William Turner of Oxford', *Walker's Quarterly* [whole issue], 11 (1923) · S. Fenwick and G. Smith, eds., *The business of watercolour: a guide to the archives of the Royal Watercolour Society* (1997) · d. cert. · parish register, Black Bourton church, 6 Jan 1767 [baptism] · parish records, Shipton-on-Cherwell, Oxfordshire, 14 Aug 1862 [burial]

Archives V&A, set of Royal Watercolour Society catalogues, with autograph annotations | Bankside Gallery, Royal Watercolour Society, MS letters, price books of annual exhibitions

Likenesses W. Turner, self-portrait, oils, AM Oxf. [*see illus.*]

Wealth at death under £3000: probate, 17 Sept 1862, *CGPLA Eng. & Wales*

Turner, William (1792–1867), diplomatist, born at Yarmouth on 5 September 1792, was the son of Richard Turner (1751–1835), lecturer, and afterwards perpetual curate of Great Yarmouth, and his second wife, Elizabeth (1761–1805), eldest daughter of Thomas Rede of Beccles. Sir George James *Turner was his younger brother. Richard Turner was a friend of George Canning, who gave William a clerkship in the Foreign Office in January 1809. In 1811 Turner was attached to the embassy of Robert Liston, and accompanied him to Constantinople. He remained in the East for five years, and during that time visited most parts of the Ottoman empire, as well as the islands and mainland of Greece. While in Asia Minor he endeavoured to emulate Leander and Lord Byron by swimming the Hellespont, and, failing in the attempt, palliated his ill success by pointing out that he had tried to swim from Asia to Europe, a far more difficult feat than Byron's passage from Europe to Asia. Byron replied in a letter to John Murray of 21 February 1821 published at the time (*Life*, ed. Moore, 80), and Turner, in a counter-rejoinder, overwhelmed his adversary with quotations from ancient and modern topographers (T. Moore, *Letters and Journals of Lord Byron, with Notices of his Life*, 2 vols., 1830, 2.817–19). Turner published a chatty account of his wanderings in 1820 as *Journal of a Tour in the Levant*.

In 1824 Turner returned to Constantinople as secretary to the British embassy. During Stratford Canning's absence, he was for eighteen months minister-plenipotentiary. On 22 October 1829 he was appointed envoy-extraordinary and minister-plenipotentiary to the republic of Colombia, and after filling that post for nine years he retired from the service. On 10 April 1824, at St George's, Hanover Square, London, Turner married Mary Anne (1797–1891), daughter and coheir of John Mansfield of Birstall. With her he had one surviving son, Mansfield, and a daughter, Mary Anne Elizabeth (1825–1894), who married Walter Stewart Broadwood. Turner died at Leamington Priors, Warwickshire, on 10 January 1867, and was buried in the vault of the parish church of Birstall in Leicestershire. A brass was erected in his memory on the north wall of the chancel.

E. I. CARLYLE, rev. H. C. G. MATTHEW

Sources FO List · H. Turner and F. Johnson, *The Turner family of Mulbarton and Great Yarmouth*, new edn (1907) · *Life of Lord Byron, with his letters and journals*, ed. T. Moore, 6 vols. (1854) · *Byron's letters and journals*, ed. L. A. Marchand, 8 (1978) · L. A. Marchand, *Byron: a biography*, 3 vols. (1957)
Archives NL Scot., corresp. with Robert Liston
Likenesses H. S. Turner, lithograph (after T. Phillips), BM, NPG
Wealth at death under £60,000: probate, 6 March 1867, *CGPLA Eng. & Wales*

Turner, Sir William (1832–1916), anatomist and university administrator, was born at 7 Friar Street, Lancaster, on 7 January 1832, the eldest surviving son of William Turner (1797–1837), upholsterer and cabinet maker, and Margaret, *née* Aldren (1793–1869). He had no recollection of his father, who died when he was five years old. His sister Mary Ellen, born in 1834, died of diphtheria at the age of four, and his brother Robert, born in 1836, died from erysipelas aged fourteen.

Education Turner was educated at a local preparatory school to the age of ten, then at a small private school run by the Revd William Shepherd at Longmarton, near Appleby, Westmorland. He left school in the Christmas vacation before his fifteenth birthday to become articled to his uncle, John Aldren, a chemist in Lancaster. His pupillage did not last long, however. His mother was related by marriage to the Johnsons, a prominent local family of surgeons, who persuaded her that William's talents would be better employed in their own profession, and in February 1847 Turner became apprenticed to Christopher Johnson jun. Besides attending to his medical duties—chiefly dispensing drugs—he also acquired a good understanding of elementary chemistry at an evening class that Johnson and his father ran at the mechanics' institute.

In 1850 Turner was released from his apprenticeship to complete his training at St Bartholomew's Hospital, London, where he took the first prizes in chemistry and botany in his first year and practical anatomy in his third year. He successfully sat the examination for the MRCS in the summer of 1853, thus qualifying for practice. However, he had set his sights on the MB degree of the University of London. In 1852 he passed the university's matriculation examination, taking the first prize in chemistry and the second place in botany, and in May 1853 St Bartholomew's

Sir William Turner (1832–1916), by Sir George Reid, in or before 1897

awarded him a two-year scholarship in anatomy, physiology, and chemistry. He passed the intermediate MB examination in August 1854, winning the gold medal in materia medica and pharmaceutical chemistry. In the course of his studies he also conducted a small amount of original research. Early in 1854 he spoke to the Abernethian Society at St Bartholomew's on 'Some of the therapeutical effects of the iodide of potassium', and in the spring of that year he performed and wrote up a chemical examination of cerebro-spinal fluid from a case of spina bifida under the care of the hospital's rising surgeon James Paget. Paget subsequently communicated Turner's paper to the Royal Society, and it was published in the society's *Proceedings*.

Teaching at Edinburgh Turner's studies were unexpectedly interrupted when John Goodsir, professor of anatomy at the University of Edinburgh, asked Paget to recommend candidates to serve as demonstrators in his large practical classes. Paget suggested Turner—initially for a junior appointment, but then, as no one more experienced was prepared to leave London for Edinburgh, for the senior demonstratorship. Turner took up the post in October 1854 at a salary of £200. He assumed responsibility for supervising the practical work in the dissecting room, for giving systematic anatomical demonstrations to augment Goodsir's lectures, and for running the demonstration classes in histology that Goodsir had instituted. He also continued to study for the London MB degree, and he successfully sat the final examination in 1857. Subsequently he began to devote more time to his own original investigations. Some of these—for instance on the muscles of the human larynx, the fossils of extinct cattle, and various aspects of pathological anatomy—were straightforwardly anatomical in character. But he also investigated and wrote on the elimination of therapeutically administered manganese from the body; on the secretory activity of the human pancreas; and, with Joseph Lister, on the structure and chemical composition of nerve fibres. As this breadth of interests suggests, Turner had not yet made a firm decision about the career he should follow. While at St Bartholomew's he had envisaged a future as a consulting physician. An opportunity to embark on such a course was presented to him early in 1861, when he was invited to apply for the post of warden to the hospital's medical college—the same post as Paget had held when Turner began his studies there. In the event he was persuaded to remain at Edinburgh when the university decided to augment his salary, hitherto paid solely by Goodsir from the class fees he received, by a further £150 per annum. Thereafter Turner was committed to a career as an academic anatomist. The increase in salary also meant an improvement in his domestic prospects, and on 21 April 1863 he married Agnes (1833–1908), the eldest daughter of Abraham Logan, farmer, of Burnhouses, Berwickshire. They had three sons and two daughters.

From 1864 Goodsir's health declined and Turner gradually took over more of his teaching. On Goodsir's death in 1867 Turner was elected his successor in the chair of anatomy, with overwhelming support from medical and scientific colleagues in Edinburgh and London and from past and present students at the university. In keeping with the traditions of the Edinburgh chair Turner did not teach anatomy simply as a preparation for surgery but as a science in its own right. He presented the details of anatomical topography within a conceptual framework which emphasized the adaptation of the parts of the human body to their various functions, and illustrated such adaptation with reference to the anatomy of other organisms. He was an early convert to the theory of evolution, which he adopted both as an explanation of adaptation and as a means of tracing the taxonomic development of anatomical function. Teaching from this point of view he was more concerned to inculcate an understanding of general principles than to impart an encyclopaedic knowledge of anatomical minutiae. He was an outstanding teacher, both of those who were destined for medical practice and of those who aspired to academic careers of their own. Among the latter were no fewer than twenty-three men who would go on to occupy chairs of anatomy in medical schools throughout the British empire. His view of anatomy as a science rather than a handicraft also prompted him to join forces with G. M. Humphry, the professor of anatomy at Cambridge, to found the *Journal of Anatomy and Pathology* in 1866. Humphry subsequently became less involved in the editorial work, and from 1875 until 1915 Turner was the senior editor.

Research The same scientific orientation was equally apparent in Turner's research. Some of his earliest work was on the variability of various structures in humans, and especially on the anatomy of supernumerary and rudimentary organs and their evolutionary relationship to corresponding structures in lower animals. In the course of this work Charles Darwin approached him for examples to illustrate his *Descent of Man*. Turner's classic studies of placentation in man and other mammals, which began in this period, established his reputation as one among the leading research anatomists in Britain, and formed the basis of the Arris and Gale lectures that he presented in 1875 and 1876 to the Royal College of Surgeons of England, of which he was elected a fellow in 1893. He also became an expert on the anatomy of whales and other marine mammals, a topic to which he first turned when a school of pilot whales visited the Firth of Forth in 1866. He dissected the great fin whale that beached at Longniddry in 1869, and subsequently built up one of the best collections of cetacean skeletons and specimens in Britain.

But the work for which Turner was best known related to the classification and evolutionary genealogy of human races. He embarked upon this project in the early 1860s, when he began investigating the detailed structure of the brains and crania of humans and animals. Other Edinburgh anatomists, including Goodsir, had taken an interest in human craniology and the light it might throw on the relationship between the mental faculties of humans and those of other animals. Turner's department thus already possessed an extensive collection of skulls, including the phrenological collection deposited there by the Henderson Trust. But Turner devoted himself to this line of research with unprecedented zeal, mobilizing an extended network of colleagues and former students to acquire a very considerable collection of fossil and recent human remains from around the world. For more than fifty years, working chiefly on skulls but also on pelvises, he endeavoured to draw up a detailed classification of the races and sub-races of humanity, and of their evolutionary and geographical interrelations. His efforts established him as one of the main architects and advocates of the biological conception of distinct human races, though he conceded that, as a result of migration and interbreeding, the facts were insufficiently clear to permit any definitive characterization of pure racial types. He was elected a fellow of the Royal Society of London in 1877, and in 1890 he served on its council. He also served twice as president of the anthropological section of the British Association for the Advancement of Science, first at Newcastle in 1889, and again in Toronto in 1897, and he was president of the entire association in 1900.

Administrative and professional activities As well as teaching and researching in his chosen discipline Turner also took a very active and prominent role in the life and affairs of his adoptive university. His main patron and guide in university politics was the eminent physician and professor of materia medica, Sir Robert Christison, with whom he first became acquainted in 1859 when he joined the newly founded university company of volunteers. Christison had been one of the most influential advocates of the 1858 Universities (Scotland) Act, which transferred control of academic business from the town council to the university's own senatus. Turner was admitted onto this body on his promotion to the chair of anatomy in 1867. It was a period of rapid expansion in university education, and Edinburgh was keen to maintain its position as the leading medical school in the British empire. In 1869 the vice-chancellor, Sir Alexander Grant, launched a campaign to raise funds for new medical school buildings. Turner was an energetic member of the extension committee from its first meeting, and eventually replaced Grant as chair of that committee following the latter's death in December 1884. By that time the new medical school buildings were nearing completion. Indeed, the anatomy department had moved in as early as 1880, and Turner was already busy organizing and cataloguing the museum. Nevertheless, he was keen to revive plans for a new academic hall, which had been dropped from the original proposals for reasons of economy, and he was instrumental in persuading the local brewer and MP, William McEwan, to cover the cost of the building, which was completed in 1897. He subsequently secured a gift from another brewer, Sir John Usher, to build an institute of public health and to endow a chair in that subject.

Turner also played an important role in the governance of the medical profession and the development of medical education on a national scale. He served on the General Medical Council as representative of the universities of Edinburgh and Aberdeen from 1873 to 1883 and, following the reconstitution of the council, of Edinburgh alone from 1886 to 1905. From 1898 to 1904 he was president of the council, the first Scottish representative to hold that office; during that period he took the lead in the difficult and contentious business of reforming the finances of the council, which had not been well managed. As a medical educationist he was a key figure in negotiations over government efforts to establish a single licensing body in each of the three divisions of the United Kingdom for doctors seeking to qualify for practice—the so-called 'single portal campaign'. In 1878 the government introduced a bill to this end, and in the following year Turner represented the university before a select committee appointed to work out the finer details of the proposed legislation. He argued that the Scottish universities should be free to establish their own curricula and run their own licensing examinations on the grounds that the training was more thorough and complete, and the standard of the examinations higher, than anything demanded by the professional licensing bodies. After a change of government sank the bill of 1878, in 1881 Turner was invited by Earl Spencer to sit on the royal commission on this issue. The majority of the commissioners reported in favour of a single portal, but Turner submitted a vigorous and detailed minority report in renewed defence of the freedom of the Scottish universities. An attempt to legislate on the lines of the majority report was effectively preempted when the royal colleges of surgeons and physicians presented a scheme for a conjoint examination to provide a complete qualification in medicine—a system

that had already been in operation in Scotland for some years. The Medical Act of 1886 did little more than endorse this arrangement, leaving Edinburgh and the other Scottish universities untouched. In the midst of his fight against the single portal proposals Turner was in 1882 elected president of the Edinburgh Royal College of Surgeons, of which he had been a fellow since 1861. His defence of university autonomy sat uncomfortably with the college's commitment to extra-academical training, however, and he declined to seek re-election for a second year as was usually the case.

Meanwhile Turner continued to rise steadily through the university's administrative hierarchy. From 1878 to 1881 he served as dean of the medical faculty. Following the passage of the Universities of Scotland Act of 1889, when the university court was reconstituted with greatly enhanced executive powers, Turner was immediately elected to this body by senatus, and served as convener of the finance committee. In 1903, on the retirement of Sir William Muir from the post of principal of the university, Turner, now over seventy years old, was appointed in his place, and became the first Englishman and the first holder of a medical chair to attain such a position at a Scottish university. He presided over a further period of rapid expansion. In 1905 the science departments moved into the site of the old City Hospital in Infirmary Street, which Turner negotiated to buy at a very moderate cost from the town council. New housing for the mathematics department was acquired in Chambers Street at about the same time. Several new lectureships and chairs were established in different departments during Turner's time as principal. He also oversaw improvements in the organization and style of teaching, including the passage of a new ordinance to reform teaching in the arts by supplementing formal lectures with tutorials, and the introduction of the three-term year. As a trustee of the Royal (Dick) Veterinary College from 1876, and chairman of the administrative board of the college from 1906, he was in large part responsible for raising the standard of teaching to a level where the university could offer degrees and doctorates in veterinary science. And in 1913 he was instrumental in brokering a new agreement with the Royal Infirmary which enabled the university to make much fuller and more efficient use of the wards for clinical teaching. Funding for this growth came from a variety of private and government bequests, but one of the most important sources was the Universities of Scotland Trust established by Andrew Carnegie in 1901. Turner was involved in discussions with Carnegie over how this trust might best benefit the Scottish universities and Scottish students, and from its inception he represented Edinburgh University on the executive committee of the trust. Probably the only form of expansion that Turner consistently opposed was the admission of women to medical education. Between 1869 and 1872 Sophia Jex-Blake and six other women unsuccessfully sought admission to the university's medical classes. Turner was among those who resisted such a move on the grounds that mixed classes would be unworkable, and as late as 1909 he reiterated this argument to the Elgin committee on the Scottish universities.

Other appointments and final years Following his appointment as principal Turner found himself invited to sit on many other educational and medical bodies. He became a governor of the Fettes Trust, chairman of the Trust for Education in the Highlands and Islands of Scotland, president of the committee of management of the St George's Training College for Women Teachers, a member of the board of governors of Morrison's academy, Crieff, and a trustee of the John Newland's Trust. He also served as a vice-president of the Royal Blind Asylum and School, and was on the board of Donaldson's Hospital for many years. He had long been active in the Royal Society of Edinburgh as a fellow from 1861, member of council from 1866, and one of the secretaries to the ordinary meetings from 1869 to 1891. In that year he was elected a vice-president, serving in this capacity to 1901; he succeeded Lord Kelvin as president in 1908, holding the office until 1913, when he became a permanent member of council. In 1909 he was granted the freedom of the City of Edinburgh, and in the same year became an honorary member of the Edinburgh Merchant Company. A knighthood was conferred on him considerably before that, in 1886, and in 1901 he was appointed KCB. He was also the recipient of honorary degrees from many universities. Turner's last years were clouded by the First World War. He was intensely patriotic, and urged the enlistment of all able-bodied students and members of the staff. But the empty quadrangles and the shrunken classes, together with the forced abandonment of his building schemes, depressed him and seemed to sap his vitality.

Turner was blessed with a vigorous constitution that enabled him to carry a heavy load of work until the very last days of his life. With his strong voice, unshakeable composure and penetrating gaze, he had no difficulty commanding attention, be it in committee or in the classroom. He was inclined to attribute his steady demeanour to the Christian faith that he retained throughout his life, for over sixty years of which he was a member of St John's Episcopal Church. Only in the winter term of 1915 did his energies begin to falter; a sudden final decline ended with his death from sudden haematemesis and heart failure on the morning of 15 February 1916 at his home, 6 Eton Terrace, Edinburgh. He was buried beside his wife in the Dean cemetery four days later after a funeral service at St John's Episcopal Church.   STEVE STURDY

Sources A. L. Turner, *Sir William Turner K.C.B., F.R.S.: a chapter in medical history* (1919) · J. A. Russell, *Proceedings of the Royal Society of Edinburgh*, 36 (1915–16), 340–71 [incl. bibliography] · *BMJ* (26 Feb 1916), 326–31 · V. G. Plarr, *Plarr's Lives of the fellows of the Royal College of Surgeons of England*, rev. D'A. Power, 2 (1930), 444–7 · *DNB* · d. cert.
Archives U. Edin. L., lecture notes and corresp. | Bodl. Oxf., letters to Acland family | FILM BFI NFTVA, current affairs footage
Likenesses W. Hole, etching, 1884, NPG, Wellcome L.; repro. in W. Hole, *Quasi cursores* (1884) · G. Reid, oils, 1897, priv. coll. · G. Reid, portrait, in or before 1897, Royal College of Surgeons, Edinburgh [*see illus.*] · J. Guthrie, oils, 1912, U. Edin. · Elliott & Fry, photograph, repro. in Russell, 'Sir William Turner', facing p. 340 · W. Graham Boss, pencil drawing, Scot. NPG
Wealth at death £71,467 17s. 5d.: confirmation, 30 March 1916, *CCI*

Turner, William Ernest Stephen (1881–1963), chemist and glass technologist, was born in Wednesbury, Staffordshire on 22 September 1881, the eldest son and second of the seven children of William George Turner and his wife, Emma Blanche Gardner, daughter of a London tradesman. His father worked, successively, as a railway porter, signalman, ironworks labourer, postman, and industrial insurance agent; he also served, throughout his working life, as deacon and elder in the Church of the Baptist Brethren in Smethwick.

From the Crocketts Lane board school in Smethwick, Turner went with a county minor scholarship to the King Edward VI Grammar School, Five Ways, Birmingham. A school-leaving scholarship took him, in 1898, to Mason College (from 1900 Birmingham University). He graduated BSc (Lond.) with first-class honours in chemistry in 1902, proceeding MSc (Birmingham) in 1904 with the Erhardt research prize. He gained his external London DSc in chemistry in 1911.

In 1904 Turner was appointed junior demonstrator and lecturer at the University College of Sheffield. His interest in applied science was revealed immediately in his course of physical chemistry lectures for metallurgy students; in response to requests from metallurgists in industry the lectures were repeated in the evenings. In 1908, Turner married Mary Isobel (d. 1939), daughter of John Marshall, a tradesman, of Birmingham. They later had two sons, including the classical scholar Eric Gardner *Turner, and two daughters.

During the spring of 1909 Turner wrote a series of articles for the *Sheffield Daily Telegraph* promoting the employment of scientists in industry. When the First World War began he proposed the formation of a technical advisory committee to assist local industry; in September 1914 a university scientific advisory committee was set up with Turner as secretary. It received many questions from the local glass plants; these led to Turner's May 1915 report which drew attention to the lack of any scientific method in the glass industry. The following month a department was established to provide courses in glass manufacture and to conduct glass research. Soon afterwards Turner introduced the term 'glass technology', with which his name became associated.

Early in 1916 the committee of the privy council for scientific and industrial research provided funds for the department, to be administered by the 'glass research delegacy'—a body composed of both industrialists and academics. The departmental research programme was framed with the solution of industrial problems in mind—one of the earlier examples of co-operation between universities and industry. Research contracts from the Glass Research Association, which required glass melting on a large scale, led to the department's move to a disused bottle works in Darnall Road in 1920. However, the association was wound up in 1925, from which time

Turner sought to bring the department back into the university area. In 1936–7 he raised funds from the industry to buy and convert a house, Elmfield, into a well-equipped home for the department. In 1916 Turner founded the Society of Glass Technology of which he was secretary in 1916–22, 1924–37, and 1938–46. He was editor of its journal until 1951. He also played a major role in the formation of the International Commission on Glass. Both institutions flourished. The commission developed a series of triennial meetings and became responsible for much international technical co-operation; Turner was the acknowledged and respected leader of these activities.

In 1918 Turner was appointed OBE in recognition of his services in organizing the application of science to the glass industry. He became FRS (1938), and was awarded an honorary DScTech degree by Sheffield in 1954. He was the only person from outside Germany to receive the Otto Schott commemoration medal (1955). In 1943 he received the silver medal of the Royal Society of Arts. Among many other positions, he was a founder fellow of the Institute of Physics, an honorary fellow of the Society of Glass Technology, and honorary president of the International Commission on Glass. He was also FSA (1958).

In early adult life Turner was active in the church and with his first wife he played an important role for many years in the Rutland Hall Settlement in Sheffield. After his first wife's death, in 1943 Turner married (Annie) Helen Nairn Monro (d. 1977), a glass-engraver. She taught in the Edinburgh College of Art and had a studio in Juniper Green, near Edinburgh. When very young Turner suffered an attack of poliomyelitis which led to atrophy of some muscles of the right arm. However, this hardly seemed to affect him; he was a keen climber and a member of the Swiss Alpine Club. He climbed in New Zealand and in the Alps, walking with his first wife, on her fifty-eighth birthday, over the Col d'Herens.

For some time after Turner's retirement from the university in 1945, he worked with Edward Meigh in the joint consulting firm Glass Technical Services and maintained his house in Sheffield. He developed his interest in glass archaeology, and wrote a number of papers on the history of glass and glass-making. His last years were spent in Juniper Green. He died on 27 October 1963 at his son's home, the rectory, Eyam, Derbyshire.

R. W. DOUGLAS, rev.

Sources R. W. Douglas, *Memoirs FRS*, 10 (1964), 325–55 · 'W. E. S. Turner memorial lecture', *Glass Technology*, 8 (1967) · private information (1981) · *CGPLA Eng. & Wales* (1964)
Likenesses W. Stoneman, photograph, 1938, NPG

Turner, Wilton George (1811–1855). *See under* Turner, Edward (1796–1837).

Turner [*married name* Paget], **Winifred** (1903–1983), sculptor, was born on 13 March 1903 in London, the younger of the two daughters of Alfred Turner (1874–1940), sculptor, and Charlotte Ann Gavin (1880/81–1938), who was seven years her husband's junior and of Irish descent. Known as Win or Winnie to friends and family, Turner was educated with her sister, Jessica, at the local convent school. The siblings went on to study at the Central School of Arts and Crafts, London, where their father had for many years held a teaching post. Winifred Turner left the Central School after a period of three years, in 1924, to enrol at the Royal Academy Schools, where she studied until 1929. Having won the Landseer scholarship, she began exhibiting at the academy as early as 1924, being awarded many prizes, including a silver medal for a bust shown in 1926.

Turner was primarily a sculptor of the female figure. The Yugoslav sculptor Ivan Mestrovic especially seems to have been highly influential in the formal conception of her work. From him, perhaps, her work derives at times an intense interest in the architectonic. Figures such as *Youth* (exh. 1934; V&A), *Thought* (exh. 1933), and *Woman and Child* (exh. 1937) are conceived with one main viewpoint in mind and are very shallow. They also demonstrate qualities of introspection and languor similar to many of Mestrovic's female figures. The Yugoslav may also have been important in Turner's references to archaic cultures, in particular the Assyrian, the faces of her figures being invariably mask-like with slanting eyes. From the work of the Swede Carl Milles, Turner may, on the other hand, have drawn the stylized yet quiet dynamism which is present in some of her figures, such as the portrayal of the dancer, *Spring* (1935; bronze cast, 1937), or *Young Girl* (1939), which has the air of a dancer at rest. (Turner was herself gifted as a dancer. Proud of her physique, she is known to have modelled herself for many of her figures.) Unlike Mestrovic, and many of her male contemporaries, Turner worked primarily as a modeller, none of her exhibited work being carved. Her most important pieces were often cast in bronze with a wide variety of patinas. Her brief foray into the medium of glazed earthenware may have been suggested by the work of Louis Richard Garbe, who had taught at Central School during Turner's time there. Later works, largely in terracotta, often feature the animals owned by the sculptor, while her female figures exhibit a rough finish and heaviness of form not evident in her earlier works.

Turner exhibited widely. Aside from her long career until 1962 as an exhibitor at the Royal Academy, she showed at the Royal Glasgow Institute; the Society of Women Artists; the Walker Art Gallery, Liverpool; and the Royal Society of Artists, Birmingham. On her marriage in 1942 to a colleague, the sculptor and medallist Humphrey Thomas Paget (1893–1974), Turner relinquished her teaching post at the Central School, which she had held since the early 1930s. Turner was elected fellow of the Royal Society of British Sculptors in 1930. Her bronze seated female figure *Thought* was purchased by the trustees of the Chantrey bequest in 1933, and is in the Tate collection. Other works of hers are held by the Ashmolean Museum, Oxford, and the Hove Museum and Art Gallery.

From the beginning of her career Turner was based in a studio adjacent to her father's at 44 Munster Road, Fulham, London, where she stayed until 1932, when she moved to Studio K, 416 Fulham Road. On the death of her father in 1940 she moved to Burwash Common, Etchingham, Sussex. Her marriage was childless. She died on 30 October 1983. HELEN SHINER

Sources N. Penny, *Alfred and Winifred Turner* (1988) [exhibition catalogue, AM Oxf.] · P. Dunford, *A biographical dictionary of women artists in Europe and America since 1850* (1989) · A. Jarman and others, eds., *Royal Academy exhibitors, 1905–1970: a dictionary of artists and their work in the summer exhibitions of the Royal Academy of Arts*, 6 vols. (1973–82), vol. 6 · J. Johnson and A. Greutzner, *The dictionary of British artists, 1880–1940* (1976), vol. 5 of *Dictionary of British art* · J. Soden and C. Baile de Laperrière, eds., *The Society of Women Artists exhibitors, 1855–1996*, 4 (1996) · R. Billcliffe, *The Royal Glasgow Institute of the Fine Arts, 1861–1989*, 4 (1992) · D. Buckman, *Dictionary of artists in Britain since 1945* (1998) · J. A. Mackay, *The dictionary of western sculptors in bronze* (1977) · K. Parkes, 'Sculpture at the Royal Academy', *Apollo*, 17 (1933), 246–7 · F. Spalding, *20th century painters and sculptors* (1990), vol. 6 of *Dictionary of British art* · *Who's who in art* (1927) · *Who's who in art* (1934) · G. M. Waters, *Dictionary of British artists, working 1900–1950* (1975) · Bénézit, *Dict.*, 4th edn, vol. 13 · Bénézit, *Dict.*, 3rd edn, vol. 10 · H. Vollmer, *Allgemeines lexikon der bildenden Künstler des XX. Jahrhunderts*, 4 (Leipzig, 1958) · box, Courtauld Inst., Conway Library · *The Royal Academy Illustrated* (1933) · *The Royal Academy Illustrated* (1935) · *The Royal Academy Illustrated* (1936) · *The Royal Academy Illustrated* (1938) · *The Royal Academy Illustrated* (1939) · *The Studio*, 110 (1935), 20 [illustration] · N. Penny, ed., *Catalogue of European sculpture in the Ashmolean Museum, 1540 to the present day*, 3 (1992) · *CGPLA Eng. & Wales* (1983)

Archives Tate collection, MSS

Likenesses A. Turner, bronze, 1927, repro. in Penny, *Alfred and Winifred Turner*; priv. coll.

Wealth at death £143,956: probate, 27 Feb 1984, *CGPLA Eng. & Wales*

Peter Turnerelli (1771/2–1839), by James Thomson, pubd 1821 (after Samuel Drummond)

Turnerelli, Edward Tracy (1813–1896). *See under* Turnerelli, Peter (1771/2–1839).

Turnerelli, Peter (1771/2–1839), sculptor, was born in Belfast, the son of Iacomo (James) Turnerelli. His grandfather was an Italian refugee whose surname was Tognarelli and who had held a title and estates at Como in northern Italy. James Turnerelli worked as a sculptor in Belfast, and from 1787 in Dublin, changing his name from Tognarelli and marrying an Irish woman. Peter Turnerelli was originally intended for the Roman Catholic priesthood and attended a school in Saul's Court, Dublin, directed by the Jesuit, Father Thomas Betagh. On the death of his mother in 1792, the family moved to London where he joined them in 1793, having given up his studies for the priesthood. He resolved to follow his father's profession and entered the Royal Academy Schools in October 1794, aged twenty-two, and was awarded a silver medal in 1799. He was also a pupil of the sculptor Peter Francis Chenu. In 1796 he visited Rome, where he was deeply influenced by the neo-classical style. Although idealized, his marble sculpture has a quality of softness associated with the tradition of Antonio Canova. On his return to London in 1797, he was commissioned by Lord Heathfield to model posthumous busts of Sir Francis Drake and General Eliot.

On the recommendation of Sir Thomas Lawrence and Benjamin West, in 1797 Turnerelli was appointed teacher of modelling to the royal princesses, a post he retained until 1801 when he was appointed sculptor-in-ordinary to the royal family. He made his début at the Royal Academy in 1802 when he exhibited a bust of the youthful Princess Charlotte, which established his reputation. He made busts of other members of the royal family, including the jubilee busts of George III in 1809 (Windsor Castle), of which eighty copies were ordered by private patrons, and the king in state robes (exh. RA, 1810). He also modelled an equestrian statue of the king, which was never realized full-size (model in Sir John Soane's Museum, London). In 1814 he was appointed sculptor to Queen Charlotte. He twice refused a knighthood: in 1801 and again when George IV ascended the throne in 1820.

Turnerelli established a highly successful practice as a sculptor—mostly of portrait busts. While deeply indebted to the neo-classical style, he introduced contemporary costume into his portraiture. He became a member of the social circle of the prince regent at Carlton House, and a friend of the duke of Sussex and Lord Palmerston. His first wife, Margaret Mary Tracy (d. 1835), whom he first met at a soirée in Dublin, was a claimant to the Tracy peerage and was believed to have been instrumental in his social success. After their marriage they lived in Newman Street, London. They had a son, Edward Tracy Turnerelli [see below]. Through his connection with royalty, Peter Turnerelli received commissions from foreign monarchs: Louis XVIII sat for his portrait in the Palais des Tuileries in Paris, and Friedrich Wilhelm III of Prussia commissioned a bust of Prince Blücher (exh. RA, 1815). Tsar Alexander I of Russia visited his studio and ordered replicas of the busts of Blücher and Count Matvey Ivanovich Platov (exh. RA, 1816) for the Hermitage in St Petersburg. The 'nuptial' busts of Princess Charlotte and Prince Leopold were exhibited at the RA in 1817; the couple sat to him in the

Royal Pavilion in Brighton and visited his studio in Newman Street for a final sitting on the day of their marriage. Other subjects included the duke of Wellington (exh. RA, 1813; India Office, London), Sir Joseph Banks (exh. RA, 1814; Royal College of Surgeons, London), and the duke of Cumberland (exh. RA, 1809; Trinity College, Dublin).

Turnerelli revisited Ireland on a number of occasions. In 1812 he modelled a head of the statesman Henry Grattan (National Gallery of Ireland, Dublin) at his home, Tinnahinch; the work was praised by Canova. He made a bust of the Revd Dr Thomas Elrington, provost of Trinity College, Dublin (exh. RA, 1813; Trinity College, Dublin), and a bust of the lawyer and statesman John Philpot Curran (exh. RA, 1815). He was in Ireland in 1818, 1829, and 1830 and executed busts of the politician Daniel O'Connell (exh. RA, 1829) and Bishop J. K. Doyle (exh. RA, 1829; Carlow Cathedral). The O'Connell bust was replicated in quantity, which earned Turnerelli over £50,000. He also exhibited at the Royal Hibernian Academy in Dublin during the 1830s. Of the number of memorials that he made, one of the finest was to the poet Robert Burns in Dumfries, paid for by a national subscription of £10,000; an engraving of it was done for the *European Magazine* (May 1821). For the Roman Catholic pro-cathedral in Cork he sculpted the memorial to Bishop Moylan. He made a fine altar frontal relief for St Mary's, the Roman Catholic pro-cathedral in Dublin, and he was most probably responsible for the memorial to Archbishop Troy (1823), also in St Mary's, as he had exhibited a bust of Troy at the RA in 1816. (Both the altar and the Troy memorial show stylistic links to the Renaissance tomb of Pope Eugene IV in San Salvatore in Lauro, Rome.) Turnerelli executed a memorial relief to his former teacher in Dublin, Father Betagh, in 1817 (formerly in the church of St Michael and St John, Dublin). Other memorials were to Sir John Hope (Westminster Abbey, London) and Lieutenant-Colonel Stuart (Canterbury Cathedral).

On the death of his wife, Margaret Mary, in 1835, Turnerelli married in that year Mary O'Connor (d. 1875), a relative of the earl of Clare; they had a daughter. Turnerelli was a prominent public figure associated with many worthy causes, being a governor of St Patrick's charity schools in London, to which he devoted time and money, and was active as an officer in the volunteer movement during the Napoleonic wars. He had a good singing voice, which may have contributed to his success in fashionable circles. Although he was rich and successful he saved little, and when he died (at home) intestate on 20 March 1839, his house in Newman Street and the contents of his studio were auctioned—purchased mainly by the firm of Manzoni, which used his moulds to produce plaster busts with his mark removed. He was buried in the graveyard of St John's Chapel, St John's Wood, London.

Edward Tracy Turnerelli (1813–1896), traveller in Russia and writer, was born on 13 October 1813 in Newman Street, London. He was sent to school in Carlow College, Ireland. He studied modelling briefly under his father at the Royal Academy, but in 1836 he went to Russia where he spent eighteen years travelling to remote parts and drawing its ancient monuments. On his return to England in 1854 he married Martha Hankey, through whom he obtained an independent income. He devoted the rest of his life to politics as a supporter of the Conservative interest. In 1878 he achieved notoriety for his 'People's Tribute'—in the form of a gold laurel wreath—for the earl of Beaconsfield in recognition of his achievements at the Congress of Berlin; however, the earl declined to accept it. He published *Tales of the Rheinish Chivalry* (1835), *Kazan, the Ancient Capital of the Tartar Khans* (1854), *What I Know of the Late Emperor Nicholas* (1855), *A Night in a Haunted House* (1859), and political pamphlets. In 1884 he published *Memories of a Life of Toil, or, The Autobiography of the Old Conservative*. He died at Leamington Spa, Warwickshire, on 24 January 1896. F. M. O'DONOGHUE, rev. JOHN TURPIN

Sources J. Gilmartin, 'Peter Turnerelli, sculptor, 1774–1839', *Quarterly Bulletin of the Irish Georgian Society*, 10/4 (1967) · W. G. Strickland, *A dictionary of Irish artists*, 2 (1913), 466–70 · H. Potterton, *Irish church monuments, 1570–1880* (1975) · J. Ingamells, ed., *A dictionary of British and Irish travellers in Italy, 1701–1800* (1997) · S. C. Hutchison, 'The Royal Academy Schools, 1768–1830', *Walpole Society*, 38 (1960–62), 123–91, esp. 38, 155 · E. T. Turnerelli, *Memories of a life of toil, or, The autobiography of the old conservative* (1884)
Likenesses J. Thomson, stipple (after S. Drummond), BM, NPG; repro. in *The European Magazine*, 1 (1821), 387 [*see illus.*]
Wealth at death £2142 6s. 10d.—E. T. Turnerelli: probate, 19 March 1896, *CGPLA Eng. & Wales*

Turnham, Robert of. See Thornham, Robert of (d. 1211).

Turnham, Stephen of. See Thornham, Stephen of (d. 1213/14).

Turnor, Sir Christopher (1607–1675), judge, was born in Milton Ernest, Bedfordshire, on 6 December 1607, the eldest son of Christopher Turnor (d. 1619) of Milton Ernest and his wife, Ellen, daughter of Thomas Samm of Pirton, Hertfordshire. He matriculated as a pensioner from Emmanuel College, Cambridge, in 1623, and entered the Middle Temple on 27 June 1626, being called to the bar on 22 November 1633. He was made joint receiver-general of south Wales on 7 March 1639. At some point around this date he married Joyce (1617–1707), daughter of Thomas Warwick of Westminster, the sister of Sir Philip Warwick MP. They had at least six sons and a daughter, the eldest child, Christopher, being born in 1639 or 1640, and all are mentioned in his will.

Turnor's estate at Milton Ernest was sequestered in 1644 on the supposition of delinquency, but the failure to prove the charge saw the estate restored to him in 1647. Following the Restoration, on 4 July 1660 he was admitted a serjeant-at-law, his sponsors being the earl of Southampton and Sir Edward Hyde (shortly to be created earl of Clarendon). On 7 July Turnor was appointed a baron of the exchequer, and on the 16th he was knighted. In October he was named to the commission of oyer and terminer charged with bringing the regicides to trial. He surrendered his receivership of south Wales on 16 June 1662. Turnor presided over the treason trials of those implicated in the Yorkshire rising of 1663. He was seen as a moderate when it came to enforcing the Conventicle Acts. Turnor served on the court set up to adjudicate on claims following the fire of London.

Turnor died in office on 19 May 1675, and was buried on 22 May at Milton Ernest, 'the place of my birth' (will, PRO, PROB 11/350, sig. 8). His widow died in November 1707. The Milton Ernest estate was sold by his sons to Sir Thomas Rolt, but it was bought by Turnor's younger brother, Sir Edmund, in 1700. Eventually it was sold to Sir George Byng. STUART HANDLEY

Sources Venn, *Alum. Cant.* · Baker, *Serjeants* · Sainty, *Judges* · will, PRO, PROB 11/350, sig. 8 · H. A. C. Sturgess, ed., *Register of admissions to the Honourable Society of the Middle Temple, from the fifteenth century to the year 1944*, 1 (1949), 117 · Burke, *Gen. GB* (1833), 300–01 · A. M. Burke, ed., *Memorials of St Margaret's Church, Westminster* (1914), 95 · *State trials*, vol. 5 · F. A. Blaydes, ed., *Bedfordshire notes and queries*, 3 (1893), 365–6 · A. F. Havighurst, 'The judiciary and politics in the reign of Charles II [pt 1]', *Law Quarterly Review*, 66 (1950), 62–78, esp. 69, 72 · *CSP dom.*, 1638–9, 540; 1668–9, 466 · *Le Neve's Pedigrees of the knights*, ed. G. W. Marshall, Harleian Society, 8 (1873), 94 · *DNB*
Likenesses M. Wright, oils, 1671, Guildhall · S. Harding, stipple (after J. M. Wright), BM, NPG; repro. in S. Harding, *Biographical mirrour* (1792) · P. Lely, oils, Stoke Rochford Hall, Lincolnshire · portrait, Lincoln's Inn, London

Turnor, Christopher Hatton (1873–1940), agricultural and social reformer, was born at Toronto, Canada, on 23 November 1873, the only child of Christopher Hatton Turnor, evangelist, and Alice Margaret, eldest daughter of Hamilton H. Killally, of Toronto; the Turnor family had been wealthy landowners who had lived at Stoke Rochford, near Grantham in England, since the second half of the seventeenth century. He was great-grandson of the antiquary Edmund Turnor.

As a youngster Turnor had been educated in a haphazard fashion while his parents, who were committed Plymouth Brethren, toured North America, from Canada to Florida, seeking converts. After his arrival in England he became a student at the Royal Agricultural College, Cirencester, before transferring to Christ Church, Oxford, from which he graduated in 1896. After leaving the university, he initially pursued a career in architecture; the Watts Picture Gallery at Compton, in Surrey, and a number of private houses were his achievements in this sphere.

In 1903, following the sudden death of his uncle Edmund Turnor, he inherited the family estates in Lincolnshire, the property being passed to Christopher by virtue of the fact that his father, the next in line to inherit, had waived his claim in favour of his son. At this stage the estates encompassed 24,000 acres in both north and south Lincolnshire, in addition to Stoke Rochford Hall, which had been built in the 1840s by his grandfather, Christopher Turnor. The estate was, however, experiencing financial difficulties, with 4000 acres of land unlet and being farmed at a loss.

Unlike many of his contemporaries Turnor was not prepared simply to enjoy the social amenities of his new position or to accept the prevailing view that there was little future for British agriculture. Instead, committed to the belief that land ownership was a trust, he helped to pioneer a new and more dynamic approach to estate management. One half of the land in hand was quickly relet, and highly qualified farm managers, one of whom was Danish, were appointed to look after the rest. Most of the

shooting was rented out, as was even the mansion house at Stoke Rochford. In 1907 Turnor married Sarah Marie Talbot, the only child of Admiral Walter Cecil Carpenter of Kipling, Northallerton, Yorkshire, second son of the eighteenth earl of Shrewsbury. The couple did not have any children. In the years after his marriage there was further rationalization of estate management, culminating in 1917 in the sale of the 6000 acre Wragby estates.

During this period Turnor was an ardent campaigner for agricultural reform and an advocate of rural regeneration, committed to the more efficient use of land. As a reform-orientated agriculturist he was closely associated with Charles Bathurst MP (later Lord Bledisloe). Both were large estate owners who considered that the traditional position and role of the aristocracy was being threatened by the new plutocracy of financiers and industrialists. In their view, landlords were failing to provide leadership in the form of the provision of scientific and economic guidance. Paternalism in its traditional form of the acceptance of non-economic rents, or a willingness to tolerate unprogressive tenants, was thought unacceptable. This, they argued, merely served to weaken the partnership between the three main agricultural classes. To Turnor and Bathurst agricultural reform and the education of the rural population was the way to alleviate Britain's problems.

During the First World War, Turnor played a key role in a number of government-inspired official investigations. In addition to lectures and seminars on agricultural and educational reform, he was a prolific writer. His best-known work was *Land Problems and National Welfare* (1911). This was followed by *Our Food Supply* (1916), *The Land and the Empire* (1917), and *The Land and its Problems* (1921). His final book, *Yeoman Calling*, was published in 1939, just before his death. Turnor was also the author of numerous pamphlets and a frequent contributor to *The Times*. An active member of a number of agricultural organizations, he was a co-founder, with his relative Algernon Turner (1845–1921), of the Central Landowners' Association from its inception. The problems of rural housing, and especially the provision of smallholdings as stepping stones for enterprising farm workers, continued to interest him.

Turnor's ideas on agricultural reform were unfortunately not widely supported either by fellow agriculturists or by the urban population. His main achievement was to devote Stoke Rochford mansion, after he had resumed occupation of it, to the hosting of summer schools for a multitude of different groups. These included the Workers' Educational Association, students, teachers, and church conferences dealing with a diverse range of social and religious questions. His pioneering role in this area was unsurpassed. Turnor died at the Imperial Hotel, Torquay, on 19 August 1940, survived by his wife; the estate was inherited by his first cousin Major Herbert Broke Turnor. JOHN MARTIN

Sources *The Times* (22 Aug 1940) · T. R. Leach, *The Turnors and their Wragby estates* (1978) · A. F. Cooper, *Agricultural policy, 1912–1936* (1989) · P. E. Dewey, *British agriculture in the First World War* (1989) · J. Franklin, 'Troops of servants: labour and planning in the country house, 1840–1914', *Victorian Studies*, 19 (1975–6), 211–39 • C. H. Turnor, *Land problems and national welfare* (1911) • C. H. Turnor, *Our food supply: perils and remedies* (1916) • C. H. Turnor, *The land and the empire* (1917) • C. H. Turnor, *Yeoman calling* (1939) • personal knowledge (1949) [*DNB*] • d. cert.

Archives Lincs. Arch., papers, incl. lectures

Wealth at death £21,739 12s. 1d.: probate, save and except settled land, 10 May 1941, *CGPLA Eng. & Wales* • £255,919 6s. 1d.: further grant, limited to settled land, 27 Sept 1941, *CGPLA Eng. & Wales*

Turnor, Edmund (*bap.* 1754, *d.* 1829), landowner and antiquary, was baptized on 14 December 1754 at the church of St Mary Magdalene, Lincoln, the eldest son of Edmund Turnor (1719/20–1805), landowner, and Mary Disney (1731/2–1818) of Stoke Rochford, Lincolnshire. His mother was the only daughter of John and Frances Disney of Swinderby and Lincoln, whose family had given its name to Norton Disney. Following his education at Stamford School he entered Trinity College, Cambridge, as a fellow-commoner in 1772; he graduated BA in 1777 and proceeded MA in 1781. By this time his family had substantially extended the estates in Lincolnshire following the purchase of Panton Hall in 1775, the reconstruction of which became an important preoccupation of his father until his death in 1805. On leaving university Turnor embarked upon a grand tour of France, Switzerland, and Italy, which fired his interest in antiquities. On returning to Stoke Rochford he continued his lifelong career of investigating and writing on various aspects of architecture and other types of antiquities. On 7 May 1795 at Nacton, Suffolk, he married Elizabeth Broke (*bap.* 1773, *d.* 1801), eldest daughter of Philip Bowes Broke and Elizabeth Beaumont of Nacton, Suffolk.

In 1773, even before going to university, Turnor had compiled and printed an informative pamphlet, *London's gratitude, or, An account of such pieces of sculpture and painting as have been placed in Guildhall at the expense of the City of London*. In 1779 he published *Chronological tables of the high sheriffs of the county of Lincoln and the knights of the shire, citizens and burgesses in parliament within the same from the earliest accounts to the present time*. His paper describing a castle at Rouen in Normandy called Le Château du Vieux Palais, built by Henry V of England, was read to the Society of Antiquaries on 1 April 1784 and printed in *Archaeologia* (7, 232–5). He was elected a fellow of the Royal Society on 15 June 1786, fellow of the Society of Antiquaries two years later, and was also a fellow of the École de Dessin at Rouen. In 1792 he presented a paper to the Society of Antiquaries, 'Extracts from the household book of Thomas Coney of Basingthorpe, co. Lincoln', which was printed in *Archaeologia* (11, 22–33). This was followed by a paper to the Royal Society, 'A narrative of the earthquake felt in Lincolnshire and the neighbouring counties on 25 September 1792', which was printed in the *Philosophical Transactions* (82, 283–8). In the following year he compiled a memoir of Sir Richard Fanshawe for the *Biographia Britannica*. In 1801 he presented a paper, 'Remarks on the military history of Bristol in the seventeenth century', to the Society of Antiquaries. His wife died on 21 January 1801, leaving one daughter, Elizabeth Edmunda.

On 22 March 1803, at St Mary's, Marylebone, Turnor married Dorothea Tucker (1776/7–1854), third daughter of Lieutenant-Colonel Martin Tucker. He had just been elected MP for the borough of Midhurst, Sussex, which he represented, as a Pittite, until the dissolution of parliament in 1806. He became high sheriff for Lincolnshire in 1810 and for a number of years was a magistrate for the area. He wrote extensively on a wide variety of topics, and his publications included *Collections for the history of the town and soke of Grantham, containing authentic memoirs of Sir Isaac Newton from Lord Portsmouth's manuscripts* (1806). He is also credited with compiling *A Short History of the Proceedings in the County of Lincoln for a Limited Exportation of Wool*, printed in 1824. In the following year he provided the Society of Antiquaries with an account of the remains of a Roman bath near Stoke in Lincolnshire, which was published in *Archaeologia* (22, 26–32). Two weeks before his death he announced similar discoveries in the same neighbourhood which had been investigated by his brother-in-law Sir Philip Vere Broke.

Turnor is best remembered for his wide-ranging antiquarian pursuits, the breadth of which inhibited him from becoming eminent in a more specialized field. Like his father, he also continued to extend the family estates. Between 1809 and 1826 he purchased several parcels of land in Panton and Wragby. In 1821 he acquired the manor of Wispington, including the impropriate, rectory, and advowson. The following year he purchased property in Horsington, and in 1827 property in Langton by Wragby. He was also responsible for founding in 1824 a school based on the principles advocated by Alexander Bell for the religious education of the poor children in his surrounding parishes. He died at Stoke Park, near Grantham, on 19 March 1829 and was buried the same day in an altar tomb, which he had designed himself, in the family vault at the church of St Andrew and St Mary at Stoke Rochford. He was survived by the daughter of his first marriage, who had married Frederick Manning, by his second wife, and by seven of their eleven children. JOHN MARTIN

Sources *GM*, 1st ser., 99/1 (1829), 566–8 • Nichols, *Lit. anecdotes* • T. R. Leach, *The Turnors and their Wragby estates* (1978) • A. R. Maddison, ed., *Lincolnshire pedigrees*, 3, Harleian Society, 52 (1904) • H. M. Colvin, 'Panton Hall', *Lincolnshire Historian*, 1/7 (1951) • *Lincoln, Rutland and Stamford Mercury* (30 Jan 1801) • *Lincoln, Rutland and Stamford Mercury* (26 May 1854) • L. Taylor, 'Turnor, Edmund', HoP, *Commons, 1790–1820* • Venn, *Alum. Cant.* • *DNB* • J. Ingamells, ed., *A dictionary of British and Irish travellers in Italy, 1701–1800* (1997) • *IGI*

Wealth at death Stoke Rochford and surrounding estates • school endowment: Nichols, *Lit. anecdotes*, 599

Turnor, Sir Edward (1616/17–1676), judge and speaker of the House of Commons, was the second son of Arthur Turnor (*d.* 1651), treasurer of the Middle Temple and serjeant-at-law, and Anne, daughter of John Jermy of Gunton, in Norfolk. He was educated at Abingdon grammar school under Dr Thomas Godwin before enrolling at Queen's College, Oxford. He matriculated from there, aged fifteen, on 9 November 1632, but does not appear to have graduated. Following an established family tradition he began his legal studies at the Middle Temple in 1633, and was called to the bar on 19 June 1640. In contrast to his elder brother, John, who was killed during the first civil

Sir Edward Turnor (1616/17–1676), by John Michael Wright?

war, Edward attempted to preserve his own neutrality throughout the conflict. At an unknown date he married Sarah (*bap.* 1624, *d.* 1651), daughter of Gerard Gore, alderman of London, with whom he had four sons, the eldest of whom was Edward *Turnour (or Turner), and two daughters. Through her he acquired the estates of Shillinglee Park, Kirdford, Sussex, and Down Place, near Godalming, in Surrey. After Sarah's death, on 4 December 1652 he married Mary (*d.* in or before 1676?), widow of William Ashton, and daughter of Henry Ewer of South Mimms, Middlesex. Though he had no children from his second marriage he became embroiled in a court case in early 1656 as the result of a dispute between his wife and John Buck over the non-payment of his stepdaughter's dowry and the custody and paternity of her children.

Having held local offices in Essex and Hertfordshire during the early years of the republic Turnor represented Essex in the three protectorate parliaments of 1654, 1656, and 1659. However, it would appear that he was no friend of the Cromwellian regime for he was excluded from the Commons in 1656. On the eve of the Restoration his fortunes changed dramatically. Having defeated Sir Harbottle Grimston in the election contest for Essex he was nominated as speaker of the House of Commons by leading Anglicans at the first meeting of the Convention Parliament in April 1660. Although his candidature was blocked by presbyterian members and Grimston, who had been returned as MP for Colchester, he was elected speaker on 25 April; Turnor gained the influential post of chairman of the elections committee. With an unprecedented number of disputed results he used his authority to favour high Anglican—as opposed to presbyterian—candidates, thereby contributing greatly to the pro-

royalist composition of, and hold over, the chamber. On 8 May he reported to the house on the preparations being made for the return of Charles II to England, and carried the draft proclamation announcing the Restoration up to the Lords. His close personal and political ties with leading financiers in the City of London expedited a £100,000 loan to the king, which effectively confirmed him in the royal favour. Honours and gifts followed swiftly. He was made king's counsel and attorney-general to the duke of York on 15 June and was knighted on 7 July 1660. Turnor was closely involved in the drafting of the Bill of Indemnity and Oblivion, and reported to the house on the clauses for excluding particular individuals from it, namely Henry Vane the younger, Arthur Heselrige, John Lambert, and Daniel Axtell, on account of their 'dangerous principles' (Helms and Hampson, 3.614). He served as prosecuting counsel during the trials of the regicides in October 1660, where he likened the spread of republicanism to the speed and virulence of the plague.

Turnor was elected to the Cavalier Parliament in February 1661 as member for Hertford, the clients of the duke of York moving to ensure that his candidature for the office of speaker would this time be successful. He was duly appointed when parliament met in May and proved himself to be a faithful servant of the crown; his addresses in parliament to the king were characterized by their florid tone and adulatory, if not slavish, nature. On 10 May 1661 he declared that monarchical government was 'certainly the best, as being nearest to Divinity itself', and thundered against the republican experiment, concluding that: 'We were sick of Reformation; Our Reformers were of all Ages, Sexes and Degrees; of all Professions and Trades. The Very Cobbler went beyond his Last … This was the Sickness and Plague of the Nation' (*JHL*, 11, 1660–61, 246). Though far from a compelling orator Turnor was inordinately proud of his parliamentary speeches and ordered them to be privately published in April 1670, to the evident fury of the printer already rewarded with the monopoly of publishing proceedings in parliament. Government sinecures and financial payments were bestowed upon Turnor, thick and fast. He received 'free gifts' of £2000 in December 1663, £5000 in July 1664, £4000 in June 1670, and £4000 in September 1674. In July 1661 he had been granted revenues from shipping along the Norfolk and Suffolk coasts in return for his maintenance of the lighthouses at Winterton Ness and Orford Ness, but he was rebuked in August 1666 for indiscriminately 'seizing the ships of the King's allies' as well as Dutch merchantmen, and later that month narrowly escaped prosecution for failing to clear the River Wye of obstructions though he had become one of the 'principal proprietors thereof' (*CSP dom.*, 1666–7, 27, 72–3). The adjournment of parliament in 1668 proved inconvenient and financially disagreeable to him. As speaker he was obliged to be attended by the mace at all times—even when the house was not in session—and he was forbidden to accept private legal briefs. However, his appeals to be released from such burdensome formalities, and professional restraints, were overruled by the Commons before its dissolution. It is conceivable that Turnor's appointments as solicitor-general, on 11 May 1670, and serjeant-at-law and lord chief baron of the exchequer, in May 1671, were intended as sops, in order to lessen the blow of a further prorogation, which had occurred in April 1670. However, Roger North later alleged that controversy had begun to cling to Sir Edward's name on account of the bribe of 50 golden pieces that Turnor had received from the East India Company in March 1666, and that his position as speaker had become increasingly untenable as a result of the parliamentary inquiry into the company's finances in 1669.

Even though Turnor resigned as speaker in February 1673 he does not seem to have forfeited his royal patronage and continued as a circuit court judge in Norfolk. He died at Bedford, after presiding at a session of the assizes, on 4 March 1676, and was accorded a public funeral. His body lay in state at his house in Chancery Lane, London, until 16 March, when it was escorted through the City by the coaches of the king, queen, duke of York, and the archbishop of Canterbury, and then driven through Hertfordshire and on into Essex, where he was buried in the chancel of Little Parndon church later that day. His wife is not mentioned in his will and may have predeceased him.

Turnor's graft and hypocrisy were mercilessly satirized by Andrew Marvell in 1671 in his *Last Instructions to a Painter*. With his 'Bright hair, fair face' Turnor was still

> obscure and dull of head
> Like knife with ivory haft and edge of lead.

Moreover, despite all his professions of high Anglican piety:

> At prayers his eyes turn up the pious white,
> But all the while his private bill's in sight
> ...
> When grievance urged, he swells like squatted toad,
> Frisks like a frog to croak a tax's load.
> (*Poems and Letters*, 1.162)

JOHN CALLOW

Sources J. A. Manning, *The lives of the speakers of the House of Commons* (1850) · M. W. Helms and G. Hampson, 'Turnor, Edward', HoP, *Commons, 1660–90*, 3.613–15 · Foss, *Judges*, vol. 7 · A. Grey, ed., *Debates of the House of Commons, from the year 1667 to the year 1694*, new edn, 10 vols. (1769), vol. 1 · *JHL*, 11–12 (1660–75) · Pepys, *Diary*, vols. 4–5, 8–10 · *The poems and letters of Andrew Marvell*, ed. H. M. Margoliouth, 1 (1927) · *The votes and orders of the Honourable House of Commons, passed Feb. 25 and 26 1662 ... together with their reasons and address ... by their speaker* (1662) · *His majesties' gracious speech. Together with the lord chancellors' [29 Dec. 1660] ... as also that of the speaker* (1660) · N. Carlisle, *An inquiry into the place and quality of the gentlemen of his majesties most honourable privy chamber* (1829) · G. H. Simpkinson, *Thomas Harrison: regicide and major-general* (1905) · *Members of parliament, part 1: parliament of England, 1213–1702* (1878) · F. J. Varley, *Major-General Thomas Harrison* (1939) · J. Peacey, ed., *The regicides and the execution of Charles I* (2001) · P. Morant, *The history and antiquities of the county of Essex*, 2 (1768) · B. Gardner, *The East India Company* (1971) · R. Hutton, *Charles the Second: king of England, Scotland and Ireland* (1989) · G. Harvey, 'Some account of the great fire in London in 1666', in D. Defoe, *A journal of the plague year* (1882) · A. P. Barclay, 'The impact of James II on the departments of the royal household', PhD diss., U. Cam., 1994 · R. North, *The lives of ... Francis North ... Dudley North ... and ... John North*, new edn, 3 vols. (1826) · *DNB* · *CSP dom., 1660–77*

Archives Essex RO, Chelmsford, assize rolls, 35/105–122 · Essex RO, Chelmsford, C 191/7/47 · Essex RO, Chelmsford, Q/SR 388/66
Likenesses M. Wright, oils, c.1671 · probably J. M. Wright, oils, Palace of Westminster, London [*see illus.*] · by or after J. M. Wright, oils, Harvard U., law school
Wealth at death £6000 to daughter and £2000 to granddaughter; remainder of estate to eldest son: Helms and Hampson, 'Turnor, Edward', 615; North, *The lives*, 97–8; *CSP dom., 1670*, 292; 1661–2, 52; 1655–6, 115; 1663–4, 398, 656; 1666–7, 27; 1671, 505

Turnor, Philip (1750/51–1799/1800), land surveyor and map maker, came from Laleham, Middlesex, and was originally engaged in farming. He first comes to notice in the records of the Hudson's Bay Company (HBC) for 1778. By this date the HBC committee in London had a tradition of developing strategies and issuing instructions for its operations more than 3000 miles away in Rupert's Land. It had recognized the need to compete effectively in the interior with the more aggressive Montreal-based Canadian fur traders; in particular to build posts far up the rivers from the company's established bay-side forts. But it lacked reliable maps with which to plan. In 1775, of its sixty or so manuscript maps and plans, very few were of the interior. Recognizing the need to produce new and reliable ones, the committee sought the advice of the astronomer William Wales FRS. Wales recommended Philip Turnor's appointment as the first of the company's inland surveyors.

Turnor's first contract with the company, of 6 May 1778, engaged him for 'Three Years' at 'Fifty Pounds per Year' (HBC records, A32/3, fol. 27). He was competent in mathematics and surveying and from the beginning his status was fairly high among HBC employees. With a salary more than five times that of a labourer on first contract, he ate at the captain's table on his first voyage to York Fort (now in Manitoba) and with the chief factor on arrival. Wales was paid 5 guineas for having recommended him.

Turnor served four three-year contracts in Rupert's Land, from August 1778 to September 1787 and August 1789 to September 1792. His first duty on reaching York Fort was to survey it, examine the fabric of its buildings, and send a report back to the London committee. Drawn in the month of his arrival, the large-scale plan was the first of at least nine maps and numerous plans he was to make for the company (HBC records, G1/109). Within a few days of completing it he was sent to Cumberland House (now in Saskatchewan). Thereafter he spent most of his time in the interior: in 1778–9 on the Saskatchewan River, in 1779–87 to the south of James Bay, and in 1789–92 at and beyond Cumberland House. He adapted quickly to travel and subsistence in the lichen woodlands and coniferous forests of which he had no previous experience, snaring birds and hunting small mammals within weeks of arrival and walking, snow-shoeing, and canoeing more than 4000 miles during his first two years. Apart from occasional snow blindness and a winter with rheumatism, he was healthy and strong.

In 1782 Turnor was appointed master at Brunswick House, at the confluence of the Opasatika and Missinaibi rivers. Between then and 1787 he mixed trading for marten, muskrat, and other pelts with occasional surveying and map making. As a master, he implemented instructions, managed the post, supervised employees, traded with Indians, and maintained correspondence, but it was as astronomer, mathematician, surveyor, cartographer, and teacher of these skills that the committee most valued him.

Between 1778 and 1782 Turnor

> prepared three original maps and several copies. He observed and calculated the astronomical locations of all the HBC's factories and posts, of the significant junctions of the interior waterways, and of important geographical features along the sea coasts, all of which he had visited.
> (Ruggles, 49)

From 1782 to 1787 Turnor devoted less time to such activities but surveyed several of the rivers draining into James Bay, usually doing so on return—downstream—journeys. Between 1789 and 1792 he led an exploring and mapping expedition into the beaver- and marten-rich Athabasca country, in which Canadians had been trading with Indians for nearly a decade but about which the HBC knew almost nothing. His observation of the latitude and longitude of Fort Chipewyan (now in Alberta), when compared with those made on the Pacific coast by Captain James Cook gave Alexander Mackenzie some real comprehension of the extent of the country through which he was to pass in 1793 in the first crossing of the continent by a European.

Turnor returned to England for the last time in October 1792 but soon afterwards the committee decided to pay him 'one guinea per week until further orders' (HBC records, A1/47, fol. 4). Between then and early 1795 he compiled several manuscript maps, of which the last is now considered one of Canada's greatest cartographic treasures. 'To the Honourable Governor … This Map of Hudson's Bay and the Rivers and Lakes Between the Atlantick and Pacifick Oceans' (HBC records, G2/32) is very large (193 cm × 259 cm). It has an exquisite cartouche attributed to Edward Dayes, the London topographical watercolourist (Turner, 8.584), and at least some of the calligraphy was by one of two artist–engraver brothers Charles and Peltro William Tomkins (ibid., 31.137). The map is a composite of information available in 1794 from Turnor's own calculations, sketches, and previously completed maps as well as those of others, fitted onto a graticule 'he himself had done so much to perfect' (Ruggles, 54). In 1795 the committee paid him £100 for the map and presented him with the HBC watch he had carried for many years (HBC records, A1/47, fol. 47). Though the map was never published, the committee gave Aaron Arrowsmith almost immediate access to it and it formed the basis of his 'Map exhibiting all the new discoveries in the interior parts of North America' (1795).

Little is known of Turnor's later life. In or about 1794 his address was Prospect Row, Dock Head, Rotherhithe, London, where he taught navigation. John Turnor, captain of an HBC sloop, is said to have been a brother (Rich, *Hudson's Bay Company*, 88–9, 98), though whether he was the John Turner who captained company trans-Atlantic supply ships between 1790 and 1816 is less clear (Cooke and Holland, 439). Philip Turnor last wrote to the company on 4 December 1799. On 26 March 1800 the London committee read a petition from his widow, Elizabeth, praying for pecuniary assistance. He had presumably married either during his furlough in 1787–9 or after his return to England in 1792.

Turnor's influence on the mapping of Rupert's Land continued after his death as a result of his surprising choice of assistant surveyor for the Athabasca expedition. In 1790, having rejected three men trained in astronomical observation, he selected **Peter Fidler** (1769–1822), surveyor and cartographer, from Bolsover, Derbyshire. Fidler, born on 16 August 1769, was the son of James and Mary Fidler, and had joined the company as a general labourer in the previous year. Reasonably well educated he had sufficient mathematical training to pick up practical astronomy quickly. He was also physically strong, keen to learn, and ambitious. Turnor trained him in surveying, field sketching, and cartography, and encouraged him to live, travel, and communicate with Indians. His wife, Mary (d. 1826), with whom he had fourteen children, was a Swampy Cree Indian. (Their long-standing union was solemnized on 14 August 1821.) Fidler succeeded Turnor as the company's chief surveyor and between 1790 and 1820 made eighty separate maps and 373 segmented sketch maps, more than any other company cartographer. Although his methods were those of Turnor he developed a distinctive map making procedure that had hitherto been used by company employees only very occasionally. He regularly asked Indians and company colleagues for descriptions and sketches of areas and routes known to them and in this way produced forty-four maps. He retired from the HBC in 1821, but stayed in Rupert's Land and died at Fort Dauphin (Dauphin, Manitoba) on 17 December 1822.

G. MALCOLM LEWIS

Sources R. I. Ruggles, *A country so interesting: the Hudson's Bay Company and two centuries of mapping, 1670–1870* (1991) · E. E. Rich, *The history of the Hudson's Bay Company, 1670–1870*, 2: 1763–1870 (1959) · records, Hudson's Bay Company Archives, Winnipeg · E. E. Rich, 'Turnor, Philip', *DCB*, vol. 4 · J. B. Tyrrell, ed., *The journals of Samuel Hearne and Philip Turnor* (1934) · E. E. Rich, ed., *Moose Fort journals, 1783–85*, Hudson's Bay Record Society, 17 (1954) · E. E. Rich, ed., *Cumberland House journals and inland journal, 1775–82: First series, 1775–79* (1951) · Manitoba Culture Heritage and Recreation, Historic Resources Branch, *Peter Fidler* (1984) · *The journals and letters of Sir Alexander Mackenzie*, ed. W. Kaye Lamb, Hakluyt Society, extra ser., 41 (1970) · C. Verner and B. Stuart-Stubbs, *The north part of America* (1979) · R. C. Harris, ed., *Historical atlas of Canada*, 1 (1987), pl. 60, 62, 67 · *The national atlas of Canada*, 4th edn (1974), 78 · J. G. MacGregor, *Peter Fidler: Canada's forgotten explorer, 1769–1822* (Calgary, AB, 1998) · J. Turner, ed., *The dictionary of art*, 34 vols. (1996), vols. 8, 31 · R. S. Allen, 'Fidler, Peter', *DCB*, vol. 6 · A. Cooke and C. Holland, *The exploration of northern Canada, 500 to 1920* (1978)

Archives NA Canada, journal | Hudson's Bay Company, Winnipeg, archives, MSS

Turnour [Turnor], **Sir Edward** (1642×7–1721), lawyer and politician, was born at Little Parndon, Essex, the eldest son of Sir Edward *Turnor (1616/17–1676), judge and speaker of the House of Commons, and his first wife, Sarah (bap. 1624, d. 1651), daughter and heir of Gerard

Gore, merchant and alderman of London. Through this marriage the family acquired Down Place, Surrey, and Shillinglee Park, Sussex, where Edward's brother Arthur made his home.

Turnour (the form in which he signed his name on his will) was admitted to the Middle Temple on 24 October 1661 and as a fellow-commoner to Christ's College, Cambridge, on 17 February 1662, when his age was given as fifteen. Knighted on 6 February 1664, he was called to the bar in 1672. In May 1667 he married Lady Isabella (d. 1690), daughter of William Keith, seventh Earl Marischal. They had seven children and lived at Great Hallingbury, Essex, purchased in 1660 by Turnour's father. Lady Isabella was buried there in 1690. In the 1690s Sir Edward, a high-Anglican tory with possible Jacobite leanings, immersed himself in party politics, a move which brought confrontation and inordinate expense. He concentrated on becoming an MP via two constituencies in Suffolk—a county with which the Turnour family retained some associations after having migrated from it in the early seventeenth century. Through rights granted to his father and grandfather, Sir Edward laid claim to a lease of three lighthouses at Winterton Ness, near Caistor, Norfolk, and two at Orford Ness, Suffolk. After 1688 he contrived to use the patronage of the latter to seek election at Aldeburgh before settling in 1692 on the neighbouring maritime borough of Orford.

Seldom venturing across the Essex/Suffolk border, Turnour relied on a network of leading tories and party agents living in Suffolk to effect his parliamentary ambitions. Their numerous reports survive among the family papers, providing a rare, detailed insight into the conduct of grass-root politics at this time. Their strenuous endeavours, however, failed to make Orford into the compliant pocket borough Turnour desired. Enormous political turmoil at the local level split the corporation into two distinct entities and electorates from 1693 to 1704. This bedevilled Sir Edward's campaigning and, for the split's duration, also involved him in expensive, irksome litigation. Moreover, as Orford's dual lights donned a political hue, allegations of negligence concerning maintenance of the lighthouses brought him into sharp conflict with Trinity House too.

Although political opposition to Turnour's candidatures was relentless and did not abate with Orford corporation's reunification in 1704, he did eventually achieve electoral success. Returned as one of Orford's two MPs on 10 January 1701, he held on to his seat until 29 January 1709 and sat again for this borough from 10 October 1710 until his death. In parliament Turnour consistently supported the tories, including voting for the tack in 1704, an attempt by high-church tories to suppress occasional conformity. He also expended much time, energy, and money battling with family matters. Among the family papers are documents concerning a long, bitter rift which commenced in the early 1690s between Sir Edward and his only surviving son, Charles (d. 1726). The cause of this, and another with his daughter Sarah, is summarized in explicit instructions

that Sir Edward gave his lawyer, Thomas Lutwyche, on 15 May 1719:

> if it should be asked why I leave my son Charles Turnour and Sarah Gee out of this my last Will let this answer suffice, because they both married themselves without my consent or leave askt, nay even contrary to my particular commands to two most begarly persons; my son's wife [Dorothea, née Fenwick] a papist, and my daughter Gee's husband [Francis] a vile proffligate wretch by which means they have, (especially my son) ruined themselves and almost undon[e] their father by continuall suites at law for almost twenty five years. (W. Sussex RO, Winterton/Shillinglee MSS, Ac.454/302)

Turnour died on 3 December 1721 and was buried at Great Hallingbury; one authority gives his age as seventy-eight. Dated 2 May 1720, his last will named his unmarried daughter Mary as his main, immediate beneficiary, she having, in Turnour's words, 'never disobeyed nor in any materiall matter disobliged me' (will). But arduous, costly disputes with those who had meant that many debts remained outstanding on his decease. Consequently, in 1727, Sir Edward's then surviving heirs obtained an act of parliament to sell some of his property. By this means Great Hallingbury was purchased in 1729 by Jacob Houblon, and Sir Edward's house no longer exists. In 1744 Turnour's great-grandson, Edward Turnour Garth Turnour, later earl of Winterton in the Irish peerage, succeeded to the remaining family estates, including Shillinglee Park.   P. E. MURRELL

Sources M. W. Helms and G. Hampson, 'Turnor, Edward', HoP, Commons, 1660–90 · R. R. Sedgwick, 'Turnor, Sir Edward', HoP, Commons, 1715–54 · P. Morant, *The history and antiquities of the county of Essex*, 2 vols. (1768) · F. G. Emmerson, *Guide to the Essex Record Office*, 2nd edn (1969) · P. E. Murrell, 'Suffolk: the political behaviour of the county and its parliamentary boroughs from the exclusion crisis to the accession of the house of Hanover', PhD diss., U. Newcastle, 1982 · W. Sussex RO, Winterton/Shillinglee papers, Ac.454 · will, W. Sussex RO, Winterton/Shillinglee MS 25/20 · *VCH Suffolk* · C. E. Welch, 'Sir E. Turnour's lighthouses at Orford', *Proceedings of the Suffolk Institute of Archaeology*, 28 (1958–60), 62–74 · C. E. Welch, 'The Turnour chapel at Little Wratting', *Proceedings of the Suffolk Institute of Archaeology*, 27 (1955–7), 37–40 · *JHC*, 21 (1727–32) · *JHL*, 23 (1726–31) · M. M. Drummond, 'Turnour, Garth', 'Turnour, Edward', HoP, Commons, 1754–90 · GEC, *Peerage*, new edn · Venn, *Alum. Cant.* · *Le Neve's Pedigrees of the knights*, ed. G. W. Marshall, Harleian Society, 8 (1873), 180 · *DNB* · *The Genealogist*, new ser., 15 (1898–9), 192 · A. I. Dasent, *The speakers of the House of Commons* (1911) · W. A. Speck, 'The House of Commons, 1702–1714: a study in political organisation', DPhil diss., U. Oxf., 1965

Archives Essex RO, Chelmsford, Turnour Papers, D/DKW · Suffolk RO, Ipswich, Orford Borough, EE5 · W. Sussex RO, Winterton/Shillinglee papers, Ac.454

Wealth at death see will, W. Sussex RO, Winterton/Shillinglee MS 25/20

Turnour, Edward, sixth Earl Winterton (1883–1962), politician, was born in London on 4 April 1883, the only child of Edward Turnour, fifth Earl Winterton (1837–1907), and his wife, Lady Georgiana Susan Hamilton (1841–1913), fifth daughter of James Hamilton, first duke of Abercorn. Educated at Eton College and at New College, Oxford, where he studied law, he had hardly begun his third year as an undergraduate when at a by-election in November 1904 he was returned to Westminster as Conservative

Edward Turnour, sixth Earl Winterton (1883–1962), by Elliott & Fry

member of parliament for the Horsham division of Sussex. Viscount Turnour (the courtesy title he bore) was not yet twenty-two and the youngest member of the house. On his father's death in 1907 he succeeded to the family honours, together with substantial estates in Sussex and Norfolk. As an Irish peer, however, he was not obliged to relinquish his seat in the Commons, which he held continuously until 1951.

Winterton was swiftly installed on the threshold of office as parliamentary private secretary to E. G. Pretyman, financial secretary to the Admiralty. In opposition after the Liberal victory of 1906 he ministered to the ailing Joseph Chamberlain. Freed from these decorous duties in 1908, he made his mark as an astute tactician and pugnacious debater. His talent for insolence and disparagement was much in demand on the tory benches during resistance to such contentious Liberal measures as the Parliament Bill of 1911 and home rule for Ireland. 'There was a little ill-temper', Winston Churchill reported to the king on 19 April 1911, 'and Lord Winterton became conspicuous.' These encounters did not deter the future first lord of the Admiralty from inviting Winterton to become a founder member of the Other Club or from establishing a lifelong though wary friendship. As much amused by journalism as by journalists, Winterton in 1909 bought an interest in, and briefly edited, a weekly newspaper called *The World*.

In the First World War Winterton served with the Sussex yeomanry in Gallipoli, with the Imperial Camel Corps in the Egyptian expeditionary force, and ultimately with T. E. Lawrence in the Hejaz operations that culminated in the fall of Damascus. He was twice mentioned in dispatches. Winterton's intense pride in having worn the king's uniform persisted to the end of his life, cutting across the less romantic loyalties of party politics. He invariably showed more respect for the opponent who had borne arms than for any colleague who had chosen to lie abed on St Crispian's day.

From 1922 to 1929, except for the brief interlude of the first Labour government, Winterton held office as parliamentary under-secretary for India and was sworn of the privy council in 1924. He received no post in the National Government of 1931 but was a delegate to the Burma round-table conference of that year and to the third India round-table conference of 1932. In concert with Churchill he pressed repeatedly for a strong defence policy to meet the growing menace of the dictators. His attachment to the Commons prompted him in 1935 to decline a United Kingdom peerage which would have becalmed him in the House of Lords. Baldwin had made the offer as a friendly gesture of regret that no place could be found for Winterton in the new cabinet. The prime minister was thus stung to anger when in May 1936 he read newspaper reports of a cabal at Shillinglee Park, Winterton's house in Sussex, attended by Churchill and other Conservative dissidents. 'This is the time of year', Baldwin observed, 'when midges come out of dirty ditches.'

Winterton returned to favour on Baldwin's retirement in 1937, when Neville Chamberlain invited him to be chancellor of the duchy of Lancaster. In March 1938 he was admitted to the cabinet as deputy to the secretary of state for air, Lord Swinton. Only ten weeks later, however, representing his department in the Commons during an angry debate on rearmament, he failed to convince the house either of the government's preparedness or of its determination to repair past neglect. A more artful politician might have pleaded that the fault lay less in his advocacy than in the realities of trying to rearm a peace-loving democracy. Winterton preferred to accept the entire blame for his poor performance and asked to be relieved of his duties at the Air Ministry. He remained chancellor of the duchy with additional duties at the Home Office. In the same year he became chairman of an intergovernmental committee for refugees, an appointment which he held until 1945. Winterton disappointed those of his friends who hoped that he would resign from the government in protest against the Munich agreement of 1938. On the contrary, his Christmas card for that year bore a photograph of Mr and Mrs Neville Chamberlain, with a comforting quotation from Horace Walpole: 'Who gives a nation peace, gives tranquillity to all.' In January 1939 he was nevertheless demoted to the sinecure office of paymaster-general without a seat in cabinet. Churchill offered him no place in the all-party coalition of 1940–45.

Winterton was glad to regain his parliamentary independence. Courteous and good-humoured outside the debating chamber, he scorned the arts of persuasion and compromise demanded of a minister at the dispatch box. He was a dedicated House of Commons man, tireless in preserving its customs and privileges, relishing interjections and points of order more than the plainer fare of legislation and supply. In the absence of an official opposition, he and a few other oddly assorted members determined that not even a wartime coalition led by Churchill should be spared critical scrutiny. Winterton's closest ally was the Labour member Emanuel Shinwell; the spectacle of patrician tory harnessed to Clydebank agitator evoked the jibe 'Arsenic and Old Lace', after a popular play of the time. More than once during the war Winterton was offered posts of dignity and importance overseas. He refused them all. But his fidelity to Westminster did bring him two rewarding duties. In 1944 he was appointed chairman of a select committee to consider the reconstruction of the Commons, destroyed by German bombs in 1941. He ensured that the chamber should be rebuilt in its traditional shape and style, whatever loss of modern convenience that might entail. And in 1945 he succeeded David Lloyd George as 'father of the house' when the former prime minister was created an earl. Later that year after the Labour victory at the general election, he was invited to join Churchill's shadow cabinet. In February 1952 he at last accepted a peerage of the United Kingdom, taking his seat in the House of Lords as Baron Turnour of Shillinglee, Sussex.

Eddie Winterton, as he was known by friends and foes alike, epitomized all the virtues and some of the supposed vices of the aristocrat in politics. He was fearless in exposing injustice or in challenging heartless bureaucracy; but he could also be quick-tempered and exceptionally offensive. The intolerance as well as the exuberance of youth persisted beyond middle age, and in the heat of controversy he would make personal allusions better left unsaid. Even while listening to others he displayed daunting mannerisms: grimly folded arms or knuckles cracking like pistol shots. When he could bear no more he exploded. If his shafts left few wounds, it was because of the affection he inspired as a 'character', almost an institution.

Winterton stood 6 feet 4 inches in height, his angular frame surmounted by a long, thin face, sharp nose, pale-blue eyes, and fair hair. In dress he favoured the high-buttoned jacket and narrow trousers of his youth. T. E. Lawrence wrote in *Seven Pillars of Wisdom* that 'Winterton's instinct joined him to the weakest and more sporting side in any choice but fox-hunting'. He was master of the Chiddingfold hunt and over the years hunted with no fewer than forty packs. At the age of seventy he sometimes spent four days out of five in the saddle. He called his favourite hunter Churchill. At the Beefsteak Club he enjoyed the company of men of letters and himself wrote three discursive volumes of memoirs.

On 28 February 1924 Winterton married Cecilia Monica Wilson (d. 1974), only daughter of Charles Henry Wellesley Wilson, second Baron Nunburnholme. There were no children. He died on 26 August 1962 at King Edward VII Hospital, Midhurst, Sussex, and was buried at Kirdford,

Sussex. He was succeeded as seventh earl by a distant kinsman, Flight Sergeant Robert Chad Turnour, of the Royal Canadian Air Force. The United Kingdom barony became extinct.

KENNETH ROSE, rev.

Sources *The Times* (28 Aug 1962) • Lord Winterton [E. Turnour], *Pre-war* (1932) • Lord Winterton [E. Turnour], *Orders of the day* (1953) • Lord Winterton [E. Turnour], *Fifty tumultuous years* (1955) • A. H. Brodrick, *Near to greatness: a life of the sixth Earl Winterton* (1965) • personal knowledge (1981) • Burke, *Peerage* (1999) • GEC, *Peerage*

Archives Bodl. Oxf., corresp., diaries, and papers | BL OIOC, letters to second earl of Lytton, MS Eur. F 160 • Bodl. RH, corresp. with Sir R. R. Welensky • CAC Cam., corresp. with Sir E. L. Spears • CUL, corresp. with Sir Samuel Hoare • HLRO, corresp. with Lord Beaverbrook • HLRO, letters to David Lloyd George • U. Reading L., corresp. with Nancy Astor | FILM BFI NFTVA, documentary footage

Likenesses W. Stoneman, two photographs, 1921–36, NPG • T. Cottrell, cigarette card, NPG • Elliott & Fry, photograph, NPG [*see illus.*] • W. Roberts, drawing, repro. in T. E. Lawrence, *The seven pillars of wisdom*, new edn (1935) • Spy [L. Ward], caricature, Hentschel-colourtype, NPG; repro. in *VF* (16 Sept 1908)

Wealth at death £160,366 11s.: probate save and except settled land, 3 April 1963, *CGPLA Eng. & Wales* • £78,822: probate limited to settled land, 14 May 1963, *CGPLA Eng. & Wales*

Turnour, George (1799–1843), orientalist, was born in Ceylon, the eldest son of George Turnour, a Ceylon civil servant, third son of Edward Turnour Garth Turnour, first earl of Winterton. His mother was Emilie, niece to the Cardinal duc de Beaussett. Turnour was educated in England. In 1818 he entered the Ceylon civil service, and began to study the Sinhala language. Through the Sinhala medium he then studied Pali, the religious language of Theravada Buddhism; at that time hardly anything was known to Europeans of the Pali language or its literature. In 1827 he obtained through the monk who was teaching him Pali a transcript of a manuscript of the commentary on the *Mahavamsa* ('Great chronicle'), the major of the two ancient Pali chronicles composed in Ceylon. His first publication about it was in the *Ceylon Almanack* of 1833. In 1836 he published at his own expense the first twenty chapters of the *Mahavamsa* with an English translation and a very long historical introduction; in 1837 he published thirty-eight chapters. This was the first publication anywhere of a Pali text of any length. He started on a second volume, but this was never published. In 1836–7 he also published several important articles in the *Journal of the Bengal Asiatic Society*. One included a translation of Buddhaghosa's account (dating from *c*.400 CE) of the first Buddhist council, held soon after the Buddha's death; Buddhists believe that the Buddhist scriptural canon was established orally on that occasion.

Turnour's greatest discovery was the identity of the promulgator of the celebrated rock edicts which are scattered over India, who calls himself Devanampiya Piyadassi. Turnour's examination of the ancient Pali chronicle, the *Dipavamsa* ('Island chronicle'), which he came upon in August 1837, showed him to be Asoka, grandson of Candragupta Maurya, the Sandrokottos of Greek historiography. He communicated this to James Prinsep, who had recently published decipherments of some of the rock edicts. Prinsep published the *Dipavamsa*, with a paper by Turnour, that very year. Through statements in the Asokan inscriptions which mention kings in Asia Minor, this established the absolute chronology of ancient India (to within a few years). Moreover, it was a great advance in estimating the date of the Buddha. The Ceylon chronicles are also the single most important source for the early history of Buddhism and of India in the period following the Buddha's death.

Turnour's literary work was carried on alongside his work in the civil service and in the latter part of his career he was a member of the supreme council of Ceylon. In 1841 he became ill and returned to Europe, where he died at Naples on 10 April 1843.   RICHARD F. GOMBRICH

Sources J. E. Tennent, *Ceylon: an account of the island, physical, historical, and topographical, with notices of its natural history, antiquities, and productions*, 3rd edn, 1 (1859), 312–17 · *Journal of the Royal Asiatic Society of Great Britain and Ireland*, 8 (1846), iv–v

Turold. See Thorold (*fl. c*.1100).

Turpin, Edmund Hart (1835–1907), organist, the eldest son of James Turpin, a lace manufacturer, and Elizabeth, daughter of Edmund Hart, was born in Nottingham on 4 May 1835. His father, an amateur musician, gave him his first lessons in music, after which he studied the organ under Charles Noble at St Mary's Church, Nottingham, and later with John Hullah and Ernst Pauer. In 1847 he was appointed organist of the Friar Lane Congregational Church in Nottingham and in 1850, he became organist of St Barnabas's Roman Catholic Cathedral, where he remained for fifteen years. He was also the bandmaster of the Nottingham corps of volunteers known as the Robin Hood Rifles. Soon, however, he was drawn to London, where he gave an organ recital at the Great Exhibition of 1851. Six years later he settled in London, although he still maintained his professional connection with Nottingham. Also in 1857 Turpin married Sarah Anne Watson, daughter of Robert Watson of Whitemoor, Nottingham. In 1860 he was appointed organist and choir director of the Catholic Apostolic Church in Gordon Square, Bloomsbury, a post which he effectively retained until his death. In 1869 he went to St George's, Bloomsbury, where he remained until his last appointment, at St Bride's, Fleet Street, in 1888.

Turpin was honorary secretary of the (Royal) College of Organists from 1875 onwards, and also acted as an administrator and examiner. The college commemorated him by a prize fund instituted in 1911. He was also elected an honorary member of the Tonic Sol-fa College (1885) and of the Royal Academy of Music (1890). He was a successful lecturer on musical subjects, and was intimately associated with London musical journalism, editing the *Musical Standard* from 1880 to 1886, and again from 1889 to 1890. For some years he was co-editor of *Musical News*, and he had connections also with the *Musical World* and the *Academic Gazette*. He edited the Student's Edition of classical piano music with marginal analyses; completed W. T. Best's edition of Bach's organ works, and prepared numerous organ arrangements and voluntaries. His own compositions included a Stabat Mater, two oratorios, two cantatas, a symphony, various concert overtures, church music of different kinds, piano music, and about twenty organ pieces.

Turpin received the degree of MusD from the archbishop of Canterbury in 1889 and was appointed warden of Trinity College of Music, London, in 1892. In 1903 his wife died after forty-six years of marriage and was buried in the Willesden cemetery. On 2 May 1905 Turpin married again, his second wife being Sarah Hobbs, the daughter of John Hobbs, a surgeon, of Bloomsbury. He died at his home at 107 Southampton Row, London, on 25 October 1907, after a fortnight's illness and was buried later that month in Highgate cemetery, Middlesex.

J. C. HADDEN, *rev.* NILANJANA BANERJI

Sources Brown & Stratton, *Brit. mus.* · *New Grove* · Grove, *Dict. mus.* (1954) · C. W. Pearce, *Biographical sketch of Edmund Hart Turpin* (1911) · *Musical Herald* (Dec 1907), 355–8 · *CGPLA Eng. & Wales* (1907)
Wealth at death £2329 17*s*. 5*d*.: probate, 19 Nov 1907, *CGPLA Eng. & Wales*

Turpin, Randolph Adolphus (1928–1966), boxer, was born on 7 June 1928 at his parents' home, 6 Willes Road, Leamington Spa, Warwickshire, the youngest of five children (three boys and two girls) of Lionel Fitzherbert Turpin, an iron-moulder at a gas stove works, and his wife, Beatrice Elizabeth Whitehouse. Lionel Turpin was a native of British Guiana who moved to Britain during the First World War, joined the infantry, and was gassed on the Somme; he eventually died from his injuries in 1929. Beatrice Turpin, a white Englishwoman, supported the family by working at a succession of low-paid jobs to eke out a meagre pension. In 1931 she married Ernest Manley, and the family settled in Warwick, where Randolph attended the West Gate council school.

Growing up in the face of racial prejudice, the Turpin boys learned to use their fists in self-defence. Randolph's elder brothers Dick and Jackie became 'booth fighters', putting on exhibition bouts at fairs and carnivals for a fistful of pennies tossed into the ring by spectators. Dick turned professional in 1937 and eventually (28 June 1948) became British middleweight champion, the first boxer of colour to hold a British professional title. Jackie became a ranked fighter in the featherweight division. Randolph's career began in 1942, when he joined the boxing section of the Leamington boys' club, started by a local policeman as a means of keeping youngsters out of trouble. He made his amateur début in March 1942, and subsequently fought more than 100 bouts, gaining national junior titles in 1943 and 1945. In 1945 he gained the Amateur Boxing Association welterweight championship. He meanwhile worked as a builder's labourer before volunteering in December 1945 for the Royal Navy, where he served as a cook at the Portsmouth naval base. In June 1946 he was a member of a British team that boxed against a United States squad selected by the Amateur Athletic Union. Shortly afterwards, in September 1946, he turned professional under the management of George Middleton. He married, on 25 January 1947, at St Peter's Roman Catholic

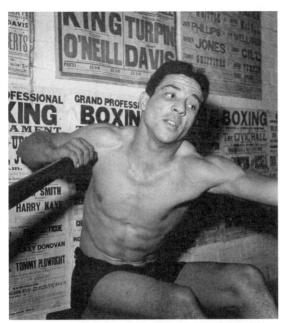

Randolph Adolphus Turpin (1928–1966), by Bert Hardy, 1949

Church, Leamington Spa, Mary Theresa (*b.* 1927/8), daughter of Matthew Paul Stack, a laboratory worker, and sister of Michael Stack, also a boxer. Their son was born later that year, but they separated in 1948.

Turpin left the navy in March 1948, and won all eight of his professional fights in the following year. Training at the Nelson gym, above a gelatine factory in Warwick, he used a regime of weight training to develop his body strength which, together with his long reach, made him a formidable fighter. On 17 October 1950 he won the British middleweight championship with a five-round victory over Croydon truck driver Albert Finch. His career really took off, however, when he sensationally knocked out Dutchman Luc van Dam in only 48 seconds at the Harringay arena on 27 February 1951, to take the European middleweight championship. By then his brawling, swinging, and slashing fighting style had earned him the publicity tag of the Leamington Licker. Subsequent victories inside the distance saw him matched with champion Sugar Ray Robinson for the world title at Earls Court, London, on 10 July 1951. The American, the four-to-one favourite, and only once defeated in 133 fights, was drained by a hectic European tour, and went down to a fifteen-round points defeat, in front of 18,000 wildly cheering British fans. As the first British fighter to hold the world middleweight title since Bob Fitzsimmons in 1891, Turpin became a national hero.

Turpin's reign lasted for only sixty-four days. In the rematch before 61,370 spectators at New York polo grounds on 12 September 1951, when Robinson was back to his best condition and sharpness, Turpin lost on a technical knock-out in the tenth round. He went on to fight in the heavier division, stopping Don Cockell in the eleventh round on 10 June 1952 to win the British and empire light heavyweight titles. On 21 October 1953 he challenged Carl

(Bobo) Olson at Madison Square Gardens for the vacant world middleweight crown. Turpin's defeat on a unanimous points decision after a controversially casual preparation—disregarding advice, he had organized his own training—marked the beginning of the decline in his fighting career. His first marriage had, meanwhile, been dissolved in June 1953 and on 15 November 1953 he married Gwyneth Price (*b.* 1925/6), who had watched his workouts at Gwrych Castle, Denbighshire. She was the daughter of Robert Owen Price, a Welsh hill farmer. They had four daughters.

Although his reflexes were becoming slower, Turpin continued to fight at the highest level until his knock-out by the Trinidadian Yolande Pompey at Birmingham on 9 September 1958. In the following month he announced his retirement. He worked as a car-breaker in a Leamington scrap metal yard and from 1959 helped to run his wife's transport café. In 1961 British boxing officials refused to let him be a sparring partner for Terry Downes, then the British middleweight champion, because of the cumulative impact of ring beatings on his mental and physical state. By then most of his fight earnings, rumoured to have been £100,000, had gone, frittered away on high living (he acquired fast cars and was a sharp dresser), failed business ventures, and, perhaps most of all, the hangers-on who exploited his generous nature. 'I was fleeced right, left and centre by those around me', he complained (*The Times*, 18 May 1966). Incidents involving women also punctuated his career: an assault charge brought by his first wife was dismissed in March 1948; an allegation of rape in 1953 was settled out of court in New York two years later; and he was cited in a divorce petition (Birtley, 99–105). In 1962 he was declared bankrupt with tax debts of £17,000. He took to circus wrestling to raise funds, but these earnings in turn led to further tax demands.

Turpin died of a self-inflicted gunshot wound to the heart at Gwen's Transport Café, 9–11 Russell Street, Leamington Spa, on 17 May 1966. His wife survived him. Conducting his funeral service, Eugene Haselden observed that 'At the height of his career Randolph was surrounded by those who regarded themselves as friends and well-wishers. But he was deserted by many as he lost his position and money' (Birtley, 145). American magazines such as *Newsweek* and *Time* dismissed the British boxer as a shell of a man who had wound up as a cook at his wife's café. The *Illustrated London News* (28 May 1966), however, recognized Turpin as 'the most exciting fighter raised in Britain for a generation'. A bronze statue of him was unveiled in Warwick in 2001 bearing an inscription which recalled his historic victory over Robinson: 'In palace, pub and parlour, the whole of Britain held its breath'.

SCOTT A. G. M. CRAWFORD

Sources J. Birtley, *The tragedy of Randolph Turpin* (1975) · *The Times* (18 May 1966), 1, 14 · *The Times* (21 May 1966), 10 · *New York Times* (18 May 1966), 3 · *ILN* (28 May 1966), 12 · *Newsweek*, 67/22 (30 May 1966), 63 · *Time*, 87/21 (27 May 1966), 96 · A. Rothe, ed., *Current Biography Yearbook* (1951), 632–3 · b. cert. · m. certs. · d. cert. · S. A. G. M. Crawford, 'Sugar Ray Robinson', *Encyclopedia of ethnic sports*, ed. G. Kirsch and O. Harris [forthcoming] · *Daily Telegraph* (11 July 2001)

Archives FILM BFI NFTVA, 'Sixty-four day hero: a boxer's tale' 17 July 1986 • BFI NFTVA, record footage • BFI NFTVA, sports footage
Likenesses B. Hardy, photograph, 1949, Hult. Arch. [*see illus.*] • photographs, repro. in Birtley, *Tragedy*

Turpin, Richard [Dick] (*bap.* **1705**, *d.* **1739**), highwayman, was baptized on 21 September 1705 at Hempstead, Essex, the fifth of six children of John Turpin (*fl. c.*1675–1739) and Mary Elizabeth Parmenter (*fl. c.*1675–1708), who were married in 1695. He was born at the Blue Bell inn (later the Rose and Crown), Hempstead, where his father, formerly a butcher, was publican.

Testimony given at his trial in 1739 stated that Richard, otherwise known as Dick Turpin, had a rudimentary education before he became a butcher and married Elizabeth (Betty) Millington (*fl. c.*1705–1737), a maidservant, about 1725. From about 1730 they lived at Buckhurst Hill, Essex, but Turpin soon became involved with a gang of deer-stealers in the royal forest of Epping, acting as their fence. The activities of the gang, led by Samuel Gregory, blacksmith, went largely unchecked until rewards for the deer-stealers' capture were increased and Gregory was caught and pilloried at Epping late in 1734.

Gregory, however, was rescued by his armed associates and they turned to housebreaking, terrorizing isolated farms and houses on the then outer fringes of London throughout the winter of 1734–5. Turpin now joined them, but when some of the gang were taken in February 1735, the youngest member, John Wheeler, turned evidence, and descriptions and rewards for the capture of the rest, including Turpin, 'a fresh coloured man, very much marked with the small pox, about five feet nine inches high … wears a blue grey coat and a light coloured wig', were posted.

By December only Turpin and Thomas Rowden, a pewterer, were left at large, the rest having been caught, tried, and executed or transported, or died in prison. They now took to highway robbery south of the Thames, but by May 1736 had separated when Rowden, adopting the alias Daniel Crispe, fled to Gloucester, where he was later captured and convicted of counterfeiting. Turpin, however, disappeared completely, although there were suggestions that he had gone to the Netherlands, which may explain why Wheeler was released from protective custody in September.

In February 1737, ostensibly upon the authorities learning of Turpin's intention to return home and rendezvous with friends, an ambush was laid at Puckeridge, Hertfordshire, and although Turpin eluded capture his wife, Elizabeth, and her companions were committed to Hertford gaol on suspicion of highway robbery, but afterwards released.

Turpin then took up with Matthew King (then, and since, erroneously identified as Tom King), whom he may have known already, and stole a racehorse called Whitestockings, which was soon traced to a stable behind the Red Lion in Whitechapel. In the ensuing ambush on 2 May, Turpin again escaped, but Matthew King was shot and later died of his wounds.

On 5 May a desperate Turpin, having shot and killed a man who attempted to capture him, anticipated the posting of a £200 reward by fleeing to Yorkshire, a prudent course, as his description had been enhanced, 'of a brown complexion … his cheek bones broad, his face thinner towards the bottom, his visage short, pretty upright, and broad about the shoulders'.

In June Rowden was recognized in Gloucester gaol and brought to Chelmsford, Essex, to stand trial for his previous offences: he was convicted on 20 July, but the death sentence was later commuted. Also, about June, the only contemporary account of Turpin as a highwayman appeared, a coarse broadsheet imaginatively titled, 'News news: great and wonderful news from London in an uproar or a hue and cry after the Great Turpin, with his escape into Ireland'.

Six months after identifying Rowden at Chelmsford, on 30 January 1738 Wheeler died unexpectedly, apparently of natural causes, and Turpin became the last member of the original Gregory Gang to remain free. During the summer of 1738 he stole horses in Lincolnshire and returned with them to Brough to sell in Yorkshire, but in July he took another stolen horse south to Hempstead, where he left it with his father in return for food and lodging. Subsequently John Turpin was charged with receiving, and spent the winter in Chelmsford gaol awaiting trial, but on 16 August his son Richard stole three more horses, the identification of two of which was to prove instrumental in his downfall. In October Turpin (in the name of John Parmen, but recorded as Palmer) was arrested for disturbing the peace and committed to the house of correction at Beverley, Yorkshire. However, when it emerged that he might be implicated in horse-stealing, he was removed to York Castle where, when evidence came to hand, he was charged.

Early in February 1739 an intercepted letter from Turpin led to his being identified in York Castle. Ironically, his father was soon afterwards released from Chelmsford gaol for having alerted the authorities to an intended breakout; but at the end of March Richard was tried and convicted, and executed at York on 7 April 1739.

Thereafter there was little promotion of Turpin's exploits until they began to appear in chapbooks about 1800, and it was at this point that the famous ride from London to York to establish an alibi, previously attributed to the highwayman William Nevison, became a feature of Turpin *Lives*. This feat of equestrian endurance was then put to good use by Harrison Ainsworth, who not only included Turpin in his 1834 novel *Rookwood* but, at the end of an enthralling ride, had Black Bess expire at York. These events immediately captured the public's imagination and were capitalized upon in Martin Colnaghi's 1836 publication of six high-quality prints of dramatic incidents in Turpin's career. These in turn secured Turpin a place in the juvenile drama, the publishers of which plagiarized the prints and, by increment, ensured his lasting fame in pottery, circus, theatre, comics, cinema, television, and advertising. Turpin therefore is the classic example of a criminal who metamorphoses into mythical hero and then, by perpetuation in entertainment, fiction, and legend, achieves immortality. This status notwithstanding, his body is reputed to be buried in St George's churchyard, York.   DEREK BARLOW

Sources D. Barlow, *Dick Turpin and the Gregory gang* (1973) · register of baptisms, Hempstead, Essex, 21 Sept 1705
Likenesses R. Grave, line engraving, BM, NPG; repro. in Caulfield, *Remarkable persons* (1820)

Turquand, William (1818/19–1894), accountant, was born in either 1818 or 1819. His father is thought to have belonged to a family of French émigrés who fled from the French Revolution, but no records of his early life have survived. The elder Turquand was one of the first official assignees to be appointed under the Bankruptcy Act of 1831 (before that he had been a City stockbroker). William also held the post of assignee in 1846–7, at 13 Old Jewry in the City of London, but soon afterwards he set up in private practice. The insolvency connection no doubt continued to be a source of profitable work for his business.

By 1852 Turquand was running a firm of 'accountants, arbitrators and referees' (*Post Office London Directory*, 1035) in partnership with a Mr Edwards. This may have been William Edwards (*d.* 1884), who from 1843 undertook the training of a number of accountants who were later to achieve success in the City. The partnership was short-lived, as about 1856 Turquand merged his share of the practice with that of Youngs & Co. The latter had been established in 1840 by John Young (*d.* 1888), the son of a farmer of Windmill, near Gordonstown, who had been joined in London by his brother Alexander Young (*d.* 1907). In 1857 the new firm of Turquand, Youngs & Co. amalgamated with J. E. Coleman & Co. During the 1840s James Edward Coleman had established a considerable reputation as a City accountant and was often appointed by the Bank of England to investigate the solvency of suspect businesses, including Trueman and Cook, colonial brokers. When giving evidence to the select committee on the Bank Acts (1857–8), Coleman calculated that his twelve largest insolvency assignments in 1857 had liabilities totalling £6,726,840.

The union of the three practices created a firm of considerable eminence under the style Coleman, Turquand, Youngs & Co., with offices in Tokenhouse Yard in the City of London. In 1861–4 Edwin Waterhouse worked as a clerk in their offices to gain experience of accountancy, and recalled how he had initially called 'at Mr Turquand's private house in Mansfield Street where I found him busy on some important railway work which had taken one of his partners to America' (*Memoirs*, 71). In an era before the establishment of professional qualifications for accountants, the partnership established a reputation for probity and, as Waterhouse wrote, gained a number of important clients:

> I was occasionally sent to the offices of the London & North Western Railway to assist in Mr Coleman's work as a public accountant in the service of the auditors. Mr Coleman was connected also with the London, Chatham & Dover Railway, then carrying out its metropolitan extensions, and I gained

not a little experience in examining into the trade claims for loss of business on change of premises. (ibid., 74)

When Coleman retired, shortly after the merger, Turquand became the senior partner; expansion resulted in a new style, Turquand, Youngs, Weise, Bishop, and Clarke, which led *The Accountant* (15 December 1888) to comment that this was 'one of the largest firms of its kind in London, indeed the world'.

Turquand rose to prominence because of his abilities as a liquidator, a fact recognized in his appointment, in 1866, as joint liquidator of Overend, Gurney & Co. The 1867 report from the select committee on Limited Liability Acts calculated that Coleman, Turquand, Youngs & Co. were currently winding up twenty-nine of the 259 companies then in liquidation and that this represented £18.4 million of the £92.1 million involved. In 1877 Turquand observed that he personally had been responsible for the liquidation of sixty-two businesses, among which were the West of England Bank, London and Colonial Bank, London and Scottish Bank, British Provident Insurance Company, Commercial and General Assurance Company, Defender Assurance Company, and Leeds Banking Company, while his firm had administered a further 140. These included the Albert Insurance Company, Collies of London, and the European Insurance Company, which took more than twenty clerks and assistants five years to complete.

The firm prospered under Turquand's leadership and its fee income rose from £19,627 in 1859 to £36,072 in 1873, although the importance of the Overend Gurney assignment revealed itself in a peak of £90,287 in 1868. The partnership was not so successful during the 1880s, when its fee income levelled at about £27,000–£28,000 per annum. By this time auditing was assuming a greater importance, but Turquand was reluctant to undertake this work and left most audit appointments to his fellow partners. John Young, for example, audited the Caledonian Railway, the Cambrian Railways, and the Great Western Railway of Canada.

In 1855 Turquand took part in an important legal case, *Royal British Bank* v. *Turquand*, which helped to establish the principle that a third party in dealing with a company need not examine its internal organizational rules in order to ensure that officers have authority for such dealings. Based upon his commercial standing in the City, Turquand assumed a leading position in the accountancy profession, and became the first president of the Institute of Chartered Accountants in England and Wales upon its formation in 1880. He had been a leading member of the Institute of Accountants in London from its foundation in 1870, when he was elected its vice-president. On the retirement of William Quilter in 1877, Turquand succeeded him as president. He gave evidence to the 1877 select committee on the Companies Acts of 1862 and 1867, but during the 1880s took a lesser role in the profession's affairs. *The Accountant* (31 March 1894, 291) described him as 'a perfect gentleman, with not only the best reputation out of his office, but … in it'.

Turquand had a wife called Ada, but nothing else is

known about his domestic life. He died aged seventy-five, on 20 March 1894, at his home, 20 Norfolk Street, Park Lane, London. EDGAR JONES

Sources E. Jones, *Accountancy and the British economy, 1840–1980: the evolution of Ernst & Whinney* (1981) · E. Jones, 'Turquand, William', *DBB* · *The Accountant* (31 March 1894) · *The Accountant* (15 Dec 1888) · *The memoirs of Edwin Waterhouse*, ed. H. E. Jones (1988) · H. Howitt and others, eds., *The history of the Institute of Chartered Accountants in England and Wales, 1880–1965, and of its founder accountancy bodies, 1870–1880* (1966) · *The Post Office London directory* (1852), 1035 · d. cert.

Archives Institute of Chartered Accountants in England and Wales, London, archive

Likenesses photograph, Price Waterhouse, London archives

Wealth at death £45,318 6s. 11d.: resworn probate, Dec 1894, CGPLA Eng. & Wales

Turrill, William Bertram

Turrill, William Bertram (1890–1961), botanist, was born at Woodstock, Oxfordshire, on 14 June 1890, the eldest of the four sons of William Banbury Turrill, provision merchant and later mayor of Woodstock, and his wife, Mary Thirza Homan, who came from a farming family. An early love of natural history was encouraged by his mother who gave him a piece of her garden to cultivate and taught him to prepare biological specimens. He was educated at Oxford high school (1903–6).

On leaving school at sixteen Turrill became a junior assistant in the Fielding herbarium of the department of botany at Oxford, under the curatorship of G. Claridge Druce. In 1909 he became a temporary assistant in the herbarium of the Royal Botanic Gardens, Kew, being appointed permanent assistant (later designated botanist) in 1914, with responsibility for several plant families including Cyperaceae, on which he specialized, and Acanthaceae. He continued his education by attending evening classes at Chelsea Polytechnic and graduated BSc (London) with first-class honours in botany in 1915. He later obtained his MSc (1922) and DSc (1928) for his work on the flora of the Balkan peninsula in which his interest had been aroused during war service (1916–18) in the Royal Army Medical Corps with the British Salonika forces in Macedonia. On 16 February 1918 he married Florence Emily (*b.* 1889/90), daughter of Arthur Homan, a draper. The marriage was particularly happy, for she shared his interests, accompanying him to society meetings and on collecting expeditions; they had no children.

After the war Turrill returned to Kew, concentrating on the floras of Europe, north Africa, and the Middle East. Between 1918 and 1939 he continued his association with Chelsea Polytechnic, conducting evening classes on plant taxonomy, plant ecology, and plant genetics. He also lectured to the student gardeners at Kew, and to botanical, agricultural, and forestry officers for the Colonial Office, many of whom later repaid his skill and enthusiasm by collecting specimens for Kew. The herbarium collections were considerably enriched also as a result of his own many expeditions, mainly in the Balkans. *Veronica turrilliana*, collected in south-eastern Bulgaria, was named in his honour.

During the Second World War Turrill returned to Oxford to take charge of the large portion of the Kew herbarium and library which had been transferred, for safe keeping, to the basement of the new Bodleian Library. During that time he also worked on a series of handbooks for the Admiralty, which described the vegetation of several countries in the war zones. In 1946 he became keeper of the herbarium and library at Kew in succession to A. D. Cotton. He retired from the post on 30 September 1957.

Early in his career Turrill advocated a broad-based approach to plant recognition and classification. He sought to include a consideration of anatomy, chemistry, cytology, ecology, and genetics, in addition to the more traditional emphasis on morphology. He was responsible for the innovation at Kew of ecological and genetical herbaria and a seed collection. In 1919 he started an experimental garden attached to the herbarium. Another experimental garden was established at the Wiltshire home of his friend and collaborator, E. M. Marsden-Jones, where Turrill carried out genetic and ecological experiments on species and variants of *Centaurea, Silene, Ranunculus*, and other genera.

Turrill's reputation as a leading authority on the flora of the Balkan peninsula was established by the publication of *The Plant Life of the Balkan Peninsula* (1929). In addition he wrote several books and well over 600 articles on botanical subjects, including *The Royal Botanic Gardens, Kew: Past and Present* (1959), and a biography (published in 1963) of J. D. Hooker. Turrill was editor of the *Botanical Magazine* from 1948 until the time of his death; an issue of the magazine (vol. 173, pt 4, 1962) was dedicated to him.

Turrill's services to botany and horticulture were recognized by numerous honours and awards. In 1955 he was appointed OBE. The Royal Horticultural Society awarded him a Veitch memorial gold medal (1953) and the Victoria medal of honour (1956). He received the gold medal of the Linnean Society (1958), of which he was vice-president (1949–50). He was president of the Kew Guild (1948–9), of section K of the British Association (1950), and of the British Ecological Society (1950–51). He was elected a fellow of the Royal Society in 1958. In addition he was a founder member and chairman of the Systematics Association.

A fast writer and an avid reader, Turrill assembled a large private library of books, pamphlets, periodicals, and newspaper clippings. Even after his retirement his capacity for lengthy and painstaking study seemed unlimited but he lacked neither a sense of humour nor generosity towards colleagues. Turrill died at his home, 26 Ennerdale Road, Richmond, Surrey, on 15 December 1961.

P. J. COOTE, *rev.*

Sources C. E. Hubbard, *Memoirs FRS*, 17 (1971), 689–712 · *The Times* (16 Dec 1961) · *The Times* (27 Dec 1961) · *WWW* · *CGPLA Eng. & Wales* (1962)

Archives RBG Kew, corresp. and papers | RBG Kew, corresp. with Victor S. Summerhayes · Rice University, Houston, Texas, Woodson Research Center, corresp. with Sir Julian Huxley

Wealth at death £19,603 17s.: probate, 28 Feb 1962, CGPLA Eng. & Wales

Turswell, Thomas (1548–1583), ecclesiastical administrator, was born at Bishop's Norton, Lincolnshire. Richard Turswell, who graduated BTh at Queens' College, Cambridge, in 1572 and became a prebendary in Lincoln Cathedral ten years later, was his brother. Having studied at Eton College, Thomas was admitted a scholar at King's College, Cambridge, on 23 August 1566 and was admitted to a fellowship on 24 August 1569. He graduated BA in 1571 and MA in 1574, being incorporated in that degree at Oxford on 14 July 1579. He is believed to have been licensed to practise medicine in 1573, and physic, or surgery, in 1578, and to have proceeded MD in 1583. He was subsequently described as 'a good surgeon and physician' (Harwood, 181). On 26 January 1576 Turswell wrote to Burghley seeking preferment to the keepership of the college library, but failed to secure the post. In the same year, with three other fellows, he was said to have slandered the provost of the college, Dr Roger Goad, and was imprisoned in the Gatehouse at Westminster as a result. His fortunes recovered, however, and he found employment as steward of the household of John Whitgift, bishop of Worcester, retaining this position after Whitgift was translated to Canterbury. On the presentation of the bishop of London he was collated to the St Paul's prebend of Portpoole on 7 December 1580. Turswell died on 8 October 1583. In his nuncupative will, made two days earlier, he had bequeathed all his goods to his father, using 'these or the like words: "from my father they came, and to him they shall go, I give him all that I have"' (PRO, PROB 11/66, fol. 42v). In their *Athenae Cantabrigienses* the Coopers attribute to Turswell three books published under the initials T. T.. Two of these are now known to be the work of Thomas Twyne, while the third appeared several years after Turswell's death. STEPHEN WRIGHT

Sources Venn, *Alum. Cant.*, 1/4.279 · *Fasti Angl., 1541–1857*, [St Paul's, London] · *CSP dom., 1547–80* · T. Harwood, *Alumni Etonenses, or, A catalogue of the provosts and fellows of Eton College and King's College, Cambridge, from the foundation in 1443 to the year 1797* (1797) · W. Sterry, ed., *The Eton College register, 1441–1698* (1943) · will, PRO, PROB 11/66, sig. 6 · Cooper, *Ath. Cantab.*, 2.101 · Foster, *Alum. Oxon.*
Wealth at death goods returned to father: will, PRO, PROB 11/66, sig. 6

Turton, John (1735–1806), physician, born in Staffordshire on 15 November 1735 was the son of John Turton (1700–1754), also a physician, originally from Wolverhampton and later resident at Adelphi Street, London, and his wife, Dorothy, only surviving child of Gregory Hickman. Dr Johnson wrote some verses to her entitled 'To Miss Hickman Playing on the Spinet'. Turton entered Queen's College, Oxford, on 23 October 1752, graduating BA on 16 June 1756, and MA on 31 May 1759. In May 1761 he obtained a Radcliffe travelling fellowship at University College, Oxford, and on 28 September 1761 began to study medicine at Leiden. While in Vienna in 1765, he fell ill, and was cared for by Lord and Lady Stormont. In return, he successfully inoculated their only daughter against smallpox. He graduated BM from University College on 11 December 1762, and DM on 27 February 1767. He was elected a fellow of the Royal Society on 17 November 1763, and admitted

on 5 March 1767. He settled in London, was admitted a candidate at the Royal College of Physicians on 24 September 1767, and elected a fellow on 30 September 1768. He was a censor in 1769, 1775, 1782, and 1788, and became an elect on 25 June 1788. He soon attained a large practice, and was physician to the queen's household in 1771, and physician-in-ordinary to the queen in 1782; in 1797 he became physician-in-ordinary to the king and to the prince of Wales.

Having grown rich from his practice, Turton resigned his post of elect in the College of Physicians and retired to Brasted Place in Kent, which he had purchased from Lord Frederick Campbell and rebuilt. He married Mary (d. 1810), the daughter of Joseph Kitchingman of Balk Hall, Thirsk. There were no children. Turton died at Brasted on 14 April 1806, and was buried in the parish church, where he was commemorated by a white marble sarcophagus. On his widow's death in 1810, Turton's real property, amounting to £9000 a year, besides £60,000 in the funds, descended by will to his relative, Edmund Peters, who assumed the name of Turton.

NORMAN MOORE, *rev.* CLAIRE L. NUTT

Sources Munk, *Roll* · Foster, *Alum. Oxon.* · *GM*, 1st ser., 76 (1806), 391, 475 · *GM*, 1st ser., 80 (1810), 288 · E. Peacock, *Index to English speaking students who have graduated at Leyden University* (1883) · J. Boswell, *The life of Samuel Johnson*, 2 vols. (1791) · Burke, *Gen. GB* (1894) · T. Thomson, *History of the Royal Society from its institution to the end of the eighteenth century* (1812) · G. De Beer and R. M. Turton, 'John Turton, FRS, 1735–1806', *Notes and Records of the Royal Society*, 12 (1956–7), 76–97
Archives Bibliothèque Publique et Universitaire, Geneva, corresp. with Charles Bonnet
Likenesses school of F. Cotes, portrait, Upsall Castle, Thirsk · marble sarcophagus, Brasted parish church, Kent
Wealth at death £9000 p.a.; plus £60,000: *DNB*

Turton, Thomas (1780–1864), bishop of Ely, born at Hatfield, Yorkshire, on 25 February 1780, was the son of Thomas Turton of Hatfield and his wife, Ann, daughter of Francis Harn of Denby. In 1801 he became a pensioner of Queens' College, Cambridge. Two years afterwards he migrated to St Catharine's College, where he held a scholarship. He was senior wrangler in the mathematical tripos of 1805, and he proceeded BA. He and Samuel Hunter Christie of Trinity College were declared equal winners of the Smith prize for mathematics and natural philosophy. In 1806 he was elected a fellow of his college, and in 1807 he was appointed a tutor. In 1808 he commenced MA, and he was a moderator (examiner) in the mathematical tripos for the years 1810, 1811, and 1812. In 1816 he took the degree of BD.

In 1822 Turton was appointed Lucasian professor of mathematics, and in 1826 he accepted the college living of Gimingham-cum-Trunch, Norfolk. He returned to the university in the following year, when he was elected regius professor of divinity on the resignation of John Kaye, bishop of Bristol. Soon afterwards he was created DD by royal mandate. He combined the divinity chair, which he held until 1842, with other church preferments, his pluralism securing him inclusion in John Wade's catalogue of abuses in church and state, *The Extraordinary Black Book*

(1832). On 5 July 1827 he was collated to the prebend of Heydour-cum-Walton in the cathedral church of Lincoln and in November 1830 he obtained the deanery of Peterborough, vacant by the promotion of James Henry Monk to the see of Gloucester and Bristol.

As a theologian Turton was a vigorous controversialist. He entered into pamphlet controversies with Edward Copleston, bishop of Llandaff, on the doctrine of predestination (1822); with Thomas Burgess (1756–1837), bishop of Salisbury, on the character of Porson (1827); with Lord Brougham on natural theology (1836); and with Cardinal Wiseman on the doctrine of the eucharist (1837). He was the author of several other polemical tracts and pamphlets, and also edited William Wilson's *Illustration of the method of explaining the New Testament by the early opinions of the Jews and Christians concerning Christ* (1838) and John Hey's *Lectures on Divinity* (1841). He was a Conservative in politics and in 1834 published a pamphlet opposing the admission of non-Anglicans to university degrees, arguing that this would harm the ability of the university to deliver orthodox religious instruction. This drew a stinging reply from the Trinity College tutor Connop Thirlwall, who exposed the inadequacy of much of the university's existing teaching in theology. Turton responded to this well-founded charge by introducing, in 1842, a voluntary theological examination, conducted by the divinity professors, for students intending to be ordained. So successful was the examination that most bishops came to require ordinands to produce certificates that they had passed it.

Turton left Cambridge in October 1842 on his appointment as dean of Westminster. In March 1845, on Sir Robert Peel's recommendation, he was made bishop of Ely, inheriting from his predecessors severe financial problems. He suffered ill health which latterly prevented him from being particularly active in diocesan affairs. Nor, being a rather shy and reserved man, was he a frequent speaker in the House of Lords. When Rowland Williams, one of his diocesan clergy, contributed an article regarded as heterodox to the collection of *Essays and Reviews* he chose not to bring a prosecution himself, but permitted another of his clergy to take out a private action against the author. His taste in the fine arts was well known, and he made a valuable collection of pictures. He was the composer of several excellent pieces of church music, two of his tunes being included in *Hymns Ancient and Modern*. Turton died unmarried at Ely House, 37 Dover Street, Piccadilly, London, on 7 January 1864, and was buried at Kensal Green cemetery in a grave adjoining that of his friend Dr Thomas Musgrave, archbishop of York. He bequeathed much of his estate to charities.

THOMPSON COOPER, *rev.* M. C. CURTHOYS

Sources Ward, *Men of the reign* · *GM*, 3rd ser., 16 (1864), 387–8 · *Daily Telegraph* (9 Jan 1864) · *Daily Telegraph* (15 Jan 1864) · *The Examiner* (16 Jan 1864), 44 · *ILN* (12 March 1864) · *Morning Post* (9 Jan 1864) · *The Times* (9 Jan 1864), 9 · D. A. Winstanley, *Early Victorian Cambridge* (1940); repr. (1955) · G. F. A. Best, *Temporal pillars: Queen Anne's bounty, the ecclesiastical commissioners, and the Church of England* (1964) · J. L. Altholz, *Anatomy of a controversy: the debate over 'Essays and Reviews', 1860–1864* (1994)

Archives BL, corresp. with Sir Robert Peel, Add. MSS 40515–40591 · Woburn Abbey, Bedfordshire, corresp. with duke of Bedford
Likenesses R. W. Sievier, marble bust, 1831, St Catharine's College, Cambridge · H. W. Pickersgill, oils, St Catharine's College, Cambridge
Wealth at death under £40,000: probate, 1864, *CGPLA Eng. & Wales*

Turton, William (1762–1835), conchologist, was born at Olveston, Gloucestershire, on 21 May 1762, the fifth child of William Turton (1731–1802), solicitor, of Olveston, and his wife, Rachel, only daughter of the Revd Andrew Cuthbert of Monmouth and, on her mother's side, a descendant of Edward, eleventh Baron Zouche. He matriculated from Oriel College, Oxford, on 28 March 1781, graduating BA on 3 February 1785, proceeding MA on 22 February 1791, and MB on 16 July 1791.

Turton began to practise as a physician in Swansea, his leisure time being devoted to the study of natural history and the publication of various works. His attention later became focused on conchology through his acquaintance with Mathias O'Kelly of Dublin. About 1797 he married a Miss Salmon; the couple had a son and three daughters. In 1809 he was elected a fellow of the Linnean Society.

From the prefaces to his books it appears that Turton was still at Swansea in 1807; between 1808 and 1817 he was known to be practising in Dublin, while in 1819 he was at Teignmouth, Devon, in 1822 at Torquay, and in 1831 at Bideford. He was author of *A Medical Glossary* (1797), *British Fauna: Containing a Compendium of the Zoology of the British Islands* (1807), and *Some Observations on Consumption* (1810). In 1816 he published 'A list of Irish shells' in the united publication *The Dublin Examiner, or, Monthly Journal of Science, Literature and Art*; it proved to be the first printed attempt at listing the Irish Mollusca. His major subsequent works comprised *A Conchological Dictionary of the British Islands*, in which he was assisted by his daughter (1819), and *A Manual of the Land and Freshwater Shells of the British Islands* (1831).

Turton also wrote, in conjunction with J. F. Kingston, the natural history portion of N. T. Carrington's *Teignmouth, Dawlish, and Torquay Guide* (1828?). Three papers on scientific subjects were also written by him for the *Zoological Journal* and the *Magazine of Natural History* between 1826 and 1834. He also published a translation of Gmelin's *Systema naturae* (1800–06), and issued a new edition of Goldsmith's *History of the Earth* (1805 and 1816) and *Luctus Nelsoniani: poems [by different authors] on the death of Lord Nelson, in Latin and English, written for the Turtonian medals* (1807).

Turton gave his collection of shells, before his *Manual* appeared, to William Clark of Bath. The shells subsequently passed into the hands of the conchologist John Gwyn Jeffreys (1809–1885), whose collections were purchased two years before his death by the American government, then placed in the National Museum at Washington. Turton died at Bideford, Devon, on 28 December 1835. A genus of bivalve shells was named Turtonia in his honour in 1849 by Forbes and Hanley.

B. B. WOODWARD, *rev.* YOLANDA FOOTE

Sources [J. Watkins and F. Shoberl], *A biographical dictionary of the living authors of Great Britain and Ireland* (1816) · *GM*, 2nd ser., 5 (1836), 557 · Desmond, *Botanists* · Foster, *Alum. Oxon.* · E. Forbes and S. Hanley, *History of British molluscs and their shells*, 4 vols. (1853), 2.81 · private information (1898) [Major H. W. Turton] · *BL cat.* · B. B. Woodward and others, eds., *Catalogue of the books, manuscripts, maps, and drawings in the British Museum (Natural History)*, 8 vols. (1903–40) · *Catalogue of scientific papers*, Royal Society, 6 (1872), 72 · H. C. G. Chesney, 'Ireland's pioneering malacologists—from dredging to drummondi', *Archives of Natural History*, 22 (1995), 321–31

Turval, Jean l'Oiseau de (*d.* **1631**). *See under* Tuvell, Daniel (*d.* 1660).

Tussaud [*née* Grosholtz], **Anna Maria** [Marie; *known as* Madame Tussaud] (*bap.* **1761**, *d.* **1850**), founder of a wax-work exhibition, was probably born in Strasbourg (where she was baptized on 7 December 1761), the posthumous daughter of Johann Grosholtz of Frankfurt, a soldier who served in the Seven Years' War, and Anne-Marie Walder, who later became housekeeper to a German-Swiss doctor, Philippe Guillaume Mathé Curtius (1737–1794), first in Bern, and then in Paris. By 1776 Curtius had started a 'cabinet de cire' (wax exhibition) in the Palais Royal, which he later extended with a separate exhibition in the boulevard du Temple. Under his auspices the young Marie learned the art of wax modelling, making her first complete portrait, that of Voltaire, at the age of seventeen; her talent impressed Madame Elizabeth, Louis XVI's sister, who invited her to Versailles to give lessons in wax modelling. During her nine-year stay there she was also able to model the king himself, Marie Antoinette, and two of their children.

Curtius became increasingly embroiled in revolutionary politics, associating with Danton, Marat, Robespierre, and others, and he prudently recalled Marie to Paris in 1789. On 12 July two of his wax busts were demanded by an angry mob for a protest march through the streets, during which the first blood of the revolution was shed. Curtius himself was personally involved in the storming of the Bastille, for which, as one of the 'vainqueurs de la Bastille' he was presented with an engraved gun by the national assembly. Both he and Marie were called upon to model some of the lifeless heads which fell from the guillotine, including those of many aristocrats whom Marie had known at Versailles, and eventually those of Robespierre and the murdered Marat. Under the reign of terror, and in the absence of Curtius, who was abroad, Marie and her mother were briefly imprisoned, together with Joséphine de Beauharnais. All had their hair cut short in preparation for the guillotine. No reason was given for their arrest, but Curtius and his household seem to have come under the protection of Collot d'Herbois, who was president of the national convention, and they were soon released.

As the reign of terror subsided, Curtius became ill, and died on 26 September 1794, leaving Marie as sole legatee of the exhibition and various properties. On 16 October 1795, Marie married François Tussaud (1769–1841), a civil engineer from a family of coppersmiths and wine producers. Three children were born to the couple: Marie Marguérite

Anna Maria Tussaud (*bap.* 1761, *d.* 1850), self-portrait, 1842

Pauline in September 1796 (who died six months later), Joseph (1798–1865), and François (1800–1873). In the aftermath of anti-revolution and war, the exhibition's popularity waned. The Tussauds' finances became severely stretched, so when an old friend offered a partnership and an opportunity to reach a new audience in England, Marie grasped it. In 1802 this unknown Frenchwoman, speaking no English, and accompanied by her four-year-old son and thirty or more wax portraits, crossed the channel. Initially her Grand European Cabinet of Figures was exhibited in the Lyceum Theatre in the Strand. Moving to Edinburgh the following year, Marie found herself treated as a grand lady among the French émigrés, and continued to enjoy great popularity. She then travelled to Dublin, and from there to other major towns in Ireland, writing to her husband in 1805 that she was now free of her business partner, and would not return to France. For the next thirty years she lived the exhausting and precarious life of an independent showman, travelling between all the large towns of Britain, and staying in each for as long as her business was successful. New figures were constantly added: among them were George III, George IV, Tsar Alexander I, Napoleon, Sir Robert Peel, and Walter Scott. The itinerant lifestyle was tough and sometimes dangerous. Marie was shipwrecked in the Irish Channel and had a narrow escape from fire in the Bristol riots of 1831. But she became successful enough to donate some of her proceeds to charitable causes, including 'the distressed peasantry of Ireland' and 'the distressed manufacturers of York'. That she took great pride in the quality of her portraiture is evident from her advertising, but she also attached importance to the instructive nature of her catalogues, in which she 'endeavoured to blend utility and amusement', stating that

> a general outline of the history of each character ... will not only greatly increase the pleasure to be derived from a mere view of the Figures, but will also convey to the minds of young Persons much biographical knowledge—a branch of education universally allowed to be of the highest importance. (*Madame Tussaud's Exhibition*)

Also instructive was the 'Adjoining Room', forerunner of the Chamber of Horrors, with its death masks, model guillotine, weapons, and bloodstained relics.

By 1822 Marie's younger son, known from this time as Francis, had abandoned his father in Paris, and come to join his mother and brother. Together, in 1835, they settled in Baker Street—the exhibition being installed in the Bazaar, Marie in no. 58, and her sons and their families nearby. As well as the wax portraits, a remarkable collection of relics was built up over the following years. Among these were an authentic blade and lunette of the guillotine, George IV's coronation robes, and many items belonging to Napoleon, including robes, his camp bed, and other furniture, together with the famous Waterloo carriage.

Marie Tussaud remained in charge of the business until the very last weeks of her life, although suffering badly at the end from asthma. A London guide of 1842 describes her thus: 'Here sits an aged lady with an accent which proclaims her Gallic origin. Were she motionless you would take her for a piece of waxwork. This is Madame Tussaud, a lady who is in herself an exhibition.' To distinguished visitors, like the duke of Wellington, she appeared talkative, except on the subject of herself and her emotions during the traumatic revolutionary years, and she is said to have consented only reluctantly to the publishing of her memoirs in 1838, in which her own lively anecdotes were set into a somewhat inaccurate historical context by Francis Hervé, a family friend. Her husband, François, made one last attempt to share in her success in 1841, but she refused to have any contact, giving her sons joint ownership of her exhibition. She died at 58 Baker Street, London, on 15 April 1850, and was buried in the Roman Catholic chapel in Pavilion Road, Chelsea, from where her remains were later removed to the crypt of St Mary's, Cadogan Gardens. Her wax self-portrait, made at the age of eighty-one, bears the marks of a hard life and the determination that carried her through it.

In 1884 the exhibition was moved to the Marylebone Road, where it has remained ever since, despite a serious fire in 1925 and bomb damage inflicted during the blitz in 1940. It became one of London's most popular attractions, with as many as 2 million visitors a year by the 1990s.

UNDINE CONCANNON

Sources *Madame Tussaud's memoirs and reminiscences of France*, ed. F. Hervé (1838) • *Madame Tussaud's exhibition* (1819) [exhibition catalogue] • P. Chapman, *The French Revolution as seen by Madame Tussaud, witness extraordinary* (1989) • P. Chapman, *Madame Tussaud in England* (1992) • P. Chapman and A. Leslie, *Madame Tussaud, waxworker extraordinary* (1978) • J. T. Tussaud, *The romance of Madame Tussaud's* (1920) • *The Times* (17 April 1850) • *ILN* (20 April 1850) • baptism cert., Alt-Sankt-Peterskirche, Strasbourg • m. cert., France • d. cert.
Archives Madame Tussaud's, London
Likenesses F. Hervé, two lithographs, 1778–1838, repro. in *Madame Tussaud's memoirs*, ed. Hervé • attrib. F. Tussaud, crayon, c.1835, NPG; copy, Madame Tussaud's, London • A. Hervé, ink silhouette, c.1840, priv. coll. • J. T. Tussaud, ink silhouette, c.1840, Madame Tussaud's, London • A. M. Tussaud, self-portrait, wax model, 1842, Madame Tussaud's, London [*see illus.*] • P. Fischer, ink sketch, 1845, Madame Tussaud's, London • P. Fischer, oils, 1845, Madame Tussaud's, London • plaster death mask, 1850, Madame Tussaud's, London • Raeburn, oils

Tusser, Thomas (c.1524–1580), writer on agriculture and poet, was born at Rivenhall, near Witham in Essex. He was the fourth son, in a family of five, of William Tusser and of Isabella, daughter of Thomas Smith of Rivenhall. The date of birth, however, remains uncertain. A date of 1515 is supported by an entry in the register of the church of St Mildred Poultry and a tablet in the church at Manningtree. The date of his birth is more probably about 1524, however, because there is clear evidence that Tusser was elected to King's College, Cambridge, in 1543, and he would have been eligible at the age of nineteen. Much of the information regarding the rest of his life comes from an autobiographical poem, first published in 1570; and while it is easy enough to determine the succession of moves, in a peripatetic and somewhat precarious existence, the exact dates are not always so clear.

At an early age Tusser was sent as a singing boy to the collegiate chapel of the castle of Wallingford in Berkshire. This was a small establishment, including as few as four choristers, which Tusser remembered as a place of ill treatment, 'abhord of sillie boies'. He was subsequently admitted to the choir of St Paul's Cathedral, where his musical education benefited from the tuition of John Redford, the organist and almoner. From St Paul's he was sent to Eton College, probably in 1540 or 1541, where the corporal punishment administered by Nicholas Udall appears to have left as much impression upon him as did his classical studies. After leaving Eton he may have spent some time in London before his election to King's. Later in 1543 he transferred to Trinity Hall as a sizar. Despite his fond memories of this institution, his stay at Cambridge may have been quite short. About 1544 he moved to court in the service of William Paget. Since Paget had himself studied at St Paul's School and Trinity Hall, it is possible that Tusser had already benefited from his patronage, perhaps as a result of a family connection. Tusser presumably served Paget as a musician, both at court and in his household at Beaudesert in Staffordshire. Although Tusser states that he spent ten years in this situation, his explanation for his departure suggests that he left earlier than this. He cites 'variance' among the nobility in the reign of Edward VI, which almost certainly refers to his patron's imprisonment in 1551–2 after the fall of the duke of Somerset.

At this time Tusser married and left the court to embark on his unstable and largely unsuccessful farming career, which took him first to Cattiwade in Suffolk. Here he introduced to the neighbourhood the culture of barley, and composed *A Hundreth Good Pointes of Husbandrie*, the first version of the book for which he is remembered. Little is known about his first wife, apart from the fact that she soon suffered health problems, which Tusser attributed to their proximity to the sea. On account of her illness they moved to Ipswich, where she died childless. Shortly after her death Tusser married a younger woman, Amy, daughter of Edmund Moon, with whom he had three sons and a daughter: Thomas, John, Edmond, and Mary. They settled first in West Dereham, Norfolk; however, he was troubled here by conflicts between local landlords, and perhaps moved more than once before finally leaving the region, probably in 1559, on the death of his patron, Sir Robert Southwell. Next they shifted to Norwich, where the dean of the cathedral, John Salisbury, procured him a living, probably as a lay clerk or singing man. However, an illness, which he attributed to 'Norwich aire', prompted a final attempt at farming, on tithe land (effectively in the possession of the church) at Fairsted, near Witham in Essex.

Tusser's husbandry manual in verse was developed by the author over the course of two decades. It was first published by Richard Tottel in 1557 as *A Hundreth Good Pointes of Husbandrie*, and dedicated to his earlier court patron, Lord Paget. The second edition of 1562 was enlarged so as to consider more fully the rural labour of women; as the title-page announces, the original text is here 'maried unto a hundreth good poyntes of huswifery'. After two further editions in this form (1570 and 1571), the text was expanded for publication in 1573 as *Five Hundreth Points of Good Husbandry United to as many of Good Huswiferie*. The expansion of material was hardly the fivefold increase that the new title suggested; however, it involved some significant additions, and effectively shaped the text into its final form. At the heart of the book is a calendar of information and advice about the farming year; in the latter part are the 'points of huswiferie', loosely arranged around a working day; and framing these principal sections are a number of miscellaneous poems, generally concerned with household management and rural customs, and including Tusser's autobiography. After some minor changes in the edition of 1580 *Five Hundreth Points of Good Husbandry* remained popular among succeeding generations. Its publication in eighteen editions between 1557 and 1599 makes it probably the biggest-selling book of poetry of the reign of Elizabeth I, and it was issued in a further five editions up to 1638.

While Tusser's poetry is simple and unpretentious, his book's didactic and polemic purposes demand closer attention. The handful of agricultural manuals previously published in England had been directed towards larger landowners, and had drawn upon classical traditions of writing on estate management. By comparison, Tusser's calendar is aimed throughout towards the tenant farmer, and deals intimately with the vicissitudes of life for smaller farmers. This point was clarified in the 1573 edition, which shifts the start of the agricultural year from August (where earlier editions had begun) to September,

and focuses immediately on the changes of tenure that would occur at this time:

> At Mihelmas lightly new fermer comes in,
> new husbandrie forceth him new to begin.

Much of his general advice is also concerned to challenge existing codes of custom and social morality, valorizing instead ideals of thrift and individualism. Most significantly, in 'A comparison betweene champion countrie and severall', he presents perhaps the first published argument in favour of enclosure written from the perspective of a tenant farmer, at a time when popular opinion was heavily weighted against the practice. In the face of the predominant contemporary ideals of moral economy, Tusser declares:

> Againe what a joie is it knowne,
> when men may be bold of their owne!

Despite the success of his agricultural manual, Tusser appears to have ceased farming himself by the early 1570s, since his third son, Edmond, was baptized at St Giles Cripplegate, on 13 March 1573. On the outbreak of plague in the city during 1573–4 he returned to Cambridge, where he was probably employed in a choir, having matriculated as a servant of Trinity Hall on 5 May 1573. Little is known about his final years, yet at some point he moved once again to London, where he died on 3 May 1580, and was buried in the church of St Mildred Poultry. John Stow records an epitaph, possibly composed by Tusser himself. Although it is generally thought that he died in poverty, perhaps a prisoner for debt, his will documents modest assets, including two small copyhold and leasehold farms, as well as books and virginals. However, the estate was encumbered by an unpaid loan of £330 to Tusser's brother William.

There is evidence to suggest that Tusser's work was read by contemporaries throughout the country, and also throughout the social order. Among the social and literary élite his reception was mixed. In 1586 William Webbe perceived Tusser as the first English georgic poet, writing within the classical tradition established by Hesiod and Virgil. Francis Meres also noted Tusser in this context, as one who had written of husbandry 'very wittily and experimentally' (Smith, 1.265, 2.323). Gabriel Harvey, who owned a copy of the 1580 edition of Tusser's book, was less generous, describing him as a poet 'for common life, and vulgar discourse' (Stern, 237). Later generations focused on the contrast between Tusser's shrewdly thrifty advice and his apparent personal failures as a farmer. Henry Peacham's *Minerva Britanna* contains the terse epigram:

> Tusser, they tell me when thou wert alive
> thou, teaching thrift, thyself couldst never thrive;
> So, like the whetstone, many men are wont
> To sharpen others when themselves are blunt.
> (Peacham, 61)

Similarly, Thomas Fuller's account in his *Worthies of England* states that nobody was 'better at the theory or worse at the practice of husbandry', and describes him as a 'stone of Sisyphus [that] could gather no moss' (Fuller, *Worthies*, 334). In following centuries Robert Southey made various notes on Tusser, and described him as a 'good, honest, homely, useful old rhymer' (*DNB*), while Sir Walter Scott praised his 'homely, pointed and quaint expression, like that of the old English proverb, which the rhyme and the alliteration tend to fix on the memory of the reader' (Tusser, ed. Grigson, 320).

Those with a practical interest in Tusser's work were more appreciative. For example, John Kay of Woodsome, compiling information and notes about his own estate management over several decades from the late sixteenth century, is consistently influenced by both the style and arguments of Tusser, whom he praises for his 'learnyd sayes' (Folger Shakespeare Library, MS X.d.445, fol. 3v). By the latter half of the seventeenth century, although his work had generally been superseded, the significance of his arguments on enclosure was recognized by Walter Blith, the foremost agricultural writer of his generation, who included Tusser's pro-enclosure poem in *The English Improver Improved* (1652). Moreover, as Scott recognized, Tusser's pithy and proverbial style was designed to be memorable, and this undoubtedly enhanced the author's reputation. At the lower end of the social order, among readers with relatively modest levels of literacy, who have understandably left far fewer records of their encounters with Tusser's book, it is fair to assume that his influence was often profound. His work was reprinted several times in each of the eighteenth, nineteenth, and twentieth centuries, though often in incomplete, revised, or incorrect editions. Although not equally reliable, the most significant editions have been those by D. Hilman (1744), W. Mavor (1812), W. Payne and S. J. Herrtage (1878), and G. Grigson (1984).   ANDREW MCRAE

Sources T. Tusser, *Five hundred points of good husbandry* (1931); facs. edn with an introduction by G. Grigson (1984) • T. Tusser, *Five hundred pointes of good husbandrie*, rev. edn, ed. W. Payne and S. J. Herrtage (1878) • Venn, *Alum. Cant.* • A. McRae, *God speed the plough: the representation of agrarian England, 1500–1660* (1996) • C. Crawley, *Trinity Hall: the history of a Cambridge college, 1350–1975* (1976) • A. Fowler, 'The beginnings of English georgic', *Renaissance genres*, ed. B. K. Lewalski (Cambridge, MA, 1986), 105–25 • L. C. Stevenson, *Praise and paradox: merchants and craftsmen in Elizabethan popular literature* (1984) • J. Thirsk, ed., *The agrarian history of England and Wales*, 4 (1967) • R. M. Schuler, 'Theory and criticism of the scientific poem in Elizabethan England', *English Literary Renaissance*, 15 (1985), 3–41 • T. Milbourn, *The history of the church of St Mildred the Virgin, Poultry* (1872) • J. Stow, *A survay of London*, rev. edn (1603); repr. with introduction by C. L. Kingsford as *A survey of London*, 2 vols. (1908), vol. 1, p. 262 • G. G. Smith, ed., *Elizabethan critical essays*, 2 vols. (1904) • V. F. Stern, *Gabriel Harvey* (1979) • H. Peacham, *Minerva Britanna* (1612) • Fuller, *Worthies* (1662) • *DNB*

Wealth at death £330 owed to him by his brother; 7 acres of copyhold land; leasehold worth 35 shillings per year; books and virginals: will, Tusser, ed. Payne and Herrtage, *Five hundred pointes*, 29–31

Tutchin, John (1660x64–1707), political writer, was possibly born on the Isle of Wight. Such few details as can be gleaned about his family background and his childhood from the columns of his political journal, *The Observator* (1702–10), suggest that he was 'Born and Bred' a gentleman, and a freeman of the City of London (*The Observator*, 3/17, 23). The same source states that Tutchin's 'Father, Grand-father, and several … Uncles were *Non-Conforming*

Ministers' (ibid., 3/32). The only other scrap of information about his youth is the suggestion that he was 'once a Member of the Academy in *Garlands Court*, in the Parish of *Stepney*' (Sharpe, 28). On 30 September 1686 Tutchin, then of St Mildred's, Bread Street, London, and Elizabeth Hickes (*b.* 1663/4, *d.* in or after 1710) of Newington Green, Middlesex, daughter of the presbyterian minister John *Hickes, were licensed to marry at St John's Coleman Street; Tutchin subsequently admitted to 'Marrying the Daughter of Mr. [John] *Hicks*', the presbyterian minister (*The Observator*, 3/32). Parish registers state that Tutchin was then aged twenty-five, though a later elegy (1707) gives him a slightly more recent birth date.

Before his marriage Tutchin had taken part in the Monmouth rebellion, and was captured and tried by Judge Jeffreys at the 'bloody assizes' held in Dorchester in autumn 1685. According to Tutchin's own account he was sentenced to seven years' imprisonment, to pay a fine of 100 marks, and to find surety for his good behaviour for the rest of his life. As a final touch Jeffreys also sentenced him to be whipped through all the market towns of Dorset once a year. Tutchin petitioned to be hanged instead. The draconian sentence meted out to Tutchin became proverbial among his contemporaries. 'Every Body knows *Tutchin* was deservedly order'd to be whip'd through the West Country Market-Towns', wrote the tory pamphleteer William Pittis, 'and that he was set at Liberty, and entertain'd by some People of no small note after the Revolution' (Pittis, 49; *Examination, Tryal and Condemnation*, 10). Among other insults Jeffreys apparently remarked upon Tutchin's poetical aspirations. 'They tell me that you are a poet', Jeffreys observed. 'I'll cap verses with you'. Tutchin, alas, was no poet, but before taking part in Monmouth's rebellion he had published *Poems on several occasions. With a pastoral [The Unfortunate Shepherd]. To which is added, a discourse of life* (1685). 'Good Poetry needs no Apology', the preface unluckily opened, 'and Bad deserves no Commendation'. Unfortunately Tutchin continued to inflict more indifferent verse on an unreceptive public, including *An heroick poem upon the late expedition of His Majesty to rescue England from popery, tyranny, and arbitrary government* (1689). It was perhaps as a consequence of this panegyric that he 'had a Place given him at the Victualling-Office; but accusing the Commissioners before the Lords of the Admiralty, and not able to make out what he charg'd 'em with, he himself was divested of his own Post' (Pittis, 49–50).

By 1699, when Tutchin was paid £12 10s. 'for reward for saving so much of the bloody pickle which drained from the casks and binns which hold the flesh at the Victualling Office and making the same serviceable for the use of the Victualling' (*Calendar of Treasury Books*, 15.134), he had apparently 'turn'd Sollicitor' (*Examination, Tryal and Condemnation*, 20). He had not yet given up writing bad verse, however, and his most notorious performance, *The Foreigners*, for which he was 'taken into the custody of a messenger' (Luttrell, 4.676), was published on 1 August 1700. Daniel Defoe accurately described the work as 'a vile abhorred pamphlet in very ill verse'. It was essentially an exercise in English xenophobia which made use of the biblical allegory invented by John Dryden for *Absalom and Achitophel* to attack William III's Dutch favourites, especially Hans Willem Bentinck, first earl of Portland. Although it was Tutchin's 'reflections upon several great men' which led to his arrest, exception could also have been taken to the radical constitutional position he assumed in line with the extreme contract theory of John Locke:

> When no Successor to the Crown's in sight,
> The Crown is certainly the People's Right.
> If Kings are made the People to enthral,
> We had much better have no King at all …

It was little wonder that *The Foreigners* was 'presented as a libel by a grand jury in the City of London on 28 August 1700' (Luttrell, 4.683) though, in the event, the attorney-general, Sir Thomas Trevor, advised the lords justices that since Tutchin had used 'covert names' ('Bentir' for Bentinck, for example), he could not be prosecuted.

Defoe answered *The Foreigners* with *The True-Born Englishman*, and thenceforth his name was inextricably linked with Tutchin's, the most well-known example occurring in Alexander Pope's satire on bad writing, *The Dunciad* (1728):

> Earless on high, stood unabash'd De Foe,
> And Tutchin flagrant from the scourge below.

During the party strife of Queen Anne's reign Tutchin and fellow whig radicals were attacked for their 'Presbyterian Eloquence' and as the 'Republican Bullies' who published 'Principles of rebellion', which appeared in *The Observator* and *The Review* (1704–13), their influential journals of opinion, which were 'the Entertainment of most Coffee houses in Town'. Charles Leslie's *Rehearsal* paper (1704–9) was published with the avowed aim of answering 'Tutchin, De Foe, and the rest of the *Scandalous Clubb*' (C. Leslie, *Rehearsal*, preface to vol. 1). To Leslie's great amusement Defoe and Tutchin often affected to quarrel, but contemporaries realized that these paper wars were carefully staged. Indeed, when Defoe was in trouble for publishing *The Shortest Way with the Dissenters* he tried to deflect criticism of his intentions by publishing a pamphlet, *A Dialogue between a Dissenter and The Observator* (1703), which was subsequently attributed to Tutchin.

Presumably Tutchin chose to call his periodical *The Observator* in conscious if ironic acknowledgement of Sir Roger L'Estrange's original journal of opinion. The first issue appeared on 1 April 1702, shortly after Queen Anne's accession to the throne. From no. 19 (24–7 June 1702) onwards Tutchin's *The Observator* began to be narrated, like L'Estrange's, in a dialogue between characters called 'Observator' and 'Countryman'. Tutchin's outspoken whig opinions were very different from L'Estrange's establishment toryism, however, and were resented by Queen Anne's tory-dominated first administration. Tutchin was quickly in trouble with the attorney-general, Sir Edward Northey, whose chance came when Tutchin was arraigned by the House of Commons for seditious libel in the issue of *The Observator* for 8–11 December 1703. On 3 January 1704 the Commons resolved that the issue 'contains Matters scandalous and malicious, reflecting upon the Proceedings of this House, and tending to the promoting Sedition in the Kingdom', and ordered that 'Tutchin the author, How the printer, and Bragg the publisher of that paper, should be taken into the custody of the serjeant at arms' (*JHC*, 14.269–79).

Tutchin absconded, and stayed in hiding until May 1704 despite the publication in February of a proclamation promising a reward for his apprehension. He was not pleased with the treatment he received on giving himself up. According to Tutchin, the secretary of state Sir Charles Hedges 'used me so very civilly, when I surrender'd my self to him upon the Proclamation, that I never think my self obliged to apply to him again' (BL, Add. MS 70261, unfoliated: Tutchin to Harley, 23 April 1705). Possibly because of his whig credentials Tutchin preferred to deal with the other secretary of state, Robert Harley, and requested that the prosecution against him be dropped and a writ of *nolle prosequi* brought in. 'I have had Notice of Tryal from the Attorney General the second sitting 4th November', he wrote to Harley on 20 October 1704.

> I think I have offered as fair as any one in my Circumstances could do. I have often told yr Honr that I would lay down the Paper [*The Observator*] provided the prosecution agst me might cease … But if I am continued to be prosecuted, I shall continue to write. (BL, Add. MS 70250, unfoliated)

Harley sent Tutchin's letter to Sir Edward Northey, explaining that 'I do not send it to You by order, but leave it to You to do in it what You think best' (BL, Add. MS 70324, fol. 38). On receiving this information Northey was minded to continue the prosecution 'by order of her Majesty signifyed to me by Mr Secretary Hedges' (BL, Add. MS 70250, unfoliated: Northey to Harley, 25 Oct 1704). Although found guilty, Tutchin survived because of a procedural error in the information against him which meant that 'all the proceedings' were declared 'null'. Northey was certain that 'somebody done it on purpose', but Lord Chief Justice Holt insisted that it was 'plain … as can be' that a genuine error had occurred (*State trials*, 14.1131, 1158). Yet there was no retrial, and Tutchin was discharged on 8 June 1705.

Tutchin's relations with Harley remain obscure. Writing to him on the subject of an alleged clandestine trade by means of which the French fleet had been victualled from England, Tutchin claimed to 'have had concerns with all the Secretaries of State for several years past' (*Portland MSS*, 4.86). Correspondence between Tutchin and the earl of Nottingham has indeed survived (*CSP dom.*, 1702–3, 580–81; 1703–4, 169, 175), and as Tutchin appeared before a committee of the House of Lords in December 1704 to give evidence in relation to his information, it appears that his intelligence was taken seriously. He appears to have been a vexatious complainant, however. In addition to protesting against the victuallers in the 1690s he made allegations of mismanagement against Nathaniel Castleton, the comptroller of the penny post office, and attacked the administration of the navy in the columns of *The Observator*. 'He's the Murderer of honest Men['s] Reputations', one contemporary complained, 'and knows no more of Irregularities committed in the *Navy* and *Victualling Offices*, unless by himself, for which he was discarded' (*The Devil Turn'd Limner, or, A Celebrated Villain Drawn to the life*, 1704, 2).

Whatever Harley thought about Tutchin, the duke of Marlborough did not take kindly to *The Observator*'s outspokenness. 'If I can't have justice done me', Marlborough wrote to Harley, 'I must find some friend that will break his and the printer's bones' (*Bath MSS*, 1.105). As with Tutchin's birth, a degree of uncertainty surrounds his death, which is reputed to have occurred on 23 September 1707 in the London queen's bench prison after he had been beaten up. He was survived by his wife, Elizabeth, who thereafter kept a girls' school at Newington Green and, in 1710, near the Nag's Head, Highgate (*Flying Post*, 12–14 Feb 1712). *An Elegy on Mr John Tutchin, Author of The Observator*, which gave his age at death as forty-three, was eloquent in praise of 'judicious *Tutchin*':

> When long by Cares his suff'ring Worth was try'd,
> He still successless took the better Side,
> And for the Cause he liv'd, a Martyr dy'd.

Such encomiums were rare, however. Typically, he was derided as 'a Senseless, starving Scribler ... Poor in his Purse, and restless in his Mind' ([W. Pittis], *The Reverse*, 1700) whose many complaints of being unjustly treated throughout his career were groundless. 'Ah! Had I Wit but equal to my Spite', he had written in a poem from *Poems on Several Occasions*, 'With what a learned Malice would I write'. Contemporaries were ready enough to acknowledge Tutchin's malice, but less inclined to grant that he had wit. Instead he was portrayed as a republican rabble-rouser and a founder member of the notorious if probably fictitious Calves' Head Club.   J. A. DOWNIE

Sources *The Observator* (1702–10) · J. A. Downie, *Robert Harley and the press: propaganda and public opinion in the age of Swift and Defoe* (1979) · L. Sonsteng Horsley, 'The trial of John Tutchin, author of *The Observator*', *Yearbook of English Studies*, 3 (1973), 124–40 · *Calndar of treasury books*, vol. 15, p. 134; vol. 17, pp. 80, 85, 87, 89, 90, 253, 269, 299, 392. · *An elegy on Mr John Tutchin, author of The Observator, who departed this life on Tuesday, the 23d of this instant September, 1707. In the 44th year of his age* (1707) · [J. Sharpe], *An appeal to the clergy of England* (1706) · N. Luttrell, *A brief historical relation of state affairs from September 1678 to April 1714*, 6 vols. (1857) · T. B. Macaulay, *The history of England from the accession of James II*, new edn, ed. C. H. Firth, 6 vols. (1913–15) · [W. Pittis], *The true-born Englishman: a satyr answer'd paragraph by paragraph* (1701) · *The examination, tryal and condemnation of Rebellion Ob[servato]r* (1703) · *Calendar of the manuscripts of the marquis of Bath preserved at Longleat, Wiltshire*, 5 vols., HMC, 58 (1904–80) · *The manuscripts of his grace the duke of Portland*, 10 vols., HMC, 29 (1891–1931), vols. 5–10 · *State trials*, vol. 14 · *DNB*
Archives BL, Add. MSS 70250, 70261, 70324
Likenesses R. Grave, line engraving, pubd 1819 (after unknown artist), BM, NPG · M. Vandergucht, line engraving, BM, NPG

Tuthill, Sir George Leman (1772–1835), physician, was born at Halesworth in Suffolk on 16 February 1772, the only son of John Tuthill, an attorney at Halesworth, and his wife, Sarah, only daughter of James Jermyn of the same place. He received his education at Bungay under Thomas Reeve, and on 3 June 1790 was admitted as a sizar at Gonville and Caius College, Cambridge; he was a scholar of the college from Michaelmas 1790 to Michaelmas 1796. He graduated BA in 1794 (fifth wrangler) and was subsequently elected to present a university address to the king.

Shortly after graduating Tuthill married Maria, daughter of Richard Smith of Halesworth. Having gone to Paris with his wife, he was included among the numerous English *détenus*; after a captivity of several years his wife, known as a great beauty (Alger, 287), was advised to make a direct appeal to the generosity of the first consul. She presented her petition to Napoleon on his return from hunting, with the result that a few days later she and her husband were on their way to England.

Tuthill then returned to Cambridge, proceeded MA in 1809, received a licence *ad practicandum* from the university dated 25 November 1812, and graduated MD in 1816. He was elected a fellow of the Royal Society in 1810, and was admitted an inceptor candidate of the Royal College of Physicians on 12 April 1813, a candidate on 30 September 1816, and a fellow on 30 September 1817. He was Goulstonian lecturer in 1818, and censor in 1819 and 1830. He was knighted on 28 April 1820.

Tuthill was physician to Westminster Hospital from 1813, and to the Bridewell and Bethlem hospitals, and he held both appointments until his death. He was known to contemporaries as a sound classical scholar and a good chemist, and he became a popular lecturer on the practice of physic. He was one of the most active members of the committee for the preparation of the ninth edition of the *Pharmacopoeia Londinensis*, in 1824, and was responsible for the language of the work itself. He produced an English version to coincide with publication of the original. He was also engaged on the *Pharmacopoeia* of 1836, but died before it appeared. Tuthill was invited to deliver the Harveian oration on 25 June 1835, and, with Sir Henry Halford and William George Maton, was active in carrying out reforms at the Royal College of Physicians in 1835, although he was a firm opponent of radicalism in the profession. Tuthill 'spoke in quick, short sentences, seldom uttering a word more than the occasion required, or omitting one that was necessary' (*GM*, 97).

Tuthill died at his home, 24 Cavendish Square, London, on 7 April 1835, and was buried at St Albans on 14 April. There is a monument to his and his wife's memory at Cransford in Suffolk. He left an only daughter, Laura Maria, married to Thomas Bowett, a solicitor in London. Tuthill's library was sold by Sothebys on 26 and 27 June 1835.   W. W. WEBB, *rev.* PATRICK WALLIS

Sources Munk, *Roll* · *GM*, 2nd ser., 4 (1835), 97 · J. G. Alger, *Englishmen in the French Revolution* (1889) · Venn, *Alum. Cant.* · W. G. Spencer, *Westminster Hospital: an outline of its history* (1924) · BL, Add. MS 19152, fols. 215–226 · BL, Add. MS 19167, fol. 401 · G. L. Tuthill, *Vindicae medicae* (1834)

Tutin, Thomas Gaskell (1908–1987), botanist, was born on 21 April 1908 in Kew, Surrey, the only son and elder child of Frank Tutin, biochemist, and his wife, Jane Ardern. He was educated at Cotham grammar school, Bristol, and Downing College, Cambridge, where he gained a third class in part one (1929) and a second in part two

(1930) of the natural sciences tripos. As an undergraduate he was much involved with the Cambridge Natural History Society and, among many other activities, he participated in a botanical expedition to the Azores in 1929. After graduation Tutin continued in Cambridge, working on fossil plants from Greenland. He went on biological expeditions to southern Spain and Spanish Morocco (1931), British Guiana (1933), and Lake Titicaca (Peru/Bolivia, 1937), the last of these resulting in his important publication on the development and stability of lake plant communities ('The hydrosere and current concepts of the climax', *Journal of Ecology*, 29, 1941).

After his return from Peru in 1938, Tutin held a part-time post as a demonstrator at King's College, London, before, in 1939, accepting an assistant lectureship in the University of Manchester. There, in addition to teaching and nocturnal fire-watching duties during the Second World War, he further developed his interests in lake algae begun during the Titicaca expedition. This led to frequent visits to the research station at Wray Castle on Lake Windermere, where he met his future wife. In 1942 Tutin joined the geographical section of the Admiralty's naval intelligence division in Cambridge, which was producing a new series of geographical handbooks for wartime use. In 1944 he was appointed lecturer in charge of the department of botany at Leicester University College. In 1947 he became the first professor of botany, and in 1957 university status was granted to Leicester by royal charter (Simmons). For the next twenty years he carried out the manifold duties of his post, conceived and developed the university botanic garden, and built up one of the more important university herbaria of flowering plants in the kingdom. In 1967 Tutin became the first occupant of the new chair of plant taxonomy in Leicester; he retired from this in 1973 and was awarded the titles of professor emeritus and university research fellow.

Shortly after the Second World War, Tutin took afternoon tea with Arthur G. Tansley, the doyen of British ecology, who suggested that a modern account of the flowering plants and ferns of Britain was urgently needed. With characteristic verve, Tutin, together with A. R. Clapham and E. F. Warburg, wrote *Flora of the British Isles* (1952; 3rd edn, 1987). At the eighth International Botanical Congress in Paris (1954), participants drew attention to the need for an overall treatment of the plants of Europe. Tutin, again, gathered together a group of colleagues who galvanized the European botanical community into producing the first comprehensive account of the higher plants of Europe. *Flora Europaea* was published in five volumes between 1964 and 1980.

Tutin wrote over sixty scientific papers and took a leading part in writing thirteen books on the plants of Britain and the rest of Europe. In 1977 he was awarded the gold medal by the Linnean Society of London, and in 1982 he was elected a fellow of the Royal Society for his considerable contributions to the furtherance of plant taxonomy. The University of Dublin awarded him an honorary ScD degree in 1979.

Tutin was of medium height, with a robust frame and a mop of grey-white hair. He enjoyed working in his garden, his glass of beer, Mozart, and, occasionally, playing his flute; always, however, there was his intellectual backbone of steel. In 1942 he married a palaeoecologist, Winifred Anne, daughter of Albert Roger Pennington, Post Office supervisor; they had a son and three daughters. She became a fellow of the Royal Society in 1979. Tutin died in Leicester on 7 October 1987. He was survived by his wife.

D. M. MOORE, *rev.*

Sources A. R. Clapham, in H. E. Street, *Essays in plant taxonomy* (1978), xi–xviii · A. D. Bradshaw, *Memoirs FRS*, 38 (1992), 361–75 · J. Simmons, *New university* (1958) · personal knowledge (1996) · private information (1996) · *CGPLA Eng. & Wales* (1987)
Likenesses photograph, repro. in Bradshaw, *Memoirs FRS*, 360
Wealth at death £89,941: probate, 8 Dec 1987, *CGPLA Eng. & Wales*

Tuttell, Thomas (*c.*1674–1702), maker of mathematical instruments, was the son of William Tuttell, a member of the Cordwainers' Company of London. He was apprenticed to Henry Wynne of the Clockmakers' Company on 2 April 1688 and freed seven years later, on 1 July 1695. The same year he set up a workshop at the sign of the King's Arms and Globe at Charing Cross, and began making and selling mathematical instruments in his own right. He advertised a full range of navigational, calculational, astronomical, and surveying instruments, and also sold globes and barometers. Between June 1697 and August 1699 he took three apprentices.

Tuttell's position as one of the foremost makers was soon established. Shortly after gaining his freedom he secured the patronage of Colonel William Parsons of the foot guards, and by 1698 his business was strong enough to have opened a new shop beside the Royal Exchange in Cornhill. More importantly, he had also received a royal appointment as mathematical instrument maker to the king.

In 1698 Tuttell published a short book, entitled *The Description and Uses of a New Contriv'd Eliptical Double Dial*, in which he described a form of analemmatic sundial which he had recently devised. While concentrating on explaining this dial (which consisted of a horizontal dial and an elliptical projection of the equatorial dial into the plane of the horizon), the book also contains a description of the universal equinoctial ring dial. Both were carefully explained by Tuttell and, as an aid to the user, he included a table of towns with their latitudes as an appendix.

In the introduction to this work, Tuttell declared his intention of writing a further book which would explain the uses of the various mathematical instruments then in use, and which he felt were not sufficiently covered in contemporary mathematical texts. This project was realized in a collaboration with James Moxon, son of the mathematician Joseph Moxon. In the 1701 edition of Joseph Moxon's *Mathematical Dictionary* James Moxon and Tuttell appended a short lexicon of mathematical instruments. Not only were the instruments described in some detail, but many of them were illustrated on a plate, very similar in style to Tuttell's later trade cards. The instruments also appeared on a set of playing cards which Tuttell issued in 1701 and which included an advertisement on the king of clubs.

At some point in 1700 Tuttell was appointed as hydrographer to the king, and during the following year he carried out surveys on the west coast of England. He was in the process of surveying the Thames when he was drowned in that river on 22 January 1702. His widow placed a notice in the *Post Boy*, describing him as being 'of Middle Stature, fair light Hair but his Head newly shaved' and requesting his body to be returned to her if it was found (*Post Boy*).

Despite his very early death, Tuttell held an important position among the makers of mathematical instruments. He was versatile enough to work not only in brass and silver, but also in wood and ivory. Those instruments of his which survive show evidence of the high quality of his workmanship. However, Tuttell was not only an instrument maker: he designed instruments and taught their use, was an able surveyor, and a competent author on mathematical subjects. In just seven years he established himself as a central figure in the mathematical community of which he was a part.   H. K. HIGTON

Sources G. Clifton, *Directory of British scientific instrument makers, 1550–1851*, ed. G. L'E. Turner (1995) · D. J. Bryden, 'A 1701 dictionary of mathematical instruments', *Making instruments count*, ed. R. G. W. Anderson, J. A. Bennett, and W. F. Ryan (1993), 365–82 · J. Moxon, *Mathematicks made easie: a mathematical dictionary*, 3rd edn (1701) · T. Tuttell, *The description and uses of a new contriv'd eliptical double dial* (1698) · *Post Boy* (31 Jan–3 Feb 1702) · T. Tuttell and W. Parsons, *Proposals … for a new pair of globes* [n.d., 1700?] [1701]

Tuttiett, Lawrence (1825–1897), hymn writer, was born at Cloyton, Devon, the son of John Tuttiett, a surgeon in the Royal Navy, and Ann Rayner. He was educated at Christ's Hospital and at King's College, London. He originally intended to devote himself to the study of medicine, but, changing his purpose, he was ordained deacon in 1848 and priest in 1849. At the beginning of his ministry he was under the influence of Charles Kingsley and F. D. Maurice, but in later life he adopted the high-church principles of E. B. Pusey. In 1848 he became curate at St Paul's, Knightsbridge, where the Tractarian William James Early Bennett was then vicar, and between 1849 and 1853 was successively curate of St Thomas and Holy Trinity churches, Ryde. He married Helen Carnegy Hunter (1823–1884); they had a son and two daughters. In 1853 Tuttiett was appointed vicar of Lea Marston in Warwickshire, and in 1870 exchanged incumbencies with the rector of St Andrews in Scotland. In 1877 he was nominated canon of St Ninian's Cathedral, Perth. He spent his last years in retirement at Pitlochry, but died on 21 May 1897 from cardiac disease at 3 Abbotsford Crescent, St Andrews, while on a visit to the town. He was buried in St Andrews.

Tuttiett is best known as a hymn writer. Much of his verse, composed on returning from visitations of the sick or burial of the dead, was conceived to express the consolatory thoughts suggested to him by what he had seen or heard. His adherence to these guidelines resulted in hymns which were characterized by a simplicity of style and a deep earnestness, including 'Oh quickly come, dread judge of all' and 'Give light, O Lord, that we may learn'. He published a number of influential collections, including *Hymns for Churchmen* (1854) and *Through the Clouds: Thoughts in Plain Verse* (1866). He also wrote hymns for children, issued as *Hymns for the Children of the Church* (1862), and published many devotional treatises, including *Germs of Thought on the Sunday Services* (1864), *Amen: its True Meaning and Proper Use* (1868), and *Meditations on the Book of Common Prayer* (1872).

E. I. CARLYLE, *rev.* LEON LITVACK

Sources J. Julian, ed., *A dictionary of hymnology*, rev. edn (1907) · M. Frost, ed., *Historical companion to 'Hymns ancient and modern'* (1962) · D. Campbell, *Hymns and hymn makers*, 5th edn (1912) · J. I. Jones and others, *The Baptist hymn book companion* · H. Martin (1962) · J. Moffatt and M. Patrick, eds., *Handbook to the church hymnary, with supplement*, 2nd edn (1935) · register of deaths, district no. 453, entry no. 77, 1884, NA Scot. [Helen Carnegy Hunter] · register of deaths, district no. 453, entry no. 56, 1897, NA Scot. · E. Routley, *An English-speaking hymnal guide* (1979)
Archives NL Scot., letters to Blackwoods
Wealth at death £1069 14s. 1d.; theological books and papers left to son: NA Scot., Cupar record of testamentary deeds, SC 20/50, vol. 76, fols. 534–9

Tutton, Alfred Edwin Howard (1864–1938), crystallographer and alpinist, was born at Stockport on 22 August 1864, the only child of James Tutton, venetian blind manufacturer, and his wife, Martha Howard. He attended the national school, Edgeley, leaving at the age of thirteen to work in the office of the town clerk of Stockport. In the evenings he attended classes at the mechanics' institute and chemistry lectures by Henry Roscoe at Owens College, Manchester. In 1883 he gained a royal exhibition to the Normal School (later Royal College) of Science and Royal School of Mines at South Kensington, where he won the Murchison medal for geology and the prizes for physics and chemistry. After a fourth year, with a teaching scholarship, he became an assistant demonstrator in chemistry, being promoted full demonstrator and lecturer in 1889.

During the years 1886 to 1892 Tutton assisted Edward Thorpe in research work on the role of phosphorus oxides in the 'phossy jaw' disease of matchmakers. The beautiful crystals of the new tetroxide (P_2O_4) turned his attention to crystallography which then, in private laboratories at his successive homes, became his life's work. He specialized in the precise measurement of the morphological, optical, elasticity, and thermal expansion constants of artificially grown crystals of various isomorphous series. One large series of hydrated double sulphates and selenates of alkali and bivalent metals came to be known as Tutton salts. He demonstrated that, in each series, these physical constants vary with the atomic weights of the replacing chemical elements.

Tutton's work was marked by the highest degree of accuracy, down to the minutest detail. A modified form of his interferometer was used to determine, in 1931, the length of the imperial standard yard in terms of the wavelength of light; his result was 1,420,210 wavelengths of the red cadmium line at 62 °F.

In 1895 Tutton was appointed inspector of technical schools under the Board of Education, which was located successively in Oxford, London, and Plymouth. While in Oxford he was awarded the degree of DSc in 1903. The previous year he had married Margaret Ethel MacLannahan, youngest daughter of William Loat of Cumnor Place, near Oxford; they had two sons and four daughters. On retiring from the Board of Education in 1924, Tutton moved to Cambridge where he lectured on crystallography until 1931 when he settled at Dallington, Sussex.

Tutton wrote five books on crystals and crystallography; his *Crystallography and Practical Crystal Measurement* (1911; 2nd edn, 2 vols., 1922) was for many years a standard treatise. His recreations were music and alpine photography. For thirty years he spent his holidays in the Alps and used many of his numerous photographs to make lantern slides for his lectures. He wrote *The Natural History of Ice and Snow, Illustrated from the Alps* (1927) and *The High Alps* (1931). He was a fellow of the Chemical Society for fifty years, was elected FRS in 1899, and was president of the Mineralogical Society from 1912 to 1915. He received the honorary degree of DSc from Manchester University in 1926. Tutton died at the Royal East Sussex Hospital at Hastings on 14 July 1938.   L. J. SPENCER, rev.

Sources *Obits. FRS*, 2 (1936–8), 621–6 · *Mineralogical Magazine*, 25 (1938–40) · *Nature*, 142 (1938), 321–2 · personal knowledge (1949) · *CGPLA Eng. & Wales* (1938)

Archives ICL, corresp. relating to Technical Optics committee; lecture notes · RS, papers · Sci. Mus., lecture notes on electricity | BL, corresp. with Macmillans, Add. MS 55224

Likenesses W. Stoneman, photograph, 1918, NPG · Maull & Fox, photograph, RS · photograph, RS · portrait, repro. in *Mineralogical Magazine* · portrait, repro. in *Obits. FRS*, 7 (Jan 1939)

Wealth at death £4100 8s. 2d.: probate, 30 Sept 1938, *CGPLA Eng. & Wales*

Tutuola, Amos (1920–1997), writer, was born at Ipose-Ake, Abeokuta, a large Yoruba-speaking town in Ogun state in south-western Nigeria, in June 1920 (he was unsure himself of the exact date of his birth). He was the son of Christian parents: his father was a cocoa farmer, and his mother and aunt told him all the folk-tales they had heard from his grandmother: the great majority of these narratives were supernatural in form and didactic in substance. He attended the Salvation Army primary school only briefly before leaving his parents' home to work as a servant for a Mr F. O. Monu, a government clerk, but when he was thirteen or fourteen Monu paid to send him to Ipose-Ake's Anglican school. When Monu was transferred to Lagos, Tutuola accompanied him and went to Lagos high school for two years. Overall, his formal education amounted to less than seven years in various schools, and in none of these schools did he stand out academically. In 1939 Tutuola's father died, and he began training as a blacksmith, a skill which enabled him to find employment as a metalworker with the Nigerian Royal Air Force at Oshodi, where he worked from 1942 until the end of the Second World War.

After the war Tutuola endured a period of unemployment, intermittently broken by short spells of work as a farm labourer, a bread seller, and a blacksmith. In 1947 he married Victoria Alake, with whom he had eight children (four sons and four daughters). In the following year he became a messenger for the labour department in Lagos. Somewhat paradoxically, he was underemployed in his new job and so began writing to relieve the boredom. While his impulse was to tell stories orally, his presence in an office compelled him to transcribe his stories onto pieces of scrap paper, though he was insistent throughout his life that he had no intention at that time of writing for publication. However, when he saw an advertisement in a local paper placed by the United Society for Christian Literature announcing its latest publications, he sent the society the manuscript of a book he had recently completed, the first draft of which was written in one frenetic forty-eight-hour period. With commendable generosity the society replied to Tutuola, advising him that it was not itself a publisher but would help him to find one. In 1952, on the recommendation of T. S. Eliot, Faber and Faber published *The Palm-Wine Drinkard*, Tutuola's most successful book. The novel, one of the first by an African writer to be written in English, tells the story of a 'drinkard' who journeys to the land of the dead to bring back his favourite wine-maker. Episodic in structure, fantastic in exposition, *The Palm-Wine Drinkard* is characterized primarily by linguistic hyperbole, but also by an unusual blend of the disgusting, the comic, and the marvellous. The novel blends fantasy with conventional realism, a feature of traditional Yoruba folk-tales, and is, undoubtedly, idiosyncratically written: 'When I saw that there was no palm-wine for me again, and nobody could tap it for me, then I thought within myself that old people were saying that the whole people who had died in this world, did not go to heaven directly, but they were living in one place somewhere in this world' (*The Palm-Wine Drinkard*, 1952, 170). Many African writers and intellectuals were contemptuous of the book, decrying it for its poor grammar and punctuation, and arguing that it pandered to Western stereotypes of African backwardness, a charge that was levelled at Tutuola throughout his career, and one that was not without substance. *The Palm-Wine Drinkard* was, however, an enormous international success, and several prominent European critics and writers, including V. S. Pritchett, Kingsley Amis, and Dylan Thomas were vocally enthusiastic about the novel; Thomas, for example, wrote: 'The writing is nearly always terse and direct, strong, wry, flat and savoury … nothing is too prodigious or too trivial to put down in this tall, devilish tale' (Lindfors, 2). *The Palm-Wine Drinkard* was turned into an opera by the Yoruba composer Kola Ogunmola, and was translated into over a dozen other languages.

Having failed to find regular employment, in 1954 Tutuola published *My Life in the Bush of Ghosts*, which he had written before *The Palm-Wine Drinkard*. In this novel an eight-year-old boy escapes a slave raid by running into the terrifying Bush of Ghosts, a fantastic world in which the boy undergoes a series of transformations and suffers a variety of experiences, invariably horrifying, before re-emerging into the normal world twenty-five years later, ready to begin adult life. Like its predecessor, the book was enthusiastically received in Europe and America but, again, dismissed by the majority of Tutuola's African peers. Tutuola's third book, *Simbi and the Satyr of the Dark Jungle*, was published in 1955: it used a young girl as its protagonist and once again utilized a quest as its central organizing principle. Over the next thirty years Tutuola produced a series of novels and collections of short stories, including *The Brave African Huntress* (1958), *The Witch–Herbalist of the Remote Town* (1981), *Yoruba Folktales* (1986), and his last published work, *The Village Witch Doctor and other Stories* (1990).

In 1956 Tutuola joined the Nigerian Broadcasting Company as a storekeeper in Ibadan, where he worked until his retirement; he moved to Ibadan in the 1980s. He was a member of the Mbari Club, the publishers' and writers' club in Ibadan, but he played no part in the intellectual life of Nigeria. Despite his international reputation, he travelled rarely and seemed uncomfortable away from home. On 13 December 1983 he spoke at the Africa Centre in London: while his reading was a great success he could not be convinced to repeat it. In 1979 he was a research fellow at the University of Ife in Ibadan, and then an associate of the international writing programme at the University of Iowa; he was also an honorary citizen of New Orleans. Heavily bespectacled and amiable in appearance, Tutuola was a slow-moving man who rarely seemed excited unless he was telling one of his stories, at which times both his features and his movements became highly animated. He was gregarious outside literary and political circles, and was always prepared to discuss his work, but he could slyly play up to those of his listeners who were expecting to meet a genuine African naïf.

None of the work which Tutuola produced after *Simbi* was as acclaimed as his early work, and while it became a critical axiom that Tutuola's powers as a writer had simply waned, the decline in his reputation is as much a cultural issue as a personal one. Gerald Moore observed of *Simbi* that its principal theme, of humanity needing to renew the energy of its world by heroic action or self-sacrifice, had for individuals and societies lost its meaning (Moore, 39). This may in large part explain why Tutuola's writing made diminishing impact over subsequent decades; his vision of a communal universe which accommodated the world of ghosts, spirits, and magic—itself derived from the Yoruba folk tradition—became less accessible to an increasingly urbanized and individualistic readership. Tutuola's work was compared at various times to that of Dante, Chaucer, Bunyan, and Homer, yet his was a unique voice, and his impact on African literature was powerful and incontestable. Tutuola died on 8 June 1997 in Ibadan.

KEVIN MCCARRON

Sources B. Lindfors, ed., *Critical perspectives on Amos Tutuola* (1975) · *The Independent* (16 June 1997) · *The Guardian* (16 June 1997) · *The Times* (16 June 1997) · G. Moore, *Seven African writers* (1962)

Tuvell [Tuvill], **Daniel** (*d.* 1660), Church of England clergyman, was perhaps a son of Michael Tuvell, Frenchman, described as a denizen, and Jone his wife, who were members of the French church in London in 1571. They lived in one of the sixteen hamlets within the precinct of St Katharine by the Tower, which included Grub Street, Shoreditch, and White Chapel. In September 1598 Daniel was admitted sizar, as born in London, to Sidney Sussex College, Cambridge, from where he graduated BA in 1601 and proceeded MA in 1607. He was vicar of St Bartholomew-the-Less, London, from 1620 to 1631, probably on the presentation of John King, diocesan bishop, and became preacher at Sutton's Hospital, Charterhouse, Clerkenwell, London, in 1630, perhaps through the patronage of John Buckeridge, who as bishop of Ely was a key governor. This post was open only to the unmarried. While there he published his only certain work, *St Pauls Threefold Cord* (1635), which reveals unqualified support for royal absolutism, which he saw as resisted only by Romanists. On 7 October 1643 he was sequestrated by parliament on charges of drunkenness, preaching favourably of the organs and new pictures in the chapel, neglecting fasts, and inviting royalist ministers to preach there. He was buried on 13 September 1660 at St Bartholomew-the-Less.

Jean l'Oiseau de Turval [John Byrde] (*d.* 1631), Church of England clergyman and author, may be responsible for other works published by 'D. T.' and attributed to Tuvell, as he used these initials. A third generation protestant, born in Paris of unknown parentage and learned in ancient and modern languages excluding English, Turval arrived in England in 1603, perhaps in the train of the marquis de Rosny, the French ambassador. He settled in London, retaining friends in the embassy. A 'D. T.', gentleman, was in the service of Lady Anne Harington, governess of Princess Elizabeth, when his secular *Essaies, Politicke and Morall* was published in 1608.

Turval was often employed by James I on secret errands to France. He translated the king's *Apologie for the Oath of Allegiance* into French, and hid for three months in Paris to get it printed there in 1609. The next year he translated extracts from Joseph Hall's works, and similarly arranged printing in Paris. His *The Dove and the Serpent* (1614), dedicated to Sir Henry Montagu, later earl of Manchester, advises on public office, negotiation, and diplomatic behaviour abroad, matters outside Daniel Tuvell's scope, and *Asylum veneris* (1616), dedicated to Lady Alice Colville, praises women, in stark contrast to Tuvell's *St Pauls Threefold Cord*.

In 1618 Turval was still on official missions to France. The next year he was naturalized as Jean l'Oiseau. By 1623 he was a royal chaplain, a position which continued under Charles I. In 1625 he was presented by his friend John Donne, dean of St Paul's Cathedral, to St Martin Orgar in the City of London, which he resigned in 1628. Three years later, by which time he was sometimes known as Byrde, Philip Herbert, earl of Pembroke, presented him to Meppershall, Bedfordshire. However, within a short time he died, probably in London. He was buried at St Martin-in-the-Fields on 26 May 1631. He was apparently unmarried.

ELIZABETH ALLEN

Sources Venn, *Alum. Cant.* · *Walker rev.*, 61 · R. E. G. Kirk and E. F. Kirk, eds., *Returns of aliens dwelling in the city and suburbs of London, from the reign of Henry VIII to that of James I*, Huguenot Society of London, 10/2 (1902), 140, 143 · A. Clarke, 'Jean Loiseau de Tourval: a Huguenot translator in England, 1603–31', *Proceedings of the Huguenot Society*, 20 (1958–64), 36–59, esp. 36–7, 40–41, 46–50, 52 · R. Newcourt, *Repertorium Ecclesiasticum*, 1 (1708), 298 · *CSP dom.*, *1611–18*, 579 · W. A. Shaw, *A history of the English church during the civil wars and under the Commonwealth, 1640–1660*, 2 (1900), 316 · G. S. Davies, *Charterhouse in London* (1921), 350

Tuzo, Sir Harry Craufurd (1917–1998), army officer, was born on 26 August 1917 in Bangalore, India, the son of Captain John Atkinson Tuzo, civil engineer, and his wife, Annie Katherine, *née* Craufurd. He was educated at Wellington College and Oriel College, Oxford, graduating with a fourth-class degree in jurisprudence in 1939.

Tuzo was commissioned into the Royal Artillery in August 1939. After only a fortnight's training he was sent to France with the 21st anti-tank regiment and in May 1940 he was part of the British expeditionary force which was evacuated from Dunkirk. He was taken to Harwich in a paddle cruiser after protecting the force's rear during the withdrawal. After working in coastal defence he made a return journey across the channel, landing at Normandy in June 1944. He took part in intense fighting across northwest Europe and was awarded the MC for bravery in supporting the guards armoured division during operation Goodwood, the armoured push east of Caen. At the end of the war, in which he was also mentioned in dispatches, he had the unusual experience of personally accepting the surrender of the German admiral who was flag officer, U-boats. On 5 October 1943 he had married Monica Patience, daughter of William Eric Salter, engineer. They had one daughter, Victoria.

Tuzo's career after 1945 alternated between staff and artillery jobs. After a period at the Staff College, Camberley, he was posted to general headquarters Far East land forces as a GSO2 (intelligence), then to the 5th regiment, Royal Horse Artillery (RHA). Following a posting as GSO2 at the school of infantry, Warminster, he commanded L battery in the 2nd regiment, RHA, at Hildesheim, West Germany, and served in the War Office before taking the 3rd regiment, RHA, to Kenya and Aden. He was appointed OBE in 1961. After a spell as assistant commandant at Sandhurst he saw action in 1963 when he was posted to the Far East to command 51st Gurkha brigade in Borneo and was involved with the SAS in incursions across the border against Indonesian forces during operation Claret. The sultan of Brunei awarded him the Dato Setia Negeri Brunei for his outstanding service. Promotion to major-general saw him appointed chief of staff of the British army of the Rhine (1967–9) and director of Royal Artillery at the Ministry of Defence (1969–71). He was knighted KCB in 1971.

Tuzo had expected to retire at this stage but fate took a hand when Lieutenant-General Vernon Erskine Crum, general officer commanding Northern Ireland, died suddenly of a heart attack. Tuzo was told by General Sir Geoffrey Baker, chief of the general staff: 'Fasten your seat belt: you are going to Northern Ireland' (Hamill, 45–6). His arrival in the province in February 1971 could scarcely have been at a less propitious time. The job was political as much as military and the Northern Ireland government at Stormont was struggling to survive as the Provisional IRA geared up for its first major offensive against the British state. Gunner Robert Curtis, the first soldier to be killed in the troubles, had just been shot dead by an IRA sniper. In the following month three Scottish soldiers—two of them teenage brothers—were executed at point-blank range after being lured by female IRA accomplices from a bar in Belfast.

Although appalled by the violence against his troops, Tuzo's sharp intellect and sense of fairness made him insist to Stormont ministers that the army's role was to act resolutely but not to assert a sectarian protestant hegemony over Roman Catholics. He soon modified his early rash prediction that the IRA could be 'finished' by March 1972 to state that while a permanent solution could not be found by military means the army could subjugate the IRA and allow the politicians to find one. But his role was a complicated military–political one and he clashed with both Brian Faulkner, the Northern Ireland prime minister, and the Royal Ulster Constabulary.

> It was a complicated situation because I was in effect a sort of Minister of Defence and Chief of Staff to two people, so far as Northern Ireland was concerned ... I worked to the Prime Minister of Northern Ireland ... and I had to report back to Westminster. (Coogan, 108)

Tuzo repeatedly resisted introducing the more draconian measures demanded by the Stormont cabinet, fearing that Northern Ireland could become the United Kingdom's Vietnam. A month before internment was introduced he told Edward Heath, the prime minister, that imprisoning suspects without trial would have a 'harmful effect'. Tuzo was not against internment in principle but recognized that the Royal Ulster Constabulary's special branch had intelligence files that were woefully out of date. Faulkner said the move would 'smash the IRA' but Tuzo was proved right. Violence swept across Northern Ireland and the perceived injustice of internment drove many moderate Catholics towards supporting the IRA. Tuzo later said that 'the error was that we were too undiscriminating ... that was where we slipped up' (Hamill, 62).

The most disastrous day of Tuzo's tumultuous time in Northern Ireland was 30 January 1972, 'bloody Sunday', when a banned civil rights march in Londonderry ended in rioting and the shooting dead by the Parachute regiment of thirteen civilians. Tuzo had wanted the army to adopt a low-key strategy that avoided clashes but he was overruled by Faulkner, who preferred the more confrontational approach of Major-General Robert Ford, the commander of land forces. The events of 'bloody Sunday' were so controversial that they eclipsed almost every other incident in some thirty years of violence.

Direct rule was imposed in March 1972, with the Stormont government relinquishing its powers to Westminster. This was welcomed by Tuzo, who had grown tired of the protestant politicians' short-sightedness and demands for the impossible. By June 1972 the 100th soldier had been killed and in the following month the IRA's no-warning bombs on 'bloody Friday' claimed the lives of nine civilians in Belfast. Tuzo seized back the initiative from the IRA with operation Motorman, the army's biggest military operation since Suez, in which 12,000 troops swept into areas of Londonderry and Belfast that the IRA had declared 'no go' for the forces of law and order. The army regained a measure of control of the 'no go' areas and the IRA was shown that the army would prove more difficult to oust than the Stormont government.

Tuzo was promoted GCB in 1973, and in the same year left Northern Ireland to take over as commander of the British army of the Rhine. His military and diplomatic skills then made him an ideal deputy supreme allied commander Europe to the American General Alexander Haig from 1976 until his retirement in 1978. He was aide-de-camp (general) to the queen from 1974 to 1977, and master gunner, St James's Park, from 1977 to 1983.

In retirement Tuzo was chairman of Marconi Defence and Space Systems (1979–83) and a director of Oceonics (1988–91). He was also active in the Royal United Services Institute (serving as chairman from 1980 to 1983) and the International Institute for Strategic Studies (of which he was a member of the council from 1978 to 1987). He chaired the Imperial War Museum Redevelopment Appeal from 1984 to 1988. Devoted to Norfolk, where he lived at Heath Farmhouse, Fakenham, he was president of the Norfolk Society (1987–92), chairman of the Fermoy Centre Foundation at King's Lynn (1982–7) and the Pensthorpe Waterfowl Trust (1988–96), and a deputy lieutenant for the county (1983–96). He was a keen sailor and amateur painter, and an enthusiast for the theatre, music, gardening, and literature.

A humane, cheerful, and resilient officer, Tuzo's sharp political brain and coolness when many around him were panicking were key factors in the army's maintaining the upper hand in Northern Ireland when civil disorder threatened to overwhelm the province. History is likely to judge him as one of the most able army commanders of the troubles. He died of heart failure at the Norfolk and Norwich Hospital, Norwich, on 7 August 1998, and was survived by his wife and daughter.   TOBY HARNDEN

Sources D. Hamill, *Pig in the middle* (1985) · T. P. Coogan, *The troubles* (1995) · P. Bishop and E. Millie, *The Provisional IRA* (1987) · M. Dewar, *The British army in N. Ireland* (1996) · P. Pringle and P. Jacobson, *Those are real bullets, aren't they?* (2000) · *The Times* (11 Aug 1998) · *The Daily Telegraph* (14 Aug 1998) · *The Guardian* (15 Aug 1998) · *The Independent* (19 Aug 1998) · *WWW* · m. cert. · d. cert.
Likenesses photograph, 1971, repro. in *The Times* · photograph, 1972, repro. in *Daily Telegraph* · photograph, 1972, repro. in *The Independent* · photograph, repro. in *The Guardian*

Tweddell, John (1769–1799), classical and archaeological scholar, was born on 1 June 1769 at Threepwood, near Hexham, the son of Francis Tweddell (1730–1805), magistrate, and Jane Westgarth of Unthank, Northumberland. Tweddell attended Hartforth School, near Richmond, Yorkshire, and studied with Dr Samuel Parr before matriculating at Trinity College, Cambridge, in March 1786,

where he was a 'fellow-collegian' of James Losh (Tweddell, *Remains*, 27). Tweddell 'carried off every prize for which he could be a candidate' including the Browne medal in 1788 and 1789, and the chancellor's classical medal in 1790 (Gunning, 2.79). He wrote 'witty epigrams', and was an accomplished mimic, imitating Thomas Erskine with particular success (ibid., 83). He graduated BA in 1790 (MA, 1793), and in 1792 published his prize compositions in Greek, Latin, and English in a volume entitled *Prolusiones juveniles*. That year he was elected a fellow of Trinity College.

Tweddell entered Lincoln's Inn in 1790 and the Middle Temple in 1792, although his ambitions aimed at politics and diplomacy. He was 'one of the early well-wishers of the [French] revolution' (Tweddell, *Remains*, 246) and was associated with the reformist Friends of the People in London. His name appears on the society's first declaration, dated 11 April 1792. Tweddell told Isabel Gunning that he was 'acquainted with almost all the leading men in opposition', including Charles Grey and James Mackintosh, and thought it 'not improbable' that he would become an MP (Paston, 328). The acquittals of Thomas Hardy and John Horne Tooke in the treason trials of 1794 gave Tweddell the 'highest gratification', and he was 'most indiscreet' in declaring his opinions (Gunning, 2.87). Between 1793 and 1795 he was frequently in company with William Godwin, whose *Political Justice* he described as 'a very able book' (Paston, 342–3), and he was present with George Dyer, William Frend, Thomas Holcroft, and James Losh when William Wordsworth met Godwin on 27 February 1795. After that meeting Tweddell dropped out of Godwin's circle. On 24 September 1795 he sailed to Hamburg to begin a tour of Europe that would take him to 'Switzerland, the North of Europe, and various parts of the East' (Tweddell, *Remains*, 9). He visited Berlin (where he met Lord Elgin), Vienna, Zürich, Moscow, St Petersburg, Stockholm, and Constantinople. In November 1796 he was the guest of Necker and Madame de Staël at Coppet near Lake Geneva.

Disappointed love for Isabel Gunning may have encouraged Tweddell's travels. His letters from Europe speak of 'painful recollections', and announce that he would be 'more happy to remain in a corner unnoticed, than to take any active part in the busy scenes of this silly world' (Tweddell, *Remains*, 47, 162–3). By 1798 he regarded the French Revolution as 'an eternal injury to the cause of freedom', and in the same year he became a vegetarian (ibid., 237, 249). While in Europe Tweddell compiled extensive journals recording his classical and archaeological researches, and hoped 'one day to shew the richest port-folio perhaps that was ever carried out of Greece, Asia, and Turkey' (ibid., 268). He arrived at Athens on 29 December 1798 and, with help from the French artist Preaux, set about copying 'every temple, and every archway … every stone, and every inscription … with the most scrupulous fidelity' (ibid., 268). His studies also detailed '*ceremonies*, and *usages*, and *dresses* of the people' of Greece (ibid., 317). While pursuing this work at Athens he died of fever on 25 July 1799; his burial in the temple of Theseus is described in Edward Clarke's *Travels* (3.533–4). In death

Tweddell became almost a mythical figure, with many laments at the genius cut off before it could show itself. Lord Byron was among those who in 1810 marked his grave with a block of marble from the Parthenon.

Some of Tweddell's papers, notes, and drawings had been left at Pera, Constantinople, in the care of Thomas Thornton, banker in the Levant Company, and these were destroyed by fire. The remainder, damaged by shipwreck in transit from Athens to Constantinople, came into the possession of Lord Elgin, British ambassador in the city. Elgin seems to have intended to ship the papers back to the Tweddell family in England, but for some reason they were never sent (although Elgin and his assistants later claimed that they had been). Between 1810 and 1816 the fate of Tweddell's papers became a subject of public scandal, and the publication of the memorial *Remains of John Tweddell* (1815) by Tweddell's brother Robert added to the controversy. Robert Tweddell claimed that of some 400 drawings by John Tweddell only 112 survived, and that the 'whole of Mr. Tweddell's MSS are still unaccounted for' (Tweddell, *Account*, 16). NICHOLAS ROE

Sources R. Tweddell, ed., *The remains of John Tweddell* (1815) · R. Tweddell, ed., *Addenda to the remains of John Tweddell* (1816) · R. Tweddell, *Account of the examination of the Elgin-box* (1816) · N. Roe, *Wordsworth and Coleridge: the radical years* (1988), 190–91, 244–8 · W. St Clair, *Lord Elgin and the marbles* (1967), 230–41 · *DNB* · G. Paston [E. M. Symonds], 'The romance of John Tweddell', *Little memoirs of the eighteenth century* (1901) · H. Gunning, *Reminiscences of the university, town, and county of Cambridge, from the year 1780*, 2 (1854), 79–92 · R. Surtees, *The history and antiquities of the county palatine of Durham*, 3 (1823), 82–3 · E. D. Clarke, *Travels in various countries of Europe, Asia and Africa*, 6 vols. (1810–23), vol. 3, pp. 532–4

Likenesses silhouette, stipple and line engraving, BM, NPG; repro. in Tweddell, ed., *Remains*

Tweddell, Ralph Hart (1843–1895), mechanical engineer and inventor of the hydraulic riveter, son of Marshall Tweddell, a shipowner, was born at South Shields on 25 May 1843, and educated at Cheltenham College, 1856–60, where he was followed by his younger brother, Marshall Tweddell (1847–1904). In 1861 he was articled to R. and W. Hawthorn of Newcastle upon Tyne, engineers. During his apprenticeship, on 9 May 1865, he took out a patent (no. 1282) for a portable hydraulic apparatus for fixing the ends of boiler tubes in tube plates. The results were so encouraging as to suggest the employment of hydraulic power for machines used in boiler construction.

In 1865 Tweddell designed a stationary hydraulic riveting machine, which he patented on 23 August 1866 (no. 2158). The plant, consisting of a pump, an accumulator, and a riveter, was first used by Thompson, Boyd & Co., of Newcastle. The work was carried out perfectly and at one-seventh the cost of hand work. The surplus power was applied to hydraulic presses for setting angle and tee irons, and it was proved that the wear and tear of the moulds and dies were greatly reduced. As it was often found difficult to bring work to the machine, Tweddell turned his attention to the design of a portable riveter. The first portable machine was made in 1871, and used by Armstrong, Mitchell & Co. at Newcastle. Two years later

the machine was employed in riveting *in situ* a lattice girder bridge which carried Primrose Street over the Great Eastern Railway at its approach to Liverpool Street Station in London. Due to the success of this work, the plant was used widely for riveting bridges. Other applications of the portable machines were soon found, such as the riveting of locomotive boilers, gun carriages, agricultural machinery, and wrought-iron underframes for railway carriages, and progress was also made in its application to the riveting of ships.

In 1874 the French government adopted Tweddell's system in their shipbuilding yard at Toulon and a similar plant was subsequently erected at the shipyard of the Forges et Chantiers de la Loire at Penhouet, part of the town of St Nazaire. The largest of the machines at Penhouet exerted 50 tons pressure, but one was constructed in 1883 for the naval arsenal at Brest with a pressure equal to 100 tons. Tweddell was responsible for major changes in the method of construction of boiler, bridge, and shipbuilding works. Not only was the work better and more reliable, but without the aid of his machinery much of it could not have been accomplished. Hydraulic riveting and the application of hydraulic power to machine tools may be said to have revolutionized engineering workshop practice. Tweddell married, on 2 August 1875, at Meopham Court, near Gravesend, Kent, Hannah Mary, third daughter of G. A. Grey of Milfield, Northumberland.

Tweddell wrote the papers, 'On machine tools and labour-saving appliances worked by hydraulic pressure' and 'Forging by hydraulic pressure'. For the former he was awarded the Telford medal and premium. He read three papers before the Institution of Mechanical Engineers, the most important being 'On the application of water pressure to shop-tools and mechanical engineering works'. The Society of Arts gave him a gold medal under the Howard Trust 'for his system of applying hydraulic power to the working of machine tools, and for the riveting and other machines which he has invented in connection with that system'. In 1890 he was awarded a Bessemer premium for a paper entitled 'The application of water pressure to machine tools and appliances'. He was a member of the French Société des Ingénieurs Civils, and he and Sir Joseph Whitworth were the only English engineers to receive a *grand prix* in the machine tool class at the Paris Exhibition of 1878. On 2 December 1878 he was elected an associate of the Institution of Civil Engineers, becoming a member on 25 February 1879. He was also a member of the Institution of Mechanical Engineers from 1867. He was a keen sportsman, and a riding accident hastened his death at his home, Meopham Court, on 3 September 1895.

G. C. BOASE, *rev.* R. C. COX

Sources *PICE*, 123 (1895–6), 437–40 · *Institution of Mechanical Engineers: Proceedings* (1895), 544–6 · *The Times* (11 Sept 1895) · E. S. Skirving, ed., *Cheltenham College register, 1841–1927* (1928), 105

Wealth at death £28,779 16s. 10d. effects in England: probate, 16 Dec 1895, CGPLA Eng. & Wales

Tweed, John (1869–1933), sculptor, was born on 21 January 1869 at 16 South Portland Street, Glasgow, the eldest of the four children of John Tweed (*c*.1810–1885), a publisher, and his second wife, Elizabeth, *née* Montgomery (*c.*1837–1908). In 1885 his father's death necessitated him leaving Hutcheson's Boys' Grammar School to run the family business. He studied part-time at Glasgow School of Art and assisted the sculptors George Lawson, James Ewing, and Pittendrigh McGillivray.

In 1890 Tweed sold his business and moved to London. He approached Hamo Thornycroft and assisted him with frieze carvings (1891–3) for the Institute of Chartered Accountants' building in Moorgate, a major example of the New Sculpture. On Thornycroft's insistence Tweed continued his artistic education at the South London Technical Art School, Lambeth, and at the Royal Academy Schools. In 1893 he visited Paris, where he intended to study with Auguste Rodin. This proved impossible, as Rodin only accepted pupils who would spend four years under his supervision. Instead he briefly studied at the École des Beaux-Arts under Alexandre Falguière before returning to London to execute a bronze relief of Jan van Riesbeeck (*in situ*) for Cecil Rhodes's residence, Groote Schuur, Cape Town, South Africa. In 1895 he married Edith Clinton, who was secretary to the Women's Suffrage Society.

Tweed obtained the Rhodes commission through the architects Edwin Lutyens and Herbert Baker. Its success led to further major works in Africa, including the Major Allan Wilson memorial (1897, View of the World Hill, Rhodes–Matopos National Park, Zimbabwe) and portrait statues of van Riesbeeck (1899, Cape Town) and Rhodes himself (1902, Bulawayo, Zimbabwe). These works resulted in Tweed being described as 'Sculptor-in-Ordinary to South Africa' (Tweed with Watson, 97). On his visits to London, Rhodes befriended Tweed, who taught him the rudiments of art history and appreciation. Their friendship suffered when Rhodes criticized his sculpture and temporarily suspended payment for his commissions, only to be threatened with legal proceedings.

In 1901 Tweed was commissioned to complete the equestrian group surmounting the Wellington monument in St Paul's Cathedral, London, which had been left unfinished since the death of its sculptor, Alfred Stevens, in 1875. Tweed's appointment provoked debate, as he was then little known and was considered suspiciously modern. Both Edward Poynter, president of the Royal Academy, and the critic M. H. Spielmann believed that the commission should have gone to an experienced, academic sculptor. The controversy deepened when the painter and critic D. S. McColl, also keeper of the Tate Gallery since 1906, who had been instrumental in securing Tweed's services, attacked him for making modifications to Stevens's designs. The monument was eventually completed in 1912, with Tweed's reputation if anything enhanced.

Tweed is best remembered for his long and close friendship with Rodin. He did much to make the diffident and awkward sculptor feel at ease in London society. Rodin frequently stayed at the Tweed family home in Cheyne Walk, Chelsea, between 1901 and 1914, and in 1902 he put a cottage and studio at Tweed's disposal at his residence at Meudon. Their closeness was indicated when Rodin told

Tweed: 'je ne vis à Londres que par vous' ('I only live in London because of you'; Tweed with Watson, 99). Tweed also did much to promote and popularize Rodin in Britain. This culminated in an exhibition of sculpture at Grosvenor House, London, in 1914, which Rodin subsequently gifted to the nation to symbolize the comradeship of France and Britain.

Somewhat unfairly, Tweed's own work takes second place to his role as the leading British 'Rodinist'. Although other significant sculptors had contacts with Rodin—for example Harry Bates, William Goscombe John, Bertram Mackennal, and Kathleen Scott—Tweed probably understood his genius better than any of them. This is indicated in the craggy surfaces of his vigorously modelled busts of Cosmo Gordon Lang and W. P. Ker (both All Souls College, Oxford) and in the impressionistic, unfinished passages of his marble busts of female models such as Lendal Tweed (Reading Museum and Art Gallery) and in his ideal sculpture. In the period between the First World War and the depression he was, moreover, a prolific and successful sculptor of public monuments. These include the lively and realistic portrait statues of Lord Clive (1917) and Lord Kitchener (1926), both in Whitehall, London, and war memorials to the King's Royal Rifle Corps, Winchester (1922), and the rifle brigade in Grosvenor Place, London (1924). Other works include the monuments to Joseph Chamberlain (1915, Westminster Abbey, London) and Field Marshal Earl Roberts (1926, St Paul's Cathedral, London). His failure to sustain a high reputation is probably because whatever its intrinsic merits, his work falls into the generation gap between the New Sculpture which preceded him and the modernism which followed.

Tweed died in a nursing home at 18 Langham Street, Great Portland Street, London, on 12 November 1933 and was buried on 14 November in Chelsea Old Church, Cheyne Walk, London. He was survived by his wife and three children. Besides Rhodes and Rodin, he was on familiar terms with Edwin Lutyens, John Singer Sargent, Hilaire Belloc, and Ramsay MacDonald. His contemporaries could find him quarrelsome, egotistical, cruel, and snobbish: Kathleen Scott, for example, observed 'what a detestable cad he was' (K. Scott, diary, entry for 13 Oct 1923, Kennet MSS, CUL). Yet to family and friends he was brave, loyal, hospitable, even loving—qualities attested in Lendal Tweed's sensitive and perceptive biography of her father, *John Tweed, Sculptor: a Memoir* (1936).

MARK STOCKER

Sources [L. Tweed and F. Watson], *John Tweed, sculptor: a memoir* (1936) · E. Radford, 'John Tweed, sculptor', *Art Journal*, new ser., 30 (1910), 41–6 · J. Newton, 'Rodin is a British institution', *Burlington Magazine*, 136 (1994), 822–8 · J. Physick, *The Wellington monument* (1970) · *John Tweed: memorial exhibition* (1934) [exhibition catalogue, Imperial Institute, London] · *DNB* · M. Stocker, 'Tweed, John', *The dictionary of art*, ed. J. Turner (1996) · J. Blackwood, *London's immortals: the complete outdoor commemorative statues* (1989) · M. H. Spielmann, *British sculpture and sculptors of to-day* (1901) · A. Borg, *War memorials: from antiquity to the present* (1991) · T. Friedman and others, eds., *The alliance of sculpture and architecture: Hamo Thornycroft, John Belcher, and the Institute of Chartered Accountants building* (1993) [exhibition catalogue, Heinz Gallery, RIBA, London, 14 Jan – 20 Feb 1993] · F. V. Grunfeld, *Rodin: a biography*, new edn (1988) ·

719 TWEEDIE, ETHEL BRILLIANA

CGPLA Eng. & Wales (1933) · L. Young, *A great task of happiness: the life of Kathleen Scott* (1995), 225 · Graves, *RA exhibitors* · CUL, Kennet MSS
Archives Musée Rodin, Paris, corresp. · Reading Museum Service, MSS | BL, corresp. with Sir Sydney Cockerell, Add. MS 52756 · Henry Moore Institute, Leeds, Thornycroft archive · V&A, D. S. McColl MSS
Likenesses Lafayette, photograph, *c.*1920, repro. in Tweed and Watson, *John Tweed* · G. C. Beresford, negative, NPG · G. C. Beresford, three photographs, NPG · C. H. Park, photograph (with Rodin), repro. in Tweed and Watson, *John Tweed*
Wealth at death £12,629 5*s.* 1*d.*: probate, 12 Dec 1933, *CGPLA Eng. & Wales*

Tweeddale. For this title name *see* Hay, John, first marquess of Tweeddale (1626–1697); Hay, John, second marquess of Tweeddale (1645–1713); Hay, John, fourth marquess of Tweeddale (1695–1762); Hay, George, eighth marquess of Tweeddale (1787–1876); Hay, Arthur, ninth marquess of Tweeddale (1824–1878).

Tweedie, Alexander (1794–1884), physician, was born in Edinburgh on 29 August 1794, the son of Alexander Tweedie and his wife, Christian Denhame, and received his early education at Edinburgh high school. In 1809 he commenced his medical studies at the University of Edinburgh, and about the same time he became a pupil of John Henry Wishart, surgeon to the Royal Infirmary. He graduated MD on 1 August 1815, and, turning his attention to surgical pathology, in 1817 he became a fellow of the Royal College of Surgeons of Edinburgh. He was then elected one of the two house surgeons to the Edinburgh Royal Infirmary.

In 1818 Tweedie commenced practice in Edinburgh, intending to devote himself to ophthalmic surgery, but in 1820 he moved south, and settled at Ely Place, London. On 25 June 1822 he was admitted a licentiate of the Royal College of Physicians. He became FRCP on 4 July 1838, held the office of conciliarius in 1853, 1854, and 1855, and was Lumleian lecturer in 1858 and 1859.

Tweedie was appointed assistant physician to the London Fever Hospital in 1822, and two years later became physician to the hospital, an office which he filled for thirty-eight years. He resigned it in 1861, when he was appointed consulting physician and one of the vice-presidents. In 1836 he was elected physician to the Foundling Hospital; he was also physician to the Standard Assurance Company, examiner in medicine at the University of London, and an honorary member of the Medical Psychological Association. He was elected a fellow of the Royal Society on 8 February 1838. In 1866 he was elected an honorary fellow of the King and Queen's College of Physicians in Ireland. Tweedie continued to practise in his rooms in Pall Mall, London, until a few years before his death, at his home, Bute Lodge, Twickenham, on 30 May 1884.

Tweedie was a voluminous writer. He contributed greatly to, and with John Conolly and John Forbes was one of the editors of, the *Cyclopaedia of Practical Medicine* (4 vols., 1831–5), which comprised treatises on the nature and treatment of diseases, materia medica and therapeutics, and medical jurisprudence. He planned and edited the *Library of Medicine*, in eight volumes, which appeared in 1840–42, and was the author of *Clinical Illustrations of Fever* (1828), and *Lectures on the Distinctive Characters, Pathology, and Treatment of Continued Fevers* (1862). Tweedie's grandson Alec was the husband of Ethel Tweedie, travel writer.

W. W. WEBB, *rev.* ANITA McCONNELL

Sources Munk, *Roll* · *The Lancet* (14 June 1884), 1101 · *Edinburgh Medical Journal*, 30 (1884–5), 191–2
Archives RCP Lond., cholera case books, Abchurch Lane, London
Likenesses E. Belli, oils, *c.*1870, RCP Lond.
Wealth at death £183,464 10*s.* 1*d.*: resworn probate, Sept 1884, *CGPLA Eng. & Wales*

Tweedie [*née* Harley], **Ethel Brilliana** [*known as* Mrs Alec Tweedie] (1861/2–1940), travel writer, was the daughter of George *Harley (1829–1896), physician, and Emma Jessie, daughter of James *Muspratt, a wealthy alkaline manufacturer. They had at least three children. Her family background was one of 'luxury and joy' (Tweedie, 1) coloured by her father's national and international scientific contacts and the wealth of her mother's family. She was educated at Queen's College, London, and in Germany, where her father had earlier worked and studied. At an early age she married Alec Tweedie, insurance broker and grandson of Alexander Tweedie, physician, and entered a life of 'still more luxury and gaiety' (Tweedie, 1). This sheltered and happy life came to an end abruptly with a series of tragic events. Her husband lost all his money when his syndicate failed; his losses turned him from a cheerful outgoing man to a cheerless one and, according to his wife, were what killed him when he died shortly thereafter. She and their sons Leslie and Harley were left with no settlement, and their predicament worsened in 1896 when her father died, also leaving her without a settlement.

Determined to bring up her sons well, even before her father's death Mrs Tweedie capitalized on her enjoyment of travel and turned to travel writing to make her living; she found a receptive public which had a taste for travel books but not yet the opportunity for travel itself. *A Girl's Ride in Iceland* (1889) was, as she explained with a mixture of pride and apology, a ride 'man fashion'. That trip set the pattern of travel followed by book—in this case perhaps her least affected book, with an appendix on geysers by her father. The visit to Iceland was followed by *A Winter Jaunt to Norway* (1894) and, perhaps her most memorable journey, *Through Finland in Carts* (1897). She then went further afield, to Sicily, Mexico, the USA, Russia, and China, and the resultant travel books, unaccountably to the late twentieth-century reader, were often popular enough to go to several cheap editions and to be translated into other languages. She dabbled in biography as well, starting by editing her father's memoirs for publication in 1899. Tragically both her sons were killed in the First World War. This removed one of the main reasons for her writing, but by then she saw herself as a professional writer and continued to turn out volumes. Her books were always rather 'anxious' to inform and 'heavily overweighted' with advice to women and girls (Middleton, 5, 9), and later on 'the melodramatic quality of her travel writing began to smack of bathos and it was only Ethel's unerring sense of

Wealth at death £19,895 13s. 1d.: probate, 24 May 1940, *CGPLA Eng. & Wales*

Tweedie, Jill Sheila (1932–1993), journalist and author, was born in Cairo on 22 May 1932, the elder child and only daughter of Patrick Graeme Tweedie, pilot, and his wife, Sheila, *née* Whittall. Her father, a Scot, later became chief inspector of accidents at the Air Ministry. Her mother came from an affluent, warm, and enormous family in Istanbul, the largest English family in the Middle East. Soon after her birth they returned to England, where her younger brother, Robbie, was born. She was sent to a variety of day schools, eight in all, 'from PNEU to GPDST' (*WWW*), though Robbie went to boarding-school and eventually Sandhurst. Neither of her parents envisaged any future for her beyond being a secretary first and a wife thereafter. Her passion for ballet saw her through her early difficulties with her father, whom she described as being 'as unacquainted with love as a Scots pine' (Tweedie, 1). By the time she was sixteen, however, it became clear that she was too tall to be a ballet dancer, and she was sent for two years to a finishing school in Switzerland, where she enjoyed the school, the girls, and the merciful absence of her parents.

Back in London, Tweedie astounded her parents by landing a job as a trainee copywriter in an advertising agency. But when after a few months she fell in love with a boy from a working-class background, they were only too happy to let her accept an invitation from one of her uncles, by then resident in Vancouver, to spend time with his family in Canada. She stayed there for six months, fell unsuitably in love again—this time with a cousin—and was dispatched home; however, she cashed in her air ticket and stopped off in Montreal instead. There she got work, initially as a reindeer in a Christmas display, later on writing for an in-store newsletter, and finally as a weather girl for a radio station. She fell in with an exotic company of expatriates, one of whom, the fiery and handsome Count Bela Cziraky (d. in or before 1993), marked her down as his future wife. By sheer persistence he persuaded her to marry him, in 1954. He took her on mad jaunts through the European castles of his relatives, while stifling her with a violently possessive love. Their firstborn son died tragically at five months, a victim of cot death, but they had two more children, Ilona and Adam. When they were three and two years old, Tweedie asked for a divorce. After many rows Cziraky appeared to agree, but then disappeared, with both children and all their joint funds, behind the iron curtain. He vowed that she would never see her children again; and when, by hiring detectives and through endless lawsuits, she was finally reunited with them in their teens, she had no language in common with them.

After the divorce Tweedie lived in England with Robert d'Ancona, a tall, blond Dutch hippy she had met in Canada, and with whom she had a son, Luke. She meanwhile worked as a freelance journalist in London. In 1970, on a promotional tour to Kenya, she met the writer and journalist Alan Brien (b. 1925). They married on Christmas eve 1973, and with him she enjoyed more than twenty years of

Ethel Brilliana Tweedie (1861/2–1940), by Sir John Lavery, 1903

admiration for herself that saved her from literary ridicule' (Robinson, 199). There can certainly be no regrets for the passing into obscurity of *Busy Days: Quotations from the Author's Works for Every Day of the Year* (1913), *Women the World Over: a Sketch both Light and Gay, Perchance both Dull and Stupid* (1914), and *My Table-Cloths* (1916), or *Mainly East* (*in Prose—perhaps Prosey*) (1922): but much of her relentless jolliness can probably be traced to her need to please. Certainly she could not afford to abandon a proven formula. She also sketched what she saw on her travels and exhibited her watercolours in several public and private galleries, mainly in London but also in Paris. Often known in mid- to later life as Mrs Alec-Tweedie, she served on numerous philanthropic and charitable committees, seeing herself increasingly as an arbiter of taste and conduct. She was a fellow of the Royal Geographical Society. She died on 15 April 1940 at her home at 60 Devonshire House, Mayfair, London. She was one of the first professional travel writers and was remarkably successful, accumulating an estate proved at just under £20,000, and though her writing now seems unattractive she claimed to have been the first woman to accomplish many feats, from riding astride to skiing.   ELIZABETH BAIGENT

Sources E. B. Tweedie, *Me and mine* (1933) · *WWW* · D. Middleton, *Victorian lady travellers* (1965) · J. Robinson, ed., *Wayward women: a guide to women travellers* (1990) · M. Morris, *The Virago book of women travellers* (1994) · J. Robinson, *Unsuitable for ladies* (1994) · d. cert.
Likenesses J. Lavery, photogravure, 1903 (after oil painting), repro. in P. Bate, *Modern Scottish painters* (1903) [see illus.] · photograph, repro. in A. Tweedie [E. B. Tweedie], 'A leap of a hundred and twenty feet', *World Wide Magazine*, 1 (1898), 572

Jill Sheila Tweedie (1932–1993), by unknown photographer

happiness. They moved house frequently, from London to rural Wales and back again, decorating home after home in startling colours. Tall, with a spectacular mane of hair, a brilliant smile, and a fiery temperament (she once threw a milk bottle through the window of a restaurant whose staff had been rude), Tweedie became 'a one-woman torchlight procession' on the London scene.

Journalistically Tweedie was riding high: by 1969 she had her own column on *The Guardian*'s women's page, as well as doing freelance writing and broadcasting. In 1971 she was named woman journalist of the year in the IPC national press awards, and she gained the Granada TV award in 1972. Her articles became compulsory reading for all *Guardian* women readers: 'she explored the tragedies of other women, or the simple, ordinary miseries of all women marooned at home with small children, demanding men, and the dreadfulness of domesticity' (*The Independent*). She could get brilliantly angry at the wrongs women suffered; she was among the first to insist that there was such a crime as rape in marriage, and her articles on the subject of women beaten up at home helped to inspire Erin Pizzey to set up the first shelter for battered women in Chiswick in 1971. She struck an immediate chord with women who, stirred by the lofty ideals of feminism, were trying frantically to align them with the messy realities of ordinary life. Her most hilarious sallies in this vein were collected in *Letters from a Faint-Hearted Feminist* (1982), followed by *More from Martha* (1983). 'She was an icon for us', many an achieving woman said of her, both at the time and later, though her attitudes often made the male-dominated *Guardian* uneasy. In 1988 her *Guardian* column ended.

Tweedie wrote two novels: *Bliss* (1984) and *Internal Affairs* (1986). These were not as admired as her journalism had been, but in 1993, after both her parents were dead, she published *Eating Children*. This hugely funny but devastating autobiography of her early years was an outstanding success. In it she admitted that her entire life had been devoted to doing and being the exact opposite of what her parents would have wanted. Following this catharsis, she thought, she could enjoy life properly at last. But in that same year she succumbed to motor neurone disease. In her last weeks she received sackfuls of letters from all over the world, and her friends flocked to see her one last time. She died at 11 Lyndhurst Gardens, Hampstead, London, on 12 November 1993. As her obituarist Sally Belfrage put it, she had 'finer qualities and worse luck than seemed possible to co-exist in one person' (*The Independent*). She was survived by her husband, Alan Brien, her daughter, Ilona, and her sons, Adam and Luke.

KATHARINE WHITEHORN

Sources *The Independent* (13 Nov 1993) · *The Times* (13 Nov 1993) · J. Tweedie, *Eating children* (1993) · G. Taylor, *Changing faces: a history of 'The Guardian', 1956–88* (1993) · L. Forgan, 'For the love of a faint-hearted feminist', *The Guardian* (18 April 2000) · *WWW*, 1991–5 · personal knowledge (2004) · private information (2004) [Alan Brien] · d. cert.

Likenesses S. Raphael, group portrait, oils, 1994 (with other *Guardian* writers), NPG · photograph, repro. in *The Independent* · photograph, News International Syndication, London [*see illus.*]

Wealth at death under £125,000: probate, 1 March 1994, *CGPLA Eng. & Wales*

Tweedie, William King (1803–1863), Free Church of Scotland minister and writer, was born at Ayr on 8 May 1803, son of John Tweedie and Janet King. Early in his life his parents emigrated to Argentina, leaving him in the care of a relative at Maybole, where he was educated. He did not see his parents again. He attended the universities of Glasgow, Edinburgh, and St Andrews before he was licensed by the presbytery of Arbroath in December 1828. In his capacity as a tutor he travelled extensively on the continent, spending the winter of 1830 in Rome, a visit which was seen as a fitting preparation for his later service as convener of the Free Church committee on popery. In July 1832 he was ordained as minister of the Scots Church, London Wall.

On 11 May 1835 Tweedie married Margaret (d. 1885), daughter of Hugh Bell of Old Garphor, Straiton, Ayrshire. They had three daughters and two sons. His eldest son, Major-General William Tweedie (1836–1914), saw active service and was severely wounded at the time of the Indian mutiny. In September 1836 Tweedie was inducted to the South parish church, Aberdeen. While there he was approached to move to the charge of North Leith, which at that time offered the second largest stipend in Scotland. Instead he transferred, in March 1842, to the Tolbooth parish, Edinburgh. The majority of the congregation left the established church, along with their minister, at the Disruption of 1843. They took the name of the Free Tolbooth Church, although they remained without a permanent and settled place of worship until, in 1858, a new building was opened in St Andrew Square.

Tweedie occupied two prominent positions with the Free Church of Scotland. In 1845 he succeeded Thomas Chalmers as convener of the Sustentation Fund Committee, serving in this capacity until his resignation on health grounds in 1847. A year later he became convener of the Foreign Missions Committee. It was in this role, a demanding but unglamorous one, that he performed his most valuable service to his church. The whole missionary effort of the Free Church was underpinned by Tweedie's voluminous correspondence. He was also secretary of the Society for the Relief of the Destitute Sick from 1843 until his death. St Andrews honoured him with a DD in 1852. While there was little in his spare but muscular frame to suggest it, his health was never good, and he suffered with a persistent cough. It was necessary for him to make a recuperative journey to the continent in 1861. He relinquished the convenership of the Foreign Missions Committee in the following year and he died at George Square, Edinburgh, after a short but painful illness, on 24 March 1863, and was buried on 28 March in the Grange cemetery, close to Thomas Chalmers.

Of the Free Church leaders of his day, Tweedie has been one of the most overlooked. A good preacher, he suffered by comparison with more brilliant contemporaries. As a writer he published much, but nothing that was considered to be profound or of lasting worth. His interest in Calvin was evidenced by his translation of a work by Albert Rilliet, under the title *Calvin and Servetus* (1846), and he published *The Life of the Rev. John Macdonald* (1849) in memory of his missionary friend. He also edited two volumes of *Select Biographies* (1845–7) for the Wodrow Society. While his industry, courtesy, and business skills were ever at the service of his church, his primary commitment was to the pastoral care of his congregation, and it was a devotion that was fully reciprocated. His position within the Free Church, at once prominent but retiring, was alluded to in his obituary in *The Witness*, which stated that

His modest nature did not allow him to bulk in the eyes of the world so much as others who wielded less moral power, but his presence was at all times hailed as an omen, and as lending weight to any cause for good.

LIONEL ALEXANDER RITCHIE

Sources J. A. Wylie, *Disruption worthies: a memorial of 1843*, ed. J. B. Gillies, new edn (1881), 481–8 · *Free Church of Scotland Monthly Record*, new ser., 10 (1 May 1863), 233 · *Fasti Scot.* · *The Witness* (26 March 1863) · J. Smith, *Our Scottish clergy*, 3rd ser. (1851), 165–72 · W. Ewing, ed., *Annals of the Free Church of Scotland, 1843–1900*, 1 (1914), 347–8 · W. Brown, *Notes and recollections of the Tolbooth Church* (1867), 76 · NA Scot., SC 70/1/116, 838–44
Archives NL Scot. · NL Scot., foreign mission committee letters | U. Edin., New Coll. L., letters to Thomas Chalmers
Likenesses portrait, repro. in Wylie, *Disruption worthies*, facing p. 481
Wealth at death £1861 6s. 1d.: probate, 15 June 1863, NA Scot., SC70/1/116, 838–44

Tweedie, William Menzies (1826–1878), portrait painter, was born in Glasgow on 19 February 1826, the son of David Tweedie, a merchant, and his wife, Mary Menzies. He studied art at Edinburgh Academy from 1842 to 1846, winning a prize for the best copy of William Etty's painting *The Combat*. In 1843 he exhibited a portrait in oils at the Royal Scottish Academy, and he continued to exhibit there, showing ten paintings between 1843 and 1875. He entered the Royal Academy Schools in London in 1846, and then studied in Paris for three years with Thomas Couture. In 1847 his *Summer* appeared at the Royal Academy, but he

did not exhibit there again until 1856, when he showed a portrait of Austen Henry Layard. He lived in Liverpool from 1856 to 1859, before settling in London. He exhibited four paintings at the British Institution between 1857 and 1860, and thirty-three at the Royal Academy, mainly portraits, including one of his father, shown in 1860, and those of the painter Thomas Faed, Samuel Wilberforce, bishop of Oxford, Prince Arthur, and Gathorne Hardy, secretary of state for war. His portrait of Francis Jeune, master of Pembroke and later bishop of Peterborough, hangs in the hall of Pembroke College, Oxford. His work declined at the end of his life, and after 1874 he was unable to get his paintings accepted by the Royal Academy. This failure affected his health, and he died on 19 March 1878 at his home, 1 Laurel Villas, Chiswick Lane, Chiswick, Middlesex, leaving a widow, Emily.

CAMPBELL DODGSON, *rev.* ANNE PIMLOTT BAKER

Sources P. J. M. McEwan, *Dictionary of Scottish art and architecture* (1994), 587 · B. Stewart and M. Cutten, *The dictionary of portrait painters in Britain up to 1920* (1997) · C. B. de Laperriere, ed., *The Royal Scottish Academy exhibitors, 1826–1990*, 4 vols. (1991), vol. 4, p. 347 · J. Halsby and P. Harris, *The dictionary of Scottish painters, 1600–1960* (1990), 218 · Wood, *Vic. painters*, 3rd edn, 1.537 · Graves, *RA exhibitors* · Boase, *Mod. Eng. biog.* · bap. reg. Scot. · CGPLA *Eng. & Wales* (1878)
Wealth at death under £200: administration, 3 April 1878, CGPLA *Eng. & Wales*

Tweedmouth. For this title name *see* Marjoribanks, Edward, second Baron Tweedmouth (1849–1909).

Tweedsmuir. For this title name *see* Buchan, John, first Baron Tweedsmuir (1875–1940); Buchan, Priscilla Jean Fortescue, Lady Tweedsmuir and Baroness Tweedsmuir of Belhelvie (1915–1978).

Twells, Leonard (*bap.* 1684, *d.* 1742), Church of England clergyman and theological writer, was baptized at Newark-on-Trent on 3 January 1684, one of at least two sons of John Twells (*d.* 1740/41), master of Newark School and grammarian. He was educated at Jesus College, Cambridge, whence he matriculated in 1701 and, as a scholar, graduated BA in 1705. He was ordained deacon in 1708, and priest in 1709, and succeeded his father as rector of Nether Wallop, Hampshire, in 1711. He relinquished this living for the vicarage of St Mary's, Marlborough, Wiltshire, in 1722, which he held until 1737.

In the 1730s Twells was a keen participant in some of the current theological debates. In *A Critical Examination of the Late New Text and Version of the New Testament* (3 parts, 1731–2), he rubbished the Greek and English edition published by the Presbyterian minister Daniel Mace. He contributed three pamphlets to the controversy started by George Reynolds, archdeacon of Lincoln, in his *Dissertation, or, Inquiry concerning the canonical authority of the gospel according to Matthew* (1732). He then crossed swords with Arthur Ashley Sykes over the interpretation of demoniacs in the gospels. He wrote a life of Edward Pococke, which he published in 1740 in his edition of Pococke's theological writings.

Twells's theological orthodoxy may have ensured his preferment to a prebend in St Paul's in 1736, and the two London livings of St Matthew's, Friday Street, and St Peter Westcheap, in 1737. He took the degree of MA at Oxford by diploma in 1738 and was created DD on 7 July 1740. He was also a lecturer of St Dunstan-in-the-West. He died in Islington on 19 February 1742, leaving a large family very destitute. He was buried at St Matthew's, Friday Street. Two volumes of his sermons were published posthumously in 1743.   THOMPSON COOPER, *rev.* S. J. SKEDD

Sources *GM*, 1st ser., 12 (1742), 107; 4th ser., 1 (1867), 209 · Venn, *Alum. Cant.* · S. Lewis, *The history and topography of the parish of St Mary, Islington* (1842), 454 · J. P. Malcolm, *Londinium redivivum*, 4 vols. (1802–7), 4.487 · J. Nichols, ed., *Bibliotheca topographica Britannica*, 3 (1790), 189 · Nichols, *Illustrations* · Nichols, *Lit. anecdotes*, 1.465–72; 2.25; 3.98; 6.454 · *N&Q*, 2nd ser., 11 (1861), 123 · B. M. Metzger, *The text of the New Testament: its transmission, corruption and restoration*, 3rd edn (1992), 111–12

Twigg, John (1748/9–1816), cook and fruiterer, is a figure about whose early life nothing is known. He was cook at the Shakespeare's Head tavern, in Covent Garden, London, having been apprenticed there, it is presumed in the 1760s. He was reputedly responsible for Admiral Augustus Keppel's huge banquet (including 108 'made' dishes—dishes requiring particular skill) to celebrate his appointment as first lord of the Admiralty in 1782. A smaller but no less extravagant dinner included among other dishes a 40 lb turbot for just five gentleman (Timbs, 427).

By 1790 Twigg was recorded in the *Universal British Directory* as a fruiterer of Covent Garden market. He is remembered by a contemporary for his assistance in purchasing medicinal herbs:

> Twigg, the fruiterer to whom Mr Justice Welch, during his magistracy had often been kind, was at times gratefully attentive to Miss Welch and her sister, Mrs Nollekens … The fruiterer was a talkative man and was called by some of his jocular friends the 'Twig of the Garden'. (Smith, 1.208–9)

Twigg appears to have lived most, if not all, of his sixty-seven years in Covent Garden. His considerable memories of the wits and gentlemen of his day were apparently collected by one John Green, but no more is known of the latter or his records. Anecdotes of Twigg's reminiscences were recorded by J. Timbs, E. J. Burford, and J. T. Smith. Twigg was buried at St Paul's Church, Covent Garden, on 9 February 1816.   FIONA LUCRAFT

Sources parish register, Covent Garden, St Paul, 9 Feb 1816, City Westm. AC [burial] · P. Barfoot and J. Wilkes, eds., *Universal British directory of trade and commerce* (1790) · J. T. Smith, *Nollekens and his times*, 2 vols. (1828) · D. Foster, 'Inns, alehouses, taverns, coffee houses etc. in and around London', *c*.1900, City Westm. AC, vol. 58 · J. Timbs, *Clubs and club life in London: with anecdotes of its famous coffee houses, hostelries, and taverns, from the seventeenth century to the present time* (1872) · E. J. Burford, *Wits, wenches and wantons* (1990) · E. B. Chancellor, *The annals of Covent Garden* (1930)

Twining, Edward Francis, Baron Twining (1899–1967), colonial governor, was born in Westminster on 29 June 1899, the second son and youngest child of William Henry Greaves Twining, vicar of St Stephen's, Rochester Row, and his wife, Agatha Georgina, fourth daughter of

Edward Francis Twining, Baron Twining (1899–1967), by Bassano, 1946

Lieutenant-Colonel Robert Bourne. It was the stuff of family legend that the Twining family, like Thomas Twining, the founder of R. Twining & Co., the tea and coffee merchants, could trace its ancestry back to the village of Twyning(e) near Tewkesbury. However, its link with the company came only when Stephan Twining, the brother of Edward Francis, secured a post with the firm and rose to be its managing director. Twining's maternal grandmother was the sister of the explorer Sir Samuel Baker.

Peter Twining (as he was known) was a provost's scholar at Lancing College, where he was friendly and likeable and showed signs of enterprise and leadership, becoming house captain, a prefect, and a sergeant in the Officers' Training Corps. At an early age he had decided to be a soldier. In 1917 he entered the Royal Military College, Sandhurst, and a year later was gazetted to the Worcestershire regiment just before the end of the war, but too late for active service. Between 1919 and the end of 1922 he served in Dublin. At the end of 1920 he was appointed battalion, subsequently brigade, intelligence officer. In June 1921 he inadvertently captured President De Valera who was immediately released and signed a truce with Lloyd George two weeks later. Twining was appointed MBE for his services in Ireland.

Seeking, as always, the unusual rather than the usual, Twining was seconded to the King's African rifles in Uganda in 1923. To normal regimental duties he preferred running a school for the children of African soldiers which sowed the seeds of a lifelong affection for Africans, and acting as battalion intelligence officer, which fulfilled his craving for constant movement untrammelled by authority. His penetrating intelligence reports brought him to the notice of those in high places in London.

After two tours in Uganda, Twining decided, at the age of twenty-nine, to transfer to the colonial administrative service. After a year's training at Oxford he was posted back to Uganda in 1929 as an assistant district commissioner. He was not a dutiful colonial officer, however: he persistently failed his language examinations, showed no signs of adapting himself to routine office work, and chafed under supervision. He was a self-confident individualist who worked best on *ad hoc* assignments carrying much personal responsibility. In 1928 Twining had married Helen Mary (d. 1975), daughter of Arthur Edmund Du Buisson JP; they had two sons. In every territory in which Twining served, his wife, known as May, a qualified doctor, played a leading role in medical and social welfare activities.

A chance to demonstrate his peculiar talents, which included a flair for showmanship, an ability to organize, and the knack of obtaining the willing co-operation of others of all races, came in 1937 when Twining was charged with organizing the local celebrations for the coronation of King George VI. This task appealed to his abiding interest in everything regal, already reflected in his ever-growing interest in crown jewels and regalia. He had, too, a natural exuberance and a capacity for bringing joy and colour into the lives of other people.

As director of labour (1939–43) in Mauritius, Twining was again faced with problems which offered a welcome challenge to his individualistic approach. He was heavily drawn into wartime intelligence work and his contribution was recognized in 1943 when he was appointed CMG. A year later he was transferred to St Lucia as administrator. The affection with which the St Lucians enfolded him was not merely a response to what he did for them but also to what he did to them. While they admired the skill with which he had bullied London into providing funds for development, they were also aware that it was Twining who had inspired them to make the most of their opportunities.

Twining was an obvious choice for the demanding governorship (1946–9) of North Borneo, which had been devastatingly impoverished by the Japanese occupation. His huge task of reconstruction and development was complicated by the traumatic break with the past, whereby the Colonial Office had replaced the chartered British North Borneo Company as the source of authority.

Before Twining's work was finished he was promoted in 1949 governor of Tanganyika, arriving in the trust territory as a newly appointed KCMG. He was governor of Tanganyika until 1958, that is for nearly nine of the last twelve years of British rule. These years were marked by a remarkably self-assured effort by the Tanganyika government to promote economic growth and to shape constitutional development in ways it judged most appropriate. To that end, Twining used the appointed native authorities, who were very often traditional chiefs, as the primary

instruments for a major use of compulsion for the promotion of rural development. When these authorities demonstrated an increasing inability to win African acquiescence to the government's programmes, Twining moved to introduce elected local councils, confident that the British district officers would be able themselves to convince the councils of the wisdom of the government's initiatives.

A further and even more dubious example of the government's determination to impose its vision on post-war Tanganyika was its vigorous promotion of 'multiracialism', that is, a sharing of political power between the African, Asian, and European communities in Tanganyika. They were, however, vastly disproportionate in size, Africans numbering over 7 million, Asians some 120,000, and Europeans 27,000. Twining devoted a good deal of his energy and time to promoting this multiracial policy. He sought to ensure to each of the minority communities the social institutions, including secondary schools, which he felt were legitimate and necessary to their continuation as separate racial communities; he gave equal representation to each community on the legislative council; he created a new multiracial tier of government between local councils and the central government; and he even required the appointment of non-African members to many African district councils. Under his leadership British constitutional policies in Tanganyika were thus in harmony with the very substantial efforts of the Colonial Office to entrench the position of the white minorities in each of the British colonies in eastern and central Africa. This effort would prove unworkable in each of these territories. That it was persistently pursued even in a country so undeniably African as Tanganyika is a measure of how out of touch the Colonial Office was with African political realities. Twining, unfortunately, was the governor who was called upon to devote his considerable talents to the impossible task of securing Tanganyikan acquiescence to this rejection of any prospect of eventual majority rule. Within several months of his replacement as governor by Sir Richard Turnbull, the effort was totally abandoned and Tanganyika was launched at breakneck speed towards its full independence in July 1961.

After his retirement in 1958 Twining was created a life peer as Baron Twining of Tanganyika and Godalming. He did not contribute much to the House of Lords, and he had never cared to be one among many. He spent six months of each year in Nairobi, where he had business and other interests. In 1960 his *History of the Crown Jewels of Europe* was published, followed in 1967 by *European Regalia*. Twining died on 21 July 1967 at his flat at 74 Ashley Gardens, Westminster, within a few hundred yards of his birthplace.

JOHN FLETCHER-COOKE, *rev.* CRANFORD PRATT

Sources D. Bates, *A gust of plumes* (1972) • C. Pratt, *The critical phase in Tanzania, 1945–1968: Nyerere and the emergence of a socialist strategy* (1976) • P. Gifford and W. R. Louis, *The transfer of power in Africa: decolonization, 1940–1960* (1982), 249–82 • personal knowledge (1981) • private information (1981, 2004) • *CGPLA Eng. & Wales* (1967) • *The Times* (24 July 1967) • WWW

Archives PRO, corresp. relating to Tanganyika, CO 967/67 | FILM BFI NFTVA, documentary footage

Likenesses Bassano, photograph, 1946, NPG [*see illus.*]
Wealth at death £30,581 0s. 0d.: probate, 1967/8, resealed, *CGPLA Eng. & Wales*

Twining, Elizabeth (1805–1889), botanic artist and social reformer, was born on 10 April 1805 at 34 Norfolk Street, the Strand, in the parish of St Clement Danes, London, the second of nine children of Richard *Twining (1772–1857) [*see under* Twining, Richard (1749–1824)], tea-merchant and banker, and his wife, Elizabeth Mary (*c.*1780–1866), daughter of Revd John Smythies, rector of All Saints, Colchester. She was the sister of William *Twining (1813–1848) [*see under* Twining, Richard (1749–1824)]. She was educated at home, chiefly by her mother. Her liberal education included lectures, visits to the theatre, parks, and gardens, as well as art lessons from the Nasmyth family. She painted miniatures and figures and made many copies from works in the Dulwich Gallery.

The first of Elizabeth Twining's many continental tours was made in her twenties; during it she recorded her travels in delightful postcard-size watercolours of landscapes and of the local flora. She was a talented portraitist of plants and flowers as well as being a competent botanist. The two-volume folio edition of her *Illustrations of the Natural Orders of Plants* (2 vols., 1849) is considered to have a place among the finest lithographic flower books of the mid-nineteenth century. The 'natural order' is that of Alphonse de Candolle, who rejected the Linnaean or 'artificial' classification. The emphasis on the appearance of mature plants and their habitat rather than their physiology is echoed not only in her art but also in her lectures on plants, which as well as having a strong geographical theme also discussed how plants were used, particularly by women. She believed botany had a place in the education of women of all social classes and her approach was that of 'mother educator', whether she was encouraging the poor to grow plants for flower shows or promoting the cultivation of window boxes in institutions such as workhouse wards, where the glory of plants could be shared by sick inmates and staff alike.

Elizabeth Twining's first experience of teaching was within her own family, where she took the main part in instructing her younger siblings, and at the age of fifteen she became a Sunday school teacher. Drawing on her later experiences as a ragged school teacher and as a workhouse visitor she concluded that her pupils received an education superior to that of children in workhouse schools. She actively supported education for middle-class girls through her work as a member of the Ladies Committee at Queen's College, where in 1865 she founded a scholarship to be awarded by the Lady Visitors. Her sister Louisa *Twining (1820–1912) credited Elizabeth, along with Lady Monteagle, Emily Taylor, and others, with the creation of a school for girls which was the foundation of Bedford College. Elizabeth Twining also taught adults at the College for Working Women and started sewing classes for the poor in Ireland during frequent visits to a cousin's estate in Connemara. She received public recognition for her philanthropic work when she was invited to give evidence to the 1860 Education Commission.

Elizabeth Twining began welfare work for mothers and families as a direct result of her contact with the mothers of her ragged school pupils. She founded and managed a temperance hall, a small nondescript building in Portugal Street, in the parish of St Clement Danes. Her Temperance Hall employed mission women and was used for activities such as the purchase of clothing, a weekly penny bank, lectures on home economics, Bible classes, and temperance meetings. Both she and her sister Louisa Twining believed that the regular meetings during which the women would pray, read, sing hymns, and do needlework were the first of their kind and led directly to the mothers' meeting movement.

Elizabeth Twining believed that the importance of her work lay in bringing rich and poor together, removing pride in the former and elevating the latter. She attributed much working-class illness, unemployment, family breakdown, and poverty to alcoholism. She was a practising member of the Church of England and belonged to the women's section of the Church of England Temperance Society. In her role as a district visitor and workhouse visitor she sought out the sick and the dying and was concerned with not only their physical welfare but also their spiritual well-being. Some of her experiences are recorded in *Leaves from the Note-Book of Elizabeth Twining* (1877), including the case of an elderly widow who died without being able to receive a visit from her son because of workhouse regulations. This incident, she believed, prompted her sister Louisa to form the Workhouse Visiting Society in 1857.

Following the death of her parents Elizabeth Twining moved from Bloomsbury to Dial House, the family country home in Twickenham. By then in her sixties, she trained young girls for domestic service and cared for retired elderly servants, all of whom resided with her in Dial House. She renovated and visited the local almshouses and established the hospital of St John's, which was opened by the duchess of Teck. The honorary consulting physician and surgeon were trained at King's College Hospital, with which she had long been associated as a subscriber and governor. It had an out-patients department and a dispensary, as well as two six-bedded wards named Richard and Elizabeth after her parents. Despite the family background in commerce and banking, the hospital had to shut temporarily because of financial and administrative difficulties, reopening in 1885. She bequeathed the hospital £2000.

In June 1881 Elizabeth Twining was presented with her portrait in recognition of all the Twining family had done for Twickenham. Through her professionalism and commitment to social work she provided the role model for her sister Louisa, her junior by fifteen years. She died unmarried on 24 December 1889 at Dial House, Twickenham, and is buried in Twickenham. She was attended in her last illness by Agnes Edginton, first matron of St John's, who had known her since early childhood and was buried with her in 1933.   THERESA DEANE

Sources E. Twining, *Leaves from the note-book of Elizabeth Twining* (1877) · L. Twining, *Some facts in the history of the Twining family from*

AD 577, 2 pts (privately printed, Salisbury, 1895) · D. Wallis, 'St John's Hospital', Twickenham Library, local studies · F. Prochaska, 'A mother's country: mothers' meetings and family welfare in Britain, 1850–1950', *History*, new ser., 74 (1989), 379–99 · P. Stageman, 'Elizabeth Twining', *The Garden*, 108 (1983), 115–17 · L. Twining, *Recollections of life and work* (1893) · A. B. Shteir, *Cultivating women, cultivating science: Flora's daughters and botany in England, 1760–1860* (1996) · T. Deane, 'Old and incapable? Louisa Twining and elderly women in Victorian Britain', *Women and aging in British society since 1500*, ed. P. Thane and L. Botelho (2001) · J. Diprose, *Some account of the parish of Saint Clement Danes*, [1] (1868), 20 · census returns for Twickenham, 1871, PRO, RG 10/1315/93; 1881, RG 11/1342/31 · d. cert.

Twining, Louisa (1820–1912), philanthropist, was born on 16 November 1820 at Norfolk Street, Strand, London, the youngest of nine children of Richard *Twining (1772–1857) [see under Twining, Richard (1749–1824)], tea merchant, and his wife, Elizabeth Mary (c.1780–1866), daughter of John Smythies, rector of All Saints, Colchester. Elizabeth *Twining and William *Twining [see under Twining, Richard] were her siblings. She was educated at home, mainly by her mother and sisters, and later attended lectures at the Royal Institution. She hated music, but showed considerable talent for drawing and had two books on Christian art published in the early 1850s, *Symbols and Emblems of Early and Medieval Christian Art* (1852) and *The Types and Figures of the Bible* (1854).

In 1853, after visiting the Strand union workhouse to see an old nurse, Twining conceived the idea of systematic visits to the workhouse by neighbourhood ladies to say prayers and converse with the inmates. She was informed that unpaid and voluntary effort was not sanctioned by the poor-law board, which viewed it as unwarrantable interference. Undeterred, and with the encouragement of her friends, she began a campaign for workhouse visiting. She believed firmly that middle-class women had a natural aptitude for helping the poor, and that they should be permitted—and encouraged—to do so. In 1855 she published *A Few Words about the Inmates of our Union Workhouses*. She began visiting other workhouses in London, the rest of England, and abroad. Through lectures, articles, and letters she earned a reputation as an expert on workhouses. She contributed a paper, 'The condition of our workhouses', the first public address on the subject, to the first congress of the National Association for the Promotion of Social Science (NAPSS) in Birmingham (1857), and followed it up with a series of letters to the *Manchester Guardian* and *The Times*. In 1858 the poor-law board relented and the Workhouse Visiting Society, with Twining as honorary secretary, was set up, affiliated to the NAPSS. The following year she gave evidence to the royal commission on education on workhouse schools, advocating industrial training for girls. In 1861 she was instrumental in setting up a home for workhouse girls sent out to service, so that they would not have to mix with women of bad character. Other homes supported by Twining were made over to the Association for Befriending Young Servants in 1878.

Reform of workhouse infirmaries was one of Twining's prime concerns, and at one time she considered training to be a nurse herself. The hardship and neglect suffered by the impoverished sick was confirmed by a report published by *The Lancet* in 1866. Louisa Twining campaigned ceaselessly for the separation of the sick, the aged, and the able-bodied in workhouses. In 1879 she became secretary of the Association for Promoting Trained Nursing in Workhouse Infirmaries and Sick Asylums, which was founded to train and supply nurses and to secure the appointment of trained matrons. In 1885 she joined and promoted Florence Nightingale's scheme to send trained nurses to the homes of the urban poor, the District Nurses Movement. In 1875 women became eligible for election as poor-law guardians. Louisa Twining was chief financial supporter of the Society for Promoting the Return of Women as Poor Law Guardians and subsequently chairwoman. She was a guardian herself in Kensington (1884–90) and Tunbridge Wells (1893–6), where she lived after retirement.

Workhouses were not Twining's only philanthropic interest. She taught classes for women in 1850 at the Working Men's College, assisted at a night school for boys, and was an adviser to the first woman inspector of pauper schools in 1873. With Angela Burdett-Coutts she established a house for art students in 1879. By 1895 she had attained the opening up of Lincoln's Inn Fields to the poor after years of campaigning. She pressed for prison reform and helped set up charitable houses for elderly, epileptic, and incurable women, to keep them out of the workhouse. She also helped set up a convalescent home for patients from the East End after the cholera epidemic of 1867. She established the need for, and secured, female matrons for London police courts and stations. She was involved in many church activities in London and abroad. A firm advocate of temperance, she believed that drink was the cause of much of the crime, vice, and misery of the poor. She was a strong supporter of women's participation in public affairs, believing that men and women should work together as equals. In 1904 she was president of the Women's Local Government Society. She was also a member of the National Society for Women's Suffrage. The presentation of an illuminated address to her in 1904 acknowledged her lifelong work in raising the whole standard of poor-law administration and in reducing prejudice against women in local government. Louisa Twining died, unmarried, at 68 Lansdowne Road, Kensington, London, on 25 September 1912, and was buried on 30 September at Kensal Green cemetery.

JANET E. GRENIER

Sources L. Twining, *Recollections of life and work* (1893) · L. Twining, *Workhouses and pauperism* (1898) · *The Times* (27 Sept 1912) · O. Banks, *The biographical dictionary of British feminists*, 1 (1985) · M. Vicinus, *Independent women: work and community for single women, 1850–1920* (1985)

Archives priv. coll. · Queen's College, London, notebooks and papers while a student · Women's Library, London, corresp. | LMA, corresp. with Henry Bonham Carter

Twining, Richard (1749–1824), tea and coffee merchant, was born at Devereux Court, the Strand, London, the second of the three sons of Daniel Twining (1713–1762), tea and coffee merchant, and his second wife, Mary (1726–1804), daughter of Richard Little, a Wisbech merchant, and half-brother of Thomas *Twining (*bap.* 1734, *d.* 1804). He was the great-grandson of Daniel Twining, a weaver who in the 1680s moved to London from Painswick, Gloucestershire, where the woollen industry was in decline. The elder Daniel's son Thomas (1675–1741) had been apprenticed to an East India merchant, and about 1706 became master of Tom's Coffee House, Devereux Court, which was frequented by such savants as the Revd Thomas Birch and the poet and physician Mark Akenside, as well as by eminent lawyers. Thomas Twining had already decided to make a special feature of tea, alongside coffee. He was a freeman of the Weavers' Company and his son Daniel was Richard Twining's father.

Richard Twining was educated at Eton College but left in 1763 to help his widowed mother, then running the business. In 1771 he married Mary, daughter of John Aldred, merchant of Norwich; they were to have five sons, three of whom later became partners, and three daughters. That year he took over the firm. As chairman of the London tea dealers by the 1780s he was regularly consulted by the prime minister, William Pitt, whose Commutation Act of 1784 reduced the tea duty from over 100 to 25 per cent, eliminated smuggling of tea, and soon led to a quadrupling of consumption.

In 1793 Twining, who had previously published three papers of *Remarks* on the company's tea trade, was elected a director of the East India Company. He played a prominent role on the company's court, putting forward a motion that prohibited directors from trading with India. After the outbreak of war that year, he helped to form the St Clement Danes Volunteers. He was promoted to lieutenant-colonel of the Royal Westminster volunteers in 1805 and was presented with a sword and two pistols in recognition of his service. An enthusiastic traveller, he kept copious journals about his experiences. He was a director of the Equitable Assurance Company, and a founder director (1803) and later chairman of the Imperial Insurance Company. In 1816 he resigned, through declining health, from the East India Company. He spent the last decade of his life at Dial House, Twickenham, Middlesex, which had been a family home for nearly a century. He died there on 23 April 1824.

Richard Twining (1772–1857), the eldest son, was born at Devereux Court on 5 May 1772 and educated under Samuel Parr at Norwich grammar school. At fifteen he joined his father in the business, and he was made a partner nine years later. In 1802 he married Elizabeth Mary (*c.*1780–1866), daughter of the Revd John Smythies. They had nine children. He was chairman of the committee of by-laws at East India House, and a member of the Society of Arts and a fellow of the Royal Society. The banking house of Richard Twining & Co. of the Strand, reputedly founded in 1824, was absorbed by Lloyds Bank in 1892. Richard Twining remained at his desk in the firm until within five

weeks of his death, at 13 Bedford Place, London, on 14 October 1857. He was succeeded by his eldest son Richard (1807–1906), who edited his grandfather's and other family correspondence.

Two of the daughters of Richard and Elizabeth Twining devoted themselves to philanthropic and educational work. These were Elizabeth *Twining (1805–1889) and Louisa *Twining (1820–1912). Both were educated at home and remained unmarried. Elizabeth Twining was the first to organize 'mothers' meetings' in London, and jointly with Emily Taylor and others founded Bedford College, London. She published *Ten Years in a Ragged School* (1857) and *Readings for Mothers' Meetings*, and wrote and painted for a number of botanical books. Louisa Twining was very active in poor-law reform, serving on the Kensington and later the Tunbridge Wells boards of guardians, between 1884 and 1896. She was appointed a lady of grace of the order of St John of Jerusalem and published writings on art and on workhouses.

Richard and Elizabeth Twining's younger son was **William Twining** (1813–1848), physician. Educated at Rugby School under Thomas Arnold, he went to Balliol College, Oxford, in 1832. He graduated BA in 1839, BM in 1840, and DM in 1842. After a visit to a pioneering asylum in Switzerland he published *Some account of cretinism and the institution for its cure, on the Abendberg near Interlachen in Switzerland* (1843). A number of asylums using this system were subsequently opened in England. William Twining died in London at 13 Bedford Place on 15 November 1848, aged thirty-five, after ten years of paralysis.

The first Richard Twining's second son, **Thomas Twining** (1776–1861), born on 27 January 1776, entered the Bengal service of the East India Company in 1792, was employed in the finance department, and became acting subaccountant-general and commissioner of the court of requests. He was later the resident at Santipur and then at Bihar, where Twining-gunge was named after him. In four *Letters* (1795–1808) he expressed his views on 'the danger of interfering in the religious opinions of the natives of India' (*DNB*). In 1893 his *Travels in India a Hundred Years Ago and a Visit to America* was published; it recorded a brief stay in the United States in 1796 on his way to England on leave. He waited on the president, George Washington, and was impressed with his courtesy and informality. He married twice, and died at Penrhyn House, London Road, Twickenham, on 25 December 1861.

His son, **Thomas Twining** (1806–1895), was an authority on technical education. Among his works were *Science for the People* (1870), *Technical Training* (1874), and *Science Made Easy* (in five parts, 1878). He was a committee member of the Society of Arts. Although his own technical museum at Twickenham was burnt down in 1871, part of his collection of technical drawings and models was donated to the Victoria and Albert Museum. He died at Penrhyn House, London Road, Twickenham on 16 February 1895.

T. A. B. CORLEY

Sources GM, 2nd ser., 31 (1849), 211 [obit. of William Twining (1813–1848)] · DNB · S. H. Twining, *The house of Twining, 1706–1956* (1956) · R. Twining, ed., *Selections from papers of the Twining family*

(1887) · L. Twining, *Some facts in the history of the Twining family from AD 577*, 2 pts (privately printed, Salisbury, 1895) · *GM*, 1st ser., 94/1 (1824), 463–4 · *GM*, 3rd ser., 3 (1857), 574 · Boase, *Mod. Eng. biog.* · S. H. G. Twining, 'Twining III, Richard', *DBB* · [A. M. Broadley], *The Twinings in three centuries, 1710–1910* (1910) · 1824, PRO, PROB 11/1686/357 · *IGI* · *WWW* · *The Times* (22 Feb 1895) [obit. of Thomas Twining, 1806–1895] · L. S. Pressnell, J. Orbell, and others, *A guide to the historical records of British banking* (1985) · *CGPLA Eng. & Wales* (1862) · d. cert. [Richard Twining] · d. cert. [Thomas Twining] · d. cert. [William Twining]

Archives BL, corresp. and papers, Add. MSS 39929–39936

Likenesses C. Turner, mezzotint, pubd 1812 (after J. J. Halls), BM, NPG · Day & Son, portrait (after M. Carpenter), BM · line drawing, repro. in Twining, *House of Twining*

Wealth at death under £40,000: will, 1824, PRO, PROB 11/1686/357 · under £12,000—Thomas Twining: will, 19 Feb 1862, *CGPLA Eng. & Wales*

Twining, Richard (1772–1857). *See under* Twining, Richard (1749–1824).

Twining, Thomas (*bap.* 1734, *d.* 1804), classical scholar and translator, was baptized on 14 December 1734 at St Clement Danes, Westminster, the only son of Daniel Twining (1713–1762), tea dealer, and his first wife, Ann March (*d.* 1743), and half-brother of Richard *Twining (1749–1824). He was educated first at Twickenham, with a view to entering his father's business, but on his revealing great aptitude for scholarship, he was sent to the Revd Palmer Smythies (1692–1776) at the Colchester Free Grammar School (where Twining's name appears in the register for 1754). He was entered at Sidney Sussex College, Cambridge, on 8 December 1755, graduated BA in 1760 and MA in 1763; he obtained a foundation scholarship in 1756 and became a fellow in 1760.

In 1761 Twining inherited a small estate at Steeple Ashton, Wiltshire, and his father's house at Twickenham in 1762, both of which he let, clearing himself from financial anxiety for the rest of his life. In 1763 he took holy orders and in 1764 he married Elizabeth Smythies (1739–1796), daughter of his former schoolmaster and his second wife, Elizabeth Brazier (1710–1802); there were no children. In 1764 Twining was appointed to the curacy of Fordham, Essex, to which the vicarage of White Notley was added by Richard Terrick, bishop of London, in 1772. In 1788 the new bishop, Robert Lowth, conferred upon him the rectory of St Mary's-at-the-Wall, Colchester, where he lived permanently from 1790 to his death.

A gifted critic, linguist, and musician since his Cambridge years, Twining first offered his scholarship to Charles Burney, whose first volume, *A General History of Music* (1776) became greatly indebted to Twining's painstaking revisions and original contributions on ancient musicology. To interests in musical theory and history he added good qualities as a performer on the violin, organ, harpsichord, and the new pianoforte. Passion for music led him to aesthetics. In 1782 he undertook a translation with full commentary of Aristotle's *Poetics*, which was first published in 1789 with the title *Aristotle's Treatise on poetry, translated, with notes on the translation, and on the original, and two dissertations, on poetical, and musical, imitation*, and was repeatedly reprinted. The work was highly praised by

Greek scholars such as C. G. Heine (1729–1812) and Samuel Parr, who believed it 'not surpassed by any translation in the English language' (Allibone, *Dict.*). The *Dissertations*, addressing the question of the nature of imitation and engaging on it the latest scholarship (that of James Harris in particular), were hailed by contemporaries as a significant progress in Aristotelian studies and were translated into German by J. G. Buhle (1792–8). Three sermons (1787, 1790, 1794) complete the list of Twining's published works.

The some 500 letters of Twining's correspondence (BL, Add. MSS 39929–39935) are only in part published. His half-brother Richard wanted to publish a selection of these, and after Twining's death, he collected and copied all letters he could retrieve from correspondents. Access was occasionally denied on the ground that 'when he wrote to Nathaniel Forster or Samuel Parr, [Twining] never thought of the Press' (Parr, quoted in *Letters*, 1.8). The letters were eventually edited and published by his great-nephew Richard Twining (1807–1906) with the title *Recreations and Studies of a Country Clergyman of the Eighteenth Century* (1882), and in a sequel entitled *Selections from the Papers of the Twining Family* (1887); Walker's edition (1991) includes new material. Some letters are in French and Italian, some contain drawings, poems, and bars of music; all are a precious source of information for eighteenth-century cultural life and enjoyable through the author's 'wit, sagacity, learning, languages ancient and modern, the best principles of criticism, and the most exquisite feelings of taste' (Parr, quoted in *Recreations*, 11f.). Twining died on 6 August 1804 at Colchester. His epitaph in St Mary's was the tribute of Samuel Parr, headmaster of Colchester School in 1777–8 and one of Twining's lifelong friends; an obituary notice was written by the other, Charles Burney.

STANLEY LANE-POOLE, *rev.* ANNA CHAHOUD

Sources Allibone, *Dict.* · Venn, *Alum. Cant.*, 2/4.258 · *IGI* · *Recreations and studies of a country clergyman of the eighteenth century: selection from the correspondence of Thomas Twining*, ed. R. Twining (1882) · *A selection of Thomas Twining's letters, 1734–1804: the record of a tranquil life*, ed. R. S. Walker, 2 vols. (1991) [incl. list of MSS collections, 23] · *The letters of Dr Charles Burney*, ed. A. Ribeiro, 1 (1991) · W. Derry, *Dr Parr: a portrait of the whig Dr Johnson* (1966), 32–4, 103, 267 · C. T. Probyn, *The sociable humanist: the life and works of James Harris, 1709–1780* (1991) · E. Olson, ed., *Aristotle's poetics and English literature: a collection of critical essays* (1965) · P. Le Huray and J. Day, eds., *Music and aesthetics in the eighteenth and early nineteenth centuries* (1981) · A. Plebe, 'La "poetica" di Aristotele in quattro commenti del settecento', *Atti dell'Accademia di Torino*, 87 (1952–3), 26–62 · J. V. Price, 'Twining, Thomas', *The dictionary of eighteenth-century British philosophers*, ed. J. W. Yolton, J. V. Price, and J. Stephens (1999) · *Fasti Angl., 1541–1857*, [St Paul's, London], 4 · *Monthly Review*, 81 (1789), 420–26, 515–22 · *Monthly Review*, new ser., 7 (1792), 121–33

Archives BL, corresp. and papers, Add. MSS 39929–39936 | Bodl. Oxf., 'Correspondence of Thomas Burgess, bishop of Salisbury', MS Engl. Lett. C. 138, fols. 125–140 · Bodl. Oxf., letters, collected by William Upcott, Montagu MS d.10, fol. 223

Likenesses J. J. Halls, oils, 1799, priv. coll. · C. Turner, mezzotint, pubd 1805 (after J. J. Halls), BM, NPG · E. Seymour, portrait (as a child)

Wealth at death inherited estates early in life: *Selection of Thomas Twining's letters*, ed. Walker, 1.4–5

Twining, Thomas (1776–1861). *See under* Twining, Richard (1749–1824).

Twining, Thomas (1806–1895). *See under* Twining, Richard (1749–1824).

Twining, William (1790–1835), military surgeon, was born in Nova Scotia, the son of the Revd William Twining, and Sarah, daughter of Joshua Wingate Weeks. He was the grandson of the Revd Griffith Twining of Pembrokeshire, who went to Nova Scotia as a missionary for the Society for the Propagation of the Gospel. Twining studied at Guy's Hospital, London, in 1808 under Sir Astley Cooper and attended the anatomy classes of Joshua Brookes, who appointed him his demonstrator. Twining became a member of the Royal College of Surgeons, and following a short stint with the Royal Navy, he joined the army as a hospital assistant, and in 1810 was posted to the British army under Wellington in the peninsula. In March 1814 he was promoted to be assistant surgeon on Lord Hill's staff, entered Paris with the allies, and was afterwards present at Waterloo. After the war he remained attached to Lord Hill until 1817, when he was stationed at Portsmouth. 1817 was also the year of his marriage to Miss Montgomery, with whom he had a daughter. In 1819 he was at the hospital at Chatham, and for a short time he was staff assistant at the cavalry depot at Maidstone. Eager to get away from garrison duty, and after turning down a posting to the West Indies and being passed over for another in Sierra Leone, Twining accepted an offer in 1821 to join Sir Edward Paget, governor of Ceylon, as his personal surgeon. When Paget was appointed commander-in-chief of the Indian army in 1823, Twining chose to accompany him to Bengal where Paget was able to help him secure a commission as an assistant surgeon in the East India Company's service. Twining did, however, retain his king's commission until 1830, making him one of the few officers or surgeons to hold company's and king's commissions simultaneously. In 1830, however, he was pressured by military authorities in London to decide between the two, which in practice meant either joining a King's regiment or relinquishing his king's commission. He chose the latter partly because his Calcutta posting had enabled him to build up a lucrative private practice.

Soon after arriving in Bengal, Twining left Paget's staff and was appointed senior permanent assistant at the general hospital at Calcutta, a post which he held until his death, combining his hospital duties with the offices of surgeon to the gaol and to the upper orphan school, Kidderpore, and a large private practice. He was also an active member of the Medical and Physical Society, in which he succeeded Dr John Adams as secretary in 1830. Twining was instrumental in establishing and later editing the society's *Transactions* and contributed a number of papers himself on subjects ranging from fever treatments to techniques for the removal of tumours. In 1828 he printed a work on *Diseases of the Spleen, Particularly … in Bengal*, followed by *A Practical Account of the Epidemic Cholera* in 1833. The first edition of Twining's most famous work,

Clinical Illustrations of the More Important Diseases of Bengal, appeared in 1832. Subsidized by the Indian government, it became a standard reference work and there even appeared a Bengali translation of this work which was intended for use in training Indian medical personnel. In 1835 a revised and enlarged edition of this work appeared. The later edition was notable for including a section dedicated to the health and diseases of the native population of India, making it one of the first British medical works in India to address in any depth the health of the Indian population. Twining's attention to the health of the Indian population, which was accompanied by an interest in Indian medicines and therapies, was not the only characteristic setting him apart. *Clinical Illustrations* also stands out because its classification of diseases broke with tradition: instead of listing diseases by their symptoms, Twining's emphasis on anatomy led him to class diseases according to the effects they had on various body organs, for example the spleen, liver, and so on. This focus on human anatomy helps to explain another characteristic of Twining, and that is his straddling of two eras in tropical hygiene and medicine. While Twining accepted some of the precepts and assumptions of those who emphasized climate as the determining factor, and who consequently suggested that there was the possibility of acclimatization for Europeans, his writings also reflect the growing impact of a racialized pathology, one in which racial differences were called upon to explain susceptibility or resistance to disease, as well as the appropriateness of particular therapies. In *Clinical Illustrations*, for example, Twining recommended not using aggressive therapies like mercury or bleeding on Indians because their constitutions were thought to be less resilient than those of Europeans. Contemporaries credited Twining with introducing many improvements in the treatment of common diseases in India, including the use of ipecacuanha in place of salivation for persons suffering from dysentery. Twining became a leading anti-mercurialist, arguing in particular against the use of mercury in the treatment of fevers and diseases of the spleen. Contemporaries described Twining as being of average height, very fit, and athletic. He was firmly committed to a regimen of moderate eating and abstention from alcohol, and lobbied incessantly for others to adopt such habits, for he saw excessive drinking and overeating as the root cause of much of the ill health plaguing the Europeans. Twining died in Calcutta on 25 August 1835, the day after his carriage had struck the buggy of another European. Hastening to assist the other party, who had suffered a badly fractured leg in the accident, Twining fatally aggravated injuries to his own chest and ruptured a blood vessel when he tried to lift the other man. His reputation as a surgeon together with the respect given to his clinical observations led the *Friend of India* (3 September 1835) to proclaim that 'we never met with a man who more fully realized the *beau ideal* of a medical man'. Twining was buried in Calcutta the day after his death. He was survived by his wife.

DOUGLAS M. PEERS

Sources *Friend of India* (3 Sept 1835) · *Calcutta Courier* (28 Aug 1835) · *India Journal of Medical Science* (Oct 1835), 376 · D. Arnold, *Colonizing the body: state medicine and epidemic disease in nineteenth-century India* (1993) · M. Harrison, '"The tender frame of man": disease, climate and racial difference in India and the West Indies, 1760–1860', *Bulletin of the History of Medicine*, 70 (1996), 68–93 · M. Harrison, 'Tropical medicine in nineteenth-century India', *British Journal for the History of Science*, 25 (1992), 299–318 · 'The late Dr. Twining', *East India United Service Journal*, 15 (Sept 1835), 268–72 · L. Twining, *Some facts in the history of the Twining family from AD 577*, 2 pts (privately printed, Salisbury, 1895) · D. G. Crawford, *A history of the Indian medical service, 1600–1913*, 2 vols. (1914) · D. G. Crawford, ed., *Roll of the Indian Medical Service, 1615–1930* (1930) · H. H. Goodeve, 'A sketch of progress of European medicine in the East', *Quarterly Journal of the Medical and Physical Society of Calcutta*, 2 (April 1837), 127–56 · K. MacKinnon, *A treatise on the public health, climate, hygiene, and prevailing diseases of Bengal and the north-west provinces* (1848) · *DNB* · *DCB*, vol. 8

Likenesses sketch (after death mask), repro. in *India Journal of Medical Science*, 2, facing p. 398

Twining, William (1813–1848). *See under* Twining, Richard (1749–1824).

Twisden [*formerly* Twysden], **Sir Thomas**, first baronet (1602–1683), judge and politician, was born on 8 January 1602 at Roydon Hall, East Peckham, Kent, the second of the five sons of Sir William Twysden (1566–1629) and his wife, Anne *Twysden (1574–1638), daughter of Sir Moyle Finch. John *Twysden and Sir Roger *Twysden were his brothers. On 8 November 1614 Twysden entered Emmanuel College, Cambridge, with his elder brother, Roger. Both brothers then studied law, Roger proceeding to Gray's Inn and Thomas to the Inner Temple in 1617 before his call to the bar in 1625.

At Roydon Hall on 26 December 1639 Twysden married Jane (*d. c.*1703), daughter of John Thomlinson of Whitby, Yorkshire, and sister of the parliamentarian officer Colonel Matthew *Tomlinson, who accompanied Charles I on the morning of his execution. Upon his marriage he changed his surname from Twysden to Twisden. Roger Twysden, having inherited their father's baronetcy, unsuccessfully promoted Thomas for a parliamentary seat at Winchelsea in the spring of 1640. During the 1640s Thomas built his legal practice, gaining notice in the law reports and earning enough income to begin buying property at West Malling in Kent, only a few miles from his ancestral home. But throughout the 1640s and 1650s Thomas and his wife lived principally with his brother at Roydon Hall, where many of their five sons and six daughters were born.

In 1642 Twisden solidified his interest in Kent when he was made town clerk and recorder of Maidstone and a county justice of the peace; in 1644 Tenterden named him town counsel. Twisden was recruited as a member of parliament for Maidstone in November 1646, sitting until Pride's Purge in December 1648. Given his lack of zeal for the new political order, Twisden was pressed to resign his place at Maidstone in 1650.

Throughout the 1640s and 1650s Twisden appeared as legal counsel in a string of politically charged cases. Though he provided advice on at least one occasion to the council of state and was made serjeant-at-law in 1654,

Sir Thomas Twisden, first baronet (1602–1683), by John Greenhill

Twisden often found himself representing those who had run afoul of the interregnum regime. Twisden proved especially prominent in the growing caseload on writs of mandamus, by which those purged from local office might regain their places, though he usually represented those making the dismissal rather than the person dismissed in such cases. Thus he helped to prevent a Cambridge schoolmaster from regaining his place with a writ of mandamus, and likewise argued against the restoration of corporate officers purged at London, Colchester, and Reading. Similarly, Twisden provided counsel in two important cases on writs of habeas corpus. The first concerned Captain John Streeter, who had been imprisoned by order of parliament for publishing seditious books. Twisden won Streeter's release by arguing that the commitment order had become void upon parliament's dissolution. In *Cony's case* of 1655 Twisden and his co-counsel, John Maynard and Wadham Windham, failed to gain their client's release after his imprisonment at the lord protector's command for refusing to pay a duty imposed without parliamentary authority. Twisden contended in the upper bench, formerly the court of king's bench, that the protector's warrant was not sufficient for a legal imprisonment, thus mirroring earlier arguments that neither the king nor his privy council could imprison without precise charges. Twisden and his companions were put in the Tower for their defiance of the lord protector, but they were released days later after making a full submission. Despite this loss, arguing prominent cases on mandamus and habeas corpus made Twisden one of the leading practitioners in a rapidly developing administrative law based on the prerogative writs.

In April 1660 Maidstone chose Twisden as one of its MPs for the Convention, and in June Twisden put aside the serjeant's coif that he had received from Cromwell and took up a new one from Charles II. Days later, on 2 July 1660, Twisden was knighted and made a justice of king's bench. Twisden served on the commission of oyer and terminer that tried the regicides in the Old Bailey, though he took little part in the proceedings. He also presided in the cases of prominent dissenters such as George Fox and John Bunyan. Though he believed that conventicles encouraged rebellions, he was often noted for his leniency toward peaceable dissenters. None the less, Twisden commanded jurors in his grand jury charges to proceed against any who defamed the Book of Common Prayer or who used alternative forms of worship. Twisden also directed jurors to inquire into all 'oppressions and misdemeanors of all manner of officers, all corruptions in judges and justices … of what quality or condition soever' (MS Rawl. c.719, fol. 26). Related to this desire to check oppressions and corruptions, Twisden argued consistently to expand king's bench's supervisory powers over lesser courts and administrative bodies using mandamus and habeas corpus, writs he had learned to use so well in the tumultuous years before 1660.

Upon the death of Sir Robert Hyde, rumours circulated that Twisden might succeed him as chief justice, but this came to nothing. On 13 June 1666 Twisden was made a baronet, taking his title from his seat at Bradbourne in East Malling. As a justice Twisden performed a number of crucial functions. In 1667 he served with the other judges in determining property claims in the wake of the fire of London. He regularly provided advice in parliament on the content of bills, for instance, by speaking against a bill that would have recognized the court of Admiralty's jurisdiction over foreign causes. Twisden agreed with the other justices in 1677 in remanding the earl of Shaftesbury after his application for release on habeas corpus, saying that king's bench had no jurisdiction over a matter in which parliament had made the commitment. By now Twisden's health had begun to fail, and many thought that he might be removed from the bench. In October 1678 he ceased acting as a justice, though by an agreement with the king he retained the title of justice and received an annual pension of £500, half his judicial salary. Twisden died on 2 January 1683 at Bradbourne and was buried in the church at East Malling, his widow surviving him by twenty years. He was succeeded to the baronetcy by his eldest son, Roger.   PAUL D. HALLIDAY

Sources *The family of Twysden and Twisden: their history and archives from an original by Sir John Ramskill Twisden*, ed. C. H. Dudley Ward (1939) · HoP, *Commons, 1660–90* · Foss, *Judges*, 7.179–84 · R. G. Hatton and C. H. Hatton, 'Notes on the family of Twysden and Twisden', *Archaeologia Cantiana*, 58 (1945), 43–67 · *CSP dom.*, 1651; 1655; 1660–61; 1664–7; 1671–2 · *Fourth report*, HMC, 3 (1874) · *Fifth report*, HMC, 4 (1876) · *Seventh report*, HMC, 6 (1879) · *Eighth report*, 1, HMC, 7 (1907–9) · *Ninth report*, 2, HMC, 8 (1884) · *Report on the manuscripts of the late Reginald Rawdon Hastings*, 4 vols., HMC, 78 (1928–47), vol. 2 · ER, vols. 82 Siderfin, 84 Keble, 86 Ventris · PRO, KB21/12–13 · Sainty, *Judges* · Venn, *Alum. Cant.* · W. A. Shaw, ed., *Calendar of treasury books*, 5, PRO (1911) · *The journal of George Fox*, rev. edn, ed. J. L. Nickalls (1952) · reports of cases, temp. Charles II, Bodl. Oxf., MS Rawl. C. 719 · reports by Twisden in the early 1670s, BL, Add. MS 10619 · will, PRO, PROB 11/373, fols. 202v–204v

Archives BL, reports, Add. MS 10619 · Harvard U., law school, commonplace book · L. Cong., commonplace book

Likenesses oils, c.1660, Inner Temple, London · oils?, c.1670, repro. in Hatton and Hatton, 'Notes on the family', 58 · painting, oils, c.1670, Bradbourne House, Kent · C. Turner, engraving, 1800–40 (after sculpture), BM · C. Turner, mezzotint, pubd 1812 (after unknown artist), BM, NPG · J. Greenhill, drawing, BM [*see illus.*] · bust, BM · mezzotint, BM · oils (after J. M. Wright), Kent Archaeological Society; on loan to East Malling Research Station, Bradbourne House, Kent

Wealth at death extensive lands to eldest son, after life interest to widow; £1000 to each of four sons; £2000 each to two daughters: will, PRO, PROB 11/373, fols. 202v–204v

Twisleton, Edward Turner Boyd (1809–1874), civil servant, born at Ceylon on 24 May 1809, was youngest son of Thomas James Twisleton (1770–1824), archdeacon of Colombo, and his second wife, Anne (*d.* 1847), daughter and coheir of Benjamin Ash of Bath. Thomas Twisleton, thirteenth Baron Saye and Sele, was his grandfather. Edward was educated at Winchester College from 1820, before matriculating at Oriel College, Oxford, in 1826; he was a scholar and exhibitioner of Trinity College, Oxford, 1826–30, graduating BA in 1829, taking first-class honours in classics, and MA in 1834, and was a fellow of Balliol College 1830–38. During this period he studied German philosophy and theology, and was strongly influenced by German Rationalism. He entered Lincoln's Inn as a student in 1831, and was called to the bar at the Inner Temple on 30 January 1835; through his whig connections he soon obtained employment on several government commissions. He was an assistant poor-law commissioner in 1839, and in 1843 was appointed a commissioner to inquire into the Scottish poor laws.

On 5 November 1845 Twisleton was nominated chief commissioner of the poor laws in Ireland, holding office during the critical period of the great famine. He was a member of the temporary relief commission set up to advise the government on measures for the relief of starvation, and became a member of the commission constituted in March 1847 to administer the delivery of cheap food under the Temporary Relief Act (the 'Soup Kitchen Act'). At first he had resolutely upheld the official line against the allowance of outdoor relief, but as the crisis worsened he came into increasing conflict with the Treasury in London. Taking the view that the poor law in Ireland lacked the resources to cope with the crisis, he pressed for financial assistance from the Treasury, which was resisted by Charles Trevelyan. The breaking point came early in 1849, when the government passed a rate-in-aid act, which effectively placed the financial burden of relief upon the Irish poor-law unions. Unwilling to implement the new act, Twisleton resigned in protest in March 1849, subsequently stating his views in his evidence to the House of Lords select committee on the Irish poor law.

Widely known in whig political and literary circles, Twisleton numbered George Cornewall Lewis and the historian H. H. Vaughan among his closest friends. After his elder brother succeeded to the barony of Saye and Sele in 1847, Twisleton was raised to the rank of a baron's son by royal warrant (1848). Visiting the American scholar George Ticknor in Boston in 1850 Twisleton met his future wife, Ellen (1819–1862), daughter of Edward Dwight, a wealthy Boston merchant. They married on 23 May 1852. Ellen Twisleton's letters to her American relatives during the early years of her marriage record the couple's extensive social engagements in the London world of letters and affairs, as well as their travels in Europe.

In the autumn of 1855, in succession to Lewis, Twisleton was made one of the executive commissioners empowered to make new statutes for the university and colleges of Oxford. His known religious heterodoxy and his sympathy towards the extension of the professoriate helped to balance the otherwise conservative and clerical tendency of the commission. A breach in his friendship with Vaughan resulted from his belief that professors should be resident in the university. In April 1859 he stood unsuccessfully as a Liberal parliamentary candidate for the borough of Cambridge, and in June 1861 became a member of the royal commission on public schools, chaired by Lord Clarendon. In 1866 he was one of the referees appointed to settle the constitutional matters in dispute between the canons and students of Christ Church, Oxford, being made an honorary student of the reformed foundation in 1869. He was elected a fellow of the University of London in 1862. From 1862 to 1870 he was a civil service commissioner, administering appointments to the service in the era of limited competition. On his retirement he was reckoned to have served on more commissions than any other man of his time.

In retirement Twisleton became interested in the controversy respecting the identity of Junius, an interest to which he had turned in his grief after the early death of his wife. He employed Charles Chabot, the handwriting expert, to report on the Junian manuscripts at the British Museum. He came to the conclusion that Philip Francis was the author of the letters, and in 1871 he published Charles Chabot's *Handwriting of Junius Professionally Investigated* (1871), to which he added a preface and collateral evidence in support of the claims of Francis. His work *The tongue not essential to speech, with illustrations of the power of speech in the African confessors* (1873) dismissed claims of miraculous phenomena, which he argued could be explained by scientific methods. Twisleton lived at 3 Rutland Gate, Hyde Park, London, but died at Boulogne on 5 October 1874 and was buried at Broughton churchyard in Oxfordshire. He had no children. M. C. CURTHOYS

Sources *Men of the time* (1872) • *ILN* (17 Oct 1874), 379 • *ILN* (5 Dec 1874), 547 • *Law Times* (24 Oct 1874), 439 • *The Times* (10 Oct 1874) • *The Times* (4 Dec 1874) • *GM*, 1st ser., 95/1 (1825), 275–6 • *GM*, 2nd ser., 27 (1847), 442 • Boase, *Mod. Eng. biog.* • E. T. Vaughan, ed., *Letters of the Hon. Mrs Edward Twisleton written to her family, 1852–1862* (1925) • C. Kinealy, *This great calamity: the Irish famine, 1845–52* (1994) • E. G. W. Bill, *University reform in nineteenth-century Oxford: a study of Henry Halford Vaughan, 1811–1885* (1973)

Archives Harvard U., Houghton L., family and personal corresp. and papers | Bodl. Oxf., corresp. with H. H. Vaughan • LPL, letters to Charles Wordsworth • NL Wales, letters to George Cornewall • NL Wales, letters to Sir G. C. Lewis
Wealth at death under £3,000: probate, 31 Oct 1874, CGPLA Eng. & Wales

Twiss, Francis (*bap.* 1759, *d.* 1827), concordance compiler, was born in Rotterdam, and baptized at the English Episcopal Church there on 5 April 1759, the sixth, and third surviving, of the eight children of Francis Twiss and his wife, Anne, *née* Hussey. The eldest child Richard *Twiss (1747–1821) survived, but the next three died in infancy. Francis Twiss the father was an English merchant from Norwich and descended from Richard, the fourth son of Richard and Frances Twiss, who had gone to co. Kerry in Ireland about 1640, resided in the castle of Castle Island, and acquired possession of Killintierna (Burke, *Gen. GB*, 1871, 1424).

Of his early life it is known only that Twiss was admitted as a pensioner to the second table at Pembroke College, Cambridge, on 30 October 1776, under the college tutors Turner and George Pretyman, but evidently remained in residence for only one year. In the early 1780s he was evidently living mainly in the London area, and acquiring a reputation as a critic of Shakespearian acting. He became a friend of John Philip Kemble, and reputedly developed 'a hopeless passion' for Kemble's sister Sarah Siddons, sufficient to draw him to Belfast to watch her performances there in 1785 (Kemble, 1.21; Parsons, 151–2, 98). He also befriended Elizabeth Inchbald, reading with her and criticizing her plays (Manvell, 33–4, 48); she described him as one 'whose integrity nothing could warp' (Parsons, 151).

Sarah Siddons was doing all she could to promote the theatrical careers of her sisters and brothers. Her sister Frances Kemble (1759–1822) appeared on stage in Bath and Bristol in 1780–81, and in London first on 6 January 1783, but critics began to find her diffidence and lack of dramatic power irritating; and the compiler of 'Theatrical intelligence' for the *Public Advertiser* became obsessively harsh about her, often reducing her to bitter weeping. To her defence came the Shakespearian commentator George Steevens, with a letter of protest published in that paper (Boaden, *Siddons*, 2.20–26), and other expressions of support and admiration. He proposed marriage, but she and her family found him 'too vehement and impracticable a suitor, too ill-tempered and capricious' (Fitzgerald, 230), and instead, on 1 May 1786, in the church of St Giles-in-the-Fields, London, Fanny married by licence Francis Twiss. Sarah wrote of him as 'a most respectable man, though of but small fortune, and I thank God that she is off the stage' (letter to the Revd Thomas Whalley, 11 Aug 1786, cited in Parsons, 152). Their offspring were Horace *Twiss (1787–1849), a daughter who died in infancy in 1789, Frances Ann (1790–1864), Amelia (1791–1852), Elizabeth (*d.* 1858), and John (1798–1866).

The Twiss family evidently remained in London until about the turn of the century, but by 1802 were resident in Bath. Sarah remained deeply attached to her sister. Mrs Hester Piozzi in a letter to Mrs Pennington of 29 April 1798 wrote that when visiting Sarah's house, 'I always meet Mr. Twiss there—a fierce Man … with a Brown Brutus Head [a fashionable wig]'. Later references were more appreciative, for example, on 21 December 1802, to 'that wise Man Mr. Twiss, with his clear straightforward Understanding' (*Piozzi Letters*, 2.491; 3.391). During this period they bore some of the brunt of the painter Thomas Lawrence's troublesome courtship of Sarah's daughter Sally.

Twiss's *A Complete Verbal Index to the Plays of Shakespeare, Adapted to All the Editions*, was published in two volumes in 1805, but of the 750 copies printed 547 were reportedly destroyed in a fire in 1807. The value of Twiss's *Complete Verbal Index* to 'all Shakespearians' was rated very highly by James Boaden in 1827. Manifestly its compilation was 'a task of the most irksome toil', demanding 'persevering diligence' (Boaden, *Siddons*, 2.102n). Doubtless it would have been for several decades more accessible, and more extensive in its references, than that of Samuel Ayscough (1790). However, its usefulness was limited, as it printed the word only, and not the line or clause in which this occurred, and it was superseded by later concordances.

In 1807, Mrs Twiss established a private school for girls in Bath, at 24 Camden Place, with the assistance of her husband and daughters. In 1803 her father Roger Kemble had bequeathed her £500, to be paid at the death of her mother, which occurred on 24 April 1807; and this doubtless financed the venture. 'A fashionable parlour-boarders' school', it was quite successful, its prospectus promising that 'The utmost attention will be paid to [the girls'] morals, conduct and manners'. The fees were relatively high, at '100 guineas per annum', with 'Entrance five guineas' (Fitzgerald, 1.231).

Frances Anne *Kemble (1809–1893), their niece, recalled her uncle as a 'grim-visaged, gaunt-figured, kind-hearted gentleman and profound scholar' (*Record of a Girlhood*, 1.21). George Hardinge described him as:

> of my height, but very thin, and stoops. His face is ghastly in the paleness of it. He takes absolute clouds of snuff, and his eyes have an ill-natured cast of acuteness in them. He is a kind of thin Dr. Johnson without his hard words (though he is often quaint in his phrase); very dogmatical, and spoilt as an *original*.   (Nichols, 3.38)

Mrs Frances Twiss died on 3 October 1822 in Bath, and Francis Twiss died on 28 April 1827 in Cheltenham. Their elder son, Horace Twiss, became a socialite, barrister, and member of parliament. The younger son rose to the rank of major-general in the army, on 5 January 1864, and became governor of the Royal Military Academy, Woolwich. Their three daughters remained unmarried.

JOHN C. ROSS

Sources J. Boaden, *Memoirs of Mrs Siddons*, 2 vols. (1827) • GM, 1st ser., 92/2 (1822), 381 • GM, 1st ser., 97/1 (1827), 476 • Nichols, *Illustrations* • C. Parsons, *The incomparable Siddons* (1909) • *The Piozzi letters: correspondence of Hester Lynch Piozzi, 1784–1821*, ed. E. A. Bloom and L. D. Bloom, 5 vols. (1989–99) • *An artist's love story: told in the letters of Sir Thomas Lawrence, Mrs Siddons and her daughters*, ed. O. G. Knapp (1904) • IGI [parish register, English Episcopal Church, Rotterdam, baptisms and marriages] • R. Manvell, *Elizabeth Inchbald: England's principal woman dramatist and independent woman of letters in 18th century London* (1987) • Highfill, Burnim & Langhans, *BDA* • F. A. Kemble, *Record of a girlhood*, rev. edn, 3 vols. (1879) • J. Boaden, *Memoirs of the life of John Philip Kemble*, 2 vols. (1825) • P. Fitzgerald, *The Kembles: an account of the Kemble family*, 2 vols. (1871) • Y. Ffrench, *Mrs. Siddons: tragic actress* (1936), repr. 1954 • C. B. Hogan, 'The Kemble family: a genealogical record, 1704–1925', *Theatre Notebook*, 30 (1976), 103–9 • B. Bourke, *A genealogical and heraldical history of the landed gentry of Great Britain & Ireland* (1871) • private information (2004) [from Dr Georgianna Ziegler, Folger] • private information (2004) [J. Ringrose, archivist, Pembroke Cam.]

Archives BL, Inchbald MSS. Add. MSS 46611; 27925; 28558

Likenesses J. Reynolds, oils, 1783, repro. in Knapp, ed., *An artist's love story* • J. Jones, mezzotint, pubd 1784 (after oil painting by J. Reynolds, 1783), BM, NPG; repro. in Knapp, ed., *An artist's love story* • J. Jones, stipple, pubd 1784 (after J. Downman), BM • J. Opie, oils, priv. coll. • miniature; in possession of Quintin Twiss's family, c.1900 • portrait

Twiss, Sir Frank Roddam (1910–1994), naval officer, was born in India on 7 July 1910, the son of Colonel Edward Kemble Twiss, Indian army officer. He entered the Royal Naval College, Dartmouth, as a cadet in 1924. He went to sea in 1927, first in the battleship *Revenge* and then in *Rodney* in her first commission. In 1932 he served in the sloop *Bideford* in the Persian Gulf and then in the battleship *Malaya* in the Home Fleet. Promoted lieutenant in 1931, he qualified as a gunnery officer in 1935 and served in the destroyer *Grenville* during the Spanish Civil War. On 28 November 1936 he married Prudence Dorothy (1915/16–1974), daughter of Admiral John de Mestre Hutchison (1862–1932); they had two sons and one daughter. In 1939 he was gunnery officer and senior staff officer of the 16th flotilla in the destroyer *Malcolm*, operating mainly in the channel. In May 1940 he was sent to Devonport Dockyard to stand by the cruiser *Trinidad* and so, to his regret, missed the epic of Dunkirk. Instead, he was given what he called the 'Gilbertian' job of taking 120 conscripts to Bath, where he was met at the station by an admiral who told him that morale was low in Bath: would Twiss's naval party march through the streets with fixed bayonets to encourage everybody? Twiss's conscripts had been civilians only a week before, but his senior gunnery instructor 'never turned a hair' (*Daily Telegraph*, 28 Jan 1994). The march took place, and morale in Bath duly rose.

In the summer of 1940 Twiss was appointed gunnery officer of the cruiser *Exeter*, which was refitting at Devonport following its famous fight against the pocket battleship *Graf Spee* off the River Plate the previous year. Her captain died on the day before she was commissioned in March 1941, which *Exeter*'s sailors took as a very bad omen. But Twiss found *Exeter* an exceptionally happy ship. In February 1942 she was one of a mixed and makeshift force of British, Dutch, American, and Australian war ships under the Dutch Admiral Karel Doorman which met a superior Japanese fleet escorting invasion convoys bound for Java. Seven allied ships were sunk. *Exeter* was damaged and went to Sourabaya for repairs. On 28 February she sailed with the destroyers *Encounter* and USS *Pope*, hoping to escape into the Indian Ocean, but early on 1 March they met another large Japanese force and all three were sunk. After twenty hours on a raft, Twiss was picked up by a Japanese destroyer and taken first to Macassar; then, with other British, American, and Dutch officers and men, he was transported in a ship infested with cockroaches to

Japan and imprisoned in a camp near Yokohama which was unknown to the Red Cross. There and in other camps they endured years of malnutrition and savage treatment. They lacked adequate clothing and medical facilities. Dysentery and beri-beri were endemic, and at one stage they were reduced to eating frogs and fungus off trees. But although they were subjected to all manner of humiliations, being forced to bow to the emperor at dawn every morning, their spirits never faltered. Twiss himself described how, when he had been ill for months with dysentery and was feeling extremely low, he was much cheered by a bird singing outside his cell. At Christmas 1942 the British contingent put on the pantomime *Cinderella*. According to the camp historian, Twiss was a 'brilliant fairy queen, complete with wings and umbrella surmounted by one large star' (*Daily Telegraph*, 28 Jan 1994). When he came home after the war, he was down to half his normal weight. He was awarded a belated DSC for the part *Exeter*'s guns had played in the battle of the Java Sea, and promoted commander.

After the war Twiss had his first command, the frigate *Porlock Bay* in the West Indies. There were few dull moments on board: the ship lost the secret wheels for her coding machine, ran all the accounts for three months using the wrong dollar exchange rate, and was battered by a hurricane in Bermuda with the commander-in-chief on board. To his horror, Twiss was then appointed 'gas' commander at HMS *Excellent*, the gunnery school in Portsmouth. They were the early days of atomic, biological, and chemical warfare, and for nearly two years Twiss had to attend 'dreary courses with the Army', and visit 'morbid doctors at Porton Down—until my finest stroke—I persuaded the Director General of Training to sell the whole caboodle to the Damage Control School' (*Daily Telegraph*, 28 Jan 1994).

In 1950, promoted captain, Twiss became commander of *Excellent*, where he ran a herd of cows, a pig farm, and a flock of chickens. Twiss loved variety, and enjoyed his stint as deputy secretary to the chiefs of staff from 1951 to 1953: it was a hectic period, when Churchill returned to power and NATO was being set up. He was then captain, fishery protection squadron, before commanding HMS *Gamecock*, the royal naval air station at Bramcote. In 1957 he took command of the cruiser *Ceylon*, which he found, he said, in a low state of morale and cleanliness. But on recommissioning with a new ship's company, *Ceylon* 'never looked back' (*Daily Telegraph*, 28 Jan 1994). Promoted rear-admiral in 1960 and vice-admiral in 1963, Twiss returned to the Admiralty as naval secretary to the first lord, Lord Carrington, who became a lifelong friend. He was then successively flag officer, flotillas, Home Fleet, and commander, Far East Fleet, at the height of the confrontation between Indonesia and Malaysia. His last appointment was as second sea lord and chief of naval personnel, with the rank of admiral, in 1967. Twiss did not forget his experience as a midshipman in *Rodney* in 1930 when there was a near-mutiny, and he sensed general unrest in the fleet. As second sea lord he told all his heads of divisions to make a point of leaving their chairs at regular intervals to go out into the ships and naval establishments and find out what the sailors were thinking.

In retirement Twiss was gentleman usher of the black rod in the House of Lords from 1970 to 1978 and serjeant-at-arms and secretary to the lord great chamberlain from 1971 to 1978. He was appointed CB in 1962, KCB in 1965, and KCVO in 1978. His first wife having died in 1974, on 19 August 1978 he married Rosemary Maitland Chilton (*b.* 1915/16), daughter of Charles Maitland Howe, a businessman, and widow of Captain Denis Chilton, naval officer.

Twiss was one of those rare men with the mental and physical resilience to resume his naval career after a prolonged ordeal in Japanese prisoner of war camps. He was gifted with an irrepressible sense of humour—he once said of Dartmouth in the 1920s that 'it was much worse than any Jap PoW camp' (*Daily Telegraph*, 28 Jan 1994). One of his fellow officers in *Malcolm* wrote of him years later, 'I regard him as one of the very few really funny men I know' (private information). He had an enormous range of friends of all age groups and from all walks of life. As one said, 'he had this marvellous sparkle about him' (ibid.). With his height and spare frame he was a dignified figure in his black rod's court dress. His eyes never properly recovered from the damage done by sea water and oil fuel from *Exeter*, and in his latter years he was blind: typically, he donated his eyes to medical research. He died of cancer at the Princess Alexandra Hospital, Wroughton, Wiltshire, on 26 January 1994; he was survived by his second wife and the three children of his first marriage. A memorial service was held at St Martin-in-the-Fields on 23 March 1994.

JOHN WINTON

Sources C. H. Bailey, ed., *Social change in the Royal Navy, 1924–70: the life and times of Admiral Sir Frank Twiss* (1996) • F. Twiss, 'Nautical almanac', typescript, [n.d.] • F. R. Twiss and N. H. Power, 'HMS *Exeter*, March 1941 – August 1945', typescript, c.1946 • F. Twiss, 'Near mutiny', *Naval Review*, 78/4 (Oct 1990) • A. J. Marder, M. Jacobsen, and J. Horsfield, *Old friends, new enemies: the Royal Navy and the imperial Japanese navy*, 2 vols. (1981–90), vol. 2 • *The Times* (28 Jan 1994) • *Daily Telegraph* (28 Jan 1994) • *WWW*, 1991–5 • private information (2004) • *Navy List* • m. cert. • d. cert.
Archives Royal Naval Museum, Portsmouth, journals and papers
Likenesses photograph, repro. in *The Times* • photograph, repro. in *Daily Telegraph*
Wealth at death £278,590: probate, 6 April 1994, *CGPLA Eng. & Wales*

Twiss, Horace (1787–1849), lawyer and politician, was the eldest son of Francis *Twiss (*bap.* 1759, *d.* 1827) and his wife, Frances Kemble (1759–1822), sister of the actress Sarah Siddons. He was probably born at Bath, was admitted as a student at the Inner Temple in 1806, and was called to the bar on 28 June 1811. He inherited the love of his mother's family for the stage. On the occasion of what amounted to her farewell to the stage, on 29 June 1812, his aunt Sarah *Siddons recited an address which he had written for her; he also assisted when she gave her 'readings from Shakespeare' (Boaden, 2.383), and he was one of the executors of her will. A satirical poem, called 'St Stephen's

Horace Twiss (1787–1849), by Abraham Wivell

acquaintance in 1804 at a debating society which met at the Crown and Rolls in Chancery Lane. He was 'the impersonation of a debating society rhetorician. … When he got into the House of Commons, though inexhaustibly fluent, his manner certainly was very flippant, factitious, and unbusinesslike' (Hardcastle, 1.143). His speech supporting the removal of the disabilities of Roman Catholics (23 March 1821), however, showed his ability and he subsequently spoke on various legal topics, particularly on those affecting the court of chancery. In 1825 he was appointed by Lord Liverpool to the posts of counsel to the Admiralty and judge-advocate of the fleet; and in Wellington's government from 1828 to 1830 he was under-secretary of war and the colonies. He vehemently opposed the introduction of the Reform Bill (1 March 1831), his speech leading to the loss of his seat in 1831. Macaulay records that when the measure passed its second reading 'the face of Twiss was as the face of a damned soul' (Trevelyan, 1.208). In 1832 he published *Conservative Reform*.

From 1831 to 1835 Twiss was out of parliament, but at the general election of 1835 he was returned as the second member for the borough of Bridport in Dorset, polling 207 votes against 199 recorded for John, first Lord Romilly. He sat for Bridport until 1837, when he was badly beaten at Nottingham, and in 1841 he was defeated at Bury St Edmunds.

During those disappointing years, while Twiss was out of parliament and out of office, he wrote for *The Times*, originating the summary of parliamentary debates and sometimes writing leaders. His *Public and Private Life of Lord Eldon* (3 vols., 1844), was a notable success, said to have made him 2000 guineas (Allibone, *Dict.*). The *Gentleman's Magazine* (June 1849) found it 'ever-entertaining'. He was rewarded for it quickly, as in October 1844 Lord Granville Charles Henry Somerset, the chancellor of the duchy of Lancaster, made him vice-chancellor of the duchy, and he enjoyed that lucrative post—effectively a pension—until his death. Twiss was known for his hospitality and wit; he entertained at first in Serle Street, Lincoln's Inn Fields; in the 1830s he lived at 5 Park Place, St James's. At the time of his death he lived in Grafton Street.

Twiss died from heart disease very suddenly while speaking at a meeting of the Rock Assurance Society at Radley's Hotel, Bridge Street, Blackfriars, London, on 4 May 1849, and was buried in the Temple church. His only child from his first marriage, Fanny Horatia Serle Twiss (*b.* 1818, *d.* 22 Jan 1874), married, first, Francis Bacon (*d.* 1840), and, second, John Thadeus *Delane, editor of *The Times*. Twiss's only son from his second marriage, Quintin William Francis Twiss, was a clerk in the Treasury.

W. P. COURTNEY, rev. H. C. G. MATTHEW

Sources GM, 1st ser., 97/1 (1827), 283 · GM, 2nd ser., 31 (1849), 649–52 · *John Bull* (12 May 1849) · F. A. Kemble, *Record of a girlhood*, 3 vols. (1878) · J. Boaden, *Memoirs of Mrs Siddons*, 2 vols. (1827) · G. O. Trevelyan, *The life and letters of Lord Macaulay*, 2 vols. (1876) · *Life of John, Lord Campbell, lord high chancellor of Great Britain*, ed. Mrs Hardcastle, 2 vols. (1881) · Allibone, *Dict.*

Archives Bodl. Oxf., corresp. | BL, corresp. with Sir Robert Peel, Add. MSS 40391–40552 · PRO NIre., corresp. with Earl Belmore · Wellcome L., corresp. with John Hodgkin

Chapel, by Horatius', which was published in 1807, is usually attributed to him, and he was known when a young man as a contributor of squibs and *jeux d'esprit* to the papers, especially to the *Morning Chronicle*. In 1812 he published *Posthumous Parodies of the Poets* (the best being of Milton) and in 1814 the lyrics for H. R. Bishop's *Scotch Melodies*. His melodrama *The Carib Chief* (1819) was well received when it was first performed, with Edmund Kean in the lead. It was said at a later date that Twiss's rise at the bar had been retarded by his social, literary, and political celebrity.

Twiss married, at Bath, on 2 August 1817, Anne Lawrence, only daughter of Colonel Serle of Montagu Place, London. She had been a pupil at his mother's school at Bath, and was the smallest woman that the actress and writer Fanny Kemble, a relative, ever saw. She was probably the Mrs Twiss who died at Cadogan Place on 20 February 1827. Twiss married, second, in 1832, Annie, daughter of the Revd Alexander Sterky (a Swiss minister and reader to the Princess Charlotte), and widow of Charles Greenwood, a Russia merchant.

Twiss went on the Oxford circuit, and rose to be one of its leaders. He afterwards practised in the equity courts. In 1825 he published *An Inquiry into the Means of Consolidating and Digesting the Laws of England*. In 1827 he became king's counsel. In 1837 he was reader of his inn, and in 1838 he was its treasurer. Twiss was attracted to politics and in 1820 he was returned to parliament, through the interest of Lord Clarendon, for the borough of Wootton Bassett in Wiltshire. He sat for it until 1830, and then from 1830 to the dissolution in April 1831 for the borough of Newport in the Isle of Wight. Lord Campbell had made his

Likenesses C. Martin, tinted pencil sketch, 1844, NPG; repro. in C. Martin, *Twelve Victorian celebrities* (1899) · A. Wivell, drawing, priv. coll. [*see illus.*]

Twiss, Richard (1747–1821), travel writer, was born on 26 April 1747 at Rotterdam, the eldest of the eight children born to Francis Twiss, an English merchant originally from Norwich but resident in the Netherlands ('from circumstances connected with his views in life', reports the *Annual Biography*'s obituary in 1822), and his wife, Anne Hussey. His younger brother was Francis *Twiss (*bap.* 1759, *d.* 1827). Possessing reasonable wealth, he indulged his enjoyment of travel after gaining some education in the Netherlands: beginning with Scotland, he then also travelled around the Netherlands, Belgium, France, Switzerland, Italy, Germany, and Bohemia, before 1770. In 1768 he visited Voltaire at Ferney; a short account of their meeting is printed (from Twiss's journal) in the *Annual Biography* (pp. 447–8). Next, after a brief spell in England, he visited Spain and Portugal during 1772–3 and published *Travels through Portugal and Spain in 1772 and 1773* (1775), which the *Monthly Review* (September 1775) criticized for its lengthy quotations from other authors. It contains, however, some humorous anecdotes, characteristic of Twiss's irreverent style. In April 1775 Samuel Johnson told Boswell that he was reading and enjoying Twiss's *Travels*, although being too lazy to cut the leaves, he had only 'read in them where the pages are open' (Boswell, *Life*, 2.345–6). Twiss's Iberian expedition was followed by a visit to Ireland, described in his *Tour in Ireland in 1775* (1776). His mildly critical views on the hygiene of Irish women provoked two anonymous satiric attacks, in laboured rhyming couplets, from Irish poet William Preston, published in Dublin in 1776 and 1777. These small octavo pamphlets (entitled *An Heroic Epistle from Donna Teresa Pinna … and An Heroic Answer, from Richard Twiss …*) poked fun also at Twiss's gallantry in the *Travels through Portugal and Spain*, and seem to have been popular: the latter was even reprinted in London in 1777 as a more opulent quarto pamphlet. Twiss's obituaries hint coyly at a more daring form of revenge on the part of the Irish, which is fully explained in *The Georgian Era* (1834), where we learn that his 'animadversions upon the character of the Irish excited the wrath of many of the natives, who retaliated, by placing his picture at the bottom of a certain chamber utensil, which, in Ireland, still goes by the name of Twiss' (Clarke, 465).

During later years Twiss seems to have travelled less. He produced two small volumes of notes on the subject of *Chess* in 1787 and 1789 (he is mentioned in chapter 9 of Maria Edgeworth's *Belinda* as an authority on chess and on Spain), but he complained that the publication left him 20 guineas out of pocket (Twiss to Douce, 18 Jan 1789, MS Douce). His most interesting work, however, is *A Trip to Paris in July and August 1792* (1793). This presents a vivid account of Revolutionary events which Twiss witnessed 'not as a politician, but as a spectator' (p. 70). His accounts of atrocities such as the massacre in the Tuileries Garden display a startling flair for reportage, while his eclectic interests make the book a fascinating repository of miscellaneous facts and opinions. His rapid departure from Paris after the events of 10 August 1792 seems to have earned him some ridicule in the contemporary English press, to which he indignantly responded in an 'Epilogue' to the *Trip*, and he wrote privately to Douce that 'for six days together I lived in expectation of being massacred and my head carried on a pike' (MS Douce d. 39, fol. 45).

Twiss was elected a fellow of the Royal Society in 1774, but withdrew from it in 1794. His obituary notice in the *Gentleman's Magazine* (April 1821) observes that he 'unfortunately entered into a speculation of making paper from straw, by which he ruined an ample hereditary fortune' (p. 284). This 'Regenerated Paper Manufacture' scheme, based at Neckenger Mill in Bermondsey, aimed to produce fresh paper out of unwanted books and papers, as well as from straw. Despite Twiss's great enthusiasm for the project (Twiss to Douce, August 1800, MS Douce), it rapidly failed, and on 1 December 1803 he noted to Douce that he was planning to publish 'one or two volumes of Miscellanies' since he is 'very little richer than Job, after he had lost everything but his patience'. The *Miscellanies* which he published in 1805 (2 vols.) are a curious collection of moral and humorous essays. The subscription list suggests that Twiss successfully generated interest in the volume: the list of subscribers included the prince of Wales, Admiral Nelson, Joseph Banks, and several other luminaries. Twiss died at his home, Warrenplace, Camden Town, on 5 March 1821. The obituary essay in the *Annual Biography* for 1822 reports that he was 'a skilful performer on the violin, and a general connoisseur, as it respected the fine arts' (p. 450).

KATHERINE TURNER

Sources *GM*, 1st ser., 91/1 (1821), 284 · *Annual Biography and Obituary*, 6 (1822), 446–50 · [Clarke], *The Georgian era: memoirs of the most eminent persons*, 3 (1834), 465 · R. Twiss, *Travels through Portugal and Spain in 1772 and 1773* (1775) · R. Twiss, *A tour in Ireland in 1775* (1776) · R. Twiss, *A trip to Paris in July and August 1792* (1793) · R. Twiss, *Miscellanies*, 2 vols. (1805) · Boswell, *Life*, 2.345–6 · *DNB* · correspondence with Francis Douce, Bodl. Oxf., Douce MS d. 39 · *IGI*

Archives Bodl. Oxf., corresp. with Francis Douce, Douce MS d. 39

Likenesses G. H. H., line engraving, 1814, Bodl. Oxf., copy of R. Twiss, *Travels through Portugal and Spain in 1772 and 1773* (1775), Douce T. subt. 5 [bound in front] · print, 1814, NPG · Mrs D. Turner, etching (after G. H. H. Harlow), BM, NPG

Twiss, Sir Travers (1809–1897), jurist, eldest son of Revd Robert Twiss LLD (*d.* 1856), and his wife, Fanny Walker, was born in Gloucester Place, Marylebone, Middlesex, on 19 March 1809. His father, who was unbeneficed, inherited an estate at Hoseley, Flintshire, from his mother, Anne Travers. Twiss matriculated on 5 April 1826 at University College, Oxford, where he gained a scholarship in 1827. He graduated BA (first class in mathematics, second class in classics) in 1830, MA in 1832, BCL by commutation in 1835, and DCL in 1841.

Twiss was elected to a fellowship of his college in 1830, which he retained until 1863, resigning it after his marriage; in 1864 he was elected to an honorary fellowship. He was bursar of the college in 1835, dean in 1837, and tutor from 1836 to 1843. It was during Twiss's time as tutor that

Sir Travers Twiss (1809–1897), by unknown engraver, pubd 1897 (after Terrasse)

in July 1838 A. P. Stanley was elected to a fellowship in preference to Mark Pattison, who later accused Twiss in his *Memoirs* of helping to arrange the election of a candidate contrary to the college statutes, a charge which Twiss vigorously denied. Unusually, he served three times as public examiner in both classics (1835–7) and in mathematics (1838–40). At the same time, Twiss began to devote his time to the study of law, political economy, and international politics. He was admitted to Lincoln's Inn in February 1835, and was called to the bar on 27 January 1840. He became bencher of his inn in January 1858. In November 1841 he was admitted to membership of the Doctors' Commons, where he acted as librarian in 1854–9, and as treasurer in 1860–61.

In the middle decades of the nineteenth century, Twiss was eminent as a university teacher, a scholar, and a practitioner in the civilian courts. In December 1841, he was elected Drummond Professor of Political Economy in succession to Herman Merivale, against whom he had stood unsuccessfully in 1837. In the election, he defeated the first holder of the chair, Nassau Senior, who would himself succeed Twiss in 1847. In contrast to Senior, Twiss was not a profound theoretician, holding the view that the doctrines of political economy were 'the conclusions of an enlarged experience', and not 'mere deductions from arbitrary premises skilfully assumed'. These views were developed in his major publication as Drummond professor, *View of the Progress of Political Economy in Europe since the Sixteenth Century* (1847), which was more a historical than an analytical work. His interest in history was also reflected by his publication of *Epitome of Niebuhr's History of Rome* (1836).

In January 1849, Twiss was appointed to the newly established chair of international law at King's College, London. He resigned the position after six years to succeed Dr Joseph Phillimore in the regius professorship of civil law at Oxford. Twiss saw his role in this post as helping to bridge the gap between the old system of legal education at Oxford, and a new one which would encourage the study of civil law in the universities as part of a preparation for the bar. He had long been a keen advocate of the reform of law studies at Oxford, urging for change as early

as 1839, in an anonymous pamphlet, *Considerations for combining the professional system with the system of public examinations in Oxford*. In 1856 he published *A letter to the vice-chancellor of the University of Oxford on the law studies of the university*. He held the post longer than he had anticipated, and resigned in 1870, to be succeeded by James Bryce.

Much of Twiss's work as a scholar was aimed at applying his historical and legal knowledge to questions of contemporary political concern. In 1851 he published *The letters apostolic of Pope Pius IX, considered with reference to the law of England and the law of Europe*, in which he argued that the papal plan to create Catholic bishoprics in England was unlawful. For Twiss, the passing of the Catholic Emancipation Bill in 1829 had been a hurried measure, which had opened the way for papal power to gain a foothold in England, which he now felt had to be resisted. Twiss remained prominent at Oxford among those who wanted to resist both Tractarian influence and any growing influence of the state over the church. He was twice invited to stand for Oxford University's parliamentary seat, once (against Gladstone) in January 1853, and again (against Sir William Heathcote) in January 1854, when Sir Robert Inglis resigned his seat. On both occasions Twiss declined to stand.

Twiss's most important work was in the field of international law. In 1846 he published *The Oregon Question Examined with Respect to Facts and the Law of Nations*, and in 1848 *The relations of the duchies of Schleswig and Holstein to the crown of Denmark and the Germanic confederation*. His major work in international law, *The Law of Nations Considered as Independent Political Communities*, was published in two parts in 1861–3. As befitted a man who was on familiar terms with Prince Metternich, Twiss felt that the system of international congresses was the most powerful organ in developing a new order of international law, and he saw advances in international law as conducing to an ever higher state of civilization. Although not as complete as the work of some other writers in the field (such as Phillimore), the book went through a number of editions, and a French translation by his friend Alphonse Rivier (2 vols., 1887–9) became a standard work on the continent. His expertise in international law and civilian jurisprudence was also much in demand in his public life at this time. In 1851 he conducted, with Dr Stephen Lushington, the statutory arbitration which determined the boundaries between New Brunswick and Canada. Twiss was also a member of a number of royal commissions, including the one appointed in 1853 to inquire into the management and government of Maynooth College. In the following decade he sat on royal commissions on the marriage laws in the United Kingdom (1865–8), on the neutrality laws (1867–8), and on the law of naturalization (1868–9). In addition, he was one of the twenty-nine commissioners appointed in 1867 to examine the conduct of public worship.

Twiss had a large practice both in the ecclesiastical and Admiralty courts. In June 1849, he was appointed commissary-general of the consistory court of Canterbury, and in March 1852 he became vicar-general of the province of Canterbury. He also held the posts of commissary-general of the archdeaconry of Suffolk and chancellor of the consistory courts of Hereford and Lincoln. After the testamentary and matrimonial jurisdiction of the ecclesiastical courts was transferred to the new civil court of probate and divorce in 1857, he was appointed QC (January 1858), along with a number of other distinguished civilians, and was given an annuity of almost £100 to compensate for the abolished offices he had held. On the promotion of Dr Lushington to the office of judge of the court of arches in July 1858, the bishop of London appointed Twiss chancellor of the diocese of London. Twiss practised with no less distinction in the Admiralty court, and was engaged in most of the prize cases which arose from captures made during the Crimean War. In September 1862, he was appointed advocate-general to the Admiralty in succession to Sir Robert Joseph Phillimore, whom he again succeeded as queen's advocate-general on 23 August 1867. He was knighted on 4 November 1867.

In August 1862 Twiss announced his marriage to Marie Pharialdé Rosalind Van Lynseele, the 22-year-old orphaned daughter of a major-general in the Polish army, Count Raoul Felix Van Lynseele, who had been brought up by guardians in Brussels. The marriage took place at the British legation in Dresden, where Twiss, as he later told A. H. Layard, 'narrowly escaped finding no clergyman, as Rev. Mr Dale, a self-supported clergyman, only returned by the same train which brought me' (BL, Add. MS 38988, fol. 288). After her marriage, Lady Twiss was twice presented at the court of St James, once in 1863 and again in 1869. Their comfortable lifestyle came to an abrupt end, however, in 1872, when a solicitor, Alexander Chaffers (1821–1899), claimed, in a statutory declaration circulated to Twiss's friends, that Lady Twiss was in fact a prostitute—Marie Pharialdé Gelas, the daughter of a carpenter, Pierre Denis, and his wife—and that she had been Twiss's mistress for three years prior to the marriage, and had also had a relationship with Chaffers himself. Twiss responded by prosecuting Chaffers in the Southwark police court for publishing a malicious libel with intent to extort money. The trial was widely reported in the press, which published Chaffers's indelicate cross-examination of Lady Twiss in considerable detail. The trial ended in great drama when on 14 March 1872, Lady Twiss departed suddenly from London, returning to the continent. It was, in effect, an admission of her true identity. Chaffers was not called upon for his defence, and the charges were withdrawn. Although the press was highly critical of Chaffers's conduct, the damage to the reputation of the Twisses was done. On 21 March 1872 Sir Travers resigned all his offices, and on 19 April the lord chamberlain announced in the *London Gazette* that Lady Twiss's presentation at court had been cancelled. She did not to return to England again until early 1882, when Chaffers attempted to prosecute her for perjury.

Henceforth, Twiss devoted himself to the study of legal history and international law. In the early 1870s, he edited for the Rolls Series *The Black Book of the Admiralty*, a collection of documents on the nature of fourteenth- and fifteenth-century admiralty law. The black book was the Admiralty's office copy of various documents, and it was thought to have disappeared at the start of the nineteenth century. When the Doctors' Commons' manuscripts ceased being available for public purposes, on the disbanding of the College of Advocates in 1858 and with the sale of its library, Twiss decided to edit a restored text of the work, which was published in 1871. Three subsequent volumes were issued (in 1873, 1874, and 1876), in which were published the Domesday of Ipswich, the customaries of Oleron and Rouen, the charter of Oleron, and the 'Customs of the sea', as well as a number of other texts on medieval maritime law. By 1874, the black book itself had been rediscovered, and in the fourth volume of his work Twiss was able to give a list of textual variations.

If Twiss's edition of the black book received high praise, his next effort for the Rolls Series—an edition of *Bracton* (*De legibus et consuetudinibus Angliae*), which appeared in six volumes between 1878 and 1883—was far less successful. The last printed edition of *Bracton* dated from 1569, and it had long been felt that a new one was needed. However, it was soon evident that Twiss's scholarly skills were not up to the task. Twiss failed to produce the best text he could from the numerous medieval copies available, and he made serious mistranslations and allowed errors and corruptions to disfigure his text. The result was heavily criticized by scholars. Sir Frederick Pollock regarded Twiss's work as 'a reproach to the learning of this country and a misfortune to the study of its history' (*Saturday Review*, 46, 1879, 154), while F. W. Maitland dismissed it as 'six volumes of rubbish' (C. H. S. Fifoot, *Frederick William Maitland*, 1971, 61–2). The definitive edition of *Bracton* thus had to wait almost another century. In the light of his obvious failings as an editor, Twiss's edition of the treatise called *Glanvill*, which had been sanctioned in 1884 and announced in the press in 1890, was suppressed.

Twiss continued in his later life to play an active part in international law circles. He was present at the inauguration in Brussels of the Association for the Reform and Codification of the Law of Nations, of which he was the English vice-president. He was also a prominent member of the Institut de Droit International (founded in 1873) and was three times its vice-president. He was also one of the editors of the *Revue de Droit International de Législation Comparée*. In 1883, he published in this journal an article entitled 'La libre navigation du Congo', in which he advocated an international protectorate for the Lower Congo and a declaration by the interested powers not to seize territory in the upper Congo. This article attracted the attention of Leopold, king of the Belgians, who used it to support his idea for an 'international association' for the region. The Congo question was ultimately referred to a west Africa conference, held in Berlin between November 1884 and February 1885, and Twiss was invited by Lord Granville, the foreign secretary, to act as unofficial adviser to the British delegation at the conference. It was the lord chancellor, Lord Selborne, Sir Julian Pauncefote, and

Twiss who largely determined the legal aspects of British policy at Berlin. In addition, Twiss played an important part in drafting and checking documents for the delegation. He also drafted the constitution of the Congo Free State for Leopold, and in 1887 was made grand commander of the order of Leopold.

Twiss continued to be a regular contributor to the periodical press to the end of his life, contributing to the *Law Quarterly Review* and the *Law Magazine and Review* as well as to the ninth edition of the *Encyclopaedia Britannica*. Difficult circumstances darkened the final years of Twiss's life, and he died on 14 January 1897 at his home, 6 Whittingstall Road, Fulham, after an attack of bronchitis. He was buried at Fulham cemetery on 20 January 1897. Among those who sent their condolences were Queen Victoria and the king of the Belgians.   MICHAEL LOBBAN

Sources *The Times* (16 Jan 1897) · *The Times* (28 April 1872) · *The Times* (19 May 1872) · *The Times* (22 May 1872) · *The Times* (29 Aug 1872) · A. Rivier, obituary, *Revue de Droit International et de Législation Comparée*, 29 (1897), 96–9 · Boase, *Mod. Eng. biog.* · *ILN* (23 Jan 1897), 110 · F. J. C. Hearnshaw, *The centenary history of King's College, London, 1828–1928* (1929) · W. R. Ward, *Victorian Oxford* (1965) · R. S. Thomson, *Fondation de l'état indépendant du Congo* (1933) · S. E. Crowe, *The Berlin West Africa Conference, 1884–85* (1942) · W. R. Louis, 'The Belgian Congo conference', *France and Britain in Africa: imperial rivalry and colonial rule*, ed. P. Gifford and W. R. Louis (1971) · G. D. Squibb, *Doctors' Commons: a history of the College of Advocates and Doctors of Law* (1977) · d. cert.
Archives Harvard U., law school, legal opinions | Bodl. Oxf., corresp. with Sir Thomas Phillipps · LPL, letters to Baroness Burdett-Coutts · LPL, corresp. with A. C. Tait
Likenesses wood-engraving (after photograph by Terrasse), NPG; repro. in *ILN* [*see illus.*]

Twiss, William (1744/5–1827), military engineer, was possibly the child of William Twiss (*d.* 1766), waterman and victualler of Gravesend, Kent, and his wife, Ann; their son William was baptized at St Anne's Church, Westminster, on 23 November 1744. Appointed to the Ordnance office at the Tower of London on 22 July 1760, Twiss worked there until May 1762 and the following July became overseer of the king's works at Gibraltar. He received a commission as practitioner engineer and ensign on 19 November 1763. In 1771, upon promotion to sub-engineer and lieutenant, he returned to England from Gibraltar and was employed on the defences of Portsmouth Dockyard. He married, in 1775, Elizabeth (1740/41–1835), daughter of Richard Wood of Hanger Hill, near Ealing, Middlesex; they had a daughter, Katherine Maria (1776–1827).

In June 1776 Twiss arrived in Canada with General Sir John Burgoyne's army and, having been appointed aide-de-camp to General William Phillips, took part in the operations to clear the insurgent Americans from Quebec province. Sir Guy Carleton, commander-in-chief in Quebec, then made him controller of works for the construction of a fleet to wrest possession of Lake Champlain from the Americans, an objective accomplished with victory at the battle of Valcour Island in October 1776. The following year, when Burgoyne opened his campaign to enter the Hudson valley, Twiss was appointed his commanding engineer, planning the siegeworks that led the Americans

to abandon Fort Ticonderoga on 5 July. Burgoyne's offensive, however, stumbled to disaster and in October 1777, following the surrender at Saratoga, Twiss became a prisoner of war; he was exchanged a few days later. Thereafter, for the next six years, Twiss was employed in strengthening the defences of Canada. He chose the site of Fort Haldimand on Lake Ontario (1778) and supervised the construction of a temporary citadel at Quebec, work on which began in 1779. Twiss also made important improvements to the navigation of the St Lawrence River, particularly by his fortified canal at Côteau-du-Lac. On 18 December 1778 he was promoted captain-lieutenant and in 1781 he became Canada's commanding engineer.

After his return to England in October 1783 Twiss was appointed secretary to the board of land and sea officers (1785), reporting on the defences of Portsmouth and Plymouth dockyards. Promoted captain on 23 March 1786, as engineer at Portsmouth (1785–92) he supervised the construction, among other fortifications, of Fort Cumberland at the entrance of Langston harbour. He then served as commanding royal engineer for the southern military district (1792–1809), and in 1794, having been promoted lieutenant-colonel, he was also appointed lieutenant-governor of the Royal Military Academy at Woolwich. During the 1790s the threat of French invasion kept Twiss busy on the south coast, and he oversaw the strengthening of the eastern defences of Dover Castle with four new bastions. In September 1799 he sailed as replacement commanding royal engineer to the duke of York's expedition to the Netherlands, the previous incumbent having been killed, and after returning home in November he was promoted colonel on 1 January 1800. He subsequently made tours of the Channel Islands (1800) and Ireland (1802) in order to report upon their defences. During the heightened danger of French invasion in 1803 he again looked to the defences of Dover and, on his recommendation, the western heights overlooking the town were fortified. He also sank the grand shaft to connect the barracks on the western heights with the town below. Appointed brigadier-general on 11 February 1804, he was instrumental in helping achieve—despite the dilatoriness of the Ordnance board—the construction between 1805 and 1808 of a chain of seventy-three Martello towers to guard landing points in Kent and Sussex.

Twiss had been promoted major-general on 30 October 1805, and on 24 June 1809 he became colonel-commandant of the corps of Royal Engineers. He was promoted lieutenant-general in 1812 and full general on 27 May 1825. After his retirement in 1810 Twiss bought a home at Myrtle Grove, Bingley, in the West Riding of Yorkshire. A man of substance, he gave £340 to Bingley national school in 1814, employed eight gardeners, and was carried about town in a sedan by two liveried servants. Twiss died aged eighty-two on 14 March 1827 at Harden Grange, Bingley, the home of his son-in-law, Walker Ferrand, who inherited his fortune worth between £7000 and £8000 a year. He was buried on 21 March in the parish church of All Saints, Bingley. The bas relief-portrait on his memorial tablet reveals Twiss to have been of strongly aviform appearance, with a great beak of a nose and a receding forehead. ALASTAIR W. MASSIE

Sources J. Philippart, ed., *The royal military calendar*, 3rd edn, 5 vols. (1820) · Royal Engineers' Library, Chatham, Conolly MSS · *DCB*, vol. 6 · C. S. Akers, 'Historical sketch of the fortifications of Dover', *Professional Papers of the Corps of Royal Engineers*, occasional papers, 12 (1886), 1–65 · H. Speight, *Chronicles and stories of Bingley and district*, 4th edn (1904) · S. Sutcliffe, *Martello towers* (1972) · S. G. P. Ward, 'Defence works in Britain, 1803–1805', *Journal of the Society for Army Historical Research*, 27 (1949), 18–37 · registers, Bingley, All Saints' Church, W. Yorks. AS, Bradford [burial], 1827, 1835 · PRO, PROB 11/924/471; PROB 11/1726/332 · register, Soho, St Anne's, 1744, City Westm. AC [baptism] · register, St Martin-in-the-Fields, 1775, City Westm. AC [marriage] · *GM*, 1st ser., 97/1 (1827), 364–5 · J. H. Turner, *Ancient Bingley* (1897)

Archives U. Durham L., letters to first Earl Grey

Likenesses memorial tablet, All Saints' Church, Bingley, West Yorkshire

Wealth at death £7000–8000 p.a.: Speight, *Chronicles*, 322

Twisse, William (1577/8–1646), theologian, was born at Speenlands in Speen, near Newbury, Berkshire, son of William Twisse, a successful clothier and grandson of an immigrant from Germany. Among his uncles were Thomas Bilson (1547–1616), warden of Winchester College and later bishop of Worcester (1596) and Winchester (1597), and the wit John Hoskins. As a youth Twisse showed remarkable intelligence; he probably also had a rebellious streak, and so his father sent him in 1590, aged twelve, to Winchester College. Twisse later admitted that he was a 'very wicked boy' at Winchester, but was converted to godly living when the 'phantom of a rakehelly boy', whom he recognized as a schoolfellow, came to him in a dream and said 'I am damned' (Wood, *Ath. Oxon.*, 3.169). In 1596 Twisse was admitted to New College, Oxford, as a probationer fellow, being admitted to the full fellowship on 11 March 1599. A student of George Abbot, later archbishop of Canterbury, he graduated BA on 14 October 1600, and proceeded MA on 12 June 1604, BD on 8 July 1612, and DD on 5 July 1614. Twisse gained the reputation of being an erudite scholar, especially in controversial theology. He assisted Sir Henry Savile in the publication of Thomas Bradwardine's *De causa Dei contra Pelagium* and preached catechetical lectures at New College on Thursdays. He also drew crowds to hear his sermons at St Aldate's in Oxford. However, Wood remarks that he was remembered by some Oxford colleagues as being 'hot headed and restless' (ibid., 3.170). Even Samuel Clarke, the puritan biographer, accounted Twisse a touch naïve and bookish.

Twisse's reputation at Oxford was confirmed in an incident of 1613 involving the baptism of a Jew. Joseph Barnet had been employed as a Hebrew tutor at Oxford and had informed Arthur Lake, the warden of New College, that he wished to convert to Christianity. A Sunday was arranged for the baptism and Twisse was asked to preach a sermon celebrating the event. However, Barnet changed his mind and tried to flee Oxford the day before his baptism. He was captured, but refused to be baptized. Twisse altered his sermon to an antisemitic theme which 'shewed God's judgment upon that perverse Nation and People [i.e. the

William Twisse (1577/8–1646), by Thomas Trotter, pubd 1783 (after unknown artist, c.1644)

Jews]' (Clarke, 14). In an age before religious tolerance, Twisse's sermon was applauded by the dons of Oxford.

Twisse's new-found standing caught the attention of James I in the summer of 1613, and he instructed that Twisse should become the chaplain to his daughter Elizabeth, princess palatine. Twisse obeyed the king and went to Heidelberg, profitably consulting with the German theologians of the city's university. However, the service turned out to be short and he returned to England after two months in Heidelberg. On 18 September the fellows of New College presented Twisse to the rectory of Newton Longvill, Buckinghamshire; he was licensed preacher in 1617. By 1615 he had married his first wife, possibly Frances, daughter of Barnabas Colnett of Combley, Isle of Wight; their eldest son, Robert, was born in late 1615 or early 1616. In October 1620 the magistrates of Newbury offered Twisse the town living, which he accepted. Although he did not neglect his flock, he spent much time studying the various controversies of the day. He seems to have been comfortable with his role as a town preacher and retiring scholar, and steadfastly refused the offer of a number of prominent positions including the provostship of Winchester, one of the prebends of Winchester Cathedral, and the divinity chair at the University of Franeker. Another reason for this lack of ambition seems to have been a desire to remain relatively free of episcopal influence. He was, however, tempted by the offer of Robert Rich, second earl of Warwick, of the living at Benefield, Northamptonshire. It promised the society of the famous godly ministers of Northamptonshire as well as a less onerous living. However, in order to leave Newbury, a crown living, Twisse needed the permission of the king. He consulted William Laud, a friend from Oxford days, who promised to support his supplication, but on the advice of Bishop John Davenant of Salisbury the king ruled against Twisse taking the position in Northamptonshire. Charles was, however, indulgent to Twisse in other matters and protected him from prosecution for not obeying the Book of Sports. Twisse or his churchwardens also defied official attempts in the 1630s to erect a railed altar at Newbury. On 11 November 1635 he seems to have married at West Meon, Hampshire, Amye, daughter of Robert *Moor (1567/8–1640), rector there, although it is conceivable that this marriage took place a decade earlier. His new father-in-law, also a product of Winchester College and New College, had been a prebendary of Winchester since 1613 and frequently clashed with Bishop Richard Neile over ceremonies.

The reason for the toleration of Twisse's puritanism was his pre-eminence as a controversialist theologian. Even the Anglican polemicist Anthony Wood described him as 'the mightiest man' in the controversies of his age (Wood, *Ath. Oxon.*, 171). Although Twisse had helped edit Bradwardine's works, his first major foray into controversy came in 1631 when he wrote a long critique of the first volume of Thomas Jackson's commentary on the creed, entitled a *Treatise of the Divine Essence and Attributes* (1628). Jackson, who was president of Corpus Christi College, Oxford, and a friend of Bishop Neile had written his commentary of the creed from a neoplatonic perspective. This work stressed the ability of humans to recognize divine truths in nature and of the human will to capture a sense of divine essence. To Twisse, schooled in the supralapsarian Calvinism of William Perkins and the rigorous logic of Aristotle and the medieval schoolmen, Jackson's work was fundamentally heretical. In *A Discourse of D. Jackson's Vanity*, Twisse stated that Jackson's thought was 'more fowle than Arminius himselfe' (p. 3). Twisse marshalled all the wordplay and syllogistic reasoning available to assail Jackson's work. It has been suggested that Twisse used 'a perverse literalness … designed to ridicule Jackson's metaphorical turn of phrase' (Hutton, 649). However, Twisse emerged from the debate a champion of Calvinist orthodoxy and a scourge of the new Pelagianism.

Twisse's attack on Jackson gave him the confidence to enter the theological controversies of the European stage. In 1632 he published *Vindiciae gratiae potestatis ac providentiae Dei*, a defence of William Perkins's predestinarianism against the critique of Jacobus Arminius. This won him great praise, and in 1639 he wrote *De scientia media*, a work attacking the Jesuits Gabriel Penothus and Francisco Suarez. This work put Twisse at the centre of the heated debate between the Jesuits and the Molinists concerning the freedom of the human will. Twisse's works characteristically stressed the divine decree of predestination and the omnipotence of divine grace and denigrated the power of the human will. This work evoked the reply of Michael Annat, the chancellor of Louvain, as well as

others. The effect of Twisse's foray into European controversy was to distinguish him as one of the most prominent theologians in England; this was especially the case among the puritans.

Twisse later put his pen to demolishing the views of John Goodwin, the Arminian 'sect master' of Coleman Street, and entered debates with the Independents Thomas Goodwin and John Cotton on their variations of the doctrine of justification. Twisse was also a friend of Joseph Mead, and in the early 1640s edited and wrote prefaces to two of Mead's works of eschatology.

In the spring of 1641 Twisse was one of the delegates to the House of Lords committee chaired by Bishop John Williams. This committee sought a critical review of the innovations of Archbishop Laud and the Durham House group, but failed to reach any profitable settlement. From the outbreak of the first civil war, Twisse allied with parliament. He remained in Newbury until the royalists captured it. Prince Rupert, its conqueror, son of Twisse's one-time employer, Elizabeth of Bohemia, failed in his courteous attempts to convince him of the virtue of supporting the king. Twisse fled Newbury for London, where he was put to parliament's service and became one of the three puritan lecturers of the parish of St Andrew Holborn.

In June 1643 Twisse was chosen as a delegate to the Westminster assembly and was subsequently elected as its prolocutor. Although Anthony Wood later charged him with falling in with the presbyterian radicals, it is clear that he was among the English divines who sought a reform of the episcopacy rather than a root and branch revolution of the church. Twisse was, however, old and sickly by the time of the assembly, and his faculties were escaping him. Robert Baillie, the Scots commissioner and presbyterian stalwart, wrote that while Twisse was 'beloved of all, and highlie esteemed', he was 'merely bookish' and 'among the unfittest of all the company for any action'. Baillie thought the appointment of Twisse a 'canny convoyance of these who guides matters for their own interest to plant such a man of purpose in the chaire' (Baillie, 2.108). Baillie also noted that Twisse did not favour extemporary prayer and had difficulty departing from the prayer book. Baillie's assessment is characteristically harsh and perhaps a little unfair; at the beginning of the debate, Twisse defended his views on the justification of faith and appealed against the stripping of the Church of England of its lands. He also upheld the Book of Common Prayer. However, in January 1645 his poor health led him to concede that he was unfit to continue in the chair of the assembly; Cornelius Burges stepped into his place as acting prolocutor.

On 30 March 1645 Twisse fainted while preaching in the pulpit of St Andrew's, Holborn. He took to his bed at his house in Holborn and died on 20 July 1646. He was buried on 24 July at Westminster Abbey in a state funeral attended by the members of both houses of parliament. Twisse's funeral sermon was preached by his lifelong friend and colleague Dr John Harris, the warden of Winchester College. The sermon was on the topic of Joshua 1:

2, 'Moses my servant is dead'. However, after the Restoration a royal proclamation ordered on 9 September 1661 that for supporting parliament Twisse's corpse, as well as the bodies of Thomas May, William Strong, and Stephen Marshall, should be disinterred and buried in a large pit in the churchyard of St Margaret's Church in Westminster.

In his will, dated 9 September 1645 and 30 June 1646, Twisse, apparently by this time again a widower, mentioned seven children: two married daughters, Elizabeth Shoen and Marie Hodges; and William, Francis or Frances, Robert, Joseph, and Constance. The inheritance of the three youngest children was placed in the hands of Twisse's aunt, Marie Moore of London. William was a fellow of New College, Oxford, between 1635 and 1650; Robert (*bap.* 1627, *d.* 1675) preached a sermon in Christ Church, Westminster, in 1665 on the martyrdom of Charles I, but was later ejected from his rectory at Buscot, Berkshire. Twisse appears to have left a fairly substantial estate; his will disposes the manor of Ashampstead in Berkshire, as well as other property. However, it appears that Twisse, deprived of the living of Newbury, suffered an acute cash flow crisis in his later years. On his deathbed parliament voted him a concession of £100 (which probably was never paid), and the assembly sent him a further £10. Twisse's children were promised a grant of £1000 by parliament at his death, but, as with so many of parliament's debts, the money was never paid. E. C. VERNON

Sources S. Clark [S. Clarke], *The lives of sundry eminent persons in this later age* (1683) · Wood, *Ath. Oxon.*, 3.169–72 · S. Hutton, 'Thomas Jackson, Oxford Platonist, and William Twisse, Aristotelian', *Journal of the History of Ideas*, 39 (1978), 635–52 · R. S. Paul, *The assembly of the Lord: politics and religion in the Westminster assembly and the 'Grand debate'* (1985) · *Hist. U. Oxf.* 4: *17th-cent. Oxf.* · *The letters and journals of Robert Baillie*, ed. D. Laing, 3 vols. (1841–2) · Foster, *Alum. Oxon.* · *Calamy rev.*, 499 · N. Tyacke, 'Anglican attitudes', *Journal of British Studies*, 35 (1996), 160 · *DNB* · *IGI*
Likenesses T. Trotter, line engraving, pubd 1783 (after unknown artist, *c.*1644), NPG [*see illus.*] · oils, Newbury parish church
Wealth at death Real estate at Ashampstead, Berkshire; other realty and personalty

Twm o'r Nant. *See* Edwards, Thomas (1738–1810).

Twm Siôn Cati. *See* Jones, Thomas (1532–1608/9).

Twort, Frederick William (1877–1950), microbiologist, was born on 22 October 1877 in Camberley, Surrey, the eldest of six sons and the second of the eleven children of Dr William Henry Twort, general practitioner, of Camberley, and his wife, Elizabeth Crampton, only child of Joseph Crampton Webster, engineer, of London. He was educated at Tomlinson's School, Woking, and St Thomas's Hospital, London, and qualified LRCP, MRCS, in 1900.

In 1901 Twort became an assistant in the clinical laboratory at St Thomas's Hospital and in December that year was appointed assistant to William Bulloch, bacteriologist at the London Hospital, Whitechapel. Here he gained valuable experience and, though occupied with much routine work, commenced innovative research. His study of bacterial fermentation of glucosides won the London University Rogers prize (jointly) in 1908. He demonstrated bacterial variability and adaptability and formulated his lifelong belief that disease-producing organisms had evolved from non-pathogenic ancestors. He also showed that the glucoside ericolin acted as a selective inhibitor of bacterial growth, thus aiding the isolation of pure cultures.

In 1909 Twort was appointed superintendent of the Brown Animal Sanatory Institution in London, where he remained until its destruction by bombing in 1944. Relative isolation suited his character and he followed his own ideas with considerable success. He demonstrated that supplementation of media with an 'essential substance' extracted from dead tubercle bacilli permitted growth of Johne's bacillus and possibly the leprosy bacillus. With his veterinary colleague George Ingram he wrote *A Monograph on Johne's Disease of Cattle* (1913).

Twort's most important contribution to microbiology was his discovery of bacteriophage. He noticed that colonies of micrococci had become transparent and that transfer of this material to a growing colony reproduced the condition. This transmissible lysis, later known as the Twort–d'Hérelle phenomenon, is of central importance to molecular biology. A paper by Twort in 1915 illustrates his cautious approach to research, as he lists several possible explanations for the phenomenon, rather than risk premature judgement. Owing to war and limited facilities he left exploitation of his discoveries to others. In the First World War he served in the Royal Army Medical Corps as temporary captain in charge of the base laboratory at Salonika in 1916, and later in Northern Ireland as bacteriologist in 1918. He married Dorothy Mary, eldest daughter of Frederick J. Banister, an architect, in 1919. They had a son and three daughters.

In 1929 Twort was elected FRS and in 1931 he became professor of bacteriology at London University. Brown Institution trust funds were never adequate, but Twort preferred impecunious independence. When, after fifteen years, a Medical Research Council grant was withdrawn, he unsuccessfully lodged a petition of right against the crown in 1937.

Twort was a reserved and somewhat unworldly man. However, over scientific matters he could be roused to considerable passion and was often tactless. He constructed much of his own research apparatus, experimented with violin making, designed novel coils to improve wireless reception, and was a keen horticulturist. He died at his home, The Wilderness, Gordon Road, Camberley, Surrey, on 20 March 1950. MICHAEL BEVAN

Sources P. Fildes, *Obits. FRS*, 7 (1950–51), 505–17 · G. Wilson, 'The Brown Animal Sanatory Institution', *Journal of Hygiene*, 82 (1979) · private information (1993)
Likenesses W. Stoneman, photograph, RS · photographs, repro. in A. Twort, *In focus, and out of step: a biography of Frederick William Twort FRS, 1877–1950* (1993)
Wealth at death £4454 17*s.* 10*d.*: probate, 19 May 1950, *CGPLA Eng. & Wales*

Twyford, Joshua (*bap.* 1640, *d.* 1729), potter, is thought to have been born at Shelton, near Stoke-on-Trent, a member of a dynastic Staffordshire potting family. He was baptized on 6 December 1640 at Stoke-on-Trent, the son of

William Twyford and his wife, Margaret. Little is known of his life apart from those legends promulgated by Simeon Shaw's *History of the Staffordshire Potteries* (1829), and repeated by Llewellyn Jewitt and others. These relied heavily on local oral history. According to Shaw, when the Dutch brothers John Philip and David Elers began, in the greatest secrecy, to make red stoneware near an excellent source of red clay at Bradwell Wood in the early 1690s, 'a person named Twyford, from Shelton, obtained employment under them, and had sufficient prudence to manifest entire carelessness and indifference to every operation he witnessed or participated' (Shaw, 119). Shaw went on to claim that both Twyford and Joshua Astbury by feigning stupidity discovered the Elerses' secrets of making red stoneware and salt-glazed stoneware, and that thereafter both 'commenced and carried forward manufactories of Red Porcelain, and White Pottery glazed with salt, amidst many small thatched dwellings in Shelton', and that 'at first both these persons made Red, Crouch, and White Stone Wares' (ibid., 121–2, 126). There is no reason to doubt that both Twyford and Astbury (a John Astbury is recorded as potter at Shelton, 1728–44) set up potteries at Shelton, perhaps in partnership and perhaps as early as 1717 (*VCH Staffordshire*, 8.164). It is also probable that they were both pioneers in new forms of Staffordshire pottery, notably the red lead-glazed earthenware with applied white sprigged decoration which was widely manufactured in Staffordshire during the 1730s and 1740s. Although modern archaeology discourages the use of the old collectors' generic term 'Astbury Ware', none the less excavations at Shelton Farm in recent years have yielded large amounts of this redware. Of Shaw's other statements, there is no proof that the Elerses employed either Twyford or Astbury, and all the present evidence points to independent, and much later, reinvention of red stoneware in Staffordshire towards the middle of the eighteenth century. As for salt-glazed stoneware, excavations on the Bradwell Wood pottery site have revealed only unglazed red stoneware; and although David Elers had learned the process of salt-glazing while residing at Cologne, it is almost certain that the Elerses' brown stoneware was confined to their pottery at Vauxhall in London. Thus the claim (which was perhaps a transposed and garbled version of John Dwight's legal action against Joshua Astbury in 1697 for stealing secrets from his Fulham pottery) that Twyford, by cunning industrial espionage, had outwitted two unpopular Dutch immigrants and thereby introduced two highly important branches of ceramic manufacture to Staffordshire is now completely disproved. He remains, however, an important if shadowy early eighteenth-century maker of Staffordshire fine earthenware and stoneware, and one whose name will always be linked with Astbury and the red earthenwares with which he is associated. He was buried at Stoke-on-Trent parish church in 1729.   ROBIN HILDYARD

Sources S. Shaw, *History of the Staffordshire potteries* (1829) · L. F. W. Jewitt, *The ceramic art of Great Britain, from pre-historic times*, 2 vols. (1878) · *VCH Staffordshire*, vol. 8 · D. Barker, *The archaeology of an 18th-century potworks: excavations at Shelton Farm* [forthcoming] · IGI

Twyford, Sir Nicholas (d. **1390/91**), goldsmith and mayor of London, may have taken his name from Twyford in Buckinghamshire—his known kinsmen included Thomas Conelee of Buckinghamshire. The most prominent and prosperous goldsmith during the period 1360–90, Twyford was frequently involved in business dealings with John of Gaunt, duke of Lancaster, and Richard II, conducting such major transactions as the sale of silver basins, pots, and other articles to the city of London for a present to the prince of Wales, to a total value of £881 10s. 2d. In 1378 he was supplier of all the Christmas and new year gifts given by Richard II at a cost of £202 5s. 4d.; in 1384 he purchased a quantity of 'old and broken vessels of white silver' for £389 11s. 8d.; in 1385 he was described as *aurifaber regis* ('King's goldsmith'). Twyford came to enjoy a level of prosperity that found him possessed of a new house in the parish of St John Zachary at his death and able to bequeath income from additional properties to the wardens of the Goldsmiths.

From 1382 Twyford is styled 'knight' in municipal records, suggesting that he was one of the city officials thus rewarded by Richard II for his loyalty during the rising of 1381. Court contacts and success in a prominent craft outside the immediate orbit of Nicholas Brembre's group of victuallers and wool staplers served as a springboard for Twyford's entry into London politics. In that sphere he maintained a cautious distance from the respective followings of Brembre and the latter's adversary, the draper John Northampton (though he was more frequently allied with Northampton). He was eventually among those leaders who forged a united front in defence of city interests when faced with conflicts between crown and aristocracy in the later 1380s, and between King Richard and the city itself in the early 1390s.

Twyford served as alderman for Coleman Street in 1375–7 and 1387–8, for Farringdon in 1378 and 1380, for Lime Street in 1383, and for Aldersgate in 1388–91. He was warden of the Goldsmiths' Company in 1358, and prime warden in 1365, 1368, 1371, and 1374. His début as an influential force in city politics occurred on 1 August 1376, when—as a member of a reformist group in which John Northampton was prominent—he endorsed removal from office of those city figures convicted during that year by the Good Parliament, and participated in a new arrangement (which was to prevail until 1384) whereby members of the common council would be chosen from craft guilds rather than wards. On 6 June 1377 he was appointed royal poll tax commissioner, and on 21 September 1377 the commonalty of the city elected him sheriff. In that capacity he came into prompt conflict with the then mayor, Nicholas Brembre, who was a grocer, when he attempted to shield a follower whom the mayor had arrested in connection with a conflict between goldsmiths and grocers (specifically, pepperers) in Cheapside. Removed from office, Twyford was immediately restored on condition of a 500 mark bond, with a group of goldsmiths, including Adam Bamme and John Fraunceys, standing surety. At the mayoral election of 13 October 1384 he was the candidate opposing Nicholas Brembre's bid for a second consecutive term. According to both the Westminster chronicler, and also to petitions later submitted to parliament, Brembre had taken the precaution of stationing armed adherents about the Guildhall. When chanting of 'Twyford! Twyford!' and 'Brembre! Brembre!' broke out between the two parties, the armed men rushed forth to disperse Twyford's followers and give the election to his rival.

Twyford must not, however, be seen only as an opponent of Brembre and that handful of victuallers and wool traders who controlled London affairs in the later fourteenth century; at times of crisis various groups and interests showed themselves well able to fashion a united front on their own behalf. With the successful initiative of the lords opposed to Richard II in and around the Merciless Parliament of December 1387 – May 1388 Brembre was effectively deserted by his own followers, meeting his death in February 1388. On 21 September 1388, mercer (and sometime Northampton supporter) Thomas Austin was elected sheriff by the commonalty. On 12 October 1388 the king sent a letter of privy seal to city officials, urging 'the peaceable election of a trusty and loyal mayor for the year coming' (Sharpe, *Calendar of Letter-Books*, H.334). The next day Twyford was elected mayor. One of his strife-reducing measures (which may not ultimately have been enforced) was to agree that the common council should be chosen by the mayor and aldermen, rather than elected by either the guilds or the wards.

Twyford died in either 1390 or 1391. No children are recorded of his marriage to Margery, who after his death married Drew Barantyn (d. 1415), also a prosperous goldsmith who was many times alderman. Twyford's will provided for anniversaries and memorials for himself and his wife, under the supervision of the rector of St John Zachary, London (where he and Margery were to be buried), and for substantial charitable bequests, as well as bequeathing lands in Tottenham and elsewhere in Middlesex to his kinsman John Twyford, esquire. Nevertheless, Barantyn was later to bequeath £60 'to the poor kinsfolk of Nicholas Twyford' (Reddaway and Walker, 279).   PAUL STROHM

Sources R. R. Sharpe, ed., *Calendar of letter-books preserved in the archives of the corporation of the City of London*, [12 vols.] (1899–1912), vols. G–H • A. H. Thomas and P. E. Jones, eds., *Calendar of plea and memoranda rolls preserved among the archives of the corporation of the City of London at the Guildhall*, 2–3 (1929–32) • R. R. Sharpe, ed., *Calendar of wills proved and enrolled in the court of husting, London, AD 1258 – AD 1688*, 2 (1890) • T. F. Reddaway, *The early history of the Goldsmiths' Company, 1327–1509*, ed. L. E. M. Walker (1975) • R. Bird, *The turbulent London of Richard II* (1949) • S. L. Thrupp, *The merchant class of medieval London, 1300–1500* (1948) • H. T. Riley, ed., *Memorials of London and London life in the XIIIth, XIVth, and XVth centuries* (1868) • L. C. Hector and B. F. Harvey, eds. and trans., *The Westminster chronicle, 1381–1394*, OMT (1982) • *Chronicon Henrici Knighton, vel Cnitthon, monachi Leycestrensis*, ed. J. R. Lumby, 2 vols., Rolls Series, 92 (1889–95) • P. Nightingale, *A medieval mercantile community: the Grocers' Company and the politics and trade of London, 1000–1485* (1995) • *RotP*, vol. 3
Wealth at death approx. £2000: will

Twyman, Frank (1876–1959), designer of optical instruments, was born at Canterbury on 17 November 1876, the seventh of nine children of George Edmund Twyman,

rope maker, and his wife, Jane Lefevre. He was educated at the Simon Langton School, Canterbury, and in 1892 went to London to attend a two-year course in electrical engineering at Finsbury Technical College, where he won the Siemens scholarship to the Central Technical College, South Kensington, later part of Imperial College. Twyman made the most of his student days. Always fond of music, he frequented concert halls and theatres, read widely, and joined societies whose lectures and activities furthered his technical and musical education. He kept fit in the gymnasium, and somehow still found time to enjoy the company of his many friends and family members living in and around London.

In 1897 Twyman obtained a post testing telephone cables with the Fowler Waring Cables Company but found night-shift work uncongenial. He left in February 1898 to become scientific assistant, at 25s. a week, to Otto Hilger, optical instrument maker, who had followed his brother Adam Hilger as head of their business in Camden Town in 1897. When Otto Hilger died in 1902 Twyman succeeded him as managing director. The company was incorporated as Adam Hilger Ltd in 1904, with Twyman continuing as managing director until 1946. He then became chairman, and took on the additional role of technical adviser to instrument making firm E. R. Watts. When the two firms were amalgamated in 1948 to form Hilger and Watts, he became a director until 1952, and served thereafter as technical adviser until his death. On 12 June 1906 Twyman married Phillipine Katherine Elisabeth (b. 1885/6), née Hilger, daughter of his former employer; they had three daughters and a son whose death in a motorcycle accident while still an undergraduate was a grievous blow.

It was from Otto Hilger that Twyman learned the fundamentals of optical design in which he himself later became an expert. When he joined Hilgers, the firm relied on two types of product: optical parts, sold mainly to rangefinder manufacturers Barr and Stroud, and specialized finished instruments, including spectrometers. Until 1910 Twyman made designs and working drawings and superintended the construction of all new instruments. Among these were the constant deviation wavelength spectrometer (1902), and the quartz spectrograph (1910) for work in the ultraviolet part of the spectrum. Before the First World War, Barr and Stroud started to make their own optical parts, which might have had grave repercussions for Hilgers. Partly in response, Twyman visited the United States to explore new markets. In due course, use of Hilgers' large quartz spectrograph by the American Brass Company helped publicize the potential of Hilger instruments for metallurgical analysis. However, at the end of the war, industrial spectroscopy was in its infancy and, to safeguard the business further, Twyman sold a significant holding in Hilgers to Thomas Cooke & Sons of York. It transpired that, unknown to Twyman, Vickers actually held the majority of the shares in Thomas Cooke and the new parent company wished to bring Hilgers into line with the rest of its organization. Twyman did not believe this to be in the best interests of his firm and, in 1926, he bought back the shares.

Twyman became an acknowledged authority in the design of optical instruments of most kinds, and he was also an expert in the means of manufacture. He had introduced the use of test or proof plates early in his association with Hilger. Between 1918 and 1923, as a result of his collaboration with Alfred Green, the foreman of the optical shop, the Michelson interferometer became the Twyman–Green interferometer, used for testing the profiles of the surfaces of optical components. The introduction of this instrument into the process of instrument testing was tremendously important and its use became universal in optical practice. Twyman was awarded the Duddell medal of the Physical Society (1927) and the John Price Wetherill medal of the Franklin Institute (1926). He was interested also in the materials of optical instruments, particularly in glass. During the First World War, in collaboration with Chance Brothers, he developed new techniques for studying the annealing of glass, based on the polarization of light, which ensured the maintenance of vital supplies which had hitherto all come from Germany. His book *Prism and Lens Making* (1943) was for many years a standard work of reference in the field.

Twyman was an approachable, friendly man. He was very interested in young people, especially in apprenticeship and apprentices, and he delighted in fine craftsmanship. Despite the expansion of his business interests, he claimed to have remained a scientist at heart and demonstrated this by freely lending new apparatus to young research workers on terms sometimes too generous even for his very tolerant business associates. His hobby was music. He once said that, had he been allowed to choose as a young man, he would have wished to become a musician. Later in life he often shut himself in his office during lunch hours and played his violin, telling visitors privileged to intrude into these sessions that he was on the way to becoming a third-class amateur instead of a third-class professional. He read widely and was a keen gardener. He was interested in the theatre, and loved a good story. Those who knew him respected him for his kindness and helpfulness, but his influence on optical design and optical manufacture is his memorial. He was president of the Optical Society (1930–31) and was a founder member of the Institute of Physics. He received the gold medal of the Society of Applied Spectroscopists of the United States in 1956. Twyman died at his home, 41 Tavistock Court, St Pancras, London, on 6 March 1959.

C. B. Allsopp, *rev.* Mari E. W. Williams

Sources F. Twyman, *An east Kent family* (1956) · *The Times* (10 March 1959) · A. C. Menzies, *Memoirs FRS*, 5 (1959), 269–79 · A. C. Menzies, *Nature*, 183 (1959), 1158–9 · d. cert. · m. cert.
Archives Sci. Mus., Adam Hilger papers
Likenesses three photographs, 1881–1953, repro. in Twyman, *An east Kent family* · photograph, 1929, repro. in *Transactions of the Optical Society*, 31 (1929–30), 113 · W. Stoneman, photograph, 1938, NPG · photograph, repro. in Menzies, *Memoirs FRS*
Wealth at death £47,741 3s. 2d.: probate, 13 May 1959, *CGPLA Eng. & Wales*

Twyn, John (*bap.* 1619, *d.* 1664), printer, was the eldest child of Robert Twyn, a yeoman of Kelshall, Hertfordshire, and his wife, Jane Warren. He was baptized at Kelshall on 14 March 1619. He was bound as an apprentice on 24 August 1633 to the London printer William Stansby and he took up his freedom in the trade on 7 September 1640. Little is known of Twyn's personal circumstances, except that he was by 1662 widowed and caring for his four small children. He was also a nonconformist of unknown hue, refusing the sacrament before he was executed as he was against the forms of the Church of England.

In 1647 Twyn became manager of the king's printing house in Edinburgh following its acquisition by the Stationers' Company. He was still resident in Scotland in 1650 but he had returned by 1658 to London, where he had premises in Cloth Fair. During his career he entered only one work in the Stationers' register, *The Three Books of Hermas* in 1661, although he was also involved in printing editions of the Bible, Hooker's *Ecclesiastical Polity*, and John Chishull's *The Danger of being Almost a Christian*.

Twyn was briefly imprisoned and he had a press seized in the early years of the Restoration. In seeking his release he pledged never to print anything against the king, but early on 7 October 1663 his premises were entered by Roger L'Estrange, Charles II's recently appointed surveyor of the press, who discovered printed sheets of *A Treatise of the Execution of Justice*, which asserted the godly duty of the people to oust the 'Bloody and Oppressing' house of Stuart (*Treatise*, 15). Twyn's trial for high treason began at the Old Bailey on 20 February 1664, accompanied by the prosecution for seditious libel of bookseller Thomas Brewster, printer Simon Dover, and bookbinder Nathan Brooks for the *Speeches and Prayers* of the regicides and, in Brewster's case, for *A Phenix, or, The Solemn League and Covenant*: the three men tried for libel were pilloried and fined.

The trial judge, Sir Robert Hyde, said the *Treatise of the Execution of Justice* was 'as High a Treason as can be Committed' (*Exact Narrative*, 31). The trial evidence and surviving pages of the seized tract (PRO, SP 29/88/76) indicate that Twyn's version was substantially similar although not identical to the 32-page edition which subsequently circulated. The *Treatise* used scriptural injunction and Biblical precedent to assert the right and duty of the people to resist a magistrate who contravened the law of God by oppressing the innocent. Charles I had 'made poor England Groan' by episcopal tyranny and illegal taxes, leading to bloody war. But now the people's war against 'Antichrist', to throw off the 'Yoak of this present Tyrant', was close at hand (*Treatise*, 15, 25–32; PRO, SP 29/88/76). Twyn denied having known the content of the book but admitted that he had agreed to print 1000 copies for the publisher Giles Calvert because he needed money. He was said to have received 40s. in part-payment, having dispatched printed sheets to Calvert's wife, Elizabeth. However, L'Estrange, supported by other witnesses, insisted that Twyn had read the book and had declared it 'mettlesome stuffe, the man was a hot fiery man that wrote it' (*Exact Narrative*, 13). It was alleged that the publication of the *Treatise* was to have been the signal for a rising by waiting rebels on 12 October. Twyn declined to reveal the author of the anonymous work. He was found guilty by a jury that included the printers Richard Royston and Thomas Roy-croft and he was sentenced by Hyde to be hanged, disem-bowelled, and quartered. Twyne was executed at Tyburn on 24 February; his head was displayed over Ludgate and his quarters over other city gates.   GEOFF KEMP

Sources *A treatise of the execution of justice* (1663?) · *An exact narrative of the tryal and condemnation of John Twyn* (1664) · *State trials*, 6.513–39 · *CSP dom.*, 1641–3, 427; 1663–4, 292, 407 · parish register, Kels-hall, Herts. ALS, D/P 60–36 · D. F. McKenzie, ed., *Stationers' Company apprentices*, [1]: 1605–1640 (1961) · Arber, *Regs. Stationers* · C. Blagden, *The Stationers' Company: a history, 1403–1959* (1960) · H. G. Aldis, *A list of books printed in Scotland before 1700* (1904) · M. Wood, ed., *Extracts from the records of the burgh of Edinburgh, 1642–1655*, [9] (1938) · P. G. Morrison, *Index of printers, publishers and booksellers in Donald Wing's 'Short-title catalogue of books … 1641–1700'* (1955) · H. R. Plomer and others, *A dictionary of the booksellers and printers who were at work in England, Scotland, and Ireland from 1641 to 1667* (1907) · Greaves & Zaller, *BDBR* · PRO, SP 29/88/76

Twyne, Brian (1581–1644), antiquary, was born at South-wark, Surrey, on or about 25 July 1581, one of four known children and the only son to reach maturity of Thomas *Twyne (1543–1613), physician, and his wife, probably Joan Pumfrett (*d.* in or after 1613), and grandson of John *Twyne (*c.*1505–1581), a notable scholar and antiquary. He probably studied at Lewes grammar school and was elected a scholar of Corpus Christi College, Oxford, on 13 December 1594, matriculating about 6 February 1596. Having graduated BA on 23 July 1599 he was unsuccess-fully recommended by his father's patron, the earl of Dor-set, for a Merton College fellowship in 1601. Although kept short of money by his father, he pursued a wide range of studies, including Hebrew, French, and Italian. Taught natural philosophy by Thomas Allen of Gloucester Hall, an acquaintance of his father and a lasting influence, he also absorbed the latest knowledge in the mathematical sciences including astronomy and navigation, and became a defender of Copernicus, Kepler, and Galileo.

Twyne proceeded MA on 9 July 1603. He was elected a probationer fellow of his college in January 1606 and the following year was involved in factional disputes with Daniel Featley. After his ordination as deacon on 20 Sep-tember and as priest on 20 December 1607, his fellowship was confirmed. Hopes of a chaplaincy to Dorset were dashed by his patron's death in April 1608. That year his only significant publication, *Antiquitatis academiae Oxonien-sis apologia*, appeared. Dedicated to Robert Sackville, sec-ond earl of Dorset, it was the first printed history of the university and sought to prove, against John Caius, that Oxford was older than Cambridge. His arguments, like those of his protagonist, were fundamentally flawed, but the work exhibited such wide reading that some attrib-uted it to Thomas Allen and Miles Windsor.

Twyne proceeded BD on 25 June 1610, and in 1612 con-sidered proceeding DD but he never did. His theological position is uncertain: although he had sided with anti-Calvinists in the non-theological faction of 1607, his note-books show him basically Calvinist years later.

In 1613 Twyne contributed verse to a volume commem-orating Sir Thomas Bodley, to whose Oxford library his father had sent books. As one of very few readers of manu-scripts there, he valued Bodley's benefaction, although he was critical of the librarian, Thomas James. On his father's death in the same year Twyne probably inherited prop-erty. Although inducted on 15 March 1614 by presentation of Richard Sackville, third earl of Dorset, to the vicarage of Rye, Sussex, he remained in Oxford almost all his life, pro-viding curates for the living. In December 1614, as a sup-porter of the newly elected president Thomas Anyan, Twyne was made Greek lecturer at Corpus. By early 1615, with an income and release from paternal pressure to marry, he could focus on antiquarian learning which had already in 1614 secured him nomination to a fruitless dele-gation for reordering university statutes.

After 1619 Twyne may have retired to Rye or Lewes for a time, but it was possibly only in 1623 that he resigned his fellowship and took up lodgings in Pennyfarthing Street, St Aldate's, which he occupied for the rest of his life. By this time he had expectations of the reversion of William Camden's new professorship in history, but Camden later told his first appointee, Degory Wheare, who in the event outlived Twyne, that this had been obtained by trickery. In 1624 a House of Commons committee found President Anyan guilty, among worse misdemeanours, of excessive lenience to Twyne for repeated drunkenness, but towards the end of Anyan's presidency, in 1627 and 1628, Twyne co-ordinated reorganization of the college archives for the safeguarding of property, which produced a thirty-volume cartulary of title deeds, and left the archives in exemplary shape.

From 1629 Twyne was the most active member of a dele-gation set up to reorder the university's statutes, produc-ing in 1631 an inventory of the archives. Having reluc-tantly and on promise of reward agreed to write a preface to the statutes, when a provisional *corpus statutorum* was printed in 1634, Twyne was troubled by Laud's innovative alterations but outraged at the rewriting of his preface by Laud's agent, Peter Turner of Merton College. He had no part in further additions made to definitive statutes pro-mulgated in August 1636, but remained largely respon-sible for arranging a code which stood for over two centur-ies. On 11 August 1634 Twyne received his reward, the new office of keeper of the archives. He threw himself into seeking royal confirmation of the university's privileges with enlargements to match those of Cambridge and to counter pretensions by the city of Oxford, his particular bugbear. The city fathers came to view him as their great-est enemy. By late August 1635 he obtained royal consent for a new charter, brought to Oxford in March 1636, but in April unsuccessfully (if without confrontation) opposed Archbishop Laud's claim of metropolitical visitation over the university. In subsequent years Twyne advised the chancellor and successive vice-chancellors on endless dis-putes with the city over courts leet, cognizance of pleas, felons' goods, the night watch, alehouses, licensing mark-ets, and related matters.

Loyal to Charles I, Twyne remained in Oxford after the outbreak of civil war and wrote an 'Account of the musterings of the University of Oxford, with other things that happened there from Aug. 9, 1642, to July 13th, 1643, inclusively', printed in 1733 by Thomas Hearne. However, despite his zeal he was never fully trusted by academic authorities: Brian Duppa, writing as vice-chancellor to Laud in 1633, had questioned his judgement, and in June 1642 Twyne found that the authentic manuscript of the statutes had been removed for safekeeping without his knowledge.

Twyne made his will on 4 July 1644 and died, unmarried, at his lodgings the same day. He was buried in Corpus Christi College chapel. His monetary bequests were small: his real wealth lay in books and manuscripts. About 350 volumes containing 750 works, including twenty incunables, went to his college, together with manuscripts; to the university, through the Bodleian Library, he left books and papers about its affairs. Although Wood suggested that some items were lost by fire and subsequent pillaging, it is unlikely that many manuscripts were lost, but most of the remaining printed books probably disappeared. A grant of administration by the prerogative court of Canterbury to a sister in 1648 suggests Twyne had estate not mentioned in his will.

Twyne's fame rests mainly on his manuscript collections, assembled by indefatigable archival research in Oxford, London, and elsewhere. These were mainly his own work although he acknowledged debts to collections by Hare, Windsor, Allen, James, and others. His championship of the university's privileges rendered him odious to townsmen, some of whom, owing to his mathematical and astrological interests, credited him with occult powers. His learning was esteemed by John Selden, William Camden, and Archbishop Ussher, all of whom consulted him. Thomas Hearne later wondered at his 'strange, unaccountable Industry' (*The Itinerary of John Leland the Antiquary*, 2.66). Wood, who used Twyne's collections extensively without giving him sufficient credit, called him 'a loving and constant friend to his mother the University and to his college, a severe student and an adorer of venerable antiquity' (Wood, *Ath. Oxon.*, 3.111). Twyne was, however, no blind bookworm. His labours had been in defence of academic property and privilege.

A. J. Hegarty

Sources CCC Oxf., MSS 254–5, 257, 263, 266–7, 280, 303–4 · Bodl. Oxf., MSS Twyne 4, 7, 9, 10, 13, 14, 15, 16, 17, 20 · Bodl. Oxf., MSS Twyne-Langbaine 1, 4 · Bodl. Oxf., MS Rawl. D. 47, 55r–56v · S. Gibson, 'Brian Twyne', *Oxoniensia*, 5 (1940), 94–114 · [H. G. S.], ed., 'Some correspondence of Brian Twyne [3 pts]', *Bodleian Quarterly Record*, 5 (1926–8), 213–18, 240–46, 269–72 · R. F. Ovenell, 'Brian Twyne's library', *Oxford Bibliographical Society*, new ser., 4 (1950), 1–42 · C. M. Woolgar, 'Two Oxford archives in the early seventeenth century', *Archives*, 16 (1983–4), 258–72 · Wood, *Ath. Oxon.*, new edn, 3.108–11 · N. Tyacke, *Anti-Calvinists: the rise of English Arminianism, c.1590–1640* (1987); repr. (1990), 64–5 · M. H. Curtis, *Oxford and Cambridge in transition, 1558–1642* (1959), 120–22, 230, 239–40, 245 · M. Feingold, *The mathematicians' apprenticeship: science, universities and society in England, 1560–1640* (1984), 28–9, 73, 133–4, 153, 155–6, 158 · JHC, 1 (1547–1628), 707 · W. H. Godfrey, 'Thomas and Brian Twyne', *Sussex Notes and Queries*, 2 (1928–9), 197–201, 229–33 · W. H. Godfrey, 'Thomas and Brian Twyne', *Sussex Notes and Queries*, 3

(1930–31), 40–42, 82–4, 250 · *The life and times of Anthony Wood*, ed. A. Clark, 5 vols., OHS, 19, 21, 26, 30, 40 (1891–1900)
Archives Bodl. Oxf., antiquarian collections and papers; astronomical and astrological papers · Bodl. Oxf., corresp. and papers, MS Gr. misc. d2 · CCC Oxf., MSS
Wealth at death £8 10s.—cash bequests; plus valuable library of books and MSS to Corpus Christi College: *Life and times of Anthony Wood*, ed. A. Clark, 4.203–4

Twyne, John (c.1505–1581), schoolmaster and antiquary, was born at Bullington, Hampshire, the son of William Twyne. He matriculated at Oxford; his college is unknown, but in 1523–4 he heard Juan Luis Vives, the Spanish humanist, lecture in Corpus Christi College, and saw Bishop Richard Fox, the founder of the college, there. In January 1525 he graduated BCL. In the same year he married Alice (1507–1567), daughter of William Peper, freeman of Canterbury.

In 1526 Twyne was resident, probably as a schoolmaster, in St Augustine's Abbey, Canterbury. After the dissolution of the monastery in 1538 he bought a house in St Paul's parish, and in 1541 he became the first headmaster of the King's School, Canterbury, which he ran with notable success for twenty years. His labours were said to have made him rich. He certainly acquired property and held civic offices in Canterbury, becoming an alderman in 1553, and serving as sheriff in 1544–5. In spring 1553 he gave some offence to the duke of Northumberland, and was summoned before the privy council. He was mayor in 1554, when the city refused to support Sir Thomas Wyatt's rebellion, and an MP for Canterbury in 1553–4. He may have held the prebend of Llandygwydd in Christ Church, Brecon, from 1558, and may also have been the John Twyne admitted to Gray's Inn in 1566. For a time he was keeper of Rivingwood Forest in Littlebourne, Kent. On relinquishing his headmastership in 1560 he leased the rectory of Preston, Kent, and lived there for some years, though he died in Canterbury.

Twyne was denounced in 1534 by a monk of St Augustine's for having twice ridden to Sandwich at Archbishop Cranmer's behest 'to read a lecture of heresy' (*LP Henry VIII*, 7, no. 1608), but in Elizabeth's reign he was suspected of Roman sympathies. No doubt these suspicions lay behind his being charged in Canterbury consistory court in 1560 with harbouring a familiar spirit, described as 'a black thing, like a great rugged dog, which would dance about the house and hurl fire about the house' (Canterbury Cathedral Library, MS Y.2.24, fol. 69v), and his being eased out of his headmastership during that year in favour of Anthony Rush, a committed protestant who later became dean of Chichester. In the same year the archdeacon of Canterbury forbade him to hold public office; he was also subsequently expelled from the aldermanry. As late as 1596 it was noted of the Catholic priest Thomas Bramston that he had been taught by Twyne. Bramston was seen as having owed his learning rather than his doctrine to his master, though Twyne had also taught the Catholic controversialist Thomas Stapleton (1535–1598) of New College and Douai. After Matthew

Parker's death in 1575 Twyne claimed that the archbishop's disfavour had cost him his forest keepership, but he seems to have escaped further sanction for recusancy, and there were probably other discordances between him and Parker. Thomas Tanner observed in his *Bibliotheca Britannico-Hibernica* (1748) that Twyne had on occasion reprobated Henry VIII, John Foxe, and Matthew Parker. Twyne's scholarship and antiquarian tastes may have made him critical of a variety of received opinions. What is certain is that he was a well-read classicist and a learned student of antiquity. His interests matched some of those of the archbishop and his household, and he was manifestly useful to Parker as a knowledgeable collector of manuscripts.

Twyne wrote several historical and biographical studies, but most remained unpublished and have been lost. In the 1530s he contributed an introduction to *The History of Kyng Boccus and Sydracke*, an exhaustive and largely fanciful compendium of general knowledge, translated into English verse from French about 1450. It is an odd text for one of Twyne's learning and general acumen to have publicized, but it was printed at the expense of Robert Saltwood, a monk of St Augustine's, and it seems likely that Twyne was obliging Saltwood. If so, his introductory remark that 'things of open goodness need no praising' may have been as much as he cared to say on that score, though he observes that the book's doctrine is sound.

Twyne's best-known work is of a very different kind. *De rebus Albionicis, Britannicis, atque Anglicis commentariorum libri duo* (1590) was published after his death by his son Thomas. It is a review of the early history of Britain, based on an after-dinner conversation at Sturry, in the summer lodgings of John Foche, the last abbot of St Augustine's. The time is about 1530. The company includes the composer John Dygon, who became prior of the house in 1535, and Nicholas Wotton, later secretary of state and dean of Canterbury. The text seems to have been revised before 1550, but after that Twyne probably did not alter it greatly. Indeed, although the symposium is a familiar literary device, there is reason to accept it as a sample of learned conversation in the abbey's last decade.

Both the setting and the opinions expressed are interesting. Foche and Twyne are robustly sceptical of the mythical history of Britain, derived from Geoffrey of Monmouth, which had prevailed in medieval England. Instead of the feudal armies and accoutrements of Brute and his Trojans, they envisage a simple society of cave dwellers, which progressed only slowly to metallurgy and other skills. The images probably came from Lucretius and Varro, but it was humanism that now made them intelligible and useful. Twyne, however, went much further. He collected Roman coins, glass, and other artefacts, pondered the Rollright Stones and Stonehenge, and noted earthworks. He made the ingenious suggestion that the Phoenicians had come to Britain in search of tin, and among other things had brought the coracle with them: a notion that beguiled much later generations. What matters about such views is not their accuracy, but the quality

of Twyne's thought, his historical sense of perspective, and his use of evidence. It was characteristic of him that he also strove to save manuscripts from the monastic libraries. He owned at least ten manuscripts from the library of Canterbury Cathedral priory, including the B manuscript of the Anglo-Saxon Chronicle, and a similar number from the library of St Augustine's. The manuscript of the *Itinerarium regis Ricardi* in the library of Corpus Christi College, Cambridge, is inscribed 'Sent from Mr Twyne'.

John and Alice Twyne had four sons and three daughters. Of the sons, Lawrence *Twyne was a civilian and fellow of All Souls, and Thomas *Twyne (1543–1613), who published *De rebus Albionicis*, was an MD and a fellow of Corpus Christi College, Oxford. Brian *Twyne (1581–1644), registrar and historian of Oxford, was Thomas's son, and left some of his grandfather's papers and manuscripts to Corpus Christi. After Alice's death Twyne married Margaret Carpenter of Canterbury on 14 November 1568. He died at Canterbury on 24 November 1581, and was buried on 30 November in the chancel of St Paul's Church, where his epitaph survives.   G. H. MARTIN

Sources DNB · Emden, *Oxf.*, 4.582–3 · T. D. Kendrick, *British antiquity* (1950) · HoP, *Commons, 1509–58*, 3.494–5 · M. R. James, *A descriptive catalogue of the manuscripts in the library of Corpus Christi College, Cambridge*, 2 vols. (1912) · T. L. Burton, ed., *Sidrak and Bokkus*, EETS, 311 (1998) · M. McKisack, *Medieval history in the Tudor age* (1971) · Tanner, *Bibl. Brit.-Hib.* · *Joannis Twini Bolingdunensis, Angli, De rebus Albionicis*, ed. T. Twyne (1590) · P. Collinson, P. N. Ramsay, and M. Sparks, eds., *A history of Canterbury Cathedral* (1995) · memorial, St Paul's Church, Canterbury · *LP Henry VIII*, 7, no. 1608 · will (draft?), CCC Oxf., MS CCLVIII · private information (2004) [M. Zell] · Canterbury Cathedral Library, MS Y.2.24
Archives CCC Cam., notes, some MSS · CCC Oxf., MSS

Twyne, Lawrence (*fl.* 1564–1588), translator, eldest son of John *Twyne (*c.*1505–1581), schoolmaster and author, and his wife, Alice (1507–1567), daughter and coheir of William Peper, was probably born at Canterbury and was educated at his father's school. He proceeded thence to All Souls College, Oxford, where he was a fellow from 1559 to 1570 and graduated BCL on 17 August 1564. In 1578 he became rector of Twineham, Sussex, where he lived for, perhaps, a decade. He married Anne, daughter of one Hoker of Southampton, with whom he had a son, John, and daughter, Anne.

Wood says that Twyne was an 'ingenious poet of his time', and wrote several copies of laudatory verses to be set before books (Wood, *Ath. Oxon.*, 1.464). One of these is at the start of his brother Thomas *Twyne's translation of Lhuyd's *Breviary of Britayne*. His main work was *The Patterne of Painefull Adventures* (1576), which tells the story of Apollonius, prince of Tyre. In the 'Epistle Dedicatory', Twyne vaunts that his work, 'which has cost me some small labour and travel … cannot but stir up the mind and sences into sundry affections' and, indeed, his translation is lively and readable. No copy of the first edition is extant, but it had several reprints, of which the third, in 1607, seems to have stirred the senses of William Shakespeare and his possible collaborator George Wilkins, who based their *Pericles*, which appeared that year, partly on Twyne's volume. In the play the poet John Gower (whose *Confessio amantis* contains a version of the story of Apollonius) appears as a chorus, and it is he, not Twyne, whom Wilkins acknowledges in his novel, *The Pattern of Adventures of Pericles, Prynce of Tyre* (1608). However, a comparison of the texts shows that *Pericles* in fact owes something to Twyne as well as Gower, and Wilkins's book, as witnessed by its title, is so close to Twyne's as to be in parts indistinguishable (on these issues, see Michael). There are some short verses in chapter 17 of Twyne's work that Tharsia, sold into slavery as a prostitute, sings to her restored father, Apollonius:

Among the harlots foule I walke
yet harlot none am I:
The rose amongst the thorns grows
and is not hurt thereby.

Twyne's reputation has been overshadowed somewhat by that of his more prolific brother, Thomas, and *The Patterne* has been several times erroneously ascribed to his sibling. ROSS KENNEDY

Sources Wood, *Ath. Oxon.*, new edn, 1.464; 2.130 · Foster, *Alum. Oxon., 1500–1714* [Lawrence Twyne] · G. L. Hennessy, *Chichester diocese clergy lists* (1900), 151 · W. Berry, *County genealogies: pedigrees of the families of the county of Hants* (1833), 222 · N. C. Michael, *Pericles: an annotated bibliography* (1987) [index, s.v. Twine] · Wood, *Ath. Oxon.: Fasti* (1815), 164 · W. C. Hazlitt, *Hand-book to the popular, poetical and dramatic literature of Great Britain* (1867), 10 · J. P. Collier, ed., *A bibliographical and critical account of the rarest books in the English language*, 2 (1865), 154, 455 · T. Corser, *Collectanea Anglo-poetica, or, A … catalogue of a … collection of early English poetry*, 1, Chetham Society, 52 (1860), 43 · T. Mommsen, *Pericles, prince of Tyre* (1857), vii · DNB

Twyne, Thomas (1543–1613), physician, was born in Canterbury, the third son of John *Twyne (*c*.1505–1581), master of Canterbury Free School, and his wife, Alice (1507–1567), daughter of William Peper. Lawrence *Twyne was his brother. He became a scholar of Corpus Christi College, Oxford, on 6 July 1560, and was elected a fellow on 9 November 1564. He graduated BA on 18 April 1564 and proceeded MA on 10 July 1568. He then studied medicine at Cambridge, where John Caius encouraged him in his studies. He married Joan Pumfrett on 6 October 1571. Brian *Twyne, the Oxford antiquary, was his son. Thomas graduated BM at Oxford on 10 July 1593, and then proceeded MD at Cambridge. He settled in Lewes, Sussex, where he acquired a large practice. Twyne was admitted a licentiate of the College of Physicians on 7 May 1596, after his patron, Lord Buckhurst, had intervened on his behalf.

Twyne was skilled in astrology and a friend of John Dee. He died at Lewes on 1 August 1613, and was buried in the chancel of the church of St Peter's and Mary's, Westout, where a brass, bearing fourteen laudatory lines of Latin verse, was erected to his memory.

Some of Twyne's works are attributed only by initials, and others are translations or editions in which it is difficult to trace his exact contribution. His book *The Schoolmaster*, published in London in 1576 and 1583, has also

been attributed to Thomas Turswell. Twyne was an undistinguished writer. His chief works are *The Breviary of Britayne* (1572); *The Garland of Godly Flowers* (1574), dedicated to Sir Nicholas Bacon; *The Wonderful Workmanship of the World* (1578), dedicated to Sir Francis Walsingham; *Physicke Against Fortune, as Well Prosperous as Adverse; Translated from F. Petrark* (1579); and *New Counsel Against the Pestilence*; translated from Peter Drouet (1578?). He also translated into English the eleventh, twelfth, and thirteenth books of the *Aeneid*, completing the work of Thomas Phaer, which was published as *The Whole xiii. Books of the Aeneidos of Virgill* in 1573, in 1584, and in 1596 in quarto. *Thomas Twyne's Discourse on the Earthquake of 1580*, edited by R. E. Ockenden, was published in 1936. He inclines to dullness in both prose and verse.

NORMAN MOORE, *rev.* RACHEL E. DAVIES

Sources Munk, *Roll* · Wood, *Ath. Oxon.* · M. A. Lower, *The worthies of Sussex* (1865), 183 · J. L. Chester and J. Foster, eds., *London marriage licences, 1521–1869* (1887)

Twysden [Twisden; *née* Finch], **Anne, Lady Twysden** (1574–1638), writer, was born on 28 February 1574 at Heneage House in London, the eldest daughter of Sir Maple, or Mayle, Finch (*d.* 1614) and Elizabeth Heneage (*d.* 1633). Her mother was created Viscountess Maidstone in 1623 and countess of Winchilsea in 1628. Anne was educated by her grandmother at the court of Queen Elizabeth, and was proficient in Latin, Italian, Spanish, and French. She was married by Alexander Nowell, dean of St Paul's, at Heneage House on 4 October 1591, to William Twysden (1566–1629) of East Peckham, Kent. Her husband was knighted in 1603 and created a baronet in 1611. He died on 8 January 1629 and was buried at East Peckham.

There were five sons and two daughters of the marriage: Roger *Twysden, second baronet (1597–1672); Elizabeth (1600–1655), who married Sir Hugh Cholmley (*d.* 1657) in 1622; Thomas *Twisden (1602–1683); Anne (1603–1670), who married Sir Christopher Yelverton (*d.* 1654) in 1630; William (1605–1641); John *Twysden (1607–1688); and Francis (1610–1675). The burden of Sir William's estate fell to Sir Roger on his death; Lady Anne's jointure was free. She succeeded to the two houses in East Peckham and Redcross Street, London. Her ladies-in-waiting, the diarist Isabella Saunder and Jane Thomlinson, married her sons Roger and Thomas in 1635 and 1639 respectively. Lady Anne refused to pay Charles I's ship-money tax, but was twice cajoled into paying by her eldest son, who also held objections to it.

Twysden composed at least one book of devotions, known as the Jennings-Bramley manuscript. This contains her own prayer compositions, scriptural passages, accounts of the devout deaths of her father, mother, and brother Sir Heneage, and a prayer composed by the latter. Sir Roger Twysden ordered a copy to be made of this manuscript, with some omissions and additions, inserting headnotes in his own hand—one of these is dated 10 November 1638 (CKS, MS U 1655 F8, p. 23). The whereabouts of the former manuscript is currently unknown, although Kemble cites from it in his 1849 edition of Roger Twysden's *Certaine Considerations upon the Government of*

England. Lady Twysden's letters are held in the British Library (BL, Add. MS 34173, fols. 9–11), and her son Roger commented of her epistolary skills:

> She had the best way of expressing her mind in writing, wth the most facilyty I ever met with in woeman indeed it might bee incredible should I say I never saw man indite better letters then I have read of hers. (BL, Add. MS 34163, fol. 80)

John Hiud's *Storie of Stories* (1632) was dedicated to her; Hiud (1578–1651) was a German friend and servant to the family for thirty-two years.

Twysden fell ill at church on Sunday 23 September 1638 and died at home in Kent on 14 October following. Her sons John and Roger both provide detailed accounts of this illness, which reveal their affection for her and her piety. She was attended by most of her children, their spouses, her grandchildren, and Hiud. Sir Roger was her executor, disposing of at least £168 (BL, Add. MS 34176, fols. 68–73). John described her as tall and fair, while Roger surmised that she 'was the handsommest woeman … I ever saw' (BL, Add. MS 34163, fol. 80), although she was lame from a fall as a child.   MARIE-LOUISE COOLAHAN

Sources BL, Add. MS 34176 · BL, Add. MS 34177 · BL, Add. MS 34163 · J. M. Kemble, introduction, in R. Twysden, *Certaine considerations upon the government of England*, ed. J. M. Kemble, CS, 45 (1849); repr. (1968) · *The family of Twysden and Twisden: their history and archives from an original by Sir John Ramskill Twisden*, ed. C. H. Dudley Ward (1939) · A. R. Cook, *A manor through four centuries* (1938)
Archives BL, Add. MSS 34163–34165, 34173–34177 · CKS, MS U 1655 F8
Likenesses plate, repro. in Dudley Ward, *The family of Twysden and Twisden*
Wealth at death £168—bequeathed to family and friends: BL, Add. MS 34176, fols. 68–73

Twysden, John (1607–1688), physician, fourth son of Sir William Twysden, first baronet (1566–1629), and Anne [*see* Twysden, Anne (1574–1638)], daughter of Sir Maple or Mayle Finch of Eastwell, Kent, and sister of Sir Heneage Finch (*d.* 1631), was born on 1 May 1607 at Roydon, Kent. Sir Roger *Twysden (1597–1672) and Sir Thomas *Twisden (1602–1683) were his brothers. John Twysden was educated at University College, Oxford, where he matriculated on 20 June 1623; he left the university without a degree and entered the Inner Temple, London, where he was called to the bar in 1634. In 1645 he was in Paris, and in 1646 graduated MD at Angers. He incorporated his degree at Oxford on 6 November 1651; in 1654 he settled in London, on 22 December was admitted a candidate of the College of Physicians, and on 20 October 1664 was elected a fellow.

Twysden's friend Walter Foster of Emmanuel College, Cambridge, passed on to him the mathematical remains of his brother Samuel Foster, after the death of the Gresham professor in 1652. Twysden's first work, in collaboration with Edmund Wingate, was published in London in 1654: it was an edition of Samuel Foster's *Elliptical, or Azimuthal Horologiography*. In 1659 he published the residue of Foster's papers, with some mathematical essays of his own, in a folio volume entitled *Miscellanea, sive, Lucubrationes mathematicae*.

During the 1660s Twysden became involved in defending the College of Physicians against the criticisms of those practitioners who were seeking to establish a separate society for 'chymical physicians'. Twysden's *Medicina veterum vindicata, or, An Answer to a Book Entitled 'Medela medicinae'* (1666) was a defence of the orthodox Galenic medical doctrines of the day against Marchamont Needham. The book, which is dedicated to Lord Chancellor Clarendon, and to the chiefs of the three courts, Keeling, Bridgman, and Hales, shows a good deal of general learning and much power of argument in its attempt to portray the chymical physicians as a revolutionary group, associated with the spirit of the republic rather than with the crown. In the same year Twysden published another book of the same kind, an *Answer to Medicina instaurata*. In 1676 Needham was defeated in an action by the Royal College of Physicians before Twysden's brother, Sir Thomas Twysden, in the court of king's bench. Twysden continued his mathematical studies, and published in 1685 *The Use of the Great Planisphere called the Analemma*.

Twysden died unmarried on 13 September 1688. He was buried on 15 September in St Margaret's Church, Westminster. Two of his letters and his account of the last illness and death of his mother are extant in the British Library (Add. MSS 34173 and 34176).

NORMAN MOORE, *rev.* PATRICK WALLIS

Sources Foster, *Alum. Oxon.* · Munk, *Roll* · C. Goodall, *The Royal College of Physicians of London founded and established by law* (1684) · T. Wotton, *The English baronets*, 1 (1727), 80–81 · J. Ward, *The lives of the professors of Gresham College* (1740) · H. J. Cook, *The decline of the old medical regime in Stuart London* (1986) · E. Hasted, *The history and topographical survey of the county of Kent*, 2nd edn, 12 vols. (1797–1801) · Wood, *Ath. Oxon.* · IGI
Archives BL, Add. MSS 34173, 34176
Likenesses oils, *c.*1650, Kent Archaeological Society; on loan to East Malling Research Station, Bradbourne House, Kent

Twysden, Sir Roger, second baronet (1597–1672), antiquary, was born at Roydon Hall, East Peckham, Kent, on 21 August 1597, the eldest child of Sir William Twysden, first baronet (1566–1629), scholar and gentleman usher of the privy chamber, and Anne (1574–1638), daughter of Sir Maple, or Mayle, Finch [*see* Twysden, Anne]. The physician John *Twysden was his younger brother.

Early life and marriage Twysden was educated at St Paul's School, and entered Emmanuel College, Cambridge, as a fellow-commoner on 8 November 1614, although he does not appear to have proceeded to a degree. He was knighted on 1 June 1620 and was admitted to Gray's Inn on 2 February 1623. He was returned as member for Winchelsea, Sussex, to the parliaments of 1625 and 1626, but there is no surviving evidence that he spoke in either.

On his father's death, on 8 January 1629, Twysden became the second baronet. His father's debts amounted to £3970, and over the following years Twysden set about improving his property, creating a park at Roydon Hall and engaging in extensive planting of trees. He kept a book in which he wrote down detailed advice on prudent estate management, including the keeping of woods which he regarded as especially important. On 27 January

Sir Roger Twysden, second baronet (1597–1672), by unknown artist, 1648

1635 Twysden married Isabella (1604/5–1657), youngest daughter of Sir Nicholas Saunder of Nonsuch in Surrey, alongside whom Twysden had served as member for Winchelsea in the 1626 parliament. By 1636 Twysden was a justice of the peace for Kent. His writings indicate that he was deeply interested in constitutional and legal issues, and in his commonplace book he recorded a debate among the Kentish gentry over the legality of ship money in February 1637. Twysden seemingly associated himself with those who cited Sir John Fortescue in support of the principle that 'the king had not an absolute power' (Fincham, 233) and he used this principle to justify his consistent refusal to pay ship money. This stance reflected a commitment to the rule of law and constitutional propriety that was highly characteristic of Twysden throughout his adult life.

Twysden and parliament, 1640–1642 Twysden wrote in 1637 that 'none could expect a Parliament, but on some great necessity not now imaginable' (Fincham, 236). However, within two years the Scottish rebellion generated just such a 'great necessity', and Twysden later claimed that 'never did any man with more earnest expectation long for a Parlyament then I did' ('Sir Roger Twysden's journal', 1.187). In February 1640 the king summoned parliament to assemble on 13 April, and Twysden was among those who were sounded out as possible candidates to represent Kent, although he initially declined. Instead, he threw his support behind Sir Henry Vane the elder, and tried to mobilize others in support of him, including Twysden's influential cousin Sir Edward Dering. Dering at first

appeared sympathetic towards Vane, but then decided to stand himself, whereupon Vane immediately withdrew. Surprised at Dering's change of mind Twysden announced his own candidature, and on 16 March 1640 he was returned together with Sir Norton Knatchbull. There is little evidence that Twysden was active in the Short Parliament, other than a fragmentary report of a speech on 4 May in which he expressed support for Vane's proposal that the Commons should vote the king subsidies in return for the ending of ship money. However, the house was unable to agree on how to proceed, the attempted compromise collapsed, and Charles dissolved the parliament the next day. Twysden later wrote that it was 'not without the great amazement of many understanding men, that (it havinge carryed it selfe with such moderation as not to have put to the question any thing might displease the king) they should be sent home without doing ought' (Sir Roger Twysden, *Certaine Considerations upon the Government of England*, ed. J. M. Kemble, CS, 1st ser., 45, 1849, 145).

Since the late sixteenth century there had been a custom in Kent that no member should represent the county in consecutive parliaments. Twysden therefore did not offer himself as a candidate for the Long Parliament, even though he was well supported, and Dering and Sir John Culpepper were returned instead. During the months that followed Twysden watched developments in the parliament with growing foreboding. Although he felt little sympathy for the Laudians he opposed the abolition of episcopacy. He was 'much troubled' by the attainder of Strafford 'by a private law (which yet no other judge was to take for a rule)' ('Sir Roger Twysden's journal', 1.195). The final straw came on 5 March 1642 when both houses passed the militia ordinance assuming command over the armed forces. Twysden felt that 'this was an imitation of the tyrants of Athens, to get an army for their defence' (ibid., 1.198), which would give parliament 'in effect all the rights of soveraignity' (ibid.).

Later that month the spring assizes at Maidstone afforded Twysden and other Kentish gentlemen of similar views an opportunity to make a public protest. Some other gentry had recently submitted a petition supporting the houses' actions, but Twysden and his allies felt that this expressed opinions 'not agreeing with the sense of the county' ('Sir Roger Twysden's journal', 1.200). Instead, they drafted an alternative petition, agreed at Maidstone on 25 March, and although Twysden did not sign the original draft he almost certainly had a hand in composing it. This petition included demands that 'the solemne Liturgy of the Church of England … established by the supream law of the land … may by your auctoryty bee enjoyed quiet and free from interruptious storms, prophanations, threats and force' (ibid., 1.206–7), and that 'episcopall government … may be preserved as the most pious, most prudent, and most safe government for the peace of the Church' (ibid.). The petition also demanded that energetic measures be taken against 'the odious and abominable scandall of schismaticall and seditious sermons and pamphletts' to prevent the 'advancing of heresy, scisme, prophanesse, libertinisme, Anabaptisme, atheisme', and that 'the pretious liberty of the subject, the common birth-right of every Englishmen, may bee … preserved intire' (ibid., 1.207–8).

MPs were highly displeased to learn of this petition, and on 28 March issued an order summoning Twysden, Dering, Sir George Strode, and Richard Spencer to appear before the house as delinquents. When they appeared on 1 April, Twysden denied that he had taken the initiative with the petition and expressed himself heartily sorry if he had offended parliament. On 9 April he was bailed on condition that he entered into a bond for £10,000, and did not move more than 10 miles from London. His uncle Francis Finch and Sir Robert Filmer acted as his two sureties, for £5000 each. On 5 May the Commons received a counter-petition from Kent, which was much more to their liking, and on 12 May Twysden was given permission to return home.

The battle of petitions continued when the summer assizes opened at Maidstone on 22 July. The Commons received information that 'some ille affected persons' in Kent were 'endeavouring to disperse rumours to the scandall of the Parlyament', whereupon they sent down fourteen members of the Commons who represented Kentish constituencies to 'preserve the said county, not onely in peace amongst themselves, but in a right understanding of the proceedings of Parlyament' ('Sir Roger Twysden's journal', 2.181–2). Twysden responded by drafting a series of instructions which informed the Commons that there was no need for such intervention and urged the house instead to give the king satisfaction on several particulars, including 'laying aside the militia till a good law may be framed', and enabling parliament to be adjourned 'to an indifferent place' (ibid., 2.187). Incensed, the Commons again summoned Twysden to appear at the bar of the house, which he did on 5 August. His bail was disallowed and he was committed to the serjeant as a prisoner, who detained him at the Three Tobacco-pipes tavern near Charing Cross. There he remained until he was bailed again on 12 September, on condition that he did not go into Kent. During his confinement his main consolation was conversations with two fellow prisoners, Sir Basil Brook and Sir Kenelm Digby. Following his release Twysden retired to his house in Redcross Street. He had obtained a passport to go to the continent, but his plans to leave England were temporarily abandoned when his kinsman, Sir John Finch, with whom he had planned to travel, was killed in a fall from his horse.

Civil war While Twysden was confined the civil war had formally begun, on 22 August. He tried to live quietly in Redcross Street and to pursue his researches into English constitutional and ecclesiastical history: in particular, he worked extensively on the records at the nearby Tower of London. But the demands of the parliamentarian war effort fell indiscriminately. Under the terms of the ordinance of 29 November, raising a loan from the city, Twysden received a ticket for £400, or a twentieth part. He pleaded vainly that he was a casual inhabitant, and therefore not liable; a few months later, officers distrained the contents of his house and 'lef nothing worth ought beehynd' ('Sir Roger Twysden's journal', 2.195).

Early in 1643 Sir Christopher Neville and others tried to persuade Twysden to join the king at Oxford, but he refused because of the dangers to his property (which lay entirely in areas controlled by parliament), his duty to his wife and five children, and the fact that he 'should bee ashamed to live in Oxford and not bee in the Army' ('Sir Roger Twysden's journal', 2.198). In May 1643 he sent his eldest son, William (1635–1697), abroad, with the intention of following as soon as possible. On 9 June he set out in disguise with some French and Portuguese traders, but got only as far as Bromley when he was recognized by his old enemy Sir Anthony Weldon and other members of the Kent county committee, who were meeting in the town that day. Twysden initially tried to conceal his identity, but Weldon declared that if he 'were not Sir Roger Twysden [he] was a rogue and ought to bee whipped' (ibid., 3.146). The next day Twysden was brought before the Commons' committee for accusations, which ordered him to be imprisoned in the Counter prison at Southwark. Among the charges levelled against him was that of carrying 'intelligence of great consequence … subtilly conveighed into nut shells' (ibid., 3.148). Twysden claimed that this charge may have originated from the fact that he wore an antidote against infection in the form of a little round ball contained in a nutshell.

Following his imprisonment Twysden's estates were sequestrated, in May 1643, and large quantities of the timber on his lands, of which he was so proud, were felled. The royalist military successes of that summer made the parliamentarians fearful of a rising in London, and on 10 August the Commons ordered Twysden and several other eminent figures to be transferred for safe custody to the *Prosperous Sarah*, one of the ships berthed in the Thames. However, by 15 August he was allowed to return to the Counter, and he then set about trying to find out by whose order, and on what grounds, he was being sequestrated. He wrote to the sequestrator-general of Kent, Thomas Dyke (23 October 1643), and to his kinsman Sir Edward Scott, who served on the county committee (30 November 1643), asking how he had offended, but neither ever replied. He petitioned the committee for sequestrations at Westminster, who referred his case to the county committee for Kent; when they failed to give any reasons that placed Twysden within the terms of the sequestration ordinance the committee for sequestrations ordered an inquiry, and temporarily stayed the felling of timber on Twysden's lands. In the meantime, in February 1644, he had been transferred from the Counter to a set of four rooms at Lambeth Palace, and there he continued the studies that were later embodied in his *Historiae Anglicanae scriptores decem*.

The sequestrations committee heard Twysden's case on 31 August 1644. The main witness against him was Sir John Sedley, who gave a highly partisan account of Twysden's activities at the Kent assizes in 1642. His wife attended on Twysden's behalf, but when the committee gave its decision she and his counsel were ordered out whereas the prosecution was allowed to remain. The committee simply ordered that the sequestration should continue without offering any reasons. Twysden's reaction was to wonder 'whither this were not wors then the Star Chamber?' ('Sir Roger Twysden's journal', 4.134). Lady Twysden submitted further petitions to the committee for sequestrations and to the Kent county committee, but to no avail, and the felling of timber on Twysden's estates resumed once again.

At this point Twysden finally admitted defeat, and early in 1645 he applied to compound as a delinquent. On 6 March his fine was set at £3000, his estate being valued (rather vindictively) at £2000 a year, and on 9 December the Commons ordered that he be bailed, whereupon he moved to a lodging in St Anne's Street, Westminster. In August 1647 he was allowed to return to Roydon Hall. However, the sequestration remained in effect because he was unable to pay his fine. On 31 May 1649, following a further petition from Twysden, his fine was reduced to £1500, at the rate of one-tenth (that is two years' income), and eventually, on 18 January 1650, he compounded for £1340. But his sufferings were not yet over. Parliament remained suspicious of him, and on 26 April 1651, amid the growing threat of a royalist invasion from Scotland, troopers searched Roydon Hall and seized such arms as they could find. They detained Twysden at Leeds Castle, near Maidstone, but finding nothing against him released him after about a week. The following September the committee for the advance of money ordered him to appear before them on 17 October to give satisfaction for the assessment of £600 originally imposed on him in November 1642. He put off his appearance on grounds of illness until 7 November when the committee reduced his fine to £450. Later that month, following payment of £225, the fine was further reduced to £400. Additional allowance was made for the fact that some of his lands were only held for life, and following his payment of another £164 18s. 6d. on 28 November Twysden's estate was discharged.

In his private journals Twysden left a meticulously detailed account of his sufferings at the hands of the parliamentarian regime. He stressed that he had absolutely no desire 'to see hys Majesty come in an absolute conqueror; (which [he] was never Cavalier enough to wish)', and he remained convinced that 'Parlyaments kept in their right bounds beeing the hapyest constitution tyme hath produced, for the preserving eyther lyberty or prerogative' ('Sir Roger Twysden's journal', 3.151–2). However, he abhorred the tyranny of those parliamentarians who,

> under pretence of maynteyning the religion of the Church of England, ... defaced (as superstitious or superfluous) all the antique monuments of pyety and devotion; ruined the cathedrals; ... denyed all former rights of monarchy; ... [and] seated in themselves an absolute power of taking from the subject all he could call hys owne, yet professing an upholding them in their lawfull rights, propryety of their goods, and liberties.   (ibid., 2.201)

Twysden's experiences during the 1640s, like those of so many others, demonstrated the profound irony that 'some who had complayned of the King's excesses in such like cases, seemed ... no lesse willing to exercise themselves this prodigious tyrany' (ibid., 4.139).

Antiquarian writings Back at Roydon Hall, during the 1650s Twysden and his family gradually rebuilt their lives and estates. Twysden lived quietly, devoting himself to his researches and writings, and to the affairs of his parish. His wife died on 11 March 1657 and was buried in East Peckham church on 17 March. Following the Restoration, on 11 September 1660 Twysden was again sworn a justice of the peace, and was reappointed to the commission of oyer and terminer; in October he was made a deputy lieutenant. He rapidly became one of the two or three leading members of the county bench and scarcely missed a meeting of the assizes or the quarter sessions from 1660 until his death in 1672. He was also appointed a commissioner under the 1660 act for confirming and restoring ministers. In the spring of 1661 he put himself forward as a candidate for the Cavalier Parliament, but his reluctance to canvass actively may explain why he lost to Sir John Tufton and Sir Thomas Peyton. Twysden was also a highly conscientious deputy lieutenant, but he resigned his commission in June 1668 rather than be associated with what he regarded as an illegal attempt by the new lord lieutenant, the duke of Richmond, to raise uniforms as well as arms for the militia. Twysden believed that the duke's demand had no basis in the Militia Act of 1662, and this episode showed that his commitment to legal propriety remained as firm as ever.

Twysden was of a deeply scholarly temperament and was especially interested in legal, constitutional, and ecclesiastical history. He numbered such scholars as Sir Simonds D'Ewes, John Selden, Sir Henry Spelman, and Sir William Dugdale among his friends. Twysden read widely in original sources, and wrote extensively: three of his works were published during his own lifetime, and others appeared posthumously. His first published work, *The Commoners Liberty, or, The English-Mans Birth-Right* (London, 1648), grew out of his own experiences of arrest and imprisonment, and drew on a range of medieval precedents from Magna Carta onwards to argue that the laws were 'the undoubted birth-right of every Englishman, the surest sanctuary any can take, and the strongest fortresse to protect the weakest' (p. 1). He concluded that 'if the Lords may try a commoner, they may judge any man's title to his lands, for no law limiting the extent of their power, but that being arbitrary, it may reach to all causes whithersoever they will stretch it' (p. 23).

The Commoners Liberty was derived from the major work on which Twysden was engaged for much of the 1640s, *Certaine Considerations upon the Government of England*. Again based on deep learning, especially in medieval legal and constitutional records, this advanced a coherent view of England as a limited monarchy. Twysden argued that the subjects' 'liberties doe well stand with the dignity and prerogative of our kings'. The laws 'afford the people sufficient liberty without any trenching on his majesty's prerogative; so that it seemes to mee there is no rule for either the liberty of the subject or the prerogative of the king but the law of the land' (p. 83). This meant that in terms of a strictly unitary (or Bodinian) theory of sovereignty, 'the kings of England were at no tyme soveraigns' (p. 88). Rather, the laws ensured that 'neither the monarchy might introduce a tyrany, nor yet fall into a popular or anarchy' (p. 181).

Another of Twysden's central interests lay in religious and ecclesiastical history. In 1652, he published the *Historiae Anglicanae scriptores decem*, a 1600-page edition of ten Latin histories compiled by such medieval English chroniclers as Simeon of Durham, Ailred of Rievaulx, and Henry Knighton. This edition formed the basis of subsequent texts of some of these chronicles edited separately for the Rolls Series. His *An historicall vindication of the Church of England in point of schism, as it stands separated from the Roman, and was reformed I. Elizabeth* (1657) offered a detailed account of the increase of papal powers over England from the Saxons to the Reformation, and argued that it was the Church of England, rather than Rome, which had held fast to the true faith. Twysden denied that the English church 'made a departure from the Church, which is the ground and pillar of truth' (p. 196). This temperate and urbane argument placed Twysden within the tradition of earlier apologists for the Church of England such as Richard Hooker and Thomas Fuller.

Twysden's other works included an unfinished treatise on the early history of monasticism entitled *The Beginners of a Monastick Life in Asia, Africa, and Europe*. This bears the date of 1 September 1661, and was printed as an appendix to the 1698 edition of Spelman's *History and Fate of Sacrilege*. Twysden also compiled, mainly between 1651 and 1653, a manuscript journal with the title 'An historicall narrative of the two houses of parliament, and either of them their committees and agents violent proceedings against Sir Roger Twysden'. This is the main source for Twysden's life during the 1640s and early 1650s, and was edited by L. B. Larking for *Archaeologia Cantiana*, 1–4 (1858–61). Twysden's scholarly activities led him to assemble a large and important collection of books and manuscripts, although most of this was dispersed in the nineteenth century when Roydon Hall passed out of the Twysden family.

Character Twysden was a gentle and scholarly person, whose absolute honesty and integrity shone throughout his life. He was most at home in exploring legal, constitutional, and ecclesiastical history. His deep commitment to due process and to the rule of law, together with a dislike of political and religious extremism, meant that he could not offer unconditional allegiance to either side in the English civil wars. He was an advocate of balance and peace in a time of turmoil and violence, and he paid a high material price for refusing to compromise his ideals. Throughout, he remained devoted to his family and magnanimous towards his enemies. Twysden's sufferings and his steadfast attachment to the known laws were typical of many moderate gentry in mid-seventeenth-century England. As Alan Everitt wrote: 'there was an oak-like stability about him … and an integrity his bitterest enemies were compelled to respect. … [He had] a certain slow-moving, deep-thinking element which, when it was

moved … could make Westminster itself tremble' (Everitt, 68–9).

From about 1665 onwards Twysden's health gradually deteriorated. On 3 November 1671 he suffered an apoplexy while travelling to petty sessions at Town Malling from which he never recovered: he grew steadily weaker and died peacefully at Roydon Hall on 27 June 1672. He was buried in East Peckham church, and it was characteristic of his careful planning and attention to detail that he had drafted the Latin wording of his own memorial tablet. The baronetcy became extinct at his death; his brother Thomas Twysden (1602–1683), of Bradbourne, was in 1666 created a baronet.   DAVID L. SMITH

Sources PRO, SP 16 [state papers domestic, Charles I] · F. W. Jessup, *Sir Roger Twysden, 1597–1672* (1965) · 'Sir Roger Twysden's journal', ed. L. B. Larking, *Archaeologia Cantiana*, 1 (1858), 184–214; 2 (1859), 175–220; 3 (1860), 145–76; 4 (1861), 131–202 · L. B. Larking, ed., *Proceedings principally in the county of Kent in connection with the parliaments called in 1640, and especially with the committee of religion appointed in that year*, CS, old ser., 80 (1862) · K. Fincham, 'The judges' decision on ship money in February 1637: the reaction of Kent', *BIHR*, 57 (1984), 230–37 · A. Everitt, *The community of Kent and the great rebellion, 1640–60* (1966) · E. S. Cope and W. H. Coates, eds., *Proceedings of the Short Parliament of 1640*, CS, 4th ser., 19 (1977) · *The Short Parliament (1640) diary of Sir Thomas Aston*, ed. J. D. Maltby, CS, 4th ser., 35 (1988) · *JHC*, 2–6 (1640–51) · M. A. E. Green, ed., *Calendar of the proceedings of the committee for advance of money, 1642–1656*, 3 vols., PRO (1888) · M. A. E. Green, ed., *Calendar of the proceedings of the committee for compounding … 1643–1660*, 5 vols., PRO (1889–92)
Archives BL, collection of family papers, Add. MSS 34147–34178 · BL, journal, corresp., and accompts, Add. MSS 34155, 34161–34167 · BL, printed edition of P. Sarpi's *Historia del Concilio Tridentino* with copious MS notes · Bodl. Oxf., estate books · CKS, diary as magistrate and papers · CKS, letters, papers, and commonplace books · LPL, collection for a history of the lieutenancy of Kent, and papers
Likenesses oils, 1648, Kent Archaeological Society; on loan to East Malling Research Station, Bradbourne House, Kent [*see illus.*] · portrait (aged fifty-one), repro. in Jessup, *Sir Roger Twysden*, frontispiece; priv. coll.
Wealth at death annual income £1000–1200: F. W. Jessup, *Sir Roger Twysden, 1597–1672*, p. 120

Twysden, Sir Thomas. See Twisden, Sir Thomas, first baronet (1602–1683).

Tyabji, Badruddin (1844–1906), judge and reformer in India, was born at Bombay on 10 October 1844, the eighth of ten children and the fifth of six sons of a Cambay merchant, Tyab Ali (also known as Tyabji Bhai Mian; 1803–1863), and his wife, Ameena (d. 1865), the daughter of a rich mullah, Meher Ali. His grandfather Bhai Mian had left Bombay after heavy losses in the great Bombay fire of 1803 but returned with Tyab Ali, initially as petty traders. Tyab Ali prospered and left a merchant house with branches in France, Karachi, and elsewhere. Since Tyab Ali was known respectfully as Tyabji Merchant, Tyabji became the English family name of his descendants though Badruddin continued to use Tyab Ali as his surname in Urdu. Tyab Ali became a deputy (aamil) to the chief mullah of his small community of Sulaimani Bohras, Gujarati converts to the Islamic Shi'i Bohra sect who had separated from other Bohras in the sixteenth century. All of Tyab Ali's sons went to England for further education or trade, the third son,

Badruddin Tyabji (1844–1906), by unknown photographer, 1891

Camruddin, being the first Indian admitted as a solicitor in England.

Badruddin began his schooling at the Dada Makba Madrassa before continuing with a westernized syllabus at the Elphinstone Institution. In April 1860 he went to England to study at the Highbury New Park College, passed the London matriculation examination and entered London University and the Middle Temple as a student in 1863. Because of deteriorating eyesight he returned to Bombay in late 1864 but resumed terms at the Middle Temple in late 1865, was called to the English bar in April 1867, and on his return to Bombay in December 1867 became the first Indian barrister in the high court of Bombay. Backed by his successful solicitor brother Camruddin, Badruddin prospered as a barrister, a success which later enabled him to support a large family and involve himself in public activities.

Badruddin had been engaged to Moti (c.1850–1905), the daughter of Sharaf Shujaat Ali, a successful China merchant from Cambay, before he first went to England. When they married on 16 January 1865 she was renamed Bibi Rahat un Nafs ('Peace of the Soul'). They had eighteen children of whom five sons and eight daughters survived Badruddin. All the children were given a westernized education with three daughters and all the sons reaching higher levels. One son joined the civil service, three sons the legal profession, and one became a civil engineer. Apart from overseeing the large family, Bibi Rahat un Nafs

was active in promoting the advancement of Indian women through the National Indian Association, and in pushing for the relaxation of purdah.

Badruddin was involved in the ferment of public activity that characterized Bombay in the 1870s and 1880s, his first major public speech in 1871 having urged reform of the municipal corporation. He was elected to the corporation in 1873 where he remained until 1886. By then he had become a member of the University of Bombay senate (1875–1905) and had been appointed to the Bombay legislative council in 1882, resigning in 1886 owing to ill health. He had spoken strongly against abolition of import duties on Manchester goods (1879), European discrimination against Indians in the Ilbert Bill agitation (1883), and the lowering of the age of entry to the Indian Civil Service examinations (1884). In these and other controversies he developed a role as one of Bombay's leaders, forming along with Pherozeshah Mehta and K. T. Telang a triumvirate representing a unity between the different communities in the city, Muslim, Parsi, and Hindu. The three met regularly in Badruddin's high court chambers to co-ordinate their public work and were largely responsible for forming the Bombay Presidency Association in 1885, a body which championed Indian interests and which hosted the first meeting of the Indian National Congress held in Bombay at the end of 1885. One of the association's delegates to the session, Badruddin was unable to attend owing to legal commitments outside Bombay. He was elected president of the third Congress session in Madras in 1887 when he tried to associate Muslims more fully with Congress, countering the opposition movement led by Sir Saiyid Ahmad Khan from Aligarh which also undercut his position among Bombay Muslims.

Badruddin was deeply concerned with matters specifically affecting Muslims. In the late 1870s he opposed Russian encroachments on Turkey in the press and at a massive public meeting of Muslims; he demanded employment of Muslims in government positions; and promoted Muslim education particularly through the modernizing Anjuman-i-Islam (Islamic Association) which he had co-founded with the Bombay Sunni leader, Muhammad Ali Rogay, and others in 1876. He eventually became its secretary and was in the last sixteen years of his life its president. The Anjuman organized meetings on issues concerning Muslims but also started a progressive school for Muslims in 1880, finally obtaining major premises near Victoria Terminus in 1893. To promote social interaction among the city's Muslims, Badruddin was instrumental in founding both the Islam Club and the Islam Gymkhana.

In June 1895 Badruddin was made a judge of the Bombay high court, the first Muslim and the third Indian to be so elevated. He sat on the original rather than the appellate side and was noted for his careful decisions. He acted as chief justice in 1903, the first Indian to do so. On his elevation he had withdrawn from public activity but agreed in 1903 to be the president of the seventeenth Mahomedan Anglo-Oriental Educational Conference which met in

Bombay for the first time. The conference had been a political and anti-Congress body based largely in northern India but Badruddin, seeing it as purely educational, used it as a modernizing tool to promote female education, attack purdah, and expand education among Muslims generally.

While on a year's furlough in London Badruddin died suddenly of a heart attack on 19 August 1906. His body was brought back to Bombay and buried in the Sulaimani Bohra cemetery on 9 October 1906. A large public meeting in January 1907 decided to set up a permanent memorial to his memory but the decision was not implemented. A portrait by Mr Haite, subscribed for by the Bombay bar, was hung in the high court.

F. H. BROWN, *rev.* JIM MASSELOS

Sources H. B Tyabji, *Badruddin Tyabji: a biography* (1952) · *The Times* (21 Aug 1906) · *Indian Magazine and Review*, 429 (Sept 1906), 237–44 · S. A. Husain, *The destiny of Indian Muslims* (1965), 44–51 · *Indian judges: biographical and critical sketches* [n.d.], 145–59 · S. P. Sen, ed., *Dictionary of national biography*, 4 vols. (1972–4), vol. 4, pp. 365–7 [India] · J. C. Masselos, *Towards nationalism: group affiliations and the politics of public associations in nineteenth century western India* (1974)
Archives National Archives of India, New Delhi, corresp. and papers | Bombay University, Fyzee collection
Likenesses photograph, 1891, repro. in Tyabji, *Badruddin Tyabji*, frontispiece [*see illus.*] · Haite, oils, Bombay High Court · photographs, priv. coll.; repro. in Tyabji, *Badruddin Tyabji*

Tydder, John. *See* Siôn Tudur (*c*.1522–1602).

Tye, Christopher (*c*.1505–1571×3), composer and poet, was probably born in East Anglia, where the name was quite common. Nothing is known of his parents or youth.

Life Suggestions that he was born about 1497 and was a chorister at King's College, Cambridge, in 1511 and 1512 cannot be verified (a choirboy Tye is listed with no forename). The first mention of Christopher Tye is in a Cambridge grace book, which records his graduation MusB in 1536 (on condition of his composing a mass), after studying the art of music for ten years, and with much practice in composition and teaching boys. Thus, if he were twenty-one years old when he began to study and to teach (in 1526), he would have been born about 1505; if younger, then a year or two later. Tye became a lay clerk at King's College in March 1537, and may indeed have been master of the choristers, for he was paid riding charges for two journeys in that year to find suitable choristers for the choir; but he had left by Michaelmas 1539 (the mundum books from Michaelmas 1537 to Michaelmas 1539 are lacking).

Where and how Tye worked during the next few years is not known, but it seems that from this time onwards his career was influenced by Richard Cox (*d.* 1581), graduate of King's College, Cambridge, and a keen religious reformer, who became archdeacon of Ely in 1541. Between 1541 and 1543 Tye was appointed organist and master of the choristers of Ely Cathedral, with an annual salary of £10. In 1545 he was granted the Cambridge degree of MusD, again being required to compose a mass; and in 1548 (Cox now dean of Christ Church and chancellor of Oxford University) Tye was incorporated DMus at Oxford. Although he

did not resign from his post at Ely, he may possibly have been absent for some or all of the years 1552–9, after which his tenure for life was formally confirmed. Cox was almoner and tutor to the young Prince Edward from 1544 to 1550 and, despite Nichol's view to the contrary, Tye may have been Edward's music tutor during these years. Samuel Rowley, author of a play concerning Henry VIII and Edward, *When you See me, you Know me* (1605), was very likely Tye's grandson. In the play Prince Edward talks of 'Doctor Tye our Musicks Lecturer'; and Rowley may have known this to be the case. Tye, indeed, has a minor part. Edward tells him:

> I oft have heard my Father merrily speake
> In your hye praise, and thus his Highnesse sayth
> England, one God, one truth, one Doctor hath
> For Musicks Art, and that is Doctor *Tye*,
> Admir'd for skill in Musickes harmonie.
> (Rowley, sig. G4*r*)

The year 1553 saw Tye's only publication, *The Actes of the Apostles*. It is dedicated to Edward, with a verse preface, in which Tye addresses the king in friendly terms, gives advice on cultivating good taste, by playing on his lute *The Actes* rather than songs of wanton love, and mentions Edward's 'dear sisters': all this suggests that Tye had been his tutor. There is, however, no evidence to support former theories that Tye also taught Mary and Elizabeth. The title-page of *The Actes* says that Tye is 'one of the Gentylmen of hys graces most honourable Chappell'. Although his name is found in no extant chapel list, he undoubtedly was a member of the Chapel Royal for Mary Tudor's coronation (Mateer, 25–6); so the *Actes* title-page is surely correct, even if his membership was somewhat occasional or honorary. Tye may have worked as a court composer during Mary's reign: a mass (*Euge bone*) was probably composed for the return of Cardinal Pole in 1554, and a motet (*Domine Deus celestis*) may be an encomium for King Philip.

Richard Cox became bishop of Ely in 1558, a year before Tye's confirmation of tenure, and in 1560 ordained him as deacon and priest. Tye resigned his cathedral post in 1561. He was appointed to the rich living of Doddington-cum-Marche, in the Isle of Ely, and in 1564 acquired two other livings in Cambridgeshire, Wilbraham Parva and Newton-cum-Capella. He appears to have taken his parochial duties lightly. Failure to pay first-fruits resulted in the Wilbraham living being immediately sequestered for some months, and following other financial shortcomings the Doddington living also was sequestered for a time. It was reported to Archbishop Parker that he was unskilful at preaching. Tye resigned the Wilbraham living in 1567 and that at Newton in 1570. He was still rector of Doddington in 1571, but had died before March 1573 when, as recorded in the bishop's register, his successor to the benefice was instituted.

Tye's will is lost, but something is known of his family. A son Peter was a scoundrel, who forged his father's signature on a letter, 'and carried it to my Lord of Canterbury, and by that means was made Minister' of Trinity Church, Ely (Strype, 577–8). Tye also had a daughter, Ellen, who married (in her brother's church) Robert *White, composer and successor of Tye at Ely Cathedral. Ellen's will names her mother, Katherine, and sisters Susan Fulke and Mary Rowley, who married Robert, probable father of the above-mentioned playwright Samuel Rowley; a third sister is implicit (a brother-in-law Thomas Hawkes is named). No portrait of Christopher Tye is known, and the only mention of his character is found in the unreliable notes on the lives of musicians made by the Oxford amateur musician Anthony Wood:

> Dr. Tye was a peevish and humoursome man, especially in his latter dayes, and sometimes playing on the organ in the chap[el] of qu. Elizab. wh. contained much musick but little delight to the ear, she would send the verger to tell him that he play'd out of tune: whereupon he sent word that her eares were out of Tune.

Paul Doe has suggested that 'he was perhaps an opportunist, who liked life at the court, was not prepared to carry his protestant principles to the extent of sharing the Marian exile of his patron, Cox, and who finally adopted the priesthood as a means of easy retirement rather than as a vocation' (Doe, 19.299).

Works Tye's skill as a poet is very modest. Only the verse text of *The Actes of the Apostles* is certainly his work. He committed half of the book of Acts (chapters 1–14) to doggerel verse in iambic heptameters, of which the following, from chapter 4, is a fair sample:

> When that the people taught they had,
> There came to them doubtles,
> Priests and rulers, as men nye mad,
> And eke the Saduces.

Thomas Warton first drew attention to *A Notable History of Nastagio and Traversari*, a story from Boccaccio's *Decameron* (fifth day, eighth tale), set to verse in the same metre and doggerel style as *Actes*, by 'C. T.', whom he plausibly considered to be Christopher Tye:

> He sawe approche with swiftie foote
> The place where he did staye,
> A dame, with scattred heares untressde
> Bereft of her araye.
> (Warton, 3.468)

In the years after his death Tye was quite well remembered, for example in Francis Meres's *Palladis tamia* of 1598, though early writers' knowledge of his music was often limited to *The Actes*. Most of the Latin church music, in particular, was known only to a few specialists until first printed in the 1970s and 1980s. Thomas Fuller, much quoted by later writers, was perhaps the first to suggest that Tye was organist to Edward VI, while Wood's anecdote has him organist to Queen Elizabeth. Giles Jacob said that Tye versified the whole of the book of Acts, 'and set part of it to musick'. Warton, while disparaging the *Actes* poetry, calls Tye 'the most notable theological versifier of these times' (Warton, 3.190). Charles Burney printed the Gloria of Tye's *Euge bone* mass, but it was another hundred years before the complete mass was first published, in 1893, by G. E. P. Arkwright, with a well-researched biographical preface.

There are many gaps in surviving knowledge of Tye's compositions. Did the composer–organist of Ely Cathedral write no keyboard music? Did the probable translator of Boccaccio's *Decameron* story compose no secular partsongs? There is no example of either genre, while of twenty-two Latin compositions, ten, for five and six voices and mostly substantial pieces, are incomplete. Even so, what remains gives a view of Tye as a thoroughly progressive composer. Works of the early 1530s, such as *Ave caput Christi*, show the current rigid and sectional votive antiphon structure (two parts, the first in triple time, the second in duple, each divided into two sections for reduced voices and one for full choir) and plentiful use of melisma. By the late 1540s prayer- and psalm-motets were replacing the votive antiphon, with flexible structures at the service of colourful texts, imitation as a basic unifying technique, lively rhythms, shorter melismas, and predominantly duple time. *Quaesumus omnipotens* and *Omnes gentes, plaudite manibus* are good respective examples. Tye was a leader in introducing these essentially continental characteristics. The Gyffard partbooks contain five shorter pieces for four voices.

There are three fine masses: *The Western Wind*, where a secular tune (a novelty in England) is made the basis of contrapuntal variations; the very progressive *Peterhouse* (also called the *Mean* mass and *Missa sine nomine*), with much reworking of motifs; and *Euge bone* for six voices, his masterpiece, which was abreast of the latest compact continental style.

Tye's eighteen English compositions are of crucial importance in laying the musical foundations for the reformed church. When, in the first years of the reign of Edward VI, choirs were ordered (as in the 1548 Lincoln Cathedral injunctions) to sing in English, with just one note to every syllable so that the words should be clearly audible, Tye was foremost in tackling the problems. His anthems are amazingly inventive, given the restrictions. A few obey the new rules meticulously; others show that a somewhat relaxed interpretation soon became acceptable. Some have chordal passages alternating with simple imitations. Repetition is an important element in many.

The Actes of the Apostles (1553) was for domestic, not church use, and there is one piece for each chapter (usually covering two stanzas, and repeating for the remaining ones). The music is deliberately simple, almost hymn-like, mostly with one or two imitations. A few pieces, with new words replacing Tye's doggerel, are still heard, such as the anthem 'O come ye servants of the Lord', and the much modified hymn tune 'Winchester New' ('While shepherds watched their flocks by night').

In consort music for viols Tye was the most prolific composer of his generation. Of thirty-one pieces, twenty-one are In nomines (William Byrd, his nearest competitor, wrote seven). Freed from the restrictions of the church and the limitations of the voice, they are splendidly imaginative. A few of the simpler pieces are close in style to his vocal writing, but most show instrumental elements: wide, unvocal ranges, 'forbidden' leaps of sevenths, tenths, and twelfths, and angular lines. Many have descriptive titles. In the one called 'Crye' there are rapid, repeated, sobbing notes, while in another the performers have to 'Trust' that it is playable, the piece being in five time.

The manuscript sources of Tye's compositions are widespread, in the libraries of some seventeen cathedrals, churches, university colleges, and other institutions. The three biggest holdings are those of the British Library (seventeen), the Bodleian (nine), and Christ Church, Oxford (six). Most would agree today that Tye's close contemporary Thomas Tallis is the finer composer, both technically and expressively. But Tye's enquiring mind, always eager to experiment and absorb, made him a composer of the greatest importance in the years of religious turmoil, and a vital fertilizer of the musical soil for the Elizabethan golden age.   NIGEL DAVISON

Sources P. Doe, 'Tye, Christopher', *New Grove* · C. Tye, *The Actes of the Apostles* (1553) · *Christopher Tye: mass to six voices 'Euge bone', with a biographical memoir*, ed. G. E. P. Arkwright (1893) · *DNB* · S. Rowley, *When you see me, you know me* (1605); repr. (1952) · I. Payne, *The provision and practice of sacred music at Cambridge colleges and selected cathedrals, c.1547–c.1646* (1993), 191, 252–3, 268, 287 · [G. Jacob], *The poetical register, or, The lives and characters of all the English poets*, 2 (1723), 216 · A. Willet, 'Epistola dedicatoria', *An harmonie upon the second booke of Samuel* (1614), fol. g3v · D. Mateer, 'The "Gyffard" part-books: composers, owners, date and provenance', *Royal Musical Association Research Chronicle*, 28 (1995), 21–50 · J. Strype, *Annals of the Reformation and establishment of religion ... during Queen Elizabeth's happy reign*, new edn, 2/2 (1824), 411–711, esp. 574–8 · *Christopher Tye, 1: English sacred music*, ed. J. Morehen, Early English Church Music, 19 (1977) · *Christopher Tye, 2: Masses*, ed. P. Doe (1980), Early English Church Music, 24 (1980) · *Christopher Tye, 3: Ritual music and motets*, ed. N. Davison, Early English Church Music, 33 (1987) · *Christopher Tye: the instrumental music*, ed. R. Weidner, Recent Researches in the Music of the Renaissance, 3 (1967) · R. Weidner, 'Tye's *Actes of the Apostles*: a reassessment', *Musical Quarterly*, 58 (1972), 242–58 · Fuller, *Worthies* (1662), 2.244 · T. Warton, *The history of English poetry*, new edn, ed. W. C. Hazlitt, 4 vols. (1871) · *Literary remains of King Edward the Sixth*, ed. J. G. Nichols, 1, Roxburghe Club, 75 (1857); repr. (1963), liv · A. Ashbee and D. Lasocki, eds., *A biographical dictionary of English court musicians, 1485–1714*, 2 (1998), 1107–9 · T. Morley, *A plain and easy introduction to practical music*, ed. R. A. Harman (1952), 123, 322 · will of Ellen White, PRO, PROB 11/58, sig. 11 · A. Wood, MS notes on the lives of musicians, Bodl. Oxf., MS Wood D 19[4] · F. Meres, *Palladis tamia: wits treasury, being the second part of wits common-wealth* (1598), fol. 288v · Burney, *Hist. mus.*, 2.589–92
Wealth at death vicar at Doddington-cum-Marche, a rich living

Tyerman, Daniel (1773–1828), missionary, was born on 19 November 1773 at Clack Farm, near Osmotherly in Yorkshire, where his parents had lived for some time. In 1790 he obtained employment in London. Coming under strong religious convictions, he entered Hoxton Academy in 1795 to prepare himself for the Congregational ministry. In 1798, the year of his marriage to Miss Rich, with whom he had a son and a daughter, he became minister at Cawsand in Cornwall, subsequently moving to Wellington in Somerset. About 1804 he officiated for a short time at Southampton, and afterwards settled at Newport in the Isle of Wight. There he was one of the first organizers of the town reading-rooms, and was secretary of the Isle of Wight Bible Society. In 1810 he married his second wife, Miss Fletcher, of Abingdon, Berkshire; they had two sons and a daughter. In these years he published several evangelical works, notably *The Importance of Domestic Discipline*

(1807); *Evangelical Hope: an Essay* (1815); and *Essay on the Wisdom of God* (1818).

In 1821 Tyerman and George Bennet of Sheffield were appointed by the London Missionary Society to visit their southern stations. They sailed from London on 2 May in the whaler *Tuscan*, and, proceeding round Cape Horn, visited Tahiti, the Leeward and Sandwich islands, and other mission stations in the south seas. In 1824 they visited New South Wales in Australia, and on the way narrowly escaped from New Zealand Maori. From Sydney, in September 1824, they sailed through the Torres Strait to Java, and thence to Singapore, Canton (Guangzhou), and Calcutta. At Serampore, in Bengal, on 3 May 1826, they met the venerable William Carey (1761–1834), who received them with much kindness. After visiting Benares, they sailed to Madras, and thence to Goa. From India they voyaged in 1827 to Mauritius and Madagascar, where the missions were firmly established under King Radama. On 30 July 1828 Tyerman, whose health had given way under the climate of southern India, died at Antananarivo in Madagascar.

The journal of Tyerman's missionary tour was published by James Montgomery, the poet, in 1831 (2nd edn, 1841). The first part was written in conjunction with George Bennet, but the latter part was entirely his own. It gives a graphic picture of the state of the London society's missions at the period.

E. I. CARLYLE, rev. H. C. G. MATTHEW

Sources *Voyages and travels around the world by the Rev. Daniel Tyerman*, ed. J. Montgomery, 2nd edn (1841) · *Congregational Magazine*, 16 (1833), 468, 513 · R. Lovett, *The history of the London Missionary Society, 1795–1895*, 2 vols. (1899) · T. Hiney, *On the missionary trail: the classic Georgian adventure of two Englishmen sent on a journey around the world, 1821–29* (2000)
Likenesses T. Blood, stipple, BM, NPG; repro. in *Evangelical Magazine* · portrait, repro. in *Voyages and travels*, ed. Montgomery

Tyerman, Donald (1908–1981), journalist and journal editor, was born on 1 March 1908 in Middlesbrough, the second of the three sons (there were no daughters) of Joseph Tyerman, an accountant, who took jobs in Kenya, and his wife, Catherine Day, who was originally a teacher. At the age of three Tyerman contracted polio and was paralysed from the neck down. He fought through ten years of hospitalization with extraordinary courage and vigour, eventually regaining control of all parts of his body except that he always had to walk with splints. He therefore went late to school but he passed through the Friends' school at Great Ayton, Coatham grammar school at Redcar, and Gateshead secondary school to Brasenose College, Oxford, with a scholarship. He achieved first-class honours in modern history (1929), and from 1930 to 1936 he was a lecturer at University College, Southampton, where he met a social science student, Margaret Charteris, daughter of Ernest Gray, a businessman; they married in 1934 and had three daughters and two sons.

In 1936 *The Economist* advertised with university appointments boards for a writer on public and economic affairs. As secretary to the appointments board at Southampton Tyerman applied for the job himself, and *The Economist* accepted him with alacrity. Throughout the Second World War he was one of the most influential journalists in England. He was deputy editor to Geoffrey Crowther at *The Economist* from 1939 to 1944 but, as Crowther was also filling many war jobs, Tyerman was quite often in charge of the paper. In 1943–4 he was also deputy editor of *The Observer*, frequently putting that paper to bed on the Saturday, having put *The Economist* to bed on the Thursday. Both papers played a major role in preparing the intellectual ground for Britain's post-war welfare state, with *The Economist* lending critical support to the crusade for central planning.

In 1944 Tyerman was lured away to be assistant editor of *The Times*, where he infuriated Winston Churchill by opposing the government's policy in Greece at the end of the war. His friends hoped Tyerman would become editor of *The Times* but by now his physical immobility was sapping his otherwise boundless energy and was making it increasingly difficult for him to edit a daily newspaper. Crowther hoped to get him the job as editor of the *News Chronicle* but he eventually succeeded Crowther as editor of *The Economist* itself (1956–65).

Tyerman's period as editor at *The Economist* cannot have been easy with Crowther constantly throwing in brilliant new ideas from the chairman's office and with the young turks whom Crowther had recruited to the paper after 1945 also being pungent rather than conventional in their opinions. Controversies over the paper's handling of the Suez conflict and the Cuban missile crisis imposed further strains. In the last issue before the election of 15 October 1964 Tyerman ended the paper's leading article: 'It does seem to *The Economist* that, on the nicest balance, the riskier choice of Labour—and Mr Wilson—will be the better choice for voters on Thursday'. This was also the view of most of his editorial writers, who thought it crucial that post-Gaitskell Labour should come back for a while into being a party of government because another spell of opposition during the 1960s could turn it into an old-time socialist party instead of a new-age responsible social democrat party.

Although Crowther and most of the rest of the board of *The Economist* did not agree with this it is not true that the contretemps over it led to Tyerman's retirement. Tyerman had decided to retire earlier in the year, and before election day in 1964 Alastair Burnet had already been approved by all concerned as his successor. Tyerman stayed on as a director of *The Economist* but he did not have the same post-editorial influence as Crowther did. He devoted more time to his extracurricular activities—on the International Press Institute, the Press Council, the Save the Children Fund, and the council of the University of Sussex. He was appointed CBE for public service in 1978. Throughout his life he was an assiduous trainer of young journalists, with a keen eye for newspaper make-up, and as brave in his integrity as in his long fight against physical disability. Tyerman died at his home, Holly Cottage, Westleton, near Saxmundham, Suffolk, on 24 April 1981; a funeral service was conducted at Westleton church four days later.　　　　　　　　　　　　NORMAN MACRAE, *rev.*

Sources *The Times* (25 April 1981) · *The Economist* (2 May 1981) · R. D. Edwards, *The pursuit of reason: The Economist, 1843–1993* (1993) · S. E. Koss, *The rise and fall of the political press in Britain*, 2 (1984) · D. Griffiths, ed., *The encyclopedia of the British press, 1422–1992* (1992) · personal knowledge (1990) · private information (1990) · *WWW* · *CGPLA Eng. & Wales* (1981)
Archives Bodl. RH, corresp. with Sir R. R. Welensky · Welwyn Garden City Central Library, corresp. with Sir Frederick Osborn | SOUND BL NSA, performance recording
Likenesses photograph, repro. in Edwards, *The pursuit of reason* · photograph, repro. in *The Times*
Wealth at death £46,307: probate, 19 June 1981, *CGPLA Eng. & Wales*

Tyers, Jonathan (1702–1767), pleasure garden proprietor, was born of unknown parents. In the early 1720s he married Elizabeth Fermor (1700–1771) whose origins and early life are also obscure. They are said to have separated in 1759, although the wording of Tyers's will does not support this supposition. Spring Gardens, later to be known as Vauxhall Gardens, which had opened in 1661, lay close to the Thames on the south bank, approximately opposite the site of Tate Britain. By the time that Tyers obtained a lease from Elizabeth Masters in 1728 (he eventually completed the purchase in 1758) the gardens had become a 'rural Brothel' (Lockman, 28), and it is to his credit that the venue was transformed into a fashionable place of evening entertainment; to those who were unable to afford a private retreat, Spring Gardens democratically offered an open invitation at a shilling a head. A series of walks, illuminated with many small lanterns, invited one to promenade; a crescent of supper boxes offered expensive fare (a plate of wafer-thin ham for 1s. and a minute roast chicken for 2s. 6d.) and also the opportunity to sit, be seen, and watch the populace go by; music could be enjoyed in the orchestra next to the Grand Walk as well as from the small ensembles dotted about the grounds.

Tyers was a man of wide cultural interests—his private house in the gardens, for example, contained a substantial art collection—and he brought these to bear in the development of Spring Gardens, employing a circle of acquaintances to contribute to the visual arts and music. Among painters, designers, and sculptors who worked for him may be counted William Hogarth, Hubert François Gravelot, Louis François Roubiliac, and the Drury Lane scene painter, Francis Hayman. Many of Hayman's compositions hung in the supper boxes, portraying various theatrical incidents. Just before the mid-century Tyers attempted to counteract the growing popularity of the rival Ranelagh Gardens by commissioning Hayman to paint four large historical canvases, the subjects of which are uncertain, for the saloon, an extension to the rotunda. Large paintings were used as vista closures to some of the walks (the ruins of the temple of Palmyra, Syria, were to be glimpsed at the termination of the South Walk) thus creating a fine theatrical effect. Tyers indulged his fondness for stage decor by creating a setting, revealed each evening by a rising curtain: an artificially lit water mill, the miller's house, and a large foaming cascade made of tin came into view accompanied by applause.

Music made the evenings the more delightful and here

again Tyers drew on his friends. Songs were one of the features of the gardens with pieces composed by Thomas and his son Michael Arne, James Hook, and James Worgan. They were published individually in the *London Magazine* and anthologies, complete with engravings of the gardens, were compiled by George Bickham (1737) and Jonathan Battishill (1761). Visitors, among them the young Mozart and George Frideric Handel, conducted and performed here and many of the popular singers of the London theatres, Sophia Baddeley, Joseph Vernon, and Frederick Charles Reinhold to mention a few, could be enjoyed. Concerts were given in the rotunda, a building equipped with the usual theatre divisions of box, pit, and gallery as well as an organ; the area under the dome was claimed to be free of vibrations. Here the house orchestra, its members made distinctive by cocked hats and livery, performed.

The energy Tyers expended on raising the tone of Spring Gardens was repaid by the quality attending: Frederick, prince of Wales, the ground landlord of the property, visited from time to time and a suitable pavilion was built for his use, bishops were to be found in the supper boxes, and Thomas Rowlandson, in his painting *Vauxhall Gardens*, drew attention to the range of visitors. By 1784 these included: Samuel Johnson, James Boswell, Mrs Thrale, Oliver Goldsmith, the duchess of Devonshire, Lady Bessborough, Admiral Paisley, Sir Henry Bate Dudley, and Mary Perdita Robinson, some of whom were known personally to Tyers.

If Spring Gardens revealed the lightness and gaiety of Tyers's taste, his private garden at Denbies, a house on the edge of Dorking, Surrey, bought from William Wakefield in 1734, shows the dark and literary side of his nature. Visitors discovered that the theatrical interest of the designer gave way to Gothic melodrama when they came across a woodland, 'Il Penseroso'. Here a hermitage contained a lectern on which was chained Edward Young's *Night Thoughts on Life, Death and Immortality* and Robert Blair's *The Grave*. Nearby, iron gates led to the 'Valley of the Shadow of Death' where the principal building, consisting of two up-ended stone coffins supporting a portico, was surmounted by human skulls.

Four children were born to Jonathan and Elizabeth Tyers: their eldest was Margaret (1724–1786), who married George Rogers of Southampton; Thomas *Tyers (1724/5–1787), the eldest son, became joint proprietor of the gardens together with his younger brother, Jonathan, who married Margaret Rogers; a second daughter, Elizabeth (1727–1802), married John Wood of Abchurch Lane. The family are shown in several of Hayman's paintings. Jonathan Tyers had made his will on 4 June 1758 with codicils dated 18 July 1758 and 6 May 1765. His wife was granted a personal estate and Thomas was paid a quarterly allowance of £200 until his mother's death in 1771. Jonathan was given £100 per annum for life. The remainder of the estate was sold to purchase government securities; the proceeds were intended for Elizabeth Tyers and to be held in trust for the daughters. Tyers died on 26 June or 1 July 1767 (reports vary) at Proprietor's House, Spring Gardens.

PAUL RANGER

Sources W. Wroth and A. E. Wroth, *The London pleasure gardens of the eighteenth century* (1896); repr. (1979) · Vauxhall Gardens, scrapbooks, Bodl. Oxf., GA Surrey c 21 · D. Coke, *The muses' bower: Vauxhall Gardens, 1728–86* (1978) · J. S. Bright, *A history of Dorking* (1884) · B. Allen, *Francis Hayman* (1987) · [J. Lockman], *A sketch of the Spring Gardens, Vaux-Hall, in a letter to a noble lord* (1751?) · B. Allen, 'Jonathan Tyers' other garden', *Journal of Garden History*, 1/3 (1981), 215–238 · J. D. Hunt, 'Theatres, gardens and garden theatres', *Essays and Studies by Members of the English Association*, new ser., 33 (1980), 95–118 · T. J. Edelstein, *Vauxhall Gardens* (1983) · *GM* · I. Reed, 'Notitia

Jonathan Tyers (1702–1767), by Francis Hayman, 1740 [with his family]

dramatica: being notes of performances on the English stage', 3 vols., BL, Add. MSS 25390–25392

Archives Bodl. Oxf., Vauxhall Gardens, scrapbooks, GA Surrey c 21 · Minet Library, Knatchbull Road, Camberwell, London, Vauxhall Gardens MSS · Museum of London, Warwick Wroth portfolio of newspaper and magazine writings relating to Vauxhall Gardens, 61. 6/3

Likenesses F. Hayman, oils, 1740, NPG [*see illus.*] · L. F. Roubiliac, marble bust, *c.*1745–1750, Birmingham Museums and Art Gallery · F. Hayman, oils, *c.*1750, Yale U. CBA, Paul Mellon collection

Wealth at death principally the Gardens, proprietor's house, contents (large art collection); Denbies manor house and extensive grounds, outside Dorking

Tyers, Thomas (1724/5–1787), writer, was the eldest son of Jonathan *Tyers (1702–1767) of Lambeth, proprietor of Vauxhall Gardens, and his wife, Elizabeth Fermor (1700–1771). He matriculated at Pembroke College, Oxford, on 13 December 1738, at the age of thirteen; he graduated BA in 1742 and MA (from Exeter College) in 1745. He was admitted from the Middle Temple to the Inner Temple in November 1753 and called to the bar on 22 June 1757. Tyers kept legal chambers in Fig Tree Court from 1760 to 1776, but 'having a handsome fortune, vivacity of temper, and eccentricity of mind, he could not confine himself to the regularity of practice' (Boswell, *Life*, 2.308). On his father's death in 1767 he became joint proprietor of Vauxhall Gardens with his brother Jonathan. He supplied the words of many of the songs sung there, wrote pastorals, and contributed an account of the gardens to Nichols's *History of Lambeth*.

Tyers had a villa at Ashtead, near Epsom, and apartments in Southampton Street, Covent Garden; he drove back and forth between them 'so that he could perpetually diversify his amusements'. In a character-sketch apparently of his own composition, he is described as 'inquisitive, talkative, full of notions and quotations, and, which is the praise of a purling stream, of no great depth' (Nichols, *Lit. anecdotes*, 8.80, 88). Boswell comments: 'He … ran about the world with a pleasant carelessness, amusing every body by his desultory conversation' (Boswell, *Life*, 2.308). Tyers's knowledge of medicine 'gave him somewhat of a propensity to hypochondriacism' (Nichols, *Lit. anecdotes*, 8.84). Among his friends were Lord Hardwicke, Bishop Lowth, and Dr John Campbell, and Boswell claims that Tyers 'lived with Dr. Johnson in as easy a manner as almost any of his very numerous acquaintance' (Boswell, *Life*, 2.309). Johnson's portrait of Tom Restless, the 'ambulatory' student who devotes little time to books, but wanders about for ideas to the coffee house and debating club, was based on Tyers (*The Idler*, no. 48). But he was actually formidably well read, and Johnson confessed that Tyers always told him 'something he did not know before' (Nichols, *Lit. anecdotes*, 8.88). It was Tyers who observed of Johnson that he always 'talked as if he was talking upon oath' (Boswell, *Life*, 2.434). Johnson told Boswell: 'Tom Tyers described me the best: "Sir (said he,) you are like a ghost: you never speak till you are spoken to".' Mrs Piozzi says that Johnson often repeated this, though Boswell noted (on information from George Steevens) that it was based on a passage from Fielding's *Tom Jones* (ibid., 5.73).

Tyers's *Political Conferences* (1780), a series of imaginary conversations between statesmen, was much praised by Boswell for its 'learning, various knowledge, and discernment of character' (Boswell, *Life*, 2.309). *An Historical Rhapsody on Mr Pope* followed in 1781; dedicated to the queen, it offered a non-chronological series of biographical anecdotes relating to Pope, and unmitigated praise for the poet throughout. *An Historical Essay on Mr Addison* (1782) was of a similar adulatory cast. Tyers gave copies of these to Johnson, and used to bind up presentation copies of his publications for the King's Library, but was otherwise concerned to limit circulation (none of his work was reviewed). *Conversations, Political and Familiar* (1784) numbered only twenty-five copies 'for the perusal of a very few friends' (Nichols, *Lit. anecdotes*, 8.81). When Johnson died in 1784, Tyers quickly drew up 'A biographical sketch of Dr Samuel Johnson'. This first appeared in the *Gentleman's Magazine*, to which Tyers was a regular contributor, in December 1784, but was expanded and corrected several times before being issued as a pamphlet in 1785. Tyers inscribed a copy for Boswell, who called him Tiresias, in a play on his name: 'Pray Mr. Boswell don't lend, lose, nor give away this biographical morsel, 1785. Tiresias is only a lute, but Boswell is a lute, and a trumpet' (Tyers, i). Boswell, who had continued to meet Tyers socially, claimed not to find much in the 'entertaining little collection of fragments', rating the Pope and Addison essays much more highly (Boswell, *Life*, 2.309); but it remains a witty and vivid account, and Tyers went on revising it until his death. Tyers drew up his will on 26 March 1785. In it he requested a quiet burial in St Paul's, Covent Garden, once 'the body begins to putrify', and made a number of large monetary bequests (three of £500, others of £100 and £50) to friends and relatives. He left the estate at Ashtead, the share in Vauxhall Gardens, and other property in Bermondsey Street, Southwark, to his brother Jonathan and sisters Margaret Rogers and Elizabeth Wood, to be divided after their deaths between his nephews and nieces, 'share and share alike'. A 'Set of resolutions' concerning health and religion also dates from 1785; at the end of the year he sold his share in Vauxhall to his brother's family. His sister Margaret Rogers died on 2 October 1786, and Tyers, a practised writer of obituaries, wrote a eulogy of her in the *Gentleman's Magazine* (1st ser., 56, 1786, 909). Tyers died at Ashtead after a lingering illness on 1 February 1787. He was unmarried. He used to give to friends a likeness of himself by I. Taylor, engraved by J. Hall.

W. W. WROTH, *rev.* PAUL BAINES

Sources Nichols, *Lit. anecdotes*, 8.79–89 · Boswell, *Life*, 2.107, 434; 3.307–9; 5.73 · T. Tyers, *Biographical sketch of Dr Samuel Johnson*, ed. G. D. Meyer (1952) · Foster, *Alum. Oxon.* · F. A. Inderwick and R. A. Roberts, eds., *A calendar of the Inner Temple records*, 5 (1936), 40, 86, 117, 171, 197, 324, 432 · S. Johnson, *The Idler*, no. 48 · *The correspondence and other papers of James Boswell relating to the making of the Life of Johnson*, ed. M. Waingrow (1969), vol. 2 of *The Yale editions of the private papers of James Boswell*, research edn (1966–), 147 · *Boswell, laird of Auchinleck, 1778–1782*, ed. J. W. Reed and F. A. Pottle (1977), vol. 11 of *The Yale editions of the private papers of James Boswell*, trade edn (1950–89), 71 · *Boswell: the applause of the jury, 1782–1785*, ed. I. S. Lustig and F. A. Pottle (1981), vol. 12 of *The Yale editions of the private* *papers of James Boswell*, trade edn (1950–89), 292, 294, 306, 315 · *London Chronicle* (1–3 Feb 1787) · *St James's Chronicle* (8–11 Jan 1785) · *GM*, 1st ser., 57 (1787), 182–4 · *N&Q*, 3rd ser., 8 (1865), 456 · *DNB* · will, PRO, PROB 11/1180, sig. 95

Archives BL, Add. MSS, letters to Lord Hardwicke

Likenesses F. Hayman, group portrait, oils, c.1740–1745, Yale U. CBA; version, 1740, NPG · J. Hall, line engraving (after portrait by I. Taylor), BM, NPG

Tylden, Sir John Maxwell (1787–1866), army officer, born at Milstead, near Sittingbourne, Kent, on 25 September 1787, was the eldest son of Richard Tylden (d. 2 Feb 1832) of Milstead Manor and his second wife, Jane, daughter of the Revd Samuel Auchmuty, rector of New York, and sister of Lieutenant-General Sir Samuel Auchmuty. William Burton *Tylden was his younger brother. He was commissioned ensign in the 43rd foot in the summer of 1804, and was promoted lieutenant on 23 November.

In 1807 Tylden served in the expedition to Montevideo and Buenos Aires as brigade major to his uncle, Sir Samuel Auchmuty. Promoted captain on 28 September 1809, in 1810 he went to Madras as aide-de-camp to Auchmuty. He accompanied him to Java, was at the capture of Fort Cornelis on 26 August 1811, and was sent home with dispatches. He received a brevet majority, and was knighted in May 1812, when he acted as proxy for Auchmuty at the installation of knights of the Bath.

Tylden joined the 1st battalion of the 43rd in the Peninsula in 1813, and was present at the battles of the Nive, Orthez, and Toulouse. In 1814 he went with his regiment to America, and took part in the unsuccessful attack on New Orleans. In the later stages of it he acted as assistant adjutant-general, Colonel Frederick Stovin having been wounded on 23 December, and he was praised in General Lambert's dispatch of 28 January 1815.

In February 1816 Tylden obtained a majority in the 3rd Buffs and was placed on half pay. On 16 July 1818 he became major in the 52nd, and on 12 August 1819 he was made brevet lieutenant-colonel. He went to Nova Scotia in 1823 in temporary command of the 52nd, but returned to England on leave in 1824, and retired from the army in June 1825. He afterwards received the silver medal for Java, and for Nive, Orthez, and Toulouse.

Tylden was a leader of the Liberal Party in east Kent. He was JP, and was made deputy lieutenant in 1852. He married, first, in 1829, Elizabeth, only daughter of the Revd Henry Lomax Walsh of Grimblesthorpe Hall, Lincoln, and they had one daughter; second, in 1842, Charlotte (1789–1858), daughter of Sir Robert Synge, bt. Tylden died at his home, Milstead Manor, on 18 May 1866.

E. M. LLOYD, rev. JAMES LUNT

Sources *GM*, 4th ser., 1 (1866) · J. Philippart, ed., *The royal military calendar*, 3 vols. (1815–16) · W. James, *Military occurrences of the late war between Great Britain and the United States of America*, 1 (1818) · W. S. Moorsom, ed., *Historical record of the fifty-second regiment (Oxfordshire light infantry), from the year 1755 to the year 1858* (1860) · Burke, *Gen. GB* (1858) · Fortescue, *Brit. army*, vol. 10 · D. B. Chidsey, *The battle of New Orleans* (1961) · D. Gates, *The Spanish ulcer: a history of the Peninsular War* (1986) · A. Harfield, *British & Indian armies in the East Indies, 1685–1935* (1984) · Boase, *Mod. Eng. biog.* · *Dod's Peerage* (1858)

Wealth at death under £12,000: probate, 15 June 1866, *CGPLA Eng. & Wales*

Tylden, Richard (1819–1855). *See under* Tylden, William Burton (1790–1854).

Tylden [Tilden; *alias* Godden], **Thomas** (1622–1688), Roman Catholic controversialist, was born Thomas Tylden (or Tilden) at Addington, Kent, in December 1622, the eldest son of William Tylden (d. 1628), a tanner of Dartford, Kent, and his wife, Parnell Godden, a widow, whose name he took as his alias. He was educated at a private school in Holborn, London, under a Mr Gill for one year before entering Queen's College, Oxford, as a commoner in 1638. In 1639 he was admitted to St John's College, Cambridge, as a pensioner. John Williams, bishop of Lincoln, wrote to the college in 1640 recommending Tylden and he was duly elected Billingsley scholar. He graduated BA in 1642.

While at St John's, Tylden befriended John Sergeant, who later converted to Catholicism and was instrumental in Tylden's conversion. Sergeant introduced Tylden to the Catholic divine George Gage, who, at the request of the two young converts, sent them with a letter of recommendation to the English College in Lisbon in November 1643. After one year spent in spiritual exercises and the study of philosophy and theology Tylden was admitted to study for holy orders. He was eventually ordained and remained at the college as a lecturer of philosophy and theology 'to the great applause of all' (Bishop John Russell in Sharratt, *Lisbon College Register*, 174–5). He became professor of theology, prefect of studies, and vice-president of the college. In 1656 he was made president of the college and according to a contemporary, through prudent administration improved the college's position. In 1660 he became doctor of divinity. In the following year he was appointed chaplain and preceptor to Princess Catherine of Braganza. In 1662 he accompanied her to England and lived in the palace of Somerset House. He was one of the witnesses to the marriage of Princess Catherine and Charles II, and shortly afterwards he was appointed treasurer to the queen's household. It is said that he taught her to speak English. According to Russell, Tylden spent his life at court as though in the cloister and 'he was very dear to the Queen and not disliked by the King' (ibid.). During this time Tylden was also involved in the administration of the English mission as a prominent member of the chapter of secular clergy in England and in May 1667 was one of the three ecclesiastics recommended by the chapter in their application to Rome for the appointment of a bishop for England. In 1673 Philip Howard, the proposed vicar apostolic for England, was not confirmed by Rome because Tylden took the dispute over the appointment to King Charles who, through the nuncio in Brussels, asked for the suspension of Howard's briefs.

In 1678, as persecution of Catholic clergy heightened, Tylden was forced to resign his post in the queen's household and went into hiding some 24 miles outside London. As persecution on account of the Popish Plot began he escaped to France, thus avoiding the fate of his servant

Lawrence Hill who was executed for his complicity in the murder of Sir Edmund Berry Godfrey. Tylden was also accused of complicity in the crime on the false testimony of Miles Prance, who swore that the corpse was concealed in Tylden's apartment. Tylden spent some months in the English convent of the Poor Clares in Rouen and then in Paris where he was employed to preach to English Catholics, now in great number in Paris. He remained in Paris until the accession of James II when he was reinstated at Somerset House as almoner and preacher to the queen dowager and chaplain as before. During this time, and until his death in 1688, Tylden collaborated with John Sergeant in writing, printing, and circulating Catholic books of devotion and replies to popular tracts, pamphlets, and books against the Catholic religion. These included published arguments with eminent bishops and divines of the Church of England such as Edward Stillingfleet, Daniel Whitby, Nicolas Stratford, William Payne, and William Jane, in which Tylden sought to refute the charge that Catholics were idolaters and that Catholic doctrines were recent inventions.

In 1686 in the presence of the king and the earl of Rochester, Tylden, with Dr Bonaventure Gifford, was chosen by James II to represent the Catholic side in a formal disputation with Dr Simon Patrick and Dr William Jane. According to Dodd, Tylden was an equal match for his opponents in his learning and was 'much superior to [th]em in his modest behaviour, which gained him great applause, even from those of the adverse party' (Dodd, 3.470). The debate was mostly concerned with the doctrine of the real presence and Tylden argued from the ancient fathers and the scholastics for the truth and authenticity of Catholic teaching on the matter. In comparing him with John Sergeant during their time at Lisbon, Russell wrote that Tylden thought philosophy should be pursued only to the extent that Christian philosophy was of help to true theology and to understanding the mysteries of faith while Sergeant was anxious to find certainty and applied himself to the new philosophies of Descartes and Digby (Sharratt, *Ushaw Magazine*, 32). This difference between Tylden and Sergeant is borne out in their controversial writings. Tylden did subscribe on Sergeant's side, however, when the orthodoxy of his works and ideas was being questioned by the Sorbonne in 1676. Tylden's most important work is *Catholicks No Idolators* (1672), a refutation of Stillingfleet which sparked off a lengthy controversy into which Daniel Whitby DD was also drawn. John Sergeant eventually took over Tylden's side in this dispute with his *Five Catholick Letters* in 1687 and 1688. Tylden died at Somerset House in November 1688 and was probably buried in the vault under the chapel there on 30 November.　　　　　　　　　　　　RUTH JORDAN

Sources M. Sharratt, ed., *Lisbon College register, 1628–1813*, Catholic RS, 72 (1991), 174–5 · M. Sharratt, 'Bishop Russell and John Sergeant', *Ushaw Magazine*, 90 (1979), 22–37 · M. Hay, *The Jesuits and the Popish Plot* (1934) · C. Dodd, *The church history of England* (1976), vol. 3, pp. 470–72 · T. Baker, *History of the college of St John the Evangelist, Cambridge*, ed. J. E. B. Mayor, 1 (1869), 525–6 · R. A. Beddard, 'James II and the Catholic challenge', *Hist. U. Oxf. 4: 17th-cent. Oxf.*, 907–54 · Wood, *Ath. Oxon.*, new edn, 4.93, 674 · J. Warner, *The history of English persecution of Catholics and the presbyterian plot*, ed. T. A. Birrell, trans. J. Bligh, 1, Catholic RS, 47 (1953), 239 · T. B. Macaulay, *The history of England from the accession of James II*, 2 (1858), 407–8 · N. Luttrell, *A brief historical relation of state affairs from September 1678 to April 1714*, 1 (1857), 391–482 · J. C. M. Weale, ed., *Registers of the Catholic chapels royal and of the Portuguese embassy chapel, 1662–1829*, Catholic RS, 38 (1941) · T. H. Clancy, *English Catholic books, 1641–1700: a bibliography*, rev. edn (1996) · DNB · G. Anstruther, *The seminary priests*, 2 (1975), 321–2

Archives Ushaw College, co. Durham, Lisbon collection, Annales (Official register of Lisbon College)

Tylden, William Burton (1790–1854), army officer, son of Richard Tylden of Milsted Manor, Kent, and his second wife, Jane, daughter of the Revd Dr Samuel Auchmuty, was born at Milsted on 8 April 1790. Sir John Maxwell *Tylden was his elder brother. After passing through the Royal Military Academy at Woolwich, Tylden received a commission as second lieutenant in the Royal Engineers on 6 November 1806, and was promoted first lieutenant on 1 May 1807. He embarked for Gibraltar on 8 January 1808, arriving on 10 March, and was employed in the revision of the fortifications. In September 1811 he went to Malta, and from there, at the end of October, to Messina. He was promoted second captain on 15 April 1812.

Tylden was commanding royal engineer, under Lord William Bentinck, at the siege of Santa Maria in the gulf of Spezzia, and at its capture on 29 March 1814, and was thanked in general orders for his exertions. He was mentioned in dispatches (*London Gazette*, 8 May 1814), and Admiral Rowley expressed his indebtedness to him for assistance to the navy at the batteries. Tylden was also commanding royal engineer of the Anglo-Sicilian army under Bentinck at the action before Genoa on 17 April, when the French were defeated, and he took part in the investment of the city and the operations which led to the surrender of the fortress on 19 April 1814. He was thanked in general orders, mentioned in dispatches (*London Gazette*, 8 May 1814), and on 23 June was promoted to the brevet rank of major. He was also appointed military secretary to Bentinck, commander-in-chief in the Mediterranean, and occupied the post until his return to England in August.

In November 1814 Tylden joined the army in the Southern Netherlands, and took charge of the defences of Antwerp. In 1815 he organized and commanded a train of eighty pontoons, with which he took part in the operations of the allies, the march to and capture of Paris, and the occupation of France. He returned to England in 1818. In June 1822 he went again to Gibraltar, and served there as second in command of the Royal Engineers until May 1823, when he returned to England, and was stationed at Portsmouth. He was promoted first captain in the Royal Engineers on 23 March 1825. In November 1830 he was appointed commanding royal engineer at Bermuda. He returned home in July 1836, and was commanding royal engineer of the eastern military district, with headquarters at Harwich. He was promoted lieutenant-colonel of

Royal Engineers on 10 January 1837. In May 1840 he went to Malta as commanding royal engineer, returning to England in October 1844, when he was appointed commanding royal engineer of the south-eastern military district and stationed at Dover. He was promoted colonel of Royal Engineers on 21 September 1850, having arrived at Corfu in June of that year as commanding royal engineer in the Ionian Islands.

From Corfu, Tylden was sent in February 1854 to join the army in the Turkish empire. He arrived at Constantinople on the 12th of that month, and on the 21st was made a brigadier-general on Lord Raglan's staff and commanding royal engineer of the army. He was busy until May with the defences of the lines of Gallipoli. On the change of base from Gallipoli to Varna, Tylden went to Varna, and when the Russians raised the siege of Silistria in the middle of June, and it was decided to invade the Crimea, he prepared the necessary works for embarking and disembarking the army and its munitions of war, and collected siege materials. During the great fire at Varna on 10 August, Tylden was chiefly instrumental in saving the town from entire destruction by protecting two large gunpowder magazines with wet blankets when the fire had reached within 30 yards of them.

Tylden went to the Crimea with the army, and took part in the battle of the Alma on 20 September 1854. Lord Raglan in his dispatch referred to him as being 'always at hand to carry out any service I might direct him to undertake'. He was taken ill with virulent cholera on the night of 21 September and died on the evening of the 22nd. He was buried in a vineyard before the army marched on the morning of the 23rd. In the orders issued on the occasion it was stated that 'no officer was ever more regretted, and deservedly so'. It was announced in the *London Gazette* of 5 July 1855 that, had Tylden survived, he would have been made a knight commander of the Bath, and in the *Gazette* of 8 September 1856 his widow was authorized to bear the same style as if her husband had been duly invested with the insignia.

Tylden had married first, at Harrietsham, Kent, on 20 August 1817, Lecilina, eldest daughter of William Baldwin of Stedehill, Kent; his second marriage, at Dover on 20 February 1851, was to Mary, widow of Captain J. H. Baldwin and eldest daughter of the Revd S. Dineley Goodyar, rector of Otterden, Kent. He had two sons with his first wife—William, curate of Stanford, Kent, and **Richard Tylden** (1819–1855), army officer, born at Stede Hill, Kent, on 22 November 1819. After passing through the Royal Military Academy at Woolwich, he received a commission as second lieutenant in the Royal Engineers on 14 December 1837, and was promoted first lieutenant on 19 March 1840 and second captain on 9 November 1846. In February 1848 he went to the Cape, where he fought with distinction in the Cape Frontier War of 1850–52, being mentioned in dispatches. He was promoted brevet major on 31 May 1853. Returning home in 1854, Tylden proceeded almost at once to serve on his father's staff in Turkey as brigade major of engineers. He went with the army to the Crimea, took part in the battle of the Alma on 20 September, and was with his father when he died on 22 September. On arrival at Sevastopol he resigned his staff appointment to share the more arduous and dangerous duties of the trenches, and on 20 October was given the command of the British right attack. On 12 December 1854 he was promoted brevet lieutenant-colonel for distinguished service. In the attack and capture of the enemy's rifle pits on 19 April 1855 Tylden distinguished himself by his gallantry, and was mentioned in dispatches. On 7 June he commanded the Royal Engineers and sappers and miners in the attack on the 'Quarries', when Garnet Wolseley served under him as an assistant engineer. Tylden was in command of the Royal Engineers and sappers and miners of the second column in the disastrous attack on the Redan on 18 June, when he was struck down by grapeshot. For his services at the rifle pits, at the 'Quarries', and at the Redan, he was on 3 July appointed aide-de-camp to the queen and promoted colonel in the army, and on 5 July he was made a companion of the Bath, military division. At the Redan he was severely wounded in both legs. His wounds were progressing favourably, and he was on his way to Malta, when he was attacked by diarrhoea, and died on 2 August 1855, the day after his arrival at Malta, where he was buried.

R. H. VETCH, *rev.* H. C. G. MATTHEW

Sources GM, 2nd ser., 44 (1855), 317 · *ILN* (16 Dec 1854) · *Morning Chronicle* (16 Aug 1855) · *The Times* (23 April 1851) · A. W. Kinglake, *The invasion of the Crimea*, 8 vols. (1863–87)

Likenesses portrait, repro. in *ILN*

Tyldesley, Sir Thomas (1612–1651), royalist army officer, was born on 3 September 1612 at Woodplumpton, the eldest of the six children of Edward Tyldesley (1582–1621) of Morleys Hall, Astley, in the parish of Leigh, Lancashire, and his wife, Elizabeth (d. 1653), daughter of Christopher Preston of Holker. He was baptized at Woodplumpton on 10 September 1612. Ten years later he entered Gray's Inn. It was clearly intended like many others of his family that he follow the traditional career of law, but destiny decreed otherwise. Little is known about his early life but the general consensus is that he served as a professional soldier in the Thirty Years' War in Germany.

In 1634 Tyldesley married Frances (d. 1691), elder daughter of Ralph Standish of Standish, with whom he had three sons and seven daughters. She was a devout Roman Catholic, so her marriage to Thomas Tyldesley was hardly surprising. Tyldesley himself was one of the leading Catholics in Caroline Lancashire. He patronized the Benedictine martyr St Ambrose Barlow, greatly encouraging his missionary activities in south Lancashire. But on 10 September 1641 Barlow was executed at Lancaster. Other members of the Tyldesley family were also sincere Roman Catholics and Thomas must have been proud of his aunt, Elizabeth Tyldesley, who from 1615 to 1654 was abbess of the Poor Clares at Gravelines in the Spanish Netherlands.

Thomas Tyldesley was one of the wealthiest gentlemen in Lancashire and according to the lay subsidy rolls his annual landed income amounted to £2050 in 1641. Much of his income came from tithes, some of which he had

Sir Thomas Tyldesley (1612–1651), by unknown artist

governor of Lichfield and early in 1646 refused to surrender the garrison as commanded, but on 10 July he finally obeyed his orders.

Tyldesley refused to compound for delinquency and took part in the second civil war of 1648. He was taken prisoner at Appleby on 9 October and allowed six months to settle his affairs and go into exile.

Tyldesley took up arms again in the third civil war of 1651. From the Isle of Man he joined the seventh earl of Derby for his invasion of Lancashire. The aim was to link up with Charles II's Scottish troops, who were quartered at Myerscough Lodge, Tyldesley's main home. That Charles resided there shows clearly that he regarded Tyldesley as a loyal and important subject. Tyldesley fought his last battle at Wigan Lane on 25 August 1651 where he made a valuable relief charge, but was either killed outright or else mortally wounded. He was buried at Leigh parish church on the same day, leaving his landed estate (worth at least £1500 p.a.) to his eldest son, Edward.

GORDON BLACKWOOD

Sources J. Lunn, *History of the Tyldesleys of Lancashire* (1966), 55, 60, 63–6, 73–89, 191 • P. R. Newman, *Royalist officers in England and Wales, 1642–1660: a biographical dictionary* (1981), 381 • *The royal martyrs* (1663), 3 • [R. Palmer, earl of Castlemaine], *A reply to the answer of the Catholique apology* (1668), appx: *a catalogue of those Catholiques that died and suffered for their loyalty*, 276 • 'The apostolic life of Ambrose Barlow, O.S.B.', *Chetham miscellanies*, ed. W. H. Rhodes, 2, Chetham Society, new ser., 63 (1908), iii–iv, vi–viii, 3, 13 • Tyldesley accounts, 1654, Lancs. RO, Lord Gerard muniments, DDGE/E/72 • Exchequer lay subsidy rolls, 1641, PRO, E 179/132/336; 132/340 • E. Robinson, *A discourse of the warr in Lancashire ... betweene King Charles and the parliament*, ed. W. Beamont, Chetham Society, 62 (1864), 19 • G. Ormerod, ed., *Tracts relating to military proceedings in Lancashire during the great civil war*, Chetham Society, 2 (1844), 21, 275 • *Articles for delivering up of Lichfield-Close* (1646), 5, 9 [Thomason tract E 345(2)] • *A list of officers claiming to the sixty thousand pounds*, 1663, PRO, SP 29/68, col. 129 • *A list of severall colonels*, PRO, SP 29/159, fol. 45 • G. R. Smith and M. Toynbee, *Leaders of the civil wars, 1642–1648*, ed. P. Young (1977), 198–9 • J. Foster, *The register of admissions to Gray's Inn, 1521–1889, together with the register of marriages in Gray's Inn chapel, 1695–1754* (privately printed, London, 1889), 168 • J. H. Stanning and J. Brownbill, eds., *The royalist composition papers*, 6, ed. J. Brownbill, Lancashire and Cheshire RS, 95 (1942), 291–2 • E. Broxap, *The great civil war in Lancashire, 1642–51*, 2nd edn (1973), 20, 28, 42, 81–6, 121, 172, 188, 191–3

Archives Lancs. RO, Lord Gerard muniments, accounts, DDGE/E/72

Likenesses J. Cochran, stipple and line engraving, BM, NPG; repro. in T. Baines, *Lancashire and Cheshire*, 2 vols. [1838] • oils, unknown collection; copyprint, NPG [*see illus.*] • portrait, repro. in Lunn, *History of the Tyldesleys*

Wealth at death £1505 p.a.; incl. £648 from tithes: Lancs. RO, DDGE/E/72: Tyldesley accounts, 18 Feb 1654

purchased from the Urmstons of Westleigh. But how much of his wealth was gained at the expense of his tenants is unclear in the absence of archival evidence.

When the first civil war began in 1642 Tyldesley loyally supported Charles I. Indeed, it was said of Tyldesley that 'there was not a man in all the County more zealous and fervent for the King's part ... not the Earle of Darbie himself' (Beamont, 19). He was certainly the animating force among the Lancashire royalists and at his own expense raised regiments of horse, foot, and dragoons for the king. Militarily, Tyldesley was extremely active. In 1642 he joined Lord Strange (afterwards seventh earl of Derby) in besieging the parliamentarian stronghold of Manchester. He then accompanied the Lancashire royalist forces who marched to Edgehill, where he served with distinction. He returned to Lancashire with Richard Molyneux of Sefton, second Viscount Molyneux of Maryborough. The return of Tyldesley and Molyneux after Edgehill led to further recruitment for the royalist cause. This army was, however, defeated at Whalley in 1643. Tyldesley then marched south with Queen Henrietta Maria and was knighted and promoted brigadier-general for his outstanding bravery at Burton upon Trent in July 1643. The following year he was sent north again with Molyneux under John Byron, first Baron Byron of Rochdale, joining forces with Prince Rupert and capturing the parliamentarian towns of Bolton and Liverpool. On 2 July Tyldesley fought alongside Rupert and Molyneux at Marston Moor, and on 18 September he was captured at Montgomery. He was then imprisoned at Eccleshall Castle before being removed to Stafford from which he escaped in late 1645. He was made

Tylecote [*née* Phythian], **Dame Mabel** (1896–1987), adult educationist, was born on 4 February 1896 in Crumpsall, Manchester, the daughter of John Ernest Phythian (1858–1935), a solicitor, journalist, and university extension lecturer, and his wife, Ada Prichard Crompton (d. 1931). She spent her childhood at Holmes Chapel in Cheshire, where she was taught by a relative, before attending Beachfield School in Wilmslow between the ages of ten and thirteen. John Phythian was a disciple of Ruskin and Morris and an active member of that distinctive Manchester élite which sought to improve social and cultural opportunities for the poor. A member of Manchester city council (1892–8), he was involved with the University Settlement, the Ancoats Art Museum, the Manchester and Salford Sanitary Association, and the Social Questions Union. Mabel Phythian's early awareness of social issues led her to follow her father's example and leave the Liberal Party for Labour at the age of eighteen. She joined the prestigious and influential Manchester University history department in 1915, graduating in 1919, and was recognized by T. F. Tout as a woman of 'first class calibre. She has keen interests, extensive knowledge, an unusual measure of enterprise and character and an exceptional amount of public spirit' (testimonial, 15 June 1922, Tylecote MSS).

Manchester University was then an exciting place for women, with a tradition in the women's department of political awareness and public service. Mabel Phythian was stimulated by the encouragement given to women by the staff and became secretary to the Women's Union as well as working with the developing Ashburne Hall for female students. An interest in academic women took her to Paris in 1921 for the international conference of the Federation of University Women. The 1920s were spent in academic study and teaching at the University of Wisconsin (1919–20), Huddersfield Technical College humanities department (1920–24), and as an assistant lecturer at Manchester University (1926–30), during which time she gained her PhD. This research in what was to remain her first love, adult education, was later published as *The Mechanics' Institutes of Lancashire and Yorkshire before 1851* (1957). The fiftieth anniversary of the admission of women to Owens College fell in 1933 and she was invited to commemorate this by a book, *The Education of Women at Manchester University 1883 to 1933* (1941), which is a landmark in the study of women in higher education. It was her work as a Workers' Educational Association (WEA) lecturer, begun at this time, which symbolized that concern for social justice and adult education which was to characterize the rest of her life. A brief but influential break from academic life was taken from 1930 to 1932 when she was warden of the Elvington Settlement on the Kent coal field, where she demonstrated, in R. H. Tawney's words, 'human sympathies and insight' (R. H. Tawney, letter, 21 July 1930, Tylecote MSS).

In 1932 Mabel Phythian married, as his second wife, Frank Edward Tylecote (*d.* 1965), a Manchester councillor and professor of medicine at Manchester University (1929–40). From 1935 to the 1950s Mabel Tylecote worked under the aegis of the Manchester University joint committee for adult education, serving as vice-president of the WEA from 1960 to 1968 and as chairwoman of the National Institute of Adult Education (1960–63). As Manchester began the immense work of slum clearance and the creation of new working-class communities in the 1930s, stimulated by the gift of the Wythenshawe estate by Ernest Simon, she became a passionate advocate of community development that not only improved housing but enhanced the quality of life, a concern traceable back to her student days when she had been involved with the

radical University Settlement in Ancoats. She was a founder of the Manchester and District New Estates Federation and became president of the National Federation of Community Associations in 1958. In the post-war years she supported the National Council for Civil Liberties and the National Council of Social Service, and was a member of the Pensions Appeal Tribunal from 1944 to 1950.

It was natural that Mabel Tylecote's academic interests, her socialism, and deep awareness of inequalities in society led to an interest in politics, but it was the depression and the appeasement of fascism which made her seek a parliamentary seat in 1938. Her political career at local and national level might be judged a failure, for she fought five parliamentary elections as a Labour candidate in three constituencies—Fylde, Middleton and Prestwich, and Norwich South—without success from 1938 to 1955, and although on Manchester city council from 1940 to 1951 and a member of Stockport council from 1956 to 1963 she was never a powerful political force. However, the significance of her participation should not be underestimated. Her national election campaigns in Lancashire and Norfolk were powerful expositions of Attleean socialism, which contributed to greater understanding of the party and the concept of politically directed social reform: 'We seek by the control of selfish interests, freedom to plan our inheritance, to create those conditions and build up those services which will give to our people at last dignified, free and happy lives' (Election pamphlet, July 1945, Tylecote MSS). Her self-confident, energetic personality did much to enhance the still insecure image of women in public life and her vigorous campaigns increased the Labour vote. In local government she was a powerful advocate of improved living conditions, provision for leisure, and greater access to education. As a very active co-opted member of the Manchester education committee from 1951 to 1977 she ensured a high profile for issues of access and support. Through years of austerity and continuing Conservatism she represented generous and enlightened reform. At a sensitive time politically she never wavered from an internationalist outlook, developing close links with German adult education after the war, advocating close cultural links with the Soviet Union, and making many contacts with adult education in Europe.

Mabel Tylecote was made DBE in 1966 for 'political and public services'. She remained closely associated with her university, but extended support to the new polytechnic in Manchester and was an active member of court, council, and governing body. In 1973 the polytechnic awarded her an honorary fellowship (a building in its successor, the Manchester Metropolitan University, commemorates her). In 1978 she became an honorary LLD of the Victoria University. Through an extremely active life of public speaking (she was a lay preacher) and laborious committee work she acted as a bridge between the older philanthropic reform of her family tradition and the concept of the welfare state. A truer estimate of her contribution than election results was demonstrated in both the respect and affection which permeated the commiserations when she lost her council seat in 1951, that of Eric

James being typical in its regret of 'the loss of someone with your knowledge and enthusiasms' (Tylecote MSS). She and her distinguished co-worker in Manchester, Lady Shena Simon, represent a key group of middle-class women, not yet given their due by historians of the women's movement, who continued the struggle after the better-known pioneers identified and recorded in her 1941 book had passed away.

Dame Mabel lived with her husband, son, and two step-children at Heaton Lodge, Stockport. Late in life she moved back to Manchester, where she died at her home, Alexandra House, 359 Wilbraham Road, Whalley Range, on 31 January 1987. She was cremated at Manchester crematorium. A. B. ROBERTSON

Sources *The Times* (3 Feb 1987) · *Manchester Evening News* (26 July 1949) · *WWW* · Manchester city council and education committee minutes, Manchester town hall, Albert Square, Manchester · Stockport council minutes, Stockport library, Wellington Road South, Stockport · JRL, Tylecote MSS
Archives JRL, corresp. and papers
Likenesses Lafayette, photograph, 1917, JRL, Tylecote MSS · photographs, JRL, Tylecote MSS
Wealth at death £34,717: probate, 16 April 1987, *CGPLA Eng. & Wales*

Tyler, Sir Charles (1760–1835), naval officer, was the son of Peter Tyler (*d.* 1763), a captain in the 52nd regiment, and his wife, Anne, daughter of Henry, eighth Lord Teynham. He entered the navy in 1771, and served for a few months on the *Barfleur*, guardship at Chatham, as servant of the captain, Andrew Snape Hamond, with whom he afterwards was in the *Arethusa*, on the North American station. In 1774 he was moved into the *Preston*, the flagship of Vice-Admiral Samuel Graves, and afterwards carrying the broad pennant of Commodore William Hotham. In 1777 he was invalided owing to an injury to his left leg, as the result of which it was 'necessary to remove the small bone, so that for two years he was unable to move except on crutches', and was left permanently lame (memorial, PRO). On 5 April 1779 he was promoted lieutenant on the *Culloden*, in which he served in the Channel Fleet until September 1780, and after that in the *Britannia*, the flagship of Vice-Admiral Darby, until April 1782, and in the *Edgar*, again with Commodore Hotham, until the end of the war. He was promoted commander on 31 December 1782, and in July 1783 commanded the armed ship *Chapman*; from 1784 to 1789 he commanded the *Trimmer*, stationed at Milford to suppress smuggling. In 1790 he commanded the *Tisiphone*, on similar service in the channel, and on 21 September 1790 was advanced to post rank. In March 1793 he was appointed to the frigate *Meleager* (32 guns), in which he went out to the Mediterranean with Lord Hood; after the capture of Calvi he was moved into the *San Fiorenzo*, one of the prizes; and in February 1795 to the *Diadem* (64 guns), in which he took part in the desultory action of 14 March.

Shortly after this Tyler was concerned in a case of peculiar importance in the history of naval discipline. A detachment of the 11th regiment was serving on board the *Diadem*, in lieu of marines, and the officer in command, Lieutenant Fitzgerald, assuming that he was independent of naval control, behaved with contempt towards his superior officers. Tyler reported the case to the admiral, who ordered a court martial. Fitzgerald denied the legality of the court, and refused to make any defence. The court overruled his objections, heard the evidence in support of the charge, and cashiered Fitzgerald. The duke of York issued an order that soldiers serving on warships were subject to military rule only. The superior naval officers protested against this, as subversive of discipline afloat and contrary to act of parliament; eventually all the soldiers were disembarked, and replaced by marines.

During late 1795 and early 1796 the *Diadem* was frequently attached to the squadron under the orders of Nelson in the Gulf of Genoa, and on the coast of Italy. Later Tyler was moved into the frigate *Aigle*, in which he captured several of the enemy's privateers in the Mediterranean, and in the channel; and on 18 July 1798, while seeking to join the squadron under Nelson, he was wrecked near Tunis. In February 1799 he was appointed to the *Warrior* (74 guns), one of the Channel Fleet, and of the fleet which in 1801 went into the Baltic under the command of Sir Hyde Parker. On returning from the Baltic, the *Warrior* was sent to Cadiz, and in January 1802 to the West Indies, one of a small squadron, under Tyler as senior officer, to watch the French expedition to San Domingo. In July the *Warrior* returned to England, and was paid off.

When the war resumed, Tyler was appointed to command a district of sea fencibles. In February 1805 he commissioned the *Tonnant* (80 guns), for service in the channel, but was afterwards sent to the fleet off Cadiz. On 21 October he served at Trafalgar, where the *Tonnant* was the fourth ship in the lee line, got early into action, and lost twenty-six killed and fifty wounded. Tyler was severely wounded by a musket-ball in the right thigh, and was granted a pension of £250. He was promoted rear-admiral on 28 April 1808, and in May hoisted his flag as second in command at Portsmouth. In June he was sent to Lisbon, and was there with Sir Charles Cotton in September to receive the surrender of the Russian fleet. From 1812 to 1815 he was commander-in-chief at the Cape of Good Hope, and his service ended with his return to England in March 1816. He was promoted vice-admiral on 4 December 1813, and admiral on 27 May 1825. He was made a KCB on 2 January 1815, and a GCB on 29 January 1833.

Tyler was twice married. His first wife was Anne (*d.* 1784), only daughter of Charles Rice RN. Charles, their son, died a captain on the retired list of the navy in 1846. Tyler married, on 25 November 1788, Margaret (*d.* 15 July 1835), daughter of Abraham Leach of Pembrokeshire. Tyler died at Beaufort Buildings, the Spa, Gloucester, on 28 September 1835.

Sir George Tyler (1792–1862), naval officer, Charles Tyler's eldest son from his second marriage, was born in Pembrokeshire, on 28 December 1792. He attended the Royal Naval College, Portsmouth, from 1806, and entered the navy in 1809. In a boat attack in Quiberon Bay in 1811 he lost his right arm. He was his father's flag lieutenant at the Cape of Good Hope, and became a commander in 1815 and a captain in 1822. He married, on 21 September 1819,

Harriet Margaret, daughter of the Right Hon. John Sullivan, and Lady Harriet, daughter of George, third earl of Buckinghamshire; they had seven sons and four daughters. From 1833 to 1840 Tyler was lieutenant-governor of the island of St Vincent. He was made a KH on 4 March 1833, and knighted again in November 1838; he became a rear-admiral in 1852, and was made vice-admiral in 1857. From February 1851 to December 1857 he was a Conservative MP for Glamorgan. He resided at Cotrel, Glamorgan. He died at Dunraven Castle, Glamorgan, on 4 June 1862.

J. K. LAUGHTON, rev. ANDREW LAMBERT

Sources D. Syrett and R. L. DiNardo, *The commissioned sea officers of the Royal Navy, 1660–1815*, rev. edn, Occasional Publications of the Navy RS, 1 (1994) • O'Byrne, *Naval biog. dict.* • *Dod's Peerage* (1858) • Burke, *Gen. GB* (1937) • WWBMP, vol. 1 • *GM*, 2nd ser., 4 (1835), 649 • *GM*, 3rd ser., 13 (1862), 116 • service book, passing certificate and memorial, PRO • J. McArthur, *Principles and practice of courts martial*, 2 vols. (1813)
Archives NMM, journals, letter-books, logs, and order books
Wealth at death under £25,000—Sir George Tyler: will, 1862

Tyler, Sir George (1792–1862). *See under* Tyler, Sir Charles (1760–1835).

Tyler, James Endell (1789–1851), Church of England clergyman, born at Monmouth on 30 January 1789, was the son of James Tyler, a solicitor in that town. He was educated at the grammar school in Monmouth, and matriculated from Oriel College, Oxford, in 1805, obtaining first-class honours in classics and second class in mathematics in 1809. Elected Michel scholar at Queen's College, he obtained a fellowship at Oriel in 1812. He graduated BA in 1809, MA in 1813, and BD in 1823. He was a university examiner from 1816 to 1818. From 1818 to 1826 he was a tutor at Oriel, under the provostship of Edward Copleston, who appointed Tyler college dean in 1822. Newman particularly identified Tyler with the policy, which the Tractarian element in the college deplored, of seeking to attract to Oriel students of wealth and rank. During this time he also held the perpetual curacy of Moreton Pinkney, Northamptonshire. In 1826 his preaching attracted the attention of Lord Liverpool, who presented him to the living of St Giles-in-the-Fields. Two years later he relinquished his fellowship, having married on 18 April 1827 Elizabeth Ann, daughter of George Griffin of Newton House, Monmouth. She died on 25 November 1830 leaving two sons—George Griffin and Edward Jones—and a daughter. He married, second, on 6 March 1834, Jane, daughter of Divie Robertson of Bedford Square, a relative of W. E. Gladstone, with whom he had a son and two daughters, Gladstone being godfather to one of them.

Besides sermons, Tyler published *Oaths: their Origin, Nature, and History* (1834; 2nd edn, 1835), which was favourably noticed in the *Quarterly Review* (61, April 1838), and *Henry of Monmouth: Memoirs of the Life and Character of Henry V* (1840), which was reckoned a useful addition to the literature on the early years of Henry's reign. He published two attacks on Roman Catholic practices, namely the worship of the Virgin Mary (1844) and of images (1847). Yet, in a classification of the opinions of the principal London

clergy prepared for J. T. Delane in 1844, Tyler was considered one of those with a leaning towards the Tractarian party. He was considered 'A very industrious clergyman: few more so. Shrewd, subtle and vigorous'; his faults were held to be that he exercised too tight a control over his parish and had 'a certain rudeness of manner' (Bodleian, MS Add. C. 290, fol. 8). He was none the less regarded with much affection by his parishioners. Endell Street, Long Acre, was named after him at their suggestion, his modesty refusing to allow it to be called Tyler Street. On 15 March 1845 Sir Robert Peel, at Copleston's suggestion, appointed him a residentiary canon of St Paul's Cathedral. Tyler died at his house in Bedford Square, London, on 5 October 1851.

M. C. CURTHOYS

Sources *GM*, 2nd ser., 37 (1852), 194–5 • T. Mozley, *Reminiscences, chiefly of Oriel College and the Oxford Movement*, 2 vols. (1882) • *GM*, 2nd ser., 1 (1834), 551 • G. C. Richards and C. L. Shadwell, *The provosts and fellows of Oriel College, Oxford* (1922) • DNB
Archives BL, corresp. with W. E. Gladstone, Add. MSS 44354–44368 • BL, corresp. with Sir Robert Peel, Add. MSS 40412–40574, *passim* • Oriel College, Oxford, letters to John Keble • St Deiniol's Library, Hawarden, letters to Sir John Gladstone
Likenesses T. Lupton, mezzotint, pubd 1833 (after G. Clint), BM • E. Clint, oils, St Giles-in-the-Fields, London • G. Clint, oils, Oriel College, Oxford

Tyler, John (d. 1724), bishop of Llandaff, is a figure whose origins remain obscure. Neither his parentage nor his early clerical career has been established. He may have been the rector of Shobdon, Herefordshire, in 1678, and of Letton Cheney, Dorset, from 1680 to 1690. He was created BA and MA from Magdalen College, Oxford, by decree on 14 April 1686, and proceeded BD on 15 May 1686. He was made a canon of Hereford in 1688, and became vicar of Brinsop, Herefordshire, in 1689 and vicar of St Peter's, Hereford, in 1690. He was also a chaplain-in-ordinary to William and Mary. He was installed as dean of Hereford on 27 September 1692, a position he continued to hold until his death, even after his elevation to the episcopal bench. He was elected to the Society for Promoting Christian Knowledge (SPCK) on 3 February 1700. On 30 November 1702 John Tyler married Sarah Rogers (d. 1726) at Llanwarne, Herefordshire. They had no children.

Tyler was consecrated as bishop of Llandaff on 30 June 1706, describing his new see in September 1706 as 'one of the poorest bishoprics in Christendom' (*London Diaries of William Nicolson*, 54), it being worth about £300 p.a. He took the oaths of allegiance and supremacy on 3 December 1706 and preached 'a very good' sermon to the House of Lords on 30 January 1707 (ibid., p. 413). He was created DD by diploma on 25 June 1707. By 1708 he was living in a house in Crutched Friars in London. He seems to have been a moderate whig churchman, supporting an amendment to the General Naturalization Bill in March 1709 which made the taking of communion in a parochial church rather than a reformed congregation a necessary condition for using the act. However, with the advent of a tory ministry under Robert Harley in 1710 his political position became more overtly whig. Harley thought him unlikely to support the ministry in an analysis made in early October 1710 and Tyler voted against the earl of

Peterborough in January 1711 when the verdict on his conduct of the war in Spain became a trial of strength between his tory supporters and the whigs. He was seen by Harley, by then earl of Oxford, as an opponent of the court in the spring of 1713, and he voted against the French commercial treaty in June 1713. In the 1714 parliament he opposed the high-church Schism Bill.

Following the Hanoverian succession Tyler voted against the earl of Oxford when the latter was impeached by the whig ministry in June 1717. He opposed the repeal of the Occasional Conformity and Schism Acts in December 1718. Tyler died on 6 or 8 July 1724 at 'a very advanced age' (*Remarks*, 242), and was buried in Hereford Cathedral. His wife was still alive in June 1726 when the SPCK agreed to send her a copy of the New Testament in Arabic which her husband had subscribed to, but she died in October or November 1726. Tyler's will bequeathed his lands in Radnorshire, Herefordshire, and Monmouthshire to John Tyler, the son of his nephew William Tyler. His stock in the Bank of England and South Sea Company was to be used to fund legacies to a host of relatives, many of them clerics.

STUART HANDLEY

Sources *Fasti Angl.* (Hardy), 1.479 • *The London diaries of William Nicolson, bishop of Carlisle, 1702–1718*, ed. C. Jones and G. Holmes (1985) • M. Clement, ed., *Correspondence and minutes of the SPCK relating to Wales, 1699–1740* (1952), 14, 296 • will, PRO, PROB 11/598, sig. 171, fols. 250*v*–251*v* • *Remarks and collections of Thomas Hearne*, ed. C. E. Doble and others, 8, OHS, 50 (1907), 242 • *The manuscripts of the House of Lords*, new ser., 12 vols. (1900–77) • C. Jones, '"The scheme lords, the necessitous lords, and the Scots lords": the earl of Oxford's management and the "party of the crown" in the House of Lords, 1711–14', *Party and management in parliament, 1660–1784*, ed. C. Jones (1984), 123–44, 160 • G. S. Holmes, *British politics in the age of Anne*, rev. edn (1987), 434 • *Tory and whig: the parliamentary papers of Edward Harley, third earl of Oxford, and William Hay, MP for Seaford, 1716–1753*, ed. S. Taylor and C. Jones (1998), 201, 207, 210 • will, PRO, PROB 11/612, sig. 246, fols. 122*r*–123*v* [Sarah Tyler, wife] • *IGI* • *The historical register*, 1 (1716)

Tyler, Margaret (*fl.* 1558–1578), translator, translated as *The Mirrour of Princely Deedes and Knighthood* (1578) the first book of a work in Spanish by Diego Ortuñez de Calahorra. This was the first English publication of a secular text translated by a woman. Her preface and dedication to Lord Thomas Howard say that she is of a 'staied age' (A4*v*) and was a 'servant' to his parents (A2*v*), the duke and second duchess of Norfolk, thus roughly between 1558 and 1564. A waiting-woman who translated romances for household entertainment, she might have been married to another literate ducal employee, perhaps the 'John Tyler, Gentleman' who copied a survey of tenant leases in 1565 (CUL, MS 5909). Her spirited preface defends a woman's right to pen secular stories: if books can be dedicated to women, they must be able to read and write books. She should not be expected to write of divinity, having no competence for it. And finally, translation is 'a matter of more heede' than of manly invention or learning (A4); she has only given 'entertainment to a stranger' (A2*v*).

LOUISE SCHLEINER

Sources D. Ortuñez de Calahorra, *The mirrour of princely deedes and knighthood*, trans. M. Tyler (1578); repr. in B. S. Travitsky and P. Cullen, eds., *The early modern Englishwoman: a facsimile library of

essential works*, 8: *Margaret Tyler*, ed. K. Coad (1996) • N. Williams, *Thomas Howard, fourth duke of Norfolk* (1964) • L. Schleiner, 'Margaret Tyler, translator and waiting woman', *English Language Notes*, 29/3 (1992), 1–8 • D. Eisenberg, *An edition of a sixteenth-century romance of chivalry: Diego Ortuñez de Calahorra's 'Espejo de principes y cavalleros'* (1971) • J. de Perrot, 'The mirrour of knighthood', *Romantic Review*, 4 (1913), 397–402 • H. Wilcox, *Women and literature in Britain* (1996)

Tyler, Margaret Lucy (1859–1943), homoeopathic practitioner, was born in London, on 9 February 1859, the third daughter of Henry Whately Tyler (1827–1908), captain in the Royal Engineers and government inspector of railways, and his wife, Margaret, daughter of Lieutenant-General Sir Charles Pasley, a generous benefactor of homoeopathy. A prolific writer, in 1884 she published a verse play in six acts entitled *Anne Boleyn*. This was followed by two pieces of fiction, *Lost Identities* (1888) and *Gentleman Jack* (1890). (Another novel, *Miss Lydd*, was published in 1931.) Relatively late in life she implemented a long-held ambition to study medicine, in order to serve the poor at the London Homoeopathic Hospital in Bloomsbury. She attended the London School of Medicine for Women, and qualified in 1903 at the age of forty-four as a licentiate of the colleges of physicians and surgeons of both Glasgow and Edinburgh, and also became MD (Brussels).

Tyler spent her entire medical career at the London Homoeopathic Hospital. In 1907, believing that homoeopathy in Britain had moved away from the principles of its founder, Samuel Hahnemann, she induced her parents to establish scholarships to enable doctors to study under Dr James Tyler Kent in the United States. He recommended single doses of high dilutions, in contrast to the repeated material doses favoured in Britain, and introduced the constitutional remedy which aimed to treat the whole person rather than just the disease. One of the first students was John Weir, who was to become physician to George VI. Within a decade the old ideas, contemptuously called 'pathological prescribing', had been swept away, and those of Kent had taken over, the result of Tyler's single-handed efforts.

In 1914 Tyler was appointed assistant physician to the children's department at the hospital. She worked with out-patients for nearly forty years, claiming her patients as her friends. She had a particular interest in children with learning difficulties, and published several articles on this subject. Although devoted to homoeopathy she was one of the few doctors at the time to practise osteopathy.

Tyler urged the need for homoeopathic education, lectured brilliantly at the hospital, and wrote a correspondence course for doctors who could not attend. She edited the *Journal of the British Homoeopathic Association* for eleven years; intended for the lay public, it served many doctors as a mine of information. In 1919 she expressed her views on political economy in *Labour—Capital—Brains*. Her best-known work was *Homoeopathic Drug Pictures* (1942), which clarified the daunting materia medica for the student, though it also possibly took Kent's constitutional ideas to extremes.

Tyler was the first woman doctor to become an eminent

homoeopath, and together with John Weir she unofficially ran the hospital for many years and may have appeared imperious to her colleagues. In later life she stopped lecturing. She would be seated alone on the dais while Sir John Weir lectured, as if overseeing the standards. Described as 'a stately dame' and as 'a big woman, motherly in figure' (private information), she had almost no social conversation, and seldom even discussed cases with her assistants.

Even when Tyler required a walking stick she refused offers of help, regarding any acceptance as a sign of weakness. Deeply religious, she believed in putting service before self. She died on 21 June 1943 at 165 Highgate Road, London, and was buried in Kensal Green cemetery.

BERNARD LEARY

Sources *Health and homoeopathy*, 1 (1943), 1,3 and 8,1 · *British Homoeopathic Journal* (1943) · J. Roberson and E. P. Hoyle, eds., *International homoeopathic medical directory, 1911–1912* [1911] · *Medical Directory* (1904) · C. Babington Smith, *Champion of homoeopathy* (1986), 69–73 · private information (2004) · b. cert. · d. cert.
Archives British Homoeopathy Association, London
Wealth at death £13,173 4s. 0d.: probate, 18 Sept 1943, CGPLA Eng. & Wales

Tyler, Thomas (1826–1902), theological and literary scholar, was born in London. Little is known of his early life, but he matriculated at King's College, London, in 1857, graduating BA in classics in 1859 and MA in 1871. He obtained prizes for Hebrew and for New Testament Greek, and soon engaged in further biblical research. He expanded an article he had contributed to the *Journal of Sacred Literature* in January 1854 into a volume called *Jehovah the Redeemer God* (1861), and discussed the New Testament interpretation of the name in a second volume, *Christ the Lord, the Revealer of God* (1863). In 1872 he joined the newly formed Society of Biblical Archaeology. In a pamphlet, *Some New Evidence as to the Date of Ecclesiastes* (1872), he first indicated exclusively from the literary point of view the influence of Greek, especially Stoic, philosophy on the teaching of the author, and assigned the composition of the work to the second century BC. Tyler developed his view in his exhaustive *Ecclesiastes, a Contribution to its Interpretation* (1874; 2nd edn, 1879; new revised edn, 1899). Here he maintained that his translation differed 'in no small degree from the Authorised Version, on which, however, it [was] to a considerable extent, based' (p. vii). Tyler also lectured and wrote on Hittite antiquities, thus helping to stimulate in England the study of the Hittite language.

Tyler made a number of contributions to Shakespearian study. He took part in the proceedings of the New Shakspere Society from its foundation in 1874. He developed a deterministic approach to Hamlet's character in his brief study *The Philosophy of 'Hamlet'* (1874), concluding that Shakespeare's view of life expressed in the play is ultimately pessimistic. In the introduction to the facsimile edition of *Shakspere's Sonnets, the First Quarto, 1609*, which Tyler edited in 1886, he, with the assistance of the Revd W. A. Harrison, vicar of St Anne's, Lambeth, first propounded

the theory that Mary Fitton was the 'dark lady' of the sonnets. He elaborated his argument in his interesting edition of *Shakespeare's Sonnets* (1890). In his substantial introduction, he also maintained that Mr. W. H. was William Herbert, earl of Pembroke, and the 'rival poet' was George Chapman. But Lady Newdigate-Newdegate in *Gossip from a Muniment Room* (1897; 2nd edn, 1898) showed from extant portraits at Arbury that Mary Fitton had a fair complexion, and Sidney Lee contested Tyler's view in his *Life of William Shakespeare* (1898). Tyler answered his critics in *The Herbert–Fitton Theory: a Reply* (1898), disputing the authenticity of the Arbury portraits. Bernard Shaw, who was an acquaintance of Tyler's, wrote *The Dark Lady of the Sonnets* (1910), partly to 'immortalise' him, although he admitted that Tyler's identification was probably mistaken ('Preface to *The Dark Lady*', 722). Tyler also edited in 1891 the facsimile issue of *The True Tragedy. The First Quarto, 1595*. He occasionally contributed to periodicals, including *The Athenaeum* and the *Modern Review*.

Tyler, who suffered from birth from a goitrous disfigurement, was of 'fair complexion, rather golden red than sandy', and had a 'rectangular figure', according to Shaw ('Preface to *The Dark Lady*', 722). For nearly half a century he frequented the British Museum reading-room. He died at the Islington Infirmary, Highgate Hill, London, unmarried and in straitened circumstances, on 19 February 1902.

W. B. OWEN, *rev.* DONALD HAWES

Sources 'Preface to *The dark lady of the sonnets*', *Prefaces by Bernard Shaw* (1934) · S. Schoenbaum, *Shakespeare's lives*, new edn (1991) · *The Times* (6 March 1902) · *The Athenaeum* (1 March 1902), 275 · Lady Newdigate-Newdegate, *Gossip from a muniment room* (1898) · *The historical record, 1836–1912: being a supplement to the calendar completed to September 1912*, University of London (1912) · *Wellesley index*, vol. 3 · d. cert.

Tyler, Walter [Wat] (*d.* 1381), leader of the peasants' revolt, was, as Froissart puts it, 'indeed a tiler of houses, an ungracious patron' (Dobson, 138). It has been generally assumed that he came from Kent. The Anonimalle chronicle states that he came from Maidstone, and a parliamentary petition of 1383–4 describes him as 'Wauter Tylere del Countes de Kent' (*RotP*, 3.175). It has been suggested, on the basis of a mysterious reference in the Dieulacres chronicle that he was Walter Culpepper, a member of the Kentish gentry, but this is extremely speculative and impossible to substantiate. Despite this evidence associating Tyler with Kent, a number of the indictments by Kentish juries taken immediately after the peasants' revolt state that he came from Essex. One claims that he was a native of Colchester. The continuation of the *Eulogium historiarum* also describes him as a 'tiler from Essex'. It is possible that Tyler was among the rebels who crossed from Essex to Kent at an early stage of the rising to help spread the disturbances. Knighton and other sources suggest that Tyler is to be identified with the enigmatic rebel leader Jack Straw. It has been generally assumed that this is erroneous, but the two names are linked so frequently that it is perhaps feasible that Jack Straw was indeed an alias adopted by Tyler.

Walter [Wat] **Tyler** (*d.* **1381**)*,* manuscript illumination [mounted, second from left]

The most famous of the leaders of the revolt of 1381, Tyler is popularly supposed to have given the signal for the rising by killing a collector of the poll tax who indecently assaulted his daughter, but the only authority for this story is John Stow, who took it from a St Albans chronicle, which is now lost. The revolt in Kent began in earnest with riots at Dartford on 4 and 5 June 1381, and further attacks at Maidstone and North Cray on the following days. The rebels then headed for Canterbury, arriving there on 10 June. By this time Tyler had emerged as one of their most prominent leaders. One indictment vividly describes how Tyler seized the sheriff of Kent, then forced him to go to a manor outside Sittingbourne and hand over his official records, which were burnt. The rebels left Canterbury and headed back towards London, going by way of Maidstone where on 11 June they stormed the royal prison and released the radical preacher John Ball. Tyler's authority continued to be recognized in Kent after he had left for London. On 13 June, a proclamation was made in the name of Tyler and John Rakestraw in the church of St John, Thanet, ordering the inhabitants of the locality to attack a local official.

The Kentish rebels assembled on Blackheath on 12 June. The following day Richard II went by boat to Rotherhithe to speak to them, but it was felt that it was unsafe for him to go ashore. Infuriated by this the rebels entered London. Tyler's role in subsequent events is unclear at key points, but it is evident that he exerted great authority. The St Albans insurgents who reached London on 14 June were uncertain as to who was the more powerful, Tyler or the king. Tyler promised the St Albans men he would come and 'shave the beards of the abbot, prior and monks' (Walsingham, *Chronicon Angliae*, 300), but stressed that they should observe his orders. This discipline of the insurgents was evident during the destruction of the Savoy Palace of John of Gaunt, duke of Lancaster, on 13 June, when they largely refrained from looting the palace. This discipline presumably reflects Tyler's influence. Froissart claims that Tyler personally killed the notorious financier Richard Lyons because he had been Lyons's servant in France

and Lyons had beaten him, but his story is not confirmed by any other source.

On 14 June the king met the rebels at Mile End, and agreed to grant them charters of freedom. While the king was away from the Tower of London, rebels entered it and seized a number of men including Simon Sudbury, the chancellor and archbishop of Canterbury, and Robert Hales, the treasurer of England and prior of the hospitallers, who were executed on Tower Hill. Tyler's role in these events is again unclear. The Anonimalle chronicle says that he was the spokesmen of the rebels at Mile End and, on receiving an assurance from the king that traitors would be punished, went to the Tower and seized those he regarded as traitors. Other chronicles suggest that Tyler was not at Mile End, but was with a group surrounding the Tower, who entered it when the king left. It has been generally assumed that the Anonimalle chronicle is mistaken in placing Tyler at Mile End, but the survival of a copy of letters of manumission for the Kentish commons apparently granted at Mile End (BL, Cotton Charter iv.51) suggests that at least some of the Kentish rebels were present there.

After Mile End a number of the rebels went home, but Tyler refused to leave London. Walsingham alleges that Tyler was hoping for a commission to kill everyone connected with the law, claiming that he boasted that within four days all laws in England would proceed from his mouth. On 15 June a further meeting took place between the king and the rebels at Smithfield. Accounts of this meeting vary considerably, to such an extent that it has been argued that the chroniclers sought to conceal a plot to kill Tyler. The most detailed report is provided by the Anonimalle chronicle. According to that source, Tyler was summoned to speak to the king by either William Walworth, the mayor of London (*d.* 1385), or Sir John Newton, the constable of Rochester Castle. Tyler rode up on a little horse, dismounted and, halfbending, shook the king's hand heartily, saying 'Brother, be of good comfort and joyful, for you shall have, in the fortnight to come, forty thousand more commons than you have at present, and we shall be good comrades' (*Anonimalle Chronicle*, 147). Tyler then outlined his demands: no law except the 'law of Winchester'; no outlawry; no one to exercise lordship except the king; the goods of the church to be divided among the laity, after suitable provision for the clergy and monks; only one bishop in England; and the abolition of villeinage and serfdom. Richard said that he would grant all he could fairly grant, saving the 'regality' of the crown.

Exactly what happened next is uncertain. It seems as if there was a deliberate attempt to pick a fight with Tyler. Tyler behaved rudely, calling for a drink and washing out his mouth in an uncouth way. He also kept his head covered in the king's presence, which offended the royal party. A member of the royal retinue said he recognized Tyler as the greatest thief and robber in Kent. Tyler tried to attack the man, so Walworth attempted to arrest him. Tyler struck at Walworth with his dagger, but the mayor was wearing armour under his cloak. Walworth then seriously wounded Tyler in the neck. Tyler fell from his horse and another member of the royal party, possibly Ralph Standish, the king's sword-bearer, dealt him a mortal blow. Tyler cried out to his followers to avenge him, and they bent back their bows and started to shoot, but Richard urged them to follow him to Clerkenwell. Walworth meanwhile rode back to London and raised the city militia, who went to Clerkenwell and surrounded the rebels. The insurgents begged for mercy. Richard pardoned them, and they were escorted out of London and allowed to go home. The dying Tyler had been taken to the nearby hospital of St Bartholomew. Walworth had him dragged out to Smithfield, where he was executed. The revolt rapidly collapsed after Tyler's death.

ANDREW PRESCOTT

Sources V. H. Galbraith, ed., *The Anonimalle chronicle, 1333 to 1381* (1927) · *Chroniques de J. Froissart*, ed. S. Luce and others, 10 (Paris, 1897) · [T. Walsingham], *Chronicon Angliae, ab anno Domini 1328 usque ad annum 1388*, ed. E. M. Thompson, Rolls Series, 64 (1874) · F. S. Haydon, ed., *Eulogium historiarum sive temporis*, 3 vols., Rolls Series, 9 (1858), vol. 3 · L. C. Hector and B. F. Harvey, eds. and trans., *The Westminster chronicle, 1381–1394*, OMT (1982) · H. T. Riley, ed., *Memorials of London and London life in the XIIIth, XIVth, and XVth centuries* (1868), 449–51 · E. Powell and G. M. Trevelyan, eds., *The peasants' rising and the Lollards* (1899) · W. E. Flaherty, 'The great rebellion in Kent of 1381 illustrated from the public records', *Archaeologia Cantiana*, 3 (1860), 65–96 · C. Barron, *Revolt in London: 11th–13th June 1381* (1981) · M. V. Clarke, *Fourteenth century studies*, ed. L. S. Sutherland and M. McKisack (1937) · J. Stow and E. Howes, *Annales, or, A generall chronicle of England … unto the end of this present yeere, 1631* (1631) · *Knighton's chronicle, 1337–1396*, ed. and trans. G. H. Martin, OMT (1995) [Lat. orig., *Chronica de eventibus Angliae a tempore regis Edgari usque mortem regis Ricardi Secundi*, with parallel Eng. text] · N. Brooks, 'The organisation and achievements of the peasants of Kent and Essex in 1381', *Studies in medieval history presented to R. H. C. Davies*, ed. H. Mayr-Harting and R. Moore (1985), 247–70 · court of king's bench, ancient indictments, PRO, KB 9/43 · R. B. Dobson, ed., *The peasants' revolt of 1381*, 2nd edn (1983) · T. Pettit, '"Here comes I Jack Straw": English folk drama and social revolt', *Folklore*, 95 (1984), 3–20 · F. W. D. Brie, 'Wat Tyler and Jack Straw', *EngHR*, 21 (1906), 106–11

Likenesses manuscript illumination, BL, Royal MS 18 E.i, fol. 175*r* [*see illus.*] · manuscript illumination, BL, Royal MS 18 E.i, fol. 165*v*; *see illus.* in Ball, John (*d.* 1381)

Tyler, William (*d.* 1801), sculptor and architect, may have been the son of William Tyler, a carver involved in the refurbishment of Leicester House, London, in 1743 for Frederick, prince of Wales. Little is known of his early life, but when applying in 1762 for the commission to carve a statue of George III in the royal exchange he described himself as 'the son and grandson of a citizen and many years student under the late Mr. Roubiliac' (City of London Records, MS 167.13). According to Joseph Nollekens, he lived 'in Dean St nearly opposite Annes Church, where his wife kept a shop and sold watch springs or something of the kind' (Farington, *Diary*, 4.1316). Tyler exhibited regularly as a sculptor at the Society of Artists, showing a model for the Wolfe monument in 1760. In 1768, with Joseph Wilton and Agostino Carlini, he was one of three sculptors to be included among the forty founder members of the Royal Academy and from 1770 exhibited various models, including one for the monument to Lord Rodney in 1784. He continued to play an active role in the academy, taking on (with George Dance) a review of its

financial affairs in 1796 and becoming, again with Dance, one of its first auditors.

Tyler's major activity as a sculptor was the production of modestly sized monuments, some to the design of architects such as Robert Adam and Henry Keene. His association with Roubiliac is evident in the subtlety with which his portrait busts are carved, including that on his monument to Samuel Vassall (*d.* 1766) in King's Chapel, Boston. His most striking work, however, is the monument to the third earl of Lichfield at Spelsbury, Oxfordshire, where Keene's inventiveness as an architect was well matched by Tyler's skills as a sculptor, the two combining to create a highly distinctive composition in which two urns are illusionistically placed within a sarcophagus. Among other monuments are those to Dean Zachary Pearce (*d.* 1774) and Martin Folkes (erected 1788), both in Westminster Abbey; like a number of his monuments, the latter was executed in collaboration with his assistant Robert Ashton.

Tyler's activity as an architect was mainly in the 1780s and 1790s, when he designed the Ordnance office in Westminster (1779–80; demolished 1805) and the Villa Maria, Kensington (*c.*1800), commissioned by the duke of Gloucester for his wife. Some of his works (including a 'sketch of General Wolfe's monument') were sold on 26 March 1770 (sale catalogue, lot 75). He died at his house in Caroline Street, Bedford Square, on 6 September 1801. While lacking the talent and authority of Wilton, Tyler played a modest but significant role in shaping the increasingly institutional practice of sculpture during the late eighteenth century, and his own monuments show both a responsiveness to current styles and a high quality of execution.

MALCOLM BAKER

Sources D. Bindman and M. Baker, *Roubiliac and the eighteenth-century monument: sculpture as theatre* (1995), 170, 221, 336 · R. Gunnis, *Dictionary of British sculptors, 1660–1851* (1953); new edn (1968) · M. Whinney, *Sculpture in Britain, 1530 to 1830*, rev. J. Physick, 2nd edn (1988), 258, 269–73, 460–61 · will, PRO, PROB 11/1363, sig. 619, fols. 147*r*–150*r*

Tylor, Alfred (1824–1884), geologist and brass-founder, was born on 26 January 1824 at Bunhill Row, St Lukes, Middlesex, the second of the six children of Joseph Tylor (1793–1852), brass-founder, and Harriet Skipper (*d.* 1851). His parents were Quakers. The anthropologist Sir Edward Burnett *Tylor was his younger brother. He was educated at Quaker schools, including those at Epping and Tottenham, near London. He left school at the age of fifteen and entered the family brass-founding business, which comprised a foundry in the City of London and an associated colliery, established by his grandfather in 1768, at Tylorstown in the Rhondda valley.

Although Tylor was an indefatigable businessman and amassed great wealth, he devoted much of his leisure time to the pursuit of geology in the company of Joseph Prestwich and Edward Forbes. He was elected a fellow of the Geological Society in 1846 and twice served on its council (1857–65 and 1867–70). A noted hydraulic geologist and geomorphologist, Tylor wrote numerous well-illustrated papers about the flow of rivers—especially relating to the erosion of valleys and the deposit of gravel beds in the Pleistocene period. To understand ancient rivers he studied modern examples. He applied mathematics to river-flow, river-form, and erosion, and he is credited with being the first person to state that a normal river profile approximates to a parabolic curve. Tylor also adopted an innovative approach to measuring rates of denudation by calculating the mean average depth by which a river basin is lowered annually. In 1853, for example, he calculated it would take 1751 and 9000 years respectively to lower the Ganges and Mississippi river basins by 1 foot. Furthermore he estimated it would take some 40,000 years to reduce the mean world land surface by 3 feet with a consequent rise in sea level of 1 foot. His work combined acute observation and meticulously argued theory. Although Charles Darwin praised his 1853 work on sea-level changes and denudation, the geologist William Whitaker and the archaeologist John Evans disagreed with his accounts of gravel deposition in England and France which appeared in 1866 and 1869. Tylor also first argued in 1853 that a pluvial period of exceptional rain followed a glacial one.

Tylor married Isabella (1823?–1906), daughter of Edward Harris, corn factor, of Stoke Newington, at the Friends' meeting-house, Winchmore Hill, Edmonton, Middlesex, on 24 April 1850. His wife was on intimate terms with several members of the royal family. The couple had two sons, including Joseph John *Tylor, and four daughters.

Tylor spent much time promoting technical education in a period when its importance was not widely recognized. His numerous writings on metallurgy were published in the United States, Canada, Sweden, and Germany, and were translated into several other languages. His final work about coloration in animals and plants appeared posthumously in 1886.

Tylor was well travelled, frequently visiting the continent, as well as Russia and the United States. He was generous, friendly, and ever ready unostentatiously to assist his equals and those less fortunate than himself. He was a friend of John Ruskin, a governor of St Bartholomew's Hospital, and a lifelong member of the Society of Friends.

Tylor suffered from diabetes mellitus for many years. He died at his home, Shepley House, Strawberry Lane, Carshalton, Surrey, on 31 December 1884, and was buried in the Quaker burial-ground, Reigate, Surrey, on 6 January 1885. He was survived by his wife, who died on 15 April 1906. In his will he provided for two London school board scholarships for children aged thirteen to sixteen and a recreational ground to be built in Carshalton.

W. H. GEORGE

Sources *Geological Magazine*, new ser., 3rd decade, 2 (1885), 142–4 · T. G. Bonney, *Quarterly Journal of the Geological Society*, 41 (1885), 42–3 · 'List of scientific papers by A. Tylor', *Geological Magazine*, new ser., 2nd decade, 2 (1875), 474–6 · *The Times* (2 Jan 1885) · *Wallington and Carshalton Herald* (10 Jan 1885) · F. W. Baxter, 'Paradise Row (Church Street), a corner of old Stoke Newington', *Hackney and Kingsland Gazette* (11 April 1924), 3 · R. J. Chorley, A. J. Dunn, and R. P. Beckinsale, *Geomorphology before Davis* (1964), vol. 1 of *The history of the study of landforms, or, The development of geomorphology* · CGPLA

Eng. & Wales (1884) · m. cert. · d. cert. · RS Friends, Lond., Book 852, p. 142

Likenesses carte-de-visite, RS Friends, Lond., picture album, T-2, p. 16, 80/N 484

Wealth at death £137,289 2s. 3d.: probate, 3 March 1885, *CGPLA Eng. & Wales*

Tylor, Sir Edward Burnett (1832–1917), anthropologist, was born on 2 October 1832 at Camberwell, Surrey, the third son of Joseph Tylor, who owned a brass foundry, and his wife, Harriet Skipper. Their second son was Alfred *Tylor, the geologist. A Quaker by birth, Tylor was educated at Grove House, Tottenham, a school belonging to the Society of Friends. His faith, which he abandoned later in life, precluded a university education, and at the age of sixteen he entered his father's foundry. In 1855, however, signs of tuberculosis required a recuperative trip to the United States, where he spent several months exploring the Mississippi river valley before going to Havana, Cuba, where, on an omnibus in 1856, he met the ethnologist and fellow Quaker Henry Christy. The two men then embarked on a four-month horseback expedition to Mexico. It was this trip, and the influence of Christy, that led Tylor to anthropology. On his return, symptoms of tuberculosis reappeared and he took a period of convalescence at Cannes, on the French riviera, where he wrote his first book: *Anahuac, or, Mexico and the Mexicans, Ancient and Modern* (1861). It is primarily a travelogue of his trip, but contains early indications of his later anthropological interests, particularly his concern as to whether the pre-conquest Aztec civilization of Mexico was due to diffusion, or borrowing, or whether it arose independently.

After the publication of *Anahuac* Tylor began to familiarize himself with the growing ethnological, linguistic, and archaeological literature, keeping numbered notebooks of his research, now located in the Balfour Library, Oxford. Developing an evolutionary perspective, he began to view culture as a continuum and to search for the origins of culture, and the laws of cultural progress. The latter, he believed, were to be found in the nature of the human mind. Consequently, in the early 1860s Tylor spent several months at the Berlin Deaf-and-Dumb Institute. By studying the language of gestures used by inmates, which they developed on their own, he hoped to discover how humans originate both language and culture. His next book, *Researches into the Early History of Mankind and the Development of Civilization* (1865), which begins with an analysis of his discoveries, is about origins and how to account for the similarity in customs and beliefs in different areas of the world. *Researches* was followed in 1866 by two articles (in the *Fortnightly Review* and *Quarterly Review*) which drew on the work of the German philologist Max Müller, in which Tylor developed further his ideas on the origin of language from interjections and imitative words. In 'The religion of savages', also published in the *Fortnightly Review* in 1866, he first outlined his theory of animism, the idea that the earliest religion began when primitive people interpreted the experience of spirits in

Sir Edward Burnett Tylor (1832–1917), by Maull & Fox, 1899

dreams and hallucinations as inhabiting or 'animating' such objects as trees and stones. In 'The survival of savage thought in modern civilization' (*Proceedings of the Royal Institute*, 1869) Tylor first used the term 'survivals': habits, metaphors, customs, and so on that have 'survived' from an earlier stage of culture and which provide clues to both the reconstruction of past states of mind, and the explanation of seemingly inexplicable practices in European civilization. Survivals became Tylor's primary tool in tracing the progress of one stage of thought to the next.

Tylor's fame rests chiefly, however, on his two-volume work *Primitive Culture: Researches into the Development of Mythology, Philosophy, Religion, Art, and Custom* (1871), which he began by providing the first anthropological definition of culture: 'Culture or Civilization, taken in its wide ethnographic sense, is that complex whole which includes knowledge, belief, art, morals, law, custom and any other capabilities and habits acquired by man as a member of society' (*Primitive Culture*, 1.1). The definition was not superseded by others until the 1920s, and in their 1952 review of definitions of the term, A. L. Kroeber and Clyde Kluckhohn comment that Tylor was deliberately establishing the science of anthropology by defining its subject matter. In the first volume of *Primitive Culture* Tylor outlined the stages of cultural progress, and refuted the commonly held idea that human beings degenerated from a savage state. The second volume he devoted

entirely to developing his theory of the evolution of religion, tracing its development from animism to polytheism, to monotheism. Shortly after the publication of *Primitive Culture* Tylor wrote a review (1872) of *Physique sociale* (1869) and *Anthropométrie* (1870) by the Belgian sociologist and statistician Adolphe Quetelet. He admired both Quetelet's use of statistics because of their objectivity, and also his sociological perspective. Quetelet's influence became evident in a two-part article that Tylor wrote for the *Contemporary Review* in 1873 entitled 'Primitive society', which focuses on morality, law, and political and social organization, and which displays a tendency toward relativism and social determinism absent from his earlier writings. In 'On a method of investigating the development of marriage' (*Journal of the Anthropological Institute*, 1889), which attempted to explain marriage practices in terms of residence patterns, Tylor pioneered the use of statistics in anthropology. The article was also one of the first to attempt to establish relationships between cultural phenomena.

In the late 1870s and the early 1880s Tylor became particularly interested in using an examination of games to trace the relationships between cultures, and many of his articles from this period, none of which is noteworthy in itself, stressed the role of diffusion in the development of culture as opposed to his earlier emphasis on independent invention. Most of his time during this period, however, was spent developing anthropology. He was instrumental in drafting the first edition of the Royal Anthropological Institute's *Notes and Queries on Anthropology for the Use of Travellers and Residents of Uncivilized Lands* (1874), and contributed eighteen sections (the largest number). He also wrote eleven articles for the ninth edition of the *Encyclopaedia Britannica*, which was published between 1875 and 1887. Tylor's last book, *Anthropology: an Introduction to the Study of Man and Civilization*, published in 1881, was the first introductory textbook on the subject and provided a survey of what was then known in the field. Over the winters of 1889–90 and 1890–91 Tylor delivered two series of ten lectures each at the University of Aberdeen, some of the first Gifford lectures. He spent the next ten years preparing them for publication; however the intended book, to be entitled 'The natural history of religion', was never published. His ideas, by this time, had lost their currency and his mental faculties had begun to fail him.

Although Tylor travelled in Mexico, spent November 1872 investigating a spiritualist group in London, and visited Pueblo villages in the south-west United States in 1884, he was, as one commentator has noted, primarily 'a navigator of books'. For the most part he culled his data from the reports of travellers and missionaries. He always attempted to corroborate this information and always carefully weighed the evidence according to his own common sense. He was, for instance, not taken in, as were some of his contemporaries, by reports of a people lacking religion. This carefulness led to a balanced view of cultural evolution and much of the secret of his success lay in his ability to elicit the universal from a multitude of particulars and to form generalizations. His eloquent style of writing gained him a wide audience.

Tylor was the only nineteenth-century anthropologist who devoted his entire time to anthropology. Nineteenth-century anthropology has been referred to as 'Mr Tylor's science', and Tylor himself as the 'father of anthropology'. He is best-known for his definition of culture and his theories of animism and survivals. Tylor was openly hostile to organized traditional religion, particularly Catholicism. He viewed anthropology as a 'reformer's science' and believed that the value of discovering the laws of cultural evolution lay in exposing 'the remains of crude old culture which have passed into harmful superstition, and to mark these out for destruction … for the good of mankind' (*Primitive Culture*, 2.453). Apart from his influence as a writer, Tylor's work as an organizer and teacher helped to establish anthropology as a legitimate field of scientific enquiry. Thus, he led the movement that resulted in the creation of an anthropological section of the British Association, and in 1884 acted as its first president. The University of Oxford awarded him the degree of DCL in 1875; he was appointed keeper of the university museum in 1883, reader in anthropology in 1884, and professor of anthropology in 1896, and was the first to hold the chair in the subject at Oxford. Tylor was also president of the Anthropological Society in 1891, and honorary fellow of Balliol College, Oxford, in 1903. He retired with the title emeritus professor in 1909, and was knighted in 1912. He became inactive in his retirement and moved to Wellington, Somerset, where he died on 2 January 1917 after a few days' illness. He was survived by his wife, Anna, daughter of Sylvanus Fox, of Wellington, whom he married in 1858. Anna was devoted to him and attended most of his lectures; they had no children.   CHRIS HOLDSWORTH

Sources R. R. Marett, *Tylor* (1936) · J. Leopold, *Culture in comparative and evolutionary perspective: E. B. Tylor and the making of primitive culture* (1980) · C. J. Holdsworth, 'The revolution in anthropology: a comparative analysis of the metaphysics of E. B. Tylor (1832–1917) and Bronislaw Malinowski (1884–1942)', DPhil diss., U. Oxf., 1994 · B. Freire-Marreco, 'A bibliography of Edward Burnett Tylor from 1861 to 1907', *Anthropological essays presented to Edward Burnett Tylor in honour of his 75th birthday*, ed. H. Balfour and others (1907) · D. L. Sills, ed., *International encyclopedia of the social sciences*, 19 vols. (1968–91) · G. W. Stocking, *Victorian anthropology* [1987] · A. Lang, 'Edward Burnett Tylor', *Anthropological essays presented to Edward Burnett Tylor in honour of his 75th birthday*, ed. H. Balfour and others (1907) · A. L. Kroeber and C. Kluckhohn, *Culture: a critical review of concepts and definitions* (1952) · DNB
Archives BL, corresp., Add. MS 50524 · Bodl. Oxf. · NHM, notebooks relating to his life by Lady Tylor · U. Oxf., Pitt Rivers Museum, papers | Oxf. U. Mus. NH, letters to Sir E. B. Poulton · Salisbury and South Wiltshire Museum, letters to A. H. L. F. Pitt-Rivers · UCL, letters to Sir Francis Galton · UCL, corresp. with G. C. Robertson
Likenesses G. Bonavia, chalk and pastel drawing, 1860, NPG · photograph, *c.*1891, Royal Anthropological Institute, London · Maull & Fox, photograph, 1899, NPG [*see illus.*] · W. E. Miller, oils, Balliol Oxf.
Wealth at death £39,517 16*s.* 1*d.*: probate, 17 Feb 1917, *CGPLA Eng. & Wales*

Tylor, Joseph John (1851–1901), engineer and Egyptologist, was born at Stoke Newington, Middlesex, on 1 February 1851, the eldest child (of two sons and four daughters) of Alfred *Tylor (1824–1884), brass-founder and geologist, and Isabella Harris (both of the Society of Friends). Sir Edward Burnett Tylor, the anthropologist, was his uncle. Joseph, after being educated at the Friends' school, Grove House, Tottenham, matriculated at London University in June 1868, and then, turning to engineering, studied at the Polytechnic School at Stuttgart, 1868–70. On returning home he entered the Bowling ironworks in Yorkshire. In February 1872 he became partner in the firm of J. Tylor & Sons, brass-founders, 2 Newgate Street, London, which had been founded by his grandfather, Joseph Tylor; on his father's death in 1884 he became senior partner. He was elected AMICE on 1 May 1877, and patented many successful inventions, particularly in connection with hydraulic meters. A Liberal in politics, he was associated with his brother-in-law William Leatham Bright and Arthur Williams in founding the National Liberal Club in 1882. He married, on 15 September 1887, Marion (*d.* 1889), third daughter of George, Lord Young, and had two sons, Alfred and George Cunnyngham.

In 1891 failing health prevented Tylor from following his profession, and he turned to Egypt and Egyptology in search of health and occupation. Here he experimented with the pictorial reproduction of the ancient sculptures and paintings of tombs and temples. His method was to divide up a wall (often irregular in form and surface) into equal spaces with stretched threads, and having photographed these without distortion, to enlarge the negatives and print them faintly. The essential outlines were then strengthened with pencil, the injuries and dirt marks on the original eliminated, and the result rephotographed for publication. In conjunction with Somers Clarke, Tylor selected al-Qab in Upper Egypt as a field for his labours, and he began a series of monographs, published between 1895 and 1900, under the general title of *Wall Drawings and Monuments of El Kab*. He died at his winter residence, Villa la Guérite, La Turbie, Alpes-Maritimes, on 5 April 1901, and was buried at Beaulieu, nearby.

F. L. GRIFFITH, *rev.*

Sources *The Times* (12 April 1901) · private information (1912) · *CGPLA Eng. & Wales* (1901) · DNB
Likenesses W. Hay, portrait, *c.*1864, priv. coll. · C. Vigor, oils, 1894, priv. coll.
Wealth at death £70,914 18*s.* 6*d.*: probate, 20 May 1901, *CGPLA Eng. & Wales*

Tymme, Thomas (*d.* 1620), translator and devotional writer, of parentage and early education unknown, seems to have studied at Cambridge under Edmund Grindal, later archbishop of Canterbury; although he never graduated, he referred in the preface to his 1577 translation of John Calvin's *Commentarie upon S. Paules Epistles to the Corinthians* to 'the benefites, which long ago in *Cambridge*, and els where since, I have receyved by your Graces preferment' (sig. ¶2*v*). Following ordination he became rector of

St Antholin, Budge Row, London, in 1566, and of Hasketon, near Woodbridge, Suffolk, in 1575, though he continued to hold the former benefice until 1592. His first translation, of John Brentius's *Newes from Ninive to Englande*, from the Latin, was published in 1570, but he first achieved significant notice four years later with his translation of Pierre de la Ramée's history of the French civil wars, *The three partes of commentaries containing the whole and perfect discourse of the civill warres of France under the raignes of Henry the Second, Frances the Second, and of Charles the Ninth*. In his preface Tymme makes clear his belief in the godly lessons concerning doctrine and behaviour contained in such a work, hoping that readers would find therein much to apply to themselves, a combination of the didactic with a pastoral hope of providing support in times of trouble reflected in Tymme's own later devotional writings. The work is prefixed by verses praising the translator by Edward Grant, headmaster of Westminster School and one of the leading classical scholars of the day, reflecting the extent of Tymme's scholarly contacts. Thomas Newton wrote commendatory lines on Tymme's *Brief Description of Hierusalem* (1595). Tymme also secured powerful patronage from, among others, the earls of Sussex, Devonshire, and Warwick (to all of whom he dedicated books), as well as Archbishop Grindal.

In 1597 Tymme published his 'cheap little illustrated history', *A Booke, Containing the True Portraiture of the Kings of England*, offering an undemanding recital of familiar views, and most remarkable for the skipping over of all matters concerning recent religious upheavals (Wright, 330). He continued to produce translations of theological works and devotional writings, which displayed his concern with prayer and instruction in the pious life. His *Poore mans pater noster, with a preparative to praier: wherto are annexed divers godly psalmes and meditations* (1598) aimed to bring such instruction to the less erudite, but more widely read was his later work *A silver watch-bell: the sound whereof is able (by the grace of God) to winne the most profane worldling, and carelesse liver ... to become a true Christian indeed that in the end he may obtaine everlasting salvation* (1605), in which Tymme set out not only an idea of a good life but a basis of good works to lead to eternal bliss. Such an approach evidently secured widespread popular approval, for the work went into a nineteenth edition by 1660. Tymme's *The Chariot of Devotion* (1618) is a good example of the defence of prayer against the monopoly of preaching in the literature of the time, designed to commend a neglected devotional form to the pious. Tymme declared that in the service of God and in worship everything should have its proper place and order, which he hoped to advance with his works of piety.

Tymme married Mary Hendy (*d.* 1657) at Hasketon on 17 July 1615; they had one son, also Thomas (*d.* 1687), who became a physician. Tymme himself died at Hasketon in April 1620, and was buried there on 29 April.

T. P. J. EDLIN

Sources L. B. Wright, *Middle class culture in Elizabethan England* (1935) · H. C. White, *English devotional literature (prose) 1600–1640* (1931) · Wood, *Ath. Oxon.*, new edn, 1.170; 2.12 · *DNB*

Tymms, Samuel (1808–1871), antiquary, was born at Camberwell, Surrey, on 27 November 1808, son of Thomas Tymms and his wife, Eliza Stuart. Little is known about his early life, except that he wrote a paper on peg tankards for the *Gentleman's Magazine* in 1827. He wrote *The Family Topographer* (7 vols., 1832–43), a guide to the counties of England, abstracted from other guidebooks. By 1842 he had moved to Suffolk. Most of his antiquarian work is closely connected with that county, especially with the town of Bury St Edmunds, where he was engaged on the staff of the *Bury Post*.

Between 1842 and 1852 Tymms was secretary to the committee that financed the restoration of the 'Norman tower' under the architectural direction of Lewis Cottingham. (The Norman tower, a twelfth-century gateway to Bury St Edmunds Abbey and bell-tower to St James's Church, was saved from possible collapse by this restoration.) He wrote a pamphlet, *The Norman Tower* (1846), for the restoration committee. On 10 July 1844 he married Mary Anne, daughter of John Jugg of Ely, Cambridgeshire. They had two sons and three daughters. The 1851 census showed the family as resident in Well Street, Bury St Edmunds.

Tymms played an important role in starting the Bury St Edmunds museum in 1847 and in developing it thereafter. He was secretary to the Suffolk Institute of Archaeology (the county archaeological society), from its foundation in 1848 until 1867. Perhaps his most important publication was *Wills and Inventories from Bury St Edmunds* (1850), a selection of wills from 1370 to 1650, which he edited for the Camden Society. This was an important study of these documents as historical sources. His *Handbook of Bury St Edmunds*, a local guide, went through nine editions between 1854 and 1916. He also wrote *The History of the Church of St Mary, Bury St Edmunds* (1854), and many articles for the *Proceedings of the Suffolk Institute of Archaeology* from 1848 to 1870. About 1840 he became a member of the New England Historic Genealogical Society, of Massachusetts, USA, and in 1853 a fellow of, and afterwards local secretary to, the Society of Antiquaries.

In 1857 Tymms moved to Lowestoft, Suffolk, where he set up in business in the High Street as a bookseller and printer. There, from 1858, he edited and published *The East Anglian, or, Notes and Queries*, a local antiquarian magazine, until his death. He died at 60 High Street, Lowestoft, on 29 April 1871, and was buried at St Margaret's Church in Lowestoft on 6 May. *The East Anglian* ceased publication on his death, but was revived between 1885 and 1910. The British Library holds a scrapbook of obituaries which Tymms compiled.

ROBERT HALLIDAY

Sources R. Halliday, 'The early history of the Bury St Edmunds museum', *Suffolk Review*, new ser., 22 (1994), 1–17 · C. H. Evelyn-White, 'Samuel Tymms FSA', *The East Anglian, or, Notes and Queries on Subjects Connected with the Counties of Suffolk, Cambridge, Essex and Norfolk*, new ser., 7 (1897–8), 65–7 · L. Dow, 'A short history of the Suffolk Institute of Archaeology', *Proceedings of the Suffolk Institute of Archaeology and Natural History*, 24 (1946–8), 129–62 · *Bury and Norwich Post* (2 May 1871) · *Bury Free Press* (6 May 1871) · *Lowestoft Observer* (6 May 1871) · *Bury and Norwich Post* (22 Dec 1842) · *Bury and Norwich Post* (7 April 1852) · *Bury and Norwich Post* (10 Nov 1852) · *Bury and*

Norwich Post (21 Feb 1855) • *Bury and Norwich Post* (22 Nov 1857) • parish register (burial), St Margaret's Church, Lowestoft • *Proceedings of the Society of Antiquaries of London*, 3 (1853–6), 42, 189
Archives BL, biographical press cuttings, incl. MS notes and additions | Suffolk RO, Bury St Edmunds, letters to second marquess of Bristol • Suffolk RO, Bury St Edmunds, letters to Hugh Pigot
Likenesses photograph, repro. in Evelyn-White, 'Samuel Tymms FSA'
Wealth at death under £1500: probate, 15 Dec 1871, *CGPLA Eng. & Wales*

Tynan [*married name* Hinkson], **Katharine** (1859–1931), poet and novelist, was born at South Richmond Street, South Circular Road, Dublin, on 23 January 1859, the fifth of the twelve children of Andrew Cullen Tynan (1829–1905), gentleman farmer, and Elizabeth O'Reilly (1831–1868/9), only daughter of Felix O'Reilly. Andrew Tynan owned Portobello Dairies in South Richmond Street. In 1868 the family moved to Whitehall, Clondalkin, the house which had belonged to John Philpott Curran, the patriot lawyer, and Tynan became a successful cattle trader and a town councillor.

A precocious child, Katharine Tynan could read by the age of three, and at five she was sent to a 'young ladies' school'. At seven she developed ulcers on her eyes, which left her purblind. In 1871 she went to the boarding-school of the Dominican Siena convent in Drogheda, leaving in 1874 because her father wanted her company. Against the rural backdrop of the Dublin mountains, he forms a frequent image in her writings. Her mother, who had become an invalid in the early 1860s, hardly features.

A nonconforming Catholic, Andrew Tynan wholeheartedly supported Parnell. His daughter, who became the first literary editor of the Parnellite *Irish Daily Independent* (even reviewing herself), shared his political convictions and joined the Ladies' Land League. Katharine Tynan's first poem, 'A Dream', appeared in September 1878 and a considerable list of poetry publications followed. Father Matthew Russell, editor of the *Irish Monthly*, became her confidant. Her early poetry betrayed the influence of English Catholics, in particular of the mystical Christina Rossetti and the aesthetic Alice Meynell, with a preference for Irish subject matter. Through Alice Meynell, she became acquainted with Francis Thompson, who praised the 'tempo rubato rhythm' of her verse, and Lionel Johnson. In 1884, Tynan fell in love with Charles Fagan, an athletic and sensitive Oxford graduate, who also wrote poetry. He died the following year. She was heart-broken and poured out her grief in unpublished poetry.

After the publication of Katharine Tynan's first collection, *Louise de la Vallière and other Poems* (1885), her father furnished a literary salon for her at Clondalkin, to which flocked the Olympians of Ireland's literary renaissance, including John O'Leary, Douglas Hyde, W. B. Yeats, and George Russell (A. E.). With Yeats she worked on *Poems and Ballads of Young Ireland* (1888) and she was the first to review his work. He, in turn, lavished praise on her second poetry collection, *Shamrocks* (1887), which contains one of the earliest attempts to make use of Ossianic material in Anglo-Irish poetry. On the instigation of his father, Yeats proposed to her on 19 July 1891, blissfully unaware that she was secretly engaged to Henry Albert Hinkson (*c*.1866–1919), who had been his exact contemporary at the Dublin high school. Hinkson was clever and handsome, a senior lay classical master at Clongowes and a classical scholar at both Trinity College, Dublin, and the Royal University.

They married on 4 May 1893 and settled in Ealing, west London. After the tragedies of bearing a stillborn child in May 1894 and the death of baby Godfrey in September 1895, Katharine bore three children—Theobald Henry (1897), Giles Aylmer (1899), and Pamela Mary (1900). *Ballads and Lyrics* (1891) deals with many of her previous themes—Ireland, nature, Celtic legends, and Catholic lore—with a more individual, less mannered, touch. *The Wind in the Trees* (1898), with its direct and somewhat imagistic celebration of nature, remains her finest book. Conjugal life brought out a depth and passion in her poetry. Her early prose, in the tradition of rural Irish fiction, is not wholly without literary merit, but the need to raise a family forced her to write too hastily.

Hinkson's lifestyle was not conducive to regular employment. He edited an anthology of verse written by members of Trinity College, produced mediocre historical adventure novels, a clever book of Irish jests, and wrote what was for many years the standard textbook on copyright. He received his law degree from the Inner Temple in 1902 but hardly contributed to the family's finances. Katharine set out to 'boil the pot', producing in all a staggering output of ninety-four novels, twenty-seven poetry collections, twenty-three collections of stories, eight volumes of memoirs, three biographies, three edited collections, two in memoria, two sundry collections, an anthology (the first to feature Joyce), a book of courtesies, a book of maxims, a history, a travelogue, and a Bible exegesis. Added to her innumerable articles, reviews, and discursive journalism, by 1908 she was earning an average income of over £60,000 in late twentieth-century currency. Nevertheless, lack of money necessitated the Hinksons' return to Ireland in 1911. Katharine befriended Lady Aberdeen, the wife of the lord lieutenant, and secured the resident magistracy of Ballinrobe, co. Mayo for her husband. Desolate in Mayo, she used her gift of expressing consolation to produce a substantial output of very popular wartime songs, which were quoted from Catholic and Anglican pulpits alike. Her sons saw active service with the Royal Irish regiment in Gallipoli and France.

After Hinkson's sudden death in 1919, Katharine moved to Dublin, living in Killiney and Shankill, before starting her wandering years, visiting France and Cologne, where life was less expensive. Several years of 'personal guesting' in Ireland followed before she settled in a flat in Wimbledon. Her daughter increasingly functioned as her extra pair of eyes. As she sustained an income with a flow of articles on love, marriage, and the decline of morals, her daughter was becoming a successful novelist under the pseudonym Peter Deane.

Katharine Tynan died of cerebral thrombosis in her flat in Wimbledon on 2 April 1931. She was buried in Kensal Green, close to her beloved Alice Meynell. Her prodigious output did not cease with her death, for several novels were published posthumously. Shortly before her death Macmillan brought out her *Collected Poems*; W. B. Yeats declined the offer to write the foreword, but her old friend A. E. obliged, and described her, aptly, as 'the earliest singer of the Irish Renaissance' with 'as much natural sunlight in her as the movement ever attained'. Inescapably, her name is forever coupled with that of Yeats; their close friendship at the onset of their literary careers has received considerable attention. More recently, Katharine Tynan has been lauded, somewhat hyperbolically, as a champion of the feminist cause. She was, foremost, a true lyrical poet, who extolled the virtues of simplicity, love of nature, love of family, and love of love.

Immensely generous, Katharine Tynan had a gift of solace and of giving that irradiates her published poetry. None the less the image of *herself* as homely and maternal was a mask: she was 'the fire upon the hearth' that never in her life lit a fire, and 'the pillar of the house' (from her poem, 'Any Woman') who ended her days in a rented flat. Her unpublished poetry affords an eloquent and moving glance into a life at times beset by depression, anxiety, and grief; it would have accorded her a more 'fashionable' place in Ireland's literary consciousness.

PETER VAN DE KAMP

Sources P. van de Kamp, 'A catalogue of the literary estate of Pamela Hinkson', PhD diss., University College Dublin, 1984 · K. Tynan, *Twenty-five years: reminiscences* (1913) · K. Tynan, *The middle years* (1916) · K. Tynan, *The years of the shadow* (1919) · K. Tynan, *The wandering years* (1922) · K. Tynan, *Memories* (1924) · K. Tynan, *Life in the occupied area* (1925) · K. Tynan, *A dog book* (1926) · K. Tynan, 'Late memoirs' (unpubd), priv. coll. · P. Hinkson, 'House of corn: Katharine Tynan, a poet's girlhood and time' (unpubd), priv. coll. · F. I. Molloney, 'Katharine Tynan: a study of her poetry', PhD diss., University of Pennsylvania, 1952 · A. C. Fallon, *Katharine Tynan* (Boston, 1979) · K. Tynan, *Irish stories, 1893–1899*, ed. P. van de Kamp (1993) · P. van de Kamp, 'Some notes on the literary estate of Pamela Hinkson', *Yeats Annual*, 4 (1986) · *Beauty and the Beast*, ed. P. Liebregts and W. Tigges (Amsterdam, 1996) · M. G. Rose, *Katharine Tynan* (Lewisburg, Pennsylvania, 1973) · *Poems of Katharine Tynan*, ed. M. Gibbon (1963) · B. Klein, 'William Butler Yeats and Katharine Tynan Hinkson: the last young Irelanders', PhD diss., U. Mich., 1990 · *W. B. Yeats letters to Katharine Tynan*, ed. R. McHugh (New York, 1953) · private information (2004) [family] · bap. cert.
Archives Bodl. Oxf. · FM Cam. · Herts. ALS · Indiana University, Bloomington, Lilly Library, corresp. and literary MSS · JRL, literary corresp. · King's School, Canterbury · NL Ire., corresp. · NL Scot. · Plunkett Foundation, Long Hanborough, Oxfordshire · priv. coll., letters · Ransom HRC, papers · Richmond Local Studies Library, London · Royal Irish Acad. · Royal Literary Fund, London · Southern Illinois University, Carbondale, corresp., literary MSS and papers · U. Lond. · U. Reading · University College, Dublin, corresp. and papers · W. Sussex RO | BL, letters to G. K. Chesterton and F. A. Chesterton, Add. MS 73240 · priv. coll., letters to Edith Oenone Somerville · U. Leeds, Brotherton L., letters to Clement Shorter
Likenesses photograph, 1886, Dublin · J. B. Yeats, oils, 1887, Hugh Lane Municipal Art Gallery, Dublin · J. B. Yeats, watercolour, 1889, priv. coll. · A. Stones, bronze head, 1990, Dublin Writers Museum · J. B. Yeats, pencil sketch
Wealth at death negligible, barring copyrights

Tynan, Kenneth Peacock (1927–1980), theatre critic, was born on 2 April 1927 at the Glenhurst Nursing Home, 319 Shaftmoor Lane, Hall Green, Birmingham, the only son of Sir Peter Peacock (1872–1948), merchant and former

Kenneth Peacock Tynan (1927–1980), by Sir Cecil Beaton, *c*.1956

mayor of Warrington, and (Letitia) Rose Tynan (1888–1961). The couple had lived as husband and wife in Birmingham, where Sir Peter was known as Mr Tynan, since 1921. He continued to maintain in some style the wife and family he had left behind in Warrington. Tynan was not told of any of this until his father's death, when he was much upset, not so much by the secret itself as that it had been kept from him. At King Edward's School, Birmingham, he had begun to acquire the enthusiasms that would shape his life. He loved music-hall, theatre, and the cinema, and could not rest until he had set down his account of any film or play or, in particular, any performance that impressed him. He acted in and directed school productions, and lured the eminent critic James Agate to come and see the result. In his last year he won a demyship at Magdalen College, Oxford, where he embarked upon a systematic campaign to outshine or outrage all contemporaries as undergraduate journalist, actor, impresario, party-giver, and (despite a stammer) debater. If Oxford had turned him into a show-off, he said later, at least it had turned him into a professional show-off. At the same time he was amassing enough serious and enthusiastic consideration of the theatre to provide him with his first book, *He that Plays the King* (1950), and a wider reputation.

After a spell as a repertory theatre director Tynan seized the chance to become a professional theatre critic. Invited by Alec Guinness to take the part of the Player King in Guinness's luckless production of *Hamlet* for the Festival of Britain, Tynan became the target of especially scornful remarks from the *Evening Standard*'s reviewer, A. Beverley Baxter. He replied with a letter to the editor so droll that according to legend he was immediately hired in Baxter's place. In fact some weeks elapsed, and he had in any case been chipping in notices to *The Spectator*, but no doubt his flair for attracting attention played its part. With the *Evening Standard* (1952–3) and to a lesser extent with the *Daily Sketch* (1953–4) Tynan established himself as a funny and scathing writer on the theatre, if still one who wanted from it heroics, illusions, and sad stories of the death of kings. It was only after he was invited to join *The Observer* in 1954 that he started to apply to drama the political convictions which he was in the process of acquiring, with characteristic intemperance, about this time. 'I doubt that I could love anyone who did not wish to see it' (*The Observer*, 13 May 1956), he affirmed in a review of John Osborne's *Look Back in Anger*, inspired as much by the play's tirades against respectability and authority as by its theatrical virtues. He went on to embrace socialism, nuclear disarmament, and the didactic drama of Bertolt Brecht.

His new-found beliefs did not prevent Tynan from remaining a socializer as well as a socialist. He had married on 25 January 1951 Elaine Rita (*b.* 1921), daughter of Samuel M. Brimberg, office equipment manufacturer, of New York. As Elaine Dundy she published three novels and a biography of the actor Peter Finch. Their Mayfair flat became a salon for celebrities passing through London, particularly from the United States. Tynan was fascinated by the outsize stars of Hollywood and Broadway. It was inevitable that he would be lured to America himself, as theatre critic of the *New Yorker*, though without severing his *Observer* connection. In the end he stayed only two years before returning to London in 1960.

Tynan was never sure that he wanted to remain a writer, much less a critic. He leapt at every chance to work in a production capacity as well. He was script editor for Ealing Films in its last years (1955–7); produced two programmes for Associated Television on the Stanislavskian method (1958) and dissent in America (1960); and edited the arts magazine *Tempo* for ABC Television (England) (1961–2). In 1963 he seized the opportunity to abandon his critic's seat altogether. The National Theatre was finally being set up with Sir Laurence Olivier as its first director. Tynan wrote to him proposing that he should be its dramaturg, or literary manager. Olivier agreed. Tynan threw himself into the task with energy and confidence. He disinterred forgotten classics, edited texts, and directly inspired such new works as Tom Stoppard's *Rosencrantz and Guildenstern are Dead* and Peter Shaffer's *Black Comedy*. These first seasons are generally regarded as having given the National's repertoire its stamp, but among the hits were one or two misfires, including a Brecht, which Tynan's critics could cite when in 1968 he clashed with the governors of the theatre over his determination to introduce *Soldiers*, by the German playwright Rolf Hochhuth. The play alleged *inter alia* that Sir Winston Churchill had ordered the death of the wartime Polish leader General Sikorski. As a former colleague of Churchill's, the National's chairman, Viscount Chandos, was adamant that the production should not go ahead. Tynan responded by mounting the play himself in the commercial theatre. This did not endear him to the board, but his eventual departure in 1973 was chiefly prompted by Olivier's retirement that year and the choice of Peter Hall, whom Tynan loathed, as his successor.

Meanwhile came the exploit which prompted mixed feelings among Tynan's friends and admirers, the revue *Oh! Calcutta!* which he devised and produced first in New York, in 1969, and then in London. He had embraced the sexual 'liberation' of the era with the same enthusiasm as he brought to its political concomitant, listing his recreations in *Who's Who* as sex and eating and in 1965 earning himself a footnote in the annals as the first Briton to say the word 'fuck' on television. *Oh! Calcutta!*'s mix of nudity and seedy humour might have been designed to shock the bourgeoisie; ironically (if inevitably) it was a success everywhere, and although Tynan complained that his royalty was only 1 per cent of the gross takings, this was enough to support, for a few years at least, an increasingly lavish lifestyle.

After some blissful years and the birth of a daughter, Tracy, Tynan's first marriage had run into trouble when he began to demand Dundy's submission to what he called 'spanking'. Though initially encouraging of her literary efforts, he also became acutely jealous when *The Dud Avocado* was a success and she embarked upon a second novel. They finally divorced in 1964. Tynan married secondly, on 30 June 1967, Kathleen Jeanette Gates (1937–1995), daughter of Matthew Halton, writer and formerly a war correspondent for the BBC and the Canadian Broadcasting Corporation. She was herself a journalist and writer. They had a daughter, Roxana, and a son, Matthew. They acquired a London house in Kensington, and somewhat late in life Tynan learned to drive and bought himself a Jaguar. Understandably, the second Mrs Tynan proved no keener than the first to share in sado-masochistic practices which only the publication of his diaries in 2001 made fully plain. Tynan took a mistress who did, and to whom he was eventually more faithful than to either wife. The marriage nevertheless jogged on, not without spells of happiness.

Tynan ventured into film production with the 1971 version of *Macbeth* directed by Roman Polanski and collaborated on a follow-up to *Oh! Calcutta!* called *Carte blanche*. But the last decade of his life was increasingly one of restless travels, unfulfilled projects, and bouts of activity alternating with periods of idleness or illness. Emphysema, first diagnosed in 1965, was steadily destroying his lungs. He now regretted the way his career had turned out and wished that he had stuck to working in the theatre or films instead of following the lonely trade of the writer. Yet it was journalism—prompted, often, by the need to raise a quick advance—that gave him a last solid achievement. Mainly for American magazines, he wrote a series of lengthy reflective profiles of actors and entertainers which, published in book form as *Show People* (1979), confirm Tynan's forte as a writer—his ability to conjure up time and place, people and performances, whether he is defining the extraordinary allure of Louise Brooks or conveying exactly what it was like to experience Donald Wolfit and Frederick Valk (two of his heroes) in a barnstorming wartime production of *Othello*.

Tynan had published two collections of theatre reviews but disappointingly few original books, despite becoming a youthful FRSL in 1956. A long-planned memoir of his

Oxford days materialized only in the form of his contribution to the television series *One Pair of Eyes* in 1968. Towards the end he was researching an autobiography, but it was not to be realized. To lessen the ravages of his illness he was now living in California. He died there at St John's Hospital, Los Angeles, on 26 July 1980 from emphysema. His remains were cremated at Rosedale, Culver City, California, on 30 July and his ashes were interred at the St Cross cemetery, Oxford, England, on 17 September that year.

Tynan was tall, slender, always elegant. In youth his habit of baring his teeth as he strove to overcome the stammer, coupled with flaring nostrils and a rather skull-like head, gave him the look of a startled rocking-horse. He matured into a relaxed and attractive human being, full of unexpected subsidiary enthusiasms (cricket, word games, bull-fighting). His conversation, as Tom Stoppard put it, always had the jingle of loose change about it. When he died it seemed that for all his aberrations he had inspired considerable affection in those who knew him. Whether or not he left any permanent mark on the theatre can never be finally settled—fashions come and go; some of those he promoted, such as Brechtian drama, were already out of favour by the time he died, doubtless due to rise again one day. All that may be said with confidence is that Tynan brought excitement, authority, and glamour to the business of writing about the theatre.

PHILIP PURSER

Sources K. H. Tynan, *The life of Kenneth Tynan* (1987) · *Kenneth Tynan: letters*, ed. K. H. Tynan (1995) · L. Olivier, *Confessions of an actor* (1984) · G. Smith, 'Peacock', *Sunday Times Magazine* (25 Aug 1963) · *The Observer* (13 May 1956) · *The diaries of Kenneth Tynan*, ed. J. Lahr (2001) · E. Dundy, *Life itself!* (2001)
Archives BL, corresp. and papers | BL, letters to Julian Holland | FILM BBC WAC · BFI NFTVA, *Reputations*, 25 July 1982 · BFI NFTVA, documentary footage · BFI NFTVA, performance footage | SOUND BL NSA, current affairs recording · BL NSA, documentary recordings · BL NSA, performance recordings
Likenesses photographs, 1955–c.1977, Hult. Arch. · C. Beaton, photograph, c.1956, NPG [*see illus.*] · B. Bury, oils, 1963, NPG · I. Kar, portrait, repro. in Tynan, *Life*, back cover

Tyndale, William (c.1494–1536), translator of the Bible and religious reformer, was born in Gloucestershire, probably in one of the villages near Dursley (possibly Stinchcombe). Landowners, wool merchants, and administrators, the prosperous family was related to the Tyndales of Northamptonshire, Essex, and Norfolk, and may have, long before, originated near the Tyne in Northumberland, as the name might suggest. The identity of Tyndale's parents is unknown, but he had two elder brothers, Richard and Edward. The latter was a considerable figure in the county; his relationship to William is confirmed by a letter from John Stokesley, then bishop of London, in 1533. A younger brother, John, was also in the wool trade.

Education Tyndale may have learned his good Latin as a child at Lady Berkeley's Grammar School at Wotton under Edge, 3 miles south-east of Stinchcombe. The first record of him, probably when he was eighteen, from which his likely date of birth may be calculated, shows him as William Hychyns (an alternative family name), graduating BA

as a member of Magdalen Hall, Oxford, on 4 July 1512. He was ordained subdeacon in that year, and proceeded to the diaconate and priesthood in London in 1515, on 24 March and 7 April respectively. He incepted as an MA at Oxford on 2 July 1515, a degree that permitted him for the first time to read theology. That this official study did not include scripture appalled him. Foxe records that he 'read privily to certain students and fellows of Magdalen College some parcel of divinity, instructing them in the knowledge and truth of the scriptures' (Foxe, ed. Pratt, 5.114–15). Erasmus, whose Oxford home some years before had been Magdalen College, and who until recently had been Lady Margaret's professor of divinity at Cambridge, published in March 1516 in Basel his *Novum instrumentum*, a new Latin translation of the New Testament, with the original Greek alongside. Although Tyndale was brought up in 'God's Gloucestershire', a county historically known for biblical preaching, the source of his vocation to the cause of reform is most likely to have been the arrival of this printing of the original Greek New Testament. It is very probable that it was from this influential volume that Tyndale led those private studies. Foxe states that Tyndale went on to Cambridge, but no contemporary record supports this.

Gloucestershire again Tyndale went back to Gloucestershire, at an unknown date. He became tutor to the children of Sir John and Lady Walsh at Little Sodbury Manor, a dozen miles south of the district of his birth. Sir John, a county squire of importance, who had been at court with the young Henry VIII (he was later twice high sheriff) had recently handed over the position of crown steward for the Berkeley estate to Edward Tyndale. Lady Walsh had been a Poyntz, a family with close connections to the Tudor court since the 1470s; Anne Walsh's nephew Nicholas, their neighbour, was close to King Henry and Queen Anne. Tyndale's duties at Little Sodbury cannot have been heavy. It is probable that he used his time to study, and even begin to translate into English, Erasmus's Greek New Testament. For the Walshes he translated Erasmus's *Enchiridion militis Christiani* into English, a book that drew them more to the reformed position, a topic of debate in the house. It is likely that this translation is lost, and is not that printed by Wynkyn de Worde in London in 1533, revised in 1534.

Tyndale appears to have been in demand in the area as a preacher (at St Mary's Green in Bristol, for example), which is not surprising given his New Testament theology and the strong commitment to Lollardy in the county. The emphasis on scripture for the people and the hostility to the corruptions in the church was common to many (including Erasmus); but that Tyndale was particularly influenced by Lollard doctrines lacks evidence. Tyndale was accused of heresy, and brought before the bishop's chancellor. Several accounts of this stormy meeting survive. One is from Tyndale himself, in the prologue to his Genesis of 1530, where he recalled that 'he threatened me grievously, and reviled me, and rated me as though I had been a dog' (*Tyndale's Old Testament*, 4). Another is in Foxe, where he is recording the narrative of the local man Richard Webb (Foxe, 514). Even Thomas More had heard enough to misreport it (More, 6/1.424). After all the shouting nothing happened.

Richard Webb also recalled that Tyndale went to visit 'an old doctor, that had been archchancellor to a bishop' living nearby. This man, identified as William Latimer by Mozley, though not conclusively, as Latimer had not held such a post, warned Tyndale that 'the pope is the very antichrist', and that if he continued to preach the scriptures 'it will cost you your life' (Foxe, ed. Pratt, 5.116–17). Tyndale's most famous Gloucestershire encounter, again told by Richard Webb, was with 'a learned man', who said 'we were better without God's law than the pope's':

> Maister Tyndale hearing that, answered him, I defy the Pope and all his laws, and said, if God spare my life ere many years, I will cause a boy that driveth the plough, shall know more of the Scripture than thou dost.   (Foxe, 514; Foxe, ed. Pratt, 4.117)

London Tyndale, already with the vocation to print the New Testament in English, and needing permission, hoped to be supported by Cuthbert Tunstall, the bishop of London. Tunstall had been highly praised by Erasmus, with whom he worked in the Low Countries on the second edition of his Greek New Testament, lending him a Greek manuscript and consulting others. He had been at Oxford with Colet, Linacre, and More (who singles him out for praise at the opening of his *Utopia*), and was known throughout Europe as a mathematician and classicist. Tyndale, probably arriving in London in the spring of 1523, had a letter of introduction from Sir John Walsh to Sir Henry Guildford, the king's controller and master of the horse, and he himself wrote to an old friend in Tunstall's service, William Hebilthwayte. All to no end: Tunstall replied, as Tyndale wrote, 'his house was full … I … understood at the last … that there was no room in my lord of London's palace to translate the new testament' (*Tyndale's Old Testament*, 5). To show his skill in Greek, Tyndale had taken with him his translation of an oration of Isocrates, which has not survived, the first recorded in English: this suggests that both Tyndale's Greek and his understanding of classical rhetoric were excellent. He was later praised by the German scholar Hermann Buschius for his mastery of seven languages: Greek, Latin, Hebrew, German, Spanish, and French, as well as English.

Tunstall, in the summer of 1523, was occupied in parliament, the first for eight years: though he snubbed Tyndale, it is observable that he did not persecute him. Tyndale stayed in London for almost a year. Foxe records him preaching in St Dunstan-in-the-West in Fleet Street. His sermons have not survived. St Dunstan-in-the-West apparently had connections with the growing reform movement, with the Poyntz family, and with merchants in the cloth trade, particularly Humphrey Monmouth, who took Tyndale into his house, where he 'studied most part of the day and of the night, at his book' (Foxe, ed. Pratt, 4.617–18, 753; Strype, 1/2.364). Tyndale, by now realizing that 'to translate the New Testament … there was no place in all England' (*Tyndale's Old Testament*, 5), left for Germany,

probably in April 1524, supported by London merchants including Monmouth, who was in serious trouble in May 1528 because of that.

Cologne, 1525 Tyndale is next recorded in Cologne in 1525, seeing through the press of Peter Quentell his English translation of the New Testament. His enemies later accused him of being with 'the arch-heretic Luther', which has led to speculation that he went to Wittenberg, for which there is no evidence, though it was not unknown for the English reformers on the continent, like John Rogers, to go there, or meet Luther, like John Frith. Mozley's ingenious suggestions about Tyndale's two visits to Hamburg, and matriculation at Wittenberg, are not persuasive. Tyndale had as his assistant, possibly instead of the later biblical translator and bishop Miles Coverdale, the Observant friar William Roy, and he may have been joined by John Frith. Peter Quentell was, like his father, an eminent printer, accepting serious work from any source. For Tyndale and Roy he had in print a long prologue and almost the whole of Matthew's gospel, when the work was stopped. He was also printing books by the strongly anti-Lutheran Cochlaeus (John Dobneck), who learned from the printers, 'after he had warmed them with wine … the secret by which England was to be brought over to the side of Luther' (Pollard, 107). He reported this to the authorities. The print-shop was raided, but Tyndale and Roy escaped up the Rhine to Worms. Dobneck said that this Lutheran New Testament, with an intended print run of 3000 or 6000, had 'got as far as the letter K', the signature that would have taken the work well into Mark. What is extant is everything up to the middle of Matthew 22, and sheets of this (or more) began to circulate in England, being the first printed Lutheran documents here. A single surviving set of finished sheets to Matthew 22, bound in the nineteenth century, is in the British Library.

The description 'Lutheran New Testament' is accurate. In appearance the pages are a smaller quarto in the style of Luther's first, 1522, 'September Testament', in layout, type, and frequency and placing of marginal notes. Two-thirds of these ninety comments are from Luther, and all are entirely expository. The text shows signs of Luther's influence in occasional word-order and vocabulary. The prologue is Luther's, cut and then expanded by Tyndale to twice the length. Tyndale's opening, and manner, is gentler than Luther's. This 'Cologne fragment' is valued most, however, for being almost the whole of the first gospel translated from the original Greek, printed in English for the first time. The words of Jesus that have chimed down the centuries appear here first—'Ask and it shall be given you: Seek and ye shall find: Knock and it shall be opened unto you'; 'Enter in at the strait gate: for wide is the gate and broad is the way that leadeth to destruction'; and many thought to be proverbial, like 'the burden and heat of the day'.

The 1526 *Worms New Testament* Tyndale and Roy arrived, probably late in 1525, in the safe Lutheran city of Worms, and the small printer Peter Schoeffer undertook an English New Testament, the first ever made, completed in

1526. This is very different from the Lutheran Cologne fragment. It is in octavo (pocket-size, like all Tyndale's books printed in his lifetime) and without prologue or marginal notes, or attribution to him. This 'bare text' had impact enough, however. Smuggled down the Rhine and into English and Scottish ports in bales of cloth, copies circulated quickly. For the first time, the whole New Testament, faithfully translated from the Greek, could be read by anyone. That this immediately alarmed the English authorities is amply testified. Tunstall himself sent out in October 1526 a prohibition of the book—'in the english tongue that pestiferous and moste pernicious poyson dispersed throughout all our dioces of London in great nomber' (Pollard, 134). He warned the booksellers. As a grand gesture, he arranged for the burning of Tyndale's New testaments at St Paul's on 27 October 1526, and himself preached the sermon on the occasion, claiming to have found 2000 errors in them, unsurprising in that Tyndale was not translating from the Latin, but an interesting comment on the position in which the Greek scholar Tunstall found himself. Tyndale later noted that the church was so devoted to the search for heresy in what he wrote that, though previously they ignored scripture, now they examined his translation so closely that they would announce to the ignorant people that it was heresy if he failed to dot an 'i'.

In considerable numbers, and to inferior standards, copies were being issued by a printer in Antwerp. Sir John Hackett, English ambassador and Wolsey's agent in the Low Countries, recorded over some months his attempts to hunt down copies there. Tunstall's chaplain wrote of 'many hundreth' burnt, 'both heir & beyonde the see' (Pollard, 125). William Warham, archbishop of Canterbury, wrote in May 1527 to all his bishops asking them to share the cost of buying up copies in order to burn them. Extant is the reply by the bishop of Norwich, Richard Nix, of 14 June 1527, sending 10 marks, offering more, and congratulating the archbishop on doing 'a gracious and a blessed deed' in burning the Testaments, for which God will highly reward him (BL, Cotton MS Vitellius B.ix, fol. 131). In November 1527 the arrest by Wolsey of the gentle Cambridge scholar Thomas Bilney heralded an onslaught against the English New testaments. Records of depositions by the many people arrested in the next year provide a profile of the first readers of Tyndale's translation.

A story told by Edward Hall in his chronicle of 1548 has been much repeated. Cuthbert Tunstall, happening to be in Antwerp, arranged with an English merchant there, Augustine Packington, to go to Tyndale to offer to buy his stock of New testaments with Tunstall's money. Though Tyndale knew they were being bought to be burnt by the bishop, he agreed: 'And so went forward the bargain, the bishop had the books, Packington had the thanks, and Tyndale had the money' (*Hall's Chronicle*, 762–3). It may well have happened: but not to Tyndale, who would never have agreed to sell New testaments for public burning. It is more likely to have been a transaction with the Antwerp 'pirate' printer of Tyndale, Christopher van Endhoven.

This 1526 Worms New Testament is rightly a treasure of English-speaking culture, for its mastery of both the Greek and English languages. Quite apart from the theological impact of these pages, many English phrases have gone into common use: 'the spirit is willing'; 'fight the good fight'; 'the powers that be'. Of Peter Schoeffer's original print run only one complete copy survives, discovered in the Stuttgart Landesbibliothek in 1996. The British Library's fine copy, for 200 years in Bristol Baptist college, lacks a title-page. St Paul's Cathedral Library's copy lacks the title-page and seventy leaves. There are no more. The volumes live on, of course, in English New testaments ever since, almost all of which, even to the present day, reflect Tyndale, many very closely. As Bishop Westcott wrote of Tyndale in 1868, 'His influence decided that our Bible should be popular and not literary, speaking in a simple dialect, and that so by its simplicity it should be endowed with permanence' (Westcott, 158).

After seeing the New Testament into print, Tyndale and Roy parted, to Tyndale's relief. He later wrote (in the prologue to his *Wicked Mammon*) of Roy's slipperiness. While in Worms, Tyndale gave to Peter Schoeffer a small book, *A Compendious Introduction, Prologue or Preface unto the Epistle of Paul to the Romans*, of which one copy survives, in the Bodleian Library. This, based loosely on Luther's *Vorrhede* to Romans in all his German New testaments, was the second printed reformed tract circulating in England. It is an exposition of Paul's doctrine of justification by faith alone. Expanded in Tyndale's 1534 revision of his New Testament, it had a large effect in England.

The Parable of the Wicked Mammon and The Obedience of a Christian Man Tyndale's movements for some years after 1526 are unrecorded, but that all his work from 1528 was published in Antwerp implies that he was living in or near that thriving port, which had strong trade connections with England and many good printers. His first two Antwerp books were from the print-shop of 'Hans Luft of Marlborow', a pseudonym of one of the biggest Antwerp printers, Martin de Keyser or Martin l'Empereur. The real Hans Luft, in Wittenberg, was Luther's prosperous printer, so de Keyser's choice of name was suggestive.

On 8 May 1528 Tyndale's *The Parable of the Wicked Mammon* was published, in his customary small octavo. It soon appeared in the records of the much sharpened interrogations in England that it provoked, and was officially banned as heretical on 24 May 1530. Following a sermon by Luther, Tyndale develops his exposition of the parable in Luke 16, known since as that of the unjust steward, to show the New Testament teaching that though good works are important, they only come naturally from true faith, as fruit comes from the tree. Overemphasis on works leads only to superstition. Lacking a title-page, the book's first four leaves are a prologue, 'William Tyndale otherwise called hychins to the reader', a declaration, as he explains, to dissociate himself from the superficial and showy William Roy.

Tyndale's most influential book outside his Bible translations, *The Obedience of a Christian Man*, came five months later, on 2 October 1528. Enemies were asserting that the reformers throughout Europe were encouraging sedition and teaching treason. Tyndale wrote to declare for the first time the two fundamental principles of the English reformers: the supreme authority of scripture in the church, and the supreme authority of the king in the state. Tyndale makes many pages of his book out of scripture, and he is scalding about the corruptions and superstitions in the church. His arguments are carefully developed, and his experiences of ordinary life are wide-ranging. Contrasted with the New Testament church and faith, he describes the sufferings of the people at the hands, especially, of monks and friars, though the whole intrusive hierarchy, as he sees it, from the pope down, is guilty of 'selling for money what God in Christ promiseth freely' (Tyndale, *Obedience*, 170). Tyndale was a master of English prose: his attacks (for example on the follies of the rival metaphysical schools of theology) make exhilarating reading, and his sympathy with the existential human condition can be moving. Like *Mammon*, the *Obedience* was widely read, and immediately banned (the bishops found and published fifty-four articles of heresy in them), and appears in records of interrogations of humble people. At the other extreme, Strype records, from Foxe's papers, a story of Anne Boleyn showing a copy to her husband-to-be, who delighted in it, and declared that 'this is a book for me and all kings to read' (Strype, 1.172-4).

The Pentateuch Somewhere in Europe, where knowledge of it was growing, Tyndale learned Hebrew: perhaps in Worms, where there were rabbinic schools. Hebrew was almost unknown in England; neither of the two scholars in Cambridge who knew Hebrew was concerned to translate. In January 1530, again from 'Hans Luft of Marlborow', copies of *The First Book of Moses called Genesis*, with a prologue, 'W. T. to the Reader', appeared in England. The five books of the Pentateuch could be bought singly or together. Each has a prologue: Exodus, Leviticus, and Deuteronomy are in Roman type; unusual words are explained after Genesis, Exodus, and Deuteronomy. The original Hebrew text was in modern English for the first time. Instead of 'Fiat lux, et facta est lux', Tyndale gave posterity 'Let there be light, and there was light', and the name of God as Jehovah. Tyndale's Hebrew was good. He used, but did not depend on, Luther's Pentateuch of 1523. Tyndale's Genesis has six marginal notes, to Luther's seventy-two. A passage in his *Obedience* declares his experience of how well Hebrew went into English. His aim was always to be clear, achieved even when the Hebrew is difficult. His skill with poetry shows what has been lost in not having his Psalms, Job, and the Prophets. Of Tyndale's 132 notes in the Pentateuch, a dozen are of one word only. Two dozen mention the pope, as 'The pope's bull slayeth more than Aaron's calf' at Exodus 32. Most are expository. Tyndale was outstanding in matching varieties of English to the differences in the Hebrew, between the tragicomedy of the fall in Genesis 3 and the long novel-like narrative of Joseph and his brothers at the end of that book.

A few lines of Foxe's last, 1576, version of *Actes and Monuments* tell of Tyndale shipwrecked on the way to Hamburg, losing everything except his life. All his work on the Pentateuch perished. He summoned Coverdale to help him, and

in Hamburg translated afresh, living in the house of Margaret Van Emmerson at a time of plague. Foxe is attractively specific, and the story has been widely noticed, but there are too many things against it for modern acceptance. Though Tyndale is at his most autobiographical in the prologue to Genesis, no records of the time mention these momentous events. With his Jonah-like rescue from the sea to disseminate the word, the story may have a trace of Tyndale's translation of that prophet from the Hebrew, printed, with a long prologue, at about this time. A single copy survives in the British Library.

Tyndale and More, and *The Practice of Prelates* In 1528 Sir Thomas More, already a seasoned antagonist of Luther in Latin, was permitted by Tunstall to read heretical books in English in order to attack Tyndale. More was determined to crush heretics, if need be by fire. In June 1529 appeared More's *Dialogue Concerning Heresies*, in the third book of which Tyndale's New Testament is demolished as heresy, and Tyndale himself vilified as worse than Luther. Essentially, More asserts that Tyndale's offence has been to give the people Paul in English, and to translate key words in their Greek meanings as 'senior', 'congregation', 'love', and 'repent', instead of the church's 'priest', 'church', 'charity', and 'do penance'.

Tyndale, to whom the attack was unexpected, replied vigorously, even page by page, in his *An Answer unto Sir Thomas More's 'Dialogue'* of 1531, at shorter length. His authority is the New Testament. He condemns the church, so absolutely defended by More, for having perverted scripture, and for the many corruptions of his day (on which More, he notes, was silent). More replied to Tyndale's *Answer* with his enormous *Confutation of Tyndale's 'Answer'*, almost 2000 heavy pages, of which the first three books were published early in 1532, and a year later the remaining six: all but the fifth book (against Barnes) attack Tyndale. Huge as it is, running to half a million words, it was never finished. Even More's devotees, including his contemporary biographer Nicholas Harpsfield, and his modern editors, agree that More is, to put it mildly, disordered. Tyndale is intemperately pilloried on almost every page ('a hell-hound in the kennel of the devil', 'discharging a filthy foam of blasphemies out of his brutish beastly mouth'). More's longest work in English does his reputation no favour. Tyndale made no further reply, but More was still attacking Tyndale in his *Apology*, and his *Debellation of Salem and Bizance*, both of 1533.

In 1530 Tyndale published, once again from 'Marborch' ('Hans Luft of Marlborow') his short *The Practice of Prelates*. The pope's conspiracy, as the old image had it, is the ivy strangling the nation's tree. 'Practice' carries also its older meaning of 'trickery'. Tyndale's attacks on the Roman hierarchy are trenchant in their rhythms, building to a sustained onslaught on the deviousness of 'Wolfsee' (Wolsey). In *Practice* there are few marginal notes: as usual, many were added in editions after his death. In the last pages Tyndale argues learnedly against King Henry's divorce of Catherine, to the king's reported anger, leading to the removal of those pages in later editions.

New Testament expositions About 1530 Tyndale expanded his prologue to the 1525 Cologne fragment to make a small, short, book, *A Pathway to the Holy Scripture*, as a guide to the New Testament to be read alongside his unannotated 1526 Worms volume. *Pathway* expounds the central doctrines of Paul in Romans, especially justification by faith alone. In September 1531 he published *An Exposition upon the First Epistle of John*. This is a section by section unfolding of John, with the decorum of a quieter tone, even in its demands for righteous love. Tyndale does, however, expound John's 'Little children, beware of images', with extended mockery of the worship of saints and their statues. Early in 1533 came his *An Exposition upon the V, VI, VII Chapters of Mathew* (that is, the sermon on the Mount), in which Tyndale contrasts the words of Christ in restoring the true meaning of God's commandments—works resulting from faith—with many corrupt practices of the church. Unpublished in Tyndale's lifetime, and first printed in 1548, was *A Brief Declaration of the Sacraments*, in which Tyndale argues that it is the inner faith of the communicant that makes the sacrament of the Lord's supper, a doctrine furiously denied by More, and for which John Frith died, and which for 450 years has been a central doctrine of the Church of England. (The book *The Supper of the Lord*, also the subject of a powerful attack by More, was not, as he thought, by Tyndale.) Also unpublished in Tyndale's lifetime, the manuscript bound with Frith's tract on the subject was Tyndale's essay on the *cause célèbre* of the will of William Tracy, in which he trusted to be saved by the merits of Christ and not by works, saints, or masses. All those printed works came from Martin de Keyser in Antwerp, as himself.

Tyndale was visited secretly in 1531 by Thomas Cromwell's emissary, Stephen Vaughan, who was the king's factor in the Netherlands. The king, it seems, had recovered from his anger at *Practice*, and had been persuaded that the country would be safer if Tyndale were in England and at court. In January 1531 Vaughan succeeded in getting a letter to Tyndale offering, on the king's authority, a safe conduct and other sureties. Tyndale, with some justification suspecting a trap, refused. As he knew, the situation in England was darkening. One evening in April 1531 Vaughan met Tyndale in a field outside Antwerp, and afterward wrote to Cromwell a long account of their conversation. Tyndale declared his strong loyalty to the king: he lived in constant poverty and danger to bring the New Testament to the king's subjects. Did the king, Tyndale asked, fear those subjects more than the clergy? Tyndale wrote to protect the king from what he termed the 'subtle demeanour' of the clergy of his realm, in particular the 'iniquitous cardinal' (namely Wolsey). Vaughan met Tyndale again in May. Tyndale movingly sent his promise that if the king would grant his people a bare text (of the scriptures, in their language), as even the emperor and other Christian princes had done, whoever made it, then he would write no more and submit himself at the feet of his royal majesty. A third meeting had the same result. Vaughan wrote twice again to Cromwell on Tyndale's behalf, with no effect. Power at court was shifting. The next emissary sent, Sir Thomas Elyot, a friend of More, went not to persuade but to arrest Tyndale.

Tyndale's 1534 New Testament The Antwerp printing house of Van Endhoven had published, by 1534, four reissues of Tyndale's 1526 Worms New Testament, in various small sizes, including sextodecimo. These printings say a good deal about the demand in Britain. In 1534 the widow of Christopher van Endhoven (who had died in London, imprisoned for printing and shipping English bibles) asked an English scholar living in Antwerp, George Joye, to oversee another edition, as the Flemish typesetters were not doing well. This he did. He also took the opportunity to make silent alterations to Tyndale's work. In particular, he altered Tyndale's English word 'resurrection', to make it 'the life after this life' and variations. Not to put his name to the changes was bad enough; but in 1533 the resurrection was the subject of debate among the English reformers.

Tyndale was already preparing his own revision of his 1526 New Testament, which was published in 1534. It shows his maturer thought, and skill, and in many ways improves on the 1526 version. He wrote for it a long prologue about translation, explaining among other things the importance of appreciating the Hebrew influence on New Testament Greek, something not widely understood before. He also wrote a second prologue, 'W. T. yet once more unto the Christian reader', in which he strongly attacked George Joye for his impertinence. Tyndale defends his own translation, and adds that Joye is free to come up with his own ideas, as long as he puts his own name to them.

This handsome small volume of 1534, well printed by de Keyser, is the English New Testament as it went forward into other sixteenth-century versions. 83 per cent of the King James (Authorized) Version New Testament is directly from Tyndale, in this 1534 revision. There are now marginal cross-references and notes, many only a single word, and acting as location-finders rather than exposition, though Tyndale clarifies and explains New Testament life and doctrine in longer notes. Revelation has twenty-two woodcuts, disturbing visualizations of the baffling text. Then follow fifteen pages containing forty Old Testament passages in English, those that were read on certain days in the services at Salisbury Cathedral, which Sarum use became a basis of the Book of Common Prayer. Each New Testament book, except Acts and Revelation, has a prologue. Those to the main Pauline epistles are important, and that to Romans is especially so: it is Tyndale again translating Luther's own *Vorrhede*, as in his 1526 *A Compendious Introduction* and *A Pathway*, but now adapting more freely. More copies of this translation have survived. One, in the British Library, was owned by Queen Anne Boleyn, with her royal name on the foredges. A revised version of this New Testament, with minor changes, was made by Tyndale in 1535.

Tyndale had made slight revisions to his translation of Genesis in a reprint of 1534. By the spring of 1535 he had certainly finished translating the historical books of the Old Testament, Joshua to 2 Chronicles, in manuscript.

Parts of these books present unusual difficulties, as for example in the 'Song of Deborah', incorporated in Judges 5, one of the oldest documents known, where the Hebrew text is corrupt and problematic: in translating it, Tyndale comes out well. His accuracy to the Hebrew in the range of tones that he can command through all these books is noteworthy.

Tyndale and Frith Frith had most probably known Tyndale in England, had been with him, with his wife and family, in the Low Countries at least, and perhaps also in Germany. Foxe prints two letters from Tyndale to Frith in the Tower in 1531, both characteristically made of scripture. The first exhorts him to courage in the likelihood of his coming martyrdom. The second, addressed to Frith under the name of 'Jacob', advises that in writing on 'Christ's body in the sacrament', dependence on the phrases of scripture would be his wisest policy; and giving him news, including assurance of his wife's support. Frith wrote of Tyndale that 'for his learning and judgement in scripture, he were more worthy to be promoted than all the bishops in England': he commended his 'faithful, clear, innocent heart' (Foxe, ed. Pratt, 5.130).

Arrest and imprisonment Tyndale had spoken to Stephen Vaughan in 1531 of his poverty, exile, absence from friends, hunger, thirst, cold, and 'the great danger wherewith I am everywhere encompassed'—all, and more, endured because he 'hoped with my labours to do honour to God' (Daniell, 213). He was relatively safe living with Thomas Poyntz and his wife in the English House in Antwerp, where John Rogers had been chaplain to the English merchants since late 1534. Poyntz was related to Lady Walsh of Little Sodbury. Tyndale could reasonably look forward to completing his translation of the Old Testament. In the spring of 1535, however, a debauched and villainous young Englishman wanting money, Henry Phillips, insinuated himself into the English House and Tyndale's trust, pretending interest in the work of Bible translation, and borrowing money from him. Phillips had gambled away money entrusted to him by his father to give to someone in London, and, full of self-pity, had fled abroad. He promised someone in authority, it is not known whom (suspicion falls on Stokesley) that he could betray Tyndale, Barnes, and Joye, for cash. On the morning of 21 May 1535, having arranged for the imperial officers to be ready, Phillips tricked Tyndale into leaving the English House. In the alley he was seized. The officers later said 'that they pitied to see his simplicity when they took him' (Foxe, ed. Pratt, 5.128). Tyndale was taken at once to the procurer-general, who immediately raided Poyntz's house and took away all Tyndale's property, including his books and papers. The Old Testament historical books in English were safely somewhere else, probably with Rogers. It is not known what further translations were removed and destroyed. Tyndale was taken to the castle of Vilvorde, outside Brussels, where he was incarcerated for the next sixteen months.

The English merchants at Antwerp, outraged at the abuse of their corporate diplomatic privilege, wrote at once to the court at Brussels and to the English government. Their ire was so well known that Phillips (as is the way with bullies) was greatly afraid: not only that the English merchants would lie in wait for him, but because his letters sent to England about the arrest of Tyndale included remarks, intended to gain favour at the emperor's court, insulting to King Henry. If they were seen by Cromwell, they would lead to his own swift arrest and death. The endeavours of the English merchants faded; the English court lost opportunities. Thomas Poyntz remained active, however. His attempts in Antwerp failing, he wrote to his brother John at the English court, saying that he believed that the king, who never had 'a truer hearted subject to his grace' than Tyndale, had written to Brussels for Tyndale's release, but did not know that his letters had been blocked, probably by Phillips. In any case, the highest political forces were against release. The holy Roman emperor, Charles V, at his court in Brussels, was in no mood to assist an English king who had just divorced his aunt.

'The king's grace', Poyntz wrote, 'should have of him at this day as high a treasure as of any one man living … there be not many perfecter men this day living, as knows God' (Daniell, 370). Cromwell meanwhile had written to two leading privy councillors in Brabant. The letters, and the attempts by Poyntz to get results from them, made a tangled skein of contacts and journeys. In the end it seemed that Poyntz had succeeded. He was told at Brussels that Tyndale would be released to him.

Phillips saw his money threatened if Tyndale, in England, talked to Cromwell, or even to the king. So he denounced Poyntz as a fellow heretic of Tyndale. Poyntz was placed under house arrest, and subjected to a three-month interrogation on more than a hundred articles. The inquisitors always arrived with Phillips at the door. Poyntz, suddenly alert to his danger, escaped and fled to England. His wife refused to join him. His business was in ruins. He lived a further twenty-six years, too poor to benefit from the inheritance of the ancestral manor in Essex. Phillips lived until 1542, travelling with increasing desperation the length of Europe, denounced by all who came to know him as a perpetual thief and traitor.

Inquisition Tyndale meanwhile had been subjected to long examination by the procurer-general. This man, Pierre Dufief, was widely known in the Low Countries for his cruelty. His zeal for hunting down heretics was fuelled by the fact that he was given a proportion of the confiscated property of his victims, and a large fee. Dufief had arranged for Tyndale's English works to be translated into, or at least summarized in, Latin, probably by Phillips.

Since Tyndale was a Lutheran, his crime was heresy. To his enemies he was the greatest English catch, and his downfall, it was believed, would remove heresy from England, and give glory to his captors. He was tried by seventeen commissioners, led by three chief accusers. At their head was the greatest heresy-hunter in Europe, Jacobus Latomus, from the new Catholic University of Louvain, a long-time opponent of Erasmus as well as of Luther. Tyndale, declining an offer of his own notary and procurer, conducted his own defence, which was not from legal manoeuvring but from scripture. Latomus wrote a detailed record, which shows him precise, and indeed courteous, as to a great scholar. This account was published in three books in 1550, six years after his death. In that he notes that Tyndale wrote his defence in a book on the proposition *sola fides justificat apud Deum* ('Faith alone justifies before God'). Tyndale's apparently frequent phrase *clavis intelligentiae salutaris sacrae scripturae* ('the key to the understanding of scripture as salvation') may supply an alternative title.

Latomus was not trying to discover whether Tyndale was a heretic. That had been determined long before: Latomus was trying to bring Tyndale back to orthodoxy, for the sake of his soul, before he was burnt. He could not avoid reproducing a good deal of what Tyndale wrote. As a result, it has been possible to reconstruct Tyndale's last, lost book in detail. It appears all of a piece with everything else he published, in its logical development, clarity, and, above all, absolute dependence on, and great knowledge of, scripture, especially Paul.

One autograph document from these months has survived in the archives of the council of Brabant. Neatly written in Latin, on one small sheet of paper, and signed 'W. Tindalus', it reveals a great deal. As the first winter approached in 1535, Tyndale wrote, most probably to the marquess of Bergen-op-Zoom (one of the councillors to whom Cromwell had written), asking him to request 'the commissary'—the procurer-general, Dufief—to let him have some of his own warmer clothing which Dufief had confiscated; what he had was worn out, and he was suffering from a perpetual cold and catarrh. Tyndale adds: 'And I ask to be allowed to have a lamp in the evening; it is indeed wearisome sitting alone in the dark.' Most urgently he asks to be permitted to have 'the Hebrew bible, Hebrew grammar, and Hebrew dictionary [that is, Reuchlin in German] that I may pass the time in that study'.

There is no evidence that any of his requests was met. Tyndale was in the prison cell for sixteen months. The notion that Tyndale spent that time in translating the historical books of the Old Testament takes no account of the mechanics of translating, nor of the absolute unlikelihood of his being allowed to continue his heretical labours, and especially not of the professional hatred felt for him by Dufief. Foxe did report, however, that in his time in prison Tyndale 'converted his keeper, the keeper's daughter, and others of his household'; others reported 'that if he were not a good Christian man, they could not tell whom to trust'; both Foxe and Hall write, too, that the procurer-general himself, Dufief no less, wrote that Tyndale was *homo doctus, pius et bonus*, that is to say, learned, godly, and good (Foxe, ed. Pratt, 5.127; *Hall's Chronicle*, 818).

Martyrdom The cold machinery of the law could not be stopped. Tyndale was condemned as a heretic early in August 1536, and probably the same day suffered the public, and ceremonial, degradation from the priesthood: the record of payments to Dufief shows the cost of arranging the elaborate ritual. A greater assembly was summoned for a morning early in October (traditionally the 6th) when in an open space outside Vilvorde Castle a stake, brushwood, and logs were prepared. Tyndale was brought out. A chain was placed round his neck. He gave the cry that Foxe records, 'Lord, open the king of England's eyes' (Foxe, ed. Pratt, 5.127). Tyndale was not burnt alive: as a mark of his distinction as a scholar, he was strangled first, and then his body was burnt.

Cromwell's agent John Hutton wrote to him from Brabant on 13 December 1536, 'They speak much of the patient sufferance of Master Tyndale at the time of his execution'. In 1550 Roger Ascham, tutor to Princess Elizabeth, rode through Vilvorde. He noted 'At the town's end is a notable solemn place of execution, where worthy William Tyndale was unworthily put to death' (Daniell, 384).

Matthew's Bible, 1537 John Rogers assembled all Tyndale's biblical translations, and a complete English Bible was printed by Matthew Crom in Antwerp, for the publishers Richard Grafton and Edward Whitchurch, with, at the foot of the title-page, the words 'Set forth with the King's most gracious licence'. Here is half the Old Testament from Tyndale, with his historical books in print for the first time. Rogers took the rest of the Old Testament and the Apocrypha from Coverdale's 1535 Bible (not made from the Hebrew). Tyndale's own 1534 New Testament in its 1535 state is printed verbatim. Rogers was a good scholar. He added many marginal notes, from Pellican's Latin commentary and from French bibles. He made few changes to Tyndale, but felt free to translate afresh the first chapters of Job, and to correct other pages of Coverdale from commentaries, from the Targums, from the Septuagint, and from the fathers.

Since the name of Tyndale the heretic could not appear, Rogers used the names of two disciples, Thomas and Matthew, and 1500 copies of Matthew's Bible were imported into England and soon sold out. Thus within months of Tyndale's martyrdom a complete English Bible, two-thirds of it Tyndale's work, and licensed by the king, was circulating in Britain. A handsome well-printed folio, it has several unusual features, especially the large and heavily ornamented initials at certain points—'IR' for John Rogers, 'RG' and 'RW' for the publishers, and, at the end of the Prophets and before the Apocrypha, 'WT', for William Tyndale. The speed of the sale of Matthew's Bible led to the initiating of its further revision as the Great Bible of 1539, to be placed in every church in the land. Thus Tyndale's work was widely read and heard. It was, moreover, handed on into successive versions in that century, notably the three Geneva versions of 1560, 1576, and 1599. King James's revisers, working between 1607 and 1611, though they made changes, went back to Tyndale afresh.

The legacy of Tyndale Tyndale was in the vanguard of the popular English Reformation. His books, especially *The*

Wicked Mammon, *The Obedience*, and his expositions of Romans, gathered to a head the widespread revulsion at the corruptions and superstitions of the church as it then was, all of which are clearly described. Scripture had to be the base for these judgements, and it was spelt out with clarity and excellent scholarship, from the original languages. From the great release that justification by faith brings to the sinner, Tyndale showed, always in the language of the New Testament, that central to a Christian's life were not curious rituals and practices, but the promises of God. He was passionate in his wish that England could be a Christian state under a Christian prince, free from the intrusions of a totally alien system stemming from the bishop of Rome.

The great change that came over England from 1526, the ability of every ordinary man, woman, and child to read and hear the whole New Testament in English, accurately rendered, was Tyndale's work, and its importance cannot be overstressed. The Vulgate was incomprehensible to the ploughboy and most of his familiars throughout the land. Now all four gospels could be read, often aloud, in their entirety, and the whole of Paul. A useful definition of the popular reformation is 'people reading Paul'. There is no shortage of evidence of the gatherings of people of all ages, all over the country, to read and hear these English scriptures—and reading meant, so often, reading aloud.

Tyndale as the first translator of Hebrew into English stands up well to informed scrutiny. His understanding of New Testament theology, and how it related to the Old Testament, pointed forward. He left Luther behind. His fresh appraisals from the Greek effectively liberated New Testament theology in English, allowing the possibility of reinterpretation in every generation, as had clearly happened in the life of the early church.

Tyndale's story as an especially significant protestant martyr was developed by Foxe in successive English editions, widely known to Elizabethan and Stuart readers. The Victorian eight volumes of *Actes and Monuments*, still standard, obscure much detail in their reliance on later editions. A resurgence of interest in Tyndale in the nineteenth century led to the first full-length biography (by Robert Demaus) and the erection of some local monuments. Foxe had also introduced John Day's 1573 volume of *The Whole Works of Tyndale, Frith, and Barnes*; they were not popularly published again until the Parker Society series of the mid-nineteenth century.

Tyndale's gift to the English language is unmeasurable. He translated into a register just above common speech, allied in its clarity to proverbs. It is a language which still speaks directly to the heart. His aims were always accuracy and clarity. King James's revisers adopted his style, and his words, for much of the Authorized Version. At a time when European scholars and professionals communicated in Latin, Tyndale insisted on being understood by ordinary people. He preferred a simple Saxon syntax of subject–verb–object. His vocabulary is predominantly Saxon, and often monosyllabic. An Oxford scholar, he was always rhetorically alert. He gave the Bible-reading nation an English plain style. It is a basis for the great Elizabethan writers, and there is truth in the remark 'without Tyndale, no Shakespeare'. It is not fanciful to see a chief agent of the energizing of the language in the sixteenth century in the constant reading of the Bible in English, of which Tyndale was the great maker. DAVID DANIELL

Sources *The acts and monuments of John Foxe*, ed. J. Pratt, [new edn], 8 vols. (1877) · J. Foxe, *Actes and monuments* (1563) · D. Daniell, *William Tyndale: a biography* (1994) · J. F. Mozley, *William Tyndale* (1937) · *Tyndale's works*, ed. H. Walter, 3 vols., Parker Society (1848–50) · *LP Henry VIII* · Emden, *Oxf.*, 4.567–9 · W. Tyndale, *The obedience of a Christian man*, ed. D. Daniell (2000) · *Tyndale's Old Testament*, ed. D. Daniell (1992) · T. Tyndale, 'Wycliffe, Queen Anne of Bohemia and the Tyndales of Hockwood, Norfolk', *Tyndale Society Journal*, 11 (1998), 36–45 · A. W. Pollard, ed., *Records of the English Bible: the documents relating to the translation and publication of the Bible in English, 1525–1611* (1911) · G. Latré, 'The 1535 Bible and its Antwerp origins', *The Bible as book: the Reformation*, ed. O. O'Sullivan (2000), 89–102 · *Hall's chronicle*, ed. H. Ellis (1809) · *Tyndale's New Testament*, ed. D. Daniell (1989) · B. Marsden, 'The Tindale–Tyndale trail in Tynedale', *Tyndale Society Journal*, 7 (1997), 8–19 · B. Marsden, 'The Tindale–Tyndale trail in Tynedale', *Tyndale Society Journal*, 8 (1997), 19–61 · St Thomas More, *A dialogue concerning heresies*, ed. T. M. C. Lawler and others, 2 vols. (1981), vol. 6 of *The Yale edition of the complete works of St Thomas More* · R. J. Wilkinson, 'Reconstructing Tyndale in Latomus: William Tyndale's last, lost book', *Reformation*, 1 (1996), 252–85, 345–400 · G. Lloyd Jones, *The discovery of Hebrew in Tudor England: a third language* (1983) · J. Nielson and R. Skousen, 'How much of the King James Bible is William Tyndale's?', *Reformation*, 3 (1998), 49–74 · B. F. Westcott, *A general view of the history of the English Bible* (1868) · J. Strype, *Ecclesiastical memorials*, 3 vols. (1721) · [W. Tyndale], *The beginning of the New Testament … 1525 … Cologne edition*, ed. A. W. Pollard (1926)

Archives National State Archives, Brussels

Likenesses E. Boehm, statue, 1884, Victoria Embankment, London · W. Dennis junior, stipple and line engraving (after unknown artist), BM, NPG · portrait, Hertford College, Oxford

Tyndall, Arthur Mannering (1881–1961), physicist, was born on 18 September 1881 at Bristol, the youngest in the family of three sons and two daughters of Henry Augustus Tyndall, a partner in the firm of Cowley and Tyndall, ironmongers, of Bristol, and his wife, Sarah Hannah Mannering, the daughter of a London linen draper. He was educated at Redland Hill House, a private school in Bristol where no science was taught except a smattering of chemistry in the last two terms. Nevertheless he entered the University College of Bristol obtaining the only scholarship offered by the city of Bristol for study there, and intending to make his career in chemistry. However, when brought into contact with the professor of physics, Arthur Chattock, who was an outstanding teacher, he decided to switch to physics; he always expressed the warmest gratitude for the inspiration which he had received from him.

Tyndall graduated BSc with second-class honours in the external London examination in 1903. In that year he was appointed assistant lecturer at Bristol; he was promoted to lecturer in 1907, and retained that post when the college became a university in 1909. In 1908 he married Lilly Mary, daughter of Frank Smith Gardner, who taught the violin at Clifton College. They had one son and two daughters. The marriage was very happy and the hospitality he and his wife provided for their numerous friends was informal and continuous.

Arthur Mannering Tyndall (1881–1961), by Sir James Gunn, 1948

Professor Chattock retired at the age of fifty in 1910. The university was unable to attract a suitable applicant to fill the chair and Tyndall became acting head of the department amid considerable public scrutiny of the university's affairs. Then, with the outbreak of war, he left the university to run an army radiological department in Hampshire, but was eventually persuaded to return to the physics department which seemed in danger of disintegrating without him.

In 1916 Tyndall met the great benefactor of Bristol physics, Henry Herbert Wills of the tobacco family, prochancellor and chairman of a special buildings committee, who was planning with the architect the details of the great hall of the university. His first contact with him was a letter to Wills as chairman of the general purposes committee about a site for some accumulators. Out of this arose a friendship, walks to work together across the Clifton downs, and ultimately Wills's desire to provide a quite exceptional building for physics in the university. Though his intentions were clear earlier, it was in March 1919 that he announced a gift of £100,000 and as much again a year later. Tyndall became Henry Overton Wills professor of physics in 1919. When H. H. Wills died in 1922 he left a further considerable sum to the university, and in the same year, together with the architect George Oatley, Tyndall visited the United States to see laboratory buildings and make plans. The H. H. Wills Physics Laboratory, on the highest point of the university's Royal Fort estate, was opened in 1927 by Sir Ernest Rutherford. It was at the time the most palatial physics laboratory in the country and was thought by many to be presumptuous in a university less than 1000 strong.

It was from the beginning Tyndall's ambition to build a research school, for he realized that this, more than imposing buildings or successful teaching, was the key to achieving a high reputation for his department. When the laboratory was opened it was much too big for the twelve members of staff and the small honours school, never more than six in the final honours year, and out of scale with anything else in the university. Tyndall's first task was to collect money for endowment and equipment. In particular he saw the appointment of a theoretician as vital to his research enterprise, and as early as 1924 he had persuaded Bristol to finance a readership for J. E. Lennard-Jones in mathematical physics. The Rockefeller foundation provided £50,000 and Melville Wills a further sum of £25,000 for a chair of theoretical physics, named after him and held in succession by Lennard-Jones and Nevill Mott. Tyndall used the considerable surplus to provide permanent positions for other members of staff and then, after 1933, to attract German refugees to Bristol. 1933 proved a watershed year for the department, the influx of very talented refugees enabling Tyndall to build a really strong school. This allowed Bristol to take part in the explosive development of physics which characterized the interwar period, a subject which earlier was centred in Cambridge and Manchester. The main achievements during Tyndall's directorship were the work on cosmic rays leading to the discovery of the mu-meson by Cecil Powell, and the strong school of solid state physics—the term was probably invented there—involving such men as H. W. B. Skinner, Harry Jones, W. Sucksmith, R. W. Gurney, H. Fröhlich, N. Mott, and, after the war, F. C. Frank and J. W. Mitchell. Tyndall always subordinated his own work and interests to those of the ambitious young men he collected round him, and his greatest pleasure lay in their success. The Nobel prize awarded in 1950 to Powell made him quite wild with joy, as did fellowships of the Royal Society and other recognitions of the quality of his colleagues' work.

Tyndall was so wrapped up in their achievements that he seemed too modest about his own personal research, but this was of considerable distinction. It was mainly in the field of the discharge of electricity in gases. In the early 1920s experiments had been made concerning the mobility of ions in gases, but the results were very discordant. Tyndall realized that this was because impurities in gases attached themselves to the ions, so that their motion was slowed down. He, with a number of young colleagues, made use of new techniques and by the middle 1920s high vacuum methods had progressed to the point where this contamination could be largely avoided. They were able to measure the mobilities of a wide range of ions, and established many of the accepted values. In 1938 he published *Mobility of Positive Ions in Gases*.

From 1940 to 1945 and again in 1946–7 Tyndall was pro-vice-chancellor and in 1944–5 acting vice-chancellor. It need hardly be said that throughout his career he took a leading part in the affairs of the university as a whole, particularly in its expansion after the war, though always he shielded his young researchers from involvement unless they wanted to be drawn in. Tyndall also took a leading part in the scientific committee work of the country. Elected into the fellowship of the Royal Society in 1933, he served on council from 1941 to 1942 and was vice-president in 1942. He was president of the Institute of Physics in 1946–8, president of the physics section of the British Association in 1952, a manager of the Royal Institution, and president in 1953 of the Science Masters' Association. In Bristol he gave most generously of his time to medical education and the National Health Service. In 1950 he was appointed CBE and in 1958 honorary LLD of his own university. He was also a DSc of both Bristol (1913) and London (1912).

When Tyndall retired in 1948 Bristol created him emeritus professor and honorary fellow. From the date of his retirement until his death he was a very active member of the editorial board of the *Philosophical Magazine*, one of the oldest scientific journals in the country (founded in 1798). It was he who carried out the day-to-day work of the journal, taking decisions on acceptance or rejection of papers contributed.

Tyndall's achievements were twofold. He presided over part of that phenomenal growth of English physics when it left its traditional home and flourished all over the country. The generosity of the Wills family gave him his opportunity, and he knew how to take it. He also worked during his whole life in what has become one of our great universities. In his department he believed that no effort was too great, and that no time should ever be judged wasted in finding out what everyone thought and in seeing that everyone was heard. Frequently the whole staff accompanied him in a Sunday walk over the Somerset hills, and, if there were any departmental difficulties, it was then that they were resolved. Bristol physics department's relatively stress free growth from small beginnings owed much to Tyndall's example in his fifty years there. But it was the creation of the H. H. Wills Physics Laboratory, and the leadership which Tyndall gave to it before and after the Second World War, which were his personal achievements, and the ones for which he would wish to be remembered.

Tyndall died suddenly at his home, 9 Henleaze Gardens, Bristol, on 29 October 1961.

NEVILL MOTT, rev. ISOBEL FALCONER

Sources N. F. Mott and C. F. Powell, *Memoirs FRS*, 8 (1962), 159–65 · S. T. Keith, 'Scientists as entrepreneurs', *Annals of Science*, 41 (1984), 335–57 · personal knowledge (1981) · private information (1981) · *CGPLA Eng. & Wales* (1962)
Archives University of Bristol, department of physics · University of Bristol Library | Nuffield Oxf., corresp. with Lord Cherwell
Likenesses J. Gunn, oils, 1948, University of Bristol, H. H. Wills Physics Laboratory [*see illus.*] · photograph, repro. in Mott and Powell, *Memoirs FRS*, facing p. 159 · photograph, RS
Wealth at death £11,611 12s. 0d.: probate, 1962, *CGPLA Eng. & Wales*

Tyndall, John (1820–1893), physicist and mountaineer, was born on 2 August 1820 at Leighlinbridge, co. Carlow, Ireland, the son of John Tyndall (1792–1847), shoemaker, constable, and Orangeman, and his wife, Sarah Macassey (d. 1867), daughter of a farmer from Ballinabranna whose maternal ancestors were Quakers.

Family and early life, 1828–1848 The Tyndalls, who claimed descent from William Tyndale, had moved to southern Ireland from Gloucestershire in the seventeenth century. Tyndall's parents were staunch protestants and committed to their son's advancement through education. In 1828 his father joined the newly established Irish constabulary and the family moved to Nurney, and then to Castlebellingham in co. Louth, where Tyndall received his schooling, returning to Leighlinbridge in 1836, where he attended the national school in Ballinabranna, latterly as a pupil teacher. Here, under John Conwill, he was taught trigonometry and surveying. Tyndall began work with the Irish Ordnance Survey in Carlow in April 1839 for 9s. a week. In 1840 he joined the survey's office in Youghal, co. Cork, where he worked as a mapper until 1842, all the while using his leisure for self-improvement and in writing short articles for the *Carlow Sentinel*.

In 1842, because of his abilities as a draughtsman, Tyndall was transferred to the English survey in Preston, Lancashire, where he joined evening classes at the mechanics' institute. Tyndall soon became critical of the survey's inefficiency and of the harsh conditions which the Irish civilian surveyors endured under their English military officers. Tyndall and others complained and were summarily dismissed in November 1843. He was then employed for three years as a railway engineer, first with the Manchester firm of Nevins and Lawton, and then with Richard Carter on the West Riding Union Railway, where he began his lifelong friendship with the young surveyor, Thomas Archer Hirst. From November 1843 Tyndall began to keep a journal in which he detailed his daily experiences, reading, and personal philosophy. Both Tyndall and Hirst were impressed by Carlyle's *Past and Present* (1843), and in Carlyle's account of Teufelsdröckh's intellectual journey towards an affirmation of the self through work and service to others following loss of faith and purpose Tyndall found a mirror of his own religious doubts, aspirations, and ideals—especially a hatred of sham and a desire for political, social, and scientific reforms.

In August 1847 Tyndall accepted an offer from George Edmondson, the newly appointed principal of Queenwood College, Stockbridge, Hampshire, to join the college staff as teacher of mathematics and surveying. Edward Frankland was lecturer in chemistry, and the two young men agreed respectively to instruct each other in chemistry and mathematics. When Queenwood failed to provide the opportunities they wished for they decided to take advantage of the excellent cheap scientific instruction to be found at the University of Marburg in Hesse. The decision was for Tyndall a momentous one. He had nothing but his surveying skills and slender savings to depend on, and his friends thought him mad for abandoning the brilliant possibilities then open to a railway engineer.

John Tyndall (1820–1893), by George Richmond, 1864

Marburg and Berlin, 1848–1851 In October 1848 Tyndall and Frankland settled at Marburg where Tyndall attended Robert Bunsen's lectures on experimental and practical chemistry, and studied mathematics and physics in the classes and laboratories of C. L. Gerling and K. H. Knoblauch. By intense application (especially in geometry and the calculus), and reading widely in German idealist philosophy while living in poverty eked out by payments for articles in English newspapers, translations for the *Philosophical Magazine*, and loans from Hirst, he accomplished in less than two years the work usually extended over three, and so graduated doctor of philosophy early in 1850. Frankland later wrote of these years: 'At Marburg he was, as a student, at the age of 29, a very conspicuous figure; the most juvenile of undergraduates in his leisure moments, but at the same time extremely industrious, genial, good-tempered and unconventional' (Eve and Creasey, 25).

Tyndall's first scientific paper, written in German, was a mathematical essay on screw surfaces which formed his inaugural dissertation when he took his degree. In conjunction with Knoblauch, Tyndall began a series of studies on diamagnetism and the magneto-optic properties of crystals that occupied him for nearly six years and which led to further publications in the *Philosophical Magazine* in 1850 and 1851. Michael Faraday had distinguished between magnetic and diamagnetic materials in the 1840s. Subsequently, the German physicist, Julius Plücker, had identified a relationship between the orientation of a crystal's magnetic and optic axes, and concluded that

magnetic poles induced forces in crystals that corresponded to magnetic or diamagnetic behaviour, or to a newly defined action on the optic axis itself. Tyndall showed that Plücker's explanation was incorrect and that a crystal's magnetic behaviour depended upon internal pressure and cleavage planes, that is, the layers into which the crystal could be split. In support of this conclusion he and Knoblauch showed how the magnetic axis of bismuth crystals could be shifted by the exertion of pressure. On a brief visit to Britain in June 1850 Tyndall read an account of his investigations at the British Association for the Advancement of Science meeting in Edinburgh, which excited interest. He afterwards returned to Marburg with Hirst for six months, and carried out a lengthy inquiry into electromagnetic attractions at short distances (*Philosophical Magazine*, April 1851).

At Easter 1851 Tyndall went to Berlin to continue his diamagnetic research in the laboratory of Gustav Magnus. Here he became acquainted with many German men of science, which led him to lifelong ties with, and admiration for, German science. Tyndall's Berlin work confirmed that diamagnetism resembled magnetism as to polarity and all other characteristics, differing from it only by the substitution of repulsion for attraction and vice versa. It confirmed Tyndall's conviction that explanations of physical properties had to be sought in the properties of molecules, though, like the majority of his contemporaries, he also invoked an ether to explain polarity. Here Tyndall's molecular physics differed from Faraday's field theory, since during the 1850s Faraday began to interpret magnetic phenomena in terms of lines of force and electric and magnetic fields. Tyndall's magnetic investigations, which firmly established him as a European physicist, were eventually revised and republished as *Researches on Diamagnetism* (1870; 3 edns).

At the Royal Institution In June 1851 Tyndall returned to Queenwood, this time as lecturer on mathematics and natural philosophy. Here he remained two years, effectively playing the role of chief master in the face of the headmaster's weakness. Although the school's laboratory gave him facilities to continue research Tyndall immediately began to seek academic positions which offered a wider scope for his abilities. On his way to the British Association meeting in Ipswich in July 1851 he made the acquaintance of T. H. Huxley, and a warm and enduring friendship resulted. They made joint applications for the chairs respectively of natural history and physics then vacant at Toronto but, in spite of excellent testimonials, they were unsuccessful. Tyndall also failed in applications for chairs at Galway and in the newly founded University of Sydney, New South Wales. Nevertheless, despite the absence of suitable employment, his talents were recognized by Faraday and Sir Edward Sabine, treasurer of the Royal Society, who moved for Tyndall's election to the society on 3 June 1852. However, when the society awarded him its royal medal for his magnetic work in 1853 Tyndall declined because of a controversy generated over the rival merits for the award of Plücker and others. Meanwhile, soon after Tyndall's departure from Berlin, Dr

Henry Bence Jones, secretary of the Royal Institution, visited that city, and, learning of Tyndall's researches and personality, invited him to give a Friday evening discourse at the Royal Institution on 11 February 1853. This lecture produced an extraordinary impression, and in May 1853 he was unanimously chosen as its professor of natural philosophy at a salary of £200 for nineteen lectures a year. Additional income was generated from lectures at the London Institution and from acting as examiner for the War Office. He also held the chair of natural philosophy at the Royal School of Mines in Jermyn Street between 1859 and 1868. The Royal Institution appointment had the special charm of making him the colleague of Faraday with whom he worked in harmony during the years that followed, despite their differences over the interpretation of magnetism, and religion. Their relationship from first to last resembled that of father and son, and Tyndall's *Faraday as a Discoverer* (1868) bears striking testimony to their attachment. Other sketches of Faraday by Tyndall were given in his *Fragments of Science* (1871; 6 edns), as well as in the Faraday entry he composed for the *Dictionary of National Biography*. Tyndall's career was now definitely marked out. To the end of his active life his best energies were devoted to the service of the Royal Institution. In 1867, when Faraday died, Tyndall succeeded him in his position as superintendent of the institution. On his own retirement in the autumn of 1887 he was elected an honorary professor.

In 1854, after attending the British Association meeting at Liverpool, Tyndall visited the slate quarries of Penrhyn in north Wales. His familiarity with the effects of pressure upon the structure of crystals led him to give special attention to the problem of slate cleavage. By careful observation and experiments with white wax and many other substances which develop cleavages in planes perpendicular to pressure, he satisfied himself that pressure (uniaxial compression) alone was sufficient to produce the cleavage of slate rocks. On 6 June 1856 he lectured on the subject at the Royal Institution and Huxley, who was present, suggested afterwards that the same cause might possibly explain the blue and white laminated structure of glacier ice described in James David Forbes's *Travels through the Alps* (1843). The friends agreed to take a holiday and inspect the glaciers together. The results of the observations made during this and two subsequent visits to Switzerland were given in Tyndall's classic work *The Glaciers of the Alps* (1860), which was based upon papers published in the Royal Society's *Philosophical Transactions*, 1857 and 1859. Tyndall, assisted by Hirst, made many measurements upon the glaciers in continuation of the work of Louis Agassiz and Forbes who had concluded that glaciers were plastic and moved like a viscous river. Tyndall was not satisfied by this plastic theory and, drawing upon the work of James and William Thomson on the lowering of the melting point of ice by pressure, he argued instead that glacier motion originated in a process of repeated fracture and regelation, that is, a process in which ice melted under pressure before refreezing. He ascribed the

veined structure to mechanical pressure, and the formation of crevasses to strains and pressures occurring in the body of the glacier. Unfortunately, in sharply criticizing Forbes's imprecise use of the term 'viscous' and in assigning to Rendu (the bishop of Annecy) priority in the development of glacier theories, Tyndall gave offence to Forbes. A long and bitter controversy followed, which effectively split the English and Scottish scientific communities and led to ructions within the Royal Society. The controversy was also to spill over into a later priority dispute concerning the first law of thermodynamics. As so often in nineteenth-century scientific disputes, both parties were partly right, though Tyndall's mechanism of fracture and regelation was later thought to be less important than the plasticity of ice under strain as suggested by Forbes.

Whether due to a sense of personal insecurity or a keen sense of justice Tyndall repeatedly took up the causes of men whom he deemed to have been unfairly treated or overlooked in respect of their scientific merits. Such lofty principles, coupled with a belligerent tone, egotism, and dogmatism, made him many enemies. In these and later disputes Tyndall was strongly supported by his friends Hirst, Huxley, Frankland, and Joseph Hooker. Their alliance was cemented in 1864 when, together with G. Busk, J. Lubbock, Herbert Spencer, and W. Spottiswoode, they formed the X-club, an informal pressure group that became actively involved in lobbying for an improved organization of science and for the creation of a powerful scientific profession.

The expedition to Switzerland, undertaken for a scientific purpose, had a secondary outcome. Tyndall was fascinated by the mountains, and from that moment forward yearly sought refreshment in the Alps when his labours in London were over. He became an accomplished mountaineer, and joined the Alpine Club in 1858. In company with F. W. Hawkins he made one of the earliest assaults upon the Matterhorn in 1860. He traversed its summit from Breuil to Zermatt in 1868. The first ascent of the Weisshorn was made by him in 1861. He climbed Mount Blanc three times for scientific purposes. Tyndall's descriptions of his alpine adventures, in which he seems to have relished danger, were not only graphic and characterized by his keen interest in scientific problems, but showed a poetical appreciation of mountain beauty in which he was approached by few Victorian alpinists. Mount Tyndall, a peak near the Matterhorn, was named after him.

Contributions to physics Tyndall's most important contribution to physics, begun in 1859, concerned radiant heat in its relation to gases and vapours. He was led from the consideration of the origin and continued existence of glaciers to investigate the part played by water vapour and other constituents of the atmosphere in producing the low temperatures which prevail in mountainous regions. Prior to 1859 no means had been found of determining by experiment, as Macedonio Melloni had done for solids and liquids, the absorption, radiation, and transmission of infra-red radiation by gases and vapours. Realizing that the effects were probably small Tyndall devised an arrangement of galvanometers and thermopiles that measured absorption differentially, using an empty test-tube as a null balance point. Unexpectedly he found that while elementary gases offered practically no obstacle to the passage of infra-red, some of the compound gases absorbed more than 80 per cent of the incident radiation. Allotropic elements came under the same rule, ozone for example being a much better absorbent of heat than oxygen. The temperature of the source of heat was found to be of importance: heat of a higher temperature was much more penetrative than heat of a lower temperature.

Tyndall explained these differences in terms of atomic structure, molecules having more degrees of freedom to vibrate than single atoms. Visible light spectroscopy had been established by Bunsen and Kirchhoff in 1859, so Tyndall was aware that he had stumbled upon an analogous method of analysis using radiant heat from the non-visible part of the spectrum. However, spectrophotometry, as it was to be called, was not to receive wide application until the 1940s. Following Balfour Stewart's work on solids and liquids Tyndall showed that the power of gases to absorb and radiate were also reciprocal. Although initially disputed by Magnus, careful measurements with purified air showed that water vapour in particular was an extremely powerful radiator and absorber. Tyndall also clearly recognized that water vapour intercepted terrestrial radiation, and that changes in its quantity would produce (and had probably caused) climatic changes. Of less long-term significance, but more spectacularly, he extended earlier research by George Stokes, although this investigation was marred by competition and disputes with a young Hungarian, C. K. Akin. Tyndall showed how infra-red radiation, focused by means of a rock salt lens, could be used to heat and ignite or cause luminescence in various substances. He saw this phenomenon of 'calorescence' as the opposite of Stokes's fluorescence. Much of this work was reported in two Bakerian lectures (1861, 1864) and led to the award of the Rumford medal in 1869. His papers on the subject were eventually gathered together in *Contributions to Molecular Physics in the Domain of Radiant Heat* (1872). This volume also included a series of striking experiments on the decomposition of vapours by light, in the course of which the blue of the firmament and the polarization of sky light—illustrated on skies artificially produced in the lecture theatre of the Royal Institution—were shown to be due to excessively fine particles floating in the atmosphere. This awe-inspiring demonstration stimulated J. W. Strutt in 1871 to develop a quantitative and mathematical explanation of why the sky is blue.

While engaged in this research Tyndall observed that a luminous beam, passing through the dust free air of his experimental tube, was invisible. It occurred to him that such a beam might be utilized to detect the presence of living germs in the atmosphere postulated by Louis Pasteur as a cause of animal and human diseases: air incompetent to scatter light, through the absence of all floating particles, he reasoned, must be free from bacteria and their germs. Numerous experiments made in 1871–2 showed

optically pure air to be incapable of developing bacterial life. In properly protected vessels infusions of fish, flesh, and vegetable, freely exposed after boiling to air rendered moteless by subsidence or by flame treatment, and declared to be so by the invisible passage of a powerful electric light, remained permanently pure and unaltered; whereas the identical liquids, exposed afterwards to ordinary dust laden air, soon swarmed with bacteria. Three extensive investigations into the behaviour of putrefactive organisms were made by Tyndall, mainly with the view of removing once and for all the possibility of spontaneous generation—a view which was still strongly maintained by the London pathologist H. Charlton Bastian. Although Bastian never conceded defeat Tyndall showed that although bacteria are killed below 100 °C, their desiccated germs—those of the hay bacillus in particular—can retain their vitality after several hours' boiling. In 1877, by a process which he called discontinuous heating, he succeeded in sterilizing nutritive liquids containing the most resistant germs. This method (later termed tyndallization in France, but pasteurization in Britain) proved of great practical value in bacteriology. Tyndall's researches led to an extensive correspondence with Pasteur; but his early admiration for the Frenchman later turned sour at Pasteur's love of adulation. In 1877 the medical faculty of Tübingen gave Tyndall the degree of MD in recognition of these researches. The original essays, written for the *Philosophical Transactions* were collected in the book *Floating Matter of the Air* (1881). He received honorary doctorates from Cambridge (1865), Edinburgh (1866), Oxford (1873), and Trinity College, Dublin (1886).

In 1866 Tyndall succeeded Faraday as scientific adviser to Trinity House and the Board of Trade. He held the post for seventeen years, resigning in 1883 during a protracted controversy concerning the elder brethren's decision to light lighthouses by oil rather than gas. His investigations on sound, originating in lectures, were extended in 1873 in an attempt to establish efficient fog signals upon British coasts. Discordant results were eventually traced to variations in atmospheric density which produced acoustic clouds that were favourable to the transmission sometimes of longer, sometimes of shorter, sound waves. A memoir on the steam siren used in experiments at South Foreland, was summarized in later editions of *Sound* (1867), in which some beautiful experiments on sensitive flames that responded to his voice were also described.

Books and lectures As a lecturer Tyndall was famed for the charm and animation of his language, for lucidity of exposition, his showmanship, and singular skill in devising and conducting interesting and exciting experimental illustrations, many of which became classics and over which he spent days in preparation and rehearsal. As a writer he did much for the diffusion and popularization of scientific knowledge. The publication of his lectures and essays in *Fragments of Science for Unscientific People* were aimed especially at making intelligible all of the dominant scientific ideas of the century. In *Heat as a Mode of*

Motion (1863) and *The Forms of Water* (1872), which was the first publication in the International Science Series, and his many other books, he promoted the evangelical cause of science to a worldwide audience. The book on *Light* (1873) gave the substance of lectures delivered in the United States in the winter of 1872–3. The proceeds of these lectures, which by judicious investment amounted in a few years to between £6000 and £7000, were devoted to fellowships at three American universities for the encouragement of science. Tyndall's works were translated into most European languages. In Germany (where Helmholtz and Wiedemann undertook the translations, and wrote prefaces) they were as popular as in Britain. Some thousands of his books were sold in America and a few translations were made into Asian languages.

To the wider public Tyndall (like Huxley) was the great exponent of scientific naturalism, a scientific world view based upon atomism, energy, evolution, and the germ theory, which challenged the hegemony of the traditional religious world view. His views upon the relation between science and theological opinions were first expressed in 1866 and 1868 in controversial critiques of contemporary views of miracles and prayer. He joined the Metaphysical Society in 1869 and provoked a year-long debate over the efficacy of prayer in 1872. Most notoriously, in his presidential address to the British Association at Belfast in 1874, he abrasively maintained the claims of science to discuss all theological questions fully and freely in all their bearings. Critics saw Tyndall as an overt materialist but, given his admiration for Carlyle and his belief in the role of imagination in science, it would be fairer to describe him as an idealist who saw matter itself pantheistically as containing the potency of life. Materialism, while an effective strategy for scientific progress, was insufficient as a personal philosophy. His protestant background and suspicion of Roman Catholicism led Tyndall to become bitterly opposed to Gladstone's policy over Irish home rule and he spent much time in the last decade of his life writing angry articles on the subject, including a spat with Gladstone himself in *The Times* in 1890.

Despite his early training in mathematics, like Faraday Tyndall avoided mathematical physics and remained a classical experimentalist who was guided by physical, not mathematical, insights. In 1902 Oliver Lodge offended Tyndall's widow by dismissing him as a poor physicist. However, at the end of the twentieth century it was judged that as an examiner, lecturer, and textbook writer on heat, light, sound, and magnetism, he did more than any other Victorian scientist to define physics as a separate scientific discipline. Only in the 1960s did physics teaching in British schools and universities depart radically from his approach. Physics aside, he was unquestionably a central figure in Victorian science.

Tyndall was of middle height, sparsely built, but with a strength, toughness, and flexibility of limb which qualified him to endure great fatigue and achieve the most difficult feats as a mountaineer. His bearded face was rather stern and strongly marked by a prominent nose and grey-blue eyes, but he bore a pleasing expression when his sympathy was touched and this was heightened by the quality of his voice.

Domestic life Tyndall had a number of love affairs in the 1840s and 1850s, but had a serious proposal of marriage rejected in 1869. It came as a shock to his friends, to whom he appeared a confirmed bachelor, when, on 29 February 1876, Tyndall married Louisa Charlotte (1845–1940), eldest daughter of Lord Claud Hamilton and Lady Elizabeth Proby of Heathfield Park, Sussex. The ceremony, witnessed by Carlyle, was conducted in Westminster Abbey by the dean, Arthur Stanley. Tyndall was fifty-two and Louisa only twenty-seven and a committed Christian. Despite their failure to have children their marriage was extremely happy. In 1877 they built a cottage (Alp Lusgen) at Bel Alp, on the northern side of the Valais, above Brieg, where they spent their summers. In 1885 they built what Tyndall called a retreat for his old age upon the summit of Hind Head, on the Surrey downs, then a very quiet district. Sleeplessness and dyspepsia—ills from which he had suffered more or less all his life—increased upon him in later years, and caused him to resign his post at the Royal Institution in March 1887. There was no pension, and apart from substantial investments, his only regular income came from acting as a gas referee. His later years were for the most part spent at Hindhead. Repeated attacks of severe illness, including phlebitis, prevented the execution of the many plans (including an autobiography) he had laid out for his retirement years. In 1893 he appeared to benefit from a three months' stay in the Alps. But an overdose of chloral, accidentally administered by Louisa instead of magnesia, brought all to a close on 4 December 1893. Following an inquest, in which a distraught Louisa was absolved from blame, the funeral service was held in Haslemere churchyard, where he was then interred, on 9 December.

Louisa, who viewed marriage to Tyndall as 'an altar on which to sacrifice one's life' (Eve and Creasey, 208), as secretary, assistant and nurse, devoted the remainder of her own life to commemorating her husband. She erected a memorial to him above Alp Lusgen in 1911, and wrote a fine memoir of him for the *Dictionary of National Biography*. She spent over forty years collecting, transcribing, and typing his letters and journals with a view to writing a definitive biography. The task proved beyond her, and the biography by Eve and Creasey based upon the materials she had lovingly collected did not appear until 1945, five years after her death.   W. H. BROCK

Sources DNB · A. S. Eve and C. H. Creasey, *Life and work of John Tyndall* (1945) · W. H. Brock, N. D. McMillan, and R. C. Mollan, eds., *John Tyndall: essays on a natural philosopher* (1981) · J. R. Friday, R. M. MacLeod, and P. Shepherd, *John Tyndall, natural philosopher: catalogue of correspondence, journals, and collected papers* (1974) [microfiche] · N. D. McMillan and J. Meehan, *John Tyndall: 'x'emplar of scientific and technological education* (1981) · R. Barton, 'John Tyndall, pantheist', *Osiris*, 2nd ser., 3 (1987), 111–34 · R. M. MacLeod, 'The X-club', *Notes and Records of the Royal Society*, 24 (1969–70), 305–22 · *The Times* (20 Aug 1940) [Louisa Tyndall] · O. Lodge, 'Tyndall', *Encyclopaedia Britannica*, 10th edn (1902–3), vol. 33, pp. 517–21

Archives BL, corresp. and literary papers, Add. MSS 53715–53716 · BL, letters, Add. MS 63092 · Hunt. L., letters · Royal Institution of Great Britain, London, corresp. and papers | Air Force Research Laboratories, Cambridge, Massachusetts, letters to Lord Rayleigh · BL, letters to T. A. Hirst, Add. MS 63092 · BL, letters to J. Pollock, Add. MS 63092 · CUL, corresp. with Lord Kelvin · CUL, letters to Sir George Stokes · ICL, corresp. with Thomas Huxley · LUL, corresp. with Herbert Spencer · RBG Kew, letters to Sir Joseph Hooker · RS, corresp. with Sir John Herschel · U. St Andr. L., corresp. with James David Forbes · UCL, letters to Sir Francis Galton · W. Sussex RO, letters to Frederick Maxse

Likenesses G. Richmond, drawing, 1864, Royal Institution of Great Britain, London [see illus.] · F. Gutekunst, photograph, 1873, NPG · T. Woolner, medallion, 1876, Royal Institution of Great Britain, London · F. E. Haig, oils, 1890–99, Royal Institution of Great Britain, London · J. McLure Hamilton, oils, 1893, NPG; related lithograph, Walker Art Gallery, Liverpool · Barraud, photograph, NPG; repro. in *Men and Women of the Day*, 2 (1889) · A. Bassano, photograph, NPG · A. Cecioni, chromolithograph caricature, NPG; repro. in *VF* (6 April 1872) · W. & D. Downey, woodburytype, NPG; repro. in W. Downey and D. Downey, *The cabinet portrait gallery*, 5 (1894) · E. Edwards, photograph, NPG; repro. in L. Reeve, ed., *Portraits of men of eminence*, 2 (1864) · Elliott & Fry, two cartes-de-visite, NPG · H. Furniss, two pen-and-ink caricature sketches, NPG · G. Jarrard, photograph, NPG · C. H. Jeens, stipple (after photograph), BM; repro. in *Nature* (1874) · Lock & Whitfield, woodburytype, NPG; repro. in T. Cooper and others, *Men of mark: a gallery of contemporary portraits* (1877) · Maull & Polyblank, carte-de-visite, NPG · P. Wood, bust, Royal Institution of Great Britain, London; posthumous · photographs, Royal Institution of Great Britain, London

Wealth at death £22,122 4s. 7d.: probate, 23 Feb 1894, *CGPLA Eng. & Wales*

Tyndall, Onesiphorus (*bap.* 1689, *d.* 1757), banker and merchant, was baptized on 28 May 1689 at Lewins Mead, Bristol, the eldest son of Onesiphorus Tyndall (1657–1748), merchant, and his wife, Elizabeth Hopper (*b.* 1661) of Loxley, Warwickshire. His father went to Bristol in 1674 from Melksham Court, Gloucestershire, and was for many years a partner in the leading Bristol merchant house of Isaac Hobhouse & Co., engaged in the West Indies trade in slaves, sugar, and tobacco. Early in the eighteenth century, Tyndall was probably apprenticed to his father in the trade of grocer and dry salter. On 6 November 1717 he married Elizabeth Cowles (1696–1730) of Bristol, and together they had four children—two sons and two daughters. The marriage ended with Elizabeth's death in December 1730, Tyndall remaining thereafter a widower. He lived for many years in the parish of Christchurch in Bristol, though in 1743 he inherited from his brother John a house in the Royal Fort, then on the northern fringes of the city, consolidating the family's close connection with the area.

Tyndall was notable for his role in the formation of the Old Bank, Bristol's first bona fide banking house, which commenced business on 1 August 1750. The date is significant, making it one of the earliest such private banks to be established in England and Wales outside London. As senior partner, Tyndall's business experience and extensive contacts, both within the Bristol region and beyond, were of great importance in securing the success of the new enterprise. Many of the early customers of the bank were drawn from the same mercantile, professional, and civic élite to which Tyndall himself belonged.

However, banking interests came to Tyndall relatively late in life, after a long and varied association with the trading activities of the port of Bristol. Widely recognized as an eminent dry salter, he also followed his father into the West Indies trade and was still listed as trading to Africa in 1755, just two years before his death. Though not especially noted for his involvement in civic duties, Tyndall, a freeman of the city of Bristol, was none the less appointed verderer and chief ranger of the forest of Kingswood, in November 1734. Like many of the eighteenth-century merchants and bankers of Bristol's emerging business class, he was also actively involved in the city's nonconformist religious society.

Tyndall died in Bristol on 30 May 1757, aged sixty-eight. He was buried at Christchurch parish church, in the same ground as his wife, on 3 June 1757. The chief beneficiary of his considerable legacy was his youngest son, Thomas Tyndall (1723–1794), who also succeeded him as a partner in the Old Bank.   IAIN S. BLACK

Sources C. H. Cave, *A history of banking in Bristol from 1750 to 1899* (privately printed, Bristol, 1899) · J. Latimer, *The annals of Bristol in the eighteenth century* (1893); repr. (1970) · W. E. Minchinton, *The Hobhouse papers, 1722–1755* (1971) · The Jeffries Collection MSS, Bristol Central Library, 758–771 · PRO, PROB 11/831/206 · parish registers, Bristol, St Werburgh · parish registers, Bristol, Christchurch · marriage licence, Bristol, 6 Nov 1717

Archives Bristol Central Library, Jeffries collection, MSS

Likenesses portrait, repro. in Cave, *History of banking in Bristol*

Wealth at death £15,300 cash legacies; excl. land, property, and shares; youngest son chief beneficiary; daughter (wife of Joshua Reynolds) given 1s., as married contrary to father's wishes: will, PRO, PROB 11/831/206

Tynemouth, John of (*d.* 1221). *See under* Tynemouth, John of (*fl.* early 13th cent.).

Tynemouth, John of (*fl.* early 13th cent.), geometer, was the author of the *Liber de curvis superficiebus Archimenidis*, a significant source of advanced Archimedean geometry. This tract in ten propositions with formal geometric demonstrations covers the major results of Archimedes's sphere measurement, including the relations for the surface and volume of the sphere, and required lemmas on the measurement of circles, cones, and cylinders. It follows the manner adopted by Archimedes in *Sphere and Cylinder*, book 1, more closely than any known alternative version then available (such as the *Verba filiorum* of the Banu Musa), but with systematic technical differences, such as to suggest dependence on a Greek adaptation of Archimedes from late antiquity. Extant in at least a dozen manuscripts (consulted by Clagett in his critical edition), and cited in the thirteenth century by Robert Grosseteste, Jordanus de Nemore, Gerard de Bruxelles, and Roger Bacon, as well as by numerous writers in the fourteenth century, the work boasted a considerable dissemination.

Taking *De curvis superficiebus* as paradigm, one finds in it idiosyncrasies of content and editorial style indicating that John of Tynemouth was responsible for editions of several other mathematical works: a revised version of

Archimedes's *De quadratura circuli* (as in Florence, Biblioteca Nazionale, Conv. soppr. MS J V 30); a recension of the anonymous *De ysoperimetris* (as in Bodl. Oxf., MS Digby 174); and two versions of an argument for the circle quadrature (one of these is also found in MS Digby 174, while the other is book 4, proposition 16, or, more extensively, propositions 14–18, of *De triangulis* by a compiler in the following of Jordanus). Furthermore, idiomatic affinities of the same kind assign to John the production of an important recension of Euclid's *Elements*, the one cited by Roger Bacon as the *editio specialis* of Adelard of Bath, and called 'Adelardian version III' by Clagett. This edition, an adaptation of the so-called 'version II' (attributed by Busard and Folkerts to Adelard's follower Robert of Chester), displays nuances of terminology and content that link it with the circle of Robert Grosseteste at Oxford, probably in the 1220s.

An attempt to identify this John of Tynemouth with a geometer known as John of London has now been abandoned. However, there was another **John of Tynemouth** (d. 1221) who was a distinguished canon lawyer in the same period as the geometer. The possibility that they were one and the same cannot be ruled out, but no explicit link has yet been traced between the legal activities of the one and the geometric pursuits of the other, and the identification must be regarded as unlikely. The canonist is recorded in 1188 as teaching in the Oxford schools, while by the late 1190s he had joined the entourage of Hubert Walter, archbishop of Canterbury, as one of the *magistri* in the latter's service. His writings show him to have been possessed of considerable canonistic learning. In 1203 he acted against Gerald of Wales in Rome as one of the archbishop's proctors, and on his way home was captured by men of Châtillon-sur-Seine in Burgundy. He alerted his captors to Gerald's imminent arrival in their parts, so ensuring that Gerald was captured as well. Gerald took his revenge by describing John as one of the clerks dearest to Archbishop Walter, with revenues from his livings worth 100 marks per annum, with the result that John was only released on payment of a heavy ransom. John is known to have been rector of Upminster by 1204 and he had also become a canon of Lincoln, holding the prebend of Langford Ecclesia, by 1206. About 1210 he became archdeacon of Oxford. One of the churchmen who remained in England during the papal interdict, John was also several times employed as a papal judge-delegate. He died in 1221.

WILBUR R. KNORR

Sources M. Clagett, ed., *Archimedes in the middle ages*, 5 vols. (1964–84), vol. 1 · M. Clagett, 'The medieval Latin translations from the Arabic of the *Elements* of Euclid, with special emphasis on the versions of Adelard of Bath', *Isis*, 44 (1953), 16–42 · W. R. Knorr, *Textual studies in ancient and medieval geometry* (1989) · W. R. Knorr, 'John of Tynemouth *alias* John of London: emerging portrait of a singular medieval mathematician', *British Journal for the History of Science*, 23 (1990), 293–330 · W. R. Knorr, 'Paraphrase editions of Latin mathematical texts: *De figuris ysoperimetris*', *Mediaeval Studies*, 52 (1990), 132–89 · W. R. Knorr, 'On a medieval circle quadrature: *De circulo quadrando*', *Historia Mathematica*, 18 (1991), 107–28 · Emden, *Oxf.*, 3.1923 · S. Kuttner, *Gratian and the schools of law* (1983) · *Gir. Camb.*, opera, vol. 3 · *The letters of Pope Innocent III (1198–1216) concerning England and Wales*, ed. C. R. Cheney and M. G. Cheney (1967) · *Fasti Angl., 1066–1300*, [Lincoln], 36, 75 · J. Brundage, *Medieval canon law* (1995), 220–21 · C. R. Cheney, *Hubert Walter* (1967), 165 · C. R. Cheney, *Pope Innocent III and England* (1976), 315 · *Robert of Chester's (?) redaction of Euclid's 'Elements', the so-called Adelard II version*, ed. H. L. L. Busard and M. Folkerts, 2 vols. (1992)

Archives Biblioteca Nazionale, Florence, Conv. soppr. MS J V 30 · Bodl. Oxf., MS Digby 174

Tynemouth [Tinmouth], **John** (*fl. c.*1350), chronicler, is a writer of whom little is known. The best medieval tradition describes him simply as vicar of Tynemouth in Northumberland. On account of references in his chronicle, the *Historia aurea*, to villages close to Wheatley in the diocese of Winchester, he might possibly be identified with a John Whetely, who was vicar of Tynemouth in the 1350s and 1360s. It is more probable, however, that our subject came from Wheatley in Yorkshire, which would explain the name, John York, which is given to the author in certain manuscripts of his work. Whatever his origins, the close connection between the vicarage at Tynemouth and the abbey of St Albans may be responsible for certain features in the manuscript tradition of the *Historia aurea*. The prior of the St Albans cell at Tynemouth appointed the vicars of Tynemouth, whose vicarage formed part of the priory church. Although Horstmann's suggestion that John Tynemouth was a St Albans monk is uncertain, it is possible that Thomas de la Mare, when prior of Tynemouth from 1341 to 1349, encouraged John Tynemouth in his work. As evidence of an early association with St Albans, an abbreviated copy of the *Historia aurea* was known to Thomas Walsingham when he was constructing the early drafts of his *Chronica majora* in the 1380s.

Apart from the *Historia aurea*, John Tynemouth wrote a *Sanctilogium*, which contains 156 lives of British saints. A single copy, presented to the St Albans cell at Redbourn in Hertfordshire by Thomas de la Mare, survives in BL, Cotton MS Tiberius E.i. John Tynemouth's main achievement, the *Historia aurea*, compiled *c.*1350, was a world history extending from the creation to 1347. In addition to a number of abbreviated versions, copies of the *Historia aurea* survive from Durham, Bury St Edmunds, and St Albans. In the *Historia aurea* (a name chosen by its author, for reasons that remain unknown) John Tynemouth gave an account of world history contained in some twenty-three chapters. Written on a larger scale than the *Polychronicon*, it lacked the coherence of Higden's work, with which its fortunes were none the less to be associated. In constructing his chronicle John Tynemouth used a short version of the *Polychronicon*, but during the fourteenth century the *Historia aurea* itself became the source of a new version of Higden's text. In certain manuscripts of the *Polychronicon* the later books of the *Historia aurea* were combined with the *Polychronicon* to provide what was in effect a new edition of the latter work. Apart from its association with the *Polychronicon* the *Historia aurea* enjoyed a modest success in its own right, and its concluding section was used in several fourteenth-century chronicles. At St Albans, however, the complete text of the *Historia aurea* does not appear to have been known until the fifteenth century, indicating that John Tynemouth himself may not have been a St Albans monk.   JOHN TAYLOR

Sources C. Horstman, ed., *Nova legenda Anglie, as collected by John of Tynemouth, J. Capgrave, and others*, 2 vols. (1901) · V. H. Galbraith, 'The *Historia aurea* of John, vicar of Tynemouth and the sources of the St. Albans chronicle (1327–1377)', *Essays in history presented to Reginald Lane Poole*, ed. H. W. C. Davis (1927), 379–95 · J. Taylor, *Fourteenth century historical literature* (1987), 103–5 · A. G. Rigg, *A history of Anglo-Latin literature, 1066–1422* (1992), 257–8

Tyrawley. For this title name *see* O'Hara, Charles, first Baron Tyrawley (d. 1724); O'Hara, James, second Baron Tyrawley and Baron Kilmaine (1681/2–1773).

Tyrconnell. For this title name *see* O'Donnell, Manus, lord of Tyrconnell (d. 1563); O'Donnell, Hugh, lord of Tyrconnell (1572–1602); O'Donnell, Rury, styled first earl of Tyrconnell (1574/5–1608); O'Donnell, Hugh Albert, styled second earl of Tyrconnell (1606–1642) [*see under* O'Donnell, Rury, styled first earl of Tyrconnell (1574/5–1608)]; Talbot, Richard, first earl of Tyrconnell and Jacobite duke of Tyrconnell (1630–1691); Talbot, Frances, duchess of Tyrconnell (1648–1731).

Tyrell family (*per. c.*1304–*c.*1510), gentry, was established in East Anglia by the beginning of the fourteenth century, although its early pedigree, including the nature of its connection with the Tyrells of the Welsh border and the south-west, is extremely uncertain. From the 1330s there were two Tyrells, Thomas Tyrell senior and **Sir Thomas** [i] **Tyrell** (d. 1382), active in Essex, who may have been brothers rather than father and son. The elder was almost certainly the son of James Tyrell (*fl.* 1304), whose land in Buttsbury he had inherited by 1332. He seems to have died in the mid-1350s. Thomas [i] and Alice, his wife, are first mentioned in 1335, when they acquired land in Great Burstead and Ramsden Cray. This was a modest beginning to what was to become a major estate in south Essex. In 1369 they secured the manor and advowson of Ramsden Cray. By this date Thomas had also acquired what later became the family's main seat, the manor of Heron in East (or Great) Horndon, Essex. He is described as 'of East Horndon' in 1363 and in the same year was licensed to empark his land there. How Thomas acquired the manor is unclear. He was not, as is usually assumed, the son of the Heron heiress. His mother was Alice Blaund—who, if the two Thomases were indeed brothers, can be identified with Alice the wife of James Tyrell mentioned in 1304. All the Tyrell pedigrees agree that the Heron heiress was called Margaret and married a James Tyrell, and although the placing of the match in the pedigrees is clearly wrong it may have a core of truth. There was a James Tyrell alive in 1344 who witnessed a release at Horndon that year. The most plausible explanation would make him the heir of Thomas senior, who died childless shortly after his father, so that his land passed to Thomas junior, as the Buttsbury land seems to have done.

Whatever the exact descent, it was the junior Thomas, Sir Thomas [i] Tyrell, who established the family securely in Essex. He did so, at least in part, through royal service.

In 1351 he was a yeoman of the crown, with a history of service to Queen Philippa and the king's daughter Isabel as well as to Edward III himself. From the early 1360s, however, his status suddenly rose, which could be linked (if the above argument is correct) with his acquisition of his nephew's land. In January 1362 he was made steward of the household and lands of the king's daughter Isabel. In 1365 he was knight of the shire for Essex, the first of five occasions on which he was to represent the county. By 1367 he was a knight. He died in 1382 and was buried at Downham, Essex, where he held a manor. His wife, Alice, survived him.

Thomas's death checked the Tyrell advance. His only known son at his death—not, as often thought (and as appears in, for example, the *History of Parliament*), his brother—was **Walter Tyrell** (*fl.* 1364). Thomas had endowed him in 1364 with lands bought for the purpose in Hampshire and Wiltshire. The transaction testifies to Thomas's wealth by that date, but it also seems to imply that Walter was then a younger son. If so, a likely candidate for Thomas's eldest son is the John Tyrell, knight, who was granted land in North Mimms, Hertfordshire, by Edward III in 1362 but who died about 1371. It is just possible that Sir John left a son, for there is no firm evidence that Walter inherited his father's Essex lands. The most that can be said is that if Walter did succeed his father, he made little impact. He is perhaps the Walter who occurs occasionally as a mainpernor in Essex until 1406, but his date of death is unknown. It was not until Walter's eldest son **Sir John Tyrell** (*c.*1382–1437) began to make his presence felt that the family resumed its advance.

John Tyrell's abilities, and perhaps some legal training, are reflected in the links which he forged, from the outset of his career, with the leading landowners in Essex. He acted as feoffee of Anne of Woodstock, the heir of *Thomas, duke of Gloucester, and her husband, William Bourchier, and also of *Humphrey, duke of Gloucester (under whom he had served in France in 1415). It was probably Gloucester who secured for him the office of steward of Clare and Thaxted during the minority of Richard, duke of York, in 1427—a connection that was to lead to service to York himself, culminating in Tyrell's appointment as the duke's receiver-general. In the same year he was appointed chief steward of the duchy of Lancaster north of the Trent. In 1431 he was made treasurer of the king's household, a post he was to hold until his death, and knighted. He sat in parliament twelve times between 1411 and 1437, and was chosen speaker on three occasions, the last time being in 1437, when he had to resign because of ill health on 19 March; he died a fortnight later on 2 April.

John Tyrell's landed wealth matched his national prominence. In 1412 he was said to be in possession only of Broomfield (his wife's dower from her first marriage) and Heron, Essex, which, if true, would mean that he had not yet inherited all his grandfather's lands, although he was later to do so. His father's Hampshire land had been settled on his widow, Eleanor, daughter and heir of Edmund Flambard of Shepreth, Cambridgeshire, and John had to wait until her death in 1422 to obtain possession. John himself made two good marriages. The first, to Alice, daughter and coheir of William Coggeshall, brought him half the Coggeshall lands at the death of William in 1426. Alice herself had died in 1422 and John had married Katherine, daughter and coheir of William Burgate of Burgate, Suffolk, and widow of Robert Stonham and John Spenser. In 1436 John's annual income was reckoned at £396, which made him the wealthiest non-aristocrat in the county. His brother Edward Tyrell (d. 1442), who had inherited the lands of their mother, Eleanor Flambard, was assessed at £135—and his estate was ultimately to come to John's heir, Thomas.

None of John's five surviving sons rivalled him in his career. At least two of his younger sons established junior branches of the family: William, who founded the Tyrells of Gipping, Suffolk, and was the father of Sir James *Tyrell, and William the younger of Beeches in Rawreth. John's heir, **Sir Thomas** [ii] **Tyrell of Heron** (c.1411–1476), followed his father into the king's service, and was a knight of the body by 1452. With the outbreak of war his sympathies remained Lancastrian. In 1460 he was among the supporters of Henry VI who held the Tower of London when the Yorkists entered the city, although he apparently suffered no recriminations after the Yorkist victory. Unlike his brother William of Gipping, who was executed for treason in 1462, Thomas co-operated with the new regime, at least to the extent of serving on the commission of the peace from 1463 until his death. His sudden appearance on other Essex commissions during the readeption suggests that he was still in some sense seen as 'Lancastrian', but he remained at least as active during Edward IV's second reign. His low profile outside Essex is likely to have been, at least in part, his own choice, for he had friends at the highest levels of the Yorkist establishment. The supervisors of his will included 'my singular good lord' Henry Bourchier, earl of Essex, Sir Thomas Montgomery (the doyen of royal household men in Essex), and the queen's kinsman Richard Haute.

With his wife, Anne, the daughter of Sir William Marney of Layer Marney, Essex, Thomas had four sons. The eldest, William, predeceased him and was buried with his wife, Alianore Darcy, at the Church of the Austin Friars, London, where Thomas's father and stepmother were also buried. Sir Thomas's heir was thus William's son **Sir Thomas** [iii] **Tyrell** (c.1453–1510?). This Thomas was an esquire of Edward IV's body by 1480, perhaps through the good offices of Sir Thomas Montgomery, for whom he was to endow prayers in his will. He transferred smoothly into the household of Richard III, and was confirmed as an esquire of the body in July 1483 at a fee of £40. He occupied the office of master of the horse at Richard's coronation, and although this is often taken as an error for James Tyrell of Gipping (d. 1502) there is no reason to assume that this was the case; Thomas is more likely to have been acting as his cousin's deputy.

Thomas [iii] Tyrell married twice and, if the unidentified brass in East Horndon church is his, had eight sons. His first wife was Anne, daughter of Walter *Devereux, first Baron Ferrers of Chartley (c.1432–1485); his second

Beatrix (d. 1513), daughter of John Cockayne of Derbyshire and widow of John Sutton of London. Thomas had entered the service of Henry VII by 1487, when he was knighted at the battle of Stoke, and was present at the battle of Blackheath, where he became a banneret. In 1509 he attended the funeral of Henry VII and was present at the coronation of his successor as master of the queen's horse, a post in which he was to be succeeded by his son and namesake. Thomas made his will on 26 August 1510 and was probably dead by the end of the year, when his name was omitted from the Essex commission of the peace. The Tyrell family's arms were: argent, two chevronels azure, a border engrailed gules crest: a peacock's tail issuing from the mouth of a boar's head, couped erect, their motto *Sans crainte.*					ROSEMARY HORROX

Sources *Chancery records* · PRO, PROB 11 · O. F. Brown, *The Tyrells of England* (1982) · G. A. Moriarty, 'The early Tyrrels of Heron in East Herndon', *New England Historical and Genealogical Register*, 109 (1955), 17–31 · H. W. King, 'Ancient wills (no. 3)', *Transactions of the Essex Archaeological Society*, 2 (1863), 75–94 · *VCH Cambridgeshire and the Isle of Ely* · *Essex feet of fines*, Essex Archaeological Society (1899–1949) · M. Stephenson, *A list of monumental brasses in the British Isles* (1926) · HoP, *Commons, 1386–1421*

Tyrell, Sir James (c.1455–1502), royal councillor, was the eldest son of William Tyrell of Gipping, Suffolk [see Tyrell family (*per. c.*1304–*c.*1510)], and his wife, Margaret, daughter of Robert Darcy of Maldon in Essex. William was executed for his involvement with John de Vere, the earl of Oxford, in a conspiracy against Edward IV in February 1462, but he was not attainted, and the custody of his land and of his heir James was bought from Cecily Neville, dowager duchess of York, by William's widow and her feoffees for £50 in March 1463. In 1471 James fought for the Yorkists at Tewkesbury, where he was knighted by Edward IV. By the following winter he was in the service of Richard, duke of Gloucester. He became a ducal councillor and feoffee, and was used by Richard on sensitive business such as conducting the dowager countess of Warwick northwards in 1473. He served under the duke in the Scottish campaigns of 1480–82 and was made banneret by him. He was the duke's nominee as chamberlain of the exchequer, and in November 1482 was commissioned to act in Gloucester's office of constable of England.

Tyrell acquired interests in the south-west through his marriage in 1469 to Anne, the daughter of John Arundel of Lanherne, Cornwall, and his first wife, Elizabeth, daughter of Thomas, Lord Morley. He was knight of the shire for Cornwall in 1478, and in June 1483 he was elected for the abortive parliament of Edward V. After Gloucester's accession Tyrell became a knight of the body, and his name was put forward as a candidate for the Garter, although he was not chosen. He was master of the king's horse and of the henchmen. He played a role in the suppression of the rebellion of Henry Stafford, the duke of Buckingham, and was one of those who escorted the captured duke to the king at Salisbury. He was rewarded with the stewardship of the duchy of Cornwall for life and with the land that he had been disputing with his wife's half-brother, the rebel

Thomas Arundel. But Richard employed him primarily in Wales, a connection already established in Edward IV's reign, when Tyrell had been the duke's sheriff of Glamorgan and steward of Morgannwg. After Buckingham's execution, Tyrell was prominent among the royal servants who were given authority to seize and administer the duke's forfeited Welsh estates and to reassert authority over the crown lands in Wales.

In spite of Tyrell's importance in Wales, Richard made him lieutenant of Guînes on 22 January 1485, during the illness of John, Lord Mountjoy; the defection to Tudor of Mountjoy's brother James Blount in the previous autumn had compromised royal control of the Calais fortresses. Tyrell was specifically charged to fulfil the post in person, and to leave south Wales to his subordinates—an order that shows the limited circle of people upon whom Richard was now prepared to rely. Tyrell was accordingly out of England when Richard was defeated at Bosworth and was able to transfer his services to Henry VII, who kept him in office at Guînes. But he lost the importance he had enjoyed under Richard III, as well as his other gains from that king, including the disputed Arundel lands. He was evidently still not fully in the king's favour in 1486. A regrant in February of two of his Welsh offices proved only temporary, and in June and July Tyrell thought it worth securing two royal pardons, one for himself and the other for himself and the Guînes garrison. But in December he was an ambassador to Maximilian, king of the Romans, and by 1488 he had again become a knight of the body. In February 1488 the king promised him compensation for his lost Welsh offices, valued by Tyrell at £3000 over three years. He was involved in the negotiations leading to the treaty of Étaples in 1492, and in 1495 he was one of the feoffees to the use of Henry VII's will.

Tyrell's downfall began obliquely. In 1499 Edmund de la Pole, earl of Suffolk, fled to Flanders and spent time with Tyrell at Guînes on the way—an episode later to be cited as the first of Tyrell's 'divers offences' against the king. Suffolk was persuaded to return to England, but fled again in the summer of 1501, and sought the help of Maximilian in making himself king. In the following spring Thomas Lovell was sent to Guînes to arrest Tyrell and a group of associates, including his son Thomas. James Tyrell was convicted of treason at the London Guildhall on 2 May and executed on 6 May. He was buried in the London church of the Austin friars, where his father was also buried. Tyrell was attainted on 25 January 1504, and the attainder was reversed on 19 April 1507.

It is as the murderer of the 'princes in the Tower'—the sons of Edward IV—that Tyrell is now usually remembered. The identification rests on a confession that Tyrell was said to have made between his condemnation and execution. No copy of the confession survives, but according to the version circulating among subsequent writers, Richard commanded the constable of the Tower, Sir Robert Brackenbury, to have the princes killed, and when Brackenbury hesitated Tyrell was sent to do the job instead—'sorrowfully', according to Polydore Vergil. The best-known version of the story is Thomas More's elaborately circumstantial account which is, however, demonstrably inaccurate in detail, notably in the lowly status assigned to Tyrell before the murder. Whatever its validity, the dissemination of Tyrell's 'confession' finally disposed of claims that the princes were still alive. If Tyrell's closeness to Richard III made him a plausible murderer, he was also (from the Tudor point of view) a very convenient one.

ROSEMARY HORROX

Sources PRO · BL · *Chancery records* · RotP · R. Horrox, *Richard III, a study of service*, Cambridge Studies in Medieval Life and Thought, 4th ser., 11 (1989) · G. Williams, ed., *Glamorgan county history*, 3: *The middle ages*, ed. T. B. Pugh (1971), 167–204 · W. R. B. Robinson, 'A letter from Sir Richard Croft to Sir Gilbert Talbot in 1486 concerning Sir James Tyrell's offices in Wales', *Historical Research*, 67 (1994), 179–89 · J. P. Yeatman, *The early genealogical history of the house of Arundel* (1882) · St Thomas More, *The history of King Richard III*, ed. R. S. Sylvester (1963), vol. 2 of *The Yale edition of the complete works of St Thomas More* · *Three books of Polydore Vergil's 'English history'*, ed. H. Ellis, CS, 29 (1844)

Tyrell, Sir John (c.1382–1437). *See under* Tyrell family (*per.* c.1304–c.1510).

Tyrell, Sir Thomas (d. 1382). *See under* Tyrell family (*per.* c.1304–c.1510).

Tyrell, Sir Thomas, of Heron (c.1411–1476). *See under* Tyrell family (*per.* c.1304–c.1510).

Tyrell, Sir Thomas (c.1453–1510?). *See under* Tyrell family (*per.* c.1304–c.1510).

Tyrell, Walter (*fl.* 1364). *See under* Tyrell family (*per.* c.1304–c.1510).

Tyrer, Henry (1858–1936), shipping agent, was born at Green Lane Farm, Ormskirk, Lancashire, on 2 March 1858, the third son among thirteen children of John Tyrer (d. 1894), a farmer, and his wife, Jane (d. 1889), née Travis. Tyrer was educated at the free grammar school in Ormskirk and left school in 1872. Deciding against agriculture as a career, he obtained a position with Alfred Murdoch & Co. in Liverpool. The firm had been active in the west African trade since 1847, and its trading in palm oil had led to the purchase of a cooperage. Tyrer learned all aspects of the business, and in 1879 he became a partner, only to leave soon after to set up his own business.

Henry Tyrer & Co. had an initial capital of only £100, but Tyrer's activities as a commission agent in the west African trade required little more as cash was usually received with each order. By taking personal care of each transaction Tyrer soon acquired a good reputation. He restored relations with Murdoch, and eventually took over his business. Tyrer then took a partner to fund further expansion, but this link ended in 1885.

Tyrer was now a general merchant, trading in goods on his own account, as well as being a commission agent. His success enabled him to marry Jane Elizabeth (1855–1936), daughter of John Porter, an estate manager, on 17 June 1885 at Rufford church near Ormskirk. Sadly both their children died at an early age. Then in 1890 Tyrer found himself in financial difficulties, and only narrowly escaped bankruptcy.

During the 1890s Tyrer made various attempts to take a more direct part in the west African shipping trade. He successively encouraged the Prince Line, the General Steam Navigation Company, and Furness Withy & Co. Ltd to provide services to west Africa for which he would act as agent. Alfred Jones dominated the west African trade, and defeated Tyrer's efforts, as he did again in 1903–4 when Tyrer organized voyages to west Africa by a ship of his own.

To compensate for these rebuffs, Tyrer diversified his business into other activities. These included agencies for short sea routes from Liverpool and the development of a small coastal trade with western Scotland. Tyrer also took advantage of the opening of the port of Preston in 1892. He was soon the leading shipping agent there, dealing with grain from Ireland, general cargo from London, and, most important of all, the woodpulp trade from Scandinavia. His own service from Preston to Brussels via London was short-lived, but was sold at a profit.

Tyrer converted his business into a limited liability company in 1914. He became governing director and six of his most long-standing employees were appointed directors. The First World War disrupted some of Tyrer's activities, but it also gave him yet another chance to take a bigger part in the west African trade. In 1916 Sir William Lever set up the Bromport Steamship Company in defiance of the west African shipping conference, and Tyrer became the agent for Bromport.

The coming of peace dealt several blows to Tyrer's business. He lost the agency for the woodpulp trade, and in 1924 the Bromport Steamship Company was wound up. However, Tyrer retained the agency for Lever's Southern Whaling and Sealing Company. In the late 1920s Tyrer was again active in the west African trade, acting for the African and Eastern Trade Corporation, and then the United African Company.

By 1930 Henry Tyrer was in his seventies, and playing a much smaller role in the running of his company. His health gradually failed and he died on 20 June 1936 at his home, Bewcastle, Latham, near Ormskirk, Lancashire. He was buried at Rufford church. Tyrer's wife survived him, but died two months later, on 25 August 1936.

ALAN G. JAMIESON

Sources P. N. Davies, *Henry Tyrer: a Liverpool shipping agent and his enterprise* (1979) · *CGPLA Eng. & Wales* (1936)
Archives Henry Tyrer & Co., Liverpool
Likenesses two photographs, repro. in Davies, *Henry Tyrer*
Wealth at death £77,661 8s. 6d.: resworn probate, 2 Oct 1936, *CGPLA Eng. & Wales*

Tyrie, James (1543–1597), Jesuit, was a younger son of David Tyrie of Drumkilbo, Perthshire. His mother was a sister of the fifth Lord Gray. Their eldest son, David, became a protestant and signed the bond of association connected with the abdication of Mary, queen of Scots. Tyrie was educated at St Andrews University and was taken abroad in 1563 by Edmund Hay, along with other future Jesuits. Briefly a student at Louvain, he decided to enter the Society of Jesus and on 19 August 1563 was admitted at Rome, where he made a good impression: 'He

is so talented and well informed that with this grounding, after hearing a little theology, he will be able to lecture' (Pollen, *Papal Negotiations*, 485). Four years later he was doing so at Paris, where he helped to establish the Collège de Clermont. He remained there for many years, teaching philosophy and divinity (as a priest from 1572, three years later as a professed Jesuit), and was latterly rector.

From Paris Tyrie corresponded with his brother David, hoping to bring the latter back to the religion he had abandoned on marriage. One letter dealing with the visibility of the church was passed on to John Knox in 1566. Knox composed a point-by-point reply, but his 'scriblit' manuscript was left aside until the same arguments, circulating more widely from other Jesuit sources, seemed to require a response. He then had it printed at St Andrews in 1572, as *An Answer to a Letter of a Jesuit Named Tyrie*. The latter quickly produced his *Refutation of ane Answer Made by Schir Johne Knox*, dated 8 March 1573, though by then both his brother and Knox were dead. His arguments against the 'invisible kirk of Scotland, not yit aucht yeir auld' (Law, 11) provoked the general assembly into setting up a committee to approve a reply, but neither then nor in 1577, when George Hay (opponent of Ninian Winzet, Edmund Hay, and James Gordon) submitted his response, was anything published. According to John Hamilton, however, the minister of Dundee had Tyrie's book burned at the market cross. Along with other Roman Catholic 'tractates' of the time, it helped the Jesuits to convert literate members of the gentry.

Tyrie was proposed for Scotland in 1584, and again a year later. In fact he never returned there, but he remained closely involved in the efforts of the Jesuit mission and was hopeful of what might be achieved through James VI. In Paris he made an important convert in Lord Claud Hamilton. Even Scots protestants were impressed by him. The early seventeenth-century author David Buchanan, who regarded the Jesuits of the French capital as a 'pestiferous race of men', reported the applause won by Tyrie during debates in the Sorbonne for his learning, sharpness, and 'stupendous memory' (Law, xxxi), and also praised his modesty, gentleness, and charity. In 1574 Andrew Melville, *en route* for Scotland from Geneva, was invited to the college at Clermont and persuaded by Tyrie to engage in public disputation over several days.

Tyrie's reputation did not rely on any body of published work, but the regard in which he was held by superiors is shown by their choosing him as one of six fathers representing the Jesuit provinces, and largely responsible, 'if not the author' (Forbes-Leith, *Pre-Reformation Scholars*, 74), for the society's first plan of studies in 1586. A treatise on the origins of Christianity in Scotland, published under the name of George Thomson at Rome in 1594, has been attributed to Tyrie. The claim has been challenged and the verdict remains not proven, but Tyrie certainly wrote an account in 1594 of how Scotland became protestant under Mary Stuart. As a Jesuit novice he had recognized the spiritual danger of literary pursuits, and he left several manuscripts behind at his untimely death. Tyrie was clear on the need for Jesuits to avoid involvement in politics, and he played no part in the disturbances which accompanied the 1590 siege of Paris. That year he was called to Rome as assistant to the general for France and Germany, succeeding Edmund Hay. The Jesuit Robert Persons (who unlike Tyrie was constantly involved in politics) blamed him for accepting James VI's claim to the English crown, for which 'it seemeth God tooke him so sodanely away to the admiration of all men' (Pollen, 'Memoirs', 208). Tyrie died at the Vatican, Rome, on 20 March 1597 and was buried there.

ALASDAIR ROBERTS

Sources T. G. Law, *Catholic tractates of the sixteenth century, 1573–1600*, STS, 45 (1901) · W. Forbes-Leith, *Pre-reformation scholars in the XVIth century* (1915) · W. Forbes-Leith, ed., *Narratives of Scottish Catholics under Mary Stuart and James VI* (1885) · 'The memoirs of Father Robert Persons', ed. J. H. Pollen, *Miscellanea, II*, Catholic RS, 2 (1906), 12–218 · J. H. Pollen, ed., *Papal negotiations with Mary queen of Scots during her reign in Scotland, 1561–1567*, Scottish History Society, 37 (1901) · J. Durkan, 'The identity of George Thomson, Catholic controversialist', *Innes Review*, 31 (1980), 45–6 · A. Bellesheim, *History of the Catholic Church in Scotland*, ed. and trans. D. O. H. Blair, 3 (1889) · J. F. S. Gordon, ed., *The Catholic church in Scotland* (1874)

Tyrone. For this title name *see* O'Neill, Conn Bacach, first earl of Tyrone (c.1482–1559); O'Neill, Hugh, second earl of Tyrone (c.1550–1616); O'Neill, Hugh, styled sixth earl of Tyrone (d. 1660/61); Power, Richard, first earl of Tyrone (1629/30–1690).

Tyrrell, Anthony (1552–1615), Roman Catholic priest and Church of England clergyman, was the son of George Tyrrell, a courtier to Queen Mary. The Tyrrells were a well-connected family of ancient lineage with property in Essex. At some point after the accession of Elizabeth, Anthony's parents decided to take their children to the Spanish Netherlands in order to avoid religious persecution in England. There they lived in considerable poverty. Anthony took a degree, perhaps at Louvain University, but could not proceed with his studies, as he wished, because he was so poor. In 1574 he returned rather impulsively to England in the company of a young man called Christopher Dryland who was later to become a Catholic priest. Tyrrell travelled around visiting his relatives in Essex, attempting to raise cash for the continuation of his studies. On 9 September 1574 he was arrested trying to embark for the continent; he spent nearly two years in prison as a result, until he was released on the orders of Lord Burghley, and he went abroad again.

Early in 1578 Tyrrell went to study at the English College, Rome; he was ordained priest and sent to England to join the mission in September 1580. On 29 April 1581 he was arrested in London and imprisoned in the Gatehouse. Towards the end of that year he managed to escape from prison in the company of John Ballard, another imprisoned priest of mercurial character. His movements over the next two years are a little unclear: there is evidence that for some of this time he was in England, especially in York and the London area, but he also may have been in Rome and Rheims in 1582 and 1583. In the spring of 1584 he and Ballard met again in England and certainly travelled abroad. They said to Catholic exiles they met on the continent that they needed a rest from the dangers of

their lives in England, and that Tyrrell wished to continue his education.

The two young priests landed in Normandy and went first to Rouen, where they visited Gertrude Tyrrell, Anthony's sister who was a Bridgettine nun. From there they travelled to Rheims to visit the English College, thence to the Jesuit seminary at Pont-à-Mousson, and so, by way of Milan, to Rome. In an account of these travels, written by Tyrrell later for the propaganda purposes of the English government, he claimed that he and Ballard had discussed the assassination of the queen with William Allen at Rheims, Owen Lewis in Milan, and in Rome with the Jesuit-general and the pope himself. All of those interviewed, with the exception of Lewis, had, even according to Tyrrell's account, expressed reservations about adopting such a course of action, although they had not forbidden it. As might be expected, the veracity of the account of these interviews given by Tyrrell has been the subject of much controversy. It seems to have a sort of authenticity about it; but on the other hand at a later date Tyrrell himself claimed it was fabricated.

From Rome, Ballard and Tyrrell returned by way of Paris, where they had discussions with Charles Paget, the agent of Mary, queen of Scots, and with other exiled conspirators. They arrived back in England at the end of 1585. Tyrrell was involved in the early part of the following year in the series of exorcisms which were being undertaken by a number of missionary priests led by William Weston largely in the house of a leading Catholic recusant, Edmund Peckham, in Buckinghamshire. He wrote a book to describe these events entitled 'The book of miracles', which seems not to have survived.

In July 1586 Tyrrell was arrested again and imprisoned for the third time. This was the turning point in his life, since he was now threatened with death. His friend Ballard was arrested shortly afterwards; he had become involved in the Babington plot, for which he was to be executed. The arrest of Ballard threatened Tyrrell, who decided rather irresolutely to become an apostate, and to co-operate in the propaganda efforts of the government. Tyrrell seems to have been emotionally unstable as well as cowardly. The government agents, led by a certain Justice Richard Young, were well able to play on his fears and desire for adventure. He was closely questioned by his captors, and he provided them with a very full account of his activities in England and abroad, naming many of his contacts. This sort of information doubtless helped government agents to bring prosecutions against a number of Catholics, and therefore contributed to their deaths. In addition, Tyrrell was transferred to a different prison, the Clink, where he was used to spy on the Catholic prisoners and provide information to the government. Young encouraged Tyrrell to win the confidence of his fellow Catholic prisoners by administering the sacraments to them; he then went to Young to report what he had learned from them, presumably from their confessions as well as from their private conversations.

While acting as a prisoner spy Tyrrell was persuaded to abandon his Catholicism, but he did so irresolutely, and recanted on several occasions. It was in August 1586, shortly after his imprisonment, that he first decided to co-operate with the government, but early the following year he was prevailed upon by an imprisoned priest, William Barlow, to recant. He relapsed shortly afterwards, and offered to become a protestant preacher. As a result, in March 1587, he was released from prison. His Catholic friends persuaded him out of this decision and collected £50 to send him abroad. It was at this point that he wrote a long, penitent account of his imprisonment and his various acts of betrayal, which was passed eventually to Robert Persons, who prepared the book for the press, but in the end decided not to publish it, perhaps because it reflected poorly not only on protestants but also on Catholics. With the funds collected for him Tyrrell travelled to Scotland and embarked for Hamburg, but then decided to return to England. In the summer of 1587 he gave the government a full account of his activities and he was placed in prison to keep him away from Catholics who might persuade him to recant. He agreed to preach at St Paul's Cross explaining his conversion to protestantism. On the day appointed he surprised his captors by giving a Catholic sermon instead, or at least starting to do so, before he was stopped. He threw copies of the sermon into the crowd, one of which survived, and was published by Catholics abroad. Imprisoned again, he finally relapsed into protestantism, and late in 1588 actually did preach his protestant sermon, which was duly printed by the government. What had intervened between his defiant theatricals on his first appearance at St Paul's Cross and his second declaration in favour of the Church of England was the defeat of the Spanish Armada, which may have strengthened his resolve.

As a reward for his protestant sermon Tyrrell was pardoned on 28 February 1589. He now became a clergyman of the Church of England. He was made rector of Dengie, by the Essex marshes, on 8 November 1589, and became vicar of the neighbouring parish of Southminster on 12 July 1591. He seems to have been in trouble for unorthodoxy as a clergyman. At some point he was married, but details of his wife are not known. In 1593 he was reported as chaplain to Lady Howard of Bindon. But in the same year he was in trouble again. He sold his benefice at Southminster for £64, and tried to arrange to travel abroad, possibly to visit his sister again, whose religious community was preparing to leave Rouen for Lisbon. It is possible that this decision to go abroad coincided with a change of religious heart. However, he was waylaid in London by some of the disreputable characters that he and Ballard had known there a few years before, and he spent much of his money frequenting a brothel. He was caught by the authorities, interviewed by his old friend Justice Young, and lodged in the Marshalsea. Once again he was released from prison, having expressed his contrition in a letter to Cecil, and he resumed his clerical career in Dengie. The next record of Tyrrell was when, in 1602, he was questioned by Dr Harsnett, chaplain to the bishop of London, about the exorcisms in which in 1586 he had become involved. His account of these events was then published by Harsnett and apparently supplied Shakespeare with material for *King Lear*.

In 1606 Tyrrell fled abroad for the last time, fearing arrest for some rather obscure involvement in the Gunpowder Plot the previous year. He probably lived in the Spanish Netherlands with his brother Robert, who was a Catholic and pensioner of the king of Spain. The final report of Tyrrell was in 1615 when he was said to have died in Naples, a Catholic.   PETER HOLMES

Sources DNB · G. Anstruther, *The seminary priests*, 1 (1969) · J. Morris, ed., *The troubles of our Catholic forefathers related by themselves*, 2 (1875) · J. H. Pollen, *Mary queen of Scots and the Babington plot*, Scottish History Society, 3rd ser., 3 (1922) · W. K. Boyd, ed., *Calendar of Scottish papers, 1585–6* (1914), 647–56 · *Miscellanea, II*, Catholic RS, 2 (1906) · *Letters of William Allen and Richard Barret, 1572–1598*, ed. P. Renold, Catholic RS, 58 (1967), 85–6, 88, 113, 115 · A. Kenny, 'A martyr manqué: the early life of Anthony Tyrrell', *Clergy Review*, new ser., 42/11 (Oct 1957), 651–68 · C. Devlin, 'An unwilling apostate: the case of Anthony Tyrrell', *The Month*, new ser., 6 (1951), 346–58 · 'Inconstant hearts: seminary priests in Essex parsonages', *Essex Recusant*, 3 (1961), 66–72 · *Calendar of the manuscripts of the most hon. the marquis of Salisbury*, 4, HMC, 9 (1892), 380, 392–3, 419, 429 · T. F. Knox and others, eds., *The first and second diaries of the English College, Douay* (1878) · *The letters and memorials of William, Cardinal Allen (1532–1594)*, ed. T. F. Knox (1882), vol. 2 of *Records of the English Catholics under the penal laws* (1878–82), 95, 135, 192, 209, 453
Archives Venerable English College, Rome, autobiography

Tyrrell, Frederick (1793–1843), surgeon, was baptized on 7 February 1794 at St Antholin's, Watling Street, London, the fourth son of Timothy Tyrrell, remembrancer of the corporation of London, and his wife, Elizabeth. He was educated at Richard Elwell's school in Hammersmith, then at King Henry VII School, Reading. In 1811 he was articled to Astley Paston Cooper, practising at the united hospitals of Guy's and St Thomas's, London.

After the battle of Waterloo, when the hospitals at Brussels were crowded with wounded men, Tyrrell, along with many others, went over to offer assistance. He was admitted a member of the Royal College of Surgeons in 1816, and in 1819 spent a year in Edinburgh. In 1820 he was appointed assistant surgeon at the London Eye Infirmary (later Moorfields Eye Hospital), and in 1822 he was elected a surgeon to St Thomas's Hospital.

Tyrrell married on 5 June 1823, at St Martin-in-the-Fields, Westminster, Frances Susanna, daughter of Samuel Lovick Cooper and a niece of Sir Astley Cooper. They lived in London in New Bridge Street and about 1840 moved to a larger house in the adjacent Chatham Place; they also resided in a country house, East Lodge, at Acton, Middlesex. When Guy's and St Thomas's medical schools were divided in 1825 Tyrrell was also lecturing on anatomy and surgery at the private Aldersgate Street school of medicine, a position he gave up a few years later on becoming lecturer on anatomy and physiology at St Thomas's Hospital.

The combination of teaching and private practice filled Tyrrell's day while increasing his reputation. His three-volume edition of Sir Astley Cooper's *Lectures on the Principles and Practice of Surgery* (1824–7), annotated with case notes, led Thomas Wakley, editor of *The Lancet*, to accuse him of copying large amounts from that journal; in the libel suit which followed Tyrrell was awarded £50 damages. Contemporaries also accused him, as a pupil and relative by marriage of Sir Astley Cooper, of profiting by favouritism. He was nevertheless regarded as an admirable surgeon and the mainstay of the departments to which he was attached. He was elected to the council of the Royal College of Surgeons in 1838, and was Arris and Gale lecturer on anatomy and physiology from 1838 to 1841. His only independent publication was *Diseases of the Eyes* (1840).

Tyrrell, who had for some time been suffering from heart disease, went to the City mart in Bartholomew's Lane, London, on 23 May 1843, intending to bid for the freehold of East Lodge. He was suddenly taken ill, collapsed, and died almost immediately.

D'A. POWER, *rev.* ANITA McCONNELL

Sources J. Hirschberg, *The history of ophthalmology*, trans. F. C. Blodi, 8a (1987), 174–85 · *The Lancet* (27 May 1843), 699 · F. G. Parsons, *The history of St Thomas's Hospital*, 3 (1936) · *The Times* (24 May 1843), 5d · d. cert.

Tyrrell, George (1861–1909), modernist Roman Catholic writer and excommunicated priest, was born on 6 February 1861 at 91 Dorset Street, Dublin, the third child and posthumous son of William Henry Tyrrell, a noted Dublin journalist, and his second wife, Mary Chamney. The Tyrrells were a well-known protestant family, who achieved success at Trinity College, Dublin, and in the professions. Tyrrell's early years were blighted by poverty and insecurity. He followed his elder brother, William, at Rathmines School. Whereas Willie became a scholar at Trinity College and at Cambridge before his early death, Tyrrell failed to win a sizarship at Trinity College and departed for London aged eighteen.

Tyrrell's early religious formation in moderate Anglicanism was at All Saints', Grangegorman, but he was also much influenced by the high-church beliefs and Christian socialism of Robert Dolling. In London he was free to pursue his growing attraction to what his family saw as 'the religion of … vulgar and uneducated classes in Ireland' (*Autobiography*, 34), accepting Roman Catholicism within two months of his arrival. Immediately, he made enquiries about joining the Jesuits. After a preliminary year teaching in Malta, he entered the noviciate at Manresa House, Roehampton. His two years as a novice were followed by three years' study of philosophy at St Mary's Hall, Stonyhurst, and three years' teaching in Malta. For a further four years he studied theology at St Beuno's College in north Wales. At the end of his third year (September 1891) he was ordained priest. With a year's tertianship at Manresa, his training as a Jesuit (of which he was later savagely critical) was complete.

For a year Tyrrell did parish work in St Helens before he was moved back to St Mary's Hall to teach philosophy. He claimed the authority of the encyclical *Aeterni patris* (1879) for teaching directly from Thomas Aquinas, rather than approved Jesuit commentators. Typically, he used conservative weapons to maintain liberty of theological interpretation. There were clashes: staff and students took sides; within two years he was moved to London to work

in the Farm Street *scriptorium* writing articles for *The Month*.

Tyrrell was a brilliant religious writer, of quicksilver wit and aggressive common sense. At a time when much Roman Catholic devotional writing was stylized and 'safe' his first full-length collection of religious meditations, *Nova et vetera* (1897), put old truths in fresh and invigorating language. He became immersed in a hectic round of letter-writing, spiritual counselling, hearing confessions, and preaching, together with his continuing work as an author. He developed a new circle of friends with broad intellectual horizons: Baron Friedrich von Hügel, Maude *Petre, Wilfrid Ward, Henri Bremond. He wrote articles and reviews regularly, together with a second full-length book of meditations and studies, *Hard Sayings* (1898). His reputation as a liberal Catholic in the tradition of Newman was at its zenith.

Among the best of Tyrrell's articles was 'The relation of theology to devotion' (*The Month*, 94, 1899, 461–73), in which he insisted on the primacy of devotion and the vivid language in which it is expressed, over the reflexive and abstract language of philosophy and theology. The second, he argued, with scholasticism in view, may clarify the misunderstandings that arise from the naïvety of the first, but

> God has revealed Himself … not to the theologian or the philosopher, but to babes, to fishermen, to peasants … and therefore He has spoken their language, leaving it to the others to translate it (at their own risk) into forms more acceptable to their taste. (ibid., 466–7)

In *External Religion* (1899) Tyrrell insisted that all church structures, such as the system of doctrine and sacraments, exist for but one purpose: the reproduction of the life of Christ in the lives of those who follow him. To these central points he returned throughout his life.

In 'A perverted devotion' (*Weekly Register*, 16 Dec 1898), Tyrrell used irony to criticize the literalistic preaching of hell by two Redemptorist writers. This article, which had been casually passed by one censor in England (his friend Joseph Thurston) was reported to Rome, where it was read by two Roman censors who condemned it out of hand. The Jesuit general insisted on disciplinary measures. Tyrrell responded by taking issue with his Roman censors. In no mood for debate, the general informed the English provincial that Tyrrell was to be banned from guiding Jesuits through the *Spiritual Exercises* of St Ignatius (his approach can be reconstructed from *The Soul's Orbit*, 1904, published under Maude Petre's name), a ban of which Tyrrell was never officially informed, though he suspected its existence. The spat ended with publication in the *Weekly Register* of a brief, non-specific avowal of orthodoxy for Tyrrell in Rome, and his retirement to the calm of the Jesuit house in Richmond, Yorkshire. He was, by mutual agreement, rusticated.

Further controversy ensued. In late 1900 the bishops of England and Wales brought out a joint pastoral letter against liberal Catholicism, which turned on an ecclesiology differentiating sharply between the *ecclesia docens* (the teaching church) and the *ecclesia discens* (the learning church), exhorting the learners to be obedient to those whose duty it was to instruct them in the faith. Tyrrell wanted to press the issue between the organic unity of the whole church including the pope, and a two-tier ecclesiology which would reinforce the authority of the pope, the curia, and the bishops over the rest of the church. For six months he wrote letters and articles opposing the joint pastoral, adopting various disguises to stir the controversy.

During the following four years of sustained study and writing Tyrrell pursued both the development of his religious philosophy and his criticism of the religious authorities. He imbibed the thought of A. F. Loisy, M. Blondel, and L. Laberthonnière. With active encouragement from von Hügel he learned German, reading protestant critics such as J. Weiss and E. Troeltsch. Only by publishing pseudonymously could he develop an interpretation of Christianity which faced the urgent intellectual difficulties he saw the Roman Catholic church refusing to address. *The Civilizing of the Matafanus* (1902, published under the name of A. R. Waller) used a fable imaginatively to explore the consciousness of Christ and the development of Christological doctrine; *Religion as a Factor of Life* (1902, published under the name Dr Ernest Engels) emphasized the centrality of the human will rather than the intellect, and the capacity of the will to be united with God. *The Church and the Future* (1903, published under the name Hilaire Bourdon) developed Tyrrell's critique of the whole Roman system, and his positive understanding of a fallible church and a human Jesus as vehicles of the immanent Spirit. Tyrrell also quietly circulated *Oil and Wine* (1902, published 1907) and *A Letter to a University Professor* (1904, published as *A Much-Abused Letter*, 1906), a distillation of letters written to intellectuals in difficulties, stressing adherence to whatever little measure of religious and moral truth the individual still holds, and the value of sacramental participation even without intellectual conviction. Under his own name Tyrrell published only *The Faith of the Millions* (1901), a selection of past essays intended to bolster his reputation for orthodoxy, and *Lex orandi* (1903), a study of the religious value of the creed which scraped past the censors—the last of Tyrrell's books to receive the *imprimatur*. Throughout this period he was much visited by more or less like-minded friends, and indefatigable in correspondence, often with people in religious or moral difficulties. He was aware, especially after the election of Pius X to the papacy in 1903, that his alienation from Rome and from his Jesuit superiors would probably end in his departure from the society. In mid-1904 he prepared a long letter asking for his release. Not until September 1905 was it finally sent.

The negotiation of Tyrrell's departure from the Jesuits was a delicate matter. Just at this time the *Corriere della Sera* published extracts from the *Letter to a University Professor* by 'an English Jesuit'. Tyrrell acknowledged authorship, and in the face of Roman censorship angrily refused to disavow what he had written. Even the pope now knew of the article, and it was on the pope's authority, in February

1906, that Tyrrell was dismissed from the Jesuits and forbidden to celebrate mass.

All hope of reconciliation ended with the publication, in July 1907, of the decree *Lamentabili* and, in September 1907, of the papal encyclical *Pascendi*, which named and characterized, and thereby created 'modernism'. The encyclical was a carefully constructed synthetic attack on positions espoused by Tyrrell and Loisy, accusing the modernist of agnosticism and immanentism, that is, of failing to do justice to the cognitive, supernatural content of revelation, and of propounding the 'synthesis of all heresies'. Immediately Tyrrell went on the offensive, savaging the encyclical in the *Giornale d'Italia* and *The Times*, the predictable result of which was his excommunication.

For the last months of his life, Tyrrell, now an avowed modernist, continued to develop his religious hermeneutic. Before his excommunication he had published *Lex credendi* (1906), a study of the Lord's prayer, and *Through Scylla and Charybdis* (1907), an important collection of essays. In 1908 it came to his notice that Cardinal Mercier, archbishop of Malines, had published a pastoral letter attacking the modernists. Tyrrell used this as a peg on which to hang *Medievalism* (1908), a masterpiece of religious polemic, written at white heat, in which he contrasts the medievalism of the religious authorities which faces none of the urgent questions of the twentieth century and the modernism of those who, in every age, cannot but seek a contemporary expression of the faith. In *Christianity at the Crossroads* (1909) he refined his position in an apparently conservative, but actually a radically innovative, direction. Following J. Weiss and A. Schweitzer, he criticized liberal protestants who excised the apocalyptic language of the earliest Christians. This rightly survived in contemporary Catholicism—but should now be interpreted with 'a frank admission of the principle of symbolism' (p. 103). The immanent Spirit will yet bring a Catholicism of the future in which the Christianity of the twentieth century will be transcended by a more inclusive and universal religion we cannot as yet discern.

This was Tyrrell's final word. Having travelled distractedly in France and Germany with Henri Bremond, he had settled in Storrington, Sussex, near Maude Petre. Here, on 6 July 1909, he became seriously ill with the last stages of Bright's (renal) disease. He received absolution and unction but not communion. Bremond arrived in time to be recognized and to give absolution before Tyrrell died on 15 July at Mulberry House, Storrington. A letter to *The Times*, drafted by von Hügel and Maude Petre, made it clear that, though he died 'fortified by the rites of the church', he did not recant his views. The bishop of Southwark immediately forebade a Roman Catholic funeral. Tyrrell was buried on 21 July, with the barest ceremony, in the Anglican churchyard at Storrington.

Shortly before the end of his life Tyrrell wrote to Arthur Boutwood, 'My own work—which I regard as done—has been to raise a question which I have failed to answer' (*George Tyrrell's Letters*, 119). The question was that of the meaning of Christianity in the modern world. Tyrrell believed passionately that Christianity should face the pressing questions of biblical criticism and natural science, though he himself was ill-equipped to deal with the detail of biblical scholarship and was naïve about its 'assured results'. He held to the vision of a generous and inclusive Catholicism that faced difficulties and nourished authentic religious devotion. His strength was in the literary communication of religious ideas. He was a superb letter-writer, witty and compassionate. Many of the reforms, intellectual, pastoral, and administrative, for which he fought, were introduced by the Roman Catholic church in the years after the Second Vatican Council (1962–5), but it is doubtful whether the institutional Roman Catholic church in any age could have contained a spiritual writer so gifted, so reckless, and so provocative.

NICHOLAS SAGOVSKY

Sources Autobiography and life of George Tyrrell, ed. M. D. Petre, 2 vols. (1912) • N. Sagovsky, 'On God's side': a life of George Tyrrell (1990) • George Tyrrell's letters, ed. M. D. Petre (1920) • M. D. Petre, Von Hügel and Tyrrell (1937) • D. G. Schultenover, George Tyrrell: in search of Catholicism (1981) • CGPLA Eng. & Wales (1909)
Archives BL, corresp. and papers, Add. MSS 52367–52382 | Archives of the British Province of the Society of Jesus, London, CD/1–4 • Archivum Romanum Societatis Iesu, Rome, AGL. 1021 'Tyrrell' • Bibliothèque Nationale, Paris, fonds Bremond • Bibliothèque Nationale, Paris, fonds Houtin • Bibliothèque Nationale, Paris, fonds Laberthonnière • Bibliothèque Nationale, Paris, fonds Loisy • BL, corresp. with Baron von Hügel, Add. MSS 44927–44931 • BL, letters to Maude Petre, Add. MSS 52367–52382, passim • BL, letters to A. R. Waller, Add. MSS 43680–43681 • Borth. Inst., corresp. with second Viscount Halifax • U. Oxf., Blackfriars Library, letters to M. A. Raffalovich • U. St Andr. L., letters to A. L. Lilley • U. St Andr. L., corresp. with Wilfrid Ward, papers
Likenesses line drawings, repro. in Autobiography, ed. Petre • photograph, repro. in Petre, Von Hügel and Tyrrell, facing p. 17
Wealth at death £475 4s.: probate, 7 Sept 1909, CGPLA Eng. & Wales • £264 12s. 7d.: administration, 1 June 1910, CGPLA Eng. & Wales

Tyrrell, George Nugent Merle (1879–1952), psychical researcher and engineer, was born at Weymouth Road, Frome, Somerset, on 23 March 1879, the son of Nugent Tyrrell, a railway engineer, and Margery Athol Back, his wife. Tyrrell was educated at Haileybury School (briefly), Seafield Engineering College, and London University, where he graduated in physics and mathematics in 1914. On 28 January 1908 he married Constance Marion Gilliat (b. 1875/6), daughter of Alfred Gilliat. They had a daughter, Kathleen Marjorie.

From 1907 to 1910 Tyrrell was employed by the English Marconi and Mexican Light and Power Company, and from 1910 to 1914 by GEC, USA. In the First World War he served in France, first as a private in the Army Service Corps, and then commissioned as a lieutenant in 1916 to serve as a signals officer with the Royal Artillery; he was twice mentioned in dispatches. After the war he became a teacher in the English public school system and also a private tutor, and he perhaps supported himself in this way while conducting psychical research. Tyrrell had joined the Society for Psychical Research (SPR) in 1908 while in

Mexico. About 1915 he made the acquaintance of a girl, Gertrude Johnson, who in 1919 was discovered to have psychic gifts. She subsequently made her home with his family, and was his main experimental subject, at first guessing playing cards accurately beyond chance.

Tyrrell's book Grades of Significance (1931) revealed his interest in the philosophical implications of the paranormal, and his awareness of metaphysical problems beneath the confident exterior of modern science. Taking as an example the writing on a page, he argued that higher levels of meaning could not be understood in terms of lower ones, and that our everyday reality was profoundly mysterious. Tyrrell resumed quantitative 'guessing' experiments with Miss Johnson in 1934, and later with other subjects, using a machine in which the subject had to locate a concealed object. This brought him into correspondence with Dr J. B. Rhine of Duke University, North Carolina, who coined the term 'extrasensory perception'. Both experimenters were obtaining results beyond chance. Year by year Tyrrell built more sophisticated devices, often using discarded post-office hardware. Tyrrell's Science and Psychical Phenomena (1938) was a fine textbook of psychical research whose impact was reduced by the war. He devoted space to both spontaneous and laboratory phenomena, but more than half the book was about mediumship and possible survival after death, in which he seems to have believed. With his clear style and broad sympathies, Tyrrell was a natural choice to write The Personality of Man (1946). This widely read and translated Pelican survey was his most successful book. The outlook and the title evoked F. W. Myers, author of Human Personality and its Survival of Bodily Death (1903), who had placed psychical and other mental phenomena in a continuum up to mystical experience. Tyrrell's paperback introduced several people to psychical research who became lifelong workers in the field.

Tyrrell's outlook changed during the Second World War. His home was bombed in the blitz and his testing machines were destroyed. He gave up experiments, having become convinced that the scientific method would never disclose the truth about the paranormal, and that the qualitative approach was superior. He joined the council of the SPR in 1938, and in 1942 gave the Myers memorial lecture to the society, about apparitions; later, in its expanded and published form, it became the standard work. Tyrrell was elected SPR president for 1945. In his presidential address, and in his later books, Homo faber (1951) and the posthumous Nature of Human Personality (1954), he argued that evolution had caused humanity to turn away from the psychic and to accept uncritically the mysteries of everyday perception. Had he fulfilled an invitation to deliver the Hibbert lectures in 1951, this theme would probably have been taken further. But an illness, which he believed to be of nervous origin, halted his work, and he died on 29 October 1952, at his home, Prospect, Blandford Road, Reigate, Surrey. He was survived by his wife.

Tyrrell's work was influential among the general public,

and continued to be cited regularly in the parapsychological literature into the twenty-first century. Its judiciousness may be contrasted with that of his sensational contemporary Harry Price. Tyrrell's respect for both the spontaneous and experimental sides of psychical research exemplified the SPR's attitude. In later years his style became somewhat didactic, and the American philosopher and psychical researcher C. J. Ducasse criticized Tyrrell's philosophical speculations quite strongly, pointing out that belief in the supernatural had always characterized human evolution.   LESLIE PRICE

Sources W. H. Salter, 'G. N. M. Tyrrell and his contributions to psychical research', *Journal of the Society of Psychical Research*, 37 (March 1953), 67–71 [with notes from G. W. Fisk (experimental work) and H. H. Price (theoretical and philosophical aspects)] · C. Sitwell, *Light*, 72 (Dec 1952) · C. A. L. Brownlow, 'Former president of S.P.R. passes', *Psychic News* (8 Nov 1952) [an appreciation of Tyrrell and his work] · b. cert. · m. cert. · d. cert. · *Biographical dictionary of parapsychology* (New York, 1964) · C. J. Ducasse, review of *The nature of human personality, Journal of Parapsychology*, 19 (1955)
Archives Duke U., Perkins L., parapsychology laboratory records, corresp. with Dr J. B. Rhine, Box 90185
Wealth at death £12,039 12s. 10d.: probate, 23 Jan 1953, *CGPLA Eng. & Wales*

Tyrrell, Sir James. *See* Tyrell, Sir James (*c*.1455–1502).

Tyrrell, James (1642–1718), political theorist and historian, was born on 5 May 1642 in Great Queen Street in the parish of St Giles-in-the-Fields, London, the eldest son of Sir Timothy Tyrrell of Shotover House near Oxford and of Elizabeth, daughter of James Ussher, archbishop of Armagh. His father was governor of Cardiff in the civil war, and his sister married Philip Hoby of Neath, son of a parliamentarian MP. The deist Charles *Blount was another brother-in-law. Tyrrell was educated at a school in Camberwell, then at Gray's Inn, where he was admitted on 7 January 1656, then at Queen's College, Oxford, whence he matriculated on 15 January 1657 and graduated MA in 1663, and finally at the Inner Temple, where he was called to the bar in 1666. He did not practise and lived off his family estate, supplemented by the profits of authorship. He went to live at Oakley, Buckinghamshire, upon his marriage in 1670 to Mary (1645–1687), daughter of Sir Michael Hutchinson of Fladbury in Worcestershire, and he served as JP and deputy lieutenant for the county of Buckinghamshire. Later he sold Oakley and moved back to Shotover to be near to the libraries in Oxford. His earliest literary venture was impeccably royalist: an edition of Ussher's *The Power Communicated by God to the Prince* (1661), prefaced by Bishop Robert Sanderson. Later he helped Richard Parr with his *Life of Ussher* (1686), contributing an appendix vindicating Ussher's churchmanship against the Laudian Peter Heylin. He visited Ireland in 1670 and 1672, and wrote an essay 'Of the Irish'.

Tyrrell was one of the closest friends of the philosopher John Locke. They met at Oxford in 1658. Sixty-seven letters between them survive, from 1677 to 1704; in these, Tyrrell took the nickname Musidore and Locke Carmelin. The relationship waxed until 1683, but was sometimes tense thereafter. Tyrrell is the source, in the margin of his copy of Locke's *Essay Concerning Human Understanding* (now in the British Library), for the often-quoted account of the origin of Locke's philosophical investigations in a discussion 'in winter 1673 as I remember being myself one of those that met there [in Locke's room] when the discourse began about the principles of morality and revealed religion'.

About 1680 a trio of authors, Tyrrell, Locke, and Algernon Sidney, wrote major works of political theory in answer to Sir Robert Filmer's defence of divine right monarchy, *Patriarcha*. Only Tyrrell's *Patriarcha non monarcha* (1681) was published at the time, anonymously. He exchanged views on Filmer with the whig lawyer William Petyt in 1680, and left to Petyt the legal-historical side of the refutation of Filmer. Like Locke, Tyrrell attacked the idea of Adam's sovereign rights as husband, father, and monarch. The Jacobite Thomas Hearne later said Tyrrell had 'shamefully deserted those good [monarchist] principles and taken up with those that are for deposing kings and taking up arms in rebellion against them' (*Remarks*). However, Tyrrell strove to distinguish his doctrine from Milton's defence of regicide and from a democratic licence for the rabble. The extent to which Locke used and modified Tyrrell's doctrines in his own *Two Treatises of Government* is a topic of debate among scholars. When Locke's book appeared in 1689 Tyrrell was the only living author named in it, and some Oxonians thought Tyrrell was the author of it.

Between 1680 and 1683 Locke frequently stayed with Tyrrell at Shotover, and stored books and papers there for safety when he fled to the Netherlands; a government spy reported on the two men as suspicious. Together they wrote a defence of liberty of conscience against Edward Stillingfleet's *Unreasonableness of Separation*, which has never been published. In 1687 Tyrrell urged Locke to publish it as an encouragement to parliament to enact toleration. This was in the reign of James II, and Tyrrell partially supported James's religious policy, if only because it offended 'the High Church men' (*Correspondence of John Locke*, 3.191). Locke was furious at Tyrrell's attempt to secure a pardon for him to return to England from exile. After the revolution of 1688–9 Tyrrell served as Locke's eyes and ears in Oxford. He reported the university's anger at the doctrines contained in Locke's *Essay Concerning Human Understanding*, and he was present (with John Toland) in the university church on 31 January 1695 at the first public attack on the *Two Treatises*. At the close of Locke's life Tyrrell arranged donations of Locke's books to the Bodleian Library. He also probably wrote the obituary of Locke which appeared in 1705 in Jeremy Collier's supplement to Louis Moreri's *Great Historical Dictionary*.

Tyrrell's literary work intensified in the 1690s. He produced an abridged translation of Richard Cumberland's *De legibus naturae* (1672), in order to vindicate the law of nature against Hobbism (*A Brief Disquisition on the Law of Nature*, 1692). His preface drew upon Locke's unpublished 'Essays on the law of nature', and locates Locke in the modern school of natural jurisprudence inaugurated by

Hugo Grotius; he sees this tradition as an instrument against Hobbist Epicureanism. Tyrrell's central axiom is that natural law is reducible to the duty to seek the common good of rational beings. His lengthy preface points towards two strands in eighteenth-century ethical thought: the hyper-rationalist insistence that morality can be reduced to mathematical propositions, and the modernized Stoicism which sought to show that morality was in harmony with both natural sociability and with the pattern of the divinely created universe.

Tyrrell next produced a thousand-page compendium of whig political doctrine, *Bibliotheca politica* (thirteen dialogues appeared during 1692–4; a fourteenth in 1702; further editions in 1701, 1718, 1727). It was a handbook of whig thought in defence of the 'late, wonderful and happy Revolution'. Copies were sent to Locke. Tyrrell attacked absolutism, defended mixed monarchy, refuted Filmer and the tory historian Robert Brady, publicized Locke's *Two Treatises*, and expounded the 'Ancient Constitution', dwelling especially on the longevity of the House of Commons since the Saxon Witengemote. He also took up the topics of trust, conquest, the meaning of St Paul's injunction to obey 'the powers that be', and the nature of oriental and European polities. The defence of the English ancient constitution also became the main theme of Tyrrell's *The General History of England*, which appeared in three volumes between 1697 and 1704, dedicated to the earl of Pembroke, and was a project apparently encouraged by William Temple. Tyrrell reached no further than Richard II. The book is largely a chronicle and catalogue of quotations, accompanied by interpretative essays, and represents a prolix refutation of Brady's case for the medieval, feudal origins of the Commons. Hearne thought Tyrrell industrious but lacking in judgement and 'tied to a party' (*Remarks*, 7.19). But Locke recommended it, along with *Patriarcha non monarcha* and *Bibliotheca politica*, in 'Some thoughts concerning reading and study for a gentleman' (1703). Tyrrell's *History* had some éclat within the eighteenth-century cult of Saxon liberty, and there were copies in colonial American libraries.

In later years Tyrrell published a further handful of tracts. These probably included *His Majesty's Government Vindicated* (1716), against George Harbin's Jacobite *Hereditary Right of the Crown of England* (1713). He hoped the Hanoverian regime would make him keeper of the records in the Tower. About 1697 the earl of Pembroke had secured for him a post in the office of the privy seal. On visits to Oxford he sparred with Hearne, who has many comments on him. In 1717 he built a Gothic temple in his park, perhaps the first intimation of the Gothic revival in England. Tyrrell died at Shotover on 7 June 1718 and was buried at Oakley church. His grandiloquent monument in the church trumpets his literary achievements: 'History of England, Political Discourses, Law of Nature, Hobbs confuted, &c &c &c'. He was, it declares, 'a man of rare integrity and gravity and wisdom [who] had never polished himself out of his sincerity, nor refined his behaviour to the prejudice of his virtue'. He left two children, James,

who became a lieutenant-general in the army and was MP for Boroughbridge from 1722 until his death in 1742, and Mary, who married Jonathan Aldworth of Ruscomb.

MARK GOLDIE

Sources J. W. Gough, 'James Tyrrell, whig historian, and friend of John Locke', *HJ*, 19 (1976), 581–610 · *The correspondence of John Locke*, ed. E. S. De Beer (1976–89) · *Remarks and collections of Thomas Hearne*, ed. C. E. Doble and others, 11 vols., OHS, 2, 7, 13, 34, 42–3, 48, 50, 65, 67, 72 (1885–1921) · Foster, *Alum. Oxon.* · Wood, *Ath. Oxon.*, new edn · D. Wootton, introduction, in J. Locke, *Political writings* (1993) · M. Goldie, 'John Locke's circle and James II', *HJ*, 35 (1992), 557–86 · J. G. A. Pocock, *The ancient constitution and the feudal law* (1987) · J. H. Franklin, *John Locke and the theory of sovereignty* (1978) · M. S. Zook, *Radical whigs and conspiratorial politics in late Stuart England* (1999) · R. J. Smith, *The Gothic bequest: medieval institutions in British thought, 1688–1863* (1987) · *Biographia Britannica, or, The lives of the most eminent persons who have flourished in Great Britain and Ireland*, 6 (1763) · J. Locke, *An essay concerning humane understanding* (1690) [annotated copy in BL]

Archives Bodl. Oxf., corresp. with J. Locke, MSS Lovelace (Locke) · Wellcome L., medical receipts

Tyrrell, Robert Yelverton (1844–1914), classical scholar, the fifth and youngest son of the Revd Henry Tyrrell, and his wife, Elizabeth Shea, was born on 21 January 1844, at Ballingarry, co. Tipperary, of which his father was vicar. He was a first cousin of George *Tyrrell, the modernist. Except for six weeks at a private school in Hume Street, Dublin, he received his education at home, where he was taught by his elder brothers. He entered Trinity College, Dublin, at the age of sixteen, carrying off the entrance prizes in classical composition. He obtained a classical scholarship in 1861 in his first year—until that date an unheard-of feat for a first-year man who was only seventeen. He graduated with a double first class in classics and logic in 1864, and obtained a fellowship in 1868 through particularly brilliant answering in classics. In 1871 he was elected professor of Latin, in 1880 regius professor of Greek, in 1899 public orator, in 1900 professor of ancient history, and in 1904 senior fellow and registrar of the college. In 1901 he was chosen as one of the first fifty members of the British Academy. In 1874 he married Ada, eldest daughter of Dr George Ferdinand Shaw, senior fellow of Trinity College, Dublin; they had three sons and three daughters. He died in Dublin on 19 September 1914 after a protracted illness.

Tyrrell produced critical editions of Sophocles (1897) and Terence (1902), and of various individual Greek and Latin plays, but his principal work was *The Correspondence of Cicero* (1879–1900), an extensive commentary in seven volumes, produced mainly in collaboration with Dr (later Professor) L. C. *Purser. He also published his Percy Turnbull lectures, delivered at Johns Hopkins University in 1893, under the title *Latin Poetry*, and a volume of *Essays on Greek Literature* (1909). Tyrrell was for many years editor of the Trinity College miscellany called *Kottabos*, to which he himself was the most brilliant and inspiring contributor; another was one of his ablest classical pupils, Oscar Wilde. It had only a short life after he resigned the editorship. He was one of the founders in 1874 of *Hermathena*, to which he remained a constant contributor to the end of his life.

Tyrrell was particularly admired by his contemporaries

for the elegance of his translations from and into Greek and Latin. He was a stimulating lecturer, with an extensive knowledge of English as well as classical literature. With his colleague, the ancient historian J. P. Mahaffy, he was influential among the younger fellows of the college as a teacher and conversationalist; and as one who took a keen interest in many forms of sport.

L. C. Purser, *rev.* Richard Smail

Sources *The Times* (21 Sept 1914) · *Hermathena*, 18 (1914–19), v–xvi · L. C. Purser, 'Robert Yelverton Tyrrell, 1844–1914', *PBA*, [7] (1915–16), 533–9 · R. B. McDowell and D. A. Webb, *Trinity College, Dublin, 1592–1952: an academic history* (1982)
Likenesses A. A. Wolmark, oils, 1907, TCD
Wealth at death £1705: probate, 10 Dec 1914, *CGPLA Ire.*

Tyrrell, Sir Thomas (1593/4–1672), judge and politician, was the third son of Sir Edward Tyrrell (d. 1606) of Thornton, Buckinghamshire, but the second son of Sir Edward and his second wife, Margaret (d. 1632), daughter of John Aston of Aston, Cheshire, and widow of Thomas Egerton. He entered the Inner Temple in 1612, being called to the bar on 13 November 1621.

Before about 1627, when his second son and heir was born, Tyrrell had married Frances (d. 1653), daughter of Thomas Saunders of Long Marston, Hertfordshire, and the widow of Richard Grenville (d. 1618) of Wotton Underwood, Buckinghamshire. They had two sons and two daughters. Tyrrell was very active in support of the parliamentary cause in the civil war, assisting John Hampden in raising forces in Buckinghamshire and serving as a colonel under the earl of Essex. His value to the parliamentarian cause was described by Sir Samuel Luke in October 1644 when he urged that Tyrrell be added to the county committee: 'it will be a great satisfaction to the gentry hereabouts, he being allied to most of them, and a man of good estate and of able parts' (*Letter Books of Sir Samuel Luke*, 47). He stood for parliament at the recruiter election in 1645, but failed to win a seat. He served on numerous local committees until 1649, but thereafter remained aloof from the regime until he served as custos of Buckinghamshire in 1654. On 14 February 1655 Tyrrell married Jane, the widow of Francis Windebank, governor of Bletchington House, Oxfordshire. They had no children. Only in 1659 did he return fully to public affairs, being elected to parliament for Aylesbury, becoming a serjeant-at-law on 16 June, and serving between June and October as a commissioner of the great seal. He served as a councillor of state (2 January – 25 February 1660), and was reappointed a commissioner of the great seal between January and May 1660.

Tyrrell was elected to the Convention for Buckinghamshire on 11 April 1660, but he had to resign his seat on 27 July, having been appointed a judge in the court of common pleas. Also in July he was again made a serjeant-at-law, and on 16th he was knighted. He was appointed to the commission of oyer and terminer in October 1660 charged with trying the regicides. On 28 August 1662 Tyrrell married Bridget (d. 1685), daughter of Sir Edward Harrington, second baronet, of Ridlington, Rutland, and widow of Sir John Gore of Gilston, Hertfordshire. Tyrrell's other

legal actions included the conference of judges held at Serjeants' Inn on 28 April 1666 to discuss the legal ramifications of Lord Morley's case. He was also named to the court set up to adjudicate between the claims consequent upon the fire of London.

Tyrrell died in office on 8 March 1672, aged seventy-eight, and was buried on the 16th at Castle Thorpe, Buckinghamshire, where a monument was erected to his memory. He was succeeded by his second son, Peter, who had been created a baronet in 1665, Tyrrell having disinherited his eldest son.   Stuart Handley

Sources HoP, *Commons, 1660–90* · Baker, *Serjeants* · Sainty, *Judges* · G. Lipscomb, *The history and antiquities of the county of Buckingham*, 4 vols. (1831–47), vol. 1, p. 600; vol. 3, p. 119; vol. 4, pp. 89–92 · Foss, *Judges*, 7.184–7 · *State trials*, 5.986 · *The letter books of Sir Samuel Luke, 1644–45*, ed. H. G. Tibbutt, Bedfordshire Historical RS, 42 (1963), 47, 57, 276 · A. M. Burke, ed., *Memorials of St Margaret's Church, Westminster* (1914), 367 · *The diary of Bulstrode Whitelocke, 1605–1675*, ed. R. Spalding, British Academy, Records of Social and Economic History, new ser., 13 (1990), 131, 178, 180, 503, 518, 520, 562, 610 · will, PRO, PROB 11/381, sig. 144 [wife, Bridget Gore]
Likenesses J. M. Wright, oils, *c.*1650–1660, Inner Temple, London

Tyrrell, William George, Baron Tyrrell (1866–1947), diplomatist, was born at Naini Tal, India, on 17 August 1866, the son of William Henry Tyrrell (d. 1895), later a judge of the high court of judicature, North-Western Provinces of India, and his wife, Julia (d. 1892), daughter of Lieutenant-Colonel John Howard Wakefield of the East India Company. His mother's sister married Prince Radolin, who was later the German ambassador at Paris at the outbreak of the First World War. Another uncle was Robert Yelveston Tyrrell, regius professor of Greek at Trinity College, Dublin, and the Revd George Tyrrell, excommunicated Roman Catholic priest, was a cousin. Tyrrell was educated at the University of Bonn, through the auspices of Prince Radolin, before going up to Balliol College, Oxford, in 1885, where he coxed one of the college boats. He received a third class in moderations (1887) but never completed his degree (though he was later made an honorary fellow of Balliol) before passing the examination for the Foreign Office in April 1889. On 22 April 1891 he married a fellow Roman Catholic, Margaret Ann (d. 1939), daughter of David *Urquhart of Braelangwell, Ross-shire, diplomatist and writer, and his wife, Harriet Angelina Fortescue, sister of Thomas Fortescue, first Baron Clermont. They had two sons and two daughters.

Tyrrell was private secretary (1896–1903) to Sir Thomas Sanderson, the permanent under-secretary, and then secretary to the committee of imperial defence (1903–4). He was promoted to assistant clerk in April 1903 and served as acting second secretary at Rome during 1904, his only foreign posting prior to his appointment as ambassador to France in 1928. Soon after his return to London a new Liberal government was formed and the new foreign secretary, Sir Edward Grey, chose Tyrrell as his précis writer, an event which proved to be the beginning of an important relationship. In May 1907 Tyrrell was promoted to senior

William George Tyrrell, Baron Tyrrell (1866–1947), by Lafayette, 1928

clerk and was appointed Grey's private secretary, a position which he held for eight critical years, becoming Grey's closest confidant. Tyrrell emerged as a figure of great influence behind the scenes of diplomacy, and would remain so almost until the end of his life. He could be a dangerous and unforgiving adversary. He did not get on with Sir Arthur Nicolson when the latter was made permanent under-secretary in November 1910, and their relationship bordered on enmity, with Tyrrell using his influence with Grey to push for Nicolson's retirement. Later Tyrrell would use his influence to have Nicolson's diplomat son, Harold, with whom he also did not get on, posted to an undesired stint in Persia.

Fluent in German and with a wide social and family network in Germany, Tyrrell none the less was one of a group of Foreign Office officials who, before 1914, warned of the growing threat from Germany, although by the eve of the final crisis he had adopted a more ameliorative view. He was equally concerned about any further expansion of Russian power and he subsequently advocated a robust policy against Bolshevism. In November 1913 Grey sent him to Washington as his personal representative to discuss matters of common interest with the new Wilson administration. His good friend the British ambassador, Cecil Spring-Rice, was very ill and Tyrrell for some weeks effectively ran the embassy. On his return to London he was probably the official closest to Grey during the July crisis and the decision to go to war in 1914.

The death of Tyrrell's younger son, Francis, a lieutenant in the Coldstream Guards, in February 1915 (his elder son Hugo, a naval officer, was killed in action in February 1918), together with the cumulative exhaustion of war work, led to a breakdown, and Tyrrell was given leave from the Foreign Office (1915–16). He returned in 1916 and, in early 1918, he was chosen to head an innovative wartime creation, the political intelligence department, an early experiment in the co-ordination of political intelligence. A magnet for outstanding intellectual ability, it was compared to the 'ministry of all the talents' and played a central role in British planning for the Paris peace conference. Tyrrell was instrumental in protecting this unconventional organization and in seeing that its product reached the highest level. It was a characteristic of his skill that he could usually make his superiors comprehend the work of Foreign Office experts. In October 1918 he was promoted to assistant under-secretary. He accompanied the British delegation to the 1919 Paris peace conference, with the rank of minister-plenipotentiary, and there he was influential in shaping the final settlement. Perhaps because of his friendship with Grey he was not an admirer of Lloyd George or of his followers, and was delighted when he fell from power.

From August 1919 to January 1920 Tyrrell accompanied Lord Grey on his unsuccessful special embassy to Washington to try to convince President Wilson to compromise with his opponents, in order to bring the United States into the League of Nations. When Sir Eyre Crowe became permanent under-secretary in November 1920 Tyrrell was made his deputy, thus forming one of the most successful partnerships in British diplomacy. Although Tyrrell served as principal adviser to the foreign secretary, Lord Curzon, at the Lausanne conference, which negotiated a final settlement with Turkey, he was dissatisfied with Curzon's leadership at the Foreign Office: he saw good relations with France as the cornerstone of British security and was unhappy with Curzon's innate distrust of France. He was also distressed by Curzon's needless harassment of Crowe, his closest friend, with whom he habitually lunched at the Travellers' Club. It is likely that Tyrrell was manoeuvring for Curzon's dismissal and was on the verge of success when the Baldwin government failed to win re-election in December 1923.

When Baldwin resumed office in November 1924, with Austen Chamberlain as foreign secretary, Tyrrell and Crowe were influential in his decision to adopt a more Francophile policy and to reintegrate Germany into international affairs. On Crowe's death, in April 1925, Tyrrell was appointed to succeed him and, together with Austen Chamberlain, he negotiated the Locarno pact, for which Chamberlain was awarded the Nobel peace prize. Tyrrell saw this as the first serious effort since the end of the war to reconstruct Europe; he developed a good working relationship with Chamberlain and influenced his European policy. A proto-European, he was a supporter of Aristide Briand's 1930 proposal for a federal Europe. He also established a close relationship with Baldwin, becoming one of his most trusted advisers and, during Baldwin's second government, spent almost a weekend a month at Chequers. British foreign policy in this period was largely determined by the triangular relationship of Baldwin, Chamberlain, and Tyrrell.

In July 1928 Tyrrell was appointed ambassador to Paris; though he had been rumoured as a possible choice for Berlin just before the First World War, he had not previously actively sought an embassy. The Paris embassy fell vacant with the retirement of Lord Crewe, and Tyrrell, with his usual good sense of timing, got Chamberlain to send him to France as the capstone of his diplomatic career. Despite his lack of experience in embassy work he was a tremendous success; his daughter Harriet's marriage at Notre Dame in April 1930, to Adrian Holman, a second secretary at the embassy, was compared to that of Mary of Scotland to the dauphin. He was undoubtedly delighted to have evaded the succession of foreign secretaries that followed Chamberlain. Positively contemptuous of Sir John Simon, he observed that, while you could load him, he still would not fire. Once, when Simon was visiting Paris and discoursing at length, Tyrrell covered his mouth to stifle a yawn, left the room, and did not return. He was equally disappointed in Ramsay MacDonald, feeling that he and Simon had allowed British credibility to be undermined on the international stage. Tyrrell retired, ostensibly on health grounds, in April 1934.

Tyrrell remained active in retirement. He was soon asked to head an unofficial British committee for relations with other countries, whose purpose was cultural propaganda and which hoped to attract foreign students to Britain. His diversions were golf, bridge, and the cinema, and he was made president of the British Board of Film Censors (1934–47). He also remained influential in foreign policy. He was concerned about the growing menace from Nazi Germany and became associated with the Friends of Europe, which sought to warn and inform the British public of the true meaning of Hitler. On taking leave of George V, having discussed the current state of the world, he replied to the king's observation that he was a pessimist, 'I was a pessimist before the last war, sir' (*The Times*). He despised Neville Chamberlain, deplored his foreign policy, and watched with despair as Britain's credibility fell even further. He had lost none of his taste for behind-the-scenes plotting, and in the spring of 1938 he was quietly advocating that Anthony Eden, Winston Churchill, and some leading Labour figures be brought into the government to prevent Chamberlain doing further damage. He viewed the Munich settlement as only purchasing an armistice from what he termed German gangsters, and he continued to press for better military preparation and conscription.

Tyrrell maintained good relations with several publishers and at times used these connections to promote support for policies he favoured but which were not being wholeheartedly embraced by government. He was friendly with Leo Maxse of the *National Review* and he wrote anonymously several articles for him on foreign affairs. He also knew H. A. Gwynne of the *Morning Post*, who worked with Tyrrell to thwart Curzon's Francophobe policies and in support of a closer relationship with Paris. Tyrrell maintained a wide network of friends and acquaintances that kept him throughout his life at the centre of events. Among his many associations was membership of the Other Club, which had been founded by Churchill and F. E. Smith.

A colleague in the Foreign Office, Owen O'Malley, described Tyrrell as 'a little man as quick as a lizard with scintillating eyes and wit and a great aversion to any work not transacted orally' (O'Malley, 45). Lewis Namier, who served in the political intelligence department, described him thus:

> complex, versatile, talkative, but exceedingly secretive, he was amiable, and even yielding on the surface, but a stubborn fighter underneath. He avoided, if he could, personal collisions, and professed a preference for 'long-range artillery': yet he disliked writing—active and restless, he shunned the drudgery of office drafts, and, cultivating the laziness which Talleyrand enjoined on diplomats, was selective even in his reading of office files. (Namier, 87)

He was noted for his mental nimbleness and quick intelligence. He could be secretive and his method was at times byzantine. He was known to drink heavily, although this had ceased by the time of his Paris embassy. He avoided whenever possible committing his views to paper. Namier recalled one instance of Tyrrell's indolence over office written work:

> An administrative question concerning our department was once submitted to Tyrrell in a long minute on the jacket of its file. Tyrrell, uninterested in the subject, initialled the minute unread. It was returned to him with the remark: 'This matter requires your decision.' Reply: 'I agree, W. T.' The decision was then obtained orally, and the jacket of the file was changed. (ibid.)

Tyrrell was appointed CB (1909), KCMG (1913), KCVO (1919), GCMG (1925), KCB (1927), and GCB (1934); he was sworn of the privy council (1928) and created Baron Tyrrell of Avon (1929). He was also awarded the cordon of the Légion d'honneur (1934). He died of bronchial pneumonia at his home, Chesham House, Chesham Place, London, on 14 March 1947. A requiem mass was held at the Brompton Oratory. He was survived by his daughter Harriet, his elder daughter, Margaret, having died in 1925 and his wife in 1939. ERIK GOLDSTEIN

Sources *DNB* · PRO, Foreign Office papers, FO 371 · PRO, Lord Tyrrell papers, FO 800/220 · private information (2004) [Sir Frank Roberts] · Z. S. Steiner, *The foreign office and foreign policy, 1898–1914* (1969) · CUL, Hardinge of Penshurst MSS · T. Hohler, *Diplomatic petrel* (1942) · D. Kelly, *The ruling few, or, The human background to diplomacy* (1952) · O. O'Malley, *The phantom caravan* (1954) · L. B. Namier, *Avenues of history* (1952) · *The memoirs of Lord Gladwyn* (1972) · K. M. Wilson, *A study in the history and politics of the Morning Post, 1905–1926* (1990) · Viscount Grey of Fallodon [E. Grey], *Twenty-five years, 1892–1916*, 1 (1925) · Prince Linchowsky, *Heading for the abyss* (1928) · CUL, Baldwin of Bewdley papers · 'Lord Tyrrell', *National Review*, 128 (1947), 258–9 · J. A. Hutcheson, *Leopold Maxse and the National Review, 1893–1914: right-wing politics and journalism in the Edwardian era* (1989) · R. White, '"Through a glass darkly": the foreign office investigation of French federalism, January–May 1930', *Statecraft* *and diplomacy in the twentieth century: essays presented to P. M. H. Bell*, ed. D. Dutton (1995) • *WWW, 1941–50* • Burke, *Peerage* • I. Elliott, ed., *The Balliol College register, 1833–1933*, 2nd edn (privately printed, Oxford, 1934) • *FO List* • *CGPLA Eng. & Wales* (1947) • *The Times* (18 March 1947)

Archives NL Scot., letters • PRO, papers, FO 800/220 | Balliol Oxf., letters to Sir Louis Mallet • Bodl. Oxf., letters to J. Bryce • Bodl. Oxf., letters to Lady Milner • Bodl. Oxf., corresp. with Lord Ponsonby of Shulbrede • Bodl. Oxf., corresp. with Sir H. Rumbold • Bodl. Oxf., corresp. with Lord Simon • CAC Cam., corresp. with Lord Lloyd • CAC Cam., corresp. with Sir E. Phipps • CAC Cam., corresp. with Sir Edward Speers • CAC Cam., corresp. with Sir C. Spring-Rice • CUL, Baldwin of Bewdley papers • CUL, corresp. with Lord Hardinge of Penshurst • Cumbria AS, Carlisle, letters to Lord Howard of Penrith • Lpool RO, corresp. with earl of Derby • NL Scot., Elibank MS • NL Scot., letters to Lord Haldane • PRO, corresp. with Sir Charles Mendl, FO 800/220 | FILM BFI NFTVA, news footage

Likenesses W. Stoneman, photograph, 1918, NPG • Lafayette, photograph, 1928, NPG [*see illus.*] • P. de Laszlo, oils, 1931, Balliol Oxf.

Wealth at death £9784 0s. 9d.: probate, 26 July 1947, *CGPLA Eng. & Wales*

Tyrwhit [*née* Oxenbridge], **Elizabeth**, **Lady Tyrwhit** (d. 1578), author and courtier, was born at Forde Place, Brede, Sussex, one of five children of Sir Goddard Oxenbridge (d. 1531) and his second wife, Anne (d. 1531), daughter of Sir Thomas Fiennes, son of Richard, Lord Dacre of Herstmonceux. From her father's first marriage, to Elizabeth, younger daughter and coheir to Sir Thomas Etchingham, Elizabeth had a half-brother, Thomas, and half-sister, Elizabeth. Elizabeth Oxenbridge married Sir Robert Tyrwhit (d. 1572) of Leighton Bromswold, Huntingdonshire, second son of Sir Robert Tyrwhit of Kettleby, Lincolnshire, and his wife, Maude, daughter of Sir Robert Taylboys, between March 1538 and August 1539. (Tyrwhit needs to be distinguished from her half-sister who also married a Robert Tyrwhit.) Elizabeth and Sir Robert had a daughter, Katherine, who married Sir Henry D'Arcy and died in 1567.

Tyrwhit's early career took place at the court of Henry VIII, where she appears in household records from 1537 on as a recipient of gifts and as a gentlewoman of the privy chamber. Her relationship with Katherine Parr was especially close, possibly because Parr was cousin by marriage to Sir Robert Tyrwhit through her own first marriage to Edward, Lord Borough. Tyrwhit shared Parr's protestant sympathies and, with others of Parr's ladies-in-waiting suspected of links to the martyr Anne Askew, was arrested by Henry in 1546. When Katherine Parr died of puerperal fever in September 1548, Tyrwhit was at her bedside. For a brief period in 1549, after the scandal surrounding the relationship between Parr's last husband, Thomas Seymour, and Princess Elizabeth in 1547–8, Tyrwhit was appointed governess to the princess in lieu of the suspect Katherine Ashley.

In recognition of her ardently Reformist leanings, Tyrwhit's husband noted that 'my wyffe is not sayne in Dyvinity, but is half a Scripture woman' (Haynes, *Collection of State Papers*, 104). Both her own work and the dedication

to her by John Feilde, rector of St Giles Cripplegate, London, of his translation of Jean de l'Espine's *Excellent Treatise of Christian Righteousness* (T. Vautrollier, 1577) support this view of her religious opinions. Tyrwhit's book, *Morning and Evening Praiers, with Divers Psalmes Himnes and Meditations* (1574), contains orders for private morning and evening prayers, with a series of 'godly prayers' and hymns appended, and appears in a unique copy held in the British Library. Another version appears in 'The second lampe' of Thomas Bentley's *Monument of Matrones* (1582). It differs substantially from the original, however, for Bentley changes not only structure, but also content and tone, by amalgamating some prayers, inserting others by different authors, and deleting some of Tyrwhit's altogether.

Of considerable interest is the volume in which Tyrwhit's original text appears, largely because a handwritten note on the flyleaf indicates that it belonged to Elizabeth I. Along with Tyrwhit's work, it contains the litany and an incomplete copy of *The Queen's Prayers* by Katherine Parr. The book's binding in enamelled gold depicts Moses raising the serpent and the judgment of Solomon on front and back covers, respectively. The former is surrounded by the phrase, 'Make the afyrye serpent an settt [*sic*] up for a sygne that as many as are bytte maye loke upon it an lyve', while the border around the latter states, 'Then the kyng ansvered an sayd gyve her the lyvyng child an slaye [it] not for she is the mother thereof.'

Tyrwhit died at her home in St John's Lane, Clerkenwell, Middlesex, and her will, dated 1577, was proved on 28 April 1578. An effigy of Elizabeth, along with those of her husband and daughter, can be found in the church of St Mary, Leighton Bromswold. PATRICIA BRACE

Sources W. D. Cooper, 'The families of Braose of Chesworth and Hoo', *Sussex Archaeological Collections*, 8 (1856), 97–131 • W. D. Cooper, 'Notices of Winchelsea in and after the fifteenth century', *Sussex Archaeological Collections*, 8 (1856), 201–34 • *CSP dom., 1547–80* • *LP Henry VIII* • M. St C. Byrne, ed., *The Lisle letters*, 6 vols. (1981) • *Notices and remains of the family of Tyrwhitt* (1872) • R. F. Hunnisett, *Sussex coroners' inquests, 1485–1558* (1985) • W. Page, *History of the county of Huntingdon* (1932) • P. W. Hill, *Illustrated guide to the church of St George's, Brede* (1964) • *A collection of state papers … left by William Cecill, Lord Burghley*, ed. S. Haynes, 1 (1740)

Likenesses effigy, after 1578, church of St Mary, Leighton Bromswold, Huntingdonshire

Wealth at death bequests: will

Tyrwhitt, Dame Mary Joan Caroline [*known as* Bovvy Tyrwhitt] (**1903–1997**), army officer, was born in Dublin on 27 December 1903, the oldest child in a family of two daughters and one son of Sir Reginald Yorke *Tyrwhitt, first baronet (1870–1951), admiral of the fleet, and his wife, Sarah Angela Mary Margaret (d. 1958), daughter of Matthew Corbally, of Rathbeale Hall, Swords, co. Dublin. Her brother, Admiral Sir St John Reginald Joseph Tyrwhitt, second baronet (1905–1961), was a Second World War destroyer commander, and second sea lord from 1959 to 1961. Bovvy Tyrwhitt was educated at the Sacred Heart Convent, Tunbridge Wells, and the Loreto convent in Gibraltar (1919–21).

Dame Mary Joan Caroline Tyrwhitt (1903–1997), by Elliott & Fry, 1951

Tyrwhitt's father was commander of the celebrated Harwich force of cruisers and destroyers during the First World War. After the armistice, at the age of fourteen, she stood watching on 20 November 1918 as her father escorted 129 surrendered German submarines into Harwich. Thereafter she accompanied her parents to Gibraltar. 'I never did any work after school in the local convent during the mornings,' she recalled, 'and so I hunted, rowed, swam and played tennis and had a jolly good time' (Terry, 89). From Gibraltar the Tyrwhitts moved to Malta, then to Scotland, and after that to Hong Kong before eventually returning to London and Admiralty House. It was all good experience for Mary Tyrwhitt, who kept herself busy as a Girl Guide leader.

Tyrwhitt's enlistment in the Auxiliary Territorial Service (ATS) was by coincidence rather than by design. She was living with her parents at Hawkhurst, Kent, when a friend asked whether she would be interested in raising an ATS platoon. 'Thank you, I'd love to', she replied, and she enrolled on 11 November 1938, two months after the ATS was established on 9 September (Terry, 97). She then set about finding twenty-three young women volunteers at Cranbrook and the platoon was affiliated to the Royal East Kent regiment (the Buffs).

When war broke out on 3 September 1939 Tyrwhitt was at the foot of Ben Nevis enjoying a walking holiday in Scotland with a friend. She hurried back to London and a week later received orders to report with her platoon to Chatham. On pay of 9s. 4d. a week she took charge of general

duties personnel and in 1940 was appointed company commander (equivalent to a captain in the army) in charge of cooks, clerks, and orderlies. Her outstanding ability marked her out for rapid promotion and she was selected to help devise a syllabus for training ATS officers. After attending a course for junior officers at the school of military administration in the New Forest, she and three other officers were posted to the War Office at Cheltenham, where they settled down to prepare a training programme. By October 1940 her team was installed at Aldermaston, ready to receive the first course of junior officers.

'We had never done any instructing before and it was a case of the blind leading the blind', she admitted.

> We had about 40 girls on that first course and in the middle of it came the most awful weather—deep snow at the beginning of November. The student officers were in new huts with very little protection and they had to walk miles for their baths and the water froze. (Terry, 138)

When the emphasis shifted to training NCOs, Tyrwhitt was posted as chief instructor to the NCOs' school, Lichfield, at the depot of the South Staffordshires. In the spring of 1942 she was transferred with the rank of chief commander (lieutenant-colonel) to command the junior officers' school at the Royal Holloway College, Egham.

After senior appointments on the staff and on regimental duty, Tyrwhitt became deputy director ATS as a controller (colonel) and on 4 May 1946 she succeeded Dame Leslie Whateley as director, with the rank of senior controller (brigadier). Her principal objective was to put forward a plan of action to transform the ATS into a permanent force. Although there was no denying that the ATS had made a valuable contribution during the war, there was considerable doubt among senior male officers whether a women's corps was a necessary part of the peacetime British army. Tyrwhitt was forthright in expressing her view that women could and should continue to play an important military role and she fought hard to enhance the status of the corps.

One of Tyrwhitt's first tasks was to bring the ATS in line with the regular army, and she established a policy committee to investigate all the matters which would have to be put before the army council, including the establishment of a penal code for ATS personnel, which was eventually approved. Two other aspects of the reorganization were the ranks held by the ATS and the recognition by the male army that ATS officers should be saluted. Tyrwhitt was adamant that her officers should have the same ranks as the men. 'You must be mad. They'll never do it!', Air-Commandant Felicity Hanbury, director of the Women's Auxiliary Air Force, exclaimed (Terry, 173). Tyrwhitt's stubbornness was rewarded in 1949 barely a month after the ATS became the Women's Royal Army Corps (WRAC) on 1 February. The Women's Royal Air Force, which succeeded the WAAF, only achieved rank parity in 1968. Later, she recalled how she had achieved this significant breakthrough for servicewomen. She was invited to an interview with the chief of the Imperial General Staff, Field

Marshal Viscount Slim, who had succeeded Lord Montgomery in 1948.

> He was my pin-up soldier of the war but, more important, he was a man you could talk to. As I sat in his office he had my memorandum on the ranks and saluting before him. He said that he wanted me to put my case again. 'I know it's been made hundreds of times but I'd like you to present it once more.' I stated it as best I could and he listened patiently. At the end he paused and then said: 'I approve.' And that was the end of that.   (Terry, 174)

Tyrwhitt also ensured that the new uniforms for the WRAC were designed by first-class designers, and eventually the queen's couturier, Norman Hartnell, was chosen to undertake this task.

Tyrwhitt was appointed OBE in 1946 and DBE in 1949. She was awarded the territorial decoration in 1950. She held the appointment of honorary aide-de-camp to George VI from 1949 to 1950. She retired in 1950 after serving the army for twelve years. After her retirement she remained a member of the WRAC council for three years, and also joined the Women's Royal Voluntary Service, of which she was assistant regional administrator in the southern region until 1965. She maintained a lifelong interest in the WRAC, and in 1988, although eighty-four years old, she became the ATS representative on the committee to arrange its fiftieth anniversary celebrations.

Mary Tyrwhitt was slight in build but a tower of strength in safeguarding the welfare of women in the corps she founded. She was resolute in her belief that women should receive equal treatment, yet modest about her own considerable achievements in ensuring the future of women in the armed forces. She had a great sense of humour and a generous disposition. She never married and lived for many years at Pewsey, Wiltshire. She died at Leamington Spa, Warwickshire, on 13 February 1997.

ROY TERRY

Sources J. M. Cowper, *The auxiliary territorial service* (1949) · R. Terry, *Women in khaki* (1988) · *Daily Telegraph* (18 March 1997) · *The Times* (31 May 1951) · *The Times* (28 Feb 1997) · personal knowledge (2004) · *WWW* · CGPLA Eng. & Wales (1997)
Archives NAM, letters from Mary, countess of Harewood
Likenesses Elliott & Fry, photograph, 1951, NPG [*see illus.*] · photograph, IWM · photograph, repro. in *Daily Telegraph*
Wealth at death £297,100: probate, 2 April 1997, CGPLA Eng. & Wales

Tyrwhitt, Sir Reginald Yorke, first baronet (1870–1951), naval officer, was born in Oxford on 10 May 1870, the fifth son of the Revd Richard St John Tyrwhitt (1827–1895), vicar of St Mary Magdalen, and the fourth with his second wife, Caroline (d. 1883), daughter of John Yorke, of Bewerley Hall, Yorkshire. He entered *Britannia* as a naval cadet in 1883, served in the *Australia* and *Ajax* for the naval manoeuvres of 1889 and 1890 respectively, and in 1892 was promoted lieutenant and appointed to the light cruiser *Cleopatra* on the North America station.

In 1896 Tyrwhitt took over the command of the *Hart*, one of the very early destroyers in the navy, and thus began a long and distinguished association with this class of ship. Towards the end of the year he was appointed first lieutenant in the *Surprise*, the commander-in-chief's yacht

in the Mediterranean, and followed that with a similar post in the *Indefatigable* on the North America station. In 1903 Tyrwhitt married Sarah Angela Mary Margaret (d. 1958), daughter of Matthew Corbally, of Rathbeale Hall, Swords, co. Dublin; they had one son and two daughters. That year, he was promoted commander and appointed to the *Aurora*, tender to the *Britannia* at Dartmouth. He commanded the destroyer *Waveney* (1904–5) and the scouts *Attentive* (1906) and *Skirmisher* (1907).

In June 1908 Tyrwhitt was promoted captain and, with a long record of destroyer command behind him, was selected in August to command the *Topaze* as captain (D) of the fourth destroyer flotilla at Portsmouth. After holding that command for two years he was made flag captain to Sir Douglas Gamble on the Mediterranean station, commanding successively the *Bacchante* and the *Good Hope*. In 1912 he returned home to command the *Bellona* as captain (D) of the second destroyer flotilla of the Home Fleet, and in 1914 was promoted commodore (T) being then in charge of all destroyer flotillas in the fleet. In addition to his main interest in destroyer tactics, Tyrwhitt was a strong supporter of the introduction of flying in the navy and his encouragement was a considerable factor in the formation of the Royal Naval Air Service.

At the outbreak of the First World War Tyrwhitt was at Harwich, flying his broad pennant in the light cruiser *Amethyst*, with the first and third destroyer flotillas in company. As commodore—and from 1918 rear-admiral—Harwich force, he served throughout the whole war in that single appointment, an indication of the Admiralty's high appreciation of the skill and leadership with which he led the force throughout the strenuous operations in which it was engaged.

It was as a war leader that Tyrwhitt really blossomed. He had in abundance the four 'aces' which make the great commander: a gift for leadership, a fertile imagination and a creative brain, an eagerness to make full use of the brains and ideas of juniors, and an offensive spirit. His were the first ships to be in action in the war when they sank the German mine-layer *Königin Luise* off the Thames estuary on 5 August 1914. Twenty-three days later the Harwich force was engaged in the Heligoland bight action, an operation jointly planned by Tyrwhitt and Roger Keyes, commanding the British submarine flotillas. Three German cruisers were sunk in the engagement, and although Tyrwhitt's ship, the *Arethusa*, was severely damaged in the action she returned safely to Sheerness where, Tyrwhitt recorded, Winston Churchill 'fairly slobbered over me'. He was created CB.

There followed the German battle cruiser raid on Scarborough and Hartlepool on 16 December 1914 when, although the sea was too rough for his destroyers, Tyrwhitt was at sea with his light cruisers and only just failed to make contact with the enemy ships. He commanded the covering force in the Heligoland bight for the naval seaplane raid on the Zeppelin sheds at Cuxhaven on 25 December 1914, and in January 1915 his Harwich force played a notable part in conjunction with the battle cruisers of Sir David Beatty at the battle of the Dogger Bank.

On intercepting the 'enemy sighted' signal on 31 May 1916 which heralded the battle of Jutland, Tyrwhitt put to sea with the Harwich force only to be recalled by signal from the Admiralty. Eventually he was permitted to sail, but arrived on the scene too late to take any part in the action. In the German fleet operation of 19 August 1916, which was to be a bombardment of Sunderland, the ships of the Harwich force were the only British vessels to sight the German fleet. Scheer, the German commander-in-chief, ordered a withdrawal before the bombardment could take place and it was as the enemy retired that Tyrwhitt sighted them. He was in chase until nightfall, but as his only chance of making an attack on them would be after the moon had risen, he was forced to draw off before bringing them to action. In uninformed circles Tyrwhitt was later criticized for failing to press an attack home, but virtual suicide was no part of his plan and his action in withdrawing was upheld by both Sir John Jellicoe and the Admiralty.

In 1917 and 1918 the Harwich force engaged in several small-scale actions, mainly off the Dutch coast or in co-operation with the destroyers of the Dover patrol, and as the covering force for naval air attacks on enemy installations. After the armistice it was Tyrwhitt's Harwich force which accepted the surrender of the German U-boats.

Tyrwhitt was appointed to the DSO in 1916 and in 1917 promoted KCB. He was created a baronet in 1919 and granted £10,000 by parliament for his services during the war. He received many foreign decorations and an honorary degree of DCL from Oxford (1919).

After the war Tyrwhitt was appointed senior officer at Gibraltar and in 1921 he returned to sea as flag officer commanding the 3rd light cruiser squadron in the Mediterranean. He was commanding officer, coast of Scotland, and admiral superintendent, Rosyth Dockyard, in 1923–5 and in 1925 was promoted vice-admiral. He was commander-in-chief, China station, from 1927 to 1929, serving there with great tact and distinction during the threat to the international settlement at Shanghai during the Chinese civil war. He was promoted admiral on relinquishing command in China and was also promoted GCB. In 1930–33 he was commander-in-chief at the Nore, becoming first and principal naval aide-de-camp to the king in 1932. In 1934, being the senior admiral on the list, he was promoted admiral of the fleet when a vacancy occurred. During the Second World War, at the age of seventy, he joined the Home Guard in 1940 and for a short time commanded the 3rd Kent battalion.

Tyrwhitt died at Ellenden, Sandhurst, Kent, on 30 May 1951, and was succeeded as second baronet by his son, St John Reginald Joseph (1905–1961), who also entered the navy, becoming second sea lord in 1959. His elder daughter, Mary *Tyrwhitt, retired as director of the Women's Royal Army Corps in 1950.   PETER KEMP, *rev.*

Sources *The Times* (31 May 1951) · *WWW* · *CGPLA Eng. & Wales* (1951)

Archives NRA, papers incl. family letters | FILM BFI NFTVA, news footage · IWM FVA, actuality footage · IWM FVA, documentary footage · IWM FVA, news footage
Likenesses F. Dodd, charcoal and watercolour drawing, 1917, IWM · G. Philpot, oils, 1918, IWM · W. Stoneman, two photographs, 1918, NPG · A. S. Cope, group portrait, oils, 1921 (*Naval officers of World War I, 1914–18*), NPG
Wealth at death £11,562 4s. 9d.: probate, 29 Aug 1951, *CGPLA Eng. & Wales*

Tyrwhitt, Richard St John (1827–1895), writer on art, was born on 19 March 1827 at Essex Street, Temple, London, the eldest son of Robert Philip Tyrwhitt (1798–1886), a Metropolitan Police magistrate and author of several legal works, and his wife, Catherine Wigley, daughter of Henry St John. He matriculated from Christ Church, Oxford, on 15 May 1845, holding a studentship from that year. He graduated BA in 1849 and MA in 1852. He was a tutor from 1852 to 1856, and rhetoric reader in 1856.

Tyrwhitt vacated his studentship following his marriage, on 22 June 1858, to Eliza Ann (*d.* 1859), daughter of John Spencer Stanhope and his wife, Lady Elizabeth. Eliza died on 8 September 1859, two days after giving birth to their son Walter Spencer Stanhope Tyrwhitt, who became a lieutenant in the Warwick militia. Ordained in 1851, from 1858 to 1872 he was vicar of St Mary Magdalen, Oxford, the gift of Christ Church. Shortly after the death of his wife Tyrwhitt set out for Europe and the Holy Land. He travelled through the Alps and on to Cairo, Jerusalem, and Constantinople, and returned to England in June 1860 via Naples and Rome. On 2 January 1861 he married a friend of his first wife: Caroline (*d.* 1883), daughter of John Yorke of Beweley Hall and Halton Place, Yorkshire; they had six children. He exhibited a number of watercolours at the Royal Academy and Suffolk Street Gallery based on this journey. Although a fairly accomplished amateur painter, Tyrwhitt failed in his application for membership of the New Watercolour Society in 1865.

Tyrwhitt was a fervent admirer of and frequent correspondent with John Ruskin, in whose favour he withdrew his candidature for the Slade professorship of fine art in 1869. Ruskin in turn admired Tyrwhitt and contributed the preface to the latter's *Christian Art and Symbolism* (1872). The critic allowed Tyrwhitt to use woodcuts and incorporate text from his own *Elements of Drawing* (1861) in Tyrwhitt's *Our Sketching Club* of 1875. Tyrwhitt published a number of other works relating to art, including *Greek and Gothic: progress and decay in the three acts of architecture, sculpture, and painting* (1881) and *An Amateur Art Book: Lectures* (1886). He also argued for the introduction of art courses at undergraduate level at Oxford and was for many years a member of the committee for the decoration of St Paul's Cathedral. In addition to his writings on art, Tyrwhitt published a number of sermons, theological tracts, and a novel, *Hugh Heron, Ch. Ch.: an Oxford Novel* (1880). He died on 6 December 1895 at his home, 62 Banbury Road, Oxford, of a cerebral haemorrhage.

DEBORAH GRAHAM-VERNON

Sources *The Times* (9 Nov 1895) · R. P. Tyrwhitt, *Notices and remains of the family of Tyrwhitt* (1862) · *The works of John Ruskin*, ed. E. T. Cook and A. Wedderburn, library edn, 39 vols. (1903–12) · T. Hilton, *John*

Ruskin: the later years (2000) · Mallalieu, *Watercolour artists* · *Hist. U. Oxf.* 7: 19th-cent. *Oxf.* pt 2 · m. certs. · d. cert. · J. Foster, *The peerage, baronetage, and knightage of the British empire* [1880–82]
Likenesses L. Carroll [C. L. Dodgson], photograph, *c.*1856, NPG
Wealth at death £34,885 1*s.* 11*d.*: probate, 20 Jan 1896, *CGPLA Eng. & Wales*

Tyrwhitt [Tirwhit], **Sir Robert** (*d.* 1428), justice, was the son of Sir William Tyrwhitt of Kettleby, Lincolnshire, and his wife, the daughter and heir of John Grovall of Harpswell. He was brought up to the law, and appears in chancery records as a JP and commissioner in Lincolnshire and Yorkshire from the early 1390s. He was created a serjeant-at-law in the 'call' of serjeants in 1396 and was appointed a king's serjeant in 1398. From 1398 to 1411 he acted as a justice of assize on the midland circuit. On 9 October 1398 he was one of those who were given power of attorney by Henry, earl of Derby (afterwards Henry IV), on his banishment, and he was also a member of the council of the duchy of Lancaster. On Henry's accession in 1399 Tyrwhitt was reappointed king's serjeant, and in 1403 was required to lend the king £100 to enable him to resist the Welsh and Scottish rebels. As a serjeant, Tyrwhitt was retained by many magnates and institutions, including John, duke of Lancaster, Richard Beauchamp, earl of Warwick, the towns of Beverley and Grimsby, the dean and chapter of Lincoln, and Selby Abbey. On 4 May 1408 he was appointed a justice of king's bench and knighted. From January 1410 until his death he acted as a trier of petitions in parliament.

In 1411 a dispute broke out between Tyrwhitt and the tenants of William, Lord Ros of Helmsley, about a right of pasture at Melton Ross, near Wrawby, Lincolnshire. It was agreed to submit the quarrel to the arbitration of Sir William Gascoigne (*d.* 1419) at Melton Ross; but on the day appointed Tyrwhitt, in spite of his judicial position, appeared at the head of 500 armed men, denied that he had ever agreed to arbitrate, and drove off Lord Ros's adherents. Tyrwhitt was summoned before parliament, where he was made to accept the award of arbitrators nominated by Ros, who determined that he should publicly apologize to Ros, and provide two fat oxen, two tuns of Gascon wine, and twelve fat sheep for consumption by the latter's tenants. Tyrwhitt nevertheless retained his position on the bench. He was, however, transferred as justice of assize from the midland circuit (which included Lincolnshire) to the northern circuit in 1412, possibly as a result of the Ros dispute. At the accession of Henry V and Henry VI he was reappointed justice of king's bench, an office he retained until his death.

Tyrwhitt and his wife, Alice, daughter of Sir Roger Kelk of Kelk, Yorkshire, had two sons: Sir William (*d.* 1451), who fought at Agincourt on 25 October 1415, was thirty years old at his father's death, and succeeded to the Kettleby property; and John (*d.* 1432), who succeeded to his grandmother's estates at Harpswell. They also had three daughters: Catherine, who married Sir John Griffith of Burton Agnes, Yorkshire, and Wichnor, Staffordshire; Maud, who married Sir William Montresor; and Cecilia, who married Sir John Newport.

Tyrwhitt died on 6 January 1428 and was buried in the chancel of Bigby church, Lincolnshire. He left his son Sir William fourteen manors in Lincolnshire, several more manors in other counties, and an inn in London. Sir William's wealth was estimated at £130 per annum in 1436. Tyrwhitt's descendants frequently served as knights of the shire and sheriffs of Lincolnshire. One of them, Sir Robert, was attached to the household of Princess (afterwards Queen) Elizabeth, his wife being her governess. His great-grandson, Sir Philip (*d.* 1624), was created a baronet of the original creation on 29 June 1611; the dignity became extinct on the death of the sixth baronet in 1760.

A. F. POLLARD, rev. EDWARD POWELL

Sources R. P. Tyrwhitt, *Some notices and remains of the family of Tyrwhitt* (1862) · *Chancery records* · C. Rawcliffe, 'Tirwhit, William', HoP, *Commons* · N. L. Ramsay, 'The English legal profession, *c.*1340–1450', PhD diss., U. Cam., 1985, civ–cv · Baker, *Serjeants* · *RotP*, vols. 3–4 · N. H. Nicolas, ed., *Proceedings and ordinances of the privy council of England*, 7 vols., RC, 26 (1834–7), vol. 1 · Rymer, *Foedera*, 2nd edn, 8.49 · J. Fortescue, *The governance of England*, ed. C. Plummer (1885) · J. H. Wylie, *History of England under Henry the Fourth*, 4 vols. (1884–98)
Wealth at death son's income est. at £130 p.a. eight years after father's death: Rawcliffe, 'Tirwhit, William'

Tyrwhitt, Robert (1735–1817), philanthropist, was born in London in January 1735, the younger son of the Revd Robert Tyrwhitt (1698–1742), canon of St Paul's Cathedral, and his wife, Elizabeth, eldest daughter of Edmund *Gibson, bishop of London. His elder brother was the philologist Thomas *Tyrwhitt. No information is available about his education before he entered Jesus College, Cambridge, in 1753. He graduated BA in 1757, and MA in 1760, and in November 1759 he was made a fellow of his college. The fellowship and his family connections indicated that he could expect early promotion in the church 'but his conscience forbade him to make use of such advantages … and he resigned his fellowship and all his expectations from the church on the delicate conviction of his mind' (*GM*). He had been influenced by the writings of Samuel Clarke but he went much further by renouncing most of the articles of the Church of England. From the time, in 1771–2, when he took part in the movement for the abolition of subscription on university graduation he was seen as part of the anti-trinitarian protest, and he associated with people hitherto foreign to him. In 1777 he resigned his fellowship, having ceased to attend the college chapel, but he continued to live in the college. This was at a financial cost but he cheerfully lived on a much reduced income until the death of his brother in 1786 allowed him the pleasure of making generous contributions to a wide range of religious and charitable causes.

In 1784 Tyrwhitt joined the unitarian-backed Society for Promoting the Knowledge of the Scriptures and contributed *Two discourses on the creation of all things by Jesus Christ; and the resurrection of the dead through the man Jesus* to its papers in 1787. This very short work became widely known as a significant expression of unitarian thinking and was often reprinted, even as late as 1844 by the British and Foreign Unitarian Association. Tyrwhitt joined the

Unitarian Society, formed in London in 1791, but withdrew when the word 'idolatrous', as applied to the worship of Jesus, was added to the preamble. From 1808 gout kept him to his rooms but it is claimed that he did not sleep outside the college for at least the last twenty years of his life. He died, unmarried, in his rooms on 25 March 1817; in his will he left £4000 stock in navy annuities to the University of Cambridge to found the Hebrew scholarships that bear his name.

ALEXANDER GORDON, rev. ALAN RUSTON

Sources GM, 1st ser., 87/1 (1817), 285–6 · Venn, Alum. Cant. · IGI · T. Lindsey, An historical view of the state of Unitarian doctrine and worship from the Reformation to our own times (1783), 492–7 · will, PRO, PROB 11/1591, sig. 219 · Monthly Repository, 12 (1817), 316 · Monthly Repository, 14 (1819), 658
Wealth at death £4000 stock in navy annuities to found scholarship: will, 1817, PRO, PROB 11/1591, sig. 219

Tyrwhitt, Thomas (1730–1786), literary editor and critic, was born in London on 27 March 1730, the eldest of four surviving children—all sons—of the Revd Dr Robert Tyrwhitt (1698–1742), rector of St James's, Westminster, and later archdeacon of London and canon of Windsor, and of Elizabeth, eldest daughter of Edmund *Gibson, bishop of London. The philanthropist Robert *Tyrwhitt was his younger brother. At the age of six Tyrwhitt was sent to school in Kensington and in 1741 he moved to Eton College where he demonstrated those talents that were to distinguish him as a scholar. On 5 May 1747 he entered Queen's College, Oxford. He graduated BA in 1750. Tyrwhitt was called to the bar at the Middle Temple in 1755, but ill health prevented him from practising. In the same year he was elected to a fellowship at Merton College, Oxford. He graduated MA in 1756 and was appointed deputy secretary at war. He held this position and his fellowship at Merton until 1762, when he was made clerk of the House of Commons in place of the late Jeremiah Dyson. This post he resigned to John Hatsell in 1768, preferring a 'private station' (GM, 56/2, 1786, 717). His philological expertise was once more exercised in a public role when he was appointed curator of the British Museum in 1784. Here, as in everything else, he was 'indefatigably diligent' in his duties so that his loss from the position on his death was 'sincerely lamented' (ibid.). He was elected a fellow of the Royal Society on 28 February 1771. For the most part, however, his life was spent in quiet devotion to the critical and literary studies that had always been his primary love.

The Gentleman's Magazine obituary of Tyrwhitt begins by observing not only that he had a knowledge of 'almost every European tongue' but that he 'was deeply conversant in the learning of Greece and Rome' (GM, 56/2, 1786, 717). Evidence of this erudition is apparent from his undergraduate years. While at Oxford he composed Translations in verse: Mr Pope's 'Messiah'; Mr Philips's 'Splendid shilling' in Latin; the 'Eighth Isthmian' of Pindar in English (1752). Characteristically of Tyrwhitt, this work was published anonymously, as was another Oxford exercise of note, An Epistle to Florio at Oxford (1749; reprinted GM, new ser., 3/2, 1835, 595–600). Florio was George Ellis of Jamaica, an Eton

classmate of Tyrwhitt and, as of 1751, a member of the house of assembly in Jamaica. Tyrwhitt's later contributions to classical scholarship demonstrate both the extent of his talents as critic and editor and the magnanimity with which he approached all undertakings. His first critical publication was Fragmenta duo Plutarchi (1773; from BL, Harley MS 5612), the importance of which, he claimed, lay not in its merit but in its inducement of further such studies (GM, 56/2, 1786, 717). Of the same nature is his anonymous Dissertatio de Babrio, fabularum Aesopearum scriptore. Inseruntur fabulae quaedam Aesopeae nunquam antehac editae, ex. Cod. MS Bodleiano. Accedunt Babrii fragmenta (1776). This 'Dissertation on Babrius as a writer of Aesopian fables' includes 'certain Aesopian tales from the Bodleian Library never before edited' and 'fragments from Babrius', whose fables, Tyrwhitt shows with Bentley-like meticulousness, were often attributed to Aesop and inserted into editions of his works. An 'auctarium' of this dissertation was appended to his edition of Orpheus in 1781. Both essay and auctarium were reprinted by T. C. Harles at Erlangen in 1785, and were included in the 1810 Fabulae Aesopicae of Franciscus de Furia. Tyrwhitt's 1781 Latin and Greek edition of poems 'On Stones' traditionally ascribed to Orpheus, Peri lithon, de lapidibus: poema Orpheo a quibusdam adscriptum, Graece et Latine, ex editione Jo. Matthiae Gesneri, was based on Gesner's edition; however, Tyrwhitt revised it and added notes, attributing the poems to the age of Constantius. Other classical authors whose works benefited from his insightful and scrupulous examination, emendation, or editing include Aeschylus, Aristophanes, Aristotle, Euripides, Polybius, and Strabo. His concerted efforts for the advancement of scholarship are also apparent in his revision of and commentary on the newly discovered Oration of Isaeus against Menecles (1785) and in his supervision of the publication of the late Samuel Musgrave's Two dissertations: 1, On the Grecian mythology; 2, An examination of Sir Isaac Newton's objection to the chronology of the Olympiads (1782). Tyrwhitt was reputedly responsible for raising a large subscription list for this work, and his own name is included among the subscribers (Nichols, Lit. anecdotes, 3.149). The extent of Tyrwhitt's contribution to classical scholarship was acknowledged by Charles Burney who listed him (alongside such names as Richard Bentley and Jeremy Markland) as one of the English Pleiades (ibid., 3.147; 4.660). Another fitting tribute is the Latin dedication to Tyrwhitt prefaced to Thomas Kidd's 1817 edition of Richard Dawes's Miscellanea critica (see the dedication and p. xvi).

As well as possessing extensive knowledge of classical languages and literature, Tyrwhitt was 'thoroughly read in the old English writers' (GM, 56/2, 1786, 717), and in an age where scholarship of early English writers and English antiquarianism was rudimentary he not only helped to further Shakespeare studies but significantly advanced the understanding and appreciation of Chaucer. In his Observations and Conjectures upon some Passages of Shakespeare (1776), Tyrwhitt recognizes the problems with editions of Shakespeare to this time by indicating his doubt about that of Samuel Johnson. Characteristically, however, he claims that his aim is not to argue with anyone but to lay out his own 'observations and conjectures upon some passages of Shakespeare, which have either been passed over in silence, or attempted, in my opinion, without success, by former commentators' (p. 3). Other insights, passed on in conversation, were afterwards used by George Steevens for the 1778 edition of Shakespeare and by Isaac Reed for the 1785 edition. Tyrwhitt was also among those few acknowledged for their help in the 1780 *Supplement to the Edition of Shakespeare's Plays Published in 1778 by Samuel Johnson and George Steevens* (p. viii), and Steevens's advertisement to the edition of 1793 relates that the second folio of Shakespeare's plays, used in the edition, came from Tyrwhitt's library. Even more notable was his work on Chaucer. His edition, *The 'Canterbury tales' of Chaucer, to which are added an essay upon his language and versification, an introductory discourse and notes in four volumes*, was published in 1775. Volume 5, containing a glossary and a life of Chaucer, was added later. Recognizing here too the carelessness of the scholarship that preceded his, Tyrwhitt 'proceeded', as he claims in the preface, 'as if his author had never been published before', collating all available manuscripts of *The Canterbury Tales* in order to make his text 'as correct as the mss within the reach of the editor would enable him to make it' (preface). He appends to this edition a list of the manuscripts consulted. Tyrwhitt's greatest contribution lies perhaps in his contextualization of Chaucer's language and of his *Tales*. He saw the necessity, he states, of enquiring 'into the state of our language and versification at the time when Chaucer wrote', as well as of examining 'the peculiarities of his style and manner of composition', and his notes and glossary focus closely on Chaucerian contexts (preface). In its own time Tyrwhitt's Chaucer was hailed 'the best edited English Classic that ever has appeared' (*GM*, 56/2, 1786, 717), while subsequent editors overlooked anything before Tyrwhitt, incorporating his work into their own.

Tyrwhitt's intimate knowledge of the language of the fourteenth and fifteenth centuries also led to his being acknowledged by contemporaries as the only real authority among those involved in the Rowley controversy. This vehement dispute erupted when Thomas Chatterton delivered to the printer Farley manuscripts of poems that he later claimed he had transcribed from the works of Thomas Rowley, a priest of Bristol in the reigns of Henry VI and Edward IV. Amid debate which grew to include the 'first scholars of the age', Tyrwhitt published anonymously in 1777 *Poems supposed to have been written at Bristol, by Thomas Rowley and others in the fifteenth century* (*GM*, 56/2, 1786, 717). This was twice republished in 1778 with the addition of his 'Appendix containing some observations upon the language of the poems tending to prove that they were written not by any ancient author, but entirely by Thomas Chatterton'. Tyrwhitt himself was reportedly 'wholly uninterested in the result of the publication' since, as always, '[m]ere truth was the object of his researches' (*GM*, 58/3, 1788, 188). In 1782, however, he was moved to publish *A vindication of the appendix to the poems called Rowley's, in reply to the answers of the dean of Exeter, Jacob*

Bryant, esquire, and a third anonymous writer, with some further observations upon those poems, and an examination of the evidence which has been produced in support of their authenticity. This thorough and searching examination of language, versification, and chronological and historical evidence closed the controversy. Where Tyrwhitt's superiority lay, W. W. Skeat suggests in his 'Essay on the Rowley poems', was not just in his knowledge of the language of Rowley's time, but in the difference between his approach and that of those writers who 'employed themselves to small purpose in ridiculing each other's notions, and in wasting time in the investigation of a few isolated words, instead of setting steadily to analyse the whole of them' (Skeat, 2.viii).

The magnanimity with which Tyrwhitt approached his scholarship extended to his relationships with all. Just as 'his censures were as void of rudeness as his erudition was free from pedantry', so his generosity was unconstrained by political or doctrinal views (Nichols, *Lit. anecdotes*, 3.150). He reportedly released the widow of the late Samuel Musgrave from a debt of several hundred pounds that her husband had borrowed from him, then corrected and undertook the patronage of one of his posthumous works, raising by subscription a considerable sum for the Musgrave children. The political views of Tyrwhitt and Musgrave could not have been more at odds, however (ibid.). A further example of Tyrwhitt's liberal help to others and encouragement of literary studies is provided by letter to Nichols's *Literary Anecdotes*. Wanting to communicate 'an instance of Mr. Tyrwhitt's benevolence and love of learning', this scholar relates how Tyrwhitt endowed upon him a considerable annual stipend enabling him to remain at college after taking his master's degree and thereby allowing him great 'literary advantages' (ibid., 9.756). Such acts, particularly in support of young men of promising abilities and application, were apparently typical of Tyrwhitt who is said to have given away £2000 in one year (*GM*, 57/1, 1787, 219). He also purchased with Matthew Duane at an auction in London in 1772 three ancient marbles from Smyrna and gave them to the British Museum, and in 1778 gave £100 towards the new buildings at Queen's College. In his will he left about 900 volumes of valuable and scarce books to the British Museum. Never of a strong constitution, he died— reputedly without an enemy and honoured by all who knew him—after a short illness at his home in Welbeck Street, Cavendish Square, London, on 15 August 1786. He was buried in the family vault in the east aisle of St George's, Windsor, on 22 August. He was unmarried.

TANYA CALDWELL

Sources *DNB* · *GM*, 1st ser., 55 (1785), 559 · *GM*, 1st ser., 56 (1786), 717–19, 905, 994 · *GM*, 1st ser., 57 (1787), 218–19 · *GM*, 2nd ser., 3 (1835), 595–600 · Nichols, *Lit. anecdotes*, 2.413–14; 3.147–51, 234; 4.660; 9.527–31, 756–7 · Nichols, *Illustrations*, 5.427; 8.220–23 · W. W. Skeat, *Chatterton's poems* (1871), 2.viii–ix · *Ricardi Dawesii miscellanea critica*, ed. T. Kidd (1817), dedication; xvi · J. Schweighaeuser, ed., *Polybii historiarum* (1789), 1.xxvi · *The letters of Horace Walpole, earl of Orford*, ed. P. Cunningham, 4 (1857), 412; 7 (1858), 279; repr. (1906) · *The letters of Samuel Johnson*, ed. B. Redford, 2 (1992), 332–3 · will, PRO, PROB 11/1145, fols. 264v–265v · Foster,

Alum. Oxon. • J. Foster, *The peerage, baronetage, and knightage of the British empire* [1880–83]
Archives Bodl. Oxf., corresp., literary MSS, and papers | BL, letters to T. Burgess, Add. MS 46487 • Bodl. Oxf., letters to Jean D'Orville • Yale U., Farmington, Lewis Walpole Library, corresp. and papers, mainly relating to Thomas Chatterton
Likenesses J. Jones, engraving, pubd 1788 (after B. Wilson) • T. Holloway, group portrait, line engraving (*Shakespearean critics*), BM; repro. in F. Malone, ed., *Shakespeare* • B. Wilson, portrait • oils, NPG
Wealth at death mortgages payable to Tyrwhitt (£2900); stocks (£2000); annuities and other assets; books left to BM: will, PRO, PROB 11/1145, sig. 457

Tysilio [St Tysilio, Suliau] (*fl. c.*600), holy man, was patron of the monastic church at Meifod in Montgomeryshire. His feast day is celebrated on 8 November. Although he is the chief saint of Powys in north-east Wales, very little relating to him survives from Wales, except for some passing notices in the vernacular *Buchedd Beuno*, an ode to him by the twelfth-century bard Cynddelw Brydydd Mawr, and material in the Welsh saints' genealogies. However, traditions about his early life and career seem to have been preserved in the Latin life of the saint Suliac (Sulinus), patron of St Suliac in east Brittany, whose feast day is 1 October. The author of this work attempted, probably incorrectly, to identify his subject with Tysilio, since the Welsh saint's name is really an extended or hypocoristic form Ty-Suliau of the name Suliau (Silio), not dissimilar to Suliac. According to these sources, Tysilio was son of *Brochfael Ysgithrog ap Cyngen, king of Powys, and of Arddun Benasgell ferch Pabo of alleged northern British descent. The genealogical connection with Brochfael, if accurate, would suggest the saint flourished in the late sixth or early seventh century. This claim that he was a member of the ruling dynasty of Powys may explain the later significance of Tysilio and his church of Meifod, burial church of the kings of Powys, although it should be recalled that royal ancestry was a very common attribute of saints in medieval Celtic hagiography.

Even in his early years Tysilio is said to have aspired to a religious life, in spite of Brochfael's disapproval, and consequently fled to the monastery at Meifod, then under Abbot Gwyddfarch. Subsequently, he moved westwards and founded the church of Llandysilio, on the Anglesey side of the Menai Strait. He remained there for seven years before returning to Meifod and succeeding Gwyddfarch as abbot. The *Buchedd Beuno* records that St Beuno visited Tysilio at Meifod. However, according to the Breton life Tysilio's dynastic connections continued to plague him, and he was forced to migrate to Brittany following the persecutions by Haiarme, the childless widow of his brother, the deceased King Iago. There is no other record elsewhere of this Iago as a son of Brochfael (who in fact was probably succeeded in the kingship by his son *Cynan Garwyn) and this whole episode may have been invented to account for the saint's migration to Brittany, and therefore to support the identification with St Suliac. He is said to have landed at the mouth of the River Rance and, following an appropriate meeting with St Malo, founded the church of St Suliac further upstream. Subsequent

attempts by members of the Meifod community to persuade Tysilio to return to Wales failed, and he is said to have died soon after. However, according to Cynddelw, Tysilio was present at the battle of Maserfelth (Maes Cogwy), possibly Oswestry, in 642 between Penda of Mercia and Oswald of Northumbria but at which Welsh tradition would also include Powysian participation in the person of Cynddylan ap Cyndrwyn. If the later chapters of the Breton life are dismissed, then it is not entirely impossible that Tysilio was still alive and active in Wales in 642; but, if he was indeed a son of Brochfael Ysgithrog, this must stretch the chronology.

Later Welsh tradition regarded Tysilio as author of some poetry preserved in the Red Book of Hergest, but this attribution is evidently incorrect. Furthermore, Archbishop James Ussher's claim that the saint wrote an 'ecclesiastical history of Britain' is equally erroneous but probably underlies his connection with the so-called *Brut Tysilio*, which was once thought to have been the source for Geoffrey of Monmouth's *Historia regum Britanniae*, but is now recognized as a fifteenth-century Welsh translation of Geoffrey's work. Not surprisingly, the Welsh cult of Tysilio is centred on Meifod, and comprises a cluster of dedications in south Denbighshire (including Llandysilio-yn-Iâl and nearby Abersili) and north Montgomeryshire (including a Llandysilio and possibly Llandysul). In addition to Llandysilio on Anglesey (as recorded in the Breton life of Suliac), churches elsewhere in Wales thought to be dedicated to Tysilio include Llandysilio on the Pembrokeshire–Carmarthenshire border, and Llandysiliogogo and possibly Llandysul in Cardiganshire. However, the Welsh saints' genealogies list a Tysul ap Corun and a Tysilio ab Enoc as two separate saints of wholly Cardiganshire ancestry; and, while these figures could account for at least some of the south-western dedications, on the other hand they may simply represent localized doublets for Tysilio of Powys.   DAVID E. THORNTON

Sources *Acta sanctorum: October*, 1 (Antwerp, 1765), 196–8 • A. W. Wade-Evans, ed. and trans., *Vitae sanctorum Britanniae et genealogiae* (1944) • P. C. Bartrum, ed., *Early Welsh genealogical tracts* (1966) • J. G. Evans, ed., *The poetry in the Red Book of Hergest* (1911) • G. H. Doble, *Saint Sulian and Saint Tyssilio*, Cornish Saints Series, 37 (1936) • E. G. Bowen, *The settlements of the Celtic saints in Wales*, 2nd edn (1956) • Cynddelw Brydydd Mawr, 'Canu Tysilio Sant', in *Gwaith Cynddelw Brydydd Mawr*, ed. N. A. Jones and A. P. Owen, 1 (1991), 15–50

Tyso, Joseph (1774–1852), Baptist minister and plantsman, was probably born in Bedfordshire. Nothing is known about his parents and early life. In 1798 he was baptized with thirteen other individuals by the Revd Stephens at Colchester where he resided, and assisted in the proclamation of the gospel. The following year he entered the Baptist college, Bristol, and in 1803, having completed his training, he was ordained pastor of the Baptist church, Helston. On 8 June 1804 he married Elizabeth Hubbard (*c.*1774–*c.*1860) at St James's Church, Colchester. In 1806 he became pastor of the Baptist church at Watchet, where he preached for the next eleven years. Their son Carey was born in 1816. The following year Tyso preached at King Street Chapel, Bristol, for nearly twelve months before becoming pastor of St Peter's Church, Wallingford, a position he retained for the next thirty years. He was a popular preacher and the increase in the size of his congregation resulted in the church's being extended in 1821.

Tyso was a prolific writer of religious tracts dealing particularly with biblical interpretations of the millennium. His seven most important tracts include *Church discipline, or, An abstract of the laws of Christ relative to the proper treatment of the members of the Christian church* (1836) and *An elucidation of the prophecies, being an exposition of the book of Daniel and the Revelation, showing that the seventy weeks, the one thousand two hundred and sixty days, and the events predicted under the seven trumpets and seven vials have not yet taken place, but that they will be accomplished within the space of about three years and a half from their commencement, and probably at no very distant period* (1838). These tracts generated considerable controversy in religious circles which led to his defending his views in pamphlets such as *The throne of David, the throne of Christ. To which is added a letter to … Dr. Harris in reply to his remarks on millenarianism in his 'Great Commission'* (1842). Tyso was one of many preachers who indulged in this form of denunciation. At this time the Church of England, which had not yet emerged from its eighteenth-century stupor, plagued by pluralism, incompetent clergy, and physical dilapidation, proved an easy prey for radical polemicists disputing theological interpretations.

Tyso was very interested in the cultivation and improvement of the genera *Anemone* and *Ranunculus*, a hobby which evolved into the establishment of initially a florist's, followed by a general nursery, business. He contributed a number of articles to a gardeners' magazine and published a catalogue of choice *Ranunculuses Grown and Sold by Rev. J. Tyso*; he produced *The Ranunculus, how to Grow it* (1847) jointly with his son, who was also interested in these plants and probably compiled a significant part of the text. In January 1848 illness compelled Tyso to resign as minister of the church; he died at Wallingford on 30 November 1852, intestate, administration being granted to his widow, Elizabeth. *A Short History of the Baptist Church at Thames Street, Wallingford* notes that his thirty-year ministry at the church was inscribed on the mural tablet as 'faithful and affectionate', a fitting epitaph for his commitment to the propagation of religious tracts and horticulture. He was buried at Wallingford on 6 December 1852.

Following Tyso's death, his son, Carey Tyso (1816–1882) continued to run the nursery until 1879, issuing periodic catalogues of anemones and ranunculuses and writing several treatises on the cultivation of these plants. Like his father he was a devout Baptist, undertaking in 1865 an analysis of 250 consecutive hymns, identifying those which he deemed unfit for public use. While his proposals were not published, it prompted him to write in 1867 a tract, *Thirty-two questions for the consideration of ministers and leaders of evangelical Christian worship*. This examined the 112 passages in the New Testament dealing with praise and prayer, and specified the questions which might improve

church services. Unlike his father, Carey was much better known for his contribution to horticulture than as a religious writer. He died on 2 February 1882 at Wallingford.

JOHN MARTIN

Sources *Baptist Magazine*, 45 (1853), 35–6 · A. R. Burt, *A short history of the Baptist church at Thames Street, Wallingford, 1794–1944* (1944) · *Baptist manual*, Baptist Society (1853) · *Gardeners' Chronicle*, new ser., 17 (1882), 233 · Baptist Union of Great Britain
Wealth at death £20

Tyson, Edward (1651–1708), physician and anatomist, was born in the parish of St Nicholas, Bristol, on 20 January 1651, the second surviving son of Edward Tyson (d. 1667), mercer and later mayor of Bristol, and Margaret, daughter of the iron master Richard *Foley (1579/80–1657) [see under Foley family (per. c.1620–1716)] of Stourbridge, Worcestershire. The Tyson family originated in Cumberland and owned a country house in Clevedon, Somerset. Edward also had six sisters. He was baptized at St Nicholas's Church, Bristol, on 14 February 1651. Little is known of his early education. He matriculated as a student commoner at Magdalen Hall, Oxford, on 10 May 1667; his father died on 20 August that year, leaving Tyson financially well provided for. Tyson studied anatomy and natural history with the naturalist Robert Plot; he also studied botany, possibly with Robert Morison. Tyson proceeded BA on 8 February 1670, and MA on 4 November 1673. Plot described some of his anatomical work in his *Natural History of Oxford-Shire* (1677), which also contains Tyson's first published work, 'On the scent-bags in poll-cats'. Tyson also continued his botanical activities, influenced by Nehemiah Grew's *The Anatomy of Vegetables Begun* (1672).

Tyson received the degree of MB in 1677 and moved to London, where he lived with his sister Sarah and brother-in-law Richard Morton (1637–1698), a well-known physician, at Grey Friar's Court, Newgate Street. There Tyson continued to pursue anatomy, and soon met Robert Hooke, who became a close friend. Early in 1678 Tyson published two papers in the *Philosophical Transactions*, both accounts of autopsies he had performed. Hooke proposed Tyson for fellowship of the Royal Society, and he was elected on 1 December 1679. Tyson also published short papers on various topics in pathology in Thomas Bartholin's *Acta medica et philosophia hafniensa*.

Tyson's first major publication was his *Phocaena, or, The Anatomy of a Porpess*, which appeared in May 1680. His preliminary discourse emphasized the importance of comparative anatomy for medicine, and outlined his natural history methods. Tyson believed in the great chain of being, the idea that all living and non-living things were hierarchically arranged, and viewed the porpoise as an intermediary figure between fish and land animals. This essay resembles the introduction, by Claude Perrault, to the Paris Academy's *Mémoires pour servir à l'histoire naturelle des animaux* (1671–6), another pioneering work on comparative anatomy, and it is unclear when Tyson read this work. Like Perrault, Tyson believed that the key to a general natural history was the accumulation of detailed accounts of individual species.

Tyson took the degree of MD at Corpus Christi College,

Edward Tyson (1651–1708), by Edmond Lilly, c.1695

Cambridge on 7 July 1680. On 30 September 1680 he was admitted as a candidate of the Royal College of Physicians, and was elected a fellow on 2 April 1683. He served as censor in 1694. In 1681 he had been elected to the first of several terms on the council of the Royal Society, and in February 1683 he was appointed anatomical curator to present dissections and experiments before the society. At the end of 1684 he was appointed to two further positions: Ventera reader in anatomy at the Company of Barber–Surgeons (succeeding William Croone) and physician to Bethlem and Bridewell hospitals. Tyson gave regular lectures at Surgeons' Hall, and manuscripts of these survive.

From 1680 onward Tyson published regularly in the *Philosophical Transactions* on natural history and on pathological cases. Notable were his description of a rattlesnake, his descriptions of tapeworms and roundworms, and his work on the scent glands of the Mexican warthog. He contributed descriptions of a shark embryo and a lumpfish to Francis Willughby's *De historia piscium* (1686), and contributed material to Samuel Collins's *Systeme of Anatomy* (1685). In 1686 he was elected to the Oxford Philosophical Society.

Tyson's only original contribution to medicine was his discovery of the preputial and coronal glands of the human penis, reported in William Cowper's *Myotomia reformata* (1694). In 1698 Tyson published (both in the *Philosophical Transactions* and as a pamphlet) his description of a female opossum. He completed an anatomy of a male opossum with Cowper in 1704.

Tyson's best-known work was his anatomy of a chimpanzee, *Orang-outang, sive homo sylvestris, or, The anatomy of a pygmie compared with that of a monkey, an ape, and a man*

(1699). The significance of this work lies not only in its detailed anatomical description, but also in its comparative aspects, for Tyson concluded that his 'pygmy' belonged in the chain of being somewhere between humans and apes, and he drew a table of comparison with both species. He concluded this work by adding a *Philological Essay Concerning the Pygmies … of the Ancients*, which Montagu termed 'the first published scientific study of the folklore of the Primates' (Montagu, 313). Tyson attempted to show that ancient references to human-like creatures in fact referred to non-human primates. The book as a whole exercised an extraordinary influence on both anthropology and popular culture in the eighteenth century.

Tyson resigned as Ventera reader in 1699, but continued to present anatomical papers to the Royal Society, some of which were published in the *Philosophical Transactions*. Many more accounts survive in manuscript. Tyson contributed an account of Bethlem Hospital to John Strype's new edition of Stow's *Survey of London*. Little is known of Tyson's term as physician at Bethlem or of his medical practice, and his historical importance lies in his pioneering work in comparative anatomy. He served as vice-president of the Royal Society in 1704. Tyson died suddenly on 1 August 1708.

Tyson had a quiet and retiring character and never married; references to his son Richard *Tyson (1680–1750) in fact refer to his nephew, a physician. Sir Samuel Garth satirized him in his poem *The Dispensary* in which Tyson is called Carus. Tyson's will, written on 8 September 1707 and proved on 17 August 1708, reveals Tyson's considerable wealth: he left annuities to six people, as well as £2000 in additional legacies. His nephew Richard was his main heir. His brother-in-law Richard Morton was executor, and William Gardiner was named a trustee. Tyson was buried on 18 August 1708 at the church of St Dionis Backchurch in Lime Street, where a monument to him was erected. This church was demolished in the nineteenth century and the monument was moved to All Hallows, Lombard Street, which was later demolished. The monument is now at All Hallows, Twickenham.

ANITA GUERRINI

Sources M. F. A. Montagu, *Edward Tyson, MD, FRS, 1650–1708, and the rise of human and comparative anatomy in England* (1943) · DSB · DNB · Munk, *Roll*

Archives Bodl. Oxf., syllabi · RCP Lond., drawings and papers | BL, Sloane MSS

Likenesses E. Lilly, oils, c.1695, RCP Lond. [*see illus.*] · E. Stanton, bust on monument, All Hallows Church, Twickenham, Middlesex · portrait, RCP Lond.

Wealth at death substantial: will, PRO

Tyson, (Dorothy Estelle) Esmé Wynne- [*née* Dorothy Estelle Esmé Innes Ripper; *pseud.* Esmé Wynne] (1898–1972), writer, was born on 29 June 1898, at 26 Stansfield Road, Stockwell, London, the only child of Harry Innes Ripper (1871–1956), a City of London stockbroker, and Minnie Maude (1874–1940), daughter of a talented amateur actor, William Pitt. Her two maternal aunts, Molly and Mona, as well as her mother, had been on the stage, encouraging her early theatrical career. Her first professional appearance was in *The Blue Bird* at the Haymarket, which made her a child star. She adopted the stage name Esmé Wynne, which she used also as a pseudonym for her early dramas. In 1912, when both were appearing in *Where the Rainbow Ends*, she befriended Noël Coward. Sharing an enthusiasm for the theatre, the teenagers performed dances in 'futurist' pyjamas and devised sketches and stories. A series of 'curtain-raisers' (Coward had played in Esmé's one-act play *The Prince's Bride*, produced on 2 February 1912) appeared under the joint *nom de plume* Esnomel: *The Last Chapter* (produced in 1917), *To Have and to Hold* (unproduced), and *Women and Whisky* (produced in 1918). Esmé also wrote lyrics to set to Coward's music; her song 'Faith' was included in his play *I'll Leave it to You* (produced in 1920).

But as the theatre had united the pair, so it divided them. Coward became famous. On 22 June 1918 Esmé married Linden Charles Tyson (1897–1977), a former army officer who was serving in the RAF; he changed his surname to Wynne-Tyson in 1919. More crucially, at twenty-four, she experienced what she called 'the mystic experience of rebirth' on reading Mary Baker Eddy's *Science and Health*, a book 'that described the *sort* of God that I *could* love' (Wynne-Tyson to Air Marshal Sir Victor Goddard, 14 July 1960, Wynne-Tyson MSS). She also became a vegetarian, and her only child, Jon, was born in 1924.

In 1926 Esmé published her first novel, *Security*, a period piece of nervy social disorder dealing with the 'lengths a woman will go to to ensure security for herself and her children when it is jeopardised by the sins of the father' (jacket copy). A friend, the novelist G. B. Stern, found it 'very subtle, very original' (G. B. Stern to E. Wynne-Tyson, 28 Oct 1926, Wynne-Tyson MSS); the *Daily Telegraph* wrote that 'very few first novels show such a mastery of style' (26 Nov 1926). Although Esmé later disparaged it as somewhat artificial, she turned it into a successful play, sold to Lee Shubert, who produced it in New York (Maxine Elliott's Theatre, 28 March 1929) and London (Savoy Theatre, 13 March 1932). Her second novel, *Quicksand* (1927), made the process in reverse, as an adaptation of her play *Little Lovers*, originally a collaboration with Coward (Aldwych Theatre, 1922). The book portrays Wynne-Tyson and Coward (its dedicatee) as Paul and Pauline Myse, talented and attractive siblings.

Esmé described her third novel, *Momus* (1928), as 'the "imagined" love affair between Bernard Shaw and Mrs Pat Campbell' (Wynne-Tyson to Goddard, 3 Feb 1961, Wynne-Tyson MSS). Reviewers found its 'brilliant effect' marred by 'pitiless cleverness in the execution' (*Times Literary Supplement*, 6 Dec 1928). Coward pointed out its various inconsistencies but agreed that it was the 'best thing you've ever done' (Coward to Wynne-Tyson, October 1928, Wynne-Tyson MSS). Esmé's early work is fraught with modern sexual mores; marriage is seldom happy; consolation is to be found in culture, or, increasingly, in religion. Such religiosity explains the 'cool welcome' for *Melody* (1929), a novel suffering, in the words of her son, from 'the common problem of how to make an essentially good person

interesting' (Wynne-Tyson). The largely autobiographical *Incense and Sweet Cane* (1930) completes the quintet. A daughter witnesses the break-up of her parents' marriage through alcoholism and violence; her tragic death reconciles them. Esmé's own marriage ended in 1930, when her husband left her for another woman; they were divorced in 1947 (he was to remarry twice).

Despite the increasing maturity of Esmé's fiction, she began to turn her back on it, as she had turned her back on the stage, although she wrote another play, *Forty Love* (Grafton Theatre, 4 October 1931). In the 1930s her writing concentrated on freelance journalism, in which her philosophical interests were beginning to dominate. *Prelude to Peace* (1936), positing a world-brotherhood educational movement, was well received by some educationists. In 1938 she met the novelist J. D. Beresford, with whom she henceforth shared an 'intense mental and working collaboration' (Wynne-Tyson, 353). Although not a Christian Scientist, Beresford was 'deeply interested in spiritual healing'. 'I found in J. D. more of the image and likeness of God … than I found in any other man' (E. Wynne-Tyson to E. N. Holstius, 3 Jan 1958, Wynne-Tyson MSS). They collaborated on ten published novels, but for contractual reasons only three bore their joint names: *Men in the Same Boat* (1943), in which seven shipwrecked men are subsequently found 'in another … existence, [each] fulfilling his own idea of happiness' (Wynne-Tyson); *The Riddle of the Tower* (1944), foreseeing industrialization as reducing human beings to mere insect status; and *The Gift* (1947), 'a beautifully etched portrait of a young man who in thought and deed practises the Christian ethics' (*Western Mail*, September 1947). The last was successful enough to go into three editions.

The post-war period had less time for Christian philosophy; none the less, after Beresford's death in 1947 Esmé continued in his tradition with *The Unity of Being* (1949) and *This is Life Eternal: the Case for Immortality* (1951). *Mithras: the Fellow in the Cap* (1958) examined, with autodidactic zeal, the sun-worshipping cult, discerning the pagan roots of Christian rites with 'disturbing conclusions about Christian orthodoxy' (J. Wynne-Tyson, 354). *The Philosophy of Compassion: the Return of the Goddess* (1962) argued that religious fundamentalists opposed to Darwinism were unable to see that Christianity is a stage in religious evolution, unfortunately become patriarchal. Indeed, *The Philosophy of Compassion* is her *Origin of Species*, in which the problems of the human condition are ascribed to male hegemony. A last work, *The Dialectics of Diotima*, was published by her son in 1969. Vivacious and quizzical, Esmé was 5 feet 5 inches tall, with green eyes and small features. She died at St Richard's Hospital, Chichester, Sussex, on 17 January 1972.

Esmé Wynne-Tyson epitomizes a particular breed of woman of the post-First World War period: self-taught and liberated to a degree; drawn to art, theatre, or literature; and challenging, in the post-war climate, both the values of the previous generation and the lack of values in their own. Writing to Coward after the publication of

Mithras in 1960, she referred to their teenage aspirations; his for theatrical success,

> mine … to 'know the Truth'. It has taken much longer, but it has happened … Your wish … has given you much pleasure in the fulfilment. Mine has given me much inward content, but the dreadful irony of mine is that, after finding the Truth … I discover that it is the very last thing the world wants to hear about. (E. Wynne-Tyson to N. Coward, 24 Feb 1960, Wynne-Tyson MSS)

But the world turned again, and in the latter years of the century her eclectic belief system, that of a 'passionate rationalist' (J. Wynne-Tyson, *Aryan Path*, April 1972), has been somewhat vindicated.　　　　　　　PHILIP HOARE

Sources private information (2004) · priv. coll., E. Wynne-Tyson MSS · J. Wynne-Tyson, 'Esmé Wynne-Tyson', *British novelists between the wars*, ed. G. M. Johnson, DLitB, 191 (1998) · P. Hoare, *Noël Coward: a biography* (1995) · WWW
Archives Boston University, Massachusetts · priv. coll. | Boston University, Massachusetts, Mugar Memorial Library, corresp. with Mrs A. M. Beesley
Likenesses photographs, priv. coll. · portraits, priv. coll.
Wealth at death £9976: probate, 16 March 1972, *CGPLA Eng. & Wales*

Tyson, Michael (1740–1780), antiquary and artist, was born on 18 November 1740 at Stamford, Lincolnshire, the only child of Michael Tyson (1711–1794), rector of St George's and afterwards dean of Stamford and archdeacon of Huntingdon, and his first wife, Elizabeth Walburge, *née* Curtis, formerly widow of Dr Simon Walburge. In December 1765 his father married Elizabeth Lucas, who died without children. Tyson was educated in Lincolnshire, entered Corpus Christi College, Cambridge, as a pensioner in October 1759 and took the degrees of BA (eleventh wrangler) in 1764, MA in 1767, and BD in 1775. He learned Greek from John Cowper, a fellow of the college, and afterwards became proficient in French, Italian, and Spanish. In September 1766 he and his college friend the antiquary Richard Gough toured Scotland and were created burgesses of Glasgow and of Inveraray. Returning to Cambridge Tyson was elected to a fellowship at Corpus in 1767, and served for some time as dean and bursar, but he tired of college life and was anxious to marry Margaret (Peggy) Wale (*bap.* 1743), one of the 'toasts' of the day, the daughter of the late Hitch Wale and his wife, Mary, of Shelford in Cambridgeshire. After a protracted engagement he vacated his fellowship and they were married on 4 July 1778 at St Benet's Church, Cambridge. Their only child, Michael Curtis Tyson, was born in May 1779 and died at the age of fourteen.

Having been ordained deacon at Whitehall Chapel in 1770 and priest at Peterborough in 1773, Tyson became vicar of Sawston, Cambridgeshire, from 1772 to 1776 and vicar of St Benet's, Cambridge, from 1773 to 1776 in which year he was Whitehall preacher. His last preferment, attended by considerable delay and legal wrangling, was to the rectory of St Mary and All Saints at Lambourne, Essex, a college living, where he was instituted on 16 March 1778, and remained until his early death.

Tyson was elected fellow of the Society of Antiquaries in June 1768 and of the Royal Society in February 1769. He was one of the Benedictines, a group of Corpus contemporaries with similar tastes in books and antiquarian researches, which included Robert Masters, James Nasmith, Richard Gough, and, though he was not a Corpus man, William Cole. Among his other friends and correspondents were Sir John Cullum, Horace Walpole, James Essex, and Samuel Henley. Cole entertained him and met him for excursions such as that to Ely Cathedral on 5 May 1768 where Bishop Hotham's coffin was opened and they saw his head. On another they travelled by water to Wicken church in July 1769 where they copied monuments and inscriptions and looked for plants since Tyson was a keen botanist. Another of his companions on expeditions around Cambridge was the botanist Israel Lyons the younger; Tyson corresponded with Thomas Gray about plants and supplied a brief account of Gray's knowledge of natural history for Mason's life of the poet. He also encouraged T. F. Forster in his early botanical studies.

Tyson published little. He wrote congratulatory verse in English for the university's collections on the accession of George III and for three similar works in the years 1760–64. A note and reproduction of an illuminated manuscript at Corpus representing Henry V was printed in *Archaeologia* and reissued separately in 1770, but William Cole also claimed to be the author. Tyson wrote and illustrated an account of the famous medieval horn at Corpus, and other pieces such as one about 'a singular fish brought by Commodore Byron from the South seas' (*Philosophical Transactions*, 1771). His studies of the progresses of Queen Elizabeth and a history of dress and fashion were contemplated but hardly begun.

Tyson enjoyed celebrity in his circle as a versatile artist and engraver especially of topographical scenes and portraits and miniatures of dead worthies such as Archbishop Parker and Browne Willis, and of his own contemporaries; he 'has left off engraving for some time, and I don't believe will ever resume it' wrote Cole in December 1775 (Walpole, 1.386). His last drawing, *The Hospital of St Petronilla at Bury* (April 1780), was engraved for the *Antiquarian Repertory* (4, 1784, 57). Gough warmly acknowledged Tyson's contribution in the preface to his *Sepulchral Monuments*, but his artistic work was largely unknown to a wide audience as he did not attempt to make money by it and it was soon forgotten. There is no adequate list of his drawings, paintings, and engravings nor any detailed study of them. The use of his drawings in architectural history remains largely undeveloped, though its importance is now acknowledged (see Lindley). John Lamb described him as an 'excellent gentleman artist' (Lamb, 408), yet a recent opinion is that his work, though 'sometimes attributed to better artists … is weakly in the Sandby tradition, rather like that of F. Grose' (Mallalieu, *Watercolour artists*, 262).

Tyson was a short man of a 'swarthy complexion … but extremely well-compacted' (Nichols, *Lit. anecdotes*, 8.210). According to Gough, his friends were concerned by his increasingly heavy drinking. He died from fever on 4 May

1780 at Brentwood and was buried on 6 May in the church at Lambourne; Richard Gough and Michael Lort were among the pall-bearers. There is no memorial to him in the church and, presumably since his father was still alive, he left a poor estate. In the summer of 1784 his widow married Isaac Crouch of the custom house. Tyson's library, which contained many foreign books and some that he had annotated, was sold by Leigh and Sotheby in 1781.   JOHN D. PICKLES

Sources Nichols, *Lit. anecdotes*, 8.204–10, 567–672 · Nichols, *Illustrations* · R. F. Scott, ed., *Admissions to the College of St John the Evangelist in the University of Cambridge*, 3: *July 1715 – November 1767* (1903), 418–19 · Walpole, *Corr.*, 1.386; 48.2705–6 · BL, Cole MSS · 'An account of an illuminated manuscript in the library of Corpus Christi College, Cambridge', *Archaeologia*, 2 (1773), 194–7 · 'Account of the horn belonging to Corpus Christi College, Cambridge', *Archaeologia*, 3 (1775), 19 · *Masters' History of the college of Corpus Christi and the Blessed Virgin Mary in the University of Cambridge*, ed. J. Lamb (1831), 407–9 · P. G. Lindley, *Gothic to Renaissance: essays on sculpture in England* (1995), 129–30, 133–4, 147–55, 171–2 · R. Gough, *Sepulchral monuments in Great Britain*, 1 (1786), 9–10 · W. M. Palmer, *William Cole of Milton* (1935), 174 · *The works, theological, medical, political and miscellaneous of John Jebb*, ed. J. Disney, 3 vols. (1787), vol. 1, p. 24 · F. Grose and others, *The antiquarian repertory*, 4 vols. (1775–84), vol. 2, p. 225; vol. 4, p. 57 · *DNB* · *IGI*
Archives BL, annotated copy of the *Iliad* · Bodl. Oxf., notes and transcriptions · Suffolk RO, Bury St Edmunds, botanical notes | BL, memoranda, corresp. with William Cole, etc. · BL, letters to R. Gough, Add. MSS 38626, 71245 · Bodl. Oxf., corresp. with Richard Gough

Tyson, Richard (1680–1750), physician, nephew of the anatomist Edward *Tyson (1651–1708), was born in Gloucestershire. He entered Pembroke College, Cambridge, on 31 October 1707, and obtained a fellowship in 1711. He graduated MB in 1710, and MD in 1715.

Tyson was elected a fellow of the Royal College of Physicians on 25 June 1718, was five times censor between 1718 and 1737, was registrar from 1723 to 1735, treasurer 1739–46, and president 1746–50. He delivered the Harveian oration in 1725. On 27 May 1725 he was elected physician to St Bartholomew's Hospital, London. He married Elizabeth Hale, of St Mary-at-Hill, at Kensington on 2 June 1720. She was the niece of the physician Richard Hale (1670–1728), a friend of Tyson's father. Tyson died on 3 January 1750 and was buried at Walton, Essex.

NORMAN MOORE, *rev.* PATRICK WALLIS

Sources Venn, *Alum. Cant.* · Munk, *Roll* · *GM*, 1st ser., 20 (1750), 43
Likenesses oils, *c.*1710–1720, RCP Lond.

Tyson, Richard (1730–1784), physician, son of Richard Tyson, physician, and great-nephew of the anatomist Edward Tyson (1651–1708), was born in the parish of St Dionis Backchurch in the City of London. He matriculated at Oriel College, Oxford, on 6 April 1747, and graduated BA on 13 October 1750, MA on 5 July 1753, MB on 30 April 1756, and MD on 15 January 1760.

Tyson was elected a fellow of the Royal College of Physicians, London, on 30 September 1761, served as censor in 1763, 1768, 1773, and 1776, and as registrar from 1774 to

1780. He was elected physician to St Bartholomew's Hospital on 5 February 1762. He lived in Queen Square, London, where he died, following a seizure, on 9 August 1784.   NORMAN MOORE, *rev.* KAYE BAGSHAW

Sources Munk, *Roll* · M. F. A. Montagu, *Edward Tyson, MD, FRS, 1650–1708, and the rise of human and comparative anatomy in England* (1943) · *GM*, 1st ser., 54 (1784), 638 · Foster, *Alum. Oxon.*
Likenesses portrait, RCP Lond.

Tytler, Alexander Fraser, Lord Woodhouselee (1747–1813), historian, was born in Edinburgh on 4 October 1747 and named Alexander Tytler, the son of William *Tytler (1711–1792), historian, and his wife, Anne Craig (d. 1783). He entered the high school in Edinburgh at the age of eight and there spent five years, becoming dux of the rector's class in his final year. In 1763 his father sent him to James Elphinston's academy in Kensington, where he stayed until 1765, when he returned to Edinburgh. At the end of 1765 he entered Edinburgh University, where he chiefly read law, in preparation for a legal career, but also attended lectures on logic, moral science, rhetoric, and *belles lettres*. In 1767 he got to know Henry Home, Lord Kames, and often accompanied that eminent judge when he went on circuit.

Tytler was called to the Scottish bar in 1770, having been admitted into the Faculty of Advocates on 23 January of that year. In the spring of 1771 he visited Paris, Flanders, and the Netherlands with his friend Kerr of Blackshiels. In the same year he published his first written work, which reflected his early interest in pastoral poetry. This was an edition of Phineas Fletcher's *Piscatory Eclogues*, with an introduction criticizing Addison's sentimentalized view of the pastoral genre. However, encouraged by Lord Kames, he soon began writing on legal matters. At Kames's suggestion he wrote a supplement to Kames's own *Dictionary of Decisions*, which appeared in 1778 as *Decisions of the Court of Session*, volumes 3 and 4. Tytler also produced lighter work, publishing articles in *The Mirror* (nos. 17, 37, 59, and 79) in 1779–80.

On 22 November 1776 Tytler married Ann (1752/3–1837), daughter and heir of William Fraser of Balnain, who brought to him the estates of Balnain and Aldourie. Tytler added the name of Fraser to his own after the marriage, which produced two daughters and three sons, the youngest of whom was the noted Scottish historian Patrick Fraser *Tytler (1791–1849).

Tytler was deeply interested in history and added an academic career to his legal one when he was appointed, jointly with John Pringle, professor of universal history at Edinburgh University on 16 February 1780. In 1786 he became full professor of civil history. As a history lecturer he brought something of a legal eye to bear on the academic discipline, insisting on a rigorous and even sceptical approach to historical evidence. His lectures were attended by, among others, Walter Scott, who remained an admirer of Tytler all his life. Tytler's lectures formed the basis of his *Plan and Outline of a Course of Lectures on Universal History*, published in 1782. Tytler was also one of the founding members of the Royal Society of Edinburgh when it was created in 1783, and he contributed several

Alexander Fraser Tytler, Lord Woodhouselee (1747–1813), by Archibald Skirving, 1798

papers to the society's transactions between 1785 and 1805, dealing with the Vikings, Scottish antiquities, the history of the society, and the nature of historical evidence.

Tytler was also extremely interested in the art of translation from foreign languages. During his life he learned Italian, Spanish, German, and French, and his essay on Petrarch (1782) included seven of the poet's sonnets, translated from the Italian. This was a popular work, appearing in new editions in 1810 and 1812. He also continued his article writing and published several items in *The Lounger* (nos. 7, 19, 24, 44, 63, 70, and 79) in the years 1785 and 1786. In 1788 he published a biography of Dr John Gregory (1724–1773).

Politically Tytler inclined to the 'new toryism' of the later eighteenth century and was closely connected to the powerful Scottish politician Henry Dundas, Lord Melville. It was through Melville's influence that he was appointed judge advocate in 1790, a now obsolete office that dealt with issues of military law in Scotland. The duties of the post were usually performed by a deputy but Tytler abandoned this practice and attended courts martial in person. The knowledge acquired in this position was used in writing his *Essay on the Military Law and the Practice of Courts-Martial*, published in 1800.

Tytler devoted the early 1790s to his interest in translation, and he dealt with the subject at length in his *Essay on the Principles of Translation*, published in 1791. Subsequent editions were published in 1797 and 1813, and a new edition was produced as recently as 1978. As Jeffrey Huntsman points out in the introduction to this edition, the

work does not constitute a major contribution to the study of linguistics but was valuable in that it laid down some general, but flexible, laws and criteria for translation. Tytler put his principles into practice in 1792, when he produced the first English translation of Schiller's *Die Räuber*, which went through four editions over the next ten years and was much admired by Scott and Coleridge. Tytler's choice of Schiller's work anticipated the appeal that sensational German literature would have in Britain in the early nineteenth century, and his interest in German is evident in his attempts to establish a course of lectures in that language at Edinburgh University.

Tytler inherited the estate of Woodhouselee, in Edinburghshire, on his father's death in 1792. As his wife had already succeeded to the estates of Balnain and Aldourie he was now comfortably wealthy. He was extremely attached to his country home and, after 1792, spent as much time there as possible, enlarging the house so as to be able to entertain his friends. Unfortunately he was struck by a severe illness in 1795, which was only prevented from becoming fatal by the skill of his friend Dr James Gregory (1753–1821). This left his health permanently impaired and he spent the next few years quietly convalescing at Woodhouselee.

Tytler was well enough to resume writing in 1798, when he produced his *Critical Examination*, of a work on Hannibal's journey across the Alps by John Whitaker. In 1799 he produced his only political work, which dealt with the proposed union with Ireland. Entitled *Ireland Profiting by Example*, it urged that Scotland had benefited immensely from the 1707 union with England and that Ireland ought to follow suit in order to derive similar benefits. This tract clearly shows Tytler's conservative, pro-government alignment, and his belief that the union of 1707 was wholly beneficial reflects the extent to which some Scots of his generation had become 'Britons' first and Scots only second.

Tytler returned to poetry in 1800, when he produced an edition of the works of the Scottish Jacobite poet Allan Ramsay, with a preface which again took issue with Addison's views on pastoral writing. He soon returned to history, however, and in 1801 brought out his *Elements of General History*, a work both popular and influential that went through four editions in his lifetime. Based on his lectures, *Elements* is essentially a broad, sweeping survey of history, from the earliest times to the eighteenth century, that reflects his political principles. Of the two major eighteenth-century Scottish historians Tytler is closer to David Hume than William Robertson, taking a markedly royalist and anti-feudal position on Scottish history and stressing the necessity of increased royal power in order to check turbulent aristocrats. He also appears to have been influenced by his father's Jacobitism, in that he gives a comparatively favourable treatment to Mary, queen of Scots, and is severe about the earl of Moray and other protestant nobles who resisted and deposed her. Tytler's last work was a biography of his old mentor Lord Kames, which appeared in 1807.

The early years of the new century saw Tytler attain the

summit of his legal career. The death of Lord Stonefield in 1801 created a vacancy on the bench of the court of session and, again through Melville's influence, Tytler was appointed to the vacant place, on 2 February 1802, as Lord Woodhouselee. On 12 March 1811 he was appointed to the justiciary bench. In 1812 he again fell ill, after returning from a trip to London in connection with some property he had inherited from his relative Sir James Craig, governor of Canada. He moved from Woodhouselee to Edinburgh to receive medical treatment but it soon became clear that there was nothing to be done. He decided to return to Woodhouselee, where he died, shortly after his arrival, on 5 January 1813. He was buried in Greyfriars churchyard in Edinburgh, outlived by his wife, who died on 16 April 1837, aged eighty-four.

Though influential in his day Tytler has not been remembered as a major contributor to historical scholarship and has received less scholarly consideration than either his father, William, or his son Patrick; indeed modern scholars seem chiefly interested in him because of his early influence on Scott. Likewise, though by all accounts an able and conscientious judge, he is not regarded as one of the great Scottish jurists. It is only in the field of translation that he is acknowledged to have some limited importance.   ALEXANDER DU TOIT

Sources J. F. Huntsman, introduction, in A. Fraser Tytler, *Essay on the principles of translation*, facs. edn (1978), ix–xlvi · A. Alison, 'Memoir of the life in writing of the Hon. Alexander Fraser Tytler, Lord Woodhouselee', *Transactions of the Royal Society of Edinburgh*, 8 (1818) · M. Ash, *The strange death of Scottish history* (1980), 22–6 · Chambers, *Scots.* (1855), 7.385–90 · W. Anderson, *The Scottish nation*, 3 (1868), 587–9 · J. Maidment, ed., *Kay's Edinburgh portraits*, 2 vols. (1885), 2.235–8 · *Memorials of his time, by Henry Cockburn* (1909); repr. with introduction by K. F. C. Miller (1974) · F. J. Grant, ed., *The Faculty of Advocates in Scotland, 1532–1943*, Scottish RS, 145 (1944), 210 · A. Bower, *The history of the University of Edinburgh*, 3 vols. (1817–30), 229–38 · A. Mackenzie, *History of the Frasers of Lovat* (1896), 571–2, 557–8 · *The Society of Writers to His Majesty's Signet with a list of the members* (1936), 351 · Burke, *Gen. GB* (1846–9), 2.1452 · C. Kidd, *Subverting Scotland's past: Scottish whig historians and the creation of an Anglo-British identity, 1689–c.1830* (1993), 108–9, 258 · L. R. Timperley, ed., *A directory of landownership in Scotland, c.1770*, Scottish RS, new ser., 5 (1976), 229 · *DNB*
Archives BL, list of portraits belonging to Tytler, Add. MS 6392 · NL Scot., commonplace books, diaries, and sketchbooks, with a memoir 'Remembrances of Woodhouselee' (1812) · NL Scot., MS 2521 · NL Scot., presented MSS, MS 2617 · NL Scot., small collections, MS 1809 · NRA, priv. coll., corresp. and papers, incl. notes for *Life of Kames* · U. Edin. L., letter, corresp., notebooks, and papers | BL, original corresp. of George Chalmers, Add. MS 22901 · BL, letters to Thomas James Matthias, Add. MS 22976 · BL, Macvey Napier papers · BL, Sherborn bequest · Bodl. Oxf., Clark papers · Bodl. Oxf., Heber family papers · Bodl. Oxf., Montagu MSS · NA Scot., letters to G. D. Home relating to *Life of Kames* · NL Scot., Constable collection · NL Scot., Lee papers · NL Scot., Leyden letters · NL Scot., letters to John MacLaurin · NL Scot., Melville papers · NL Scot., Erskine Murray papers · NL Scot., Watson collection · U. Edin., Laing collection
Likenesses J. Lee, drawing, 1798, U. Edin. · A. Skirving, pastel drawing, 1798, priv. coll. [*see illus.*] · group portrait, 1808 (*The Diamond Beetle Case*), repro. in Maidment, ed., *Kay's Edinburgh portraits*, vol. 2 · C. Picart, stipple (after H. Raeburn), BM, NPG; repro. in H. Raeburn, *Contemporary portraits* (1813)
Wealth at death estate of Woodhouselee, Edinburghshire, valued at £300: valuation roll · probably estate of Balnain; probably

estate of Aldourie: Timperley, ed., *Directory of landownership in Scotland*, 229; Mackenzie, *History of the Frasers*

Tytler, Christian Helen Fraser- [*née* Christian Helen Shairp] (1897–1995), army officer, was born in Elie, Fife, on 23 August 1897, the only daughter and youngest of three children of John Campbell Shairp (1858–1913), advocate and sheriff, of Houston, Uphall, Linlithgow, and his wife, Harriet Caroline (d. 1949), the third daughter in a family of five daughters and two sons of Lieutenant-Colonel Sir Thomas Erskine, second baronet, army officer, of Cambo, Fife. Her two older brothers, Norman (b. 1891) and John (b. 1894), both served with the Ayrshire yeomanry during the First World War; Norman died on active service on 13 October 1918. She was educated at home by a governess, and then joined the Foreign Office, in which she worked as a clerical officer from 1917 to 1919. In the latter year she attended the peace conference at Versailles. There she met, and on 19 June 1919 married, Neil Fraser-Tytler (1889–1937), a colonel in the Inverness-shire Royal Horse Artillery. He was the second and only surviving son in a family of two sons and one daughter of Lieutenant-Colonel Edward Grant Fraser-Tytler, army officer, of Aldourie and Balnain, Inverness-shire, and his first wife, Edith Adriana, daughter of Sir Charles Selwyn, lord justice of appeal. They had two daughters.

Between the wars Christian lived at her husband's home, Aldourie Castle, Loch Ness (and believed in the existence of the Loch Ness monster). After her husband's death she joined the ATS, which had been formed in 1938 to replace the women's army corps, which had done sterling work in the First World War but had subsequently been disbanded.

Fraser-Tytler served at the War Office from 1939 to 1943 as a member of the staff of the adjutant-general, Sir Ronald Adam; she became a controller in 1940. With Dame Helen Gwynne-Vaughan she reorganized the service and was appointed director of organization, ATS. She established and ran AG16, the department responsible for recruiting and organizing the rapidly expanding ATS. A major problem in those early days was deciding which tasks could be managed successfully by women, and, once decisions had been taken, ensuring that suitable appointments and postings were arranged. This was an area in which there was considerable divergence of opinion in the army but where Fraser-Tytler's tact and insight proved invaluable. Her achievements were recognized by her appointment as CBE (military) in 1941. Hers was one of the first honours conferred on a woman during the war.

By 1943 the need for, and soon the indispensability of, women on anti-aircraft sites was unmistakable. ATS staff were serving in anti-aircraft command in a variety of tasks from clerical to transport and cooking, but were regarded as particularly valuable in the mixed anti-aircraft batteries of 200 men and 200 women. With the arrival of flying bombs (V1s) and rockets (V2s) many of these anti-aircraft units had to be hastily deployed on coastal sites where conditions were far from satisfactory, a fact noted by the press, among other critics. At least one MP, Tom Driberg, encouraged ATS women to express their complaints. In

1943 Fraser-Tytler was appointed deputy director ATS in anti-aircraft command, and in the next two years she had to deal with this and similar problems, which involved endless travelling to gun sites, mostly in remote areas. Her duties also included escorting the queen (later Queen Elizabeth, the queen mother) and the princess royal to anti-aircraft units where ATS people were serving, and to bomb-damaged areas.

After demobilization Fraser-Tytler returned to Aldourie Castle, where she indulged her passion for fishing. She became a JP and ran the ATS in Ross and Cromarty and Inverness-shire, as well as serving on the Scottish council of the Young Women's Christian Association, and representing Scotland on the national council. She also founded the local branch of the women's rural institute (the Scottish Women's Institute).

Although a strong woman, with powerful organizational abilities, Christian Fraser-Tytler was far from the conventional idea of a female brigadier, and always remained charming and elegant. She died at St Andrews on 30 June 1995 and was survived by her two daughters, Ann (b. 1920), who married Sir David Erskine, fifth baronet, and Mary Hermione (b. 1922), who married Rear-Admiral Sir Patrick Morgan.   PHILIP WARNER

Sources *Daily Telegraph* (24 July 1995) · *The Independent* (19 July 1995) · *The Times* (13 July 1995) · ATS records, Army Records Centre, Bourne Avenue, Hayes, Middlesex · WWW · Burke, *Peerage* · Burke, *Gen. GB*
Likenesses photograph, repro. in *The Times* · photograph, repro. in *The Independent*
Wealth at death £233,324.90: confirmation, 12 June 1996, NA Scot., SC/CO 925/9

Tytler, Henry William (1752/3–1808), translator and physician, was born at Fern near Brechin, Forfarshire, the son of George Tytler (1705/6–1785), minister of Fern, and his wife, Janet Robertson (d. 1795); he was the younger brother of James *Tytler (1745–1804). He published *The Works of Callimachus Translated into English Verse* (dated 1793), with a preface by the earl of Buchan, said to be the first translation of a Greek poet into English published by a native of Scotland. His model was avowedly Pope's *Iliad*, in which he had steeped himself by way of preparation; he rendered Callimachus's *Hymns* and *Lock of Berenice* into heroic couplets, the epigrams into rhymed tetrameters. In 1797 he published *Paedotrophia, or, The Art of Nursing and Rearing Children*, translated from the sixteenth-century Latin of Scévole de Sainte-Marthe. Pope was again the model, Tytler explaining that he had avoided the 'low disgusting phrases' of the previous translator; he used his professional knowledge to supply medical and historical notes on the text; his preface compares Sainte-Marthe, not wholly to his disadvantage, with Virgil. He also published a 'Voyage from the Cape of Good Hope' and some other miscellaneous poems, and completed a translation of the longest poem in classical Latin, Silius Italicus's *Punica*, posthumously published in two volumes at Calcutta in 1828. He died in Edinburgh on 22 July 1808.
                                    RICHARD JENKYNS

Sources H. Tytler, *The works of Callimachus translated into English verse* (1793) · W. Anderson, *The Scottish nation*, 3 (1877), 593 · *Fasti Scot.*, new edn, 5.397 · *GM*, 1st ser., 78 (1808), 852 · *British Critic*, 11 (1798), 70–72 · *N&Q*, 12th ser., 11 (1922), 510

Tytler, James [*called* Balloon Tytler] (1745–1804), balloonist and radical, was born on 17 December 1745 at the manse at Fern, Forfarshire, the fourth child of George Tytler (1705/6–1785), Church of Scotland minister in the presbytery of Brechin, and his wife, Janet Robertson (d. 1795). His brother Henry William *Tytler was a noted physician and translator. He was educated at the local parish school and possibly at Aberdeen University, which he claimed to have left before the age of fifteen. Tytler was then apprenticed to a Mr Ogilvie, a Forfar surgeon, before in 1763 he entered Edinburgh University, where he studied under William Cullen, from whom he gained a lifelong interest in experimental chemistry. Funds for his education were raised by work as a surgeon on a whaling ship, the *Royal Bounty*, in which he sailed to Greenland in mid-1765. On his return Tytler became involved with members of the Glasite religious sect, through which he met Elizabeth, daughter of James Rattray, writer to the signet, whom he married some time after 27 October 1765; the couple had five sons.

Tytler now began the first of several periods of piecemeal work, financial hardship, and exile in Newcastle upon Tyne to escape the debtors' prison. In 1772 the family returned to Edinburgh, where Tytler bolstered his meagre income as an apothecary with a series of small-scale publishing ventures, beginning in January 1774 with the short-lived *Gentleman and Lady's Magazine*. Later that year he published two works on theology which revealed his antipathy to Humean scepticism and religious factionalism, a conviction that now prompted his break with the Glasites. More significant than the content of these works was the fact that Tytler produced both on a home-made printing press, evidence of the innovation and resourcefulness that he brought to many of his scientific and (often unsuccessful) money-making schemes over the next three decades. About this time his wife, Elizabeth, left to establish herself as a grocer in the Canongate area of the city. The couple were divorced in 1788, by when Tytler had been involved in two further relationships; the first was with the sister of John Cairns, a local butcher; the second, after her death in or before 1782, was with Jean Aitkenhead (1739/40–1834), with whom he had two children and lived for the rest of his life.

In 1776, through his new literary connections, Tytler was appointed editor of the second edition of Andrew Bell's and Colin Macfarquhar's *Encyclopaedia Britannica*. Under Tytler's editorship the collection was enlarged from three to ten volumes (many of the new entries being written by Tytler) and published between 1777 and 1784. Though steady work, the editorship was not well paid. Tytler and his family now lodged at Duddingston near Edinburgh in the home of a washerwoman on whose upturned tub Tytler composed hundreds of encyclopaedia articles. His talent for abridgement coupled with his ongoing penury prompted further publishing schemes in

James Tytler (1745–1804), by Hannah Crowninshield, 1804

these years, notably a reduced version of the twenty-volume *Universal History* as the *General History of All Nations, Ancient and Modern* (only one volume of which appeared) and a self-printed translation of Virgil's *Eclogues*.

Tytler's enterprise next found expression in the balloon mania which swept Britain following the Montgolfier brothers' successful flight at Versailles in September 1783. Though now virtually unknown in the history of ballooning, Tytler was the first Briton to make a successful ascent (27 August 1784), predating by several weeks the flights of the Italian Vincenzo Lunardi in London and the first English aeronaut, James Sadler from Oxford. Tytler's obscurity undoubtedly owes much to the mixed fortunes he enjoyed during his four attempts at manned flight, the relatively short ground distance covered, and the bathetic conclusion of his much-publicized final flight (11 October 1784), when his balloon crashed before hundreds of paying spectators at Edinburgh's Comely Gardens. Nevertheless, by this date Tytler had twice left the ground in a craft of his own design and construction, becoming on 27 August, as the *Edinburgh Advertiser* reported next day, the 'first person in Great Britain to have navigated the air' when at a height of 350 feet he flew for half a mile across the city (Fergusson, 77). But what little coverage Tytler received in August was soon forgotten following Sadler's landmark flight on 4 October (over 6 miles at 3600 feet) and the triumphant display given by Lunardi on a visit to Edinburgh a year later. Subsequent discussions of ballooning in the *Scots Magazine* (November 1805) made no reference to Tytler, though his achievement was recognized in Lunardi's *Account of Five Aerial Voyages in Scotland* (1786).

After his brief career as an aeronaut Tytler returned to a life of hack-journalism, scientific invention, and debt. In 1788 he fled again to England, after which there is no record of his movements until he returned to Edinburgh three years later to begin his final periodical, the *Historical Register* (last edition July 1792). Born perhaps of his long-running belief in religious liberty or a sense of injustice surrounding his literary and scientific career, Tytler now became increasingly interested in the radical cause in Scotland. In 1792 he joined the Society of the Friends of the People, a constitutional reform society to promote non-violent opposition to Pitt's administration. However, his hostility to the ministry's actions, notably its proclamation against seditious writings, led him to advocate more extreme political reform and to make personal attacks on leading personalities such as the lord advocate, Robert Dundas. In November 1792 Tytler fell foul of the targets of his abuse after his essay 'To the people and their friends' had denounced the House of Commons as a 'vile junto of aristocrats', and had called on readers to petition George III to replace existing MPs with representatives of 'good understanding and character' and to withhold paying their taxes should the demand be ignored (Fergusson, 125–6). Tytler was arrested and charged with seditious libel on 4 December 1792, the first person in Edinburgh to be detained as part of the government's crackdown on Scotland's radical societies. Faced with a court appearance in the new year, Tytler left the city for Belfast; there he was joined by Jean Aitkenhead, and from there he published pamphlets attacking Thomas Paine's deism.

Tytler's final years were spent in Salem, Massachusetts, where he emigrated with his family in 1795. Here, at Cat Cove near Salem Neck, he eked out a living through journalism and literary compilations such as his poorly received *Treatise on the Plague and Yellow Fever* (1799). Disappointment led increasingly to drink, and it was when inebriated that he fell and drowned near his home on 9 January 1804. His body was discovered and buried two days later at the East Meeting-House, Salem.

MEG RUSSELL

Sources DNB · J. Fergusson, *Balloon Tytler* (1972) · N. J. Gossman, 'Tytler, James (1745–1804)', *BDMBR*, vol. 1 · J. Kay, *A series of original portraits and caricature etchings … with biographical sketches and illustrative anecdotes*, ed. [H. Paton and others], 1 (1837), 86–9 · L. T. C. Rolt, *The aeronauts: a history of ballooning, 1783–1903* (1966) · R. Meek, *Biographical sketch of the life of James Tytler* (1805)
Likenesses H. Crowninshield, watercolour, 1804, Essex Institute, Salem, Massachusetts [*see illus.*] · portrait, 1804, repro. in Fergusson, *Balloon Tytler* · J. Kay, group portrait, etching, BM

Tytler, Patrick Fraser (1791–1849), historian, was born at 108 Princes Street, Edinburgh, on 30 August 1791, the youngest of four children of Alexander Fraser *Tytler (1747–1813), advocate and later judge with the title of Lord Woodhouselee, and of his wife, Ann (1752/3–1837), eldest daughter and heir of William Fraser of Balnain, Inverness-shire.

The Tytlers were a distinguished legal and academic family typical of contemporary Edinburgh, enlightened in outlook and tory in politics; Patrick would in later life

Patrick Fraser Tytler (1791–1849), by Sir John Watson-Gordon

thank God he had not a drop of whig blood in his veins. His parents encouraged him to develop his interests in a happy, indulgent home that freely offered its hospitality to the city's literati. Walter Scott took the little Tytlers on story-telling walks; the Revd John Lee (1779–1859), afterwards principal of the university, was Patrick's private tutor. Tytler also attended Edinburgh high school until 1808, when he was sent to Chobham House, a school in Surrey, to improve his Latin. He returned in 1810 to enrol in the University of Edinburgh, where he studied law and classics, and he was called to the Scottish bar on 3 July 1813. He would practise until 1832, never with great diligence or enthusiasm. A minor legal post awarded him in 1816, king's counsel in exchequer, paid £150 a year for more rewarding pursuits. While still a bachelor he took two foreign tours. In the company of his cousins the Alison brothers, William the pioneer of reform in public health and Archibald the historian, he went to Paris in the summer of 1814. Four years later he visited Norway. On 30 March 1826 he married Rachel (d. 15 April 1835), second daughter of Thomas Hog of Newliston, Linlithgowshire, and of his second wife, Mary Stewart. They had two sons and one daughter.

Up to about the time of his first marriage, Tytler was unsure whether to devote himself to literature or history. He had made attempts at drama and poetry, none particularly promising. He contributed to *Blackwood's Edinburgh Magazine* from 1817, but was deterred from doing more by dislike of its most popular feature, the scurrilous 'Chaldee' manuscripts. Tytler developed into an earnest young man, unsparing in self-examination and relentless in efforts to raise his own moral character, as notebooks and

diaries attest. In his outer life this rigour ran in two channels, in his practice of episcopalian piety and in his obsessively disciplined scholarship, both of which he regarded as spiritual exercises. Except for a bit of fishing and shooting, he had no interests apart from these, and he looked the part he had chosen in life. His brother-in-law John Hog wrote: 'He seemed so much older than he really was. He was singularly pale and old looking, a circumstance which I have since attributed to his elevated forehead, which … gave him the appearance of premature baldness' (Burgon, 182).

There was in Tytler, in other words, not a great deal of scope for literary fancy, and almost inevitably history came to dominate his other interests, at first in the form of biography. He followed his earliest published work, *The Life of the Admirable Crichton of Cluny* (1819) with a *Life of Sir Thomas Craig* (1823) and a *Life of Wicliff* (1826). In 1823 he helped to found the Bannatyne Club for the publication of Scottish muniments. With his father-in-law and Adam Urquhart he edited the club's volume of *The Memoirs of the War in Scotland and Ireland, 1689–1691* by General Hugh Mackay (1833).

Meanwhile a turning point for Tytler had come in 1823, while he was staying at Abbotsford as a guest of Walter Scott, who proposed to him that he should write a new history of Scotland. There had been no major one since William Robertson's of 1759. A vast amount of lost information was becoming available again from the herculean labours of Thomas Thomson (1768–1852), depute clerk register and another leading light of the Bannatyne Club, who had spent twenty years reducing to order the chaotic public records of Scotland. It was now clear that they would permit the entire history of the country to be rewritten, and Scott was anxious for a man energetic, talented, and youthful enough to take on the job. For Tytler it proved indeed to be his life's work.

In the way he executed Scott's commission, Tytler helped bring about something of a revolution in British historical method. He did not yet aspire to raise his discipline to fully scientific status, in the manner of the German school founded by Leopold von Ranke later in the century. But he insisted on the primacy of personal research in original sources, and the superiority of these to published memoirs, partisan manifestos, popular memories, and the programmatic morality of the author as the material or the organizing principle of historiography. Utterly dedicated to his task, Tytler set future historians a high example of objectivity in his painstaking scrutiny and strict evaluation of relevant documents. If in writing them up he was understandably inclined to show off the fruits of his exertions, and include a good deal of repetitive or tenuously related citation, he has at least by his unwavering reliability saved many successors from enduring again the tedium to which he so willingly submitted himself.

Tytler began this great enterprise, after finishing other work in hand, in 1826. A mere two years later the first volume appeared, opening with the reign of Alexander III (1249–86); Scott, in the *Quarterly Review* of November 1829, regretted that it did not go back further. The rest followed in eight instalments. The last, carrying the narrative down to the union of the crowns in 1603, came out in 1843. As publication proceeded, Tytler, who so prided himself on his impartiality, felt pained to discover that the true history of Scotland he was toiling to reveal by no means met with universal acceptance. He relished demolishing old legends, only to find that his public preferred comforting national myths.

There was no special problem with the earlier volumes, which covered subjects such as the wars of independence, on which all Scots could agree. But Tytler ran into trouble as soon as he moved into the more sensitive early modern era. For example, he came across evidence in the state paper office that seemed to implicate the reformer John Knox in the murder of David Rizzio, the favourite of Mary, queen of Scots. For that he was berated by Thomas McCrie (1797–1875), son of Knox's biographer, a minister of the same name, in an issue of December 1840 of *The Witness*, the organ of the evangelical wing of the Church of Scotland. Attacks on Tytler sharpened as his treatment of the later periods unfolded. Preserved in the Laing papers at Edinburgh University Library (La. II. 494) is a letter from a fellow historian, Mark Napier, which abused his lack of patriotism over sixteen pages, each punctuated at the foot by the injunction 'Read on, you bitch!' A more cogent summation of this increasingly hostile reception appeared with Patrick Fraser's survey of the completed work *Tytler's History Examined* (1848), the collection in book form of critical articles previously published in the *North British Review*. He objected that the whole had been written from an aristocratic, tory, episcopalian point of view, underrating the role of the Scottish people. The scholar who placed objectivity above everything thus stood accused of deliberate bias. The reproach bruised Tytler. A generation earlier, his mentor Scott had in the Waverley novels succeeded in the literary depiction of a Scotland informed by many of the values they shared, yet in a way that won fulsome assent from his readers. Tytler, trying to do the same on a factual plane, failed. But perhaps, in a changed Scotland of bourgeois politics and sectarian religion, that synthesis was no longer possible.

At least in a personal sense, however, this casting out of Tytler sent him off in fresh directions where he could still seek fulfilment. On the whigs' coming to power in 1830, he had lost his legal post. In 1836 their partisan habits of patronage caused him to be passed over as historiographer royal of Scotland in favour of a manifestly inferior scholar, George Brodie. Meanwhile, free to devote all his time to research, he had been going often to London, drawn there by the fact that, for the later centuries he was working on, Scottish and English affairs grew ever more entangled. Lord Melville, tory political manager of Scotland, had originally arranged for his admission to the state paper office. But the whig authorities gratuitously tried to keep him out on the absurd pretext that someone writing Scottish history should not be allowed into English archives. His refusal to truckle to this outrageous treatment, and the respect he was winning among English scholars, brought in 1836 a revision of policy on the public records. The commission in charge of them, after taking evidence from Tytler among others, agreed to the principle of authorized access and to a programme of publication. It adopted his proposal of concentrating in the first instance on lists and calendars of documents, rather than on the inevitably slow and expensive reproduction of full texts.

With his labours keeping him so much in London, Tytler decided in 1837, after the death of his first wife, to settle there permanently. More and more, too, he turned to English history, writing a *Life of King Henry VIII* (1837) and *England under the Reign of Edward VI and Mary* (1839). On 11 August 1845 he married an Englishwoman, Anastasia (*d.* 1857), daughter of Thomson Bonar of Camden Place, Kent. Once the final volume of his *History of Scotland* was out in 1843, Queen Victoria invited him to Windsor Castle to help Prince Albert arrange the royal historical miniatures. He penned for her a paper, afterwards published in a limited edition (1843), *Historical Notes on the Lennox or Darnley Jewel*. In 1844 he was granted a pension from the civil list.

Tytler never returned to Scotland, except for brief holidays, and never deigned to frame a systematic retort to his detractors at home. Exile and silence were a strange fate for a man who wanted nothing more than to write the definitive history of his country. On 24 December 1849 Tytler died at Malvern, but was brought back for burial on 29 December in his family's lair in the churchyard of Greyfriars, Edinburgh. The general rejection of his work marked the end of efforts to consolidate the achievement of Scott with a tory academic narrative of the Scottish past. The field was left clear for whigs and radicals who, by the time of Peter Hume Brown at the turn of the century, monopolized the historiography of Scotland.

MICHAEL FRY

Sources J. W. Burgon, *Portrait of a Christian gentleman* (1859) · A. Tytler, *Reminiscences of Patrick Fraser Tytler* (1854) · M. Ash, *The strange death of Scottish history* (1980) · G. Seton, *A history of the family of Seton during eight centuries*, 2 vols. (1896) · **Archives** Aldourie Castle, Inverness-shire, muniments · BL, poems, genealogical notes and corresp., Add. MS 39523 · NRA, priv. coll., corresp. and papers · U. Edin. L., corresp. and papers | NL Scot., Bannatyne Club minute books · U. Edin. L., letters to David Laing · **Likenesses** M. S. Carpenter, oils, *c.*1845, NPG · W. Drummond, lithograph, BM; repro. in *Athenaeum portraits* (1836) · R. J. Lane, lithograph, NPG · J. Watson-Gordon, oil study, Scot. NPG · J. Watson-Gordon, oils, Scot. NPG [*see illus.*] · **Wealth at death** 1,336 8*s.* 9*d.*—inventory; £1500 India government security; £ 6306 2*s.* 7*d.* additional estate: Edinburgh, 1850

Tytler, Sarah. *See* Keddie, Henrietta (1827–1914).

Tytler, William (1711–1792), lawyer and historian, was born in Edinburgh on 12 October 1711, the eighth of the twelve children of Alexander Tytler, writer to the signet, and Jane, the daughter of William Leslie, an Aberdeen merchant. He was educated at Edinburgh high school, and at Edinburgh University where he studied law. He was apprenticed to William Forbes and became a member of the Society of Writers to the Signet on 5 October 1742, subsequently serving as treasurer between 1788 and 1792. In September 1745 he married Anne (d. 1783), daughter of James Craig, a solicitor of Costerton, and they had eight children. He acquired the estate of Woodhouselee, about 6 miles from Edinburgh.

In 1760 Tytler published *An historical and critical enquiry into the evidence produced by the earls of Murray and Morton against Mary, queen of Scots*, which was generally well received by reviewers who included Samuel Johnson in the *Gentleman's Magazine* and Tobias Smollett in the *Critical Review*. It was republished five times (including French translations). This work was in part a critique of earlier scholarship by William Robertson and David Hume; Robertson remained on friendly terms with Tytler, while Hume did not. Tytler was an original member and vice-president of the Society of Scottish Antiquaries founded by David Erskine, eleventh earl of Buchan, in November 1780, and he published 'A dissertation on the marriage of Mary to the earl of Bothwell' (1792), as well as a number of other articles on various subjects, in the society's transactions, *Archaeologia Scotica*. Aside from the *Enquiry* he is best remembered for his edition of *The Poetical Remains of James the First, King of Scotland* (1783), which contained the first known printed text of 'The Kingis Quair' from a manuscript rediscovered in the Bodleian Library ten years earlier at the instigation of Thomas Percy.

Tytler was a well-known member of Edinburgh's polite, literary society. He was a member of the Select Society (1754–c.1763) and a member and director of the Edinburgh Musical Society (founded 1728); he was himself a harpsichordist and flautist. He contributed an article to *The Lounger* (16, 1786), entitled 'Defects of modern female education in teaching the duties of a wife'. A widower, he died at Woodhouselee on 12 September 1792, survived by three of his children, Alexander Fraser *Tytler, Patrick, and Christina.   A. J. G. MACKAY, rev. SARAH COUPER

Sources H. MacKenzie, 'A short account of the life and writings of William Tytler', *Transactions of the Royal Society of Edinburgh*, 4/1 (1798), (17–34) · 'Short characteristical notices of the late William Tytler', *The Bee*, 13 (1793), 1–11 · J. W. Burgon, *The portrait of a Christian gentleman: a memoir of Patrick Fraser Tytler* (1859), 3–8 · [F. J. Grant], *A history of the Society of Writers to Her Majesty's Signet* (1890), 206 · W. Smellie, *Account of the institution and progress of the Society of the Antiquaries of Scotland* (1782), 3, 19 · W. Steven, *The history of the high school of Edinburgh* (1849), 212 · T. Royle, *The mainstream companion to Scottish literature* (1993), 317 · 'Memoirs of William Tytler', *Scots Magazine*, 63 (1801), 155–6 · Allibone, *Dict.* · J. Dwyer, *Virtuous discourse: sensibility and community in late eighteenth-century Scotland* (1987)
Likenesses J. Jones, mezzotint, pubd 1790 (after H. Raeburn), BM · J. Edgar, group portrait, wash drawing, c.1854, Scot. NPG · I. Beugo, engraving (after H. Raeburn), repro. in 'Memoirs of William Tytler' · R. Scott, engraving (after H. Raeburn), repro. in 'Short characteristical notices of the late William Tytler'

Ua Braín, Tigernach (d. 1088), abbot of Clonmacnoise and supposed annalist, as well as heading that major Irish midland monastery was also abbot of the somewhat less important Roscommon. His name has been misleadingly attached to the so-called annals of Tigernach on account of a note in Oxford, Bodleian Library, MS Rawlinson B.488,

the sole surviving manuscript of the annals for the period after the emperor Antoninus Pius. Under 1088, the year in which the annals of Ulster records his death, the manuscript (of the fourteenth century) has a note saying that Tigernach wrote the text up to that point. This does not make it clear whether he was simply the scribe or also the annalist; the second is perhaps the more likely. In another set of annals, *Chronicum Scotorum*, he is said to have been 'the heir of Ciarán and of Commán', namely abbot of both Clonmacnoise and Roscommon, and to have belonged to the Síl Muiredaig, the descendants of Muiredach Muillethan (d. 702), the ruling dynasty of the Connachta. The Uí Braín were a branch that had no share in the kingship enjoyed by their kinsmen but had, instead, gone into the church. The earliest attested member of the Uí Braín to be abbot of Clonmacnoise died in 989; another who was abbot of Roscommon died in 1170 and yet another in 1234; the ecclesiastical prominence of the Uí Braín was, therefore, long-standing. Clonmacnoise had had property within Connacht ever since the seventh century; and in the eleventh was the pre-eminent church of the province. Tigernach's abbacy was an example of the close link between Clonmacnoise, itself in Mide, and the Connachta; it could maintain close relations with the rulers of two provinces because they were normally in alliance. Annals, such as those which pass under the name of Tigernach, were carried forward by a succession of annalists; Tigernach Ua Braín may have been one such, but the importance of his office and his own distinguished family background give the annals of Tigernach for the generation before 1088 an added interest.

T. M. CHARLES-EDWARDS

Sources W. Stokes, ed., 'The annals of Tigernach [8 pts]', *Revue Celtique*, 16 (1895), 374–419; 17 (1896), 6–33, 119–263, 337–420; 18 (1897), 9–59, 150–97, 267–303, 374–91; pubd sep. (1993) · *Ann. Ulster* · W. M. Hennessy, ed. and trans., *Chronicum Scotorum: a chronicle of Irish affairs*, Rolls Series, 46 (1866) · P. Walsh, 'The annals attributed to Tigernach', *Irish Historical Studies*, 2 (1940–41), 154–9 · K. Grabowski and D. Dumville, *Chronicles and annals of mediaeval Ireland and Wales: the Clonmacnoise-group texts* (1984) · K. W. Hughes, *Early Christian Ireland: introduction to the sources* (1972), chap. 4
Archives Bodl. Oxf., MS Rawl. B.488

Ua Briain, Domnall Mór [Donal O'Brien] (d. **1194**), king of Thomond, was the son of Toirdelbach Ua Briain (d. 1167), king of Thomond. He became king in 1168, blinding his brother, Brian, in the same year. His marriage to Órlaith, daughter of Diarmait Mac Murchada (d. 1171), king of Leinster, may be presumed to have taken place following his accession and Mac Murchada's return from exile with Anglo-Norman mercenaries. In 1170 Mac Murchada sent Anglo-Norman forces to assist Ua Briain in repelling an invasion by Ruaidrí Ua Conchobair, king of Connacht, and contender for the high-kingship. The following year Ruaidrí took hostages from Domnall and they besieged the Anglo-Norman garrison in Dublin together; but subsequently Ua Briain campaigned in Osraige with his brother-in-law, Richard fitz Gilbert, earl of Pembroke and lord of Striguil, known as Strongbow. On Henry II's arrival, Ua Briain submitted to him, thereby rejecting the high-kingship of Ruaidrí Ua Conchobair.

In 1173 Ua Briain destroyed the castle of Kilkenny following the retreat to Waterford by the Anglo-Norman garrison in advance of his forces and the next year he overcame an Anglo-Norman raiding party at Thurles, which suffered heavy casualties. In 1175 he treacherously slew a son of Mac Gilla Pátraic, king of Osraige, and blinded dynastic rivals, Diarmait and Mathgamain Ua Briain, in his residence at Caislén Uí Chonaing (Castleconnell, Limerick). Ruaidri Ua Conchobair took retaliatory action for this deed by attempting to remove Ua Briain from the kingship of Thomond. Ruaidrí may have sought to use the treaty of Windsor, negotiated with Henry II in 1175, to wrest control of the city of Limerick from Domnall; but the Anglo-Norman garrison (which installed itself in Limerick in 1175) abandoned the city to Ua Briain in 1176 and Limerick was not retaken by Anglo-Normans until after his death. The importance of his control of Limerick is evidenced by his use of the title king of Limerick in his charters; he was described likewise by Gerald of Wales and in the so-called *Song of Dermot and the Earl*. During the expedition to Ireland of John, son of Henry II, in 1185, the Anglo-Norman garrison of Ardfinnan was twice attacked and suffered fatalities at Ua Briain's hands, although he himself incurred casualties inflicted by the Anglo-Norman garrison of Tibberaghny. In 1192 he won a significant military victory over an Anglo-Norman force at Thurles and in 1193 the castle of Briginis (Breckinish Island in the Shannon estuary) was built by Anglo-Normans 'with the consent of Ua Briain' as a check on Domnall Mac Carthaig, king of Desmond.

An original charter in favour of the Cistercian abbey of Holycross, which Ua Briain founded, survives, as well as a charter-text in favour of Brictius, bishop of Limerick. He was responsible for embellishing St Mary's Cathedral in Limerick as well as the cathedral church of St Flannan, Killaloe, of which his brother, Consaidín, was bishop from 1179 to 1194. Ua Briain successfully reconstituted the kingship of Thomond, which had been seriously weakened following the defeat incurred by his father, Toirdelbach, at the battle of Móin Mór in 1151. In 1177 Henry II made a speculative grant of the 'kingdom of Limerick' to Philip de Briouze but it remained unrealized during Domnall's lifetime. He retained his kingdom intact against incursions by the Meic Carthaig of Desmond, the Meic Gilla Pátraic of Osraige, and the Uí Conchobair of Connacht, as well as by Anglo-Normans. Some annals style him king of Munster at his death in 1194. Domnall's death was followed by bitter disputes between his three sons. It was ultimately the second of these, Donnchad Cairprech *Ó Briain, who established himself as king of Thomond, while his elder brother, Muirchertach Finn, became king of Limerick.

M. T. FLANAGAN

Sources S. Mac Airt, ed. and trans., *The annals of Inisfallen* (1951) · W. Stokes, ed., 'The annals of Tigernach [8 pts]', *Revue Celtique*, 16 (1895), 374–419; 17 (1896), 6–33, 119–263, 337–420; 18 (1897), 9–59, 150–97, 267–303, 374–91; pubd sep. (1993) · *AFM* · Giraldus Cambrensis, *Expugnatio Hibernica / The conquest of Ireland*, ed. and trans. A. B. Scott and F. X. Martin (1978), 52–3, 92–3, 138–9, 148–9, 160–63, 166–7, 234–5, 236–7 · G. H. Orpen, ed. and trans., *The song of Dermot and the earl* (1892), lines 1758, 2035–46, 2093, 2100, 2130, 2156, 3346, 3385, 3399 · S. Ó hInnse, ed. and trans., *Miscellaneous Irish annals, AD 1114–1437* (1947) · J. T. Gilbert, ed., *Facsimiles of national manuscripts of Ireland*, 4 vols. in 5 (1874–84), vol. 2, no. 62 · J. MacCaffrey, ed., *The Black Book of Limerick* (1907), 34 · M. C. Dobbs, ed. and trans., 'The Ban-shenchus [pt 2]', *Revue Celtique*, 48 (1931), 163–234, esp. 233 · A. Gwynn and D. F. Gleeson, *A history of the diocese of Killaloe* (1962), 166–8

Ua Briain, Muirchertach [Murtagh O'Brien] (*c.*1050–1119), king of Munster and high-king of Ireland, was of the Dál Cais dynasty of north Munster and was the son of Toirdelbach *Ua Briain (1009–1086) and Derbfhorgaill (*d.* 1098), daughter of Tadc Mac Gilla Pádraig, king of Osraige. According to the uncorroborated statement of the annals of Ulster, he was born in 1050. Like his great-grandfather Brian Bóruma, Muirchertach tried to make the idea of the high-kingship of Ireland a political reality. He secured his position in the south, and extended Uí Briain control into the midlands and Connacht for a time, but failed to bring to heel Domnall Ua Lochlainn, king of Cenél nEógain in the north. His control of Dublin, his activities in the Irish Sea region, and his courtship of Armagh's clerics all played a part, and he also made use of propaganda: the *Cogad Gáedel re Gallaib* ('War of the Irish with the foreigners') presented Brian Bóruma as the nation's defence against the viking onslaught and Muirchertach as his worthy successor. The national extent of his aspirations is seen in his ruthless treatment of weaker kingdoms and his dealings with the church. He presided over the early formal stages of ecclesiastical reform and the attempt to create a national, diocesan institution.

Muirchertach Ua Briain and his family As the eleventh century progressed and competition among the major dynasties intensified, the Norse towns became increasingly important in the struggle for power. Toirdelbach Ua Briain made Limerick in the west his capital and in 1075 appointed Muirchertach ruler of Dublin in the east. But when Toirdelbach sent his forces north under Muirchertach, they suffered defeat at Ard Monainn. Toirdelbach realized that a more cautious approach was required. A master of the policy of divide and rule, he tried to keep the Cenél nEógain in check by supporting their rivals, the Ulaid. This had some success, but the events of 1084 showed Muirchertach that it would not do as a long-term strategy.

In that year Muirchertach defeated Donnchad Ua Ruairc of Connacht at the battle of Móin Cruinneoige. Among the casualties on Ua Ruairc's side was Cennétig Ua Briain whose grandfather, Donnchad mac Briain, had been ousted from the kingship of Munster by Toirdelbach. Cennétig, as Toirdelbach's bitter opponent, was appointed king of Telach Óc by the Cenél nEógain in response to Toirdelbach's support for the Ulaid. His fighting on behalf of Ua Ruairc was an ominous sign, for it indicated that Domnall Ua Lochlainn, king of Cenél nEógain, had reached an understanding with Ua Ruairc. The capable Domnall was a problem with which Muirchertach would have to deal directly.

This was forcefully brought home to Muirchertach Ua

Briain after his father's death in 1086. Munster was divided between three of Toirdelbach's sons: Muirchertach, Tadc, and their half-brother Diarmait. Tadc outlived his father by a month, but despite being given control over Waterford and its hinterland, Diarmait continued to cause trouble for Muirchertach, who was trying to establish himself in the south. He defeated Donnchad, king of Leinster, in 1087 but two naval expeditions against Connacht failed. Domnall Ua Lochlainn reacted quickly. The alliance with Connacht materialized and the combined forces marched into north Munster, destroying Kincora, the Uí Briain stronghold. Muirchertach was preoccupied with events in the east where Munster dominance had declined since the death of Toirdelbach. A fleet sent to settle his score with Connacht was trapped by Ruaidrí Ua Conchobair, king of Connacht, and Domnall Ua Maíl Shechnaill, king of Meath, who together marched into north Munster. This was the second major attack into the Uí Briain heartland in two years. Muirchertach had no choice but to agree to peace terms with Domnall Ua Lochlainn.

The struggle for the high-kingship In 1092 Ruaidrí Ua Conchobair was blinded by the Uí Flaithbertaig. This was a major development. Muirchertach Ua Briain moved decisively and attacked Connacht, expelling the Uí Chonchobair, and appointing a puppet king. With Connacht under Muirchertach's control and ruled by an appointee with no traditional rights, the king of Meath recognized that the political map was being redrawn in Muirchertach's favour and submitted to him.

These signs of Ua Briain's growing power caused alarm in the north. The inevitable confrontation between Domnall Ua Lochlainn and Muirchertach occurred at Dublin in 1094. Domnall, supported by the Ulaid, by Ua Maíl Shechnaill of Meath, and by a fleet of ninety ships supplied by Godred (or Gofraid), Norse king of Dublin and the Isles (that is, Man and the islands off the west Scottish coast), routed the Munster forces. However the Ulaid— one-time allies of the Uí Briain—remembered their old loyalties and Domnall's alliance dissolved. Muirchertach then took measures against Dublin and Meath. He expelled Meath's rulers and, to ensure future compliance, divided the kingdom and appointed two puppet kings. This was a highly significant development. Meath was an ancient kingdom, but Muirchertach's casual disdain revealed a new attitude to kingship. No matter how venerable their titles, the rights of lesser kings were to be subordinated to the ambitions of the dominant dynasties in competition for the kingship of all Ireland. Godred was banished from Dublin and died in 1095. Bereft of their leader, the nobles of the Isles dispatched an embassy to Muirchertach requesting a regent to serve for Godred's son's minority. Dublin led the Munster kings deep into the politics of the Irish Sea province and this request is the measure of their success in establishing overlordship here. Muirchertach sent Domnall, son of his brother Tadc, to Dublin: Domnall's mother was the daughter of the former Norse king of Man, Echmarcach Mac Ragnaill, who accompanied Donnchad mac Briain, Muirchertach's

great-uncle, on his pilgrimage to Rome in 1064. Muirchertach then asserted his authority over Connacht in the west by expelling the dynasty to which the Uí Chonchobair belonged and set up Domnall Ua Ruairc as king. The high point of Muirchertach's career followed these successes. The Munster king who could force acknowledgement of his supremacy in the north would be rewarded with recognition as king of all Ireland. Control of the eastern seaboard and Irish Sea trade would bring rewards of a material nature. Muirchertach redoubled his efforts against Domnall Ua Lochlainn in the north. However, in the east, his growing power caused the king of Norway, Magnus Barelegs, to be anxious about his interests in the region and he arrived in 1098 to defend them.

The hostility between Muirchertach Ua Briain and Domnall Ua Lochlainn entered a new phase with Muirchertach on the offensive. He led his army north in 1097 but, as happened repeatedly in later attacks, the abbot of Armagh intervened. In 1101 Muirchertach assembled an army from Munster, Leinster, Connacht, Meath, and Osraige and boldly asserted his supremacy by destroying Ailech, the Cenél nEógain capital, and returning along the Slige Midluachra, the ancient route from Ulster to Tara. However, he failed to force Domnall into submission. Magnus of Norway reappeared on a second expedition in 1102. His arrival on the Isle of Man and his designs on Dublin brought him too close for Munster comfort. But Magnus realized that if he were to make gains in Ireland, there were easier pickings in the north. He reached some understanding with Muirchertach, symbolized by the marriage of his son, Sigurd, to Muirchertach's daughter, and both Muirchertach and Magnus launched co-ordinated campaigns northward in 1103.

Muirchertach's and Domnall's forces faced each other for a week when Muirchertach imprudently split his army, sending one contingent south, while he himself with another harried the surrounding territories, perhaps in an attempt to draw out Domnall. In his absence, Domnall decisively defeated the remaining contingent in the battle of Mag Coba, on 5 August. Magnus was killed in a separate skirmish with the Ulaid. These campaigns of the early twelfth century were the closest Muirchertach would come to achieving his ambition of imposing his authority on the whole of Ireland.

Foreign and ecclesiastical engagements As part of their development of the notion of *imperium*, kings of England laid claim to Dublin and, by extension, to much of Ireland. Control of Dublin led the Munster kings in the opposite direction and Muirchertach Ua Briain was drawn deep into Welsh politics. A succession of Welsh rulers, including Rhys ap Tewdwr, king of Deheubarth, his son Gruffudd (who remained under Muirchertach's protection in Ireland until c.1115), Cadwgan ap Bleddyn, king of Powys, and his son Owain, sought Munster support and, in difficult times, refuge in Ireland. Gruffudd ap Cynan was born in Dublin and left in 1075 when Muirchertach ruled it. He gained control of Gwynedd with the help of a Waterford fleet. Among the Norman invaders against whom the Welsh sought Munster help was Robert de Bellême, earl of

Shrewsbury. By 1102 Robert was gathering support for his challenge to Henry I. He sent Gerald of Windsor to Ireland to seek Muirchertach's assistance. The agreement was formalized with the marriage of Robert's brother, Arnulf de Montgomery, to another of Muirchertach's daughters. A letter survives from Muirchertach to Archbishop Anselm of Canterbury, thanking him for intervening with Henry on behalf of his son-in-law after Robert's failure.

This period also saw the attempt to reorganize the church. Muirchertach presided over the synods of Cashel (1101) and Ráith Bressail (1111). Important measures were adopted at Cashel to free the church from secular control. As a token of support, Muirchertach gave the Rock of Cashel, a site of great symbolic significance, to the church. His motives have been long debated. Cashel was associated with the Eóganachta, the dynasty ousted by the Uí Briain. In handing over Cashel Muirchertach was neutralizing its political associations. However, at a time when a diocesan church was emerging, the grant was a shrewd move if Muirchertach wanted an ecclesiastical office of first importance situated in his territories. His generosity paid dividends, for the Synod of Ráith Bressail legislated for the creation of a diocesan organization, with metropolitan sees at Armagh and Cashel. Muirchertach took an active role in important ecclesiastical appointments, seeing to the promotion of men of proven ability and reforming zeal like Bishop Domnall Ua hÉnna of Killaloe and Máel Muire Ua Dúnáin, 'preeminent bishop in Munster'. He was probably involved in the selection of Donngus (Donatus) Ua hAingli and Samuel Ua hAingli as bishops of Dublin and his name appears on the letter to Anselm requesting the consecration of Máel Ísa (Malchus) Ua hAinmire as first bishop of Waterford in 1096. After 1111 Máel Ísa became the first archbishop of Cashel. Muirchertach was also behind the appointment of Gilla Espaig (Gilbertus) as first bishop of Limerick and had a hand in the consecration in Munster of Cellach (Celsus) Mac Áeda as bishop of Armagh in 1106.

Death and achievement Muirchertach Ua Briain's advance suffered a rude check after he fell gravely ill in 1114. Domnall Ua Lochlainn and Toirdelbach Ua Conchobair of Connacht mustered a great army and defeated the Munstermen. However, the allies quarrelled, and Domnall had no choice but to treat for a year's truce. Muirchertach faced an internal challenge from his own half-brother Diarmait, who deposed him. He recovered somewhat the following year and imprisoned Diarmait in Limerick, before marching into Leinster and then into Meath. In 1118—the year Diarmait died in Cork—Ua Conchobair led his army into Munster. He applied Muirchertach's device for dealing with troublesome kingdoms to Munster and divided Munster between Tadc Mac Carthaigh and Diarmait's sons. Muirchertach's sons (at least one of whom, Domnall, was born of his father's union with Derbfhorgaill, daughter of Ua Laidcnen, king of Airgialla) were thereby excluded from the kingship. Muirchertach, who entered the monastery of Lismore, Waterford, as a penitent in 1116, died in March 1119 (the sources give variously the 8th, the 10th, and the 12th) and was buried at Killaloe, Clare.

The reign of Muirchertach Ua Briain marked the apogee of Uí Briain influence in Munster, and of Munster dominance in Ireland. He was one of the first Irish kings to make his power felt outside Ireland, in the Irish Sea region, Wales, and western Scotland: King Edgar of Scotland was moved to send him the tribute of 'a camel, a beast of wondrous size' (annals of Inisfallen, s.a. 1105). He played a vital role in the creation of the national institution of the church, and in his correspondence Anselm of Canterbury referred to him as king of Ireland. A similar ambition with regard to the institution of kingship guided his actions in expelling weaker dynasties, dividing their kingdoms, and promoting puppet kings. Indeed, the complex web of alliance and counter-alliance that characterized the politics of his time is symptomatic not of a state of anarchy, but of the trauma that precedes the emergence of a new order.

DAMIAN BRACKEN

Sources AFM · S. Mac Airt, ed. and trans., *The annals of Inisfallen* (1951) · *Ann. Ulster* · S. Ó hInnse, ed. and trans., *Miscellaneous Irish annals, AD 1114–1437* (1947) · D. Murphy, ed., *The annals of Clonmacnoise*, trans. C. Mageoghagan (1896); facs. edn (1993) · W. Stokes, ed., 'The annals of Tigernach [8 pts]', *Revue Celtique*, 16 (1895), 374–419; 17 (1896), 6–33, 119–263, 337–420; 18 (1897), 9–59, 150–97, 267–303, 374–91; pubd sep. (1993) · W. M. Hennessy, ed. and trans., *Chronicon Scotorum: a chronicle of Irish affairs*, Rolls Series, 46 (1866) · W. M. Hennessy, ed. and trans., *The annals of Loch Cé: a chronicle of Irish affairs from AD 1014 to AD 1590*, 2 vols., Rolls Series, 54 (1871) · J. M. MacGrath and S. H. O'Grady, eds. and trans., 'Senchas Síl Bhriain', in S. Mac Ruaidhrí Mac Craith, *Caithréim Thoirdhealbaigh / The triumphs of Turlough*, ed. S. H. O'Grady, 2 vols, ITS, 26–7 (1929), vol. 1, pp. 171–92; vol. 2, pp. 181–202 · M. C. Dobbs, ed. and trans., 'The Ban-shenchus [3 pts]', *Revue Celtique*, 47 (1930), 283–339; 48 (1931), 163–234; 49 (1932), 437–89 · J. Ryan, 'The O'Briens in Munster after Clontarf', *North Munster Antiquarian Journal*, 2 (1940–41), 141–52; 3 (1942–3), 1–152 · 'The Dalcassians', *North Munster Antiquarian Journal*, 3 (1942–3), 189–202 · D. Ó Corráin, *Ireland before the Normans* (1972) · A. Candon, 'Muirchertach Ua Briain, politics, and naval activity in the Irish Sea, 1075 to 1119', *Keimelia: studies in medieval archaeology and history in memory of Tom Delaney*, ed. G. Mac Niocaill and P. F. Wallace (1988) · S. Duffy, 'Irishmen and Islesmen in the kingdoms of Dublin and Man, 1052–1171', *Ériu*, 43 (1992), 93–133 · A. Gwynn, *The Irish church in the eleventh and twelfth centuries*, ed. G. O'Brien (1992) · S. Duffy, *Ireland in the middle ages* (1997) · S. Duffy, 'Ostmen, Irish, and Welsh in the eleventh century', *Peritia*, 9 (1995), 378–96 · A. Candon, 'Barefaced effrontery: secular and ecclesiastical politics in early twelfth-century Ireland', *Seanchas Ardmhacha*, 14 (1990–91), 1–25 · F. J. Byrne, *Irish kings and high-kings* (1973) · D. Ó Cróinín, *Early medieval Ireland, 400–1200* (1995) · M. T. Flanagan, *Irish society, Anglo-Norman settlers, Angevin kingship: interactions in Ireland in the late twelfth century* (1989) · E. Curtis, 'Muchertach O'Brien, high king of Ireland, and his Norman son-in-law, Arnulf de Montgomery, c.1100', *Journal of the Royal Society of Antiquaries of Ireland*, 6th ser., 11 (1921), 116–24 · D. Ó Corráin, 'Foreign connections and domestic policies: Killaloe and the Uí Briain in twelfth-century hagiography', *Ireland in early mediaeval Europe*, ed. D. Whitelock, R. McKitterick, and D. Dumville (1982) · D. Ó Corráin, 'Mael Muire Ua Dúnáin (1040–1117), reformer', *Folia Gaedelica*, ed. P. de Brún, S. Ó Coileáin, and P. Ó Riain (1983) · M. Richter, *Medieval Ireland, the enduring tradition* (1988)

Ua Briain, Toirdelbach [Turlough O'Brien] (**1009–1086**), king of Munster, was the son of Tadc mac Briain, and grandson of *Brian Bóruma. His mother was Mór, daughter of Gilla Brigte Ua Maíl Muaid (d. 1071), king of Cenél Fiachach. The death of Brian Bóruma in 1014 and the dispute for succession among his sons, Donnchad *Mac Briain and Tadc, weakened the Uí Briain. Donnchad had Tadc, Toirdelbach's father, assassinated in 1023 so as to become king of Munster. His enemy, the dynamic Diarmait mac Máel na mBó, emerged as king of Leinster. Diarmait encouraged opposition to Donnchad by supporting his rival and nephew, Toirdelbach. Toirdelbach united Diarmait's hostility to Donnchad with that of Áed Ua Conchobair, king of Connacht. Donnchad was caught between Diarmait in the south-east and Áed in the northwest. Combined assaults began in the mid-1050s. In 1063 Donnchad succumbed and left on pilgrimage to Rome, where he died. Toirdelbach Ua Briain became king of Munster with Diarmait's backing but his ability in co-ordinating opposition to Donnchad showed he would be more than Diarmait's creature. This explains Diarmait's continued involvement in Munster: capable allies require careful management.

Toirdelbach Ua Briain sought to control Connacht by encouraging competition between the Uí Conchobair and Uí Ruairc. Manipulating these dissensions prepared him for events in Leinster. The death of Diarmait mac Máel na mBó in 1072 was unexpected, but Toirdelbach may not have been unprepared, for the king of Leinster was by then an old man. Toirdelbach's direction of events shows the full extent of his considerable strength and ability. He moved quickly and, by promoting rival candidates, fractured the power base Diarmait had created. He consolidated his position in the south by installing his sons Diarmait and Muirchertach *Ua Briain as duces in the viking ports of Waterford and Dublin and made Limerick his capital. By 1075 Ireland south of a line from Dublin in the east to Limerick in the west was firmly under his control. He now turned his attention northward.

Ua Briain extended control over Meath in 1073 following the death of its king, Conchobar Ua Máel Shechnaill. However, the limits of his power were demonstrated in 1075 when he ventured further north and was defeated by the Airgialla. A more cautious policy was needed. Northern opposition could be contained by encouraging rivalry between the Cenél nEógain and the Ulaid. The Ulaid had been in alliance with Diarmait mac Máel na mBó. It was natural for them to transfer that allegiance to Toirdelbach, his successor as leader in the south. He received Donnsléibe Ua hEochada and Áed Meránach Ua hEochada of the Ulaid in Limerick. At this time the Cenél nEógain promoted Conchobar Ua Briain and, later, his brother Cennétig, grandsons of Donnchad Mac Briain and Toirdelbach's rivals, to their kingship. The presence of these Uí Briain in the north is therefore symptomatic, not of Toirdelbach's power but of the complex web of strategic alliances that was very much a feature of the power structure in Ireland. If Toirdelbach planned on fragmenting the Ulster polity by promoting the Ulaid, the Cenél nEógain responded by making kings of Toirdelbach's enemies. But despite his capable manipulation of political

tensions, Toirdelbach failed in 1079 to recognize the opportunity presented by the arrival of a number of Jews at his court. The purpose of their journey was probably commercial but he chose not to use their capital to finance his ambitions and 'they were sent back again over the sea' (annals of Inisfallen, s.a. 1079).

In 1080 Máel Shechnaill, king of Meath, submitted to Toirdelbach Ua Briain as security against Donnchad Ua Ruairc of Connacht. In 1084 the Munstermen marched into Meath. Ua Ruairc launched a successful counter-attack into Munster and pushed as far as Leinster. Toirdelbach's son Muirchertach defeated him near Leixlip and brought his severed head to Limerick as a trophy. Cennétig Ua Briain, fighting on Ua Ruairc's side, was among the casualties. Toirdelbach fell ill in the following year and suffered the loss of his hair. He died on 14 July 1086 at Kincora (in what is now Clare) and, despite his failure in the north, the annals of Ulster style him king of Ireland in his obit. The same dignity is accorded him in letters from Pope Gregory VII and Archbishop Lanfranc of Canterbury, who wanted him to support church reform. The entry in the annals of St Mary's Abbey, Dublin, recording the selection of Donngus (Donatus) as bishop of Dublin in 1085 by Terdylvacus, king of Ireland (Gilbert, 250), reflects Toirdelbach's controlling interest and also represents the beginnings of the movement for ecclesiastical reform under royal patronage in the south. His title was disputed among his sons Diarmait, Tadc, and Muirchertach. Derbfhorgaill (d. 1098), daughter of Tadc Mac Gilla Pádraig, was mother of Tadc, and of Muirchertach, who succeeded Toirdelbach. Diarmait's mother was Dubchoblaig of the Uí Chennselaig, rulers of Leinster. Gormlaith (d. 1076), daughter of Ua Fógarta of southern Éile, is also recorded as one of Toirdelbach's wives.

Toirdelbach Ua Briain's expert reading of the political landscape and quick, decisive reaction to political developments re-established the Uí Briain of Dál Cais as the dominant dynasty in Ireland. As competition increased and access to power became limited to fewer dynasties, the exploitation of internal rivalry became an important means for powerful men to direct affairs in rival kingdoms. This manipulation of tensions was a constant feature of Toirdelbach's career; he was himself subjected to it and used his enemies' difficulties to good effect.

DAMIAN BRACKEN

Sources W. M. Hennessy, ed. and trans., *Chronicum Scotorum: a chronicle of Irish affairs*, Rolls Series, 46 (1866) · W. M. Hennessy, ed. and trans., *The annals of Loch Cé: a chronicle of Irish affairs from AD 1014 to AD 1590*, 2 vols., Rolls Series, 54 (1871) · S. Mac Airt, ed. and trans., *The annals of Inisfallen* (1951) · *The letters of Lanfranc, archbishop of Canterbury*, ed. and trans. H. Clover and M. Gibson, OMT (1979) · *Ann. Ulster* · T. W. Moody and others, eds., *A new history of Ireland, 9: Maps, genealogies, lists* (1984) · D. Murphy, ed., *The annals of Clonmacnoise*, trans. C. Mageoghagan (1896); facs. edn (1993) · J. T. Gilbert, ed., *Chartularies of St Mary's Abbey, Dublin: with the register of its house at Dunbrody and annals of Ireland*, 2 vols., Rolls Series, 80 (1884) · AFM · F. J. Byrne, *Irish kings and high-kings* (1973) · A. Gwynn, *The Irish church in the eleventh and twelfth centuries*, ed. G. O'Brien (1992) · J. Hogan, 'The Ua Briain kingship in Telach Óc', *Féil-sgríbhinn Eóin Mhic Néill*, ed. J. Ryan [E. Ua Riain] (1940) · D. Ó Corráin, *Ireland before the Normans* (1972) · D. Ó Corráin, 'The career of Diarmait Mac Máel na mBó, king of Leinster', *Journal of Old Wexford Society*, 3 (1970–71), 27–35 · D. Ó Cróinín, *Early medieval Ireland, 400–1200* (1995) · J. Ryan, 'The O'Briens in Munster after Clontarf', *North Munster Antiquarian Journal*, 2 (1940–41), 141–52; 3 (1942–3), 1–152 · 'The Dalcassians', *North Munster Antiquarian Journal*, 3 (1942–3), 189–202

Ua Brolcháin, Flaithbertach (*d.* 1175), abbot of Derry and head of Columban churches in Ireland, was an important exponent of ecclesiastical reform in twelfth-century Ireland. The Uí Brolcháin were of the Cenél nEógain of the northern Uí Néill, but Flaithbertach's precise genealogical affiliation is not certain. Occasional reference to him as *mac in epscuip hUí Bhrolcháin* (that is, 'son of the bishop Ua Brolcháin') suggests he was perhaps son of Máel Coluim Ua Brolcháin (*d.* 1122), or of Máel Brigte Ua Brolcháin (*d.* 1139), both styled 'bishop of Armagh' in the annals. He succeeded as abbot of Derry and *coarb*, or successor, of Colum Cille on the death of Máel Ísu Ua Branáin in 1150 and probably had the support of Gilla Meic Liac, reformist archbishop of Armagh and himself ex-abbot of Derry, as well as that of Muirchertach Mac Lochlainn, king of Cenél nEógain. Indeed, his success was very much linked to the patronage of Mac Lochlainn, and Ua Brolcháin's genealogical connection with the Cenél nEógain (traditional supporters of Derry) was doubtless important in this regard. The title *coarb* of Colum Cille had previously been bestowed on the abbots of Kells, not Derry, so clearly Ua Brolcháin's succession marked an important moment.

From the start Flaithbertach Ua Brolcháin was active in asserting his jurisdiction as *coarb*, initially in the north of Ireland where Mac Lochlainn's influence extended. In 1150 he made a circuit (*cuairt*) of Cenél nEógain, receiving tribute from Mac Lochlainn. This was followed in the next year by a circuit of Síl Cathasaig (in what is now co. Antrim), receiving tribute for its ruler Cú Ulad Ua Lainn, and in 1153 of Dál Cairpre and Uí Eachach Ulad (in modern co. Down), with tribute from the ruler Ua Duinn Sléibe. By 1157 Mac Lochlainn had achieved the status 'king of Ireland', and Ua Brolcháin's situation was duly enhanced. Thus, in the very next year, at the Synod of Breemount, Meath, presided over by Gilla Meic Liac and the papal legate Gilla Críst Ua Connairche, he was recognized as head of all Columban churches in Ireland and given 'a chair', that is, status equivalent to a bishop. This was evidently an attempt by Gilla Meic Liac to make the relationship of the *coarb* of Colum Cille to his churches analogous to that of a bishop to his diocese. In 1161 at an assembly of clerics and laymen at Dervor, Meath, Mac Lochlainn confirmed Ua Brolcháin's jurisdiction over the Columban churches in Meath and Leinster (said thus to be free from exaction of secular dues); and in the same year he made a circuit of Osraige, thus confirming his jurisdiction in southern Ireland. In 1164, Ua Brolcháin was invited by Somarlaide (Sumerled) Mac Gillai Adomnáin, king of Argyll and the Isles, to become abbot of Iona. Since such a move would have disrupted the new organization being established in Ireland, it was opposed by Gilla Meic Liac and Mac Lochlainn and was never realized.

Flaithbertach Ua Brolcháin was also noted for extensive architectural work at Derry, in collaboration with his patron Mac Lochlainn. As early as 1155 the door of Derry church was made at his behest, but the main work was done between 1162 and 1164. In 1162 over eighty houses at Derry were demolished to enable the construction of an enclosing wall around the main ecclesiastical site. In 1163 a lime-kiln (*tene-aeil*), measuring 60 feet square, was constructed in the space of twenty days. Finally, in 1164 the great church (*tempull mór*), measuring 90 feet in length, was built in just forty days by Ua Brolcháin and Mac Lochlainn. It seems that some of this work may have been in vain, for Derry suffered serious burning in 1166, ironically the same year that Mac Lochlainn was slain. Ua Brolcháin sought to have his secular patron interred at Derry, but was overruled, since it was traditional for the Cenél nEógain kings to be buried at Armagh. Little is heard of Flaithbertach Ua Brolcháin after this point and he himself died in 1175, in the *dubreicles* or 'dark church' at Derry, following an unknown illness.   DAVID E. THORNTON

Sources W. M. Hennessy and B. MacCarthy, eds., *Annals of Ulster, otherwise, annals of Senat*, 4 vols. (1887–1901), vol. 2 · *AFM* · M. Herbert, *Iona, Kells, and Derry: the history and hagiography of the monastic familia of Columba* (1988) · A. Gwynn, *The Irish church in the eleventh and twelfth centuries*, ed. G. O'Brien (1992)

Ua Caráin, Gilla in Choimded [Gilbertus; Gilbert O'Caran] (*d.* 1180?), archbishop of Armagh, had previously been bishop of Raphoe; Gilla in Choimded means 'Servant of the Lord'. The date of his accession as bishop of Raphoe is not known, but it had certainly occurred by 1156–7 when he witnessed a charter of Muirchertach Mac Lochlainn, king of Cenél nEógain and claimant to the high-kingship of Ireland, in favour of the Cistercian abbey of Newry, in which he was styled bishop of Tír Conaill, a territory which was coterminous with the bishopric of Raphoe. Since no bishop of Tír Conaill (the land of the Cenél Conaill) or Raphoe is listed as having been present at the Synod of Kells, 1152, Ua Caráin may have been consecrated by the papal legate, Cardinal Giovanni Paparo, immediately after that synod. He is listed as swearing fealty to Henry II in 1172, his forename latinized as Gilbertus. He was translated to the see of Armagh about 1175. In 1177 he was taken prisoner at the capture of Downpatrick by John de Courcy, when he was in the company of Máel Sechlainn Mac Lochlainn bearing the *Canóin Phátraic* (believed to refer to the manuscript now known as the Book of Armagh), but was released shortly afterwards. The date of his death is not known, but it may be deduced to have been earlier than February 1180, when a charter witnessed by Lorcán Ua Tuathail, archbishop of Dublin, as papal legate (who is known to have left for England in that month), was also witnessed by Ua Caráin's successor, 'T' (Tommaltach, or Thomas), archbishop of Armagh. The text of a charter issued by Ua Caráin confirmed Ballyboghill, Dublin, formerly held by his predecessor Cellach (archbishop of Armagh from 1105 to 1129), to St Mary's Abbey, Dublin.   M. T. FLANAGAN

Sources Dugdale, *Monasticon*, new edn, vol. 6 · J. T. Gilbert, ed., *Chartularies of St Mary's Abbey, Dublin: with the register of its house at Dunbrody and annals of Ireland*, 2 vols., Rolls Series, 80 (1884), vol. 1, pp. 141, 147, 153, 416; vol. 2, p. 28 · W. M. Hennessy, ed. and trans., *The annals of Loch Cé: a chronicle of Irish affairs from AD 1014 to AD 1590*, 1, Rolls Series, 54 (1871) · W. M. Hennessy and B. MacCarthy, eds., *Annals of Ulster, otherwise, annals of Senat*, 4 vols. (1887–1901), vol. 2, p. 197 · S. Ó hInnse, ed. and trans., *Miscellaneous Irish annals, AD 1114–1437* (1947), s.a. 1178. 2 (recte 1177) · M. P. Sheehy, ed., *Pontificia Hibernica: medieval papal chancery documents concerning Ireland, 640–1261*, 2 (1965), no. 18a, p. 4 · G. Keating, *Foras feasa ar Éirinn / The history of Ireland*, ed. D. Comyn and P. S. Dinneen, 3, ITS, 9 (1908), 316–17 · W. Stubbs, ed., *Gesta regis Henrici secundi Benedicti abbatis: the chronicle of the reigns of Henry II and Richard I, AD 1169–1192*, 2 vols., Rolls Series, 49 (1867), 1.26 · *Chronica magistri Rogeri de Hovedene*, ed. W. Stubbs, 2, Rolls Series, 51 (1869), 30 · A. Gwynn, 'Saint Lawrence O'Toole as legate in Ireland (1179–80)', *Analecta Bollandiana*, 68 (1950), 223–40, esp. 235

Ua Cerbaill, Máel Suthain [Maolsuthain O'Carroll] (*d.* 1010), ecclesiastic, entitled in his obit 'chief scholar of Ireland', was one of the principal supporters of Brian Bóruma, king successively of Dál Cais, Munster, and all Ireland. The names of his parents are unrecorded. Máel Suthain died in Achad Deó, Aghadoe, just to the north of Lough Leane in the west of Munster. This gives some weight to the claim made in a later addition to his obit in the annals of Ulster and in the annals of the four masters that he was also king of the Eóganacht Locha Léin (in the past, the leading dynasty of west Munster). He would thus have been following a tradition, long established in Munster, of combining high ecclesiastical office with kingship. The Uí Cherbaill were one of the kindreds which supplied kings of the Eóganacht Locha Léin in the eleventh century, so this addition may be true. Máel Suthain is, however, best known as the person who made an addition to the Book of Armagh on behalf of Brian:

> Saint Patrick, when going to heaven, ordered that the whole fruit of his labour, as well of baptism and of causes as of alms, should be paid to the apostolic city which in Irish is named Ardd Macha. So I have found in the books of the Irish. I, namely Calvus Perennis [the Latinate form of Máel Suthain], have written in the sight of Brian, emperor of the Irish, and what I have written he has confirmed for all the kings of Cashel.　(Kenney, 354)

The addition is likely to have been made in 1005, when Brian went on campaign to Armagh and left 20 ounces of gold on Patrick's altar and departed, 'taking with him the sureties of the men of Ireland' (*Ann. Ulster*, s.a. 1005).

The title here given to Brian echoes the imperial titulature of tenth-century kings of England and may well be a direct imitation. It is uncertain whether Brian had aspirations to extend his supremacy over the *Scotti* of North Britain, as the choice of 'emperor of the Irish' (*Scotti*) rather than 'of Ireland' as his title allows. What is certain is that Brian, by adopting a role as lay patron of Armagh and acknowledging Armagh's rights to revenue in virtue of its status as the apostolic city, effectively another Rome for the Irish, was making a statement which was seen as a corollary of his own status as 'emperor of the Irish'. There is a probably contemporary entry in the annals of Ulster (at this date an Armagh chronicle) stating that, in 1014, after Brian had been killed at the battle of Clontarf, the heir of Patrick (that is, the abbot of Armagh) came and removed the bodies of Brian

and of his son Murchad to Armagh, buried them in a new tomb (like Christ), and 'for twelve nights the community of Patrick waked the bodies in honour of the buried king' (*Ann. Ulster*, s.a. 1014, 2). The community of Patrick, for their part, gave Brian exceptional honours.

Although Máel Suthain Ua Cerbaill accompanied Brian on his major expedition of 1005 to establish his overlordship over Ireland, he was not the most powerful cleric in Munster. That status was reserved for Brian's brother, Marcán, son of Cennéitig, a pluralist on a grand scale as abbot of Terryglass, Inis Celtra, and Killaloe, and described by one annalist as 'head of Munster so far as the clergy are concerned' (*Chronicum Scotorum*, s.a. 1008, *recte* 1010). Máel Suthain was, however, personally close to Brian, if those sources which describe him as his confessor are correct. Moreover, his power in west Munster would have helped to ensure that Brian had no serious opposition in that region. A poem on ecclesiastical and secular rank is attributed to him. He was also remembered in a short late-medieval tale which told how he was saved from hell by three pupils who came back from the dead to inform him that he was currently destined to perdition for three reasons: for the number of personal interpretations of scripture he had invented, for the number of women with whom he had had sex, and for giving up reciting the *Altus prosator* attributed to St Columba. He reformed on all three counts and was saved.

Máel Suthain Ua Cerbaill should be distinguished from a namesake whose death in 1031 is recorded in the annals of Ulster and the annals of the four masters. It remains unclear whether the latter source is correct in saying that this Máel Suthain Ua Cerbaill, rather than his presumably older contemporary, was confessor to Brian Bóruma.

T. M. CHARLES-EDWARDS

Sources *Ann. Ulster* · S. Mac Airt, ed. and trans., *The annals of Inisfallen* (1951) · W. M. Hennessy, ed. and trans., *Chronicum Scotorum: a chronicle of Irish affairs*, Rolls Series, 46 (1866) · K. Meyer, 'Siebenteilung alle geistlichen und weltlichen Rangstufen', *Zeitschrift für Celtische Philologie*, 5 (1905), 498 · J. Vendryes, 'L'aventure de Maelsuthain', *Revue Celtique*, 35 (1914), 203–11 · A. Gwynn, 'Brian in Armagh, 1005', *Seanchas Ardmhacha*, 9 (1978–9), 35–50 · J. F. Kenney, *The sources for the early history of Ireland* (1929), nos. 144, 620 · R. Sharpe, 'Palaeographical considerations in the study of the Patrician documents in the Book of Armagh', *Scriptorium*, 36 (1982), 28 · AFM, 2nd edn

Ua Conchobair, Áed [Aedh O'Connor, Áed in Gaí Bernaig] (*d.* 1067), king of Connacht, was the son of Tadc in Eich Gil (*d.* 1030), a member of the Síl Muiredaig branch of Uí Briúin Aí. He first appears in the historical record in 1036, when he slew his father's killer, but the kingship of eastern Connacht was held at this point by Art Uallach Ua Ruairc of Uí Briúin Bréifne. Áed killed one of the latter's sons in 1039 (and another in 1047) and can be regarded as king of east Connacht following the death of Art Uallach in 1046. He extended his rule in 1051, when he blinded the king of west Connacht, whom he had held captive for a year, and thereupon took up residence in the west, probably on an island in Lough Corrib.

Ua Conchobair now engaged in inter-provincial warfare, invading north Munster in 1051, felling the Tree of

Mag Adair, the Dál Cais inauguration site; and although pursued by Donnchad mac Briain Bóraime, the claimant to the high-kingship, he went unpunished, and indeed killed the latter's son at about this time. He raided here again in 1054, and ravaged Lorrha in 1058. Remarkably, Donnchad submitted to him in 1059, the annals recording a strange story for 1061, that Áed demolished Kincora and broke the wall of the well, eating its two salmon.

However, 1061 saw a resurgence of opposition from west Connacht, by the Uí Fhlaithbertaig of Uí Briúin Seola, who deposed Áed Ua Conchobair from the kingship, having ousted him from his base on Lough Corrib. Although he regained power, returning to Cruachu bearing the head of his defeated rival, his position was weakened and he submitted to the king of the northern Uí Néill, Ardgar Mac Lochlainn, in 1063. In 1065, however, he defeated Ua Ruairc of Bréifne and Ua Cellaig of Uí Maine after they had plundered Clonmacnoise, the annals suggesting that Áed was its patron. Although the Leinster–Munster alliance headed by Diarmait mac Máel na mBó and Toirdelbach Ua Briain is said to have paid him 30 ounces of gold for mutual aid in 1066, Áed's last triumph was his successful resistance to their invasion of Connacht in the following year.

Ua Conchobair was killed a week later at the battle of Turlach Adnaig in Galway (receiving a particularly glowing obit in the annals of Tigernach), by Áed, son of Art Uallach Ua Ruairc, who succeeded him as king of Connacht. His wife was Caillech Cáemgein, daughter of Ócán Ua Fallamain; a family of that name provided minor lords of Clann Uadach in Roscommon. With her he had his son Ruaidrí *Ua Conchobair, who recovered the kingship before 1076.   SEÁN DUFFY

Sources AFM · Ann. Ulster · W. Stokes, ed., 'The annals of Tigernach [8 pts]', Revue Celtique, 16 (1895), 374–419; 17 (1896), 6–33, 119–263, 337–420; 18 (1897), 9–59, 150–97, 267–303, 374–91; pubd sep. (1993) · S. Mac Airt, ed. and trans., The annals of Inisfallen (1951) · D. Murphy, ed., The annals of Clonmacnoise, trans. C. Mageoghagan (1896); facs. edn (1993) · R. O'Flaherty, A chorographical description of west or H-Iar Connaught, ed. J. Hardiman (1846) · M. C. Dobbs, ed. and trans., 'The Ban-shenchus [3 pts]', Revue Celtique, 47 (1930), 283–339; 48 (1931), 163–234; 49 (1932), 437–89

Ua Conchobair, Ruaidrí [Roderic O'Connor, Ruaidrí na Saide Buide] (d. 1118), king of Connacht, was the son of Áed *Ua Conchobair (d. 1067), a member of the Síl Muiredaig branch of Uí Briúin Aí, and of Caillech Cáemgein, daughter of Ócán Ua Fallamain, probably of Clann Uadach in Roscommon. He first appears on record in 1076, described as king of Connacht, submitting to the Munster king, Toirdelbach Ua Briain, who expelled him from kingship three years later. He killed the king of west Connacht, Áed Ua Flaithbertaig, in 1079 and a family rival, Cathal Ua Conchobair, in 1082. At the battle of Conachail in 1087, assisted by the clergy of Clonmacnoise bearing the relics of St Ciarán, he defeated his father's vanquisher, Áed Ua Ruairc, thereby securing his family's hold on the kingship. By this stage he had probably married the first of at least four wives, the daughter of Ua hEgra of Luigne, who bore him at least one daughter.

In 1088 Ua Conchobair fended off a land and sea invasion by Muirchertach Ua Briain, whose forces he slaughtered, and retaliated with three raids on Munster; then he submitted at Ráith Cruachan to Ua Briain's rival for the high-kingship, Domnall Mac Lochlainn of Ailech, joining him on another such raid. In 1089 Ua Briain felled the sacred tree at Ruadbethach in Galway, though Ua Conchobair also blocked Ua Briain's attempted passage up the Shannon and joined forces with Domnall Ua Maíl Shechnaill of Mide on a retaliatory naval raid, attacking Munster again in the two succeeding years. Clearly a threat to the authority of Muirchertach Ua Briain, Ua Conchobair was present when the latter gave hostages to Mac Lochlainn in 1090, joining him in his submission. However, his promising career was brought to a halt in 1092 when he was treacherously blinded by Flaithbertach Ua Flaithbertaig of west Connacht, his foster son with whom he had entered bonds of baptismal sponsorship on seven occasions. Revenge for the deed came when Ua Flaithbertaig was murdered six years later.

Ua Briain took advantage of Ruaidrí Ua Conchobair's plight to raid Connacht in 1092, though his invasion of the province two years later was unsuccessful. In 1093, Ruaidrí's son Niall was killed by the Conmaicne; and in 1094 another son, Tadc (whose mother was a daughter of Éicnechán Ua Cuind of Muinter Gilgain, Longford), triumphed over their enemies in west Connacht at the battle of Fidnacha, though he was himself treacherously killed in 1097 by one of his own followers. Another son, Conchobar, was killed in or before 1103, by his own foster brother, a member of Clann Chosraig of Uí Briúin Seola.

Thereafter another son of Ruaidrí Ua Conchobair, Domnall—whose mother was a daughter of Ua Conaing of Dál Cais—came to prominence, participating as king of Connacht in Ua Briain's Mag Coba campaign of 1103; but the latter deposed him in 1106, whereupon the most famous of Ruaidrí's sons, Toirdelbach Mór *Ua Conchobair (whose mother, Mór (d. 1088), was the daughter of Toirdelbach Ua Briain) was inaugurated as king and ruled until his death in 1156. Little is known of their father, Ruaidrí, throughout all this time, other than that he died in Clonmacnoise in 1118; he may well have retired there after his blinding.   SEÁN DUFFY

Sources AFM · Ann. Ulster · W. Stokes, ed., 'The annals of Tigernach [8 pts]', Revue Celtique, 16 (1895), 374–419; 17 (1896), 6–33, 119–263, 337–420; 18 (1897), 9–59, 150–97, 267–303, 374–91; pubd sep. (1993) · S. Mac Airt, ed. and trans., The annals of Inisfallen (1951) · W. M. Hennessy, ed. and trans., Chronicum Scotorum: a chronicle of Irish affairs, Rolls Series, 46 (1866) · D. Murphy, ed., The annals of Clonmacnoise, trans. C. Mageoghagan (1896); facs. edn (1993) · M. C. Dobbs, ed. and trans., 'The Ban-shenchus [3 pts]', Revue Celtique, 47 (1930), 283–339; 48 (1931), 163–234; 49 (1932), 437–89

Ua Conchobair, Ruaidrí [Rory O'Connor] (c.1116–1198), high-king of Ireland, was the son of Toirdelbach *Ua Conchobair (1088–1156), king of Connacht and high-king, and of Caillech Dé, daughter of Ua hEidin, king of Uí Fiachrach Aidne.

Early years Ruaidrí is first mentioned in 1136 when, aged about twenty, he was imprisoned by his father despite being under the protection of ecclesiastical sureties. In 1143 he was again taken prisoner by his brother, Conchobar, acting under the authority of their father, suggesting that Ruaidrí already by that stage was bidding for succession to the kingship of Connacht. Conchobar was killed in 1144, while another brother, Tadg, died shortly after, following which Ruaidrí was released from captivity through the intercession of the clergy. He may have been regarded as successor designate to the kingship from that date. In 1147 he led a great raid into Dartraige (in what is now co. Leitrim), and in a separate incident instigated the capture of a rival dynast, Domnall Ua Conchobair, by Toirdelbach Ua Briain, king of Thomond. In 1153, as part of his father's campaign against Muirchertach Mac Lochlainn, king of Cenél nEógain, and contender for the high-kingship, Ruaidrí was in command of the battalions of west Connacht, when his camp at Fardrum (Westmeath) suffered a surprise attack from Mac Lochlainn's army.

Succession to kingship On his father's death in 1156 Ruaidrí Ua Conchobair succeeded as king of Connacht, moving quickly to secure his position by blinding his brother Brian Breifnech and taking two other brothers, Brian Luignech and Muirchertach Muimnech, as prisoners. In 1157, while Muirchertach Mac Lochlainn, newly acknowledged as high-king, was campaigning to assert his dominance in Munster, Ruaidrí hosted into Cenél nEógain in his absence, thereby signifying his intention to contest the high-kingship against Mac Lochlainn; Ruaidrí then moved on to campaign himself in Munster, restoring Toirdelbach Ua Briain as king of Thomond, exacting hostages from Diarmait Mac Carthaig, king of Desmond, and retaining a large fleet on the Shannon, actions intended as a direct challenge to Mac Lochlainn's high-kingship. In 1158 Ruaidrí sent a marauding fleet to Cenél nEógain. In 1159 his erection of a new bridge at Athlone, which afforded ready access into Mide, led to conflict at the site with Donnchad Ua Máelsechlainn, king of Mide, at which Ruaidrí's son and potential successor (*rídamna*), Áed, lost his life. Later in the same year Ua Conchobair led an army against Muirchertach Mac Lochlainn to Ardee (Louth), where, however, he suffered a decisive defeat which Mac Lochlainn followed up with raiding in Connacht, destroying a series of strongholds. In 1160 a meeting between Mac Lochlainn and Ruaidrí at Assaroe (Donegal) concluded without a truce. In 1161 Ruaidrí hosted into Leinster and installed his own nominees in the north Leinster kingships of Uí Fáeláin and Uí Failge at the expense of Diarmait Mac Murchada, provincial king of Leinster. Ruaidrí subsequently gave four hostages to Muirchertach Mac Lochlainn as high-king in return for a derogated overlordship of Bréifne, Conmaicne, the western half of Mide, and the southern half of Ireland, though in 1162 Diarmait Ua Máelsechlainn paid 100 ounces of gold for the restoration to him of west Mide. In 1164, continuing with his father's policy of encastellation, Ua Conchobair erected a castle at Tuam and in 1166 he endowed a new gold reliquary for the shrine of St Manchán of Mohill (Leitrim), again imitative of his father's patronage of ecclesiastical art.

High-kingship Following the assassination of Muirchertach Mac Lochlainn in 1166 Ruaidrí Ua Conchobair and Diarmait Mac Murchada, king of Leinster, emerged as the main contenders for the high-kingship. The decisive turning point in Ruaidrí's favour was the wresting of control of the city of Dublin from Mac Murchada, who was exiled on 1 August 1166. Ua Conchobair was acknowledged as high-king at a major convention at Athlone in 1166, at which the allegiance of Dublin was secured by a stipend of 4000 cows from Ruaidrí. In 1167 and 1168 he celebrated the traditional fair of Tailtiu at the ancient assembly site of Teltown (Meath) as a ceremonial assertion of his high-kingship. Another assembly at Athboy in 1167 was attended by the archbishops of Armagh, Tuam, and Dublin, and the kings of Bréifne, Airgialla, Ulaid, Mide, and Dublin, whose combined forces reputedly numbered thirteen thousand horsed soldiers. Ua Conchobair had not yet, however, secured recognition from Cenél nEógain and, in pursuit of that objective, he dispatched a fleet to Derry and himself led a near national army into Cenél nEógain, where he effected a partition between the rival lineages of Mac Lochlainn and Ua Néill, with Niall Mac Lochlainn receiving the northern portion and Áed Ua Néill that south of Slieve Gullion. In 1168 the new kings of Cenél nEógain, accompanied by the abbot of Derry, were received by Ruaidrí at Athlone and accepted stipend. In 1169 he donated an annual stipend of ten cows to support the teaching of students from Ireland and Scotland, a gesture intended to secure endorsement of his high-kingship from the primatial church of Armagh.

Anglo-Norman intervention Ruaidrí Ua Conchobair's failure to prevent the return to Leinster in the autumn of 1167 of Diarmait Mac Murchada with Anglo-Norman mercenaries and the latter's recovery of his patrimonial kingdom of Uí Chennselaig (south Leinster) was to have momentous consequences: the Anglo-Norman commentator, Gerald of Wales, depicts Diarmait Mac Murchada on his return as determined 'to bring Connacht under his control together with the kingship of all Ireland' (Giraldus Cambrensis, 52). Ruaidrí was content to host into Leinster and to exact compensation on behalf of his ally, Tigernán *Ua Ruairc, king of Bréifne, for Mac Murchada's abduction of the latter's wife in 1152, and to take hostages, including Mac Murchada's legitimate son and potential successor, Conchobar. Ruaidrí was too preoccupied with asserting his authority in Munster, which he invaded and partitioned in 1168 between Domnall Ua Briain, king of Thomond, and Diarmait Mac Carthaig, king of Desmond, and in Mide, which he divided in 1169, assigning the eastern portion to Tigernán Ua Ruairc of Bréifne and retaining the western half himself. In 1170 Ruaidrí sought to penetrate Domnall Ua Briain's kingdom of Thomond, but the latter stalled the attempt by securing the assistance of an Anglo-Norman force provided by Diarmait Mac Murchada, who was his father-in-law. Following Ua Conchobair's failure to prevent Mac Murchada's capture of Dublin in September 1170 with the assistance of Richard fitz Gilbert, earl of Pembroke and lord of Striguil (known as Strongbow), Ruaidrí executed Mac Murchada's hostaged son,

Conchobar. After Mac Murchada's death in May 1171, Ruaidrí besieged Dublin but again failed to dislodge the Anglo-Norman garrison, which succeeded in mounting a surprise sortie on his decamped army and lifting his blockade. The claim made by Gerald of Wales that Ruaidrí submitted to Henry II during the latter's expedition to Ireland in 1171–2 is contradicted by the evidence both of the Irish annals and of other Anglo-Norman chroniclers. Henry may have planned an expedition against Connacht in the summer of 1172, but, if so, it was pre-empted by the rebellion of his son, which determined his withdrawal from Ireland shortly before Easter 1172. Henry's grants before his departure from Ireland of the lordships of Leinster and of Meath to Richard fitz Gilbert and Hugh de Lacy respectively and the consequent removal of these two former provincial kingdoms from the orbit of influence of Ruaidrí Ua Conchobair effectively marked the end of his high-kingship. In 1173 Ruaidrí's son, Conchobar Máenmaige, led a battalion from Connacht to aid Domnall Ua Briain in dislodging an Anglo-Norman garrison in Kilkenny, and in 1174 assisted Domnall in his victory over Anglo-Normans at Thurles, thereby demonstrating his capacities as prospective successor to the kingship of Connacht. Ruaidrí himself led a major offensive into Mide in 1174, with the Connacht army augmented by forces from the kings of Cenél Conaill, Cenél nEógain, Bréifne, Ulaid, and Airgialla, where he destroyed the newly erected Anglo-Norman strongholds at Trim and Duleek and raided as far as the confines of Dublin. It had little permanent effect, however, since in 1175 the castles were rebuilt and Anglo-Norman control of Mide was demonstrated by raiding as far as the Shannon.

Treaty of Windsor The failure of Ruaidrí Ua Conchobair to achieve any permanent gain from that expedition, coupled with the difficulties of maintaining dominance over Ua Briain of Thomond, may have determined the strategy embodied in the treaty of Windsor: it was concluded on 6 October 1175 between Henry II and Ruaidrí with Cadla Ua Dubhtaig, archbishop of Tuam, Cantordis, abbot of Clonfert, and Master Laurence, his chancellor, acting as Ruaidrí's proxies. Henry II arrogated to himself overlordship of Leinster and Meath, while Ruaidrí was to be over-king of the remainder of Ireland. Ua Conchobair became the liegeman of Henry and 'king under him', a position he was to retain as long as he should faithfully serve Henry and 'be ready at his service as his man' (Rymer, *Foedera*, 1.31–2). Ruaidrí's main obligations as a subordinate of Henry were to collect and transmit tribute and to punish rebellious subordinates, but he was also entitled to seek military support from Henry II's garrisons in Ireland. The key clause in the treaty from Ruaidrí's standpoint may have been the right afforded him to call on the constable of the king of England for military assistance. Shortly before 1 October 1175, that is even before the treaty had been formally ratified, Ua Conchobair secured an Anglo-Norman force to plunder Domnall Ua Briain's capital of Limerick, a key fortified gateway on the Shannon between Thomond and Connacht. However, when the Anglo-Norman garrison withdrew from Limerick in

1176, Ruaidrí was obliged to reach an accommodation with Ua Briain. In 1177 an Anglo-Norman contingent from the Dublin garrison was invited into Connacht by Murchad, son of Ruaidrí, who undertook to lead it to the capital, Tuam, while Ruaidrí was absent on circuit in west Connacht (the annals of Boyle also implicate Conchobar Máenmaige). The attack was repulsed, and Murchad subsequently was blinded in punishment by his father. In 1178 a foraging party of Hugh de *Lacy (d. 1186), first Anglo-Norman lord of Meath, turned back at Clonmacnoise for fear of Ruaidrí. In 1179 a synod was convened at Clonfert by Lorcán Ua Tuathail (Laurence O'Toole), archbishop of Dublin and native papal legate, to proclaim the decrees of the Third Lateran Council, which he had attended. Lorcán was instrumental in securing the translation in early 1180 of Ruaidrí's nephew Tommaltach Ua Conchobair, bishop of Elphin, to the primatial see of Armagh. This act implied that Ruaidrí claimed a right to present to ecclesiastical offices that reflected his continued claim to the high-kingship. It was shortly after the installation of Tommaltach that Lorcán, who had witnessed the treaty of Windsor, travelled to England to negotiate with Henry II on Ruaidrí's behalf, delivering a son as a hostage. Whether this mission should be linked to the treaty of Windsor is uncertain, since it is unclear how long it was deemed to be in operation. About 1180 a daughter of Ruaidrí Ua Conchobair married Hugh de Lacy, the alliance, no doubt, intended to stabilize Ruaidrí's eastern frontier, but it may have contributed to Ruaidrí's difficulties with Henry, whose permission for the marriage Lacy had not sought.

Abdication and later years In 1183 Ruaidrí Ua Conchobair retired from the kingship of Connacht and was replaced by his son, Conchobar Máenmaige. In 1185, however, Ruaidrí attempted to recover the kingship by concluding an alliance with Domnall Ua Briain, king of Thomond, and securing the help of an Anglo-Norman force. This resulted in a temporary division of Connacht between himself and Conchobar Máenmaige, who, however, deposed him again. In 1188 John de Courcy hosted into Connacht, accompanied by two other sons of Ruaidrí, rivals of Conchobar Máenmaige, possibly with the intention of supporting Ruaidrí's restoration; but Conchobar Máenmaige repulsed their forces decisively. When Conchobar Máenmaige was assassinated the following year, supporters of Ruaidrí staged another attempt to reinstate him, but it was his half-brother, Cathal Croibhdhearg *Ó Conchobhair, who succeeded in taking the kingship. In 1191 Ruaidrí unsuccessfully sought aid in Cenél Conaill, Cenél nEógain, Ulaid, among the Anglo-Normans in Meath, and in Munster to recover the kingship; eventually he was recalled from Munster by members of his kindred (the Síl Muiredaig) and allocated lands in Uí Fiachrach Aidne and Cenél Áeda na hEchtge in south Connacht. He died at Cong on 2 December 1198, aged eighty-two, and was buried on the left-hand side of the high altar at Clonmacnoise, his remains being reinterred in a stone coffin in 1207. The annals of Loch Cé and of Connacht, in recording the death of his son Áed in 1233, attribute the loss of the kingship of Connacht by his successors to the fact that the pope had offered Ruaidrí an allowance of six married wives provided that he desisted from all other women, but that he had refused to accept. The criticism seems more appropriate to his father, Toirdelbach, for whom six wives can be named. The only wife of Ruaidrí known by name is Dub Coblaid (d. 1181), daughter of Tigernán Ua Ruairc, king of Bréifne, reflective of the strong political alliance between Tigernán and Ruaidrí.

Ruaidrí Ua Conchobair's assumption of the high-kingship in 1166, although initially spectacularly successful, was compromised by Anglo-Norman incursion into Ireland from 1167 onwards and his failure to retain control over events in Leinster. His negotiation of the treaty of Windsor with Henry II inaugurated the first partition of Ireland between native and incomer and spelt the end of an indigenous high-kingship of Ireland. Just as Ruaidrí had challenged his own father for the regnal succession during the latter's reign, so he, in turn, was seriously undermined by intra-familial dissension and prospective successors bidding for power and after 1183 never recovered his position.   M. T. FLANAGAN

Sources M. T. Flanagan, *Irish society, Anglo-Norman settlers, Angevin kingship: interactions in Ireland in the late twelfth century* (1989) · W. Stokes, ed., 'The annals of Tigernach [8 pts]', *Revue Celtique*, 16 (1895), 374–419; 17 (1896), 6–33, 119–263, 337–420; 18 (1897), 9–59, 150–97, 267–303, 374–91; pubd sep. (1993) · W. M. Hennessy and B. MacCarthy, eds., *Annals of Ulster, otherwise, annals of Senat*, 4 vols. (1887–1901) · W. M. Hennessy, ed. and trans., *The annals of Loch Cé: a chronicle of Irish affairs from AD 1014 to AD 1590*, 2 vols., Rolls Series, 54 (1871) · AFM · Giraldus Cambrensis, *Expugnatio Hibernica / The conquest of Ireland*, ed. and trans. A. B. Scott and F. X. Martin (1978), 25, 41–5, 50–53, 69, 79–83, 95–7, 139–41, 149–51, 163, 183, 237 · G. H. Orpen, ed. and trans., *The song of Dermot and the earl* (1892), lines 1134–60, 1570–1635, 1746–1957, 3238–3304 · H. Perros, 'Crossing the Shannon frontier: Connacht and the Anglo-Normans, 1170–1224', *Colony and frontier in medieval Ireland: essays presented to J. F. Lydon*, ed. T. Barry and others (1995), 117–38 · W. Stubbs, ed., *Gesta regis Henrici secundi Benedicti abbatis: the chronicle of the reigns of Henry II and Richard I, AD 1169–1192*, 2 vols., Rolls Series, 49 (1867), 1.25–6, 29–30, 102–3, 270 · *Chronica magistri Rogeri de Hovedene*, ed. W. Stubbs, 2, Rolls Series, 51 (1869), 30, 84–5, 253 · A. M. Freeman, ed., 'The annals in Cotton MS Titus A XXV [pts 2–3]', *Revue Celtique*, 42 (1925), 283–305; 43 (1926), 358–84 · R. O'Flaherty, *Ogygia, seu, Rerum Hibernicarum chronologia* (1685), 441–2 · *Radulfi de Diceto … opera historica*, ed. W. Stubbs, 1: 1148–79, Rolls Series, 68 (1876), 348 · *The historical works of Gervase of Canterbury*, ed. W. Stubbs, 1: *The chronicle of the reigns of Stephen, Henry II, and Richard I*, Rolls Series, 73 (1879), 235 · D. Murphy, ed., *The annals of Clonmacnoise*, trans. C. Mageoghagan (1896); facs. edn (1993), 196, 213 · C. Plummer, ed., 'Vie et miracles de S. Laurent, archevêque de Dublin', *Analecta Bollandiana*, 33 (1914), 121–86 · A. Gwynn, 'Tomaltach Ua Conchobair, coarb of Patrick (1181–1201)', *Seanchas Ardmhacha*, 8 (1975–7), 231–74 · M. C. Dobbs, ed. and trans., 'The Ban-shenchus [pt 2]', *Revue Celtique*, 48 (1931), 163–234, esp. 191, 234 · Rymer, *Foedera*, new edn, 1.131–2 · A. M. Freeman, ed. and trans., *Annála Connacht / The annals of Connacht* (1944); repr. (1970), 47

Ua Conchobair, Toirdelbach Mór [Turlough the Great O'Connor] (1088–1156), high-king of Ireland, held from *c*.1120 that precarious supremacy over most other rulers in Ireland which justified native historians in styling a series of dominant kings during the eleventh and twelfth centuries 'high-kings with opposition'. Toirdelbach was born in Connacht, the son of Ruaidrí *Ua Conchobair (d. 1118; also known as Ruaidrí na Saide Buide, or 'Rory of the Yellow Bitch'), king of Connacht, and Mór (d. 1088), daughter of Toirdelbach Mór *Ua Briain (d. 1086), king of Munster and 'high-king with opposition'. As 'Toirdelbach' was then very much an Ua Briain family name, the subject of this article was presumably called after his maternal grandfather, significantly so, in that Ua Briain had played a part in the defeat and death of Ruaidrí na Saide Buide's father in 1067, before forcing Ruaidrí himself to submit in 1076. The marriage of Ruaidrí and Mór may have been brief. She died the year of her son Toirdelbach's birth, having earlier borne a daughter to another husband, Máelsechlainn Ua Máelsechlainn, king of Meath (d. 1087).

Also in 1088, Ruaidrí changed allegiance to the rival northern high-king, Domnall Mac Lochlainn of Tír Eoghain (d. 1121), and joined him on an invasion of Munster, razing the Ua Briain palace of Kincora, while Connacht was invaded by Toirdelbach Ua Briain's son and heir, Muirchertach. Four years later Ruaidrí was blinded by the rebellious king of west Connacht, Ua Flaithbertaig, and in 1093 Muirchertach Ua Briain temporarily banished the whole Ua Conchobair family into Tír Eoghain, and installed in their patrimony a puppet-king from south Connacht, Gilla na nóeb Ua hEidin (d. 1100). The Ua Conchobair dynasty fought back, challenged not only by Ua Flaithbertaig, but by the Ua Ruairc king of east Connacht or Bréifne, who also aspired to kingship of the whole province. In 1106 Domnall son of Ruaidrí Ua Conchobair was declared to be deposed by his own subjects and his eighteen-year-old half-brother Toirdelbach was installed by Muirchertach Ua Briain, his maternal uncle, at 'Áth an termoinn' (perhaps near Termonbarry, Roscommon) as local ruler of the Ua Conchobair homeland of Síl Muiredaig (approximately what is now co. Roscommon and north-east co. Galway). The same year Muirchertach Ua Briain forcibly installed into the kingship of neighbouring Meath Murchad Ua Máelsechlainn, the father of Órlaith (d. 1115) and Tailtiu (d. 1127/1129), two early wives among the many, named and unnamed, of Toirdelbach Ua Conchobair.

In his first recorded campaigns as king of the Síl Muiredaig against Ua Fergail of Conmaicne (modern co. Longford) in 1110 and against Termonn Da Beoóc (St Patrick's Purgatory) and Lough Erne in 1111, Toirdelbach Ua Conchobair appears aligned with his maternal uncle, Ua Briain, and his father-in-law, Ua Maelsechlainn, against Ua Ruairc of Bréifne and Domnall Mac Lochlainn, overlord of the north of Ireland, who inflicted a great raid on Connacht in 1110. However, in 1114 the high-king, Muirchertach Ua Briain, fell sick, and Toirdelbach, together with Murchad Ua Maelsechlainn, changed allegiance to Domnall Mac Lochlainn and joined him in an invasion of the Ua Briain homeland as far as Tulla, Clare, where Toirdelbach was instrumental in arranging a year's peace between Muirchertach's usurping brother, Diarmait Ua Briain, and the northern army. Subsequently the partially cured Muirchertach attempted to recover power by invading Leinster and Meath, while Ua Conchobair had to overcome a rebellion in Connacht led by his brother Domnall with Ua Fergail and Ua Briain support. No sooner was his brother captured than Toirdelbach himself was laid low for some time by an assassination attempt in west Connacht at Áth Bó, near Tuam. Yet this widespread opposition in itself marks the extension of Toirdelbach's rule from his family homeland of Síl Muiredaig to the whole province of Connacht. Before the end of 1115 he had delivered punishing raids against the Ua Briain territory of Thomond or north Munster, ravaged the Ua Fergail land of Conmaicne and the western part of Meath using a fleet on the River Shannon, and pressurized Murchad Ua Maelsechlainn into submission. At the close of this campaign he fasted at the church of Clonmacnoise and presented the community with a gilded drinking horn, a silver chalice, and a gilded copper paten.

Continuing Ua Briain dynastic strife allowed Toirdelbach Ua Conchobair to invade Thomond and destroy the palace of Kincora in 1116 (releasing all prisoners taken on the campaign in honour of St Flannán, patron saint of Killaloe). On the death of Diarmait Ua Briain, acting king of Munster, in 1118, Toirdelbach led the armies of Connacht, Bréifne, and Meath southwards as far as Glanmire, Cork, ostensibly to restore Muirchertach Ua Briain to power. Instead he concluded a treaty with Tadc Mac Carthaig to divide the province, allotting Desmond or south Munster to Mac Carthaig and Thomond to the sons of Diarmait Ua Briain. Subsequently Ua Conchobair joined Murchad Ua Maelsechlainn in subduing the province of Leinster and the Ostman kingdom of Dublin; and in 1119 he used the forces of Leinster to complete the subjugation of Munster, Muirchertach Ua Briain having finally died after five years of illness. This death revived Domnall Mac Lochlainn's claims to high-kingship, supported by Murchad Ua Maelsechlainn, king of Meath. In 1120 Ua Conchobair's initial attacks on Ua Maelsechlainn were halted by Mac Lochlainn's entry into Meath with an army, and Toirdelbach came to terms. Later in the year he built two bridges across the Shannon and one over the River Suck to facilitate raids from Connacht into Meath. He expelled Ua Maelsechlainn to the north, then celebrated the fair of Tailtiu, an obsolete ceremonial assembly traditionally associated with the high-kingship of Ireland.

Ua Conchobair's overlordship had to be strenuously maintained. In 1121 he invaded Munster to reimpose his settlement, causing 'the people of Munster to cry aloud' (*Annals of Tigernach*, 42), even plundering the reformed monastery of Lismore. Next year Énna Mac Murchada, king of Leinster, submitted. In 1123 Toirdelbach took hostages from the new king of Desmond, Cormac Mac Carthaig, but remained threatened until this king's death in 1138 by Mac Carthaig's persistent ambition to unite all Munster under his rule and exercise overlordship in Osraige and Leinster. Ua Conchobair responded to a revolt in 1124 by Ua Maelsechlainn, Mac Murchada, Mac Carthaig, and Tigernán Ua Ruairc, the new king of

Bréifne, by ravaging Meath, killing Mac Carthaig's hostages, and building three 'castles' in Connacht, at Dunlo (near Ballinasloe), at Galway, and at Collooney in Sligo. Public works were a feature of Ua Conchobair's reign, including, in 1129, a canal cut to drain the River Suck. Another characteristic was the division of subject territories and the imposition of nominated kings. In 1125 he joined with Ua Ruairc to banish Ua Maelsechlainn and divide the kingdom of Meath into three. Following the death of Énna Mac Murchada in 1126, he appointed his own son Conchobar Ua Conchobair king over Dublin and Leinster. When Leinster revolted the next year, Toirdelbach imposed another king of his choice there. However, in 1131 Cormac Mac Carthaig made a joint attack on Connacht with Conchobar Mac Lochlainn (*d*. 1136), king of the north, and although Ua Conchobair repelled them, his power was effectively reduced to his own province for some years. His own son Conchobar Ua Conchobair, as king of Síl Muiredaig, and his vassal Ua Cellaig actually submitted to Murchad Ua Maelsechlainn, king of Meath, in 1135. By 1138 Toirdelbach recovered somewhat, invading Meath again in alliance with Ua Ruairc and Donnchad Ua Cearbaill, king of Airgialla. In 1140 he erected bridges across the Shannon at Athlone and Lanesborough; and the next year Murchad Ua Maelsechlainn renewed his submission. Then in 1143 Ua Conchobair arrested Ua Maelsechlainn, apparently for collaboration with Munster, and imposed his own son Conchobar Ua Conchobar as king over Meath. Six months later Conchobar was assassinated by a Meath chieftain, whereupon Toirdelbach, after a battle 'like the Day of Judgement', exacted a fine of 400 cows and divided Meath at first between Ua Ruairc, Diarmait Mac Murchada, and an Ua Maelsechlainn prince, then between Murchad Ua Maelsechlainn and a kinsman.

Toirdelbach Ua Conchobair's relations with his other sons seem less affectionate. He allowed Conchobar to blind another son, Áed (whose mother was Derbforgaill (*d*. 1151), daughter of Domnall Mac Lochlainn), and he imprisoned his eventual heir, Ruaidrí *Ua Conchobair, in 1136 and again in 1143, though forced to release him by the lay and clerical guarantors of the prince's original safe conduct. This was not the only occasion Ua Conchobair responded to clerical influence. He granted a great tribute to a relic of the Holy Cross brought to Ireland in 1123, and enshrined a portion at Roscommon; he ordered the construction of the Cross of Cong to house the same, or a similar relic; he endowed and walled the ecclesiastical settlement of Tuam in 1127 and hosted a metropolitan visitation of Connacht by the reformed archbishop of Armagh, Gelasius, in 1140 and again in 1151; and in his will he left 160 ounces of gold, 60 marks of silver, and all his moveable property, except weapons and drinking-horns, to various churches. The last years of Toirdelbach's life were made eventful by the rise of Muirchertach (*d*. 1166), grandson of Domnall Mac Lochlainn, to rule the north and claim high-kingship of Ireland from *c*.1149. In 1150 Ua Conchobair yielded hostages to Mac Lochlainn, receiving in exchange a portion of Meath. He immediately commenced a war of conquest against Toirdelbach Ua Briain (*d.* 1167) culminating in a victory at Móin Mór (1152), followed by Ua Conchobair's redivision of Munster in 1153 between Mac Carthaig and Ua Briain kings, before Muirchertach Mac Lochlainn intervened to force the restoration of Toirdelbach Ua Briain. An inconclusive war broke out in 1154 between Mac Lochlainn and Toirdelbach Ua Conchobair, now ably assisted by his son Ruaidrí. The rivalry was settled in Mac Lochlainn's favour by the death of Toirdelbach in 1156 at the age of sixty-eight. He was buried at Clonmacnoise, and his son Ruaidrí succeeded him as king of Connacht, and after 1166 as high-king, though another son, Cathal Croibhdhearg *Ó Conchobhair, became ancestor of the main Ó Conchobair line in post-Norman times.   KATHARINE SIMMS

Sources J. Ryan, *Toirdelbach O Conchubair, 1088–1156* (1966) · G. H. Orpen, *Ireland under the Normans*, 4 vols. (1911–20), vol. 1, pp. 41–60 · F. J. Byrne, 'The trembling sod: Ireland in 1169', *A new history of Ireland*, ed. T. W. Moody and others, 2: *Medieval Ireland, 1169–1534* (1987), 33–6; repr. with corrections (1993) · W. Stokes, ed., 'The annals of Tigernach [pts 5–6]', *Revue Celtique*, 18 (1897), 9–59, 150–97 · S. Ó hInnse, ed. and trans., *Miscellaneous Irish annals, AD 1114–1437* (1947) · *AFM*, vol. 2 · S. Mac Airt, ed. and trans., *The annals of Inisfallen* (1951) · *Ann. Ulster* · W. M. Hennessy, ed. and trans., *The annals of Loch Cé: a chronicle of Irish affairs from AD 1014 to AD 1590*, 1, Rolls Series, 54 (1871) · D. Murphy, ed., *The annals of Clonmacnoise*, trans. C. Mageoghagan (1896); facs. edn (1993) · M. Ní Bhrolcháin, 'The prose Banshenchus', PhD diss., University College, Galway, 1981 · M. Dillon, 'The inauguration of O'Conor', *Medieval studies presented to Aubrey Gwynn*, ed. J. A. Watt, J. B. Morrall, and F. X. Martin (1961), 186–202 **Wealth at death** bequeathed property to churches; moveable wealth incl. 160 ounces of gold, 60 marks of refined silver; horses; cattle; raiment; weapons; drinking horns; chessboards and gaming pieces; books; quivers; slings: Stokes, ed., 'Annals of Tigernach'

Ua Diummusaig, Diarmait [Dermot O'Dempsey] (*d.* 1193), king of Uí Failge, was son of Cú Broga Ua Diummusaig of Clann Máel Ugra, slain in 1162 at Killeigh, Offaly, by Máel Sechlainn mac Congailig Ua Conchobair, king of Uí Failge. The surname Ua Diummusaig derived from Diummasach, an eleventh-century dynast of Clann Máel Ugra which, in turn, derived its name from the mid-ninth-century Máel Ugrai. The Clann Máel Ugra claimed descent from Rus Failge, the eponymous ancestor of the Uí Failge, and were therefore considered to be a branch of the Uí Failge, the overkingship of which generally was monopolized by the Uí Conchobair Failge. The lands of the Clann Máel Ugra were situated along either side of the River Barrow in Laois and Offaly. Diarmait probably succeeded to the kingship of Clann Máel Ugra in 1162 and subsequently gained control also of the overkingship of Uí Failge, possibly because of dynastic rivalry among the Uí Conchobair Failge following the death of Máel Sechlainn Ua Conchobair at the hands of the Clann Máel Ugra in 1164.

In 1173 Diarmait Ua Diummusaig, who occurs as king of Uí Failge in the so-called *Song of Dermot and the Earl*, mounted an attack on an Anglo-Norman raiding party in Uí Failge led by Richard fitz Gilbert, earl of Pembroke and lord of Striguil, known as Strongbow. As the Anglo-Normans passed through a narrow defile, their rearguard

was attacked and, among others, Strongbow's son-in-law, Robert de Quincy, was killed. Ua Diummusaig is styled *rex Offalie* ('king of Uí Failge') in a charter which he issued to a Benedictine (later Cistercian) community between 1177 and 1181, which granted the early Irish ecclesiastical site of Monasterevin (or Mainister Eimhin), reputedly founded by St Eimin in the sixth century and also known as Rosglas, in Kildare. The charter states that the grant was made with the assent of Muirchertach Ua Conchobair, suggesting that he may have been Diarmait's successor designate in the kingship of Uí Failge. Diarmait Ua Diummusaig died in 1193. His son, Máel Sechlainn, was killed in 1216 by the Uí Máel Muaid in Fir Chell along with followers of Meiler fitz Henry.   M. T. FLANAGAN

Sources *AFM*, s.a. 1162, 1163, 1164, 1193, 1216 · D. Murphy, ed., *The annals of Clonmacnoise*, trans. C. Mageoghagan (1896); facs. edn (1993), 228 · M. A. O'Brien, ed., *Corpus genealogiarum Hiberniae* (Dublin, 1962), 336–7, 432 · Dugdale, *Monasticon*, new edn, vol. 6 · G. H. Orpen, ed. and trans., *The song of Dermot and the earl* (1892), lines 2774–816 · W. M. Hennessy, ed. and trans., *The annals of Loch Cé: a chronicle of Irish affairs from AD 1014 to AD 1590*, 2 vols., Rolls Series, 54 (1871), s.a. 1193 · W. M. Hennessy and B. MacCarthy, eds., *Annals of Ulster, otherwise, annals of Senat*, 4 vols. (1887–1901), s.a. 1193 · W. Stokes, ed., 'The annals of Tigernach [8 pts]', *Revue Celtique*, 16 (1895), 374–419; 17 (1896), 6–33, 119–263, 337–420; 18 (1897), 9–59, 150–97, 267–303, 374–91; pubd sep. (1993), s.a. 1162, 1164 · J. Carney, ed., *Topographical poems by Seaán Mór Ó Dubhagáin and Giolla-na-naomhh Ó hUidhrin* (1943), l.988

Ua Domhnaill, Pádraic. *See* O'Donnell, Patrick (1856–1927).

Ua Duinn, Gilla na Náemh [Gillernew O'Dunne] (1102/3–1160), historian and poet, was *fer légind* (literally 'man of learning') the head of a church school, at Inis Clothrann (Inchcleraun, or Quaker Island, in Lough Ree, Longford) around the time when this early Christian foundation of St Diarmait was to be reorganized as St Mary's Augustinian priory. He is a late and well-documented example of an Irish ecclesiastical scholar whose high reputation derived from his vernacular works on secular history. A notable example was his *Cóiced Laigen na lecht ríg*, a long poem with a contemporary copy in the Book of Leinster, listing the Christian kings of Leinster to his own day, the length of their reigns, and the manner of their deaths, and ending with a eulogy of Diarmait Mac Murchada (*d.* 1171). In this and other compositions of his, which include a poem on the *dindshenchus* or place-name lore of Slíab Fúait (Slieve Gullion in Armagh), the last verse claims authorship for the 'discerning', or 'erudite' Ua Duinn. The seventeenth-century manuscript, CUL, Add. MS 3084, which contains two of his poems, calls him a 'sage in history and bardic poetry'. Recording his death at Inis Clothrann on 17 December 1160, in the fifty-eighth year of his age, the annals imply he was eloquent and pious, and hail him as Ireland's chief author in history and poetry, *aenollam na nGaedhel*, '[the best] bardic teacher, or master-poet, of the Irish people'.   KATHARINE SIMMS

Sources W. Stokes, ed., 'The annals of Tigernach [pt 6]', *Revue Celtique*, 18 (1897), 150–97, esp. 191 · *AFM*, 2.1136–7 · P. De Brún and M. Herbert, eds., *Catalogue of Irish manuscripts in Cambridge libraries* (1986), 13–14 · A. Gwynn and R. N. Hadcock, *Medieval religious houses:*

Ireland (1970) • E. Gwynn, ed. and trans., *The metrical dindshenchas*, 4, Royal Irish Academy: Todd Lecture Series, 11 (1924), 166–9, 419–21 • S. O'Grady, R. Flower, and M. Dillon, eds., *Catalogue of Irish manuscripts in the British Library (formerly British Museum)*, 2 vols. (1926–53); repr. (1992), 83 • R. I. Best and others, eds., *The Book of Leinster, formerly Lebar na Núachongbála*, 6 vols. (1954–83), vol. 1, pp. 135–44 • CUL, Add. MS 3084

Archives CUL, Add. MS 3084

Ua Gormáin, Máel Muire [Marianus O'Gorman] (*d.* 1181?), abbot of Knock, may possibly be equated with the Máel Muire Ua Dúnáin, abbot of the same Augustinian house, dedicated to St Peter and St Paul, who died in 1181. He is remembered as author of *Félire húi Gormáin* ('The martyrology of Ua Gormáin') which survives in Brussels, Bibliothèque Royale, MSS 5100–5104, fols. 124–97, transcribed about 1630 by Michael O'Clery, one of the four masters. Little is known of his life. He was a member of a prominent ecclesiastical family, probably related to the Óengus Ua Gormáin, abbot of Bangor, who died in Lismore in 1123, to the Máel Cáemgein Ua Gormáin, former abbot of Termonfeckin, who died as master of the monastic school of Louth in 1164, and to the Flann Ua Gormáin, chief lector of Armagh, who died in 1174 described as 'a learned sage, versed in sacred and profane philosophy, after having spent twenty-one years of study in France and England and twenty other years in directing and governing the schools of Ireland' (*AFM*, s.a. 1174).

The preface to Ua Gormáin's martyrology states that it was written after Ruaidrí Ua Conchobair became high-king of Ireland (in 1166) but before the death of the archbishop of Armagh, Gilla Meic Liac (in 1174). John Colgan, in his *Acta sanctorum … Hiberniae* of 1645, added that it was written *c.*1167. The martyrology does, however, contain a record of the feast days of Archbishop Gilla Meic Liac and of Gilla Mo Chaidbeo, superior of the abbey of St Peter and St Paul at Armagh, both of whom died in March 1174, though these may possibly have been later insertions.

Ua Gormáin explains in the preface his motivation in compiling the martyrology as being to secure a place in heaven for himself and for anyone who sings it, and also because he is unhappy that the earlier and better-known martyrology of Óengus the Culdee (*Félire Oengusso*) has included so few of the saints of Ireland and of elsewhere and arranges them frequently under the wrong feast day. His own martyrology, which is in verse and in Irish, consists of 2780 lines in the strict metre known as *rinnaird mór*, and is important because it contains the names and feast days of almost as many Irish saints as non-Irish saints (a total of about 3450 persons, biblical, continental, English, British, and Irish). It is therefore an important record of the early Irish church, and since its object was to bring Irish hagiology and the Irish church calendar into greater harmony with those of the rest of Christendom, it may be regarded as a product of the reforms then taking place in the Irish church.

The martyrology of Donegal (*Félire na naomh nÉrennach*), the last and largest of the calendars of Irish saints, places Máel Muire Ua Gormáin's own feast day at 3 July, though there is no record of his formal canonization by the apostolic see.

SEÁN DUFFY

Sources *Félire húi Gormáin / The martyrology of Gorman*, ed. and trans. W. Stokes, HBS, 9 (1895) • J. F. Kenney, *The sources for the early history of Ireland* (1929) • *AFM* • J. Hennig, 'Studies in the Latin texts of the *Martyrology of Tallaght*, of *Félire Oengusso*, and of *Félire húi Gormáin*', *Proceedings of the Royal Irish Academy*, 69C (1970), 45–112 • J. Colgan, *Acta sanctorum veteris et maioris Scotiae seu Hiberniae* (Louvain, 1645); facs. edn with introduction by B. Jennings, *The Acta sanctorum Hiberniae of John Colgan* (Dublin, 1948), 737 • D'Arbois de Jubainville, 'Le martyrologie d'O'Gorman', *Analecta Bollandiana*, 13 (1894), 193–6 • M. O'Clery, *The martyrology of Donegal: a calendar of the saints of Ireland*, ed. J. H. Todd and W. Reeves, trans. J. O'Donovan (1864)

Archives Royal Library of Belgium, Brussels, MS 5100–5104, fols. 124–97

Ua hAingliu, Donngus [Donatus O'Haingli, Donatus] (*d.* 1095), bishop of Dublin, used the Latin name Donatus when he was consecrated by Lanfranc, archbishop of Canterbury, in the sixteenth year of his pontificate (that is, some time after 29 August 1085), 'at the request and choice of Terdyluacus [Toirdelbach Ua Briain], king of Ireland, and the bishops of Ireland, and the clergy and people of the city of Dublin' (Gilbert, 2.250). He made a profession of obedience: 'I, Donatus, bishop-elect of the church of Dublin in Ireland, promise canonical obedience to you Lanfranc, archbishop of Canterbury, and to your successors' (Richter, no. 42). According to the *Acta Lanfranci*, Donngus had been a monk of Christ Church, Canterbury; he returned to Ireland following his consecration with (not extant) letters of exhortation to the kings and clergy of Ireland. A subsequent letter of Lanfranc's successor, Anselm, reveals that Lanfranc had given Donngus books, vestments, and ornaments for the church of Dublin.

Donngus died of pestilence on 22 November 1095 and was succeeded by his nephew, **Samuel Ua hAingliu** [Samuel O'Haingli] (*d.* 1121), who had been trained as a monk at St Albans and was consecrated by Anselm in the church of Winchester on 27 April 1096, making a profession of obedience to him as *totius Britanniae primas* ('primate of all Britain'). According to Eadmer, Samuel was elected by the clergy and people of Dublin with the assent of 'Murierdach' (Muirchertach Ua Briain, king of Munster, overlord of Dublin, and claimant to the high-kingship of Ireland), to whom Anselm sent a letter following Samuel's consecration. Later in the same year, Samuel signed the petition of the clergy and people of Waterford to Anselm requesting consecration of Máel Isú Ua hAinmire as bishop of Waterford. About 1101–2, Anselm, in a letter to Samuel transmitted to him via Máel Isú Ua hAinmire, made various complaints about his conduct, including: that objects given by Lanfranc to his uncle, Donngus, on the testimony of the monks of Canterbury, were not a personal gift but for the use of the church of Dublin; that he had expelled certain monks from the church of Dublin, who were willing to return but he had refused to readmit them; and that he should desist from having his cross carried before him on journeys since this was a right reserved to archbishops who had been confirmed with the pall from the pope. Samuel appears to have been claiming archiepiscopal status. He died on 4 July 1121. A sepulchral monument in St Michan's Church, Dublin, which has been suggested as his, is certainly not contemporaneous with his death.   M. T. FLANAGAN

Sources M. Richter, ed., *Canterbury professions*, CYS, 67 (1973), nos. 42, 51 · 'Epistolae Anselmi', ed. F. S. Schmitt, *S. Anselmi Cantuariensis archiepiscopi opera omnia*, 3–5 (1938–61), epp. 201, 277, 278, 427, 435 · *Eadmeri Historia novorum in Anglia*, ed. M. Rule, Rolls Series, 81 (1884), 73–4, 76–7 · J. Earle, ed., *Two of the Saxon chronicles parallel: with supplementary extracts from the others*, rev. C. Plummer, 1 (1892), 290 · S. Mac Airt, ed. and trans., *The annals of Inisfallen* (1951) · *Ann. Ulster* · W. Stokes, ed., 'The annals of Tigernach [8 pts]', *Revue Celtique*, 16 (1895), 374–419; 17 (1896), 6–33, 119–263, 337–420; 18 (1897), 9–59, 150–97, 267–303, 374–91; pubd sep. (1993) · J. T. Gilbert, ed., *Chartularies of St Mary's Abbey, Dublin: with the register of its house at Dunbrody and annals of Ireland*, 2, Rolls Series, 80 (1884), 250–51, 254 · *The whole works of … James Ussher*, ed. C. R. Elrington and J. H. Todd, 17 vols. (1847–64), vol. 4, pp. 518–19, 528–31 · J. C. Crosthwaite, ed., *The book of obits and martyrology of the cathedral church … Dublin*, Irish Archaeological Society, 4 (1844), xxxii, 31, 51 · J. Hunt, *Irish medieval figure sculpture, 1200–1600*, 2 vols. (1974), vol. 1, no. 42 · *AFM*

Ua hAingliu, Samuel (d. 1121). *See under* Ua hAingliu, Donngus (d. 1095).

Ua hAonghusa, Uilliam. *See* Hennessy, William Maunsell (1828/9–1889).

Ua Lochlainn, Domnall [Domhnall O'Lochlainn] (1048–1121), king of Cenél nEógain, was the son of Ardgar Mac Lochlainn, who led a major plundering expedition into Connacht in 1062, died as king of Ailech in 1064 at Telach Óc (Tullaghoge in Tyrone), and was buried at Armagh in the mausoleum of the kings. Domnall first married Bébinn (d. 1110), daughter of Cennétig Ua Briain (a member of the Uí Briain of Munster, who had briefly been king of Telach Óc, the inauguration site of Cenél nEógain, from 1078 but was killed in battle in 1084). His second wife was Benmide, daughter of Conchobar Ua Máel Shechlainn, king of Mide. From 1083 Domnall Ua Lochlainn was king of Cenél nEógain (or king of Ailech, after the fortress at Greenan in Donegal), and he inaugurated his kingship in that year by undertaking a *crech ríg*, or royal prey, in Conaille (modern co. Louth) and distributing stipends to the men of Fernmag. He aimed throughout his career to secure the dominance of his lineage within Cenél nEógain, to assert lordship in the north of Ireland over the kingdom of Ulaid on his eastern frontier and over Cenél Conaill to the west, and to challenge Muirchertach Ua Briain for the high-kingship of Ireland. In order to make such a challenge to the Munster king, he needed not only to achieve a clear hegemony in the north but also to subdue, or ally with, the kings of Connacht and Mide: that is, he needed to rally the whole of Leth Cuinn, the northern half of Ireland, against Munster. He sometimes came close to attaining his ambition, but his power was, in the end, too fragile.

Domnall Ua Lochlainn early demonstrated the scale of his ambitions by leading an army into Connacht in 1088, securing the submission of Ruaidrí Ua Conchobair, king of the province, who then hosted with him to Munster to challenge Muirchertach Ua Briain; Limerick and other fortresses were burnt and the Ua Briain residence at Kincora (in Clare) was razed. Two years later he even secured hostages from Ua Briain himself and from Domnaill Ua Máel Shechlainn, king of Mide, as well as from Ua Conchobair. This was the high point of his reign, the moment at which he seemed to be the new high-king; but he never established himself in that position. In the very next year, 1091, he had to deal with opposition from a neighbouring king: he slew Donnsléibe Ua hEochada, king of Ulaid, in a military encounter at Belach Goirt in Iubair (Gortinure in Londonderry). The site of the engagement shows that the king of the Ulaid was the aggressor.

After this early success there were several distinct phases to Ua Lochlainn's reign. First, from 1094 to 1103 he was engaged in a war of invasion and counter-invasion, in which Ua Briain held, perhaps increasingly, the upper hand. The Munster-led army invaded the north, while Ua Lochlainn never, in this period, repeated his invasion of Munster of 1090; instead, he was obliged to resort to extreme acts of violence to try to retain control over the Ulaid and Cenél Conaill, blinding Áed Ua Canannáin, king of Cenél Conaill, in 1093 and cutting down the tree under which the kings of Ulster were traditionally inaugurated in 1099. That his challenge to Ua Briain survived owed something to the traditional Cenél nEógain alliance with Armagh; in 1097 an invasion by Ua Briain was halted at Fid Conaill in Louth and a truce negotiated by the head of the church of Armagh, Domnall mac Amalgada; another invasion in 1099 ended in a further truce arranged by Domnall; in 1100 he also negotiated a settlement between Ua Lochlainn and the captive king of the Ulaid.

A major crisis for Ua Lochlainn came in 1103 after Ua Briain had invaded the north in 1101, on which occasion he had avenged Ua Lochlainn's 1090 destruction of Kincora by pillaging Ailech, after which yet another year's truce was arranged by the head of the church of Armagh in 1102. The situation was complicated by the appearance of Magnus, king of Norway, in the Irish Sea and an alliance between Magnus and Ua Briain, also in 1102. The next year the Ulaid revolted against Ua Lochlainn; Ua Briain brought an army north to give them aid, basing himself at Mag Coba (in west Down). After an inconclusive stand-off at Armagh, in August Ua Briain divided his forces, keeping some in Mag Coba, and leading others on a raid into Dál nAraidi (local opponents of the Ulaid); this raid was expensive in casualties, and Ua Lochlainn meanwhile attacked and defeated the detachments left in Mag Coba, compelling Ua Briain to withdraw. Magnus landed in Down, where he was killed in a skirmish, also in August. Ua Briain's grand combination of the forces of Munster, Leinster (including Osraige), together, probably, with Magnus of Norway, had ended in defeat.

After 1103 there was a phase in which Ua Lochlainn's control of the north was now reasonably secure. Ua Briain, however, still controlled Mide and was thus the leading king in Ireland. In the period 1111–13, however, there were further difficulties with the Ulaid, leading to Ua Lochlainn dividing the province between different rulers; at the same period he appears to have placed his son Niall in the kingship of Cenél Conaill. In 1114 Ua Briain fell ill, and Ua Lochlainn could then pursue his ambitions in the southern half of Ireland, in abeyance since 1088. His control on the north was now much more secure than it had been at the beginning of his reign. Moreover, Ua Lochlainn had also negotiated an alliance with Toirdelbach Ua Conchobair, king of Connacht: Ua Lochlainn's daughter, Mór (*d.* 1122), is named as Ua Conchobair's wife, while another daughter, Derbfhorgaill (*d.* 1151), bore Ua Conchobair three sons, Domnall, Áed, and Cathal.

Yet, in the final years of his life, after the death of Muirchertach Ua Briain in 1119, Ua Lochlainn's place as chief challenger to the power of Munster was taken by Ua Conchobair. In 1120 Ua Lochlainn mounted an expedition to assist Murchad Ua Máel Shechlainn, king of Mide 'against Connacht' (*Annals of Loch Cé*, s.a. 1120). Domnall Ua Lochlainn died aged seventy-three on 9 February 1121 at Derry, where he was buried. He is styled 'high-king of Ireland' in his obituary notice in the annals of Ulster (compiled at Armagh and consequently favourable to Cenél nEógain). His patronage of Armagh is illustrated by the endowment of a shrine for St Patrick's bell, which bears the inscription 'Or[oit] do Domhnall U Lachlaind lasin dernad in clocsa' ('a prayer for Domnall Ua Lochlainn by whom this bell was made').

Domnall Ua Lochlainn's second wife, Benmide, was the mother of Niall, killed in 1119, aged twenty-eight, by the Cenél Móen (a branch of Cenél nEógain located around Lifford in Donegal). A son, Muirchertach, was killed 'unjustly', according to the annals of Ulster, in 1114. Domnall's son Conchobar, who directly succeeded him, was slain by the men of Mag nÍtha in 1136. Another son, Magnus, was slain in 1128 or 1129.   M. T. FLANAGAN

Sources *Ann. Ulster* · S. Mac Airt, ed. and trans., *The annals of Inisfallen* (1951) · *AFM* · W. M. Hennessy, ed. and trans., *The annals of Loch Cé: a chronicle of Irish affairs from AD 1014 to AD 1590*, 2 vols., Rolls Series, 54 (1871) · M. Ryan, ed., *Treasures of Ireland: Irish art 3000 BC – 1500 AD* (1983), no. 79a–b [exhibition catalogue] · M. C. Dobbs, ed. and trans., 'The Ban-shenchus [pt 2]', *Revue Celtique*, 48 (1931), 163–234, esp. 191, 197 · J. Hogan, 'The Ua Briain kingship in Telach Óc', *Féilsgribhinn Eóin Mhic Néill*, ed. J. Ryan (1940), 406–44 · W. Stokes, ed., 'The annals of Tigernach [8 pts]', *Revue Celtique*, 16 (1895), 374–419; 17 (1896), 6–33, 119–263, 337–420; 18 (1897), 9–59, 150–97, 267–303, 374–91; pubd sep. (1993) · W. M. Hennessy, ed. and trans., *Chronicum Scotorum: a chronicle of Irish affairs*, Rolls Series, 46 (1866) · S. Ó hInnse, ed. and trans., *Miscellaneous Irish annals, AD 1114–1437* (1947), s.a. 1119, 1120, 1121

Ualtéir na bPaidrín. *See* Butler, Walter, eleventh earl of Ormond and fourth earl of Ossory (1559–1633).

Ua Mordha, Ruaidhrí Caoch. *See* O'More, Rory Caoch MacConnell (*d.* 1545), *under* O'More, Rory Oge (*c.*1540–1578).

Ua Mordha, Ruaidhri Óg. *See* O'More, Rory Oge (*c.*1540–1578).

Ua Mordha, Uaithne MacRuaidhri. *See* O'More, Owny MacRory (*b.* in or before 1577, *d.* 1600).

Ua Néill, Flaithbertach [Flaithbheartach O'Neill, Flaithbertach an Trostáin] (*d.* **1036**), king of Ailech, was a member of the Cenél nEógain branch of the northern Uí Néill, and the son of Muirchertach (*d.* 977), son of *Domnall ua Néill (*d.* 980), high-king of Ireland, and of Cres Cumal, a lady of the Uí Maine of Connacht. He succeeded to the kingship of Ailech following the premature death of his uncle Áed in 1004, and in 1005 and 1007 is found raiding in Lecale, Down, and doing battle against the Ulaid. He may have submitted to the high-king, Brian Bóruma, on the latter's northern campaign of 1005, but refused submission on that of the following year (though at some point he married Brian's daughter, Bé Binn, who bore him his sons Áed and Domnall). When he ventured south to Conailli Muirthemne in 1006 he was opposed by the former high-king, Máel Sechnaill mac Domnaill of the southern Uí Néill, and lost 200 men; but he raided successfully as far south as Brega in 1009.

Ua Néill continued to build up his northern power base by blinding and killing an Inishowen lord in 1009, and, having in 1010 made a renewed submission at Armagh to Brian Bóruma (who brought Flaithbertach's hostages home to Kincora), he raided westwards in Cenél Conaill in the following year in the company of Brian's son Murchad, and eastwards in Ulaid, where he burnt Duneight. In 1012 he was back in east Ulster plundering Ards, and led two western campaigns against Cenél Conaill. Máel Sechnaill took advantage of his absence on one of these to raid the Cenél nEógain inauguration site at Telach Óc, but offered no opposition to Flaithbertach when he campaigned near Kells, Meath, a year later.

In 1015, following the death of Brian Bóruma, Ua Néill assisted Máel Sechnaill in his campaign to recover the high-kingship, burning Dublin and Uí Chennselaig in the south-east, setting up a new king over Leinster, and plundering neighbouring Osraige. Five years later he helped secure the hostages of Connacht for Máel Sechnaill; but after the latter's death in 1022 he began to interfere again in the late high-king's sphere of influence. In 1025 he took an army south to Brega and to the area ruled by the Hiberno-Norse of Dublin, taking hostages and effectively securing his dominance over them. Although he was repulsed by a member of Máel Sechnaill's dynasty, he returned to Meath a year later and seized from the Hiberno-Norse the crannóg site at Inishmot.

This is the last military engagement at which Flaithbertach Ua Néill's presence is recorded, although the army of Cenél nEógain did raid Ulaid in 1027 and Cenél Conaill in 1028. He must have been very elderly at this stage, a full fifty years after the death of his father, and in the following year went 'on his pilgrimage' to Armagh, thereby abdicating. In spite of his advanced years, in 1030 he became the latest in a succession of recent Irish lords to visit Rome (as a result of which he acquired his nickname, Flaithbertach an Trostáin, 'Flaithbertach of the Pilgrim's Staff'), returning safely within a year. His son Domnall had died in 1027 and he was succeeded by another son, Áed, whom he joined in plundering Inishowen in 1031; but Áed too died, in 1033, forcing Flaithbertach out of his retirement, an annalist reporting that 'the north of Ireland submitted to him on account of seniority' (annals of Inisfallen, s.a. 1034). However, he died in 1036 'after a good life and penance' (*AFM*, s.a. 1036). The kingship of Cenél nEógain and Ailech passed out of his direct line at this point, and no one of the surname Ua Néill held it again until it was recovered by Flaithbertach's direct descendant, Áed in Macáem Tóinlesc, in 1167.   SEÁN DUFFY

Sources *AFM* · *Ann. Ulster* · S. Mac Airt, ed. and trans., *The annals of Inisfallen* (1951) · W. M. Hennessy, ed. and trans., *The annals of Loch Cé: a chronicle of Irish affairs from AD 1014 to AD 1590*, 2 vols., Rolls Series, 54 (1871) · W. M. Hennessy, ed. and trans., *Chronicum Scotorum: a chronicle of Irish affairs*, Rolls Series, 46 (1866) · W. Stokes, ed., 'The annals of Tigernach [8 pts]', *Revue Celtique*, 16 (1895), 374–419; 17 (1896), 6–33, 119–263, 337–420; 18 (1897), 9–59, 150–97, 267–303, 374–91; pubd sep. (1993) · M. C. Dobbs, ed. and trans., 'The Banshenchus [pt 3]', *Revue Celtique*, 49 (1932), 437–89, esp. 189, 228 · 'The O'Clery book of genealogies', ed. S. Pender, *Analecta Hibernica*, 18 (1951), 1–195

Ua Ruairc, Tigernán [Tiernan O'Rourke] (*d.* 1172), king of Bréifne, was the son of Áed, king of Bréifne (*d.* 1122), and is first mentioned as king of Bréifne in 1124. His mother was Aillend, daughter of Ua Baígelláin of Fir Manach, who was also mother of Donnchad Ua Cerbaill, king of Airgialla (*d.* 1168), with whom he later competed to expand into the area of what is now co. Louth.

In 1125 Ua Ruairc submitted to Toirdelbach Ua Conchobair, king of Connacht, contender for the high-kingship, and effective overlord of Ireland, who deposed Murchad Ua Máelsechlainn, king of Mide (*d.* 1153), and allocated a quarter-portion of Mide to him. Eight years later, however, in 1133, Ua Ruairc took part in a grand alliance against Ua Conchobair, fighting alongside Ua Máelsechlainn and destroying the bridge and castle at Athlone. In 1137 he and Ua Máelsechlainn placed a fleet of between 140 and 200 ships on the River Shannon at Lough Ree, against Ua Conchobair. In the next year, however, Ua Ruairc switched his support back to Ua Conchobair, while Ua Máelsechlainn concluded an alliance with Diarmait Mac Murchada, king of Leinster, and the Hiberno-Norse of Dublin. After renewed conflict Ua Conchobair divided east Mide between Mac Murchada and Ua Ruairc in 1144.

In a further political shift, Ua Ruairc in 1149 submitted to Muirchertach Mac Lochlainn, king of Tír Eoghain, a rising power and contender for the high-kingship against Ua Conchobair; and the following year Mac Lochlainn effected a tripartite division of Mide between Ua Conchobair, Ua Ruairc, and Donnchad Ua Cerbaill, king of Airgialla. In 1152 Mac Lochlainn, having concluded an alliance with Ua Conchobair and Mac Murchada, invaded Bréifne and temporarily deposed Ua Ruairc from the kingship in favour of a collateral, Áed, son of Gilla Braite Ua Ruairc (*d.* 1176). It was on this occasion that Mac Murchada carried off Ua Ruairc's wife, Derbforgaill (*d.* 1193), daughter of Murchad Ua Máelsechlainn, as a calculated political insult. Ua Ruairc was restored by Ua Conchobair, who in 1153 led an army into Leinster which brought Derbforgaill back to Bréifne. Nevertheless, Mac Lochlainn 'compelled the men of Bréifne to submit to him' (*Annála ríoghachta Éireann*, s.a. 1154). In 1156 Ua Ruairc negotiated a peace

with Toirdelbach Ua Conchobair; but following the latter's death, he was defeated at Liss Luigdi, Meath, by Mac Murchada, accompanied by the Hiberno-Norse of Dublin.

Ua Ruairc attended the consecration of the church of Mellifont in 1157, a ceremony which endorsed the high-kingship of Muirchertach Mac Lochlainn and at which Derbforgaill donated gold, altar cloths, and vessels. In 1159 Ua Ruairc swore mutual oaths with Ruaidrí Ua Conchobair, who had succeeded his father, Toirdelbach, as king of Connacht in 1156 and who married Ua Ruairc's daughter Dub Coblaid (*d.* 1181); the two then hosted together against Mac Lochlainn, who retaliated by attempting to expel Ua Ruairc from Mide. The next year, when Mac Lochlainn sought hostages from Ua Ruairc, Ua Conchobair led an army to support his ally. One of Ua Ruairc's sons, Máelsechlainn, was killed in 1162 and another, Sitric, in 1165 in renewed warfare between the men of Mide and of Bréifne. In 1166 he hosted with Ua Conchobair to Dublin city, which submitted, and into Leinster against Diarmait Mac Murchada, on whom they inflicted a defeat. While Ua Conchobair moved on to campaign in Tír Conaill, Ua Ruairc's army, probably as part of a co-ordinated strategy, invaded Tír Eoghain, where Muirchertach Mac Lochlainn was routed and killed. Ua Ruairc then returned to Leinster and drove Mac Murchada into exile, ostensibly in vengeance for the abduction of his wife. In 1167, following Mac Murchada's return, Ua Conchobair and Ua Ruairc hosted into Leinster and obliged him to submit to Ua Conchobair as high-king and pay 100 ounces of gold to Ua Ruairc in compensation for his wife's abduction.

Two years later, in 1169, Ua Conchobair apportioned the eastern half of Mide to Ua Ruairc, retaining the western half himself. Ua Ruairc subsequently accompanied Ua Conchobair to Leinster where hostages were taken from Mac Murchada, who, his forces augmented by additional Norman mercenaries, then raided in Mide and Bréifne and secured the submission of east Mide. As Mac Murchada's position strengthened, Ua Ruairc made his acknowledgement of Ruaidrí Ua Conchobair's high-kingship conditional on the execution of the hostages whom Ua Conchobair held from Mac Murchada. Following Mac Murchada's death about May 1171, Ua Ruairc hosted with Ua Conchobair to besiege the Anglo-Norman garrison in Dublin and, in an engagement with Miles de Cogan, Ua Ruairc's son (and almost certainly his successor designate), Áed Manach, was killed. At Christmas 1171 Ua Ruairc submitted to Henry II at Dublin. He was killed by Hugh de Lacy at Tlachtga (Hill of Ward, Meath) in 1172, a rival dynast, Domnall, son of Annach Ua Ruairc, being in the company of Lacy; the dead man was decapitated, his head fixed on a gate of Dublin city, and his body hung by the feet from a gibbet. Áed, son of Gilla Braite Ua Ruairc, succeeded him as king.

Tigernán Ua Ruairc was involved in partitions of Mide in 1124, 1144, 1150, and 1169 and his designation by Gerald of Wales as 'king of the men of Mide' reflected his expansion into Meath, where he erected bases at Kells (to the church of which he made grants of land, recorded in the Book of Kells) and Slane. His encroachments into Meath were the real source of the tension between himself and Mac Murchada which occasioned the abduction of Derbforgaill, as Mac Murchada sought to extend the borders of Leinster into the same area. Ua Ruairc's territorial expansion was reflected at the Synod of Kells in 1152, when the dioceses of Bréifne (later Kilmore), with a see at Kells, and of Ardagh were created, the latter coterminous with his sub-kingdom of Conmaicne. Despite Ua Ruairc's shifting alliances between claimants for the high-kingship, Diarmait Mac Murchada remained his constant and implacable enemy. The sizeable overkingship of Bréifne which he had assembled, extending from the mouth of the Erne to the mouth of the Boyne, collapsed following his death; his conquests in Meath came under the control of Hugh de Lacy; and the see of Kells was extinguished and absorbed into the Anglo-Norman diocese of Meath.

M. T. FLANAGAN

Sources W. Stokes, ed., 'The annals of Tigernach [8 pts]', *Revue Celtique*, 16 (1895), 374–419; 17 (1896), 6–33, 119–263, 337–420; 18 (1897), 9–59, 150–97, 267–303, 374–91; pubd sep. (1993) · *AFM*, 2nd edn · *Ann. Ulster*, s.a. 1122, 1125, 1128 · W. M. Hennessy and B. MacCarthy, eds., *Annals of Ulster, otherwise, annals of Senat*, 4 vols. (1887–1901), vol. 2, pp. 1157, 1159, 1162, 1165–6, 1170–2 · Giraldus Cambrensis, *Expugnatio Hibernica / The conquest of Ireland*, ed. and trans. A. B. Scott and F. X. Martin (1978), 25, 69, 85, 91, 95, 113–15 · G. H. Orpen, ed. and trans., *The song of Dermot and the earl* (1892), lines 23–125 · M. C. Dobbs, ed. and trans., 'The Ban-shenchus [pt 2]', *Revue Celtique*, 48 (1931), 163–234, esp. 191 · P. Fox, ed., *The Book of Kells, MS 58, Trinity College Library, Dublin: commentary* (1990), 155, 161, 163 · D. Murphy, ed., *The annals of Clonmacnoise*, trans. C. Mageoghagan (1896); facs. edn (1993), 198, 200, 204, 205, 206, 214 · S. Ó hInnse, ed. and trans., *Miscellaneous Irish annals, AD 1114–1437* (1947), s.a. 1123, 1124, 1158, 1165, 1171, 1172, 1173 · M. T. Flanagan, *Irish society, Anglo-Norman settlers, Angevin kingship: interactions in Ireland in the late twelfth century* (1989)

Ubaldini, Petruccio (*fl.* 1545–1599), calligrapher and writer, claimed Florentine citizenship, though he cannot be traced in Florence. The names of his parents and his date of birth are unknown. However, he was possibly born in the Florentine state, his mother may have been a Petrucci, and he may have been the illegitimate son of a noble Ubaldini. In youth he acquired a knowledge of Latin, and his professional skill implies apprenticeship as a copyist and illuminator. By 1545 he was on the Scottish borders in Henry VIII's army under Edward Seymour, earl of Hertford. On royal orders he visited Venice, but by 1549, recalled, he was again in England, one of an Italian contingent garrisoning Haddington Castle against the Scots. In 1550 he freely translated into Italian, supplemented by personal experience, Hector Boece's *Chronicle of Scotland*, probably utilizing the Latin text printed in 1526 (Corpus Christi College, Oxford, L., MS CCXLVI). That year he sought a post in royal service on the evidence of his compilation of moral aphorisms from various sources, copied in fine script for the use of Edward VI (BL, Royal MS 17.A.xxiv). He probably also tried to gain employment at the court of wards as a clerk, his 'Un libro d'esemplari scritto l'anno 1550' (BL, Royal MS 14.A.i), comprising finely

copied extracts of correspondence, dedicated to Sir Nicholas Bacon, the court's attorney.

Thwarted in bids for a congenial post in England, Ubaldini probably left for Venice. There his 'Relatione delle cose del regno d'Inghilterra' (National Library, Vienna, MS Foscarini 184.6626), dated 1551, though perhaps commissioned by the Venetian *signoria*, appears to have brought no permanent post. In Venice in September 1552 he copied an annotated translation from the Greek: 'The art of living' attributed to Cebes of Thebes (Bibl. Laurenziana, Florence, MS Plut. lxxvi.78); the Italian translation was seemingly by Francesco Angelo Coccio, the annotations by Ubaldini. It was dedicated to Cosimo (I) de' Medici, duke of Florence, and the work's present location implies the duke received it. The text's nature and presentation parallel Ubaldini's earlier attempt to enter the service of Edward VI, and so it was presumably a quest for ducal service. Nothing is known of Ubaldini during the next decade; perhaps he obtained employment in the ducal chancery and then acquired Florentine citizenship (the minute of a grand ducal letter to Ubaldini dated 21 July 1588 suggests this).

Ubaldini returned to London in 1562, possibly deeming his talents more likely to be rewarded than previously, as Italian culture was by then held in higher esteem. His writings indicate that he remained at heart a Roman Catholic (despite recent suggestions, his travels could testify to his being a protestant), and the timing of his return may have been influenced by the moderation of the Elizabethan religious settlement. Initially he taught Italian, acted in Italian comedies performed at court, transcribed official letters destined for foreign powers, and above all copied texts in fine script and illuminated them. On 21 January 1566 he married Anne Lawrence, with whom he had at least one son (who signed himself Lodovico Petrucci). By 1565 Ubaldini had renewed contact with the court circle, acknowledging as a patron Henry Fitzalan, twelfth earl of Arundel, for whom he copied on vellum a Latin psalter in folio, illuminated with Arundel arms facing a miniature of King David in prayer (BL, Royal MS 2.B.ix); in 1576 he dedicated to Arundel and presumably presented to him the transcript on paper of his Italian version of 1550 of Boece's 'Chronicle' (BL, Royal MS 13.A. viii). About 1577 Sir Nicholas Bacon, the lord keeper, commissioned Ubaldini to copy, as a gift for the Lady Lumley, the classical and scriptural dicta in Latin painted in his gallery, enhancing his Gorhambury house (BL, Royal MS 17.A.xxiii).

This task was undertaken when Ubaldini's livelihood was precarious. In May 1574 debts had caused him to petition Lord Burghley, the lord high treasurer, for financial assistance from the crown; one can suppose the manuscript sent to Arundel in 1576 was a plea for money. That year, no doubt with like motive, he presented Elizabeth I with his 'Le vite delle donne illustri del regno d'Inghilterra et del regno di Scotia' (now lost). Symptomatic of the crisis he faced that same year, he revised and transcribed his 1551 account of England as 'Relatione delle cose del regno d'Inghilterra' (Bibl. Statale, Lucca, MS 308). This work, stressing that Ubaldini was a Florentine citizen in an apparent quest for Florentine service, reflects the author's disappointment with his London prospects; understandably his 'Relatione' was highly critical of the city's hospices for the poor and its poor-law relief. The following year Ubaldini's financial situation was somewhat ameliorated by an annual state pension from the queen; in gratitude he presented her with his 'Le vite et i fatti di sei donne illustri' (BL, Royal MS 14.A.xix). Even so, in 1578 the privy council insisted that he compound his debts with creditors, which saved him from arrest; the queen's support was probably paramount, as at new year 1579 he presented her with a book on vellum written and illuminated by him as a gift, and this brought a royal gift in exchange (similar reciprocal exchanges are recorded for 1585 and 1589). In 1580 he presented the queen with an illuminated Latin prayer book.

The year 1579 marked a turning point in Ubaldini's career: there is no evidence of debt then or subsequently. External threats to England, and Ubaldini's Italian background, rendered him suitable for occasional diplomatic missions. He seemingly visited Ireland in the autumn of 1580 and wrote an account of the repulse of the Hispano-Italico invasion of co. Kerry (BL, Add. MS 48082, fols. 87–121). He was resident in Shoreditch by 1586, and on 31 October of that year a passport was issued for him to visit the Low Countries, presumably on state business. In 1588, having interviewed Drake, he compiled for Lord Howard of Effingham his 'Commentario del successo dell'Armata Spagnola nell'assalir l'Inghilterra l'anno 1588' (BL, Royal MS 14.A.x), and the following year he dedicated an elaborated narrative to Sir Christopher Hatton: 'Commentario della impresa fatta contra il regno d'Inghilterra dal re Cattolico l'anno 1588' (BL, Royal MS 14.A.xi). In 1588 he sent the grand duke of Tuscany a copy of his printed *Descrittione del regno di Scozia*, and the next year a manuscript entitled 'Discorso della genealogia, et discendenza della casa dei Medici' (Arch. di Stato, Florence, Miscell. medicea, filza 145), prepared some years previously for presentation to Catherine de' Medici, presumably on a mission to France never undertaken. In 1594 he presented the queen with a short treatise on different taxation methods (BL, MS Lansdowne 98, art. 22), a theme that she encouraged him to develop.

Ubaldini acquired financial remuneration from his contact with London printers: from 1581 from John Wolfe, who also turned to him in an advisory capacity, and from 1592 from Richard Field, who printed nine of Ubaldini's titles. Though these were not the first works in Italian printed in England, they testify to the aristocracy's facility with that language. His publications, while rather superficial and in terms of their historical content more poetry than truth, were interesting, easy to read, and topical. Four were writings that Ubaldini had presented in manuscript, such as his free translation of Boece's 'Chronicle', dedicated to Sir Christopher Hatton, the earl of Leicester, and Sir Francis Walsingham, printed with the date 1 January 1588 as *Descrittione del regno di Scozia* at 'Anversa' (a fiction for John Wolfe, London), and *Le vite delle donne illustri del regno d'Inghilterra & del regno di Scotia* (1591), known in

two states, one with a dedication to the queen. Ubaldini's account of the Armada was understandably well received. It was printed not in Italian, but in English and also in Latin for the continental market (both published by Wolfe with engraved maps by Augustine Ryther, 1590). Between 1584 and 1587 Ubaldini assisted Wolfe in printing several of Machiavelli's works (being on the index of prohibited books their fictitious place of printing was also given as 'Anversa'). The first work by Ubaldini published by Field was *Parte prima delle brevi dimostrationi et precetti ne i quali si trattano diversi propositi morali, politici & iconomici* (1592), which harked back to his presentation manuscripts for Edward VI and Duke Cosimo. Field subsequently printed Ubaldini's works of both Italian and broader interest, previously unknown: *Lo stato delle tre corti ... della corte romana, del regno di Napoli, & nelli stati del gran duca di Thoscana* (1594); *La militia del gran duca di Toscana* (1597); *Scelta di alcune attioni ... occorsi tra alcune nationi differenti del mondo* (1595); and his *Rime* (1596). The first of his books printed by Wolfe in 1581 was *La vita di Carlo Magno Imperadore*, a topic of interest reflected in the broader 'Un libro della forma et regola dell'eleggere et coronare gl'imperadori' (BL, Royal MS 14.S.viii), dedicated and presented to the queen and embellished with two of his sonnets. Charlemagne's biography was reprinted as *Di nuevo corretta* by Field in 1599, and, on the assumption that these corrections were the author's, it is the last testimony of his existence. There is no record of his will, and the date of his death is unknown.

CECIL H. CLOUGH

Sources G. Pellegrini, *Un fiorentino alla corte d'Inghilterra nel cinquecento: Petruccio Ubaldini* (1967) · F. Bugliani, 'Petruccio Ubaldini's account of England', *Renaissance Studies*, 8 (1994), 175–97 · A. M. Crinò, 'Come Petruccio Ubaldini vede lo schisma d'Inghilterra', *Studi offerti a Roberto Ridolfi*, ed. B. Maracchi Biagiarelli and D. E. Rhodes (1973), 223–36 · A. M. Crinò, 'Il testo di quella che Petruccio Ubaldini considerava la redazione definitiva della sua "Relatione d'Inghilterra"', *Annali della Scuola Normale Superiore di Pisa*, 3rd ser., 9 (1979), 641–771 · F. Bugliani, 'La questione ubaldiniana', *Lingua e letteratura*, 17 (1991), 160–76 · STC, 1475–1640, 2.413 · M. G. Bellorini, 'Le pubblicazioni italiane dell'editore londinese John Wolfe, 1580–1591', *Miscellanea*, 1 (1971), 17–65 · H. R. Hoppe, 'John Wolfe: printer and publisher, 1579–1601', *The Library*, 4th ser., 14 (1933–4), 241–88 · K. M. Lea, *Italian popular comedy*, 2 (1934), 362–3 · J. W. Bradley, *A dictionary of miniaturists, illuminators, calligraphers and copyists*, 3 (1889), 331–2 · H. Walpole, *Anecdotes of painting in England: with some account of the principal artists*, ed. R. N. Wornum, new edn, 3 vols. (1888), vol. 1, pp. 169–71; vol. 3, pp. 132, 134 · P. Ubaldini, *Descrittione del regno di Scotia*, ed. A. Coventry (1829), v–vii

Uber [*née* Corbin], **Elizabeth** [Betty] (1906–1983), badminton player, was born at 17 Prince of Wales Road, Carshalton, Surrey, on 2 June 1906, the daughter of Gerald Corbin, a commercial clerk and later a stockbroker, and his wife, Mary Ethel Johnson (1887–1947). Her father served in the army during the First World War but was invalided out and died at an early age (by 1925) as a result of his injuries. Betty had a convent education and followed a short career in retailing. From an early age she was a skilful racket player. While she made her distinctive mark in badminton, she was also recognized as a very able lawn tennis player: she won the junior championships of Great Britain in 1923 and played at Wimbledon regularly between

1929 and 1946. During this time she played six times in the ladies' singles, and was a competitor in the ladies' doubles on eleven occasions and in the mixed doubles on eight occasions. It is thought that lack of good local tennis courts was a key factor in her development as a badminton player. Her exceptional progress in the game was also very much due to tuition from her husband, Herbert Septimus (Bertie) Uber (1883–1969), a manufacturer and importer of elastic web for corsets, whom she married on 12 September 1925. They had at least one daughter. Bertie was himself an outstanding badminton player and earned twenty-two England caps between 1920 and 1932.

With guidance from her husband, Betty Uber graduated quickly from the 'shy ladies' court at her club and was soon competing at the highest level. Her forte was in the mixed doubles. She won the All England title in this event a record eight times in the nine years 1930–38, the singles title in 1935, and the ladies' doubles four times. She made thirty-seven international appearances between 1926 and 1951, and the achievement of winning every one of her first fifty international matches will be very hard to beat. As a player she was highly respected for her sportsmanship and modesty. She was an outstanding ambassador for badminton and made a significant contribution to popularizing the game. On court she was adept at analysing her opponents' strengths and weaknesses and using this assessment to her advantage. Her play was characterized by accuracy and impressive defence and it was her exceptional ability to return the shuttle against the fiercest of smashes that made her such a formidable opponent in the mixed doubles.

In 1936 Betty and Bertie Uber wrote *Badminton* and in 1949 Betty wrote *That Badminton Racket*. She also gave a cup for the ladies' world team badminton championship. The Uber cup competition, which was won in its first year, 1956, by the USA, remains a much coveted prize. The Badminton Association of England acknowledged Betty's outstanding contribution to badminton, on and off the court, by electing her an honorary vice-president. She died on 30 April 1983 at the General Hospital, Poole, Dorset, and is buried in the graveyard of All Saints' Church in Branksome Park, Poole. MARGARET WHITEHEAD

Sources P. Davis, *The encyclopaedia of badminton* (1987) · *Badminton Gazette* (Oct 1956) · *Badminton Now* (May–June 1983) · B. Adams, *The badminton story* (1980) · material, Wimbledon Lawn Tennis Museum · b. cert. · m. cert. · d. cert. · private information (2004)
Archives FILM BBC WAC
Wealth at death £325,900: probate, 16 June 1983, *CGPLA Eng. & Wales*

Uchtryd. *See* Uthred (*d.* 1148).

Udall, Ephraim (*bap.* 1587?, *d.* 1647), Church of England clergyman and religious controversialist, was baptized at Kingston upon Thames, Surrey, on 3 or 7 February 1587 (or possibly 1588), the son of John *Udall (*c.*1560–1592/3), preacher in the parish. He matriculated from Emmanuel College, Cambridge, in 1606, graduating BA in 1610 and proceeding MA in 1614. In 1615 he was presented by Sir Francis Vincent of Stoke d'Abernon, Surrey, to the perpetual curacy of Teddington, which he held until 1626. In

1634 he was appointed rector of St Augustine by St Paul, Watling Street, London.

Roger Ley's life of Udall describes him as 'the son of Udall the great schismatic in Queen Elizabeth's time, but wholly dissimilar to his father' (BL, Stowe MS 76, fol. 344). He rejected his father's nonconformity in favour of a more moderate brand of churchmanship, conforming to the ceremonies of the Church of England while strongly emphasizing the importance of the preaching ministry. At St Augustine's he preached a weekly lecture on Tuesday afternoons, and he was praised after his death as 'a most judicious and industrious Preacher' who had made 'many thousand Converts' in London (Reeve, 6). In his pamphlet *Good Workes, if they be Well Handled* (1641) he argued that the preaching ministry in London should be funded by an increase in rents and tithes, so as to remove the need for parochial lectureships supported by 'an arbitrary and benevolent maintenance'. In a companion work, *Communion Comlinesse* (1641), he set out his views on the administration of communion, complaining that the new fashion of 'building the Pewes so much higher and closer than heretofore' made it impossible for most people to see the outward actions of the minister at the communion table. He rejected the Laudian practice of setting the table altarwise against the east wall of the chancel and proposed as an alternative that the table should be placed in the middle of the chancel and railed on all four sides. This removed the need for ministers to 'goe up and down the church, reaching and stretching, rending and tearing themselves in long Pewes, to hold forth the Elements over foure or five persons' or 'to stride and straddle over the laps of Maids and Women: a most indecent thing'.

Udall was probably the author of another pamphlet containing proposals for ecclesiastical reform, *Directions Propounded, and Humbly Presented to the High Court of Parliament* (1642), attributed in some editions to Archbishop James Ussher but in others to 'a Reverend and Learned Divine now resident in London'. This work outlined a system of modified episcopacy in which bishops were to be placed under synodical authority, and made various suggestions for the revision of the Book of Common Prayer, including the substitution of the term 'minister' for 'priest', the omission of the Apocrypha from the calendrical lessons, and the alteration of the Sternhold and Hopkins version of the metrical psalms to remove 'superfluous bodges' and 'homely phrases'. Udall's moderation, implicit in these proposals for limited reform, brought him into suspicion as an enemy to parliament. In *Communion Comlinesse* he noted that some persons in his parish were attempting 'to get hands to a Petition against me'; and in the preface to his sermon *The Good of Peace and Ill of Warre* (1642) he complained that some people had come to hear him on purpose 'to catch upon something they expected would fall from mee, for which they might call mee in question, and bring mee into trouble'. The sermon avoided any open criticism of parliament, but warned against 'pestilent and destructive spirits' and ended with a prayer that God 'would stirre up in the hearts of Prince and Parliament the studious desire and endeavour of pacification'.

Udall's most controversial work was his pamphlet *Noli me tangere* (1642), which denounced parliamentary plans for the alienation of cathedral lands and the abolition of tithes, and called instead for the letting of cathedral lands on shorter leases, and at higher rents, in order to increase prebendal income and remove the need for pluralism. On 29 June 1643 he was sequestered from his rectory for 'charging the Parliament with Sacriledge' in *Noli me tangere* and for affirming 'that the great reformers of the Church now were Hypocrites' (White, sig. C1r). According to Robert Chestlin, the sequestration was carried out with exceptional harshness, Udall's bedridden wife, Philippa (*d.* in or after 1647), being 'turned out of doores, and left in the streets' (Chestlin, sig. G3r). By 1646 he had apparently retired to Greenstead, Essex (BL, Add. MS 34712, fol. 203). His final work, 'A briefe survey of the clergy lands', does not appear to have been printed, but survives in a manuscript copy (Bodl. Oxf., MS Bodley 307) transcribed for Sir Henry Spelman. It consists of an attack on lay impropriations, directed particularly at 'the tradesmen of our Citties' whose 'riches and fulnes is so great, that they are ready to purchase al the Clergy Lands left remaining, and to divide the spoile among themselves'. A postscript states that Udall circulated the tract among his friends but left it unfinished 'by reason of sicknes and distractions'.

Udall died in London, probably on 20 May 1647, and was buried on 24 May at St Michael-le-Querne, Paternoster Row, notwithstanding instructions in his will that his body was to be buried in the chancel of All Hallows, Honey Lane, Cheapside. The parishioners of St Augustine's granted £10 towards the cost of his funeral. His funeral sermon, published as *Lazarus his Rest* (1647), was preached by Thomas Reeve, who stated that Udall had expressly forbidden him to publish 'anything that passed between us in private concerning his spirituall scrutiny', but praised his 'sweet, affable, courteous disposition' and described him as 'one of the gentlest persons that ever trod your streets' (Reeve). In his will Udall left his sermon notes to his 'very loving friend' John Powle, on condition that he 'put none of them into print'.   ARNOLD HUNT

Sources J. White, *The first century of scandalous, malignant priests* (1643) · [Chestlin], *Persecutio undecima: the churches eleventh persecution* (1648) · T. Reeve, *Lazarus his rest* (1647) · will, PRO, PROB 11/200, sig. 118 · R. Ley, 'Gesta Britannica', BL, Stowe MS 76, fol. 344 · *Walker rev.* · *JHC*, 3 (1642–4) · Venn, *Alum. Cant.* · *IGI* [parish register, Kingston upon Thames]
Archives BL, letter to his cousin William Walker, Add. MS 34712, fol. 203
Wealth at death over £20: will, PRO, PROB 11/200, sig. 118

Udall, John (*c.*1560–1592/3), religious controversialist, was born of humble parents early in Elizabeth's reign. He matriculated as a sizar at Christ's College, Cambridge, in 1578, and proceeded BA from Trinity College in 1581 and MA in 1584. At Cambridge he made the acquaintance of John Penry. Ordained deacon at Bromley and granted a preaching licence by Grindal, but significantly not proceeding to the priesthood, in 1584 he took up the post of lecturer at Kingston upon Thames. Very early in his ministry the London printer Robert Waldegrave brought out two small volumes of expository sermons, *Obedience to the Gospell*, specifically intended for 'the Congregation of Christes people, imbracing the trueth of the Gospell' at Kingston upon Thames, and *Amendment of Life*, dedicated to Charles, Lord Howard of Effingham. He followed these with *Peter's Fall*, probably in 1585, and *The True Remedie against Famine and Warres: five sermons … preached in the time of the dearth, 1586* (1588?), dedicated to Francis, earl of Bedford, and Ambrose, earl of Warwick, respectively. 'Three sermons out of the second chapter of the prophesie of Esay', apparently never issued separately, but included in his posthumously published *Certaine Sermons, Taken out of Several Places of Scripture* (1596), may also date from this time.

This constant preaching soon seems to have had a marked effect upon the parish, and as early as 1586 John Hone, the archdeacon of Surrey, was asserting that 'certaine newfangled people' of the town had introduced 'new ceremonies, new forme of prayer, new feasts and fasting dayes, private meetinges, singeing of psalmes, and lectures or readings, and interspersing [interpreting?] of scriptures in private houses, contrary to the lawes and customes of this church of England' (Peel, 2.39–40). After a brief period in prison in September 1586, Udall was summoned to appear before the bishop of Winchester on a series of charges, one of them that of having taught 'that there oughte to be in the church a pastor, deacon, and elder elected by the congregation' (ibid., 2.40). Udall bitterly resented his silencing at the hands of the ecclesiastical authorities, declaring to the vicar of Kingston 'it was best for them not to stopp his mouth: for yf they did, he would then sett himself to writing, and geve the Bishoppes suche a blowe as they never had lyke in their lyves' (Arber, 83). No less provocatively, he sent details of his prosecutors to John Field for inclusion in his 'register'.

Whereas all Udall's published writings up to 1586 had been largely confined to spiritual matters, during the next year and a half he turned to far more explicitly polemical works. In April 1588, the same month as he had printed John Penry's *An exhortation unto the governours and people of her maiesties countrie of Wales, to labor earnestly to have the preaching of the gospell planted among them*, Robert Waldegrave published anonymously *The state of the Church of England laid open in a conference between Diotrephes a bishop, Tertullus a papist, Demetrius a usurer, Pandochus an innkeeper, and Paul a preacher of the word of God*. Usually known as *Diotrephes*, in its dramatic format this discourse closely resembled *A pleasaunt dialogue betweene a souldior of Barwicke and an English chaplaine*, written by Anthony Gilby soon after the vestiarian controversy but not published until 1581. Heedless of the consequences, it castigated the bishops who had stopped 'the mouth of the sheepeheards, and set at libertie the ravening wolves', and turned 'the foxes among the lambes' (Udall, *Diotrephes*, 8). The publication of this tract precipitated a raid upon Waldegrave's house and the destruction of his press. He moved what type he could salvage to Mrs Crane's house in Aldermanbury, and then in the late summer or early autumn of 1588, on a new press procured by John Penry, Waldegrave brought out at Mrs Crane's country estate at East Molesey another anonymous work, *A demonstration of the truth of that discipline, which Christ hath prescribed in his Word, for the government of his church, in all times and places, until the end of the world*. Prefaced by a further virulent onslaught upon 'the supposed governours of the Church of England', this tract, with remorseless logic, supported by biblical proof texts together with refutations of objections, set out chapter by chapter the constituent parts of a divinely ordained form of church government by pastors, doctors, deacons, and elders. In October 1588 the clandestine press produced *The Epistle*, the first of the Marprelate tracts.

The see of Durham and the archiepiscopate of York being both opportunely vacant, the president of the council in the north, the third earl of Huntingdon, passed on to Udall a 'call' from 'some that feared God in Newcastle upon Tyne', and so, having been instrumental in introducing Penry to Waldegrave, and having helped his friend distribute *The Epistle*, towards the end of 1588 Udall left Kingston for the north of England. At Newcastle he 'joyned in the ministry of the word there with two godly men, Master Houldesworth the pastor, and Master Bamford a teacher' (Arber, 170). As a token of his thankfulness for Huntingdon's protection Udall dedicated his next book of sermons, *The Combate betweene Christ and the Devill* (1588?), to the earl. During his Newcastle ministry he made a visit to Scotland and preached with acclaim in St Giles's Cathedral before James VI and the general assembly. When John Penry fled England after the capture of the Marprelate press near Manchester in August 1589, he called on Udall as he passed through Newcastle *en route* for Edinburgh.

No more than a month or two later Udall received a letter from the lord chamberlain in the name of the privy council summoning him to London, and he obediently set out on 29 December, arriving in London on 9 January 1590. At his formal examination on 13 January he admitted having gone to Mrs Crane's house at East Molesey while Waldegrave's press was operating there, but, arguing that at the common law no man could be required to incriminate himself, refused to say whether he had written *Diotrephes* or the *Demonstration of Discipline*. After six months of close imprisonment in the Gatehouse, on 23 July 1590 he appeared at the assizes at Croydon, indicted under the statute of 23 Elizabeth for writing 'a wicked, scandalous libel' called the *Demonstration of Discipline*, and was found guilty. His sentence having been respited, he was offered a pardon if he would confess to being the author of the *Demonstration*, which contained seditious matters against the queen and the laws ecclesiastical, as tending to erect a new form of church government contrary to law. This he refused to do, offering instead an alternative submission in which he defended the substance of the doctrine expressed in the book, while admitting that the manner of writing might be thought worthy of blame.

Udall's pleas for pardon having failed, he appeared for sentence at the Lent assizes of 1591. He again contended that the *Demonstration* spoke of the queen's person 'but in Duty and Honour' and questioned whether 'the drawing of it from her Royal Person to the Bishops, as being part of her Body politick, be not a violent depraving and wresting of the statute' (Neal, 1.405–6). Despite all his entreaties he was sentenced to death, though the judges gave order for the penalty to be withheld until the queen's pleasure should be known. Alexander Nowell, the dean of St Paul's, and Lancelot Andrewes attempted to persuade him to sign a submission, but once more he refused, producing instead a confession of faith in which, while he allowed that the Church of England was 'a part of the true, visible Church, the Word and Sacraments being truly dispensed', he insisted that 'the Church rightly reformed ought to be governed ecclesiastically by Ministers, assisted by Elders, as in the foreign reformed churches' (ibid., 1.407). With his declaration of faith he sent a new request to the queen, that if she could not pardon him she would commute his sentence to banishment. Much concerned over Udall's fate, at this juncture Penry prevailed upon the Scottish ministers to bring his case to the notice of James VI, who wrote to Elizabeth asking for Udall's life to be spared. In 1592 some English merchants offered to appoint Udall a chaplain to their factors in Syria or Guinea, and the earl of Essex had a draft pardon drawn up in which Udall was required not to return to England without licence from the queen. But Elizabeth never signed the pardon, and Udall died in prison about the turn of the year and was buried in the churchyard of St George's, Southwark. He left a wife (name unknown) and young family. One son, Ephraim *Udall, after studying at Cambridge between 1606 and 1614, became perpetual curate of Teddington in 1615, and rector of St Augustine, Watling Street, London, in 1634.

After Udall's death, in addition to *Certaine Sermons* (1596), two others of his works were published posthumously, *A Commentarie upon the Lamentations of Jeremy* (1593) and *The key of the holy tongue: wherein is conteined, first the Hebrue grammar (in a manner) woord for woord out of P. Martinius … Englished … by John Udall* (1593). CLAIRE CROSS

Sources J. Udall, *Obedience to the gospell: two sermons, conteyning fruitfull matter* (1584) · J. Udall, *Amendment of life: three sermons upon Acts 2 verses 37, 38* (1584) · J. Udall, *Peters fall: two sermons upon the historie of Peters denying Christ* (1585?) · J. Udall, *The true remedie against famine and warres: five sermons upon the firste chapter of the prophesis of Joel … preached in the time of the dearth, 1586* [n.d., 1588?] · J. Udall, *The combate between Christ and the devill: foure sermons upon the temptations of Christ in the wildernes by Satan* (1588?) · E. Arber, ed., *An introductory sketch to the Martin Marprelate controversy, 1588–1590* (1879) · D. Neal, *The history of the puritans or protestant nonconformists*, 1 (1755) · A. Peel, ed., *The seconde parte of a register*, 2 (1915) · Venn, *Alum. Cant.*, 1/4 · W. Pierce, *An historical introduction to the Marprelate tracts* (1908) · W. Pierce, *John Penry, his life, times and writings* (1923) · P. Collinson, *The Elizabethan puritan movement* (1967) · P. Collinson, *The religion of protestants* (1982) · P. Collinson, *Godly people: essays on English protestantism and puritanism* (1983) · P. Collinson, 'Ecclesiastical vitriol: religious satire in the 1590s and the invention of puritanism', *The reign of Elizabeth I: court and culture in the last decade*, ed.

J. Guy (1995), 150–70 • L. H. Carlson, *Martin Marprelate, gentleman: Master Job Throkmorton laid open in his colors* (1981), xvii–xxi • C. Cross, *The puritan earl: the life of Henry Hastings, third earl of Huntingdon* (1966)

Udall [Yevedale], **Nicholas** (1504–1556), schoolmaster and playwright, was born about Christmas 1504, in Holy Rood parish, Southampton. Nothing is known of his family, although a 'John Owdale' was the Southampton steward in 1505. Similarly, nothing is known of his exact relationship to the numerous, and prosperous, Uvedale family of Hampshire, although such a connection almost certainly exists.

Early career In 1517 Udall entered Winchester College and in 1520 he was admitted to the newly established Corpus Christi College at Oxford. In May 1524 he received his bachelor of arts degree, and in September 1524 he became a probationary fellow of the college, serving the customary two years in this capacity, and lecturing to younger students, before being made a full fellow in 1526. Between 1526 and 1529 there are records of payments to him for delivering lectures on Greek and logic. However, in the years 1527–8 Udall was among those accused of being involved in a ring of distributors of banned Lutheran works to Oxford undergraduates. There is no specific record of punishment for Udall on this occasion, and he was probably among those who were merely forced to file past a bonfire, throwing onto it their heretical books.

Udall left Oxford in 1529, and nothing certain is known of his movements for the next few years. It has been suggested by Edgerton that the intervening period was spent at a continental university, but hard evidence is lacking, and it is possible that he was an usher at St Anthony's School. Udall was certainly in London by 31 May 1533, the date of the pageant celebrating the coronation of Anne Boleyn, since both Udall and his friend John Leland contributed to the pageant. Udall's contributions were staged at Cornhill and Leadenhall, and involve numerous staging effects and speaking parts for child actors: they are, in effect, miniature interludes.

In February 1534 Udall published his first important work, *Floures for Latine Spekynge*, a Latin textbook. Udall's book marked an advance on previous 'vulgars', such as that of William Horman, in that it contained the conversational Latin modelled closely on the idiomatic usages of Terence, rather than the stilted classroom phrases invented for earlier vulgars. *Floures for Latine Spekynge* was reprinted several times over the next fifty years, and was a standard school text over the same period. Further evidence of Udall's interest in learning and teaching takes the form of his personal copy of Thomas Linacre's *De emendata structura Latini sermonis* (1525), heavily annotated. In June 1534 he was appointed as headmaster of Eton, a 'poorly paid but honorable post' (Edgerton, 31).

Thomas Tusser, one of Udall's pupils, describing his time at Eton in a section of his *Five Hundreth Points of Good Husbandry* (1575), singled out Udall as representative of its brutality:

fifty-three stripes given to me at once I had
For fault but small, or none at all.
See, Udall, see, the mercy of thee, to me, poor lad.
(Edgerton, 32)

From this it has been suggested that Udall was a sadistic teacher. However, he is not the only headmaster of Eton from the period to have been described as a keen flogger, so that it is not clear if Tusser's complaint is against Udall or against the school. In 1537 there are records of Udall's being paid for putting on performances of plays at court. In the same year, rather puzzlingly, Udall was appointed vicar of Braintree, Essex, and a letter from Eton describes him as 'late Scholemastre' (Edgerton, 34). However, Udall certainly continued in post at Eton after this date.

On 12 March 1541 John Hoorde, late scholar of Eton, gave evidence to the privy council confessing that he had been involved in a robbery at the school. On the same day William Emlar, a London goldsmith, was also arrested, charged with buying 'certain images of silver and other plate' stolen from Eton. The following day Thomas Cheney, another of Udall's pupils, also confessed to involvement in the robbery. On 14 March Udall himself was brought in for questioning, and confessed 'that he did commit buggery with the said cheney, sundry times heretofore' (Edgerton, 38). The connection between the buggery and the theft is not clear, and the hopeful suggestion of Udall's most recent biographer, that it was a clerical error for 'burglary', has not met with much approval. Under the 1534 buggery statute, of which Udall appears to have been only the second man to fall foul, the offence was potentially punishable by death.

Udall was committed to the Marshalsea prison, and it is unclear how long he stayed there. About this date he wrote a long letter to an unidentified patron, apologizing for his behaviour and pleading to be restored to his job at Eton. Candidates for this patron include Thomas Wriothesley, John Udall, Robert Aldridge, and Richard Cox. It has been plausibly suggested—on the basis of verses by John Leland—that Udall then travelled to the north of England, presumably to stay with this or another patron.

In September 1542 Udall returned to public prominence with the publication of his *Apophthegmes*. The book was a translation of selections from Erasmus's anthology, with Udall's own additions and comments. In 1543 Udall was appointed to lead a group of scholars, under the patronage of Queen Katherine Parr, in the task of translating *The Paraphrase of Erasmus upon the New Testament*. Udall's own personal contribution appears to include translating the paraphrase of Luke, and perhaps also of Matthew and Acts. In 1545 the work on Luke was printed and in a preface Udall thanked Katherine Parr for her patronage. On 30 March 1546 he and three others were awarded by Katherine rights to the benefice of the church of Hartyng, Sussex, which all of them quickly sold on.

Udall's whole career is punctuated by a series of long-running lawsuits. From 1538 until 1545 he was in dispute with Henry Creede, a clothman of Wilton, over a loan of £20 that Creede had made him: this dispute even caused Udall to be declared 'outlawed' from 1538 to 1545. In 1544

Udall loaned Edward Clement, a Somerset gentleman, £50, and then himself took out loans from Thomas Day, a London wax chandler, and Herman Evans, an Oxford bookseller. Clement failed to repay Udall and litigation between the various parties continued until at least 1550. On 10 June 1546 Udall borrowed £10 from William Martyn, gentleman, of London, to be repaid when his own income rose above a certain level. This loan, too, eventually resulted in a lawsuit for non-repayment, in 1554.

Under Edward VI The accession of Edward VI was good for Udall, who by 1548 had established a reputation as a protestant propagandist. On 29 June 1548 the bishop of Winchester, Stephen Gardiner, preached before the young king concerning the limits of royal power to enforce religious change, and Udall was among those requested to make a record of what Gardiner said, this evidence being later used in Gardiner's 1550 trial. Udall has also been credited with 'An answer to the articles of the comoners of Devonsheir and Cornwall', a manuscript tract written in 1549 in response to the uprising of feeling in the west country against the Book of Common Prayer. However, the identification of Udall as the author is uncertain. In 1549 Udall was appointed tutor to Edward Courtenay, a great-grandson of Edward IV and therefore a long-term prisoner in the Tower of London.

In 1550 Udall was granted special privileges by the privy council to print a translation of the tract on the eucharist by Pietro Martire Vermigli (known as Peter Martyr). This translation, *A Discource or Traictise of Petur Martyr*, appeared in 1550, with Udall named as the publisher 'Cum Privilegiis ad Imprimendum solum': what this meant in practice has been much debated, but it seems that Udall was, in effect, playing the role of entrepreneur. The privy council had also granted him rights over the printing of English bibles, which he does not appear to have made use of. Thus, Udall is an interesting figure in publishing history.

Udall's activities in 1551 include contributions to books of Latin elegies on Martin Bucer and on Henry and Charles Brandon, two sons of the widowed duchess of Suffolk. He also worked on revisions and expansions for a second edition of *The Paraphrase of Erasmus*, which was printed the following year. In December he was appointed canon of St George's Chapel at Windsor Castle. Quickly, Udall was once again involved in controversy, since in July 1552 the dean and canons of Windsor were visited by a royal commission investigating allegations of theft of jewels and vessels. Udall himself was exonerated, as he had been away preaching when the sales took place, but several of his colleagues were punished. During this period he prepared for the press *Compendiosa totius anatomiae delineatio* (1552), an English edition of the anatomical textbook of Thomas Gemini, with numerous engravings: Udall did more than merely translate the accompanying text, since he also expanded it considerably. This important medical text was dedicated to the king.

Yet another lawsuit flared up in March 1553. It appears that Udall had negotiated a fee from his former landlord, John Grenebery, in exchange for Udall's obtaining for him (via the offices of his friend and former student the humanist Thomas Wilson) the post of caterer to English troops at Calais. The promised post never materialized, and Grenebery sued Udall for the return of half the fee. In the same month Udall was appointed rector of Calborne, on the Isle of Wight, a position commanding an income of £300–400 a year.

Under Mary I Scholars disagree about the effect of Mary's accession on Udall's fortunes. Some point to his loss of the rectory of Calborne and, in time, of the post at Windsor. Others put more stress on the fact that Mary herself had participated in the translation of Erasmus's *Paraphrases*; on Udall's alleged involvement in attempting to extract a recantation from the future protestant martyr Thomas Mountain; and on continuing evidence of favour at court. For instance, a warrant dated 13 December 1554 directs the master of the revels to supply Udall with the requisites for staging a play at court, since he 'hath at soondrie seasons convenient heretofore showed, and myndeth hereafter to showe, his diligence in setting foorth of Dialogues and Enterludes before us for our regal disporte and recreation' (Edgerton, 66). It is tempting to link this to Udall's resumed teaching activities. The will of Stephen Gardiner, by now lord chancellor, was proved on 12 November 1555. It refers to Udall as Gardiner's 'schoolmaster', perhaps referring to Gardiner's household of young scholars, but perhaps indicating that Udall had already succeeded Alexander Nowell as headmaster of Westminster School, a post which he held until the school's reabsorption under Mary into the refounded monastery of Westminster. Udall died about a month after this event, and the burial of 'Nicholas Yevedale' is recorded in the registers of St Margaret's, Westminster, under the date 23 December 1556. The parish registers contain records of several other people bearing similar surnames, including a 'Katherine Woddall' buried twelve days earlier, but there is nothing to demonstrate how any of them might be related to Nicholas.

Udall's drama Udall's most enduring reputation, however, is as a dramatist. The one extant play that is certainly by him is *Ralph Roister Doister*, universally recognized as a seminal text of early English comedy, fusing elements from Latin comedy together with a native English tradition. Its attribution to Udall, and indeed its survival at all, hangs by a very thin thread. The comedy survived to the nineteenth century in a single copy, lacking its title-page or any indication of authorship. *Rauf Ruyster Duster* was licensed for printing in 1566: it is possible that the sole surviving copy dates from this printing. The attribution depends on act III, scene iv, where the hero sends Dame Custance a letter which turns out to be ambiguously punctuated, so that depending on the emphases with which it is read, it can yield two entirely opposite and contradictory meanings. In the third edition of *The Rule of Reason* (1553), this letter was quoted by Udall's friend Thomas Wilson as an example of the importance of punctuation, and Wilson ascribes it, and the 'enterlude' from which it comes, to Udall.

Udall's play, then, was written at the very latest by January 1554, although there remains uncertainty about whether it was written for Mary's court, or for Edward's. The eponymous central character is a bragging soldier, who is an example of the Plautine type of the *miles gloriosus* given a particularly English flavour. Egged on by his parasite, Matthew Merygreeke, he spends the play in a series of farcical attempts to woo Mistress Custance, who is not at all interested. He even attempts an assault on her house, but is driven back by her and her doughty maids. The climax of the play threatens for a moment to become more serious, as Mistress Custance's betrothed, Gawain Goodluck, returns from sea and is suspicious that his betrothed has been unfaithful to him, but the situation is resolved and Goodluck and Custance are reunited at last. In its five-act structure and its use of character types, it links itself to classical drama: and yet the execution of it is distinctly vernacular.

Also probably by Udall is *Respublica*, a play that certainly was written under Mary in 1553. It is an avowedly allegorical play, about the threat to Lady Respublica posed by 'Avarice, *alias* Policy', 'Insolence, *alias* Authority', 'Oppression, *alias* Reformation', and 'Adulation, *alias* Honesty'. Each of these is an allegorical character within the action, Avarice fulfilling what is explicitly described as the role of the Vice. In the last of the ten scenes, Lady Nemesis arrives *ex machina* to impose order and save Respublica: again, the classical and the vernacular traditions combine to interesting effect.

Beyond this, it is harder to recover the 'many comedies' with which Udall was credited by Bale. The most likely candidate is a rather earlier play, *Thersytes*, printed in 1561 and first performed on 12 October 1537. This is a comic interlude in which the eponymous hero boasts about his illustrious deeds at Troy, while obtaining a new set of armour from Mulciber the smith: he is soon engaged in, and losing, a surreal battle with a snail. Udall's name has also been linked with *Placidas*, a lost play on the subject of St Eustace performed at Braintree in 1534, but this is untenable, based as it is on an incorrect date for Udall's appointment as vicar there (Chambers, 2.451). Udall was credited by John Bale with having written a *tragoedia de papatu*, a 'tragedy of the papacy'. This has been taken as a garbled allusion to John Ponet's 1549 translation from Bernardino Occhino of a dialogue bearing a similar title. A now-lost play called 'Ezechias' was performed for Queen Elizabeth on 8 August 1564 at Cambridge University, and this too was written by Udall. A. R. Moon collected together the surviving evidence concerning its plot and performance, and proposed, plausibly, that it could be identified with the missing tragedy of the papacy.

Udall is an important figure in the history of British education, and to a lesser extent in the history of sexuality. (He figures as a sinister homosexual in Ford Madox Ford's *The Fifth Queen*, 1906.) He was an influential humanist, and charted an interesting—and still debated—course through the religious politics of the Reformation. But his main legacy is as a writer of some of the originary texts of Renaissance English drama.   MATTHEW STEGGLE

Sources W. L. Edgerton, *Nicholas Udall* (1965) • A. R. Moon, 'Nicholas Udall's lost tragedy "Ezechias"', *TLS* (19 April 1928), 289 • S. J. Kunitz and H. Haycraft, eds., *British authors before 1800: a biographical dictionary* (1952) • M. Axton, ed., *Three Tudor classical interludes* (1982) • E. K. Chambers, *The medieval stage*, 2 vols. (1903)

Udall [Uvedale], **William** [*pseud.* William Stranguage] (*fl. c.*1595–1636), historian and informer, was born into the influential Udall (or Uvedale) family, active in and around the echelons of power. According to his own recollections, he had a very good education and a Catholic upbringing in Worcestershire, Staffordshire, and Warwickshire. However, for the most part, his early years are hazy. His first marriage, while living in Ireland, was to a Fitzgerald; given that they had six children by 1601, the couple must have been married some time in the early 1590s. Except for two children, his loved ones starved to death by 1604. He married again some time after 1613 a 'Mrs. Udall of Gunpowder Alley', a known Catholic bookseller who died in 1623.

Udall's first accomplishment was as a spy for Lord Burghley in the 1590s. In this role he participated in the captures of the earl of Essex, Christopher Blount, and Everard Digby. However, these ties in addition to his knowledge of certain people's activities earned him many enemies both in Ireland and England. In 1599 he was accused of treason, deported back to England, and locked away in the Gatehouse prison until 1604. After he left prison, Udall shifted his activity to informing on recusant Catholics, clandestine presses, and importers of continental religious works.

Udall's other achievement was his *Historie of the Life and Death of Mary Stuart, Queene of Scotland* (1612), the first account of the Scottish queen in English, translated from Sir William Camden's *Britannia* (1600). Udall probably adopted the pseudonym of William Stranguage for the first edition of the book partly because of his own recent troubles with the English government, but principally out of fear of reprisals from James I, who was censoring works relating to his mother. In this way he hoped to avoid retaliation by his enemies at court. In the second edition of 1624 and the third edition of 1636 the author is William Udall or Uvedale.

Udall's later years are a mystery and his exact date of death remains unknown.   DAVID J. DUNCAN

Sources E. G. Atkinson, ed., *Calendar 1600, March–October* (1903) • *CSP Ire.* • *Calendar of the manuscripts of the most hon. the marquis of Salisbury*, 24 vols., HMC, 9 (1883–1976), vols. 7–23 • P. R. Harris, 'The reports of William Udall, informer, 1605–1612 [pts 1–2]', *Recusant History*, 8 (1965–6), 192–249, 252–84 • F. Edwards, *Guy Fawkes: the real story of the Gunpowder Plot?* (1969) • J. Featherstone and F. Bengsten, 'Adventurers, diplomats and inquisitors: the life and times of Armigel and William Waad, 1511 to 1623', dialspace.dial.pipex. com/town/walk/acw43/waad01, 25 Nov 2000 • H. Trevor-Roper, *Queen Elizabeth's first historian: William Camden and the beginnings of English civil history*, Neale Lectures in English History (1971) • *DNB*
Archives Hatfield House, Hertfordshire, letter collection pertaining to Udall's activities

Ude, Louis-Eustache (d. 1846), chef, became a celebrated figure in England in the later 1820s, but little definite is known of his earlier life and circumstances. However, he was French and for a time had been a cook at the court of Louis XVI. He says in the preface to his book, *The French Cook* (1813), that he has had 'upwards of forty years practice' (Ude, vi) of his vocation, so he must have begun working in kitchens in the 1770s, somewhere near the beginning in 1774 of the doomed king's reign. He is unlikely to have continued as the king's chef much beyond the flight to Varennes in 1791, and certainly not after the king was guillotined in 1793. In the standard French work (*Dictionnaire Universal de cuisine*, vol. 4, 1892, p. 1803) Joseph Favre wrote that Ude was *maître d'hôtel* to Napoleon's mother, Princess Letitia Bonaparte, for two years. There is, however, a tradition that he fled from the terror to England.

In any case, Ude became chef to Charles William Molyneux, created earl of Sefton in 1771, of whom Joseph Favre says 'this very rich lord, who was regarded as the king of English Epicureans, recompensed the services of his cook by leaving him an annual income of one hundred pounds sterling (2500 francs)' (Favre, 4.1803). There is a story that he left Sefton's service because a guest once added more pepper to his soup. Ude became the chef at the United Service Club, 'where his dinners were acknowledged to be better than any other Club could boast' (Humphreys, 221). The duke of York, 'the soldier's friend', subsequently employed Ude; and it was to the duke's memory that he dedicated the 1828 edition of his cookery book. Ude then became chef at Watier's Club.

First published in London in 1813, Ude's *The French Cook* was undoubtedly a great success, going through numerous editions. Although it was not, as Favre argued, the first culinary work to appear in London, there is some truth in the claim that Ude was 'one of the first to popularize haute cuisine in London' (Favre, vol. 4, p. 1803). The saying, 'Coquus nascitur non fit'—'cooks are born, not made'—is attributed to him, and in the section of the book entitled 'Advice to cooks' he wrote that 'Music, dancing, fencing, painting, and mechanics in general, possess professors under twenty years of age, whereas, in the first line of cooking, pre-eminence never occurs under thirty' (Ude, xix). He also insists that cookery is the most difficult and demanding of the sciences; that there are few good cooks, though many who claim to be; and that a properly qualified cook can be 'placed in the rank of artists' (ibid., xxix).

One well-known quotation attributed to Ude is: 'It is very remarkable, that in France, where there is but one religion, the sauces are infinitely varied, whilst in England, where the different sects are innumerable, there is, we may say, but one single sauce' (www.clairvision.org/ UdeSauceQuote). He certainly did write that 'sauces … are the soul of Cookery' (Ude, xxiii) and also that 'Cookery in England, when it is well done, is superior to that of any in the world' (ibid., xxiv). 'How many marriages', he asks rhetorically, 'have been the consequences of meeting at dinner? How much good fortune has been the result of a good supper?' (ibid.). In an essay, 'On cookery', in the 1828 Philadelphia edition of *The French Cook*, Ude says

The Ladies of England are unfavourably disposed towards our art … It is particularly the case with them (and indeed it is so in some measure with our own sex) that they are not

introduced to their parent's table till their palates have been completely benumbed by the strict diet observed in the Nursery and Boarding-Schools. (ibid., xxvii)

One of Ude's most celebrated dishes was conceived while in the service of the earl of Sefton. This was 'an entrée of soft roes of mackerel baked in butter and served with a cream sauce' (Blyth, 105). Another exquisite culinary concoction, first produced for the young Lord George Bentinck, was 'a most delicious sweet made with fresh stoned cherries, and which he christened *Boudin de cerises à la Bentinck*' (ibid.).

Ude's fame was at its height during the ten years in which he served as chef at Crockford's, the famous gaming club opened in 1828 at 50 St James's by William *Crockford. His appointment was announced by the *Public Ledger* in glowing terms: 'Mr Ude of culinary celebrity is engaged by Mr Crockford, to superintend the *cuisine* of his vast establishment … Mr Ude is fitting up a house for his own family contiguous to the scene of his official duties, in Albemarle Street' (Humphreys, 227). Ude had married Barbe Lucot on 4 April 1821 at St George's, Hanover Square; and they lived in Albemarle Street until his death.

At a time when club food consisted chiefly of boiled fowl, mutton, and roast beef, Ude's more refined cooking put Crockford's on the culinary map. He had been enticed to work for the club by the then enormous salary of £1200—out of which he had to pay all his assistant chefs and kitchen staff—and by the prospect of feeding the distinguished and important men who were members. Ude had also expressly obtained 'the freedom to order whatever he liked and to cook in whatever manner he chose' (Blyth, 104).

Conscious of the brilliance of his art, Ude would rage at any who failed to appreciate the privilege. One evening he charged a member 2*s.* for a red mullet and 6*d.* for an exquisite sauce, but exploded with anger when the diner objected to paying for the sauce as well. 'The imbecile must think that red mullets come out of the sea with my sauce in their pockets', he protested (Blyth, 115–16).

Ude's reign at Crockford's ended in 1838 after a fierce disagreement with the management. 'There has been a row at Crockfords, and Ude dismissed', Benjamin Disraeli informed his sister Sarah on 13 October 1838. 'He told the Committee that he was worth £4,000 a year' (Monypenny, 39–40). Ude retired, but confessed to Lord Wombwell that he was very miserable and sat all day at home doing nothing. When Wombwell recommended the exercise of his art for the gratification of his own appetite, Ude replied: 'Bah! … I have not been into my kitchen once, I hate the sight of my kitchen. I dine on roast mutton dressed by a cookmaid!' Asked about Crockford's, Ude admitted that 'I love that Club, though they are ingrats' (ibid.).

Ude remained in London until his death at Albemarle Street on 10 April 1846. His wife survived him. Reporting his death, the *Gentleman's Magazine* described Ude as 'the celebrated *chef de cuisine* at Crockfords, and author of a popular cookery-book, to which his portrait is prefixed' (*GM*, 25, 1846, 663). PAUL LEVY and ROBERT BROWN

Sources L.-E. Ude, *The French cook*, facsimile edn of 1828 Philadelphia edn (New York, 1978) • S. Mennell, *All manners of food: eating and taste in England and France from the middle ages to the present* (1985) • *GM*, 2nd ser., 25 (1846) • J. Favre, *Dictionnaire universal de cuisine*, 4 vols. (Paris, 1883–94) • www.clairvision.org/UdeSauceQuote • W. F. Monypenny, *The life of Benjamin Disraeli*, 2 (1912) • H. Blyth, *Hell and hazard, or, William Crockford versus the gentlemen of England* (1969) • A. L. Humphreys, *Crockfords* (1953) • J. Timbs, *Clubs and club life in London* (1872)
Likenesses portrait, repro. in L.-E. Ude, *The French cook* (1813)

Ufford, Sir Ralph (d. 1346), justiciar of Ireland, was a younger son of Robert Ufford, Lord Ufford (1279–1316), and Cicely (d. 1325), daughter of Robert de Valoignes. His elder brother, Robert *Ufford, was created earl of Suffolk in 1337. Their grandfather, Robert of *Ufford (d. 1298), had been justiciar of Ireland under Edward I. In 1324 Ralph Ufford was going overseas in the service of the earl of Kent. Probably in 1335 or 1336 he was with the king in Scotland, and played a part in the defence of Perth. By 1337 he had been knighted. His career advanced rapidly during the early campaigns of the Hundred Years' War. He was overseas with the king as a household knight in 1338–40. By September 1342 he had become a banneret, and was promised £200 a year until he obtained land or rents to that value; a month later he was going abroad once more, with three knights, eleven esquires, and eight mounted archers. In May 1343 he had an additional £100 to maintain his status. These signs of favour were confirmed by his marriage, which had taken place by June 1343, to the king's cousin, *Matilda of Lancaster (d. 1377), widow of William de Burgh, earl of Ulster. Her daughter Elizabeth, who was heir both to the vast Irish lordships of the de Burghs and to the lands of her grandmother, Elizabeth de *Clare, in England, Wales, and Ireland, was already betrothed to the king's son, *Lionel. It was therefore not surprising that in 1344 Ufford was made justiciar of Ireland; his appointment foreshadowed that of Lionel himself and of successive Mortimer earls of Ulster.

Ufford's justiciarship, though militarily effective, was politically stormy; for Edward III's relations with the magnates it proved cathartic. The justiciar was provided with an English retinue of 40 knights and other men-at-arms and 200 archers. This force allowed him some freedom of manoeuvre; but it led to jealousies over patronage, reflected in the Dublin annalist's condemnation of him for 'spurning, with a few exceptions, the local inhabitants (*indigeni*)' (Gilbert, 2.385). His association with absentee proprietors also produced tensions. Shortly after his arrival at Dublin in July 1344 he rode south to Munster. There he struck two blows against the interests of the earl of Desmond, Maurice fitz Thomas Fitzgerald, asserting royal lordship over Youghal and Inchiquin in Cork, into which Desmond had intruded after the death of Giles Badlesmere in 1338; and awarding custody of the Ormond lordships, for which Desmond had been negotiating with the king, to the dowager countess of Ormond and her husband, Thomas Dagworth. On his return to Dublin he assured Edward III that the 'outrageous riots' in Munster had been stamped out, and that the Irish of Leinster, whom he had raided on his return journey, 'do not walk so

tall now as they did' (Sayles, *Documents*, 181). In March 1345 he went north, losing horses, baggage, and treasure as he fought his way through the Moiry Pass into Ulster, where he acted with equal decisiveness, deposing one branch of the Ó Néill dynasty and installing another.

The consequences of Ufford's earlier actions now were apparent in a rising by the earl of Desmond. In the summer of 1345 Ufford moved again into Munster, steadily gathering support; by October he had more than 2000 men in pay. Desmond's castles fell before his onslaught; his seneschal, William Grant, was hanged, drawn, and quartered, while the outlawed earl fled to the Irish. Before this Ufford had sent one of his knights back to Dublin where he effected the arrest—by trickery, according to the Dublin annalist—of the earl of Kildare, Maurice fitz Thomas Fitzgerald (d. 1390), who had failed to come to his support. Kildare was imprisoned, and the liberty of Kildare resumed into the king's hand. The removal of the earls left a political vacuum. After Ufford's death the king rehabilitated them, and each was appointed justiciar during the 1350s.

Early in 1346 Ufford fell ill, spending his last weeks with the hospitallers at Kilmainham, where he died on 9 April. The Dublin annalist, whose sentiments lay with the local élites, condemned his rule as oppressive, sarcastically describing his body, which his widow took to England for burial, as 'this treasure, scarcely to be reckoned among saintly relics' (Gilbert, 2.388). Friar Clyn, writing at Kilkenny, within the Ormond orbit, shows no such hostility. Ralph Ufford was buried at Campsey Ash in Suffolk, where in 1347 his wife endowed a chantry to provide prayers for his soul. At his death he held lands in Dorset and Berkshire. His heir for such of these as had not been granted to him and the heirs male of his body, was his daughter, Matilda, presumably the child with whom his wife was said to be pregnant in November 1345.   **ROBIN FRAME**

Sources Chancery records • PRO • NA Ire. • J. T. Gilbert, ed., *Chartularies of St Mary's Abbey, Dublin: with the register of its house at Dunbrody and annals of Ireland*, 2, Rolls Series, 80 (1884) • R. Frame, 'The justiciarship of Ralph Ufford: warfare and politics in fourteenth-century Ireland', *Studia Hibernica*, 13 (1973) • R. Frame, *English lordship in Ireland, 1318–1361* (1982) • A. J. Otway-Ruthven, *A history of medieval Ireland* (1968) • *The annals of Ireland by Friar John Clyn and Thady Dowling: together with the annals of Ross*, ed. R. Butler, Irish Archaeological Society (1849) • G. O. Sayles, ed., *Documents on the affairs of Ireland before the king's council*, IMC (1979) • *The wardrobe book of William de Norwell*, ed. M. Lyon and others (1983) • G. O. Sayles, ed., 'The legal proceedings against the first earl of Desmond', *Analecta Hibernica*, 23 (1966), 1–47 • *CIPM*, 8, no. 629
Wealth at death see *CIPM*

Ufford, Sir Robert of (b. in or before 1235, d. 1298), justiciar of Ireland, came from Ufford in Suffolk where, at the time of his death, he held military subtenancies from both the bishop of Ely and the earl of Norfolk. These holdings were probably inherited from his father before 1256, but his father's name is unknown. Ufford had entered the service of the Lord Edward by 1257 when he went with him to Wales on a military expedition. He travelled overseas with Edward in July 1261 and was with him at Boulogne in January 1264. It was at Edward's request that

Henry III pardoned Ufford some Jewish debts in 1261. Later evidence indicates that some time before his murder in 1271 Henry of Almain had granted him a rent of £50 a year for life payable out of property belonging to the honour of Tickhill, which in 1280 he exchanged with Edward I for custody of the castle and town of Orford in Suffolk. This suggests that at some time during the 1260s Ufford had entered Henry's service.

It was, however, Ufford's former patron, Edward, who appointed him justiciar of Ireland in 1268. During his first period as justiciar (1268–70) legislation was enacted for uniform weights and measures in Ireland. He was also responsible for the erection of a new castle at Roscommon. Soon after his return from Ireland Ufford received a protection as a crusader and he probably accompanied Edward to the Holy Land. In June 1276 he was reappointed to the Irish justiciarship. This time he remained in office for over five years and was only replaced in November 1281 because illness prevented him from performing the duties of his office. Ufford led successful expeditions against the resurgent native Irish in the Wicklow Mountains in 1277 and in Offaly in 1278, and was involved in the prolonged but ultimately fruitless negotiations which began in 1276 or 1277 for a general extension of English law to the native Irish who lived within the ambit of the English lordship. His second period as justiciar is also associated with the enactment in 1278 in the Irish parliament of a series of statutes for the lordship. Ufford's brother, Master John of Ufford, joined him in Ireland late in 1280 or early in 1281 and it was presumably to his brother that John owed his appointment to the archdeaconry of Annadown and his subsequent election to the see of Annadown. The temporalities of the see had been united with those of the archbishopric of Tuam some fifty years before and despite travelling to Rome to press his claims John resigned c.1289 without ever taking possession of his see.

Ufford was twice married. His first wife, Mary, whom he married in 1272 or 1273, was the widow of William de Say. She was the mother of his son and heir, Robert, and was still living in August 1280. He had married his second wife, Joan, by 1286 or 1287. She was the mother of his son Thomas and was still living in 1307. Robert also had a daughter, Margaret, and in 1292 acquired the marriage of Edmund, the son and heir of a minor tenant-in-chief, Roger de Colevile of Byham, in order to arrange a marriage between them. Ufford died in early September 1298.

PAUL BRAND

Sources Chancery records · H. S. Sweetman and G. F. Handcock, eds., Calendar of documents relating to Ireland, 5 vols., PRO (1875–86) · GEC, Peerage, new edn · H. G. Richardson and G. O. Sayles, The Irish parliament in the middle ages (1952)
Wealth at death see CIPM, 3, no. 469

Ufford, Robert, first earl of Suffolk (1298–1369), magnate and soldier, was the second, but eldest surviving, son and heir of Robert Ufford, Lord Ufford of Ufford, Suffolk (1279–1316), and Cicely (d. 1325), daughter and coheir of Robert de Valoignes (d. 1325). Sir Ralph *Ufford (d. 1346) was his younger brother. He was born on 9 August 1298. Since he was a minor at his father's death, the family estates were

taken into royal custody; his marriage was granted to Walter Norwich (d. 1329), the treasurer of the exchequer, to whose daughter, Margaret, widow of Thomas Cailly, Lord Cailly, Robert was subsequently married between 2 July and 13 November 1324. On 19 May 1318 he was granted seisin of his inheritance, having given homage while still under age.

Early career In 1324 Ufford joined the military force led by the earl of Kent to Gascony; he was still abroad when the crown granted him seisin of his mother's lands in August 1325. His political affiliations during the events that led up to the deposition of Edward II in 1327 are obscure, but he clearly ingratiated himself with the new regime of Edward III, attending the king on his mission to Amiens in 1329 to perform homage for his French possessions, and becoming a banneret of the royal household by 1330. In May 1330 he was honoured with a grant for life of the royal castle and town of Orford, Suffolk.

Ufford sided with the king against the overbearing dominance of Roger Mortimer, earl of March, and took part in the ambush of Mortimer at Nottingham Castle in October 1330. Rewards followed fast. The parliament of November–December 1330 approved the king's grant to him of £200 in land for his contribution to the downfall of Mortimer; in 1331 Edward III started to make good this promise with gifts of land. Ufford also received a special pardon for his involvement in the killings of Sir Hugh Turplington and Richard Monmouth during the Nottingham coup, and was appointed keeper of the forests south of the Trent (1330–35). Later he served for a year as steward of the royal household (1336–7). His first personal summons to parliament in 1332 confirmed his status and prominence as a close associate and adviser of Edward III.

Ufford took part in the Scottish campaigns of the mid-1330s (serving with a retinue of forty-three men-at-arms on the expedition of 1335), and was appointed to treat for peace with the Scots in November 1335. It was the outbreak of war with France in 1337, however, that provided the real breakthrough in his career. On 16 March 1337, in parliament, Edward III declared his intention of restocking the ranks of the English high aristocracy in preparation for the impending Anglo-French hostilities, and appointed six new earls and a duke, bestowing on Ufford the title of earl of Suffolk. To support his new dignity the earl was granted extensive estates in Suffolk and Norfolk (including the lordship of Eye), promised a number of other estates when they fell in to the crown, and in the interim allowed annuities from the exchequer to bring his total endowment to the value of 1000 marks a year (£666 13s. 4d.).

Service in war Ufford's elevation to the peerage not only demonstrated the king's personal confidence in his abilities; it also, in effect, obliged him to play a leading part in Edward's enterprise against the French. The earl was joint admiral of the northern fleet in March–August 1337, at a moment when extensive plans were being made for the mobilization of shipping; later in the year he was dispatched to the continent on an important embassy to treat variously with the king's prospective enemy, Philippe VI, and his potential ally, the German emperor. By November 1338 Suffolk had joined Edward III at Antwerp, only to be dispatched once more on a mission to the French court. However, he returned to the king's side in time to take part in the first major military engagement of the war, the English invasion of the Cambrésis in September 1339, during which Suffolk himself led the successful attack on Beaumetz and took a prominent part in the preparations for the abortive battle at Buironfosse. After the failure of that campaign Suffolk was charged to treat for an alliance with the count of Flanders and the Flemish estates.

When the king returned to England early in 1340 to plead with parliament for further resources, the earls of Suffolk and Salisbury agreed to remain in the Low Countries as surety for Edward's outstanding debts to his allies. During the king's absence, however, they launched an attack on the pro-French town of Lille; they were said to have acted rashly in the engagement, as a result of which they were taken captive and sent to Paris to be held in custody. The truce of Esplechin of September 1340 allowed for their release, but only after the payment of heavy ransoms: Edward III himself contributed £500 to secure Suffolk's freedom.

Suffolk was back in England by mid-January 1341. He did not apparently involve himself in the public quarrel that had recently broken out between Edward III and John Stratford, archbishop of Canterbury, over the conduct of the war, though he is recorded as a member of the committee set up in the parliament of April–May 1341 to investigate the issue at the heart of Stratford's grievances against the king: the right of peers to trial before the lords in parliament. Whatever Suffolk's private sympathies, he remained publicly committed to the king: he was present at the great council in October where Edward rescinded the political concessions wrung from him in the previous parliament; and although it is not known whether Suffolk took part in the king's winter expedition into Scotland, he was certainly one of the group of loyal noblemen who turned out in a show of solidarity at the tournament held at Dunstable to mark the end of that campaign in February 1342. He took part in the expedition to Brittany in the autumn of 1342 with a retinue of fifty-five men-at-arms. In 1343 he was commissioned as an ambassador to Avignon; back in England in 1344, he was reappointed admiral of the north (1344–7).

Suffolk took part in the great expedition of 1346–7, landing with the king at St Vaast-la-Hougue in Normandy, and accompanying the army *en route* for its engagement with the French: according to Froissart, Suffolk was one of the notables who advised Edward III on the suitability of the battleground at Crécy. He fought in the prince of Wales's division and, according to Walsingham, distinguished himself by his bravery. He went on to participate in the siege of Calais (1347), and thereafter appeared in all the principal campaigns and engagements of this phase of the Hundred Years' War: the naval battle off Winchelsea in 1350; the campaign of 1355–6 led by Edward, the Black

Prince, which culminated in the battle of Poitiers; and the Rheims campaign of 1359–60. In the early stages of the French war Suffolk, like other members of the high aristocracy, had been forced to invest large sums of his own money in the king's enterprises in return for uncertain promises of repayment from the crown. At Poitiers, however, where Walsingham once more claims that he acted with conspicuous valour, Suffolk experienced some of the fruits of victory, taking 3000 florins as his share of the ransom of the count of Auxerre. His career in diplomacy continued up to, and beyond, the Anglo-French peace of 1360: in 1362 he took part in the negotiations for the marriage of Edmund of Langley to the daughter of the count of Flanders.

Family matters Throughout his career Ufford seems to have retained quite close connections in East Anglia, especially in Suffolk where his family had originated. His marriage, and particularly his comital endowment, very much strengthened his holdings in Suffolk and Norfolk; it is likely that Eye, Suffolk, was his principal place of residence in the region. He was regularly appointed to a range of royal commissions in Suffolk and Norfolk, including (during the last twenty years of his life) the notional presidency of the peace sessions in both counties. However, the true extent of his involvement in local government and politics, and of his contacts with the East Anglian nobility and gentry, remains obscure.

Ufford's marriage to Margaret produced a large family. The eldest son, Robert, himself took an active part in the French wars, but died childless and before his father, so that the comital title passed, in due course, to the next son, William [see Ufford, William, second earl of Suffolk]. Joan, the eldest daughter, was betrothed to marry her father's ward, John de St Philibert, but the marriage did not take place. Three other daughters all married well: Cecily [see under Willoughby family of Eresby] to William, Lord Willoughby of Eresby, Catherine to Robert, Lord Scales, and Margaret to William, Lord Ferrers of Groby. The other known daughter, Maud, entered the house of Augustinian canonesses at Campsey Ash, Suffolk, with which the Uffords had a long-standing connection. Suffolk's wife died on 2 April 1368 and was buried at Campsey. Her demise, and his own advanced age, no doubt precipitated the earl's decision to make his will on 29 June 1368; he died on 4 November 1369. Under the terms of his will he was to be buried at Campsey in a tomb to be placed in the arcade between the chapel of St Nicholas and the high altar. Robert Ufford was also remembered as a patron of the Premonstratensian abbey at Leiston, Suffolk: he supported the community's application to the pope to remove itself from an unsuitable position near the sea, and may have contributed to the expense of rebuilding the house on its new site, though the surviving remains date from a later campaign in the 1380s.

Relations with the crown Suffolk's service with the Black Prince in the campaigns of 1346–7 and 1355–6 was the natural product of a much longer association between the two men. Suffolk may have been in the prince's service as early as 1337–8; in 1353 he was regarded as his principal councillor. The relationship is, however, curiously elusive, possibly because of the considerable age gap between the two men. A certain sense of detachment may also, to a lesser extent, have characterized Suffolk's relations with Edward III. In comparison with another of the king's friends elevated to an earldom in 1337, William Montagu, earl of Salisbury (d. 1344), Robert Ufford received only relatively modest patronage. Perhaps this was because he spent little time with the king: the witness lists to royal charters suggest that his attendances at court and council were relatively sparse in comparison with two other members of the same group, William de Bohun, earl of Northampton (d. 1360), and William Clinton, earl of Huntingdon (d. 1354). On the other hand, the king did not forget or neglect loyalty: although Ufford was not among the founder members of the Order of the Garter at its inception in 1348, he and Bohun filled the first two vacancies to arise in the membership in 1349. Suffolk's bequest to his eldest son of the sword with which the king had bestowed on him the title of earl hints at an enduring affection between Ufford and Edward III. The contemporary chronicler Geoffrey Baker claims that Suffolk was distinguished by the strenuous deeds he undertook from youth to advanced age. Although such a judgement was fairly conventional, it provides some hint of the consistent and significant role undertaken by the earl in public life over some four eventful decades of the fourteenth century.   W. M. ORMROD

Sources GEC, *Peerage* · *DNB* · *Chancery records* · *CIPM*, 6, no. 58; 12, no. 424 · *VCH Suffolk* · R. Mortimer, ed., *Leiston Abbey Cartulary and Butley Priory charters*, Suffolk Charters, 1 (1979) · *Œuvres de Froissart: chroniques*, ed. K. de Lettenhove, 25 vols. (Brussels, 1867–77) · *Thomae Walsingham, quondam monachi S. Albani, historia Anglicana*, ed. H. T. Riley, 2 vols., pt 1 of *Chronica monasterii S. Albani*, Rolls Series, 28 (1863–4) · 'Annales Ricardi secundi et Henrici quarti, regum Angliae', *Johannis de Trokelowe et Henrici de Blaneforde … chronica et annales*, ed. H. T. Riley, pt 3 of *Chronica monasterii S. Albani*, Rolls Series, 28 (1866), 155–420 · *Chronicon Galfridi le Baker de Swynebroke*, ed. E. M. Thompson (1889) · F. Devon, ed. and trans., *Issues of the exchequer: being payments made out of his majesty's revenue, from King Henry III to King Henry VI inclusive*, RC (1837) · exchequer, king's remembrancer, accounts various, PRO, E 101 · N. H. Nicolas, ed., *Testamenta vetusta: being illustrations from wills*, 1 (1826), 73–4
Wealth at death see *CIPM*, 12

Ufford, William, second earl of Suffolk (*c.*1339–1382), magnate, was the fourth but eldest surviving son of Robert *Ufford, first earl of Suffolk (1298–1369), and of his wife, Margaret Norwich (d. 1368), eventual heir in her issue to the Norwich family.

Inheritance and early career   Ufford's early life is ill-recorded, for until the last three years of his father's life he had at least two elder brothers living, which also explains why he needed to make his own way through military activity and by marriage. In the latter he was successful, presumably through his father: by 14 July 1361 he had married the twelve-year-old Joan Montagu (1349–1375), whose mother Alice was daughter and coheir to *Thomas of Brotherton, earl of Norfolk. Joan was in effect heir to half the estate (her sister became a nun at Barking),

and Ufford came into the lands in 1362 and 1363, following the deaths of his wife's father, brother, and stepmother, and her own coming of age: they included the castles of Framlingham and Bungay with thirteen East Anglian manors and other property. This may have been the basis on which he was summoned to the parliaments of 1365 and 1366 in the lifetime of his father.

Direct evidence for Ufford's military career only begins in the autumn of 1367, when he was going overseas, probably on crusade to Prussia, with his exact contemporary and later companion-in-arms, Thomas *Beauchamp, soon to be earl of Warwick. However, it may be conjectured that Ufford, like Beauchamp, accompanied his father to France in 1355–6 and 1359–60, and perhaps was knighted with the sons of other earls and lords in July 1355. Earlier in 1367 Ufford had been a commissioner of array in Norfolk and Suffolk. After the death of his father, on 4 November 1369, he played a part in the desultory and unsuccessful campaigns of the 1370s. In July 1370 he and Warwick escorted King Charles of Navarre from Cherbourg to England and back. In 1372 Suffolk was summoned to serve in Edward III's abortive expedition to relieve Thouars. In the next year he and Warwick were the marshals for the *chevauchée* led by John of Gaunt, duke of Lancaster, through France from Calais to Bordeaux, where they arrived in January 1374, returning to England in April. In or after July 1375 Suffolk was made a knight of the Garter, filling the stall once occupied by his elder brother Thomas until the latter's death, probably in Spain in 1367. In the second half of 1376 Suffolk was briefly admiral of the north. In 1378 he was leading his retinue, again with Warwick (now his brother-in-law) and other earls, first in early summer at sea around Normandy where he fought an engagement, then (under Gaunt) at the unsuccessful siege of St Malo. In the autumn of 1380 he was on the Scottish border with Gaunt, who was then lieutenant of the march; he and Warwick were commissioners under him to settle disputes and enforce the truce.

Suffolk was similarly present and active at important national political events. In parliaments he was usually trier of overseas petitions, and in the Good Parliament of 1376 he was chosen by the shire knights to be on the committee of twelve lords to discuss their grievances with them, as was Warwick. Given his proximity to Gaunt both militarily and locally, it is more likely that he was a neutral figure respected by all parties than someone openly critical of the government; Walsingham describes the qualifications for the four earls on the committee as distinction in loyalty, strength of mind, and wealth. Suffolk was entertained to dinner with many other earls and barons (but not Gaunt) by the Commons at the end of the parliament. Perhaps his appointment as admiral was an attempt to placate the Commons with someone acceptable to all parties; if so, Michael de la Pole's appointment to the office in November was part of Gaunt's *revanche*. Nevertheless, on 25 January 1377 Suffolk was at court with Prince Richard, Gaunt, and other earls for the entertainment put on for them by the city of London. Suffolk was also at the great council summoned by Edward in April, and at court for the St George's day celebrations at Windsor.

National and local politics At the coronation of Richard II on 16 July 1377 Suffolk bore the sceptre, having carried the king on his shoulders from the palace to the abbey. In April 1378 he was one of the guarantors of the treaty between Richard and the duke of Brittany, and in October of that year he was appointed to the third continual council of the minority; payments to him suggest fairly assiduous attendance. Again, he was probably a neutral and respected figure rather than overtly committed to any particular faction, highly suitable to a conciliar regime whose first priority was harmony. The poor performance of this administration in handling the war led the Commons successfully to demand an end to councils in January 1380, but Suffolk continued to be present at court for some important business: he confirmed the treaty of March 1380 with the duke of Brittany, and that with Wenceslas, king of the Romans, for the king's marriage to his sister, Anne, in April 1381. In the quarrel between Gaunt and Henry Percy, earl of Northumberland, in the latter half of 1381 Suffolk played a mediating role, and at the council at Berkhamsted in October went surety with Warwick for Northumberland's appearance at the parliament of November to resolve the matter. In that parliament, his last, he was on the committee to intercommune with the Commons, and was on the broadly based commission to investigate the household.

Suffolk's apparently central and consensual position in these years may be symptomatic of Gaunt's attempts to build a cohesive noble group in the search for political stability. Suffolk's military co-operation with Gaunt and Warwick was matched by dynastic ties: by June 1376 Suffolk had married Isabel, who was probably Warwick's sister, and the mother of the heiress Elizabeth Lestrange whose marriage Gaunt held; she was probably then placed in the countess's household. The connection between the Ufford and Lancastrian families went back a generation, to Suffolk's father and uncles and Gaunt's father-in-law, and it was now continued not only in national politics but also at a local level. There was some overlap between their affinities: Richard, Lord Scrope (chancellor during the third continual council), and Sir Robert Swillington, two Lancastrian retainers, were Suffolk's chief executors, and Swillington was one of his regular feoffees. Other Lancastrian officers and retainers also worked on behalf of Suffolk in his land dealings, and received legacies from him.

This connection provided part of the basis for Suffolk's active exercise of local authority in Norfolk and Suffolk, where Gaunt was rarely active. The estates Suffolk inherited from his father in 1369 comprised the paternal inheritance built up by his father's ancestors through royal service and marriage, enormously supplemented by the lands granted by Edward III to his father in the 1330s, including Orford Castle and the honour of Eye. To these Suffolk added not only his wife's earldom of Norfolk estates (the other half of which were in the hands of an heiress, Margaret Brotherton), but also the inheritance of

his mother's family, the Norwiches, through his Huntingfield and Brews cousins. Together with the co-operation of Gaunt and his affinity, all this gave Suffolk a solid base for exercising local authority as the pre-eminent magnate active in the region. He therefore appears as the natural leader of East Anglian society during his tenure of the earldom, epitomized by his almost continuous headship of the Norfolk and Suffolk peace commissions, which also included various of his relatives and retainers.

The peasants' revolt It was therefore natural that Suffolk should play a leading part in the suppression of the rebellion of 1381 in East Anglia. Although his role has always been overshadowed by that played by Henry Despenser, bishop of Norwich, who violently suppressed the Norfolk rebellion, Suffolk met no resistance when he went to Bury St Edmunds with 500 lances, and he was left to clear up afterwards. It is true that Suffolk's initial actions were somewhat ignominious, in that, in Walsingham's account, he had to flee from the Norfolk rebels, led by Geoffrey Lister, who threatened to force him to lead them so as to legitimize their revolt. Alerted over dinner, he immediately donned the disguise of a groom and escaped to St Albans, going by roundabout ways to avoid gatherings of the commons. Thence he reached the king at the Tower of London. Suffolk was, however, right to adopt this course of action: Lister, now acting as 'king of the commons', forced some prominent lords and knights to serve him, whereas Suffolk was now free to be commissioned to arrest the insurgents, and by 23 June he was back in Bury. Then he set to work to round up and try the rebels, which occupied him through Suffolk and Norfolk for more than a month, re-establishing his own control of the county at the head of its gentry. His own property and associates had suffered in the marauding: court rolls and deeds were burnt at various of his manors, and Mettingham Castle, the Norwich family residence that he inherited in 1380, was plundered by the rebels of goods worth over £1000.

Death and dispositions Suffolk was commissioned again in December 1381 to put down unlawful meetings and riots in Norfolk and Suffolk, during the prorogation of the parliament. During the next session, however, on 15 February 1382, after consulting with the knights of the shires who had chosen him for this role, he entered Westminster Hall jovially and feeling nothing amiss, and was ascending the steps to the chamber to which the lords had withdrawn when he collapsed and died. Walsingham reported that the consternation this caused was unprecedented, among not only the great men of the realm but also all the 'mediocres' and 'pauperes' because he had been amiable to everyone throughout his life (a further indication of his consensual political position). His removal from the scene came when Richard II's attempts to gain independence threatened a fragile consensus, and Suffolk's absence may have contributed to the ensuing political fragmentation, although it also relieved him of the difficult choices that later confronted Warwick and Arundel.

Suffolk's estates were dispersed: the honour of Eye and the other properties which had been granted in tail male with the earldom in 1337 reverted to the crown, with some reserved in dower to Countess Isabel, and the earldom of Norfolk lands, in default of heirs from his marriage to Joan, were united with the moiety held by her aunt Margaret *Brotherton, who had recently been styled countess of Norfolk. In accordance with the earl's will, most of the Ufford patrimony ultimately devolved on the Willoughbys, the senior coheirs.

Suffolk was buried, probably on 23 February, that is, eight days after his death as requested in his will, in the family mausoleum, Campsey Priory, an Augustinian nunnery in south-east Suffolk, between Framlingham and Orford, in the chapel of St Nicholas behind his father and mother, under, he requested, a marble tomb. He left money to all the friaries in East Anglia and to the twelve religious houses of which he was patron, and his executors endowed other religious houses such as the London Charterhouse and Bury St Edmunds in his memory, as well as Brusyard Abbey, a house of Franciscan minoresses founded by his aunt. But his main focus was on Campsey, where his sister was a nun and where many members of his family, including both his wives, had been buried. All five of his known children predeceased him, enabling his executors to use some of his property for a lasting memorial to the family, in the form of two additional nuns, and a secular college of five priests in the priory, to pray for the two earls and their wives.   BENJAMIN THOMPSON

Sources R. E. C. Waters, *Genealogical memoirs of the extinct family of Chester of Chicheley*, 2 vols. (1878), 322–42 · register of William Courtenay, LPL, fol. 191 [printed in *De Scales Peerage case*, House of Lords (1856–), 112–21] · *CIPM*, 10–15, esp. 15, nos. 599–624 · *Chancery records* · *Thomae Walsingham, quondam monachi S. Albani, historia Anglicana*, ed. H. T. Riley, 2 vols., pt 1 of *Chronica monasterii S. Albani*, Rolls Series, 28 (1863–4) · V. H. Galbraith, ed., *The Anonimalle chronicle, 1333 to 1381* (1927) · *Chroniques de J. Froissart*, ed. S. Luce and others, 15 vols. (Paris, 1869–1975) · A. Goodman, *John of Gaunt: the exercise of princely power in fourteenth-century Europe* (1992) · *DNB* · GEC, *Peerage*, new edn, 12/1.429–34 · R. B. Dobson, ed., *The peasants' revolt of 1381* (1970) · Rymer, *Foedera*, vols. 3–4 · *VCH Suffolk*, vol. 2 · L. C. Hector and B. F. Harvey, eds. and trans., *The Westminster chronicle, 1381–1394*, OMT (1982)
Archives BL, deeds · Norfolk RO, deeds · Suffolk RO, deeds
Wealth at death approx. £2000–£3000 p.a.? and goods: *CIPM*, 15 Edward III, 599–624

Ughtred, Sir Anthony (*d.* 1534), soldier, was the third son of Sir Robert Ughtred (*d.* 1487) and Katherine, daughter of Sir William Eure of Stokesley, Yorkshire. Based in Yorkshire, the lineage of the Ughtreds extended back to the early thirteenth century; it was, however, Sir Thomas Ughtred, summoned to the House of Lords in April 1344, who assured their place as one of the leading families in the area. Anthony Ughtred served both Henry VII and Henry VIII as a soldier and military administrator. He took part in Edward Poynings's campaign to subdue Ulster, leading a troop of twenty-seven soldiers in 1496. Knighted at Eltham in 1512, he participated in Edmund Howard's naval expedition to Brittany in August 1512 and as captain of the *Mary James* distinguished himself in the raid on Brest. He accompanied King Henry to France in July 1513 and was appointed marshal of Tournai after the city's fall

in September, at which post he remained until February 1515.

For the next seventeen years Ughtred served as captain of Berwick. Few appointments were more challenging. As the most northerly of England's garrison towns Berwick played a key role in the defence of the Anglo-Scottish border. In 1522 and 1523 the duke of Albany's threatened invasions of England both centred on Berwick, and on the former occasion Albany's force, which included twenty-four pieces of artillery, came within 18 miles of the town. Responsible for organizing Berwick's defences, Ughtred was also entrusted with intelligence gathering and played a key role in the frequent negotiations that took place between the two countries. In August 1532 he exchanged one outpost for another, replacing Sir Hugh Vaughan at the Château de Mont-Orgueil as captain and governor of Jersey, a position he held until his death. At an unknown date he married Elizabeth Seymour, sister to Jane, Henry VIII's third wife, with whom he had at least one son, Henry, born in Jersey. Ughtred died in Jersey on 6 October 1534 and was buried in the chapel of St George, Château de Mont-Orgueil. His wife survived him.

LUKE MACMAHON

Sources *LP Henry VIII* · S. G. Ellis, *Tudor frontiers and noble power: the making of the British state* (1995) · J. Gairdner, ed., *Letters and papers illustrative of the reigns of Richard III and Henry VII*, 2 vols., Rolls Series, 24 (1861–3) · GEC, *Peerage* · S. de Carteret, *Chroniques des Îles de Jersey, Guernesey, Auregny et Serk* (1832)

Ughtred, Thomas, first Lord Ughtred (1291/2–1365), soldier, was the son and heir of Robert Ughtred of Scarborough, a landowner with extensive holdings in Yorkshire, and of Isabel of Steeton. He was born in 1291 or 1292, being eighteen years of age at his father's death in 1310. He married, before January 1329, Margaret, daughter of Brian Burdon of Kexby. Having probably fought at Bannockburn in 1314, Ughtred subsequently served regularly in the Scottish wars. On 8 June 1319 he was appointed commissioner of array for Yorkshire, an office he frequently filled during Edward II's reign; and a few months later he served at the siege of Berwick. In October 1320 he sat in parliament as knight of the shire for Yorkshire. He sided with the king against Thomas, earl of Lancaster, and on 14 March 1322 was empowered to arrest any of the earl's adherents in Yorkshire. Having had custody of Scarborough Castle for a few weeks late in 1321, he was made constable of Pickering Castle in March of the following year. During the summer of 1322 he participated in Edward II's ill-fated Scottish campaign. He was taken prisoner by the Scots, after a courageous feat of arms, at the battle of Byland (14 October 1322). In a letter written from captivity Ughtred begged the king to help secure his release, emphasizing that, as an old enemy of the Scots, he feared the wrath of Robert I. On 23 February 1323 Edward duly granted his household knight the custody of the manor of Bentley, Yorkshire, during the minority of the heir of Payn de Tibetot, to help meet the expense of his ransom; and in the following month Ughtred is recorded as going to Scotland to release his hostages. He was summoned to a great council that met at Westminster in late May 1324. On 14 April 1328 he was placed on a commission of oyer and terminer in Yorkshire, and in the years that followed he was often appointed to peace commissions and other posts in local administration. He again represented his county in parliament in November 1330 and March 1332 (and possibly in June 1344 as well).

In 1332 Ughtred accompanied Edward Balliol and the disinherited lords in their invasion of Scotland. The expedition landed at Kinghorn and defeated the Scots at Dupplin Moor on 11 August. Following Ughtred's gallant defence of Roxburgh Bridge Balliol granted him, on 20 October, the forfeited lands of Sir John Stewart, principally the manor of Bunkle, Berwickshire. Ughtred appears to have fought at Halidon Hill on 19 July 1333, and in the summer of 1334, following the Scots' rising, Balliol sent him to Edward III with a request for help. He served in Scotland, as a captain, during the winter of 1334–5, the summer of 1335, and, again during the following two years, now as a banneret. On 12 March 1337 he set out from Hull, with a retinue of 240 men, to take command of Perth. An indenture dated 4 August 1338 allowed him a garrison of 460 men in time of peace and 800 in time of war, although, in truth, these were unrealistic manpower targets. Within a few months Ughtred, aggrieved that his troops were not adequately supplied, asked to be relieved of his command. He was assured that victuals would be sent, but Perth was besieged and Ughtred was compelled to surrender on 17 August 1339. This led to aspersions on his courage, and there followed in October an inquiry in parliament, in which Ughtred vigorously defended his conduct and succeeded in clearing his name.

In July 1340, as Edward III was preparing to besiege Tournai, Ughtred was attached to a secondary force, led by Robert of Artois, that attempted to take St Omer. Although the expedition was unsuccessful, Ughtred's English archers distinguished themselves in the confused fighting outside St Omer on 26 July. Having returned from France, he continued to see active service against the Scots, as during the winter of 1341–2, but he was as much concerned with his own affairs at this time. In February 1342 he obtained a licence to crenellate his manors at Kexby and Moor Monkton, Yorkshire, while a surviving carpenter's contract shows that, in the previous year, he had embarked on building work at another of his Yorkshire properties, probably Brandsby. Ughtred was summoned to parliament on 20 April 1344 and took part in Edward III's continental expeditions in 1345–7. Serving under Thomas Beauchamp, earl of Warwick (d. 1369), Ughtred was sub-marshal of the royal army that landed in Normandy in July 1346 and won the battle of Crécy on 26 August. He was also present for part of the siege of Calais, during which, on 20 March 1347, he was granted an annuity of £200 by the king. From 28 November 1349 this was reduced to £100 a year, with £50 supplements payable when Ughtred attended the king with a retinue, as he did on a number of occasions during the 1350s. These duties were combined with continuing public responsibilities in his home county; and he was also summoned regularly to parliaments and great councils from 20 November 1348 to 4 December 1364. His last campaign in France was in 1359–60, when he brought to Edward III's army a retinue of 19 men-at-arms and 20 archers. At about this time Ughtred was admitted into the Order of the Garter, and occupied the stall vacated on the death of Sir Henry Eam. He died in 1365, aged about seventy-three, and was buried in Catton church, Yorkshire. Ughtred was succeeded by his son Thomas, who like his father was militarily active in Scotland and France. It was probably the son who served as knight of the shire for Yorkshire in 1352, but he was never summoned to parliament. He died in 1401.

ANDREW AYTON

Sources A. Ayton, 'Sir Thomas Ughtred and the Edwardian military revolution', *The age of Edward III*, ed. J. S. Bothwell (2001), 107–32 · GEC, *Peerage* · PRO, SC 1; E 101 · *Chancery records* · BL, Cotton MSS · BL, Stowe MSS · *CDS*, vol. 5 · G. F. Beltz, *Memorials of the most noble order of the Garter* (1841), 107–10 · *Report of the Lords committees … for all matters touching the dignity of a peer of the realm*, 4 (1829) · G. Wrottesley, *Crécy and Calais* (1897); repr. (1898) · R. Nicholson, *Edward III and the Scots: the formative years of a military career, 1327–1335* (1965) · J. Sumption, *The Hundred Years War*, 1 (1990) · N. B. Lewis, 'An early fourteenth-century contract for military service', *BIHR*, 20 (1943–5), 111–18 · L. F. Salzman, *Building in England down to 1540*, rev. edn (1967), appx D, no. 1 · J. Barbour, *The Bruce*, ed. A. A. M. Duncan (1997), 686–9

Archives PRO, ancient correspondence, SC 1 · PRO, various indentures and financial accounts, E 101

Uglow, Euan Ernest Richard (1932–2000), artist, was born at 73 Hinton Road, Brixton, London, on 10 March 1932, the middle child in the family of three children of Ernest William Uglow (1904–1978), chief accountant in a firm of mantle manufacturers, and his wife, Elizabeth Jane Williams (1905–1991). Although both parents were Londoners, the Uglows came originally from Cornwall, while Elizabeth Williams was from Ebbw Vale in Wales. Growing up during the Second World War was hazardous, and the children were evacuated first to Cornwall and then to Wales, before being reunited in Surrey. The Uglows were then bombed out of their new home in Ewell East, and moved back to London. Throughout these upheavals Uglow demonstrated an unwavering devotion to art, and at the age of fifteen began to attend Camberwell School of Arts and Crafts.

Uglow was fortunate in the teaching at Camberwell, coming under the inspiring tutelage of the painters Victor Pasmore, Claude Rogers, and William Coldstream and the sculptor Karel Vogel. Coldstream was particularly influential, instilling in Uglow the desire to enquire into the nature of appearances through studied observation and analysis, which information was conveyed onto the canvas through a complex system of mark-making and monocular measurement, in order accurately to capture shapes, colours, and proportions in a realist manner. When Coldstream was appointed professor of fine art at the Slade School of Fine Art, it seemed natural for Uglow to follow him there for a period of further study (1951–4).

Uglow was a supremely gifted student, winning bursaries and scholarships and impressing his teachers with his dedication. They, in turn, responded to him with warmth and encouragement; Thomas Monnington, later president of the Royal Academy, even bought Uglow his first motorbike. In his twenties Uglow developed the lifelong habit of making pilgrimages to see specific works of art. He was much involved with the art of the past—particularly with such masters as Piero della Francesca, Poussin, and Chardin. One of his last trips was to Bucharest to see a painting by Domenico Veneziano.

Balding, bearded, and bespectacled, Uglow had a priestly look, clad as he usually was in dark velours and corduroy, with open-toed sandals. He was precise in his habits. His life revolved around painting, and therefore around models, who were rigorously timetabled. He painted every day while the light lasted, and some nights. Friends were discouraged from dropping in until 6.30 p.m., but after that Uglow was a warm and generous host, plying his guests with well-chosen wines and home-cooked foods. The conversation could be far-ranging but tended to be confined to the broad field of the plastic arts, about which Uglow had firm and well thought-out opinions.

Uglow married on 30 December 1963 (Veronica) Clare (b. 1944), a student of painting and the daughter of Charles O'Brien, an air force officer. But neither Uglow's temperament nor his demanding studio routine were suited to marriage, and the couple separated in the summer of 1966. He continued to have close friendships with women, but none were permitted to move into his studio home. This was a mews house in Battersea, which Uglow had reconstructed from its dirt floor up when he moved into it in 1959. It remained his home for the rest of his life. He liked to make things, and had passed his national service as a conscientious objector in farming and in the building trade, helping to restore a Wren City church. He often built the furniture and props required in his pictures, and always made the distinctive frames for his paintings, though not for his drawings. He also liked tools and implements, owned a duck press, and would wield a large magnifying glass to examine things in detail. As a student he had relished motorbikes and fast cars, and had once owned an Allard racing car, but he gave up such distractions when he determined to focus his energies exclusively on his work. He read sparingly and possessed a radio but no television.

Uglow is considered primarily a painter of nudes, though he also painted ravishing still lifes and landscapes. A slow and meticulous worker, he rarely finished more than two or three paintings a year. His first London solo exhibition was in 1961 at Helen Lessore's fabled Beaux Arts Gallery, and from 1977 he showed regularly with Browse and Darby. There were two retrospective exhibitions at the Whitechapel Gallery, in 1974 and 1989, and one commercial exhibition in New York, in 1993. Uglow's reputation survived the fall from fashion in the 1970s of figurative art and increased steadily during his lifetime; at the time of his death he was hailed in *The Observer* as 'Britain's greatest figurative artist'. He was a painter of considerable originality, a maker of images extreme in structure

and colour, of distilled sensuality and frozen movement, dedicated to what he saw as pictorial truth and beauty.

Although shy, Uglow was convivial when not working. He claimed never to go out but, by dint of careful arrangement, managed in fact to be remarkably sociable. His close friend Craigie Aitchison was one of the few for whom he would rearrange his plans, but most were happy to defer to his wishes. Thursday evenings were devoted to dinner with one set of friends, Fridays to another. Friday daytime was reserved for teaching at the Slade. Even when dreadfully debilitated by chemotherapy at the end of his life, and made self-conscious by the falling out of his remaining hair, he continued to teach. When asked why, he replied that he felt a duty to give something back since he had been treated so well himself as a student. He avoided honours, was neither professor nor Royal Academician, though he did serve as a trustee at the National Gallery (1990–95). He was respected, feared, and loved by his students, and if his strict methods of teaching did tend to turn out disciples, he was nevertheless always ready to admire good work done by very different kinds of artists. His extensive network of former pupils, friends, and former models was increasingly demanding, not merely at Christmas time when he made highly individual cards (one year casting a 'key of life' in lead, another year painting on a dried gingko leaf) in an edition of several hundreds. But work always came first, until, with the rapid onset of the cancer that was to kill him, he could no longer paint. He died in St Thomas's Hospital, London, on 31 August 2000, and his body was cremated at the Robin Hood crematorium, Kent, on 8 September.

ANDREW LAMBIRTH

Sources personal knowledge (2004) · private information (2004) · *Encounters* (2000) [exhibition catalogue, National Gallery, 2000] · *Euan Uglow* (1989) [exhibition catalogue, Whitechapel Gallery, London, 1989] · b. cert. · d. cert. · *Daily Telegraph* (1 Sept 2000) · *The Scotsman* (1 Sept 2000) · *The Guardian* (1 Sept 2000) · *The Times* (1 Sept 2000) · *The Independent* (8 Sept 2000)
Archives priv. coll.
Likenesses photograph, 2000, repro. in *The Times* · B. Bernard, photograph, repro. in *The Independent* · J. Hill, photograph, repro. in *The Guardian*

Uhlman, (Nancy) Diana Joyce (1912–1999). *See under* Uhlman, Manfred (1901–1985).

Uhlman, Manfred [Fred] (1901–1985), writer and painter, was born on 19 January 1901 in Stuttgart, Germany, the first of two children of Ludwig Uhlman (1869–c.1943), textile merchant, and his wife, Johanna Grombacher (1879–c.1943). His father, a descendant of an old-established Jewish family in Stuttgart, and his mother were killed in the concentration camp Theresienstadt. Uhlman grew up in Stuttgart. He studied law in Freiburg, Munich, and Tübingen, finishing with a doctorate in 1925. In 1927 he started to work as an attorney in Stuttgart. In the same year he joined the local group of the Social Democrat Party of Germany, became its official legal representative in 1932, working with Kurt Schumacher, later the party's president, and campaigned for the party in Württemberg in 1933. In March of that year, after a warning that his arrest was imminent because of his political adherence, he emigrated to Paris. There, unable to work as a lawyer and encouraged by André Lhôte, a French art critic, and Paul Westheim, a German refugee art historian, who had promoted unknown talents in the Weimar republic, Uhlman started to paint successfully in a naïve and colourful style, such as in *Au palais des gourmands* (1935; priv. coll.). His first exhibition took place at the Galerie Le Niveau, Paris, in 1936. While he was staying in Spain in 1936 the civil war broke out. Uhlman emigrated to Britain, where he began assisting refugees from Nazism, for which he is still remembered. He was supported by Diana Page Croft [*see below*], whom he had met in Spain and married on 4 November 1936. They found guarantors and accommodation for the refugees and even put their own home at the disposal of the photomontagist John Heartfield for six years. In 1938 Uhlman co-founded the only German artistic association of refugees in Britain, the Freier Deutscher Kulturbund, which shortly after its foundation moved into his house in Hampstead, London. At the beginning of July 1940 Uhlman, together with further refugees, was interned at Ascot and then at the Hutchinson camp, Isle of Man, where he met the Dadaist Kurt Schwitters, who portrayed him in a naturalistic way reading (1945; Hatton Gallery, University of Newcastle upon Tyne). During his internment his first child, Caroline, was born. After Uhlman's release in December 1940 he lived with his family in Bambers Green, Essex, where his son Francis was born in 1943; he returned to London in 1944. He continued to paint and had one-man exhibitions, including those at the Leicester Galleries (December 1941) and Redfern Gallery (1943), both in London. After 1945 he became internationally known, exhibiting, for example, at the Graphisches Kabinett, Bremen (1954). He also published his drawings, produced while interned, under the title *Captivity* (1946), and *An Artist in North Wales* (1947). North Wales inspired him for many of his landscape paintings, such as *North Wales* (1958; priv. coll.). From the late 1940s he wrote an autobiography, *The Making of an Englishman* (1960), and several novels, which have been translated into twelve languages. The most successful is *Reunion* (1971), a book about a German-Jewish childhood in Stuttgart in the early 1930s, which was made into a film by Harold Pinter with the same title in 1989. Although Uhlman was a member of the London Group he never really belonged to the art establishment. He died in the Royal Free Hospital, Hampstead, London, on 11 April 1985, his wife and their two children surviving him, and was buried in Yarpole, Herefordshire. His paintings are in private and public collections, such as the Hereford City Art Gallery and the Ben Uri Gallery, London. The Fred and Diana Uhlman collection of African sculptures was donated to the Hatton Gallery, University of Newcastle upon Tyne.

Uhlman's wife, **(Nancy) Diana Joyce Uhlman** [*née* Nancy Diana Joyce Page Croft] (1912–1999), art gallery administrator, was born in South Kensington, London, on 31 March 1912, the second daughter of Henry Page *Croft, first Baron Croft (1881–1947), politician, and his wife, Nancy Beatrice (*d.* 1949), daughter of Robert Hudson Borwick, first Baron Borwick. She attended St James's School, West Malvern, and finishing schools in Paris and Florence, and was presented at court. Rebelling against her father's conservatism, in 1936 she greeted the Jarrow marchers on their arrival in London. While holidaying in Spain the same year she met Uhlman. Her father strongly disapproved of their marriage. They helped the republican Spanish cause and she was joint secretary of the Artists' Refugee Committee, which helped artists from Germany and central Europe, including Oskar Kokoschka. From 1947 to 1957 she was secretary and administrator of the Artists' International Association, a Soho gallery which helped the careers of Edward Ardizzone and David Gentleman, among others. In the 1950s she was instrumental in saving the Croft ancestral home, the largely fourteenth-century Croft Castle, Herefordshire, from demolition. She died of cancer at the Wye Valley Nuffield Hospital, Venns Lane, Hereford, on 14 November 1999, and was survived by her son and daughter.   JUTTA VINZENT

Sources F. Uhlman, *The making of an Englishman* (1960) · F. Whitford, 'Fred Uhlman: a profile', *Studio International*, 189 (1975), 155–6 · *Recent paintings by Fred Uhlman* (1942) [exhibition catalogue, Leicester Galleries, London, Dec 1941] · F. Uhlman, *Captivity* (1946) · F. Uhlman and C. Williams-Ellis, *An artist in north Wales* [1947] [pictures by F. Uhlman and commentary by C. Williams-Ellis] · private information (2004) [D. Uhlman] · A. Koestler, introduction, in F. Uhlman, *Reunion* (1994) · H. Pinter, *The comfort of strangers and other screenplays* (1990), 54–99 · E. Frommhold, *Kunst im Widerstand: Malerei, Graphik, Plastik, 1922–35* (1968), 576 · I. Grose, introduction, *Jewish artists of Great Britain, 1845–1945* (1978), 64 [exhibition catalogue, Belgrave Gallery, London, 15 March – 16 April 1978] · H. A. Strauss and W. Röder, eds., *Biographisches Handbuch der deutschsprachigen Emigration nach 1933 / International biographical dictionary of central European émigrés, 1933–1945*, 2 (1983), 1179 · *Kunst im Exil in Großbritannien, 1933–1945*, Neue Gesellschaft für Bildende Kunst Berlin, ed. [H. Krug and M. Nungesser] (Berlin, 1986), 157f. [exhibition catalogue, Orangerie des Schlosses Charlottenburg, Berlin, 10 Jan – 23 Feb 1986] · F. Uhlman, *Exhibition of paintings and drawings*, ed. Friends of Herefordshire Museums and Arts (1981) [exhibition catalogue, Hereford City Art Gallery, 6–27 June 1981] · *CGPLA Eng. & Wales* (1985) · Burke, *Peerage* [Diana Uhlman] · *Daily Telegraph* (29 Nov 1999) · d. cert. [Diana Uhlman]
Archives SOUND IWM SA, 'Artists in an age of conflict'
Likenesses K. Schwitters, oils, 1945, U. Newcastle, Hatton Gallery
Wealth at death £240,474: probate, 23 Oct 1985, *CGPLA Eng. & Wales*

Uhtred (*fl.* 757–777). *See under* Hwicce, kings of the (*act. c.*670–*c.*780).

Uhtred, earl of Bamburgh (*d.* 1016), magnate, was the son of Waltheof (*fl. c.*994–1006) and an unknown mother. Waltheof was probably the son of Eadwulf, the son of Oswulf (*d.* 966), the son of *Ealdred of Bamburgh (*d.* 933?); the family had ruled Bernicia (Northumbria north of the Tyne) since the Scandinavian invasion and settlement of the late ninth century. The northern part of their earldom (Lothian) was ceded to the Scots, probably by 973. Uhtred, together with the entire population of the land lying between the rivers Tees and Coquet, assisted Aldhun, bishop of the Community of St Cuthbert, in clearing the site at Durham and relocating the episcopal see from

Chester-le-Street in 995. According to the *De obsessione Dunelmi*, a Durham tract on the history of the earldom of Northumbria, the principal theme of which was the right of Durham to certain estates, Uhtred married Aldhun's daughter, Ecgfrida, probably at about this time. The marriage brought Uhtred certain vills of the church of St Cuthbert, namely Barmpton, Skirningham, Elton, Carlton, School Aycliffe, and Monk Hesleden in the south of co. Durham. This marriage has been seen as part of the church of St Cuthbert's policy of recruiting allies, although the earl would also have gained from an alliance with this powerful ecclesiastical institution. Uhtred was to retain control of these vills as long as he lived honourably in marriage with Ecgfrida.

During an attack on Durham by Malcolm II, king of Scots, Uhtred's father, Waltheof, described as being of great age and thus unable to lead the counter-attack, shut himself up in the fortress at Bamburgh, leaving the resistance to the Scots to his son, whom the *De obsessione* describes as a young man of great energy and skilled in warfare. Leading a force composed of troops from both Bernicia and York, Uhtred defeated the Scots. The severed heads of the Scots were washed by women, who received payment of a cow each, and fixed on stakes to Durham's walls. Uhtred's victory brought him to the attention of Æthelred II who recognized him as earl even though Waltheof seems still to have been alive, adding the earldom of York in succession to the Mercian Ælfhelm. The king's grant effectively reunited the two parts of Northumbria under the earls of Bamburgh. In this respect Uhtred may have been seen as a political counterweight to the Scandinavians at York who may still have harboured thoughts of a separate Scandinavian-dominated north.

On his return from Æthelred's court, probably about 1006, Uhtred dismissed Ecgfrida and Bishop Aldhun recovered the aforementioned vills. Uhtred then married Sige, daughter of Styr, son of Ulf, in an attempt to bolster his power in the southern portion of his combined earldom by uniting with the leader of Æthelred's supporters in York. According to the *De obsessione*, the marriage was contracted on the understanding that Uhtred would kill Styr's enemy Thurbrand. Similarly, the marriage of Uhtred's first wife, Ecgfrida, to Kilvert, son of the Yorkshire thegn Ligulf, may also have been an attempt by Uhtred's ally, Aldhun, to establish political support in Yorkshire. Shortly after Swein Forkbeard's invasion in 1013, Uhtred and the northern nobles submitted to the Danish king. It seems that Æthelred was successful in recovering Uhtred's loyalty, possibly through the latter's marriage to his daughter Ælfgifu. Uhtred remained faithful to the West Saxon cause despite Cnut's promise of substantial rewards, and accompanied Edmund Ironside on campaign in Staffordshire, Cheshire, and Shrewsbury against Eadric Streona. Cnut replied by invading Northumbria, forcing Uhtred to submit. Summoned to Cnut's court and granted safe conduct, Uhtred was murdered by Thurbrand Hold, presumably that enemy of Styr. Forty of Uhtred's men were slaughtered with him at Wiheal, identified as Wighill, near Tadcaster, in Yorkshire. Although a comparatively late source puts Uhtred at the battle of Carham leading the English to defeat by the Scots in 1018, it is now generally accepted that this was an error and that his death occurred in 1016.

Uhtred was succeeded at Bamburgh by his brother Eadulf Cudel 'a very lazy and cowardly man' (Symeon of Durham, *Opera*, 1.218), and at York by Erik, son of Hákon, *jarl* of Hlathir (Trondheim). Uhtred had two sons: Ealdred, his son with Ecgfrida, succeeded Eadulf Cudel as earl; Eadulf, his son with Sige, succeeded Ealdred. His daughter with Ælfgifu, Ealdgyth, married Maldred, son of Crinan, and their son, Cospatric, also became earl. Uhtred's murder at the hands of Thurbrand Hold initiated a series of killings involving the two families which continued into the 1070s. WILLIAM M. AIRD

Sources Symeon of Durham, *Opera* · C. R. Hart, *The early charters of northern England and the north midlands* (1975) · *ASC*, s.a. 1013, 1016 · John of Worcester, *Chron.* · B. Meehan, 'The siege of Durham, the battle of Carham and the cession of Lothian', *SHR*, 55 (1976), 1–19 · W. E. Kapelle, *The Norman conquest of the north: the region and its transformation, 1000–1135* (1979) · C. J. Morris, *Marriage and murder in eleventh-century Northumbria: a study of De obsessione Dunelmi*, Borthwick Papers, 82 (1992) · M. K. Lawson, *Cnut: the Danes in England in the early eleventh century* (1993) · A. Williams, *The English and the Norman conquest* (1995) · A. Campbell, ed. and trans., *Encomium Emmae reginae*, CS, 3rd ser., 72 (1949) · S. Keynes, *The diplomats of Æthelred II* (1980)

Uhtred. *See* Boldon, Uthred (c.1320–1397).

Uidhir, Aodh Mág. *See* Maguire, Sir Hugh, lord of Fermanagh (d. 1600).

Ulecot, Philip of. *See* Oldcoates, Sir Philip of (d. 1220).

Ulf Fenisc (*fl.* 1066), magnate, was a major landholder in England in 1066. According to Domesday Book he was a king's thegn with land in nine counties that rendered £394 annually; only two other laymen below the rank of earl had more valuable estates. Most of his property was in Lincolnshire (£190), Yorkshire (£88), and Nottinghamshire (£49), counties in which he had jurisdictional rights; but in Nottinghamshire he had the exceptional privilege of retaining the third penny of royal revenues normally reserved for the earl. It is therefore remarkable that he rarely, if ever, attested charters of Edward the Confessor.

There is little doubt that the byname Fenisc, recorded in several Domesday entries, meant 'from [the Danish island of] Fyn'. It is not known when he came to England or how he acquired his property. The church at Aldborough in Yorkshire, one of his most valuable properties, has a mid-eleventh-century inscription 'Ulf had this church built for himself and for the soul of Gunvara', probably his wife (Okasha, 147). He is not named as one of those who rebelled against William the Conqueror, but a few years after the conquest most of his property was held by Gilbert of Ghent. P. H. SAWYER

Sources P. A. Clarke, *The English nobility under Edward the Confessor* (1994) · E. Okasha, *A handlist of Anglo-Saxon non-runic inscriptions* (1971) · P. Sawyer, *Scandinavians and the English in the Viking age* (1994), 22

Ulfcytel [Ulfcytel Snillingr] (*d.* **1016**), soldier, is of unknown family and origin, though his name suggests Scandinavian descent. According to the 'Supplement to *Jómsvíkinga saga*', preserved in the late fourteenth-century *Flateyjarbók*, his wife was Wulfhild, the daughter of King *Æthelred II; she is said to have later married his killer, Earl *Thorkell the Tall. This late source is of only questionable authority, however. Ulfcytel's byname Snillingr (meaning 'the Valiant') occurs only in Norse sources but is consistent with his portrayal in the Anglo-Saxon Chronicle, where he is singled out for his heroic resistance to the vikings. In 1004 Ulfcytel, in consultation with a council of East Anglian magnates, attempted to purchase peace from the Danish King Swein Forkbeard, whose attack upon Norwich had caught them by surprise. When the Danes broke the truce and burnt Thetford, Ulfcytel raised what forces he could and attacked. The Danes gained a pyrrhic victory; badly mauled, they withdrew to their ships. Six years later, on 5 May 1010, Ulfcytel led the combined forces of East Anglia and Cambridgeshire against another Danish army at 'Ringmere' about 5 miles northeast of Thetford, and again suffered defeat in a hard-fought battle. His shattered forces could offer no further resistance to the Danes, who freely harried East Anglia over the next three months. Ulfcytel died fighting the Danes at 'Assandun' on 18 October 1016. The 'Supplement to *Jómsvíkinga saga*' claims that Thorkell the Tall slew him to avenge his brother's death. Snorri Sturluson (*d.* 1241), on the other hand, names Erik of Hlathir, another of Cnut's earls, as his slayer. It is impossible to determine which—if either—account is true.

Ulfcytel apparently performed the duties of ealdorman in East Anglia and is referred to as 'earl' in twelfth-century Anglo-Norman sources. To the skald Sigvatr, East Anglia was 'Ulfkel's land'. There is, however, no contemporary evidence that he was ever formally invested with the office of ealdorman. He appears as a king's *minister* ('thegn') in the witness lists of charters between 1002 and 1016, and may have been the 'Ulfketel' who donated five estates in Suffolk to Bury St Edmunds at about this time. From 1013 until his death he attested as the first of the *ministri*, immediately after the ealdormen and before the king's other thegns. The Anglo-Saxon Chronicle (s.a. 1016) follows this same convention in noting his name among the list of prominent men who fell at 'Assandun'.

Although Ulfcytel was on the losing side of all three battles he fought against the Danes, his tenacity and fierce courage won him the respect of his enemies and the admiration of the author of this section of the Anglo-Saxon Chronicle. Of his defeat in 1004 the chronicler observed, 'There the flower of the East Anglian people was killed. But if their full strength had been there, the Danes would never have got back to their ships; as they themselves said that they never met worse fighting in England than Ulfcytel dealt to them' (*ASC*, s.a. 1004, texts C, D).

RICHARD ABELS

Sources *ASC*, s.a. 1004, 1010, 1016 [texts C, D, E] • John of Worcester, *Chron.* • M. Ashdown, *English and Norse documents relating to the reign of Ethelred the Unready* (1930), 159, 165, 177, 225, 291 • A. Campbell, 'Supplement to *Jómsvíkinga saga*', *Encomium Emmae reginae*, ed. and trans. A. Campbell, CS, 3rd ser., 72 (1949), 91–3 • *AS chart.*, S 854, 900, 901, 906, 907, 910, 911, 912, 915, 916, 918, 922, 926, 931, 933, 935, 1219 • A. J. Robertson, ed. and trans., *Anglo-Saxon charters*, 2nd edn (1956), 146–7, 392 • R. G. Poole, *Viking poems on war and peace: a study in skaldic narrative* (1991), 88, 113, 115 • C. Hart, *The Danelaw* (1992), 525–6 • E. A. Freeman, *The history of the Norman conquest of England*, 6 vols. (1867–79), vol. 1, pp. 350–52, 378, 431

Ullathorne, William [*name in religion* Bernard] (**1806–1889**), vicar apostolic of the western district and Roman Catholic bishop of Birmingham, was born in Pocklington in the East Riding of Yorkshire, on 7 May 1806, eldest of the ten children of William Ullathorne, a highly successful general trader in Pocklington, and his wife, Hannah, *née* Longstaff, of Lincolnshire. His father, who was of modest Yorkshire stock, was an Old English Catholic or recusant, who was distantly related to St Thomas More; his mother had converted to Catholicism on their marriage.

Ullathorne grew up conscious of sectarian divisions in local society and of restrictions on Catholic practice; the family worshipped in a tiny gentry mission chapel staffed by a French émigré priest. He described himself as a child as 'a heavy, clumsy urchin … with large, blobbing eyes' (*Devil is a Jackass*, 7). He was a bookish child, whose first great literary passion was *Robinson Crusoe*, to which he partly attributed his love for the sea. From an early age he had weak eyes, perhaps exacerbated by voracious reading in poor light, and wore spectacles. Below average height and stocky, he was described by his opponent Cardinal Manning later in life as 'that busy little Yorkshireman'.

Ullathorne attended the village school at Burnby, Yorkshire, until, when he was nine or ten, the family moved to Scarborough, where he soon left Mr Hornsey's school to help in the family business. His religious education was nearly as scant as his formal schooling. Mass was only available once in six weeks and Catholics gathered for prayers (often led by William's father) on the intervening Sundays. Living in Scarborough fed the boy's dreams of seafaring and his reluctant parents let him go to sea at the age of fifteen. By his own account, he set forth as cabin boy on the brig *Leghorn* and later on *Anne's Resolution*, with scarcely a thought for religion (though he had brought a few devotional books with him on ship, including Challoner's *Garden of the Soul*). When the ship's mate, a Catholic, took him to mass while they were docked at the Baltic port of Memel, however, he experienced a sort of conversion which 'turned my heart completely round on myself' (*Autobiography*, 34). He immediately gave up the seafaring life and returned home. Although he had still not been confirmed or received communion, the influence of one of his father's acquaintances enabled him to be accepted by the Benedictine college of St Gregory's, Downside, near Bath. This unlikely potential monk embarked on the adventure which was to take him both into a monastic cloister and to the ends of the earth.

Ullathorne's religious education began in earnest after his entry at Downside in February 1823. His voracious reading habits were now turned to this purpose and he was pushed through his education rapidly. On 5 April 1825 he made his first vows as a monk and on 24 September 1831 he was ordained priest. Through the influence of the school's headmaster William Polding, who became his mentor at Downside, he was invited by the newly appointed vicar apostolic of Mauritius, William Morris (himself a Downside Benedictine), to join in the missionary enterprise much needed in the developing colonies of Australia. Only a year after his ordination, on 16 September 1832, he set sail for New South Wales as vicar-general with a government salary of £200 per annum. Sir Richard Bourke, the governor of New South Wales, had asked the British government for a priest with real authority to settle disputes. Ullathorne proved to have 'the support of both church and state and the personal talents to establish an institutional infrastructure to underpin this ministry' (Collins, fol. 72), and he successfully raised large funds for the mission in Lancashire, finding many other supporters through the success of his pamphlet *The Catholic Mission in Australasia* (1837). He also became a convinced opponent of transportation; he published *The Horrors of Transportation* in 1837 and was a key witness before the Molesworth parliamentary select committee of 1838. By the late 1830s he had managed to place the church on an organized and firm footing and had shown himself to be the major contributor to the transformation of the Australian church from a primarily convict chaplaincy to an institution active both in urban areas and in the rapidly expanding frontier territory.

In 1840 Ullathorne's poor health led him to decline appointments as bishop of Hobart and bishop of Adelaide, and he returned to England and to his monastery. Rather than readjust to the quiet rhythms of monastic life, he seized the opportunity to take over the mission at Coventry. There he not only developed a thriving congregation and built a fine church and missionary priory, but he met the person who was to be his greatest ally and friend, Margaret *Hallahan. She became his assistant at Coventry and, under his guidance, founded the sisters of the third order of St Dominic. When, in 1845, Ullathorne could resist episcopal appointment no longer and accepted the post of vicar apostolic of the western district, Margaret Hallahan and her small community went with him, setting up their own missionary campaigns and programme of social outreach. Ullathorne was consecrated bishop on 21 June 1846.

Ullathorne's short period as vicar apostolic based in Bristol (1845–8) was difficult and contentious. It was dominated by disputes over the college at Prior Park, near Bath, which had proved a major financial drain on the district and whose affairs he tried to help to regulate in negotiations with Rome. His skills in negotiation were also called upon by the other vicars apostolic of England and Wales who had become convinced that the time was ripe to restore episcopal government for the Catholic community but who needed to persuade the Vatican of their case. Upon the successful re-establishment of the English Catholic hierarchy in September 1850, Ullathorne was appointed bishop of Birmingham, having been translated as vicar apostolic of the midland district, incorporating more or less the same territory, in 1848.

From 1850 Ullathorne, like many other of the new bishops, but particularly urged forward by Hallahan, was preoccupied with the desire to restore full Catholic life to his diocese. He often expressed the belief that missionary arrangements which had evolved during the recusant period should be regarded as temporary expedients to be replaced as quickly as possible by the regular forms of ecclesiastical life common to Catholic countries on the continent. His main priorities, once the restoration of the episcopal hierarchy had been accomplished, were to restore cathedral chapters and then to establish ecclesiastical seminaries. By quickly establishing permanent councils of clerical advisers in his diocese after 1850, he made clear his determination as a bishop to put into practice what he had learned from Australia and the western district: that order and financial stringency were the only means of securing a stable future for the church. His ideal was a purely ecclesiastical seminary for priestly training which, like his own diocesan college at Oscott, would separate clerical students from lay pupils. In 1873 he achieved this ideal through the creation of St Bernard's Seminary in Olton, though after his death the school closed and seminary education returned to Oscott College.

Ullathorne was a dominant figure in the new hierarchy, one of the few with practical experience and skills in missionary enterprise, learned in the hard school of Australia. Although outspoken and direct, his opinions were often more moderate and wise than those of more strident bishops. At the First Vatican Council (1869–70), for example, he was much praised as a balanced and fair-minded participant who steered a middle course between the twin extremes of ultramontane and liberal Catholic opinion. His position on the great debate at the council on the definition of papal infallibility reflected his preoccupation with the role and character of the episcopate. As he wrote to J. H. Newman, 'I should not oppose a calm and moderate definition *provided* it was duly balanced by strengthening the authority of the episcopate' (C. Butler, *The Vatican Council*, 1930, 1.216). His anxiety about the episcopate in relation to the primacy and infallibility of the pope proved to be prescient, as it was to dog the church for a century, re-emerging in the debates of the Second Vatican Council (1962–5).

There was something of a paradox in the tough, outspoken, Yorkshire-bred bishop, who was opposed as Archbishop Wiseman's successor at Westminster on the grounds that he would be dropping his aitches all over London and was said to have exclaimed 'the devil's an ass!' on his deathbed (Butler, 2.295). Throughout his life he retained that romantic streak which had led him to go to sea as a young boy and which drew him to the novels of Walter Scott, inspired him to cross the world as a missionary, and helped to form his deep attachment to the monastic life. Although he rarely followed the life of the cloister, he declared the monastic life to be 'the grandest expression the world has seen of that elevation of the soul to which men may ascend through the power of grace', and he remained deeply attached to the Benedictine tradition, believing monks to 'belong to the grand poetry of life' (W. B. Ullathorne, *Ecclesiastical Discourses*, 1876). As he stated in his *Discourse on Benedictine Saints* (1875), his training in that tradition shaped much of his clerical career and his life was punctuated with yearnings to return to the monastery. When pleading with Pope Pius IX in 1862 to be released from his episcopal duties, he was told: 'Stand to your place. Persevere until death. You have yet many things to do' (Butler, 1.234). Ullathorne died, following a brief period of retirement and appointment as titular archbishop of Cabasa, at Oscott College, Birmingham, on 21 March 1889. He was buried in the church of St Dominic at Stone, Staffordshire, the home of the community of Margaret Hallahan's Dominican sisters.

Ullathorne's role and influence in Victorian Catholicism has long been overshadowed by that of Newman, Wiseman, and H. E. Manning. Yet his influence was widely felt, however seldom recognized in retrospective historical writings. A strong oral tradition about the first bishop of Birmingham has survived at least a hundred years, and his ecclesiastical structures, as well as their underlying principles, bore fruit in abundance. Perhaps his most lasting achievement in the life of the church was his careful handling and sympathetic encouragement of Newman. Their relationship began with what Newman called 'preliminary boxing bouts' (*The Letters and Diaries of John Henry Newman*, ed. C. S. Dessain, 1961–77, 12.337), before they learned to understand one another, and matured into a 'friendship and confidence that have enriched my life', as Ullathorne expressed it in his last book, dedicated to Newman (W. B. Ullathorne, *Christian Patience*, 1886, dedication). The theological influence which Newman was able to exert on the church of his own time and the century which followed was in great measure due to the mediation and protection of his stalwart bishop.

JUDITH F. CHAMP

Sources W. B. Ullathorne, *The autobiography of Archbishop Ullathorne*, 2 vols. (1891–2) · *The devil is a jackass, being the dying words of the autobiographer, William Bernard Ullathorne, 1806–1889*, ed. L. Madigan (1995) · C. Butler, *The life and times of Bishop Ullathorne*, 2 vols. (1926) · P. Collins, 'William Bernard Ullathorne and the foundation of Australian Catholicism, 1815–40', PhD diss., Australian National University, 1989 · J. Champ, ed., *Oscott College, 1838–1988: a volume of commemorative essays* (1988) · T. S. Suttor, 'Ullathorne, William Bernard', *AusDB*, vol. 2 · M. Heimann, *Catholic devotion in Victorian England* (1995)

Archives Birm. CA, autobiography [copy] · Birmingham House, Birmingham Roman Catholic archdiocesan archives, corresp. and papers · Clifton Roman Catholic diocese, Bristol, account of work in the western district · English College, Rome · English Congregation of Dominican Sisters, corresp. and papers · NRA, priv. coll., corresp. and papers · Stanbrook Abbey, Worcestershire, letters | Birmingham Oratory, letters to Newman · Downside Abbey Archives, Bath, corresp. and papers relating to Downside Abbey · Georgetown University, Washington, DC, Lauinger Library, corresp., mainly relating to his notes on the education question 1857 · Southwark Roman Catholic Diocese, London, letters to Wiseman and Grant · St Dominic's Convent, Stone, Staffordshire, letters to Hallahan · Ushaw College, Durham, corresp. relating to Ushaw College · Westm. DA, corresp. relating to Prior Park College, Bath · Westm. DA, letters to Wiseman

Likenesses Burchett, oils, 1852, Downside Abbey, near Bath · J. R. Herbert, oils, *c*.1860–1869, Oscott College, Birmingham · photograph, *c*.1880; copies, Oscott College, Birmingham · photograph (in death); copies, Oscott College, Birmingham

Wealth at death £279 7*s*. 8*d*.: probate, 24 June 1889, *CGPLA Eng. & Wales*

Ullerston, Richard (*d.* 1423), theological controversialist, probably came from Ulverston in Lancashire. Ordained priest in 1384, he became a fellow of Queen's College, Oxford, in 1391 and lived there continually until July 1402, acting as bursar (1391–2) and treasurer (1396–7), and also as chancellor's commissary in 1394. By 1401 he had a doctorate in theology. In 1402 Archbishop Richard Scrope of York (*d.* 1405) gave him the vicarage of Silkston, Yorkshire, after which he continued to live in Oxford, sometimes renting a room in Queen's College. He was commissary again in 1407–8. Many of his extant works are products of his routine lectures; for instance *Defensorium dotacionis ecclesie* (after March 1401), a defence of endowment against the Lollards, where Wyclif's *Trialogus* is probably one of his targets. The defence is largely based on Uthred Boldon (*d.* 1397) and was presented to Archbishop Thomas Arundel of Canterbury (*d.* 1414). While wholly orthodox, it is unusual in its refusal to defend *sacerdotium* against *regnum*, as Uthred did, or to argue that modern tithes can be justified from the Old Testament. Also in 1401, in a work later reused by the Lollards, he defended translation of the Bible into the vernacular. The debate in Oxford, to which Ullerston's determination was a contribution, was doubtless prompted by the translation undertaken by Wyclif's followers and disseminated through the Lollard movement, though neither Ullerston nor the surviving opposing text written the same year by William Butler mentions this association overtly. Ullerston's contribution is marked by a greater sophistication concerning the linguistic problems of translation than is found in other near contemporary discussions, even if the impossibility of translating without some degree of interpretation is only partly admitted. Another of Ullerston's disputations survives in outline from 1402–3.

In Advent 1403, at the request of his friend Richard Courtenay (*d.* 1415), Ullerston wrote for the prince of Wales *De officio militari*, a conventional work on knightly duty. In 1408, in preparation for the English attendance at the Council of Pisa, which was intended to end the great schism and reform the church, he wrote, at the suggestion of Robert Hallum, bishop of Salisbury (*d.* 1417), sixteen *Petitiones Ricardi quoad reformationem ecclesie militantis*, which were presented to Henry IV at the suggestion of the royal confessor, Roger Coringham. His most important work, the *Petitiones*, based on authorities that include the writings of Robert Grosseteste (*d.* 1253) attacks papal overcentralization, in favour of episcopal power, and is very critical about papal dispensations, exemptions, and privileges. Ullerston did not attend Pisa but Hallum was a leader of the English group there and at Constance, and there is evidence for Ullerston's influence on English thinking still at the time of the latter council. In 1410 Ullerston wrote *De symbolo*, now lost, which defended Alexander V (*r.* 1409–10), elected pope following the Council of Pisa, against the charge that he was Antichrist. In 1412 he exchanged Silkston for Little Steeping in Lincoln diocese, but was still living in Oxford, presenting Henry Chichele (*d.* 1443), now archbishop of Canterbury, with his lectures on the psalter (now lost), delivered in 1415. In the latter year he also issued a commentary on the canticles usually attached to the psalter, using Richard Rolle's work on the same texts. In 1416 Hallum obtained for him a canonry with the prebend of Axford in Salisbury. He moved to live there and his last known writing is a sermon on the canonization of St Osmund, delivered in May 1416. In June 1423 he exchanged Little Steeping for the rectory of Chilmark in Wiltshire. In his will, made in August 1423, he asked to be buried 'before the angelic visitation on the south side of the choir' of Salisbury Cathedral (*Register of Henry Chichele*, 257). He was dead by 12 September 1423.

MARGARET HARVEY

Sources M. Harvey, 'English views on the reforms to be undertaken in the general councils (1400–1418) with special reference to the proposals made by Richard Ullerston', DPhil diss., U. Oxf., 1964 · Emden, *Oxf.*, 2.1928–9 · A. Hudson, 'The debate on Bible translation, Oxford 1401', *EngHR*, 90 (1975), 1–18 · M. Harvey, *Solutions to the schism: a study of some English attitudes 1378 to 1409* (1983) · M. Harvey, *England, Rome, and the papacy, 1417–1464: the study of a relationship* (1993) · A. R. Malden, *The canonisation of St Osmund*, Wilts RS, 2 (1901), appx 2 · H. van der Hardt, *Magnum Oecumenicum Constancientie Concilium*, 4 vols. (1700), vol. 1, cols. 1126–71 · E. F. Jacob, ed., *The register of Henry Chichele, archbishop of Canterbury, 1414–1443*, 2, CYS, 42 (1937) **Archives** Österreichische Nationalbibliothek, Vienna, MS 4133, fols. 195r–207v · BL, MS Lansdowne 409 · Bodl. Oxf., MS Lyell 20 · CCC Cam., MS 177 · CCC Oxf., MS 280 · CCC Oxf., MS 183 · Exeter Cathedral, MS D&C 3516 · Magd. Oxf., MSS 115, 89 · Merton Oxf., MS 193 · Staatsbibliothek, Berlin, Theol. Lat. fol. 580, fols. 375r–401v · Trinity Cam., MS B.15.25

Ullman, Elisabeth Maria Martha (1907–1985). *See under* Laban, Rudolf Jean-Baptiste Attila (1879–1958).

Ullmann, Stephen (1914–1976), linguist and university teacher, was born on 13 June 1914 in Hungary, where his father, István Ullmann, was a senior civil servant. Ullmann read modern languages at the University of Budapest, from where he obtained a doctorate at the early age of twenty-two. In 1939 he married Susan Gáspár, with whom he had one son (Michael) and two daughters (Diana and Patricia). Stephen and Susan Ullmann left Hungary for the United Kingdom in 1939 and became permanently domiciled there as British citizens.

From 1940 to 1946 Ullmann was employed by the BBC Monitoring Service. In 1946 he joined the University of Glasgow as lecturer in Romance philology and general linguistics, and was promoted to a senior lectureship in 1950, having been awarded the degree of DLitt in 1949. From Glasgow he moved to the University of Leeds, where he was successively professor of Romance philology (1953–64) and of French language and Romance philology (1964–8). From 1968 until his death he held the chair of Romance

languages at the University of Oxford, and was simultaneously fellow of Trinity College. His international reputation earned him invitations to undertake lecture tours in many European countries, in North America, and in India, and he held visiting professorships at the universities of Toronto (1964 and 1966) and Michigan (1965), and at the Australian National University (1974). From 1970 to 1976 he was president of the Philological Society.

Ullmann's scholarly interests were broad and his knowledge encyclopaedic, but his research and publications fell into two main areas. The first was semantics, to which he had been introduced by one of his teachers at the University of Budapest, Zoltán Gombocz, and in which he did much pioneering work at a time when the study of meaning was somewhat neglected by theoretical linguists. Following the posthumous publication of Ferdinand de Saussure's *Cours de linguistique générale* in 1916, theoretical linguistics, until then almost exclusively historical in its orientation, became primarily synchronic and descriptive. Recognizing this, Ullmann justifiably contended that semantics had largely escaped the impact of this revolution, since it continued to be concerned above all with the study of changes in meaning. The one significant exception to this generalization, he observed, was the development in Germany by Jost Trier and others, in the 1920s and the early 1930s, of the theory of semantic fields. It was largely through Ullmann's publications some two decades later that this approach to the study of meaning became more widely known to Western scholarship.

Ullmann's approach to semantics was first set out at length in 1951 in *The Principles of Semantics*. There he presents his view of the essence of the subject at that point in its development, and maintains a balance between descriptive and historical aspects. It had been preceded earlier in the same year by a more popular book on meaning and language, *Words and their Use*, which avoids discussion of theory.

Following closely on *Principles*, Ullmann's *Précis de sémantique française* (1953) makes explicit its aim to present the principles of semantics to a wider public by applying them to French, although the audience envisaged, unlike that of *Words and their Use*, is clearly academic. This time the balance was tipped much more towards the synchronic side. Despite its apparently modest intentions, this book contains much that is new in comparison with its predecessor and develops considerably further some of the ideas contained in the author's earlier writings—notably on synonymy, polysemy, and homonymy, and the problems involved in distinguishing between the last two of these. 'Motivation' in language is also extensively discussed. Taking as his starting point Saussure's insistence on the essentially arbitrary nature of the linguistic sign, under which view the relationship between a word and its meaning is entirely conventional, Ullmann aims to show that, on the contrary, the meaning attached to a linguistic symbol can be motivated at three different levels—the phonetic (in cases where it is possible to speak of onomatopoeia or sound symbolism), the morphological (where complex forms are understood from a knowledge of the meaning of their component parts), and the semantic (where words take on new meanings because of perceived similarities between entities, as when one speaks, for instance, of the 'head' of an institution). A further point of discussion is the way in which it is possible to distinguish between 'intellectual' and 'affective' meaning, because of the existence in all languages of devices for conveying emotional overtones. Arguing that the presence of these various features occurs in different proportions in different languages, Ullmann developed his theory of semantic typology, showing in this context that French is typologically different from, say, German. Consideration of typology later led him to prepare a paper on semantic universals (1963).

In *Semantics: an Introduction to the Science of Meaning* (1962) there is less theoretical discussion, the book being intended mainly for non-specialists. The main themes of the two earlier books are taken up again, but discussed in language rather less technical. There is an attempt, too, to show how the subject had developed since the publication of his first major book, for Ullmann was always at pains to present his own theories in the broader context.

Somewhat unusually for a general linguist, Ullmann concerned himself extensively with language as used in literature as well as with what one might by contrast refer to as everyday, non-creative language. Many points in his books and articles on semantics are illustrated with quotations from literary works, especially poetry. Where such items occur, one is not far removed from a discussion of style. It is therefore not surprising that the second of his two principal research interests should be stylistics. Ullmann is sometimes held to have worked first in semantics and then turned his allegiance mainly to stylistics. In fact the two strands run in parallel throughout his published work, with articles in both spheres first appearing in the mid-1940s. The closeness of the two in his mind is symbolized by the titles of his two books of collected papers, *Language and Style* (1964) and *Meaning and Style* (1973). His stylistic work was first directed to French poetry, and there are early articles on Racine, Hugo, Leconte de Lisle, Vigny, and Musset. Later he turned his attention to the novel, and this is the subject of his two books *Style in the French Novel* (1957) and *The Image in the French Novel: Gide, Alain-Fournier, Proust, Camus* (1960). The first alternates between the treatment of a theme (for example, word order) over a number of novels and an analysis of some aspect of a single novel: in the book as a whole, twenty novels by seventeen authors, mostly belonging to the nineteenth century, are examined. In his work on style Ullmann aimed to construct a bridge between the type of stylistics which is concerned with the expressive resources of a language as a whole and the type which looks at the variety of the language that is the particular creation of a given author. His own studies, however, concentrate on the latter. In the first of the two books, he looked at the linguistic world presented in a single novel, while the second was more concerned with the linguistic world of an author's total output.

In both his domains of endeavour—semantics and stylistics—Ullmann was something of a pioneer. This was not in the sense that he was a creator of the disciplines, but in the sense that, in the first case, he did much to revive an important and neglected area of linguistics, and, in the second, he did much to strengthen a fledgeling subject. He was zealous in promoting both, seeing the former as 'the youngest branch of modern linguistics' (*The Principles of Semantics*, 1) and the latter as the 'new science of style' (*Style in the French Novel*, vii). He did not strive solely for novelty or originality. His extraordinarily wide reading had given him not only an exceptional knowledge of those who had contributed studies on topics germane to his interests, but also an appreciation of the value of their work. His own research was never conducted in isolation, for he had total familiarity with the work of his contemporaries. When reviewing the work of others, he always attempted, even where he disagreed with the trend of a book's argument, to highlight what was positive and insightful.

Stephen Ullmann died on 10 January 1976 of a coronary thrombosis in the Evans Lane post office, near his home in Kidlington, Oxfordshire. He was described by those who knew him as a dominating presence who at the same time was shy and modest, as a man who was generous with his time to students and colleagues, as a brilliant and inspiring lecturer who yet suffered from stage fright, and as an academic who worked in fields that encouraged controversy but who made no enemies.   R. E. ASHER

Sources 'Professor Stephen Ullmann: an eminent Romance philologist', *The Times* (14 Jan 1976), 16 • T. E. Hope, 'Stephen Ullmann (1914–76)', *French Studies*, 30 (1976), 245–6 • T. E. Hope, 'Stephen Ullmann (1914–76)', *Language, meaning and style: essays in memory of Stephen Ullmann*, ed. T. E. Hope and others (1981), 1–4 • T. E. Hope, 'Publications of Stephen Ullmann', *Language, meaning and style: essays in memory of Stephen Ullmann*, ed. T. E. Hope and others (1981), 157–66 • R. E. Asher and J. M. Y. Simpson, eds., *The encyclopedia of language and linguistics* (1994), 9.4828–9 • Y. Malkiel, 'Stephen Ullmann (1914–76)', *Romance Philology*, 30 (1976–7), 481–6 • d. cert. • *WW*
Wealth at death £4745: probate, 10 March 1976, *CGPLA Eng. & Wales*

Ullmann, Walter (1910–1983), historian, was born on 29 November 1910 at 5 Rathausstrasse, Pulkau, Lower Austria, the elder son of Rudolf Ullmann (*d.* 1932), a country doctor, and his wife, Leopoldine, *née* Apfelthaler (*d.* 1949). With the outbreak of war in 1914 both his parents went to serve on the Serbian front, taking their barely four-year-old son with them. After the war Ullmann attended the *Gymnasium* at Horn, went to the University of Vienna in 1929 to read jurisprudence, and transferred in 1931 to the University of Innsbruck, where he graduated JUD in 1933.

German and Austrian law degrees were then far broader than their English equivalents: Ullmann was required to take courses not only in Roman and canon law but also in legal history and modern history, economics, and related humanities and social sciences. This training placed law firmly in a historical and social context. When Ullmann began to practise as a criminal lawyer in the judicial service, he also started a parallel research project on the legal aspects of criminal psychology. Modern psychological theory was one line of attack, but he also began to trace the genealogy of modern jurisprudential thought on the topic back through the jurists of the eighteenth and seventeenth centuries to the medieval commentators on Roman law whom they cited. He discovered that medieval views threw little light on modern ones, but became so absorbed by the former that he chose to write his *Habilitationschrift* on the medieval doctrine of criminal attempt. The nature of his legal training meant that he approached the doctrine of the commentators in its own, medieval terms.

Meanwhile, the twentieth century was overtaking Ullmann. He had not endeared himself to the Nazi fifth column in Austria: working on pre-trial investigation, he had continued, with characteristic inflexibility, to prosecute Nazi criminals vigorously. Soon after *Anschluss* in March 1938 he had to flee to Britain. The discovery that an ancestor had been Jewish made his position even more parlous. He had already corresponded with several members of the Cambridge law faculty. A Cambridge committee for the support of refugee scholars now enabled him to begin work there. The collections of glossators, commentators, and canonists in the Wren Library of Trinity College soon led him into fields other than medieval concepts of *mens rea*. He became particularly interested in the neglected Neapolitan commentator Lucas da Penna. He was intrigued by Lucas's use of theologians and philosophers in his commentary on Justinian's *Code*. He saw Lucas as sharing his own view that law should not be an entirely discrete discipline, and could only be properly understood in relation to a much wider framework of ideas and beliefs. Lucas was to be the subject of Ullmann's first book, *The Medieval Idea of Law as Represented by Lucas da Penna* (1946).

In 1939 Ullmann became a master at Ratcliffe College, a Roman Catholic boarding-school in Leicestershire. He was briefly interned on the Isle of Man with other enemy aliens, and, on his release, allowed to volunteer for military service. On 23 November 1940 he married (Mary) Elizabeth Finnemore Knapp (*b.* 1916), a former Cambridge undergraduate whom he had taught German; she was the daughter of Harold John Knapp, bank manager. On their wedding day, when he was allowed out of barracks only for the day because of an invasion scare, she and her new husband spent the afternoon correcting the proofs of an article. His military career, in the Pioneer Corps, was not distinguished, but he found his duties on the sanitary fatigue compatible with academic work. In 1942 he returned to schoolmastering, and also became involved in the re-education of German prisoners of war. While working on Lucas, he came across Baldus's *consilium* of 1378 on the legality of Pope Urban VI's election. As a lawyer he had been trained to apply legal rules to events, but in this case the event had occasioned the Great Schism. The schism had sharpened the dialectical conflict between those canonists who thought the church a papal monarchy, and those who argued that it should be ruled by a general council, representing all the faithful. Two opposed interpretations of the origin of authority within the church

could be derived from the same canonical sources. This conflict emerged in the middle ages not only in the ecclesiastical sphere; much of Ullmann's subsequent work was to be concerned with the conflict's secular manifestations, with the ultimate triumph, in the West, of the 'ascending' over the 'descending' theory.

By the time that *The Origins of the Great Schism* was published, in 1948, Ullmann was a lecturer at the University of Leeds. In that year he gave the Maitland memorial lectures in Cambridge, published in 1949 as *Medieval Papalism*. This book worked backwards from *Origins* to explore the papal monarchical view of the proper relations between pope and emperor, as expressed by thirteenth- and fourteenth-century canonists. In the same year Ullmann was appointed to a lectureship in Cambridge. After some remarkable essays, chiefly concerned with the conflicts between the Hohenstaufen and the papacy, he published in 1955 his most important book, *The growth of papal government in the middle ages: a study in the ideological relations of clerical to lay power*. It demonstrated how the theory of papal monarchy was present, in potential, from the pontificate of Leo I in the mid-fifth century, and how its logic was worked out in the West during the early middle ages and was eventually expressed in its fully realized form in the twelfth century, in Gratian, just before the period covered by *Medieval Papalism*. The book seemed to conclude with the triumph of hierocratic over anti-hierocratic thought.

But the mole of history was busy grubbing away: Ullmann went on to argue, in *Principles of Government and Politics in the Middle Ages* (1961), that the rediscovery of Aristotle's *Ethics* and *Politics* in the thirteenth century presented those who sought a degree of lay autonomy with incontrovertible authorities to counter those of the hierocrats. At the same time the 'ascending theme' appeared in canonist form, with the early conciliarists, and in Romanist form, above all in the work of Bartolus. The antithetical logics of 'ascending' and 'descending' had long been dialectically embodied in medieval monarchy, which combined a theocratic element with what Ullmann, at his most Germanic, termed a feudal or popular element. The rediscovery of Aristotle and the developments in Roman and canon law gave theoretical bite to this popular element. In his view, the ultimate triumph of this element in the West was the essence of Renaissance humanism, a case he was later to develop with uncompromising verve in *The Medieval Foundations of Renaissance Humanism* (1977). Many critics judged *Principles* to be overschematic, particularly in its reification of feudalism. It is true that Ullmann remained a continental civilian, and never got to grips with the distinct, arcane logic of English common law. It is also true that he considered that he had a public duty to synthesize his research in accessible form, and that the nuances of his vast number of articles tended to be smoothed over in the books he published during the 1960s and 1970s.

One exception was *The Carolingian Renaissance and the Idea of Kingship* (1969), which examined in more detail the theocratization of medieval monarchy in the West. In

Ullmann's view this had 'stunted' the Germanic monarch's 'sovereignty' by subordinating him to the jurisdiction of the priesthood. The king's rebirth through royal anointing reflected that of the whole of Frankish society, and the Christian form in which *Romanitas* was reborn made a definitive breach with Byzantium inevitable. Again the interpretation was open to detailed criticism, but there was no doubt about its boldness and power. It was this renaissance which the humanism of the more familiar Renaissance reversed, when it buried theocracy and resurrected populism.

Another was Ullman's last major project, a study of the pontificate of Gelasius I, published in 1981. In this he did not confine himself to Gelasius's pontificate, but re-examined in more detail than ever before the development of papal ideology from the beginnings to the end of the fifth century, by when, he argued, the foundations for the papal hierocratic system had all been laid. With his last book, therefore, he returned to the origins of the system the study of which had been the main focus of his scholarly life; and he also returned to writing in German.

Recognition had come despite Ullman's being outside the mainstream of British medievalism, although some thought it came late: he was awarded a readership in 1957, the degree of LittD in 1958, a fellowship of Trinity College in 1959, an *ad hominem* chair in 1966, fellowship of the British Academy in 1968, and the chair of medieval history in 1972. He was probably the most prolific British medievalist since the Second World War, not only in terms of publications but also in terms of research students. His belief in the public duties of a historian, probably a result of his own raw experience of twentieth-century history, made him an enthusiastic popularizer—he gave radio talks on improbable subjects such as John of Paris and the king's grace—and a scourge of what Maitland had termed 'aimless medievalism'. He could be superbly tactless: 'modern medievalists—and not all of them are obtuse—', he parenthesized before the great and good assembled for his inaugural lecture as professor of medieval history. The tactlessness arose from a total—and very un-English— inability to conceal his passions. It was his passionate engagement with medieval history which made him such a dramatic and captivating lecturer. His Austrian accent remained thick but, far from making his lectures difficult to follow, it seemed to imbue them with a metrical cadence. He was the sort of figure around whom legends readily formed: that while working as a petrol pump attendant he had conversed in Latin with a motorist who turned out to be W. W. Buckland, the regius professor of civil law; that he had once been a mechanic on a motor-racing circuit; that he had been court-martialled for dereliction of guard duty in order to work on Bartolus; that he kept a compact copy of the *corpus iuris canonici* for use in bed. Like most legends, each had a kernel of truth. One story was recounted, with a tell-tale twinkle behind the spectacles, by Ullmann himself. As a student in Vienna, he had sometimes worked as an extra at the opera. Playing the part of a warrior in a performance of *Lohengrin*, he had become fascinated by the way in which the swan glided onto the stage. He leant over surreptitiously, in order to ascertain the nature of the inner mechanism which was propelling it, and his helmet and wig slipped from his head, jamming the rails along which the swan was moving, and bringing both the performance and his operatic career to an abrupt halt. On an ideological plane, that search for inner mechanisms was what defined his approach to medieval history. It was his belief in their explanatory force which differentiated him from those educated in the tradition of Anglo-Saxon empiricism.

Ullmann retired in 1978, but continued to supervise until a few days before his death. He and his wife had two sons. He remained a devout Catholic throughout his life, although he always claimed that this was irrelevant to his approach to history. He died from cancer at his home, 128 Queen Edith's Way, Cambridge, on 18 January 1983, and was buried six days later in Cambridge city cemetery. His wife survived him.   GEORGE GARNETT

Sources W. Ullmann, speech given at his retirement dinner in Cambridge, 29 Nov 1978 · J. A. Watt, 'Walter Ullmann, 1910–1983', *PBA*, 74 (1988), 483–509 · E. Ullmann, *Walter Ullmann: a tale of two cultures* (1990) · B. Tierney and P. Linehan, eds., *Authority and power: studies on medieval law and government, presented to Walter Ullmann on his seventieth birthday* (1980), 255–74 [bibliography covering the years 1940–79] · W. Ullmann, *Law and jurisdiction in the middle ages*, ed. G. Garnett (1988), xv–xviii [bibliography covering the years 1980–88] · H. Chadwick, 'Walter Ullmann, 1910–1983', *Cambridge Review* (18 Nov 1983), 212–13 · H. Fuhrmann, 'Walter Ullmann, 29/11/1910–18/1/1983', *Jahrbuch der Bayerischen Akademie der Wissenschaften* (1983), 198–201 · J. Gilchrist, 'Walter Ullmann', *Zeitschrift der Savigny-Stiftung für Rechtsgeschichte*, 70 (1984), 465–8 [kanonistische Abteilung] · m. cert.
Archives Trinity Cam.
Likenesses photograph, repro. in Watt, 'Walter Ullman', facing p. 483 · photograph, repro. in Tierney and Linehan, eds., *Authority and power*, frontispiece
Wealth at death £17,621: probate, 30 March 1983, *CGPLA Eng. & Wales*

Ullock, William (1617/18–1667), headmaster, was the son of Richard Ullock, husbandman, of Tallantaire, near Cockermouth, Cumberland. After spending three years at Repton School, Derbyshire, under Thomas Whitehead, on 29 June 1635, aged seventeen, he was admitted sizar to St John's College, Cambridge, where his tutor was Henry Masterson, whose brother John was also educated at Repton. Ullock graduated BA in 1639 and proceeded MA in 1642.

Having been an usher at Repton from 1637, in 1642 Ullock became headmaster, at a salary of £40 per annum. Under him the school was maintained and 'heightened', increasing in numbers from about 60 to 300, with a considerable contingent of boys being sent to his old college. However, Ullock was said not to be strong on discipline, and in 1652 a dispute between the school and its neighbours, headed by Gilbert Thacker, concerning alleged trespasses and annoyances by the boys came to court. Not only had the scholars apparently caused inconvenience by playing football around Thacker's house, but they had also disposed of refuse inappropriately and 'untrussed' near the causeway between the two properties. Despite arbitration, proceedings dragged on during the remainder of Ullock's tenure. Ullock died on 13 May 1667 and was buried at Repton. He was survived by his son William, who graduated BA from St John's College, Cambridge, in 1672 and became a clergyman in Kent.   W. JOHNSON

Sources Venn, *Alum. Cant.* · J. C. Cox, *Memorials of old Derbyshire* (1907) · A. Macdonald, *A short history of Repton* (1929) · M. Messiter, ed., *Repton School register, 1557–1910* (1910) · R. O'Day, *Education and society, 1500–1800* (1982) · *VCH Derbyshire* · B. Thomas, ed., *Repton, 1557–1957* (1957)

Ullswater. For this title name *see* Lowther, James William, first Viscount Ullswater (1855–1949).

Ulpius Marcellus (*fl.* **178–184**). *See under* Roman officials (*act.* AD 43–410).

Ulster. For this title name *see* Lacy, Hugh de, earl of Ulster (*d.* 1242); Burgh, Walter de, first earl of Ulster (*d.* 1271); Burgh, Richard de, second earl of Ulster (*b.* in or after 1259, *d.* 1326); Burgh, William de, third earl of Ulster (1312–1333); Matilda of Lancaster, countess of Ulster (*d.* 1377); Mortimer, Edmund (III), third earl of March and earl of Ulster (1352–1381); Mortimer, Roger (VII), fourth earl of March and sixth earl of Ulster (1374–1398); Mortimer, Edmund (V), fifth earl of March and seventh earl of Ulster (1391–1425).

Ulster, saints of (*act. c.*400–*c.*650), were the foci of religious life in the north of Ireland. 'Ulster' is here an early medieval counterpart to the province of Ulster (consisting of the nine modern counties of Antrim, Down, Donegal, Londonderry, Tyrone, Fermanagh, Cavan, Monaghan, and Armagh); a tenth county, Louth, now part of Leinster, was part of Ulster until the mid-eighth century. A loss of territory, partly beyond the reach of historical record but recent enough to have left traces, left the province of Ulster confined to the lands east of the River Bann. The eastern part of co. Londonderry was lost in the late sixth century, most of co. Louth not until the battle of Faughart in 735. The lands said to have been lost to the Ulstermen were principally the kingdoms of the Airgialla; these covered most of the central counties of Londonderry, Tyrone, Fermanagh, Monaghan, and Armagh. The far northwest, Donegal, and parts of Londonderry and Tyrone, belonged to the two great northern branches of the Uí Néill, Cenél Conaill and Cenél nEógain, claiming descent from Conall and Éogan, two sons of Niall Noígíallach. The wider political context of northern saints' cults in the pre-viking period was, therefore, a long-term shift in power from the Ulstermen to the Uí Néill.

Sources The sources are relatively good. Apart from texts which cover the whole of Ireland, such as the ninth-century martyrologies of Tallaght and Óengus the Culdee, the Patrician material, especially Tírechán's *Collectanea* from the late seventh century and the tripartite life from *c.*900, reveals the ambitions of the community of Patrick in the northern half of Ireland. Patrick's principal church of Armagh and supposed burial church of Saul were situated in the lands of the Airgialla and the Ulstermen respectively. A section of the fourteenth-century Codex Salmanticensis contains a fragment of a legendary of northern saints—brief lives in the order of the saints' feast days in the calendar. The surviving lives come from August and the beginning of September. If the entire text had been preserved, there would have been exceptionally good information on northern saints. The textual history of this legendary has not been fully investigated; the standard view is that it consists of lives abbreviated not long before the date of the manuscript, using earlier texts of unknown and probably different dates.

There is a serious possibility that some lives in the legendary preserve information from the eighth century. An example is Inis Caín Dega (Inishkeen on the border of counties Monaghan and Louth), the church of **Daig mac Cairill** (*d.* 587), whose feast day is 18 August. The life associates Daig with the Ciannacht Breg, a kingdom which then stretched from the south of Louth to the Liffey. The saints' genealogies, however, make him a great-great-grandson of Éogan mac Néill, the eponymous ancestor of Cenél nEógain. Once this pedigree was accepted as true, Cenél nEógain would be 'the kindred of the patron-saint' (*érlam*), normally enjoying a prior right to provide the abbot to the church. In the genealogies, however, the Cenél nEógain pedigree is associated with the assertion that Daig was smith to *Ciarán of Clonmacnoise [*see under* Meath, saints of], as **Assicus** [Tassach] (*fl. c.*480) of Racoon, co. Donegal, or Raholp, co. Down, feast day 14 April, was smith to Patrick. Both claims were designed to make the saints and their churches part of the *familiae* of the saints concerned; Daig mac Cairill is explicitly said to have granted his church to Ciarán. In the genealogies, therefore, Inis Caín Dega was part of a network linking the great midland church of Clonmacnoise with Cenél nEógain. Yet the connection with Clonmacnoise is also in the life of Daig, in which there is no mention of any association of him with Cenél nEógain. The life's attribution of Daig to the Ciannacht Breg appears to stem from a period before Cenél nEógain gained power over Conailli Muirthemne, the kingdom within which Inis Caín Dega was situated, as a result of the battle of Faughart in 735. A parallel case is the female saint, Femme, said in the genealogies to be a sister of Daig. A note in the martyrology of Óengus the Culdee places her in the church of Ernaide in Mag nÍtha, namely Urney, south-west of Strabane, in the late medieval rural deanery of Moghy (Mag nÍtha). Mag nÍtha was conquered by Cenél nEógain from Cenél Conaill during the 730s. The one genealogical fiction, therefore, served to buttress Cenél nEógain claims to two churches in kingdoms conquered in the same decade. The subjection of Inis Caín Dega to Clonmacnoise, acknowledged both in the life and in the genealogies, presumably dates from no later than the first half of the eighth century and survived the establishment of Cenél nEógain power in what had been the southernmost kingdom of the Ulstermen. Presumably it survived because Cenél nEógain wished to gain influence in a major church of the midlands. Daig's mother is named in the tract 'On the mothers of the saints' as Dediu, granddaughter of Dubthach moccu Lugair, the legendary representative of the poets who embraced Christianity; she was also believed to be the mother of other saints, including Diarmait of Inis Clothrann, so that Daig's maternal descent gave Inishkeen an alliance with several other churches.

The saints of Ulster east of the River Bann In what is now counties Antrim and Down, there were three main early political groups of kingdoms: the Cruithni of south and west Antrim and west Down; the Dál Fiatach of East Down; and the Dál Riata of north-east Antrim, east of the River Bush and north of Glenarm. The political hopes of Dál Riata lay increasingly in Argyll and elsewhere in Scotland, rather than in their Irish homeland—a shift of power which had a harmful effect on their main Irish church at Armoy (Airther Maige) and on the cult of its saint, **Olcán** (*fl.* 5th cent.), whose feast day is 20 February. The *familia* of Patrick had had high hopes of Olcán and Dál Riata, as shown by Tírechán's statement, late in the seventh century, that Patrick had given Olcán a portion of the relics of Peter and Paul and other saints, one of the proudest possessions of Armagh. The investment, however, was a failure: the tripartite life records that lands belonging to Armoy had been taken by force and given to Mac Nisse of Connor and Senán of Inis Cathaig (an error for Senán of Láthrach Briúin). The general pattern of these events is confirmed by a fragment of a life of Columba of Iona written by Cumméne Find, abbot from 657 to 669, which laments that Dál Riata was being subjected to its enemies.

From the mid-seventh century the heavyweight powers were a branch of the Cruithni, Dál nAraidi, whose oldest lands lay near Antrim Town, and Dál Fiatach, around Downpatrick. The most powerful churches in local politics were, among the Cruithni, Connor (Conderi, Condaire), and, among Dál Fiatach, Nendrum (Nóendruimm). A principal saint of the Cruithni was thus **Mac Nisse mac Faíbrig** (*d.* 507/8) of Connor, feast day 3 September, and of Dál Fiatach **Mo Chóe mac Luacháin** (*d.* 497) of Nendrum, feast day 23 June. The tensions in the relationship of local east Ulster churches are well brought out by the story of Patrick's relationship with Míliucc maccu Buain (Bóin), his master when a slave, and his friend **Díchu mac Trichim** (*fl.* 5th cent.) of Dál Fiatach, whose feast day of 29 April appears first in the twelfth-century martyrology of Gorman. Dál mBuain (to which Míliucc maccu Buain belonged) was the ruling group of the area around Broughshane and Ballymena; in the genealogies of the saints and in origin legends about Lough Neagh it is associated with its neighbour to the south, Dál Sailni, the people of Mac Nisse of Connor, Senán of Láthrach Briúin, and Colmán Elo—of Lynally, but also described in a version of his life as the 'second patron-saint of Connor'. The descendants of Díchu, however, were the principal ecclesiastical family of Saul and then of Downpatrick up to the ninth century: the story of their gift of the land at Saul to Patrick established their claim as 'the kindred of the land'—a claim that should have prevailed against all others since the patron saint, Patrick, had no heirs by blood. Downpatrick, originally a royal fort, became a church in the mid-eighth century. Since the strong likelihood is that Patrick was a slave in what is now co. Mayo,

the role of Míliucc maccu Buain is fictional. Moreover, Patrick's failure to convert Míliucc is explicitly contrasted with his conversion of Díchu mac Trichim in Muirchú's late seventh-century life of Patrick. The fiction, therefore, served to advance one Ulster ecclesiastical kindred, the descendants of Díchu, at the expense of two kindreds that were closely related to each other.

Local background to the story emerges from the dossier of another Ulster saint, **Do Biu mac Comgaill** [Do Bí, Mo Biu, Mo Bí] (*fl.* 5th cent.?) of Inis Causcraid (Inch, Down), whose feast day is 22 July but whose obit is unrecorded. The parallel variations in the name forms make it probable that the patron of Inis Causcraid in the martyrologies is the saint ascribed to Dál mBuain in the genealogies. His church is the early predecessor of the Cistercian abbey founded by John de Courcy about 1180 as a refuge for the displaced monks of Carrick. Inis Causcraid was a mile to the north-west of Downpatrick, the main early 'seat of kingship' for Dál Fiatach; similarly, Saul, the home of the Uí Díchon, Díchu mac Trichim's descendants, was 2 miles to the north-east. The topography suggests, therefore, that the implicit message of the story was an attack on those associated with Dál mBuain. The two churches of Inis Causcraid and Saul were potential rivals to be the local church of the royal fort at Downpatrick. The descendants of Díchu at Saul had one handicap balanced by some major advantages. Díchu had no serious early cult: he was not included in the martyrology of Tallaght or that of Óengus, although his feast day (29 April) was included in the much later martyrology of Donegal. On the other hand, the late seventh-century life of Patrick by Muirchú had asserted Saul's claims to be the burial place of Patrick, the apostle of the Irish. The first target of the story about Míliucc maccu Buain may have been Inis Causcraid, but, given the close connection between Dál mBuain and Dál Sailni and the topography associated with Patrick's time as a slave, Connor may also have been implicated.

As for Mo Chóe of Nendrum, the tripartite life has a story suggesting an alliance between the community of Patrick and Nendrum, concealing the truth that Nendrum was, in reality, a greater church by far than Saul. The genealogies of the saints connect Mo Chóe with Dál mBuain through his mother, Brónach, daughter of Míliucc maccu Buain. Both Nendrum and Connor were episcopal churches, and their bishops were among the leading churchmen from the northern half of Ireland to whom the pope-elect John wrote in 640.

Influential in a rather different mode were two churches situated close to each other but belonging to different kingdoms: Bangor (Bennchor) and Movilla (Mag mBili). Both had strong intellectual traditions, while Bangor, and probably also Movilla, had wide links with other major monasteries, such as Iona. Admittedly the founder of Bangor, **Comgall mac Sétnai** (511/516–602), who was born, according to different texts, either in 511 or 516, and whose feast day is 10 May, belonged to Dál nAraidi; Adomnán associated him with the Cruithni, just as Columba of Iona was the great saint of the Uí Néill. Moreover, some of the daughter churches of Bangor confirm its status among the Cruithni: Antrim (Óentreb) was within the leading kingdom of Dál nAraidi, Mag Line; Camus (Cambas), on the west bank of the Bann 3 miles south-south-east of Coleraine, probably dated from the period before the Cruithni lost control of the lands immediately west of the Bann. Yet Bangor's influence also extended much further. The annals of Ulster record what appears to have been a prolonged visit to Britain by Máel Rubai, abbot of Bangor, beginning in 671 and leading to the foundation of Applecross (Aporcrosan) in Wester Ross in 673. In the southern coastal region of Wexford, in one of the kingdoms of the Uí Bairrche, the monastery of Ard Crema also belonged to the *familia* of Comgall. Members of the communities of Antrim and Applecross were to be promoted to the abbacy of Bangor (in 613, 728, and 802), according to the annals of Ulster, demonstrating that the links between these houses were enduring. *Columbanus's ascetic exile from Ireland (*c.*591), after some years as a monk of Bangor under Comgall, led to equally enduring links with Bobbio, in the Apennines south of the Lombard capital at Pavia, but not, apparently, with his earlier foundation at Luxeuil on the southern side of the Vosges. The intellectual culture of Bangor in the time of Comgall is attested by Columbanus's two surviving hymns, one of them preserved in the antiphonary of Bangor, a late seventh-century manuscript written at Bangor and later taken to Bobbio, that also contains a poem listing the abbots of Bangor up to the late seventh century. The prestige of the community emerges clearly from a comparison of the obits of its abbots in the annals of Ulster and the martyrologies of Tallaght and Óengus: all the early abbots have their obits noted in the annals (then written on Iona) and with one or two possible exceptions all the early abbots were commemorated in the martyrologies. Among them, for example, is the **Sillán moccu Mind** [Mo Sinu] (*d.* 610), feast day 28 February, who is recorded as having a particular expertise in arithmetical computation. The obits demonstrate that abbots were not recruited exclusively from within the Dál nAraidi (Comgall's kinsmen); again Bangor was more of a pan-Irish community than was either Connor or Nendrum. To judge by the annals and martyrologies, Bangor was the greatest monastery of Ulster, followed by its close neighbour Movilla, and then by Nendrum. It may not be an accident that the two leading houses, Bangor and Movilla, were close to the boundary between the Cruithni and Dál Fiatach, as well as being close to each other: they may have been placed there deliberately to assist peace-keeping.

The monastery of Movilla (Mag mBili) was founded by **Findbarr moccu Fiatach** [Vinnianus] (*d.* 579), whose feast day is 10 September. None of the Irish collections of saints' lives contains his life. The only extant life is a brief text contained in John Tynemouth's fourteenth-century *Nova legenda Anglie*, derived from Welsh sources. It is intriguing that the stanza on Findbarr in the martyrology of Óengus says that he came to Ireland 'with [scriptural] law across the wind-swept sea' (Stokes, *Félire Óengusso*, 10 September). He is there described as a *suí*, by which is normally meant a scriptural scholar. In the martyrology of

Tallaght, the source used by Óengus, there are two separate entries under 10 September, first Finnio maccu Fiatach and then Findbarr Maige Bili. It is likely that Óengus was working solely from the second entry, since the phrase *maccu Fiatach* would have suggested to him that Findbarr was a native of what is now co. Down and did not come to Ireland from across the sea; also, he uses the full name form, Findbarr, rather than the pet name Finnio. At the beginning of the ninth century, therefore, Irish scholars may have been having difficulty reconciling two personae for the founder of Movilla: one was that of a member of the local ruling group, Dál Fiatach; the other was that of a foreign scriptural scholar. In the genealogies, Findbarr is even ascribed to the same branch of Dál Fiatach as Díchu mac Trichim of Saul. Of course, these two personae might be reconciled, either by supposing that the foreign scholar was adopted into Dál Fiatach (full adoption was recognized in Irish law) or by supposing that a native of Ulster had gone abroad for his education.

Two earlier pieces of evidence lend further weight to these suspicions. First, Findbarr's name in his obit (very probably from the Iona annals) is *Vinnianus episcopus*. The initial V-rather than F-suggests a Briton rather than an Irishman; it also terms him 'son of a descendant of Fiatach', but this designation was probably added later to the original obit (it involves a reinterpretation of *maccu* as *macc uí*). Secondly, Adomnán gives the teacher of Columba of Iona three name forms, Findbarr, Finnio, and Vinnianus, using the Irish full name, an Irish pet name, and a Latin version of a British name. Unless an unnecessary emendation is made to Adomnán's text, moreover, this Findbarr was still alive as an old man in 563, which means that he cannot be identified with *Finnián mac Findloga, or Finnian of Clonard [*see under* Meath, saints of], who died of the great plague in 549 or 551. This casts doubt on the claim advanced in the life of Finnian of Clonard that Columba had been his pupil. The particular interest of the question lies partly in the indirect light the learning of the pupil, Columba, stressed by Dallán Forgaill's *Amra Choluim Chille*, may throw on the learning of the teacher. Columbanus refers in one of his letters to correspondence between Vennianus (a variant of Vinnianus) and Gildas. Since Columbanus's time at Bangor, a few miles north of Movilla, probably overlapped with the last years of Findbarr's life, it is plausible to suppose that Gildas's correspondent was the saint of Movilla. A further strong possibility is that Findbarr was the Vinnian who composed a penitential deriving from the British tradition of penitentials (exemplified by Gildas's penitential) and subsequently used by Columbanus. The upshot, then, is that Findbarr was probably British; that his learning was derived partly from Britain and was reflected in enduring British contacts; that he was the teacher of Columba and influenced Columbanus; and, finally, that he made Movilla one of the major episcopal churches of Ulster. He was the last great British missionary in sixth-century Ireland.

Female saints were relatively common east of the Bann

but their cults were, on the whole, only of local significance. A good example is **Brónach** (*fl.* 5th–6th cent.?) of Kilbroney, whose feast day is 2 April. Her church, Cell Brónche, became the parish church of Glenn Sechis, the valley running down to Rostrevor, co. Down. The old church was sufficiently important to be marked by a high cross. A similar figure was **Ercnat ingen Dáire** (*fl.* 5th–6th cent.) of Dún dá Én, later the parish of Duneane (including the modern village of Toome, co. Antrim). Her cult seems to have declined in the viking period: she was important enough to be commemorated *c.*800 by Óengus the Culdee in the verse he devoted to the saints of 8 January, but she was not included in the genealogies of the saints. To judge by similar churches elsewhere, Cell Brónche and Dún dá Én are likely to have been founded as nunneries—or, at least, churches served by one or more nuns—but were also pastoral centres with a priest or priests attached.

A quite different church and cult was that of Mo Ninne (Dar Ercae, Monenna, Modwenna) [*see* Moninne], founder of Killevy (Cell Shléibe on the north-west slopes of Slieve Gullion in south Armagh). Her floruit was placed by her first life within the first half of the sixth century; her feast day is 6 July. Mo Ninne was said to be the principal female saint of Ireland after St Brigit, a claim to which the only possible rival was the west Munster saint, *Íte [*see under* Munster, saints of], of Killeedy, Limerick: not only is Mo Ninne's feast day in all the Irish martyrologies, but she is included in the genealogies and a life is preserved in the late fourteenth-century compilation Codex Salmanticensis. A later, eleventh-century, life by Conchubranus was then the basis of a further life by Geoffrey of Burton: St Modwenna was established as the patron saint of Burton. Her cult was thus exceptionally powerful for a female saint and quite exceptional also in being extended to England. The first life, was, however, firmly anchored in the area of her birth and her principal foundation, Killevy. Moreover the political geography is early: Killevy, south-west of Newry, was treated as part of the province of Ulster, as is Mag Muirthemne, the central plain of co. Louth. Mo Ninne is presented as one of the principal saints, perhaps *the* principal saint, of three neighbouring territories, Mag Coba (west Down), Conailli Muirthemne (around Dundalk), and Cuailnge (the Carlingford peninsula). The first life does not confine her to these territories: instead she is presented as a pilgrim who later returned home. Not surprisingly she was said to have spent some time with St Brigit, but she also travelled to the south of Leinster to become the disciple of St Ibar of Becc-Ériu (Beggerin Island on the north side of Wexford harbour). The difference, therefore, between Killevy and the churches of Brónach and Ercnat was that Killevy continued over a considerable period to sustain a full community of nuns, while the other churches were probably local pastoral centres run by a combination of one or more nuns and a priest. The nuns of Killbroney and Duneane may have been in possession of their churches, but a major part of their role was to support a priest.

The saints west of the Bann and east of the Foyle In the lands of the Airgialla stretching from Lough Foyle to the southern part of co. Monaghan, there was usually not more than one major church in each kingdom capable of sustaining the level of cult likely to produce a saint's life. So, for example, **Éogan mac Dega** (*fl.* late 6th cent.) of Ardstraw, feast day 23 August, was the saint of the kingdom known after its ruling dynasty as Uí Fhiachrach Arda Sratha (Ard Sratha, 'the Upper Part of the Vale' of the Mourne and Foyle, gave its name to the modern town of Ardstraw, 10 miles south of Strabane in the north-west of co. Tyrone, the site of Éogan's monastery). His church was the episcopal see of the kingdom, but *c.*700 it also had ambitions to acquire control of churches outside the boundaries of the kingdom. Tírechán says that the community of Ardstraw claimed Assicus, Patrick's smith, buried in the church of Ráith Cungi in the south of co. Donegal. Although, therefore, the cult was solidly based in the principal church of a middle-ranking kingdom, it was by no means confined within that kingdom's borders. Éogan is said in his life to have founded Cell na Manach in Cualu (the area stretching southwards from Dublin, along the east side of the Dublin and Wicklow Mountains as far south as Wicklow Town and thus including Glendalough). This accords with his pedigree in the genealogies of the saints which attributes him to Dál Messin Corb, a Leinster group of declining political fortunes which came, by the ninth century, to be settled between Wicklow and Arklow. Although unsuccessful in secular terms, Dál Messin Corb had one outstanding saint in *Cóemgen (Kevin) of Glendalough [*see under* Leinster, saints of]; Éogan is said to have been his foster father. The life also gives Éogan, as one of the leading Airgiallan saints, significant connections with other northern patron saints, which even extended east across the River Bann and so into the territory that remained part of Ulster after its early medieval contraction. He was particular closely connected with his neighbour Tigernach of Clones and with Coirpre, bishop and patron of Coleraine; more remote connections included Comgall of Bangor and Cainnech of Aghaboe.

Mac Caírthinn of Clogher, Tigernach of Clones, and Mo Laisse of Devenish were the principal saints of south-west Tyrone and co. Monaghan. Their churches all belonged to the two kingdoms ruled by the Uí Chremthainn: Fernmag, approximately from Clones to Monaghan Town (ruled by the branch of the Uí Chremthainnz known as Uí Nad Sluaig), and the area around Clogher, ruled by the other branch, Síl nDaimíni. In between their principal areas of influence, on less good land on the edge of Slieve Beagh in the north-west of co. Monaghan, was a small area whose principal saint was a nun, Damnat of Tedavnet (Tech nDamnat, 'The House of Damnat'). Mo Laisse, Mac Caírthinn, and Tigernach all received due honour in lives written in their principal churches and preserved in the late medieval collections; Damnat's memory is preserved, other than in place names, only in the martyrologies and in the genealogies of the saints.

The feast day of **Mac Caírthinn mac Cainnig** [Áed mac Caírthinn] (*d.* 506) is 24 March. The Codex Salmanticensis preserves the latter part of a life, from the point at which Mac Caírthinn left his teacher (unnamed in the surviving text) and went to found Clogher. Almost all the rest of the life is determined by the situation of the monastery: it was to be founded facing the royal seat. The life thus gives an elaborate story involving three main characters, the king who remained a pagan subject to the influence of druids, his queen, and his son, both of whom were presented as ready to receive the preaching of the saint. A miracle achieves two purposes, the rescuing of the saint when the king's son was sent, albeit unwilling, to expel him from the site chosen for the monastery, and the safeguarding of the sleeping boy so that he could return unharmed to his parents. The king was then only too pleased to let Mac Caírthinn remain where he was. The surviving part of the life thus justified the role of Clogher as the principal church of the kingdom, a church which was also episcopal. It was not arguing a controversial case: Clogher was known as 'Clogher of the Sons of Daimíne', that is to say, it was closely identified with the dynasty and the kingdom. In the twelfth century it would become the diocesan church of the whole area, including both Clones and Devenish.

The most interesting aspect of Mac Caírthinn's dossier is his genealogy. Since the beginning of his life is lost, this is only in the genealogies of the saints. Given the close identification of the church with the kingdom, it might have been expected that the saint would have been claimed by the royal dynasty. Yet he is said to have belonged to the Cruithni and his pedigree fails to connect him even with the major dynasty of Dál nAraidi (the Uí Chóelbad). There is room for suspicion, therefore, that the genealogical connections of Mac Caírthinn are early, going back to a period before the River Bann had become a major boundary separating the Cruithni to the east from the Airgialla to the west.

If Mac Caírthinn was the dominant saint of Síl nDaimíni, **Tigernach mac Coirpri** (d. 549) of Clones, whose feast day is 4 April, held a similar position in Fernmag. There is, however, one major difference: whereas Clogher was at the secular centre of the kingdom, Clones was further away from the seat of kingship, a crannog that took its name from Lough nUaithne (Lough Oony near Smithborough). The topographical advantage that Clogher held in the northern kingdom of the Uí Chremthainn was held in Fernmag by Druim Snechtae (Drumsnat), said to have been the first foundation of *Mo Lua moccu Óche [see under Munster, saints of] after he had left Bangor, and thus before his major foundation of Clonfertmulloe. Tigernach's western scope of activity within Fernmag is also seen in the foundation—earlier than that at Clones—at Galloon Island (Gabáil-liúin) on Upper Lough Erne (3¼ miles south-west of Newtown Butler, co. Fermanagh). This remained important since the site contains the shafts of two high crosses. Lough Erne was the western boundary of the Uí Chremthainn kingdoms, so that Tigernach's churches were, unlike Clogher, clearly peripheral in secular terms.

One of the themes in the life of Tigernach (evidently written for his last and principal foundation at Clones) was his relationship with the more advantageously situated Clogher, represented as a seat of kings as well as a monastery. For the life, the dynasty of the Uí Chremthainn had not yet split into the two branches, Uí Nad Sluaig and Síl nDaimíni. Tigernach, like Mac Caírthinn, was of alien paternity: his father, Coirpre, was one of the soldiers of Eochaid (Eochu), king of all the Uí Chremthainn, with his seat near Clogher, but was himself a Leinsterman (of the Uí Bairrche, as the genealogies reveal). His mother, however, Der Fraích, was Eochaid's daughter. Not surprisingly, the king had not given his daughter in marriage to an alien retainer; Der Fraích had fallen in love with Coirpre and had given herself to him. Once Tigernach was born, Coirpre acknowledged paternity and removed his son to Leinster, where Brigit met the pair and gave the child his name: 'Because he is the sister's son of many lords and kings, he will be called Tigernach [princely]' (translated from the Latin in Heist, 108). Brigit received the child from the font and thus became his godmother, an example of a custom notably rare among the Irish, who were much more concerned with fosterage than with godparenthood. Both Tigernach and Éogan of Ardstraw had, therefore, strong links with Leinster, but whereas those of Éogan were with the less powerful Dál Messin Corb and with Cóemgen of Glendalough, those of Tigernach were with Brigit of Kildare and, via his father's pedigree, with the Uí Bairrche. The life has no precise details on Tigernach's Leinster connections; such as are available are in the Leinster genealogies, which place the saint among the Uí Briúin, one of 'the three free kindreds of the Uí Bairrche', but not in the royal kindred, to which, by contrast, Mo Dímmóc of Killeshin did belong. In particular, the life fails to name the first foundation of the saint, a monastery within the kingdom of the Uí Bairrche. For the life, the saint's career before his return to his mother's country is a series of journeys enhancing the status of the patron—to 'Rosnat' in Britain for his education, where his teacher prophesied that he would found a distinguished church in the native land of his mother, to Rome for relics, and a subsequent stay in Leinster where it is the connection with Brigit that matters most. It was Brigit who not only became his godmother but also commanded him to be consecrated bishop.

Once Tigernach had returned to the lands of the Uí Chremthainn, his mother's people, the concern of the life was to situate the saint in relation to the royal dynasty and neighbouring churches before allowing him to make any new foundations. His mother's father, the king, 'driven by carnal love' (Plummer, *Vitae sanctorum*, vol. 2, referring to the love of kinsman for kinsman, *condalbae*), wished to give him Clogher itself and to drive out the incumbent bishop. Tigernach was properly appalled by this proposal and removed himself to an unnamed and presumably small church on a mountain nearby (possibly Slieve Beagh). There his reputation as an ascetic grew, while he performed a significant miracle in bringing back to life Doach, archbishop of Armagh; the effect was 'a perpetual alliance' between their churches. Once these arrangements had been made, Tigernach was instructed by an angel to go to the limits of the kingdom ruled by his maternal grandfather where he founded Galloon. Subsequently Tigernach was said to be moved by divine grace to grant Galloon to Comgall of Bangor and to remove himself 'not far to the east to a broader and more fertile piece of land' (ibid.). There he founded Clones, and with the foundation the life takes Tigernach first into 'a quasi-eremitic life' of contemplation, encouraged by blindness, and then to a death attended by the angels who would conduct his soul to heaven.

If Clones was in a peripheral position within the lands of the Uí Chremthainn, Devenish (Daiminis) near Enniskillen, the church of **Mo Laisse mac Nad Froích** [Laisrén, Laisrianus] (d. 564), whose feast day is 12 September, was even more remote. The Latin and Irish lives both imply that Devenish was in an area subject to the Síl nDaiméni branch of the Uí Chremthainn, but the Irish life contains at the end an account of the wanderings of a people called the Dartrige. The explanation is given by an annal entry for 869 in *Chronicum Scotorum* giving the obit of Martan of the Dartrige of Daiminis, abbot of Clonmacnoise and Daiminis. Devenish, therefore, was situated within the client people of Dartrige, who, in the later middle ages, would take over the area formerly known as Fernmag, while the Uí Nad Sluaig, rulers of Fernmag, moved further southeast, into south Monaghan, where the barony of Farney is named after their later lands. The Latin life does not give Mo Laisse's descent; in the genealogies of the saints his pedigree makes him a member of the Uí Chóelbad, the most powerful dynasty among the Cruithin of counties Antrim and Down. The Irish life, on the other hand, claims that Mo Laisse belonged to the Éoganachta of Munster and also gives a story about his birth taken straight from an origin legend of the Éoganachta; the explanation for this change may lie in the legend given at the end of the Irish life according to which the Dartrige were exiles from Munster. The lives are largely taken up with a series of miracle stories, with no obvious structure, punctuated by major incidents in the saint's career: his education under Finnian of Clonard, his triumph over a pagan king called Conall Derg (of Síl nDaiméni according to the Irish life), and by a pilgrimage to Rome on his own behalf and also on behalf of his foster brother, Máedóc of Ferns. From Rome he brought back relics of Peter and Paul, Laurence, and Clement, thus rivalling Armagh, and placed them in his cemetery, so that all those buried on Devenish would be as if buried in Rome. Before a brief account of his death, the life records his acting as confessor to Columba and as commanding him to go into exile so that he might win as many souls from damnation as he had, by bringing about the battle of Cúl Dreimne, caused to be sent to hell. 'And thus arose the practice that all the heirs of St Columba should show reverence and respect to the heirs of St Lasrén' (Plummer, *Vitae sanctorum*, vol. 2).

When Tigernach refused to accede to the king's proposal that he should be installed in Clogher, the incumbent bishop having been expelled, he retired for a time

onto a neighbouring mountain. Damnat, however, the saint of Tech nDamnat (Tedavnet), was known as Damnat of Slieve Beagh, the mountain which Tigernach is likely to have adopted as a temporary retreat. Caldavnet (on the edge of Slieve Beagh) is also named after her. The enshrined *bachall* or staff of St Damnat was kept by the Ó Luain family until the last of the line sold it to George Petrie (d. 1866); it is now in the National Museum of Ireland in Dublin. She has been confused with *Dympna, the saint of Geel in Flanders. Damnat, however, is the best example among the Airgialla of the type of local female saint of which, east of the Bann, Brónach and Ercnat were excellent instances. As Ercnat's church was in heavily wooded land near the boundary between two kingdoms and Brónach's church served a mountain valley remote from all centres of power, there is a contrast between the great churches, Devenish to the west, Clogher to the north, Clones to the south-west, and the lesser church of Tedavnet, lying on the wetter soils of northern Fernmag towards Slieve Beagh.

The saints west of the Foyle West of the Foyle and the Mourne were the lands of Cenél Conaill and Cenél nÉogain, the latter expanding, especially in the course of the eighth and ninth centuries, into former Airgiallan territory. Both these dynasties were branches of the Uí Néill, and their great saint was *Columba of Iona, who had churches at Derry and Drumhome and on Tory Island. Another saint of almost equal rank was *Adomnán, whose church at Raphoe lay within the minor Uí Néill kingdom of Cenél nÉndai. An Uí Néill saint who was not abbot of Iona was *Áed mac Bricc [see under Meath, saints of], whose main churches lay in the midlands, at Rahugh and Killare, but who also had a church at Slieve League. With competition of this calibre it is hardly surprising that the north-west had almost no other major saints.

One church which appears to have been of some importance, especially to judge by the sculpture surviving on the site and by the relics of the saint, **Muru mac Feradaig** [Mura] (fl. c.600–c.650), was Fahan on the east (Inishowen) side of Lough Swilly. Although Muru's floruit was the first half of the seventh century, his obit is unrecorded and he was not included in the martyrologies of Tallaght and Óengus. His feast day (12 March) is first given in the twelfth-century martyrology of Gorman. On the other hand he is given a prominent place among the saints of Cenél nÉogain in the genealogies of the saints. The only surviving narrative about him is a late Middle Irish (perhaps twelfth-century) text included in the fragmentary annals of Ireland, in which the saint appears as a friend and confessor of Áed Uaridnach, Cenél nÉogain king of Tara from 605 to 612. The bell associated with Muru is in the Wallace Collection in London, while his staff is in the National Museum in Dublin. In terms of relics and sculpture, therefore, the cult of the saint would appear to have been vigorous, which only makes more puzzling the virtual absence of textual evidence for someone who was, after all, one of the principal saints of an outstandingly powerful and enduring royal dynasty.

T. M. CHARLES-EDWARDS

Sources *Ann. Ulster* · S. Mac Airt, ed. and trans., *The annals of Inisfallen* (1951) · *AFM* · W. M. Hennessy, ed. and trans., *Chronicum Scotorum: a chronicle of Irish affairs*, Rolls Series, 46 (1866) · D. Murphy, ed., *The annals of Clonmacnoise*, trans. C. Mageoghagan (1896); facs. edn (1993) · W. Stokes, ed., 'The annals of Tigernach [8 pts]', *Revue Celtique*, 16 (1895), 374–419; 17 (1896), 6–33, 119–263, 337–420; 18 (1897), 9–59, 150–97, 267–303, 374–91; pubd sep. (1993) · R. I. Best and H. J. Lawlor, eds., *The martyrology of Tallaght*, HBS, 68 (1931) · *Félire Óengusso Céli Dé | The martyrology of Oengus the Culdee*, ed. and trans. W. Stokes, HBS, 29 (1905) · W. Stokes, ed., *The Martyrology of Gormán*, HBS, 9 (1895) · M. O'Clery, *The martyrology of Donegal: a calendar of the saints of Ireland*, ed. J. H. Todd and W. Reeves, trans. J. O'Donovan (1864) · K. Meyer, ed., 'The Laud (610) genealogies and tribal histories', *Zeitschrift für Celtische Philologie*, 8 (1911), 291–338, 418–19 · M. A. O'Brien, ed., *Corpus genealogiarum Hiberniae* (Dublin, 1962) · P. Ó Riain, ed., *Corpus genealogiarum sanctorum Hiberniae* (Dublin, 1985) · W. W. Heist, ed., *Vitae sanctorum Hiberniae ex codice Salmanticensi nunc Bruxellensi* (Brussels, 1965) · C. Plummer, ed., *Vitae sanctorum Hiberniae* (1910) · C. Plummer, ed. and trans., *Bethada náem nÉrenn | Lives of Irish saints*, 2 vols. (1922) · W. Stokes, ed., *Lives of the saints from the Book of Lismore*, 2 vols. (1890) · F. J. Byrne, *Irish kings and high-kings* (1973) · A. Gwynn and R. N. Hadcock, *Medieval religious houses: Ireland* (1988) · E. Hogan, ed., *Onomasticon Goedelicum, locorum et tribuum Hiberniae et Scotiae* (1910) · J. F. Kenney, *The sources for the early history of Ireland* (1929); repr. (1979) · Lord Killanin and M. V. Duignan, *Shell guide to Ireland* (1962) · T. W. Moody and others, eds., *A new history of Ireland*, 9: *Maps, genealogies, lists* (1984) · C. Plummer, 'A tentative catalogue of Irish hagiography', *Miscellanea Hagiographica Hibernica* (1925) · R. Sharpe, *Medieval Irish saints' lives: an introduction to the 'Vitae sanctorum Hiberniae'* (1991) · S. H. O'Grady, ed., *Betha Mholaise Dhaiminse*, *Silva Gadelica* (1892), 17–37 · W. Reeves, *The ecclesiastical antiquities of Down, Connor, and Dromore* (1847) · J. O'Donovan, ed., *Three fragments of Irish annals* (1860)

Ultán moccu Chonchobair (d. 657). *See under* Meath, saints of (*act. c.*400–*c.*900).

Umfraville, de, family (*per. c.*1100–1245), barons, became prominent among the ruling families of England's border with Scotland by virtue of their strategically important lordships of Prudhoe and Redesdale. But it cannot be said for certain either where they came from, though Offranville near Dieppe seems their likeliest place of origin, or when they were first established in the north. It is possible that they were related to Umfravilles active in Glamorgan in the years on either side of 1100, but no connection besides the name has been established between them. Family tradition, as presented in an early thirteenth-century lawsuit, named Robert 'with the beard' as the first Umfraville lord of Prudhoe, and described him as having come 'to the conquest of England' (Thompson, 30–31). Excavations at Prudhoe have revealed substantial fortifications there datable to the late eleventh century, when Anglo-Norman lords were beginning to establish themselves on and north of the Tyne. But there is nothing to connect these defences with an Umfraville, and in any case the tale of generations recorded in 1207 makes Robert *cum barba* identical with the man traditionally named as Robert [ii] de Umfraville. Since early thirteenth-century exchequer returns date the establishment of the Umfravilles to the reign of Henry I, it seems highly probable that the first Robert never existed, and that later tradition had made two men out of one.

The true **Robert** [i] **de Umfraville** (*fl. c.*1120–*c.*1145),

therefore, was the one ensconced in Northumberland by 1130, when he was pardoned an exchequer debt of 40*s*. It is in keeping with Henry I's policy for the settlement of the north that he should have been given Prudhoe, just south of the Tyne on a commanding position on the route from Carlisle to Newcastle, and the wild valley of Redesdale, the latter by the service of keeping it from thieves. At the same time he was acquiring interests in Scotland. About 1120 Robert witnessed the foundation charter of Earl David, later David I, for Selkirk, and between then and the mid-1140s he witnessed other charters for David and his son Prince Henry. It seems likely that lands at Kinnaird and Dunipace, Stirlingshire, disposed of by his descendants, had been first granted to Robert [i].

The Scottish connection was maintained in the following generation. It is highly likely that Robert [i] had two sons, of whom the elder, **Odinel** [i] **de Umfraville** (*fl. c.*1145–*c.*1166), was his father's heir in England but nevertheless witnessed several times in Scotland for David I and Malcolm IV, for the latter's brother William as earl of Northumberland, and for Bishop Robert of St Andrews. He was with Henry II in Cumberland in 1158, while in Northumberland his activities included giving judgment some time before 1162 at Welton over lands at Burradon and Widdrington, and litigating in 1156 against William de Vescy, lord of Alnwick. He is probably last recorded in 1166, holding two knights' fees in Yorkshire. He was outlived by **Gilbert de Umfraville** (*fl. c.*1140–*c.*1175), without much doubt his younger brother, who made his career almost entirely in Scotland. He established close links with Prince Henry, whose constable he was by the early 1140s, and witnessed charters in England and Scotland both for Henry and for the prince's two sons. He accompanied Malcolm IV to France in 1159, and was constable to Malcolm's brother William before the latter became king. He retained links with Northumberland, witnessing three charters there, two of them alongside his presumed brother Odinel, but his territorial interests were essentially Scottish. His confirming Malcolm IV's grant to Kelso Abbey of the church of Keith Marischal, Haddingtonshire, may indicate that he extended them.

The direct line continued with **Odinel** [ii] **de Umfraville** (*d.* 1182), who for a while maintained his family's cross-border connections. He was raised in the household of William the Lion's father, and witnessed charters for William himself. According to Jordan Fantosme the Scottish king expected Odinel to join him in war against Henry II in 1173, and was furious when disillusioned:

> I'll be damned or excommunicated or shamed and discomfited, if I grant truce or respite to Odinel's castle; rather will I utterly destroy his happiness and his pleasure. Earl Henry, my father, held him dear and brought him up, but before the end of the day he will regret setting eyes on me. (*Fantosme's Chronicle*, 44–7)

Odinel's *caput* at Prudhoe withstood a fierce attack in 1173, and though his subsidiary castle at Harbottle was captured in the following year, Prudhoe once more held out. Odinel himself escaped to raise a relieving force, before taking part in the battle at Alnwick on 13 July in which

King William was captured. The damage to his lands had been such that he had to be paid £20 to enable him to garrison Prudhoe afterwards. He had earlier married Alice, daughter of the justiciar Richard de *Lucy, who brought him the Suffolk manor of Thorney Green. In 1177 he was present in London when Henry II arbitrated between the kings of Castile and Navarre, but remained essentially a northern magnate—he is named as 'the most powerful of the potentates of Northumberland' in the miracles of St Oswin (Dugdale, *Monasticon*, 3.311), which describe him commandeering the serfs of Tynemouth Abbey to work on his castle's roofs. The context for this activity was probably the building of a new keep at Prudhoe, datable to the period after the Anglo-Scottish war. A benefactor to Hexham and Newminster, Odinel died in 1182, when his estates in Northumberland alone were valued at nearly £60 per annum; his estates elsewhere, in Yorkshire, Suffolk, and Rutland, may have doubled that.

Odinel [ii] had four or five sons and at least three daughters; the latter's marriages enhanced the position of the Umfravilles among the Northumbrian baronage. Their father's heir was his eldest son, **Robert [ii] de Umfraville** (d. in or before 1195), who was perhaps only just of age when his father died, since he was given 100s. to maintain himself from the issues of his inheritance, while 40s. were spent on clothes for his siblings. Robert litigated over his family's Rutland estates and confirmed his father's grant to Newminster in return for 20 marks, while about 1185 he settled lands in Redesdale on his sister Alice and her husband, William Bertram of Mitford. But there is no evidence that Robert [ii] married, and when he died, before Michaelmas 1195, his heir was his brother **Richard de Umfraville** (d. 1226), who paid £100 both for his brother's lands and for the remission of Richard I's ill will because he had failed to go to Normandy. Like his father he was principally concerned with his northern interests, and engaged in a good deal of litigation in defence of them, including an important, and successful, action against Eustace de Vescy of Alnwick over a Northumbrian wardship.

Such a clash notwithstanding, Richard de Umfraville and Eustace de Vescy were political allies in resisting King John. Umfraville suffered like other northern barons from John's exactions. His scutages were assessed at 50 marks in 1201, 120 marks in 1204, and 40 marks in 1205, and in the latter year he also owed 100 marks for his share of the Lucy inheritance. By 1212 his links to men like Vescy, and perhaps also his resentment, had brought him under intense suspicion, for on 24 August he undertook to hand over to John his four sons and Prudhoe Castle; these, with all his lands, would face the consequences if Richard took part in treasonable discussion or activity. In late spring 1213 he joined the army that the king assembled at Dover, and in May 1215 he was among the northern barons to whom the king claimed he wanted to be reconciled. But his loyalty was not to be won. In the following year he was reported to be in arms against John, and on 13 March 1216 all his lands were given to the loyalist Hugh de Balliol.

Richard de Umfraville had made his peace with Henry III's minority government by 26 October 1217, and on 3 November order was given that Prudhoe be restored to him. He then proceeded to trouble the still precarious peace by engaging in a prolonged dispute with the former loyalist Philip of Oldcotes. In July 1218 he complained that Oldcotes had built a castle at Natterton, detrimental to his own at Prudhoe. Oldcotes retaliated by claiming that Umfraville had strengthened his other castle at Harbottle, in breach of a government prohibition, and secured an order on 25 July 1220 that the work be undone. This in turn led to Umfraville's appeal to Hubert de Burgh, setting out the importance of Harbottle—'it is situated on the Scottish march towards the great waste, to the great utility of the realm' (Shirley, 1.140–41)—and demanding that the order be revoked. Eventually he had his way, and thereafter he supported the regime: he was present in the king's army at the siege of Bedford in 1224. In Northumberland he continued to promote his family's position, quarrelling so violently with the see of York in its liberty of Hexham that he found it necessary to give the vill and church of Throckington to Archbishop Gray. Then or later he was a benefactor to Hexham Abbey, as he was to Newminster. With a wife whose identity is unknown he had at least four sons and two daughters.

Richard de Umfraville died in 1226, and was succeeded by his eldest son, **Sir Gilbert de Umfraville** (d. 1245), who paid a baronial relief of £100 in the following year. Gilbert had all his father's energy, but kept out of controversy. Knighted by 1228, he went to Brittany with Henry III in 1230, and three times formed part of the escort for Alexander II's visits to England. In 1237 he witnessed the treaty of York. He served the crown as a forest justice, but also continued to consolidate his local authority, to the extent that his liberty in Northumberland was compared to that of the bishop of Durham, and he was described as holding Redesdale 'by royal power' (*Liber feodarum*, 2.1121). He cultivated good relations with his northern neighbours, witnessing a number of their charters. His first wife, Theophania, was a member of the Balliol family; she brought him Mickley as her portion in a match that may also have been intended to heal the divisions caused by the civil war. Gilbert abandoned a nebulous claim to Wooler, inherited from his grandfather, in favour of Robert de Muschamp, and is recorded as sending a horse as a gift to Robert fitz Meldred, lord of Raby. A benefactor to Newminster and Hexham, he confirmed and extended his grandfather's grant to Kelso Abbey of the tithe of horses from Redesdale Forest.

Horses were an important source of wealth for Gilbert de Umfraville, from Northumbrian estates that were prosperous when he died. His inquisition post mortem records mills, fisheries, and breweries, the pasturing of hundreds of sheep and cattle, and a substantial dependent population. As his grant to Kelso shows, he had retained his family's Scottish connections, and after Theophania died he married in 1243 Maud (or Matilda), daughter of Malcolm, earl of Angus, and widow of John Comyn. He may have been earl of Angus in his wife's right. Maud was the mother of Gilbert's only son, another Gilbert de *Umfraville. When the elder Gilbert died early in 1245, to be buried in Hexham Abbey, Matthew Paris hailed him as 'a distinguished baron, the guardian and outstanding flower of the northern parts of England' (Paris, *Chron.*, 4.415). No less strikingly, the two greatest laymen in the realm after the king, Richard of Cornwall and Simon de Montfort, competed for the wardship of Gilbert's infant heir. Simon won, with a proffer of 10,000 marks, which the king subsequently remitted. Montfort is reckoned to have profited to the tune of £330 per annum as a result. The marriage to Maud transformed the position of the Umfravilles. The two Gilberts had become more than leading northern barons, they were outstanding figures among the Anglo-Scottish nobility.   HENRY SUMMERSON

Sources Chancery records • Pipe rolls • J. Hodgson, *A history of Northumberland*, 3 pts in 7 vols. (1820–58), pt 3, vols. 2–3 • chancery, inquisitions post mortem, PRO, C 132/3, no. 9 • M. H. Dodds, ed., *A history of Northumberland*, 12 (1926) • G. W. S. Barrow, ed., *The charters of King David I* (1999) • G. W. S. Barrow, ed., *Regesta regum Scottorum*, 1–2 (1960–71) • A. M. Oliver, ed., *Northumberland and Durham deeds from the Dodsworth MSS*, Newcastle upon Tyne Record Series, 7 (1929) • P. Oliver, ed., *Feet of fines, Northumberland and Durham*, Newcastle upon Tyne Record Series, 10 (1931) • A. H. Thompson, ed., *Northumberland pleas, 1198–1272*, Newcastle upon Tyne Record Series, 2 (1922) • J. T. Fowler, ed., *Chartularium abbathiae de novo monasterio*, SurtS, 66 (1878) • Paris, *Chron.*, vol. 4 • W. P. Hedley, *Northumberland families*, 1, Society of Antiquaries of Newcastle upon Tyne, Record Series (1968) • L. Keen, 'The Umfravilles, the castle and the barony of Prudhoe, Northumberland', *Anglo-Norman Studies*, 5 (1982), 165–84 • GEC, *Peerage*, 1.146 • *Jordan Fantosme's chronicle*, ed. R. C. Johnston (1981) • I. J. Sanders, *English baronies: a study of their origin and descent, 1086–1327* (1960) • L. C. Loyd, *The origins of some Anglo-Norman families*, ed. C. T. Clay and D. C. Douglas, Harleian Society, 103 (1951) • H. C. M. Lyte, ed., *Liber feodorum: the book of fees*, 2 (1923), 2 • H. Hall, ed., *The Red Book of the Exchequer*, 3 vols., Rolls Series, 99 (1896) • Dugdale, *Monasticon*, vol. 3 • W. W. Shirley, ed., *Royal and other historical letters illustrative of the reign of Henry III*, 1, Rolls Series, 27 (1862), 1 • J. R. Maddicott, *Simon de Montfort* (1994) • C. Roberts, ed., *Excerpta è rotulis finium in Turri Londinensi asservatis, Henrico Tertio rege, AD 1216–1272*, 1, RC, 32 (1835)

Wealth at death by 1245 est. value £330 p.a.: Maddicott, *Simon de Montfort*, 55

Umfraville, Gilbert de (*fl. c.*1140–*c.*1175). *See under* Umfraville, de, family (*per. c.*1100–1245).

Umfraville, Sir Gilbert de (d. 1245). *See under* Umfraville, de, family (*per. c.*1100–1245).

Umfraville, Gilbert de, seventh earl of Angus (1244?–1307), baron, was the son and heir of Sir Gilbert de *Umfraville [see under Umfraville, de, family (*per. c.*1100–1245)] and Matilda (Maud), heir to the Scottish earldom of Angus. This Matilda had previously been married to John Comyn, who took the title of earl of Angus during his lifetime. The title then passed to her second husband, who died in April 1245. The Umfravilles had come originally from Normandy and acquired a considerable estate in England, most notably the barony of Prudhoe with its castle and the liberty of Redesdale and Coquetdale, all in Northumberland. For 10,000 marks the wardship of the young Gilbert was granted to Simon de Montfort, earl of Leicester, under whose influence his charge joined the barons in their revolt against Henry III. However, Earl

Simon's death at the battle of Evesham in 1265, by when Gilbert had joined the royalists, presumably released the young man from his obligation to pay Montfort 1200 marks for entry to his inheritance on reaching his majority.

In 1295 Gilbert was summoned to the English parliament as Lord Umfraville, although his Scottish title of earl of Angus was sometimes also used as a courtesy in English royal writs. He served with Edward I in Wales in 1277 and also in Gascony in 1294. Although Earl Gilbert was clearly in possession of his Scottish earldom, including custody of the royal castles of Dundee and Forfar, he does not seem to have played much part in Scottish affairs, although he could lay claim to be one of the seven ancient Celtic earls who allegedly had the right to elect a king of Scots. This claim naturally took on a greater importance after the untimely death of Alexander III in 1286. Earl Gilbert was given custody of Dundee and Forfar castles and in 1290 attended the parliament held at Birgham to ratify the marriage contract between Margaret, the Maid of Norway, and Edward, Prince of Wales. After the death of the Maid, he, along with other keepers of royal castles, professed himself unsure of King Edward's right to take them into his hands until a new king was chosen, but he was soon persuaded and did homage to the English king as lord superior of Scotland. Earl Gilbert, like so many of his peers, was quite at ease with the idea of holding important lands and offices in more than one kingdom, though it was not long before such an outlook become untenable.

With the outbreak of war between England and Scotland in 1296, Umfraville remained loyal to King Edward. He went north with the English army in the same year, having again paid homage to the English king as earl of Angus, along with Patrick, earl of March and Dunbar, and Robert (VI) de Brus and his son, Robert Bruce, later king of Scots. An unsavoury incident occurred at this time between Angus's eldest son and heir, Gilbert, and Sir Hugh Lowther, a royal servant. It is not known why the young Gilbert attacked Lowther, but he was certainly made to give due satisfaction for the incident.

Earl Gilbert went north again in 1298 and, along with Earl Patrick of Dunbar, played a crucial role in that year's campaign. The English had advanced far into Lothian, where they could find no provisions, since the Scots had burnt the crops and driven off all cattle in the area; supplies sent north by ship were not sufficient to stem the rising tide of starvation and, to cap it all, there was no sign of the Scottish army. In the nick of time, these two 'Scottish' earls arrived with news of the whereabouts of Wallace and his men, and Edward's army marched forward to victory at Falkirk. Earl Gilbert continued to play his part in Anglo-Scottish affairs, attending a meeting at York in July 1299 to consider the state of English garrisons in Scotland; but since he was now in his late fifties, the turn of the century saw him entering semi-retirement. He was summoned to the Carlisle parliament of early 1307 but died in the same year. His wife was Elizabeth, third daughter of Alexander *Comyn, earl of Buchan, and Elizabeth de

Quincy. Gilbert and Elizabeth were buried in a magnificent tomb in Hexham Priory, where their effigies can still be seen.

The couple had three sons, the eldest of whom, Gilbert, died in 1303 without children from his marriage to Margaret, daughter of Thomas de Clare. The youngest, Thomas, was appointed Edward I's constable of the royal castle of Dundee in 1304 once English control was again established north of the Forth. He and a number of his men from the Dundee garrison gave chase to William Wallace 'beneath' Ironside, a hill behind Dundee, in September 1304; this was the Scottish leader's last recorded skirmish before his final capture in August 1305, and perhaps forms a flimsy basis for the claim made by a fifteenth-century chronicler, John Hardyng, that Gilbert de Umfraville, earl of Angus, took Wallace prisoner, defeated Bruce in battle, and was regent of Scotland north of the Forth. Alas, Earl Gilbert's career was far more ordinary.

Robert Umfraville, eighth earl of Angus (*c.*1277–1325) was the second son of Gilbert de Umfraville and Elizabeth Comyn. Having survived his elder brother, Robert succeeded to his father's estates in both England and Scotland when aged about thirty. He proved a loyal and energetic supporter of Edward II, and was given positions of considerable responsibility, including that of a royal lieutenant in Scotland in 1308 and keeper of the march in 1310. He regularly served on commissions for negotiating truces between 1307 and 1313, while he also seems to have maintained his family's control of the royal castle of Dundee, before its capture by King Robert in 1312.

As might be expected, Angus fought for Edward II at the battle of Bannockburn. Having survived the battle itself, Earl Robert fled from the carnage as a member of the earl of Hereford's cavalry troop, seeking refuge in the English-held castle of Bothwell, on the Clyde. The constable, a Scot, decided that now was the time to declare his allegiance to King Robert and promptly handed over his very important prisoners. Angus seems to have been released just over a year later, when he was admitted to Edward II's household as a banneret. He returned to duty on the borders where he was empowered to receive 'rebels' to the

king's peace. In 1319 he took part in the unsuccessful English siege of Berwick and seems to have remained active in the king's service: though his loyalty was stretched by the activities of the Despensers, as earl of Angus he none the less sat in judgment on Thomas of Lancaster in March 1322, even though he had formerly been a retainer of the earl's. King Robert I appears to have deprived Angus of his Scottish lands after Bannockburn, but the earldom itself was not granted out until the end of his reign, when it was given to Sir John Stewart of Bonkil. By 1389 it had passed to an illegitimate branch of the Douglas family. Robert Umfraville died in March 1325, and was buried, not with his parents in the family chapel at Hexham, but in the Cistercian abbey of Newminster. He had married twice: his first wife was Lucy, daughter of William of Kyme, from whom the Umfravilles acquired a large amount of land in Lincolnshire and Yorkshire, including Kyme Castle; his second wife, Eleanor, may have been a kinswoman of the Clares, earls of Gloucester. Robert and Lucy produced two children, their son and heir, Gilbert, and a daughter, Elizabeth; Robert and Eleanor had two sons, Robert and Thomas.

Gilbert Umfraville, ninth earl of Angus (1309/10–1381), was the son and heir of Robert Umfraville and Lucy Kyme and was fifteen years old when his father died in 1325. Although he was accorded the title of earl of Angus when summoned to the English parliament, his Scottish inheritance remained forfeited until the campaigns of Edward Balliol provided an opportunity to try to win it back. He was therefore present at all the major battles of the period: Dupplin (1332), Halidon Hill (1333), and Nevilles Cross (1346). After this last battle, he received the submission of the pro-Bruce garrison in Roxburgh Castle. Umfraville also attested forged letters purporting to have been granted in 1333 by the boy-king, David II, asserting that Scotland was held of the English kings; in this document he was not only described as earl of Angus and lord of Prudhoe, but also as marshal of Scotland.

In his Scottish activities Angus was closely associated with Sir Henry Percy (*d.* 1352), who was the chief English commissioner in the north. In 1346 Percy wrote to the

Gilbert de Umfraville, seventh earl of Angus (1244?–1307), tomb effigy [with his wife, Elizabeth]

chancellor, John Offord, complaining that Angus's name had been omitted from the latest commission for the keeping of the eastern border; it is not clear whether this was a mistake, or whether Angus had earned Edward III's displeasure in some way.

Having finally lost his Scottish inheritance with the cessation of Edward III's interest in Scotland in the 1350s, and David II's return to his throne, Umfraville concentrated on his interests in Northumberland and those parts of southern Scotland still in English hands. He married twice. His first marriage, to Joan, daughter of Sir Robert Willoughby of Eresby, produced three sons, but none of them outlived their parents. His second marriage, to Matilda Lucy, heir to her brother Anthony Lucy, brought the Umfravilles the honour of Cockermouth and estates in Cumberland. There were no children of the marriage. In 1375 Henry, Lord Percy (1341–1408) [see Percy, Henry, first earl of Northumberland] persuaded Umfraville to make over to him, probably by sale, a considerable portion of his inheritance, including the castle and barony of Prudhoe. When Gilbert died, on 6 January 1381, part of the Umfraville estate went to his niece Eleanor Tailboys, who married Sir Gilbert Burowden. But Matilda retained Cockermouth and the Northumberland barony of Langley, and when, later in 1381, she married Percy, who was now earl of Northumberland, these, too, passed to the Percys. However, in 1375 the liberty of Redesdale had been settled by an entail on the two sons of Gilbert's father's second marriage. The elder, Robert, died before Gilbert, but Thomas was still alive, and now inherited Redesdale.

Sir Thomas Umfraville (*d.* 1387) was the youngest son of Robert Umfraville, eighth earl of Angus, and his second wife, Eleanor. Although he inherited Redesdale from his half-brother Gilbert in 1381, these lands were insufficient to maintain him in the style to which the main branch of the family were accustomed, and he was never summoned to parliament. However, he seems to have acquired the barony of Kyme, the inheritance of his father's first wife, even though this was never mentioned in the entail of 1375, and through this he inherited Redesdale. He married Joan, daughter of Adam Roddam. Their two sons, Thomas and Robert *Umfraville, enjoyed a higher profile than their father, the former sitting in parliament as the member for Northumberland, and the latter becoming a knight of the Garter. The older Thomas died on 21 May 1387, only five years after his entry to Redesdale.   FIONA WATSON

Sources CDS, vols. 1–5 · J. Stevenson, ed., *Documents illustrative of the history of Scotland*, 2 vols. (1870) · F. Palgrave, ed., *Documents and records illustrating the history of Scotland*, 1 (1887) · G. W. S. Barrow, *Robert Bruce and the community of the realm of Scotland*, 3rd edn (1988) · J. Hodgson, *A history of Northumberland*, 1/2 (1827); repr. (1973) · W. P. Hedley, *Northumberland families*, 1, Society of Antiquaries of Newcastle upon Tyne, Record Series (1968) · GEC, *Peerage*, new edn, vol. 1 · RotP · *Chancery records* · Rymer, *Foedera*, new edn · *The chronicle of Walter of Guisborough*, ed. H. Rothwell, CS, 3rd ser., 89 (1957) · Paris, *Chron.* · J. R. Maddicott, *Simon de Montfort* (1994) · C. Given-Wilson, *The English nobility in the late middle ages* (1987)
Likenesses tomb effigy, Hexham Priory [see illus.]

Umfraville, Gilbert, ninth earl of Angus (1309/10–1381). *See under* Umfraville, Gilbert de, seventh earl of Angus (1244?–1307).

Umfraville, Sir Gilbert (1390–1421). *See under* Umfraville, Sir Robert (*d.* 1437).

Umfraville, Sir Ingram de (*d.* in or after 1321), baron, was certainly a descendant of the Umfraville family of Prudhoe, Northumberland, though his exact parentage is obscure. He was perhaps born about 1260, since in 1279 he or a namesake sought from Edward I the lands of his late father Robert, perhaps the younger brother of Gilbert de Umfraville, earl of Angus (*d.* 1245). However, Robert was born before 1212 and died before 1257, dates which make him a somewhat unlikely father to Ingram and his younger brothers. Although he was said to have been married to a daughter of Ingram de Balliol of Urr (in Kirkcudbrightshire) and Redcastle (in Angus), Ingram de Umfraville was given a Balliol forename, and his mother or grandmother must have been Ingram de Balliol's sister or daughter; he himself assumed the Balliol of Redcastle arms.

Knighted and in receipt of an annual fee of 20 merks from Alexander III, Umfraville was not among the barons who acknowledged Margaret, the Maid of Norway, as heir presumptive to that king in 1284, and, apart from his fee, is not mentioned during the period of guardianship (1286–91). He accepted Edward I's overlordship at Norham on 13 June 1291, and was named an auditor in the Great Cause by Balliol; he was present at King John's homage to Edward at Newcastle on 26 December 1292, when he was named eighth of sixteen barons, and witnessed a charter of John at Dundee, 23 February 1293. But he was not among the eighteen Scottish magnates summoned to serve Edward in Gascony in June 1294, and in July 1295, when a parliament at Stirling deprived King John of power, Umfraville was probably not one of the council of twelve then appointed, for he was one of four commissioners sent to France to conclude an alliance with Philippe IV. Probably he was still in France during Edward I's invasion and the Scots' defeat at Dunbar in 1296, but he had returned by 28 June, when he surrendered Dumbarton Castle; his homage to Edward at the end of August calls him 'of the county of Ayr' and the order to restore his lands was sent to the sheriffs of Berwick and Ayr. It is not clear how he acquired these lands, some apparently in Carrick.

Umfraville was one of sixteen Scottish nobles ordered by the English to support the guardian, Brian Fitzalan on 26 September 1297, in response to the Scottish victory at Stirling Bridge (11 September); he had not supported Robert Bruce's rising (June 1297), nor that of Wallace, but he must have deserted the English and was probably active against them in 1298. In February 1299, on the recent death of Ingram de Balliol, Edward I gave all his lands to one coheir, Henry Percy, because the other, Ingram de Umfraville, was the king's enemy and rebel. In August of that year, when the Scots invaded Ettrick Forest, Umfraville was named first as their leader, in a host which included several earls and the two guardians, Robert Bruce, earl of Carrick (the future Robert I), and John Comyn the younger. As a result of the guardians' bitter quarrel, the Scots named William Lamberton, bishop of St Andrews, as principal guardian and Umfraville as sheriff of Roxburgh (a castle in English hands) with 100 horse and 1500 foot (a large force for the Scots) to attack the border.

The following May, 1300, another quarrel, between the bishop and Comyn, led to Umfraville being chosen to replace Carrick as guardian; if this act was not as inconsequential as it seems at first sight, Umfraville must have been seen as a peace-keeper with influence over the volatile Comyn. In the first half of 1301 a truce allowed the Scots to contact King John, who appointed John Soulis as guardian; in September Umfraville and Soulis led a large force in attacking Lochmaben, unsuccessfully. In 1302 a delegation of six, including Umfraville, went to Paris in a desperate but unsuccessful search for continued French support. The war was renewed and in 1303 Edward I reconquered southern Scotland. When the Scottish leaders submitted in February 1304, Umfraville was still in France, and in July Edward I would offer no safe conduct to him, Soulis, or James Stewart until Wallace was handed over to him. Umfraville returned, perhaps after Wallace's taking (3 August 1305); his lands were restored in October 1305 for a fine of his rents for five years—the longest period imposed on any of the Scottish leaders—and in March 1306 he was in Liddesdale, as one of Edward I's captains. He had been driven from his patriotic role by the murder of John Comyn at the hands of Carrick's followers.

In the years that followed Umfraville played a minor role as an English commander in south-west Scotland; in August 1308 he was made guardian of Galloway and was keeper of Caerlaverock Castle; he and it disappear in 1310–11, when he may have been taken prisoner. With other Scots he attended Edward II's parliament, probably in August 1312, to advise on Scottish affairs. On 24 June 1314 he was taken prisoner at Bannockburn and despite leave a month later to his brother William and others to seek money for his ransom in France, he remained in Scotland for six years. At some point before 1320, Robert I had Ingram de Balliol's barony of Redcastle partitioned to give Umfraville his moiety (Robert kept Percy's half); it is clearly implied that Umfraville had made terms, and this is confirmed by finding his name fifteenth in the long list of nobles who petitioned Pope John XXII on 6 April 1320, a document sponsored by the government (the declaration of Arbroath).

Not long after, in August 1320, a major conspiracy against Robert I was revealed, and among those tried and executed was Sir David Brechin, who had not been party to it, but had had guilty knowledge of it. Moved by his execution, states Barbour in *The Bruce*, Umfraville sought Robert's leave to return to England, which was chivalrously granted. The role of Umfraville in that poem is indeed remarkable. He is said to have gone to Perth with Valence in 1306 and instructed the latter in a successful ruse to catch the Scots unawares; he sent Carrick men to kill Bruce by subterfuge; as commander in Galloway he

had a red bonnet on a spear carried before him as token that he was the most chivalrous knight; he advised Edward II on the morn of Bannockburn to play the 'feigned withdrawal' strategy, but was rebuffed by an over-confident king; on his departure from Scotland he advised Edward to make a long truce so that the Scots would lose their military skills, advice which in 1323 Edward took, though to no profit. Barbour had some written source, perhaps a treatise on chivalry, which portrayed Umfraville as a wily but chivalrous tactician. Barbour's story of his departure from Scotland fits with his recorded arrival at Edward II's court in December 1320, when he disingenuously claimed that he had never made peace with Robert I. Edward gave him generous gifts and, in February 1321, leave to depart to France—the last that is heard of Ingram de Umfraville. His career epitomizes the conflicting claims to loyalty which beset a minor Scottish baron in 1290–1314; Edward I could not win him for the English, but Robert I did.

In 1346 a namesake, described as 'Scot', fought on the English side at Nevilles Cross, and for thirty years served Edward III on the border; he was perhaps a great-nephew of the earlier Ingram. The name of the latter's wife is not known; in 1296 he had two daughters, Eve and Isabel, but since no son is recorded, he probably had none.

A. A. M. DUNCAN

Sources W. P. Hedley, *Northumberland families*, 1, Society of Antiquaries of Newcastle upon Tyne, Record Series (1968), 211 · J. Hodgson, *A history of Northumberland*, 3 pts in 7 vols. (1820–58), pt 2, vol. 1, p. 31 · *CDS*, vol. 2, nos. 155–6, 325, 328, 348, 594, 853, 884, 1060, 1220, 1574, 1656, 1696, 1931, 1961, 1978; vol. 3, nos. 95, 121, 235, 302, 373–4, 435, 694, 721 · J. Barbour, *The Bruce*, ed. A. A. M. Duncan (1997), 91, 215–17, 347–53, 471–3, 702–9 · G. W. S. Barrow, *Robert Bruce and the community of the realm of Scotland*, 3rd edn (1988), 64, 106, 112–14, 124, 129–30, 379

Umfraville, Odinel de (*d.* 1182). *See under* Umfraville, de, family (*per. c.*1100–1245).

Umfraville, Odinel de (*fl. c.*1145–*c.*1166). *See under* Umfraville, de, family (*per. c.*1100–1245).

Umfraville, Richard de (*d.* 1226). *See under* Umfraville, de, family (*per. c.*1100–1245).

Umfraville, Robert de (*fl. c.*1120–*c.*1145). *See under* Umfraville, de, family (*per. c.*1100–1245).

Umfraville, Robert de (*d.* in or before 1195). *See under* Umfraville, de, family (*per. c.*1100–1245).

Umfraville, Robert, eighth earl of Angus (*c.*1277–1325). *See under* Umfraville, Gilbert de, seventh earl of Angus (1244?–1307).

Umfraville, Sir Robert (*d.* 1437), soldier, was the younger son of Sir Thomas *Umfraville (*d.* 1387) [*see under* Umfraville, Gilbert de, seventh earl of Angus], lord of Redesdale, and his wife, Joan Roddam. According to the chronicler John Hardyng, who later entered his service, Robert Umfraville fought for the Percys at the battle of Otterburn in 1388, and he may also have led a raid into Scotland in 1390, the first of many such. In the 1390s he began to be involved in government commissions in Northumberland, and in 1401 was sheriff of the county. He was quickly involved in the renewed Anglo-Scottish hostilities that followed the deposition of Richard II; Hardyng records successful forays and fights in 1399 and 1400, and also claims that Umfraville was present at the battle of Homildon Hill in 1402. Henry IV appreciated his value; on 14 December 1402 he retained him for life with an annuity of £40, and probably also knighted him, thereby helping to ensure his loyalty against the Percys, his former lords. In 1404 it was agreed that the earl of Northumberland should transfer the command of Berwick to Umfraville, and in 1405 the latter also received the command of Warkworth Castle and a life grant of the lordship of Langley. In 1405 he rallied to the earl of Westmorland against Archbishop Scrope's rising, and was again made sheriff of Northumberland. At the same time he was active in the defence of the borders, his expertise making him a valued adviser to John, duke of Lancaster, the warden of the east march. His services received further recognition in September 1408 when he was made a knight of the Garter—a notable honour for a younger son without obvious prospects.

On 4 September 1407 Umfraville attended the enthronement of Bishop Thomas Langley in Durham Cathedral. With him was his nephew **Sir Gilbert Umfraville** (1390–1421), the son of Robert's elder brother, Sir Thomas Umfraville (c.1362–1391), and his wife, Agnes. He was born at Harbottle on 18 October 1390, and his father's death soon afterwards, on 12 February 1391, led to a prolonged minority. Gilbert's wardship was granted first to Edward, earl of Rutland, then to Ralph Neville, Baron Neville of Raby and later first earl of Westmorland, who married him to his daughter Anne. The descent of the Umfraville estates was complicated by earlier marriages and entails. Gilbert Umfraville (d. 1381), styled earl of Angus, had conveyed some to the Percys and entailed the rest on his half-brothers, one of whom was the younger Gilbert's grandfather. Some estates which had passed with Earl Gilbert's widow, Maud, to her second husband, the first earl of Northumberland, reverted to her first husband's family on her death in 1398. At first the Percys retained custody, but after 1403 Kyme in Lincolnshire was entrusted to the earl of Dunbar, Redesdale to Sir Robert Umfraville. Gilbert spent some time in the north, training for war under his uncle's supervision. When the two men led a fierce raid into Teviotdale in 1408, according to Hardyng:

> The wyves swere by seynt Rynyan and yelpe
> This olde dogge hath grete joy to bayte his whelpe.
> (BL, Lansdowne MS 204, fol. 208)

Shortly afterwards, again according to Hardyng, Gilbert jousted with distinction at Lille before returning to Northumberland, where he and Sir Robert raided round Jedburgh. His going north may also have been connected with his being granted livery of Harbottle Castle and the lordship of Redesdale on 10 January 1410, though not yet of full age. An energetic warrior, Gilbert Umfraville took part in the English expedition to France of 1411–12, distinguishing himself in the Anglo-Burgundian victory at St Cloud on 10 November 1411. The campaign had been planned by Prince Henry, with whom Gilbert became closely associated. A knight of the king's chamber in 1413, he was bequeathed a golden bowl in Henry V's will of 1415.

Sir Gilbert Umfraville served in France in 1415, as did his uncle. Confirmed in his annuity by Henry V (and later by Henry VI), Sir Robert had continued to fight the Scots on land and sea. In 1410, as lieutenant in the north of the admiral Sir Thomas Beaufort, he led a devastating raid on shipping in the Firth of Forth. On 11 July 1411 he was given custody of Roxburgh Castle for six years. Nevertheless he was suspected of harbouring a residual loyalty to the Percys, whose heir had taken refuge in Scotland, and thus of being sympathetic to the Southampton plot of 1415, whose aims included a Percy restoration. There is no certain evidence of Umfraville's involvement in the conspiracy; indeed, when the Scots invaded in late July he routed them. But King Henry was taking no chances, and Sir Robert was relieved of Roxburgh and on 5 August summoned to the king. As a result he was present on the Agincourt campaign that autumn. In France again in the following year, this time under a formal indenture, he was back on the borders in 1417, conducting a successful defence of Berwick against the 'foul raid' led by the duke of Albany. Then in the next two years he revenged this truce-breaking attack with a series of savage raids into Scotland.

Meanwhile Sir Gilbert Umfraville had been distinguishing himself in France. Having fought at Harfleur and Agincourt, he took part in a number of the sieges that marked the subjugation of Normandy, including those of Caen, Nully-Lévêque, Pont de l'Arche, and particularly Rouen, where he is said to have been prominent in the negotiations preceding the surrender of the city. According to the *Brut*, a number of citizens approached the English lines to plead for access to the king, and on Umfraville's identifying himself, 'thei thankid God and oure Lady that thei had mette with hym, for he was of the old blode of that contre of Normandye' (*Brut: England*, 2.404). This story, like the grant to Umfraville of the lordship of Offranville, supposedly his family's place of origin, may reflect King Henry's desire to present his claim to Normandy as the recovery of a lost possession rather than an act of conquest. Umfraville received a number of other lordships, and was at various times captain of Caen, Pontoise, Eu, and Melun. In 1419–20 he also acted as an ambassador to the French court, in negotiations for peace and Henry's marriage to Princess Catherine. According to the first version of Hardyng's chronicle, Sir Gilbert took part in the jousting that formed part of the Christmas celebrations in 1420, and 'dyd call Hym erle of Kyme' (BL, Lansdowne MS 204, fol. 213v). The title is puzzling, and may have puzzled Hardyng himself, since in the second version of his chronicle Umfraville is said to have acquired it by acclamation in France in 1411—'proclaymed was erle of Kyme' (*Chronicle*, ed. Ellis, 367). It certainly had no official status; Umfraville is never more than 'lord of Kyme' in government records. Yet the style is recorded in a number of chronicles, French and English. In all likelihood he was so dubbed from his principal lordship in deference to his descent from a comital family—in Scotland, where the lordship of Kyme probably meant little, he seems instead to have been known as 'earl of Redesdale' (Bower, 8.121).

If Sir Gilbert Umfraville had hopes of a formal earldom they were dashed by his death at the battle of Baugé on 22 March 1421. According to Hardyng he was a member of a small company led by the duke of Clarence, whom he vainly tried to dissuade from attacking a much larger force of French and Scots. Clarence's pursuit of glory brought disaster on himself and his followers, and Umfraville was among those killed with him. His body was recovered and brought back to England, but its place of burial is unrecorded. He left an estate valued at almost exactly £400, mostly from estates in Lincolnshire. He had no children from his marriage to Anne Neville, and made no will. His administrator was his uncle Sir Robert, who inherited Redesdale as well as Kyme, thereby acquiring a territorial base in Northumberland to replace Langley, lost when the Percys were restored in 1414.

Sir Robert Umfraville was active on the borders for the rest of his long career, usually as the second earl of Northumberland's lieutenant on the east march. He attended all the major assemblies arranged to negotiate truces, and occasionally went on embassies to Scotland. He also helped to keep the peace within Northumberland, being closely involved in the resolution of the quarrel between the Heron and Manners families that threatened the peace of the county between 1428 and 1431. A feoffee for Sir William Heron in 1427, after the latter was killed Umfraville supported his widow's claims for justice and helped to negotiate a settlement, attending the final ceremony of reconciliation at Newcastle on 24 May 1431. A widely respected figure in the north, Umfraville was a friend of Prior Wessington of Durham, becoming a member (with his wife, Isabella, recorded for the first time on this occasion) of the Durham confraternity on 3 July 1419. He demonstrated his secular loyalties and religious devotion together when, under a licence granted on 27 June 1428, he gave the manor of Farnacres, south-west of Newcastle, to endow a chantry for himself and his wife, for Henry IV and Henry V, and for all past, present, and future knights of the Garter. Having received his last commission to negotiate an Anglo-Scottish truce on 14 March 1436, Umfraville died on 27 January 1437 and was buried in Newminster Abbey. His widow died on 31 December 1438 and was interred beside him. They had no children, and their lands passed under entail to Sir Robert's cousin William Tailboys.

At the time of Umfraville's death England and Scotland were at war, and his Northumbrian lands were said to have been made worthless by Scottish ravages. In the previous year his lands in Northumberland, Yorkshire, Lincolnshire, and the bishopric of Durham had been valued together at £400 per annum, but probably that was essentially the value of his Lincolnshire estates. In peacetime some 27,600 acres of moorland pasture in and around Redesdale might have been expected to be profitable. But the winnings of war, often referred to by Hardyng, were doubtless also considerable. The chronicler celebrated his dead lord as:

> a Jewell for a kynge,
> In wyse consayle and knyghtly dede of werre.
> (BL, Lansdowne MS 204, fol. 221v)

and held him up as an example to the young Henry VI. Such praise might seem excessive, had not the council written to Sir Robert in the king's name in 1426, acknowledging his 'great and notable services ... to your most renowned honour and praise and to the advantage of us and our whole realm' (*Proceedings ... of the Privy Council, 1422–9*, 205–6). Such eulogies suggest that Sir Robert Umfraville was a worthy last representative of a family that had been prominent on the Anglo-Scottish borders since the early twelfth century. HENRY SUMMERSON

Sources chancery, inquisitions post mortem, PRO, Henry V, C138/60 no. 56; Henry VI, C139/83, no. 57 · BL, Lansdowne MS 204 · exchequer, king's remembrancer, lay subsidy rolls, PRO, E 179/158/38 · BL, Add. Charters 11445, 3512–3514 · exchequer, king's remembrancer, accounts various, PRO, E101/69/8, no. 540 · *The chronicle of John Hardyng*, ed. H. Ellis (1812) · C. A. Cole, ed., *Memorials of Henry the Fifth, king of England*, Rolls Series, 11 (1858) · F. W. D. Brie, ed., *The Brut, or, The chronicles of England*, 2 vols., EETS, 131, 136 (1906–8), 2 · *Chronique de Jean Le Fèvre, Seigneur de Saint-Remy*, ed. F. Morand, 2 vols. (Paris, 1876–81) · B. Williams, ed., 'Chronique de Normandie', *Henrici quinti, Angliae regis, gesta, cum chronica Neustriae, Gallice*, EHS, 12 (1850) · W. Bower, *Scotichronicon*, ed. D. E. R. Watt and others, new edn, 9 vols. (1987–98), vol. 8 · *A collection of the chronicles and ancient histories of Great Britain ... by John de Wavrin*, trans. W. Hardy and E. L. C. P. Hardy, 3 vols., Rolls Series, 40 (1864–91) · T. Hearne, ed., *Duo rerum Anglicarum scriptores veteres*, 2 vols. (1732), vol. 1 · C. L. Kingsford, ed., *The first English life of King Henry the Fifth* (1911) · T. Walsingham, *The St Albans chronicle, 1406–1420*, ed. V. H. Galbraith (1937) · F. Taylor and J. S. Roskell, eds. and trans., *Gesta Henrici quinti / The deeds of Henry the Fifth*, OMT (1975) · *The obituary roll of William Ebchester and John Burnby, priors of Durham*, ed. [J. Raine], SurtS, 31 (1856) · *RotS*, vol. 2 · *CIPM*, 19, no. 1005 · *Report of the Deputy Keeper of the Public Records*, 41 (1880); 42 (1881); 44 (1883) · Chancery records · N. H. Nicolas, ed., *Proceedings and ordinances of the privy council of England*, 7 vols., RC, 26 (1834–7), vols. 1–4 · *CDS*, vols. 4–5 · Rymer, *Foedera*, 3rd edn, vols. 3–4 · *GEC, Peerage*, 1.151–2 · HoP, *Commons, 1386–1421*, 4.686–8 · *A history of Northumberland*, Northumberland County History Committee, 15 vols. (1893–1940), vols. 5, 11 · M. H. Dodds, ed., *A history of Northumberland*, 15 (1940) · E. F. Jacob, ed., *The register of Henry Chichele, archbishop of Canterbury, 1414–1443*, 2, CYS, 42 (1937) · J. T. Fowler, ed., *Chartularium abbathiae de novo monasterio*, SurtS, 66 (1878) · J. C. Hodgson, *A history of Northumberland*, pt 2, vol. 2 (1832) · R. B. Dobson, *Durham Priory, 1400–1450*, Cambridge Studies in Medieval Life and Thought, 3rd ser., 6 (1973) · R. L. Storey, *Thomas Langley and the bishopric of Durham, 1406–1437* (1961) · G. L. Harriss, *Cardinal Beaufort: a study of Lancastrian ascendancy and decline* (1988) · C. Given-Wilson, *The royal household and the king's affinity: service, politics and finance in England, 1360–1413* (1986) · R. A. Griffiths, *The reign of King Henry VI: the exercise of royal authority, 1422–1461* (1981) · T. B. Pugh, *Henry V and the Southampton plot of 1415*, Southampton RS, 30 (1988) · H. E. L. Collins, *The order of the Garter, 1348–1461* (2000)

Wealth at death approx. £400 in lands: PRO, E 179/158/38 · approx. £400 in lands; Sir Gilbert Umfraville: PRO, C 138/60, no. 56

Umfraville, Sir Thomas (d. 1387). *See under* Umfraville, Gilbert de, seventh earl of Angus (1244?–1307).

Umfreville [*alias* Fell], **Charles** (1687–1763), Roman Catholic priest, born in England, the son of Charles Umfraville, was of French descent; he used the alias of Fell in England.

After studying philosophy and divinity at the *communauté* of Monsieur Duvieux he was sent to St Gregory's seminary at Paris in 1707. Later in the year he went to Douai to learn English and to complete his course of scholastic theology, although his later opponents spoke of his poor English. In 1709 he returned to Paris, and in 1713 was ordained priest. He was created DD in 1716. Shortly afterwards he went on the English mission and resided principally in London, where he devoted his leisure time to the compilation of *The lives of saints, collected from authentick records of church history, with a full account of the other festivals throughout the year, to which is prefixed a treatise on the moveable feasts and fasts of the church*, published anonymously in four volumes in 1729. A second edition appeared in 1750. Robert Witham, the president of Douai, wrote observations on this work and denounced it at Rome, his principal complaint being that Umfreville had taken his *Lives* chiefly from Bachlet, and had recorded few miracles. The publication of the *Lives* involved Umfreville in such pecuniary difficulties that when he was required to give a statement of his accounts of the London clergy funds, for which he was a deputy during the period 1728–57, he was found to owe £1272. Of this sum he was unable to pay more than 10d. in the pound in 1731. In the following year his irregular election as a member of the chapter gave rise to much contention, and to some publications. The case was decided against him on appeal. In 1755 he was named superior of St Gregory's, Paris, but declined the office on account of health and age. He died in Gray's Inn on 22 October 1763, and was buried five days later in St Pancras churchyard.

THOMPSON COOPER, *rev.* G. BRADLEY

Sources G. Anstruther, *The seminary priests*, 3 (1976), 236 · D. A. Bellenger, ed., *English and Welsh priests, 1558–1800* (1984), 117 · Gillow, *Lit. biog. hist.*, 2.238 · J. Kirk, *Biographies of English Catholics in the eighteenth century*, ed. J. H. Pollen and E. Burton (1909), 78 · E. H. Burton, ed., 'The register book of St Gregory's College, Paris, 1667–1786', *Miscellanea, XI*, Catholic RS, 19 (1917), 93–160, esp. 118, 121 · F. Blom and others, *English Catholic books, 1701–1800: a bibliography* (1996), 1034–6

Wealth at death see will, 29 Dec 1758, quoted in Anstruther, *Seminary priests*, 893 n. 490

Umfreville, Edward (*bap.* 1702?, *d.* 1786), collector of legal manuscripts, was probably baptized on 24 November 1702 at the Temple Church, London, the eldest son of Edward Umfreville (*d.* 1739), a minor exchequer official, and his wife, Mary. His family was supposedly descended from an ancient Northumbrian family which had fallen into obscurity. He may have been a grandson of Edward Umfreville (1638–1691), bencher of the Middle Temple and unsuccessful claimant to the barony of Umfreville. Upon his admission to the Inner Temple in January 1723 he was described as the son of Edward Umfreville of the Inner Temple, gentleman, as was his brother William in 1734, though no record can be found of their father's admission to the inn, and the reference may simply be to his occupation of a chamber in Inner Temple Lane. The son was called to the bar in 1727, but devoted himself to historical studies and is not known to have engaged in legal practice on his own behalf. In 1741 he was living in Johnson's Court, Fleet Street.

It is not clear how Umfreville managed to acquire his enormous collection of legal manuscripts, though they seem mostly to have been bought at auction in his earlier days. His concentration was on paper manuscripts, which sold for a few pence or shillings a volume, and his was probably the largest collection of its kind ever made, including more than eighty volumes of unpublished law reports and readings. He was well known in antiquarian circles, and was elected a fellow of the Society of Antiquaries in 1745, but later resigned from the society 'in disgust' together with his friend Dr Richard Rawlinson. By 1748 he had fallen into such financial difficulties that his inn pardoned him all his 'amercements' since call, and in 1758 he was obliged to sell a considerable part of his library, including 257 manuscripts, for the benefit of his creditors. Many of these manuscripts came into the Lansdowne collection and are now in the British Library. In 1792, after his widow's death, another 1000 law manuscripts were sold at auction, and these formed the basis of the collection of Francis Hargrave, also in the British Library. A good many other manuscripts still exist, with his 'E. U.' ownership inscription and notes in his spidery hand, which cannot be located in the sale catalogues. Though his annotations show him to have been learned in legal history and deeply knowledgeable about legal manuscripts, Umfreville's only publication was *Lex coronatoria* (1761). This treatise on the law relating to coroners was prompted by his appointment in 1754 as a coroner for Middlesex, an office which he held until his death at Islington on 17 June 1786. In 1760 he was invited to become a bencher of the Inner Temple, but declined. Nothing is known about Umfreville's wife except that she died at Lambeth on 22 March 1791. His son and heir, Neville, was admitted to the Inner Temple in 1748.

J. H. BAKER

Sources J. H. B. [J. H. Baker], 'Umfreville, Edward', *Biographical dictionary of the common law*, ed. A. W. B. Simpson (1984) · Inner Temple, London · *GM*, 1st ser., 9 (1739), 554 · *GM*, 1st ser., 24 (1754), 48 · *GM*, 1st ser., 56 (1786), 530 · BL, Add. MS 4256, fol. 12 · notes, BL, MSS Hargrave and Lansdowne · *A catalogue of a genuine collection of law, and other printed books and manuscripts* (1758) [sale catalogue, Samuel Paterson, London, 13 Feb 1758] · *A catalogue of the valuable law manuscripts and books of the late Edward Umfreville* (Leigh and Sotheby, March 1792) · W. Musgrave, *Obituary prior to 1800*, ed. G. J. Armytage, 1, Harleian Society, 44 (1899) · IGI

Umphelby, Fanny (1788–1852), author, was born at Knowles's Court in the parish of St Mary Magdalen, Old Fish Street, Doctors' Commons, London, the daughter of Joseph Umphelby, a merchant. She lived for many years at Leatherhead, Surrey, and died at Bow, London, on 9 April 1852. No contemporary obituaries have been found, and acknowledgement of her accomplishments is entirely due to the entry by her nephew Robert Avey Ward in the *Dictionary of National Biography* (1899).

In 1825 Miss Umphelby published *262 Questions and Answers, or, The Children's Guide to Knowledge … by a Lady*. The advertisement to the first edition led some to attribute its authorship to her sister Ann (Mrs Robert Ward), but Mrs Ward's son Robert, one of the earliest users of the book, affirmed that the 'lady' was his aunt Fanny. Its focus was on the 'most commonplace subjects', which are either taken for granted or sometimes misunderstood by children. Its question-and-answer format, like other school catechisms, such as Mangnall's or Pinnock's, popular in the first (and frequently reprinted into the last) quarter of the nineteenth century, required children to learn answers to an adult's questions: 'Are there not many things in [the world] you would like to know about?' 'Yes, very much.' *The Child's Guide to Knowledge*, as it was known in later editions, did more perhaps than some of its contemporaries to 'habituate [pupils] to enquiry, by tracing the connection and bearing of one subject on another'. Much supplemented and updated, first by her nephew and later by others, *The Child's Guide* reached a sixtieth edition in 1900. Miss Umphelby's *A Guide to Jewish History, Ceremonies, Manners and Customs* (1834) was intended for use in schools and as a 'Sunday book' in families, but had nothing of her earlier book's success.   Susan Drain

Sources *DNB* · will, PROB 11/2135/450

Unaipon, David (1872–1967), writer and promoter of Aboriginal rights, was born on 28 September 1872 at Point McLeay Mission, South Australia, the fourth of the nine children of James Ngunaitponi. His father was a Yaralde man of the Lower Murray River and had been the first Aboriginal Christian convert in the region. He befriended the Free Church of Scotland missionary James Reid on his arrival in 1861 and quickly became a key intermediary between Europeans and his own people. James Ngunaitponi assisted the missionary George Taplin with his ethnographic and linguistic research but remained a steadfast Christian. He was also one of the first literate Aboriginal people in South Australia and corresponded with Reid's mentor, the Scottish philanthropist Henrietta Smith, *née* Erskine. David Unaipon grew up in a mission environment, with only slight exposure to the traditional culture of his people. He was heavily influenced by the mission schoolteacher, Walter Hutley, who provoked his interest in popular science, introducing him to unsolved mysteries of the philosopher's stone and perpetual motion. In 1885, with his parents' permission, Unaipon was taken into the Kanmantoo home of the pastoralist C. B. Young, a patron of the mission. There he was introduced to classical literature, folk tales, Greek, and Latin.

On his return to Point McLeay, Unaipon joined other literate, talented young Ngarrindjeri men seeking alternatives to the mission's limited employment opportunities. He avoided physical work such as shearing, fishing, or farming by working as a bookkeeper in the mission store. Adept on the mission organ, he accompanied performances of the young men's Band of Hope, reciting verse as well. During the 1890s Unaipon's relations with mission authorities deteriorated, but now he had befriended several influential members of Adelaide society. These associations later enabled him to avoid the full effect of legislation restricting Aboriginal freedom of movement.

On 4 January 1901 Unaipon married Catherine Carter, *née* Sumner, a Tangani woman. Their son, De Witt Talmage, was born later in the year and named after an American evangelist. Unaipon's was an unhappy marriage and from this point his mission home served mainly as a base for his frequent travels. His speaking skills were in demand from church groups eager to regard him as living vindication of the mission endeavour, and he addressed large congregations in Melbourne, Sydney, and Adelaide. His social and political message was conservative, often reflecting the views of the Aborigines' Friends' Association (AFA) which ran the Point McLeay Mission; he considered that Aboriginal people should be brought into the mainstream of Australian society through enlightened paternalism and that, like him, they would respond to the effect of a favourable environment and Christian influence. He proclaimed: 'Look at me and you will see what the Bible can do.'

In 1910 Unaipon accompanied the Point McLeay glee club to Hobart to participate in Tasmanian centenary commemorations. His troupe impersonated Tasmanian Aborigines; Unaipon played the organ. He did not share the views of the emerging voice of Aboriginal activism arising from eastern Australia, and in 1938 he rejected calls for involvement in a national day of mourning. In 1928 he led a delegation from Point McLeay calling for the reinstatement of the AFA control of the mission, which had become administered by the government after 1910. During the 1920s he supported the utopian scheme of a model Aboriginal state proposed for central Australia, but criticized attempts to insulate Aboriginal people from European contact by creating reserves. He and another moderate, the lay preacher James Noble, were suggested as Aboriginal representatives for federal parliament.

Precocious and self-possessed in his urbanity, Unaipon subverted popular notions of an inarticulate and primitive Aboriginality. When steamerloads of tourists visited Point McLeay to see the natives, Unaipon demonstrated his perpetual motion prototype machine, lecturing the visitors on Aboriginal astronomy, botany, and bushcraft, and calling for donations. The press hailed him, perhaps ironically, as the Black Leonardo. Unaipon took out nine patent applications between 1909 and 1944. His particular interest lay in converting rotary to linear motion, and he drew inspiration from the flight of the boomerang. He produced a prototype of a shearing handpiece after 1910, but the device did not go into production.

Unaipon was called upon to advise anthropologists, particularly during the 1914 meeting of the Australasian Association for the Advancement of Science; these interviews encouraged his interest in Aboriginal and European mythology. He began gathering Aboriginal legends while working in the country in South Australia, Victoria, and New South Wales as an itinerant pedlar for the AFA. During the 1920s he signed a contract with the publishers Angus and Robertson for a book of children's Aboriginal stories. He submitted several, but they baulked at his blend of fairy tale, popular science, Aboriginal legend, and Christian morality. He published two stories with AFA support, becoming the first Aboriginal author in print, but Angus and Robertson transferred the rights in his collection to William Ramsay Smith, who edited and published them without acknowledgement as *Myths and Legends of the Australian Aborigines* (1930).

Unaipon lived until the age of ninety-four, dying at Point McLeay on 8 February 1967. In 1992 his portrait appeared on the Australian $50 note. Now remembered for his writings, Unaipon achieved his main impact through public speaking, delivering a potent message that his people were actors in the historical present, not in a primitive past.   PHILIP JONES

Sources J. B. Beston, 'David Unaipon, the first Aboriginal writer', *Southerly*, 3 (1979), 334–50 · J. Horner, *Vote Ferguson for Aboriginal freedom* (Sydney, 1974) · G. Jenkin, *Conquest of the Ngarrindjeri* (1979) · P. Jones, 'Unaipon, David', *AusDB*, vol. 12 · A. Markus, *Blood from a stone* (Sydney, 1988) · C. Mattingley and K. Hampton, eds., *Survival in our own land* (1988) · L. A. Murray, 'Ngunaitponi: the story of Hungarrda', *The new Oxford book of Australian verse*, ed. L. A. Murray (1986) · G. Rowe, *Sketches of outstanding Aborigines* (1956) · J. H. Sexton, 'Is the Australian Aborigine a "degraded creature"? An interview with one of them', *Australian Board of Missions Review*, 2 (1912), 174–5 · W. Ramsay Smith, *Myths and legends of the Australian Aboriginals* (1930) · G. Taplin, *The folklore, manners, customs and languages of the South Australian Aborigines* (1879) · D. Unaipon, 'The story of the Mungingee', *The Home* (1925), 43 · D. Unaipon, *Native legends* (1928) · D. Unaipon, 'My life story', *Annual Report* [Aborigines' Friends' Association] (1951) · D. Unaipon, *Legendary tales of the Australian Aborigines*, ed. S. Muecke and A. Shoemaker (2001) · *The Advertiser* [Adelaide] (12 April 1907) · *The Advertiser* [Adelaide] (27 April 1914) · *The Advertiser* [Adelaide] (9 Nov 1936) · *The Advertiser* [Adelaide] (9 Feb 1967) · *The Bible in the World* (1 Aug 1911) · *The News* [Adelaide] (22 July 1959) · *The Observer* [Adelaide] (10 Oct 1925) · *The Register* [Adelaide] (14 July 1926) · South Australian Museum Archives, Adelaide, M. Angas MSS, N. B. Tindale MSS · State RO, Adelaide, GRG 19; 24; 52 · George Taplin Journal, State Library of South Australia, Adelaide, Mortlock Library of South Australiana, Aborigines' Friends' Association Records · D. Unaipon, MSS of 'Legendary tales of the Australian Aborigines', 1924–5, Mitchell L., NSW · J. Mathew papers, Australian Institute of Aboriginal and Torres Strait Islander Studies, Canberra · Commonwealth Patents Office, Canberra

Uncas (d. c.1682), leader of the Mohegan Indians, was born into the Mohegan tribe in present-day New England, the son of Oweneco, a Mohegan sachem, and Meekump. Little is known about the early life of Uncas and his family background. He later claimed to be descended from the sachems of neighbouring tribes, including the powerful Pequot and Narragansett. The Mohegan were originally part of the Pequot, who numbered about 6000 in 1620 and controlled present-day south-eastern Connecticut from the Nehantic River eastward to the border of Rhode Island.

Uncas's marriage to a daughter of the Pequot sachem Tatobem in 1626 was not enough to quell disputes over hunting grounds and authority between the two tribes. In 1634 Tatobem attempted to reassert his authority in a region where American Indians, Dutch, and English settlers all vied for power, but was killed. His son Sassacus succeeded him, but was unpopular and lost many of his followers. Among them was Uncas, who led a group of followers to a site on what is now the Thames River in Connecticut. About 12 miles downriver at its mouth was Sassacus and the main Pequot group.

Uncas attempted to refashion himself as an independent leader through a dangerous game of switching alliances—playing off the Pequot, Narragansett, and English. In 1636 he focused his attention on an alliance with the puritan colonists, spreading rumours among them of an imminent Pequot attack. John Winthrop jun., governor of Connecticut, believed the stories and issued the Pequot with a provoking ultimatum, which essentially demanded that they become tributaries. The conflict erupted into what has become known as the Pequot War of 1637. The decisive blow came to the Pequot when Captain John Mason led ninety heavily armed colonists and seventy Mohegan warriors under Uncas in a surprise attack against the Pequot settlement at Mystic River. The main force and 500 allied Narragansett warriors surrounded and destroyed the settlement, killing almost all the 700 inhabitants. The English-led force suffered only sixteen men killed or wounded. When the main Pequot force arrived, its demoralized warriors surrendered in droves. Sassacus fled to the Mohawk, who killed him. The surviving Pequot were either killed, absorbed into neighbouring tribes, or sold into slavery.

The victory sealed the alliance between Uncas and Connecticut, but also created a rivalry between the Mohegan and larger Narragansett. Uncas won Connecticut's favour by ceding all the territory of the Mohegan's tributary tribes. In return Connecticut worked to undermine the authority of the Narragansett and its leader, Miantonomo, over its tributary tribes. In 1643 war erupted between the Mohegan and Narragansett. Connecticut sided with the Mohegan, who captured Miantonomo, who made the unwise decision to wear a borrowed suit of armour in battle. Despite receiving offers of marriage to Miantonomo's daughter, Uncas handed the Narragansett leader over to the English. Unable to execute him owing to a matter of jurisdiction, the English handed him back to Uncas, who executed him.

Uncas remained loyal to the English, regularly paying tribute, deferring to their authority, and answering their summons. The English generally turned a blind eye to Mohegan raids on neighbouring American Indians, and Uncas led warriors into battle against England's enemies. Many Mohegan also converted to Christianity, receiving the label 'praying Indians'. Often condemned as a collaborator, traitor, or aggressive man, Uncas was perhaps the most successful leader at surviving a most tumultuous period. Of all the major New England tribes, the Mohegan alone managed to retain a portion of their original land. Uncas died at the settlement on what became Uncas Hill in Connecticut about 1682. The Mohegan are sometimes referred to as Unkus (Uncas) after their great leader, whose name the town of Uncasville in Connecticut bears. James Fenimore Cooper also chose the name Uncas for the main character of his novel *The Last of the Mohicans*.

TROY O. BICKHAM

Sources M. E. Perry, 'Uncas', *ANB* · I. K. Steele, *Warpaths: invasions of North America* (1994) · P. Vincentius, *A true relation of the late battell fought in New England and the salvages* (1638) · V. F. Voight, *Uncas: sachem of the wolf people* (1939) · F. Jennings, *The invasion of America:*

Indians, colonialism, and the chant of conquest (1975) · N. Salisbury, *Manitou and providence: Indians, Europeans, and the making of New England, 1500–1643* (1982) · A. A. Cave, *The Pequot War* (1996)

Uncle Mac. *See* McCulloch, Derek Ivor Breashur (1897–1967).

Underdowne, Thomas (*fl.* 1566–1577), poet and translator, was the son of Steven Underdowne; however, Thomas Warton's claim that Underdowne was born in Oxford and Anthony Wood's that he 'spent time in [Oxford] university, but left it without a degree' cannot be confirmed, though certainly his classical knowledge points to university study (Wood, *Ath. Oxon.*, 1.430–31). Underdowne was the first to produce an English translation of the third-century work *Aethiopica* by the Syrian Heliodorus, calling it *An Aethiopian Historie* (*c*.1569).

Underdowne's first original work, *The Excellent Historye of Theseus and Ariadne* (1566), an Ovidian narrative composed in fourteeners, hardly bears out the fervid misogyny of its preface. His knowledge of the *Aethiopica* at this stage is shown when Ariadne cites Theagenes for his exemplary faithfulness to Cariclea. Underdowne used the same verse form for his translation *Ovid his Invective Against Ibis* (1569) in which the poetic text is interspersed by narrative annotations which draw upon an extensive range of literary and mythographical sources. Enlivened by the occasional moral comment and frank colloquialism—'Hippomenes … as he passed through a grove … was by motion of *Venus*, so sharpe sette, that even there he muste needes have to doe with his wife' (sig. G 6r)—it demonstrates that zest for lively narrative abundantly evident in *An Aethiopian Historie*.

This more successful translation was entered to Underdowne's friend (as he was described in the 1587 edition), the publisher Francis Coldock, in the Stationers' register for 1568–9; it was published without a date and revised by Underdowne for a second edition in 1577. Heliodorus's prose romance, with its Mediterranean and North African settings, embodying elements of epic and tragedy in its interlocking narrative structure, was, for Underdowne, 'the most honest … historie of love' (*Aethiopian Historie*, ¶ 3r). He translated Stanislaus Warschewiczki's Latin version (Basel, 1551) of Heliodorus's Greek, perpetuated its errors and introduced more of his own, but invigorated the narrative with the robustness of Elizabethan English: '[Demeneta] lawfully married hath a husband, and yet playeth the naughtipack' (ibid., ¶ 20). Side-notes include Latin quotations and Underdowne's own moral pronouncements, some on commendable qualities in rulers 'imitated of none, or very few at this day' (ibid., ¶ 252). Three more editions followed before 1622.

Underdowne's version may well variously have prompted Abraham Fraunce's paraphrase in hexameters of the story's opening scene (published as *The Countesse of Pembroke's Yuychurch* in 1591); helped influence aspects of character presentation, episode, and narrative structure in both old and revised versions of Sir Philip Sidney's *Arcadia*

and in Robert Greene's *Pandosto* (1588) and *Menaphon* (1589); suggested details in Spenser's depiction of the temple of Isis in *The Faerie Queene* (v.vii.14; compare *Aethiopian Historie*, ¶ 28); provided Shakespeare's Orsino with an impassioned reference to Thyamis, 'the Egyptian thief' (Shakespeare, *Twelfth Night*, v.i.116–17); influenced Posthumus's dream and other elements in the final act of *Cymbeline*; and started a brief vogue for plays about the story's heroine: a lost court 'play of Cariclea' (1583) and the anonymous *The White Aethiopian*.

After William Barrett's revision which supposedly 'cleered [it] from the barbarisms of antiquity' (Barrett, sig. A2v), Underdowne's translation disappeared from print until Charles Whibley republished it in 1895 as Heliodorus's 'best hope of immortality' in the face of imminent neglect: 'Underdowne … understood the language of Romance, and if he did not translate his author, he replaced him with a piece of prose as rich in invention as it is ingenious in style' (Whibley, xxix).

DAVID FREEMAN

Sources *DNB* · *STC, 1475–1640* · *Thomas Warton's History of English poetry*, ed. D. Fairer, 4 vols. (1998) · Wood, *Ath. Oxon.*, new edn · Foster, *Alum. Oxon.* · Arber, *Regs. Stationers* · Heliodorus, *Ethiopian story*, trans. W. Lamb (1961) · B. P. Reardon, *The form of Greek romance* (1991) · S. L. Wolff, *The Greek romances in Elizabethan prose fiction* (1912) · C. S. Lewis, *English literature in the sixteenth century* (1954) · P. Sidney, *The countess of Pembroke's Arcadia: the old 'Arcadia'*, ed. J. Robertson (1973) · P. Sidney, *The countess of Pembroke's Arcadia: the new 'Arcadia'*, ed. V. Skretkowicz (1987) · E. Spenser, *The faerie queene*, ed. A. C. Hamilton (1977) · W. Shakespeare, *Twelfth night*, ed. J. M. Lothian and T. W. Craik (1975) · W. Shakespeare, *Cymbeline*, ed. J. M. Nosworthy (1955) · A. Feuillerat, ed., *Documents relating to the office of the revels in the time of Queen Elizabeth* (1908); repr. (1963) · W. Barrett, *Heliodorus his Aethiopian history* (1622) · C. Whibley, preface, in Heliodorus, *An Aethiopian history*, trans. T. Underdowne (1895)

Underhill, Cave (1634–1713), actor, was the son of Nicholas Underhill (*d.* 1652), citizen, draper, and theatre musician of London, and his wife, Sara. The registers of the Merchant Taylors' School, London, to which Cave Underhill was admitted in 1645, record the date of his birth as 17 March 1634 (though they are in error about his father's trade); he was baptized at St Andrew's, Holborn, on 23 March, and the parish register calls his father a 'musitionor', resident in Robin Hood Court, just to the south of the church, off Shoe Lane. Cave Underhill began acting in 1660, and had a fifty-year career on the stage, specializing in comic roles, and especially in eccentric and stupid characters. His emergence as a performer in John Rhodes's company at the Cockpit in Drury Lane no doubt owed something to his father, who may have trained him as a musician, and who had been associated with both the Blackfriars and the Cockpit playhouses before the interregnum, as had John Rhodes; like Underhill senior, Rhodes was a freeman of the Drapers' Company.

Underhill had two short-lived marriages before he became a prominent actor: on 31 August 1655 he married Sarah Kitter, with whom he had two children before she died in 1657. He had remarried by 1661; his second wife, a woman named Rebecca, gave birth to their daughter of

Cave Underhill (1634–1713), by Robert Bing [as Obadiah in *The Committee* by Sir Robert Howard]

in *Romeo and Juliet*, and the title role in *The Cutter of Coleman Street* (Cowley). At court in 1662 he acted the title role in *Ignoramus*, an English version of a Latin academic comedy of 1615 (Ruggle). He was Diego in *The Adventures of Five Hours* (Tuke), Peralta in *The Slighted Maid* (Stapleton), Tetrick in *The Stepmother* (Stapleton), the Parson in *A Witty Combat* (Porter), the Duke of Bedford in *Henry V* (Boyle), Palmer in *The Comical Revenge* (Etherege), Cunopes in *The Rivals* (*The Two Noble Kinsmen* as adapted by Davenant), and Gardiner in *Henry VIII* (Shakespeare and Fletcher). Theatres were closed, first for plague, then because of the great fire, in 1665 and 1666; thereafter Underhill played Old Moody in *Sir Martin Mar-All* (Dryden), Trincalo in *The Tempest* (see above), Jodelet in *The Man's the Master* (Davenant), Timothy in *Sir Solomon* (Caryl), Pedagog in *Mr. Anthony* (Boyle), and Sir Adam Meredith in *The Six Days' Adventure* (Howard). In 1671 the Duke's Company moved to their new theatre in Dorset Garden, where Underhill played, among others, Sir Simon Softhead in *The Citizen Turned Gentleman* (Ravenscroft), Justice Clodpate in *Epsom Wells* (Shadwell), the Tutor in *The Reformation* (Arrowsmith), Fullham in *The Morning Ramble* (Payne), Booby in *The Country Wit* (Crowne), Snarl in *The Virtuoso* (Shadwell), Sanco in *The Wrangling Lovers* (Ravenscroft), Jacomo in *The Libertine* (Shadwell), Old Jollyman in *Madame Fickle* (D'Urfey), Blunt in *The Rover* (Behn), and Phaeax in *Timon of Athens* (Shakespeare adapted by Shadwell).

With the formation of the United Company in 1682 Underhill began to act at the Drury Lane playhouse. His parts in new productions there were the Curate in *The Duke of Guise* (Dryden), Daredevil in *The Atheist* (Otway), a Plebeian in *Julius Caesar*, the Cook in *The Bloody Brother* (Fletcher and Massinger), Hothead in *Sir Courtly Nice* (Crowne), Don Diego in *The Banditti* (D'Urfey), Dr Baliardo in *The Emperor of the Moon* (Behn), Lolpoop in *The Squire of Alsatia* (Shadwell), a Soldier in *The Injured Lovers* (Mountfort), Old Ranter in *The English Friar* (Crowne), Oldwit in *Bury Fair* (Shadwell), Bernardo in *The Amorous Bigot* (Shadwell), Mufti Abdalla in *Don Sebastian* (Dryden), Guzman in *The Successful Strangers* (Mountfort), Timerous Cornet in *The Widow Ranter* (Behn), Smug in *The Merry Devil of Edmonton* (anonymous), Sassafras in *Greenwich Park* (Mountfort), Sir Rowland Rakehell in *Love for Money* (D'Urfey), Justice Shallow in *The Merry Wives of Windsor*, Sir John Oldfop in *Win her and Take her* (partly (?) by Underhill himself), Hiarbas in *Regulus* (Crowne), Dryrub in *The Maid's Last Prayer* (Southerne), Setter in *The Old Bachelor* (Congreve), Stockjob in *The Richmond Heiress* (D'Urfey), Sir Maurice Meanwell in *The Female Vertuosos* (Wright), Lopez in *Love Triumphant* (Dryden), Sancho in the second part of *Don Quixote* (D'Urfey), Sampson in *The Fatal Marriage* (Southerne), and Sir Barnaby Buffler in *The Canterbury Guests* (Ravenscroft).

Underhill joined his old colleague Betterton in the independent company of actors formed in April 1695, and played at the theatre in Lincoln's Inn Fields, beginning with the role of Sir Sampson Legend in Congreve's *Love for Love*. Thereafter he took the roles of Sir Topewell Clownish in *Love's a Jest* (Motteux), Sir Thomas Testie in *The Country*

the same name in that year. Rebecca died late in 1662. He married at least twice more. On 17 November 1664 he married a widow named Elizabeth Robinson, who died in 1673. By 1683 or 1684 he was married to a second woman named Sarah: three of their children were baptized at St Andrew's, Holborn, between 1684 and 1687. A son named after him was born in 1685; he predeceased his father in 1709, and was buried in his native parish. Underhill appears to have lived within or near the district where he was born for most of his life.

The acting company formed by John Rhodes early in 1660 became the nucleus of the Duke's Company, founded later in that year under the management of Sir William Davenant, of which Underhill became a member; he subsequently joined the United Company of 1682, and then the independent company led by Thomas Betterton in 1695. Many of his stage roles are known: he was the first Blunt in *The Rover*, Sir Sampson Legend in *Love for Love*, and Sir Wilfull Witwoud in *The Way of the World*. He was renowned for certain Shakespearian comic roles, including the Gravedigger in *Hamlet*, which he acted for the entire length of his career, and Trincalo in the version of *The Tempest* adapted by Dryden and Davenant, a name which he acquired as a nickname.

The parts that Underhill acted before 1665 at the theatre in Lincoln's Inn Fields, the first house of the Duke's Company, included Sir Morgly Thwack in *The Wits* (Davenant), the Gravedigger in *Hamlet*, Feste in *Twelfth Night*, Gregory

Wake (Doggett), Sir Toby Cusifle in *The She-Gallants* (Granville), Alderman Whim in *The Lover's Luck* (Dilke), the Doctor in *The Anatomist* (Ravenscroft), Cacafogo in *Rule a Wife and have a Wife* (Fletcher), Bevis in *The City Lady* (Dilke), Sir Blunder Bosse in *The Intrigues at Versailles* (D'Urfey), Flywife in *The Innocent Mistress* (Pix), Sir Wealthy Plainder in *The Pretenders* (Dilke), Sir Wilfull Witwoud in *The Way of the World* (Congreve), Merryman in *The Amorous Widow* (Betterton), Obadiah in *The Committee* (Howard), and Kent in *King Lear* (Shakespeare adapted by Tate).

Underhill acted less frequently as he grew older, but he continued to perform occasionally in his famous roles until he was in his mid-seventies. After his company had moved to the Queen's Theatre in the Haymarket in 1705 Underhill played Sir Joslin in *She Would if she Could* (Etherege). A performance of *Hamlet* for his benefit at Drury Lane in June 1709, in which he appeared in his traditional role of the Gravedigger, was advertised by Sir Richard Steele in *The Tatler* of 31 May.

Apart from Steele's notice of Underhill's acting, which praises his understated and natural style, accounts of his character and qualities as a performer survive from Thomas Brown (1702), Colley Cibber (1740), and Anthony Aston (1748), of which the second seems the most balanced, and least facetious or exaggerated. Cibber, who probably saw something of his later career, judged Underhill to be:

> a correct and natural Comedian, his particular Excellence was in Characters that may be called Still-life, I mean the Stiff, the Heavy, and the Stupid; to these he gave the exactest and the most expressive colours, and in some of them look'd as if it were not in the power of human Passions to alter a Feature of them … His Face was full and long; from his Crown to the end of his Nose was the shorter half of it, so that the Disproportion of his lower Features, when soberly compos'd, with an unwandering Eye hanging over them, threw him into the most lumpish, moping Mortal that ever made beholders merry! (Highfill, Burnim & Langhans, *BDA*)

Aston believed Underhill was more admired by his fellow actors than by the audience, and though he thought him the 'most contained actor I ever saw' conceded that he had no rivals in his 'dry, heavy, downright Way in Low Comedy' (ibid.).

Underhill's artistic success does not seem to have been rewarded by any great degree of prosperity. He was sued for debt on a number of occasions, and in 1677 arrested and imprisoned. His income from his profession, however, was probably at its highest at about the middle of his career. He was one of the original sharing actors in the agreement made with Davenant in November 1660 at the foundation of the Duke's Company; later he held one and a half shares, for some years had a small capital share in the Dorset Garden theatre, and at one point held three-quarters of an actor's share in the United Company. He signed an agreement as a sharer in the Lincoln's Inn Fields Company in March 1695. An estimate given of his basic salary in 1694–5 quoted £150 per year; by 1703 he would seem to have drawn about half that amount annually, plus a guinea for each of his performances. The announcement of his benefit performance of *Hamlet* in 1709 claimed

that he had lost £2500, and was acting to recoup what he could; a further benefit performance, of *The Tempest*, with Underhill as Trincalo, followed at Drury Lane in May 1710. Satires from the 1680s onwards accuse Underhill of intemperance and wastefulness. A *Satyr on the Players* (1684) had it that:

> Roaring Mad Cave is ye Reproach o'the Age;
> Scandall to all, but ye leud shameless stage.
> (Highfill, Burnim & Langhans, *BDA*)

In Brown's *Letters from the Dead to the Living* Anthony Leigh described Underhill as 'a good sociable sort of Drunkard, and a pretty little pedling sort of Whoremaster' (ibid.). It is hard to tell what truth lies behind these claims, and to what extent the stories of his frequent drunkenness arise from his portrayal of that state on the stage, in a number of his celebrated roles. Similarly, it is difficult to assess the facts of the case in the formal complaints about profanity and obscenity in a number of performances in 1700–01 in which Underhill, with a number of other actors, was involved: one of them was of *Love for Love*. It is known, however, that on 4 July 1662 Underhill was fined 3s. 4d. for his part in an affray at the theatre in which a messenger was beaten.

At the end of his life Underhill was living in Carter Lane, south of St Paul's. He was buried at St Andrew's, Holborn, the parish church at which he had been baptized, on 26 May 1713.   JOHN H. ASTINGTON

Sources DNB · Highfill, Burnim & Langhans, *BDA* · J. Milhous and R. D. Hume, eds., *A register of English theatrical documents, 1660–1737*, 2 vols. (1991) · L. Hutson, *The Commonwealth and Restoration stage* (1928) · A. Nicoll, *A history of English drama, 1660–1900*, 1 (1952) · C. B. Hogan, *Shakespeare in the theatre, 1701–1800*, 1 (1952) · G. Ashton, K. A. Burnim, and A. Wilton, *Pictures in the Garrick Club: a catalogue* (1997) · Mrs E. P. Hart, ed., *Merchant Taylors' School register, 1561–1934*, 2 vols. (1936) · A. Ashbee and D. Lasocki, eds., *A biographical dictionary of English court musicians, 1485–1714*, 2 vols. (1998) · C. Cibber, *An apology for the life of Mr. Colley Cibber* (1740) · parish register, Holborn, St Andrew's, 1623–42, GL, MS 6667/1 [baptism] · IGI · manuscript records of Drapers' company

Likenesses J. Faber junior, mezzotint, 1712 (after R. Bing), BM, NPG; repro. in Cibber, *Apology* · W. Parsons, reversed etching, 1825 (after R. Bing), repro. in Highfill, Burnim & Langhans, *BDA* · R. Bing, oils (as Obadiah in *The committee*), Garr. Club [*see illus.*]

Underhill, Edward (b. 1512, d. in or after 1576), courtier and religious radical, known as the Hot Gospeller, was born into a prominent west midland family, the eldest son of Thomas Underhill (d. 1518x20) of Hunningham, Warwickshire, and his wife, Anne Winter, of Huddington, Worcestershire. His uncle William Underhill was a former clerk of the House of Commons, and his maternal step-grandmother was the daughter of Sir George Throckmorton of Coughton. His cousin Gilbert Winter was a gentleman usher to Princess Elizabeth. He inherited a lease at Eatington, Warwickshire, from his father, and later came into other property from his brother Ralph and his aunt Jane Winter. His background and connections did much to shape Underhill's career. In 1539 he moved to London, and in that year was appointed a gentleman pensioner to Henry VIII. In 1543 he served as a gentleman-at-arms at the siege of Landrecy in Hainault under Sir Richard Cromwell. On the latter's recommendation he took part in the 1544 invasion of France among the personal troops of Henry VIII. In 1545 he sold his family's Hunningham estate in order to provide for court expenses that were not covered by an annual salary of 70 marks. He acquired a reputation for profligate spending habits and joined a group of gamblers that included the Staffordshire landowner Sir Ralph Bagnall. Gambling losses and financial indiscretion may have accounted for the eventual sale of a large part of his inheritance.

During the reign of Edward VI, Underhill displayed an evangelical fervency that earned him a reputation as a 'hot gospeller'. In 1547 he removed the pyx from the altar of Stratford-le-Bow parish church, and narrowly escaped death at the hands of the Catholic women of Stepney. He thrived at the court of the boy king, which was filled with like-minded protestant scholars, poets, and translators, people like John Cheke, Miles Coverdale, Thomas Sternhold, Ann Cooke, Philip Gerrard, and John Philpot. Underhill's accusation that Sir Miles Partridge and Sir Thomas Palmer, two notable soldiers, were covert 'papists' caused great offence. Underhill also used his position at court to promote the publication of protestant books in London. When John Day, the well-known evangelical printer, was harassed by the lord mayor of London, Sir John Gresham, for printing a vitriolic anti-Catholic satire by Luke Shepherd, *John Bon and Mast Person* (1547), Underhill intervened on behalf of the author and printer by handing the mayor a copy and informing him that 'ther is many off them in the courte' (Nichols, 172). In response to pressure from the king's court, the mayoral court permitted the continued operation of Day's press and thus the circulation of *John Bon and Mast Person* among a wide readership.

During the winter of 1549–50 Underhill participated in the defence of Boulogne as controller of the ordnance under the second earl of Huntingdon. Soon after his return to England he incurred the resentment of London woodmongers by exposing their questionable business practices in dealings with the ordnance department. During the controversy over episcopal vestments in 1550–51 he earned the praise and confidence of Bishop John Hooper, an opponent of vestments, and John Dudley, duke of Northumberland, by nailing an impassioned defence of Hooper on a gate at St Paul's Cathedral. In addition to Dudley, Underhill's friends and protectors included John Russell, first earl of Bedford, and his son Francis, Lord Russell. In 1553 Underhill became a member of parliament and during the same year Lady Jane Grey, then nominal queen of England, stood as godmother to one of his daughters.

Underhill's fortunes were to change, however, with the accession of Mary I on 19 July 1553. Having published an anti-Catholic ballad, he underwent arrest and interrogation before the privy council. That he was punished only by a month in Newgate was probably due to sympathizers among his examiners, notably the earl of Bedford and the second earl of Sussex. While he was in prison Francis Russell was among his benefactors. He was released on the grounds of illness on 5 September, through the efforts of his kinsman John Throckmorton (Sir George's seventh

son), and of the earl of Bedford, whose eldest son Underhill had saved from drowning in the River Thames. He recovered his place as a gentleman-at-arms, lost in the previous autumn, by defending Queen Mary during Wyatt's rebellion in February 1554, and he retained his position as a gentleman pensioner. After attending the queen at Winchester when she married Philip of Spain on 25 July 1555, he tried to hinder the growing persecution of protestants by bricking up evangelical tracts in his possession behind a wall at his dwelling at Limehouse. For this service Underhill may have turned to his friend Henry Daunce, the bricklayer preacher of Whitechapel, a nearby district of London. Far from abandoning his religious zeal on the failure of the protestant cause, Underhill, although a courtier and personal bodyguard to the queen, allowed groups of religious reformers to meet with impunity. No doubt his personal loyalty to Mary and the influence of his many powerful patrons contributed to his unusual position, as one who retained a position of trust at the court of the Roman Catholic queen and yet used it for fairly undisguised evangelical activities. His memoirs document his unyielding religious fervency in a very lively manner.

After his appointment as master of the common hunt by Elizabeth I, Underhill took part in the suppression of a public disturbance in London on 12 May 1562. He is said to have lived to a considerable age, but no evidence survives concerning his later life. He is included in a list of gentlemen-at-arms compiled in 1558, but he is not known to have served at court after 1566, and seems to have spent his last years at Bagginton, Warwickshire. He is last recorded in 1576. Underhill married his wife, Joan, the daughter of Thomas Peryns, a London merchant, and widow of the evangelical Ralph Downes, on 17 November 1546 at St Antholin in Budge Row, London. She died in 1562. They had five sons and seven daughters. Thomas Underhill, like his father, was a fervent protestant, commemorated by an annual sermon in St Mary's, Warwick. Little evidence supports the conjecture that William Shakespeare composed a verse epitaph for his son Anthony in 1587.

J. G. Nichols published a fragment of Underhill's account of his examination and imprisonment in *The Chronicle of Queen Jane and Queen Mary* (1850), before making the entire text available as part of his *Narratives of the Reformation*, published by the Camden Society in 1859. Portions of Underhill's narrative provided details for Agnes Strickland's *Queens of England* (1840–48) and also for Harrison Ainsworth's novel *The Tower of London* (1840).

JOHN N. KING

Sources HoP, *Commons, 1509–58*, 3.505–6 · DNB · STC, 1475–1640 · J. N. King, *English Reformation literature: the Tudor origins of the protestant tradition* (1982) · S. Brigden, *London and the Reformation* (1989) · J. G. Nichols, ed., *Narratives of the days of the Reformation*, CS, old ser., 77 (1859)

Underhill, Edward Bean (1813–1901), missionary society secretary and writer, born at St Aldates, Oxford, on 4 October 1813, was one of seven children of Michael Underhill, a grocer of Oxford, and his wife, Eleanor, *née* Scrivener. After education at a school in Oxford set up by James

Edward Bean Underhill (1813–1901), by unknown engraver, pubd 1863

Hinton, Baptist minister, Underhill engaged in business as a grocer in Beaumont Street, Oxford, from 1828 until 1843. In 1836 he married Sophia Ann (*d.* 1850), daughter of Samuel Collingwood, printer to Oxford University. They had three daughters. Owing to the ill health of his wife he then moved to Avening, near Stroud, Gloucestershire, where he devoted himself to study of the history of the Baptist denomination. In 1845 he founded the Hanserd Knollys Society for the publication of works by early Baptist writers. Of the ten volumes which appeared, Underhill edited seven, two with elaborate introductions on the seventeenth-century history of the denomination. On account of these volumes he deserves to be remembered as one of the earliest historians of Baptist origins in England. In 1848 he became proprietor and editor of the *Baptist Record*, to which he contributed historical papers.

After the magazine ceased publication in June 1849, Underhill became joint secretary of the Baptist Missionary Society (July 1849). He was sole secretary from 1869 to 1876, and honorary secretary from 1876 until his death. The society's work grew steadily under his guidance. He visited the missionary centres of the society, and during a long stay in India and Ceylon from October 1854 to February 1857 acquired a full knowledge of Indian problems, which he placed at the disposal of the committee of the House of Commons on the affairs of India in 1859. On his India tour, Underhill was accompanied by his second wife, Emily (*d.* 1869), eldest daughter of John Lee *Benham, of London, whom he had married on 17 November 1852. His Indian tour gave him first-hand experience of the problems of dependence which afflicted the Baptist churches (as other churches) in north India, and was the source of a sustained attempt which he made a decade later to reform the society's India policy. Although this attempt met with

only limited success, Underhill was one of the first missionary strategists in the nineteenth century to emphasize the crucial importance of a self-supporting church and perceive the need for more fluid patterns of missionary evangelism which enabled missionaries to live alongside the Hindu population. He was also a champion of the role of Serampore College in providing a broad but advanced Christian education within Bengal, and fought a successful campaign within the society in the 1890s to save the college from threatened closure.

After visiting the West Indies in 1859, Underhill published *The West Indies: their Social and Religious Condition* (1862), the historical importance of which is evidenced by its republication in 1970 by the Negro Universities Press. Subsequently he took part in the violent controversy over the treatment of the black population in Jamaica. Under the title of *The Exposition of Abuses in Jamaica* he published in 1865 a letter, exposing the cruelty of the planters, which he had addressed to Edward Cardwell, the colonial secretary (5 January 1865). A rising of the local population followed in October. The governor, Edward John Eyre, denounced Underhill's pamphlet as an incitement to sedition, and with his champions attempted vehemently to impugn Underhill's accuracy.

In 1869 Underhill made a further deputation journey, to the Cameroons, in an attempt to resolve differences between the leading Baptist missionary Alfred Saker and his colleagues. Owing in large measure to the sympathy evoked by the sudden death in the course of the visit of Emily Underhill on 22 December 1869, his objective was substantially achieved. On his return he devoted himself to missionary organization and literary work, writing, besides magazine articles and accounts of Baptist missions, biographies of J. M. Phillippo (1881), Edward Steane DD (1883), Alfred Saker (1884), and J. Wenger DD (1886). A collection of his papers on missionary subjects was published in 1896 under the title *Principles and Methods of Missionary Labour.*

On 17 July 1872 Underhill married his third wife, Mary, daughter of Alfred Pigeon, distiller, of London. She survived Underhill, and died on 2 December 1908. In 1873 he became president of the Baptist Union; in 1876 he was made treasurer of the Bible Translation Society, and in 1880 treasurer of Regent's Park College, having been a member of its committee since 1857; in 1886 he was elected president of the London Baptist Association. In 1870 the honorary degree of LLD was conferred on him by Rochester University, USA. He died at his home in London, Derwent Lodge, Thurlow Road, Hampstead, on 11 May 1901, and was buried at Hampstead cemetery.

W. B. OWEN, *rev.* BRIAN STANLEY

Sources C. Hall, *Civilising subjects: metropole and colony in the English imagination, 1830–1867* (2002) · E. A. Payne, *The great succession* (c.1938) · B. Stanley, *The history of the Baptist Missionary Society, 1792–1992* (1992) · *Missionary Herald* (July 1901), 347–53 · E. C. Starr, ed., *A Baptist bibliography*, 24 (1976), 92–6 · *CGPLA Eng. & Wales* (1901)

Archives Regent's Park College, Oxford, Angus Library, corresp. and papers · SOAS

Likenesses stipple, pubd 1863, NPG [*see illus.*] · portrait, Baptist House, Didcot, Oxfordshire

Wealth at death £14,749 2s. 10d.: probate, 10 July 1901, *CGPLA Eng. & Wales*

Underhill [*married name* Stuart Moore], **Evelyn Maud Bosworth** (1875–1941), religious writer and spiritual director, was born on 6 December 1875 at Graisley Hill, 183 Penn Road, Wolverhampton, the only child of Sir Arthur Underhill (1850–1939), barrister and a bencher of Lincoln's Inn, and his wife, Alice Lucy Ironmonger (1850–1924), the youngest daughter of Moses Ironmonger, mayor of Wolverhampton, and his second wife, Elizabeth. She was educated at home and for a few years at Sandgate House, a boarding-school in Folkestone. In 1893 she attended the ladies' department of King's College, London, in Kensington Square, where she studied history, languages, art, and botany. Beginning in 1898 she travelled to Italy, where through art and architecture she came, by 'a sort of gradual unconscious growing into an understanding of things' (Menzies, 2.11). Italy was for her 'the holy land of Europe', a place medicinal to the soul. She published several essays as a young girl, and in 1902 her first book, a satirical poem about the law, which was followed by three novels and subsequently by two books of poetry. After her marriage, on 3 July 1907, to Hubert Stuart Moore (1869–1951), a childhood friend, she moved to 50 Campden Hill Square, London, where she lived until a year before her death. There she entertained her barrister husband's colleagues and her many friends. She and her husband shared an interest in yachting with Arthur Underhill. She was a bookbinder, avid gardener, and lover of cats. Having no children, she gave considerable attention to her parents, whom she visited every day.

Although baptized and confirmed in the Church of England, the Underhill parents had no interest in religion; neither did Hubert Moore. Evelyn Underhill's religious sensibilities were ignited aesthetically during her travels to Italy. In 1904 she participated in the order of the Golden Dawn, a fellowship dedicated to ritual spiritualism, and was influenced by Arthur Waite and the Flemish writer Maurice Maeterlinck. Her fascination with spiritualism was short-lived, and she turned to a study of mysticism. Counselled by Robert Hugh Benson, she decided to enter the Roman Catholic church, but she postponed this move because of both her fiancé's opposition and the papal condemnation of modernism, a movement with which she felt allied. The year she married, she began work on her 500-page 'big book'. Based on 1000 sources, *Mysticism: a Study of the Nature and Development of Man's Spiritual Consciousness* (1911) became the standard introduction to the topic in the English language for the next fifty years. She continued to write articles and books on mysticism and to edit mystical texts.

During the First World War, Evelyn Underhill worked at the Admiralty in naval intelligence. These were difficult years, and by her own subsequent account in a letter to the Roman Catholic theologian and her spiritual director, Friedrich von Hügel, she 'went to pieces' (Underhill, *Fragments*, 108). By 1919 she had become a practising Anglican, and soon afterwards sought the counsel of Hügel, who urged her to be more Christocentric in her devotion and

Evelyn Maud Bosworth Underhill (1875–1941), by Powys Evans

incarnational in her work, sending her to serve the poor of North Kensington. After Hügel's death in 1925, Walter Howard Frere and Reginald Somerset Ward served as her spiritual directors. By giving the Upton lecture in religion at Manchester College, Oxford, in 1921/2, subsequently published as *The Life of the Spirit and the Life of Today*, she became the first woman outside lecturer in religion at Oxford University. In this she subjected the experiences of spiritual life to the conclusions of modern psychology. She found participation in the Church of England difficult until 1924, when she began to serve as a retreat conductor. This work and that of spiritual guidance became her vocation for the rest of her life. As an unassuming, attentive, and highly dedicated woman, she was particularly well suited for this work. She gave a retreat for clergy in 1926 and became the first woman to conduct a retreat in Canterbury Cathedral in 1927. She usually gave seven retreats a year, and was especially active at the Retreat House at Pleshey, Essex. Her last major work was *Worship* (1936), a pioneering study of the human response to the divine, in which she displayed her ecumenical spirit and appreciation for the variety of religious expressions. During this time she became interested in the Orthodox communion and joined the Fellowship of St Alban and St Sergius.

Underhill's written corpus was large; she was the author or editor of thirty-nine books and more than 350 articles and reviews, many of which were written for *The Spectator*, where she served as theological editor, and for *Time and*

Tide. She wrote two books under the pseudonym John Cordelier. Acclaimed within Anglicanism, Evelyn Underhill was also honoured as a fellow of King's College, London, in 1927, and the University of Aberdeen awarded her the honorary degree of doctor of divinity in 1939. In that same year she became a pacifist. She joined the Anglican Pacifist Fellowship and wrote several pamphlets and articles on this topic. This vocational commitment to help Christians forgive their enemies continued even during the blitz.

Through her writing on mysticism and the spiritual life and her work as a retreat conductor and spiritual guide, Evelyn Underhill made a pioneering contribution to the understanding of human consciousness and its orientation toward the divine. Afflicted with asthma for many years, she died at home, at 12 Hampstead Square, on 15 June 1941, of a cerebral haemorrhage, and was buried in the churchyard at St John's parish church, Hampstead, on 19 June 1941.   DANA GREENE

Sources D. Greene, *Evelyn Underhill: artist of the infinite life* (1990) · M. Cropper, *Evelyn Underhill* (1958) · C. J. R. Armstrong, *Evelyn Underhill (1875–1941)* (1975) · A. Callahan, *Evelyn Underhill: spirituality for daily living* (1997) · A. Loades, *Evelyn Underhill* (1997) · E. Underhill, *The letters of Evelyn Underhill*, ed. C. Williams (1943) · E. Underhill, *Fragments from an inner life: the notebooks of Evelyn Underhill*, ed. D. Greene (1993) · E. Underhill, *Modern guide to the ancient quest for the holy*, ed. D. Greene (1988) [incl. bibliography] · E. Underhill, *Ways of the spirit*, ed. G. Brame (1990) · T. Johnson, 'Evelyn Underhill's pneumatology: origins and implications', *Downside Review*, 116 (1998), 109–36 · E. Underhill, to F. von Hügel, 21 Dec 1921, U. St Andr. L., special collections department, Underhill–von Hügel MSS · *CGPLA Eng. & Wales* (1941) · b. cert. · m. cert. · d. cert. · L. Menzies, 'A biography of Evelyn Underhill', 1954, U. St Andr. L., special collections department, 2.11 · will, 1 May 1940, King's Lond., Evelyn Underhill MSS, folder 44 · parish register (baptism), Wolverhampton, St John's Church, 30 Dec 1875 · parish register (burial), Hampstead, St John's Church, 19 June 1941
Archives King's Lond., papers, incl. articles, corresp., sermons, sketches, and watercolours · U. St Andr. L., special collections department, Underhill–von Hügel MSS | U. St Andr. L., letters to Margaret Robinson
Likenesses H. Smith, drawing, 1932, repro. in *The Bookman* [supplement] (Dec 1932) · Vandyk, photograph, 1933, repro. in Underhill, *Letters* · P. Evans, drawing, NPG [*see illus.*]
Wealth at death £13,610 2s. 5d.: probate, 29 Oct 1941, *CGPLA Eng. & Wales*

Underhill, John (1544/5–1592), bishop of Oxford, was born at The Cross inn in Cornmarket Street, Oxford, the son of Thomas Underhill, innholder and freeman of Oxford, and his wife, Elizabeth. He entered Winchester College in 1556, aged eleven, and was elected a fellow of New College, Oxford, in 1561; he graduated BA in 1564, and proceeded MA in 1568 and DTh in 1581. In 1570 he was appointed praelector in moral philosophy and in 1575 a proctor of the university. His university career gained from a chaplaincy to the chancellor, Robert Dudley, earl of Leicester, who induced a reluctant congregation to give him a second term as proctor. In 1576, when New College's visitor Robert Horne, bishop of Winchester, and his delegate Thomas Bilson proposed to adjourn their visitation, Underhill and three other fellows objected on the grounds

that this tended to establish a perpetual visitation in derogation of collegiate authority, and were promptly expelled. Leicester's influence and threats of litigation restored Underhill; the same influence overbore two elections by Lincoln College of a member of their own as rector and imposed the outsider Underhill in June 1577. Underhill became vice-chancellor of the university in 1584, the year after the visit to Oxford of the cosmopolitan philosopher Giordano Bruno, when he (it seems) was 'the poor doctor' whom Bruno claimed to have baffled in disputation and left 'a fish out of water' (Bruno, 187).

In 1581 the crown presented Underhill to the rectory of Thornton-le-Moors, Cheshire (valued at £24 7s. 8d.), along with a royal chaplaincy and probably a sub-almonership (he has often been recorded as almoner, but is not officially listed as such). Martin Marprelate suggests Underhill as almoner for the foolish household that he attributes to Archbishop Whitgift and adds that such 'serve thee for no other use, but to work thy ruin and to bewray their own shame and miserable ignorance' (Pierce, 333). The crown presented Underhill in 1585 to Northop, Flintshire, void by the death of Nicholas Robinson, bishop of Bangor, but he probably resigned this and kept a more appropriate living of Robinson's, the Oxfordshire rectory of Witney (valued at £47 9s. 4d. p.a.). He was also joint vicar of Bampton, Oxfordshire, between 1581 and 1585.

Underhill was recommended to the see of Oxford (vacant for twenty years) by Sir Francis Walsingham, according to Harington 'of pure devotion to the leases' of episcopal property thus made renewable—'persuading him to take it as in the way to a better; but God knows it was out of his way every way' (Harington, 149). William Fleetwood, writing to the earl of Derby, associated Underhill's election more with the profit of Robert Devereux, earl of Essex. Elected on 8 December 1589 and consecrated six days later, Underhill only received the see's temporalities, assessed at £481 11s. p.a., in October 1590, generously back-dated two years but in practice depleted by an enforced and disadvantageous exchange of all the episcopal manors except Hook Norton for impropriated ecclesiastical benefices (a resource harder to exploit, especially for an absentee). Essex had procured Underhill a licence to hold the Lincoln rectorship, Thornton, and Witney *in commendam* for life; but this was probably insurance before the temporalities were released, since Thornton received a new incumbent in July 1590 and Lincoln a new rector (Richard Kilbye) in December. It is probably significant, however, that, when Underhill still owed over £343 in first fruits, the queen discharged him under the privy seal 'forasmuch as the revenewes and proffitts of the same … bishopprick ar but smal' (not a problem paying pro rata, if he had really received full value) and so that he might 'be the better able to kepe good hospitalitie according to his degree and serve God and us more quietlie' (PRO, E337/11, m. 139).

The Oxford register of ordinations records, 'their are no orders entered in the tyme of John Underhill … bishop of Oxford for that he never came into his dioces after his consecration' (Oxfordshire Archives, Oxf. dioc. d. 105, p. 263).

All signs of him are in London—appearing at the exchequer in Michaelmas term 1590 to seek to delay payment, assisting at the consecration at Lambeth of John Coldwell as bishop of Salisbury (like Underhill, allegedly nominated for others' financial gain) in December 1591. Underhill, according to Whitgift's register, died on 1 May 1592; according to Harington, 'at Greenwich, in much discontent and poverty', although his nephews were said to have inherited something. He was buried in the cathedral that he had neglected. Thomas Churchyard's epitaph for him praises his life 'in chaste content and single wise', but implies that one explanation for the poverty was Underhill's wish to

> Hold house and table in such state, as though his seat had bin,
> As great as any his estate, whose wealth comes flowing in.
> (Churchyard, 8)

—a curious echo of the problems funding hospitality cited in the queen's first fruits discharge, and perhaps of his insistence on arriving at Lincoln College that the rector's stables be greatly expanded. His university career may have led him to expect more preferment than he ever achieved. JULIAN LOCK

Sources V. Green, *The commonwealth of Lincoln College, 1427–1977* (1979) · J. Harington, *A briefe view of the state of the Church of England* (1653), 148–51 · J. H. Morison, *The Underhills of Warwickshire … an essay in family history* (1932), 210–12 · P. Williams, 'Elizabethan Oxford: state, church and university', *Hist. U. Oxf.* 3: *Colleg. univ.*, 397–440 · F. O. White, *Lives of the Elizabethan bishops of the Anglican church* (1898) · F. Heal, *Of prelates and princes: a study of the economic and social position of the Tudor episcopate* (1980), 227, 250n, 278 · H. Rashdall and R. S. Rait, *New College* (1901) · Wood, *Ath. Oxon.*, new edn, 2.830–32 · T. F. Kirby, *Winchester scholars: a list of the wardens, fellows, and scholars of … Winchester College* (1888), 134 · signet office, privy seal docquet books, PRO, SO 3/1 · exchequer, first fruits office, composition books, PRO, E334/9–11 · exchequer, first fruits office, plea rolls, PRO, E337/11, m. 139 · faculty office register, LPL, F.I/B, fols. 142v–143r · Archbishop John Whitgift's register, LPL · Oxford episcopal register, 1543–1601, Oxfordshire Archives, Oxf. dioc. d. 105, p. 263 · R. Horne, bishop's register, Hants. RO, Winchester diocesan records, 21M65.A1/26, fols. 109ff. [incl. visitation of New College, 1576] · E. Lodge, *Illustrations of British history, biography, and manners*, 2nd edn, 2 (1838), 353 · G. Bruno, *The 'cena de le ceneri': the Ash Wednesday supper*, ed. and trans. E. A. Gosselin and L. S. Lerner (1977), 187 · N. Orsini, 'Appunti su Giordano Bruno in Inghilterra: l'avversario di Oxford', *Giornale Critico della Filosofia Italiana*, 2nd ser., 5 (1937), 41–3 · F. A. Yates, *Giordano Bruno and the hermetic tradition* (1964), 206–10 · *The Marprelate tracts, 1588–1589*, ed. W. Pierce (1911) · L. H. Carlson, *Martin Marprelate, gentleman: Master Job Throkmorton laid open in his colors* (1981) · P. E. McCullough, *Sermons at court: politics and religion in Elizabethan and Jacobean preaching* (1998), 70 [incl. CD-ROM] · H. E. Salter, *Survey of Oxford*, 1, ed. W. A. Pantin, OHS, 14 (1960), 7–12 · T. Churchyard, *A feaste full of sad cheere* (1592)

Wealth at death died 'in poverty': Harington, *A briefe view*, 149

Underhill, John (*c*.1608–1672), soldier and colonist in America, was born in Bergen op Zoom in the Netherlands to John Underhill of Warwickshire, a soldier who died in October 1608, and Honor Pauley of St Ives parish, Cornwall. He married Helena de Hooch (*d*. 1658) at The Hague on 12 December 1628. His marriage record identifies him as an *adelhorst* (cadet) in the guard of the prince of Orange,

and thus he may have seen service in the Dutch campaigns of the late 1620s. In 1630 Underhill emigrated to Massachusetts Bay with the rank of captain to help train the colony's militia. He took an active part in the war against the Pequot nation on the Connecticut coast in 1636–7. In the summer of 1636 he accompanied an expedition against the Pequot and Block Island peoples. That campaign was inconclusive, but on 26 May 1637 he co-commanded a successful surprise attack on a fortified Pequot village, in which 400 to 700 Pequot men, women, and children were killed. Underhill published an account of his experiences entitled *Newes from America* (1638). After returning to Boston, Underhill clashed with Massachusetts authorities over his support for the radical antinomian faction. The court punished his dissent in November 1637 with disfranchisement and forfeiture of his military office. A year later, still openly defiant and suspected of adultery with a neighbour's wife, he was banished from the colony.

Underhill moved to the New Hampshire settlements and became president of the governing board of magistrates at Dover in 1639, styling himself 'governor' to annoy his former colleagues at Massachusetts. His chastening came in 1640: the Boston church excommunicated him in February for refusing to reconcile with them, and he lost his New Hampshire seat the following month. In despair he considered suicide, but the church lifted its sentence in September, following Underhill's public repentance made 'in his worst clothes (being accustomed to take great pride in his bravery and neatness)' (*Journal of John Winthrop*, 334), and the court rescinded his banishment. Nevertheless, he moved to Connecticut in 1642 to try his fortunes there. When another Indian war broke out in the neighbouring colony of New Netherland, Underhill accepted a captaincy from Governor Kieft in September 1643. He plied his old craft with vigour, ravaging native groups on Long Island and reprising his 1637 exploit by attacking and burning a Native American village near Stamford, with the loss of 500 Native American lives.

Though rewarded for his service, Underhill was expelled from the Dutch colony in 1653 during England's naval war with the Netherlands. He seized this latest opportunity, and obtained a commission from Rhode Island colony to harry the Dutch. At the war's conclusion he moved to the New Haven settlements on Long Island. His wife, Helena, died in 1658; she had borne him at least three children: Deborah, Elizabeth, and John. On 16 January 1659 he married Elizabeth Feake (*née* Fones, formerly Winthrop); they had five more children: Deborah, Nathaniel, Hannah, Elizabeth, and David. His second wife was a Quaker, and he may have adopted that faith before his death. When New Netherland fell to the English in 1664, he served as a deputy for Oyster Bay and as high constable for Queens county. His health declining, he was excused from military service in 1671, and died on 21 September 1672 at his estate at Killingworth, Oyster Bay, aged sixty-three, and was buried at Oyster Bay.

LEN TRAVERS

Sources H. C. Shelley, *John Underhill, captain of New England and New Netherland* (1932) · *The journal of John Winthrop, 1630–1649*, ed. R. S. Dunn, J. Savage, and L. Yeandle (1996) · H. Macey Jr, 'Captain John Underhill revised', *New York Genealogical and Biographical Record*, 127/1 (1996), 22–3 · L. Effingham de Forest, *Captain John Underhill, gentleman soldier of fortune* (1934) · C. F. Adams, *Three episodes of Massachusetts history*, [2nd edn], 2 vols. (1892), vol. 2
Archives Mass. Hist. Soc., corresp.
Likenesses oils, priv. coll.; repro. in Shelley, *John Underhill*

Underwood, (George Claude) Leon (1890–1975), artist and art teacher, was born on 25 December 1890 at 145 Percy Road, Shepherd's Bush, London, the eldest of three children (all sons) of (Theodore) George Black Underwood, fine art dealer, and his wife, Rose Ellen Cornelius, dressmaker. Educated at St Michael's primary school, Paddington, and for three years at Hampden Gurney Church of England School, Tyburn, he started work at his father's shop in Praed Street at the age of fifteen. Three generations of Underwoods had been antiquaries and numismatists, and George Underwood wished his eldest son to follow the family trade. However, his exposure to prints—particularly Blake's—inspired Leon with the desire for an artistic career. He left home in 1907 to lodge with a publican, William Goody, at Dulwich. Goody supported Underwood by paying his fees at the Polytechnic School of Art, Regent Street, where he enrolled in 1907. His talent was never in doubt, but his independence of mind and disregard of academic convention led to clashes with art school officials throughout his career as a student, and later as a teacher. In 1910 he won a scholarship to the Royal College of Art, where he studied until 1913. Although he won prizes at the student-run sketch club, he was constantly at odds with the principal, Augustus Spencer. He failed his painting diploma, but passed at a re-sit in 1914.

Underwood spent most of 1914 at Ravanica, near Minsk, Poland (now Belarus), with Edward Armitage, a friend from the Polytechnic. Returning home via Scandinavia on the outbreak of war, they enlisted in the Royal Horse Artillery. They transferred to the 2nd London field battery in 1915, and the following year Underwood was seconded to the Royal Engineers (camouflage division), rising to the rank of captain in 1917. Attacks of gastroenteritis in 1918 and influenza in 1919 permanently altered his naturally plump features, leaving him gaunt. On 3 January 1917 he had married Mary Louise (1890–1978), art teacher, daughter of John Coleman, a railway-carriage upholsterer. They had two sons and a daughter.

In 1919 Underwood took a lease on 12 Girdler's Road, off Brook Green, Hammersmith, which would be his home, studio, and school until his death. He spent a refresher year in Henry Tonks's life class at the Slade School of Fine Art. As he went there on an ex-serviceman's grant, he was ineligible for the prix de Rome, but in 1920 he won the special premium for ex-services students. He baulked at the conditions for the award, which stipulated that the recipient make a study trip to Rome. After lengthy bargaining he persuaded the board to let him spend the money on an expedition to Iceland. In the mean time he joined the staff of the Royal College—numbering Barbara Hepworth among his pupils—and in 1921 opened his own Brook

(George Claude) Leon Underwood (1890–1975), self-portrait, 1921

Green School of Drawing. Students included Henry Moore, Eileen Agar, Blair Hughes-Stanton, and Gertrude Hermes. The pupils, together with other young artists and intellectuals in the Hammersmith and Chiswick neighbourhood, formed a lively and creative coterie. They enjoyed fancy-dress parties at Girdler's Road, but also forged artistic alliances. From this Brook Green circle emerged in 1925 the English Wood-Engraving Society, and in 1931 a short-lived review, *The Island*, which carried artwork by Moore, Agar, and Laurence Bradshaw as well as Underwood's own woodcuts and writings. He was moreover a founder member of the Seven and Five Society, and of the National Society, but he never maintained any institutional commitment for long, and he resisted the regimentation of artistic life. He also avoided developing an 'Underwood style', preferring that each work of art should embody the qualities characteristic of its medium.

Underwood encouraged his pupils to sketch quickly, registering movement as well as outline, as he did in his own drawings. His large figure tableaux in oils, such as *Venus in Kensington Gardens* (1921) and *Peasantry* (1922), are, by contrast, elaborate in composition and relatively static. His etchings—portraits and rural studies executed in 1921 and 1922—and his wood-engravings drew the attention of John Knewstub, director of the Chenil Galleries, Chelsea. Here Underwood had his first exhibitions, and Knewstub arranged the first showing of his sculpture, at the Alpine Club Gallery (1924). A self-taught sculptor, Underwood followed the practice of Henri Gaudier-Brzeska and Jacob Epstein by carving directly into stone or wood. The 1924 exhibition met a mixed reception in the press. The only critic convinced of his worth at this time was R. H. Wilenski, in whose book *Draughtsmen* (1924) Underwood featured.

Meanwhile, Underwood travelled: to Iceland in 1923, and to the painted caves at Altamira, Spain, in 1925. In the United States of America (1925–6) he illustrated books, all for New York publishers, including his own children's rhymes, *Animalia* (1926), and his novel *The Siamese Cat* (1928). An expedition to Mexico (1928) with the American writer Phillips Russell resulted in the book *Red Tiger* (1929), which was richly illustrated with Underwood's drawings and colour lino-cuts. The Mexican experience was to furnish subjects and exuberant colours for many more paintings and prints.

Underwood was now at work on large wood-carvings loaded with esoteric symbolism: *Regenesis* (1930–31) and *The Cathedral* (1930–32). After creating a handful of experimental pictures in a surrealist idiom, he abandoned painting in favour of sculpture in 1932, though he continued to produce watercolour landscapes and countless life drawings. His book *Art for Heaven's Sake* (1934) expounded his views on the sterility of abstract art and the primacy of imagination. These ideas were embodied in the Carrara marble *Mindslave* (1934), subtitled *The Mind in Abject Subordination to the Intellect*. *Mindslave* and *The Cathedral* were prominent in a retrospective at the Leicester Galleries, Leicester Square (1934). The critics were again divided, but Underwood was learning to look elsewhere for appreciation. Fellow sculptors who admired his work at this period included Frank Dobson, Eric Kennington, and John Skeaping. The *African Madonna* (1935) in lignum vitae, commissioned for a school in Johannesburg, was, however, his last major carving.

During the Second World War, Underwood was assigned to the civil defence camouflage establishment at Leamington Spa, without being selected as a war artist. The British Council sent him on a lecture tour of west Africa in 1945, and he went on to write three books about the art of that region, which a new generation of 'primitivist' artists read eagerly. Africa prompted a return to painting, with new rhythmic and geometrical methods of composition. About 1948 he began casting his own bronzes in the studio, often using improvised equipment. He slit and flayed his sculptures to reveal the inner cavities of the hollow cast. These dynamic late bronzes were exhibited by several West End dealers between 1953 and 1973. Underwood shared his interest in the techniques of metal sculpture with such younger artists as Reg Butler, and he now enthused a new generation of students: John Bunting, John Mills, Philip Turner. He accepted commissions for sculptures and murals from corporate and ecclesiastical patrons. His bronze *Pursuit of Ideas* (1960) was commissioned for a housing estate by the London county council. He began to receive critical attention on the continent

when the Antwerp Biennale (1959) exhibited *Mindslave*. This was the occasion of Underwood's meeting Ossip Zadkine; later they would visit one another's studios. A 1962 exhibition in New York led to an interview with *Time* magazine. A retrospective was held at the Minories, Colchester (1969), and Christopher Neve wrote a monograph on Underwood in 1974.

Nevertheless, Underwood resented his neglect by the art establishment when honours were being heaped on his contemporaries. His disappointment, compounded by the early death of his younger son, John, in 1972, coincided with the wane of his artistic powers. His last and most ambitious book, surveying art's interaction with science and religion from Altamira to what he saw as the present decline, remained unfinished despite two decades' work. Underwood died at the Hostel of God, Clapham, on 9 October 1975 and was cremated at Mortlake.

There were two posthumous exhibitions of Underwood's work at the National Museum of Wales, Cardiff: 'Mexico and After' (1979) and 'Pure Plastic Rhythm' (1993). A volume of his wood-engravings was published in 1986, and a catalogue raisonné of his sculpture was included in a monograph by B. Whitworth (2000). Art historians now acknowledge the influence Underwood exercised through teaching and writing, though his *œuvre* itself has received scant academic attention. The Tate collection, the Victoria and Albert Museum, the Ashmolean Museum, Oxford, and the National Museum and Gallery of Wales, Cardiff, all hold some of his works.

BEN WHITWORTH

Sources C. Neve, *Leon Underwood* (1974) • B. Whitworth, *The sculpture of Leon Underwood* (2000) • DNB • WW (1973) • private information (2004) • b. cert. • m. cert. • d. cert. • census returns, 1891 • parish registers, St Luke's Shepherd's Bush
Archives Courtauld Inst., scrapbooks incl. press cuttings • Henry Moore Institute, Leeds • Tate collection, address book, letter, MSS, and notebook | Tate collection, corresp. with J. Rothenstein • Tate collection, letters to R. H. Wilenski, incl. proof of *Art for heaven's sake* • V&A NAL, questionnaire completed for Kineton Parkes
Likenesses L. Underwood, self-portrait, etching, 1921, NPG [*see illus.*] • W. Rothenstein, chalk drawing, 1922, NPG • L. Underwood, self-portrait, oils, *c.*1947, priv. coll. • C. Ware, photograph, 1961, Hult. Arch. • L. Underwood, self-portrait, etching, Bradford City Art Gallery • photograph, repro. in Neve, *Leon Underwood*, figs. 2, 87 • photographs, repro. in Whitworth, *Sculpture of Leon Underwood*
Wealth at death £32,455: probate, 17 March 1976, CGPLA Eng. & Wales

Underwood, Michael (1737–1820), man-midwife and surgeon, was born at West Molsey, Surrey, on 29 September 1737, one of the four sons of John Underwood, who was possibly a clockmaker, and his wife, Dorothy. After being educated first in West Molsey, and then at Kensington, in 1754 he was apprenticed to the surgeon Sir Caesar Hawkins and spent a number of years as house pupil at St George's Hospital, London. After further study in Paris he received the diploma of the Company of Surgeons on 4 October 1764 and established himself in practice at St Margaret's Street, Cavendish Square. It is thought that

Underwood married about this time, and, although the name of his wife is unknown, it is known that he was the father of at least five children. Underwood became friendly with the physician Richard Warren who was instrumental in his being appointed physician to the princess of Wales; Underwood attended the birth of Princess Charlotte on 7 January 1796. Not surprisingly, the move into royal circles did wonders for Underwood's fortunes and 'Having been thus brought conspicuously into notice, his practice rapidly increased, and the road to wealth was opened to him with all its allurements' (Maloney, 294).

However, it appears that material success made Underwood uneasy. A Calvinistic Methodist and a follower of George Whitefield, he recorded his spiritual concerns in a diary which ran to 122 volumes. A heavily edited version appeared in 1823 as *Extracts from the Diary of the Late Michael Underwood*. According to its editor:

> it was the constant practice of [Underwood] to commit to paper the occurrences of each day, for his own personal gratification; thus every minute domestic circumstance, as well as every professional visit, was regularly noted; but his grand object appears to have been that of recording his own religious impressions and religious experiences.   (Maloney, 293)

In 1766 Underwood was elected surgeon practising midwifery at the British Lying-in Hospital, where he also lectured. He published *A Treatise upon Ulcers of the Legs* (1783) and *Surgical Tracts on Ulcers of the Legs* (1784). The work for which he is most remembered is *A Treatise on the Diseases of Children*, first published in 1784, which gave the first description of poliomyelitis. The award to Underwood in 1784 by the Royal College of Physicians of the licence in midwifery brought him into conflict with the Company of Surgeons who fined him 20 guineas for obtaining the licence in midwifery without first gaining their permission. Suffering from what appears to be depression, Underwood retired from practice in 1801. Underwood died at Knightsbridge, where he lived, on 14 March 1820. He had directed that his body should be interred in his vault in 'the Revd. Mr Whitefield's Chapel, in Tottenham Court Road, by the side of my late dear wife and children' (Maloney, 291).   MICHAEL BEVAN

Sources W. J. Maloney, 'Michael Underwood: a surgeon practising midwifery from 1764 to 1784', *Journal of the History of Medicine and Allied Sciences*, 5 (1950), 289–314 · Munk, *Roll* · *GM*, 1st ser., 90/1 (1820), 286
Likenesses J. Zoffany?, portrait, priv. coll.; repro. in Maloney, 'Michael Underwood'
Wealth at death details of will: Maloney, 'Michael Underwood'

Underwood [née Montgomery Cuninghame], **Pamela Richenda Cubitt** (1910–1978), florist and nurserywoman, was born on 10 March 1910 at Ballyfair, co. Kildare, the daughter of Colonel Sir Thomas Andrew Alexander Montgomery Cuninghame, tenth baronet DSO (1877–1945), and his first wife, Alice Frances Denison des Voeux. Her father served in the army until 1919, when he was posted abroad on Foreign Office duties; he spent little time in England from then until his death in 1945. Tutored in her father's interests, Pamela Montgomery Cuninghame had short spells of schooling interspersed with long periods of travel and residence in various southern European countries, recalling that 'as a girl I had wandered over many of the foothills surrounding the Mediterranean and had often been sent clambering up cliffs collecting bits and pieces for the garden' (Underwood, 9). Naturally good at languages, she became secretary to Sir Eustace Percy MP before marrying Captain Thomas Abdy Combe (*b.* 1894/5) of the Grenadier Guards on 20 June 1932 at St George's Church in Hanover Square. They had two daughters, Susan (*b.* 1936) and Elizabeth (*b.* 1939), and divorced in 1941. On 20 June 1942 she married her second husband, Captain Desmond Fitzgerald Underwood (*b.* 1891/2), subsequently press officer at the Admiralty; their only child, John Weston Underwood, was born in 1943.

Pamela Underwood's nursery—growing carnations and outdoor tomatoes—was started about this time at Ramparts Farm, Braiswick, Colchester, Essex. Despairing of Dutch competition and the low rainfall of Essex, she began to specialize in the artemesias, helichrysums, lavender, santolina, senecio, and verbascums, the silver-leaved, scented, and drought-tolerant plants familiar from her Mediterranean wanderings. In this she was encouraged by her father just before he died, and gained inspiration from her young neighbours Andrew and Beth Chatto. Success came from her hard work, the superb quality of her plants, and exhibits at shows, and from her untiring encouragement of flower clubs all over Britain—she was a founder of Colchester Flower Club and chairman for many years. In 1970 she was awarded the Royal Horticultural Society's Veitch memorial medal in recognition of the unfailing high standards of the plants she exhibited at the Chelsea and Westminster shows, which had already won a series of Banksian medals. Her book, *Grey and Silver Plants* (1971), appeared under the name Mrs Desmond Underwood. She was a woman of high standards and great courage; tall, with a loud voice, with her 'slightly stooping figure, ash gently drifting down the front of her London suit from the inevitable cigarette held between her lips, her fine eyes half closed against the smoke' (Chatto) is the image recalled by Beth Chatto and remembered by many who met her, and bought her plants, at the shows. In 1977 for the queen's silver jubilee, Underwood supplied and planted a silver garden at Buckingham Palace as the Royal Horticultural Society's celebratory gift; in the same year she was awarded the Victoria medal of honour, horticulture's highest accolade. She had become affectionately known among gardeners as the Silver Queen. Underwood died on 30 April 1978, her death certified at Essex County Hospital at Colchester. Her great gift to twentieth-century gardeners, her revival of her silver 'weeds', lives on, part of constantly renewed flower settings and plantings by other hands.   JANE BROWN

Sources Mrs D. Underwood [P. R. C. Underwood], *Grey and silver plants* (1971) · private information (2004) [John Underwood, son] · B. Chatto, 'Mrs Desmond Underwood: the Silver Queen', *Hortus*, 2 (1988) · *The Times* (5 May 1978), 16g · b. cert. · m. cert. [Thomas Abdy Combe] · m. cert. [Desmond Fitzgerald Underwood] · d. cert.
Wealth at death £42,007: probate, 2 Nov 1978, *CGPLA Eng. & Wales*

Underwood, Thomas Richard (1772–1835), watercolour painter and geologist, was born on 24 February 1772 at 43 Lamb's Conduit Street, Holborn, London, the only son of Thomas Underwood (d. 1808) and his wife, Susannah (d. 1804/5). Nothing is known of his early education or training in watercolour drawing. At an early age, he married Jane Eleanor Stageldoir, a dancer at Drury Lane, and they had at least two children. There was a separation before 1803.

In company with Turner, Girtin, and many others Underwood worked regularly at the home of Dr Monro, and from 1789 to 1802 he exhibited regularly at the Royal Academy. He was a founder member of the Sketching Society (known as 'the Brothers'). In 1792 he was appointed draughtsman-in-ordinary to the Society of Antiquaries who have a number of his original drawings—engravings of some of these appeared in *Archaeologia* (vols. 11–14). The range of subjects depicted in his works suggests he travelled widely in England and Wales. His circle of acquaintances also included Wordsworth, Coleridge (to whom he was known as Subligno), Southey, and the Wedgwood brothers Josiah, John, and Thomas, possibly through their connection with Dr Beddoes' Pneumatic Institute in Bristol.

In 1800, Underwood became a proprietor of the newly founded Royal Institution, and the following year he pressed Count Rumford to appoint Humphry Davy assistant lecturer there. Shortly after Davy's appointment, he and Underwood holidayed together in Penzance. In 1802, after the treaty of Amiens, he made a visit to France. The following year he agreed at the last minute, as a substitute for Coleridge, to return as secretary–companion to Thomas Wedgwood. They reached Geneva before turning back. Some time after the resumption of hostilities on 16 May 1803 the pair were parted; Wedgwood escaped, but Underwood was arrested at Calais and detained in France until 1814. During this period his financial support was provided by the Wedgwood family through their Paris banker.

For a time Underwood lived with some degree of freedom in Paris until the English were ordered to Verdun. He then went into hiding until 1806 when, with the help of *tribun* Pictet, he was allowed to return to Paris and study at the Louvre. On several occasions he secured a passport to travel to Rigny Ussé and to Roucy to draw landscapes. In Paris he renewed his acquaintance with Rumford, who had settled at Auteuil, and made friendships with many scientists, including Ampère, Humboldt, Thenard, Gay-Lussac, and the Brongniarts. When Napoleon gave Davy special permission to travel through France in 1813, Underwood acted as his escort, introducing him to the scientific community, enabling him to acquire some iodine, taking him to meetings of learned societies and accompanying him to the empress Josephine at Malmaison.

Early in 1814, the allies invaded France and during the siege of Paris it was only the intervention of the empress that allowed Underwood to remain in the city. During the first four months of 1814 he kept a journal of the siege, which was later published in the *London Magazine*, 1825, under the title 'The journal of a détenu'; it gives a unique account of Paris under siege. His detention came to an end with the entry of the allies into Paris and in June he left for England. However, he soon returned to France and made Paris his home for the rest of his life.

With his knowledge of Paris and his friendly manner, Underwood was uniquely placed to welcome visiting English scientists and introduce them to their French counterparts, as may be seen from his correspondence with Adam Sedgwick (1822–9) and Thomas Webster (1820–27) particularly. Underwood's letters were full of the latest scientific intelligence: books about to be published; papers read to learned societies; the current state of scientific debate; opinions on contemporaries. On his frequent visits to England he carried geological specimens and letters which aided the rapid exchange of knowledge, especially the correspondence between Faraday and Ampère on electro-magnetism.

Underwood's own scientific interests seem to have centred on the field of geology, especially the extinct volcanoes of Auvergne and the geology of the Paris basin. His letters to Sedgwick contain carefully drawn and densely annotated sections which reveal him as an accomplished geologist. In London he was a member of the Royal Institution and a member (later fellow) of the Geological Society; in Paris he was a member of the Société Philomathique, the Société Géologique, and the Société Linnéenne. He died on 11 July 1835 at Chamarande, near Paris, and was buried there. The principal beneficiary of his estate in England was his daughter, Eleanor Gawan, and in France his sole executor, one Marie Dassau.

D. L. GARDINER and K. R. GARDINER

Sources T. R. Underwood, 'The journal of a détenu', *London Magazine* (1825), 1–35, 237–56, 385–404, 485–517 • *Memoirs and recollections of the late Abraham Raimbach*, ed. M. T. S. Raimbach (1843) • W. A. Smeaton, 'Notes on British art, 5', *Apollo*, 83 (1966) [*Thomas Richard Underwood*] • A. de Montaiglon, *Archives de l'art* (1862) • J. Challinor, 'Some correspondence of Thomas Webster', *Annals of Science*, 17/3 (1961); 18/3 (1962); 19/1 (1963); 19/4 (1963) • J. A. Paris, *The life of Sir Humphry Davy, Bart. LLD*, 2 vols. (1831) • *Collected letters of Samuel Taylor Coleridge*, ed. E. L. Griggs, 2 (1956) • J. Evans, *A history of the Society of Antiquaries* (1956) • J. G. Alger, *Napoleon's British visitors and captives* (1904) • R. R. Litchfield, *Tom Wedgwood, the first photographer* (1903) • H. Bence Jones, *The Royal Institution, its founder and its first professors* (1871) • Dr Guillemard, 'Girtin's Sketching Club', *Connoisseur*, 63 (1922), 189–95

Archives CUL, Sedgwick archive, Add. MS 7652 • Keele University, Wedgwood archive • U. Wales, Aberystwyth, Webster archive

Wealth at death disposed of property in Chatham and Paris; detailed bequests totalled £1300: will, PRO, PROB 11/1850

Unknown Warrior, the [the Unknown Soldier] (d. 1914?), an unidentified British soldier of the First World War, was buried in Westminster Abbey as a symbolic representative of the British and dominion servicemen who died in that war. About 9 per cent of British males under forty-five died in the conflict, and some northern towns whose pals' battalions were devastated on the Somme or elsewhere lost an even higher proportion. Mortality rates were highest among junior officers, leaving the social and educational élite heavily depleted; of the undergraduates who matriculated at Oxford University in 1913, 31 per cent were killed. The scale of the slaughter and the nature of the war meant that over 300,000 British and dominion dead had no known grave; large numbers of those buried in war graves were unidentified, hence the words inscribed on headstones, 'a soldier of the Great War known unto God'.

The war deaths left British society bereaved, trying to come to terms with what had occurred. About 3 million people lost a close relative, and many more lost members of their extended family, sweethearts, fiancés, and friends, including comrades-in-arms. Some historians, more arithmetical than sensitive, later argued against the concept of a 'lost generation'; to contemporaries it was the reality. Mourning and commemoration took many forms, private and public. Some succumbed to spiritualism but more, like Kipling, refused the road to En-dor. War shrines were improvised, and after the war permanent memorials were erected. The British authorities—for reasons of practicality, expense, and equality—forbade repatriation of war corpses, and in Flanders and elsewhere the Imperial War Graves Commission organized the cemeteries, the 'silent cities', to which some of the bereaved went on pilgrimages.

The impetus for the repatriation and reburial of a symbolic unknown serviceman is usually attributed to the Revd David *Railton, an Anglican army chaplain on the western front. Seeing the inscription 'An Unknown British Soldier (of the Black Watch)' on a grave in a garden near Armentières in 1916, he suggested the idea to Douglas Haig, but received no reply. In August 1920 he wrote to Herbert Edward Ryle, dean of Westminster, proposing that a soldier selected from among those with no known grave should be brought back to England and interred in Westminster Abbey 'to represent all those who fell' (Gavaghan, 9). Railton asked that such a request be put to the king. Fearing that it would 'reopen the war wound which time is gradually healing' (Blythe, 8), George V disliked the idea, and it took the intervention of the prime minister, Lloyd George, to win over the monarch. The matter was then delegated to a cabinet committee chaired by Curzon, who decided on most of the ensuing ceremony.

With the second anniversary of the armistice imminent, the procedure was hurried, and apparently no accurate record was kept. As a result there are conflicting accounts of what was done. On 9 November 1920, army working parties exhumed four (according to some accounts six) bodies of unidentified British soldiers from the areas of the Somme, Aisne, Arras, and Ypres. They were taken to a makeshift chapel at St Pol where, covered and concealed, one was chosen by Brigadier-General Louis John Wyatt, GOC British forces, France and Flanders, and so became the Unknown Warrior. Specially guarded and honoured, he was taken to Boulogne, where he was placed in a casket made of oak from Hampton Court, and taken by HM destroyer *Verdun* to Dover. There the coffin was placed in the passenger luggage van which had previously carried the bodies of nurse Edith Cavell and Captain Charles Fryatt. Crowds awaited the special train at stations *en route* and at Victoria Station.

On armistice day, 11 November 1920, draped with a union flag, the coffin of the Unknown Warrior was placed on a gun carriage at Victoria and, attended by Beatty, Haig, and other admirals, field marshals, and generals, processed through immense and silent crowds to the new Cenotaph in Whitehall. The king, as chief mourner, placed a wreath on the coffin. It was taken to Westminster Abbey where, at a short funeral service attended by the king, cabinet ministers, about a thousand war-bereaved women, and a guard of honour of Victoria Cross holders and others, it was entombed just inside the west entrance. The grave was filled with earth from the main battlefields and initially left covered with the union flag. For the *Manchester Guardian* on 11 November the gathering of holders of the Victoria Cross on that occasion was 'a little democracy of valour' (Ayerst, 393). During that day and those following possibly a million people came: the queue was almost continuous until the grave was sealed on the night of 17 November. It was one of the most striking public demonstrations in British history. In 1921 the present black Belgian marble gravestone, its inscription composed by Dean Ryle, was placed over the tomb. Ryle's inscription declared: 'Beneath this stone rests the body of a British warrior unknown by name or rank brought from France to lie among the most illustrious of the land'.

Predictably the popular press speculated on the identity of the Unknown Warrior. The Curzon committee apparently intended that a corpse from 1914 should be exhumed, and the chosen one was probably a regular army soldier of the original 'contemptible' British expeditionary force, and therefore a young unmarried man in his twenties or possibly an older married reservist recalled from civilian life to the colours. He might have been a Territorial, since the London Scottish and other Territorial units were at the western front from September 1914. He was not navy or air force, a 'new army' volunteer, conscript, or dominion soldier. Yet the Unknown Warrior transcended his former life: he 'stood in for all the missing dead' (Bourke, 237) as a focus of grief and mourning, a surrogate body for those whose beloved one had no known grave.

Railton wanted him called the Unknown Comrade. 'Warrior' was chosen, the designation being intended to cover all branches of the services (though he was often called the Unknown Soldier), all ranks, and both British and dominion dead. Contemporary accounts emphasized his classless, rankless inclusivity. *The Times* stated that he was 'an emblem of "the plain man", of the masses of the people' (Bourke, 250). The vicar of All Hallows', East India Dock, wrote that the Unknown Warrior was 'a symbol of the highest ideal' and his grave 'the glorious tomb of every lad who understands what England in her most exalted and unselfish mood stood for and stands for' (Connelly, 145). The inscription records:

> Thus are commemorated the many multitudes who during the Great War of 1914–1918 gave the most that man can give, life itself, for God, for king and country; for loved ones, home

and empire; for the sacred cause of justice and the freedom of the world.

Those who paid their respects to the grave were likened to pilgrims journeying to a saint's shrine. Although an afterthought to the Cenotaph, the tomb of the Unknown Warrior fulfilled a need that the latter, inherently empty, could not. Bereaved women were especially attracted to the tomb, though former servicemen apparently felt little towards it.

The idea of reburying a symbolic unknown soldier was not new in 1916. Unknown soldiers had been commemorated after the American Civil War, and there had been proposals in France for such a burial following the Franco-Prussian War. Colonel Clive Wigram, private secretary to the king, wrote in December 1920 that the idea had been in existence for some time, and had originated in France. The French Unknown Soldier was buried on the same day as the British, the American in 1921, and others later. The Americans entombed unknown soldiers from their later wars. The Australian Unknown Soldier was buried at Canberra in 1993, the Canadian Unknown Soldier in Ottawa in 2000. None the less, in Britain the Unknown Warrior remains representative of the British and Commonwealth servicemen who died in the First World War and in subsequent wars.   ROGER T. STEARN

Sources M. Gavaghan, *The story of the unknown warrior: 11 November 1920* (1997) · A. Gregory, *The silence of memory: armistice day, 1919–1946* (1994) · R. Blythe, *The age of illusion: England in the twenties and thirties, 1919–1940* (1963) · J. Winter, *Sites of memory, sites of mourning: the Great War in European cultural history* (1995) · J. Bourke, *Dismembering the male: men's bodies, Britain and the Great War* (1996) · *Annual Register* (1920), pt 1, pp. 125–6 · I. F. W. Beckett, *The Great War, 1914–1918* (2001) · M. Connelly, *The Great War, memory and ritual: commemoration in the City and east London, 1916–1939* (2002) · D. Cannadine, 'War and death, grief and mourning in modern Britain', *Mirrors of mortality: studies in the social history of death*, ed. J. Whaley (1981), 187–242 · T. Wilson, *The myriad faces of war: Britain and the Great War, 1914–1918* (1988) · 'En-dor', *Rudyard Kipling's verse: inclusive edition, 1885–1918*, 417–18 · S. C. Hurst, *The silent cities: an illustrated guide to the war cemeteries and memorials to the 'missing' in France and Flanders: 1914–1918* (1929) · D. Ayerst, ed., *The Guardian omnibus, 1821–1971* (1973)

Unna, Percy John Henry (1878–1950), mountaineer and conservationist, was born on 18 January 1878 at 12 Lancaster Gate, London, the fourth son and seventh of the seven children of Ferdinand Unna (1816–1898), merchant, and his wife, Friederike Ruben (*c.*1830–1901). His parents were both born in Hamburg, Germany. Ferdinand became a partner in the firm of Openshaw, Unna & Co., which traded in England and South Africa. The Unnas lived in Cape Town and Manchester, before moving to London in the late 1850s. Ferdinand Unna successfully applied for naturalization in 1861.

Unna was educated at Eton College (1891–6) and Trinity College, Cambridge (1896–9), where he graduated with a first-class degree in mechanical sciences and where he, like many others, developed a taste for mountaineering. He was working as a civil engineer at Grangemouth when he joined the Alpine Club (1904) and Scottish Mountaineering Club (1905). He served in the Royal Naval Volunteer Reserve as a lieutenant-commander in home waters and

Egypt during the First World War. After the war he became involved in developing equipment for Alpine Club expeditions. He designed a high-altitude stove for use on the early Everest expeditions and, with Captain John Percy Farrar and Captain George Ingle Finch, designed the first mountain oxygen apparatus, which was used on the 1922 and 1924 Everest expeditions. He was, however, more closely involved with the Scottish club, and became its president in 1936. With another member, Arthur W. Russell, law agent for the National Trust for Scotland (founded 1931), and the club secretary, Alexander C. Harrison, Unna organized fund-raising among mountaineers throughout Britain to acquire the mountainous parts of Glencoe for the trust in 1935. In 1936, pursuing a suggestion of James M. Wordie, the geologist and polar explorer, Unna again raised funds to secure the estate of Dalness (which included Buachaille Etive Mor and the Glen Etive hills). In both cases Unna made large personal contributions. These purchases were completed in 1937 during Unna's presidency and in a letter from the club to the trust dated 23 November 1937 he recommended ten principles for 'the management of mountainous country acquired for the use of the public' (*Scottish Mountaineering Club Journal*, April 1945, 261) and expressed the hope that they should be applied to other similar tracts of land in Britain. These principles, sometimes known as Unna's Rules, endorsed a minimalist approach to management aimed at preserving the primitive state of the mountains. Perhaps the core principle—and certainly the one which presents the most difficulty for managers—was number 4: 'That the hills should not be made easier or safer to climb', advice that proscribes the provision of new roads, paths, bridges, waymarks, shelters, and places of refreshment. Unna gave other more direct proofs of his abhorrence of mountain 'furniture', being the sole objector to the erection of a Ben Nevis mountain indicator (*Scottish Mountaineering Club Journal*, April 1926, 283), and founding a mysterious Gadarene Club, which had as its sole object the destruction of superfluous waymarking cairns. In a letter protesting about these (*Fell and Rock Climbing Club Journal*, 1942), Unna claimed that he had 'managed to level out from three to four hundred of these ugly piles on but half a dozen Lakeland hills, and I appeal to fellow members to complete the work'. Unna's principles focused on preserving primitiveness and hazard, and on the goal of unrestricted public access, while conserving landscape value and mountain beauty.

Unna's munificence to the National Trust for Scotland continued throughout his life. In 1944 he bought Kintail estate (containing the famous Five Sisters) and in 1950 his funds were used to purchase the Ben Lawers estate, which includes the summits of the group and their southern and western slopes, which are of great botanical importance because of their rich arctic-alpine flora.

When attending a Scottish Mountaineering Club meet at Dalmally on 27 December 1950, Unna fell while climbing on nearby Ben Eunaich and died from head injuries. He was climbing alone—at his own slow pace—because of heart problems, and it may have been these which caused the fall. He was buried in Pennyfuir cemetery, close to Oban. His will donated his libraries and art works to public collections, and left the residue of his considerable estate to the National Trust for Scotland to be used in the purchase of further mountain properties. His mountainous country fund was used by the trust to assist the purchases of Goatfell (1958), Grey Mare's Tail (1962), Torridon (1967), and several others.

Unna was self-effacing and modest. His enormous contributions in time and money to the National Trust for Scotland in its formative years were made under the strictest possible anonymity. His libraries (navigational, mountaineering, and engineering) were offered to the London Library, the Cambridge Alpine Club and University Mountaineering Club, and the Institute of Civil Engineering respectively, with the condition that 'no marks of identification or ownership be placed'. He even shunned photography: most photographs show him turning away from the prying lens, or deliberately moving his head. Neither is much known of his character, since he wrote so little, though his obituarists and other commentators mention impish humour and a fondness for radical opinions and for good-natured but determined argument.

Despite Unna's efforts at concealment, it is now acknowledged that the mountain heritage of Scotland owes more to the perception and generosity of this Englishman of German-Jewish descent than it does to any of its natives; and Unna's place in the movement to preserve mountains from damaging development is also assured. His simple but far-sighted principles were endorsed and championed in the decades following his death by mountain writers such as William H. (Bill) Murray and Rennie McOwan; they govern the management policies of the National Trust for Scotland and anticipated many features of present-day wilderness management around the world.   ROBIN N. CAMPBELL

Sources will of Percy J. H. Unna · G. S. Russell, 'Glencoe & Dalness: how it all began', *Heritage Scotland* (autumn 1987), 10 · R. McOwan, 'Man of the mountains', *Heritage Scotland* (spring 2000), 30–32 · *Fell and Rock Climbing Club Journal* (1942) · P. J. H. Unna, 'Preservation of Scottish mountain land for the nation', *Scottish Mountaineering Club Journal* (April 1945), 261–2 · W. N. Ling, 'Percy John Henry Unna', *Scottish Mountaineering Club Journal* (April 1951), 338–9 · W. N. Ling, 'Percy John Henry Unna', *Alpine Journal* (May 1951), 116–17 · N. S. Finzi, 'Percy J. H. Unna', *Alpine Journal* (May 1951), 117–18 · P. J. H. Unna, 'The oxygen equipment of the 1922 Everest expedition', *Alpine Journal* (May 1922), 235–50 · NL Scot., Unna MS Acc. 11538/275 · b. cert.
Archives NL Scot., Acc. 11538/275
Wealth at death £152,875 17s. 8d.: probate, certified Edinburgh, 1951, *CCI*

Unstead, Robert John (1915–1988), historian, was born at Firth Dene, Stanhope Road, Deal, Kent, on 21 November 1915, the son of Charles Edmund Unstead, a Post Office clerk and telegraphist, and his wife, Elizabeth Nightingale. He later told how he 'took up writing seriously at the age of 9' (Unstead), when he was awarded the East Kent Wolf Cubs' prize for an essay on the British empire. Educated at Dover grammar school (1926–33), he won a scholarship to Cambridge but could not afford to go and instead trained as a teacher at Goldsmiths' College, London (1933–6). The proceeds of the sale of a couple of short stories to an evening newspaper paid for an engagement ring and he married Florence Margaret Thomas (b. 1917) on 27 May 1939 at St George the Martyr's Church, Deal; she was a chemist's assistant and the daughter of Oswald Frederick Thomas, a collier. They had three daughters. He taught from 1936 to 1940, when he joined the RAF and became a sector controller on combined operations in Normandy, Greece, and Italy. In 1946 he was appointed headmaster of Norton Road primary school, Letchworth, and in 1951 of the Grange School, Letchworth, where he remained until 1957. Thereafter he concentrated on writing.

Unstead reviewed for the *Times Educational Supplement*, producing protests from publishers as he scorned the turgid, matter-of-fact approach of many contemporary textbooks, declaring most history books to be written in a way calculated to put children off the subject for the rest of their lives. The publishers A. and C. Black took up his challenge and his *Looking at History*, published in four books (1953), constituted a new approach to the teaching of history in primary schools. As he remarked in the foreword to the *Middle Ages* volume, 'You will not find very much about kings, queens and battles in this book … this is a book about everyday people and things'. Unstead wrote what might be termed 'inclusive history'; his book *Castles* in 1970, for example, also dealt with fortified houses used in border warfare, showed how and why castles were built, defended, and attacked, and included a chapter entitled 'How to visit a castle'. He aimed to stimulate the reader's imagination about life as it was lived. The *Times Literary Supplement* wrote of him that 'his narrative is always clear and his style direct and forceful'. He was also concerned for accuracy and possessed of a passionate patriotism. On the cover of book 4 of *England: a History* (1963) he reproduced John Piper's window from the new Coventry Cathedral, and his philosophy was encapsulated in the book's foreword:

> at a time when it is fashionable in some quarters to belittle England's achievements in the past and to doubt her place in the future, I have tried to show that whereas England has often acted foolishly or badly, her history shows the persistence of ideals which good men have lived by since Alfred's day.

The popularity of Unstead's books—over 8 million copies were sold of *Looking at History* alone—was based on perhaps two things above all else: his capacity for simplification, which was compared with Arthur Mee's in an earlier generation, and his recognition that most twentieth-century children preferred an illustrator's impression of a historical event to an authentic contemporary picture. His books were richly illustrated so as to bring history to life; his texts were tautly written. In more than fifty books he covered many civilizations ancient and modern—Greece and Rome, Egypt, the British empire, Australia especially—and he was able to make children's reference books, like the generously illustrated *History of the English-Speaking World* (1972), as fascinating as fiction. The books were often keenly priced and they sold exceptionally well;

they appealed to children and teachers as basic texts and as sources for the topics and projects so popular in primary and middle schools in the 1960s and 1970s. To Unstead's delight, they were sometimes bought as Christmas and birthday presents.

Many of Unstead's titles were published overseas and this led to invitations to the United States, east Africa, and Australia, for example. His most ambitious work, *A History of the World* (1983), was targeted at a wider readership and was also a decided success. A small boy at a prep school wrote sorrowfully to ask whether Unstead could write a series about the ancient world which he had to study. The result was *Looking at Ancient History* (1959)—another bestseller.

Unstead was a modest and humorous man who aroused much affection by his balance between heart and brain which put people of diverse backgrounds at ease. He worked hard for his fellow authors: he was founder and chairman of the Educational Writers' Group of the Society of Authors (1965–8); a member of the Council of East Anglian Writers (1976–88); and he campaigned vigorously for the Public Lending Right. He remained interested in education long after he left teaching, and was a governor of Leiston middle school (1973–85). He gave freely of his time to young authors in particular and retained to the end a boyish enthusiasm as well as an outspokenness which marked him as an honest man and a sincere friend. He accepted philosophically that his early ambition to become a high-flown literary critic and novelist was not to be fulfilled. At the time of his death, from heart failure, at Ipswich Hospital, on 5 May 1988, he was working on a new book on the 1940s with his youngest daughter Sue, a children's publisher.

A keen golfer and gardener, a devoted follower of cricket, Unstead was above all a family man. He was survived by his wife and their three daughters. In the words of Sean Lang in *Teaching History*, 'not one single writer of children's history has yet even approached the eminence or creative productivity, never mind the affectionate esteem, which were the hallmarks of R. J. Unstead' (Lang, 26). He was deservedly promoted by his publishers as 'the young person's historian'. As he remarked in his Dean lecture to Goldsmiths' College, in 1985, he 'wanted children to begin to understand that the past was different from the present and that it is unfair to judge people of the past by the standards and ideas of to-day' (Unstead).

G. R. BATHO

Sources S. Lang, '"Mr History": the achievement of R. J. Unstead reconsidered', *Teaching History*, 58 (Jan 1990), 24–6 · *The Times* (5 May 1988) · *Daily Telegraph* (9 May 1988) · 'R. J. Unstead, British children's writer', *Annual Obituary* (1988), 265–7 · private information (2004) [Florence Unstead] · b. cert. · m. cert. · d. cert. · Historical Association textbook collection, U. Durham, School of Education [G. R. Batho] · R. J. Unstead, Dean lecture, Goldsmiths College, London, 1985, priv. coll.

Wealth at death £128,380: probate, 3 Aug 1988, *CGPLA Eng. & Wales*

Unton [Umpton], **Sir Henry** (*c.*1558–1596), diplomat and soldier, was born at Wadley, the second son of Sir Edward Unton (*d.* 1583) of Wadley, near Faringdon, Berkshire, and

Sir Henry Unton (*c.*1558–1596), by unknown artist

his wife, Anne *Dudley (1538–1587) [*see under* Seymour, Jane], the eldest daughter of Edward *Seymour, duke of Somerset, and widow of John Dudley, earl of Warwick.

Family and education Sir Edward Unton belonged to a Berkshire family that traced its pedigree to the time of Edward IV. He had been knighted at Queen Elizabeth's coronation in January 1559 and was sheriff of the county in 1567–8. He owned property in Oxfordshire, including the borough of Burford, and in 1566 was chosen at a by-election to serve as a knight of the shire there. In the elections to the parliament of 1571, despite his distinguished marriage and clear protestant leanings, Sir Edward Unton was defeated in a bitter contest to be the junior knight in his native Berkshire. The defeat led to an affray at the October quarter sessions when a man was killed. His principal opponent, Sir Henry Norris, subsequently brought a case against him in Star Chamber. The following year, however, with Norris about to be elevated to the peerage, he was successful in becoming Berkshire's senior county MP and he entertained the queen at Wadley in July 1574, presenting her with a lavish gift. The same year one of his sons (William) joined him as the junior county MP for Berkshire in a by-election. Sir Edward died on 16 September 1583 and was buried in Faringdon church. The privy council declared his wife, who was always known as the countess of Warwick, of unsound mind in October 1582. She died in February 1588. The elder son, Edward, succeeded his father as county MP in 1584 and 1586. He then accompanied the earl of Essex on the Portugal voyage in 1589 and died at Plymouth on his return.

Henry Unton was educated, like his elder brother, at Oriel College, Oxford, where he supplicated for a BA in October 1573. He became a student of the Middle Temple in 1575 and then went on a European tour. Whereas a fragment of his father's itinerary for his tour of 1563–4 survives in the British Library, Henry Unton's peregrinations must be deduced from scattered records: he visited the French Midi (where he met Henri de Montmorency-Damville, the influential governor of Languedoc), Padua, and Venice. By then his father's preferred son, Henry, had returned to marry the young and rich Dorothy Wroughton (d. 1634), eldest daughter and heir of Sir Thomas Wroughton of Broad Hinton, Wiltshire, in 1580. His father had instructed him 'to govern himself' by Walsingham's advice and 'those of the religion' and, at the time of his father's death, Unton looked to him for an office (Nichols, li). However, it would be with the assistance of the earl of Leicester and through the chancellor, Sir Christopher Hatton, his 'friend in any thinge' concerning his 'benefitt, honor or reputacion', and in whose service he had been 'first bred up', that he would also secure advancement (Correspondence, 58). He was appointed the royal keeper of Cornbury Park in Oxfordshire in 1583 and elected MP for New Woodstock in 1584 (probably with the support of Leicester and Sir Henry Lee, the high steward), and he was most likely the Umpton who intervened in the debate on a Cloth Bill with mercantile realism. He served as JP in Oxfordshire from c.1583, becoming its deputy lieutenant from 1587 to 1593. He was afterwards a JP and deputy lieutenant for Berkshire from 1593.

In June 1586 Unton accompanied William Hatton, the chancellor's nephew and heir and Unton's lifetime friend, to the Netherlands carrying a letter from Burghley to Leicester. They distinguished themselves militarily during the duke of Parma's attack on Zutphen on 22 September 1586, when Sir Philip Sidney was fatally wounded. Leicester knighted them on 29 September and accompanied their return to England with a commendatory dispatch to Walsingham on their courage. They were among the twelve knights of Sidney's 'kindred and friends' at his funeral in St Paul's.

Diplomatic career For the next period Unton was mainly occupied in managing his inherited estates, buying two further manors in Berkshire to consolidate his influence. It is possible, but unproven, that he accompanied his brother on the Portugal expedition in 1589. By 1591, however, with Leicester and Walsingham dead, Unton's appointment as resident ambassador to France in July that year was probably the result of the influence of Hatton and Robert Cecil. As his accompanying letters of instruction (dated 24 July 1591) made clear, he was sent to ensure that the army of the French king, Henri IV, was fully deployed alongside the English expeditionary forces under the earl of Essex in Normandy and Sir John Norris in Brittany. He was also to secure the repayment of debts due to the English crown and to oversee the interests of English merchants. He went with an elaborate retinue that required forty-six post-horses to transport it to Dover.

After arriving in Dieppe on 4 August, he promptly succumbed to a 'yellow jaundice', from which he required over a month and the services of a London physician to recover. During that period the queen proposed to withdraw the Normandy forces. When Unton (who had been instructed to stay in Normandy until Henri IV arrived) exceeded his instructions and journeyed in military armour to his first audience with Henri IV at Vervins in Picardy in October, the queen delivered a stinging rebuke. Unton was left to apologize lamely for his 'want of experience' (Correspondence, 115).

Unton was impressed with Henri IV and the respect was mutual. He reminded Burghley that the French king was juggling with inadequate resources to fight a civil war on numerous fronts, which explained in large measure his failure to intervene more promptly in Normandy. In November 1591 the French king finally arrived to lay siege to Rouen, and Unton accompanied the French army regularly until his recall in May 1592. He was 'close by' when Henri IV was wounded at the skirmish at Aumale (Correspondence, 291). In the spring of 1592 he issued a challenge to a duel to the young Charles, duke of Guise, who was reported to have spoken 'impudently, indiscreetly and overboldly' of Queen Elizabeth (Fuller, Worthies, 1811, 1.91–2). Nothing transpired, although Unton is said to have reissued the challenge three times. He also took part in the skirmish at Yvetot on 21 April 1592, where his servants took one Spaniard captive and killed another. By then, however, the Normandy campaign had run its unsuccessful course. Seriously alarmed at the French king's enthusiasm for a personal meeting with the English queen, Essex pleaded on Unton's behalf for his release. The warrant was issued on 4 May 1592 and he returned to court on the following 17 June. The embassy cost him dearly. He was forced to retain a large retinue 'for my garde and safety' and to the 'excessive dearnes of this countrey occasioned by warres', where 'Intelligences were never so deare', were added the costs of horses—he lost eleven in the journey to the king at Vervins alone. He complained bitterly of the 'discomodities of a runninge campe, wherein we have neither lodginge nor good victualls' and, on 18 January 1592, he had all his money and clothing stolen, leaving him with only the nightshirt he was wearing (Correspondence, 243, 244, 256). The queen's sympathies were distinctly lukewarm: 'she did bothe pittie, and yett thought strange howe it should be doane, you having soe many servants' (ibid., 282).

Doubtless with these debts in mind, Unton sued for profitable office with greater urgency, turning to Essex for assistance and breaking with Cecil. This latter alienation probably contributed to Unton's nemesis at the parliament of 1593, to which he had been returned as the senior knight for Berkshire. He sought an active role and was appointed to several committees. But it was on the subsidy committee that he made his main contribution, supporting a triple subsidy in early March on the grounds of the known menace of Spain and the papacy and the needs of 'preserving a brave and worthy king of our religion' in France. At the same time he defended the rights of the

Commons to make the decision on their own and accused an unnamed minister of preparing a list of trouble-makers in the Commons for the queen. Cecil energetically defended himself and Elizabeth reacted with extraordinary hostility. As Essex reported directly to Unton, she 'startles at your name, chargeth you with popularity and hath every particular of your speeches in Parliament without book' (*Salisbury MSS*, 4.68; dated 24 October 'about 1590' in the calendar, but clearly later). Unton was left without hopes of court office and trying to mend his fences with Cecil, suing 'that I may depend on you after the old manner and end where I began' (ibid., 4.362).

The earl of Essex became the focus of Unton's prospective fortune. He acted as his property manager in Berkshire and Oxfordshire and enjoyed familiar relationships with him. It was Essex who secured his reappointment as resident ambassador in France in December 1595. (His pay was dated from 30 November and he may have left court on that date, awaiting his instructions to be forwarded the following month; Bell, 100.) The original draft of his instructions bears corrections by Cecil and Burghley and is endorsed 16 December 1595. He also carried additional 'remembrances' from Cecil, two further sets of instructions, and a private autograph letter from the queen (PRO, SP 78/16, fols. 113, 129, 131, 151). With Henri IV actively negotiating a peace with the duke of Mayenne, the fears of English ministers that this would be succeeded by a French peace with Spain were far from unfounded. Unton's mission was to sustain French enmities with Spain, but he was given next to nothing with which to do so beyond the queen's new-found interest in meeting the French king, if he still 'had a meaning to have stepped over into England' (Murdin, 707). On the contrary, he was to give the French king the unpalatable news that she would withdraw her remaining troops in Brittany and to explain her reluctance to come to his assistance in Picardy. Essex, who dispatched his secret advice to France (dated 23 December 1595), hoped to use the mission, however, to wrong-foot Cecil and others who doubted the dangers of a separate French peace with Spain. Unton met Henri IV at Coucy-le-Château on the Flemish border for his main initial audience on 13 February 1596. Despite a characteristically elaborate display of affection from Henri IV towards Unton and his English sovereign (the latter involving a cameo portrait of the queen that the king begged him for), the French council reacted badly to Unton's message, calling it a 'discours du foin' (ibid., 706).

Unton was humiliated by the mission, 'wishing I had spent twice as much as my Jorney will cost, that I had not been employed therein'. His friends back home had already made it known that he was a 'disgraced man'. He accompanied the French king to the siege of Spanish forces at La Fère and promptly fell dangerously ill with 'a violent, burning Fever' (Murdin, 701, 730). The French king visited him in person on 14 March, despite being advised not to do so because it appeared to be the contagious 'purple fever' (*Salisbury MSS*, 6.99). Although he rallied for a while, Unton died just over a week later, on 23 March

1596. On 1 April, Henri IV sent the queen a generous appreciation of her ambassador's virtues. Unton's body was taken to London in a black ship and transported on a baron's hearse (since he died an ambassador) to Wadley to be buried in Faringdon church with elaborate pomp on 8 July. A substantial monument there, damaged subsequently during the civil war and rebuilt afterwards on the west transept of the church, was erected in his memory by his widow.

Unton was a lover of music, an accomplished linguist, and a literary patron. His library was inventoried at his death and contained 220 volumes. In 1581 Charles Merbury acknowledged that 'he was not a little incouraged' by Unton in preparing his *Briefe Discourse of Royall Monarchie*, an early sketch of Bodinian ideas in English, to which Unton also supplied a preface. Robert Ashley, the son of a Middle Temple friend of Unton, dedicated his Latin translation of Du Bartas's *L'Uranie, ou, Muse celeste* to him in 1589. Matthew Gwinne served him as his physician in France and Thomas Edmondes was apprenticed as secretary to Unton's embassies. A copious collection of Latin verse was published in his memory by Thomas Wright, his chaplain in France (*Funebria … H. Untoni*, Oxford, 1596). He was a scrupulous and observant traveller, keeping a diary (parts of which survive) of 'all the places of our marchinghe and in campaigne, and of the enemy, and of all other things of valewe' in France in 1591–2 (*Correspondence*, 322). He may well have composed, or had cause to have written, the interesting 'Government of France', a detailed account of the nature of French government that appears to date from his second embassy (PRO, SP 78/16, fols. 211–26). He certainly wrote a 'Discourse of ambassages', or a treatise on being a good ambassador, which is now lost. He received an honorary MA from the University of Oxford along with William Hatton on 14 July 1590. His dispatches were studied by Dudley Carleton, John Chamberlain, and others in the early seventeenth century as exemplary of the diplomatic art that England's continental engagement in the 1590s had remarkably cultivated.

Unton died intestate without direct heirs and left an encumbered estate with debts said to have amounted to £23,000. His personal possessions were valued at £1446. His sister Cicely, wife of John Wentworth, was granted letters of administration of his affairs. Disputes over the inheritance between her and the three daughters of his sister Anne and Valentine Knightley were only finally settled by an act of parliament in 1597. His widow retained Faringdon and other properties during her lifetime. She retired to Broad Hinton, where Dudley Carleton reported her mourning Unton's death, 'her voice tuned with a mournful accent, and her cupboards (instead of casting bottles) adorned with prayer-books and epitaphs' (*CSP dom.*, 1595–7, 265).

The most famous and highly unusual portrait of Unton was acquired by the National Portrait Gallery in 1884. It was commissioned by Unton's widow and completed by an unknown artist after the monument in Faringdon church had been erected. A horizontal panel measuring 740 by 1632 cm, at its centre is a portrait of Unton writing at a table on which the cameo jewel of the queen that he had shown to Henri IV is visible. This is surrounded by a sequential narrative of his career flanked by the figures of Fame and Death in the top right-hand and left-hand corners respectively. The scenes include his birth, his studies at Oxford and his European tour, the masque celebrating his marriage, his embassies, and his death and burial.

M. GREENGRASS

Sources *The correspondence of Sir Henry Unton, knt: ambassador from Queen Elizabeth to Henry IV, king of France*, ed. J. Stevenson (1847) • J. G. Nichols, *The Unton inventories: with a memoir of the family of Unton*, Berkshire Archaeological Society (1841) • W. Murdin, *A collection of state papers relating to affairs in the reign of Queen Elizabeth from the year 1571 to 1596* (1759) • T. Birch, *Memoirs of the reign of Queen Elizabeth, from the year 1581 till her death*, 2 vols. (1744) • *Calendar of the manuscripts of the most hon. the marquis of Salisbury*, 24 vols., HMC, 9 (1883–1976), vols. 4–6 • HoP, *Commons, 1558–1603* • R. B. Wernham, ed., *List and analysis of state papers, foreign series* (1964–2000), 1592–3 • R. B. Wernham, ed., *List and analysis of state papers, foreign series* (1964–2000), Jan–Dec1595 • *CSP dom.*, 1581–95 • G. M. Bell, *A handlist of British diplomatic representatives, 1509–1688*, Royal Historical Society Guides and Handbooks, 16 (1990) • R. B. Wernham, *After the Armada: Elizabethan England and the struggle for western Europe, 1588–1595* (1984) • P. E. J. Hammer, *The polarisation of Elizabethan politics: the political career of Robert Devereux, 2nd earl of Essex, 1585–1597* (1999)
Archives BL, letterbook, Add. MS 38137 • BL, manuscript collections, Cotton MSS | BL, Cotton MSS, Caligula E. vii–ix; Titus B. ii • BL, Lansdowne MS 68 • BL, Add. MS 4114–4117 • BL, Stowe MS 166 • Bodl. Oxf., MS 3498 • HMC, Hatfield House, Hertfordshire, Salisbury [Hatfield] MSS • LPL, MS 651 • PRO, SP 78/25–28; 35–7
Likenesses oils, *c*.1596, NPG • M. Gheeraerts the younger, portrait • oils, Arundel Castle, West Sussex [*see illus.*] • panel, NPG • portrait; formerly priv. coll., 1899

Unwin, George (1870–1925), historian, was born at 2 Brook Street West, Stockport, Cheshire, on 7 May 1870, the eldest of the six children of Edward Unwin, innkeeper, and his wife, Priscilla, *née* Whitaker (*d.* 1919), of a local nonconformist tradesman's family. Having attended the Edgeley Wesleyan day school in the town, he left at thirteen to work in the office of Carrington's hat firm, where he wrote for his employer speeches and letters to the press.

In 1890 Unwin won a scholarship to the University College of South Wales and Monmouthshire, Cardiff; he lodged with an uncle and had to skimp on £20 per annum. Three years later, a classical scholarship took him to Lincoln College, Oxford; in 1897 he gained a first in Greats and a bursary from Oriel College for six months' residence in Germany. There he studied economic history under Gustav Schmoller, reacted against Schmoller's championing of the state, and acquired a cosmopolitan outlook.

In 1899, after his return to England, he became secretary to Leonard Henry, first Baron Courtney, a Liberal politician and convinced individualist. Courtney's mistrust of imperialism, so destructive of indigenous cultural heritages, complemented Unwin's view that the mainspring of progress in society was to be found in voluntary associations of people for the common good, whether in guild, trade union, or chapel.

On 7 March 1902 Unwin married Frances Mabelle (*b.* 1869/70), an artist and third daughter of the Revd Mark Guy Pearse, a prominent Wesleyan minister whose biography she later wrote (1930). They had no children. His

first full-length book, *Industrial Organization in the Sixteenth and Seventeenth Centuries* (1904), analysed the growth of corporate and other bodies in England, with plentiful cross-references to similar continental arrangements. He was elected a fellow of the Royal Historical Society in 1906.

In 1908, the year in which he published—again in a European context—*The Gilds and Companies of London*, Unwin was appointed a lecturer in economic history at Edinburgh University. The harsh climate took its toll on his slight frame, weakened by the undernourishment of his earlier years, and in 1910 he accepted the professorship of economic history at Manchester, the only chair of that subject in the British empire. He projected full-scale works on several topics, but most remained unwritten. For he was a man with a mission, resolved to carry his ideas about voluntary groups and the social geology of towns to as many intra- and extra-mural audiences as possible. He regularly rewrote his lectures, pasting new versions over the old until each sheet had the thickness of cardboard. If many listeners were baffled by his complex train of thought, they became inspired by his enthusiasm. He was at his best with graduate students, being supervisor or mentor to, among others, Richard Henry Tawney, Thomas Southcliffe Ashton, and Alfred Powell Wadsworth.

A small man, with a triangular face and lofty brow fronting an outsize brain, Unwin had an elfin quality which was emphasized by his semi-ironic, if sometimes passionate, way of talking. In the First World War, regarding violence as abhorrent, he joined the Union of Democratic Control and other peace-seeking groups, but did his bit by covering for absent colleagues with extra teaching and administration. He also stepped up his extension lectures and classes.

Prematurely aged by the war, insomniac, dyspeptic, and increasingly deaf, Unwin remained industrious in peacetime. No less prolific of new ideas for books, he published two, partly written by others: *Finance and Trade under Edward III* (1918) and *Samuel Oldknow and the Arkwrights* (1924). The latter, in portraying the firm and its industry as growing organisms, marked him out as the forerunner of a coming academic discipline. In the words of H. M. Larson, there 'he came to the very threshold of business history' (*Guide to Business History*, 1948, 14).

Unwin's weak heart was by then inflicting on him spells of physical exhaustion; as a pick-me-up, he relied on long-vacation visits to continental cities, whose histories he enjoyed tracing. During the summer of 1924, however, atrocious weather in Italy terminally weakened him. Mentally buoyant and a music-lover to the last, on his deathbed he and his wife resolutely sang their way through Handel's *Messiah*. His heart gave out on 30 January 1925, at his home, 47 Heaton Road, Withington, Manchester. His widow subsequently wrote a life (1928) of the Bristol philanthropist Ada Vachell.

T. A. B. CORLEY

Sources R. H. Tawney, Introductory memoir, in *Studies in economic history: the collected papers of George Unwin*, ed. R. H. Tawney (1927) • T. S. Ashton, Introduction, in G. Unwin, *Industrial organization in the* *sixteenth and seventeenth centuries* (1963) • R. H. Tawney, *Economic Journal*, 35 (1925), 156–7 • *Manchester City News* (30 Jan 1925) • *The Times* (2 Feb 1925) • *The Times* (7 Feb 1925) • G. W. Daniels, *George Unwin: a memorial lecture* (1926) • T. S. Ashton, 'Recollections of four British economic historians', *Banca Nazionale del Lavoro Quarterly Review*, 158 (Sept 1986), 337–52 • *Lancashire: biographies, rolls of honour* (1917), 386 • b. cert. • m. cert. • d. cert.

Archives JRL, papers, incl. material on Bolton

Likenesses photograph, 1913, repro. in, ed., *Studies in economic history*

Wealth at death £4003 13s. 7d.: probate, 1 April 1925, *CGPLA Eng. & Wales*

Unwin, (Emma) Jane Catherine Cobden (1851–1947), suffragist and radical, was born on 28 April 1851 at Westbourne Terrace, London, the fourth of the six children of Richard *Cobden (1804–1865), radical politician and statesman, and his wife, Catherine Anne (1815–1877), the youngest daughter of Hugh Williams, timber merchant, of Machynlleth, Montgomeryshire, and his wife, Elinor. After the death of their elder brother in Germany in 1856, Cobden's daughters formed a remarkable sisterhood in late Victorian and Edwardian Britain. The eldest sister, Kate (1844–1916), married Richard Fisher, a Sussex neighbour, who was to become a valuable recruit to the Cobden Club set up in 1866 in honour of their father. Ellen Millicent Ashburner (1848–1914), having married and then divorced (in 1899) the artist Walter Sickert, was to write several novels redolent of her father's life. Jane's younger sister (Julia Sarah) Anne Cobden-*Sanderson (1853–1926), the wife of the Arts and Crafts bookbinder and printer Thomas J. Cobden-Sanderson, gravitated towards the Independent Labour Party and was to be imprisoned as a suffragette in 1906. Only the short life of Lucy Elizabeth Margaret (1861–1891) was to prove relatively uneventful.

Having grown up in the shadow of a remarkable politician to whom they had been very close, on Cobden's premature death the sisters, and their mother, were left with a keen desire to protect his memory. Jane, educated intermittently by governesses and at small private schools in London, Southport, and Paris, became the most intimately involved in the family manoeuvres which led to the discontinuance of the edition of Cobden's correspondence which his political friends (also in large part the family's financial benefactors) had wished to publish and to its replacement by John Morley's *Life of Cobden*, published in 1881. After the death of their mother, the Cobden sisters, living independently in London, found many friendships among their father's political allies, but expanded into an artistic and literary cultural milieu which included the novelist George MacDonald and William and Jane Morris. Also among Jane's friends were several early advocates of women's suffrage, and in 1875 she decided 'No more aimless wanderings abroad for me, I shall enter into the Women's Suffrage Campaign and so have a real interest in life' (diary, Cobden MS 1071). This resolution took some years to mature, but from 1880, after several more extensive journeys abroad, especially to Algiers, Jane Cobden played an active role in women's Liberal politics, especially promoting women's suffrage within the Women's Liberal Federation. In 1888 she supported the majority of members of the National Union of Women's Suffrage Societies, who favoured continued agitation through the Liberal Party, and as a founder member of the Women's Suffrage League she and Lady Sandhurst were the first women elected to the new London county council in 1889. Prematurely white-haired, quietly dressed, but striking in appearance, Jane sat for Bow and Bromley, where George Lansbury had ably managed her election. However, the legality of her position was questioned in a series of actions brought by Walter de Souza, with the result that, while she continued to serve on the council until 1892, she faced financial penalties and was not able to vote at its meetings; only in 1907 would women acquire full rights in local government.

Jane Cobden remained active in the suffrage cause (she represented the Women's Franchise League at the World Congress of Representative Women in Chicago in 1893), but she was never a single-issue politician. In the 1880s she had also taken up with enthusiasm the cause of Irish home rule. She visited Ireland several times, most prominently in 1887 as part of the English women's mission to Ireland, and she lectured extensively in England for the Home Rule Union. She also took up the claims and supported the families of many prisoners and evicted tenants in Ireland, the 'victims' of English misgovernment. Many of her father's friends had become Unionists, but one of them, Thomas Bayley Potter, warmly approved her conduct, for 'You are true to the living and just instincts of your father. … You know your father's heart better than John Bright does' (Potter to Jane Cobden, 27 Oct 1887, Cobden MS 1065).

Like many women's activists at this period, Jane Cobden had regarded marriage as secondary to a fulfilling career, but on 9 February 1892, at the relatively late age of forty-one, she became the wife of Thomas Fisher *Unwin (1848–1935), a leading avant-garde publisher (at this time he published Conrad, Ibsen, Somerset Maugham, Nietzsche, and Olive Schreiner) and keen alpinist. Their marriage was one of genuine affection and devotion, even if on occasion The Jane, as she was known at the press, exercised an intrusive interest in its work. With Unwin, too, she was ready to take up a variety of causes, including international arbitration, Congo reform, and the rights of native peoples, and during the Second South African War she acted as secretary to the women's section of the pro-Boer South African Conciliation Committee. Most notably, ever anxious to advance her father's political principles, in 1903 she took up the defence of free trade against Chamberlain's tariff reform crusade, coining the term the 'hungry forties' and vindicating it in an evocative and brilliantly successful tract of that title. This, together with other numerous contributions from the Fisher Unwin press, did much to turn free trade into a progressive Edwardian cause. Fostered by the Fisher Unwins, the cult of Cobden burgeoned in his centenary year (1904), with his old Sussex home, Dunford House, becoming a much-visited 'shrine'. Jane Cobden Unwin also took a keen interest in the neighbouring village of Heyshott, especially its working men's Cobden Club, which she had helped found in 1879. In 1913 she published *The Land Hunger: Life under Monopoly*, a minor addition to the literature of Edwardian land reform, but one which did not repeat the success of its predecessor; significantly, her sister Anne (there was some jealousy between them) had preferred to enlist their father's memory on the side of land nationalization.

Jane Cobden Unwin was a woman of sentiment and enthusiasm who took up (and sometimes speedily dropped) causes with a fire which brooked no opposition. In the years immediately before the First World War she acted on behalf of the wives and children of strikers in east London and Dublin as well as appealing on behalf of starving Arab women and children in Tripoli. She also acted as secretary of the Emma Cons memorial committee (Cons had also served on the LCC), its funds ultimately going to the Old Vic, originally set up by Cons as a coffee music-hall but turned into a theatre of national repute by Cons's niece, Lilian Baylis. During the First World War, Jane's strong interest in South Africa revived, and within the Anti-Slavery and Aborigines' Protection Society she became an inconveniently outspoken opponent of the segregation policy embodied in the Native Land Act of 1913. After the war she also took up with great personal generosity the cause of the victims of the Black and Tans, remaining a leading British sympathizer with the cause of Irish freedom.

Jane Cobden Unwin's idealism also led to her presenting Cobden's former home to the London School of Economics (LSE) in 1919, hoping thereby to inspire a new generation with her passions; she was, however, speedily disappointed, Beatrice Webb recording 'the poor lady, because she cannot ensure that the use of the place corresponds to her dreams, is regretting the gift' (B. Webb, diary, 2 May 1923); in 1923 the school sold Dunford back to the Fisher Unwins, although Jane remained a governor of the LSE until 1928. Dunford House instead now became a significant centre for international meetings devoted to the Cobdenite causes of free trade, peace, and goodwill, with a series of conferences and lectures, enlisting the help of valuable recruits such as F. W. Hirst and the American internationalist N. M. Butler. Jane also spent much time obsessively arranging and rearranging Cobden's papers before gradually and selectively depositing them in the British Museum. Following Fisher Unwin's death in 1935, Jane Cobden Unwin, now in her eighties, led an increasingly solitary life at her home, Oatscroft, near Dunford House, but occasionally wrote to the press on Cobdenite points. She died at Whitehanger Nursing Home in Fenhurst, Surrey, on 7 July 1947.   A. C. HOWE

Sources W. Sussex RO, Cobden papers · University of Bristol Library, Jane Cobden Unwin MSS · BL, Jane Cobden Unwin MSS, Add. MS 52416 · P. Hollis, *Ladies elect: women in English local government, 1865–1914* (1987) · S. Millar, 'Middle class women and public politics in the late nineteenth and early twentieth century: a study of the Cobden sisters', MA diss., U. Sussex, 1985 · J. Schneer, 'Politics and feminism in "Outcast London": George Lansbury and Jane Cobden's campaign for the first LCC', *Journal of British Studies*, 30 (1991), 63–82 · BLPES, London School of Economics archives · Beatrice Webb diaries, BLPES, Passfield MSS · S. Unwin, *The truth about a publisher* (1960) · *Midhurst Times* (12 July 1947) · J. S. Rogers, *Cobden and his Kate: the story of a marriage* (1990) · CGPLA Eng. & Wales (1947)

Archives BL, papers, Add. MS 52416 · NRA, papers · University of Bristol Library, corresp. and papers · W. Sussex RO, Cobden MSS | BLPES, LSE archives · BLPES, Lansbury MSS

Likenesses E. Osborn, photograph, c.1888 (after portrait), University of Bristol Library, Jane Cobden Unwin MSS · pencil sketch, 1890, W. Sussex RO, Cobden MSS, 802; repro. in *The Illustrated American*

Wealth at death £13,791 12s. 11d.: probate, 7 Oct 1947, CGPLA Eng. & Wales

Unwin [*née* Cawthorne], **Mary** (*bap.* 1723, *d.* 1796), friend of William Cowper, was baptized on 21 July 1723 at Downham, Isle of Ely, Cambridgeshire, the daughter of William Cawthorne, a draper of Ely who retired to Huntingdon, and Jane Tingey. In 1744 Mary married Morley Unwin (1703–1767), son of Thomas and Martha Unwin, a clergyman who had been educated at Queens' College, Cambridge. Ordained, and appointed master of the free school in Huntingdon in 1729, he served also as lecturer to the two churches in that town. Unwin gave up these posts in 1743 when he was presented to the rectory of Grimston in Norfolk, an appointment which enabled his marriage. It was there that Mary Unwin's two children were born (William Cawthorne Unwin [*see below*]; Susanna, 1747–1835). The isolation of the place, and its lack of good society, told upon her, however, and in 1748 she persuaded her husband to return to Huntingdon.

In September 1765, through her son William, Mary Unwin became acquainted with William *Cowper (1731–1800), and their common commitment to evangelical principles and piety quickly led to friendship. In November, Cowper took up residence in her home as a paying guest. With him and her children Mary Unwin now spent her days in serious conversation, playing the harpsichord for the singing of hymns, and in rural walks. This idyllic existence ended abruptly on 2 July 1767 when Morley Unwin died after being thrown from his horse. Mary Unwin decided immediately to move her household to some place where an evangelical clergyman officiated, and at Michaelmas travelled with Susanna and Cowper to Olney in north Buckinghamshire, where John Newton was curate. Here they finally took up residence in a house fronting on the market square. In 1772 Susanna's engagement to Matthew Powley, vicar of Dewsbury in Yorkshire, threatened to leave her mother without a chaperone; the obvious solution was for Cowper to marry Mary Unwin, and they became engaged. But Cowper, bound by secret vows to his cousin Theodora, could not go through with this. He had always seen Mary rather as a maternal figure, sent to replace in some degree the mother he had lost (Cowper to Mrs Cowper, 11 March 1766).

Cowper broke down completely in January 1773, falling into a state of despair from which he never fully recovered. From this time onwards, Mary Unwin's household lived permanently on suicide watch. Her care enabled Cowper slowly to return to something like an outwardly normal life; she encouraged his interests in drawing, gardening, and especially in writing verse. In 1786

Lady Hesketh, Cowper's cousin, provided the means to enable Mary Unwin to move with Cowper to a better house in the nearby village of Weston Underwood, closer to their friends the Throckmortons of Weston Hall. In 1791 Mary Unwin suffered the first of a series of strokes; a visit to William Hayley's home in Sussex in 1792 did not bring the hoped-for improvement, and by the autumn of 1793 her movements and speech were severely impaired. In 1795 the Revd John Johnson, Cowper's cousin, took charge of her and of Cowper, caring for them in his home, latterly at East Dereham in Norfolk. There Mary Unwin died on 17 December 1796. She was buried in the parish church on 23 December, with a memorial inscription by William Hayley.

Mary Unwin's son, **William Cawthorne Unwin** (1745–1786), was born at Grimston, Norfolk, on 15 March 1745. He was educated at Charterhouse School, and Christ's College, Cambridge (BA and second chancellor's medal for classical studies, 1765; MA, 1767). Unwin was ordained deacon in December 1767, and the following year undertook with success the curacy of Comberton, Cambridgeshire. In his will Morley Unwin had entrusted the material arrangements of his son's career to his brother John (d. 1789), a successful ecclesiastical lawyer, and two months after his ordination as priest in May 1769 William was presented by the bishop of London to the combined rectories of Stock and Ramsden Bellhouse, near Chelmsford, Essex, where John Unwin owned property and the advowson. Probably through his uncle's influence, William was elected a governor of Christ's Hospital school in London in 1779. In the following year he overcame his scruples against pluralism to accept further patronage from his uncle in the shape of the neighbouring rectory of Ramsden Crays. While he may have owed his position to his uncle's wealth and influence, he proved to be a conscientious parish minister.

Unwin's humanity is evidenced by his successful campaign to have the county gaol heated in winter. In a sermon on Romans 13: 7, *The Sinfulness of Buying Run-Goods* (1773), he courageously presents civil and religious arguments against smuggling, then a popular practice in Essex. His argument against the drinking of contraband tea reveals acute observation of social gradations in a provincial town. The evil does not end with his readers' dishonest enjoyment:

> your Children and Maid-servants must have their Tea too, once, if not twice, a day; and mark the consequences:—your Children, as unable to buy Tea of the fair Trader as yourselves, are brought up in the iniquity you have taught them; while the Servants marrying, and surrounded with a poor family, will rather let themselves and their children want decent clothing, than go without their Tea. (*The Sinfulness of Buying Run-Goods*, 15)

His tract, *Friendly Reproof and Instruction to those that Seldom Attend Public Worship*, was distributed by the SPCK, and reached a seventh edition by 1788. In 1786, while travelling with his friend Henry Thornton, he contracted a 'putrid fever' (typhus), and died at Winchester on 29 November. Cowper composed a Latin epitaph for his burial place in Winchester Cathedral, but it was dropped in favour of an English one (Cowper to W. Park, 17 May 1793; *GM*, 63, 1793, 217).

William Unwin married (before 31 March 1770) Anne Shuttleworth (d. 1825). They had three children: John (1775–1843), Mary Anne or Marianne (1779–1799), and William (1781–c.1800). His decision to educate his sons at home rather than at a public school is celebrated in Cowper's dedication of *Tirocinium* (1785). John was admitted to Queens' College, Cambridge, in 1792 (BA, 1797); in 1804, when he married, he was working at the Treasury. Seven years after his father's death he proposed to visit his grandmother at Weston Underwood, but she felt unable to sustain the emotional strain, and Cowper wrote a gently worded letter to put him off (29 October 1793). A few days later, Cowper paid his final tribute to his beloved companion in the lines 'To Mary'. JOHN D. BAIRD

Sources *The letters and prose writings of William Cowper*, ed. J. King and C. Ryskamp, 5 vols. (1979–86) · Venn, *Alum. Cant.* · *DNB* · R. E. Spiller, 'A new biographical source for William Cowper', *Publications of the Modern Language Association of America*, 42 (1927), 956 · C. Ryskamp, *William Cowper of the Inner Temple, esq.: a study of his life and works to the year 1768* (1959), 167–70 · *IGI* · J. Peile, *Biographical register of Christ's College, 1505–1905, and of the earlier foundation, God's House, 1448–1505*, ed. [J. A. Venn], 2 (1913) · E. P. Gibson, *The annals of Ramsden Bellhouse*, ed. F. W. Austen (1927), 7, 31–2 · C. Unwin, *The Unwin family … genealogical tree*, rev. J. D. Unwin and R. Jennings (privately printed, London, 1947) · *GM*, 1st ser., 56 (1786), 1094, 1116 · *GM*, 1st ser., 57 (1787), 3, 637 · *GM*, 1st ser., 63 (1793), 217

Likenesses R. Cooper, stipple, 1823 (after A. Devis, c.1750), BM, NPG; repro. in *Private correspondence of William Cowper*, ed. J. Johnson, 2 vols. (1824), vol. 2 · H. Robinson, stipple, pubd 1836 (after W. Harvey), NPG · H. Robinson, stipple, pubd 1836 (William Cawthorne Unwin; after drawing by W. Harvey; after Gainsborough), NPG; repro. in *The works of William Cowper*, ed. R. Southey, 15 vols. (1835–7), vol. 2

Wealth at death over £5500 for his children's education; to John £2500; to William £1000 and 'my property in the Orphan Stock'; to Mary Ann £2000; remainder left widow adequately provided for; William Cawthorne Unwin: will, 22 Dec 1786

Unwin, Nora Spicer (1907–1982), wood-engraver and illustrator, was born on 22 February 1907 in Tolworth, Surrey, the youngest, with her twin sister, Nancy, of five children of George Soundy Unwin (d. 1950) and Eleanor Mary, *née* Eady. The Unwin family had been involved in printing and publishing for several generations, founding a printing company (Unwin Brothers) and two different publishing houses (T. Fisher Unwin and later George Allen and Unwin) in the nineteenth and early twentieth centuries, and from an early age the children were exposed to the processes of book-making. Nora attended Surbiton high school, and went on to study at Leon Underwood's studio in London (1923–5), the Kingston School of Art (1925–7), and the Royal College of Art (1927–31). During her childhood wood-engraving had begun a vigorous revival and was used not only for the production of prints but also for book illustration. Her artistic training included various techniques, of which wood-engraving and book illustration were the most important for her future career.

In 1925, while still at college, Unwin received her first commission, from her great-uncle, the publisher T. Fisher Unwin, for a black and white drawing for the dust jacket for a children's book by Edith Nesbit (*Five of Us and Madeline*). Many of her engravings depict scenes from nature, and one of the early books she illustrated in this way was Charles Elton's *Exploring the Animal World* (Allen and Unwin) in 1933; in the same year she illustrated the Allen and Unwin Christmas catalogue with cartoon-like pen sketches. She also engraved prints and from 1930 entered the annual exhibitions of the Society of Wood Engravers. In 1932 she was admitted as an associate of the Royal College of Art, and in 1933 became an associate of the Royal Society of Painter-Etchers and Engravers and a fellow in 1946. During her lifetime she made more than 200 wood-engravings, many of which were used for book illustrations. Unwin was also a watercolourist and used other techniques for her book illustrations, but it is on her engravings that her reputation rests. In 1938 Campbell Dodgson, keeper of prints and drawings at the British Museum, chose her engraving *Antelope and Young* as the cover illustration for *Prints of the Year 1938*, which guaranteed her recognition as one of the country's leading wood-engravers. Her work after that date, done mostly in North America, only added to her stature.

In 1937, through her sister Nancy, Unwin met Elizabeth Yates, an American writer who was living in London with her husband William McGreal. Though this relationship was at first a purely professional one, with Yates and Unwin collaborating on magazine articles and children's books, it blossomed into a solid partnership and a lifelong friendship with both Yates and her husband. After the American couple returned to the United States in 1939, Unwin spent the war years in England, caring for children who had been evacuated to the countryside for its relative safety. Fortunately this gave her time to continue engraving and illustrating books, and with Gwendy Caroe, the mother of the children she was looking after, she wrote and illustrated *Lucy and the Little Red Horse* (1943). It was through Yates that Unwin obtained her first American commission in 1942, to illustrate *Under the Little Fir*, and in 1949 Unwin accepted an invitation for an extended stay with her friends in New Hampshire. She lived in New England for the rest of her life, with just short visits back to her family and friends in England.

In the United States, Unwin illustrated many more books, her best perhaps being the twenty-five engravings she did for John Kieran's *Footnotes on Nature* (1947). She also produced many engravings, and for many years taught wood-engraving at the Sharon Arts Center, Sharon, New Hampshire, and in various other schools and centres in New England. She wrote at least fourteen books for children, exhibited at Sharon and at many other galleries including the Print Club of Albany, New York, and at the Boston Atheneum. In 1952 she was elected to the Society of American Graphic Artists, and in 1953 was admitted as an associate of the National Academy of Design in New York, the American counterpart of the Royal Academy. In 1976 she was elected a full lifetime academician for her outstanding work as a graphic artist and engraver; this placed her firmly in the front rank of her profession. Predeceased by her sister Nancy in 1980, Nora Unwin died, unmarried, in Wayland, Massachusetts, on 5 January 1982. There is a major collection of her engravings at the Sharon Center, and she donated correspondence and books to the McCain Library at the University of Southern Mississippi.

ALAN HORNE

Sources L. C. McGoldrick, *Nora S. Unwin: artist and wood engraver* (1990) · *The Times* (18 Jan 1982) · A. Garrett, *A history of British wood engraving* (1978) · A. Garrett, ed., *British wood engraving of the 20th century: a personal view* (1980) · www.lib.usm.edu/~degrum/html/research/findaids/unwin.htm, 15 Feb 2000 · T. Balston, *English wood-engraving, 1900–1950* (1951)
Archives Sharon Arts Center, Sharon, New Hampshire · University of Oregon, Eugene, notebooks | University of Southern Mississippi, de Grummond collection

Unwin, Sir Raymond (1863–1940), engineer, architect, and town planner, was the younger son of William Unwin (1827–1900) and his wife, Elizabeth Sully, of a family from Bridgwater, Somerset, with shipping interests in the Welsh coal trade. His father had inherited a tannery at Rotherham, Yorkshire, and it was at Whiston, near Rotherham, that Raymond was born on 2 November 1863. In 1874 William Unwin, whose mother had the reputation of being a local bluestocking, gave up his management of the tannery business and moved with his family to Oxford. There he enrolled in middle age for a degree as an unattached student, before transferring in 1877 to Balliol College and graduating in the following year. Unwin senior became a private tutor, frequented progressive circles, and made the acquaintance of Arnold Toynbee and the Revd Samuel Barnett, promoter of the settlement movement and other charitable projects in the East End of London. Raymond was devoted to his father and owned a framed photograph of him inscribed: 'One who leaned upon the rod of duty'. Oxford also exerted a lasting influence upon him: he attended Magdalen College School, heard Ruskin and Morris lecture, and imbibed the subtle and accretive virtues of the city's topography.

Early career Unwin contemplated entering the Church of England, as his elder brother William did. But he was diverted (to his father's disappointment) into a life of social activism, reputedly on the advice of Samuel Barnett, who bade him ask himself which concerned him more, humanity's sinfulness or its unhappiness. Another influence may have been his friendship with the charismatic radical and homosexual Edward Carpenter, who had left the church and after some years as a university extension lecturer settled in the Sheffield and Chesterfield area from 1878. After declining a scholarship offered at Magdalen College, Unwin in 1881 took up an engineering apprenticeship with an affiliate of the Staveley Coal and Iron Company at Chesterfield. This was the home town of a brother-in-law of his father, Robert Parker (1828–1901), branch manager of the Sheffield Banking Company. Among Parker's children Unwin became intimate with his two cousins Ethel (1865–1949), his future wife, and (Richard) Barry *Parker (1867–1947), his future partner. A formal engagement with Ethel was forbidden until 1891, because of Unwin's *risqué* friends and socialist ideals; they were eventually married (by civil ceremony) in 1893.

Sir Raymond Unwin (1863–1940), by George Charles Beresford, 1922

Unwin spent much time in the 1880s at the 'simple life' community founded at Millthorpe near Chesterfield by Carpenter, who described him in retrospect as 'a young man of cultured antecedents … healthy, democratic, vegetarian' (E. Carpenter, *My Days and Dreams*, 1916, 131–2). But for two years from early 1885 he worked as an engineering draughtsman in Manchester. Here he threw himself into political agitation. He became branch secretary of William Morris's newly founded Socialist League, met Morris himself and Ford Madox Brown (then completing his paintings for Manchester town hall), contributed to the league's magazine, *Commonweal*, and made other political friends, notably Bruce Glasier (1859–1920), who stimulated his interest in architecture.

The failure of the league's Manchester branch, coupled with growing self-education in co-operative theory, converted Unwin to a reformist and technical view of socialist progress, which he never henceforward abandoned. He found new political outlets in the Ancoats Brotherhood (founded in 1889) and the Labour church (established in 1891). In 1887 Unwin returned to the Staveley Coal and Iron Company as chief draughtsman, at first designing mining equipment, then grappling with the poor standards of layout and facility offered by the company's colliery housing. This led in 1894 to Unwin's first formal collaboration with Barry Parker (then fresh from his articles as an architectural pupil) on the design of a simple church for the mining community of Barrow Hill. Unwin devised the strategy and layout and Parker the aesthetic detail; and such, as a rule, was to be the division of labour in their later working relationship.

Architectural partnership There followed the formal architectural partnership of Parker and Unwin, run between the brothers-in-law on an easy and amicable basis between 1896 and 1914. It was at first based in Buxton, whither the Parker family had now moved. Housing was always the focus: initially the internal planning of the middle-class home or artisan's house, then the grouping of small houses, and finally complete suburban and civic layouts, as Unwin's mastery of all sides of 'the housing

question' grew. The partners' early practice consisted largely of arts and crafts homes for progressive businessmen, furnished with ample living-rooms and inglenooks in the manner of M. H. Baillie-Scott or C. F. A. Voysey. But in *The Art of Building a Home*, which they published in 1901, such designs alternate with picturesque, communal groups of working-class cottages round an open green, with plans offering bigger living-rooms at the expense of the outmoded front parlour.

In 1902 appeared the first of Unwin's planning tracts, *Cottage Plans and Common Sense*, which declared war on back extensions and called for lower housing densities. In the next year, following a talk by him at the Garden City Association's Bournville conference, Parker and Unwin secured their first important planning commission. This was for laying out suburban factory housing at New Earswick, York, for the Quaker cocoa manufacturer Joseph Rowntree, in response to the impassioned report of his son Seebohm Rowntree on social conditions in York, *Poverty: a Study of Town Life* (1901). At New Earswick the design of the cottage housing itself, in a rationalized vernacular manner, was still the partners' main focus. Not so at Letchworth, the first garden city, with a target population of 33,000, the plan for which Parker and Unwin won in a limited competition promoted by Ebenezer Howard's Garden City Association later in 1903. The concept of the self-sufficient garden city promoted by Howard in *Garden Cities of Tomorrow* (1898–1902) having been entirely diagrammatic, Unwin was in effect asked to endow Letchworth with an image and identity. This raised issues of industrial and civic planning, phasing, and investment on a scale that no British architect had hitherto faced. The plan was revised in 1905–6, when work at Letchworth commenced. The housing areas got the earliest attention, Unwin tackling road layout, grouping, plot size, style, and supervision with originality and a remarkable perception of the complex issues. But Letchworth's civic centre, which was allotted an axial approach perhaps derived from Wren's plan for rebuilding London, grew too slowly for the ideas of Parker and Unwin to be carried through, and remains a grave disappointment.

Despite Unwin's critical role at Letchworth, where he lived between 1904 and 1906, he never identified wholly with Howard's obsession with autonomous garden cities on virgin sites detached from metropolitan influence, and indeed left further work at Letchworth to Parker after 1914. His main concern henceforward was the general improvement of housing standards. He took on numerous commissions and consultancies for garden suburbs and co-partnership housing on the outskirts of cities— many of them curtailed by the First World War. Much the most successful was Hampstead Garden Suburb, Middlesex, first formulated in 1905 but commenced to a radically revised plan only in 1907. Here Unwin's mature grasp of the aesthetics of picturesque housing layout (in which the ideas of the Austrian planner Camillo Sitte and study of German medieval towns played a strong part) and a fine, accessible location on the fringes of Hampstead Heath helped the project to success. He also had the doughty support of the suburb's chief promoter, Henrietta Barnett, wife of Unwin's early mentor Samuel Barnett, in securing a private act of parliament to circumvent irksome building by-laws. This enabled the Parker and Unwin office to realize the most sophisticated of all their plans, ringing the changes on short rows of houses with deep gardens, culs-de-sac, open courts, advanced and recessed frontage lines, boundary hedges, a varied geometry of open spaces, 'vista-stoppers' for sight-lines, and skewed road junctions. Again, however, the centre, in part entrusted to Edwin Lutyens and commenced only after the housing was well advanced, remains an uncompleted hole in the suburb's heart. The Unwins moved in 1906 to Wyldes, a farmhouse on the southern edge of Hampstead Garden Suburb, which remained their home until his death.

Town planning The garden suburb as envisioned by Parker and Unwin (rather than the garden city as adumbrated by Howard) spread internationally with notable speed, in particular to Germany, Belgium, and the United States. A key to this was Unwin's book *Town Planning in Practice* (1909), a shrewd concoction which combined technical information, quaint medievalizing sketches, and even qualified homage to the formal 'City Beautiful' movement of American origin, which Unwin by no means disdained. Many consultancies and invitations followed, and in 1910 he organized the Town Planning conference of the Royal Institute of British Architects. This represented the peak of the British garden city movement's international influence.

After the passing of the Housing and Town Planning Act of 1909, which promised much but delivered little, Unwin's chief ambition became to create a national planning framework for imaginative, low-density housing. His personal credo was set out in the pamphlet *Nothing Gained by Overcrowding* (1912), which sought to show that, because of the heavy price of road making, 'by-law' development in terraces at high density cost almost as much as low-density garden suburb development at between twelve and fifteen dwellings per acre with all the houses round the edges of a large block and generous internal common gardens. The economic assumptions in this document are questionable. But it commanded huge moral authority, led between the world wars to the American housing 'superblock', and was still a force in what became known as 'perimeter planning' in 1960s Britain.

In December 1914, some months after dissolving his partnership with Parker, Unwin embarked on a public career by taking over from Thomas Adams as chief town planning inspector to the Local Government Board. His hope was to push through planning schemes formulated under the 1909 act. But in July 1915 he was seconded as chief housing architect to the wartime Ministry of Munitions. This marked the start of Unwin's influential alliance with Christopher Addison, then minister of munitions, and a renewed connection with Seebohm Rowntree. Teams under Unwin built munitions housing at

Gretna and Eastriggs on the Solway Firth and at Mancot Royal, near Chester, which prefigured the plainer manner of cottage housing after 1918.

In July 1917, with Addison now minister of reconstruction, Unwin was appointed to the Local Government Board's Tudor Walters committee. Its task was to report on 'the methods of securing economy and despatch' in providing working-class dwellings across the country after the war. By now it was clear to Unwin that adequate housing for the nation could not be secured without a concerted municipal programme, based on the direct subvention from central government that had been signally missing at Letchworth and in the garden suburbs. His was the dominant hand in the bold, progressivist tone of the Tudor Walters report, published in October 1918, which called for obligatory state provision of housing via local authorities. In June 1919 the Ministry of Health took over housing responsibilities from the Local Government Board, with Addison as its head. Addison immediately pushed through the Housing and Town Planning Act of 1919, which endorsed the Tudor Walters recommendations and ushered in universal local-authority housing. It was accompanied by a *Housing Manual* largely drafted by Unwin, now chief housing architect to the Ministry of Health, with layouts and house plans following simplified models of the Parker and Unwin idiom. In tandem with all this, Unwin encouraged the infant Building Research Board (now the building research establishment) to experiment with new structural and material solutions for the coming housing programmes.

The high expectations of the 1919 Housing Act went unfulfilled: inflation savagely reduced the number of houses constructed, and Addison crumbled under the strain. Nevertheless, nearly 200,000 dwellings were built, and the model of development prescribed by Unwin survived the Addison Act and was endorsed with less generous space standards in the 'Wheatley' Housing (Financial Provisions) Act of 1924. Down to his retirement from the ministry in December 1928, Unwin continued to work persuasively with successive ministers of health, notably Neville Chamberlain, for his ideal of well-planned, low-density housing.

For the remainder of his life Unwin called indefatigably for a wider vision of planning, turning his experience to issues of city size, shape, land values, compensation, and transport. An immediate focus was the unwieldy, 45-strong, Greater London regional planning committee, inaugurated by Chamberlain to bring coherence to London's inexorable growth. Unwin had already studied metropolitan planning in some depth during the First World War, in collaboration with the London Society. Between 1929 and 1933 he acted as the committee's full-time technical adviser and wrote the bulk of its reports. His recommendations for a regional planning authority made no headway in a period of slump, but he made a trenchant case for a London green belt and satellite towns. Both were to be fulfilled: the former by piecemeal purchase and negotiation after Labour won the London county council in 1934, the latter after Unwin's death, following the report of the royal commission on the distribution of the industrial population (to which he gave evidence) and the New Towns Act of 1946.

Later years Unwin was president of the Royal Institute of British Architects from 1931 to 1933, received the institute's gold medal in 1937, and was knighted in 1932. He was president of the Town Planning Institute in 1915, and of the International Federation for Housing and Town Planning between 1928 and 1931. He travelled much in his later years, notably to the United States, where his daughter, Peggy, had married Curtice Hitchcock, a member of Woodrow Wilson's peace delegation. His contacts with Lewis Mumford, Clarence Stein, and other American planners were close, and he was marginally involved in the planning of Radburn, New Jersey, in 1928. He took a close interest in President Franklin D. Roosevelt's New Deal housing programmes, and met the Roosevelts in the course of a Rockefeller-funded international housing commission in 1934. From 1936 Unwin accepted a visiting professorship for four months of the year at Columbia University, New York, where his manner in the studio was appreciated. Stranded in 1939 by the outbreak of war, he was still in the United States when he fell ill and died at Old Lyme, Connecticut, on 28 June 1940, aged seventy-six. His ashes were eventually interred at Crosthwaite church, Cumberland.

It may be claimed that Raymond Unwin had a greater beneficial effect on more people's lives than any other British architect. Creative ideas for improving cottage plans and housing layout had been developed, notably in the factory villages of Bournville and Port Sunlight, before he adopted them. But he fought for them and refined them at every technical and political level, and succeeded in carrying through a national and to some extent international revolution in housing standards. Adamant in his zeal for the benefits of low-density planning as against either undisciplined sprawl or multi-storey flats in cities (which he consistently opposed), he won his case through quiet powers of persuasion united with technical concentration.

Unwin's approach to planning touched a deep and enduring chord in English attitudes towards the home. But it was unfortunate that his campaign against the high costs of road making in housing development should have coincided with the coming of the automobile, to the growth of which, despite his advocacy of the separation and screening of arterial roads by means of 'parkways', he could offer no fully developed response. Though not an intellectual of the stature of Patrick Geddes nor a romantic idealist of such transcendental vision as Ebenezer Howard (he enjoyed friendships with both), Unwin ranks beside them as one of three commanding British planners of the twentieth century, and the most practically productive of all three. All architect–planners of the next generation were indebted to his ideas, most notably in Britain, Patrick Abercrombie. The Parker and Unwin office also trained a whole generation of architects whose skills

in designing low-density housing persisted, so long as the garden city and new town ideal remained dynamic.

Lewis Mumford described Unwin as 'politically gifted, dispassionate, reasoned, always a bit of a Quaker, a sound practical man due to his apprenticeship as an engineer' (Miller, *Raymond Unwin*, 226). He derived his aesthetic instincts from William Morris's later beliefs in plainness, usefulness, and a good English garden; he had no feeling for architectural modernism, though he appreciated its rationalizing ambitions. He had unbounded respect for a sober and neighbourly style of family life, which he thought it his duty to promote. Tweedy in dress, mustachioed, with a good shock of hair, Unwin had a mild but persistent manner; he made friends easily but was rarely passionate. Though not a strict pacifist during the First World War, he maintained his socialist and internationalist beliefs and was a member of the group which led to the founding of the League of Nations Union. A frugal but hospitable routine and a largely vegetarian table were maintained by the Unwins at Wyldes; Ethel (Ettie) Unwin was a member of the Society of Friends, dressed in Liberty style, and unremittingly knitted or embroidered. There were two children: Edward (1894–1936), who became an architect and helped his father on his Greater London work but died of cancer, to his parents' great grief; and Margaret (Peggy) Curtice Hitchcock (1899–1982).

ANDREW SAINT

Sources M. Miller, *Raymond Unwin: garden cities and town planning* (1992) · M. Miller, *Letchworth: the first garden city* (1989) · C. B. Purdom, *The building of satellite towns* (1949) · F. Jackson, *Sir Raymond Unwin: architect, planner and visionary* (1985) · 'Report of the committee appointed to consider questions of building construction', *Parl. papers* (1918), 7.391, Cd 9191 · C. B. Purdom, *Life over again* (1951) · G. E. Cherry, *Pioneers in British planning* (1981) · *DNB*
Archives First Garden City Heritage Museum, Letchworth, papers and architectural drawings · NRA, priv. coll., family MSS, corresp. · RIBA BAL, corresp., working papers · University of Manchester, school of planning and landscape | Bodl. Oxf., letters to Gilbert Murray · First Garden City Heritage Museum, Letchworth, Letchworth collections · Hampstead Garden Suburb Trust, archives · Keele University Library, LePlay Collection, corresp. and minute book entries as member of Sociological Society committees · LMA, minutes of Greater London regional planning committee · NL Scot., corresp. with Patrick Geddes · PRO, files of Local Government Board, Ministry of Health, Ministry of Munitions, etc. · Welwyn Garden City Central Library, corresp. with Frederic Osborn
Likenesses G. C. Beresford, photograph, 1922, NPG [*see illus.*] · G. Clausen, oils, 1933, RIBA · photographs, repro. in Miller, *Raymond Unwin*, frontispiece, 13, 233 · photographs, First Garden City Heritage Museum, Letchworth
Wealth at death £8229 3s. 2d.: probate, 31 Dec 1940, *CGPLA Eng. & Wales*

Unwin, Rayner Stephens (1925–2000), publisher and writer, was born on 23 December 1925 at 6 Windmill Hill, Hampstead, the third of the four children of Sir Stanley *Unwin (1884–1968), publisher, and his wife, (Alice) Mary, née Storr (1883–1971). At the age of ten Rayner was asked by his father to review a new book by J. R. R. Tolkien: he was paid 1s. for his reader's report that ensured publication for *The Hobbit*. Educated at Abbotsholme School, Derbyshire, from 1936 to 1942, at seventeen Unwin became a book salesman for Basil Blackwell in Oxford. During the Second World War he served in the Far East as a sub-lieutenant in the Royal Naval Volunteer Reserve. After demobilization he went up to Trinity College, Oxford, where he graduated BA in 1949. He spent the academic year 1949–50 as a Fulbright scholar at Harvard University and was awarded a master's degree in English. In 1951 he joined Allen and Unwin at a salary of £35 per week.

In 1953 Unwin edited *The Gulf of Years: Letters from John Ruskin to Kathleen Olander* and in 1954 he published his critical study of the peasant poetry of England, *The Rural Muse*, which included the work of James Thomson, George Crabbe, John Clare, and Stephen Duck. *The Defeat of John Hawkins* (1960), Unwin's elegant, entertaining, and popular history of the Elizabethan navigator, became a Pelican paperback. Groomed as his father's successor when his elder brother David turned to writing children's books, Rayner Unwin essentially gave up his academic work for the business of publishing. David Unwin, in his memoir *Fifty Years with Father* (1982), wrote: 'I have always felt guilty at my defection, for by taking my place Rayner sacrificed his own promising career as an author' (D. Unwin, 116).

On 3 April 1952 Unwin married Carol Margaret, *née* Curwen (*b.* 1924), a children's nurse and daughter of Harold Spedding Curwen (1885–1949), master printer and proprietor of the Curwen Press, and his wife, Freda Margaret, *née* Simpson (1888–1974). Rayner and Carol had known each other since childhood, their fathers having been contemporaries at Abbotsholme. After their marriage they lived for a time in a tiny flat above the Allen and Unwin offices in Museum Street, London. They had one son and three daughters.

At the time that Unwin joined the firm it was thriving on its export business, the range of titles it published, and the reputation of his father as one of the leading lights of the trade. Rayner Unwin learned the business from the ground up, starting off being 'the-man-who-looks-after-the-booksellers'-queries' (Potter, 89). As an editor he quickly became involved in one of the firm's great successes: just as he had been crucial to the publication of *The Hobbit*, so was he the prime mover in 'the sixteen-year saga' to bring Tolkien's epic *The Lord of the Rings* (1954–5) into print. He negotiated, cajoled, and even nurtured the man he came to see as 'his' author.

Unwin triggered the necessary updating of the firm's management procedures, many of them instituted in the 1920s. Although far the youngest member of staff, the only senior executive under forty, Unwin had what he called the 'very flattering trust' of his father (Potter, 81). He used this trust to make reforms at an administrative level and also to see through the publication of such potentially controversial—yet highly successful—books as the *Kama Sutra*. When Stanley Unwin died in 1968, his son inherited a backlist that ran to 2500 titles covering an extraordinarily wide range.

It is this range, however, that has been blamed for the demise of George Allen and Unwin. The 1970s were a decade of flagging confidence caused by inflation, new technology, and internal difficulties within the firm. By the

1980s the company's £8 million turnover was good, but small compared with that of other publishers at the time. Unwin admitted that he should have studied America more closely, taken what he had seen happening there in the 1970s more seriously for, in the 1980s, 'the same winds of change crossed the Atlantic [and] the City grew to dominate British publishing' (R. Unwin, 180). In 1986 he merged the firm with Bell and Hyman to create Unwin Hyman, becoming its non-executive chairman alongside Robin Hyman as managing director. In 1989 a crisis was precipitated when Hyman became seriously ill and plunging profits coincided with a bid made for the company by HarperCollins, the 'sharks' as he called them. In 1990, and against his wishes, the firm was eventually sold to HarperCollins. The day before the contract was finalized he resigned in protest.

Unwin was extremely candid about his role in the collapse of the firm: 'The children of pioneers do not necessarily do well to follow closely in their father's footsteps' (R. Unwin, 22). The decline and eventual fall of the company affected him deeply and he said: 'I feel I have betrayed my father.' Some argued that Unwin was more 'scholar than businessman, more editor than salesman' (Norrie, 4), and Unwin himself may have concurred: 'I never had the confidence, which my father instinctively possessed, to manage a Company with assurance' (R. Unwin, 137). Yet his directorship of his father's charity, the Stanley Unwin Foundation, founded in 1968, demonstrated not only business acumen but foresight and shrewd management. With the funds it generated, Unwin purchased the vacant Wandsworth town hall, which he renamed Book House, and installed there the Book Trust, an amalgamation of the National Book League and the Publishers' Association training and education sector. He was also chairman of Unwin Enterprises, an investment company, and a director of Allen and Unwin (Australia), which secured its independence—and thus the continuation of the imprint—in 1990.

Awarded the CBE in 1977, Unwin served on the Publishers' Association council from 1965 to 1985, holding the posts of treasurer (1969), president (1971), and vice-president (1973). He was chairman of the British Council publishers' advisory committee from 1981 to 1988 and president of the Book Trade Benevolent Society from 1989 to 1995. As an executive of the committee of the National Life Story Collection, the oral history archive housed at the British Library, Unwin was keen that the experiences of ordinary members of the publishing world be recorded in the book trade lives project. He was also involved in the life of his village, being chairman of the Little Missenden festival from 1981 to 1988.

In 1995 Unwin published *A Winter Away from Home*, his study of the Arctic voyages of the sixteenth-century Dutch explorer William Barents. His *George Allen & Unwin: a Remembrancer* (1999) is perhaps his most significant written contribution to literary and publishing history. An engaging and evocative narrative, it was clearly a means of catharsis for Unwin. Moreover, it can be described as both an elegy and an indictment: an elegy to, as he put it, a 'style of book publishing that has now, regrettably, almost totally vanished' (R. Unwin, viii), and an indictment of ruthless, multimedia conglomerates. His son Merlin carried on the tradition of small, independent publisher, when, after working for Allen and Unwin, he set up his own company, Merlin Unwin Books, specializing in fishing and country interests.

A tall man with a rather large pear-shaped nose, heavy eyebrows, and, in later years, thinning hair that was sometimes awry, Unwin had a witty sense of humour reinforced by his jolly, shoulder-shrugging laugh. He was enormously proud of his thirteen grandchildren. He loved birds, mountains, walking, and tending his large garden at Little Missenden, where he also kept sheep. He especially loved trekking in the Himalayas, which he regarded as spiritual food for the soul. On his last visit to Allen and Unwin (Australia) in July 2000 to celebrate the company's tenth anniversary, he stopped in Canada on his way home for 'a glimpse of the Calgary Stampede' and 'three magic days walking in the mountains' near Lake Louise in the Rockies (private information). A member of the Garrick Club, he spent the weekdays at his flat near Covent Garden and the weekends at his home in Buckinghamshire.

Rayner Unwin died of cancer on 23 November 2000 at the Hospice of St Francis, 27 Shrublands Road, Berkhamsted, Hertfordshire. He was cremated on 1 December and his ashes were scattered by his daughter and his good friend Sherpa Tschering Dorie in the foothills of the Himalayas.   JANE POTTER

Sources R. Unwin, *George Allen and Unwin: a remembrancer* (1999) · J. Potter, interview with Rayner Unwin, *Publishing History*, 41 (1997) · *The Times* (25 Nov 2000) · *The Guardian* (27 Nov 2000) · *Daily Telegraph* (5 Dec 2000) · personal knowledge (2004) · private information (2004) · I. Norrie, *Publishing News* (1 Dec 2000), 4 · D. Unwin, *Fifty years with father* (1982) · b. cert. · m. cert. · d. cert.
Archives SOUND BL NSA, documentary recordings

Unwin, Sir Stanley (1884–1968), publisher, was born on 19 December 1884 at Handen Road, Lee, south-east London, the youngest of the nine children of Edward Unwin (1840–1933), printer and the son of Jacob Unwin, the founder of the printing firm of Unwin Brothers, and his wife, Elizabeth (1840–1921), the daughter of James Spicer, of the paper firm of that name. Unwin was brought up in a devoutly nonconformist atmosphere and was educated at the School for Sons of Missionaries at Blackheath, then at Abbotsholme School, Derbyshire, from 1897 to 1899. He left after two years, the burning down of his father's printing works at Chilworth in Surrey having led to financial straits.

The young Unwin then joined a ship and insurance broker in Crosby Square in the City of London as an office boy but he left after a few years in order to spend time in Germany, primarily in Leipzig, in 1903. During his nine months there he gained his first experience as a publisher in the German book trade, which proved an influential ingredient in his career since he was, and remained, the only London publisher of any distinction with a genuine

Sir Stanley Unwin (1884–1968), by unknown photographer, 1956

understanding of any book trade outside his own country.

In 1904 Unwin joined his father's youngest stepbrother, T. Fisher Unwin, in Paternoster Buildings. The older man was himself a leading and successful publisher and something of a doyen of literary London. Under him Unwin rapidly learned the craft of publishing, specializing in contracts and the marketing of foreign rights. So successful was he that he embarked on discussions, which proved abortive, about a jointly owned company with his relative. For Unwin at twenty-eight, knowledgeable, confident, impatient, there was no alternative but to start his own firm. Following a world tour with his future brother-in-law, chronicled in *Two Young Men See the World* (1934), he bought the firm of George Allen & Co., which had recently gone bankrupt. In 1911 George Allen had merged with Swan Sonnenschein, 'one of the great seminal publishers of the books of ideas … The books they had were simply staggering: Marx, Shaw, George Moore, Freud; you name it, they had it' (Potter, 92). Unwin went back twice to the receiver before purchasing George Allen and he had looked very carefully at the lists of both firms. George Allen was essentially 'a one-author publisher: Ruskin, and Ruskin and Ruskin', so 'it must have been the Swan

Sonnenschein bits that attracted him' (ibid., 92–3). However, the date on which George Allen and Unwin Ltd was founded was not auspicious: 4 August 1914. The fact that he started trading on the day the First World War was declared made Unwin even more determined 'to see what I could do with it, war or no war' (S. Unwin, 131).

On 19 December 1914 Unwin married (Alice) Mary Storr (1883–1971), daughter of Rayner Storr, an auctioneer. They had four children: Elizabeth Spicer (*b. d.* 1916), David Storr (*b.* 1918), who became a noted children's author, Ruth Severn (1920–1998), and Rayner Stephens *Unwin (1925–2000).

To be called up for military service would have been a complete disaster for the newly established publisher; in any case Unwin was from the start a confirmed pacifist. When it was clear that he could no longer be exempt from duty, he decided that it 'was essential for me to do whatever I could conscientiously do' (S. Unwin, 138). He served as a member of the voluntary aid detachment London I and passed not only the required examinations in first aid, home nursing, and hygiene, but advanced exams in all three. He was summoned during air raids, participated in the recovery of a downed Zeppelin, and acted as a porter at Charing Cross Hospital, all of which is recorded in his book *The Work of V.A.D., London I, During the War* (1920).

In addition to his pacifism Unwin staunchly opposed censorship in any form and was particularly incensed by what he saw as the mindless restrictions imposed by the Defence of the Realm Act. Accordingly he was not afraid of courting controversy to support the free flow of ideas. He published books by and about conscientious objectors, in the face of much public hostility. Many booksellers refused to stock Mrs Henry Hobhouse's '*I Appeal unto Caesar*' (1915), so readers had to go to the Allen and Unwin offices in Museum Street to procure copies. Unwin calculated that the book, which was referred to in parliament, sold in the thousands but the experience 'was an uphill fight with the book trade which I have never forgotten' (S. Unwin, 155). He also published Bertrand Russell's *The Principles of Social Reconstruction* (1916), a bold move because Russell was already notorious for his pacifism and 'unpatriotic' opinions. Other influential books included *The Framework of Lasting Peace* (1917), edited by Leonard Woolf. Unwin himself was deeply concerned about the nature of the peace to be concluded, but expressed concern most effectively through his publications, which included Woolf's *International Government* (1916), George Lansbury's *Your Part in Poverty* (1917), and *A Century of British Foreign Policy* (1918) by G. P. Gooch and J. H. B. Masterman.

Unwin relied heavily on a circle of advisers, whose opinions he solicited when the publication of a book was in question or likely to cause controversy. Gilbert Murray and G. Lowes Dickinson were frequently called upon and it was through the advocacy of Professor J. H. Muirhead, editor of the Library of Philosophy, that Russell joined the Allen and Unwin list, though Muirhead disagreed with much of Russell's philosophy. Another helper was A. R. Orage, editor of the *New Age*, through whom Unwin acquired the Russian philosopher–mystic George Gurdjieff, as well as Edwin Muir, Ramiro de Maetzu, and A. J. Penty. Unwin was also able to pick up authors from other small publishers who failed where he was succeeding. Such authors included Benedetto Croce, August Strindberg, Albert Sorel, James Elroy Flecker, Jules Romains, and J. C. Squire.

While Unwin published some important translations of Russian classics and a number of fine novels, fiction was not outstanding on his list. His main interests remained serious works of scholarship, with some topical relevance or at least with the possibility of a wide sale to the literate public. Such a publication was Russell's *The Practice and Theory of Bolshevism* (1920). The immediate post-war period was a productive one for Unwin, for many leading authors, literary and academic, joined the firm's list—Arthur Waley, Sidney J. Webb, G. D. H. Cole, R. H. Tawney, and H. W. Nevinson. Though Unwin never published George Bernard Shaw, he published books about him, which occasioned a heated correspondence with the playwright.

Unwin quickly built his own formidable list of authors, established himself as a spokesman on the affairs of the British book trade not only within Britain but all over the world, and became a public personality in his own right. In 1926 he published *The Truth about Publishing*, which became the most authoritative textbook on the subject for generations of people entering the book trade. It was regularly updated in his lifetime and is still in print, though some criticize it for setting down all the facts but leaving out the fun. At first sight this is a real criticism and it is true that Unwin himself rarely played the traditional role of entertainer of budding geniuses sometimes thought to be the only function of literary publishers. He was a hard-headed man who disliked spending his money—even small sums—on what he regarded as trivial matters, and he acquired, and kept, his authors in a truly professional manner. With Russell, for instance, a respectful distance was maintained: 'Like the Victorian aristocrat that he was Russell regarded my father as a tradesman who knew his job and respected him for it, and father never attempted to encroach upon or alter that social situation' (R. Unwin, 45).

In 1933 Unwin became president of the Publishers' Association and was a passionate upholder of the net book agreement, of co-operation between publishers and booksellers, in particular as represented by the Society of Bookmen and the National Book League, and of international copyright conventions. He championed the British Council and served on its executive committee. Unwin also fought against America's discriminatory tariffs and regulations and took every opportunity to 'preach' a doctrine of more equitable terms. But his book trade interests went beyond publishing. When the bookseller W. J. Bryce ran into financial difficulties, Unwin purchased the assets from the receiver and created a new company with Bryce and I. P. M. Chambers as directors and installed them 'in a corner of my building in Museum Street on favourable terms' (S. Unwin, 242).

Unwin had strong links with the Fabian Society and in the inter-war years published many left-wing books, including the work of Harold J. Laski and of Leon Trotsky. Another aspect of his character, developed by his parents with their clear religious beliefs, concerned his strong non-sectarian Christian convictions. These led him to publish for C. F. Andrews and through him the works of several Indian authors, including M. K. Gandhi. In 1936 he published one of the best-sellers of the period—*Mathematics for the Million*—followed by *Science for the Citizen* (1938), both by Lancelot Hogben. He also published the Icelandic Nobel prize-winning author Hallond Laxness's *Salka Valka* (1936) and *Independent People* (1945) and numerous books by the Czechoslovak writer Karel Capek. When Unwin discovered that Ford Madox Ford was in need of financial help, he offered to publish his books. All Ford's last works, including *The March of Literature* (1939), were issued under the Allen and Unwin imprint.

In 1937, acting on the recommendation of his young son Rayner, Unwin published J. R. R. Tolkien's *The Hobbit*. Sixteen years later the firm at last published the 'sequel', the epic *The Lord of the Rings* (1954–5), and the success of Tolkien's writing, as well as his subsequent fanatical worldwide readership, was due in no small part to the author–publisher relationship that existed between Tolkien, Stanley Unwin, and later Rayner Unwin.

In 1937 Unwin, along with W. G. Taylor (Dent) and G. Wren Howard (Cape), took control of the Bodley Head Ltd. The firm was insolvent at the time of John Lane's death in 1925, and tenders were eventually invited for the purchase of the firm. Unwin felt that 'it would be amusing to run the John Lane business co-operatively with two of my competitors … something new in publishing' (S. Unwin, 244). For the Bodley Head, Unwin also acquired the firms of Boriswood & Co. Ltd, R. Cobden Sanderson Ltd, Martin Hopkinson & Co. Ltd, and Gerald Howe Ltd.

During the 1930s Unwin was only too well aware of the growing threat from the Nazis and their persecution of the Jews. He urged his publisher friend Dr Horovitz, proprietor of the Phaidon Verlag, to leave Austria and, in order to save the firm, he set about purchasing it. His ownership of the famous art-publishing house infuriated the German authorities, who at one stage issued a directive that 'Disputes with Mr Unwin are not desired' (S. Unwin, 225). Unwin later learned that his name was on the notorious Gestapo 'black list'.

Along with other publishers and booksellers Unwin helped to rescue the wholesaler Simpkin Marshall after its business, including its entire stock of 6 million books, was destroyed in the blitz. He worked in London throughout the war, narrowly escaping bombs: 'When the raids were at their worst,' he wrote, 'it was my practice to put on a record of Dvorak's *New World Symphony* at full blast so that I could hear nothing else' (S. Unwin, 253). This was not his only eccentricity, which arose more from his single-minded wish to get on with his life and work than from any intention to astonish or amuse. When his cousin Philip was shown the manuscript of his autobiography and ventured to say that the many stories told of Unwin's triumphs could have been tempered with one or two instances where he had not been entirely right or justified, Unwin replied, 'You don't expect me to start writing fiction at my age, do you?' At the office he opened the post himself every day, even on bank holidays. At his Hampstead home tennis was his passion—every Saturday and Sunday afternoon, winter and summer, men's doubles only. When he moved house late in life, the tennis court was completed before the house so that no interruption need be experienced.

Unwin was knighted in 1946 and created KCMG in 1966. Aberdeen University honoured him with an honorary degree of LLD in 1945. He also received decorations from France (officier de l'Académie Française), Czechoslovakia (order of the White Lion), and Iceland (knight of the order of the Falcon).

Later successes from Unwin's firm included *The Kon-Tiki Expedition* by Thor Heyerdahl (1950), acquired in Oslo by his nephew Philip. It was the firm's first blockbuster, enabling it 'to change into an altogether higher key of success and prosperity' (P. Unwin, 146) and to offer a pension scheme for its employees for the first time. In this period Unwin travelled widely on business—to New Zealand by way of the USA, Canada, India, and the Middle East—and in 1954 completed fifty years in the book trade. He sold the Bodley Head in 1957 and, as formerly, he continued his interest in the activities of the Publishers' Association and the International Publishers' Association as well as the British Council. Nor with his advancing years was there any diminution in his involvement with the numerous charities he supported or in his overriding interest in the firm that he had built from so little and the books that appeared under his imprint. The concept of retirement 'was entirely alien' to Stanley Unwin (P. Unwin, 153). At seventy-six, true to his belief in the free flow of books and his rejection of censorship in any form, Unwin appeared as a witness for the defence in the *Lady Chatterley* trial in 1960. In that year he published his autobiography, *The Truth about a Publisher*. He rarely missed a day in the office and attended every Allen and Unwin board meeting until two months before his death. Shortly before he died he signed a deed establishing the Stanley Unwin Foundation, a charity to promote book-trade education. It was later used by his son Rayner to establish the Book Trust, a merger of the National Book League and the Publishers' Association training and education sector.

When Stanley Unwin died in London on 13 October 1968, at University College Hospital, he was widely recognized as one of the architects of the British, and indeed the international, book trade; as a publisher of the highest standards of probity in business matters as well as in the quality of the books he published; and as a personality, not without weaknesses, reasonably self-righteous, but one who had contributed importantly to the life and well-being of his country over half a century.

ROBIN DENNISTON

Sources personal knowledge (2004) · private information (1981) [Rayner Unwin] · S. Unwin, *The truth about a publisher* (1960) · R. Unwin, *George Allen & Unwin: a remembrancer* (1999) · J. Potter, interview, Rayner Unwin, *Publishing History*, 41 (1997) · P. Unwin, *The publishing Unwins* (1972)

Archives PRO, report on his visit to Europe, BW2/333 | BL, letters to Albert Mansbridge, Add. MS 65259 · Bodl. Oxf., corresp. with L. G. Curtis · Bodl. Oxf., corresp. with Gilbert Murray · U. Birm. L., corresp. with W. H. Dawson · University of Bristol Library, corresp. and statements relating to trial of *Lady Chatterley's lover*

Likenesses W. Stoneman, photograph, 1946, NPG · photograph, 1956, NPG [*see illus.*] · G. Argent, photograph, 1968, NPG · O. Kokoschka, oils, Book Trust at Book House, Wandsworth, London · photograph, NPG

Wealth at death £233,514: probate, 10 March 1969, *CGPLA Eng. & Wales*

Unwin, Thomas Fisher (1848–1935), publisher, was born on 24 January 1848 at 33 Lowgate Hill, London, the son of Jacob Unwin (1802–1855), and his wife, Isobel, *née* Hall. He was born into a family of printers and publishers: his father had founded the Gresham Press, and his mother was from the Miller family, who had published the *Cheap Magazine*. He attended the City of London School, and in 1892 married Jane Cobden (1851–1947) [*see* Unwin, (Emma) Jane Catherine Cobden], daughter of the politician Richard Cobden.

After serving with Jackson, Walford, and Hodder, Unwin started his own London business in 1882 in Holborn Viaduct, buying Marshall, Japp & Co. for £1000. He established himself at 11 Paternoster Building in 1883. Annual profits averaged between £600 and £700 until about 1900, and the firm moved to Adelphi Terrace in 1905. By 1912 the business had expanded so much that it was taking in profits of £6000, and in 1920 it became a company. Unwin was considered generous to unknown writers but was notorious for refusing to increase the pay of those whose careers took off, and so although he published some of the most experimental writers of the period, many of them eventually left Unwin when they became famous: H. G. Wells, John Galsworthy, Somerset Maugham, Joseph Conrad, George Moore, and Ford Madox Ford. Unwin also first published the work of several aesthete poets and playwrights, including John Davidson, May Crommelin, Graham Rosamund Tomson, and Katherine Tynan. The risk of publishing unknown writers was balanced by the republishing of popular writers; Unwin handled colonial editions for publishers and acted as author's agent, serializing fiction for publication in the United States, for a 10 per cent commission.

What distinguished the firm of Unwin was its publication of many series and its launching of new writers. Series ranged widely in subject from popular literature (prose and poetry), to history, to current politics and social issues of the day. The Pseudonym Library was a series of eighteen-pence books, stiff-covered and paper-bound, and its writers included John Oliver Hobbes (Pearl Craigie), John Buchan, Mrs Humphry Ward, Edith Nesbit Bland, William Henry Hudson, Mark Rutherford (William Hale White), Vernon Lee (Violet Paget), Ouida (Louise de La Ramée), and Ethel M. Dell. Never one to flinch from controversy, Unwin also published the first novel of Olive Schreiner, *Trooper Peter Halket of Mashonaland* (1897), which attacked the Chartered Company, and accused Cecil Rhodes of murdering Matabele (Ndebele) envoys.

The Story of the Nations Library, to which distinguished historians contributed, reflected Unwin's interests in foreign writers, liberalism, free trade, international affairs, and in combating the persecution of minorities. These books also reflected his wife's interests in abolition and suffrage. He published historical and political subjects by controversial writers such as Wilfrid Scawen Blunt. Unwin, who was pro-Boer, saw through publication the *Memoirs* (1902) of former South African President Stephanus Kruger. He also supported the Aborigines Protection Society, publishing E. D. Morel's *Red Rubber* (1906, 1907). His press also issued Annie Besant's *Autobiography* (1893), Freud's *The Psychopathology of Everyday Life* (1914) and *Wit and its Relation to the Unconscious* (1916), works by Karl Besant, and translations of Russian novels by Constance Garnett.

Many of Unwin's interests are evident from his publishing lists, but they are also seen in his many memberships and affiliations. He was not only a joint founder of the Publishers' Association (1896) but he was also joint founder and treasurer of the Friends of Russian Freedom and a member of the South African Conciliation Committee. He served both as treasurer of the library committee and chair of the political and economic circle for the National Liberal Club; he was also vice-president of the West Sussex Liberal Association, and governor of Dunford House (Cobden Memorial). His commitment to public service can been seen, too, in his founding of the Johnson Club, his treasurership of the Cobden Club, and his serving at various points as governor of Johnson House, the London School of Economics, and Carlyle House.

By 1917 Unwin's firm had published twenty-seven series, including the Autonym Library, Independent Novels, the Welsh Library, the Idle Hours series, the Children's Library, and the Literary History series. Unwin's First Novel series included *Whose Body?* by Dorothy L. Sayers (1912). The New Irish Library, co-published with Sealy, Bryers, and Walker in Dublin, published works by W. B. Yeats. The Reformer's Bookshelf series issued *The Political Writings of Richard Cobden*, and Edward Carpenter's controversial *Towards Democracy* (1892). The Mermaid series reprinted rare Jacobean and Restoration plays in new scholarly editions costing half a crown; participating editors included Havelock Ellis (general editor), J. A. Symonds, A. C. Swinburne, Ernest Rhys, Edmund Gosse, Herbert Horne, and Arthur Symons.

The firm's periodicals also exemplify the internationalism that Unwin promoted in line with his liberalism and interest in world politics: *Revue Bleue*, *Independent Review* (October 1903 to March 1907), and *Compolis: an International Review* (1896–8). The latter was edited by F. Ortmans and featured such writers as Andrew Lang, W. Lebknecht (a close friend of Marx and Engels), G. B. Shaw, Henry James, Yeats, Conrad, George Gissing, Rudyard Kipling, George Meredith, Anatole France, Israel Zangwill, Tolstoy, and Edmund Gosse.

Unwin himself was tall and upright in bearing; family

members commented on his distinguished stature and characteristic erect carriage, and he was described by his nephew Philip Unwin variously as looking 'as if his neck and torso were encased in plaster' (P. Unwin, 39), and looking 'like a horse with a bearing rein' (ibid., 3). His irascible personality was well known in the publishing business, as were his sometimes eccentric habits, such as spitting in public. Although he was not really athletic, he had a keen interest in mountaineering, and once climbed the Matterhorn. His dress was consistent throughout his life, including his floppy, yellow bow-tie; even in old age he sported a full beard, and his piercing blue eyes lost none of their clarity. Unfortunately his publishing business lacked his vigorous stamina, and its final years were marked by financial decline. In 1926 Unwin retired to his Sussex home, and the firm merged with Ernest Benn Ltd. Unwin died of bronchitis on 6 February 1935 at his home, Oatscroft, Heyshott Road, Midhurst, Sussex.

JULIE F. CODELL

Sources J. F. Codell, 'T. Fisher Unwin', *British literary publishing houses, 1820–1880*, ed. P. Anderson and J. Rose, DLitB, 106 (1991), 304–11 · P. Unwin, *The publishing Unwins* (1972) · *George Moore in transition: letters to T. Fisher Unwin and Lena Milman, 1894–1910*, ed. H. E. Gerber (1968) · C. de Saint Victor, 'Cosmopolis', *British literary magazines*, ed. A. Sullivan, [3]: *The Victorian and Edwardian age, 1837–1913* (1984), 85–92 · *WWW*, 1929–40, 1379 · S. Unwin, *The truth about a publisher* (1960) · b. cert. · d. cert.

Archives University of Bristol Library, corresp. and papers · W. Sussex RO, corresp. and publishing papers | Bishopsgate Institute, London, letters to George Howell · CUL, corresp. with Lord Hardinge · King's Cam., letters to Oscar Browning

Unwin, William Cawthorne (1745–1786). *See under* Unwin, Mary (*bap.* 1723, *d.* 1796).

Unwin, William Cawthorne (1838–1933), civil and mechanical engineer, was born at Great Coggeshall, Essex, on 12 December 1838, the eldest son of William Jordan Unwin (1811–1877), pastor of the Congregational chapel at Woodbridge, Suffolk, and later principal of the Congregational theological college at Homerton, and his wife, Eliza Davey (*d.* 1872), daughter of J. Bailey Tailer, of Woodbridge. He attended the City of London School (1848–54) and studied science for a year at New College, St John's Wood, London, passing the London matriculation examination in 1855 with honours in chemistry, and after study in the evenings he graduated with a BSc (London) in 1861.

In 1856, by personal introduction, Unwin obtained his first appointment as scientific assistant in Manchester to William Fairbairn. During the next six years he assisted Fairbairn in important researches, including those on the strength of boiler flues, on the laws governing the density and expansion of steam at higher temperatures, and on the properties of saturated steam. Unwin took a leading part in the trials of the Fay and Newall continuous mechanical railway brakes in 1859, which resulted in the general application of continuous brakes to all passenger rolling-stock. He was also largely concerned with Fairbairn's famous early experiments on the fatigue of wrought iron girders (1860–62), and the work of the

William Cawthorne Unwin (1838–1933), by Harold Speed, 1920

Admiralty special committee on iron for shipbuilding. In 1862 Unwin became works manager to Messrs Williamson & Brothers, of Kendal, but continued to correspond with Fairbairn on technical matters. At Kendal he was concerned with the construction of turbines and waterwheels and began work on hydraulics. In the winter of 1864–5 he gave to the Royal Engineers at Chatham, on Fairbairn's recommendation, his first engineering lecture. In 1866 he returned to Manchester as manager of the engine department of the Fairbairn Engineering Company.

Unwin's inclination was towards teaching, and in 1867 he returned to Homerton. Between 1868 and 1871 he prepared and delivered five different courses of lectures to the Royal Engineers on a wide range of civil and mechanical engineering subjects. In 1869 he was appointed an instructor in marine engineering at the Royal School of Naval Architecture and Marine Engineering at South Kensington, forerunner of the Royal Naval College, Greenwich.

The Royal Indian Engineering College was opened at Cooper's Hill, Englefield Green, Surrey, in 1871, to train engineers for the public services in India. Unwin was appointed professor of hydraulics and mechanical engineering in 1872. Here, in addition to his teaching duties, he carried out much original work and published several books, including *The Elements of Machine Design* (1877).

In 1884 the Central Institution of the City and Guilds of London was being completed and Unwin was appointed professor of civil and mechanical engineering. He served as dean of the college from 1885 to 1896 and again from

1902 to 1904. When the college was incorporated into London University in 1900 he became the first London University professor of engineering and was a leader in the advancement of engineering education and training.

In 1890 Unwin was appointed, by the promoters of the Niagara Falls Power Company, secretary of the international commission established to assess the competitive designs for the first major hydro-electric power scheme. He took a prominent part in the development of the project and was appointed one of the three foreign consulting engineers to the company. In connection with this work he visited the United States of America in 1892 and subsequent years, as well as Germany and France, but declined an invitation to go to America permanently in charge of the work.

At the same time Unwin took a prominent part from 1890 in the introduction and application of the internal combustion engine. His 1897 report on the diesel engine was an accurate forecast of its development. He took up in 1893 the study of the stability of masonry dams for the water storage reservoirs then under construction for hydro-electric power schemes for India, the Coolgardie water pipeline, and others. In his last paper before retiring from his professorship in 1904 he developed the principles and formulae that have since been used generally for determining flow in gas mains. He undertook some of the earliest work for the engineering standards committee and established dimensions for standard tensile test pieces.

After 1904, when he attended the International Engineering Congress at St Louis, Unwin continued to be consulted on important projects and to give his services freely for the advancement of engineering practice. He took a principal part in the masonry dam controversy of 1905–8, when his practical rational analyses were vindicated fully against the incorrect mathematical premises of his opponents. He was a British representative at the meeting in New York of the International Society for the Testing of Materials in 1912. He was a principal influence in fixing membership qualifications by examination for the leading technical institutions. For many years he gave much time to this work, in addition to serving on the governing bodies of London University, Imperial College, and the City and Guilds College. During the First World War, Unwin served on a number of technical committees of the Ministry of Munitions, and continued to serve thereafter occasionally on government committees and to produce original contributions on engineering and educational problems. He was the first recipient, in 1921, of the Kelvin medal. His last important work was a report for the consulting engineers on the stresses in the Mersey Tunnel in 1922.

Unwin's technical interests were remarkably widespread and he attained eminence in all. He was elected FRS in 1886 and received the honorary degree of LLD from Edinburgh University in 1905. He was president of the Institution of Civil Engineers in 1911 and of the Institution of Mechanical Engineers in 1915; he was an honorary member of eight technical societies, and wrote numerous papers, lectures, and addresses. He died, unmarried, at his home, 7 Palace Gate Mansions, 29 Palace Gate, Kensington, London, on 17 March 1933.

E. G. WALKER, rev. JOHN BOSNELL

Sources E. G. Walker, *The life and work of William Cawthorne Unwin* (1947) [with bibliography] · J. S. Wilson, *Obits. FRS*, 1 (1932–5), 167–78 · *PICE*, 236 (1932–3), 514–19 · *Institution of Mechanical Engineers: Proceedings*, 124 (1933), 789 · *Transactions of the American Society of Civil Engineers*, 99 (1934), 361 · *The Times* (18 March 1933) · personal knowledge (1949) · b. cert. · d. cert. · *CGPLA Eng. & Wales* (1933)
Archives ICL, corresp. and papers
Likenesses W. Water, oils, 1914, Inst. CE · H. Speed, oils, 1920, Institution of Mechanical Engineers, London [*see illus.*] · A. Legros, etching, ICL · photograph, repro. in Wilson, *Obits. FRS*
Wealth at death £26,331 7s. 10d.: resworn probate, 19 May 1933, *CGPLA Eng. & Wales*

Unwona (d. 800×03), bishop of Leicester, succeeded Eadberht as sixth bishop of that see some time between 781 and 785. He was present at a legatine council in 787 and, from 788, attests at least four genuine charters of Offa, king of Mercia, and two of Cenwulf in 798 and 799. Unwona may be identical with the 'Speratus' to whom Alcuin addressed a letter of 796 concerning the succession to the Mercian throne. This 'Speratus' was a royal adviser of some importance and Unwona's increasing prominence in the witness lists of Mercian charters and ecclesiastical synods certainly supports the view that he brought the bishopric of Leicester to its highest position of influence in the Anglo-Saxon period.

Unwona's almost unique name should not lead to a confusion with the tenth-century priest called Unwona whom Matthew Paris mentions in connection with St Albans Abbey. Bishop Unwona died between 800 and 803, his successor, Werenberht, having been appointed by the latter year.

A. F. POLLARD, rev. MARIOS COSTAMBEYS

Sources D. A. Bullough, 'What had Ingeld to do with Lindisfarne?', *Anglo-Saxon England*, 22 (1993), 93–125 · E. Dümmler, ed., *Epistolae Karolini aevi*, MGH Epistolae [quarto], 4 (Berlin, 1895), no. 124 · E. B. Fryde and others, eds., *Handbook of British chronology*, 3rd edn, Royal Historical Society Guides and Handbooks, 2 (1986) · *AS chart.*, S 128, 139, 146, 153, 154, 1430 · *Gesta abbatum monasterii Sancti Albani, a Thoma Walsingham*, ed. H. T. Riley, 3 vols., pt 4 of *Chronica monasterii S. Albani*, Rolls Series, 28 (1867–9), vol. 1

Upcott, William (1779–1845), antiquary and autograph collector, was born on 15 June 1779 in London, the only child of the artist Ozias *Humphry (1742–1810) and Delly Wickers (d. 1786), daughter of an Oxford shopkeeper. Five days later he was baptized as William Upcott Humphry, but the patronymic was never used, and both Humphry and Upcott habitually referred to their relationship as that of godfather and godson. In September 1779 Upcott and his mother moved to Oxford, and after her death in December 1786 the boy continued there with his grandmother; Humphry provided some financial assistance, and may have paid for his schooling. In two autobiographical accounts (Huntington MSS Up 693 and 697) Upcott lists eight schools that he attended for periods ranging from a few months to three years; apart from Witney grammar school, all were dame-schools or private seminaries in or near Oxford. Early in 1797 Upcott left Oxford for London, having with his father's assistance secured an apprenticeship with the Piccadilly bookseller John Wright. Three years later he transferred to the shop of Robert Harding Evans in Pall Mall, remaining there until his election on 24 April 1806 as sub-librarian at the new London Institution, where he served under first Richard Porson and later William Maltby.

By then Upcott was already a keen collector of coins, trade tokens, and engravings, and at his father's death in March 1810 he inherited not only a number of Humphry's original paintings and drawings but also his extensive correspondence with artists, writers, and men of affairs. According to Upcott's note of 1835 in the first of the bound volumes of these letters (now in the library of the Royal Academy), it was this bequest that inspired him to concentrate his collecting activity on autographs, and by 1816 he could declare to Dawson Turner that 'the disease … that has the strongest hold of my inclinations, is the autographic mania' (*GM*, 2nd ser., 26, 1846, 476). In this he was a considerable pioneer, for although several late eighteenth-century collectors had accumulated autographs alongside their books and engravings, none had approached the pursuit with Upcott's single-mindedness.

Early in 1813 Upcott was introduced by the antiquary William Bray to Mary, Lady Evelyn, who engaged him to catalogue the library at Wotton, the Evelyn family home in Surrey. There the two men uncovered in a cabinet John Evelyn's famous 'Kalendarium' or diary; Upcott helped Bray to edit the first edition (1818) and in 1825 himself edited Evelyn's *Miscellaneous Works*. During his time at Wotton he also helped himself to a large number of papers and printed books from the library. After Lady Evelyn's death Upcott sanctioned the publication of an anecdote in which it was stated that she had assured him he was 'welcome to lay aside any [manuscripts] that might add to his own collection' (T. F. Dibdin, *The Library Companion*, 1824, 553); recent research, however, has established not only that Lady Evelyn had no legal authority to make such a grant, but that in May 1815 she demanded the return of all the material Upcott had taken. He failed to restore the property, and it was not until his posthumous sale that the Evelyn family could recover a portion of the manuscripts.

Upcott is said to have collaborated in writing an 1816 *Biographical Dictionary of the Living Authors of Great Britain and Ireland*, and in 1818 he published his three-volume *Bibliographical Account of the Principal Works Relating to English Topography*. In the mid-1820s he helped to re-establish the Guildhall Library, and by the end of the decade Upcott's own collections had provided the primary material for S. W. Singer's edition of the correspondence of the second earl of Clarendon (1828) and Joseph Hunter's edition of the papers of Ralph Thoresby (1830). New acquisitions continued to pour into his rooms at the London Institution, but in May 1833 he was the victim of a burglary in which gold and silver coins and other curiosities, valued

by Upcott at £400, were taken; his friends obtained 555 signatories to a petition urging compensation on the grounds that he had 'faithfully served the Institution during a period of more than twenty-seven years', and on 10 April 1834 he was awarded £500. Less than two months later, however, a special committee of the board of management, convened in early May to investigate the domestic arrangements of the institution, recommended that Upcott's employment should cease as of midsummer day; in reply Upcott tendered his resignation (effective 9 June), apologizing for the 'Annoyances caused by my Household to others' and the 'general ill Effect of their Conduct upon the Character of the Establishment' (Munby, 18). No further details of the affair are known, although Joseph Hunter recorded privately at the time that Upcott had been 'dismissed in disgrace … for some immoral practice or other, the particulars of which I have not heard' (BL, Add. MS 36527, fol. 193).

At the time of his resignation Upcott was already involved in abortive negotiations for the sale of his collections, first with the Guildhall Library and later with the state paper office and the British Museum. Other potential customers included the duke of Sussex, Sir Thomas Phillipps, and even the Library of Congress in Washington, DC, but although many items were sold over the last eleven years of Upcott's life (for example, the manuscript of Thomas Chatterton's *Amphitryon*, which went to the British Museum in 1841), the bulk of his autographs, prints, and books remained with him at Autograph Cottage, as he named his home at 102 Upper Street, Islington. Here he entertained fellow collectors and the more casually curious, never tiring of displaying his treasures: 'every inch of wall was covered with paintings, drawings, and prints', wrote Dawson Turner in 1846, and 'not only every drawer, shelf, box, and cupboard was crammed, but every table and chair groaned under its load of books, portraits, autographs, and newspaper cuttings' (*GM*, 2nd ser., 26, 1846, 473). In 1836 Upcott printed a private catalogue of his manuscripts and in 1844 exhibited a large selection at the Liverpool Mechanics' Institution, again with a printed catalogue. Over the following year his health declined severely and he was troubled by hallucinations. He died at home in Upper Street on 23 September 1845, after a two-week illness occasioned by a journey from Liverpool to London in an open second-class railway carriage; he was buried on 1 October at Kensal Green cemetery. He had never married, and his will of 1833 named as his principal legatee Miss Anne Berry, who at the time of his death was living in Lewisham.

Upcott's collections were dispersed in three London sales of June 1846, making just under £4100 in all. The portion containing the manuscripts and autograph letters—the latter estimated at some 32,000 items—realized nearly £2421. Upcott's extensive collections relating to the topography of Great Britain were purchased for the British Museum (BL, Add. MSS 15921–15929), and a number of items were repossessed at considerable expense by the Evelyn family; the greater part of the remainder were divided among private enthusiasts, members of a new and enduring cult that Upcott's relentless 'autographic mania' had served largely to inspire.

JANET ING FREEMAN

Sources A. N. L. Munby, *The cult of the autograph letter in England* (1962) · *Memoirs of Thomas Dodd, William Upcott, and George Stubbs* (1879) · W. G. Hiscock, 'John Evelyn's library at Christ Church', *TLS* (6 April 1951), 220 · autobiographical letters of William Upcott: Upcott to Miss E. Peckover, 15/6/1808, and Upcott to Miss Temple, 21/1/1822, Hunt. L., Huntington MS Up 693; Huntington MS Up 697 · S. Adams, 'The papers of Robert Dudley, earl of Leicester, 1: The Browne-Evelyn collection', *Archives*, 20 (1992), 63–85 · *John Evelyn in the British Library* (1995), 64–71 · G. C. Williams, *The life and works of Ozias Humphry* (1918) · Charles Britiffe Smith's MS life of Upcott (and other materials in this manuscript including letters from Upcott), BL, Add. MS 21113, fols. 4–11
Archives BL, corresp. and papers, Add. MS 15951 · CUL, corresp. · Harvard U., corresp. and antiquarian collections · Hunt. L., corresp. · RA, papers · U. Edin. L., corresp. · UCL, memorandum book and corresp., Ogden MS 93 | BL, autograph and antiquarian collections, Add. MSS 21113, 28653–28654, 38728–38730 · BL, bibliographical collections relating to topography of Great Britain, Add. MSS 15921–15929 · BL, diary, Add. MS 32558 · BL, letters to J. Hunter, Add. MS 24876 · Bodl. Oxf., autograph collection · Bodl. Oxf., letters to John Dunkin · Bodl. Oxf., letters to Sir Thomas Phillipps · Trinity Cam., letters to Dawson Turner · W. Yorks. AS, Leeds, Yorkshire Archaeological Society, collection of letters to Ralph Thoresby · Yale U., collections
Likenesses T. Bragg, line engraving, 1818 (after drawing by W. Behnes), BM, NPG; repro. in Munby, *Cult of the autograph letter*, facing p. 20 · lithograph, 1835 (after L. Schmid), BM, NPG · H. S. Turner, lithograph, 1836; copy BL, Add. MS 37967, fol. 38 · G. P. Harding, lithograph, pubd 1837, BM, NPG; repro. in A. N. L. Munby, *The formation of the Phillipps library up to the year 1840* (1954), facing p. 86 · Day & Haghe, lithograph (after G. P. Harding; signed by Upcott, 1837) · Nethercliff, engraving (after lithograph by H. S. Turner)

Upfield, Arthur William (1890–1964), author and traveller, was born on 1 September 1890, at 88 North Street, Gosport, Hampshire, the eldest of the five sons of a draper, James Upfield, and his wife, Annie, *née* Barmore. During childhood he lived sometimes with his parents, sometimes with his grandparents, and attended a series of different schools in Gosport. Although he began writing novels in his spare time, his academic success was minimal. Articled at sixteen to an estate agent, he failed his examinations two years later and was shipped off by his exasperated father to Australia.

In reaction against the boredom of clerical work, Upfield took a job as boundary rider in interior New South Wales. He quickly gained a liking for the bush, and worked at a variety of jobs, including drover, farmhand, bullock-wagon driver, and cook. His patriotism caused him to join the Australian Imperial Force in August 1914, and he endured campaigns in Flanders and Gallipoli. He married an English nurse, Anne Douglas; they had one son, Arthur James. However, the marriage failed and he returned to Australia and resumed his wandering life. Although his wife and son came out to join him in Western Australia in the early 1930s, the reconciliation attempt failed. However, they were never divorced.

While working in southern Queensland, Upfield met Leon Wood, whose white mother and Aboriginal father had abandoned him at birth, but whose abilities had brought him employment by the Queensland police. Upfield had begun writing a detective story, but had set it aside and instead written a thriller, *The House of Cain* (1928). Their second meeting inspired him to model his central character on Leon; the result was Napoleon Bonaparte, the half-Aboriginal detective who made his earliest appearance in *The Barrakee Mystery* (1929) and was subsequently to be featured in twenty-eight further crime novels; these have been repeatedly republished and featured on radio and television. Upfield published three other novels, but these did not find a significant readership. In 1933 he became a staff writer for the *Melbourne Herald* and wrote for that newspaper a serial, *The Great Melbourne Cup Mystery*; this was eventually republished in book form in 1996. He was also a contributor to *World Wide Magazine* and *Walkabout*.

For the second Bonaparte novel, *The Sands of Windee* (1931), Upfield conceived an effective technique for the disposal of a corpse. He described this to a group that included an itinerant swagman, Snowy Rowles: to Upfield's great dismay, the method was used by Rowles while committing three murders in Western Australia. Upfield's account of this episode, *The Murchison Murders*, was published obscurely in the 1930s and republished in 1987.

Upfield's burgeoning career as a writer did not prevent him from travelling. In 1948 he headed a 5000 mile long Australian Geographical Society tour in Western Australia. Indeed, there were few parts of Australia that he did not visit. In most of his novels, the setting is integral to the plot; one is even set, not onshore, but in the swordfishing grounds of the Tasman Sea (*The Mystery of Swordfish Reef*, 1939). The most urban is *An Author Bites the Dust* (1948), which contains a thinly disguised self-portrait and expresses his rancour at his shabby treatment by the Australian literary establishment.

Upfield's strength, however, lies in his depiction of the Australian outback—its topography, its erratic weather patterns, its unique fauna, and its equally unique human inhabitants. Usually his male characters are of the pioneer breed that was already vanishing; whether good or evil, they are always strongly drawn. Some of his female characters, like the formidable Mary Answerth and her manipulating sister in *Venom House* (1952), or the streetwise policewoman Alice McGorr in *Murder must Wait* (1953) and *The Battling Prophet* (1956), are equally well drawn; but his heroines tend to be idealized and insipid. A particular virtue is Upfield's percipient and sympathetic characterization of Australia's Aboriginal peoples. His knowledge of their beliefs and traditions, and his regret at the erosion of these through the indifference or antipathy of most white settlers, give his writing an especial relevance and poignancy.

In his later years Upfield enjoyed the companionship of Jessica Uren, with whom he lived at Airey Inlet, Victoria, and at Bermagui and Bowral, New South Wales. She tended him during his last illness; he died in Bowral on 13 February 1964.

WILLIAM A. S. SARJEANT

Sources J. Hawke, *Follow my dust: a biography of Arthur Upfield* (1957) • R. B. Browne, *The spirit of Australia: the crime fiction of Arthur W. Upfield* (1988) • W. A. S. Sarjeant, 'The great Australian detective', *Armchair Detective*, 12/2 (1979), 99–105 • W. A. S. Sarjeant, 'The great Australian detective', *Armchair Detective*, 12/4 (1979), 358–9 • *Bony Bulletin* [ed. Philip T. Asdell, 33 issues] (1981–90) • I. H. Godden, 'Arthur W. Upfield: a heart often broken', *CADS: Crime and Detective Stories*, 23 (1994), 3–7 • B. Donaldson, 'Arthur William Upfield', *Armchair Detective*, 8/1 (1974), 1–11 • B. Donaldson, 'Upfield, Arthur William', *Twentieth-century crime and mystery writers*, ed. J. M. Reilly (1980), 1406–9 • b. cert.

Likenesses photographs, repro. in Hawke, *Follow my dust*

Upham, Charles Hazlitt (1908–1994), army officer, was born on 21 September 1908 in Gloucester Street, Christchurch, New Zealand, the only son of four children of John Hazlitt Upham, barrister and solicitor, and his wife, Agatha Mary, *née* Coates. A quiet, reserved boy, Upham was a boarder at Waihi preparatory school, Winchester, South Canterbury, between 1917 and 1922 and at Christ's College, Christchurch, from 1923 until 1927. A love of the land saw him complete a diploma of agriculture at Canterbury Agricultural College, Lincoln, in 1930. For six years he worked on high country sheep stations of the South Island as shepherd, musterer, and farm manager. Here he gained an eye for country, great physical endurance, a complete indifference to personal comfort, and a vocabulary of expletives that coloured his language regardless of company or occasion. In 1937 he joined the valuation department as assistant district valuer in Timaru, and in 1939 he returned to Canterbury Agricultural College to complete a diploma in valuation and farm management. An unlikely civil servant, he was described by a contemporary as an 'experienced, educated, well-bred rough diamond' (Sandford, 24).

Upham enlisted in the second New Zealand expeditionary force (2NZEF) in September 1939 and was posted to the 20th infantry battalion. Older than his fellows, of wiry build and average height, Upham stood out for his piercing blue eyes and his practical attention to weapon handling, fieldcraft, and tactics. Promoted temporary lance-corporal, he refused a recommendation to attend an officer cadet training unit (OCTU) in the belief that it would prevent his going overseas with the battalion. Promoted sergeant in December 1939, Upham sailed for Egypt with the advance party of 2NZEF in the same month. In Egypt he attended an OCTU and was commissioned on 2 November 1940, passing out bottom of his course. Upham was posted as a platoon commander to C company, 20th battalion, made up of hard no-nonsense men from the west coast of the South Island, and won their respect because he never demanded anything of them that he had not already mastered himself, and in situations of risk, always placed himself at the front.

Upham served with the New Zealand division in Greece in March 1941 and was evacuated with his battalion to Crete in April. His platoon was part of the night counter-attack on Maleme airfield on 22 May and fought its way forward against a German defence strongly organized in depth. He used his favourite weapon, the hand grenade, to destroy a series of machine gun posts. Daylight stopped

Charles Hazlitt Upham (1908–1994), by unknown photographer, 1941

further progress and after carrying out a wounded man under fire, Upham and his platoon sergeant covered 600 yards of open ground to extract an isolated company from the edge of the airfield.

Weak with dysentery, Upham was slightly wounded by mortar shrapnel in the arm which he had his platoon sergeant remove with a knife rather than leave his platoon. At Galatos on 25 May he led his platoon in smashing a German attack, and was again wounded by a spent bullet in the foot. After the retreat to the evacuation port at Sphakia an exhausted Upham led his platoon up the steep hills to eliminate a German penetration that threatened the force headquarters. Evacuated to Egypt, he was awarded the Victoria Cross for his exceptional gallantry on Crete. Deeply distressed by being singled out for recognition, Upham had to be ordered to wear the ribbon on his battle-dress.

Promoted lieutenant on 2 November 1941 and captain on 8 May 1942, Upham was later to be awarded a bar to the Victoria Cross for his gallantry and leadership as a company commander in June–July 1942. During the battle at Minqâr Qaim on 27 June and the breakout of the New Zealand division on 27/28 June, Upham led his company as part of the night infantry attack which, with hand grenade and bayonet, carved its way through a mass of German transport and men. Upham and one of his soldiers were seen wiping out a truckload of German soldiers with hand grenades. Upham was wounded in both arms from grenade fragments, but insisted on remaining with his company.

In the disastrous New Zealand attack on Ruweisat Ridge on the night 14/15 July 1942 Upham's company was fired on by an enemy strongpoint. Upham personally eliminated one of the machine gun posts despite his left arm being shattered below the elbow by a bullet. Semiconscious, he stayed with his company until the position was secured, before consenting to his evacuation to the RAP. With his arm in splints he rejoined his company, and was again severely wounded. Unable to walk, he was captured when his company, now reduced to six survivors, was overrun by German armour. Gravely wounded, he was sent to a prison hospital in Italy, and once his health improved he began a series of increasingly bold attempts to escape. This continued after he was sent to Germany, and in 1944 he became the only New Zealand combatant officer to be transferred to the camp at Colditz Castle for habitual escapees.

Liberated in April 1945, Upham was reunited with his fiancée, Mary Eileen (Molly) McTamney, a New Zealand nurse serving in Britain to whom he had become engaged in 1938, and they were married in Britain on 20 June 1945. He returned to New Zealand and in September 1945 was notified of the award of a bar to his Victoria Cross. Upham was only the third man and the only combatant officer to receive such recognition. Once again he found public attention difficult to deal with, and turned down a gesture by his fellow citizens to present him with £10,000 towards the purchase of a farm; the money was used to establish a scholarship fund for the sons of servicemen.

In late 1945 Upham purchased a farm at Parnassus, North Canterbury, which he successfully farmed, while raising a family of three daughters, before retiring to Christchurch in 1994. He died in Christchurch on 22 November 1994 and was accorded a funeral with full military honours in Christchurch Cathedral. Selflessness and singleness of purpose personified, Charles Upham represented all that was best in the New Zealand soldier of the Second World War. CHRISTOPHER PUGSLEY

Sources K. Sandford, *Mark of the lion* (1962) · D. J. C. Pringle and W. A. Glue, *Armoured regiment* (1957) · J. A. B. Crawford, 'Upham, Charles Hazlitt', *DNZB*, vol. 5 · J. T. Burrows, *Pathway among men* (1974) · M. Lambert, ed., *Who's who in New Zealand* (1991) · H. Kippenberger, *Infantry brigadier* (1949) · I. McGibbon, ed., *The Oxford companion to New Zealand military history* (2000) · A. H. McLintock, ed., *An encyclopaedia of New Zealand*, 3 vols. (1966) · *The Times* (23 Nov 1994) · J. E. R. Wood, *Detour: the story of Oflag IVC* (1946) · m. cert.
Archives Archives New Zealand, Wellington, war archives, narrative and war diaries, 20th infantry battalion, 2NZEF · New Zealand defence forces headquarters, private bag, Wellington, personal file, base records | FILM Archives New Zealand, Wellington · New Zealand Film Archive, Wellington, New Zealand · TVNZ Film Archive, Wellington, New Zealand | SOUND NL NZ, Turnbull L., NZ Oral History Archives, interviews Captain Charles Upham VC and Bar · Radio New Zealand Sound Archives, Christchurch, New Zealand, interviews Captain C. H. Upham
Likenesses photograph, 1941, NL NZ, Turnbull L. [*see illus.*] · P. MacIntyre, oils (as second lieutenant), Archives New Zealand, Wellington, National Collection of War Art · P. MacIntyre, watercolour (as second lieutenant), Archives New Zealand, Wellington, National Collection of War Art · J. F. Watton, portrait (as captain), repro. in Wood, *Detour*

Upham, Edward (1776–1834), bookseller and orientalist, the third son of Charles Upham (1739–1807), mayor of Exeter in 1796, was born at Exeter. He made a career as a bookseller in Exeter; his brother John carried on a similar business in Bath. Upham became a member of the corporation, was sheriff in 1807, and mayor of Exeter in 1809. He married, on 25 August 1801, Mary (*d.* 19 Oct 1829), daughter of John Hoblyn, vicar of Newton St Cyres and Padstow.

Upham retired early in order to devote his time to literary pursuits. One laborious and useful task was the completion of the *Index to the Rolls of Parliament* (1278–1503), commenced by John Strachey and John Pridden, which Upham completed after Pridden's death in 1825 and published in 1832. He was the author of two exotic novels, *Rameses: an Egyptian Tale* (3 vols., 1824, with extensive historical notes) and *Karmath: an Arabian Tale* (1827), but these made little lasting impression. He was better remembered for his academic works on the East, such as *History of the Ottoman Empire from its Establishment till the Year 1828* (2 vols., 1829), and especially for his study of Buddhist Ceylon: *The History and Doctrine of Buddhism* (1829, illustrated with drawings acquired in Ceylon by Sir Alexander Johnston). He also edited the translations of three important native histories of Ceylon, *The Mahávansi, the Rájá-Ratnácari, and the Rájá-vali* (3 vols., 1833), although he did not himself know Sinhalese. His contemporaries were impressed by his erudition and by his piety.

Upham was a member of the Royal Asiatic Society, and a fellow of the Society of Antiquaries of London. Towards the end of his life he lived at Dawlish, where he was one of the charity trustees. He moved to Bath, where he died on 24 January 1834 after several years of ill health.

H. R. TEDDER, *rev.* R. S. SIMPSON

Sources private information (1899) · *GM*, 2nd ser., 1 (1834), 336 · *The Athenaeum* (1 Feb 1834), 88

Upington, Sir Thomas (1845–1898), politician and lawyer in Cape Colony, born at Mallow, co. Cork, on 28 October 1845, was the son of Samuel Upington (*d.* 1875) of Lisleigh House, co. Cork, and Mary, *née* Tarrant. He was educated at schools in Mallow and Cloyne, and at Trinity College, Dublin, graduating BA in 1865. He was called to the Irish bar in 1867, and a few years later was made a queen's counsel, having been appointed secretary to the Irish lord chancellor, Thomas O'Hagan. In 1872 he married Mary (or May), daughter of John Guerin of Edenhill, co. Cork; they had two daughters and three sons.

In 1874 Upington settled in Cape Colony, was in 1878 elected to the representative assembly, and in the same year, on the fall of the Molteno ministry, became attorney-general in Gordon Sprigg's administration, and a prominent politician, identified with Sir Bartle Frere's policy of federation; he resigned in 1881, and became leader of the opposition in the Cape parliament. In 1883 he was chosen to defend Patrick O'Donnell, who had shot the informer James Carey, but O'Donnell was extradited and Upington returned the brief.

In 1884 Upington became premier, taking office as attorney-general, with Gordon Sprigg as his treasurer. Vigorous retrenchment had to be combined with such forward movement as the annexation of Walfish Bay. J. A. Froude interviewed Upington (by the latter's desire) during the term of his ministry, and was impressed by his opposition to Sir Charles Warren's expedition on the ground that it would widen the breach between the English and the Dutch, who were ultimately loyal to British sovereignty believing that it would be infinitely less irksome than any other (Froude, 65–7).

In 1886 Upington resigned the premiership in favour of Sir Gordon Sprigg, but continued in the cabinet as attorney-general until 1890. He was appointed puisne judge in the supreme court of the Cape in 1892, but resumed the attorney-generalship in succession to W. P. Schreiner in 1896. He was on the commission appointed to inquire into native laws and customs of the colony, and was a delegate at the colonial conference in 1887, when he was made a KCMG. He died at Breda Street, Cape Town, on 10 December 1898, and was buried in the Maitland (Woltemade) cemetery. His wife survived him. Upington, on the Orange River, and a district in Bechuanaland were named after him.　　THOMAS SECCOMBE, rev. LYNN MILNE

Sources The Times (12 Dec 1898) • A. Wilmot, The history of our own times in South Africa, 3 vols. (1897) • Argus Annual and Cape of Good Hope Directory (1898), 128 • Walford, County families (1898) • DSAB • J. A. Froude, Oceana, or, England and her colonies (1886), 65–7 • Debrett's Peerage (1924)

Archives Rhodes University, Grahamstown, South Africa, Cory Library for Historical Research, corresp., incl. with John Gordon Spring

Likenesses C. Winch, lithograph, Law Library, Cape Town

Upjohn, Gerald Ritchie, Baron Upjohn (1903–1971), judge, was born in Wimbledon, Surrey, on 25 February 1903, the younger son and youngest of five children of William Henry Upjohn KC (1853–1941), of Annesley House, Lyndhurst, Hampshire, and his wife, Lucy Martha (d. 1943), daughter of Rees Williams, small landowner of independent means, of Aberdâr. Upjohn's father was a well-known leading counsel with a large practice, whose considerable reputation as lawyer and advocate was somewhat marred by an irascibility which he notably failed to control. But the ill temper for which the father was noted did not characterize his relations with his younger son. These were warm, and Upjohn owed much to his father's solicitous attention to his training for a legal career.

Upjohn was educated at Eton College and (as an exhibitioner) at Trinity College, Cambridge, where he gained a first class in the mechanical sciences tripos in 1925 and a first class in part two of the law tripos the following year. Thereafter he worked in solicitors' and accountants' offices and also in the mining industry, and he served pupillages in both common law and Chancery chambers.

On being called to the bar (Lincoln's Inn) in 1929, Upjohn quickly acquired a large and varied practice. He had good looks, a distinguished presence, fine manners, a beautifully modulated voice, a first-class and penetrating brain,

and a capacity for hard work. He rapidly became a persuasive and lucid advocate.

Upjohn joined the Welsh Guards immediately on the outbreak of war in September 1939, and served from 1941 to 1943 as technical adjutant in the rank of captain, of the 2nd (armoured) battalion. In 1943 he was appointed, in the rank of colonel, chief legal adviser of the Allied Control Commission (Italy), and in the same year he was one of the rare wartime recipients of a silk gown. In 1944 he was promoted to brigadier on appointment as vice-president of the Allied Control Commission. He was mentioned in dispatches. For his services to the control commission, he was appointed CBE (1945) and an officer of the US legion of merit (1946).

In 1945 Upjohn returned to practice at the bar. Success as leading counsel was immediate. His presence, his legal scholarship, at once comprehensive and distinguished, and his ability to master a complicated brief impressed judges and solicitors alike. In addition to a busy practice he undertook a remarkably wide variety of duties. In 1948 Upjohn was a member of the three-man tribunal appointed, after rumours of widespread corruption had attracted much sensational publicity, to inquire into allegations reflecting on the official conduct of ministers of the crown and other public servants. The villain of the piece was the egregious Sydney Stanley, a man who profited from smoothing the lives of businessmen whose activities were hampered by the multitude of regulations and controls of the immediate post-war world. After sitting for twenty-seven days and hearing evidence from fifty-eight witnesses the tribunal, chaired by Sir George Lynskey, found that Stanley had indeed made 'benefactions' to John Belcher, a junior minister at the Board of Trade. Although the gifts were in fact modest, Stanley had achieved his objective of putting Belcher in his debt and Stanley was able to boast of his ability to use his contact to get results. The tribunal stuck to its fact-finding brief and declined to give any general guidance to public servants about their conduct in dealing with personal friends.

Upjohn was treasurer of the bar council from 1946 to 1951 and served as a member of the (Evershed) committee on the practice and procedure of the Supreme Court (1947–51). He was an ideal committee man, always master of his subject, courteous and patient, and with an enviable capacity for well-timed interventions.

Upjohn was an exceptionally sociable man who greatly enjoyed the company of both men and women. He had a host of friends, and the burdens of his arduous professional life were eased by their company. His marriage in 1947 to Marjorie Dorothy Bertha (Bubbles), daughter of Major Ernest Murray Lucas, was exceptionally happy. She survived him, but there were no children.

When Upjohn was appointed a Chancery judge and knighted in 1951, he defined courtesy and silence as two of the greatest judicial attributes. These he displayed throughout his career. He was an admirable judge at first instance, patient, courteous, and attentive. He earned a reputation as an outstanding judge of fact, while his reported decisions on such matters as the creation of easements and the circumstances in which contractual obligations in respect of the use of land are enforceable by those not party to the original transaction made contributions of permanent value to property law. In 1956 Upjohn was also appointed a judge of the newly created restrictive trade practices court.

Upjohn was appointed a lord justice of appeal and sworn of the privy council in 1960, but his rapid promotion to the House of Lords in November 1963 as Baron Upjohn meant that he had little opportunity to make a great impact on the Court of Appeal. The eight years in which he served as a lord of appeal in ordinary were, in contrast, remarkably fruitful. Upjohn delivered many impressive judgments dealing lucidly with a wide range of issues. The period was one of great importance for the highest appellate court, not least because it was often necessary to decide whether the unorthodox doctrines brilliantly and persuasively expounded by Lord Denning could be accepted. Upjohn opted for orthodoxy. Thus, Upjohn's learned opinion in *National Provincial Bank* v. *Ainsworth* (1965) demonstrated conclusively that the notion that a wife could assert a so-called equity entitling her to stay in the husband's property against the wishes of a purchaser or mortgagee was inconsistent with fundamental principles of property law. Upjohn believed the solution lay in legislation; and the Matrimonial Homes Act was enacted in 1967. Similarly, in *Pettitt* v. *Pettitt* (1962) Upjohn ridiculed the notion that the legislature which in 1882 enacted section 17 of the Married Women's Property Act could have intended to allow county court judges to deal with the property entitlements of husband and wife as they thought fit rather than in accordance with recognized principles of law and equity. Again a solution was found in legislation.

The very high rates of taxation imposed in the post-war period had led to many ingenious attempts to minimize their impact; and the law lords frequently found themselves obliged to analyse basic legal concepts to determine the effectiveness of such schemes. So in a series of cases the question was whether a settlement of property gave so wide a discretion to the trustees as to make it unenforceable; and Upjohn's penetrating analysis in *Re Gulbenkian* (1970) was significant in bringing about the rationalization of the law. He also made important contributions to the law of contract, notably in the *Suisse Atlantique* case (1966), where his analysis of the consequences of a breach of a contractual term was influential. In *Beswick* v. *Beswick* (1968) Upjohn's judgment upheld the principle (now modified by the Contracts (Rights of Third Parties) Act of 1999) that only the parties to a contract could sue on it, while allowing equitable remedies to avoid the harsh consequences which would otherwise have followed on the facts of that case.

The fact that Upjohn believed in orthodoxy did not mean that he was reactionary in outlook; and in *Conway* v. *Rimmer* (1968) he was able to confine within comparatively narrow limits claims by the crown to privilege in the disclosure of material relevant to the case. It is true that in *Rondel* v. *Worsley* (1969) Upjohn, having demolished the basis upon which claims to immunity from suits for professional negligence by barristers was traditionally based, yet concurred in the view that public policy required that advocates enjoy such an immunity. The fact that thirty years later the House of Lords took a different view may be held to demonstrate that perceptions of the public interest can change in a comparatively short period.

Upjohn was a devoted member of Lincoln's Inn. He was elected a bencher in 1948 and served as treasurer in 1965. For eleven years from 1954 he was chairman of the inn's finance committee.

Upjohn served as fellow on the governing body of Eton College from 1963 until his death; and he was also a valued governor of Felsted School. From 1954 to 1964 he was chairman of the St George's Hospital medical school. He was a prominent freemason. His recreations were fishing, sailing, and gardening. He died on 27 January 1971 at the London Clinic, Devonshire Place.

HILARY MAGNUS, *rev.* S. M. CRETNEY

Sources *The Times* (28–30 Jan 1971); (4 Feb 1971) · personal knowledge (1986) · private information (1986) · law reports, 1945–73 · *WWW* · *Report of the [Lynskey] tribunal*, Cmd. 7616 (1949) · *Records of the Honourable Society of Lincoln's Inn: the black books*, 6 (1914–65)
Archives FILM BFI NFTVA, news footage
Likenesses photograph, 1943?, Lincoln's Inn, London · I. Pannett, pastel drawing, priv. coll.
Wealth at death £199,657: probate, 5 March 1971, *CGPLA Eng. & Wales*

Upper Ossory. For this title name *see* Fitzpatrick, Barnaby, second baron of Upper Ossory (*c.*1535–1581).

Upton, Arthur (1633–1706), politician, was born on 31 May 1633 on the family estate of Castle Upton (formerly Castle Norton) at Templepatrick, co. Antrim, the eldest son of Captain Henry Upton (*b.* 1592, *d.* in or after 1641), landowner, and Mary (*fl.* 1600–1650), daughter of Sir Hugh Clotworthy, of Antrim Castle. His father was the younger son of a Devon squire who had arrived in Ireland with the earl of Essex in 1599; his mother also came from a notable planter family and was a sister of Sir John Clotworthy (later first Viscount Massereene). Comparatively little is known of the Upton family before the Ulster rising in 1641, except for the fact that their tenants included substantial numbers of native Irish Catholics, whom they did their best to protect during the 1640s. When the rising broke out Henry Upton raised a troop of cavalry in defence of the beleaguered settler communities, a troop that eventually came under authority of the Scottish covenanter army. Whatever the precise religious beliefs of the family had hitherto been, by 1653 Arthur Upton, who had succeeded his father in the estates, was identifiable as a Presbyterian. By the same year he was married to Dorothy (*c.*1633–1717), daughter of Michael Beresford of Coleraine, co. Londonderry. Upton refused the Cromwellian engagement and was one of those Ulster landowners ordered by proclamation in 1653 to remove to Munster. However, this requirement was not enforced, and by 1657 Upton had re-established himself in the good opinion of the protectorate regime sufficiently to be appointed sheriff of his county.

After the Restoration, Upton was elected to Charles II's Irish parliament as MP for Carrickfergus. He was among the adventurers and soldiers, recipients of parcels of the estates of the marquess of Antrim, who petitioned the crown in 1662 against the grant of a proviso which would restore to Antrim any of his former properties. The failure of this agitation, allegedly resulting in the loss of everything Upton had gained by the Cromwellian confiscations, enraged him to such an extent that he determined to vote in principle against the Bill of Explanation in 1665, and did so even though his was the only negative given in the Irish House of Commons. He had been one of a number of Presbyterians removed from the commission of the peace by the duke of Ormond's government in Ireland after the failure of Captain Blood's plot in 1663, but worked his way back into favour under viceroys who were more indulgent of nonconformity; in all probability he was the Upton of Templepatrick who served as sheriff of co. Antrim again in 1672, and in 1673 and 1678 he was named a local commissioner for receiving arms from Catholics under the proclamations for disarmament.

At the revolution of 1688 Upton was prominent among the Williamite faction in Ulster. Having in December 1688 forwarded to Dublin Castle evidence of a supposed plot to massacre protestants, in the form of an anonymous letter captured at Comber, co. Down, he attended the meeting of protestant gentry convened at Antrim Castle in January 1689 by the second Viscount Massereene, and was elected to the council of the voluntary association in co. Antrim. He raised a regiment of foot from among his tenants, but their military record was not inspiring. They formed part of the Williamite force routed by the Jacobites in March 1689 at the break of Dromore. Naturally Upton was among the protestant rebels attainted by King James's Irish parliament. In the following November, Upton was sent to accompany two Presbyterian ministers to London to deliver a loyal address to William and Mary from the Ulster Presbyterians. The three men subsequently took the opportunity to petition the king and queen for relief for the suffering Presbyterian clergy. Subsequently Upton was elected to William's Irish parliaments, for Antrim borough (1692–3) and co. Antrim (1695–9). He did not cut much of a figure in the Commons and did not stand for re-election in 1703, retiring in favour of his eldest surviving son, Clotworthy *Upton, who took over his mantle of principal lay spokesman for the Ulster Presbyterians. Despite his commitment to the Presbyterian cause Arthur Upton had not once attended the General Synod of Ulster since its establishment in 1691. But in 1705 he signed a petition to the Irish parliament protesting at the effects of the imposition of the sacramental test clause in the 1704 Popery Act. This was his last public act. He died in June 1706 (his will, dated 1 January 1706, was proved on 30 June). The Belfast Presbyterian minister James Kirkpatrick published a verse panegyric the following year, which began:

Great Upton to the highest bliss is borne;
He leaves a nation here below to mourn.
(Kirkpatrick, *An Essay*, 3)

This was hyperbole by any standard. Upton's wife survived him. The couple had eight sons and four daughters, of whom at least the first three sons predeceased their father, one, Arthur, at the battle of Aughrim in 1691. The daughters were married into local landed families or to members of the Presbyterian merchant community in Belfast, and at least one of his surviving sons also set up in trade in the town. Two of the younger sons, Thomas (a king's counsel in Ireland and for a time recorder of Londonderry) and John, also sat in the Irish House of Commons; the latter, who eventually conformed to the established church, was the father of the first Lord Templetown.   D. W. HAYTON

Sources W. H. Upton, *Upton family records* (1893), 13, 41, 89, 110–12 · J. Lodge, *The peerage of Ireland*, rev. M. Archdall, rev. edn, 7 (1789), 152–7 · J. S. Reid and W. D. Killen, *History of the Presbyterian church in Ireland*, new edn, 2–3 (1867) · J. Kirkpatrick, *An essay by way of elegy, on the Hond. Arthur Upton esq., of Castle-Upton* (1707) · J. Kirkpatrick, *An historical essay upon the loyalty of Presbyterians* (1713), 405, 563 · *CSP Ire., 1660–69* · *CSP dom., 1679–80* · *The manuscripts of the marquis of Ormonde*, [old ser.], 3 vols., HMC, 36 (1895–1909), vol. 2 · *The journals of the House of Commons of the kingdom of Ireland*, 2nd edn, 2 (1763) · *Records of the General Synod of Ulster, from 1691 to 1820*, 1 (1890) · R. Gillespie, *Colonial Ulster: the settlement of east Ulster, 1600–1641* (1985), 59 · D. Stevenson, *Scottish covenanters and Irish confederates* (1981), 74 · *DNB*

Upton, Charles Barnes (1831–1920), Unitarian minister and tutor, was born on 19 November 1831 at Portsea in Hampshire, son of Henry Upton, a bookbinder. His early education was undertaken by Dr J. R. Beard, his uncle, at his school in Manchester. In September 1853, at the age of twenty-one, Upton was enrolled at Manchester New College, which had just moved from Manchester to Gordon Square in London. Here he studied for the Unitarian ministry, taking his BA degree at the University of London in 1857. The following year he won a Hibbert scholarship which enabled him to continue his studies after completing his ministerial training and to gain a BSc in 1862. On 11 July 1863 he married Louisa, daughter of Charles Elcock, a captain in the merchant navy. Although they had no children, they enjoyed thirty-four years of happily married life. In 1867 he received an invitation to become the minister of the Ancient Chapel at Toxteth Park in Liverpool, where he remained until 1875, when he was invited back to his old college as professor of philosophy to work alongside James Martineau, the principal. When Manchester College was relocated to Oxford in 1889 he moved with it, and remained on the staff until his retirement in 1903.

Upton was not an original philosopher, but he was a competent teacher and perceptive reviewer, whose main achievement was to popularize the philosophy of James Martineau, his former tutor and colleague. His major work was his contribution to the *Life and Letters of James Martineau* (1902), which he wrote with James Drummond. Upton's section of this book was later published separately under the title *Dr Martineau's Philosophy* (1905). This was an able work which did justice to a complex philosopher. His other major work was the publication of his Hibbert lectures delivered in 1893, *The Bases of Religious Belief*. Here again he acknowledged his dependence upon Martineau and dedicated the book to him. He strongly argued in this work for the doctrine of human freedom, which was a theme constantly found in his lectures and other writings.

Upton was a gentle and quiet man, who read widely and spent much time as a conscientious teacher, a preacher in the college chapel, and a writer of reviews for *The Inquirer*, the Unitarian newspaper. He was a sociable person who enjoyed company and receiving guests, both friends and former students, at his home, St George's, Littlemore, which had been the residence of John Henry Newman after he resigned from the living of St Mary's. Upton died in his home on 21 November 1920. His chief interest outside his academic work was the cultivation of fruit trees in his garden at Littlemore. There is a fine portrait of him by Leslie Brooke in the small dining-room at Manchester College, which captures something of his unselfish and loving character. There is also a memorial plaque to him in the college chapel.   RALPH WALLER

Sources *The Inquirer* (27 Nov 1920) · *The Inquirer* (26 June 1897) · *The Inquirer* (17 June 1916) · *The Inquirer* (2 Dec 1876) · H. McLachlan, *The Ancient Chapel of Toxteth: an address at the 334th anniversary* (1952) · H. McLachlan, *The Unitarian movement in the religious life of England: its contribution to thought and learning, 1700–1900* (1934) · V. D. Davies, *A history of Manchester College* (1932) · *DNB* · Harris Man. Oxf., Upton papers
Archives Harris Man. Oxf., MSS
Likenesses L. Brooke, oils, Harris Man. Oxf.
Wealth at death £25,868 0s. 3d.: probate, 31 Jan 1921, *CGPLA Eng. & Wales*

Upton, Clotworthy (1665–1725), politician and religious activist, was born on 6 January 1665, the fourth but eldest surviving son of Arthur *Upton (1633–1706), landowner and politician, of Castle Upton, Templepatrick, co. Antrim, and his wife, Dorothy (*b. c.*1643, *d.* in or after 1717), daughter of Michael Beresford of Coleraine, co. Londonderry. The first Upton to arrive in Ireland had been Henry, a captain in Essex's army in 1598, who had married into the planter family of the Clotworthys, viscounts Massereene. Although of English descent, the Uptons had by the late seventeenth century become strict Presbyterians. In 1689 Arthur Upton was active in organizing local resistance to James II, while Clotworthy raised a troop and joined King William at the siege of Limerick, where he fell into the hands of the Jacobites and was for a time held prisoner. Prior to the rising of 1688 he had been entered at the Middle Temple, and he may have been the Mr Upton who was admitted in 1702 to the King's Inns in Dublin, although there is no record of his ever having practised law.

Elected to the Irish parliament in 1695 for the borough of Newtownards, Upton succeeded his father in 1703 as MP for co. Antrim. In the Irish House of Commons he was always ready to speak in defence of his fellow Presbyterians. He strongly opposed the imposition of the sacramental test in 1704 and subsequently fought a lone battle for its repeal, so that he came to be recognized as 'the chief lay Dissenter in Ireland' (Bishop John Evans to Archbishop William Wake, 30 April 1717, Christ Church, Oxford, Wake MS 12). In 1715 he was sent to England by the general synod to solicit the repeal of the test, but returned empty-handed. A second mission in 1717, with toleration the objective, was similarly unsuccessful. But Upton badgered his friends in England, and in 1719 secured a promise from Lord Sunderland to instruct the new viceroy, the duke of Bolton, to push for repeal of the test. However, Upton could only watch helplessly as first the proposed repeal was abandoned, then ministerial proposals for a toleration bill were undermined by the Irish parliamentary opposition. The outcome, a limited toleration and a partial retrospective indemnity over the test, was bitterly disappointing.

In his religion Upton was staunchly orthodox, and he may have been responsible for the appointment as minister for Templepatrick of the arch-conservative William Livingston. When conflict broke out within the general synod on the issue of subscription to the Westminster confession, Upton weighed in on the subscribing side. In 1722 he brought before the synod a 'charge' against the non-subscribers, claiming that one of their pamphlets proved them guilty of 'holding a principle that opens a door for letting in error and heresy' (Wodrow Letters Quarto 20, fol. 305). This affair rumbled on for two years and came to an unsatisfactory conclusion in 1724 when Upton was unable to attend the synod to prosecute his accusations, detained in Dublin on what was perhaps a diplomatic pretext.

Upton was married three times, and each marriage was tragically brief: in 1692 to Lady Mary Boyle (*d.* 1695), daughter of Roger Boyle, second earl of Orrery, and Mary Sackville; in 1706 to Mary (*d.* 1707), daughter of William Stewart of Killymoon, co. Tyrone; and finally, about November 1712, to Jane (*d.* 1713), daughter of John Ormsby of Athlacca, co. Limerick, who, before she died, gave birth to his only child, a daughter, Jane. He died at his home, Castle Upton, on 3 September 1725, after a short illness, when an infection in his leg became gangrenous. According to Livingston, he was 'lamented by men of all distinctions. The Tories and Jacobites say he was a fair and generous adversary, and the papists express a great concern for him, for … he protected them from some severities in the House of Commons' (Witherow, 207–8). He was succeeded at Castle Upton by his brother John, an army officer and a conformist, and father of the first Baron Templetown. By a settlement made shortly before his death Clotworthy Upton left a fortune of £6000 p.a. to his daughter, who after her marriage was created *suo jure* Baroness Langford. Livingston, and his successors in the Presbyterian ministry of Templepatrick, received a legacy of £8 per annum.

D. W. HAYTON

Sources *Miscellanea Genealogica et Heraldica*, 2nd ser., 4 (1890–91), 46–7 · Burke, *Peerage* (1907), 1628 · *Records of the General Synod of Ulster, from 1691 to 1820*, 3 vols. (1890–98) · letters, NL Scot., Wodrow MSS Quarto 20–21, Octavo 3 · T. Witherow, *Historical and literary* *memorials of presbyterianism in Ireland, 1623–1731* (1879), 206–8 · J. S. Reid and W. D. Killen, *History of the Presbyterian church in Ireland*, new edn, 3 vols. (1867) · J. C. Beckett, *Protestant dissent in Ireland, 1687–1780* (1948) · D. W. Hayton, 'Ireland and the English ministers, 1707–16', DPhil diss., U. Oxf., 1975 · state papers (Ireland), PRO, SP 63/366–380 · Christ Church Oxf., Wake MSS 12–13 · Surrey HC, Midleton MSS 1248/2–4 · W. D. Killen, *History of congregations of the Presbyterian church in Ireland* (1879)

Archives BL, Add. MS 61640 · BL, Stowe MS 228 · priv. coll., Bolton MSS

Wealth at death £6000 p.a.; also entailed estates: NL Scot., Wodrow MSS Quarto 21, fol. 182, William Livingston to Robert Wodrow, 3 Sept 1725

Upton, Edward (*d.* 1419?), logician and preacher, is likely to have come from the diocese of Winchester. He is first mentioned as having succeeded William Hamsterly as principal of St Edmund Hall, Oxford, in 1384, although it is likely that he had matriculated at Oxford earlier. He remained principal until 1390, perhaps resigning his office in consequence of an incident in the previous year, when the manciple of St Edmund's and others created a serious disturbance in the town. Upton studied theology and philosophy at Oxford, became a master of arts, and rented a school from Exeter College from 1390 to 1392. While at Exeter he wrote *De probationibus propositionum*, included in Bodl. Oxf., MS Bodley 676 (SC 2593, fols. 38–49v), and *De actione interiori elementorum simplicium*, included in Oxford, Corpus Christi College, MS 116, (fols. 117v–178), as well as two other brief logical tractates contained in Worcester Cathedral Library, MS F.118 (fols. 43v–45v and 85). Upton is known mostly for his innovative work in propositional logic and simple supposition; and he appears to have been influential among Oxford philosophers of the fifteenth century, for his name appears regularly on registers and library lists into the sixteenth century.

De probationibus propositionum is an instance of 'probatione' literature, which was concerned with proving sentences. There were two kinds of treatises in the genre: those proving truth conditions of composite, or molecular, sentences and those concerned with non-composite, atomic, sentences. This second group is divisible into, first, those that establish truth conditions by listing requirements that the subject and predicate terms of atomic sentences have to meet, and second, those that establish truth through rigorous analysis of the atomic terms. *De probationibus* comes into the second category. This genre of literature is likely to have been used in conjunction with 'insolubilia' in order to guide students in their analysis of how terms have meaning and refer to extra-mental objects. Upton shows how one must break a statement down into two or more properties which more accurately reflect its meaning. The analysis is of one term taken at a time, and not of the relation of subject to predicate, which means that the work is as much concerned with proving terms as it is with proving propositions. Upton pays particular attention to 'resoluble' proofs, which include universal and particular or indefinite affirmations and negations ('All men run'), and

'exponible' proofs, where such statements are modified comparatively, positively, or exclusively ('All men except Socrates run'). He also examines 'officiable' proofs, which involve modal operators ('All men can run').

On 20 December 1399 Upton was granted letters dimissory to proceed to higher orders and was ordained subdeacon to title of University College two months later, on 22 February 1400; he is recorded as having been a resident of University College until 1402. By the late 1390s, Wycliffism had become a serious threat to the authority of the church and efforts by bishops to regain and reassert their control over the laity mounted as the heresy spread. Philip Repingdon, bishop of Lincoln (*d.* 1424), gathered a group of doctors and masters of theology to combat Wycliffism in his diocese. Upton was in this group, along with Dr Thomas Duffield, chancellor of Lincoln, and two future chancellors of Oxford, William Truegoff and Thomas Chace. Wycliffism was particularly troublesome in Buckinghamshire, where Wyclif had been rector at Ludgershall from 1368 to 1374, and Repingdon seems to have felt that a preacher of similar dialectical skill was needed to undermine Wyclif's influence. Upton was appointed to the rectory of the first portion of Waddesdon in Buckinghamshire on 20 March 1399 and began his work there on 25 January 1401. Repingdon appears to have been satisfied with Upton's preaching in Waddesdon, for he granted him licence to preach in the archdeaconries of Buckingham, Oxford, and Northampton on 13 December 1418. But it is doubtful whether Upton had the chance to enjoy this privilege, for no further mention is made of his activities after this; and since John Castell was appointed to succeed him at Waddesdon on 4 February 1419, it is reasonable to conclude that Upton died in early January 1419.

STEPHEN E. LAHEY

Sources Emden, *Oxf.*, 3.1932 · A. B. Emden, *An Oxford hall in medieval times: being the early history of St Edmund Hall* (1927) · J. N. D. Kelly, *St Edmund Hall: almost seven hundred years* (1989) · M. Archer, ed., *The register of Bishop Philip Repingdon, 1405–1419*, 3, Lincoln RS, 74 (1982) · register of Henry Beaufort, Lincs. Arch., episcopal register 13 · P. V. Spade and E. J. Ashworth, 'Logic in late medieval Oxford', *Hist. U. Oxf.* 2: *Late med. Oxf.*, 35–64 · J. D. North, 'Astronomy and mathematics', *Hist. U. Oxf.* 2: *Late med. Oxf.*, 103–74 · J. M. Fletcher, 'Developments in the faculty of arts, 1370–1520', *Hist. U. Oxf.* 2: *Late med. Oxf.*, 315–45, esp. 341 · J. K. Floyer, ed., *Catalogue of manuscripts preserved in … Worcester Cathedral*, rev. S. G. Hamilton, Worcestershire Historical Society (1905), 89 · J. I. Catto, 'Wyclif and Wycliffism at Oxford, 1356–1430', *Hist. U. Oxf.* 2: *Late med. Oxf.*, 175–261, esp. 254–5 · G. Lipscomb, *The history and antiquities of the county of Buckingham*, 4 vols. (1831–47), vol. 1

Archives Bodl. Oxf., MS Bodley 676 (SC 2593), fols. 38–49v · CCC Oxf., MS 116, fols. 117v–178 · Worcester Cathedral Library, MS F.118, fols. 43v–45v, 85

Upton, Florence Kate (1873–1922), illustrator and artist, was born on 22 February 1873 in Flushing, Long Island, New York, USA, the second of four children of Thomas Harborough Upton (1835–1889), a confidential clerk in the American Exchange Bank, and his wife, Bertha (1849–1912), the daughter of John W. Hudson, an architect. Florence's parents were both English, but they married in

Florence Kate Upton (1873–1922), by Elliott & Fry, 1912

patented her creation she had no control over its extensive marketing. In addition to illustrating a volume of Bertha's verse, *Little Hearts* (1897), Florence tried twice more to produce Golliwogg-free books, neither of which was a success. The second of these, *The Adventures of Borbee and the Wisp* (1908), was the only work that she produced on her own.

The bold, adventurous Golliwogg had a prodigious appeal, with his strange mix of cultural elements: black and white monochrome features against bright minstrel clothing, paws rather than hands or feet, and grotesque features—hair standing on end in fright, shocked eyes, and engorged lips. But despite his initially disturbing appearance, he is an endearing character, full of bold, child-like plans (many with a contemporary feel, involving polar adventures, bicycling, and airships, for example), who encounters many set-backs but, with the help of his five companion dolls, Peg, Sarah Jane, Meg, Weg, and Midget, always emerges victorious. His power has been celebrated by such luminaries as the art critic Sir Kenneth Clark. The dolls themselves, including Golliwogg, were sold at auction at Christies in 1917, along with the original artwork, and the proceeds were used to equip an ambulance for the front in France. The dolls were subsequently displayed at Chequers, the prime minister's country residence, but are now on display at the Bethnal Green Museum of Childhood. The generic 'golliwog' subsequently became infamous as a racist icon, and has largely disappeared from public view.

Florence Upton did not depend on the Golliwogg, though. She used the proceeds from the first books to train as an artist, first at the Art Students League in New York (1897–1900), then in Paris (1901–6) at the Académie Colarossi, spending her summers taking classes at the village of Egmond aan den Hoef in Holland. In each case, she took the whole family with her, and helped to support them. But in 1906, when the rest of the family went back to America, Florence set herself up in London, first in Chelsea and then in Westminster in 1909, moving to her final address, 21 Great College Street, in 1910.

Though Upton is now neglected as an artist, her biographers, Edith Lyttelton (1926) and Norma S. Davis (1992), stress her contemporary reputation, first as a genre painter, then as a portraitist. Her work was exhibited, among other places, at the salon of the Société Nationale des Beaux Arts, where she was made a *sociétaire*; at the international exhibition in Nantes in 1905, where she won a medal of honour; at the Royal Salon, London; and in various exhibitions in Germany, Holland, and America. In 1912 she held a one-woman show at her studio in Westminster.

Adaline Piper, a contemporary artist, wrote an appreciation of Florence Upton shortly after her death, in which she recalls the artist with her long, brown hair, in her prime, 'like a wild rose, tall and slender, with blue eyes' (Piper, 487). Florence never married, being something of a loner, and suffered bouts of depression, though Lyttelton says that she was more outgoing after becoming involved

New York in 1870, where her father had emigrated. Florence had one elder sister (Ethel), and a younger sister (Alice) and brother (Desmond). When Florence was sixteen, their father suddenly died, an event that ended her schooling and triggered her career as an illustrator.

In 1893 the family returned to the maternal family home in Hampstead, England, where Florence Upton pursued her artistic career with cartoons in *Punch* and elsewhere, and made her début as a book illustrator for Ernest Beckman's *Pax and Carlino: a Story* (1894). However, her breakthrough came in the following year. A children's story about some Dutch dolls suddenly came to life when an old black doll was found that the girls had forgotten on a previous visit. Their mother composed verses for the story, which Florence illustrated. It was rejected by two publishers before being accepted by J. W. Allen, of Longmans, Green & Co., who noted its popularity with his own children. The title on the book's cover was *The Adventures of Two Dutch Dolls*, the crucial addition of 'Golliwogg' appearing only on the title-page.

Florence and Bertha Upton produced twelve further Golliwogg titles, on an almost annual basis, the last being *The Golliwogg in the African Jungle* (1909). Towards the end of this period the books' popularity declined, although that of the character itself did not. Many others took him up, most famously Debussy in his piece 'The Golliwogg's Cakewalk' (1908). The more common spelling, 'golliwog', then became the norm, probably to avoid accusations of copyright infringement, but since Florence had never in spiritualism. Though she was brought up as an Episcopalian, a vision of her dead mother turned her in a spiritualist direction in 1916. Thereafter, she filled some twenty-two books with automatic writing, later turning to automatic utterance. She supposedly helped many grieving parents during the war by doing psychic portraits of their lost loved ones. She died at her home in Westminster on 15 October 1922, after suffering from carcinoma of the gall bladder. She was buried in Hampstead cemetery, and the inscription on the headstone of her grave says of her that 'she was possessed of a gift of fantasy and created the golliwog to the unfading delight of generations of children' (*The Times*, 31 Jan 1997, 19).   DAVID RUDD

Sources N. S. Davis, *A lark ascends: Florence Kate Upton, artist and illustrator* (1992) • E. Lyttelton, *Florence Upton: painter* (1926) • A. Piper, 'Florence K. Upton, painter: an appreciation of her work', *American Magazine of Art*, 14 (1923), 487–92 • *The Times* (31 Jan 1997), 19 • G. D. Little, 'Bertha Upton and Florence K. Upton', *British children's writers, 1880–1914*, ed. L. M. Zaidman, DLitB, 141 (1994), 284–91 • H. W. Peet, 'Birth of the Golliwogg', *John O'London's Weekly* (22 Dec 1950), 697 • E. Osborne, 'The birth of Golliwogg', *Junior Bookshelf*, 12 (1948), 159–65 • K. Clark, *Another part of the wood* (1974) • d. cert. • *WWW*

Archives Bethnal Green Museum of Childhood, London, Renier Collection

Likenesses Vandyk, photograph, 1896, repro. in Lyttelton, *Florence Upton* • Elliott & Fry, photograph, 1912, repro. in Lyttelton, *Florence Upton* [*see illus.*]

Wealth at death £798 0s. 11d.: probate, 11 Jan 1923, CGPLA Eng. & Wales

Upton, James (1671–1749), schoolmaster, was born at Wilmslow, Cheshire, on 10 December 1671, the son of John Upton of Wilmslow, who was reported by Thomas Hearne to have been gardener to Sir Philip Sydenham. He was educated at Eton College from 1687 and matriculated from King's College, Cambridge, in 1694. He graduated BA in 1698, MA in 1701, and was a fellow of his college from 1696 to 1697 and was ordained deacon (1697). At the request of Dr John Newborough, the headmaster, he returned to Eton as an assistant master about 1698. It was probably in 1700 that he married Mary, daughter of Mr Proctor, a boarding master at Eton; they had six sons and two daughters.

Ordained priest at Lincoln in 1701, Upton was presented in the same year to the rectory of Brimpton, near Yeovil, by the Sydenham family. He acted briefly as chaplain to the duke of St Albans before being appointed headmaster of Ilminster grammar school in 1704. He made a name for himself locally by reviving the fortunes of his school and in 1712 he was persuaded to take on the headship of another failing school, Taunton grammar school. Taking many of his pupils with him, he found the school buildings in a dilapidated state but, nothing daunted, he succeeded in transforming the school. At the height of its reputation the school had over 200 pupils and, according to Joshua Toulmin, was the largest provincial school in England. He had gained another preferment from the Sydenhams in 1711 when he exchanged Brimpton for the rectory of Monksilver, near Taunton, and he also acquired the living at Plympton in Devon, which he held until his death. He served as chaplain to Lord Poulett, gave up

Monksilver in 1717, and was appointed in 1731 to the vicarage of Bishop's Hull, a neighbouring parish to Taunton in which the school was situated.

Upton made his mark as a competent classical scholar early on with an edition of Theodore Gulston's *Poetics of Aristotle* (1623), which he published at Cambridge in 1696. He published a selection of passages from Greek authors in 1701 which was used at Eton, and an edition of Dionysius of Halicarnassus in 1702 (reprinted 1728 and 1747). His most notable work was his sympathetic edition of Roger Ascham's *The Schoolmaster* (1711; reprinted 1743, 1761, 1815), which he claimed he had rescued from 'Darkness and Obscurity' (preface). Upton was also the author of a couple of published sermons. He died on 13 August 1749 at Bishop's Hull, where he was buried; he was survived by his wife.

Upton's second son, **John Upton** (1707–1760), Church of England clergyman, born at Taunton, was educated by his father and at Merton College, Oxford, whence he matriculated on 5 March 1725, aged seventeen. In 1728 he was elected fellow of Exeter College, Oxford, whence he graduated BA (1730) and MA (1732). He resigned his fellowship in February 1737 after being admitted prebendary of Rochester the previous month. He had held, successively, the rectory of Seavington with Dinnington, Somerset (in the gift of his father's patron, Lord Poulett), the rectory of Great Rissington, Gloucestershire (presented by Earl Talbot), and the sinecure rectory of Landrillo, Denbighshire. An accomplished classical and literary scholar, he published an excellent edition of Arrian's *Epictetus* in two volumes (1739–41); a new edition, with glossary and notes, of Spenser's *Faerie Queen* (2 vols., 1758); and some critical observations on the plays of Shakespeare and Ben Jonson. Upton died unmarried at Taunton on 2 or 9 December 1760.   E. C. MARCHANT, *rev.* S. J. SKEDD

Sources W. Sterry, ed., *The Eton College register, 1441–1698* (1943), 342 • Venn, *Alum. Cant.* • J. Toulmin, *The history of Taunton, in the county of Somerset*, ed. J. Savage, new edn (1822), 202–3 • *Miscellanea Genealogica et Heraldica*, 2nd ser., 3 (1888–9), 167 • R. Bush, *The book of Taunton* (1977) • private information (1937) [A. T. Wicks] • C. W. Boase, ed., *Registrum Collegii Exoniensis*, new edn, OHS, 27 (1894), 137 • *GM*, 1st ser., 30 (1760), 594 • will, PRO, PROB 11/775, sig. 359 [will of James Upton] • N. Carlisle, *A concise description of the endowed grammar schools in England and Wales*, 2 (1818), 432

Archives Som. ARS, commonplace book

Likenesses stipple (John Upton; after J. Collyer), BM; repro. in S. Harding and E. Harding, *Shakespeare illustrated* (1793)

Wealth at death bequeathed three estates; plus other bequests: will, PRO, PROB 11/775, fols. 33v–34r

Upton, John (1707–1760). *See under* Upton, James (1671–1749).

Upton, Nicholas (c.1400–1457), cleric, lawyer, and writer on warfare and heraldry, was probably the second son of John and Elizabeth Upton who came from Portlinch, near Newton, Devon. Claims that he was born in Somerset are dubious. Enrolled as a scholar of Winchester in 1409 with the alias Helyer, he then went to Oxford as a scholar of New College on 16 December 1413 and became a fellow in 1415. He graduated as a bachelor of civil law in 1421 and of canon law in 1427, eventually becoming a doctor of canon law in March 1439. Among the benefices he acquired were the rectory of Chedzoy, Somerset (August 1427 – September 1434), a canonry of Wells Cathedral (April 1431 – January 1452), the rectory of Stapleford, Wiltshire (29 September 1434 – March 1443), the rectory of Fawley, Hampshire (1440), and a canonry of St Paul's, London (10 April 1443 – May 1446). Two papal dispensations in 1434 and 1440 allowed him to hold some of these benefices concurrently. On 6 September 1442 he became the master of St Nicholas's Hospital in Salisbury, and was made precentor of the cathedral (14 May 1446) where he delivered 'erudite sermons', according to later testimony. From June 1452 to May 1453 he acted as one of the proctors of the dean and chapter seeking the canonization of Bishop Osmund (d. 1099) in Rome, a protracted and costly venture which finally achieved its goal in 1457—but not before Upton had been withdrawn from Rome, leaving rents unpaid, to cut down on the mission's expenses.

Upton's career had been far from exclusively clerical. In 1421 he had joined the retinue of Thomas Montagu, earl of Salisbury (d. 1428), in France, serving probably in bureaucratic, heraldic, and possibly in priestly capacities. At the battle of Verneuil (August 1424), he gave a certain gentleman a coat of arms displaying oxen, gelded beasts, to betoken an unfortunate injury to the gentleman's 'privy parts'. Salisbury may well have helped Upton's clerical career: the advowson of Chedzoy lay in his gift. The loss of his patron to a freak cannon ball at the siege of Orléans in 1428 did not end Upton's military career. In 1430 he took part in Cardinal Beaufort's proposed crusade against the Hussites (which was diverted to France) and he was in the retinue of Sir John Tiptoft in 1431. Although he returned to England to become canon of Wells, his military and heraldic career was not forgotten. In 1436 he, and others, were commissioned to take the muster of a certain retinue at Southampton. Much later, in 1449, he was asked to organize the heraldic aspects of Walter Hungerford's funeral in Salisbury Cathedral because of his known involvement, as executor, in the burial of his former patron, the earl of Salisbury. Upton also acquired two other powerful patrons: Humphrey, duke of Gloucester, and William de la Pole, duke of Suffolk, who had also served with Salisbury. Both may have helped Upton acquire lucrative benefices: Suffolk presented Upton to the rectory of Stapleford. Through Suffolk, Upton seems to have been drawn into a circle of courtiers who by 1449 were popularly blamed for social injustices and the disastrous war effort in France. On 3 June 1449 Upton helped save one such courtier, Robert Hungerford, Lord Moleyns, from being set upon in a Salisbury city inn, by escorting him to safety under the protection of the host. In June 1450, during Jack Cade's revolt against Suffolk's rule, Upton's house in Salisbury was sacked.

All aspects of his career—clerical, legal, and military—were brought to bear in Upton's famed work *De studio militari*. Written in 1447 and dedicated to Humphrey, duke of Gloucester, it is a treatise, in four parts, on heraldry and the arts of war, drawing heavily on a tradition of heraldic

and legal writing, but also reflecting contemporary concerns. The first book elaborates a view of nobility and knighthood that recognizes the importance of virtue, but which also attaches importance (as Bartolo da Sassoferrato had done) to princely authority in the granting of arms. Upton voices the topos of the decline of chivalry, as well as contemporary aristocratic concern that too many low-born men were acquiring arms in wartime. The second book discusses various types and laws of war (using Giovanni da Legnano's *Tractatus de bello*), a theme carried over into the fourth book with treatment of Henry V's campaign statutes. For the third book, on the colours of heraldry, Upton relies, though not slavishly, on the treatise of Johannes de Bado Aureo (possibly Bishop John Trevor of St Asaph's). The fourth draws also on French treatises and especially on encyclopaedias (such as Bartholomaeus Anglicus's *De proprietatibus rerum*) for the meaning of heraldic signs (animals, birds, fish, flowers, and ordinaries); but the extended list, in 195 sections, also reflects a growing demand for (and disputes over) coats of arms. Some subjects make for reminiscence on youthful pranks: Upton recalls how he was required by his lord Salisbury to give, to an unnamed gentleman, arms displaying partridges, because these birds symbolized sodomy and deceit. Others elicit more serious social criticism: the cat toys with its prey, Upton writes, in the same way that men in England, perverting the jury system, play with and then devour the poor.

Upton died early in 1457 and was probably buried in Salisbury Cathedral: a commission on 15 February saw to the collection of his goods and debts.

ANDREW BROWN and CRAIG WALKER

Sources N. Upton, *De studio militari*, ed. C. Bissaeus (1654) · N. Upton, 'De studio militari', trans. J. Blount, *c.*1500, Bodl. Oxf., MS Eng. misc. d. 227 · F. P. Barnard, *The essential portions of Nicholas Upton's 'De studio militari'* (1931) · Emden, *Oxf.*, vol. 3 · A. R. Malden, *The canonization of St Osmund* (1901) · *CPR, 1425–36*, 184, 444, 536; *1436–41*, 369 · Salisbury Cathedral muniments, chapter act books, register of John Burgh, 1447–57, fols. 1, 23v–24 · *Report of the Deputy Keeper of the Public Records*, 48 (1887), 267, 272, 275 · J. Stevenson, ed., *Letters and papers illustrative of the wars of the English in France during the reign of Henry VI, king of England*, 1, Rolls Series, 22 (1861), 464–7 · J. Prince, *Danmonii orientales illustres, or, The worthies of Devon* (1701) · R. Dennys, *The heraldic imagination* (1975) · A. R. Wagner, *Heralds and heraldry in the middle ages* (1935) · M. H. Keen, 'The debate over nobility: Dante, Nicholas Upton and Bartholus', *The culture of Christendom*, ed. M.-A. Meyer (1993), 257–68 · J. N. Hare, 'The Wiltshire risings of 1450: politics and economic discontent in mid-fifteenth-century England', *Southern History*, 4 (1982), 13–31

Archives BL, Upton's 'De studio militari', Add. MS 30946 · BL, Upton's 'De studio militari', Cotton MS Nero ciii · Bodl. Oxf., Upton's 'De studio militari', MS Holkham misc. 31 · Coll. Arms, Upton's 'De studio militari', MS Arundel 64 · FM Cam., Upton's 'De studio militari', MS 324 | BL, Harleian MSS, 3504 and 6106 · Bodl. Oxf., Rawlinson MSS, B 20, B 107 · Trinity College, Oxford, MS xxxvi

Upton, Sir Nicholas (*b.* in or before **1513**, *d.* **1551**), knight of the hospital of St John of Jerusalem, was the third son of Nicholas Upton (*d.* 1533) of Northolme by Wainfleet, a Lincolnshire gentleman, and his first wife, Alice. His father subsequently married Margaret Sutton of Burton by Lincoln, who was the niece, sister, and mother of knights of

St John (hospitallers). The younger Nicholas was received into the English *langue* or 'tongue' (branch) of the order in Malta in July 1531, when he must have been at least eighteen. His admission was probably arranged either by his stepbrother Thomas Coppledike or by his step-uncle John Sutton, both of whom were hospitaller preceptors, in charge of houses of the order, and with whom he maintained a correspondence. Upton remained in Malta for some years, making three tours of duty on the order's galleys between 1532 and 1537. He then served under William Tyrrell, who had been appointed captain of the order's great galleon in 1537. In early 1539 he returned home from Marseilles, where the galleon was then stationed, by way of Calais, carrying news of the great Christian defeat by the Ottoman Turks at Prevesa in the previous autumn, in which several hospitaller vessels had taken part.

By October Upton had returned to Malta, and after the dissolution of the order in England in May 1540, along with two other Englishmen he elected to remain there. In September 1541 he was granted a small pension by the order to supplement his income. The exiles kept in touch with developments at home, and despite his loyalty to the order Upton was investigated by the Inquisition in April 1546 for possessing prohibited English tracts and books. In the following year he was nevertheless appointed preceptor of Ribston (Yorkshire) and licensed to return home. On Edward VI's refusal to restore the order's lands he was forced back to Malta, where he entertained Gerald Fitzgerald, the claimant to the earldom of Kildare, who was conspiring with the order and Cardinal Pole to raise rebellion in Ireland. In November 1548 he was appointed turcopolier, a dignity which gave him responsibility for the coastguard and a seat on the order's councils. Renewed evidence of the favour in which he was held was provided by his appointment as castellan of Birgu in 1549. It was in this capacity that Upton led a force of cavalry to victory over Turkish raiders attacking Malta in July 1551. He expired on 16 July in the moment of triumph, overcome by his corpulence and by the strain of fighting all day in the summer heat. He was buried in the church of St Laurence in Birgu. G. J. O'MALLEY

Sources H. P. Scicluna, ed., *The book of deliberations of the venerable tongue of England, 1523–1567* (1949) · *LP Henry VIII* · National Library of Malta, archives of the knights, vols. 85–8, 287–8, 420–21 · G. Bosio, *Dell'istoria della sacra religione e ill.ma militia di San Giovanni Gierosolimitano*, 3 (1602) · A. R. Maddison, ed., *Lincolnshire pedigrees*, 3, Harleian Society, 52 (1904) · A. Mifsud, *Knights hospitallers of the ven. tongue of England in Malta* (1914) · Cathedral Archives, Mdina, Malta, archivum inquisitionis Melitensis, vol. 1A, case 1, fols. 13r–17r

Wealth at death 200 florins of Rhodes: annual pension from 1541; annuity of 10 marks under father's will: National Library of Malta, archives of the knights, 86, fol. 118v; Maddison, ed., *Lincolnshire pedigrees*

ʿUrabi [ʿArabī], **Ahmad Muhammad** [Aḥmad Muḥammad ʿUrabī; *known as* Arabi Pasha] (**1841–1911**), army officer and politician in Egypt, was born on 31 March 1841 (7 Safar 1257 according to the Islamic calendar) in the village of Huriyyah Razna, near the delta town of Zaqaziq, the second of four sons and six daughters of al-Sayyid

Ahmad Muhammad ʿUrabi (1841–1911), by unknown engraver, pubd 1882 (after N. Fettel & Co.)

Muhammad ʿUrabi (*d.* 1848), religious scholar and graduate of the famous Cairo mosque-university of al-Azhar, and al-Sayyida Fatima Sulayman, one of his three wives. ʿUrabi claimed descent from the family of the Prophet Muhammad through a thirteenth-century Iraqi settler in Egypt, though the lineage is disputed. Both parents were native Egyptians of peasant extraction.

At the age of five ʿUrabi entered the Koranic school in the village, where he studied under his father for three years before his father's death of cholera, and then under his elder brother Muhammad's tuition until the age of twelve. He then entered the University of al-Azhar in Cairo, where for two years he was exposed to the rudiments of the Islamic sciences. He abandoned his religious studies in 1854 when the new governor of Egypt, Saʿid Pasha, opened the military to the sons of village headmen. Seizing the new opportunity, ʿUrabi enlisted as a common soldier on 6 December 1854.

In the ten years of Saʿid Pasha's reign (*r.* 1854–63), ʿUrabi enjoyed rapid promotion to officer grade. Within six years he was the first native-born Egyptian to reach the rank of *kaymakam*, or lieutenant-colonel, thanks to the patronage of Saʿid Pasha and the French general under whom he served, Süleyman Pasha. Just before Saʿid's death ʿUrabi travelled in the governor's retinue to visit the Islamic holy city of Medina in Arabia. In later life he was to look back on this period of royal patronage and rapid promotion as the happiest days of his life.

With the accession of Ismaʿil (*r.* 1863–79), native-born officers found promotion obstructed by the Turco-Circassian élites favoured by the new governor. ʿUrabi was court-martialled for insubordination following a dispute with a Circassian brigadier, Hushrev Pasha, and sentenced to twenty-one days' imprisonment. While ʿUrabi successfully appealed the decision, he earned the enmity of the minister of war. The ambitious ʿUrabi received no promotions in the reign of Ismaʿil, in spite of his service in the Abyssinian campaign (1876). He was seconded to the civil service for three years (1867–70), during which time he married Karima, a lower member of the khedival household. Karima was a milk-sister to the wife of Khedive

Tawfiq, Ismaʿil's son and successor, and served as wet-nurse to Prince Ilhami Pasha. This was not a unique honour: three of the six conspirators later exiled to Ceylon with ʿUrabi had also married women of the royal household.

It was in the reign of Khedive Tawfiq (r. 1879–92) that ʿUrabi was promoted to his highest rank of full colonel, and during this period he entered the political arena. The economy of Egypt had been largely in British and French hands since 1876, when the Egyptian treasury had been unable to honour its commitments to foreign creditors. In order to satisfy its European creditors, the Egyptian government began to make cuts in expenditure, which led to pay arrears and the threat of reductions in the size of the army that touched native-born Egyptian soldiers and officers.

In July 1880 the khedive issued a decree limiting military service to four years, which was interpreted by ʿUrabi and his fellow officers as a means of preventing native-born Egyptians from ever reaching officer rank. ʿUrabi led a group of dissident officers who began to petition the khedive to appoint an Egyptian as minister of war. In January 1881 government plans to arrest ʿUrabi and his fellows were leaked to the dissidents, who instructed their soldiers to mutiny. When, on 1 February 1881, ʿUrabi and two colleagues were arrested, their troops stormed the ministry of war, seized the military judges, and released their commanders. Tawfiq defused the crisis by appointing the dissidents' candidate as minister of war, though relations between the military and the khedive continued to deteriorate. The dissident officers made common cause with members of the national assembly and landed élites with grievances against European influence or the khedive's rule. These grievances were presented in a military demonstration before the viceregal palace on 9 September 1881 in which Tawfiq was forced to concede to demands for representative government and an enlarged army. ʿUrabi then claimed to speak on behalf of Egyptian interests rather than just those of the army.

ʿUrabi's anti-European agitation turned against Tawfiq, who was accused of subservience to the powers. This point seemed reinforced by the Anglo-French joint note of 8 January 1882, written by French foreign minister Léon Gambetta, in which the two powers undertook to preserve the khedive on his throne. The initiative had the opposite effect to that intended, raising objections from Egypt's suzerain, the Ottoman sultan, and discrediting Tawfiq and his government. The ʿUrabists capitalized on the Gambetta note to force a change of cabinet in February 1882 in which ʿUrabi was appointed minister of war.

Civil order in Egypt began to break down as the military and the khedive became rival poles of authority. Britain and France, fearing for their financial interests in Egypt, dispatched a joint fleet to prop up the khedive. They demanded the resignation of the cabinet on 25 May, calling in particular for ʿUrabi to withdraw from Egypt to reduce tensions. ʿUrabi responded by denouncing Tawfiq for betraying his country to foreign interests. Tawfiq retreated from Cairo to his palace in Alexandria to be closer to the protection of the European fleet, leaving Egypt under ʿUrabi's effective control. Tensions between Egyptians and Europeans erupted in riots in Alexandria (11 June). ʿUrabi ordered the building of shore defences to protect Alexandria from attack by sea, which elicited repeated demands from Sir Beauchamp Seymour, the commander of the British fleet in Alexandria, that construction be halted. This led to a series of ultimata and to the bombardment of Alexandria. The French, unwilling to take military action, withdrew their naval squadron and on 11 July the British fleet opened fire, marking the beginning of the British intervention in Egypt which would ultimately lead to a seventy-four-year occupation.

ʿUrabi, in control of Cairo and most of Egypt, responded to the British occupation of Alexandria by calling for a general conscription and declaring war on Britain. He obtained a religious ruling (fatwa) from al-Azhar calling for Tawfiq's deposal as a traitor to his country and religion for bringing about a foreign occupation. Tawfiq, confined to Alexandria and its hinterlands, backed by the British, declared ʿUrabi a rebel. This dual authority crisis endured until Sir Garnet Wolseley landed a British force of 20,000 men, who routed ʿUrabi's army near the Suez Canal at Tell al-Kebir (13 September 1882). ʿUrabi was arrested two days later and subsequently tried for treason, along with a number of his leading supporters. His cause was taken up by a number of sympathetic Britons, particularly Wilfrid Scawen Blunt, who arranged for an English lawyer, A. M. Broadley, to undertake the defence of the group which came to be known as 'Arabi and his friends'. On 3 December 1882 ʿUrabi pleaded guilty to the charge of rebellion and had his death sentence commuted to perpetual exile, along with six of his colleagues. They and their families were shipped at British expense on a chartered steamer, the Mareotis, to Ceylon.

After nineteen years in exile ʿUrabi was pardoned by Khedive ʿAbbas II (r. 1892–1914) and returned to Egypt on 1 October 1901. In his final years he declined all political activity and applied himself to preserving his rightful place in Egyptian history. He wrote his memoirs and gave autobiographical essays to his friend W. S. Blunt to publish in English and to Jurji Zaydan to publish in his Arabic biographical dictionary of luminaries of the nineteenth century. He died at his home on Jawhar al-Qaʾid Street in the Munira district of Cairo, after nine months' illness, on 21 September 1911 and was buried the same day in the Imam al-Shafiʿi mosque.   EUGENE ROGAN

Sources Ahmad Muhammad ʿUrabi, *Mudhakkirat ʿUrabi*, 2 vols. (Dar al-Hilal, 1953) · Jurji Zaydan, *Tarajim mashahir al-sharq*, 1 (Cairo, 1910), 254–80 · W. S. Blunt, *Secret history of the English occupation of Egypt: being a personal narrative of events* (1922) · A. M. Broadley, *How we defended Arabi and his friends* (1884) · A. al-Rafiʿi, *Al-thawra al-ʿUrabiyya* (1949) · P. J. Vatikiotis, *The history of Egypt*, 3rd edn (1985) · A. Schölch, *Egypt for the Egyptians: the socio-political crisis in Egypt, 1878–1882* (1981); trans. of *Ägypten den Ägyptern! Die politische und gesellschaftliche Krise der Jahre 1878–1882 in Ägypten* (1972) · J. R. I. Cole, *Colonialism and revolution in the Middle East* (1993) · *al-Jaridah* [Cairo] (21 Sept 1911) · *al-Muqattam* [Cairo] (21 Sept 1911)
Archives Egyptian National Archives, Cairo, Mahafiz al-thawra al-ʿUrabiyya · Egyptian National Archives, Cairo, Mukatabat ʿArabi, corresp. [Arabic correspondence]

Likenesses engraving, pubd 1882 (after N. Fettel & Co.), NPG [*see illus.*] · photographs, repro. in Jurji Zaydan, *Tarajim mashahir al-sharq* · photographs and lithographs, repro. in Broadley, *How we defended Arabi*

Wealth at death essentially nothing; all possessions confiscated by the state after conviction: ʿUrabi, *Mudhakkirat*; Broadley, *How we defended Arabi*

Urard [Airard] **mac Coise** [Erard Maccoisse] (*d.* 983x1023), Gaelic poet, is recorded in the annals of Ulster and the annals of Tigernach as having died in 990. Other annals record dates of 983 and 988 and even as late as 1023 in the seventeenth-century compilation, the annals of the four masters. The discrepancy has given rise to considerable uncertainty, especially since another poet, the similarly named *Airbertach mac Coise, the lector and *erenagh* of Ros Ailithir (Ross Carbery), died in 1016. While there may have been two poets named Urard mac Coise, it seems most likely that the later date arises from confusion with Airbertach mac Coise, the author of a long geographical poem, *Ro fessa hi curp domuin dúir*, preserved in the twelfth-century Book of Leinster. It is possible that some of the poems ascribed to Urard, composed not long after 1000, were in fact the work of Airbertach or others. Urard's posthumous fame, and later poems retrospectively authored on him, make this an attractive theory.

While a small number of Urard's poems seem to survive, his fame mainly rested on the prose tale *Airec menman Uraird maic Coise* ('The stratagem of Urard mac Coise'). Urard's authorship of this tale has been generally accepted and a composition date of some time before 980 has been plausibly suggested. The *Airec menman* tale is a third-person narrative in which Urard describes how Cenél nÉogain raiders carry off his possessions and destroy his home at 'Clártha' (probably Clare, in Westmeath). The poet decides to exact compensation by visiting Domnall mac Muirchertaig (*d.* 980), the Cenél nÉogain king of Tara. Domnall welcomes Urard and asks him for news. The word for both news and stories is the same, *scéla*, and Urard cleverly accepts this opening by listing all the tales he knows. This tale list is, in fact, an important piece of evidence proving the existence of versions of certain narratives by the end of the tenth century. Moreover, it delineates the repertory expected of an *ollam*, the highest grade of *fili* or professional poet. The last of Urard's titles is *Orgain cathrach Maíl Milscothaig* ('The destruction of the fort of Máel Milscothach'). The king has never heard this tale and asks Urard to recite it. As the tale progresses, it becomes clear that Máel Milscothach, Máel of the Sweet Words, is in fact Urard himself. Máel Milscothach successfully seeks reparation at the court of the king of Tara, following the destruction of his home. At the dénouement of this tale within a tale, Urard tells Domnall that he is indeed that king. Domnall, taking the hint, apprehends the wrongdoers and brings the nobles of Cenél nÉogain together. The latter compensate the poet for his loss. Furthermore, at a council of professional poets and judges, the king attempts to fix the compensation and honour price owed to a poet. The matter is eventually handed over to Flann, the lector of Clonmacnoise. Since the annals of

Tigernach mention that Urard died in penitence at Clonmacnoise, it is possible that he may have had links with the monastery. In any event, Flann decides that Urard should receive complete compensation for his losses, as well as an honour price equal to the king of Tara. This ruling should, furthermore, apply to every *ollam*.

It has been argued that this tale represents an attempt by the *filid*, the professional poets, to force back changes in Irish society inimical to the status of their order. It has been convincingly shown, however, that the claims set forth in *Airec menman* are innovatory and an attempt to enhance further the high status of the *filid*. Eighth-century legal material, dealing with the status of *filid*, assigns to an *ollam* an honour price equivalent to a petty king. The plea in *Airec menman*, that this should be replaced with an honour price equivalent to the king of Tara, reflects the profound changes that were transforming ninth- and tenth-century Irish society. The petty kingdoms were sinking to the level of lordships in an area of wider authority. The overkings, with greater economic resources, had become the most significant lay patrons. For a poet such as Urard, it was important to take advantage of this and become associated with the greater kings.

Urard's reputation as the confidant of great kings was such that the chief poet of the annals became associated not only with Domnall mac Muirchertaig, but with his immediate successor in the high-kingship, Máel Sechnaill mac Domnaill (*d.* 1022), the last southern Uí Néill king of Tara. In these, late, sources, Urard is awarded the revenues of Ireland for a year by Máel Sechnaill, a paradigm of generosity. A poem in praise of Máel Sechnaill is retrospectively authored on Urard. Moreover, a version of this tale is contained in the seventeenth-century annals of Clonmacnoise.

Urard was imagined as the ideal *fili*. Ironically, this image was self-created. It was eagerly perpetuated by Urard's *fili* successors for many generations; a version of *Airec menman* was written as late as the end of the sixteenth century, on the eve of the destruction of the *filid*. For six centuries Urard mac Coise was an eloquent supporter of the privileges of the professional poets.

ELVA JOHNSTON

Sources O. Bergin, ed., 'A dialogue between Donnchad son of Brian and Mac Coisse', *Ériu*, 9 (1921–3), 175–80 · M. E. Byrne, ed., 'Airec menman Uraird maic Coisse', *Anecdota from Irish manuscripts*, ed. O. J. Bergin and others, 2 (1908), 42–76 · W. M. Hennessy, ed. and trans., *Chronicum Scotorum: a chronicle of Irish affairs*, Rolls Series, 46 (1866) · E. Knott, ed., *The bardic poems of Tadhg Dall Ó Huiginn* (1922), poem no. 3 · *Ann. Ulster* · K. Meyer, ed. and trans., *Fianaigecht: being a collection of hitherto unedited Irish poems and tales* (1910); repr. (1937); another edn (1993) · G. Murphy, ed., *Early Irish lyrics* (1956) · D. Murphy, ed., *The annals of Clonmacnoise*, trans. C. Mageoghagan (1896); facs. edn (1993) · *AFM* · W. Stokes, ed., 'The annals of Tigernach [8 pts]', *Revue Celtique*, 16 (1895), 374–419; 17 (1896), 6–33, 119–263, 337–420; 18 (1897), 9–59, 150–97, 267–303, 374–91; pubd sep. (1993) · L. Breatnach, *Uraicecht na riar: the poetic grades in early Irish law*, Early Irish Law Series, 2 (1987) · J. Carney, 'Notes on early Irish verse', *Éigse*, 13 (1969–70), 291–312 · P. Mac Cana, *The learned tales of medieval Ireland* (1980)

Urban [Gwrgan] (d. **1134**), bishop of Llandaff, has been identified as a priest of the church of Worcester, and was also known by the Welsh name Gwrgan, though it is uncertain whether he was of Welsh or English extraction; of his brothers, two were known by Welsh names and two by French names. He was closely linked with the ecclesiastical community at Llancarfan, had served Bishop Herewald as archdeacon, and was intimately aware of local traditions. He was consecrated as bishop in Glamorgan by Archbishop Anselm on 11 August 1107 and owed his appointment to Henry I. He was one of the first group of bishops appointed under the procedure agreed between Henry and the papacy, which became operative in 1107. The see in south-east Wales had probably been vacant since 1104. Because of the long vacancy, the clergy and people of the area wrote to Anselm asking him to consecrate Urban. Their letter was not a local production, but was based on exemplars available at Canterbury. There is no evidence that Norman influence, within the lordship of Glamorgan, lay behind his appointment.

Urban attended provincial synods regularly, was often associated with the consecration of new bishops, and was occasionally to be found at Henry I's court in England and Normandy. He was responsible for the consolidation of his diocese, though he failed in his ambition to extend its boundaries. The conflicts over these issues first emerge in documents dating from 1119 onwards. He had two main concerns. The first was to protect his diocese against despoliation by Norman settlers, who had taken advantage of Herewald's age and the early years of his own episcopate to occupy manors and churches within the diocese. The second was to claim jurisdiction over areas in the dioceses of Hereford and St David's. On these issues Urban sought the support of provincial councils and of the papal curia. In 1119 he travelled to France and gained a sympathetic hearing from Calixtus II at Soissons and at the Council of Rheims. From that year onwards his bishopric was called with increasing consistency the diocese of Llandaff. Calixtus II and, later, Honorius II addressed the leading magnates of the area to persuade them to restore possessions of the see, and pressed the bishops of Hereford and St David's to restore churches and territories claimed by Urban in Ergyng (Archenfield), Ystrad Yw, Gower, Cydweli, and Cantref Bychan.

Urban continued to press his claims at the Council of London over which the papal legate, Giovanni da Crema, presided in 1125. As a result, the legate visited Llandaff, noted the poverty to which despoliation had reduced the diocese, and commended the new cathedral being built there. Two years later Urban renewed his pleading at another council in London, and in 1128 he travelled to Rome to make his case there. The new pope, Honorius II, was favourably inclined to his cause; Urban's opponents, Richard of Hereford and Bernard of St David's, failed to appear, and judgment was given in his favour. But in April 1129 Bernard of St David's appeared at Rome with a reasonable answer to Urban's complaints, and it was Urban's turn to be summoned to answer charges. His friends at

Rome wrote in cautious terms. Innocent II, at first well disposed, was markedly less sympathetic after the appointment in 1131 of Robert de Béthune as bishop of Hereford. It was argued that the diocese of Hereford should not suffer because its bishop had died during the course of litigation, and concessions made to Urban were suspended. Urban was summoned to answer at the Council of Rheims in 1131. Bernard of St David's appeared, while Urban was prevented by illness from attending, and the case was remitted to judges-delegate in England, who eventually decided against Urban. He set out for Rome for the last time in 1134, and died on the journey, some time before 9 October. He had failed in his attempts to enlarge his diocese, but its existing boundaries were confirmed; it was now recognized as much more than a territorial diocese limited to Glamorgan.

A local problem was to define the rights of the bishop and the lord of Glamorgan. This was resolved in 1126 by a detailed agreement between Urban and Robert, earl of Gloucester, drawn up in Henry I's presence at Woodstock. At Llandaff, Urban had found a very small church and determined to give the diocese an imposing cathedral. The work, in hand by April 1120, is mentioned in 1125, but its completion is not recorded. The dedication of the church to St Euddogwy was extended to include St Peter, as a link with the European church, and St Dyfrig, whose churches in Herefordshire Urban was anxious to claim. Whether he also added the name of St Teilo to bolster his claims to churches with this dedication in the diocese of St David's has been widely debated.

Under Urban's direction the final recension of the Book of Llandaff was drawn up. This collection of historical material included much bearing upon the possessions of the diocese. In earlier recensions, its contents had been amended and inflated, and in Urban's episcopate it was adapted and used to provide the evidence for his claims to a wider jurisdiction. The future bishop of Llandaff, *Nicholas ap Gwrgan, has sometimes been identified as Urban's son.									DAVID WALKER

Sources J. C. Davies, ed., *Episcopal acts and cognate documents relating to Welsh dioceses, 1066–1272*, 2, Historical Society of the Church in Wales, 3 (1948) · J. G. Evans and J. Rhys, eds., *The text of the Book of Llan Dâv reproduced from the Gwysaney manuscript* (1893) · A. W. Haddan and W. Stubbs, eds., *Councils and ecclesiastical documents relating to Great Britain and Ireland*, 1 (1869) · G. T. Clark, ed., *Cartae et alia munimenta quae ad dominium de Glamorgancia pertinent*, ed. G. L. Clark, 6 vols. (1910), vol. 1 · *Reg. RAN*, vol. 2 · D. Crouch, ed., *Llandaff episcopal acta, 1140–1287*, South Wales and Monmouth RS, 5 (1988) · W. Davies, *The Llandaff charters* (1979) · W. Davies, 'St Mary's Worcester and the *Liber Landavensis*', *Journal of the Society of Archivists*, 4 (1970–73), 459–85 · J. E. Lloyd, *A history of Wales from the earliest times to the Edwardian conquest*, 3rd edn, 2 vols. (1939)

Urban, Charles (1867–1942), film producer, was born on 15 April 1867 in Cincinnati, Ohio, the second eldest of the ten children of Joseph Urban, a sign painter, and his wife, Anna Sophie (1846–1887), daughter of Heinrich Glatz of Königsberg and his wife, Pauline. His parents were part of the German community in Cincinnati. There he went to school until fifteen (by which time he had Anglicized his first name, Carl), after which he worked in stationery shops, before graduating to successful book agent. In 1889 he moved to Detroit, where he opened a stationery shop, and became interested in Edison phonographs. In 1895 he became manager of a phonograph and Kinetoscope parlour, the Kinetoscope being the Edison peepshow device that introduced motion picture films. In 1896 Urban acquired the agency rights to the Edison Vitascope film projector for Michigan, and soon joined Edison film agents Maguire and Baucus of New York. By August 1897 he was in London as manager of Maguire and Baucus in Britain, controlling Edison's European interests.

Urban flourished in his new country. He brought with him a highly reliable projector, the Bioscope, which proved to be the cornerstone of his fortune. Maguire and Baucus moved to Warwick Court, London, and renamed itself the Warwick Trading Company, a name that became renowned for its reliable product and emphasis on actuality, news, and travel film. Warwick cameramen were soon travelling the globe to bring moving images to audiences new to this world of wonders. The pioneer band included John Avery (Urban's brother-in-law), F. Ormiston-Smith, and, most celebrated among them, Joseph Rosenthal, who filmed scenes from the Second South African War. The ebullient but pushy Urban outstripped his steadier colleagues, and broke away in 1903 to form the Charles Urban Trading Company.

Urban continued to build a reputation, always boasting the educational benefits of his product. He became a figurehead for the British film industry, famed for his bold promotions, sure sense of style, and his trademark cigars (his alarming habit of dropping ash while editing inflammable film became legendary). He was proudest of his achievements in colour cinematography. In 1901 inventor Edward Turner interested him in a potential three-colour cinematography system. Initial results were unsatisfactory, and shortly afterwards Turner died, but Urban acquired the patent rights and set his associate George Albert *Smith (1864–1959) to work on the project. After futile experiments with three colour filters, in 1906 Smith discovered that a two-colour system would reproduce most of the spectrum adequately, and Kinemacolor was invented, the first natural colour film process.

Urban moved to Urbanora House, Wardour Street (the first film business in what has remained the heart of the British film industry), where he gave the first demonstration of Kinemacolor in May 1908. Kinemacolor, brilliantly and exclusively marketed via the Natural Color Kinematograph Company, became Urban's greatest triumph, and in particular the extensive colour film record of the Delhi durbar, held in 1911 to celebrate the coronation of George V, was the sensation of London. But the downturn in Urban's fortunes had begun. In December 1913 a legal challenge to the Kinemacolor patent was launched by William Friese-Greene, anxious to promote his own Biocolour system. The petition was dismissed, but reversed on appeal in March 1914, a decision upheld when taken to the

House of Lords in March 1915. Urban had lost his precious, and ultimately indefensible, monopoly on colour films.

Urban became a naturalized British citizen in 1907. He was married twice, first to Julia Lamereux Avery on 20 December 1888; the marriage ended in divorce in 1908. On 22 February 1910 he married Ada Aline Jones, née Gorecki (1868–1937), whose money supported much of the Kinemacolor venture. Urban adopted her daughter from her previous marriage, Anna Marguerite. He had no children of his own.

With the outbreak of war, Urban used his persuasive powers to interest British officialdom in the propagandist power of the cinema, and in late 1915 produced *Britain Prepared*, a documentary feature on Britain's military strength, made for the Wellington House cinema committee. Urban was then sent to the USA to promote this and other British war films. After returning briefly to Britain in the summer of 1916 to edit the masterly documentary feature *The Battle of the Somme*, Urban moved his business interests to the USA, where he worked with an engineer called Henry Joy on an improved colour system, to be called Kinekrom, and continued to promote British propaganda films in the USA. This latter activity yielded mixed results, causing some embarrassment to his British masters when Urban made an ill-judged approach to the Hearst press (which was widely seen to support the German cause), but he continued to handle British war films in the USA to the end of the war, and edited a propaganda newsreel, *Official War Review*.

Urban sought to expand his activities in the USA after the war, and conceived of a hugely ambitious scheme to bring all his various activities and huge film library together under one roof at Stanford White's imposing Cosmopolitan Magazine Building in Irvington-on-Hudson, New York, which he renamed the Urban Institute. While enthusiastically launching his plan in 1922 for a kind of audio-visual encyclopaedia, Urban was blind to the fact that a library of largely outdated short interest films would never find the necessary bookings to support such an ambitious venture, and it all collapsed into bankruptcy in 1924.

Around 1930 Urban returned to Britain. He continued for a while to pursue chimerical further fortunes, but in 1937 he donated all of his papers to the Science Museum, and the following year retired to Brighton. There he befriended once more G. A. Smith, the Kinemacolor inventor from whom he had become estranged in 1910. He died on 29 August 1942, in a nursing home at 12 Dyke Road, Brighton. He was cremated at Brighton crematorium on 1 September.

Charles Urban was a dangerous man to know. He was a financial liability to many, was quick to find fault and slow to take blame, and possessed all the abrasive qualities of the get-rich-quick businessmen of his era. But he inspired as much loyalty and friendship as he did enmity, and was genuine in his belief in the importance and educational value of films. He put money behind this belief, and was admirably generous in supporting experimentation. If film has any lasting value, it will arguably be as a medium of record, and Charles Urban's central role as an enthusiastic producer of actuality film in the first years of the twentieth century makes him a truly noteworthy cinema pioneer. LUKE MCKERNAN

Sources Sci. Mus., Urban MSS · C. Urban, 'A Yank in Britain', 1942, priv. coll. [unpublished memoir] · *A Yank in Britain: the lost memoirs of Charles Urban, film pioneer*, ed. L. McKernan (1999) · D. B. Thomas, *The first colour motion pictures* (1969) · 'Charles Urban', *The Cine-Technician* (Nov–Dec 1942), 124–5 · R. Low, *The history of the British film*, 2: *1906–1914* (1949) · R. Brown, '"England is not big enough …": American rivalry in the early English film business: the case of Warwick v. Urban, 1903', *Film History*, 10 (1998), 21–34 · J. Barnes, *The beginnings of the cinema in England, 1894–1901*, 5 vols. (1976–97) · C. Urban, 'A terse history of natural colour cinema kinematography', 1921, Sci. Mus., Urban MSS, 9/1 · T. Ramsaye, *A million and one nights: a history of the motion picture*, 2 vols. (1926) · 'Cinema pioneer passes', *Brighton and Hove Herald* (5 Sept 1942), 1 · S. Herbert and L. McKernan, eds., *Who's who of Victorian cinema: a worldwide survey* (1996) · R. Low, *The history of the British film*, 1: *1896–1906* (1948) · CGPLA Eng. & Wales (1943) · IGI · d. cert. [Ada Aline Jones] · m. cert. [Ada Aline Jones] · divorce records, PRO
Archives Sci. Mus., memoirs; papers | FILM BFI NFTVA, 'Picturing Charles Urban', c.1921 · BFI NFTVA, documentary footage
Likenesses photographs, Sci. Mus. · photographs, BFI
Wealth at death £466 14s. 3d.: probate, 12 Feb 1943, CGPLA Eng. & Wales

Ure, Alexander, first Baron Strathclyde (1853–1928), lawyer and politician, was the second son of John Ure of Cairndhu, Helensburgh, merchant and a distinguished lord provost of Glasgow, and his wife, Isabella, daughter of John Gibb of Glasgow. He was born in Glasgow on 24 February 1853, and educated at Larchfield Academy, Helensburgh, and at Glasgow University, graduating MA in 1872, BL in 1874, and LLB in 1878; he was made an honorary LLD by the university in 1907. In 1878 he was admitted a member of the Faculty of Advocates and began his career at the Scottish bar. In the following year he married Margaret McDowall, daughter of Thomas Steven, iron merchant in Glasgow. They had one daughter, who died in 1918.

Success came early to Ure, and for him there was no weary waiting for briefs. His influential connection with the west of Scotland, the source of most of the lucrative commercial litigations in the Parliament House, and a natural gift of robust and telling advocacy secured for him from the outset a steady flow of business. After only fourteen years of junior practice he 'gave up writing', the step which then marked the transition of a Scottish advocate to senior rank, and, on the institution of a roll of queen's counsel for Scotland in 1897, he was one of the first new Scottish silks. For ten years after his call to the bar (1878–88) Ure held the lecturership of constitutional law and history in Glasgow University, but this appointment, which did not require him to live in the city, did not interfere with his professional advancement. Like so many ambitious young advocates he took to politics, and he was a strong Gladstonian home ruler. His first attempt to enter parliament as a candidate for West Perthshire in 1892 was unsuccessful. He also failed in 1893 to secure election for Linlithgowshire, but at the general election in 1895 he was

Alexander Ure, first Baron Strathclyde (1853–1928), by Sir Benjamin Stone, 1897

returned as a Liberal for that constituency which he continued to represent until his elevation to the bench in 1913. From 1905 to 1909 he was solicitor-general for Scotland, and in the latter year he succeeded Lord Shaw (afterwards Lord Craigmyle) as lord advocate and was sworn of the privy council.

Ure's activities during his tenure of the lord advocateship brought him to prominence. It was a period of political high tension, and Lloyd George's budget for 1909–10 was the storm centre. Ure threw himself into the fray with characteristic energy and devoted himself to advocating the taxation of land values. His physical vigour, his ubiquity, and his powers of relentless rhetoric rendered him an invaluable party henchman. His comments on Unionist policy with respect to old-age pensions brought upon him a severe rebuke by A. J. Balfour, who, at a meeting in the Constitutional Club on 26 October 1909, charged him with having been guilty of a 'frigid and calculated lie'. The phrase, singularly inappropriate to Ure's sanguine temperament, passed into currency, and its imputation was not entirely dispelled by Ure's brilliant defence of himself in the House of Commons on 3 November 1909. It was in that year also that Ure conducted the prosecution in the trial of Oscar Slater for murder, and secured from the jury a verdict of guilty by a majority of nine to six. The death sentence was commuted, but the verdict gave rise to a prolonged agitation, which a somewhat inconclusive departmental inquiry failed to satisfy; it was not finally set at rest until, in July 1928, after Slater's liberation, his conviction was reviewed and quashed by the High Court of Justiciary under the Criminal Appeal Act.

In 1913 Ure succeeded Lord Dunedin as lord justice-general for Scotland and lord president of the Court of Session, and in 1914 was raised to the peerage under the title of Baron Strathclyde of Sandyford, co. Lanark. The transition from party polemics to the dispassionate atmosphere of the judiciary was abrupt, but it was achieved with remarkable success, for the new lord president proved from the first an efficient and capable judge, courteous, attentive, and alert. He always had an eye to the practical issue, and his judgments were models of clarity. But the easy certitude which stood him in such good stead in his political career was a less suitable endowment for a judge, and his reported opinions exhibit little of that balanced discussion of legal principles which best contributes to the elucidation and advancement of the law. Undoubtedly Ure was better as an advocate than as a judge, though in neither capacity was he learned in the technical sense. He particularly excelled in cross-examination, where his direct methods and his masterful style found full scope. He had a quite admirable gift, too, of lucid exposition, aided by a retentive memory, which enabled him to handle intricate matters with enviable facility. Sometimes, however, his invincible optimism led him to see both facts and law as he wished them to be rather than as they were.

Ure's mental vigour found its counterpart in his physical constitution, and he was an intrepid yachtsman, and an untiring walker. On one occasion he tramped from Edinburgh to London, and on another from London to Land's End. During the First World War he rendered valuable service in the promotion of the Scottish War Savings Association, in recognition of which he was made a GCB in 1917.

In 1920 Ure was compelled by ill health to resign from the bench, and he retired to Cairndhu, the family house on the Clyde at Helensburgh. It was characteristic of him that he gave up the pension to which he was entitled, but with which his private means enabled him to dispense. In 1921 he published a pleasantly written biographical study of Lord Fullerton, a learned senator of the college of justice, for whom he had a great admiration. He died at Helensburgh on 2 October 1928, and the peerage became extinct; he was survived by his wife.

MACMILLAN, rev. H. C. G. MATTHEW

Sources The Times (3 Oct 1928) · The Scotsman (3 Oct 1928) · Glasgow Herald (3 Oct 1928) · personal knowledge (1937)
Archives FILM BFI NFTVA, actuality footage
Likenesses B. Stone, photograph, 1897, NPG [see illus.]
Wealth at death £150,180 18s. 1d.: confirmation, 2 Feb 1929, CGPLA Eng. & Wales

Ure, Andrew (1778–1857), chemist, was born in New Street, Glasgow, on 18 May 1778, the son of Alexander Ure, cheesemonger of New Street, and his wife, Anne. From an early age he showed a 'combative and rancorous disposition' (Farrar, 299). He graduated MD from Glasgow University in 1801 and served, briefly, as an army surgeon in

Andrew Ure (1778–1857), by unknown artist, c.1820

Scotland. In 1804 he succeeded George Birkbeck in the chair of natural philosophy at Anderson's Institution. Ure gave evening lectures on chemistry and mechanics, which he encouraged working men and women to attend. The lectures were most successful, attracting audiences of up to 500; they later inspired the foundation of mechanics institutions throughout Britain, and also of the École des Arts et Métiers in Paris.

In 1807 Ure married Catherine Monteath, of Greenock. A year later he became director of the short-lived Garnet Hill observatory, run by the Glasgow Society for Promoting Astronomical Observations. In 1814 he gave vacation lectures at Belfast Academical Institution but these were not as successful as those at Glasgow. However, while in Ireland, Ure also worked as a consultant for the Irish linen board. Here he devised his 'alkalimeter' for volumetric estimates of the true alkali contents of various substances used in the linen industry. His innovation was to use solutions of acids and alkalis in such concentrations that they could be expressed in terms of their chemical equivalents. This led him, eventually, to the concept of normality in volumetric analysis. Zealous in his pursuit of new scientific and industrial knowledge, he toured Britain and the continent. He also built up a reputation as a highly competent practical chemist, and in this capacity did his most useful chemical work: his density composition tables for aqueous acids were quoted up to the end of the nineteenth century.

In 1818 Ure caused a sensation when he used a large voltaic pile to activate the muscles of an executed murderer; to the alarm of onlookers, the corpse was, literally, galvanized into apparent life. Early in the same year his wife,

Catherine, with whom he had had two sons (one of whom became a London surgeon) and a daughter, had become the mistress of Granville Sharpe Pattison, professor of anatomy at Anderson's Institution. There followed, in 1819, a much publicized divorce. Pattison was not, however, Ure's only opponent at that time; Ure was beginning a polemic against his fellow chemists that made him notorious. Among those with whom he quarrelled vehemently was Thomas Thomson, regius professor of chemistry at Glasgow University.

In 1821 Ure's first major book, his *Dictionary of Chemistry*, appeared. It was designed to replace William Nicholson's *Dictionary*, by then out of date. He insisted, in the article 'Equivalents', that William Higgins had originated the atomic theory, and dismissed Dalton's claims. In his next book, *A New System of Geology* (1829), Ure attempted to reconcile the biblical flood with the facts of geology and zoology, by boldly proposing a second, post-diluvial, Creation. Less contentious was his inference that the flood must have been accompanied by a series of fine rainbows. His geological knowledge was deficient, however, and the book was severely criticized.

Ure's links with Anderson's Institution weakened as his other interests grew and as his feuds escalated. In May 1830 he resigned from the chair of natural philosophy and, in September, from the institution altogether. He went to London, where he set up as probably the first consulting chemist in Britain, willing to advise on any scientific question and to act as an expert witness in the courts. He also took commissions from the government, and toured industrial areas in Belgium and France.

On one summer's tour of Lancashire, Cheshire, and Derbyshire in the early 1830s, Ure was most impressed by the huge textile mills. Staffed mainly by women and children, with the minimum of skilled labour and equipped with elaborate machines, the mills produced immense quantities of yarn and fabric. His observations inspired his most memorable work, *The Philosophy of Manufactures* (1835), which dealt with four textile industries: cotton, wool, linen, and silk. The salient feature of the new industry that Arkwright had pioneered was, he wrote, the 'decomposing [of] a process into its constituents and embodying each part in an automatic machine' (p. 22). Adam Smith's eulogy of the division of labour was, he argued, out of date. Indeed, the lesson of what Ure called 'the automatic factory' was that human skill had been banished. Employees were merely machine minders. What had happened in textiles must happen in all manufacturing industries. Machines would displace labour and skill. He recognized that in addition to mechanical innovations there had been major, and irreversible, changes in social and commercial organization. The factory system required that the immemorial rural custom, whereby people worked when it suited them, must go. Everyone must go to work at a fixed time and leave at a fixed time. Ure vigorously defended the new factories against numerous criticisms, particularly those from landowners. He considered that earnings in Lancashire cotton mills were far higher than those in agriculture, and conditions were incomparably better than those in coalmines.

Ure held that the freedoms to innovate, to invest, and to trade that Britain enjoyed had encouraged this development. France, where the state, following Colbert, interfered in industry, lagged behind. The main hindrances to progress, in Britain, were trade unions—combinations of workers whose aims were to increase wages and to exclude outsiders. He showed to his own satisfaction that such combinations defeat their own ends. According to Ure, trade union leaders were evilly disposed while employers were usually long-suffering philanthropists.

Ure's comments on social conditions were sometimes patently absurd. He once claimed that workers in cotton mills were less liable to cholera than the rest of the population and that working at a temperature of 150 °F was not harmful. Such ills as afflicted the workers were due to their inordinate taste for bacon. He advocated the education of mill children but held that the aim of such education must be moral and classes should be held in Sunday schools so that work in the mills was not interrupted. Ure's *Philosophy* influenced both Marx and Engels, who devoted considerable space to its examination and severely criticized its apologetic for the factory system.

In 1836 Ure published his *Account of the Cotton Industry*. It was to have been the first of a series of books on different industries but in the event was the only one published. His scholarship is slightly suspect: the descriptions of many machines are cryptic to the point of being unintelligible, and Ure's own understanding may be doubted. In 1839 he produced his final major work, *Dictionary of Arts, Mines and Manufactures*, with contributions from various authorities. Its fifth edition, in 1860, was by Robert Hunt, keeper of mining records. Henry Watts had been asked to produce a new edition of Ure's *Dictionary of Chemistry*, to be a companion to Hunt's edition of the *Dictionary of Arts, Manufactures and Mines*. However, the rise of organic chemistry and, indeed, the 'complete revolution', since 1831, had made it almost impossible 'to adapt any matter written so long ago to the existing requirements of the sciences' (*Dictionary of Chemistry*, 1863, 1. v). A completely new work was essential. The new edition, under Watts's name, came out in 1863. In it Watts refers to Dalton's atomic theory and makes no mention of Higgins.

Ure was elected FRS in 1822. In 1834 he became consulting analyst to the board of customs and in 1840 he played a leading part in the foundation of the Pharmaceutical Society. He died in London on 2 January 1857 and was buried in Highgate cemetery. DONALD CARDWELL

Sources W. V. Farrar, 'Andrew Ure, FRS, and the philosophy of manufactures', *Notes and Records of the Royal Society*, 27 (1972–3), 299–324 · E. L. Scott, 'Ure, Andrew', *DSB*, 13.547–8 · W. S. C. Copeman, 'Andrew Ure, MD', *Proceedings of the Royal Society of Medicine*, 44 (1951), 655–62 · M. Berg, *The machinery question and the making of political economy, 1815–1848* (1980) · E. P. Thompson, *The making of the English working class*, new edn (1968); repr. (1980) · K. Marx, *Capital: a critique of political economy*, 3rd edn, ed. F. Engels, trans. S. Moore and E. Aveling, 2 vols. (1970), vol. 1 · F. Engels, *The condition of the working class in England*, ed. D. McLellan (1993)

Archives RCP Lond., papers · University of Strathclyde, Glasgow, corresp. | NRA Scotland, Ewart MSS, letters to Sir Thomas Makdougall-Brisbane

Likenesses watercolour drawing, c.1820, NPG [see illus.] · D. Macnee, oils, 1837, V&A · R. Roffe, stipple, pubd 1837 (after D. Macnee), NPG · T. Bridgford, lithograph, BM · C. Cook, stipple (after photograph by W. L. Diamond), BM · portrait, repro. in Farrar, 'Andrew Ure', facing p. 300

Ure, David (*bap.* 1749, *d.* 1798), naturalist and local historian, was born in Glasgow and baptized there on 30 March 1749. He was the eldest of nine children of Patrick Ure (also known as Peter Urie; *b.* c.1720, *d.* after 1783), weaver, and his wife, Isabell Malcolm. After attending the Glasgow grammar school, he worked as a weaver before and after matriculating at Glasgow University in 1770. After graduating MA in 1776, he studied divinity (teaching meanwhile in various schools) and was licensed as a preacher by Glasgow presbytery on 11 June 1783. Soon afterwards, Ure was appointed as assistant to the ageing minister of East Kilbride in Lanarkshire. During the seven years he spent there he cultivated an interest, first manifested in his student days, in the scientific observation of natural phenomena. His collection of specimens achieved local fame, and in 1788 he was elected as a corresponding member of the Natural History Society of Edinburgh. His hopes of succeeding the parish minister, who died in 1790, were disappointed. Ure is said to have walked to Newcastle upon Tyne, where he was for a time assistant minister to one of the Scottish Presbyterian congregations. He soon returned to Scotland. Before leaving East Kilbride he had established contact with John Sinclair, who had just launched his *Statistical Account of Scotland*. Not only did Ure write for this the accounts of East Kilbride, Rutherglen, and Killearn, he also became a member of Sinclair's editorial staff, playing a significant part in preparing the later volumes for publication. He contributed to the surveys commissioned by Sinclair as president of the board of agriculture and internal improvement, writing substantial accounts of agricultural conditions in Dunbartonshire, Roxburghshire, and Kinross-shire. Ure had other patrons too. John Anderson, professor of natural philosophy at Glasgow, saw him as the appropriate candidate for the chair of natural history in Anderson's Institution to be founded after his (and, in the event, after Ure's) death. And the eccentric but enlightened David Erskine, earl of Buchan, presented Ure to his first and only parish, as minister of Uphall, Linlithgowshire. Ordained in July 1796, Ure ministered there for less than two years. He died of dropsy at Strathbrock manse, Uphall, on 28 March 1798 and was buried in the Erskine family vault at St Nicholas Kirk, Strathbrock, Uphall, where a stone was erected outside the church door to commemorate him.

It is above all for his *History of Rutherglen and East-Kilbride* (1793) that Ure deserves to be remembered. The book has value for local history, but is chiefly significant as a pioneering work in geology, and especially in palaeontology: it contains the earliest illustrations of Scottish fossils. Ure has been called the father of palaeontology in Scotland; and it is clear that his lead was followed and his work respected in the nineteenth century. It can indeed still attract interest today. In detail and in methodology it was of course soon left behind; but Ure's more professional successors looked back admiringly to 'a breadth of mind and an accuracy of observation … which were not equalled in his native country at the time' (Duns, 19).

J. H. BURNS

Sources J. Headrick, 'Biographical sketch of the late Rev. David Ure', *Scots Magazine and Edinburgh Literary Miscellany*, 70 (1808), 903–5 · J. Gray, *Biographical notice of the Rev. David Ure: with an examination … of his 'History of Rutherglen and East Kilbride'* (Glasgow, 1865) [incl. repr. of Headrick] · D. Ure, *The history of Rutherglen and East-Kilbride: published with a view to promote the study of antiquity and natural history* (1793); repr. (1991) [with repr. of Gray] · J. H. Burns, 'David Ure (1749–1798): "Breadth of Mind and Accuracy of Observation"', *Glasgow Naturalist*, 22 (1993), 259–75 · W. I. Addison, ed., *The matriculation albums of the University of Glasgow from 1728 to 1858* (1913) · W. I. Addison, *A roll of graduates of the University of Glasgow from 31st December 1727 to 31st December 1897* (1898) · *Fasti Scot.*, new edn, 1.234 · T. Davidson, 'The carboniferous system in Scotland characterized by its brachiopoda', *The Geologist*, 2 (1859), 461–77 · *The lithology of Edinburgh, by the late John Fleming*, ed. J. Duns (1859), 1–104 · W. Ross, *Busby and its neighbourhood, including the parishes of Carmunnock, East Kilbride, Mearns, and Cathcart* (1883) · J. Primrose, *Strathbrock, or, The history and antiquities of the parish of Uphall* (1898) · T. E. Niven, *East Kilbride: the history of parish and village* (1965) · parish register, High Kirk, Glasgow · testament dative, 18 April 1799, NA Scot. · presbytery minutes, Linlithgow, West Lothian

Archives NL Scot., letters and notebooks; notes on antiquities and surnames, Adv. MSS 16.1.11–12; 16.2.10–11

Wealth at death Lord Buchan and other heritors of Uphall parish owed him £5 of stipend; papers, books, specimens: testament dative, 18 April 1799, NA Scot.

Ure, Joan. *See* Clark, Elizabeth Thomson (1918–1978).

Ure, Mary Eileen (1933–1975), actress, was born on 18 February 1933 at 17 Kelvinside Terrace South, Glasgow, daughter of Colin McGregor Ure, engineer, and his wife, Edith Hannah Eileen Willis Swinburne. She was educated at the Mount School, York, and trained at the Central School of Speech Training and Dramatic Art, making her first stage appearance in 1954 in Alan Melville's *Simon and Laura* at the Opera House, Manchester. She made her name as Amanda in Jean Anouilh's *Time Remembered* in her London début at the Lyric, Hammersmith, in December 1954, a production that included Paul Scofield, with whom she went on to play Ophelia to his Hamlet in Peter Brook's production. Before opening at the Phoenix Theatre in December 1955, the company took *Hamlet* to the Moscow Art Theatre for two weeks: the nunnery scene was televised for Russian television, with Mary Ure playing opposite a Russian actor, each speaking in their own language. In 1956, at the Royal Court Theatre, she played Abigail Williams in the first London production of Arthur Miller's *The Crucible*.

Mary Ure was cast as Alison, opposite Kenneth Haigh playing Jimmy Porter, in the original production of John Osborne's *Look Back in Anger*, put on by the English Stage Company at the Royal Court Theatre in 1956, the play that established Osborne as the original 'angry young man', and started a vogue for 'kitchen sink' drama. She also starred in the film of the play, in 1957, opposite Richard Burton. In 1957 she married John *Osborne (1929–1994), the second of his five wives: the marriage ended in divorce in 1963 and the relationship was chronicled by Osborne in the second volume of his autobiography, *Almost a Gentleman* (1991). For Ure *Look Back in Anger* was followed by a part in Arthur Miller's *A View from the Bridge* at the Comedy Theatre, a very successful production that ran from October 1956 until April 1957, directed by Peter Brook. After starring in the 1957 Broadway production of *Look Back in Anger*, she did a season at the Shakespeare Memorial Theatre, Stratford upon Avon, in 1959, playing Titania to Robert Hardy's Oberon in Peter Hall's production of *A Midsummer Night's Dream*, and Desdemona to Paul Robeson's Othello. Following this, in 1960 she replaced Claire Bloom in Jean Giradoux's *Duel of Angels* in Boston, playing opposite Vivien Leigh, before touring the United States. Back in London in 1960, at the Royal Court, she again took the part of Abigail Williams in *The Crucible*, and Beatrice in Thomas Middleton's *The Changeling* in 1961. The cast of *The Changeling* included Robert *Shaw (1927–1978), whom she married in 1963: it was his second marriage also. They had two sons and two daughters.

Although Ure left the stage in 1961 for several years, by then she was an established film actress, after roles in *Storm over the Nile* (1955), *Windom's Way* (1957), and *Sons and Lovers* (1960), and her film career continued with *The Mind Benders* (1963), *The Luck of Ginger Coffey* (1964), *Custer of the West* (1966), *Where Eagles Dare* (1968), and *A Reflection of Fear* (1973). She returned to the stage briefly in 1967 in Tennessee Williams's *Two Character Play*, and was in the cast of the Broadway production of Harold Pinter's *Old Times* (1971–2).

Blonde and beautiful, Mary Ure was often cast in the role of an innocent victim. She returned to the London stage on 2 April 1975 in *The Exorcism* at the Comedy Theatre, but died from a fatal overdose on 3 April after celebrating the successful opening of the play.

ANNE PIMLOTT BAKER

Sources J. Osborne, *Almost a gentleman: an autobiography*, 2 (1991) · D. Quinlan, *Quinlan's film stars* (1981) · J. P. Wearing, *The London stage, 1890–1959* (1976–93) · J. C. Trewin, *Paul Scofield* (1956) · *The Times* (4 April 1975) · WW · b. cert.
Likenesses photograph, 1954 (with Paul Scofield), repro. in Trewin, *Paul Scofield*, 89 · photograph, repro. in *The Times* · photographs, Hult. Arch. · photographs, repro. in Osborne, *Almost a gentleman*, nos. 12 and 24

Uri, Joannes (1726–1796), orientalist, was born at Körös in Hungary, and studied oriental languages under Jans Jacob Schultens at Leiden, where he took the degrees of PhD and DD. In 1761 he published a short treatise on Hebrew etymology, *Prima decas originum Hebraearum genuinarum*, and also (for the Leiden Library) an edition of the Arabic poem 'Burda' in honour of the prophet Muhammad with a Latin translation and further notes on Hebrew etymology. In 1766 Uri was invited, on the advice of Sir Joseph Yorke (later Baron Dover), to catalogue the 30,000 oriental manuscripts at the Bodleian Library, Oxford. After twenty years' preparation the catalogue appeared (1787) bearing the title *Bibliothecae Bodleianae codd. manuscriptorum orientalium videlicet Hebraeorum, Chaldaicorum, Syriacorum, &c., catalogus*. The work contained a number of errors,

many of which were corrected in a second volume by Alexander Nicoll (first part published in 1821) and by Edward Bouverie Pusey (part 2 published, after Nicoll's death, in 1835). While at Oxford, Uri published an edition of some Persian and Turkish letters, *Epistolae Turcicae et narrationes Persicae* (1771), and also a short commentary on Daniel's weeks (1788) with some other cruces of Old Testament exegesis. He is said to have given instruction in the oriental languages at Oxford, the theologian and orientalist Joseph White being his most distinguished pupil. In old age Uri was discharged by the delegates of the university press, but was provided for by the kindness of Henry Kett of Trinity College and others. He died at his lodgings in Oxford on 18 October 1796.

D. S. MARGOLIOUTH, *rev.* PHILIP CARTER

Sources *GM*, 1st ser., 66 (1796), 884 · *GM*, 1st ser., 95/2 (1825), 184 · *The life and labours of Adam Clarke* (1834) · I. Goldziher, *Uri János* (Budapest, 1908) · W. D. Macray, *Annals of the Bodleian Library, Oxford* (1868)

Urie, Robert (*bap.* **1713**, *d.* **1771**), printer and bookseller, was the son of John Urie of Holmhead and his second wife, Isobel Murdoch. He was baptized in Cathcart, near Glasgow, on 19 December 1713. John Urie was apparently a man of some importance, since the witnesses to his marriages and to the baptisms of his children were the owners of substantial estates in the area. A Robert Urie who took a Greek class at Glasgow University in 1728 may have been John Urie's son, but the entry in the matriculation album is one of the few from which the Christian name and designation of the signatory's father are omitted.

Urie is known to have served an apprenticeship with Alexander Millar, merchant and printer in Glasgow, and was admitted burgess and guild brother by this right on 28 July 1748. He first appears as a printer in 1740, when a number of books were printed and sold by Robert Urie & Co. at their printing house in the Gallowgate. He and his partners, Andrew Stalker and Alexander Carlile, booksellers, published the *Glasgow Journal*, which first appeared in July 1741. The partnership appears to have been dissolved in 1747. Robert Urie & Co. printed a number of books in that year, but the *Scots Magazine* for November contains the announcement of the publication of the second edition of Henry Guthry's *Memoirs*, printed by Robert Urie. Thereafter he printed alone. Advertisements show his address to have been in the foot of the Salt-mercat. He remained there throughout his career.

During the period in which Urie printed in partnership his work was unremarkable, but afterwards it underwent a marked change. Influenced, no doubt, by Andrew and Robert Foulis, he acquired new type, rid himself of cluttered title-pages, printed on good quality paper, and generally raised the standard of his work. He did not, however, attempt to compete with the fine folios of the Foulises but confined himself almost entirely to the printing of octavos and duodecimos. In 1750 he produced in those formats what may be considered his finest works, a Greek New Testament and an edition of George Buchanan's *Psalms*. Urie printed regularly until 1757, in which year the first books bearing the imprint 'Printed for Robert Urie' were issued from what was clearly his press. After 1759 he printed only occasionally. It is probable that he devoted himself to bookselling and publishing, and left the printing to William Smith, another Millar apprentice, who worked with Urie and, at his death, succeeded him. The arrangement must have been in the nature of a partnership, though not formalized as such, since Urie left no printing materials in his will.

Not the least interesting feature of Urie's career is his choice of titles for publication. If these reflect his own taste he was a man of some culture with an inclination towards philosophy, history, and poetry, and with little of his contemporaries' interest in sermons. He published very few of the Greek and Latin classics in the original languages, once again, perhaps, not wishing to compete with the Foulis press. The 1750s, and even more the 1760s, revealed an interest in the books of the French Enlightenment, particularly translations of the works of Voltaire: Urie published more than twenty of these, many within a year of their first translation into English. Other authors who feature prominently are Vertot, Fenelon, d'Alembert, Formey, and Rousseau.

Robert Urie died, unmarried, of the palsy, on 9 February 1771 in Glasgow, and was buried that month in the city's Ramshorn churchyard. In his will, which was recorded on 6 December 1771, his half-sister Isobel Urie, widow of the deceased William Anderson, was named executor dative as nearest of kin. The will shows him to have been a prosperous man. The sale of his books in sheets realized £2000 sterling, and more than £900 sterling was owed to him by booksellers and others, the latter sum including nearly £300 owed to him in Virginia and Jamaica.

R. A. GILLESPIE

Sources H. A. McLean, *Robert Urie, printer in Glasgow, c.1711–1771* (1914) • R. A. Gillespie, 'The parentage of Robert Urie, printer in Glasgow', *Bibliothek*, 5 (1967), 38–40 • will, recorded 6 Dec 1771, NA Scot. • parish register (baptism), Cathcart, 19 Dec 1713 • parish register (death), Glasgow, 9 Feb 1771 • R. Renwick, ed., *Extracts from the records of the burgh of Glasgow, AD 1760–1780*, 7 (1912) • *The burgesses and guild brethren of Glasgow, 1573–1750*, Scottish Records Society (1925) • W. I. Addison, ed., *The matriculation albums of the University of Glasgow from 1728 to 1858* (1913) • factory legal deed, Alexander Carlile to John Carlile, 6 April 1748, Mitchell L., Glas., Glasgow City Archives, B/O/15/5945 • *Scots Magazine*, 9 (Nov 1747) • *Scots Magazine*, 33 (1771), 110 • *Glasgow Journal* (7–14 Feb 1771)
Wealth at death £2900 value of his books in sheets and monies due to him: will, 1771, NA Scot.

Urien Rheged [Urien ap Cynfarch] (*fl. c.*560–*c.*580), king of Rheged, was the son of Cynfarch Oer ap Meirchion Gul, a descendant of Coel Hen ('Old King Cole') and also, according to later Welsh genealogies, of Nyfain, daughter of Brychan of Brycheiniog in south Wales. Urien ruled the north British kingdom of Rheged in the second half of the sixth century. The exact extent of Rheged is unknown, though it seems to have straddled either side of the Solway Firth, as far west as Stranraer in Galloway on the (modern) Scottish side and incorporating Carlisle on the (modern)

English side. In addition, it had possibly extended further south-east along the Eden valley and over the Pennines to Catterick in what is now Yorkshire. Details of Urien's life and rule are limited to a handful of brief notices and some allusions in early Welsh poetry. Much incidental information, such as the identification of his wife as Modron ferch Afallach and the name of his bard Tristfardd, is without doubt unreliable.

Urien Rheged appears to have been the foremost of the northern British rulers who fought, ultimately unsuccessfully, against the expanding Northumbrian kingdoms of Bernicia and Deira. In one later Welsh poem Urien is called 'lord of Christendom', no doubt owing to his opposition to these pagan English. His allies against the Northumbrians included Rhydderch Hen, king of Strathclyde, Gwallog ap Llinog (whom some today would locate in Elfed in Yorkshire), and a Morgan (possibly Morgan Mwynfawr). Relations between these British rulers were not always amicable, despite the common threat. Urien's sons Owain and Pasgen seem to have fought Dunod ap Pabo (another northern ruler), and another son, Elffin, fought Gwallog. Indeed, Urien's eventual death was not at English hands but at the instigation of his erstwhile ally Morgan. According to the *Historia Brittonum* Urien and his allies fought the Bernician successors of King Ida, most notably Theodoric (*supp. r.* 572–9) and Hussa (*supp. r.* 585–92). There are some problems with the chronology of these events as Urien's death is placed in Theodoric's reign which would mean he could not have fought Hussa, at least after he had succeeded to the kingship. The fortunes of Urien and his sons against Theodoric fluctuated, but they eventually were able to besiege him on Lindisfarne for three days and nights. At this point, however, Morgan, jealous of Urien's predominant position among the British kings, arranged for the assassination of his rival. Later Welsh tradition named Urien's killer as one Llofen Llaw Ddifro ('Llofen of the Exiled Hand') and located the deed at a site which has been identified with Ross Law, on the mainland opposite Lindisfarne. It is possible that the encounters between Urien's sons and the other British rulers date from after this treacherous deed. Urien was probably succeeded by his son Owain. Another son, Rhun, was remembered in Welsh tradition for having baptized King Edwin of Northumbria and his daughter Eanflæd.

DAVID E. THORNTON

Sources T. Mommsen, ed., 'Historia Brittonum', *Chronica minora saec. IV. V. VI. VII.*, 3, MGH Auctores Antiquissimi, 13 (Berlin, 1898), 111–222 • P. C. Bartrum, ed., *Early Welsh genealogical tracts* (1966) • R. Bromwich, ed. and trans., *Trioedd ynys Prydein: the Welsh triads*, 2nd edn (1978) • *The poems of Taliesin*, ed. I. Williams, trans. J. E. Caerwyn-Williams (1968) [Welsh orig. *Canu Taliesin* (1960)] • I. Williams, ed., *Canu Llywarch Hen* (1935); pbk edn (1978) • A. P. Smyth, *Warlords and holy men: Scotland, AD 80–1000* (1984)

Urmston [*née* Hughes], **Harriett Elizabeth Hughes** (1828–1897), missionary, was born on 20 January 1828 at Clapham Common, Surrey, the fifth of six daughters of William Hughes Hughes (1792–1874), MP for Oxford, and his wife, Maria, *née* Field (*d.* 1870). She lived at the family's summer home at Ryde, Isle of Wight, until she was eighteen, receiving her education from a governess. Her future husband, Henry Brabazon Urmston (1829–1898), son of Sir James Brabazon Urmston, was accepted as a cadet by the East India Company. He sailed for Bengal in 1847; in September 1850 Harriett left England and the couple married at the military station, Barrackpore, on 15 November 1850. They remained in India, with two furloughs home, until 1875.

As the wife of a military officer and, after 1854, a civilian, Harriett's life was a series of relocations. With a growing family she often had little time for direct mission work; instead, the Urmstons opened their home to Anglican missionaries of the Church Missionary Society, as well as to local clergymen. Harriett made her convictions known by refusing to attend balls, the theatre, or the races. She derived spiritual sustenance from a long-running correspondence with Mary Kershaw, a Yorkshire invalid and active supporter of mission work; they began writing to each other in 1869 and the friendship was to end only on Harriett's death.

Harriett Urmston found an opportunity for full-time missionary activity when her husband was sent to Rawalpindi as deputy commissioner in 1868. They remained there until 1874. By the terms of a neutrality proclamation, she was not permitted to evangelize among the people of India; in the cantonment were British soldiers, and instead she began a mothers' meeting for soldiers' wives, which in turn became a meeting for soldiers. Her services combined newly popular Sankey hymns and a sermon on a biblical text. Her practical exhortations proved popular and many were converted by her. Her unashamed ministry to any who would listen earned her the epithet 'Holy Mary'.

Poor health forced the Urmstons' return to England in 1875 and they settled in Southsea, Hampshire. Harriett became involved with the Zenana, Bible, and Medical Mission and between 1875 and 1884 addressed more than 300 meetings on its behalf. She visited the dockyard dining halls to lecture on temperance and, at the behest of Frederick Charrington (1850–1936), preached thirteen times at the Assembly Hall, Mile End, in east London, in 1878–9. In one year, 1877, she gave 276 addresses at which a total of 32,700 people were present. She was frequently invited to preach at local mission halls. In 1885 the Urmstons moved to Maidstone, Kent, where she regularly visited about eighty households in the parish.

Harriett Urmston blended biblical knowledge, fervent piety, spiritual authority, and practical knowledge. Her forthrightness, especially in later life, earned her some reproach, but her biographer dismisses this as an (albeit unfortunate) product of her great zeal. She died from typhoid at her home, Ardenlee, Maidstone, on 4 September 1897. She was survived by her husband and six of their eight children: Mary Grace (1853–1933), Gertrude Elizabeth (1858–1916), Arthur Brabazon (b. 1861), Robert Bruce Brabazon (b. 1862), Beatrice Brabazon (b. 1864), and Florence Macan (b. 1866). The eldest son, Henry Brabazon (1851–1888), was killed on the Afghan frontier; and the second son, Herbert Edwardes (1855–1885), died after being invalided out of the Royal Navy.

L. E. LAUER

Sources G. Everard, ed., *The starry crown: a sketch of the life work of Harriett E. H. Urmston* (1898) • Burke, *Gen. GB* (1939) • *CGPLA Eng. & Wales* (1897)
Likenesses engravings, repro. in Everard, ed., *Starry crown*
Wealth at death £2686 7s. 0d.: probate, 30 Oct 1897, *CGPLA Eng. & Wales*

Urquhart, David (1805–1877), diplomatist and writer, was born at Braelangwell, Cromarty, on the Black Isle peninsula in Scotland, the second son of David Urquhart (1748–1811) and his second wife, Margaret Hunter (d. 1839), the daughter of an Edinburgh merchant. Shortly after her husband's death Mrs Urquhart took her son to be educated abroad. Urquhart firstly attended the college of Sorèze (a former Benedictine school in France), then spent a year studying in Geneva, before rounding off his education travelling with a tutor through Spain. His mother also introduced him to a number of her acquaintances who were to prove useful to him in later life, including the philosopher Jeremy Bentham and Sir Herbert Taylor, former private secretary to George III and Queen Charlotte, and later private secretary to William IV. In 1821 Urquhart returned to Britain, where he spent six months learning farming methods and a further three months working at Woolwich arsenal. In October 1822 he went to St John's College, Oxford, where he read classics; he did not complete his degree, however, and left Oxford after two years when his mother ran into financial difficulties and proved unable to support his studies.

Urquhart in Greece and the Balkans, 1827–1834 On leaving Oxford, encouraged by Bentham's Hellenism and having begun learning Turkish and modern Greek, Urquhart decided to volunteer his services in the Greek war of independence. Eventually, at the beginning of 1827, after several delays, he and his elder half-brother Charles travelled to Marseilles to join the London Greek Committee's naval expedition to Greece under the command of Lord Cochrane. Urquhart remained in Greece for two and a half years, first serving on the brig *Sauveur*, before being given the rank of lieutenant on board the frigate *Hellas*. The *Hellas* was involved in the siege of Scio, at which Urquhart was severely wounded. He remained in Greece as the war drew to a close at the end of 1828, but in November of the following year, restless, without much money, and on the look-out for a possible diplomatic or consular appointment, Urquhart visited Constantinople, and then three months later travelled back through Albania and the borderlands between Greece and Turkey. From here he inundated Bentham and Sir Herbert Taylor with reports on conditions at the Greek frontier, in the hope that the British government would take notice of his expertise. Some of these reports appeared in the *Morning Courier* during 1831, and Taylor also brought them to the attention of William IV, to whom Urquhart was presented when he returned to Britain. This publicity paid off, for in November 1831 Urquhart was chosen to accompany Sir Stratford

David Urquhart (1805–1877), by unknown photographer, *c.*1874

Canning on his mission to Constantinople to negotiate a final settlement of the Greek boundary.

As aide to Canning, Urquhart's main mission in 1832 was to travel to Scutari in Albania in order to cultivate the support of the Turkish sultan's most influential adviser, Reschid Pasha. But during this time he became convinced of the reforming character of the Turkish regime, and of the threat posed by Russian intervention in the region. Back in Constantinople in February 1832, Urquhart went native, moving out of the embassy quarter and adopting Turkish dress, and on his return to London in the summer of 1832 he urged the Foreign Office to reconsider its refusal to ally with the Turkish sultan against Egypt. He discussed his views with William IV in January 1833 and the king ordered Urquhart to send on to the Foreign Office a memorandum detailing their conversation. In the memorandum Urquhart denied that the Turkish empire was about to collapse, and emphasized the commercial opportunities that awaited Britain should she give aid to the sultan. If Britain did not intervene, he warned, Turkey would ally with Russia and the resources of the region would be at the tsar's disposal. In May, Russia did indeed give support to the sultan, and as public disquiet over Russia's designs grew, Urquhart dashed off a volume, published in July, detailing Turkey's state of progress, entitled *Turkey and its Resources*. The book was well received, and at the end of the summer the foreign secretary, Lord Palmerston, agreed that Urquhart should undertake a secret commercial mission to examine the possibilities for British trade in the Balkans, Turkey, Persia, southern Russia, and Afghanistan.

Urquhart's commercial enquiries came to a halt once he reached Constantinople in December 1833. Encouraged by the British ambassador, Viscount Ponsonby, Urquhart remained in the capital for the next year. His *Turkey and its Resources* was translated into Turkish and Urquhart was presented to the sultan. He gained the confidence of the Turkish government, and his mission passed from being exclusively commercial to overtly political, and in his reports to London he began to call for British support for the sultan and to propose possible treaty negotiations. In July 1834 Urquhart embarked on a yacht tour around the Black Sea, visiting the Circassian tribes who were fighting off Russian attempts to incorporate them within the empire. When Palmerston learned of Urquhart's trip to Circassia three months later, he decided to order an end to his mission, on the grounds that he was wasting time as well as causing diplomatic embarrassment. Ponsonby entered a plea of support on behalf of Urquhart, Palmerston reversed his decision, and in December suggested to William IV that Urquhart be appointed consul at Constantinople. By then Urquhart was already *en route* for Britain again. He turned down the appointment, aiming instead to restart the domestic publicity campaign of support for Turkey.

Unfortunately, on his arrival back in London Urquhart found the tories in government and the duke of Wellington at the Foreign Office. The duke refused to accede to Urquhart's demand for intervention against Russia, but Urquhart carried on with publicizing the Turkish cause. A pamphlet he had co-written with Ponsonby, entitled *England, France, Russia and Turkey*, was published in December 1834 and went through five editions very quickly, receiving positive reviews. So encouraged was Urquhart by this favourable reception that he established a weekly periodical, *The Portfolio*, in which he published copies of secret Russian dispatches which had been given to him by Polish émigrés and by Ponsonby. *The Portfolio* commenced publication in November 1835. In September, with the whigs now again in office, Urquhart was appointed secretary of embassy at Constantinople, but he did not leave for Turkey until March 1836. In the meantime, as well as producing *The Portfolio*, he became involved in unofficial negotiations aimed at increasing Anglo-Turkish trade. In February 1836 he submitted a draft treaty to the Foreign Office. This treaty stipulated a reduction of import duties between the two countries, removal of other trade prohibitions, and freedom of transit by sea and land through Turkey. The Board of Trade proved reluctant to give Turkey favourable terms in preference to Russia, and Urquhart's proposals were not taken up, although, to his eternal chagrin, the substance of his draft, without any lowering of British import duties, became the basis of the Anglo-Turkish commercial treaty of 1838.

The *Vixen* affair, 1834 Shortly after this set-back Urquhart left to take up his new position in Constantinople, where he found his role rather limited. Ponsonby wanted him to remain in London, and Palmerston had no intention of allowing Urquhart to become involved in tariff negotiations. He took up Circassian claims once more, concocting an attempt to break the Russian embargo on international trade along the Black Sea coast. At the end of October 1836, encouraged by Urquhart, the British schooner *Vixen* flouted the Russian embargo by sailing to the Circassian coast. As Urquhart had anticipated, a Russian warship seized the *Vixen*, and Ponsonby urged Palmerston to send a fleet into the Black Sea. Not only did Britain not intervene, but in March 1837 Palmerston recalled Urquhart from Constantinople, and in June charged him with a breach of official secrecy and dismissed him from the service. Ponsonby was implicated in the *Vixen* affair, and Urquhart always claimed that Palmerston himself had known of the plan, but it was Urquhart who was made to shoulder full responsibility; and with the death of William IV, he had no powerful ally to defend him.

Urquhart and British politics Urquhart's diplomatic career lay in ruins as a result of the *Vixen* affair, and for the rest of his life he neither forgave nor forgot Palmerston's role, nor that of the Foreign Office and the diplomatic service more generally. His reputation as a Turcophile writer still intact, in 1838 Urquhart wrote a two-volume account of his decade in the Near East, *The Spirit of the East*, a celebration of the parochial and patriarchal structure of Turkish society, and the simple faith embodied in Islam (Urquhart noted that as a 'Presbyterian and a Calvinist, I consider Islam nearer in dogma to the true Church' (xxv)). At the end of 1838 he made a short tour of north-east England and Scotland, warning merchants and chambers of commerce of the dangers of leaving commerce in the hands of statesmen and diplomats. Through these meetings Urquhart came into contact with various men who were to prove lifelong acolytes—such as Charles Attwood and Robert Monteith—as well as ex-members of some of the political unions (in Birmingham and Newcastle) and, in 1839, with delegates to the Chartist convention in London. Urquhart impressed some of the Chartists with his call for the restitution of the powers of English local government, but most of his efforts were devoted to establishing associations or committees for investigating treaties and diplomatic correspondence. Over the next few years these associations, as well as the Colonial Society, which Urquhart joined in 1842, protested through petitions and pamphlets against British policy towards China, Afghanistan, and the Levant, and against the American annexation of Texas. In 1843 Urquhart revived *The Portfolio*, which continued publication for a further two years (it was then reprinted during the 1860s).

Urquhart unsuccessfully contested Sheffield at the 1841 general election, and then stood at Stafford, this time successfully, in the general election of July 1847. At Stafford he stood as an independent, taking as his colours the Circassian flag, supporting free trade, and opposing the 1844 Bank Charter Act. Once in parliament Urquhart repeatedly called for Palmerston's conduct of foreign policy to be investigated by the House of Commons. He spoke frequently on foreign affairs in the 1848 parliamentary session, and also called for a reduction of national expenditure and the repeal of the union with Ireland. Urquhart also opposed the whig government's public health measures, which he felt were inimical to the spirit of English municipal government. By the end of the 1848 session Urquhart was clearly losing interest in parliament. He spent the remainder of the year travelling in Spain and Morocco. These travels were written up as a two-volume memoir published in 1850, entitled *The Pillars of Hercules*. In 1849 he left Britain again, this time to visit Lebanon (of which he produced a two-volume account in 1860) and later Turkey, where he met up with the exiled Hungarian leader Lajos Kossuth. Urquhart returned for some of the parliamentary session of 1851, but he did not contest the Stafford seat in the general election the following year.

Turcophilia and the Crimean War With the revival of public interest in the eastern question during the summer of 1853, Urquhart's expertise as a leading Turcophile was in demand once more. In August he began a series of regular articles for the *Morning Advertiser*, most of which were quickly reprinted in book form, and he spoke at a series of meetings in the midlands. He denounced Russia's designs on Turkey and the Danubian grain region, and argued that the Foreign Office was under Russian influence. In his opinion only the monarchy remained immune from Russian intrigue, and for this reason he called for the restitution of the full powers of the privy council. He also insisted that the negotiations between the powers over Turkey—so-called 'secret diplomacy'—should be made public, and he called for non-intervention by the other European powers in Turkish affairs, pointing out that Turkey, under a progressive regime, was capable of defending itself. At the beginning of 1854 Urquhart joined with various London radicals in establishing the Association for the Protection of Turkey and other Countries from Partition, and in June 1854 he considered contesting Lord John Russell's City of London seat. However, once Britain had declared war on Russia, Urquhart's pro-Turkish, non-interventionist stance was completely eclipsed by a more vociferous war mood. Although several foreign affairs committees were established during 1854 and 1855 along the lines of the associations that he had formed in the early 1840s, most of them were far more supportive of the war and of the fortunes of European nationalism than Urquhart. Differences of opinion between Urquhart and many of the committees reached a climax at a conference held in Birmingham in July 1855.

Marriage, later years, and death In September 1854 Urquhart married Harriet Angelina Fortescue (1824–1889), the sister of Chichester Fortescue MP (later Baron Carlingford). Urquhart's persistent attacks on Palmerston during 1855 caused considerable embarrassment to Fortescue, who, at the time, was serving in Palmerston's administration as a lord of the Treasury. Harriet aided Urquhart in his work, writing under the pseudonym Caritas, and after his death converted to Catholicism. They had three sons and two daughters, and until the mid-1860s resided mainly at Rickmansworth, where Urquhart installed a Turkish bath, a device which he helped popularize in Britain, despite the death of his son William in the steam room in February 1858. Their second surviving son was Francis Fortescue *Urquhart.

As the Crimean War drew to a close Urquhart's campaign for the reform of foreign policy gathered new momentum. His defence of natural law and the ancient constitution was clearly set out in two works published in 1855: *Public Opinion* and *Familiar Words*, and the influential *Free Press* (later entitled the *Diplomatic Review*), a natural successor to *The Portfolio*, began publication later in the same year. In 1857, in the aftermath of the British bombardment of Canton (Guangzhou) and the Indian mutiny, many more foreign affairs committees were established, and virtually all of these looked upon Urquhart as a messianic presence and devoted themselves to the study of international law, particularly maritime law. In 1864 Urquhart left Britain permanently for health reasons and divided his time between Montreux and Nice, where he spent the winters, and the chalet des Mélèzes in St Gervais on Mont Blanc, where he resided during the summers. In his later years he became a strong supporter of Pope Pius IX, seeing in him the embodiment of international law and natural justice against the doctrines of the eastern Orthodox church. Along with his friend Monteith he travelled to Rome in 1869 and made various appeals to the Vatican Council.

Urquhart died in Naples on 16 May 1877, *en route* home from a visit to Egypt. He was buried at Clarens, Montreux. Urquhart was worshipped as a seer by many of his followers in the foreign affairs committees, but dismissed as something of a crank by most of his political contemporaries. His monomania over Palmerston's treachery and collusion, and his eccentric championing of all matters 'eastern' (late in life he led a campaign to abolish handshaking and replace it with the customary Turkish salutation), tended to undermine his well earned reputation as the leading Turcophile writer of his generation, and as one of the best-informed critics of British foreign policy in the age of Palmerston.   MILES TAYLOR

Sources *Pall Mall Gazette* (30 May 1877) • M. C. Bishop, *Memoir of Mrs Urquhart* (1897) • G. Robinson, *David Urquhart* (1920) • C. Bailey, *Frances Fortescue Urquhart* (1936) • G. H. Bolsover, 'David Urquhart and the eastern question, 1833–1837', *Journal of Modern History*, 8 (1936), 444–67 • H. Tayler, *History of the Urquhart family* (1946) • C. K. Webster, 'Urquhart, Ponsonby and Palmerston', *EngHR*, 62 (1947), 327–51 • O. W. Hewett, *Strawberry fair: a biography of Frances, Countess Waldegrave, 1821–1879* (1956) • M. H. Jenks, 'The activities and influence of David Urquhart, 1833–1856, with special reference to the affairs of the Near East', PhD diss., U. Lond., 1964 • B. Aspinwall, 'David Urquhart, Robert Montieth and the Catholic church: a search for justice and peace', *Innes Review*, 31 (1980), 57–70 • M. Taylor, 'The old radicalism and the new: David Urquhart and the politics of opposition, 1832–1867', *Currents of radicalism: popular radicalism, organised labour, and party politics in Britain, 1850–1914*, ed. E. F. Biagini and A. J. Reid (1991), 23–43 • M. Lamb, 'The making of a Russophobe: David Urquhart—the formative years, 1825–1835', *International History Review*, 3 (1981), 330–57 • M. Lamb, 'Writing up the eastern question in 1835-6', *International History Review*, 15 (1993), 239–68 • *CGPLA Eng. & Wales* (1877)

Archives Balliol Oxf., corresp. and papers • Wellcome L., corresp. and papers relating to Turkish baths | Bodl. Oxf., letters to Benjamin Disraeli • NA Scot., corresp. with Sir John McNeill • Som. ARS, corresp. with Lord Calingford • U. Durham L., letters to Viscount Ponsonby • U. Southampton L., corresp. with Lord Palmerston, etc.
Likenesses photograph, *c.*1874, repro. in Robinson, *David Urquhart*, frontispiece [*see illus.*]
Wealth at death under £2000: probate, 28 July 1877, *CGPLA Eng. & Wales*

Urquhart, Francis Fortescue, of Urquhart [nicknamed Sligger] (**1868–1934**), bachelor don, was born on 1 September 1868 at 21 Malagnou, Geneva, the third (second surviving) son and fifth (last) child of David *Urquhart (1805–1877), diplomatist and writer on international affairs, and his wife, Harriet Angelina Fortescue (1824–1889), also a writer. Her brother Chichester *Fortescue, Baron Carlingford, was a father figure during Francis Urquhart's youth: the name Fortescue was added at Carlingford's request when he died childless in 1898.

Urquhart's childhood home was in Montreux, with summers at the Chalet des Mélèzes, which his father had built in 1865, 1000 metres above St Gervais-les-Bains, in the French Alps. His mother became a Roman Catholic in 1877, and he was educated in that tradition at Hodder Place near Stonyhurst (1879–80), Beaumont College in Old Windsor (1881–6), and Stonyhurst College (1886–9). In 1889 he took an external London BA in classics. Urquhart entered Balliol College, Oxford, as an exhibitioner in 1890: he won the Stanhope historical essay prize, took a first in modern history (1894), and was elected to a tutorial fellowship in 1896. The first Catholic tutor in Oxford since the Reformation, and a pious one at that, his presence did much to reconcile conservative Catholics with the university; but he did not seek converts, which helped to settle the suspicions of conservative Anglicans.

Urquhart lived in Balliol for nearly forty years, holding office as junior dean (1896–1907), domestic bursar (1907–19), and dean (1918–34). A conscientious but uninspiring tutor, his interests were more in art and architecture than literature or history, and he made no contributions of his own to historical scholarship. He took little part in university affairs except the development of the Oxford Catholic chaplaincy—he was instrumental in the appointment of his friend R. A. Knox as chaplain in 1926. Nevertheless, he became one of the best-known and most warmly remembered dons of his time. His main role, recalled L. E. Jones, 'was social, not pedagogic … he appeared to have endless leisure for loitering in the Quad by day and gossiping in his rooms by night' (Jones, 33). Late in the evening during term time his rooms above Balliol's back gate became an informal salon for undergraduates of all sorts to mix and talk. In vacations he often took a chosen few with him touring, and every summer except 1915–18 he invited groups of a dozen or so to stay with him at his father's chalet, which became known as the Chalet des Anglais. He had first taken a reading party there in 1891; in 1896 he bought the chalet from his elder brother, David Urquhart (1855–1928). It burnt down in 1906 while he was on a trip round the world, but he had it rebuilt. Between 1891 and

1931, when his health failed, he had about 300 chalet guests for a week or two of morning reading and afternoon mountain walks. About half were Balliol undergraduates, including C. V. Connolly, L. P. Hartley, J. S. Huxley, F. S. Kelly, M. Harold Macmillan, and W. T. Monckton, but other colleges were also well represented—by T. S. R. Boase and R. J. G. Boothby (both Magdalen); R. H. S. Crossman, W. G. Hayter, J. P. R. Maud, J. H. A. Sparrow (all New College); and Q. McG. Hogg (Christ Church).

Urquhart had a slim, athletic frame, blue eyes, and a handsome, smooth face with heavy, slightly pouting lips; his hair was thick and curly—light brown in youth, white later. The nickname Sligger, by which he was generally known after about 1892, was derived from 'sleek one' through 'slicker'. He liked handsome young men, and photographing them, but was probably celibate. Only one special relationship is evident, with Stephen Hewett (1893–1916), whose letters from the trenches he edited for publication. Walter Pater may have used Urquhart as the model for some features of the subject in *Emerald Uthwart* (1892). Anthony Powell, a pupil of Urquhart's, placed his recurrent character Sillery in a setting based on Urquhart's salon, but denied otherwise drawing on him.

Urquhart died of lung disease at the Acland Nursing Home, Oxford, on 18 September 1934, and was buried in Wolvercote cemetery three days later after a solemn requiem mass at the church of St Aloysius. He left most of his £15,000 English estate to Balliol. In 1959 lord Lyon king of arms accepted that the chiefship of the clan Urquhart had been vested in him (1928–34), and had passed on his death to his distant American cousin Wilkins Fisk Urquhart of that ilk (1896–1976). Urquhart bequeathed the Chalet des Anglais to his Balliol friend R. A. B. Mynors. At the close of the twentieth century it was still being used for undergraduate reading parties.   JOHN JONES

Sources C. Bailey, *Francis Fortescue Urquhart: a memoir* (1936) · G. Robinson, *David Urquhart* (1920) · M. C. Bishop, *Memoir of Mrs Urquhart* (1897) · *The Times* (19 Sept 1934) · *The Universe* (21 Sept 1934) · unpublished material, Balliol Oxf. · W. Drumm, *The Old Palace: the Catholic chaplaincy at Oxford* (1991) · S. H. Hewett, *A scholar's letters from the front*, ed. F. F. Urquhart (1918) · L. E. Jones, *An Edwardian youth* (1956) · A. Powell, *Journals, 1982–1986* (1995), 273 · A. Powell, *Infants of the spring* (1976), 151 · E. Waugh, *Ronald Knox* (1959) · J. Fortescue, *A history of the family of Fortescue*, ed. T. Fortescue, 2nd edn (1880), 132 · b. cert. · d. cert.
Archives Balliol Oxf., photograph albums | Balliol Oxf., The Chalet Book · Balliol Oxf., Chalet de Mélèzes Collection
Likenesses W. W. Russell, oils, *c.*1926, Balliol Oxf. · S. Elwes, oils, *c.*1929, Stonyhurst College, Lancashire · J. R. Merton, oils, *c.*1932, Balliol Oxf. · photographs, Balliol Oxf.
Wealth at death £15,139 0s. 10d.: probate, 4 Dec 1934, *CGPLA Eng. & Wales*

Urquhart, Frederick Burrows (1912–1995),

writer, was born on 12 July 1912 at 8 Palmerston Place Lane, Edinburgh, first among the three sons of Frederick Burrows Urquhart (d. 1958), a chauffeur, and Agnes, née Harrower. His father was unfit for war service and became in turn chauffeur to a series of wealthy men. Urquhart's childhood was spent in Edinburgh, Granton, Perthshire, Wigtownshire, and Wardie. He thus attended the village schools of Torryburn, Styx, Perthshire, and Kirkcolm,

before progressing to Stranraer High School and Broughton Academy, Edinburgh. The last he disliked, and he left school at fifteen to work in an Edinburgh bookshop, thus beginning a lifelong professional connection with books; he claimed that this was the best university for an aspiring writer. An avid film and theatre fan, he nourished ambitions in both these directions, as he related in his memoir of his early days, 'My many splendoured pavilion' (1979), but above all, in his seven years in the bookshop, he wrote. His first two novels, aside from being handwritten and betraying inexperience, were marked by a strong homosexual interest and were repeatedly refused by publishers; they remained unpublished, in manuscript, in the National Library of Scotland into the twenty-first century. His first published novel was *Time will Knit* (1938). This was followed by *The Ferret was Abraham's Daughter* (1949) and *Jezebel's Dust* (1951). The first of his novels to deal with a homosexual theme was *Palace of Green Days*, not published until 1979. It was in many ways autobiographical and the first of a projected series that did not materialize. It treats the childhoods of a young girl and her brother, the children of a chauffeur. The sister is film- and theatre-crazy, and the brother notably drawn to sewing doll's dresses rather than to toy trains and guns—definitely 'feminine' in his tastes. The book treats this apparently cross-gender feeling—and a fair amount of child sexual abuse—unsensationally, even matter-of-factly. The promised sequel, with the boy reaching puberty, was never published; Urquhart felt that an audience was not yet ready.

Fred Urquhart is best known and most widely admired among a small body of critical cognoscenti for his short stories. Short-story writers are too easily overlooked, and Urquhart was very seriously neglected by the larger book-reading public. He was successful from the thirties to the sixties and prominent in all the fashionable literary magazines of the time, excelling both in pathos and comedy, but almost none of his stories remained long in print. Alexander Reid described him as 'Scotland's leading short story writer of the century' (Roberts, vii). Stevie Smith and others drew attention to the unusual understanding and effectiveness of his treatment of women and to the polish of his 'diamond style' (ibid.).

It was early in his career that Urquhart earned tributes to his understanding of unhappy or frustrated women—the girl dying of TB, deserted by her lover, in 'We never died in winter'; or 'Sweat', where the girl tries to disguise the effects of working in a basement sweatshop only to disgust her admirer by the crudity and ineffectiveness of her cheap perfume.

Urquhart was living in Cupar at the start of the Second World War, and his observations of relations between the local girls and incoming Polish soldiers informed his subject matter in 'The laundry girl and the Pole' and a number of other works. But the war, in which both his brothers served, clarified for Urquhart his (non-religious) conscientious objection to fighting. As a result he was sent as farm labourer and secretary to Bent Farm, Laurencekirk. He lost 3 stone over four years there, no small matter for a man of his slight build. Auchencairn was his fictional name for the town in the Howe of the Mearns where he set his fine stories of the agricultural north-east of Scotland—such as 'The prisoners', 'The red stot', and 'The last sister'—which have borne comparison with Grassic Gibbon and Jessie Kesson. In 1967–8 Rupert Hart-Davis published a two-volume 'collected' edition of the stories (in fact generously selected) entitled *The Dying Stallion* and *The Ploughing Match*.

As Graeme Roberts has pointed out, later treatments of the theme of romantic yearning tend to be more 'robustly comic' (Roberts, ix), like the wall-eyed servant lass in 'Beautiful music' with her dung-splashed legs and fingers like 'red rationed sausages'. But Gillian Ferguson points out how completely Urquhart could capture both admirable and unattractive sides of Scottish womanly submissiveness: 'He raises what might seem the surrender of the ego, or unattractive acquiescence to powerlessness, to nobility, wisdom' (Macpherson, 29). The same is true of his treatment of children, old people, the desperate, and the lonely. He supplies an important documentary insight into the mid-twentieth-century period and especially civilian life during the war, whether writing about pub life or family life, Polish soldiers or GI brides, the impact of the new National Health Service, the Co-op, the pictures, or the erring milkman. Despite his long residence in England, Urquhart told Hugh Macpherson: 'On the whole I still think in Scots, and very often what I have done is I've found a situation in England and transferred it up to Scotland for the story' (ibid., 28).

After the war Urquhart gravitated to London's Soho, where he met and enjoyed a sexually more liberated society than he had known in Scotland. He resumed his career in the world of books, he was a scout for Walt Disney and a reader for a literary agency, for MGM, and for a number of publishers. He also edited a number of books on varied subjects, from a cartoon biography and a book of horses to several collections of short stories.

In 1946 Urquhart met his life partner, Peter Wyndham Allen (1908–1990), who had been a dancer. In 'Forty-three years: a benediction', written after Allen's death, he finally felt able to speak about their love, celebrating their life together in a 'happy homosexual marriage', first in London and latterly in a cottage in the middle of Ashdown Forest. This was an idyll in which Urquhart was writer, editor, and earner, and for the most part Allen was carer and kept house. Early in the 1990s Urquhart, now diabetic and subject to minor strokes, returned to Scotland to live in Musselburgh, near his brother Morris. But undaunted he proceeded to write more stories, add polish to the autobiography that he had been long composing, and at last attempt a mature, open, and sexually complex novel; this he developed from a short story that he had published, 'Robert/Hilda', which can be found in Carl MacDougall's anthology of Scottish short stories, *The Devil and the Giro* (1989). It begins: 'After she died Robert Greenlees took to dressing up in his wife's clothes'. Robert and Hilda had led an apparently harmonious married life but 'he'd been dominated enough all his life by women, and he wanted a

change'. Recapitulation of the marriage involves a masterly compressed social history, after which the narrative returns to a present where Robert, now regularly dressed and made-up as a woman, persuades his son to take him out to a pub. There a contemporary, George, admiringly buys Robert/Hilda a drink, and by the end of the story the two are planning to set up house together. Once Urquhart felt free to write about eccentric sexual preference he did so convincingly, although again unsensationally and matter-of-factly.

Urquhart died in Roodlands General Hospital, Haddington, East Lothian, on 2 December 1995. On his death his papers were deposited in Edinburgh University Library, and it is to be hoped that among these will be found a final version of 'Robert/Hilda and George', the novel. Its publication would be an important vindication of a very neglected Scottish fiction writer. ISOBEL MURRAY

Sources F. Urquhart, 'Forty-three years: a benediction', *The ghost of Liberace: new writing Scotland*, ed. A. L. Kennedy and H. Whyte, 11 (1993) · F. Urquhart, 'My many splendoured pavilion', *As I remember*, ed. M. Lindsay (1979) · J. G. Roberts, ed., *Fred Urquhart: full score* (1989) · A. Bold, ed., *Scotland: a literary guide* (1989) · I. Murray, 'Fred Urquhart at 80', *The Scotsman* (11 July 1992), 9 · H. Macpherson, 'Scottish writers: Fred Urquhart', *Scottish Book Collector*, 3/3 (1992), 27–30 · personal knowledge (2004) · b. cert. · d. cert.
Archives NL Scot., MSS and unpublished material · Ransom HRC, corresp. and literary papers · U. Edin. L., corresp. and papers | NL Scot., letters to Alexander Reid · U. Edin. L., letters to R. Greacen · U. Edin. L., corresp. with John Ryder and Herta Ryder
Likenesses photographs, repro. in Macpherson, 'Scottish writers'

Urquhart, Mary Sinclair [Molly] (1906–1977), actress, was born in Glasgow on 21 January 1906, the eldest of the family of three daughters and a son of William Urquhart (1875–1956), ship's engineer, and his wife, Ann McCallum (b. 1874), a Post Office clerk. Both parents had moved from the highlands to work in Glasgow, where they married. The family lived at 27 Caird Drive, Dowanhill, and attended Gardner Street Presbyterian Church.

Mary was a lively child who took delight in singing round the piano and learning highland dancing to her father's chanter. Her party piece was 'Cockles and mussels', telling the sad tale of Molly Malone, and she became known as Molly from then on. She attended Dowanhill primary school and Church Street School, leaving at fourteen to work in the civil service in the telephone exchange. Her abiding passion was still acting and she saved her money to pay for elocution lessons from a renowned teacher, Percival Steeds at the Athenaeum in Glasgow. At sixteen she joined a local drama club and by her twenties she had become an accomplished amateur. Her work attracted the attention of R. F. Pollock, a Glasgow businessman with a real passion for theatre. Inspired by Theodore Komisarjevsky's Chekhov season in London in 1926, he chose a group of players, gave each actor a meticulously annotated script of *The Three Sisters*, and rehearsed them for ten weeks. Urquhart played the part of Irena. The play was presented for a week's private performances and received admiring reviews.

In 1934 Urquhart made her professional début in Glasgow's Theatre Royal, playing Effie Deans in a roistering stage version of Sir Walter Scott's *Heart of Midlothian*, directed by Millard Shevlin. She used her full name, Mary S. Urquhart. During this time she became engaged to William McIntosh (1900–1959) from Inverness-shire, a member of the Glasgow police force. He totally understood that acting was essential to her happiness, and they married on 1 August 1934. In 1935–6 Molly worked with the Cambridge Festival Theatre, then in 1936–7 with the Sheldon-Browne company in Gourock. She gained valuable experience from these engagements but realized that in order to work in Scotland she would have to find a theatre space and form her own company.

Urquhart found a suitable building in Rutherglen, a small royal burgh outside Glasgow. A disused church, it had a square interior with pews seating about 250 people. John Paterson, founder of a famous oatcake firm, was the owner. Impressed that Urquhart had saved £300 towards the venture, more than he had when he started, he rented the building to her for a nominal figure. The theatre was to be called the MSU (after her initials). She saw this as a place where young amateur actors who wanted to become professional could gain experience. She planned a season of weekly repertory, and all of her company rehearsed in the evenings after their day's work was done. Her family and friends helped in every way, adapting the building and making scenery and costumes. One day, as she took off her overalls and put on some make-up to meet the press, someone quipped, 'Star by night, char by day' (Murdoch, 65). The play chosen for the opening was Merton Hodge's *The Wind and the Rain*, an entertaining story of student life. The leading roles were played by Eileen Herlie, Andrew Crawford, and Archie Duncan, with Molly directing and playing the landlady.

The people of Rutherglen rallied round the theatre and after a successful opening night on 2 May 1939, audiences grew steadily. Her husband took the accounts in hand, and with the support of the company on stage, backstage, and in the box office, Urquhart ran the theatre until 1944, in spite of the war, the black-out, and the lack of any public subsidy. However, she did allow herself a few weeks off in September 1943 for the birth of her son, James Urquhart McIntosh. Over 100 plays were presented in the theatre, from G. B. Shaw to James Bridie, and with several modern comedies, pantomimes, and new plays by Scottish dramatists. Actors who gained experience on that little stage included Duncan Macrae, Gordon Jackson, and the young Nicholas Parsons, who said of Molly: 'She gave us real experience of walking the boards, learning one's job the hard, the only way' (Murdoch, 122–3).

In 1944 when the Paterson family decided to sell the building for £2000 Molly had to accept that the price was beyond her means. The little theatre in its five brief years had been an important chapter in Scottish dramatic history. However, Molly Urquhart was invited to join a new venture, the Citizens' Theatre, established in Glasgow by James Bridie. Her first part was the lead in J. B. Priestley's *Bull Market*, a comedy about a chambermaid who became a millionaire. Translating the dialogue from Yorkshire to Scots she gave a triumphant performance, in the central role, described by the author as 'truly magnificent and vital' (Murdoch, 130). Urquhart became a permanent member of the Citizens' Company and worked there, on and off, from 1944 to 1957. She was supremely happy, especially when she got parts that allowed her to give full rein to her very Scottish style of acting. These included Mrs Grant in Bridie's *The Forrigan Reel*, Mary Paterson in *The Anatomist* (also by Bridie), and Dame Sensualitie in David Lindsay's *The Thrie Estaites* at the Edinburgh festival. In this last she was magnificent: beautifully gowned, she advanced into the assembly halls and made the old Scots words ring out with warmth and humour. In Bridie's pantomime *The Tintock Cup* she played a redoubtable principal boy, stopping the show with a song written by Stanley Baxter, 'Tatty Bacchante—I'm everyone's auntie'.

In 1945 Molly Urquhart's first London appearance was in James Bridie's *The Forrigan Reel* in Sadler's Wells. The company was headed by Alistair Sim, with whom she again appeared in Bridie's *Dr. Angelus* (Phoenix Theatre, 1947) and *The Anatomist* (Westminster Theatre, 1948). Her inclusion in *Who's Who in the Theatre* followed in 1951.

In 1957 Molly Urquhart appeared in *The Nun's Story*, a film by Fred Zinnemann; she also had roles in several of his later films, including *A Man for All Seasons* (1966). She had made the acquaintance of Dame Peggy Ashcroft in *The Nun's Story* and she was invited to join her in a play called *The Coast of Coromandel*. During rehearsals she got word, on 9 January 1959, that her husband had suffered an aneurism while at the wheel of his car and had died instantly. Now a widow with a sixteen-year-old son, Molly Urquhart subsequently undertook television and film work whenever possible. She played in *The Flying Swan*, a television series with Margaret Lockwood, and *The Very Merry Widow* with Moira Lister, taking the part of a Scottish housekeeper in both series. In 1962 she appeared in the Sean O'Casey season at the Mermaid Theatre and also worked in a series of Scottish comedies with Jimmy Logan in his New Metropole Theatre in Glasgow.

In her latter years Molly Urquhart continued her lifelong residence in Glasgow, and spent as much time as possible with her family in Wester Ross and on Loch Lomondside. Shortly after she made her final appearance in Fred Zinnemann's film of *Julia* in 1977, she became ill and, following an operation for cancer, died in the Southern General Hospital, Glasgow, on 5 October 1977. She was buried in Arrochar churchyard, Loch Long. She was a lady at the heart of Scottish theatre and an inspiration to many young actors. Perhaps Dame Peggy Ashcroft summed up her essential spirit: 'She was like the sun coming into the room' (Murdoch, 243).   HELEN MURDOCH

Sources H. Murdoch, *Travelling hopefully: the story of Molly Urquhart* (1981) · D. Campbell, *Playing for Scotland* (1996), 127–35 · U. Glas. L., special collections department, Scottish Theatre Archive · personal knowledge (2004) · private information (2004) · d. cert.
Archives U. Glas., Scottish Theatre archive, papers | U. Glas., Scottish Theatre archive, Citizens' Theatre documents | FILM BFI NFTVA, performance footage
Likenesses photographs, U. Glas. L., Scottish Theatre Archive

Urquhart, Robert Elliott [Roy] (1901–1988), army officer, was born in Shepperton on 28 November 1901, the eldest in the family of three sons and one daughter of Alexander Urquhart MD, physician, and his wife, Isabel Gillespie. After attending St Paul's School and the Royal Military College, Sandhurst, he was commissioned as a second lieutenant in the Highland light infantry in 1920. Two years at the Staff College, Camberley (1936–7), were followed by staff appointments in India—staff captain (1938), deputy adjutant and quartermaster-general at army headquarters (1939–40), and deputy assistant adjutant-general and assistant adjutant and quartermaster-general, 3rd division (1940–41), until he was given command of the 2nd battalion of the Duke of Cornwall's light infantry in 1941. In 1942 he became general staff officer grade 1 of the 51st Highland division and went through the campaign in north Africa which destroyed the Afrika Korps. He was given command of 231st brigade in Malta in 1943, and its distinguished performance in Sicily and Italy brought him appointment to the DSO.

Urquhart was then brigadier general staff of 12th corps and was chosen in 1944 for command of the 1st airborne division. He led it in operation Market Garden, which was designed to cross three main river obstacles in the Netherlands in September 1944 and to join up with 30th corps arriving from the south, to swing through into the German industrial heartland. Since Urquhart was over 6 feet tall, of robust build, and possibly at forty-two rather too old for parachuting, he moved into battle by glider. He faced immediate difficulties. British troops arrived in a piecemeal fashion over three days and had to move 5 miles to their allotted positions around Arnhem. Their route was blocked by German armour reorganizing after Normandy, and, to compound the difficulties, the Germans captured the plans of the entire operation on the body of an American soldier shot down in a glider. Communications were rarely satisfactory and the weather was atrocious, making air support and replenishment difficult. The worst stroke of ill luck was Urquhart's enforced absence (he was obliged to take refuge in the attic of a house surrounded by German troops) from his headquarters for thirty-six hours soon after his arrival, when decisive command was imperative and was lacking. Urquhart made mistakes: the high ground at Wester Bouwing, for example, dominating the divisional bridgehead, and the heavy ferry at Heveadorp were never secured, but he fought a great battle. The high morale of the troops under his command reflected his own, but the battle of Arnhem was a defeat for the British and the advance of 30th corps was delayed. The remnants of Urquhart's division, withdrawn on 25 September 1944 across the lower Rhine, numbered some 2600 men of the 10,000 he had brought in.

Urquhart, appointed CB after Arnhem (1944), was next used to command an *ad hoc* airborne force, styled 1st airborne division, which was sent to Norway to rescue King Haakon, but his division was never reconstituted and was disbanded in November 1945. He became a colonel in 1945 and major-general in 1946. He was awarded the Netherlands Bronze Lion (1944) and Norwegian order of St Olaf (1945).

Urquhart's career thereafter puzzled and disappointed many who knew his qualities. For fourteen months while the Territorial Army was being reorganized he was its director-general (1945–6). He was general officer commanding, 16th airborne division, Territorial Army (1947–8), and commander, lowland district (1948–50). In 1950 he was given command of 17th Gurkha division in Malaya and in the same year became general officer commanding, Malaya. He moved to Austria in 1952 for three years as general officer commanding-in-chief of British troops, in an agreeable if uninspiring assignment which was his last in the service. From 1954 he was colonel of his regiment, the Highland light infantry, but when the army council decreed its amalgamation with the Royal Scots Fusiliers in 1957 he became embroiled in a disagreement which concerned style, title, and above all dress. Would the new regiment be in kilt or trews? The two colonels negotiated an agreement, with the lord Lyon's support, that the kilt should be worn with the tartan dress Erskine. The War Office insisted on trews and both colonels had to go (1958).

After Urquhart's retirement from the army in December 1955 he lived for some years at Drymen in Stirlingshire and thereafter at Bigram, Port of Menteith, nearby. In 1957 he joined the Davy and United Engineering Co., where his sound judgement and administrative experience found useful scope, first as personnel manager and then as director, in an industrial environment whose technical aspects were not perhaps among his deepest interests. He moved into complete retirement in 1970.

In 1939 Urquhart, always known as Roy, married Pamela, daughter of Brigadier William Edmund Hunt Condon, of the Indian army. They had one son and three daughters. Urquhart died on 13 December 1988 at his home in Port of Menteith. He was survived by his wife.

J. W. HACKETT, *rev.*

Sources R. E. Urquhart, *Arnhem* (1958) · J. Hackett, *I was a stranger* (1977) · *The Times* (15 Dec 1988) · *The Independent* (19 Dec 1988) · personal knowledge (1996) · private information (1996)
Likenesses photograph, repro. in *The Independent* · photograph, repro. in *The Times*

Urquhart [Urchard], **Sir Thomas, of Cromarty** (1611–1660), author and translator, was the eldest son of Sir Thomas Urquhart of Cromarty (1582–1642) and Christian Elphinston (*b.* 1590), fourth daughter of Alexander, fourth Lord Elphinston. He records, on the death of his father, that he had been 'bequeathed five brethren, all men, and two sisters' (*Works*, 340). He was probably born in the family's town house in Banff or in the old castle of Cromarty but no records of the event remain.

The Urquharts were an influential family who held the heritable sheriffdom of Cromarty and owned extensive estates in the area. The author's own grandfather Henry succeeded his great-grandfather Walter on 11 May 1607. The elder Sir Thomas was highly esteemed by James I, who knighted him in 1617. He was also the first Urquhart to

Sir Thomas Urquhart of Cromarty (1611–1660), by George Glover, 1641

probable that he was abroad at this time, seeking to complement academic theory with the experience offered by travel. Certainly, his later writings reflect a broad, detailed knowledge of European geography and customs. In one context, he claims to have visited sixteen countries; in another he boasts that his fluency in French, Spanish, and Italian allows him to pass himself off as a native in these countries.

When describing such events, Urquhart regularly assumes for himself the status of Scotland's martial and academic champion, reminding the outside world that the current unheroic, presbyterian age is only a temporary aberration in that nation's proud history. When later celebrating the 'admirable' James Crichton in his prose romance *The Jewel* he therefore immortalizes a hero in his own image. Only Crichton's amorous exploits have no parallel in Urquhart's unapologetic mirroring of his own heroism.

Family troubles If the late 1620s and early 1630s were indeed spent in foreign lands, family troubles soon demanded Urquhart's return. His father fell into debt and in the mid-1630s his son's name appears regularly in documents outlining claims made by creditors. Although the *Annals of Banff* confirm that Sir Thomas senior had received his lands unburdened by any debts, by 1632 he was borrowing £20,000 from one of his neighbours, William Rig of Adernie. On 29 June 1636 he even sold to Rig £2000 worth of annual rent from the Cromarty estates in order to delay full repayment.

Although Thomas later excuses his father's conduct as deriving from too strict an adherence to the principle of honesty, the two men certainly fell out at this time. Indeed, Thomas and his younger brothers were charged with 'putting violent hands' on him and holding him in an upper chamber of Cromarty Castle, named the 'Inner Dortour' (Tayler, 38). After some legal wrangling, however, the justiciary court resolved the family dispute amicably.

This truce did not endure. On 25 January 1637, when Alexander Dunbar of Westfield and Katherine Dunbar, widow of David Brodie, raised a case against Urquhart senior for non-payment of a debt of 5000 merks, he was outlawed by the privy council. Lands as well as money were under threat. In July 1637 Patrick Smith of Braco seized part of the Cromarty estates in lieu of financial recompense. Urquhart senior, however, had earlier gained from Charles I a year's protection against claims of this sort. Ironically, it is the text of a letter confirming this grant under the great seal on 1 June 1637 which also reveals the father blaming his sons' 'undewtifull carriage and behaviour' for his own situation (*Sir Thomas Urquhart … : the Jewel*, 4). By 25 July, however, harmonious family relations had been restored, suggesting that, at least among their own, the Urquharts were as incapable of sustaining anger as they were prone to exhibit it.

National events also played a part in re-establishing family unity. The *History of Scots Affairs* records that, in Cromarty, the Urquharts were the only noble family holding episcopalian views and were 'environed with covenanters as neighbours' (Gordon, 1.61). The elder Sir

abandon the Catholic faith. As a determined episcopalian, however, he remained a royalist, refusing to sign the covenant of 1638.

Education and early years The elder Sir Thomas also ensured a good education for his son. The future author was admitted to King's College, Aberdeen, in 1622 and although, like many others in his day, he did not graduate, he profited from the teaching he received, later paying handsome tributes to the regent, Alexander Lunan, and to his tutor, William Setoun, 'a very able preacher truly, and a good scholar' (*Works*, 263).

George Glover's engraved portraits of Urquhart claim to represent him '*ad vivum*' (from life). They depict an elegant cavalier, slim and handsome with long flowing locks. Yet the many autobiographical passages in his writing say nothing of love or marriage. Even the allegorical settings for the portraits define his fame in martial and artistic terms alone. In one, he hovers between hell and heaven, on Mount Parnassus, accepting from the muses a set of wreaths, celebrating medium ('invention, sweetnes, stile') and message ('judgment, learning, wit'). In the other, a cherub hands him a laurel crown 'For Armes and Artes'.

After his studies at university Urquhart's name disappears from Scottish records for about ten years. It seems

Thomas not only refused to sign the covenant in 1638, he went to Ellon in support of the alternative 'king's covenant'. Thomas himself, designated as 'the young laird of Cromartie', is listed among those who staged a counter-raid against some covenanters on 10 May 1638. As the *Memorialls of the Trubles* note, this was 'the first blood that wes drawin' in the civil war north of the border (Spalding, 1.181). When the northern confederate forces were defeated on 13 May 1639 at the Trott of Turiff, he sailed from Aberdeen to England and the court of Charles I.

Early works The 1640s saw Urquhart established as both courtier and author. On his own evidence, he was in attendance on Charles by 27 November 1639, when the bishop of Ross presented the king with a copy of Spottiswoode's *History of the Church of Scotland*. Versifying was a good way of becoming noticed within the courtly game and so Urquhart's two collections of epigrams, 'Apollo and the Muses' (1640; unpublished) and *Epigrams: Divine and Moral* (1641) may sign political ambition as much as an enthusiasm for versifying. Certainly, each of the ten books in the first collection is dedicated to a different, named courtier. Its 1103 poems, which the author claims to have completed in thirteen weeks, include both serious and witty examples of the epigrammatic mode. The manuscript is retained in the Osborn collection of the Beinecke Library at Yale University.

Neither of these early verse collections even remotely suggests the imaginative power and rhythmical subtlety of Urquhart's later prose. Arguably, the second set of epigrams, printed by Barnard Alsop and Thomas Fawcet in 1641, is even less inspired than the first. Dedicated to James, third marquess of Hamilton, these verses shun wit entirely. While their moral tone cannot be faulted their artistic value remains questionable as the following couplet, advocating the 'true nature of human wealth', illustrates,

> And hee, whose heart is discontented, is
> But a poore wretch, though all the world were his.
> (*Works*, 9)

On 7 April 1641 Urquhart was knighted by Charles I in the gallery at Whitehall. In 1642 he returned to Cromarty following the death of his father. Although Urquhart dates the death in August 1642, the *Annals of Banff* (2.418) already describe his father as 'umquhill' on 14 June. After dealing with his creditors, the author claims to have spent the next three years abroad although there is evidence of the occasional return to London, in order to safeguard his British interests.

On 9 May 1644 Urquhart was resident in London again. When ordered 'to be brought up in custody to pay his assessment' he is described as having lodgings in Clare Street (Willcock, 45). And he was still resident in the capital in 1645, when seeing his third book through the press. Fulsomely dedicated to his mother, this was his geometric and logarithmic treatise, *The trissotetras, or, A most exquisite table for resolving all manner of triangles … with greater facility than ever hitherto hath been practised*. The vast range of his proclaimed expertise is at once announced—mathematics, morals, metaphysics are all grist to his mill. Tonally, a

stridently confident authorial persona is established, while the expansiveness of his style warns readers that even in a work whose proposed aim is brevity he will live up to the name of Parresiastes, which he attributes to himself in his own genealogy of the Urquharts, the *Pantochronochanon* (*Works*, 172). As a self-proclaimed 'freespeaker', he writes originally and copiously, even when his subject is mathematical. Indeed, he uses over two hundred words, many of them coinages, to 'simplify' Pythagoras's proposition that 'The square of the hypotenuse of a right-angled triangle is equal to the sum of the squares on the other two sides'. Stylistic and verbal eccentricity, however, is usually matched by keen market awareness. This work, he notes, will aid no fewer than eleven major occupations ranging from navigation to planetary theory. His capacity for self-advertisement bore fruit; the *Trissotetras* was reprinted in 1646.

By then, Sir Thomas was back in Cromarty Castle. His early success in holding off creditors had proved shortlived. Led by Leslie of Findrassie, they made claims on him at a time when his episcopalian beliefs were also bringing him into conflict with local presbyterian clergy. On 31 March 1647 Sir Robert Farquhar of Mounie apprised the title and estate of Cromarty. He also replaced him as sheriff of Cromarty.

But it was national rather than local politics which led to the nadir in Urquhart's fortunes. Under the engagement of December 1647 an unlikely alliance between Scottish royalists and presbyterians offered support to the king. Under this agreement Urquhart attended his local committee of war on 18 April 1648 and joined the engagers' army which was subsequently defeated at Preston in August. When Charles was executed on 30 January 1649 Sir Thomas was again prominent among those lairds who sought to gain the northern counties in the royalist cause. Indeed, there is a persuasive stylistic case for supposing that he drafted the highly rhetorical letter of protest which that group sent to the commissioners of the general assembly. Defeat at Balvenie in May resulted in the collapse of the rebellion and on 14 November Urquhart wrote in a more contrite manner to the assembly, asking how he might be reconciled with them. In the event, his 'dangerous opinions' were noted but, in summer 1650, his conduct was excused (*Sir Thomas Urquhart … : the Jewel*, 38, n. 35).

Imprisonment and major works The desire not to offend again may account for Urquhart's absence from the Scottish army, defeated at Dunbar on 3 September 1650. But when Charles II landed at Scone in January 1651 and the assembly rescinded its act against royalist 'malignants' in May of that year, 'the house of Cromarty was put in a posture of defence' (Tayler, 52) and its owner rallied to the standard again. In marching south to eventual defeat at Worcester on 3 September 1653 Urquhart also marched into the major crisis of his own eventful life. As he recalls in the introductions to his three major prose works of 1652 and 1653, defeat and imprisonment coincided with the loss of those literary manuscripts which he had optimistically packed, intending to have them printed in London after a royalist victory. Of the 'sixscore and eight quires and a half', which he meticulously records, only one, 'together with two other loose sheets', was rescued from Worcester's rain-soaked streets (*Works*, 189–90).

Urquhart optimistically claims that this meant the loss of 'a hundred severall bookes, on subjects never hitherto thought upon by any' (*Works*, 312). He set about minimizing this tragedy by redrafting the rescued material. As a result, 1652 saw the publishing of his family genealogy, *Pantochronochanon, or, A Peculiar Promptuary of Time* and *Ekskubalauron, or, The Discovery of a most Exquisite Jewel*. The latter vindicates Scottish heroism against the malignancy of presbyterianism 'by running through all the eminent Scots Urquhart could remember or invent' (Reid, 195). *Logopandecteision, or, An Introduction to the Universal Language* appeared in 1653. It complements the earlier research of Francis Lodwick and Samuel Hartlib by providing a full description of his universal language. In addition to these, an epistolary account of the civil war period, 'Written in answer to a Letter sent from a Gentleman in Scotland to a friend of his in London', and printed by Richard Moore in 1653, has sometimes been attributed to Urquhart. Its argument is anticipated in its lengthy title—*Reason why the supreme authority of the three nations (for the time) is not in the PARLIAMENT but in the new-established council of state consisting of His Excellence the Lord General Cromwell, and the honourable assessors*. While the pungent and satirical letter is consistent with Urquhart's known views and exhibits some of his stylistic and verbal preferences, the ascription remains dubious.

The verbal inventiveness of *Trissotetras* transfers itself to all of Sir Thomas's later original writing, as does its egotistical pragmatism. The literary products of his imprisonment in different, highly fanciful ways offer praise of their author's lineage and genius as a means of pleading the case for his release. The genealogy in the *Promptuary*, after all, stretches back to Adam. Exaggeration is matched to euphuistic diction within strange, hybrid literary forms. In *The Jewel*, for example, a third-person narrator, identified as the author himself and employing a style which makes Sir Philip Sidney's *Arcadia* seem understated, introduces a meandering defence of past Scottish heroism with an unapologetic account of his own genius. Finally, there is in each an unresolved tension between the personal and political levels of argument. While the petition in all three necessarily accommodates itself to Cromwell's puritanism, the evidence presented—genealogical, heroic, or linguistic—is at once royalist, hierarchical, and anti-presbyterian. It is an eccentric form of political allegory, which allows tenor and vehicle to contradict each other so unapologetically.

This evidence helps to explain why Urquhart's original writing has, until recently, been underestimated. Only *The Jewel*, which has some claim to be regarded as the first extant Scottish prose romance, has been given any serious critical attention. Even it introduces the Arcadian mode in such an eccentric manner as to make its example at once tangential and inimitable. Literary historians may be forgiven, therefore, for preferring the later *Aretina* of George MacKenzie as a safer source for fictive prose north of the Tweed.

Rabelais and final years Urquhart's reputation, therefore, is still based on his last literary endeavour—his translation of Rabelais. *The first book [and 'The second book'] of the works of Mr. Francis Rabelais, doctor in physick … now faithfully translated into English by S.T.U.C.* appeared in 1653 and was reprinted in 1664. The third volume appeared in 1693. Pierre Motteux' commentaries and editions (with translations of books 4–5) followed in 1694 and 1708. Between 1737 and 1900 Sir Theodore Martin, Henry Morley, and Charles Whibley were among those so impressed by Urquhart's version that they re-edited it. It fully deserves this enthusiastic reception. In Rabelais, Urquhart found a writer whose style and imagination matched his own. Both 'cultivated a taste for a copious, robust and original vocabulary. To each of them, imagination … furnished a rare selection of racy words in extraordinary abundance' (Roe, 11).

After 1653 Urquhart may have continued working on the unfinished third book of his Rabelais but no additional 'quaint discourses' have been preserved. Lyall provides evidence which suggests that he may again have sought refuge abroad. Certainly two of his letters place him in Middelburg, Zeeland, in September 1655 and again in July 1658 (*Sir Thomas Urquhart … : the Jewel*, 10). That he died abroad is also likely. Scottish records place this event between 4 May 1660 (when an Aberdeenshire notary witnesses his written consent to a sale of land) and early August of the same year, when his brother Alexander was designated sheriff of Cromarty. This dating is consistent with the account favoured in Urquhart family history: that this resolute royalist, whose life had been blighted by a Commonwealth parenthesis in English history, expired on a hearty burst of laughter on hearing of Charles II's restoration to the throne. Urquhart would surely have rejoiced in this epitaph. Believing that the 'conceptions and words' set down by microcosmic man serve only as 'representatives of what in the whole world is comprehended' he consistently viewed his fictive treatises as 'importing beyond' actuality to the higher truths of what might and ought to be (*Works*, 305).

Indeed, love of words or, in his own terms, a 'logofascinated spirit' (*Works*, 231) is the only true romance revealed by Urquhart's life and letters. As these 'metonymical, ironical, metaphysical and synecdochical instruments of elocution' (ibid., 292) are in English and praise 'the incorporation of both nations into one' (ibid., 179), his imaginative prose still sits uncomfortably within a Scottish literary canon which tends to prefer linguistic and political separatism (K. Wittig, *Scottish Tradition in Literature*, 1957, 3–4). There are signs that these parameters are now broadening, however, in a way which may allow this self-proclaimed universal genius to take his rightful place not only as a worthy successor to Gavin Douglas in that country's impressive roll of creative translators but as the first herald of a tradition in prose romance which would lead eventually to Walter Scott.

R. D. S. JACK

Sources *Sir Thomas Urquhart of Cromarty: the jewel*, ed. R. D. S. Jack and R. J. Lyall (1983) · H. Tayler, *The history of the family of Urquhart* (1946) · J. Willcock, *Sir Thomas Urquhart of Cromartie, knight* (1899) · *The works of Sir Thomas Urquhart of Cromarty, knight*, ed. T. Maitland, Maitland Club, 30 (1834) · *DNB* · D. Reid, 'Prose after Knox', *The history of Scottish literature*, ed. C. Craig, 1: *Origins to 1660*, ed. R. D. S. Jack (1988), 183–98 · J. Gordon, *History of Scots affairs from 1637–1641*, ed. J. Robertson and G. Grub, 1, Spalding Club, 1 (1841) · J. Spalding, *Memorialls of the trubles in Scotland and in England, AD 1624 – AD 1645*, ed. J. Stuart, 1, Spalding Club, [21] (1850) · F. C. Roe, *Sir Thomas Urquhart and Rabelais* (1957) · R. Boston, *The admirable Urquhart* (1975) · W. Cramond, ed., *Annals of Banff*, 2 (1893) · M. Spiller, 'Poetry after the union, 1603–1660', *The history of Scottish literature*, ed. C. Craig, 1: *Origins to 1660*, ed. R. D. S. Jack (1988), 141–62
Archives Yale U., James S. Osborn Collection, unpublished epigrams
Likenesses G. Glover, engraving, 1640, Scot. NPG · G. Glover, line engraving, 1641, BM, NPG [*see illus.*] · engraving facsimile, 1646

Urquhart, Thomas (d. 1698?), violin maker, is of unknown origins. Tradition has it that he went to London from Scotland at the invitation of Charles II, but there is no evidence for this. Nor is there any basis for the birth date of 1625 given by Vannes. Surviving instruments suggest that he was active from 1648 through to about 1680. It is recorded that a Thomas Urquhart was buried at St Giles-in-the-Fields, London, in 1698 and this may have been the violin maker.

One of the earliest important English violin makers, Urquhart probably studied with Jacob Rayman (fl. 1620–1650) and may, in turn, have taught Edward Pamphilon (fl. 1670–1690). (The widely held assumption that he also taught Barak Norman (1651–c.1724) has now been discounted.) The labels in his instruments indicate that (like Pamphilon) he had his workshop on London Bridge. His violins have the high arching characteristic of the Stainer school and follow two distinct patterns, one small and one large. His instruments have been praised for their fine workmanship and sweet (though somewhat small) sound. Their varnish has often been described as equal to that on Cremonese instruments from the same period.

PETER WALLS

Sources S. Sadie, ed., *The new Grove dictionary of musical instruments*, 3 vols. (1984) · C. Bearke and J. Dilworth, 'Urquhart, Thomas', *New Grove*, 2nd edn · B. W. Harvey, *The violin family and its makers in the British Isles: an illustrated history and directory* (1995) · W. Henley, *Universal dictionary of violin and bow makers*, 5 vols. (1959–60) · L. W. Lütgendorff, *Die geigen un Lautenmacher vom Mittelalter bis zur Gegenwart*, 3 vols. (Nendeln, Liechtenstein, 1922); repr. (1968) · R. Vannes, *Dictionnaire universel des luthiers*, 3 vols. (Paris, 1972); repr. (1981) · W. M. Morris, *British violin makers: a biographical dictionary of British makers of stringed instruments*, 2nd edn (1920) · W. Sandys and S. A. Forster, *The history of the violin* (1864)

Urquhart, William Pollard- (1815–1871), writer, the eldest child of William Dutton Pollard (1789–1839) of Kinturk, Castlepollard, co. Westmeath, and his second wife,

Louisa Anne, eldest daughter of Admiral Sir Thomas *Pakenham, was born at Kinturk, Castlepollard, on 19 June 1815. He was educated at Harrow School and at Trinity College, Cambridge, graduating BA as eighteenth wrangler in 1838, and MA in 1843. He kept his terms at the Inner Temple, but was never called to the bar. In 1840 he was gazetted high sheriff of co. Westmeath, and in 1846, on his marriage on 20 August to Mary Isabella, only daughter of William Urquhart of Craigston Castle, Aberdeenshire, he added by royal licence the name of Urquhart. He sat in parliament for County Westmeath as a Liberal from 1852 to 1857, and from 1859 to his death.

Pollard-Urquhart's family connections with Irish and Scottish land encouraged him to publish on the subject. From 1850 he wrote quite regularly, chiefly on rural political economy and taxation, his works including *Agricultural Distress and its Remedies* (1850), *Essays on Subjects of Political Economy* (1850), *The substitution of direct for indirect taxation necessary to carry out the policy of free trade* (1851), *A short account of the Prussian land credit companies, with suggestions for the formation of a land credit company in Ireland* (1853), *The Currency Question and the Bank Charter Committees of 1857 and 1858* (1860), and *Dialogues on Taxation, Local and Imperial* (1867). He was less happy in his biography of Francisco Sforza (2 vols., 1852). Pollard-Urquhart died at 19 Brunswick Terrace, Brighton, on 1 June 1871.

G. C. BOASE, rev. H. C. G. MATTHEW

Sources Venn, *Alum. Cant.* · *ILN* (10 June 1871), 579 · Boase, *Mod. Eng. biog.* · Burke, *Gen. GB* (1886)

Urry [Hurry], **Sir John** (d. 1650), army officer, was the son of John Urry of Pitfichie, Monymusk parish, Aberdeenshire, and his wife, Mariora Cameraria (Marian Chamberlain), of Coullie in the same parish. He spent some years in foreign military service, probably in Germany. He returned to Scotland about 1639 and received the rank of lieutenant-colonel in the covenanters' army (in accordance with their policy of seconding local leaders with skilled soldiers). In October 1641 he was asked to join the plot against the marquess of Hamilton and the earls of Argyll and Lanark, known as the 'incident'. William Murray of the royal household and the earl of Crawford with other Scottish royalist nobles and colonels Cochrane of Cochrane and Alexander Stewart aimed to exile or kill Hamilton, Argyll, and Lanark. The conspirators unsuccessfully attempted to enlist Urry, who realized the importance of gathering information to thwart it. On 11 October Urry revealed all he knew about the plot to the lord general, Alexander Leslie, as did Lieutenant-Colonel Robert Home and Captain William Stewart (both of Cochrane's regiment). Rumour connected the king to the plot, which he strenuously denied, although his efforts against the five members indicate that the suspicion had some justification.

On the outbreak of the English civil war Urry joined the parliamentarians, and in June 1642 received command of the fourth troop of horse designated for Irish service under Philip, Lord Wharton. He took part in the battle of Edgehill, and at the fight at Brentford on 12 November 'for his stoutness and wisdom was much cryed up by the Londoners' (*Letters and Journals of Robert Baillie*, 2.56). At the start of 1643 he was nominated a major of cavalry under the earl of Bedford. However, owing to a personal pique, probably because he had not received a higher rank, he deserted to the royalists and provided them with very useful military information. He played a large part in securing the royalist success at Chalgrove on 18 June, and was knighted at Oxford as a consequence on the same day. On 25 June he sacked West Wycombe, and on 1 January 1644 he was reported dead at Oxford, of an old wound; but on 18 February he had moved northward with Prince Rupert. He fought in the royalist right flank cavalry at Marston Moor. In August 1644, despairing of success for the royalists, he fled to Sir William Waller's parliamentarian army at Shrewsbury. He planned to return to Scotland where the estates had already forfeited his possessions. Waller sent him to London, where the committee of both kingdoms ordered him into custody. On Waller's word, and on the statement of the army committee that his professional skill would be useful, he was allowed to rejoin the parliamentarian army on parole on 30 October. He had hopes of bringing over a superior leader to himself, probably his fellow Scot the earl of Brentford, whom he unsuccessfully attempted to cajole in November after the second battle of Newbury.

A little later Urry joined the army of the solemn league and covenant under the earl of Leven in north-east England. On 27 February 1645 the Scottish estates made him a major-general of horse and foot in Scotland and a colonel of dragoons. On 8 March he was sent into the highlands against Montrose, as major-general and cavalry commander under Lieutenant-General William Baillie, who disliked him. He took Aberdeen from the royalists on the 15th by surprise, but abandoned it the next day. His unsuccessful pursuit of Montrose after the sack of Dundee earned him Baillie's further disdain. Urry continued north in the pursuit of the royalists. Finally utilizing his commission as colonel of dragoons for Aberdeenshire and Banffshire, he transformed 400 infantry levies into horsemen. His army consisted of 1200 foot, and 160 horse plus the dragoons. North of the Grampians he joined with the earls of Seaforth and Sutherland and other local covenanters to hunt down Montrose. On 9 May he attempted a surprise attack on Montrose, but his initial success ended in disastrous defeat at Auldearn, near Nairn. With 100 cavalry he rejoined Baillie at Strathbogie, but soon after relinquished his command on grounds of ill health. The estates passed an act of approbation for his military services on 11 July. On 7 August they granted him a reward of £500 for killing Donald Farquharson during the March attack on Aberdeen.

Urry returned to the king's side by joining Montrose, for which he was excluded from the pardon offered by the estates to royalists. In August 1646 the covenanter Major-General John Middleton offered him a permit to leave Scotland, but fearful of the covenanters, he sailed with Montrose to the continent on 3 September.

In 1648 Urry, against the command of the Scottish committee of estates, joined the train of the prince of Wales, then accompanied the duke of Hamilton's army to England, where he was wounded and fell prisoner after 18 August. He escaped to the continent again, where he linked up with Montrose. He sailed with the marquess to the royalist base on Orkney in 1650. From there Montrose ordered him to land in Caithness with 300 men and stop the earl of Sutherland from taking that county. Urry landed on 9 April at the Ord of Caithness, and continued to serve with Montrose throughout his last brief campaign. He commanded the royalist centre at Carbisdale, where he was wounded in the cheek and taken prisoner. He was beheaded at Edinburgh on 29 May, maintaining a brave and constant demeanour at the end of a vacillating career. Urry serves as the exemplar of the professional soldier, who followed the fortunes of war as opposed to maintaining firm allegiance to a cause or idea. He left five children, who, on 31 October 1658 received a certificate of gentility from Charles II.　　　　EDWARD M. FURGOL

Sources Clarendon, *Hist. rebellion* · *The letters and journals of Robert Baillie*, ed. D. Laing, 3 vols., Bannatyne Club, 73 (1841–2) · *CSP dom.*, 1641–4 · *Fourth report*, HMC, 3 (1874) · *APS* · G. Wishart, *The memoirs of James, marquis of Montrose, 1639–1650*, ed. and trans. A. D. Murdoch and H. F. M. Simpson (1893) · J. Spalding, *Memorialls of the trubles in Scotland and in England, AD 1624 – AD 1645*, ed. J. Stuart, 2 vols., Spalding Club, [21, 23] (1850–51) · J. Turner, *Memoirs of his own life and times, 1632–1670*, ed. T. Thomson, Bannatyne Club, 28 (1829) · P. Gordon, *A short abridgement of Britane's distemper*, ed. J. Dunn, Spalding Club, 10 (1844) · C. H. Firth, 'The battle of Marston Moor', *TRHS*, new ser., 12 (1898), 17–79, esp. 17–19 · S. R. Gardiner, *History of the great civil war, 1642–1649*, new edn, 4 vols. (1893) · F. J. Cowan, *Montrose: for covenant and king* (1977) · BL, Add. MS 15856, fol. 89b · C. Russell, *The fall of the British monarchies, 1637–1642* (1991) · *DNB*

Urry, John (1666–1715), literary editor, was born in Dublin, the son of William Urry and Jane Scott. William Urry was appointed major of the royal guards in Scotland at the Restoration. He was of Scottish family, and his brother, Sir John *Urry or Hurry, was a prominent officer in the civil war. The younger John Urry matriculated from Christ Church, Oxford, on 30 June 1682, was elected to a studentship, and graduated BA in 1686. He was a man of strong loyalist principles, and bore arms against Monmouth during the rebellion. On the accession of William III he refused the oath of supremacy and lost his studentship.

The first indication of Urry's interest in medieval textual scholarship is the edition of Gavin Douglas's *Eneydos* published in Edinburgh in 1710 which acknowledges in the preface the help of 'the worthy Mr. John Urry of Christ-Church. Oxon'. Towards the end of the following year a new edition of Chaucer was projected, and Urry, much against his inclination, was persuaded to undertake it, chiefly through the urgency of the dean of Christ Church, Francis Atterbury, afterwards bishop of Rochester. On 25 July 1714 Urry obtained a patent for the exclusive right of printing Chaucer's works for fourteen years, and on 17 December assigned it to Barnaby Bernard Lintot, who issued proposals for publishing the undertaking in January 1715 (*GM*, 49, 1779, 438). Before the work was completed, Urry died unmarried on 18 March 1715, and was buried the following day in Christ Church Cathedral at Oxford. Thomas Hearne gives an account of his death (*Remarks*, 5.33–6).

After his death Thomas Ainsworth of Christ Church, who had already been employed under Urry in transcribing part of the text of Chaucer, was thought the best qualified to proceed with the edition. He died in August 1719, and the work was finally revised by Timothy and William Thomas, the former a graduate of Christ Church, and appeared in 1721 under the title *The Works of Geoffrey Chaucer, Compared with the Former Editions, and many Valuable MSS.* This was the first collected edition of Chaucer to be printed in roman type. The life of Chaucer prefixed to the volume was the work of the Revd John Dart, corrected and revised by Timothy Thomas. The glossary appended was also mainly compiled by Thomas.

The text of Urry's edition has often been criticized by subsequent editors for its frequent conjectural emendations, mainly to make it conform to his sense of Chaucer's metre. The justice of such criticisms should not obscure his achievement. His is the first edition of Chaucer for nearly a hundred and fifty years to consult any manuscripts and is the first since that of William Thynne in 1534 to seek systematically to assemble a substantial number of manuscripts to establish his text. It is also the first edition to offer descriptions of the manuscripts of Chaucer's works, and the first to print texts of 'Gamelyn' and 'The Tale of Beryn', works ascribed to, but not by, Chaucer.

Urry was a friend of Thomas Hearne, who styles him a 'thorough pac'd scholar' and a 'truly worthy and virtuous, as well as ingenious, gentleman'. A portrait of Urry, engraved by N. Pigné, is prefixed to the work.

E. I. CARLYLE, *rev.* A. S. G. EDWARDS

Sources W. L. Alderson and A. C. Henderson, *Chaucer and Augustan scholarship* (1970) · *Remarks and collections of Thomas Hearne*, ed. C. E. Doble and others, 5, OHS, 42 (1901), 33–6 · Foster, *Alum. Oxon.*
Likenesses N. Pigné, line engraving, BM, NPG; repro. in *The works of Chaucer* (1721)

Urse d'Abetot. *See* Abetot, Urse d' (*c.*1040–1108).

Ursula [St Ursula] (*fl.* mid-5th cent.), martyr, was venerated at Cologne, but is traditionally supposed to be of British birth. Although various legends—*vitae, passiones, miracula,* accounts of translations—form the predominant body of source material, there does exist a concrete object with which consideration of Ursula has often begun. This is a memorial stone, in the church now dedicated to St Ursula in Cologne, which bears an inscription purporting to explain that one Clematius, an Eastern Christian, had restored that church, which was already sanctified by the bodies of several anonymous virgin martyrs. The inscription seems to date from about 400, and there is nothing inherently impossible in it. But there is no mention of an Ursula here, nor in most of several early medieval continental calendars and litanies in which these virgins, sometimes specified as eleven, are commemorated.

The saint's name first appears, as Ursola and eighth in a list of the eleven virgins, in a litany datable to 946–62.

Soon thereafter (969–76) comes the earliest narrative source to specify her as principal heroine, a *historia* which begins 'Fuit tempore pervetusto in partibus Brittanniae [*sic*]' ('In the earliest time, there was in the regions of Britain'). This gives her a British royal father (unnamed) and contains the main elements of the fully developed legend: her dismay at a projected marriage; her setting to sea in a flotilla of eleven ships, each holding a thousand virgins; their adventures on land as well as water; and their final martyrdom at Cologne (in this story at the hands of Huns, though in other versions there is wide variance as to the persecutors, and therefore as to the putative date of the martyrdom). The expansion from eleven to eleven thousand virgins is most plausibly explained by a misreading of 'XI m[artyres] v[irgines]' as 'XI m[illia] v[irgines]'. Subsequent elaboration, spurred by discoveries of supposed relics around Cologne, added names for her father (Deonotus) and for at least some of the enormous number of virgins, explanations as to how children and even men came to be part of the sailing party, and eventually a totally fictitious pope, Cyriacus. This last detail is part of an overwrought narrative transmitted to, and then through, the twelfth-century German mystic Elisabeth of Schönau. Of particular British interest is the use of a version of the basic story in Geoffrey of Monmouth's *Historia regum Britanniae, c.*1140 (5.xii–xvi). Some of his details seem to be taken from what came to be the most widely used *passio*, an eleventh-century composition beginning 'Regnante Domino', but only one of the edited manuscripts of his work (and that probably of the thirteenth century) contains Ursula's name.

If there is any substance at all to the linkage between the virgin martyrs commemorated in Clematius's stone at Cologne and the original St Ursula, and if she was indeed of British origin, its context should be sought in the Roman Britain. That the legends make her father a king may be only a convention of the genre, but it is also conceivable that someone who came to be known as Ursula was born in circumstances which St Patrick would have recognized in the mid-fifth century: those of the sub- or client-kingdoms in northern and western Britain, ruled over by Christian kings like the Coroticus he addressed in a famous letter. Such a hypothesis is about all that can be offered towards securing her identity as British. It seems about equally likely that she had her initial fame solely on the continent and that she is (as a named martyr) totally imaginary. It may be relevant that Bede did not celebrate her life as he did those of two other Romano-British saints, Alban and Ninian (though he nowhere mentions Patrick). In the catalogue of British saints, then, there seems to be little place for an Ursula. It is only when the medieval hagiographers get to work on her that she becomes a figure who can be treated at any length: but by then she is thoroughly and impenetrably legendary.

RICHARD W. PFAFF

Sources *Acta sanctorum: October*, 9 (Brussels, 1858), 73–303, esp. 154–63 · 'Historia SS. Ursulae et sociarum ejus', *Analecta Bollandiana*, 3 (1884), 5–20 · W. Levison, *Das Werden der Ursula-*

Legende (1928) · M. Coens, 'Les vierges martyres de Cologne', *Analecta Bollandiana*, 47 (1929), 89–110 · M. Tout, 'The legend of St Ursula and the eleven thousand virgins', *Historical essays by members of the Owens College, Manchester*, ed. T. F. Tout and J. Tait (1902), 17–56 · J. S. P. Tatlock, *The legendary history of Britain: Geoffrey of Monmouth's Historia regum Britanniae and its early vernacular versions* (1950), 236–41 · A. L. Clark, *Elisabeth of Schönau: a twelfth-century visionary* (1992), 37–40
Likenesses painted representation, before 1450, Dombild, Cologne · H. Memling, portrait series, 1486, shrine of St Ursula, Bruges · V. Carpaccio, nine portraits, *c.*1495, academy, Venice · fourteen portraits, Wallraf Richartz Museum, Cologne · representations, Ursula church, Cologne

Urswick, Christopher (1448?–1522), courtier, diplomat, and ecclesiastic, was the son of John Urswick and his wife, lay brother and sister of the Cistercian abbey of Furness in Lancashire. On 14 January 1486 he put his age at thirty-six; his memorial brass gives it as seventy-three at death. Educated at Cambridge, with the support of the Stanley family (who were powerful in Furness), he was fellow of King's Hall (1470–71), MA (1479), licenciate in canon law (1482), and doctor of canon and civil law (before 4 February 1486). On 26 November 1485 he became warden of King's Hall (he had vacated the office by 24 April 1488), and in 1499–1500 was given a present of wine and sweetmeats by the university. By 14 June 1474, when he received a pardon for all offences committed before 8 June, he had lived in Troston, Suffolk, and in London; during 1475/6 he rented a room, as a mature commoner, in University College, Oxford.

Urswick was ordained subdeacon on 16 April 1468 and on 23 May 1472 priest, in York. He was in Rome on 16 March 1480, and may have stayed there or elsewhere in Italy until 25 January 1481. Perhaps through the Stanley connection he had attracted the attention of Lady Margaret Beaufort (d. 1509), who became his patron for the remainder of her life; she presented him in 1482 to his first living—Puttenham, Huntingdonshire—and made him her chaplain and confessor. Margaret apparently involved Urswick in the negotiations between herself and John Morton (d. 1500), then bishop of Ely, designed to lead to the marriage of her son, the future Henry VII. Urswick deposed in January 1486 that he had known Henry well for fifteen or sixteen years, and Elizabeth of York for about four. He may have visited Morton and Henry in Brittany, and have fled to Flanders after the failure of Buckingham's rebellion in October 1483; in the following year Morton sent him to warn Henry in Vannes of Richard III's moves against him. Urswick accompanied Henry on his flight to the French court, was envoy to Henry Percy, earl of Northumberland (d. 1489), and was appointed Henry's chaplain and confessor. He landed with Henry at Milford Haven on 7 August 1485, and accompanied him to Shrewsbury and to Bosworth. He was rewarded with the prebend of St Stephen's, Westminster (21 September), and promoted three days later to the influential position of king's clerk and almoner. He was subsequently granted the prebend of Chiswick in St Paul's Cathedral (20 February 1486) and presented to the rectories of All Hallows-the-Great, London (9 March 1487), and Chedzoy, Somerset (1487–8).

He held many other benefices, offices, and prebends, being dispensed as royal almoner from the need to reside in some.

Urswick was dispatched to the curia on 4 February 1486 and admitted to the confraternity of the English hospice in Rome on 11 June; he had returned to England by November. He was appointed on 10 March 1488 to the embassy for peace with Spain and the match between Prince Arthur (d. 1502) and Katherine of Aragon (d. 1536); in May and December 1488 and in October 1492 he was in France; he was in Scotland in March and later in 1492 and in 1493, treating for peace with England. In May 1489 he was entrusted with £155 to distribute among the envoys of the king of the Romans. Early in 1493 he was again in Rome; he left on 1 April but returned there in June. He may have gone to Sicily, since he had come with a commission to invest the future Alfonso II of Naples with the Garter. Urswick's last ambassadorship abroad was to Maximilian, king of the Romans, at Augsburg in April 1496, but in 1500 he was present at the meeting in Calais of Henry VII and Maximilian's son, the archduke, Philip the Fair.

Urswick was dean of York (1488–94), canon and prebendary of St George's Chapel, Windsor (1492–6), registrar of the Order of the Garter (by 1492), and dean of Windsor (1496–1505). There is no evidence to support suggestions that he declined the see of Norwich in 1499. By that time he had begun to drop out of active participation in public affairs, and on 5 November 1502 was inducted into the living of St Augustine's, Hackney, Middlesex, which he held until death. From semi-retirement there he was sometimes present at court, and occasionally served on commissions; he was executor of various wills (including that of Henry VII); he opposed anti-clericalism, and asserted the church's liberties.

Concern for the church was Urswick's chief point of contact with the Tudor humanist movement. When Erasmus (d. 1536) first visited England in 1499 he was probably introduced to Urswick by their common friends John Colet (d. 1519) and Thomas More (d. 1535): meetings once attributed to 1483 and 1503 are imaginary. Erasmus included Urswick among his English dedicatees: for his translation of the *Somnium, sive, Gallus* in 1506 Urswick gave him a reliable horse. When it died in 1516, Erasmus sued long and unsuccessfully for another, enlisting friends in support and sending his *Novum instrumentum* and his edition of St Jerome to Urswick. To More and to Polydore Vergil (d. 1555), Urswick supplied information about Richard III; he is named in the manuscript of Polydore's *Anglica historia* (1512–13), but not in the printed edition (Basel, 1534). Cuthbert Tunstall (d. 1559) was remembered in his will. Given these associates, Urswick's name might be expected to figure in the admission book of Doctors' Commons in London, but does not.

Between 1503 and about 1520 Urswick and Colet were the most frequent English employers of Pieter Meghen (1466–1540), the one-eyed Brabantine who later wrote magnificent books for Wolsey and Henry VIII. Meghen's manuscripts for Urswick include miscellanies of texts by St Gregory of Nazianzus, Pseudo-Ambrose, and others on the dignity of the priesthood, Celso Maffei on the liberties of the church (printed by Richard Pynson, 1505, perhaps at Urswick's instance), meditations by Savonarola, and a pair of Luther's early sermons. For Urswick as executor of Sir John Huddleston (*c*.1440–1512), another native of Furness, Meghen wrote two large illuminated codices, as gifts to the Cistercian abbey of Hayles, Gloucestershire: a psalter (1514) and George of Trebizond's version of St John Chrysostom upon St Matthew (1517). Nothing Urswick himself wrote survives except four letters and annotations in books. Some of his books bear presentation inscriptions to the Dominicans of Lancaster and to St George's Chapel, Windsor: they include classical, patristic, legal, scholastic, and humanist authors.

As royal almoner Urswick was in constant attendance on the king. He was an intimate of Sir Reginald Bray (*d.* 1503); their devices and Urswick's motto 'Mi[sericordi]a' appear in the roof bosses of St George's Chapel, Windsor, rebuilt under their direction. A chapel in St George's was named for Urswick, and he rebuilt the deanery. To Henry, second baron Daubeney, son of Bray's confederate Sir Giles, Urswick gave Cicero's *De officiis*, written by Meghen, with a prefatory letter in which he recommends to Henry his father's example. Urswick also rebuilt St Augustine's, Hackney (destroyed in 1798), and its rectory, where he died on 21 March 1522. He was buried in the church. His will of 10 October 1521 (codicil 28 December) was proved on 11 April 1522. His tomb, of the Easter sepulchre type in the Tudor Perpendicular style, and a memorial floor-brass with a factotum image of him, are now in St John's, Hackney.

As Henry VII's trusted personal agent Urswick was one of the clerics whose administrative and rhetorical skills helped to establish and consolidate the Tudor regime. Less important politically and more retiring than his contemporaries Morton and Richard Fox (*d.* 1528), he is mentioned as an example of diffidence in 1624 by Robert Burton (*Anatomy of Melancholy*, I.iii.1.ii). He appears briefly in Shakespeare's *Richard III* (IV.v). Urswick was not quite a humanist, even of the north European evangelical sort, though he had humanist interests and a sympathetic understanding of humanist ideas and ideals.

J. B. TRAPP

Sources will, PRO, PROB 11/20, sig. 23 · Emden, *Cam.*, 605–6, 685 · Emden, *Oxf.*, 3.1905–6 · *CEPR letters*, 14.17–20 · *Opus epistolarum Des. Erasmi Roterodami*, ed. P. S. Allen and others, 12 vols. (1906–58) · *The correspondence of Erasmus*, ed. and trans. R. A. B. Mynors and others, 22 vols. (1974–94) [letters 193, 416, 451–2, 455, 467–8, 474, 481, 499, 785, 786] · *Fasti Angl., 1300–1541*, [Monastic cathedrals], 29n · S. L. Ollard, *Fasti Wyndesorienses: the deans and canons of Windsor* (privately printed, Windsor, 1950) · J. N. Dalton, ed., *The manuscripts of St George's Chapel, Windsor Castle* (1957) · B. Cherry, 'An early sixteenth-century London tomb design', *Architectural History*, 27 (1984), 86–94 · P. G. Bietenholz and T. B. Deutscher, eds., *Contemporaries of Erasmus: a biographical register*, 3 (1987), 357–60 · J. B. Trapp, *Erasmus, Colet and More: the early Tudor humanists and their books* (1991), 13–29 · *Australian Book Collector*, 36 (1992), 12–14 · J. I. Catto, 'Scholars and studies in Renaissance Oxford', *Hist. U. Oxf.* 2: *Late med. Oxf.*, 769–84 · memorial brass, St John's, Hackney

Archives BL · Bodl. Oxf. · Wells Cathedral

Likenesses factotum memorial brass effigy, St John's Church, Hackney

Wealth at death see will, PRO, PROB 11/20, sig. 23

Urswick, Sir Thomas (*c.*1415–1479), lawyer, belonged to a Lancashire family, and was most likely the son of Sir Thomas Urswick of Badsworth and his wife, Joan, the daughter of Roger Hertforth of Badsworth. He attended Gray's Inn in London, and probably gave readings there in 1441 and 1448—dates which suggest, in the light of better documented career patterns, that he was born *c.*1415. In 1452 he was appointed serjeant and attorney to the duchy of Lancaster at Lancaster, but he also pursued a career in the south of England, for in 1449 he was elected MP for Midhurst in Sussex, and in January 1452 was referred to as a citizen of London. On 27 June 1453 he was appointed common sergeant of the city, and in July 1454 defended its interests in the court of common pleas. On 3 October 1454 he became recorder of London, and in that capacity was a member of the city's delegation which in February 1461 negotiated with Queen Margaret at Barnet, to prevent her northern troops from pillaging London after the second battle of St Albans.

Later in 1461 Urswick was elected one of London's four MPs, a position he was to hold again in 1463, 1467, and 1470. Both before and after 1461 he is often recorded acting as an arbitrator, an executor, a feoffee to uses, and a commissioner of oyer and terminer, while in 1467 he received a fee of 26*s.* 8*d.* as an apprentice-at-law retained to be of the queen's council, and he continued to be retained in the same capacity by the duchy of Lancaster. Although he sat in the parliament of Henry VI's readeption in 1470, he showed notable Yorkist sympathies in the following year, first on 11 April, when he was one of the leading citizens who admitted Edward IV to London, and again in May, when he was prominent in London's resistance to Thomas Fauconberg. For these services he was knighted by the king, and on 22 May 1471 was appointed chief baron of the exchequer, receiving 110 marks and two robes yearly as well as the usual fee. He resigned as recorder of London, and the citizens, too, rewarded him, with the grant of a pipe of wine yearly.

Urswick's name seldom appears in the year-books; he owed his elevation primarily to his political services. For the same reason he was appointed to commissions of the peace in several midland counties during the 1470s, and was clearly active in that role; in July 1477, for instance, he presided at a sessions of the peace at Worcester. He was also appointed to commissions of the peace for Essex, where he accumulated a substantial estate, based on his manor of Marks; he was probably largely instrumental in Havering's obtaining a charter of privileges in 1465, and took advantage of his involvement to ensure that Marks was included in the liberty thus created. An inventory made there at the time of his death records a substantial and handsomely furnished house, containing twenty rooms. As well as fine clothes, hangings, and plate, Urswick owned a number of books, including Froissart's *Chronicles* in French, Mandeville's *Travels* in English, and a copy of the *Canterbury Tales*. He was married twice, first to a member of the Needham family, with whom he had at least one daughter, and second, in or before 1457, to Isabel Rich, daughter of a London mercer, with whom he had four sons and eight daughters. All his sons predeceased him, and when Urswick died, on 19 March 1479, his heirs were his five surviving daughters. He was buried in the church of St Peter and St Paul, Dagenham, where a brass commemorates him and his family.

HENRY SUMMERSON

Sources T. A. Urwick and W. Urwick, eds., *Records of the family of Urswyk, Urswick or Urwick* (1893), 63–80 · J. C. Wedgwood and A. D. Holt, *History of parliament*, 1: *Biographies of the members of the Commons house, 1439–1509* (1936), 897–8 · *Chancery records* (RC) · PRO, CIPM, C140/73 no. 11 · Exchequer, king's remembrancer, inventories of goods and chattels, PRO, E 154/2/2 · P. E. Jones, ed., *Calendar of plea and memoranda rolls preserved among the archives of the corporation of the City of London at the Guildhall*, 5: *1437–1457* (1954) · R. Fabyan, *The new chronicles of England and France*, ed. H. Ellis, new edn (1811) · J. Warkworth, *A chronicle of the first thirteen years of the reign of King Edward the Fourth*, ed. J. O. Halliwell, CS, old ser., 10 (1839) · A. H. Thomas and I. D. Thornley, eds., *The great chronicle of London* (1938) · A. R. Myers, 'The household of Queen Elizabeth Woodville, 1466–7', *Crown, household, and parliament in fifteenth century England*, ed. C. H. Clough (1985), 251–318 · R. Somerville, *History of the duchy of Lancaster, 1265–1603* (1953) · S. E. Thorne and J. H. Baker, eds., *Readings and moots at the inns of court in the fifteenth century*, 1, SeldS, 71 (1954) · B. H. Putnam, ed., *Proceedings before the justices of the peace in the fourteenth and fifteenth centuries* (1938), 426–7 · *An inventory of the historical monuments in Essex*, Royal Commission for Historical Monuments (England), 2 (1921) · *VCH Essex*, 5.275–7
Likenesses brass effigy, St Peter and St Paul Church, Dagenham, Essex · drawing (after brass effigy), repro. in Urwick, *Records of the family of Urswyck*, facing p. 72
Wealth at death £315 5s. 5½d.—value of goods and chattels: PRO, E 154/2/2

Urwick, Lyndall Fownes (1891–1983), management consultant, was born on 3 March 1891 at Northwood, north Malvern, Leigh, Worcestershire, the only child of Henry Urwick (1859–1931) and his wife, Annis (1862–1948), daughter of Elias Lyndall Whitby (1833–1911), glove manufacturer and leather dresser of Yeovil. His father was a partner in the Malvern and Worcester glove-making firm of Fownes Brothers, which had been founded by an ancestor in 1777; as a Liberal Party fund-raiser he was knighted in 1915. Through his mother Lyndall Urwick was first cousin of Sir Lionel Whitby.

Initially schooled locally in Malvern, Urwick went on to Boxgrove School, Guildford, and then to Repton School, from where he gained an open history exhibition to New College, Oxford, in 1910. After graduating he joined Fownes Brothers in 1913 and was a partner between 1916 and 1920. Having volunteered for military service in 1914, he became an administrative staff officer and reached the rank of major in 1918, when he received the MC and was appointed OBE. He afterwards felt that he had survived the trenches for a purpose, and was disappointed when other people did not recognize this. While serving in Belgium he read *Shop Management* (1903) by Frederick W. Taylor, the American who first systematically formulated and applied the principles of scientific management. Although Urwick had reservations about the ruthless application of Taylor's ideas in Britain, he became the

leading European proponent of Taylorism, and was ultimately its historian. Later he was employers' secretary of the joint industrial council of the glove-making industry (1919–20) and a volunteer with the Schools and Services Co-operative Supply Association; he also joined the National Institute of Industrial Psychology.

In 1922 Urwick was recruited by Seebohm Rowntree to improve the organization of Rowntree's confectionery business in York. His textbook *Organising a Sales Office* (1928) is an account of his managerial reforms at Rowntrees. He lectured at the management conferences sponsored by Rowntree at Oxford, and became the first honorary secretary (1926–8) of the management research groups intended by Rowntree to be a national forum for business managers to discuss their work. Many businessmen doubted that management could be taught as a subject, and Urwick endured widespread suspicion of his pioneering ideas. He was a forceful, attractive public speaker (he shared his father's gift in amateur theatricals) and he wrote in a lucid prose.

In *The Meaning of Rationalisation* (1929) Urwick advocated the industrial rationalization movement as a means of applying scientific method to economic life and thus of raising human productive efficiency. Urwick believed in the inter-war period that the greatest failure of contemporary management was in distribution, and in 1931 he published a study of European and American practice in this area. Another work, *The Management of Tomorrow* (1933), was more philosophical in presentation than his specialized textbooks, but it had a long-term influence on British managerial thinking. His ideas about organization and leadership were deeply influenced by his early soldiering. In the 1920s he urged the need for a college of managerial education which was equivalent to the staff colleges of the fighting services. Significantly his idea resulted in the Administrative Staff College when it came to fruition in 1948.

In 1928 Urwick was appointed director of the International Management Institute at Geneva (partly financed by the International Labour Office and the Twentieth Century Fund, USA). Established to promote the principles of scientific management, this institute was the first international management body and it involved Urwick in innumerable meetings in Europe and the USA. He was rapporteur général of the International Distribution Commission (1932) and general secretary of the International Committee of Scientific Management (1932–5). After the institute's funding collapsed, he founded in 1934 the management consultancy Urwick, Orr, & Partners—only the fourth consultancy of its kind in Britain. Hitherto the rigid, peremptory attitudes of American management consultants operating in Britain had been provocative in some workplaces. Urwick tempered Taylorism to British susceptibilities and adjusted his advice to the needs of individual client companies. Indeed he desired major social adjustments so that workers and managers could accommodate the demands of mechanization, and he favoured joint consultation, profit-sharing, and a formal reapportioning of authority between managers and staff.

Urwick Orr commanded a worldwide reputation and for many years was unequalled among British consultancies. Urwick was its chairman (1934–61), managing partner (1945–51), and president (1963–83).

Taylorite principles of organization and methods were crucial to Urwick's faith that, with scrupulously defined procedures, management techniques could be refined almost to scientific exactitude. During 1940–42 Urwick advised the Treasury on the application of organization and methods. Often abrasive when he felt he was being frustrated, he clashed with Sir Horace Wilson, head of the civil service, over civil service reforms. Some of his ideas on improving governmental efficiency by management specialization were implemented by Sir Derek Rayner after 1979. Urwick, who was commissioned in 1942 as a lieutenant-colonel and who retained his military title in civilian life, was deputy director of the petroleum warfare department (1942–4) and chairman of the departmental committee on education for management (1945).

Together with Edward Brech, Urwick compiled three authoritative volumes entitled *The Making of Scientific Management* (1945–8). Among other public work, Urwick was a council member of the British Institute of Management (1947–52), chairman of the Anglo-American productivity team on education for management (1951), and master of the Glovers' Company. He was honoured with professional medals and honorary degrees, chiefly in countries other than his own; universities in Canada, the USA, and Australia invited him as a visiting professor in business administration. He published prolifically during this period.

On 31 March 1923 Urwick married a medical student, Joan Wilhelmina (1901–1984), daughter of James Pirch Bedford, of the Indian Civil Service. From this marriage, which was dissolved in 1938, there was a son and a daughter. Urwick married second, on 27 September 1941, Beatrice Helen Fitzhardinge (b. 1908), daughter of Major Hugh Munro Warrand, army officer, and sister of Sir Hugh Munro-Lucas-Tooth of Teananich, first baronet. They adopted a son and a daughter. Beatrice Urwick had Australian connections, and after Urwick relinquished the chairmanship of his consultancy they emigrated to Sydney. Urwick died in Australia on 5 December 1983 at Longueville, Sydney, New South Wales, and was cremated there shortly afterwards. RICHARD DAVENPORT-HINES

Sources private information (2004) · E. F. L. Brech, 'L. F. Urwick', *International encyclopedia of business and management*, ed. M. Warner (1996) · R. M. Thomas, *The British philosophy of administration* (1978) · *The Times* (8/10 Dec 1983) · *The Times* (20 Dec 1983) · R. M. Thomas, 'Urwick, Lyndall Fownes', *DBB* · L. F. Urwick and E. Brech, *The making of scientific management*, 3 vols. (1945–8) · b. cert. · m. certs.
Archives Henley Management College · PowerGen Library, corresp., lecture notes, articles, and papers | London, Urwick, Orr & Partners MSS
Likenesses photograph, c.1960, repro. in Thomas, 'Urwick, Lyndall Fownes' · photographs, priv. coll.
Wealth at death £22,107—in England and Wales: Australian probate sealed in England, 12 Feb 1985, *CGPLA Eng. & Wales*

Urwick, Thomas (1727–1807), Independent minister, was born on 8 December 1727 at Shelton, near Shrewsbury, the second son of Samuel Urwick (1687–1773), a farmer, and his wife, Sarah Wright (1697–1788). His parents were dissenters who were attracted to the ministry of Job Orton at Shrewsbury. He was educated at Shrewsbury grammar school, and following preparation for the ministry by Orton he went to Philip Doddridge's academy at Northampton in 1747. After Doddridge's death in 1751, instead of completing his ministerial training at Daventry Academy under Caleb Ashworth with the rest of Doddridge's students he went to the University of Glasgow, where he was a Dr Williams's Trust scholar; he matriculated in 1752. In 1754 he became assistant pastor at the Angel Street Chapel, Worcester. He declined the offer to become its minister, and Dr John Allen was appointed in 1760. When Allen retired in 1764 Urwick agreed to succeed him, an office which 'he discharged with so much acceptance and usefulness, that few ministers were ever more beloved by their hearers' (W. Urwick, 105). He married Mary Smith (1725/6–1791), a member of the congregation, in Worcester in 1767; there were no children.

Urwick resigned in 1775 to the regret of the congregation, seeking a quiet retirement in the ministry of a small congregation at Narborough, Leicestershire.

> A new and handsome house was erected for him, to the expense of which he himself contributed. But he and Mrs Urwick not finding such a retirement to meet their expectation, he was prevailed upon by some intimate friends to accept an invitation to Clapham … There his sphere of usefulness was enlarged. (*Monthly Repository*, March 1807, 161)

He followed Philip Furneaux in the ministry of Grafton Square Chapel, Clapham, without an assistant, and became widely accepted as an influential leader in the Independent denomination.

> His sermons although not brilliant, were well composed; and though so plain as to suit the meanest capacities, were not below the attention of learned and critical hearers, though they cost him but little pains. Few persons indeed ever composed such good discourses as his with so much ease; and few set so small a value on their own compositions. (ibid., 161)

Urwick became a trustee of both Dr Williams's and the Coward trusts. 'With his appointment [to the Coward Trust] the Trust entered on a period of much needed stability' (Thompson, 32). He was seen by many as a dissenter of the old school, being the last living pupil of Doddridge. However his theological position was uncertain: 'his religious opinions were by no means what are called orthodox, nor could he, we apprehend, be justly said to believe in a Trinity in any sense. But also he did not oppose that doctrine' (*Monthly Repository*, April 1807, 215). He retired from his ministry a few years before his death but continued to preach. The story is told of him that in a Clapham shop he found a woman much distressed, as her young son had secretly enlisted in the navy. Urwick knew the admiral involved and used his influence to secure the boy's release. The boy was Joseph Lancaster, who became an educational pioneer.

Urwick died at his home at Balham Hill after a brief illness on 26 February 1807, and was buried with his wife, who predeceased him, in Clapham parish churchyard. Unusually for a dissenting minister, his will suggests that he owned quite extensive property. ALAN RUSTON

Sources W. Urwick, *Nonconformity in Worcester* (1897), 103–9 • T. A. Urwick and W. Urwick, eds., *Records of the family of Urswyk, Urswick or Urwick* (1893), 212–14 • *Monthly Repository*, 2 (1807), 161–2, 215–16 • J. H. Thompson, *A history of the Coward Trust: the first two hundred and fifty years, 1738–1988* (1998), 32 • *DNB* • *GM*, 1st ser., 77 (1807), 282, 371–3 • *Calendar of the correspondence of Philip Doddridge*, ed. G. F. Nuttall, HMC, JP 26 (1979), 1504, 1509, 1537 • C. Surman, index, DWL, card U.48 • J. Waddington, *Surrey Congregational history* (1866), 186 • biographical recollections, DWL, Walter Wilson MSS, vol. K4 • W. D. Jeremy, *The Presbyterian Fund and Dr Daniel Williams's Trust* (1885), 173 • will, 1807, PRO, PROB 11/1460, sig. 353
Likenesses pastel drawing, DWL • portrait, repro. in Urwick, *Nonconformity in Worcester*
Wealth at death see will, PRO, PROB 11/1460, sig. 353, reproduced with comments in Urwick, *Nonconformity in Worcester*, 116–17

Urwick, William (1791–1868), Congregational minister, was born on 8 December 1791 in Shrewsbury, the only son and youngest child in the family of three of William Urwick (1750–1799) and his wife, Ellinor (1757–1853), daughter of his uncle Joshua Eddowes, a printer. He was educated at the Red House School, Worcester, under Thomas Belsher, and in 1812 entered Hoxton Academy to study for the Independent ministry under Dr Robert Simpson. In 1815 he was invited to become minister at Sligo, and was ordained there on 19 June 1816. He married Sarah (1791–1852), daughter of Thomas Cooke of Shrewsbury, on 16 June 1818. Of their ten children, three daughters and two sons survived early childhood. At Sligo Urwick was active in attempts to convert Roman Catholics, and served as secretary of the famine committee in 1824–5.

In 1826 Urwick became minister of the congregation at York Street, Dublin. The chapel had been built in 1808 by the Countess of Huntingdon's Connexion, and although it was a large building, seating 1600, Urwick filled it to capacity. Small of stature, with a clear, bell-like voice, he acquired the sobriquets 'Multum in Parvo' and 'the Little Giant'. A pioneer of the temperance movement, for years he was the only minister in Dublin who took the pledge. In 1829 he published *The Evils, Occasions, and Cure of Intemperance*, a tract urging total abstinence on moral principles.

In 1831 Urwick issued a reply to Edward Irving's Christological views, *The True Nature of Christ's Person and Atonement Stated*, and in the following year was appointed professor of dogmatics and pastoral theology in the Dublin Theological Institute, an office he combined with his pastorate at York Street for twenty years. Dartmouth College, New Hampshire, awarded him a DD in 1832. He preached throughout Ireland, and founded an Irish Congregational home mission, of which he was honorary secretary for some years. He fought vigorously for home rule in church matters, in opposition to the Irish Evangelical Society of London. He was one of the founders of the Evangelical Alliance, inaugurated at Liverpool in 1845, attended its meetings regularly, and spoke in Paris in 1855 and in Geneva in 1862.

Urwick's two chief works appeared in 1839: *The Saviour's Right to Divine Worship*, which took the form of letters to

James Armstrong discussing the Unitarian controversy, and *The Second Advent*, in which he opposed premillennial teaching. In 1852 he published *The Triple Crown*, a history of 'the papacy, its power, course, and doom'. He also wrote a memoir of his friend Thomas Kelly, the hymn writer. In 1862, the bicentenary of the nonconformist evictions of 1662, he wrote *Independency in Dublin in the Olden Time*, an account of the lives of Samuel Winter, provost of Trinity College, Dublin (1650–60), John Rogers of St Bride's, John Murcot, and Samuel Mather. In March 1866 he published *Christ's World School*, essays in verse on Matthew 28: 18–20, and he left two other poems, 'The inheritance of the saints' and 'My Sligo Ministry', in manuscript. His last book, *Biographic Sketches of James Digges La Touche* (1868), the patron of Sunday schools in Ireland, appeared posthumously, and *A Father's Letters to his Son on Coming of Age* was published by the Religious Tract Society in 1874.

Urwick died on 16 July 1868 at his home, 40 Rathmines Road, Rathmines, co. Dublin, and was buried in Mount Jerome cemetery, Dublin. His son, William *Urwick, who followed him into the ministry, published a *Life and Letters* of his father in 1870.

WILLIAM URWICK, *rev.* ANNE PIMLOTT BAKER

Sources T. A. Urwick and W. Urwick, eds., *Records of the family of Urswyk, Urswick or Urwick* (1893) • R. Tudur Jones, *Congregationalism in England, 1662–1962* (1962) • W. Urwick, ed., *The life and letters of William Urwick* (1870) • Boase, *Mod. Eng. biog.*
Archives DWL, corresp. with Dublin Theological Academy
Likenesses J. Cochran, stipple (after photograph by Maull & Polyblank), NG Ire. • portrait?, repro. in Urwick, ed., *Life and letters*, frontispiece
Wealth at death under £2000 in England: probate, 14 Oct 1868, *CGPLA Ire.* • under £6000 in Ireland: probate, 14 Oct 1868, *CGPLA Ire.*

Urwick, William (1826–1905), Congregational minister and writer, born at Sligo on 8 March 1826, was the second son of William *Urwick (1791–1868) who soon moved to Dublin as minister of York Street Chapel. His mother was Sarah (1791–1852), daughter of Thomas Cooke of Shrewsbury. William junior attended Trinity College, Dublin, graduating BA in 1848 (MA 1851). He then proceeded to the Lancashire Independent college, Manchester, where he studied under Robert Vaughan and Samuel Davidson. He was ordained at Hatherlow, Cheshire, on 19 June 1851 and in this industrial village he served as a Congregational minister for twenty-three years. He was a devoted pastor, and for a long period secretary of the Cheshire Congregational Union; he ran evening classes for young men, and advocated total abstinence principles which he had adopted at an early age. He also translated German works for Clarke's Foreign Theological Library. His *History of Cheshire Nonconformity*, published in 1864, was not well received, being criticized as unfair to Unitarianism and as a medley of disjointed scraps of information collected together with no serious attempt at historical analysis. In 1874 Urwick moved to London where he occupied the chair of Hebrew and Old Testament exegesis at New College; *The Servant of Jehovah* (1877), a commentary on Isaiah 52–3, is a product of these years. In 1880 he received an invitation to the pulpit of Spicer Street Chapel, St Albans.

He accepted, though he continued to reside in London. He rebuilt the Spicer Street Sunday schools and was active in temperance work in the city. While at St Albans he became embroiled in educational controversies—writing *The Nonconformists and the Education Act* in 1872—and was involved in conflict with high Anglicans and Roman Catholics. He also published a *History of Hertfordshire Nonconformity* (1884). Though this begins oddly with a chapter on St Alban, it soon takes up its proper theme, and is considered superior both to his Cheshire history and a later work on Worcestershire nonconformity (1897). In 1892 he published a very valuable account of the early years of Trinity College, Dublin. Besides his historical works and his commentary Urwick published a life of his father (1870), *Ecumenical Councils* (1870), *The Errors of Ritualism* (1872), *The Papacy and the Bible* (1874—in controversy with Kenelm Vaughan), and *Bible Truths and Church Errors* (1888—an attempt to claim John Bunyan for Congregationalism). He edited his father's *Biographic Sketches of James Digges La Touche* (1868) and T. A. Urwick's *Records of the Family of Urwick* (1893). Urwick resigned his pastorate in 1895. His wife, Sophia (*née* Hunter), of Manchester, died two years later and he died on a visit to his sisters in the old family home at 40 Rathmines Road, Rathmines, co. Dublin, on 20 August 1905 and was buried in Dublin. The Urwicks had four sons and five daughters.

ALEXANDER GORDON, rev. IAN SELLERS

Sources *Congregational Year Book* (1906) · *The Times* (28 Aug 1905) · Lancashire Independent College, report for 1905 · T. A. Urwick and W. Urwick, eds., *Records of the family of Urswyk, Urswick or Urwick* (1893) · DWL, London New College MSS
Archives DWL, London New College MSS
Likenesses J. Cochran, stipple (after photograph by Maull & Polyblank), NPG · portrait, repro. in *Congregational Year Book* (1905)
Wealth at death £13,933 12s. 7d.: probate, 21 Oct 1905, *CGPLA Eng. & Wales*

Urwin, Charles Henry [Harry] (1915–1996), trade unionist, was born on 24 February 1915 at 16 Dean Street, Witton Gilbert, co. Durham, the son of Thomas Urwin, coalminer, and his wife, Lydia, *née* Spark. He was educated at a Durham county council school until the age of fourteen, when he followed his father down the pit. After three years underground he felt the need to 'escape the dust' and migrated to Coventry, finding work as a welder in the machine tool trade, serving the burgeoning local car industry. There he joined the Transport and General Workers' Union (TGWU), became a shop steward, and married a local girl, Hilda Pinfold (*d.* 1996), daughter of Thomas Pinfold, lawyer, on 31 May 1941. They had one daughter, Marion.

In 1947 Urwin became a full-time union official and seven years later he succeeded Jack Jones as secretary of the Coventry district. In 1959 he moved to Birmingham as a regional officer and in 1963 he was appointed secretary of the midlands region, again in succession to Jones. In 1969, when Jones was elected general secretary, Urwin became deputy secretary of the union and was elected in the same year to the general council of the Trades Union Congress (TUC). He served on the social insurance, education, and economic committees, and chaired the organization (subsequently employment policy and organization) committee, from 1973. When Labour returned to office in 1974, he was appointed to a large number of public bodies, including the Manpower Services Commission (1974–9), the National Enterprise Board (1975–9), the Energy Commission (1977–9), the Advisory, Conciliation, and Arbitration Service (1978–80), and the standing committee on pay comparability (1979–80). He was also a member of the conference arrangements committee of the Labour Party.

Urwin was undoubtedly the most influential and respected member of the TUC general council who was never a general secretary. His unique position was the consequence of two factors: first, his lifelong friendship and alliance with Jack Jones, the visionary and proactive leader of the TGWU, who was in effective command of Britain's largest union from the mid-1960s until his retirement in 1978, and secondly, the fact that Urwin excelled in every job he was given, especially where his pragmatism and persuasiveness complemented and reinforced the more adamantine leadership style of Jones. It used to be said that the twin capped figures of Jones and Urwin could be seen at soccer matches on Saturday afternoons, arguing furiously about something before and after the game; but remarkably they never argued in public. Together they were often irresistible.

This unflagging duo pursued a range of initiatives. Within the union they launched a much more aggressive recruitment policy, based on the development of workplace bargaining by shop stewards. In general council elections they organized support for like-minded candidates from other unions, who would follow their policy lead. Within the Labour Party they campaigned for the 'TUC–Labour Party Liaison Committee', to decide the contents of the next election manifesto. A central feature was to be a pledge to repeal 'all Tory anti-union laws', in exchange for TUC assistance with any future wage–price explosion. By 1974 there were gains on all fronts. TGWU membership was approaching 2 million. Workplace bargaining by shop stewards became the dominant mode in most of private industry. Sympathetic majorities ensured that Labour's election programme met with the duo's approval.

When in 1975 the explosion arrived, the Jones–Urwin coalition did not try to evade its responsibilities. Congress agreed and delivered three years of pay restraint, during which the annual rate of increase in earnings was cut by more than half—from 20 per cent to 8.5 per cent. Unfortunately the government was unable to arrest the impact on prices of a continually declining exchange rate, so that by 1977 workers were experiencing a 7 per cent cut in real wages. With unanswerable logic, and their usual persistence, Jones and Urwin argued for what they termed 'an orderly return to free collective bargaining'. But the government had stopped listening. They were pursuing the chimera of 'single digit' inflation. And when, in what he subsequently termed a 'somewhat relaxed New Year broadcast', the prime minister admitted that this would require a '5 per cent pay limit', an unbridgeable gap opened between the cabinet and the TUC. The result was a series of industrial disputes which *The Sun* newspaper was the first to term 'The Winter of Discontent'. As a result Labour lost both the fight against inflation and the election of May 1979. By this time Jones had retired as general secretary, and had been succeeded by Moss Evans, in 1978.

Curiously enough, to judge from their memoirs, only one member of the cabinet of the day later admitted to a significant share of the blame for the 'winter of discontent'. The chancellor, Dennis Healey, confessed that the insistence on a 5 per cent pay limit, without any help from the TUC, could best be described as a fatal attack of hubris. More doubtfully, he also suggested that a figure of 9 per cent might have avoided most strikes, reduced inflation, and even won the election. Perhaps. What is certain is that through all the bitterness and recrimination, Urwin retained his cool. He never stopped trying to find a way out, even if it meant negotiating with those he thought most responsible for destroying his life's work. He was rewarded with continued popularity and even greater respect. As tempers rose his mixture of realism tempered by raillery never seemed to offend. Yet he could also be monumentally obstinate. After once receiving his TUC expenses in the form of a cheque that 'bounced', he invariably insisted on cash in a brown envelope. He never moved to London, despite the rule that said all national officers should do so, slipping off to his beloved Walsall whenever he could.

Following his retirement in 1980 Urwin led a relatively quiet life in Walsall. He died at his home there, 4 Leacliffe Way, Aldridge, on 10 February 1996, of heart disease. His wife, Hilda, died a month later. They were survived by their daughter, Marion.   WILLIAM McCARTHY

Sources D. Healey, *The time of my life* (1989) · J. Jones, *Union man* (1986) · J. Callaghan, *Time and chance* (1987) · J. Barnett, *Inside the treasury* (1982) · P. Whitehead, *The writing on the wall* (1981) · *T&GWU Record* (March 1996) · *Annual report*, general council of the TUC (1996) · *The Guardian* (22 Feb 1996) · *The Times* (24 Feb 1996) · *WWW* · personal knowledge (2004) · private information (2004) · b. cert. · m. cert. · d. cert.
Likenesses photograph, repro. in *The Guardian* · photograph, repro. in *The Times*
Wealth at death £178,186: probate, 7 Oct 1996, CGPLA Eng. & Wales

Urwin, William [Will] (d. **1695**), coffee-house keeper, is of unknown parentage, and nothing is known of his early life or education. At an unknown date he opened a coffee house which subsequently became the most famous in London of its time. It was well established as early as February 1664, when Samuel Pepys found the poet John Dryden and 'all the wits of the town' engaged in their 'very witty and pleasant discourse' (Pepys, 5.37). The coffee house became known as John Dryden's favourite place to relax and socialize. Aspirant poets and playwrights flocked to the coffee house, desiring to find a seat next to

Dryden with the hope that the great man would notice and appreciate their way with words. Dryden's enemies also knew that they could find him at 'Will's', and the poet was beaten by some ruffians outside the coffee house on the night of 18 December 1679, perhaps at the instigation of John Wilmot, earl of Rochester. It was at Will's that William Congreve's skilful Latin and Greek translations brought him into favour with Dryden's circle and thus launched his literary career; he later succeeded Dryden as the doyen of the London literati at Will's.

Less is known about Urwin himself. He did not become a full paying member of the parish poor rate in St Paul's, Covent Garden, until 1675. In 1672 he joined with more than 140 other coffee-house keepers to sign a remarkable petition to Thomas Osborne, earl of Danby and lord high treasurer of England, in which they complained of their harassment by agents of the crown, despite their possession of licences obtained in good faith and by virtue of statutory authority. Although his coffee house was implicated as one of several gathering places for the conspirators in the Rye House plot of 1683, Urwin's business continued to prosper. In the 1680s he could afford to pay £55 per year to the excise collectors for his coffee sales, but the charge was sufficiently onerous to make him think it worth petitioning directly to the excise commissioners for relief. By 1693 Urwin was paying a full pound to the poor rate, a sure sign that he had attained a secure standing within the parish, but when he died, in 1695, his widow (whose name is unknown) was unable to maintain the payments, and she died not long afterwards. The coffee house continued to function, and Joseph Addison and Richard Steele revived its fame in their *Tatler* and *Spectator* papers (1709–12), though Steele remarked in the first *Tatler* (12 April 1709) that it was 'very much altered' since Dryden's time:

> where you used to see songs, epigrams, and satires in the hands of every man you met, you have now only a pack of cards; and instead of cavils about the turn of expression, the elegance of the style, and the like, the learned now dispute only about the truth of the game.   (Bond, 1.19)

Jonathan Swift's judgement on the state of wit at the post-Dryden coffee house was even more damning. He thought that 'the worst conversation I ever remember to have heard in my life', was to be found there; self-important playwrights 'entertained one another with their trifling composures' before 'an humble audience of young students from the inns of court, or the universities', who, having 'listened to these oracles, … returned home with great contempt for law and philosophy, their heads filled with trash, under the name of politeness, criticism, and belles lettres' (*Prose Writings*, 4.90). It was perhaps this disappointment with the state of wit at Will's that prompted Addison and Steele to remove their coterie to Button's Coffee House on Russell Street in Covent Garden in 1712–13. By the mid-eighteenth century Will's Coffee House had regained its lustre in the imagination of England's literati, however, as witness the remarks of 28 June 1763 in James Boswell's London journal and Samuel Johnson's of 15 May

1776 in Boswell's *Life of Johnson*. In the early nineteenth century Lord Macaulay immortalized Will's place in Augustan culture with his evocative description of the coffee house in the third chapter of his *History of England* (1848).   BRIAN COWAN

Sources B. Lillywhite, *London coffee houses* (1963), 655–9 · A. Ellis, *The penny universities: a history of the coffee-houses* (1956), 58–69 · H. B. Wheatley and P. Cunningham, *London past and present*, 3 vols. (1891), vol. 3, pp. 516–17 · B. Cowan, 'The social life of coffee: commercial culture and metropolitan society in early modern England, 1600–1720', PhD diss., Princeton University, 2000 · D. F. Bond, ed., *The Tatler*, 1 (1987), 19 · *The prose writings of Jonathan Swift*, ed. H. Davis and others, 4: *A proposal for correcting the English tongue* (1957), 90 · M. Novak, *William Congreve* (1971), 27 · *William Congreve: letters and documents*, ed. J. C. Hodges (1964), 4, 190–95 · Pepys, *Diary*, 5.37; 8.363 · Bodl. Oxf., MS Don c. 37, fol. 276v · churchwarden's accounts, St Paul's, Covent Garden, City Westm. AC · W. A. Shaw, ed., *Calendar of treasury books*, 7, PRO (1916), 889 · *Boswell's London journal, 1762–63*, ed. F. A. Pottle (1950), vol. 1 of *The Yale editions of the private papers of James Boswell*, trade edn (1950–89), 286 · J. Boswell, *Life of Johnson*, ed. R. W. Chapman, rev. J. D. Fleeman, new edn (1970); repr. with introduction by P. Rogers (1980), 770 · T. B. Macaulay, *The history of England from the accession of James II*, new edn, 3 vols. (1906); repr. (1967), vol. 1, p. 289 · 'To Will's Coffeehouse', 1691, BL, Harley MS 7319, fol. 366r · *A paquet from Will's* (1701) · *Urania's temple, or, A satyr upon the silent-poets* (1695) · *A satyr against wit* (1700) · R. Blackmore, *Discommendatory verses, on those which are truly commendatory, on the author of the two 'Arthurs' and the 'Satyr against wit'* [1700]

Usher, James (1720–1771), Roman Catholic priest and schoolmaster, was born in co. Dublin, the son of Gilbert Usher (*d.* 1725), a gentleman farmer of Bridgend and Balsoon, co. Meath, and later of Ramsgrange, co. Wexford, and his wife, Mary. Gilbert Usher drowned in the River Boyne when James was five years old, and Mary Usher subsequently married Terence Callaghan. Brought up a Roman Catholic, Usher appears to have been educated at Trinity College, Dublin, whence he graduated AM. From 1745 to 1748 he worked as a gentleman farmer on his property at Cannycourt, near Calliaghstown, co. Meath, but, not meeting with success, he opened a linen draper's shop in Dublin. About 1747 he married Jane Fitzsimons, with whom he had four children. Following her death he gave up his failing business and took holy orders in the Roman Catholic church. He provided for his children's education by sending his three sons—Gilbert, Marcus, and Joseph—to the Collège des Lombards, in Paris, and his daughter to a convent, where she died soon afterwards.

Usher then moved to London, and inherited a legacy of £300 from Charles Molloy (*d.* 1767), a writer for the opposition journals *Mist's Weekly Journal* and *Fog's Weekly Journal*. This enabled him to open a school for Roman Catholic boys at Kensington Gravel Pits in January 1769, in partnership with his friend John Walker (1732–1807), whom he had converted to Roman Catholicism. Walker subsequently withdrew from the undertaking, and Usher became sole master of the school.

Usher published several works, including two philosophical treatises: *A New System of Philosophy, Founded on the Universal Operations of Nature* (1764) and *An Introduction to the Theory of the Human Mind* (1771). His only controversial work was *A Free Examination of the Common Methods Employed to Prevent the Growth of Popery* (1766), which appeared originally as a series of letters signed 'A Free Thinker' in the *Public Ledger*. Usher robustly denied that his fellow Catholics posed a political threat in England, and accused the protestant press of whipping up anti-Catholic prejudices in the country. He provoked retaliatory pamphlets from Benjamin Pye (1767) and Donald Grant, vicar of Hutton Rudby, Yorkshire (1771). His most popular publication was *Clio, or, A Discourse on Taste, Addressed to a Young Lady* (1767), which had run to a fourth edition by 1803.

Usher conducted his school until his death, which occurred, probably in Paddington, London, between 17 December 1771, when he made his will, and 24 December, when probate was granted to his eldest son, Gilbert.

THOMPSON COOPER, *rev.* S. J. SKEDD

Sources W. B. Wright, *The Ussher memoirs* (1889) · *European Magazine*, 29 (March 1796), 151 · T. Green, *Extracts from the diary of a lover of literature* (1810), 128 · J. Milner, 'A brief account of the life of the late R. Rev. Richard Challoner', in R. Challoner, *The grounds of the old religion*, 5th edn (1798) · will, PRO, PROB 11/973, sig. 504

Usher, Richard (1785–1843), clown and theatre designer, was the son of the owner of a 'mechanical exhibition' who travelled in the north of England and in Ireland. From an early age he shared in the management of this exhibition. He inherited his father's talent for constructing curious contrivances, and a spirit of adventure soon led him to set up business on his own account. With a friend he gave exhibitions in Newcastle, Manchester, Liverpool, and other large towns. On one of these occasions, according to *The Era*, he attracted the attention of Mr Banks, the proprietor of the Liverpool Amphitheatre, who asked him to perform in a Christmas pantomime in 1807. Two years later John Astley, the manager of Astley's Amphitheatre, engaged Usher, who soon became a favourite with metropolitan audiences—particularly during his annual benefits, when extraordinary feats were known to take place. The most remarkable of these occurred in 1828, when in a washing tub drawn by geese he sailed down the Thames from Westminster to Waterloo Bridge. He was then to have proceeded in a car drawn by eight cats to the Coburg Theatre, but the crowd in the Waterloo Road made this impossible, and he was carried to the theatre on the shoulders of several watermen. Usher married, as his second wife, Elizabeth Pincott, *née* Wallack, a sister of the actor James William Wallack (1795–1864), who by her first marriage was the mother of the actress Leonora *Wigan [*see under* Wigan, Alfred Sydney].

Usher was known as the John Kemble of his art, and his career was comparable in its success to that of Joseph Grimaldi. His manner was irresistibly comic and his jokes were original. He created several stock pantomimes. In his later career he gave up clowning and confined himself to the invention of stage properties and the design of theatres. When William Batty purchased Astley's in 1842 with a view to rebuilding the theatre (fire had twice damaged it during the previous year), he declared, 'Dicky Usher [is] the only man that could do it' (*The Era*, 1 Oct 1843, 6). Batty had the theatre redesigned according to Usher's plans and models. The excitement of witnessing the successful completion of his work, it was said, precipitated Usher's illness. He died of dropsy at Hercules Buildings, Lambeth, London, on 23 September 1843, survived by his wife and family.   G. C. BOASE, *rev.* BRENDA ASSAEL

Sources *The Era* (1 Oct 1843), 6 · Hall, *Dramatic ports.* · d. cert.
Likenesses coloured portrait, 1811 · portrait, 1811 · three prints, Harvard TC · woodcut

PICTURE CREDITS

Tonson, Jacob, the elder (1655/6–1736)—© National Portrait Gallery, London

Tonyn, Patrick (1725–1804)—© National Portrait Gallery, London

Tooke, John Horne (1736–1812)—© National Portrait Gallery, London

Toole, John Lawrence (1830–1906)—Garrick Club / the art archive

Topham, Mirabel Dorothy (1891–1980)—© Empics

Toplady, Augustus Montague (1740–1778)—© National Portrait Gallery, London

Torrens, Sir Henry (1779–1828)—© National Portrait Gallery, London

Torrens, Robert (1780?–1864)—photograph courtesy of the State Library of South Australia; SLSA B7557

Torry, Patrick (1763–1852)—© National Portrait Gallery, London

Tosti, Sir (Francesco) Paolo (1846–1916)—© National Portrait Gallery, London

Toulmin, Joshua (1740–1815)—Ashmolean Museum, Oxford

Tout, Thomas Frederick (1855–1929)—© National Portrait Gallery, London

Tovey, Sir Donald Francis (1875–1940)—© Estate of Sir William Rothenstein / National Portrait Gallery, London

Townley, Charles (1737–1805)—Towneley Hall Art Gallery & Museum, Burnley / Bridgeman Art Library

Townsend, Charles Harrison (1851–1928)—Art Workers' Guild

Townsend, Sir John Sealy Edward (1868–1957)—© Royal Society; photograph National Portrait Gallery, London

Townsend, Mary Elizabeth (1841–1918)—Girls' Friendly Society

Townsend, Meredith White (1831–1911)—V&A Images, The Victoria and Albert Museum

Townsend, Peter Woolridge (1914–1995)—© News International Newspapers Ltd

Townshend, Caroline, suo jure Baroness Greenwich (1717–1794)—in the collection of the Duke of Buccleuch and Queensberry KT; photograph courtesy National Gallery of Scotland

Townshend, Charles, second Viscount Townshend (1674–1738)—© National Portrait Gallery, London

Townshend, Charles (1725–1767)—private collection

Townshend, Chauncy Hare (1798–1868)—V&A Images, The Victoria and Albert Museum

Townshend, Etheldreda, Viscountess Townshend (c.1708–1788)—photograph by courtesy Sotheby's Picture Library, London

Townshend, George, first Marquess Townshend (1724–1807)—Art Gallery of Ontario, Toronto, Gift of Rueben Wells Leonard Estate, 1948

Townshend, Horatio, first Viscount Townshend (bap. 1630, d. 1687)—© National Museums and Galleries of Wales

Towse, Sir (Ernest) Beachcroft Beckwith (1864–1948)—© National Portrait Gallery, London

Toynbee, Arnold (1852–1883)—© National Portrait Gallery, London

Toynbee, Arnold Joseph (1889–1975)—© Karsh / Camera Press; collection National Portrait Gallery, London

Toynbee, Charlotte Maria (1841–1931)—private collection

Toynbee, Joseph (1815–1866)—© National Portrait Gallery, London

Toynbee, Paget Jackson (1855–1932)—© National Portrait Gallery, London

Toynbee, (Theodore) Philip (1916–1981)—© Jane Bown

Tradescant, John, the elder (d. 1638)—Ashmolean Museum, Oxford

Traill, Henry Duff (1842–1900)—© National Portrait Gallery, London

Trapp, John (1601–1669)—© National Portrait Gallery, London

Traquair, Phoebe Anna (1852–1936)—Scottish National Portrait Gallery

Travers, Benjamin (1783–1858)—reproduced by kind permission of the President and Council of the Royal College of Surgeons of England. Photograph: Photographic Survey, Courtauld Institute of Art, London

Travers, Benjamin (1886–1980)—© National Portrait Gallery, London

Travers, Morris William (1872–1961)—© National Portrait Gallery, London

Travis, Sir Edward Wilfrid Harry (1888–1956)—© National Portrait Gallery, London

Trease, (Robert) Geoffrey (1909–1998)—© reserved; News International Syndication; photograph National Portrait Gallery, London

Treby, Sir George (bap. 1644, d. 1700)—© National Portrait Gallery, London

Tree, Sir Herbert Beerbohm (1852–1917)—© National Portrait Gallery, London

Tree, (Anna) Maria (1801/2–1862)—Garrick Club / the art archive

Treece, Henry William (1911–1966)—David Lee Photography Ltd., Barton-upon-Humber

Trefusis, Violet (1894–1972)—© ADAGP, Paris, and DACS, London, 2004; collection National Portrait Gallery, London

Trelawney, Charles (1653–1731)—© The Trustees of the Holburne Museum of Art, Bath

Trelawny, Edward John (1792–1881)—© National Portrait Gallery, London

Trelawny, Sir Jonathan, third baronet (1650–1721)—© National Portrait Gallery, London

Treloar, Sir William Purdie, baronet (1843–1923)—© National Portrait Gallery, London

Trench, Anthony Chenevix- (1919–1979)—© National Portrait Gallery, London

Trench, Francis Chenevix (1805–1886)—© National Portrait Gallery, London

Trench, Richard Chenevix (1807–1886)—Representative Body of the Church of Ireland

Trench, Richard Le Poer, second earl of Clancarty (1767–1837)—© National Portrait Gallery, London

Trenchard, Hugh Montague, first Viscount Trenchard (1873–1956)—The Imperial War Museum, London

Trend, Burke Frederick St John, Baron Trend (1914–1987)—© National Portrait Gallery, London

Trevelyan, Sir Charles Edward, first baronet (1807–1886)—© National Portrait Gallery, London

Trevelyan, Sir Charles Philips, third baronet (1870–1958)—© Estate of Sir William Rothenstein / National Portrait Gallery, London

Trevelyan, George Macaulay (1876–1962)—© reserved; The Master and Fellows, Trinity College, Cambridge

Trevelyan, Sir George Otto, second baronet (1838–1928)—The Master and Fellows, Trinity College, Cambridge

Trevelyan, Humphrey, Baron Trevelyan (1905–1985)—© National Portrait Gallery, London

Trevelyan, Paulina Jermyn, Lady Trevelyan (1816–1866)—National Trust Photographic Library

Treves, Sir Frederick, baronet (1853–1923)—© National Portrait Gallery, London

Trevithick, Richard (1771–1833)—Science & Society Picture Library

Trimmer, Sarah (1741–1810)—© National Portrait Gallery, London

Trimnell, Charles (bap. 1663, d. 1723)—photograph: The Paul Mellon Centre for Studies in British Art

Trinder, Thomas Edward (1909–1989)—Getty Images – Baron

Tripe, Linnaeus (1822–1902)—The British Library

Trocchi, Alexander Whitelaw Robertson (1925–1984)—Estate of Alex Trocchi

Trollope, Anthony (1815–1882)—© National Portrait Gallery, London

Trollope, Frances (1779–1863)—© National Portrait Gallery, London

Trollope, George Haward (1845–1929)—Skanska

Trollope, Sir Henry (1756–1839)—© National Portrait Gallery, London

Trollope, Theodosia (1812x19–1865)—Boston Public Library / Rare Books Department - courtesy of the Trustees

Trollope, Thomas Adolphus (1810–1892)—© Bodleian Library, University of Oxford

Trotter, Wilfred Batten Lewis (1872–1939)—reproduced by kind permission of the President and Council of the Royal College of Surgeons of London

Troubridge, Sir Ernest Charles Thomas (1862–1926)—© National Portrait Gallery, London

Troubridge, Sir Thomas, first baronet (c.1758–1807)—© reserved

Troubridge, Sir Thomas Hope (1895–1949)—© National Portrait Gallery, London

Troup, Sir Charles Edward (1857–1941)—© National Portrait Gallery, London

Trumbull, Sir William (1639–1716)—© National Portrait Gallery, London

Tryon, Sir George (1832–1893)—© National Portrait Gallery, London

Tryon, Thomas (1634–1703)—© National Portrait Gallery, London

T'Serclaes, Baroness Elizabeth Blackall de (1884–1978)—© National Portrait Gallery, London

Tuck, Mary (1928–1996)—© reserved; News International Syndication; photograph National Portrait Gallery, London

Tucker, Alfred Robert (1849–1914)—© National Portrait Gallery, London

Tucker, St George (1752–1827)—in the collection of the Corcoran Gallery of Art

Tuckwell, Gertrude Mary (1861–1951)—© National Portrait Gallery, London

Tuke, Anthony William (1897–1975)—© National Portrait Gallery, London

Tuke, Sir Brian (d. 1545)—Andrew W. Mellon Collection, Photograph © 2004 Board of Trustees, National Gallery of Art, Washington

Tuke, Daniel Hack (1827–1895)—Wellcome Library, London

Tuke, Henry Scott (1858–1929)—© Royal Institution of Cornwall

Tuke, James Hack (1819–1896)—© National Portrait Gallery, London

Tuke, Mabel Kate (1871–1962)—© reserved; private collection; photograph Museum of London / National Portrait Gallery, London

Tuke, Dame Margaret Janson (1862–1947)—© National Portrait Gallery, London / Oxford University Press

Tull, Jethro (bap. 1674, d. 1741)—Royal Agricultural Society of England

Tull, Walter Daniel John (1888–1918)—courtesy of Mr Philip Vasili

Tullis, Julia Elissa May (1939–1986)—Alpine Club Photo Library, London

Tulloch, John (1823–1886)—The Royal Collection © 2004 HM Queen Elizabeth II

Tunstal, Cuthbert (1474–1559)—private collection. Photograph: Photographic Survey, Courtauld Institute of Art, London

Tupper, Sir Charles, first baronet (1821–1915)—© National Portrait Gallery, London

Tupper, Martin Farquhar (1810–1889)—© National Portrait Gallery, London

Turbervill, Edith Picton- (1872–1960)—by kind permission of the Estate of Sir Cedric Morris; photograph courtesy Sotheby's Picture Library, London

Turing, Alan Mathison (1912–1954)—© National Portrait Gallery, London

Turnbull, William Barclay David Donald (1811–1863)—Ashmolean Museum, Oxford

Turner, Anne (1576–1615)—© National Portrait Gallery, London

Turner, Sir Ben (1863–1942)—by permission of the People's History Museum

Turner, Benjamin Brecknell (1815–1894)—Benjamin Brecknell Turner Descendants' Private Collection

Turner, Charles (1774–1857)—© National Portrait Gallery, London

Turner, Cuthbert Hamilton (1860–1930)—© National Portrait Gallery, London

Turner, Daniel (1667–1741)—© National Portrait Gallery, London

Turner, Dame Eva (1892–1990)—photograph by Maurice Seymour, courtesy of Ronald Seymour. Print from Royal Opera House Archives

Turner, Francis (1637–1700)—by permission of the Master and Fellows of St John's College, Cambridge

Turner, George Grey (1877–1951)—Wellcome Library, London

Turner, Sir James (b. c.1615, d. in or after 1689)—© National Portrait Gallery, London

Turner, Joseph Mallord William (1775–1851)—© Tate, London, 2004

Turner, Sharon (1768–1847)—© National Portrait Gallery, London

Turner, Thomas (bap. 1592, d. 1672)—© National Portrait Gallery, London

Turner, William [of Oxford] (1789–1862)—Ashmolean Museum, Oxford

Turner, Sir William (1832–1916)—reproduced with the kind permission of the Royal College of Surgeons of Edinburgh

Turnerelli, Peter (1771/2–1839)—© National Portrait Gallery, London

Turnor, Sir Edward (1616/17–1676)—Palace of Westminster Collection

Turnour, Edward, sixth Earl Winterton (1883–1962)—© National Portrait Gallery, London

Turpin, Randolph Adolphus (1928–1966)—Getty Images – Bert Hardy

Tussaud, Anna Maria (bap. 1761, d. 1850)—Madame Tussaud's Archives, London

Tweedie, Ethel Brilliana (1861/2–1940)—by courtesy of Felix Rosenstiel's Widow & Son Ltd., London, on behalf of the Estate of Sir John Lavery; photograph National Portrait Gallery, London

Tweedie, Jill Sheila (1932–1993)—© News International Syndication; photograph National Portrait Gallery, London

Twining, Edward Francis, Baron Twining (1899–1967)—© National Portrait Gallery, London

Twisden, Sir Thomas, first baronet (1602–1683)—© Copyright The British Museum

Twiss, Horace (1787–1849)—private collection

Twiss, Sir Travers (1809–1897)—© National Portrait Gallery, London

Twisse, William (1577/8–1646)—© National Portrait Gallery, London

Twysden, Sir Roger, second baronet (1597–1672)—© National Portrait Gallery, London

Tyabji, Badruddin (1844–1906)—© reserved

Tyers, Jonathan (1702–1767)—© National Portrait Gallery, London

Tyldesley, Sir Thomas (1612–1651)—© National Portrait Gallery, London

Tyler, Walter [Wat] (d. 1381)—The British Library

Tylor, Sir Edward Burnett (1832–1917)—© National Portrait Gallery, London

Tynan, Kenneth Peacock (1927–1980)—© Cecil Beaton Archive, Sotheby's; collection National Portrait Gallery, London

Tyndall, Arthur Mannering (1881–1961)—Estate of the Artist; Bristol University

Tyndall, John (1820–1893)—Royal Institution, London / Bridgeman Art Library

Tyrrell, William George, Baron Tyrrell (1866–1947)—© National Portrait Gallery, London

Tyrwhitt, Dame Mary Joan Caroline (1903–1997)—© National Portrait Gallery, London

Tyson, Edward (1651–1708)—by permission of the Royal College of Physicians, London

Tytler, Alexander Fraser, Lord Woodhouselee (1747–1813)—in a private Scottish collection; photograph courtesy the Scottish National Portrait Gallery

Tytler, James (1745–1804)—photography courtesy Peabody Essex Museum

Tytler, Patrick Fraser (1791–1849)—Scottish National Portrait Gallery

Umfraville, Gilbert de, seventh earl of Angus (1244?–1307)—RJL Smith of Much Wenlock

Underhill, Cave (1634–1713)—Garrick Club / the art archive

Underhill, Edward Bean (1813–1901)—© National Portrait Gallery, London

Underhill, Evelyn Maud Bosworth (1875–1941)—© Estate of Powys Evans; collection National Portrait Gallery, London

Underwood, (George Claude) Leon (1890–1975)—© Estate of Leon Underwood; collection National Portrait Gallery, London

Unton, Sir Henry (c.1558–1596)—reproduced by kind permission of His Grace the Duke of Norfolk. Photograph: Photographic Survey, Courtauld Institute of Art, London

Unwin, Sir Raymond (1863–1940)—© National Portrait Gallery, London

Unwin, Sir Stanley (1884–1968)—© reserved; collection National Portrait Gallery, London

Unwin, William Cawthorne (1838–1933)—© reserved; Institution of Mechanical Engineers

Upham, Charles Hazlitt (1908–1994)—Alexander Turnbull Library, National Library of New Zealand, Te Puna Matauranga o Aotearoa (F-6981-1/2-DA)

Upton, Florence Kate (1873–1922)—© National Portrait Gallery, London

ʿUrabi, Ahmad Muhammad (1841–1911)—© National Portrait Gallery, London

Ure, Alexander, first Baron Strathclyde (1853–1928)—© National Portrait Gallery, London

Ure, Andrew (1778–1857)—© National Portrait Gallery, London

Urquhart, David (1805–1877)—© National Portrait Gallery, London

Urquhart, Sir Thomas, of Cromarty (1611–1660)—© National Portrait Gallery, London